Profiles
of
Florida

2008

Profiles
of
Florida

A UNIVERSAL REFERENCE BOOK

Grey House
Publishing

PUBLISHER: Leslie Mackenzie
EDITOR: David Garoogian
EDITORIAL DIRECTOR: Laura Mars-Proietti
RESEARCH ASSISTANTS: Michael Marturana; Karen Stevens

MARKETING DIRECTOR: Jessica Moody

Grey House Publishing, Inc.
185 Millerton Road
Millerton, NY 12546
518.789.8700
FAX 518.789.0545
www.greyhouse.com
e-mail: books @greyhouse.com

First edition published 2005
Second edition published 2008
Printed in the USA

ISBN: 978-1-59237-354-3
ISSN: 1941-1952

Table of Contents

Introduction

Welcome to the second edition of *Profiles of Florida - Facts, Figures & Statistics for 941 Populated Places in Florida.* As with the other titles in our *State Profiles* series, we built this work using content from Grey House Publishing's award-winning *Profiles of America* - a 4-volume compilation of data on more than 42,000 places in the United States. We have updated and included the Florida chapter from *Profiles of America,* and added entire fresh chapters of demographic information and ranking sections, so that *Profiles of Florida* is the most comprehensive portrait of the state of Florida ever published.

> "*Profiles of Florida* is a comprehensive portrait of the economic and social condition of the state. This book includes a wide variety of data including answers to frequently asked demographic and economic questions. Small businesses...rely heavily on this...data. This is an excellent reference tool for all types of libraries."
>
> *Journal of Business & Finance Librarianship*

This second edition provides data on all populated communities and counties in the state of Florida for which the US Census provides individual statistics. It includes seven major sections that cover everything from **Education** to **Ethnic Backgrounds** to **Climate**. All sections include **Comparative Statistics** or **Rankings**, and full-color **Maps** at the back of the book provide valuable information in a quickly processed, visual format. Here's an overview of each section:

1. Profiles

This section, organized by county, gives detailed profiles of 941 places plus 67 counties, and is based on the 2000 Census. This core Census data has been so extensively updated, however, that nearly 80% of this section has 2007 numbers. In addition, we have added current government statistics and original research, so that these profiles pull together statistical and descriptive information on every Census-recognized place in the state. Major fields of information include:

Geography	*Housing*	*Education*	*Religion*
Ancestry	*Transportation*	*Population*	*Climate*
Economy	*Industry*	*Health*	

In addition to place profiles, this section includes an **Alphabetical Place Index** and **Comparative Statistics** that compare Florida's 100 largest communities by dozens of data points.

2. Education

This section begins with an **Educational State Profile,** summarizing number of schools, students, diplomas granted and educational dollars spent. Following the state profile are **School District Rankings** on 16 topics ranging from *Teacher/Student Ratios* to *High School Drop-Out Rates.* Following these rankings are statewide *National Assessment of Educational Progress (NAEP)* results and data from the *Florida Comprehensive Assessment Test (FCAT)* - an overview of student performance by subject, including easy-to-read charts and graphs.

3. Ancestry

This section provides a detailed look at the ancestral and racial makeup of Florida. 217 ethnic categories are ranked three ways: 1) by number, based on all places regardless of population; 2) by percent, based on all places regardless of population; 3) by percent, based on places with populations of 10,000 or more. You will discover, for example, that Altamonte Springs has the greatest number of *Egyptians* in the state (204), and that 22.2% of the population of North Palm Beach are of *Irish* ancestry.

4. Hispanic Population

This section defines Florida's Hispanic population by 23 Hispanic backgrounds from *Argentinian* to *Venezuelan.* It ranks each of 15 categories, from Median Age to Median Home Value, by each Hispanic background. For example, you'll see that Gainesville has the highest percentage of *Cubans* who speak

English-only at home (36.3%), and that Coral Gables has the highest percentage of *Puerto Ricans* who are four-year college graduates (63.5%).

5. Asian Population
Similar in format to the section on Hispanic Population, this section defines Florida's Asian population by 21 Asian backgrounds from *Bangladeshi* to *Vietnamese.* It ranks each of 14 categories, from Median Age to Median Home Value, by each Asian background. You will learn that *Filipinos* in Miramar have a median household income of $88,334 and that 75.8% of *Vietnamese* in Pinellas Park are high-school graduates.

6. Weather
This important topic is explored in detail in this section, which includes a *State Summary,* a *map* of the state's weather stations, and profiles of both *National and Cooperative Weather Stations.* In addition, you'll find *Weather Station Rankings,* where you'll see that, over the 30-year recorded period, Key West International Airport reported the lowest annual precipitation with 39.3 inches.

This section also includes current *Storm* data, with the most destructive weather events ranked by both fatalities and property damage, from 1982-2007. Here you will learn that Hurricane Wilma caused $10 billion in property damage in South Florida in October 2005 and that an F3 tornado was responsible for 25 fatalities in Intercession City in February 1998.

7. Maps
For a more visual point of view, there are 16 full-color maps of Florida at the back of the book. They provide information on topics such as Populated Places, Transportation and Physical Features, Core-Based Statistical Areas and Counties, Population Demographics, Household Size, Median Age, Income, Median Home Values, Educational Attainment, and another look at who voted for George Bush in 2004.

Note: The extensive **User's Guide** that follows this Introduction is segmented into six sections and examines, in some detail, each data field in the individual profiles and comparative sections for all chapters. It provides sources for all data points and statistical definitions as necessary.

User's Guide: Profiles

PLACES COVERED

All 67 counties.

402 incorporated municipalities. Municipalities are incorporated as either cities, towns or villages.

484 census designated places (CDP). The U.S. Bureau of the Census defines a CDP as "a statistical entity, defined for each decennial census according to Census Bureau guidelines, comprising a densely settled concentration of population that is not within an incorporated place, but is locally identified by a name. CDPs are delineated cooperatively by state and local officials and the Census Bureau, following Census Bureau guidelines. Beginning with Census 2000 there are no size limits."

55 unincorporated communities. The communities included have both their own zip code and statistics for their ZIP Code Tabulation Area (ZCTA) available from the Census Bureau. They are referred to as "postal areas." A ZCTA is a statistical entity developed by the Census Bureau to approximate the delivery area for a US Postal Service 5-digit or 3-digit ZIP Code in the US and Puerto Rico. A ZCTA is an aggregation of census blocks that have the same predominant ZIP Code associated with the mailing addresses in the Census Bureau's Master Address File. Thus, the Postal Service's delivery areas have been adjusted to encompass whole census blocks so that the Census Bureau can tabulate census data for the ZCTAs. ZCTAs do not include all ZIP Codes used for mail delivery and therefore do not precisely depict the area within which mail deliveries associated with that ZIP Code occur. Additionally, some areas that are known by a unique name, although they are part of a larger incorporated place, are also included as "postal areas."

Important Notes

- Unincorporated communities that span multiple zip codes are not included in this book.
- In Florida, most school districts serve an entire county. In each community profile, only school districts that have schools that are physically located within the community are shown. In addition, statistics for each school district cover the entire district, regardless of the physical location of the schools within the district.
- Special care should be taken when interpreting certain statistics for communities containing large colleges or universities. College students were counted as residents of the area in which they were living while attending college (as they have been since the 1950 census). One effect this may have is skewing the figures for population, income, housing, and educational attainment.
- Some information (e.g. unemployment rates) is available for both counties and individual communities. Other information is available for just counties (e.g. election results), or just individual communities (e.g. local newspapers).
- Some statistical information is available only for larger communities. In addition, the larger places are more apt to have services such as newspapers, airports, school districts, etc.
- For the most complete information on any community, you should also check the entry for the county in which the community is located. In addition, more information and services will be listed under the larger places in the county.
- For a more in-depth discussion of geographic areas, please refer to the Census Bureau's Geographic Areas Reference Manual at http://www.census.gov/geo/www/garm.html.

DATA SOURCES

CENSUS 2000

The parts of the data which are from the 2000 Decennial Census are from the following sources: *U.S. Bureau of the Census, Census of Population and Housing, 2000: Summary Files 1 and 3*. Summary File 3 (SF 3) consists of 813 detailed tables of Census 2000 social, economic and housing characteristics compiled from a sample of approximately 19 million housing units (about 1 in 6 households) that received the Census 2000 long-form questionnaire. Summary File 1 (SF 1) contains 286 tables focusing on age, sex, households, families, and housing units. This file presents 100-percent population and housing figures for the total population, for 63 race categories, and for many other race and Hispanic or Latino categories.

Comparing SF 3 Estimates with Corresponding Values in SF 1

As in earlier censuses, the responses from the sample of households reporting on long forms must be weighted to reflect the entire population. Specifically, each responding household represents, on average, six or seven other households who reported using short forms.

One consequence of the weighting procedures is that each estimate based on the long form responses has an associated confidence interval. These confidence intervals are wider (as a percentage of the estimate) for geographic areas with smaller populations and for characteristics that occur less frequently in the area being examined (such as the proportion of people in poverty in a middle-income neighborhood).

In order to release as much useful information as possible, statisticians must balance a number of factors. In particular, for Census 2000, the Bureau of the Census created weighting areas—geographic areas from which about two hundred or more long forms were completed—which are large enough to produce good quality estimates. If smaller weighting areas had been used, the confidence intervals around the estimates would have been significantly wider, rendering many estimates less useful due to their lower reliability.

The disadvantage of using weighting areas this large is that, for smaller geographic areas within them, the estimates of characteristics that are also reported on the short form will not match the counts reported in SF 1. Examples of these characteristics are the total number of people, the number of people reporting specific racial categories, and the number of housing units. The official values for items reported on the short form come from SF 1 and SF 2.

The differences between the long form estimates in SF 3 and values in SF 1 are particularly noticeable for the smallest places, tracts, and block groups. The long form estimates of total population and total housing units in SF 3 will, however, match the SF 1 counts for larger geographic areas such as counties and states, and will be essentially the same for medium and large cities.

SF 1 gives exact numbers even for very small groups and areas, whereas SF 3 gives estimates for small groups and areas such as tracts and small places that are less exact. The goal of SF 3 is to identify large differences among areas or large changes over time. Estimates for small areas and small population groups often do exhibit large changes from one census to the next, so having the capability to measure them is worthwhile.

2006 Estimates and 2011 Projections

Some 2000 Census data has been updated with data provided by Claritas. Founded in 1971, Claritas is the industry leader in applied demography and the preeminent provider of small-area demographic estimates.

PHYSICAL CHARACTERISTICS

Place Type: Lists the type of place (city, town, village, borough, special city, CDP, township, plantation, gore, district, grant, location, reservation, or postal area). *Source: U.S. Bureau of the Census, Census of Population and Housing, 2000: Summary File 1 and U.S. Postal Service, City State File.*

Land and Water Area: Land and water area in square miles. *Source: U.S. Bureau of the Census, Census of Population and Housing, 2000: Summary File 1.*

Latitude and Longitude: Latitude and longitude in degrees. *Source: U.S. Bureau of the Census, Census of Population and Housing, 2000: Summary File 1.*

Elevation: Elevation in feet. *Source: U.S. Geological Survey, Geographic Names Information System (GNIS).*

HISTORY

History: Historical information. *Source: Columbia University Press, The Columbia Gazetteer of North America; Original research.*

POPULATION

Population: 1990 and 2000 figures are a 100% count of population. 2006 estimates and 2011 projections were provided by Claritas. *Source: Claritas; U.S. Bureau of the Census, Census of Population and Housing, 2000: Summary File 1.*

Population by Race: 2007 estimates includes the U.S. Bureau of the Census categories of White alone; Black alone; Asian alone; and Hispanic of any race. Alone refers to the fact that these figures are not in combination with any other race. 2007 data for American Indian/Alaska Native and Native Hawaiian/Other Pacific Islander was not available.

The concept of race, as used by the Census Bureau, reflects self-identification by people according to the race or races with which they most closely identify. These categories are socio-political constructs and should not be interpreted as being scientific or anthropological in nature. Furthermore, the race categories include both racial and national-origin groups.

- **White.** A person having origins in any of the original peoples of Europe, the Middle East, or North Africa. It includes people who indicate their race as "White" or report entries such as Irish, German, Italian, Lebanese, Near Easterner, Arab, or Polish.
- **Black or African American.** A person having origins in any of the Black racial groups of Africa. It includes people who indicate their race as "Black, African American, or Negro," or provide written entries such as African American, Afro-American, Kenyan, Nigerian, or Haitian.
- **Asian.** A person having origins in any of the original peoples of the Far East, Southeast Asia, or the Indian subcontinent including, for example, Cambodia, China, India, Japan, Korea, Malaysia, Pakistan, the Philippine Islands, Thailand, and Vietnam. It includes "Asian Indian," "Chinese," "Filipino," "Korean," "Japanese," "Vietnamese," and "Other Asian."
- **Hispanic.** The data on the Hispanic or Latino population, which was asked of all people, were derived from answers to long-form questionnaire Item 5, and short-form questionnaire Item 7. The terms "Spanish," "Hispanic origin," and "Latino" are used interchangeably. Some respondents identify with all three terms, while others may identify with only one of these three specific terms. Hispanics or Latinos who identify with the terms "Spanish," "Hispanic," or "Latino" are those who classify themselves in one of the specific Hispanic or Latino categories listed on the questionnaire — "Mexican," "Puerto Rican," or "Cuban" — as well as those who indicate that they are "other Spanish, Hispanic, or Latino." People who do not identify with one of the specific origins listed on the questionnaire but indicate that they are "other Spanish, Hispanic, or Latino" are those whose origins are from Spain, the Spanish-speaking countries of Central or South America, the Dominican Republic, or people identifying themselves generally as Spanish, Spanish-American, Hispanic, Hispano, Latino, and so on. All write-in responses to the "other Spanish/Hispanic/Latino" category were coded. Origin can be viewed as the heritage, nationality group, lineage, or country of birth of the person or the person's parents or ancestors before their arrival in the United States. People who identify their origin as Spanish, Hispanic, or Latino may be of any race.

Population Density: 2007 population estimates divided by the land area in square miles. *Source: Claritas, U.S. Bureau of the Census, Census of Population and Housing, 2000: Summary File 1.*

Average Household Size: Average household size was calculated by dividing the total population by the total number of households. Figures are 2007 estimates. *Source: Claritas.*

Median Age: Figures are 2007 estimates. *Source: Claritas.*

Male/Female Ratio: Number of males per 100 females. Figures are 2007 estimates. *Source: Claritas.*

Marital Status: Percentage of population never married, now married, widowed, or divorced. *Source: U.S. Bureau of the Census, Census of Population and Housing, 2000: Summary File 3.*

The marital status classification refers to the status at the time of enumeration. Data on marital status are tabulated only for the population 15 years old and over. Each person was asked whether they were "Now married," "Widowed," "Divorced," or "Never married." Couples who live together (for example, people in common-law marriages) were able to report the marital status they considered to be the most appropriate.

- **Never married**. Never married includes all people who have never been married, including people whose only marriage(s) was annulled.
- **Now married.** All people whose current marriage has not ended by widowhood or divorce. This category includes people defined as "separated."
- **Widowed**. This category includes widows and widowers who have not remarried.
- **Divorced.** This category includes people who are legally divorced and who have not remarried.

Foreign Born: Percentage of population who were not U.S. citizens at birth. Foreign-born people are those who indicated they were either a U.S. citizen by naturalization or they were not a citizen of the United States. *Source: U.S. Bureau of the Census, Census of Population and Housing, 2000: Summary File 3.*

Ancestry: Largest ancestry groups reported (up to five). Includes multiple ancestries. *Source: U.S. Bureau of the Census, Census of Population and Housing, 2000: Summary File 3.*

The data represent self-classification by people according to the ancestry group or groups with which they most closely identify. Ancestry refers to a person's ethnic origin or descent, "roots," heritage, or the place of birth of the person, the person's parents, or their ancestors before their arrival in the United States. Some ethnic identities, such as Egyptian or Polish, can be traced to geographic areas outside the United States, while other ethnicities such as Pennsylvania German or Cajun evolved in the United States.

The ancestry question was intended to provide data for groups that were not included in the Hispanic origin and race questions. Therefore, although data on all groups are collected, the ancestry data shown in these tabulations are for non-Hispanic and non-race groups. Hispanic and race groups are included in the "Other groups" category for the ancestry tables in these tabulations.

The ancestry question allowed respondents to report one or more ancestry groups, although only the first two were coded. If a response was in terms of a dual ancestry, for example, "Irish English," the person was assigned two codes, in this case one for Irish and another for English. However, in certain cases, multiple responses such as "French Canadian," "Greek Cypriote," and "Scotch Irish" were assigned a single code reflecting their status as unique groups. If a person reported one of these unique groups in addition to another group, for example, "Scotch Irish English," resulting in three terms, that person received one code for the unique group (Scotch-Irish) and another one for the remaining group (English). If a person reported "English Irish French," only English and Irish were coded. Certain combinations of ancestries where the ancestry group is a part of another, such as "German-Bavarian," were coded as a single ancestry using the more specific group (Bavarian). Also, responses such as "Polish-American" or "Italian-American" were coded and tabulated as a single entry (Polish or Italian).

The Census Bureau accepted "American" as a unique ethnicity if it was given alone, with an ambiguous response, or with state names. If the respondent listed any other ethnic identity such as "Italian-American," generally the "American" portion of the response was not coded. However, distinct groups such as "American Indian," "Mexican American," and "African American" were coded and identified separately because they represented groups who considered themselves different from those who reported as "Indian," "Mexican," or "African," respectively.

The data is based on the total number of ancestries reported and coded. Thus, the sum of the counts in this type of presentation is not the total population but the total of all responses.

ECONOMY

Unemployment Rate: Data as of November 2007. Includes all civilians age 16 or over who were unemployed and looking for work. *Source: U.S. Department of Labor, Bureau of Labor Statistics, Local Area Unemployment Statistics (http://www.bls.gov/lau/home.htm).*

Total Civilian Labor Force: Data as of November 2007. Includes all civilians age 16 or over who were either employed, or unemployed and looking for work. *Source: U.S. Department of Labor, Bureau of Labor Statistics, Local Area Unemployment Statistics (http://www.bls.gov/lau/home.htm).*

Single-Family Building Permits Issued: Building permits issued for new single-family housing units in 2006. *Source: U.S. Census Bureau, Manufacturing and Construction Division (http://www.census.gov/const/www/permitsindex.html).*

Multi-Family Building Permits Issued: Building permits issued for new multi-family housing units in 2006. *Source: U.S. Census Bureau, Manufacturing and Construction Division (http://www.census.gov/const/www/permitsindex.html).*

Statistics on housing units authorized by building permits include housing units issued in local permit-issuing jurisdictions by a building or zoning permit. Not all areas of the country require a building or zoning permit. The statistics only represent those areas that do require a permit. Current surveys indicate that construction is undertaken for all but a very small percentage of housing units authorized by building permits. A major portion typically get under way during the month of permit issuance and most of the remainder begin within the three following months. Because of this lag, the housing unit authorization statistics do not represent the number of units actually put into construction for the period shown, and should therefore not be directly interpreted as "housing starts."

Statistics are based upon reports submitted by local building permit officials in response to a mail survey. They are obtained using Form C-404 const/www/c404.pdf, "Report of New Privately-Owned Residential Building or Zoning Permits Issued." When a report is not received, missing data are either (1) obtained from the Survey of Use of Permits (SUP) which is used to collect information on housing starts, or (2) imputed based on the assumption that the ratio of current month authorizations to those of a year ago should be the same for reporting and non-reporting places.

Employment by Occupation: Percentage of the employed civilian population 16 years and over in management, professional, service, sales, farming, construction, and production occupations. *Source: U.S. Bureau of the Census, Census of Population and Housing, 2000: Summary File 3.*

- **Management** includes management, business, and financial operations occupations:
    Management occupations, except farmers and farm managers
    Farmers and farm managers
    Business and financial operations occupations:
        Business operations specialists
        Financial specialists

- **Professional** includes professional and related occupations:
    Computer and mathematical occupations
    Architecture and engineering occupations:
        Architects, surveyors, cartographers, and engineers
        Drafters, engineering, and mapping technicians
    Life, physical, and social science occupations
    Community and social services occupations
    Legal occupations
    Education, training, and library occupations
    Arts, design, entertainment, sports, and media occupations
    Healthcare practitioners and technical occupations:
        Health diagnosing and treating practitioners and technical occupations
        Health technologists and technicians

- **Service** occupations include:
    Healthcare support occupations
    Protective service occupations:
        Fire fighting, prevention, and law enforcement workers, including supervisors

           Other protective service workers, including supervisors
           Food preparation and serving related occupations
           Building and grounds cleaning and maintenance occupations
           Personal care and service occupations

- **Sales** and office occupations include:
  Sales and related occupations
  Office and administrative support occupations

- **Farming,** fishing, and forestry occupations

- **Construction,** extraction, and maintenance occupations include:
  Construction and extraction occupations:
      Supervisors, construction, and extraction workers
      Construction trades workers
      Extraction workers
  Installation, maintenance, and repair occupations

- **Production,** transportation, and material moving occupations include:
  Production occupations
  Transportation and material moving occupations:
      Supervisors, transportation, and material moving workers
      Aircraft and traffic control occupations
      Motor vehicle operators
      Rail, water, and other transportation occupations
      Material moving workers

INCOME

Per Capita Income: Per capita income is the mean income computed for every man, woman, and child in a particular group. It is derived by dividing the total income of a particular group by the total population in that group. Per capita income is rounded to the nearest whole dollar. Figures shown are 2007 estimates. *Source: Claritas.*

Median Household Income: Includes the income of the householder and all other individuals 15 years old and over in the household, whether they are related to the householder or not. The median divides the income distribution into two equal parts: one-half of the cases falling below the median income and one-half above the median. For households, the median income is based on the distribution of the total number of households including those with no income. Median income for households is computed on the basis of a standard distribution and is rounded to the nearest whole dollar. Figures shown are 2007 estimates. *Source: Claritas.*

Average Household Income: Average household income is obtained by dividing total household income by the total number of households. Figures shown are 2007 estimates. *Source: Claritas.*

Percent of Households with Income of $100,000 or more: Figures shown are 2007 estimates. *Source: Claritas.*

Poverty Rate: Percentage of population with income in 1999 below the poverty level. Based on individuals for whom poverty status is determined. Poverty status was determined for all people except institutionalized people, people in military group quarters, people in college dormitories, and unrelated individuals under 15 years old. *Source: U.S. Bureau of the Census, Census of Population and Housing, 2000: Summary File 3.*

The poverty status of families and unrelated individuals in 1999 was determined using 48 thresholds (income cutoffs) arranged in a two-dimensional matrix. The matrix consists of family size (from 1 person to 9 or more people) cross-classified by presence and number of family members under 18 years old (from no children present to 8 or more children present). Unrelated individuals and 2-person families were further differentiated by the age of the reference person (RP) (under 65 years old and 65 years old and over).

To determine a person's poverty status, one compares the person's total family income with the poverty threshold appropriate for that person's family size and composition. If the total income of that person's family is less than the threshold appropriate for that family, then the person is considered poor, together with every member of his or her family. If a person is not living with anyone related by birth, marriage, or adoption, then the person's own income is compared with his or her poverty threshold.

TAXES

Total City Taxes Per Capita: Total city taxes collected divided by the population of the city. *Source: U.S. Bureau of the Census, State and Local Government Finances, 2004-05 (http://www.census.gov/govs/www/estimate.html).*

Taxes include:

- Property Taxes
- Sales and Gross Receipts Taxes
- Federal Customs Duties
- General Sales and Gross Receipts Taxes
- Selective Sales Taxes (alcoholic beverages; amusements; insurance premiums; motor fuels; pari-mutuels; public utilities; tobacco products; other)
- License Taxes (alcoholic beverages; amusements; corporations in general; hunting and fishing; motor vehicles motor vehicle operators; public utilities; occupation and business, NEC; other)
- Income Taxes (individual income; corporation net income; other)
- Death and Gift
- Documentary & Stock Transfer
- Severance
- Taxes, NEC

Total City Property Taxes Per Capita: Total city property taxes collected divided by the population of the city. *Source: U.S. Bureau of the Census, State and Local Government Finances, 2004-05 (http://www.census.gov/govs/www/estimate.html).*

Property Taxes include general property taxes, relating to property as a whole, taxed at a single rate or at classified rates according to the class of property. Property refers to real property (e.g. land and structures) as well as personal property; personal property can be either tangible (e.g. automobiles and boats) or intangible (e.g. bank accounts and stocks and bonds). Special property taxes, levied on selected types of property (e.g. oil and gas properties, house trailers, motor vehicles, and intangibles) and subject to rates not directly related to general property tax rates. Taxes based on income produced by property as a measure of its value on the assessment date.

EDUCATION

Educational Attainment: Figures shown are 2007 estimates and show the percent of population age 25 and over with a:

- **High school diploma (including GED) or higher:** includes people whose highest degree was a high school diploma or its equivalent, people who attended college but did not receive a degree, and people who received a college, university, or professional degree. People who reported completing the 12th grade but not receiving a diploma are not high school graduates.
- **Bachelor's degree or higher**
- **Master's degree or higher:** Master's degrees include the traditional MA and MS degrees and field-specific degrees, such as MSW, MEd, MBA, MLS, and Meng. *Source: Claritas.*

School Districts: Lists the name of each school district, the grade range (PK=pre-kindergarten; KG=kindergarten), the student enrollment, and the district headquarters' phone number. In each community profile, only school districts that have schools that are physically located within the community are shown. In addition, statistics for each school district cover the entire district, regardless of the physical location of the schools within the district. *Source: U.S. Department of Education, National Center for Educational Statistics, Directory of Public Elementary and Secondary Education Agencies, 2005-06.*

Four-year Colleges: Lists the name of each four-year college, the type of institution (private or public; for-profit or non-profit; religious affiliation; historically black), the total student enrollment (Fall 2006), the general telephone number, and the annual tuition (including fees) for full-time, first-time undergraduate students (in-state and out-of-state). *Source: U.S. Department of Education, National Center for Educational Statistics, IPEDS College Data, 2006-07.*

Two-year Colleges: Lists the name of each two-year college, the type of institution (private or public; for-profit or non-profit; religious affiliation; historically black), the total student enrollment (Fall 2006), the general telephone number, and the annual tuition (including fees) for full-time, first-time undergraduate students (in-state and out-of-state). *Source: U.S. Department of Education, National Center for Educational Statistics, IPEDS College Data, 2006-07.*

Vocational/Technical Schools: Lists the name of each vocational/technical school, the type of institution (private or public; for-profit or non-profit; religious affiliation; historically black), the total student enrollment (Fall 2006), the general telephone number, and the annual tuition and fees for full-time students. *Source: U.S. Department of Education, National Center for Educational Statistics, IPEDS College Data, 2006-07.*

HOUSING

Homeownership Rate: Percentage of housing units that are owner-occupied. Figures shown are 2007 estimates. *Source: Claritas.*

Median Home Value: Median value of all owner-occupied housing units as reported by the owner. Figures shown are 2007 estimates. *Source: Claritas.*

Median Rent: Median monthly contract rent on specified renter-occupied and specified vacant-for-rent units. Specified renter-occupied and specified vacant-for-rent units exclude 1-family houses on 10 acres or more. Contract rent is the monthly rent agreed to or contracted for, regardless of any furnishings, utilities, fees, meals, or services that may be included. For vacant units, it is the monthly rent asked for the rental unit at the time of enumeration. *Source: U.S. Bureau of the Census, Census of Population and Housing, 2000: Summary File 3.*

Median Age of Housing: Median age of housing was calculated by subtracting median year structure built from 2000 (e.g. if the median year structure built is 1967, the median age of housing in that area is 33 years—2000 minus 1967). Year structure built refers to when the building was first constructed, not when it was remodeled, added to, or converted. For housing units under construction that met the housing unit definition—that is, all exterior windows, doors, and final usable floors were in place—the category "1999 or 2000" was used for tabulations. For mobile homes, houseboats, RVs, etc, the manufacturer's model year was assumed to be the year built. The data relate to the number of units built during the specified periods that were still in existence at the time of enumeration. *Source: U.S. Bureau of the Census, Census of Population and Housing, 2000: Summary File 3.*

HOSPITALS

Lists the hospital name and the number of licensed beds. *Source: Grey House Publishing, Directory of Hospital Personnel, 2007.*

SAFETY

Violent Crime Rate: Number of violent crimes reported per 10,000 population. Violent crimes include murder, forcible rape, robbery, and aggravated assault. *Source: Federal Bureau of Investigation, Uniform Crime Reports 2006 (http://www.fbi.gov/ucr/ucr.htm).*

Property Crime Rate: Number of property crimes reported per 10,000 population. Property crimes include burglary, larceny-theft, and motor vehicle theft. *Source: Federal Bureau of Investigation, Uniform Crime Reports 2006 (http://www.fbi.gov/ucr/ucr.htm).*

NEWSPAPERS

Lists the name, type and circulation of daily and weekly newspapers. Includes newspapers with offices located in the community profiled. *Source: BurrellesLuce MediaContacts 2006 (http://www.burrellesluce.com/MediaConnect).*

TRANSPORTATION

Commute to Work: Percentage of workers 16 years old and over that use the following means of transportation to commute to work: car; public transportation; walk; work from home. *Source: U.S. Bureau of the Census, Census of Population and Housing, 2000: Summary File 3.*

The means of transportation data for some areas may show workers using modes of public transportation that are not available in those areas (e.g. subway or elevated riders in a metropolitan area where there actually is no subway or elevated service). This result is largely due to people who worked during the reference week at a location that was different from their usual place of work (such as people away from home on business in an area where subway service was available) and people who used more than one means of transportation each day but whose principal means was unavailable where they lived (e.g. residents of non-metropolitan areas who drove to the fringe of a metropolitan area and took the commuter railroad most of the distance to work).

Travel Time to Work: Travel time to work for workers 16 years old and over. Reported for the following intervals: less than 15 minutes; 15 to 30 minutes; 30 to 45 minutes; 45 to 60 minutes; 60 minutes or more. *Source: U.S. Bureau of the Census, Census of Population and Housing, 2000: Summary File 3.*

Travel time to work refers to the total number of minutes that it usually took the person to get from home to work each day during the reference week. The elapsed time includes time spent waiting for public transportation, picking up passengers in carpools, and time spent in other activities related to getting to work.

Amtrak: Indicates if Amtrak service is available. Please note that the cities being served continually change. *Source: National Railroad Passenger Corporation, Amtrak National Timetable, 2008 (www.amtrak.com).*

AIRPORTS

Lists the local airport(s) along with type of service and hub size. *Source: U.S. Department of Transportation, Bureau of Transportation Statistics (http://www.bts.gov).*

ADDITIONAL INFORMATION CONTACTS

The following phone numbers are provided as sources of additional information: Chambers of Commerce; Economic Development Agencies; Boards of Realtors; Convention & Visitors Bureaus. Efforts have been made to provide the most recent area codes. However, area code changes may have occurred in listed numbers. *Source: Original research.*

INFORMATION FOR COUNTIES

PHYSICAL CHARACTERISTICS

Physical Location: Describes the physical location of the county. *Source: Columbia University Press, The Columbia Gazetteer of North America and original research.*

Land and Water Area: Land and water area in square miles. *Source: U.S. Bureau of the Census, Census of Population and Housing, 2000: Summary File 1.*

Time Zone: Lists the time zone. *Source: Original research.*

Year Organized: Year the county government was organized. *Source: National Association of Counties (www.naco.org).*

County Seat: Lists the county seat. If a county has more than one seat, then both are listed. *Source: National Association of Counties (www.naco.org).*

Metropolitan Area: Indicates the metropolitan area the county is located in. Also lists all the component counties of that metropolitan area. The Office of Management and Budget (OMB) defines metropolitan and micropolitan statistical areas. The current definitions are as of December 2006. *Source: U.S. Bureau of the Census (http://www.census.gov/population/www/estimates/metrodef.html).*

Climate: Includes all weather stations located within the county. Indicates the station name and elevation as well as the monthly average high and low temperatures, average precipitation, and average snowfall. The period of record is generally 1970-1999, however, certain weather stations contain averages going back as far as 1900. *Source: Grey House Publishing, Weather America: A Thirty-Year Summary of Statistical Weather Data and Rankings, 2001.*

POPULATION

Population: 1990 and 2000 figures are a 100% count of population. 2006 estimates and 2011 projections were provided by Claritas. *Source: Claritas; U.S. Bureau of the Census, Census of Population and Housing, 2000: Summary File 1.*

Population by Race: 2007 estimates includes the U.S. Bureau of the Census categories of White alone; Black alone; Asian alone; and Hispanic of any race. Alone refers to the fact that these figures are not in combination with any other race. 2007 data for American Indian/Alaska Native and Native Hawaiian/Other Pacific Islander was not available.

The concept of race, as used by the Census Bureau, reflects self-identification by people according to the race or races with which they most closely identify. These categories are socio-political constructs and should not be interpreted as being scientific or anthropological in nature. Furthermore, the race categories include both racial and national-origin groups.

- **White.** A person having origins in any of the original peoples of Europe, the Middle East, or North Africa. It includes people who indicate their race as "White" or report entries such as Irish, German, Italian, Lebanese, Near Easterner, Arab, or Polish.
- **Black or African American.** A person having origins in any of the Black racial groups of Africa. It includes people who indicate their race as "Black, African American, or Negro," or provide written entries such as African American, Afro-American, Kenyan, Nigerian, or Haitian.
- **Asian.** A person having origins in any of the original peoples of the Far East, Southeast Asia, or the Indian subcontinent including, for example, Cambodia, China, India, Japan, Korea, Malaysia, Pakistan, the Philippine Islands, Thailand, and Vietnam. It includes "Asian Indian," "Chinese," "Filipino," "Korean," "Japanese," "Vietnamese," and "Other Asian."
- **Hispanic.** The data on the Hispanic or Latino population, which was asked of all people, were derived from answers to long-form questionnaire Item 5, and short-form questionnaire Item 7. The terms "Spanish," "Hispanic origin," and "Latino" are used interchangeably. Some respondents identify with all three terms, while others may identify with only one of these three specific terms. Hispanics or Latinos who identify with the terms "Spanish," "Hispanic," or "Latino" are those who classify themselves in one of the specific Hispanic or Latino categories listed on the questionnaire — "Mexican," "Puerto Rican," or "Cuban" — as well as those who indicate that they are "other Spanish, Hispanic, or Latino." People who do not identify with one of the specific origins listed on the questionnaire but indicate that they are "other

Spanish, Hispanic, or Latino" are those whose origins are from Spain, the Spanish-speaking countries of Central or South America, the Dominican Republic, or people identifying themselves generally as Spanish, Spanish-American, Hispanic, Hispano, Latino, and so on. All write-in responses to the "other Spanish/Hispanic/Latino" category were coded. Origin can be viewed as the heritage, nationality group, lineage, or country of birth of the person or the person's parents or ancestors before their arrival in the United States. People who identify their origin as Spanish, Hispanic, or Latino may be of any race.

Population Density: 2007 population estimate divided by the land area in square miles. *Source: Claritas; U.S. Bureau of the Census, Census of Population and Housing, 2000: Summary File 1.*

Average Household Size: Average household size was calculated by dividing the total population by the total number of households. Figures are 2007 estimates. *Source: Claritas.*

Median Age: Figures are 2007 estimates. *Source: Claritas.*

Male/Female Ratio: Number of males per 100 females. Figures are 2007 estimates. *Source: Claritas.*

RELIGION

Religion: Lists the largest religious groups (up to five) based on the number of adherents divided by the population of the county. Adherents are defined as "all members, including full members, their children and the estimated number of other regular participants who are not considered as communicant, confirmed or full members." The data is based on a study of 149 religious bodies sponsored by the Association of Statisticians of American Religious Bodies. The 149 bodies reported 268,254 congregations and 141,371,963 adherents. *Source: Glenmary Research Center, Religious Congregations & Membership in the United States 2000.*

ECONOMY

Unemployment Rate: Data as of November 2007. Includes all civilians age 16 or over who were unemployed and looking for work. *Source: U.S. Department of Labor, Bureau of Labor Statistics, Local Area Unemployment Statistics (http://www.bls.gov/lau/home.htm).*

Total Civilian Labor Force: Data as of November 2007. Includes all civilians age 16 or over who were either employed, or unemployed and looking for work. *Source: U.S. Department of Labor, Bureau of Labor Statistics, Local Area Unemployment Statistics (http://www.bls.gov/lau/home.htm).*

Leading Industries: Lists the three largest industries (excluding government) based on the number of employees. *Source: U.S. Bureau of the Census, County Business Patterns 2005 (http://www.census.gov/epcd/cbp/view/cbpview.html).*

Farms: The total number of farms and the total acreage they occupy. *Source: U.S. Department of Agriculture, National Agricultural Statistics Service, 2002 Census of Agriculture (http://www.nass.usda.gov/census).*

Companies that Employ 500 or more persons: The numbers of companies that employ 500 or more persons. Includes private employers only. *Source: U.S. Bureau of the Census, County Business Patterns 2005 (http://www.census.gov/epcd/cbp/view/cbpview.html).*

Companies that Employ 100 - 499 persons: The numbers of companies that employ 100 - 499 persons. Includes private employers only. *Source: U.S. Bureau of the Census, County Business Patterns 2005 (http://www.census.gov/epcd/cbp/view/cbpview.html).*

Companies that Employ 1 - 99 persons: The numbers of companies that employ 1 - 99 persons. Includes private employers only. *Source: U.S. Bureau of the Census, County Business Patterns 2005 (http://www.census.gov/epcd/cbp/view/cbpview.html)*

Black-Owned Businesses: Number of businesses that are majority-owned by a Black or African-American person(s). Majority ownership is defined as having 51 percent or more of the stock or equity in the business. Black or African American is defined as a person having origins in any of the black racial groups of Africa, including those who consider themselves to be "Haitian." *Source: U.S. Bureau of the Census, 2002 Economic Census, Survey of Business Owners: Black-Owned Firms, 2002 (http://www.census.gov/csd/sbo/index.html).*

Asian-Owned Businesses: Number of businesses that are majority-owned by an Asian person(s). Majority ownership is defined as having 51 percent or more of the stock or equity in the business. *Source: U.S. Bureau of the Census, 2002 Economic Census, Survey of Business Owners: Black-Owned Firms, 2002 (http://www.census.gov/csd/sbo/index.html).*

Hispanic-Owned Businesses: Number of businesses that are majority-owned by a person(s) of Hispanic or Latino origin. Majority ownership is defined as having 51 percent or more of the stock or equity in the business. Hispanic or Latino origin is defined as a person of Cuban, Mexican, Puerto Rican, South or Central American, or other Spanish culture or origin, regardless of race. *Source: U.S. Bureau of the Census, 2002 Economic Census, Survey of Business Owners: Hispanic-Owned Firms, 2002 (http://www.census.gov/csd/sbo/index.html).*

Women-Owned Businesses: Number of businesses that are majority-owned by a woman. Majority ownership is defined as having 51 percent or more of the stock or equity in the business. *Source: U.S. Bureau of the Census, 2002 Economic Census, Survey of Business Owners: Women-Owned Firms, 2002 (http://www.census.gov/csd/sbo/index.html).*

The Survey of Business Owners (SBO), formerly known as the Surveys of Minority- and Women-Owned Business Enterprises (SMOBE/SWOBE), provides statistics that describe the composition of U.S. businesses by gender, Hispanic or Latino origin, and race. Additional statistics include owner's age, education level, veteran status, and primary function in the business; family- and home-based businesses; types of customers and workers; and sources of financing for expansion, capital improvements, or start-up. Economic policymakers in federal, state and local governments use the SBO data to understand conditions of business success and failure by comparing census-to-census changes in business performances and by comparing minority-/nonminority- and women-/men-owned businesses.

Retail Sales per Capita: Total dollar amount of estimated retail sales divided by the estimated population of the county in 2007. *Source: Editor & Publisher Market Guide 2007*

Single-Family Building Permits Issued: Building permits issued for new, single-family housing units in 2006. *Source: U.S. Census Bureau, Manufacturing and Construction Division (http://www.census.gov/const/www/permitsindex.html).*

Multi-Family Building Permits Issued: Building permits issued for new, multi-family housing units in 2006. *Source: U.S. Census Bureau, Manufacturing and Construction Division (http://www.census.gov/const/www/permitsindex.html).*

Statistics on housing units authorized by building permits include housing units issued in local permit-issuing jurisdictions by a building or zoning permit. Not all areas of the country require a building or zoning permit. The statistics only represent those areas that do require a permit. Current surveys indicate that construction is undertaken for all but a very small percentage of housing units authorized by building permits. A major portion typically get under way during the month of permit issuance and most of the remainder begin within the three following months. Because of this lag, the housing unit authorization statistics do not represent the number of units actually put into construction for the period shown, and should therefore not be directly interpreted as "housing starts."

Statistics are based upon reports submitted by local building permit officials in response to a mail survey. They are obtained using Form C-404 const/www/c404.pdf, "Report of New Privately-Owned Residential Building or Zoning Permits Issued." When a report is not received, missing data are either (1) obtained from the Survey of Use of Permits (SUP) which is used to collect information on housing starts, or (2) imputed based on the assumption that the ratio of current month authorizations to those of a year ago should be the same for reporting and non-reporting places.

INCOME

Per Capita Income: Per capita income is the mean income computed for every man, woman, and child in a particular group. It is derived by dividing the total income of a particular group by the total population in that group. Per capita income is rounded to the nearest whole dollar. Figures shown are 2007 estimates. *Source: Claritas.*

Median Household Income: Includes the income of the householder and all other individuals 15 years old and over in the household, whether they are related to the householder or not. The median divides the income distribution into two equal parts: one-half of the cases falling below the median income and one-half above the median. For households, the median income is based on the distribution of the total number of households including those with no income. Median income for households is computed on the basis of a standard distribution and is rounded to the nearest whole dollar. Figures shown are 2007 estimates. *Source: Claritas.*

Average Household Income: Average household income is obtained by dividing total household income by the total number of households. Figures shown are 2007 estimates. *Source: Claritas.*

Percent of Households with Income of $100,000 or more: Figures shown are 2007 estimates. *Source: Claritas.*

Poverty Rate: Estimated percentage of population with income in 2005 below the poverty level. *Source: U.S. Bureau of the Census, Small Area Income & Poverty Estimates.*

Bankruptcy Rate: The personal bankruptcy filing rate is the number of bankruptcies per thousand residents in 2006. Personal bankruptcy filings include both Chapter 7 (liquidations) and Chapter 13 (reorganizations) based on the county of residence of the filer. *Source: Federal Deposit Insurance Corporation, Regional Economic Conditions (http://www2.fdic.gov/recon/index.html).*

TAXES

Total County Taxes Per Capita: Total county taxes collected divided by the population of the county. *Source: U.S. Bureau of the Census, State and Local Government Finances, 2004-05 (http://www.census.gov/govs/www/estimate.html).*

Taxes include:
- Property Taxes
- Sales and Gross Receipts Taxes
- Federal Customs Duties
- General Sales and Gross Receipts Taxes
- Selective Sales Taxes (alcoholic beverages; amusements; insurance premiums; motor fuels; pari-mutuels; public utilities; tobacco products; other)
- License Taxes (alcoholic beverages; amusements; corporations in general; hunting and fishing; motor vehicles motor vehicle operators; public utilities; occupation and business, NEC; other)
- Income Taxes (individual income; corporation net income; other)
- Death and Gift
- Documentary & Stock Transfer
- Severance
- Taxes, NEC

Total County Property Taxes Per Capita: Total county property taxes collected divided by the population of the county. *Source: U.S. Bureau of the Census, State and Local Government Finances, 2004-05 (http://www.census.gov/govs/www/estimate.html).*

Property Taxes include general property taxes, relating to property as a whole, taxed at a single rate or at classified rates according to the class of property. Property refers to real property (e.g. land and structures) as well as personal property; personal property can be either tangible (e.g. automobiles and boats) or intangible (e.g. bank accounts and stocks and bonds). Special property taxes, levied on selected types of property (e.g. oil and gas properties, house trailers, motor vehicles, and intangibles) and subject to rates not directly related to general property tax rates. Taxes based on income produced by property as a measure of its value on the assessment date.

EDUCATION

Educational Attainment: Figures shown are 2007 estimates and show the percent of population age 25 and over with a:

- **High school diploma (including GED) or higher:** includes people whose highest degree was a high school diploma or its equivalent, people who attended college but did not receive a degree, and people who received a college, university, or professional degree. People who reported completing the 12th grade but not receiving a diploma are not high school graduates.
- **Bachelor's degree or higher**
- **Master's degree or higher:** Master's degrees include the traditional MA and MS degrees and field-specific degrees, such as MSW, MEd, MBA, MLS, and Meng. *Source: Claritas.*

HOUSING

Homeownership Rate: Percentage of housing units that are owner-occupied. Figures shown are 2007 estimates. *Source: Claritas.*

Median Home Value: Median value of all owner-occupied housing units as reported by the owner. Figures shown are 2007 estimates. *Source: Claritas.*

Median Rent: Median monthly contract rent on specified renter-occupied and specified vacant-for-rent units. Specified renter-occupied and specified vacant-for-rent units exclude 1-family houses on 10 acres or more. Contract rent is the monthly rent agreed to or contracted for, regardless of any furnishings, utilities, fees, meals, or services that may be included. For vacant units, it is the monthly rent asked for the rental unit at the time of enumeration. *Source: U.S. Bureau of the Census, Census of Population and Housing, 2000: Summary File 3.*

Median Age of Housing: Median age of housing was calculated by subtracting median year structure built from 2000 (e.g. if the median year structure built is 1967, the median age of housing in that area is 33 years — 2000 minus 1967). Year structure built refers to when the building was first constructed, not when it was remodeled, added to, or converted. For housing units under construction that met the housing unit definition—that is, all exterior windows, doors, and final usable floors were in place—the category "1999 or 2000" was used for tabulations. For mobile homes, houseboats, RVs, etc, the manufacturer's model year was assumed to be the year built. The data relate to the number of units built during the specified periods that were still in existence at the time of enumeration. *Source: U.S. Bureau of the Census, Census of Population and Housing, 2000: Summary File 3.*

HEALTH AND VITAL STATISTICS

Birth Rate: Estimated number of births per 10,000 population in 2006. *Source: U.S. Census Bureau, Population Estimates, July 1, 2005 - July 1 , 2006 (http://www.census.gov/popest/births.html).*

Death Rate: Estimated number of deaths per 10,000 population in 2006. *Source: U.S. Census Bureau, Population Estimates, July 1, 2005 - July 1 , 2006 (http://www.census.gov/popest/births.html).*

Age-adjusted Cancer Mortality Rate: Number of age-adjusted deaths from cancer per 100,000 population in 2004. Cancer is defined as International Classification of Disease (ICD) codes C00 - D48.9 Neoplasms. *Source: Centers for Disease Control, CDC Wonder (http://wonder.cdc.gov).*

Age-adjusted death rates are weighted averages of the age-specific death rates, where the weights represent a fixed population by age. They are used because the rates of almost all causes of death vary by age. Age adjustment is a technique for "removing" the effects of age from crude rates, so as to allow meaningful comparisons across populations with different underlying age structures. For example, comparing the crude rate of heart disease in New York to that of California is misleading, because the relatively older population in New York will lead to a higher crude death rate, even if the age-specific rates of heart disease in New York and California are the same. For such a comparison, age-adjusted rates would be preferable. Age-adjusted rates should be viewed as relative indexes rather than as direct or actual measures of mortality risk.

Death rates based on counts of twenty or less (<=20) are flagged as "Unreliable". Death rates based on fewer than three years of data for counties with populations of less than 100,000 in the 1990 Census counts, are also flagged as "Unreliable" if the number of deaths is five or less (<=5).

Air Quality Index: The percentage of days in 2006 the AQI fell into the Good (0-50), Moderate (51-100), Unhealthy for Sensitive Groups (101-150), and Unhealthy (151+) ranges. Data covers January 2006 through December 2006. Counties with less than 100 days of air quality data were excluded. *Source: Air Quality Index Report, 2006, U.S. Environmental Protection Agency, Office of Air and Radiation (http://www.epa.gov/oar).*

The AQI is an index for reporting daily air quality. It tells you how clean or polluted your air is, and what associated health concerns you should be aware of. The AQI focuses on health effects that can happen within a few hours or days after breathing polluted air. EPA uses the AQI for five major air pollutants regulated by the Clean Air Act: ground-level ozone, particulate matter, carbon monoxide, sulfur dioxide, and nitrogen dioxide. For each of these pollutants, EPA has established national air quality standards to protect against harmful health effects.

The AQI runs from 0 to 500. The higher the AQI value, the greater the level of air pollution and the greater the health danger. For example, an AQI value of 50 represents good air quality and little potential to affect public health, while an AQI value over 300 represents hazardous air quality. An AQI value of 100 generally corresponds to the national air quality standard for the pollutant, which is the level EPA has set to protect public health. So, AQI values below 100 are generally thought of as satisfactory. When AQI values are above 100, air quality is considered to be unhealthy—at first for certain sensitive groups of people, then for everyone as AQI values get higher. Each category corresponds to a different level of health concern. For example, when the AQI for a pollutant is between 51 and 100, the health concern is "Moderate." Here are the six levels of health concern and what they mean:

- "Good" The AQI value for your community is between 0 and 50. Air quality is considered satisfactory and air pollution poses little or no risk.
- "Moderate" The AQI for your community is between 51 and 100. Air quality is acceptable; however, for some pollutants there may be a moderate health concern for a very small number of individuals. For example, people who are unusually sensitive to ozone may experience respiratory symptoms.
- "Unhealthy for Sensitive Groups" Certain groups of people are particularly sensitive to the harmful effects of certain air pollutants. This means they are likely to be affected at lower levels than the general public. For example, children and adults who are active outdoors and people with respiratory disease are at greater risk from exposure to ozone, while people with heart disease are at greater risk from carbon monoxide. Some people may be sensitive to more than one pollutant. When AQI values are between 101 and 150, members of sensitive groups may experience health effects. The general public is not likely to be affected when the AQI is in this range.
- "Unhealthy" AQI values are between 151 and 200. Everyone may begin to experience health effects. Members of sensitive groups may experience more serious health effects.
- "Very Unhealthy" AQI values between 201 and 300 trigger a health alert, meaning everyone may experience more serious health effects.
- "Hazardous" AQI values over 300 trigger health warnings of emergency conditions. The entire population is more likely to be affected.

Number of Physicians: The number of active, non-federal physicians per 10,000 population in 2005. *Source: Area Resource File (ARF). June 2007. U.S. Department of Health and Human Services, Health Resources and Services Administration, Bureau of Health Professions, Rockville, MD.*

Number of Hospital Beds: The number of hospital beds per 10,000 population in 2004. *Source: Area Resource File (ARF). June 2007. U.S. Department of Health and Human Services, Health Resources and Services Administration, Bureau of Health Professions, Rockville, MD.*

Number of Hospital Admissions: The number of hospital admissions per 10,000 population in 2004. *Source: Area Resource File (ARF). June 2007. U.S. Department of Health and Human Services, Health Resources and Services Administration, Bureau of Health Professions, Rockville, MD.*

ELECTIONS

Elections: 2004 Presidential election results. *Source: Dave Leip's Atlas of U.S. Presidential Elections (http://www.uselectionatlas.org).*

NATIONAL AND STATE PARKS

Lists National and State parks located in the area. *Source: U.S. Geological Survey, Geographic Names Information System.*

ADDITIONAL INFORMATION CONTACTS

The following phone numbers are provided as sources of additional information: Chambers of Commerce; Economic Development Agencies; Boards of Realtors; Convention & Visitors Bureaus. Efforts have been made to provide the most recent area codes. However, area code changes may have occurred in listed numbers. *Source: Original research.*

User's Guide: Education

School District Rankings

Number of Schools: Total number of schools in the district. *Source: U.S. Department of Education, National Center for Education Statistics, Common Core of Data, Public Elementary/Secondary School Universe Survey: School Year 2005-2006.*

Number of Teachers: Teachers are defined as individuals who provide instruction to pre-kindergarten, kindergarten, grades 1 through 12, or ungraded classes, or individuals who teach in an environment other than a classroom setting, and who maintain daily student attendance records. Numbers reported are full-time equivalents (FTE). *Source: U.S. Department of Education, National Center for Education Statistics, Common Core of Data, Local Education Agency (School District) Universe Survey: School Year 2005-2006.*

Number of Students: A student is an individual for whom instruction is provided in an elementary or secondary education program that is not an adult education program and is under the jurisdiction of a school, school system, or other education institution. *Sources: U.S. Department of Education, National Center for Education Statistics, Common Core of Data, Local Education Agency (School District) Universe Survey: School Year 2005-2006 and Public Elementary/Secondary School Universe Survey: School Year 2005-2006*

Individual Education Program (IEP) Students: A written instructional plan for students with disabilities designated as special education students under IDEA-Part B. The written instructional plan includes a statement of present levels of educational performance of a child; statement of annual goals, including short-term instructional objectives; statement of specific educational services to be provided and the extent to which the child will be able to participate in regular educational programs; the projected date for initiation and anticipated duration of services; the appropriate objectives, criteria and evaluation procedures; and the schedules for determining, on at least an annual basis, whether instructional objectives are being achieved. *Source: U.S. Department of Education, National Center for Education Statistics, Common Core of Data, Local Education Agency (School District) Universe Survey: School Year 2005-2006*

English Language Learner (ELL) Students: Formerly referred to as Limited English Proficient (LEP). Students being served in appropriate programs of language assistance (e.g., English as a Second Language, High Intensity Language Training, bilingual education). Does not include pupils enrolled in a class to learn a language other than English. Also Limited-English-Proficient students are individuals who were not born in the United States or whose native language is a language other than English; or individuals who come from environments where a language other than English is dominant; or individuals who are American Indians and Alaskan Natives and who come from environments where a language other than English has had a significant impact on their level of English language proficiency; and who, by reason thereof, have sufficient difficulty speaking, reading, writing, or understanding the English language, to deny such individuals the opportunity to learn successfully in classrooms where the language of instruction is English or to participate fully in our society. *Source: U.S. Department of Education, National Center for Education Statistics, Common Core of Data, Local Education Agency (School District) Universe Survey: School Year 2005-2006*

Migrant Students: A migrant student as defined under federal regulation 34 CFR 200.40: 1) (a) Is younger than 22 (and has not graduated from high school or does not hold a high school equivalency certificate), but (b), if the child is too young to attend school-sponsored educational programs, is old enough to benefit from an organized instructional program; and 2) A migrant agricultural worker or a migrant fisher or has a parent, spouse, or guardian who is a migrant agricultural worker or a migrant fisher; and 3) Performs, or has a parent, spouse, or guardian who performs qualifying agricultural or fishing employment as a principal means of livelihood; and 4) Has moved within the preceding 36 months to obtain or to accompany or join a parent, spouse, or guardian to obtain, temporary or seasonal employment in agricultural or fishing work; and 5) Has moved from one school district to another; or in a state that is comprised of a single school district, has moved from one administrative area to another within such district; or resides in a school district of more than 15,000 square miles, and migrates a distance of 20 miles or more to a temporary residence to engage in a fishing activity. Provision 5 currently applies only to Alaska. *Note: Data covers the 2004-2005 school year. Source: U.S. Department of Education, National Center for Education Statistics, Common Core of Data, Public Elementary/Secondary School Universe Survey: School Year 2005-2006*

Students Eligible for Free Lunch Program: The free lunch program is defined as a program under the National School Lunch Act that provides cash subsidies for free lunches to students based on family size and income criteria. *Source: U.S. Department of Education, National Center for Education Statistics, Common Core of Data, Public Elementary/Secondary School Universe Survey: School Year 2005-2006*

Students Eligible for Reduced-Price Lunch Program: A student who is eligible to participate in the Reduced-Price Lunch Program under the National School Lunch Act. *Source: U.S. Department of Education, National Center for Education Statistics, Common Core of Data, Public Elementary/Secondary School Universe Survey: School Year 2005-2006*

Student/Teacher Ratio: The number of students divided by the number of teachers (FTE). See Number of Students and Number of Teachers above for for information.

Student/Librarian Ratio: The number of students divided by the number of library and media support staff. Library and media support staff are defined as staff members who render other professional library and media services; also includes library aides and those involved in library/media support. Their duties include selecting, preparing, caring for, and making available to instructional staff, equipment, films, filmstrips, transparencies, tapes, TV programs, and similar materials maintained separately or as part of an instructional materials center. Also included are activities in the audio-visual center, TV studio, related-work-study areas, and services provided by audio-visual personnel. Numbers are based on full-time equivalents. *Source: U.S. Department of Education, National Center for Education Statistics, Common Core of Data, Local Education Agency (School District) Universe Survey: School Year 2005-2006.*

Student/Counselor Ratio: The number of students divided by the number of guidance counselors. Guidance counselors are professional staff assigned specific duties and school time for any of the following activities in an elementary or secondary setting: counseling with students and parents; consulting with other staff members on learning problems; evaluating student abilities; assisting students in making educational and career choices; assisting students in personal and social development; providing referral assistance; and/or working with other staff members in planning and conducting guidance programs for students. The state applies its own standards in apportioning the aggregate of guidance counselors/directors into the elementary and secondary level components. Numbers reported are full-time equivalents. *Source: U.S. Department of Education, National Center for Education Statistics, Common Core of Data, Local Education Agency (School District) Universe Survey: School Year 2005-2006.*

Current Spending per Student: Expenditure for Instruction, Support Services, and Other Elementary/Secondary Programs. Includes salaries, employee benefits, purchased services, and supplies, as well as payments made by states on behalf of school districts. Also includes transfers made by school districts into their own retirement system. Excludes expenditure for Non-Elementary/Secondary Programs, debt service, capital outlay, and transfers to other governments or school districts. This item is formally called "Current Expenditures for Public Elementary/Secondary Education."

Instruction: Includes payments from all funds for salaries, employee benefits, supplies, materials, and contractual services for elementary/secondary instruction. It excludes capital outlay, debt service, and interfund transfers for elementary/secondary instruction. Instruction covers regular, special, and vocational programs offered in both the regular school year and summer school. It excludes instructional support activities as well as adult education and community services. Instruction salaries includes salaries for teachers and teacher aides and assistants.

Support Services: Relates to support services functions (series 2000) defined in Financial Accounting for Local and State School Systems (National Center for Education Statistics 2000). Includes payments from all funds for salaries, employee benefits, supplies, materials, and contractual services. It excludes capital outlay, debt service, and interfund transfers. It includes expenditure for the following functions:

- Business/Central/Other Support Services
- General Administration
- Instructional Staff Support
- Operation and Maintenance
- Pupil Support Services
- Pupil Transportation Services
- School Administration
- Nonspecified Support Services

Values shown are dollars per pupil per year. They were calculated by dividing the total dollar amounts by the fall membership. Fall membership is comprised of the total student enrollment on October 1 (or the closest school day to October 1) for all grade levels (including prekindergarten and kindergarten) and ungraded pupils. Membership includes students both present and absent on the measurement day. *Source: U.S. Department of Education, National Center for Education Statistics, Common Core of Data, School District Finance Survey (F-33), Fiscal Year 2005.*

Number of Diploma Recipients: A student who has received a diploma during the previous school year or subsequent summer school. This category includes regular diploma recipients and other diploma recipients. A High School Diploma is a formal document certifying the successful completion of a secondary school program prescribed by the state education agency or other appropriate body. *Note: The National Center for Education Statistics has not released more current district level data due to privacy issues. Source: U.S. Department of Education, National Center for Education Statistics, Common Core of Data, Local Education Agency (School District) Universe Survey: School Year 2002-2003. State data covers the 2004-2005 school year and comes from the Common Core of Data, State Nonfiscal Survey of Public Elementary/Secondary Education, 2005-06.*

High School Drop-out Rate: A dropout is a student who was enrolled in school at some time during the previous school year; was not enrolled at the beginning of the current school year; has not graduated from high school or completed a state or district approved educational program; and does not meet any of the following exclusionary conditions: has transferred to another public school district, private school, or state- or district-approved educational program; is temporarily absent due to suspension or school-approved illness; or has died. The values shown cover grades 9 through 12. *Note: The National Center for Education Statistics has not released more current district level data due to privacy issues. Source: U.S. Department of Education, National Center for Education Statistics, Common Core of Data, Local Education Agency Universe Dropout File: School Year 2001-2002*

Note: n/a indicates data not available.

State Educational Profile

Please refer to the District Rankings section in the front of this User's Guide for an explanation of data for all items except for the following:

Average Salary: The average teacher salary in 2004-2005. *Source: American Federation of Teachers, Survey & Analysis of Teacher Salary Trends 2005*

College Entrance Exam Scores:

Scholastic Aptitude Test (SAT). *Note: The College Board strongly discourages the comparison or ranking of states on the basis of SAT scores alone. Source: The College Board, Mean SAT Reasoning Test™ Critical Reading, Math, and Writing Scores by State, with Changes for Selected Years, 2006*

American College Testing Program (ACT). *ACT, 2006 Average ACT Scores by State*

National Assessment of Educational Progress (NAEP)

The National Assessment of Educational Progress (NAEP), also known as "the Nation's Report Card," is the only nationally representative and continuing assessment of what America's students know and can do in various subject areas. As a result of the "No Child Left Behind" legislation, all states are required to participate in NAEP. For more information, visit the U.S. Department of Education, National Center for Education Statistics at http://nces.ed.gov/nationsreportcard.

Florida Comprehensive Assessment Test (FCAT)

The Florida Comprehensive Assessment Test (FCAT) is part of Florida's overall plan to increase student achievement by implementing higher standards. The FCAT, administered to students in Grades 3-11, contains two basic components: criterion-referenced tests (CRT), measuring selected benchmarks in Mathematics, Reading, Science, and Writing from the Sunshine State Standards (SSS); and norm-referenced tests (NRT) in Reading and Mathematics, measuring individual student performance against national norms. For more information, visit the Florida Department of Education at http://www.fldoe.org.

User's Guide: Ancestry

Places Covered

The ranking tables are based on 886 places in Florida (except where noted). Places covered fall into one of the following categories:

402 incorporated municipalities. Municipalities are incorporated as either cities, towns or villages.

484 census designated places (CDP). The U.S. Bureau of the Census defines a CDP as "a statistical entity, defined for each decennial census according to Census Bureau guidelines, comprising a densely settled concentration of population that is not within an incorporated place, but is locally identified by a name. CDPs are delineated cooperatively by state and local officials and the Census Bureau, following Census Bureau guidelines. Beginning with Census 2000 there are no size limits."

Source of Data

The ancestries shown in this chapter were compiled from three different sections of the 2000 Census: Race; Hispanic Origin; and Ancestry. While the ancestries are sorted alphabetically for ease-of-use, it's important to note the origin of each piece of data. Data for Race and Hispanic Origin was taken from Summary File 1 (SF1) while Ancestry data was taken from Summary File 3 (SF3). The distinction is important because SF1 contains the 100-percent data, which is the information compiled from the questions asked of all people and about every housing unit. SF3 was compiled from a sample of approximately 19 million housing units (about 1 in 6 households) that received the Census 2000 long-form questionnaire.

Ancestries Based on Race

The data on race were derived from answers to the question on race that was asked of all people. The concept of race, as used by the Census Bureau, reflects self-identification by people according to the race or races with which they most closely identify. These categories are sociopolitical constructs and should not be interpreted as being scientific or anthropological in nature. Furthermore, the race categories include both racial and national-origin groups.

If an individual did not provide a race response, the race or races of the householder or other household members were assigned using specific rules of precedence of household relationship. For example, if race was missing for a natural-born child in the household, then either the race or races of the householder, another natural-born child, or the spouse of the householder were assigned. If race was not reported for anyone in the household, the race or races of a householder in a previously processed household were assigned.

African-American/Black:
  Not Hispanic
  Hispanic
Alaska Native tribes, specified:
  Alaska Athabascan
  Aleut
  Eskimo
  Tlingit-Haida
  All other tribes
Alaska Native tribes, not specified
American Indian or Alaska Native
  tribes, not specified
American Indian tribes, specified:
  Apache
  Blackfeet
  Cherokee
  Cheyenne
  Chickasaw
  Chippewa
  Choctaw
  Colville
  Comanche
  Cree

Creek
Crow
Delaware
Houma
Iroquois
Kiowa
Latin American Indians
Lumbee
Menominee
Navajo
Osage
Ottawa
Paiute
Pima
Potawatomi
Pueblo
Puget Sound Salish
Seminole
Shoshone
Sioux
Tohono O'Odham
Ute
Yakama

Yaqui
Yuman
All other tribes
American Indian tribes,
  not specified
Asian:
  Bangladeshi
  Cambodian
  Chinese, except Taiwanese
  Filipino
  Hmong
  Indian
  Indonesian
  Japanese
  Korean
  Laotian
  Malaysian
  Pakistani
  Sri Lankan
  Taiwanese
  Thai
  Vietnamese
  Other Asian, specified

Other Asian, not specified
Hawaii Native/Pacific Islander:
  Melanesian:
    Fijian
    Other Melanesian
  Micronesian:
    Guamanian/Chamorro
    Other Micronesian
  Polynesian:
    Native Hawaiian
    Samoan
    Tongan
    Other Polynesian
  Other Pacific Islander,
    specified
  Other Pacific Islander,
    not specified
White:
  Not Hispanic
  Hispanic

African American or Black: A person having origins in any of the Black racial groups of Africa. It includes people who indicate their race as "Black, African Am., or Negro," or provide written entries such as African American, Afro American, Kenyan, Nigerian, or Haitian.

American Indian or Alaska Native: A person having origins in any of the original peoples of North and South America (including Central America) and who maintain tribal affiliation or community attachment. It includes people who classified themselves as described below.

American Indian - Includes people who indicated their race as "American Indian," entered the name of an Indian tribe, or reported such entries as Canadian Indian, French American Indian, or Spanish-American Indian.

Respondents who identified themselves as American Indian were asked to report their enrolled or principal tribe. Therefore, tribal data in tabulations reflect the written entries reported on the questionnaires. Some of the entries (for example, Iroquois, Sioux, Colorado River, and Flathead) represent nations or reservations. The information on tribe is based on self identification and therefore does not reflect any designation of federally or state-recognized tribe. Information on American Indian tribes is presented in summary files. The information for Census 2000 is derived from the American Indian Tribal Classification List for the 1990 census that was updated based on a December 1997 Federal Register Notice, entitled "Indian Entities Recognized and Eligible to Receive Service From the United States Bureau of Indian Affairs," Department of the Interior, Bureau of Indian Affairs, issued by the Office of Management and Budget.

Alaska Native - Includes written responses of Eskimos, Aleuts, and Alaska Indians, as well as entries such as Arctic Slope, Inupiat, Yupik, Alutiiq, Egegik, and Pribilovian. The Alaska tribes are the Alaskan Athabascan, Tlingit, and Haida. The information for Census 2000 is based on the American Indian Tribal Classification List for the 1990 census, which was expanded to list the individual Alaska Native Villages when provided as a written response for race.

Asian: A person having origins in any of the original peoples of the Far East, Southeast Asia, or the Indian subcontinent including, for example, Cambodia, China, India, Japan, Korea, Malaysia, Pakistan, the Philippine Islands, Thailand, and Vietnam. It includes "Asian Indian," "Chinese," "Filipino," "Korean," "Japanese," "Vietnamese," and "Other Asian."

Asian Indian - Includes people who indicated their race as "Asian Indian" or identified themselves as Bengalese, Bharat, Dravidian, East Indian, or Goanese.

Chinese - Includes people who indicate their race as "Chinese" or who identify themselves as Cantonese, or Chinese American.

Filipino - Includes people who indicate their race as "Filipino" or who report entries such as Philipino, Philipine, or Filipino American.

Japanese - Includes people who indicate their race as "Japanese" or who report entries such as Nipponese or Japanese American.

Korean - Includes people who indicate their race as "Korean" or who provide a response of Korean American.

Vietnamese - Includes people who indicate their race as "Vietnamese" or who provide a response of Vietnamese American.

Cambodian - Includes people who provide a response such as Cambodian or Cambodia.

Hmong - Includes people who provide a response such as Hmong, Laohmong, or Mong.

Laotian - Includes people who provide a response such as Laotian, Laos, or Lao.

Thai - Includes people who provide a response such as Thai, Thailand, or Siamese.

Other Asian - Includes people who provide a response of Bangladeshi; Bhutanese; Burmese; Indochinese; Indonesian; Iwo Jiman; Madagascar; Malaysian; Maldivian; Nepalese; Okinawan; Pakistani; Singaporean; Sri Lankan; or Other Asian, specified and Other Asian, not specified.

Native Hawaiian or Other Pacific Islander: A person having origins in any of the original peoples of Hawaii, Guam, Samoa, or other Pacific Islands. It includes people who indicate their race as "Native Hawaiian," "Guamanian or Chamorro," "Samoan," and "Other Pacific Islander."

Native Hawaiian - Includes people who indicate their race as "Native Hawaiian" or who identify themselves as "Part Hawaiian" or "Hawaiian."

Guamanian or Chamorro - Includes people who indicate their race as such, including written entries of Chamorro or Guam.

Samoan - Includes people who indicate their race as "Samoan" or who identify themselves as American Samoan or Western Samoan.

Other Pacific Islander - Includes people who provide a write-in response of a Pacific Islander group, such as Carolinian, Chuukese (Trukese), Fijian, Kosraean, Melanesian, Micronesian, Northern Mariana Islander, Palauan, Papua New Guinean, Pohnpeian, Polynesian, Solomon Islander, Tahitian, Tokelauan, Tongan, Yapese, or Pacific Islander, not specified.

White: A person having origins in any of the original peoples of Europe, the Middle East, or North Africa. It includes people who indicate their race as "White" or report entries such as Irish, German, Italian, Lebanese, Near Easterner, Arab, or Polish.

Ancestries Based on Hispanic Origin

Hispanic or Latino:	Salvadoran	Argentinean	Uruguayan
Central American:	Other Central American	Bolivian	Venezuelan
Costa Rican	Cuban	Chilean	Other South American
Guatemalan	Dominican Republic	Colombian	Other Hispanic/Latino
Honduran	Mexican	Ecuadorian	
Nicaraguan	Puerto Rican	Paraguayan	
Panamanian	South American:	Peruvian	

The data on the Hispanic or Latino population were derived from answers to a question that was asked of all people. The terms "Spanish," "Hispanic origin," and "Latino" are used interchangeably. Some respondents identify with all three terms while others may identify with only one of these three specific terms. Hispanics or Latinos who identify with the terms "Spanish," "Hispanic," or "Latino" are those who classify themselves in one of the specific Spanish, Hispanic, or Latino categories listed on the questionnaire ("Mexican," "Puerto Rican," or "Cuban") as well as those who indicate that they are "other Spanish/Hispanic/Latino." People who do not identify with one of the specific origins listed on the questionnaire but indicate that they are "other Spanish, Hispanic, or Latino" are those whose origins are from Spain, the Spanish-speaking countries of Central or South America, the Dominican Republic, or people identifying themselves generally as Spanish, Spanish-American, Hispanic, Hispano, Latino, and so on. All write-in responses to the "other Spanish/Hispanic/Latino" category were coded.

Origin can be viewed as the heritage, nationality group, lineage, or country of birth of the person or the person's parents or ancestors before their arrival in the United States. People who identify their origin as Spanish, Hispanic, or Latino may be of any race.

In all cases where the origin of households, families, or occupied housing units is classified as Spanish, Hispanic, or Latino, the origin of the householder is used. If an individual could not provide a Hispanic origin response, their origin was assigned using specific rules of precedence of household relationship. For example, if origin was missing for a natural-born daughter in the household, then either the origin of the householder, another natural-born child, or spouse of the householder was assigned. If Hispanic origin was not reported for anyone in the household, the Hispanic origin of a householder in a previously processed household with the same race was assigned.

Other Ancestries

Acadian/Cajun	Moroccan	French, except Basque	Scottish
Afghan	Palestinian	French Canadian	Serbian
African, Subsaharan:	Syrian	German	Slavic
African	Other Arab	German Russian	Slovak
Cape Verdean	Armenian	Greek	Slovene
Ethiopian	Assyrian/Chaldean/Syriac	Guyanese	Soviet Union
Ghanian	Australian	Hungarian	Swedish
Kenyan	Austrian	Icelander	Swiss
Liberian	Basque	Iranian	Turkish
Nigerian	Belgian	Irish	Ukrainian
Senegalese	Brazilian	Israeli	United States or American
Sierra Leonean	British	Italian	Welsh
Somalian	Bulgarian	Latvian	West Indian, excluding Hispanic:
South African	Canadian	Lithuanian	Bahamian
Sudanese	Carpatho Rusyn	Luxemburger	Barbadian
Ugandan	Celtic	Macedonian	Belizean
Zairian	Croatian	Maltese	Bermudan
Zimbabwean	Cypriot	New Zealander	British West Indian
Other Subsaharan African	Czech	Northern European	Dutch West Indian
Albanian	Czechoslovakian	Norwegian	Haitian
Alsatian	Danish	Pennsylvania German	Jamaican
Arab:	Dutch	Polish	Trinidadian and
Arab/Arabic	Eastern European	Portuguese	Tobagonian
Egyptian	English	Romanian	U.S. Virgin Islander
Iraqi	Estonian	Russian	West Indian
Jordanian	European	Scandinavian	Other West Indian
Lebanese	Finnish	Scotch-Irish	Yugoslavian

The data on ancestry were derived from answers to long-form questionnaire Item 10, which was asked of a sample of the population. The data represent self-classification by people according to the ancestry group or groups with which they most closely identify. Ancestry refers to a person's ethnic origin or descent, "roots," heritage, or the place of birth of the person, the person's parents, or their ancestors before their arrival in the United States. Some ethnic identities, such as Egyptian or Polish, can be traced to geographic areas outside the United States, while other ethnicities, such as Pennsylvania German or Cajun, evolved in the United States.

The intent of the ancestry question was not to measure the degree of attachment the respondent had to a particular ethnicity. For example, a response of "Irish" might reflect total involvement in an Irish community or only a memory of ancestors several generations removed from the individual. Also, the question was intended to provide data for groups that were not included in the Hispanic origin and race questions. Official Hispanic origin data come from long-form questionnaire Item 5, and official race data come from long-form questionnaire Item 6. Therefore, although data on all groups are collected, the ancestry data shown in these tabulations are for non-Hispanic and non-race groups.

The ancestry question allowed respondents to report one or more ancestry groups, although only the first two were coded. If a response was in terms of a dual ancestry, for example, "Irish English," the person was assigned two codes, in this case one for Irish and another for English. However, in certain cases, multiple responses such as "French Canadian," "Greek Cypriote," and "Scotch Irish" were assigned a single code reflecting their status as unique groups. If a person reported one of these unique groups in addition to another group, for example, "Scotch Irish English," resulting in three terms, that person received one code for the unique group (Scotch-Irish) and another one for the remaining group (English). If a person reported "English Irish French," only English and Irish were coded. Certain combinations of ancestries where the ancestry group is a part of another, such as "German-Bavarian," were coded as a single ancestry using the more specific group (Bavarian). Also, responses such as "Polish-American" or "Italian-American" were coded and tabulated as a single entry (Polish or Italian).

The Census Bureau accepted "American" as a unique ethnicity if it was given alone, with an ambiguous response, or with state names. If the respondent listed any other ethnic identity such as "Italian-American," generally the "American" portion of the response was not coded. However, distinct groups such as "American Indian," "Mexican American," and "African American" were coded and identified separately because they represented groups who considered themselves different from those who reported as "Indian," "Mexican," or "African," respectively.

Census 2000 tabulations on ancestry are presented using two types of data presentations — one using total people as the base, and the other using total responses as the base. This chapter uses total responses as the base and includes the total number of ancestries reported and coded. If a person reported a multiple ancestry such as "French Danish," that response was counted twice in the tabulations — once in the French category and again in the Danish category. Thus, the sum of the counts in this type of presentation is not the total population but the total of all responses.

An automated coding system was used for coding ancestry in Census 2000. This greatly reduced the potential for error associated with a clerical review. Specialists with knowledge of the subject matter reviewed, edited, coded, and resolved inconsistent or incomplete responses. The code list used in Census 2000, containing over 1,000 categories, reflects the results of the Census Bureau's experience with the 1990 ancestry question, research, and consultation with many ethnic experts. Many decisions were made to determine the classification of responses. These decisions affected the grouping of the tabulated data. For example, the Italian category includes the responses of Sicilian and Tuscan, as well as a number of other responses.

Although some people consider religious affiliation a component of ethnic identity, the ancestry question was not designed to collect any information concerning religion. Thus, if a religion was given as an answer to the ancestry question, it was listed in the "Other groups" category which is not shown in this chapter.

Ancestry should not be confused with a person's place of birth, although a person's place of birth and ancestry may be the same.

Ranking Section

In the ranking section of this chapter, each ancestry has three tables. The first table shows the top 10 places sorted by number (based on all places, regardless of population), the second table shows the top 10 places sorted by percent (based on all places, regardless of population), the third table shows the top 10 places sorted by percent (based on places with populations of 10,000 or more).

Within each table, column one displays the place name, the state, and the county (if a place spans more than one county, the county that holds the majority of the population is shown). Column two displays the number of people reporting each ancestry, and column three is the percent of the total population reporting each ancestry. For tables representing ancestries based on race or Hispanic origin, the 100-percent population figure from SF1 is used to calculate the value in the "%" column. For all other ancestries the sample population figure from SF3 is used to calculate the value in the "%" column.

Alphabetical Ancestry Cross-Reference Guide

Acadian/Cajun
Afghan
African *See African, sub-Saharan: African*
African American/Black
African American/Black: Hispanic
African American/Black: Not Hispanic
African, sub-Saharan
African, sub-Saharan: African
African, sub-Saharan: Cape Verdean
African, sub-Saharan: Ethiopian
African, sub-Saharan: Ghanian
African, sub-Saharan: Kenyan
African, sub-Saharan: Liberian
African, sub-Saharan: Nigerian
African, sub-Saharan: Other
African, sub-Saharan: Senegalese
African, sub-Saharan: Sierra Leonean
African, sub-Saharan: Somalian
African, sub-Saharan: South African
African, sub-Saharan: Sudanese
African, sub-Saharan: Ugandan
African, sub-Saharan: Zairian
African, sub-Saharan: Zimbabwean
Alaska Athabascan *See Alaska Native: Alaska Athabascan*
Alaska Native tribes, not specified
Alaska Native tribes, specified
Alaska Native: Alaska Athabascan
Alaska Native: Aleut
Alaska Native: All other tribes
Alaska Native: Eskimo
Alaska Native: Tlingit-Haida
Albanian
Aleut *See Alaska Native: Aleut*
Alsatian
American *See United States or American*
American Indian or Alaska Native tribes, not specified
American Indian tribes, not specified
American Indian tribes, specified
American Indian: All other tribes
American Indian: Apache
American Indian: Blackfeet
American Indian: Cherokee
American Indian: Cheyenne
American Indian: Chickasaw
American Indian: Chippewa
American Indian: Choctaw
American Indian: Colville
American Indian: Comanche
American Indian: Cree
American Indian: Creek
American Indian: Crow
American Indian: Delaware
American Indian: Houma
American Indian: Iroquois
American Indian: Kiowa
American Indian: Latin American Indians
American Indian: Lumbee
American Indian: Menominee
American Indian: Navajo
American Indian: Osage
American Indian: Ottawa
American Indian: Paiute
American Indian: Pima
American Indian: Potawatomi
American Indian: Pueblo
American Indian: Puget Sound Salish
American Indian: Seminole
American Indian: Shoshone

American Indian: Sioux
American Indian: Tohono O'Odham
American Indian: Ute
American Indian: Yakama
American Indian: Yaqui
American Indian: Yuman
Apache *See American Indian: Apache*
Arab
Arab/Arabic *See Arab: Arab/Arabic*
Arab: Arab/Arabic
Arab: Egyptian
Arab: Iraqi
Arab: Jordanian
Arab: Lebanese
Arab: Moroccan
Arab: Other
Arab: Palestinian
Arab: Syrian
Argentinean *See Hispanic: Argentinean*
Armenian
Asian
Asian: Bangladeshi
Asian: Cambodian
Asian: Chinese, except Taiwanese
Asian: Filipino
Asian: Hmong
Asian: Indian
Asian: Indonesian
Asian: Japanese
Asian: Korean
Asian: Laotian
Asian: Malaysian
Asian: Other Asian, not specified
Asian: Other Asian, specified
Asian: Pakistani
Asian: Sri Lankan
Asian: Taiwanese
Asian: Thai
Asian: Vietnamese
Assyrian/Chaldean/Syriac
Australian
Austrian
Bahamian *See West Indian: Bahamian, excluding Hispanic*
Bangladeshi *See Asian: Bangladeshi*
Barbadian *See West Indian: Barbadian, excluding Hispanic*
Basque
Belgian
Belizean *See West Indian: Belizean, excluding Hispanic*
Bermudan *See West Indian: Bermudan, excluding Hispanic*
Blackfeet *See American Indian: Blackfeet*
Bolivian *See Hispanic: Bolivian*
Brazilian
British
British West Indian *See West Indian: British West Indian, excluding Hispanic*
Bulgarian
Cambodian *See Asian: Cambodian*
Canadian
Cape Verdean *See African, sub-Saharan: Cape Verdean*
Carpatho Rusyn
Celtic
Central American: *See Hispanic: Central American*
Cherokee *See American Indian: Cherokee*

Cheyenne *See American Indian: Cheyenne*
Chickasaw *See American Indian: Chickasaw*
Chilean *See Hispanic: Chilean*
Chinese, except Taiwanese *See Asian: Chinese, except Taiwanese*
Chippewa *See American Indian: Chippewa*
Choctaw *See American Indian: Choctaw*
Colombian *See Hispanic: Colombian*
Colville *See American Indian: Colville*
Comanche *See American Indian: Comanche*
Costa Rican *See Hispanic: Costa Rican*
Cree *See American Indian: Cree*
Creek *See American Indian: Creek*
Croatian
Crow *See American Indian: Crow*
Cuban *See Hispanic: Cuban*
Cypriot
Czech
Czechoslovakian
Danish
Delaware *See American Indian: Delaware*
Dominican Republic *See Hispanic: Dominican Republic*
Dutch
Dutch West Indian *See West Indian: Dutch West Indian, excluding Hispanic*
Eastern European
Ecuadorian *See Hispanic: Ecuadorian*
Egyptian *See Arab: Egyptian*
English
Eskimo *See Alaska Native: Eskimo*
Estonian
Ethiopian *See African, sub-Saharan: Ethiopian*
European
Fijian *See Hawaii Native/Pacific Islander: Fijian*
Filipino *See Asian: Filipino*
Finnish
French Canadian
French, except Basque
German
German Russian
Ghanian *See African, sub-Saharan: Ghanian*
Greek
Guamanian or Chamorro *See Hawaii Native/Pacific Islander: Guamanian or Chamorro*
Guatemalan *See Hispanic: Guatemalan*
Guyanese
Haitian *See West Indian: Haitian, excluding Hispanic*
Hawaii Native/Pacific Islander
Hawaii Native/Pacific Islander: Fijian
Hawaii Native/Pacific Islander: Guamanian or Chamorro
Hawaii Native/Pacific Islander: Melanesian
Hawaii Native/Pacific Islander: Micronesian
Hawaii Native/Pacific Islander: Native Hawaiian
Hawaii Native/Pacific Islander: Other Melanesian
Hawaii Native/Pacific Islander: Other Micronesian

Hawaii Native/Pacific Islander: Other Pacific Islander, not specified
Hawaii Native/Pacific Islander: Other Pacific Islander, specified
Hawaii Native/Pacific Islander: Other Polynesian
Hawaii Native/Pacific Islander: Polynesian
Hawaii Native/Pacific Islander: Samoan
Hawaii Native/Pacific Islander: Tongan
Hispanic or Latino
Hispanic: Argentinean
Hispanic: Bolivian
Hispanic: Central American
Hispanic: Chilean
Hispanic: Colombian
Hispanic: Costa Rican
Hispanic: Cuban
Hispanic: Dominican Republic
Hispanic: Ecuadorian
Hispanic: Guatemalan
Hispanic: Honduran
Hispanic: Mexican
Hispanic: Nicaraguan
Hispanic: Other
Hispanic: Other Central American
Hispanic: Other South American
Hispanic: Panamanian
Hispanic: Paraguayan
Hispanic: Peruvian
Hispanic: Puerto Rican
Hispanic: Salvadoran
Hispanic: South American
Hispanic: Uruguayan
Hispanic: Venezuelan
Hmong *See Asian: Hmong*
Honduran *See Hispanic: Honduran*
Houma *See American Indian: Houma*
Hungarian
Icelander
Indian, American *See American Indian*
Indian, Asian *See Asian: Indian*
Indonesian *See Asian: Indonesian*
Iranian
Iraqi *See Arab: Iraqi*
Irish
Iroquois *See American Indian: Iroquois*
Israeli
Italian
Jamaican *See West Indian: Jamaican, excluding Hispanic*
Japanese *See Asian: Japanese*
Jordanian *See Arab: Jordanian*
Kenyan *See African, sub-Saharan: Kenyan*
Kiowa *See American Indian: Kiowa*
Korean *See Asian: Korean*
Laotian *See Asian: Laotian*
Latin American Indians *See American Indian: Latin American Indians*
Latino *See Hispanic or Latino*
Latvian
Lebanese *See Arab: Lebanese*
Liberian *See African, sub-Saharan: Liberian*
Lithuanian
Lumbee *See American Indian: Lumbee*
Luxemburger
Macedonian
Malaysian *See Asian: Malaysian*
Maltese
Melanesian: *See Hawaii Native/Pacific Islander: Melanesian*

Menominee *See American Indian: Menominee*
Mexican *See Hispanic: Mexican*
Micronesian: *See Hawaii Native/Pacific Islander: Micronesian*
Moroccan *See Arab: Moroccan*
Native Hawaiian *See Hawaii Native/Pacific Islander: Native Hawaiian*
Navajo *See American Indian: Navajo*
New Zealander
Nicaraguan *See Hispanic: Nicaraguan*
Nigerian *See African, sub-Saharan: Nigerian*
Northern European
Norwegian
Osage *See American Indian: Osage*
Ottawa *See American Indian: Ottawa*
Paiute *See American Indian: Paiute*
Pakistani *See Asian: Pakistani*
Palestinian *See Arab: Palestinian*
Panamanian *See Hispanic: Panamanian*
Paraguayan *See Hispanic: Paraguayan*
Pennsylvania German
Peruvian *See Hispanic: Peruvian*
Pima *See American Indian: Pima*
Polish
Polynesian: *See Hawaii Native/Pacific Islander: Polynesian*
Portuguese
Potawatomi *See American Indian: Potawatomi*
Pueblo *See American Indian: Pueblo*
Puerto Rican *See Hispanic: Puerto Rican*
Puget Sound Salish *See American Indian: Puget Sound Salish*
Romanian
Russian
Salvadoran *See Hispanic: Salvadoran*
Samoan *See Hawaii Native/Pacific Islander: Samoan*
Scandinavian
Scotch-Irish
Scottish
Seminole *See American Indian: Seminole*
Senegalese *See African, sub-Saharan: Senegalese*
Serbian
Shoshone *See American Indian: Shoshone*
Sierra Leonean *See African, sub-Saharan: Sierra Leonean*
Sioux *See American Indian: Sioux*
Slavic
Slovak
Slovene
Somalian *See African, sub-Saharan: Somalian*
South African *See African, sub-Saharan: South African*
South American: *See Hispanic: South American*
Soviet Union
Sri Lankan *See Asian: Sri Lankan*
sub-Saharan African *See African, sub-Saharan*
Sudanese *See African, sub-Saharan: Sudanese*
Swedish
Swiss
Syrian *See Arab: Syrian*
Taiwanese *See Asian: Taiwanese*
Thai *See Asian: Thai*

Tlingit-Haida *See Alaska Native: Tlingit-Haida*
Tohono O'Odham *See American Indian: Tohono O'Odham*
Tongan *See Hawaii Native/Pacific Islander: Tongan*
Trinidadian and Tobagonian *See West Indian: Trinidadian and Tobagonian, excluding Hispanic*
Turkish
U.S. Virgin Islander *See West Indian: U.S. Virgin Islander, excluding Hispanic*
Ugandan *See African, sub-Saharan: Ugandan*
Ukrainian
United States or American
Uruguayan *See Hispanic: Uruguayan*
Ute *See American Indian: Ute*
Venezuelan *See Hispanic: Venezuelan*
Vietnamese *See Asian: Vietnamese*
Welsh
West Indian, excluding Hispanic
West Indian: Bahamian, excluding Hispanic
West Indian: Barbadian, excluding Hispanic
West Indian: Belizean, excluding Hispanic
West Indian: Bermudan, excluding Hispanic
West Indian: British West Indian, excluding Hispanic
West Indian: Dutch West Indian, excluding Hispanic
West Indian: Haitian, excluding Hispanic
West Indian: Jamaican, excluding Hispanic
West Indian: Other, excluding Hispanic
West Indian: Trinidadian and Tobagonian, excluding Hispanic
West Indian: U.S. Virgin Islander, excluding Hispanic
West Indian: West Indian, excluding Hispanic
White
White: Hispanic
White: Not Hispanic
Yakama *See American Indian: Yakama*
Yaqui *See American Indian: Yaqui*
Yugoslavian
Yuman *See American Indian: Yuman*
Zairian *See African, sub-Saharan: Zairian*
Zimbabwean *See African, sub-Saharan: Zimbabwean*

User's Guide: Hispanic Population

Places Covered

Ranking tables cover all counties and all places in Florida with populations of 10,000 or more.

Source of Data

CENSUS 2000

Data for this chapter was derived from following source: *U.S. Bureau of the Census, Census of Population and Housing, 2000: Summary File 4*. Summary File 4 (SF 4) contains sample data, which is the information compiled from the questions asked of a sample (generally 1-in-6) of all people and housing units. Summary File 4 is repeated or iterated for the total population and 335 additional population groups. This chapter focuses on the following 24 population groups:

Hispanic or Latino (of any race)
    Central American
        Costa Rican
        Guatemalan
        Honduran
        Nicaraguan
        Panamanian
        Salvadoran
    Cuban
    Dominican (Dominican Republic)
    Mexican
    Puerto Rican
    South American
        Argentinian
        Bolivian
        Chilean
        Colombian
        Ecuadorian
        Paraguayan
        Peruvian
        Uruguayan
        Venezuelan
    Spaniard
    Other Hispanic or Latino

Please note that the above list only includes Spanish-speaking population groups. Groups such as Brazilian are not classified as Hispanic by the Bureau of the Census because they primarily speak Portugese.

In order for any of the tables for a specific group to be shown in Summary File 4, the data must meet a minimum population threshold. For Summary File 4, all tables are repeated for each race group, American Indian and Alaska Native tribe, and Hispanic or Latino group if the 100-percent count of people of that specific group in a particular geographic area is 100 or more. There also must be 50 or more unweighted people of that specific group in a particular geographic area. For example, if there are 100 or more 100-percent people tabulated as Chilean in County A, and there are 50 or more unweighted people, then all matrices for Chilean are shown in SF 4 for County A.

To maintain confidentiality, the Census Bureau applies statistical procedures that introduce some uncertainty into data for small geographic areas with small population groups. Therefore, tables may contain both sampling and nonsampling error.

In an iterated file such as SF 4, the universes *households, families,* and *occupied housing units* are classified by the race or ethnic group of the householder. In any population table where there is no note, the universe classification is always based on the race or ethnicity of the person. In all housing tables, the universe classification is based on the race or ethnicity of the householder.

Comparing SF 4 Estimates with Corresponding Values in SF 1 and SF 2

As in earlier censuses, the responses from the sample of households reporting on long forms must be weighted to reflect the entire population. Specifically, each responding household represents, on average, six or seven other households who reported using short forms. One consequence of the weighting procedures is that each estimate based on the long form responses has an associated confidence interval. These confidence intervals are wider (as a percentage of the estimate) for geographic areas with smaller populations and for characteristics that occur less frequently in the area being examined (such as the proportion of people in poverty in a middle-income neighborhood). In order to release as much useful information as possible, statisticians must balance a number of factors. In particular, for Census 2000, the Bureau of the Census created weighting areas—geographic areas from which about two hundred or more long forms were completed—which are large enough to produce good quality estimates. If smaller weighting areas had been used, the confidence intervals around the estimates would have been significantly wider, rendering many estimates less useful due to their lower reliability. The disadvantage of using weighting areas this large is that, for smaller geographic areas within them, the estimates of characteristics that are also reported on the short form will not match the counts reported in SF 1 or SF 2. Examples of these characteristics are the total number of people, the number of people reporting specific racial categories, and the number of housing units. The official values for items reported on the short form come from SF 1 and SF 2. The differences between the long form estimates in SF 4 and values in SF 1 or SF 2 are particularly noticeable for the smallest places, tracts, and block groups. The long form estimates of total population and total housing units in SF 4 will, however, match the SF 1 and SF 2 counts for larger geographic areas such as counties and states, and will be essentially the same for medium and large cities. This phenomenon also occurred for the 1990 Census, although in that case, the weighting areas included relatively small places. As a result, the long form estimates matched the short form counts for those places, but the confidence intervals around the estimates of characteristics collected only on the long form were often significantly wider (as a percentage of the estimate). SF 1 gives exact numbers even for very small groups and areas; whereas, SF 4 gives estimates for small groups and areas such as tracts and small places that are less exact. The goal of SF 4 is to identify large differences among areas or large changes over time. Estimates for small areas and small population groups often do exhibit large changes from one census to the next, so having the capability to measure them is worthwhile.

Topics

POPULATION

Total Population: Sample count of total population.

Hispanic Population: The data on the Hispanic or Latino population, which was asked of all people, were derived from answers to long-form questionnaire Item 5, and short-form questionnaire Item 7. The terms "Spanish," "Hispanic origin," and "Latino" are used interchangeably. Some respondents identify with all three terms, while others may identify with only one of these three specific terms. Hispanics or Latinos who identify with the terms "Spanish," "Hispanic," or "Latino" are those who classify themselves in one of the specific Hispanic or Latino categories listed on the questionnaire — "Mexican," "Puerto Rican," or "Cuban" — as well as those who indicate that they are "other Spanish, Hispanic, or Latino." People who do not identify with one of the specific origins listed on the questionnaire but indicate that they are "other Spanish, Hispanic, or Latino" are those whose origins are from Spain, the Spanish-speaking countries of Central or South America, the Dominican Republic, or people identifying themselves generally as Spanish, Spanish-American, Hispanic, Hispano, Latino, and so on. All write-in responses to the "other Spanish/Hispanic/Latino" category were coded. Origin can be viewed as the heritage, nationality group, lineage, or country of birth of the person or the person's parents or ancestors before their arrival in the United States. People who identify their origin as Spanish, Hispanic, or Latino may be of any race.

Population groups whose primary language is not Spanish are not classified as Hispanic by the Bureau of the Census and are not included in this chapter (eg. Brazilian).

AGE

Median Age: Divides the age distribution into two equal parts: one-half of the cases falling below the median age and one-half above the median. Median age is computed on the basis of a single year of age standard distribution.

The data on age, which was asked of all people, were derived from answers to the long-form questionnaire Item 4 and short-form questionnaire Item 6. The age classification is based on the age of the person in complete years as of April 1, 2000. The age of the person usually was derived from their date of birth information. Their reported age was used only when date of birth information was unavailable.

HOUSEHOLD SIZE

Average Household Size: A measure obtained by dividing the number of people in households by the total number of households (or householders). In cases where household members are tabulated by race or Hispanic origin, household members are classified by the race or Hispanic origin of the householder rather than the race or Hispanic origin of each individual. Average household size is rounded to the nearest hundredth.

LANGUAGE SPOKEN AT HOME

English Only: Number and percentage of population 5 years and over who report speaking English-only at home.

Spanish: Number and percentage of population 5 years and over who report speaking Spanish at home.

Language spoken at home data were derived from answers to long-form questionnaire Items 11a and 11b, which were asked of a sample of the population. Data were edited to include in tabulations only the population 5 years old and over. Questions 11a and 11b referred to languages spoken at home in an effort to measure the current use of languages other than English. People who knew languages other than English but did not use them at home or who only used them elsewhere were excluded. Most people who reported speaking a language other than English at home also speak English. The questions did not permit determination of the primary or dominant language of people who spoke both English and another language.

FOREIGN-BORN

Foreign Born: Number and percentage of population who were not U.S. citizens at birth. Foreign-born people are those who indicated they were either a U.S. citizen by naturalization or they were not a citizen of the United States.

Foreign-Born Naturalized Citizens: Number and percentage of population who were not U.S. citizens at birth but became U.S. citizens by naturalization.

The data on place of birth were derived from answers to long-form questionnaire Item 12 which was asked of a sample of the population. Respondents were asked to report the U.S. state, Puerto Rico, U.S. Island Area, or foreign country where they were born. People not reporting a place of birth were assigned the state or country of birth of another family member or their residence 5 years earlier, or were imputed the response of another person with similar characteristics. People born outside the United States were asked to report their place of birth according to current international boundaries. Since numerous changes in boundaries of foreign countries have occurred in the last century, some people may have reported their place of birth in terms of boundaries that existed at the time of their birth or emigration, or in accordance with their own national preference.

EDUCATIONAL ATTAINMENT

High School Graduates: Number and percentage of the population age 25 and over who have a high school diploma or higher. This category includes people whose highest degree was a high school diploma or its equivalent, people who attended college but did not receive a degree, and people who received a college, university, or professional degree. People who reported completing the 12th grade but not receiving a diploma are not high school graduates.

4-Years College Graduates: Number and percentage of the population age 25 and over who have a 4-year college, university, or professional degree.

Data on educational attainment were derived from answers to long-form questionnaire Item 9, which was asked of a sample of the population. Data on attainment are tabulated for the population 25 years old and over.

The order in which degrees were listed on the questionnaire suggested that doctorate degrees were "higher" than professional school degrees, which were "higher" than master's degrees. The question included instructions for people currently enrolled in school to report the level of the previous grade attended or the highest degree received. Respondents who did not report educational attainment or enrollment level were assigned the attainment of a person of the same age, race, Hispanic or Latino origin, occupation and sex, where possible, who resided in the same or a nearby area. Respondents who filled more than one box were edited to the highest level or degree reported.

The question included a response category that allowed respondents to report completing the 12th grade without receiving a high school diploma. It allowed people who received either a high school diploma or the equivalent (Test of General Educational Development—G.E.D.) and did not attend college, to be reported as "high school graduate(s)." The category "Associate degree" included people whose highest degree is an associate degree, which generally requires 2 years of college level work and is either in an occupational program that prepares them for a specific occupation, or an academic program primarily in the arts and sciences. The course work may or may not be transferable to a bachelor's degree. Master's degrees include the traditional MA and MS degrees and field-specific degrees, such as MSW, MEd, MBA, MLS, and MEng. Some examples of professional degrees include medicine, dentistry, chiropractic, optometry, osteopathic medicine, pharmacy, podiatry, veterinary medicine, law, and theology. Vocational and technical training such as barber school training; business, trade, technical, and vocational schools; or other training for a specific trade, are specifically excluded.

INCOME AND POVERTY

Median Household Income (in dollars): Includes the income of the householder and all other individuals 15 years old and over in the household, whether they are related to the householder or not. The median divides the income distribution into two equal parts: one-half of the cases falling below the median income and one-half above the median. For households, the median income is based on the distribution of the total number of households including those with no income. Median income for households is computed on the basis of a standard distribution and is rounded to the nearest whole dollar.

Per Capita Income (in dollars): Per capita income is the mean income computed for every man, woman, and child in a particular group. It is derived by dividing the total income of a particular group by the total population in that group. Per capita income is rounded to the nearest whole dollar.

The data on income in 1999 were derived from answers to long-form questionnaire Items 31 and 32, which were asked of a sample of the population 15 years old and over. "Total income" is the sum of the amounts reported separately for wage or salary income; net self-employment income; interest, dividends, or net rental or royalty income or income from estates and trusts; social security or railroad retirement income; Supplemental Security Income (SSI); public assistance or welfare payments; retirement, survivor, or disability pensions; and all other income.

Receipts from the following sources are not included as income: capital gains, money received from the sale of property (unless the recipient was engaged in the business of selling such property); the value of income "in kind" from food stamps, public housing subsidies, medical care, employer contributions for individuals, etc.; withdrawal of bank deposits; money borrowed; tax refunds; exchange of money between relatives living in the same household; and gifts and lump-sum inheritances, insurance payments, and other types of lump-sum receipts.

The eight types of income reported in the census are defined as follows:

Wage or salary income. Wage or salary income includes total money earnings received for work performed as an employee during the calendar year 1999. It includes wages, salary, armed forces pay, commissions, tips, piece-rate payments, and cash bonuses earned before deductions were made for taxes, bonds, pensions, union dues, etc.

Self-employment income. Self-employment income includes both farm and nonfarm self-employment income. Nonfarm self-employment income includes net money income (gross receipts minus expenses) from one's own business, professional enterprise, or partnership. Gross receipts include the value of all goods sold and services rendered. Expenses include costs of goods purchased, rent, heat, light, power, depreciation charges, wages and salaries paid, business taxes (not personal income taxes), etc. Farm self-employment income includes net money income (gross receipts minus operating expenses) from the operation of a farm by a person on his or her own account, as an owner, renter, or sharecropper. Gross receipts include the value of all products sold, government farm programs, money received from the rental of farm equipment to others, and incidental receipts from the sale of wood, sand, gravel, etc. Operating expenses include cost of feed, fertilizer, seed, and other farming supplies, cash wages paid to farmhands, depreciation charges, cash rent, interest on farm mortgages, farm building repairs, farm taxes (not state and federal personal income taxes), etc. The value of fuel, food, or other farm products used for family living is not included as part of net income.

Interest, dividends, or net rental income. Interest, dividends, or net rental income includes interest on savings or bonds, dividends from stockholdings or membership in associations, net income from rental of property to others and receipts from boarders or lodgers, net royalties, and periodic payments from an estate or trust fund.

Social Security income. Social security income includes social security pensions and survivors benefits, permanent disability insurance payments made by the Social Security Administration prior to deductions for medical insurance, and railroad retirement insurance checks from the U.S. government. Medicare reimbursements are not included.

Supplemental Security Income (SSI). Supplemental Security Income (SSI) is a nationwide U.S. assistance program administered by the Social Security Administration that guarantees a minimum level of income for needy aged, blind, or disabled individuals. The census questionnaire for Puerto Rico asked about the receipt of SSI; however, SSI is not a federally administered program in Puerto Rico. Therefore, it is probably not being interpreted by most respondents as the same as SSI in the United States. The only way a resident of Puerto Rico could have appropriately reported SSI would have been if they lived in the United States at any time during calendar year 1999 and received SSI.

Public assistance income. Public assistance income includes general assistance and Temporary Assistance to Needy Families (TANF). Separate payments received for hospital or other medical care (vendor payments) are excluded. This does not include Supplemental Security Income (SSI).

Retirement income. Retirement income includes: (1) retirement pensions and survivor benefits from a former employer; labor union; or federal, state, or local government; and the U.S. military; (2) income from workers' compensation; disability income from companies or unions; federal, state, or local government; and the U.S. military; (3) periodic receipts from annuities and insurance; and (4) regular income from IRA and KEOGH plans. This does not include social security income.

All other income. All other income includes unemployment compensation, Veterans' Administration (VA) payments, alimony and child support, contributions received periodically from people not living in the household, military family allotments, and other kinds of periodic income other than earnings.

Poverty Status: Number and percentage of population with income in 1999 below the poverty level. Based on individuals for whom poverty status is determined. Poverty status was determined for all people except institutionalized people, people in military group quarters, people in college dormitories, and unrelated individuals under 15 years old.

The poverty status of families and unrelated individuals in 1999 was determined using 48 thresholds (income cutoffs) arranged in a two dimensional matrix. The matrix consists of family size (from 1 person to 9 or more people) cross-classified by presence and number of family members under 18 years old (from no children present to 8 or more children present). Unrelated individuals and 2-person families were further differentiated by the age of the reference person (RP) (under 65 years old and 65 years old and over).

To determine a person's poverty status, one compares the person's total family income with the poverty threshold appropriate for that person's family size and composition. If the total income of that person's family is less than the threshold appropriate for that family, then the person is considered poor, together with every member of his or her family. If a person is not living with anyone related by birth, marriage, or adoption, then the person's own income is compared with his or her poverty threshold.

HOUSING

Homeownership: Number and percentage of housing units that are owner-occupied.

The data on tenure, which was asked at all occupied housing units, were obtained from answers to long-form questionnaire Item 33, and short-form questionnaire Item 2. All occupied housing units are classified as either owner occupied or renter occupied.

A housing unit is owner occupied if the owner or co-owner lives in the unit even if it is mortgaged or not fully paid for. The owner or co-owner must live in the unit and usually is Person 1 on the questionnaire. The unit is "Owned by you or someone in this household with a mortgage or loan" if it is being purchased with a mortgage or some other debt arrangement, such as a deed of trust, trust deed, contract to purchase, land contract, or purchase agreement. The unit is also considered owned with a mortgage if it is built on leased land and there is a mortgage on the unit. Mobile homes occupied by owners with installment loans balances are also included in this category.

Median Gross Rent (in dollars): Median monthly gross rent on specified renter-occupied and specified vacant-for-rent units. Specified renter-occupied and specified vacant-for-rent units exclude 1-family houses on 10 acres or more.

The data on gross rent were obtained from answers to long-form questionnaire Items 45a-d, which were asked on a sample basis. Gross rent is the contract rent plus the estimated average monthly cost of utilities (electricity, gas, water and sewer) and fuels (oil, coal, kerosene, wood, etc.) if these are paid by the renter (or paid for the renter by someone else). Gross rent is intended to eliminate differentials that result from varying practices with respect to the inclusion of utilities and fuels as part of the rental payment. The estimated costs of utilities and fuels are reported on an annual basis but are converted to monthly figures for the tabulations. Renter units occupied without payment of cash rent are shown separately as "No cash rent" in the tabulations.

Housing units that are renter occupied without payment of cash rent are shown separately as "No cash rent" in census data products. The unit may be owned by friends or relatives who live elsewhere and who allow occupancy without charge. Rent-free houses or apartments may be provided to compensate caretakers, ministers, tenant farmers, sharecroppers, or others.

Contract rent is the monthly rent agreed to or contracted for, regardless of any furnishings, utilities, fees, meals, or services that may be included. For vacant units, it is the monthly rent asked for the rental unit at the time of enumeration.

If the contract rent includes rent for a business unit or for living quarters occupied by another household, only that part of the rent estimated to be for the respondent's unit was included. Excluded was any rent paid for additional units or for business premises.

If a renter pays rent to the owner of a condominium or cooperative, and the condominium fee or cooperative carrying charge also is paid by the renter to the owner, the condominium fee or carrying charge was included as rent.

If a renter receives payments from lodgers or roomers who are listed as members of the household, the rent without deduction for any payments received from the lodgers or roomers was to be reported. The respondent was to report the rent agreed to or contracted for even if paid by someone else such as friends or relatives living elsewhere, a church or welfare agency, or the government through subsidies or vouchers.

The median divides the rent distribution into two equal parts: one-half of the cases falling below the median contract rent and one-half above the median. Median contract rents are computed on the basis of a standard distribution and are rounded to the nearest whole dollar. Units reported as "No cash rent" are excluded.

Median Home Value (in dollars): Reported by the owner of specified owner-occupied or specified vacant-for-sale housing units. Specified owner-occupied and specified vacant-for-sale housing units include only 1-family houses on less than 10 acres without a business or medical office on the property. The data for "specified units" exclude mobile homes, houses with a business or medical office, houses on 10 or more acres, and housing units in multi-unit buildings.

The data on value (also referred to as "price asked" for vacant units) were obtained from answers to long-form questionnaire Item 51, which was asked on a sample basis at owner-occupied housing units and units that were being bought, or vacant for sale at the time of enumeration. Value is the respondent's estimate of how much the property (house and lot, mobile home and lot, or condominium unit) would sell for if it were for sale. If the house or mobile home was owned or being bought, but the land on which it sits was not, the respondent was asked to estimate the combined value of the house or mobile home and the land. For vacant units, value was the price asked for the property. Value was tabulated separately for all owner-occupied and vacant-for-sale housing units, owner-occupied and vacant-for-sale mobile homes, and specified owner-occupied and specified vacant-for-sale housing units.

The median divides the value distribution into two equal parts: one-half of the cases falling below the median value of the property (house and lot, mobile home and lot, or condominium unit) and one-half above the median. Median values are computed on the basis of a standard distribution and are rounded to the nearest hundred dollars.

User's Guide: Asian Population

Places Covered

Ranking tables cover all counties and places in Florida with Asian and/or Native Hawaiian and other Pacific Islander residents.

Source of Data

CENSUS 2000

Data for this chapter was derived from following source: *U.S. Bureau of the Census, Census of Population and Housing, 2000: Summary File 4*. Summary File 4 (SF 4) contains sample data, which is the information compiled from the questions asked of a sample (generally 1-in-6) of all people and housing units. Summary File 4 is repeated or iterated for the total population and 335 additional population groups. This chapter focuses on the following 23 population groups:

Asian
    Asian Indian
    Bangladeshi
    Cambodian
    Chinese (except Taiwanese)
    Filipino
    Hmong
    Indonesian
    Japanese
    Korean
    Laotian
    Malaysian
    Pakistani
    Sri Lankan
    Taiwanese
    Thai
    Vietnamese
Native Hawaiian and Other Pacific Islander
    Fijian
    Guamanian or Chamorro
    Hawaiian, Native
    Samoan
    Tongan

Please note that this chapter only includes people who responded to the question on race by indicating only one race. These people are classified by the Census Bureau as the race *alone* population. For example, respondents reporting a single detailed Asian group, such as Korean or Filipino, would be included in the Asian *alone* population. Respondents reporting more than one detailed Asian group, such as Chinese and Japanese or Asian Indian and Chinese and Vietnamese would also be included in the Asian *alone* population. This is because all of the detailed groups in these example combinations are part of the larger Asian race category. The same criteria apply to the Native Hawaiian and Other Pacific Islander groups.

In order for any of the tables for a specific group to be shown in Summary File 4, the data must meet a minimum population threshold. For Summary File 4, all tables are repeated for each race group, American Indian and Alaska Native tribe, and Hispanic or Latino group if the 100-percent count of people of that specific group in a particular geographic area is 100 or more. There also must be 50 or more unweighted people of that specific group in a particular geographic area. For example, if there are 100 or more 100-percent people tabulated as Korean in County A, and there are 50 or more unweighted people, then all matrices for Korean are shown in SF 4 for County A.

To maintain confidentiality, the Census Bureau applies statistical procedures that introduce some uncertainty into data for small geographic areas with small population groups. Therefore, tables may contain both sampling and nonsampling error.

In an iterated file such as SF 4, the universes *households, families,* and *occupied housing units* are classified by the race or ethnic group of the householder. In any population table where there is no note, the universe classification is always based on the race or ethnicity of the person. In all housing tables, the universe classification is based on the race or ethnicity of the householder.

Comparing SF 4 Estimates with Corresponding Values in SF 1 and SF 2

As in earlier censuses, the responses from the sample of households reporting on long forms must be weighted to reflect the entire population. Specifically, each responding household represents, on average, six or seven other households who reported using short forms. One consequence of the weighting procedures is that each estimate based on the long form responses has an associated confidence interval. These confidence intervals are wider (as a percentage of the estimate) for geographic areas with smaller populations and for characteristics that occur less frequently in the area being examined (such as the proportion of people in poverty in a middle-income neighborhood). In order to release as much useful information as possible, statisticians must balance a number of factors. In particular, for Census 2000, the Bureau of the Census created weighting areas—geographic areas from which about two hundred or more long forms were completed—which are large enough to produce good quality estimates. If smaller weighting areas had been used, the confidence intervals around the estimates would have been significantly wider, rendering many estimates less useful due to their lower reliability. The disadvantage of using weighting areas this large is that, for smaller geographic areas within them, the estimates of characteristics that are also reported on the short form will not match the counts reported in SF 1 or SF 2. Examples of these characteristics are the total number of people, the number of people reporting specific racial categories, and the number of housing units. The official values for items reported on the short form come from SF 1 and SF 2. The differences between the long form estimates in SF 4 and values in SF 1 or SF 2 are particularly noticeable for the smallest places, tracts, and block groups. The long form estimates of total population and total housing units in SF 4 will, however, match the SF 1 and SF 2 counts for larger geographic areas such as counties and states, and will be essentially the same for medium and large cities. This phenomenon also occurred for the 1990 Census, although in that case, the weighting areas included relatively small places. As a result, the long form estimates matched the short form counts for those places, but the confidence intervals around the estimates of characteristics collected only on the long form were often significantly wider (as a percentage of the estimate). SF 1 gives exact numbers even for very small groups and areas; whereas, SF 4 gives estimates for small groups and areas such as tracts and small places that are less exact. The goal of SF 4 is to identify large differences among areas or large changes over time. Estimates for small areas and small population groups often do exhibit large changes from one census to the next, so having the capability to measure them is worthwhile.

Topics

POPULATION

Total Population: Sample count of total population of all races.

Asian Population: A person having origins in any of the original peoples of the Far East, Southeast Asia, or the Indian subcontinent including, for example, Cambodia, China, India, Japan, Korea, Malaysia, Pakistan, the Philippine Islands, Thailand, and Vietnam. It includes Asian Indian, Bangladeshi, Cambodian, Chinese (except Taiwanese), Filipino, Hmong, Indonesian, Japanese, Korean, Laotian, Malaysian, Pakistani, Sri Lankan, Taiwanese, Thai, and Vietnamese.

Native Hawaiian or Other Pacific Islander (NHPI) Population: A person having origins in any of the original peoples of Hawaii, Guam, Samoa, or other Pacific Islands. It includes people who indicate their race as Fijian, Guamanian or Chamorro, Native Hawaiian, Samoan, and Tongan.

The data on race, which was asked of all people, were derived from answers to long-form questionnaire Item 6 and short-form questionnaire Item 8. The concept of race, as used by the Census Bureau, reflects self-identification by people according to the race or races with which they most closely identify. These categories are socio-political constructs and should not be interpreted as being scientific or anthropological in nature. Furthermore, the race categories include both racial and national-origin groups.

If an individual did not provide a race response, the race or races of the householder or other household members were assigned using specific rules of precedence of household relationship. For example, if race was missing for a natural-born child in the household, then either the race or races of the householder, another natural-born child, or the spouse of the householder were assigned. If race was not reported for anyone in the household, the race or races of a householder in a previously processed household were assigned.

AGE

Median Age: Divides the age distribution into two equal parts: one-half of the cases falling below the median age and one-half above the median. Median age is computed on the basis of a single year of age standard distribution.

The data on age, which was asked of all people, were derived from answers to the long-form questionnaire Item 4 and short-form questionnaire Item 6. The age classification is based on the age of the person in complete years as of April 1, 2000. The age of the person usually was derived from their date of birth information. Their reported age was used only when date of birth information was unavailable.

HOUSEHOLD SIZE

Average Household Size: A measure obtained by dividing the number of people in households by the total number of households (or householders). In cases where household members are tabulated by race or Hispanic origin, household members are classified by the race or Hispanic origin of the householder rather than the race or Hispanic origin of each individual. Average household size is rounded to the nearest hundredth.

LANGUAGE SPOKEN AT HOME

English Only: Number and percentage of population 5 years and over who report speaking English-only at home.

Language spoken at home data were derived from answers to long-form questionnaire Items 11a and 11b, which were asked of a sample of the population. Data were edited to include in tabulations only the population 5 years old and over. Questions 11a and 11b referred to languages spoken at home in an effort to measure the current use of languages other than English. People who knew languages other than English but did not use them at home or who only used them elsewhere were excluded. Most people who reported speaking a language other than English at home also speak English. The questions did not permit determination of the primary or dominant language of people who spoke both English and another language.

FOREIGN-BORN

Foreign Born: Number and percentage of population who were not U.S. citizens at birth. Foreign-born people are those who indicated they were either a U.S. citizen by naturalization or they were not a citizen of the United States.

Foreign-Born Naturalized Citizens: Number and percentage of population who were not U.S. citizens at birth but became U.S. citizens by naturalization.

The data on place of birth were derived from answers to long-form questionnaire Item 12 which was asked of a sample of the population. Respondents were asked to report the U.S. state, Puerto Rico, U.S. Island Area, or foreign country where they were born. People not reporting a place of birth were assigned the state or country of birth of another family member or their residence 5 years earlier, or were imputed the response of another person with similar characteristics. People born outside the United States were asked to report their place of birth according to current international boundaries. Since numerous changes in boundaries of foreign countries have occurred in the last century, some people may have reported their place of birth in terms of boundaries that existed at the time of their birth or emigration, or in accordance with their own national preference.

EDUCATIONAL ATTAINMENT

High School Graduates: Number and percentage of the population age 25 and over who have a high school diploma or higher. This category includes people whose highest degree was a high school diploma or its equivalent, people who attended college but did not receive a degree, and people who received a college, university, or professional degree. People who reported completing the 12th grade but not receiving a diploma are not high school graduates.

Four-Year College Graduates: Number and percentage of the population age 25 and over who have a 4-year college, university, or professional degree.

Data on educational attainment were derived from answers to long-form questionnaire Item 9, which was asked of a sample of the population. Data on attainment are tabulated for the population 25 years old and over.

The order in which degrees were listed on the questionnaire suggested that doctorate degrees were "higher" than professional school degrees, which were "higher" than master's degrees. The question included instructions for people currently enrolled in school to report the level of the previous grade attended or the highest degree received. Respondents who did not report educational attainment or enrollment level were assigned the attainment of a person of the same age, race, Hispanic or Latino origin, occupation and sex, where possible, who resided in the same or a nearby area. Respondents who filled more than one box were edited to the highest level or degree reported.

The question included a response category that allowed respondents to report completing the 12th grade without receiving a high school diploma. It allowed people who received either a high school diploma or the equivalent (Test of General Educational Development—G.E.D.) and did not attend college, to be reported as "high school graduate(s)." The category "Associate degree" included people whose highest degree is an associate degree, which generally requires 2 years of college level work and is either in an occupational program that prepares them for a specific occupation, or an academic program primarily in the arts and sciences. The course work may or may not be transferable to a bachelor's degree. Master's degrees include the traditional MA and MS degrees and field-specific degrees, such as MSW, MEd, MBA, MLS, and MEng. Some examples of professional degrees include medicine, dentistry, chiropractic, optometry, osteopathic medicine, pharmacy, podiatry, veterinary medicine, law, and theology. Vocational and technical training such as barber school training; business, trade, technical, and vocational schools; or other training for a specific trade, are specifically excluded.

INCOME AND POVERTY

Median Household Income (in dollars): Includes the income of the householder and all other individuals 15 years old and over in the household, whether they are related to the householder or not. The median divides the income distribution into two equal parts: one-half of the cases falling below the median income and one-half above the median. For households, the median income is based on the distribution of the total number of households including those with no income. Median income for households is computed on the basis of a standard distribution and is rounded to the nearest whole dollar.

Per Capita Income (in dollars): Per capita income is the mean income computed for every man, woman, and child in a particular group. It is derived by dividing the total income of a particular group by the total population in that group. Per capita income is rounded to the nearest whole dollar.

The data on income in 1999 were derived from answers to long-form questionnaire Items 31 and 32, which were asked of a sample of the population 15 years old and over. "Total income" is the sum of the amounts reported separately for wage or salary income; net self-employment income; interest, dividends, or net rental or royalty income or income from estates and trusts; social security or railroad retirement income; Supplemental Security Income (SSI); public assistance or welfare payments; retirement, survivor, or disability pensions; and all other income.

Receipts from the following sources are not included as income: capital gains, money received from the sale of property (unless the recipient was engaged in the business of selling such property); the value of income "in kind" from food stamps, public housing subsidies, medical care, employer contributions for individuals, etc.; withdrawal of bank deposits; money borrowed; tax refunds; exchange of money between relatives living in the same household; and gifts and lump-sum inheritances, insurance payments, and other types of lump-sum receipts.

The eight types of income reported in the census are defined as follows:

Wage or salary income. Wage or salary income includes total money earnings received for work performed as an employee during the calendar year 1999. It includes wages, salary, armed forces pay, commissions, tips, piece-rate payments, and cash bonuses earned before deductions were made for taxes, bonds, pensions, union dues, etc.

Self-employment income. Self-employment income includes both farm and nonfarm self-employment income. Nonfarm self-employment income includes net money income (gross receipts minus expenses) from one's own business, professional enterprise, or partnership. Gross receipts include the value of all goods sold and services rendered. Expenses include costs of goods purchased, rent, heat, light, power, depreciation charges, wages and salaries paid, business taxes (not personal income taxes), etc. Farm self-employment income includes net money income (gross receipts minus operating expenses) from the operation of a farm by a person on his or her own account, as an owner, renter, or sharecropper. Gross receipts include the value of all products sold, government farm programs, money received from the rental of farm equipment to others, and incidental receipts from the sale of wood, sand, gravel, etc. Operating expenses include cost of feed, fertilizer, seed, and other farming supplies, cash wages paid to farmhands, depreciation charges, cash rent, interest on farm mortgages, farm building repairs, farm taxes (not state and federal personal income taxes), etc. The value of fuel, food, or other farm products used for family living is not included as part of net income.

Interest, dividends, or net rental income. Interest, dividends, or net rental income includes interest on savings or bonds, dividends from stockholdings or membership in associations, net income from rental of property to others and receipts from boarders or lodgers, net royalties, and periodic payments from an estate or trust fund.

Social Security income. Social security income includes social security pensions and survivors benefits, permanent disability insurance payments made by the Social Security Administration prior to deductions for medical insurance, and railroad retirement insurance checks from the U.S. government. Medicare reimbursements are not included.

Supplemental Security Income (SSI). Supplemental Security Income (SSI) is a nationwide U.S. assistance program administered by the Social Security Administration that guarantees a minimum level of income for needy aged, blind, or disabled individuals. The census questionnaire for Puerto Rico asked about the receipt of SSI; however, SSI is not a federally administered program in Puerto Rico. Therefore, it is probably not being interpreted by most respondents as the same as SSI in the United States. The only way a resident of Puerto Rico could have appropriately reported SSI would have been if they lived in the United States at any time during calendar year 1999 and received SSI.

Public assistance income. Public assistance income includes general assistance and Temporary Assistance to Needy Families (TANF). Separate payments received for hospital or other medical care (vendor payments) are excluded. This does not include Supplemental Security Income (SSI).

Retirement income. Retirement income includes: (1) retirement pensions and survivor benefits from a former employer; labor union; or federal, state, or local government; and the U.S. military; (2) income from workers' compensation; disability income from companies or unions; federal, state, or local government; and the U.S. military; (3) periodic receipts from annuities and insurance; and (4) regular income from IRA and KEOGH plans. This does not include social security income.

All other income. All other income includes unemployment compensation, Veterans' Administration (VA) payments, alimony and child support, contributions received periodically from people not living in the household, military family allotments, and other kinds of periodic income other than earnings.

Poverty Status: Number and percentage of population with income in 1999 below the poverty level. Based on individuals for whom poverty status is determined. Poverty status was determined for all people except institutionalized people, people in military group quarters, people in college dormitories, and unrelated individuals under 15 years old.

The poverty status of families and unrelated individuals in 1999 was determined using 48 thresholds (income cutoffs) arranged in a two dimensional matrix. The matrix consists of family size (from 1 person to 9 or more people) cross-classified by presence and number of family members under 18 years old (from no children present to 8 or more children present). Unrelated individuals and 2-person families were further differentiated by the age of the reference person (RP) (under 65 years old and 65 years old and over).

To determine a person's poverty status, one compares the person's total family income with the poverty threshold appropriate for that person's family size and composition. If the total income of that person's family is less than the threshold appropriate for that family, then the person is considered poor, together with every member of his or her family. If a person is not living with anyone related by birth, marriage, or adoption, then the person's own income is compared with his or her poverty threshold.

HOUSING

Homeownership: Number and percentage of housing units that are owner-occupied.

The data on tenure, which was asked at all occupied housing units, were obtained from answers to long-form questionnaire Item 33, and short-form questionnaire Item 2. All occupied housing units are classified as either owner occupied or renter occupied.

A housing unit is owner occupied if the owner or co-owner lives in the unit even if it is mortgaged or not fully paid for. The owner or co-owner must live in the unit and usually is Person 1 on the questionnaire. The unit is "Owned by you or someone in this household with a mortgage or loan" if it is being purchased with a mortgage or some other debt arrangement, such as a deed of trust, trust deed, contract to purchase, land contract, or purchase agreement. The unit is also considered owned with a mortgage if it is built on leased land and there is a mortgage on the unit. Mobile homes occupied by owners with installment loans balances are also included in this category.

Median Gross Rent (in dollars): Median monthly gross rent on specified renter-occupied and specified vacant-for-rent units. Specified renter-occupied and specified vacant-for-rent units exclude 1-family houses on 10 acres or more.

The data on gross rent were obtained from answers to long-form questionnaire Items 45a-d, which were asked on a sample basis. Gross rent is the contract rent plus the estimated average monthly cost of utilities (electricity, gas, water and sewer) and fuels (oil, coal, kerosene, wood, etc.) if these are paid by the renter (or paid for the renter by someone else). Gross rent is intended to eliminate differentials that result from varying practices with respect to the inclusion of utilities and fuels as part of the rental payment. The estimated costs of utilities and fuels are reported on an annual basis but are converted to monthly figures for the tabulations. Renter units occupied without payment of cash rent are shown separately as "No cash rent" in the tabulations.

Housing units that are renter occupied without payment of cash rent are shown separately as "No cash rent" in census data products. The unit may be owned by friends or relatives who live elsewhere and who allow occupancy without charge. Rent-free houses or apartments may be provided to compensate caretakers, ministers, tenant farmers, sharecroppers, or others.

Contract rent is the monthly rent agreed to or contracted for, regardless of any furnishings, utilities, fees, meals, or services that may be included. For vacant units, it is the monthly rent asked for the rental unit at the time of enumeration.

If the contract rent includes rent for a business unit or for living quarters occupied by another household, only that part of the rent estimated to be for the respondent's unit was included. Excluded was any rent paid for additional units or for business premises.

If a renter pays rent to the owner of a condominium or cooperative, and the condominium fee or cooperative carrying charge also is paid by the renter to the owner, the condominium fee or carrying charge was included as rent.

If a renter receives payments from lodgers or roomers who are listed as members of the household, the rent without deduction for any payments received from the lodgers or roomers was to be reported. The respondent was to report the rent agreed to or contracted for even if paid by someone else such as friends or relatives living elsewhere, a church or welfare agency, or the government through subsidies or vouchers.

The median divides the rent distribution into two equal parts: one-half of the cases falling below the median contract rent and one-half above the median. Median contract rents are computed on the basis of a standard distribution and are rounded to the nearest whole dollar. Units reported as "No cash rent" are excluded.

Median Home Value (in dollars): Reported by the owner of specified owner-occupied or specified vacant-for-sale housing units. Specified owner-occupied and specified vacant-for-sale housing units include only 1-family houses on less than 10 acres without a business or medical office on the property. The data for "specified units" exclude mobile homes, houses with a business or medical office, houses on 10 or more acres, and housing units in multi-unit buildings.

The data on value (also referred to as "price asked" for vacant units) were obtained from answers to long-form questionnaire Item 51, which was asked on a sample basis at owner-occupied housing units and units that were being bought, or vacant for sale at the time of enumeration. Value is the respondent's estimate of how much the property (house and lot, mobile home and lot, or condominium unit) would sell for if it were for sale. If the house or mobile home was owned or being bought, but the land on which it sits was not, the respondent was asked to estimate the combined value of the house or mobile home and the land. For vacant units, value was the price asked for the property. Value was tabulated separately for all owner-occupied and vacant-for-sale housing units, owner-occupied and vacant-for-sale mobile homes, and specified owner-occupied and specified vacant-for-sale housing units.

The median divides the value distribution into two equal parts: one-half of the cases falling below the median value of the property (house and lot, mobile home and lot, or condominium unit) and one-half above the median. Median values are computed on the basis of a standard distribution and are rounded to the nearest hundred dollars.

User's Guide: Climate

Inclusion Criteria — How the Data and Stations Were Selected

There were two central goals in the preparation of the climate chapter. The first was to select those data elements which would have the broadest possible use by the greatest range of potential users. For most of the National Weather Service stations there is a substantial quantity and variety of climatological data that is collected, however for the majority of stations the data is more limited. After evaluating the available data set, the editors chose nine temperature measures, five precipitation measures, and heating and cooling degree days — sixteen key data elements that are widely requested and are believed to be of the greatest general interest.

The second goal was to provide data for as many weather stations as possible. Although there are over 10,000 stations in the United States, not every station collects data for both precipitation and temperature, and even among those that do, the data is not always complete for the last thirty years. As the editors used a different methodology than that of NCDC to compute data, a formal data sufficiency criteria was devised and applied to the source tapes in order to select stations for inclusion.

Sources of the Data

The data in the climate chapter is compiled from several sources. The majority comes from the original National Climactic Data Center computer tapes (TD-3220 Summary of Month Co-Operative). This data was used to create the entire table for each Cooperative station and part of each National Weather Service station. The remainder of the data for each NWS station comes from the International Station Meteorological Climate Summary, Version 4.0, September 1996, which is also available from the NCDC.

NCDC has two main classes or types of weather stations; first order stations which are staffed by professional meteorologists and cooperative stations which are staffed by volunteers. In the climate chapter all first order stations operated by the National Weather Service are included, as well as every cooperative station that met our selection criteria.

Potential cautions in using *Weather America*

First, as with any statistical reference work of this type, users need to be aware of the source of the data. The information here comes from NOAA, and it is the most comprehensive and reliable core data available. Although it is the best, it is not perfect. Most weather stations are staffed by volunteers, times of observation sometimes vary, stations occasionally are moved (especially over a thirty year period), equipment is changed or upgraded, and all of these factors affect the uniformity of the data. the climate chapter does not attempt to correct for these factors, and is not intended for either climatologists or atmospheric scientists. Users with concerns about data collection and reporting protocols are both referred to NCDC technical documentation, and also, they are perhaps better served by using the original computer tapes themselves as well.

Second, users need to be aware of the methodology used, which is described later in this User's Guide. Although this methodology has produced fully satisfactory results, it is not directly compatible with other methodologies, hence variances in the results published here and those which appear in other publications will doubtlessly arise.

Third, is the trap of that informal logical fallacy known as "hasty generalization," and its corollaries. This may involve presuming the future will be like the past (specifically, next year will be an average year), or it may involve misunderstanding the limitations of an arithmetic average, but more interestingly, it may involve those mistakes made most innocently by generalizing informally on too broad a basis. As weather is highly localized, the data should be taken in that context. A weather station collects data about climatic conditions at that spot, and that spot may or may not be an effective paradigm for an entire town or area. For example, the weather station in Burlington, Vermont is located at the airport about 3 miles east of the center of town. Most of Burlington is a lot closer to Lake Champlain, and that should mean to a careful user that there could be a significant difference between the temperature readings gathered at the weather station and readings that might be gathered at City Hall downtown. How much would this difference be? How could it be estimated? There are no answers here for these sorts of questions, but it is important for users of this book to raise them for themselves. (It is interesting to note that similar situations abound across the country. For example, compare different readings for the multiple stations in San Francisco, CA or for those around New York City.)

Our source of data has been consistent, so has our methodology. The data has been computed and reported consistently as well. As a result, the climate chapter should prove valuable to the careful and informed reader.

Weather Station Tables

The weather station tables are grouped by type (National Weather Service and Cooperative) and then arranged alphabetically. The station name is almost always a place name, and is shown here just as it appears in NCDC data. The station name is followed by the county in which the station is located, the elevation of the station (at the time beginning of the thirty year period) and the latitude and longitude.

The National Weather Service Station tables contain 30 data elements which were compiled from two different sources, the International Station Meteorological Climate Summary (ISMCS) and NCDC TD-3220 data tapes. The following 14 elements are from the ISMCS: maximum precipitation, minimum precipitation, maximum 24-hour precipitation, maximum snowfall, maximum 24-hour snowfall, thunderstorm days, foggy days, predominant sky cover, relative humidity (morning and afternoon), dewpoint, wind speed and direction, and maximum wind gust. The remaining 16 elements come from the TD-3220 data tapes. The period of record (POR) for data from the TD-3220 data tapes is 1970-1999. The POR for ISMCS data varies from station to station.

Weather Elements (National Weather Service and Cooperative Stations)

The following elements were compiled by the editor from the NCDC TD-3220 data tapes using a period of record of 1970-1999.

The average temperatures (maximum, minimum, and mean) are the average (see Methodology below) of those temperatures for all available values for a given month. For example, for a given station the average maximum temperature for July is the arithmetic average of all available maximum July temperatures for that station. (Maximum means the highest recorded temperature, minimum means the lowest recorded temperature, and mean means an arithmetic average temperature.)

The extreme maximum temperature is the highest temperature recorded in each month over the period 1970-1999. The extreme minimum temperature is the lowest temperature recorded in each month over the same time period.

The days for maximum temperature and minimum temperature are the average number of days those criteria were met for all available instances. The symbol >= means greater than or equal to, the symbol <= means less than or equal to. For example, for a given station, the number of days the maximum temperature was greater than or equal to 90°F in July, is just an arithmetic average of the number of days in all the available Julys for that station.

Heating and cooling degree days are based on the median temperature for a given day and its variance from 65°F. For example, for a given station if the day's high temperature was 50°F and the day's low temperature was 30°F, the median (midpoint) temperature was 40°F. 40°F is 25 degrees below 65°F, hence on this day there would be 25 heating degree days. The also applies for cooling degree days. For example, for a given station if the day's high temperature was 80°F and the day's low temperature was 70°F, the median (midpoint) temperature was 75°F. 75°F is 10 degrees above 65°F, hence on this day there would be 10 cooling degree days. All heating and/or cooling degree days in a month are summed for the month giving respective totals for each element for that month. These sums for a given month for a given station over the past thirty years are again summed and then arithmetically averaged. It should be noted that the heating and cooling degree days do not cancel each other out. It is possible to have both for a given station in the same month.

Precipitation data is computed the same as heating and cooling degree days. Mean precipitation and mean snowfall are arithmetic averages of cumulative totals for the month. All available values for the thirty year period for a given month for a given station are summed and then divided by the number of values. The same is true for days of greater than or equal to 0.1" and 1.0" of precipitation, and days of greater than or equal to 1.0" of snow depth on the ground. The word trace appears for precipitation and snowfall amounts that are too small to measure.

Finally, remember that all values presented in the tables and the rankings are averages of available data (see Methodology below) for that specific data element for the last thirty years (1970-1999).

Weather Elements (National Weather Service Stations Only)

The following elements were taken directly from the International Station Meteorological Climate Summary. The periods of records vary per station.

Maximum precipitation, minimum precipitation, maximum 24-hour precipitation, maximum snowfall, maximum 24-hour snowfall, thunderstorm days, foggy days, relative humidity (morning and afternoon), dewpoint, prevailing wind speed and direction, and maximum wind gust are all self-explanatory.

The word trace appears for precipitation and snowfall amounts that are too small to measure.

Predominant sky cover contains four possible entries: CLR (clear); SCT (scattered); BRK (broken); and OVR (overcast).

How Cooperative Stations Were Selected

The basic criteria is that a station must have data for temperature, precipitation, heating and cooling degree days of sufficient quantity in order to create a meaningful average. More specifically, the definition of sufficiency here has two parts. First, there must be 22 values for a given data element (with the exception of cooling degree days which required only 14 values in order to be considered sufficient- more about this later), and second, eight of the sixteen elements included in the table must pass this sufficiency test. For example, in regard to average maximum temperature (the first element on every data table), a given station needs to have a value for every month of at least 22 of the last thirty years in order to meet the criteria, and, in addition, every station included must have at least eight of the sixteen elements at least this minimal level of completeness in order to fulfill the criteria. By using this procedure, 3,933 stations met these requirements and are included here.

Methodology

The following discussion applies only to data compiled from the NCDC TD-3220 data tapes.

The climate chapter is based on an arithmetic average of all available data for a specific data element at a given station. For example, the average maximum daily high temperature during July for Pontiac, New York was abstracted from NCDC source tapes for the thirty Julys, starting in July, 1970 and ending in July, 1999. These thirty figures were then summed and divided by thirty to produce an arithmetic average. As might be expected, there were not thirty values for every data element on every table. For a variety of reasons, NCDC data is sometimes incomplete. Thus the following standards were established.

For those data elements where there were 26-30 values, the data was taken to be essentially complete and an average was computed. For data elements where there were 22-25 values, the data was taken as being partly complete but still valid enough to use to compute an average. Such averages are shown in ***bold italic*** type to indicate that there was less than 26 values. For the few data elements where there were not even 22 values, no average was computed and 'na' appears in the space. If any of the twelve months for a given data element reported a value of 'na', no annual average was computed and the annual average was reported as 'na' as well.

This procedure was followed for 15 of the 16 data elements. The one exception is cooling degree days. The collection of this data began in 1980 so the following standards were adopted: for those data elements where there were 17-20 values, the data was taken to be essentially complete and an average was computed. For data elements where there were 14-16 values, the data was taken as being partly complete but still valid enough to use to compute an average. Such averages are shown in ***bold italic*** type to indicate that there was 14-16 values. For the few data elements where there were not even 14 values, no average was computed and 'na' appears in the space. If any of the twelve months for a given data element reported a value of 'na', no annual average was computed and the annual average was reported as 'na' as well.

Thus the basic computational methodology of the climate chapter is to provide an arithmetic average. Because of this, such a pure arithmetic average is somewhat different from the special type of average (called a "normal") which NCDC procedures produces and appears in federal publications.

Perhaps the best outline of the contrasting normalization methodology is found in the following paragraph (which appears as part of an NCDC technical document titled, CLIM81 1961-1990 NORMALS TD-9641 prepared by Lewis France of NCDC in May, 1992):

Normals have been defined as the arithmetic mean of a climatological element computed over a long time period. International agreements eventually led to the decision that the appropriate time period would be three consecutive decades (Guttman, 1989). The data record should be consistent (have no changes in location, instruments, observation practices, etc.; these are identified here as "exposure changes") and have no missing values so a normal will reflect the actual average climatic conditions. If any significant exposure changes have occurred, the data record is said to be "inhomogeneous," and the normal may not reflect a true climatic average. Such data need to be adjusted to remove the nonclimatic inhomogeneities. The resulting (adjusted) record is then said to be "homogeneous." If no exposure changes have occurred at a station, the normal is calculated simply by averaging the appropriate 30 values from the 1961-1990 record.

In the main, there are two "inhomogeneities" that NCDC is correcting for with normalization: adjusting for variances in time of day of observation (at the so-called First Order stations data is based on midnight to midnight observation times and this practice is not necessarily followed at cooperative stations which are staffed by volunteers), and second, estimating data that is either missing or incongruent.

A long discussion of the normalization process is not required here but a short note concerning comparative results of the two methodologies is appropriate.

When the editors first started compiling the climate chapter a concern arose because the normalization process would not be replicated: would our methodology produce strikingly different results than NCDC's? To allay concerns, results of the two processes were compared for the time period normalized results are available (1961-1990). In short, what was found was that the answer to this question is no. Never-the-less, users should be aware that because of both the time period covered (1970-1999) and the methodology used, data in the climate chapter is not compatible with data from other sources.

area of 94.88 square miles, and is located in the Eastern Time Zone. The county was founded in 1824. County seat is Gainesville.

Alachua County is part of the Gainesville, FL Metropolitan Statistical Area. The entire metro area includes: Alachua County, FL; Gilchrist County, FL

Weather Station: High Springs										Elevation: 62 feet		
	Jan	Feb	Mar	Apr	May	Jun	Jul	Aug	Sep	Oct	Nov	Dec
High	68	72	78	83	89	92	93	92	90	83	77	71
Low	40	43	49	53	62	69	71	71	68	58	49	43
Precip	4.4	3.8	4.5	3.4	3.8	6.8	7.3	8.2	4.4	3.1	2.2	2.7
Snow	tr	0.0	0.0	0.0	0.0	0.0	0.0	0.0	0.0	0.0	0.0	0.0

High and Low temperatures in degrees Fahrenheit; Precipitation and Snow in inches

Population: 181,596 (1990); 217,955 (2000); 235,806 (2007); 254,760 (2012 projected); Race: 71.4% White, 19.9% Black, 4.4% Asian, 6.5% Hispanic of any race (2007); Density: 269.7 persons per square mile (2007); Average household size: 2.42 (2007); Median age: 29.9 (2007); Males per 100 females: 95.2 (2007).
Religion: Five largest groups: 11.2% Southern Baptist Convention, 7.3% Catholic Church, 5.4% The United Methodist Church, 1.1% Episcopal Church, 1.1% Presbyterian Church (U.S.A.) (2000).
Economy: Unemployment rate: 3.1% (11/2007); Total civilian labor force: 127,868 (11/2007); Leading industries: 23.3% health care and social assistance; 16.9% retail trade; 12.8% accommodation & food services (2005); Farms: 1,493 totaling 222,728 acres (2002); Companies that employ 500 or more persons: 11 (2005); Companies that employ 100 to 499 persons: 109 (2005); Companies that employ less than 100 persons: 5,611 (2005); Black-owned businesses: 866 (2002); Hispanic-owned businesses: 955 (2002); Asian-owned businesses: 430 (2002); Women-owned businesses: 5,068 (2002); Retail sales per capita: $15,658 (2007). Single-family building permits issued: 1,009 (2006); Multi-family building permits issued: 940 (2006).
Income: Per capita income: $23,268 (2007); Median household income: $37,616 (2007); Average household income: $55,261 (2007); Percent of households with income of $100,000 or more: 13.5% (2007); Poverty rate: 21.8% (2005); Bankruptcy rate: 0.85% (2006).
Taxes: Total county taxes per capita: $478 (2005); County property taxes per capita: $365 (2005).
Education: Percent of population age 25 and over with: High school diploma (including GED) or higher: 88.4% (2007); Bachelor's degree or higher: 39.4% (2007); Master's degree or higher: 19.2% (2007).
Housing: Homeownership rate: 57.2% (2007); Median home value: $159,816 (2007); Median rent: $465 per month (2000); Median age of housing: 20 years (2000).
Health: Birth rate: 121.7 per 10,000 population (2006); Death rate: 70.4 per 10,000 population (2006); Age-adjusted cancer mortality rate: 197.3 deaths per 100,000 population (2004); Air Quality Index: 89.6% good, 10.4% moderate, 0.0% unhealthy for sensitive individuals, 0.0% unhealthy (percent of days in 2006); Number of physicians: 82.2 per 10,000 population (2005); Hospital beds: 79.2 per 10,000 population (2004); Hospital admissions: 3,046.1 per 10,000 population (2004).
Elections: 2004 Presidential election results: 42.9% Bush, 56.1% Kerry, 0.5% Nader, 0.3% Badnarik;
National and State Parks: Devils Millhopper Geological State Park; Dudley Farm Historic State Park; Marjorie Kinnan Rawlings Historic State Park; Paynes Prairie Preserve State Park; San Felasco Hammock Preserve State Park; Sunland Center State Park
Additional Information Contacts
Alachua County Government . . . . (352) 374-5210
   http://www.co.alachua.fl.us
Alachua Chamber of Commerce . . . . (386) 462-3333
   http://www.alachua.com
City of Alachua . . . . (386) 462-1231
   http://www.cityofalachua.com
Fort White Chamber of Commerce . . . . (386) 462-8277
Gainesville Chamber of Commerce . . . . (352) 334-7100
   http://www.gainesvillechamber.com
High Springs Chamber of Commerce . . . . (904) 454-3120
   http://www.highsprings.com
Newberry Chamber of Commerce . . . . (352) 472-6611
   http://www.newberrychamber.com

water area of 0.153 square miles. Located at 29.77° N. Lat.; 82.48° W. Long. Elevation is 138 feet.
History: Alachua was founded in 1884 when the Atlantic Coast Line Railroad was built through the area. The town became a shipping point for tobacco, cotton, and winter vegetables, and later for watermelons.
Population: 4,825 (1990); 6,098 (2000); 7,284 (2007); 8,283 (2012 projected); Race: 71.1% White, 24.1% Black, 1.9% Asian, 4.6% Hispanic of any race (2007); Density: 252.1 persons per square mile (2007); Average household size: 2.48 (2007); Median age: 36.7 (2007); Males per 100 females: 88.6 (2007); Marriage status: 25.8% never married, 53.4% now married, 9.8% widowed, 11.1% divorced (2000); Foreign born: 3.3% (2000); Ancestry (includes multiple ancestries): 35.0% Other groups, 12.6% Irish, 9.6% German, 8.3% English, 5.9% United States or American (2000).
Economy: Single-family building permits issued: 116 (2006); Multi-family building permits issued: 2 (2006); Employment by occupation: 10.7% management, 24.7% professional, 18.3% services, 28.0% sales, 1.2% farming, 6.0% construction, 11.1% production (2000).
Income: Per capita income: $23,756 (2007); Median household income: $47,669 (2007); Average household income: $58,779 (2007); Percent of households with income of $100,000 or more: 14.7% (2007); Poverty rate: 16.0% (2000).
Taxes: Total city taxes per capita: $432 (2005); City property taxes per capita: $288 (2005).
Education: Percent of population age 25 and over with: High school diploma (including GED) or higher: 84.1% (2007); Bachelor's degree or higher: 28.5% (2007); Master's degree or higher: 11.6% (2007).
School District(s)
Alachua County School District (PK-12)
   2005-06 Enrollment: 29,259 . . . . (352) 955-7880
Housing: Homeownership rate: 78.0% (2007); Median home value: $159,744 (2007); Median rent: $299 per month (2000); Median age of housing: 17 years (2000).
Safety: Violent crime rate: 105.4 per 10,000 population; Property crime rate: 529.7 per 10,000 population (2006).
Transportation: Commute to work: 92.3% car, 0.0% public transportation, 1.7% walk, 3.9% work from home (2000); Travel time to work: 20.1% less than 15 minutes, 39.6% 15 to 30 minutes, 32.2% 30 to 45 minutes, 4.2% 45 to 60 minutes, 3.9% 60 minutes or more (2000)
Additional Information Contacts
Alachua Chamber of Commerce . . . . (386) 462-3333
   http://www.alachua.com
City of Alachua . . . . (386) 462-1231
   http://www.cityofalachua.com
Fort White Chamber of Commerce . . . . (386) 462-8277

ARCHER (city). Covers a land area of 2.375 square miles and a water area of 0 square miles. Located at 29.53° N. Lat.; 82.52° W. Long. Elevation is 92 feet.
History: First called Deer Hammock, Archer was founded in 1859 and named for Brigadier General James J. Archer, a Confederate leader. Among the early settlers was a group of Quakers from Ohio, attracted by the citrus groves.
Population: 1,456 (1990); 1,289 (2000); 1,173 (2007); 1,235 (2012 projected); Race: 53.5% White, 44.2% Black, 0.3% Asian, 2.7% Hispanic of any race (2007); Density: 493.8 persons per square mile (2007); Average household size: 2.57 (2007); Median age: 30.6 (2007); Males per 100 females: 82.7 (2007); Marriage status: 29.6% never married, 46.5% now married, 10.1% widowed, 13.8% divorced (2000); Foreign born: 2.3% (2000); Ancestry (includes multiple ancestries): 39.5% Other groups, 13.3% United States or American, 9.4% Irish, 7.6% English, 7.3% German (2000).
Economy: Employment by occupation: 7.6% management, 13.6% professional, 24.9% services, 29.0% sales, 0.8% farming, 12.6% construction, 11.5% production (2000).
Income: Per capita income: $15,488 (2007); Median household income: $32,115 (2007); Average household income: $39,841 (2007); Percent of households with income of $100,000 or more: 6.4% (2007); Poverty rate: 21.6% (2000).
Education: Percent of population age 25 and over with: High school diploma (including GED) or higher: 74.7% (2007); Bachelor's degree or higher: 11.6% (2007); Master's degree or higher: 4.3% (2007).

$95,577 (2007); Median rent: $305 per month (2000); Median age of housing: 24 years (2000).

Transportation: Commute to work: 90.8% car, 0.0% public transportation, 2.7% walk, 2.3% work from home (2000); Travel time to work: 12.8% less than 15 minutes, 32.9% 15 to 30 minutes, 41.0% 30 to 45 minutes, 9.8% 45 to 60 minutes, 3.4% 60 minutes or more (2000)

GAINESVILLE (city). County seat. Covers a land area of 48.182 square miles and a water area of 0.921 square miles. Located at 29.66° N. Lat.; 82.33° W. Long. Elevation is 177 feet.

History: A settlement called Hog Town grew up around a trading post established here in 1830. The town was named Gainesville in 1853 for General Edmund P. Gaines, a Seminole War leader, and was settled by cotton planters from Georgia, Alabama, and the Carolinas. The University of Florida opened in 1853 in Gainesville, and in 1905 several State-supported schools were consolidated with it.

Population: 90,519 (1990); 95,447 (2000); 97,244 (2007); 101,406 (2012 projected); Race: 65.1% White, 25.0% Black, 5.3% Asian, 7.3% Hispanic of any race (2007); Density: 2,018.2 persons per square mile (2007); Average household size: 2.49 (2007); Median age: 27.6 (2007); Males per 100 females: 95.8 (2007); Marriage status: 49.1% never married, 37.1% now married, 4.7% widowed, 9.1% divorced (2000); Foreign born: 8.7% (2000); Ancestry (includes multiple ancestries): 31.1% Other groups, 12.6% German, 10.7% Irish, 9.9% English, 5.6% United States or American (2000).

Economy: Unemployment rate: 3.0% (11/2007); Total civilian labor force: 59,483 (11/2007); Single-family building permits issued: 147 (2006); Multi-family building permits issued: 576 (2006); Employment by occupation: 10.7% management, 35.2% professional, 17.6% services, 26.3% sales, 0.3% farming, 4.4% construction, 5.5% production (2000).

Income: Per capita income: $20,195 (2007); Median household income: $32,466 (2007); Average household income: $48,650 (2007); Percent of households with income of $100,000 or more: 10.9% (2007); Poverty rate: 26.7% (2000).

Taxes: Total city taxes per capita: $337 (2005); City property taxes per capita: $166 (2005).

Education: Percent of population age 25 and over with: High school diploma (including GED) or higher: 87.9% (2007); Bachelor's degree or higher: 43.2% (2007); Master's degree or higher: 22.2% (2007).

School District(s)
Alachua County School District (PK-12)
   2005-06 Enrollment: 29,259 . . . . (352) 955-7880
University of Florida Laboratory School (PK-12)
   2005-06 Enrollment: 1,159 . . . . (352) 392-1554

Four-year College(s)
City College Branch Campus (Private, Not-for-profit)
   Fall 2006 Enrollment: 222 . . . . (352) 335-4000
   2006-07 Tuition: In-state $8,559; Out-of-state $8,559
University of Florida (Public)
   Fall 2006 Enrollment: 50,912. (352) 392-3261
   2006-07 Tuition: In-state $3,206; Out-of-state $17,791

Two-year College(s)
Santa Fe Community College (Public)
   Fall 2006 Enrollment: 14,012. (352) 395-5000
   2006-07 Tuition: In-state $1,604; Out-of-state $6,061

Housing: Homeownership rate: 48.5% (2007); Median home value: $145,197 (2007); Median rent: $457 per month (2000); Median age of housing: 26 years (2000).

Hospitals: Malcom Randall VA Medical Center (323 beds); North Florida Regional Medical Center (278 beds); Shands AGH (367 beds); Shands Rehab Hospital (40 beds); Shands at University of Florida (570 beds); Shands at Vista (81 beds)

Safety: Violent crime rate: 99.1 per 10,000 population; Property crime rate: 523.9 per 10,000 population (2006).

Newspapers: The Gainesville Sun (Circulation 48,467); The Record (General - Circulation 5,000)

Transportation: Commute to work: 82.0% car, 3.2% public transportation, 5.6% walk, 3.1% work from home (2000); Travel time to work: 43.2% less than 15 minutes, 43.2% 15 to 30 minutes, 7.7% 30 to 45 minutes, 2.6% 45 to 60 minutes, 3.3% 60 minutes or more (2000); Amtrak: Service available.

Airports: Gainesville Regional (primary service)

HAWTHORNE (city). Aka Hawthorn. Covers a land area of 3.203 square miles and a water area of 0.150 square miles. Located at 29.59° N. Lat.; 82.08° W. Long. Elevation is 148 feet.

History: Hawthorne was incorporated in 1890 and named for James M. Hawthorn (no "e"), the owner of the site.

Population: 1,495 (1990); 1,415 (2000); 1,287 (2007); 1,343 (2012 projected); Race: 48.7% White, 49.5% Black, 0.1% Asian, 1.4% Hispanic of any race (2007); Density: 401.8 persons per square mile (2007); Average household size: 2.52 (2007); Median age: 35.6 (2007); Males per 100 females: 88.2 (2007); Marriage status: 25.6% never married, 47.9% now married, 13.5% widowed, 12.9% divorced (2000); Foreign born: 1.2% (2000); Ancestry (includes multiple ancestries): 30.5% Other groups, 14.1% United States or American, 8.7% English, 7.9% Irish, 6.4% German (2000).

Economy: Employment by occupation: 8.1% management, 17.7% professional, 24.4% services, 23.4% sales, 0.0% farming, 11.7% construction, 14.6% production (2000).

Income: Per capita income: $16,109 (2007); Median household income: $30,000 (2007); Average household income: $40,652 (2007); Percent of households with income of $100,000 or more: 5.1% (2007); Poverty rate: 23.8% (2000).

Education: Percent of population age 25 and over with: High school diploma (including GED) or higher: 71.7% (2007); Bachelor's degree or higher: 10.8% (2007); Master's degree or higher: 5.6% (2007).

School District(s)
Alachua County School District (PK-12)
   2005-06 Enrollment: 29,259 . . . . (352) 955-7880
Putnam County School District (PK-12)
   2005-06 Enrollment: 12,456 . . . . (386) 329-0510

Housing: Homeownership rate: 72.4% (2007); Median home value: $96,892 (2007); Median rent: $269 per month (2000); Median age of housing: 31 years (2000).

Transportation: Commute to work: 91.3% car, 2.0% public transportation, 3.7% walk, 2.4% work from home (2000); Travel time to work: 21.8% less than 15 minutes, 19.8% 15 to 30 minutes, 34.0% 30 to 45 minutes, 17.3% 45 to 60 minutes, 7.1% 60 minutes or more (2000)

HIGH SPRINGS (city). Covers a land area of 18.454 square miles and a water area of 0.030 square miles. Located at 29.82° N. Lat.; 82.59° W. Long. Elevation is 66 feet.

History: High Springs began as a trading post in 1885, and was named for a hilltop spring. It grew as a center for an agricultural area where tobacco, corn, and peanuts were raised.

Population: 3,390 (1990); 3,863 (2000); 4,682 (2007); 5,364 (2012 projected); Race: 78.7% White, 18.2% Black, 0.4% Asian, 5.7% Hispanic of any race (2007); Density: 253.7 persons per square mile (2007); Average household size: 2.41 (2007); Median age: 38.8 (2007); Males per 100 females: 88.0 (2007); Marriage status: 20.1% never married, 55.2% now married, 10.6% widowed, 14.1% divorced (2000); Foreign born: 3.5% (2000); Ancestry (includes multiple ancestries): 24.5% Other groups, 12.2% German, 11.6% English, 10.4% United States or American, 9.3% Irish (2000).

Economy: Employment by occupation: 9.0% management, 22.4% professional, 16.8% services, 29.1% sales, 0.7% farming, 10.7% construction, 11.4% production (2000).

Income: Per capita income: $20,548 (2007); Median household income: $39,819 (2007); Average household income: $49,323 (2007); Percent of households with income of $100,000 or more: 8.2% (2007); Poverty rate: 12.0% (2000).

Education: Percent of population age 25 and over with: High school diploma (including GED) or higher: 82.2% (2007); Bachelor's degree or higher: 15.3% (2007); Master's degree or higher: 5.1% (2007).

School District(s)
Alachua County School District (PK-12)
   2005-06 Enrollment: 29,259 . . . . (352) 955-7880

Housing: Homeownership rate: 80.0% (2007); Median home value: $121,636 (2007); Median rent: $370 per month (2000); Median age of housing: 21 years (2000).

Safety: Violent crime rate: 35.5 per 10,000 population; Property crime rate: 459.0 per 10,000 population (2006).

Newspapers: The High Springs Herald (General - Circulation 5,000)

Transportation: Commute to work: 94.8% car, 0.4% public transportation, 1.1% walk, 2.0% work from home (2000); Travel time to work: 19.7% less than 15 minutes, 32.1% 15 to 30 minutes, 34.1% 30 to 45 minutes, 11.1% 45 to 60 minutes, 3.0% 60 minutes or more (2000)
Additional Information Contacts
High Springs Chamber of Commerce . . . . (904) 454-3120
  http://www.highsprings.com

LA CROSSE (town). Covers a land area of 1.338 square miles and a water area of 0 square miles. Located at 29.84° N. Lat.; 82.40° W. Long. Elevation is 144 feet.
Population: 122 (1990); 143 (2000); 148 (2007); 155 (2012 projected); Race: 81.1% White, 16.2% Black, 0.0% Asian, 10.8% Hispanic of any race (2007); Density: 110.6 persons per square mile (2007); Average household size: 2.28 (2007); Median age: 46.9 (2007); Males per 100 females: 105.6 (2007); Marriage status: 35.1% never married, 49.5% now married, 2.7% widowed, 12.6% divorced (2000); Foreign born: 0.0% (2000); Ancestry (includes multiple ancestries): 32.3% Other groups, 16.2% United States or American, 10.8% German, 10.8% Irish, 4.6% French (except Basque) (2000).
Economy: Employment by occupation: 0.0% management, 26.4% professional, 15.1% services, 22.6% sales, 3.8% farming, 11.3% construction, 20.8% production (2000).
Income: Per capita income: $13,733 (2007); Median household income: $26,071 (2007); Average household income: $31,269 (2007); Percent of households with income of $100,000 or more: 0.0% (2007); Poverty rate: 28.5% (2000).
Education: Percent of population age 25 and over with: High school diploma (including GED) or higher: 65.5% (2007); Bachelor's degree or higher: 13.3% (2007); Master's degree or higher: 5.3% (2007).
Housing: Homeownership rate: 86.2% (2007); Median home value: $100,000 (2007); Median rent: $n/a per month (2000); Median age of housing: 19 years (2000).
Transportation: Commute to work: 88.7% car, 0.0% public transportation, 5.7% walk, 5.7% work from home (2000); Travel time to work: 26.0% less than 15 minutes, 28.0% 15 to 30 minutes, 16.0% 30 to 45 minutes, 24.0% 45 to 60 minutes, 6.0% 60 minutes or more (2000)

MICANOPY (town). Covers a land area of 1.034 square miles and a water area of 0.046 square miles. Located at 29.50° N. Lat.; 82.28° W. Long. Elevation is 125 feet.
History: Micanopy was named for the Seminole chief Micanope. Settlement began in 1817 when land was granted to Don Fernando de la Maza Arredondo of Cuba.
Population: 693 (1990); 653 (2000); 612 (2007); 602 (2012 projected); Race: 68.6% White, 27.9% Black, 0.3% Asian, 2.3% Hispanic of any race (2007); Density: 591.8 persons per square mile (2007); Average household size: 2.06 (2007); Median age: 45.7 (2007); Males per 100 females: 98.1 (2007); Marriage status: 24.0% never married, 48.6% now married, 12.6% widowed, 14.7% divorced (2000); Foreign born: 3.5% (2000); Ancestry (includes multiple ancestries): 25.8% Other groups, 15.1% United States or American, 10.4% English, 7.9% German, 6.6% Irish (2000).
Economy: Employment by occupation: 9.0% management, 26.5% professional, 18.7% services, 24.0% sales, 0.0% farming, 6.9% construction, 15.0% production (2000).
Income: Per capita income: $28,664 (2007); Median household income: $35,893 (2007); Average household income: $59,066 (2007); Percent of households with income of $100,000 or more: 15.2% (2007); Poverty rate: 15.7% (2000).
Education: Percent of population age 25 and over with: High school diploma (including GED) or higher: 76.3% (2007); Bachelor's degree or higher: 29.0% (2007); Master's degree or higher: 13.5% (2007).
School District(s)
Alachua County School District (PK-12)
  2005-06 Enrollment: 29,259 . . . . (352) 955-7880
Housing: Homeownership rate: 68.7% (2007); Median home value: $116,429 (2007); Median rent: $359 per month (2000); Median age of housing: 34 years (2000).
Transportation: Commute to work: 90.4% car, 0.0% public transportation, 1.6% walk, 4.5% work from home (2000); Travel time to work: 13.4% less than 15 minutes, 54.4% 15 to 30 minutes, 26.2% 30 to 45 minutes, 2.3% 45 to 60 minutes, 3.7% 60 minutes or more (2000)

NEWBERRY (city). Covers a land area of 44.916 square miles and a water area of 1.055 square miles. Located at 29.64° N. Lat.; 82.60° W. Long. Elevation is 75 feet.
History: Newberry developed as a shipping center for the watermelons grown on nearby farms.
Population: 2,683 (1990); 3,316 (2000); 4,187 (2007); 4,889 (2012 projected); Race: 84.3% White, 13.2% Black, 0.4% Asian, 2.9% Hispanic of any race (2007); Density: 93.2 persons per square mile (2007); Average household size: 2.53 (2007); Median age: 34.2 (2007); Males per 100 females: 92.6 (2007); Marriage status: 22.3% never married, 56.9% now married, 7.9% widowed, 12.9% divorced (2000); Foreign born: 3.6% (2000); Ancestry (includes multiple ancestries): 22.2% Other groups, 13.0% United States or American, 12.7% Irish, 11.9% English, 8.0% German (2000).
Economy: Single-family building permits issued: 12 (2006); Multi-family building permits issued: 0 (2006); Employment by occupation: 9.1% management, 16.6% professional, 16.0% services, 30.6% sales, 0.6% farming, 15.2% construction, 11.9% production (2000).
Income: Per capita income: $19,091 (2007); Median household income: $39,654 (2007); Average household income: $48,358 (2007); Percent of households with income of $100,000 or more: 9.3% (2007); Poverty rate: 12.8% (2000).
Education: Percent of population age 25 and over with: High school diploma (including GED) or higher: 79.4% (2007); Bachelor's degree or higher: 13.9% (2007); Master's degree or higher: 4.7% (2007).
School District(s)
Alachua County School District (PK-12)
  2005-06 Enrollment: 29,259 . . . . (352) 955-7880
Housing: Homeownership rate: 81.0% (2007); Median home value: $126,661 (2007); Median rent: $330 per month (2000); Median age of housing: 17 years (2000).
Transportation: Commute to work: 94.4% car, 0.8% public transportation, 1.1% walk, 2.1% work from home (2000); Travel time to work: 17.0% less than 15 minutes, 26.3% 15 to 30 minutes, 40.9% 30 to 45 minutes, 9.5% 45 to 60 minutes, 6.3% 60 minutes or more (2000)
Additional Information Contacts
Newberry Chamber of Commerce . . . . (352) 472-6611
  http://www.newberrychamber.com

WALDO (city). Covers a land area of 1.719 square miles and a water area of 0 square miles. Located at 29.79° N. Lat.; 82.17° W. Long. Elevation is 167 feet.
History: Waldo developed as a shipping center, with produce from around Lake Santa Fe brought by steamer on a canal constructed in 1870, and transferred to the Seaboard Air Line Railway at Waldo.
Population: 924 (1990); 821 (2000); 815 (2007); 835 (2012 projected); Race: 76.7% White, 12.0% Black, 0.9% Asian, 2.8% Hispanic of any race (2007); Density: 474.0 persons per square mile (2007); Average household size: 2.26 (2007); Median age: 36.0 (2007); Males per 100 females: 95.9 (2007); Marriage status: 25.9% never married, 49.5% now married, 9.5% widowed, 15.1% divorced (2000); Foreign born: 1.4% (2000); Ancestry (includes multiple ancestries): 27.9% United States or American, 26.7% Other groups, 9.1% English, 7.9% German, 5.3% Irish (2000).
Economy: Single-family building permits issued: 0 (2006); Multi-family building permits issued: 0 (2006); Employment by occupation: 5.8% management, 12.2% professional, 25.1% services, 31.5% sales, 0.6% farming, 16.5% construction, 8.3% production (2000).
Income: Per capita income: $17,276 (2007); Median household income: $28,370 (2007); Average household income: $39,003 (2007); Percent of households with income of $100,000 or more: 3.3% (2007); Poverty rate: 16.7% (2000).
Education: Percent of population age 25 and over with: High school diploma (including GED) or higher: 72.8% (2007); Bachelor's degree or higher: 9.1% (2007); Master's degree or higher: 3.7% (2007).
School District(s)
Alachua County School District (PK-12)
  2005-06 Enrollment: 29,259 . . . . (352) 955-7880
Housing: Homeownership rate: 69.5% (2007); Median home value: $79,211 (2007); Median rent: $327 per month (2000); Median age of housing: 31 years (2000).
Safety: Violent crime rate: 12.7 per 10,000 population; Property crime rate: 114.1 per 10,000 population (2006).
Transportation: Commute to work: 92.9% car, 0.6% public transportation, 4.0% walk, 1.2% work from home (2000); Travel time to work: 11.2% less

than 15 minutes, 35.4% 15 to 30 minutes, 34.2% 30 to 45 minutes, 12.7% 45 to 60 minutes, 6.5% 60 minutes or more (2000); Amtrak: Service available.

Baker County

Located in northern Florida; bounded on the north by Georgia; includes part of Okefenokee Swamp and Osceola National Forest. Covers a land area of 585.21 square miles, a water area of 3.67 square miles, and is located in the Eastern Time Zone. The county was founded in 1861. County seat is Macclenny.

Baker County is part of the Jacksonville, FL Metropolitan Statistical Area. The entire metro area includes: Baker County, FL; Clay County, FL; Duval County, FL; Nassau County, FL; St. Johns County, FL

Population: 18,486 (1990); 22,259 (2000); 24,787 (2007); 26,362 (2012 projected); Race: 84.9% White, 13.1% Black, 0.5% Asian, 2.4% Hispanic of any race (2007); Density: 42.4 persons per square mile (2007); Average household size: 3.09 (2007); Median age: 34.6 (2007); Males per 100 females: 111.3 (2007).
Religion: Five largest groups: 14.2% Southern Baptist Convention, 3.6% Assemblies of God, 2.3% The United Methodist Church, 2.3% The Church of Jesus Christ of Latter-day Saints, 2.2% Church of God (Cleveland, Tennessee) (2000).
Economy: Unemployment rate: 3.8% (11/2007); Total civilian labor force: 11,776 (11/2007); Leading industries: 32.2% health care and social assistance; 18.3% transportation & warehousing; 11.8% retail trade (2005); Farms: 204 totaling 18,061 acres (2002); Companies that employ 500 or more persons: 2 (2005); Companies that employ 100 to 499 persons: 6 (2005); Companies that employ less than 100 persons: 373 (2005); Black-owned businesses: n/a (2002); Hispanic-owned businesses: n/a (2002); Asian-owned businesses: n/a (2002); Women-owned businesses: 197 (2002); Retail sales per capita: $6,988 (2007). Single-family building permits issued: 226 (2006); Multi-family building permits issued: 0 (2006).
Income: Per capita income: $18,442 (2007); Median household income: $47,154 (2007); Average household income: $54,952 (2007); Percent of households with income of $100,000 or more: 9.9% (2007); Poverty rate: 14.5% (2005); Bankruptcy rate: 1.63% (2006).
Education: Percent of population age 25 and over with: High school diploma (including GED) or higher: 72.0% (2007); Bachelor's degree or higher: 8.4% (2007); Master's degree or higher: 3.0% (2007).
Housing: Homeownership rate: 81.6% (2007); Median home value: $131,321 (2007); Median rent: $310 per month (2000); Median age of housing: 19 years (2000).
Health: Birth rate: 158.3 per 10,000 population (2006); Death rate: 63.5 per 10,000 population (2006); Age-adjusted cancer mortality rate: 223.3 deaths per 100,000 population (2004); Air Quality Index: 95.1% good, 4.9% moderate, 0.0% unhealthy for sensitive individuals, 0.0% unhealthy (percent of days in 2006); Number of physicians: 6.5 per 10,000 population (2005); Hospital beds: 28.4 per 10,000 population (2004); Hospital admissions: 539.4 per 10,000 population (2004).
Elections: 2004 Presidential election results: 77.7% Bush, 21.9% Kerry, 0.2% Nader, 0.1% Badnarik
National and State Parks: Osceola National Forest
Additional Information Contacts
Baker County Government . . . . (904) 259-3613
   http://www.bakercountyfl.org
Baker County Chamber of Commerce. . . . . (904) 259-6433
   http://www.bakerchamberfl.com

Baker County Communities

GLEN SAINT MARY (town). Covers a land area of 0.420 square
miles and a water area of 0 square miles. Located at 30.27° N. Lat.; 82.16° W. Long. Elevation is 131 feet.
Population: 504 (1990); 473 (2000); 511 (2007); 534 (2012 projected); Race: 97.8% White, 0.6% Black, 0.8% Asian, 3.1% Hispanic of any race (2007); Density: 1,217.6 persons per square mile (2007); Average household size: 2.57 (2007); Median age: 32.4 (2007); Males per 100 females: 91.4 (2007); Marriage status: 20.2% never married, 57.7% now married, 6.4% widowed, 15.7% divorced (2000); Foreign born: 1.3% (2000); Ancestry (includes multiple ancestries): 34.4% United States or American, 11.1% Other groups, 6.0% Irish, 4.2% English, 2.2% Scotch-Irish (2000).

Economy: Employment by occupation: 10.5% management, 11.4% professional, 27.6% services, 25.2% sales, 4.3% farming, 9.0% construction, 11.9% production (2000).
Income: Per capita income: $16,248 (2007); Median household income: $34,022 (2007); Average household income: $41,721 (2007); Percent of households with income of $100,000 or more: 6.5% (2007); Poverty rate: 18.2% (2000).
Education: Percent of population age 25 and over with: High school diploma (including GED) or higher: 68.1% (2007); Bachelor's degree or higher: 6.1% (2007); Master's degree or higher: 1.0% (2007).
School District(s)
Baker County School District (PK-12)
   2005-06 Enrollment: 4,775 . . . . (904) 259-0401
Housing: Homeownership rate: 67.8% (2007); Median home value: $81,875 (2007); Median rent: $345 per month (2000); Median age of housing: 22 years (2000).
Transportation: Commute to work: 91.8% car, 0.0% public transportation, 2.9% walk, 0.5% work from home (2000); Travel time to work: 33.8% less than 15 minutes, 26.6% 15 to 30 minutes, 22.2% 30 to 45 minutes, 4.8% 45 to 60 minutes, 12.6% 60 minutes or more (2000)

MACCLENNY (city). County seat. Covers a land area of 3.291 square
miles and a water area of 0 square miles. Located at 30.28° N. Lat.; 82.12° W. Long. Elevation is 131 feet.
History: MacClenny had an early reputation as Florida's "Gretna Green" for its many quick weddings. It was said that when the judge was absent, his wife would perform the ceremony.
Population: 4,070 (1990); 4,459 (2000); 4,765 (2007); 4,984 (2012 projected); Race: 73.7% White, 23.8% Black, 0.8% Asian, 3.4% Hispanic of any race (2007); Density: 1,447.8 persons per square mile (2007); Average household size: 2.83 (2007); Median age: 30.9 (2007); Males per 100 females: 94.6 (2007); Marriage status: 18.1% never married, 58.8% now married, 7.9% widowed, 15.2% divorced (2000); Foreign born: 1.3% (2000); Ancestry (includes multiple ancestries): 21.2% Other groups, 15.1% United States or American, 9.3% Irish, 7.1% English, 6.1% German (2000).
Economy: Single-family building permits issued: 119 (2006); Multi-family building permits issued: 0 (2006); Employment by occupation: 8.5% management, 17.6% professional, 22.8% services, 24.2% sales, 0.5% farming, 13.0% construction, 13.6% production (2000).
Income: Per capita income: $17,488 (2007); Median household income: $37,619 (2007); Average household income: $46,395 (2007); Percent of households with income of $100,000 or more: 5.3% (2007); Poverty rate: 20.9% (2000).
Education: Percent of population age 25 and over with: High school diploma (including GED) or higher: 71.8% (2007); Bachelor's degree or higher: 14.2% (2007); Master's degree or higher: 5.4% (2007).
School District(s)
Baker County School District (PK-12)
   2005-06 Enrollment: 4,775 . . . . (904) 259-0401
Housing: Homeownership rate: 67.2% (2007); Median home value: $131,545 (2007); Median rent: $348 per month (2000); Median age of housing: 26 years (2000).
Hospitals: Ed Fraser Memorial Hospital (25 beds); Northeast Florida State Hospital (553 beds)
Newspapers: The Baker County Press (General - Circulation 5,400)
Transportation: Commute to work: 93.4% car, 0.0% public transportation, 0.9% walk, 3.3% work from home (2000); Travel time to work: 39.6% less than 15 minutes, 16.3% 15 to 30 minutes, 19.8% 30 to 45 minutes, 17.5% 45 to 60 minutes, 6.7% 60 minutes or more (2000)
Additional Information Contacts
Baker County Chamber of Commerce. . . . . (904) 259-6433
   http://www.bakerchamberfl.com

SANDERSON (unincorporated postal area, zip code 32087). Covers a
land area of 110.442 square miles and a water area of 0.756 square miles. Located at 30.39° N. Lat.; 82.26° W. Long. Elevation is 156 feet.
History: Sanderson was named in 1859 for an early settler.
Population: 3,331 (2000); Race: 76.9% White, 21.3% Black, 0.0% Asian, 2.9% Hispanic of any race (2000); Density: 30.2 persons per square mile (2000); Age: 34.7% under 18, 8.6% over 64 (2000); Marriage status: 27.6% never married, 53.8% now married, 6.9% widowed, 11.7% divorced (2000); Foreign born: 0.0% (2000); Ancestry (includes multiple ancestries): 28.7% Other groups, 25.2% United States or American, 9.8% Irish, 3.7% German, 3.4% English (2000).

Economy: Employment by occupation: 5.5% management, 9.5% professional, 23.4% services, 22.9% sales, 2.4% farming, 17.4% construction, 19.0% production (2000).
Income: Per capita income: $13,887 (2000); Median household income: $34,432 (2000); Poverty rate: 16.1% (2000).
Education: Percent of population age 25 and over with: High school diploma (including GED) or higher: 69.7% (2000); Bachelor's degree or higher: 3.4% (2000).
Housing: Homeownership rate: 79.6% (2000); Median home value: $70,500 (2000); Median rent: $280 per month (2000); Median age of housing: 19 years (2000).
Transportation: Commute to work: 97.0% car, 0.7% public transportation, 0.0% walk, 1.8% work from home (2000); Travel time to work: 8.9% less than 15 minutes, 27.6% 15 to 30 minutes, 21.7% 30 to 45 minutes, 14.2% 45 to 60 minutes, 27.5% 60 minutes or more (2000)

Bay County

Located in northwestern Florida; bounded on the south by the Gulf of Mexico. Covers a land area of 763.68 square miles, a water area of 269.60 square miles, and is located in the Central Time Zone. The county was founded in 1913. County seat is Panama City.

Bay County is part of the Panama City-Lynn Haven, FL Metropolitan Statistical Area. The entire metro area includes: Bay County, FL

Weather Station: Panama City 5 NE   Elevation: 29 feet

	Jan	Feb	Mar	Apr	May	Jun	Jul	Aug	Sep	Oct	Nov	Dec
High	63	65	71	77	84	88	90	90	88	80	73	65
Low	40	42	48	54	62	69	72	71	68	56	48	41
Precip	6.0	4.9	6.2	3.9	4.0	6.1	8.9	7.5	6.2	3.7	4.6	4.1
Snow	tr	tr	0.0	0.0	0.0	0.0	0.0	0.0	0.0	0.0	0.0	0.0

High and Low temperatures in degrees Fahrenheit; Precipitation and Snow in inches

Population: 126,994 (1990); 148,217 (2000); 165,965 (2007); 177,709 (2012 projected); Race: 83.1% White, 11.3% Black, 1.8% Asian, 3.3% Hispanic of any race (2007); Density: 217.3 persons per square mile (2007); Average household size: 2.44 (2007); Median age: 39.5 (2007); Males per 100 females: 98.2 (2007).
Religion: Five largest groups: 18.8% Southern Baptist Convention, 6.5% The United Methodist Church, 4.7% Catholic Church, 2.6% Assemblies of God, 1.0% Lutheran Church—Missouri Synod (2000).
Economy: Unemployment rate: 4.0% (11/2007); Total civilian labor force: 87,555 (11/2007); Leading industries: 17.1% retail trade; 15.8% health care and social assistance; 15.1% accommodation & food services (2005); Farms: 116 totaling 10,863 acres (2002); Companies that employ 500 or more persons: 7 (2005); Companies that employ 100 to 499 persons: 82 (2005); Companies that employ less than 100 persons: 4,541 (2005); Black-owned businesses: 377 (2002); Hispanic-owned businesses: 153 (2002); Asian-owned businesses: 494 (2002); Women-owned businesses: 3,071 (2002); Retail sales per capita: $16,548 (2007). Single-family building permits issued: 920 (2006); Multi-family building permits issued: 2,156 (2006).
Income: Per capita income: $23,103 (2007); Median household income: $43,586 (2007); Average household income: $55,815 (2007); Percent of households with income of $100,000 or more: 11.7% (2007); Poverty rate: 13.7% (2005); Bankruptcy rate: 1.32% (2006).
Taxes: Total county taxes per capita: $368 (2005); County property taxes per capita: $294 (2005).
Education: Percent of population age 25 and over with: High school diploma (including GED) or higher: 81.5% (2007); Bachelor's degree or higher: 18.0% (2007); Master's degree or higher: 6.7% (2007).
Housing: Homeownership rate: 69.5% (2007); Median home value: $163,702 (2007); Median rent: $442 per month (2000); Median age of housing: 19 years (2000).
Health: Birth rate: 146.4 per 10,000 population (2006); Death rate: 87.8 per 10,000 population (2006); Age-adjusted cancer mortality rate: 199.3 deaths per 100,000 population (2004); Air Quality Index: 86.0% good, 14.0% moderate, 0.0% unhealthy for sensitive individuals, 0.0% unhealthy (percent of days in 2006); Number of physicians: 20.9 per 10,000 population (2005); Hospital beds: 38.4 per 10,000 population (2004); Hospital admissions: 1,892.2 per 10,000 population (2004).
Elections: 2004 Presidential election results: 71.2% Bush, 28.1% Kerry, 0.5% Nader, 0.1% Badnarik
National and State Parks: Camp Helen State Park; Pine Log State Forest; Saint Andrews State Park

Additional Information Contacts
Bay County Government . . . . (850) 747-5100
  http://www.co.bay.fl.us
City of Callaway . . . . (850) 871-6000
  http://www.cityofcallaway.com
City of Lynn Haven. . . . . (850) 265-2121
  http://www.cityoflynnhaven.com
City of Panama City Beach . . . . (850) 233-5100
  http://www.pcbgov.com
City of Springfield. . . . . (850) 872-7570
  http://www.springfieldfl.org
Panama City Chamber of Commerce . . . . (850) 785-5206
  http://www.panamacity.org

Bay County Communities

CALLAWAY (city). Aka Calloway. Covers a land area of 5.685 square miles and a water area of 0.412 square miles. Located at 30.14° N. Lat.; 85.57° W. Long. Elevation is 33 feet.
Population: 13,001 (1990); 14,233 (2000); 14,363 (2007); 14,541 (2012 projected); Race: 70.1% White, 20.8% Black, 3.3% Asian, 4.4% Hispanic of any race (2007); Density: 2,526.3 persons per square mile (2007); Average household size: 2.52 (2007); Median age: 35.1 (2007); Males per 100 females: 99.1 (2007); Marriage status: 23.0% never married, 58.7% now married, 5.1% widowed, 13.2% divorced (2000); Foreign born: 5.9% (2000); Ancestry (includes multiple ancestries): 30.2% Other groups, 13.9% United States or American, 10.4% Irish, 10.0% German, 8.4% English (2000).
Economy: Single-family building permits issued: 67 (2006); Multi-family building permits issued: 2 (2006); Employment by occupation: 7.4% management, 15.9% professional, 21.8% services, 31.9% sales, 0.6% farming, 10.0% construction, 12.4% production (2000).
Income: Per capita income: $20,037 (2007); Median household income: $42,681 (2007); Average household income: $50,429 (2007); Percent of households with income of $100,000 or more: 8.4% (2007); Poverty rate: 11.6% (2000).
Education: Percent of population age 25 and over with: High school diploma (including GED) or higher: 83.1% (2007); Bachelor's degree or higher: 14.0% (2007); Master's degree or higher: 5.5% (2007).
Housing: Homeownership rate: 64.7% (2007); Median home value: $161,630 (2007); Median rent: $417 per month (2000); Median age of housing: 18 years (2000).
Transportation: Commute to work: 96.0% car, 0.4% public transportation, 0.9% walk, 1.6% work from home (2000); Travel time to work: 24.1% less than 15 minutes, 54.2% 15 to 30 minutes, 12.8% 30 to 45 minutes, 2.6% 45 to 60 minutes, 6.3% 60 minutes or more (2000)
Additional Information Contacts
City of Callaway . . . . (850) 871-6000
  http://www.cityofcallaway.com

CEDAR GROVE (town). Covers a land area of 9.375 square miles and a water area of 0 square miles. Located at 30.21° N. Lat.; 85.60° W. Long. Elevation is 33 feet.
Population: 4,329 (1990); 5,367 (2000); 5,856 (2007); 6,204 (2012 projected); Race: 80.8% White, 14.0% Black, 1.9% Asian, 3.2% Hispanic of any race (2007); Density: 624.6 persons per square mile (2007); Average household size: 2.54 (2007); Median age: 34.6 (2007); Males per 100 females: 93.2 (2007); Marriage status: 22.2% never married, 56.2% now married, 5.7% widowed, 15.9% divorced (2000); Foreign born: 3.0% (2000); Ancestry (includes multiple ancestries): 21.7% United States or American, 19.1% Other groups, 10.0% Irish, 8.8% German, 6.8% English (2000).
Economy: Employment by occupation: 4.4% management, 10.6% professional, 24.3% services, 29.4% sales, 0.4% farming, 17.9% construction, 13.0% production (2000).
Income: Per capita income: $17,057 (2007); Median household income: $33,914 (2007); Average household income: $43,134 (2007); Percent of households with income of $100,000 or more: 5.9% (2007); Poverty rate: 19.0% (2000).
Education: Percent of population age 25 and over with: High school diploma (including GED) or higher: 72.3% (2007); Bachelor's degree or higher: 8.3% (2007); Master's degree or higher: 3.2% (2007).
Housing: Homeownership rate: 67.6% (2007); Median home value: $105,988 (2007); Median rent: $378 per month (2000); Median age of housing: 17 years (2000).

Safety: Violent crime rate: 18.8 per 10,000 population; Property crime rate: 201.4 per 10,000 population (2006).
Transportation: Commute to work: 93.0% car, 0.7% public transportation, 1.1% walk, 2.0% work from home (2000); Travel time to work: 37.0% less than 15 minutes, 41.7% 15 to 30 minutes, 14.6% 30 to 45 minutes, 4.3% 45 to 60 minutes, 2.5% 60 minutes or more (2000)

FOUNTAIN (unincorporated postal area, zip code 32438). Covers a land area of 72.899 square miles and a water area of 0.280 square miles. Located at 30.48° N. Lat.; 85.41° W. Long. Elevation is 184 feet.

Population: 3,365 (2000); Race: 94.6% White, 0.6% Black, 1.9% Asian, 4.1% Hispanic of any race (2000); Density: 46.2 persons per square mile (2000); Age: 27.2% under 18, 9.6% over 64 (2000); Marriage status: 15.8% never married, 65.5% now married, 5.7% widowed, 13.0% divorced (2000); Foreign born: 3.1% (2000); Ancestry (includes multiple ancestries): 25.3% United States or American, 15.2% Other groups, 14.2% German, 12.1% Irish, 6.1% English (2000).
Economy: Employment by occupation: 4.0% management, 5.3% professional, 21.9% services, 27.6% sales, 0.5% farming, 23.8% construction, 16.8% production (2000).
Income: Per capita income: $12,267 (2000); Median household income: $25,465 (2000); Poverty rate: 28.9% (2000).
Education: Percent of population age 25 and over with: High school diploma (including GED) or higher: 59.1% (2000); Bachelor's degree or higher: 4.6% (2000).
Housing: Homeownership rate: 90.3% (2000); Median home value: $42,500 (2000); Median rent: $278 per month (2000); Median age of housing: 18 years (2000).
Transportation: Commute to work: 93.8% car, 0.0% public transportation, 0.0% walk, 1.2% work from home (2000); Travel time to work: 9.1% less than 15 minutes, 11.2% 15 to 30 minutes, 48.5% 30 to 45 minutes, 19.7% 45 to 60 minutes, 11.5% 60 minutes or more (2000)

HILAND PARK (CDP). Covers a land area of 1.133 square miles and a water area of 0 square miles. Located at 30.20° N. Lat.; 85.62° W. Long. Elevation is 36 feet.

Population: 1,016 (1990); 999 (2000); 1,039 (2007); 1,068 (2012 projected); Race: 90.2% White, 6.5% Black, 2.1% Asian, 1.7% Hispanic of any race (2007); Density: 917.3 persons per square mile (2007); Average household size: 2.62 (2007); Median age: 40.0 (2007); Males per 100 females: 97.2 (2007); Marriage status: 18.1% never married, 49.7% now married, 8.5% widowed, 23.7% divorced (2000); Foreign born: 3.4% (2000); Ancestry (includes multiple ancestries): 20.4% United States or American, 15.9% Other groups, 6.9% Irish, 5.7% German, 4.4% English (2000).
Economy: Employment by occupation: 10.4% management, 18.3% professional, 20.3% services, 26.6% sales, 0.0% farming, 19.5% construction, 4.8% production (2000).
Income: Per capita income: $20,454 (2007); Median household income: $45,116 (2007); Average household income: $53,352 (2007); Percent of households with income of $100,000 or more: 10.4% (2007); Poverty rate: 19.3% (2000).
Education: Percent of population age 25 and over with: High school diploma (including GED) or higher: 83.0% (2007); Bachelor's degree or higher: 17.2% (2007); Master's degree or higher: 4.9% (2007).
Housing: Homeownership rate: 77.8% (2007); Median home value: $106,250 (2007); Median rent: $370 per month (2000); Median age of housing: 22 years (2000).
Transportation: Commute to work: 90.6% car, 0.0% public transportation, 6.1% walk, 1.3% work from home (2000); Travel time to work: 35.7% less than 15 minutes, 33.4% 15 to 30 minutes, 14.7% 30 to 45 minutes, 13.6% 45 to 60 minutes, 2.6% 60 minutes or more (2000)

LAGUNA BEACH (CDP). Covers a land area of 2.558 square miles and a water area of 0.141 square miles. Located at 30.25° N. Lat.; 85.94° W. Long. Elevation is 23 feet.

Population: 1,886 (1990); 2,909 (2000); 4,062 (2007); 4,762 (2012 projected); Race: 93.3% White, 1.4% Black, 1.9% Asian, 1.5% Hispanic of any race (2007); Density: 1,588.2 persons per square mile (2007); Average household size: 2.10 (2007); Median age: 47.2 (2007); Males per 100 females: 97.8 (2007); Marriage status: 21.1% never married, 56.2% now married, 6.4% widowed, 16.2% divorced (2000); Foreign born: 2.3% (2000); Ancestry (includes multiple ancestries): 17.8% English, 17.1% German, 17.0% United States or American, 16.0% Other groups, 11.8% Irish (2000).

Economy: Employment by occupation: 10.3% management, 12.1% professional, 22.5% services, 25.1% sales, 0.0% farming, 19.6% construction, 10.4% production (2000).
Income: Per capita income: $25,598 (2007); Median household income: $42,139 (2007); Average household income: $53,792 (2007); Percent of households with income of $100,000 or more: 9.6% (2007); Poverty rate: 14.8% (2000).
Education: Percent of population age 25 and over with: High school diploma (including GED) or higher: 84.6% (2007); Bachelor's degree or higher: 21.0% (2007); Master's degree or higher: 5.8% (2007).
Housing: Homeownership rate: 69.5% (2007); Median home value: $207,784 (2007); Median rent: $491 per month (2000); Median age of housing: 20 years (2000).
Transportation: Commute to work: 91.5% car, 0.8% public transportation, 1.5% walk, 1.1% work from home (2000); Travel time to work: 31.0% less than 15 minutes, 31.3% 15 to 30 minutes, 25.2% 30 to 45 minutes, 8.0% 45 to 60 minutes, 4.5% 60 minutes or more (2000)

LOWER GRAND LAGOON (CDP). Covers a land area of 2.174 square miles and a water area of 0.517 square miles. Located at 30.15° N. Lat.; 85.76° W. Long. Elevation is 10 feet.

Population: 3,323 (1990); 4,082 (2000); 4,452 (2007); 4,689 (2012 projected); Race: 95.0% White, 1.7% Black, 0.8% Asian, 4.4% Hispanic of any race (2007); Density: 2,047.9 persons per square mile (2007); Average household size: 1.93 (2007); Median age: 44.5 (2007); Males per 100 females: 103.8 (2007); Marriage status: 27.4% never married, 47.6% now married, 9.2% widowed, 15.9% divorced (2000); Foreign born: 6.8% (2000); Ancestry (includes multiple ancestries): 15.2% German, 14.6% English, 14.6% Irish, 11.8% Other groups, 8.5% United States or American (2000).
Economy: Employment by occupation: 12.9% management, 14.3% professional, 23.1% services, 30.8% sales, 1.2% farming, 12.1% construction, 5.5% production (2000).
Income: Per capita income: $21,287 (2007); Median household income: $32,997 (2007); Average household income: $41,044 (2007); Percent of households with income of $100,000 or more: 6.2% (2007); Poverty rate: 16.3% (2000).
Education: Percent of population age 25 and over with: High school diploma (including GED) or higher: 89.7% (2007); Bachelor's degree or higher: 21.2% (2007); Master's degree or higher: 6.4% (2007).
Housing: Homeownership rate: 52.2% (2007); Median home value: $177,500 (2007); Median rent: $515 per month (2000); Median age of housing: 17 years (2000).
Transportation: Commute to work: 91.6% car, 0.0% public transportation, 2.4% walk, 2.3% work from home (2000); Travel time to work: 39.4% less than 15 minutes, 42.6% 15 to 30 minutes, 13.3% 30 to 45 minutes, 1.5% 45 to 60 minutes, 3.1% 60 minutes or more (2000)

LYNN HAVEN (city). Covers a land area of 8.150 square miles and a water area of 1.378 square miles. Located at 30.24° N. Lat.; 85.64° W. Long. Elevation is 13 feet.

Population: 10,502 (1990); 12,451 (2000); 15,481 (2007); 17,427 (2012 projected); Race: 85.4% White, 9.7% Black, 1.8% Asian, 2.4% Hispanic of any race (2007); Density: 1,899.4 persons per square mile (2007); Average household size: 2.49 (2007); Median age: 39.1 (2007); Males per 100 females: 93.5 (2007); Marriage status: 19.9% never married, 61.6% now married, 6.4% widowed, 12.2% divorced (2000); Foreign born: 2.8% (2000); Ancestry (includes multiple ancestries): 17.2% Other groups, 14.9% United States or American, 14.4% Irish, 12.9% German, 11.6% English (2000).
Economy: Single-family building permits issued: 84 (2006); Multi-family building permits issued: 0 (2006); Employment by occupation: 12.7% management, 22.9% professional, 14.2% services, 29.6% sales, 0.6% farming, 9.7% construction, 10.3% production (2000).
Income: Per capita income: $25,213 (2007); Median household income: $50,334 (2007); Average household income: $62,703 (2007); Percent of households with income of $100,000 or more: 15.6% (2007); Poverty rate: 7.2% (2000).
Education: Percent of population age 25 and over with: High school diploma (including GED) or higher: 86.0% (2007); Bachelor's degree or higher: 22.7% (2007); Master's degree or higher: 8.0% (2007).
School District(s)
Bay County School District (PK-12)
    2005-06 Enrollment: 27,147 . . . . (850) 872-7700

Housing: Homeownership rate: 77.1% (2007); Median home value: $187,780 (2007); Median rent: $417 per month (2000); Median age of housing: 19 years (2000).
Safety: Violent crime rate: 167.5 per 10,000 population; Property crime rate: 226.5 per 10,000 population (2006).
Transportation: Commute to work: 95.1% car, 0.1% public transportation, 1.5% walk, 1.5% work from home (2000); Travel time to work: 35.6% less than 15 minutes, 48.0% 15 to 30 minutes, 12.1% 30 to 45 minutes, 1.4% 45 to 60 minutes, 2.9% 60 minutes or more (2000)
Additional Information Contacts
City of Lynn Haven.................................(850) 265-2121
  http://www.cityoflynnhaven.com

MEXICO BEACH (city). Covers a land area of 1.308 square miles and a water area of 0.015 square miles. Located at 29.94° N. Lat.; 85.40° W. Long. Elevation is 13 feet.
Population: 1,012 (1990); 1,017 (2000); 1,308 (2007); 1,494 (2012 projected); Race: 94.3% White, 1.8% Black, 1.1% Asian, 2.1% Hispanic of any race (2007); Density: 999.7 persons per square mile (2007); Average household size: 1.90 (2007); Median age: 57.0 (2007); Males per 100 females: 97.6 (2007); Marriage status: 11.0% never married, 64.7% now married, 10.3% widowed, 14.0% divorced (2000); Foreign born: 3.4% (2000); Ancestry (includes multiple ancestries): 22.8% United States or American, 19.0% German, 15.3% Irish, 14.2% English, 12.3% Other groups (2000).
Economy: Single-family building permits issued: 7 (2006); Multi-family building permits issued: 0 (2006); Employment by occupation: 18.4% management, 14.9% professional, 16.2% services, 27.4% sales, 0.5% farming, 12.0% construction, 10.6% production (2000).
Income: Per capita income: $25,864 (2007); Median household income: $36,441 (2007); Average household income: $49,029 (2007); Percent of households with income of $100,000 or more: 11.9% (2007); Poverty rate: 11.5% (2000).
Education: Percent of population age 25 and over with: High school diploma (including GED) or higher: 83.9% (2007); Bachelor's degree or higher: 19.1% (2007); Master's degree or higher: 6.5% (2007).
Housing: Homeownership rate: 73.9% (2007); Median home value: $205,000 (2007); Median rent: $484 per month (2000); Median age of housing: 20 years (2000).
Safety: Violent crime rate: 41.3 per 10,000 population; Property crime rate: 354.8 per 10,000 population (2006).
Transportation: Commute to work: 86.8% car, 0.0% public transportation, 5.9% walk, 5.3% work from home (2000); Travel time to work: 46.2% less than 15 minutes, 28.5% 15 to 30 minutes, 13.4% 30 to 45 minutes, 7.0% 45 to 60 minutes, 4.8% 60 minutes or more (2000)

PANAMA CITY (city). County seat. Covers a land area of 20.519 square miles and a water area of 6.171 square miles. Located at 30.17° N. Lat.; 85.66° W. Long. Elevation is 26 feet.
History: In 1909 Panama City was united in incorporation with St. Andrews and Millville. St. Andrews had been a flourishing community in the early 1800's, when homesteaders who came during the Revolutionary War established indigo plantations and engaged in lumbering and fishing. Growth came to Panama City with the founding of paper mills in 1931.
Population: 36,193 (1990); 36,417 (2000); 36,923 (2007); 37,375 (2012 projected); Race: 71.7% White, 22.8% Black, 1.6% Asian, 4.4% Hispanic of any race (2007); Density: 1,799.5 persons per square mile (2007); Average household size: 2.43 (2007); Median age: 37.8 (2007); Males per 100 females: 95.7 (2007); Marriage status: 23.5% never married, 53.8% now married, 8.2% widowed, 14.5% divorced (2000); Foreign born: 3.2% (2000); Ancestry (includes multiple ancestries): 25.9% Other groups, 12.9% United States or American, 10.3% Irish, 9.8% German, 9.1% English (2000).
Economy: Unemployment rate: 4.0% (11/2007); Total civilian labor force: 18,560 (11/2007); Employment by occupation: 10.9% management, 21.2% professional, 20.8% services, 27.7% sales, 0.4% farming, 8.6% construction, 10.4% production (2000).
Income: Per capita income: $21,357 (2007); Median household income: $37,292 (2007); Average household income: $51,039 (2007); Percent of households with income of $100,000 or more: 10.3% (2007); Poverty rate: 17.2% (2000).
Taxes: Total city taxes per capita: $645 (2005); City property taxes per capita: $210 (2005).

Education: Percent of population age 25 and over with: High school diploma (including GED) or higher: 79.6% (2007); Bachelor's degree or higher: 19.2% (2007); Master's degree or higher: 7.5% (2007).
School District(s)
Bay County School District (PK-12)
  2005-06 Enrollment: 27,147 ....(850) 872-7700
Four-year College(s)
Gooding Institute of Nurse Anesthesia (Public)
  Fall 2006 Enrollment: 39 ....(850) 747-6918
Two-year College(s)
Gulf Coast Community College (Public)
  Fall 2006 Enrollment: 6,152 ....(850) 769-1551
  2006-07 Tuition: In-state $2,006; Out-of-state $6,805
Tom P Haney Technical Center (Public)
  Fall 2006 Enrollment: 377 ....(850) 747-5500
Housing: Homeownership rate: 57.6% (2007); Median home value: $145,210 (2007); Median rent: $435 per month (2000); Median age of housing: 31 years (2000).
Hospitals: 325th Medical Group (AETC) (25 beds); Bay Medical Center (413 beds); Gulf Coast Medical Center (176 beds)
Safety: Violent crime rate: 106.0 per 10,000 population; Property crime rate: 563.3 per 10,000 population (2006).
Newspapers: The News Herald (Circulation 32,350)
Transportation: Commute to work: 93.9% car, 0.7% public transportation, 1.6% walk, 2.2% work from home (2000); Travel time to work: 44.1% less than 15 minutes, 40.2% 15 to 30 minutes, 10.3% 30 to 45 minutes, 2.6% 45 to 60 minutes, 2.8% 60 minutes or more (2000)
Airports: Panama City-Bay Co International (primary service); Tyndall AFB (primary service)
Additional Information Contacts
Panama City Chamber of Commerce ....(850) 785-5206
  http://www.panamacity.org

PANAMA CITY BEACH (city). Covers a land area of 6.943 square miles and a water area of 0.100 square miles. Located at 30.20° N. Lat.; 85.85° W. Long. Elevation is 10 feet.
History: Panama City Beach developed as a resort and fishing center in an area where English soldiers were given land grants in the late 1700's.
Population: 4,306 (1990); 7,671 (2000); 11,903 (2007); 14,556 (2012 projected); Race: 95.3% White, 1.3% Black, 0.8% Asian, 3.2% Hispanic of any race (2007); Density: 1,714.5 persons per square mile (2007); Average household size: 2.13 (2007); Median age: 47.1 (2007); Males per 100 females: 100.4 (2007); Marriage status: 15.7% never married, 63.0% now married, 6.9% widowed, 14.5% divorced (2000); Foreign born: 4.1% (2000); Ancestry (includes multiple ancestries): 17.8% English, 17.4% German, 14.8% Irish, 11.1% United States or American, 8.1% Other groups (2000).
Economy: Single-family building permits issued: 51 (2006); Multi-family building permits issued: 1,346 (2006); Employment by occupation: 13.8% management, 18.8% professional, 20.4% services, 29.3% sales, 0.2% farming, 9.3% construction, 8.2% production (2000).
Income: Per capita income: $30,267 (2007); Median household income: $50,872 (2007); Average household income: $64,369 (2007); Percent of households with income of $100,000 or more: 14.7% (2007); Poverty rate: 5.0% (2000).
Education: Percent of population age 25 and over with: High school diploma (including GED) or higher: 87.4% (2007); Bachelor's degree or higher: 24.6% (2007); Master's degree or higher: 9.0% (2007).
School District(s)
Bay County School District (PK-12)
  2005-06 Enrollment: 27,147 ....(850) 872-7700
Housing: Homeownership rate: 72.9% (2007); Median home value: $212,689 (2007); Median rent: $589 per month (2000); Median age of housing: 14 years (2000).
Safety: Violent crime rate: 79.7 per 10,000 population; Property crime rate: 704.3 per 10,000 population (2006).
Transportation: Commute to work: 90.3% car, 0.0% public transportation, 5.0% walk, 3.0% work from home (2000); Travel time to work: 48.0% less than 15 minutes, 30.5% 15 to 30 minutes, 15.0% 30 to 45 minutes, 2.8% 45 to 60 minutes, 3.7% 60 minutes or more (2000)
Additional Information Contacts
City of Panama City Beach ....(850) 233-5100
  http://www.pcbgov.com

PARKER (city). Covers a land area of 1.941 square miles and a water area of 0.488 square miles. Located at 30.13° N. Lat.; 85.60° W. Long. Elevation is 20 feet.

Population: 4,559 (1990); 4,623 (2000); 4,717 (2007); 4,809 (2012 projected); Race: 77.2% White, 15.2% Black, 2.9% Asian, 2.8% Hispanic of any race (2007); Density: 2,430.1 persons per square mile (2007); Average household size: 2.27 (2007); Median age: 39.6 (2007); Males per 100 females: 97.6 (2007); Marriage status: 20.3% never married, 55.9% now married, 6.9% widowed, 16.8% divorced (2000); Foreign born: 5.1% (2000); Ancestry (includes multiple ancestries): 21.4% United States or American, 21.0% Other groups, 12.3% Irish, 10.6% German, 10.0% English (2000).

Economy: Employment by occupation: 9.5% management, 17.8% professional, 21.8% services, 25.5% sales, 0.6% farming, 14.8% construction, 10.0% production (2000).

Income: Per capita income: $23,779 (2007); Median household income: $44,966 (2007); Average household income: $54,081 (2007); Percent of households with income of $100,000 or more: 10.9% (2007); Poverty rate: 12.2% (2000).

Education: Percent of population age 25 and over with: High school diploma (including GED) or higher: 82.3% (2007); Bachelor's degree or higher: 18.0% (2007); Master's degree or higher: 5.9% (2007).

Housing: Homeownership rate: 61.9% (2007); Median home value: $151,346 (2007); Median rent: $449 per month (2000); Median age of housing: 24 years (2000).

Safety: Violent crime rate: 27.4 per 10,000 population; Property crime rate: 267.3 per 10,000 population (2006).

Transportation: Commute to work: 93.1% car, 0.5% public transportation, 2.2% walk, 2.4% work from home (2000); Travel time to work: 30.4% less than 15 minutes, 47.2% 15 to 30 minutes, 11.8% 30 to 45 minutes, 4.3% 45 to 60 minutes, 6.4% 60 minutes or more (2000)

PRETTY BAYOU (CDP). Covers a land area of 1.974 square miles and a water area of 0.141 square miles. Located at 30.19° N. Lat.; 85.69° W. Long. Elevation is 13 feet.

Population: 3,685 (1990); 3,519 (2000); 3,489 (2007); 3,457 (2012 projected); Race: 93.2% White, 3.1% Black, 1.3% Asian, 2.1% Hispanic of any race (2007); Density: 1,767.4 persons per square mile (2007); Average household size: 2.44 (2007); Median age: 48.8 (2007); Males per 100 females: 94.6 (2007); Marriage status: 16.7% never married, 62.0% now married, 9.9% widowed, 11.4% divorced (2000); Foreign born: 2.7% (2000); Ancestry (includes multiple ancestries): 17.1% German, 16.3% English, 14.2% United States or American, 10.1% Irish, 8.9% Other groups (2000).

Economy: Employment by occupation: 12.7% management, 23.9% professional, 15.5% services, 30.0% sales, 1.0% farming, 6.3% construction, 10.6% production (2000).

Income: Per capita income: $29,516 (2007); Median household income: $54,343 (2007); Average household income: $71,892 (2007); Percent of households with income of $100,000 or more: 19.4% (2007); Poverty rate: 6.0% (2000).

Education: Percent of population age 25 and over with: High school diploma (including GED) or higher: 84.8% (2007); Bachelor's degree or higher: 28.2% (2007); Master's degree or higher: 11.3% (2007).

Housing: Homeownership rate: 82.2% (2007); Median home value: $243,952 (2007); Median rent: $433 per month (2000); Median age of housing: 27 years (2000).

Transportation: Commute to work: 96.0% car, 0.0% public transportation, 0.4% walk, 3.2% work from home (2000); Travel time to work: 47.0% less than 15 minutes, 41.4% 15 to 30 minutes, 6.2% 30 to 45 minutes, 1.1% 45 to 60 minutes, 4.3% 60 minutes or more (2000)

SPRINGFIELD (city). Covers a land area of 3.962 square miles and a water area of 0.162 square miles. Located at 30.16° N. Lat.; 85.61° W. Long. Elevation is 26 feet.

Population: 9,120 (1990); 8,810 (2000); 8,861 (2007); 8,924 (2012 projected); Race: 63.2% White, 26.0% Black, 4.8% Asian, 4.1% Hispanic of any race (2007); Density: 2,236.5 persons per square mile (2007); Average household size: 2.54 (2007); Median age: 33.3 (2007); Males per 100 females: 91.7 (2007); Marriage status: 24.6% never married, 54.4% now married, 7.2% widowed, 13.8% divorced (2000); Foreign born: 5.0% (2000); Ancestry (includes multiple ancestries): 32.2% Other groups, 14.1% United States or American, 10.0% Irish, 7.4% English, 5.9% German (2000).

Economy: Employment by occupation: 8.7% management, 12.6% professional, 24.9% services, 26.5% sales, 0.3% farming, 15.2% construction, 13.8% production (2000).

Income: Per capita income: $15,696 (2007); Median household income: $33,702 (2007); Average household income: $39,584 (2007); Percent of households with income of $100,000 or more: 2.1% (2007); Poverty rate: 21.5% (2000).

Education: Percent of population age 25 and over with: High school diploma (including GED) or higher: 69.0% (2007); Bachelor's degree or higher: 7.8% (2007); Master's degree or higher: 2.1% (2007).

Housing: Homeownership rate: 59.9% (2007); Median home value: $111,031 (2007); Median rent: $376 per month (2000); Median age of housing: 27 years (2000).

Safety: Violent crime rate: 97.9 per 10,000 population; Property crime rate: 442.6 per 10,000 population (2006).

Transportation: Commute to work: 97.7% car, 0.1% public transportation, 0.5% walk, 1.2% work from home (2000); Travel time to work: 31.6% less than 15 minutes, 48.0% 15 to 30 minutes, 15.4% 30 to 45 minutes, 2.5% 45 to 60 minutes, 2.5% 60 minutes or more (2000)

Additional Information Contacts

City of Springfield . . . . (850) 872-7570
   http://www.springfieldfl.org

TYNDALL AFB (CDP). Covers a land area of 14.574 square miles and a water area of 0.064 square miles. Located at 30.07° N. Lat.; 85.57° W. Long.

Population: 4,321 (1990); 2,757 (2000); 2,272 (2007); 2,009 (2012 projected); Race: 73.2% White, 14.1% Black, 3.1% Asian, 11.0% Hispanic of any race (2007); Density: 155.9 persons per square mile (2007); Average household size: 4.27 (2007); Median age: 22.0 (2007); Males per 100 females: 124.7 (2007); Marriage status: 28.0% never married, 69.4% now married, 0.7% widowed, 1.9% divorced (2000); Foreign born: 4.6% (2000); Ancestry (includes multiple ancestries): 29.9% Other groups, 15.2% German, 10.4% Irish, 10.3% United States or American, 6.0% Italian (2000).

Economy: Employment by occupation: 6.3% management, 25.1% professional, 22.0% services, 39.5% sales, 0.0% farming, 4.4% construction, 2.7% production (2000).

Income: Per capita income: $13,793 (2007); Median household income: $39,800 (2007); Average household income: $49,041 (2007); Percent of households with income of $100,000 or more: 5.3% (2007); Poverty rate: 3.6% (2000).

Education: Percent of population age 25 and over with: High school diploma (including GED) or higher: 96.7% (2007); Bachelor's degree or higher: 22.3% (2007); Master's degree or higher: 7.8% (2007).

School District(s)

Bay County School District (PK-12)
   2005-06 Enrollment: 27,147 . . . . (850) 872-7700

Housing: Homeownership rate: 1.3% (2007); Median home value: $325,000 (2007); Median rent: $694 per month (2000); Median age of housing: 33 years (2000).

Transportation: Commute to work: 91.3% car, 0.0% public transportation, 3.6% walk, 1.8% work from home (2000); Travel time to work: 66.3% less than 15 minutes, 26.7% 15 to 30 minutes, 6.1% 30 to 45 minutes, 0.5% 45 to 60 minutes, 0.5% 60 minutes or more (2000)

UPPER GRAND LAGOON (CDP). Covers a land area of 8.248 square miles and a water area of 7.674 square miles. Located at 30.17° N. Lat.; 85.75° W. Long.

Population: 7,855 (1990); 10,889 (2000); 12,678 (2007); 13,871 (2012 projected); Race: 93.0% White, 1.5% Black, 1.9% Asian, 3.1% Hispanic of any race (2007); Density: 1,537.1 persons per square mile (2007); Average household size: 2.33 (2007); Median age: 41.5 (2007); Males per 100 females: 103.9 (2007); Marriage status: 19.8% never married, 62.9% now married, 5.0% widowed, 12.3% divorced (2000); Foreign born: 3.8% (2000); Ancestry (includes multiple ancestries): 16.6% United States or American, 15.8% English, 15.0% Irish, 13.5% German, 10.7% Other groups (2000).

Economy: Employment by occupation: 15.4% management, 19.6% professional, 22.5% services, 26.1% sales, 1.0% farming, 8.2% construction, 7.2% production (2000).

Income: Per capita income: $29,460 (2007); Median household income: $48,511 (2007); Average household income: $67,663 (2007); Percent of households with income of $100,000 or more: 18.1% (2007); Poverty rate: 9.6% (2000).

Education: Percent of population age 25 and over with: High school diploma (including GED) or higher: 88.0% (2007); Bachelor's degree or higher: 23.1% (2007); Master's degree or higher: 9.2% (2007).
Housing: Homeownership rate: 69.5% (2007); Median home value: $238,321 (2007); Median rent: $525 per month (2000); Median age of housing: 14 years (2000).
Transportation: Commute to work: 92.3% car, 0.0% public transportation, 1.9% walk, 4.4% work from home (2000); Travel time to work: 49.6% less than 15 minutes, 33.6% 15 to 30 minutes, 11.9% 30 to 45 minutes, 1.7% 45 to 60 minutes, 3.2% 60 minutes or more (2000)

YOUNGSTOWN (unincorporated postal area, zip code 32466).
Covers a land area of 123.232 square miles and a water area of 0.178 square miles. Located at 30.37° N. Lat.; 85.52° W. Long. Elevation is 88 feet.
Population: 5,546 (2000); Race: 93.5% White, 1.3% Black, 0.3% Asian, 1.5% Hispanic of any race (2000); Density: 45.0 persons per square mile (2000); Age: 28.5% under 18, 8.0% over 64 (2000); Marriage status: 17.1% never married, 65.4% now married, 5.6% widowed, 11.9% divorced (2000); Foreign born: 2.8% (2000); Ancestry (includes multiple ancestries): 27.3% United States or American, 17.3% Other groups, 11.8% Irish, 9.7% English, 8.0% German (2000).
Economy: Employment by occupation: 9.3% management, 12.4% professional, 14.9% services, 24.9% sales, 0.7% farming, 19.1% construction, 18.6% production (2000).
Income: Per capita income: $14,899 (2000); Median household income: $35,000 (2000); Poverty rate: 12.0% (2000).
Education: Percent of population age 25 and over with: High school diploma (including GED) or higher: 73.7% (2000); Bachelor's degree or higher: 5.7% (2000).

School District(s)
Bay County School District (PK-12)
    2005-06 Enrollment: 27,147 . . . . (850) 872-7700
Housing: Homeownership rate: 91.3% (2000); Median home value: $84,000 (2000); Median rent: $433 per month (2000); Median age of housing: 14 years (2000).
Transportation: Commute to work: 93.0% car, 0.8% public transportation, 0.8% walk, 3.0% work from home (2000); Travel time to work: 11.1% less than 15 minutes, 35.0% 15 to 30 minutes, 31.7% 30 to 45 minutes, 12.4% 45 to 60 minutes, 9.8% 60 minutes or more (2000)

Bradford County

Located in northern Florida; bounded on the south by the Santa Fe River. Covers a land area of 293.13 square miles, a water area of 6.91 square miles, and is located in the Eastern Time Zone. The county was founded in 1858. County seat is Starke.
Population: 22,515 (1990); 26,088 (2000); 28,693 (2007); 30,519 (2012 projected); Race: 75.0% White, 22.0% Black, 0.7% Asian, 3.0% Hispanic of any race (2007); Density: 97.9 persons per square mile (2007); Average household size: 3.07 (2007); Median age: 37.4 (2007); Males per 100 females: 133.3 (2007).
Religion: Five largest groups: 33.8% Southern Baptist Convention, 4.0% The United Methodist Church, 2.5% Church of God (Cleveland, Tennessee), 1.4% The Church of Jesus Christ of Latter-day Saints, 1.3% Presbyterian Church (U.S.A.) (2000).
Economy: Unemployment rate: 3.4% (11/2007); Total civilian labor force: 12,449 (11/2007); Leading industries: 19.4% accommodation & food services; 19.0% health care and social assistance; 18.3% retail trade (2005); Farms: 378 totaling 44,819 acres (2002); Companies that employ 500 or more persons: 0 (2005); Companies that employ 100 to 499 persons: 11 (2005); Companies that employ less than 100 persons: 442 (2005); Black-owned businesses: n/a (2002); Hispanic-owned businesses: n/a (2002); Asian-owned businesses: n/a (2002); Women-owned businesses: 406 (2002); Retail sales per capita: $10,299 (2007). Single-family building permits issued: 124 (2006); Multi-family building permits issued: 0 (2006).
Income: Per capita income: $16,331 (2007); Median household income: $39,094 (2007); Average household income: $48,663 (2007); Percent of households with income of $100,000 or more: 7.6% (2007); Poverty rate: 15.9% (2005); Bankruptcy rate: 1.09% (2006).
Taxes: Total county taxes per capita: $284 (2005); County property taxes per capita: $181 (2005).

Education: Percent of population age 25 and over with: High school diploma (including GED) or higher: 74.3% (2007); Bachelor's degree or higher: 8.3% (2007); Master's degree or higher: 3.3% (2007).
Housing: Homeownership rate: 79.1% (2007); Median home value: $135,853 (2007); Median rent: $323 per month (2000); Median age of housing: 23 years (2000).
Health: Birth rate: 119.8 per 10,000 population (2006); Death rate: 93.4 per 10,000 population (2006); Age-adjusted cancer mortality rate: 190.9 deaths per 100,000 population (2004); Number of physicians: 5.0 per 10,000 population (2005); Hospital beds: 9.1 per 10,000 population (2004); Hospital admissions: 374.2 per 10,000 population (2004).
Elections: 2004 Presidential election results: 69.6% Bush, 29.9% Kerry, 0.3% Nader, 0.1% Badnarik
Additional Information Contacts
Bradford County Government . . . . (904) 964-6280
    http://www.bradford-co-fla.org
City of Starke . . . . (904) 964-5027
Starke Chamber of Commerce . . . . (904) 964-5278
    http://www.northfloridachamber.com

Bradford County Communities

BROOKER (town). Covers a land area of 0.525 square miles and a water area of 0 square miles. Located at 29.88° N. Lat.; 82.33° W. Long. Elevation is 128 feet.
Population: 312 (1990); 352 (2000); 377 (2007); 394 (2012 projected); Race: 96.6% White, 1.1% Black, 0.0% Asian, 3.4% Hispanic of any race (2007); Density: 718.4 persons per square mile (2007); Average household size: 2.83 (2007); Median age: 40.5 (2007); Males per 100 females: 89.4 (2007); Marriage status: 27.1% never married, 59.7% now married, 7.5% widowed, 5.8% divorced (2000); Foreign born: 0.0% (2000); Ancestry (includes multiple ancestries): 12.0% United States or American, 10.8% Other groups, 9.4% German, 7.9% Irish, 5.6% English (2000).
Economy: Employment by occupation: 6.0% management, 9.9% professional, 13.9% services, 27.8% sales, 4.6% farming, 25.8% construction, 11.9% production (2000).
Income: Per capita income: $21,913 (2007); Median household income: $47,500 (2007); Average household income: $62,030 (2007); Percent of households with income of $100,000 or more: 9.8% (2007); Poverty rate: 14.0% (2000).
Education: Percent of population age 25 and over with: High school diploma (including GED) or higher: 64.1% (2007); Bachelor's degree or higher: 9.5% (2007); Master's degree or higher: 3.8% (2007).

School District(s)
Bradford County School District (PK-12)
    2005-06 Enrollment: 3,831 . . . . (904) 966-6018
Housing: Homeownership rate: 82.7% (2007); Median home value: $91,667 (2007); Median rent: $275 per month (2000); Median age of housing: 27 years (2000).
Transportation: Commute to work: 93.4% car, 1.3% public transportation, 2.0% walk, 1.3% work from home (2000); Travel time to work: 6.7% less than 15 minutes, 36.9% 15 to 30 minutes, 32.9% 30 to 45 minutes, 3.4% 45 to 60 minutes, 20.1% 60 minutes or more (2000)

HAMPTON (city). Covers a land area of 1.033 square miles and a water area of 0 square miles. Located at 29.86° N. Lat.; 82.13° W. Long. Elevation is 151 feet.
Population: 317 (1990); 431 (2000); 521 (2007); 584 (2012 projected); Race: 83.5% White, 15.0% Black, 0.0% Asian, 2.1% Hispanic of any race (2007); Density: 504.1 persons per square mile (2007); Average household size: 2.64 (2007); Median age: 37.9 (2007); Males per 100 females: 98.9 (2007); Marriage status: 23.7% never married, 47.6% now married, 13.4% widowed, 15.4% divorced (2000); Foreign born: 1.6% (2000); Ancestry (includes multiple ancestries): 16.7% German, 12.8% Other groups, 11.6% French (except Basque), 10.4% English, 8.1% United States or American (2000).
Economy: Employment by occupation: 10.2% management, 9.6% professional, 24.0% services, 19.8% sales, 3.6% farming, 15.0% construction, 18.0% production (2000).
Income: Per capita income: $15,841 (2007); Median household income: $29,306 (2007); Average household income: $40,051 (2007); Percent of households with income of $100,000 or more: 7.1% (2007); Poverty rate: 26.6% (2000).

Education: Percent of population age 25 and over with: High school diploma (including GED) or higher: 65.0% (2007); Bachelor's degree or higher: 2.7% (2007); Master's degree or higher: 1.5% (2007).
School District(s)
Bradford County School District (PK-12)
 2005-06 Enrollment: 3,831 . . . . (904) 966-6018
Housing: Homeownership rate: 79.2% (2007); Median home value: $85,000 (2007); Median rent: $228 per month (2000); Median age of housing: 26 years (2000).
Transportation: Commute to work: 96.4% car, 0.0% public transportation, 3.6% walk, 0.0% work from home (2000); Travel time to work: 27.4% less than 15 minutes, 22.6% 15 to 30 minutes, 16.7% 30 to 45 minutes, 10.1% 45 to 60 minutes, 23.2% 60 minutes or more (2000)

LAWTEY (city). Covers a land area of 1.376 square miles and a water area of 0 square miles. Located at 30.04° N. Lat.; 82.07° W. Long. Elevation is 161 feet.
History: Lawtey grew as a shipping center for strawberries raised in Bradford County.
Population: 663 (1990); 656 (2000); 798 (2007); 884 (2012 projected); Race: 67.7% White, 28.8% Black, 0.0% Asian, 2.1% Hispanic of any race (2007); Density: 580.1 persons per square mile (2007); Average household size: 2.48 (2007); Median age: 32.5 (2007); Males per 100 females: 98.5 (2007); Marriage status: 23.8% never married, 57.1% now married, 9.2% widowed, 9.9% divorced (2000); Foreign born: 2.1% (2000); Ancestry (includes multiple ancestries): 24.9% United States or American, 23.1% Other groups, 8.0% German, 7.3% Irish, 6.6% English (2000).
Economy: Employment by occupation: 6.4% management, 14.5% professional, 23.6% services, 28.2% sales, 2.3% farming, 11.4% construction, 13.6% production (2000).
Income: Per capita income: $17,240 (2007); Median household income: $29,483 (2007); Average household income: $42,725 (2007); Percent of households with income of $100,000 or more: 6.5% (2007); Poverty rate: 22.8% (2000).
Education: Percent of population age 25 and over with: High school diploma (including GED) or higher: 66.0% (2007); Bachelor's degree or higher: 8.3% (2007); Master's degree or higher: 2.2% (2007).
School District(s)
Bradford County School District (PK-12)
 2005-06 Enrollment: 3,831 . . . . (904) 966-6018
Housing: Homeownership rate: 70.2% (2007); Median home value: $114,516 (2007); Median rent: $269 per month (2000); Median age of housing: 23 years (2000).
Safety: Violent crime rate: 0.0 per 10,000 population; Property crime rate: 186.8 per 10,000 population (2006).
Transportation: Commute to work: 99.1% car, 0.0% public transportation, 0.0% walk, 0.9% work from home (2000); Travel time to work: 19.0% less than 15 minutes, 30.1% 15 to 30 minutes, 18.5% 30 to 45 minutes, 26.4% 45 to 60 minutes, 6.0% 60 minutes or more (2000)

STARKE (city). County seat. Covers a land area of 6.664 square miles and a water area of 0 square miles. Located at 29.94° N. Lat.; 82.10° W. Long. Elevation is 164 feet.
History: Starke was named for Starke Perry, governor of Florida from 1857-1861, and grew as the seat of Bradford County with strawberry growing and truck gardening as early industries.
Population: 5,226 (1990); 5,593 (2000); 5,860 (2007); 6,058 (2012 projected); Race: 65.0% White, 31.5% Black, 1.5% Asian, 2.8% Hispanic of any race (2007); Density: 879.4 persons per square mile (2007); Average household size: 2.78 (2007); Median age: 36.3 (2007); Males per 100 females: 90.6 (2007); Marriage status: 23.3% never married, 47.3% now married, 12.7% widowed, 16.6% divorced (2000); Foreign born: 3.5% (2000); Ancestry (includes multiple ancestries): 30.8% Other groups, 10.9% United States or American, 9.9% English, 7.8% German, 7.8% Irish (2000).
Economy: Employment by occupation: 8.4% management, 12.9% professional, 27.0% services, 25.0% sales, 1.6% farming, 12.4% construction, 12.7% production (2000).
Income: Per capita income: $15,117 (2007); Median household income: $30,793 (2007); Average household income: $40,162 (2007); Percent of households with income of $100,000 or more: 6.9% (2007); Poverty rate: 23.9% (2000).
Education: Percent of population age 25 and over with: High school diploma (including GED) or higher: 77.0% (2007); Bachelor's degree or higher: 11.3% (2007); Master's degree or higher: 4.9% (2007).

School District(s)
Bradford County School District (PK-12)
 2005-06 Enrollment: 3,831 . . . . (904) 966-6018
Clay County School District (PK-12)
 2005-06 Enrollment: 32,605 . . . . (904) 284-6510
Vocational/Technical School(s)
Bradford-Union Area Career Technical Center (Public)
 Fall 2006 Enrollment: 148 . . . . (904) 966-6764
 2006-07 Tuition: $1,050
Housing: Homeownership rate: 65.5% (2007); Median home value: $120,647 (2007); Median rent: $311 per month (2000); Median age of housing: 30 years (2000).
Hospitals: Shands at Starke (49 beds)
Safety: Violent crime rate: 99.3 per 10,000 population; Property crime rate: 279.3 per 10,000 population (2006).
Newspapers: Bradford County Telegraph (General - Circulation 9,500)
Transportation: Commute to work: 91.4% car, 0.5% public transportation, 2.6% walk, 0.7% work from home (2000); Travel time to work: 43.2% less than 15 minutes, 24.0% 15 to 30 minutes, 11.6% 30 to 45 minutes, 11.2% 45 to 60 minutes, 10.0% 60 minutes or more (2000)
Additional Information Contacts
City of Starke . . . . (904) 964-5027
Starke Chamber of Commerce . . . . (904) 964-5278
 http://www.northfloridachamber.com

Brevard County

Located in central Florida, on the Atlantic coast; bounded on the east by barrier beaches; drained by the St. Johns River in the western marshy peat area. Covers a land area of 1,018.19 square miles, a water area of 538.76 square miles, and is located in the Eastern Time Zone. The county was founded in 1844. County seat is Titusville.

Brevard County is part of the Palm Bay-Melbourne-Titusville, FL Metropolitan Statistical Area. The entire metro area includes: Brevard County, FL

Weather Station: Melbourne Regional Airport   Elevation: 32 feet

	Jan	Feb	Mar	Apr	May	Jun	Jul	Aug	Sep	Oct	Nov	Dec
High	72	73	77	81	85	89	90	90	88	83	78	73
Low	51	52	57	61	67	71	72	73	72	68	61	54
Precip	2.5	2.5	3.0	2.1	4.1	5.7	5.4	5.7	7.2	4.7	3.1	2.3
Snow	0.0	0.0	0.0	0.0	0.0	0.0	0.0	0.0	0.0	0.0	0.0	0.0

High and Low temperatures in degrees Fahrenheit; Precipitation and Snow in inches

Weather Station: Titusville   Elevation: 29 feet

	Jan	Feb	Mar	Apr	May	Jun	Jul	Aug	Sep	Oct	Nov	Dec
High	70	72	77	81	86	90	92	91	89	83	78	73
Low	48	50	55	59	65	70	72	72	71	65	58	51
Precip	2.5	2.8	3.8	2.8	3.7	6.2	7.3	7.5	6.8	4.4	3.5	2.5
Snow	tr	0.0	0.0	0.0	0.0	0.0	0.0	0.0	0.0	0.0	0.0	0.0

High and Low temperatures in degrees Fahrenheit; Precipitation and Snow in inches

Population: 398,978 (1990); 476,230 (2000); 546,599 (2007); 597,055 (2012 projected); Race: 84.8% White, 9.3% Black, 1.8% Asian, 6.4% Hispanic of any race (2007); Density: 536.8 persons per square mile (2007); Average household size: 2.36 (2007); Median age: 43.4 (2007); Males per 100 females: 96.4 (2007).
Religion: Five largest groups: 16.8% Catholic Church, 6.4% Southern Baptist Convention, 4.0% The United Methodist Church, 1.3% Independent, Charismatic Churches, 1.2% Presbyterian Church (U.S.A.) (2000).
Economy: Unemployment rate: 4.6% (11/2007); Total civilian labor force: 264,348 (11/2007); Leading industries: 15.9% retail trade; 14.2% health care and social assistance; 11.2% manufacturing (2005); Farms: 555 totaling 187,570 acres (2002); Companies that employ 500 or more persons: 29 (2005); Companies that employ 100 to 499 persons: 237 (2005); Companies that employ less than 100 persons: 13,358 (2005); Black-owned businesses: 1,474 (2002); Hispanic-owned businesses: 1,532 (2002); Asian-owned businesses: 1,313 (2002); Women-owned businesses: 12,501 (2002); Retail sales per capita: $14,070 (2007). Single-family building permits issued: 3,967 (2006); Multi-family building permits issued: 1,077 (2006).
Income: Per capita income: $25,969 (2007); Median household income: $47,059 (2007); Average household income: $60,859 (2007); Percent of

households with income of $100,000 or more: 14.9% (2007); Poverty rate: 10.1% (2005); Bankruptcy rate: 1.00% (2006).

Taxes: Total county taxes per capita: $396 (2005); County property taxes per capita: $334 (2005).

Education: Percent of population age 25 and over with: High school diploma (including GED) or higher: 86.6% (2007); Bachelor's degree or higher: 23.9% (2007); Master's degree or higher: 8.5% (2007).

Housing: Homeownership rate: 75.3% (2007); Median home value: $194,255 (2007); Median rent: $516 per month (2000); Median age of housing: 19 years (2000).

Health: Birth rate: 104.7 per 10,000 population (2006); Death rate: 106.8 per 10,000 population (2006); Age-adjusted cancer mortality rate: 193.1 deaths per 100,000 population (2004); Air Quality Index: 91.8% good, 7.9% moderate, 0.3% unhealthy for sensitive individuals, 0.0% unhealthy (percent of days in 2006); Number of physicians: 21.5 per 10,000 population (2005); Hospital beds: 33.4 per 10,000 population (2004); Hospital admissions: 1,304.5 per 10,000 population (2004).

Elections: 2004 Presidential election results: 57.7% Bush, 41.6% Kerry, 0.5% Nader, 0.2% Badnarik

National and State Parks: Canaveral National Seashore; Merritt Island National Wildlife Refuge; Saint Johns National Wildlife Refuge

Additional Information Contacts

Brevard County Government . . . . (321) 633-2000
   http://www.countygovt.brevard.fl.us
City of Cape Canaveral . . . . (321) 868-1221
   http://www.myflorida.com/cape
City of Cocoa . . . . (321) 639-7550
   http://www.cocoafl.org
City of Cocoa Beach . . . . (321) 868-3286
   http://www.cityofcocoabeach.com
City of Indian Harbour Beach . . . . (321) 773-7212
   http://www.indianharbourbeach.org
City of Rockledge . . . . (321) 690-3978
   http://www.cityofrockledge.org
City of Satellite Beach . . . . (321) 773-4407
   http://www.satellitebeach.org
City of West Melbourne . . . . (321) 727-7700
   http://www.westmelbourne.org
Cocoa Beach Chamber of Commerce . . . . (321) 459-2200
   http://www.cocoabeachchamber.com
Melbourne Chamber of Commerce . . . . (321) 724-5400
   http://www.melpb-chamber.org
Palm Bay Area Chamber of Commerce. . . . . (321) 724-5400
   http://www.melpb-chamber.org
Space Coast Economic Development Commerce. . . . . (321) 269-3221
Titusville Chamber of Commerce. . . . . (321) 267-3036
   http://www.titusville.org

Brevard County Communities

CAPE CANAVERAL (city). Aka Port Canaveral. Covers a land area of 2.331 square miles and a water area of 0.017 square miles. Located at 28.38° N. Lat.; 80.60° W. Long. Elevation is 10 feet.

Population: 8,007 (1990); 8,829 (2000); 10,970 (2007); 12,464 (2012 projected); Race: 94.1% White, 1.3% Black, 2.2% Asian, 4.3% Hispanic of any race (2007); Density: 4,706.6 persons per square mile (2007); Average household size: 1.71 (2007); Median age: 48.8 (2007); Males per 100 females: 108.8 (2007); Marriage status: 25.2% never married, 44.3% now married, 8.5% widowed, 22.0% divorced (2000); Foreign born: 7.8% (2000); Ancestry (includes multiple ancestries): 22.0% German, 16.4% Irish, 15.4% English, 12.2% Other groups, 8.3% Italian (2000).

Economy: Single-family building permits issued: 14 (2006); Multi-family building permits issued: 28 (2006); Employment by occupation: 13.2% management, 18.7% professional, 20.4% services, 24.7% sales, 0.4% farming, 12.8% construction, 9.8% production (2000).

Income: Per capita income: $28,302 (2007); Median household income: $36,294 (2007); Average household income: $48,316 (2007); Percent of households with income of $100,000 or more: 8.8% (2007); Poverty rate: 11.6% (2000).

Education: Percent of population age 25 and over with: High school diploma (including GED) or higher: 87.0% (2007); Bachelor's degree or higher: 25.7% (2007); Master's degree or higher: 7.9% (2007).

School District(s)

Brevard County School District (PK-12)
   2005-06 Enrollment: 74,824 . . . . (321) 631-1911

Housing: Homeownership rate: 50.5% (2007); Median home value: $186,661 (2007); Median rent: $497 per month (2000); Median age of housing: 24 years (2000).

Transportation: Commute to work: 88.5% car, 1.0% public transportation, 3.1% walk, 2.8% work from home (2000); Travel time to work: 36.2% less than 15 minutes, 32.4% 15 to 30 minutes, 17.6% 30 to 45 minutes, 4.9% 45 to 60 minutes, 8.9% 60 minutes or more (2000)

Additional Information Contacts

City of Cape Canaveral . . . . (321) 868-1221
   http://www.myflorida.com/cape

COCOA (city). Aka Cocoa-Rockledge. Covers a land area of 7.459 square miles and a water area of 2.065 square miles. Located at 28.36° N. Lat.; 80.74° W. Long. Elevation is 36 feet.

History: Cocoa was incorporated in 1895 and named for the coco plum growing in the area. It grew as a popular fishing spot, both from the Indian River bridge and in the ocean surf, and as a citrus shipping center.

Population: 17,762 (1990); 16,412 (2000); 16,598 (2007); 16,883 (2012 projected); Race: 57.9% White, 35.6% Black, 1.0% Asian, 7.3% Hispanic of any race (2007); Density: 2,225.3 persons per square mile (2007); Average household size: 2.32 (2007); Median age: 36.8 (2007); Males per 100 females: 91.8 (2007); Marriage status: 27.8% never married, 46.8% now married, 8.8% widowed, 16.5% divorced (2000); Foreign born: 5.8% (2000); Ancestry (includes multiple ancestries): 36.5% Other groups, 9.6% German, 9.1% United States or American, 9.0% Irish, 8.7% English (2000).

Economy: Single-family building permits issued: 57 (2006); Multi-family building permits issued: 0 (2006); Employment by occupation: 6.6% management, 15.7% professional, 21.7% services, 27.9% sales, 0.1% farming, 12.5% construction, 15.5% production (2000).

Income: Per capita income: $18,031 (2007); Median household income: $30,175 (2007); Average household income: $41,460 (2007); Percent of households with income of $100,000 or more: 7.3% (2007); Poverty rate: 24.1% (2000).

Education: Percent of population age 25 and over with: High school diploma (including GED) or higher: 75.9% (2007); Bachelor's degree or higher: 14.0% (2007); Master's degree or higher: 4.5% (2007).

School District(s)

Brevard County School District (PK-12)
   2005-06 Enrollment: 74,824 . . . . (321) 631-1911

Two-year College(s)

Brevard Community College (Public)
   Fall 2006 Enrollment: 13,670. (321) 632-1111
   2006-07 Tuition: In-state $1,626; Out-of-state $5,928

Housing: Homeownership rate: 58.8% (2007); Median home value: $138,388 (2007); Median rent: $403 per month (2000); Median age of housing: 32 years (2000).

Safety: Violent crime rate: 231.6 per 10,000 population; Property crime rate: 674.5 per 10,000 population (2006).

Transportation: Commute to work: 93.1% car, 0.6% public transportation, 2.5% walk, 0.8% work from home (2000); Travel time to work: 26.1% less than 15 minutes, 42.1% 15 to 30 minutes, 21.7% 30 to 45 minutes, 4.4% 45 to 60 minutes, 5.7% 60 minutes or more (2000)

Additional Information Contacts

City of Cocoa . . . . (321) 639-7550
   http://www.cocoafl.org

COCOA BEACH (city). Covers a land area of 4.891 square miles and a water area of 10.149 square miles. Located at 28.33° N. Lat.; 80.61° W. Long. Elevation is 12 feet.

History: Cocoa Beach began as a small ocean resort built on a dune ridge along the shore.

Population: 12,083 (1990); 12,482 (2000); 12,490 (2007); 12,665 (2012 projected); Race: 95.9% White, 0.8% Black, 1.3% Asian, 2.8% Hispanic of any race (2007); Density: 2,553.7 persons per square mile (2007); Average household size: 1.85 (2007); Median age: 57.0 (2007); Males per 100 females: 99.1 (2007); Marriage status: 17.2% never married, 58.0% now married, 11.5% widowed, 13.3% divorced (2000); Foreign born: 8.6% (2000); Ancestry (includes multiple ancestries): 18.5% Irish, 18.4% German, 16.1% English, 9.3% Italian, 8.2% Other groups (2000).

Economy: Single-family building permits issued: 19 (2006); Multi-family building permits issued: 15 (2006); Employment by occupation: 18.1% management, 25.9% professional, 15.0% services, 26.5% sales, 0.5% farming, 5.7% construction, 8.3% production (2000).

Income: Per capita income: $35,685 (2007); Median household income: $49,576 (2007); Average household income: $65,923 (2007); Percent of

diploma (including GED) or higher: 93.5% (2007); Bachelor's degree or higher: 33.6% (2007); Master's degree or higher: 11.6% (2007).

School District(s)
Brevard County School District (PK-12)
  2005-06 Enrollment: 74,824 . . . . (321) 631-1911
Housing: Homeownership rate: 72.8% (2007); Median home value: $277,887 (2007); Median rent: $555 per month (2000); Median age of housing: 27 years (2000).
Hospitals: Cape Canaveral Hospital (150 beds)
Safety: Violent crime rate: 98.1 per 10,000 population; Property crime rate: 835.1 per 10,000 population (2006).
Transportation: Commute to work: 91.2% car, 0.6% public transportation, 2.2% walk, 3.5% work from home (2000); Travel time to work: 34.8% less than 15 minutes, 31.0% 15 to 30 minutes, 19.1% 30 to 45 minutes, 7.1% 45 to 60 minutes, 8.1% 60 minutes or more (2000)
Airports: Patrick AFB
Additional Information Contacts
City of Cocoa Beach . . . . (321) 868-3286
  http://www.cityofcocoabeach.com

COCOA WEST (CDP).
Covers a land area of 4.281 square miles and a water area of 0 square miles. Located at 28.36° N. Lat.; 80.76° W. Long.
Population: 6,048 (1990); 5,921 (2000); 5,787 (2007); 5,842 (2012 projected); Race: 52.2% White, 42.8% Black, 0.3% Asian, 5.1% Hispanic of any race (2007); Density: 1,351.7 persons per square mile (2007); Average household size: 2.59 (2007); Median age: 33.8 (2007); Males per 100 females: 98.4 (2007); Marriage status: 26.9% never married, 46.4% now married, 7.9% widowed, 18.8% divorced (2000); Foreign born: 2.9% (2000); Ancestry (includes multiple ancestries): 39.5% Other groups, 12.0% United States or American, 8.7% German, 8.2% English, 7.4% Irish (2000).
Economy: Employment by occupation: 8.6% management, 9.8% professional, 22.7% services, 25.4% sales, 1.2% farming, 19.2% construction, 13.2% production (2000).
Income: Per capita income: $14,659 (2007); Median household income: $31,015 (2007); Average household income: $37,889 (2007); Percent of households with income of $100,000 or more: 4.2% (2007); Poverty rate: 26.8% (2000).
Education: Percent of population age 25 and over with: High school diploma (including GED) or higher: 66.0% (2007); Bachelor's degree or higher: 6.7% (2007); Master's degree or higher: 1.4% (2007).
Housing: Homeownership rate: 59.7% (2007); Median home value: $115,030 (2007); Median rent: $422 per month (2000); Median age of housing: 31 years (2000).
Transportation: Commute to work: 93.5% car, 0.0% public transportation, 1.8% walk, 1.1% work from home (2000); Travel time to work: 25.4% less than 15 minutes, 39.8% 15 to 30 minutes, 20.7% 30 to 45 minutes, 5.1% 45 to 60 minutes, 8.9% 60 minutes or more (2000)

GRANT (unincorporated postal area, zip code 32949).
Covers a land area of 2.077 square miles and a water area of 0 square miles. Located at 27.93° N. Lat.; 80.55° W. Long. Elevation is 8 feet.
Population: 735 (2000); Race: 93.3% White, 3.2% Black, 0.0% Asian, 1.8% Hispanic of any race (2000); Density: 353.9 persons per square mile (2000); Age: 18.3% under 18, 19.4% over 64 (2000); Marriage status: 12.7% never married, 78.3% now married, 4.7% widowed, 4.3% divorced (2000); Foreign born: 0.0% (2000); Ancestry (includes multiple ancestries): 20.7% German, 9.6% Scotch-Irish, 9.1% United States or American, 8.4% Other groups, 7.8% Italian (2000).
Economy: Employment by occupation: 10.3% management, 16.6% professional, 18.8% services, 31.0% sales, 4.1% farming, 10.7% construction, 8.5% production (2000).
Income: Per capita income: $24,906 (2000); Median household income: $36,875 (2000); Poverty rate: 16.8% (2000).
Education: Percent of population age 25 and over with: High school diploma (including GED) or higher: 73.5% (2000); Bachelor's degree or higher: 15.0% (2000).
Housing: Homeownership rate: 80.4% (2000); Median home value: $143,500 (2000); Median rent: $364 per month (2000); Median age of housing: 22 years (2000).
Transportation: Commute to work: 90.2% car, 0.0% public transportation, 0.0% walk, 9.8% work from home (2000); Travel time to work: 25.0% less

---

INDIALANTIC (town).
Covers a land area of 1.036 square miles and a water area of 0.201 square miles. Located at 28.08° N. Lat.; 80.56° W. Long. Elevation is 13 feet.
Population: 2,844 (1990); 2,944 (2000); 3,124 (2007); 3,292 (2012 projected); Race: 96.6% White, 0.4% Black, 0.8% Asian, 2.7% Hispanic of any race (2007); Density: 3,014.3 persons per square mile (2007); Average household size: 2.20 (2007); Median age: 48.0 (2007); Males per 100 females: 98.6 (2007); Marriage status: 23.1% never married, 58.3% now married, 7.3% widowed, 11.3% divorced (2000); Foreign born: 5.9% (2000); Ancestry (includes multiple ancestries): 18.9% German, 18.5% English, 16.4% Irish, 13.7% Italian, 5.5% Other groups (2000).
Economy: Single-family building permits issued: 2 (2006); Multi-family building permits issued: 0 (2006); Employment by occupation: 14.1% management, 40.1% professional, 8.0% services, 22.2% sales, 0.5% farming, 10.5% construction, 4.5% production (2000).
Income: Per capita income: $50,114 (2007); Median household income: $80,199 (2007); Average household income: $110,097 (2007); Percent of households with income of $100,000 or more: 37.4% (2007); Poverty rate: 2.3% (2000).
Education: Percent of population age 25 and over with: High school diploma (including GED) or higher: 95.6% (2007); Bachelor's degree or higher: 51.7% (2007); Master's degree or higher: 24.6% (2007).

School District(s)
Brevard County School District (PK-12)
  2005-06 Enrollment: 74,824 . . . . (321) 631-1911
Housing: Homeownership rate: 78.9% (2007); Median home value: $362,609 (2007); Median rent: $660 per month (2000); Median age of housing: 30 years (2000).
Safety: Violent crime rate: 25.6 per 10,000 population; Property crime rate: 294.1 per 10,000 population (2006).
Transportation: Commute to work: 90.5% car, 0.0% public transportation, 1.5% walk, 6.3% work from home (2000); Travel time to work: 45.6% less than 15 minutes, 38.8% 15 to 30 minutes, 9.4% 30 to 45 minutes, 1.4% 45 to 60 minutes, 4.8% 60 minutes or more (2000)

INDIAN HARBOUR BEACH (city).
Covers a land area of 2.140 square miles and a water area of 0.491 square miles. Located at 28.15° N. Lat.; 80.59° W. Long. Elevation is 10 feet.
Population: 6,995 (1990); 8,152 (2000); 8,438 (2007); 8,710 (2012 projected); Race: 94.5% White, 1.1% Black, 1.9% Asian, 4.5% Hispanic of any race (2007); Density: 3,943.7 persons per square mile (2007); Average household size: 2.16 (2007); Median age: 48.8 (2007); Males per 100 females: 91.3 (2007); Marriage status: 17.7% never married, 60.3% now married, 10.3% widowed, 11.7% divorced (2000); Foreign born: 7.3% (2000); Ancestry (includes multiple ancestries): 20.5% German, 18.1% English, 16.1% Irish, 11.1% Other groups, 9.5% Italian (2000).
Economy: Single-family building permits issued: 6 (2006); Multi-family building permits issued: 13 (2006); Employment by occupation: 17.2% management, 29.8% professional, 10.8% services, 27.5% sales, 0.0% farming, 9.3% construction, 5.4% production (2000).
Income: Per capita income: $35,094 (2007); Median household income: $50,560 (2007); Average household income: $75,734 (2007); Percent of households with income of $100,000 or more: 21.0% (2007); Poverty rate: 5.5% (2000).
Education: Percent of population age 25 and over with: High school diploma (including GED) or higher: 93.8% (2007); Bachelor's degree or higher: 39.3% (2007); Master's degree or higher: 17.5% (2007).

School District(s)
Brevard County School District (PK-12)
  2005-06 Enrollment: 74,824 . . . . (321) 631-1911
Housing: Homeownership rate: 74.6% (2007); Median home value: $252,690 (2007); Median rent: $591 per month (2000); Median age of housing: 26 years (2000).
Safety: Violent crime rate: 16.3 per 10,000 population; Property crime rate: 101.4 per 10,000 population (2006).
Transportation: Commute to work: 91.4% car, 0.0% public transportation, 0.9% walk, 4.1% work from home (2000); Travel time to work: 26.5% less than 15 minutes, 49.7% 15 to 30 minutes, 14.0% 30 to 45 minutes, 4.5% 45 to 60 minutes, 5.3% 60 minutes or more (2000)
Additional Information Contacts
City of Indian Harbour Beach . . . . (321) 773-7212
  http://www.indianharbourbeach.org

JUNE PARK (CDP). Covers a land area of 3.729 square miles and a water area of 0 square miles. Located at 28.07° N. Lat.; 80.68° W. Long. Elevation is 26 feet.
Population: 3,714 (1990); 4,367 (2000); 4,891 (2007); 5,284 (2012 projected); Race: 95.7% White, 1.1% Black, 1.7% Asian, 3.3% Hispanic of any race (2007); Density: 1,311.5 persons per square mile (2007); Average household size: 2.48 (2007); Median age: 45.1 (2007); Males per 100 females: 99.8 (2007); Marriage status: 17.4% never married, 66.1% now married, 7.0% widowed, 9.5% divorced (2000); Foreign born: 3.5% (2000); Ancestry (includes multiple ancestries): 22.4% German, 15.6% English, 15.0% Irish, 11.8% Other groups, 10.9% United States or American (2000).
Economy: Employment by occupation: 13.9% management, 17.8% professional, 14.5% services, 29.3% sales, 0.3% farming, 12.8% construction, 11.5% production (2000).
Income: Per capita income: $27,118 (2007); Median household income: $52,438 (2007); Average household income: $67,087 (2007); Percent of households with income of $100,000 or more: 17.9% (2007); Poverty rate: 4.9% (2000).
Education: Percent of population age 25 and over with: High school diploma (including GED) or higher: 81.8% (2007); Bachelor's degree or higher: 16.6% (2007); Master's degree or higher: 8.8% (2007).
Housing: Homeownership rate: 90.7% (2007); Median home value: $220,148 (2007); Median rent: $429 per month (2000); Median age of housing: 27 years (2000).
Transportation: Commute to work: 93.2% car, 0.0% public transportation, 0.5% walk, 2.5% work from home (2000); Travel time to work: 37.4% less than 15 minutes, 42.1% 15 to 30 minutes, 9.3% 30 to 45 minutes, 5.1% 45 to 60 minutes, 6.2% 60 minutes or more (2000)

MALABAR (town). Covers a land area of 10.631 square miles and a water area of 2.582 square miles. Located at 27.99° N. Lat.; 80.58° W. Long. Elevation is 23 feet.
History: Malabar developed around a sawmill, and was named for Cape Malabar on the African coast.
Population: 1,977 (1990); 2,622 (2000); 2,776 (2007); 2,898 (2012 projected); Race: 91.9% White, 4.2% Black, 1.3% Asian, 2.4% Hispanic of any race (2007); Density: 261.1 persons per square mile (2007); Average household size: 2.48 (2007); Median age: 45.8 (2007); Males per 100 females: 105.5 (2007); Marriage status: 18.2% never married, 63.6% now married, 8.2% widowed, 10.1% divorced (2000); Foreign born: 7.4% (2000); Ancestry (includes multiple ancestries): 19.3% English, 18.3% German, 15.1% Irish, 14.2% United States or American, 10.3% Other groups (2000).
Economy: Single-family building permits issued: 28 (2006); Multi-family building permits issued: 0 (2006); Employment by occupation: 11.8% management, 24.1% professional, 15.4% services, 23.5% sales, 0.7% farming, 17.9% construction, 6.6% production (2000).
Income: Per capita income: $31,055 (2007); Median household income: $61,776 (2007); Average household income: $76,804 (2007); Percent of households with income of $100,000 or more: 25.8% (2007); Poverty rate: 10.7% (2000).
Education: Percent of population age 25 and over with: High school diploma (including GED) or higher: 85.8% (2007); Bachelor's degree or higher: 21.2% (2007); Master's degree or higher: 7.5% (2007).
Housing: Homeownership rate: 92.0% (2007); Median home value: $277,811 (2007); Median rent: $450 per month (2000); Median age of housing: 17 years (2000).
Transportation: Commute to work: 94.2% car, 1.0% public transportation, 0.7% walk, 3.5% work from home (2000); Travel time to work: 32.3% less than 15 minutes, 43.2% 15 to 30 minutes, 18.4% 30 to 45 minutes, 0.8% 45 to 60 minutes, 5.3% 60 minutes or more (2000)

MELBOURNE (city). Covers a land area of 30.197 square miles and a water area of 5.292 square miles. Located at 28.11° N. Lat.; 80.63° W. Long. Elevation is 20 feet.
History: Melbourne was named for the Australian city by a resident who had immigrated from there. Melbourne attracted hunting parties going up the St. Johns River, as well as fresh and salt-water fishermen.
Population: 61,834 (1990); 71,382 (2000); 77,266 (2007); 81,907 (2012 projected); Race: 81.8% White, 10.6% Black, 2.8% Asian, 7.6% Hispanic of any race (2007); Density: 2,558.7 persons per square mile (2007); Average household size: 2.28 (2007); Median age: 41.1 (2007); Males per 100 females: 95.3 (2007); Marriage status: 24.3% never married, 53.3% now married, 9.0% widowed, 13.5% divorced (2000); Foreign born: 7.8%

(2000); Ancestry (includes multiple ancestries): 20.2% Other groups, 16.7% German, 14.7% Irish, 12.8% English, 8.2% Italian (2000).
Economy: Unemployment rate: 4.5% (11/2007); Total civilian labor force: 39,818 (11/2007); Single-family building permits issued: 315 (2006); Multi-family building permits issued: 197 (2006); Employment by occupation: 10.9% management, 20.5% professional, 18.2% services, 28.9% sales, 0.3% farming, 10.2% construction, 11.0% production (2000).
Income: Per capita income: $22,888 (2007); Median household income: $39,542 (2007); Average household income: $51,320 (2007); Percent of households with income of $100,000 or more: 10.1% (2007); Poverty rate: 11.5% (2000).
Taxes: Total city taxes per capita: $469 (2005); City property taxes per capita: $180 (2005).
Education: Percent of population age 25 and over with: High school diploma (including GED) or higher: 85.6% (2007); Bachelor's degree or higher: 21.9% (2007); Master's degree or higher: 7.6% (2007).

School District(s)
Brevard County School District (PK-12)
    2005-06 Enrollment: 74,824 . . . . (321) 631-1911
Four-year College(s)
Florida Institute of Technology (Private, Not-for-profit)
    Fall 2006 Enrollment: 4,741. . . . . (321) 674-8000
    2006-07 Tuition: In-state $27,540; Out-of-state $27,540
Florida Metropolitan University-Melbourne (Private, For-profit)
    Fall 2006 Enrollment: 912 . . . . (321) 253-2929
    2006-07 Tuition: In-state $10,820; Out-of-state $10,820
Housing: Homeownership rate: 62.0% (2007); Median home value: $175,175 (2007); Median rent: $510 per month (2000); Median age of housing: 21 years (2000).
Hospitals: Circles of Care (52 beds); Devereux Florida Treatment Network (122 beds); HealthSouth Sea Pines Rehabilitation Hospital (80 beds); Holmes Regional Medical Center (468 beds); Wuesthoff Medical Center - Melbourne (65 beds)
Safety: Violent crime rate: 113.4 per 10,000 population; Property crime rate: 514.5 per 10,000 population (2006).
Newspapers: Bay Bulletin (General - Circulation 30,524); Florida Today (Circulation 94,118); The Press Tribune (General - Circulation 38,022); The Times (General - Circulation 52,778)
Transportation: Commute to work: 94.3% car, 0.3% public transportation, 1.9% walk, 1.9% work from home (2000); Travel time to work: 36.2% less than 15 minutes, 43.3% 15 to 30 minutes, 11.5% 30 to 45 minutes, 4.0% 45 to 60 minutes, 5.0% 60 minutes or more (2000)
Airports: Melbourne International (primary service)
Additional Information Contacts
Melbourne Chamber of Commerce . . . . (321) 724-5400
    http://www.melpb-chamber.org

MELBOURNE BEACH (town). Covers a land area of 1.028 square miles and a water area of 0.255 square miles. Located at 28.06° N. Lat.; 80.56° W. Long. Elevation is 10 feet.
Population: 3,021 (1990); 3,335 (2000); 3,252 (2007); 3,264 (2012 projected); Race: 97.0% White, 0.1% Black, 1.0% Asian, 3.0% Hispanic of any race (2007); Density: 3,162.8 persons per square mile (2007); Average household size: 2.34 (2007); Median age: 48.2 (2007); Males per 100 females: 103.8 (2007); Marriage status: 15.6% never married, 64.6% now married, 7.9% widowed, 11.9% divorced (2000); Foreign born: 6.5% (2000); Ancestry (includes multiple ancestries): 16.9% German, 16.8% Irish, 16.5% English, 12.6% Italian, 7.3% Other groups (2000).
Economy: Single-family building permits issued: 2 (2006); Multi-family building permits issued: 0 (2006); Employment by occupation: 22.5% management, 29.8% professional, 10.8% services, 27.2% sales, 0.4% farming, 6.8% construction, 2.6% production (2000).
Income: Per capita income: $37,443 (2007); Median household income: $64,135 (2007); Average household income: $87,601 (2007); Percent of households with income of $100,000 or more: 23.2% (2007); Poverty rate: 3.8% (2000).
Education: Percent of population age 25 and over with: High school diploma (including GED) or higher: 93.9% (2007); Bachelor's degree or higher: 44.2% (2007); Master's degree or higher: 20.6% (2007).

School District(s)
Brevard County School District (PK-12)
    2005-06 Enrollment: 74,824 . . . . (321) 631-1911
Housing: Homeownership rate: 84.2% (2007); Median home value: $366,384 (2007); Median rent: $622 per month (2000); Median age of housing: 30 years (2000).

Safety: Violent crime rate: 3.0 per 10,000 population; Property crime rate: 124.6 per 10,000 population (2006).
Transportation: Commute to work: 90.1% car, 0.0% public transportation, 1.9% walk, 5.8% work from home (2000); Travel time to work: 28.4% less than 15 minutes, 40.6% 15 to 30 minutes, 18.0% 30 to 45 minutes, 5.2% 45 to 60 minutes, 7.9% 60 minutes or more (2000)

MELBOURNE VILLAGE (town). Covers a land area of 0.570 square miles and a water area of 0 square miles. Located at 28.08° N. Lat.; 80.66° W. Long. Elevation is 23 feet.

Population: 591 (1990); 706 (2000); 760 (2007); 795 (2012 projected); Race: 98.8% White, 0.0% Black, 0.5% Asian, 1.4% Hispanic of any race (2007); Density: 1,334.2 persons per square mile (2007); Average household size: 2.24 (2007); Median age: 49.5 (2007); Males per 100 females: 95.4 (2007); Marriage status: 16.3% never married, 60.9% now married, 11.2% widowed, 11.6% divorced (2000); Foreign born: 5.6% (2000); Ancestry (includes multiple ancestries): 22.9% English, 20.1% German, 15.6% Irish, 12.0% United States or American, 7.9% Italian (2000).
Economy: Single-family building permits issued: 3 (2006); Multi-family building permits issued: 0 (2006); Employment by occupation: 20.7% management, 36.5% professional, 8.4% services, 22.4% sales, 0.0% farming, 5.4% construction, 6.7% production (2000).
Income: Per capita income: $32,766 (2007); Median household income: $51,429 (2007); Average household income: $73,243 (2007); Percent of households with income of $100,000 or more: 18.8% (2007); Poverty rate: 6.4% (2000).
Education: Percent of population age 25 and over with: High school diploma (including GED) or higher: 95.1% (2007); Bachelor's degree or higher: 42.0% (2007); Master's degree or higher: 18.6% (2007).
Housing: Homeownership rate: 90.0% (2007); Median home value: $273,438 (2007); Median rent: $584 per month (2000); Median age of housing: 37 years (2000).
Safety: Violent crime rate: 14.0 per 10,000 population; Property crime rate: 98.0 per 10,000 population (2006).
Transportation: Commute to work: 91.9% car, 0.0% public transportation, 0.7% walk, 6.8% work from home (2000); Travel time to work: 35.3% less than 15 minutes, 50.2% 15 to 30 minutes, 8.4% 30 to 45 minutes, 2.5% 45 to 60 minutes, 3.6% 60 minutes or more (2000)

MERRITT ISLAND (CDP). Covers a land area of 17.651 square miles and a water area of 29.400 square miles. Located at 28.35° N. Lat.; 80.68° W. Long. Elevation is 3 feet.

History: Merritt Island was named for an early settler who received the entire island as a land grant from Spain about 1800. The town of Merritt Island developed as the chief trading center on the island.
Population: 32,886 (1990); 36,090 (2000); 37,565 (2007); 38,955 (2012 projected); Race: 89.4% White, 5.2% Black, 2.0% Asian, 5.1% Hispanic of any race (2007); Density: 2,128.2 persons per square mile (2007); Average household size: 2.38 (2007); Median age: 44.8 (2007); Males per 100 females: 96.2 (2007); Marriage status: 19.6% never married, 58.3% now married, 9.0% widowed, 13.1% divorced (2000); Foreign born: 6.4% (2000); Ancestry (includes multiple ancestries): 19.6% German, 16.0% English, 15.5% Irish, 14.4% Other groups, 8.7% Italian (2000).
Economy: Employment by occupation: 13.9% management, 25.6% professional, 15.6% services, 25.9% sales, 0.5% farming, 9.1% construction, 9.5% production (2000).
Income: Per capita income: $28,838 (2007); Median household income: $50,654 (2007); Average household income: $67,942 (2007); Percent of households with income of $100,000 or more: 19.9% (2007); Poverty rate: 9.4% (2000).
Education: Percent of population age 25 and over with: High school diploma (including GED) or higher: 88.6% (2007); Bachelor's degree or higher: 28.8% (2007); Master's degree or higher: 10.4% (2007).
School District(s)
Brevard County School District (PK-12)
    2005-06 Enrollment: 74,824 . . . . (321) 631-1911
Vocational/Technical School(s)
Academy of Cosmetology (Private, For-profit)
    Fall 2006 Enrollment: 79 . . . . (321) 452-8490
    2006-07 Tuition: $8,200
Housing: Homeownership rate: 75.4% (2007); Median home value: $258,938 (2007); Median rent: $503 per month (2000); Median age of housing: 30 years (2000).

Transportation: Commute to work: 94.2% car, 0.3% public transportation, 1.2% walk, 2.8% work from home (2000); Travel time to work: 33.0% less than 15 minutes, 38.4% 15 to 30 minutes, 16.7% 30 to 45 minutes, 5.8% 45 to 60 minutes, 6.2% 60 minutes or more (2000)
Additional Information Contacts
Cocoa Beach Chamber of Commerce . . . . (321) 459-2200
    http://www.cocoabeachchamber.com

MICCO (CDP). Covers a land area of 9.405 square miles and a water area of 0.263 square miles. Located at 27.87° N. Lat.; 80.51° W. Long. Elevation is 23 feet.

History: Micco grew as a center for citrus growing and commercial fishing. The Sebastian River Bridge near Micco was the scene in 1924 of a confrontation between the Ashley gang, who had been robbing banks for 14 years, and the deputy sheriffs. This was the end of the Ashley gang.
Population: 8,757 (1990); 9,498 (2000); 9,490 (2007); 9,574 (2012 projected); Race: 98.6% White, 0.2% Black, 0.1% Asian, 2.0% Hispanic of any race (2007); Density: 1,009.0 persons per square mile (2007); Average household size: 1.79 (2007); Median age: 69.0 (2007); Males per 100 females: 88.8 (2007); Marriage status: 8.5% never married, 65.2% now married, 16.4% widowed, 10.0% divorced (2000); Foreign born: 5.0% (2000); Ancestry (includes multiple ancestries): 19.9% German, 18.9% Irish, 16.2% English, 10.4% Italian, 6.4% United States or American (2000).
Economy: Employment by occupation: 8.4% management, 11.3% professional, 19.0% services, 33.6% sales, 1.9% farming, 12.5% construction, 13.4% production (2000).
Income: Per capita income: $25,266 (2007); Median household income: $33,978 (2007); Average household income: $45,138 (2007); Percent of households with income of $100,000 or more: 6.2% (2007); Poverty rate: 10.1% (2000).
Education: Percent of population age 25 and over with: High school diploma (including GED) or higher: 77.4% (2007); Bachelor's degree or higher: 10.4% (2007); Master's degree or higher: 4.2% (2007).
Housing: Homeownership rate: 91.8% (2007); Median home value: $131,648 (2007); Median rent: $517 per month (2000); Median age of housing: 17 years (2000).
Transportation: Commute to work: 91.8% car, 0.4% public transportation, 2.2% walk, 2.7% work from home (2000); Travel time to work: 33.6% less than 15 minutes, 30.2% 15 to 30 minutes, 26.0% 30 to 45 minutes, 3.8% 45 to 60 minutes, 6.3% 60 minutes or more (2000)

MIMS (CDP). Covers a land area of 19.797 square miles and a water area of 5.913 square miles. Located at 28.66° N. Lat.; 80.84° W. Long. Elevation is 33 feet.

Population: 9,064 (1990); 9,147 (2000); 10,006 (2007); 10,681 (2012 projected); Race: 87.3% White, 10.0% Black, 0.2% Asian, 2.0% Hispanic of any race (2007); Density: 505.4 persons per square mile (2007); Average household size: 2.49 (2007); Median age: 43.2 (2007); Males per 100 females: 98.8 (2007); Marriage status: 20.7% never married, 58.4% now married, 8.6% widowed, 12.4% divorced (2000); Foreign born: 2.2% (2000); Ancestry (includes multiple ancestries): 19.0% Other groups, 16.4% United States or American, 11.8% German, 11.1% English, 10.5% Irish (2000).
Economy: Employment by occupation: 7.9% management, 17.9% professional, 18.2% services, 26.5% sales, 0.5% farming, 17.1% construction, 11.9% production (2000).
Income: Per capita income: $20,474 (2007); Median household income: $41,747 (2007); Average household income: $50,702 (2007); Percent of households with income of $100,000 or more: 9.1% (2007); Poverty rate: 15.6% (2000).
Education: Percent of population age 25 and over with: High school diploma (including GED) or higher: 77.3% (2007); Bachelor's degree or higher: 11.1% (2007); Master's degree or higher: 3.4% (2007).
School District(s)
Brevard County School District (PK-12)
    2005-06 Enrollment: 74,824 . . . . (321) 631-1911
Housing: Homeownership rate: 86.0% (2007); Median home value: $137,448 (2007); Median rent: $412 per month (2000); Median age of housing: 25 years (2000).
Transportation: Commute to work: 97.4% car, 0.0% public transportation, 0.9% walk, 1.0% work from home (2000); Travel time to work: 27.4% less than 15 minutes, 32.5% 15 to 30 minutes, 23.5% 30 to 45 minutes, 9.4% 45 to 60 minutes, 7.2% 60 minutes or more (2000)

PALM BAY (city).
Covers a land area of 63.645 square miles and a water area of 3.105 square miles. Located at 27.98° N. Lat.; 80.65° W. Long. Elevation is 16 feet.

Population: 62,587 (1990); 79,413 (2000); 97,251 (2007); 109,542 (2012 projected); Race: 77.1% White, 14.1% Black, 1.9% Asian, 11.9% Hispanic of any race (2007); Density: 1,528.0 persons per square mile (2007); Average household size: 2.58 (2007); Median age: 38.0 (2007); Males per 100 females: 95.7 (2007); Marriage status: 21.5% never married, 59.9% now married, 6.5% widowed, 12.0% divorced (2000); Foreign born: 9.5% (2000); Ancestry (includes multiple ancestries): 21.9% Other groups, 17.9% German, 14.6% Irish, 10.1% English, 9.2% Italian (2000).

Economy: Unemployment rate: 5.3% (11/2007); Total civilian labor force: 48,306 (11/2007); Single-family building permits issued: 1,764 (2006); Multi-family building permits issued: 7 (2006); Employment by occupation: 9.6% management, 19.8% professional, 18.8% services, 27.5% sales, 0.2% farming, 12.1% construction, 12.1% production (2000).

Income: Per capita income: $19,843 (2007); Median household income: $42,480 (2007); Average household income: $50,922 (2007); Percent of households with income of $100,000 or more: 8.1% (2007); Poverty rate: 9.5% (2000).

Taxes: Total city taxes per capita: $433 (2005); City property taxes per capita: $188 (2005).

Education: Percent of population age 25 and over with: High school diploma (including GED) or higher: 83.8% (2007); Bachelor's degree or higher: 16.6% (2007); Master's degree or higher: 4.8% (2007).

School District(s)
Brevard County School District (PK-12)
    2005-06 Enrollment: 74,824 . . . . (321) 631-1911

Vocational/Technical School(s)
Academy of Cosmetology-Palm Bay (Private, For-profit)
    Fall 2006 Enrollment: 64 . . . . (321) 951-0595
    2006-07 Tuition: $8,200

Housing: Homeownership rate: 75.8% (2007); Median home value: $168,061 (2007); Median rent: $536 per month (2000); Median age of housing: 15 years (2000).

Safety: Violent crime rate: 63.7 per 10,000 population; Property crime rate: 332.7 per 10,000 population (2006).

Transportation: Commute to work: 95.6% car, 0.4% public transportation, 0.4% walk, 2.1% work from home (2000); Travel time to work: 19.4% less than 15 minutes, 47.1% 15 to 30 minutes, 21.0% 30 to 45 minutes, 6.7% 45 to 60 minutes, 5.8% 60 minutes or more (2000)

Additional Information Contacts
Palm Bay Area Chamber of Commerce. . . . . (321) 724-5400
    http://www.melpb-chamber.org

PALM SHORES (town).
Covers a land area of 0.494 square miles and a water area of 0 square miles. Located at 28.19° N. Lat.; 80.66° W. Long. Elevation is 13 feet.

Population: 310 (1990); 794 (2000); 909 (2007); 975 (2012 projected); Race: 81.5% White, 6.9% Black, 5.1% Asian, 6.4% Hispanic of any race (2007); Density: 1,841.4 persons per square mile (2007); Average household size: 2.44 (2007); Median age: 45.5 (2007); Males per 100 females: 99.3 (2007); Marriage status: 16.0% never married, 66.4% now married, 4.9% widowed, 12.8% divorced (2000); Foreign born: 14.6% (2000); Ancestry (includes multiple ancestries): 19.4% German, 17.5% Other groups, 16.7% English, 16.1% Irish, 7.0% French (except Basque) (2000).

Economy: Single-family building permits issued: 1 (2006); Multi-family building permits issued: 0 (2006); Employment by occupation: 21.2% management, 20.7% professional, 15.9% services, 28.7% sales, 0.0% farming, 4.8% construction, 8.8% production (2000).

Income: Per capita income: $29,406 (2007); Median household income: $60,441 (2007); Average household income: $71,855 (2007); Percent of households with income of $100,000 or more: 24.2% (2007); Poverty rate: 9.3% (2000).

Education: Percent of population age 25 and over with: High school diploma (including GED) or higher: 92.0% (2007); Bachelor's degree or higher: 23.3% (2007); Master's degree or higher: 7.9% (2007).

Housing: Homeownership rate: 82.3% (2007); Median home value: $218,878 (2007); Median rent: $475 per month (2000); Median age of housing: 8 years (2000).

Transportation: Commute to work: 93.2% car, 0.0% public transportation, 1.5% walk, 4.1% work from home (2000); Travel time to work: 21.8% less

PATRICK AFB (unincorporated postal area, zip code 32925).
Covers a land area of 3.134 square miles and a water area of 0 square miles. Located at 28.17° N. Lat.; 80.58° W. Long.

Population: 2,137 (2000); Race: 61.1% White, 21.8% Black, 3.3% Asian, 12.9% Hispanic of any race (2000); Density: 681.9 persons per square mile (2000); Age: 38.7% under 18, 0.1% over 64 (2000); Marriage status: 25.0% never married, 69.7% now married, 0.0% widowed, 5.3% divorced (2000); Foreign born: 4.0% (2000); Ancestry (includes multiple ancestries): 44.5% Other groups, 11.2% German, 9.8% United States or American, 9.4% Irish, 2.9% Italian (2000).

Economy: Employment by occupation: 12.2% management, 22.0% professional, 16.9% services, 42.2% sales, 0.0% farming, 4.1% construction, 2.6% production (2000).

Income: Per capita income: $12,547 (2000); Median household income: $40,282 (2000); Poverty rate: 4.2% (2000).

Education: Percent of population age 25 and over with: High school diploma (including GED) or higher: 97.2% (2000); Bachelor's degree or higher: 13.9% (2000).

Housing: Homeownership rate: 0.7% (2000); Median home value: $22,500 (2000); Median rent: $708 per month (2000); Median age of housing: 4 years (2000).

Transportation: Commute to work: 90.1% car, 0.0% public transportation, 4.2% walk, 4.2% work from home (2000); Travel time to work: 52.6% less than 15 minutes, 22.1% 15 to 30 minutes, 19.9% 30 to 45 minutes, 4.2% 45 to 60 minutes, 1.3% 60 minutes or more (2000)

PORT SAINT JOHN (CDP).
Covers a land area of 3.818 square miles and a water area of 0 square miles. Located at 28.47° N. Lat.; 80.78° W. Long. Elevation is 26 feet.

Population: 8,933 (1990); 12,112 (2000); 13,328 (2007); 14,262 (2012 projected); Race: 89.0% White, 6.1% Black, 0.8% Asian, 4.3% Hispanic of any race (2007); Density: 3,490.4 persons per square mile (2007); Average household size: 2.77 (2007); Median age: 38.7 (2007); Males per 100 females: 99.5 (2007); Marriage status: 17.8% never married, 63.5% now married, 4.9% widowed, 13.8% divorced (2000); Foreign born: 2.8% (2000); Ancestry (includes multiple ancestries): 17.6% German, 16.3% Irish, 14.6% Other groups, 13.6% English, 10.2% United States or American (2000).

Economy: Employment by occupation: 10.6% management, 22.9% professional, 15.3% services, 26.5% sales, 0.0% farming, 11.2% construction, 13.4% production (2000).

Income: Per capita income: $21,651 (2007); Median household income: $52,606 (2007); Average household income: $57,467 (2007); Percent of households with income of $100,000 or more: 11.1% (2007); Poverty rate: 6.6% (2000).

Education: Percent of population age 25 and over with: High school diploma (including GED) or higher: 88.6% (2007); Bachelor's degree or higher: 15.4% (2007); Master's degree or higher: 4.3% (2007).

Housing: Homeownership rate: 86.9% (2007); Median home value: $168,511 (2007); Median rent: $614 per month (2000); Median age of housing: 14 years (2000).

Transportation: Commute to work: 96.9% car, 0.1% public transportation, 0.8% walk, 1.4% work from home (2000); Travel time to work: 14.3% less than 15 minutes, 52.0% 15 to 30 minutes, 20.8% 30 to 45 minutes, 6.6% 45 to 60 minutes, 6.3% 60 minutes or more (2000)

ROCKLEDGE (city).
Covers a land area of 10.703 square miles and a water area of 1.476 square miles. Located at 28.32° N. Lat.; 80.73° W. Long. Elevation is 23 feet.

Population: 16,297 (1990); 20,170 (2000); 24,946 (2007); 28,228 (2012 projected); Race: 79.2% White, 15.8% Black, 2.0% Asian, 4.3% Hispanic of any race (2007); Density: 2,330.6 persons per square mile (2007); Average household size: 2.52 (2007); Median age: 42.4 (2007); Males per 100 females: 91.6 (2007); Marriage status: 19.6% never married, 62.0% now married, 6.9% widowed, 11.5% divorced (2000); Foreign born: 4.6% (2000); Ancestry (includes multiple ancestries): 21.1% Other groups, 16.7% German, 14.4% English, 13.7% Irish, 7.9% United States or American (2000).

Economy: Single-family building permits issued: 97 (2006); Multi-family building permits issued: 244 (2006); Employment by occupation: 14.2% management, 23.6% professional, 15.1% services, 28.7% sales, 0.1% farming, 7.2% construction, 11.1% production (2000).

Income: Per capita income: $25,530 (2007); Median household income: $53,651 (2007); Average household income: $63,497 (2007); Percent of households with income of $100,000 or more: 15.9% (2007); Poverty rate: 6.5% (2000).

Education: Percent of population age 25 and over with: High school diploma (including GED) or higher: 87.4% (2007); Bachelor's degree or higher: 24.2% (2007); Master's degree or higher: 8.4% (2007).

School District(s)
Brevard County School District (PK-12)
    2005-06 Enrollment: 74,824 . . . . (321) 631-1911

Housing: Homeownership rate: 82.2% (2007); Median home value: $192,235 (2007); Median rent: $587 per month (2000); Median age of housing: 20 years (2000).

Hospitals: Wuesthoff Health Systems (295 beds)

Safety: Violent crime rate: 25.1 per 10,000 population; Property crime rate: 292.0 per 10,000 population (2006).

Transportation: Commute to work: 95.1% car, 0.3% public transportation, 0.8% walk, 2.7% work from home (2000); Travel time to work: 30.2% less than 15 minutes, 35.7% 15 to 30 minutes, 22.9% 30 to 45 minutes, 5.7% 45 to 60 minutes, 5.5% 60 minutes or more (2000)

Additional Information Contacts
City of Rockledge. . . . . (321) 690-3978
    http://www.cityofrockledge.org

SATELLITE BEACH (city).
Covers a land area of 2.376 square miles and a water area of 0.989 square miles. Located at 28.17° N. Lat.; 80.59° W. Long. Elevation is 13 feet.

Population: 9,840 (1990); 9,577 (2000); 9,800 (2007); 10,077 (2012 projected); Race: 94.3% White, 1.1% Black, 1.7% Asian, 3.6% Hispanic of any race (2007); Density: 4,124.4 persons per square mile (2007); Average household size: 2.37 (2007); Median age: 47.7 (2007); Males per 100 females: 95.4 (2007); Marriage status: 19.0% never married, 62.6% now married, 8.0% widowed, 10.3% divorced (2000); Foreign born: 5.2% (2000); Ancestry (includes multiple ancestries): 20.4% German, 18.4% English, 17.9% Irish, 10.5% Italian, 8.2% Other groups (2000).

Economy: Single-family building permits issued: 40 (2006); Multi-family building permits issued: 0 (2006); Employment by occupation: 12.6% management, 30.3% professional, 15.4% services, 27.3% sales, 0.1% farming, 7.4% construction, 6.8% production (2000).

Income: Per capita income: $31,372 (2007); Median household income: $61,604 (2007); Average household income: $74,145 (2007); Percent of households with income of $100,000 or more: 21.9% (2007); Poverty rate: 4.5% (2000).

Education: Percent of population age 25 and over with: High school diploma (including GED) or higher: 95.6% (2007); Bachelor's degree or higher: 37.6% (2007); Master's degree or higher: 14.4% (2007).

School District(s)
Brevard County School District (PK-12)
    2005-06 Enrollment: 74,824 . . . . (321) 631-1911

Housing: Homeownership rate: 83.4% (2007); Median home value: $273,322 (2007); Median rent: $648 per month (2000); Median age of housing: 28 years (2000).

Safety: Violent crime rate: 31.1 per 10,000 population; Property crime rate: 252.6 per 10,000 population (2006).

Transportation: Commute to work: 92.0% car, 0.0% public transportation, 2.0% walk, 3.6% work from home (2000); Travel time to work: 29.2% less than 15 minutes, 45.1% 15 to 30 minutes, 14.0% 30 to 45 minutes, 4.2% 45 to 60 minutes, 7.5% 60 minutes or more (2000)

Additional Information Contacts
City of Satellite Beach . . . . (321) 773-4407
    http://www.satellitebeach.org

SHARPES (CDP).
Covers a land area of 2.983 square miles and a water area of 3.303 square miles. Located at 28.44° N. Lat.; 80.76° W. Long. Elevation is 20 feet.

Population: 3,348 (1990); 3,415 (2000); 3,373 (2007); 3,438 (2012 projected); Race: 90.3% White, 3.9% Black, 0.8% Asian, 3.7% Hispanic of any race (2007); Density: 1,130.6 persons per square mile (2007); Average household size: 2.25 (2007); Median age: 44.1 (2007); Males per 100 females: 98.8 (2007); Marriage status: 18.7% never married, 55.6% now married, 7.8% widowed, 17.8% divorced (2000); Foreign born: 2.0% (2000); Ancestry (includes multiple ancestries): 18.4% United States or American, 17.2% Other groups, 17.0% Irish, 17.0% German, 9.7% English (2000).

Economy: Employment by occupation: 10.6% management, 12.7% professional, 17.9% services, 29.4% sales, 0.9% farming, 18.2% construction, 10.3% production (2000).

Income: Per capita income: $19,958 (2007); Median household income: $30,965 (2007); Average household income: $44,325 (2007); Percent of households with income of $100,000 or more: 9.9% (2007); Poverty rate: 18.7% (2000).

Education: Percent of population age 25 and over with: High school diploma (including GED) or higher: 78.1% (2007); Bachelor's degree or higher: 13.6% (2007); Master's degree or higher: 4.5% (2007).

School District(s)
Brevard County School District (PK-12)
    2005-06 Enrollment: 74,824 . . . . (321) 631-1911

Housing: Homeownership rate: 77.4% (2007); Median home value: $91,944 (2007); Median rent: $410 per month (2000); Median age of housing: 24 years (2000).

Transportation: Commute to work: 93.7% car, 0.0% public transportation, 2.1% walk, 3.0% work from home (2000); Travel time to work: 23.8% less than 15 minutes, 41.3% 15 to 30 minutes, 24.1% 30 to 45 minutes, 4.8% 45 to 60 minutes, 6.0% 60 minutes or more (2000)

SOUTH PATRICK SHORES (CDP).
Aka Amherst. Covers a land area of 2.058 square miles and a water area of 1.669 square miles. Located at 28.20° N. Lat.; 80.60° W. Long. Elevation is 10 feet.

Population: 10,298 (1990); 8,913 (2000); 8,550 (2007); 8,467 (2012 projected); Race: 90.8% White, 2.7% Black, 2.2% Asian, 6.0% Hispanic of any race (2007); Density: 4,154.9 persons per square mile (2007); Average household size: 2.41 (2007); Median age: 44.1 (2007); Males per 100 females: 98.1 (2007); Marriage status: 17.2% never married, 66.3% now married, 6.1% widowed, 10.4% divorced (2000); Foreign born: 6.0% (2000); Ancestry (includes multiple ancestries): 20.4% German, 17.6% Irish, 15.4% Other groups, 15.1% English, 9.2% Italian (2000).

Economy: Employment by occupation: 12.3% management, 26.4% professional, 18.7% services, 23.9% sales, 0.3% farming, 10.2% construction, 8.2% production (2000).

Income: Per capita income: $28,508 (2007); Median household income: $54,769 (2007); Average household income: $68,627 (2007); Percent of households with income of $100,000 or more: 16.3% (2007); Poverty rate: 4.6% (2000).

Education: Percent of population age 25 and over with: High school diploma (including GED) or higher: 91.9% (2007); Bachelor's degree or higher: 30.3% (2007); Master's degree or higher: 12.3% (2007).

Housing: Homeownership rate: 71.7% (2007); Median home value: $251,136 (2007); Median rent: $672 per month (2000); Median age of housing: 34 years (2000).

Transportation: Commute to work: 93.6% car, 0.5% public transportation, 1.0% walk, 2.5% work from home (2000); Travel time to work: 30.4% less than 15 minutes, 38.0% 15 to 30 minutes, 21.5% 30 to 45 minutes, 5.0% 45 to 60 minutes, 5.1% 60 minutes or more (2000)

TITUSVILLE (city).
County seat. Covers a land area of 21.256 square miles and a water area of 4.651 square miles. Located at 28.59° N. Lat.; 80.82° W. Long. Elevation is 10 feet.

History: Titusville was named for Colonel H.T. Titus, an early resident. It was a flourishing port in the 1880's, situated at the head of navigation on the Indian River. A railroad with wooden tracks, powered by mules, carried goods inland.

Population: 39,970 (1990); 40,670 (2000); 44,760 (2007); 47,890 (2012 projected); Race: 81.5% White, 14.3% Black, 1.1% Asian, 4.6% Hispanic of any race (2007); Density: 2,105.8 persons per square mile (2007); Average household size: 2.32 (2007); Median age: 42.2 (2007); Males per 100 females: 91.7 (2007); Marriage status: 20.0% never married, 56.7% now married, 10.0% widowed, 13.3% divorced (2000); Foreign born: 4.8% (2000); Ancestry (includes multiple ancestries): 19.4% Other groups, 16.7% German, 13.4% Irish, 12.4% English, 8.9% United States or American (2000).

Economy: Unemployment rate: 4.3% (11/2007); Total civilian labor force: 20,914 (11/2007); Single-family building permits issued: 288 (2006); Multi-family building permits issued: 72 (2006); Employment by occupation: 10.1% management, 23.5% professional, 16.7% services, 25.9% sales, 0.1% farming, 10.8% construction, 13.0% production (2000).

Income: Per capita income: $22,712 (2007); Median household income: $40,852 (2007); Average household income: $52,105 (2007); Percent of households with income of $100,000 or more: 11.4% (2007); Poverty rate: 12.4% (2000).

Taxes: Total city taxes per capita: $352 (2005); City property taxes per capita: $183 (2005).
Education: Percent of population age 25 and over with: High school diploma (including GED) or higher: 84.6% (2007); Bachelor's degree or higher: 19.5% (2007); Master's degree or higher: 6.0% (2007).

School District(s)
Brevard County School District (PK-12)
   2005-06 Enrollment: 74,824 . . . . (321) 631-1911
Housing: Homeownership rate: 68.5% (2007); Median home value: $155,173 (2007); Median rent: $445 per month (2000); Median age of housing: 27 years (2000).
Hospitals: Parrish Medical Center (210 beds)
Safety: Violent crime rate: 80.0 per 10,000 population; Property crime rate: 364.5 per 10,000 population (2006).
Transportation: Commute to work: 94.6% car, 0.3% public transportation, 1.8% walk, 2.0% work from home (2000); Travel time to work: 35.4% less than 15 minutes, 30.1% 15 to 30 minutes, 19.2% 30 to 45 minutes, 8.8% 45 to 60 minutes, 6.6% 60 minutes or more (2000)
Airports: Space Coast Regional
Additional Information Contacts
Space Coast Economic Development Commerce. . . . . (321) 269-3221
Titusville Chamber of Commerce. . . . . (321) 267-3036
  http://www.titusville.org

WEST MELBOURNE (city).
Covers a land area of 7.823 square miles and a water area of 0.017 square miles. Located at 28.07° N. Lat.; 80.66° W. Long. Elevation is 30 feet.
Population: 8,881 (1990); 9,824 (2000); 15,068 (2007); 18,461 (2012 projected); Race: 90.6% White, 2.1% Black, 3.1% Asian, 5.8% Hispanic of any race (2007); Density: 1,926.0 persons per square mile (2007); Average household size: 2.11 (2007); Median age: 48.6 (2007); Males per 100 females: 87.1 (2007); Marriage status: 18.1% never married, 54.9% now married, 13.9% widowed, 13.1% divorced (2000); Foreign born: 8.3% (2000); Ancestry (includes multiple ancestries): 18.6% German, 17.9% English, 15.8% Irish, 13.3% Other groups, 10.0% United States or American (2000).
Economy: Single-family building permits issued: 142 (2006); Multi-family building permits issued: 0 (2006); Employment by occupation: 12.8% management, 29.1% professional, 11.5% services, 27.0% sales, 0.0% farming, 7.6% construction, 12.0% production (2000).
Income: Per capita income: $28,325 (2007); Median household income: $43,848 (2007); Average household income: $58,827 (2007); Percent of households with income of $100,000 or more: 13.4% (2007); Poverty rate: 7.8% (2000).
Education: Percent of population age 25 and over with: High school diploma (including GED) or higher: 87.3% (2007); Bachelor's degree or higher: 25.0% (2007); Master's degree or higher: 8.7% (2007).

School District(s)
Brevard County School District (PK-12)
   2005-06 Enrollment: 74,824 . . . . (321) 631-1911
Housing: Homeownership rate: 71.7% (2007); Median home value: $175,282 (2007); Median rent: $544 per month (2000); Median age of housing: 18 years (2000).
Safety: Violent crime rate: 13.7 per 10,000 population; Property crime rate: 231.9 per 10,000 population (2006).
Transportation: Commute to work: 93.6% car, 0.3% public transportation, 2.5% walk, 1.8% work from home (2000); Travel time to work: 43.7% less than 15 minutes, 38.9% 15 to 30 minutes, 11.2% 30 to 45 minutes, 2.3% 45 to 60 minutes, 3.9% 60 minutes or more (2000)
Additional Information Contacts
City of West Melbourne . . . . (321) 727-7700
  http://westmelbourne.org

Broward County

Located in southern Florida, on the Atlantic coast. Covers a land area of 1,205.40 square miles, a water area of 114.24 square miles, and is located in the Eastern Time Zone. The county was founded in 1915. County seat is Fort Lauderdale.

Broward County is part of the Miami-Fort Lauderdale-Pompano Beach, FL Metropolitan Statistical Area. The entire metro area includes: Fort Lauderdale-Pompano Beach-Deerfield Beach, FL Metropolitan Division (Broward County, FL); Miami-Miami Beach-Kendall, FL Metropolitan

Division (Miami-Dade County, FL); West Palm Beach-Boca Raton-Boynton Beach, FL Metropolitan Division (Palm Beach County, FL)

Weather Station: Fort Lauderdale   Elevation: 13 feet

	Jan	Feb	Mar	Apr	May	Jun	Jul	Aug	Sep	Oct	Nov	Dec
High	76	77	79	82	86	88	90	90	89	85	81	78
Low	59	59	63	66	71	74	75	76	75	72	66	61
Precip	3.0	2.8	3.0	3.8	6.4	9.9	6.6	7.0	8.3	6.2	4.6	2.5
Snow	0.0	0.0	0.0	0.0	0.0	0.0	0.0	0.0	0.0	0.0	0.0	0.0

High and Low temperatures in degrees Fahrenheit; Precipitation and Snow in inches

Population: 1,255,488 (1990); 1,623,018 (2000); 1,789,095 (2007); 1,896,854 (2012 projected); Race: 64.5% White, 23.9% Black, 2.9% Asian, 23.0% Hispanic of any race (2007); Density: 1,484.2 persons per square mile (2007); Average household size: 2.52 (2007); Median age: 38.9 (2007); Males per 100 females: 94.5 (2007).
Religion: Five largest groups: 21.1% Catholic Church, 13.1% Jewish Estimate, 3.6% Southern Baptist Convention, 1.1% The United Methodist Church, 0.8% Presbyterian Church in America (2000).
Economy: Unemployment rate: 3.9% (11/2007); Total civilian labor force: 994,428 (11/2007); Leading industries: 15.8% retail trade; 13.0% health care and social assistance; 10.6% accommodation & food services (2005); Farms: 494 totaling 23,741 acres (2002); Companies that employ 500 or more persons: 73 (2005); Companies that employ 100 to 499 persons: 1,004 (2005); Companies that employ less than 100 persons: 56,545 (2005); Black-owned businesses: 22,065 (2002); Hispanic-owned businesses: 29,627 (2002); Asian-owned businesses: 6,279 (2002); Women-owned businesses: 54,889 (2002); Retail sales per capita: $18,683 (2007). Single-family building permits issued: 3,550 (2006); Multi-family building permits issued: 3,166 (2006).
Income: Per capita income: $26,995 (2007); Median household income: $48,980 (2007); Average household income: $67,651 (2007); Percent of households with income of $100,000 or more: 18.5% (2007); Poverty rate: 11.2% (2005); Bankruptcy rate: 1.23% (2006).
Taxes: Total county taxes per capita: $479 (2005); County property taxes per capita: $402 (2005).
Education: Percent of population age 25 and over with: High school diploma (including GED) or higher: 82.3% (2007); Bachelor's degree or higher: 25.1% (2007); Master's degree or higher: 8.9% (2007).
Housing: Homeownership rate: 70.1% (2007); Median home value: $242,449 (2007); Median rent: $676 per month (2000); Median age of housing: 23 years (2000).
Health: Birth rate: 137.5 per 10,000 population (2006); Death rate: 87.7 per 10,000 population (2006); Age-adjusted cancer mortality rate: 178.1 deaths per 100,000 population (2004); Air Quality Index: 87.4% good, 12.1% moderate, 0.5% unhealthy for sensitive individuals, 0.0% unhealthy (percent of days in 2006); Number of physicians: 26.0 per 10,000 population (2005); Hospital beds: 32.3 per 10,000 population (2004); Hospital admissions: 1,344.9 per 10,000 population (2004).
Elections: 2004 Presidential election results: 34.6% Bush, 64.2% Kerry, 0.5% Nader, 0.2% Badnarik
National and State Parks: Hugh Taylor Birch State Park; John U Lloyd Beach State Park; Pan-American State Park
Additional Information Contacts
Broward County Government . . . . (954) 357-7585
  http://www.co.broward.fl.us
British American Chamber of Commerce . . . . (407) 428-6226
Christian Chamber of Commerce . . . . (954) 972-9256
City of Coconut Creek . . . . (954) 973-6770
  http://www.creekgov.net
City of Cooper City. . . . . (954) 434-4300
  http://www.coopercityfl.org
City of Coral Springs . . . . (954) 344-1000
  http://www.coralsprings.org
City of Dania Beach . . . . (954) 924-6800
  http://www.ci.dania-beach.fl.us
City of Deerfield Beach . . . . (954) 480-4200
  http://www.deerfield-beach.com
City of Hallandale Beach . . . . (954) 457-1300
  http://www.hallandalebeach.org
City of Lauderdale Lakes . . . . (954) 535-2700
  http://www.lauderdalelakes.org
City of Lauderhill . . . . (954) 730-3010
  http://www.lauderhill-fl.gov
City of Lighthouse Point . . . . (954) 943-6500
  http://www.lighthousepoint.com

City of Margate. . . . . (954) 972-6454
   http://www.margatefl.com
City of Miramar. . . . . (954) 602-3011
   http://www.ci.miramar.fl.us
City of North Lauderdale . . . . (954) 722-0900
   http://www.nlauderdale.org
City of Oakland Park . . . . (954) 630-4200
   http://oaklandparkfl.org
City of Parkland . . . . (954) 753-5040
   http://www.cityofparkland.org
City of Plantation . . . . (954) 797-2200
   http://www.plantation.org
City of Pompano Beach . . . . (954) 786-4600
   http://www.mypompanobeach.org
City of Sunrise . . . . (954) 741-2580
   http://www.sunrisefl.gov
City of Tamarac . . . . (954) 597-3505
   http://www.tamarac.org
City of Weston . . . . (954) 385-2000
   http://www.westonfl.org
City of Wilton Manors. . . . . (954) 390-2100
   http://www.wiltonmanors.com
Coconut Creek Chamber of Commerce. . . . . (954) 295-2711
   http://www.coconutcreek.net
Davie-Cooper City Chamber of Commerce . . . . (954) 581-0790
   http://www.davie-coopercity.org
Deerfield Beach Chamber of Commerce . . . . (954) 427-1050
   http://www.deerfieldchamber.com
Florida-Israel Chamber . . . . (561) 620-9288
   http://www.floridaisraelchamber.org
Fort Lauderdale Chamber of Commerce . . . . (954) 462-6000
   http://www.ftlchamber.com
Greater Dania Chamber of Commerce . . . . (954) 926-2323
   http://www.greaterdania.org
Greater Hollywood Chamber of Commerce. . . . . (954) 923-4000
   http://www.hollywoodchamber.org
Greater Pompano Beach Chamber . . . . (954) 941-2940
   http://www.pompanobeachchamber.com
Lauderdale By-The-Sea Chamber . . . . (954) 776-1000
   http://www.lbts.com
North Broward Chamber of Commerce . . . . (954) 972-0818
   http://www.browardbiz.com
Oakland Park-Wilton Chamber . . . . (954) 568-7755
   http://www.opwmchamber.org
Pembroke Pines Chamber of Commerce . . . . (954) 432-9808
   http://www.ppines.com
Plantation Chamber of Commerce. . . . . (954) 587-1410
   http://www.plantationchamber.org
Sunrise Chamber of Commerce . . . . (954) 741-3300
   http://www.sunrisechamber.org
Tamarac Chamber of Commerce . . . . (954) 722-1520
   http://www.tamaracchamber.org
Town of Davie . . . . (954) 797-1000
   http://www.davie-fl.gov

Broward County Communities

BONNIE LOCK-WOODSETTER NORTH (CDP). Covers a land area of 0.479 square miles and a water area of 0 square miles. Located at 26.28° N. Lat.; 80.13° W. Long. Elevation is 13 feet.
Population: 3,398 (1990); 4,275 (2000); 4,655 (2007); 4,915 (2012 projected); Race: 31.9% White, 40.1% Black, 3.3% Asian, 22.4% Hispanic of any race (2007); Density: 9,722.1 persons per square mile (2007); Average household size: 3.48 (2007); Median age: 29.6 (2007); Males per 100 females: 103.3 (2007); Marriage status: 31.9% never married, 53.5% now married, 4.5% widowed, 10.1% divorced (2000); Foreign born: 42.9% (2000); Ancestry (includes multiple ancestries): 30.3% Other groups, 20.2% Haitian, 6.2% German, 6.1% United States or American, 5.5% Brazilian (2000).
Economy: Employment by occupation: 8.1% management, 8.2% professional, 25.0% services, 34.8% sales, 0.0% farming, 13.0% construction, 10.9% production (2000).
Income: Per capita income: $16,033 (2007); Median household income: $44,041 (2007); Average household income: $55,095 (2007); Percent of

households with income of $100,000 or more: 12.6% (2007); Poverty rate: 10.7% (2000).
Education: Percent of population age 25 and over with: High school diploma (including GED) or higher: 69.0% (2007); Bachelor's degree or higher: 12.4% (2007); Master's degree or higher: 3.6% (2007).
Housing: Homeownership rate: 68.1% (2007); Median home value: $177,155 (2007); Median rent: $639 per month (2000); Median age of housing: 24 years (2000).
Transportation: Commute to work: 95.3% car, 2.0% public transportation, 0.5% walk, 0.4% work from home (2000); Travel time to work: 19.0% less than 15 minutes, 40.6% 15 to 30 minutes, 27.3% 30 to 45 minutes, 6.9% 45 to 60 minutes, 6.2% 60 minutes or more (2000)

BOULEVARD GARDENS (CDP). Covers a land area of 0.263 square miles and a water area of 0 square miles. Located at 26.12° N. Lat.; 80.18° W. Long.
Population: 1,515 (1990); 1,415 (2000); 1,355 (2007); 1,308 (2012 projected); Race: 1.6% White, 94.1% Black, 0.5% Asian, 3.0% Hispanic of any race (2007); Density: 5,148.6 persons per square mile (2007); Average household size: 3.10 (2007); Median age: 30.6 (2007); Males per 100 females: 97.2 (2007); Marriage status: 42.5% never married, 34.0% now married, 12.4% widowed, 11.1% divorced (2000); Foreign born: 10.1% (2000); Ancestry (includes multiple ancestries): 77.6% Other groups, 4.3% Jamaican, 2.8% United States or American, 1.9% Haitian, 0.9% Hungarian (2000).
Economy: Employment by occupation: 8.7% management, 7.5% professional, 29.3% services, 12.6% sales, 0.0% farming, 21.5% construction, 20.3% production (2000).
Income: Per capita income: $16,245 (2007); Median household income: $25,183 (2007); Average household income: $50,372 (2007); Percent of households with income of $100,000 or more: 10.3% (2007); Poverty rate: 37.4% (2000).
Education: Percent of population age 25 and over with: High school diploma (including GED) or higher: 51.8% (2007); Bachelor's degree or higher: 6.4% (2007); Master's degree or higher: 3.6% (2007).
Housing: Homeownership rate: 64.5% (2007); Median home value: $157,813 (2007); Median rent: $399 per month (2000); Median age of housing: 38 years (2000).
Transportation: Commute to work: 71.9% car, 17.9% public transportation, 10.1% walk, 0.0% work from home (2000); Travel time to work: 12.2% less than 15 minutes, 31.7% 15 to 30 minutes, 36.1% 30 to 45 minutes, 17.4% 45 to 60 minutes, 2.6% 60 minutes or more (2000)

BROADVIEW PARK (CDP). Covers a land area of 0.978 square miles and a water area of 0.044 square miles. Located at 26.09° N. Lat.; 80.20° W. Long. Elevation is 16 feet.
Population: 6,109 (1990); 6,798 (2000); 7,221 (2007); 7,515 (2012 projected); Race: 61.8% White, 19.6% Black, 2.3% Asian, 53.1% Hispanic of any race (2007); Density: 7,381.5 persons per square mile (2007); Average household size: 3.30 (2007); Median age: 31.9 (2007); Males per 100 females: 107.8 (2007); Marriage status: 31.5% never married, 52.1% now married, 5.3% widowed, 11.1% divorced (2000); Foreign born: 36.9% (2000); Ancestry (includes multiple ancestries): 49.3% Other groups, 10.5% United States or American, 6.5% German, 6.2% Irish, 5.1% English (2000).
Economy: Employment by occupation: 5.2% management, 11.0% professional, 17.9% services, 26.3% sales, 0.7% farming, 20.0% construction, 18.9% production (2000).
Income: Per capita income: $15,960 (2007); Median household income: $44,450 (2007); Average household income: $51,857 (2007); Percent of households with income of $100,000 or more: 9.2% (2007); Poverty rate: 14.8% (2000).
Education: Percent of population age 25 and over with: High school diploma (including GED) or higher: 62.4% (2007); Bachelor's degree or higher: 7.2% (2007); Master's degree or higher: 3.6% (2007).
Housing: Homeownership rate: 60.4% (2007); Median home value: $192,785 (2007); Median rent: $547 per month (2000); Median age of housing: 39 years (2000).
Transportation: Commute to work: 92.3% car, 4.0% public transportation, 0.8% walk, 1.2% work from home (2000); Travel time to work: 15.6% less than 15 minutes, 46.4% 15 to 30 minutes, 21.9% 30 to 45 minutes, 9.2% 45 to 60 minutes, 6.9% 60 minutes or more (2000)

BROADVIEW-POMPANO PARK (CDP). Covers a land area of 0.594 square miles and a water area of 0 square miles. Located at 26.20° N. Lat.; 80.21° W. Long. Elevation is 13 feet.

Population: 4,156 (1990); 5,314 (2000); 5,611 (2007); 5,822 (2012 projected); Race: 52.3% White, 24.5% Black, 4.0% Asian, 45.9% Hispanic of any race (2007); Density: 9,447.9 persons per square mile (2007); Average household size: 3.52 (2007); Median age: 30.6 (2007); Males per 100 females: 104.4 (2007); Marriage status: 28.4% never married, 52.5% now married, 5.9% widowed, 13.2% divorced (2000); Foreign born: 40.7% (2000); Ancestry (includes multiple ancestries): 43.1% Other groups, 9.3% Irish, 7.6% Italian, 7.1% United States or American, 7.0% Haitian (2000).

Economy: Employment by occupation: 9.0% management, 9.2% professional, 17.6% services, 22.0% sales, 0.0% farming, 22.5% construction, 19.8% production (2000).

Income: Per capita income: $14,373 (2007); Median household income: $40,750 (2007); Average household income: $50,548 (2007); Percent of households with income of $100,000 or more: 8.7% (2007); Poverty rate: 15.5% (2000).

Education: Percent of population age 25 and over with: High school diploma (including GED) or higher: 62.6% (2007); Bachelor's degree or higher: 5.9% (2007); Master's degree or higher: 1.8% (2007).

Housing: Homeownership rate: 76.6% (2007); Median home value: $170,673 (2007); Median rent: $700 per month (2000); Median age of housing: 33 years (2000).

Transportation: Commute to work: 96.0% car, 0.0% public transportation, 0.4% walk, 2.0% work from home (2000); Travel time to work: 19.6% less than 15 minutes, 40.7% 15 to 30 minutes, 26.8% 30 to 45 minutes, 7.4% 45 to 60 minutes, 5.5% 60 minutes or more (2000)

BROWARD ESTATES (CDP). Covers a land area of 0.517 square miles and a water area of 0 square miles. Located at 26.12° N. Lat.; 80.19° W. Long. Elevation is 3 feet.

Population: 3,631 (1990); 3,416 (2000); 3,294 (2007); 3,169 (2012 projected); Race: 0.8% White, 96.5% Black, 0.4% Asian, 1.5% Hispanic of any race (2007); Density: 6,375.3 persons per square mile (2007); Average household size: 3.41 (2007); Median age: 33.0 (2007); Males per 100 females: 89.0 (2007); Marriage status: 34.7% never married, 47.6% now married, 7.7% widowed, 10.0% divorced (2000); Foreign born: 5.5% (2000); Ancestry (includes multiple ancestries): 74.6% Other groups, 2.8% Jamaican, 2.6% Haitian, 1.6% United States or American, 1.2% African (2000).

Economy: Employment by occupation: 5.3% management, 11.8% professional, 21.5% services, 30.6% sales, 0.0% farming, 11.2% construction, 19.6% production (2000).

Income: Per capita income: $14,923 (2007); Median household income: $42,458 (2007); Average household income: $50,415 (2007); Percent of households with income of $100,000 or more: 11.6% (2007); Poverty rate: 23.2% (2000).

Education: Percent of population age 25 and over with: High school diploma (including GED) or higher: 61.6% (2007); Bachelor's degree or higher: 9.9% (2007); Master's degree or higher: 4.0% (2007).

Housing: Homeownership rate: 82.6% (2007); Median home value: $175,216 (2007); Median rent: $575 per month (2000); Median age of housing: 40 years (2000).

Transportation: Commute to work: 94.8% car, 4.2% public transportation, 0.5% walk, 0.6% work from home (2000); Travel time to work: 22.1% less than 15 minutes, 44.2% 15 to 30 minutes, 23.0% 30 to 45 minutes, 4.5% 45 to 60 minutes, 6.2% 60 minutes or more (2000)

CARVER RANCHES (CDP). Covers a land area of 0.674 square miles and a water area of 0 square miles. Located at 25.99° N. Lat.; 80.19° W. Long. Elevation is 10 feet.

Population: 3,882 (1990); 4,299 (2000); 5,085 (2007); 5,583 (2012 projected); Race: 2.1% White, 96.0% Black, 0.0% Asian, 2.5% Hispanic of any race (2007); Density: 7,542.3 persons per square mile (2007); Average household size: 3.25 (2007); Median age: 30.0 (2007); Males per 100 females: 87.8 (2007); Marriage status: 38.3% never married, 41.6% now married, 8.7% widowed, 11.4% divorced (2000); Foreign born: 5.8% (2000); Ancestry (includes multiple ancestries): 72.8% Other groups, 5.3% United States or American, 2.5% Bahamian, 2.4% African, 1.6% Haitian (2000).

Economy: Employment by occupation: 3.3% management, 14.4% professional, 24.8% services, 24.5% sales, 0.0% farming, 9.6% construction, 23.5% production (2000).

$30,717 (2007); Average household income: $35,026 (2007); Percent of households with income of $100,000 or more: 1.7% (2007); Poverty rate: 25.3% (2000).

Education: Percent of population age 25 and over with: High school diploma (including GED) or higher: 65.6% (2007); Bachelor's degree or higher: 5.8% (2007); Master's degree or higher: 1.6% (2007).

Housing: Homeownership rate: 61.2% (2007); Median home value: $192,713 (2007); Median rent: $532 per month (2000); Median age of housing: 32 years (2000).

Transportation: Commute to work: 89.8% car, 4.9% public transportation, 2.6% walk, 0.7% work from home (2000); Travel time to work: 22.2% less than 15 minutes, 36.6% 15 to 30 minutes, 28.6% 30 to 45 minutes, 6.5% 45 to 60 minutes, 6.1% 60 minutes or more (2000)

CHAMBERS ESTATES (CDP). Covers a land area of 0.551 square miles and a water area of 0 square miles. Located at 26.05° N. Lat.; 80.20° W. Long. Elevation is 3 feet.

Population: 3,073 (1990); 3,556 (2000); 3,939 (2007); 4,140 (2012 projected); Race: 69.3% White, 16.5% Black, 2.2% Asian, 36.9% Hispanic of any race (2007); Density: 7,151.3 persons per square mile (2007); Average household size: 2.70 (2007); Median age: 34.7 (2007); Males per 100 females: 96.5 (2007); Marriage status: 26.3% never married, 50.6% now married, 5.3% widowed, 17.8% divorced (2000); Foreign born: 24.9% (2000); Ancestry (includes multiple ancestries): 32.0% Other groups, 10.6% Italian, 10.3% United States or American, 8.9% Irish, 8.4% German (2000).

Economy: Employment by occupation: 6.6% management, 16.0% professional, 17.6% services, 30.8% sales, 2.3% farming, 10.2% construction, 16.5% production (2000).

Income: Per capita income: $21,619 (2007); Median household income: $45,864 (2007); Average household income: $58,293 (2007); Percent of households with income of $100,000 or more: 14.2% (2007); Poverty rate: 12.8% (2000).

Education: Percent of population age 25 and over with: High school diploma (including GED) or higher: 78.7% (2007); Bachelor's degree or higher: 15.5% (2007); Master's degree or higher: 5.5% (2007).

Housing: Homeownership rate: 56.8% (2007); Median home value: $204,672 (2007); Median rent: $680 per month (2000); Median age of housing: 27 years (2000).

Transportation: Commute to work: 86.0% car, 5.1% public transportation, 1.8% walk, 4.7% work from home (2000); Travel time to work: 23.7% less than 15 minutes, 32.5% 15 to 30 minutes, 30.5% 30 to 45 minutes, 5.8% 45 to 60 minutes, 7.6% 60 minutes or more (2000)

CHULA VISTA (CDP). Covers a land area of 0.088 square miles and a water area of 0 square miles. Located at 26.10° N. Lat.; 80.18° W. Long.

Population: 524 (1990); 573 (2000); 621 (2007); 653 (2012 projected); Race: 58.9% White, 20.1% Black, 2.7% Asian, 46.4% Hispanic of any race (2007); Density: 7,073.3 persons per square mile (2007); Average household size: 2.82 (2007); Median age: 35.5 (2007); Males per 100 females: 107.0 (2007); Marriage status: 25.9% never married, 50.7% now married, 8.3% widowed, 15.1% divorced (2000); Foreign born: 36.4% (2000); Ancestry (includes multiple ancestries): 31.5% Other groups, 12.6% German, 9.1% Irish, 4.3% French (except Basque), 3.4% West Indian (2000).

Economy: Employment by occupation: 2.6% management, 9.1% professional, 3.9% services, 28.0% sales, 0.0% farming, 25.0% construction, 31.5% production (2000).

Income: Per capita income: $16,526 (2007); Median household income: $37,750 (2007); Average household income: $46,648 (2007); Percent of households with income of $100,000 or more: 3.2% (2007); Poverty rate: 21.5% (2000).

Education: Percent of population age 25 and over with: High school diploma (including GED) or higher: 60.2% (2007); Bachelor's degree or higher: 1.5% (2007); Master's degree or higher: 1.5% (2007).

Housing: Homeownership rate: 60.0% (2007); Median home value: $221,296 (2007); Median rent: $519 per month (2000); Median age of housing: 28 years (2000).

Transportation: Commute to work: 96.9% car, 0.0% public transportation, 0.0% walk, 0.0% work from home (2000); Travel time to work: 29.3% less than 15 minutes, 41.8% 15 to 30 minutes, 28.9% 30 to 45 minutes, 0.0% 45 to 60 minutes, 0.0% 60 minutes or more (2000)

COCONUT CREEK (city).

Covers a land area of 11.546 square miles and a water area of 0.238 square miles. Located at 26.27° N. Lat.; 80.18° W. Long. Elevation is 7 feet.

History: Named for its abundance of coconut palms and canals. Site of major suburban development since 1980.

Population: 27,509 (1990); 43,566 (2000); 49,339 (2007); 52,965 (2012 projected); Race: 78.3% White, 10.3% Black, 3.6% Asian, 18.2% Hispanic of any race (2007); Density: 4,273.2 persons per square mile (2007); Average household size: 2.24 (2007); Median age: 41.6 (2007); Males per 100 females: 88.5 (2007); Marriage status: 17.6% never married, 60.3% now married, 11.4% widowed, 10.7% divorced (2000); Foreign born: 18.3% (2000); Ancestry (includes multiple ancestries): 24.4% Other groups, 13.5% Italian, 10.7% German, 10.2% Irish, 6.8% Polish (2000).

Economy: Unemployment rate: 3.5% (11/2007); Total civilian labor force: 27,203 (11/2007); Single-family building permits issued: 132 (2006); Multi-family building permits issued: 0 (2006); Employment by occupation: 17.9% management, 19.7% professional, 12.9% services, 33.8% sales, 0.3% farming, 8.7% construction, 6.7% production (2000).

Income: Per capita income: $29,515 (2007); Median household income: $52,395 (2007); Average household income: $65,896 (2007); Percent of households with income of $100,000 or more: 17.9% (2007); Poverty rate: 7.1% (2000).

Education: Percent of population age 25 and over with: High school diploma (including GED) or higher: 87.8% (2007); Bachelor's degree or higher: 27.9% (2007); Master's degree or higher: 9.2% (2007).

School District(s)
Broward County School District (PK-12)

2005-06 Enrollment: 274,591 . . . . (754) 321-2600

Two-year College(s)
Atlantic Technical Center (Public)

Fall 2006 Enrollment: 746 . . . . (754) 321-5100

Housing: Homeownership rate: 74.5% (2007); Median home value: $210,716 (2007); Median rent: $824 per month (2000); Median age of housing: 13 years (2000).

Safety: Violent crime rate: 20.7 per 10,000 population; Property crime rate: 219.9 per 10,000 population (2006).

Transportation: Commute to work: 95.1% car, 0.7% public transportation, 0.5% walk, 2.8% work from home (2000); Travel time to work: 17.3% less than 15 minutes, 43.2% 15 to 30 minutes, 27.4% 30 to 45 minutes, 7.4% 45 to 60 minutes, 4.7% 60 minutes or more (2000)

Additional Information Contacts

City of Coconut Creek . . . . (954) 973-6770
  http://www.creekgov.net
Coconut Creek Chamber of Commerce . . . . (954) 295-2711
  http://www.coconutcreek.net
North Broward Chamber of Commerce . . . . (954) 972-0818
  http://www.browardbiz.com

COLLIER MANOR-CRESTHAVEN (CDP).

Covers a land area of 1.158 square miles and a water area of 0 square miles. Located at 26.26° N. Lat.; 80.10° W. Long. Elevation is 13 feet.

Population: 7,322 (1990); 7,741 (2000); 7,754 (2007); 7,809 (2012 projected); Race: 66.8% White, 18.9% Black, 1.3% Asian, 21.1% Hispanic of any race (2007); Density: 6,693.6 persons per square mile (2007); Average household size: 2.60 (2007); Median age: 37.2 (2007); Males per 100 females: 104.9 (2007); Marriage status: 27.4% never married, 53.3% now married, 6.0% widowed, 13.3% divorced (2000); Foreign born: 22.2% (2000); Ancestry (includes multiple ancestries): 23.3% Other groups, 15.0% Italian, 14.3% German, 14.2% Irish, 9.3% English (2000).

Economy: Employment by occupation: 5.3% management, 10.1% professional, 21.9% services, 25.5% sales, 0.0% farming, 21.9% construction, 15.3% production (2000).

Income: Per capita income: $18,151 (2007); Median household income: $41,250 (2007); Average household income: $47,179 (2007); Percent of households with income of $100,000 or more: 6.2% (2007); Poverty rate: 11.1% (2000).

Education: Percent of population age 25 and over with: High school diploma (including GED) or higher: 76.5% (2007); Bachelor's degree or higher: 10.7% (2007); Master's degree or higher: 3.2% (2007).

Housing: Homeownership rate: 71.2% (2007); Median home value: $179,393 (2007); Median rent: $586 per month (2000); Median age of housing: 37 years (2000).

Transportation: Commute to work: 94.3% car, 1.2% public transportation, 1.3% walk, 1.7% work from home (2000); Travel time to work: 27.9% less

than 15 minutes, 46.5% 15 to 30 minutes, 23.5% 30 to 45 minutes, 1.1% 45 to 60 minutes, 3.4% 60 minutes or more (2000)

COOPER CITY (city).

Covers a land area of 6.346 square miles and a water area of 0.350 square miles. Located at 26.04° N. Lat.; 80.29° W. Long. Elevation is 7 feet.

Population: 21,193 (1990); 27,939 (2000); 29,812 (2007); 31,084 (2012 projected); Race: 85.3% White, 4.3% Black, 5.3% Asian, 20.6% Hispanic of any race (2007); Density: 4,697.5 persons per square mile (2007); Average household size: 3.13 (2007); Median age: 37.0 (2007); Males per 100 females: 94.6 (2007); Marriage status: 22.0% never married, 66.7% now married, 3.5% widowed, 7.8% divorced (2000); Foreign born: 16.9% (2000); Ancestry (includes multiple ancestries): 26.8% Other groups, 14.7% German, 13.9% Irish, 12.5% Italian, 8.4% English (2000).

Economy: Unemployment rate: 2.9% (11/2007); Total civilian labor force: 18,514 (11/2007); Single-family building permits issued: 1 (2006); Multi-family building permits issued: 0 (2006); Employment by occupation: 18.1% management, 27.2% professional, 12.8% services, 29.3% sales, 0.1% farming, 6.8% construction, 5.7% production (2000).

Income: Per capita income: $33,096 (2007); Median household income: $89,685 (2007); Average household income: $103,577 (2007); Percent of households with income of $100,000 or more: 42.0% (2007); Poverty rate: 3.2% (2000).

Education: Percent of population age 25 and over with: High school diploma (including GED) or higher: 92.2% (2007); Bachelor's degree or higher: 38.4% (2007); Master's degree or higher: 15.0% (2007).

School District(s)
Broward County School District (PK-12)

2005-06 Enrollment: 274,591 . . . . (754) 321-2600

Housing: Homeownership rate: 92.4% (2007); Median home value: $339,588 (2007); Median rent: $831 per month (2000); Median age of housing: 15 years (2000).

Safety: Violent crime rate: 28.8 per 10,000 population; Property crime rate: 187.4 per 10,000 population (2006).

Transportation: Commute to work: 95.5% car, 0.1% public transportation, 0.5% walk, 3.3% work from home (2000); Travel time to work: 17.1% less than 15 minutes, 34.8% 15 to 30 minutes, 27.8% 30 to 45 minutes, 12.2% 45 to 60 minutes, 8.1% 60 minutes or more (2000)

Additional Information Contacts

City of Cooper City . . . . (954) 434-4300
  http://www.coopercityfl.org

CORAL SPRINGS (city).

Covers a land area of 23.909 square miles and a water area of 0.237 square miles. Located at 26.27° N. Lat.; 80.25° W. Long. Elevation is 10 feet.

History: Named for the local natural springs. Has grown rapidly along with the South Florida and Fort Lauderdale area. The population of Coral Springs nearly doubled between 1980 and 1990. Incorporated 1963.

Population: 78,602 (1990); 117,549 (2000); 129,132 (2007); 136,677 (2012 projected); Race: 74.1% White, 13.5% Black, 4.5% Asian, 22.1% Hispanic of any race (2007); Density: 5,401.0 persons per square mile (2007); Average household size: 2.99 (2007); Median age: 34.5 (2007); Males per 100 females: 95.6 (2007); Marriage status: 25.5% never married, 60.2% now married, 4.1% widowed, 10.3% divorced (2000); Foreign born: 21.3% (2000); Ancestry (includes multiple ancestries): 26.8% Other groups, 14.2% Italian, 11.9% German, 11.3% Irish, 6.5% United States or American (2000).

Economy: Unemployment rate: 3.4% (11/2007); Total civilian labor force: 77,595 (11/2007); Single-family building permits issued: 76 (2006); Multi-family building permits issued: 22 (2006); Employment by occupation: 18.7% management, 20.8% professional, 12.8% services, 32.9% sales, 0.1% farming, 7.6% construction, 7.0% production (2000).

Income: Per capita income: $28,946 (2007); Median household income: $66,396 (2007); Average household income: $85,989 (2007); Percent of households with income of $100,000 or more: 28.4% (2007); Poverty rate: 8.0% (2000).

Taxes: Total city taxes per capita: $357 (2005); City property taxes per capita: $212 (2005).

Education: Percent of population age 25 and over with: High school diploma (including GED) or higher: 89.8% (2007); Bachelor's degree or higher: 34.5% (2007); Master's degree or higher: 11.9% (2007).

School District(s)
Broward County School District (PK-12)

2005-06 Enrollment: 274,591 . . . . (754) 321-2600

$365,318 (2007); Median rent: $806 per month (2000); Median age of housing: 14 years (2000).

Hospitals: Coral Springs Medical Center (200 beds)

Safety: Violent crime rate: 22.3 per 10,000 population; Property crime rate: 225.2 per 10,000 population (2006).

Newspapers: Coral Springs-Parkland Forum (General - Circulation 30,000); Jewish Journal - Broward Central (General, Jewish - Circulation 25,000); Margate-Coconut Creek Forum (General - Circulation 22,000); Sunrise Forum (General - Circulation 19,000); Tamarac-North Lauderdale Forum (General - Circulation 25,000)

Transportation: Commute to work: 92.7% car, 1.0% public transportation, 1.2% walk, 3.9% work from home (2000); Travel time to work: 23.5% less than 15 minutes, 30.0% 15 to 30 minutes, 28.0% 30 to 45 minutes, 11.1% 45 to 60 minutes, 7.4% 60 minutes or more (2000)

Additional Information Contacts
City of Coral Springs . . . . (954) 344-1000
   http://www.coralsprings.org

COUNTRY ESTATES (CDP). Covers a land area of 3.999 square miles and a water area of 0 square miles. Located at 26.04° N. Lat.; 80.40° W. Long.

Population: 1,824 (1990); 1,910 (2000); 2,525 (2007); 2,908 (2012 projected); Race: 89.3% White, 4.0% Black, 1.5% Asian, 25.7% Hispanic of any race (2007); Density: 631.3 persons per square mile (2007); Average household size: 3.45 (2007); Median age: 38.8 (2007); Males per 100 females: 106.5 (2007); Marriage status: 20.2% never married, 68.2% now married, 0.9% widowed, 10.6% divorced (2000); Foreign born: 14.5% (2000); Ancestry (includes multiple ancestries): 35.5% Other groups, 20.2% Irish, 15.3% Italian, 14.8% German, 8.9% English (2000).

Economy: Employment by occupation: 23.0% management, 23.1% professional, 14.5% services, 24.1% sales, 0.7% farming, 10.6% construction, 4.0% production (2000).

Income: Per capita income: $38,591 (2007); Median household income: $108,929 (2007); Average household income: $130,365 (2007); Percent of households with income of $100,000 or more: 56.8% (2007); Poverty rate: 4.2% (2000).

Education: Percent of population age 25 and over with: High school diploma (including GED) or higher: 86.9% (2007); Bachelor's degree or higher: 29.7% (2007); Master's degree or higher: 10.4% (2007).

Housing: Homeownership rate: 98.6% (2007); Median home value: $597,444 (2007); Median rent: $n/a per month (2000); Median age of housing: 16 years (2000).

Transportation: Commute to work: 86.2% car, 0.0% public transportation, 0.7% walk, 12.4% work from home (2000); Travel time to work: 8.7% less than 15 minutes, 29.7% 15 to 30 minutes, 31.9% 30 to 45 minutes, 21.7% 45 to 60 minutes, 8.0% 60 minutes or more (2000)

DANIA BEACH (city). Aka Dania. Covers a land area of 6.090 square miles and a water area of 0.221 square miles. Located at 26.05° N. Lat.; 80.15° W. Long. Elevation is 5 feet.

Population: 18,021 (1990); 20,061 (2000); 21,896 (2007); 23,097 (2012 projected); Race: 67.0% White, 24.3% Black, 2.1% Asian, 17.5% Hispanic of any race (2007); Density: 3,595.5 persons per square mile (2007); Average household size: 2.23 (2007); Median age: 41.1 (2007); Males per 100 females: 101.1 (2007); Marriage status: 30.2% never married, 45.4% now married, 8.2% widowed, 16.2% divorced (2000); Foreign born: 18.1% (2000); Ancestry (includes multiple ancestries): 29.9% Other groups, 12.4% Italian, 10.2% Irish, 9.7% German, 7.1% United States or American (2000).

Economy: Single-family building permits issued: 103 (2006); Multi-family building permits issued: 24 (2006); Employment by occupation: 12.0% management, 15.1% professional, 19.4% services, 29.6% sales, 0.1% farming, 12.1% construction, 11.7% production (2000).

Income: Per capita income: $25,011 (2007); Median household income: $41,827 (2007); Average household income: $55,099 (2007); Percent of households with income of $100,000 or more: 13.7% (2007); Poverty rate: 18.3% (2000).

Education: Percent of population age 25 and over with: High school diploma (including GED) or higher: 78.0% (2007); Bachelor's degree or higher: 17.5% (2007); Master's degree or higher: 5.2% (2007).

School District(s)
Broward County School District (PK-12)
   2005-06 Enrollment: 274,591 . . . . (754) 321-2600

Key College (Private, For-profit)
   Fall 2006 Enrollment: 101 . . . . (954) 923-4440
   2006-07 Tuition: In-state $8,985; Out-of-state $8,985

Housing: Homeownership rate: 57.7% (2007); Median home value: $216,241 (2007); Median rent: $599 per month (2000); Median age of housing: 26 years (2000).

Safety: Violent crime rate: 76.9 per 10,000 population; Property crime rate: 502.6 per 10,000 population (2006).

Transportation: Commute to work: 88.8% car, 3.2% public transportation, 2.5% walk, 2.7% work from home (2000); Travel time to work: 30.1% less than 15 minutes, 38.9% 15 to 30 minutes, 19.1% 30 to 45 minutes, 6.4% 45 to 60 minutes, 5.5% 60 minutes or more (2000)

Additional Information Contacts
City of Dania Beach . . . . (954) 924-6800
   http://www.ci.dania-beach.fl.us
Greater Dania Chamber of Commerce . . . . (954) 926-2323
   http://www.greaterdania.org

DAVIE (town). Covers a land area of 33.428 square miles and a water area of 0.741 square miles. Located at 26.08° N. Lat.; 80.28° W. Long. Elevation is 3 feet.

Population: 54,493 (1990); 75,720 (2000); 85,081 (2007); 91,137 (2012 projected); Race: 82.4% White, 6.2% Black, 3.6% Asian, 26.9% Hispanic of any race (2007); Density: 2,545.2 persons per square mile (2007); Average household size: 2.70 (2007); Median age: 36.2 (2007); Males per 100 females: 96.0 (2007); Marriage status: 25.5% never married, 55.1% now married, 5.7% widowed, 13.6% divorced (2000); Foreign born: 17.5% (2000); Ancestry (includes multiple ancestries): 28.2% Other groups, 14.0% Irish, 13.7% German, 12.5% Italian, 7.5% English (2000).

Economy: Unemployment rate: 3.3% (11/2007); Total civilian labor force: 50,735 (11/2007); Single-family building permits issued: 510 (2006); Multi-family building permits issued: 71 (2006); Employment by occupation: 14.8% management, 19.3% professional, 15.3% services, 30.0% sales, 0.3% farming, 11.6% construction, 8.8% production (2000).

Income: Per capita income: $27,403 (2007); Median household income: $55,254 (2007); Average household income: $73,743 (2007); Percent of households with income of $100,000 or more: 23.1% (2007); Poverty rate: 9.8% (2000).

Taxes: Total city taxes per capita: $552 (2005); City property taxes per capita: $317 (2005).

Education: Percent of population age 25 and over with: High school diploma (including GED) or higher: 84.5% (2007); Bachelor's degree or higher: 26.2% (2007); Master's degree or higher: 9.8% (2007).

School District(s)
Broward County School District (PK-12)
   2005-06 Enrollment: 274,591 . . . . (754) 321-2600
Four-year College(s)
Trinity International University (Private, Not-for-profit, Evangelical Free Church of America)
   Fall 2006 Enrollment: 280 . . . . (954) 382-6400
Two-year College(s)
McFatter Technical Center (Public)
   Fall 2006 Enrollment: 767 . . . . (754) 321-5700
   2006-07 Tuition: In-state $1,873; Out-of-state $7,048
Vocational/Technical School(s)
ASM Beauty World Academy (Private, For-profit)
   Fall 2006 Enrollment: 169 . . . . (954) 321-8411
   2006-07 Tuition: $7,470

Housing: Homeownership rate: 76.5% (2007); Median home value: $255,629 (2007); Median rent: $711 per month (2000); Median age of housing: 17 years (2000).

Safety: Violent crime rate: 34.5 per 10,000 population; Property crime rate: 334.6 per 10,000 population (2006).

Newspapers: Miramar Community News (General - Circulation 100,000); Plantation Community News (General - Circulation 23,000)

Transportation: Commute to work: 93.7% car, 0.9% public transportation, 1.2% walk, 2.6% work from home (2000); Travel time to work: 19.1% less than 15 minutes, 36.4% 15 to 30 minutes, 26.6% 30 to 45 minutes, 9.9% 45 to 60 minutes, 8.0% 60 minutes or more (2000)

Additional Information Contacts
Davie-Cooper City Chamber of Commerce . . . . (954) 581-0790
   http://www.davie-coopercity.org
Town of Davie . . . . (954) 797-1000
   http://www.davie-fl.gov

DEERFIELD BEACH (city). Covers a land area of 13.425 square miles and a water area of 1.502 square miles. Located at 26.30° N. Lat.; 80.12° W. Long. Elevation is 13 feet.

History: Named for the abundance of local deer. Incorporated 1925.
Population: 55,289 (1990); 64,583 (2000); 65,940 (2007); 67,072 (2012 projected); Race: 75.1% White, 15.9% Black, 1.8% Asian, 12.5% Hispanic of any race (2007); Density: 4,911.7 persons per square mile (2007); Average household size: 2.07 (2007); Median age: 45.4 (2007); Males per 100 females: 88.5 (2007); Marriage status: 23.5% never married, 50.8% now married, 13.5% widowed, 12.3% divorced (2000); Foreign born: 22.7% (2000); Ancestry (includes multiple ancestries): 23.2% Other groups, 10.8% Irish, 10.6% Italian, 9.6% German, 7.2% English (2000).
Economy: Unemployment rate: 3.6% (11/2007); Total civilian labor force: 39,762 (11/2007); Single-family building permits issued: 138 (2006); Multi-family building permits issued: 0 (2006); Employment by occupation: 15.3% management, 15.4% professional, 18.8% services, 30.3% sales, 0.5% farming, 10.3% construction, 9.4% production (2000).
Income: Per capita income: $26,746 (2007); Median household income: $39,456 (2007); Average household income: $54,540 (2007); Percent of households with income of $100,000 or more: 12.4% (2007); Poverty rate: 12.5% (2000).
Education: Percent of population age 25 and over with: High school diploma (including GED) or higher: 79.5% (2007); Bachelor's degree or higher: 21.2% (2007); Master's degree or higher: 6.6% (2007).

School District(s)
Broward County School District (PK-12)
　　2005-06 Enrollment: 274,591 . . . . (754) 321-2600
Housing: Homeownership rate: 70.8% (2007); Median home value: $172,610 (2007); Median rent: $718 per month (2000); Median age of housing: 23 years (2000).
Safety: Violent crime rate: 72.3 per 10,000 population; Property crime rate: 333.7 per 10,000 population (2006).
Newspapers: Deerfield Beach/Lighthouse Point Observer (General - Circulation 27,500); Hi-Riser/Broward (General - Circulation 18,500); Jewish Journal - Broward South (Jewish - Circulation 26,000)
Transportation: Commute to work: 93.4% car, 1.2% public transportation, 1.4% walk, 2.4% work from home (2000); Travel time to work: 24.3% less than 15 minutes, 45.0% 15 to 30 minutes, 20.9% 30 to 45 minutes, 5.4% 45 to 60 minutes, 4.4% 60 minutes or more (2000); Amtrak: Service available.

Additional Information Contacts
City of Deerfield Beach . . . . (954) 480-4200
　　http://www.deerfield-beach.com
Deerfield Beach Chamber of Commerce . . . . (954) 427-1050
　　http://www.deerfieldchamber.com
Florida-Israel Chamber . . . . (561) 620-9288
　　http://www.floridaisraelchamber.org

EDGEWATER (CDP). Covers a land area of 0.230 square miles and a water area of 0 square miles. Located at 26.06° N. Lat.; 80.20° W. Long.

Population: 766 (1990); 803 (2000); 732 (2007); 737 (2012 projected); Race: 87.2% White, 1.9% Black, 0.7% Asian, 18.2% Hispanic of any race (2007); Density: 3,185.4 persons per square mile (2007); Average household size: 2.29 (2007); Median age: 44.3 (2007); Males per 100 females: 112.2 (2007); Marriage status: 24.6% never married, 48.4% now married, 11.4% widowed, 15.6% divorced (2000); Foreign born: 15.7% (2000); Ancestry (includes multiple ancestries): 27.6% Other groups, 20.3% Irish, 18.1% German, 11.4% United States or American, 11.0% European (2000).
Economy: Employment by occupation: 15.1% management, 0.0% professional, 24.5% services, 20.4% sales, 0.0% farming, 25.8% construction, 14.2% production (2000).
Income: Per capita income: $19,781 (2007); Median household income: $30,976 (2007); Average household income: $45,250 (2007); Percent of households with income of $100,000 or more: 11.3% (2007); Poverty rate: 23.3% (2000).
Education: Percent of population age 25 and over with: High school diploma (including GED) or higher: 75.4% (2007); Bachelor's degree or higher: 6.6% (2007); Master's degree or higher: 1.2% (2007).

School District(s)
Volusia County School District (PK-12)
　　2005-06 Enrollment: 65,281 . . . . (386) 734-7190

$313,115 (2007); Median rent: $654 per month (2000); Median age of housing: 31 years (2000).
Transportation: Commute to work: 97.2% car, 0.0% public transportation, 0.0% walk, 2.8% work from home (2000); Travel time to work: 27.8% less than 15 minutes, 43.7% 15 to 30 minutes, 17.2% 30 to 45 minutes, 4.9% 45 to 60 minutes, 6.5% 60 minutes or more (2000)

ESTATES OF FORT LAUDERDALE (CDP). Covers a land area of 0.316 square miles and a water area of 0.088 square miles. Located at 26.05° N. Lat.; 80.18° W. Long.

Population: 1,666 (1990); 1,791 (2000); 1,926 (2007); 2,022 (2012 projected); Race: 84.9% White, 5.1% Black, 2.1% Asian, 18.0% Hispanic of any race (2007); Density: 6,094.4 persons per square mile (2007); Average household size: 2.08 (2007); Median age: 49.3 (2007); Males per 100 females: 82.9 (2007); Marriage status: 17.7% never married, 58.5% now married, 13.0% widowed, 10.8% divorced (2000); Foreign born: 22.4% (2000); Ancestry (includes multiple ancestries): 21.6% Italian, 14.0% Other groups, 10.9% Irish, 9.8% German, 7.3% English (2000).
Economy: Employment by occupation: 20.7% management, 10.7% professional, 19.7% services, 30.4% sales, 0.0% farming, 11.2% construction, 7.2% production (2000).
Income: Per capita income: $25,511 (2007); Median household income: $38,864 (2007); Average household income: $53,004 (2007); Percent of households with income of $100,000 or more: 9.8% (2007); Poverty rate: 7.5% (2000).
Education: Percent of population age 25 and over with: High school diploma (including GED) or higher: 73.6% (2007); Bachelor's degree or higher: 13.6% (2007); Master's degree or higher: 4.4% (2007).
Housing: Homeownership rate: 88.3% (2007); Median home value: $162,788 (2007); Median rent: $706 per month (2000); Median age of housing: 24 years (2000).
Transportation: Commute to work: 89.4% car, 1.4% public transportation, 1.5% walk, 6.3% work from home (2000); Travel time to work: 32.4% less than 15 minutes, 46.7% 15 to 30 minutes, 15.3% 30 to 45 minutes, 1.9% 45 to 60 minutes, 3.7% 60 minutes or more (2000)

FORT LAUDERDALE (city). County seat. Covers a land area of 31.729 square miles and a water area of 4.287 square miles. Located at 26.13° N. Lat.; 80.14° W. Long. Elevation is 3 feet.

History: The town of Fort Lauderdale was built on the site of a fort constructed in 1838 and named for its commander, Major William Lauderdale. It developed as a popular winter headquarters for yachtsmen and fishermen.
Population: 149,908 (1990); 152,397 (2000); 166,763 (2007); 176,239 (2012 projected); Race: 61.0% White, 30.4% Black, 1.2% Asian, 11.6% Hispanic of any race (2007); Density: 5,255.9 persons per square mile (2007); Average household size: 2.21 (2007); Median age: 41.4 (2007); Males per 100 females: 110.8 (2007); Marriage status: 35.3% never married, 43.3% now married, 7.3% widowed, 14.0% divorced (2000); Foreign born: 21.7% (2000); Ancestry (includes multiple ancestries): 27.5% Other groups, 10.4% German, 10.3% Irish, 8.2% English, 7.6% Italian (2000).
Economy: Unemployment rate: 3.8% (11/2007); Total civilian labor force: 95,186 (11/2007); Single-family building permits issued: 289 (2006); Multi-family building permits issued: 1,021 (2006); Employment by occupation: 15.5% management, 17.9% professional, 20.1% services, 27.4% sales, 0.3% farming, 9.1% construction, 9.8% production (2000).
Income: Per capita income: $32,371 (2007); Median household income: $45,479 (2007); Average household income: $70,455 (2007); Percent of households with income of $100,000 or more: 18.4% (2007); Poverty rate: 17.7% (2000).
Taxes: Total city taxes per capita: $880 (2005); City property taxes per capita: $535 (2005).
Education: Percent of population age 25 and over with: High school diploma (including GED) or higher: 78.8% (2007); Bachelor's degree or higher: 27.8% (2007); Master's degree or higher: 10.4% (2007).

School District(s)
Broward County School District (PK-12)
　　2005-06 Enrollment: 274,591 . . . . (754) 321-2600
Four-year College(s)
Atlantic Institute of Oriental Medicine (Private, Not-for-profit)
　　Fall 2006 Enrollment: 94 . . . . (954) 763-9840

Fall 2006 Enrollment: 575 .... (954) 476-9300
  2006-07 Tuition: In-state $14,880; Out-of-state $14,880
Keiser College-Ft Lauderdale (Private, For-profit)
  Fall 2006 Enrollment: 9,639 .... (954) 776-4476
  2006-07 Tuition: In-state $12,440; Out-of-state $12,440
Nova Southeastern University (Private, Not-for-profit)
  Fall 2006 Enrollment: 25,960 .... (954) 262-7300
  2006-07 Tuition: In-state $18,650; Out-of-state $18,650
The Art Institute of Fort Lauderdale Inc (Private, For-profit)
  Fall 2006 Enrollment: 3,058 .... (954) 463-3000
  2006-07 Tuition: In-state $18,325; Out-of-state $18,325
Two-year College(s)
ATI Career Training Center (Private, For-profit)
  Fall 2006 Enrollment: 685 .... (954) 973-4760
Broward Community College (Public)
  Fall 2006 Enrollment: 30,607 .... (954) 201-7400
  2006-07 Tuition: In-state $1,675; Out-of-state $5,809
Sanford-Brown Institute (Private, For-profit)
  Fall 2006 Enrollment: 635 .... (954) 308-7400
Vocational/Technical School(s)
Coral Ridge Nurses Assistant Training School Inc (Private, For-profit)
  Fall 2006 Enrollment: 20 .... (954) 561-2022
  2006-07 Tuition: $7,650
Florida Academy of Health & Beauty (Private, For-profit)
  Fall 2006 Enrollment: 54 .... (954) 563-9098
  2006-07 Tuition: In-state $5,750; Out-of-state $5,750
National School of Technology (Private, For-profit)
  Fall 2006 Enrollment: 542 .... (954) 630-0066
  2006-07 Tuition: $10,042
Housing: Homeownership rate: 54.9% (2007); Median home value: $317,292 (2007); Median rent: $577 per month (2000); Median age of housing: 35 years (2000).
Hospitals: Atlantic Shores Hospital (72 beds); Broward General Medical Center (744 beds); Florida Medical Center (459 beds); Fort Lauderdale Hospital (100 beds); HealthSouth Sunrise Rehabilitation Hospital (108 beds); Holy Cross Hospital (597 beds); Imperial Point Medical Center (204 beds); Kindred Hospital-Ft Lauderdale (70 beds); North Ridge Medical Center (332 beds)
Safety: Violent crime rate: 98.9 per 10,000 population; Property crime rate: 583.8 per 10,000 population (2006).
Newspapers: Broward Daily Business Review (Circulation 10,000); City Link (Alternative, General - Circulation 56,000); El Heraldo de Broward (Hispanic - Circulation 22,000); New Times - Broward/Palm Beach (Alternative, General - Circulation 70,000); South Florida Sun-Sentinel (Circulation 282,538); The Broward Times (Black, General - Circulation 25,000); Westside Gazette (General - Circulation 65,000)
Transportation: Commute to work: 86.5% car, 4.9% public transportation, 2.4% walk, 3.8% work from home (2000); Travel time to work: 29.7% less than 15 minutes, 38.5% 15 to 30 minutes, 19.7% 30 to 45 minutes, 5.8% 45 to 60 minutes, 6.4% 60 minutes or more (2000); Amtrak: Service available.
Airports: Fort Lauderdale Executive; Fort Lauderdale/Hollywood International (primary service/large hub)
Additional Information Contacts
British American Chamber of Commerce .... (407) 428-6226
Christian Chamber of Commerce .... (954) 972-9256
Fort Lauderdale Chamber of Commerce .... (954) 462-6000
  http://www.ftlchamber.com
Lauderdale By-The-Sea Chamber .... (954) 776-1000
  http://www.lbts.com

FRANKLIN PARK (CDP). Covers a land area of 0.068 square miles and a water area of 0 square miles. Located at 26.13° N. Lat.; 80.17° W. Long. Elevation is 3 feet.
Population: 1,099 (1990); 943 (2000); 957 (2007); 975 (2012 projected); Race: 0.6% White, 97.1% Black, 0.0% Asian, 2.0% Hispanic of any race (2007); Density: 14,022.6 persons per square mile (2007); Average household size: 3.06 (2007); Median age: 23.6 (2007); Males per 100 females: 86.9 (2007); Marriage status: 51.3% never married, 40.0% now married, 1.8% widowed, 6.9% divorced (2000); Foreign born: 2.7% (2000);

construction, 21.6% production (2000).
Income: Per capita income: $9,514 (2007); Median household income: $27,292 (2007); Average household income: $29,089 (2007); Percent of households with income of $100,000 or more: 0.0% (2007); Poverty rate: 38.2% (2000).
Education: Percent of population age 25 and over with: High school diploma (including GED) or higher: 50.2% (2007); Bachelor's degree or higher: 0.0% (2007); Master's degree or higher: 0.0% (2007).
Housing: Homeownership rate: 8.9% (2007); Median home value: $118,750 (2007); Median rent: $394 per month (2000); Median age of housing: 42 years (2000).
Transportation: Commute to work: 83.5% car, 16.5% public transportation, 0.0% walk, 0.0% work from home (2000); Travel time to work: 19.5% less than 15 minutes, 36.7% 15 to 30 minutes, 17.2% 30 to 45 minutes, 6.4% 45 to 60 minutes, 20.2% 60 minutes or more (2000)

GODFREY ROAD (CDP). Covers a land area of 0.216 square miles and a water area of 0 square miles. Located at 26.29° N. Lat.; 80.22° W. Long.
Population: 69 (1990); 172 (2000); 180 (2007); 184 (2012 projected); Race: 77.2% White, 0.0% Black, 0.0% Asian, 12.8% Hispanic of any race (2007); Density: 832.7 persons per square mile (2007); Average household size: 3.10 (2007); Median age: 45.2 (2007); Males per 100 females: 93.5 (2007); Marriage status: 39.1% never married, 60.9% now married, 0.0% widowed, 0.0% divorced (2000); Foreign born: 22.1% (2000); Ancestry (includes multiple ancestries): 32.9% Irish, 26.3% Italian, 17.8% Hungarian, 15.5% Other groups, 8.5% French Canadian (2000).
Economy: Employment by occupation: 9.6% management, 25.4% professional, 21.9% services, 35.1% sales, 0.0% farming, 7.9% construction, 0.0% production (2000).
Income: Per capita income: $38,782 (2007); Median household income: $90,385 (2007); Average household income: $110,043 (2007); Percent of households with income of $100,000 or more: 41.4% (2007); Poverty rate: 0.0% (2000).
Education: Percent of population age 25 and over with: High school diploma (including GED) or higher: 69.5% (2007); Bachelor's degree or higher: 39.8% (2007); Master's degree or higher: 9.4% (2007).
Housing: Homeownership rate: 98.3% (2007); Median home value: $891,667 (2007); Median rent: $n/a per month (2000); Median age of housing: 22 years (2000).
Transportation: Commute to work: 71.1% car, 0.0% public transportation, 0.0% walk, 28.9% work from home (2000); Travel time to work: 9.9% less than 15 minutes, 50.6% 15 to 30 minutes, 13.6% 30 to 45 minutes, 0.0% 45 to 60 minutes, 25.9% 60 minutes or more (2000)

GOLDEN HEIGHTS (CDP). Covers a land area of 0.051 square miles and a water area of 0 square miles. Located at 26.14° N. Lat.; 80.17° W. Long. Elevation is 7 feet.
Population: 533 (1990); 501 (2000); 519 (2007); 533 (2012 projected); Race: 1.2% White, 93.1% Black, 1.0% Asian, 0.8% Hispanic of any race (2007); Density: 10,185.7 persons per square mile (2007); Average household size: 2.82 (2007); Median age: 39.5 (2007); Males per 100 females: 95.1 (2007); Marriage status: 26.2% never married, 43.9% now married, 14.2% widowed, 15.8% divorced (2000); Foreign born: 2.6% (2000); Ancestry (includes multiple ancestries): 87.5% Other groups, 2.6% African, 1.5% United States or American, 1.3% Jamaican, 0.7% Egyptian (2000).
Economy: Employment by occupation: 8.3% management, 19.3% professional, 18.9% services, 28.9% sales, 3.0% farming, 11.3% construction, 10.3% production (2000).
Income: Per capita income: $22,731 (2007); Median household income: $55,000 (2007); Average household income: $64,117 (2007); Percent of households with income of $100,000 or more: 19.6% (2007); Poverty rate: 11.6% (2000).
Education: Percent of population age 25 and over with: High school diploma (including GED) or higher: 60.1% (2007); Bachelor's degree or higher: 25.1% (2007); Master's degree or higher: 10.3% (2007).
Housing: Homeownership rate: 85.3% (2007); Median home value: $178,783 (2007); Median rent: $525 per month (2000); Median age of housing: 36 years (2000).

GREEN MEADOW (CDP). Covers a land area of 2.090 square miles and a water area of 0.006 square miles. Located at 26.05° N. Lat.; 80.36° W. Long.

Population: 1,592 (1990); 1,874 (2000); 2,091 (2007); 2,224 (2012 projected); Race: 87.7% White, 3.9% Black, 3.5% Asian, 26.7% Hispanic of any race (2007); Density: 1,000.5 persons per square mile (2007); Average household size: 3.38 (2007); Median age: 39.2 (2007); Males per 100 females: 101.4 (2007); Marriage status: 18.9% never married, 71.8% now married, 2.9% widowed, 6.4% divorced (2000); Foreign born: 11.7% (2000); Ancestry (includes multiple ancestries): 27.2% Other groups, 17.2% German, 16.8% Italian, 7.8% Irish, 6.7% English (2000).
Economy: Employment by occupation: 18.9% management, 24.3% professional, 6.6% services, 34.0% sales, 1.0% farming, 8.2% construction, 6.9% production (2000).
Income: Per capita income: $37,682 (2007); Median household income: $95,301 (2007); Average household income: $127,496 (2007); Percent of households with income of $100,000 or more: 46.0% (2007); Poverty rate: 0.6% (2000).
Education: Percent of population age 25 and over with: High school diploma (including GED) or higher: 93.2% (2007); Bachelor's degree or higher: 20.8% (2007); Master's degree or higher: 10.3% (2007).
Housing: Homeownership rate: 98.5% (2007); Median home value: $575,725 (2007); Median rent: $2,000+ per month (2000); Median age of housing: 21 years (2000).
Transportation: Commute to work: 99.3% car, 0.0% public transportation, 0.0% walk, 0.7% work from home (2000); Travel time to work: 15.9% less than 15 minutes, 24.9% 15 to 30 minutes, 32.6% 30 to 45 minutes, 16.9% 45 to 60 minutes, 9.7% 60 minutes or more (2000)

HALLANDALE (city). Aka Hallandale Beach. Covers a land area of 4.210 square miles and a water area of 0.345 square miles. Located at 25.98° N. Lat.; 80.14° W. Long. Elevation is 10 feet.
History: Named for the country of Holland by early Hollander settler. Settled 1897. Incorporated 1927.
Population: 30,997 (1990); 34,282 (2000); 35,594 (2007); 36,590 (2012 projected); Race: 72.8% White, 18.1% Black, 1.3% Asian, 26.3% Hispanic of any race (2007); Density: 8,454.7 persons per square mile (2007); Average household size: 1.94 (2007); Median age: 52.0 (2007); Males per 100 females: 87.1 (2007); Marriage status: 20.4% never married, 50.3% now married, 16.4% widowed, 12.9% divorced (2000); Foreign born: 36.1% (2000); Ancestry (includes multiple ancestries): 33.9% Other groups, 9.2% Italian, 5.9% German, 5.4% United States or American, 5.1% Russian (2000).
Economy: Unemployment rate: 4.5% (11/2007); Total civilian labor force: 17,372 (11/2007); Single-family building permits issued: 12 (2006); Multi-family building permits issued: 181 (2006); Employment by occupation: 12.4% management, 15.3% professional, 20.5% services, 32.4% sales, 0.1% farming, 8.3% construction, 11.0% production (2000).
Income: Per capita income: $24,938 (2007); Median household income: $33,331 (2007); Average household income: $47,637 (2007); Percent of households with income of $100,000 or more: 9.4% (2007); Poverty rate: 16.8% (2000).
Education: Percent of population age 25 and over with: High school diploma (including GED) or higher: 73.2% (2007); Bachelor's degree or higher: 19.8% (2007); Master's degree or higher: 8.1% (2007).

School District(s)
Broward County School District (PK-12)
    2005-06 Enrollment: 274,591 . . . . (754) 321-2600
Four-year College(s)
Academy for Element Acupuncture (Private, Not-for-profit)
    Fall 2006 Enrollment: 79 . . . . (954) 456-6336
Housing: Homeownership rate: 66.5% (2007); Median home value: $176,781 (2007); Median rent: $578 per month (2000); Median age of housing: 28 years (2000).
Safety: Violent crime rate: 104.0 per 10,000 population; Property crime rate: 418.7 per 10,000 population (2006).
Transportation: Commute to work: 88.2% car, 4.3% public transportation, 2.8% walk, 3.2% work from home (2000); Travel time to work: 24.2% less than 15 minutes, 34.7% 15 to 30 minutes, 23.7% 30 to 45 minutes, 8.8% 45 to 60 minutes, 8.7% 60 minutes or more (2000)

HILLSBORO BEACH (town). Covers a land area of 0.436 square miles and a water area of 1.199 square miles. Located at 26.29° N. Lat.; 80.07° W. Long. Elevation is 13 feet.
Population: 1,748 (1990); 2,163 (2000); 2,326 (2007); 2,437 (2012 projected); Race: 98.9% White, 0.3% Black, 0.2% Asian, 2.4% Hispanic of any race (2007); Density: 5,329.9 persons per square mile (2007); Average household size: 1.67 (2007); Median age: 64.7 (2007); Males per 100 females: 82.3 (2007); Marriage status: 9.4% never married, 63.4% now married, 14.6% widowed, 12.6% divorced (2000); Foreign born: 14.0% (2000); Ancestry (includes multiple ancestries): 17.4% German, 16.3% Italian, 14.3% English, 11.8% Irish, 7.0% Other groups (2000).
Economy: Single-family building permits issued: 0 (2006); Multi-family building permits issued: 0 (2006); Employment by occupation: 38.7% management, 13.0% professional, 6.6% services, 34.5% sales, 0.0% farming, 3.8% construction, 3.5% production (2000).
Income: Per capita income: $55,502 (2007); Median household income: $57,048 (2007); Average household income: $92,477 (2007); Percent of households with income of $100,000 or more: 24.7% (2007); Poverty rate: 8.0% (2000).
Education: Percent of population age 25 and over with: High school diploma (including GED) or higher: 94.7% (2007); Bachelor's degree or higher: 39.7% (2007); Master's degree or higher: 14.1% (2007).
Housing: Homeownership rate: 90.4% (2007); Median home value: $374,613 (2007); Median rent: $1,169 per month (2000); Median age of housing: 29 years (2000).
Safety: Violent crime rate: 12.7 per 10,000 population; Property crime rate: 76.0 per 10,000 population (2006).
Transportation: Commute to work: 83.4% car, 0.0% public transportation, 1.7% walk, 12.0% work from home (2000); Travel time to work: 29.5% less than 15 minutes, 39.9% 15 to 30 minutes, 21.7% 30 to 45 minutes, 5.1% 45 to 60 minutes, 3.8% 60 minutes or more (2000)

HILLSBORO PINES (CDP). Covers a land area of 0.224 square miles and a water area of 0 square miles. Located at 26.32° N. Lat.; 80.19° W. Long.
Population: 95 (1990); 406 (2000); 488 (2007); 540 (2012 projected); Race: 92.0% White, 3.3% Black, 1.0% Asian, 4.5% Hispanic of any race (2007); Density: 2,175.5 persons per square mile (2007); Average household size: 2.90 (2007); Median age: 39.5 (2007); Males per 100 females: 105.9 (2007); Marriage status: 22.7% never married, 57.1% now married, 6.4% widowed, 13.7% divorced (2000); Foreign born: 5.6% (2000); Ancestry (includes multiple ancestries): 30.7% Italian, 17.1% English, 15.1% Irish, 11.8% Polish, 11.8% German (2000).
Economy: Employment by occupation: 30.7% management, 12.2% professional, 5.0% services, 26.1% sales, 0.0% farming, 18.1% construction, 8.0% production (2000).
Income: Per capita income: $29,908 (2007); Median household income: $72,778 (2007); Average household income: $86,875 (2007); Percent of households with income of $100,000 or more: 27.4% (2007); Poverty rate: 1.6% (2000).
Education: Percent of population age 25 and over with: High school diploma (including GED) or higher: 91.9% (2007); Bachelor's degree or higher: 16.5% (2007); Master's degree or higher: 0 (2007).
Housing: Homeownership rate: 86.9% (2007); Median home value: $375,000 (2007); Median rent: $605 per month (2000); Median age of housing: 24 years (2000).
Transportation: Commute to work: 92.8% car, 0.0% public transportation, 3.6% walk, 3.6% work from home (2000); Travel time to work: 12.4% less than 15 minutes, 45.2% 15 to 30 minutes, 25.3% 30 to 45 minutes, 3.3% 45 to 60 minutes, 13.7% 60 minutes or more (2000)

HILLSBORO RANCHES (CDP). Covers a land area of 0.100 square miles and a water area of 0 square miles. Located at 26.32° N. Lat.; 80.18° W. Long.
Population: 13 (1990); 47 (2000); 55 (2007); 60 (2012 projected); Race: 94.5% White, 0.0% Black, 0.0% Asian, 0.0% Hispanic of any race (2007); Density: 551.9 persons per square mile (2007); Average household size: 3.06 (2007); Median age: 41.2 (2007); Males per 100 females: 103.7 (2007); Marriage status: 0.0% never married, 0.0% now married, 100.0% widowed, 0.0% divorced (2000); Foreign born: 0.0% (2000); **Income:** Per capita income: $10,000 (2007); Median household income: $30,909 (2007);

Housing: Homeownership rate: 77.8% (2007); Median home value: $1,000,000 (2007); Median rent: $n/a per month (2000); Median age of housing: 21 years (2000).

HOLLYWOOD (city).
Covers a land area of 27.340 square miles and a water area of 3.456 square miles. Located at 26.02° N. Lat.; 80.17° W. Long. Elevation is 10 feet.

History: Named for Joseph W. Young, the city's founder, who had come with his associaes from California to establish a resort town. The town of Hollywood was founded in 1921 and planned as a winter resort town, founded during the real estate boom and promoted vigorously by its developers.

Population: 121,944 (1990); 139,357 (2000); 144,774 (2007); 148,736 (2012 projected); Race: 71.9% White, 15.3% Black, 2.5% Asian, 31.3% Hispanic of any race (2007); Density: 5,295.3 persons per square mile (2007); Average household size: 2.39 (2007); Median age: 40.3 (2007); Males per 100 females: 95.6 (2007); Marriage status: 25.5% never married, 50.7% now married, 9.5% widowed, 14.4% divorced (2000); Foreign born: 26.3% (2000); Ancestry (includes multiple ancestries): 33.5% Other groups, 9.5% Italian, 9.1% Irish, 8.6% German, 7.0% United States or American (2000).

Economy: Unemployment rate: 4.0% (11/2007); Total civilian labor force: 81,830 (11/2007); Single-family building permits issued: 69 (2006); Multi-family building permits issued: 106 (2006); Employment by occupation: 13.0% management, 18.4% professional, 16.9% services, 29.7% sales, 0.4% farming, 11.6% construction, 10.0% production (2000).

Income: Per capita income: $25,377 (2007); Median household income: $43,310 (2007); Average household income: $60,137 (2007); Percent of households with income of $100,000 or more: 14.3% (2007); Poverty rate: 13.2% (2000).

Taxes: Total city taxes per capita: $590 (2005); City property taxes per capita: $365 (2005).

Education: Percent of population age 25 and over with: High school diploma (including GED) or higher: 79.5% (2007); Bachelor's degree or higher: 21.8% (2007); Master's degree or higher: 8.4% (2007).

School District(s)
Broward County School District (PK-12)
    2005-06 Enrollment: 274,591 . . . . (754) 321-2600

Two-year College(s)
Sheridan Technical Center (Public)
    Fall 2006 Enrollment: 1,262 . . . . (754) 321-5400

Vocational/Technical School(s)
Ross Medical Education Center (Private, For-profit)
    Fall 2006 Enrollment: 38 . . . . (954) 963-0043
    2006-07 Tuition: $9,430

Housing: Homeownership rate: 62.5% (2007); Median home value: $233,506 (2007); Median rent: $619 per month (2000); Median age of housing: 32 years (2000).

Hospitals: Hollywood Pavilion (46 beds); Memorial Regional Hospital (684 beds); Memorial Regional Hospital South (324 beds)

Safety: Violent crime rate: 49.8 per 10,000 population; Property crime rate: 422.3 per 10,000 population (2006).

Transportation: Commute to work: 90.8% car, 3.1% public transportation, 1.8% walk, 2.8% work from home (2000); Travel time to work: 22.5% less than 15 minutes, 37.4% 15 to 30 minutes, 24.5% 30 to 45 minutes, 9.1% 45 to 60 minutes, 6.5% 60 minutes or more (2000); Amtrak: Service available.

Additional Information Contacts
Greater Hollywood Chamber of Commerce. . . . . (954) 923-4000
    http://www.hollywoodchamber.org

IVANHOE ESTATES (CDP).
Covers a land area of 0.210 square miles and a water area of 0.011 square miles. Located at 26.05° N. Lat.; 80.34° W. Long.

Population: 269 (1990); 279 (2000); 341 (2007); 379 (2012 projected); Race: 63.9% White, 12.6% Black, 13.5% Asian, 25.5% Hispanic of any race (2007); Density: 1,624.4 persons per square mile (2007); Average household size: 4.06 (2007); Median age: 30.1 (2007); Males per 100 females: 104.2 (2007); Marriage status: 24.2% never married, 59.5% now married, 4.6% widowed, 11.8% divorced (2000); Foreign born: 15.0%

construction, 5.2% production (2000).

Income: Per capita income: $38,996 (2007); Median household income: $132,955 (2007); Average household income: $158,304 (2007); Percent of households with income of $100,000 or more: 78.6% (2007); Poverty rate: 2.0% (2000).

Education: Percent of population age 25 and over with: High school diploma (including GED) or higher: 95.8% (2007); Bachelor's degree or higher: 37.6% (2007); Master's degree or higher: 12.7% (2007).

Housing: Homeownership rate: 98.8% (2007); Median home value: $812,500 (2007); Median rent: $n/a per month (2000); Median age of housing: 14 years (2000).

Transportation: Commute to work: 92.7% car, 0.0% public transportation, 0.0% walk, 7.3% work from home (2000); Travel time to work: 42.7% less than 15 minutes, 32.6% 15 to 30 minutes, 21.3% 30 to 45 minutes, 3.4% 45 to 60 minutes, 0.0% 60 minutes or more (2000)

KENDALL GREEN (CDP).
Covers a land area of 0.477 square miles and a water area of 0 square miles. Located at 26.26° N. Lat.; 80.12° W. Long. Elevation is 20 feet.

Population: 2,781 (1990); 3,084 (2000); 3,288 (2007); 3,440 (2012 projected); Race: 23.4% White, 53.1% Black, 1.0% Asian, 17.8% Hispanic of any race (2007); Density: 6,895.7 persons per square mile (2007); Average household size: 3.45 (2007); Median age: 30.5 (2007); Males per 100 females: 104.2 (2007); Marriage status: 36.8% never married, 44.7% now married, 5.7% widowed, 12.8% divorced (2000); Foreign born: 36.8% (2000); Ancestry (includes multiple ancestries): 26.6% Other groups, 23.0% Haitian, 7.8% German, 6.7% United States or American, 4.0% English (2000).

Economy: Employment by occupation: 7.0% management, 8.9% professional, 34.2% services, 21.8% sales, 0.0% farming, 15.4% construction, 12.8% production (2000).

Income: Per capita income: $13,307 (2007); Median household income: $41,228 (2007); Average household income: $45,961 (2007); Percent of households with income of $100,000 or more: 4.0% (2007); Poverty rate: 22.7% (2000).

Education: Percent of population age 25 and over with: High school diploma (including GED) or higher: 60.8% (2007); Bachelor's degree or higher: 7.2% (2007); Master's degree or higher: 2.1% (2007).

Housing: Homeownership rate: 64.7% (2007); Median home value: $167,756 (2007); Median rent: $566 per month (2000); Median age of housing: 32 years (2000).

Transportation: Commute to work: 92.1% car, 2.6% public transportation, 1.4% walk, 0.6% work from home (2000); Travel time to work: 23.5% less than 15 minutes, 42.9% 15 to 30 minutes, 25.1% 30 to 45 minutes, 5.4% 45 to 60 minutes, 3.1% 60 minutes or more (2000)

LAKE FOREST (CDP).
Covers a land area of 0.654 square miles and a water area of 0.065 square miles. Located at 25.97° N. Lat.; 80.18° W. Long. Elevation is 7 feet.

Population: 4,812 (1990); 4,994 (2000); 5,179 (2007); 5,318 (2012 projected); Race: 49.5% White, 30.3% Black, 1.2% Asian, 40.0% Hispanic of any race (2007); Density: 7,923.5 persons per square mile (2007); Average household size: 3.33 (2007); Median age: 32.8 (2007); Males per 100 females: 96.0 (2007); Marriage status: 27.7% never married, 57.4% now married, 5.8% widowed, 9.2% divorced (2000); Foreign born: 31.4% (2000); Ancestry (includes multiple ancestries): 40.7% Other groups, 8.5% German, 8.2% United States or American, 6.6% Italian, 6.2% Irish (2000).

Economy: Employment by occupation: 8.4% management, 13.1% professional, 20.0% services, 29.7% sales, 0.4% farming, 12.5% construction, 16.0% production (2000).

Income: Per capita income: $14,268 (2007); Median household income: $38,146 (2007); Average household income: $46,830 (2007); Percent of households with income of $100,000 or more: 5.2% (2007); Poverty rate: 15.4% (2000).

Education: Percent of population age 25 and over with: High school diploma (including GED) or higher: 72.1% (2007); Bachelor's degree or higher: 10.4% (2007); Master's degree or higher: 3.5% (2007).

Housing: Homeownership rate: 85.4% (2007); Median home value: $186,680 (2007); Median rent: $626 per month (2000); Median age of housing: 41 years (2000).

LAUDERDALE LAKES (city).
Covers a land area of 3.590 square miles and a water area of 0.051 square miles. Located at 26.17° N. Lat.; 80.20° W. Long. Elevation is 7 feet.

Population: 27,341 (1990); 31,705 (2000); 32,461 (2007); 32,914 (2012 projected); Race: 16.3% White, 74.1% Black, 1.0% Asian, 6.0% Hispanic of any race (2007); Density: 9,042.7 persons per square mile (2007); Average household size: 2.67 (2007); Median age: 34.6 (2007); Males per 100 females: 83.9 (2007); Marriage status: 32.2% never married, 45.9% now married, 11.0% widowed, 10.9% divorced (2000); Foreign born: 40.5% (2000); Ancestry (includes multiple ancestries): 35.3% Other groups, 17.9% Jamaican, 15.0% Haitian, 5.7% United States or American, 2.5% Italian (2000).

Economy: Unemployment rate: 4.7% (11/2007); Total civilian labor force: 14,809 (11/2007); Single-family building permits issued: 0 (2006); Multi-family building permits issued: 0 (2006); Employment by occupation: 5.3% management, 14.8% professional, 26.8% services, 27.3% sales, 0.3% farming, 11.7% construction, 13.8% production (2000).

Income: Per capita income: $14,738 (2007); Median household income: $30,181 (2007); Average household income: $38,725 (2007); Percent of households with income of $100,000 or more: 4.5% (2007); Poverty rate: 22.5% (2000).

Education: Percent of population age 25 and over with: High school diploma (including GED) or higher: 67.9% (2007); Bachelor's degree or higher: 12.7% (2007); Master's degree or higher: 4.4% (2007).

School District(s)
Broward County School District (PK-12)
    2005-06 Enrollment: 274,591 . . . . (754) 321-2600

Two-year College(s)
Medvance Institute of Fort Lauderdale (Private, For-profit)
    Fall 2006 Enrollment: 301 . . . . (954) 587-7100

Vocational/Technical School(s)
Concorde Career Institute (Private, For-profit)
    Fall 2006 Enrollment: 306 . . . . (954) 731-8880
    2006-07 Tuition: $10,799
School of Health Careers (Private, For-profit)
    Fall 2006 Enrollment: 401 . . . . (954) 777-0083
    2006-07 Tuition: $11,995
Superior Career Institute (Private, For-profit)
    Fall 2006 Enrollment: 68 . . . . (954) 741-0088
    2006-07 Tuition: $7,300

Housing: Homeownership rate: 62.4% (2007); Median home value: $124,097 (2007); Median rent: $596 per month (2000); Median age of housing: 25 years (2000).

Safety: Violent crime rate: 125.5 per 10,000 population; Property crime rate: 439.7 per 10,000 population (2006).

Transportation: Commute to work: 90.2% car, 7.1% public transportation, 1.2% walk, 0.8% work from home (2000); Travel time to work: 11.5% less than 15 minutes, 42.5% 15 to 30 minutes, 29.5% 30 to 45 minutes, 8.3% 45 to 60 minutes, 8.2% 60 minutes or more (2000)

Additional Information Contacts
City of Lauderdale Lakes . . . . (954) 535-2700
    http://www.lauderdalelakes.org

LAUDERDALE-BY-THE-SEA (town).
Covers a land area of 0.505 square miles and a water area of 0.726 square miles. Located at 26.19° N. Lat.; 80.09° W. Long. Elevation is 10 feet.

Population: 2,990 (1990); 2,563 (2000); 2,647 (2007); 2,733 (2012 projected); Race: 94.8% White, 1.2% Black, 1.5% Asian, 7.3% Hispanic of any race (2007); Density: 5,238.5 persons per square mile (2007); Average household size: 1.68 (2007); Median age: 55.0 (2007); Males per 100 females: 101.1 (2007); Marriage status: 18.1% never married, 49.3% now married, 13.1% widowed, 19.5% divorced (2000); Foreign born: 16.2% (2000); Ancestry (includes multiple ancestries): 21.3% Irish, 17.3% Italian, 13.5% German, 13.2% English, 8.7% Other groups (2000).

Economy: Employment by occupation: 26.1% management, 22.3% professional, 10.4% services, 27.4% sales, 0.0% farming, 6.1% construction, 7.6% production (2000).

Income: Per capita income: $33,920 (2007); Median household income: $40,372 (2007); Average household income: $57,043 (2007); Percent of

Housing: Homeownership rate: 61.2% (2007); Median home value: $445,178 (2007); Median rent: $675 per month (2000); Median age of housing: 36 years (2000).

Safety: Violent crime rate: 36.1 per 10,000 population; Property crime rate: 295.5 per 10,000 population (2006).

Transportation: Commute to work: 76.5% car, 3.1% public transportation, 8.1% walk, 9.5% work from home (2000); Travel time to work: 28.3% less than 15 minutes, 37.7% 15 to 30 minutes, 21.2% 30 to 45 minutes, 6.6% 45 to 60 minutes, 6.2% 60 minutes or more (2000)

LAUDERHILL (city).
Covers a land area of 7.296 square miles and a water area of 0.037 square miles. Located at 26.16° N. Lat.; 80.23° W. Long. Elevation is 3 feet.

Population: 49,135 (1990); 57,585 (2000); 59,078 (2007); 60,156 (2012 projected); Race: 26.6% White, 64.6% Black, 1.7% Asian, 8.3% Hispanic of any race (2007); Density: 8,097.5 persons per square mile (2007); Average household size: 2.53 (2007); Median age: 36.0 (2007); Males per 100 females: 86.3 (2007); Marriage status: 30.3% never married, 48.5% now married, 9.7% widowed, 11.5% divorced (2000); Foreign born: 33.8% (2000); Ancestry (includes multiple ancestries): 33.8% Other groups, 17.0% Jamaican, 8.8% Haitian, 7.5% United States or American, 3.8% Italian (2000).

Economy: Unemployment rate: 4.4% (11/2007); Total civilian labor force: 31,002 (11/2007); Single-family building permits issued: 163 (2006); Multi-family building permits issued: 0 (2006); Employment by occupation: 10.1% management, 16.1% professional, 20.0% services, 32.3% sales, 0.3% farming, 10.4% construction, 10.8% production (2000).

Income: Per capita income: $18,722 (2007); Median household income: $35,593 (2007); Average household income: $46,679 (2007); Percent of households with income of $100,000 or more: 7.9% (2007); Poverty rate: 17.8% (2000).

Education: Percent of population age 25 and over with: High school diploma (including GED) or higher: 76.2% (2007); Bachelor's degree or higher: 16.4% (2007); Master's degree or higher: 5.4% (2007).

School District(s)
Broward County School District (PK-12)
    2005-06 Enrollment: 274,591 . . . . (754) 321-2600

Vocational/Technical School(s)
Florida Education Center (Private, For-profit)
    Fall 2006 Enrollment: 189 . . . . (954) 797-6140
    2006-07 Tuition: $11,750

Housing: Homeownership rate: 60.8% (2007); Median home value: $154,539 (2007); Median rent: $614 per month (2000); Median age of housing: 23 years (2000).

Safety: Violent crime rate: 104.1 per 10,000 population; Property crime rate: 387.0 per 10,000 population (2006).

Transportation: Commute to work: 90.9% car, 5.3% public transportation, 1.0% walk, 1.5% work from home (2000); Travel time to work: 14.2% less than 15 minutes, 40.2% 15 to 30 minutes, 28.9% 30 to 45 minutes, 9.5% 45 to 60 minutes, 7.1% 60 minutes or more (2000)

Additional Information Contacts
City of Lauderhill . . . . (954) 730-3010
    http://www.lauderhill-fl.gov

LAZY LAKE (village).
Covers a land area of 0.024 square miles and a water area of 0 square miles. Located at 26.15° N. Lat.; 80.14° W. Long. Elevation is 3 feet.

Population: 33 (1990); 38 (2000); 37 (2007); 35 (2012 projected); Race: 75.7% White, 18.9% Black, 0.0% Asian, 2.7% Hispanic of any race (2007); Density: 1,534.7 persons per square mile (2007); Average household size: 3.08 (2007); Median age: 40.8 (2007); Males per 100 females: 184.6 (2007); Marriage status: 69.4% never married, 11.1% now married, 0.0% widowed, 19.4% divorced (2000); Foreign born: 7.7% (2000); Ancestry (includes multiple ancestries): 28.2% German, 28.2% Irish, 15.4% Dutch, 12.8% Other groups, 10.3% Swiss (2000).

Economy: Employment by occupation: 16.7% management, 23.3% professional, 10.0% services, 6.7% sales, 0.0% farming, 23.3% construction, 20.0% production (2000).

Income: Per capita income: $40,270 (2007); Median household income: $150,000 (2007); Average household income: $124,167 (2007); Percent of

diploma (including GED) or higher: 100.0% (2007); Bachelor's degree or higher: 44.4% (2007); Master's degree or higher: 18.5% (2007).
Housing: Homeownership rate: 66.7% (2007); Median home value: $916,667 (2007); Median rent: $950 per month (2000); Median age of housing: 40 years (2000).
Transportation: Commute to work: 70.0% car, 23.3% public transportation, 0.0% walk, 6.7% work from home (2000); Travel time to work: 10.7% less than 15 minutes, 64.3% 15 to 30 minutes, 25.0% 30 to 45 minutes, 0.0% 45 to 60 minutes, 0.0% 60 minutes or more (2000)

LEISUREVILLE (CDP).
Covers a land area of 0.218 square miles and a water area of 0 square miles. Located at 26.26° N. Lat.; 80.12° W. Long.
Population: 1,034 (1990); 1,147 (2000); 1,238 (2007); 1,284 (2012 projected); Race: 74.4% White, 16.2% Black, 0.8% Asian, 5.7% Hispanic of any race (2007); Density: 5,672.2 persons per square mile (2007); Average household size: 1.62 (2007); Median age: 67.2 (2007); Males per 100 females: 76.9 (2007); Marriage status: 8.1% never married, 48.0% now married, 32.5% widowed, 11.3% divorced (2000); Foreign born: 25.4% (2000); Ancestry (includes multiple ancestries): 21.8% German, 17.0% English, 11.8% Italian, 9.9% Irish, 8.6% Haitian (2000).
Economy: Employment by occupation: 4.1% management, 13.8% professional, 41.8% services, 30.5% sales, 0.0% farming, 2.2% construction, 7.5% production (2000).
Income: Per capita income: $21,401 (2007); Median household income: $27,992 (2007); Average household income: $34,725 (2007); Percent of households with income of $100,000 or more: 3.7% (2007); Poverty rate: 6.1% (2000).
Education: Percent of population age 25 and over with: High school diploma (including GED) or higher: 66.0% (2007); Bachelor's degree or higher: 12.8% (2007); Master's degree or higher: 6.2% (2007).
Housing: Homeownership rate: 88.5% (2007); Median home value: $112,748 (2007); Median rent: $525 per month (2000); Median age of housing: 33 years (2000).
Transportation: Commute to work: 87.9% car, 2.2% public transportation, 2.9% walk, 7.0% work from home (2000); Travel time to work: 18.2% less than 15 minutes, 64.9% 15 to 30 minutes, 7.9% 30 to 45 minutes, 6.5% 45 to 60 minutes, 2.4% 60 minutes or more (2000)

LIGHTHOUSE POINT (city).
Covers a land area of 2.293 square miles and a water area of 0.108 square miles. Located at 26.27° N. Lat.; 80.08° W. Long. Elevation is 3 feet.
Population: 10,378 (1990); 10,767 (2000); 11,189 (2007); 11,505 (2012 projected); Race: 95.9% White, 0.7% Black, 1.0% Asian, 6.0% Hispanic of any race (2007); Density: 4,879.0 persons per square mile (2007); Average household size: 2.11 (2007); Median age: 47.9 (2007); Males per 100 females: 93.4 (2007); Marriage status: 15.1% never married, 62.2% now married, 9.9% widowed, 12.8% divorced (2000); Foreign born: 13.6% (2000); Ancestry (includes multiple ancestries): 19.0% Irish, 17.7% Italian, 16.6% German, 15.0% English, 10.1% Other groups (2000).
Economy: Single-family building permits issued: 110 (2006); Multi-family building permits issued: 0 (2006); Employment by occupation: 20.9% management, 20.2% professional, 12.4% services, 32.3% sales, 0.4% farming, 8.7% construction, 5.0% production (2000).
Income: Per capita income: $44,901 (2007); Median household income: $63,261 (2007); Average household income: $94,702 (2007); Percent of households with income of $100,000 or more: 28.9% (2007); Poverty rate: 5.0% (2000).
Education: Percent of population age 25 and over with: High school diploma (including GED) or higher: 90.5% (2007); Bachelor's degree or higher: 36.5% (2007); Master's degree or higher: 12.9% (2007).
Housing: Homeownership rate: 83.8% (2007); Median home value: $452,753 (2007); Median rent: $698 per month (2000); Median age of housing: 34 years (2000).
Safety: Violent crime rate: 12.2 per 10,000 population; Property crime rate: 204.3 per 10,000 population (2006).
Transportation: Commute to work: 89.5% car, 1.2% public transportation, 1.0% walk, 6.3% work from home (2000); Travel time to work: 28.7% less than 15 minutes, 40.4% 15 to 30 minutes, 20.6% 30 to 45 minutes, 4.8% 45 to 60 minutes, 5.4% 60 minutes or more (2000)
Additional Information Contacts

LOCH LOMOND (CDP).
Covers a land area of 0.225 square miles and a water area of 0 square miles. Located at 26.27° N. Lat.; 80.13° W. Long.
Population: 2,848 (1990); 3,537 (2000); 3,577 (2007); 3,621 (2012 projected); Race: 34.9% White, 34.2% Black, 1.1% Asian, 28.5% Hispanic of any race (2007); Density: 15,888.9 persons per square mile (2007); Average household size: 2.60 (2007); Median age: 31.1 (2007); Males per 100 females: 118.5 (2007); Marriage status: 34.2% never married, 52.4% now married, 2.5% widowed, 10.9% divorced (2000); Foreign born: 58.5% (2000); Ancestry (includes multiple ancestries): 39.6% Other groups, 18.6% Haitian, 14.1% Brazilian, 4.4% German, 3.3% English (2000).
Economy: Employment by occupation: 3.1% management, 5.8% professional, 28.5% services, 19.5% sales, 0.0% farming, 27.5% construction, 15.6% production (2000).
Income: Per capita income: $11,817 (2007); Median household income: $24,528 (2007); Average household income: $30,076 (2007); Percent of households with income of $100,000 or more: 1.6% (2007); Poverty rate: 30.7% (2000).
Education: Percent of population age 25 and over with: High school diploma (including GED) or higher: 64.1% (2007); Bachelor's degree or higher: 11.3% (2007); Master's degree or higher: 5.6% (2007).
Housing: Homeownership rate: 15.6% (2007); Median home value: $70,417 (2007); Median rent: $577 per month (2000); Median age of housing: 27 years (2000).
Transportation: Commute to work: 81.4% car, 7.3% public transportation, 1.2% walk, 1.2% work from home (2000); Travel time to work: 20.1% less than 15 minutes, 44.7% 15 to 30 minutes, 24.0% 30 to 45 minutes, 1.4% 45 to 60 minutes, 9.9% 60 minutes or more (2000)

MARGATE (city).
Covers a land area of 8.808 square miles and a water area of 0.173 square miles. Located at 26.24° N. Lat.; 80.21° W. Long. Elevation is 10 feet.
Population: 42,985 (1990); 53,909 (2000); 55,768 (2007); 57,095 (2012 projected); Race: 69.1% White, 17.9% Black, 3.7% Asian, 21.7% Hispanic of any race (2007); Density: 6,331.6 persons per square mile (2007); Average household size: 2.41 (2007); Median age: 41.1 (2007); Males per 100 females: 91.5 (2007); Marriage status: 21.7% never married, 56.4% now married, 11.3% widowed, 10.6% divorced (2000); Foreign born: 22.0% (2000); Ancestry (includes multiple ancestries): 27.6% Other groups, 12.8% Italian, 11.2% German, 11.2% Irish, 6.5% English (2000).
Economy: Unemployment rate: 4.0% (11/2007); Total civilian labor force: 30,721 (11/2007); Single-family building permits issued: 10 (2006); Multi-family building permits issued: 0 (2006); Employment by occupation: 12.1% management, 15.4% professional, 15.4% services, 34.5% sales, 0.1% farming, 12.5% construction, 9.9% production (2000).
Income: Per capita income: $22,772 (2007); Median household income: $44,496 (2007); Average household income: $54,716 (2007); Percent of households with income of $100,000 or more: 11.8% (2007); Poverty rate: 8.4% (2000).
Education: Percent of population age 25 and over with: High school diploma (including GED) or higher: 80.2% (2007); Bachelor's degree or higher: 17.1% (2007); Master's degree or higher: 5.7% (2007).
School District(s)
Broward County School District (PK-12)
   2005-06 Enrollment: 274,591 . . . . (754) 321-2600
Vocational/Technical School(s)
Margate School of Beauty Inc (Private, For-profit)
   Fall 2006 Enrollment: n/a. . . . . (954) 972-9630
Housing: Homeownership rate: 79.9% (2007); Median home value: $188,109 (2007); Median rent: $720 per month (2000); Median age of housing: 22 years (2000).
Hospitals: Northwest Medical Center (215 beds)
Safety: Violent crime rate: 34.4 per 10,000 population; Property crime rate: 169.6 per 10,000 population (2006).
Newspapers: Senior News (General, Senior Citizen - Circulation 20,000)
Transportation: Commute to work: 94.4% car, 1.3% public transportation, 0.9% walk, 1.8% work from home (2000); Travel time to work: 18.6% less than 15 minutes, 36.4% 15 to 30 minutes, 30.2% 30 to 45 minutes, 9.0% 45 to 60 minutes, 5.8% 60 minutes or more (2000)
Additional Information Contacts
City of Margate. . . . . (954) 972-6454
   http://www.margatefl.com

MELROSE PARK (CDP). Covers a land area of 0.903 square miles and a water area of 0 square miles. Located at 26.11° N. Lat.; 80.19° W. Long. Elevation is 7 feet.

Population: 6,477 (1990); 7,114 (2000); 7,188 (2007); 7,268 (2012 projected); Race: 6.4% White, 85.3% Black, 0.7% Asian, 3.3% Hispanic of any race (2007); Density: 7,959.0 persons per square mile (2007); Average household size: 3.72 (2007); Median age: 30.7 (2007); Males per 100 females: 96.5 (2007); Marriage status: 38.8% never married, 48.7% now married, 4.0% widowed, 8.5% divorced (2000); Foreign born: 37.5% (2000); Ancestry (includes multiple ancestries): 35.1% Other groups, 22.5% Jamaican, 15.9% Haitian, 4.7% United States or American, 2.5% Irish (2000).

Economy: Employment by occupation: 5.7% management, 15.4% professional, 24.1% services, 27.1% sales, 0.0% farming, 10.5% construction, 17.1% production (2000).

Income: Per capita income: $16,386 (2007); Median household income: $55,273 (2007); Average household income: $60,481 (2007); Percent of households with income of $100,000 or more: 11.7% (2007); Poverty rate: 15.7% (2000).

Education: Percent of population age 25 and over with: High school diploma (including GED) or higher: 66.1% (2007); Bachelor's degree or higher: 8.4% (2007); Master's degree or higher: 1.6% (2007).

Housing: Homeownership rate: 82.6% (2007); Median home value: $217,611 (2007); Median rent: $504 per month (2000); Median age of housing: 41 years (2000).

Transportation: Commute to work: 90.5% car, 5.9% public transportation, 1.4% walk, 1.0% work from home (2000); Travel time to work: 12.9% less than 15 minutes, 43.1% 15 to 30 minutes, 28.0% 30 to 45 minutes, 6.4% 45 to 60 minutes, 9.5% 60 minutes or more (2000)

MIAMI GARDENS (CDP). Covers a land area of 0.405 square miles and a water area of 0 square miles. Located at 25.97° N. Lat.; 80.20° W. Long. Elevation is 7 feet.

Population: 2,506 (1990); 2,706 (2000); 2,462 (2007); 2,431 (2012 projected); Race: 44.3% White, 35.1% Black, 1.9% Asian, 47.2% Hispanic of any race (2007); Density: 6,071.6 persons per square mile (2007); Average household size: 3.30 (2007); Median age: 34.1 (2007); Males per 100 females: 101.1 (2007); Marriage status: 25.9% never married, 55.9% now married, 6.6% widowed, 11.7% divorced (2000); Foreign born: 44.1% (2000); Ancestry (includes multiple ancestries): 64.3% Other groups, 6.8% United States or American, 6.5% Jamaican, 4.9% Irish, 3.7% Haitian (2000).

Economy: Employment by occupation: 9.4% management, 11.0% professional, 18.9% services, 21.8% sales, 1.0% farming, 20.8% construction, 17.1% production (2000).

Income: Per capita income: $12,304 (2007); Median household income: $37,985 (2007); Average household income: $40,607 (2007); Percent of households with income of $100,000 or more: 4.0% (2007); Poverty rate: 14.0% (2000).

Education: Percent of population age 25 and over with: High school diploma (including GED) or higher: 62.9% (2007); Bachelor's degree or higher: 7.8% (2007); Master's degree or higher: 1.3% (2007).

School District(s)
Dade County School District (PK-12)
    2005-06 Enrollment: 368,933 . . . . (305) 995-1430
Four-year College(s)
Florida Memorial University (Private, Not-for-profit, Historically black, Baptist)
    Fall 2006 Enrollment: 1,867 . . . . (305) 626-3600
    2006-07 Tuition: In-state $12,254; Out-of-state $12,254
Saint Thomas University (Private, Not-for-profit, Roman Catholic)
    Fall 2006 Enrollment: 2,517 . . . . (305) 625-6000
    2006-07 Tuition: In-state $18,750; Out-of-state $18,750

Housing: Homeownership rate: 83.8% (2007); Median home value: $176,768 (2007); Median rent: $519 per month (2000); Median age of housing: 40 years (2000).

Safety: Violent crime rate: 184.7 per 10,000 population; Property crime rate: 621.2 per 10,000 population (2006).

Transportation: Commute to work: 92.1% car, 1.1% public transportation, 2.1% walk, 1.5% work from home (2000); Travel time to work: 14.7% less than 15 minutes, 36.9% 15 to 30 minutes, 28.8% 30 to 45 minutes, 9.6% 45 to 60 minutes, 10.0% 60 minutes or more (2000)

MIRAMAR (city). Covers a land area of 29.499 square miles and a water area of 1.501 square miles. Located at 25.97° N. Lat.; 80.28° W. Long. Elevation is 7 feet.

History: Named for the Spanish translations of "look, behold!" and "sea". Incorporated 1955.

Population: 40,663 (1990); 72,739 (2000); 114,073 (2007); 139,680 (2012 projected); Race: 41.4% White, 43.6% Black, 3.6% Asian, 37.5% Hispanic of any race (2007); Density: 3,867.0 persons per square mile (2007); Average household size: 3.23 (2007); Median age: 32.1 (2007); Males per 100 females: 92.6 (2007); Marriage status: 27.6% never married, 58.1% now married, 4.2% widowed, 10.1% divorced (2000); Foreign born: 40.7% (2000); Ancestry (includes multiple ancestries): 47.8% Other groups, 15.5% Jamaican, 6.0% Haitian, 4.9% United States or American, 3.9% German (2000).

Economy: Unemployment rate: 4.0% (11/2007); Total civilian labor force: 59,278 (11/2007); Single-family building permits issued: 397 (2006); Multi-family building permits issued: 566 (2006); Employment by occupation: 12.9% management, 18.4% professional, 16.3% services, 33.1% sales, 0.4% farming, 9.2% construction, 9.9% production (2000).

Income: Per capita income: $22,422 (2007); Median household income: $61,503 (2007); Average household income: $72,174 (2007); Percent of households with income of $100,000 or more: 21.4% (2007); Poverty rate: 8.2% (2000).

Education: Percent of population age 25 and over with: High school diploma (including GED) or higher: 83.3% (2007); Bachelor's degree or higher: 22.8% (2007); Master's degree or higher: 7.1% (2007).

School District(s)
Broward County School District (PK-12)
    2005-06 Enrollment: 274,591 . . . . (754) 321-2600
Two-year College(s)
Le Cordon Bleu College of Culinary Arts-Miami (Private, For-profit)
    Fall 2006 Enrollment: 669 . . . . (954) 628-4400
    2006-07 Tuition: In-state $33,250; Out-of-state $33,250

Housing: Homeownership rate: 81.6% (2007); Median home value: $283,994 (2007); Median rent: $694 per month (2000); Median age of housing: 16 years (2000).

Safety: Violent crime rate: 51.2 per 10,000 population; Property crime rate: 296.9 per 10,000 population (2006).

Transportation: Commute to work: 94.7% car, 1.5% public transportation, 0.9% walk, 1.9% work from home (2000); Travel time to work: 12.1% less than 15 minutes, 32.0% 15 to 30 minutes, 31.9% 30 to 45 minutes, 14.3% 45 to 60 minutes, 9.6% 60 minutes or more (2000)

Additional Information Contacts
City of Miramar . . . . (954) 602-3011
    http://www.ci.miramar.fl.us

NORTH ANDREWS GARDENS (CDP). Aka North Andrews Terrace. Covers a land area of 1.087 square miles and a water area of 0 square miles. Located at 26.19° N. Lat.; 80.14° W. Long. Elevation is 7 feet.

Population: 8,968 (1990); 9,656 (2000); 9,728 (2007); 9,821 (2012 projected); Race: 76.6% White, 8.0% Black, 1.4% Asian, 39.2% Hispanic of any race (2007); Density: 8,949.3 persons per square mile (2007); Average household size: 2.83 (2007); Median age: 37.4 (2007); Males per 100 females: 105.0 (2007); Marriage status: 27.2% never married, 53.6% now married, 6.0% widowed, 13.2% divorced (2000); Foreign born: 24.6% (2000); Ancestry (includes multiple ancestries): 30.2% Other groups, 16.5% Irish, 11.9% Italian, 11.1% German, 9.5% United States or American (2000).

Economy: Employment by occupation: 10.9% management, 8.7% professional, 19.6% services, 28.2% sales, 0.2% farming, 20.7% construction, 11.7% production (2000).

Income: Per capita income: $19,349 (2007); Median household income: $48,909 (2007); Average household income: $54,650 (2007); Percent of households with income of $100,000 or more: 8.5% (2007); Poverty rate: 8.6% (2000).

Education: Percent of population age 25 and over with: High school diploma (including GED) or higher: 74.4% (2007); Bachelor's degree or higher: 9.6% (2007); Master's degree or higher: 2.5% (2007).

Housing: Homeownership rate: 85.3% (2007); Median home value: $203,924 (2007); Median rent: $743 per month (2000); Median age of housing: 39 years (2000).

Transportation: Commute to work: 92.5% car, 2.1% public transportation, 1.3% walk, 1.3% work from home (2000); Travel time to work: 29.4% less

NORTH LAUDERDALE (city).
Covers a land area of 3.878 square miles and a water area of 0.033 square miles. Located at 26.21° N. Lat.; 80.22° W. Long. Elevation is 10 feet.

Population: 26,844 (1990); 32,264 (2000); 36,089 (2007); 38,584 (2012 projected); Race: 37.9% White, 44.9% Black, 3.0% Asian, 25.1% Hispanic of any race (2007); Density: 9,305.4 persons per square mile (2007); Average household size: 3.04 (2007); Median age: 31.3 (2007); Males per 100 females: 95.0 (2007); Marriage status: 32.9% never married, 51.6% now married, 4.7% widowed, 10.8% divorced (2000); Foreign born: 34.9% (2000); Ancestry (includes multiple ancestries): 36.9% Other groups, 11.4% Jamaican, 8.0% United States or American, 6.9% Italian, 6.9% Haitian (2000).

Economy: Unemployment rate: 3.5% (11/2007); Total civilian labor force: 24,214 (11/2007); Single-family building permits issued: 243 (2006); Multi-family building permits issued: 0 (2006); Employment by occupation: 10.2% management, 13.4% professional, 19.1% services, 31.7% sales, 0.2% farming, 13.8% construction, 11.7% production (2000).

Income: Per capita income: $16,555 (2007); Median household income: $43,376 (2007); Average household income: $50,384 (2007); Percent of households with income of $100,000 or more: 7.3% (2007); Poverty rate: 13.7% (2000).

Education: Percent of population age 25 and over with: High school diploma (including GED) or higher: 77.7% (2007); Bachelor's degree or higher: 13.6% (2007); Master's degree or higher: 3.1% (2007).

School District(s)
Broward County School District (PK-12)
  2005-06 Enrollment: 274,591 . . . . (754) 321-2600

Housing: Homeownership rate: 63.9% (2007); Median home value: $198,033 (2007); Median rent: $696 per month (2000); Median age of housing: 21 years (2000).

Safety: Violent crime rate: 74.5 per 10,000 population; Property crime rate: 218.3 per 10,000 population (2006).

Transportation: Commute to work: 94.1% car, 2.6% public transportation, 0.6% walk, 1.9% work from home (2000); Travel time to work: 13.9% less than 15 minutes, 40.1% 15 to 30 minutes, 31.3% 30 to 45 minutes, 7.5% 45 to 60 minutes, 7.3% 60 minutes or more (2000)

Additional Information Contacts
City of North Lauderdale . . . . (954) 722-0900
  http://www.nlauderdale.org

OAK POINT (CDP).
Covers a land area of 0.041 square miles and a water area of 0 square miles. Located at 26.04° N. Lat.; 80.18° W. Long.

Population: 172 (1990); 145 (2000); 156 (2007); 163 (2012 projected); Race: 92.9% White, 0.0% Black, 0.0% Asian, 1.3% Hispanic of any race (2007); Density: 3,843.9 persons per square mile (2007); Average household size: 3.06 (2007); Median age: 47.8 (2007); Males per 100 females: 90.2 (2007); Marriage status: 18.1% never married, 77.1% now married, 0.0% widowed, 4.9% divorced (2000); Foreign born: 4.4% (2000); Ancestry (includes multiple ancestries): 25.3% United States or American, 25.3% Ukrainian, 13.9% Russian, 10.1% Polish, 9.5% German (2000).

Economy: Employment by occupation: 0.0% management, 73.1% professional, 11.5% services, 15.4% sales, 0.0% farming, 0.0% construction, 0.0% production (2000).

Income: Per capita income: $73,894 (2007); Median household income: $175,000 (2007); Average household income: $226,029 (2007); Percent of households with income of $100,000 or more: 76.5% (2007); Poverty rate: 0.0% (2000).

Education: Percent of population age 25 and over with: High school diploma (including GED) or higher: 100.0% (2007); Bachelor's degree or higher: 84.8% (2007); Master's degree or higher: 70.5% (2007).

Housing: Homeownership rate: 100.0% (2007); Median home value: $875,000 (2007); Median rent: $n/a per month (2000); Median age of housing: 16 years (2000).

Transportation: Commute to work: 100.0% car, 0.0% public transportation, 0.0% walk, 0.0% work from home (2000); Travel time to work: 30.8% less than 15 minutes, 46.2% 15 to 30 minutes, 23.1% 30 to 45 minutes, 0.0% 45 to 60 minutes, 0.0% 60 minutes or more (2000)

OAKLAND PARK (city).
Covers a land area of 6.301 square miles and a water area of 0.604 square miles. Located at 26.17° N. Lat.; 80.14° W. Long. Elevation is 3 feet.

Average household size: 2.32 (2007); Median age: 37.5 (2007); Males per 100 females: 108.9 (2007); Marriage status: 35.6% never married, 43.9% now married, 5.2% widowed, 15.2% divorced (2000); Foreign born: 29.6% (2000); Ancestry (includes multiple ancestries): 32.4% Other groups, 10.3% German, 9.6% Irish, 8.0% Italian, 7.4% Haitian (2000).

Economy: Unemployment rate: 3.6% (11/2007); Total civilian labor force: 20,573 (11/2007); Single-family building permits issued: 166 (2006); Multi-family building permits issued: 0 (2006); Employment by occupation: 10.3% management, 16.2% professional, 21.3% services, 27.0% sales, 0.2% farming, 11.8% construction, 13.2% production (2000).

Income: Per capita income: $22,071 (2007); Median household income: $41,028 (2007); Average household income: $50,550 (2007); Percent of households with income of $100,000 or more: 9.2% (2007); Poverty rate: 16.5% (2000).

Education: Percent of population age 25 and over with: High school diploma (including GED) or higher: 78.2% (2007); Bachelor's degree or higher: 21.4% (2007); Master's degree or higher: 6.6% (2007).

School District(s)
Broward County School District (PK-12)
  2005-06 Enrollment: 274,591 . . . . (754) 321-2600
Vocational/Technical School(s)
ATI Career Training Center (Private, For-profit)
  Fall 2006 Enrollment: 685 . . . . (954) 563-5899
  2006-07 Tuition: $24,010

Housing: Homeownership rate: 51.3% (2007); Median home value: $217,900 (2007); Median rent: $606 per month (2000); Median age of housing: 29 years (2000).

Safety: Violent crime rate: 156.3 per 10,000 population; Property crime rate: 760.0 per 10,000 population (2006).

Transportation: Commute to work: 89.9% car, 4.4% public transportation, 2.3% walk, 2.0% work from home (2000); Travel time to work: 26.1% less than 15 minutes, 42.7% 15 to 30 minutes, 19.2% 30 to 45 minutes, 6.3% 45 to 60 minutes, 5.7% 60 minutes or more (2000)

Additional Information Contacts
City of Oakland Park . . . . (954) 630-4200
  http://oaklandparkfl.org
Oakland Park-Wilton Chamber . . . . (954) 568-7755
  http://www.opwmchamber.org

PALM AIRE (CDP).
Covers a land area of 0.223 square miles and a water area of 0 square miles. Located at 26.20° N. Lat.; 80.19° W. Long. Elevation is 10 feet.

Population: 1,411 (1990); 1,539 (2000); 1,686 (2007); 1,778 (2012 projected); Race: 75.9% White, 15.8% Black, 1.4% Asian, 21.9% Hispanic of any race (2007); Density: 7,552.3 persons per square mile (2007); Average household size: 2.86 (2007); Median age: 37.6 (2007); Males per 100 females: 104.9 (2007); Marriage status: 20.6% never married, 63.9% now married, 6.0% widowed, 9.6% divorced (2000); Foreign born: 15.4% (2000); Ancestry (includes multiple ancestries): 30.7% Other groups, 15.6% Italian, 15.5% German, 12.1% Irish, 9.6% English (2000).

Economy: Employment by occupation: 16.7% management, 20.6% professional, 9.2% services, 24.3% sales, 0.0% farming, 18.1% construction, 11.1% production (2000).

Income: Per capita income: $23,880 (2007); Median household income: $64,485 (2007); Average household income: $68,242 (2007); Percent of households with income of $100,000 or more: 21.7% (2007); Poverty rate: 7.9% (2000).

Education: Percent of population age 25 and over with: High school diploma (including GED) or higher: 87.8% (2007); Bachelor's degree or higher: 20.5% (2007); Master's degree or higher: 9.8% (2007).

Housing: Homeownership rate: 94.2% (2007); Median home value: $240,909 (2007); Median rent: $1,125 per month (2000); Median age of housing: 26 years (2000).

Transportation: Commute to work: 97.9% car, 1.1% public transportation, 0.0% walk, 0.9% work from home (2000); Travel time to work: 25.2% less than 15 minutes, 42.4% 15 to 30 minutes, 19.1% 30 to 45 minutes, 4.1% 45 to 60 minutes, 9.1% 60 minutes or more (2000)

PARKLAND (city).
Covers a land area of 10.198 square miles and a water area of 0.579 square miles. Located at 26.31° N. Lat.; 80.24° W. Long. Elevation is 13 feet.

household size: 3.20 (2007); Median age: 34.5 (2007); Males per 100 females: 98.6 (2007); Marriage status: 16.9% never married, 75.1% now married, 2.9% widowed, 5.0% divorced (2000); Foreign born: 16.7% (2000); Ancestry (includes multiple ancestries): 22.2% Other groups, 16.4% Italian, 12.9% German, 12.5% Irish, 9.3% United States or American (2000).

Economy: Single-family building permits issued: 326 (2006); Multi-family building permits issued: 56 (2006); Employment by occupation: 26.2% management, 25.1% professional, 7.4% services, 32.0% sales, 0.2% farming, 3.5% construction, 5.4% production (2000).

Income: Per capita income: $49,967 (2007); Median household income: $118,974 (2007); Average household income: $160,011 (2007); Percent of households with income of $100,000 or more: 61.0% (2007); Poverty rate: 2.4% (2000).

Education: Percent of population age 25 and over with: High school diploma (including GED) or higher: 94.2% (2007); Bachelor's degree or higher: 53.1% (2007); Master's degree or higher: 19.4% (2007).

School District(s)
Broward County School District (PK-12)
    2005-06 Enrollment: 274,591 . . . . (754) 321-2600

Housing: Homeownership rate: 88.8% (2007); Median home value: $654,196 (2007); Median rent: $958 per month (2000); Median age of housing: 6 years (2000).

Safety: Violent crime rate: 11.5 per 10,000 population; Property crime rate: 122.1 per 10,000 population (2006).

Transportation: Commute to work: 91.6% car, 0.4% public transportation, 0.1% walk, 7.1% work from home (2000); Travel time to work: 18.4% less than 15 minutes, 35.2% 15 to 30 minutes, 28.2% 30 to 45 minutes, 9.4% 45 to 60 minutes, 8.8% 60 minutes or more (2000)

Additional Information Contacts
City of Parkland . . . . (954) 753-5040
  http://www.cityofparkland.org

PEMBROKE PARK (town). Aka Pembroke. Covers a land area of 1.411 square miles and a water area of 0.365 square miles. Located at 25.98° N. Lat.; 80.17° W. Long. Elevation is 3 feet.

Population: 5,240 (1990); 6,299 (2000); 7,078 (2007); 7,445 (2012 projected); Race: 31.8% White, 58.2% Black, 0.8% Asian, 17.7% Hispanic of any race (2007); Density: 5,017.8 persons per square mile (2007); Average household size: 2.38 (2007); Median age: 33.4 (2007); Males per 100 females: 87.7 (2007); Marriage status: 32.1% never married, 44.8% now married, 9.4% widowed, 13.7% divorced (2000); Foreign born: 28.6% (2000); Ancestry (includes multiple ancestries): 39.2% Other groups, 7.9% Jamaican, 7.0% United States or American, 6.5% Italian, 6.0% German (2000).

Economy: Single-family building permits issued: 0 (2006); Multi-family building permits issued: 0 (2006); Employment by occupation: 4.7% management, 16.1% professional, 21.9% services, 31.1% sales, 0.0% farming, 13.8% construction, 12.4% production (2000).

Income: Per capita income: $14,309 (2007); Median household income: $23,754 (2007); Average household income: $33,902 (2007); Percent of households with income of $100,000 or more: 4.5% (2007); Poverty rate: 24.0% (2000).

Education: Percent of population age 25 and over with: High school diploma (including GED) or higher: 69.8% (2007); Bachelor's degree or higher: 7.0% (2007); Master's degree or higher: 2.4% (2007).

School District(s)
Broward County School District (PK-12)
    2005-06 Enrollment: 274,591 . . . . (754) 321-2600

Housing: Homeownership rate: 44.6% (2007); Median home value: $96,311 (2007); Median rent: $625 per month (2000); Median age of housing: 24 years (2000).

Safety: Violent crime rate: 129.0 per 10,000 population; Property crime rate: 786.7 per 10,000 population (2006).

Transportation: Commute to work: 95.1% car, 1.9% public transportation, 0.6% walk, 0.3% work from home (2000); Travel time to work: 24.0% less than 15 minutes, 38.6% 15 to 30 minutes, 22.0% 30 to 45 minutes, 6.8% 45 to 60 minutes, 8.7% 60 minutes or more (2000)

PEMBROKE PINES (city). Covers a land area of 33.054 square miles and a water area of 1.382 square miles. Located at 26.01° N. Lat.; 80.31° W. Long. Elevation is 7 feet.

Population: 66,095 (1990); 137,427 (2000); 149,322 (2007); 157,001 (2012 projected); Race: 68.0% White, 17.9% Black, 4.6% Asian, 38.3% Hispanic of any race (2007); Density: 4,517.5 persons per square mile (2007); Average household size: 2.67 (2007); Median age: 38.1 (2007); Males per 100 females: 88.0 (2007); Marriage status: 20.9% never married, 60.7% now married, 7.8% widowed, 10.6% divorced (2000); Foreign born: 29.0% (2000); Ancestry (includes multiple ancestries): 42.2% Other groups, 9.4% Italian, 8.2% Irish, 8.1% German, 6.1% United States or American (2000).

Economy: Unemployment rate: 3.5% (11/2007); Total civilian labor force: 85,079 (11/2007); Single-family building permits issued: 5 (2006); Multi-family building permits issued: 103 (2006); Employment by occupation: 18.4% management, 22.3% professional, 12.5% services, 32.2% sales, 0.2% farming, 7.3% construction, 7.2% production (2000).

Income: Per capita income: $28,210 (2007); Median household income: $61,542 (2007); Average household income: $75,031 (2007); Percent of households with income of $100,000 or more: 24.7% (2007); Poverty rate: 5.4% (2000).

Taxes: Total city taxes per capita: $465 (2005); City property taxes per capita: $215 (2005).

Education: Percent of population age 25 and over with: High school diploma (including GED) or higher: 87.8% (2007); Bachelor's degree or higher: 28.6% (2007); Master's degree or higher: 10.1% (2007).

School District(s)
Broward County School District (PK-12)
    2005-06 Enrollment: 274,591 . . . . (754) 321-2600
Florida State University Laboratory School (PK-12)
    2005-06 Enrollment: 2,321 . . . . (850) 245-3700

Housing: Homeownership rate: 80.7% (2007); Median home value: $272,847 (2007); Median rent: $856 per month (2000); Median age of housing: 10 years (2000).

Hospitals: Memorial Hospital Pembroke (149 beds); Memorial Hospital West (220 beds); South Florida State Hospital (350 beds)

Safety: Violent crime rate: 23.7 per 10,000 population; Property crime rate: 319.5 per 10,000 population (2006).

Newspapers: Observer (General - Circulation 10,000)

Transportation: Commute to work: 94.6% car, 0.9% public transportation, 0.6% walk, 3.0% work from home (2000); Travel time to work: 13.4% less than 15 minutes, 29.5% 15 to 30 minutes, 31.2% 30 to 45 minutes, 16.7% 45 to 60 minutes, 9.1% 60 minutes or more (2000)

Additional Information Contacts
Pembroke Pines Chamber of Commerce . . . . (954) 432-9808
  http://www.ppines.com

PINE ISLAND RIDGE (CDP). Covers a land area of 0.782 square miles and a water area of 0.006 square miles. Located at 26.09° N. Lat.; 80.27° W. Long. Elevation is 7 feet.

Population: 5,230 (1990); 5,199 (2000); 5,943 (2007); 6,434 (2012 projected); Race: 92.6% White, 1.7% Black, 2.0% Asian, 13.2% Hispanic of any race (2007); Density: 7,599.5 persons per square mile (2007); Average household size: 1.78 (2007); Median age: 57.1 (2007); Males per 100 females: 78.3 (2007); Marriage status: 16.4% never married, 52.6% now married, 17.3% widowed, 13.7% divorced (2000); Foreign born: 20.0% (2000); Ancestry (includes multiple ancestries): 20.6% Other groups, 14.0% Italian, 10.9% Irish, 10.4% German, 10.2% United States or American (2000).

Economy: Employment by occupation: 16.8% management, 23.1% professional, 11.3% services, 38.3% sales, 0.0% farming, 2.8% construction, 7.7% production (2000).

Income: Per capita income: $29,093 (2007); Median household income: $39,863 (2007); Average household income: $51,859 (2007); Percent of households with income of $100,000 or more: 10.0% (2007); Poverty rate: 3.5% (2000).

Education: Percent of population age 25 and over with: High school diploma (including GED) or higher: 87.7% (2007); Bachelor's degree or higher: 26.3% (2007); Master's degree or higher: 9.2% (2007).

Housing: Homeownership rate: 86.1% (2007); Median home value: $179,979 (2007); Median rent: $728 per month (2000); Median age of housing: 18 years (2000).

Transportation: Commute to work: 91.6% car, 0.0% public transportation, 1.2% walk, 3.2% work from home (2000); Travel time to work: 22.6% less than 15 minutes, 43.5% 15 to 30 minutes, 20.5% 30 to 45 minutes, 9.0% 45 to 60 minutes, 4.3% 60 minutes or more (2000)

PLANTATION (city). Covers a land area of 21.738 square miles and a water area of 0.193 square miles. Located at 26.12° N. Lat.; 80.24° W. Long. Elevation is 3 feet.

History: Named for its history as the plantation of Frederick C. Peters. Incorporated 1953.

Population: 66,997 (1990); 82,934 (2000); 85,549 (2007); 87,416 (2012 projected); Race: 71.0% White, 18.7% Black, 3.7% Asian, 17.4% Hispanic of any race (2007); Density: 3,935.5 persons per square mile (2007); Average household size: 2.50 (2007); Median age: 39.3 (2007); Males per 100 females: 91.5 (2007); Marriage status: 25.2% never married, 57.7% now married, 6.5% widowed, 10.7% divorced (2000); Foreign born: 22.4% (2000); Ancestry (includes multiple ancestries): 26.8% Other groups, 10.8% German, 10.2% Irish, 8.9% Italian, 8.0% United States or American (2000).

Economy: Unemployment rate: 3.2% (11/2007); Total civilian labor force: 53,917 (11/2007); Single-family building permits issued: 38 (2006); Multi-family building permits issued: 201 (2006); Employment by occupation: 18.7% management, 24.2% professional, 12.0% services, 32.2% sales, 0.1% farming, 6.5% construction, 6.2% production (2000).

Income: Per capita income: $33,025 (2007); Median household income: $62,619 (2007); Average household income: $82,200 (2007); Percent of households with income of $100,000 or more: 27.2% (2007); Poverty rate: 6.4% (2000).

Taxes: Total city taxes per capita: $461 (2005); City property taxes per capita: $276 (2005).

Education: Percent of population age 25 and over with: High school diploma (including GED) or higher: 91.0% (2007); Bachelor's degree or higher: 36.6% (2007); Master's degree or higher: 13.5% (2007).

School District(s)

Broward County School District (PK-12)
    2005-06 Enrollment: 274,591 . . . . (754) 321-2600

Four-year College(s)

University of Phoenix-South Florida Campus (Private, For-profit)
    Fall 2006 Enrollment: 3,114 . . . . (954) 382-5303
    2006-07 Tuition: In-state $10,808; Out-of-state $10,808

Housing: Homeownership rate: 71.7% (2007); Median home value: $307,854 (2007); Median rent: $851 per month (2000); Median age of housing: 19 years (2000).

Hospitals: Columbia Westside Regional Medical Center (224 beds); Plantation General Hospital (264 beds)

Safety: Violent crime rate: 30.0 per 10,000 population; Property crime rate: 420.3 per 10,000 population (2006).

Transportation: Commute to work: 93.9% car, 1.2% public transportation, 0.6% walk, 3.4% work from home (2000); Travel time to work: 22.1% less than 15 minutes, 37.0% 15 to 30 minutes, 25.9% 30 to 45 minutes, 9.2% 45 to 60 minutes, 5.8% 60 minutes or more (2000)

Additional Information Contacts

City of Plantation . . . . (954) 797-2200
    http://www.plantation.org
Plantation Chamber of Commerce. . . . . (954) 587-1410
    http://www.plantationchamber.org

POMPANO BEACH (city). Covers a land area of 20.553 square miles and a water area of 1.601 square miles. Located at 26.23° N. Lat.; 80.12° W. Long. Elevation is 13 feet.

History: Named for the abundance of fish found along its coast. Incorporated 1908.

Population: 72,400 (1990); 78,191 (2000); 81,277 (2007); 83,506 (2012 projected); Race: 65.8% White, 25.1% Black, 1.0% Asian, 14.2% Hispanic of any race (2007); Density: 3,954.6 persons per square mile (2007); Average household size: 2.21 (2007); Median age: 43.7 (2007); Males per 100 females: 98.4 (2007); Marriage status: 27.0% never married, 49.8% now married, 10.5% widowed, 12.7% divorced (2000); Foreign born: 20.3% (2000); Ancestry (includes multiple ancestries): 29.3% Other groups, 9.7% German, 9.7% Irish, 8.9% Italian, 6.5% English (2000).

Economy: Unemployment rate: 3.8% (11/2007); Total civilian labor force: 52,733 (11/2007); Single-family building permits issued: 334 (2006); Multi-family building permits issued: 178 (2006); Employment by occupation: 13.5% management, 15.1% professional, 18.5% services, 30.0% sales, 0.5% farming, 11.4% construction, 11.0% production (2000).

Income: Per capita income: $27,475 (2007); Median household income: $41,622 (2007); Average household income: $59,059 (2007); Percent of households with income of $100,000 or more: 14.0% (2007); Poverty rate: 17.0% (2000).

capita: $342 (2005).

Education: Percent of population age 25 and over with: High school diploma (including GED) or higher: 77.6% (2007); Bachelor's degree or higher: 22.0% (2007); Master's degree or higher: 7.2% (2007).

School District(s)

Broward County School District (PK-12)
    2005-06 Enrollment: 274,591 . . . . (754) 321-2600

Four-year College(s)

Florida College of Natural Health (Private, For-profit)
    Fall 2006 Enrollment: 265 . . . . (954) 975-6400
Florida Metropolitan University (Private, For-profit)
    Fall 2006 Enrollment: 1,912 . . . . (954) 783-7339
    2006-07 Tuition: In-state $10,440; Out-of-state $10,440

Vocational/Technical School(s)

Florida Barber Academy (Private, For-profit)
    Fall 2006 Enrollment: 145 . . . . (954) 781-6066
    2006-07 Tuition: $5,800

Housing: Homeownership rate: 63.1% (2007); Median home value: $215,872 (2007); Median rent: $630 per month (2000); Median age of housing: 27 years (2000).

Hospitals: North Broward Medical Center (409 beds)

Safety: Violent crime rate: 129.0 per 10,000 population; Property crime rate: 470.6 per 10,000 population (2006).

Newspapers: Boca Thursday (General - Circulation 27,000); Boynton Beach Times (General - Circulation 27,000); Deerfield Beach/Lighthouse Point Thursday Times (General - Circulation 20,000); Delray Thursday Times (General - Circulation 19,000); Jewish Journal - Palm Beach South (General, Jewish - Circulation 22,000); Jewish Journal Broward North (General, Jewish - Circulation 21,000); Jewish Journal-Dade (General, Jewish - Circulation 20,000); The Jewish Journal-Palm Beach North (General, Jewish - Circulation 22,000); The Pompano Pelican (General - Circulation 10,000); West Boca Times (General - Circulation 24,000)

Transportation: Commute to work: 89.7% car, 2.7% public transportation, 2.2% walk, 2.6% work from home (2000); Travel time to work: 25.9% less than 15 minutes, 41.5% 15 to 30 minutes, 21.5% 30 to 45 minutes, 5.4% 45 to 60 minutes, 5.7% 60 minutes or more (2000)

Additional Information Contacts

City of Pompano Beach . . . . (954) 786-4600
    http://www.mypompanobeach.org
Greater Pompano Beach Chamber . . . . (954) 941-2940
    http://www.pompanobeachchamber.com

POMPANO BEACH HIGHLANDS (CDP). Covers a land area of 1.345 square miles and a water area of 0 square miles. Located at 26.28° N. Lat.; 80.10° W. Long. Elevation is 13 feet.

Population: 6,104 (1990); 6,505 (2000); 6,554 (2007); 6,620 (2012 projected); Race: 68.3% White, 13.1% Black, 3.1% Asian, 30.7% Hispanic of any race (2007); Density: 4,871.2 persons per square mile (2007); Average household size: 2.87 (2007); Median age: 35.6 (2007); Males per 100 females: 107.1 (2007); Marriage status: 27.1% never married, 53.7% now married, 5.1% widowed, 14.1% divorced (2000); Foreign born: 22.0% (2000); Ancestry (includes multiple ancestries): 32.5% Other groups, 14.3% Irish, 13.0% German, 10.5% Italian, 7.7% United States or American (2000).

Economy: Employment by occupation: 8.2% management, 13.5% professional, 18.3% services, 27.2% sales, 0.3% farming, 20.5% construction, 12.0% production (2000).

Income: Per capita income: $15,922 (2007); Median household income: $36,659 (2007); Average household income: $45,729 (2007); Percent of households with income of $100,000 or more: 6.0% (2007); Poverty rate: 12.9% (2000).

Education: Percent of population age 25 and over with: High school diploma (including GED) or higher: 74.1% (2007); Bachelor's degree or higher: 10.5% (2007); Master's degree or higher: 4.1% (2007).

Housing: Homeownership rate: 75.1% (2007); Median home value: $195,708 (2007); Median rent: $668 per month (2000); Median age of housing: 39 years (2000).

Transportation: Commute to work: 90.0% car, 3.0% public transportation, 0.0% walk, 3.7% work from home (2000); Travel time to work: 29.1% less than 15 minutes, 38.4% 15 to 30 minutes, 21.9% 30 to 45 minutes, 5.3% 45 to 60 minutes, 5.4% 60 minutes or more (2000)

POMPANO ESTATES (CDP).
Covers a land area of 0.544 square miles and a water area of 0 square miles. Located at 26.28° N. Lat.; 80.11° W. Long. Elevation is 16 feet.

Population: 3,286 (1990); 3,367 (2000); 3,103 (2007); 2,962 (2012 projected); Race: 25.3% White, 59.7% Black, 0.2% Asian, 11.7% Hispanic of any race (2007); Density: 5,707.4 persons per square mile (2007); Average household size: 3.59 (2007); Median age: 29.5 (2007); Males per 100 females: 93.6 (2007); Marriage status: 35.6% never married, 46.3% now married, 7.4% widowed, 10.7% divorced (2000); Foreign born: 36.4% (2000); Ancestry (includes multiple ancestries): 32.6% Other groups, 31.3% Haitian, 4.6% United States or American, 3.2% German, 2.5% Italian (2000).

Economy: Employment by occupation: 6.4% management, 12.0% professional, 22.9% services, 27.3% sales, 1.2% farming, 14.0% construction, 16.2% production (2000).

Income: Per capita income: $13,035 (2007); Median household income: $31,319 (2007); Average household income: $45,049 (2007); Percent of households with income of $100,000 or more: 7.1% (2007); Poverty rate: 32.5% (2000).

Education: Percent of population age 25 and over with: High school diploma (including GED) or higher: 58.3% (2007); Bachelor's degree or higher: 10.0% (2007); Master's degree or higher: 2.3% (2007).

Housing: Homeownership rate: 63.9% (2007); Median home value: $166,054 (2007); Median rent: $496 per month (2000); Median age of housing: 26 years (2000).

Transportation: Commute to work: 93.4% car, 1.1% public transportation, 0.3% walk, 2.3% work from home (2000); Travel time to work: 20.1% less than 15 minutes, 45.4% 15 to 30 minutes, 23.5% 30 to 45 minutes, 4.1% 45 to 60 minutes, 6.9% 60 minutes or more (2000)

RAMBLEWOOD EAST (CDP).
Covers a land area of 0.093 square miles and a water area of 0 square miles. Located at 26.28° N. Lat.; 80.24° W. Long.

Population: 1,103 (1990); 1,395 (2000); 1,520 (2007); 1,597 (2012 projected); Race: 85.7% White, 3.9% Black, 2.2% Asian, 30.3% Hispanic of any race (2007); Density: 16,270.8 persons per square mile (2007); Average household size: 1.75 (2007); Median age: 43.3 (2007); Males per 100 females: 75.1 (2007); Marriage status: 21.1% never married, 42.8% now married, 25.1% widowed, 11.0% divorced (2000); Foreign born: 27.4% (2000); Ancestry (includes multiple ancestries): 33.4% Other groups, 13.0% Russian, 10.8% Italian, 7.9% Polish, 6.5% United States or American (2000).

Economy: Employment by occupation: 9.2% management, 15.3% professional, 14.1% services, 35.1% sales, 0.0% farming, 14.4% construction, 11.9% production (2000).

Income: Per capita income: $21,253 (2007); Median household income: $25,547 (2007); Average household income: $37,175 (2007); Percent of households with income of $100,000 or more: 4.1% (2007); Poverty rate: 14.4% (2000).

Education: Percent of population age 25 and over with: High school diploma (including GED) or higher: 76.0% (2007); Bachelor's degree or higher: 14.8% (2007); Master's degree or higher: 7.2% (2007).

Housing: Homeownership rate: 74.2% (2007); Median home value: $90,697 (2007); Median rent: $539 per month (2000); Median age of housing: 24 years (2000).

Transportation: Commute to work: 98.2% car, 1.8% public transportation, 0.0% walk, 0.0% work from home (2000); Travel time to work: 21.2% less than 15 minutes, 27.0% 15 to 30 minutes, 30.5% 30 to 45 minutes, 6.3% 45 to 60 minutes, 15.1% 60 minutes or more (2000)

RAVENSWOOD ESTATES (CDP).
Covers a land area of 0.166 square miles and a water area of 0 square miles. Located at 26.05° N. Lat.; 80.17° W. Long.

Population: 929 (1990); 960 (2000); 1,192 (2007); 1,341 (2012 projected); Race: 89.4% White, 2.9% Black, 3.1% Asian, 9.6% Hispanic of any race (2007); Density: 7,168.9 persons per square mile (2007); Average household size: 2.23 (2007); Median age: 47.1 (2007); Males per 100 females: 93.8 (2007); Marriage status: 15.5% never married, 65.4% now married, 6.2% widowed, 12.9% divorced (2000); Foreign born: 18.5% (2000); Ancestry (includes multiple ancestries): 17.0% Italian, 15.1% German, 15.1% Irish, 12.3% Other groups, 10.7% Canadian (2000).

Economy: Employment by occupation: 11.1% management, 8.0% professional, 19.0% services, 35.2% sales, 0.0% farming, 22.2% construction, 4.6% production (2000).

$48,537 (2007); Average household income: $53,315 (2007); Percent of households with income of $100,000 or more: 9.7% (2007); Poverty rate: 8.8% (2000).

Education: Percent of population age 25 and over with: High school diploma (including GED) or higher: 69.0% (2007); Bachelor's degree or higher: 7.7% (2007); Master's degree or higher: 2.7% (2007).

Housing: Homeownership rate: 89.5% (2007); Median home value: $142,945 (2007); Median rent: $589 per month (2000); Median age of housing: 17 years (2000).

Transportation: Commute to work: 91.5% car, 0.0% public transportation, 0.0% walk, 4.4% work from home (2000); Travel time to work: 16.8% less than 15 minutes, 47.3% 15 to 30 minutes, 29.0% 30 to 45 minutes, 5.1% 45 to 60 minutes, 1.8% 60 minutes or more (2000)

RIVERLAND VILLAGE (CDP).
Covers a land area of 0.325 square miles and a water area of 0 square miles. Located at 26.09° N. Lat.; 80.19° W. Long.

Population: 2,077 (1990); 2,108 (2000); 2,167 (2007); 2,212 (2012 projected); Race: 77.5% White, 10.1% Black, 1.7% Asian, 37.3% Hispanic of any race (2007); Density: 6,658.4 persons per square mile (2007); Average household size: 2.89 (2007); Median age: 39.8 (2007); Males per 100 females: 106.0 (2007); Marriage status: 19.8% never married, 60.2% now married, 2.2% widowed, 17.8% divorced (2000); Foreign born: 27.7% (2000); Ancestry (includes multiple ancestries): 39.3% Other groups, 9.5% Irish, 8.3% English, 7.7% Italian, 6.7% German (2000).

Economy: Employment by occupation: 14.6% management, 11.3% professional, 20.9% services, 27.2% sales, 0.0% farming, 11.4% construction, 14.7% production (2000).

Income: Per capita income: $22,100 (2007); Median household income: $58,580 (2007); Average household income: $63,768 (2007); Percent of households with income of $100,000 or more: 13.2% (2007); Poverty rate: 5.5% (2000).

Education: Percent of population age 25 and over with: High school diploma (including GED) or higher: 81.0% (2007); Bachelor's degree or higher: 17.7% (2007); Master's degree or higher: 3.4% (2007).

Housing: Homeownership rate: 92.4% (2007); Median home value: $239,668 (2007); Median rent: $838 per month (2000); Median age of housing: 40 years (2000).

Transportation: Commute to work: 91.7% car, 3.4% public transportation, 0.8% walk, 3.2% work from home (2000); Travel time to work: 20.0% less than 15 minutes, 46.4% 15 to 30 minutes, 20.2% 30 to 45 minutes, 9.6% 45 to 60 minutes, 3.8% 60 minutes or more (2000)

ROCK ISLAND (CDP).
Covers a land area of 0.614 square miles and a water area of 0 square miles. Located at 26.15° N. Lat.; 80.18° W. Long. Elevation is 3 feet.

Population: 3,538 (1990); 3,076 (2000); 3,047 (2007); 3,051 (2012 projected); Race: 2.1% White, 95.6% Black, 0.2% Asian, 1.1% Hispanic of any race (2007); Density: 4,964.4 persons per square mile (2007); Average household size: 3.17 (2007); Median age: 32.6 (2007); Males per 100 females: 86.8 (2007); Marriage status: 32.6% never married, 47.9% now married, 8.4% widowed, 11.1% divorced (2000); Foreign born: 6.0% (2000); Ancestry (includes multiple ancestries): 69.5% Other groups, 8.7% Jamaican, 3.7% United States or American, 2.5% African, 1.1% Bahamian (2000).

Economy: Employment by occupation: 5.2% management, 14.3% professional, 19.7% services, 31.7% sales, 0.0% farming, 9.0% construction, 20.2% production (2000).

Income: Per capita income: $14,289 (2007); Median household income: $34,464 (2007); Average household income: $44,198 (2007); Percent of households with income of $100,000 or more: 8.3% (2007); Poverty rate: 21.7% (2000).

Education: Percent of population age 25 and over with: High school diploma (including GED) or higher: 63.3% (2007); Bachelor's degree or higher: 9.2% (2007); Master's degree or higher: 1.9% (2007).

Housing: Homeownership rate: 73.5% (2007); Median home value: $172,460 (2007); Median rent: $461 per month (2000); Median age of housing: 31 years (2000).

Transportation: Commute to work: 93.3% car, 4.1% public transportation, 0.0% walk, 1.4% work from home (2000); Travel time to work: 11.7% less than 15 minutes, 63.7% 15 to 30 minutes, 13.6% 30 to 45 minutes, 4.4% 45 to 60 minutes, 6.5% 60 minutes or more (2000)

ROLLING OAKS (CDP). Covers a land area of 2.529 square miles and a water area of <.001 square miles. Located at 26.04° N. Lat.; 80.38° W. Long.
Population: 1,209 (1990); 1,291 (2000); 1,599 (2007); 1,792 (2012 projected); Race: 87.3% White, 5.0% Black, 0.8% Asian, 35.4% Hispanic of any race (2007); Density: 632.2 persons per square mile (2007); Average household size: 3.40 (2007); Median age: 39.7 (2007); Males per 100 females: 97.4 (2007); Marriage status: 24.9% never married, 66.1% now married, 3.6% widowed, 5.4% divorced (2000); Foreign born: 16.9% (2000); Ancestry (includes multiple ancestries): 39.4% Other groups, 16.7% English, 14.9% Italian, 11.8% United States or American, 10.0% Irish (2000).
Economy: Employment by occupation: 19.2% management, 19.4% professional, 24.7% services, 23.5% sales, 0.0% farming, 9.3% construction, 4.0% production (2000).
Income: Per capita income: $44,270 (2007); Median household income: $107,692 (2007); Average household income: $150,612 (2007); Percent of households with income of $100,000 or more: 55.1% (2007); Poverty rate: 7.3% (2000).
Education: Percent of population age 25 and over with: High school diploma (including GED) or higher: 86.8% (2007); Bachelor's degree or higher: 30.3% (2007); Master's degree or higher: 10.9% (2007).
Housing: Homeownership rate: 98.1% (2007); Median home value: $680,632 (2007); Median rent: $n/a per month (2000); Median age of housing: 21 years (2000).
Transportation: Commute to work: 91.0% car, 0.0% public transportation, 0.0% walk, 9.0% work from home (2000); Travel time to work: 6.2% less than 15 minutes, 36.5% 15 to 30 minutes, 22.6% 30 to 45 minutes, 21.6% 45 to 60 minutes, 13.1% 60 minutes or more (2000)

ROOSEVELT GARDENS (CDP). Covers a land area of 0.317 square miles and a water area of 0 square miles. Located at 26.14° N. Lat.; 80.18° W. Long.
Population: 2,231 (1990); 1,923 (2000); 2,074 (2007); 2,172 (2012 projected); Race: 0.6% White, 97.9% Black, 0.0% Asian, 0.2% Hispanic of any race (2007); Density: 6,544.7 persons per square mile (2007); Average household size: 2.88 (2007); Median age: 30.1 (2007); Males per 100 females: 90.4 (2007); Marriage status: 40.3% never married, 35.7% now married, 10.5% widowed, 13.5% divorced (2000); Foreign born: 3.5% (2000); Ancestry (includes multiple ancestries): 81.0% Other groups, 2.6% Jamaican, 1.4% West Indian, 1.2% United States or American, 0.9% Trinidadian and Tobagonian (2000).
Economy: Employment by occupation: 2.4% management, 7.0% professional, 32.8% services, 21.4% sales, 1.7% farming, 12.5% construction, 22.2% production (2000).
Income: Per capita income: $10,840 (2007); Median household income: $22,798 (2007); Average household income: $31,226 (2007); Percent of households with income of $100,000 or more: 1.9% (2007); Poverty rate: 33.2% (2000).
Education: Percent of population age 25 and over with: High school diploma (including GED) or higher: 55.6% (2007); Bachelor's degree or higher: 3.0% (2007); Master's degree or higher: 0.0% (2007).
Housing: Homeownership rate: 39.4% (2007); Median home value: $146,250 (2007); Median rent: $501 per month (2000); Median age of housing: 31 years (2000).
Transportation: Commute to work: 83.5% car, 8.9% public transportation, 1.5% walk, 0.0% work from home (2000); Travel time to work: 10.0% less than 15 minutes, 46.5% 15 to 30 minutes, 27.0% 30 to 45 minutes, 6.1% 45 to 60 minutes, 10.4% 60 minutes or more (2000)

ROYAL PALM RANCHES (CDP). Covers a land area of 0.292 square miles and a water area of 0 square miles. Located at 26.04° N. Lat.; 80.27° W. Long.
Population: 209 (1990); 294 (2000); 340 (2007); 370 (2012 projected); Race: 84.1% White, 0.9% Black, 5.9% Asian, 23.2% Hispanic of any race (2007); Density: 1,166.3 persons per square mile (2007); Average household size: 3.30 (2007); Median age: 40.2 (2007); Males per 100 females: 109.9 (2007); Marriage status: 16.8% never married, 70.5% now married, 1.8% widowed, 10.9% divorced (2000); Foreign born: 17.3% (2000); Ancestry (includes multiple ancestries): 32.2% German, 27.9% United States or American, 24.3% Other groups, 16.6% Italian, 10.6% Irish (2000).

Economy: Employment by occupation: 29.3% management, 20.4% professional, 5.4% services, 29.3% sales, 0.0% farming, 0.0% construction, 15.6% production (2000).
Income: Per capita income: $44,544 (2007); Median household income: $135,938 (2007); Average household income: $147,039 (2007); Percent of households with income of $100,000 or more: 65.0% (2007); Poverty rate: 0.0% (2000).
Education: Percent of population age 25 and over with: High school diploma (including GED) or higher: 92.6% (2007); Bachelor's degree or higher: 26.4% (2007); Master's degree or higher: 19.4% (2007).
Housing: Homeownership rate: 99.0% (2007); Median home value: $625,000 (2007); Median rent: $n/a per month (2000); Median age of housing: 17 years (2000).
Transportation: Commute to work: 78.2% car, 15.0% public transportation, 6.8% walk, 0.0% work from home (2000); Travel time to work: 12.2% less than 15 minutes, 8.8% 15 to 30 minutes, 40.8% 30 to 45 minutes, 38.1% 45 to 60 minutes, 0.0% 60 minutes or more (2000)

SAINT GEORGE (CDP). Covers a land area of 0.449 square miles and a water area of 0 square miles. Located at 26.13° N. Lat.; 80.19° W. Long.
Population: 2,626 (1990); 2,450 (2000); 2,286 (2007); 2,219 (2012 projected); Race: 1.3% White, 97.2% Black, 0.0% Asian, 1.6% Hispanic of any race (2007); Density: 5,094.8 persons per square mile (2007); Average household size: 3.24 (2007); Median age: 34.1 (2007); Males per 100 females: 91.0 (2007); Marriage status: 36.3% never married, 40.7% now married, 10.3% widowed, 12.7% divorced (2000); Foreign born: 12.1% (2000); Ancestry (includes multiple ancestries): 72.4% Other groups, 7.4% Jamaican, 1.3% Haitian, 1.0% Barbadian, 0.9% United States or American (2000).
Economy: Employment by occupation: 2.6% management, 12.6% professional, 23.4% services, 31.7% sales, 0.0% farming, 15.5% construction, 14.2% production (2000).
Income: Per capita income: $17,914 (2007); Median household income: $48,080 (2007); Average household income: $58,089 (2007); Percent of households with income of $100,000 or more: 15.3% (2007); Poverty rate: 10.9% (2000).
Education: Percent of population age 25 and over with: High school diploma (including GED) or higher: 68.1% (2007); Bachelor's degree or higher: 10.2% (2007); Master's degree or higher: 2.7% (2007).
Housing: Homeownership rate: 86.8% (2007); Median home value: $180,357 (2007); Median rent: $528 per month (2000); Median age of housing: 38 years (2000).
Transportation: Commute to work: 91.6% car, 6.6% public transportation, 0.0% walk, 0.9% work from home (2000); Travel time to work: 18.1% less than 15 minutes, 38.4% 15 to 30 minutes, 28.6% 30 to 45 minutes, 6.7% 45 to 60 minutes, 8.2% 60 minutes or more (2000)

SEA RANCH LAKES (village). Covers a land area of 0.181 square miles and a water area of 0.044 square miles. Located at 26.20° N. Lat.; 80.09° W. Long. Elevation is 10 feet.
Population: 619 (1990); 1,392 (2000); 1,543 (2007); 1,628 (2012 projected); Race: 97.0% White, 1.6% Black, 0.6% Asian, 11.1% Hispanic of any race (2007); Density: 8,523.6 persons per square mile (2007); Average household size: 2.01 (2007); Median age: 57.2 (2007); Males per 100 females: 84.6 (2007); Marriage status: 10.8% never married, 64.4% now married, 13.0% widowed, 11.9% divorced (2000); Foreign born: 15.1% (2000); Ancestry (includes multiple ancestries): 20.5% German, 16.9% Irish, 16.4% Italian, 12.6% English, 7.5% Russian (2000).
Economy: Single-family building permits issued: 0 (2006); Multi-family building permits issued: 0 (2006); Employment by occupation: 27.6% management, 30.9% professional, 0.8% services, 33.9% sales, 0.0% farming, 2.5% construction, 4.3% production (2000).
Income: Per capita income: $62,474 (2007); Median household income: $59,946 (2007); Average household income: $125,354 (2007); Percent of households with income of $100,000 or more: 30.0% (2007); Poverty rate: 7.0% (2000).
Education: Percent of population age 25 and over with: High school diploma (including GED) or higher: 93.4% (2007); Bachelor's degree or higher: 53.5% (2007); Master's degree or higher: 24.4% (2007).
Housing: Homeownership rate: 90.6% (2007); Median home value: $555,168 (2007); Median rent: $1,034 per month (2000); Median age of housing: 24 years (2000).
Safety: Violent crime rate: 12.9 per 10,000 population; Property crime rate: 193.8 per 10,000 population (2006).

Transportation: Commute to work: 92.1% car, 2.5% public transportation, 0.0% walk, 5.4% work from home (2000); Travel time to work: 24.2% less than 15 minutes, 40.8% 15 to 30 minutes, 18.3% 30 to 45 minutes, 9.6% 45 to 60 minutes, 7.0% 60 minutes or more (2000)

SUNRISE (city). Aka City of Sunrise. Covers a land area of 18.202 square miles and a water area of 0.229 square miles. Located at 26.15° N. Lat.; 80.28° W. Long. Elevation is 5 feet.
Population: 64,675 (1990); 85,779 (2000); 90,378 (2007); 93,484 (2012 projected); Race: 61.4% White, 25.5% Black, 3.8% Asian, 23.3% Hispanic of any race (2007); Density: 4,965.2 persons per square mile (2007); Average household size: 2.58 (2007); Median age: 37.7 (2007); Males per 100 females: 89.7 (2007); Marriage status: 24.1% never married, 55.2% now married, 10.0% widowed, 10.7% divorced (2000); Foreign born: 28.1% (2000); Ancestry (includes multiple ancestries): 33.8% Other groups, 10.3% Italian, 8.0% Jamaican, 7.4% Irish, 7.4% German (2000).
Economy: Unemployment rate: 3.8% (11/2007); Total civilian labor force: 50,620 (11/2007); Single-family building permits issued: 18 (2006); Multi-family building permits issued: 500 (2006); Employment by occupation: 13.1% management, 18.6% professional, 15.7% services, 34.1% sales, 0.1% farming, 8.9% construction, 9.5% production (2000).
Income: Per capita income: $21,214 (2007); Median household income: $46,371 (2007); Average household income: $54,525 (2007); Percent of households with income of $100,000 or more: 11.4% (2007); Poverty rate: 9.7% (2000).
Taxes: Total city taxes per capita: $579 (2005); City property taxes per capita: $309 (2005).
Education: Percent of population age 25 and over with: High school diploma (including GED) or higher: 84.0% (2007); Bachelor's degree or higher: 20.3% (2007); Master's degree or higher: 6.6% (2007).

School District(s)

Broward County School District (PK-12)
    2005-06 Enrollment: 274,591 . . . . (754) 321-2600
Housing: Homeownership rate: 73.6% (2007); Median home value: $212,751 (2007); Median rent: $759 per month (2000); Median age of housing: 19 years (2000).
Safety: Violent crime rate: 46.2 per 10,000 population; Property crime rate: 362.9 per 10,000 population (2006).
Transportation: Commute to work: 94.8% car, 1.7% public transportation, 1.1% walk, 1.8% work from home (2000); Travel time to work: 20.3% less than 15 minutes, 33.2% 15 to 30 minutes, 28.2% 30 to 45 minutes, 10.9% 45 to 60 minutes, 7.3% 60 minutes or more (2000)
Additional Information Contacts
City of Sunrise . . . . (954) 741-2580
    http://www.sunrisefl.gov
Sunrise Chamber of Commerce . . . . (954) 741-3300
    http://www.sunrisechamber.org

SUNSHINE ACRES (CDP). Covers a land area of 1.028 square miles and a water area of 0 square miles. Located at 26.05° N. Lat.; 80.29° W. Long.
Population: 894 (1990); 827 (2000); 882 (2007); 919 (2012 projected); Race: 84.9% White, 6.8% Black, 2.5% Asian, 11.9% Hispanic of any race (2007); Density: 858.1 persons per square mile (2007); Average household size: 3.53 (2007); Median age: 38.8 (2007); Males per 100 females: 108.5 (2007); Marriage status: 20.4% never married, 68.4% now married, 3.8% widowed, 7.3% divorced (2000); Foreign born: 16.7% (2000); Ancestry (includes multiple ancestries): 26.1% Other groups, 23.0% German, 20.3% English, 17.0% Irish, 15.3% Italian (2000).
Economy: Employment by occupation: 11.9% management, 16.1% professional, 23.2% services, 32.2% sales, 3.1% farming, 8.6% construction, 4.9% production (2000).
Income: Per capita income: $32,899 (2007); Median household income: $85,714 (2007); Average household income: $114,870 (2007); Percent of households with income of $100,000 or more: 38.8% (2007); Poverty rate: 4.3% (2000).
Education: Percent of population age 25 and over with: High school diploma (including GED) or higher: 82.3% (2007); Bachelor's degree or higher: 29.8% (2007); Master's degree or higher: 8.8% (2007).
Housing: Homeownership rate: 96.8% (2007); Median home value: $620,690 (2007); Median rent: $n/a per month (2000); Median age of housing: 19 years (2000).
Transportation: Commute to work: 87.9% car, 0.0% public transportation, 8.0% walk, 2.6% work from home (2000); Travel time to work: 27.6% less

than 15 minutes, 35.8% 15 to 30 minutes, 12.9% 30 to 45 minutes, 0.0% 45 to 60 minutes, 23.6% 60 minutes or more (2000)

SUNSHINE RANCHES (CDP). Covers a land area of 4.171 square miles and a water area of 0 square miles. Located at 26.04° N. Lat.; 80.32° W. Long. Elevation is 3 feet.
Population: 1,405 (1990); 1,704 (2000); 2,380 (2007); 2,811 (2012 projected); Race: 89.8% White, 4.1% Black, 0.7% Asian, 23.0% Hispanic of any race (2007); Density: 570.6 persons per square mile (2007); Average household size: 3.14 (2007); Median age: 41.3 (2007); Males per 100 females: 94.1 (2007); Marriage status: 15.6% never married, 71.7% now married, 7.0% widowed, 5.7% divorced (2000); Foreign born: 19.4% (2000); Ancestry (includes multiple ancestries): 29.4% Other groups, 15.3% Italian, 13.0% Irish, 11.8% United States or American, 10.2% German (2000).
Economy: Employment by occupation: 28.9% management, 22.6% professional, 10.7% services, 26.4% sales, 2.5% farming, 3.0% construction, 5.9% production (2000).
Income: Per capita income: $43,762 (2007); Median household income: $109,965 (2007); Average household income: $136,435 (2007); Percent of households with income of $100,000 or more: 57.5% (2007); Poverty rate: 2.1% (2000).
Education: Percent of population age 25 and over with: High school diploma (including GED) or higher: 90.8% (2007); Bachelor's degree or higher: 42.2% (2007); Master's degree or higher: 19.6% (2007).
Housing: Homeownership rate: 94.5% (2007); Median home value: $866,803 (2007); Median rent: $1,875 per month (2000); Median age of housing: 18 years (2000).
Transportation: Commute to work: 90.0% car, 0.0% public transportation, 1.1% walk, 8.9% work from home (2000); Travel time to work: 8.9% less than 15 minutes, 34.4% 15 to 30 minutes, 29.0% 30 to 45 minutes, 12.8% 45 to 60 minutes, 14.9% 60 minutes or more (2000)

TAMARAC (city). Covers a land area of 11.391 square miles and a water area of 0.502 square miles. Located at 26.20° N. Lat.; 80.24° W. Long. Elevation is 10 feet.
Population: 45,366 (1990); 55,588 (2000); 60,269 (2007); 63,445 (2012 projected); Race: 73.4% White, 16.2% Black, 1.9% Asian, 21.6% Hispanic of any race (2007); Density: 5,290.7 persons per square mile (2007); Average household size: 2.05 (2007); Median age: 49.8 (2007); Males per 100 females: 83.0 (2007); Marriage status: 17.3% never married, 55.7% now married, 16.0% widowed, 11.0% divorced (2000); Foreign born: 21.3% (2000); Ancestry (includes multiple ancestries): 29.8% Other groups, 10.9% Italian, 9.1% United States or American, 7.9% Irish, 7.7% German (2000).
Economy: Unemployment rate: 4.5% (11/2007); Total civilian labor force: 29,382 (11/2007); Single-family building permits issued: 254 (2006); Multi-family building permits issued: 26 (2006); Employment by occupation: 13.2% management, 15.2% professional, 15.7% services, 36.0% sales, 0.1% farming, 10.6% construction, 9.0% production (2000).
Income: Per capita income: $24,337 (2007); Median household income: $38,780 (2007); Average household income: $49,558 (2007); Percent of households with income of $100,000 or more: 9.1% (2007); Poverty rate: 8.9% (2000).
Education: Percent of population age 25 and over with: High school diploma (including GED) or higher: 83.8% (2007); Bachelor's degree or higher: 17.0% (2007); Master's degree or higher: 5.8% (2007).

School District(s)

Broward County School District (PK-12)
    2005-06 Enrollment: 274,591 . . . . (754) 321-2600
Housing: Homeownership rate: 80.5% (2007); Median home value: $198,011 (2007); Median rent: $720 per month (2000); Median age of housing: 21 years (2000).
Hospitals: University Hospital & Medical Center (317 beds)
Safety: Violent crime rate: 27.4 per 10,000 population; Property crime rate: 200.4 per 10,000 population (2006).
Transportation: Commute to work: 94.2% car, 1.7% public transportation, 1.0% walk, 1.9% work from home (2000); Travel time to work: 19.9% less than 15 minutes, 36.2% 15 to 30 minutes, 29.2% 30 to 45 minutes, 8.3% 45 to 60 minutes, 6.4% 60 minutes or more (2000)
Additional Information Contacts
City of Tamarac . . . . (954) 597-3505
    http://www.tamarac.org
Tamarac Chamber of Commerce . . . . (954) 722-1520
    http://www.tamaracchamber.org

TEDDER (CDP). Covers a land area of 0.278 square miles and a water area of 0 square miles. Located at 26.28° N. Lat.; 80.12° W. Long. Elevation is 16 feet.

Population: 1,686 (1990); 2,079 (2000); 2,080 (2007); 1,944 (2012 projected); Race: 27.8% White, 49.8% Black, 1.2% Asian, 20.5% Hispanic of any race (2007); Density: 7,469.2 persons per square mile (2007); Average household size: 4.23 (2007); Median age: 33.7 (2007); Males per 100 females: 103.1 (2007); Marriage status: 40.7% never married, 45.1% now married, 6.2% widowed, 8.1% divorced (2000); Foreign born: 35.2% (2000); Ancestry (includes multiple ancestries): 34.5% Other groups, 25.1% Haitian, 7.2% German, 4.9% United States or American, 4.7% Irish (2000).

Economy: Employment by occupation: 8.7% management, 11.0% professional, 22.9% services, 27.9% sales, 0.8% farming, 10.9% construction, 17.8% production (2000).

Income: Per capita income: $11,060 (2007); Median household income: $42,778 (2007); Average household income: $44,233 (2007); Percent of households with income of $100,000 or more: 2.6% (2007); Poverty rate: 18.2% (2000).

Education: Percent of population age 25 and over with: High school diploma (including GED) or higher: 50.7% (2007); Bachelor's degree or higher: 8.7% (2007); Master's degree or higher: 2.8% (2007).

Housing: Homeownership rate: 82.1% (2007); Median home value: $185,750 (2007); Median rent: $586 per month (2000); Median age of housing: 35 years (2000).

Transportation: Commute to work: 97.0% car, 2.1% public transportation, 0.0% walk, 0.0% work from home (2000); Travel time to work: 25.5% less than 15 minutes, 49.9% 15 to 30 minutes, 18.5% 30 to 45 minutes, 5.5% 45 to 60 minutes, 0.6% 60 minutes or more (2000)

TERRA MAR (CDP). Covers a land area of 0.373 square miles and a water area of 0 square miles. Located at 26.21° N. Lat.; 80.09° W. Long. Elevation is 3 feet.

Population: 3,072 (1990); 2,631 (2000); 2,859 (2007); 3,015 (2012 projected); Race: 96.8% White, 0.9% Black, 0.2% Asian, 6.6% Hispanic of any race (2007); Density: 7,665.6 persons per square mile (2007); Average household size: 1.65 (2007); Median age: 61.1 (2007); Males per 100 females: 90.5 (2007); Marriage status: 15.4% never married, 55.1% now married, 14.3% widowed, 15.2% divorced (2000); Foreign born: 22.5% (2000); Ancestry (includes multiple ancestries): 16.4% German, 14.8% Italian, 12.1% Irish, 10.3% English, 8.7% Other groups (2000).

Economy: Employment by occupation: 14.3% management, 23.2% professional, 12.2% services, 37.0% sales, 0.0% farming, 7.9% construction, 5.4% production (2000).

Income: Per capita income: $50,232 (2007); Median household income: $55,074 (2007); Average household income: $83,013 (2007); Percent of households with income of $100,000 or more: 23.7% (2007); Poverty rate: 8.2% (2000).

Education: Percent of population age 25 and over with: High school diploma (including GED) or higher: 88.7% (2007); Bachelor's degree or higher: 37.9% (2007); Master's degree or higher: 17.3% (2007).

Housing: Homeownership rate: 76.8% (2007); Median home value: $361,111 (2007); Median rent: $1,074 per month (2000); Median age of housing: 30 years (2000).

Transportation: Commute to work: 88.2% car, 1.1% public transportation, 2.5% walk, 8.2% work from home (2000); Travel time to work: 19.6% less than 15 minutes, 37.6% 15 to 30 minutes, 28.2% 30 to 45 minutes, 10.4% 45 to 60 minutes, 4.2% 60 minutes or more (2000)

TWIN LAKES (CDP). Covers a land area of 0.260 square miles and a water area of 0.006 square miles. Located at 26.18° N. Lat.; 80.15° W. Long. Elevation is 3 feet.

Population: 1,786 (1990); 1,875 (2000); 1,900 (2007); 1,970 (2012 projected); Race: 65.9% White, 24.8% Black, 2.1% Asian, 21.1% Hispanic of any race (2007); Density: 7,307.1 persons per square mile (2007); Average household size: 2.91 (2007); Median age: 37.4 (2007); Males per 100 females: 113.2 (2007); Marriage status: 26.5% never married, 60.2% now married, 3.7% widowed, 9.6% divorced (2000); Foreign born: 21.9% (2000); Ancestry (includes multiple ancestries): 19.8% Other groups, 15.3% English, 14.6% German, 14.1% United States or American, 10.0% Irish (2000).

Economy: Employment by occupation: 15.6% management, 15.7% professional, 11.0% services, 30.1% sales, 0.0% farming, 17.6% construction, 10.0% production (2000).

$46,515 (2007); Average household income: $56,212 (2007); Percent of households with income of $100,000 or more: 10.4% (2007); Poverty rate: 8.9% (2000).

Education: Percent of population age 25 and over with: High school diploma (including GED) or higher: 72.5% (2007); Bachelor's degree or higher: 12.7% (2007); Master's degree or higher: 3.6% (2007).

Housing: Homeownership rate: 78.7% (2007); Median home value: $223,908 (2007); Median rent: $597 per month (2000); Median age of housing: 34 years (2000).

Transportation: Commute to work: 92.8% car, 1.1% public transportation, 0.0% walk, 4.5% work from home (2000); Travel time to work: 33.5% less than 15 minutes, 34.6% 15 to 30 minutes, 23.0% 30 to 45 minutes, 3.1% 45 to 60 minutes, 5.7% 60 minutes or more (2000)

UTOPIA (CDP). Covers a land area of 0.307 square miles and a water area of 0 square miles. Located at 25.98° N. Lat.; 80.20° W. Long.

Population: 660 (1990); 714 (2000); 687 (2007); 695 (2012 projected); Race: 15.9% White, 65.5% Black, 0.4% Asian, 28.8% Hispanic of any race (2007); Density: 2,238.9 persons per square mile (2007); Average household size: 2.72 (2007); Median age: 30.2 (2007); Males per 100 females: 95.7 (2007); Marriage status: 39.9% never married, 42.4% now married, 5.0% widowed, 12.7% divorced (2000); Foreign born: 31.4% (2000); Ancestry (includes multiple ancestries): 65.9% Other groups, 12.6% Jamaican, 8.1% United States or American, 4.0% British West Indian, 2.1% U.S. Virgin Islander (2000).

Economy: Employment by occupation: 2.0% management, 14.0% professional, 16.4% services, 38.4% sales, 0.0% farming, 12.4% construction, 16.8% production (2000).

Income: Per capita income: $14,447 (2007); Median household income: $24,346 (2007); Average household income: $39,229 (2007); Percent of households with income of $100,000 or more: 4.7% (2007); Poverty rate: 28.4% (2000).

Education: Percent of population age 25 and over with: High school diploma (including GED) or higher: 58.4% (2007); Bachelor's degree or higher: 5.3% (2007); Master's degree or higher: 0.0% (2007).

Housing: Homeownership rate: 34.4% (2007); Median home value: $133,553 (2007); Median rent: $560 per month (2000); Median age of housing: 25 years (2000).

Transportation: Commute to work: 84.2% car, 13.3% public transportation, 2.5% walk, 0.0% work from home (2000); Travel time to work: 14.5% less than 15 minutes, 48.1% 15 to 30 minutes, 31.1% 30 to 45 minutes, 6.2% 45 to 60 minutes, 0.0% 60 minutes or more (2000)

VILLAGE PARK (CDP). Covers a land area of 0.178 square miles and a water area of 0 square miles. Located at 26.19° N. Lat.; 80.20° W. Long.

Population: 566 (1990); 895 (2000); 859 (2007); 859 (2012 projected); Race: 70.1% White, 8.8% Black, 5.6% Asian, 32.5% Hispanic of any race (2007); Density: 4,827.8 persons per square mile (2007); Average household size: 1.96 (2007); Median age: 47.5 (2007); Males per 100 females: 111.1 (2007); Marriage status: 18.0% never married, 44.2% now married, 14.8% widowed, 23.0% divorced (2000); Foreign born: 28.0% (2000); Ancestry (includes multiple ancestries): 27.2% Other groups, 15.8% Italian, 13.9% German, 11.9% Irish, 7.6% Canadian (2000).

Economy: Employment by occupation: 0.0% management, 6.5% professional, 18.4% services, 33.5% sales, 0.0% farming, 28.8% construction, 12.9% production (2000).

Income: Per capita income: $18,862 (2007); Median household income: $29,688 (2007); Average household income: $36,992 (2007); Percent of households with income of $100,000 or more: 2.5% (2007); Poverty rate: 16.4% (2000).

Education: Percent of population age 25 and over with: High school diploma (including GED) or higher: 64.3% (2007); Bachelor's degree or higher: 11.6% (2007); Master's degree or higher: 5.0% (2007).

Housing: Homeownership rate: 91.8% (2007); Median home value: $15,597 (2007); Median rent: $421 per month (2000); Median age of housing: 25 years (2000).

Transportation: Commute to work: 85.9% car, 9.1% public transportation, 2.6% walk, 0.0% work from home (2000); Travel time to work: 20.3% less than 15 minutes, 33.8% 15 to 30 minutes, 21.4% 30 to 45 minutes, 7.9% 45 to 60 minutes, 16.6% 60 minutes or more (2000)

WASHINGTON PARK (CDP). Covers a land area of 0.398 square miles and a water area of 0.017 square miles. Located at 26.13° N. Lat.; 80.17° W. Long. Elevation is 3 feet.

Population: 1,524 (1990); 1,257 (2000); 1,297 (2007); 1,319 (2012 projected); Race: 0.1% White, 97.8% Black, 0.2% Asian, 0.7% Hispanic of any race (2007); Density: 3,262.7 persons per square mile (2007); Average household size: 3.02 (2007); Median age: 34.3 (2007); Males per 100 females: 90.7 (2007); Marriage status: 37.4% never married, 45.1% now married, 6.7% widowed, 10.7% divorced (2000); Foreign born: 9.1% (2000); Ancestry (includes multiple ancestries): 74.5% Other groups, 8.3% Jamaican, 6.9% United States or American, 1.0% Bahamian, 0.4% Belizean (2000).

Economy: Employment by occupation: 5.7% management, 12.7% professional, 32.8% services, 12.3% sales, 1.5% farming, 14.4% construction, 20.6% production (2000).

Income: Per capita income: $12,429 (2007); Median household income: $26,597 (2007); Average household income: $37,576 (2007); Percent of households with income of $100,000 or more: 6.1% (2007); Poverty rate: 28.5% (2000).

Education: Percent of population age 25 and over with: High school diploma (including GED) or higher: 51.1% (2007); Bachelor's degree or higher: 9.8% (2007); Master's degree or higher: 3.4% (2007).

Housing: Homeownership rate: 64.8% (2007); Median home value: $164,085 (2007); Median rent: $525 per month (2000); Median age of housing: 32 years (2000).

Transportation: Commute to work: 95.0% car, 5.0% public transportation, 0.0% walk, 0.0% work from home (2000); Travel time to work: 15.8% less than 15 minutes, 37.0% 15 to 30 minutes, 31.1% 30 to 45 minutes, 7.8% 45 to 60 minutes, 8.4% 60 minutes or more (2000)

WEST KEN-LARK (CDP). Covers a land area of 0.486 square miles and a water area of 0 square miles. Located at 26.14° N. Lat.; 80.19° W. Long.

Population: 3,413 (1990); 3,412 (2000); 3,423 (2007); 3,445 (2012 projected); Race: 1.2% White, 96.4% Black, 0.1% Asian, 2.4% Hispanic of any race (2007); Density: 7,048.1 persons per square mile (2007); Average household size: 3.46 (2007); Median age: 29.0 (2007); Males per 100 females: 87.5 (2007); Marriage status: 42.0% never married, 39.7% now married, 10.2% widowed, 8.2% divorced (2000); Foreign born: 3.9% (2000); Ancestry (includes multiple ancestries): 85.3% Other groups, 1.2% Jamaican, 0.8% Haitian, 0.5% West Indian, 0.4% African (2000).

Economy: Employment by occupation: 3.8% management, 11.0% professional, 29.1% services, 26.1% sales, 0.9% farming, 12.6% construction, 16.6% production (2000).

Income: Per capita income: $12,392 (2007); Median household income: $34,667 (2007); Average household income: $40,863 (2007); Percent of households with income of $100,000 or more: 2.3% (2007); Poverty rate: 33.3% (2000).

Education: Percent of population age 25 and over with: High school diploma (including GED) or higher: 51.8% (2007); Bachelor's degree or higher: 4.4% (2007); Master's degree or higher: 2.6% (2007).

Housing: Homeownership rate: 74.3% (2007); Median home value: $171,172 (2007); Median rent: $294 per month (2000); Median age of housing: 34 years (2000).

Transportation: Commute to work: 92.1% car, 5.6% public transportation, 1.6% walk, 0.0% work from home (2000); Travel time to work: 17.5% less than 15 minutes, 42.9% 15 to 30 minutes, 25.9% 30 to 45 minutes, 4.7% 45 to 60 minutes, 9.0% 60 minutes or more (2000)

WESTON (city). Covers a land area of 23.762 square miles and a water area of 2.516 square miles. Located at 26.10° N. Lat.; 80.38° W. Long. Elevation is 3 feet.

Population: 10,099 (1990); 49,286 (2000); 67,538 (2007); 78,734 (2012 projected); Race: 83.9% White, 5.2% Black, 4.1% Asian, 38.4% Hispanic of any race (2007); Density: 2,842.3 persons per square mile (2007); Average household size: 3.07 (2007); Median age: 34.7 (2007); Males per 100 females: 94.4 (2007); Marriage status: 19.2% never married, 70.6% now married, 3.3% widowed, 6.9% divorced (2000); Foreign born: 28.0% (2000); Ancestry (includes multiple ancestries): 40.7% Other groups, 9.8% Italian, 9.2% German, 7.9% Irish, 6.8% United States or American (2000).

Economy: Unemployment rate: 2.9% (11/2007); Total civilian labor force: 35,828 (11/2007); Single-family building permits issued: 11 (2006); Multi-family building permits issued: 0 (2006); Employment by occupation:

0.0% farming, 3.2% construction, 4.6% production (2000).

Income: Per capita income: $43,902 (2007); Median household income: $98,168 (2007); Average household income: $134,580 (2007); Percent of households with income of $100,000 or more: 49.0% (2007); Poverty rate: 5.0% (2000).

Taxes: Total city taxes per capita: $383 (2005); City property taxes per capita: $119 (2005).

Education: Percent of population age 25 and over with: High school diploma (including GED) or higher: 95.7% (2007); Bachelor's degree or higher: 52.7% (2007); Master's degree or higher: 22.0% (2007).

School District(s)
Broward County School District (PK-12)
   2005-06 Enrollment: 274,591 . . . . (754) 321-2600

Four-year College(s)
American Intercontinental University (Private, For-profit)
   Fall 2006 Enrollment: 1,871 . . . . (954) 446-6100
   2006-07 Tuition: In-state $16,223; Out-of-state $16,223

Housing: Homeownership rate: 83.6% (2007); Median home value: $454,205 (2007); Median rent: $969 per month (2000); Median age of housing: 5 years (2000).

Hospitals: Cleveland Clinic Hospital (150 beds)

Safety: Violent crime rate: 14.4 per 10,000 population; Property crime rate: 144.8 per 10,000 population (2006).

Newspapers: Pembroke Pines Community News (General - Circulation 27,000); Weston Community News (General - Circulation 18,000)

Transportation: Commute to work: 91.9% car, 0.6% public transportation, 0.8% walk, 5.7% work from home (2000); Travel time to work: 17.3% less than 15 minutes, 25.9% 15 to 30 minutes, 29.6% 30 to 45 minutes, 16.9% 45 to 60 minutes, 10.4% 60 minutes or more (2000)

Additional Information Contacts
City of Weston . . . . (954) 385-2000
   http://www.westonfl.org

WILTON MANORS (city). Aka Wilton Manor. Covers a land area of 1.943 square miles and a water area of 0 square miles. Located at 26.15° N. Lat.; 80.14° W. Long. Elevation is 7 feet.

Population: 11,804 (1990); 12,697 (2000); 12,755 (2007); 12,861 (2012 projected); Race: 72.4% White, 17.4% Black, 2.0% Asian, 12.9% Hispanic of any race (2007); Density: 6,565.1 persons per square mile (2007); Average household size: 2.15 (2007); Median age: 42.8 (2007); Males per 100 females: 124.2 (2007); Marriage status: 38.4% never married, 39.2% now married, 6.7% widowed, 15.7% divorced (2000); Foreign born: 20.5% (2000); Ancestry (includes multiple ancestries): 19.9% Other groups, 14.1% Irish, 13.3% German, 12.1% English, 9.1% Italian (2000).

Economy: Single-family building permits issued: 19 (2006); Multi-family building permits issued: 50 (2006); Employment by occupation: 12.5% management, 15.8% professional, 19.4% services, 30.8% sales, 0.1% farming, 10.5% construction, 10.8% production (2000).

Income: Per capita income: $28,189 (2007); Median household income: $48,449 (2007); Average household income: $58,933 (2007); Percent of households with income of $100,000 or more: 14.2% (2007); Poverty rate: 15.4% (2000).

Education: Percent of population age 25 and over with: High school diploma (including GED) or higher: 83.8% (2007); Bachelor's degree or higher: 25.0% (2007); Master's degree or higher: 8.3% (2007).

School District(s)
Broward County School District (PK-12)
   2005-06 Enrollment: 274,591 . . . . (754) 321-2600

Housing: Homeownership rate: 58.2% (2007); Median home value: $322,261 (2007); Median rent: $566 per month (2000); Median age of housing: 35 years (2000).

Safety: Violent crime rate: 58.1 per 10,000 population; Property crime rate: 505.5 per 10,000 population (2006).

Transportation: Commute to work: 88.2% car, 4.2% public transportation, 2.1% walk, 3.9% work from home (2000); Travel time to work: 33.1% less than 15 minutes, 39.7% 15 to 30 minutes, 16.4% 30 to 45 minutes, 5.5% 45 to 60 minutes, 5.3% 60 minutes or more (2000)

Additional Information Contacts
City of Wilton Manors . . . . (954) 390-2100
   http://www.wiltonmanors.com

Calhoun County

Located in northwestern Florida; lowland area, drained by the Chipola River; bounded on the east by the Apalachicola River. Covers a land area of 567.31 square miles, a water area of 7.03 square miles, and is located in the Central Time Zone. The county was founded in 1838. County seat is Blountstown.

Population: 11,011 (1990); 13,017 (2000); 13,815 (2007); 14,589 (2012 projected); Race: 79.7% White, 15.9% Black, 0.5% Asian, 4.6% Hispanic of any race (2007); Density: 24.4 persons per square mile (2007); Average household size: 2.85 (2007); Median age: 36.9 (2007); Males per 100 females: 117.7 (2007).

Religion: Five largest groups: 17.4% Southern Baptist Convention, 4.0% The United Methodist Church, 2.6% International Pentecostal Holiness Church, 2.5% Church of God (Cleveland, Tennessee), 1.6% Assemblies of God (2000).

Economy: Unemployment rate: 3.6% (11/2007); Total civilian labor force: 5,453 (11/2007); Leading industries: 24.8% retail trade; 24.4% health care and social assistance; 15.7% construction (2005); Farms: 151 totaling 49,107 acres (2002); Companies that employ 500 or more persons: 0 (2005); Companies that employ 100 to 499 persons: 3 (2005); Companies that employ less than 100 persons: 231 (2005); Black-owned businesses: n/a (2002); Hispanic-owned businesses: n/a (2002); Asian-owned businesses: n/a (2002); Women-owned businesses: n/a (2002); Retail sales per capita: $9,635 (2007). Single-family building permits issued: 40 (2006); Multi-family building permits issued: 0 (2006).

Income: Per capita income: $14,260 (2007); Median household income: $30,714 (2007); Average household income: $40,064 (2007); Percent of households with income of $100,000 or more: 5.7% (2007); Poverty rate: 21.2% (2005); Bankruptcy rate: 1.27% (2006).

Education: Percent of population age 25 and over with: High school diploma (including GED) or higher: 69.2% (2007); Bachelor's degree or higher: 7.6% (2007); Master's degree or higher: 3.0% (2007).

Housing: Homeownership rate: 80.6% (2007); Median home value: $116,130 (2007); Median rent: $248 per month (2000); Median age of housing: 21 years (2000).

Health: Birth rate: 120.8 per 10,000 population (2006); Death rate: 105.9 per 10,000 population (2006); Age-adjusted cancer mortality rate: 220.7 deaths per 100,000 population (2004); Number of physicians: 6.0 per 10,000 population (2005); Hospital beds: 19.2 per 10,000 population (2004); Hospital admissions: 417.3 per 10,000 population (2004).

Elections: 2004 Presidential election results: 63.4% Bush, 35.5% Kerry, 0.6% Nader, 0.1% Badnarik

Additional Information Contacts
Calhoun County Government . . . . (904) 674-4545
  http://www.calhounco.org
Calhoun Chamber of Commerce . . . . (850) 674-4519
  http://www.calhounco.org

Calhoun County Communities

ALTHA (town). Covers a land area of 1.426 square miles and a water area of 0.040 square miles. Located at 30.57° N. Lat.; 85.12° W. Long. Elevation is 203 feet.

History: Altha grew as a farming community with a cotton gin and gristmill. Corn, rice, pecans, and Satsuma oranges were grown in the area.

Population: 497 (1990); 506 (2000); 472 (2007); 479 (2012 projected); Race: 94.7% White, 0.4% Black, 0.2% Asian, 8.5% Hispanic of any race (2007); Density: 331.0 persons per square mile (2007); Average household size: 2.42 (2007); Median age: 38.3 (2007); Males per 100 females: 95.0 (2007); Marriage status: 26.5% never married, 48.6% now married, 10.6% widowed, 14.3% divorced (2000); Foreign born: 4.1% (2000); Ancestry (includes multiple ancestries): 39.7% United States or American, 12.9% Irish, 12.9% Other groups, 12.0% German, 4.5% English (2000).

Economy: Employment by occupation: 6.9% management, 12.2% professional, 21.6% services, 24.5% sales, 4.1% farming, 20.8% construction, 9.8% production (2000).

Income: Per capita income: $17,076 (2007); Median household income: $33,088 (2007); Average household income: $41,333 (2007); Percent of households with income of $100,000 or more: 6.2% (2007); Poverty rate: 17.3% (2000).

Taxes: Total city taxes per capita: $186 (2005); City property taxes per capita: $0 (2005).

Education: Percent of population age 25 and over with: High school diploma (including GED) or higher: 70.8% (2007); Bachelor's degree or higher: 7.9% (2007); Master's degree or higher: 2.8% (2007).

School District(s)
Calhoun County School District (PK-12)
  2005-06 Enrollment: 2,313 . . . . (850) 674-5927
Housing: Homeownership rate: 67.7% (2007); Median home value: $94,444 (2007); Median rent: $255 per month (2000); Median age of housing: 27 years (2000).

Safety: Violent crime rate: 19.2 per 10,000 population; Property crime rate: 153.8 per 10,000 population (2006).

Transportation: Commute to work: 89.2% car, 0.8% public transportation, 4.2% walk, 4.6% work from home (2000); Travel time to work: 25.8% less than 15 minutes, 39.3% 15 to 30 minutes, 13.5% 30 to 45 minutes, 10.9% 45 to 60 minutes, 10.5% 60 minutes or more (2000)

BLOUNTSTOWN (city). County seat. Covers a land area of 3.186 square miles and a water area of 0.009 square miles. Located at 30.44° N. Lat.; 85.04° W. Long. Elevation is 62 feet.

History: Blountstown was founded in 1823 and named for Seminole chief John Blount. Incorporated in 1925, the town developed as a lumber center along the Apalachicola River.

Population: 2,541 (1990); 2,444 (2000); 2,345 (2007); 2,395 (2012 projected); Race: 66.2% White, 30.7% Black, 0.4% Asian, 0.9% Hispanic of any race (2007); Density: 736.1 persons per square mile (2007); Average household size: 2.64 (2007); Median age: 43.2 (2007); Males per 100 females: 78.2 (2007); Marriage status: 25.1% never married, 50.4% now married, 14.0% widowed, 10.5% divorced (2000); Foreign born: 2.1% (2000); Ancestry (includes multiple ancestries): 33.0% Other groups, 18.2% United States or American, 6.3% English, 4.0% Irish, 3.6% German (2000).

Economy: Single-family building permits issued: 0 (2006); Multi-family building permits issued: 0 (2006); Employment by occupation: 10.3% management, 18.1% professional, 25.6% services, 25.3% sales, 2.7% farming, 8.4% construction, 9.7% production (2000).

Income: Per capita income: $13,660 (2007); Median household income: $26,192 (2007); Average household income: $34,884 (2007); Percent of households with income of $100,000 or more: 5.1% (2007); Poverty rate: 24.3% (2000).

Education: Percent of population age 25 and over with: High school diploma (including GED) or higher: 70.6% (2007); Bachelor's degree or higher: 11.8% (2007); Master's degree or higher: 6.0% (2007).

School District(s)
Calhoun County School District (PK-12)
  2005-06 Enrollment: 2,313 . . . . (850) 674-5927
Housing: Homeownership rate: 72.7% (2007); Median home value: $141,528 (2007); Median rent: $248 per month (2000); Median age of housing: 32 years (2000).

Hospitals: Calhoun-Liberty Hospital (36 beds)

Safety: Violent crime rate: 24.3 per 10,000 population; Property crime rate: 202.1 per 10,000 population (2006).

Newspapers: County Record (General - Circulation 3,000)

Transportation: Commute to work: 91.6% car, 1.7% public transportation, 5.6% walk, 0.0% work from home (2000); Travel time to work: 46.6% less than 15 minutes, 15.6% 15 to 30 minutes, 15.9% 30 to 45 minutes, 9.3% 45 to 60 minutes, 12.6% 60 minutes or more (2000)

Additional Information Contacts
Calhoun Chamber of Commerce . . . . (850) 674-4519
  http://www.calhounco.org

CLARKSVILLE (unincorporated postal area, zip code 32430). Covers a land area of 95.111 square miles and a water area of 0 square miles. Located at 30.43° N. Lat.; 85.24° W. Long. Elevation is 112 feet.

Population: 1,037 (2000); Race: 98.2% White, 0.0% Black, 0.0% Asian, 0.0% Hispanic of any race (2000); Density: 10.9 persons per square mile (2000); Age: 20.3% under 18, 18.6% over 64 (2000); Marriage status: 13.3% never married, 62.2% now married, 9.6% widowed, 15.0% divorced (2000); Foreign born: 0.9% (2000); Ancestry (includes multiple ancestries): 26.6% United States or American, 15.5% Other groups, 9.3% Irish, 6.5% German, 5.3% English (2000).

Economy: Employment by occupation: 8.6% management, 13.0% professional, 21.1% services, 20.4% sales, 2.5% farming, 27.1% construction, 7.4% production (2000).

Income: Per capita income: $17,622 (2000); Median household income: $32,670 (2000); Poverty rate: 5.3% (2000).

Education: Percent of population age 25 and over with: High school diploma (including GED) or higher: 83.4% (2000); Bachelor's degree or higher: 4.8% (2000).

School District(s)
Calhoun County School District (PK-12)

　2005-06 Enrollment: 2,313 . . . . (850) 674-5927

Housing: Homeownership rate: 90.4% (2000); Median home value: $56,700 (2000); Median rent: $225 per month (2000); Median age of housing: 19 years (2000).

Transportation: Commute to work: 91.7% car, 0.0% public transportation, 0.0% walk, 6.8% work from home (2000); Travel time to work: 12.5% less than 15 minutes, 46.4% 15 to 30 minutes, 28.1% 30 to 45 minutes, 3.1% 45 to 60 minutes, 9.9% 60 minutes or more (2000)

KINARD (unincorporated postal area, zip code 32449). Covers a land area of 58.177 square miles and a water area of 1.345 square miles. Located at 30.28° N. Lat.; 85.21° W. Long. Elevation is 75 feet.

Population: 562 (2000); Race: 85.6% White, 0.0% Black, 0.0% Asian, 0.0% Hispanic of any race (2000); Density: 9.7 persons per square mile (2000); Age: 19.3% under 18, 19.7% over 64 (2000); Marriage status: 8.7% never married, 73.9% now married, 8.7% widowed, 8.7% divorced (2000); Foreign born: 0.0% (2000); Ancestry (includes multiple ancestries): 40.5% United States or American, 12.2% Other groups, 5.4% English, 4.2% German, 3.3% Irish (2000).

Economy: Employment by occupation: 10.4% management, 13.2% professional, 22.6% services, 23.1% sales, 9.0% farming, 14.2% construction, 7.5% production (2000).

Income: Per capita income: $10,731 (2000); Median household income: $20,787 (2000); Poverty rate: 24.0% (2000).

Education: Percent of population age 25 and over with: High school diploma (including GED) or higher: 57.7% (2000); Bachelor's degree or higher: 4.6% (2000).

Housing: Homeownership rate: 84.1% (2000); Median home value: $42,400 (2000); Median rent: $300 per month (2000); Median age of housing: 25 years (2000).

Transportation: Commute to work: 90.0% car, 0.0% public transportation, 3.0% walk, 7.0% work from home (2000); Travel time to work: 30.5% less than 15 minutes, 25.7% 15 to 30 minutes, 16.6% 30 to 45 minutes, 17.1% 45 to 60 minutes, 10.2% 60 minutes or more (2000)

Charlotte County

Located in southern Florida, on the Gulf of Mexico. Covers a land area of 693.60 square miles, a water area of 165.51 square miles, and is located in the Eastern Time Zone. The county was founded in 1921. County seat is Punta Gorda.

Charlotte County is part of the Punta Gorda, FL Metropolitan Statistical Area. The entire metro area includes: Charlotte County, FL

Weather Station: Punta Gorda 4 ESE　　　　　　　　Elevation: 19 feet

	Jan	Feb	Mar	Apr	May	Jun	Jul	Aug	Sep	Oct	Nov	Dec
High	74	76	80	84	89	91	92	92	91	86	81	76
Low	52	53	57	60	66	71	73	73	72	66	60	54
Precip	2.3	2.4	3.0	1.7	3.4	8.5	7.7	7.8	6.6	3.1	1.9	1.8
Snow	0.0	0.0	0.0	0.0	0.0	0.0	0.0	0.0	0.0	0.0	0.0	0.0

High and Low temperatures in degrees Fahrenheit; Precipitation and Snow in inches

Population: 110,975 (1990); 141,627 (2000); 158,635 (2007); 169,992 (2012 projected); Race: 91.2% White, 5.3% Black, 1.1% Asian, 4.4% Hispanic of any race (2007); Density: 228.7 persons per square mile (2007); Average household size: 2.22 (2007); Median age: 53.4 (2007); Males per 100 females: 92.0 (2007).

Religion: Five largest groups: 18.4% Catholic Church, 3.0% The United Methodist Church, 2.4% Southern Baptist Convention, 1.8% Jewish Estimate, 1.4% Presbyterian Church (U.S.A.) (2000).

Economy: Unemployment rate: 5.9% (11/2007); Total civilian labor force: 70,741 (11/2007); Leading industries: 24.1% retail trade; 22.2% health care and social assistance; 12.1% construction (2005); Farms: 284 totaling 191,529 acres (2002); Companies that employ 500 or more persons: 4 (2005); Companies that employ 100 to 499 persons: 49 (2005); Companies that employ less than 100 persons: 3,885 (2005); Black-owned businesses: 229 (2002); Hispanic-owned businesses: n/a (2002); Asian-owned businesses: n/a (2002); Women-owned businesses: 3,539 (2002); Retail sales per capita: $12,723 (2007). Single-family building permits issued: 3,052 (2006); Multi-family building permits issued: 1,283 (2006).

Income: Per capita income: $25,282 (2007); Median household income: $41,993 (2007); Average household income: $55,497 (2007); Percent of households with income of $100,000 or more: 10.9% (2007); Poverty rate: 9.6% (2005); Bankruptcy rate: 0.95% (2006).

Taxes: Total county taxes per capita: $781 (2005); County property taxes per capita: $451 (2005).

Education: Percent of population age 25 and over with: High school diploma (including GED) or higher: 82.5% (2007); Bachelor's degree or higher: 18.0% (2007); Master's degree or higher: 6.8% (2007).

Housing: Homeownership rate: 84.4% (2007); Median home value: $190,151 (2007); Median rent: $520 per month (2000); Median age of housing: 17 years (2000).

Health: Birth rate: 75.6 per 10,000 population (2006); Death rate: 149.9 per 10,000 population (2006); Age-adjusted cancer mortality rate: 164.0 deaths per 100,000 population (2004); Number of physicians: 22.2 per 10,000 population (2005); Hospital beds: 46.0 per 10,000 population (2004); Hospital admissions: 1,777.3 per 10,000 population (2004).

Elections: 2004 Presidential election results: 55.7% Bush, 42.9% Kerry, 0.7% Nader, 0.2% Badnarik

National and State Parks: Don Pedro Island State Park; Island Bay National Wildlife Refuge; Port Charlotte Beach State Park; Stump Pass Beach State Park

Additional Information Contacts

Charlotte County Government . . . . (941) 743-1200
　http://www.charlottecountyfl.com
Economic Development Council . . . . (941) 627-3023
　http://www.pureeconomics.org
Port Charlotte Chamber of Commerce . . . . (941) 627-2222
　http://www.charlottecountychamber.org
Punta Gorda Chamber of Commerce . . . . (941) 639-3720
　http://www.puntagorda-chamber.com
Southwest Florida Tourist Info . . . . (941) 639-0007

Charlotte County Communities

CHARLOTTE HARBOR (CDP). Covers a land area of 2.181 square miles and a water area of 0.038 square miles. Located at 26.96° N. Lat.; 82.06° W. Long. Elevation is 3 feet.

History: Charlotte Harbor was established as a fishing village at the mouth of the Peace River. The name probably refers to the Calusa tribe which formerly inhabited this area.

Population: 3,061 (1990); 3,647 (2000); 3,879 (2007); 3,979 (2012 projected); Race: 91.4% White, 4.2% Black, 1.8% Asian, 4.6% Hispanic of any race (2007); Density: 1,778.2 persons per square mile (2007); Average household size: 2.07 (2007); Median age: 70.8 (2007); Males per 100 females: 74.4 (2007); Marriage status: 11.3% never married, 51.9% now married, 29.0% widowed, 7.7% divorced (2000); Foreign born: 4.9% (2000); Ancestry (includes multiple ancestries): 15.9% English, 14.3% German, 11.9% Irish, 10.9% United States or American, 8.9% Other groups (2000).

Economy: Employment by occupation: 1.3% management, 24.2% professional, 20.9% services, 32.8% sales, 1.3% farming, 11.9% construction, 7.6% production (2000).

Income: Per capita income: $25,820 (2007); Median household income: $32,517 (2007); Average household income: $47,113 (2007); Percent of households with income of $100,000 or more: 5.6% (2007); Poverty rate: 10.3% (2000).

Education: Percent of population age 25 and over with: High school diploma (including GED) or higher: 73.1% (2007); Bachelor's degree or higher: 15.5% (2007); Master's degree or higher: 6.2% (2007).

School District(s)
Charlotte County School District (PK-12)

　2005-06 Enrollment: 17,507 . . . . (941) 255-0808

Housing: Homeownership rate: 63.8% (2007); Median home value: $123,278 (2007); Median rent: $626 per month (2000); Median age of housing: 20 years (2000).

Transportation: Commute to work: 95.2% car, 0.0% public transportation, 2.4% walk, 0.9% work from home (2000); Travel time to work: 42.6% less than 15 minutes, 31.9% 15 to 30 minutes, 14.2% 30 to 45 minutes, 6.5% 45 to 60 minutes, 4.7% 60 minutes or more (2000)

CHARLOTTE PARK (CDP). Covers a land area of 1.211 square miles and a water area of 0.155 square miles. Located at 26.90° N. Lat.; 82.04° W. Long. Elevation is 3 feet.

Population: 2,101 (1990); 2,182 (2000); 2,426 (2007); 2,434 (2012 projected); Race: 97.7% White, 0.3% Black, 0.2% Asian, 2.7% Hispanic of any race (2007); Density: 2,003.0 persons per square mile (2007); Average household size: 1.87 (2007); Median age: 65.2 (2007); Males per 100 females: 96.4 (2007); Marriage status: 10.2% never married, 64.9% now married, 12.0% widowed, 12.9% divorced (2000); Foreign born: 4.9% (2000); Ancestry (includes multiple ancestries): 26.3% German, 19.1% English, 18.9% Irish, 5.2% Other groups, 5.2% Italian (2000).
Economy: Employment by occupation: 5.7% management, 20.6% professional, 17.9% services, 29.0% sales, 1.2% farming, 13.5% construction, 12.0% production (2000).
Income: Per capita income: $23,164 (2007); Median household income: $31,049 (2007); Average household income: $43,260 (2007); Percent of households with income of $100,000 or more: 5.4% (2007); Poverty rate: 6.8% (2000).
Education: Percent of population age 25 and over with: High school diploma (including GED) or higher: 82.4% (2007); Bachelor's degree or higher: 16.6% (2007); Master's degree or higher: 3.6% (2007).
Housing: Homeownership rate: 90.8% (2007); Median home value: $159,375 (2007); Median rent: $533 per month (2000); Median age of housing: 23 years (2000).
Transportation: Commute to work: 88.7% car, 0.0% public transportation, 0.0% walk, 8.1% work from home (2000); Travel time to work: 53.5% less than 15 minutes, 22.7% 15 to 30 minutes, 4.4% 30 to 45 minutes, 6.9% 45 to 60 minutes, 12.6% 60 minutes or more (2000)

CLEVELAND (CDP). Covers a land area of 5.496 square miles and a water area of 0.050 square miles. Located at 26.95° N. Lat.; 81.99° W. Long. Elevation is 7 feet.
Population: 2,896 (1990); 3,268 (2000); 3,395 (2007); 3,518 (2012 projected); Race: 97.4% White, 0.5% Black, 0.3% Asian, 1.9% Hispanic of any race (2007); Density: 617.8 persons per square mile (2007); Average household size: 2.09 (2007); Median age: 52.4 (2007); Males per 100 females: 99.8 (2007); Marriage status: 15.3% never married, 60.0% now married, 13.2% widowed, 11.5% divorced (2000); Foreign born: 4.4% (2000); Ancestry (includes multiple ancestries): 22.4% German, 21.6% English, 11.1% Irish, 9.8% United States or American, 5.2% Italian (2000).
Economy: Employment by occupation: 9.2% management, 11.5% professional, 23.5% services, 29.7% sales, 0.5% farming, 11.8% construction, 13.9% production (2000).
Income: Per capita income: $26,459 (2007); Median household income: $37,569 (2007); Average household income: $55,212 (2007); Percent of households with income of $100,000 or more: 8.8% (2007); Poverty rate: 8.4% (2000).
Education: Percent of population age 25 and over with: High school diploma (including GED) or higher: 82.4% (2007); Bachelor's degree or higher: 15.6% (2007); Master's degree or higher: 5.8% (2007).
Housing: Homeownership rate: 83.4% (2007); Median home value: $114,773 (2007); Median rent: $439 per month (2000); Median age of housing: 23 years (2000).
Transportation: Commute to work: 95.3% car, 0.8% public transportation, 0.0% walk, 1.9% work from home (2000); Travel time to work: 31.3% less than 15 minutes, 35.0% 15 to 30 minutes, 17.0% 30 to 45 minutes, 9.6% 45 to 60 minutes, 7.2% 60 minutes or more (2000)

GROVE CITY (CDP). Covers a land area of 1.270 square miles and a water area of 0.057 square miles. Located at 26.91° N. Lat.; 82.32° W. Long. Elevation is 10 feet.
Population: 2,057 (1990); 2,092 (2000); 2,186 (2007); 2,253 (2012 projected); Race: 96.7% White, 0.6% Black, 1.2% Asian, 1.1% Hispanic of any race (2007); Density: 1,721.6 persons per square mile (2007); Average household size: 1.99 (2007); Median age: 56.4 (2007); Males per 100 females: 102.4 (2007); Marriage status: 9.6% never married, 63.0% now married, 11.0% widowed, 16.4% divorced (2000); Foreign born: 4.5% (2000); Ancestry (includes multiple ancestries): 19.1% German, 17.0% English, 14.0% United States or American, 12.9% Irish, 5.7% Polish (2000).
Economy: Employment by occupation: 6.1% management, 15.1% professional, 28.1% services, 25.3% sales, 0.0% farming, 16.2% construction, 9.1% production (2000).
Income: Per capita income: $25,055 (2007); Median household income: $37,549 (2007); Average household income: $49,791 (2007); Percent of households with income of $100,000 or more: 10.4% (2007); Poverty rate: 9.6% (2000).

Education: Percent of population age 25 and over with: High school diploma (including GED) or higher: 79.3% (2007); Bachelor's degree or higher: 12.5% (2007); Master's degree or higher: 5.1% (2007).
Housing: Homeownership rate: 82.5% (2007); Median home value: $149,738 (2007); Median rent: $490 per month (2000); Median age of housing: 25 years (2000).
Transportation: Commute to work: 93.0% car, 1.2% public transportation, 0.8% walk, 4.6% work from home (2000); Travel time to work: 39.0% less than 15 minutes, 26.1% 15 to 30 minutes, 17.9% 30 to 45 minutes, 12.1% 45 to 60 minutes, 4.8% 60 minutes or more (2000)

HARBOUR HEIGHTS (CDP). Covers a land area of 2.196 square miles and a water area of 0.014 square miles. Located at 26.99° N. Lat.; 82.00° W. Long. Elevation is 10 feet.
Population: 2,498 (1990); 2,873 (2000); 3,060 (2007); 3,321 (2012 projected); Race: 91.1% White, 4.6% Black, 1.1% Asian, 5.9% Hispanic of any race (2007); Density: 1,393.4 persons per square mile (2007); Average household size: 2.30 (2007); Median age: 49.5 (2007); Males per 100 females: 86.7 (2007); Marriage status: 14.8% never married, 70.6% now married, 7.4% widowed, 7.2% divorced (2000); Foreign born: 7.9% (2000); Ancestry (includes multiple ancestries): 19.5% German, 13.4% Italian, 10.8% Irish, 10.0% United States or American, 9.8% English (2000).
Economy: Employment by occupation: 12.9% management, 19.2% professional, 12.8% services, 34.6% sales, 0.0% farming, 12.4% construction, 8.1% production (2000).
Income: Per capita income: $26,980 (2007); Median household income: $51,531 (2007); Average household income: $61,935 (2007); Percent of households with income of $100,000 or more: 15.5% (2007); Poverty rate: 2.7% (2000).
Education: Percent of population age 25 and over with: High school diploma (including GED) or higher: 86.3% (2007); Bachelor's degree or higher: 19.1% (2007); Master's degree or higher: 5.8% (2007).
Housing: Homeownership rate: 85.8% (2007); Median home value: $223,538 (2007); Median rent: $485 per month (2000); Median age of housing: 16 years (2000).
Transportation: Commute to work: 96.3% car, 0.6% public transportation, 0.0% walk, 2.4% work from home (2000); Travel time to work: 32.9% less than 15 minutes, 42.1% 15 to 30 minutes, 10.0% 30 to 45 minutes, 6.9% 45 to 60 minutes, 8.2% 60 minutes or more (2000)

MANASOTA KEY (CDP). Covers a land area of 1.065 square miles and a water area of 1.660 square miles. Located at 26.92° N. Lat.; 82.36° W. Long.
Population: 1,395 (1990); 1,345 (2000); 1,404 (2007); 1,453 (2012 projected); Race: 99.0% White, 0.2% Black, 0.4% Asian, 1.4% Hispanic of any race (2007); Density: 1,318.6 persons per square mile (2007); Average household size: 1.74 (2007); Median age: 67.6 (2007); Males per 100 females: 82.6 (2007); Marriage status: 4.0% never married, 75.0% now married, 13.7% widowed, 7.4% divorced (2000); Foreign born: 7.0% (2000); Ancestry (includes multiple ancestries): 23.5% German, 19.9% English, 13.4% Irish, 10.2% Scottish, 8.3% Polish (2000).
Economy: Employment by occupation: 15.6% management, 27.9% professional, 17.8% services, 19.0% sales, 3.1% farming, 5.5% construction, 11.0% production (2000).
Income: Per capita income: $41,337 (2007); Median household income: $48,178 (2007); Average household income: $71,740 (2007); Percent of households with income of $100,000 or more: 17.1% (2007); Poverty rate: 4.7% (2000).
Education: Percent of population age 25 and over with: High school diploma (including GED) or higher: 93.2% (2007); Bachelor's degree or higher: 35.3% (2007); Master's degree or higher: 16.1% (2007).
Housing: Homeownership rate: 80.6% (2007); Median home value: $376,571 (2007); Median rent: $657 per month (2000); Median age of housing: 18 years (2000).
Transportation: Commute to work: 75.2% car, 0.0% public transportation, 8.0% walk, 13.2% work from home (2000); Travel time to work: 47.3% less than 15 minutes, 29.0% 15 to 30 minutes, 1.8% 30 to 45 minutes, 12.7% 45 to 60 minutes, 9.2% 60 minutes or more (2000)

PLACIDA (unincorporated postal area, zip code 33946). Covers a land area of 3.446 square miles and a water area of 0.019 square miles. Located at 26.84° N. Lat.; 82.28° W. Long. Elevation is 3 feet.
History: Placida was built around an ancient Indian mound, with fishing as the primary occupation.

Population: 1,064 (2000); Race: 99.4% White, 0.0% Black, 0.0% Asian, 0.0% Hispanic of any race (2000); Density: 308.8 persons per square mile (2000); Age: 8.6% under 18, 47.5% over 64 (2000); Marriage status: 3.8% never married, 85.7% now married, 6.2% widowed, 4.3% divorced (2000); Foreign born: 3.8% (2000); Ancestry (includes multiple ancestries): 30.6% German, 24.3% English, 12.1% Irish, 7.2% Scottish, 6.5% Italian (2000).
Economy: Employment by occupation: 24.4% management, 26.3% professional, 3.8% services, 32.7% sales, 0.0% farming, 8.3% construction, 4.5% production (2000).
Income: Per capita income: $43,383 (2000); Median household income: $64,141 (2000); Poverty rate: 4.7% (2000).
Education: Percent of population age 25 and over with: High school diploma (including GED) or higher: 95.3% (2000); Bachelor's degree or higher: 40.6% (2000).
Housing: Homeownership rate: 97.8% (2000); Median home value: $264,300 (2000); Median rent: $225 per month (2000); Median age of housing: 14 years (2000).
Transportation: Commute to work: 66.7% car, 0.0% public transportation, 0.0% walk, 22.0% work from home (2000); Travel time to work: 7.7% less than 15 minutes, 62.4% 15 to 30 minutes, 16.2% 30 to 45 minutes, 13.7% 45 to 60 minutes, 0.0% 60 minutes or more (2000)

PORT CHARLOTTE (CDP).
Covers a land area of 22.269 square miles and a water area of 1.590 square miles. Located at 26.99° N. Lat.; 82.10° W. Long. Elevation is 3 feet.
History: Planned residential community— one of several on a peninsula once owned by the Vanderbilt family. The town's population quadrupled between 1970 and 1990.
Population: 41,534 (1990); 46,451 (2000); 47,745 (2007); 48,841 (2012 projected); Race: 86.4% White, 8.5% Black, 1.4% Asian, 7.3% Hispanic of any race (2007); Density: 2,144.0 persons per square mile (2007); Average household size: 2.29 (2007); Median age: 47.5 (2007); Males per 100 females: 88.9 (2007); Marriage status: 15.8% never married, 61.8% now married, 11.8% widowed, 10.5% divorced (2000); Foreign born: 9.6% (2000); Ancestry (includes multiple ancestries): 19.3% German, 15.9% Irish, 12.6% English, 12.4% Other groups, 10.4% Italian (2000).
Economy: Employment by occupation: 8.0% management, 17.1% professional, 22.4% services, 29.5% sales, 0.2% farming, 13.1% construction, 9.8% production (2000).
Income: Per capita income: $20,850 (2007); Median household income: $37,346 (2007); Average household income: $47,503 (2007); Percent of households with income of $100,000 or more: 8.1% (2007); Poverty rate: 10.1% (2000).
Education: Percent of population age 25 and over with: High school diploma (including GED) or higher: 79.2% (2007); Bachelor's degree or higher: 14.8% (2007); Master's degree or higher: 6.0% (2007).

School District(s)
Charlotte County School District (PK-12)
   2005-06 Enrollment: 17,507 . . . . (941) 255-0808
Two-year College(s)
Charlotte Technical Center (Public)
   Fall 2006 Enrollment: 905 . . . . (941) 255-7500
   2006-07 Tuition: In-state $2,344; Out-of-state $9,292
Housing: Homeownership rate: 80.5% (2007); Median home value: $165,862 (2007); Median rent: $535 per month (2000); Median age of housing: 21 years (2000).
Hospitals: Fawcett Memorial Hospital (238 beds); Peace River Regional Medical Center (212 beds)
Newspapers: Charlotte Sun Herald (Circulation 39,332)
Transportation: Commute to work: 95.0% car, 0.3% public transportation, 0.6% walk, 2.4% work from home (2000); Travel time to work: 42.6% less than 15 minutes, 35.0% 15 to 30 minutes, 10.1% 30 to 45 minutes, 6.7% 45 to 60 minutes, 5.6% 60 minutes or more (2000); Amtrak: Service available.
Additional Information Contacts
Economic Development Council . . . . (941) 627-3023
   http://www.pureeconomics.org
Port Charlotte Chamber of Commerce . . . . (941) 627-2222
   http://www.charlottecountychamber.org

PUNTA GORDA (city).
County seat. Covers a land area of 14.162 square miles and a water area of 4.314 square miles. Located at 26.91° N. Lat.; 82.04° W. Long. Elevation is 3 feet.
History: The name of Punta Gorda is Spanish for "flat point," referring to its location on the peninsula extending into Charlotte Harbor. The town was

first named for Isaac Trabue of Kentucky, who purchased land here in 1880 and built a hotel and pier.
Population: 10,931 (1990); 14,344 (2000); 16,745 (2007); 18,364 (2012 projected); Race: 95.0% White, 2.4% Black, 1.2% Asian, 2.6% Hispanic of any race (2007); Density: 1,182.4 persons per square mile (2007); Average household size: 1.99 (2007); Median age: 64.5 (2007); Males per 100 females: 89.4 (2007); Marriage status: 6.6% never married, 74.8% now married, 10.6% widowed, 8.0% divorced (2000); Foreign born: 7.8% (2000); Ancestry (includes multiple ancestries): 23.7% German, 17.7% English, 16.8% Irish, 8.6% Italian, 6.7% Other groups (2000).
Economy: Single-family building permits issued: 67 (2006); Multi-family building permits issued: 174 (2006); Employment by occupation: 15.4% management, 18.7% professional, 18.3% services, 32.8% sales, 0.0% farming, 6.5% construction, 8.3% production (2000).
Income: Per capita income: $38,534 (2007); Median household income: $55,728 (2007); Average household income: $76,069 (2007); Percent of households with income of $100,000 or more: 19.3% (2007); Poverty rate: 6.5% (2000).
Taxes: Total city taxes per capita: $564 (2005); City property taxes per capita: $288 (2005).
Education: Percent of population age 25 and over with: High school diploma (including GED) or higher: 91.0% (2007); Bachelor's degree or higher: 33.0% (2007); Master's degree or higher: 12.9% (2007).
School District(s)
Charlotte County School District (PK-12)
   2005-06 Enrollment: 17,507 . . . . (941) 255-0808
Housing: Homeownership rate: 88.8% (2007); Median home value: $395,695 (2007); Median rent: $481 per month (2000); Median age of housing: 16 years (2000).
Hospitals: Charlotte Regional Medical Center (208 beds)
Safety: Violent crime rate: 26.4 per 10,000 population; Property crime rate: 255.2 per 10,000 population (2006).
Transportation: Commute to work: 86.9% car, 0.0% public transportation, 1.0% walk, 9.2% work from home (2000); Travel time to work: 44.5% less than 15 minutes, 31.6% 15 to 30 minutes, 12.6% 30 to 45 minutes, 6.1% 45 to 60 minutes, 5.2% 60 minutes or more (2000)
Additional Information Contacts
Punta Gorda Chamber of Commerce . . . . (941) 639-3720
   http://www.puntagorda-chamber.com
Southwest Florida Tourist Info . . . . (941) 639-0007

ROTONDA (CDP).
Covers a land area of 11.005 square miles and a water area of 0.179 square miles. Located at 26.88° N. Lat.; 82.27° W. Long. Elevation is 10 feet.
Population: 3,576 (1990); 6,574 (2000); 8,671 (2007); 9,969 (2012 projected); Race: 97.8% White, 0.6% Black, 0.4% Asian, 1.8% Hispanic of any race (2007); Density: 787.9 persons per square mile (2007); Average household size: 2.06 (2007); Median age: 62.5 (2007); Males per 100 females: 89.8 (2007); Marriage status: 7.3% never married, 74.5% now married, 10.1% widowed, 8.1% divorced (2000); Foreign born: 9.2% (2000); Ancestry (includes multiple ancestries): 22.0% German, 17.0% Irish, 13.6% English, 11.9% Italian, 6.0% French (except Basque) (2000).
Economy: Employment by occupation: 10.2% management, 20.3% professional, 23.8% services, 31.8% sales, 0.8% farming, 6.6% construction, 6.4% production (2000).
Income: Per capita income: $26,403 (2007); Median household income: $45,617 (2007); Average household income: $54,042 (2007); Percent of households with income of $100,000 or more: 10.8% (2007); Poverty rate: 4.0% (2000).
Education: Percent of population age 25 and over with: High school diploma (including GED) or higher: 87.4% (2007); Bachelor's degree or higher: 22.3% (2007); Master's degree or higher: 7.2% (2007).
Housing: Homeownership rate: 84.0% (2007); Median home value: $246,326 (2007); Median rent: $495 per month (2000); Median age of housing: 12 years (2000).
Transportation: Commute to work: 93.2% car, 0.0% public transportation, 0.8% walk, 5.9% work from home (2000); Travel time to work: 22.5% less than 15 minutes, 41.2% 15 to 30 minutes, 20.0% 30 to 45 minutes, 10.3% 45 to 60 minutes, 6.0% 60 minutes or more (2000)

ROTONDA WEST (unincorporated postal area, zip code 33947).
Covers a land area of 14.442 square miles and a water area of 0.015 square miles. Located at 26.88° N. Lat.; 82.26° W. Long.
Population: 5,238 (2000); Race: 96.6% White, 0.4% Black, 0.3% Asian, 2.1% Hispanic of any race (2000); Density: 362.7 persons per square mile

(2000); Age: 13.9% under 18, 40.9% over 64 (2000); Marriage status: 9.0% never married, 75.2% now married, 7.8% widowed, 8.0% divorced (2000); Foreign born: 8.5% (2000); Ancestry (includes multiple ancestries): 21.3% German, 18.0% Irish, 12.4% Italian, 12.2% English, 6.9% United States or American (2000).

Economy: Employment by occupation: 8.5% management, 20.7% professional, 27.0% services, 32.5% sales, 1.0% farming, 5.5% construction, 5.0% production (2000).

Income: Per capita income: $20,777 (2000); Median household income: $40,967 (2000); Poverty rate: 3.0% (2000).

Education: Percent of population age 25 and over with: High school diploma (including GED) or higher: 87.8% (2000); Bachelor's degree or higher: 21.7% (2000).

School District(s)

Charlotte County School District (PK-12)

    2005-06 Enrollment: 17,507 . . . . (941) 255-0808

Housing: Homeownership rate: 88.9% (2000); Median home value: $112,600 (2000); Median rent: $568 per month (2000); Median age of housing: 12 years (2000).

Transportation: Commute to work: 95.4% car, 0.0% public transportation, 0.9% walk, 3.6% work from home (2000); Travel time to work: 22.5% less than 15 minutes, 41.0% 15 to 30 minutes, 21.3% 30 to 45 minutes, 9.6% 45 to 60 minutes, 5.6% 60 minutes or more (2000)

SOLANA (CDP). Covers a land area of 1.713 square miles and a water area of 0.058 square miles. Located at 26.94° N. Lat.; 82.02° W. Long. Elevation is 3 feet.

Population: 1,046 (1990); 1,011 (2000); 863 (2007); 798 (2012 projected); Race: 91.8% White, 4.9% Black, 1.5% Asian, 3.0% Hispanic of any race (2007); Density: 503.9 persons per square mile (2007); Average household size: 2.21 (2007); Median age: 39.5 (2007); Males per 100 females: 102.6 (2007); Marriage status: 25.0% never married, 43.5% now married, 12.2% widowed, 19.4% divorced (2000); Foreign born: 2.0% (2000); Ancestry (includes multiple ancestries): 22.8% German, 17.9% United States or American, 16.9% Irish, 10.3% Italian, 9.6% English (2000).

Economy: Employment by occupation: 5.2% management, 10.7% professional, 24.7% services, 24.9% sales, 0.0% farming, 22.5% construction, 12.0% production (2000).

Income: Per capita income: $17,315 (2007); Median household income: $26,071 (2007); Average household income: $38,216 (2007); Percent of households with income of $100,000 or more: 6.1% (2007); Poverty rate: 19.7% (2000).

Education: Percent of population age 25 and over with: High school diploma (including GED) or higher: 73.1% (2007); Bachelor's degree or higher: 12.8% (2007); Master's degree or higher: 2.4% (2007).

Housing: Homeownership rate: 62.7% (2007); Median home value: $111,298 (2007); Median rent: $418 per month (2000); Median age of housing: 29 years (2000).

Transportation: Commute to work: 83.6% car, 0.0% public transportation, 2.5% walk, 5.1% work from home (2000); Travel time to work: 35.9% less than 15 minutes, 38.3% 15 to 30 minutes, 14.8% 30 to 45 minutes, 5.6% 45 to 60 minutes, 5.3% 60 minutes or more (2000)

Citrus County

Located in central Florida; bounded on the west by the Gulf of Mexico, and on the north and east by the Withlacoochee River; includes a swampy coast and the Homosassa Islands. Covers a land area of 583.81 square miles, a water area of 189.34 square miles, and is located in the Eastern Time Zone. The county was founded in 1887. County seat is Inverness.

Citrus County is part of the Homosassa Springs, FL Micropolitan Statistical Area. The entire metro area includes: Citrus County, FL

Weather Station: Inverness 3 SE   Elevation: 39 feet

	Jan	Feb	Mar	Apr	May	Jun	Jul	Aug	Sep	Oct	Nov	Dec
High	70	72	77	82	88	91	92	91	90	84	77	72
Low	44	46	51	56	63	70	71	72	70	62	53	47
Precip	3.6	3.1	4.3	2.4	3.5	7.3	6.9	7.8	5.9	2.7	2.3	2.6
Snow	0.0	0.0	0.0	0.0	0.0	0.0	0.0	0.0	0.0	0.0	0.0	0.0

High and Low temperatures in degrees Fahrenheit; Precipitation and Snow in inches

Population: 93,515 (1990); 118,085 (2000); 137,796 (2007); 151,182 (2012 projected); Race: 93.9% White, 2.8% Black, 1.1% Asian, 3.6% Hispanic of any race (2007); Density: 236.0 persons per square mile

(2007); Average household size: 2.25 (2007); Median age: 50.6 (2007); Males per 100 females: 92.5 (2007).

Religion: Five largest groups: 14.5% Catholic Church, 5.6% Southern Baptist Convention, 3.5% The United Methodist Church, 1.6% Church of God (Cleveland, Tennessee), 1.3% Presbyterian Church in America (2000).

Economy: Unemployment rate: 5.1% (11/2007); Total civilian labor force: 58,554 (11/2007); Leading industries: 23.1% health care and social assistance; 21.1% retail trade; 11.1% construction (2005); Farms: 432 totaling 47,209 acres (2002); Companies that employ 500 or more persons: 4 (2005); Companies that employ 100 to 499 persons: 38 (2005); Companies that employ less than 100 persons: 2,793 (2005); Black-owned businesses: n/a (2002); Hispanic-owned businesses: 277 (2002); Asian-owned businesses: 210 (2002); Women-owned businesses: 2,840 (2002); Retail sales per capita: $11,662 (2007). Single-family building permits issued: 2,056 (2006); Multi-family building permits issued: 41 (2006).

Income: Per capita income: $21,743 (2007); Median household income: $36,518 (2007); Average household income: $48,524 (2007); Percent of households with income of $100,000 or more: 8.5% (2007); Poverty rate: 13.3% (2005); Bankruptcy rate: 1.58% (2006).

Taxes: Total county taxes per capita: $521 (2005); County property taxes per capita: $388 (2005).

Education: Percent of population age 25 and over with: High school diploma (including GED) or higher: 78.6% (2007); Bachelor's degree or higher: 13.4% (2007); Master's degree or higher: 5.0% (2007).

Housing: Homeownership rate: 86.0% (2007); Median home value: $132,416 (2007); Median rent: $388 per month (2000); Median age of housing: 16 years (2000).

Health: Birth rate: 69.5 per 10,000 population (2006); Death rate: 151.9 per 10,000 population (2006); Age-adjusted cancer mortality rate: 201.4 deaths per 100,000 population (2004); Air Quality Index: 90.9% good, 9.1% moderate, 0.0% unhealthy for sensitive individuals, 0.0% unhealthy (percent of days in 2006); Number of physicians: 18.5 per 10,000 population (2005); Hospital beds: 23.0 per 10,000 population (2004); Hospital admissions: 1,324.1 per 10,000 population (2004).

Elections: 2004 Presidential election results: 56.9% Bush, 42.1% Kerry, 0.7% Nader, 0.2% Badnarik.

National and State Parks: Crystal River State Archaeological Site; Fort Cooper State Park; Homosassa Springs Wildlife State Park; Withlacoochee Trail State Park; Yulee Sugar Mill Ruins Historic State Park

Additional Information Contacts

Citrus County Government . . . . (352) 341-6400
    http://www.bocc.citrus.fl.us
Citrus County Chamber of Commerce . . . . (352) 795-3149
    http://www.citruscountychamber.com
City of Inverness . . . . (352) 726-2611
    http://www.inverness-fl.gov
Crystal River Chamber of Commerce . . . . (352) 795-3149
    http://www.citruscountychamber.com
Homosassa Chamber of Commerce . . . . (352) 628-2666
    http://www.citruscountychamber.com
Nature Coast Visitors Guide . . . . (352) 726-7700
    http://www.ncvg.com

Citrus County Communities

BEVERLY HILLS (CDP). Covers a land area of 2.846 square miles and a water area of 0 square miles. Located at 28.91° N. Lat.; 82.45° W. Long. Elevation is 102 feet.

Population: 7,015 (1990); 8,317 (2000); 8,655 (2007); 8,956 (2012 projected); Race: 94.4% White, 2.5% Black, 0.8% Asian, 5.9% Hispanic of any race (2007); Density: 3,040.8 persons per square mile (2007); Average household size: 1.94 (2007); Median age: 67.1 (2007); Males per 100 females: 82.1 (2007); Marriage status: 9.1% never married, 63.0% now married, 18.4% widowed, 9.5% divorced (2000); Foreign born: 9.2% (2000); Ancestry (includes multiple ancestries): 19.8% German, 16.5% Irish, 13.8% English, 12.5% Italian, 8.3% Other groups (2000).

Economy: Employment by occupation: 3.4% management, 11.3% professional, 33.9% services, 24.8% sales, 0.7% farming, 11.4% construction, 14.4% production (2000).

Income: Per capita income: $17,692 (2007); Median household income: $27,798 (2007); Average household income: $34,164 (2007); Percent of households with income of $100,000 or more: 2.4% (2007); Poverty rate: 12.4% (2000).

Education: Percent of population age 25 and over with: High school diploma (including GED) or higher: 77.2% (2007); Bachelor's degree or higher: 11.3% (2007); Master's degree or higher: 4.5% (2007).
Housing: Homeownership rate: 87.0% (2007); Median home value: $96,927 (2007); Median rent: $453 per month (2000); Median age of housing: 20 years (2000).
Newspapers: Beverly Hills Visitor (General - Circulation 10,600)
Transportation: Commute to work: 94.5% car, 0.3% public transportation, 2.3% walk, 1.8% work from home (2000); Travel time to work: 33.7% less than 15 minutes, 35.9% 15 to 30 minutes, 20.4% 30 to 45 minutes, 2.4% 45 to 60 minutes, 7.6% 60 minutes or more (2000)

BLACK DIAMOND (CDP).

Covers a land area of 3.780 square miles and a water area of 0 square miles. Located at 28.91° N. Lat.; 82.49° W. Long. Elevation is 56 feet.
Population: 309 (1990); 694 (2000); 914 (2007); 1,043 (2012 projected); Race: 91.8% White, 0.4% Black, 7.4% Asian, 1.2% Hispanic of any race (2007); Density: 241.8 persons per square mile (2007); Average household size: 2.67 (2007); Median age: 62.8 (2007); Males per 100 females: 82.8 (2007); Marriage status: 6.0% never married, 69.7% now married, 22.6% widowed, 1.8% divorced (2000); Foreign born: 16.0% (2000); Ancestry (includes multiple ancestries): 17.8% Other groups, 15.8% English, 9.4% Irish, 7.2% Italian, 6.9% German (2000).
Economy: Employment by occupation: 12.1% management, 57.8% professional, 6.0% services, 24.1% sales, 0.0% farming, 0.0% construction, 0.0% production (2000).
Income: Per capita income: $66,046 (2007); Median household income: $131,048 (2007); Average household income: $169,656 (2007); Percent of households with income of $100,000 or more: 63.7% (2007); Poverty rate: 3.7% (2000).
Education: Percent of population age 25 and over with: High school diploma (including GED) or higher: 83.5% (2007); Bachelor's degree or higher: 37.1% (2007); Master's degree or higher: 13.4% (2007).
Housing: Homeownership rate: 97.1% (2007); Median home value: $559,524 (2007); Median rent: $n/a per month (2000); Median age of housing: 4 years (2000).
Transportation: Commute to work: 87.1% car, 0.0% public transportation, 0.0% walk, 12.9% work from home (2000); Travel time to work: 26.7% less than 15 minutes, 73.3% 15 to 30 minutes, 0.0% 30 to 45 minutes, 0.0% 45 to 60 minutes, 0.0% 60 minutes or more (2000)

CITRUS HILLS (CDP).

Covers a land area of 9.798 square miles and a water area of 0 square miles. Located at 28.88° N. Lat.; 82.42° W. Long. Elevation is 115 feet.
Population: 2,291 (1990); 4,029 (2000); 5,355 (2007); 6,248 (2012 projected); Race: 90.4% White, 1.4% Black, 6.3% Asian, 4.3% Hispanic of any race (2007); Density: 546.6 persons per square mile (2007); Average household size: 2.26 (2007); Median age: 58.2 (2007); Males per 100 females: 92.8 (2007); Marriage status: 9.7% never married, 81.1% now married, 5.4% widowed, 3.8% divorced (2000); Foreign born: 11.0% (2000); Ancestry (includes multiple ancestries): 16.9% Irish, 16.8% English, 16.8% German, 12.5% Other groups, 11.6% Italian (2000).
Economy: Employment by occupation: 14.2% management, 30.6% professional, 12.7% services, 26.2% sales, 0.0% farming, 5.7% construction, 10.6% production (2000).
Income: Per capita income: $32,626 (2007); Median household income: $55,866 (2007); Average household income: $73,812 (2007); Percent of households with income of $100,000 or more: 19.1% (2007); Poverty rate: 6.5% (2000).
Education: Percent of population age 25 and over with: High school diploma (including GED) or higher: 89.7% (2007); Bachelor's degree or higher: 27.1% (2007); Master's degree or higher: 9.2% (2007).
Housing: Homeownership rate: 92.1% (2007); Median home value: $256,355 (2007); Median rent: $729 per month (2000); Median age of housing: 9 years (2000).
Transportation: Commute to work: 93.4% car, 0.0% public transportation, 0.0% walk, 5.2% work from home (2000); Travel time to work: 32.5% less than 15 minutes, 44.4% 15 to 30 minutes, 13.8% 30 to 45 minutes, 3.4% 45 to 60 minutes, 5.8% 60 minutes or more (2000)

CITRUS SPRINGS (CDP).

Covers a land area of 21.274 square miles and a water area of 0 square miles. Located at 28.99° N. Lat.; 82.46° W. Long. Elevation is 95 feet.
Population: 3,058 (1990); 4,157 (2000); 5,993 (2007); 7,167 (2012 projected); Race: 92.6% White, 1.9% Black, 1.1% Asian, 6.9% Hispanic of

any race (2007); Density: 281.7 persons per square mile (2007); Average household size: 2.35 (2007); Median age: 49.9 (2007); Males per 100 females: 89.3 (2007); Marriage status: 12.6% never married, 67.0% now married, 12.2% widowed, 8.2% divorced (2000); Foreign born: 4.9% (2000); Ancestry (includes multiple ancestries): 19.2% German, 14.3% Irish, 13.9% Italian, 11.2% Other groups, 11.1% English (2000).
Economy: Employment by occupation: 9.9% management, 24.4% professional, 16.3% services, 29.7% sales, 0.5% farming, 6.2% construction, 13.0% production (2000).
Income: Per capita income: $19,449 (2007); Median household income: $35,363 (2007); Average household income: $45,442 (2007); Percent of households with income of $100,000 or more: 6.0% (2007); Poverty rate: 7.8% (2000).
Education: Percent of population age 25 and over with: High school diploma (including GED) or higher: 76.9% (2007); Bachelor's degree or higher: 11.2% (2007); Master's degree or higher: 5.2% (2007).

School District(s)
Citrus County School District (PK-12)
    2005-06 Enrollment: 15,720 . . . . (352) 726-1931
Housing: Homeownership rate: 90.8% (2007); Median home value: $140,441 (2007); Median rent: $437 per month (2000); Median age of housing: 16 years (2000).
Transportation: Commute to work: 93.9% car, 1.2% public transportation, 0.0% walk, 3.5% work from home (2000); Travel time to work: 20.6% less than 15 minutes, 43.4% 15 to 30 minutes, 20.9% 30 to 45 minutes, 6.7% 45 to 60 minutes, 8.4% 60 minutes or more (2000)

CRYSTAL RIVER (city).

Covers a land area of 5.696 square miles and a water area of 0.574 square miles. Located at 28.90° N. Lat.; 82.59° W. Long. Elevation is 7 feet.
History: The town of Crystal River grew as a fish, oyster, and lumber center. It was established in an area of springs, some of them crystal clear.
Population: 4,069 (1990); 3,485 (2000); 3,594 (2007); 3,671 (2012 projected); Race: 83.2% White, 12.5% Black, 1.8% Asian, 4.6% Hispanic of any race (2007); Density: 630.9 persons per square mile (2007); Average household size: 2.32 (2007); Median age: 48.3 (2007); Males per 100 females: 92.0 (2007); Marriage status: 19.5% never married, 56.4% now married, 10.0% widowed, 14.2% divorced (2000); Foreign born: 3.1% (2000); Ancestry (includes multiple ancestries): 20.1% Other groups, 16.2% English, 15.2% Irish, 12.7% German, 6.4% Italian (2000).
Economy: Single-family building permits issued: 10 (2006); Multi-family building permits issued: 3 (2006); Employment by occupation: 8.4% management, 25.9% professional, 14.5% services, 27.1% sales, 1.2% farming, 9.9% construction, 12.9% production (2000).
Income: Per capita income: $28,734 (2007); Median household income: $41,494 (2007); Average household income: $63,995 (2007); Percent of households with income of $100,000 or more: 18.3% (2007); Poverty rate: 9.9% (2000).
Education: Percent of population age 25 and over with: High school diploma (including GED) or higher: 80.7% (2007); Bachelor's degree or higher: 23.5% (2007); Master's degree or higher: 8.9% (2007).

School District(s)
Citrus County School District (PK-12)
    2005-06 Enrollment: 15,720 . . . . (352) 726-1931
Housing: Homeownership rate: 70.3% (2007); Median home value: $146,094 (2007); Median rent: $345 per month (2000); Median age of housing: 22 years (2000).
Hospitals: Seven Rivers Regional Medical Center (128 beds)
Safety: Violent crime rate: 103.8 per 10,000 population; Property crime rate: 876.8 per 10,000 population (2006).
Newspapers: Citrus County Chronicle (Circulation 27,168)
Transportation: Commute to work: 96.3% car, 0.0% public transportation, 0.8% walk, 2.8% work from home (2000); Travel time to work: 50.5% less than 15 minutes, 31.2% 15 to 30 minutes, 10.9% 30 to 45 minutes, 3.2% 45 to 60 minutes, 4.2% 60 minutes or more (2000)
Additional Information Contacts
Crystal River Chamber of Commerce . . . . (352) 795-3149
    http://www.citruscountychamber.com

FLORAL CITY (CDP).

Covers a land area of 23.326 square miles and a water area of 1.593 square miles. Located at 28.74° N. Lat.; 82.29° W. Long. Elevation is 62 feet.
History: Floral City was established at the south end of Lake Tsala Apopka as a center for sportsmen who came to the nearby lakes and hunting grounds.

Population: 4,268 (1990); 4,989 (2000); 5,766 (2007); 6,295 (2012 projected); Race: 95.6% White, 2.1% Black, 0.2% Asian, 3.6% Hispanic of any race (2007); Density: 247.2 persons per square mile (2007); Average household size: 2.28 (2007); Median age: 47.4 (2007); Males per 100 females: 92.4 (2007); Marriage status: 14.4% never married, 64.9% now married, 9.6% widowed, 11.1% divorced (2000); Foreign born: 1.9% (2000); Ancestry (includes multiple ancestries): 24.7% German, 16.6% English, 13.1% Irish, 8.9% Other groups, 8.8% United States or American (2000).
Economy: Employment by occupation: 8.0% management, 17.1% professional, 20.3% services, 26.3% sales, 3.2% farming, 17.4% construction, 7.7% production (2000).
Income: Per capita income: $18,469 (2007); Median household income: $32,699 (2007); Average household income: $41,599 (2007); Percent of households with income of $100,000 or more: 5.1% (2007); Poverty rate: 15.1% (2000).
Education: Percent of population age 25 and over with: High school diploma (including GED) or higher: 74.3% (2007); Bachelor's degree or higher: 7.8% (2007); Master's degree or higher: 2.7% (2007).
School District(s)
Citrus County School District (PK-12)
   2005-06 Enrollment: 15,720 . . . . (352) 726-1931
Housing: Homeownership rate: 89.3% (2007); Median home value: $114,789 (2007); Median rent: $358 per month (2000); Median age of housing: 19 years (2000).
Transportation: Commute to work: 89.8% car, 0.9% public transportation, 1.7% walk, 5.3% work from home (2000); Travel time to work: 16.0% less than 15 minutes, 38.2% 15 to 30 minutes, 17.1% 30 to 45 minutes, 15.3% 45 to 60 minutes, 13.5% 60 minutes or more (2000)

HERNANDO (CDP).
Covers a land area of 31.478 square miles and a water area of 3.900 square miles. Located at 28.92° N. Lat.; 82.37° W. Long. Elevation is 56 feet.
History: Hernando was settled on the west shore of Lake Tsala Apopka in 1881, and named for Hernando de Soto, who had crossed through this area in the 1500's.
Population: 6,281 (1990); 8,253 (2000); 9,661 (2007); 10,636 (2012 projected); Race: 94.5% White, 2.8% Black, 0.8% Asian, 2.2% Hispanic of any race (2007); Density: 306.9 persons per square mile (2007); Average household size: 2.24 (2007); Median age: 47.6 (2007); Males per 100 females: 96.3 (2007); Marriage status: 14.1% never married, 62.7% now married, 9.0% widowed, 14.2% divorced (2000); Foreign born: 3.0% (2000); Ancestry (includes multiple ancestries): 21.0% German, 16.0% English, 15.5% Irish, 11.3% United States or American, 10.1% Other groups (2000).
Economy: Employment by occupation: 6.7% management, 14.1% professional, 19.7% services, 26.0% sales, 0.3% farming, 18.4% construction, 14.7% production (2000).
Income: Per capita income: $18,255 (2007); Median household income: $34,562 (2007); Average household income: $40,908 (2007); Percent of households with income of $100,000 or more: 4.5% (2007); Poverty rate: 15.4% (2000).
Education: Percent of population age 25 and over with: High school diploma (including GED) or higher: 73.1% (2007); Bachelor's degree or higher: 9.0% (2007); Master's degree or higher: 1.9% (2007).
School District(s)
Citrus County School District (PK-12)
   2005-06 Enrollment: 15,720 . . . . (352) 726-1931
Housing: Homeownership rate: 83.5% (2007); Median home value: $98,258 (2007); Median rent: $346 per month (2000); Median age of housing: 19 years (2000).
Transportation: Commute to work: 92.1% car, 0.0% public transportation, 2.6% walk, 3.8% work from home (2000); Travel time to work: 20.8% less than 15 minutes, 42.7% 15 to 30 minutes, 18.7% 30 to 45 minutes, 5.5% 45 to 60 minutes, 12.2% 60 minutes or more (2000)

HOMOSASSA (CDP).
Covers a land area of 7.946 square miles and a water area of 0.435 square miles. Located at 28.78° N. Lat.; 82.61° W. Long. Elevation is 4 feet.
Population: 2,576 (1990); 2,294 (2000); 2,568 (2007); 2,766 (2012 projected); Race: 98.4% White, 0.1% Black, 0.0% Asian, 0.8% Hispanic of any race (2007); Density: 323.2 persons per square mile (2007); Average household size: 2.03 (2007); Median age: 58.2 (2007); Males per 100 females: 99.1 (2007); Marriage status: 11.8% never married, 63.6% now married, 10.0% widowed, 14.6% divorced (2000); Foreign born: 1.5%

(2000); Ancestry (includes multiple ancestries): 23.5% German, 18.4% English, 16.1% Irish, 6.5% Other groups, 6.0% Polish (2000).
Economy: Employment by occupation: 10.2% management, 19.0% professional, 17.1% services, 32.0% sales, 4.5% farming, 13.4% construction, 3.8% production (2000).
Income: Per capita income: $25,157 (2007); Median household income: $43,022 (2007); Average household income: $50,684 (2007); Percent of households with income of $100,000 or more: 10.5% (2007); Poverty rate: 10.8% (2000).
Education: Percent of population age 25 and over with: High school diploma (including GED) or higher: 83.6% (2007); Bachelor's degree or higher: 17.2% (2007); Master's degree or higher: 7.1% (2007).
School District(s)
Citrus County School District (PK-12)
   2005-06 Enrollment: 15,720 . . . . (352) 726-1931
Housing: Homeownership rate: 88.6% (2007); Median home value: $213,760 (2007); Median rent: $448 per month (2000); Median age of housing: 18 years (2000).
Transportation: Commute to work: 92.9% car, 0.0% public transportation, 0.0% walk, 5.7% work from home (2000); Travel time to work: 21.2% less than 15 minutes, 39.6% 15 to 30 minutes, 24.1% 30 to 45 minutes, 6.1% 45 to 60 minutes, 8.9% 60 minutes or more (2000)
Additional Information Contacts
Homosassa Chamber of Commerce . . . . (352) 628-2666
   http://www.citruscountychamber.com

HOMOSASSA SPRINGS (CDP).
Covers a land area of 25.843 square miles and a water area of 0 square miles. Located at 28.80° N. Lat.; 82.55° W. Long. Elevation is 7 feet.
History: Homosassa Springs was established at the site of springs which were used to form a natural aquarium as part of a Federal fish preserve. This was the location of a hunting lodge operated by baseball pitcher Dazzy Vance.
Population: 10,235 (1990); 12,458 (2000); 14,173 (2007); 15,341 (2012 projected); Race: 95.8% White, 1.1% Black, 0.7% Asian, 2.9% Hispanic of any race (2007); Density: 548.4 persons per square mile (2007); Average household size: 2.38 (2007); Median age: 41.9 (2007); Males per 100 females: 98.1 (2007); Marriage status: 16.5% never married, 60.0% now married, 9.5% widowed, 14.0% divorced (2000); Foreign born: 2.7% (2000); Ancestry (includes multiple ancestries): 21.1% German, 17.4% Irish, 15.2% English, 11.4% United States or American, 10.4% Other groups (2000).
Economy: Employment by occupation: 5.9% management, 12.7% professional, 21.4% services, 25.9% sales, 1.4% farming, 16.5% construction, 16.3% production (2000).
Income: Per capita income: $16,714 (2007); Median household income: $32,734 (2007); Average household income: $39,805 (2007); Percent of households with income of $100,000 or more: 4.2% (2007); Poverty rate: 13.3% (2000).
Education: Percent of population age 25 and over with: High school diploma (including GED) or higher: 73.4% (2007); Bachelor's degree or higher: 6.8% (2007); Master's degree or higher: 2.7% (2007).
Housing: Homeownership rate: 83.5% (2007); Median home value: $91,807 (2007); Median rent: $369 per month (2000); Median age of housing: 15 years (2000).
Transportation: Commute to work: 96.7% car, 0.3% public transportation, 0.4% walk, 1.4% work from home (2000); Travel time to work: 30.3% less than 15 minutes, 41.9% 15 to 30 minutes, 14.1% 30 to 45 minutes, 4.1% 45 to 60 minutes, 9.7% 60 minutes or more (2000)

INVERNESS (city).
County seat. Covers a land area of 7.286 square miles and a water area of 0.818 square miles. Located at 28.83° N. Lat.; 82.34° W. Long. Elevation is 49 feet.
History: Inverness, on Lake Tsala Apopka, was named by an early settler for his home town in Scotland. The town developed as the marketing center for a large rural area where citrus growing, truck farming, beekeeping, and dairying were early occupations.
Population: 5,913 (1990); 6,789 (2000); 7,024 (2007); 7,180 (2012 projected); Race: 91.2% White, 5.5% Black, 0.7% Asian, 5.7% Hispanic of any race (2007); Density: 964.0 persons per square mile (2007); Average household size: 2.13 (2007); Median age: 51.2 (2007); Males per 100 females: 78.4 (2007); Marriage status: 17.2% never married, 51.8% now married, 16.4% widowed, 14.6% divorced (2000); Foreign born: 3.7% (2000); Ancestry (includes multiple ancestries): 16.4% German, 13.8%

Irish, 13.2% English, 12.7% Other groups, 8.7% United States or American (2000).
Economy: Single-family building permits issued: 54 (2006); Multi-family building permits issued: 4 (2006); Employment by occupation: 7.9% management, 19.2% professional, 23.8% services, 27.0% sales, 0.7% farming, 10.7% construction, 10.8% production (2000).
Income: Per capita income: $20,417 (2007); Median household income: $30,898 (2007); Average household income: $42,114 (2007); Percent of households with income of $100,000 or more: 6.3% (2007); Poverty rate: 14.8% (2000).
Education: Percent of population age 25 and over with: High school diploma (including GED) or higher: 74.2% (2007); Bachelor's degree or higher: 12.1% (2007); Master's degree or higher: 4.3% (2007).

School District(s)
Citrus County School District (PK-12)
  2005-06 Enrollment: 15,720 . . . . (352) 726-1931
Vocational/Technical School(s)
Withlacoochee Technical Institute (Public)
  Fall 2006 Enrollment: 370 . . . . (352) 726-2430
  2006-07 Tuition: $1,282
Housing: Homeownership rate: 67.7% (2007); Median home value: $118,984 (2007); Median rent: $371 per month (2000); Median age of housing: 17 years (2000).
Hospitals: Citrus Memorial Hospital (171 beds)
Transportation: Commute to work: 87.4% car, 2.2% public transportation, 6.4% walk, 3.7% work from home (2000); Travel time to work: 50.2% less than 15 minutes, 21.4% 15 to 30 minutes, 9.0% 30 to 45 minutes, 7.8% 45 to 60 minutes, 11.6% 60 minutes or more (2000)
Additional Information Contacts
Citrus County Chamber of Commerce. . . . . (352) 795-3149
  http://www.citruscountychamber.com
City of Inverness . . . . (352) 726-2611
  http://www.inverness-fl.gov
Nature Coast Visitors Guide . . . . (352) 726-7700
  http://www.ncvg.com

INVERNESS HIGHLANDS NORTH (CDP). Covers a land area of 1.917 square miles and a water area of 0.018 square miles. Located at 28.86° N. Lat.; 82.37° W. Long.
Population: 1,162 (1990); 1,470 (2000); 1,687 (2007); 1,829 (2012 projected); Race: 88.3% White, 9.0% Black, 0.4% Asian, 3.3% Hispanic of any race (2007); Density: 880.0 persons per square mile (2007); Average household size: 2.37 (2007); Median age: 39.8 (2007); Males per 100 females: 90.0 (2007); Marriage status: 16.6% never married, 62.4% now married, 8.7% widowed, 12.4% divorced (2000); Foreign born: 2.7% (2000); Ancestry (includes multiple ancestries): 19.6% Irish, 15.6% German, 12.6% Other groups, 11.3% English, 10.2% United States or American (2000).
Economy: Employment by occupation: 7.6% management, 6.2% professional, 30.3% services, 29.8% sales, 1.2% farming, 14.1% construction, 10.9% production (2000).
Income: Per capita income: $15,873 (2007); Median household income: $31,726 (2007); Average household income: $37,609 (2007); Percent of households with income of $100,000 or more: 4.4% (2007); Poverty rate: 14.0% (2000).
Education: Percent of population age 25 and over with: High school diploma (including GED) or higher: 69.9% (2007); Bachelor's degree or higher: 4.8% (2007); Master's degree or higher: 0.0% (2007).
Housing: Homeownership rate: 92.7% (2007); Median home value: $105,795 (2007); Median rent: $479 per month (2000); Median age of housing: 18 years (2000).
Transportation: Commute to work: 94.4% car, 0.0% public transportation, 1.1% walk, 3.2% work from home (2000); Travel time to work: 58.4% less than 15 minutes, 23.3% 15 to 30 minutes, 8.2% 30 to 45 minutes, 6.2% 45 to 60 minutes, 4.0% 60 minutes or more (2000)

INVERNESS HIGHLANDS SOUTH (CDP). Covers a land area of 5.642 square miles and a water area of 0.012 square miles. Located at 28.79° N. Lat.; 82.33° W. Long.
Population: 4,828 (1990); 5,781 (2000); 6,503 (2007); 7,002 (2012 projected); Race: 94.2% White, 2.4% Black, 1.1% Asian, 6.1% Hispanic of any race (2007); Density: 1,152.5 persons per square mile (2007); Average household size: 2.26 (2007); Median age: 47.2 (2007); Males per 100 females: 89.2 (2007); Marriage status: 12.5% never married, 66.0% now married, 12.4% widowed, 9.0% divorced (2000); Foreign born: 5.8%

(2000); Ancestry (includes multiple ancestries): 22.3% German, 18.3% Italian, 17.3% Irish, 13.3% Other groups, 11.6% English (2000).
Economy: Employment by occupation: 4.6% management, 21.3% professional, 23.9% services, 25.5% sales, 0.0% farming, 13.3% construction, 11.5% production (2000).
Income: Per capita income: $20,997 (2007); Median household income: $33,295 (2007); Average household income: $47,257 (2007); Percent of households with income of $100,000 or more: 7.9% (2007); Poverty rate: 9.0% (2000).
Education: Percent of population age 25 and over with: High school diploma (including GED) or higher: 78.9% (2007); Bachelor's degree or higher: 11.3% (2007); Master's degree or higher: 5.1% (2007).
Housing: Homeownership rate: 90.0% (2007); Median home value: $131,361 (2007); Median rent: $425 per month (2000); Median age of housing: 16 years (2000).
Transportation: Commute to work: 95.3% car, 0.0% public transportation, 0.5% walk, 2.1% work from home (2000); Travel time to work: 41.2% less than 15 minutes, 28.4% 15 to 30 minutes, 17.0% 30 to 45 minutes, 6.5% 45 to 60 minutes, 7.0% 60 minutes or more (2000)

LECANTO (CDP). Covers a land area of 27.045 square miles and a water area of 0.009 square miles. Located at 28.84° N. Lat.; 82.48° W. Long. Elevation is 46 feet.
Population: 3,432 (1990); 5,161 (2000); 6,327 (2007); 7,072 (2012 projected); Race: 91.6% White, 4.8% Black, 0.8% Asian, 3.5% Hispanic of any race (2007); Density: 233.9 persons per square mile (2007); Average household size: 2.72 (2007); Median age: 45.0 (2007); Males per 100 females: 105.8 (2007); Marriage status: 17.4% never married, 61.0% now married, 11.1% widowed, 10.6% divorced (2000); Foreign born: 5.0% (2000); Ancestry (includes multiple ancestries): 17.2% Irish, 16.3% German, 14.6% English, 12.1% Other groups, 8.9% United States or American (2000).
Economy: Employment by occupation: 12.2% management, 13.7% professional, 18.5% services, 28.5% sales, 0.4% farming, 13.8% construction, 12.9% production (2000).
Income: Per capita income: $21,996 (2007); Median household income: $46,423 (2007); Average household income: $55,503 (2007); Percent of households with income of $100,000 or more: 10.4% (2007); Poverty rate: 9.1% (2000).
Education: Percent of population age 25 and over with: High school diploma (including GED) or higher: 75.6% (2007); Bachelor's degree or higher: 12.3% (2007); Master's degree or higher: 4.7% (2007).
School District(s)
Citrus County School District (PK-12)
  2005-06 Enrollment: 15,720 . . . . (352) 726-1931
Housing: Homeownership rate: 85.8% (2007); Median home value: $150,478 (2007); Median rent: $405 per month (2000); Median age of housing: 14 years (2000).
Transportation: Commute to work: 89.9% car, 0.0% public transportation, 3.6% walk, 4.7% work from home (2000); Travel time to work: 29.0% less than 15 minutes, 45.0% 15 to 30 minutes, 9.2% 30 to 45 minutes, 6.5% 45 to 60 minutes, 10.4% 60 minutes or more (2000)

PINE RIDGE (CDP). Covers a land area of 25.235 square miles and a water area of 0 square miles. Located at 28.94° N. Lat.; 82.47° W. Long. Elevation is 95 feet.
Population: 3,374 (1990); 5,490 (2000); 7,198 (2007); 8,324 (2012 projected); Race: 93.3% White, 3.1% Black, 2.3% Asian, 3.6% Hispanic of any race (2007); Density: 285.2 persons per square mile (2007); Average household size: 2.34 (2007); Median age: 59.3 (2007); Males per 100 females: 88.3 (2007); Marriage status: 9.1% never married, 72.5% now married, 11.2% widowed, 7.3% divorced (2000); Foreign born: 11.8% (2000); Ancestry (includes multiple ancestries): 19.3% German, 15.9% Irish, 14.2% English, 9.6% Italian, 7.1% Other groups (2000).
Economy: Employment by occupation: 11.9% management, 27.0% professional, 21.0% services, 24.0% sales, 0.0% farming, 9.1% construction, 7.0% production (2000).
Income: Per capita income: $28,199 (2007); Median household income: $52,311 (2007); Average household income: $64,731 (2007); Percent of households with income of $100,000 or more: 15.5% (2007); Poverty rate: 5.9% (2000).
Education: Percent of population age 25 and over with: High school diploma (including GED) or higher: 82.8% (2007); Bachelor's degree or higher: 24.0% (2007); Master's degree or higher: 8.5% (2007).

SUGARMILL WOODS (CDP). Covers a land area of 26.369 square miles and a water area of 0.001 square miles. Located at 28.73° N. Lat.; 82.52° W. Long. Elevation is 82 feet.

Population: 4,073 (1990); 6,409 (2000); 8,698 (2007); 10,190 (2012 projected); Race: 96.8% White, 1.4% Black, 1.1% Asian, 1.7% Hispanic of any race (2007); Density: 329.9 persons per square mile (2007); Average household size: 2.09 (2007); Median age: 64.9 (2007); Males per 100 females: 91.8 (2007); Marriage status: 7.9% never married, 76.2% now married, 9.8% widowed, 6.1% divorced (2000); Foreign born: 5.2% (2000); Ancestry (includes multiple ancestries): 25.6% German, 19.4% English, 17.0% Irish, 9.4% Italian, 5.6% Other groups (2000).

Economy: Employment by occupation: 18.6% management, 16.3% professional, 16.7% services, 30.1% sales, 0.0% farming, 10.2% construction, 8.2% production (2000).

Income: Per capita income: $28,187 (2007); Median household income: $49,402 (2007); Average household income: $58,853 (2007); Percent of households with income of $100,000 or more: 12.7% (2007); Poverty rate: 6.4% (2000).

Education: Percent of population age 25 and over with: High school diploma (including GED) or higher: 88.7% (2007); Bachelor's degree or higher: 20.9% (2007); Master's degree or higher: 8.2% (2007).

Housing: Homeownership rate: 92.8% (2007); Median home value: $193,353 (2007); Median rent: $586 per month (2000); Median age of housing: 13 years (2000).

Transportation: Commute to work: 94.8% car, 0.0% public transportation, 0.7% walk, 4.5% work from home (2000); Travel time to work: 14.0% less than 15 minutes, 46.5% 15 to 30 minutes, 23.4% 30 to 45 minutes, 5.1% 45 to 60 minutes, 11.0% 60 minutes or more (2000)

Clay County

Located in northeastern Florida; bounded on the east by the St. Johns River; includes many small lakes. Covers a land area of 601.11 square miles, a water area of 42.59 square miles, and is located in the Eastern Time Zone. The county was founded in 1858. County seat is Green Cove Springs.

Clay County is part of the Jacksonville, FL Metropolitan Statistical Area. The entire metro area includes: Baker County, FL; Clay County, FL; Duval County, FL; Nassau County, FL; St. Johns County, FL

Population: 105,986 (1990); 140,814 (2000); 178,873 (2007); 205,422 (2012 projected); Race: 84.0% White, 8.7% Black, 2.4% Asian, 5.8% Hispanic of any race (2007); Density: 297.6 persons per square mile (2007); Average household size: 2.74 (2007); Median age: 37.2 (2007); Males per 100 females: 97.6 (2007).

Religion: Five largest groups: 18.0% Southern Baptist Convention, 9.7% Catholic Church, 4.5% The United Methodist Church, 1.6% Episcopal Church, 1.2% Presbyterian Church (U.S.A.) (2000).

Economy: Unemployment rate: 3.8% (11/2007); Total civilian labor force: 91,652 (11/2007); Leading industries: 25.0% retail trade; 15.6% health care and social assistance; 12.8% accommodation & food services (2005); Farms: 340 totaling 78,542 acres (2002); Companies that employ 500 or more persons: 2 (2005); Companies that employ 100 to 499 persons: 58 (2005); Companies that employ less than 100 persons: 3,531 (2005); Black-owned businesses: 433 (2002); Hispanic-owned businesses: 319 (2002); Asian-owned businesses: 364 (2002); Women-owned businesses: 3,155 (2002); Retail sales per capita: $11,715 (2007). Single-family building permits issued: 1,336 (2006); Multi-family building permits issued: 1,076 (2006).

Income: Per capita income: $25,380 (2007); Median household income: $57,110 (2007); Average household income: $69,202 (2007); Percent of households with income of $100,000 or more: 18.6% (2007); Poverty rate: 8.1% (2005); Bankruptcy rate: 1.86% (2006).

Taxes: Total county taxes per capita: $484 (2005); County property taxes per capita: $284 (2005).

per 100,000 population (2004); Number of physicians: 19.4 per 10,000 population (2005); Hospital beds: 17.7 per 10,000 population (2004); Hospital admissions: 836.7 per 10,000 population (2004).

Elections: 2004 Presidential election results: 76.2% Bush, 23.3% Kerry, 0.3% Nader, 0.1% Badnarik.

National and State Parks: Camp Blanding State Wildlife Management Area; Mike Roess Gold Head Branch State Park

Additional Information Contacts

Clay County Government . . . . (904) 284-6300
   http://www.claycountygov.com
City of Green Cove Springs . . . . (904) 529-2200
   http://www.greencovesprings.com
Clay County Development Authority . . . . (904) 264-7373
   http://www.clayedo.com
Orange Park Chamber of Commerce . . . . (904) 264-2651
   http://www.claychamber.org
Town of Orange Park . . . . (904) 278-3018
   http://www.townoforangepark.com

Clay County Communities

ASBURY LAKE (CDP). Covers a land area of 3.361 square miles and a water area of 0.246 square miles. Located at 30.05° N. Lat.; 81.81° W. Long. Elevation is 33 feet.

Population: 2,072 (1990); 2,228 (2000); 3,135 (2007); 3,766 (2012 projected); Race: 96.6% White, 0.4% Black, 0.9% Asian, 1.6% Hispanic of any race (2007); Density: 932.7 persons per square mile (2007); Average household size: 2.67 (2007); Median age: 46.0 (2007); Males per 100 females: 101.5 (2007); Marriage status: 15.8% never married, 72.4% now married, 3.7% widowed, 8.1% divorced (2000); Foreign born: 0.4% (2000); Ancestry (includes multiple ancestries): 19.2% German, 16.3% Irish, 16.2% United States or American, 13.8% English, 9.1% Other groups (2000).

Economy: Employment by occupation: 9.3% management, 19.3% professional, 5.7% services, 39.1% sales, 0.0% farming, 16.5% construction, 10.0% production (2000).

Income: Per capita income: $30,474 (2007); Median household income: $75,000 (2007); Average household income: $81,237 (2007); Percent of households with income of $100,000 or more: 28.7% (2007); Poverty rate: 3.8% (2000).

Education: Percent of population age 25 and over with: High school diploma (including GED) or higher: 92.5% (2007); Bachelor's degree or higher: 20.2% (2007); Master's degree or higher: 9.6% (2007).

Housing: Homeownership rate: 96.4% (2007); Median home value: $218,893 (2007); Median rent: $625 per month (2000); Median age of housing: 21 years (2000).

Transportation: Commute to work: 91.9% car, 1.6% public transportation, 0.0% walk, 5.9% work from home (2000); Travel time to work: 6.6% less than 15 minutes, 16.8% 15 to 30 minutes, 17.5% 30 to 45 minutes, 38.8% 45 to 60 minutes, 20.3% 60 minutes or more (2000)

BELLAIR-MEADOWBROOK TERRACE (CDP). Covers a land area of 5.603 square miles and a water area of 0 square miles. Located at 30.17° N. Lat.; 81.74° W. Long.

Population: 15,606 (1990); 16,539 (2000); 17,965 (2007); 19,185 (2012 projected); Race: 71.6% White, 15.8% Black, 4.2% Asian, 8.9% Hispanic of any race (2007); Density: 3,206.1 persons per square mile (2007); Average household size: 2.46 (2007); Median age: 35.3 (2007); Males per 100 females: 94.9 (2007); Marriage status: 24.1% never married, 58.9% now married, 4.7% widowed, 12.3% divorced (2000); Foreign born: 6.4% (2000); Ancestry (includes multiple ancestries): 26.7% Other groups, 12.1% German, 11.0% Irish, 10.8% United States or American, 10.3% English (2000).

Economy: Employment by occupation: 12.3% management, 16.2% professional, 17.6% services, 31.8% sales, 0.1% farming, 11.8% construction, 10.1% production (2000).

Income: Per capita income: $25,101 (2007); Median household income: $46,729 (2007); Average household income: $60,948 (2007); Percent of

Transportation: Commute to work: 95.5% car, 0.1% public transportation, 1.5% walk, 1.6% work from home (2000); Travel time to work: 23.9% less than 15 minutes, 34.9% 15 to 30 minutes, 26.3% 30 to 45 minutes, 9.4% 45 to 60 minutes, 5.6% 60 minutes or more (2000)

GREEN COVE SPRINGS (city). County seat. Covers a land area of 6.816 square miles and a water area of 2.633 square miles. Located at 29.99° N. Lat.; 81.68° W. Long. Elevation is 16 feet.

History: Green Cove Springs was established around a spring and developed as a fashionable spa in the late 1870's and 1880's. Prominent property owners here were Gail Borden, condensed milk manufacturer, and J.C. Penney, department store owner. Nearby, Penney built the Penney Farms Memorial Home Community for retired religious leaders of all denominations.

Population: 4,646 (1990); 5,378 (2000); 6,209 (2007); 6,833 (2012 projected); Race: 68.9% White, 26.0% Black, 0.6% Asian, 7.4% Hispanic of any race (2007); Density: 910.9 persons per square mile (2007); Average household size: 2.58 (2007); Median age: 40.0 (2007); Males per 100 females: 101.1 (2007); Marriage status: 18.7% never married, 60.2% now married, 8.3% widowed, 12.8% divorced (2000); Foreign born: 5.4% (2000); Ancestry (includes multiple ancestries): 26.7% Other groups, 10.8% English, 9.5% United States or American, 9.3% Irish, 9.2% German (2000).

Economy: Single-family building permits issued: 55 (2006); Multi-family building permits issued: 0 (2006); Employment by occupation: 8.3% management, 13.4% professional, 19.1% services, 25.7% sales, 0.6% farming, 14.7% construction, 18.2% production (2000).

Income: Per capita income: $21,854 (2007); Median household income: $39,360 (2007); Average household income: $54,318 (2007); Percent of households with income of $100,000 or more: 14.4% (2007); Poverty rate: 19.1% (2000).

Education: Percent of population age 25 and over with: High school diploma (including GED) or higher: 76.4% (2007); Bachelor's degree or higher: 16.3% (2007); Master's degree or higher: 6.3% (2007).

School District(s)
Clay County School District (PK-12)
   2005-06 Enrollment: 32,605 . . . . (904) 284-6510

Housing: Homeownership rate: 70.8% (2007); Median home value: $128,673 (2007); Median rent: $322 per month (2000); Median age of housing: 26 years (2000).

Safety: Violent crime rate: 124.4 per 10,000 population; Property crime rate: 413.7 per 10,000 population (2006).

Transportation: Commute to work: 88.9% car, 0.6% public transportation, 2.4% walk, 2.2% work from home (2000); Travel time to work: 33.9% less than 15 minutes, 23.0% 15 to 30 minutes, 20.6% 30 to 45 minutes, 15.8% 45 to 60 minutes, 6.8% 60 minutes or more (2000)

Additional Information Contacts
City of Green Cove Springs . . . . (904) 529-2200
   http://www.greencovesprings.com

KEYSTONE HEIGHTS (city). Covers a land area of 4.544 square miles and a water area of 0.085 square miles. Located at 29.78° N. Lat.; 82.03° W. Long. Elevation is 141 feet.

History: Keystone Heights developed as a resort town in the lake region. First known as Brookly, it was renamed in 1922 by J.J. Lawrence of Pennsylvania for his home Keystone State.

Population: 1,321 (1990); 1,349 (2000); 1,382 (2007); 1,405 (2012 projected); Race: 94.4% White, 0.7% Black, 0.7% Asian, 3.5% Hispanic of any race (2007); Density: 304.1 persons per square mile (2007); Average household size: 2.55 (2007); Median age: 37.8 (2007); Males per 100 females: 89.1 (2007); Marriage status: 22.9% never married, 57.6% now married, 8.7% widowed, 10.9% divorced (2000); Foreign born: 2.1% (2000); Ancestry (includes multiple ancestries): 18.3% English, 15.1% German, 12.7% Irish, 10.5% United States or American, 8.2% Other groups (2000).

diploma (including GED) or higher: 90.4% (2007); Bachelor's degree or higher: 20.3% (2007); Master's degree or higher: 6.7% (2007).

School District(s)
Clay County School District (PK-12)
   2005-06 Enrollment: 32,605 . . . . (904) 284-6510

Housing: Homeownership rate: 83.2% (2007); Median home value: $129,167 (2007); Median rent: $431 per month (2000); Median age of housing: 27 years (2000).

Newspapers: Lake Region Monitor (General - Circulation 2,175)

Transportation: Commute to work: 92.6% car, 0.0% public transportation, 3.2% walk, 3.5% work from home (2000); Travel time to work: 36.0% less than 15 minutes, 14.7% 15 to 30 minutes, 20.1% 30 to 45 minutes, 18.6% 45 to 60 minutes, 10.7% 60 minutes or more (2000)

LAKESIDE (CDP). Covers a land area of 15.155 square miles and a water area of 2.264 square miles. Located at 30.13° N. Lat.; 81.76° W. Long. Elevation is 66 feet.

Population: 29,137 (1990); 30,927 (2000); 33,811 (2007); 36,215 (2012 projected); Race: 81.9% White, 9.7% Black, 2.9% Asian, 7.1% Hispanic of any race (2007); Density: 2,231.1 persons per square mile (2007); Average household size: 2.77 (2007); Median age: 36.8 (2007); Males per 100 females: 96.2 (2007); Marriage status: 20.7% never married, 64.4% now married, 4.4% widowed, 10.6% divorced (2000); Foreign born: 5.7% (2000); Ancestry (includes multiple ancestries): 20.8% Other groups, 14.7% German, 12.4% Irish, 11.9% United States or American, 10.9% English (2000).

Economy: Employment by occupation: 15.1% management, 19.3% professional, 12.2% services, 32.8% sales, 0.1% farming, 11.4% construction, 9.2% production (2000).

Income: Per capita income: $23,944 (2007); Median household income: $56,496 (2007); Average household income: $66,128 (2007); Percent of households with income of $100,000 or more: 17.1% (2007); Poverty rate: 4.5% (2000).

Education: Percent of population age 25 and over with: High school diploma (including GED) or higher: 90.0% (2007); Bachelor's degree or higher: 21.8% (2007); Master's degree or higher: 7.0% (2007).

Housing: Homeownership rate: 77.3% (2007); Median home value: $155,393 (2007); Median rent: $609 per month (2000); Median age of housing: 18 years (2000).

Transportation: Commute to work: 94.3% car, 0.2% public transportation, 0.8% walk, 2.9% work from home (2000); Travel time to work: 17.9% less than 15 minutes, 26.8% 15 to 30 minutes, 28.9% 30 to 45 minutes, 18.1% 45 to 60 minutes, 8.3% 60 minutes or more (2000)

MIDDLEBURG (CDP). Covers a land area of 18.284 square miles and a water area of 0 square miles. Located at 30.05° N. Lat.; 81.90° W. Long. Elevation is 33 feet.

History: Middleburg was a shipping port for cotton in the 1840's, where sea-going vessels could enter Black Creek.

Population: 6,223 (1990); 10,338 (2000); 12,781 (2007); 14,558 (2012 projected); Race: 91.9% White, 4.1% Black, 0.6% Asian, 3.4% Hispanic of any race (2007); Density: 699.0 persons per square mile (2007); Average household size: 2.88 (2007); Median age: 35.3 (2007); Males per 100 females: 99.5 (2007); Marriage status: 21.6% never married, 63.3% now married, 4.0% widowed, 11.1% divorced (2000); Foreign born: 2.2% (2000); Ancestry (includes multiple ancestries): 14.4% United States or American, 14.2% German, 13.4% English, 13.1% Irish, 12.7% Other groups (2000).

Economy: Employment by occupation: 10.2% management, 11.3% professional, 15.0% services, 32.0% sales, 0.8% farming, 16.5% construction, 14.2% production (2000).

Income: Per capita income: $21,269 (2007); Median household income: $52,436 (2007); Average household income: $61,210 (2007); Percent of households with income of $100,000 or more: 12.1% (2007); Poverty rate: 9.2% (2000).

Education: Percent of population age 25 and over with: High school diploma (including GED) or higher: 80.9% (2007); Bachelor's degree or higher: 8.8% (2007); Master's degree or higher: 2.3% (2007).

School District(s)
Clay County School District (PK-12)
  2005-06 Enrollment: 32,605 . . . . (904) 284-6510

Housing: Homeownership rate: 88.5% (2007); Median home value: $126,957 (2007); Median rent: $453 per month (2000); Median age of housing: 11 years (2000).

Transportation: Commute to work: 97.0% car, 0.0% public transportation, 0.8% walk, 1.3% work from home (2000); Travel time to work: 10.5% less than 15 minutes, 20.0% 15 to 30 minutes, 26.7% 30 to 45 minutes, 20.0% 45 to 60 minutes, 22.8% 60 minutes or more (2000)

ORANGE PARK (town).

Covers a land area of 3.896 square miles and a water area of 1.655 square miles. Located at 30.16° N. Lat.; 81.70° W. Long. Elevation is 13 feet.

History: Orange Park was established on land granted to Zephaniah Kingsley in 1790 by Spain. In the early 1800's Kingsley owned much land on Fort George Island and engaged in an active slave trade, bringing slaves from Africa in his own ships. Orange Park was founded on part of the original Kingsley plantation.

Population: 9,491 (1990); 9,081 (2000); 9,112 (2007); 9,221 (2012 projected); Race: 79.4% White, 13.0% Black, 2.8% Asian, 6.3% Hispanic of any race (2007); Density: 2,339.0 persons per square mile (2007); Average household size: 2.56 (2007); Median age: 44.7 (2007); Males per 100 females: 92.3 (2007); Marriage status: 19.3% never married, 60.7% now married, 8.7% widowed, 11.3% divorced (2000); Foreign born: 5.8% (2000); Ancestry (includes multiple ancestries): 18.7% Other groups, 16.6% English, 14.6% German, 12.5% Irish, 11.1% United States or American (2000).

Economy: Single-family building permits issued: 6 (2006); Multi-family building permits issued: 4 (2006); Employment by occupation: 12.0% management, 21.3% professional, 15.4% services, 29.4% sales, 0.0% farming, 11.0% construction, 11.0% production (2000).

Income: Per capita income: $27,206 (2007); Median household income: $52,163 (2007); Average household income: $67,103 (2007); Percent of households with income of $100,000 or more: 17.0% (2007); Poverty rate: 7.5% (2000).

Education: Percent of population age 25 and over with: High school diploma (including GED) or higher: 87.6% (2007); Bachelor's degree or higher: 25.6% (2007); Master's degree or higher: 10.4% (2007).

School District(s)
Clay County School District (PK-12)
  2005-06 Enrollment: 32,605 . . . . (904) 284-6510

Four-year College(s)
Florida Metropolitan University-Orange Park (Private, For-profit)
  Fall 2006 Enrollment: 725 . . . . (904) 264-9122
  2006-07 Tuition: In-state $10,320; Out-of-state $10,320

Two-year College(s)
North Florida Institute (Private, For-profit)
  Fall 2006 Enrollment: 348 . . . . (904) 269-7086

Housing: Homeownership rate: 65.1% (2007); Median home value: $174,027 (2007); Median rent: $554 per month (2000); Median age of housing: 25 years (2000).

Hospitals: Orange Park Medical Center (224 beds)

Safety: Violent crime rate: 62.0 per 10,000 population; Property crime rate: 321.6 per 10,000 population (2006).

Newspapers: Clay Today (General - Circulation 10,000); The Jax Air News (General - Circulation 12,000)

Transportation: Commute to work: 91.6% car, 0.9% public transportation, 2.8% walk, 3.4% work from home (2000); Travel time to work: 27.9% less than 15 minutes, 29.8% 15 to 30 minutes, 27.6% 30 to 45 minutes, 10.8% 45 to 60 minutes, 3.9% 60 minutes or more (2000)

Additional Information Contacts
Clay County Development Authority . . . . (904) 264-7373
  http://www.clayedo.com
Orange Park Chamber of Commerce . . . . (904) 264-2651
  http://www.claychamber.org
Town of Orange Park. . . . . (904) 278-3018
  http://www.townoforangepark.com

PENNEY FARMS (town).

Covers a land area of 1.399 square miles and a water area of 0 square miles. Located at 29.98° N. Lat.; 81.81° W. Long. Elevation is 95 feet.

Population: 660 (1990); 580 (2000); 625 (2007); 660 (2012 projected); Race: 91.8% White, 6.9% Black, 0.2% Asian, 0.6% Hispanic of any race (2007); Density: 446.9 persons per square mile (2007); Average household size: 2.06 (2007); Median age: 76.9 (2007); Males per 100 females: 68.0 (2007); Marriage status: 9.3% never married, 68.0% now married, 17.0% widowed, 5.8% divorced (2000); Foreign born: 5.2% (2000); Ancestry (includes multiple ancestries): 28.9% English, 14.3% German, 8.6% United States or American, 6.1% Scotch-Irish, 5.8% Other groups (2000).

Economy: Single-family building permits issued: 6 (2006); Multi-family building permits issued: 0 (2006); Employment by occupation: 6.6% management, 35.5% professional, 18.4% services, 25.0% sales, 3.9% farming, 6.6% construction, 3.9% production (2000).

Income: Per capita income: $26,637 (2007); Median household income: $40,952 (2007); Average household income: $50,806 (2007); Percent of households with income of $100,000 or more: 9.2% (2007); Poverty rate: 16.4% (2000).

Education: Percent of population age 25 and over with: High school diploma (including GED) or higher: 93.6% (2007); Bachelor's degree or higher: 56.5% (2007); Master's degree or higher: 33.9% (2007).

Housing: Homeownership rate: 32.9% (2007); Median home value: $126,190 (2007); Median rent: $392 per month (2000); Median age of housing: 37 years (2000).

Transportation: Commute to work: 88.2% car, 0.0% public transportation, 2.6% walk, 6.6% work from home (2000); Travel time to work: 35.2% less than 15 minutes, 36.6% 15 to 30 minutes, 15.5% 30 to 45 minutes, 12.7% 45 to 60 minutes, 0.0% 60 minutes or more (2000)

Collier County

Located in southern Florida, on the Gulf of Mexico; swampy area, including the Everglades and Ten Thousand Islands. Covers a land area of 2,025.34 square miles, a water area of 279.59 square miles, and is located in the Eastern Time Zone. The county was founded in 1923. County seat is East Naples.

Collier County is part of the Naples-Marco Island, FL Metropolitan Statistical Area. The entire metro area includes: Collier County, FL

Weather Station: Immokalee 3 NNW										Elevation: 32 feet	
	Jan	Feb	Mar	Apr	May	Jun	Jul	Aug	Sep	Oct	Nov	Dec
High	76	78	82	85	89	91	92	91	90	86	82	78
Low	52	53	56	59	65	70	72	72	72	66	60	54
Precip	2.3	2.3	3.0	2.4	4.2	7.9	7.0	7.5	6.4	2.8	2.3	1.8
Snow	0.0	0.0	0.0	0.0	0.0	0.0	0.0	0.0	0.0	0.0	0.0	0.0

High and Low temperatures in degrees Fahrenheit; Precipitation and Snow in inches

Weather Station: Naples										Elevation: 3 feet	
	Jan	Feb	Mar	Apr	May	Jun	Jul	Aug	Sep	Oct	Nov	Dec
High	77	78	81	84	88	90	92	92	91	88	83	78
Low	54	55	58	62	67	72	73	73	73	68	62	56
Precip	2.1	2.2	2.5	2.0	4.3	8.2	8.0	7.7	8.2	3.7	2.0	1.5
Snow	0.0	0.0	0.0	0.0	0.0	0.0	0.0	0.0	0.0	0.0	0.0	0.0

High and Low temperatures in degrees Fahrenheit; Precipitation and Snow in inches

Population: 152,099 (1990); 251,377 (2000); 329,495 (2007); 389,401 (2012 projected); Race: 83.2% White, 5.0% Black, 0.9% Asian, 25.4% Hispanic of any race (2007); Density: 162.7 persons per square mile (2007); Average household size: 2.42 (2007); Median age: 43.4 (2007); Males per 100 females: 101.8 (2007).

Religion: Five largest groups: 19.3% Catholic Church, 3.8% Southern Baptist Convention, 2.1% The United Methodist Church, 1.7% Presbyterian Church (U.S.A.), 1.7% Jewish Estimate (2000).

Economy: Unemployment rate: 4.7% (11/2007); Total civilian labor force: 158,664 (11/2007); Leading industries: 18.4% retail trade; 14.9% accommodation & food services; 14.7% construction (2005); Farms: 273 totaling 180,852 acres (2002); Companies that employ 500 or more persons: 8 (2005); Companies that employ 100 to 499 persons: 171 (2005); Companies that employ less than 100 persons: 10,325 (2005); Black-owned businesses: 565 (2002); Hispanic-owned businesses: 3,123 (2002); Asian-owned businesses: 259 (2002); Women-owned businesses: 8,279 (2002); Retail sales per capita: $19,338 (2007). Single-family building permits issued: 2,829 (2006); Multi-family building permits issued: 1,959 (2006).

Income: Per capita income: $35,186 (2007); Median household income: $55,984 (2007); Average household income: $84,581 (2007); Percent of

households with income of $100,000 or more: 23.7% (2007); Poverty rate: 9.6% (2005); Bankruptcy rate: 0.49% (2006).

Taxes: Total county taxes per capita: $899 (2005); County property taxes per capita: $694 (2007).

Education: Percent of population age 25 and over with: High school diploma (including GED) or higher: 82.8% (2007); Bachelor's degree or higher: 28.9% (2007); Master's degree or higher: 10.2% (2007).

Housing: Homeownership rate: 77.3% (2007); Median home value: $365,397 (2007); Median rent: $669 per month (2000); Median age of housing: 13 years (2000).

Health: Birth rate: 134.7 per 10,000 population (2006); Death rate: 77.3 per 10,000 population (2006); Age-adjusted cancer mortality rate: 143.3 deaths per 100,000 population (2004); Air Quality Index: 97.0% good, 3.0% moderate, 0.0% unhealthy for sensitive individuals, 0.0% unhealthy (percent of days in 2006); Number of physicians: 25.9 per 10,000 population (2005); Hospital beds: 21.2 per 10,000 population (2004); Hospital admissions: 1,171.8 per 10,000 population (2004).

Elections: 2004 Presidential election results: 65.0% Bush, 34.1% Kerry, 0.5% Nader, 0.1% Badnarik

National and State Parks: Barefoot Beach State Preserve; Big Cypress National Preserve; Collier-Seminole State Park; Delnor-Wiggins Pass State Park; Fakahatchee Strand Preserve State Park

Additional Information Contacts

Collier County Government . . . . (239) 252-8999
   http://www.colliergov.net
Golden Gate Area Chamber of Commerce . . . . (239) 352-0508
   http://www.goldengateonline.com
Immokalee Chamber of Commerce. . . . . (941) 657-3237
   http://www.immokaleechamber.org
Marco Island Chamber of Commerce . . . . (941) 394-7549
   http://www.marcoislandchamber.org
Naples Area Chamber of Commerce. . . . . (941) 455-3100
   http://www.napleschamber.org

Collier County Communities

CHOKOLOSKEE (CDP). Covers a land area of 0.280 square miles and a water area of 0 square miles. Located at 25.81° N. Lat.; 81.36° W. Long. Elevation is 10 feet.

Population: 347 (1990); 404 (2000); 493 (2007); 569 (2012 projected); Race: 97.6% White, 0.0% Black, 0.0% Asian, 4.5% Hispanic of any race (2007); Density: 1,763.4 persons per square mile (2007); Average household size: 2.17 (2007); Median age: 50.1 (2007); Males per 100 females: 95.6 (2007); Marriage status: 5.2% never married, 75.0% now married, 5.5% widowed, 14.3% divorced (2000); Foreign born: 2.7% (2000); Ancestry (includes multiple ancestries): 50.3% United States or American, 10.9% English, 10.5% German, 8.9% Irish, 3.5% Hungarian (2000).

Economy: Employment by occupation: 11.1% management, 17.6% professional, 31.7% services, 23.6% sales, 4.5% farming, 4.0% construction, 7.5% production (2000).

Income: Per capita income: $23,347 (2007); Median household income: $37,262 (2007); Average household income: $50,705 (2007); Percent of households with income of $100,000 or more: 10.6% (2007); Poverty rate: 1.6% (2000).

Education: Percent of population age 25 and over with: High school diploma (including GED) or higher: 69.7% (2007); Bachelor's degree or higher: 13.7% (2007); Master's degree or higher: 3.7% (2007).

Housing: Homeownership rate: 84.1% (2007); Median home value: $178,750 (2007); Median rent: $333 per month (2000); Median age of housing: 27 years (2000).

Transportation: Commute to work: 81.4% car, 0.0% public transportation, 9.0% walk, 0.0% work from home (2000); Travel time to work: 72.4% less than 15 minutes, 12.1% 15 to 30 minutes, 8.0% 30 to 45 minutes, 4.0% 45 to 60 minutes, 3.5% 60 minutes or more (2000)

EVERGLADES (city). Aka Everglades City. Covers a land area of 0.933 square miles and a water area of 0.252 square miles. Located at 25.85° N. Lat.; 81.38° W. Long.

History: The city of Everglades developed on the Barron River, inland from the western boundary of the Everglades, as the seat of Collier County.

Population: 321 (1990); 479 (2000); 588 (2007); 682 (2012 projected); Race: 93.0% White, 2.0% Black, 0.9% Asian, 8.8% Hispanic of any race (2007); Density: 630.0 persons per square mile (2007); Average household size: 2.04 (2007); Median age: 57.0 (2007); Males per 100 females: 104.9

(2007); Marriage status: 11.4% never married, 71.7% now married, 5.8% widowed, 11.0% divorced (2000); Foreign born: 4.8% (2000); Ancestry (includes multiple ancestries): 17.2% German, 16.2% English, 14.9% Irish, 10.4% Other groups, 8.7% United States or American (2000).

Economy: Single-family building permits issued: 15 (2006); Multi-family building permits issued: 0 (2006); Employment by occupation: 7.1% management, 11.7% professional, 27.4% services, 26.9% sales, 13.7% farming, 4.6% construction, 8.6% production (2000).

Income: Per capita income: $25,497 (2007); Median household income: $39,000 (2007); Average household income: $52,057 (2007); Percent of households with income of $100,000 or more: 6.9% (2007); Poverty rate: 6.0% (2000).

Education: Percent of population age 25 and over with: High school diploma (including GED) or higher: 83.2% (2007); Bachelor's degree or higher: 17.9% (2007); Master's degree or higher: 6.4% (2007).

School District(s)

Collier County School District (PK-12)
   2005-06 Enrollment: 42,105 . . . . (239) 377-0212

Housing: Homeownership rate: 79.2% (2007); Median home value: $256,250 (2007); Median rent: $510 per month (2000); Median age of housing: 22 years (2000).

Transportation: Commute to work: 77.4% car, 0.0% public transportation, 13.8% walk, 5.6% work from home (2000); Travel time to work: 63.6% less than 15 minutes, 17.9% 15 to 30 minutes, 4.3% 30 to 45 minutes, 9.8% 45 to 60 minutes, 4.3% 60 minutes or more (2000)

Airports: Everglades Airpark

GOLDEN GATE (CDP). Aka Golden Gate Estates. Covers a land area of 4.036 square miles and a water area of 0.038 square miles. Located at 26.18° N. Lat.; 81.70° W. Long. Elevation is 10 feet.

Population: 14,116 (1990); 20,951 (2000); 22,869 (2007); 24,862 (2012 projected); Race: 68.4% White, 13.4% Black, 0.8% Asian, 55.2% Hispanic of any race (2007); Density: 5,665.9 persons per square mile (2007); Average household size: 3.30 (2007); Median age: 29.8 (2007); Males per 100 females: 115.0 (2007); Marriage status: 32.1% never married, 53.9% now married, 3.3% widowed, 10.7% divorced (2000); Foreign born: 33.5% (2000); Ancestry (includes multiple ancestries): 37.6% Other groups, 9.4% German, 7.8% Irish, 7.4% United States or American, 5.8% Haitian (2000).

Economy: Employment by occupation: 6.8% management, 9.4% professional, 25.0% services, 23.7% sales, 0.5% farming, 22.1% construction, 12.5% production (2000).

Income: Per capita income: $15,881 (2007); Median household income: $43,878 (2007); Average household income: $52,198 (2007); Percent of households with income of $100,000 or more: 8.4% (2007); Poverty rate: 14.1% (2000).

Education: Percent of population age 25 and over with: High school diploma (including GED) or higher: 68.2% (2007); Bachelor's degree or higher: 11.0% (2007); Master's degree or higher: 3.0% (2007).

Housing: Homeownership rate: 56.3% (2007); Median home value: $231,645 (2007); Median rent: $639 per month (2000); Median age of housing: 15 years (2000).

Transportation: Commute to work: 92.9% car, 0.3% public transportation, 1.6% walk, 1.6% work from home (2000); Travel time to work: 17.7% less than 15 minutes, 53.9% 15 to 30 minutes, 21.9% 30 to 45 minutes, 3.2% 45 to 60 minutes, 3.3% 60 minutes or more (2000)

GOODLAND (CDP). Aka Collier City. Covers a land area of 0.212 square miles and a water area of 0.190 square miles. Located at 25.92° N. Lat.; 81.64° W. Long. Elevation is 7 feet.

Population: 348 (1990); 320 (2000); 388 (2007); 446 (2012 projected); Race: 98.5% White, 0.5% Black, 0.5% Asian, 2.3% Hispanic of any race (2007); Density: 1,833.3 persons per square mile (2007); Average household size: 1.70 (2007); Median age: 54.3 (2007); Males per 100 females: 110.9 (2007); Marriage status: 13.8% never married, 49.2% now married, 14.8% widowed, 22.2% divorced (2000); Foreign born: 0.0% (2000); Ancestry (includes multiple ancestries): 18.6% Irish, 17.6% German, 11.8% English, 11.3% Czech, 7.2% Scottish (2000).

Economy: Employment by occupation: 23.8% management, 0.0% professional, 32.1% services, 15.5% sales, 0.0% farming, 19.0% construction, 9.5% production (2000).

Income: Per capita income: $28,189 (2007); Median household income: $31,957 (2007); Average household income: $47,971 (2007); Percent of households with income of $100,000 or more: 10.1% (2007); Poverty rate: 14.0% (2000).

Housing: Homeownership rate: 76.8% (2007); Median home value: $457,317 (2007); Median rent: $604 per month (2000); Median age of housing: 29 years (2000).
Transportation: Commute to work: 89.2% car, 0.0% public transportation, 0.0% walk, 0.0% work from home (2000); Travel time to work: 91.9% less than 15 minutes, 0.0% 15 to 30 minutes, 0.0% 30 to 45 minutes, 8.1% 45 to 60 minutes, 0.0% 60 minutes or more (2000)

IMMOKALEE (CDP).
Covers a land area of 8.070 square miles and a water area of 0.008 square miles. Located at 26.42° N. Lat.; 81.42° W. Long. Elevation is 33 feet.
History: A sawmill was built in Immokalee in 1884, at the location of an Episcopal Indian Mission School. The area was first known as Gopher Ridge. The name of Immokalee is of Indian origin meaning "tumbling water."
Population: 14,317 (1990); 19,763 (2000); 20,095 (2007); 20,924 (2012 projected); Race: 32.3% White, 16.7% Black, 0.2% Asian, 75.5% Hispanic of any race (2007); Density: 2,490.2 persons per square mile (2007); Average household size: 4.29 (2007); Median age: 25.9 (2007); Males per 100 females: 130.7 (2007); Marriage status: 43.8% never married, 47.9% now married, 3.3% widowed, 5.1% divorced (2000); Foreign born: 45.8% (2000); Ancestry (includes multiple ancestries): 60.8% Other groups, 10.8% Haitian, 3.3% United States or American, 0.9% Irish, 0.5% English (2000).
Economy: Employment by occupation: 6.9% management, 4.5% professional, 20.5% services, 12.7% sales, 27.0% farming, 14.8% construction, 13.5% production (2000).
Income: Per capita income: $9,795 (2007); Median household income: $28,545 (2007); Average household income: $37,519 (2007); Percent of households with income of $100,000 or more: 5.0% (2007); Poverty rate: 39.8% (2000).
Education: Percent of population age 25 and over with: High school diploma (including GED) or higher: 23.7% (2007); Bachelor's degree or higher: 2.1% (2007); Master's degree or higher: 0.4% (2007).
School District(s)
Collier County School District (PK-12)
   2005-06 Enrollment: 42,105 . . . . (239) 377-0212
Housing: Homeownership rate: 38.3% (2007); Median home value: $127,461 (2007); Median rent: $327 per month (2000); Median age of housing: 20 years (2000).
Transportation: Commute to work: 73.6% car, 18.2% public transportation, 6.3% walk, 1.3% work from home (2000); Travel time to work: 23.7% less than 15 minutes, 17.5% 15 to 30 minutes, 22.2% 30 to 45 minutes, 16.1% 45 to 60 minutes, 20.5% 60 minutes or more (2000)
Airports: Immokalee
Additional Information Contacts
Immokalee Chamber of Commerce. . . . . (941) 657-3237
   http://www.immokaleechamber.org

LELY (CDP).
Covers a land area of 1.462 square miles and a water area of 0.011 square miles. Located at 26.10° N. Lat.; 81.73° W. Long. Elevation is 7 feet.
Population: 2,993 (1990); 3,857 (2000); 4,909 (2007); 5,737 (2012 projected); Race: 95.3% White, 1.1% Black, 0.8% Asian, 7.2% Hispanic of any race (2007); Density: 3,358.6 persons per square mile (2007); Average household size: 1.85 (2007); Median age: 65.2 (2007); Males per 100 females: 85.4 (2007); Marriage status: 7.4% never married, 65.0% now married, 18.0% widowed, 9.6% divorced (2000); Foreign born: 5.8% (2000); Ancestry (includes multiple ancestries): 21.2% German, 20.8% Irish, 17.3% English, 11.8% Italian, 5.8% Other groups (2000).
Economy: Employment by occupation: 20.3% management, 21.2% professional, 13.6% services, 30.6% sales, 0.0% farming, 7.1% construction, 7.3% production (2000).
Income: Per capita income: $34,152 (2007); Median household income: $48,080 (2007); Average household income: $60,206 (2007); Percent of households with income of $100,000 or more: 13.7% (2007); Poverty rate: 6.3% (2000).
Education: Percent of population age 25 and over with: High school diploma (including GED) or higher: 89.3% (2007); Bachelor's degree or higher: 27.9% (2007); Master's degree or higher: 10.9% (2007).

Transportation: Commute to work: 95.1% car, 0.0% public transportation, 1.6% walk, 3.3% work from home (2000); Travel time to work: 30.9% less than 15 minutes, 42.3% 15 to 30 minutes, 22.8% 30 to 45 minutes, 3.0% 45 to 60 minutes, 1.0% 60 minutes or more (2000)

LELY RESORT (CDP).
Covers a land area of 5.226 square miles and a water area of 0.004 square miles. Located at 26.08° N. Lat.; 81.70° W. Long. Elevation is 7 feet.
Population: 56 (1990); 1,426 (2000); 2,683 (2007); 3,572 (2012 projected); Race: 75.1% White, 11.6% Black, 0.5% Asian, 42.7% Hispanic of any race (2007); Density: 513.4 persons per square mile (2007); Average household size: 2.39 (2007); Median age: 35.7 (2007); Males per 100 females: 108.6 (2007); Marriage status: 20.4% never married, 65.5% now married, 8.2% widowed, 5.9% divorced (2000); Foreign born: 19.0% (2000); Ancestry (includes multiple ancestries): 21.9% Other groups, 16.8% German, 14.6% Irish, 14.2% Italian, 7.6% Polish (2000).
Economy: Employment by occupation: 5.7% management, 13.6% professional, 15.8% services, 45.6% sales, 0.0% farming, 8.1% construction, 11.1% production (2000).
Income: Per capita income: $34,105 (2007); Median household income: $56,800 (2007); Average household income: $81,408 (2007); Percent of households with income of $100,000 or more: 19.2% (2007); Poverty rate: 6.9% (2000).
Education: Percent of population age 25 and over with: High school diploma (including GED) or higher: 88.3% (2007); Bachelor's degree or higher: 32.3% (2007); Master's degree or higher: 11.7% (2007).
Housing: Homeownership rate: 60.9% (2007); Median home value: $370,062 (2007); Median rent: $717 per month (2000); Median age of housing: 3 years (2000).
Transportation: Commute to work: 95.9% car, 0.0% public transportation, 0.0% walk, 4.1% work from home (2000); Travel time to work: 33.6% less than 15 minutes, 44.8% 15 to 30 minutes, 17.2% 30 to 45 minutes, 2.0% 45 to 60 minutes, 2.5% 60 minutes or more (2000)

MARCO ISLAND (city).
Covers a land area of 10.574 square miles and a water area of 6.522 square miles. Located at 25.94° N. Lat.; 81.71° W. Long. Elevation is 5 feet.
Population: 9,772 (1990); 14,879 (2000); 17,990 (2007); 20,554 (2012 projected); Race: 97.3% White, 0.4% Black, 0.8% Asian, 7.0% Hispanic of any race (2007); Density: 1,701.3 persons per square mile (2007); Average household size: 2.07 (2007); Median age: 60.1 (2007); Males per 100 females: 98.3 (2007); Marriage status: 9.5% never married, 73.6% now married, 8.2% widowed, 8.7% divorced (2000); Foreign born: 12.3% (2000); Ancestry (includes multiple ancestries): 23.4% German, 19.3% Irish, 14.9% English, 13.4% Italian, 5.3% Other groups (2000).
Economy: Single-family building permits issued: 73 (2006); Multi-family building permits issued: 0 (2006); Employment by occupation: 18.8% management, 17.0% professional, 20.0% services, 32.8% sales, 0.4% farming, 6.2% construction, 4.8% production (2000).
Income: Per capita income: $49,605 (2007); Median household income: $66,803 (2007); Average household income: $102,133 (2007); Percent of households with income of $100,000 or more: 31.2% (2007); Poverty rate: 5.4% (2000).
Education: Percent of population age 25 and over with: High school diploma (including GED) or higher: 92.7% (2007); Bachelor's degree or higher: 37.0% (2007); Master's degree or higher: 13.3% (2007).
School District(s)
Collier County School District (PK-12)
   2005-06 Enrollment: 42,105 . . . . (239) 377-0212
Housing: Homeownership rate: 87.4% (2007); Median home value: $688,303 (2007); Median rent: $785 per month (2000); Median age of housing: 16 years (2000).
Safety: Violent crime rate: 9.2 per 10,000 population; Property crime rate: 126.4 per 10,000 population (2006).
Newspapers: Marco Island Eagle (General - Circulation 7,938)
Transportation: Commute to work: 86.3% car, 0.2% public transportation, 2.6% walk, 8.7% work from home (2000); Travel time to work: 62.9% less than 15 minutes, 16.2% 15 to 30 minutes, 10.4% 30 to 45 minutes, 4.6% 45 to 60 minutes, 5.9% 60 minutes or more (2000)
Airports: Marco Island
Additional Information Contacts

NAPLES (city). Covers a land area of 12.025 square miles and a water area of 2.379 square miles. Located at 26.15° N. Lat.; 81.79° W. Long. Elevation is 3 feet.

History: Naples was laid out as a winter resort in the 1880's, and named for the Italian city. The resort flourished after the railroad reached Naples.

Population: 19,903 (1990); 20,976 (2000); 22,439 (2007); 24,134 (2012 projected); Race: 91.2% White, 5.2% Black, 0.5% Asian, 3.4% Hispanic of any race (2007); Density: 1,866.0 persons per square mile (2007); Average household size: 1.92 (2007); Median age: 61.8 (2007); Males per 100 females: 87.9 (2007); Marriage status: 11.9% never married, 65.6% now married, 12.1% widowed, 10.4% divorced (2000); Foreign born: 8.9% (2000); Ancestry (includes multiple ancestries): 20.0% German, 18.7% English, 15.5% Irish, 7.3% Italian, 6.9% Other groups (2000).

Economy: Single-family building permits issued: 96 (2006); Multi-family building permits issued: 48 (2006); Employment by occupation: 26.5% management, 17.9% professional, 14.0% services, 30.4% sales, 0.2% farming, 6.4% construction, 4.6% production (2000).

Income: Per capita income: $64,763 (2007); Median household income: $75,200 (2007); Average household income: $124,294 (2007); Percent of households with income of $100,000 or more: 38.8% (2007); Poverty rate: 5.9% (2000).

Education: Percent of population age 25 and over with: High school diploma (including GED) or higher: 92.9% (2007); Bachelor's degree or higher: 45.1% (2007); Master's degree or higher: 15.5% (2007).

School District(s)
Collier County School District (PK-12)
    2005-06 Enrollment: 42,105 . . . . (239) 377-0212

Four-year College(s)
Ave Maria University (Private, Not-for-profit, Roman Catholic)
    Fall 2006 Enrollment: 367 . . . . (239) 280-2500
    2006-07 Tuition: In-state $15,805; Out-of-state $15,805
International College (Private, Not-for-profit)
    Fall 2006 Enrollment: 1,640 . . . . (239) 513-1122
    2006-07 Tuition: In-state $10,100; Out-of-state $10,100

Vocational/Technical School(s)
Lorenzo Walker Institute of Technology (Public)
    Fall 2006 Enrollment: 793 . . . . (239) 377-0900
    2006-07 Tuition: $1,923

Housing: Homeownership rate: 79.8% (2007); Median home value: $918,600 (2007); Median rent: $621 per month (2000); Median age of housing: 24 years (2000).

Hospitals: NCH Healthcare System (446 beds); Physicians Regional Medical Center (83 beds); Willough at Naples (92 beds)

Safety: Violent crime rate: 24.0 per 10,000 population; Property crime rate: 389.1 per 10,000 population (2006).

Newspapers: Everglades Echo (General - Circulation 1,000); Golden Gate Gazette (General - Circulation 7,000); Naples Daily News (Circulation 66,976)

Transportation: Commute to work: 79.1% car, 0.5% public transportation, 4.3% walk, 12.6% work from home (2000); Travel time to work: 58.0% less than 15 minutes, 31.2% 15 to 30 minutes, 5.8% 30 to 45 minutes, 2.2% 45 to 60 minutes, 2.8% 60 minutes or more (2000)

Airports: Naples Municipal (primary service)

Additional Information Contacts
Golden Gate Area Chamber of Commerce . . . . (239) 352-0508
    http://www.goldengateonline.com
Naples Area Chamber of Commerce . . . . (941) 455-3100
    http://www.napleschamber.org

NAPLES MANOR (CDP). Covers a land area of 0.693 square miles and a water area of 0.013 square miles. Located at 26.09° N. Lat.; 81.72° W. Long. Elevation is 3 feet.

Population: 3,022 (1990); 5,186 (2000); 6,292 (2007); 7,183 (2012 projected); Race: 36.2% White, 12.2% Black, 0.0% Asian, 84.6% Hispanic of any race (2007); Density: 9,078.9 persons per square mile (2007); Average household size: 5.03 (2007); Median age: 26.0 (2007); Males per 100 females: 129.6 (2007); Marriage status: 34.1% never married, 59.6% now married, 2.1% widowed, 4.3% divorced (2000); Foreign born: 52.9% (2000); Ancestry (includes multiple ancestries): 58.2% Other groups, 9.2% Haitian, 2.3% United States or American, 1.7% German, 1.1% English (2000).

Income: Per capita income: $12,434 (2007); Median household income: $48,519 (2007); Average household income: $62,488 (2007); Percent of households with income of $100,000 or more: 15.5% (2007); Poverty rate: 26.5% (2000).

Education: Percent of population age 25 and over with: High school diploma (including GED) or higher: 32.1% (2007); Bachelor's degree or higher: 2.1% (2007); Master's degree or higher: 0.5% (2007).

Housing: Homeownership rate: 63.3% (2007); Median home value: $199,865 (2007); Median rent: $547 per month (2000); Median age of housing: 17 years (2000).

Transportation: Commute to work: 94.7% car, 0.5% public transportation, 1.4% walk, 0.0% work from home (2000); Travel time to work: 14.2% less than 15 minutes, 46.6% 15 to 30 minutes, 33.2% 30 to 45 minutes, 4.3% 45 to 60 minutes, 1.8% 60 minutes or more (2000)

NAPLES PARK (CDP). Covers a land area of 1.216 square miles and a water area of 0 square miles. Located at 26.26° N. Lat.; 81.80° W. Long. Elevation is 13 feet.

Population: 6,302 (1990); 6,741 (2000); 6,944 (2007); 7,316 (2012 projected); Race: 86.2% White, 2.3% Black, 1.3% Asian, 29.6% Hispanic of any race (2007); Density: 5,708.2 persons per square mile (2007); Average household size: 2.43 (2007); Median age: 37.1 (2007); Males per 100 females: 111.9 (2007); Marriage status: 26.0% never married, 53.2% now married, 6.4% widowed, 14.4% divorced (2000); Foreign born: 18.6% (2000); Ancestry (includes multiple ancestries): 21.5% Other groups, 16.1% Irish, 15.6% German, 13.6% Italian, 10.0% English (2000).

Economy: Employment by occupation: 10.0% management, 10.8% professional, 25.4% services, 26.3% sales, 0.0% farming, 19.2% construction, 8.3% production (2000).

Income: Per capita income: $23,284 (2007); Median household income: $44,656 (2007); Average household income: $56,470 (2007); Percent of households with income of $100,000 or more: 9.3% (2007); Poverty rate: 7.8% (2000).

Education: Percent of population age 25 and over with: High school diploma (including GED) or higher: 83.0% (2007); Bachelor's degree or higher: 18.1% (2007); Master's degree or higher: 4.5% (2007).

Housing: Homeownership rate: 63.2% (2007); Median home value: $317,218 (2007); Median rent: $691 per month (2000); Median age of housing: 22 years (2000).

Transportation: Commute to work: 89.6% car, 0.2% public transportation, 1.3% walk, 3.9% work from home (2000); Travel time to work: 30.4% less than 15 minutes, 48.5% 15 to 30 minutes, 16.3% 30 to 45 minutes, 2.8% 45 to 60 minutes, 2.0% 60 minutes or more (2000)

OCHOPEE (unincorporated postal area, zip code 34141). Covers a land area of 1,221.159 square miles and a water area of 156.272 square miles. Located at 25.87° N. Lat.; 81.16° W. Long. Elevation is 6 feet.

History: Ochopee developed as the center for tomato farms in a swampy region. Marsh buggies, with wheels 8-10 feet high, were developed here to operate within the swamps, on land or on water.

Population: 128 (2000); Race: 44.4% White, 37.0% Black, 0.0% Asian, 0.0% Hispanic of any race (2000); Density: 0.1 persons per square mile (2000); Age: 48.1% under 18, 14.8% over 64 (2000); Marriage status: 2.9% never married, 78.1% now married, 0.0% widowed, 19.0% divorced (2000); Foreign born: 1.9% (2000); Ancestry (includes multiple ancestries): 15.7% Other groups, 13.0% Italian, 9.3% United States or American, 6.5% German, 5.6% Scotch-Irish (2000).

Economy: Employment by occupation: 0.0% management, 0.0% professional, 61.5% services, 38.5% sales, 0.0% farming, 0.0% construction, 0.0% production (2000).

Income: Per capita income: $13,381 (2000); Median household income: $36,328 (2000); Poverty rate: 5.1% (2000).

Education: Percent of population age 25 and over with: High school diploma (including GED) or higher: 64.3% (2000); Bachelor's degree or higher: 16.1% (2000).

School District(s)
Collier County School District (PK-12)
    2005-06 Enrollment: 42,105 . . . . (239) 377-0212

Housing: Homeownership rate: 83.3% (2000); Median home value: $75,000 (2000); Median rent: $475 per month (2000); Median age of housing: 26 years (2000).

0.0% walk, 23.1% work from home (2000); Travel time to work: 70.0% less than 15 minutes, 0.0% 15 to 30 minutes, 30.0% 30 to 45 minutes, 0.0% 45 to 60 minutes, 0.0% 60 minutes or more (2000)

ORANGETREE (CDP).
Covers a land area of 4.424 square miles and a water area of 0.007 square miles. Located at 26.28° N. Lat.; 81.58° W. Long. Elevation is 13 feet.

Population: 221 (1990); 950 (2000); 1,882 (2007); 2,527 (2012 projected); Race: 94.4% White, 1.4% Black, 0.2% Asian, 13.6% Hispanic of any race (2007); Density: 425.5 persons per square mile (2007); Average household size: 2.99 (2007); Median age: 34.4 (2007); Males per 100 females: 101.7 (2007); Marriage status: 8.8% never married, 79.8% now married, 2.2% widowed, 9.2% divorced (2000); Foreign born: 5.0% (2000); Ancestry (includes multiple ancestries): 21.3% Other groups, 18.8% Irish, 17.2% English, 16.9% German, 10.2% Italian (2000).

Economy: Employment by occupation: 16.9% management, 24.5% professional, 24.3% services, 23.9% sales, 0.0% farming, 5.3% construction, 5.1% production (2000).

Income: Per capita income: $27,970 (2007); Median household income: $72,938 (2007); Average household income: $83,688 (2007); Percent of households with income of $100,000 or more: 33.9% (2007); Poverty rate: 1.7% (2000).

Education: Percent of population age 25 and over with: High school diploma (including GED) or higher: 91.9% (2007); Bachelor's degree or higher: 24.1% (2007); Master's degree or higher: 12.1% (2007).

Housing: Homeownership rate: 96.3% (2007); Median home value: $380,085 (2007); Median rent: $345 per month (2000); Median age of housing: 3 years (2000).

Transportation: Commute to work: 91.1% car, 0.0% public transportation, 2.6% walk, 5.0% work from home (2000); Travel time to work: 13.8% less than 15 minutes, 22.9% 15 to 30 minutes, 29.0% 30 to 45 minutes, 16.9% 45 to 60 minutes, 17.4% 60 minutes or more (2000)

PELICAN BAY (CDP).
Covers a land area of 3.242 square miles and a water area of 0.175 square miles. Located at 26.23° N. Lat.; 81.80° W. Long. Elevation is 13 feet.

Population: 2,035 (1990); 5,686 (2000); 8,293 (2007); 10,223 (2012 projected); Race: 98.9% White, 0.1% Black, 0.7% Asian, 1.4% Hispanic of any race (2007); Density: 2,558.2 persons per square mile (2007); Average household size: 1.86 (2007); Median age: 68.4 (2007); Males per 100 females: 85.8 (2007); Marriage status: 6.2% never married, 79.0% now married, 9.4% widowed, 5.3% divorced (2000); Foreign born: 10.8% (2000); Ancestry (includes multiple ancestries): 21.9% German, 19.4% English, 17.1% Irish, 9.4% Italian, 4.3% Other groups (2000).

Economy: Employment by occupation: 30.8% management, 15.6% professional, 3.0% services, 47.3% sales, 0.0% farming, 3.2% construction, 0.0% production (2000).

Income: Per capita income: $89,424 (2007); Median household income: $109,294 (2007); Average household income: $165,341 (2007); Percent of households with income of $100,000 or more: 53.9% (2007); Poverty rate: 2.8% (2000).

Education: Percent of population age 25 and over with: High school diploma (including GED) or higher: 95.1% (2007); Bachelor's degree or higher: 60.0% (2007); Master's degree or higher: 22.4% (2007).

Housing: Homeownership rate: 94.5% (2007); Median home value: $936,711 (2007); Median rent: $1,082 per month (2000); Median age of housing: 8 years (2000).

Transportation: Commute to work: 74.2% car, 0.6% public transportation, 3.7% walk, 19.9% work from home (2000); Travel time to work: 53.8% less than 15 minutes, 32.4% 15 to 30 minutes, 9.2% 30 to 45 minutes, 0.9% 45 to 60 minutes, 3.8% 60 minutes or more (2000)

PINE RIDGE (CDP).
Covers a land area of 1.767 square miles and a water area of 0.092 square miles. Located at 26.23° N. Lat.; 81.79° W. Long. Elevation is 10 feet.

Population: 1,983 (1990); 1,965 (2000); 2,153 (2007); 2,346 (2012 projected); Race: 95.8% White, 1.9% Black, 0.7% Asian, 4.9% Hispanic of any race (2007); Density: 1,218.2 persons per square mile (2007); Average household size: 2.41 (2007); Median age: 43.8 (2007); Males per 100 females: 92.7 (2007); Marriage status: 11.9% never married, 65.2% now married, 8.1% widowed, 14.7% divorced (2000); Foreign born: 7.6% (2000); Ancestry (includes multiple ancestries): 19.8% English, 17.5% German, 8.7% Other groups, 8.6% Irish, 8.2% United States or American (2000).

professional, 4.1% services, 47.6% sales, 0.0% farming, 8.9% construction, 5.4% production (2000).

Income: Per capita income: $56,051 (2007); Median household income: $69,023 (2007); Average household income: $134,835 (2007); Percent of households with income of $100,000 or more: 38.8% (2007); Poverty rate: 1.9% (2000).

Education: Percent of population age 25 and over with: High school diploma (including GED) or higher: 93.0% (2007); Bachelor's degree or higher: 44.7% (2007); Master's degree or higher: 17.3% (2007).

Housing: Homeownership rate: 85.4% (2007); Median home value: $934,579 (2007); Median rent: $893 per month (2000); Median age of housing: 19 years (2000).

Transportation: Commute to work: 92.1% car, 0.0% public transportation, 2.4% walk, 3.3% work from home (2000); Travel time to work: 43.8% less than 15 minutes, 45.0% 15 to 30 minutes, 2.6% 30 to 45 minutes, 2.4% 45 to 60 minutes, 6.2% 60 minutes or more (2000)

PLANTATION ISLAND (CDP).
Covers a land area of 0.587 square miles and a water area of 0 square miles. Located at 25.84° N. Lat.; 81.36° W. Long.

Population: 129 (1990); 202 (2000); 250 (2007); 289 (2012 projected); Race: 100.0% White, 0.0% Black, 0.0% Asian, 6.4% Hispanic of any race (2007); Density: 425.9 persons per square mile (2007); Average household size: 2.14 (2007); Median age: 48.1 (2007); Males per 100 females: 106.6 (2007); Marriage status: 26.5% never married, 54.7% now married, 6.6% widowed, 12.2% divorced (2000); Foreign born: 0.5% (2000); Ancestry (includes multiple ancestries): 28.6% United States or American, 19.7% Irish, 18.3% German, 12.7% English, 7.5% Other groups (2000).

Economy: Employment by occupation: 5.4% management, 17.4% professional, 31.5% services, 9.8% sales, 8.7% farming, 9.8% construction, 17.4% production (2000).

Income: Per capita income: $25,450 (2007); Median household income: $42,500 (2007); Average household income: $54,380 (2007); Percent of households with income of $100,000 or more: 12.0% (2007); Poverty rate: 14.6% (2000).

Education: Percent of population age 25 and over with: High school diploma (including GED) or higher: 83.9% (2007); Bachelor's degree or higher: 12.0% (2007); Master's degree or higher: 2.1% (2007).

Housing: Homeownership rate: 91.5% (2007); Median home value: $222,115 (2007); Median rent: $325 per month (2000); Median age of housing: 21 years (2000).

Transportation: Commute to work: 92.0% car, 0.0% public transportation, 2.3% walk, 5.7% work from home (2000); Travel time to work: 67.1% less than 15 minutes, 2.4% 15 to 30 minutes, 4.9% 30 to 45 minutes, 8.5% 45 to 60 minutes, 17.1% 60 minutes or more (2000)

VINEYARDS (CDP).
Covers a land area of 2.261 square miles and a water area of 0 square miles. Located at 26.22° N. Lat.; 81.72° W. Long. Elevation is 10 feet.

Population: 980 (1990); 2,232 (2000); 4,998 (2007); 6,840 (2012 projected); Race: 97.8% White, 0.9% Black, 0.3% Asian, 2.4% Hispanic of any race (2007); Density: 2,210.3 persons per square mile (2007); Average household size: 2.17 (2007); Median age: 58.7 (2007); Males per 100 females: 89.5 (2007); Marriage status: 7.1% never married, 79.6% now married, 5.5% widowed, 7.9% divorced (2000); Foreign born: 9.2% (2000); Ancestry (includes multiple ancestries): 20.2% German, 16.3% Irish, 14.6% Italian, 14.1% English, 5.2% Polish (2000).

Economy: Employment by occupation: 22.4% management, 13.3% professional, 13.0% services, 46.0% sales, 0.0% farming, 0.0% construction, 5.4% production (2000).

Income: Per capita income: $72,803 (2007); Median household income: $106,076 (2007); Average household income: $157,068 (2007); Percent of households with income of $100,000 or more: 53.0% (2007); Poverty rate: 6.9% (2000).

Education: Percent of population age 25 and over with: High school diploma (including GED) or higher: 96.0% (2007); Bachelor's degree or higher: 51.3% (2007); Master's degree or higher: 15.6% (2007).

Housing: Homeownership rate: 94.9% (2007); Median home value: $592,694 (2007); Median rent: $1,344 per month (2000); Median age of housing: 5 years (2000).

Transportation: Commute to work: 81.6% car, 0.0% public transportation, 1.7% walk, 13.8% work from home (2000); Travel time to work: 14.6% less than 15 minutes, 62.9% 15 to 30 minutes, 16.0% 30 to 45 minutes, 3.1% 45 to 60 minutes, 3.3% 60 minutes or more (2000)

Located in northern Florida; bounded on the north by Georgia, on the west by the Suwanee River; includes part of the Okefenokee Swamp and Osceola National Forest. Covers a land area of 797.05 square miles, a water area of 3.99 square miles, and is located in the Eastern Time Zone. The county was founded in 1832. County seat is Lake City.

Columbia County is part of the Lake City, FL Micropolitan Statistical Area. The entire metro area includes: Columbia County, FL

Weather Station: Lake City 2 E   Elevation: 193 feet

	Jan	Feb	Mar	Apr	May	Jun	Jul	Aug	Sep	Oct	Nov	Dec
High	64	68	74	80	86	90	91	91	88	81	74	67
Low	42	44	50	55	62	68	71	71	68	59	51	44
Precip	4.5	3.8	5.1	3.3	3.8	6.8	6.7	7.4	4.6	2.9	2.4	3.0
Snow	tr	0.0	0.0	0.0	0.0	0.0	0.0	0.0	0.0	0.0	0.0	0.0

High and Low temperatures in degrees Fahrenheit; Precipitation and Snow in inches

Population: 42,613 (1990); 56,513 (2000); 64,565 (2007); 69,289 (2012 projected); Race: 79.1% White, 17.4% Black, 0.8% Asian, 3.7% Hispanic of any race (2007); Density: 81.0 persons per square mile (2007); Average household size: 2.66 (2007); Median age: 37.6 (2007); Males per 100 females: 103.6 (2007).
Religion: Five largest groups: 17.3% Southern Baptist Convention, 4.2% Catholic Church, 4.0% The United Methodist Church, 1.9% The Church of Jesus Christ of Latter-day Saints, 1.6% Church of God (Cleveland, Tennessee) (2000).
Economy: Unemployment rate: 3.7% (11/2007); Total civilian labor force: 31,074 (11/2007); Leading industries: 21.0% health care and social assistance; 18.5% retail trade; 12.6% accommodation & food services (2005); Farms: 688 totaling 90,227 acres (2002); Companies that employ 500 or more persons: 4 (2005); Companies that employ 100 to 499 persons: 22 (2005); Companies that employ less than 100 persons: 1,298 (2005); Black-owned businesses: 136 (2002); Hispanic-owned businesses: n/a (2002); Asian-owned businesses: n/a (2002); Women-owned businesses: 1,107 (2002); Retail sales per capita: $16,315 (2007). Single-family building permits issued: 467 (2006); Multi-family building permits issued: 6 (2006).
Income: Per capita income: $17,224 (2007); Median household income: $35,170 (2007); Average household income: $45,163 (2007); Percent of households with income of $100,000 or more: 7.4% (2007); Poverty rate: 19.0% (2005); Bankruptcy rate: 1.18% (2006).
Education: Percent of population age 25 and over with: High school diploma (including GED) or higher: 74.3% (2007); Bachelor's degree or higher: 10.8% (2007); Master's degree or higher: 4.0% (2007).
Housing: Homeownership rate: 77.8% (2007); Median home value: $138,846 (2007); Median rent: $344 per month (2000); Median age of housing: 18 years (2000).
Health: Birth rate: 134.2 per 10,000 population (2006); Death rate: 95.7 per 10,000 population (2006); Age-adjusted cancer mortality rate: 193.0 deaths per 100,000 population (2004); Air Quality Index: 93.1% good, 6.9% moderate, 0.0% unhealthy for sensitive individuals, 0.0% unhealthy (percent of days in 2006); Number of physicians: 15.5 per 10,000 population (2005); Hospital beds: 83.5 per 10,000 population (2004); Hospital admissions: 2,441.4 per 10,000 population (2004).
Elections: 2004 Presidential election results: 67.1% Bush, 32.1% Kerry, 0.4% Nader, 0.2% Badnarik
National and State Parks: O'Leno State Park; River Rise Preserve State Park

Additional Information Contacts
Columbia County Government . . . . (386) 755-4100
  http://www.columbiacountyfla.com
City of Lake City . . . . (386) 758-5427
  http://www.ci.lake-city.fl.us
Lake City Chamber of Commerce . . . . (386) 752-3690
  http://www.lakecitychamber.com

Columbia County Communities

FIVE POINTS (CDP). Covers a land area of 2.582 square miles and a water area of 0 square miles. Located at 30.21° N. Lat.; 82.64° W. Long. Elevation is 164 feet.
Population: 1,108 (1990); 1,362 (2000); 1,583 (2007); 1,688 (2012 projected); Race: 78.6% White, 19.3% Black, 0.4% Asian, 2.8% Hispanic of any race (2007); Density: 613.2 persons per square mile (2007); Average

females: 142.4 (2007); Marriage status: 12.8% never married, 46.1% now married, 13.3% widowed, 27.8% divorced (2000); Foreign born: 1.5% (2000); Ancestry (includes multiple ancestries): 19.0% United States or American, 10.5% Other groups, 3.5% English, 2.8% Irish, 1.7% French (except Basque) (2000).
Economy: Employment by occupation: 2.5% management, 6.0% professional, 26.8% services, 21.1% sales, 0.0% farming, 12.7% construction, 31.0% production (2000).
Income: Per capita income: $7,474 (2007); Median household income: $17,738 (2007); Average household income: $22,602 (2007); Percent of households with income of $100,000 or more: 1.6% (2007); Poverty rate: 43.8% (2000).
Education: Percent of population age 25 and over with: High school diploma (including GED) or higher: 50.0% (2007); Bachelor's degree or higher: 2.8% (2007); Master's degree or higher: 1.4% (2007).
Housing: Homeownership rate: 61.2% (2007); Median home value: $71,667 (2007); Median rent: $259 per month (2000); Median age of housing: 25 years (2000).
Transportation: Commute to work: 85.0% car, 0.0% public transportation, 1.8% walk, 0.0% work from home (2000); Travel time to work: 53.1% less than 15 minutes, 33.3% 15 to 30 minutes, 4.4% 30 to 45 minutes, 2.2% 45 to 60 minutes, 7.0% 60 minutes or more (2000)

FORT WHITE (town). Covers a land area of 2.313 square miles and a water area of 0 square miles. Located at 29.92° N. Lat.; 82.71° W. Long. Elevation is 69 feet.
History: The original Fort White, for which the town was named, was built during the Seminole Wars. The town of Fort White developed as a turkey-farming center.
Population: 381 (1990); 409 (2000); 492 (2007); 542 (2012 projected); Race: 48.4% White, 48.6% Black, 0.8% Asian, 4.9% Hispanic of any race (2007); Density: 212.7 persons per square mile (2007); Average household size: 2.63 (2007); Median age: 37.3 (2007); Males per 100 females: 78.9 (2007); Marriage status: 35.5% never married, 44.5% now married, 11.3% widowed, 8.7% divorced (2000); Foreign born: 0.0% (2000); Ancestry (includes multiple ancestries): 33.9% Other groups, 27.9% United States or American, 5.3% German, 4.8% English, 4.6% Irish (2000).
Economy: Employment by occupation: 8.9% management, 23.3% professional, 25.3% services, 26.7% sales, 0.0% farming, 6.8% construction, 8.9% production (2000).
Income: Per capita income: $15,803 (2007); Median household income: $31,375 (2007); Average household income: $41,578 (2007); Percent of households with income of $100,000 or more: 7.5% (2007); Poverty rate: 26.8% (2000).
Education: Percent of population age 25 and over with: High school diploma (including GED) or higher: 69.5% (2007); Bachelor's degree or higher: 11.4% (2007); Master's degree or higher: 3.8% (2007).

School District(s)
Columbia County School District (PK-12)
  2005-06 Enrollment: 9,957 . . . . (386) 755-8000
Housing: Homeownership rate: 78.6% (2007); Median home value: $105,921 (2007); Median rent: $325 per month (2000); Median age of housing: 18 years (2000).
Transportation: Commute to work: 92.4% car, 0.0% public transportation, 4.1% walk, 1.4% work from home (2000); Travel time to work: 37.8% less than 15 minutes, 20.3% 15 to 30 minutes, 18.9% 30 to 45 minutes, 18.9% 45 to 60 minutes, 4.2% 60 minutes or more (2000)

LAKE CITY (city). County seat. Covers a land area of 10.563 square miles and a water area of 0.520 square miles. Located at 30.19° N. Lat.; 82.64° W. Long. Elevation is 194 feet.
History: Before 1859, Lake City was known as Alligator. From 1883 to 1905, this was the location of the State Agricultural College. Lumber, naval stores (rosin and turpentine used for calking ships), and tobacco were the basis of Lake City's early economy.
Population: 10,198 (1990); 9,980 (2000); 10,486 (2007); 10,747 (2012 projected); Race: 55.0% White, 41.5% Black, 1.3% Asian, 3.9% Hispanic of any race (2007); Density: 992.7 persons per square mile (2007); Average household size: 2.46 (2007); Median age: 37.1 (2007); Males per 100 females: 92.3 (2007); Marriage status: 27.4% never married, 45.9% now married, 12.8% widowed, 13.9% divorced (2000); Foreign born: 3.1% (2000); Ancestry (includes multiple ancestries): 37.8% Other groups, 11.9% United States or American, 7.3% German, 6.7% English, 5.8% Irish (2000).

$29,106 (2007); Average household income: $40,220 (2007); Percent of households with income of $100,000 or more: 7.3% (2007); Poverty rate: 20.5% (2000).
Education: Percent of population age 25 and over with: High school diploma (including GED) or higher: 75.3% (2007); Bachelor's degree or higher: 15.3% (2007); Master's degree or higher: 7.2% (2007).

School District(s)
Columbia County School District (PK-12)
   2005-06 Enrollment: 9,957 . . . . (386) 755-8000
Two-year College(s)
Lake City Community College (Public)
   Fall 2006 Enrollment: 2,639. . . . . (386) 752-1822
   2006-07 Tuition: In-state $2,979; Out-of-state $7,638
Housing: Homeownership rate: 54.4% (2007); Median home value: $125,604 (2007); Median rent: $359 per month (2000); Median age of housing: 32 years (2000).
Hospitals: Lake City Medical Center (75 beds); Shands at Lake Shore (99 beds); Veterans Affairs Medical Center (319 beds)
Safety: Violent crime rate: 167.6 per 10,000 population; Property crime rate: 771.9 per 10,000 population (2006).
Newspapers: Lake City Reporter (Circulation 8,184)
Transportation: Commute to work: 93.5% car, 0.0% public transportation, 1.5% walk, 2.6% work from home (2000); Travel time to work: 60.8% less than 15 minutes, 19.7% 15 to 30 minutes, 9.3% 30 to 45 minutes, 4.6% 45 to 60 minutes, 5.7% 60 minutes or more (2000); Amtrak: Service available.
Additional Information Contacts
City of Lake City. . . . . (386) 758-5427
   http://www.ci.lake-city.fl.us
Lake City Chamber of Commerce . . . . (386) 752-3690
   http://www.lakecitychamber.com

LULU (unincorporated postal area, zip code 32061). Covers a land area of 12.609 square miles and a water area of 0 square miles. Located at 30.10° N. Lat.; 82.50° W. Long. Elevation is 155 feet.
Population: 146 (2000); Race: 94.2% White, 0.0% Black, 0.0% Asian, 0.0% Hispanic of any race (2000); Density: 11.6 persons per square mile (2000); Age: 15.3% under 18, 16.8% over 64 (2000); Marriage status: 11.5% never married, 74.6% now married, 0.0% widowed, 13.9% divorced (2000); Foreign born: 0.0% (2000); Ancestry (includes multiple ancestries): 33.6% United States or American, 17.5% Other groups, 7.3% German, 7.3% Irish, 5.8% English (2000).
Economy: Employment by occupation: 18.2% management, 0.0% professional, 22.7% services, 50.0% sales, 0.0% farming, 9.1% construction, 0.0% production (2000).
Income: Per capita income: $19,290 (2000); Median household income: $45,469 (2000); Poverty rate: 10.2% (2000).
Education: Percent of population age 25 and over with: High school diploma (including GED) or higher: 92.6% (2000); Bachelor's degree or higher: 7.4% (2000).
Housing: Homeownership rate: 100.0% (2000); Median home value: $55,000 (2000); Median rent: $n/a per month (2000); Median age of housing: 17 years (2000).
Transportation: Commute to work: 100.0% car, 0.0% public transportation, 0.0% walk, 0.0% work from home (2000); Travel time to work: 9.1% less than 15 minutes, 79.5% 15 to 30 minutes, 0.0% 30 to 45 minutes, 0.0% 45 to 60 minutes, 11.4% 60 minutes or more (2000)

WATERTOWN (CDP). Covers a land area of 2.391 square miles and a water area of 0.060 square miles. Located at 30.18° N. Lat.; 82.60° W. Long. Elevation is 187 feet.
History: Watertown developed as a center for lumbering, with railroad spur lines bringing logs to the sawmills.
Population: 3,069 (1990); 2,837 (2000); 2,832 (2007); 2,885 (2012 projected); Race: 66.7% White, 30.6% Black, 0.3% Asian, 2.0% Hispanic of any race (2007); Density: 1,184.2 persons per square mile (2007); Average household size: 2.40 (2007); Median age: 40.7 (2007); Males per 100 females: 93.4 (2007); Marriage status: 21.6% never married, 54.7% now married, 8.2% widowed, 15.4% divorced (2000); Foreign born: 1.2% (2000); Ancestry (includes multiple ancestries): 33.5% Other groups,

Income: Per capita income: $15,825 (2007); Median household income: $31,899 (2007); Average household income: $38,043 (2007); Percent of households with income of $100,000 or more: 3.1% (2007); Poverty rate: 17.1% (2000).
Education: Percent of population age 25 and over with: High school diploma (including GED) or higher: 75.7% (2007); Bachelor's degree or higher: 7.5% (2007); Master's degree or higher: 3.1% (2007).
Housing: Homeownership rate: 72.9% (2007); Median home value: $111,338 (2007); Median rent: $296 per month (2000); Median age of housing: 31 years (2000).
Transportation: Commute to work: 89.9% car, 0.0% public transportation, 4.8% walk, 1.3% work from home (2000); Travel time to work: 51.7% less than 15 minutes, 24.3% 15 to 30 minutes, 13.1% 30 to 45 minutes, 4.4% 45 to 60 minutes, 6.5% 60 minutes or more (2000)

De Soto County

Located in south central Florida; partly swampy with many small lakes, drained by the Peace River. Covers a land area of 637.27 square miles, a water area of 2.23 square miles, and is located in the Eastern Time Zone. The county was founded in 1887. County seat is Arcadia.

De Soto County is part of the Arcadia, FL Micropolitan Statistical Area. The entire metro area includes: DeSoto County, FL

Weather Station: Arcadia											Elevation: 62 feet	
	Jan	Feb	Mar	Apr	May	Jun	Jul	Aug	Sep	Oct	Nov	Dec
High	74	75	80	84	89	91	92	91	90	86	80	75
Low	49	50	54	57	63	69	71	71	70	64	57	52
Precip	2.2	2.6	3.3	1.7	4.2	8.0	7.4	7.0	6.8	2.9	2.1	1.8
Snow	0.0	0.0	0.0	0.0	0.0	0.0	0.0	0.0	0.0	0.0	0.0	0.0

High and Low temperatures in degrees Fahrenheit; Precipitation and Snow in inches

Population: 23,865 (1990); 32,209 (2000); 34,382 (2007); 34,934 (2012 projected); Race: 70.8% White, 11.3% Black, 0.5% Asian, 32.7% Hispanic of any race (2007); Density: 54.0 persons per square mile (2007); Average household size: 3.02 (2007); Median age: 34.9 (2007); Males per 100 females: 134.3 (2007).
Religion: Five largest groups: 15.0% Southern Baptist Convention, 5.2% The United Methodist Church, 2.6% Catholic Church, 1.5% Church of God (Cleveland, Tennessee), 1.4% Assemblies of God (2000).
Economy: Unemployment rate: 5.6% (11/2007); Total civilian labor force: 15,213 (11/2007); Leading industries: 24.8% retail trade; 20.2% health care and social assistance; 8.8% accommodation & food services (2005); Farms: 1,153 totaling 388,177 acres (2002); Companies that employ 500 or more persons: 0 (2005); Companies that employ 100 to 499 persons: 5 (2005); Companies that employ less than 100 persons: 489 (2005); Black-owned businesses: n/a (2002); Hispanic-owned businesses: 129 (2002); Asian-owned businesses: n/a (2002); Women-owned businesses: n/a (2002); Retail sales per capita: $9,274 (2007). Single-family building permits issued: 167 (2006); Multi-family building permits issued: 20 (2006).
Income: Per capita income: $15,548 (2007); Median household income: $34,983 (2007); Average household income: $45,243 (2007); Percent of households with income of $100,000 or more: 6.6% (2007); Poverty rate: 21.4% (2005); Bankruptcy rate: 0.74% (2006).
Education: Percent of population age 25 and over with: High school diploma (including GED) or higher: 64.0% (2007); Bachelor's degree or higher: 8.6% (2007); Master's degree or higher: 3.3% (2007).
Housing: Homeownership rate: 75.8% (2007); Median home value: $116,381 (2007); Median rent: $364 per month (2000); Median age of housing: 20 years (2000).
Health: Birth rate: 128.8 per 10,000 population (2006); Death rate: 96.0 per 10,000 population (2006); Age-adjusted cancer mortality rate: 165.1 deaths per 100,000 population (2004); Number of physicians: 8.3 per 10,000 population (2005); Hospital beds: 14.1 per 10,000 population (2004); Hospital admissions: 752.9 per 10,000 population (2004).
Elections: 2004 Presidential election results: 58.1% Bush, 41.1% Kerry, 0.5% Nader, 0.1% Badnarik
Additional Information Contacts
De Soto County Government. . . . . (863) 993-4800
   http://www.co.desoto.fl.us

De Soto County Communities

ARCADIA (city). County seat. Covers a land area of 4.038 square miles and a water area of 0.006 square miles. Located at 27.21° N. Lat.; 81.86° W. Long. Elevation is 59 feet.

History: Arcadia developed as the center of a cattle area, with numerous cow camps in the vicinity giving the town a frontier atmosphere in the early 1900's.

Population: 6,490 (1990); 6,604 (2000); 6,612 (2007); 6,494 (2012 projected); Race: 60.8% White, 25.8% Black, 1.2% Asian, 28.7% Hispanic of any race (2007); Density: 1,637.6 persons per square mile (2007); Average household size: 3.02 (2007); Median age: 31.2 (2007); Males per 100 females: 111.9 (2007); Marriage status: 31.5% never married, 50.6% now married, 6.1% widowed, 11.7% divorced (2000); Foreign born: 15.9% (2000); Ancestry (includes multiple ancestries): 50.5% Other groups, 11.6% United States or American, 8.4% English, 6.2% German, 5.9% Irish (2000).

Economy: Employment by occupation: 4.7% management, 16.2% professional, 22.5% services, 17.9% sales, 17.1% farming, 11.2% construction, 10.3% production (2000).

Income: Per capita income: $13,241 (2007); Median household income: $27,541 (2007); Average household income: $38,827 (2007); Percent of households with income of $100,000 or more: 4.8% (2007); Poverty rate: 25.9% (2000).

Education: Percent of population age 25 and over with: High school diploma (including GED) or higher: 64.0% (2007); Bachelor's degree or higher: 9.9% (2007); Master's degree or higher: 3.5% (2007).

School District(s)
Desoto County School District (PK-12)
    2005-06 Enrollment: 4,942 . . . . (863) 494-4222

Housing: Homeownership rate: 61.1% (2007); Median home value: $111,638 (2007); Median rent: $351 per month (2000); Median age of housing: 33 years (2000).

Hospitals: DeSoto Memorial Hospital (49 beds)

Safety: Violent crime rate: 96.3 per 10,000 population; Property crime rate: 339.7 per 10,000 population (2006).

Newspapers: DeSoto Sun Herald (Circulation 3,900)

Transportation: Commute to work: 91.5% car, 1.5% public transportation, 2.3% walk, 1.7% work from home (2000); Travel time to work: 39.7% less than 15 minutes, 25.0% 15 to 30 minutes, 22.3% 30 to 45 minutes, 6.7% 45 to 60 minutes, 6.3% 60 minutes or more (2000)

Additional Information Contacts
Arcadia Chamber of Commerce . . . . (863) 494-4033
    http://www.desotochamber.net
City of Arcadia . . . . (863) 494-4114
    http://www.cityofarcadia.org

SOUTHEAST ARCADIA (CDP). Covers a land area of 7.305 square miles and a water area of 0 square miles. Located at 27.19° N. Lat.; 81.85° W. Long.

Population: 4,143 (1990); 6,064 (2000); 5,740 (2007); 5,401 (2012 projected); Race: 66.9% White, 3.7% Black, 0.5% Asian, 59.9% Hispanic of any race (2007); Density: 785.7 persons per square mile (2007); Average household size: 3.30 (2007); Median age: 29.7 (2007); Males per 100 females: 146.1 (2007); Marriage status: 22.1% never married, 64.1% now married, 6.0% widowed, 7.7% divorced (2000); Foreign born: 32.1% (2000); Ancestry (includes multiple ancestries): 39.6% Other groups, 15.4% United States or American, 6.0% German, 5.6% English, 4.2% Irish (2000).

Economy: Employment by occupation: 2.8% management, 5.3% professional, 16.9% services, 14.1% sales, 40.0% farming, 10.7% construction, 10.2% production (2000).

Income: Per capita income: $13,124 (2007); Median household income: $31,343 (2007); Average household income: $43,127 (2007); Percent of households with income of $100,000 or more: 6.2% (2007); Poverty rate: 33.8% (2000).

Education: Percent of population age 25 and over with: High school diploma (including GED) or higher: 53.5% (2007); Bachelor's degree or higher: 4.6% (2007); Master's degree or higher: 1.1% (2007).

work: 27.3% less than 15 minutes, 25.6% 15 to 30 minutes, 31.4% 30 to 45 minutes, 6.3% 45 to 60 minutes, 9.3% 60 minutes or more (2000)

Dixie County

Located in northern Florida; swampy area, bounded on the south and west by the Gulf of Mexico, and on the east by the Suwannee River. Covers a land area of 704.01 square miles, a water area of 159.65 square miles, and is located in the Eastern Time Zone. The county was founded in 1921. County seat is Cross City.

Weather Station: Cross City 2 WNW   Elevation: 39 feet

	Jan	Feb	Mar	Apr	May	Jun	Jul	Aug	Sep	Oct	Nov	Dec
High	65	68	74	79	85	89	90	90	88	82	74	68
Low	40	43	49	53	60	67	70	70	68	57	49	42
Precip	4.5	3.6	4.7	3.5	3.2	6.3	8.9	9.8	5.8	3.0	2.4	3.4
Snow	0.0	0.0	0.0	0.0	0.0	0.0	0.0	0.0	0.0	0.0	0.0	0.0

High and Low temperatures in degrees Fahrenheit; Precipitation and Snow in inches

Population: 10,585 (1990); 13,827 (2000); 15,381 (2007); 16,722 (2012 projected); Race: 88.2% White, 9.5% Black, 0.3% Asian, 2.2% Hispanic of any race (2007); Density: 21.8 persons per square mile (2007); Average household size: 2.65 (2007); Median age: 40.6 (2007); Males per 100 females: 116.6 (2007).

Religion: Five largest groups: 30.8% Southern Baptist Convention, 3.7% The United Methodist Church, 2.2% International Pentecostal Holiness Church, 2.0% Church of God (Cleveland, Tennessee), 1.4% The Church of Jesus Christ of Latter-day Saints (200

Economy: Unemployment rate: 4.2% (11/2007); Total civilian labor force: 5,962 (11/2007); Leading industries: 35.7% manufacturing; 17.6% retail trade; 11.5% health care and social assistance (2005); Farms: 215 totaling 31,249 acres (2002); Companies that employ 500 or more persons: 0 (2005); Companies that employ 100 to 499 persons: 2 (2005); Companies that employ less than 100 persons: 199 (2005); Black-owned businesses: n/a (2002); Hispanic-owned businesses: n/a (2002); Asian-owned businesses: n/a (2002); Women-owned businesses: 142 (2002); Retail sales per capita: $4,799 (2007). Single-family building permits issued: 71 (2006); Multi-family building permits issued: 12 (2006).

Income: Per capita income: $16,409 (2007); Median household income: $30,533 (2007); Average household income: $42,077 (2007); Percent of households with income of $100,000 or more: 6.6% (2007); Poverty rate: 24.0% (2005); Bankruptcy rate: 0.80% (2006).

Education: Percent of population age 25 and over with: High school diploma (including GED) or higher: 65.7% (2007); Bachelor's degree or higher: 6.6% (2007); Master's degree or higher: 3.1% (2007).

Housing: Homeownership rate: 87.1% (2007); Median home value: $100,829 (2007); Median rent: $231 per month (2000); Median age of housing: 19 years (2000).

Health: Birth rate: 130.3 per 10,000 population (2006); Death rate: 129.6 per 10,000 population (2006); Age-adjusted cancer mortality rate: 259.3 deaths per 100,000 population (2004); Number of physicians: 4.1 per 10,000 population (2005); Hospital beds: 0.0 per 10,000 population (2004); Hospital admissions: 0.0 per 10,000 population (2004).

Elections: 2004 Presidential election results: 68.8% Bush, 30.4% Kerry, 0.5% Nader, 0.1% Badnarik

National and State Parks: Lower Suwannee National Wildlife Refuge

Additional Information Contacts
Dixie County Government . . . . (352) 498-1206

Cross City Chamber of Commerce . . . . (352) 498-5454
    http://www.dixiecounty.org

Dixie County Communities

CROSS CITY (town). County seat. Covers a land area of 1.897 square miles and a water area of 0 square miles. Located at 29.63° N. Lat.; 83.12° W. Long. Elevation is 39 feet.

History: Cross City developed as a timber, turpentine, and fishing center, with cold-storage plants that prepared fish for shipment to northern markets.

Population: 2,041 (1990); 1,775 (2000); 1,521 (2007); 1,555 (2012 projected); Race: 68.6% White, 29.4% Black, 0.7% Asian, 0.9% Hispanic of any race (2007); Density: 801.7 persons per square mile (2007); Average household size: 2.55 (2007); Median age: 33.8 (2007); Males per 100 females: 85.0 (2007); Marriage status: 23.4% never married, 51.7% now married, 14.7% widowed, 10.3% divorced (2000); Foreign born: 1.1% (2000); Ancestry (includes multiple ancestries): 25.8% Other groups, 15.3% United States or American, 7.1% English, 5.6% German, 4.4% Irish (2000).
Economy: Employment by occupation: 8.6% management, 14.2% professional, 18.7% services, 21.1% sales, 6.3% farming, 9.8% construction, 21.4% production (2000).
Income: Per capita income: $13,768 (2007); Median household income: $22,065 (2007); Average household income: $34,446 (2007); Percent of households with income of $100,000 or more: 5.2% (2007); Poverty rate: 27.2% (2000).
Education: Percent of population age 25 and over with: High school diploma (including GED) or higher: 64.6% (2007); Bachelor's degree or higher: 7.4% (2007); Master's degree or higher: 2.2% (2007).

School District(s)
Dixie County School District (PK-12)
    2005-06 Enrollment: 2,144 . . . . (352) 498-6131
Housing: Homeownership rate: 69.6% (2007); Median home value: $90,208 (2007); Median rent: $222 per month (2000); Median age of housing: 28 years (2000).
Safety: Violent crime rate: 59.8 per 10,000 population; Property crime rate: 647.4 per 10,000 population (2006).
Newspapers: Dixie County Advocate (General - Circulation 3,200)
Transportation: Commute to work: 91.9% car, 0.0% public transportation, 1.9% walk, 1.4% work from home (2000); Travel time to work: 55.5% less than 15 minutes, 15.8% 15 to 30 minutes, 7.2% 30 to 45 minutes, 4.0% 45 to 60 minutes, 17.4% 60 minutes or more (2000)
Additional Information Contacts
Cross City Chamber of Commerce . . . . (352) 498-5454
    http://www.dixiecounty.org

HORSESHOE BEACH (town). Covers a land area of 0.203 square miles and a water area of 0.041 square miles. Located at 29.44° N. Lat.; 83.28° W. Long. Elevation is 7 feet.
Population: 252 (1990); 206 (2000); 164 (2007); 171 (2012 projected); Race: 93.3% White, 6.7% Black, 0.0% Asian, 0.0% Hispanic of any race (2007); Density: 807.3 persons per square mile (2007); Average household size: 2.41 (2007); Median age: 48.7 (2007); Males per 100 females: 86.4 (2007); Marriage status: 20.6% never married, 66.1% now married, 7.3% widowed, 6.1% divorced (2000); Foreign born: 0.0% (2000); Ancestry (includes multiple ancestries): 24.8% United States or American, 16.3% Irish, 7.9% English, 5.9% German, 4.0% Other groups (2000).
Economy: Single-family building permits issued: 14 (2006); Multi-family building permits issued: 12 (2006); Employment by occupation: 24.7% management, 2.7% professional, 8.2% services, 23.3% sales, 21.9% farming, 11.0% construction, 8.2% production (2000).
Income: Per capita income: $22,607 (2007); Median household income: $38,750 (2007); Average household income: $54,522 (2007); Percent of households with income of $100,000 or more: 8.8% (2007); Poverty rate: 22.3% (2000).
Education: Percent of population age 25 and over with: High school diploma (including GED) or higher: 73.9% (2007); Bachelor's degree or higher: 7.2% (2007); Master's degree or higher: 2.7% (2007).
Housing: Homeownership rate: 89.7% (2007); Median home value: $162,500 (2007); Median rent: $375 per month (2000); Median age of housing: 17 years (2000).
Transportation: Commute to work: 80.8% car, 0.0% public transportation, 8.2% walk, 0.0% work from home (2000); Travel time to work: 69.9% less than 15 minutes, 9.6% 15 to 30 minutes, 6.8% 30 to 45 minutes, 4.1% 45 to 60 minutes, 9.6% 60 minutes or more (2000)

OLD TOWN (unincorporated postal area, zip code 32680). Covers a land area of 115.124 square miles and a water area of 2.006 square miles. Located at 29.64° N. Lat.; 82.99° W. Long. Elevation is 23 feet.
History: Old Town, once known as Suwannee Oldtown, was built on the site of a large Creek village. An early industry was a moss factory where Spanish moss was prepared for use in mattresses and upholstering.
Population: 7,748 (2000); Race: 97.3% White, 0.3% Black, 0.5% Asian, 1.8% Hispanic of any race (2000); Density: 67.3 persons per square mile (2000); Age: 22.0% under 18, 20.9% over 64 (2000); Marriage status:

16.7% never married, 61.9% now married, 9.1% widowed, 12.3% divorced (2000); Foreign born: 2.1% (2000); Ancestry (includes multiple ancestries): 21.7% United States or American, 11.0% Irish, 9.8% German, 9.4% English, 8.9% Other groups (2000).
Economy: Employment by occupation: 7.7% management, 11.0% professional, 20.1% services, 24.7% sales, 4.5% farming, 14.3% construction, 17.7% production (2000).
Income: Per capita income: $13,200 (2000); Median household income: $24,131 (2000); Poverty rate: 19.1% (2000).
Education: Percent of population age 25 and over with: High school diploma (including GED) or higher: 62.6% (2000); Bachelor's degree or higher: 6.7% (2000).

School District(s)
Dixie County School District (PK-12)
    2005-06 Enrollment: 2,144 . . . . (352) 498-6131
Housing: Homeownership rate: 91.0% (2000); Median home value: $66,700 (2000); Median rent: $245 per month (2000); Median age of housing: 17 years (2000).
Transportation: Commute to work: 91.3% car, 0.5% public transportation, 0.0% walk, 6.4% work from home (2000); Travel time to work: 29.5% less than 15 minutes, 31.1% 15 to 30 minutes, 14.4% 30 to 45 minutes, 6.2% 45 to 60 minutes, 18.9% 60 minutes or more (2000)

Duval County

Located in northeastern Florida; partly swampy area, bounded on the east by the Atlantic Ocean; includes Little Talbot Island; drained by the St. Johns River. Covers a land area of 773.67 square miles, a water area of 144.57 square miles, and is located in the Eastern Time Zone. The county was founded in 1822. County seat is Jacksonville.

Duval County is part of the Jacksonville, FL Metropolitan Statistical Area. The entire metro area includes: Baker County, FL; Clay County, FL; Duval County, FL; Nassau County, FL; St. Johns County, FL

Weather Station: Jacksonville Beach									Elevation: 9 feet		
	Jan	Feb	Mar	Apr	May	Jun	Jul	Aug	Sep	Oct	Nov	Dec
High	64	66	71	77	83	87	90	88	86	80	72	67
Low	46	48	54	59	66	72	74	74	73	66	56	50
Precip	3.7	3.0	4.1	2.8	3.1	5.7	5.2	6.1	7.1	5.2	2.3	2.8
Snow	tr	tr	0.0	0.0	0.0	0.0	0.0	0.0	0.0	0.0	0.0	tr

High and Low temperatures in degrees Fahrenheit; Precipitation and Snow in inches

Weather Station: Jacksonville Int'l Airport									Elevation: 22 feet		
	Jan	Feb	Mar	Apr	May	Jun	Jul	Aug	Sep	Oct	Nov	Dec
High	65	68	74	79	85	90	92	91	87	80	73	67
Low	42	44	50	55	63	69	72	72	69	60	51	44
Precip	3.7	3.4	4.2	3.1	3.5	5.4	6.0	7.0	7.6	4.0	2.3	2.6
Snow	tr	tr	tr	tr	0.0	tr	0.0	0.0	0.0	0.0	0.0	tr

High and Low temperatures in degrees Fahrenheit; Precipitation and Snow in inches

Population: 672,971 (1990); 778,879 (2000); 859,684 (2007); 930,011 (2012 projected); Race: 61.9% White, 30.1% Black, 3.3% Asian, 5.6% Hispanic of any race (2007); Density: 1,111.2 persons per square mile (2007); Average household size: 2.51 (2007); Median age: 35.7 (2007); Males per 100 females: 94.7 (2007).
Religion: Five largest groups: 18.4% Southern Baptist Convention, 8.3% Catholic Church, 3.7% The United Methodist Church, 1.7% Presbyterian Church (U.S.A.), 1.7% Episcopal Church (2000).
Economy: Unemployment rate: 4.2% (11/2007); Total civilian labor force: 444,975 (11/2007); Leading industries: 12.7% retail trade; 12.4% health care and social assistance; 12.3% finance & insurance (2005); Farms: 382 totaling 31,241 acres (2002); Companies that employ 500 or more persons: 83 (2005); Companies that employ 100 to 499 persons: 609 (2005); Companies that employ less than 100 persons: 23,094 (2005); Black-owned businesses: 6,164 (2002); Hispanic-owned businesses: 2,431 (2002); Asian-owned businesses: 1,941 (2002); Women-owned businesses: 17,733 (2002); Retail sales per capita: $17,733 (2007). Single-family building permits issued: 6,450 (2006); Multi-family building permits issued: 3,633 (2006).
Income: Per capita income: $25,024 (2007); Median household income: $47,675 (2007); Average household income: $62,255 (2007); Percent of households with income of $100,000 or more: 15.0% (2007); Poverty rate: 12.1% (2005); Bankruptcy rate: 2.34% (2006).

Education: Percent of population age 25 and over with: High school diploma (including GED) or higher: 83.1% (2007); Bachelor's degree or higher: 22.2% (2007); Master's degree or higher: 6.9% (2007).

Housing: Homeownership rate: 64.1% (2007); Median home value: $157,627 (2007); Median rent: $508 per month (2000); Median age of housing: 25 years (2000).

Health: Birth rate: 162.0 per 10,000 population (2006); Death rate: 87.7 per 10,000 population (2006); Age-adjusted cancer mortality rate: 230.5 deaths per 100,000 population (2004); Air Quality Index: 83.6% good, 16.2% moderate, 0.3% unhealthy for sensitive individuals, 0.0% unhealthy (percent of days in 2006); Number of physicians: 32.3 per 10,000 population (2005); Hospital beds: 32.6 per 10,000 population (2004); Hospital admissions: 1,590.6 per 10,000 population (2004).

Elections: 2004 Presidential election results: 57.8% Bush, 41.6% Kerry, 0.3% Nader, 0.2% Badnarik

National and State Parks: Big Talbot Island State Park; Fort Caroline National Memorial; Fort George Island Cultural State Park; Kingsley Plantation State Historical Site; Little Talbot Island State Park; Yellow Bluff Fort Historic State Park

Additional Information Contacts

Duval County Government. . . . . (904) 630-2039
  http://www.coj.net/default.htm
City of Atlantic Beach. . . . . (904) 247-5800
  http://www.ci.atlantic-beach.fl.us
City of Jacksonville Beach . . . . (904) 247-6100
  http://www.jacksonvillebeach.org
City of Neptune Beach. . . . . (904) 270-2400
  http://www.ci.neptune-beach.fl.us
Jacksonville Beach Chamber of Commerce . . . . (904) 249-3868
  http://www.myjaxchamber.com
Jacksonville Chamber of Commerce . . . . (904) 366-6600
  http://www.myjaxchamber.com

Duval County Communities

ATLANTIC BEACH (city). Covers a land area of 3.730 square miles and a water area of 9.252 square miles. Located at 30.33° N. Lat.; 81.40° W. Long. Elevation is 10 feet.

History: Named for the city's location on the Atlantic Ocean. Atlantic Beach developed as a summer resort, particularly for Jacksonville residents.

Population: 11,639 (1990); 13,368 (2000); 13,736 (2007); 14,310 (2012 projected); Race: 82.4% White, 12.4% Black, 1.7% Asian, 5.5% Hispanic of any race (2007); Density: 3,682.9 persons per square mile (2007); Average household size: 2.29 (2007); Median age: 41.5 (2007); Males per 100 females: 94.8 (2007); Marriage status: 24.5% never married, 55.2% now married, 7.0% widowed, 13.2% divorced (2000); Foreign born: 5.6% (2000); Ancestry (includes multiple ancestries): 19.7% Other groups, 15.7% German, 14.2% English, 13.3% Irish, 7.9% United States or American (2000).

Economy: Single-family building permits issued: 58 (2006); Multi-family building permits issued: 0 (2006); Employment by occupation: 15.9% management, 23.8% professional, 15.9% services, 24.2% sales, 0.5% farming, 9.8% construction, 9.9% production (2000).

Income: Per capita income: $35,736 (2007); Median household income: $56,063 (2007); Average household income: $81,001 (2007); Percent of households with income of $100,000 or more: 26.4% (2007); Poverty rate: 8.8% (2000).

Education: Percent of population age 25 and over with: High school diploma (including GED) or higher: 88.7% (2007); Bachelor's degree or higher: 37.3% (2007); Master's degree or higher: 16.1% (2007).

School District(s)

Duval County School District (PK-12)
  2005-06 Enrollment: 129,486 . . . . (904) 390-2115

Housing: Homeownership rate: 65.7% (2007); Median home value: $295,661 (2007); Median rent: $620 per month (2000); Median age of housing: 21 years (2000).

Safety: Violent crime rate: 44.6 per 10,000 population; Property crime rate: 352.8 per 10,000 population (2006).

Transportation: Commute to work: 89.4% car, 2.3% public transportation, 2.3% walk, 3.0% work from home (2000); Travel time to work: 25.9% less than 15 minutes, 27.2% 15 to 30 minutes, 28.7% 30 to 45 minutes, 12.2% 45 to 60 minutes, 6.0% 60 minutes or more (2000)

Additional Information Contacts

City of Atlantic Beach. . . . . (904) 247-5800
  http://www.ci.atlantic-beach.fl.us

BALDWIN (town). Covers a land area of 2.130 square miles and a water area of 0.002 square miles. Located at 30.30° N. Lat.; 81.97° W. Long. Elevation is 85 feet.

History: Baldwin was once called Thigpen, but was renamed for Dr. A.S. Baldwin who arranged for the railroad to be built in the area in 1860. The Seaboard Air Line Railway established its freight yards in Baldwin.

Population: 1,456 (1990); 1,634 (2000); 1,467 (2007); 1,495 (2012 projected); Race: 69.1% White, 28.8% Black, 0.8% Asian, 0.9% Hispanic of any race (2007); Density: 688.9 persons per square mile (2007); Average household size: 2.49 (2007); Median age: 33.8 (2007); Males per 100 females: 87.1 (2007); Marriage status: 27.5% never married, 47.1% now married, 9.3% widowed, 16.1% divorced (2000); Foreign born: 1.3% (2000); Ancestry (includes multiple ancestries): 34.4% Other groups, 11.2% Irish, 10.8% United States or American, 7.9% English, 7.1% German (2000).

Economy: Single-family building permits issued: 8 (2006); Multi-family building permits issued: 0 (2006); Employment by occupation: 5.3% management, 8.9% professional, 21.2% services, 24.2% sales, 0.3% farming, 15.2% construction, 25.0% production (2000).

Income: Per capita income: $18,688 (2007); Median household income: $36,471 (2007); Average household income: $46,466 (2007); Percent of households with income of $100,000 or more: 8.6% (2007); Poverty rate: 17.7% (2000).

Education: Percent of population age 25 and over with: High school diploma (including GED) or higher: 67.2% (2007); Bachelor's degree or higher: 5.3% (2007); Master's degree or higher: 2.2% (2007).

School District(s)

Duval County School District (PK-12)
  2005-06 Enrollment: 129,486 . . . . (904) 390-2115

Housing: Homeownership rate: 65.6% (2007); Median home value: $97,083 (2007); Median rent: $285 per month (2000); Median age of housing: 25 years (2000).

Transportation: Commute to work: 92.8% car, 0.0% public transportation, 3.5% walk, 1.5% work from home (2000); Travel time to work: 21.9% less than 15 minutes, 28.3% 15 to 30 minutes, 33.7% 30 to 45 minutes, 6.7% 45 to 60 minutes, 9.3% 60 minutes or more (2000)

JACKSONVILLE (special city). County seat. Covers a land area of 757.678 square miles and a water area of 116.649 square miles. Located at 30.31° N. Lat.; 81.66° W. Long. Elevation is 16 feet.

History: Jacksonville was established in 1822 on the north bank of the St. Johns River, where a settlement named Cowford had grown up around a rowboat ferry maintained by John Brady. The new town was named Jacksonville in honor of Florida's governor, General Andrew Jackson. Growth was slow until 1842, when steamship service began and Jacksonville began to ship lumber and cotton from its harbor. Badly damaged by the Civil War, Jacksonville was rebuilt as a winter resort during the Reconstruction period.

Population: 635,221 (1990); 735,617 (2000); 814,629 (2007); 882,596 (2012 projected); Race: 60.4% White, 31.4% Black, 3.4% Asian, 5.7% Hispanic of any race (2007); Density: 1,075.2 persons per square mile (2007); Average household size: 2.54 (2007); Median age: 35.4 (2007); Males per 100 females: 94.5 (2007); Marriage status: 26.5% never married, 53.9% now married, 6.3% widowed, 13.3% divorced (2000); Foreign born: 5.9% (2000); Ancestry (includes multiple ancestries): 35.5% Other groups, 9.6% German, 9.3% United States or American, 9.0% Irish, 8.5% English (2000).

Economy: Unemployment rate: 4.1% (11/2007); Total civilian labor force: 417,148 (11/2007); Single-family building permits issued: 6,291 (2006); Multi-family building permits issued: 3,521 (2006); Employment by occupation: 13.6% management, 17.6% professional, 14.0% services, 32.6% sales, 0.2% farming, 9.5% construction, 12.4% production (2000).

Income: Per capita income: $24,492 (2007); Median household income: $47,137 (2007); Average household income: $61,475 (2007); Percent of households with income of $100,000 or more: 14.5% (2007); Poverty rate: 12.2% (2000).

Taxes: Total city taxes per capita: $829 (2005); City property taxes per capita: $416 (2005).

Education: Percent of population age 25 and over with: High school diploma (including GED) or higher: 82.7% (2007); Bachelor's degree or higher: 21.5% (2007); Master's degree or higher: 6.6% (2007).

St. Johns County School District (PK-12)
2005-06 Enrollment: 24,403 . . . . (904) 819-7502

Four-year College(s)

Edward Waters College (Private, Not-for-profit, Historically black, African Methodist Episcopal)
Fall 2006 Enrollment: 842 . . . . (904) 470-8000
2006-07 Tuition: In-state $9,176; Out-of-state $9,176

Florida Coastal School of Law (Private, For-profit)
Fall 2006 Enrollment: 1,278. . . . . (904) 680-7700

Florida Metropolitan University-Jacksonville (Private, For-profit)
Fall 2006 Enrollment: 900 . . . . (904) 731-4949
2006-07 Tuition: In-state $10,440; Out-of-state $10,440

ITT Technical Institute-Jacksonville (Private, For-profit)
Fall 2006 Enrollment: 539 . . . . (904) 573-9100
2006-07 Tuition: In-state $14,880; Out-of-state $14,880

Jacksonville University (Private, Not-for-profit)
Fall 2006 Enrollment: 3,093. . . . . (904) 256-8000
2006-07 Tuition: In-state $21,200; Out-of-state $21,200

Jones College-Jacksonville (Private, Not-for-profit)
Fall 2006 Enrollment: 539 . . . . (904) 743-1122
2006-07 Tuition: In-state $6,690; Out-of-state $6,690

Remington College-Jacksonville Campus (Private, For-profit)
Fall 2006 Enrollment: 226 . . . . (904) 296-3435
2006-07 Tuition: In-state $12,825; Out-of-state $12,825

Trinity Baptist College (Private, Not-for-profit, Baptist)
Fall 2006 Enrollment: 358 . . . . (904) 596-2400
2006-07 Tuition: In-state $5,850; Out-of-state $5,850

University of North Florida (Public)
Fall 2006 Enrollment: 15,954. (904) 620-1000
2006-07 Tuition: In-state $2,682; Out-of-state $12,084

University of Phoenix-North Florida Campus (Private, For-profit)
Fall 2006 Enrollment: 2,210. . . . . (904) 636-6645
2006-07 Tuition: In-state $10,808; Out-of-state $10,808

Two-year College(s)

Florida Community College at Jacksonville (Public)
Fall 2006 Enrollment: 22,732. (904) 632-3000
2006-07 Tuition: In-state $1,714; Out-of-state $6,118

Florida Technical College of Jacksonville Inc (Private, For-profit)
Fall 2006 Enrollment: 107 . . . . (904) 724-2229

Heritage Institute-Jacksonville (Private, For-profit)
Fall 2006 Enrollment: 252 . . . . (904) 332-0910

Sanford-Brown Institute (Private, For-profit)
Fall 2006 Enrollment: 249 . . . . (904) 363-6221

Stenotype Institute of Jacksonville Inc (Private, For-profit)
Fall 2006 Enrollment: 417 . . . . (904) 398-4141
2006-07 Tuition: In-state $10,800; Out-of-state $10,800

Vocational/Technical School(s)

Commercial Diving Academy (Private, For-profit)
Fall 2006 Enrollment: 60 . . . . (904) 766-7736
2006-07 Tuition: In-state $13,800; Out-of-state $13,800

Concorde Career Institute (Private, For-profit)
Fall 2006 Enrollment: 440 . . . . (904) 725-0525
2006-07 Tuition: $10,721

Jacksonville Beauty Institute (Private, For-profit)
Fall 2006 Enrollment: 64 . . . . (904) 768-9001
2006-07 Tuition: $9,995

Normandy Beauty School of Jacksonville (Private, For-profit)
Fall 2006 Enrollment: 58 . . . . (904) 786-6250
2006-07 Tuition: $5,100

North Florida Institute-Jacksonville (Private, For-profit)
Fall 2006 Enrollment: 241 . . . . (904) 443-6300
2006-07 Tuition: $12,000

Riverside Hairstyling Academy (Private, For-profit)
Fall 2006 Enrollment: 91 . . . . (904) 398-0502
2006-07 Tuition: $8,000

Southeastern School of Neuromuscular & Massage Therapy-Jacksonville (Private, For-profit)
Fall 2006 Enrollment: 25 . . . . (904) 448-9499
2006-07 Tuition: $9,170

2006-07 Tuition: $12,440

Housing: Homeownership rate: 64.2% (2007); Median home value: $153,560 (2007); Median rent: $501 per month (2000); Median age of housing: 25 years (2000).

Hospitals: Baptist Medical Center (601 beds); Baptist Medical Center Beaches (146 beds); Brooks Health System (143 beds); Columbia Memorial Hospital of Jacksonville (353 beds); Mayo Clinic; Shands at Jacksonville (696 beds); Specialty Hospital (107 beds); St. Luke's Hospital (289 beds); St. Vincent's Medical Center (528 beds); Ten Broeck Hospital (99 beds); US Naval Hospital (176 beds)

Safety: Violent crime rate: 83.7 per 10,000 population; Property crime rate: 541.6 per 10,000 population (2006).

Newspapers: Financial News and Daily Record (Circulation 5,400); Florida Star (Black - Circulation 3,000); Jacksonville Advocate (Black, General - Circulation 36,000); Jacksonville Free Press (Black, General - Circulation 36,230); Mandarin News & St. Johns River Pilot (General - Circulation 5,000); The Florida Times-Union (Circulation 169,093); The Veteran Voice (General - Circulation 10,000)

Transportation: Commute to work: 92.6% car, 2.1% public transportation, 1.8% walk, 1.9% work from home (2000); Travel time to work: 21.2% less than 15 minutes, 43.7% 15 to 30 minutes, 24.1% 30 to 45 minutes, 6.4% 45 to 60 minutes, 4.6% 60 minutes or more (2000); Amtrak: Service available.

Airports: Craig Municipal; Herlong; Jacksonville International (primary service/medium hub); Jacksonville NAS /Towers Field/ (primary service/medium hub)

Additional Information Contacts
Jacksonville Chamber of Commerce . . . . (904) 366-6600
http://www.myjaxchamber.com

JACKSONVILLE BEACH (city). Covers a land area of 7.682 square miles and a water area of 14.281 square miles. Located at 30.28° N. Lat.; 81.39° W. Long. Elevation is 10 feet.

History: Named for Andrew Jackson, seventh President of the United States. Jacksonville Beach developed as part of a large ocean front resort area, with a mile-long boardwalk and other amusements.

Population: 17,842 (1990); 20,990 (2000); 22,734 (2007); 24,424 (2012 projected); Race: 91.0% White, 4.0% Black, 1.7% Asian, 3.9% Hispanic of any race (2007); Density: 2,959.4 persons per square mile (2007); Average household size: 2.07 (2007); Median age: 41.7 (2007); Males per 100 females: 100.5 (2007); Marriage status: 27.3% never married, 50.9% now married, 7.0% widowed, 14.8% divorced (2000); Foreign born: 4.4% (2000); Ancestry (includes multiple ancestries): 15.9% Irish, 15.5% English, 13.0% German, 13.0% Other groups, 8.0% Italian (2000).

Economy: Single-family building permits issued: 74 (2006); Multi-family building permits issued: 112 (2006); Employment by occupation: 15.4% management, 23.0% professional, 16.0% services, 28.0% sales, 0.8% farming, 10.2% construction, 6.6% production (2000).

Income: Per capita income: $34,547 (2007); Median household income: $56,514 (2007); Average household income: $70,939 (2007); Percent of households with income of $100,000 or more: 21.6% (2007); Poverty rate: 7.2% (2000).

Education: Percent of population age 25 and over with: High school diploma (including GED) or higher: 89.9% (2007); Bachelor's degree or higher: 30.0% (2007); Master's degree or higher: 9.3% (2007).

School District(s)

Duval County School District (PK-12)
2005-06 Enrollment: 129,486 . . . . (904) 390-2115

Housing: Homeownership rate: 60.2% (2007); Median home value: $258,573 (2007); Median rent: $636 per month (2000); Median age of housing: 25 years (2000).

Safety: Violent crime rate: 90.3 per 10,000 population; Property crime rate: 660.0 per 10,000 population (2006).

Newspapers: Sun Times Weekly (General - Circulation 11,000); The Beaches Leader (General - Circulation 22,500)

Transportation: Commute to work: 91.9% car, 1.0% public transportation, 1.7% walk, 3.9% work from home (2000); Travel time to work: 31.0% less than 15 minutes, 29.8% 15 to 30 minutes, 27.0% 30 to 45 minutes, 8.4% 45 to 60 minutes, 3.7% 60 minutes or more (2000)

Additional Information Contacts

NEPTUNE BEACH (city). Covers a land area of 2.449 square miles and a water area of 4.386 square miles. Located at 30.31° N. Lat.; 81.40° W. Long. Elevation is 10 feet.

History: Neptune Beach was once a part of Jacksonville Beach, but later incorporated on its own.

Population: 6,813 (1990); 7,270 (2000); 7,118 (2007); 7,186 (2012 projected); Race: 95.5% White, 0.5% Black, 1.2% Asian, 2.6% Hispanic of any race (2007); Density: 2,906.8 persons per square mile (2007); Average household size: 2.17 (2007); Median age: 42.6 (2007); Males per 100 females: 103.4 (2007); Marriage status: 24.6% never married, 51.7% now married, 6.3% widowed, 17.4% divorced (2000); Foreign born: 3.9% (2000); Ancestry (includes multiple ancestries): 16.3% German, 13.7% Other groups, 13.7% English, 13.6% Irish, 9.9% United States or American (2000).

Economy: Single-family building permits issued: 19 (2006); Multi-family building permits issued: 0 (2006); Employment by occupation: 19.5% management, 28.3% professional, 12.7% services, 26.7% sales, 0.9% farming, 6.8% construction, 5.1% production (2000).

Income: Per capita income: $36,033 (2007); Median household income: $64,433 (2007); Average household income: $78,053 (2007); Percent of households with income of $100,000 or more: 24.9% (2007); Poverty rate: 2.5% (2000).

Taxes: Total city taxes per capita: $321 (2005); City property taxes per capita: $193 (2005).

Education: Percent of population age 25 and over with: High school diploma (including GED) or higher: 93.3% (2007); Bachelor's degree or higher: 40.1% (2007); Master's degree or higher: 13.3% (2007).

School District(s)

Duval County School District (PK-12)

    2005-06 Enrollment: 129,486 . . . . (904) 390-2115

Housing: Homeownership rate: 64.1% (2007); Median home value: $290,256 (2007); Median rent: $660 per month (2000); Median age of housing: 29 years (2000).

Safety: Violent crime rate: 29.4 per 10,000 population; Property crime rate: 398.0 per 10,000 population (2006).

Transportation: Commute to work: 94.5% car, 1.1% public transportation, 0.2% walk, 1.8% work from home (2000); Travel time to work: 27.1% less than 15 minutes, 27.9% 15 to 30 minutes, 26.6% 30 to 45 minutes, 12.1% 45 to 60 minutes, 6.3% 60 minutes or more (2000)

Additional Information Contacts

City of Neptune Beach . . . . (904) 270-2400
    http://www.ci.neptune-beach.fl.us

Escambia County

Located in northwestern Florida; bounded on the north by Alabama, on the west by the Perdido River and the Alabama border, on the south by the Gulf of Mexico, and on the east by the Escambia River. Covers a land area of 662.35 square miles, a water area of 213.21 square miles, and is located in the Central Time Zone. The county was founded in 1822. County seat is Pensacola.

Escambia County is part of the Pensacola-Ferry Pass-Brent, FL Metropolitan Statistical Area. The entire metro area includes: Escambia County, FL; Santa Rosa County, FL

Weather Station: Pensacola Regional Airport   Elevation: 111 feet

	Jan	Feb	Mar	Apr	May	Jun	Jul	Aug	Sep	Oct	Nov	Dec
High	61	64	70	76	83	89	90	90	87	79	70	64
Low	43	45	52	58	66	72	74	74	71	60	51	45
Precip	5.4	4.9	6.5	3.9	4.7	6.6	8.0	7.0	5.6	4.4	4.2	4.0
Snow	tr	tr	tr	0.0	0.0	0.0	tr	0.0	0.0	0.0	0.0	tr

High and Low temperatures in degrees Fahrenheit; Precipitation and Snow in inches

Population: 262,441 (1990); 294,410 (2000); 301,476 (2007); 307,694 (2012 projected); Race: 70.0% White, 23.1% Black, 2.4% Asian, 3.0% Hispanic of any race (2007); Density: 455.2 persons per square mile (2007); Average household size: 2.60 (2007); Median age: 37.3 (2007); Males per 100 females: 98.5 (2007).

assistance; 16.0% retail trade; 10.7% administration, support, waste management, remediation services (2005); Farms: 674 totaling 64,581 acres (2002); Companies that employ 500 or more persons: 19 (2005); Companies that employ 100 to 499 persons: 135 (2005); Companies that employ less than 100 persons: 6,830 (2005); Black-owned businesses: n/a (2002); Hispanic-owned businesses: 350 (2002); Asian-owned businesses: 534 (2002); Women-owned businesses: 6,120 (2002); Retail sales per capita: $15,745 (2007). Single-family building permits issued: 1,218 (2006); Multi-family building permits issued: 666 (2006).

Income: Per capita income: $22,506 (2007); Median household income: $42,022 (2007); Average household income: $55,416 (2007); Percent of households with income of $100,000 or more: 11.7% (2007); Poverty rate: 15.9% (2005); Bankruptcy rate: 1.53% (2006).

Taxes: Total county taxes per capita: $495 (2005); County property taxes per capita: $288 (2005).

Education: Percent of population age 25 and over with: High school diploma (including GED) or higher: 82.5% (2007); Bachelor's degree or higher: 21.3% (2007); Master's degree or higher: 7.4% (2007).

Housing: Homeownership rate: 67.9% (2007); Median home value: $130,782 (2007); Median rent: $443 per month (2000); Median age of housing: 24 years (2000).

Health: Birth rate: 139.4 per 10,000 population (2006); Death rate: 106.3 per 10,000 population (2006); Age-adjusted cancer mortality rate: 203.2 deaths per 100,000 population (2004); Air Quality Index: 70.4% good, 28.5% moderate, 1.1% unhealthy for sensitive individuals, 0.0% unhealthy (percent of days in 2006); Number of physicians: 27.8 per 10,000 population (2005); Hospital beds: 45.4 per 10,000 population (2004); Hospital admissions: 1,860.7 per 10,000 population (2004).

Elections: 2004 Presidential election results: 65.3% Bush, 33.7% Kerry, 0.4% Nader, 0.2% Badnarik

National and State Parks: Big Lagoon State Park; Fort Pickens State Park; Fort Pickens State Park Aquatic Preserve; Perdido Key State Park; Tarkiln Bayou Preserve State Park

Additional Information Contacts

Escambia County Government . . . . (850) 595-4900
    http://www.co.escambia.fl.us
Pensacola Chamber of Commerce . . . . (850) 438-4081
    http://www.pensacolachamber.com
Pensacola Convention & Visitors Bureau . . . . (850) 434-1234
    http://www.visitpensacola.com

Escambia County Communities

BELLVIEW (CDP). Aka Belleview. Covers a land area of 11.822 square miles and a water area of 0.061 square miles. Located at 30.46° N. Lat.; 87.30° W. Long. Elevation is 89 feet.

Population: 19,386 (1990); 21,201 (2000); 22,042 (2007); 22,736 (2012 projected); Race: 77.1% White, 14.8% Black, 3.4% Asian, 2.6% Hispanic of any race (2007); Density: 1,864.4 persons per square mile (2007); Average household size: 2.53 (2007); Median age: 38.4 (2007); Males per 100 females: 91.4 (2007); Marriage status: 21.4% never married, 58.0% now married, 6.2% widowed, 14.4% divorced (2000); Foreign born: 4.1% (2000); Ancestry (includes multiple ancestries): 24.8% Other groups, 13.6% United States or American, 13.0% German, 11.0% Irish, 10.4% English (2000).

Economy: Employment by occupation: 9.8% management, 17.1% professional, 15.5% services, 31.4% sales, 0.5% farming, 11.7% construction, 13.9% production (2000).

Income: Per capita income: $21,580 (2007); Median household income: $44,970 (2007); Average household income: $54,662 (2007); Percent of households with income of $100,000 or more: 9.8% (2007); Poverty rate: 10.2% (2000).

Education: Percent of population age 25 and over with: High school diploma (including GED) or higher: 83.3% (2007); Bachelor's degree or higher: 13.7% (2007); Master's degree or higher: 5.5% (2007).

Housing: Homeownership rate: 76.3% (2007); Median home value: $117,898 (2007); Median rent: $489 per month (2000); Median age of housing: 20 years (2000).

Transportation: Commute to work: 95.7% car, 0.6% public transportation, 0.5% walk, 2.1% work from home (2000); Travel time to work: 21.0% less

BRENT (CDP). Aka Brentwood. Covers a land area of 10.437 square miles and a water area of 0.087 square miles. Located at 30.47° N. Lat.; 87.24° W. Long. Elevation is 112 feet.

Population: 21,389 (1990); 22,257 (2000); 20,980 (2007); 20,222 (2012 projected); Race: 54.8% White, 38.6% Black, 2.7% Asian, 1.9% Hispanic of any race (2007); Density: 2,010.1 persons per square mile (2007); Average household size: 3.17 (2007); Median age: 26.3 (2007); Males per 100 females: 83.0 (2007); Marriage status: 38.9% never married, 43.8% now married, 6.0% widowed, 11.2% divorced (2000); Foreign born: 2.9% (2000); Ancestry (includes multiple ancestries): 35.0% Other groups, 8.7% United States or American, 5.3% German, 5.1% Irish, 4.2% English (2000).

Economy: Employment by occupation: 6.0% management, 17.8% professional, 21.6% services, 30.5% sales, 0.5% farming, 11.2% construction, 12.4% production (2000).

Income: Per capita income: $13,177 (2007); Median household income: $31,461 (2007); Average household income: $38,982 (2007); Percent of households with income of $100,000 or more: 5.2% (2007); Poverty rate: 24.5% (2000).

Education: Percent of population age 25 and over with: High school diploma (including GED) or higher: 73.8% (2007); Bachelor's degree or higher: 11.8% (2007); Master's degree or higher: 4.2% (2007).

Housing: Homeownership rate: 63.2% (2007); Median home value: $91,497 (2007); Median rent: $389 per month (2000); Median age of housing: 31 years (2000).

Transportation: Commute to work: 77.7% car, 3.3% public transportation, 15.2% walk, 1.7% work from home (2000); Travel time to work: 46.1% less than 15 minutes, 35.2% 15 to 30 minutes, 11.8% 30 to 45 minutes, 2.4% 45 to 60 minutes, 4.4% 60 minutes or more (2000)

CANTONMENT (unincorporated postal area, zip code 32533). Covers a land area of 76.107 square miles and a water area of 0.126 square miles. Located at 30.60° N. Lat.; 87.32° W. Long. Elevation is 150 feet.

Population: 23,889 (2000); Race: 84.8% White, 11.3% Black, 0.7% Asian, 1.6% Hispanic of any race (2000); Density: 313.9 persons per square mile (2000); Age: 28.1% under 18, 10.3% over 64 (2000); Marriage status: 20.0% never married, 65.0% now married, 4.3% widowed, 10.7% divorced (2000); Foreign born: 2.0% (2000); Ancestry (includes multiple ancestries): 21.4% Other groups, 16.1% United States or American, 9.8% Irish, 9.5% English, 8.9% German (2000).

Economy: Employment by occupation: 12.1% management, 19.2% professional, 14.0% services, 29.3% sales, 0.2% farming, 12.7% construction, 12.4% production (2000).

Income: Per capita income: $19,852 (2000); Median household income: $44,191 (2000); Poverty rate: 11.1% (2000).

Education: Percent of population age 25 and over with: High school diploma (including GED) or higher: 83.5% (2000); Bachelor's degree or higher: 18.1% (2000).

School District(s)
Escambia County School District (PK-12)
   2005-06 Enrollment: 43,953 . . . . (850) 469-6130

Housing: Homeownership rate: 86.6% (2000); Median home value: $107,200 (2000); Median rent: $374 per month (2000); Median age of housing: 16 years (2000).

Transportation: Commute to work: 94.5% car, 0.3% public transportation, 1.0% walk, 3.1% work from home (2000); Travel time to work: 21.2% less than 15 minutes, 43.2% 15 to 30 minutes, 23.2% 30 to 45 minutes, 6.1% 45 to 60 minutes, 6.3% 60 minutes or more (2000)

CENTURY (town). Aka South Flomaton. Covers a land area of 3.281 square miles and a water area of 0.061 square miles. Located at 30.97° N. Lat.; 87.26° W. Long. Elevation is 85 feet.

History: Century was named for the establishment in January 1900 of a large sawmill around which the settlement grew.

Population: 1,989 (1990); 1,714 (2000); 1,765 (2007); 1,834 (2012 projected); Race: 39.1% White, 56.3% Black, 0.8% Asian, 2.3% Hispanic of any race (2007); Density: 538.0 persons per square mile (2007); Average household size: 2.45 (2007); Median age: 31.7 (2007); Males per 100 females: 83.5 (2007); Marriage status: 27.7% never married, 49.9% now married, 11.3% widowed, 11.2% divorced (2000); Foreign born: 1.1% (2000); Ancestry (includes multiple ancestries): 45.4% Other groups,

professional, 21.5% services, 20.7% sales, 0.0% farming, 16.3% construction, 24.3% production (2000).

Income: Per capita income: $14,407 (2007); Median household income: $27,935 (2007); Average household income: $35,316 (2007); Percent of households with income of $100,000 or more: 4.3% (2007); Poverty rate: 30.1% (2000).

Education: Percent of population age 25 and over with: High school diploma (including GED) or higher: 63.4% (2007); Bachelor's degree or higher: 5.5% (2007); Master's degree or higher: 1.9% (2007).

School District(s)
Escambia County School District (PK-12)
   2005-06 Enrollment: 43,953 . . . . (850) 469-6130

Housing: Homeownership rate: 70.6% (2007); Median home value: $67,500 (2007); Median rent: $198 per month (2000); Median age of housing: 30 years (2000).

Transportation: Commute to work: 90.3% car, 2.8% public transportation, 2.5% walk, 2.7% work from home (2000); Travel time to work: 36.4% less than 15 minutes, 19.1% 15 to 30 minutes, 23.0% 30 to 45 minutes, 12.5% 45 to 60 minutes, 9.1% 60 minutes or more (2000)

ENSLEY (CDP). Covers a land area of 12.337 square miles and a water area of 0 square miles. Located at 30.52° N. Lat.; 87.27° W. Long. Elevation is 131 feet.

Population: 17,308 (1990); 18,752 (2000); 19,823 (2007); 20,607 (2012 projected); Race: 63.5% White, 31.2% Black, 1.3% Asian, 2.6% Hispanic of any race (2007); Density: 1,606.7 persons per square mile (2007); Average household size: 2.43 (2007); Median age: 37.4 (2007); Males per 100 females: 91.4 (2007); Marriage status: 23.3% never married, 54.7% now married, 7.2% widowed, 14.8% divorced (2000); Foreign born: 3.1% (2000); Ancestry (includes multiple ancestries): 36.3% Other groups, 11.4% United States or American, 9.6% Irish, 8.9% German, 8.0% English (2000).

Economy: Employment by occupation: 8.4% management, 15.3% professional, 17.4% services, 29.7% sales, 0.4% farming, 15.1% construction, 13.6% production (2000).

Income: Per capita income: $20,060 (2007); Median household income: $36,910 (2007); Average household income: $48,577 (2007); Percent of households with income of $100,000 or more: 8.1% (2007); Poverty rate: 15.7% (2000).

Education: Percent of population age 25 and over with: High school diploma (including GED) or higher: 78.8% (2007); Bachelor's degree or higher: 14.0% (2007); Master's degree or higher: 3.8% (2007).

Housing: Homeownership rate: 68.0% (2007); Median home value: $112,361 (2007); Median rent: $406 per month (2000); Median age of housing: 21 years (2000).

Transportation: Commute to work: 94.3% car, 0.7% public transportation, 1.5% walk, 2.0% work from home (2000); Travel time to work: 26.7% less than 15 minutes, 47.6% 15 to 30 minutes, 16.2% 30 to 45 minutes, 2.4% 45 to 60 minutes, 7.2% 60 minutes or more (2000)

FERRY PASS (CDP). Covers a land area of 14.084 square miles and a water area of 0.018 square miles. Located at 30.51° N. Lat.; 87.20° W. Long. Elevation is 131 feet.

Population: 24,919 (1990); 27,176 (2000); 28,296 (2007); 29,259 (2012 projected); Race: 80.2% White, 13.5% Black, 2.0% Asian, 2.9% Hispanic of any race (2007); Density: 2,009.2 persons per square mile (2007); Average household size: 2.27 (2007); Median age: 39.7 (2007); Males per 100 females: 87.2 (2007); Marriage status: 26.3% never married, 50.7% now married, 10.1% widowed, 13.0% divorced (2000); Foreign born: 4.3% (2000); Ancestry (includes multiple ancestries): 19.5% Other groups, 13.4% German, 12.1% United States or American, 11.0% Irish, 10.9% English (2000).

Economy: Employment by occupation: 11.6% management, 23.8% professional, 16.0% services, 30.8% sales, 0.2% farming, 9.3% construction, 8.3% production (2000).

Income: Per capita income: $25,963 (2007); Median household income: $43,679 (2007); Average household income: $56,651 (2007); Percent of households with income of $100,000 or more: 11.4% (2007); Poverty rate: 12.1% (2000).

Education: Percent of population age 25 and over with: High school diploma (including GED) or higher: 87.5% (2007); Bachelor's degree or higher: 29.7% (2007); Master's degree or higher: 11.8% (2007).

$141,170 (2007); Median rent: $523 per month (2000); Median age of housing: 17 years (2000).

Transportation: Commute to work: 94.4% car, 0.6% public transportation, 0.8% walk, 2.0% work from home (2000); Travel time to work: 28.7% less than 15 minutes, 49.0% 15 to 30 minutes, 15.5% 30 to 45 minutes, 2.4% 45 to 60 minutes, 4.4% 60 minutes or more (2000)

GONZALEZ (CDP). Aka Roberts. Covers a land area of 15.287 square miles and a water area of 0.054 square miles. Located at 30.57° N. Lat.; 87.29° W. Long. Elevation is 151 feet.

History: Gonzalez was first settled in the early 1800's and named for Don Manuel Gonzalez who had a land grant here. The town grew as a trading center for farmers.

Population: 7,949 (1990); 11,365 (2000); 12,641 (2007); 13,525 (2012 projected); Race: 85.2% White, 9.8% Black, 1.8% Asian, 2.1% Hispanic of any race (2007); Density: 826.9 persons per square mile (2007); Average household size: 2.72 (2007); Median age: 39.4 (2007); Males per 100 females: 94.9 (2007); Marriage status: 20.8% never married, 65.4% now married, 4.0% widowed, 9.8% divorced (2000); Foreign born: 2.9% (2000); Ancestry (includes multiple ancestries): 22.6% Other groups, 13.2% United States or American, 10.5% German, 10.1% Irish, 8.6% English (2000).

Economy: Employment by occupation: 11.7% management, 22.1% professional, 14.9% services, 30.6% sales, 0.0% farming, 10.7% construction, 10.0% production (2000).

Income: Per capita income: $26,085 (2007); Median household income: $59,314 (2007); Average household income: $71,043 (2007); Percent of households with income of $100,000 or more: 18.5% (2007); Poverty rate: 8.0% (2000).

Education: Percent of population age 25 and over with: High school diploma (including GED) or higher: 89.2% (2007); Bachelor's degree or higher: 20.9% (2007); Master's degree or higher: 6.3% (2007).

School District(s)
Escambia County School District (PK-12)
   2005-06 Enrollment: 43,953 . . . . (850) 469-6130

Housing: Homeownership rate: 86.0% (2007); Median home value: $172,175 (2007); Median rent: $390 per month (2000); Median age of housing: 16 years (2000).

Transportation: Commute to work: 94.3% car, 0.5% public transportation, 0.9% walk, 3.2% work from home (2000); Travel time to work: 23.5% less than 15 minutes, 43.5% 15 to 30 minutes, 24.5% 30 to 45 minutes, 4.1% 45 to 60 minutes, 4.4% 60 minutes or more (2000)

GOULDING (CDP). Covers a land area of 1.231 square miles and a water area of 0 square miles. Located at 30.43° N. Lat.; 87.23° W. Long. Elevation is 82 feet.

History: Goulding developed as an industrial community with fertilizer factories and a chemical plant manufacturing rosin.

Population: 4,159 (1990); 4,484 (2000); 4,218 (2007); 4,071 (2012 projected); Race: 27.7% White, 69.2% Black, 0.7% Asian, 2.1% Hispanic of any race (2007); Density: 3,427.1 persons per square mile (2007); Average household size: 3.54 (2007); Median age: 41.2 (2007); Males per 100 females: 137.5 (2007); Marriage status: 41.3% never married, 33.5% now married, 15.2% widowed, 10.0% divorced (2000); Foreign born: 0.7% (2000); Ancestry (includes multiple ancestries): 40.7% Other groups, 3.9% African, 3.6% United States or American, 3.0% German, 2.5% Irish (2000).

Economy: Employment by occupation: 2.0% management, 7.8% professional, 30.1% services, 17.5% sales, 0.0% farming, 16.9% construction, 25.6% production (2000).

Income: Per capita income: $9,671 (2007); Median household income: $16,159 (2007); Average household income: $25,206 (2007); Percent of households with income of $100,000 or more: 3.0% (2007); Poverty rate: 30.4% (2000).

Education: Percent of population age 25 and over with: High school diploma (including GED) or higher: 57.5% (2007); Bachelor's degree or higher: 7.6% (2007); Master's degree or higher: 3.0% (2007).

Housing: Homeownership rate: 49.2% (2007); Median home value: $64,324 (2007); Median rent: $240 per month (2000); Median age of housing: 39 years (2000).

Transportation: Commute to work: 84.1% car, 7.7% public transportation, 6.0% walk, 0.8% work from home (2000); Travel time to work: 42.8% less than 15 minutes, 31.1% 15 to 30 minutes, 14.4% 30 to 45 minutes, 8.6% 45 to 60 minutes, 3.1% 60 minutes or more (2000)

MCDAVID (unincorporated postal area, zip code 32568). Covers a land area of 216.066 square miles and a water area of 0.157 square miles. Located at 30.87° N. Lat.; 87.47° W. Long. Elevation is 34 feet.

History: McDavid grew as a center for naval stores (rosen and turpentine used in calking boats).

Population: 3,225 (2000); Race: 84.8% White, 9.6% Black, 0.0% Asian, 0.8% Hispanic of any race (2000); Density: 14.9 persons per square mile (2000); Age: 26.3% under 18, 14.3% over 64 (2000); Marriage status: 19.6% never married, 64.8% now married, 5.6% widowed, 10.0% divorced (2000); Foreign born: 0.1% (2000); Ancestry (includes multiple ancestries): 23.1% United States or American, 18.3% Other groups, 6.4% German, 5.0% Irish, 4.7% English (2000).

Economy: Employment by occupation: 6.6% management, 16.1% professional, 16.7% services, 23.8% sales, 1.8% farming, 18.2% construction, 17.0% production (2000).

Income: Per capita income: $15,054 (2000); Median household income: $35,533 (2000); Poverty rate: 14.3% (2000).

Education: Percent of population age 25 and over with: High school diploma (including GED) or higher: 70.9% (2000); Bachelor's degree or higher: 7.1% (2000).

Housing: Homeownership rate: 88.1% (2000); Median home value: $70,700 (2000); Median rent: $260 per month (2000); Median age of housing: 23 years (2000).

Transportation: Commute to work: 93.1% car, 0.0% public transportation, 0.8% walk, 2.6% work from home (2000); Travel time to work: 15.4% less than 15 minutes, 28.5% 15 to 30 minutes, 21.7% 30 to 45 minutes, 18.0% 45 to 60 minutes, 16.5% 60 minutes or more (2000)

MOLINO (CDP). Covers a land area of 6.969 square miles and a water area of 0.029 square miles. Located at 30.72° N. Lat.; 87.32° W. Long. Elevation is 36 feet.

History: Molino was settled about 1820 and developed around the sawmills that had operated here as early as 1812.

Population: 1,192 (1990); 1,312 (2000); 1,425 (2007); 1,508 (2012 projected); Race: 69.6% White, 26.2% Black, 0.6% Asian, 1.1% Hispanic of any race (2007); Density: 204.5 persons per square mile (2007); Average household size: 2.72 (2007); Median age: 37.4 (2007); Males per 100 females: 103.9 (2007); Marriage status: 24.3% never married, 57.2% now married, 9.3% widowed, 9.3% divorced (2000); Foreign born: 0.4% (2000); Ancestry (includes multiple ancestries): 26.8% Other groups, 19.8% United States or American, 8.6% German, 7.2% Irish, 6.4% English (2000).

Economy: Employment by occupation: 4.4% management, 11.2% professional, 19.9% services, 17.0% sales, 2.0% farming, 18.5% construction, 27.1% production (2000).

Income: Per capita income: $18,707 (2007); Median household income: $43,649 (2007); Average household income: $50,873 (2007); Percent of households with income of $100,000 or more: 12.2% (2007); Poverty rate: 12.7% (2000).

Education: Percent of population age 25 and over with: High school diploma (including GED) or higher: 69.0% (2007); Bachelor's degree or higher: 4.9% (2007); Master's degree or higher: 0.3% (2007).

School District(s)
Escambia County School District (PK-12)
   2005-06 Enrollment: 43,953 . . . . (850) 469-6130

Housing: Homeownership rate: 84.9% (2007); Median home value: $91,250 (2007); Median rent: $285 per month (2000); Median age of housing: 25 years (2000).

Transportation: Commute to work: 96.8% car, 0.0% public transportation, 1.8% walk, 0.0% work from home (2000); Travel time to work: 13.1% less than 15 minutes, 26.8% 15 to 30 minutes, 47.4% 30 to 45 minutes, 6.4% 45 to 60 minutes, 6.3% 60 minutes or more (2000)

MYRTLE GROVE (CDP). Covers a land area of 6.604 square miles and a water area of 0 square miles. Located at 30.42° N. Lat.; 87.30° W. Long. Elevation is 75 feet.

Population: 17,402 (1990); 17,211 (2000); 17,389 (2007); 17,658 (2012 projected); Race: 70.0% White, 17.8% Black, 5.1% Asian, 4.7% Hispanic of any race (2007); Density: 2,633.1 persons per square mile (2007); Average household size: 2.71 (2007); Median age: 33.6 (2007); Males per 100 females: 103.7 (2007); Marriage status: 28.6% never married, 53.3% now married, 6.0% widowed, 12.2% divorced (2000); Foreign born: 5.5% (2000); Ancestry (includes multiple ancestries): 33.1% Other groups, 12.4% Irish, 12.4% German, 9.5% United States or American, 9.2% English (2000).

Economy: Employment by occupation: 11.6% management, 17.7% professional, 18.3% services, 27.9% sales, 0.3% farming, 11.8% construction, 12.4% production (2000).

Income: Per capita income: $21,171 (2007); Median household income: $38,422 (2007); Average household income: $48,205 (2007); Percent of households with income of $100,000 or more: 7.7% (2007); Poverty rate: 14.2% (2000).

Education: Percent of population age 25 and over with: High school diploma (including GED) or higher: 84.2% (2007); Bachelor's degree or higher: 18.4% (2007); Master's degree or higher: 6.1% (2007).

Housing: Homeownership rate: 59.8% (2007); Median home value: $116,210 (2007); Median rent: $486 per month (2000); Median age of housing: 24 years (2000).

Transportation: Commute to work: 82.8% car, 0.8% public transportation, 13.4% walk, 1.4% work from home (2000); Travel time to work: 29.3% less than 15 minutes, 49.6% 15 to 30 minutes, 12.8% 30 to 45 minutes, 3.4% 45 to 60 minutes, 4.8% 60 minutes or more (2000)

PENSACOLA (city). County seat. Covers a land area of 22.696 square miles and a water area of 16.958 square miles. Located at 30.43° N. Lat.; 87.20° W. Long. Elevation is 102 feet.

History: Spanish and French forts and settlements were built around Pensacola Bay for several centuries. After Florida became a British colony in 1763, a town was laid out, which surrendered in 1781 to the Spanish. In 1814 both Spanish and British flags flew over Pensacola. When Florida was transfered to the United States in 1821, Andrew Jackson became provisional governor of the territory and took up residence in Pensacola, which was chartered as a city in 1822. Development began in earnest after the Civil War, when Pensacola's landlocked harbor was visited by ships from around the world.

Population: 58,906 (1990); 56,255 (2000); 53,700 (2007); 52,303 (2012 projected); Race: 64.1% White, 30.9% Black, 1.9% Asian, 2.2% Hispanic of any race (2007); Density: 2,366.1 persons per square mile (2007); Average household size: 2.24 (2007); Median age: 42.1 (2007); Males per 100 females: 88.9 (2007); Marriage status: 29.6% never married, 48.0% now married, 8.7% widowed, 13.6% divorced (2000); Foreign born: 3.6% (2000); Ancestry (includes multiple ancestries): 33.4% Other groups, 11.0% English, 10.5% German, 10.0% Irish, 7.7% United States or American (2000).

Economy: Unemployment rate: 3.7% (11/2007); Total civilian labor force: 26,648 (11/2007); Single-family building permits issued: 104 (2006); Multi-family building permits issued: 0 (2006); Employment by occupation: 13.3% management, 25.0% professional, 17.9% services, 26.8% sales, 0.6% farming, 7.7% construction, 8.7% production (2000).

Income: Per capita income: $25,627 (2007); Median household income: $40,622 (2007); Average household income: $57,173 (2007); Percent of households with income of $100,000 or more: 12.6% (2007); Poverty rate: 16.1% (2000).

Taxes: Total city taxes per capita: $614 (2005); City property taxes per capita: $251 (2005).

Education: Percent of population age 25 and over with: High school diploma (including GED) or higher: 85.0% (2007); Bachelor's degree or higher: 32.9% (2007); Master's degree or higher: 12.0% (2007).

School District(s)
Escambia County School District (PK-12)
  2005-06 Enrollment: 43,953 . . . . (850) 469-6130
Santa Rosa County School District (PK-12)
  2005-06 Enrollment: 25,038 . . . . (850) 983-5010
Four-year College(s)
The University of West Florida (Public)
  Fall 2006 Enrollment: 9,819 . . . . (850) 474-2000
  2006-07 Tuition: In-state $2,860; Out-of-state $13,702
Two-year College(s)
Florida Institute of Ultrasound Inc (Private, For-profit)
  Fall 2006 Enrollment: 67 . . . . (850) 478-7611
George Stone Career Center (Public)
  Fall 2006 Enrollment: 741 . . . . (850) 941-6200
Pensacola Junior College (Public)
  Fall 2006 Enrollment: 10,208. . . . . (850) 484-1000
  2006-07 Tuition: In-state $1,581; Out-of-state $5,698
Virginia College at Pensacola (Private, For-profit)
  Fall 2006 Enrollment: 224 . . . . (850) 436-8444
  2006-07 Tuition: In-state $8,460; Out-of-state $8,460

Housing: Homeownership rate: 63.9% (2007); Median home value: $148,639 (2007); Median rent: $455 per month (2000); Median age of housing: 33 years (2000).

Hospitals: Baptist Hospital (546 beds); Naval Hospital-Pensacola (65 beds); Sacred Heart Health System (449 beds); West Florida Regional Medical Center (531 beds)

Safety: Violent crime rate: 92.1 per 10,000 population; Property crime rate: 530.0 per 10,000 population (2006).

Newspapers: Escambia Sun Press (General - Circulation 4,800); Pensacola News Journal (Circulation 64,675); Pensacola Voice (Black - Circulation 36,584)

Transportation: Commute to work: 91.6% car, 2.1% public transportation, 1.7% walk, 3.0% work from home (2000); Travel time to work: 39.4% less than 15 minutes, 41.8% 15 to 30 minutes, 11.6% 30 to 45 minutes, 2.7% 45 to 60 minutes, 4.5% 60 minutes or more (2000); Amtrak: Service available.

Airports: Pensacola Regional (primary service/small hub)

Additional Information Contacts
Pensacola Chamber of Commerce . . . . (850) 438-4081
  http://www.pensacolachamber.com
Pensacola Convention & Visitors Bureau . . . . (850) 434-1234
  http://www.visitpensacola.com

WARRINGTON (CDP). Covers a land area of 6.572 square miles and a water area of 1.936 square miles. Located at 30.38° N. Lat.; 87.29° W. Long. Elevation is 52 feet.

Population: 15,984 (1990); 15,207 (2000); 13,500 (2007); 12,609 (2012 projected); Race: 67.8% White, 25.2% Black, 1.9% Asian, 3.0% Hispanic of any race (2007); Density: 2,054.3 persons per square mile (2007); Average household size: 2.27 (2007); Median age: 37.7 (2007); Males per 100 females: 92.6 (2007); Marriage status: 24.5% never married, 50.3% now married, 8.6% widowed, 16.6% divorced (2000); Foreign born: 3.4% (2000); Ancestry (includes multiple ancestries): 30.7% Other groups, 14.5% United States or American, 10.3% German, 9.6% Irish, 9.0% English (2000).

Economy: Employment by occupation: 9.2% management, 13.8% professional, 22.1% services, 28.6% sales, 0.5% farming, 14.7% construction, 11.1% production (2000).

Income: Per capita income: $21,683 (2007); Median household income: $36,122 (2007); Average household income: $49,176 (2007); Percent of households with income of $100,000 or more: 8.2% (2007); Poverty rate: 20.6% (2000).

Education: Percent of population age 25 and over with: High school diploma (including GED) or higher: 78.9% (2007); Bachelor's degree or higher: 14.6% (2007); Master's degree or higher: 4.7% (2007).

Housing: Homeownership rate: 61.9% (2007); Median home value: $97,165 (2007); Median rent: $381 per month (2000); Median age of housing: 41 years (2000).

Transportation: Commute to work: 89.8% car, 3.4% public transportation, 1.2% walk, 2.7% work from home (2000); Travel time to work: 29.6% less than 15 minutes, 40.4% 15 to 30 minutes, 18.5% 30 to 45 minutes, 5.2% 45 to 60 minutes, 6.3% 60 minutes or more (2000)

WEST PENSACOLA (CDP). Covers a land area of 7.367 square miles and a water area of 0.076 square miles. Located at 30.42° N. Lat.; 87.26° W. Long. Elevation is 89 feet.

Population: 22,074 (1990); 21,939 (2000); 20,867 (2007); 20,195 (2012 projected); Race: 48.5% White, 43.0% Black, 3.5% Asian, 2.6% Hispanic of any race (2007); Density: 2,832.6 persons per square mile (2007); Average household size: 2.43 (2007); Median age: 35.2 (2007); Males per 100 females: 91.4 (2007); Marriage status: 29.1% never married, 44.5% now married, 9.6% widowed, 16.8% divorced (2000); Foreign born: 4.6% (2000); Ancestry (includes multiple ancestries): 37.6% Other groups, 10.2% United States or American, 7.1% Irish, 5.8% German, 5.5% English (2000).

Economy: Employment by occupation: 5.2% management, 12.3% professional, 26.0% services, 25.0% sales, 1.0% farming, 15.1% construction, 15.4% production (2000).

Income: Per capita income: $14,663 (2007); Median household income: $27,579 (2007); Average household income: $35,225 (2007); Percent of households with income of $100,000 or more: 3.8% (2007); Poverty rate: 25.3% (2000).

Education: Percent of population age 25 and over with: High school diploma (including GED) or higher: 69.4% (2007); Bachelor's degree or higher: 8.1% (2007); Master's degree or higher: 2.1% (2007).

Housing: Homeownership rate: 56.6% (2007); Median home value: $69,011 (2007); Median rent: $381 per month (2000); Median age of housing: 40 years (2000).
Transportation: Commute to work: 90.5% car, 3.3% public transportation, 1.8% walk, 1.9% work from home (2000); Travel time to work: 33.6% less than 15 minutes, 41.1% 15 to 30 minutes, 16.4% 30 to 45 minutes, 3.6% 45 to 60 minutes, 5.3% 60 minutes or more (2000)

Flagler County

Located in northeastern Florida; swampy area, bounded on the east by the Atlantic Ocean, and on the west by Crescent Lake. Covers a land area of 485.00 square miles, a water area of 85.77 square miles, and is located in the Eastern Time Zone. The county was founded in 1917. County seat is Bunnell.

Flagler County is part of the Palm Coast, FL Metropolitan Statistical Area. The entire metro area includes: Flagler County, FL

Population: 28,701 (1990); 49,832 (2000); 86,326 (2007); 112,809 (2012 projected); Race: 86.2% White, 9.1% Black, 1.7% Asian, 6.9% Hispanic of any race (2007); Density: 178.0 persons per square mile (2007); Average household size: 2.33 (2007); Median age: 45.3 (2007); Males per 100 females: 94.8 (2007).
Religion: Five largest groups: 21.1% Catholic Church, 5.4% Southern Baptist Convention, 3.4% The United Methodist Church, 1.2% Episcopal Church, 1.2% Evangelical Lutheran Church in America (2000).
Economy: Unemployment rate: 5.9% (11/2007); Total civilian labor force: 34,792 (11/2007); Leading industries: 17.6% construction; 15.8% retail trade; 12.8% accommodation & food services (2005); Farms: 100 totaling 68,364 acres (2002); Companies that employ 500 or more persons: 5 (2005); Companies that employ 100 to 499 persons: 13 (2005); Companies that employ less than 100 persons: 1,735 (2005); Black-owned businesses: 164 (2002); Hispanic-owned businesses: 159 (2002); Asian-owned businesses: n/a (2002); Women-owned businesses: 1,701 (2002); Retail sales per capita: $8,336 (2007). Single-family building permits issued: 1,499 (2006); Multi-family building permits issued: 340 (2006).
Income: Per capita income: $26,421 (2007); Median household income: $47,651 (2007); Average household income: $61,233 (2007); Percent of households with income of $100,000 or more: 14.0% (2007); Poverty rate: 9.6% (2005); Bankruptcy rate: 1.59% (2006).
Education: Percent of population age 25 and over with: High school diploma (including GED) or higher: 85.6% (2007); Bachelor's degree or higher: 20.3% (2007); Master's degree or higher: 7.4% (2007).
Housing: Homeownership rate: 84.6% (2007); Median home value: $216,731 (2007); Median rent: $592 per month (2000); Median age of housing: 11 years (2000).
Health: Birth rate: 84.1 per 10,000 population (2006); Death rate: 92.4 per 10,000 population (2006); Age-adjusted cancer mortality rate: 185.8 deaths per 100,000 population (2004); Number of physicians: 11.3 per 10,000 population (2005); Hospital beds: 11.8 per 10,000 population (2004); Hospital admissions: 751.1 per 10,000 population (2004).
Elections: 2004 Presidential election results: 51.0% Bush, 48.3% Kerry, 0.5% Nader, 0.1% Badnarik
National and State Parks: Bulow Plantation Ruins Historic State Park; Gamble Rogers Memorial State Recreation Area; Relay State Wildlife Management Area; Washington Oaks Gardens State Park
Additional Information Contacts
Flagler County Government . . . . (386) 437-7414
　http://www.flaglercounty.org
City of Palm Coast . . . . (386) 986-3700
　http://www.ci.palm-coast.fl.us
Flagler Beach Chamber of Commerce . . . . (904) 439-0995
　http://www.flaglercounty.com

Flagler County Communities

BEVERLY BEACH (town). Covers a land area of 0.358 square miles and a water area of 0.030 square miles. Located at 29.51° N. Lat.; 81.14° W. Long. Elevation is 16 feet.
Population: 312 (1990); 547 (2000); 800 (2007); 998 (2012 projected); Race: 96.3% White, 0.4% Black, 0.3% Asian, 0.1% Hispanic of any race (2007); Density: 2,233.8 persons per square mile (2007); Average household size: 1.70 (2007); Median age: 62.2 (2007); Males per 100 females: 94.6 (2007); Marriage status: 9.3% never married, 59.7% now

married, 20.5% widowed, 10.5% divorced (2000); Foreign born: 4.3% (2000); Ancestry (includes multiple ancestries): 22.0% German, 17.5% English, 14.0% Irish, 9.6% Italian, 7.9% United States or American (2000).
Economy: Single-family building permits issued: 1 (2006); Multi-family building permits issued: 0 (2006); Employment by occupation: 8.6% management, 15.0% professional, 17.9% services, 30.0% sales, 0.0% farming, 20.7% construction, 7.9% production (2000).
Income: Per capita income: $25,125 (2007); Median household income: $33,359 (2007); Average household income: $42,675 (2007); Percent of households with income of $100,000 or more: 6.2% (2007); Poverty rate: 8.7% (2000).
Education: Percent of population age 25 and over with: High school diploma (including GED) or higher: 79.5% (2007); Bachelor's degree or higher: 16.6% (2007); Master's degree or higher: 6.5% (2007).
Housing: Homeownership rate: 84.9% (2007); Median home value: $102,532 (2007); Median rent: $392 per month (2000); Median age of housing: 16 years (2000).
Transportation: Commute to work: 89.7% car, 0.0% public transportation, 7.4% walk, 2.9% work from home (2000); Travel time to work: 33.3% less than 15 minutes, 46.2% 15 to 30 minutes, 8.3% 30 to 45 minutes, 6.1% 45 to 60 minutes, 6.1% 60 minutes or more (2000)

BUNNELL (city). County seat. Covers a land area of 4.664 square miles and a water area of 0 square miles. Located at 29.46° N. Lat.; 81.25° W. Long. Elevation is 20 feet.
History: Bunnell developed as a lumber and turpentine town, situated in a potato-growing area. Another early industry was the cutting and shipping of palmetto leaves for use in Palm Sunday services.
Population: 1,911 (1990); 2,122 (2000); 4,055 (2007); 5,435 (2012 projected); Race: 74.9% White, 19.9% Black, 1.4% Asian, 6.8% Hispanic of any race (2007); Density: 869.5 persons per square mile (2007); Average household size: 2.31 (2007); Median age: 38.6 (2007); Males per 100 females: 96.1 (2007); Marriage status: 33.2% never married, 43.5% now married, 9.8% widowed, 13.5% divorced (2000); Foreign born: 2.2% (2000); Ancestry (includes multiple ancestries): 34.3% Other groups, 9.3% German, 8.5% English, 8.1% Irish, 6.0% Italian (2000).
Economy: Single-family building permits issued: 5 (2006); Multi-family building permits issued: 0 (2006); Employment by occupation: 6.4% management, 11.3% professional, 24.3% services, 24.9% sales, 1.6% farming, 15.0% construction, 16.5% production (2000).
Income: Per capita income: $17,980 (2007); Median household income: $27,771 (2007); Average household income: $40,110 (2007); Percent of households with income of $100,000 or more: 7.6% (2007); Poverty rate: 22.5% (2000).
Education: Percent of population age 25 and over with: High school diploma (including GED) or higher: 75.0% (2007); Bachelor's degree or higher: 11.7% (2007); Master's degree or higher: 2.7% (2007).
School District(s)
Flagler County School District (PK-12)
　2005-06 Enrollment: 9,698 . . . . (386) 437-7526
Housing: Homeownership rate: 73.2% (2007); Median home value: $125,069 (2007); Median rent: $332 per month (2000); Median age of housing: 26 years (2000).
Newspapers: The Flagler/Palm Coast News Tribune (General - Circulation 9,635)
Transportation: Commute to work: 90.0% car, 2.6% public transportation, 4.4% walk, 2.3% work from home (2000); Travel time to work: 38.8% less than 15 minutes, 37.9% 15 to 30 minutes, 13.1% 30 to 45 minutes, 5.0% 45 to 60 minutes, 5.2% 60 minutes or more (2000)
Airports: Flagler County

FLAGLER BEACH (city). Covers a land area of 3.683 square miles and a water area of 0.402 square miles. Located at 29.47° N. Lat.; 81.12° W. Long. Elevation is 10 feet.
Population: 3,882 (1990); 4,954 (2000); 6,155 (2007); 7,122 (2012 projected); Race: 97.5% White, 0.6% Black, 0.9% Asian, 2.5% Hispanic of any race (2007); Density: 1,671.2 persons per square mile (2007); Average household size: 1.90 (2007); Median age: 52.4 (2007); Males per 100 females: 95.8 (2007); Marriage status: 15.3% never married, 60.4% now married, 12.0% widowed, 12.2% divorced (2000); Foreign born: 6.1% (2000); Ancestry (includes multiple ancestries): 19.7% Irish, 16.6% German, 16.5% English, 8.0% United States or American, 7.9% Italian (2000).

Education: Percent of population age 25 and over with: High school diploma (including GED) or higher: 90.0% (2007); Bachelor's degree or higher: 31.5% (2007); Master's degree or higher: 12.0% (2007).

School District(s)

Flagler County School District (PK-12)

    2005-06 Enrollment: 9,698 . . . . (386) 437-7526

Housing: Homeownership rate: 71.4% (2007); Median home value: $274,196 (2007); Median rent: $500 per month (2000); Median age of housing: 18 years (2000).

Safety: Violent crime rate: 37.1 per 10,000 population; Property crime rate: 507.3 per 10,000 population (2006).

Transportation: Commute to work: 89.5% car, 1.4% public transportation, 3.1% walk, 3.8% work from home (2000); Travel time to work: 29.4% less than 15 minutes, 39.4% 15 to 30 minutes, 17.9% 30 to 45 minutes, 8.8% 45 to 60 minutes, 4.5% 60 minutes or more (2000)

Additional Information Contacts

Flagler Beach Chamber of Commerce . . . . (904) 439-0995

    http://www.flaglercounty.com

MARINELAND (town). Covers a land area of 0.340 square miles and a water area of 0 square miles. Located at 29.66° N. Lat.; 81.21° W. Long. Elevation is 7 feet.

Population: 21 (1990); 6 (2000); 8 (2007); 10 (2012 projected); Race: 100.0% White, 0.0% Black, 0.0% Asian, 0.0% Hispanic of any race (2007); Density: 23.5 persons per square mile (2007); Average household size: 2.00 (2007); Median age: 30.0 (2007); Males per 100 females: 100.0 (2007); Marriage status: 66.7% never married, 33.3% now married, 0.0% widowed, 0.0% divorced (2000); Foreign born: 71.4% (2000); Ancestry (includes multiple ancestries): 71.4% Russian, 28.6% Welsh (2000).

Economy: Single-family building permits issued: 1 (2006); Multi-family building permits issued: 0 (2006); Employment by occupation: 0.0% management, 100.0% professional, 0.0% services, 0.0% sales, 0.0% farming, 0.0% construction, 0.0% production (2000).

Income: Per capita income: $18,750 (2007); Median household income: $40,000 (2007); Average household income: $37,500 (2007); Percent of households with income of $100,000 or more: 0.0% (2007); Poverty rate: 0.0% (2000).

Education: Percent of population age 25 and over with: High school diploma (including GED) or higher: 100.0% (2007); Bachelor's degree or higher: 100.0% (2007); Master's degree or higher: 33.3% (2007).

Housing: Homeownership rate: 0.0% (2007); Median home value: $n/a (2007); Median rent: $375 per month (2000); Median age of housing: 32 years (2000).

Transportation: Commute to work: 66.7% car, 0.0% public transportation, 33.3% walk, 0.0% work from home (2000); Travel time to work: 100.0% less than 15 minutes, 0.0% 15 to 30 minutes, 0.0% 30 to 45 minutes, 0.0% 45 to 60 minutes, 0.0% 60 minutes or more (2000)

PALM COAST (city). Covers a land area of 50.715 square miles and a water area of 0.981 square miles. Located at 29.53° N. Lat.; 81.22° W. Long. Elevation is 3 feet.

Population: 16,998 (1990); 32,732 (2000); 58,540 (2007); 77,162 (2012 projected); Race: 83.2% White, 11.2% Black, 2.1% Asian, 8.6% Hispanic of any race (2007); Density: 1,154.3 persons per square mile (2007); Average household size: 2.39 (2007); Median age: 44.8 (2007); Males per 100 females: 93.2 (2007); Marriage status: 12.9% never married, 70.8% now married, 9.2% widowed, 7.2% divorced (2000); Foreign born: 12.5% (2000); Ancestry (includes multiple ancestries): 17.5% Other groups, 16.9% Irish, 15.9% German, 15.3% Italian, 11.9% English (2000).

Economy: Unemployment rate: 5.8% (11/2007); Total civilian labor force: 27,812 (11/2007); Single-family building permits issued: 1,283 (2006); Multi-family building permits issued: 298 (2006); Employment by occupation: 12.5% management, 15.6% professional, 20.6% services, 29.9% sales, 0.1% farming, 10.6% construction, 10.8% production (2000).

Income: Per capita income: $26,030 (2007); Median household income: $49,371 (2007); Average household income: $61,893 (2007); Percent of households with income of $100,000 or more: 13.5% (2007); Poverty rate: 7.5% (2000).

$220,115 (2007); Median rent: $655 per month (2000); Median age of housing: 10 years (2000).

Hospitals: Memorial Hospital Flagler (81 beds)

Transportation: Commute to work: 94.2% car, 0.7% public transportation, 0.7% walk, 2.9% work from home (2000); Travel time to work: 36.6% less than 15 minutes, 29.1% 15 to 30 minutes, 20.0% 30 to 45 minutes, 6.7% 45 to 60 minutes, 7.6% 60 minutes or more (2000)

Additional Information Contacts

City of Palm Coast . . . . (386) 986-3700

    http://www.ci.palm-coast.fl.us

Franklin County

Located in northwestern Florida; bounded on the south by the Gulf of Mexico, on the west by the Apalachicola River, and on the east by the Ochlockonee River; includes St. Vincent, St. George, and Dog Islands, enclosing St. Vincent Sound, Apalachicola Bay, and St. George Sound. Covers a land area of 544.34 square miles, a water area of 493.14 square miles, and is located in the Eastern Time Zone. The county was founded in 1832. County seat is Apalachicola.

Weather Station: Apalachicola Municipal Airport   Elevation: 19 feet

	Jan	Feb	Mar	Apr	May	Jun	Jul	Aug	Sep	Oct	Nov	Dec
High	62	65	70	76	83	88	90	89	87	80	72	65
Low	44	47	52	58	66	72	74	74	71	61	53	47
Precip	4.9	3.8	5.0	3.1	2.9	4.3	7.1	7.9	6.6	4.4	3.5	3.6
Snow	tr	tr	tr	0.0	0.0	0.0	0.0	0.0	0.0	0.0	0.0	tr

High and Low temperatures in degrees Fahrenheit; Precipitation and Snow in inches

Population: 8,967 (1990); 11,057 (2000); 10,675 (2007); 11,527 (2012 projected); Race: 83.8% White, 13.8% Black, 0.4% Asian, 2.7% Hispanic of any race (2007); Density: 19.6 persons per square mile (2007); Average household size: 2.34 (2007); Median age: 44.0 (2007); Males per 100 females: 93.4 (2007).

Religion: Five largest groups: 6.9% Southern Baptist Convention, 5.6% The United Methodist Church, 4.7% Assemblies of God, 4.0% Church of God (Cleveland, Tennessee), 2.1% International Pentecostal Holiness Church (2000).

Economy: Unemployment rate: 3.4% (11/2007); Total civilian labor force: 5,136 (11/2007); Leading industries: 23.9% accommodation & food services; 19.1% retail trade; 11.8% full-service restaurants (2005); Farms: 20 totaling n/a acres (2002); Companies that employ 500 or more persons: 0 (2005); Companies that employ 100 to 499 persons: 0 (2005); Companies that employ less than 100 persons: 357 (2005); Black-owned businesses: n/a (2002); Hispanic-owned businesses: n/a (2002); Asian-owned businesses: n/a (2002); Women-owned businesses: n/a (2002); Retail sales per capita: $13,749 (2007); Single-family building permits issued: 225 (2006); Multi-family building permits issued: 0 (2006).

Income: Per capita income: $21,219 (2007); Median household income: $34,563 (2007); Average household income: $47,659 (2007); Percent of households with income of $100,000 or more: 7.8% (2007); Poverty rate: 18.3% (2005); Bankruptcy rate: 0.58% (2006).

Education: Percent of population age 25 and over with: High school diploma (including GED) or higher: 69.8% (2007); Bachelor's degree or higher: 13.5% (2007); Master's degree or higher: 6.9% (2007).

Housing: Homeownership rate: 79.8% (2007); Median home value: $177,712 (2007); Median rent: $300 per month (2000); Median age of housing: 21 years (2000).

Health: Birth rate: 137.4 per 10,000 population (2006); Death rate: 90.6 per 10,000 population (2006); Age-adjusted cancer mortality rate: 215.7 deaths per 100,000 population (2004); Number of physicians: 8.9 per 10,000 population (2005); Hospital beds: 24.8 per 10,000 population (2004); Hospital admissions: 935.0 per 10,000 population (2004).

Elections: 2004 Presidential election results: 58.5% Bush, 40.5% Kerry, 0.6% Nader, 0.1% Badnarik

National and State Parks: Dr Julian G Bruce Saint George Island State Park; Fort Gadsden State Historic Site; Fort Gadsden State Park; John Gorrie Museum State Park; Saint Vincent National Wildlife Refuge

Additional Information Contacts

Franklin County Communities

APALACHICOLA (city). County seat. Covers a land area of 1.879 square miles and a water area of 0.780 square miles. Located at 29.72° N. Lat.; 84.99° W. Long. Elevation is 13 feet.

History: Apalachicola was founded in 1821 at the mouth of the Apalachicola (of Indian origin meaning "people on the other side") River. The town was incorporated as West Point in 1827, and renamed Apalachicola in 1831. This was a major cotton shipping port on the Gulf of Mexico until the Civil War, after which fishing became the dominant industry.

Population: 2,602 (1990); 2,334 (2000); 2,177 (2007); 2,285 (2012 projected); Race: 73.4% White, 24.8% Black, 0.6% Asian, 1.9% Hispanic of any race (2007); Density: 1,158.6 persons per square mile (2007); Average household size: 2.20 (2007); Median age: 43.5 (2007); Males per 100 females: 78.7 (2007); Marriage status: 26.8% never married, 47.9% now married, 12.3% widowed, 13.0% divorced (2000); Foreign born: 1.5% (2000); Ancestry (includes multiple ancestries): 41.2% Other groups, 7.8% Irish, 7.2% English, 6.1% United States or American, 6.0% German (2000).

Economy: Single-family building permits issued: 6 (2006); Multi-family building permits issued: 0 (2006); Employment by occupation: 9.8% management, 15.6% professional, 27.5% services, 21.2% sales, 5.9% farming, 5.6% construction, 14.4% production (2000).

Income: Per capita income: $18,311 (2007); Median household income: $29,697 (2007); Average household income: $40,225 (2007); Percent of households with income of $100,000 or more: 7.0% (2007); Poverty rate: 25.3% (2000).

Education: Percent of population age 25 and over with: High school diploma (including GED) or higher: 70.0% (2007); Bachelor's degree or higher: 15.6% (2007); Master's degree or higher: 4.2% (2007).

School District(s)

Franklin County School District (PK-12)

   2005-06 Enrollment: 1,371 . . . . (850) 653-8831

Housing: Homeownership rate: 68.9% (2007); Median home value: $190,000 (2007); Median rent: $303 per month (2000); Median age of housing: 40 years (2000).

Hospitals: George E. Weems Memorial Hospital (25 beds)

Safety: Violent crime rate: 8.4 per 10,000 population; Property crime rate: 374.1 per 10,000 population (2006).

Newspapers: The Apalachicola Times (General - Circulation 4,500); The Carrabelle Times (General - Circulation 1,500)

Transportation: Commute to work: 87.5% car, 0.2% public transportation, 5.4% walk, 3.3% work from home (2000); Travel time to work: 72.0% less than 15 minutes, 13.7% 15 to 30 minutes, 6.1% 30 to 45 minutes, 1.7% 45 to 60 minutes, 6.5% 60 minutes or more (2000)

Additional Information Contacts

Apalachicola Bay Chamber of Commerce . . . . (850) 653-9419
   http://www.apalachicolabay.org

CARRABELLE (city). Covers a land area of 3.731 square miles and a water area of 1.078 square miles. Located at 29.85° N. Lat.; 84.66° W. Long. Elevation is 26 feet.

History: Carrabelle grew as a resort and fishing village, shipping shrimp, oysters, and fish to northern markets.

Population: 1,219 (1990); 1,303 (2000); 1,280 (2007); 1,320 (2012 projected); Race: 92.7% White, 4.6% Black, 0.2% Asian, 2.0% Hispanic of any race (2007); Density: 343.0 persons per square mile (2007); Average household size: 2.25 (2007); Median age: 41.0 (2007); Males per 100 females: 88.0 (2007); Marriage status: 16.9% never married, 55.5% now married, 9.4% widowed, 18.2% divorced (2000); Foreign born: 1.6% (2000); Ancestry (includes multiple ancestries): 22.1% United States or American, 15.1% Irish, 11.2% Other groups, 6.7% English, 6.0% German (2000).

Economy: Employment by occupation: 6.9% management, 10.5% professional, 28.1% services, 25.1% sales, 4.2% farming, 15.6% construction, 9.7% production (2000).

Income: Per capita income: $17,443 (2007); Median household income: $30,500 (2007); Average household income: $39,070 (2007); Percent of

2005-06 Enrollment: 1,371 . . . . (850) 653-8831

Housing: Homeownership rate: 73.9% (2007); Median home value: $148,311 (2007); Median rent: $251 per month (2000); Median age of housing: 25 years (2000).

Safety: Violent crime rate: 30.5 per 10,000 population; Property crime rate: 350.6 per 10,000 population (2006).

Transportation: Commute to work: 91.2% car, 0.0% public transportation, 5.3% walk, 2.5% work from home (2000); Travel time to work: 43.5% less than 15 minutes, 19.3% 15 to 30 minutes, 26.5% 30 to 45 minutes, 5.0% 45 to 60 minutes, 5.7% 60 minutes or more (2000)

Additional Information Contacts

Carrabelle Chamber of Commerce . . . . (850) 697-2585
   http://www.carrabelle.org

EASTPOINT (CDP). Covers a land area of 7.331 square miles and a water area of 0 square miles. Located at 29.74° N. Lat.; 84.87° W. Long. Elevation is 7 feet.

Population: 1,577 (1990); 2,158 (2000); 2,309 (2007); 2,521 (2012 projected); Race: 96.9% White, 0.7% Black, 0.3% Asian, 1.9% Hispanic of any race (2007); Density: 314.9 persons per square mile (2007); Average household size: 2.59 (2007); Median age: 36.4 (2007); Males per 100 females: 85.8 (2007); Marriage status: 15.9% never married, 58.1% now married, 7.9% widowed, 18.1% divorced (2000); Foreign born: 1.9% (2000); Ancestry (includes multiple ancestries): 21.5% Irish, 21.4% United States or American, 13.4% Other groups, 11.3% English, 8.0% German (2000).

Economy: Employment by occupation: 5.9% management, 6.8% professional, 22.4% services, 15.0% sales, 20.5% farming, 12.6% construction, 16.6% production (2000).

Income: Per capita income: $18,508 (2007); Median household income: $39,589 (2007); Average household income: $47,893 (2007); Percent of households with income of $100,000 or more: 4.2% (2007); Poverty rate: 12.1% (2000).

Education: Percent of population age 25 and over with: High school diploma (including GED) or higher: 64.0% (2007); Bachelor's degree or higher: 8.3% (2007); Master's degree or higher: 3.1% (2007).

School District(s)

Franklin County School District (PK-12)

   2005-06 Enrollment: 1,371 . . . . (850) 653-8831

Housing: Homeownership rate: 83.7% (2007); Median home value: $131,447 (2007); Median rent: $196 per month (2000); Median age of housing: 17 years (2000).

Transportation: Commute to work: 93.8% car, 0.8% public transportation, 1.4% walk, 1.4% work from home (2000); Travel time to work: 41.2% less than 15 minutes, 39.2% 15 to 30 minutes, 11.7% 30 to 45 minutes, 0.0% 45 to 60 minutes, 7.9% 60 minutes or more (2000)

Gadsden County

Located in northwestern Florida; bounded on the north by Georgia, on the east and south by the Ochlockonee River and Lake Talquin, and on the west by the Apalachicola River. Covers a land area of 516.13 square miles, a water area of 12.35 square miles, and is located in the Eastern Time Zone. The county was founded in 1823. County seat is Quincy.

Gadsden County is part of the Tallahassee, FL Metropolitan Statistical Area. The entire metro area includes: Gadsden County, FL; Jefferson County, FL; Leon County, FL; Wakulla County, FL

Weather Station: Quincy 3 SSW   Elevation: 242 feet

	Jan	Feb	Mar	Apr	May	Jun	Jul	Aug	Sep	Oct	Nov	Dec
High	62	66	72	78	85	89	91	90	87	80	72	65
Low	40	42	49	54	62	68	71	71	67	57	49	43
Precip	5.7	4.5	6.2	3.6	4.8	5.6	6.9	5.6	3.7	3.4	3.5	3.6
Snow	tr	tr	tr	0.0	0.0	0.0	0.0	0.0	0.0	0.0	0.0	0.0

High and Low temperatures in degrees Fahrenheit; Precipitation and Snow in inches

Population: 41,105 (1990); 45,087 (2000); 47,518 (2007); 49,715 (2012 projected); Race: 38.8% White, 56.0% Black, 0.4% Asian, 8.3% Hispanic of

any race (2007); Density: 92.1 persons per square mile (2007); Average household size: 2.79 (2007); Median age: 36.0 (2007); Males per 100 females: 90.5 (2007).
Religion: Five largest groups: 15.0% Southern Baptist Convention, 4.1% The United Methodist Church, 3.9% National Primitive Baptist Convention, USA, 1.7% Presbyterian Church (U.S.A.), 0.9% Catholic Church (2000).
Economy: Unemployment rate: 4.6% (11/2007); Total civilian labor force: 21,656 (11/2007); Leading industries: 33.0% health care and social assistance; 14.9% retail trade; 13.6% manufacturing (2005); Farms: 343 totaling 68,140 acres (2002); Companies that employ 500 or more persons: 1 (2005); Companies that employ 100 to 499 persons: 14 (2005); Companies that employ less than 100 persons: 647 (2005); Black-owned businesses: 328 (2002); Hispanic-owned businesses: n/a (2002); Asian-owned businesses: n/a (2002); Women-owned businesses: 424 (2002); Retail sales per capita: $6,631 (2007). Single-family building permits issued: 458 (2006); Multi-family building permits issued: 0 (2006).
Income: Per capita income: $17,382 (2007); Median household income: $36,899 (2007); Average household income: $46,486 (2007); Percent of households with income of $100,000 or more: 7.7% (2007); Poverty rate: 17.7% (2005); Bankruptcy rate: 2.12% (2006).
Education: Percent of population age 25 and over with: High school diploma (including GED) or higher: 70.1% (2007); Bachelor's degree or higher: 12.7% (2007); Master's degree or higher: 5.0% (2007).
Housing: Homeownership rate: 78.3% (2007); Median home value: $111,487 (2007); Median rent: $271 per month (2000); Median age of housing: 22 years (2000).
Health: Birth rate: 155.2 per 10,000 population (2006); Death rate: 97.5 per 10,000 population (2006); Age-adjusted cancer mortality rate: 204.0 deaths per 100,000 population (2004); Number of physicians: 8.2 per 10,000 population (2005); Hospital beds: 220.7 per 10,000 population (2004); Hospital admissions: 434.8 per 10,000 population (2004).
Elections: 2004 Presidential election results: 29.8% Bush, 69.7% Kerry, 0.3% Nader, 0.1% Badnarik
National and State Parks: Bear Creek State Park; Lake Talquin State Park
Additional Information Contacts
Gadsden County Government . . . . (850) 875-8650
　http://www.gadsdengov.net
City of Quincy . . . . (850) 627-7681
　http://www.myquincy.net
Quincy Chamber of Commerce . . . . (850) 627-9231
　http://www.gadsdencc.com

Gadsden County Communities

CHATTAHOOCHEE (city). Covers a land area of 5.454 square miles and a water area of 0.187 square miles. Located at 30.69° N. Lat.; 84.84° W. Long. Elevation is 236 feet.
History: The name of Chattahoochee is of Indian origin meaning "marked rock."
Population: 4,382 (1990); 3,287 (2000); 3,829 (2007); 4,165 (2012 projected); Race: 51.4% White, 45.9% Black, 1.1% Asian, 3.6% Hispanic of any race (2007); Density: 702.1 persons per square mile (2007); Average household size: 3.42 (2007); Median age: 41.3 (2007); Males per 100 females: 124.0 (2007); Marriage status: 27.9% never married, 52.8% now married, 8.8% widowed, 10.5% divorced (2000); Foreign born: 1.1% (2000); Ancestry (includes multiple ancestries): 29.4% Other groups, 12.8% United States or American, 5.0% English, 3.9% Irish, 2.8% German (2000).
Economy: Employment by occupation: 11.4% management, 21.4% professional, 30.4% services, 18.7% sales, 0.0% farming, 9.6% construction, 8.5% production (2000).
Income: Per capita income: $15,958 (2007); Median household income: $33,125 (2007); Average household income: $43,956 (2007); Percent of households with income of $100,000 or more: 7.4% (2007); Poverty rate: 26.1% (2000).
Education: Percent of population age 25 and over with: High school diploma (including GED) or higher: 68.2% (2007); Bachelor's degree or higher: 13.4% (2007); Master's degree or higher: 7.4% (2007).
School District(s)
Gadsden County School District (PK-12)
　2005-06 Enrollment: 6,710 . . . . (850) 627-9651
Housing: Homeownership rate: 62.3% (2007); Median home value: $84,083 (2007); Median rent: $240 per month (2000); Median age of housing: 40 years (2000).

Hospitals: Florida State Hospital (1137 beds)
Safety: Violent crime rate: 153.3 per 10,000 population; Property crime rate: 214.1 per 10,000 population (2006).
Newspapers: Twin City News (General - Circulation 2,000)
Transportation: Commute to work: 91.7% car, 0.0% public transportation, 2.8% walk, 3.1% work from home (2000); Travel time to work: 54.4% less than 15 minutes, 7.9% 15 to 30 minutes, 14.0% 30 to 45 minutes, 12.5% 45 to 60 minutes, 11.2% 60 minutes or more (2000)

GREENSBORO (town). Covers a land area of 1.010 square miles and a water area of 0 square miles. Located at 30.56° N. Lat.; 84.74° W. Long. Elevation is 269 feet.
Population: 586 (1990); 619 (2000); 520 (2007); 528 (2012 projected); Race: 51.3% White, 33.3% Black, 2.1% Asian, 45.8% Hispanic of any race (2007); Density: 514.6 persons per square mile (2007); Average household size: 2.89 (2007); Median age: 29.1 (2007); Males per 100 females: 97.0 (2007); Marriage status: 28.3% never married, 59.0% now married, 6.3% widowed, 6.3% divorced (2000); Foreign born: 23.7% (2000); Ancestry (includes multiple ancestries): 63.2% Other groups, 21.3% United States or American, 2.3% English, 1.0% Irish, 0.5% African (2000).
Economy: Employment by occupation: 3.3% management, 9.1% professional, 17.1% services, 21.8% sales, 15.3% farming, 15.6% construction, 17.8% production (2000).
Income: Per capita income: $14,202 (2007); Median household income: $36,176 (2007); Average household income: $41,028 (2007); Percent of households with income of $100,000 or more: 3.3% (2007); Poverty rate: 24.3% (2000).
Education: Percent of population age 25 and over with: High school diploma (including GED) or higher: 63.2% (2007); Bachelor's degree or higher: 10.1% (2007); Master's degree or higher: 4.1% (2007).
School District(s)
Gadsden County School District (PK-12)
　2005-06 Enrollment: 6,710 . . . . (850) 627-9651
Housing: Homeownership rate: 70.0% (2007); Median home value: $81,111 (2007); Median rent: $358 per month (2000); Median age of housing: 42 years (2000).
Safety: Violent crime rate: 240.0 per 10,000 population; Property crime rate: 624.0 per 10,000 population (2006).
Transportation: Commute to work: 98.5% car, 0.0% public transportation, 0.4% walk, 0.0% work from home (2000); Travel time to work: 9.5% less than 15 minutes, 45.8% 15 to 30 minutes, 27.1% 30 to 45 minutes, 11.4% 45 to 60 minutes, 6.2% 60 minutes or more (2000)

GRETNA (city). Covers a land area of 1.885 square miles and a water area of 0 square miles. Located at 30.61° N. Lat.; 84.66° W. Long. Elevation is 299 feet.
Population: 2,058 (1990); 1,709 (2000); 1,890 (2007); 2,018 (2012 projected); Race: 8.1% White, 83.1% Black, 0.2% Asian, 15.4% Hispanic of any race (2007); Density: 1,002.7 persons per square mile (2007); Average household size: 3.28 (2007); Median age: 29.2 (2007); Males per 100 females: 92.5 (2007); Marriage status: 44.1% never married, 40.8% now married, 6.0% widowed, 9.1% divorced (2000); Foreign born: 6.8% (2000); Ancestry (includes multiple ancestries): 84.4% Other groups, 1.1% African, 0.8% United States or American, 0.4% English, 0.4% French (except Basque) (2000).
Economy: Single-family building permits issued: 0 (2006); Multi-family building permits issued: 0 (2006); Employment by occupation: 4.0% management, 10.3% professional, 33.7% services, 18.7% sales, 7.2% farming, 9.3% construction, 16.8% production (2000).
Income: Per capita income: $10,530 (2007); Median household income: $28,598 (2007); Average household income: $34,493 (2007); Percent of households with income of $100,000 or more: 2.9% (2007); Poverty rate: 30.6% (2000).
Education: Percent of population age 25 and over with: High school diploma (including GED) or higher: 59.3% (2007); Bachelor's degree or higher: 5.6% (2007); Master's degree or higher: 0.9% (2007).
School District(s)
Gadsden County School District (PK-12)
　2005-06 Enrollment: 6,710 . . . . (850) 627-9651
Housing: Homeownership rate: 80.9% (2007); Median home value: $68,750 (2007); Median rent: $234 per month (2000); Median age of housing: 26 years (2000).
Transportation: Commute to work: 97.3% car, 0.4% public transportation, 1.2% walk, 0.0% work from home (2000); Travel time to work: 19.3% less

than 15 minutes, 38.3% 15 to 30 minutes, 21.6% 30 to 45 minutes, 15.6% 45 to 60 minutes, 5.2% 60 minutes or more (2000)

HAVANA (town). Covers a land area of 1.857 square miles and a water area of 0 square miles. Located at 30.62° N. Lat.; 84.41° W. Long. Elevation is 236 feet.
History: Havana, named for the Cuban city, grew in an area of tobacco farms and cypress lumber and shingle mills.
Population: 1,654 (1990); 1,713 (2000); 1,714 (2007); 1,760 (2012 projected); Race: 43.4% White, 55.3% Black, 0.1% Asian, 1.5% Hispanic of any race (2007); Density: 923.1 persons per square mile (2007); Average household size: 2.34 (2007); Median age: 40.9 (2007); Males per 100 females: 84.3 (2007); Marriage status: 31.3% never married, 48.3% now married, 12.3% widowed, 8.1% divorced (2000); Foreign born: 0.2% (2000); Ancestry (includes multiple ancestries): 50.7% Other groups, 7.4% United States or American, 4.7% Irish, 4.3% English, 2.6% German (2000).
Economy: Employment by occupation: 8.4% management, 19.0% professional, 22.4% services, 33.8% sales, 0.6% farming, 8.1% construction, 7.7% production (2000).
Income: Per capita income: $22,725 (2007); Median household income: $34,868 (2007); Average household income: $50,881 (2007); Percent of households with income of $100,000 or more: 8.7% (2007); Poverty rate: 16.3% (2000).
Education: Percent of population age 25 and over with: High school diploma (including GED) or higher: 70.3% (2007); Bachelor's degree or higher: 16.9% (2007); Master's degree or higher: 4.5% (2007).

School District(s)
Gadsden County School District (PK-12)
    2005-06 Enrollment: 6,710 . . . . (850) 627-9651
Housing: Homeownership rate: 70.9% (2007); Median home value: $131,944 (2007); Median rent: $287 per month (2000); Median age of housing: 35 years (2000).
Safety: Violent crime rate: 115.6 per 10,000 population; Property crime rate: 398.8 per 10,000 population (2006).
Newspapers: Havana Herald (General - Circulation 3,100)
Transportation: Commute to work: 94.0% car, 0.0% public transportation, 4.0% walk, 1.4% work from home (2000); Travel time to work: 21.0% less than 15 minutes, 31.2% 15 to 30 minutes, 32.3% 30 to 45 minutes, 10.9% 45 to 60 minutes, 4.5% 60 minutes or more (2000)

MIDWAY (city). Covers a land area of 3.835 square miles and a water area of 0 square miles. Located at 30.49° N. Lat.; 84.46° W. Long. Elevation is 200 feet.
Population: 1,028 (1990); 1,446 (2000); 1,844 (2007); 2,126 (2012 projected); Race: 4.3% White, 94.8% Black, 0.3% Asian, 0.7% Hispanic of any race (2007); Density: 480.9 persons per square mile (2007); Average household size: 2.87 (2007); Median age: 29.7 (2007); Males per 100 females: 82.8 (2007); Marriage status: 37.0% never married, 43.4% now married, 7.8% widowed, 11.8% divorced (2000); Foreign born: 1.2% (2000); Ancestry (includes multiple ancestries): 80.8% Other groups, 1.1% United States or American, 1.1% African, 0.4% Irish, 0.1% Scotch-Irish (2000).
Economy: Single-family building permits issued: 289 (2006); Multi-family building permits issued: 0 (2006); Employment by occupation: 3.2% management, 9.7% professional, 30.7% services, 24.6% sales, 0.9% farming, 11.4% construction, 19.6% production (2000).
Income: Per capita income: $14,330 (2007); Median household income: $31,148 (2007); Average household income: $41,160 (2007); Percent of households with income of $100,000 or more: 3.9% (2007); Poverty rate: 31.3% (2000).
Education: Percent of population age 25 and over with: High school diploma (including GED) or higher: 59.5% (2007); Bachelor's degree or higher: 5.6% (2007); Master's degree or higher: 1.1% (2007).
Housing: Homeownership rate: 80.7% (2007); Median home value: $120,635 (2007); Median rent: $218 per month (2000); Median age of housing: 16 years (2000).
Transportation: Commute to work: 98.4% car, 0.2% public transportation, 0.0% walk, 1.4% work from home (2000); Travel time to work: 7.7% less than 15 minutes, 48.1% 15 to 30 minutes, 30.6% 30 to 45 minutes, 8.8% 45 to 60 minutes, 4.7% 60 minutes or more (2000)

QUINCY (city). County seat. Covers a land area of 7.619 square miles and a water area of 0.012 square miles. Located at 30.58° N. Lat.; 84.58° W. Long. Elevation is 207 feet.

History: Quincy was settled about 1824 by tobacco planters. After the Civil War, many people of Swedish descent settled in Quincy.
Population: 7,468 (1990); 6,982 (2000); 6,858 (2007); 6,847 (2012 projected); Race: 28.6% White, 65.0% Black, 0.4% Asian, 10.8% Hispanic of any race (2007); Density: 900.2 persons per square mile (2007); Average household size: 2.54 (2007); Median age: 33.8 (2007); Males per 100 females: 81.3 (2007); Marriage status: 28.6% never married, 45.1% now married, 13.4% widowed, 12.9% divorced (2000); Foreign born: 4.8% (2000); Ancestry (includes multiple ancestries): 61.4% Other groups, 7.7% United States or American, 4.4% Irish, 4.1% English, 2.5% German (2000).
Economy: Employment by occupation: 12.7% management, 15.4% professional, 21.6% services, 26.9% sales, 1.3% farming, 8.4% construction, 13.7% production (2000).
Income: Per capita income: $17,334 (2007); Median household income: $32,661 (2007); Average household income: $43,834 (2007); Percent of households with income of $100,000 or more: 7.1% (2007); Poverty rate: 19.1% (2000).
Taxes: Total city taxes per capita: $280 (2005); City property taxes per capita: $71 (2005).
Education: Percent of population age 25 and over with: High school diploma (including GED) or higher: 72.6% (2007); Bachelor's degree or higher: 14.5% (2007); Master's degree or higher: 5.7% (2007).

School District(s)
Gadsden County School District (PK-12)
    2005-06 Enrollment: 6,710 . . . . (850) 627-9651
Housing: Homeownership rate: 72.0% (2007); Median home value: $110,638 (2007); Median rent: $299 per month (2000); Median age of housing: 35 years (2000).
Safety: Violent crime rate: 115.3 per 10,000 population; Property crime rate: 644.1 per 10,000 population (2006).
Newspapers: Gadsden County Times (General - Circulation 6,000)
Transportation: Commute to work: 94.5% car, 1.1% public transportation, 2.3% walk, 1.8% work from home (2000); Travel time to work: 39.6% less than 15 minutes, 18.7% 15 to 30 minutes, 23.4% 30 to 45 minutes, 12.6% 45 to 60 minutes, 5.7% 60 minutes or more (2000)
Additional Information Contacts
City of Quincy. . . . . (850) 627-7681
    http://www.myquincy.net
Quincy Chamber of Commerce . . . . (850) 627-9231
    http://www.gadsdencc.com

Gilchrist County

Located in northern Florida; bounded on the north by the Santa Fe River, and on the west by the Suwannee River; includes many small lakes. Covers a land area of 348.89 square miles, a water area of 6.58 square miles, and is located in the Eastern Time Zone. The county was founded in 1925. County seat is Trenton.

Gilchrist County is part of the Gainesville, FL Metropolitan Statistical Area. The entire metro area includes: Alachua County, FL; Gilchrist County, FL

Population: 9,667 (1990); 14,437 (2000); 16,831 (2007); 18,469 (2012 projected); Race: 90.7% White, 6.5% Black, 0.3% Asian, 3.9% Hispanic of any race (2007); Density: 48.2 persons per square mile (2007); Average household size: 2.82 (2007); Median age: 36.9 (2007); Males per 100 females: 107.3 (2007).
Religion: Five largest groups: 32.0% Southern Baptist Convention, 2.7% Churches of Christ, 1.7% The United Methodist Church, 1.3% Church of God (Cleveland, Tennessee), 1.1% The American Baptist Association (2000).
Economy: Unemployment rate: 4.2% (11/2007); Total civilian labor force: 7,822 (11/2007); Leading industries: 21.7% health care and social assistance; 17.5% retail trade; 16.3% manufacturing (2005); Farms: 408 totaling 81,489 acres (2002); Companies that employ 500 or more persons: 0 (2005); Companies that employ 100 to 499 persons: 2 (2005); Companies that employ less than 100 persons: 258 (2005); Black-owned businesses: n/a (2002); Hispanic-owned businesses: n/a (2002); Asian-owned businesses: n/a (2002); Women-owned businesses: n/a (2002); Retail sales per capita: $6,006 (2007). Single-family building permits issued: 92 (2006); Multi-family building permits issued: 0 (2006).
Income: Per capita income: $16,547 (2007); Median household income: $35,365 (2007); Average household income: $46,170 (2007); Percent of households with income of $100,000 or more: 6.5% (2007); Poverty rate: 13.7% (2005); Bankruptcy rate: 1.19% (2006).

Education: Percent of population age 25 and over with: High school diploma (including GED) or higher: 72.2% (2007); Bachelor's degree or higher: 9.4% (2007); Master's degree or higher: 3.1% (2007).
Housing: Homeownership rate: 86.1% (2007); Median home value: $127,192 (2007); Median rent: $299 per month (2000); Median age of housing: 15 years (2000).
Health: Birth rate: 127.5 per 10,000 population (2006); Death rate: 86.6 per 10,000 population (2006); Age-adjusted cancer mortality rate: 134.7 deaths per 100,000 population (2004); Number of physicians: 3.0 per 10,000 population (2005); Hospital beds: 0.0 per 10,000 population (2004); Hospital admissions: 0.0 per 10,000 population (2004).
Elections: 2004 Presidential election results: 70.4% Bush, 28.8% Kerry, 0.5% Nader, 0.2% Badnarik
Additional Information Contacts
Gilchrist County Government . . . . (352) 463-3170
   http://gilchrist.fl.us
Bell Chamber of Commerce . . . . (352) 463-3467
   http://www.gilchristcounty.com
Gilchrist County Chamber of Commerce . . . . (352) 463-3467
   http://www.gilchristcounty.com

Gilchrist County Communities

BELL (town). Covers a land area of 1.634 square miles and a water area of 0 square miles. Located at 29.75° N. Lat.; 82.86° W. Long. Elevation is 69 feet.
Population: 280 (1990); 349 (2000); 386 (2007); 411 (2012 projected); Race: 94.8% White, 2.8% Black, 0.0% Asian, 1.6% Hispanic of any race (2007); Density: 236.2 persons per square mile (2007); Average household size: 2.76 (2007); Median age: 35.0 (2007); Males per 100 females: 89.2 (2007); Marriage status: 26.8% never married, 55.8% now married, 5.1% widowed, 12.3% divorced (2000); Foreign born: 2.0% (2000); Ancestry (includes multiple ancestries): 25.5% United States or American, 14.0% Irish, 11.5% Other groups, 7.4% German, 5.2% French (except Basque) (2000).
Economy: Employment by occupation: 5.8% management, 9.5% professional, 16.8% services, 30.7% sales, 6.6% farming, 10.2% construction, 20.4% production (2000).
Income: Per capita income: $14,573 (2007); Median household income: $34,615 (2007); Average household income: $40,179 (2007); Percent of households with income of $100,000 or more: 6.4% (2007); Poverty rate: 17.2% (2000).
Education: Percent of population age 25 and over with: High school diploma (including GED) or higher: 67.9% (2007); Bachelor's degree or higher: 11.8% (2007); Master's degree or higher: 2.8% (2007).
School District(s)
Gilchrist County School District (PK-12)
   2005-06 Enrollment: 2,858 . . . . (352) 463-3200
Housing: Homeownership rate: 77.1% (2007); Median home value: $111,458 (2007); Median rent: $281 per month (2000); Median age of housing: 18 years (2000).
Transportation: Commute to work: 89.8% car, 1.5% public transportation, 0.7% walk, 1.5% work from home (2000); Travel time to work: 34.8% less than 15 minutes, 25.2% 15 to 30 minutes, 6.7% 30 to 45 minutes, 16.3% 45 to 60 minutes, 17.0% 60 minutes or more (2000)
Additional Information Contacts
Bell Chamber of Commerce . . . . (352) 463-3467
   http://www.gilchristcounty.com

TRENTON (city). County seat. Covers a land area of 2.594 square miles and a water area of 0 square miles. Located at 29.61° N. Lat.; 82.81° W. Long. Elevation is 52 feet.
Population: 1,363 (1990); 1,617 (2000); 1,954 (2007); 2,186 (2012 projected); Race: 83.8% White, 13.9% Black, 0.6% Asian, 2.0% Hispanic of any race (2007); Density: 753.3 persons per square mile (2007); Average household size: 2.64 (2007); Median age: 38.2 (2007); Males per 100 females: 85.0 (2007); Marriage status: 21.9% never married, 50.0% now married, 16.1% widowed, 12.0% divorced (2000); Foreign born: 1.7% (2000); Ancestry (includes multiple ancestries): 22.8% Other groups, 20.6% United States or American, 13.0% Irish, 8.4% English, 8.1% German (2000).
Economy: Employment by occupation: 4.6% management, 15.8% professional, 23.8% services, 30.8% sales, 3.8% farming, 9.1% construction, 12.1% production (2000).

Income: Per capita income: $15,189 (2007); Median household income: $29,676 (2007); Average household income: $39,298 (2007); Percent of households with income of $100,000 or more: 3.9% (2007); Poverty rate: 20.4% (2000).
Education: Percent of population age 25 and over with: High school diploma (including GED) or higher: 60.3% (2007); Bachelor's degree or higher: 8.0% (2007); Master's degree or higher: 3.1% (2007).
School District(s)
Gilchrist County School District (PK-12)
   2005-06 Enrollment: 2,858 . . . . (352) 463-3200
Housing: Homeownership rate: 68.2% (2007); Median home value: $88,600 (2007); Median rent: $279 per month (2000); Median age of housing: 26 years (2000).
Safety: Violent crime rate: 32.9 per 10,000 population; Property crime rate: 351.1 per 10,000 population (2006).
Newspapers: Gilchrist County Journal (General - Circulation 4,000)
Transportation: Commute to work: 93.8% car, 0.0% public transportation, 4.1% walk, 1.5% work from home (2000); Travel time to work: 49.8% less than 15 minutes, 16.0% 15 to 30 minutes, 12.2% 30 to 45 minutes, 13.9% 45 to 60 minutes, 8.1% 60 minutes or more (2000)
Additional Information Contacts
Gilchrist County Chamber of Commerce . . . . (352) 463-3467
   http://www.gilchristcounty.com

Glades County

Located in southern Florida; bounded on the east by Lake Okeechobee; crossed by the Caloosahatchee River. Covers a land area of 773.64 square miles, a water area of 212.79 square miles, and is located in the Eastern Time Zone. The county was founded in 1921. County seat is Moore Haven.

Weather Station: Moore Haven Lock 1   Elevation: 32 feet

	Jan	Feb	Mar	Apr	May	Jun	Jul	Aug	Sep	Oct	Nov	Dec
High	74	76	80	83	88	90	92	91	90	85	80	75
Low	52	52	57	61	66	71	72	73	72	67	60	54
Precip	2.1	2.1	3.3	2.2	3.8	7.2	6.7	6.9	6.1	3.1	1.9	1.6
Snow	0.0	0.0	0.0	0.0	0.0	0.0	0.0	0.0	0.0	0.0	0.0	0.0

High and Low temperatures in degrees Fahrenheit; Precipitation and Snow in inches

Population: 7,617 (1990); 10,576 (2000); 11,045 (2007); 11,205 (2012 projected); Race: 76.3% White, 10.3% Black, 0.4% Asian, 18.1% Hispanic of any race (2007); Density: 14.3 persons per square mile (2007); Average household size: 2.74 (2007); Median age: 41.6 (2007); Males per 100 females: 121.7 (2007).
Religion: Five largest groups: 16.1% Catholic Church, 11.6% Southern Baptist Convention, 2.1% The United Methodist Church, 0.9% Church of God (Cleveland, Tennessee), 0.7% Christian Churches and Churches of Christ (2000).
Economy: Unemployment rate: 4.7% (11/2007); Total civilian labor force: 4,708 (11/2007); Leading industries: 13.2% manufacturing; 10.6% accommodation & food services; 0.0% forestry, fishing, hunting, and agriculture support (2005); Farms: 231 totaling 407,950 acres (2002); Companies that employ 500 or more persons: 0 (2005); Companies that employ 100 to 499 persons: 1 (2005); Companies that employ less than 100 persons: 76 (2005); Black-owned businesses: n/a (2002); Hispanic-owned businesses: n/a (2002); Asian-owned businesses: n/a (2002); Women-owned businesses: n/a (2002); Retail sales per capita: $6,060 (2007). Single-family building permits issued: 73 (2006); Multi-family building permits issued: 0 (2006).
Income: Per capita income: $18,254 (2007); Median household income: $36,160 (2007); Average household income: $47,522 (2007); Percent of households with income of $100,000 or more: 9.3% (2007); Poverty rate: 15.2% (2005); Bankruptcy rate: 0.45% (2006).
Education: Percent of population age 25 and over with: High school diploma (including GED) or higher: 69.5% (2007); Bachelor's degree or higher: 9.7% (2007); Master's degree or higher: 4.2% (2007).
Housing: Homeownership rate: 81.6% (2007); Median home value: $118,550 (2007); Median rent: $386 per month (2000); Median age of housing: 19 years (2000).
Health: Birth rate: 80.1 per 10,000 population (2006); Death rate: 99.7 per 10,000 population (2006); Age-adjusted cancer mortality rate: 181.2 deaths per 100,000 population (2004); Number of physicians: 1.8 per 10,000 population (2005); Hospital beds: 0.0 per 10,000 population (2004); Hospital admissions: 0.0 per 10,000 population (2004).

Elections: 2004 Presidential election results: 58.3% Bush, 41.0% Kerry, 0.4% Nader, 0.1% Badnarik

Additional Information Contacts

Glades County Government . . . . (863) 946-6000
   http://www.myglades.com

Glades County Chamber of Commerce. . . . . (863) 946-0440
   http://www.gladesonline.com

Glades County Communities

BUCKHEAD RIDGE (CDP). Covers a land area of 1.304 square miles and a water area of 0.104 square miles. Located at 27.13° N. Lat.; 80.89° W. Long. Elevation is 13 feet.

Population: 1,279 (1990); 1,390 (2000); 1,476 (2007); 1,511 (2012 projected); Race: 98.2% White, 0.1% Black, 0.1% Asian, 0.7% Hispanic of any race (2007); Density: 1,132.3 persons per square mile (2007); Average household size: 1.98 (2007); Median age: 64.3 (2007); Males per 100 females: 103.0 (2007); Marriage status: 11.7% never married, 65.6% now married, 11.1% widowed, 11.6% divorced (2000); Foreign born: 0.0% (2000); Ancestry (includes multiple ancestries): 24.5% United States or American, 15.1% German, 14.9% English, 10.6% Irish, 5.0% French (except Basque) (2000).

Economy: Employment by occupation: 9.8% management, 16.3% professional, 18.1% services, 27.1% sales, 0.0% farming, 15.2% construction, 13.4% production (2000).

Income: Per capita income: $19,443 (2007); Median household income: $28,600 (2007); Average household income: $38,468 (2007); Percent of households with income of $100,000 or more: 7.5% (2007); Poverty rate: 19.4% (2000).

Education: Percent of population age 25 and over with: High school diploma (including GED) or higher: 72.1% (2007); Bachelor's degree or higher: 7.4% (2007); Master's degree or higher: 3.3% (2007).

Housing: Homeownership rate: 89.1% (2007); Median home value: $127,298 (2007); Median rent: $429 per month (2000); Median age of housing: 19 years (2000).

Transportation: Commute to work: 91.1% car, 0.0% public transportation, 0.0% walk, 3.1% work from home (2000); Travel time to work: 12.1% less than 15 minutes, 58.1% 15 to 30 minutes, 12.1% 30 to 45 minutes, 1.9% 45 to 60 minutes, 15.7% 60 minutes or more (2000)

MOORE HAVEN (city). County seat. Covers a land area of 1.084 square miles and a water area of 0.066 square miles. Located at 26.83° N. Lat.; 81.09° W. Long. Elevation is 13 feet.

History: Moore Haven grew on the southwestern shore of Lake Okeechobee as a trading and shipping center for produce and catfish.

Population: 1,432 (1990); 1,635 (2000); 1,522 (2007); 1,494 (2012 projected); Race: 58.9% White, 23.7% Black, 0.5% Asian, 30.6% Hispanic of any race (2007); Density: 1,404.5 persons per square mile (2007); Average household size: 2.82 (2007); Median age: 34.7 (2007); Males per 100 females: 105.1 (2007); Marriage status: 31.1% never married, 57.4% now married, 3.8% widowed, 7.7% divorced (2000); Foreign born: 13.4% (2000); Ancestry (includes multiple ancestries): 44.4% Other groups, 11.9% United States or American, 6.8% Irish, 6.0% English, 5.4% German (2000).

Economy: Single-family building permits issued: 0 (2006); Multi-family building permits issued: 0 (2006); Employment by occupation: 3.8% management, 8.2% professional, 18.5% services, 21.5% sales, 6.5% farming, 17.8% construction, 23.8% production (2000).

Income: Per capita income: $13,734 (2007); Median household income: $29,734 (2007); Average household income: $37,639 (2007); Percent of households with income of $100,000 or more: 4.5% (2007); Poverty rate: 23.8% (2000).

Education: Percent of population age 25 and over with: High school diploma (including GED) or higher: 61.3% (2007); Bachelor's degree or higher: 6.6% (2007); Master's degree or higher: 2.7% (2007).

School District(s)

Glades County School District (PK-12)
   2005-06 Enrollment: 1,237 . . . . (863) 946-2083

Housing: Homeownership rate: 75.9% (2007); Median home value: $79,375 (2007); Median rent: $347 per month (2000); Median age of housing: 19 years (2000).

Transportation: Commute to work: 91.3% car, 1.5% public transportation, 2.4% walk, 2.2% work from home (2000); Travel time to work: 43.7% less than 15 minutes, 26.4% 15 to 30 minutes, 12.8% 30 to 45 minutes, 5.9% 45 to 60 minutes, 11.2% 60 minutes or more (2000)

Additional Information Contacts

Glades County Chamber of Commerce . . . . (863) 946-0440
   http://www.gladesonline.com

Gulf County

Located in northwestern Florida; swampy area, bounded on the south and west by the Gulf of Mexico, and on the east by the Apalachicola River. Covers a land area of 554.60 square miles, a water area of 190.00 square miles, and is located in the Central/Eastern Time Zone. The county was founded in 1925. County seat is Port Saint Joe.

Population: 11,504 (1990); 13,332 (2000); 15,498 (2007); 17,015 (2012 projected); Race: 83.3% White, 13.9% Black, 0.5% Asian, 1.7% Hispanic of any race (2007); Density: 27.9 persons per square mile (2007); Average household size: 2.66 (2007); Median age: 41.7 (2007); Males per 100 females: 119.3 (2007).

Religion: Five largest groups: 26.9% Southern Baptist Convention, 6.9% The United Methodist Church, 4.5% Assemblies of God, 2.4% International Pentecostal Holiness Church, 2.1% Catholic Church (2000).

Economy: Unemployment rate: 3.7% (11/2007); Total civilian labor force: 6,869 (11/2007); Leading industries: 15.7% health care and social assistance; 15.5% retail trade; 12.5% manufacturing (2005); Farms: 30 totaling 4,521 acres (2002); Companies that employ 500 or more persons: 0 (2005); Companies that employ 100 to 499 persons: 2 (2005); Companies that employ less than 100 persons: 320 (2005); Black-owned businesses: n/a (2002); Hispanic-owned businesses: n/a (2002); Asian-owned businesses: n/a (2002); Women-owned businesses: 409 (2002); Retail sales per capita: $6,150 (2007). Single-family building permits issued: 235 (2006); Multi-family building permits issued: 0 (2006).

Income: Per capita income: $18,063 (2007); Median household income: $36,488 (2007); Average household income: $46,525 (2007); Percent of households with income of $100,000 or more: 7.2% (2007); Poverty rate: 17.6% (2005); Bankruptcy rate: 0.85% (2006).

Education: Percent of population age 25 and over with: High school diploma (including GED) or higher: 72.6% (2007); Bachelor's degree or higher: 10.0% (2007); Master's degree or higher: 3.6% (2007).

Housing: Homeownership rate: 81.6% (2007); Median home value: $155,870 (2007); Median rent: $316 per month (2000); Median age of housing: 21 years (2000).

Health: Birth rate: 101.1 per 10,000 population (2006); Death rate: 110.4 per 10,000 population (2006); Age-adjusted cancer mortality rate: 226.6 deaths per 100,000 population (2004); Number of physicians: 7.2 per 10,000 population (2005); Hospital beds: 21.9 per 10,000 population (2004); Hospital admissions: 664.1 per 10,000 population (2004).

Elections: 2004 Presidential election results: 66.0% Bush, 33.1% Kerry, 0.6% Nader, 0.1% Badnarik

National and State Parks: Constitution Convention Museum State Park; Dead Lakes State Park; Saint Joseph Peninsula State Park; T H Stone Memorial Saint Joseph Peninsula State Park

Additional Information Contacts

Gulf County Government . . . . (850) 229-6106
   http://www.gulfcountygovernment.com

Port St. Joe Chamber of Commerce . . . . (850) 227-1223
   http://www.gulfchamber.org

Wewahitchka Chamber of Commerce . . . . (850) 639-2130
   http://www.wewahitchka.com

Gulf County Communities

PORT SAINT JOE (city). County seat. Covers a land area of 3.321 square miles and a water area of 0 square miles. Located at 29.80° N. Lat.; 85.29° W. Long. Elevation is 7 feet.

History: Port St. Joe developed on the shore of St. Josephs Bay around a paper mill, opened in 1938, and plants manufacturing fish oil and fertilizers.

Population: 4,044 (1990); 3,644 (2000); 4,022 (2007); 4,375 (2012 projected); Race: 77.6% White, 21.1% Black, 0.3% Asian, 0.3% Hispanic of any race (2007); Density: 1,211.2 persons per square mile (2007); Average household size: 2.55 (2007); Median age: 44.1 (2007); Males per 100 females: 92.3 (2007); Marriage status: 19.8% never married, 57.4% now married, 12.4% widowed, 10.5% divorced (2000); Foreign born: 2.3% (2000); Ancestry (includes multiple ancestries): 34.5% Other groups, 13.6% United States or American, 10.6% Irish, 6.5% English, 5.0% German (2000).

Economy: Employment by occupation: 9.6% management, 20.5% professional, 23.0% services, 24.9% sales, 0.0% farming, 13.6% construction, 8.5% production (2000).
Income: Per capita income: $19,679 (2007); Median household income: $39,014 (2007); Average household income: $49,266 (2007); Percent of households with income of $100,000 or more: 6.3% (2007); Poverty rate: 13.0% (2000).
Education: Percent of population age 25 and over with: High school diploma (including GED) or higher: 81.1% (2007); Bachelor's degree or higher: 14.6% (2007); Master's degree or higher: 4.4% (2007).

School District(s)
Gulf County School District (PK-12)
    2005-06 Enrollment: 2,177 . . . . (850) 229-8256
Housing: Homeownership rate: 77.1% (2007); Median home value: $177,857 (2007); Median rent: $261 per month (2000); Median age of housing: 36 years (2000).
Safety: Violent crime rate: 60.1 per 10,000 population; Property crime rate: 207.5 per 10,000 population (2006).
Newspapers: Panhandle Beacon (General - Circulation 13,500); Panhandle Hook & Trigger (General - Circulation 13,500); The Star (General - Circulation 4,800)
Transportation: Commute to work: 95.1% car, 0.0% public transportation, 2.7% walk, 1.4% work from home (2000); Travel time to work: 59.8% less than 15 minutes, 11.9% 15 to 30 minutes, 9.6% 30 to 45 minutes, 7.8% 45 to 60 minutes, 10.9% 60 minutes or more (2000)
Additional Information Contacts
Port St. Joe Chamber of Commerce . . . . (850) 227-1223
    http://www.gulfchamber.org

WEWAHITCHKA (city). Covers a land area of 6.207 square miles and a water area of 1.221 square miles. Located at 30.11° N. Lat.; 85.19° W. Long. Elevation is 46 feet.
History: The name of Wewahitchka is of Indian origin meaning "water eyes," perhaps referring to two nearby small lakes of the same size. The town was known as a producer of tupelo honey made from the tupelo or cotton-gum trees that grow in the swamps.
Population: 1,779 (1990); 1,722 (2000); 1,878 (2007); 2,022 (2012 projected); Race: 91.5% White, 5.5% Black, 1.3% Asian, 0.6% Hispanic of any race (2007); Density: 302.6 persons per square mile (2007); Average household size: 2.39 (2007); Median age: 39.4 (2007); Males per 100 females: 92.2 (2007); Marriage status: 19.6% never married, 58.0% now married, 10.3% widowed, 12.1% divorced (2000); Foreign born: 1.5% (2000); Ancestry (includes multiple ancestries): 20.4% United States or American, 15.1% Other groups, 14.4% Irish, 8.3% English, 5.9% European (2000).
Economy: Employment by occupation: 7.2% management, 16.4% professional, 26.2% services, 21.3% sales, 0.3% farming, 16.1% construction, 12.4% production (2000).
Income: Per capita income: $18,302 (2007); Median household income: $33,009 (2007); Average household income: $43,768 (2007); Percent of households with income of $100,000 or more: 8.3% (2007); Poverty rate: 19.2% (2000).
Education: Percent of population age 25 and over with: High school diploma (including GED) or higher: 68.5% (2007); Bachelor's degree or higher: 8.3% (2007); Master's degree or higher: 3.2% (2007).

School District(s)
Gulf County School District (PK-12)
    2005-06 Enrollment: 2,177 . . . . (850) 229-8256
Housing: Homeownership rate: 75.4% (2007); Median home value: $115,761 (2007); Median rent: $222 per month (2000); Median age of housing: 25 years (2000).
Transportation: Commute to work: 90.6% car, 0.0% public transportation, 4.0% walk, 3.8% work from home (2000); Travel time to work: 41.3% less than 15 minutes, 11.5% 15 to 30 minutes, 21.5% 30 to 45 minutes, 15.7% 45 to 60 minutes, 10.0% 60 minutes or more (2000)
Additional Information Contacts
Wewahitchka Chamber of Commerce . . . . (850) 639-2130
    http://www.wewahitchka.com

Hamilton County

Located in northern Florida; bounded on the north by Georgia, on the south and east by the Suwannee River, and on the west by the Withlacoochee River; flatwoods area with swamps in the east; drained by the Alapaha River. Covers a land area of 514.86 square miles, a water area of 4.45

square miles, and is located in the Eastern Time Zone. The county was founded in 1827. County seat is Jasper.

Weather Station: Jasper | | | | | | | | | | Elevation: 144 feet
	Jan	Feb	Mar	Apr	May	Jun	Jul	Aug	Sep	Oct	Nov	Dec
High	64	67	74	79	86	90	92	91	89	81	74	66
Low	38	41	47	53	60	67	70	70	66	55	47	41
Precip	5.0	4.1	5.3	3.5	3.4	6.0	5.7	6.5	3.9	2.9	2.8	3.5
Snow	tr	tr	tr	0.0	0.0	0.0	0.0	0.0	0.0	0.0	0.0	tr

High and Low temperatures in degrees Fahrenheit; Precipitation and Snow in inches

Population: 10,930 (1990); 13,327 (2000); 14,268 (2007); 15,106 (2012 projected); Race: 59.9% White, 35.8% Black, 0.3% Asian, 8.7% Hispanic of any race (2007); Density: 27.7 persons per square mile (2007); Average household size: 3.22 (2007); Median age: 35.8 (2007); Males per 100 females: 152.0 (2007).
Religion: Five largest groups: 16.3% Southern Baptist Convention, 3.3% The United Methodist Church, 3.3% Church of God (Cleveland, Tennessee), 1.6% Christian Churches and Churches of Christ, 1.0% Presbyterian Church (U.S.A.) (2000).
Economy: Unemployment rate: 4.9% (11/2007); Total civilian labor force: 4,782 (11/2007); Leading industries: 19.5% retail trade; 13.7% health care and social assistance; 4.9% construction (2005); Farms: 239 totaling 52,027 acres (2002); Companies that employ 500 or more persons: 1 (2005); Companies that employ 100 to 499 persons: 2 (2005); Companies that employ less than 100 persons: 185 (2005); Black-owned businesses: n/a (2002); Hispanic-owned businesses: n/a (2002); Asian-owned businesses: n/a (2002); Women-owned businesses: n/a (2002); Retail sales per capita: $6,533 (2007). Single-family building permits issued: 40 (2006); Multi-family building permits issued: 0 (2006).
Income: Per capita income: $11,838 (2007); Median household income: $28,359 (2007); Average household income: $37,240 (2007); Percent of households with income of $100,000 or more: 3.7% (2007); Poverty rate: 26.6% (2005); Bankruptcy rate: 0.49% (2006).
Education: Percent of population age 25 and over with: High school diploma (including GED) or higher: 62.7% (2007); Bachelor's degree or higher: 7.0% (2007); Master's degree or higher: 2.0% (2007).
Housing: Homeownership rate: 78.2% (2007); Median home value: $98,947 (2007); Median rent: $209 per month (2000); Median age of housing: 20 years (2000).
Health: Birth rate: 143.5 per 10,000 population (2006); Death rate: 92.9 per 10,000 population (2006); Age-adjusted cancer mortality rate: 282.4 deaths per 100,000 population (2004); Air Quality Index: 99.7% good, 0.3% moderate, 0.0% unhealthy for sensitive individuals, 0.0% unhealthy (percent of days in 2006); Number of physicians: 7.2 per 10,000 population (2005); Hospital beds: 29.9 per 10,000 population (2004); Hospital admissions: 579.8 per 10,000 population (2004).
Elections: 2004 Presidential election results: 55.0% Bush, 44.5% Kerry, 0.3% Nader, 0.0% Badnarik
National and State Parks: Big Shoals State Park; Stephen Foster Folk Culture Center State Park; Suwannee River State Park
Additional Information Contacts
Hamilton County Government . . . . (386) 792-1288
    http://www.hamiltoncountyflorida.com
Jasper Chamber of Commerce . . . . (386) 792-1300
    http://www.hamiltoncountyflorida.com/cd_chamber.aspx

Hamilton County Communities

JASPER (city). County seat. Covers a land area of 1.954 square miles and a water area of 0 square miles. Located at 30.51° N. Lat.; 82.95° W. Long. Elevation is 151 feet.
History: Jasper was established as a trading post in 1830 by families from South Carolina and Georgia, and was named for Sergeant William Jasper, a Revolutionary War soldier. Cotton was grown here, as well as tobacco.
Population: 2,105 (1990); 1,780 (2000); 1,581 (2007); 1,532 (2012 projected); Race: 55.0% White, 42.4% Black, 0.5% Asian, 3.8% Hispanic of any race (2007); Density: 809.3 persons per square mile (2007); Average household size: 2.30 (2007); Median age: 33.6 (2007); Males per 100 females: 80.3 (2007); Marriage status: 29.9% never married, 44.2% now married, 14.6% widowed, 11.4% divorced (2000); Foreign born: 0.8% (2000); Ancestry (includes multiple ancestries): 50.4% Other groups, 11.6% United States or American, 7.4% English, 4.9% Irish, 3.2% German (2000).

Economy: Employment by occupation: 9.1% management, 13.3% professional, 25.0% services, 24.4% sales, 2.0% farming, 5.5% construction, 20.8% production (2000).
Income: Per capita income: $14,651 (2007); Median household income: $20,903 (2007); Average household income: $33,765 (2007); Percent of households with income of $100,000 or more: 4.7% (2007); Poverty rate: 37.4% (2000).
Education: Percent of population age 25 and over with: High school diploma (including GED) or higher: 65.5% (2007); Bachelor's degree or higher: 12.3% (2007); Master's degree or higher: 3.2% (2007).

School District(s)
Hamilton County School District (PK-12)
   2005-06 Enrollment: 2,017 . . . . (386) 792-6501
Housing: Homeownership rate: 59.8% (2007); Median home value: $100,446 (2007); Median rent: $185 per month (2000); Median age of housing: 32 years (2000).
Hospitals: Trinity Community Hospital (42 beds)
Newspapers: The Jasper News (General - Circulation 2,300)
Transportation: Commute to work: 86.8% car, 0.0% public transportation, 6.2% walk, 1.4% work from home (2000); Travel time to work: 44.8% less than 15 minutes, 22.7% 15 to 30 minutes, 18.9% 30 to 45 minutes, 8.9% 45 to 60 minutes, 4.7% 60 minutes or more (2000)
Additional Information Contacts
Jasper Chamber of Commerce . . . . (386) 792-1300
  http://www.hamiltoncountyflorida.com/cd_chamber.aspx

JENNINGS (town). Covers a land area of 1.806 square miles and a water area of 0 square miles. Located at 30.60° N. Lat.; 83.10° W. Long. Elevation is 141 feet.
History: Jennings was named for George Jennings who settled here in the 1840's. For a time, Jennings was a cotton shipping center.
Population: 747 (1990); 833 (2000); 806 (2007); 819 (2012 projected); Race: 42.6% White, 39.5% Black, 1.2% Asian, 33.9% Hispanic of any race (2007); Density: 446.4 persons per square mile (2007); Average household size: 2.86 (2007); Median age: 33.6 (2007); Males per 100 females: 104.6 (2007); Marriage status: 26.8% never married, 54.1% now married, 7.2% widowed, 11.9% divorced (2000); Foreign born: 18.3% (2000); Ancestry (includes multiple ancestries): 56.9% Other groups, 6.6% United States or American, 4.2% German, 3.6% English, 2.8% Irish (2000).
Economy: Employment by occupation: 9.4% management, 10.6% professional, 22.1% services, 13.3% sales, 21.1% farming, 4.8% construction, 18.7% production (2000).
Income: Per capita income: $16,280 (2007); Median household income: $29,630 (2007); Average household income: $43,316 (2007); Percent of households with income of $100,000 or more: 7.1% (2007); Poverty rate: 30.8% (2000).
Education: Percent of population age 25 and over with: High school diploma (including GED) or higher: 53.0% (2007); Bachelor's degree or higher: 4.2% (2007); Master's degree or higher: 0.2% (2007).

School District(s)
Hamilton County School District (PK-12)
   2005-06 Enrollment: 2,017 . . . . (386) 792-6501
Housing: Homeownership rate: 63.5% (2007); Median home value: $71,842 (2007); Median rent: $196 per month (2000); Median age of housing: 23 years (2000).
Transportation: Commute to work: 72.2% car, 9.7% public transportation, 0.3% walk, 3.0% work from home (2000); Travel time to work: 34.6% less than 15 minutes, 31.8% 15 to 30 minutes, 26.5% 30 to 45 minutes, 2.2% 45 to 60 minutes, 5.0% 60 minutes or more (2000)

WHITE SPRINGS (town). Covers a land area of 1.836 square miles and a water area of 0.002 square miles. Located at 30.33° N. Lat.; 82.75° W. Long. Elevation is 112 feet.
History: White Springs was founded in 1826 on the Suwannee River, and grew as a health resort around medicinal springs. During the Civil War, the White Springs area was considered a place of refuge, where many plantation owners lived in safety from Union invasion.
Population: 823 (1990); 819 (2000); 894 (2007); 961 (2012 projected); Race: 33.1% White, 66.0% Black, 0.0% Asian, 0.6% Hispanic of any race (2007); Density: 486.8 persons per square mile (2007); Average household size: 2.33 (2007); Median age: 33.5 (2007); Males per 100 females: 92.7 (2007); Marriage status: 30.0% never married, 49.8% now married, 9.3% widowed, 10.8% divorced (2000); Foreign born: 1.4% (2000); Ancestry (includes multiple ancestries): 56.8% Other groups, 10.4% United States or American, 3.7% English, 2.8% German, 2.8% Irish (2000).

Economy: Employment by occupation: 3.3% management, 14.2% professional, 29.7% services, 15.3% sales, 6.7% farming, 14.7% construction, 16.1% production (2000).
Income: Per capita income: $14,304 (2007); Median household income: $24,744 (2007); Average household income: $33,301 (2007); Percent of households with income of $100,000 or more: 2.1% (2007); Poverty rate: 22.6% (2000).
Education: Percent of population age 25 and over with: High school diploma (including GED) or higher: 69.5% (2007); Bachelor's degree or higher: 9.0% (2007); Master's degree or higher: 2.6% (2007).

School District(s)
Hamilton County School District (PK-12)
   2005-06 Enrollment: 2,017 . . . . (386) 792-6501
Housing: Homeownership rate: 73.4% (2007); Median home value: $93,750 (2007); Median rent: $163 per month (2000); Median age of housing: 28 years (2000).
Safety: Violent crime rate: 96.5 per 10,000 population; Property crime rate: 289.5 per 10,000 population (2006).
Transportation: Commute to work: 89.5% car, 0.0% public transportation, 5.9% walk, 1.7% work from home (2000); Travel time to work: 15.5% less than 15 minutes, 43.4% 15 to 30 minutes, 28.4% 30 to 45 minutes, 3.4% 45 to 60 minutes, 9.2% 60 minutes or more (2000)

Hardee County

Located in central Florida; rolling terrain, partly swampy, with many small lakes; drained by the Peace River. Covers a land area of 637.30 square miles, a water area of 1.03 square miles, and is located in the Eastern Time Zone. The county was founded in 1921. County seat is Wauchula.

Hardee County is part of the Wauchula, FL Micropolitan Statistical Area. The entire metro area includes: Hardee County, FL

Weather Station: Wauchula   Elevation: 59 feet

	Jan	Feb	Mar	Apr	May	Jun	Jul	Aug	Sep	Oct	Nov	Dec
High	74	76	80	84	89	91	92	92	91	86	80	75
Low	50	51	54	58	64	70	71	72	71	65	57	52
Precip	2.4	2.7	3.5	2.3	4.0	8.0	8.1	7.3	6.0	2.7	2.1	2.0
Snow	tr	0.0	0.0	0.0	0.0	0.0	0.0	0.0	0.0	0.0	0.0	0.0

High and Low temperatures in degrees Fahrenheit; Precipitation and Snow in inches

Population: 19,499 (1990); 26,938 (2000); 27,941 (2007); 28,325 (2012 projected); Race: 67.6% White, 8.5% Black, 0.5% Asian, 40.6% Hispanic of any race (2007); Density: 43.8 persons per square mile (2007); Average household size: 3.42 (2007); Median age: 32.4 (2007); Males per 100 females: 127.6 (2007).
Religion: Five largest groups: 34.2% Southern Baptist Convention, 18.4% Catholic Church, 3.6% The United Methodist Church, 3.1% Church of God (Cleveland, Tennessee), 2.6% Christian Churches and Churches of Christ (2000).
Economy: Unemployment rate: 4.2% (11/2007); Total civilian labor force: 13,308 (11/2007); Leading industries: 26.5% health care and social assistance, 10.7% retail trade; 8.9% accommodation & food services (2005); Farms: 1,142 totaling 346,191 acres (2002); Companies that employ 500 or more persons: 0 (2005); Companies that employ 100 to 499 persons: 5 (2005); Companies that employ less than 100 persons: 407 (2005); Black-owned businesses: n/a (2002); Hispanic-owned businesses: n/a (2002); Asian-owned businesses: n/a (2002); Women-owned businesses: 510 (2002); Retail sales per capita: $7,253 (2007). Single-family building permits issued: 216 (2006); Multi-family building permits issued: 0 (2006).
Income: Per capita income: $14,112 (2007); Median household income: $34,323 (2007); Average household income: $47,073 (2007); Percent of households with income of $100,000 or more: 7.6% (2007); Poverty rate: 24.6% (2005); Bankruptcy rate: 0.77% (2006).
Education: Percent of population age 25 and over with: High school diploma (including GED) or higher: 58.2% (2007); Bachelor's degree or higher: 8.3% (2007); Master's degree or higher: 2.8% (2007).
Housing: Homeownership rate: 73.3% (2007); Median home value: $114,462 (2007); Median rent: $334 per month (2000); Median age of housing: 24 years (2000).
Health: Birth rate: 168.4 per 10,000 population (2006); Death rate: 75.1 per 10,000 population (2006); Age-adjusted cancer mortality rate: 146.6 deaths per 100,000 population (2004); Number of physicians: 3.2 per 10,000 population (2005); Hospital beds: 0.0 per 10,000 population (2004); Hospital admissions: 0.0 per 10,000 population (2004).

0.5% Nader, 0.1% Badnarik
National and State Parks: Paynes Creek Historic State Park
Additional Information Contacts
Hardee County Government . . . . (863) 773-6952
   http://www.hardeecounty.net
Hardee County Chamber of Commerce . . . . (863) 773-6967
   http://www.hardeecc.com

Hardee County Communities

BOWLING GREEN (city). Covers a land area of 1.416 square miles and a water area of 0.002 square miles. Located at 27.63° N. Lat.; 81.82° W. Long. Elevation is 118 feet.
History: The settlement here was first called Utica. It became Bowling Green in the late 1880's, when farmers from Bowling Green, Kentucky, purchased the land.
Population: 1,880 (1990); 2,892 (2000); 2,659 (2007); 2,594 (2012 projected); Race: 55.0% White, 10.9% Black, 0.9% Asian, 49.3% Hispanic of any race (2007); Density: 1,877.5 persons per square mile (2007); Average household size: 3.65 (2007); Median age: 29.1 (2007); Males per 100 females: 112.4 (2007); Marriage status: 31.3% never married, 55.1% now married, 5.3% widowed, 8.3% divorced (2000); Foreign born: 23.9% (2000); Ancestry (includes multiple ancestries): 46.4% Other groups, 10.3% United States or American, 3.6% German, 3.6% Irish, 2.4% English (2000).
Economy: Employment by occupation: 5.2% management, 8.3% professional, 16.3% services, 11.4% sales, 28.5% farming, 12.3% construction, 18.0% production (2000).
Income: Per capita income: $11,902 (2007); Median household income: $32,411 (2007); Average household income: $42,009 (2007); Percent of households with income of $100,000 or more: 5.1% (2007); Poverty rate: 30.5% (2000).
Education: Percent of population age 25 and over with: High school diploma (including GED) or higher: 47.6% (2007); Bachelor's degree or higher: 6.1% (2007); Master's degree or higher: 2.1% (2007).
School District(s)
Hardee County School District (PK-12)
   2005-06 Enrollment: 5,146 . . . . (863) 773-9058
Housing: Homeownership rate: 73.4% (2007); Median home value: $98,444 (2007); Median rent: $316 per month (2000); Median age of housing: 26 years (2000).
Safety: Violent crime rate: 53.7 per 10,000 population; Property crime rate: 228.4 per 10,000 population (2006).
Transportation: Commute to work: 92.0% car, 2.6% public transportation, 2.3% walk, 0.5% work from home (2000); Travel time to work: 28.5% less than 15 minutes, 27.4% 15 to 30 minutes, 22.5% 30 to 45 minutes, 7.0% 45 to 60 minutes, 14.6% 60 minutes or more (2000)

ONA (unincorporated postal area, zip code 33865). Covers a land area of 140.742 square miles and a water area of 0.336 square miles. Located at 27.43° N. Lat.; 81.93° W. Long. Elevation is 90 feet.
Population: 681 (2000); Race: 86.8% White, 5.1% Black, 0.0% Asian, 12.5% Hispanic of any race (2000); Density: 4.8 persons per square mile (2000); Age: 17.1% under 18, 12.8% over 64 (2000); Marriage status: 19.0% never married, 65.9% now married, 6.8% widowed, 8.3% divorced (2000); Foreign born: 4.4% (2000); Ancestry (includes multiple ancestries): 27.2% Other groups, 21.9% Irish, 14.7% United States or American, 9.0% English, 7.2% German (2000).
Economy: Employment by occupation: 0.0% management, 20.5% professional, 22.8% services, 20.5% sales, 5.1% farming, 16.1% construction, 15.0% production (2000).
Income: Per capita income: $14,252 (2000); Median household income: $23,750 (2000); Poverty rate: 29.0% (2000).
Education: Percent of population age 25 and over with: High school diploma (including GED) or higher: 48.7% (2000); Bachelor's degree or higher: 10.8% (2000).
Housing: Homeownership rate: 65.1% (2000); Median home value: $62,900 (2000); Median rent: $275 per month (2000); Median age of housing: 24 years (2000).
Transportation: Commute to work: 79.9% car, 0.0% public transportation, 0.0% walk, 20.1% work from home (2000); Travel time to work: 26.1% less than 15 minutes, 20.7% 15 to 30 minutes, 35.5% 30 to 45 minutes, 7.9% 45 to 60 minutes, 9.9% 60 minutes or more (2000)

WAUCHULA (city). County seat. Covers a land area of 2.616 square miles and a water area of 0 square miles. Located at 27.54° N. Lat.; 81.81° W. Long. Elevation is 112 feet.
History: Wauchula began as Fort Hartsuff, built during the Seminole Wars. Wauchula was known as a supplier of frog's legs, gathered at night from the surrounding swamps and shipped to markets in the north.
Population: 3,400 (1990); 4,368 (2000); 4,570 (2007); 4,632 (2012 projected); Race: 67.3% White, 4.4% Black, 0.4% Asian, 49.6% Hispanic of any race (2007); Density: 1,746.8 persons per square mile (2007); Average household size: 3.13 (2007); Median age: 29.9 (2007); Males per 100 females: 104.9 (2007); Marriage status: 27.4% never married, 53.8% now married, 9.8% widowed, 9.0% divorced (2000); Foreign born: 19.6% (2000); Ancestry (includes multiple ancestries): 42.9% Other groups, 16.9% United States or American, 6.1% Irish, 5.8% English, 3.5% German (2000).
Economy: Employment by occupation: 5.4% management, 9.4% professional, 17.0% services, 22.1% sales, 22.2% farming, 10.8% construction, 13.1% production (2000).
Income: Per capita income: $11,618 (2007); Median household income: $28,699 (2007); Average household income: $35,241 (2007); Percent of households with income of $100,000 or more: 4.0% (2007); Poverty rate: 25.0% (2000).
Education: Percent of population age 25 and over with: High school diploma (including GED) or higher: 56.3% (2007); Bachelor's degree or higher: 7.6% (2007); Master's degree or higher: 3.7% (2007).
School District(s)
Hardee County School District (PK-12)
   2005-06 Enrollment: 5,146 . . . . (863) 773-9058
Housing: Homeownership rate: 60.0% (2007); Median home value: $112,775 (2007); Median rent: $352 per month (2000); Median age of housing: 32 years (2000).
Hospitals: Florida Hospital Wauchula (25 beds)
Safety: Violent crime rate: 77.3 per 10,000 population; Property crime rate: 450.8 per 10,000 population (2006).
Newspapers: The Herald Advocate (General - Circulation 5,300)
Transportation: Commute to work: 90.9% car, 2.1% public transportation, 4.0% walk, 1.5% work from home (2000); Travel time to work: 44.7% less than 15 minutes, 12.0% 15 to 30 minutes, 22.3% 30 to 45 minutes, 6.0% 45 to 60 minutes, 15.0% 60 minutes or more (2000)
Additional Information Contacts
Hardee County Chamber of Commerce . . . . (863) 773-6967
   http://www.hardeecc.com

ZOLFO SPRINGS (town). Covers a land area of 1.510 square miles and a water area of 0 square miles. Located at 27.49° N. Lat.; 81.79° W. Long. Elevation is 66 feet.
History: Zolfo Springs was named for its large sulphur spring, by Italian laborers employed on the construction of the Atlantic Coast Line Railroad. Zolfo is Italian for sulphur.
Population: 1,219 (1990); 1,641 (2000); 1,576 (2007); 1,588 (2012 projected); Race: 64.2% White, 2.5% Black, 0.1% Asian, 61.3% Hispanic of any race (2007); Density: 1,043.5 persons per square mile (2007); Average household size: 3.37 (2007); Median age: 29.4 (2007); Males per 100 females: 107.1 (2007); Marriage status: 26.2% never married, 58.4% now married, 7.2% widowed, 8.1% divorced (2000); Foreign born: 27.2% (2000); Ancestry (includes multiple ancestries): 53.0% Other groups, 8.0% English, 7.9% United States or American, 4.3% German, 3.6% Irish (2000).
Economy: Employment by occupation: 4.6% management, 8.7% professional, 14.8% services, 18.5% sales, 24.2% farming, 17.3% construction, 11.9% production (2000).
Income: Per capita income: $12,829 (2007); Median household income: $30,484 (2007); Average household income: $42,965 (2007); Percent of households with income of $100,000 or more: 6.2% (2007); Poverty rate: 27.3% (2000).
Education: Percent of population age 25 and over with: High school diploma (including GED) or higher: 45.8% (2007); Bachelor's degree or higher: 3.1% (2007); Master's degree or higher: 1.0% (2007).
School District(s)
Hardee County School District (PK-12)
   2005-06 Enrollment: 5,146 . . . . (863) 773-9058
Housing: Homeownership rate: 75.2% (2007); Median home value: $94,865 (2007); Median rent: $358 per month (2000); Median age of housing: 19 years (2000).

5.2% walk, 0.7% work from home (2000); Travel time to work: 36.7% less than 15 minutes, 21.2% 15 to 30 minutes, 23.0% 30 to 45 minutes, 9.3% 45 to 60 minutes, 9.8% 60 minutes or more (2000)

Hendry County

Located in southern Florida; Everglades area, crossed by the Caloosahatchee River. Covers a land area of 1,152.53 square miles, a water area of 37.26 square miles, and is located in the Eastern Time Zone. The county was founded in 1923. County seat is Labelle.

Hendry County is part of the Clewiston, FL Micropolitan Statistical Area. The entire metro area includes: Hendry County, FL

Weather Station: Clewiston U.S. Engineers   Elevation: 19 feet

	Jan	Feb	Mar	Apr	May	Jun	Jul	Aug	Sep	Oct	Nov	Dec
High	73	75	80	84	88	90	92	91	90	85	80	75
Low	54	56	59	63	68	72	73	73	73	69	64	57
Precip	2.2	2.1	3.0	2.1	4.7	7.2	6.5	6.4	4.9	3.0	2.3	1.5
Snow	0.0	0.0	0.0	0.0	0.0	0.0	0.0	0.0	0.0	0.0	0.0	0.0

High and Low temperatures in degrees Fahrenheit; Precipitation and Snow in inches

Weather Station: La Belle   Elevation: 13 feet

	Jan	Feb	Mar	Apr	May	Jun	Jul	Aug	Sep	Oct	Nov	Dec
High	na	78	82	86	na	92	na	na	na	87	na	na
Low	na	52	55	59	64	69	na	na	na	65	na	na
Precip	2.4	2.2	3.3	2.3	4.1	8.9	7.7	7.8	6.3	3.4	2.3	1.7
Snow	tr	0.0	0.0	0.0	0.0	0.0	0.0	0.0	0.0	0.0	0.0	0.0

High and Low temperatures in degrees Fahrenheit; Precipitation and Snow in inches

Population: 25,773 (1990); 36,210 (2000); 39,845 (2007); 41,904 (2012 projected); Race: 65.0% White, 12.8% Black, 0.5% Asian, 47.1% Hispanic of any race (2007); Density: 34.6 persons per square mile (2007); Average household size: 3.34 (2007); Median age: 29.9 (2007); Males per 100 females: 126.4 (2007).
Religion: Five largest groups: 8.2% Southern Baptist Convention, 3.6% Catholic Church, 2.9% The United Methodist Church, 2.5% Assemblies of God, 2.3% Church of God (Cleveland, Tennessee) (2000).
Economy: Unemployment rate: 7.5% (11/2007); Total civilian labor force: 18,956 (11/2007); Leading industries: 22.7% retail trade; 17.1% health care and social assistance; 13.4% manufacturing (2005); Farms: 456 totaling 552,352 acres (2002); Companies that employ 500 or more persons: 0 (2005); Companies that employ 100 to 499 persons: 9 (2005); Companies that employ less than 100 persons: 581 (2005); Black-owned businesses: n/a (2002); Hispanic-owned businesses: n/a (2002); Asian-owned businesses: n/a (2002); Women-owned businesses: 290 (2002); Retail sales per capita: $9,502 (2007). Single-family building permits issued: 282 (2006); Multi-family building permits issued: 2 (2006).
Income: Per capita income: $14,906 (2007); Median household income: $37,487 (2007); Average household income: $47,753 (2007); Percent of households with income of $100,000 or more: 7.8% (2007); Poverty rate: 22.2% (2005); Bankruptcy rate: 0.69% (2006).
Education: Percent of population age 25 and over with: High school diploma (including GED) or higher: 53.6% (2007); Bachelor's degree or higher: 8.3% (2007); Master's degree or higher: 2.2% (2007).
Housing: Homeownership rate: 72.5% (2007); Median home value: $107,137 (2007); Median rent: $380 per month (2000); Median age of housing: 18 years (2000).
Health: Birth rate: 168.6 per 10,000 population (2006); Death rate: 74.1 per 10,000 population (2006); Age-adjusted cancer mortality rate: 175.8 deaths per 100,000 population (2004); Number of physicians: 5.6 per 10,000 population (2005); Hospital beds: 6.6 per 10,000 population (2004); Hospital admissions: 261.3 per 10,000 population (2004).
Elections: 2004 Presidential election results: 58.9% Bush, 40.5% Kerry, 0.2% Nader, 0.1% Badnarik
Additional Information Contacts
Hendry County Government . . . . (863) 675-5220
   http://www.hendryfla.net
City of Clewiston . . . . (863) 983-1484
   http://www.clewiston-fl.gov
Clewiston Chamber of Commerce . . . . (863) 983-7979
   http://www.clewiston.org

Hendry County Communities

CLEWISTON (city). Covers a land area of 4.678 square miles and a water area of 0.021 square miles. Located at 26.75° N. Lat.; 80.93° W. Long. Elevation is 16 feet.
History: Clewiston began in 1921 as a construction camp for the Moore Haven-Clewiston Railroad. The Clewiston Company Sugar Mill was built here to process sugar cane.
Population: 6,085 (1990); 6,460 (2000); 7,232 (2007); 7,681 (2012 projected); Race: 77.2% White, 11.1% Black, 1.3% Asian, 46.0% Hispanic of any race (2007); Density: 1,546.1 persons per square mile (2007); Average household size: 2.97 (2007); Median age: 32.2 (2007); Males per 100 females: 106.9 (2007); Marriage status: 26.3% never married, 57.4% now married, 7.4% widowed, 8.9% divorced (2000); Foreign born: 22.0% (2000); Ancestry (includes multiple ancestries): 50.1% Other groups, 12.2% United States or American, 7.0% German, 6.9% English, 6.7% Irish (2000).
Economy: Single-family building permits issued: 66 (2006); Multi-family building permits issued: 2 (2006); Employment by occupation: 11.7% management, 17.4% professional, 14.6% services, 20.5% sales, 9.1% farming, 13.3% construction, 13.4% production (2000).
Income: Per capita income: $16,092 (2007); Median household income: $38,010 (2007); Average household income: $47,356 (2007); Percent of households with income of $100,000 or more: 8.7% (2007); Poverty rate: 18.8% (2000).
Education: Percent of population age 25 and over with: High school diploma (including GED) or higher: 65.2% (2007); Bachelor's degree or higher: 13.8% (2007); Master's degree or higher: 3.8% (2007).
School District(s)
Hendry County School District (PK-12)
   2005-06 Enrollment: 7,604 . . . . (863) 674-4642
Housing: Homeownership rate: 66.5% (2007); Median home value: $132,994 (2007); Median rent: $382 per month (2000); Median age of housing: 26 years (2000).
Hospitals: Hendry Regional Medical Center (66 beds)
Safety: Violent crime rate: 82.3 per 10,000 population; Property crime rate: 363.3 per 10,000 population (2006).
Newspapers: The Clewiston News (General - Circulation 3,400); The Sun (General - Circulation 1,900)
Transportation: Commute to work: 86.9% car, 4.9% public transportation, 3.6% walk, 2.7% work from home (2000); Travel time to work: 56.4% less than 15 minutes, 16.4% 15 to 30 minutes, 19.5% 30 to 45 minutes, 2.2% 45 to 60 minutes, 5.5% 60 minutes or more (2000)
Additional Information Contacts
City of Clewiston . . . . (863) 983-1484
   http://www.clewiston-fl.gov
Clewiston Chamber of Commerce . . . . (863) 983-7979
   http://www.clewiston.org

HARLEM (CDP). Covers a land area of 0.968 square miles and a water area of 0 square miles. Located at 26.73° N. Lat.; 80.95° W. Long. Elevation is 20 feet.
Population: 3,053 (1990); 2,730 (2000); 2,159 (2007); 2,108 (2012 projected); Race: 4.4% White, 92.5% Black, 0.2% Asian, 4.4% Hispanic of any race (2007); Density: 2,230.9 persons per square mile (2007); Average household size: 3.07 (2007); Median age: 25.2 (2007); Males per 100 females: 92.6 (2007); Marriage status: 50.9% never married, 35.6% now married, 6.4% widowed, 7.0% divorced (2000); Foreign born: 10.7% (2000); Ancestry (includes multiple ancestries): 75.3% Other groups, 6.6% Jamaican, 1.5% German, 1.4% African, 1.3% United States or American (2000).
Economy: Employment by occupation: 0.8% management, 12.8% professional, 26.9% services, 16.0% sales, 4.7% farming, 15.5% construction, 23.2% production (2000).
Income: Per capita income: $9,514 (2007); Median household income: $21,900 (2007); Average household income: $29,176 (2007); Percent of households with income of $100,000 or more: 2.1% (2007); Poverty rate: 40.4% (2000).
Education: Percent of population age 25 and over with: High school diploma (including GED) or higher: 47.6% (2007); Bachelor's degree or higher: 2.4% (2007); Master's degree or higher: 0.0% (2007).

LABELLE (city). County seat. Covers a land area of 3.468 square miles and a water area of 0.086 square miles. Located at 26.76° N. Lat.; 81.43° W. Long. Elevation is 13 feet.

History: La Belle was named by Captain Francis Asbury Hendry (for whom the county was named) for his two daughters, Laura and Belle. The town developed around a sawmill and as a shipping point for cattle.

Population: 2,745 (1990); 4,210 (2000); 4,803 (2007); 5,148 (2012 projected); Race: 72.8% White, 8.0% Black, 0.4% Asian, 41.6% Hispanic of any race (2007); Density: 1,384.9 persons per square mile (2007); Average household size: 2.96 (2007); Median age: 34.9 (2007); Males per 100 females: 107.7 (2007); Marriage status: 20.7% never married, 59.2% now married, 10.2% widowed, 9.9% divorced (2000); Foreign born: 19.6% (2000); Ancestry (includes multiple ancestries): 42.5% Other groups, 10.4% United States or American, 8.6% English, 8.3% German, 6.9% Irish (2000).

Economy: Single-family building permits issued: 12 (2006); Multi-family building permits issued: 0 (2006); Employment by occupation: 9.6% management, 13.2% professional, 13.9% services, 26.1% sales, 12.2% farming, 14.2% construction, 10.8% production (2000).

Income: Per capita income: $16,984 (2007); Median household income: $37,480 (2007); Average household income: $48,854 (2007); Percent of households with income of $100,000 or more: 9.0% (2007); Poverty rate: 18.0% (2000).

Education: Percent of population age 25 and over with: High school diploma (including GED) or higher: 61.0% (2007); Bachelor's degree or higher: 11.8% (2007); Master's degree or higher: 4.8% (2007).

School District(s)
Glades County School District (PK-12)
    2005-06 Enrollment: 1,237 . . . . (863) 946-2083
Hendry County School District (PK-12)
    2005-06 Enrollment: 7,604 . . . . (863) 674-4642

Housing: Homeownership rate: 75.2% (2007); Median home value: $95,565 (2007); Median rent: $422 per month (2000); Median age of housing: 19 years (2000).

Newspapers: Caloosa Belle (General - Circulation 6,500); Immokalee Bulletin (General - Circulation 3,500)

Transportation: Commute to work: 90.7% car, 5.1% public transportation, 1.9% walk, 0.9% work from home (2000); Travel time to work: 46.3% less than 15 minutes, 13.5% 15 to 30 minutes, 15.1% 30 to 45 minutes, 10.7% 45 to 60 minutes, 14.3% 60 minutes or more (2000)

Additional Information Contacts
La Belle Chamber of Commerce . . . . (863) 675-0125
    http://members.aol.com/browne/chamber.html

PORT LA BELLE (CDP). Covers a land area of 8.615 square miles and a water area of 0.002 square miles. Located at 26.74° N. Lat.; 81.39° W. Long. Elevation is 10 feet.

Population: 1,997 (1990); 3,050 (2000); 3,478 (2007); 3,712 (2012 projected); Race: 69.3% White, 7.4% Black, 0.6% Asian, 52.9% Hispanic of any race (2007); Density: 403.7 persons per square mile (2007); Average household size: 3.54 (2007); Median age: 27.3 (2007); Males per 100 females: 122.5 (2007); Marriage status: 31.2% never married, 58.1% now married, 4.5% widowed, 6.3% divorced (2000); Foreign born: 33.8% (2000); Ancestry (includes multiple ancestries): 48.2% Other groups, 8.3% Irish, 6.2% United States or American, 5.0% German, 4.1% English (2000).

Economy: Employment by occupation: 5.5% management, 7.1% professional, 13.9% services, 19.9% sales, 30.3% farming, 9.5% construction, 13.9% production (2000).

Income: Per capita income: $15,510 (2007); Median household income: $38,559 (2007); Average household income: $52,248 (2007); Percent of households with income of $100,000 or more: 9.6% (2007); Poverty rate: 22.5% (2000).

Education: Percent of population age 25 and over with: High school diploma (including GED) or higher: 54.1% (2007); Bachelor's degree or higher: 8.2% (2007); Master's degree or higher: 2.1% (2007).

Hernando County

Located in west central Florida; bounded on the east by the Withlacoochee River, and on the west by the Gulf of Mexico; lowland area with marshy coast and small lakes. Covers a land area of 478.31 square miles, a water area of 110.77 square miles, and is located in the Eastern Time Zone. The county was founded in 1843. County seat is Brooksville.

Hernando County is part of the Tampa-St. Petersburg-Clearwater, FL Metropolitan Statistical Area. The entire metro area includes: Hernando County, FL; Hillsborough County, FL; Pasco County, FL; Pinellas County, FL

Weather Station: Brooksville Chin Hill   Elevation: 239 feet

	Jan	Feb	Mar	Apr	May	Jun	Jul	Aug	Sep	Oct	Nov	Dec
High	71	73	78	82	88	90	91	90	89	84	78	72
Low	49	50	55	59	65	70	72	72	70	64	56	51
Precip	3.4	3.4	4.4	2.7	3.4	7.0	6.9	8.5	6.1	2.4	2.4	2.5
Snow	0.0	0.0	0.0	0.0	0.0	0.0	0.0	0.0	0.0	0.0	0.0	0.0

High and Low temperatures in degrees Fahrenheit; Precipitation and Snow in inches

Weather Station: Weeki Wachee   Elevation: 19 feet

	Jan	Feb	Mar	Apr	May	Jun	Jul	Aug	Sep	Oct	Nov	Dec
High	70	72	77	82	87	90	92	91	90	85	79	73
Low	44	46	51	56	62	69	71	71	69	61	53	46
Precip	3.8	3.2	4.2	2.5	3.0	5.9	8.3	7.6	6.5	2.3	2.1	2.5
Snow	0.0	0.0	0.0	0.0	0.0	0.0	0.0	0.0	0.0	0.0	0.0	0.0

High and Low temperatures in degrees Fahrenheit; Precipitation and Snow in inches

Population: 101,115 (1990); 130,802 (2000); 161,872 (2007); 180,920 (2012 projected); Race: 91.4% White, 4.6% Black, 0.9% Asian, 7.9% Hispanic of any race (2007); Density: 338.4 persons per square mile (2007); Average household size: 2.34 (2007); Median age: 46.3 (2007); Males per 100 females: 91.9 (2007).

Religion: Five largest groups: 26.7% Catholic Church, 4.5% Southern Baptist Convention, 3.1% The United Methodist Church, 1.7% Assemblies of God, 1.2% Evangelical Lutheran Church in America (2000).

Economy: Unemployment rate: 6.2% (11/2007); Total civilian labor force: 62,258 (11/2007); Leading industries: 21.8% retail trade; 19.8% health care and social assistance; 12.6% accommodation & food services (2005); Farms: 617 totaling 65,315 acres (2002); Companies that employ 500 or more persons: 5 (2005); Companies that employ 100 to 499 persons: 39 (2005); Companies that employ less than 100 persons: 3,098 (2005); Black-owned businesses: n/a (2002); Hispanic-owned businesses: n/a (2002); Asian-owned businesses: 144 (2002); Women-owned businesses: 2,190 (2002); Retail sales per capita: $11,250 (2007). Single-family building permits issued: 2,862 (2006); Multi-family building permits issued: 275 (2006).

Income: Per capita income: $22,000 (2007); Median household income: $39,519 (2007); Average household income: $51,185 (2007); Percent of households with income of $100,000 or more: 8.4% (2007); Poverty rate: 11.8% (2005); Bankruptcy rate: 1.66% (2006).

Taxes: Total county taxes per capita: $476 (2005); County property taxes per capita: $345 (2005).

Education: Percent of population age 25 and over with: High school diploma (including GED) or higher: 78.7% (2007); Bachelor's degree or higher: 12.7% (2007); Master's degree or higher: 4.6% (2007).

Housing: Homeownership rate: 86.9% (2007); Median home value: $151,251 (2007); Median rent: $453 per month (2000); Median age of housing: 15 years (2000).

Health: Birth rate: 90.9 per 10,000 population (2006); Death rate: 134.6 per 10,000 population (2006); Age-adjusted cancer mortality rate: 210.4 deaths per 100,000 population (2004); Number of physicians: 14.6 per 10,000 population (2005); Hospital beds: 28.6 per 10,000 population (2004); Hospital admissions: 1,573.6 per 10,000 population (2004).

Elections: 2004 Presidential election results: 52.9% Bush, 46.2% Kerry, 0.6% Nader, 0.1% Badnarik

National and State Parks: Chassahowitzka National Wildlife Refuge

Hernando County Communities

BAYPORT (CDP). Covers a land area of 0.663 square miles and a water area of 0 square miles. Located at 28.54° N. Lat.; 82.64° W. Long. Elevation is 3 feet.
Population: 30 (1990); 36 (2000); 37 (2007); 36 (2012 projected); Race: 94.6% White, 5.4% Black, 0.0% Asian, 0.0% Hispanic of any race (2007); Density: 55.8 persons per square mile (2007); Average household size: 2.18 (2007); Median age: 51.5 (2007); Males per 100 females: 85.0 (2007); Marriage status: 0.0% never married, 75.0% now married, 0.0% widowed, 25.0% divorced (2000); Foreign born: 0.0% (2000); Ancestry (includes multiple ancestries): 66.7% English, 41.7% German, 33.3% Other groups, 25.0% Scotch-Irish (2000).
Economy: Employment by occupation: 31.6% management, 36.8% professional, 0.0% services, 0.0% sales, 0.0% farming, 31.6% construction, 0.0% production (2000).
Income: Per capita income: $12,500 (2007); Median household income: $35,500 (2007); Average household income: $27,206 (2007); Percent of households with income of $100,000 or more: 0.0% (2007); Poverty rate: 25.0% (2000).
Education: Percent of population age 25 and over with: High school diploma (including GED) or higher: 100.0% (2007); Bachelor's degree or higher: 25.8% (2007); Master's degree or higher: 25.8% (2007).
Housing: Homeownership rate: 82.4% (2007); Median home value: $137,500 (2007); Median rent: $n/a per month (2000); Median age of housing: 19 years (2000).
Transportation: Commute to work: 68.4% car, 0.0% public transportation, 0.0% walk, 31.6% work from home (2000); Travel time to work: 61.5% less than 15 minutes, 38.5% 15 to 30 minutes, 0.0% 30 to 45 minutes, 0.0% 45 to 60 minutes, 0.0% 60 minutes or more (2000)

BROOKRIDGE (CDP). Covers a land area of 2.027 square miles and a water area of 0 square miles. Located at 28.54° N. Lat.; 82.49° W. Long. Elevation is 62 feet.
Population: 2,805 (1990); 3,279 (2000); 3,753 (2007); 4,059 (2012 projected); Race: 98.4% White, 0.3% Black, 0.3% Asian, 1.5% Hispanic of any race (2007); Density: 1,851.6 persons per square mile (2007); Average household size: 1.77 (2007); Median age: 72.0 (2007); Males per 100 females: 81.8 (2007); Marriage status: 3.5% never married, 71.5% now married, 19.1% widowed, 5.9% divorced (2000); Foreign born: 4.6% (2000); Ancestry (includes multiple ancestries): 19.7% German, 17.2% English, 13.0% Irish, 6.9% Italian, 5.9% United States or American (2000).
Economy: Employment by occupation: 5.9% management, 6.6% professional, 15.3% services, 46.0% sales, 0.0% farming, 10.3% construction, 15.8% production (2000).
Income: Per capita income: $21,235 (2007); Median household income: $29,695 (2007); Average household income: $36,572 (2007); Percent of households with income of $100,000 or more: 2.5% (2007); Poverty rate: 5.7% (2000).
Education: Percent of population age 25 and over with: High school diploma (including GED) or higher: 74.0% (2007); Bachelor's degree or higher: 10.6% (2007); Master's degree or higher: 5.5% (2007).
Housing: Homeownership rate: 97.0% (2007); Median home value: $91,630 (2007); Median rent: $508 per month (2000); Median age of housing: 15 years (2000).
Transportation: Commute to work: 97.6% car, 0.0% public transportation, 0.0% walk, 2.4% work from home (2000); Travel time to work: 32.0% less than 15 minutes, 46.6% 15 to 30 minutes, 6.6% 30 to 45 minutes, 4.4% 45 to 60 minutes, 10.4% 60 minutes or more (2000)

BROOKSVILLE (city). County seat. Covers a land area of 4.943 square miles and a water area of 0.027 square miles. Located at 28.55° N. Lat.; 82.38° W. Long. Elevation is 203 feet.
History: Brooksville was named for Preston Brooks, a U.S. congressman from South Carolina. In the 1870's Brooksville was a stopover on the stage line from Gainesville to Tampa.

American (2000).
Economy: Single-family building permits issued: 68 (2006); Multi-family building permits issued: 176 (2006); Employment by occupation: 10.7% management, 20.8% professional, 22.4% services, 21.3% sales, 0.3% farming, 11.1% construction, 13.3% production (2000).
Income: Per capita income: $19,004 (2007); Median household income: $29,608 (2007); Average household income: $40,718 (2007); Percent of households with income of $100,000 or more: 5.2% (2007); Poverty rate: 21.5% (2000).
Education: Percent of population age 25 and over with: High school diploma (including GED) or higher: 76.1% (2007); Bachelor's degree or higher: 14.4% (2007); Master's degree or higher: 5.0% (2007).
School District(s)
Hernando County School District (PK-12)
    2005-06 Enrollment: 20,666 . . . . (352) 797-7001
Housing: Homeownership rate: 65.2% (2007); Median home value: $69,080 (2007); Median rent: $345 per month (2000); Median age of housing: 22 years (2000).
Hospitals: Brooksville Regional Hospital (120 beds); Oak Hill Hospital (204 beds); Spring Brook Hospital (60 beds)
Safety: Violent crime rate: 95.3 per 10,000 population; Property crime rate: 534.4 per 10,000 population (2006).
Newspapers: Hernando Today (Circulation 16,395)
Transportation: Commute to work: 93.6% car, 0.4% public transportation, 3.1% walk, 2.0% work from home (2000); Travel time to work: 44.7% less than 15 minutes, 30.2% 15 to 30 minutes, 10.0% 30 to 45 minutes, 5.2% 45 to 60 minutes, 9.9% 60 minutes or more (2000)
Additional Information Contacts
Brooksville Chamber of Commerce . . . . (352) 796-0697
    http://www.hernandochamber.com
City of Brooksville . . . . (352) 544-5400
    http://www.ci.brooksville.fl.us

HERNANDO BEACH (CDP). Covers a land area of 3.915 square miles and a water area of 0.057 square miles. Located at 28.48° N. Lat.; 82.65° W. Long. Elevation is 3 feet.
Population: 1,788 (1990); 2,185 (2000); 2,397 (2007); 2,516 (2012 projected); Race: 97.0% White, 0.3% Black, 0.8% Asian, 3.1% Hispanic of any race (2007); Density: 612.3 persons per square mile (2007); Average household size: 2.19 (2007); Median age: 53.3 (2007); Males per 100 females: 98.4 (2007); Marriage status: 12.2% never married, 66.9% now married, 8.8% widowed, 12.1% divorced (2000); Foreign born: 5.7% (2000); Ancestry (includes multiple ancestries): 24.9% German, 15.0% English, 13.9% Other groups, 13.5% Irish, 12.5% Italian (2000).
Economy: Employment by occupation: 15.0% management, 23.6% professional, 13.2% services, 27.9% sales, 3.8% farming, 10.6% construction, 6.0% production (2000).
Income: Per capita income: $32,831 (2007); Median household income: $58,622 (2007); Average household income: $71,868 (2007); Percent of households with income of $100,000 or more: 22.2% (2007); Poverty rate: 6.6% (2000).
Education: Percent of population age 25 and over with: High school diploma (including GED) or higher: 86.9% (2007); Bachelor's degree or higher: 22.2% (2007); Master's degree or higher: 12.5% (2007).
Housing: Homeownership rate: 91.4% (2007); Median home value: $264,844 (2007); Median rent: $553 per month (2000); Median age of housing: 16 years (2000).
Transportation: Commute to work: 91.8% car, 0.0% public transportation, 0.0% walk, 5.5% work from home (2000); Travel time to work: 9.3% less than 15 minutes, 38.7% 15 to 30 minutes, 26.3% 30 to 45 minutes, 6.1% 45 to 60 minutes, 19.7% 60 minutes or more (2000)

HIGH POINT (CDP). Covers a land area of 2.940 square miles and a water area of 0.033 square miles. Located at 28.54° N. Lat.; 82.52° W. Long.
Population: 2,947 (1990); 2,973 (2000); 3,213 (2007); 3,360 (2012 projected); Race: 97.7% White, 0.2% Black, 0.5% Asian, 3.5% Hispanic of

Irish, 9.2% United States or American, 9.0% English, 6.8% Italian (2000).

Economy: Employment by occupation: 6.7% management, 9.9% professional, 18.2% services, 36.5% sales, 0.0% farming, 10.8% construction, 18.0% production (2000).

Income: Per capita income: $20,395 (2007); Median household income: $29,514 (2007); Average household income: $39,287 (2007); Percent of households with income of $100,000 or more: 5.0% (2007); Poverty rate: 7.4% (2000).

Education: Percent of population age 25 and over with: High school diploma (including GED) or higher: 70.0% (2007); Bachelor's degree or higher: 5.6% (2007); Master's degree or higher: 2.8% (2007).

Housing: Homeownership rate: 93.7% (2007); Median home value: $83,494 (2007); Median rent: $441 per month (2000); Median age of housing: 18 years (2000).

Transportation: Commute to work: 94.9% car, 1.5% public transportation, 0.0% walk, 1.1% work from home (2000); Travel time to work: 29.9% less than 15 minutes, 45.2% 15 to 30 minutes, 11.1% 30 to 45 minutes, 4.4% 45 to 60 minutes, 9.3% 60 minutes or more (2000)

HILL 'N DALE (CDP).

Covers a land area of 0.509 square miles and a water area of 0 square miles. Located at 28.52° N. Lat.; 82.29° W. Long. Elevation is 108 feet.

Population: 1,324 (1990); 1,436 (2000); 1,463 (2007); 1,479 (2012 projected); Race: 61.0% White, 32.4% Black, 0.6% Asian, 12.0% Hispanic of any race (2007); Density: 2,876.4 persons per square mile (2007); Average household size: 3.02 (2007); Median age: 28.2 (2007); Males per 100 females: 90.5 (2007); Marriage status: 28.2% never married, 53.2% now married, 4.9% widowed, 13.7% divorced (2000); Foreign born: 4.4% (2000); Ancestry (includes multiple ancestries): 28.2% Other groups, 18.0% United States or American, 15.3% German, 9.2% Irish, 8.2% English (2000).

Economy: Employment by occupation: 3.9% management, 13.7% professional, 22.4% services, 21.8% sales, 2.6% farming, 19.0% construction, 16.6% production (2000).

Income: Per capita income: $13,526 (2007); Median household income: $41,220 (2007); Average household income: $40,749 (2007); Percent of households with income of $100,000 or more: 1.2% (2007); Poverty rate: 18.5% (2000).

Education: Percent of population age 25 and over with: High school diploma (including GED) or higher: 70.7% (2007); Bachelor's degree or higher: 10.5% (2007); Master's degree or higher: 0.0% (2007).

Housing: Homeownership rate: 82.9% (2007); Median home value: $91,849 (2007); Median rent: $466 per month (2000); Median age of housing: 20 years (2000).

Transportation: Commute to work: 100.0% car, 0.0% public transportation, 0.0% walk, 0.0% work from home (2000); Travel time to work: 22.2% less than 15 minutes, 25.5% 15 to 30 minutes, 25.4% 30 to 45 minutes, 6.3% 45 to 60 minutes, 20.5% 60 minutes or more (2000)

ISTACHATTA (CDP).

Covers a land area of 0.129 square miles and a water area of 0.020 square miles. Located at 28.66° N. Lat.; 82.27° W. Long. Elevation is 59 feet.

Population: 76 (1990); 65 (2000); 68 (2007); 70 (2012 projected); Race: 94.1% White, 5.9% Black, 0.0% Asian, 4.4% Hispanic of any race (2007); Density: 528.8 persons per square mile (2007); Average household size: 1.89 (2007); Median age: 58.1 (2007); Males per 100 females: 100.0 (2007); Marriage status: 18.9% never married, 81.1% now married, 0.0% widowed, 0.0% divorced (2000); Foreign born: 0.0% (2000); Ancestry (includes multiple ancestries): 49.2% Other groups, 36.1% German, 29.5% Irish (2000).

Economy: Employment by occupation: 0.0% management, 100.0% professional, 0.0% services, 0.0% sales, 0.0% farming, 0.0% construction, 0.0% production (2000).

Income: Per capita income: $14,890 (2007); Median household income: $27,000 (2007); Average household income: $28,125 (2007); Percent of households with income of $100,000 or more: 0.0% (2007); Poverty rate: 29.5% (2000).

Education: Percent of population age 25 and over with: High school diploma (including GED) or higher: 41.9% (2007); Bachelor's degree or higher: 0.0% (2007); Master's degree or higher: 0.0% (2007).

work: 0.0% less than 15 minutes, 100.0% 15 to 30 minutes, 0.0% 30 to 45 minutes, 0.0% 45 to 60 minutes, 0.0% 60 minutes or more (2000)

LAKE LINDSEY (CDP).

Covers a land area of 0.022 square miles and a water area of 0 square miles. Located at 28.63° N. Lat.; 82.36° W. Long. Elevation is 98 feet.

Population: 59 (1990); 49 (2000); 52 (2007); 53 (2012 projected); Race: 100.0% White, 0.0% Black, 0.0% Asian, 0.0% Hispanic of any race (2007); Density: 2,341.9 persons per square mile (2007); Average household size: 2.08 (2007); Median age: 42.5 (2007); Males per 100 females: 100.0 (2007); Marriage status: 0.0% never married, 33.3% now married, 43.3% widowed, 23.3% divorced (2000); Foreign born: 0.0% (2000); Ancestry (includes multiple ancestries): 15.9% Norwegian, 15.9% German, 13.6% Irish (2000).

Economy: Employment by occupation: 0.0% management, 41.2% professional, 35.3% services, 0.0% sales, 0.0% farming, 23.5% construction, 0.0% production (2000).

Income: Per capita income: $11,923 (2007); Median household income: $30,500 (2007); Average household income: $24,800 (2007); Percent of households with income of $100,000 or more: 0.0% (2007); Poverty rate: 15.9% (2000).

Education: Percent of population age 25 and over with: High school diploma (including GED) or higher: 83.8% (2007); Bachelor's degree or higher: 0.0% (2007); Master's degree or higher: 0.0% (2007).

Housing: Homeownership rate: 80.0% (2007); Median home value: $33,750 (2007); Median rent: $375 per month (2000); Median age of housing: 20 years (2000).

Transportation: Commute to work: 100.0% car, 0.0% public transportation, 0.0% walk, 0.0% work from home (2000); Travel time to work: 0.0% less than 15 minutes, 58.8% 15 to 30 minutes, 41.2% 30 to 45 minutes, 0.0% 45 to 60 minutes, 0.0% 60 minutes or more (2000)

MASARYKTOWN (CDP).

Covers a land area of 1.059 square miles and a water area of 0 square miles. Located at 28.44° N. Lat.; 82.46° W. Long. Elevation is 62 feet.

Population: 675 (1990); 920 (2000); 1,231 (2007); 1,439 (2012 projected); Race: 94.0% White, 0.3% Black, 0.6% Asian, 11.1% Hispanic of any race (2007); Density: 1,162.4 persons per square mile (2007); Average household size: 2.39 (2007); Median age: 42.1 (2007); Males per 100 females: 94.5 (2007); Marriage status: 9.5% never married, 63.0% now married, 7.2% widowed, 20.3% divorced (2000); Foreign born: 6.7% (2000); Ancestry (includes multiple ancestries): 24.1% German, 10.6% Other groups, 10.0% Irish, 10.0% Italian, 9.1% English (2000).

Economy: Employment by occupation: 12.4% management, 8.5% professional, 18.9% services, 17.3% sales, 0.0% farming, 21.5% construction, 21.5% production (2000).

Income: Per capita income: $19,938 (2007); Median household income: $45,079 (2007); Average household income: $42,471 (2007); Percent of households with income of $100,000 or more: 0.0% (2007); Poverty rate: 13.8% (2000).

Education: Percent of population age 25 and over with: High school diploma (including GED) or higher: 76.3% (2007); Bachelor's degree or higher: 8.5% (2007); Master's degree or higher: 4.2% (2007).

Housing: Homeownership rate: 82.1% (2007); Median home value: $87,245 (2007); Median rent: $238 per month (2000); Median age of housing: 29 years (2000).

Transportation: Commute to work: 92.4% car, 0.0% public transportation, 0.0% walk, 5.0% work from home (2000); Travel time to work: 11.5% less than 15 minutes, 41.3% 15 to 30 minutes, 25.5% 30 to 45 minutes, 3.1% 45 to 60 minutes, 18.5% 60 minutes or more (2000)

NOBLETON (CDP).

Covers a land area of 0.197 square miles and a water area of 0.012 square miles. Located at 28.64° N. Lat.; 82.26° W. Long. Elevation is 59 feet.

Population: 186 (1990); 160 (2000); 185 (2007); 202 (2012 projected); Race: 99.5% White, 0.0% Black, 0.0% Asian, 2.2% Hispanic of any race (2007); Density: 939.0 persons per square mile (2007); Average household size: 2.03 (2007); Median age: 47.0 (2007); Males per 100 females: 115.1 (2007); Marriage status: 0.0% never married, 69.0% now married, 9.5% widowed, 21.4% divorced (2000); Foreign born: 0.0% (2000); Ancestry

construction, 48.5% production (2000).

Income: Per capita income: $18,189 (2007); Median household income: $32,115 (2007); Average household income: $36,978 (2007); Percent of households with income of $100,000 or more: 2.2% (2007); Poverty rate: 50.8% (2000).

Education: Percent of population age 25 and over with: High school diploma (including GED) or higher: 67.6% (2007); Bachelor's degree or higher: 2.2% (2007); Master's degree or higher: 1.4% (2007).

Housing: Homeownership rate: 91.2% (2007); Median home value: $71,667 (2007); Median rent: $n/a per month (2000); Median age of housing: 25 years (2000).

Transportation: Commute to work: 72.7% car, 0.0% public transportation, 0.0% walk, 27.3% work from home (2000); Travel time to work: 33.3% less than 15 minutes, 37.5% 15 to 30 minutes, 29.2% 30 to 45 minutes, 0.0% 45 to 60 minutes, 0.0% 60 minutes or more (2000)

NORTH BROOKSVILLE (CDP).

Covers a land area of 2.763 square miles and a water area of 0.002 square miles. Located at 28.56° N. Lat.; 82.40° W. Long. Elevation is 157 feet.

Population: 1,438 (1990); 1,461 (2000); 1,441 (2007); 1,438 (2012 projected); Race: 86.7% White, 8.7% Black, 1.3% Asian, 4.1% Hispanic of any race (2007); Density: 521.5 persons per square mile (2007); Average household size: 2.62 (2007); Median age: 36.2 (2007); Males per 100 females: 89.6 (2007); Marriage status: 23.9% never married, 52.0% now married, 8.5% widowed, 15.6% divorced (2000); Foreign born: 2.7% (2000); Ancestry (includes multiple ancestries): 20.3% United States or American, 15.6% Other groups, 6.6% Italian, 6.5% English, 6.0% Irish (2000).

Economy: Employment by occupation: 4.4% management, 12.0% professional, 21.5% services, 24.8% sales, 1.4% farming, 20.0% construction, 15.9% production (2000).

Income: Per capita income: $15,928 (2007); Median household income: $31,196 (2007); Average household income: $39,501 (2007); Percent of households with income of $100,000 or more: 5.8% (2007); Poverty rate: 13.7% (2000).

Education: Percent of population age 25 and over with: High school diploma (including GED) or higher: 68.2% (2007); Bachelor's degree or higher: 8.9% (2007); Master's degree or higher: 3.9% (2007).

Housing: Homeownership rate: 70.4% (2007); Median home value: $97,895 (2007); Median rent: $387 per month (2000); Median age of housing: 25 years (2000).

Transportation: Commute to work: 95.3% car, 0.0% public transportation, 1.3% walk, 1.1% work from home (2000); Travel time to work: 53.6% less than 15 minutes, 23.6% 15 to 30 minutes, 11.3% 30 to 45 minutes, 1.0% 45 to 60 minutes, 10.5% 60 minutes or more (2000)

NORTH WEEKI WACHEE (CDP).

Covers a land area of 7.357 square miles and a water area of 0.931 square miles. Located at 28.54° N. Lat.; 82.56° W. Long.

Population: 2,009 (1990); 4,253 (2000); 6,276 (2007); 7,535 (2012 projected); Race: 95.3% White, 1.7% Black, 0.8% Asian, 7.8% Hispanic of any race (2007); Density: 853.0 persons per square mile (2007); Average household size: 2.27 (2007); Median age: 51.6 (2007); Males per 100 females: 96.1 (2007); Marriage status: 10.3% never married, 72.8% now married, 8.5% widowed, 8.4% divorced (2000); Foreign born: 3.8% (2000); Ancestry (includes multiple ancestries): 18.9% German, 18.2% Irish, 13.3% English, 13.0% Italian, 11.7% United States or American (2000).

Economy: Employment by occupation: 16.4% management, 20.1% professional, 13.8% services, 27.2% sales, 0.7% farming, 13.1% construction, 8.7% production (2000).

Income: Per capita income: $26,806 (2007); Median household income: $38,924 (2007); Average household income: $60,851 (2007); Percent of households with income of $100,000 or more: 15.4% (2007); Poverty rate: 5.9% (2000).

Education: Percent of population age 25 and over with: High school diploma (including GED) or higher: 81.2% (2007); Bachelor's degree or higher: 16.6% (2007); Master's degree or higher: 4.4% (2007).

Housing: Homeownership rate: 90.1% (2007); Median home value: $170,263 (2007); Median rent: $487 per month (2000); Median age of housing: 10 years (2000).

PINE ISLAND (CDP).

Covers a land area of 0.068 square miles and a water area of 0 square miles. Located at 28.57° N. Lat.; 82.65° W. Long. Elevation is 3 feet.

Population: 53 (1990); 64 (2000); 66 (2007); 66 (2012 projected); Race: 83.3% White, 13.6% Black, 0.0% Asian, 0.0% Hispanic of any race (2007); Density: 975.2 persons per square mile (2007); Average household size: 2.20 (2007); Median age: 46.0 (2007); Males per 100 females: 94.1 (2007); Marriage status: 12.7% never married, 40.0% now married, 18.2% widowed, 29.1% divorced (2000); Foreign born: 0.0% (2000); Ancestry (includes multiple ancestries): 50.9% German, 21.8% Swedish, 21.8% Irish, 20.0% Dutch, 18.2% English (2000).

Economy: Employment by occupation: 0.0% management, 0.0% professional, 0.0% services, 100.0% sales, 0.0% farming, 0.0% construction, 0.0% production (2000).

Income: Per capita income: $19,735 (2007); Median household income: $49,000 (2007); Average household income: $43,417 (2007); Percent of households with income of $100,000 or more: 0.0% (2007); Poverty rate: 20.0% (2000).

Education: Percent of population age 25 and over with: High school diploma (including GED) or higher: 100.0% (2007); Bachelor's degree or higher: 21.6% (2007); Master's degree or higher: 0.0% (2007).

Housing: Homeownership rate: 73.3% (2007); Median home value: $240,000 (2007); Median rent: $625 per month (2000); Median age of housing: 17 years (2000).

Transportation: Commute to work: 100.0% car, 0.0% public transportation, 0.0% walk, 0.0% work from home (2000); Travel time to work: 0.0% less than 15 minutes, 0.0% 15 to 30 minutes, 0.0% 30 to 45 minutes, 0.0% 45 to 60 minutes, 100.0% 60 minutes or more (2000)

RIDGE MANOR (CDP).

Covers a land area of 8.718 square miles and a water area of 0.309 square miles. Located at 28.49° N. Lat.; 82.18° W. Long. Elevation is 69 feet.

Population: 3,339 (1990); 4,108 (2000); 4,622 (2007); 4,937 (2012 projected); Race: 93.8% White, 2.7% Black, 0.4% Asian, 4.9% Hispanic of any race (2007); Density: 530.1 persons per square mile (2007); Average household size: 2.40 (2007); Median age: 42.1 (2007); Males per 100 females: 97.4 (2007); Marriage status: 17.3% never married, 61.4% now married, 9.7% widowed, 11.6% divorced (2000); Foreign born: 3.5% (2000); Ancestry (includes multiple ancestries): 16.8% Irish, 14.7% German, 14.0% United States or American, 13.8% English, 13.5% Other groups (2000).

Economy: Employment by occupation: 8.6% management, 16.0% professional, 16.7% services, 27.7% sales, 0.0% farming, 11.2% construction, 19.8% production (2000).

Income: Per capita income: $18,522 (2007); Median household income: $33,505 (2007); Average household income: $44,542 (2007); Percent of households with income of $100,000 or more: 7.0% (2007); Poverty rate: 15.1% (2000).

Education: Percent of population age 25 and over with: High school diploma (including GED) or higher: 72.5% (2007); Bachelor's degree or higher: 9.1% (2007); Master's degree or higher: 2.5% (2007).

Housing: Homeownership rate: 87.0% (2007); Median home value: $117,727 (2007); Median rent: $410 per month (2000); Median age of housing: 19 years (2000).

Transportation: Commute to work: 93.7% car, 0.5% public transportation, 0.8% walk, 1.7% work from home (2000); Travel time to work: 14.0% less than 15 minutes, 42.3% 15 to 30 minutes, 14.3% 30 to 45 minutes, 9.2% 45 to 60 minutes, 20.1% 60 minutes or more (2000)

SOUTH BROOKSVILLE (CDP).

Covers a land area of 3.506 square miles and a water area of 0.056 square miles. Located at 28.54° N. Lat.; 82.39° W. Long. Elevation is 115 feet.

Population: 1,387 (1990); 1,376 (2000); 1,363 (2007); 1,366 (2012 projected); Race: 57.2% White, 37.4% Black, 0.7% Asian, 8.1% Hispanic of any race (2007); Density: 388.8 persons per square mile (2007); Average household size: 2.43 (2007); Median age: 32.3 (2007); Males per 100 females: 86.7 (2007); Marriage status: 17.5% never married, 51.3% now married, 12.8% widowed, 18.5% divorced (2000); Foreign born: 0.0% (2000); Ancestry (includes multiple ancestries): 40.9% Other groups,

14.9% United States or American, 9.9% German, 6.6% Irish, 5.8% Nigerian (2000).

Economy: Employment by occupation: 5.5% management, 11.2% professional, 29.1% services, 19.6% sales, 0.0% farming, 17.5% construction, 17.0% production (2000).

Income: Per capita income: $18,309 (2007); Median household income: $33,911 (2007); Average household income: $44,483 (2007); Percent of households with income of $100,000 or more: 5.9% (2007); Poverty rate: 16.1% (2000).

Education: Percent of population age 25 and over with: High school diploma (including GED) or higher: 62.4% (2007); Bachelor's degree or higher: 6.2% (2007); Master's degree or higher: 2.0% (2007).

Housing: Homeownership rate: 72.2% (2007); Median home value: $97,353 (2007); Median rent: $373 per month (2000); Median age of housing: 30 years (2000).

Transportation: Commute to work: 98.4% car, 0.0% public transportation, 0.0% walk, 1.6% work from home (2000); Travel time to work: 32.6% less than 15 minutes, 40.3% 15 to 30 minutes, 13.6% 30 to 45 minutes, 3.8% 45 to 60 minutes, 9.7% 60 minutes or more (2000)

SPRING HILL (CDP). Covers a land area of 53.134 square miles and a water area of 1.706 square miles. Located at 28.47° N. Lat.; 82.54° W. Long. Elevation is 213 feet.

Population: 50,663 (1990); 69,078 (2000); 90,586 (2007); 103,687 (2012 projected); Race: 91.4% White, 4.0% Black, 1.1% Asian, 10.3% Hispanic of any race (2007); Density: 1,704.9 persons per square mile (2007); Average household size: 2.42 (2007); Median age: 44.6 (2007); Males per 100 females: 91.2 (2007); Marriage status: 16.0% never married, 64.7% now married, 10.1% widowed, 9.2% divorced (2000); Foreign born: 6.7% (2000); Ancestry (includes multiple ancestries): 19.7% German, 18.0% Italian, 17.0% Irish, 12.8% Other groups, 11.0% English (2000).

Economy: Employment by occupation: 8.2% management, 17.5% professional, 19.3% services, 30.7% sales, 0.5% farming, 12.5% construction, 11.3% production (2000).

Income: Per capita income: $20,769 (2007); Median household income: $39,792 (2007); Average household income: $49,925 (2007); Percent of households with income of $100,000 or more: 7.5% (2007); Poverty rate: 9.5% (2000).

Education: Percent of population age 25 and over with: High school diploma (including GED) or higher: 79.2% (2007); Bachelor's degree or higher: 11.9% (2007); Master's degree or higher: 4.1% (2007).

School District(s)

Hernando County School District (PK-12)

  2005-06 Enrollment: 20,666 . . . . (352) 797-7001

Pasco County School District (PK-12)

  2005-06 Enrollment: 60,846 . . . . (813) 794-2651

Housing: Homeownership rate: 86.6% (2007); Median home value: $158,712 (2007); Median rent: $510 per month (2000); Median age of housing: 14 years (2000).

Hospitals: Spring Hill Regional Hospital (124 beds)

Transportation: Commute to work: 96.3% car, 0.1% public transportation, 0.5% walk, 2.2% work from home (2000); Travel time to work: 27.6% less than 15 minutes, 36.6% 15 to 30 minutes, 16.0% 30 to 45 minutes, 7.1% 45 to 60 minutes, 12.8% 60 minutes or more (2000)

SPRING LAKE (CDP). Covers a land area of 3.375 square miles and a water area of 0.107 square miles. Located at 28.48° N. Lat.; 82.30° W. Long. Elevation is 220 feet.

Population: 304 (1990); 327 (2000); 388 (2007); 426 (2012 projected); Race: 97.4% White, 0.0% Black, 1.5% Asian, 9.8% Hispanic of any race (2007); Density: 115.0 persons per square mile (2007); Average household size: 2.60 (2007); Median age: 42.4 (2007); Males per 100 females: 87.4 (2007); Marriage status: 14.4% never married, 49.5% now married, 7.9% widowed, 28.2% divorced (2000); Foreign born: 4.1% (2000); Ancestry (includes multiple ancestries): 28.4% German, 23.5% United States or American, 16.0% English, 12.3% Irish, 10.8% Polish (2000).

Economy: Employment by occupation: 8.2% management, 4.1% professional, 10.2% services, 68.4% sales, 0.0% farming, 9.2% construction, 0.0% production (2000).

Income: Per capita income: $23,192 (2007); Median household income: $57,500 (2007); Average household income: $60,034 (2007); Percent of households with income of $100,000 or more: 9.4% (2007); Poverty rate: 3.4% (2000).

Education: Percent of population age 25 and over with: High school diploma (including GED) or higher: 84.0% (2007); Bachelor's degree or higher: 5.1% (2007); Master's degree or higher: 5.1% (2007).

Housing: Homeownership rate: 93.3% (2007); Median home value: $313,415 (2007); Median rent: $n/a per month (2000); Median age of housing: 15 years (2000).

Transportation: Commute to work: 100.0% car, 0.0% public transportation, 0.0% walk, 0.0% work from home (2000); Travel time to work: 0.0% less than 15 minutes, 66.3% 15 to 30 minutes, 7.1% 30 to 45 minutes, 18.4% 45 to 60 minutes, 8.2% 60 minutes or more (2000)

TIMBER PINES (CDP). Covers a land area of 2.378 square miles and a water area of 0 square miles. Located at 28.46° N. Lat.; 82.60° W. Long. Elevation is 13 feet.

Population: 3,008 (1990); 5,840 (2000); 6,375 (2007); 6,712 (2012 projected); Race: 98.5% White, 0.6% Black, 0.4% Asian, 0.8% Hispanic of any race (2007); Density: 2,681.3 persons per square mile (2007); Average household size: 1.77 (2007); Median age: 72.5 (2007); Males per 100 females: 82.4 (2007); Marriage status: 2.0% never married, 82.0% now married, 13.0% widowed, 3.0% divorced (2000); Foreign born: 5.0% (2000); Ancestry (includes multiple ancestries): 26.0% German, 18.2% Irish, 17.9% English, 9.7% Italian, 6.9% Polish (2000).

Economy: Employment by occupation: 3.1% management, 31.5% professional, 6.8% services, 38.0% sales, 0.0% farming, 11.6% construction, 8.9% production (2000).

Income: Per capita income: $37,974 (2007); Median household income: $51,923 (2007); Average household income: $67,226 (2007); Percent of households with income of $100,000 or more: 12.8% (2007); Poverty rate: 2.6% (2000).

Education: Percent of population age 25 and over with: High school diploma (including GED) or higher: 89.9% (2007); Bachelor's degree or higher: 23.8% (2007); Master's degree or higher: 9.5% (2007).

Housing: Homeownership rate: 97.4% (2007); Median home value: $227,060 (2007); Median rent: $703 per month (2000); Median age of housing: 9 years (2000).

Transportation: Commute to work: 88.0% car, 0.0% public transportation, 0.0% walk, 12.0% work from home (2000); Travel time to work: 31.2% less than 15 minutes, 39.2% 15 to 30 minutes, 3.2% 30 to 45 minutes, 0.0% 45 to 60 minutes, 26.4% 60 minutes or more (2000)

WEEKI WACHEE (city). Aka Weekiwachee Springs. Covers a land area of 1.015 square miles and a water area of 0.024 square miles. Located at 28.51° N. Lat.; 82.57° W. Long. Elevation is 33 feet.

Population: 53 (1990); 12 (2000); 16 (2007); 19 (2012 projected); Race: 100.0% White, 0.0% Black, 0.0% Asian, 0.0% Hispanic of any race (2007); Density: 15.8 persons per square mile (2007); Average household size: 2.67 (2007); Median age: 21.0 (2007); Males per 100 females: 220.0 (2007); Marriage status: 0.0% never married, 100.0% now married, 0.0% widowed, 0.0% divorced (2000); Foreign born: 0.0% (2000); Ancestry (includes multiple ancestries): 22.2% German, 22.2% Irish, 22.2% Other groups, 11.1% Italian, 11.1% French (except Basque) (2000).

Economy: Single-family building permits issued: 8 (2006); Multi-family building permits issued: 0 (2006); Employment by occupation: 0.0% management, 40.0% professional, 20.0% services, 0.0% sales, 0.0% farming, 0.0% construction, 40.0% production (2000).

Income: Per capita income: $13,594 (2007); Median household income: $35,000 (2007); Average household income: $36,250 (2007); Percent of households with income of $100,000 or more: 0.0% (2007); Poverty rate: 55.6% (2000).

Education: Percent of population age 25 and over with: High school diploma (including GED) or higher: 85.7% (2007); Bachelor's degree or higher: 42.9% (2007); Master's degree or higher: 0.0% (2007).

Housing: Homeownership rate: 83.3% (2007); Median home value: $81,667 (2007); Median rent: $475 per month (2000); Median age of housing: 17 years (2000).

Transportation: Commute to work: 80.0% car, 0.0% public transportation, 0.0% walk, 20.0% work from home (2000); Travel time to work: 0.0% less than 15 minutes, 0.0% 15 to 30 minutes, 0.0% 30 to 45 minutes, 50.0% 45 to 60 minutes, 50.0% 60 minutes or more (2000)

WEEKI WACHEE GARDENS (CDP). Covers a land area of 1.386 square miles and a water area of 0.011 square miles. Located at 28.53° N. Lat.; 82.62° W. Long. Elevation is 3 feet.

Population: 1,170 (1990); 1,140 (2000); 1,215 (2007); 1,254 (2012 projected); Race: 97.4% White, 0.3% Black, 0.1% Asian, 1.6% Hispanic of

any race (2007); Density: 876.7 persons per square mile (2007); Average household size: 2.01 (2007); Median age: 53.7 (2007); Males per 100 females: 107.3 (2007); Marriage status: 12.3% never married, 71.4% now married, 7.6% widowed, 8.7% divorced (2000); Foreign born: 3.4% (2000); Ancestry (includes multiple ancestries): 17.0% German, 16.6% English, 13.8% Other groups, 12.0% Irish, 8.3% United States or American (2000).
Economy: Employment by occupation: 17.1% management, 12.1% professional, 18.6% services, 25.6% sales, 1.5% farming, 12.9% construction, 12.3% production (2000).
Income: Per capita income: $25,337 (2007); Median household income: $35,682 (2007); Average household income: $50,884 (2007); Percent of households with income of $100,000 or more: 6.8% (2007); Poverty rate: 9.0% (2000).
Education: Percent of population age 25 and over with: High school diploma (including GED) or higher: 92.8% (2007); Bachelor's degree or higher: 17.4% (2007); Master's degree or higher: 6.1% (2007).
Housing: Homeownership rate: 87.8% (2007); Median home value: $159,683 (2007); Median rent: $420 per month (2000); Median age of housing: 24 years (2000).
Transportation: Commute to work: 94.8% car, 0.0% public transportation, 0.0% walk, 1.7% work from home (2000); Travel time to work: 21.6% less than 15 minutes, 34.9% 15 to 30 minutes, 22.5% 30 to 45 minutes, 7.3% 45 to 60 minutes, 13.7% 60 minutes or more (2000)

Highlands County

Located in south central Florida, partly in the Everglades; bounded on the east by the Kissimmee River; rolling terrain with many lakes, including Lake Istokpoga. Covers a land area of 1,028.27 square miles, a water area of 78.01 square miles, and is located in the Eastern Time Zone. The county was founded in 1921. County seat is Sebring.

Highlands County is part of the Sebring, FL Micropolitan Statistical Area. The entire metro area includes: Highlands County, FL

Weather Station: Archbold Bio Station   Elevation: 137 feet

	Jan	Feb	Mar	Apr	May	Jun	Jul	Aug	Sep	Oct	Nov	Dec
High	74	76	81	85	90	92	93	93	91	87	81	76
Low	48	48	53	56	62	67	68	69	69	63	57	51
Precip	2.4	2.5	3.5	2.3	4.1	7.9	7.8	7.5	6.4	3.1	2.1	1.9
Snow	tr	0.0	0.0	0.0	0.0	0.0	0.0	0.0	0.0	0.0	0.0	0.0

High and Low temperatures in degrees Fahrenheit; Precipitation and Snow in inches

Weather Station: Avon Park 2 W   Elevation: 150 feet

	Jan	Feb	Mar	Apr	May	Jun	Jul	Aug	Sep	Oct	Nov	Dec
High	72	75	79	84	88	91	92	92	90	85	79	75
Low	48	50	55	59	65	70	71	72	71	64	57	51
Precip	2.6	2.5	3.2	2.2	3.8	8.2	7.1	7.2	6.0	3.1	2.3	1.8
Snow	tr	0.0	0.0	0.0	0.0	0.0	0.0	0.0	0.0	0.0	0.0	0.0

High and Low temperatures in degrees Fahrenheit; Precipitation and Snow in inches

Population: 68,432 (1990); 87,366 (2000); 96,397 (2007); 102,039 (2012 projected); Race: 82.1% White, 9.2% Black, 1.2% Asian, 15.8% Hispanic of any race (2007); Density: 93.7 persons per square mile (2007); Average household size: 2.36 (2007); Median age: 47.6 (2007); Males per 100 females: 96.3 (2007).
Religion: Five largest groups: 11.1% Southern Baptist Convention, 5.3% Catholic Church, 4.7% The United Methodist Church, 2.0% Seventh-day Adventist Church, 1.4% Associate Reformed Presbyterian Church (2000).
Economy: Unemployment rate: 5.1% (11/2007); Total civilian labor force: 43,725 (11/2007); Leading industries: 23.8% health care and social assistance; 20.0% retail trade; 13.1% accommodation & food services (2005); Farms: 1,035 totaling 576,900 acres (2002); Companies that employ 500 or more persons: 3 (2005); Companies that employ 100 to 499 persons: 19 (2005); Companies that employ less than 100 persons: 2,071 (2005); Black-owned businesses: n/a (2002); Hispanic-owned businesses: 416 (2002); Asian-owned businesses: n/a (2002); Women-owned businesses: 1,596 (2002); Retail sales per capita: $11,348 (2007). Single-family building permits issued: 1,415 (2006); Multi-family building permits issued: 125 (2006).
Income: Per capita income: $19,469 (2007); Median household income: $34,367 (2007); Average household income: $45,558 (2007); Percent of households with income of $100,000 or more: 7.3% (2007); Poverty rate: 16.6% (2005); Bankruptcy rate: 0.94% (2006).

Education: Percent of population age 25 and over with: High school diploma (including GED) or higher: 75.0% (2007); Bachelor's degree or higher: 13.8% (2007); Master's degree or higher: 5.3% (2007).
Housing: Homeownership rate: 80.4% (2007); Median home value: $105,970 (2007); Median rent: $372 per month (2000); Median age of housing: 18 years (2000).
Health: Birth rate: 103.8 per 10,000 population (2006); Death rate: 140.9 per 10,000 population (2006); Age-adjusted cancer mortality rate: 176.8 deaths per 100,000 population (2004); Air Quality Index: 94.8% good, 5.2% moderate, 0.0% unhealthy for sensitive individuals, 0.0% unhealthy (percent of days in 2006); Number of physicians: 17.9 per 10,000 population (2005); Hospital beds: 26.9 per 10,000 population (2004); Hospital admissions: 1,695.9 per 10,000 population (2004).
Elections: 2004 Presidential election results: 62.4% Bush, 37.0% Kerry, 0.5% Nader, 0.1% Badnarik
National and State Parks: Highlands Hammock State Park; Lake June-in-Winter Scrub State Park
Additional Information Contacts

Highlands County Government . . . . (863) 386-6517
   http://www.hcbcc.net
Avon Park Chamber of Commerce . . . . (863) 453-3350
   http://www.apfla.com
City of Avon Park . . . . (863) 452-4400
   http://avonpark.cc
City of Sebring . . . . (863) 471-5100
Lake Placid Chamber of Commerce . . . . (863) 465-4331
   http://www.lpfla.com
Sebring Chamber of Commerce . . . . (863) 385-8448
   http://www.sebringflchamber.com

Highlands County Communities

AVON PARK (city). Covers a land area of 4.638 square miles and a water area of 1.017 square miles. Located at 27.59° N. Lat.; 81.50° W. Long. Elevation is 151 feet.
History: Avon Park was established in 1886 by the Florida Development Company. O.M. Crosby, president of the company, brought settlers from England who named the town for the Avon River in England. The town declined between 1885 and 1912, when construction of the Atlantic Coast Line Railroad brought new growth. Avon Park was incorporated in 1913.
Population: 8,134 (1990); 8,542 (2000); 8,424 (2007); 8,520 (2012 projected); Race: 56.0% White, 29.2% Black, 0.8% Asian, 25.6% Hispanic of any race (2007); Density: 1,816.4 persons per square mile (2007); Average household size: 2.73 (2007); Median age: 33.8 (2007); Males per 100 females: 99.6 (2007); Marriage status: 27.2% never married, 52.0% now married, 11.6% widowed, 9.2% divorced (2000); Foreign born: 14.3% (2000); Ancestry (includes multiple ancestries): 43.0% Other groups, 10.1% United States or American, 8.1% German, 7.3% Irish, 7.3% English (2000).
Economy: Single-family building permits issued: 7 (2006); Multi-family building permits issued: 25 (2006); Employment by occupation: 5.1% management, 9.5% professional, 26.7% services, 18.9% sales, 15.9% farming, 9.2% construction, 14.7% production (2000).
Income: Per capita income: $12,939 (2007); Median household income: $25,269 (2007); Average household income: $34,636 (2007); Percent of households with income of $100,000 or more: 4.0% (2007); Poverty rate: 27.6% (2000).
Education: Percent of population age 25 and over with: High school diploma (including GED) or higher: 62.1% (2007); Bachelor's degree or higher: 7.8% (2007); Master's degree or higher: 2.9% (2007).

School District(s)
Highlands County School District (PK-12)
   2005-06 Enrollment: 12,049 . . . . (863) 471-5564
Polk County School District (PK-12)
   2005-06 Enrollment: 86,292 . . . . (863) 534-0521
Two-year College(s)
South Florida Community College (Public)
   Fall 2006 Enrollment: 2,414 . . . . (863) 453-6661
   2006-07 Tuition: In-state $2,048; Out-of-state $7,692
Housing: Homeownership rate: 60.8% (2007); Median home value: $71,855 (2007); Median rent: $349 per month (2000); Median age of housing: 31 years (2000).
Safety: Violent crime rate: 127.5 per 10,000 population; Property crime rate: 400.1 per 10,000 population (2006).

LAKE PLACID (town).
Covers a land area of 2.565 square miles and a water area of 0.270 square miles. Located at 27.29° N. Lat.; 81.36° W. Long. Elevation is 151 feet.

History: Lake Placid was called Lake Stearns when it was founded in 1924 as part of a land and citrus orchard development. It was later named for the Lake Placid Club of New York, which founded a branch here.

Population: 1,386 (1990); 1,668 (2000); 1,643 (2007); 1,671 (2012 projected); Race: 73.9% White, 9.5% Black, 1.0% Asian, 39.5% Hispanic of any race (2007); Density: 640.5 persons per square mile (2007); Average household size: 2.61 (2007); Median age: 32.6 (2007); Males per 100 females: 99.6 (2007); Marriage status: 22.8% never married, 56.6% now married, 7.0% widowed, 13.6% divorced (2000); Foreign born: 26.7% (2000); Ancestry (includes multiple ancestries): 47.2% Other groups, 9.7% German, 9.6% English, 8.1% United States or American, 6.2% Irish (2000).

Economy: Employment by occupation: 6.6% management, 9.5% professional, 20.5% services, 13.0% sales, 22.9% farming, 14.2% construction, 13.3% production (2000).

Income: Per capita income: $12,706 (2007); Median household income: $23,735 (2007); Average household income: $33,172 (2007); Percent of households with income of $100,000 or more: 5.4% (2007); Poverty rate: 34.7% (2000).

Education: Percent of population age 25 and over with: High school diploma (including GED) or higher: 57.2% (2007); Bachelor's degree or higher: 7.1% (2007); Master's degree or higher: 2.2% (2007).

School District(s)
Highlands County School District (PK-12)
    2005-06 Enrollment: 12,049 . . . . (863) 471-5564

Housing: Homeownership rate: 49.3% (2007); Median home value: $107,143 (2007); Median rent: $334 per month (2000); Median age of housing: 20 years (2000).

Hospitals: Florida Hospital Lake Placid (50 beds)

Safety: Violent crime rate: 176.4 per 10,000 population; Property crime rate: 595.4 per 10,000 population (2006).

Newspapers: Lake Placid Journal (General - Circulation 6,500)

Transportation: Commute to work: 90.6% car, 0.9% public transportation, 5.2% walk, 1.7% work from home (2000); Travel time to work: 34.6% less than 15 minutes, 42.9% 15 to 30 minutes, 17.1% 30 to 45 minutes, 1.8% 45 to 60 minutes, 3.7% 60 minutes or more (2000)

Additional Information Contacts
Lake Placid Chamber of Commerce . . . . (863) 465-4331
    http://www.lpfla.com

LORIDA (unincorporated postal area, zip code 33857).
Covers a land area of 161.488 square miles and a water area of 0.785 square miles. Located at 27.39° N. Lat.; 81.14° W. Long. Elevation is 49 feet.

Population: 1,645 (2000); Race: 88.6% White, 8.0% Black, 0.0% Asian, 5.2% Hispanic of any race (2000); Density: 10.2 persons per square mile (2000); Age: 20.0% under 18, 28.2% over 64 (2000); Marriage status: 22.1% never married, 57.6% now married, 9.1% widowed, 11.1% divorced (2000); Foreign born: 2.2% (2000); Ancestry (includes multiple ancestries): 21.5% German, 21.3% Other groups, 16.2% Irish, 13.3% United States or American, 8.1% English (2000).

Economy: Employment by occupation: 0.0% management, 9.0% professional, 15.8% services, 27.6% sales, 14.8% farming, 8.1% construction, 24.6% production (2000).

Income: Per capita income: $12,998 (2000); Median household income: $23,500 (2000); Poverty rate: 16.8% (2000).

Education: Percent of population age 25 and over with: High school diploma (including GED) or higher: 62.9% (2000); Bachelor's degree or higher: 8.4% (2000).

Housing: Homeownership rate: 78.0% (2000); Median home value: $91,200 (2000); Median rent: $369 per month (2000); Median age of housing: 22 years (2000).

W. Long. Elevation is 128 feet.

Population: 2,045 (1990); 3,054 (2000); 3,239 (2007); 3,335 (2012 projected); Race: 86.6% White, 6.7% Black, 1.5% Asian, 15.0% Hispanic of any race (2007); Density: 177.0 persons per square mile (2007); Average household size: 2.28 (2007); Median age: 48.6 (2007); Males per 100 females: 93.4 (2007); Marriage status: 9.4% never married, 72.6% now married, 10.8% widowed, 7.3% divorced (2000); Foreign born: 7.5% (2000); Ancestry (includes multiple ancestries): 15.3% Other groups, 13.8% German, 11.8% United States or American, 10.9% Irish, 10.4% English (2000).

Economy: Employment by occupation: 11.9% management, 13.8% professional, 23.7% services, 29.4% sales, 1.7% farming, 6.6% construction, 13.0% production (2000).

Income: Per capita income: $19,685 (2007); Median household income: $35,302 (2007); Average household income: $44,901 (2007); Percent of households with income of $100,000 or more: 7.1% (2007); Poverty rate: 6.0% (2000).

Education: Percent of population age 25 and over with: High school diploma (including GED) or higher: 78.0% (2007); Bachelor's degree or higher: 12.9% (2007); Master's degree or higher: 3.6% (2007).

Housing: Homeownership rate: 84.9% (2007); Median home value: $140,389 (2007); Median rent: $451 per month (2000); Median age of housing: 15 years (2000).

Transportation: Commute to work: 98.5% car, 0.0% public transportation, 0.5% walk, 0.0% work from home (2000); Travel time to work: 32.0% less than 15 minutes, 38.9% 15 to 30 minutes, 12.6% 30 to 45 minutes, 7.0% 45 to 60 minutes, 9.5% 60 minutes or more (2000)

SEBRING (city).
County seat. Covers a land area of 5.132 square miles and a water area of 5.875 square miles. Located at 27.49° N. Lat.; 81.44° W. Long. Elevation is 135 feet.

History: Sebring was founded in 1912 by George Eugene Sebring, a pottery manufacturer from Ohio who purchased the townsite and laid out the city with streets radiating from a central park.

Population: 9,238 (1990); 9,667 (2000); 9,745 (2007); 9,883 (2012 projected); Race: 72.4% White, 16.7% Black, 0.9% Asian, 14.7% Hispanic of any race (2007); Density: 1,898.9 persons per square mile (2007); Average household size: 2.48 (2007); Median age: 40.5 (2007); Males per 100 females: 93.8 (2007); Marriage status: 23.1% never married, 48.5% now married, 15.2% widowed, 13.2% divorced (2000); Foreign born: 7.5% (2000); Ancestry (includes multiple ancestries): 29.5% Other groups, 11.6% German, 10.7% Irish, 10.3% United States or American, 8.8% English (2000).

Economy: Single-family building permits issued: 60 (2006); Multi-family building permits issued: 69 (2006); Employment by occupation: 10.0% management, 12.8% professional, 21.0% services, 29.4% sales, 5.3% farming, 9.4% construction, 12.2% production (2000).

Income: Per capita income: $16,348 (2007); Median household income: $26,147 (2007); Average household income: $39,003 (2007); Percent of households with income of $100,000 or more: 6.3% (2007); Poverty rate: 23.5% (2000).

Education: Percent of population age 25 and over with: High school diploma (including GED) or higher: 67.4% (2007); Bachelor's degree or higher: 13.8% (2007); Master's degree or higher: 6.1% (2007).

School District(s)
Highlands County School District (PK-12)
    2005-06 Enrollment: 12,049 . . . . (863) 471-5564

Housing: Homeownership rate: 58.8% (2007); Median home value: $87,885 (2007); Median rent: $359 per month (2000); Median age of housing: 31 years (2000).

Hospitals: Florida Hospital Heartland Medical Center (111 beds); Highlands Regional Medical Center (126 beds)

Safety: Violent crime rate: 81.1 per 10,000 population; Property crime rate: 531.7 per 10,000 population (2006).

Newspapers: Highlands Today (Circulation 41,200); The News-Sun (General - Circulation 18,100)

Transportation: Commute to work: 92.1% car, 0.6% public transportation, 3.6% walk, 1.3% work from home (2000); Travel time to work: 45.0% less

SYLVAN SHORES (CDP).

Covers a land area of 2.231 square miles and a water area of 0.584 square miles. Located at 27.31° N. Lat.; 81.35° W. Long.

Population: 2,067 (1990); 2,424 (2000); 2,322 (2007); 2,292 (2012 projected); Race: 94.7% White, 2.4% Black, 0.2% Asian, 7.2% Hispanic of any race (2007); Density: 1,040.7 persons per square mile (2007); Average household size: 2.11 (2007); Median age: 62.2 (2007); Males per 100 females: 87.7 (2007); Marriage status: 10.4% never married, 70.0% now married, 13.4% widowed, 6.2% divorced (2000); Foreign born: 5.7% (2000); Ancestry (includes multiple ancestries): 16.7% United States or American, 15.9% German, 15.2% Irish, 13.6% English, 13.0% Other groups (2000).

Economy: Employment by occupation: 7.9% management, 13.7% professional, 25.4% services, 31.4% sales, 8.0% farming, 8.7% construction, 4.9% production (2000).

Income: Per capita income: $20,230 (2007); Median household income: $33,932 (2007); Average household income: $42,705 (2007); Percent of households with income of $100,000 or more: 5.0% (2007); Poverty rate: 11.2% (2000).

Education: Percent of population age 25 and over with: High school diploma (including GED) or higher: 78.1% (2007); Bachelor's degree or higher: 9.3% (2007); Master's degree or higher: 2.8% (2007).

Housing: Homeownership rate: 94.2% (2007); Median home value: $94,167 (2007); Median rent: $468 per month (2000); Median age of housing: 19 years (2000).

Transportation: Commute to work: 88.0% car, 0.0% public transportation, 2.9% walk, 9.1% work from home (2000); Travel time to work: 51.1% less than 15 minutes, 28.6% 15 to 30 minutes, 11.0% 30 to 45 minutes, 0.6% 45 to 60 minutes, 8.6% 60 minutes or more (2000)

VENUS (unincorporated postal area, zip code 33960).

Covers a land area of 176.301 square miles and a water area of 0.172 square miles. Located at 27.05° N. Lat.; 81.39° W. Long. Elevation is 105 feet.

History: The community of Venus was named for the Roman goddess of gardens and beauty.

Population: 701 (2000); Race: 90.5% White, 3.7% Black, 3.8% Asian, 7.5% Hispanic of any race (2000); Density: 4.0 persons per square mile (2000); Age: 22.0% under 18, 18.2% over 64 (2000); Marriage status: 15.1% never married, 70.2% now married, 5.2% widowed, 9.5% divorced (2000); Foreign born: 6.6% (2000); Ancestry (includes multiple ancestries): 21.0% United States or American, 13.8% Other groups, 10.7% Irish, 7.5% English, 6.6% Scotch-Irish (2000).

Economy: Employment by occupation: 12.8% management, 5.6% professional, 4.9% services, 23.4% sales, 14.8% farming, 14.8% construction, 23.7% production (2000).

Income: Per capita income: $16,981 (2000); Median household income: $27,875 (2000); Poverty rate: 22.5% (2000).

Education: Percent of population age 25 and over with: High school diploma (including GED) or higher: 62.4% (2000); Bachelor's degree or higher: 7.8% (2000).

School District(s)

Glades County School District (PK-12)
2005-06 Enrollment: 1,237 . . . . (863) 946-2083

Housing: Homeownership rate: 84.1% (2000); Median home value: $27,800 (2000); Median rent: $332 per month (2000); Median age of housing: 22 years (2000).

Transportation: Commute to work: 87.7% car, 0.0% public transportation, 7.6% walk, 4.7% work from home (2000); Travel time to work: 31.8% less than 15 minutes, 14.0% 15 to 30 minutes, 30.7% 30 to 45 minutes, 5.7% 45 to 60 minutes, 17.8% 60 minutes or more (2000)

Hillsborough County

Located in western Florida, on the Gulf Coast; bounded on the south and partly on the west by Tampa Bay; drained by the Hillsboro River; includes many small lakes. Covers a land area of 1,050.91 square miles, a water area of 215.31 square miles, and is located in the Eastern Time Zone. The county was founded in 1834. County seat is Tampa.

	Jan	Feb	Mar	Apr	May	Jun	Jul	Aug	Sep	Oct	Nov	Dec
High	73	75	79	84	89	91	92	91	90	85	80	75
Low	49	51	55	59	65	70	72	72	71	65	57	51
Precip	2.7	3.2	3.6	2.1	3.8	7.0	7.4	7.8	6.6	2.4	2.1	2.6
Snow	0.0	0.0	0.0	0.0	0.0	0.0	0.0	0.0	0.0	0.0	0.0	0.0

High and Low temperatures in degrees Fahrenheit; Precipitation and Snow in inches

Weather Station: Tampa Int'l Airport   Elevation: 16 feet

	Jan	Feb	Mar	Apr	May	Jun	Jul	Aug	Sep	Oct	Nov	Dec
High	71	72	77	82	87	90	91	91	89	84	78	73
Low	51	52	57	61	68	73	75	75	73	66	59	53
Precip	2.3	2.8	3.0	1.8	3.0	5.4	6.3	7.7	6.5	2.3	1.6	2.3
Snow	tr	0.0	tr	tr	0.0	0.0	tr	0.0	0.0	0.0	0.0	tr

High and Low temperatures in degrees Fahrenheit; Precipitation and Snow in inches

Population: 834,054 (1990); 998,948 (2000); 1,168,651 (2007); 1,288,921 (2012 projected); Race: 71.9% White, 16.0% Black, 2.9% Asian, 21.9% Hispanic of any race (2007); Density: 1,112.0 persons per square mile (2007); Average household size: 2.53 (2007); Median age: 36.3 (2007); Males per 100 females: 97.1 (2007).

Religion: Five largest groups: 16.6% Catholic Church, 10.3% Southern Baptist Convention, 3.3% The United Methodist Church, 2.0% Jewish Estimate, 1.0% Presbyterian Church (U.S.A.) (2000).

Economy: Unemployment rate: 4.2% (11/2007); Total civilian labor force: 616,436 (11/2007); Leading industries: 13.3% retail trade; 11.9% health care and social assistance; 9.1% finance & insurance (2005); Farms: 2,969 totaling 284,910 acres (2002); Companies that employ 500 or more persons: 98 (2005); Companies that employ 100 to 499 persons: 830 (2005); Companies that employ less than 100 persons: 30,977 (2005); Black-owned businesses: 4,330 (2002); Hispanic-owned businesses: 10,719 (2002); Asian-owned businesses: 3,051 (2002); Women-owned businesses: 22,076 (2002); Retail sales per capita: $19,470 (2007). Single-family building permits issued: 8,639 (2006); Multi-family building permits issued: 2,815 (2006).

Income: Per capita income: $26,153 (2007); Median household income: $48,032 (2007); Average household income: $65,375 (2007); Percent of households with income of $100,000 or more: 16.9% (2007); Poverty rate: 13.0% (2005); Bankruptcy rate: 1.75% (2006).

Taxes: Total county taxes per capita: $728 (2005); County property taxes per capita: $482 (2005).

Education: Percent of population age 25 and over with: High school diploma (including GED) or higher: 81.4% (2007); Bachelor's degree or higher: 25.9% (2007); Master's degree or higher: 8.7% (2007).

Housing: Homeownership rate: 65.1% (2007); Median home value: $181,067 (2007); Median rent: $532 per month (2000); Median age of housing: 20 years (2000).

Health: Birth rate: 145.7 per 10,000 population (2006); Death rate: 78.1 per 10,000 population (2006); Age-adjusted cancer mortality rate: 195.7 deaths per 100,000 population (2004); Air Quality Index: 66.3% good, 32.3% moderate, 1.1% unhealthy for sensitive individuals, 0.3% unhealthy (percent of days in 2006); Number of physicians: 31.5 per 10,000 population (2005); Hospital beds: 34.2 per 10,000 population (2004); Hospital admissions: 1,429.4 per 10,000 population (2004).

Elections: 2004 Presidential election results: 53.0% Bush, 46.2% Kerry, 0.4% Nader, 0.2% Badnarik

National and State Parks: Alafia River State Park; Egmont Key National Wildlife Refuge; Hillsborough River State Park; Little Manatee River State Park; Skyway Fishing Pier State Park; Ybor City Museum State Park

Additional Information Contacts

Hillsborough County Government . . . . (813) 272-5750
    http://www.hillsboroughcounty.org
Apollo Beach Chamber of Commerce . . . . (813) 645-1366
    http://www.apollobeachchamber.com
Brandon Chamber of Commerce . . . . (813) 689-1221
    http://www.brandonchamber.com
City of Plant City . . . . (813) 659-4200
    http://www.plantcitygov.com
City of Temple Terrace . . . . (813) 989-7100
    http://www.templeterrace.com
Greater Riverview Chamber . . . . (813) 234-5944
    http://www.riverviewchamber.com

Hispanic Chamber of Commerce . . . . (813) 414-9411
  http://www.tampahispanicchamber.com
North Tampa Chamber of Commerce . . . . (813) 980-6966
  http://www.northtampachamber.com
Plant City Chamber of Commerce . . . . (813) 754-3707
  http://www.plantcity.org
Ruskin Chamber of Commerce . . . . (813) 645-3808
  http://www.ruskinchamber.org
Seffner Chamber of Commerce . . . . (813) 627-8686
  http://www.seffnerchamber.com
South Tampa Chamber of Commerce . . . . (813) 637-0156
  http://www.southtampachamber.org
Sun City Chamber of Commerce . . . . (813) 634-5111
  http://www.suncitycenterchamber.org
Tampa Chamber of Commerce . . . . (813) 228-7777
  http://www.tampachamber.com
Town 'n' Country Chamber of Commerce . . . . (813) 884-5344
  http://www.oldsmarchamber.com
West Tampa Chamber of Commerce . . . . (813) 253-2056
  http://www.westtampachamber.com
Ybor City Chamber of Commerce . . . . (813) 248-3712
  http://www.ybor.org

Hillsborough County Communities

APOLLO BEACH (CDP). Covers a land area of 5.690 square miles and a water area of 0.215 square miles. Located at 27.77° N. Lat.; 82.41° W. Long. Elevation is 3 feet.
Population: 6,025 (1990); 7,444 (2000); 8,816 (2007); 9,781 (2012 projected); Race: 91.8% White, 1.1% Black, 1.8% Asian, 9.9% Hispanic of any race (2007); Density: 1,549.5 persons per square mile (2007); Average household size: 2.31 (2007); Median age: 48.7 (2007); Males per 100 females: 100.3 (2007); Marriage status: 11.7% never married, 69.1% now married, 7.5% widowed, 11.8% divorced (2000); Foreign born: 7.8% (2000); Ancestry (includes multiple ancestries): 18.6% German, 16.5% Other groups, 16.1% Irish, 15.1% English, 7.6% Italian (2000).
Economy: Employment by occupation: 19.9% management, 18.8% professional, 9.4% services, 33.4% sales, 0.2% farming, 7.7% construction, 10.6% production (2000).
Income: Per capita income: $34,615 (2007); Median household income: $59,708 (2007); Average household income: $80,033 (2007); Percent of households with income of $100,000 or more: 26.1% (2007); Poverty rate: 4.1% (2000).
Education: Percent of population age 25 and over with: High school diploma (including GED) or higher: 88.0% (2007); Bachelor's degree or higher: 21.9% (2007); Master's degree or higher: 7.9% (2007).
School District(s)
Hillsborough County School District (PK-12)
  2005-06 Enrollment: 189,469 . . . . (813) 272-4050
Housing: Homeownership rate: 87.6% (2007); Median home value: $259,477 (2007); Median rent: $525 per month (2000); Median age of housing: 19 years (2000).
Transportation: Commute to work: 93.7% car, 0.2% public transportation, 0.4% walk, 4.3% work from home (2000); Travel time to work: 19.8% less than 15 minutes, 33.2% 15 to 30 minutes, 24.5% 30 to 45 minutes, 15.0% 45 to 60 minutes, 7.4% 60 minutes or more (2000)
Additional Information Contacts
Apollo Beach Chamber of Commerce . . . . (813) 645-1366
  http://www.apollobeachchamber.com

BLOOMINGDALE (CDP). Covers a land area of 7.829 square miles and a water area of 0.065 square miles. Located at 27.88° N. Lat.; 82.26° W. Long. Elevation is 52 feet.
Population: 14,129 (1990); 19,839 (2000); 22,147 (2007); 23,862 (2012 projected); Race: 85.1% White, 8.1% Black, 2.9% Asian, 8.6% Hispanic of any race (2007); Density: 2,828.8 persons per square mile (2007); Average household size: 2.95 (2007); Median age: 36.7 (2007); Males per 100 females: 98.1 (2007); Marriage status: 19.5% never married, 70.1% now married, 2.5% widowed, 7.9% divorced (2000); Foreign born: 6.5% (2000); Ancestry (includes multiple ancestries): 20.9% Other groups, 19.3% German, 16.2% Irish, 14.7% English, 8.7% Italian (2000).
Economy: Employment by occupation: 21.6% management, 24.5% professional, 10.1% services, 32.3% sales, 0.1% farming, 6.0% construction, 5.4% production (2000).

Income: Per capita income: $33,130 (2007); Median household income: $82,307 (2007); Average household income: $97,850 (2007); Percent of households with income of $100,000 or more: 37.7% (2007); Poverty rate: 3.3% (2000).
Education: Percent of population age 25 and over with: High school diploma (including GED) or higher: 94.9% (2007); Bachelor's degree or higher: 38.1% (2007); Master's degree or higher: 13.8% (2007).
Housing: Homeownership rate: 87.7% (2007); Median home value: $240,043 (2007); Median rent: $664 per month (2000); Median age of housing: 12 years (2000).
Transportation: Commute to work: 93.2% car, 1.0% public transportation, 0.5% walk, 4.3% work from home (2000); Travel time to work: 14.3% less than 15 minutes, 33.8% 15 to 30 minutes, 28.8% 30 to 45 minutes, 13.7% 45 to 60 minutes, 9.5% 60 minutes or more (2000)

BOYETTE (CDP). Covers a land area of 6.601 square miles and a water area of 0.288 square miles. Located at 27.84° N. Lat.; 82.28° W. Long. Elevation is 82 feet.
Population: 3,451 (1990); 5,895 (2000); 10,140 (2007); 12,865 (2012 projected); Race: 86.7% White, 7.0% Black, 1.5% Asian, 10.0% Hispanic of any race (2007); Density: 1,536.2 persons per square mile (2007); Average household size: 3.04 (2007); Median age: 36.3 (2007); Males per 100 females: 101.4 (2007); Marriage status: 19.0% never married, 63.9% now married, 5.8% widowed, 11.3% divorced (2000); Foreign born: 5.5% (2000); Ancestry (includes multiple ancestries): 19.9% Other groups, 16.8% German, 14.5% Irish, 13.4% English, 11.8% United States or American (2000).
Economy: Employment by occupation: 14.9% management, 18.1% professional, 8.3% services, 35.0% sales, 0.0% farming, 10.8% construction, 12.8% production (2000).
Income: Per capita income: $25,234 (2007); Median household income: $67,451 (2007); Average household income: $76,748 (2007); Percent of households with income of $100,000 or more: 25.7% (2007); Poverty rate: 5.9% (2000).
Education: Percent of population age 25 and over with: High school diploma (including GED) or higher: 84.0% (2007); Bachelor's degree or higher: 20.8% (2007); Master's degree or higher: 6.5% (2007).
Housing: Homeownership rate: 90.3% (2007); Median home value: $226,025 (2007); Median rent: $1,008 per month (2000); Median age of housing: 12 years (2000).
Transportation: Commute to work: 93.2% car, 0.9% public transportation, 0.9% walk, 4.6% work from home (2000); Travel time to work: 11.4% less than 15 minutes, 39.1% 15 to 30 minutes, 33.4% 30 to 45 minutes, 10.4% 45 to 60 minutes, 5.7% 60 minutes or more (2000)

BRANDON (CDP). Covers a land area of 28.719 square miles and a water area of 0.568 square miles. Located at 27.93° N. Lat.; 82.28° W. Long. Elevation is 46 feet.
History: Named for John Brandon, who moved to Florida in 1857 and homesteaded at this place in 1874. Experienced significant developmental and population growth, particularly due to the construction of new highways connecting it to other Florida urban centers.
Population: 57,304 (1990); 77,895 (2000); 95,468 (2007); 107,570 (2012 projected); Race: 75.2% White, 13.3% Black, 3.0% Asian, 17.6% Hispanic of any race (2007); Density: 3,324.2 persons per square mile (2007); Average household size: 2.64 (2007); Median age: 35.4 (2007); Males per 100 females: 95.2 (2007); Marriage status: 22.9% never married, 62.3% now married, 4.4% widowed, 10.4% divorced (2000); Foreign born: 7.6% (2000); Ancestry (includes multiple ancestries): 27.1% Other groups, 14.4% German, 12.5% Irish, 11.4% English, 8.5% United States or American (2000).
Economy: Employment by occupation: 15.3% management, 21.5% professional, 12.1% services, 34.9% sales, 0.3% farming, 7.2% construction, 8.7% production (2000).
Income: Per capita income: $26,296 (2007); Median household income: $58,602 (2007); Average household income: $68,852 (2007); Percent of households with income of $100,000 or more: 17.6% (2007); Poverty rate: 5.4% (2000).
Education: Percent of population age 25 and over with: High school diploma (including GED) or higher: 89.2% (2007); Bachelor's degree or higher: 26.0% (2007); Master's degree or higher: 7.5% (2007).
School District(s)
Hillsborough County School District (PK-12)
  2005-06 Enrollment: 189,469 . . . . (813) 272-4050

Housing: Homeownership rate: 70.4% (2007); Median home value: $189,666 (2007); Median rent: $630 per month (2000); Median age of housing: 16 years (2000).
Hospitals: Brandon Regional Hospital (277 beds)
Newspapers: South Tampa News (General - Circulation 34,000)
Transportation: Commute to work: 94.8% car, 0.5% public transportation, 1.0% walk, 3.1% work from home (2000); Travel time to work: 22.9% less than 15 minutes, 34.5% 15 to 30 minutes, 25.8% 30 to 45 minutes, 10.8% 45 to 60 minutes, 6.0% 60 minutes or more (2000)
Additional Information Contacts
Brandon Chamber of Commerce . . . . (813) 689-1221
  http://www.brandonchamber.com

CHEVAL (CDP). Covers a land area of 6.683 square miles and a water area of 0.161 square miles. Located at 28.14° N. Lat.; 82.51° W. Long. Elevation is 59 feet.
Population: 3,544 (1990); 7,602 (2000); 10,007 (2007); 11,640 (2012 projected); Race: 82.2% White, 5.7% Black, 7.2% Asian, 17.2% Hispanic of any race (2007); Density: 1,497.3 persons per square mile (2007); Average household size: 2.27 (2007); Median age: 37.9 (2007); Males per 100 females: 96.3 (2007); Marriage status: 22.5% never married, 58.6% now married, 5.7% widowed, 13.2% divorced (2000); Foreign born: 8.9% (2000); Ancestry (includes multiple ancestries): 25.9% Other groups, 17.5% German, 14.0% English, 13.2% Irish, 11.0% Italian (2000).
Economy: Employment by occupation: 23.1% management, 21.4% professional, 6.9% services, 36.7% sales, 0.7% farming, 4.6% construction, 6.8% production (2000).
Income: Per capita income: $42,264 (2007); Median household income: $65,035 (2007); Average household income: $95,904 (2007); Percent of households with income of $100,000 or more: 29.5% (2007); Poverty rate: 4.9% (2000).
Education: Percent of population age 25 and over with: High school diploma (including GED) or higher: 91.0% (2007); Bachelor's degree or higher: 41.2% (2007); Master's degree or higher: 12.8% (2007).
Housing: Homeownership rate: 44.4% (2007); Median home value: $372,097 (2007); Median rent: $631 per month (2000); Median age of housing: 10 years (2000).
Transportation: Commute to work: 96.5% car, 0.0% public transportation, 0.1% walk, 2.6% work from home (2000); Travel time to work: 11.1% less than 15 minutes, 34.2% 15 to 30 minutes, 31.6% 30 to 45 minutes, 16.2% 45 to 60 minutes, 7.0% 60 minutes or more (2000)

CITRUS PARK (CDP). Covers a land area of 10.572 square miles and a water area of 0.315 square miles. Located at 28.07° N. Lat.; 82.55° W. Long. Elevation is 43 feet.
Population: 15,020 (1990); 20,226 (2000); 24,558 (2007); 27,573 (2012 projected); Race: 78.0% White, 8.6% Black, 3.9% Asian, 26.1% Hispanic of any race (2007); Density: 2,322.8 persons per square mile (2007); Average household size: 2.79 (2007); Median age: 36.1 (2007); Males per 100 females: 97.3 (2007); Marriage status: 21.9% never married, 62.0% now married, 4.5% widowed, 11.5% divorced (2000); Foreign born: 11.8% (2000); Ancestry (includes multiple ancestries): 30.6% Other groups, 14.1% German, 11.0% Irish, 10.8% English, 10.4% United States or American (2000).
Economy: Employment by occupation: 17.2% management, 20.6% professional, 10.6% services, 35.8% sales, 0.3% farming, 7.2% construction, 8.4% production (2000).
Income: Per capita income: $27,390 (2007); Median household income: $64,607 (2007); Average household income: $76,199 (2007); Percent of households with income of $100,000 or more: 23.3% (2007); Poverty rate: 6.3% (2000).
Education: Percent of population age 25 and over with: High school diploma (including GED) or higher: 85.9% (2007); Bachelor's degree or higher: 29.2% (2007); Master's degree or higher: 7.9% (2007).
Housing: Homeownership rate: 83.7% (2007); Median home value: $198,285 (2007); Median rent: $636 per month (2000); Median age of housing: 14 years (2000).
Transportation: Commute to work: 94.2% car, 0.7% public transportation, 0.7% walk, 3.8% work from home (2000); Travel time to work: 14.6% less than 15 minutes, 40.8% 15 to 30 minutes, 28.4% 30 to 45 minutes, 10.9% 45 to 60 minutes, 5.3% 60 minutes or more (2000)

DOVER (CDP). Covers a land area of 2.613 square miles and a water area of 0.029 square miles. Located at 27.99° N. Lat.; 82.21° W. Long. Elevation is 102 feet.

Population: 2,606 (1990); 2,798 (2000); 2,855 (2007); 2,894 (2012 projected); Race: 74.9% White, 0.6% Black, 0.8% Asian, 64.9% Hispanic of any race (2007); Density: 1,092.5 persons per square mile (2007); Average household size: 3.78 (2007); Median age: 28.7 (2007); Males per 100 females: 114.0 (2007); Marriage status: 27.4% never married, 60.7% now married, 3.7% widowed, 8.3% divorced (2000); Foreign born: 29.5% (2000); Ancestry (includes multiple ancestries): 46.8% Other groups, 16.7% United States or American, 8.4% English, 4.4% German, 4.1% Irish (2000).
Economy: Employment by occupation: 4.9% management, 7.2% professional, 15.5% services, 15.5% sales, 11.9% farming, 28.8% construction, 16.2% production (2000).
Income: Per capita income: $11,213 (2007); Median household income: $34,570 (2007); Average household income: $40,967 (2007); Percent of households with income of $100,000 or more: 3.6% (2007); Poverty rate: 28.0% (2000).
Education: Percent of population age 25 and over with: High school diploma (including GED) or higher: 46.7% (2007); Bachelor's degree or higher: 3.8% (2007); Master's degree or higher: 1.7% (2007).
School District(s)
Hillsborough County School District (PK-12)
  2005-06 Enrollment: 189,469 . . . . (813) 272-4050
Housing: Homeownership rate: 70.3% (2007); Median home value: $106,860 (2007); Median rent: $411 per month (2000); Median age of housing: 25 years (2000).
Transportation: Commute to work: 94.7% car, 0.0% public transportation, 0.0% walk, 1.6% work from home (2000); Travel time to work: 34.0% less than 15 minutes, 34.9% 15 to 30 minutes, 19.7% 30 to 45 minutes, 8.6% 45 to 60 minutes, 2.7% 60 minutes or more (2000)

EAST LAKE-ORIENT PARK (CDP). Covers a land area of 4.380 square miles and a water area of 0.276 square miles. Located at 27.97° N. Lat.; 82.37° W. Long.
Population: 6,171 (1990); 5,703 (2000); 5,543 (2007); 5,461 (2012 projected); Race: 56.1% White, 34.4% Black, 0.6% Asian, 15.7% Hispanic of any race (2007); Density: 1,265.5 persons per square mile (2007); Average household size: 2.81 (2007); Median age: 34.5 (2007); Males per 100 females: 97.8 (2007); Marriage status: 25.6% never married, 54.5% now married, 6.3% widowed, 13.6% divorced (2000); Foreign born: 6.5% (2000); Ancestry (includes multiple ancestries): 39.9% Other groups, 11.5% United States or American, 7.1% German, 6.9% Irish, 3.3% English (2000).
Economy: Employment by occupation: 4.1% management, 10.1% professional, 15.9% services, 30.9% sales, 0.6% farming, 13.8% construction, 24.7% production (2000).
Income: Per capita income: $16,890 (2007); Median household income: $38,910 (2007); Average household income: $47,316 (2007); Percent of households with income of $100,000 or more: 8.3% (2007); Poverty rate: 14.6% (2000).
Education: Percent of population age 25 and over with: High school diploma (including GED) or higher: 66.6% (2007); Bachelor's degree or higher: 7.5% (2007); Master's degree or higher: 1.8% (2007).
Housing: Homeownership rate: 76.6% (2007); Median home value: $116,095 (2007); Median rent: $434 per month (2000); Median age of housing: 33 years (2000).
Transportation: Commute to work: 91.3% car, 1.1% public transportation, 2.5% walk, 2.7% work from home (2000); Travel time to work: 25.7% less than 15 minutes, 42.6% 15 to 30 minutes, 19.0% 30 to 45 minutes, 6.4% 45 to 60 minutes, 6.4% 60 minutes or more (2000)

EGYPT LAKE-LETO (CDP). Covers a land area of 5.969 square miles and a water area of 0.217 square miles. Located at 28.01° N. Lat.; 82.50° W. Long. Elevation is 43 feet.
Population: 28,830 (1990); 32,782 (2000); 35,830 (2007); 38,183 (2012 projected); Race: 71.1% White, 9.8% Black, 4.4% Asian, 54.6% Hispanic of any race (2007); Density: 6,002.3 persons per square mile (2007); Average household size: 2.39 (2007); Median age: 34.0 (2007); Males per 100 females: 96.6 (2007); Marriage status: 29.9% never married, 50.1% now married, 5.2% widowed, 14.8% divorced (2000); Foreign born: 27.3% (2000); Ancestry (includes multiple ancestries): 54.6% Other groups, 7.6% German, 6.8% Irish, 6.3% Italian, 5.5% United States or American (2000).
Economy: Employment by occupation: 11.2% management, 14.8% professional, 15.5% services, 35.4% sales, 0.1% farming, 9.1% construction, 13.7% production (2000).

$38,969 (2007); Average household income: $48,211 (2007); Percent of households with income of $100,000 or more: 7.7% (2007); Poverty rate: 14.4% (2000).
Education: Percent of population age 25 and over with: High school diploma (including GED) or higher: 76.6% (2007); Bachelor's degree or higher: 19.0% (2007); Master's degree or higher: 6.7% (2007).
Housing: Homeownership rate: 44.3% (2007); Median home value: $157,142 (2007); Median rent: $559 per month (2000); Median age of housing: 22 years (2000).
Transportation: Commute to work: 94.6% car, 0.9% public transportation, 1.6% walk, 1.9% work from home (2000); Travel time to work: 27.5% less than 15 minutes, 42.0% 15 to 30 minutes, 21.5% 30 to 45 minutes, 5.3% 45 to 60 minutes, 3.7% 60 minutes or more (2000)

FISH HAWK (CDP).
Covers a land area of 16.345 square miles and a water area of 0.060 square miles. Located at 27.85° N. Lat.; 82.20° W. Long. Elevation is 62 feet.
Population: 1,232 (1990); 1,991 (2000); 6,540 (2007); 9,427 (2012 projected); Race: 88.8% White, 5.7% Black, 0.6% Asian, 7.5% Hispanic of any race (2007); Density: 400.1 persons per square mile (2007); Average household size: 2.88 (2007); Median age: 36.5 (2007); Males per 100 females: 98.3 (2007); Marriage status: 13.5% never married, 71.7% now married, 3.1% widowed, 11.6% divorced (2000); Foreign born: 4.4% (2000); Ancestry (includes multiple ancestries): 18.1% Other groups, 13.7% Irish, 11.7% German, 9.9% Italian, 9.7% English (2000).
Economy: Employment by occupation: 25.1% management, 22.3% professional, 9.8% services, 22.4% sales, 0.0% farming, 6.9% construction, 13.6% production (2000).
Income: Per capita income: $34,933 (2007); Median household income: $86,321 (2007); Average household income: $100,689 (2007); Percent of households with income of $100,000 or more: 37.7% (2007); Poverty rate: 3.3% (2000).
Education: Percent of population age 25 and over with: High school diploma (including GED) or higher: 86.7% (2007); Bachelor's degree or higher: 32.3% (2007); Master's degree or higher: 18.4% (2007).
Housing: Homeownership rate: 91.7% (2007); Median home value: $309,889 (2007); Median rent: $565 per month (2000); Median age of housing: 4 years (2000).
Transportation: Commute to work: 89.4% car, 1.1% public transportation, 1.3% walk, 7.0% work from home (2000); Travel time to work: 10.5% less than 15 minutes, 27.4% 15 to 30 minutes, 39.9% 30 to 45 minutes, 18.4% 45 to 60 minutes, 3.9% 60 minutes or more (2000)

GIBSONTON (CDP).
Aka East Tampa. Covers a land area of 12.851 square miles and a water area of 0.836 square miles. Located at 27.83° N. Lat.; 82.37° W. Long. Elevation is 7 feet.
History: Gibsonton was settled along the southern bank of the Alafia River, and named for the pioneer Gibson family.
Population: 8,017 (1990); 8,752 (2000); 12,245 (2007); 14,531 (2012 projected); Race: 86.2% White, 2.3% Black, 0.9% Asian, 23.4% Hispanic of any race (2007); Density: 952.8 persons per square mile (2007); Average household size: 2.93 (2007); Median age: 31.1 (2007); Males per 100 females: 104.6 (2007); Marriage status: 25.4% never married, 54.1% now married, 6.3% widowed, 14.2% divorced (2000); Foreign born: 7.4% (2000); Ancestry (includes multiple ancestries): 23.4% Other groups, 11.9% German, 9.5% United States or American, 8.8% Irish, 5.5% English (2000).
Economy: Employment by occupation: 11.9% management, 7.8% professional, 11.9% services, 25.2% sales, 3.1% farming, 20.2% construction, 20.0% production (2000).
Income: Per capita income: $19,241 (2007); Median household income: $42,644 (2007); Average household income: $56,160 (2007); Percent of households with income of $100,000 or more: 10.6% (2007); Poverty rate: 18.3% (2000).
Education: Percent of population age 25 and over with: High school diploma (including GED) or higher: 65.7% (2007); Bachelor's degree or higher: 10.0% (2007); Master's degree or higher: 3.6% (2007).
School District(s)
Hillsborough County School District (PK-12)
    2005-06 Enrollment: 189,469 . . . . (813) 272-4050
Housing: Homeownership rate: 62.7% (2007); Median home value: $124,864 (2007); Median rent: $444 per month (2000); Median age of housing: 20 years (2000).

2.8% walk, 2.4% work from home (2000); Travel time to work: 21.6% less than 15 minutes, 41.1% 15 to 30 minutes, 21.0% 30 to 45 minutes, 10.9% 45 to 60 minutes, 5.4% 60 minutes or more (2000)

GREATER CARROLLWOOD (CDP).
Covers a land area of 9.569 square miles and a water area of 0.715 square miles. Located at 28.05° N. Lat.; 82.51° W. Long.
Population: 29,062 (1990); 33,519 (2000); 35,861 (2007); 37,812 (2012 projected); Race: 80.9% White, 7.1% Black, 4.2% Asian, 24.5% Hispanic of any race (2007); Density: 3,747.5 persons per square mile (2007); Average household size: 2.35 (2007); Median age: 38.8 (2007); Males per 100 females: 92.7 (2007); Marriage status: 23.9% never married, 58.5% now married, 4.4% widowed, 13.2% divorced (2000); Foreign born: 13.5% (2000); Ancestry (includes multiple ancestries): 31.0% Other groups, 13.9% German, 12.7% Irish, 10.2% English, 8.9% Italian (2000).
Economy: Employment by occupation: 18.8% management, 25.4% professional, 10.5% services, 33.8% sales, 0.1% farming, 4.6% construction, 6.7% production (2000).
Income: Per capita income: $31,685 (2007); Median household income: $55,613 (2007); Average household income: $74,332 (2007); Percent of households with income of $100,000 or more: 21.1% (2007); Poverty rate: 5.0% (2000).
Education: Percent of population age 25 and over with: High school diploma (including GED) or higher: 91.8% (2007); Bachelor's degree or higher: 42.3% (2007); Master's degree or higher: 14.7% (2007).
Housing: Homeownership rate: 70.3% (2007); Median home value: $209,161 (2007); Median rent: $646 per month (2000); Median age of housing: 17 years (2000).
Transportation: Commute to work: 94.3% car, 0.6% public transportation, 1.0% walk, 3.0% work from home (2000); Travel time to work: 19.1% less than 15 minutes, 41.1% 15 to 30 minutes, 27.5% 30 to 45 minutes, 8.2% 45 to 60 minutes, 4.1% 60 minutes or more (2000)

GREATER NORTHDALE (CDP).
Covers a land area of 7.897 square miles and a water area of 0.554 square miles. Located at 28.09° N. Lat.; 82.52° W. Long.
Population: 17,957 (1990); 20,461 (2000); 22,682 (2007); 24,336 (2012 projected); Race: 82.8% White, 6.5% Black, 4.5% Asian, 19.7% Hispanic of any race (2007); Density: 2,872.2 persons per square mile (2007); Average household size: 2.59 (2007); Median age: 37.6 (2007); Males per 100 females: 92.9 (2007); Marriage status: 25.7% never married, 58.9% now married, 4.3% widowed, 11.2% divorced (2000); Foreign born: 12.0% (2000); Ancestry (includes multiple ancestries): 27.0% Other groups, 16.7% German, 14.9% Irish, 11.5% English, 11.0% Italian (2000).
Economy: Employment by occupation: 19.3% management, 24.5% professional, 10.5% services, 35.3% sales, 0.1% farming, 4.5% construction, 5.8% production (2000).
Income: Per capita income: $29,898 (2007); Median household income: $64,715 (2007); Average household income: $76,842 (2007); Percent of households with income of $100,000 or more: 22.2% (2007); Poverty rate: 4.7% (2000).
Education: Percent of population age 25 and over with: High school diploma (including GED) or higher: 92.0% (2007); Bachelor's degree or higher: 33.9% (2007); Master's degree or higher: 9.3% (2007).
Housing: Homeownership rate: 71.7% (2007); Median home value: $219,601 (2007); Median rent: $711 per month (2000); Median age of housing: 15 years (2000).
Transportation: Commute to work: 94.1% car, 0.7% public transportation, 1.1% walk, 3.5% work from home (2000); Travel time to work: 16.0% less than 15 minutes, 33.5% 15 to 30 minutes, 31.9% 30 to 45 minutes, 12.3% 45 to 60 minutes, 6.3% 60 minutes or more (2000)

GREATER SUN CENTER (CDP).
Covers a land area of 12.526 square miles and a water area of 0.284 square miles. Located at 27.71° N. Lat.; 82.36° W. Long. Elevation is 49 feet.
Population: 10,697 (1990); 16,321 (2000); 19,492 (2007); 21,773 (2012 projected); Race: 98.5% White, 0.2% Black, 0.6% Asian, 1.8% Hispanic of any race (2007); Density: 1,556.2 persons per square mile (2007); Average household size: 1.72 (2007); Median age: 74.9 (2007); Males per 100 females: 76.5 (2007); Marriage status: 2.7% never married, 72.3% now married, 19.4% widowed, 5.6% divorced (2000); Foreign born: 6.5% (2000); Ancestry (includes multiple ancestries): 22.9% German, 20.5% English, 14.7% Irish, 5.7% United States or American, 5.0% Italian (2000).

professional, 13.1% services, 37.8% sales, 1.0% farming, 1.0% construction, 12.1% production (2000).
Income: Per capita income: $32,643 (2007); Median household income: $42,290 (2007); Average household income: $51,897 (2007); Percent of households with income of $100,000 or more: 8.8% (2007); Poverty rate: 4.6% (2000).
Education: Percent of population age 25 and over with: High school diploma (including GED) or higher: 89.2% (2007); Bachelor's degree or higher: 29.0% (2007); Master's degree or higher: 11.4% (2007).
Housing: Homeownership rate: 90.1% (2007); Median home value: $163,702 (2007); Median rent: $1,357 per month (2000); Median age of housing: 15 years (2000).
Transportation: Commute to work: 86.8% car, 0.0% public transportation, 1.1% walk, 5.7% work from home (2000); Travel time to work: 52.3% less than 15 minutes, 21.2% 15 to 30 minutes, 14.6% 30 to 45 minutes, 8.6% 45 to 60 minutes, 3.4% 60 minutes or more (2000)

KEYSTONE (CDP).
Covers a land area of 36.079 square miles and a water area of 3.164 square miles. Located at 28.12° N. Lat.; 82.58° W. Long. Elevation is 39 feet.
Population: 6,412 (1990); 14,627 (2000); 21,682 (2007); 26,281 (2012 projected); Race: 88.5% White, 4.7% Black, 3.3% Asian, 10.8% Hispanic of any race (2007); Density: 601.0 persons per square mile (2007); Average household size: 2.80 (2007); Median age: 39.6 (2007); Males per 100 females: 99.8 (2007); Marriage status: 17.2% never married, 73.8% now married, 3.1% widowed, 5.8% divorced (2000); Foreign born: 8.2% (2000); Ancestry (includes multiple ancestries): 20.4% German, 18.9% Other groups, 14.9% English, 13.9% Irish, 12.1% Italian (2000).
Economy: Employment by occupation: 25.4% management, 22.8% professional, 8.0% services, 31.8% sales, 0.5% farming, 5.3% construction, 6.2% production (2000).
Income: Per capita income: $44,167 (2007); Median household income: $98,414 (2007); Average household income: $123,502 (2007); Percent of households with income of $100,000 or more: 48.9% (2007); Poverty rate: 2.4% (2000).
Education: Percent of population age 25 and over with: High school diploma (including GED) or higher: 94.9% (2007); Bachelor's degree or higher: 43.3% (2007); Master's degree or higher: 13.3% (2007).
Housing: Homeownership rate: 94.6% (2007); Median home value: $369,602 (2007); Median rent: $800 per month (2000); Median age of housing: 6 years (2000).
Transportation: Commute to work: 90.4% car, 0.1% public transportation, 0.4% walk, 7.3% work from home (2000); Travel time to work: 8.5% less than 15 minutes, 32.9% 15 to 30 minutes, 37.6% 30 to 45 minutes, 13.6% 45 to 60 minutes, 7.4% 60 minutes or more (2000)

LAKE MAGDALENE (CDP).
Covers a land area of 10.576 square miles and a water area of 1.109 square miles. Located at 28.08° N. Lat.; 82.47° W. Long. Elevation is 46 feet.
Population: 28,791 (1990); 28,755 (2000); 29,545 (2007); 30,394 (2012 projected); Race: 83.2% White, 7.4% Black, 3.0% Asian, 17.8% Hispanic of any race (2007); Density: 2,793.6 persons per square mile (2007); Average household size: 2.33 (2007); Median age: 40.8 (2007); Males per 100 females: 92.7 (2007); Marriage status: 24.3% never married, 56.4% now married, 6.5% widowed, 12.8% divorced (2000); Foreign born: 9.7% (2000); Ancestry (includes multiple ancestries): 23.6% Other groups, 15.1% German, 13.5% Irish, 11.9% English, 8.3% Italian (2000).
Economy: Employment by occupation: 14.4% management, 23.9% professional, 11.7% services, 36.0% sales, 0.1% farming, 6.7% construction, 7.2% production (2000).
Income: Per capita income: $31,644 (2007); Median household income: $49,770 (2007); Average household income: $72,616 (2007); Percent of households with income of $100,000 or more: 18.3% (2007); Poverty rate: 7.2% (2000).
Education: Percent of population age 25 and over with: High school diploma (including GED) or higher: 89.2% (2007); Bachelor's degree or higher: 33.8% (2007); Master's degree or higher: 11.4% (2007).
Housing: Homeownership rate: 70.0% (2007); Median home value: $191,680 (2007); Median rent: $560 per month (2000); Median age of housing: 20 years (2000).
Transportation: Commute to work: 95.0% car, 0.6% public transportation, 0.7% walk, 2.8% work from home (2000); Travel time to work: 18.6% less than 15 minutes, 38.7% 15 to 30 minutes, 26.7% 30 to 45 minutes, 10.1% 45 to 60 minutes, 5.8% 60 minutes or more (2000)

LITHIA (unincorporated postal area, zip code 33547).
Covers a land area of 190.922 square miles and a water area of 0.605 square miles. Located at 27.78° N. Lat.; 82.15° W. Long. Elevation is 105 feet.
Population: 8,527 (2000); Race: 94.6% White, 0.3% Black, 0.4% Asian, 6.5% Hispanic of any race (2000); Density: 44.7 persons per square mile (2000); Age: 27.2% under 18, 9.1% over 64 (2000); Marriage status: 19.0% never married, 65.2% now married, 6.6% widowed, 9.2% divorced (2000); Foreign born: 4.1% (2000); Ancestry (includes multiple ancestries): 19.9% Other groups, 12.4% German, 11.1% Irish, 10.4% English, 9.5% United States or American (2000).
Economy: Employment by occupation: 15.4% management, 14.2% professional, 11.3% services, 26.0% sales, 0.8% farming, 14.2% construction, 18.1% production (2000).
Income: Per capita income: $20,284 (2000); Median household income: $47,907 (2000); Poverty rate: 9.1% (2000).
Education: Percent of population age 25 and over with: High school diploma (including GED) or higher: 79.9% (2000); Bachelor's degree or higher: 14.5% (2000).
School District(s)
Hillsborough County School District (PK-12)
   2005-06 Enrollment: 189,469 . . . . (813) 272-4050
Housing: Homeownership rate: 90.2% (2000); Median home value: $123,300 (2000); Median rent: $391 per month (2000); Median age of housing: 15 years (2000).
Transportation: Commute to work: 94.0% car, 1.3% public transportation, 0.7% walk, 3.4% work from home (2000); Travel time to work: 10.2% less than 15 minutes, 30.2% 15 to 30 minutes, 36.6% 30 to 45 minutes, 13.5% 45 to 60 minutes, 9.5% 60 minutes or more (2000)

LUTZ (CDP).
Covers a land area of 21.470 square miles and a water area of 2.056 square miles. Located at 28.13° N. Lat.; 82.46° W. Long. Elevation is 69 feet.
Population: 13,403 (1990); 17,081 (2000); 20,303 (2007); 22,546 (2012 projected); Race: 90.4% White, 3.9% Black, 1.8% Asian, 10.1% Hispanic of any race (2007); Density: 945.6 persons per square mile (2007); Average household size: 2.67 (2007); Median age: 40.1 (2007); Males per 100 females: 99.9 (2007); Marriage status: 22.1% never married, 63.6% now married, 5.2% widowed, 9.2% divorced (2000); Foreign born: 5.5% (2000); Ancestry (includes multiple ancestries): 19.0% Other groups, 18.1% German, 16.4% Irish, 14.8% English, 10.1% United States or American (2000).
Economy: Employment by occupation: 20.5% management, 24.8% professional, 8.6% services, 31.3% sales, 0.1% farming, 9.1% construction, 5.6% production (2000).
Income: Per capita income: $36,611 (2007); Median household income: $74,488 (2007); Average household income: $97,490 (2007); Percent of households with income of $100,000 or more: 34.2% (2007); Poverty rate: 6.0% (2000).
Education: Percent of population age 25 and over with: High school diploma (including GED) or higher: 90.0% (2007); Bachelor's degree or higher: 34.6% (2007); Master's degree or higher: 13.6% (2007).
School District(s)
Hillsborough County School District (PK-12)
   2005-06 Enrollment: 189,469 . . . . (813) 272-4050
Pasco County School District (PK-12)
   2005-06 Enrollment: 60,846 . . . . (813) 794-2651
Housing: Homeownership rate: 86.7% (2007); Median home value: $243,277 (2007); Median rent: $533 per month (2000); Median age of housing: 18 years (2000).
Newspapers: Brandon/Valrico Community News (General - Circulation 20,000); Carrollwood/Northdale/Cheval (General - Circulation 26,000); Riverview/Fishhawk/Apollo Beach Community News (General - Circulation 12,000); Temple Terrace Beacon (General - Circulation 22,000); The Laker (General - Circulation 15,000)
Transportation: Commute to work: 94.4% car, 0.0% public transportation, 0.4% walk, 4.0% work from home (2000); Travel time to work: 14.7% less than 15 minutes, 37.2% 15 to 30 minutes, 30.6% 30 to 45 minutes, 12.2% 45 to 60 minutes, 5.3% 60 minutes or more (2000)

MANGO (CDP).
Covers a land area of 4.588 square miles and a water area of 0.068 square miles. Located at 27.98° N. Lat.; 82.30° W. Long. Elevation is 52 feet.
Population: 8,700 (1990); 8,842 (2000); 10,217 (2007); 11,191 (2012 projected); Race: 84.7% White, 7.0% Black, 1.0% Asian, 13.0% Hispanic of

any race (2007); Density: 2,226.8 persons per square mile (2007); Average household size: 2.65 (2007); Median age: 33.7 (2007); Males per 100 females: 101.5 (2007); Marriage status: 25.1% never married, 51.3% now married, 6.5% widowed, 17.1% divorced (2000); Foreign born: 3.5% (2000); Ancestry (includes multiple ancestries): 25.1% Other groups, 13.4% Irish, 13.0% United States or American, 12.0% German, 7.8% English (2000).

Economy: Employment by occupation: 6.5% management, 9.4% professional, 17.5% services, 32.0% sales, 0.4% farming, 17.6% construction, 16.6% production (2000).

Income: Per capita income: $18,122 (2007); Median household income: $39,060 (2007); Average household income: $47,928 (2007); Percent of households with income of $100,000 or more: 7.7% (2007); Poverty rate: 12.6% (2000).

Education: Percent of population age 25 and over with: High school diploma (including GED) or higher: 74.0% (2007); Bachelor's degree or higher: 7.9% (2007); Master's degree or higher: 1.6% (2007).

Housing: Homeownership rate: 66.1% (2007); Median home value: $127,495 (2007); Median rent: $466 per month (2000); Median age of housing: 21 years (2000).

Transportation: Commute to work: 93.4% car, 0.5% public transportation, 1.4% walk, 1.6% work from home (2000); Travel time to work: 24.5% less than 15 minutes, 41.1% 15 to 30 minutes, 19.3% 30 to 45 minutes, 7.3% 45 to 60 minutes, 7.8% 60 minutes or more (2000)

PALM RIVER-CLAIR MEL (CDP). Covers a land area of 11.705 square miles and a water area of 0.005 square miles. Located at 27.92° N. Lat.; 82.37° W. Long.

Population: 15,990 (1990); 17,589 (2000); 20,185 (2007); 22,012 (2012 projected); Race: 50.7% White, 36.3% Black, 1.7% Asian, 28.0% Hispanic of any race (2007); Density: 1,724.4 persons per square mile (2007); Average household size: 2.85 (2007); Median age: 31.7 (2007); Males per 100 females: 95.5 (2007); Marriage status: 27.6% never married, 51.5% now married, 6.3% widowed, 14.6% divorced (2000); Foreign born: 11.9% (2000); Ancestry (includes multiple ancestries): 53.1% Other groups, 9.6% United States or American, 6.0% German, 5.2% Irish, 5.0% English (2000).

Economy: Employment by occupation: 8.4% management, 11.9% professional, 16.1% services, 28.3% sales, 0.6% farming, 11.9% construction, 22.8% production (2000).

Income: Per capita income: $18,265 (2007); Median household income: $41,034 (2007); Average household income: $52,023 (2007); Percent of households with income of $100,000 or more: 9.9% (2007); Poverty rate: 17.4% (2000).

Education: Percent of population age 25 and over with: High school diploma (including GED) or higher: 69.5% (2007); Bachelor's degree or higher: 11.8% (2007); Master's degree or higher: 3.7% (2007).

Housing: Homeownership rate: 72.4% (2007); Median home value: $132,268 (2007); Median rent: $474 per month (2000); Median age of housing: 26 years (2000).

Transportation: Commute to work: 93.8% car, 1.9% public transportation, 0.9% walk, 1.2% work from home (2000); Travel time to work: 27.0% less than 15 minutes, 42.0% 15 to 30 minutes, 20.3% 30 to 45 minutes, 5.6% 45 to 60 minutes, 5.2% 60 minutes or more (2000)

PEBBLE CREEK (CDP). Covers a land area of 2.979 square miles and a water area of 0.005 square miles. Located at 28.15° N. Lat.; 82.34° W. Long. Elevation is 49 feet.

Population: 1,665 (1990); 4,824 (2000); 6,853 (2007); 8,188 (2012 projected); Race: 78.0% White, 8.3% Black, 8.9% Asian, 12.5% Hispanic of any race (2007); Density: 2,300.8 persons per square mile (2007); Average household size: 2.76 (2007); Median age: 36.9 (2007); Males per 100 females: 95.4 (2007); Marriage status: 19.1% never married, 67.9% now married, 4.6% widowed, 8.3% divorced (2000); Foreign born: 10.4% (2000); Ancestry (includes multiple ancestries): 21.2% Other groups, 14.8% German, 11.6% English, 11.2% Irish, 10.1% Italian (2000).

Economy: Employment by occupation: 21.4% management, 32.6% professional, 10.9% services, 25.8% sales, 0.0% farming, 4.6% construction, 4.6% production (2000).

Income: Per capita income: $34,076 (2007); Median household income: $79,552 (2007); Average household income: $93,973 (2007); Percent of households with income of $100,000 or more: 34.0% (2007); Poverty rate: 1.7% (2000).

Education: Percent of population age 25 and over with: High school diploma (including GED) or higher: 92.6% (2007); Bachelor's degree or higher: 48.0% (2007); Master's degree or higher: 17.8% (2007).

Housing: Homeownership rate: 83.7% (2007); Median home value: $247,237 (2007); Median rent: $780 per month (2000); Median age of housing: 8 years (2000).

Transportation: Commute to work: 94.4% car, 0.0% public transportation, 0.6% walk, 4.0% work from home (2000); Travel time to work: 17.1% less than 15 minutes, 27.1% 15 to 30 minutes, 31.5% 30 to 45 minutes, 15.1% 45 to 60 minutes, 9.2% 60 minutes or more (2000)

PLANT CITY (city). Covers a land area of 22.630 square miles and a water area of 0.121 square miles. Located at 28.01° N. Lat.; 82.12° W. Long. Elevation is 128 feet.

History: Named for Henry B. Plant, owner of the South Florida Railroad. Plant City was called Ichepucksassa at first, and later changed to Cork by an Irish postmaster. When the town was incorporated in 1885 it was renamed for Plant, who had extended his South Florida Railroad to this area the year before. Strawberries were a leading product of Plant City.

Population: 23,296 (1990); 29,915 (2000); 31,872 (2007); 33,456 (2012 projected); Race: 67.9% White, 15.1% Black, 1.1% Asian, 23.7% Hispanic of any race (2007); Density: 1,408.4 persons per square mile (2007); Average household size: 2.73 (2007); Median age: 33.3 (2007); Males per 100 females: 94.9 (2007); Marriage status: 22.5% never married, 58.0% now married, 7.4% widowed, 12.1% divorced (2000); Foreign born: 9.8% (2000); Ancestry (includes multiple ancestries): 37.4% Other groups, 11.3% Irish, 11.0% German, 10.7% English, 9.2% United States or American (2000).

Economy: Unemployment rate: 4.3% (11/2007); Total civilian labor force: 15,403 (11/2007); Single-family building permits issued: 328 (2006); Multi-family building permits issued: 15 (2006); Employment by occupation: 10.9% management, 14.6% professional, 15.3% services, 28.1% sales, 2.5% farming, 10.1% construction, 18.5% production (2000).

Income: Per capita income: $22,301 (2007); Median household income: $46,389 (2007); Average household income: $60,592 (2007); Percent of households with income of $100,000 or more: 13.2% (2007); Poverty rate: 14.7% (2000).

Taxes: Total city taxes per capita: $396 (2005); City property taxes per capita: $211 (2005).

Education: Percent of population age 25 and over with: High school diploma (including GED) or higher: 71.4% (2007); Bachelor's degree or higher: 16.8% (2007); Master's degree or higher: 5.5% (2007).

School District(s)
Hillsborough County School District (PK-12)
    2005-06 Enrollment: 189,469 . . . . (813) 272-4050

Housing: Homeownership rate: 65.9% (2007); Median home value: $161,412 (2007); Median rent: $445 per month (2000); Median age of housing: 20 years (2000).

Hospitals: South Florida Baptist Hospital (147 beds)

Safety: Violent crime rate: 98.8 per 10,000 population; Property crime rate: 568.8 per 10,000 population (2006).

Transportation: Commute to work: 94.7% car, 0.4% public transportation, 1.2% walk, 2.0% work from home (2000); Travel time to work: 34.6% less than 15 minutes, 30.6% 15 to 30 minutes, 21.8% 30 to 45 minutes, 7.5% 45 to 60 minutes, 5.5% 60 minutes or more (2000)

Additional Information Contacts
City of Plant City . . . . (813) 659-4200
    http://www.plantcitygov.com
Plant City Chamber of Commerce . . . . (813) 754-3707
    http://www.plantcity.org

PROGRESS VILLAGE (CDP). Covers a land area of 3.366 square miles and a water area of 0 square miles. Located at 27.89° N. Lat.; 82.36° W. Long. Elevation is 16 feet.

Population: 2,495 (1990); 2,482 (2000); 3,058 (2007); 3,455 (2012 projected); Race: 14.7% White, 81.3% Black, 0.3% Asian, 4.3% Hispanic of any race (2007); Density: 908.5 persons per square mile (2007); Average household size: 2.81 (2007); Median age: 34.8 (2007); Males per 100 females: 86.0 (2007); Marriage status: 31.5% never married, 47.0% now married, 13.0% widowed, 8.5% divorced (2000); Foreign born: 2.2% (2000); Ancestry (includes multiple ancestries): 74.2% Other groups, 2.6% Italian, 2.5% African, 1.4% Jamaican, 1.0% Irish (2000).

Economy: Employment by occupation: 2.7% management, 11.3% professional, 21.6% services, 38.3% sales, 0.0% farming, 7.3% construction, 18.7% production (2000).

Income: Per capita income: $15,673 (2007); Median household income: $36,524 (2007); Average household income: $44,011 (2007); Percent of

households with income of $100,000 or more: 5.2% (2007); Poverty rate: 18.4% (2000).
Education: Percent of population age 25 and over with: High school diploma (including GED) or higher: 69.2% (2007); Bachelor's degree or higher: 6.7% (2007); Master's degree or higher: 1.1% (2007).
Housing: Homeownership rate: 83.2% (2007); Median home value: $113,810 (2007); Median rent: $459 per month (2000); Median age of housing: 35 years (2000).
Transportation: Commute to work: 95.7% car, 2.5% public transportation, 0.9% walk, 0.9% work from home (2000); Travel time to work: 19.6% less than 15 minutes, 28.1% 15 to 30 minutes, 31.6% 30 to 45 minutes, 10.1% 45 to 60 minutes, 10.6% 60 minutes or more (2000)

RIVERVIEW (CDP).
Covers a land area of 9.144 square miles and a water area of 0.289 square miles. Located at 27.87° N. Lat.; 82.32° W. Long. Elevation is 16 feet.
History: Riverview was settled in 1856 on the Alafia River. First known as Peru, it developed as a center for truck gardening and citrus products.
Population: 6,843 (1990); 12,035 (2000); 17,905 (2007); 21,739 (2012 projected); Race: 79.9% White, 12.4% Black, 2.0% Asian, 12.2% Hispanic of any race (2007); Density: 1,958.1 persons per square mile (2007); Average household size: 2.70 (2007); Median age: 37.2 (2007); Males per 100 females: 98.4 (2007); Marriage status: 17.4% never married, 66.4% now married, 5.3% widowed, 11.0% divorced (2000); Foreign born: 4.5% (2000); Ancestry (includes multiple ancestries): 22.3% Other groups, 17.9% German, 11.1% English, 11.0% Irish, 10.3% United States or American (2000).
Economy: Employment by occupation: 17.9% management, 16.7% professional, 14.0% services, 32.0% sales, 0.4% farming, 8.6% construction, 10.5% production (2000).
Income: Per capita income: $30,654 (2007); Median household income: $65,043 (2007); Average household income: $82,571 (2007); Percent of households with income of $100,000 or more: 29.0% (2007); Poverty rate: 6.8% (2000).
Education: Percent of population age 25 and over with: High school diploma (including GED) or higher: 87.3% (2007); Bachelor's degree or higher: 26.8% (2007); Master's degree or higher: 8.3% (2007).
School District(s)
Hillsborough County School District (PK-12)
    2005-06 Enrollment: 189,469 . . . . (813) 272-4050
Housing: Homeownership rate: 79.4% (2007); Median home value: $235,554 (2007); Median rent: $559 per month (2000); Median age of housing: 14 years (2000).
Transportation: Commute to work: 93.9% car, 0.2% public transportation, 1.0% walk, 3.4% work from home (2000); Travel time to work: 18.7% less than 15 minutes, 42.7% 15 to 30 minutes, 24.4% 30 to 45 minutes, 10.0% 45 to 60 minutes, 4.2% 60 minutes or more (2000)
Additional Information Contacts
Greater Riverview Chamber . . . . (813) 234-5944
    http://www.riverviewchamber.com

RUSKIN (CDP).
Covers a land area of 14.238 square miles and a water area of 1.184 square miles. Located at 27.71° N. Lat.; 82.43° W. Long. Elevation is 3 feet.
History: Ruskin was founded in 1910 as a socialist colony by George M. Miller, a Chicago lawyer and educator, and named for John Ruskin, English author and critic. Ruskin developed as a cooperative tomato-growing settlement at the mouth of the Little Manatee River.
Population: 7,762 (1990); 8,321 (2000); 10,628 (2007); 12,198 (2012 projected); Race: 75.0% White, 1.5% Black, 0.5% Asian, 44.8% Hispanic of any race (2007); Density: 746.4 persons per square mile (2007); Average household size: 2.81 (2007); Median age: 34.7 (2007); Males per 100 females: 105.6 (2007); Marriage status: 24.1% never married, 56.3% now married, 7.1% widowed, 12.4% divorced (2000); Foreign born: 13.3% (2000); Ancestry (includes multiple ancestries): 35.3% Other groups, 14.0% German, 9.6% English, 9.1% Irish, 7.6% United States or American (2000).
Economy: Employment by occupation: 7.7% management, 10.9% professional, 22.0% services, 20.2% sales, 8.4% farming, 15.0% construction, 15.8% production (2000).
Income: Per capita income: $15,522 (2007); Median household income: $33,892 (2007); Average household income: $43,313 (2007); Percent of households with income of $100,000 or more: 5.9% (2007); Poverty rate: 17.1% (2000).

Education: Percent of population age 25 and over with: High school diploma (including GED) or higher: 61.8% (2007); Bachelor's degree or higher: 7.3% (2007); Master's degree or higher: 3.0% (2007).
School District(s)
Hillsborough County School District (PK-12)
    2005-06 Enrollment: 189,469 . . . . (813) 272-4050
Housing: Homeownership rate: 72.2% (2007); Median home value: $134,754 (2007); Median rent: $434 per month (2000); Median age of housing: 22 years (2000).
Hospitals: Columbia South Bay Hospital (112 beds); South Bay Hospital (112 beds)
Transportation: Commute to work: 93.5% car, 0.7% public transportation, 1.1% walk, 0.8% work from home (2000); Travel time to work: 36.8% less than 15 minutes, 28.3% 15 to 30 minutes, 13.5% 30 to 45 minutes, 10.9% 45 to 60 minutes, 10.5% 60 minutes or more (2000)
Additional Information Contacts
Ruskin Chamber of Commerce . . . . (813) 645-3808
    http://www.ruskinchamber.org

SEFFNER (CDP).
Covers a land area of 3.615 square miles and a water area of 0.111 square miles. Located at 27.99° N. Lat.; 82.27° W. Long. Elevation is 69 feet.
Population: 5,371 (1990); 5,467 (2000); 5,440 (2007); 5,503 (2012 projected); Race: 90.1% White, 3.2% Black, 1.4% Asian, 10.6% Hispanic of any race (2007); Density: 1,504.8 persons per square mile (2007); Average household size: 2.53 (2007); Median age: 38.9 (2007); Males per 100 females: 96.5 (2007); Marriage status: 21.8% never married, 58.6% now married, 6.8% widowed, 12.9% divorced (2000); Foreign born: 4.9% (2000); Ancestry (includes multiple ancestries): 22.3% Other groups, 15.0% German, 13.1% United States or American, 11.9% English, 11.2% Irish (2000).
Economy: Employment by occupation: 10.8% management, 16.3% professional, 14.2% services, 34.9% sales, 0.0% farming, 12.5% construction, 11.3% production (2000).
Income: Per capita income: $23,918 (2007); Median household income: $47,771 (2007); Average household income: $59,669 (2007); Percent of households with income of $100,000 or more: 15.1% (2007); Poverty rate: 4.6% (2000).
Education: Percent of population age 25 and over with: High school diploma (including GED) or higher: 78.0% (2007); Bachelor's degree or higher: 13.7% (2007); Master's degree or higher: 3.1% (2007).
School District(s)
Hillsborough County School District (PK-12)
    2005-06 Enrollment: 189,469 . . . . (813) 272-4050
Housing: Homeownership rate: 80.1% (2007); Median home value: $164,583 (2007); Median rent: $515 per month (2000); Median age of housing: 22 years (2000).
Transportation: Commute to work: 93.3% car, 0.6% public transportation, 2.3% walk, 2.4% work from home (2000); Travel time to work: 20.4% less than 15 minutes, 45.7% 15 to 30 minutes, 21.2% 30 to 45 minutes, 6.1% 45 to 60 minutes, 6.5% 60 minutes or more (2000)
Additional Information Contacts
Seffner Chamber of Commerce . . . . (813) 627-8686
    http://www.seffnerchamber.com

TAMPA (city).
County seat. Covers a land area of 112.065 square miles and a water area of 58.534 square miles. Located at 27.97° N. Lat.; 82.46° W. Long. Elevation is 3 feet.
History: A post office called Tampa Bay was established in 1831 near the site of Fort Brooke, which had been built in 1823. Tampa became the center of a cattle industry, but activities of the Civil War caused severe damage. Rebuilding and expansion began about 1884 when Henry Plant's narrow-gauge South Florida Railroad reached Tampa, and when the Hillsborough River was bridged. Tampa was a deep-water port, shipping phosphate and cigars. Henry Plant, seeking to outdo Henry Flagler on the east coast, built the extravagant Tampa Bay Hotel in 1891 to establish Tampa as a winter resort.
Population: 279,960 (1990); 303,447 (2000); 332,025 (2007); 354,374 (2012 projected); Race: 60.8% White, 27.3% Black, 2.9% Asian, 22.6% Hispanic of any race (2007); Density: 2,962.8 persons per square mile (2007); Average household size: 2.41 (2007); Median age: 35.6 (2007); Males per 100 females: 97.3 (2007); Marriage status: 31.0% never married, 47.4% now married, 7.6% widowed, 14.0% divorced (2000); Foreign born: 12.2% (2000); Ancestry (includes multiple ancestries): 42.3% Other

167,604 (11/2007); Single-family building permits issued: 1,940 (2006); Multi-family building permits issued: 985 (2006); Employment by occupation: 13.8% management, 20.2% professional, 16.3% services, 30.1% sales, 0.2% farming, 8.6% construction, 10.9% production (2000).

Income: Per capita income: $25,634 (2007); Median household income: $40,377 (2007); Average household income: $60,794 (2007); Percent of households with income of $100,000 or more: 14.3% (2007); Poverty rate: 18.1% (2000).

Taxes: Total city taxes per capita: $748 (2005); City property taxes per capita: $348 (2005).

Education: Percent of population age 25 and over with: High school diploma (including GED) or higher: 77.7% (2007); Bachelor's degree or higher: 26.5% (2007); Master's degree or higher: 9.5% (2007).

School District(s)
Hillsborough County School District (PK-12)
  2005-06 Enrollment: 189,469 . . . . (813) 272-4050

Four-year College(s)
Argosy University-Tampa Campus (Private, For-profit)
  Fall 2006 Enrollment: 660 . . . . (813) 246-4419
Florida Metropolitan University-Brandon (Private, For-profit)
  Fall 2006 Enrollment: 4,374. . . . . (813) 621-0041
  2006-07 Tuition: In-state $10,440; Out-of-state $10,440
Florida Metropolitan University-Tampa (Private, For-profit)
  Fall 2006 Enrollment: 1,242. . . . . (813) 879-6000
  2006-07 Tuition: In-state $10,440; Out-of-state $10,440
ITT Technical Institute-Tampa (Private, For-profit)
  Fall 2006 Enrollment: 627 . . . . (813) 885-2244
  2006-07 Tuition: In-state $14,880; Out-of-state $14,880
International Academy of Design and Technology (Private, For-profit)
  Fall 2006 Enrollment: 2,174. . . . . (813) 881-0007
  2006-07 Tuition: In-state $18,480; Out-of-state $18,480
Remington College-Tampa Campus (Private, For-profit)
  Fall 2006 Enrollment: 467 . . . . (813) 935-5700
  2006-07 Tuition: In-state $12,875; Out-of-state $12,875
The University of Tampa (Private, Not-for-profit)
  Fall 2006 Enrollment: 5,381. . . . . (813) 253-3333
  2006-07 Tuition: In-state $19,628; Out-of-state $19,628
University of South Florida (Public)
  Fall 2006 Enrollment: 43,636. (813) 974-2011
  2006-07 Tuition: In-state $3,416; Out-of-state $16,115

Two-year College(s)
Brewster Technical Center (Public)
  Fall 2006 Enrollment: 218 . . . . (813) 276-5448
D G Erwin Technical Center (Public)
  Fall 2006 Enrollment: 213 . . . . (813) 231-1800
  2006-07 Tuition: In-state $2,017; Out-of-state $8,002
Gulf Coast College (Private, For-profit)
  Fall 2006 Enrollment: 101 . . . . (813) 620-1446
  2006-07 Tuition: In-state $10,860; Out-of-state $10,860
Hillsborough Community College (Public)
  Fall 2006 Enrollment: 21,293. (813) 253-7000
  2006-07 Tuition: In-state $2,380; Out-of-state $8,678
Sanford-Brown Institute (Private, For-profit)
  Fall 2006 Enrollment: 421 . . . . (813) 621-0072

Vocational/Technical School(s)
Artistic Nails and Beauty Academy (Private, For-profit)
  Fall 2006 Enrollment: 100 . . . . (813) 654-4529
  2006-07 Tuition: $10,050
Concorde Career Institute (Private, For-profit)
  Fall 2006 Enrollment: 433 . . . . (813) 874-0094
  2006-07 Tuition: $10,690
Manhattan Hair (Private, For-profit)
  Fall 2006 Enrollment: 828 . . . . (813) 258-0505
  2006-07 Tuition: $9,500
Suncoast II the Tampa Bay School of Massage Therapy LLC (Private, For-profit)
  Fall 2006 Enrollment: 94 . . . . (813) 879-1500
  2006-07 Tuition: $6,800

Housing: Homeownership rate: 54.8% (2007); Median home value: $163,856 (2007); Median rent: $486 per month (2000); Median age of housing: 34 years (2000).

Hospital-Central Tampa (102 beds); Memorial Hospital of Tampa (180 beds); Northside Mental Health Center (16 beds); Shriners Hospitals for Children (60 beds); St. Joseph's Hospital (521 beds); Tampa General Healthcare; Town and Country Hospital (201 beds); University Community Hospital (551 beds); University Community Hospital of Carrollwood (120 beds)

Safety: Violent crime rate: 115.8 per 10,000 population; Property crime rate: 566.8 per 10,000 population (2006).

Newspapers: Florida Sentinel-Bulletin (Black, General - Circulation 23,000); La Gaceta (Hispanic - Circulation 18,000); Nuevo Siglo (Hispanic - Circulation 22,000); Tampa Tribune (Circulation 238,176); The Florida Dollar Stretcher (Black - Circulation 8,300); The Free Press (General - Circulation 1,500); Town 'n Country News (General - Circulation 23,700)

Transportation: Commute to work: 90.3% car, 2.7% public transportation, 2.3% walk, 2.6% work from home (2000); Travel time to work: 30.1% less than 15 minutes, 41.6% 15 to 30 minutes, 18.5% 30 to 45 minutes, 4.9% 45 to 60 minutes, 4.9% 60 minutes or more (2000); Amtrak: Service available.

Airports: Tampa International (primary service/large hub); Vandenberg (primary service/large hub)

Additional Information Contacts
Hispanic Chamber of Commerce. (813) 414-9411
  http://www.tampahispanicchamber.com
North Tampa Chamber of Commerce . . . . (813) 980-6966
  http://www.northtampachamber.com
South Tampa Chamber of Commerce. . . . . (813) 637-0156
  http://www.southtampachamber.org
Tampa Chamber of Commerce . . . . (813) 228-7777
  http://www.tampachamber.com
West Tampa Chamber of Commerce . . . . (813) 253-2056
  http://www.westtampachamber.com
Ybor City Chamber of Commerce . . . . (813) 248-3712
  http://www.ybor.org

TEMPLE TERRACE (city). Covers a land area of 6.856 square miles and a water area of 0.075 square miles. Located at 28.04° N. Lat.; 82.38° W. Long. Elevation is 59 feet.

Population: 18,960 (1990); 20,918 (2000); 21,973 (2007); 22,976 (2012 projected); Race: 74.7% White, 14.7% Black, 3.2% Asian, 14.2% Hispanic of any race (2007); Density: 3,205.1 persons per square mile (2007); Average household size: 2.33 (2007); Median age: 36.0 (2007); Males per 100 females: 93.1 (2007); Marriage status: 27.7% never married, 53.9% now married, 6.0% widowed, 12.4% divorced (2000); Foreign born: 11.6% (2000); Ancestry (includes multiple ancestries): 25.3% Other groups, 15.5% German, 12.3% English, 11.8% Irish, 8.3% Italian (2000).

Economy: Single-family building permits issued: 97 (2006); Multi-family building permits issued: 0 (2006); Employment by occupation: 17.0% management, 29.1% professional, 10.0% services, 32.4% sales, 0.1% farming, 5.1% construction, 6.3% production (2000).

Income: Per capita income: $29,091 (2007); Median household income: $48,865 (2007); Average household income: $67,468 (2007); Percent of households with income of $100,000 or more: 18.9% (2007); Poverty rate: 7.2% (2000).

Education: Percent of population age 25 and over with: High school diploma (including GED) or higher: 90.4% (2007); Bachelor's degree or higher: 43.3% (2007); Master's degree or higher: 17.1% (2007).

School District(s)
Hillsborough County School District (PK-12)
  2005-06 Enrollment: 189,469 . . . . (813) 272-4050

Four-year College(s)
Florida College (Private, Not-for-profit)
  Fall 2006 Enrollment: 513 . . . . (813) 988-5131
  2006-07 Tuition: In-state $11,380; Out-of-state $11,380
University of Phoenix-West Florida Campus (Private, For-profit)
  Fall 2006 Enrollment: 2,646. . . . . (813) 626-7911
  2006-07 Tuition: In-state $10,808; Out-of-state $10,808

Housing: Homeownership rate: 58.8% (2007); Median home value: $192,798 (2007); Median rent: $631 per month (2000); Median age of housing: 19 years (2000).

Safety: Violent crime rate: 52.4 per 10,000 population; Property crime rate: 439.4 per 10,000 population (2006).

45 to 60 minutes, 4.3% 60 minutes or more (2000)
Additional Information Contacts
City of Temple Terrace . . . . (813) 989-7100
    http://www.templeterrace.com

THONOTOSASSA (CDP).
Covers a land area of 16.665 square miles and a water area of 1.303 square miles. Located at 28.05° N. Lat.; 82.29° W. Long. Elevation is 33 feet.
History: In 1846 William Miley laid out a homestead at the site of Thonotosassa, on the lake named by the early inhabitants as the "place of many flints." Orange groves here had been started by seeds dropped in 1835 by Major Dade and his troops.
Population: 5,960 (1990); 6,091 (2000); 6,813 (2007); 7,352 (2012 projected); Race: 90.5% White, 4.0% Black, 0.5% Asian, 8.2% Hispanic of any race (2007); Density: 408.8 persons per square mile (2007); Average household size: 2.76 (2007); Median age: 37.1 (2007); Males per 100 females: 99.4 (2007); Marriage status: 20.9% never married, 58.4% now married, 5.3% widowed, 15.4% divorced (2000); Foreign born: 4.3% (2000); Ancestry (includes multiple ancestries): 19.0% Other groups, 16.1% United States or American, 14.4% German, 11.0% English, 7.9% Irish (2000).
Economy: Employment by occupation: 10.9% management, 11.7% professional, 15.6% services, 31.1% sales, 0.0% farming, 14.8% construction, 15.9% production (2000).
Income: Per capita income: $22,764 (2007); Median household income: $53,711 (2007); Average household income: $61,788 (2007); Percent of households with income of $100,000 or more: 13.6% (2007); Poverty rate: 16.0% (2000).
Education: Percent of population age 25 and over with: High school diploma (including GED) or higher: 73.2% (2007); Bachelor's degree or higher: 11.1% (2007); Master's degree or higher: 3.5% (2007).
School District(s)
Hillsborough County School District (PK-12)
    2005-06 Enrollment: 189,469 . . . . (813) 272-4050
Housing: Homeownership rate: 76.2% (2007); Median home value: $143,857 (2007); Median rent: $483 per month (2000); Median age of housing: 17 years (2000).
Transportation: Commute to work: 90.9% car, 0.3% public transportation, 1.8% walk, 4.9% work from home (2000); Travel time to work: 15.2% less than 15 minutes, 46.2% 15 to 30 minutes, 27.4% 30 to 45 minutes, 5.2% 45 to 60 minutes, 6.0% 60 minutes or more (2000)

TOWN 'N' COUNTRY (CDP).
Covers a land area of 23.673 square miles and a water area of 0.744 square miles. Located at 28.01° N. Lat.; 82.57° W. Long. Elevation is 3 feet.
Population: 60,978 (1990); 72,523 (2000); 78,961 (2007); 84,039 (2012 projected); Race: 73.4% White, 9.8% Black, 4.0% Asian, 37.1% Hispanic of any race (2007); Density: 3,335.4 persons per square mile (2007); Average household size: 2.46 (2007); Median age: 36.9 (2007); Males per 100 females: 96.1 (2007); Marriage status: 27.2% never married, 54.2% now married, 5.3% widowed, 13.3% divorced (2000); Foreign born: 17.6% (2000); Ancestry (includes multiple ancestries): 39.9% Other groups, 13.2% German, 10.3% Irish, 8.2% English, 7.3% Italian (2000).
Economy: Employment by occupation: 14.2% management, 17.1% professional, 14.4% services, 34.5% sales, 0.2% farming, 7.8% construction, 11.9% production (2000).
Income: Per capita income: $24,196 (2007); Median household income: $46,901 (2007); Average household income: $59,393 (2007); Percent of households with income of $100,000 or more: 12.8% (2007); Poverty rate: 8.6% (2000).
Education: Percent of population age 25 and over with: High school diploma (including GED) or higher: 83.0% (2007); Bachelor's degree or higher: 24.1% (2007); Master's degree or higher: 6.9% (2007).
Housing: Homeownership rate: 64.2% (2007); Median home value: $164,997 (2007); Median rent: $626 per month (2000); Median age of housing: 19 years (2000).
Transportation: Commute to work: 93.7% car, 1.3% public transportation, 1.1% walk, 2.3% work from home (2000); Travel time to work: 21.1% less than 15 minutes, 39.8% 15 to 30 minutes, 24.8% 30 to 45 minutes, 8.1% 45 to 60 minutes, 6.2% 60 minutes or more (2000)
Additional Information Contacts

UNIVERSITY (CDP).
Covers a land area of 3.870 square miles and a water area of 0.012 square miles. Located at 28.07° N. Lat.; 82.43° W. Long.
Population: 23,760 (1990); 30,736 (2000); 32,339 (2007); 33,800 (2012 projected); Race: 45.0% White, 37.5% Black, 4.4% Asian, 23.6% Hispanic of any race (2007); Density: 8,355.5 persons per square mile (2007); Average household size: 2.23 (2007); Median age: 28.8 (2007); Males per 100 females: 99.6 (2007); Marriage status: 49.1% never married, 31.7% now married, 6.4% widowed, 12.8% divorced (2000); Foreign born: 15.0% (2000); Ancestry (includes multiple ancestries): 46.8% Other groups, 6.7% German, 6.1% Irish, 4.5% United States or American, 4.1% English (2000).
Economy: Employment by occupation: 7.5% management, 19.5% professional, 20.9% services, 32.5% sales, 0.4% farming, 9.7% construction, 9.5% production (2000).
Income: Per capita income: $14,621 (2007); Median household income: $23,986 (2007); Average household income: $30,195 (2007); Percent of households with income of $100,000 or more: 2.5% (2007); Poverty rate: 31.3% (2000).
Education: Percent of population age 25 and over with: High school diploma (including GED) or higher: 75.0% (2007); Bachelor's degree or higher: 22.2% (2007); Master's degree or higher: 7.3% (2007).
Housing: Homeownership rate: 11.9% (2007); Median home value: $100,820 (2007); Median rent: $481 per month (2000); Median age of housing: 20 years (2000).
Transportation: Commute to work: 87.0% car, 3.3% public transportation, 5.6% walk, 0.8% work from home (2000); Travel time to work: 26.4% less than 15 minutes, 33.7% 15 to 30 minutes, 23.8% 30 to 45 minutes, 9.2% 45 to 60 minutes, 6.9% 60 minutes or more (2000)

VALRICO (CDP).
Part of the Census Designated Place of Brandon. Covers a land area of 5.592 square miles and a water area of 0.085 square miles. Located at 27.94° N. Lat.; 82.24° W. Long. Elevation is 56 feet.
Population: 5,174 (1990); 6,582 (2000); 9,898 (2007); 12,067 (2012 projected); Race: 85.7% White, 4.3% Black, 1.8% Asian, 18.0% Hispanic of any race (2007); Density: 1,769.9 persons per square mile (2007); Average household size: 2.47 (2007); Median age: 39.7 (2007); Males per 100 females: 96.4 (2007); Marriage status: 17.5% never married, 62.7% now married, 9.6% widowed, 10.2% divorced (2000); Foreign born: 6.9% (2000); Ancestry (includes multiple ancestries): 19.3% Other groups, 14.9% German, 13.8% United States or American, 11.4% Irish, 9.4% English (2000).
Economy: Employment by occupation: 14.1% management, 15.5% professional, 12.1% services, 31.1% sales, 1.9% farming, 9.8% construction, 15.5% production (2000).
Income: Per capita income: $25,203 (2007); Median household income: $47,041 (2007); Average household income: $61,986 (2007); Percent of households with income of $100,000 or more: 15.4% (2007); Poverty rate: 7.5% (2000).
Education: Percent of population age 25 and over with: High school diploma (including GED) or higher: 77.4% (2007); Bachelor's degree or higher: 18.8% (2007); Master's degree or higher: 4.7% (2007).
School District(s)
Hillsborough County School District (PK-12)
    2005-06 Enrollment: 189,469 . . . . (813) 272-4050
Housing: Homeownership rate: 78.7% (2007); Median home value: $168,004 (2007); Median rent: $562 per month (2000); Median age of housing: 16 years (2000).
Transportation: Commute to work: 92.5% car, 0.9% public transportation, 0.7% walk, 4.2% work from home (2000); Travel time to work: 22.7% less than 15 minutes, 36.6% 15 to 30 minutes, 26.4% 30 to 45 minutes, 8.4% 45 to 60 minutes, 6.0% 60 minutes or more (2000)

WESTCHASE (CDP).
Covers a land area of 10.748 square miles and a water area of 0.050 square miles. Located at 28.05° N. Lat.; 82.61° W. Long. Elevation is 16 feet.
Population: 2,070 (1990); 11,116 (2000); 22,028 (2007); 28,988 (2012 projected); Race: 83.8% White, 6.0% Black, 5.7% Asian, 12.7% Hispanic of any race (2007); Density: 2,049.4 persons per square mile (2007); Average household size: 2.66 (2007); Median age: 35.1 (2007); Males per 100 females: 96.6 (2007); Marriage status: 16.6% never married, 73.2% now married, 3.7% widowed, 6.6% divorced (2000); Foreign born: 9.6% (2000);

German, 16.9% Irish, 12.7% English, 11.6% Italian (2000).
Economy: Employment by occupation: 27.8% management, 27.3% professional, 6.6% services, 30.5% sales, 0.0% farming, 4.3% construction, 3.5% production (2000).
Income: Per capita income: $45,832 (2007); Median household income: $98,383 (2007); Average household income: $121,798 (2007); Percent of households with income of $100,000 or more: 49.0% (2007); Poverty rate: 2.4% (2000).
Education: Percent of population age 25 and over with: High school diploma (including GED) or higher: 96.2% (2007); Bachelor's degree or higher: 50.1% (2007); Master's degree or higher: 15.3% (2007).
Housing: Homeownership rate: 88.4% (2007); Median home value: $345,833 (2007); Median rent: $832 per month (2000); Median age of housing: 4 years (2000).
Transportation: Commute to work: 93.3% car, 0.1% public transportation, 0.0% walk, 5.3% work from home (2000); Travel time to work: 13.0% less than 15 minutes, 32.3% 15 to 30 minutes, 34.6% 30 to 45 minutes, 14.1% 45 to 60 minutes, 6.0% 60 minutes or more (2000)

WIMAUMA (CDP). Covers a land area of 8.423 square miles and a water area of 0.389 square miles. Located at 27.71° N. Lat.; 82.31° W. Long. Elevation is 102 feet.
Population: 4,249 (1990); 4,246 (2000); 5,796 (2007); 6,817 (2012 projected); Race: 39.2% White, 5.2% Black, 0.3% Asian, 80.8% Hispanic of any race (2007); Density: 688.1 persons per square mile (2007); Average household size: 4.47 (2007); Median age: 24.7 (2007); Males per 100 females: 115.2 (2007); Marriage status: 30.6% never married, 56.0% now married, 4.5% widowed, 8.9% divorced (2000); Foreign born: 30.1% (2000); Ancestry (includes multiple ancestries): 58.2% Other groups, 3.7% United States or American, 3.7% German, 3.1% English, 2.5% African (2000).
Economy: Employment by occupation: 3.8% management, 6.1% professional, 19.8% services, 15.6% sales, 13.9% farming, 14.4% construction, 26.4% production (2000).
Income: Per capita income: $10,860 (2007); Median household income: $40,990 (2007); Average household income: $46,250 (2007); Percent of households with income of $100,000 or more: 6.8% (2007); Poverty rate: 31.7% (2000).
Education: Percent of population age 25 and over with: High school diploma (including GED) or higher: 38.0% (2007); Bachelor's degree or higher: 0.5% (2007); Master's degree or higher: 0.5% (2007).
School District(s)
Hillsborough County School District (PK-12)
    2005-06 Enrollment: 189,469 . . . . (813) 272-4050
Housing: Homeownership rate: 60.3% (2007); Median home value: $128,091 (2007); Median rent: $251 per month (2000); Median age of housing: 17 years (2000).
Transportation: Commute to work: 93.9% car, 2.2% public transportation, 1.2% walk, 0.0% work from home (2000); Travel time to work: 22.0% less than 15 minutes, 40.5% 15 to 30 minutes, 21.0% 30 to 45 minutes, 12.3% 45 to 60 minutes, 4.3% 60 minutes or more (2000)

Holmes County

Located in northwestern Florida; bounded on the north by Alabama, and on the east by Holmes Creek; drained by the Choctawhatchee River. Covers a land area of 482.45 square miles, a water area of 6.26 square miles, and is located in the Central Time Zone. The county was founded in 1848. County seat is Bonifay.
Population: 15,778 (1990); 18,564 (2000); 19,331 (2007); 19,842 (2012 projected); Race: 89.3% White, 6.5% Black, 0.4% Asian, 2.9% Hispanic of any race (2007); Density: 40.1 persons per square mile (2007); Average household size: 2.63 (2007); Median age: 38.5 (2007); Males per 100 females: 114.9 (2007).
Religion: Five largest groups: 35.4% Southern Baptist Convention, 9.9% Assemblies of God, 4.4% The United Methodist Church, 1.3% The Church of Jesus Christ of Latter-day Saints, 1.1% Catholic Church (2000).
Economy: Unemployment rate: 3.5% (11/2007); Total civilian labor force: 9,134 (11/2007); Leading industries: 30.7% health care and social assistance; 18.4% retail trade; 8.8% accommodation & food services (2005); Farms: 672 totaling 90,875 acres (2002); Companies that employ 500 or more persons: 0 (2005); Companies that employ 100 to 499 persons: 2 (2005); Companies that employ less than 100 persons: 287 (2005); Black-owned businesses: n/a (2002); Hispanic-owned businesses:

businesses: 224 (2002); Retail sales per capita: $4,085 (2007).
Single-family building permits issued: 97 (2006); Multi-family building permits issued: 0 (2006).
Income: Per capita income: $16,889 (2007); Median household income: $33,126 (2007); Average household income: $43,628 (2007); Percent of households with income of $100,000 or more: 6.5% (2007); Poverty rate: 21.9% (2005); Bankruptcy rate: 1.45% (2006).
Education: Percent of population age 25 and over with: High school diploma (including GED) or higher: 65.1% (2007); Bachelor's degree or higher: 8.6% (2007); Master's degree or higher: 3.0% (2007).
Housing: Homeownership rate: 82.2% (2007); Median home value: $115,045 (2007); Median rent: $273 per month (2000); Median age of housing: 22 years (2000).
Health: Birth rate: 131.7 per 10,000 population (2006); Death rate: 115.1 per 10,000 population (2006); Age-adjusted cancer mortality rate: 186.3 deaths per 100,000 population (2004); Air Quality Index: 94.2% good, 5.6% moderate, 0.3% unhealthy for sensitive individuals, 0.0% unhealthy (percent of days in 2006); Number of physicians: 5.8 per 10,000 population (2005); Hospital beds: 13.2 per 10,000 population (2004); Hospital admissions: 551.7 per 10,000 population (2004).
Elections: 2004 Presidential election results: 77.3% Bush, 21.8% Kerry, 0.5% Nader, 0.2% Badnarik.
National and State Parks: Ponce de Leon Springs State Park
Additional Information Contacts
Holmes County Government . . . . (850) 547-1119
    http://www.holmescountyonline.com
Holmes County Chamber of Commerce . . . . (850) 547-4682
    http://www.holmescountyonline.com

Holmes County Communities

BONIFAY (city). County seat. Covers a land area of 3.619 square miles and a water area of 0 square miles. Located at 30.79° N. Lat.; 85.68° W. Long. Elevation is 135 feet.
History: Bonifay was established on Holmes Creek as a center for cattle, sheep, and hog farmers.
Population: 2,868 (1990); 4,078 (2000); 3,976 (2007); 3,870 (2012 projected); Race: 65.4% White, 27.6% Black, 1.1% Asian, 6.9% Hispanic of any race (2007); Density: 1,098.7 persons per square mile (2007); Average household size: 3.90 (2007); Median age: 35.0 (2007); Males per 100 females: 196.7 (2007); Marriage status: 32.7% never married, 39.9% now married, 11.4% widowed, 16.0% divorced (2000); Foreign born: 4.2% (2000); Ancestry (includes multiple ancestries): 29.0% Other groups, 23.9% United States or American, 7.5% Irish, 6.7% English, 5.0% German (2000).
Economy: Employment by occupation: 7.8% management, 16.6% professional, 23.4% services, 21.2% sales, 1.0% farming, 12.0% construction, 18.0% production (2000).
Income: Per capita income: $12,087 (2007); Median household income: $25,559 (2007); Average household income: $41,587 (2007); Percent of households with income of $100,000 or more: 10.4% (2007); Poverty rate: 21.7% (2000).
Education: Percent of population age 25 and over with: High school diploma (including GED) or higher: 59.4% (2007); Bachelor's degree or higher: 10.1% (2007); Master's degree or higher: 4.1% (2007).
School District(s)
Holmes County School District (PK-12)
    2005-06 Enrollment: 3,389 . . . . (850) 547-9341
Housing: Homeownership rate: 62.6% (2007); Median home value: $133,544 (2007); Median rent: $247 per month (2000); Median age of housing: 30 years (2000).
Hospitals: Doctors Memorial Hospital (34 beds)
Safety: Violent crime rate: 7.3 per 10,000 population; Property crime rate: 174.1 per 10,000 population (2006).
Transportation: Commute to work: 89.1% car, 0.0% public transportation, 6.1% walk, 4.0% work from home (2000); Travel time to work: 42.1% less than 15 minutes, 22.8% 15 to 30 minutes, 13.0% 30 to 45 minutes, 5.0% 45 to 60 minutes, 17.1% 60 minutes or more (2000)
Additional Information Contacts
Holmes County Chamber of Commerce . . . . (850) 547-4682
    http://www.holmescountyonline.com

ESTO (town). Covers a land area of 2.202 square miles and a water area of 0.151 square miles. Located at 30.98° N. Lat.; 85.64° W. Long. Elevation is 233 feet.

Population: 253 (1990); 356 (2000); 369 (2007); 375 (2012 projected); Race: 90.2% White, 3.0% Black, 0.0% Asian, 3.8% Hispanic of any race (2007); Density: 167.5 persons per square mile (2007); Average household size: 2.41 (2007); Median age: 38.2 (2007); Males per 100 females: 113.3 (2007); Marriage status: 20.1% never married, 58.6% now married, 9.6% widowed, 11.6% divorced (2000); Foreign born: 0.0% (2000); Ancestry (includes multiple ancestries): 14.1% Irish, 14.1% United States or American, 13.2% English, 12.9% Other groups, 1.4% Dutch (2000).

Economy: Employment by occupation: 10.3% management, 5.6% professional, 15.0% services, 28.0% sales, 0.9% farming, 18.7% construction, 21.5% production (2000).

Income: Per capita income: $18,760 (2007); Median household income: $36,563 (2007); Average household income: $45,245 (2007); Percent of households with income of $100,000 or more: 4.6% (2007); Poverty rate: 12.5% (2000).

Education: Percent of population age 25 and over with: High school diploma (including GED) or higher: 66.1% (2007); Bachelor's degree or higher: 6.2% (2007); Master's degree or higher: 2.5% (2007).

Housing: Homeownership rate: 83.7% (2007); Median home value: $92,500 (2007); Median rent: $275 per month (2000); Median age of housing: 25 years (2000).

Transportation: Commute to work: 96.9% car, 0.0% public transportation, 2.1% walk, 0.0% work from home (2000); Travel time to work: 9.3% less than 15 minutes, 27.8% 15 to 30 minutes, 23.7% 30 to 45 minutes, 25.8% 45 to 60 minutes, 13.4% 60 minutes or more (2000)

NOMA (town). Covers a land area of 1.094 square miles and a water area of 0 square miles. Located at 30.98° N. Lat.; 85.61° W. Long. Elevation is 180 feet.

Population: 222 (1990); 213 (2000); 222 (2007); 227 (2012 projected); Race: 77.9% White, 19.4% Black, 0.0% Asian, 2.3% Hispanic of any race (2007); Density: 202.9 persons per square mile (2007); Average household size: 2.29 (2007); Median age: 39.3 (2007); Males per 100 females: 98.2 (2007); Marriage status: 30.2% never married, 47.9% now married, 12.4% widowed, 9.5% divorced (2000); Foreign born: 0.9% (2000); Ancestry (includes multiple ancestries): 37.9% Other groups, 20.5% United States or American, 2.7% Irish, 2.3% English, 2.3% French (except Basque) (2000).

Economy: Employment by occupation: 2.5% management, 6.2% professional, 28.4% services, 18.5% sales, 0.0% farming, 11.1% construction, 33.3% production (2000).

Income: Per capita income: $14,583 (2007); Median household income: $30,833 (2007); Average household income: $33,376 (2007); Percent of households with income of $100,000 or more: 0.0% (2007); Poverty rate: 18.3% (2000).

Education: Percent of population age 25 and over with: High school diploma (including GED) or higher: 47.3% (2007); Bachelor's degree or higher: 3.3% (2007); Master's degree or higher: 0.0% (2007).

Housing: Homeownership rate: 78.4% (2007); Median home value: $65,455 (2007); Median rent: $172 per month (2000); Median age of housing: 23 years (2000).

Transportation: Commute to work: 93.4% car, 0.0% public transportation, 5.3% walk, 1.3% work from home (2000); Travel time to work: 12.0% less than 15 minutes, 36.0% 15 to 30 minutes, 28.0% 30 to 45 minutes, 12.0% 45 to 60 minutes, 12.0% 60 minutes or more (2000)

PONCE DE LEON (town). Covers a land area of 4.953 square miles and a water area of 0.011 square miles. Located at 30.72° N. Lat.; 85.93° W. Long. Elevation is 62 feet.

History: Ponce de Leon is on the site of Ponce de Leon Springs, one of many "fountains of youth" named for the Spanish explorer.

Population: 428 (1990); 457 (2000); 567 (2007); 636 (2012 projected); Race: 89.9% White, 3.0% Black, 0.0% Asian, 3.7% Hispanic of any race (2007); Density: 114.5 persons per square mile (2007); Average household size: 2.23 (2007); Median age: 43.1 (2007); Males per 100 females: 94.2 (2007); Marriage status: 14.0% never married, 64.0% now married, 9.3% widowed, 12.6% divorced (2000); Foreign born: 2.7% (2000); Ancestry (includes multiple ancestries): 24.7% United States or American, 17.3% Other groups, 12.8% Irish, 9.7% English, 7.6% German (2000).

Economy: Employment by occupation: 7.4% management, 5.3% professional, 24.7% services, 31.6% sales, 4.7% farming, 18.9% construction, 7.4% production (2000).

$30,952 (2007); Average household income: $40,177 (2007); Percent of households with income of $100,000 or more: 2.4% (2007); Poverty rate: 19.3% (2000).

Education: Percent of population age 25 and over with: High school diploma (including GED) or higher: 67.4% (2007); Bachelor's degree or higher: 2.6% (2007); Master's degree or higher: 0.5% (2007).

School District(s)

Holmes County School District (PK-12)

   2005-06 Enrollment: 3,389 . . . . (850) 547-9341

Housing: Homeownership rate: 75.6% (2007); Median home value: $93,333 (2007); Median rent: $243 per month (2000); Median age of housing: 24 years (2000).

Transportation: Commute to work: 97.9% car, 0.0% public transportation, 1.1% walk, 1.1% work from home (2000); Travel time to work: 34.0% less than 15 minutes, 29.3% 15 to 30 minutes, 16.5% 30 to 45 minutes, 3.7% 45 to 60 minutes, 16.5% 60 minutes or more (2000)

WESTVILLE (town). Covers a land area of 7.274 square miles and a water area of 0.178 square miles. Located at 30.76° N. Lat.; 85.85° W. Long. Elevation is 69 feet.

Population: 257 (1990); 221 (2000); 248 (2007); 263 (2012 projected); Race: 98.4% White, 0.0% Black, 0.4% Asian, 1.6% Hispanic of any race (2007); Density: 34.1 persons per square mile (2007); Average household size: 2.30 (2007); Median age: 35.8 (2007); Males per 100 females: 87.9 (2007); Marriage status: 14.6% never married, 66.1% now married, 7.0% widowed, 12.3% divorced (2000); Foreign born: 0.0% (2000); Ancestry (includes multiple ancestries): 41.1% United States or American, 10.0% English, 9.5% Other groups, 5.6% Scottish, 3.5% Irish (2000).

Economy: Employment by occupation: 0.0% management, 14.1% professional, 16.5% services, 15.3% sales, 5.9% farming, 23.5% construction, 24.7% production (2000).

Income: Per capita income: $16,462 (2007); Median household income: $32,727 (2007); Average household income: $37,801 (2007); Percent of households with income of $100,000 or more: 2.8% (2007); Poverty rate: 13.9% (2000).

Education: Percent of population age 25 and over with: High school diploma (including GED) or higher: 69.3% (2007); Bachelor's degree or higher: 6.0% (2007); Master's degree or higher: 1.8% (2007).

Housing: Homeownership rate: 87.0% (2007); Median home value: $91,667 (2007); Median rent: $225 per month (2000); Median age of housing: 33 years (2000).

Transportation: Commute to work: 95.2% car, 0.0% public transportation, 0.0% walk, 0.0% work from home (2000); Travel time to work: 9.6% less than 15 minutes, 30.1% 15 to 30 minutes, 18.1% 30 to 45 minutes, 14.5% 45 to 60 minutes, 27.7% 60 minutes or more (2000)

Indian River County

Located in central Florida; bounded on the east by the Atlantic Ocean; coastal lowland area with a barrier beach enclosing Indian River Lagoon; includes Lake Wilmington. Covers a land area of 503.23 square miles, a water area of 113.69 square miles, and is located in the Eastern Time Zone. The county was founded in 1925. County seat is Vero Beach.

Indian River County is part of the Sebastian-Vero Beach, FL Metropolitan Statistical Area. The entire metro area includes: Indian River County, FL

Population: 90,208 (1990); 112,947 (2000); 134,055 (2007); 149,527 (2012 projected); Race: 86.4% White, 8.2% Black, 0.9% Asian, 9.2% Hispanic of any race (2007); Density: 266.4 persons per square mile (2007); Average household size: 2.28 (2007); Median age: 46.5 (2007); Males per 100 females: 94.6 (2007).

Religion: Five largest groups: 26.7% Catholic Church, 6.0% Southern Baptist Convention, 3.7% The United Methodist Church, 2.4% United Church of Christ, 2.4% Episcopal Church (2000).

Economy: Unemployment rate: 6.0% (11/2007); Total civilian labor force: 61,703 (11/2007); Leading industries: 21.8% retail trade; 17.3% health care and social assistance; 9.9% construction (2005); Farms: 480 totaling 191,333 acres (2002); Companies that employ 500 or more persons: 3 (2005); Companies that employ 100 to 499 persons: 55 (2005); Companies that employ less than 100 persons: 3,966 (2005); Black-owned businesses: 346 (2002); Hispanic-owned businesses: 527 (2002); Asian-owned businesses: 184 (2002); Women-owned businesses: 2,649 (2002); Retail sales per capita: $15,341 (2007). Single-family building permits issued: 2,839 (2006); Multi-family building permits issued: 304 (2006).

$45,839 (2007); Average household income: $70,299 (2007); Percent of households with income of $100,000 or more: 16.5% (2007); Poverty rate: 11.7% (2005); Bankruptcy rate: 0.55% (2006).

Taxes: Total county taxes per capita: $778 (2005); County property taxes per capita: $545 (2005).

Education: Percent of population age 25 and over with: High school diploma (including GED) or higher: 81.0% (2007); Bachelor's degree or higher: 22.5% (2007); Master's degree or higher: 7.7% (2007).

Housing: Homeownership rate: 78.4% (2007); Median home value: $196,510 (2007); Median rent: $521 per month (2000); Median age of housing: 17 years (2000).

Health: Birth rate: 101.9 per 10,000 population (2006); Death rate: 163.3 per 10,000 population (2006); Age-adjusted cancer mortality rate: 186.9 deaths per 100,000 population (2004); Number of physicians: 27.6 per 10,000 population (2005); Hospital beds: 44.5 per 10,000 population (2004); Hospital admissions: 1,516.1 per 10,000 population (2004).

Elections: 2004 Presidential election results: 60.1% Bush, 39.0% Kerry, 0.5% Nader, 0.2% Badnarik

National and State Parks: Pelican Island National Wildlife Refuge; Sebastian Inlet State Park

Additional Information Contacts

Indian River County Government . . . . (772) 567-8000
   http://www.ircgov.com
Indian River County Chamber . . . . (772) 567-3491
   http://www.indianriverchamber.com
Sebastian Chamber of Commerce . . . . (561) 589-5969
   http://www.sebastianchamber.com

Indian River County Communities

FELLSMERE (city). Covers a land area of 5.302 square miles and a water area of 0.103 square miles. Located at 27.76° N. Lat.; 80.59° W. Long. Elevation is 23 feet.

Population: 2,143 (1990); 3,813 (2000); 5,110 (2007); 5,957 (2012 projected); Race: 55.3% White, 5.0% Black, 0.1% Asian, 86.1% Hispanic of any race (2007); Density: 963.8 persons per square mile (2007); Average household size: 4.39 (2007); Median age: 27.4 (2007); Males per 100 females: 135.3 (2007); Marriage status: 24.2% never married, 67.5% now married, 4.3% widowed, 4.0% divorced (2000); Foreign born: 39.3% (2000); Ancestry (includes multiple ancestries): 59.2% Other groups, 3.5% United States or American, 2.5% English, 2.2% Irish, 2.0% German (2000).

Economy: Single-family building permits issued: 23 (2006); Multi-family building permits issued: 0 (2006); Employment by occupation: 4.2% management, 4.7% professional, 17.9% services, 12.6% sales, 28.7% farming, 14.7% construction, 17.1% production (2000).

Income: Per capita income: $11,305 (2007); Median household income: $36,655 (2007); Average household income: $44,841 (2007); Percent of households with income of $100,000 or more: 6.8% (2007); Poverty rate: 24.3% (2000).

Education: Percent of population age 25 and over with: High school diploma (including GED) or higher: 29.3% (2007); Bachelor's degree or higher: 1.7% (2007); Master's degree or higher: 0.5% (2007).

School District(s)

Indian River County School District (PK-12)
   2005-06 Enrollment: 17,099 . . . . (772) 564-3150

Four-year College(s)

Reformation International College (Private, Not-for-profit, Reformed Presbyterian Church)
   Fall 2006 Enrollment: n/a . . . . (772) 571-8833
   2006-07 Tuition: In-state $4,500; Out-of-state $4,500
Reformation International Theological Seminary (Private, Not-for-profit, Reformed Presbyterian Church)
   Fall 2006 Enrollment: n/a . . . . (772) 571-8833
   2006-07 Tuition: In-state $1,800; Out-of-state $1,800

Housing: Homeownership rate: 69.9% (2007); Median home value: $120,803 (2007); Median rent: $396 per month (2000); Median age of housing: 16 years (2000).

Safety: Violent crime rate: 26.6 per 10,000 population; Property crime rate: 125.0 per 10,000 population (2006).

Transportation: Commute to work: 90.2% car, 4.7% public transportation, 1.8% walk, 0.1% work from home (2000); Travel time to work: 24.1% less than 15 minutes, 32.8% 15 to 30 minutes, 32.9% 30 to 45 minutes, 3.3% 45 to 60 minutes, 6.8% 60 minutes or more (2000)

FLORIDA RIDGE (CDP). Covers a land area of 10.798 square miles and a water area of 1.784 square miles. Located at 27.57° N. Lat.; 80.39° W. Long. Elevation is 20 feet.

Population: 12,218 (1990); 15,217 (2000); 18,781 (2007); 21,370 (2012 projected); Race: 84.0% White, 12.2% Black, 0.9% Asian, 5.3% Hispanic of any race (2007); Density: 1,739.4 persons per square mile (2007); Average household size: 2.33 (2007); Median age: 42.9 (2007); Males per 100 females: 92.6 (2007); Marriage status: 17.1% never married, 61.1% now married, 9.8% widowed, 12.0% divorced (2000); Foreign born: 7.2% (2000); Ancestry (includes multiple ancestries): 19.1% Other groups, 16.0% Irish, 15.4% English, 14.4% German, 8.3% United States or American (2000).

Economy: Employment by occupation: 9.3% management, 12.9% professional, 23.0% services, 28.3% sales, 1.4% farming, 13.5% construction, 11.5% production (2000).

Income: Per capita income: $22,778 (2007); Median household income: $42,217 (2007); Average household income: $53,137 (2007); Percent of households with income of $100,000 or more: 8.8% (2007); Poverty rate: 9.5% (2000).

Education: Percent of population age 25 and over with: High school diploma (including GED) or higher: 80.4% (2007); Bachelor's degree or higher: 18.0% (2007); Master's degree or higher: 6.1% (2007).

Housing: Homeownership rate: 82.3% (2007); Median home value: $154,835 (2007); Median rent: $535 per month (2000); Median age of housing: 17 years (2000).

Transportation: Commute to work: 96.3% car, 0.3% public transportation, 0.6% walk, 1.5% work from home (2000); Travel time to work: 29.6% less than 15 minutes, 54.2% 15 to 30 minutes, 12.2% 30 to 45 minutes, 2.2% 45 to 60 minutes, 1.9% 60 minutes or more (2000)

GIFFORD (CDP). Covers a land area of 7.049 square miles and a water area of 0.455 square miles. Located at 27.67° N. Lat.; 80.41° W. Long. Elevation is 13 feet.

History: Gifford was named for F. Charles Gifford, who selected the site for Vero Beach, just south of Gifford.

Population: 6,278 (1990); 7,599 (2000); 9,070 (2007); 10,195 (2012 projected); Race: 43.7% White, 52.7% Black, 0.3% Asian, 9.3% Hispanic of any race (2007); Density: 1,286.8 persons per square mile (2007); Average household size: 2.39 (2007); Median age: 38.6 (2007); Males per 100 females: 83.9 (2007); Marriage status: 26.4% never married, 51.1% now married, 11.1% widowed, 11.4% divorced (2000); Foreign born: 8.4% (2000); Ancestry (includes multiple ancestries): 51.0% Other groups, 6.1% English, 5.2% German, 5.2% United States or American, 4.4% Irish (2000).

Economy: Employment by occupation: 7.5% management, 13.1% professional, 28.8% services, 21.9% sales, 5.7% farming, 7.1% construction, 16.0% production (2000).

Income: Per capita income: $26,019 (2007); Median household income: $35,970 (2007); Average household income: $61,378 (2007); Percent of households with income of $100,000 or more: 14.5% (2007); Poverty rate: 23.4% (2000).

Education: Percent of population age 25 and over with: High school diploma (including GED) or higher: 58.8% (2007); Bachelor's degree or higher: 17.0% (2007); Master's degree or higher: 6.0% (2007).

Housing: Homeownership rate: 52.4% (2007); Median home value: $242,021 (2007); Median rent: $323 per month (2000); Median age of housing: 14 years (2000).

Transportation: Commute to work: 90.6% car, 1.0% public transportation, 1.6% walk, 3.5% work from home (2000); Travel time to work: 45.4% less than 15 minutes, 35.6% 15 to 30 minutes, 14.3% 30 to 45 minutes, 2.1% 45 to 60 minutes, 2.6% 60 minutes or more (2000)

INDIAN RIVER SHORES (town). Covers a land area of 5.174 square miles and a water area of 1.985 square miles. Located at 27.70° N. Lat.; 80.38° W. Long. Elevation is 6 feet.

Population: 2,315 (1990); 3,448 (2000); 3,694 (2007); 3,824 (2012 projected); Race: 98.5% White, 0.1% Black, 1.0% Asian, 0.9% Hispanic of any race (2007); Density: 713.9 persons per square mile (2007); Average household size: 1.84 (2007); Median age: 69.3 (2007); Males per 100 females: 85.6 (2007); Marriage status: 3.4% never married, 78.4% now married, 12.5% widowed, 5.7% divorced (2000); Foreign born: 4.6% (2000); Ancestry (includes multiple ancestries): 27.9% English, 20.7% German, 16.7% Irish, 6.5% Scottish, 5.8% United States or American (2000).

building permits issued: 0 (2006); Employment by occupation: 34.8% management, 24.7% professional, 3.4% services, 31.2% sales, 1.6% farming, 3.4% construction, 0.9% production (2000).

Income: Per capita income: $107,581 (2007); Median household income: $128,329 (2007); Average household income: $198,009 (2007); Percent of households with income of $100,000 or more: 61.7% (2007); Poverty rate: 2.2% (2000).

Education: Percent of population age 25 and over with: High school diploma (including GED) or higher: 98.9% (2007); Bachelor's degree or higher: 53.9% (2007); Master's degree or higher: 18.9% (2007).

Housing: Homeownership rate: 95.9% (2007); Median home value: $1 million+ (2007); Median rent: $533 per month (2000); Median age of housing: 17 years (2000).

Safety: Violent crime rate: 0.0 per 10,000 population; Property crime rate: 97.0 per 10,000 population (2006).

Transportation: Commute to work: 82.0% car, 1.1% public transportation, 0.0% walk, 15.9% work from home (2000); Travel time to work: 38.5% less than 15 minutes, 46.9% 15 to 30 minutes, 7.5% 30 to 45 minutes, 5.8% 45 to 60 minutes, 1.3% 60 minutes or more (2000)

NORTH BEACH (CDP).
Covers a land area of 3.088 square miles and a water area of 7.246 square miles. Located at 27.79° N. Lat.; 80.41° W. Long. Elevation is 7 feet.

Population: 156 (1990); 243 (2000); 290 (2007); 323 (2012 projected); Race: 98.3% White, 0.7% Black, 0.0% Asian, 2.4% Hispanic of any race (2007); Density: 93.9 persons per square mile (2007); Average household size: 2.57 (2007); Median age: 52.1 (2007); Males per 100 females: 105.7 (2007); Marriage status: 8.1% never married, 91.9% now married, 0.0% widowed, 0.0% divorced (2000); Foreign born: 6.8% (2000); Ancestry (includes multiple ancestries): 24.4% English, 22.6% German, 18.6% Irish, 16.3% United States or American, 10.9% Norwegian (2000).

Economy: Employment by occupation: 26.6% management, 2.5% professional, 0.0% services, 58.2% sales, 0.0% farming, 6.3% construction, 6.3% production (2000).

Income: Per capita income: $62,397 (2007); Median household income: $68,125 (2007); Average household income: $160,133 (2007); Percent of households with income of $100,000 or more: 38.9% (2007); Poverty rate: 0.0% (2000).

Education: Percent of population age 25 and over with: High school diploma (including GED) or higher: 100.0% (2007); Bachelor's degree or higher: 45.2% (2007); Master's degree or higher: 13.9% (2007).

Housing: Homeownership rate: 89.4% (2007); Median home value: $1 million+ (2007); Median rent: $n/a per month (2000); Median age of housing: 5 years (2000).

Transportation: Commute to work: 96.2% car, 0.0% public transportation, 0.0% walk, 3.8% work from home (2000); Travel time to work: 10.5% less than 15 minutes, 55.3% 15 to 30 minutes, 9.2% 30 to 45 minutes, 10.5% 45 to 60 minutes, 14.5% 60 minutes or more (2000)

ORCHID (town).
Covers a land area of 1.230 square miles and a water area of 0.614 square miles. Located at 27.77° N. Lat.; 80.41° W. Long. Elevation is 3 feet.

Population: 10 (1990); 140 (2000); 167 (2007); 186 (2012 projected); Race: 100.0% White, 0.0% Black, 0.0% Asian, 0.6% Hispanic of any race (2007); Density: 135.8 persons per square mile (2007); Average household size: 1.99 (2007); Median age: 61.0 (2007); Males per 100 females: 103.7 (2007); Marriage status: 0.0% never married, 98.5% now married, 0.0% widowed, 1.5% divorced (2000); Foreign born: 2.9% (2000); Ancestry (includes multiple ancestries): 30.4% English, 29.0% German, 17.4% Irish, 6.5% Norwegian, 5.1% Scotch-Irish (2000).

Economy: Single-family building permits issued: 3 (2006); Multi-family building permits issued: 0 (2006); Employment by occupation: 52.9% management, 20.6% professional, 0.0% services, 17.6% sales, 8.8% farming, 0.0% construction, 0.0% production (2000).

Income: Per capita income: $160,150 (2007); Median household income: $312,500 (2007); Average household income: $318,393 (2007); Percent of households with income of $100,000 or more: 76.2% (2007); Poverty rate: 0.0% (2000).

Taxes: Total city taxes per capita: $1,449 (2005); City property taxes per capita: $1,099 (2005).

Education: Percent of population age 25 and over with: High school diploma (including GED) or higher: 98.7% (2007); Bachelor's degree or higher: 75.2% (2007); Master's degree or higher: 20.3% (2007).

Housing: Homeownership rate: 95.2% (2007); Median home value: $1 million+ (2007); Median rent: $625 per month (2000); Median age of housing: 2 years (2000).

Transportation: Commute to work: 64.7% car, 0.0% public transportation, 0.0% walk, 35.3% work from home (2000); Travel time to work: 31.8% less than 15 minutes, 40.9% 15 to 30 minutes, 27.3% 30 to 45 minutes, 0.0% 45 to 60 minutes, 0.0% 60 minutes or more (2000)

ROSELAND (CDP).
Covers a land area of 1.987 square miles and a water area of 1.185 square miles. Located at 27.83° N. Lat.; 80.48° W. Long. Elevation is 20 feet.

Population: 1,651 (1990); 1,775 (2000); 1,845 (2007); 1,926 (2012 projected); Race: 96.5% White, 0.3% Black, 1.4% Asian, 1.5% Hispanic of any race (2007); Density: 928.5 persons per square mile (2007); Average household size: 2.04 (2007); Median age: 54.6 (2007); Males per 100 females: 93.8 (2007); Marriage status: 14.2% never married, 60.9% now married, 11.1% widowed, 13.8% divorced (2000); Foreign born: 3.9% (2000); Ancestry (includes multiple ancestries): 17.3% Irish, 13.4% German, 12.4% United States or American, 10.2% Other groups, 10.2% English (2000).

Economy: Employment by occupation: 10.1% management, 15.1% professional, 21.5% services, 21.0% sales, 4.1% farming, 13.3% construction, 14.8% production (2000).

Income: Per capita income: $22,717 (2007); Median household income: $31,688 (2007); Average household income: $45,800 (2007); Percent of households with income of $100,000 or more: 11.1% (2007); Poverty rate: 18.7% (2000).

Education: Percent of population age 25 and over with: High school diploma (including GED) or higher: 72.2% (2007); Bachelor's degree or higher: 10.8% (2007); Master's degree or higher: 4.3% (2007).

Housing: Homeownership rate: 81.1% (2007); Median home value: $158,904 (2007); Median rent: $609 per month (2000); Median age of housing: 24 years (2000).

Transportation: Commute to work: 90.3% car, 0.0% public transportation, 2.6% walk, 4.9% work from home (2000); Travel time to work: 30.7% less than 15 minutes, 28.2% 15 to 30 minutes, 30.0% 30 to 45 minutes, 4.9% 45 to 60 minutes, 6.1% 60 minutes or more (2000)

SEBASTIAN (city).
Covers a land area of 12.620 square miles and a water area of 0.927 square miles. Located at 27.78° N. Lat.; 80.48° W. Long. Elevation is 20 feet.

History: Sebastian began as a trading post on the Atlantic Coast, named for St. Sebastian. It developed as a tourist destination.

Population: 10,282 (1990); 16,181 (2000); 21,425 (2007); 25,074 (2012 projected); Race: 92.9% White, 3.9% Black, 0.7% Asian, 5.1% Hispanic of any race (2007); Density: 1,697.7 persons per square mile (2007); Average household size: 2.32 (2007); Median age: 46.8 (2007); Males per 100 females: 92.7 (2007); Marriage status: 15.5% never married, 64.6% now married, 9.5% widowed, 10.4% divorced (2000); Foreign born: 6.8% (2000); Ancestry (includes multiple ancestries): 19.8% German, 14.9% Irish, 13.7% English, 13.7% Italian, 10.1% Other groups (2000).

Economy: Single-family building permits issued: 317 (2006); Multi-family building permits issued: 6 (2006); Employment by occupation: 9.9% management, 14.0% professional, 26.0% services, 27.1% sales, 0.7% farming, 13.8% construction, 8.5% production (2000).

Income: Per capita income: $23,801 (2007); Median household income: $47,709 (2007); Average household income: $55,101 (2007); Percent of households with income of $100,000 or more: 9.6% (2007); Poverty rate: 6.3% (2000).

Education: Percent of population age 25 and over with: High school diploma (including GED) or higher: 83.2% (2007); Bachelor's degree or higher: 14.3% (2007); Master's degree or higher: 4.2% (2007).

School District(s)
Indian River County School District (PK-12)
    2005-06 Enrollment: 17,099 . . . . (772) 564-3150

Housing: Homeownership rate: 87.3% (2007); Median home value: $203,110 (2007); Median rent: $599 per month (2000); Median age of housing: 12 years (2000).

Hospitals: Sebastian River Medical Center (129 beds)

Safety: Violent crime rate: 25.5 per 10,000 population; Property crime rate: 256.3 per 10,000 population (2006).

Transportation: Commute to work: 93.4% car, 0.0% public transportation, 0.4% walk, 4.3% work from home (2000); Travel time to work: 24.5% less than 15 minutes, 50.8% 15 to 30 minutes, 16.3% 30 to 45 minutes, 3.7% 45 to 60 minutes, 4.6% 60 minutes or more (2000)

SOUTH BEACH (CDP). Covers a land area of 2.701 square miles and a water area of 4.188 square miles. Located at 27.59° N. Lat.; 80.33° W. Long.

Population: 2,754 (1990); 3,457 (2000); 4,127 (2007); 4,625 (2012 projected); Race: 97.9% White, 0.8% Black, 1.1% Asian, 1.8% Hispanic of any race (2007); Density: 1,527.9 persons per square mile (2007); Average household size: 2.10 (2007); Median age: 60.8 (2007); Males per 100 females: 92.9 (2007); Marriage status: 7.7% never married, 81.1% now married, 8.3% widowed, 3.0% divorced (2000); Foreign born: 4.3% (2000); Ancestry (includes multiple ancestries): 26.0% English, 19.2% Irish, 18.8% German, 7.6% Italian, 5.0% French (except Basque) (2000).

Economy: Employment by occupation: 26.5% management, 37.7% professional, 4.0% services, 23.9% sales, 0.0% farming, 2.6% construction, 5.2% production (2000).

Income: Per capita income: $90,717 (2007); Median household income: $132,960 (2007); Average household income: $188,040 (2007); Percent of households with income of $100,000 or more: 63.1% (2007); Poverty rate: 3.4% (2000).

Education: Percent of population age 25 and over with: High school diploma (including GED) or higher: 97.4% (2007); Bachelor's degree or higher: 58.3% (2007); Master's degree or higher: 26.4% (2007).

Housing: Homeownership rate: 95.8% (2007); Median home value: $745,866 (2007); Median rent: $625 per month (2000); Median age of housing: 16 years (2000).

Transportation: Commute to work: 79.6% car, 0.0% public transportation, 1.0% walk, 17.5% work from home (2000); Travel time to work: 47.8% less than 15 minutes, 35.7% 15 to 30 minutes, 6.7% 30 to 45 minutes, 3.4% 45 to 60 minutes, 6.4% 60 minutes or more (2000)

VERO BEACH (city). County seat. Covers a land area of 11.073 square miles and a water area of 1.853 square miles. Located at 27.64° N. Lat.; 80.39° W. Long. Elevation is 13 feet.

History: Vero Beach, extending across the Indian River to the ocean, developed as a citrus shipping point. In 1916 bones were found that were believed to be prehistoric, leading to the naming of the "Vero Beach Man." Though it was later thought that the bones were of more recent origin, other excavations revealed the remains of a mastodon.

Population: 17,403 (1990); 17,705 (2000); 16,995 (2007); 16,824 (2012 projected); Race: 91.7% White, 3.6% Black, 1.8% Asian, 8.1% Hispanic of any race (2007); Density: 1,534.8 persons per square mile (2007); Average household size: 2.04 (2007); Median age: 47.5 (2007); Males per 100 females: 94.3 (2007); Marriage status: 21.3% never married, 53.8% now married, 11.1% widowed, 13.8% divorced (2000); Foreign born: 8.8% (2000); Ancestry (includes multiple ancestries): 17.9% Irish, 16.4% German, 16.1% English, 11.4% Other groups, 8.7% Italian (2000).

Economy: Employment by occupation: 12.5% management, 20.9% professional, 19.8% services, 27.3% sales, 0.8% farming, 11.0% construction, 7.6% production (2000).

Income: Per capita income: $37,938 (2007); Median household income: $43,671 (2007); Average household income: $76,829 (2007); Percent of households with income of $100,000 or more: 19.4% (2007); Poverty rate: 9.1% (2000).

Taxes: Total city taxes per capita: $625 (2005); City property taxes per capita: $229 (2005).

Education: Percent of population age 25 and over with: High school diploma (including GED) or higher: 84.0% (2007); Bachelor's degree or higher: 31.2% (2007); Master's degree or higher: 10.5% (2007).

School District(s)

Indian River County School District (PK-12)

    2005-06 Enrollment: 17,099 . . . . (772) 564-3150

Housing: Homeownership rate: 64.7% (2007); Median home value: $258,919 (2007); Median rent: $509 per month (2000); Median age of housing: 27 years (2000).

Hospitals: HealthSouth Treasure Coast Rehabilitation Hospital (90 beds); Indian River Hospital for Emotional & Behavioral Health (54 beds); Indian River Memorial Hospital (335 beds)

Safety: Violent crime rate: 43.8 per 10,000 population; Property crime rate: 369.7 per 10,000 population (2006).

Newspapers: Vero Beach Press-Journal (Circulation 32,712)

Transportation: Commute to work: 90.1% car, 0.5% public transportation, 3.0% walk, 4.4% work from home (2000); Travel time to work: 55.7% less

VERO BEACH SOUTH (CDP). Covers a land area of 10.337 square miles and a water area of 0.568 square miles. Located at 27.62° N. Lat.; 80.41° W. Long.

Population: 16,920 (1990); 20,362 (2000); 23,295 (2007); 25,498 (2012 projected); Race: 93.4% White, 2.8% Black, 1.2% Asian, 4.3% Hispanic of any race (2007); Density: 2,253.6 persons per square mile (2007); Average household size: 2.33 (2007); Median age: 42.7 (2007); Males per 100 females: 92.6 (2007); Marriage status: 17.2% never married, 62.3% now married, 8.7% widowed, 11.8% divorced (2000); Foreign born: 6.1% (2000); Ancestry (includes multiple ancestries): 19.4% Irish, 17.3% German, 15.8% English, 10.2% Other groups, 10.0% United States or American (2000).

Economy: Employment by occupation: 12.6% management, 17.6% professional, 19.8% services, 31.0% sales, 1.1% farming, 10.1% construction, 7.8% production (2000).

Income: Per capita income: $25,361 (2007); Median household income: $44,075 (2007); Average household income: $58,862 (2007); Percent of households with income of $100,000 or more: 13.3% (2007); Poverty rate: 7.6% (2000).

Education: Percent of population age 25 and over with: High school diploma (including GED) or higher: 86.2% (2007); Bachelor's degree or higher: 21.7% (2007); Master's degree or higher: 6.3% (2007).

Housing: Homeownership rate: 76.1% (2007); Median home value: $191,315 (2007); Median rent: $531 per month (2000); Median age of housing: 18 years (2000).

Transportation: Commute to work: 94.4% car, 0.0% public transportation, 1.1% walk, 2.8% work from home (2000); Travel time to work: 44.9% less than 15 minutes, 40.6% 15 to 30 minutes, 8.7% 30 to 45 minutes, 1.7% 45 to 60 minutes, 4.2% 60 minutes or more (2000)

WABASSO (CDP). Covers a land area of 2.423 square miles and a water area of 0 square miles. Located at 27.74° N. Lat.; 80.43° W. Long. Elevation is 13 feet.

History: Wabasso was named for Ossabaw Island, Georgia, but the name is spelled backwards. Wabasso developed as a citrus growing and packing area.

Population: 864 (1990); 918 (2000); 1,075 (2007); 1,188 (2012 projected); Race: 79.0% White, 5.9% Black, 1.9% Asian, 17.2% Hispanic of any race (2007); Density: 443.6 persons per square mile (2007); Average household size: 2.20 (2007); Median age: 42.8 (2007); Males per 100 females: 118.9 (2007); Marriage status: 14.9% never married, 47.7% now married, 19.6% widowed, 17.8% divorced (2000); Foreign born: 20.9% (2000); Ancestry (includes multiple ancestries): 17.8% Other groups, 15.5% United States or American, 14.5% Irish, 11.3% German, 7.4% English (2000).

Economy: Employment by occupation: 14.4% management, 6.6% professional, 19.5% services, 13.2% sales, 17.1% farming, 17.4% construction, 12.0% production (2000).

Income: Per capita income: $25,110 (2007); Median household income: $31,053 (2007); Average household income: $54,959 (2007); Percent of households with income of $100,000 or more: 8.6% (2007); Poverty rate: 25.9% (2000).

Education: Percent of population age 25 and over with: High school diploma (including GED) or higher: 60.8% (2007); Bachelor's degree or higher: 12.5% (2007); Master's degree or higher: 2.2% (2007).

Housing: Homeownership rate: 62.7% (2007); Median home value: $189,286 (2007); Median rent: $507 per month (2000); Median age of housing: 28 years (2000).

Transportation: Commute to work: 91.9% car, 2.1% public transportation, 6.0% walk, 0.0% work from home (2000); Travel time to work: 21.9% less than 15 minutes, 45.2% 15 to 30 minutes, 19.8% 30 to 45 minutes, 3.0% 45 to 60 minutes, 10.2% 60 minutes or more (2000)

WABASSO BEACH (CDP). Covers a land area of 1.178 square miles and a water area of 0.016 square miles. Located at 27.76° N. Lat.; 80.40° W. Long. Elevation is 10 feet.

Population: 523 (1990); 1,075 (2000); 1,490 (2007); 1,789 (2012 projected); Race: 99.1% White, 0.1% Black, 0.1% Asian, 1.1% Hispanic of any race (2007); Density: 1,264.5 persons per square mile (2007); Average household size: 1.88 (2007); Median age: 64.7 (2007); Males per 100

Economy: Employment by occupation: 23.9% management, 30.9% professional, 7.0% services, 32.9% sales, 0.0% farming, 0.0% construction, 5.3% production (2000).
Income: Per capita income: $63,243 (2007); Median household income: $82,920 (2007); Average household income: $119,131 (2007); Percent of households with income of $100,000 or more: 38.7% (2007); Poverty rate: 1.4% (2000).
Education: Percent of population age 25 and over with: High school diploma (including GED) or higher: 97.3% (2007); Bachelor's degree or higher: 60.6% (2007); Master's degree or higher: 22.4% (2007).
Housing: Homeownership rate: 92.2% (2007); Median home value: $526,452 (2007); Median rent: $847 per month (2000); Median age of housing: 13 years (2000).
Transportation: Commute to work: 91.7% car, 0.0% public transportation, 0.0% walk, 4.3% work from home (2000); Travel time to work: 14.6% less than 15 minutes, 65.6% 15 to 30 minutes, 14.2% 30 to 45 minutes, 0.0% 45 to 60 minutes, 5.6% 60 minutes or more (2000)

WEST VERO CORRIDOR (CDP). Covers a land area of 4.962 square miles and a water area of 0 square miles. Located at 27.64° N. Lat.; 80.49° W. Long. Elevation is 20 feet.

Population: 6,605 (1990); 7,695 (2000); 9,071 (2007); 10,110 (2012 projected); Race: 97.4% White, 0.3% Black, 0.7% Asian, 3.9% Hispanic of any race (2007); Density: 1,828.1 persons per square mile (2007); Average household size: 1.77 (2007); Median age: 72.3 (2007); Males per 100 females: 79.2 (2007); Marriage status: 7.7% never married, 63.7% now married, 20.5% widowed, 8.1% divorced (2000); Foreign born: 6.0% (2000); Ancestry (includes multiple ancestries): 20.2% German, 18.8% English, 18.4% Irish, 8.6% United States or American, 8.4% Italian (2000).
Economy: Employment by occupation: 10.6% management, 14.4% professional, 25.6% services, 28.7% sales, 1.9% farming, 9.8% construction, 8.9% production (2000).
Income: Per capita income: $27,414 (2007); Median household income: $38,149 (2007); Average household income: $48,176 (2007); Percent of households with income of $100,000 or more: 6.6% (2007); Poverty rate: 7.3% (2000).
Education: Percent of population age 25 and over with: High school diploma (including GED) or higher: 83.3% (2007); Bachelor's degree or higher: 18.8% (2007); Master's degree or higher: 6.6% (2007).
Housing: Homeownership rate: 78.9% (2007); Median home value: $108,731 (2007); Median rent: $1,113 per month (2000); Median age of housing: 15 years (2000).
Transportation: Commute to work: 89.6% car, 0.0% public transportation, 1.2% walk, 5.7% work from home (2000); Travel time to work: 36.6% less than 15 minutes, 45.1% 15 to 30 minutes, 10.1% 30 to 45 minutes, 2.4% 45 to 60 minutes, 5.7% 60 minutes or more (2000)

WINTER BEACH (CDP). Covers a land area of 6.887 square miles and a water area of 0.013 square miles. Located at 27.71° N. Lat.; 80.42° W. Long. Elevation is 10 feet.

Population: 647 (1990); 965 (2000); 1,145 (2007); 1,295 (2012 projected); Race: 96.9% White, 1.0% Black, 1.1% Asian, 2.4% Hispanic of any race (2007); Density: 166.3 persons per square mile (2007); Average household size: 2.52 (2007); Median age: 48.5 (2007); Males per 100 females: 100.9 (2007); Marriage status: 14.6% never married, 68.5% now married, 5.6% widowed, 11.4% divorced (2000); Foreign born: 3.2% (2000); Ancestry (includes multiple ancestries): 19.6% German, 15.8% English, 15.7% Irish, 15.3% Italian, 9.9% Other groups (2000).
Economy: Employment by occupation: 21.1% management, 17.6% professional, 17.2% services, 26.0% sales, 1.5% farming, 5.7% construction, 10.8% production (2000).
Income: Per capita income: $45,269 (2007); Median household income: $93,006 (2007); Average household income: $113,709 (2007); Percent of households with income of $100,000 or more: 44.8% (2007); Poverty rate: 2.2% (2000).
Education: Percent of population age 25 and over with: High school diploma (including GED) or higher: 86.6% (2007); Bachelor's degree or higher: 30.3% (2007); Master's degree or higher: 9.2% (2007).
Housing: Homeownership rate: 87.0% (2007); Median home value: $441,667 (2007); Median rent: $363 per month (2000); Median age of housing: 15 years (2000).

Jackson County

Located in northwestern Florida; bounded on the north by Alabama, and on the east by the Chattahoochee River and the Georgia border. Covers a land area of 915.64 square miles, a water area of 38.94 square miles, and is located in the Central Time Zone. The county was founded in 1822. County seat is Marianna.

Population: 41,375 (1990); 46,755 (2000); 50,184 (2007); 52,755 (2012 projected); Race: 69.2% White, 27.3% Black, 0.5% Asian, 3.6% Hispanic of any race (2007); Density: 54.8 persons per square mile (2007); Average household size: 2.79 (2007); Median age: 38.4 (2007); Males per 100 females: 115.2 (2007).
Religion: Five largest groups: 22.9% Southern Baptist Convention, 5.8% The United Methodist Church, 5.0% Assemblies of God, 2.1% National Association of Free Will Baptists, 1.1% The Church of Jesus Christ of Latter-day Saints (2000).
Economy: Unemployment rate: 3.8% (11/2007); Total civilian labor force: 21,971 (11/2007); Leading industries: 20.8% retail trade; 17.2% health care and social assistance; 11.9% accommodation & food services (2005); Farms: 920 totaling 226,890 acres (2002); Companies that employ 500 or more persons: 0 (2005); Companies that employ 100 to 499 persons: 14 (2005); Companies that employ less than 100 persons: 833 (2005); Black-owned businesses: n/a (2002); Hispanic-owned businesses: n/a (2002); Asian-owned businesses: n/a (2002); Women-owned businesses: 660 (2002); Retail sales per capita: $13,729 (2007). Single-family building permits issued: 179 (2006); Multi-family building permits issued: 2 (2006).
Income: Per capita income: $16,835 (2007); Median household income: $35,178 (2007); Average household income: $45,999 (2007); Percent of households with income of $100,000 or more: 8.1% (2007); Poverty rate: 16.9% (2005); Bankruptcy rate: 1.32% (2006).
Education: Percent of population age 25 and over with: High school diploma (including GED) or higher: 69.0% (2007); Bachelor's degree or higher: 12.6% (2007); Master's degree or higher: 4.8% (2007).
Housing: Homeownership rate: 78.6% (2007); Median home value: $131,257 (2007); Median rent: $270 per month (2000); Median age of housing: 24 years (2000).
Health: Birth rate: 118.5 per 10,000 population (2006); Death rate: 107.1 per 10,000 population (2006); Age-adjusted cancer mortality rate: 210.9 deaths per 100,000 population (2004); Number of physicians: 8.6 per 10,000 population (2005); Hospital beds: 21.2 per 10,000 population (2004); Hospital admissions: 695.0 per 10,000 population (2004).
Elections: 2004 Presidential election results: 61.2% Bush, 38.1% Kerry, 0.4% Nader, 0.1% Badnarik
National and State Parks: Florida Caverns State Park; Three Rivers State Park
Additional Information Contacts
Jackson County Government . . . . (850) 482-9633
　　http://www.jacksoncountyfl.com
City of Marianna . . . . (850) 482-4353
　　http://www.cityofmarianna.com
Graceville Chamber of Commerce . . . . (850) 263-4289
　　http://www.graceville.org
Jackson County Chamber of Commerce . . . . (850) 482-8060
　　http://www.jacksoncounty.com

Jackson County Communities

ALFORD (town). Covers a land area of 1.284 square miles and a water area of 0.023 square miles. Located at 30.69° N. Lat.; 85.39° W. Long. Elevation is 148 feet.

History: Alford was settled in an area of pecan groves.
Population: 472 (1990); 466 (2000); 512 (2007); 540 (2012 projected); Race: 95.5% White, 2.3% Black, 0.0% Asian, 2.1% Hispanic of any race (2007); Density: 398.8 persons per square mile (2007); Average household size: 2.33 (2007); Median age: 36.8 (2007); Males per 100 females: 83.5 (2007); Marriage status: 20.7% never married, 57.3% now married, 8.8% widowed, 13.2% divorced (2000); Foreign born: 2.0% (2000); Ancestry (includes multiple ancestries): 12.7% Irish, 12.4% Other groups, 10.0% United States or American, 8.0% English, 5.2% German (2000).

Economy: Employment by occupation: 7.2% management, 4.6% professional, 26.3% services, 26.8% sales, 0.0% farming, 21.6% construction, 13.4% production (2000).
Income: Per capita income: $14,922 (2007); Median household income: $21,000 (2007); Average household income: $34,727 (2007); Percent of households with income of $100,000 or more: 5.0% (2007); Poverty rate: 36.9% (2000).
Education: Percent of population age 25 and over with: High school diploma (including GED) or higher: 53.4% (2007); Bachelor's degree or higher: 2.8% (2007); Master's degree or higher: 0.6% (2007).
Housing: Homeownership rate: 84.5% (2007); Median home value: $93,333 (2007); Median rent: $273 per month (2000); Median age of housing: 26 years (2000).
Transportation: Commute to work: 92.6% car, 0.0% public transportation, 2.1% walk, 4.2% work from home (2000); Travel time to work: 17.1% less than 15 minutes, 44.8% 15 to 30 minutes, 25.4% 30 to 45 minutes, 3.3% 45 to 60 minutes, 9.4% 60 minutes or more (2000)

BASCOM (town). Covers a land area of 0.236 square miles and a water area of 0 square miles. Located at 30.92° N. Lat.; 85.11° W. Long. Elevation is 141 feet.
Population: 90 (1990); 106 (2000); 122 (2007); 131 (2012 projected); Race: 100.0% White, 0.0% Black, 0.0% Asian, 0.0% Hispanic of any race (2007); Density: 516.0 persons per square mile (2007); Average household size: 2.54 (2007); Median age: 43.1 (2007); Males per 100 females: 106.8 (2007); Marriage status: 20.5% never married, 67.9% now married, 11.5% widowed, 0.0% divorced (2000); Foreign born: 0.0% (2000); Ancestry (includes multiple ancestries): 28.8% United States or American, 10.8% Other groups, 6.3% English, 4.5% Irish, 1.8% German (2000).
Economy: Employment by occupation: 2.1% management, 8.3% professional, 39.6% services, 14.6% sales, 0.0% farming, 22.9% construction, 12.5% production (2000).
Income: Per capita income: $16,230 (2007); Median household income: $36,429 (2007); Average household income: $41,250 (2007); Percent of households with income of $100,000 or more: 4.2% (2007); Poverty rate: 6.3% (2000).
Education: Percent of population age 25 and over with: High school diploma (including GED) or higher: 64.6% (2007); Bachelor's degree or higher: 5.1% (2007); Master's degree or higher: 5.1% (2007).
Housing: Homeownership rate: 89.6% (2007); Median home value: $119,643 (2007); Median rent: $250 per month (2000); Median age of housing: 35 years (2000).
Transportation: Commute to work: 100.0% car, 0.0% public transportation, 0.0% walk, 0.0% work from home (2000); Travel time to work: 41.7% less than 15 minutes, 43.8% 15 to 30 minutes, 14.6% 30 to 45 minutes, 0.0% 45 to 60 minutes, 0.0% 60 minutes or more (2000)

CAMPBELLTON (town). Covers a land area of 0.889 square miles and a water area of 0.010 square miles. Located at 30.94° N. Lat.; 85.39° W. Long. Elevation is 184 feet.
History: Campbellton had its beginnings during the English occupation (1763-1783). Later, a grain elevator, lumber mill, and a grist mill processing corn and peanuts were established.
Population: 202 (1990); 212 (2000); 206 (2007); 208 (2012 projected); Race: 29.1% White, 70.4% Black, 0.0% Asian, 0.5% Hispanic of any race (2007); Density: 231.6 persons per square mile (2007); Average household size: 2.31 (2007); Median age: 43.1 (2007); Males per 100 females: 100.0 (2007); Marriage status: 28.8% never married, 51.7% now married, 15.1% widowed, 4.4% divorced (2000); Foreign born: 0.4% (2000); Ancestry (includes multiple ancestries): 29.5% Other groups, 7.0% United States or American, 4.1% German, 2.6% Irish, 1.5% British (2000).
Economy: Employment by occupation: 0.0% management, 10.5% professional, 26.3% services, 25.3% sales, 7.4% farming, 7.4% construction, 23.2% production (2000).
Income: Per capita income: $17,937 (2007); Median household income: $28,750 (2007); Average household income: $41,517 (2007); Percent of households with income of $100,000 or more: 7.9% (2007); Poverty rate: 16.6% (2000).
Education: Percent of population age 25 and over with: High school diploma (including GED) or higher: 56.3% (2007); Bachelor's degree or higher: 2.8% (2007); Master's degree or higher: 1.4% (2007).
Housing: Homeownership rate: 79.8% (2007); Median home value: $97,000 (2007); Median rent: $213 per month (2000); Median age of housing: 24 years (2000).

Transportation: Commute to work: 95.6% car, 4.4% public transportation, 0.0% walk, 0.0% work from home (2000); Travel time to work: 16.5% less than 15 minutes, 31.9% 15 to 30 minutes, 28.6% 30 to 45 minutes, 18.7% 45 to 60 minutes, 4.4% 60 minutes or more (2000)

COTTONDALE (town). Covers a land area of 1.516 square miles and a water area of 0.178 square miles. Located at 30.79° N. Lat.; 85.37° W. Long. Elevation is 131 feet.
History: Cottondale developed as a farming, fishing, and hunting center. Early Cottondale residents claimed that the fish in their streams and lakes were so assertive, fishermen had to hide behind trees while baiting their hooks.
Population: 900 (1990); 869 (2000); 875 (2007); 885 (2012 projected); Race: 71.5% White, 23.2% Black, 0.7% Asian, 6.7% Hispanic of any race (2007); Density: 577.1 persons per square mile (2007); Average household size: 2.27 (2007); Median age: 36.4 (2007); Males per 100 females: 88.6 (2007); Marriage status: 27.8% never married, 49.1% now married, 12.8% widowed, 10.3% divorced (2000); Foreign born: 1.2% (2000); Ancestry (includes multiple ancestries): 22.0% Other groups, 15.8% United States or American, 8.6% Irish, 4.0% German, 3.3% English (2000).
Economy: Employment by occupation: 4.1% management, 26.2% professional, 24.3% services, 20.5% sales, 2.8% farming, 8.8% construction, 13.2% production (2000).
Income: Per capita income: $14,411 (2007); Median household income: $24,740 (2007); Average household income: $32,753 (2007); Percent of households with income of $100,000 or more: 3.6% (2007); Poverty rate: 27.4% (2000).
Education: Percent of population age 25 and over with: High school diploma (including GED) or higher: 61.7% (2007); Bachelor's degree or higher: 12.3% (2007); Master's degree or higher: 4.9% (2007).
School District(s)
Jackson County School District (PK-12)
    2005-06 Enrollment: 7,394 . . . . (850) 482-1200
Housing: Homeownership rate: 63.6% (2007); Median home value: $107,552 (2007); Median rent: $239 per month (2000); Median age of housing: 24 years (2000).
Transportation: Commute to work: 89.9% car, 0.0% public transportation, 5.5% walk, 4.5% work from home (2000); Travel time to work: 37.1% less than 15 minutes, 27.6% 15 to 30 minutes, 21.8% 30 to 45 minutes, 8.5% 45 to 60 minutes, 5.1% 60 minutes or more (2000)

GRACEVILLE (city). Covers a land area of 4.297 square miles and a water area of 0.100 square miles. Located at 30.95° N. Lat.; 85.51° W. Long. Elevation is 151 feet.
Population: 2,680 (1990); 2,402 (2000); 2,358 (2007); 2,377 (2012 projected); Race: 71.5% White, 25.7% Black, 0.2% Asian, 2.2% Hispanic of any race (2007); Density: 548.8 persons per square mile (2007); Average household size: 2.57 (2007); Median age: 36.5 (2007); Males per 100 females: 86.8 (2007); Marriage status: 24.3% never married, 54.1% now married, 12.3% widowed, 9.3% divorced (2000); Foreign born: 1.1% (2000); Ancestry (includes multiple ancestries): 20.5% Other groups, 15.0% United States or American, 7.4% Irish, 6.3% English, 4.2% African (2000).
Economy: Employment by occupation: 8.6% management, 25.0% professional, 26.7% services, 20.3% sales, 0.4% farming, 7.6% construction, 11.4% production (2000).
Income: Per capita income: $17,910 (2007); Median household income: $28,488 (2007); Average household income: $45,286 (2007); Percent of households with income of $100,000 or more: 9.4% (2007); Poverty rate: 20.7% (2000).
Education: Percent of population age 25 and over with: High school diploma (including GED) or higher: 73.2% (2007); Bachelor's degree or higher: 21.8% (2007); Master's degree or higher: 8.1% (2007).
School District(s)
Holmes County School District (PK-12)
    2005-06 Enrollment: 3,389 . . . . (850) 547-9341
Jackson County School District (PK-12)
    2005-06 Enrollment: 7,394 . . . . (850) 482-1200
Four-year College(s)
The Baptist College of Florida (Private, Not-for-profit, Southern Baptist)
    Fall 2006 Enrollment: 595 . . . . (850) 263-3261
    2006-07 Tuition: In-state $7,200; Out-of-state $7,200
Housing: Homeownership rate: 57.0% (2007); Median home value: $131,250 (2007); Median rent: $189 per month (2000); Median age of housing: 30 years (2000).

Safety: Violent crime rate: 0.0 per 10,000 population; Property crime rate: 308.4 per 10,000 population (2006).

Newspapers: The Graceville News (General - Circulation 1,700)

Transportation: Commute to work: 92.1% car, 0.0% public transportation, 5.8% walk, 1.7% work from home (2000); Travel time to work: 46.0% less than 15 minutes, 17.5% 15 to 30 minutes, 23.7% 30 to 45 minutes, 7.0% 45 to 60 minutes, 5.8% 60 minutes or more (2000)

Additional Information Contacts

Graceville Chamber of Commerce. . . . . (850) 263-4289
http://www.graceville.org

GRAND RIDGE (town). Covers a land area of 2.171 square miles and a water area of 0.090 square miles. Located at 30.71° N. Lat.; 85.01° W. Long. Elevation is 128 feet.

Population: 741 (1990); 792 (2000); 816 (2007); 833 (2012 projected); Race: 93.1% White, 2.8% Black, 0.0% Asian, 1.7% Hispanic of any race (2007); Density: 375.9 persons per square mile (2007); Average household size: 2.51 (2007); Median age: 37.4 (2007); Males per 100 females: 93.8 (2007); Marriage status: 22.5% never married, 58.8% now married, 7.1% widowed, 11.6% divorced (2000); Foreign born: 0.8% (2000); Ancestry (includes multiple ancestries): 24.5% United States or American, 17.6% Other groups, 11.6% Irish, 8.0% German, 6.7% English (2000).

Economy: Employment by occupation: 9.7% management, 18.3% professional, 22.2% services, 22.2% sales, 0.6% farming, 11.4% construction, 15.8% production (2000).

Income: Per capita income: $17,880 (2007); Median household income: $37,625 (2007); Average household income: $44,892 (2007); Percent of households with income of $100,000 or more: 5.8% (2007); Poverty rate: 16.5% (2000).

Education: Percent of population age 25 and over with: High school diploma (including GED) or higher: 75.6% (2007); Bachelor's degree or higher: 8.8% (2007); Master's degree or higher: 4.1% (2007).

School District(s)

Jackson County School District (PK-12)

   2005-06 Enrollment: 7,394 . . . . (850) 482-1200

Housing: Homeownership rate: 80.9% (2007); Median home value: $117,378 (2007); Median rent: $233 per month (2000); Median age of housing: 22 years (2000).

Transportation: Commute to work: 94.4% car, 0.0% public transportation, 1.4% walk, 2.2% work from home (2000); Travel time to work: 19.1% less than 15 minutes, 42.3% 15 to 30 minutes, 25.7% 30 to 45 minutes, 4.6% 45 to 60 minutes, 8.3% 60 minutes or more (2000)

GREENWOOD (town). Covers a land area of 4.795 square miles and a water area of 0 square miles. Located at 30.87° N. Lat.; 85.16° W. Long. Elevation is 115 feet.

Population: 612 (1990); 735 (2000); 665 (2007); 675 (2012 projected); Race: 63.6% White, 29.0% Black, 1.5% Asian, 3.0% Hispanic of any race (2007); Density: 138.7 persons per square mile (2007); Average household size: 2.46 (2007); Median age: 35.1 (2007); Males per 100 females: 90.5 (2007); Marriage status: 17.1% never married, 58.4% now married, 14.0% widowed, 10.5% divorced (2000); Foreign born: 2.2% (2000); Ancestry (includes multiple ancestries): 23.0% Other groups, 22.2% United States or American, 8.6% German, 8.4% English, 7.6% Irish (2000).

Economy: Employment by occupation: 8.2% management, 17.7% professional, 27.0% services, 26.3% sales, 0.0% farming, 5.1% construction, 15.7% production (2000).

Income: Per capita income: $18,760 (2007); Median household income: $33,800 (2007); Average household income: $44,537 (2007); Percent of households with income of $100,000 or more: 6.7% (2007); Poverty rate: 17.8% (2000).

Education: Percent of population age 25 and over with: High school diploma (including GED) or higher: 80.5% (2007); Bachelor's degree or higher: 13.9% (2007); Master's degree or higher: 7.1% (2007).

Housing: Homeownership rate: 79.3% (2007); Median home value: $112,255 (2007); Median rent: $310 per month (2000); Median age of housing: 25 years (2000).

Transportation: Commute to work: 97.5% car, 0.0% public transportation, 1.4% walk, 1.1% work from home (2000); Travel time to work: 29.1% less than 15 minutes, 47.8% 15 to 30 minutes, 14.0% 30 to 45 minutes, 1.8% 45 to 60 minutes, 7.2% 60 minutes or more (2000)

JACOB CITY (city). Aka Jacobs. Covers a land area of 3.099 square miles and a water area of 0.134 square miles. Located at 30.89° N. Lat.; 85.41° W. Long.

Population: 261 (1990); 281 (2000); 275 (2007); 275 (2012 projected); Race: 6.9% White, 93.1% Black, 0.0% Asian, 0.0% Hispanic of any race (2007); Density: 88.7 persons per square mile (2007); Average household size: 2.78 (2007); Median age: 35.2 (2007); Males per 100 females: 84.6 (2007); Marriage status: 28.0% never married, 57.5% now married, 9.3% widowed, 5.2% divorced (2000); Foreign born: 0.0% (2000); Ancestry (includes multiple ancestries): 76.9% Other groups, 3.3% United States or American, 1.5% African (2000).

Economy: Employment by occupation: 0.0% management, 0.0% professional, 39.7% services, 14.1% sales, 2.6% farming, 12.8% construction, 30.8% production (2000).

Income: Per capita income: $12,727 (2007); Median household income: $27,083 (2007); Average household income: $35,354 (2007); Percent of households with income of $100,000 or more: 2.0% (2007); Poverty rate: 26.0% (2000).

Education: Percent of population age 25 and over with: High school diploma (including GED) or higher: 70.2% (2007); Bachelor's degree or higher: 4.7% (2007); Master's degree or higher: 1.8% (2007).

Housing: Homeownership rate: 88.9% (2007); Median home value: $80,000 (2007); Median rent: $171 per month (2000); Median age of housing: 13 years (2000).

Transportation: Commute to work: 100.0% car, 0.0% public transportation, 0.0% walk, 0.0% work from home (2000); Travel time to work: 7.1% less than 15 minutes, 18.6% 15 to 30 minutes, 51.4% 30 to 45 minutes, 20.0% 45 to 60 minutes, 2.9% 60 minutes or more (2000)

MALONE (town). Covers a land area of 3.129 square miles and a water area of 0 square miles. Located at 30.95° N. Lat.; 85.16° W. Long. Elevation is 141 feet.

Population: 988 (1990); 2,007 (2000); 2,267 (2007); 2,460 (2012 projected); Race: 40.0% White, 53.1% Black, 0.1% Asian, 11.0% Hispanic of any race (2007); Density: 724.4 persons per square mile (2007); Average household size: 6.77 (2007); Median age: 36.9 (2007); Males per 100 females: 443.6 (2007); Marriage status: 13.8% never married, 72.7% now married, 9.1% widowed, 4.4% divorced (2000); Foreign born: 0.6% (2000); Ancestry (includes multiple ancestries): 10.0% Other groups, 4.4% United States or American, 2.9% English, 2.4% Irish, 2.0% German (2000).

Economy: Employment by occupation: 12.1% management, 18.9% professional, 26.9% services, 21.5% sales, 2.7% farming, 8.4% construction, 9.4% production (2000).

Income: Per capita income: $7,179 (2007); Median household income: $34,833 (2007); Average household income: $46,619 (2007); Percent of households with income of $100,000 or more: 6.0% (2007); Poverty rate: 10.8% (2000).

Education: Percent of population age 25 and over with: High school diploma (including GED) or higher: 44.2% (2007); Bachelor's degree or higher: 6.5% (2007); Master's degree or higher: 1.7% (2007).

School District(s)

Jackson County School District (PK-12)

   2005-06 Enrollment: 7,394 . . . . (850) 482-1200

Housing: Homeownership rate: 79.4% (2007); Median home value: $127,381 (2007); Median rent: $204 per month (2000); Median age of housing: 35 years (2000).

Transportation: Commute to work: 92.4% car, 0.0% public transportation, 3.8% walk, 3.1% work from home (2000); Travel time to work: 31.6% less than 15 minutes, 30.5% 15 to 30 minutes, 24.5% 30 to 45 minutes, 6.4% 45 to 60 minutes, 7.1% 60 minutes or more (2000)

MARIANNA (city). County seat. Covers a land area of 8.028 square miles and a water area of 0.029 square miles. Located at 30.77° N. Lat.; 85.23° W. Long. Elevation is 167 feet.

History: Marianna was founded in 1829 on the Chipola River, and named for two daughters of a pioneer merchant. The town developed as the center of an agricultural area growing peanuts, corn, cotton, pecans, and fruit.

Population: 6,332 (1990); 6,230 (2000); 6,143 (2007); 6,230 (2012 projected); Race: 55.6% White, 41.1% Black, 1.1% Asian, 3.5% Hispanic of any race (2007); Density: 765.2 persons per square mile (2007); Average household size: 2.62 (2007); Median age: 35.2 (2007); Males per 100 females: 95.3 (2007); Marriage status: 31.2% never married, 44.7% now married, 14.3% widowed, 9.9% divorced (2000); Foreign born: 3.1% (2000); Ancestry (includes multiple ancestries): 34.2% Other groups, 13.2% United States or American, 4.9% English, 4.8% Irish, 3.6% German (2000).

Economy: Employment by occupation: 9.8% management, 24.6% professional, 25.0% services, 25.1% sales, 0.7% farming, 3.9% construction, 11.0% production (2000).

Income: Per capita income: $15,366 (2007); Median household income: $27,145 (2007); Average household income: $38,802 (2007); Percent of households with income of $100,000 or more: 5.5% (2007); Poverty rate: 28.5% (2000).

Education: Percent of population age 25 and over with: High school diploma (including GED) or higher: 74.6% (2007); Bachelor's degree or higher: 20.6% (2007); Master's degree or higher: 8.3% (2007).

School District(s)

Dozier/Okeechobee (PK-12)
   2005-06 Enrollment: 420 . . . . (850) 638-6222
Jackson County School District (PK-12)
   2005-06 Enrollment: 7,394 . . . . (850) 482-1200

Four-year College(s)

Chipola College (Public)
   Fall 2006 Enrollment: 2,051 . . . . (850) 526-2761
   2006-07 Tuition: In-state $2,137; Out-of-state $6,100

Housing: Homeownership rate: 58.3% (2007); Median home value: $126,311 (2007); Median rent: $277 per month (2000); Median age of housing: 42 years (2000).

Hospitals: Jackson Hospital (100 beds)

Safety: Violent crime rate: 94.0 per 10,000 population; Property crime rate: 369.8 per 10,000 population (2006).

Newspapers: Jackson County Floridan (Circulation 6,413)

Transportation: Commute to work: 93.4% car, 0.3% public transportation, 2.6% walk, 2.1% work from home (2000); Travel time to work: 59.2% less than 15 minutes, 20.3% 15 to 30 minutes, 9.8% 30 to 45 minutes, 2.6% 45 to 60 minutes, 8.1% 60 minutes or more (2000)

Additional Information Contacts

City of Marianna . . . . (850) 482-4353
   http://www.cityofmarianna.com
Jackson County Chamber of Commerce . . . . (850) 482-8060
   http://www.jacksoncounty.com

SNEADS (town). Covers a land area of 4.422 square miles and a water area of 0.211 square miles. Located at 30.71° N. Lat.; 84.92° W. Long. Elevation is 118 feet.

Population: 1,746 (1990); 1,919 (2000); 2,015 (2007); 2,086 (2012 projected); Race: 78.8% White, 16.4% Black, 0.1% Asian, 4.8% Hispanic of any race (2007); Density: 455.7 persons per square mile (2007); Average household size: 2.36 (2007); Median age: 37.9 (2007); Males per 100 females: 95.8 (2007); Marriage status: 23.6% never married, 57.2% now married, 8.0% widowed, 11.3% divorced (2000); Foreign born: 1.0% (2000); Ancestry (includes multiple ancestries): 31.6% United States or American, 20.6% Other groups, 7.3% English, 3.5% Irish, 3.3% German (2000).

Economy: Employment by occupation: 8.6% management, 21.9% professional, 27.8% services, 16.4% sales, 0.5% farming, 13.1% construction, 11.8% production (2000).

Income: Per capita income: $18,505 (2007); Median household income: $34,868 (2007); Average household income: $43,662 (2007); Percent of households with income of $100,000 or more: 6.1% (2007); Poverty rate: 17.2% (2000).

Education: Percent of population age 25 and over with: High school diploma (including GED) or higher: 75.1% (2007); Bachelor's degree or higher: 10.2% (2007); Master's degree or higher: 4.4% (2007).

School District(s)

Jackson County School District (PK-12)
   2005-06 Enrollment: 7,394 . . . . (850) 482-1200

Housing: Homeownership rate: 75.5% (2007); Median home value: $109,375 (2007); Median rent: $234 per month (2000); Median age of housing: 26 years (2000).

Safety: Violent crime rate: 10.1 per 10,000 population; Property crime rate: 141.7 per 10,000 population (2006).

Transportation: Commute to work: 97.4% car, 0.0% public transportation, 1.8% walk, 0.8% work from home (2000); Travel time to work: 45.9% less than 15 minutes, 21.2% 15 to 30 minutes, 18.1% 30 to 45 minutes, 7.9% 45 to 60 minutes, 6.9% 60 minutes or more (2000)

Jefferson County

Located in northwestern Florida; bounded on the north by Georgia, on the south by the Gulf of Mexico, and on the east by the Aucilla River; lowland area, partly swampy, with Lake Miccosukee in the north. Covers a land area of 597.74 square miles, a water area of 38.91 square miles, and is located in the Eastern Time Zone. The county was founded in 1827. County seat is Monticello.

Jefferson County is part of the Tallahassee, FL Metropolitan Statistical Area. The entire metro area includes: Gadsden County, FL; Jefferson County, FL; Leon County, FL; Wakulla County, FL

Weather Station: Monticello 3 W								Elevation: 144 feet			
	Jan	Feb	Mar	Apr	May	Jun	Jul	Aug	Sep	Oct	Nov	Dec
High	62	66	72	78	85	89	91	90	87	80	72	65
Low	38	41	47	52	60	67	70	69	66	54	46	40
Precip	5.6	4.6	6.0	3.6	4.1	5.7	6.7	6.8	4.5	3.4	3.6	3.9
Snow	tr	tr	tr	0.0	0.0	0.0	0.0	0.0	0.0	0.0	0.0	tr

High and Low temperatures in degrees Fahrenheit; Precipitation and Snow in inches

Population: 11,296 (1990); 12,902 (2000); 14,673 (2007); 15,888 (2012 projected); Race: 61.5% White, 35.5% Black, 0.4% Asian, 4.0% Hispanic of any race (2007); Density: 24.5 persons per square mile (2007); Average household size: 2.81 (2007); Median age: 40.4 (2007); Males per 100 females: 128.1 (2007).

Religion: Five largest groups: 17.8% Southern Baptist Convention, 7.0% The United Methodist Church, 2.5% International Pentecostal Holiness Church, 2.1% Episcopal Church, 1.2% Catholic Church (2000).

Economy: Unemployment rate: 3.1% (11/2007); Total civilian labor force: 7,149 (11/2007); Leading industries: 20.2% health care and social assistance; 19.3% retail trade; 11.0% construction (2005); Farms: 418 totaling 132,727 acres (2002); Companies that employ 500 or more persons: 0 (2005); Companies that employ 100 to 499 persons: 2 (2005); Companies that employ less than 100 persons: 265 (2005); Black-owned businesses: n/a (2002); Hispanic-owned businesses: n/a (2002); Asian-owned businesses: n/a (2002); Women-owned businesses: n/a (2002); Retail sales per capita: $6,078 (2007); Single-family building permits issued: 100 (2006); Multi-family building permits issued: 0 (2006).

Income: Per capita income: $19,574 (2007); Median household income: $38,635 (2007); Average household income: $52,706 (2007); Percent of households with income of $100,000 or more: 11.1% (2007); Poverty rate: 18.7% (2005); Bankruptcy rate: 1.70% (2006).

Education: Percent of population age 25 and over with: High school diploma (including GED) or higher: 72.7% (2007); Bachelor's degree or higher: 16.5% (2007); Master's degree or higher: 5.8% (2007).

Housing: Homeownership rate: 81.1% (2007); Median home value: $127,313 (2007); Median rent: $293 per month (2000); Median age of housing: 20 years (2000).

Health: Birth rate: 128.8 per 10,000 population (2006); Death rate: 100.8 per 10,000 population (2006); Age-adjusted cancer mortality rate: 203.8 deaths per 100,000 population (2004); Number of physicians: 2.1 per 10,000 population (2005); Hospital beds: 0.0 per 10,000 population (2004); Hospital admissions: 0.0 per 10,000 population (2004).

Elections: 2004 Presidential election results: 44.1% Bush, 55.3% Kerry, 0.4% Nader, 0.1% Badnarik

Additional Information Contacts

Jefferson County Government . . . . (850) 342-0218
   http://www.co.jefferson.fl.us
Monticello Chamber of Commerce . . . . (850) 997-5552
   http://monticellojeffersonfl.com

Jefferson County Communities

LAMONT (unincorporated postal area, zip code 32336). Covers a land area of 80.203 square miles and a water area of 0.922 square miles. Located at 30.41° N. Lat.; 83.82° W. Long. Elevation is 63 feet.

History: Lamont was first called Lick Skillet, but was changed in 1890 by residents who desired a more dignified name and chose that of Vice-President Cornelius Lamont, who had been a recent visitor in the town.

Population: 1,130 (2000); Race: 49.2% White, 49.3% Black, 0.8% Asian, 0.0% Hispanic of any race (2000); Density: 14.1 persons per square mile (2000); Age: 20.0% under 18, 13.9% over 64 (2000); Marriage status: 33.3% never married, 49.6% now married, 8.0% widowed, 9.1% divorced (2000); Foreign born: 0.0% (2000); Ancestry (includes multiple ancestries): 53.2% Other groups, 9.0% English, 7.3% Irish, 7.2% United States or American, 5.3% German (2000).

Economy: Employment by occupation: 11.4% management, 5.4% professional, 27.0% services, 27.8% sales, 2.1% farming, 17.6% construction, 8.7% production (2000).
Income: Per capita income: $18,044 (2000); Median household income: $26,667 (2000); Poverty rate: 31.9% (2000).
Education: Percent of population age 25 and over with: High school diploma (including GED) or higher: 57.1% (2000); Bachelor's degree or higher: 8.6% (2000).
Housing: Homeownership rate: 85.3% (2000); Median home value: $79,600 (2000); Median rent: $158 per month (2000); Median age of housing: 17 years (2000).
Transportation: Commute to work: 95.0% car, 2.9% public transportation, 0.0% walk, 0.0% work from home (2000); Travel time to work: 18.0% less than 15 minutes, 24.3% 15 to 30 minutes, 34.8% 30 to 45 minutes, 16.8% 45 to 60 minutes, 6.1% 60 minutes or more (2000)

MONTICELLO (city). County seat. Covers a land area of 3.380 square miles and a water area of 0 square miles. Located at 30.54° N. Lat.; 83.86° W. Long. Elevation is 233 feet.
History: Monticello was founded in the early 1800's by planters from Georgia and the Carolinas, and named for Thomas Jefferson's home in Virginia. The courthouse built in the center of the town was modeled on Jefferson's house.
Population: 2,641 (1990); 2,533 (2000); 2,785 (2007); 2,948 (2012 projected); Race: 46.0% White, 51.5% Black, 1.0% Asian, 2.3% Hispanic of any race (2007); Density: 824.0 persons per square mile (2007); Average household size: 2.62 (2007); Median age: 40.0 (2007); Males per 100 females: 93.5 (2007); Marriage status: 30.0% never married, 45.4% now married, 11.7% widowed, 12.9% divorced (2000); Foreign born: 0.9% (2000); Ancestry (includes multiple ancestries): 49.5% Other groups, 9.7% United States or American, 7.4% English, 5.4% Irish, 3.4% German (2000).
Economy: Employment by occupation: 12.0% management, 15.5% professional, 21.2% services, 24.4% sales, 5.5% farming, 9.5% construction, 11.7% production (2000).
Income: Per capita income: $17,314 (2007); Median household income: $32,237 (2007); Average household income: $44,993 (2007); Percent of households with income of $100,000 or more: 8.3% (2007); Poverty rate: 22.2% (2000).
Education: Percent of population age 25 and over with: High school diploma (including GED) or higher: 74.7% (2007); Bachelor's degree or higher: 21.4% (2007); Master's degree or higher: 9.0% (2007).

School District(s)
Jefferson County School District (PK-12)
    2005-06 Enrollment: 1,379 . . . . (850) 342-0100
Housing: Homeownership rate: 68.8% (2007); Median home value: $114,693 (2007); Median rent: $279 per month (2000); Median age of housing: 38 years (2000).
Safety: Violent crime rate: 127.5 per 10,000 population; Property crime rate: 251.1 per 10,000 population (2006).
Newspapers: Monticello News (General - Circulation 3,000)
Transportation: Commute to work: 95.7% car, 0.8% public transportation, 0.8% walk, 1.5% work from home (2000); Travel time to work: 42.9% less than 15 minutes, 9.1% 15 to 30 minutes, 22.2% 30 to 45 minutes, 20.9% 45 to 60 minutes, 4.9% 60 minutes or more (2000)
Additional Information Contacts
Monticello Chamber of Commerce . . . . (850) 997-5552
  http://monticellojeffersonfl.com

Lafayette County

Located in northern Florida; bounded on the east and northeast by the Suwanee River; swampy area, with many small lakes. Covers a land area of 542.84 square miles, a water area of 5.08 square miles, and is located in the Eastern Time Zone. The county was founded in 1856. County seat is Mayo.

Weather Station: Mayo										Elevation: 62 feet	
	Jan	Feb	Mar	Apr	May	Jun	Jul	Aug	Sep	Oct	Nov	Dec
High	65	69	75	81	87	91	92	92	89	82	75	67
Low	40	43	49	54	62	69	71	71	68	57	49	42
Precip	5.0	3.7	5.1	3.2	3.2	5.9	7.7	8.1	4.7	3.1	2.6	3.3
Snow	tr	0.0	0.0	0.0	0.0	0.0	0.0	0.0	0.0	0.0	0.0	0.0

High and Low temperatures in degrees Fahrenheit; Precipitation and Snow in inches

Population: 5,578 (1990); 7,022 (2000); 8,272 (2007); 9,141 (2012 projected); Race: 75.0% White, 17.1% Black, 0.2% Asian, 12.5% Hispanic

of any race (2007); Density: 15.2 persons per square mile (2007); Average household size: 3.41 (2007); Median age: 34.5 (2007); Males per 100 females: 168.1 (2007).
Religion: Five largest groups: 41.2% Southern Baptist Convention, 4.0% The United Methodist Church, 2.6% Church of God (Cleveland, Tennessee), 1.7% Assemblies of God, 1.1% Churches of Christ (2000).
Economy: Unemployment rate: 3.1% (11/2007); Total civilian labor force: 2,893 (11/2007); Leading industries: 24.5% health care and social assistance; 19.1% retail trade; 8.9% accommodation & food services (2005); Farms: 195 totaling 91,988 acres (2002); Companies that employ 500 or more persons: 0 (2005); Companies that employ 100 to 499 persons: 0 (2005); Companies that employ less than 100 persons: 94 (2005); Black-owned businesses: n/a (2002); Hispanic-owned businesses: n/a (2002); Asian-owned businesses: n/a (2002); Women-owned businesses: n/a (2002); Retail sales per capita: $2,929 (2007). Single-family building permits issued: 26 (2006); Multi-family building permits issued: 0 (2006).
Income: Per capita income: $14,196 (2007); Median household income: $33,569 (2007); Average household income: $44,683 (2007); Percent of households with income of $100,000 or more: 5.9% (2007); Poverty rate: 23.6% (2005); Bankruptcy rate: -1.00% (2006).
Education: Percent of population age 25 and over with: High school diploma (including GED) or higher: 67.9% (2007); Bachelor's degree or higher: 7.0% (2007); Master's degree or higher: 2.7% (2007).
Housing: Homeownership rate: 80.8% (2007); Median home value: $130,876 (2007); Median rent: $296 per month (2000); Median age of housing: 23 years (2000).
Health: Birth rate: 124.3 per 10,000 population (2006); Death rate: 109.4 per 10,000 population (2006); Age-adjusted cancer mortality rate: 334.6 deaths per 100,000 population (2004); Number of physicians: 2.5 per 10,000 population (2005); Hospital beds: 0.0 per 10,000 population (2004); Hospital admissions: 0.0 per 10,000 population (2004).
Elections: 2004 Presidential election results: 74.0% Bush, 25.4% Kerry, 0.3% Nader, 0.0% Badnarik
National and State Parks: Troy Spring State Park
Additional Information Contacts
Lafayette County Government . . . . (386) 294-1600

Lafayette County Chamber of Commerce . . . . (904) 294-2705

Lafayette County Communities

DAY (unincorporated postal area, zip code 32013). Covers a land area of 1.016 square miles and a water area of 0 square miles. Located at 30.19° N. Lat.; 83.29° W. Long. Elevation is 85 feet.
Population: 58 (2000); Race: 100.0% White, 0.0% Black, 0.0% Asian, 0.0% Hispanic of any race (2000); Density: 57.1 persons per square mile (2000); Age: 0.0% under 18, 0.0% over 64 (2000); Marriage status: 11.8% never married, 88.2% now married, 0.0% widowed, 0.0% divorced (2000); Foreign born: 0.0% (2000); Ancestry (includes multiple ancestries): 100.0% United States or American (2000).
Economy: Employment by occupation: 0.0% management, 0.0% professional, 23.5% services, 0.0% sales, 0.0% farming, 76.5% construction, 0.0% production (2000).
Income: Per capita income: $10,826 (2000); Median household income: $20,481 (2000); Poverty rate: 0.0% (2000).
Education: Percent of population age 25 and over with: High school diploma (including GED) or higher: 100.0% (2000); Bachelor's degree or higher: 0.0% (2000).
Housing: Homeownership rate: 100.0% (2000); Median home value: $n/a (2000); Median rent: $n/a per month (2000); Median age of housing: 17 years (2000).
Transportation: Commute to work: 100.0% car, 0.0% public transportation, 0.0% walk, 0.0% work from home (2000); Travel time to work: 0.0% less than 15 minutes, 100.0% 15 to 30 minutes, 0.0% 30 to 45 minutes, 0.0% 45 to 60 minutes, 0.0% 60 minutes or more (2000)

MAYO (town). County seat. Covers a land area of 0.817 square miles and a water area of 0 square miles. Located at 30.05° N. Lat.; 83.17° W. Long. Elevation is 89 feet.
Population: 917 (1990); 988 (2000); 1,078 (2007); 1,151 (2012 projected); Race: 58.5% White, 25.0% Black, 0.0% Asian, 25.7% Hispanic of any race (2007); Density: 1,319.3 persons per square mile (2007); Average household size: 2.95 (2007); Median age: 33.6 (2007); Males per 100 females: 105.7 (2007); Marriage status: 21.1% never married, 56.4% now

married, 10.0% widowed, 12.5% divorced (2000); Foreign born: 16.4% (2000); Ancestry (includes multiple ancestries): 44.8% Other groups, 14.7% United States or American, 5.7% English, 3.6% Irish, 1.8% German (2000).
Economy: Employment by occupation: 5.9% management, 9.2% professional, 29.9% services, 9.5% sales, 19.9% farming, 5.9% construction, 19.7% production (2000).
Income: Per capita income: $15,064 (2007); Median household income: $29,211 (2007); Average household income: $43,033 (2007); Percent of households with income of $100,000 or more: 7.1% (2007); Poverty rate: 34.6% (2000).
Education: Percent of population age 25 and over with: High school diploma (including GED) or higher: 52.5% (2007); Bachelor's degree or higher: 6.1% (2007); Master's degree or higher: 1.0% (2007).

School District(s)

Lafayette County School District (PK-12)
    2005-06 Enrollment: 1,058 . . . . (386) 294-4107
Housing: Homeownership rate: 68.9% (2007); Median home value: $103,788 (2007); Median rent: $266 per month (2000); Median age of housing: 24 years (2000).
Newspapers: Mayo Free Press (General - Circulation 1,700)
Transportation: Commute to work: 89.4% car, 0.0% public transportation, 2.6% walk, 1.3% work from home (2000); Travel time to work: 47.1% less than 15 minutes, 28.3% 15 to 30 minutes, 13.9% 30 to 45 minutes, 2.1% 45 to 60 minutes, 8.6% 60 minutes or more (2000)
Additional Information Contacts
Lafayette County Chamber of Commerce . . . . (904) 294-2705

Lake County

Located in central Florida; bounded on the northeast by the St. Johns River; rolling terrain with many lakes; includes part of Apopka and Ocala National Forests. Covers a land area of 953.15 square miles, a water area of 203.25 square miles, and is located in the Eastern Time Zone. The county was founded in 1887. County seat is Tavares.

Lake County is part of the Orlando-Kissimmee, FL Metropolitan Statistical Area. The entire metro area includes: Lake County, FL; Orange County, FL; Osceola County, FL; Seminole County, FL

Weather Station: Clermont 7 S — Elevation: 108 feet

	Jan	Feb	Mar	Apr	May	Jun	Jul	Aug	Sep	Oct	Nov	Dec
High	70	73	78	83	88	90	92	91	89	83	77	72
Low	49	51	55	59	65	70	72	72	71	65	58	52
Precip	3.2	2.7	4.0	2.2	3.8	7.9	6.8	6.9	5.8	2.5	2.4	2.4
Snow	tr	tr	0.0	0.0	0.0	0.0	0.0	0.0	0.0	0.0	0.0	0.0

High and Low temperatures in degrees Fahrenheit; Precipitation and Snow in inches

Weather Station: Lisbon — Elevation: 65 feet

	Jan	Feb	Mar	Apr	May	Jun	Jul	Aug	Sep	Oct	Nov	Dec
High	69	71	77	81	87	90	91	91	89	83	76	70
Low	47	49	53	58	65	71	72	72	71	63	55	49
Precip	3.4	3.0	4.2	2.8	4.2	6.1	5.5	6.3	5.6	2.6	2.5	2.6
Snow	tr	tr	0.0	0.0	0.0	0.0	0.0	0.0	0.0	0.0	0.0	0.0

High and Low temperatures in degrees Fahrenheit; Precipitation and Snow in inches

Population: 152,104 (1990); 210,528 (2000); 287,348 (2007); 336,938 (2012 projected); Race: 84.5% White, 8.7% Black, 1.5% Asian, 9.9% Hispanic of any race (2007); Density: 301.5 persons per square mile (2007); Average household size: 2.38 (2007); Median age: 44.5 (2007); Males per 100 females: 94.4 (2007).
Religion: Five largest groups: 12.2% Southern Baptist Convention, 9.1% Catholic Church, 4.7% The United Methodist Church, 2.5% Presbyterian Church (U.S.A.), 1.2% Church of God (Cleveland, Tennessee) (2000).
Economy: Unemployment rate: 4.4% (11/2007); Total civilian labor force: 128,858 (11/2007); Leading industries: 20.0% retail trade; 18.5% health care and social assistance; 11.8% construction (2005); Farms: 1,798 totaling 180,245 acres (2002); Companies that employ 500 or more persons: 7 (2005); Companies that employ 100 to 499 persons: 106 (2005); Companies that employ less than 100 persons: 6,103 (2005); Black-owned businesses: 797 (2002); Hispanic-owned businesses: 636 (2002); Asian-owned businesses: 361 (2002); Women-owned businesses: 5,238 (2002); Retail sales per capita: $12,057 (2007). Single-family building permits issued: 5,637 (2006); Multi-family building permits issued: 472 (2006).

Income: Per capita income: $23,823 (2007); Median household income: $43,462 (2007); Average household income: $56,235 (2007); Percent of households with income of $100,000 or more: 11.8% (2007); Poverty rate: 11.4% (2005); Bankruptcy rate: 1.57% (2006).
Taxes: Total county taxes per capita: $397 (2005); County property taxes per capita: $240 (2005).
Education: Percent of population age 25 and over with: High school diploma (including GED) or higher: 80.4% (2007); Bachelor's degree or higher: 17.2% (2007); Master's degree or higher: 5.4% (2007).
Housing: Homeownership rate: 82.0% (2007); Median home value: $160,236 (2007); Median rent: $424 per month (2000); Median age of housing: 16 years (2000).
Health: Birth rate: 110.0 per 10,000 population (2006); Death rate: 111.4 per 10,000 population (2006); Age-adjusted cancer mortality rate: 176.1 deaths per 100,000 population (2004); Air Quality Index: 92.4% good, 7.6% moderate, 0.0% unhealthy for sensitive individuals, 0.0% unhealthy (percent of days in 2006); Number of physicians: 17.4 per 10,000 population (2005); Hospital beds: 27.2 per 10,000 population (2004); Hospital admissions: 1,248.8 per 10,000 population (2004).
Elections: 2004 Presidential election results: 60.0% Bush, 38.9% Kerry, 0.5% Nader, 0.2% Badnarik
National and State Parks: General James A. Van Fleet Trail State Park; Hontoon Island State Park; Lake Griffin State Park; Lake Louisa State Park
Additional Information Contacts
Lake County Government . . . . (352) 742-4100
    http://www.lakecountyfl.gov
Astor Chamber of Commerce . . . . (352) 759-2679
    http://www.astorchamber.com
City of Clermont . . . . (352) 241-9248
    http://cityofclermont.com
City of Eustis . . . . (352) 483-5430
    http://www.eustis.org
City of Leesburg . . . . (352) 728-9700
    http://www.ci.leesburg.fl.us
City of Minneola . . . . (352) 394-3598
    http://www.minneola.us
City of Mount Dora . . . . (352) 735-7100
    http://ci.mount-dora.fl.us
City of Tavares . . . . (352) 742-6209
    http://www.tavares.org
Clermont Chamber of Commerce . . . . (352) 394-4191
    http://www.southlakechamber-fl.com
East Lake County Chamber of Commerce . . . . (352) 383-8801
    http://elcchamber.com
Eustis Chamber of Commerce . . . . (352) 357-3434
    http://www.eustischamber.org
Lady Lake Chamber of Commerce . . . . (352) 753-6029
    http://ladylakechamber.com
Leesburg Area Chamber of Commerce . . . . (352) 787-2131
    http://www.leesburgchamber.com
Mount Dora Chamber of Commerce . . . . (352) 383-2165
    http://www.mountdora.com
Tavares Chamber of Commerce . . . . (352) 343-2531
    http://www.tavareschamber.com
Town of Lady Lake . . . . (352) 751-1500
    http://www.ladylake.org
Umatilla Chamber of Commerce . . . . (352) 669-3511
    http://www.umatillachamber.org

Lake County Communities

ALTOONA (CDP). Covers a land area of 0.448 square miles and a water area of 0.056 square miles. Located at 28.96° N. Lat.; 81.64° W. Long. Elevation is 98 feet.
Population: 52 (1990); 88 (2000); 111 (2007); 123 (2012 projected); Race: 97.3% White, 0.0% Black, 0.0% Asian, 2.7% Hispanic of any race (2007); Density: 247.9 persons per square mile (2007); Average household size: 2.31 (2007); Median age: 43.8 (2007); Males per 100 females: 91.4 (2007); Marriage status: 7.0% never married, 74.0% now married, 0.0% widowed, 19.0% divorced (2000); Foreign born: 0.0% (2000); Ancestry (includes multiple ancestries): 30.7% United States or American, 18.4% Other groups, 8.8% Irish (2000).
Economy: Employment by occupation: 0.0% management, 0.0% professional, 56.8% services, 0.0% sales, 22.7% farming, 0.0% construction, 20.5% production (2000).

Income: Per capita income: $24,392 (2007); Median household income: $64,000 (2007); Average household income: $56,406 (2007); Percent of households with income of $100,000 or more: 6.3% (2007); Poverty rate: 0.0% (2000).
Education: Percent of population age 25 and over with: High school diploma (including GED) or higher: 85.7% (2007); Bachelor's degree or higher: 1.2% (2007); Master's degree or higher: 1.2% (2007).
School District(s)
Lake County School District (PK-12)
    2005-06 Enrollment: 36,117 . . . . (352) 253-6510
Housing: Homeownership rate: 68.8% (2007); Median home value: $117,500 (2007); Median rent: $296 per month (2000); Median age of housing: 26 years (2000).
Transportation: Commute to work: 77.3% car, 0.0% public transportation, 22.7% walk, 0.0% work from home (2000); Travel time to work: 22.7% less than 15 minutes, 0.0% 15 to 30 minutes, 77.3% 30 to 45 minutes, 0.0% 45 to 60 minutes, 0.0% 60 minutes or more (2000)

ASTATULA (town). Covers a land area of 2.186 square miles and a water area of 0.016 square miles. Located at 28.71° N. Lat.; 81.73° W. Long. Elevation is 95 feet.
Population: 1,064 (1990); 1,298 (2000); 1,717 (2007); 1,987 (2012 projected); Race: 83.5% White, 2.0% Black, 0.3% Asian, 24.8% Hispanic of any race (2007); Density: 785.4 persons per square mile (2007); Average household size: 2.63 (2007); Median age: 36.6 (2007); Males per 100 females: 93.1 (2007); Marriage status: 17.5% never married, 66.9% now married, 6.9% widowed, 8.6% divorced (2000); Foreign born: 11.5% (2000); Ancestry (includes multiple ancestries): 23.0% Other groups, 18.2% United States or American, 16.3% German, 12.8% English, 8.7% Irish (2000).
Economy: Employment by occupation: 8.3% management, 9.5% professional, 22.3% services, 20.1% sales, 9.5% farming, 12.7% construction, 17.6% production (2000).
Income: Per capita income: $19,212 (2007); Median household income: $39,397 (2007); Average household income: $50,440 (2007); Percent of households with income of $100,000 or more: 8.4% (2007); Poverty rate: 8.0% (2000).
Education: Percent of population age 25 and over with: High school diploma (including GED) or higher: 65.8% (2007); Bachelor's degree or higher: 4.0% (2007); Master's degree or higher: 1.8% (2007).
School District(s)
Lake County School District (PK-12)
    2005-06 Enrollment: 36,117 . . . . (352) 253-6510
Housing: Homeownership rate: 85.0% (2007); Median home value: $114,796 (2007); Median rent: $400 per month (2000); Median age of housing: 16 years (2000).
Transportation: Commute to work: 91.3% car, 0.6% public transportation, 0.4% walk, 5.2% work from home (2000); Travel time to work: 20.7% less than 15 minutes, 45.2% 15 to 30 minutes, 18.1% 30 to 45 minutes, 8.1% 45 to 60 minutes, 7.9% 60 minutes or more (2000)

ASTOR (CDP). Covers a land area of 2.465 square miles and a water area of 0.004 square miles. Located at 29.16° N. Lat.; 81.53° W. Long. Elevation is 3 feet.
Population: 1,283 (1990); 1,487 (2000); 1,698 (2007); 1,850 (2012 projected); Race: 95.5% White, 0.9% Black, 0.0% Asian, 16.7% Hispanic of any race (2007); Density: 688.9 persons per square mile (2007); Average household size: 2.35 (2007); Median age: 47.3 (2007); Males per 100 females: 96.8 (2007); Marriage status: 17.0% never married, 62.1% now married, 8.6% widowed, 12.2% divorced (2000); Foreign born: 8.0% (2000); Ancestry (includes multiple ancestries): 17.0% Other groups, 11.9% English, 9.6% German, 9.3% Irish, 8.6% United States or American (2000).
Economy: Employment by occupation: 6.4% management, 9.2% professional, 18.9% services, 29.4% sales, 9.5% farming, 14.1% construction, 12.4% production (2000).
Income: Per capita income: $17,142 (2007); Median household income: $35,179 (2007); Average household income: $40,315 (2007); Percent of households with income of $100,000 or more: 4.6% (2007); Poverty rate: 12.5% (2000).
Education: Percent of population age 25 and over with: High school diploma (including GED) or higher: 69.7% (2007); Bachelor's degree or higher: 11.6% (2007); Master's degree or higher: 2.5% (2007).

Housing: Homeownership rate: 84.3% (2007); Median home value: $106,974 (2007); Median rent: $335 per month (2000); Median age of housing: 19 years (2000).
Transportation: Commute to work: 90.1% car, 0.0% public transportation, 3.8% walk, 5.2% work from home (2000); Travel time to work: 47.1% less than 15 minutes, 10.1% 15 to 30 minutes, 10.1% 30 to 45 minutes, 10.0% 45 to 60 minutes, 22.7% 60 minutes or more (2000)
Additional Information Contacts
Astor Chamber of Commerce . . . . (352) 759-2679
    http://www.astorchamber.com

CITRUS RIDGE (CDP). Covers a land area of 46.845 square miles and a water area of 3.741 square miles. Located at 28.33° N. Lat.; 81.64° W. Long.
Population: 4,090 (1990); 12,015 (2000); 25,387 (2007); 34,277 (2012 projected); Race: 80.9% White, 4.8% Black, 3.7% Asian, 25.4% Hispanic of any race (2007); Density: 541.9 persons per square mile (2007); Average household size: 2.41 (2007); Median age: 38.5 (2007); Males per 100 females: 97.6 (2007); Marriage status: 23.5% never married, 63.5% now married, 4.3% widowed, 8.7% divorced (2000); Foreign born: 12.2% (2000); Ancestry (includes multiple ancestries): 24.1% Other groups, 15.6% German, 13.1% Irish, 11.2% Italian, 9.7% English (2000).
Economy: Employment by occupation: 16.7% management, 15.3% professional, 24.3% services, 28.7% sales, 0.2% farming, 6.5% construction, 8.2% production (2000).
Income: Per capita income: $25,501 (2007); Median household income: $52,615 (2007); Average household income: $61,394 (2007); Percent of households with income of $100,000 or more: 12.2% (2007); Poverty rate: 5.2% (2000).
Education: Percent of population age 25 and over with: High school diploma (including GED) or higher: 89.2% (2007); Bachelor's degree or higher: 18.8% (2007); Master's degree or higher: 2.6% (2007).
Housing: Homeownership rate: 78.1% (2007); Median home value: $189,290 (2007); Median rent: $572 per month (2000); Median age of housing: 4 years (2000).
Transportation: Commute to work: 95.5% car, 0.1% public transportation, 1.6% walk, 2.2% work from home (2000); Travel time to work: 14.1% less than 15 minutes, 47.7% 15 to 30 minutes, 24.6% 30 to 45 minutes, 8.8% 45 to 60 minutes, 4.7% 60 minutes or more (2000)

CLERMONT (city). Covers a land area of 10.486 square miles and a water area of 0.979 square miles. Located at 28.54° N. Lat.; 81.75° W. Long. Elevation is 141 feet.
History: Clermont was named for Clermont, France, the birthplace of A.F. Wrotnoski, one of its founders. Diatomite was mined near Clermont and used in the manufacture of moisture-proof tops for salt shakers.
Population: 7,208 (1990); 9,333 (2000); 16,164 (2007); 20,532 (2012 projected); Race: 82.9% White, 10.7% Black, 1.6% Asian, 9.3% Hispanic of any race (2007); Density: 1,541.5 persons per square mile (2007); Average household size: 2.26 (2007); Median age: 49.3 (2007); Males per 100 females: 90.0 (2007); Marriage status: 18.2% never married, 62.0% now married, 11.4% widowed, 8.4% divorced (2000); Foreign born: 6.5% (2000); Ancestry (includes multiple ancestries): 19.9% Other groups, 19.8% German, 13.2% Irish, 12.9% English, 7.3% Italian (2000).
Economy: Employment by occupation: 14.0% management, 17.8% professional, 22.5% services, 25.6% sales, 0.5% farming, 9.3% construction, 10.4% production (2000).
Income: Per capita income: $26,285 (2007); Median household income: $46,310 (2007); Average household income: $58,705 (2007); Percent of households with income of $100,000 or more: 12.7% (2007); Poverty rate: 7.8% (2000).
Education: Percent of population age 25 and over with: High school diploma (including GED) or higher: 86.9% (2007); Bachelor's degree or higher: 24.0% (2007); Master's degree or higher: 7.4% (2007).
School District(s)
Lake County School District (PK-12)
    2005-06 Enrollment: 36,117 . . . . (352) 253-6510
Housing: Homeownership rate: 74.8% (2007); Median home value: $211,875 (2007); Median rent: $505 per month (2000); Median age of housing: 19 years (2000).
Hospitals: South Lake Hospital (80 beds)
Safety: Violent crime rate: 108.4 per 10,000 population; Property crime rate: 557.9 per 10,000 population (2006).
Newspapers: South Lake Press (General - Circulation 3,000)

Transportation: Commute to work: 90.1% car, 0.9% public transportation, 3.8% walk, 4.4% work from home (2000); Travel time to work: 28.8% less than 15 minutes, 19.1% 15 to 30 minutes, 30.5% 30 to 45 minutes, 15.0% 45 to 60 minutes, 6.7% 60 minutes or more (2000)

Additional Information Contacts

City of Clermont . . . . (352) 241-9248
  http://cityofclermont.com
Clermont Chamber of Commerce . . . . (352) 394-4191
  http://www.southlakechamber-fl.com

EUSTIS (city).
Covers a land area of 8.354 square miles and a water area of 1.285 square miles. Located at 28.85° N. Lat.; 81.68° W. Long. Elevation is 69 feet.

History: Named for General Abram Eustis, a military leader in the Seminole Wars. Eustis was first known as Highlands and then as Pendryville. The town was settled in 1876 when A.S. Pendry planted a citrus grove and opened a hotel in which the post office was established.

Population: 13,440 (1990); 15,106 (2000); 17,145 (2007); 18,590 (2012 projected); Race: 74.7% White, 19.0% Black, 0.9% Asian, 11.1% Hispanic of any race (2007); Density: 2,052.3 persons per square mile (2007); Average household size: 2.35 (2007); Median age: 41.4 (2007); Males per 100 females: 85.5 (2007); Marriage status: 19.2% never married, 56.8% now married, 12.9% widowed, 11.2% divorced (2000); Foreign born: 4.3% (2000); Ancestry (includes multiple ancestries): 25.1% Other groups, 14.5% English, 13.5% German, 12.1% Irish, 9.7% United States or American (2000).

Economy: Single-family building permits issued: 210 (2006); Multi-family building permits issued: 102 (2006); Employment by occupation: 11.3% management, 20.7% professional, 19.3% services, 25.1% sales, 1.7% farming, 10.2% construction, 11.7% production (2000).

Income: Per capita income: $20,776 (2007); Median household income: $36,924 (2007); Average household income: $48,020 (2007); Percent of households with income of $100,000 or more: 9.6% (2007); Poverty rate: 15.3% (2000).

Education: Percent of population age 25 and over with: High school diploma (including GED) or higher: 78.0% (2007); Bachelor's degree or higher: 18.1% (2007); Master's degree or higher: 5.8% (2007).

School District(s)
Lake County School District (PK-12)
  2005-06 Enrollment: 36,117 . . . . (352) 253-6510

Vocational/Technical School(s)
Lake Technical Center (Public)
  Fall 2006 Enrollment: 887 . . . . (352) 589-2250
  2006-07 Tuition: $2,732

Housing: Homeownership rate: 69.8% (2007); Median home value: $141,517 (2007); Median rent: $401 per month (2000); Median age of housing: 22 years (2000).

Safety: Violent crime rate: 35.6 per 10,000 population; Property crime rate: 208.6 per 10,000 population (2006).

Transportation: Commute to work: 96.8% car, 0.0% public transportation, 0.4% walk, 2.5% work from home (2000); Travel time to work: 36.4% less than 15 minutes, 32.6% 15 to 30 minutes, 11.3% 30 to 45 minutes, 9.4% 45 to 60 minutes, 10.3% 60 minutes or more (2000)

Additional Information Contacts

City of Eustis . . . . (352) 483-5430
  http://www.eustis.org
Eustis Chamber of Commerce . . . . (352) 357-3434
  http://www.eustischamber.org

FERNDALE (CDP).
Covers a land area of 2.732 square miles and a water area of 0.107 square miles. Located at 28.61° N. Lat.; 81.70° W. Long. Elevation is 102 feet.

Population: 103 (1990); 233 (2000); 319 (2007); 376 (2012 projected); Race: 96.6% White, 0.6% Black, 0.0% Asian, 4.7% Hispanic of any race (2007); Density: 116.8 persons per square mile (2007); Average household size: 2.75 (2007); Median age: 37.2 (2007); Males per 100 females: 93.3 (2007); Marriage status: 11.6% never married, 69.7% now married, 3.0% widowed, 15.7% divorced (2000); Foreign born: 4.2% (2000); Ancestry (includes multiple ancestries): 20.1% German, 18.4% Italian, 17.7% United States or American, 14.6% Irish, 12.2% Other groups (2000).

Economy: Employment by occupation: 19.4% management, 9.7% professional, 10.3% services, 26.5% sales, 10.3% farming, 7.1% construction, 16.8% production (2000).

Income: Per capita income: $28,636 (2007); Median household income: $71,667 (2007); Average household income: $78,750 (2007); Percent of

households with income of $100,000 or more: 15.5% (2007); Poverty rate: 0.0% (2000).

Education: Percent of population age 25 and over with: High school diploma (including GED) or higher: 64.3% (2007); Bachelor's degree or higher: 12.2% (2007); Master's degree or higher: 0.0% (2007).

Housing: Homeownership rate: 85.3% (2007); Median home value: $162,500 (2007); Median rent: $n/a per month (2000); Median age of housing: 18 years (2000).

Transportation: Commute to work: 82.6% car, 0.0% public transportation, 0.0% walk, 4.5% work from home (2000); Travel time to work: 10.8% less than 15 minutes, 37.8% 15 to 30 minutes, 18.9% 30 to 45 minutes, 16.9% 45 to 60 minutes, 15.5% 60 minutes or more (2000)

FRUITLAND PARK (city).
Covers a land area of 2.917 square miles and a water area of 0.752 square miles. Located at 28.85° N. Lat.; 81.91° W. Long. Elevation is 108 feet.

History: Fruitland Park was founded in 1876 by Major O.P. Rooks, and named for the Fruitland Nurseries of Georgia, which specialized in rare fruits and flowers.

Population: 3,029 (1990); 3,186 (2000); 3,624 (2007); 3,925 (2012 projected); Race: 83.4% White, 10.9% Black, 2.3% Asian, 3.8% Hispanic of any race (2007); Density: 1,242.3 persons per square mile (2007); Average household size: 2.65 (2007); Median age: 35.0 (2007); Males per 100 females: 94.4 (2007); Marriage status: 21.0% never married, 57.9% now married, 7.9% widowed, 13.2% divorced (2000); Foreign born: 3.8% (2000); Ancestry (includes multiple ancestries): 18.0% Other groups, 14.5% Irish, 12.1% English, 11.8% German, 10.0% United States or American (2000).

Economy: Single-family building permits issued: 83 (2006); Multi-family building permits issued: 4 (2006); Employment by occupation: 9.8% management, 17.2% professional, 18.2% services, 28.5% sales, 1.2% farming, 11.9% construction, 13.3% production (2000).

Income: Per capita income: $20,028 (2007); Median household income: $44,957 (2007); Average household income: $52,980 (2007); Percent of households with income of $100,000 or more: 8.1% (2007); Poverty rate: 10.2% (2000).

Education: Percent of population age 25 and over with: High school diploma (including GED) or higher: 82.6% (2007); Bachelor's degree or higher: 9.7% (2007); Master's degree or higher: 2.8% (2007).

School District(s)
Lake County School District (PK-12)
  2005-06 Enrollment: 36,117 . . . . (352) 253-6510

Housing: Homeownership rate: 73.5% (2007); Median home value: $130,078 (2007); Median rent: $398 per month (2000); Median age of housing: 26 years (2000).

Safety: Violent crime rate: 24.7 per 10,000 population; Property crime rate: 277.6 per 10,000 population (2006).

Newspapers: Lake News (General - Circulation 21,500)

Transportation: Commute to work: 96.2% car, 0.6% public transportation, 1.8% walk, 0.3% work from home (2000); Travel time to work: 38.2% less than 15 minutes, 38.1% 15 to 30 minutes, 12.0% 30 to 45 minutes, 5.3% 45 to 60 minutes, 6.5% 60 minutes or more (2000)

Additional Information Contacts

Leesburg Area Chamber of Commerce . . . . (352) 787-2131
  http://www.leesburgchamber.com

GRAND ISLAND (unincorporated postal area, zip code 32735).
Covers a land area of 5.092 square miles and a water area of 0.910 square miles. Located at 28.89° N. Lat.; 81.74° W. Long. Elevation is 106 feet.

History: Grand Island was settled in the late 1880's and named because the several lakes that surrounded it made it seem like an island.

Population: 2,532 (2000); Race: 96.0% White, 0.9% Black, 1.6% Asian, 3.2% Hispanic of any race (2000); Density: 497.3 persons per square mile (2000); Age: 19.0% under 18, 34.3% over 64 (2000); Marriage status: 5.9% never married, 77.7% now married, 9.1% widowed, 7.2% divorced (2000); Foreign born: 4.3% (2000); Ancestry (includes multiple ancestries): 17.3% German, 15.9% English, 15.7% United States or American, 14.5% Irish, 13.4% Other groups (2000).

Economy: Employment by occupation: 14.4% management, 23.9% professional, 15.5% services, 33.2% sales, 0.0% farming, 10.2% construction, 2.9% production (2000).

Income: Per capita income: $21,360 (2000); Median household income: $33,948 (2000); Poverty rate: 4.5% (2000).

Education: Percent of population age 25 and over with: High school diploma (including GED) or higher: 84.6% (2000); Bachelor's degree or higher: 15.4% (2000).
Housing: Homeownership rate: 94.7% (2000); Median home value: $90,300 (2000); Median rent: $367 per month (2000); Median age of housing: 12 years (2000).
Transportation: Commute to work: 93.9% car, 0.0% public transportation, 0.0% walk, 4.8% work from home (2000); Travel time to work: 25.7% less than 15 minutes, 47.2% 15 to 30 minutes, 8.6% 30 to 45 minutes, 7.2% 45 to 60 minutes, 11.4% 60 minutes or more (2000)

GROVELAND (city).
Covers a land area of 2.631 square miles and a water area of 0.394 square miles. Located at 28.55° N. Lat.; 81.85° W. Long. Elevation is 102 feet.
History: Groveland was named for the large citrus groves that surrounded it when it was founded in the early 1900's. It was first called Taylorville, and was renamed Groveland in 1911. Many of Groveland's early residents were of Swedish descent.
Population: 2,405 (1990); 2,360 (2000); 3,795 (2007); 4,725 (2012 projected); Race: 66.2% White, 18.4% Black, 0.9% Asian, 23.6% Hispanic of any race (2007); Density: 1,442.7 persons per square mile (2007); Average household size: 2.75 (2007); Median age: 32.6 (2007); Males per 100 females: 99.5 (2007); Marriage status: 28.0% never married, 54.0% now married, 7.1% widowed, 10.8% divorced (2000); Foreign born: 5.9% (2000); Ancestry (includes multiple ancestries): 34.1% Other groups, 15.6% United States or American, 12.5% German, 9.7% Irish, 7.1% English (2000).
Economy: Single-family building permits issued: 479 (2006); Multi-family building permits issued: 0 (2006); Employment by occupation: 8.1% management, 8.3% professional, 22.7% services, 25.7% sales, 3.4% farming, 15.9% construction, 15.9% production (2000).
Income: Per capita income: $17,345 (2007); Median household income: $37,152 (2007); Average household income: $47,767 (2007); Percent of households with income of $100,000 or more: 8.3% (2007); Poverty rate: 18.8% (2000).
Education: Percent of population age 25 and over with: High school diploma (including GED) or higher: 68.6% (2007); Bachelor's degree or higher: 8.6% (2007); Master's degree or higher: 3.2% (2007).

School District(s)
Lake County School District (PK-12)
    2005-06 Enrollment: 36,117 . . . . (352) 253-6510
Housing: Homeownership rate: 68.0% (2007); Median home value: $143,901 (2007); Median rent: $351 per month (2000); Median age of housing: 30 years (2000).
Safety: Violent crime rate: 22.7 per 10,000 population; Property crime rate: 302.3 per 10,000 population (2006).
Transportation: Commute to work: 95.1% car, 0.2% public transportation, 0.8% walk, 2.2% work from home (2000); Travel time to work: 29.5% less than 15 minutes, 28.4% 15 to 30 minutes, 18.7% 30 to 45 minutes, 13.1% 45 to 60 minutes, 10.3% 60 minutes or more (2000)

HOWEY-IN-THE-HILLS (town).
Aka Howey. Covers a land area of 1.768 square miles and a water area of 0.086 square miles. Located at 28.71° N. Lat.; 81.77° W. Long. Elevation is 121 feet.
Population: 726 (1990); 956 (2000); 1,191 (2007); 1,335 (2012 projected); Race: 96.5% White, 0.7% Black, 1.1% Asian, 3.5% Hispanic of any race (2007); Density: 673.5 persons per square mile (2007); Average household size: 2.40 (2007); Median age: 46.0 (2007); Males per 100 females: 97.2 (2007); Marriage status: 16.2% never married, 68.3% now married, 5.9% widowed, 9.6% divorced (2000); Foreign born: 5.4% (2000); Ancestry (includes multiple ancestries): 21.1% German, 18.6% English, 14.8% United States or American, 13.0% Irish, 8.1% Other groups (2000).
Economy: Single-family building permits issued: 6 (2006); Multi-family building permits issued: 0 (2006); Employment by occupation: 16.2% management, 21.2% professional, 11.9% services, 30.6% sales, 0.5% farming, 10.3% construction, 9.4% production (2000).
Income: Per capita income: $28,403 (2007); Median household income: $56,914 (2007); Average household income: $68,201 (2007); Percent of households with income of $100,000 or more: 18.1% (2007); Poverty rate: 5.7% (2000).
Education: Percent of population age 25 and over with: High school diploma (including GED) or higher: 87.4% (2007); Bachelor's degree or higher: 27.7% (2007); Master's degree or higher: 8.3% (2007).

Housing: Homeownership rate: 84.5% (2007); Median home value: $201,271 (2007); Median rent: $583 per month (2000); Median age of housing: 29 years (2000).
Safety: Violent crime rate: 0.0 per 10,000 population; Property crime rate: 41.2 per 10,000 population (2006).
Transportation: Commute to work: 88.0% car, 0.0% public transportation, 1.9% walk, 8.5% work from home (2000); Travel time to work: 24.0% less than 15 minutes, 37.6% 15 to 30 minutes, 16.2% 30 to 45 minutes, 12.1% 45 to 60 minutes, 10.1% 60 minutes or more (2000)

LADY LAKE (town).
Covers a land area of 6.618 square miles and a water area of 0.135 square miles. Located at 28.92° N. Lat.; 81.93° W. Long. Elevation is 85 feet.
Population: 8,917 (1990); 11,828 (2000); 13,139 (2007); 14,076 (2012 projected); Race: 93.8% White, 4.1% Black, 0.5% Asian, 2.9% Hispanic of any race (2007); Density: 1,985.2 persons per square mile (2007); Average household size: 1.88 (2007); Median age: 69.8 (2007); Males per 100 females: 87.2 (2007); Marriage status: 6.8% never married, 73.7% now married, 13.4% widowed, 6.1% divorced (2000); Foreign born: 4.6% (2000); Ancestry (includes multiple ancestries): 19.1% German, 18.2% English, 15.2% Irish, 10.2% United States or American, 7.5% Italian (2000).
Economy: Single-family building permits issued: 54 (2006); Multi-family building permits issued: 0 (2006); Employment by occupation: 7.1% management, 12.6% professional, 26.4% services, 29.8% sales, 0.3% farming, 11.4% construction, 12.4% production (2000).
Income: Per capita income: $25,373 (2007); Median household income: $37,840 (2007); Average household income: $47,337 (2007); Percent of households with income of $100,000 or more: 5.8% (2007); Poverty rate: 8.4% (2000).
Education: Percent of population age 25 and over with: High school diploma (including GED) or higher: 82.4% (2007); Bachelor's degree or higher: 12.3% (2007); Master's degree or higher: 5.0% (2007).

School District(s)
Lake County School District (PK-12)
    2005-06 Enrollment: 36,117 . . . . (352) 253-6510
Housing: Homeownership rate: 91.5% (2007); Median home value: $137,072 (2007); Median rent: $431 per month (2000); Median age of housing: 11 years (2000).
Safety: Violent crime rate: 23.8 per 10,000 population; Property crime rate: 246.5 per 10,000 population (2006).
Newspapers: The Daily Sun (Circulation 18,900)
Transportation: Commute to work: 91.4% car, 0.7% public transportation, 1.8% walk, 2.2% work from home (2000); Travel time to work: 39.9% less than 15 minutes, 36.6% 15 to 30 minutes, 12.3% 30 to 45 minutes, 5.3% 45 to 60 minutes, 5.9% 60 minutes or more (2000)
Additional Information Contacts
Lady Lake Chamber of Commerce . . . . (352) 753-6029
    http://ladylakechamber.com
Town of Lady Lake. . . . . (352) 751-1500
    http://www.ladylake.org

LAKE KATHRYN (CDP).
Covers a land area of 2.800 square miles and a water area of 0.069 square miles. Located at 29.01° N. Lat.; 81.49° W. Long. Elevation is 59 feet.
Population: 861 (1990); 845 (2000); 973 (2007); 1,060 (2012 projected); Race: 94.5% White, 1.1% Black, 0.6% Asian, 2.5% Hispanic of any race (2007); Density: 347.5 persons per square mile (2007); Average household size: 2.41 (2007); Median age: 40.5 (2007); Males per 100 females: 108.4 (2007); Marriage status: 28.5% never married, 41.9% now married, 10.1% widowed, 19.5% divorced (2000); Foreign born: 0.0% (2000); Ancestry (includes multiple ancestries): 30.6% Irish, 25.2% Other groups, 20.8% German, 12.7% Italian, 6.8% United States or American (2000).
Economy: Employment by occupation: 4.0% management, 9.3% professional, 30.8% services, 20.7% sales, 0.0% farming, 17.6% construction, 17.6% production (2000).
Income: Per capita income: $9,738 (2007); Median household income: $18,953 (2007); Average household income: $23,453 (2007); Percent of households with income of $100,000 or more: 0.0% (2007); Poverty rate: 36.9% (2000).
Education: Percent of population age 25 and over with: High school diploma (including GED) or higher: 45.5% (2007); Bachelor's degree or higher: 0.0% (2007); Master's degree or higher: 0.0% (2007).

$74,038 (2007); Median rent: $390 per month (2000); Median age of housing: 25 years (2000).

Transportation: Commute to work: 100.0% car, 0.0% public transportation, 0.0% walk, 0.0% work from home (2000); Travel time to work: 4.0% less than 15 minutes, 33.5% 15 to 30 minutes, 7.9% 30 to 45 minutes, 42.7% 45 to 60 minutes, 11.9% 60 minutes or more (2000)

LAKE MACK-FOREST HILLS (CDP). Covers a land area of
4.737 square miles and a water area of 0.302 square miles. Located at 28.99° N. Lat.; 81.42° W. Long. Elevation is 69 feet.

Population: 923 (1990); 989 (2000); 1,107 (2007); 1,185 (2012 projected); Race: 92.8% White, 0.1% Black, 1.2% Asian, 7.0% Hispanic of any race (2007); Density: 233.7 persons per square mile (2007); Average household size: 2.45 (2007); Median age: 38.3 (2007); Males per 100 females: 100.2 (2007); Marriage status: 18.5% never married, 56.5% now married, 7.0% widowed, 18.0% divorced (2000); Foreign born: 2.1% (2000); Ancestry (includes multiple ancestries): 14.9% German, 11.9% Irish, 11.8% Other groups, 7.8% English, 6.4% United States or American (2000).

Economy: Employment by occupation: 6.1% management, 4.0% professional, 12.5% services, 10.6% sales, 7.7% farming, 39.1% construction, 19.9% production (2000).

Income: Per capita income: $15,117 (2007); Median household income: $29,894 (2007); Average household income: $37,024 (2007); Percent of households with income of $100,000 or more: 3.8% (2007); Poverty rate: 10.3% (2000).

Education: Percent of population age 25 and over with: High school diploma (including GED) or higher: 55.8% (2007); Bachelor's degree or higher: 0.8% (2007); Master's degree or higher: 0.8% (2007).

Housing: Homeownership rate: 81.9% (2007); Median home value: $68,387 (2007); Median rent: $288 per month (2000); Median age of housing: 23 years (2000).

Transportation: Commute to work: 100.0% car, 0.0% public transportation, 0.0% walk, 0.0% work from home (2000); Travel time to work: 6.6% less than 15 minutes, 33.8% 15 to 30 minutes, 21.8% 30 to 45 minutes, 19.7% 45 to 60 minutes, 18.1% 60 minutes or more (2000)

LEESBURG (city). Covers a land area of 18.666 square miles and a
water area of 5.779 square miles. Located at 28.81° N. Lat.; 81.88° W. Long. Elevation is 95 feet.

History: Named for the Lee family of New York, the town's founders. Leesburg was founded in 1856 in an area that produced citrus fruit, berries, grapes, and watermelons.

Population: 15,039 (1990); 15,956 (2000); 18,532 (2007); 20,253 (2012 projected); Race: 60.0% White, 33.6% Black, 2.4% Asian, 6.5% Hispanic of any race (2007); Density: 992.8 persons per square mile (2007); Average household size: 2.33 (2007); Median age: 39.5 (2007); Males per 100 females: 84.7 (2007); Marriage status: 22.5% never married, 48.6% now married, 14.3% widowed, 14.5% divorced (2000); Foreign born: 5.6% (2000); Ancestry (includes multiple ancestries): 29.9% Other groups, 11.8% English, 11.8% German, 8.3% United States or American, 7.5% Irish (2000).

Economy: Single-family building permits issued: 471 (2006); Multi-family building permits issued: 194 (2006); Employment by occupation: 8.7% management, 16.2% professional, 24.1% services, 26.2% sales, 1.6% farming, 11.5% construction, 11.8% production (2000).

Income: Per capita income: $17,782 (2007); Median household income: $27,825 (2007); Average household income: $40,312 (2007); Percent of households with income of $100,000 or more: 5.4% (2007); Poverty rate: 19.8% (2000).

Education: Percent of population age 25 and over with: High school diploma (including GED) or higher: 72.1% (2007); Bachelor's degree or higher: 13.9% (2007); Master's degree or higher: 5.3% (2007).

School District(s)
Lake County School District (PK-12)
    2005-06 Enrollment: 36,117 . . . . (352) 253-6510
Four-year College(s)
Beacon College (Private, Not-for-profit)
    Fall 2006 Enrollment: 112 . . . . (352) 787-7660
    2006-07 Tuition: In-state $25,700; Out-of-state $25,700
Two-year College(s)
Lake-Sumter Community College (Public)
    Fall 2006 Enrollment: 3,641. . . . . (352) 787-3747
    2006-07 Tuition: In-state $2,008; Out-of-state $7,552

$109,598 (2007); Median rent: $380 per month (2000); Median age of housing: 26 years (2000).

Hospitals: Leesburg Regional Medical Center (294 beds)

Safety: Violent crime rate: 152.0 per 10,000 population; Property crime rate: 655.4 per 10,000 population (2006).

Newspapers: Daily Commercial (Circulation 29,718)

Transportation: Commute to work: 91.6% car, 0.7% public transportation, 3.5% walk, 1.7% work from home (2000); Travel time to work: 50.6% less than 15 minutes, 29.2% 15 to 30 minutes, 12.0% 30 to 45 minutes, 3.7% 45 to 60 minutes, 4.5% 60 minutes or more (2000)

Airports: Leesburg Regional

Additional Information Contacts

City of Leesburg . . . . (352) 728-9700
    http://www.ci.leesburg.fl.us

LISBON (CDP). Covers a land area of 1.883 square miles and a water
area of 0.098 square miles. Located at 28.88° N. Lat.; 81.78° W. Long. Elevation is 69 feet.

Population: 179 (1990); 273 (2000); 350 (2007); 403 (2012 projected); Race: 85.7% White, 0.0% Black, 0.0% Asian, 17.4% Hispanic of any race (2007); Density: 185.8 persons per square mile (2007); Average household size: 2.57 (2007); Median age: 41.4 (2007); Males per 100 females: 108.3 (2007); Marriage status: 20.3% never married, 47.6% now married, 19.3% widowed, 12.8% divorced (2000); Foreign born: 6.7% (2000); Ancestry (includes multiple ancestries): 29.6% United States or American, 11.3% English, 11.3% German, 7.9% Other groups, 3.3% Italian (2000).

Economy: Employment by occupation: 8.4% management, 16.8% professional, 10.5% services, 28.4% sales, 2.1% farming, 15.8% construction, 17.9% production (2000).

Income: Per capita income: $14,336 (2007); Median household income: $27,000 (2007); Average household income: $36,893 (2007); Percent of households with income of $100,000 or more: 7.4% (2007); Poverty rate: 7.5% (2000).

Education: Percent of population age 25 and over with: High school diploma (including GED) or higher: 61.5% (2007); Bachelor's degree or higher: 5.1% (2007); Master's degree or higher: 0.0% (2007).

Housing: Homeownership rate: 77.2% (2007); Median home value: $99,167 (2007); Median rent: $340 per month (2000); Median age of housing: 10 years (2000).

Transportation: Commute to work: 100.0% car, 0.0% public transportation, 0.0% walk, 0.0% work from home (2000); Travel time to work: 16.8% less than 15 minutes, 48.4% 15 to 30 minutes, 34.7% 30 to 45 minutes, 0.0% 45 to 60 minutes, 0.0% 60 minutes or more (2000)

MASCOTTE (city). Covers a land area of 2.429 square miles and a
water area of 0.389 square miles. Located at 28.57° N. Lat.; 81.88° W. Long. Elevation is 135 feet.

History: Mascotte developed around a railroad station as a trading center for citrus growers.

Population: 1,973 (1990); 2,687 (2000); 4,607 (2007); 5,843 (2012 projected); Race: 49.2% White, 4.8% Black, 1.0% Asian, 60.5% Hispanic of any race (2007); Density: 1,896.6 persons per square mile (2007); Average household size: 3.31 (2007); Median age: 27.3 (2007); Males per 100 females: 117.0 (2007); Marriage status: 28.6% never married, 56.0% now married, 4.2% widowed, 11.2% divorced (2000); Foreign born: 24.9% (2000); Ancestry (includes multiple ancestries): 48.7% Other groups, 13.9% United States or American, 5.8% German, 5.4% Irish, 5.1% English (2000).

Economy: Single-family building permits issued: 100 (2006); Multi-family building permits issued: 0 (2006); Employment by occupation: 5.3% management, 6.9% professional, 17.8% services, 17.1% sales, 11.7% farming, 25.9% construction, 15.2% production (2000).

Income: Per capita income: $15,512 (2007); Median household income: $44,765 (2007); Average household income: $51,121 (2007); Percent of households with income of $100,000 or more: 8.0% (2007); Poverty rate: 15.7% (2000).

Education: Percent of population age 25 and over with: High school diploma (including GED) or higher: 52.7% (2007); Bachelor's degree or higher: 5.7% (2007); Master's degree or higher: 1.1% (2007).

School District(s)
Lake County School District (PK-12)
    2005-06 Enrollment: 36,117 . . . . (352) 253-6510

$141,296 (2007); Median rent: $416 per month (2000); Median age of housing: 11 years (2000).
Safety: Violent crime rate: 16.9 per 10,000 population; Property crime rate: 165.1 per 10,000 population (2006).
Transportation: Commute to work: 91.3% car, 0.0% public transportation, 0.9% walk, 0.5% work from home (2000); Travel time to work: 10.3% less than 15 minutes, 29.0% 15 to 30 minutes, 21.7% 30 to 45 minutes, 20.0% 45 to 60 minutes, 19.1% 60 minutes or more (2000)

MINNEOLA (city).
Covers a land area of 3.055 square miles and a water area of 0.173 square miles. Located at 28.57° N. Lat.; 81.74° W. Long. Elevation is 98 feet.
Population: 2,028 (1990); 5,435 (2000); 9,975 (2007); 12,808 (2012 projected); Race: 82.6% White, 7.9% Black, 2.5% Asian, 18.4% Hispanic of any race (2007); Density: 3,265.0 persons per square mile (2007); Average household size: 2.86 (2007); Median age: 34.0 (2007); Males per 100 females: 96.6 (2007); Marriage status: 17.5% never married, 71.0% now married, 3.9% widowed, 7.6% divorced (2000); Foreign born: 7.9% (2000); Ancestry (includes multiple ancestries): 19.4% Other groups, 16.0% German, 13.7% English, 12.4% Irish, 6.6% United States or American (2000).
Economy: Single-family building permits issued: 35 (2006); Multi-family building permits issued: 0 (2006); Employment by occupation: 13.8% management, 20.3% professional, 16.6% services, 28.5% sales, 0.3% farming, 11.7% construction, 8.7% production (2000).
Income: Per capita income: $23,538 (2007); Median household income: $55,347 (2007); Average household income: $67,280 (2007); Percent of households with income of $100,000 or more: 17.8% (2007); Poverty rate: 6.1% (2000).
Education: Percent of population age 25 and over with: High school diploma (including GED) or higher: 84.4% (2007); Bachelor's degree or higher: 23.5% (2007); Master's degree or higher: 4.6% (2007).
Housing: Homeownership rate: 80.5% (2007); Median home value: $202,500 (2007); Median rent: $581 per month (2000); Median age of housing: 5 years (2000).
Transportation: Commute to work: 96.5% car, 0.0% public transportation, 0.9% walk, 1.2% work from home (2000); Travel time to work: 23.8% less than 15 minutes, 17.2% 15 to 30 minutes, 36.8% 30 to 45 minutes, 16.7% 45 to 60 minutes, 5.4% 60 minutes or more (2000)
Additional Information Contacts
City of Minneola . . . . (352) 394-3598
   http://www.minneola.us

MONTVERDE (town).
Covers a land area of 1.571 square miles and a water area of 0.206 square miles. Located at 28.59° N. Lat.; 81.67° W. Long. Elevation is 108 feet.
History: Montverde developed as the center of a grape-growing area.
Population: 888 (1990); 882 (2000); 1,177 (2007); 1,372 (2012 projected); Race: 96.0% White, 2.1% Black, 0.4% Asian, 2.2% Hispanic of any race (2007); Density: 749.3 persons per square mile (2007); Average household size: 2.47 (2007); Median age: 42.9 (2007); Males per 100 females: 97.5 (2007); Marriage status: 9.6% never married, 71.5% now married, 7.2% widowed, 11.7% divorced (2000); Foreign born: 3.4% (2000); Ancestry (includes multiple ancestries): 25.6% German, 19.9% English, 15.7% Irish, 10.6% Italian, 8.2% United States or American (2000).
Economy: Employment by occupation: 14.2% management, 17.4% professional, 11.0% services, 31.2% sales, 1.1% farming, 13.3% construction, 11.7% production (2000).
Income: Per capita income: $25,484 (2007); Median household income: $53,750 (2007); Average household income: $62,883 (2007); Percent of households with income of $100,000 or more: 13.4% (2007); Poverty rate: 5.3% (2000).
Education: Percent of population age 25 and over with: High school diploma (including GED) or higher: 84.1% (2007); Bachelor's degree or higher: 14.4% (2007); Master's degree or higher: 5.0% (2007).
Housing: Homeownership rate: 86.0% (2007); Median home value: $194,940 (2007); Median rent: $504 per month (2000); Median age of housing: 18 years (2000).
Transportation: Commute to work: 88.8% car, 0.0% public transportation, 5.2% walk, 4.0% work from home (2000); Travel time to work: 19.8% less than 15 minutes, 16.6% 15 to 30 minutes, 36.1% 30 to 45 minutes, 17.1% 45 to 60 minutes, 10.4% 60 minutes or more (2000)

MOUNT DORA (city).
Covers a land area of 4.917 square miles and a water area of 0.844 square miles. Located at 28.80° N. Lat.; 81.64° W. Long. Elevation is 144 feet.
History: Mount Dora was founded in 1882 on the shores of Lake Dora, named for Dora Ann Drawdy who lived in the area. The South Florida Chautauqua was established at Mount Dora in 1885.
Population: 7,670 (1990); 9,418 (2000); 11,483 (2007); 12,854 (2012 projected); Race: 74.6% White, 20.3% Black, 1.1% Asian, 10.9% Hispanic of any race (2007); Density: 2,335.3 persons per square mile (2007); Average household size: 2.24 (2007); Median age: 47.0 (2007); Males per 100 females: 87.1 (2007); Marriage status: 17.0% never married, 60.2% now married, 12.1% widowed, 10.7% divorced (2000); Foreign born: 5.4% (2000); Ancestry (includes multiple ancestries): 25.3% Other groups, 14.3% English, 14.2% German, 13.0% Irish, 8.6% United States or American (2000).
Economy: Single-family building permits issued: 199 (2006); Multi-family building permits issued: 0 (2006); Employment by occupation: 16.8% management, 21.5% professional, 14.4% services, 22.5% sales, 3.3% farming, 10.6% construction, 10.8% production (2000).
Income: Per capita income: $25,831 (2007); Median household income: $40,486 (2007); Average household income: $57,389 (2007); Percent of households with income of $100,000 or more: 12.9% (2007); Poverty rate: 15.6% (2000).
Education: Percent of population age 25 and over with: High school diploma (including GED) or higher: 82.0% (2007); Bachelor's degree or higher: 27.7% (2007); Master's degree or higher: 10.6% (2007).
School District(s)
Lake County School District (PK-12)
   2005-06 Enrollment: 36,117 . . . . (352) 253-6510
Housing: Homeownership rate: 65.6% (2007); Median home value: $200,591 (2007); Median rent: $487 per month (2000); Median age of housing: 22 years (2000).
Safety: Violent crime rate: 83.1 per 10,000 population; Property crime rate: 401.1 per 10,000 population (2006).
Newspapers: Eustis News (General - Circulation 1,500); Tavares Citizen (General - Circulation 1,000); The Mount Dora Topic (General - Circulation 1,500)
Transportation: Commute to work: 89.5% car, 1.1% public transportation, 2.4% walk, 5.5% work from home (2000); Travel time to work: 35.7% less than 15 minutes, 27.2% 15 to 30 minutes, 21.5% 30 to 45 minutes, 8.0% 45 to 60 minutes, 7.7% 60 minutes or more (2000)
Additional Information Contacts
City of Mount Dora . . . . (352) 735-7100
   http://ci.mount-dora.fl.us
Mount Dora Chamber of Commerce . . . . (352) 383-2165
   http://www.mountdora.com

MOUNT PLYMOUTH (CDP).
Covers a land area of 2.784 square miles and a water area of 0.144 square miles. Located at 28.79° N. Lat.; 81.53° W. Long. Elevation is 79 feet.
Population: 2,221 (1990); 2,814 (2000); 3,822 (2007); 4,468 (2012 projected); Race: 88.7% White, 5.6% Black, 1.9% Asian, 6.7% Hispanic of any race (2007); Density: 1,372.9 persons per square mile (2007); Average household size: 2.56 (2007); Median age: 38.9 (2007); Males per 100 females: 95.1 (2007); Marriage status: 19.4% never married, 59.0% now married, 6.5% widowed, 15.1% divorced (2000); Foreign born: 4.1% (2000); Ancestry (includes multiple ancestries): 20.1% Other groups, 16.5% German, 13.1% English, 10.3% United States or American, 10.3% Irish (2000).
Economy: Employment by occupation: 12.9% management, 16.5% professional, 13.1% services, 34.0% sales, 2.7% farming, 12.6% construction, 8.2% production (2000).
Income: Per capita income: $19,957 (2007); Median household income: $45,864 (2007); Average household income: $51,124 (2007); Percent of households with income of $100,000 or more: 5.8% (2007); Poverty rate: 6.6% (2000).
Education: Percent of population age 25 and over with: High school diploma (including GED) or higher: 78.9% (2007); Bachelor's degree or higher: 14.0% (2007); Master's degree or higher: 5.7% (2007).
Housing: Homeownership rate: 89.8% (2007); Median home value: $157,401 (2007); Median rent: $627 per month (2000); Median age of housing: 14 years (2000).
Transportation: Commute to work: 93.5% car, 0.0% public transportation, 2.6% walk, 2.6% work from home (2000); Travel time to work: 11.8% less

Elevation is 85 feet.

History: Okahumpka was founded in 1885 by Reverend Edmund Snyder of Pennsylvania. It grew as a lumber and turpentine community.

Population: 95 (1990); 251 (2000); 383 (2007); 471 (2012 projected); Race: 99.0% White, 0.5% Black, 0.0% Asian, 1.3% Hispanic of any race (2007); Density: 1,600.9 persons per square mile (2007); Average household size: 2.25 (2007); Median age: 40.5 (2007); Males per 100 females: 103.7 (2007); Marriage status: 16.9% never married, 48.3% now married, 9.3% widowed, 25.6% divorced (2000); Foreign born: 0.0% (2000); Ancestry (includes multiple ancestries): 36.3% Other groups, 22.1% United States or American, 17.2% English, 13.2% Irish, 6.9% German (2000).

Economy: Employment by occupation: 0.0% management, 0.0% professional, 29.3% services, 29.3% sales, 0.0% farming, 26.0% construction, 15.4% production (2000).

Income: Per capita income: $12,689 (2007); Median household income: $19,643 (2007); Average household income: $28,588 (2007); Percent of households with income of $100,000 or more: 0.0% (2007); Poverty rate: 31.4% (2000).

Education: Percent of population age 25 and over with: High school diploma (including GED) or higher: 67.7% (2007); Bachelor's degree or higher: 0.0% (2007); Master's degree or higher: 0.0% (2007).

Housing: Homeownership rate: 66.5% (2007); Median home value: $78,750 (2007); Median rent: $375 per month (2000); Median age of housing: 18 years (2000).

Transportation: Commute to work: 100.0% car, 0.0% public transportation, 0.0% walk, 0.0% work from home (2000); Travel time to work: 7.3% less than 15 minutes, 86.2% 15 to 30 minutes, 0.0% 30 to 45 minutes, 0.0% 45 to 60 minutes, 6.4% 60 minutes or more (2000)

PAISLEY (CDP). Covers a land area of 3.282 square miles and a water area of 0.148 square miles. Located at 28.98° N. Lat.; 81.53° W. Long. Elevation is 72 feet.

Population: 572 (1990); 734 (2000); 869 (2007); 962 (2012 projected); Race: 96.4% White, 0.0% Black, 0.9% Asian, 2.0% Hispanic of any race (2007); Density: 264.8 persons per square mile (2007); Average household size: 2.30 (2007); Median age: 44.4 (2007); Males per 100 females: 99.8 (2007); Marriage status: 10.8% never married, 54.1% now married, 14.4% widowed, 20.7% divorced (2000); Foreign born: 4.7% (2000); Ancestry (includes multiple ancestries): 29.4% Other groups, 22.1% United States or American, 16.6% Irish, 16.5% German, 5.6% English (2000).

Economy: Employment by occupation: 7.5% management, 10.4% professional, 25.4% services, 29.1% sales, 1.9% farming, 10.8% construction, 14.9% production (2000).

Income: Per capita income: $15,967 (2007); Median household income: $32,115 (2007); Average household income: $36,706 (2007); Percent of households with income of $100,000 or more: 5.8% (2007); Poverty rate: 17.4% (2000).

Education: Percent of population age 25 and over with: High school diploma (including GED) or higher: 83.4% (2007); Bachelor's degree or higher: 5.7% (2007); Master's degree or higher: 3.9% (2007).

School District(s)

Lake County School District (PK-12)

   2005-06 Enrollment: 36,117 . . . . (352) 253-6510

Housing: Homeownership rate: 87.0% (2007); Median home value: $110,776 (2007); Median rent: $325 per month (2000); Median age of housing: 19 years (2000).

Transportation: Commute to work: 95.1% car, 4.9% public transportation, 0.0% walk, 0.0% work from home (2000); Travel time to work: 15.7% less than 15 minutes, 23.9% 15 to 30 minutes, 26.1% 30 to 45 minutes, 16.4% 45 to 60 minutes, 17.9% 60 minutes or more (2000)

PINE LAKES (CDP). Covers a land area of 1.551 square miles and a water area of 0.181 square miles. Located at 28.94° N. Lat.; 81.42° W. Long. Elevation is 49 feet.

Population: 533 (1990); 755 (2000); 864 (2007); 937 (2012 projected); Race: 94.1% White, 1.6% Black, 0.2% Asian, 3.7% Hispanic of any race (2007); Density: 557.1 persons per square mile (2007); Average household size: 2.63 (2007); Median age: 34.1 (2007); Males per 100 females: 103.8 (2007); Marriage status: 26.7% never married, 52.4% now married, 5.9%

construction, 28.4% production (2000).

Income: Per capita income: $14,716 (2007); Median household income: $31,813 (2007); Average household income: $38,647 (2007); Percent of households with income of $100,000 or more: 4.0% (2007); Poverty rate: 32.4% (2000).

Education: Percent of population age 25 and over with: High school diploma (including GED) or higher: 60.2% (2007); Bachelor's degree or higher: 4.3% (2007); Master's degree or higher: 2.1% (2007).

Housing: Homeownership rate: 80.2% (2007); Median home value: $84,545 (2007); Median rent: $275 per month (2000); Median age of housing: 21 years (2000).

Transportation: Commute to work: 90.3% car, 5.1% public transportation, 4.6% walk, 0.0% work from home (2000); Travel time to work: 0.0% less than 15 minutes, 24.1% 15 to 30 minutes, 31.3% 30 to 45 minutes, 15.4% 45 to 60 minutes, 29.2% 60 minutes or more (2000)

PITTMAN (CDP). Covers a land area of 1.283 square miles and a water area of 0.017 square miles. Located at 28.99° N. Lat.; 81.64° W. Long. Elevation is 69 feet.

Population: 169 (1990); 192 (2000); 241 (2007); 275 (2012 projected); Race: 78.4% White, 15.4% Black, 0.0% Asian, 9.5% Hispanic of any race (2007); Density: 187.9 persons per square mile (2007); Average household size: 2.84 (2007); Median age: 37.5 (2007); Males per 100 females: 117.1 (2007); Marriage status: 41.0% never married, 28.2% now married, 0.0% widowed, 30.8% divorced (2000); Foreign born: 0.0% (2000); Ancestry (includes multiple ancestries): 43.6% Other groups, 16.7% English, 15.4% Irish, 14.1% Swiss, 12.8% German (2000).

Economy: Employment by occupation: 0.0% management, 0.0% professional, 32.4% services, 0.0% sales, 38.2% farming, 0.0% construction, 29.4% production (2000).

Income: Per capita income: $8,963 (2007); Median household income: $18,906 (2007); Average household income: $25,412 (2007); Percent of households with income of $100,000 or more: 0.0% (2007); Poverty rate: 28.2% (2000).

Education: Percent of population age 25 and over with: High school diploma (including GED) or higher: 36.1% (2007); Bachelor's degree or higher: 16.5% (2007); Master's degree or higher: 0.0% (2007).

Housing: Homeownership rate: 83.5% (2007); Median home value: $116,848 (2007); Median rent: $n/a per month (2000); Median age of housing: 23 years (2000).

Transportation: Commute to work: 100.0% car, 0.0% public transportation, 0.0% walk, 0.0% work from home (2000); Travel time to work: 0.0% less than 15 minutes, 70.6% 15 to 30 minutes, 0.0% 30 to 45 minutes, 0.0% 45 to 60 minutes, 29.4% 60 minutes or more (2000)

SILVER LAKE (CDP). Covers a land area of 2.449 square miles and a water area of 0.607 square miles. Located at 28.83° N. Lat.; 81.79° W. Long. Elevation is 66 feet.

Population: 1,569 (1990); 1,882 (2000); 2,366 (2007); 2,688 (2012 projected); Race: 87.4% White, 3.7% Black, 6.3% Asian, 3.3% Hispanic of any race (2007); Density: 966.1 persons per square mile (2007); Average household size: 2.30 (2007); Median age: 46.5 (2007); Males per 100 females: 93.6 (2007); Marriage status: 20.8% never married, 59.9% now married, 8.8% widowed, 10.4% divorced (2000); Foreign born: 4.2% (2000); Ancestry (includes multiple ancestries): 19.7% English, 13.5% German, 11.6% United States or American, 10.6% Irish, 9.7% Other groups (2000).

Economy: Employment by occupation: 17.7% management, 23.3% professional, 3.7% services, 41.8% sales, 2.2% farming, 6.5% construction, 4.7% production (2000).

Income: Per capita income: $31,716 (2007); Median household income: $56,327 (2007); Average household income: $72,854 (2007); Percent of households with income of $100,000 or more: 23.4% (2007); Poverty rate: 8.8% (2000).

Education: Percent of population age 25 and over with: High school diploma (including GED) or higher: 91.1% (2007); Bachelor's degree or higher: 30.0% (2007); Master's degree or higher: 11.7% (2007).

Housing: Homeownership rate: 76.8% (2007); Median home value: $252,249 (2007); Median rent: $457 per month (2000); Median age of housing: 15 years (2000).

SORRENTO (CDP).

Covers a land area of 1.294 square miles and a water area of 0.016 square miles. Located at 28.80° N. Lat.; 81.56° W. Long. Elevation is 69 feet.

Population: 828 (1990); 765 (2000); 975 (2007); 1,107 (2012 projected); Race: 89.4% White, 0.5% Black, 0.0% Asian, 24.9% Hispanic of any race (2007); Density: 753.4 persons per square mile (2007); Average household size: 2.76 (2007); Median age: 35.5 (2007); Males per 100 females: 106.1 (2007); Marriage status: 20.9% never married, 59.2% now married, 9.5% widowed, 10.3% divorced (2000); Foreign born: 0.0% (2000); Ancestry (includes multiple ancestries): 21.0% United States or American, 15.2% English, 14.0% Irish, 12.1% Other groups, 11.7% German (2000).

Economy: Employment by occupation: 3.0% management, 9.0% professional, 20.6% services, 24.4% sales, 12.1% farming, 16.2% construction, 14.6% production (2000).

Income: Per capita income: $17,972 (2007); Median household income: $44,300 (2007); Average household income: $49,639 (2007); Percent of households with income of $100,000 or more: 7.6% (2007); Poverty rate: 2.2% (2000).

Education: Percent of population age 25 and over with: High school diploma (including GED) or higher: 54.5% (2007); Bachelor's degree or higher: 7.2% (2007); Master's degree or higher: 3.6% (2007).

School District(s)
Lake County School District (PK-12)
    2005-06 Enrollment: 36,117 . . . . (352) 253-6510

Housing: Homeownership rate: 72.8% (2007); Median home value: $117,659 (2007); Median rent: $388 per month (2000); Median age of housing: 28 years (2000).

Transportation: Commute to work: 100.0% car, 0.0% public transportation, 0.0% walk, 0.0% work from home (2000); Travel time to work: 23.4% less than 15 minutes, 46.2% 15 to 30 minutes, 14.8% 30 to 45 minutes, 8.1% 45 to 60 minutes, 7.4% 60 minutes or more (2000)

Additional Information Contacts
East Lake County Chamber of Commerce . . . . (352) 383-8801
    http://www.elcchamber.com

TAVARES (city).

County seat. Covers a land area of 7.089 square miles and a water area of 0.356 square miles. Located at 28.80° N. Lat.; 81.73° W. Long. Elevation is 75 feet.

History: Tavares was founded in 1875 by Alexander St.Clair Abrams and named for one of his Spanish ancestors. Abrahms planned the town as a resort community, but later built lumber mills and a cigar factory.

Population: 8,022 (1990); 9,700 (2000); 11,950 (2007); 13,426 (2012 projected); Race: 85.8% White, 9.3% Black, 1.6% Asian, 5.3% Hispanic of any race (2007); Density: 1,685.7 persons per square mile (2007); Average household size: 2.11 (2007); Median age: 56.1 (2007); Males per 100 females: 90.9 (2007); Marriage status: 15.0% never married, 59.9% now married, 12.8% widowed, 12.4% divorced (2000); Foreign born: 3.8% (2000); Ancestry (includes multiple ancestries): 18.2% German, 15.3% Other groups, 14.8% English, 10.3% United States or American, 9.8% Irish (2000).

Economy: Single-family building permits issued: 264 (2006); Multi-family building permits issued: 24 (2006); Employment by occupation: 10.8% management, 16.9% professional, 22.0% services, 28.1% sales, 0.6% farming, 10.7% construction, 10.9% production (2000).

Income: Per capita income: $23,689 (2007); Median household income: $35,101 (2007); Average household income: $47,928 (2007); Percent of households with income of $100,000 or more: 7.4% (2007); Poverty rate: 10.3% (2000).

Education: Percent of population age 25 and over with: High school diploma (including GED) or higher: 78.0% (2007); Bachelor's degree or higher: 14.0% (2007); Master's degree or higher: 4.2% (2007).

School District(s)
Lake County School District (PK-12)
    2005-06 Enrollment: 36,117 . . . . (352) 253-6510

Housing: Homeownership rate: 80.1% (2007); Median home value: $113,379 (2007); Median rent: $411 per month (2000); Median age of housing: 22 years (2000).

Hospitals: Florida Hospital Waterman (204 beds)

Safety: Violent crime rate: 43.2 per 10,000 population; Property crime rate: 220.9 per 10,000 population (2006).

City of Tavares . . . . (352) 742-6209
    http://www.tavares.org
Tavares Chamber of Commerce . . . . (352) 343-2531
    http://www.tavareschamber.com

UMATILLA (city).

Covers a land area of 2.541 square miles and a water area of 0.516 square miles. Located at 28.93° N. Lat.; 81.66° W. Long. Elevation is 98 feet.

Population: 2,450 (1990); 2,214 (2000); 2,635 (2007); 2,912 (2012 projected); Race: 92.2% White, 3.6% Black, 0.5% Asian, 6.8% Hispanic of any race (2007); Density: 1,037.2 persons per square mile (2007); Average household size: 2.57 (2007); Median age: 39.1 (2007); Males per 100 females: 90.5 (2007); Marriage status: 18.3% never married, 57.7% now married, 14.2% widowed, 9.8% divorced (2000); Foreign born: 2.9% (2000); Ancestry (includes multiple ancestries): 22.5% United States or American, 12.7% Irish, 11.7% English, 11.2% German, 10.1% Other groups (2000).

Economy: Single-family building permits issued: 0 (2006); Multi-family building permits issued: 0 (2006); Employment by occupation: 8.6% management, 14.1% professional, 19.9% services, 24.2% sales, 2.6% farming, 13.0% construction, 17.4% production (2000).

Income: Per capita income: $19,100 (2007); Median household income: $33,409 (2007); Average household income: $47,927 (2007); Percent of households with income of $100,000 or more: 9.7% (2007); Poverty rate: 11.9% (2000).

Education: Percent of population age 25 and over with: High school diploma (including GED) or higher: 72.9% (2007); Bachelor's degree or higher: 10.8% (2007); Master's degree or higher: 5.0% (2007).

School District(s)
Lake County School District (PK-12)
    2005-06 Enrollment: 36,117 . . . . (352) 253-6510

Housing: Homeownership rate: 69.3% (2007); Median home value: $123,459 (2007); Median rent: $323 per month (2000); Median age of housing: 26 years (2000).

Safety: Violent crime rate: 141.2 per 10,000 population; Property crime rate: 345.5 per 10,000 population (2006).

Newspapers: North Lake Outpost (General - Circulation 2,500)

Transportation: Commute to work: 95.7% car, 0.0% public transportation, 0.9% walk, 2.0% work from home (2000); Travel time to work: 33.2% less than 15 minutes, 35.9% 15 to 30 minutes, 15.0% 30 to 45 minutes, 7.3% 45 to 60 minutes, 8.6% 60 minutes or more (2000)

Additional Information Contacts
Umatilla Chamber of Commerce . . . . (352) 669-3511
    http://www.umatillachamber.org

YALAHA (CDP).

Covers a land area of 6.250 square miles and a water area of 8.640 square miles. Located at 28.74° N. Lat.; 81.81° W. Long. Elevation is 75 feet.

Population: 1,168 (1990); 1,175 (2000); 1,723 (2007); 2,079 (2012 projected); Race: 85.0% White, 7.7% Black, 1.3% Asian, 7.8% Hispanic of any race (2007); Density: 275.7 persons per square mile (2007); Average household size: 2.19 (2007); Median age: 51.4 (2007); Males per 100 females: 94.5 (2007); Marriage status: 16.3% never married, 63.3% now married, 11.5% widowed, 8.9% divorced (2000); Foreign born: 1.5% (2000); Ancestry (includes multiple ancestries): 23.2% German, 18.4% English, 15.7% Other groups, 11.3% Irish, 9.5% United States or American (2000).

Economy: Employment by occupation: 14.5% management, 12.3% professional, 21.1% services, 32.1% sales, 4.7% farming, 6.2% construction, 9.1% production (2000).

Income: Per capita income: $20,461 (2007); Median household income: $34,329 (2007); Average household income: $44,451 (2007); Percent of households with income of $100,000 or more: 8.1% (2007); Poverty rate: 11.2% (2000).

Education: Percent of population age 25 and over with: High school diploma (including GED) or higher: 87.5% (2007); Bachelor's degree or higher: 23.4% (2007); Master's degree or higher: 2.7% (2007).

Housing: Homeownership rate: 89.1% (2007); Median home value: $191,827 (2007); Median rent: $450 per month (2000); Median age of housing: 26 years (2000).

Transportation: Commute to work: 88.8% car, 1.5% public transportation, 1.1% walk, 3.7% work from home (2000); Travel time to work: 16.6% less than 15 minutes, 24.2% 15 to 30 minutes, 32.9% 30 to 45 minutes, 11.4% 45 to 60 minutes, 15.0% 60 minutes or more (2000)

Lee County

Located in southwestern Florida, on the Gulf of Mexico; lowland area, drained by the Caloosahatchee River; bordered by a chain of barrier islands and lagoons. Covers a land area of 803.63 square miles, a water area of 408.26 square miles, and is located in the Eastern Time Zone. The county was founded in 1887. County seat is Fort Myers.

Lee County is part of the Cape Coral-Fort Myers, FL Metropolitan Statistical Area. The entire metro area includes: Lee County, FL

Weather Station: Fort Myers Page Field   Elevation: 13 feet

	Jan	Feb	Mar	Apr	May	Jun	Jul	Aug	Sep	Oct	Nov	Dec
High	75	76	80	85	89	91	92	92	90	86	81	77
Low	54	55	59	63	68	73	74	75	74	69	62	56
Precip	2.4	2.1	3.3	1.6	3.6	9.7	9.0	9.6	7.8	2.5	1.8	1.6
Snow	0.0	0.0	0.0	0.0	0.0	0.0	0.0	0.0	0.0	0.0	0.0	0.0

High and Low temperatures in degrees Fahrenheit; Precipitation and Snow in inches

Population: 335,113 (1990); 440,888 (2000); 579,463 (2007); 678,958 (2012 projected); Race: 84.3% White, 7.3% Black, 1.1% Asian, 15.4% Hispanic of any race (2007); Density: 721.1 persons per square mile (2007); Average household size: 2.32 (2007); Median age: 43.5 (2007); Males per 100 females: 97.3 (2007).
Religion: Five largest groups: 17.1% Catholic Church, 4.1% Southern Baptist Convention, 3.1% Assemblies of God, 2.9% The United Methodist Church, 1.6% Presbyterian Church (U.S.A.) (2000).
Economy: Unemployment rate: 5.4% (11/2007); Total civilian labor force: 296,640 (11/2007); Leading industries: 18.8% retail trade; 15.3% construction; 13.4% health care and social assistance (2005); Farms: 643 totaling 126,484 acres (2002); Companies that employ 500 or more persons: 14 (2005); Companies that employ 100 to 499 persons: 275 (2005); Companies that employ less than 100 persons: 15,801 (2005); Black-owned businesses: 1,300 (2002); Hispanic-owned businesses: 2,050 (2002); Asian-owned businesses: 901 (2002); Women-owned businesses: 12,360 (2002); Retail sales per capita: $18,939 (2007). Single-family building permits issued: 14,700 (2006); Multi-family building permits issued: 4,046 (2006).
Income: Per capita income: $29,287 (2007); Median household income: $48,714 (2007); Average household income: $67,508 (2007); Percent of households with income of $100,000 or more: 16.2% (2007); Poverty rate: 9.5% (2005); Bankruptcy rate: 0.88% (2006).
Taxes: Total county taxes per capita: $717 (2005); County property taxes per capita: $534 (2005).
Education: Percent of population age 25 and over with: High school diploma (including GED) or higher: 83.0% (2007); Bachelor's degree or higher: 21.6% (2007); Master's degree or higher: 7.7% (2007).
Housing: Homeownership rate: 77.4% (2007); Median home value: $232,669 (2007); Median rent: $554 per month (2000); Median age of housing: 17 years (2000).
Health: Birth rate: 113.0 per 10,000 population (2006); Death rate: 100.6 per 10,000 population (2006); Age-adjusted cancer mortality rate: 163.3 deaths per 100,000 population (2004); Air Quality Index: 93.4% good, 6.6% moderate, 0.0% unhealthy for sensitive individuals, 0.0% unhealthy (percent of days in 2006); Number of physicians: 21.5 per 10,000 population (2005); Hospital beds: 31.1 per 10,000 population (2004); Hospital admissions: 1,515.3 per 10,000 population (2004).
Elections: 2004 Presidential election results: 59.9% Bush, 39.0% Kerry, 0.6% Nader, 0.2% Badnarik
National and State Parks: Caloosahatchee National Wildlife Refuge; Caloosahatchee River State Park; Cayo Costa State Park; Gasparilla Island State Park; J N Darling National Wildlife Refuge; Koreshan State Historic Site; Lovers Key State Park; Matlacha Pass National Wildlife Refuge; Mound Key Archaeological State Park; Pine Island National Wildlife Refuge
Additional Information Contacts
Lee County Government . . . . (239) 335-2259
  http://www.lee-county.com
Bonita Springs Chamber of Commerce . . . . (941) 992-2943
  http://www.bonitaspringschamber.com

Cape Coral Chamber of Commerce . . . . (941) 549-6900
  http://www.capecoralchamber.com
Christian Chamber of Commerce . . . . (239) 481-1411
  http://www.ccswf.org
City of Sanibel . . . . (239) 472-4135
  http://www.mysanibel.com
Estero Chamber of Commerce . . . . (239) 931-0931
  http://www.leechamber.com
Fort Myers Beach Chamber of Commerce . . . . (941) 454-7500
  http://www.fortmyersbeach.org
Fort Myers Chamber of Commerce . . . . (239) 278-4001
  http://www.chamber-swflorida.com
Greater Pine Island Chamber . . . . (239) 283-0888
  http://www.pineislandchamber.org
Hispanic Chamber of Commerce . . . . (239) 334-3190
Lehigh Acres Chamber of Commerce . . . . (239) 369-3322
  http://www.lehighacreschamber.org
SW Florida Chamber of Commerce . . . . (239) 278-4001
  http://www.chamber-swflorida.com
Sanibel-Captiva Chamber of Commerce . . . . (239) 472-1080
  http://www.sanibel-captiva.org
Town of Fort Myers Beach . . . . (239) 765-0202

Lee County Communities

ALVA (CDP). Covers a land area of 17.952 square miles and a water area of 0.843 square miles. Located at 26.71° N. Lat.; 81.62° W. Long. Elevation is 16 feet.
History: Alva developed along the Caloosahatchee River as a trading center for turkey farmers.
Population: 1,904 (1990); 2,182 (2000); 2,575 (2007); 2,882 (2012 projected); Race: 89.4% White, 2.5% Black, 0.2% Asian, 8.9% Hispanic of any race (2007); Density: 143.4 persons per square mile (2007); Average household size: 2.35 (2007); Median age: 45.9 (2007); Males per 100 females: 98.5 (2007); Marriage status: 13.0% never married, 65.6% now married, 9.0% widowed, 12.5% divorced (2000); Foreign born: 2.8% (2000); Ancestry (includes multiple ancestries): 19.5% English, 18.9% German, 15.2% United States or American, 15.1% Irish, 6.8% Other groups (2000).
Economy: Employment by occupation: 11.2% management, 16.2% professional, 14.4% services, 23.0% sales, 1.6% farming, 23.5% construction, 10.2% production (2000).
Income: Per capita income: $30,961 (2007); Median household income: $51,111 (2007); Average household income: $72,742 (2007); Percent of households with income of $100,000 or more: 17.8% (2007); Poverty rate: 7.8% (2000).
Education: Percent of population age 25 and over with: High school diploma (including GED) or higher: 81.9% (2007); Bachelor's degree or higher: 17.7% (2007); Master's degree or higher: 6.5% (2007).
School District(s)
Lee County School District (PK-12)
  2005-06 Enrollment: 71,210 . . . . (239) 337-8301
Housing: Homeownership rate: 92.6% (2007); Median home value: $231,471 (2007); Median rent: $343 per month (2000); Median age of housing: 21 years (2000).
Transportation: Commute to work: 96.7% car, 0.6% public transportation, 0.9% walk, 1.1% work from home (2000); Travel time to work: 11.2% less than 15 minutes, 28.5% 15 to 30 minutes, 41.0% 30 to 45 minutes, 8.2% 45 to 60 minutes, 11.1% 60 minutes or more (2000)

BOKEELIA (CDP). Covers a land area of 8.846 square miles and a water area of 0.016 square miles. Located at 26.68° N. Lat.; 82.14° W. Long. Elevation is 3 feet.
Population: 1,491 (1990); 1,997 (2000); 2,150 (2007); 2,294 (2012 projected); Race: 97.4% White, 0.3% Black, 0.4% Asian, 26.3% Hispanic of any race (2007); Density: 243.0 persons per square mile (2007); Average household size: 2.19 (2007); Median age: 49.6 (2007); Males per 100 females: 112.5 (2007); Marriage status: 15.0% never married, 71.7% now married, 7.5% widowed, 5.8% divorced (2000); Foreign born: 13.0% (2000); Ancestry (includes multiple ancestries): 20.5% English, 20.5% Other groups, 16.5% German, 9.2% United States or American, 8.0% Irish (2000).
Economy: Employment by occupation: 10.8% management, 15.1% professional, 13.4% services, 27.9% sales, 12.7% farming, 9.4% construction, 10.8% production (2000).

Income: Per capita income: $30,834 (2007); Median household income: $45,536 (2007); Average household income: $67,439 (2007); Percent of households with income of $100,000 or more: 16.1% (2007); Poverty rate: 17.6% (2000).
Education: Percent of population age 25 and over with: High school diploma (including GED) or higher: 81.2% (2007); Bachelor's degree or higher: 17.5% (2007); Master's degree or higher: 6.4% (2007).
Housing: Homeownership rate: 81.8% (2007); Median home value: $218,095 (2007); Median rent: $339 per month (2000); Median age of housing: 19 years (2000).
Newspapers: Pine Island Eagle (General - Circulation 8,500)
Transportation: Commute to work: 80.2% car, 2.9% public transportation, 2.1% walk, 8.9% work from home (2000); Travel time to work: 30.8% less than 15 minutes, 23.6% 15 to 30 minutes, 25.5% 30 to 45 minutes, 7.2% 45 to 60 minutes, 13.0% 60 minutes or more (2000)

BONITA SPRINGS (city). Covers a land area of 35.289 square miles and a water area of 5.717 square miles. Located at 26.35° N. Lat.; 81.79° W. Long. Elevation is 10 feet.
Population: 17,511 (1990); 32,797 (2000); 40,311 (2007); 45,953 (2012 projected); Race: 83.4% White, 0.6% Black, 0.5% Asian, 28.3% Hispanic of any race (2007); Density: 1,142.3 persons per square mile (2007); Average household size: 2.19 (2007); Median age: 53.1 (2007); Males per 100 females: 105.2 (2007); Marriage status: 14.0% never married, 68.8% now married, 8.1% widowed, 9.1% divorced (2000); Foreign born: 16.0% (2000); Ancestry (includes multiple ancestries): 20.5% German, 19.4% Other groups, 14.8% English, 13.6% Irish, 6.2% United States or American (2000).
Economy: Unemployment rate: 4.2% (11/2007); Total civilian labor force: 19,892 (11/2007); Single-family building permits issued: 747 (2006); Multi-family building permits issued: 329 (2006); Employment by occupation: 13.2% management, 11.4% professional, 21.7% services, 27.2% sales, 1.8% farming, 18.0% construction, 6.8% production (2000).
Income: Per capita income: $42,609 (2007); Median household income: $58,633 (2007); Average household income: $93,212 (2007); Percent of households with income of $100,000 or more: 25.2% (2007); Poverty rate: 6.7% (2000).
Education: Percent of population age 25 and over with: High school diploma (including GED) or higher: 84.6% (2007); Bachelor's degree or higher: 27.5% (2007); Master's degree or higher: 10.1% (2007).
School District(s)
Lee County School District (PK-12)
    2005-06 Enrollment: 71,210 . . . . (239) 337-8301
Housing: Homeownership rate: 83.6% (2007); Median home value: $315,941 (2007); Median rent: $631 per month (2000); Median age of housing: 11 years (2000).
Newspapers: Bonita Banner (General - Circulation 30,000)
Transportation: Commute to work: 89.6% car, 0.5% public transportation, 1.6% walk, 5.8% work from home (2000); Travel time to work: 30.9% less than 15 minutes, 35.2% 15 to 30 minutes, 23.4% 30 to 45 minutes, 6.1% 45 to 60 minutes, 4.5% 60 minutes or more (2000)
Additional Information Contacts
Bonita Springs Chamber of Commerce . . . . (941) 992-2943
    http://www.bonitaspringschamber.com

BUCKINGHAM (CDP). Covers a land area of 18.964 square miles and a water area of <.001 square miles. Located at 26.65° N. Lat.; 81.73° W. Long. Elevation is 10 feet.
Population: 3,134 (1990); 3,742 (2000); 4,415 (2007); 4,850 (2012 projected); Race: 91.8% White, 2.7% Black, 0.7% Asian, 7.3% Hispanic of any race (2007); Density: 232.8 persons per square mile (2007); Average household size: 2.78 (2007); Median age: 42.0 (2007); Males per 100 females: 110.3 (2007); Marriage status: 27.8% never married, 56.9% now married, 4.7% widowed, 10.7% divorced (2000); Foreign born: 3.4% (2000); Ancestry (includes multiple ancestries): 18.8% German, 15.9% Irish, 15.2% English, 11.4% Other groups, 11.4% United States or American (2000).
Economy: Employment by occupation: 11.0% management, 19.7% professional, 10.7% services, 22.6% sales, 1.0% farming, 22.0% construction, 13.0% production (2000).
Income: Per capita income: $25,263 (2007); Median household income: $60,447 (2007); Average household income: $69,351 (2007); Percent of households with income of $100,000 or more: 21.7% (2007); Poverty rate: 16.8% (2000).

Education: Percent of population age 25 and over with: High school diploma (including GED) or higher: 74.6% (2007); Bachelor's degree or higher: 14.1% (2007); Master's degree or higher: 4.4% (2007).
Housing: Homeownership rate: 90.1% (2007); Median home value: $317,143 (2007); Median rent: $491 per month (2000); Median age of housing: 17 years (2000).
Transportation: Commute to work: 92.6% car, 0.2% public transportation, 2.9% walk, 4.2% work from home (2000); Travel time to work: 18.3% less than 15 minutes, 41.0% 15 to 30 minutes, 30.6% 30 to 45 minutes, 5.8% 45 to 60 minutes, 4.3% 60 minutes or more (2000)

BURNT STORE MARINA (CDP). Covers a land area of 1.221 square miles and a water area of 0.206 square miles. Located at 26.76° N. Lat.; 82.05° W. Long. Elevation is 7 feet.
Population: 283 (1990); 1,271 (2000); 2,571 (2007); 3,436 (2012 projected); Race: 98.5% White, 1.1% Black, 0.1% Asian, 0.7% Hispanic of any race (2007); Density: 2,105.5 persons per square mile (2007); Average household size: 1.87 (2007); Median age: 63.5 (2007); Males per 100 females: 96.1 (2007); Marriage status: 4.1% never married, 81.9% now married, 6.1% widowed, 7.9% divorced (2000); Foreign born: 8.4% (2000); Ancestry (includes multiple ancestries): 27.0% German, 19.0% English, 16.9% Irish, 10.1% Italian, 7.7% United States or American (2000).
Economy: Employment by occupation: 17.8% management, 28.3% professional, 14.0% services, 29.7% sales, 0.0% farming, 6.6% construction, 3.5% production (2000).
Income: Per capita income: $54,018 (2007); Median household income: $70,127 (2007); Average household income: $100,930 (2007); Percent of households with income of $100,000 or more: 30.1% (2007); Poverty rate: 3.6% (2000).
Education: Percent of population age 25 and over with: High school diploma (including GED) or higher: 93.5% (2007); Bachelor's degree or higher: 40.1% (2007); Master's degree or higher: 16.4% (2007).
Housing: Homeownership rate: 94.5% (2007); Median home value: $418,396 (2007); Median rent: $894 per month (2000); Median age of housing: 8 years (2000).
Transportation: Commute to work: 71.2% car, 0.0% public transportation, 2.2% walk, 17.0% work from home (2000); Travel time to work: 26.2% less than 15 minutes, 29.8% 15 to 30 minutes, 15.1% 30 to 45 minutes, 20.0% 45 to 60 minutes, 8.9% 60 minutes or more (2000)

CAPE CORAL (city). Covers a land area of 105.188 square miles and a water area of 9.910 square miles. Located at 26.64° N. Lat.; 81.98° W. Long. Elevation is 3 feet.
History: Cape Coral has a cultural center and a historical Museum The city's population more than doubled between 1980 and 1990, and it was the fastest-growing city in the U.S. during that decade. Incorporated 1970.
Population: 75,507 (1990); 102,286 (2000); 153,992 (2007); 189,594 (2012 projected); Race: 88.7% White, 3.3% Black, 1.2% Asian, 15.0% Hispanic of any race (2007); Density: 1,464.0 persons per square mile (2007); Average household size: 2.51 (2007); Median age: 39.8 (2007); Males per 100 females: 96.1 (2007); Marriage status: 17.0% never married, 64.6% now married, 7.1% widowed, 11.3% divorced (2000); Foreign born: 8.7% (2000); Ancestry (includes multiple ancestries): 20.9% German, 15.9% Irish, 13.5% Other groups, 13.1% Italian, 11.9% English (2000).
Economy: Unemployment rate: 5.4% (11/2007); Total civilian labor force: 83,691 (11/2007); Single-family building permits issued: 3,727 (2006); Multi-family building permits issued: 770 (2006); Employment by occupation: 12.2% management, 16.3% professional, 16.5% services, 32.3% sales, 0.3% farming, 12.8% construction, 9.5% production (2000).
Income: Per capita income: $25,641 (2007); Median household income: $52,607 (2007); Average household income: $64,047 (2007); Percent of households with income of $100,000 or more: 14.0% (2007); Poverty rate: 7.0% (2000).
Taxes: Total city taxes per capita: $589 (2005); City property taxes per capita: $314 (2005).
Education: Percent of population age 25 and over with: High school diploma (including GED) or higher: 85.5% (2007); Bachelor's degree or higher: 17.3% (2007); Master's degree or higher: 5.6% (2007).
School District(s)
Lee County School District (PK-12)
    2005-06 Enrollment: 71,210 . . . . (239) 337-8301
Two-year College(s)
Lee County High Tech Center North (Public)
    Fall 2006 Enrollment: 184 . . . . (239) 574-4440

Housing: Homeownership rate: 80.4% (2007); Median home value: $248,494 (2007); Median rent: $588 per month (2000); Median age of housing: 15 years (2000).

Hospitals: Lee Memorial Health System (281 beds)

Safety: Violent crime rate: 28.5 per 10,000 population; Property crime rate: 344.7 per 10,000 population (2006).

Newspapers: Cape Coral Daily Breeze (Circulation 3,500)

Transportation: Commute to work: 94.7% car, 0.5% public transportation, 0.7% walk, 2.8% work from home (2000); Travel time to work: 25.5% less than 15 minutes, 41.4% 15 to 30 minutes, 21.1% 30 to 45 minutes, 5.8% 45 to 60 minutes, 6.2% 60 minutes or more (2000)

Additional Information Contacts

Cape Coral Chamber of Commerce . . . . (941) 549-6900
  http://www.capecoralchamber.com
Greater Pine Island Chamber . . . . (239) 283-0888
  http://www.pineislandchamber.org

CAPTIVA (CDP).
Covers a land area of 1.242 square miles and a water area of 9.254 square miles. Located at 26.51° N. Lat.; 82.19° W. Long. Elevation is 3 feet.

Population: 469 (1990); 379 (2000); 379 (2007); 390 (2012 projected); Race: 97.6% White, 0.0% Black, 1.1% Asian, 1.3% Hispanic of any race (2007); Density: 305.3 persons per square mile (2007); Average household size: 1.98 (2007); Median age: 58.2 (2007); Males per 100 females: 98.4 (2007); Marriage status: 7.5% never married, 59.1% now married, 15.5% widowed, 17.9% divorced (2000); Foreign born: 10.2% (2000); Ancestry (includes multiple ancestries): 35.7% English, 30.1% German, 20.2% Irish, 13.0% Italian, 9.7% Scottish (2000).

Economy: Employment by occupation: 52.5% management, 11.5% professional, 11.5% services, 9.4% sales, 0.0% farming, 2.9% construction, 12.2% production (2000).

Income: Per capita income: $70,218 (2007); Median household income: $83,796 (2007); Average household income: $139,332 (2007); Percent of households with income of $100,000 or more: 40.8% (2007); Poverty rate: 0.0% (2000).

Education: Percent of population age 25 and over with: High school diploma (including GED) or higher: 92.9% (2007); Bachelor's degree or higher: 34.4% (2007); Master's degree or higher: 8.9% (2007).

Housing: Homeownership rate: 79.6% (2007); Median home value: $1 million+ (2007); Median rent: $875 per month (2000); Median age of housing: 16 years (2000).

Transportation: Commute to work: 65.5% car, 0.0% public transportation, 0.0% walk, 30.2% work from home (2000); Travel time to work: 47.4% less than 15 minutes, 27.8% 15 to 30 minutes, 0.0% 30 to 45 minutes, 24.7% 45 to 60 minutes, 0.0% 60 minutes or more (2000)

CHARLESTON PARK (CDP).
Covers a land area of 0.122 square miles and a water area of 0 square miles. Located at 26.70° N. Lat.; 81.58° W. Long. Elevation is 13 feet.

Population: 251 (1990); 411 (2000); 510 (2007); 585 (2012 projected); Race: 1.2% White, 96.5% Black, 0.0% Asian, 4.1% Hispanic of any race (2007); Density: 4,193.5 persons per square mile (2007); Average household size: 3.54 (2007); Median age: 22.7 (2007); Males per 100 females: 86.1 (2007); Marriage status: 44.4% never married, 39.1% now married, 0.0% widowed, 16.5% divorced (2000); Foreign born: 5.4% (2000); Ancestry (includes multiple ancestries): 93.8% Other groups, 2.0% Haitian, 1.2% Jamaican (2000).

Economy: Employment by occupation: 3.1% management, 14.9% professional, 37.3% services, 14.3% sales, 0.0% farming, 15.5% construction, 14.9% production (2000).

Income: Per capita income: $10,515 (2007); Median household income: $32,778 (2007); Average household income: $37,240 (2007); Percent of households with income of $100,000 or more: 0.0% (2007); Poverty rate: 18.1% (2000).

Education: Percent of population age 25 and over with: High school diploma (including GED) or higher: 48.5% (2007); Bachelor's degree or higher: 4.3% (2007); Master's degree or higher: 0.0% (2007).

Housing: Homeownership rate: 54.2% (2007); Median home value: $116,071 (2007); Median rent: $192 per month (2000); Median age of housing: 25 years (2000).

Transportation: Commute to work: 100.0% car, 0.0% public transportation, 0.0% walk, 0.0% work from home (2000); Travel time to work: 3.7% less than 15 minutes, 42.9% 15 to 30 minutes, 26.1% 30 to 45 minutes, 24.2% 45 to 60 minutes, 3.1% 60 minutes or more (2000)

CYPRESS LAKE (CDP).
Covers a land area of 3.977 square miles and a water area of 0.004 square miles. Located at 26.53° N. Lat.; 81.90° W. Long. Elevation is 3 feet.

Population: 10,491 (1990); 12,072 (2000); 15,151 (2007); 17,448 (2012 projected); Race: 95.4% White, 1.4% Black, 0.8% Asian, 6.2% Hispanic of any race (2007); Density: 3,809.9 persons per square mile (2007); Average household size: 1.85 (2007); Median age: 54.9 (2007); Males per 100 females: 84.8 (2007); Marriage status: 15.8% never married, 58.6% now married, 13.4% widowed, 12.1% divorced (2000); Foreign born: 6.8% (2000); Ancestry (includes multiple ancestries): 23.1% German, 17.5% Irish, 17.5% English, 8.7% Italian, 7.4% United States or American (2000).

Economy: Employment by occupation: 15.5% management, 19.8% professional, 19.1% services, 32.3% sales, 0.4% farming, 7.5% construction, 5.5% production (2000).

Income: Per capita income: $27,599 (2007); Median household income: $39,851 (2007); Average household income: $50,771 (2007); Percent of households with income of $100,000 or more: 9.0% (2007); Poverty rate: 7.2% (2000).

Education: Percent of population age 25 and over with: High school diploma (including GED) or higher: 90.7% (2007); Bachelor's degree or higher: 27.6% (2007); Master's degree or higher: 9.7% (2007).

Housing: Homeownership rate: 79.7% (2007); Median home value: $199,314 (2007); Median rent: $662 per month (2000); Median age of housing: 17 years (2000).

Transportation: Commute to work: 93.3% car, 0.4% public transportation, 0.8% walk, 4.2% work from home (2000); Travel time to work: 30.8% less than 15 minutes, 44.7% 15 to 30 minutes, 16.2% 30 to 45 minutes, 4.7% 45 to 60 minutes, 3.7% 60 minutes or more (2000)

EAST DUNBAR (CDP).
Covers a land area of 0.797 square miles and a water area of 0.010 square miles. Located at 26.63° N. Lat.; 81.84° W. Long.

Population: 2,485 (1990); 1,935 (2000); 2,043 (2007); 2,151 (2012 projected); Race: 4.1% White, 90.6% Black, 0.0% Asian, 4.4% Hispanic of any race (2007); Density: 2,562.8 persons per square mile (2007); Average household size: 2.99 (2007); Median age: 29.3 (2007); Males per 100 females: 93.5 (2007); Marriage status: 41.7% never married, 33.0% now married, 10.8% widowed, 14.6% divorced (2000); Foreign born: 1.1% (2000); Ancestry (includes multiple ancestries): 78.1% Other groups, 7.3% United States or American, 0.7% Haitian, 0.6% Irish, 0.6% African (2000).

Economy: Employment by occupation: 4.3% management, 11.6% professional, 32.5% services, 14.5% sales, 1.1% farming, 9.8% construction, 26.4% production (2000).

Income: Per capita income: $11,119 (2007); Median household income: $24,596 (2007); Average household income: $33,148 (2007); Percent of households with income of $100,000 or more: 4.8% (2007); Poverty rate: 37.3% (2000).

Education: Percent of population age 25 and over with: High school diploma (including GED) or higher: 52.5% (2007); Bachelor's degree or higher: 5.9% (2007); Master's degree or higher: 2.5% (2007).

Housing: Homeownership rate: 61.8% (2007); Median home value: $88,125 (2007); Median rent: $394 per month (2000); Median age of housing: 27 years (2000).

Transportation: Commute to work: 92.6% car, 2.2% public transportation, 1.0% walk, 0.0% work from home (2000); Travel time to work: 38.9% less than 15 minutes, 32.5% 15 to 30 minutes, 16.2% 30 to 45 minutes, 5.9% 45 to 60 minutes, 6.4% 60 minutes or more (2000)

ESTERO (CDP).
Covers a land area of 21.085 square miles and a water area of 0.048 square miles. Located at 26.43° N. Lat.; 81.80° W. Long. Elevation is 13 feet.

History: In 1894 Estero was the site of the Koreshan Unity, a religious cooperative community established here by Cyrus R. Teed.

Population: 4,028 (1990); 9,503 (2000); 17,353 (2007); 22,412 (2012 projected); Race: 96.3% White, 0.8% Black, 0.5% Asian, 4.3% Hispanic of any race (2007); Density: 823.0 persons per square mile (2007); Average household size: 2.00 (2007); Median age: 61.1 (2007); Males per 100 females: 92.9 (2007); Marriage status: 9.6% never married, 75.1% now married, 7.6% widowed, 7.6% divorced (2000); Foreign born: 7.4% (2000); Ancestry (includes multiple ancestries): 22.7% German, 15.4% English, 13.1% Irish, 8.5% United States or American, 7.7% Italian (2000).

Economy: Employment by occupation: 18.1% management, 19.4% professional, 18.8% services, 31.2% sales, 0.3% farming, 8.2% construction, 4.0% production (2000).

Income: Per capita income: $53,542 (2007); Median household income: $67,259 (2007); Average household income: $106,766 (2007); Percent of households with income of $100,000 or more: 34.4% (2007); Poverty rate: 3.2% (2000).

Education: Percent of population age 25 and over with: High school diploma (including GED) or higher: 89.8% (2007); Bachelor's degree or higher: 34.9% (2007); Master's degree or higher: 11.6% (2007).

School District(s)
Lee County School District (PK-12)
    2005-06 Enrollment: 71,210 . . . . (239) 337-8301

Housing: Homeownership rate: 88.4% (2007); Median home value: $363,072 (2007); Median rent: $683 per month (2000); Median age of housing: 6 years (2000).

Transportation: Commute to work: 90.8% car, 0.1% public transportation, 1.2% walk, 4.8% work from home (2000); Travel time to work: 24.1% less than 15 minutes, 35.5% 15 to 30 minutes, 26.5% 30 to 45 minutes, 8.3% 45 to 60 minutes, 5.6% 60 minutes or more (2000)

Additional Information Contacts
Estero Chamber of Commerce . . . . (239) 931-0931
    http://www.leechamber.com

FORT MYERS (city). County seat. Covers a land area of 31.829 square miles and a water area of 8.591 square miles. Located at 26.63° N. Lat.; 81.85° W. Long. Elevation is 10 feet.

History: Fort Myers began as a fort built by Federal troops in 1839 and named for Colonel Abraham C. Myers, then chief quartermaster in Florida. The community that grew up around the fort became an agricultural center and a headquarters for sportsmen fishing for tarpon. Thomas Edison came to Fort Myers in 1886 looking for a suitable fiber for the incandescent lamp he was developing. Edison continued to spend his winters here, along with his friend, Henry Ford, who bought an estate adjoining Edison's.

Population: 45,222 (1990); 48,208 (2000); 55,227 (2007); 60,968 (2012 projected); Race: 50.6% White, 35.7% Black, 1.3% Asian, 20.8% Hispanic of any race (2007); Density: 1,735.1 persons per square mile (2007); Average household size: 2.49 (2007); Median age: 31.7 (2007); Males per 100 females: 100.6 (2007); Marriage status: 33.6% never married, 43.2% now married, 8.8% widowed, 14.5% divorced (2000); Foreign born: 13.4% (2000); Ancestry (includes multiple ancestries): 38.5% Other groups, 10.7% German, 8.0% English, 7.7% Irish, 6.4% United States or American (2000).

Economy: Unemployment rate: 4.6% (11/2007); Total civilian labor force: 31,580 (11/2007); Single-family building permits issued: 1,435 (2006); Multi-family building permits issued: 1,188 (2006); Employment by occupation: 8.1% management, 17.5% professional, 23.4% services, 27.5% sales, 1.1% farming, 12.7% construction, 9.8% production (2000).

Income: Per capita income: $19,605 (2007); Median household income: $32,425 (2007); Average household income: $47,395 (2007); Percent of households with income of $100,000 or more: 9.1% (2007); Poverty rate: 21.8% (2000).

Taxes: Total city taxes per capita: $775 (2005); City property taxes per capita: $411 (2005).

Education: Percent of population age 25 and over with: High school diploma (including GED) or higher: 70.9% (2007); Bachelor's degree or higher: 18.0% (2007); Master's degree or higher: 6.4% (2007).

School District(s)
Lee County School District (PK-12)
    2005-06 Enrollment: 71,210 . . . . (239) 337-8301

Four-year College(s)
Edison College (Public)
    Fall 2006 Enrollment: 10,474. . . . . (239) 489-9300
    2006-07 Tuition: In-state $2,091; Out-of-state $7,934
Florida Gulf Coast University (Public)
    Fall 2006 Enrollment: 8,279. . . . . (239) 590-1000
    2006-07 Tuition: In-state $3,565; Out-of-state $15,486
Southwest Florida College (Private, Not-for-profit)
    Fall 2006 Enrollment: 1,985. . . . . (239) 939-4766
    2006-07 Tuition: In-state $8,700; Out-of-state $8,700

Two-year College(s)
Lee County High Tech Center Central (Public)
    Fall 2006 Enrollment: 538 . . . . (239) 334-4544

Vocational/Technical School(s)
Heritage Institute-Ft Myers (Private, For-profit)
    Fall 2006 Enrollment: 236 . . . . (239) 936-5822
    2006-07 Tuition: $16,220

Sunstate Academy (Private, For-profit)
    Fall 2006 Enrollment: 182 . . . . (239) 278-1311
    2006-07 Tuition: $11,550

Housing: Homeownership rate: 37.8% (2007); Median home value: $167,703 (2007); Median rent: $508 per month (2000); Median age of housing: 26 years (2000).

Hospitals: Gulf Coast Hospital (107 beds); Lee Memorial Health System (948 beds); Southwest Florida Regional Medical Center (400 beds)

Safety: Violent crime rate: 157.7 per 10,000 population; Property crime rate: 489.8 per 10,000 population (2006).

Newspapers: Community Voice (Black - Circulation 12,000); News-Press (Circulation 102,134)

Transportation: Commute to work: 90.0% car, 2.3% public transportation, 3.4% walk, 1.8% work from home (2000); Travel time to work: 33.5% less than 15 minutes, 38.9% 15 to 30 minutes, 15.6% 30 to 45 minutes, 5.8% 45 to 60 minutes, 6.1% 60 minutes or more (2000); Amtrak: Service available.

Airports: Page Field; Southwest Florida International (primary service/medium hub)

Additional Information Contacts
Christian Chamber of Commerce . . . . (239) 481-1411
    http://www.ccswf.org
Fort Myers Chamber of Commerce . . . . (239) 278-4001
    http://www.chamber-swflorida.com
Hispanic Chamber of Commerce. (239) 334-3190
SW Florida Chamber of Commerce. . . . . (239) 278-4001
    http://www.chamber-swflorida.com

FORT MYERS BEACH (town). Covers a land area of 2.864 square miles and a water area of 3.291 square miles. Located at 26.43° N. Lat.; 81.92° W. Long. Elevation is 3 feet.

Population: 5,836 (1990); 6,561 (2000); 6,926 (2007); 7,333 (2012 projected); Race: 95.3% White, 0.1% Black, 0.5% Asian, 6.4% Hispanic of any race (2007); Density: 2,418.4 persons per square mile (2007); Average household size: 1.87 (2007); Median age: 59.3 (2007); Males per 100 females: 99.8 (2007); Marriage status: 13.0% never married, 64.6% now married, 10.6% widowed, 11.8% divorced (2000); Foreign born: 8.8% (2000); Ancestry (includes multiple ancestries): 21.2% German, 18.1% English, 17.0% Irish, 7.0% Italian, 6.9% United States or American (2000).

Economy: Single-family building permits issued: 18 (2006); Multi-family building permits issued: 64 (2006); Employment by occupation: 15.2% management, 14.8% professional, 23.4% services, 29.2% sales, 0.2% farming, 11.1% construction, 6.1% production (2000).

Income: Per capita income: $44,046 (2007); Median household income: $60,620 (2007); Average household income: $82,353 (2007); Percent of households with income of $100,000 or more: 25.4% (2007); Poverty rate: 7.2% (2000).

Education: Percent of population age 25 and over with: High school diploma (including GED) or higher: 90.4% (2007); Bachelor's degree or higher: 26.9% (2007); Master's degree or higher: 9.7% (2007).

School District(s)
Lee County School District (PK-12)
    2005-06 Enrollment: 71,210 . . . . (239) 337-8301

Housing: Homeownership rate: 77.3% (2007); Median home value: $451,739 (2007); Median rent: $642 per month (2000); Median age of housing: 22 years (2000).

Newspapers: Fort Myers Beach Bulletin (General - Circulation 14,000); Fort Myers Beach Observer (General - Circulation 16,000)

Transportation: Commute to work: 78.7% car, 2.4% public transportation, 7.0% walk, 7.3% work from home (2000); Travel time to work: 38.7% less than 15 minutes, 25.3% 15 to 30 minutes, 20.6% 30 to 45 minutes, 11.0% 45 to 60 minutes, 4.4% 60 minutes or more (2000)

Additional Information Contacts
Fort Myers Beach Chamber of Commerce . . . . (941) 454-7500
    http://www.fortmyersbeach.org
Town of Fort Myers Beach. . . . . (239) 765-0202

FORT MYERS SHORES (CDP). Covers a land area of 2.146 square miles and a water area of 0.316 square miles. Located at 26.71° N. Lat.; 81.73° W. Long. Elevation is 10 feet.

Population: 5,460 (1990); 5,793 (2000); 6,046 (2007); 6,306 (2012 projected); Race: 76.4% White, 6.0% Black, 2.2% Asian, 32.3% Hispanic of any race (2007); Density: 2,817.1 persons per square mile (2007); Average household size: 2.65 (2007); Median age: 33.6 (2007); Males per 100 females: 95.9 (2007); Marriage status: 20.2% never married, 60.4% now

married, 8.4% widowed, 11.0% divorced (2000); Foreign born: 6.5% (2000); Ancestry (includes multiple ancestries): 25.4% Other groups, 16.6% German, 13.0% United States or American, 11.1% Irish, 9.4% English (2000).
Economy: Employment by occupation: 7.9% management, 13.0% professional, 18.8% services, 30.5% sales, 0.2% farming, 20.0% construction, 9.6% production (2000).
Income: Per capita income: $21,312 (2007); Median household income: $43,299 (2007); Average household income: $56,564 (2007); Percent of households with income of $100,000 or more: 10.3% (2007); Poverty rate: 8.2% (2000).
Education: Percent of population age 25 and over with: High school diploma (including GED) or higher: 74.1% (2007); Bachelor's degree or higher: 12.6% (2007); Master's degree or higher: 5.1% (2007).
Housing: Homeownership rate: 79.3% (2007); Median home value: $188,445 (2007); Median rent: $452 per month (2000); Median age of housing: 23 years (2000).
Transportation: Commute to work: 97.4% car, 1.4% public transportation, 0.0% walk, 0.2% work from home (2000); Travel time to work: 18.9% less than 15 minutes, 39.4% 15 to 30 minutes, 30.3% 30 to 45 minutes, 5.2% 45 to 60 minutes, 6.3% 60 minutes or more (2000)

GATEWAY (CDP). Covers a land area of 8.551 square miles and a water area of 0.152 square miles. Located at 26.57° N. Lat.; 81.75° W. Long. Elevation is 23 feet.
Population: 46 (1990); 2,943 (2000); 5,709 (2007); 7,530 (2012 projected); Race: 92.9% White, 2.3% Black, 2.7% Asian, 3.7% Hispanic of any race (2007); Density: 667.6 persons per square mile (2007); Average household size: 2.52 (2007); Median age: 40.9 (2007); Males per 100 females: 97.9 (2007); Marriage status: 10.1% never married, 77.8% now married, 4.0% widowed, 8.0% divorced (2000); Foreign born: 7.4% (2000); Ancestry (includes multiple ancestries): 19.5% German, 15.4% Irish, 11.1% Italian, 11.0% English, 10.2% Other groups (2000).
Economy: Employment by occupation: 25.3% management, 26.7% professional, 9.0% services, 33.3% sales, 0.4% farming, 2.7% construction, 2.7% production (2000).
Income: Per capita income: $54,573 (2007); Median household income: $112,628 (2007); Average household income: $137,737 (2007); Percent of households with income of $100,000 or more: 58.8% (2007); Poverty rate: 0.9% (2000).
Education: Percent of population age 25 and over with: High school diploma (including GED) or higher: 96.9% (2007); Bachelor's degree or higher: 48.1% (2007); Master's degree or higher: 17.0% (2007).
Housing: Homeownership rate: 92.1% (2007); Median home value: $400,614 (2007); Median rent: $1,121 per month (2000); Median age of housing: 4 years (2000).
Transportation: Commute to work: 92.7% car, 0.0% public transportation, 1.3% walk, 5.1% work from home (2000); Travel time to work: 16.3% less than 15 minutes, 51.8% 15 to 30 minutes, 20.5% 30 to 45 minutes, 2.3% 45 to 60 minutes, 9.1% 60 minutes or more (2000)

HARLEM HEIGHTS (CDP). Covers a land area of 0.794 square miles and a water area of 0 square miles. Located at 26.51° N. Lat.; 81.92° W. Long. Elevation is 3 feet.
Population: 433 (1990); 1,065 (2000); 1,619 (2007); 2,040 (2012 projected); Race: 45.7% White, 29.1% Black, 0.2% Asian, 66.9% Hispanic of any race (2007); Density: 2,039.2 persons per square mile (2007); Average household size: 3.47 (2007); Median age: 29.5 (2007); Males per 100 females: 103.9 (2007); Marriage status: 43.2% never married, 34.3% now married, 6.9% widowed, 15.6% divorced (2000); Foreign born: 1.7% (2000); Ancestry (includes multiple ancestries): 92.7% Other groups, 1.8% United States or American, 1.0% Irish, 1.0% German (2000).
Economy: Employment by occupation: 0.0% management, 7.3% professional, 38.4% services, 31.3% sales, 0.0% farming, 12.3% construction, 10.6% production (2000).
Income: Per capita income: $11,455 (2007); Median household income: $37,719 (2007); Average household income: $39,796 (2007); Percent of households with income of $100,000 or more: 3.2% (2007); Poverty rate: 27.5% (2000).
Education: Percent of population age 25 and over with: High school diploma (including GED) or higher: 48.7% (2007); Bachelor's degree or higher: 3.6% (2007); Master's degree or higher: 0.0% (2007).
Housing: Homeownership rate: 82.8% (2007); Median home value: $123,394 (2007); Median rent: $341 per month (2000); Median age of housing: 21 years (2000).

Transportation: Commute to work: 97.6% car, 0.0% public transportation, 0.0% walk, 0.0% work from home (2000); Travel time to work: 38.0% less than 15 minutes, 23.5% 15 to 30 minutes, 27.6% 30 to 45 minutes, 8.2% 45 to 60 minutes, 2.6% 60 minutes or more (2000)

IONA (CDP). Covers a land area of 7.131 square miles and a water area of 3.077 square miles. Located at 26.51° N. Lat.; 81.95° W. Long. Elevation is 7 feet.
Population: 9,565 (1990); 11,756 (2000); 13,862 (2007); 15,522 (2012 projected); Race: 96.2% White, 0.4% Black, 0.8% Asian, 7.1% Hispanic of any race (2007); Density: 1,943.9 persons per square mile (2007); Average household size: 1.92 (2007); Median age: 56.8 (2007); Males per 100 females: 93.3 (2007); Marriage status: 11.9% never married, 65.9% now married, 11.3% widowed, 10.9% divorced (2000); Foreign born: 7.3% (2000); Ancestry (includes multiple ancestries): 25.1% German, 16.8% English, 15.8% Irish, 8.8% United States or American, 7.3% Other groups (2000).
Economy: Employment by occupation: 16.9% management, 20.0% professional, 19.3% services, 26.7% sales, 0.4% farming, 7.8% construction, 8.9% production (2000).
Income: Per capita income: $41,844 (2007); Median household income: $45,151 (2007); Average household income: $80,400 (2007); Percent of households with income of $100,000 or more: 19.6% (2007); Poverty rate: 10.0% (2000).
Education: Percent of population age 25 and over with: High school diploma (including GED) or higher: 86.7% (2007); Bachelor's degree or higher: 27.6% (2007); Master's degree or higher: 10.7% (2007).
Housing: Homeownership rate: 80.3% (2007); Median home value: $223,249 (2007); Median rent: $580 per month (2000); Median age of housing: 16 years (2000).
Transportation: Commute to work: 90.5% car, 0.2% public transportation, 2.0% walk, 4.8% work from home (2000); Travel time to work: 34.1% less than 15 minutes, 38.3% 15 to 30 minutes, 18.1% 30 to 45 minutes, 6.1% 45 to 60 minutes, 3.4% 60 minutes or more (2000)

LEHIGH ACRES (CDP). Covers a land area of 94.887 square miles and a water area of 1.094 square miles. Located at 26.60° N. Lat.; 81.63° W. Long. Elevation is 20 feet.
Population: 22,352 (1990); 33,430 (2000); 47,986 (2007); 58,233 (2012 projected); Race: 76.5% White, 12.6% Black, 1.1% Asian, 23.2% Hispanic of any race (2007); Density: 505.7 persons per square mile (2007); Average household size: 2.68 (2007); Median age: 35.3 (2007); Males per 100 females: 97.0 (2007); Marriage status: 17.3% never married, 63.2% now married, 9.2% widowed, 10.3% divorced (2000); Foreign born: 9.3% (2000); Ancestry (includes multiple ancestries): 22.4% Other groups, 15.1% German, 12.4% Irish, 11.9% United States or American, 10.6% English (2000).
Economy: Employment by occupation: 9.0% management, 12.9% professional, 19.0% services, 30.5% sales, 0.2% farming, 16.3% construction, 12.1% production (2000).
Income: Per capita income: $20,386 (2007); Median household income: $46,708 (2007); Average household income: $54,282 (2007); Percent of households with income of $100,000 or more: 8.6% (2007); Poverty rate: 7.7% (2000).
Education: Percent of population age 25 and over with: High school diploma (including GED) or higher: 77.1% (2007); Bachelor's degree or higher: 11.2% (2007); Master's degree or higher: 4.3% (2007).
School District(s)
Lee County School District (PK-12)
    2005-06 Enrollment: 71,210 . . . . (239) 337-8301
Housing: Homeownership rate: 84.0% (2007); Median home value: $184,616 (2007); Median rent: $513 per month (2000); Median age of housing: 17 years (2000).
Hospitals: Lehigh Regional Medical Center (88 beds)
Newspapers: Lehigh Acres News Star (General - Circulation 14,000)
Transportation: Commute to work: 95.2% car, 0.4% public transportation, 0.7% walk, 2.5% work from home (2000); Travel time to work: 18.9% less than 15 minutes, 30.7% 15 to 30 minutes, 32.3% 30 to 45 minutes, 11.1% 45 to 60 minutes, 7.0% 60 minutes or more (2000)
Additional Information Contacts
Lehigh Acres Chamber of Commerce . . . . (239) 369-3322
    http://www.lehighacreschamber.org

LOCHMOOR WATERWAY ESTATES (CDP). Covers a land area of 2.230 square miles and a water area of 0.528 square miles. Located at 26.64° N. Lat.; 81.91° W. Long. Elevation is 3 feet.
Population: 3,671 (1990); 3,858 (2000); 4,188 (2007); 4,496 (2012 projected); Race: 93.8% White, 1.4% Black, 2.1% Asian, 6.6% Hispanic of any race (2007); Density: 1,877.8 persons per square mile (2007); Average household size: 2.31 (2007); Median age: 46.9 (2007); Males per 100 females: 94.8 (2007); Marriage status: 15.8% never married, 66.9% now married, 8.1% widowed, 9.1% divorced (2000); Foreign born: 5.4% (2000); Ancestry (includes multiple ancestries): 21.8% German, 16.8% Irish, 15.9% English, 7.9% Italian, 7.7% Other groups (2000).
Economy: Employment by occupation: 15.0% management, 21.5% professional, 13.2% services, 30.3% sales, 0.0% farming, 12.6% construction, 7.4% production (2000).
Income: Per capita income: $36,468 (2007); Median household income: $58,645 (2007); Average household income: $84,242 (2007); Percent of households with income of $100,000 or more: 24.4% (2007); Poverty rate: 3.2% (2000).
Education: Percent of population age 25 and over with: High school diploma (including GED) or higher: 89.3% (2007); Bachelor's degree or higher: 28.6% (2007); Master's degree or higher: 9.3% (2007).
Housing: Homeownership rate: 86.7% (2007); Median home value: $253,139 (2007); Median rent: $511 per month (2000); Median age of housing: 23 years (2000).
Transportation: Commute to work: 95.6% car, 0.8% public transportation, 0.4% walk, 3.1% work from home (2000); Travel time to work: 26.5% less than 15 minutes, 49.5% 15 to 30 minutes, 17.7% 30 to 45 minutes, 2.0% 45 to 60 minutes, 4.3% 60 minutes or more (2000)

MATLACHA (CDP). Covers a land area of 0.151 square miles and a water area of <.001 square miles. Located at 26.63° N. Lat.; 82.07° W. Long. Elevation is 3 feet.
Population: 742 (1990); 735 (2000); 778 (2007); 822 (2012 projected); Race: 97.3% White, 0.0% Black, 0.3% Asian, 2.7% Hispanic of any race (2007); Density: 5,164.2 persons per square mile (2007); Average household size: 1.78 (2007); Median age: 58.2 (2007); Males per 100 females: 106.4 (2007); Marriage status: 13.6% never married, 63.8% now married, 11.0% widowed, 11.6% divorced (2000); Foreign born: 2.7% (2000); Ancestry (includes multiple ancestries): 29.5% German, 17.8% Irish, 15.0% English, 11.4% Italian, 8.0% Other groups (2000).
Economy: Employment by occupation: 18.8% management, 17.1% professional, 19.9% services, 27.7% sales, 3.1% farming, 6.5% construction, 6.8% production (2000).
Income: Per capita income: $35,228 (2007); Median household income: $46,346 (2007); Average household income: $62,574 (2007); Percent of households with income of $100,000 or more: 9.6% (2007); Poverty rate: 9.2% (2000).
Education: Percent of population age 25 and over with: High school diploma (including GED) or higher: 90.2% (2007); Bachelor's degree or higher: 17.7% (2007); Master's degree or higher: 8.1% (2007).
Housing: Homeownership rate: 74.0% (2007); Median home value: $283,696 (2007); Median rent: $488 per month (2000); Median age of housing: 29 years (2000).
Transportation: Commute to work: 87.0% car, 0.0% public transportation, 3.8% walk, 7.5% work from home (2000); Travel time to work: 38.9% less than 15 minutes, 30.4% 15 to 30 minutes, 14.4% 30 to 45 minutes, 0.0% 45 to 60 minutes, 16.3% 60 minutes or more (2000)

MATLACHA ISLES-MATLACHA SHORES (CDP). Covers a land area of 0.218 square miles and a water area of 0.186 square miles. Located at 26.63° N. Lat.; 82.06° W. Long.
Population: 193 (1990); 304 (2000); 431 (2007); 515 (2012 projected); Race: 97.7% White, 0.0% Black, 0.7% Asian, 0.7% Hispanic of any race (2007); Density: 1,972.9 persons per square mile (2007); Average household size: 1.87 (2007); Median age: 58.4 (2007); Males per 100 females: 113.4 (2007); Marriage status: 8.1% never married, 72.7% now married, 4.8% widowed, 14.4% divorced (2000); Foreign born: 7.4% (2000); Ancestry (includes multiple ancestries): 34.7% German, 18.5% United States or American, 12.2% English, 11.8% Irish, 10.7% French (except Basque) (2000).
Economy: Employment by occupation: 22.8% management, 20.5% professional, 13.4% services, 33.9% sales, 0.0% farming, 3.1% construction, 6.3% production (2000).

Income: Per capita income: $28,306 (2007); Median household income: $40,259 (2007); Average household income: $52,814 (2007); Percent of households with income of $100,000 or more: 7.4% (2007); Poverty rate: 4.8% (2000).
Education: Percent of population age 25 and over with: High school diploma (including GED) or higher: 95.0% (2007); Bachelor's degree or higher: 41.0% (2007); Master's degree or higher: 10.6% (2007).
Housing: Homeownership rate: 80.1% (2007); Median home value: $263,571 (2007); Median rent: $481 per month (2000); Median age of housing: 22 years (2000).
Transportation: Commute to work: 88.2% car, 0.0% public transportation, 0.0% walk, 11.8% work from home (2000); Travel time to work: 5.4% less than 15 minutes, 34.8% 15 to 30 minutes, 35.7% 30 to 45 minutes, 17.0% 45 to 60 minutes, 7.1% 60 minutes or more (2000)

MCGREGOR (CDP). Covers a land area of 2.563 square miles and a water area of 1.528 square miles. Located at 26.56° N. Lat.; 81.91° W. Long.
Population: 6,504 (1990); 7,136 (2000); 8,983 (2007); 10,355 (2012 projected); Race: 94.1% White, 1.5% Black, 2.3% Asian, 5.0% Hispanic of any race (2007); Density: 3,504.7 persons per square mile (2007); Average household size: 2.13 (2007); Median age: 51.9 (2007); Males per 100 females: 94.2 (2007); Marriage status: 11.7% never married, 67.2% now married, 10.8% widowed, 10.3% divorced (2000); Foreign born: 7.9% (2000); Ancestry (includes multiple ancestries): 21.6% German, 16.7% English, 14.8% Irish, 9.0% Italian, 8.2% Other groups (2000).
Economy: Employment by occupation: 18.4% management, 29.2% professional, 10.5% services, 32.1% sales, 0.0% farming, 4.7% construction, 5.0% production (2000).
Income: Per capita income: $47,340 (2007); Median household income: $67,192 (2007); Average household income: $100,891 (2007); Percent of households with income of $100,000 or more: 32.5% (2007); Poverty rate: 3.3% (2000).
Education: Percent of population age 25 and over with: High school diploma (including GED) or higher: 93.7% (2007); Bachelor's degree or higher: 49.7% (2007); Master's degree or higher: 19.3% (2007).
Housing: Homeownership rate: 89.3% (2007); Median home value: $334,550 (2007); Median rent: $624 per month (2000); Median age of housing: 22 years (2000).
Transportation: Commute to work: 93.8% car, 0.0% public transportation, 0.2% walk, 5.3% work from home (2000); Travel time to work: 32.8% less than 15 minutes, 47.3% 15 to 30 minutes, 14.8% 30 to 45 minutes, 3.0% 45 to 60 minutes, 2.1% 60 minutes or more (2000)

NORTH FORT MYERS (CDP). Covers a land area of 52.621 square miles and a water area of 1.967 square miles. Located at 26.70° N. Lat.; 81.88° W. Long. Elevation is 3 feet.
Population: 34,213 (1990); 40,214 (2000); 46,669 (2007); 51,779 (2012 projected); Race: 94.0% White, 1.8% Black, 0.7% Asian, 5.4% Hispanic of any race (2007); Density: 886.9 persons per square mile (2007); Average household size: 2.00 (2007); Median age: 59.1 (2007); Males per 100 females: 92.3 (2007); Marriage status: 11.6% never married, 64.4% now married, 13.2% widowed, 10.8% divorced (2000); Foreign born: 4.2% (2000); Ancestry (includes multiple ancestries): 20.0% German, 15.7% English, 14.0% Irish, 10.0% United States or American, 8.1% Other groups (2000).
Economy: Employment by occupation: 9.4% management, 14.0% professional, 17.2% services, 30.6% sales, 0.4% farming, 16.7% construction, 11.7% production (2000).
Income: Per capita income: $24,672 (2007); Median household income: $39,150 (2007); Average household income: $49,071 (2007); Percent of households with income of $100,000 or more: 8.4% (2007); Poverty rate: 9.9% (2000).
Education: Percent of population age 25 and over with: High school diploma (including GED) or higher: 80.2% (2007); Bachelor's degree or higher: 14.3% (2007); Master's degree or higher: 5.9% (2007).
School District(s)
Lee County School District (PK-12)
    2005-06 Enrollment: 71,210 . . . . (239) 337-8301
Housing: Homeownership rate: 86.9% (2007); Median home value: $124,823 (2007); Median rent: $480 per month (2000); Median age of housing: 18 years (2000).
Transportation: Commute to work: 92.2% car, 0.9% public transportation, 1.2% walk, 3.5% work from home (2000); Travel time to work: 23.0% less

OLGA (CDP). Covers a land area of 4.249 square miles and a water area of 0.153 square miles. Located at 26.71° N. Lat.; 81.70° W. Long. Elevation is 3 feet.

Population: 1,163 (1990); 1,398 (2000); 1,869 (2007); 2,225 (2012 projected); Race: 82.2% White, 4.1% Black, 1.8% Asian, 17.8% Hispanic of any race (2007); Density: 439.9 persons per square mile (2007); Average household size: 2.72 (2007); Median age: 33.5 (2007); Males per 100 females: 98.6 (2007); Marriage status: 17.9% never married, 64.8% now married, 9.2% widowed, 8.1% divorced (2000); Foreign born: 6.2% (2000); Ancestry (includes multiple ancestries): 24.6% Other groups, 14.5% German, 14.1% English, 10.1% United States or American, 7.9% Irish (2000).

Economy: Employment by occupation: 14.8% management, 13.5% professional, 17.1% services, 27.6% sales, 0.8% farming, 19.0% construction, 7.2% production (2000).

Income: Per capita income: $29,576 (2007); Median household income: $63,835 (2007); Average household income: $80,345 (2007); Percent of households with income of $100,000 or more: 17.0% (2007); Poverty rate: 4.0% (2000).

Education: Percent of population age 25 and over with: High school diploma (including GED) or higher: 83.6% (2007); Bachelor's degree or higher: 15.4% (2007); Master's degree or higher: 5.6% (2007).

Housing: Homeownership rate: 83.6% (2007); Median home value: $195,292 (2007); Median rent: $471 per month (2000); Median age of housing: 17 years (2000).

Transportation: Commute to work: 94.4% car, 0.0% public transportation, 0.0% walk, 4.6% work from home (2000); Travel time to work: 13.9% less than 15 minutes, 31.8% 15 to 30 minutes, 27.7% 30 to 45 minutes, 7.2% 45 to 60 minutes, 19.3% 60 minutes or more (2000)

PAGE PARK (CDP). Covers a land area of 0.277 square miles and a water area of 0 square miles. Located at 26.57° N. Lat.; 81.86° W. Long. Elevation is 13 feet.

Population: 610 (1990); 524 (2000); 466 (2007); 483 (2012 projected); Race: 79.2% White, 4.5% Black, 0.2% Asian, 33.5% Hispanic of any race (2007); Density: 1,681.6 persons per square mile (2007); Average household size: 2.17 (2007); Median age: 33.6 (2007); Males per 100 females: 154.6 (2007); Marriage status: 28.5% never married, 42.1% now married, 2.6% widowed, 26.8% divorced (2000); Foreign born: 8.6% (2000); Ancestry (includes multiple ancestries): 21.7% German, 20.7% Other groups, 14.8% United States or American, 12.5% English, 10.7% French (except Basque) (2000).

Economy: Employment by occupation: 3.3% management, 9.5% professional, 22.5% services, 31.4% sales, 0.0% farming, 18.0% construction, 15.4% production (2000).

Income: Per capita income: $14,383 (2007); Median household income: $24,662 (2007); Average household income: $31,174 (2007); Percent of households with income of $100,000 or more: 1.9% (2007); Poverty rate: 13.2% (2000).

Education: Percent of population age 25 and over with: High school diploma (including GED) or higher: 77.2% (2007); Bachelor's degree or higher: 2.4% (2007); Master's degree or higher: 0.0% (2007).

Housing: Homeownership rate: 19.1% (2007); Median home value: $120,833 (2007); Median rent: $393 per month (2000); Median age of housing: 44 years (2000).

Transportation: Commute to work: 84.6% car, 2.1% public transportation, 6.6% walk, 0.0% work from home (2000); Travel time to work: 42.0% less than 15 minutes, 38.7% 15 to 30 minutes, 13.3% 30 to 45 minutes, 2.1% 45 to 60 minutes, 3.9% 60 minutes or more (2000)

PALMONA PARK (CDP). Covers a land area of 0.830 square miles and a water area of 0 square miles. Located at 26.68° N. Lat.; 81.89° W. Long. Elevation is 10 feet.

Population: 1,392 (1990); 1,353 (2000); 1,332 (2007); 1,375 (2012 projected); Race: 92.3% White, 0.2% Black, 1.3% Asian, 22.9% Hispanic of any race (2007); Density: 1,605.6 persons per square mile (2007); Average household size: 2.41 (2007); Median age: 30.1 (2007); Males per 100 females: 115.2 (2007); Marriage status: 25.5% never married, 57.9% now married, 4.8% widowed, 11.8% divorced (2000); Foreign born: 4.0% (2000); Ancestry (includes multiple ancestries): 24.0% German, 23.0% Other groups, 16.9% Irish, 11.9% United States or American, 11.1% English (2000).

Income: Per capita income: $16,074 (2007); Median household income: $23,594 (2007); Average household income: $38,786 (2007); Percent of households with income of $100,000 or more: 5.3% (2007); Poverty rate: 21.1% (2000).

Education: Percent of population age 25 and over with: High school diploma (including GED) or higher: 64.8% (2007); Bachelor's degree or higher: 3.7% (2007); Master's degree or higher: 1.6% (2007).

Housing: Homeownership rate: 55.8% (2007); Median home value: $106,875 (2007); Median rent: $424 per month (2000); Median age of housing: 27 years (2000).

Transportation: Commute to work: 85.3% car, 4.8% public transportation, 0.0% walk, 3.6% work from home (2000); Travel time to work: 33.9% less than 15 minutes, 48.7% 15 to 30 minutes, 10.6% 30 to 45 minutes, 6.8% 45 to 60 minutes, 0.0% 60 minutes or more (2000)

PINE ISLAND CENTER (CDP). Covers a land area of 4.298 square miles and a water area of 0.007 square miles. Located at 26.63° N. Lat.; 82.12° W. Long. Elevation is 3 feet.

Population: 1,395 (1990); 1,721 (2000); 1,989 (2007); 2,213 (2012 projected); Race: 95.5% White, 0.0% Black, 0.4% Asian, 3.8% Hispanic of any race (2007); Density: 462.8 persons per square mile (2007); Average household size: 2.27 (2007); Median age: 44.0 (2007); Males per 100 females: 104.8 (2007); Marriage status: 11.9% never married, 62.8% now married, 10.4% widowed, 14.9% divorced (2000); Foreign born: 0.9% (2000); Ancestry (includes multiple ancestries): 23.5% German, 17.1% Irish, 14.7% English, 10.4% United States or American, 7.3% French (except Basque) (2000).

Economy: Employment by occupation: 12.0% management, 16.5% professional, 12.5% services, 31.2% sales, 10.0% farming, 11.0% construction, 6.8% production (2000).

Income: Per capita income: $25,520 (2007); Median household income: $49,352 (2007); Average household income: $57,945 (2007); Percent of households with income of $100,000 or more: 15.0% (2007); Poverty rate: 9.6% (2000).

Education: Percent of population age 25 and over with: High school diploma (including GED) or higher: 88.2% (2007); Bachelor's degree or higher: 19.1% (2007); Master's degree or higher: 5.7% (2007).

Housing: Homeownership rate: 79.5% (2007); Median home value: $208,333 (2007); Median rent: $433 per month (2000); Median age of housing: 16 years (2000).

Transportation: Commute to work: 93.0% car, 0.0% public transportation, 0.0% walk, 4.7% work from home (2000); Travel time to work: 16.2% less than 15 minutes, 18.7% 15 to 30 minutes, 36.8% 30 to 45 minutes, 13.5% 45 to 60 minutes, 14.8% 60 minutes or more (2000)

PINE MANOR (CDP). Covers a land area of 0.425 square miles and a water area of 0 square miles. Located at 26.57° N. Lat.; 81.87° W. Long. Elevation is 10 feet.

Population: 3,166 (1990); 3,785 (2000); 4,131 (2007); 4,481 (2012 projected); Race: 55.3% White, 21.7% Black, 0.5% Asian, 63.6% Hispanic of any race (2007); Density: 9,715.4 persons per square mile (2007); Average household size: 3.16 (2007); Median age: 27.0 (2007); Males per 100 females: 121.0 (2007); Marriage status: 32.2% never married, 44.4% now married, 5.5% widowed, 17.8% divorced (2000); Foreign born: 27.9% (2000); Ancestry (includes multiple ancestries): 43.2% Other groups, 13.2% Irish, 8.1% United States or American, 8.0% German, 4.0% English (2000).

Economy: Employment by occupation: 3.9% management, 7.3% professional, 30.8% services, 18.5% sales, 1.2% farming, 25.9% construction, 12.4% production (2000).

Income: Per capita income: $10,260 (2007); Median household income: $26,903 (2007); Average household income: $30,334 (2007); Percent of households with income of $100,000 or more: 1.1% (2007); Poverty rate: 32.6% (2000).

Education: Percent of population age 25 and over with: High school diploma (including GED) or higher: 54.5% (2007); Bachelor's degree or higher: 7.2% (2007); Master's degree or higher: 4.3% (2007).

Housing: Homeownership rate: 16.1% (2007); Median home value: $89,222 (2007); Median rent: $423 per month (2000); Median age of housing: 29 years (2000).

Transportation: Commute to work: 84.2% car, 5.7% public transportation, 3.1% walk, 1.0% work from home (2000); Travel time to work: 23.4% less

PINELAND (CDP). Covers a land area of 0.922 square miles and a water area of 0 square miles. Located at 26.66° N. Lat.; 82.14° W. Long. Elevation is 20 feet.

Population: 309 (1990); 444 (2000); 478 (2007); 509 (2012 projected); Race: 97.5% White, 0.0% Black, 0.0% Asian, 2.5% Hispanic of any race (2007); Density: 518.6 persons per square mile (2007); Average household size: 2.07 (2007); Median age: 57.1 (2007); Males per 100 females: 95.1 (2007); Marriage status: 10.0% never married, 72.0% now married, 5.3% widowed, 12.7% divorced (2000); Foreign born: 4.9% (2000); Ancestry (includes multiple ancestries): 23.6% English, 14.6% German, 13.9% Irish, 8.6% United States or American, 6.3% Scotch-Irish (2000).

Economy: Employment by occupation: 19.2% management, 52.6% professional, 8.3% services, 13.5% sales, 6.4% farming, 0.0% construction, 0.0% production (2000).

Income: Per capita income: $34,629 (2007); Median household income: $68,654 (2007); Average household income: $71,656 (2007); Percent of households with income of $100,000 or more: 19.5% (2007); Poverty rate: 3.0% (2000).

Education: Percent of population age 25 and over with: High school diploma (including GED) or higher: 95.6% (2007); Bachelor's degree or higher: 34.9% (2007); Master's degree or higher: 17.1% (2007).

Housing: Homeownership rate: 86.1% (2007); Median home value: $408,333 (2007); Median rent: $575 per month (2000); Median age of housing: 16 years (2000).

Transportation: Commute to work: 87.2% car, 0.0% public transportation, 8.3% walk, 4.5% work from home (2000); Travel time to work: 45.6% less than 15 minutes, 0.0% 15 to 30 minutes, 27.5% 30 to 45 minutes, 21.5% 45 to 60 minutes, 5.4% 60 minutes or more (2000)

PUNTA RASSA (CDP). Covers a land area of 2.356 square miles and a water area of 2.139 square miles. Located at 26.51° N. Lat.; 81.99° W. Long. Elevation is 3 feet.

History: Punta Rassa was established on the site of a military post built in 1837, and used again during the Civil War. The townsite of Punta Rassa was surveyed in 1866 by the International Ocean Telegraph Company, which established cable service between the U.S. and Cuba.

Population: 1,493 (1990); 1,731 (2000); 2,173 (2007); 2,514 (2012 projected); Race: 98.8% White, 0.6% Black, 0.3% Asian, 0.4% Hispanic of any race (2007); Density: 922.5 persons per square mile (2007); Average household size: 1.65 (2007); Median age: 79.9 (2007); Males per 100 females: 67.4 (2007); Marriage status: 6.9% never married, 58.0% now married, 31.3% widowed, 3.8% divorced (2000); Foreign born: 3.6% (2000); Ancestry (includes multiple ancestries): 30.0% English, 28.7% German, 8.9% Scottish, 8.5% Irish, 4.6% French (except Basque) (2000).

Economy: Employment by occupation: 12.1% management, 21.1% professional, 3.4% services, 63.4% sales, 0.0% farming, 0.0% construction, 0.0% production (2000).

Income: Per capita income: $50,749 (2007); Median household income: $55,150 (2007); Average household income: $80,734 (2007); Percent of households with income of $100,000 or more: 26.0% (2007); Poverty rate: 1.9% (2000).

Education: Percent of population age 25 and over with: High school diploma (including GED) or higher: 95.8% (2007); Bachelor's degree or higher: 52.0% (2007); Master's degree or higher: 18.7% (2007).

Housing: Homeownership rate: 43.0% (2007); Median home value: $477,885 (2007); Median rent: $1,074 per month (2000); Median age of housing: 21 years (2000).

Transportation: Commute to work: 86.0% car, 0.0% public transportation, 2.7% walk, 5.4% work from home (2000); Travel time to work: 23.9% less than 15 minutes, 42.4% 15 to 30 minutes, 28.4% 30 to 45 minutes, 2.9% 45 to 60 minutes, 2.5% 60 minutes or more (2000)

SAINT JAMES CITY (CDP). Covers a land area of 14.602 square miles and a water area of 0.168 square miles. Located at 26.53° N. Lat.; 82.09° W. Long. Elevation is 3 feet.

History: St. James City was settled in 1887 on Pine Island by a group of New Englanders, and developed as a resort. When the resort deteriorated, it was purchased by a sisal hemp company which began the manufacture of rope.

Population: 3,364 (1990); 4,105 (2000); 4,806 (2007); 5,362 (2012 projected); Race: 98.6% White, 0.2% Black, 0.3% Asian, 1.2% Hispanic of any race (2007); Density: 329.1 persons per square mile (2007); Average

(2000); Ancestry (includes multiple ancestries): 23.6% German, 17.9% Irish, 17.4% English, 9.4% United States or American, 6.0% French (except Basque) (2000).

Economy: Employment by occupation: 11.7% management, 17.6% professional, 19.8% services, 30.6% sales, 3.3% farming, 8.7% construction, 8.3% production (2000).

Income: Per capita income: $32,976 (2007); Median household income: $45,134 (2007); Average household income: $61,957 (2007); Percent of households with income of $100,000 or more: 13.7% (2007); Poverty rate: 4.3% (2000).

Education: Percent of population age 25 and over with: High school diploma (including GED) or higher: 83.4% (2007); Bachelor's degree or higher: 17.6% (2007); Master's degree or higher: 6.8% (2007).

Housing: Homeownership rate: 91.9% (2007); Median home value: $220,000 (2007); Median rent: $629 per month (2000); Median age of housing: 19 years (2000).

Transportation: Commute to work: 86.1% car, 0.0% public transportation, 3.5% walk, 6.9% work from home (2000); Travel time to work: 36.4% less than 15 minutes, 15.8% 15 to 30 minutes, 23.2% 30 to 45 minutes, 20.2% 45 to 60 minutes, 4.4% 60 minutes or more (2000)

SAN CARLOS PARK (CDP). Covers a land area of 4.856 square miles and a water area of 0.209 square miles. Located at 26.47° N. Lat.; 81.81° W. Long. Elevation is 16 feet.

Population: 11,272 (1990); 16,317 (2000); 20,235 (2007); 23,115 (2012 projected); Race: 90.2% White, 2.1% Black, 0.9% Asian, 15.2% Hispanic of any race (2007); Density: 4,167.4 persons per square mile (2007); Average household size: 2.79 (2007); Median age: 33.2 (2007); Males per 100 females: 103.9 (2007); Marriage status: 21.5% never married, 60.8% now married, 4.3% widowed, 13.4% divorced (2000); Foreign born: 5.9% (2000); Ancestry (includes multiple ancestries): 25.5% German, 17.5% Irish, 14.2% Other groups, 11.1% Italian, 10.2% English (2000).

Economy: Employment by occupation: 10.3% management, 14.7% professional, 19.3% services, 29.9% sales, 0.2% farming, 15.5% construction, 10.1% production (2000).

Income: Per capita income: $21,913 (2007); Median household income: $53,696 (2007); Average household income: $61,033 (2007); Percent of households with income of $100,000 or more: 12.4% (2007); Poverty rate: 8.0% (2000).

Education: Percent of population age 25 and over with: High school diploma (including GED) or higher: 85.5% (2007); Bachelor's degree or higher: 13.7% (2007); Master's degree or higher: 4.6% (2007).

Housing: Homeownership rate: 79.5% (2007); Median home value: $222,085 (2007); Median rent: $612 per month (2000); Median age of housing: 13 years (2000).

Transportation: Commute to work: 96.8% car, 0.1% public transportation, 0.7% walk, 1.7% work from home (2000); Travel time to work: 16.1% less than 15 minutes, 44.6% 15 to 30 minutes, 26.6% 30 to 45 minutes, 7.8% 45 to 60 minutes, 4.9% 60 minutes or more (2000)

SANIBEL (city). Covers a land area of 17.207 square miles and a water area of 15.958 square miles. Located at 26.44° N. Lat.; 82.08° W. Long. Elevation is 3 feet.

Population: 5,468 (1990); 6,064 (2000); 6,042 (2007); 6,160 (2012 projected); Race: 97.4% White, 1.0% Black, 0.5% Asian, 2.1% Hispanic of any race (2007); Density: 351.1 persons per square mile (2007); Average household size: 1.95 (2007); Median age: 60.3 (2007); Males per 100 females: 90.9 (2007); Marriage status: 8.7% never married, 74.2% now married, 8.7% widowed, 8.5% divorced (2000); Foreign born: 7.4% (2000); Ancestry (includes multiple ancestries): 21.2% German, 21.2% English, 15.2% Irish, 7.9% Italian, 6.8% United States or American (2000).

Economy: Single-family building permits issued: 16 (2006); Multi-family building permits issued: 0 (2006); Employment by occupation: 28.5% management, 16.1% professional, 14.0% services, 29.6% sales, 0.2% farming, 5.2% construction, 6.6% production (2000).

Income: Per capita income: $70,904 (2007); Median household income: $95,724 (2007); Average household income: $138,372 (2007); Percent of households with income of $100,000 or more: 47.7% (2007); Poverty rate: 3.2% (2000).

Education: Percent of population age 25 and over with: High school diploma (including GED) or higher: 96.0% (2007); Bachelor's degree or higher: 54.9% (2007); Master's degree or higher: 22.3% (2007).

Lee County School District (PK-12)
2005-06 Enrollment: 71,210 . . . . (239) 337-8301

Housing: Homeownership rate: 86.6% (2007); Median home value: $902,134 (2007); Median rent: $929 per month (2000); Median age of housing: 21 years (2000).

Safety: Violent crime rate: 3.2 per 10,000 population; Property crime rate: 160.3 per 10,000 population (2006).

Newspapers: Captiva Current (General - Circulation 2,000); Island Reporter (General - Circulation 45,000); Island Sun (General - Circulation 12,000); Sanibel-Captiva Chronicle (General - Circulation 7,000)

Transportation: Commute to work: 78.0% car, 0.4% public transportation, 3.7% walk, 13.0% work from home (2000); Travel time to work: 54.4% less than 15 minutes, 26.2% 15 to 30 minutes, 10.3% 30 to 45 minutes, 5.9% 45 to 60 minutes, 3.3% 60 minutes or more (2000)

Additional Information Contacts
City of Sanibel . . . . (239) 472-4135
http://www.mysanibel.com
Sanibel-Captiva Chamber of Commerce . . . . (239) 472-1080
http://www.sanibel-captiva.org

SUNCOAST ESTATES (CDP). Covers a land area of 2.688 square miles and a water area of 0 square miles. Located at 26.71° N. Lat.; 81.86° W. Long. Elevation is 16 feet.

Population: 4,469 (1990); 4,867 (2000); 5,321 (2007); 5,729 (2012 projected); Race: 92.7% White, 1.2% Black, 0.2% Asian, 9.0% Hispanic of any race (2007); Density: 1,979.8 persons per square mile (2007); Average household size: 2.63 (2007); Median age: 32.1 (2007); Males per 100 females: 110.6 (2007); Marriage status: 21.8% never married, 50.8% now married, 7.6% widowed, 19.8% divorced (2000); Foreign born: 2.7% (2000); Ancestry (includes multiple ancestries): 18.6% German, 17.3% Irish, 16.4% United States or American, 15.5% Other groups, 8.9% English (2000).

Economy: Employment by occupation: 3.3% management, 6.5% professional, 22.4% services, 26.2% sales, 1.0% farming, 27.9% construction, 12.6% production (2000).

Income: Per capita income: $13,427 (2007); Median household income: $31,158 (2007); Average household income: $35,264 (2007); Percent of households with income of $100,000 or more: 4.0% (2007); Poverty rate: 23.4% (2000).

Education: Percent of population age 25 and over with: High school diploma (including GED) or higher: 60.5% (2007); Bachelor's degree or higher: 3.9% (2007); Master's degree or higher: 1.8% (2007).

Housing: Homeownership rate: 61.9% (2007); Median home value: $84,356 (2007); Median rent: $426 per month (2000); Median age of housing: 22 years (2000).

Transportation: Commute to work: 95.1% car, 2.2% public transportation, 1.2% walk, 0.9% work from home (2000); Travel time to work: 19.8% less than 15 minutes, 42.0% 15 to 30 minutes, 19.8% 30 to 45 minutes, 8.4% 45 to 60 minutes, 10.0% 60 minutes or more (2000)

THREE OAKS (CDP). Covers a land area of 1.296 square miles and a water area of 0 square miles. Located at 26.46° N. Lat.; 81.79° W. Long. Elevation is 16 feet.

Population: 665 (1990); 2,255 (2000); 3,141 (2007); 3,782 (2012 projected); Race: 94.1% White, 0.3% Black, 2.2% Asian, 7.7% Hispanic of any race (2007); Density: 2,423.0 persons per square mile (2007); Average household size: 3.03 (2007); Median age: 33.3 (2007); Males per 100 females: 98.4 (2007); Marriage status: 16.5% never married, 75.1% now married, 2.2% widowed, 6.3% divorced (2000); Foreign born: 3.9% (2000); Ancestry (includes multiple ancestries): 26.9% Irish, 21.8% English, 19.3% German, 14.7% Other groups, 11.1% Italian (2000).

Economy: Employment by occupation: 17.1% management, 22.3% professional, 11.1% services, 32.4% sales, 0.6% farming, 9.1% construction, 7.4% production (2000).

Income: Per capita income: $31,631 (2007); Median household income: $86,630 (2007); Average household income: $93,789 (2007); Percent of households with income of $100,000 or more: 35.9% (2007); Poverty rate: 1.6% (2000).

Education: Percent of population age 25 and over with: High school diploma (including GED) or higher: 95.3% (2007); Bachelor's degree or higher: 35.1% (2007); Master's degree or higher: 13.0% (2007).

Housing: Homeownership rate: 95.4% (2007); Median home value: $329,890 (2007); Median rent: $1,125 per month (2000); Median age of housing: 7 years (2000).

Transportation: Commute to work: 97.0% car, 0.5% public transportation, 0.0% walk, 2.4% work from home (2000); Travel time to work: 25.8% less than 15 minutes, 38.1% 15 to 30 minutes, 31.3% 30 to 45 minutes, 3.3% 45 to 60 minutes, 1.5% 60 minutes or more (2000)

TICE (CDP). Covers a land area of 1.140 square miles and a water area of 0.132 square miles. Located at 26.67° N. Lat.; 81.81° W. Long. Elevation is 16 feet.

Population: 3,971 (1990); 4,538 (2000); 4,664 (2007); 4,786 (2012 projected); Race: 56.1% White, 15.7% Black, 1.0% Asian, 59.2% Hispanic of any race (2007); Density: 4,089.8 persons per square mile (2007); Average household size: 2.98 (2007); Median age: 30.2 (2007); Males per 100 females: 113.8 (2007); Marriage status: 31.8% never married, 46.0% now married, 7.9% widowed, 14.3% divorced (2000); Foreign born: 17.7% (2000); Ancestry (includes multiple ancestries): 47.3% Other groups, 10.2% United States or American, 7.3% English, 5.6% German, 5.6% Irish (2000).

Economy: Employment by occupation: 5.3% management, 8.6% professional, 23.8% services, 18.7% sales, 2.1% farming, 23.9% construction, 17.7% production (2000).

Income: Per capita income: $13,205 (2007); Median household income: $28,881 (2007); Average household income: $39,304 (2007); Percent of households with income of $100,000 or more: 5.0% (2007); Poverty rate: 33.1% (2000).

Education: Percent of population age 25 and over with: High school diploma (including GED) or higher: 53.2% (2007); Bachelor's degree or higher: 5.3% (2007); Master's degree or higher: 1.5% (2007).

Housing: Homeownership rate: 59.9% (2007); Median home value: $131,088 (2007); Median rent: $441 per month (2000); Median age of housing: 34 years (2000).

Transportation: Commute to work: 91.0% car, 0.9% public transportation, 0.5% walk, 2.2% work from home (2000); Travel time to work: 22.6% less than 15 minutes, 39.2% 15 to 30 minutes, 19.1% 30 to 45 minutes, 10.6% 45 to 60 minutes, 8.4% 60 minutes or more (2000)

VILLAS (CDP). Covers a land area of 4.686 square miles and a water area of 0.119 square miles. Located at 26.55° N. Lat.; 81.86° W. Long. Elevation is 10 feet.

Population: 9,898 (1990); 11,346 (2000); 13,391 (2007); 14,980 (2012 projected); Race: 90.1% White, 3.1% Black, 1.5% Asian, 11.7% Hispanic of any race (2007); Density: 2,857.4 persons per square mile (2007); Average household size: 1.96 (2007); Median age: 43.7 (2007); Males per 100 females: 91.7 (2007); Marriage status: 23.6% never married, 51.4% now married, 12.4% widowed, 12.6% divorced (2000); Foreign born: 9.0% (2000); Ancestry (includes multiple ancestries): 20.4% German, 17.3% English, 15.3% Irish, 11.6% Other groups, 10.1% Italian (2000).

Economy: Employment by occupation: 14.0% management, 18.3% professional, 18.8% services, 31.1% sales, 0.3% farming, 8.8% construction, 8.7% production (2000).

Income: Per capita income: $29,112 (2007); Median household income: $44,789 (2007); Average household income: $56,182 (2007); Percent of households with income of $100,000 or more: 10.1% (2007); Poverty rate: 6.5% (2000).

Education: Percent of population age 25 and over with: High school diploma (including GED) or higher: 87.3% (2007); Bachelor's degree or higher: 28.0% (2007); Master's degree or higher: 8.8% (2007).

Housing: Homeownership rate: 61.7% (2007); Median home value: $198,630 (2007); Median rent: $665 per month (2000); Median age of housing: 20 years (2000).

Transportation: Commute to work: 91.6% car, 0.5% public transportation, 2.4% walk, 3.9% work from home (2000); Travel time to work: 35.9% less than 15 minutes, 43.1% 15 to 30 minutes, 13.2% 30 to 45 minutes, 3.8% 45 to 60 minutes, 4.0% 60 minutes or more (2000)

WHISKEY CREEK (CDP). Covers a land area of 1.601 square miles and a water area of 0 square miles. Located at 26.57° N. Lat.; 81.89° W. Long. Elevation is 10 feet.

Population: 5,063 (1990); 4,806 (2000); 5,638 (2007); 6,303 (2012 projected); Race: 94.3% White, 2.1% Black, 0.9% Asian, 4.2% Hispanic of any race (2007); Density: 3,521.8 persons per square mile (2007); Average household size: 2.18 (2007); Median age: 48.8 (2007); Males per 100 females: 89.3 (2007); Marriage status: 15.1% never married, 62.5% now married, 12.6% widowed, 9.7% divorced (2000); Foreign born: 5.3% (2000); Ancestry (includes multiple ancestries): 18.8% German, 16.2%

Irish, 15.9% English, 10.8% United States or American, 9.9% Other groups (2000).

Economy: Employment by occupation: 16.5% management, 27.1% professional, 14.1% services, 26.0% sales, 0.9% farming, 9.3% construction, 6.1% production (2000).

Income: Per capita income: $33,141 (2007); Median household income: $56,667 (2007); Average household income: $72,254 (2007); Percent of households with income of $100,000 or more: 20.5% (2007); Poverty rate: 2.2% (2000).

Education: Percent of population age 25 and over with: High school diploma (including GED) or higher: 90.3% (2007); Bachelor's degree or higher: 33.5% (2007); Master's degree or higher: 11.9% (2007).

Housing: Homeownership rate: 93.4% (2007); Median home value: $247,828 (2007); Median rent: $542 per month (2000); Median age of housing: 23 years (2000).

Transportation: Commute to work: 94.9% car, 0.0% public transportation, 0.5% walk, 3.6% work from home (2000); Travel time to work: 32.7% less than 15 minutes, 44.4% 15 to 30 minutes, 12.1% 30 to 45 minutes, 3.1% 45 to 60 minutes, 7.6% 60 minutes or more (2000)

Leon County

Located in northwestern Florida; bounded on the north by Georgia, and on the west by the Ochlockonee River and Lake Talquin; includes many lakes and part of Apalachicola National Forest. Covers a land area of 666.74 square miles, a water area of 35.04 square miles, and is located in the Eastern Time Zone. The county was founded in 1824. County seat is Tallahassee.

Leon County is part of the Tallahassee, FL Metropolitan Statistical Area. The entire metro area includes: Gadsden County, FL; Jefferson County, FL; Leon County, FL; Wakulla County, FL

Weather Station: Tallahassee Municipal Airport   Elevation: 52 feet

	Jan	Feb	Mar	Apr	May	Jun	Jul	Aug	Sep	Oct	Nov	Dec
High	64	67	74	80	86	91	92	91	89	81	73	66
Low	39	41	47	52	61	68	71	71	68	56	47	41
Precip	5.5	4.7	6.7	3.7	5.1	7.0	8.4	7.1	4.8	3.4	3.8	4.1
Snow	tr	tr	tr	0.0	0.0	tr	tr	0.0	tr	0.0	0.0	tr

High and Low temperatures in degrees Fahrenheit; Precipitation and Snow in inches

Population: 192,493 (1990); 239,452 (2000); 263,605 (2007); 289,950 (2012 projected); Race: 64.3% White, 30.1% Black, 2.5% Asian, 4.2% Hispanic of any race (2007); Density: 395.4 persons per square mile (2007); Average household size: 2.41 (2007); Median age: 31.7 (2007); Males per 100 females: 92.1 (2007).

Religion: Five largest groups: 12.5% Southern Baptist Convention, 5.7% Catholic Church, 4.7% The United Methodist Church, 2.2% National Primitive Baptist Convention, USA, 2.0% Episcopal Church (2000).

Economy: Unemployment rate: 3.2% (11/2007); Total civilian labor force: 144,531 (11/2007); Leading industries: 17.8% retail trade; 15.6% health care and social assistance; 14.1% accommodation & food services (2005); Farms: 281 totaling 74,004 acres (2002); Companies that employ 500 or more persons: 5 (2005); Companies that employ 100 to 499 persons: 131 (2005); Companies that employ less than 100 persons: 7,168 (2005); Black-owned businesses: 1,777 (2002); Hispanic-owned businesses: 541 (2002); Asian-owned businesses: 561 (2002); Women-owned businesses: 5,414 (2002); Retail sales per capita: $16,532 (2007). Single-family building permits issued: 1,301 (2006); Multi-family building permits issued: 588 (2006).

Income: Per capita income: $25,460 (2007); Median household income: $44,152 (2007); Average household income: $60,606 (2007); Percent of households with income of $100,000 or more: 15.9% (2007); Poverty rate: 17.2% (2005); Bankruptcy rate: 1.23% (2006).

Taxes: Total county taxes per capita: $504 (2005); County property taxes per capita: $358 (2005).

Education: Percent of population age 25 and over with: High school diploma (including GED) or higher: 89.3% (2007); Bachelor's degree or higher: 42.4% (2007); Master's degree or higher: 18.0% (2007).

Housing: Homeownership rate: 57.3% (2007); Median home value: $172,616 (2007); Median rent: $489 per month (2000); Median age of housing: 18 years (2000).

Health: Birth rate: 135.5 per 10,000 population (2006); Death rate: 64.3 per 10,000 population (2006); Age-adjusted cancer mortality rate: 198.8 deaths per 100,000 population (2004); Air Quality Index: 85.2% good, 14.8% moderate, 0.0% unhealthy for sensitive individuals, 0.0% unhealthy

(percent of days in 2006); Number of physicians: 26.9 per 10,000 population (2005); Hospital beds: 33.5 per 10,000 population (2004); Hospital admissions: 1,465.9 per 10,000 population (2004).

Elections: 2004 Presidential election results: 37.8% Bush, 61.5% Kerry, 0.3% Nader, 0.2% Badnarik

National and State Parks: Alfred B Maclay Gardens State Park; Killearn Gardens State Park; Lake Jackson Mounds Archaeological State Park; Natural Bridge Battlefield Historic State Park

Additional Information Contacts

Leon County Government . . . . (850) 606-5302
  http://www.leoncountyfl.gov
Tallahassee Chamber of Commerce . . . . (850) 224-8116
  http://www.talchamber.com

Leon County Communities

TALLAHASSEE (city). County seat. Covers a land area of 95.708 square miles and a water area of 2.544 square miles. Located at 30.45° N. Lat.; 84.27° W. Long. Elevation is 203 feet.

History: Tallahassee was selected as the capital of Florida in 1824, before any town existed on the site. Settlers came in rapidly, however, and Tallahassee was incorporated as a city in 1825. The city became the center of an aristocratic society that made its money from cotton. Politics and education shaped the course of life for the residents, who set their calendars by the convening of the state legislature and by the opening of the school term.

Population: 128,014 (1990); 150,624 (2000); 166,141 (2007); 182,811 (2012 projected); Race: 57.8% White, 35.6% Black, 3.2% Asian, 4.9% Hispanic of any race (2007); Density: 1,735.9 persons per square mile (2007); Average household size: 2.30 (2007); Median age: 29.2 (2007); Males per 100 females: 90.8 (2007); Marriage status: 49.2% never married, 37.2% now married, 4.3% widowed, 9.3% divorced (2000); Foreign born: 5.5% (2000); Ancestry (includes multiple ancestries): 34.1% Other groups, 9.4% German, 9.2% English, 8.8% Irish, 5.3% United States or American (2000).

Economy: Unemployment rate: 3.3% (11/2007); Total civilian labor force: 91,396 (11/2007); Single-family building permits issued: 804 (2006); Multi-family building permits issued: 588 (2006); Employment by occupation: 15.3% management, 30.7% professional, 15.4% services, 28.7% sales, 0.1% farming, 4.6% construction, 5.2% production (2000).

Income: Per capita income: $22,960 (2007); Median household income: $35,236 (2007); Average household income: $51,781 (2007); Percent of households with income of $100,000 or more: 12.1% (2007); Poverty rate: 24.7% (2000).

Taxes: Total city taxes per capita: $425 (2005); City property taxes per capita: $134 (2005).

Education: Percent of population age 25 and over with: High school diploma (including GED) or higher: 89.9% (2007); Bachelor's degree or higher: 45.1% (2007); Master's degree or higher: 19.7% (2007).

School District(s)

Florida A&M Laboratory School (PK-12)
  2005-06 Enrollment: 519 . . . . (850) 599-3325
Florida State University Laboratory School (PK-12)
  2005-06 Enrollment: 2,321 . . . . (850) 245-3700
Leon County School District (PK-12)
  2005-06 Enrollment: 32,191 . . . . (850) 487-7147

Four-year College(s)

Flagler College-Tallahassee (Private, Not-for-profit)
  Fall 2006 Enrollment: 411 . . . . (850) 201-8070
Florida Agricultural and Mechanical University (Public, Historically black)
  Fall 2006 Enrollment: 11,907. . . . . (850) 599-3000
  2006-07 Tuition: In-state $3,274; Out-of-state $15,196
Florida State University (Public)
  Fall 2006 Enrollment: 39,973 . . . . (850) 644-2525
  2006-07 Tuition: In-state $3,307; Out-of-state $16,439

Two-year College(s)

Lively Technical Center (Public)
  Fall 2006 Enrollment: 1,055. . . . . (850) 487-7555
Tallahassee Community College (Public)
  Fall 2006 Enrollment: 12,732. . . . . (850) 201-6200
  2006-07 Tuition: In-state $1,645; Out-of-state $1,645

Vocational/Technical School(s)

North Florida Cosmetology Institute (Private, For-profit)
  Fall 2006 Enrollment: 81 . . . . (850) 878-5269
  2006-07 Tuition: $6,250

Housing: Homeownership rate: 44.2% (2007); Median home value: $167,326 (2007); Median rent: $490 per month (2000); Median age of housing: 21 years (2000).

Hospitals: Capital Regional Medical Center (198 beds); HealthSouth Rehabilitation Hospital of Tallahassee (76 beds); Tallahassee Memorial Health Care Foundation (770 beds)

Safety: Violent crime rate: 100.2 per 10,000 population; Property crime rate: 478.3 per 10,000 population (2006).

Newspapers: Capital Outlook (Black, General, Religious - Circulation 15,000); Tallahassee Democrat (Circulation 51,285)

Transportation: Commute to work: 91.3% car, 2.4% public transportation, 2.6% walk, 2.4% work from home (2000); Travel time to work: 37.6% less than 15 minutes, 45.4% 15 to 30 minutes, 12.3% 30 to 45 minutes, 2.0% 45 to 60 minutes, 2.7% 60 minutes or more (2000); Amtrak: Service available.

Airports: Tallahassee Regional (primary service/small hub)

Additional Information Contacts

Tallahassee Chamber of Commerce . . . . (850) 224-8116
  http://www.talchamber.com

WOODVILLE (CDP). Covers a land area of 6.426 square miles and a water area of 0 square miles. Located at 30.30° N. Lat.; 84.25° W. Long. Elevation is 33 feet.

Population: 2,760 (1990); 3,006 (2000); 3,062 (2007); 3,289 (2012 projected); Race: 77.1% White, 20.1% Black, 0.1% Asian, 2.8% Hispanic of any race (2007); Density: 476.5 persons per square mile (2007); Average household size: 2.48 (2007); Median age: 38.4 (2007); Males per 100 females: 97.2 (2007); Marriage status: 20.8% never married, 62.8% now married, 4.1% widowed, 12.3% divorced (2000); Foreign born: 2.7% (2000); Ancestry (includes multiple ancestries): 31.8% Other groups, 16.5% United States or American, 8.3% Irish, 7.5% French (except Basque), 6.8% English (2000).

Economy: Employment by occupation: 10.0% management, 17.5% professional, 14.7% services, 31.4% sales, 0.0% farming, 12.9% construction, 13.4% production (2000).

Income: Per capita income: $24,006 (2007); Median household income: $46,607 (2007); Average household income: $59,424 (2007); Percent of households with income of $100,000 or more: 15.4% (2007); Poverty rate: 10.7% (2000).

Education: Percent of population age 25 and over with: High school diploma (including GED) or higher: 75.2% (2007); Bachelor's degree or higher: 17.8% (2007); Master's degree or higher: 7.8% (2007).

School District(s)

Leon County School District (PK-12)
    2005-06 Enrollment: 32,191 . . . . (850) 487-7147

Housing: Homeownership rate: 83.4% (2007); Median home value: $108,255 (2007); Median rent: $373 per month (2000); Median age of housing: 17 years (2000).

Transportation: Commute to work: 96.2% car, 0.0% public transportation, 0.0% walk, 3.0% work from home (2000); Travel time to work: 13.6% less than 15 minutes, 43.9% 15 to 30 minutes, 28.1% 30 to 45 minutes, 11.3% 45 to 60 minutes, 3.2% 60 minutes or more (2000)

Levy County

Located in northern Florida; bounded partly on the south and west by the Gulf of Mexico, on the northwest by the Suwannee River, and on the south by the Withlacoochee River; flatwoods area, with many small lakes. Covers a land area of 1,118.38 square miles, a water area of 293.94 square miles, and is located in the Eastern Time Zone. The county was founded in 1845. County seat is Bronson.

Weather Station: Usher Tower											Elevation: 32 feet	
	Jan	Feb	Mar	Apr	May	Jun	Jul	Aug	Sep	Oct	Nov	Dec
High	68	71	77	82	88	91	92	91	90	84	76	70
Low	43	46	51	55	62	68	70	71	69	59	51	45
Precip	4.6	3.5	4.8	3.7	3.1	6.7	8.5	10.2	6.4	3.0	2.5	3.3
Snow	0.0	tr	0.0	0.0	0.0	0.0	0.0	0.0	0.0	0.0	0.0	0.0

High and Low temperatures in degrees Fahrenheit; Precipitation and Snow in inches

Population: 25,923 (1990); 34,450 (2000); 38,921 (2007); 42,113 (2012 projected); Race: 85.7% White, 10.6% Black, 0.6% Asian, 5.6% Hispanic of any race (2007); Density: 34.8 persons per square mile (2007); Average household size: 2.44 (2007); Median age: 41.2 (2007); Males per 100 females: 93.9 (2007).

Religion: Five largest groups: 21.0% Southern Baptist Convention, 3.8% The United Methodist Church, 2.0% Catholic Church, 1.9% Church of God (Cleveland, Tennessee), 1.8% Churches of Christ (2000).

Economy: Unemployment rate: 4.4% (11/2007); Total civilian labor force: 17,566 (11/2007); Leading industries: 24.5% retail trade; 15.4% accommodation & food services; 10.7% manufacturing (2005); Farms: 897 totaling 180,314 acres (2002); Companies that employ 500 or more persons: 0 (2005); Companies that employ 100 to 499 persons: 7 (2005); Companies that employ less than 100 persons: 782 (2005); Black-owned businesses: n/a (2002); Hispanic-owned businesses: n/a (2002); Asian-owned businesses: n/a (2002); Women-owned businesses: 635 (2002); Retail sales per capita: $11,239 (2007). Single-family building permits issued: 275 (2006); Multi-family building permits issued: 3 (2006).

Income: Per capita income: $17,468 (2007); Median household income: $31,884 (2007); Average household income: $42,420 (2007); Percent of households with income of $100,000 or more: 6.5% (2007); Poverty rate: 19.4% (2005); Bankruptcy rate: 1.33% (2006).

Education: Percent of population age 25 and over with: High school diploma (including GED) or higher: 73.9% (2007); Bachelor's degree or higher: 10.4% (2007); Master's degree or higher: 3.8% (2007).

Housing: Homeownership rate: 83.9% (2007); Median home value: $119,967 (2007); Median rent: $307 per month (2000); Median age of housing: 17 years (2000).

Health: Birth rate: 114.9 per 10,000 population (2006); Death rate: 121.0 per 10,000 population (2006); Age-adjusted cancer mortality rate: 242.4 deaths per 100,000 population (2004); Number of physicians: 6.3 per 10,000 population (2005); Hospital beds: 10.8 per 10,000 population (2004); Hospital admissions: 364.4 per 10,000 population (2004).

Elections: 2004 Presidential election results: 62.5% Bush, 36.5% Kerry, 0.6% Nader, 0.2% Badnarik.

National and State Parks: Cedar Key Museum State Park; Cedar Key Scrub State Reserve; Cedar Key State Memorial; Cedar Keys National Wildlife Refuge; Fanning Springs State Park; Gulf Hammock State Wildlife Management Area; Manatee Springs State Park

Additional Information Contacts

Levy County Government . . . . (352) 486-5100

Bronson Chamber of Commerce . . . . (352) 486-1003
  http://www.bronsonchamber.com
Cedar Key Chamber of Commerce . . . . (352) 543-5600
  http://www.cedarkey.org
Chiefland Chamber of Commerce . . . . (352) 493-1849
  http://www.chieflandchamber.com
Inglis Chamber of Commerce . . . . (352) 447-3383
Williston Chamber of Commerce . . . . (352) 528-5552
  http://www.willistonfl.com

Levy County Communities

ANDREWS (CDP). Covers a land area of 6.827 square miles and a water area of 0 square miles. Located at 29.53° N. Lat.; 82.88° W. Long. Elevation is 49 feet.

Population: 462 (1990); 708 (2000); 862 (2007); 974 (2012 projected); Race: 96.6% White, 1.5% Black, 0.0% Asian, 3.6% Hispanic of any race (2007); Density: 126.3 persons per square mile (2007); Average household size: 2.36 (2007); Median age: 40.2 (2007); Males per 100 females: 100.9 (2007); Marriage status: 10.2% never married, 73.5% now married, 4.0% widowed, 12.4% divorced (2000); Foreign born: 2.1% (2000); Ancestry (includes multiple ancestries): 22.1% Irish, 13.2% English, 12.1% German, 11.3% Other groups, 8.6% United States or American (2000).

Economy: Employment by occupation: 2.1% management, 0.0% professional, 18.5% services, 44.4% sales, 0.0% farming, 15.4% construction, 19.6% production (2000).

Income: Per capita income: $14,208 (2007); Median household income: $31,708 (2007); Average household income: $33,555 (2007); Percent of households with income of $100,000 or more: 0.0% (2007); Poverty rate: 18.2% (2000).

Education: Percent of population age 25 and over with: High school diploma (including GED) or higher: 76.7% (2007); Bachelor's degree or higher: 3.8% (2007); Master's degree or higher: 0.0% (2007).

Housing: Homeownership rate: 83.0% (2007); Median home value: $116,189 (2007); Median rent: $366 per month (2000); Median age of housing: 13 years (2000).

Transportation: Commute to work: 96.3% car, 0.0% public transportation, 0.0% walk, 3.7% work from home (2000); Travel time to work: 31.7% less

than 15 minutes, 34.0% 15 to 30 minutes, 15.1% 30 to 45 minutes, 3.9% 45 to 60 minutes, 15.4% 60 minutes or more (2000)

BRONSON (town). County seat. Covers a land area of 3.949 square miles and a water area of 0.089 square miles. Located at 29.44° N. Lat.; 82.63° W. Long. Elevation is 59 feet.

History: Bronson was originally called Chunky Pond, and adopted the name of Bronson from an early settler when it was incorporated in 1884.
Population: 875 (1990); 964 (2000); 1,044 (2007); 1,117 (2012 projected); Race: 73.7% White, 21.2% Black, 0.5% Asian, 10.7% Hispanic of any race (2007); Density: 264.4 persons per square mile (2007); Average household size: 2.57 (2007); Median age: 32.3 (2007); Males per 100 females: 84.1 (2007); Marriage status: 30.0% never married, 50.6% now married, 6.7% widowed, 12.7% divorced (2000); Foreign born: 0.0% (2000); Ancestry (includes multiple ancestries): 38.0% Other groups, 11.4% United States or American, 10.0% Irish, 8.3% English, 5.7% German (2000).
Economy: Employment by occupation: 6.4% management, 14.2% professional, 24.5% services, 25.5% sales, 1.0% farming, 10.1% construction, 18.3% production (2000).
Income: Per capita income: $14,986 (2007); Median household income: $29,868 (2007); Average household income: $38,534 (2007); Percent of households with income of $100,000 or more: 3.4% (2007); Poverty rate: 27.2% (2000).
Education: Percent of population age 25 and over with: High school diploma (including GED) or higher: 61.3% (2007); Bachelor's degree or higher: 6.3% (2007); Master's degree or higher: 2.3% (2007).
School District(s)
Levy County School District (PK-12)
    2005-06 Enrollment: 6,284 . . . . (352) 486-5231
Housing: Homeownership rate: 74.4% (2007); Median home value: $93,636 (2007); Median rent: $321 per month (2000); Median age of housing: 19 years (2000).
Newspapers: Levy County Journal (General - Circulation 1,200)
Transportation: Commute to work: 89.6% car, 0.0% public transportation, 4.4% walk, 2.1% work from home (2000); Travel time to work: 31.7% less than 15 minutes, 22.0% 15 to 30 minutes, 32.3% 30 to 45 minutes, 11.4% 45 to 60 minutes, 2.6% 60 minutes or more (2000)
Additional Information Contacts
Bronson Chamber of Commerce . . . . (352) 486-1003
    http://www.bronsonchamber.com

CEDAR KEY (city). Aka Cedar Keys. Covers a land area of 0.914 square miles and a water area of 1.129 square miles. Located at 29.14° N. Lat.; 83.04° W. Long. Elevation is 10 feet.

History: Cedar Key developed on an island three miles off the west coast of Florida in the Gulf of Mexico. First a fishing village, it later became a port and railroad transfer point to south Florida. The Atlantic, Gulf & West Indies Transit Company railroad was extended to Cedar Key in 1860.
Population: 707 (1990); 790 (2000); 902 (2007); 987 (2012 projected); Race: 97.1% White, 0.3% Black, 0.6% Asian, 2.1% Hispanic of any race (2007); Density: 987.3 persons per square mile (2007); Average household size: 1.89 (2007); Median age: 55.8 (2007); Males per 100 females: 92.7 (2007); Marriage status: 15.4% never married, 60.5% now married, 8.7% widowed, 15.5% divorced (2000); Foreign born: 4.5% (2000); Ancestry (includes multiple ancestries): 20.3% English, 18.2% German, 16.4% Irish, 12.1% United States or American, 6.2% Other groups (2000).
Economy: Single-family building permits issued: 6 (2006); Multi-family building permits issued: 0 (2006); Employment by occupation: 11.9% management, 20.6% professional, 17.7% services, 27.9% sales, 8.4% farming, 5.8% construction, 7.6% production (2000).
Income: Per capita income: $26,081 (2007); Median household income: $36,563 (2007); Average household income: $49,319 (2007); Percent of households with income of $100,000 or more: 10.5% (2007); Poverty rate: 11.1% (2000).
Education: Percent of population age 25 and over with: High school diploma (including GED) or higher: 87.2% (2007); Bachelor's degree or higher: 34.4% (2007); Master's degree or higher: 15.8% (2007).
School District(s)
Levy County School District (PK-12)
    2005-06 Enrollment: 6,284 . . . . (352) 486-5231
Housing: Homeownership rate: 77.1% (2007); Median home value: $277,551 (2007); Median rent: $394 per month (2000); Median age of housing: 20 years (2000).
Safety: Violent crime rate: 10.3 per 10,000 population; Property crime rate: 154.0 per 10,000 population (2006).

Newspapers: Cedar Key Beacon (General - Circulation 1,800)
Transportation: Commute to work: 70.3% car, 0.0% public transportation, 7.3% walk, 16.6% work from home (2000); Travel time to work: 70.0% less than 15 minutes, 5.9% 15 to 30 minutes, 3.5% 30 to 45 minutes, 7.3% 45 to 60 minutes, 13.2% 60 minutes or more (2000)
Additional Information Contacts
Cedar Key Chamber of Commerce . . . . (352) 543-5600
    http://www.cedarkey.org

CHIEFLAND (city). Covers a land area of 3.911 square miles and a water area of 0 square miles. Located at 29.48° N. Lat.; 82.86° W. Long. Elevation is 33 feet.

History: The town of Chiefland began when Florida was a Territory, and became a shipping center for turpentine, rosin, livestock, and peanuts.
Population: 1,924 (1990); 1,993 (2000); 2,155 (2007); 2,272 (2012 projected); Race: 61.8% White, 31.0% Black, 3.5% Asian, 4.3% Hispanic of any race (2007); Density: 551.0 persons per square mile (2007); Average household size: 2.45 (2007); Median age: 31.5 (2007); Males per 100 females: 81.1 (2007); Marriage status: 26.7% never married, 43.7% now married, 15.8% widowed, 13.8% divorced (2000); Foreign born: 2.8% (2000); Ancestry (includes multiple ancestries): 33.2% Other groups, 10.6% United States or American, 6.3% English, 5.7% German, 4.1% Irish (2000).
Economy: Single-family building permits issued: 3 (2006); Multi-family building permits issued: 0 (2006); Employment by occupation: 6.6% management, 15.9% professional, 22.2% services, 30.0% sales, 3.8% farming, 9.1% construction, 12.3% production (2000).
Income: Per capita income: $13,269 (2007); Median household income: $21,667 (2007); Average household income: $31,649 (2007); Percent of households with income of $100,000 or more: 2.7% (2007); Poverty rate: 36.8% (2000).
Education: Percent of population age 25 and over with: High school diploma (including GED) or higher: 64.7% (2007); Bachelor's degree or higher: 9.5% (2007); Master's degree or higher: 1.8% (2007).
School District(s)
Levy County School District (PK-12)
    2005-06 Enrollment: 6,284 . . . . (352) 486-5231
Housing: Homeownership rate: 54.7% (2007); Median home value: $108,505 (2007); Median rent: $240 per month (2000); Median age of housing: 23 years (2000).
Safety: Violent crime rate: 169.0 per 10,000 population; Property crime rate: 920.2 per 10,000 population (2006).
Newspapers: Chiefland Citizen (General - Circulation 3,650); Tri-County Bulletin (General - Circulation 22,000)
Transportation: Commute to work: 92.0% car, 0.0% public transportation, 4.3% walk, 1.3% work from home (2000); Travel time to work: 50.0% less than 15 minutes, 22.8% 15 to 30 minutes, 11.1% 30 to 45 minutes, 8.3% 45 to 60 minutes, 7.8% 60 minutes or more (2000)
Additional Information Contacts
Chiefland Chamber of Commerce . . . . (352) 493-1849
    http://www.chieflandchamber.com

EAST BRONSON (CDP). Covers a land area of 11.462 square miles and a water area of 0 square miles. Located at 29.45° N. Lat.; 82.59° W. Long.

Population: 620 (1990); 1,075 (2000); 1,292 (2007); 1,429 (2012 projected); Race: 83.7% White, 6.3% Black, 0.2% Asian, 15.9% Hispanic of any race (2007); Density: 112.7 persons per square mile (2007); Average household size: 2.69 (2007); Median age: 35.2 (2007); Males per 100 females: 92.3 (2007); Marriage status: 17.9% never married, 67.7% now married, 5.8% widowed, 8.6% divorced (2000); Foreign born: 2.2% (2000); Ancestry (includes multiple ancestries): 18.5% Irish, 13.3% English, 13.2% Other groups, 11.0% German, 9.6% United States or American (2000).
Economy: Employment by occupation: 7.8% management, 17.4% professional, 22.3% services, 13.3% sales, 0.0% farming, 22.6% construction, 16.5% production (2000).
Income: Per capita income: $14,044 (2007); Median household income: $30,057 (2007); Average household income: $37,723 (2007); Percent of households with income of $100,000 or more: 5.2% (2007); Poverty rate: 15.2% (2000).
Education: Percent of population age 25 and over with: High school diploma (including GED) or higher: 60.5% (2007); Bachelor's degree or higher: 6.5% (2007); Master's degree or higher: 1.6% (2007).

Housing: Homeownership rate: 89.2% (2007); Median home value: $87,500 (2007); Median rent: $358 per month (2000); Median age of housing: 13 years (2000).

Transportation: Commute to work: 97.3% car, 0.0% public transportation, 0.0% walk, 2.7% work from home (2000); Travel time to work: 1.6% less than 15 minutes, 18.4% 15 to 30 minutes, 40.5% 30 to 45 minutes, 29.9% 45 to 60 minutes, 9.7% 60 minutes or more (2000)

EAST WILLISTON (CDP). Covers a land area of 3.110 square miles and a water area of 0 square miles. Located at 29.38° N. Lat.; 82.41° W. Long.

Population: 790 (1990); 966 (2000); 986 (2007); 1,006 (2012 projected); Race: 9.0% White, 87.6% Black, 0.0% Asian, 2.8% Hispanic of any race (2007); Density: 317.0 persons per square mile (2007); Average household size: 2.77 (2007); Median age: 30.0 (2007); Males per 100 females: 76.1 (2007); Marriage status: 41.7% never married, 35.2% now married, 9.3% widowed, 13.9% divorced (2000); Foreign born: 1.6% (2000); Ancestry (includes multiple ancestries): 68.8% Other groups, 5.4% Irish, 2.4% English, 1.7% German, 1.6% United States or American (2000).

Economy: Employment by occupation: 10.2% management, 13.8% professional, 36.2% services, 15.3% sales, 2.8% farming, 4.0% construction, 17.8% production (2000).

Income: Per capita income: $16,435 (2007); Median household income: $28,684 (2007); Average household income: $45,520 (2007); Percent of households with income of $100,000 or more: 13.5% (2007); Poverty rate: 28.7% (2000).

Education: Percent of population age 25 and over with: High school diploma (including GED) or higher: 73.0% (2007); Bachelor's degree or higher: 10.5% (2007); Master's degree or higher: 3.3% (2007).

Housing: Homeownership rate: 70.8% (2007); Median home value: $113,571 (2007); Median rent: $272 per month (2000); Median age of housing: 21 years (2000).

Transportation: Commute to work: 94.4% car, 0.0% public transportation, 1.4% walk, 2.5% work from home (2000); Travel time to work: 37.7% less than 15 minutes, 22.3% 15 to 30 minutes, 29.9% 30 to 45 minutes, 4.3% 45 to 60 minutes, 5.8% 60 minutes or more (2000)

FANNING SPRINGS (city). Aka Suwannee River. Covers a land area of 3.557 square miles and a water area of 0.138 square miles. Located at 29.58° N. Lat.; 82.92° W. Long. Elevation is 32 feet.

Population: 496 (1990); 737 (2000); 880 (2007); 984 (2012 projected); Race: 84.7% White, 7.2% Black, 0.5% Asian, 13.3% Hispanic of any race (2007); Density: 247.4 persons per square mile (2007); Average household size: 2.34 (2007); Median age: 36.1 (2007); Males per 100 females: 96.4 (2007); Marriage status: 16.8% never married, 56.6% now married, 9.4% widowed, 17.1% divorced (2000); Foreign born: 6.3% (2000); Ancestry (includes multiple ancestries): 14.4% Irish, 14.2% Other groups, 9.4% United States or American, 8.7% German, 8.2% English (2000).

Economy: Employment by occupation: 10.6% management, 10.6% professional, 24.5% services, 24.5% sales, 7.4% farming, 16.7% construction, 5.6% production (2000).

Income: Per capita income: $12,841 (2007); Median household income: $21,905 (2007); Average household income: $30,053 (2007); Percent of households with income of $100,000 or more: 1.3% (2007); Poverty rate: 30.5% (2000).

Education: Percent of population age 25 and over with: High school diploma (including GED) or higher: 65.5% (2007); Bachelor's degree or higher: 13.5% (2007); Master's degree or higher: 5.6% (2007).

Housing: Homeownership rate: 64.6% (2007); Median home value: $87,250 (2007); Median rent: $273 per month (2000); Median age of housing: 17 years (2000).

Transportation: Commute to work: 90.3% car, 0.0% public transportation, 3.2% walk, 2.8% work from home (2000); Travel time to work: 51.0% less than 15 minutes, 27.1% 15 to 30 minutes, 13.8% 30 to 45 minutes, 3.3% 45 to 60 minutes, 4.8% 60 minutes or more (2000)

INGLIS (town). Covers a land area of 3.653 square miles and a water area of 0.017 square miles. Located at 29.03° N. Lat.; 82.66° W. Long. Elevation is 16 feet.

Population: 1,241 (1990); 1,491 (2000); 1,501 (2007); 1,523 (2012 projected); Race: 98.6% White, 0.0% Black, 0.5% Asian, 2.7% Hispanic of any race (2007); Density: 410.9 persons per square mile (2007); Average household size: 2.19 (2007); Median age: 47.0 (2007); Males per 100 females: 97.2 (2007); Marriage status: 16.1% never married, 57.5% now married, 8.8% widowed, 17.6% divorced (2000); Foreign born: 1.7%

(2000); Ancestry (includes multiple ancestries): 17.2% German, 17.0% English, 14.4% United States or American, 13.3% Irish, 8.2% Other groups (2000).

Economy: Employment by occupation: 12.0% management, 13.8% professional, 13.4% services, 21.5% sales, 3.5% farming, 17.5% construction, 18.3% production (2000).

Income: Per capita income: $17,079 (2007); Median household income: $28,158 (2007); Average household income: $37,369 (2007); Percent of households with income of $100,000 or more: 5.4% (2007); Poverty rate: 22.3% (2000).

Education: Percent of population age 25 and over with: High school diploma (including GED) or higher: 73.1% (2007); Bachelor's degree or higher: 9.8% (2007); Master's degree or higher: 2.3% (2007).

School District(s)

Levy County School District (PK-12)
   2005-06 Enrollment: 6,284 . . . . (352) 486-5231

Housing: Homeownership rate: 78.6% (2007); Median home value: $104,573 (2007); Median rent: $232 per month (2000); Median age of housing: 18 years (2000).

Safety: Violent crime rate: 48.8 per 10,000 population; Property crime rate: 250.3 per 10,000 population (2006).

Transportation: Commute to work: 87.8% car, 0.4% public transportation, 4.2% walk, 5.4% work from home (2000); Travel time to work: 32.6% less than 15 minutes, 28.2% 15 to 30 minutes, 22.9% 30 to 45 minutes, 7.8% 45 to 60 minutes, 8.4% 60 minutes or more (2000)

Additional Information Contacts
Inglis Chamber of Commerce . . . . (352) 447-3383

MANATTEE ROAD (CDP). Covers a land area of 14.305 square miles and a water area of 0 square miles. Located at 29.50° N. Lat.; 82.92° W. Long. Elevation is 30 feet.

Population: 1,618 (1990); 1,937 (2000); 1,951 (2007); 1,969 (2012 projected); Race: 95.9% White, 2.4% Black, 0.0% Asian, 2.2% Hispanic of any race (2007); Density: 136.4 persons per square mile (2007); Average household size: 2.23 (2007); Median age: 49.2 (2007); Males per 100 females: 93.7 (2007); Marriage status: 17.9% never married, 60.1% now married, 10.9% widowed, 11.1% divorced (2000); Foreign born: 0.5% (2000); Ancestry (includes multiple ancestries): 15.8% German, 14.7% Other groups, 12.4% English, 12.2% United States or American, 10.5% Irish (2000).

Economy: Employment by occupation: 1.2% management, 9.5% professional, 15.2% services, 32.8% sales, 1.6% farming, 23.9% construction, 15.8% production (2000).

Income: Per capita income: $17,405 (2007); Median household income: $25,773 (2007); Average household income: $38,853 (2007); Percent of households with income of $100,000 or more: 4.3% (2007); Poverty rate: 21.1% (2000).

Education: Percent of population age 25 and over with: High school diploma (including GED) or higher: 71.5% (2007); Bachelor's degree or higher: 8.5% (2007); Master's degree or higher: 1.9% (2007).

Housing: Homeownership rate: 91.1% (2007); Median home value: $105,220 (2007); Median rent: $263 per month (2000); Median age of housing: 16 years (2000).

Transportation: Commute to work: 88.9% car, 2.8% public transportation, 1.6% walk, 6.7% work from home (2000); Travel time to work: 30.7% less than 15 minutes, 27.1% 15 to 30 minutes, 15.2% 30 to 45 minutes, 8.6% 45 to 60 minutes, 18.5% 60 minutes or more (2000)

MORRISTON (unincorporated postal area, zip code 32668). Covers a land area of 151.141 square miles and a water area of 0.521 square miles. Located at 29.28° N. Lat.; 82.51° W. Long. Elevation is 63 feet.

Population: 3,881 (2000); Race: 93.7% White, 2.1% Black, 0.4% Asian, 2.9% Hispanic of any race (2000); Density: 25.7 persons per square mile (2000); Age: 21.3% under 18, 17.1% over 64 (2000); Marriage status: 18.6% never married, 61.8% now married, 10.1% widowed, 9.6% divorced (2000); Foreign born: 2.8% (2000); Ancestry (includes multiple ancestries): 17.6% German, 15.8% United States or American, 14.4% Irish, 13.2% Other groups, 12.0% English (2000).

Economy: Employment by occupation: 11.7% management, 7.3% professional, 19.1% services, 24.1% sales, 3.8% farming, 19.7% construction, 14.3% production (2000).

Income: Per capita income: $15,088 (2000); Median household income: $27,476 (2000); Poverty rate: 16.5% (2000).

Education: Percent of population age 25 and over with: High school diploma (including GED) or higher: 76.9% (2000); Bachelor's degree or higher: 7.9% (2000).

Housing: Homeownership rate: 91.8% (2000); Median home value: $107,500 (2000); Median rent: $313 per month (2000); Median age of housing: 13 years (2000).

Transportation: Commute to work: 92.3% car, 0.0% public transportation, 0.5% walk, 5.7% work from home (2000); Travel time to work: 6.7% less than 15 minutes, 32.4% 15 to 30 minutes, 27.5% 30 to 45 minutes, 17.1% 45 to 60 minutes, 16.2% 60 minutes or more (2000)

OTTER CREEK (town).

Covers a land area of 1.428 square miles and a water area of 0.021 square miles. Located at 29.32° N. Lat.; 82.77° W. Long. Elevation is 26 feet.

History: Otter were hunted in the vicinity of Otter Creek through the 1800's, but the economy of the town developed around lumber. The manufacturing of hardwood slats for fruit crates was an early industry.

Population: 136 (1990); 121 (2000); 128 (2007); 133 (2012 projected); Race: 93.0% White, 2.3% Black, 0.0% Asian, 4.7% Hispanic of any race (2007); Density: 89.6 persons per square mile (2007); Average household size: 2.21 (2007); Median age: 50.3 (2007); Males per 100 females: 109.8 (2007); Marriage status: 16.7% never married, 59.8% now married, 7.8% widowed, 15.7% divorced (2000); Foreign born: 0.0% (2000); Ancestry (includes multiple ancestries): 22.0% English, 10.1% United States or American, 9.2% German, 8.3% Other groups, 7.3% Irish (2000).

Economy: Single-family building permits issued: 0 (2006); Multi-family building permits issued: 0 (2006); Employment by occupation: 0.0% management, 0.0% professional, 15.9% services, 31.8% sales, 11.4% farming, 13.6% construction, 27.3% production (2000).

Income: Per capita income: $12,090 (2007); Median household income: $19,500 (2007); Average household income: $26,681 (2007); Percent of households with income of $100,000 or more: 0.0% (2007); Poverty rate: 20.2% (2000).

Education: Percent of population age 25 and over with: High school diploma (including GED) or higher: 56.9% (2007); Bachelor's degree or higher: 2.9% (2007); Master's degree or higher: 2.9% (2007).

Housing: Homeownership rate: 82.8% (2007); Median home value: $75,000 (2007); Median rent: $n/a per month (2000); Median age of housing: 30 years (2000).

Transportation: Commute to work: 97.7% car, 0.0% public transportation, 2.3% walk, 0.0% work from home (2000); Travel time to work: 11.4% less than 15 minutes, 29.5% 15 to 30 minutes, 18.2% 30 to 45 minutes, 18.2% 45 to 60 minutes, 22.7% 60 minutes or more (2000)

WILLISTON (city).

Covers a land area of 6.061 square miles and a water area of 0.019 square miles. Located at 29.38° N. Lat.; 82.44° W. Long. Elevation is 75 feet.

History: Williston developed around limestone deposits from which rock is quarried.

Population: 2,279 (1990); 2,297 (2000); 2,411 (2007); 2,506 (2012 projected); Race: 69.3% White, 26.6% Black, 0.8% Asian, 4.7% Hispanic of any race (2007); Density: 397.8 persons per square mile (2007); Average household size: 2.72 (2007); Median age: 37.1 (2007); Males per 100 females: 88.1 (2007); Marriage status: 23.0% never married, 54.4% now married, 11.6% widowed, 11.0% divorced (2000); Foreign born: 3.2% (2000); Ancestry (includes multiple ancestries): 27.5% Other groups, 18.1% United States or American, 9.7% Irish, 7.9% German, 7.7% English (2000).

Economy: Single-family building permits issued: 13 (2006); Multi-family building permits issued: 0 (2006); Employment by occupation: 10.1% management, 12.7% professional, 21.6% services, 29.0% sales, 3.0% farming, 10.9% construction, 12.7% production (2000).

Income: Per capita income: $15,173 (2007); Median household income: $30,685 (2007); Average household income: $40,790 (2007); Percent of households with income of $100,000 or more: 5.4% (2007); Poverty rate: 22.6% (2000).

Education: Percent of population age 25 and over with: High school diploma (including GED) or higher: 69.0% (2007); Bachelor's degree or higher: 10.2% (2007); Master's degree or higher: 3.6% (2007).

School District(s)

Levy County School District (PK-12)
  2005-06 Enrollment: 6,284 . . . . (352) 486-5231

Housing: Homeownership rate: 68.5% (2007); Median home value: $117,782 (2007); Median rent: $318 per month (2000); Median age of housing: 28 years (2000).

Hospitals: Nature Coast Regional Hospital (40 beds)

Safety: Violent crime rate: 164.7 per 10,000 population; Property crime rate: 717.6 per 10,000 population (2006).

Transportation: Commute to work: 92.8% car, 0.0% public transportation, 5.7% walk, 0.7% work from home (2000); Travel time to work: 45.0% less than 15 minutes, 17.4% 15 to 30 minutes, 26.8% 30 to 45 minutes, 7.1% 45 to 60 minutes, 3.7% 60 minutes or more (2000)

Additional Information Contacts

Williston Chamber of Commerce . . . . (352) 528-5552
  http://www.willistonfl.com

WILLISTON HIGHLANDS (CDP).

Covers a land area of 11.241 square miles and a water area of 0 square miles. Located at 29.33° N. Lat.; 82.53° W. Long.

Population: 853 (1990); 1,386 (2000); 1,864 (2007); 2,187 (2012 projected); Race: 91.8% White, 5.3% Black, 0.3% Asian, 5.5% Hispanic of any race (2007); Density: 165.8 persons per square mile (2007); Average household size: 2.30 (2007); Median age: 45.5 (2007); Males per 100 females: 97.5 (2007); Marriage status: 17.4% never married, 64.9% now married, 5.4% widowed, 12.3% divorced (2000); Foreign born: 1.8% (2000); Ancestry (includes multiple ancestries): 19.4% United States or American, 15.7% German, 12.2% Other groups, 9.7% Irish, 5.9% English (2000).

Economy: Employment by occupation: 7.1% management, 12.1% professional, 21.5% services, 27.6% sales, 0.0% farming, 20.2% construction, 11.5% production (2000).

Income: Per capita income: $16,270 (2007); Median household income: $28,324 (2007); Average household income: $37,395 (2007); Percent of households with income of $100,000 or more: 5.2% (2007); Poverty rate: 21.1% (2000).

Education: Percent of population age 25 and over with: High school diploma (including GED) or higher: 77.3% (2007); Bachelor's degree or higher: 8.9% (2007); Master's degree or higher: 1.9% (2007).

Housing: Homeownership rate: 89.8% (2007); Median home value: $118,067 (2007); Median rent: $375 per month (2000); Median age of housing: 14 years (2000).

Transportation: Commute to work: 96.1% car, 0.0% public transportation, 0.0% walk, 2.1% work from home (2000); Travel time to work: 7.2% less than 15 minutes, 24.1% 15 to 30 minutes, 31.6% 30 to 45 minutes, 31.4% 45 to 60 minutes, 5.6% 60 minutes or more (2000)

YANKEETOWN (town).

Covers a land area of 7.824 square miles and a water area of 12.481 square miles. Located at 29.03° N. Lat.; 82.72° W. Long. Elevation is 10 feet.

History: Yankeetown was founded by Judge A.F. Knotts as a sportsmen's resort.

Population: 635 (1990); 629 (2000); 689 (2007); 735 (2012 projected); Race: 96.2% White, 0.0% Black, 1.3% Asian, 0.7% Hispanic of any race (2007); Density: 88.1 persons per square mile (2007); Average household size: 2.00 (2007); Median age: 57.0 (2007); Males per 100 females: 103.2 (2007); Marriage status: 9.3% never married, 65.4% now married, 7.8% widowed, 17.5% divorced (2000); Foreign born: 4.5% (2000); Ancestry (includes multiple ancestries): 20.7% German, 19.9% English, 12.2% Other groups, 10.7% Irish, 6.0% Scotch-Irish (2000).

Economy: Employment by occupation: 13.1% management, 25.3% professional, 20.5% services, 11.8% sales, 5.2% farming, 12.7% construction, 11.4% production (2000).

Income: Per capita income: $28,229 (2007); Median household income: $38,871 (2007); Average household income: $56,541 (2007); Percent of households with income of $100,000 or more: 12.2% (2007); Poverty rate: 12.5% (2000).

Education: Percent of population age 25 and over with: High school diploma (including GED) or higher: 83.8% (2007); Bachelor's degree or higher: 26.0% (2007); Master's degree or higher: 14.1% (2007).

School District(s)

Levy County School District (PK-12)
  2005-06 Enrollment: 6,284 . . . . (352) 486-5231

Housing: Homeownership rate: 82.8% (2007); Median home value: $190,972 (2007); Median rent: $365 per month (2000); Median age of housing: 29 years (2000).

Transportation: Commute to work: 86.0% car, 0.0% public transportation, 3.1% walk, 9.6% work from home (2000); Travel time to work: 24.2% less than 15 minutes, 37.2% 15 to 30 minutes, 22.2% 30 to 45 minutes, 4.8% 45 to 60 minutes, 11.6% 60 minutes or more (2000)

Liberty County

Located in northwestern Florida; bounded on the east by the Ochlockonee River, and on the west by the Apalachicola River; partly in Apalachicola National Forest. Covers a land area of 835.87 square miles, a water area of 7.29 square miles, and is located in the Eastern Time Zone. The county was founded in 1855. County seat is Bristol.

Population: 5,569 (1990); 7,021 (2000); 7,885 (2007); 8,411 (2012 projected); Race: 75.1% White, 18.9% Black, 0.2% Asian, 6.9% Hispanic of any race (2007); Density: 9.4 persons per square mile (2007); Average household size: 3.13 (2007); Median age: 34.8 (2007); Males per 100 females: 153.9 (2007).

Religion: Five largest groups: 23.0% Southern Baptist Convention, 11.3% The Church of Jesus Christ of Latter-day Saints, 3.4% Assemblies of God, 3.3% Church of God (Cleveland, Tennessee), 2.2% The United Methodist Church (2000).

Economy: Unemployment rate: 2.8% (11/2007); Total civilian labor force: 3,813 (11/2007); Leading industries: 10.1% logging; 8.7% retail trade; 0.0% insurance agencies & brokerages (2005); Farms: 67 totaling 9,900 acres (2002); Companies that employ 500 or more persons: 0 (2005); Companies that employ 100 to 499 persons: 3 (2005); Companies that employ less than 100 persons: 79 (2005); Black-owned businesses: n/a (2002); Hispanic-owned businesses: n/a (2002); Asian-owned businesses: n/a (2002); Women-owned businesses: n/a (2002); Retail sales per capita: $3,106 (2007). Single-family building permits issued: 22 (2006); Multi-family building permits issued: 0 (2006).

Income: Per capita income: $19,465 (2007); Median household income: $33,588 (2007); Average household income: $48,190 (2007); Percent of households with income of $100,000 or more: 8.6% (2007); Poverty rate: 21.6% (2005); Bankruptcy rate: 0.64% (2006).

Education: Percent of population age 25 and over with: High school diploma (including GED) or higher: 65.2% (2007); Bachelor's degree or higher: 7.0% (2007); Master's degree or higher: 3.2% (2007).

Housing: Homeownership rate: 82.0% (2007); Median home value: $113,801 (2007); Median rent: $265 per month (2000); Median age of housing: 22 years (2000).

Health: Birth rate: 125.9 per 10,000 population (2006); Death rate: 81.0 per 10,000 population (2006); Age-adjusted cancer mortality rate: 261.5 (Unreliable as per CDC) deaths per 100,000 population (2004); Number of physicians: 0.0 per 10,000 population (2005); Hospital beds: 0.0 per 10,000 population (2004); Hospital admissions: 0.0 per 10,000 population (2004).

Elections: 2004 Presidential election results: 63.8% Bush, 35.4% Kerry, 0.5% Nader, 0.1% Badnarik.

National and State Parks: Torreya State Park

Additional Information Contacts
Liberty County Government . . . . (850) 643-5404
   http://www.libertycountyflorida.com
Bristol Chamber of Commerce . . . . (850) 643-2359
   http://www.libertycountyflorida.com

Liberty County Communities

BRISTOL (city). County seat. Covers a land area of 1.634 square miles and a water area of 0 square miles. Located at 30.42° N. Lat.; 84.97° W. Long. Elevation is 174 feet.

History: Bristol was founded about 1850, when it was called Riddeysville. The name was changed in 1858.

Population: 778 (1990); 845 (2000); 921 (2007); 949 (2012 projected); Race: 83.8% White, 3.8% Black, 0.0% Asian, 10.4% Hispanic of any race (2007); Density: 563.6 persons per square mile (2007); Average household size: 2.53 (2007); Median age: 37.7 (2007); Males per 100 females: 92.7 (2007); Marriage status: 18.8% never married, 54.4% now married, 14.4% widowed, 12.5% divorced (2000); Foreign born: 4.5% (2000); Ancestry (includes multiple ancestries): 39.7% United States or American, 15.2% Other groups, 8.8% Irish, 6.5% English, 5.0% German (2000).

Economy: Single-family building permits issued: 1 (2006); Multi-family building permits issued: 0 (2006); Employment by occupation: 7.9% management, 16.5% professional, 18.6% services, 19.2% sales, 7.9% farming, 14.8% construction, 15.1% production (2000).

Income: Per capita income: $20,777 (2007); Median household income: $37,778 (2007); Average household income: $51,360 (2007); Percent of households with income of $100,000 or more: 9.1% (2007); Poverty rate: 19.8% (2000).

Education: Percent of population age 25 and over with: High school diploma (including GED) or higher: 74.2% (2007); Bachelor's degree or higher: 20.9% (2007); Master's degree or higher: 11.2% (2007).

School District(s)
Liberty County School District (PK-12)
   2005-06 Enrollment: 1,396 . . . . (850) 643-2275
Housing: Homeownership rate: 72.3% (2007); Median home value: $116,204 (2007); Median rent: $233 per month (2000); Median age of housing: 29 years (2000).
Newspapers: The Calhoun-Liberty Journal (General - Circulation 5,000)
Transportation: Commute to work: 93.5% car, 0.0% public transportation, 2.7% walk, 3.1% work from home (2000); Travel time to work: 37.6% less than 15 minutes, 24.1% 15 to 30 minutes, 14.2% 30 to 45 minutes, 7.4% 45 to 60 minutes, 16.7% 60 minutes or more (2000)

Additional Information Contacts
Bristol Chamber of Commerce . . . . (850) 643-2359
   http://www.libertycountyflorida.com

HOSFORD (unincorporated postal area, zip code 32334). Covers a land area of 147.569 square miles and a water area of 0.025 square miles. Located at 30.38° N. Lat.; 84.77° W. Long. Elevation is 95 feet.

Population: 1,548 (2000); Race: 98.3% White, 0.0% Black, 0.0% Asian, 0.0% Hispanic of any race (2000); Density: 10.5 persons per square mile (2000); Age: 25.8% under 18, 10.0% over 64 (2000); Marriage status: 20.8% never married, 52.6% now married, 9.6% widowed, 17.0% divorced (2000); Foreign born: 0.0% (2000); Ancestry (includes multiple ancestries): 29.6% United States or American, 22.7% Other groups, 9.3% Irish, 8.1% German, 6.2% English (2000).

Economy: Employment by occupation: 10.1% management, 7.2% professional, 17.1% services, 28.4% sales, 2.2% farming, 23.4% construction, 11.6% production (2000).

Income: Per capita income: $20,140 (2000); Median household income: $33,831 (2000); Poverty rate: 16.1% (2000).

Education: Percent of population age 25 and over with: High school diploma (including GED) or higher: 60.3% (2000); Bachelor's degree or higher: 4.8% (2000).

School District(s)
Liberty County School District (PK-12)
   2005-06 Enrollment: 1,396 . . . . (850) 643-2275
Housing: Homeownership rate: 82.0% (2000); Median home value: $76,500 (2000); Median rent: $268 per month (2000); Median age of housing: 20 years (2000).
Transportation: Commute to work: 95.3% car, 0.0% public transportation, 0.6% walk, 3.3% work from home (2000); Travel time to work: 22.3% less than 15 minutes, 21.9% 15 to 30 minutes, 17.2% 30 to 45 minutes, 17.9% 45 to 60 minutes, 20.6% 60 minutes or more (2000)

Madison County

Located in northern Florida; bounded on the north by Georgia, on the west by the Aucilla River, on the northeast by the Withlacoochee River, and on the southeast by the Suwannee River; includes many lakes. Covers a land area of 691.79 square miles, a water area of 24.00 square miles, and is located in the Eastern Time Zone. The county was founded in 1827. County seat is Madison.

Population: 16,563 (1990); 18,733 (2000); 19,520 (2007); 20,306 (2012 projected); Race: 57.5% White, 40.2% Black, 0.4% Asian, 4.6% Hispanic of any race (2007); Density: 28.2 persons per square mile (2007); Average household size: 2.76 (2007); Median age: 36.8 (2007); Males per 100 females: 110.9 (2007).

Religion: Five largest groups: 29.4% Southern Baptist Convention, 7.9% The United Methodist Church, 1.6% National Primitive Baptist Convention, USA, 1.0% Church of God (Cleveland, Tennessee), 0.8% Catholic Church (2000).

Economy: Unemployment rate: 5.5% (11/2007); Total civilian labor force: 7,102 (11/2007); Leading industries: 23.9% health care and social assistance; 21.5% retail trade; 21.4% manufacturing (2005); Farms: 529 totaling 156,995 acres (2002); Companies that employ 500 or more persons: 0 (2005); Companies that employ 100 to 499 persons: 6 (2005); Companies that employ less than 100 persons: 322 (2005); Black-owned businesses: n/a (2002); Hispanic-owned businesses: n/a (2002); Asian-owned businesses: n/a (2002); Women-owned businesses: n/a (2002); Retail sales per capita: $6,475 (2007). Single-family building permits issued: 89 (2006); Multi-family building permits issued: 0 (2006).

Income: Per capita income: $15,416 (2007); Median household income: $31,064 (2007); Average household income: $41,929 (2007); Percent of households with income of $100,000 or more: 5.8% (2007); Poverty rate: 23.8% (2005); Bankruptcy rate: 1.51% (2006).
Education: Percent of population age 25 and over with: High school diploma (including GED) or higher: 68.5% (2007); Bachelor's degree or higher: 10.0% (2007); Master's degree or higher: 3.6% (2007).
Housing: Homeownership rate: 79.1% (2007); Median home value: $108,203 (2007); Median rent: $237 per month (2000); Median age of housing: 23 years (2000).
Health: Birth rate: 128.6 per 10,000 population (2006); Death rate: 126.5 per 10,000 population (2006); Age-adjusted cancer mortality rate: 288.1 deaths per 100,000 population (2004); Number of physicians: 5.8 per 10,000 population (2005); Hospital beds: 16.3 per 10,000 population (2004); Hospital admissions: 500.0 per 10,000 population (2004).
Elections: 2004 Presidential election results: 50.5% Bush, 48.8% Kerry, 0.5% Nader, 0.1% Badnarik
Additional Information Contacts
Madison County Government . . . . (850) 973-3179
  http://www.madisoncountyfl.com
Madison Chamber of Commerce. . . . . (850) 973-2788
  http://www.madisonfl.org

Madison County Communities

GREENVILLE (town). Covers a land area of 1.314 square miles and a water area of 0 square miles. Located at 30.46° N. Lat.; 83.63° W. Long. Elevation is 98 feet.
History: Greenville was founded about 1850. It was first known as Sandy Ford, and later as Station Five for its location as the fifth railroad station east of Tallahassee. The town was later named for Greenville, South Carolina, the former home of many residents.
Population: 950 (1990); 837 (2000); 763 (2007); 785 (2012 projected); Race: 22.8% White, 76.9% Black, 0.1% Asian, 0.1% Hispanic of any race (2007); Density: 580.6 persons per square mile (2007); Average household size: 2.46 (2007); Median age: 34.6 (2007); Males per 100 females: 85.6 (2007); Marriage status: 35.1% never married, 43.1% now married, 12.6% widowed, 9.2% divorced (2000); Foreign born: 0.4% (2000); Ancestry (includes multiple ancestries): 60.6% Other groups, 8.1% United States or American, 7.4% Irish, 4.3% English, 2.8% German (2000).
Economy: Employment by occupation: 9.7% management, 10.8% professional, 22.6% services, 25.1% sales, 0.0% farming, 6.1% construction, 25.8% production (2000).
Income: Per capita income: $14,073 (2007); Median household income: $25,192 (2007); Average household income: $34,637 (2007); Percent of households with income of $100,000 or more: 4.5% (2007); Poverty rate: 32.9% (2000).
Education: Percent of population age 25 and over with: High school diploma (including GED) or higher: 52.6% (2007); Bachelor's degree or higher: 9.0% (2007); Master's degree or higher: 3.4% (2007).
School District(s)
Madison County School District (PK-12)
  2005-06 Enrollment: 3,211 . . . . (850) 973-5022
Housing: Homeownership rate: 73.5% (2007); Median home value: $72,800 (2007); Median rent: $167 per month (2000); Median age of housing: 32 years (2000).
Transportation: Commute to work: 91.0% car, 0.0% public transportation, 6.5% walk, 0.7% work from home (2000); Travel time to work: 31.0% less than 15 minutes, 31.8% 15 to 30 minutes, 19.1% 30 to 45 minutes, 7.9% 45 to 60 minutes, 10.1% 60 minutes or more (2000)

LEE (town). Covers a land area of 1.223 square miles and a water area of 0.003 square miles. Located at 30.41° N. Lat.; 83.30° W. Long. Elevation is 89 feet.
Population: 330 (1990); 352 (2000); 359 (2007); 368 (2012 projected); Race: 95.3% White, 3.1% Black, 0.3% Asian, 4.2% Hispanic of any race (2007); Density: 293.5 persons per square mile (2007); Average household size: 2.62 (2007); Median age: 37.5 (2007); Males per 100 females: 99.4 (2007); Marriage status: 22.4% never married, 57.6% now married, 6.0% widowed, 14.0% divorced (2000); Foreign born: 0.0% (2000); Ancestry (includes multiple ancestries): 29.1% Other groups, 18.0% United States or American, 10.6% Irish, 9.7% German, 8.9% Scotch-Irish (2000).
Economy: Single-family building permits issued: 1 (2006); Multi-family building permits issued: 0 (2006); Employment by occupation: 5.9%

management, 27.1% professional, 9.3% services, 22.0% sales, 7.6% farming, 1.7% construction, 26.3% production (2000).
Income: Per capita income: $19,833 (2007); Median household income: $33,438 (2007); Average household income: $51,971 (2007); Percent of households with income of $100,000 or more: 9.5% (2007); Poverty rate: 26.5% (2000).
Education: Percent of population age 25 and over with: High school diploma (including GED) or higher: 74.0% (2007); Bachelor's degree or higher: 11.0% (2007); Master's degree or higher: 8.4% (2007).
School District(s)
Madison County School District (PK-12)
  2005-06 Enrollment: 3,211 . . . . (850) 973-5022
Housing: Homeownership rate: 76.6% (2007); Median home value: $82,273 (2007); Median rent: $242 per month (2000); Median age of housing: 25 years (2000).
Transportation: Commute to work: 88.5% car, 0.0% public transportation, 3.5% walk, 4.4% work from home (2000); Travel time to work: 26.9% less than 15 minutes, 50.9% 15 to 30 minutes, 8.3% 30 to 45 minutes, 8.3% 45 to 60 minutes, 5.6% 60 minutes or more (2000)

MADISON (city). County seat. Covers a land area of 2.530 square miles and a water area of 0.047 square miles. Located at 30.46° N. Lat.; 83.41° W. Long. Elevation is 194 feet.
History: Madison was settled in 1838 by planters from South Carolina who grew sea-island cotton here.
Population: 3,428 (1990); 3,061 (2000); 2,998 (2007); 3,027 (2012 projected); Race: 36.1% White, 61.9% Black, 0.6% Asian, 3.2% Hispanic of any race (2007); Density: 1,184.8 persons per square mile (2007); Average household size: 2.41 (2007); Median age: 31.6 (2007); Males per 100 females: 85.7 (2007); Marriage status: 28.8% never married, 45.1% now married, 13.7% widowed, 12.4% divorced (2000); Foreign born: 1.0% (2000); Ancestry (includes multiple ancestries): 45.9% Other groups, 9.4% English, 6.0% United States or American, 4.0% Scotch-Irish, 1.6% German (2000).
Economy: Single-family building permits issued: 12 (2006); Multi-family building permits issued: 0 (2006); Employment by occupation: 7.7% management, 18.1% professional, 26.8% services, 21.6% sales, 0.8% farming, 5.4% construction, 19.6% production (2000).
Income: Per capita income: $11,934 (2007); Median household income: $18,088 (2007); Average household income: $27,203 (2007); Percent of households with income of $100,000 or more: 1.8% (2007); Poverty rate: 39.9% (2000).
Education: Percent of population age 25 and over with: High school diploma (including GED) or higher: 63.3% (2007); Bachelor's degree or higher: 18.1% (2007); Master's degree or higher: 7.4% (2007).
School District(s)
Madison County School District (PK-12)
  2005-06 Enrollment: 3,211 . . . . (850) 973-5022
Two-year College(s)
North Florida Community College (Public)
  Fall 2006 Enrollment: 1,239. (904) 973-2288
  2006-07 Tuition: In-state $1,860; Out-of-state $6,630
Housing: Homeownership rate: 56.9% (2007); Median home value: $109,579 (2007); Median rent: $218 per month (2000); Median age of housing: 33 years (2000).
Hospitals: Madison County Memorial Hospital (31 beds)
Safety: Violent crime rate: 98.6 per 10,000 population; Property crime rate: 576.4 per 10,000 population (2006).
Newspapers: Enterprise-Recorder (General - Circulation 4,000)
Transportation: Commute to work: 91.0% car, 0.0% public transportation, 7.5% walk, 0.0% work from home (2000); Travel time to work: 59.0% less than 15 minutes, 24.0% 15 to 30 minutes, 6.4% 30 to 45 minutes, 6.3% 45 to 60 minutes, 4.3% 60 minutes or more (2000); Amtrak: Service available.
Additional Information Contacts
Madison Chamber of Commerce. . . . . (850) 973-2788
  http://www.madisonfl.org

PINETTA (unincorporated postal area, zip code 32350). Covers a land area of 36.601 square miles and a water area of 0.410 square miles. Located at 30.59° N. Lat.; 83.32° W. Long. Elevation is 148 feet.
Population: 1,173 (2000); Race: 82.8% White, 14.6% Black, 0.0% Asian, 0.0% Hispanic of any race (2000); Density: 32.0 persons per square mile (2000); Age: 29.1% under 18, 11.5% over 64 (2000); Marriage status: 24.9% never married, 51.2% now married, 8.1% widowed, 15.7% divorced (2000); Foreign born: 1.4% (2000); Ancestry (includes multiple ancestries):

17.0% English, 16.1% Other groups, 11.8% United States or American, 10.8% Irish, 5.5% German (2000).
Economy: Employment by occupation: 4.5% management, 10.8% professional, 27.0% services, 16.2% sales, 2.4% farming, 16.2% construction, 22.9% production (2000).
Income: Per capita income: $16,006 (2000); Median household income: $29,750 (2000); Poverty rate: 12.1% (2000).
Education: Percent of population age 25 and over with: High school diploma (including GED) or higher: 72.6% (2000); Bachelor's degree or higher: 6.0% (2000).

School District(s)

Madison County School District (PK-12)
    2005-06 Enrollment: 3,211 . . . . (850) 973-5022
Housing: Homeownership rate: 83.0% (2000); Median home value: $35,000 (2000); Median rent: $199 per month (2000); Median age of housing: 17 years (2000).
Transportation: Commute to work: 96.0% car, 0.0% public transportation, 2.8% walk, 1.2% work from home (2000); Travel time to work: 6.7% less than 15 minutes, 43.2% 15 to 30 minutes, 31.2% 30 to 45 minutes, 4.5% 45 to 60 minutes, 14.5% 60 minutes or more (2000)

Manatee County

Located in western Florida, on the Gulf of Mexico; bounded on the west by Tampa Bay; drained by the Manatee and Myakka Rivers; includes several lakes, part of Sarasota Bay, Anna Maria Key, and other small islands. Covers a land area of 741.03 square miles, a water area of 151.72 square miles, and is located in the Eastern Time Zone. The county was founded in 1855. County seat is Bradenton.

Manatee County is part of the Sarasota-Bradenton-Venice, FL Metropolitan Statistical Area. The entire metro area includes: Manatee County, FL; Sarasota County, FL

Weather Station: Bradenton 5 ESE — Elevation: 19 feet

	Jan	Feb	Mar	Apr	May	Jun	Jul	Aug	Sep	Oct	Nov	Dec
High	73	74	78	82	87	90	92	91	90	85	80	74
Low	50	51	56	59	65	71	72	73	72	65	58	52
Precip	3.0	2.7	3.5	1.8	3.0	7.4	8.5	9.4	7.2	3.0	2.3	2.4
Snow	0.0	0.0	0.0	0.0	0.0	0.0	0.0	0.0	0.0	0.0	0.0	0.0

High and Low temperatures in degrees Fahrenheit; Precipitation and Snow in inches

Weather Station: Parrish — Elevation: 59 feet

	Jan	Feb	Mar	Apr	May	Jun	Jul	Aug	Sep	Oct	Nov	Dec
High	73	74	78	83	88	90	91	91	90	85	80	75
Low	50	51	55	59	64	70	72	72	71	65	58	52
Precip	2.9	3.2	3.2	2.0	3.2	7.2	7.5	8.7	7.4	2.9	2.3	2.3
Snow	tr	0.0	0.0	0.0	0.0	0.0	0.0	0.0	0.0	0.0	0.0	0.0

High and Low temperatures in degrees Fahrenheit; Precipitation and Snow in inches

Population: 211,707 (1990); 264,002 (2000); 317,306 (2007); 354,361 (2012 projected); Race: 84.4% White, 8.5% Black, 1.3% Asian, 12.4% Hispanic of any race (2007); Density: 428.2 persons per square mile (2007); Average household size: 2.35 (2007); Median age: 43.1 (2007); Males per 100 females: 94.9 (2007).
Religion: Five largest groups: 13.3% Catholic Church, 8.0% Southern Baptist Convention, 3.1% The United Methodist Church, 1.5% Jewish Estimate, 1.2% Presbyterian Church (U.S.A.) (2000).
Economy: Unemployment rate: 4.2% (11/2007); Total civilian labor force: 156,858 (11/2007); Leading industries: 18.5% retail trade; 14.3% health care and social assistance; 12.0% manufacturing (2005); Farms: 852 totaling 301,231 acres (2002); Companies that employ 500 or more persons: 10 (2005); Companies that employ 100 to 499 persons: 118 (2005); Companies that employ less than 100 persons: 7,397 (2005); Black-owned businesses: 503 (2002); Hispanic-owned businesses: 1,486 (2002); Asian-owned businesses: n/a (2002); Women-owned businesses: 6,302 (2002); Retail sales per capita: $14,896 (2007). Single-family building permits issued: 2,565 (2006); Multi-family building permits issued: 1,001 (2006).
Income: Per capita income: $26,833 (2007); Median household income: $45,955 (2007); Average household income: $62,104 (2007); Percent of households with income of $100,000 or more: 14.9% (2007); Poverty rate: 10.3% (2005); Bankruptcy rate: 1.00% (2006).
Taxes: Total county taxes per capita: $613 (2005); County property taxes per capita: $487 (2005).

Education: Percent of population age 25 and over with: High school diploma (including GED) or higher: 82.2% (2007); Bachelor's degree or higher: 21.9% (2007); Master's degree or higher: 7.6% (2007).
Housing: Homeownership rate: 74.9% (2007); Median home value: $216,072 (2007); Median rent: $539 per month (2000); Median age of housing: 21 years (2000).
Health: Birth rate: 119.2 per 10,000 population (2006); Death rate: 108.1 per 10,000 population (2006); Age-adjusted cancer mortality rate: 172.4 deaths per 100,000 population (2004); Air Quality Index: 90.7% good, 9.0% moderate, 0.3% unhealthy for sensitive individuals, 0.0% unhealthy (percent of days in 2006); Number of physicians: 21.6 per 10,000 population (2005); Hospital beds: 27.4 per 10,000 population (2004); Hospital admissions: 1,125.9 per 10,000 population (2004).
Elections: 2004 Presidential election results: 56.6% Bush, 42.7% Kerry, 0.5% Nader, 0.1% Badnarik
National and State Parks: De Soto National Memorial; Lake Manatee State Park; Madira Bickel Mound State Archaeological Site; Passage Key National Wildlife Refuge
Additional Information Contacts
Manatee County Government . . . . (941) 745-3700
    http://www.co.manatee.fl.us
Anna Maria Island Chamber of Commerce . . . . (941) 778-1541
    http://amichamber.org
Bradenton Chamber of Commerce . . . . (941) 748-3411
    http://www.manateechamber.com
Palmetto Convention & Visitors Bureau . . . . (941) 748-3411
    http://www.manateechamber.com

Manatee County Communities

ANNA MARIA (city). Covers a land area of 0.776 square miles and a water area of 0.210 square miles. Located at 27.53° N. Lat.; 82.73° W. Long. Elevation is 3 feet.
History: Anna Maria developed as a resort at the northern end of Anna Maria Key.
Population: 1,754 (1990); 1,814 (2000); 1,577 (2007); 1,610 (2012 projected); Race: 97.5% White, 0.4% Black, 0.4% Asian, 2.4% Hispanic of any race (2007); Density: 2,032.8 persons per square mile (2007); Average household size: 1.99 (2007); Median age: 56.6 (2007); Males per 100 females: 91.4 (2007); Marriage status: 15.3% never married, 63.2% now married, 12.1% widowed, 9.4% divorced (2000); Foreign born: 5.0% (2000); Ancestry (includes multiple ancestries): 22.0% German, 20.9% English, 17.2% Irish, 10.3% United States or American, 6.4% French (except Basque) (2000).
Economy: Single-family building permits issued: 5 (2006); Multi-family building permits issued: 0 (2006); Employment by occupation: 12.7% management, 23.1% professional, 20.3% services, 29.9% sales, 1.4% farming, 6.3% construction, 6.3% production (2000).
Income: Per capita income: $35,461 (2007); Median household income: $45,500 (2007); Average household income: $70,609 (2007); Percent of households with income of $100,000 or more: 17.2% (2007); Poverty rate: 10.5% (2000).
Education: Percent of population age 25 and over with: High school diploma (including GED) or higher: 93.2% (2007); Bachelor's degree or higher: 39.7% (2007); Master's degree or higher: 15.6% (2007).
Housing: Homeownership rate: 79.0% (2007); Median home value: $596,535 (2007); Median rent: $743 per month (2000); Median age of housing: 30 years (2000).
Transportation: Commute to work: 82.6% car, 0.0% public transportation, 2.7% walk, 9.1% work from home (2000); Travel time to work: 34.3% less than 15 minutes, 27.5% 15 to 30 minutes, 19.5% 30 to 45 minutes, 8.0% 45 to 60 minutes, 10.7% 60 minutes or more (2000)

BAYSHORE GARDENS (CDP). Covers a land area of 3.559 square miles and a water area of 0.024 square miles. Located at 27.43° N. Lat.; 82.57° W. Long. Elevation is 13 feet.
Population: 17,191 (1990); 17,350 (2000); 19,344 (2007); 20,791 (2012 projected); Race: 84.8% White, 6.3% Black, 1.5% Asian, 13.4% Hispanic of any race (2007); Density: 5,435.0 persons per square mile (2007); Average household size: 2.08 (2007); Median age: 42.6 (2007); Males per 100 females: 90.2 (2007); Marriage status: 19.7% never married, 52.3% now married, 14.1% widowed, 13.9% divorced (2000); Foreign born: 7.9% (2000); Ancestry (includes multiple ancestries): 18.6% German, 16.3% English, 14.8% Other groups, 12.8% Irish, 11.3% United States or American (2000).

Economy: Employment by occupation: 7.7% management, 13.6% professional, 16.9% services, 30.5% sales, 0.3% farming, 13.5% construction, 17.5% production (2000).
Income: Per capita income: $20,088 (2007); Median household income: $33,601 (2007); Average household income: $41,709 (2007); Percent of households with income of $100,000 or more: 4.8% (2007); Poverty rate: 10.1% (2000).
Education: Percent of population age 25 and over with: High school diploma (including GED) or higher: 78.7% (2007); Bachelor's degree or higher: 12.6% (2007); Master's degree or higher: 3.7% (2007).
Housing: Homeownership rate: 67.7% (2007); Median home value: $144,834 (2007); Median rent: $498 per month (2000); Median age of housing: 27 years (2000).
Transportation: Commute to work: 94.3% car, 0.7% public transportation, 3.0% walk, 0.9% work from home (2000); Travel time to work: 29.7% less than 15 minutes, 45.4% 15 to 30 minutes, 17.7% 30 to 45 minutes, 2.9% 45 to 60 minutes, 4.4% 60 minutes or more (2000)

BRADENTON (city). County seat. Covers a land area of 12.108 square miles and a water area of 2.335 square miles. Located at 27.48° N. Lat.; 82.57° W. Long. Elevation is 3 feet.
History: Dr. Joseph Braden built a house here in 1854, and when the post office was established in 1878, the town was named for him. At first the name was spelled Braidentown, later changed to Bradentown, and in 1924 to Bradenton.
Population: 43,699 (1990); 49,504 (2000); 54,934 (2007); 59,082 (2012 projected); Race: 75.6% White, 15.5% Black, 1.1% Asian, 15.2% Hispanic of any race (2007); Density: 4,537.0 persons per square mile (2007); Average household size: 2.31 (2007); Median age: 40.5 (2007); Males per 100 females: 92.4 (2007); Marriage status: 22.4% never married, 52.7% now married, 12.3% widowed, 12.6% divorced (2000); Foreign born: 8.5% (2000); Ancestry (includes multiple ancestries): 24.8% Other groups, 14.9% German, 12.0% English, 10.9% Irish, 6.7% United States or American (2000).
Economy: Unemployment rate: 4.0% (11/2007); Total civilian labor force: 27,446 (11/2007); Single-family building permits issued: 221 (2006); Multi-family building permits issued: 38 (2006); Employment by occupation: 10.0% management, 18.0% professional, 19.5% services, 26.3% sales, 1.8% farming, 10.6% construction, 13.7% production (2000).
Income: Per capita income: $22,790 (2007); Median household income: $39,876 (2007); Average household income: $50,683 (2007); Percent of households with income of $100,000 or more: 8.7% (2007); Poverty rate: 13.6% (2000).
Education: Percent of population age 25 and over with: High school diploma (including GED) or higher: 80.4% (2007); Bachelor's degree or higher: 20.8% (2007); Master's degree or higher: 7.4% (2007).

School District(s)
Manatee County School District (PK-12)
    2005-06 Enrollment: 41,351 . . . . (941) 708-8770
Four-year College(s)
Florida College of Natural Health (Private, For-profit)
    Fall 2006 Enrollment: 182 . . . . (941) 744-1244
Two-year College(s)
Manatee Community College (Public)
    Fall 2006 Enrollment: 9,080. (941) 752-5000
    2006-07 Tuition: In-state $2,091; Out-of-state $7,708
Manatee Technical Institute (Public)
    Fall 2006 Enrollment: 1,169. (941) 751-7900
Vocational/Technical School(s)
Bradenton Beauty and Barber Academy (Private, For-profit)
    Fall 2006 Enrollment: 129 . . . . (941) 761-4400
    2006-07 Tuition: $9,700
Housing: Homeownership rate: 61.3% (2007); Median home value: $189,179 (2007); Median rent: $562 per month (2000); Median age of housing: 23 years (2000).
Hospitals: Blake Medical Center (383 beds); Lakewood Ranch Medical Center (120 beds); Manatee Glens Hospital (47 beds); Manatee Memorial Hospital (319 beds)
Safety: Violent crime rate: 74.8 per 10,000 population; Property crime rate: 481.5 per 10,000 population (2006).
Newspapers: Bradenton Herald (Circulation 51,113)
Transportation: Commute to work: 93.1% car, 1.0% public transportation, 1.4% walk, 2.3% work from home (2000); Travel time to work: 30.5% less than 15 minutes, 41.7% 15 to 30 minutes, 17.3% 30 to 45 minutes, 5.4%

45 to 60 minutes, 5.0% 60 minutes or more (2000); Amtrak: Service available.
Airports: Sarasota/Bradenton International (primary service/small hub)
Additional Information Contacts
Bradenton Chamber of Commerce . . . . (941) 748-3411
    http://www.manateechamber.com

BRADENTON BEACH (city). Covers a land area of 0.548 square miles and a water area of 0.549 square miles. Located at 27.47° N. Lat.; 82.70° W. Long.
Population: 1,657 (1990); 1,482 (2000); 1,481 (2007); 1,515 (2012 projected); Race: 98.2% White, 0.3% Black, 0.1% Asian, 2.0% Hispanic of any race (2007); Density: 2,703.0 persons per square mile (2007); Average household size: 1.81 (2007); Median age: 51.7 (2007); Males per 100 females: 104.3 (2007); Marriage status: 21.8% never married, 47.1% now married, 10.5% widowed, 20.7% divorced (2000); Foreign born: 3.4% (2000); Ancestry (includes multiple ancestries): 28.0% German, 17.5% English, 16.4% Irish, 7.5% Other groups, 6.4% United States or American (2000).
Economy: Single-family building permits issued: 1 (2006); Multi-family building permits issued: 25 (2006); Employment by occupation: 15.4% management, 18.0% professional, 25.4% services, 23.7% sales, 0.0% farming, 12.2% construction, 5.3% production (2000).
Income: Per capita income: $26,195 (2007); Median household income: $37,881 (2007); Average household income: $47,311 (2007); Percent of households with income of $100,000 or more: 8.7% (2007); Poverty rate: 7.3% (2000).
Education: Percent of population age 25 and over with: High school diploma (including GED) or higher: 85.2% (2007); Bachelor's degree or higher: 24.5% (2007); Master's degree or higher: 11.4% (2007).
Housing: Homeownership rate: 57.1% (2007); Median home value: $280,882 (2007); Median rent: $618 per month (2000); Median age of housing: 34 years (2000).
Safety: Violent crime rate: 50.4 per 10,000 population; Property crime rate: 497.8 per 10,000 population (2006).
Transportation: Commute to work: 89.9% car, 0.0% public transportation, 2.4% walk, 3.3% work from home (2000); Travel time to work: 29.1% less than 15 minutes, 35.5% 15 to 30 minutes, 21.3% 30 to 45 minutes, 5.6% 45 to 60 minutes, 8.5% 60 minutes or more (2000)

CORTEZ (CDP). Covers a land area of 2.193 square miles and a water area of 2.942 square miles. Located at 27.46° N. Lat.; 82.67° W. Long. Elevation is 3 feet.
History: Cortez developed as a fishing village.
Population: 4,509 (1990); 4,491 (2000); 4,824 (2007); 5,097 (2012 projected); Race: 97.8% White, 0.2% Black, 0.7% Asian, 1.7% Hispanic of any race (2007); Density: 2,199.5 persons per square mile (2007); Average household size: 1.85 (2007); Median age: 62.1 (2007); Males per 100 females: 92.1 (2007); Marriage status: 8.2% never married, 67.8% now married, 13.9% widowed, 10.1% divorced (2000); Foreign born: 6.5% (2000); Ancestry (includes multiple ancestries): 22.8% German, 16.8% English, 14.8% Irish, 9.4% United States or American, 7.1% Other groups (2000).
Economy: Employment by occupation: 9.8% management, 16.5% professional, 11.7% services, 38.5% sales, 1.9% farming, 11.8% construction, 9.9% production (2000).
Income: Per capita income: $30,680 (2007); Median household income: $41,291 (2007); Average household income: $56,801 (2007); Percent of households with income of $100,000 or more: 14.0% (2007); Poverty rate: 9.4% (2000).
Education: Percent of population age 25 and over with: High school diploma (including GED) or higher: 84.9% (2007); Bachelor's degree or higher: 22.2% (2007); Master's degree or higher: 8.4% (2007).
Housing: Homeownership rate: 85.1% (2007); Median home value: $232,726 (2007); Median rent: $529 per month (2000); Median age of housing: 25 years (2000).
Transportation: Commute to work: 90.6% car, 0.5% public transportation, 0.6% walk, 5.9% work from home (2000); Travel time to work: 26.1% less than 15 minutes, 46.1% 15 to 30 minutes, 17.5% 30 to 45 minutes, 2.8% 45 to 60 minutes, 7.5% 60 minutes or more (2000)

ELLENTON (CDP). Covers a land area of 3.668 square miles and a water area of 1.140 square miles. Located at 27.52° N. Lat.; 82.52° W. Long. Elevation is 10 feet.

History: It was in the Gamble plantation house in Ellenton that Judah Philip Benjamin, Secretary of State of the Confederacy, took refuge at the end of the Civil War. Federal gunboats came to Tampa Bay searching for Benjamin, but he disguised himself and sailed for England under the noses of the Federal officers.

Population: 2,597 (1990); 3,142 (2000); 3,948 (2007); 4,503 (2012 projected); Race: 86.9% White, 6.0% Black, 0.6% Asian, 12.9% Hispanic of any race (2007); Density: 1,076.4 persons per square mile (2007); Average household size: 2.25 (2007); Median age: 43.5 (2007); Males per 100 females: 90.3 (2007); Marriage status: 11.8% never married, 65.4% now married, 11.1% widowed, 11.7% divorced (2000); Foreign born: 6.2% (2000); Ancestry (includes multiple ancestries): 19.1% German, 14.3% Irish, 13.2% Other groups, 11.5% English, 11.0% United States or American (2000).

Economy: Employment by occupation: 7.3% management, 25.2% professional, 12.2% services, 25.3% sales, 2.1% farming, 15.0% construction, 12.9% production (2000).

Income: Per capita income: $21,158 (2007); Median household income: $35,840 (2007); Average household income: $47,163 (2007); Percent of households with income of $100,000 or more: 7.0% (2007); Poverty rate: 8.7% (2000).

Education: Percent of population age 25 and over with: High school diploma (including GED) or higher: 83.4% (2007); Bachelor's degree or higher: 11.7% (2007); Master's degree or higher: 2.6% (2007).

Housing: Homeownership rate: 75.2% (2007); Median home value: $182,935 (2007); Median rent: $508 per month (2000); Median age of housing: 21 years (2000).

Transportation: Commute to work: 89.3% car, 0.0% public transportation, 2.2% walk, 5.5% work from home (2000); Travel time to work: 37.6% less than 15 minutes, 32.8% 15 to 30 minutes, 16.8% 30 to 45 minutes, 7.5% 45 to 60 minutes, 5.3% 60 minutes or more (2000)

HOLMES BEACH (city). Covers a land area of 1.621 square miles and a water area of 0.110 square miles. Located at 27.51° N. Lat.; 82.71° W. Long. Elevation is 3 feet.

Population: 4,800 (1990); 4,966 (2000); 5,494 (2007); 5,739 (2012 projected); Race: 98.1% White, 0.2% Black, 0.4% Asian, 1.7% Hispanic of any race (2007); Density: 3,389.2 persons per square mile (2007); Average household size: 1.91 (2007); Median age: 54.8 (2007); Males per 100 females: 91.4 (2007); Marriage status: 12.3% never married, 58.5% now married, 13.3% widowed, 15.9% divorced (2000); Foreign born: 5.4% (2000); Ancestry (includes multiple ancestries): 20.7% German, 17.4% Irish, 15.0% English, 9.8% Italian, 7.1% Other groups (2000).

Economy: Single-family building permits issued: 25 (2006); Multi-family building permits issued: 0 (2006); Employment by occupation: 13.8% management, 16.1% professional, 23.9% services, 27.5% sales, 0.5% farming, 8.4% construction, 9.8% production (2000).

Income: Per capita income: $34,765 (2007); Median household income: $49,952 (2007); Average household income: $66,573 (2007); Percent of households with income of $100,000 or more: 16.1% (2007); Poverty rate: 3.6% (2000).

Education: Percent of population age 25 and over with: High school diploma (including GED) or higher: 92.7% (2007); Bachelor's degree or higher: 29.2% (2007); Master's degree or higher: 11.0% (2007).

School District(s)
Manatee County School District (PK-12)
   2005-06 Enrollment: 41,351 . . . . (941) 708-8770

Housing: Homeownership rate: 67.9% (2007); Median home value: $465,304 (2007); Median rent: $648 per month (2000); Median age of housing: 28 years (2000).

Safety: Violent crime rate: 23.1 per 10,000 population; Property crime rate: 316.2 per 10,000 population (2006).

Transportation: Commute to work: 84.9% car, 0.5% public transportation, 4.8% walk, 8.1% work from home (2000); Travel time to work: 38.6% less than 15 minutes, 25.3% 15 to 30 minutes, 16.8% 30 to 45 minutes, 7.0% 45 to 60 minutes, 12.3% 60 minutes or more (2000)

Additional Information Contacts
Anna Maria Island Chamber of Commerce . . . . (941) 778-1541
   http://amichamber.org

MEMPHIS (CDP). Covers a land area of 3.162 square miles and a water area of 0 square miles. Located at 27.54° N. Lat.; 82.56° W. Long. Elevation is 20 feet.

Population: 6,733 (1990); 7,264 (2000); 7,758 (2007); 8,198 (2012 projected); Race: 46.9% White, 39.4% Black, 0.4% Asian, 26.6% Hispanic

of any race (2007); Density: 2,453.3 persons per square mile (2007); Average household size: 2.93 (2007); Median age: 32.0 (2007); Males per 100 females: 99.4 (2007); Marriage status: 30.1% never married, 51.2% now married, 8.0% widowed, 10.7% divorced (2000); Foreign born: 11.6% (2000); Ancestry (includes multiple ancestries): 48.0% Other groups, 7.7% German, 5.5% English, 5.4% Irish, 4.2% United States or American (2000).

Economy: Employment by occupation: 5.9% management, 13.4% professional, 20.9% services, 26.3% sales, 2.7% farming, 12.6% construction, 18.1% production (2000).

Income: Per capita income: $17,493 (2007); Median household income: $39,605 (2007); Average household income: $48,738 (2007); Percent of households with income of $100,000 or more: 7.1% (2007); Poverty rate: 20.7% (2000).

Education: Percent of population age 25 and over with: High school diploma (including GED) or higher: 62.4% (2007); Bachelor's degree or higher: 13.6% (2007); Master's degree or higher: 5.5% (2007).

Housing: Homeownership rate: 74.7% (2007); Median home value: $159,835 (2007); Median rent: $416 per month (2000); Median age of housing: 22 years (2000).

Transportation: Commute to work: 93.0% car, 0.8% public transportation, 1.9% walk, 2.1% work from home (2000); Travel time to work: 23.9% less than 15 minutes, 47.3% 15 to 30 minutes, 20.6% 30 to 45 minutes, 4.8% 45 to 60 minutes, 3.4% 60 minutes or more (2000)

MYAKKA CITY (unincorporated postal area, zip code 34251). Covers a land area of 298.597 square miles and a water area of 0.282 square miles. Located at 27.39° N. Lat.; 82.23° W. Long. Elevation is 44 feet.

History: Myakka City grew as a trading center for truck farmers and citrus growers. The name Myakka is of Indian origin meaning "very large," referring to the river here.

Population: 4,239 (2000); Race: 97.4% White, 0.0% Black, 1.1% Asian, 13.7% Hispanic of any race (2000); Density: 14.2 persons per square mile (2000); Age: 30.2% under 18, 6.0% over 64 (2000); Marriage status: 15.2% never married, 73.8% now married, 2.3% widowed, 8.8% divorced (2000); Foreign born: 4.2% (2000); Ancestry (includes multiple ancestries): 13.4% English, 12.9% German, 11.3% United States or American, 10.9% Irish, 8.6% Other groups (2000).

Economy: Employment by occupation: 12.3% management, 14.4% professional, 19.2% services, 23.2% sales, 3.4% farming, 18.8% construction, 8.8% production (2000).

Income: Per capita income: $24,143 (2000); Median household income: $54,216 (2000); Poverty rate: 2.6% (2000).

Education: Percent of population age 25 and over with: High school diploma (including GED) or higher: 78.4% (2000); Bachelor's degree or higher: 11.9% (2000).

School District(s)
Manatee County School District (PK-12)
   2005-06 Enrollment: 41,351 . . . . (941) 708-8770

Housing: Homeownership rate: 86.0% (2000); Median home value: $145,100 (2000); Median rent: $419 per month (2000); Median age of housing: 12 years (2000).

Transportation: Commute to work: 92.3% car, 0.0% public transportation, 0.5% walk, 7.3% work from home (2000); Travel time to work: 9.6% less than 15 minutes, 21.1% 15 to 30 minutes, 37.3% 30 to 45 minutes, 20.4% 45 to 60 minutes, 11.7% 60 minutes or more (2000)

PALMETTO (city). Covers a land area of 4.316 square miles and a water area of 0.134 square miles. Located at 27.52° N. Lat.; 82.57° W. Long. Elevation is 10 feet.

History: Palmetto developed on the north bank of the Manatee River as a packing and shipping center for fruits and vegetables. Palmetto's river-front harbor sheltered both fishing and pleasure boats.

Population: 9,534 (1990); 12,571 (2000); 13,895 (2007); 14,868 (2012 projected); Race: 74.6% White, 10.4% Black, 0.5% Asian, 34.4% Hispanic of any race (2007); Density: 3,219.7 persons per square mile (2007); Average household size: 2.83 (2007); Median age: 34.0 (2007); Males per 100 females: 102.0 (2007); Marriage status: 22.0% never married, 56.9% now married, 9.5% widowed, 11.6% divorced (2000); Foreign born: 13.3% (2000); Ancestry (includes multiple ancestries): 29.9% Other groups, 11.5% German, 11.3% English, 10.1% United States or American, 7.9% Irish (2000).

Economy: Single-family building permits issued: 51 (2006); Multi-family building permits issued: 197 (2006); Employment by occupation: 6.8% management, 14.3% professional, 20.2% services, 21.1% sales, 5.6% farming, 14.2% construction, 17.8% production (2000).

diploma (including GED) or higher: 66.3% (2007); Bachelor's degree or higher: 11.4% (2007); Master's degree or higher: 4.5% (2007).

School District(s)

Manatee County School District (PK-12)

   2005-06 Enrollment: 41,351 . . . . (941) 708-8770

Housing: Homeownership rate: 71.2% (2007); Median home value: $162,606 (2007); Median rent: $400 per month (2000); Median age of housing: 26 years (2000).

Safety: Violent crime rate: 208.9 per 10,000 population; Property crime rate: 610.0 per 10,000 population (2006).

Transportation: Commute to work: 90.5% car, 0.7% public transportation, 3.6% walk, 3.2% work from home (2000); Travel time to work: 30.1% less than 15 minutes, 37.5% 15 to 30 minutes, 23.6% 30 to 45 minutes, 5.1% 45 to 60 minutes, 3.6% 60 minutes or more (2000)

Additional Information Contacts

Palmetto Convention & Visitors Bureau . . . . (941) 748-3411
   http://www.manateechamber.com

PARRISH (unincorporated postal area, zip code 34219). Covers a land area of 80.450 square miles and a water area of 6.030 square miles. Located at 27.57° N. Lat.; 82.40° W. Long. Elevation is 44 feet.

History: Parrish developed as a citrus-fruit and vegetable shipping center.

Population: 5,812 (2000); Race: 93.4% White, 3.2% Black, 0.7% Asian, 5.6% Hispanic of any race (2000); Density: 72.2 persons per square mile (2000); Age: 18.3% under 18, 23.1% over 64 (2000); Marriage status: 13.1% never married, 74.0% now married, 6.4% widowed, 6.5% divorced (2000); Foreign born: 5.9% (2000); Ancestry (includes multiple ancestries): 18.9% German, 15.4% English, 13.5% Irish, 13.2% Other groups, 12.1% United States or American (2000).

Economy: Employment by occupation: 17.8% management, 18.7% professional, 13.9% services, 26.1% sales, 3.1% farming, 10.8% construction, 9.7% production (2000).

Income: Per capita income: $26,496 (2000); Median household income: $51,250 (2000); Poverty rate: 8.2% (2000).

Education: Percent of population age 25 and over with: High school diploma (including GED) or higher: 88.2% (2000); Bachelor's degree or higher: 23.0% (2000).

Housing: Homeownership rate: 92.2% (2000); Median home value: $178,400 (2000); Median rent: $439 per month (2000); Median age of housing: 7 years (2000).

Transportation: Commute to work: 89.0% car, 0.2% public transportation, 2.2% walk, 6.7% work from home (2000); Travel time to work: 19.9% less than 15 minutes, 37.6% 15 to 30 minutes, 28.1% 30 to 45 minutes, 10.0% 45 to 60 minutes, 4.4% 60 minutes or more (2000)

SAMOSET (CDP). Covers a land area of 1.927 square miles and a water area of 0 square miles. Located at 27.47° N. Lat.; 82.54° W. Long. Elevation is 30 feet.

Population: 3,135 (1990); 3,440 (2000); 3,743 (2007); 3,956 (2012 projected); Race: 50.8% White, 32.6% Black, 0.1% Asian, 27.9% Hispanic of any race (2007); Density: 1,942.3 persons per square mile (2007); Average household size: 3.11 (2007); Median age: 29.7 (2007); Males per 100 females: 99.8 (2007); Marriage status: 31.0% never married, 46.9% now married, 8.0% widowed, 14.1% divorced (2000); Foreign born: 6.0% (2000); Ancestry (includes multiple ancestries): 40.1% Other groups, 9.0% United States or American, 7.8% English, 5.2% Irish, 4.9% German (2000).

Economy: Employment by occupation: 2.2% management, 6.9% professional, 16.5% services, 27.1% sales, 1.3% farming, 24.6% construction, 21.5% production (2000).

Income: Per capita income: $13,298 (2007); Median household income: $35,000 (2007); Average household income: $40,704 (2007); Percent of households with income of $100,000 or more: 2.6% (2007); Poverty rate: 22.5% (2000).

Education: Percent of population age 25 and over with: High school diploma (including GED) or higher: 58.5% (2007); Bachelor's degree or higher: 5.2% (2007); Master's degree or higher: 2.6% (2007).

Housing: Homeownership rate: 71.0% (2007); Median home value: $147,283 (2007); Median rent: $393 per month (2000); Median age of housing: 29 years (2000).

SOUTH BRADENTON (CDP). Covers a land area of 4.460 square miles and a water area of 0.078 square miles. Located at 27.45° N. Lat.; 82.57° W. Long. Elevation is 20 feet.

Population: 20,264 (1990); 21,587 (2000); 23,065 (2007); 24,273 (2012 projected); Race: 85.5% White, 6.8% Black, 1.7% Asian, 13.4% Hispanic of any race (2007); Density: 5,171.8 persons per square mile (2007); Average household size: 2.02 (2007); Median age: 43.0 (2007); Males per 100 females: 89.8 (2007); Marriage status: 23.3% never married, 47.2% now married, 14.0% widowed, 15.5% divorced (2000); Foreign born: 9.0% (2000); Ancestry (includes multiple ancestries): 17.9% Other groups, 16.4% German, 14.0% English, 12.8% Irish, 8.0% United States or American (2000).

Economy: Employment by occupation: 6.5% management, 11.1% professional, 21.5% services, 30.4% sales, 1.4% farming, 10.6% construction, 18.4% production (2000).

Income: Per capita income: $19,081 (2007); Median household income: $30,699 (2007); Average household income: $38,198 (2007); Percent of households with income of $100,000 or more: 3.7% (2007); Poverty rate: 13.0% (2000).

Education: Percent of population age 25 and over with: High school diploma (including GED) or higher: 75.4% (2007); Bachelor's degree or higher: 13.2% (2007); Master's degree or higher: 3.8% (2007).

Housing: Homeownership rate: 59.6% (2007); Median home value: $119,080 (2007); Median rent: $488 per month (2000); Median age of housing: 26 years (2000).

Transportation: Commute to work: 93.8% car, 0.6% public transportation, 2.0% walk, 2.1% work from home (2000); Travel time to work: 36.2% less than 15 minutes, 43.3% 15 to 30 minutes, 13.7% 30 to 45 minutes, 2.5% 45 to 60 minutes, 4.4% 60 minutes or more (2000)

WEST BRADENTON (CDP). Aka Rosedale. Covers a land area of 1.365 square miles and a water area of 0.064 square miles. Located at 27.50° N. Lat.; 82.61° W. Long. Elevation is 16 feet.

Population: 4,562 (1990); 4,444 (2000); 4,667 (2007); 4,877 (2012 projected); Race: 96.3% White, 0.9% Black, 1.0% Asian, 3.0% Hispanic of any race (2007); Density: 3,419.4 persons per square mile (2007); Average household size: 2.61 (2007); Median age: 41.1 (2007); Males per 100 females: 92.4 (2007); Marriage status: 17.0% never married, 65.7% now married, 5.9% widowed, 11.3% divorced (2000); Foreign born: 3.7% (2000); Ancestry (includes multiple ancestries): 23.4% German, 14.7% Irish, 13.9% English, 9.2% United States or American, 8.3% Other groups (2000).

Economy: Employment by occupation: 11.6% management, 26.2% professional, 17.0% services, 27.0% sales, 0.8% farming, 9.7% construction, 7.7% production (2000).

Income: Per capita income: $32,038 (2007); Median household income: $61,315 (2007); Average household income: $83,672 (2007); Percent of households with income of $100,000 or more: 22.0% (2007); Poverty rate: 5.2% (2000).

Education: Percent of population age 25 and over with: High school diploma (including GED) or higher: 89.3% (2007); Bachelor's degree or higher: 29.5% (2007); Master's degree or higher: 12.7% (2007).

Housing: Homeownership rate: 89.9% (2007); Median home value: $245,122 (2007); Median rent: $750 per month (2000); Median age of housing: 30 years (2000).

Transportation: Commute to work: 95.1% car, 0.0% public transportation, 1.0% walk, 2.9% work from home (2000); Travel time to work: 31.2% less than 15 minutes, 45.7% 15 to 30 minutes, 13.9% 30 to 45 minutes, 7.4% 45 to 60 minutes, 1.8% 60 minutes or more (2000)

WEST SAMOSET (CDP). Covers a land area of 1.372 square miles and a water area of 0 square miles. Located at 27.47° N. Lat.; 82.55° W. Long. Elevation is 39 feet.

Population: 3,819 (1990); 5,507 (2000); 6,367 (2007); 6,989 (2012 projected); Race: 50.7% White, 33.1% Black, 0.7% Asian, 31.7% Hispanic of any race (2007); Density: 4,640.5 persons per square mile (2007); Average household size: 3.09 (2007); Median age: 29.1 (2007); Males per 100 females: 96.0 (2007); Marriage status: 32.1% never married, 46.3% now married, 11.9% widowed, 9.6% divorced (2000); Foreign born: 12.0%

(2000); Ancestry (includes multiple ancestries): 47.5% Other groups, 9.2% United States or American, 7.6% German, 5.8% Irish, 3.9% English (2000).
Economy: Employment by occupation: 1.2% management, 5.7% professional, 18.3% services, 20.9% sales, 2.4% farming, 16.2% construction, 35.4% production (2000).
Income: Per capita income: $12,840 (2007); Median household income: $32,614 (2007); Average household income: $38,961 (2007); Percent of households with income of $100,000 or more: 3.7% (2007); Poverty rate: 18.8% (2000).
Education: Percent of population age 25 and over with: High school diploma (including GED) or higher: 56.9% (2007); Bachelor's degree or higher: 6.7% (2007); Master's degree or higher: 2.2% (2007).
Housing: Homeownership rate: 39.1% (2007); Median home value: $117,844 (2007); Median rent: $529 per month (2000); Median age of housing: 26 years (2000).
Transportation: Commute to work: 95.2% car, 1.8% public transportation, 1.6% walk, 0.0% work from home (2000); Travel time to work: 29.7% less than 15 minutes, 42.9% 15 to 30 minutes, 17.2% 30 to 45 minutes, 2.3% 45 to 60 minutes, 8.0% 60 minutes or more (2000)

WHITFIELD (CDP). Covers a land area of 1.404 square miles and a water area of 0.020 square miles. Located at 27.41° N. Lat.; 82.56° W. Long. Elevation is 16 feet.
Population: 3,246 (1990); 2,984 (2000); 3,065 (2007); 3,156 (2012 projected); Race: 91.3% White, 5.2% Black, 0.9% Asian, 7.6% Hispanic of any race (2007); Density: 2,182.6 persons per square mile (2007); Average household size: 2.36 (2007); Median age: 44.5 (2007); Males per 100 females: 97.1 (2007); Marriage status: 20.9% never married, 63.0% now married, 5.4% widowed, 10.7% divorced (2000); Foreign born: 16.9% (2000); Ancestry (includes multiple ancestries): 23.5% German, 15.0% English, 13.0% Irish, 12.1% Other groups, 9.6% French (except Basque) (2000).
Economy: Employment by occupation: 11.5% management, 20.3% professional, 17.4% services, 23.2% sales, 0.0% farming, 13.8% construction, 13.8% production (2000).
Income: Per capita income: $28,949 (2007); Median household income: $56,752 (2007); Average household income: $68,410 (2007); Percent of households with income of $100,000 or more: 15.2% (2007); Poverty rate: 6.3% (2000).
Education: Percent of population age 25 and over with: High school diploma (including GED) or higher: 88.4% (2007); Bachelor's degree or higher: 26.5% (2007); Master's degree or higher: 11.7% (2007).
Housing: Homeownership rate: 87.3% (2007); Median home value: $283,086 (2007); Median rent: $599 per month (2000); Median age of housing: 27 years (2000).
Transportation: Commute to work: 94.2% car, 0.0% public transportation, 0.0% walk, 5.8% work from home (2000); Travel time to work: 37.2% less than 15 minutes, 43.8% 15 to 30 minutes, 12.5% 30 to 45 minutes, 2.8% 45 to 60 minutes, 3.8% 60 minutes or more (2000)

Marion County

Located in north central Florida; drained by the Oklawaha River; includes Lakes Weir and Kerr, and Ocala National Forest. Covers a land area of 1,578.86 square miles, a water area of 84.15 square miles, and is located in the Eastern Time Zone. The county was founded in 1844. County seat is Ocala.

Marion County is part of the Ocala, FL Metropolitan Statistical Area. The entire metro area includes: Marion County, FL

Weather Station: Ocala   Elevation: 72 feet

	Jan	Feb	Mar	Apr	May	Jun	Jul	Aug	Sep	Oct	Nov	Dec
High	70	73	78	83	88	91	92	92	90	84	77	72
Low	46	47	52	56	63	69	71	71	69	61	54	47
Precip	3.6	3.3	4.2	2.9	3.8	7.1	6.4	6.1	5.5	2.8	2.4	2.7
Snow	tr	tr	0.0	0.0	0.0	0.0	0.0	0.0	0.0	0.0	0.0	0.0

High and Low temperatures in degrees Fahrenheit; Precipitation and Snow in inches

Population: 194,833 (1990); 258,916 (2000); 317,593 (2007); 359,606 (2012 projected); Race: 83.1% White, 11.3% Black, 1.0% Asian, 8.3% Hispanic of any race (2007); Density: 201.2 persons per square mile (2007); Average household size: 2.40 (2007); Median age: 43.5 (2007); Males per 100 females: 94.0 (2007).

Religion: Five largest groups: 11.5% Catholic Church, 9.3% Southern Baptist Convention, 4.0% The United Methodist Church, 1.4% Presbyterian Church (U.S.A.), 1.3% Church of God (Cleveland, Tennessee) (2000).
Economy: Unemployment rate: 5.0% (11/2007); Total civilian labor force: 136,853 (11/2007); Leading industries: 19.9% retail trade; 16.1% health care and social assistance; 10.9% manufacturing (2005); Farms: 2,930 totaling 270,562 acres (2002); Companies that employ 500 or more persons: 10 (2005); Companies that employ 100 to 499 persons: 99 (2005); Companies that employ less than 100 persons: 6,783 (2005); Black-owned businesses: 1,201 (2002); Hispanic-owned businesses: n/a (2002); Asian-owned businesses: 258 (2002); Women-owned businesses: 5,390 (2002); Retail sales per capita: $14,241 (2007). Single-family building permits issued: 6,753 (2006); Multi-family building permits issued: 310 (2006).
Income: Per capita income: $21,065 (2007); Median household income: $37,795 (2007); Average household income: $49,891 (2007); Percent of households with income of $100,000 or more: 8.8% (2007); Poverty rate: 13.6% (2005); Bankruptcy rate: 1.37% (2006).
Taxes: Total county taxes per capita: $486 (2005); County property taxes per capita: $267 (2005).
Education: Percent of population age 25 and over with: High school diploma (including GED) or higher: 78.5% (2007); Bachelor's degree or higher: 13.7% (2007); Master's degree or higher: 5.1% (2007).
Housing: Homeownership rate: 80.9% (2007); Median home value: $126,053 (2007); Median rent: $404 per month (2000); Median age of housing: 16 years (2000).
Health: Birth rate: 111.6 per 10,000 population (2006); Death rate: 123.0 per 10,000 population (2006); Age-adjusted cancer mortality rate: 220.0 deaths per 100,000 population (2004); Air Quality Index: 90.7% good, 9.3% moderate, 0.0% unhealthy for sensitive individuals, 0.0% unhealthy (percent of days in 2006); Number of physicians: 16.7 per 10,000 population (2005); Hospital beds: 23.3 per 10,000 population (2004); Hospital admissions: 1,256.3 per 10,000 population (2004).
Elections: 2004 Presidential election results: 58.2% Bush, 41.0% Kerry, 0.5% Nader, 0.2% Badnarik
National and State Parks: Ocala National Forest; Rainbow Springs State Park; Silver River State Park
Additional Information Contacts
Marion County Government . . . . (352) 671-5604
    http://www.marioncountyfl.org
Belleview Chamber of Commerce . . . . (352) 245-2178
    http://www.ocalacc.com
Dunnellon Chamber of Commerce . . . . (352) 489-2320
    http://www.dunnellonchamber.org
Lake Weir Chamber of Commerce . . . . (352) 288-3751
Ocala Chamber of Commerce . . . . (352) 629-8051
    http://www.ocalacc.com

Marion County Communities

ANTHONY (unincorporated postal area, zip code 32617). Covers a land area of 20.077 square miles and a water area of 0.090 square miles. Located at 29.31° N. Lat.; 82.10° W. Long. Elevation is 85 feet.
Population: 3,546 (2000); Race: 83.2% White, 14.5% Black, 0.0% Asian, 4.8% Hispanic of any race (2000); Density: 176.6 persons per square mile (2000); Age: 25.6% under 18, 11.1% over 64 (2000); Marriage status: 24.6% never married, 59.2% now married, 5.3% widowed, 10.9% divorced (2000); Foreign born: 3.9% (2000); Ancestry (includes multiple ancestries): 28.3% Other groups, 13.2% United States or American, 11.5% Irish, 10.4% German, 9.5% English (2000).
Economy: Employment by occupation: 11.8% management, 13.6% professional, 17.0% services, 25.7% sales, 1.7% farming, 14.1% construction, 16.0% production (2000).
Income: Per capita income: $15,483 (2000); Median household income: $38,627 (2000); Poverty rate: 13.4% (2000).
Education: Percent of population age 25 and over with: High school diploma (including GED) or higher: 72.0% (2000); Bachelor's degree or higher: 10.6% (2000).

School District(s)
Marion County School District (PK-12)
    2005-06 Enrollment: 41,205 . . . . (352) 671-7702
Housing: Homeownership rate: 83.1% (2000); Median home value: $93,100 (2000); Median rent: $398 per month (2000); Median age of housing: 17 years (2000).

Transportation: Commute to work: 91.2% car, 0.0% public transportation, 3.3% walk, 2.9% work from home (2000); Travel time to work: 14.7% less than 15 minutes, 48.4% 15 to 30 minutes, 26.6% 30 to 45 minutes, 6.2% 45 to 60 minutes, 4.1% 60 minutes or more (2000)

BELLEVIEW (city). Covers a land area of 1.825 square miles and a water area of 0.002 square miles. Located at 29.06° N. Lat.; 82.05° W. Long. Elevation is 79 feet.
History: Belleview developed around an area of citrus and pecan groves, with fruit packing plants and lumber mills.
Population: 3,310 (1990); 3,478 (2000); 3,645 (2007); 3,792 (2012 projected); Race: 90.2% White, 4.5% Black, 0.7% Asian, 10.4% Hispanic of any race (2007); Density: 1,997.0 persons per square mile (2007); Average household size: 2.14 (2007); Median age: 41.6 (2007); Males per 100 females: 90.1 (2007); Marriage status: 20.4% never married, 45.7% now married, 16.8% widowed, 17.2% divorced (2000); Foreign born: 3.5% (2000); Ancestry (includes multiple ancestries): 21.3% Other groups, 15.5% German, 14.2% Irish, 10.3% United States or American, 10.1% French (except Basque) (2000).
Economy: Single-family building permits issued: 56 (2006); Multi-family building permits issued: 46 (2006); Employment by occupation: 4.5% management, 16.6% professional, 15.1% services, 31.1% sales, 0.0% farming, 14.2% construction, 18.4% production (2000).
Income: Per capita income: $19,099 (2007); Median household income: $30,232 (2007); Average household income: $39,331 (2007); Percent of households with income of $100,000 or more: 3.2% (2007); Poverty rate: 12.3% (2000).
Education: Percent of population age 25 and over with: High school diploma (including GED) or higher: 73.7% (2007); Bachelor's degree or higher: 8.4% (2007); Master's degree or higher: 3.4% (2007).

School District(s)
Marion County School District (PK-12)
    2005-06 Enrollment: 41,205 . . . . (352) 671-7702
Housing: Homeownership rate: 68.6% (2007); Median home value: $96,548 (2007); Median rent: $361 per month (2000); Median age of housing: 20 years (2000).
Safety: Violent crime rate: 74.0 per 10,000 population; Property crime rate: 686.0 per 10,000 population (2006).
Newspapers: Voice of South Marion (General - Circulation 2,800)
Transportation: Commute to work: 89.6% car, 0.0% public transportation, 2.4% walk, 5.1% work from home (2000); Travel time to work: 26.1% less than 15 minutes, 37.9% 15 to 30 minutes, 24.5% 30 to 45 minutes, 4.2% 45 to 60 minutes, 7.3% 60 minutes or more (2000)
Additional Information Contacts
Belleview Chamber of Commerce . . . . (352) 245-2178
    http://www.ocalacc.com

CITRA (unincorporated postal area, zip code 32113). Covers a land area of 88.893 square miles and a water area of 3.659 square miles. Located at 29.39° N. Lat.; 82.09° W. Long. Elevation is 75 feet.
History: Citra was founded in the early 1880's. The pineapple orange was developed near here.
Population: 6,891 (2000); Race: 81.4% White, 15.6% Black, 0.6% Asian, 2.8% Hispanic of any race (2000); Density: 77.5 persons per square mile (2000); Age: 22.8% under 18, 17.5% over 64 (2000); Marriage status: 19.0% never married, 57.1% now married, 6.5% widowed, 17.4% divorced (2000); Foreign born: 2.4% (2000); Ancestry (includes multiple ancestries): 21.5% Other groups, 19.0% United States or American, 9.9% Irish, 8.7% German, 6.8% English (2000).
Economy: Employment by occupation: 9.8% management, 10.4% professional, 20.8% services, 26.3% sales, 4.3% farming, 15.6% construction, 12.7% production (2000).
Income: Per capita income: $15,948 (2000); Median household income: $30,045 (2000); Poverty rate: 19.1% (2000).
Education: Percent of population age 25 and over with: High school diploma (including GED) or higher: 69.9% (2000); Bachelor's degree or higher: 7.2% (2000).

School District(s)
Marion County School District (PK-12)
    2005-06 Enrollment: 41,205 . . . . (352) 671-7702
Housing: Homeownership rate: 83.6% (2000); Median home value: $66,400 (2000); Median rent: $358 per month (2000); Median age of housing: 19 years (2000).
Transportation: Commute to work: 91.7% car, 0.0% public transportation, 1.2% walk, 5.2% work from home (2000); Travel time to work: 11.4% less

than 15 minutes, 37.7% 15 to 30 minutes, 37.1% 30 to 45 minutes, 8.6% 45 to 60 minutes, 5.3% 60 minutes or more (2000)

DUNNELLON (city). Covers a land area of 7.048 square miles and a water area of 0.381 square miles. Located at 29.05° N. Lat.; 82.45° W. Long. Elevation is 49 feet.
History: Dunnellon was established on the Withlacoochee River, and grew after 1889 as a center for the mining and shipping of phosphate and limestone rock. Before that, Dunnellon was a trading center for planters and stockmen of the surrounding areas.
Population: 1,741 (1990); 1,898 (2000); 2,128 (2007); 2,309 (2012 projected); Race: 86.0% White, 11.0% Black, 0.5% Asian, 2.3% Hispanic of any race (2007); Density: 301.9 persons per square mile (2007); Average household size: 1.97 (2007); Median age: 50.6 (2007); Males per 100 females: 81.7 (2007); Marriage status: 15.1% never married, 52.7% now married, 17.6% widowed, 14.6% divorced (2000); Foreign born: 3.9% (2000); Ancestry (includes multiple ancestries): 17.9% Other groups, 17.6% German, 15.4% English, 11.5% Irish, 11.0% United States or American (2000).
Economy: Single-family building permits issued: 20 (2006); Multi-family building permits issued: 0 (2006); Employment by occupation: 8.3% management, 21.8% professional, 16.4% services, 21.7% sales, 1.9% farming, 10.5% construction, 19.5% production (2000).
Income: Per capita income: $22,352 (2007); Median household income: $31,901 (2007); Average household income: $43,960 (2007); Percent of households with income of $100,000 or more: 9.9% (2007); Poverty rate: 15.5% (2000).
Education: Percent of population age 25 and over with: High school diploma (including GED) or higher: 84.1% (2007); Bachelor's degree or higher: 13.9% (2007); Master's degree or higher: 5.4% (2007).

School District(s)
Marion County School District (PK-12)
    2005-06 Enrollment: 41,205 . . . . (352) 671-7702
Housing: Homeownership rate: 71.1% (2007); Median home value: $125,129 (2007); Median rent: $358 per month (2000); Median age of housing: 23 years (2000).
Safety: Violent crime rate: 79.8 per 10,000 population; Property crime rate: 254.5 per 10,000 population (2006).
Newspapers: Riverland News (General - Circulation 3,100)
Transportation: Commute to work: 91.9% car, 0.0% public transportation, 3.2% walk, 3.3% work from home (2000); Travel time to work: 38.0% less than 15 minutes, 19.3% 15 to 30 minutes, 23.4% 30 to 45 minutes, 13.8% 45 to 60 minutes, 5.4% 60 minutes or more (2000)
Additional Information Contacts
Dunnellon Chamber of Commerce . . . . (352) 489-2320
    http://www.dunnellonchamber.org

FORT MCCOY (unincorporated postal area, zip code 32134). Covers a land area of 225.356 square miles and a water area of 12.896 square miles. Located at 29.40° N. Lat.; 81.83° W. Long. Elevation is 75 feet.
Population: 7,950 (2000); Race: 95.9% White, 0.9% Black, 1.6% Asian, 2.1% Hispanic of any race (2000); Density: 35.3 persons per square mile (2000); Age: 20.2% under 18, 22.9% over 64 (2000); Marriage status: 12.2% never married, 62.5% now married, 12.2% widowed, 13.2% divorced (2000); Foreign born: 3.1% (2000); Ancestry (includes multiple ancestries): 15.3% United States or American, 14.1% German, 13.9% Other groups, 13.3% Irish, 11.5% English (2000).
Economy: Employment by occupation: 10.8% management, 7.3% professional, 16.1% services, 23.7% sales, 1.1% farming, 21.6% construction, 19.5% production (2000).
Income: Per capita income: $15,582 (2000); Median household income: $28,195 (2000); Poverty rate: 16.2% (2000).
Education: Percent of population age 25 and over with: High school diploma (including GED) or higher: 72.6% (2000); Bachelor's degree or higher: 8.1% (2000).

School District(s)
Marion County School District (PK-12)
    2005-06 Enrollment: 41,205 . . . . (352) 671-7702
Housing: Homeownership rate: 88.5% (2000); Median home value: $62,500 (2000); Median rent: $334 per month (2000); Median age of housing: 21 years (2000).
Transportation: Commute to work: 95.6% car, 0.7% public transportation, 0.4% walk, 2.9% work from home (2000); Travel time to work: 13.5% less than 15 minutes, 12.4% 15 to 30 minutes, 34.0% 30 to 45 minutes, 21.9% 45 to 60 minutes, 18.2% 60 minutes or more (2000)

MCINTOSH (town). Covers a land area of 0.696 square miles and a water area of 0 square miles. Located at 29.44° N. Lat.; 82.22° W. Long. Elevation is 108 feet.

History: McIntosh developed in an area of citrus and pecan groves.

Population: 411 (1990); 453 (2000); 568 (2007); 655 (2012 projected); Race: 96.0% White, 3.5% Black, 0.0% Asian, 2.5% Hispanic of any race (2007); Density: 816.1 persons per square mile (2007); Average household size: 1.98 (2007); Median age: 52.9 (2007); Males per 100 females: 83.8 (2007); Marriage status: 14.8% never married, 62.7% now married, 7.5% widowed, 15.0% divorced (2000); Foreign born: 1.9% (2000); Ancestry (includes multiple ancestries): 15.8% Other groups, 13.7% English, 13.7% German, 11.6% Irish, 7.9% United States or American (2000).

Economy: Employment by occupation: 8.8% management, 29.3% professional, 6.3% services, 35.6% sales, 0.0% farming, 8.8% construction, 11.2% production (2000).

Income: Per capita income: $29,353 (2007); Median household income: $45,357 (2007); Average household income: $58,092 (2007); Percent of households with income of $100,000 or more: 13.2% (2007); Poverty rate: 6.3% (2000).

Education: Percent of population age 25 and over with: High school diploma (including GED) or higher: 91.2% (2007); Bachelor's degree or higher: 26.9% (2007); Master's degree or higher: 14.4% (2007).

School District(s)
Marion County School District (PK-12)
    2005-06 Enrollment: 41,205 . . . . (352) 671-7702

Housing: Homeownership rate: 79.8% (2007); Median home value: $152,155 (2007); Median rent: $395 per month (2000); Median age of housing: 25 years (2000).

Transportation: Commute to work: 99.0% car, 0.0% public transportation, 0.0% walk, 0.0% work from home (2000); Travel time to work: 11.2% less than 15 minutes, 41.0% 15 to 30 minutes, 40.5% 30 to 45 minutes, 2.4% 45 to 60 minutes, 4.9% 60 minutes or more (2000)

OCALA (city). County seat. Covers a land area of 38.633 square miles and a water area of 0 square miles. Located at 29.18° N. Lat.; 82.13° W. Long. Elevation is 69 feet.

History: Ocala began as a trading post established in 1825, and used during the Seminole Wars as a military post. The town became a trading and shipping center for truck gardeners and for phosphate and limestone mining companies.

Population: 42,851 (1990); 45,943 (2000); 50,721 (2007); 54,553 (2012 projected); Race: 71.2% White, 21.9% Black, 1.9% Asian, 8.4% Hispanic of any race (2007); Density: 1,312.9 persons per square mile (2007); Average household size: 2.48 (2007); Median age: 37.5 (2007); Males per 100 females: 92.6 (2007); Marriage status: 23.7% never married, 51.5% now married, 10.1% widowed, 14.6% divorced (2000); Foreign born: 4.6% (2000); Ancestry (includes multiple ancestries): 26.9% Other groups, 13.2% German, 11.8% Irish, 11.1% English, 6.8% United States or American (2000).

Economy: Unemployment rate: 4.1% (11/2007); Total civilian labor force: 24,043 (11/2007); Single-family building permits issued: 612 (2006); Multi-family building permits issued: 192 (2006); Employment by occupation: 11.7% management, 20.1% professional, 18.9% services, 27.1% sales, 0.8% farming, 9.4% construction, 12.0% production (2000).

Income: Per capita income: $20,735 (2007); Median household income: $35,601 (2007); Average household income: $49,684 (2007); Percent of households with income of $100,000 or more: 9.7% (2007); Poverty rate: 18.1% (2000).

Taxes: Total city taxes per capita: $513 (2005); City property taxes per capita: $282 (2005).

Education: Percent of population age 25 and over with: High school diploma (including GED) or higher: 79.6% (2007); Bachelor's degree or higher: 19.6% (2007); Master's degree or higher: 7.6% (2007).

School District(s)
Marion County School District (PK-12)
    2005-06 Enrollment: 41,205 . . . . (352) 671-7702
Four-year College(s)
Webster College (Private, For-profit)
    Fall 2006 Enrollment: 401 . . . . (352) 629-1941
    2006-07 Tuition: In-state $10,205; Out-of-state $10,205
Two-year College(s)
Central Florida Community College (Public)
    Fall 2006 Enrollment: 5,825. . . . . (352) 873-5800
    2006-07 Tuition: In-state $1,631; Out-of-state $5,906

    Fall 2006 Enrollment: 307 . . . . (352) 671-7200

Housing: Homeownership rate: 56.3% (2007); Median home value: $127,923 (2007); Median rent: $430 per month (2000); Median age of housing: 24 years (2000).

Hospitals: Munroe Regional Medical Center (421 beds); Ocala Regional Medical Center (200 beds)

Safety: Violent crime rate: 141.9 per 10,000 population; Property crime rate: 649.0 per 10,000 population (2006).

Newspapers: Mahogany Revue (General, Hispanic - Circulation 30,000); Star-Banner (Circulation 49,660)

Transportation: Commute to work: 93.1% car, 0.4% public transportation, 2.1% walk, 2.6% work from home (2000); Travel time to work: 45.0% less than 15 minutes, 38.8% 15 to 30 minutes, 8.4% 30 to 45 minutes, 3.1% 45 to 60 minutes, 4.7% 60 minutes or more (2000); Amtrak: Service available.

Airports: Ocala Regional/Jim Taylor Field

Additional Information Contacts
Ocala Chamber of Commerce . . . . (352) 629-8051
    http://www.ocalacc.com

REDDICK (town). Covers a land area of 1.245 square miles and a water area of 0 square miles. Located at 29.37° N. Lat.; 82.19° W. Long. Elevation is 72 feet.

Population: 554 (1990); 571 (2000); 655 (2007); 719 (2012 projected); Race: 50.7% White, 40.0% Black, 0.0% Asian, 11.0% Hispanic of any race (2007); Density: 526.1 persons per square mile (2007); Average household size: 2.79 (2007); Median age: 30.4 (2007); Males per 100 females: 97.3 (2007); Marriage status: 35.1% never married, 45.5% now married, 6.6% widowed, 12.8% divorced (2000); Foreign born: 6.7% (2000); Ancestry (includes multiple ancestries): 43.9% Other groups, 16.4% United States or American, 10.9% German, 6.3% Swedish, 5.1% English (2000).

Economy: Employment by occupation: 2.9% management, 10.0% professional, 22.9% services, 20.8% sales, 13.8% farming, 13.8% construction, 15.8% production (2000).

Income: Per capita income: $19,492 (2007); Median household income: $42,875 (2007); Average household income: $54,330 (2007); Percent of households with income of $100,000 or more: 11.5% (2007); Poverty rate: 18.3% (2000).

Education: Percent of population age 25 and over with: High school diploma (including GED) or higher: 70.6% (2007); Bachelor's degree or higher: 8.0% (2007); Master's degree or higher: 4.0% (2007).

School District(s)
Marion County School District (PK-12)
    2005-06 Enrollment: 41,205 . . . . (352) 671-7702

Housing: Homeownership rate: 77.0% (2007); Median home value: $105,114 (2007); Median rent: $350 per month (2000); Median age of housing: 29 years (2000).

Transportation: Commute to work: 91.2% car, 0.0% public transportation, 5.0% walk, 2.1% work from home (2000); Travel time to work: 32.1% less than 15 minutes, 20.9% 15 to 30 minutes, 38.0% 30 to 45 minutes, 5.6% 45 to 60 minutes, 3.4% 60 minutes or more (2000)

SILVER SPRINGS SHORES (CDP). Covers a land area of 4.774 square miles and a water area of 0.057 square miles. Located at 29.10° N. Lat.; 82.01° W. Long. Elevation is 95 feet.

Population: 6,421 (1990); 6,690 (2000); 7,464 (2007); 8,063 (2012 projected); Race: 57.1% White, 33.5% Black, 1.8% Asian, 14.4% Hispanic of any race (2007); Density: 1,563.3 persons per square mile (2007); Average household size: 2.30 (2007); Median age: 40.8 (2007); Males per 100 females: 82.1 (2007); Marriage status: 15.0% never married, 60.6% now married, 13.5% widowed, 10.9% divorced (2000); Foreign born: 18.1% (2000); Ancestry (includes multiple ancestries): 29.6% Other groups, 9.9% Jamaican, 9.5% Irish, 9.3% German, 8.5% Italian (2000).

Economy: Employment by occupation: 6.8% management, 18.5% professional, 17.8% services, 28.8% sales, 0.9% farming, 9.5% construction, 17.7% production (2000).

Income: Per capita income: $14,329 (2007); Median household income: $26,733 (2007); Average household income: $32,761 (2007); Percent of households with income of $100,000 or more: 3.7% (2007); Poverty rate: 12.0% (2000).

Education: Percent of population age 25 and over with: High school diploma (including GED) or higher: 75.2% (2007); Bachelor's degree or higher: 10.8% (2007); Master's degree or higher: 5.0% (2007).

Housing: Homeownership rate: 73.9% (2007); Median home value: $93,467 (2007); Median rent: $458 per month (2000); Median age of housing: 21 years (2000).
Transportation: Commute to work: 95.7% car, 1.3% public transportation, 0.4% walk, 0.4% work from home (2000); Travel time to work: 19.8% less than 15 minutes, 44.6% 15 to 30 minutes, 21.4% 30 to 45 minutes, 8.0% 45 to 60 minutes, 6.3% 60 minutes or more (2000)

WEIRSDALE (unincorporated postal area, zip code 32195). Covers a land area of 24.367 square miles and a water area of 2.343 square miles. Located at 29.00° N. Lat.; 81.89° W. Long. Elevation is 97 feet.
History: Weirsdale was established as a resort on the shores of Lake Weir, with citrus packing plants providing for the early economy of the town.
Population: 3,181 (2000); Race: 84.8% White, 11.7% Black, 2.4% Asian, 3.4% Hispanic of any race (2000); Density: 130.5 persons per square mile (2000); Age: 24.0% under 18, 16.4% over 64 (2000); Marriage status: 15.5% never married, 64.3% now married, 7.0% widowed, 13.2% divorced (2000); Foreign born: 5.9% (2000); Ancestry (includes multiple ancestries): 21.0% Other groups, 17.3% German, 11.9% Irish, 11.0% English, 9.6% United States or American (2000).
Economy: Employment by occupation: 8.3% management, 15.7% professional, 16.7% services, 27.6% sales, 2.4% farming, 16.8% construction, 12.4% production (2000).
Income: Per capita income: $21,543 (2000); Median household income: $40,410 (2000); Poverty rate: 13.7% (2000).
Education: Percent of population age 25 and over with: High school diploma (including GED) or higher: 70.9% (2000); Bachelor's degree or higher: 14.0% (2000).

School District(s)
Marion County School District (PK-12)
    2005-06 Enrollment: 41,205 . . . . (352) 671-7702
Housing: Homeownership rate: 82.1% (2000); Median home value: $95,500 (2000); Median rent: $327 per month (2000); Median age of housing: 16 years (2000).
Transportation: Commute to work: 95.3% car, 0.0% public transportation, 2.4% walk, 1.6% work from home (2000); Travel time to work: 22.2% less than 15 minutes, 25.4% 15 to 30 minutes, 31.9% 30 to 45 minutes, 14.0% 45 to 60 minutes, 6.5% 60 minutes or more (2000)

Martin County

Located in southeastern Florida; bounded on the west by Lake Okeechobee, and on the east by the Atlantic Ocean and Jupiter Island. Covers a land area of 555.62 square miles, a water area of 197.18 square miles, and is located in the Eastern Time Zone. The county was founded in 1925. County seat is Stuart.

Martin County is part of the Port St. Lucie, FL Metropolitan Statistical Area. The entire metro area includes: Martin County, FL; St. Lucie County, FL

Weather Station: Stuart 1 S										Elevation: 9 feet		
	Jan	Feb	Mar	Apr	May	Jun	Jul	Aug	Sep	Oct	Nov	Dec
High	75	76	79	82	86	89	90	90	89	85	80	77
Low	55	55	60	64	69	73	74	74	74	70	64	58
Precip	3.1	3.4	4.6	2.8	5.4	6.9	6.3	6.4	8.2	6.4	4.2	2.7
Snow	0.0	0.0	0.0	0.0	0.0	0.0	0.0	0.0	0.0	0.0	0.0	0.0

High and Low temperatures in degrees Fahrenheit; Precipitation and Snow in inches

Population: 100,900 (1990); 126,731 (2000); 143,801 (2007); 156,609 (2012 projected); Race: 88.3% White, 5.3% Black, 0.7% Asian, 9.4% Hispanic of any race (2007); Density: 258.8 persons per square mile (2007); Average household size: 2.30 (2007); Median age: 47.5 (2007); Males per 100 females: 97.4 (2007).
Religion: Five largest groups: 28.0% Catholic Church, 3.8% The United Methodist Church, 3.2% Southern Baptist Convention, 2.9% Episcopal Church, 1.7% Jewish Estimate (2000).
Economy: Unemployment rate: 4.6% (11/2007); Total civilian labor force: 68,181 (11/2007); Leading industries: 20.1% retail trade; 14.4% health care and social assistance; 12.2% accommodation & food services (2005); Farms: 418 totaling 206,198 acres (2002); Companies that employ 500 or more persons: 4 (2005); Companies that employ 100 to 499 persons: 79 (2005); Companies that employ less than 100 persons: 4,931 (2005); Black-owned businesses: 304 (2002); Hispanic-owned businesses: 669 (2002); Asian-owned businesses: n/a (2002); Women-owned businesses: 3,923 (2002); Retail sales per capita: $20,104 (2007). Single-family

building permits issued: 936 (2006); Multi-family building permits issued: 28 (2006).
Income: Per capita income: $32,910 (2007); Median household income: $49,578 (2007); Average household income: $74,531 (2007); Percent of households with income of $100,000 or more: 20.2% (2007); Poverty rate: 9.8% (2005); Bankruptcy rate: 0.49% (2006).
Taxes: Total county taxes per capita: $979 (2005); County property taxes per capita: $769 (2005).
Education: Percent of population age 25 and over with: High school diploma (including GED) or higher: 85.5% (2007); Bachelor's degree or higher: 26.6% (2007); Master's degree or higher: 9.0% (2007).
Housing: Homeownership rate: 80.2% (2007); Median home value: $264,395 (2007); Median rent: $557 per month (2000); Median age of housing: 18 years (2000).
Health: Birth rate: 98.6 per 10,000 population (2006); Death rate: 130.1 per 10,000 population (2006); Age-adjusted cancer mortality rate: 180.9 deaths per 100,000 population (2004); Number of physicians: 28.9 per 10,000 population (2005); Hospital beds: 22.4 per 10,000 population (2004); Hospital admissions: 1,196.4 per 10,000 population (2004).
Elections: 2004 Presidential election results: 57.1% Bush, 41.7% Kerry, 0.6% Nader, 0.2% Badnarik
National and State Parks: Hobe Sound National Wildlife Refuge; Jonathan Dickinson State Park; Saint Lucie Inlet Preserve State Park; Seabranch Preserve State Park
Additional Information Contacts
Martin County Government . . . . (772) 288-5420
    http://www.martin.fl.us
Hobe Sound Chamber of Commerce. . . . . (772) 546-4724
    http://www.hobesound.org
Indiantown Chamber of Commerce . . . . (772) 597-3984
    http://www.indiantownfl.org
Jensen Beach Chamber of Commerce . . . . (772) 334-3444
    http://www.jensenbeachchamber.org
Palm City Chamber of Commerce . . . . (561) 286-8121
    http://www.palmcitychamber.com
Stuart Chamber of Commerce . . . . (772) 287-1088
    http://www.goodnature.org

Martin County Communities

HOBE SOUND (CDP). Covers a land area of 5.462 square miles and a water area of 0.265 square miles. Located at 27.07° N. Lat.; 80.14° W. Long. Elevation is 20 feet.
Population: 11,507 (1990); 11,376 (2000); 11,536 (2007); 11,799 (2012 projected); Race: 91.3% White, 5.9% Black, 0.7% Asian, 2.9% Hispanic of any race (2007); Density: 2,112.1 persons per square mile (2007); Average household size: 2.19 (2007); Median age: 51.0 (2007); Males per 100 females: 94.2 (2007); Marriage status: 14.5% never married, 62.4% now married, 11.5% widowed, 11.6% divorced (2000); Foreign born: 4.8% (2000); Ancestry (includes multiple ancestries): 17.6% German, 15.1% Irish, 14.1% English, 11.1% Other groups, 8.6% United States or American (2000).
Economy: Employment by occupation: 15.4% management, 15.2% professional, 21.9% services, 25.2% sales, 0.7% farming, 11.7% construction, 9.9% production (2000).
Income: Per capita income: $25,048 (2007); Median household income: $41,391 (2007); Average household income: $54,287 (2007); Percent of households with income of $100,000 or more: 13.2% (2007); Poverty rate: 5.5% (2000).
Education: Percent of population age 25 and over with: High school diploma (including GED) or higher: 82.7% (2007); Bachelor's degree or higher: 23.1% (2007); Master's degree or higher: 7.9% (2007).

School District(s)
Martin County School District (PK-12)
    2005-06 Enrollment: 17,917 . . . . (772) 219-1200
Four-year College(s)
Hobe Sound Bible College (Private, Not-for-profit, Wesleyan)
    Fall 2006 Enrollment: 136 . . . . (772) 546-5534
    2006-07 Tuition: In-state $4,200; Out-of-state $4,200
Housing: Homeownership rate: 80.6% (2007); Median home value: $183,084 (2007); Median rent: $529 per month (2000); Median age of housing: 18 years (2000).
Transportation: Commute to work: 89.0% car, 0.0% public transportation, 2.7% walk, 4.3% work from home (2000); Travel time to work: 36.2% less

45 to 60 minutes, 6.7% 60 minutes or more (2000)

Additional Information Contacts

Hobe Sound Chamber of Commerce.................. (772) 546-4724
  http://www.hobesound.org

INDIANTOWN (CDP).

Covers a land area of 5.969 square miles and a water area of 0 square miles. Located at 27.02° N. Lat.; 80.47° W. Long. Elevation is 33 feet.

Population: 4,794 (1990); 5,588 (2000); 6,029 (2007); 6,418 (2012 projected); Race: 45.0% White, 16.6% Black, 0.2% Asian, 54.3% Hispanic of any race (2007); Density: 1,010.1 persons per square mile (2007); Average household size: 3.47 (2007); Median age: 30.1 (2007); Males per 100 females: 121.3 (2007); Marriage status: 31.1% never married, 54.5% now married, 5.7% widowed, 8.6% divorced (2000); Foreign born: 32.1% (2000); Ancestry (includes multiple ancestries): 52.1% Other groups, 4.8% United States or American, 4.1% English, 4.0% Irish, 3.7% German (2000).

Economy: Employment by occupation: 6.1% management, 9.8% professional, 31.3% services, 13.6% sales, 9.9% farming, 12.6% construction, 16.8% production (2000).

Income: Per capita income: $11,661 (2007); Median household income: $32,912 (2007); Average household income: $40,474 (2007); Percent of households with income of $100,000 or more: 3.9% (2007); Poverty rate: 23.8% (2000).

Education: Percent of population age 25 and over with: High school diploma (including GED) or higher: 52.3% (2007); Bachelor's degree or higher: 10.0% (2007); Master's degree or higher: 4.7% (2007).

School District(s)

Martin County School District (PK-12)
  2005-06 Enrollment: 17,917 .... (772) 219-1200

Housing: Homeownership rate: 67.1% (2007); Median home value: $146,898 (2007); Median rent: $389 per month (2000); Median age of housing: 19 years (2000).

Transportation: Commute to work: 87.7% car, 2.9% public transportation, 0.0% walk, 1.8% work from home (2000); Travel time to work: 25.2% less than 15 minutes, 23.0% 15 to 30 minutes, 22.2% 30 to 45 minutes, 14.0% 45 to 60 minutes, 15.6% 60 minutes or more (2000)

Additional Information Contacts

Indiantown Chamber of Commerce .... (772) 597-3984
  http://www.indiantownfl.org

JENSEN BEACH (CDP).

Covers a land area of 7.246 square miles and a water area of 0.880 square miles. Located at 27.23° N. Lat.; 80.23° W. Long. Elevation is 7 feet.

Population: 10,320 (1990); 11,100 (2000); 11,761 (2007); 12,364 (2012 projected); Race: 94.7% White, 2.5% Black, 0.5% Asian, 3.5% Hispanic of any race (2007); Density: 1,623.0 persons per square mile (2007); Average household size: 2.19 (2007); Median age: 45.6 (2007); Males per 100 females: 95.7 (2007); Marriage status: 18.1% never married, 57.5% now married, 10.5% widowed, 13.9% divorced (2000); Foreign born: 4.5% (2000); Ancestry (includes multiple ancestries): 20.9% German, 19.9% Irish, 17.2% English, 12.8% Italian, 9.5% Other groups (2000).

Economy: Employment by occupation: 14.4% management, 16.2% professional, 20.1% services, 26.9% sales, 0.5% farming, 13.2% construction, 8.7% production (2000).

Income: Per capita income: $25,765 (2007); Median household income: $42,124 (2007); Average household income: $56,072 (2007); Percent of households with income of $100,000 or more: 11.5% (2007); Poverty rate: 8.3% (2000).

Education: Percent of population age 25 and over with: High school diploma (including GED) or higher: 86.6% (2007); Bachelor's degree or higher: 20.1% (2007); Master's degree or higher: 5.7% (2007).

School District(s)

Martin County School District (PK-12)
  2005-06 Enrollment: 17,917 .... (772) 219-1200

Housing: Homeownership rate: 76.5% (2007); Median home value: $199,387 (2007); Median rent: $518 per month (2000); Median age of housing: 22 years (2000).

Transportation: Commute to work: 94.1% car, 0.4% public transportation, 0.9% walk, 3.4% work from home (2000); Travel time to work: 29.6% less than 15 minutes, 43.3% 15 to 30 minutes, 15.1% 30 to 45 minutes, 5.4% 45 to 60 minutes, 6.6% 60 minutes or more (2000)

Additional Information Contacts

Jensen Beach Chamber of Commerce .... (772) 334-3444
  http://www.jensenbeachchamber.org

JUPITER ISLAND (town).

Covers a land area of 2.719 square miles and a water area of 0.900 square miles. Located at 27.05° N. Lat.; 80.11° W. Long. Elevation is 10 feet.

Population: 549 (1990); 620 (2000); 702 (2007); 763 (2012 projected); Race: 93.2% White, 1.0% Black, 0.1% Asian, 7.0% Hispanic of any race (2007); Density: 258.1 persons per square mile (2007); Average household size: 2.15 (2007); Median age: 61.0 (2007); Males per 100 females: 86.2 (2007); Marriage status: 15.2% never married, 59.5% now married, 15.8% widowed, 9.5% divorced (2000); Foreign born: 25.8% (2000); Ancestry (includes multiple ancestries): 28.5% English, 13.2% Irish, 11.1% Other groups, 6.3% German, 5.6% Portuguese (2000).

Economy: Single-family building permits issued: 15 (2006); Multi-family building permits issued: 0 (2006); Employment by occupation: 29.5% management, 13.8% professional, 40.7% services, 11.3% sales, 3.3% farming, 1.1% construction, 0.4% production (2000).

Income: Per capita income: $155,030 (2007); Median household income: $381,757 (2007); Average household income: $317,469 (2007); Percent of households with income of $100,000 or more: 74.9% (2007); Poverty rate: 8.1% (2000).

Education: Percent of population age 25 and over with: High school diploma (including GED) or higher: 95.0% (2007); Bachelor's degree or higher: 48.3% (2007); Master's degree or higher: 15.6% (2007).

Housing: Homeownership rate: 92.0% (2007); Median home value: $1 million+ (2007); Median rent: $617 per month (2000); Median age of housing: 25 years (2000).

Safety: Violent crime rate: 29.8 per 10,000 population; Property crime rate: 253.0 per 10,000 population (2006).

Transportation: Commute to work: 23.6% car, 1.5% public transportation, 28.2% walk, 37.5% work from home (2000); Travel time to work: 50.6% less than 15 minutes, 30.2% 15 to 30 minutes, 6.2% 30 to 45 minutes, 4.3% 45 to 60 minutes, 8.6% 60 minutes or more (2000)

NORTH RIVER SHORES (CDP).

Covers a land area of 1.300 square miles and a water area of 0.629 square miles. Located at 27.22° N. Lat.; 80.27° W. Long. Elevation is 3 feet.

Population: 3,238 (1990); 3,101 (2000); 3,074 (2007); 3,065 (2012 projected); Race: 97.1% White, 0.7% Black, 0.7% Asian, 2.5% Hispanic of any race (2007); Density: 2,365.0 persons per square mile (2007); Average household size: 2.16 (2007); Median age: 49.6 (2007); Males per 100 females: 91.2 (2007); Marriage status: 15.2% never married, 62.7% now married, 9.8% widowed, 12.3% divorced (2000); Foreign born: 2.8% (2000); Ancestry (includes multiple ancestries): 27.1% German, 20.3% Irish, 18.5% English, 14.9% Italian, 4.9% Other groups (2000).

Economy: Employment by occupation: 13.8% management, 26.6% professional, 16.5% services, 28.6% sales, 0.0% farming, 9.9% construction, 4.7% production (2000).

Income: Per capita income: $31,775 (2007); Median household income: $46,940 (2007); Average household income: $68,189 (2007); Percent of households with income of $100,000 or more: 19.3% (2007); Poverty rate: 5.3% (2000).

Education: Percent of population age 25 and over with: High school diploma (including GED) or higher: 88.8% (2007); Bachelor's degree or higher: 24.8% (2007); Master's degree or higher: 9.3% (2007).

Housing: Homeownership rate: 83.8% (2007); Median home value: $200,794 (2007); Median rent: $590 per month (2000); Median age of housing: 25 years (2000).

Transportation: Commute to work: 87.3% car, 0.5% public transportation, 1.7% walk, 8.2% work from home (2000); Travel time to work: 38.3% less than 15 minutes, 41.2% 15 to 30 minutes, 10.2% 30 to 45 minutes, 4.8% 45 to 60 minutes, 5.5% 60 minutes or more (2000)

OCEAN BREEZE PARK (town).

Covers a land area of 0.171 square miles and a water area of 0.039 square miles. Located at 27.24° N. Lat.; 80.22° W. Long. Elevation is 7 feet.

Population: 519 (1990); 463 (2000); 469 (2007); 475 (2012 projected); Race: 97.4% White, 2.3% Black, 0.0% Asian, 1.7% Hispanic of any race (2007); Density: 2,741.6 persons per square mile (2007); Average household size: 1.38 (2007); Median age: 71.0 (2007); Males per 100 females: 81.1 (2007); Marriage status: 8.2% never married, 41.2% now married, 27.7% widowed, 22.8% divorced (2000); Foreign born: 4.4% (2000); Ancestry (includes multiple ancestries): 23.1% English, 20.4% German, 14.2% Irish, 8.9% United States or American, 4.9% Italian (2000).

Economy: Single-family building permits issued: 0 (2006); Multi-family building permits issued: 0 (2006); Employment by occupation: 8.2%

management, 9.4% professional, 24.7% services, 29.4% sales, 0.0% farming, 8.2% construction, 20.0% production (2000).
Income: Per capita income: $18,417 (2007); Median household income: $17,589 (2007); Average household income: $25,404 (2007); Percent of households with income of $100,000 or more: 3.2% (2007); Poverty rate: 15.3% (2000).
Education: Percent of population age 25 and over with: High school diploma (including GED) or higher: 75.8% (2007); Bachelor's degree or higher: 15.9% (2007); Master's degree or higher: 4.3% (2007).
Housing: Homeownership rate: 90.3% (2007); Median home value: $24,766 (2007); Median rent: $241 per month (2000); Median age of housing: 34 years (2000).
Transportation: Commute to work: 84.3% car, 0.0% public transportation, 13.3% walk, 0.0% work from home (2000); Travel time to work: 33.7% less than 15 minutes, 48.2% 15 to 30 minutes, 13.3% 30 to 45 minutes, 0.0% 45 to 60 minutes, 4.8% 60 minutes or more (2000)

PALM CITY (CDP). Covers a land area of 14.634 square miles and a
water area of 1.949 square miles. Located at 27.17° N. Lat.; 80.27° W. Long. Elevation is 7 feet.
Population: 11,139 (1990); 20,097 (2000); 25,793 (2007); 29,707 (2012 projected); Race: 95.1% White, 1.7% Black, 1.3% Asian, 3.6% Hispanic of any race (2007); Density: 1,762.6 persons per square mile (2007); Average household size: 2.38 (2007); Median age: 48.1 (2007); Males per 100 females: 92.9 (2007); Marriage status: 11.3% never married, 71.9% now married, 7.5% widowed, 9.4% divorced (2000); Foreign born: 5.6% (2000); Ancestry (includes multiple ancestries): 19.1% German, 17.3% Irish, 16.8% English, 14.9% Italian, 7.8% United States or American (2000).
Economy: Employment by occupation: 17.9% management, 24.1% professional, 14.3% services, 32.4% sales, 0.2% farming, 6.1% construction, 5.0% production (2000).
Income: Per capita income: $40,738 (2007); Median household income: $72,022 (2007); Average household income: $96,402 (2007); Percent of households with income of $100,000 or more: 32.4% (2007); Poverty rate: 3.7% (2000).
Education: Percent of population age 25 and over with: High school diploma (including GED) or higher: 93.5% (2007); Bachelor's degree or higher: 35.8% (2007); Master's degree or higher: 11.6% (2007).
School District(s)
Martin County School District (PK-12)
   2005-06 Enrollment: 17,917 . . . . (772) 219-1200
Housing: Homeownership rate: 86.2% (2007); Median home value: $378,993 (2007); Median rent: $817 per month (2000); Median age of housing: 11 years (2000).
Transportation: Commute to work: 92.4% car, 0.4% public transportation, 0.6% walk, 5.5% work from home (2000); Travel time to work: 27.5% less than 15 minutes, 43.2% 15 to 30 minutes, 16.4% 30 to 45 minutes, 5.8% 45 to 60 minutes, 7.2% 60 minutes or more (2000)
Additional Information Contacts
Palm City Chamber of Commerce . . . . (561) 286-8121
   http://www.palmcitychamber.com

PORT SALERNO (CDP). Aka Salerno. Covers a land area of 3.618
square miles and a water area of 0.399 square miles. Located at 27.14° N. Lat.; 80.19° W. Long. Elevation is 13 feet.
Population: 7,786 (1990); 10,141 (2000); 11,453 (2007); 12,429 (2012 projected); Race: 87.3% White, 7.0% Black, 1.0% Asian, 10.9% Hispanic of any race (2007); Density: 3,165.8 persons per square mile (2007); Average household size: 2.25 (2007); Median age: 44.3 (2007); Males per 100 females: 94.3 (2007); Marriage status: 16.7% never married, 62.1% now married, 9.1% widowed, 12.1% divorced (2000); Foreign born: 6.5% (2000); Ancestry (includes multiple ancestries): 18.6% German, 17.5% Other groups, 17.1% Irish, 15.3% English, 9.5% Italian (2000).
Economy: Employment by occupation: 14.3% management, 14.2% professional, 19.3% services, 27.6% sales, 0.8% farming, 13.9% construction, 10.0% production (2000).
Income: Per capita income: $28,266 (2007); Median household income: $43,953 (2007); Average household income: $63,002 (2007); Percent of households with income of $100,000 or more: 15.2% (2007); Poverty rate: 9.6% (2000).
Education: Percent of population age 25 and over with: High school diploma (including GED) or higher: 85.3% (2007); Bachelor's degree or higher: 21.7% (2007); Master's degree or higher: 5.6% (2007).

Housing: Homeownership rate: 73.8% (2007); Median home value: $205,623 (2007); Median rent: $559 per month (2000); Median age of housing: 18 years (2000).
Transportation: Commute to work: 93.8% car, 0.6% public transportation, 1.0% walk, 2.9% work from home (2000); Travel time to work: 28.0% less than 15 minutes, 38.8% 15 to 30 minutes, 21.6% 30 to 45 minutes, 5.7% 45 to 60 minutes, 5.9% 60 minutes or more (2000)

RIO (CDP). Covers a land area of 0.400 square miles and a water area of
0.507 square miles. Located at 27.21° N. Lat.; 80.24° W. Long. Elevation is 3 feet.
Population: 1,054 (1990); 1,028 (2000); 965 (2007); 983 (2012 projected); Race: 97.1% White, 0.7% Black, 0.4% Asian, 2.2% Hispanic of any race (2007); Density: 2,411.1 persons per square mile (2007); Average household size: 2.09 (2007); Median age: 48.1 (2007); Males per 100 females: 102.3 (2007); Marriage status: 20.5% never married, 56.5% now married, 8.2% widowed, 14.7% divorced (2000); Foreign born: 1.0% (2000); Ancestry (includes multiple ancestries): 28.8% German, 16.4% Irish, 14.8% English, 13.3% Italian, 5.9% Dutch (2000).
Economy: Employment by occupation: 11.1% management, 30.2% professional, 19.1% services, 14.1% sales, 1.9% farming, 14.9% construction, 8.6% production (2000).
Income: Per capita income: $31,746 (2007); Median household income: $49,405 (2007); Average household income: $66,453 (2007); Percent of households with income of $100,000 or more: 13.4% (2007); Poverty rate: 11.9% (2000).
Education: Percent of population age 25 and over with: High school diploma (including GED) or higher: 85.4% (2007); Bachelor's degree or higher: 32.9% (2007); Master's degree or higher: 11.4% (2007).
Housing: Homeownership rate: 76.6% (2007); Median home value: $223,214 (2007); Median rent: $375 per month (2000); Median age of housing: 19 years (2000).
Transportation: Commute to work: 89.3% car, 0.0% public transportation, 0.0% walk, 5.8% work from home (2000); Travel time to work: 35.1% less than 15 minutes, 53.5% 15 to 30 minutes, 5.8% 30 to 45 minutes, 0.0% 45 to 60 minutes, 5.6% 60 minutes or more (2000)

SEWALL'S POINT (town). Covers a land area of 1.233 square miles
and a water area of 2.903 square miles. Located at 27.19° N. Lat.; 80.19° W. Long. Elevation is 20 feet.
Population: 1,588 (1990); 1,946 (2000); 2,235 (2007); 2,440 (2012 projected); Race: 98.3% White, 0.8% Black, 0.4% Asian, 2.1% Hispanic of any race (2007); Density: 1,812.5 persons per square mile (2007); Average household size: 2.62 (2007); Median age: 48.0 (2007); Males per 100 females: 98.1 (2007); Marriage status: 12.0% never married, 77.1% now married, 4.2% widowed, 6.7% divorced (2000); Foreign born: 6.5% (2000); Ancestry (includes multiple ancestries): 20.8% Irish, 20.1% German, 19.3% English, 13.8% Italian, 6.1% Other groups (2000).
Economy: Single-family building permits issued: 5 (2006); Multi-family building permits issued: 0 (2006); Employment by occupation: 25.3% management, 34.4% professional, 8.1% services, 25.1% sales, 0.0% farming, 2.4% construction, 4.7% production (2000).
Income: Per capita income: $54,808 (2007); Median household income: $101,322 (2007); Average household income: $143,605 (2007); Percent of households with income of $100,000 or more: 50.6% (2007); Poverty rate: 4.3% (2000).
Education: Percent of population age 25 and over with: High school diploma (including GED) or higher: 96.6% (2007); Bachelor's degree or higher: 59.9% (2007); Master's degree or higher: 26.5% (2007).
Housing: Homeownership rate: 94.8% (2007); Median home value: $857,639 (2007); Median rent: $1,792 per month (2000); Median age of housing: 19 years (2000).
Safety: Violent crime rate: 9.6 per 10,000 population; Property crime rate: 105.1 per 10,000 population (2006).
Transportation: Commute to work: 88.2% car, 0.0% public transportation, 0.3% walk, 9.9% work from home (2000); Travel time to work: 37.3% less than 15 minutes, 34.9% 15 to 30 minutes, 9.4% 30 to 45 minutes, 8.6% 45 to 60 minutes, 9.8% 60 minutes or more (2000)

STUART (city). County seat. Covers a land area of 6.306 square miles
and a water area of 2.220 square miles. Located at 27.19° N. Lat.; 80.24° W. Long. Elevation is 10 feet.
History: Stuart developed as a fishing center, with shark fishing predominating. All parts of the shark were valuable, the flesh, hides, teeth,

bones, livers, fins, and eyes each having a market. Tiger, sand, nurse, hammerhead, and shovel-nose sharks were found in the waters here.
Population: 13,235 (1990); 14,633 (2000); 15,992 (2007); 17,115 (2012 projected); Race: 80.6% White, 12.6% Black, 0.8% Asian, 9.1% Hispanic of any race (2007); Density: 2,536.0 persons per square mile (2007); Average household size: 2.03 (2007); Median age: 47.4 (2007); Males per 100 females: 90.6 (2007); Marriage status: 21.6% never married, 46.6% now married, 16.5% widowed, 15.3% divorced (2000); Foreign born: 8.0% (2000); Ancestry (includes multiple ancestries): 19.5% Other groups, 15.7% Irish, 14.7% German, 14.2% English, 9.9% Italian (2000).
Economy: Single-family building permits issued: 8 (2006); Multi-family building permits issued: 8 (2006); Employment by occupation: 10.2% management, 19.4% professional, 19.8% services, 28.6% sales, 0.7% farming, 10.0% construction, 11.2% production (2000).
Income: Per capita income: $23,166 (2007); Median household income: $32,809 (2007); Average household income: $43,972 (2007); Percent of households with income of $100,000 or more: 7.4% (2007); Poverty rate: 11.2% (2000).
Education: Percent of population age 25 and over with: High school diploma (including GED) or higher: 80.7% (2007); Bachelor's degree or higher: 21.2% (2007); Master's degree or higher: 7.8% (2007).

School District(s)
Martin County School District (PK-12)
    2005-06 Enrollment: 17,917 . . . . (772) 219-1200

Vocational/Technical School(s)
Medvance Institute-Stuart (Private, For-profit)
    Fall 2006 Enrollment: 156 . . . . (772) 221-9799
    2006-07 Tuition: $12,495

Housing: Homeownership rate: 61.2% (2007); Median home value: $150,416 (2007); Median rent: $576 per month (2000); Median age of housing: 24 years (2000).
Hospitals: Martin Memorial Medical Center (236 beds)
Safety: Violent crime rate: 59.9 per 10,000 population; Property crime rate: 515.9 per 10,000 population (2006).
Newspapers: Flashes (General - Circulation 60,000); The Stuart News (Circulation 41,170)
Transportation: Commute to work: 91.5% car, 0.6% public transportation, 2.5% walk, 3.3% work from home (2000); Travel time to work: 43.5% less than 15 minutes, 28.9% 15 to 30 minutes, 16.8% 30 to 45 minutes, 5.0% 45 to 60 minutes, 5.9% 60 minutes or more (2000)
Airports: Witham Field
Additional Information Contacts
Stuart Chamber of Commerce . . . . (772) 287-1088
    http://www.goodnature.org

Miami-Dade County

Covers a land area of 1,946.06 square miles, a water area of 485.19 square miles, and is located in the Eastern Time Zone. The county was founded in 1836. County seat is Miami.

Miami-Dade County is part of the Miami-Fort Lauderdale-Pompano Beach, FL Metropolitan Statistical Area. The entire metro area includes: Fort Lauderdale-Pompano Beach-Deerfield Beach, FL Metropolitan Division (Broward County, FL); Miami-Miami Beach-Kendall, FL Metropolitan Division (Miami-Dade County, FL); West Palm Beach-Boca Raton-Boynton Beach, FL Metropolitan Division (Palm Beach County, FL)

Weather Station: Hialeah											Elevation: 9 feet	
	Jan	Feb	Mar	Apr	May	Jun	Jul	Aug	Sep	Oct	Nov	Dec
High	77	78	81	83	87	89	91	91	89	86	82	78
Low	58	59	64	67	71	75	76	76	75	71	67	61
Precip	2.5	2.3	3.2	3.8	6.3	10.4	7.0	9.0	8.9	6.4	3.8	2.4
Snow	0.0	0.0	0.0	0.0	0.0	0.0	0.0	0.0	0.0	0.0	0.0	0.0

High and Low temperatures in degrees Fahrenheit; Precipitation and Snow in inches

Weather Station: Miami Beach											Elevation: 3 feet	
	Jan	Feb	Mar	Apr	May	Jun	Jul	Aug	Sep	Oct	Nov	Dec
High	74	75	77	79	83	86	87	88	86	83	79	76
Low	63	64	67	70	74	77	78	79	78	75	70	66
Precip	2.5	2.2	2.2	2.7	5.0	6.9	3.3	5.2	6.9	4.6	3.4	2.0
Snow	0.0	0.0	0.0	0.0	0.0	0.0	0.0	0.0	0.0	0.0	0.0	0.0

High and Low temperatures in degrees Fahrenheit; Precipitation and Snow in inches

Weather Station: Miami Int'l Airport											Elevation: 32 feet	
	Jan	Feb	Mar	Apr	May	Jun	Jul	Aug	Sep	Oct	Nov	Dec
High	76	77	80	83	86	88	90	90	88	85	81	77
Low	60	61	65	68	72	76	77	77	76	73	68	63
Precip	2.0	2.1	2.6	3.3	5.8	8.6	5.8	8.5	8.3	5.7	3.4	2.0
Snow	0.0	0.0	0.0	0.0	tr	0.0	0.0	0.0	0.0	0.0	0.0	0.0

High and Low temperatures in degrees Fahrenheit; Precipitation and Snow in inches

Weather Station: Tamiami Trail 40 Mile Bend											Elevation: 13 feet	
	Jan	Feb	Mar	Apr	May	Jun	Jul	Aug	Sep	Oct	Nov	Dec
High	78	79	82	86	89	91	92	92	91	87	83	79
Low	57	57	60	63	67	72	74	75	75	71	65	59
Precip	1.9	2.0	2.3	2.4	5.0	8.5	7.6	6.9	6.6	4.5	2.3	1.6
Snow	0.0	0.0	0.0	0.0	0.0	0.0	0.0	0.0	0.0	0.0	0.0	0.0

High and Low temperatures in degrees Fahrenheit; Precipitation and Snow in inches

Population: 1,937,094 (1990); 2,253,362 (2000); 2,430,421 (2007); 2,575,235 (2012 projected); Race: 70.3% White, 19.2% Black, 1.4% Asian, 61.3% Hispanic of any race (2007); Density: 1,248.9 persons per square mile (2007); Average household size: 2.94 (2007); Median age: 37.6 (2007); Males per 100 females: 93.9 (2007).
Religion: Five largest groups: 24.1% Catholic Church, 5.5% Jewish Estimate, 3.6% Southern Baptist Convention, 0.8% Seventh-day Adventist Church, 0.8% The United Methodist Church (2000).
Economy: Unemployment rate: 3.7% (11/2007); Total civilian labor force: 1,212,356 (11/2007); Leading industries: 13.8% retail trade; 13.3% health care and social assistance; 10.5% accommodation & food services (2005); Farms: 2,244 totaling 90,373 acres (2002); Companies that employ 500 or more persons: 125 (2005); Companies that employ 100 to 499 persons: 1,195 (2005); Companies that employ less than 100 persons: 72,946 (2005); Black-owned businesses: 28,335 (2002); Hispanic-owned businesses: 163,187 (2002); Asian-owned businesses: 6,729 (2002); Women-owned businesses: 88,168 (2002); Retail sales per capita: $14,214 (2007). Single-family building permits issued: 6,548 (2006); Multi-family building permits issued: 13,469 (2006).
Income: Per capita income: $20,859 (2007); Median household income: $41,131 (2007); Average household income: $60,485 (2007); Percent of households with income of $100,000 or more: 14.8% (2007); Poverty rate: 17.9% (2005); Bankruptcy rate: -1.00% (2006).
Taxes: Total county taxes per capita: $709 (2005); County property taxes per capita: $485 (2005).
Education: Percent of population age 25 and over with: High school diploma (including GED) or higher: 68.2% (2007); Bachelor's degree or higher: 21.8% (2007); Master's degree or higher: 9.3% (2007).
Housing: Homeownership rate: 58.1% (2007); Median home value: $252,487 (2007); Median rent: $572 per month (2000); Median age of housing: 27 years (2000).
Health: Birth rate: 142.7 per 10,000 population (2006); Death rate: 79.1 per 10,000 population (2006); Age-adjusted cancer mortality rate: 161.5 deaths per 100,000 population (2004); Air Quality Index: 87.4% good, 12.3% moderate, 0.3% unhealthy for sensitive individuals, 0.0% unhealthy (percent of days in 2006); Number of physicians: 34.3 per 10,000 population (2005); Hospital beds: 37.1 per 10,000 population (2004); Hospital admissions: 1,448.7 per 10,000 population (2004).
Elections: 2004 Presidential election results: 46.6% Bush, 52.9% Kerry, 0.3% Nader, 0.1% Badnarik
National and State Parks: Bill Baggs Cape Florida State Park; Biscayne National Park; Grossman Hammock State Park; Oleta River State Park; The Barnacle Historic State Park
Additional Information Contacts
Miami-Dade County Government . . . . (305) 375-4419
    http://miamidade.gov
Allapattah Chamber of Commerce . . . . (305) 638-0280
Argentine Florida Chamber . . . . (305) 357-8047
    http://www.argentinaflorida.org
Aventura Chamber of Commerce . . . . (305) 935-2131
    http://www.aventura.org
Brazilian-American Chamber . . . . (954) 965-1184
    http://www.brazilchamber.org
British American Chamber of Commerce . . . . (305) 377-0992
    http://www.baccsouthflorida.org
Central America Us Chamber . . . . (305) 569-9113
    http://www.centralamerica.us
Chile-US Chamber of Commerce . . . . (305) 447-0908
    http://www.chileus.org

City of Aventura . . . . (305) 466-8900
 http://www.cityofaventura.com
City of Coral Gables . . . . (305) 460-5209
 http://www.citybeautiful.net
City of Florida City . . . . (305) 242-8132
 http://www.floridacityfl.us
City of Hialeah Gardens . . . . (305) 558-4114
 http://www.cityofhialeahgardens.org
City of Homestead . . . . (305) 224-4400
 http://ci.homestead.fl.us
City of Miami Beach . . . . (305) 673-7411
 http://web.miamibeachfl.gov
City of Miami Springs . . . . (305) 805-5000
 http://www.miamisprings-fl.gov
City of North Bay Village . . . . (305) 756-7171
 http://www.nbvillage.com
City of North Miami . . . . (305) 893-6511
 http://www.northmiamifl.gov
City of North Miami Beach . . . . (305) 947-7581
 http://ci.north-miami-beach.fl.us
City of Opa-locka . . . . (305) 688-4611
 http://www.opalockafl.gov
City of South Miami . . . . (305) 663-6338
 http://www.cityofsouthmiami.net
City of Sunny Isles Beach . . . . (305) 947-0606
 http://www.sibfl.net
City of Sweetwater . . . . (305) 485-4528
 http://www.cityofsweetwater.fl.gov
City of West Miami . . . . (305) 266-1122
Coconut Grove Chamber of Commerce . . . . (305) 446-9900
 http://www.coconutgrove.com
Colombian American Chamber . . . . (305) 446-2542
 http://www.colombiachamber.com
Coral Gables Chamber of Commerce . . . . (305) 446-1657
 http://www.coralgableschamber.org
Doral-Airport West Chamber . . . . (305) 244-1641
 http://www.dawcc.org
Ecuadorian-American Chamber . . . . (305) 539-0010
 http://www.ecuachamber.com
Florida Gold Coast Chamber . . . . (305) 866-6020
 http://www.flgoldcc.org
French-American Chamber of Commerce . . . . (305) 442-2277
Greater Miami Chamber of Commerce . . . . (305) 350-7700
 http://www.greatermiami.com
Greater Miami Convention & Visitors Bureau . . . . . . (305) 539-3000
 http://www.gmcvb.com
Greater Miami Shores Chamber . . . . (305) 754-5466
 http://www.miamishores.com
Greater North Miami Chamber . . . . (305) 891-7811
 http://www.northmiamichamber.com
Homestead-Florida City Chamber . . . . (305) 247-2332
 http://www.chamberinaction.com
Italy America Chamber of Commerce . . . . (305) 577-9868
 http://www.iacc-miami.com
Key Biscayne Chamber of Commerce . . . . (305) 361-5207
 http://www.keybiscaynechamber.org
Korean American Chamber of Commerce . . . . (305) 468-1718
 http://www.abicc.org/kaccmiami
Latin Chamber of Commerce . . . . (305) 674-1414
 http://www.miamibeach.org
Miami Beach Chamber of Commerce . . . . (305) 672-1270
 http://www.miamibeachchamber.com
Miami International Chamber . . . . (305) 861-2000
Miami-Dade Chamber of Commerce . . . . (305) 751-8648
 http://www.m-dcc.org
Nicaraguan-American Chamber of Commerce . . . . . (305) 994-2460
 http://www.naccflorida.com
North Dade Chamber of Commerce . . . . (305) 690-9123
 http://www.thechamber.cc
North Miami Beach Chamber of Commerce . . . . . . (305) 653-1200
 http://www.nmbchamber.com
Peruvian U.S. Chamber of Commerce . . . . (305) 349-5000
 http://www.peruvianchamber.org
Puerto Rico Convention Bureau . . . . (305) 471-0202
 http://www.meetpuertorico.com

South Beach Hispanic Chamber . . . . (305) 534-1903
 http://sobechamber.tripod.com
South Miami Chamber of Commerce . . . . (305) 275-0091
 http://chambersouth.com
Swedish American Chamber of Commerce . . . . (305) 443-3558
 http://www.sacc-florida.com
Town of Bay Harbor Islands . . . . (305) 866-6241
 http://www.bayharborislands.org
United States-Mexico Chamber of Commerce . . . . . (305) 379-6090
 http://www.usmcoc.org
Venezuelan American Chamber . . . . (305) 728-7042
 http://www.venezuelanchamber.org
Village of Key Biscayne . . . . (305) 365-5511
 http://vkb.key-biscayne.fl.us
Village of Miami Shores . . . . (305) 795-2207
 http://www.miamishoresvillage.com
Village of Pinecrest . . . . (305) 234-2121
 http://ci.pinecrest.fl.us
Women's Chamber of Commerce . . . . (305) 446-6660
 http://www.womenschamberofcommerce.org

Miami-Dade County Communities

ANDOVER (CDP). Covers a land area of 1.676 square miles and a water area of 0.112 square miles. Located at 25.96° N. Lat.; 80.20° W. Long. Elevation is 3 feet.
Population: 6,251 (1990); 8,489 (2000); 9,290 (2007); 9,973 (2012 projected); Race: 21.7% White, 70.5% Black, 1.0% Asian, 18.8% Hispanic of any race (2007); Density: 5,542.3 persons per square mile (2007); Average household size: 2.49 (2007); Median age: 35.5 (2007); Males per 100 females: 80.5 (2007); Marriage status: 32.7% never married, 42.9% now married, 7.6% widowed, 16.8% divorced (2000); Foreign born: 35.8% (2000); Ancestry (includes multiple ancestries): 45.7% Other groups, 16.6% Jamaican, 6.3% Haitian, 4.2% United States or American, 3.4% Bahamian (2000).
Economy: Employment by occupation: 11.2% management, 20.1% professional, 17.3% services, 32.6% sales, 0.1% farming, 8.4% construction, 10.3% production (2000).
Income: Per capita income: $17,317 (2007); Median household income: $32,585 (2007); Average household income: $42,925 (2007); Percent of households with income of $100,000 or more: 6.0% (2007); Poverty rate: 15.8% (2000).
Education: Percent of population age 25 and over with: High school diploma (including GED) or higher: 75.4% (2007); Bachelor's degree or higher: 16.0% (2007); Master's degree or higher: 4.9% (2007).
Housing: Homeownership rate: 47.5% (2007); Median home value: $165,586 (2007); Median rent: $541 per month (2000); Median age of housing: 25 years (2000).
Transportation: Commute to work: 91.1% car, 6.6% public transportation, 0.9% walk, 0.3% work from home (2000); Travel time to work: 9.7% less than 15 minutes, 40.4% 15 to 30 minutes, 30.2% 30 to 45 minutes, 10.1% 45 to 60 minutes, 9.7% 60 minutes or more (2000)

AVENTURA (city). Covers a land area of 2.704 square miles and a water area of 0.806 square miles. Located at 25.96° N. Lat.; 80.13° W. Long. Elevation is 3 feet.
Population: 15,376 (1990); 25,267 (2000); 31,506 (2007); 35,884 (2012 projected); Race: 92.4% White, 2.1% Black, 1.4% Asian, 28.0% Hispanic of any race (2007); Density: 11,652.1 persons per square mile (2007); Average household size: 1.83 (2007); Median age: 54.7 (2007); Males per 100 females: 81.3 (2007); Marriage status: 19.3% never married, 53.6% now married, 15.8% widowed, 11.3% divorced (2000); Foreign born: 36.8% (2000); Ancestry (includes multiple ancestries): 30.8% Other groups, 11.9% Russian, 8.9% United States or American, 7.5% Polish, 4.7% German (2000).
Economy: Unemployment rate: 3.1% (11/2007); Total civilian labor force: 15,006 (11/2007); Single-family building permits issued: 4 (2006); Multi-family building permits issued: 179 (2006); Employment by occupation: 25.4% management, 23.1% professional, 9.5% services, 36.2% sales, 0.1% farming, 2.7% construction, 2.9% production (2000).
Income: Per capita income: $45,721 (2007); Median household income: $51,235 (2007); Average household income: $83,633 (2007); Percent of households with income of $100,000 or more: 24.6% (2007); Poverty rate: 9.1% (2000).

Taxes: Total city taxes per capita: $700 (2005); City property taxes per capita: $345 (2005).
Education: Percent of population age 25 and over with: High school diploma (including GED) or higher: 89.5% (2007); Bachelor's degree or higher: 39.0% (2007); Master's degree or higher: 16.4% (2007).

School District(s)
Dade County School District (PK-12)
   2005-06 Enrollment: 368,933 . . . . (305) 995-1430
Housing: Homeownership rate: 71.7% (2007); Median home value: $275,241 (2007); Median rent: $1,145 per month (2000); Median age of housing: 15 years (2000).
Hospitals: Aventura Hospital and Medical Center (407 beds)
Safety: Violent crime rate: 20.1 per 10,000 population; Property crime rate: 581.2 per 10,000 population (2006).
Transportation: Commute to work: 89.6% car, 2.0% public transportation, 1.8% walk, 5.7% work from home (2000); Travel time to work: 22.7% less than 15 minutes, 28.4% 15 to 30 minutes, 27.1% 30 to 45 minutes, 15.2% 45 to 60 minutes, 6.7% 60 minutes or more (2000)
Additional Information Contacts
City of Aventura . . . . (305) 466-8900
  http://www.cityofaventura.com

BAL HARBOUR (village). Covers a land area of 0.338 square miles and a water area of 0.251 square miles. Located at 25.89° N. Lat.; 80.12° W. Long. Elevation is 3 feet.
Population: 3,045 (1990); 3,305 (2000); 3,014 (2007); 2,971 (2012 projected); Race: 93.6% White, 1.8% Black, 1.0% Asian, 30.3% Hispanic of any race (2007); Density: 8,929.3 persons per square mile (2007); Average household size: 1.75 (2007); Median age: 57.7 (2007); Males per 100 females: 75.8 (2007); Marriage status: 14.3% never married, 53.9% now married, 19.6% widowed, 12.2% divorced (2000); Foreign born: 40.0% (2000); Ancestry (includes multiple ancestries): 30.2% Other groups, 12.0% Russian, 8.9% Polish, 6.4% Irish, 6.2% French (except Basque) (2000).
Economy: Single-family building permits issued: 3 (2006); Multi-family building permits issued: 0 (2006); Employment by occupation: 33.0% management, 29.6% professional, 8.2% services, 24.6% sales, 0.0% farming, 2.2% construction, 2.4% production (2000).
Income: Per capita income: $65,070 (2007); Median household income: $55,429 (2007); Average household income: $112,934 (2007); Percent of households with income of $100,000 or more: 30.7% (2007); Poverty rate: 9.2% (2000).
Education: Percent of population age 25 and over with: High school diploma (including GED) or higher: 89.5% (2007); Bachelor's degree or higher: 46.0% (2007); Master's degree or higher: 21.1% (2007).
Housing: Homeownership rate: 49.2% (2007); Median home value: $957,865 (2007); Median rent: $1,068 per month (2000); Median age of housing: 29 years (2000).
Safety: Violent crime rate: 21.0 per 10,000 population; Property crime rate: 222.4 per 10,000 population (2006).
Transportation: Commute to work: 78.4% car, 2.2% public transportation, 6.4% walk, 12.5% work from home (2000); Travel time to work: 27.8% less than 15 minutes, 25.7% 15 to 30 minutes, 33.7% 30 to 45 minutes, 3.0% 45 to 60 minutes, 9.8% 60 minutes or more (2000)

BAY HARBOR ISLANDS (town). Covers a land area of 0.371 square miles and a water area of 0.241 square miles. Located at 25.88° N. Lat.; 80.13° W. Long. Elevation is 3 feet.
Population: 4,703 (1990); 5,146 (2000); 5,123 (2007); 5,187 (2012 projected); Race: 89.3% White, 2.0% Black, 1.4% Asian, 46.7% Hispanic of any race (2007); Density: 13,813.4 persons per square mile (2007); Average household size: 2.03 (2007); Median age: 44.3 (2007); Males per 100 females: 81.5 (2007); Marriage status: 23.3% never married, 48.7% now married, 11.0% widowed, 17.0% divorced (2000); Foreign born: 39.3% (2000); Ancestry (includes multiple ancestries): 44.1% Other groups, 9.5% Russian, 7.4% Italian, 6.9% Polish, 6.4% German (2000).
Economy: Single-family building permits issued: 3 (2006); Multi-family building permits issued: 60 (2006); Employment by occupation: 18.9% management, 25.5% professional, 15.3% services, 31.4% sales, 0.0% farming, 4.9% construction, 4.0% production (2000).
Income: Per capita income: $32,156 (2007); Median household income: $43,226 (2007); Average household income: $65,139 (2007); Percent of households with income of $100,000 or more: 14.0% (2007); Poverty rate: 13.1% (2000).

Education: Percent of population age 25 and over with: High school diploma (including GED) or higher: 87.7% (2007); Bachelor's degree or higher: 35.4% (2007); Master's degree or higher: 14.4% (2007).
Housing: Homeownership rate: 53.0% (2007); Median home value: $261,957 (2007); Median rent: $743 per month (2000); Median age of housing: 37 years (2000).
Safety: Violent crime rate: 25.1 per 10,000 population; Property crime rate: 152.5 per 10,000 population (2006).
Transportation: Commute to work: 84.9% car, 3.5% public transportation, 6.1% walk, 5.2% work from home (2000); Travel time to work: 18.6% less than 15 minutes, 36.4% 15 to 30 minutes, 30.4% 30 to 45 minutes, 9.2% 45 to 60 minutes, 5.5% 60 minutes or more (2000)
Additional Information Contacts
Town of Bay Harbor Islands. . . . . (305) 866-6241
  http://www.bayharborislands.org

BISCAYNE PARK (village). Covers a land area of 0.635 square miles and a water area of 0 square miles. Located at 25.88° N. Lat.; 80.18° W. Long. Elevation is 7 feet.
History: Incorporated 1932.
Population: 3,068 (1990); 3,269 (2000); 2,940 (2007); 2,989 (2012 projected); Race: 67.6% White, 22.0% Black, 2.6% Asian, 31.8% Hispanic of any race (2007); Density: 4,629.0 persons per square mile (2007); Average household size: 2.62 (2007); Median age: 39.7 (2007); Males per 100 females: 93.8 (2007); Marriage status: 25.5% never married, 56.6% now married, 8.0% widowed, 9.8% divorced (2000); Foreign born: 34.6% (2000); Ancestry (includes multiple ancestries): 34.5% Other groups, 12.7% English, 10.3% Haitian, 8.0% Italian, 8.0% Irish (2000).
Economy: Single-family building permits issued: 0 (2006); Multi-family building permits issued: 0 (2006); Employment by occupation: 13.1% management, 24.5% professional, 11.7% services, 36.6% sales, 0.0% farming, 6.4% construction, 7.7% production (2000).
Income: Per capita income: $26,579 (2007); Median household income: $55,982 (2007); Average household income: $69,646 (2007); Percent of households with income of $100,000 or more: 18.6% (2007); Poverty rate: 12.0% (2000).
Education: Percent of population age 25 and over with: High school diploma (including GED) or higher: 85.3% (2007); Bachelor's degree or higher: 34.0% (2007); Master's degree or higher: 12.8% (2007).
Housing: Homeownership rate: 70.4% (2007); Median home value: $289,899 (2007); Median rent: $609 per month (2000); Median age of housing: 47 years (2000).
Safety: Violent crime rate: 15.7 per 10,000 population; Property crime rate: 257.8 per 10,000 population (2006).
Transportation: Commute to work: 93.1% car, 0.0% public transportation, 0.5% walk, 5.7% work from home (2000); Travel time to work: 20.5% less than 15 minutes, 30.5% 15 to 30 minutes, 34.5% 30 to 45 minutes, 12.1% 45 to 60 minutes, 2.4% 60 minutes or more (2000)

BROWNSVILLE (CDP). Covers a land area of 2.294 square miles and a water area of 0.003 square miles. Located at 25.82° N. Lat.; 80.24° W. Long. Elevation is 10 feet.
Population: 15,607 (1990); 14,393 (2000); 14,876 (2007); 15,357 (2012 projected); Race: 7.7% White, 88.0% Black, 0.0% Asian, 11.5% Hispanic of any race (2007); Density: 6,485.7 persons per square mile (2007); Average household size: 2.98 (2007); Median age: 28.9 (2007); Males per 100 females: 85.0 (2007); Marriage status: 48.4% never married, 27.3% now married, 10.7% widowed, 13.6% divorced (2000); Foreign born: 9.7% (2000); Ancestry (includes multiple ancestries): 74.6% Other groups, 3.8% United States or American, 2.1% African, 1.9% Bahamian, 0.8% Jamaican (2000).
Economy: Employment by occupation: 4.3% management, 9.7% professional, 31.9% services, 27.4% sales, 0.3% farming, 10.5% construction, 15.9% production (2000).
Income: Per capita income: $9,896 (2007); Median household income: $18,136 (2007); Average household income: $29,393 (2007); Percent of households with income of $100,000 or more: 2.8% (2007); Poverty rate: 42.7% (2000).
Education: Percent of population age 25 and over with: High school diploma (including GED) or higher: 53.4% (2007); Bachelor's degree or higher: 4.9% (2007); Master's degree or higher: 2.2% (2007).
Housing: Homeownership rate: 40.4% (2007); Median home value: $131,215 (2007); Median rent: $324 per month (2000); Median age of housing: 39 years (2000).

BUNCHE PARK (CDP).
Covers a land area of 0.758 square miles and a water area of 0 square miles. Located at 25.92° N. Lat.; 80.23° W. Long. Elevation is 3 feet.

Population: 4,388 (1990); 3,972 (2000); 3,864 (2007); 3,835 (2012 projected); Race: 2.4% White, 94.4% Black, 0.2% Asian, 5.2% Hispanic of any race (2007); Density: 5,097.5 persons per square mile (2007); Average household size: 2.94 (2007); Median age: 37.7 (2007); Males per 100 females: 85.7 (2007); Marriage status: 31.7% never married, 39.8% now married, 15.7% widowed, 12.9% divorced (2000); Foreign born: 7.5% (2000); Ancestry (includes multiple ancestries): 72.6% Other groups, 3.3% Bahamian, 2.5% United States or American, 2.4% Haitian, 2.1% African (2000).

Economy: Employment by occupation: 6.5% management, 15.5% professional, 27.7% services, 26.5% sales, 0.0% farming, 10.3% construction, 13.4% production (2000).

Income: Per capita income: $12,776 (2007); Median household income: $27,559 (2007); Average household income: $37,207 (2007); Percent of households with income of $100,000 or more: 6.6% (2007); Poverty rate: 27.0% (2000).

Education: Percent of population age 25 and over with: High school diploma (including GED) or higher: 60.8% (2007); Bachelor's degree or higher: 8.8% (2007); Master's degree or higher: 2.4% (2007).

Housing: Homeownership rate: 80.2% (2007); Median home value: $145,532 (2007); Median rent: $583 per month (2000); Median age of housing: 44 years (2000).

Transportation: Commute to work: 87.8% car, 8.6% public transportation, 1.0% walk, 2.0% work from home (2000); Travel time to work: 15.0% less than 15 minutes, 33.8% 15 to 30 minutes, 32.0% 30 to 45 minutes, 8.8% 45 to 60 minutes, 10.4% 60 minutes or more (2000)

CAROL CITY (CDP).
Covers a land area of 7.625 square miles and a water area of 0.113 square miles. Located at 25.94° N. Lat.; 80.27° W. Long. Elevation is 7 feet.

Population: 53,331 (1990); 59,443 (2000); 62,519 (2007); 65,440 (2012 projected); Race: 40.1% White, 49.5% Black, 0.5% Asian, 45.9% Hispanic of any race (2007); Density: 8,199.4 persons per square mile (2007); Average household size: 3.64 (2007); Median age: 33.2 (2007); Males per 100 females: 92.6 (2007); Marriage status: 33.2% never married, 50.9% now married, 4.9% widowed, 10.9% divorced (2000); Foreign born: 37.2% (2000); Ancestry (includes multiple ancestries): 70.8% Other groups, 5.2% Jamaican, 4.8% United States or American, 2.3% Haitian, 0.8% African (2000).

Economy: Employment by occupation: 6.6% management, 13.2% professional, 19.6% services, 29.9% sales, 0.3% farming, 11.6% construction, 18.9% production (2000).

Income: Per capita income: $14,237 (2007); Median household income: $42,896 (2007); Average household income: $50,921 (2007); Percent of households with income of $100,000 or more: 8.1% (2007); Poverty rate: 16.5% (2000).

Education: Percent of population age 25 and over with: High school diploma (including GED) or higher: 61.1% (2007); Bachelor's degree or higher: 9.7% (2007); Master's degree or higher: 3.7% (2007).

School District(s)
Dade County School District (PK-12)
    2005-06 Enrollment: 368,933 . . . . (305) 995-1430

Housing: Homeownership rate: 82.4% (2007); Median home value: $191,317 (2007); Median rent: $620 per month (2000); Median age of housing: 27 years (2000).

Transportation: Commute to work: 94.1% car, 3.2% public transportation, 0.4% walk, 0.9% work from home (2000); Travel time to work: 11.7% less than 15 minutes, 33.5% 15 to 30 minutes, 33.8% 30 to 45 minutes, 11.5% 45 to 60 minutes, 9.4% 60 minutes or more (2000)

CORAL GABLES (city).
Covers a land area of 13.133 square miles and a water area of 24.024 square miles. Located at 25.72° N. Lat.; 80.27° W. Long. Elevation is 10 feet.

History: Named for the town's first house, which had gables decorated with coral rock. Coral Gables developed quickly in the mid-1920s through the advertising of George Merrick, its founder. The University of Miami was established here in 1926.

married, 6.0% widowed, 10.6% divorced (2000); Foreign born: 37.9% (2000); Ancestry (includes multiple ancestries): 54.0% Other groups, 7.4% English, 7.0% German, 5.7% Irish, 5.3% Italian (2000).

Economy: Unemployment rate: 2.2% (11/2007); Total civilian labor force: 25,857 (11/2007); Single-family building permits issued: 63 (2006); Multi-family building permits issued: 153 (2006); Employment by occupation: 25.1% management, 34.8% professional, 9.4% services, 25.3% sales, 0.0% farming, 2.5% construction, 2.9% production (2000).

Income: Per capita income: $52,464 (2007); Median household income: $78,045 (2007); Average household income: $130,013 (2007); Percent of households with income of $100,000 or more: 40.4% (2007); Poverty rate: 6.9% (2000).

Taxes: Total city taxes per capita: $1,694 (2005); City property taxes per capita: $1,119 (2005).

Education: Percent of population age 25 and over with: High school diploma (including GED) or higher: 91.6% (2007); Bachelor's degree or higher: 58.2% (2007); Master's degree or higher: 30.8% (2007).

School District(s)
Dade County School District (PK-12)
    2005-06 Enrollment: 368,933 . . . . (305) 995-1430

Four-year College(s)
University of Miami (Private, Not-for-profit)
    Fall 2006 Enrollment: 15,670 . . . . (305) 284-2211
    2006-07 Tuition: In-state $31,288; Out-of-state $31,288

Housing: Homeownership rate: 65.2% (2007); Median home value: $732,933 (2007); Median rent: $694 per month (2000); Median age of housing: 42 years (2000).

Safety: Violent crime rate: 27.1 per 10,000 population; Property crime rate: 489.3 per 10,000 population (2006).

Newspapers: Coral Gables Gazette (General - Circulation 8,600)

Transportation: Commute to work: 83.7% car, 2.9% public transportation, 6.7% walk, 5.5% work from home (2000); Travel time to work: 29.1% less than 15 minutes, 40.2% 15 to 30 minutes, 21.1% 30 to 45 minutes, 5.9% 45 to 60 minutes, 3.7% 60 minutes or more (2000)

Additional Information Contacts

Central America Us Chamber . . . . (305) 569-9113
    http://www.centralamerica.us
Chile-US Chamber of Commerce . . . . (305) 447-0908
    http://www.chileus.org
City of Coral Gables . . . . (305) 460-5209
    http://www.citybeautiful.net
Colombian American Chamber . . . . (305) 446-2542
    http://www.colombiachamber.com
Coral Gables Chamber of Commerce . . . . (305) 446-1657
    http://www.coralgableschamber.org
French-American Chamber of Commerce . . . . (305) 442-2277
Puerto Rico Convention Bureau . . . . (305) 471-0202
    http://www.meetpuertorico.com
Swedish American Chamber of Commerce . . . . (305) 443-3558
    http://www.sacc-florida.com
Venezuelan American Chamber . . . . (305) 728-7042
    http://www.venezuelanchamber.org

CORAL TERRACE (CDP).
Covers a land area of 3.429 square miles and a water area of 0.019 square miles. Located at 25.74° N. Lat.; 80.30° W. Long. Elevation is 3 feet.

Population: 23,255 (1990); 24,380 (2000); 24,247 (2007); 24,421 (2012 projected); Race: 93.7% White, 1.3% Black, 0.5% Asian, 84.0% Hispanic of any race (2007); Density: 7,071.2 persons per square mile (2007); Average household size: 3.18 (2007); Median age: 43.4 (2007); Males per 100 females: 90.2 (2007); Marriage status: 21.8% never married, 57.5% now married, 8.7% widowed, 12.0% divorced (2000); Foreign born: 66.1% (2000); Ancestry (includes multiple ancestries): 79.5% Other groups, 2.4% United States or American, 1.7% Irish, 1.7% German, 1.7% English (2000).

Economy: Employment by occupation: 11.9% management, 14.7% professional, 15.0% services, 35.1% sales, 0.4% farming, 9.0% construction, 13.9% production (2000).

Income: Per capita income: $18,464 (2007); Median household income: $45,494 (2007); Average household income: $58,146 (2007); Percent of

households with income of $100,000 or more: 14.3% (2007); Poverty rate: 11.2% (2000).
Education: Percent of population age 25 and over with: High school diploma (including GED) or higher: 62.1% (2007); Bachelor's degree or higher: 17.9% (2007); Master's degree or higher: 7.6% (2007).
Housing: Homeownership rate: 70.5% (2007); Median home value: $313,941 (2007); Median rent: $627 per month (2000); Median age of housing: 42 years (2000).
Transportation: Commute to work: 92.0% car, 2.7% public transportation, 1.2% walk, 3.1% work from home (2000); Travel time to work: 17.5% less than 15 minutes, 39.9% 15 to 30 minutes, 30.7% 30 to 45 minutes, 5.7% 45 to 60 minutes, 6.3% 60 minutes or more (2000)

COUNTRY CLUB (CDP).
Covers a land area of 4.312 square miles and a water area of 0.196 square miles. Located at 25.93° N. Lat.; 80.31° W. Long. Elevation is 3 feet.
Population: 23,164 (1990); 36,310 (2000); 41,861 (2007); 46,032 (2012 projected); Race: 62.7% White, 21.3% Black, 2.0% Asian, 65.6% Hispanic of any race (2007); Density: 9,707.8 persons per square mile (2007); Average household size: 2.85 (2007); Median age: 32.3 (2007); Males per 100 females: 90.7 (2007); Marriage status: 29.3% never married, 55.3% now married, 4.0% widowed, 11.5% divorced (2000); Foreign born: 47.0% (2000); Ancestry (includes multiple ancestries): 72.7% Other groups, 3.8% United States or American, 3.1% Haitian, 2.1% Irish, 2.1% Italian (2000).
Economy: Employment by occupation: 14.2% management, 17.3% professional, 13.9% services, 35.4% sales, 0.1% farming, 7.6% construction, 11.5% production (2000).
Income: Per capita income: $18,595 (2007); Median household income: $41,844 (2007); Average household income: $52,778 (2007); Percent of households with income of $100,000 or more: 8.9% (2007); Poverty rate: 13.1% (2000).
Education: Percent of population age 25 and over with: High school diploma (including GED) or higher: 80.2% (2007); Bachelor's degree or higher: 23.2% (2007); Master's degree or higher: 7.4% (2007).
Housing: Homeownership rate: 44.9% (2007); Median home value: $217,470 (2007); Median rent: $726 per month (2000); Median age of housing: 14 years (2000).
Transportation: Commute to work: 94.8% car, 1.7% public transportation, 0.7% walk, 1.9% work from home (2000); Travel time to work: 12.4% less than 15 minutes, 31.3% 15 to 30 minutes, 32.4% 30 to 45 minutes, 14.7% 45 to 60 minutes, 9.2% 60 minutes or more (2000)

COUNTRY WALK (CDP).
Covers a land area of 2.746 square miles and a water area of 0.009 square miles. Located at 25.63° N. Lat.; 80.43° W. Long. Elevation is 7 feet.
Population: 2,327 (1990); 10,653 (2000); 16,866 (2007); 20,944 (2012 projected); Race: 77.2% White, 10.3% Black, 2.2% Asian, 65.4% Hispanic of any race (2007); Density: 6,141.2 persons per square mile (2007); Average household size: 3.38 (2007); Median age: 32.9 (2007); Males per 100 females: 91.8 (2007); Marriage status: 21.0% never married, 67.7% now married, 2.6% widowed, 8.7% divorced (2000); Foreign born: 42.6% (2000); Ancestry (includes multiple ancestries): 65.4% Other groups, 6.4% German, 4.7% Jamaican, 4.5% Italian, 4.3% Irish (2000).
Economy: Employment by occupation: 20.9% management, 22.9% professional, 11.0% services, 32.4% sales, 0.2% farming, 5.3% construction, 7.2% production (2000).
Income: Per capita income: $24,287 (2007); Median household income: $73,868 (2007); Average household income: $81,572 (2007); Percent of households with income of $100,000 or more: 26.7% (2007); Poverty rate: 4.8% (2000).
Education: Percent of population age 25 and over with: High school diploma (including GED) or higher: 88.3% (2007); Bachelor's degree or higher: 31.4% (2007); Master's degree or higher: 11.9% (2007).
Housing: Homeownership rate: 92.2% (2007); Median home value: $298,183 (2007); Median rent: $917 per month (2000); Median age of housing: 6 years (2000).
Transportation: Commute to work: 92.8% car, 2.6% public transportation, 0.8% walk, 2.9% work from home (2000); Travel time to work: 8.7% less than 15 minutes, 26.3% 15 to 30 minutes, 26.6% 30 to 45 minutes, 16.9% 45 to 60 minutes, 21.5% 60 minutes or more (2000)

CUTLER (CDP).
Covers a land area of 6.727 square miles and a water area of 0.024 square miles. Located at 25.62° N. Lat.; 80.32° W. Long. Elevation is 10 feet.

Population: 15,548 (1990); 17,390 (2000); 17,667 (2007); 18,130 (2012 projected); Race: 89.0% White, 3.7% Black, 2.9% Asian, 32.5% Hispanic of any race (2007); Density: 2,626.2 persons per square mile (2007); Average household size: 3.08 (2007); Median age: 40.3 (2007); Males per 100 females: 94.6 (2007); Marriage status: 20.6% never married, 68.4% now married, 3.9% widowed, 7.1% divorced (2000); Foreign born: 23.7% (2000); Ancestry (includes multiple ancestries): 35.0% Other groups, 12.4% English, 12.2% German, 11.8% Irish, 7.9% Italian (2000).
Economy: Employment by occupation: 26.5% management, 30.2% professional, 8.7% services, 25.7% sales, 0.0% farming, 4.7% construction, 4.2% production (2000).
Income: Per capita income: $49,849 (2007); Median household income: $127,917 (2007); Average household income: $153,060 (2007); Percent of households with income of $100,000 or more: 63.8% (2007); Poverty rate: 5.2% (2000).
Education: Percent of population age 25 and over with: High school diploma (including GED) or higher: 92.9% (2007); Bachelor's degree or higher: 55.7% (2007); Master's degree or higher: 23.2% (2007).
Housing: Homeownership rate: 88.2% (2007); Median home value: $599,391 (2007); Median rent: $584 per month (2000); Median age of housing: 28 years (2000).
Transportation: Commute to work: 91.6% car, 2.7% public transportation, 0.3% walk, 4.4% work from home (2000); Travel time to work: 14.0% less than 15 minutes, 32.8% 15 to 30 minutes, 27.5% 30 to 45 minutes, 14.0% 45 to 60 minutes, 11.7% 60 minutes or more (2000)

CUTLER RIDGE (CDP).
Covers a land area of 4.753 square miles and a water area of 0.111 square miles. Located at 25.58° N. Lat.; 80.34° W. Long. Elevation is 10 feet.
History: Named for Dr. C.F. Cutler of Massachusetts, who built a settlement and mill here in 1884. The town has grown and developed since the 1970s, and a large shopping center was constructed here. Sustained major devastation in 1992 when Hurricane Andrew struck; rebuilding effort completed by mid-1990s.
Population: 21,268 (1990); 24,781 (2000); 26,801 (2007); 28,435 (2012 projected); Race: 72.1% White, 16.4% Black, 1.5% Asian, 45.7% Hispanic of any race (2007); Density: 5,638.4 persons per square mile (2007); Average household size: 3.00 (2007); Median age: 36.0 (2007); Males per 100 females: 93.2 (2007); Marriage status: 24.6% never married, 57.4% now married, 6.5% widowed, 11.5% divorced (2000); Foreign born: 26.5% (2000); Ancestry (includes multiple ancestries): 49.4% Other groups, 8.6% Irish, 8.5% United States or American, 8.2% German, 5.7% English (2000).
Economy: Employment by occupation: 14.4% management, 18.1% professional, 13.0% services, 33.5% sales, 0.2% farming, 12.0% construction, 8.7% production (2000).
Income: Per capita income: $21,424 (2007); Median household income: $50,356 (2007); Average household income: $63,098 (2007); Percent of households with income of $100,000 or more: 16.2% (2007); Poverty rate: 11.5% (2000).
Education: Percent of population age 25 and over with: High school diploma (including GED) or higher: 82.1% (2007); Bachelor's degree or higher: 19.8% (2007); Master's degree or higher: 7.6% (2007).
Housing: Homeownership rate: 68.5% (2007); Median home value: $245,890 (2007); Median rent: $551 per month (2000); Median age of housing: 30 years (2000).
Transportation: Commute to work: 92.5% car, 3.0% public transportation, 0.7% walk, 2.3% work from home (2000); Travel time to work: 18.4% less than 15 minutes, 27.8% 15 to 30 minutes, 22.7% 30 to 45 minutes, 15.1% 45 to 60 minutes, 15.9% 60 minutes or more (2000)

DORAL (CDP).
Covers a land area of 13.163 square miles and a water area of 0.478 square miles. Located at 25.80° N. Lat.; 80.35° W. Long. Elevation is 3 feet.
Population: 6,267 (1990); 20,438 (2000); 31,143 (2007); 38,231 (2012 projected); Race: 85.9% White, 1.7% Black, 4.6% Asian, 75.0% Hispanic of any race (2007); Density: 2,365.9 persons per square mile (2007); Average household size: 2.77 (2007); Median age: 34.4 (2007); Males per 100 females: 96.6 (2007); Marriage status: 20.4% never married, 69.5% now married, 1.7% widowed, 8.5% divorced (2000); Foreign born: 62.6% (2000); Ancestry (includes multiple ancestries): 72.6% Other groups, 5.4% Italian, 3.3% United States or American, 2.6% Brazilian, 2.5% Irish (2000).
Economy: Single-family building permits issued: 475 (2006); Multi-family building permits issued: 602 (2006); Employment by occupation: 30.4% management, 19.4% professional, 7.1% services, 32.9% sales, 0.3% farming, 3.4% construction, 6.5% production (2000).

Income: Per capita income: $33,347 (2007); Median household income: $65,404 (2007); Average household income: $92,204 (2007); Percent of households with income of $100,000 or more: 28.8% (2007); Poverty rate: 11.7% (2000).
Taxes: Total city taxes per capita: $977 (2005); City property taxes per capita: $605 (2005).
Education: Percent of population age 25 and over with: High school diploma (including GED) or higher: 92.1% (2007); Bachelor's degree or higher: 49.0% (2007); Master's degree or higher: 20.5% (2007).

School District(s)
Dade County School District (PK-12)
    2005-06 Enrollment: 368,933 . . . . (305) 995-1430
Housing: Homeownership rate: 62.9% (2007); Median home value: $386,368 (2007); Median rent: $870 per month (2000); Median age of housing: 7 years (2000).
Safety: Violent crime rate: 56.6 per 10,000 population; Property crime rate: 1,192.1 per 10,000 population (2006).
Transportation: Commute to work: 93.0% car, 0.8% public transportation, 1.9% walk, 4.1% work from home (2000); Travel time to work: 30.8% less than 15 minutes, 39.6% 15 to 30 minutes, 19.9% 30 to 45 minutes, 6.1% 45 to 60 minutes, 3.6% 60 minutes or more (2000)

EAST PERRINE (CDP). Covers a land area of 1.974 square miles and a water area of 0 square miles. Located at 25.60° N. Lat.; 80.34° W. Long. Elevation is 13 feet.
Population: 6,526 (1990); 7,079 (2000); 7,058 (2007); 7,181 (2012 projected); Race: 71.0% White, 16.9% Black, 2.1% Asian, 37.0% Hispanic of any race (2007); Density: 3,575.6 persons per square mile (2007); Average household size: 3.12 (2007); Median age: 36.9 (2007); Males per 100 females: 91.1 (2007); Marriage status: 26.4% never married, 56.9% now married, 6.3% widowed, 10.4% divorced (2000); Foreign born: 30.2% (2000); Ancestry (includes multiple ancestries): 42.0% Other groups, 10.0% German, 9.8% United States or American, 8.2% Irish, 5.9% Jamaican (2000).
Economy: Employment by occupation: 17.3% management, 26.9% professional, 14.9% services, 24.4% sales, 0.0% farming, 10.5% construction, 6.0% production (2000).
Income: Per capita income: $28,512 (2007); Median household income: $73,038 (2007); Average household income: $88,571 (2007); Percent of households with income of $100,000 or more: 34.7% (2007); Poverty rate: 7.8% (2000).
Education: Percent of population age 25 and over with: High school diploma (including GED) or higher: 83.7% (2007); Bachelor's degree or higher: 31.0% (2007); Master's degree or higher: 12.6% (2007).
Housing: Homeownership rate: 74.8% (2007); Median home value: $356,977 (2007); Median rent: $627 per month (2000); Median age of housing: 27 years (2000).
Transportation: Commute to work: 89.6% car, 5.0% public transportation, 1.0% walk, 3.1% work from home (2000); Travel time to work: 21.5% less than 15 minutes, 24.1% 15 to 30 minutes, 22.1% 30 to 45 minutes, 15.2% 45 to 60 minutes, 17.1% 60 minutes or more (2000)

EL PORTAL (village). Covers a land area of 0.425 square miles and a water area of 0 square miles. Located at 25.85° N. Lat.; 80.19° W. Long. Elevation is 7 feet.
Population: 2,457 (1990); 2,505 (2000); 2,374 (2007); 2,319 (2012 projected); Race: 26.9% White, 60.4% Black, 0.8% Asian, 24.0% Hispanic of any race (2007); Density: 5,588.2 persons per square mile (2007); Average household size: 3.06 (2007); Median age: 39.3 (2007); Males per 100 females: 96.8 (2007); Marriage status: 38.9% never married, 39.9% now married, 7.7% widowed, 13.5% divorced (2000); Foreign born: 37.2% (2000); Ancestry (includes multiple ancestries): 42.3% Other groups, 22.1% Haitian, 8.1% Jamaican, 4.3% United States or American, 2.7% German (2000).
Economy: Single-family building permits issued: 2 (2006); Multi-family building permits issued: 0 (2006); Employment by occupation: 17.6% management, 17.6% professional, 23.3% services, 26.8% sales, 0.0% farming, 5.2% construction, 9.5% production (2000).
Income: Per capita income: $19,860 (2007); Median household income: $50,657 (2007); Average household income: $59,919 (2007); Percent of households with income of $100,000 or more: 15.4% (2007); Poverty rate: 22.2% (2000).
Education: Percent of population age 25 and over with: High school diploma (including GED) or higher: 75.3% (2007); Bachelor's degree or higher: 23.1% (2007); Master's degree or higher: 9.5% (2007).

Housing: Homeownership rate: 77.0% (2007); Median home value: $236,528 (2007); Median rent: $609 per month (2000); Median age of housing: 48 years (2000).
Safety: Violent crime rate: 52.7 per 10,000 population; Property crime rate: 397.1 per 10,000 population (2006).
Transportation: Commute to work: 86.5% car, 10.2% public transportation, 1.1% walk, 1.6% work from home (2000); Travel time to work: 14.7% less than 15 minutes, 41.2% 15 to 30 minutes, 28.3% 30 to 45 minutes, 8.4% 45 to 60 minutes, 7.3% 60 minutes or more (2000)

FISHER ISLAND (CDP). Covers a land area of 0.343 square miles and a water area of 0 square miles. Located at 25.76° N. Lat.; 80.14° W. Long. Elevation is 10 feet.
Population: 204 (1990); 467 (2000); 464 (2007); 417 (2012 projected); Race: 92.7% White, 2.4% Black, 2.6% Asian, 10.1% Hispanic of any race (2007); Density: 1,353.9 persons per square mile (2007); Average household size: 2.15 (2007); Median age: 51.6 (2007); Males per 100 females: 97.4 (2007); Marriage status: 14.1% never married, 71.2% now married, 7.5% widowed, 7.2% divorced (2000); Foreign born: 27.7% (2000); Ancestry (includes multiple ancestries): 15.9% Russian, 13.3% English, 10.0% Other groups, 8.8% Iranian, 8.6% United States or American (2000).
Economy: Employment by occupation: 60.4% management, 26.6% professional, 7.9% services, 0.0% sales, 0.0% farming, 0.0% construction, 5.0% production (2000).
Income: Per capita income: $139,639 (2007); Median household income: $310,811 (2007); Average household income: $299,965 (2007); Percent of households with income of $100,000 or more: 69.9% (2007); Poverty rate: 0.0% (2000).
Education: Percent of population age 25 and over with: High school diploma (including GED) or higher: 97.2% (2007); Bachelor's degree or higher: 68.0% (2007); Master's degree or higher: 50.3% (2007).
Housing: Homeownership rate: 89.8% (2007); Median home value: $1 million+ (2007); Median rent: $1,698 per month (2000); Median age of housing: 11 years (2000).
Transportation: Commute to work: 56.8% car, 0.0% public transportation, 13.7% walk, 5.0% work from home (2000); Travel time to work: 52.3% less than 15 minutes, 31.1% 15 to 30 minutes, 16.7% 30 to 45 minutes, 0.0% 45 to 60 minutes, 0.0% 60 minutes or more (2000)

FLORIDA CITY (city). Covers a land area of 3.219 square miles and a water area of 0 square miles. Located at 25.45° N. Lat.; 80.48° W. Long. Elevation is 3 feet.
History: Florida City was incorporated in 1913. It was first called Detroit, but the postal authorities insisted on a different name.
Population: 5,896 (1990); 7,843 (2000); 11,123 (2007); 13,510 (2012 projected); Race: 30.5% White, 52.0% Black, 0.7% Asian, 38.6% Hispanic of any race (2007); Density: 3,455.0 persons per square mile (2007); Average household size: 3.65 (2007); Median age: 22.8 (2007); Males per 100 females: 95.7 (2007); Marriage status: 39.4% never married, 38.8% now married, 12.5% widowed, 9.4% divorced (2000); Foreign born: 20.9% (2000); Ancestry (includes multiple ancestries): 72.1% Other groups, 5.8% Haitian, 2.4% United States or American, 1.8% African, 1.0% Italian (2000).
Economy: Single-family building permits issued: 143 (2006); Multi-family building permits issued: 0 (2006); Employment by occupation: 6.0% management, 11.9% professional, 26.2% services, 24.8% sales, 4.9% farming, 9.3% construction, 16.9% production (2000).
Income: Per capita income: $8,572 (2007); Median household income: $18,646 (2007); Average household income: $30,478 (2007); Percent of households with income of $100,000 or more: 2.5% (2007); Poverty rate: 43.3% (2000).
Taxes: Total city taxes per capita: $571 (2005); City property taxes per capita: $233 (2005).
Education: Percent of population age 25 and over with: High school diploma (including GED) or higher: 44.2% (2007); Bachelor's degree or higher: 6.9% (2007); Master's degree or higher: 2.0% (2007).

School District(s)
Dade County School District (PK-12)
    2005-06 Enrollment: 368,933 . . . . (305) 995-1430
Housing: Homeownership rate: 41.8% (2007); Median home value: $146,758 (2007); Median rent: $431 per month (2000); Median age of housing: 18 years (2000).
Safety: Violent crime rate: 296.8 per 10,000 population; Property crime rate: 1,319.7 per 10,000 population (2006).

Transportation: Commute to work: 88.7% car, 4.6% public transportation, 1.6% walk, 3.9% work from home (2000); Travel time to work: 29.1% less than 15 minutes, 25.0% 15 to 30 minutes, 22.4% 30 to 45 minutes, 8.2% 45 to 60 minutes, 15.2% 60 minutes or more (2000)

Additional Information Contacts

City of Florida City . . . . (305) 242-8132
  http://www.floridacityfl.us

FOUNTAINBLEAU (CDP). Covers a land area of 4.403 square miles and a water area of 0.114 square miles. Located at 25.77° N. Lat.; 80.34° W. Long. Elevation is 3 feet.
Population: 46,661 (1990); 59,549 (2000); 64,389 (2007); 68,359 (2012 projected); Race: 87.3% White, 2.0% Black, 1.8% Asian, 87.6% Hispanic of any race (2007); Density: 14,623.9 persons per square mile (2007); Average household size: 2.87 (2007); Median age: 37.6 (2007); Males per 100 females: 87.6 (2007); Marriage status: 26.3% never married, 55.3% now married, 6.0% widowed, 12.3% divorced (2000); Foreign born: 73.1% (2000); Ancestry (includes multiple ancestries): 86.2% Other groups, 2.5% United States or American, 1.7% Italian, 0.8% German, 0.5% Irish (2000).
Economy: Employment by occupation: 13.0% management, 14.4% professional, 15.7% services, 37.6% sales, 0.2% farming, 6.7% construction, 12.4% production (2000).
Income: Per capita income: $16,899 (2007); Median household income: $40,212 (2007); Average household income: $48,487 (2007); Percent of households with income of $100,000 or more: 7.8% (2007); Poverty rate: 14.2% (2000).
Education: Percent of population age 25 and over with: High school diploma (including GED) or higher: 70.0% (2007); Bachelor's degree or higher: 22.2% (2007); Master's degree or higher: 10.4% (2007).
Housing: Homeownership rate: 51.3% (2007); Median home value: $184,245 (2007); Median rent: $705 per month (2000); Median age of housing: 18 years (2000).
Transportation: Commute to work: 92.0% car, 3.0% public transportation, 1.2% walk, 2.1% work from home (2000); Travel time to work: 15.9% less than 15 minutes, 41.5% 15 to 30 minutes, 27.0% 30 to 45 minutes, 9.6% 45 to 60 minutes, 6.0% 60 minutes or more (2000)

GLADEVIEW (CDP). Covers a land area of 2.541 square miles and a water area of 0 square miles. Located at 25.84° N. Lat.; 80.23° W. Long. Elevation is 10 feet.
Population: 15,637 (1990); 14,468 (2000); 12,563 (2007); 11,520 (2012 projected); Race: 23.1% White, 69.4% Black, 0.2% Asian, 29.1% Hispanic of any race (2007); Density: 4,944.5 persons per square mile (2007); Average household size: 3.39 (2007); Median age: 26.8 (2007); Males per 100 females: 88.5 (2007); Marriage status: 47.8% never married, 32.2% now married, 9.5% widowed, 10.5% divorced (2000); Foreign born: 20.1% (2000); Ancestry (includes multiple ancestries): 74.4% Other groups, 2.2% United States or American, 1.5% Haitian, 1.0% African, 1.0% Bahamian (2000).
Economy: Employment by occupation: 4.2% management, 13.0% professional, 24.8% services, 24.7% sales, 0.5% farming, 9.0% construction, 23.8% production (2000).
Income: Per capita income: $8,603 (2007); Median household income: $17,946 (2007); Average household income: $28,102 (2007); Percent of households with income of $100,000 or more: 3.0% (2007); Poverty rate: 52.8% (2000).
Education: Percent of population age 25 and over with: High school diploma (including GED) or higher: 51.3% (2007); Bachelor's degree or higher: 4.2% (2007); Master's degree or higher: 1.1% (2007).
Housing: Homeownership rate: 43.6% (2007); Median home value: $103,464 (2007); Median rent: $278 per month (2000); Median age of housing: 38 years (2000).
Transportation: Commute to work: 80.9% car, 14.3% public transportation, 3.0% walk, 0.7% work from home (2000); Travel time to work: 16.0% less than 15 minutes, 34.5% 15 to 30 minutes, 31.4% 30 to 45 minutes, 7.5% 45 to 60 minutes, 10.6% 60 minutes or more (2000)

GLENVAR HEIGHTS (CDP). Covers a land area of 4.210 square miles and a water area of 0.175 square miles. Located at 25.70° N. Lat.; 80.31° W. Long. Elevation is 13 feet.
Population: 14,823 (1990); 16,243 (2000); 16,179 (2007); 16,325 (2012 projected); Race: 87.2% White, 2.9% Black, 2.8% Asian, 63.3% Hispanic of any race (2007); Density: 3,843.2 persons per square mile (2007); Average household size: 2.29 (2007); Median age: 39.8 (2007); Males per 100 females: 88.1 (2007); Marriage status: 31.3% never married, 50.1% now

married, 6.5% widowed, 12.1% divorced (2000); Foreign born: 45.4% (2000); Ancestry (includes multiple ancestries): 61.6% Other groups, 6.3% German, 5.5% English, 4.7% Irish, 4.2% Italian (2000).
Economy: Employment by occupation: 17.0% management, 25.8% professional, 13.1% services, 32.1% sales, 0.0% farming, 5.2% construction, 6.8% production (2000).
Income: Per capita income: $30,934 (2007); Median household income: $46,462 (2007); Average household income: $70,502 (2007); Percent of households with income of $100,000 or more: 19.3% (2007); Poverty rate: 12.7% (2000).
Education: Percent of population age 25 and over with: High school diploma (including GED) or higher: 87.4% (2007); Bachelor's degree or higher: 40.5% (2007); Master's degree or higher: 18.9% (2007).
Housing: Homeownership rate: 52.9% (2007); Median home value: $374,515 (2007); Median rent: $650 per month (2000); Median age of housing: 28 years (2000).
Transportation: Commute to work: 85.6% car, 6.5% public transportation, 1.5% walk, 4.8% work from home (2000); Travel time to work: 19.7% less than 15 minutes, 34.1% 15 to 30 minutes, 27.3% 30 to 45 minutes, 10.5% 45 to 60 minutes, 8.4% 60 minutes or more (2000)

GOLDEN BEACH (town). Covers a land area of 0.341 square miles and a water area of 0.059 square miles. Located at 25.96° N. Lat.; 80.12° W. Long. Elevation is 10 feet.
Population: 771 (1990); 919 (2000); 939 (2007); 953 (2012 projected); Race: 95.5% White, 0.3% Black, 1.1% Asian, 25.2% Hispanic of any race (2007); Density: 2,751.3 persons per square mile (2007); Average household size: 3.37 (2007); Median age: 37.1 (2007); Males per 100 females: 96.0 (2007); Marriage status: 20.4% never married, 66.8% now married, 4.8% widowed, 8.1% divorced (2000); Foreign born: 31.3% (2000); Ancestry (includes multiple ancestries): 31.2% Other groups, 11.9% United States or American, 11.0% Italian, 9.0% Russian, 7.4% Polish (2000).
Economy: Single-family building permits issued: 1 (2006); Multi-family building permits issued: 0 (2006); Employment by occupation: 35.6% management, 25.4% professional, 5.1% services, 29.8% sales, 0.0% farming, 1.5% construction, 2.5% production (2000).
Income: Per capita income: $64,742 (2007); Median household income: $156,481 (2007); Average household income: $217,894 (2007); Percent of households with income of $100,000 or more: 63.1% (2007); Poverty rate: 8.1% (2000).
Taxes: Total city taxes per capita: $4,815 (2005); City property taxes per capita: $3,987 (2005).
Education: Percent of population age 25 and over with: High school diploma (including GED) or higher: 96.4% (2007); Bachelor's degree or higher: 60.2% (2007); Master's degree or higher: 27.1% (2007).
Housing: Homeownership rate: 93.5% (2007); Median home value: $1 million+ (2007); Median rent: $1,469 per month (2000); Median age of housing: 26 years (2000).
Safety: Violent crime rate: 32.6 per 10,000 population; Property crime rate: 162.9 per 10,000 population (2006).
Transportation: Commute to work: 83.9% car, 0.0% public transportation, 0.0% walk, 15.6% work from home (2000); Travel time to work: 25.0% less than 15 minutes, 30.0% 15 to 30 minutes, 31.9% 30 to 45 minutes, 10.3% 45 to 60 minutes, 2.8% 60 minutes or more (2000)

GOLDEN GLADES (CDP). Covers a land area of 4.917 square miles and a water area of 0.065 square miles. Located at 25.91° N. Lat.; 80.19° W. Long. Elevation is 3 feet.
Population: 25,312 (1990); 32,623 (2000); 33,426 (2007); 34,349 (2012 projected); Race: 20.0% White, 68.1% Black, 1.3% Asian, 16.9% Hispanic of any race (2007); Density: 6,798.3 persons per square mile (2007); Average household size: 3.39 (2007); Median age: 32.6 (2007); Males per 100 females: 89.6 (2007); Marriage status: 35.6% never married, 46.7% now married, 6.9% widowed, 10.9% divorced (2000); Foreign born: 45.3% (2000); Ancestry (includes multiple ancestries): 36.4% Other groups, 32.0% Haitian, 5.4% Jamaican, 5.2% United States or American, 1.9% German (2000).
Economy: Employment by occupation: 7.0% management, 14.9% professional, 25.7% services, 29.0% sales, 0.3% farming, 10.6% construction, 12.6% production (2000).
Income: Per capita income: $12,251 (2007); Median household income: $30,995 (2007); Average household income: $40,617 (2007); Percent of households with income of $100,000 or more: 5.6% (2007); Poverty rate: 20.9% (2000).

Education: Percent of population age 25 and over with: High school diploma (including GED) or higher: 63.4% (2007); Bachelor's degree or higher: 12.4% (2007); Master's degree or higher: 4.8% (2007).
Housing: Homeownership rate: 53.2% (2007); Median home value: $203,602 (2007); Median rent: $549 per month (2000); Median age of housing: 35 years (2000).
Transportation: Commute to work: 88.0% car, 8.7% public transportation, 0.7% walk, 1.4% work from home (2000); Travel time to work: 14.5% less than 15 minutes, 35.0% 15 to 30 minutes, 31.1% 30 to 45 minutes, 9.9% 45 to 60 minutes, 9.5% 60 minutes or more (2000)

GOULDS (CDP).
Covers a land area of 2.964 square miles and a water area of 0.002 square miles. Located at 25.56° N. Lat.; 80.38° W. Long. Elevation is 10 feet.
History: Goulds grew around a packing plant that shipped citrus fruits, potatoes, and other truck garden produce.
Population: 7,284 (1990); 7,453 (2000); 10,219 (2007); 12,051 (2012 projected); Race: 17.6% White, 74.0% Black, 0.5% Asian, 20.8% Hispanic of any race (2007); Density: 3,447.8 persons per square mile (2007); Average household size: 3.35 (2007); Median age: 25.4 (2007); Males per 100 females: 86.3 (2007); Marriage status: 45.1% never married, 34.0% now married, 8.0% widowed, 12.9% divorced (2000); Foreign born: 15.2% (2000); Ancestry (includes multiple ancestries): 69.8% Other groups, 4.8% United States or American, 3.7% Jamaican, 2.5% Haitian, 1.8% Bahamian (2000).
Economy: Employment by occupation: 9.0% management, 15.9% professional, 26.5% services, 28.1% sales, 0.8% farming, 9.9% construction, 9.8% production (2000).
Income: Per capita income: $9,835 (2007); Median household income: $23,266 (2007); Average household income: $32,951 (2007); Percent of households with income of $100,000 or more: 3.4% (2007); Poverty rate: 43.6% (2000).
Education: Percent of population age 25 and over with: High school diploma (including GED) or higher: 50.8% (2007); Bachelor's degree or higher: 6.9% (2007); Master's degree or higher: 2.2% (2007).
Housing: Homeownership rate: 44.2% (2007); Median home value: $190,872 (2007); Median rent: $369 per month (2000); Median age of housing: 28 years (2000).
Transportation: Commute to work: 86.4% car, 9.5% public transportation, 0.6% walk, 1.4% work from home (2000); Travel time to work: 19.7% less than 15 minutes, 35.6% 15 to 30 minutes, 21.3% 30 to 45 minutes, 9.1% 45 to 60 minutes, 14.4% 60 minutes or more (2000)

HIALEAH (city).
Covers a land area of 19.241 square miles and a water area of 0.501 square miles. Located at 25.86° N. Lat.; 80.29° W. Long. Elevation is 7 feet.
History: Named for the Seminole-Creek translations of "prairie" and "pretty". Hialeah was founded in the early 1920s by James Bright, a Missouri ranchman. In 1931 Joe Smoot built the Hialeah Park race track, attracting tourists in the Greater Miami area.
Population: 188,005 (1990); 226,419 (2000); 219,483 (2007); 217,593 (2012 projected); Race: 88.1% White, 2.6% Black, 0.4% Asian, 91.5% Hispanic of any race (2007); Density: 11,406.8 persons per square mile (2007); Average household size: 3.24 (2007); Median age: 40.0 (2007); Males per 100 females: 93.0 (2007); Marriage status: 22.3% never married, 58.5% now married, 7.3% widowed, 11.8% divorced (2000); Foreign born: 72.1% (2000); Ancestry (includes multiple ancestries): 85.0% Other groups, 2.6% United States or American, 0.7% Italian, 0.6% German, 0.5% Irish (2000).
Economy: Unemployment rate: 4.8% (11/2007); Total civilian labor force: 101,015 (11/2007); Single-family building permits issued: 12 (2006); Multi-family building permits issued: 231 (2006); Employment by occupation: 7.5% management, 9.0% professional, 14.2% services, 30.7% sales, 0.3% farming, 14.3% construction, 24.0% production (2000).
Income: Per capita income: $13,295 (2007); Median household income: $32,595 (2007); Average household income: $41,988 (2007); Percent of households with income of $100,000 or more: 6.1% (2007); Poverty rate: 18.6% (2000).
Taxes: Total city taxes per capita: $485 (2005); City property taxes per capita: $210 (2005).
Education: Percent of population age 25 and over with: High school diploma (including GED) or higher: 50.0% (2007); Bachelor's degree or higher: 10.4% (2007); Master's degree or higher: 4.4% (2007).

School District(s)
Dade County School District (PK-12)
   2005-06 Enrollment: 368,933 . . . . (305) 995-1430
Two-year College(s)
College of Business and Technology-Hialeah Campus (Private, For-profit)
   Fall 2006 Enrollment: 71 . . . . (305) 273-4499
   2006-07 Tuition: In-state $10,224; Out-of-state $10,224
Florida National College (Private, For-profit)
   Fall 2006 Enrollment: 1,796. . . . . (305) 821-3333
   2006-07 Tuition: In-state $10,670; Out-of-state $10,670
National School of Technology Inc (Private, For-profit)
   Fall 2006 Enrollment: 606 . . . . (305) 558-9500
Vocational/Technical School(s)
Advance Science Institute (Private, For-profit)
   Fall 2006 Enrollment: 125 . . . . (305) 827-5452
   2006-07 Tuition: $6,600
American Advanced Technicians Institute (Private, For-profit)
   Fall 2006 Enrollment: 183 . . . . (305) 362-5519
   2006-07 Tuition: $6,650
Beauty Schools of America (Private, For-profit)
   Fall 2006 Enrollment: 470 . . . . (305) 362-9003
   2006-07 Tuition: $9,939
Compu-Med Vocational Careers Corp (Private, For-profit)
   Fall 2006 Enrollment: 594 . . . . (305) 888-9200
   2006-07 Tuition: $4,700
Florida National College Training Center (Private, For-profit)
   Fall 2006 Enrollment: 88 . . . . (305) 231-3326
   2006-07 Tuition: In-state $10,670; Out-of-state $10,670
La Belle Beauty School (Private, For-profit)
   Fall 2006 Enrollment: 380 . . . . (305) 558-0562
   2006-07 Tuition: $8,495
Total International Career Institute (Private, For-profit)
   Fall 2006 Enrollment: 11 . . . . (305) 681-6622
   2006-07 Tuition: In-state $5,000; Out-of-state $5,000
Housing: Homeownership rate: 50.8% (2007); Median home value: $226,794 (2007); Median rent: $537 per month (2000); Median age of housing: 27 years (2000).
Hospitals: Palmetto General Hospital (360 beds); Southern Winds Hospital (72 beds)
Safety: Violent crime rate: 56.3 per 10,000 population; Property crime rate: 386.9 per 10,000 population (2006).
Newspapers: El Sol de Hialeah (Hispanic - Circulation 24,000); La Voz Calle (Hispanic - Circulation 25,000)
Transportation: Commute to work: 93.1% car, 2.9% public transportation, 1.6% walk, 1.1% work from home (2000); Travel time to work: 18.4% less than 15 minutes, 38.4% 15 to 30 minutes, 27.8% 30 to 45 minutes, 8.4% 45 to 60 minutes, 6.9% 60 minutes or more (2000)

HIALEAH GARDENS (city).
Covers a land area of 2.460 square miles and a water area of 0.065 square miles. Located at 25.87° N. Lat.; 80.34° W. Long. Elevation is 7 feet.
Population: 7,713 (1990); 19,297 (2000); 24,029 (2007); 27,278 (2012 projected); Race: 87.7% White, 2.2% Black, 0.6% Asian, 92.7% Hispanic of any race (2007); Density: 9,769.8 persons per square mile (2007); Average household size: 3.45 (2007); Median age: 36.2 (2007); Males per 100 females: 93.5 (2007); Marriage status: 21.4% never married, 63.1% now married, 4.6% widowed, 10.9% divorced (2000); Foreign born: 70.1% (2000); Ancestry (includes multiple ancestries): 88.9% Other groups, 1.9% United States or American, 1.1% Italian, 0.3% English, 0.3% German (2000).
Economy: Single-family building permits issued: 101 (2006); Multi-family building permits issued: 64 (2006); Employment by occupation: 11.7% management, 8.7% professional, 11.8% services, 32.8% sales, 0.1% farming, 11.0% construction, 23.9% production (2000).
Income: Per capita income: $16,528 (2007); Median household income: $47,161 (2007); Average household income: $56,616 (2007); Percent of households with income of $100,000 or more: 12.0% (2007); Poverty rate: 13.3% (2000).
Education: Percent of population age 25 and over with: High school diploma (including GED) or higher: 60.0% (2007); Bachelor's degree or higher: 13.4% (2007); Master's degree or higher: 6.2% (2007).
School District(s)
Dade County School District (PK-12)
   2005-06 Enrollment: 368,933 . . . . (305) 995-1430

Housing: Homeownership rate: 75.6% (2007); Median home value: $212,227 (2007); Median rent: $617 per month (2000); Median age of housing: 9 years (2000).
Safety: Violent crime rate: 31.1 per 10,000 population; Property crime rate: 388.8 per 10,000 population (2006).
Transportation: Commute to work: 92.9% car, 2.0% public transportation, 1.4% walk, 1.8% work from home (2000); Travel time to work: 13.9% less than 15 minutes, 39.3% 15 to 30 minutes, 28.8% 30 to 45 minutes, 10.7% 45 to 60 minutes, 7.2% 60 minutes or more (2000)
Additional Information Contacts
City of Hialeah Gardens............................ (305) 558-4114
  http://www.cityofhialeahgardens.org

HOMESTEAD (city). Covers a land area of 14.284 square miles and a water area of 0.093 square miles. Located at 25.47° N. Lat.; 80.46° W. Long. Elevation is 3 feet.
History: Named for its history as an area open to homesteading by the U.S. government. Homestead developed as the trading center of the Redlands fruit and winter-vegetable area when the railroad arrived in 1904. In 1912 Colonel H.W. Johnston came to Homestead from Kentucky, and became interested in horticulture. On his estate he planted more than 8,000 varieties of tropical plants and trees, including more than 1,500 varieties of palms.
Population: 28,451 (1990); 31,909 (2000); 46,428 (2007); 56,016 (2012 projected); Race: 63.2% White, 20.1% Black, 0.9% Asian, 57.0% Hispanic of any race (2007); Density: 3,250.4 persons per square mile (2007); Average household size: 3.12 (2007); Median age: 29.4 (2007); Males per 100 females: 103.2 (2007); Marriage status: 36.7% never married, 48.5% now married, 4.8% widowed, 10.0% divorced (2000); Foreign born: 36.0% (2000); Ancestry (includes multiple ancestries): 62.2% Other groups, 5.2% United States or American, 4.8% Haitian, 4.2% Irish, 4.0% German (2000).
Economy: Unemployment rate: 3.2% (11/2007); Total civilian labor force: 21,675 (11/2007); Single-family building permits issued: 991 (2006); Multi-family building permits issued: 662 (2006); Employment by occupation: 7.0% management, 10.3% professional, 19.7% services, 21.4% sales, 14.3% farming, 17.5% construction, 9.8% production (2000).
Income: Per capita income: $13,409 (2007); Median household income: $30,916 (2007); Average household income: $40,914 (2007); Percent of households with income of $100,000 or more: 6.2% (2007); Poverty rate: 31.8% (2000).
Taxes: Total city taxes per capita: $421 (2005); City property taxes per capita: $150 (2005).
Education: Percent of population age 25 and over with: High school diploma (including GED) or higher: 53.8% (2007); Bachelor's degree or higher: 11.1% (2007); Master's degree or higher: 3.5% (2007).
School District(s)
Dade County School District (PK-12)
  2005-06 Enrollment: 368,933 .... (305) 995-1430
Housing: Homeownership rate: 40.8% (2007); Median home value: $179,059 (2007); Median rent: $444 per month (2000); Median age of housing: 19 years (2000).
Hospitals: Homestead Hospital (120 beds)
Safety: Violent crime rate: 229.6 per 10,000 population; Property crime rate: 688.5 per 10,000 population (2006).
Newspapers: South Dade News Leader (General - Circulation 15,000)
Transportation: Commute to work: 90.2% car, 2.9% public transportation, 1.6% walk, 1.0% work from home (2000); Travel time to work: 23.8% less than 15 minutes, 27.7% 15 to 30 minutes, 22.9% 30 to 45 minutes, 10.0% 45 to 60 minutes, 15.5% 60 minutes or more (2000)
Airports: Homestead AFB; Homestead General Aviation
Additional Information Contacts
City of Homestead .... (305) 224-4400
  http://ci.homestead.fl.us
Homestead-Florida City Chamber .... (305) 247-2332
  http://www.chamberinaction.com

HOMESTEAD BASE (CDP). Covers a land area of 4.353 square miles and a water area of 0 square miles. Located at 25.49° N. Lat.; 80.39° W. Long.
Population: 5,169 (1990); 446 (2000); 492 (2007); 527 (2012 projected); Race: 50.4% White, 38.0% Black, 0.8% Asian, 53.9% Hispanic of any race (2007); Density: 113.0 persons per square mile (2007); Average household size: 24.60 (2007); Median age: 30.1 (2007); Males per 100 females: 99.2 (2007); Marriage status: 40.0% never married, 41.6% now married, 7.9% widowed, 10.4% divorced (2000); Foreign born: 19.8% (2000); Ancestry

(includes multiple ancestries): 44.0% Other groups, 10.6% United States or American, 3.0% Nigerian, 2.5% Italian, 1.7% German (2000).
Economy: Employment by occupation: 17.3% management, 0.0% professional, 26.7% services, 30.7% sales, 10.7% farming, 14.7% construction, 0.0% production (2000).
Income: Per capita income: $8,504 (2007); Median household income: $50,000 (2007); Average household income: $97,000 (2007); Percent of households with income of $100,000 or more: 30.0% (2007); Poverty rate: 65.5% (2000).
Education: Percent of population age 25 and over with: High school diploma (including GED) or higher: 30.3% (2007); Bachelor's degree or higher: 6.6% (2007); Master's degree or higher: 3.6% (2007).
Housing: Homeownership rate: 0.0% (2007); Median home value: $n/a (2007); Median rent: $175 per month (2000); Median age of housing: 35 years (2000).
Transportation: Commute to work: 37.3% car, 48.0% public transportation, 0.0% walk, 0.0% work from home (2000); Travel time to work: 0.0% less than 15 minutes, 21.3% 15 to 30 minutes, 0.0% 30 to 45 minutes, 14.7% 45 to 60 minutes, 64.0% 60 minutes or more (2000)

INDIAN CREEK (village). Covers a land area of 0.424 square miles and a water area of 0.029 square miles. Located at 25.87° N. Lat.; 80.13° W. Long. Elevation is 7 feet.
Population: 44 (1990); 33 (2000); 25 (2007); 27 (2012 projected); Race: 100.0% White, 0.0% Black, 0.0% Asian, 8.0% Hispanic of any race (2007); Density: 59.0 persons per square mile (2007); Average household size: 2.50 (2007); Median age: 51.3 (2007); Males per 100 females: 127.3 (2007); Marriage status: 24.1% never married, 58.6% now married, 6.9% widowed, 10.3% divorced (2000); Foreign born: 55.9% (2000); Ancestry (includes multiple ancestries): 35.3% Other groups, 20.6% Dutch, 11.8% Brazilian, 11.8% Russian, 11.8% German (2000).
Economy: Single-family building permits issued: 0 (2006); Multi-family building permits issued: 0 (2006); Employment by occupation: 35.3% management, 29.4% professional, 23.5% services, 11.8% sales, 0.0% farming, 0.0% construction, 0.0% production (2000).
Income: Per capita income: $58,200 (2007); Median household income: $67,500 (2007); Average household income: $145,500 (2007); Percent of households with income of $100,000 or more: 40.0% (2007); Poverty rate: 29.4% (2000).
Education: Percent of population age 25 and over with: High school diploma (including GED) or higher: 90.0% (2007); Bachelor's degree or higher: 30.0% (2007); Master's degree or higher: 10.0% (2007).
Housing: Homeownership rate: 80.0% (2007); Median home value: $1 million+ (2007); Median rent: $n/a per month (2000); Median age of housing: 37 years (2000).
Safety: Violent crime rate: 0.0 per 10,000 population; Property crime rate: 0.0 per 10,000 population (2006).
Transportation: Commute to work: 76.5% car, 0.0% public transportation, 11.8% walk, 11.8% work from home (2000); Travel time to work: 13.3% less than 15 minutes, 73.3% 15 to 30 minutes, 13.3% 30 to 45 minutes, 0.0% 45 to 60 minutes, 0.0% 60 minutes or more (2000)

ISLANDIA (city). Covers a land area of 6.452 square miles and a water area of 59.941 square miles. Located at 25.38° N. Lat.; 80.23° W. Long. Elevation is 3 feet.
Population: 13 (1990); 6 (2000); 16 (2007); 22 (2012 projected); Race: 100.0% White, 0.0% Black, 0.0% Asian, 0.0% Hispanic of any race (2007); Density: 2.5 persons per square mile (2007); Average household size: 2.00 (2007); Median age: 33.8 (2007); Males per 100 females: 128.6 (2007); Marriage status: 50.0% never married, 50.0% now married, 0.0% widowed, 0.0% divorced (2000); Foreign born: 0.0% (2000); Ancestry (includes multiple ancestries): 50.0% Dutch, 50.0% German, 33.3% United States or American, 16.7% Norwegian, 16.7% Irish (2000).
Economy: Employment by occupation: 0.0% management, 0.0% professional, 100.0% services, 0.0% sales, 0.0% farming, 0.0% construction, 0.0% production (2000).
Income: Per capita income: $37,344 (2007); Median household income: $56,667 (2007); Average household income: $74,688 (2007); Percent of households with income of $100,000 or more: 37.5% (2007); Poverty rate: 0.0% (2000).
Education: Percent of population age 25 and over with: High school diploma (including GED) or higher: 100.0% (2007); Bachelor's degree or higher: 100.0% (2007); Master's degree or higher: 0.0% (2007).

Housing: Homeownership rate: 0.0% (2007); Median home value: $n/a (2007); Median rent: $525 per month (2000); Median age of housing: 7 years (2000).
Transportation: Commute to work: 66.7% car, 0.0% public transportation, 0.0% walk, 0.0% work from home (2000); Travel time to work: 0.0% less than 15 minutes, 66.7% 15 to 30 minutes, 0.0% 30 to 45 minutes, 0.0% 45 to 60 minutes, 33.3% 60 minutes or more (2000)

IVES ESTATES (CDP). Covers a land area of 2.646 square miles and a water area of 0.153 square miles. Located at 25.96° N. Lat.; 80.18° W. Long. Elevation is 10 feet.
Population: 13,531 (1990); 17,586 (2000); 18,143 (2007); 18,683 (2012 projected); Race: 44.2% White, 40.7% Black, 4.9% Asian, 27.2% Hispanic of any race (2007); Density: 6,856.4 persons per square mile (2007); Average household size: 2.58 (2007); Median age: 37.2 (2007); Males per 100 females: 84.6 (2007); Marriage status: 29.0% never married, 49.2% now married, 7.6% widowed, 14.2% divorced (2000); Foreign born: 40.7% (2000); Ancestry (includes multiple ancestries): 41.0% Other groups, 14.1% Haitian, 5.7% Jamaican, 5.3% United States or American, 4.1% Russian (2000).
Economy: Employment by occupation: 11.7% management, 21.7% professional, 16.7% services, 35.0% sales, 0.1% farming, 6.2% construction, 8.7% production (2000).
Income: Per capita income: $18,836 (2007); Median household income: $40,839 (2007); Average household income: $48,309 (2007); Percent of households with income of $100,000 or more: 6.7% (2007); Poverty rate: 8.6% (2000).
Education: Percent of population age 25 and over with: High school diploma (including GED) or higher: 84.9% (2007); Bachelor's degree or higher: 26.6% (2007); Master's degree or higher: 8.9% (2007).
Housing: Homeownership rate: 75.4% (2007); Median home value: $167,700 (2007); Median rent: $695 per month (2000); Median age of housing: 19 years (2000).
Transportation: Commute to work: 93.8% car, 1.4% public transportation, 1.1% walk, 2.5% work from home (2000); Travel time to work: 14.1% less than 15 minutes, 38.7% 15 to 30 minutes, 29.7% 30 to 45 minutes, 9.9% 45 to 60 minutes, 7.5% 60 minutes or more (2000)

KENDALE LAKES (CDP). Covers a land area of 8.173 square miles and a water area of 0.430 square miles. Located at 25.70° N. Lat.; 80.41° W. Long. Elevation is 3 feet.
Population: 48,524 (1990); 56,901 (2000); 57,577 (2007); 58,813 (2012 projected); Race: 87.6% White, 1.9% Black, 1.6% Asian, 82.0% Hispanic of any race (2007); Density: 7,045.1 persons per square mile (2007); Average household size: 3.19 (2007); Median age: 37.7 (2007); Males per 100 females: 90.2 (2007); Marriage status: 23.9% never married, 58.4% now married, 6.4% widowed, 11.4% divorced (2000); Foreign born: 58.8% (2000); Ancestry (includes multiple ancestries): 79.4% Other groups, 2.8% United States or American, 2.3% Italian, 1.8% German, 1.7% English (2000).
Economy: Employment by occupation: 14.6% management, 16.8% professional, 13.1% services, 37.9% sales, 0.2% farming, 7.9% construction, 9.5% production (2000).
Income: Per capita income: $19,697 (2007); Median household income: $49,363 (2007); Average household income: $62,295 (2007); Percent of households with income of $100,000 or more: 14.6% (2007); Poverty rate: 10.3% (2000).
Education: Percent of population age 25 and over with: High school diploma (including GED) or higher: 78.6% (2007); Bachelor's degree or higher: 22.9% (2007); Master's degree or higher: 9.9% (2007).
Housing: Homeownership rate: 79.2% (2007); Median home value: $233,658 (2007); Median rent: $755 per month (2000); Median age of housing: 21 years (2000).
Transportation: Commute to work: 93.1% car, 2.1% public transportation, 1.1% walk, 3.3% work from home (2000); Travel time to work: 11.2% less than 15 minutes, 26.4% 15 to 30 minutes, 28.7% 30 to 45 minutes, 17.3% 45 to 60 minutes, 16.5% 60 minutes or more (2000)

KENDALL (CDP). Covers a land area of 16.126 square miles and a water area of 0.216 square miles. Located at 25.66° N. Lat.; 80.35° W. Long. Elevation is 13 feet.
Population: 69,644 (1990); 75,226 (2000); 74,666 (2007); 75,254 (2012 projected); Race: 87.0% White, 3.6% Black, 2.8% Asian, 58.1% Hispanic of any race (2007); Density: 4,630.1 persons per square mile (2007); Average household size: 2.67 (2007); Median age: 39.7 (2007); Males per 100

females: 89.0 (2007); Marriage status: 25.8% never married, 55.7% now married, 6.1% widowed, 12.4% divorced (2000); Foreign born: 42.6% (2000); Ancestry (includes multiple ancestries): 59.3% Other groups, 5.7% German, 5.4% United States or American, 5.1% Italian, 5.0% Irish (2000).
Economy: Employment by occupation: 18.7% management, 26.2% professional, 11.8% services, 32.8% sales, 0.1% farming, 5.2% construction, 5.3% production (2000).
Income: Per capita income: $31,133 (2007); Median household income: $57,060 (2007); Average household income: $82,127 (2007); Percent of households with income of $100,000 or more: 24.9% (2007); Poverty rate: 8.6% (2000).
Education: Percent of population age 25 and over with: High school diploma (including GED) or higher: 88.2% (2007); Bachelor's degree or higher: 40.4% (2007); Master's degree or higher: 17.4% (2007).

School District(s)
Dade County School District (PK-12)
    2005-06 Enrollment: 368,933 . . . . (305) 995-1430
Housing: Homeownership rate: 66.1% (2007); Median home value: $325,039 (2007); Median rent: $712 per month (2000); Median age of housing: 24 years (2000).
Transportation: Commute to work: 89.5% car, 4.5% public transportation, 1.0% walk, 4.2% work from home (2000); Travel time to work: 17.4% less than 15 minutes, 29.7% 15 to 30 minutes, 25.3% 30 to 45 minutes, 14.8% 45 to 60 minutes, 12.8% 60 minutes or more (2000)

KENDALL WEST (CDP). Covers a land area of 3.390 square miles and a water area of 0.259 square miles. Located at 25.70° N. Lat.; 80.44° W. Long.
Population: 16,857 (1990); 38,034 (2000); 47,803 (2007); 54,570 (2012 projected); Race: 84.6% White, 3.1% Black, 1.1% Asian, 84.4% Hispanic of any race (2007); Density: 14,100.1 persons per square mile (2007); Average household size: 3.35 (2007); Median age: 33.5 (2007); Males per 100 females: 90.4 (2007); Marriage status: 25.1% never married, 59.6% now married, 4.0% widowed, 11.4% divorced (2000); Foreign born: 59.4% (2000); Ancestry (includes multiple ancestries): 82.8% Other groups, 2.5% United States or American, 2.1% Italian, 1.6% German, 1.2% English (2000).
Economy: Employment by occupation: 12.5% management, 15.0% professional, 15.7% services, 37.6% sales, 0.2% farming, 9.7% construction, 9.4% production (2000).
Income: Per capita income: $17,115 (2007); Median household income: $44,008 (2007); Average household income: $57,018 (2007); Percent of households with income of $100,000 or more: 12.9% (2007); Poverty rate: 15.4% (2000).
Education: Percent of population age 25 and over with: High school diploma (including GED) or higher: 76.9% (2007); Bachelor's degree or higher: 21.8% (2007); Master's degree or higher: 8.7% (2007).
Housing: Homeownership rate: 64.3% (2007); Median home value: $249,464 (2007); Median rent: $691 per month (2000); Median age of housing: 13 years (2000).
Transportation: Commute to work: 92.3% car, 3.1% public transportation, 0.6% walk, 2.1% work from home (2000); Travel time to work: 8.5% less than 15 minutes, 20.8% 15 to 30 minutes, 30.4% 30 to 45 minutes, 19.5% 45 to 60 minutes, 20.7% 60 minutes or more (2000)

KEY BISCAYNE (village). Covers a land area of 1.277 square miles and a water area of 0.115 square miles. Located at 25.69° N. Lat.; 80.16° W. Long. Elevation is 3 feet.
Population: 8,854 (1990); 10,507 (2000); 10,126 (2007); 10,055 (2012 projected); Race: 94.8% White, 0.4% Black, 1.1% Asian, 53.3% Hispanic of any race (2007); Density: 7,926.7 persons per square mile (2007); Average household size: 2.49 (2007); Median age: 42.6 (2007); Males per 100 females: 88.8 (2007); Marriage status: 20.1% never married, 64.3% now married, 5.9% widowed, 9.7% divorced (2000); Foreign born: 50.4% (2000); Ancestry (includes multiple ancestries): 53.5% Other groups, 9.4% German, 6.9% English, 6.0% Italian, 4.8% Irish (2000).
Economy: Single-family building permits issued: 16 (2006); Multi-family building permits issued: 0 (2006); Employment by occupation: 37.9% management, 24.4% professional, 6.7% services, 27.8% sales, 0.2% farming, 0.9% construction, 2.0% production (2000).
Income: Per capita income: $59,473 (2007); Median household income: $99,907 (2007); Average household income: $148,003 (2007); Percent of households with income of $100,000 or more: 50.0% (2007); Poverty rate: 8.3% (2000).

Education: Percent of population age 25 and over with: High school diploma (including GED) or higher: 95.0% (2007); Bachelor's degree or higher: 65.4% (2007); Master's degree or higher: 31.5% (2007).

School District(s)

Dade County School District (PK-12)

    2005-06 Enrollment: 368,933 . . . . (305) 995-1430

Housing: Homeownership rate: 70.3% (2007); Median home value: $885,644 (2007); Median rent: $1,609 per month (2000); Median age of housing: 25 years (2000).

Safety: Violent crime rate: 5.8 per 10,000 population; Property crime rate: 275.9 per 10,000 population (2006).

Newspapers: The Islander News (General - Circulation 3,800)

Transportation: Commute to work: 85.2% car, 1.7% public transportation, 2.0% walk, 9.4% work from home (2000); Travel time to work: 23.4% less than 15 minutes, 45.6% 15 to 30 minutes, 21.8% 30 to 45 minutes, 4.8% 45 to 60 minutes, 4.4% 60 minutes or more (2000)

Additional Information Contacts

Key Biscayne Chamber of Commerce . . . . (305) 361-5207
    http://www.keybiscaynechamber.org

Village of Key Biscayne . . . . (305) 365-5511
    http://vkb.key-biscayne.fl.us

LAKE LUCERNE (CDP). Covers a land area of 2.615 square miles and a water area of 0.014 square miles. Located at 25.96° N. Lat.; 80.25° W. Long. Elevation is 3 feet.

Population: 9,478 (1990); 9,132 (2000); 10,351 (2007); 11,252 (2012 projected); Race: 10.5% White, 83.6% Black, 0.3% Asian, 14.9% Hispanic of any race (2007); Density: 3,958.5 persons per square mile (2007); Average household size: 3.46 (2007); Median age: 29.8 (2007); Males per 100 females: 88.8 (2007); Marriage status: 39.7% never married, 43.3% now married, 5.2% widowed, 11.9% divorced (2000); Foreign born: 20.0% (2000); Ancestry (includes multiple ancestries): 66.4% Other groups, 6.2% Jamaican, 5.3% United States or American, 3.1% Haitian, 2.6% Bahamian (2000).

Economy: Employment by occupation: 5.9% management, 13.6% professional, 19.7% services, 30.8% sales, 0.6% farming, 10.2% construction, 19.1% production (2000).

Income: Per capita income: $14,258 (2007); Median household income: $38,372 (2007); Average household income: $47,604 (2007); Percent of households with income of $100,000 or more: 8.6% (2007); Poverty rate: 16.5% (2000).

Education: Percent of population age 25 and over with: High school diploma (including GED) or higher: 63.2% (2007); Bachelor's degree or higher: 8.7% (2007); Master's degree or higher: 1.8% (2007).

Housing: Homeownership rate: 63.9% (2007); Median home value: $176,625 (2007); Median rent: $497 per month (2000); Median age of housing: 30 years (2000).

Transportation: Commute to work: 91.2% car, 6.9% public transportation, 0.4% walk, 0.4% work from home (2000); Travel time to work: 10.2% less than 15 minutes, 33.2% 15 to 30 minutes, 32.9% 30 to 45 minutes, 11.6% 45 to 60 minutes, 12.1% 60 minutes or more (2000)

LAKES BY THE BAY (CDP). Covers a land area of 4.852 square miles and a water area of 0.099 square miles. Located at 25.57° N. Lat.; 80.33° W. Long. Elevation is 3 feet.

Population: 5,615 (1990); 9,055 (2000); 12,732 (2007); 15,240 (2012 projected); Race: 70.9% White, 16.5% Black, 2.7% Asian, 52.4% Hispanic of any race (2007); Density: 2,624.0 persons per square mile (2007); Average household size: 2.81 (2007); Median age: 34.4 (2007); Males per 100 females: 94.8 (2007); Marriage status: 21.6% never married, 62.5% now married, 4.4% widowed, 11.6% divorced (2000); Foreign born: 30.3% (2000); Ancestry (includes multiple ancestries): 54.5% Other groups, 8.0% Irish, 6.4% German, 5.4% United States or American, 4.2% Italian (2000).

Economy: Employment by occupation: 16.8% management, 20.0% professional, 13.2% services, 34.4% sales, 0.1% farming, 7.7% construction, 7.8% production (2000).

Income: Per capita income: $24,324 (2007); Median household income: $57,352 (2007); Average household income: $68,417 (2007); Percent of households with income of $100,000 or more: 19.8% (2007); Poverty rate: 10.1% (2000).

Education: Percent of population age 25 and over with: High school diploma (including GED) or higher: 84.1% (2007); Bachelor's degree or higher: 26.9% (2007); Master's degree or higher: 9.7% (2007).

Housing: Homeownership rate: 64.2% (2007); Median home value: $274,387 (2007); Median rent: $716 per month (2000); Median age of housing: 11 years (2000).

Transportation: Commute to work: 95.3% car, 1.7% public transportation, 0.9% walk, 1.2% work from home (2000); Travel time to work: 14.8% less than 15 minutes, 26.9% 15 to 30 minutes, 26.0% 30 to 45 minutes, 16.9% 45 to 60 minutes, 15.3% 60 minutes or more (2000)

LEISURE CITY (CDP). Covers a land area of 3.413 square miles and a water area of 0.019 square miles. Located at 25.49° N. Lat.; 80.43° W. Long. Elevation is 7 feet.

Population: 19,378 (1990); 22,152 (2000); 27,643 (2007); 31,420 (2012 projected); Race: 65.9% White, 17.6% Black, 0.7% Asian, 68.3% Hispanic of any race (2007); Density: 8,098.7 persons per square mile (2007); Average household size: 3.73 (2007); Median age: 27.9 (2007); Males per 100 females: 100.1 (2007); Marriage status: 32.3% never married, 54.9% now married, 3.8% widowed, 9.0% divorced (2000); Foreign born: 39.4% (2000); Ancestry (includes multiple ancestries): 73.9% Other groups, 5.1% United States or American, 3.5% Haitian, 3.0% Irish, 2.9% German (2000).

Economy: Employment by occupation: 5.7% management, 10.0% professional, 21.4% services, 24.9% sales, 8.2% farming, 16.2% construction, 13.7% production (2000).

Income: Per capita income: $11,126 (2007); Median household income: $33,721 (2007); Average household income: $41,465 (2007); Percent of households with income of $100,000 or more: 4.8% (2007); Poverty rate: 25.0% (2000).

Education: Percent of population age 25 and over with: High school diploma (including GED) or higher: 49.8% (2007); Bachelor's degree or higher: 7.2% (2007); Master's degree or higher: 2.6% (2007).

School District(s)

Dade County School District (PK-12)

    2005-06 Enrollment: 368,933 . . . . (305) 995-1430

Housing: Homeownership rate: 63.8% (2007); Median home value: $182,278 (2007); Median rent: $417 per month (2000); Median age of housing: 23 years (2000).

Transportation: Commute to work: 94.8% car, 2.0% public transportation, 1.2% walk, 0.8% work from home (2000); Travel time to work: 19.8% less than 15 minutes, 34.0% 15 to 30 minutes, 22.3% 30 to 45 minutes, 11.0% 45 to 60 minutes, 12.9% 60 minutes or more (2000)

MEDLEY (town). Covers a land area of 3.778 square miles and a water area of 0.520 square miles. Located at 25.85° N. Lat.; 80.33° W. Long. Elevation is 7 feet.

Population: 663 (1990); 1,098 (2000); 1,048 (2007); 1,041 (2012 projected); Race: 78.8% White, 8.2% Black, 3.1% Asian, 74.5% Hispanic of any race (2007); Density: 277.4 persons per square mile (2007); Average household size: 3.01 (2007); Median age: 41.7 (2007); Males per 100 females: 96.6 (2007); Marriage status: 20.4% never married, 56.1% now married, 5.4% widowed, 18.2% divorced (2000); Foreign born: 62.1% (2000); Ancestry (includes multiple ancestries): 72.4% Other groups, 4.4% United States or American, 2.4% Irish, 1.1% German, 0.7% Italian (2000).

Economy: Single-family building permits issued: 6 (2006); Multi-family building permits issued: 0 (2006); Employment by occupation: 4.5% management, 7.0% professional, 34.1% services, 14.2% sales, 0.6% farming, 21.8% construction, 17.9% production (2000).

Income: Per capita income: $15,508 (2007); Median household income: $27,857 (2007); Average household income: $42,866 (2007); Percent of households with income of $100,000 or more: 5.7% (2007); Poverty rate: 20.0% (2000).

Education: Percent of population age 25 and over with: High school diploma (including GED) or higher: 50.3% (2007); Bachelor's degree or higher: 8.4% (2007); Master's degree or higher: 5.1% (2007).

Housing: Homeownership rate: 68.4% (2007); Median home value: $67,222 (2007); Median rent: $550 per month (2000); Median age of housing: 20 years (2000).

Safety: Violent crime rate: 167.1 per 10,000 population; Property crime rate: 3,509.7 per 10,000 population (2006).

Transportation: Commute to work: 89.0% car, 2.0% public transportation, 7.1% walk, 0.0% work from home (2000); Travel time to work: 24.6% less than 15 minutes, 48.4% 15 to 30 minutes, 14.7% 30 to 45 minutes, 7.9% 45 to 60 minutes, 4.2% 60 minutes or more (2000)

MIAMI (city). County seat. Covers a land area of 35.673 square miles and a water area of 19.593 square miles. Located at 25.78° N. Lat.; 80.22° W. Long. Elevation is 7 feet.

History: Miami owes its beginning to Julia S. Tuttle, who purchased property on both sides of the Miami River about 1870, and to Henry Flagler, who joined with her in 1896 to create a resort town and attact tourists and vacationers. Many people came for the game fishing. The first land boom occurred in the mid-1920's, when Florida real estate became prized across America, and skyrocketed in cost.

Population: 358,843 (1990); 362,470 (2000); 398,228 (2007); 426,446 (2012 projected); Race: 68.7% White, 19.7% Black, 0.7% Asian, 67.8% Hispanic of any race (2007); Density: 11,163.3 persons per square mile (2007); Average household size: 2.69 (2007); Median age: 40.0 (2007); Males per 100 females: 99.2 (2007); Marriage status: 32.2% never married, 46.7% now married, 8.3% widowed, 12.8% divorced (2000); Foreign born: 59.5% (2000); Ancestry (includes multiple ancestries): 71.3% Other groups, 5.0% Haitian, 3.1% United States or American, 1.4% Italian, 1.2% German (2000).

Economy: Unemployment rate: 4.0% (11/2007); Total civilian labor force: 173,413 (11/2007); Single-family building permits issued: 133 (2006); Multi-family building permits issued: 7,348 (2006); Employment by occupation: 10.4% management, 13.4% professional, 22.1% services, 26.2% sales, 0.5% farming, 13.6% construction, 13.8% production (2000).

Income: Per capita income: $17,720 (2007); Median household income: $27,277 (2007); Average household income: $46,332 (2007); Percent of households with income of $100,000 or more: 9.6% (2007); Poverty rate: 28.5% (2000).

Taxes: Total city taxes per capita: $841 (2005); City property taxes per capita: $489 (2005).

Education: Percent of population age 25 and over with: High school diploma (including GED) or higher: 53.3% (2007); Bachelor's degree or higher: 16.7% (2007); Master's degree or higher: 8.0% (2007).

School District(s)
Dade County School District (PK-12)
   2005-06 Enrollment: 368,933 . . . . (305) 995-1430

Four-year College(s)
Acupuncture and Massage College (Private, For-profit)
   Fall 2006 Enrollment: 206 . . . . (305) 595-9500
   2006-07 Tuition: In-state $12,000; Out-of-state $12,000
Ai Miami International University of Art and Design (Private, For-profit)
   Fall 2006 Enrollment: 2,550. . . . . (305) 428-5700
   2006-07 Tuition: In-state $25,280; Out-of-state $25,280
Barry University (Private, Not-for-profit, Roman Catholic)
   Fall 2006 Enrollment: 8,882. . . . . (800) 756-6000
   2006-07 Tuition: In-state $24,000; Out-of-state $24,000
Carlos Albizu University-Miami Campus (Private, Not-for-profit)
   Fall 2006 Enrollment: 1,079. . . . . (305) 593-1223
   2006-07 Tuition: In-state $11,109; Out-of-state $11,109
City College (Private, Not-for-profit)
   Fall 2006 Enrollment: 269 . . . . (305) 666-9242
   2006-07 Tuition: In-state $9,840; Out-of-state $9,840
Florida College of Natural Health (Private, For-profit)
   Fall 2006 Enrollment: 204 . . . . (305) 597-9599
Florida International University (Public)
   Fall 2006 Enrollment: 37,997. . . . . (305) 348-2000
   2006-07 Tuition: In-state $3,130; Out-of-state $15,528
ITT Technical Institute-Miami (Private, For-profit)
   Fall 2006 Enrollment: 557 . . . . (305) 477-3080
   2006-07 Tuition: In-state $14,880; Out-of-state $14,880
Jones College-Miami Campus (Private, Not-for-profit)
   Fall 2006 Enrollment: 94 . . . . (305) 275-9996
   2006-07 Tuition: In-state $6,690; Out-of-state $6,690
Miami Dade College (Public)
   Fall 2006 Enrollment: 51,329. . . . . (305) 237-8888
   2006-07 Tuition: In-state $1,655; Out-of-state $5,490
Saint John Vianney College Seminary (Private, Not-for-profit, Roman Catholic)
   Fall 2006 Enrollment: 56 . . . . (305) 223-4561
   2006-07 Tuition: In-state $17,000; Out-of-state $17,000

Two-year College(s)
ATI Career Training Center (Private, For-profit)
   Fall 2006 Enrollment: 805 . . . . (305) 591-3060
   2006-07 Tuition: In-state $11,703; Out-of-state $11,703
ATI College of Health (Private, For-profit)
   Fall 2006 Enrollment: 966 . . . . (305) 628-1000
   2006-07 Tuition: In-state $32,000; Out-of-state $32,000

Brown Mackie College-Miami (Private, For-profit)
   Fall 2006 Enrollment: 368 . . . . (305) 341-6600
   2006-07 Tuition: In-state $11,472; Out-of-state $11,472
College of Business and Technology (Private, For-profit)
   Fall 2006 Enrollment: 93 . . . . (305) 273-4499
   2006-07 Tuition: In-state $10,224; Out-of-state $10,224
College of Business and Technology-Flagler Campus (Private, For-profit)
   Fall 2006 Enrollment: 158 . . . . (305) 273-4499
   2006-07 Tuition: In-state $10,224; Out-of-state $10,224
Dade Medical Institute (Private, For-profit)
   Fall 2006 Enrollment: 98 . . . . (305) 644-1171
Florida Career College (Private, For-profit)
   Fall 2006 Enrollment: 3,666. . . . . (305) 553-6065
   2006-07 Tuition: In-state $13,320; Out-of-state $13,320
George T Baker Aviation School (Public)
   Fall 2006 Enrollment: 444 . . . . (305) 871-3143
   2006-07 Tuition: In-state $1,800; Out-of-state $1,800
Lindsey Hopkins Technical Education Center (Public)
   Fall 2006 Enrollment: 1,011. . . . . (305) 324-6070
Medvance Institute-Miami (Private, For-profit)
   Fall 2006 Enrollment: 164 . . . . (305) 596-5553
National School of Technology Inc (Private, For-profit)
   Fall 2006 Enrollment: 825 . . . . (305) 949-9500
National School of Technology Inc (Private, For-profit)
   Fall 2006 Enrollment: 466 . . . . (305) 893-0005
Professional Training Centers (Private, For-profit)
   Fall 2006 Enrollment: 424 . . . . (305) 220-4120
Robert Morgan Educational Center (Public)
   Fall 2006 Enrollment: 1,477. . . . . (305) 253-9920
   2006-07 Tuition: In-state $2,333; Out-of-state $9,292

Vocational/Technical School(s)
Advanced Technical Centers (Private, Not-for-profit)
   Fall 2006 Enrollment: n/a. . . . . (305) 871-2820
   2006-07 Tuition: $3,250
Beauty Schools of America (Private, For-profit)
   Fall 2006 Enrollment: 571 . . . . (305) 267-6604
   2006-07 Tuition: $9,939
Florida Education Institute (Private, For-profit)
   Fall 2006 Enrollment: 203 . . . . (305) 263-9990
   2006-07 Tuition: $6,625
International Training Careers (Private, Not-for-profit)
   Fall 2006 Enrollment: 309 . . . . (305) 263-9696
   2006-07 Tuition: $8,720
La Belle Beauty Academy (Private, For-profit)
   Fall 2006 Enrollment: 276 . . . . (305) 649-2800
   2006-07 Tuition: $8,495
Mercy Hospital School of Practical Nursing (Private, Not-for-profit, Roman Catholic)
   Fall 2006 Enrollment: 91 . . . . (305) 285-2777
   2006-07 Tuition: $5,190
Miami-Dade County Public Schools-The English Center (Public)
   Fall 2006 Enrollment: 498 . . . . (305) 445-7731
   2006-07 Tuition: $1,731
New Concept Massage and Beauty School (Private, For-profit)
   Fall 2006 Enrollment: 20 . . . . (305) 642-3020
   2006-07 Tuition: $7,500
New Professions Technical Institute (Private, For-profit)
   Fall 2006 Enrollment: 418 . . . . (305) 461-2223
   2006-07 Tuition: $4,040
Nouvelle Institute (Private, For-profit)
   Fall 2006 Enrollment: 401 . . . . (305) 643-3360
   2006-07 Tuition: $6,287
Praxis Institute (Private, For-profit)
   Fall 2006 Enrollment: 285 . . . . (305) 642-4104
   2006-07 Tuition: $5,400
South Florida Institute of Technology (Private, For-profit)
   Fall 2006 Enrollment: 295 . . . . (305) 649-2050
   2006-07 Tuition: $4,350
Technical Career Institute (Private, For-profit)
   Fall 2006 Enrollment: 693 . . . . (305) 261-5511
   2006-07 Tuition: In-state $8,700; Out-of-state $8,700

Housing: Homeownership rate: 35.0% (2007); Median home value: $267,085 (2007); Median rent: $473 per month (2000); Median age of housing: 37 years (2000).

Coral Gables Hospital (273 beds); HealthSouth Doctors' Hospital (285 beds); Hialeah Hospital (378 beds); Jackson Memorial Hospital (1498 beds); Jackson South Community Hospital (205 beds); Kendall Medical Center (412 beds); Mercy Health Systems (483 beds); Miami Childrens Hospital (268 beds); Miami Heart Institute and Medical Center (278 beds); Miami Jewish Home & Hospital for the Aged @ Douglas Gardens (494 beds); Miami Veterans Affairs Medical Center (415 beds); Mount Sinai Medical Center (701 beds); North Shore Medical Center (357 beds); Palm Springs General Hospital (247 beds); Pan American Hospital (146 beds); South Miami Hospital (336 beds); University of Miami Hospital & Clinics (40 beds); University of Miami, Bascom Palmer Eye Institute (100 beds); Villa Maria Rehabilitation Hospital (272 beds); Westchester General Hospital (160 beds)

Safety: Violent crime rate: 150.9 per 10,000 population; Property crime rate: 516.3 per 10,000 population (2006).

Newspapers: Catalyst (General - Circulation 3,000); Diario las Americas (Circulation 69,100); El Especial (Hispanic, Senior Citizen - Circulation 35,000); El Nuevo Herald (Circulation 90,264); El Nuevo Patria (Hispanic - Circulation 28,000); El Popular (General, Hispanic - Circulation 50,000); Falcon Times (General - Circulation 2,000); Florida Newspaper (General - Circulation 20,000); Florida Review Newspaper (General - Circulation 32,000); Miami Daily Business Review (Circulation 10,000); Miami New Times (Alternative, General - Circulation 105,000); Prensa Grafica (Hispanic - Circulation 31,000); River Cities Gazette (General - Circulation 12,000); Sabor Magazine (Hispanic - Circulation 28,000); The Miami Herald (Circulation 306,943); The Miami Times (Black - Circulation 28,170); The Weekly News - TWN (Gay/Lesbian - Circulation 22,500)

Transportation: Commute to work: 80.8% car, 11.4% public transportation, 3.7% walk, 2.1% work from home (2000); Travel time to work: 20.0% less than 15 minutes, 38.9% 15 to 30 minutes, 24.8% 30 to 45 minutes, 6.6% 45 to 60 minutes, 9.6% 60 minutes or more (2000); Amtrak: Service available.

Airports: Dade-Collier Training and Transition; Kendall-Tamiami Executive; Miami (commercial service); Miami International (primary service/large hub); Opa Locka (primary service/large hub)

Additional Information Contacts

Allapattah Chamber of Commerce	(305) 638-0280
Argentine Florida Chamber	(305) 357-8047
http://www.argentinaflorida.org	
Aventura Chamber of Commerce	(305) 935-2131
http://www.aventura.org	
Brazilian-American Chamber	(954) 965-1184
http://www.brazilchamber.org	
British American Chamber of Commerce	(305) 377-0992
http://www.baccsouthflorida.org	
Coconut Grove Chamber of Commerce	(305) 446-9900
http://www.coconutgrove.com	
Doral-Airport West Chamber	(305) 244-1641
http://www.dawcc.org	
Ecuadorian-American Chamber	(305) 539-0010
http://www.ecuachamber.com	
Florida Gold Coast Chamber	(305) 866-6020
http://www.flgoldcc.org	
Greater Miami Chamber of Commerce	(305) 350-7700
http://www.greatermiami.com	
Greater Miami Convention & Visitors Bureau	(305) 539-3000
http://www.gmcvb.com	
Italy America Chamber of Commerce	(305) 577-9868
http://www.iacc-miami.com	
Korean American Chamber of Commerce	(305) 468-1718
http://www.abicc.org/kaccmiami	
Latin Chamber of Commerce	(305) 674-1414
http://www.miamibeach.org	
Nicaraguan-American Chamber of Commerce	(305) 994-2460
http://www.naccflorida.com	
North Dade Chamber of Commerce	(305) 690-9123
http://www.thechamber.cc	
Peruvian U.S. Chamber of Commerce	(305) 349-5000
http://www.peruvianchamber.org	
United States-Mexico Chamber of Commerce	(305) 379-6090
http://www.usmcoc.org	
Women's Chamber of Commerce	(305) 446-6660
http://www.womenschamberofcommerce.org	

MIAMI BEACH (city). Covers a land area of 7.033 square miles and a water area of 11.675 square miles. Located at 25.81° N. Lat.; 80.13° W. Long. Elevation is 3 feet.

History: Named for the Mayaimi Indian tribe. Miami Beach was made suitable for settlement by John S. Collins, a New Jersey horticulturist who first planted an avocado grove here. Collins dredged a canal, and organized the Miami Beach Improvement Company. A bridge across the bay to Miami was completed in 1913, and in 1915 Miami Beach was incorporated as a city.

Population: 92,639 (1990); 87,933 (2000); 88,233 (2007); 89,932 (2012 projected); Race: 87.6% White, 3.3% Black, 1.4% Asian, 56.7% Hispanic of any race (2007); Density: 12,544.7 persons per square mile (2007); Average household size: 1.93 (2007); Median age: 42.6 (2007); Males per 100 females: 105.1 (2007); Marriage status: 35.4% never married, 41.8% now married, 8.8% widowed, 14.0% divorced (2000); Foreign born: 55.5% (2000); Ancestry (includes multiple ancestries): 54.1% Other groups, 5.0% Italian, 5.0% United States or American, 4.3% German, 3.7% Russian (2000).

Economy: Unemployment rate: 2.8% (11/2007); Total civilian labor force: 50,354 (11/2007); Single-family building permits issued: 23 (2006); Multi-family building permits issued: 285 (2006); Employment by occupation: 17.7% management, 22.5% professional, 21.1% services, 26.9% sales, 0.2% farming, 4.8% construction, 6.8% production (2000).

Income: Per capita income: $33,734 (2007); Median household income: $35,994 (2007); Average household income: $64,446 (2007); Percent of households with income of $100,000 or more: 16.1% (2007); Poverty rate: 21.8% (2000).

Taxes: Total city taxes per capita: $1,911 (2005); City property taxes per capita: $1,078 (2005).

Education: Percent of population age 25 and over with: High school diploma (including GED) or higher: 78.8% (2007); Bachelor's degree or higher: 33.5% (2007); Master's degree or higher: 15.8% (2007).

School District(s)

Dade County School District (PK-12)
    2005-06 Enrollment: 368,933 . . . . (305) 995-1430

Four-year College(s)

Miami Ad School (Private, For-profit)
    Fall 2006 Enrollment: 176 . . . . (305) 538-3193
    2006-07 Tuition: In-state $14,300; Out-of-state $14,300
Talmudic College of Florida (Private, Not-for-profit, Jewish)
    Fall 2006 Enrollment: 44 . . . . (305) 534-7050
    2006-07 Tuition: In-state $7,500; Out-of-state $7,500
Yeshivah Gedolah Rabbinical College (Private, Not-for-profit, Jewish)
    Fall 2006 Enrollment: 46 . . . . (305) 653-8770
    2006-07 Tuition: In-state $8,000; Out-of-state $8,000

Housing: Homeownership rate: 36.7% (2007); Median home value: $324,455 (2007); Median rent: $581 per month (2000); Median age of housing: 37 years (2000).

Safety: Violent crime rate: 124.7 per 10,000 population; Property crime rate: 848.0 per 10,000 population (2006).

Transportation: Commute to work: 67.7% car, 11.4% public transportation, 10.3% walk, 5.4% work from home (2000); Travel time to work: 27.5% less than 15 minutes, 37.3% 15 to 30 minutes, 22.5% 30 to 45 minutes, 6.0% 45 to 60 minutes, 6.8% 60 minutes or more (2000)

Additional Information Contacts

City of Miami Beach	(305) 673-7411
http://web.miamibeachfl.gov	
Miami Beach Chamber of Commerce	(305) 672-1270
http://www.miamibeachchamber.com	
Miami International Chamber	(305) 861-2000
South Beach Hispanic Chamber	(305) 534-1903
http://sobechamber.tripod.com	

MIAMI LAKES (CDP). Covers a land area of 5.957 square miles and a water area of 0.431 square miles. Located at 25.91° N. Lat.; 80.32° W. Long. Elevation is 3 feet.

Population: 14,033 (1990); 22,676 (2000); 24,636 (2007); 26,227 (2012 projected); Race: 89.5% White, 2.8% Black, 1.9% Asian, 75.2% Hispanic of any race (2007); Density: 4,135.4 persons per square mile (2007); Average household size: 2.92 (2007); Median age: 37.8 (2007); Males per 100 females: 92.8 (2007); Marriage status: 22.6% never married, 60.9% now married, 5.5% widowed, 10.9% divorced (2000); Foreign born: 47.6% (2000); Ancestry (includes multiple ancestries): 73.7% Other groups, 4.3% Irish, 3.8% United States or American, 3.8% German, 3.5% Italian (2000).

Economy: Single-family building permits issued: 65 (2006); Multi-family building permits issued: 0 (2006); Employment by occupation: 21.2% management, 21.1% professional, 7.7% services, 37.4% sales, 0.2% farming, 3.8% construction, 8.4% production (2000).
Income: Per capita income: $31,853 (2007); Median household income: $70,902 (2007); Average household income: $92,547 (2007); Percent of households with income of $100,000 or more: 30.5% (2007); Poverty rate: 4.9% (2000).
Education: Percent of population age 25 and over with: High school diploma (including GED) or higher: 84.4% (2007); Bachelor's degree or higher: 35.0% (2007); Master's degree or higher: 14.7% (2007).

School District(s)
Dade County School District (PK-12)
    2005-06 Enrollment: 368,933 . . . . (305) 995-1430
Two-year College(s)
Miami Lakes Educational Center (Public)
    Fall 2006 Enrollment: 1,597. . . . . (305) 557-1100
    2006-07 Tuition: In-state $1,993; Out-of-state $7,933
Housing: Homeownership rate: 75.3% (2007); Median home value: $346,645 (2007); Median rent: $806 per month (2000); Median age of housing: 17 years (2000).
Safety: Violent crime rate: 35.7 per 10,000 population; Property crime rate: 404.5 per 10,000 population (2006).
Newspapers: Miami Laker (General - Circulation 27,000)
Transportation: Commute to work: 94.6% car, 1.1% public transportation, 0.2% walk, 3.7% work from home (2000); Travel time to work: 21.1% less than 15 minutes, 29.8% 15 to 30 minutes, 26.3% 30 to 45 minutes, 15.5% 45 to 60 minutes, 7.3% 60 minutes or more (2000)

MIAMI SHORES (village). Covers a land area of 2.455 square miles and a water area of 1.274 square miles. Located at 25.86° N. Lat.; 80.18° W. Long. Elevation is 7 feet.

History: Separated from Miami in 1932. Barry University is here.
Population: 9,891 (1990); 10,380 (2000); 10,140 (2007); 10,077 (2012 projected); Race: 63.3% White, 24.3% Black, 2.7% Asian, 27.3% Hispanic of any race (2007); Density: 4,129.9 persons per square mile (2007); Average household size: 2.94 (2007); Median age: 39.3 (2007); Males per 100 females: 95.2 (2007); Marriage status: 27.4% never married, 54.8% now married, 6.3% widowed, 11.5% divorced (2000); Foreign born: 27.7% (2000); Ancestry (includes multiple ancestries): 35.7% Other groups, 11.8% Irish, 9.3% Haitian, 9.2% German, 8.0% Italian (2000).
Economy: Single-family building permits issued: 0 (2006); Multi-family building permits issued: 0 (2006); Employment by occupation: 20.9% management, 28.8% professional, 15.3% services, 23.4% sales, 0.3% farming, 5.8% construction, 5.6% production (2000).
Income: Per capita income: $30,203 (2007); Median household income: $69,037 (2007); Average household income: $87,867 (2007); Percent of households with income of $100,000 or more: 31.1% (2007); Poverty rate: 8.8% (2000).
Education: Percent of population age 25 and over with: High school diploma (including GED) or higher: 88.3% (2007); Bachelor's degree or higher: 42.3% (2007); Master's degree or higher: 17.9% (2007).

School District(s)
Dade County School District (PK-12)
    2005-06 Enrollment: 368,933 . . . . (305) 995-1430
Housing: Homeownership rate: 89.5% (2007); Median home value: $371,286 (2007); Median rent: $679 per month (2000); Median age of housing: 47 years (2000).
Safety: Violent crime rate: 61.7 per 10,000 population; Property crime rate: 624.0 per 10,000 population (2006).
Transportation: Commute to work: 89.7% car, 2.9% public transportation, 1.9% walk, 4.8% work from home (2000); Travel time to work: 19.6% less than 15 minutes, 44.2% 15 to 30 minutes, 26.0% 30 to 45 minutes, 4.8% 45 to 60 minutes, 5.4% 60 minutes or more (2000)
Additional Information Contacts
Greater Miami Shores Chamber . . . . (305) 754-5466
    http://www.miamishores.com
Miami-Dade Chamber of Commerce . . . . (305) 751-8648
    http://www.m-dcc.org
Village of Miami Shores . . . . (305) 795-2207
    http://www.miamishoresvillage.com

MIAMI SPRINGS (city). Covers a land area of 2.938 square miles and a water area of 0.041 square miles. Located at 25.82° N. Lat.; 80.29° W. Long. Elevation is 3 feet.

History: Named for the Mayaimi Indian tribe. Incorporated 1926.
Population: 13,268 (1990); 13,712 (2000); 12,949 (2007); 12,684 (2012 projected); Race: 91.0% White, 2.0% Black, 0.9% Asian, 68.6% Hispanic of any race (2007); Density: 4,407.1 persons per square mile (2007); Average household size: 2.77 (2007); Median age: 41.8 (2007); Males per 100 females: 92.6 (2007); Marriage status: 23.5% never married, 54.4% now married, 9.2% widowed, 12.9% divorced (2000); Foreign born: 43.6% (2000); Ancestry (includes multiple ancestries): 65.7% Other groups, 7.0% German, 6.3% Irish, 5.8% English, 4.3% United States or American (2000).
Economy: Single-family building permits issued: 5 (2006); Multi-family building permits issued: 0 (2006); Employment by occupation: 16.2% management, 18.5% professional, 11.1% services, 33.1% sales, 0.1% farming, 10.5% construction, 10.5% production (2000).
Income: Per capita income: $28,287 (2007); Median household income: $60,925 (2007); Average household income: $77,740 (2007); Percent of households with income of $100,000 or more: 23.4% (2007); Poverty rate: 9.7% (2000).
Education: Percent of population age 25 and over with: High school diploma (including GED) or higher: 82.4% (2007); Bachelor's degree or higher: 26.7% (2007); Master's degree or higher: 10.5% (2007).

School District(s)
Dade County School District (PK-12)
    2005-06 Enrollment: 368,933 . . . . (305) 995-1430
Housing: Homeownership rate: 64.6% (2007); Median home value: $347,260 (2007); Median rent: $547 per month (2000); Median age of housing: 44 years (2000).
Safety: Violent crime rate: 32.1 per 10,000 population; Property crime rate: 332.3 per 10,000 population (2006).
Transportation: Commute to work: 92.2% car, 1.9% public transportation, 1.2% walk, 3.8% work from home (2000); Travel time to work: 28.6% less than 15 minutes, 43.1% 15 to 30 minutes, 20.5% 30 to 45 minutes, 4.0% 45 to 60 minutes, 3.9% 60 minutes or more (2000)
Additional Information Contacts
City of Miami Springs . . . . (305) 805-5000
    http://www.miamisprings-fl.gov

NARANJA (CDP). Covers a land area of 1.520 square miles and a water area of 0.148 square miles. Located at 25.51° N. Lat.; 80.42° W. Long. Elevation is 7 feet.

History: Virtually destroyed by Hurricane Andrew in 1992.
Population: 5,790 (1990); 4,034 (2000); 5,725 (2007); 6,913 (2012 projected); Race: 37.1% White, 52.4% Black, 1.0% Asian, 36.0% Hispanic of any race (2007); Density: 3,767.4 persons per square mile (2007); Average household size: 3.50 (2007); Median age: 24.9 (2007); Males per 100 females: 92.3 (2007); Marriage status: 42.2% never married, 40.5% now married, 5.6% widowed, 11.7% divorced (2000); Foreign born: 23.3% (2000); Ancestry (includes multiple ancestries): 71.4% Other groups, 4.0% Haitian, 3.5% Jamaican, 2.5% United States or American, 2.5% Trinidadian and Tobagonian (2000).
Economy: Employment by occupation: 8.6% management, 7.9% professional, 31.3% services, 33.1% sales, 0.8% farming, 11.4% construction, 7.0% production (2000).
Income: Per capita income: $7,603 (2007); Median household income: $19,741 (2007); Average household income: $24,786 (2007); Percent of households with income of $100,000 or more: 1.3% (2007); Poverty rate: 50.5% (2000).
Education: Percent of population age 25 and over with: High school diploma (including GED) or higher: 53.4% (2007); Bachelor's degree or higher: 5.2% (2007); Master's degree or higher: 1.9% (2007).

School District(s)
Dade County School District (PK-12)
    2005-06 Enrollment: 368,933 . . . . (305) 995-1430
Housing: Homeownership rate: 32.8% (2007); Median home value: $132,877 (2007); Median rent: $430 per month (2000); Median age of housing: 21 years (2000).
Transportation: Commute to work: 79.5% car, 15.0% public transportation, 3.2% walk, 1.0% work from home (2000); Travel time to work: 17.7% less than 15 minutes, 29.7% 15 to 30 minutes, 25.4% 30 to 45 minutes, 13.1% 45 to 60 minutes, 14.0% 60 minutes or more (2000)

NORLAND (CDP). Covers a land area of 3.610 square miles and a water area of 0.040 square miles. Located at 25.94° N. Lat.; 80.21° W. Long. Elevation is 7 feet.

Population: 22,084 (1990); 22,995 (2000); 22,854 (2007); 23,118 (2012 projected); Race: 11.4% White, 80.7% Black, 1.0% Asian, 9.5% Hispanic of

any race (2007); Density: 6,330.3 persons per square mile (2007); Average household size: 3.40 (2007); Median age: 31.7 (2007); Males per 100 females: 86.0 (2007); Marriage status: 36.3% never married, 46.3% now married, 5.9% widowed, 11.5% divorced (2000); Foreign born: 39.2% (2000); Ancestry (includes multiple ancestries): 42.2% Other groups, 21.1% Jamaican, 12.1% Haitian, 3.8% United States or American, 2.2% Bahamian (2000).
Economy: Employment by occupation: 7.9% management, 15.0% professional, 26.2% services, 28.5% sales, 0.3% farming, 10.3% construction, 11.9% production (2000).
Income: Per capita income: $14,196 (2007); Median household income: $38,655 (2007); Average household income: $47,226 (2007); Percent of households with income of $100,000 or more: 6.5% (2007); Poverty rate: 16.0% (2000).
Education: Percent of population age 25 and over with: High school diploma (including GED) or higher: 69.5% (2007); Bachelor's degree or higher: 12.4% (2007); Master's degree or higher: 4.2% (2007).
Housing: Homeownership rate: 65.5% (2007); Median home value: $189,686 (2007); Median rent: $546 per month (2000); Median age of housing: 36 years (2000).
Transportation: Commute to work: 88.1% car, 7.9% public transportation, 2.0% walk, 1.6% work from home (2000); Travel time to work: 14.4% less than 15 minutes, 32.8% 15 to 30 minutes, 31.9% 30 to 45 minutes, 11.0% 45 to 60 minutes, 9.9% 60 minutes or more (2000)

NORTH BAY VILLAGE (city). Covers a land area of 0.332 square miles and a water area of 0.505 square miles. Located at 25.84° N. Lat.; 80.15° W. Long. Elevation is 7 feet.
Population: 5,383 (1990); 6,733 (2000); 8,267 (2007); 9,325 (2012 projected); Race: 78.7% White, 5.2% Black, 3.7% Asian, 57.1% Hispanic of any race (2007); Density: 24,884.6 persons per square mile (2007); Average household size: 2.21 (2007); Median age: 39.0 (2007); Males per 100 females: 100.8 (2007); Marriage status: 31.9% never married, 48.6% now married, 5.1% widowed, 14.4% divorced (2000); Foreign born: 54.1% (2000); Ancestry (includes multiple ancestries): 52.5% Other groups, 6.7% Italian, 6.2% Brazilian, 5.0% United States or American, 4.7% German (2000).
Economy: Single-family building permits issued: 1 (2006); Multi-family building permits issued: 52 (2006); Employment by occupation: 13.5% management, 20.1% professional, 19.3% services, 31.6% sales, 0.0% farming, 5.7% construction, 9.7% production (2000).
Income: Per capita income: $24,173 (2007); Median household income: $39,526 (2007); Average household income: $53,056 (2007); Percent of households with income of $100,000 or more: 11.0% (2007); Poverty rate: 12.9% (2000).
Education: Percent of population age 25 and over with: High school diploma (including GED) or higher: 86.5% (2007); Bachelor's degree or higher: 29.3% (2007); Master's degree or higher: 11.9% (2007).
School District(s)
Dade County School District (PK-12)
    2005-06 Enrollment: 368,933 . . . . (305) 995-1430
Housing: Homeownership rate: 29.1% (2007); Median home value: $237,336 (2007); Median rent: $776 per month (2000); Median age of housing: 34 years (2000).
Safety: Violent crime rate: 20.7 per 10,000 population; Property crime rate: 249.3 per 10,000 population (2006).
Transportation: Commute to work: 88.6% car, 5.2% public transportation, 2.7% walk, 2.9% work from home (2000); Travel time to work: 12.9% less than 15 minutes, 40.9% 15 to 30 minutes, 35.3% 30 to 45 minutes, 5.5% 45 to 60 minutes, 5.3% 60 minutes or more (2000)
Additional Information Contacts
City of North Bay Village . . . . (305) 756-7171
    http://www.nbvillage.com

NORTH MIAMI (city). Covers a land area of 8.458 square miles and a water area of 1.531 square miles. Located at 25.89° N. Lat.; 80.18° W. Long. Elevation is 7 feet.
History: Named for its location north of Miami. Substantial retail development since the 1980s. Incorporated 1926.
Population: 50,721 (1990); 59,880 (2000); 57,614 (2007); 56,907 (2012 projected); Race: 31.1% White, 57.9% Black, 1.7% Asian, 23.6% Hispanic of any race (2007); Density: 6,812.0 persons per square mile (2007); Average household size: 3.01 (2007); Median age: 33.5 (2007); Males per 100 females: 92.8 (2007); Marriage status: 37.2% never married, 47.1% now married, 6.3% widowed, 9.4% divorced (2000); Foreign born: 48.5%

(2000); Ancestry (includes multiple ancestries): 34.2% Other groups, 31.1% Haitian, 5.5% United States or American, 3.1% Jamaican, 2.4% German (2000).
Economy: Unemployment rate: 4.0% (11/2007); Total civilian labor force: 28,363 (11/2007); Single-family building permits issued: 3 (2006); Multi-family building permits issued: 3 (2006); Employment by occupation: 9.2% management, 15.0% professional, 25.0% services, 28.5% sales, 0.0% farming, 8.4% construction, 13.8% production (2000).
Income: Per capita income: $15,361 (2007); Median household income: $31,860 (2007); Average household income: $45,494 (2007); Percent of households with income of $100,000 or more: 7.8% (2007); Poverty rate: 23.9% (2000).
Taxes: Total city taxes per capita: $405 (2005); City property taxes per capita: $244 (2005).
Education: Percent of population age 25 and over with: High school diploma (including GED) or higher: 66.9% (2007); Bachelor's degree or higher: 15.8% (2007); Master's degree or higher: 6.8% (2007).
School District(s)
Dade County School District (PK-12)
    2005-06 Enrollment: 368,933 . . . . (305) 995-1430
Four-year College(s)
Johnson & Wales University-Florida Campus (Private, Not-for-profit)
    Fall 2006 Enrollment: 2,215. . . . . (305) 892-7000
    2006-07 Tuition: In-state $20,826; Out-of-state $20,826
Housing: Homeownership rate: 50.5% (2007); Median home value: $186,207 (2007); Median rent: $547 per month (2000); Median age of housing: 35 years (2000).
Safety: Violent crime rate: 111.2 per 10,000 population; Property crime rate: 623.1 per 10,000 population (2006).
Transportation: Commute to work: 83.2% car, 10.6% public transportation, 2.7% walk, 2.0% work from home (2000); Travel time to work: 15.6% less than 15 minutes, 32.9% 15 to 30 minutes, 32.0% 30 to 45 minutes, 10.3% 45 to 60 minutes, 9.1% 60 minutes or more (2000)
Additional Information Contacts
City of North Miami . . . . (305) 893-6511
    http://www.northmiamifl.gov
Greater North Miami Chamber. . . . . (305) 891-7811
    http://www.northmiamichamber.com

NORTH MIAMI BEACH (city). Covers a land area of 4.955 square miles and a water area of 0.335 square miles. Located at 25.93° N. Lat.; 80.17° W. Long. Elevation is 10 feet.
History: Named for its location north of Miami Beach. North Miami Beach was first known as Fulford, for an early settler. The town changed its name in the hope of becoming more closely associated with Miami Beach. The North Miami Zoo was established here.
Population: 34,812 (1990); 40,786 (2000); 39,548 (2007); 39,235 (2012 projected); Race: 43.7% White, 40.9% Black, 3.9% Asian, 33.8% Hispanic of any race (2007); Density: 7,980.8 persons per square mile (2007); Average household size: 2.99 (2007); Median age: 36.2 (2007); Males per 100 females: 92.2 (2007); Marriage status: 31.6% never married, 49.9% now married, 7.2% widowed, 11.3% divorced (2000); Foreign born: 49.7% (2000); Ancestry (includes multiple ancestries): 43.2% Other groups, 19.3% Haitian, 6.0% United States or American, 5.4% Jamaican, 3.0% Italian (2000).
Economy: Unemployment rate: 4.2% (11/2007); Total civilian labor force: 19,456 (11/2007); Single-family building permits issued: 84 (2006); Multi-family building permits issued: 0 (2006); Employment by occupation: 9.0% management, 13.0% professional, 22.6% services, 32.1% sales, 0.1% farming, 10.2% construction, 13.0% production (2000).
Income: Per capita income: $15,677 (2007); Median household income: $34,619 (2007); Average household income: $46,489 (2007); Percent of households with income of $100,000 or more: 7.3% (2007); Poverty rate: 20.5% (2000).
Education: Percent of population age 25 and over with: High school diploma (including GED) or higher: 68.6% (2007); Bachelor's degree or higher: 14.3% (2007); Master's degree or higher: 5.9% (2007).
School District(s)
Dade County School District (PK-12)
    2005-06 Enrollment: 368,933 . . . . (305) 995-1430
Housing: Homeownership rate: 61.7% (2007); Median home value: $193,064 (2007); Median rent: $573 per month (2000); Median age of housing: 36 years (2000).
Hospitals: Parkway Regional Medical Center (382 beds)

rate: 552.5 per 10,000 population (2006).
Transportation: Commute to work: 86.6% car, 9.5% public transportation, 1.3% walk, 1.6% work from home (2000); Travel time to work: 18.3% less than 15 minutes, 32.1% 15 to 30 minutes, 28.5% 30 to 45 minutes, 11.1% 45 to 60 minutes, 10.0% 60 minutes or more (2000)
Additional Information Contacts
City of North Miami Beach . . . . (305) 947-7581
   http://ci.north-miami-beach.fl.us
North Miami Beach Chamber of Commerce . . . . (305) 653-1200
   http://www.nmbchamber.com

OJUS (CDP).

Covers a land area of 2.786 square miles and a water area of 0.491 square miles. Located at 25.95° N. Lat.; 80.15° W. Long. Elevation is 10 feet.
History: Named for the Indian translation of "plentiful," referring to the vegetation in the area. Ojus began as a trading post.
Population: 15,141 (1990); 16,642 (2000); 16,907 (2007); 17,291 (2012 projected); Race: 81.4% White, 8.8% Black, 2.0% Asian, 41.4% Hispanic of any race (2007); Density: 6,068.3 persons per square mile (2007); Average household size: 2.31 (2007); Median age: 44.8 (2007); Males per 100 females: 86.4 (2007); Marriage status: 21.3% never married, 56.2% now married, 11.0% widowed, 11.6% divorced (2000); Foreign born: 41.6% (2000); Ancestry (includes multiple ancestries): 40.5% Other groups, 7.5% Russian, 7.0% United States or American, 5.0% Polish, 4.8% Italian (2000).
Economy: Employment by occupation: 18.1% management, 20.9% professional, 16.9% services, 32.4% sales, 0.0% farming, 5.4% construction, 6.3% production (2000).
Income: Per capita income: $27,195 (2007); Median household income: $37,418 (2007); Average household income: $62,103 (2007); Percent of households with income of $100,000 or more: 16.3% (2007); Poverty rate: 13.5% (2000).
Education: Percent of population age 25 and over with: High school diploma (including GED) or higher: 80.6% (2007); Bachelor's degree or higher: 29.7% (2007); Master's degree or higher: 15.0% (2007).
Housing: Homeownership rate: 84.7% (2007); Median home value: $130,363 (2007); Median rent: $569 per month (2000); Median age of housing: 32 years (2000).
Transportation: Commute to work: 90.4% car, 3.1% public transportation, 2.1% walk, 4.3% work from home (2000); Travel time to work: 22.0% less than 15 minutes, 32.2% 15 to 30 minutes, 26.9% 30 to 45 minutes, 11.9% 45 to 60 minutes, 7.1% 60 minutes or more (2000)

OLYMPIA HEIGHTS (CDP).

Covers a land area of 2.722 square miles and a water area of 0.291 square miles. Located at 25.72° N. Lat.; 80.34° W. Long. Elevation is 7 feet.
Population: 13,268 (1990); 13,452 (2000); 13,204 (2007); 13,263 (2012 projected); Race: 93.8% White, 1.0% Black, 0.7% Asian, 80.0% Hispanic of any race (2007); Density: 4,850.4 persons per square mile (2007); Average household size: 3.27 (2007); Median age: 43.9 (2007); Males per 100 females: 92.3 (2007); Marriage status: 21.4% never married, 59.4% now married, 7.8% widowed, 11.4% divorced (2000); Foreign born: 58.7% (2000); Ancestry (includes multiple ancestries): 75.9% Other groups, 3.6% Irish, 2.9% United States or American, 2.7% German, 2.6% English (2000).
Economy: Employment by occupation: 11.2% management, 16.1% professional, 14.9% services, 33.1% sales, 0.0% farming, 11.9% construction, 12.7% production (2000).
Income: Per capita income: $21,590 (2007); Median household income: $58,425 (2007); Average household income: $69,088 (2007); Percent of households with income of $100,000 or more: 20.2% (2007); Poverty rate: 6.9% (2000).
Education: Percent of population age 25 and over with: High school diploma (including GED) or higher: 69.0% (2007); Bachelor's degree or higher: 20.8% (2007); Master's degree or higher: 9.0% (2007).
Housing: Homeownership rate: 86.5% (2007); Median home value: $328,957 (2007); Median rent: $809 per month (2000); Median age of housing: 42 years (2000).
Transportation: Commute to work: 94.9% car, 1.7% public transportation, 0.7% walk, 1.9% work from home (2000); Travel time to work: 15.9% less than 15 minutes, 34.6% 15 to 30 minutes, 31.0% 30 to 45 minutes, 11.1% 45 to 60 minutes, 7.5% 60 minutes or more (2000)

OPA-LOCKA (city).

Covers a land area of 4.331 square miles and a water area of 0.143 square miles. Located at 25.90° N. Lat.; 80.25° W. Long. Elevation is 7 feet.
Population: 15,283 (1990); 14,951 (2000); 15,800 (2007); 16,681 (2012 projected); Race: 25.8% White, 66.4% Black, 0.2% Asian, 31.7% Hispanic of any race (2007); Density: 3,647.9 persons per square mile (2007); Average household size: 3.06 (2007); Median age: 27.3 (2007); Males per 100 females: 85.9 (2007); Marriage status: 43.8% never married, 38.1% now married, 4.8% widowed, 13.2% divorced (2000); Foreign born: 23.6% (2000); Ancestry (includes multiple ancestries): 68.8% Other groups, 3.0% United States or American, 2.6% Jamaican, 2.4% Haitian, 1.3% African (2000).
Economy: Single-family building permits issued: 38 (2006); Multi-family building permits issued: 37 (2006); Employment by occupation: 6.4% management, 9.1% professional, 21.2% services, 30.0% sales, 2.6% farming, 11.8% construction, 18.9% production (2000).
Income: Per capita income: $10,395 (2007); Median household income: $20,670 (2007); Average household income: $30,649 (2007); Percent of households with income of $100,000 or more: 3.8% (2007); Poverty rate: 35.2% (2000).
Education: Percent of population age 25 and over with: High school diploma (including GED) or higher: 52.4% (2007); Bachelor's degree or higher: 5.4% (2007); Master's degree or higher: 2.4% (2007).
School District(s)
Dade County School District (PK-12)
   2005-06 Enrollment: 368,933 . . . . (305) 995-1430
Housing: Homeownership rate: 34.5% (2007); Median home value: $148,879 (2007); Median rent: $395 per month (2000); Median age of housing: 35 years (2000).
Safety: Violent crime rate: 266.4 per 10,000 population; Property crime rate: 993.2 per 10,000 population (2006).
Newspapers: Lion's Tale (General - Circulation 2,000)
Transportation: Commute to work: 84.4% car, 10.2% public transportation, 3.3% walk, 0.5% work from home (2000); Travel time to work: 16.6% less than 15 minutes, 33.0% 15 to 30 minutes, 30.1% 30 to 45 minutes, 12.1% 45 to 60 minutes, 8.3% 60 minutes or more (2000)
Additional Information Contacts
City of Opa-locka . . . . (305) 688-4611
   http://www.opalockafl.gov

OPA-LOCKA NORTH (CDP).

Covers a land area of 2.174 square miles and a water area of 0.114 square miles. Located at 25.92° N. Lat.; 80.26° W. Long.
Population: 6,568 (1990); 6,224 (2000); 6,764 (2007); 7,214 (2012 projected); Race: 24.7% White, 69.5% Black, 0.6% Asian, 24.9% Hispanic of any race (2007); Density: 3,111.7 persons per square mile (2007); Average household size: 4.06 (2007); Median age: 25.9 (2007); Males per 100 females: 90.0 (2007); Marriage status: 38.5% never married, 44.7% now married, 4.7% widowed, 12.0% divorced (2000); Foreign born: 24.5% (2000); Ancestry (includes multiple ancestries): 65.6% Other groups, 6.4% Jamaican, 3.3% United States or American, 2.7% Haitian, 2.1% African (2000).
Economy: Employment by occupation: 4.3% management, 16.6% professional, 22.5% services, 31.2% sales, 0.0% farming, 9.1% construction, 16.3% production (2000).
Income: Per capita income: $11,992 (2007); Median household income: $39,043 (2007); Average household income: $46,389 (2007); Percent of households with income of $100,000 or more: 6.8% (2007); Poverty rate: 19.9% (2000).
Education: Percent of population age 25 and over with: High school diploma (including GED) or higher: 62.1% (2007); Bachelor's degree or higher: 7.5% (2007); Master's degree or higher: 3.0% (2007).
Housing: Homeownership rate: 66.7% (2007); Median home value: $170,152 (2007); Median rent: $588 per month (2000); Median age of housing: 38 years (2000).
Transportation: Commute to work: 82.3% car, 6.9% public transportation, 7.4% walk, 2.4% work from home (2000); Travel time to work: 17.8% less than 15 minutes, 29.4% 15 to 30 minutes, 29.5% 30 to 45 minutes, 8.9% 45 to 60 minutes, 14.4% 60 minutes or more (2000)

PALM SPRINGS NORTH (CDP).

Covers a land area of 0.692 square miles and a water area of 0.098 square miles. Located at 25.93° N. Lat.; 80.33° W. Long. Elevation is 3 feet.

Population: 5,300 (1990); 5,460 (2000); 5,029 (2007); 4,795 (2012 projected); Race: 92.4% White, 0.7% Black, 0.5% Asian, 72.9% Hispanic of any race (2007); Density: 7,262.8 persons per square mile (2007); Average household size: 3.37 (2007); Median age: 38.1 (2007); Males per 100 females: 95.3 (2007); Marriage status: 22.1% never married, 64.9% now married, 4.7% widowed, 8.3% divorced (2000); Foreign born: 36.6% (2000); Ancestry (includes multiple ancestries): 69.0% Other groups, 8.0% Irish, 6.0% United States or American, 4.8% English, 4.2% German (2000).
Economy: Employment by occupation: 10.9% management, 14.3% professional, 11.1% services, 38.8% sales, 0.0% farming, 14.0% construction, 10.9% production (2000).
Income: Per capita income: $24,597 (2007); Median household income: $73,567 (2007); Average household income: $81,994 (2007); Percent of households with income of $100,000 or more: 28.0% (2007); Poverty rate: 4.4% (2000).
Education: Percent of population age 25 and over with: High school diploma (including GED) or higher: 69.1% (2007); Bachelor's degree or higher: 15.7% (2007); Master's degree or higher: 5.4% (2007).
Housing: Homeownership rate: 93.2% (2007); Median home value: $312,360 (2007); Median rent: $951 per month (2000); Median age of housing: 34 years (2000).
Transportation: Commute to work: 95.1% car, 1.5% public transportation, 1.0% walk, 1.2% work from home (2000); Travel time to work: 13.8% less than 15 minutes, 30.0% 15 to 30 minutes, 33.0% 30 to 45 minutes, 13.8% 45 to 60 minutes, 9.5% 60 minutes or more (2000)

PALMETTO ESTATES (CDP). Covers a land area of 2.124 square miles and a water area of 0.024 square miles. Located at 25.62° N. Lat.; 80.36° W. Long. Elevation is 10 feet.
Population: 12,293 (1990); 13,675 (2000); 13,964 (2007); 14,383 (2012 projected); Race: 38.4% White, 47.1% Black, 2.6% Asian, 34.7% Hispanic of any race (2007); Density: 6,573.4 persons per square mile (2007); Average household size: 3.47 (2007); Median age: 33.7 (2007); Males per 100 females: 92.5 (2007); Marriage status: 31.5% never married, 53.2% now married, 5.2% widowed, 10.2% divorced (2000); Foreign born: 41.2% (2000); Ancestry (includes multiple ancestries): 52.5% Other groups, 17.3% Jamaican, 4.1% United States or American, 3.4% Haitian, 3.2% German (2000).
Economy: Employment by occupation: 10.2% management, 19.7% professional, 18.9% services, 32.8% sales, 0.0% farming, 10.7% construction, 7.7% production (2000).
Income: Per capita income: $18,657 (2007); Median household income: $54,326 (2007); Average household income: $64,076 (2007); Percent of households with income of $100,000 or more: 14.9% (2007); Poverty rate: 10.9% (2000).
Education: Percent of population age 25 and over with: High school diploma (including GED) or higher: 81.5% (2007); Bachelor's degree or higher: 20.2% (2007); Master's degree or higher: 8.5% (2007).
Housing: Homeownership rate: 83.5% (2007); Median home value: $229,672 (2007); Median rent: $655 per month (2000); Median age of housing: 27 years (2000).
Transportation: Commute to work: 93.2% car, 4.1% public transportation, 0.7% walk, 1.2% work from home (2000); Travel time to work: 15.7% less than 15 minutes, 34.4% 15 to 30 minutes, 21.1% 30 to 45 minutes, 12.8% 45 to 60 minutes, 16.0% 60 minutes or more (2000)

PINECREST (village). Covers a land area of 7.538 square miles and a water area of 0.013 square miles. Located at 25.66° N. Lat.; 80.30° W. Long. Elevation is 3 feet.
Population: 17,810 (1990); 19,055 (2000); 19,568 (2007); 20,225 (2012 projected); Race: 90.1% White, 1.6% Black, 4.9% Asian, 35.1% Hispanic of any race (2007); Density: 2,595.9 persons per square mile (2007); Average household size: 3.14 (2007); Median age: 39.3 (2007); Males per 100 females: 92.9 (2007); Marriage status: 21.5% never married, 67.3% now married, 4.7% widowed, 6.6% divorced (2000); Foreign born: 27.6% (2000); Ancestry (includes multiple ancestries): 41.7% Other groups, 9.9% English, 8.6% German, 6.9% Russian, 6.7% Irish (2000).
Economy: Single-family building permits issued: 61 (2006); Multi-family building permits issued: 0 (2006); Employment by occupation: 25.3% management, 34.7% professional, 7.5% services, 27.7% sales, 0.1% farming, 2.1% construction, 2.6% production (2000).
Income: Per capita income: $55,858 (2007); Median household income: $126,800 (2007); Average household income: $174,731 (2007); Percent of households with income of $100,000 or more: 59.7% (2007); Poverty rate: 4.1% (2000).

Education: Percent of population age 25 and over with: High school diploma (including GED) or higher: 94.1% (2007); Bachelor's degree or higher: 61.3% (2007); Master's degree or higher: 31.3% (2007).
Housing: Homeownership rate: 82.2% (2007); Median home value: $885,326 (2007); Median rent: $696 per month (2000); Median age of housing: 35 years (2000).
Safety: Violent crime rate: 15.9 per 10,000 population; Property crime rate: 319.0 per 10,000 population (2006).
Transportation: Commute to work: 86.7% car, 3.9% public transportation, 0.8% walk, 7.4% work from home (2000); Travel time to work: 20.6% less than 15 minutes, 27.3% 15 to 30 minutes, 32.2% 30 to 45 minutes, 12.6% 45 to 60 minutes, 7.3% 60 minutes or more (2000)
Additional Information Contacts
Village of Pinecrest . . . . (305) 234-2121
  http://ci.pinecrest.fl.us

PINEWOOD (CDP). Covers a land area of 1.717 square miles and a water area of 0.177 square miles. Located at 25.87° N. Lat.; 80.21° W. Long. Elevation is 7 feet.
Population: 15,518 (1990); 16,523 (2000); 16,830 (2007); 17,171 (2012 projected); Race: 20.9% White, 67.4% Black, 0.3% Asian, 25.8% Hispanic of any race (2007); Density: 9,800.2 persons per square mile (2007); Average household size: 3.34 (2007); Median age: 30.8 (2007); Males per 100 females: 92.7 (2007); Marriage status: 40.2% never married, 44.9% now married, 6.6% widowed, 8.4% divorced (2000); Foreign born: 38.1% (2000); Ancestry (includes multiple ancestries): 47.6% Other groups, 25.7% Haitian, 5.5% United States or American, 3.4% Jamaican, 1.8% Bahamian (2000).
Economy: Employment by occupation: 5.1% management, 10.2% professional, 30.2% services, 26.2% sales, 0.0% farming, 9.1% construction, 19.3% production (2000).
Income: Per capita income: $10,193 (2007); Median household income: $25,374 (2007); Average household income: $33,648 (2007); Percent of households with income of $100,000 or more: 2.8% (2007); Poverty rate: 33.5% (2000).
Education: Percent of population age 25 and over with: High school diploma (including GED) or higher: 49.8% (2007); Bachelor's degree or higher: 5.8% (2007); Master's degree or higher: 1.3% (2007).
Housing: Homeownership rate: 47.9% (2007); Median home value: $163,531 (2007); Median rent: $482 per month (2000); Median age of housing: 36 years (2000).
Transportation: Commute to work: 86.4% car, 11.8% public transportation, 0.5% walk, 0.5% work from home (2000); Travel time to work: 10.2% less than 15 minutes, 39.8% 15 to 30 minutes, 30.4% 30 to 45 minutes, 8.5% 45 to 60 minutes, 11.1% 60 minutes or more (2000)

PRINCETON (CDP). Covers a land area of 7.347 square miles and a water area of 0.004 square miles. Located at 25.53° N. Lat.; 80.39° W. Long. Elevation is 10 feet.
History: Princeton was known as Modello until 1905, when a sawmill was established by several Princeton graduates who renamed the town for their university.
Population: 7,073 (1990); 10,090 (2000); 14,361 (2007); 17,260 (2012 projected); Race: 53.5% White, 31.9% Black, 0.9% Asian, 54.3% Hispanic of any race (2007); Density: 1,954.6 persons per square mile (2007); Average household size: 3.80 (2007); Median age: 28.0 (2007); Males per 100 females: 96.1 (2007); Marriage status: 33.3% never married, 55.2% now married, 5.4% widowed, 6.2% divorced (2000); Foreign born: 28.5% (2000); Ancestry (includes multiple ancestries): 73.9% Other groups, 3.7% German, 2.8% United States or American, 2.7% Irish, 2.7% Italian (2000).
Economy: Employment by occupation: 11.0% management, 14.4% professional, 18.8% services, 27.8% sales, 2.9% farming, 13.9% construction, 11.1% production (2000).
Income: Per capita income: $14,007 (2007); Median household income: $45,554 (2007); Average household income: $52,478 (2007); Percent of households with income of $100,000 or more: 9.4% (2007); Poverty rate: 23.8% (2000).
Education: Percent of population age 25 and over with: High school diploma (including GED) or higher: 68.1% (2007); Bachelor's degree or higher: 11.9% (2007); Master's degree or higher: 3.7% (2007).
Housing: Homeownership rate: 69.0% (2007); Median home value: $194,078 (2007); Median rent: $480 per month (2000); Median age of housing: 14 years (2000).
Transportation: Commute to work: 95.0% car, 1.8% public transportation, 0.5% walk, 1.8% work from home (2000); Travel time to work: 18.1% less

RICHMOND HEIGHTS (CDP).
Covers a land area of 1.655 square miles and a water area of 0 square miles. Located at 25.63° N. Lat.; 80.37° W. Long. Elevation is 10 feet.

Population: 8,583 (1990); 8,479 (2000); 8,058 (2007); 7,893 (2012 projected); Race: 14.0% White, 80.1% Black, 0.8% Asian, 15.9% Hispanic of any race (2007); Density: 4,869.9 persons per square mile (2007); Average household size: 3.16 (2007); Median age: 35.5 (2007); Males per 100 females: 84.7 (2007); Marriage status: 30.7% never married, 49.9% now married, 8.7% widowed, 10.7% divorced (2000); Foreign born: 12.8% (2000); Ancestry (includes multiple ancestries): 81.8% Other groups, 2.8% Jamaican, 2.7% United States or American, 1.5% African, 1.2% Bahamian (2000).

Economy: Employment by occupation: 7.5% management, 19.9% professional, 22.4% services, 30.6% sales, 0.2% farming, 7.2% construction, 12.3% production (2000).

Income: Per capita income: $18,227 (2007); Median household income: $44,087 (2007); Average household income: $56,558 (2007); Percent of households with income of $100,000 or more: 13.7% (2007); Poverty rate: 15.1% (2000).

Education: Percent of population age 25 and over with: High school diploma (including GED) or higher: 72.8% (2007); Bachelor's degree or higher: 15.3% (2007); Master's degree or higher: 5.3% (2007).

Housing: Homeownership rate: 83.4% (2007); Median home value: $179,585 (2007); Median rent: $537 per month (2000); Median age of housing: 33 years (2000).

Transportation: Commute to work: 89.3% car, 7.0% public transportation, 2.0% walk, 0.7% work from home (2000); Travel time to work: 17.2% less than 15 minutes, 31.9% 15 to 30 minutes, 24.3% 30 to 45 minutes, 12.7% 45 to 60 minutes, 13.9% 60 minutes or more (2000)

RICHMOND WEST (CDP).
Covers a land area of 4.179 square miles and a water area of 0.088 square miles. Located at 25.61° N. Lat.; 80.42° W. Long. Elevation is 7 feet.

Population: 6,224 (1990); 28,082 (2000); 36,786 (2007); 42,751 (2012 projected); Race: 77.4% White, 7.7% Black, 1.9% Asian, 77.2% Hispanic of any race (2007); Density: 8,803.5 persons per square mile (2007); Average household size: 3.69 (2007); Median age: 31.8 (2007); Males per 100 females: 95.6 (2007); Marriage status: 20.5% never married, 68.0% now married, 3.0% widowed, 8.4% divorced (2000); Foreign born: 45.6% (2000); Ancestry (includes multiple ancestries): 79.4% Other groups, 5.4% United States or American, 3.4% Jamaican, 2.7% Italian, 2.2% Irish (2000).

Economy: Employment by occupation: 15.1% management, 16.7% professional, 14.5% services, 36.7% sales, 0.4% farming, 8.7% construction, 7.9% production (2000).

Income: Per capita income: $21,097 (2007); Median household income: $67,679 (2007); Average household income: $77,904 (2007); Percent of households with income of $100,000 or more: 22.0% (2007); Poverty rate: 5.6% (2000).

Education: Percent of population age 25 and over with: High school diploma (including GED) or higher: 83.0% (2007); Bachelor's degree or higher: 22.5% (2007); Master's degree or higher: 7.7% (2007).

Housing: Homeownership rate: 93.8% (2007); Median home value: $270,039 (2007); Median rent: $929 per month (2000); Median age of housing: 4 years (2000).

Transportation: Commute to work: 95.8% car, 1.1% public transportation, 0.2% walk, 2.3% work from home (2000); Travel time to work: 8.5% less than 15 minutes, 22.8% 15 to 30 minutes, 27.6% 30 to 45 minutes, 17.4% 45 to 60 minutes, 23.7% 60 minutes or more (2000)

SCOTT LAKE (CDP).
Covers a land area of 3.289 square miles and a water area of 0.059 square miles. Located at 25.93° N. Lat.; 80.23° W. Long. Elevation is 7 feet.

Population: 14,588 (1990); 14,401 (2000); 14,054 (2007); 14,013 (2012 projected); Race: 4.7% White, 90.6% Black, 0.4% Asian, 5.9% Hispanic of any race (2007); Density: 4,272.8 persons per square mile (2007); Average household size: 3.53 (2007); Median age: 32.6 (2007); Males per 100 females: 87.2 (2007); Marriage status: 36.0% never married, 47.2% now married, 5.8% widowed, 11.0% divorced (2000); Foreign born: 24.1% (2000); Ancestry (includes multiple ancestries): 59.8% Other groups, 13.0% Jamaican, 5.5% Haitian, 2.2% United States or American, 1.5% Bahamian (2000).

Income: Per capita income: $17,627 (2007); Median household income: $53,665 (2007); Average household income: $61,639 (2007); Percent of households with income of $100,000 or more: 15.5% (2007); Poverty rate: 16.4% (2000).

Education: Percent of population age 25 and over with: High school diploma (including GED) or higher: 75.7% (2007); Bachelor's degree or higher: 16.9% (2007); Master's degree or higher: 5.6% (2007).

Housing: Homeownership rate: 87.3% (2007); Median home value: $195,122 (2007); Median rent: $714 per month (2000); Median age of housing: 35 years (2000).

Transportation: Commute to work: 91.4% car, 6.0% public transportation, 0.5% walk, 1.2% work from home (2000); Travel time to work: 13.5% less than 15 minutes, 34.3% 15 to 30 minutes, 31.3% 30 to 45 minutes, 11.9% 45 to 60 minutes, 9.0% 60 minutes or more (2000)

SOUTH MIAMI (city).
Covers a land area of 2.295 square miles and a water area of <.001 square miles. Located at 25.71° N. Lat.; 80.29° W. Long. Elevation is 10 feet.

History: Named for its location south of Miami. South Miami was first called Larkins for a man who operated a store here in the early days of the town. South Miami developed around a tomato packing plant and as a shipping center for citrus fruit and truck crops.

Population: 10,438 (1990); 10,741 (2000); 11,316 (2007); 11,858 (2012 projected); Race: 72.4% White, 22.0% Black, 1.1% Asian, 40.4% Hispanic of any race (2007); Density: 4,931.1 persons per square mile (2007); Average household size: 2.52 (2007); Median age: 39.7 (2007); Males per 100 females: 93.4 (2007); Marriage status: 31.5% never married, 46.8% now married, 6.1% widowed, 15.6% divorced (2000); Foreign born: 30.3% (2000); Ancestry (includes multiple ancestries): 54.9% Other groups, 6.5% Irish, 6.1% German, 5.9% English, 4.5% United States or American (2000).

Economy: Single-family building permits issued: 19 (2006); Multi-family building permits issued: 0 (2006); Employment by occupation: 15.0% management, 27.8% professional, 12.4% services, 34.5% sales, 0.0% farming, 4.3% construction, 5.9% production (2000).

Income: Per capita income: $28,263 (2007); Median household income: $48,459 (2007); Average household income: $70,829 (2007); Percent of households with income of $100,000 or more: 23.6% (2007); Poverty rate: 17.1% (2000).

Education: Percent of population age 25 and over with: High school diploma (including GED) or higher: 81.1% (2007); Bachelor's degree or higher: 37.7% (2007); Master's degree or higher: 18.3% (2007).

School District(s)
Dade County School District (PK-12)
   2005-06 Enrollment: 368,933 . . . . (305) 995-1430

Housing: Homeownership rate: 61.4% (2007); Median home value: $375,647 (2007); Median rent: $609 per month (2000); Median age of housing: 40 years (2000).

Hospitals: Larkin Community Hospital (112 beds)

Safety: Violent crime rate: 86.5 per 10,000 population; Property crime rate: 678.4 per 10,000 population (2006).

Newspapers: Aventura News (General - Circulation 25,000); Coral Gables News (General - Circulation 15,000); Doral Tribune (General - Circulation 10,000); Kendall Gazette (General - Circulation 18,000); Pinecrest Tribune (General - Circulation 15,000); South Miami News (General - Circulation 7,500); Sunny Isles Beach Sun (General - Circulation 6,000)

Transportation: Commute to work: 84.6% car, 6.8% public transportation, 2.9% walk, 4.3% work from home (2000); Travel time to work: 23.0% less than 15 minutes, 33.1% 15 to 30 minutes, 27.5% 30 to 45 minutes, 7.8% 45 to 60 minutes, 8.7% 60 minutes or more (2000)

Additional Information Contacts
City of South Miami . . . . (305) 663-6338
   http://www.cityofsouthmiami.net
South Miami Chamber of Commerce . . . . (305) 275-0091
   http://chambersouth.com

SOUTH MIAMI HEIGHTS (CDP).
Covers a land area of 4.929 square miles and a water area of 0.004 square miles. Located at 25.58° N. Lat.; 80.38° W. Long. Elevation is 10 feet.

Population: 30,030 (1990); 33,522 (2000); 35,794 (2007); 37,792 (2012 projected); Race: 57.1% White, 27.7% Black, 1.7% Asian, 61.4% Hispanic of any race (2007); Density: 7,261.3 persons per square mile (2007); Average household size: 3.44 (2007); Median age: 32.8 (2007); Males per

100 females: 93.4 (2007); Marriage status: 30.8% never married, 51.2% now married, 6.2% widowed, 11.8% divorced (2000); Foreign born: 44.1% (2000); Ancestry (includes multiple ancestries): 71.3% Other groups, 5.7% Jamaican, 4.4% United States or American, 1.7% English, 1.6% German (2000).
Economy: Employment by occupation: 8.5% management, 9.8% professional, 22.6% services, 30.8% sales, 0.6% farming, 14.2% construction, 13.5% production (2000).
Income: Per capita income: $13,962 (2007); Median household income: $39,642 (2007); Average household income: $47,781 (2007); Percent of households with income of $100,000 or more: 8.7% (2007); Poverty rate: 17.2% (2000).
Education: Percent of population age 25 and over with: High school diploma (including GED) or higher: 61.3% (2007); Bachelor's degree or higher: 9.1% (2007); Master's degree or higher: 3.4% (2007).
Housing: Homeownership rate: 62.5% (2007); Median home value: $197,553 (2007); Median rent: $518 per month (2000); Median age of housing: 25 years (2000).
Transportation: Commute to work: 91.0% car, 3.9% public transportation, 1.8% walk, 1.7% work from home (2000); Travel time to work: 17.3% less than 15 minutes, 31.4% 15 to 30 minutes, 23.5% 30 to 45 minutes, 12.8% 45 to 60 minutes, 14.9% 60 minutes or more (2000)

SUNNY ISLES BEACH (city). Covers a land area of 1.006 square miles and a water area of 0.401 square miles. Located at 25.94° N. Lat.; 80.12° W. Long. Elevation is 3 feet.

Population: 11,740 (1990); 15,315 (2000); 16,665 (2007); 17,804 (2012 projected); Race: 90.5% White, 2.4% Black, 1.6% Asian, 46.5% Hispanic of any race (2007); Density: 16,573.7 persons per square mile (2007); Average household size: 1.93 (2007); Median age: 52.2 (2007); Males per 100 females: 87.4 (2007); Marriage status: 19.7% never married, 51.3% now married, 15.7% widowed, 13.3% divorced (2000); Foreign born: 56.8% (2000); Ancestry (includes multiple ancestries): 41.7% Other groups, 9.5% Russian, 5.9% Italian, 5.0% Polish, 4.9% United States or American (2000).
Economy: Single-family building permits issued: 1 (2006); Multi-family building permits issued: 1,349 (2006); Employment by occupation: 20.8% management, 19.0% professional, 11.7% services, 37.5% sales, 0.5% farming, 5.0% construction, 5.5% production (2000).
Income: Per capita income: $30,985 (2007); Median household income: $36,763 (2007); Average household income: $59,556 (2007); Percent of households with income of $100,000 or more: 13.0% (2007); Poverty rate: 14.7% (2000).
Taxes: Total city taxes per capita: $975 (2005); City property taxes per capita: $519 (2005).
Education: Percent of population age 25 and over with: High school diploma (including GED) or higher: 79.1% (2007); Bachelor's degree or higher: 28.4% (2007); Master's degree or higher: 12.5% (2007).
Housing: Homeownership rate: 59.0% (2007); Median home value: $263,363 (2007); Median rent: $833 per month (2000); Median age of housing: 25 years (2000).
Safety: Violent crime rate: 22.3 per 10,000 population; Property crime rate: 332.2 per 10,000 population (2006).
Transportation: Commute to work: 86.1% car, 3.8% public transportation, 3.5% walk, 4.5% work from home (2000); Travel time to work: 13.5% less than 15 minutes, 29.0% 15 to 30 minutes, 29.0% 30 to 45 minutes, 16.4% 45 to 60 minutes, 12.1% 60 minutes or more (2000)
Additional Information Contacts
City of Sunny Isles Beach . . . . (305) 947-0606
  http://www.sibfl.net

SUNSET (CDP). Covers a land area of 3.558 square miles and a water area of 0.013 square miles. Located at 25.70° N. Lat.; 80.35° W. Long. Elevation is 7 feet.

Population: 15,810 (1990); 17,150 (2000); 16,537 (2007); 16,300 (2012 projected); Race: 92.3% White, 1.2% Black, 2.0% Asian, 74.9% Hispanic of any race (2007); Density: 4,648.3 persons per square mile (2007); Average household size: 3.13 (2007); Median age: 40.2 (2007); Males per 100 females: 91.5 (2007); Marriage status: 25.0% never married, 57.4% now married, 6.8% widowed, 10.8% divorced (2000); Foreign born: 50.7% (2000); Ancestry (includes multiple ancestries): 74.4% Other groups, 4.6% German, 3.8% Italian, 3.5% Irish, 3.4% United States or American (2000).
Economy: Employment by occupation: 19.3% management, 21.9% professional, 13.0% services, 32.8% sales, 0.0% farming, 6.8% construction, 6.1% production (2000).

Income: Per capita income: $28,794 (2007); Median household income: $70,365 (2007); Average household income: $88,214 (2007); Percent of households with income of $100,000 or more: 30.7% (2007); Poverty rate: 7.1% (2000).
Education: Percent of population age 25 and over with: High school diploma (including GED) or higher: 81.6% (2007); Bachelor's degree or higher: 30.6% (2007); Master's degree or higher: 11.1% (2007).
Housing: Homeownership rate: 79.0% (2007); Median home value: $363,371 (2007); Median rent: $696 per month (2000); Median age of housing: 29 years (2000).
Transportation: Commute to work: 92.5% car, 2.0% public transportation, 0.6% walk, 4.2% work from home (2000); Travel time to work: 14.4% less than 15 minutes, 32.6% 15 to 30 minutes, 29.1% 30 to 45 minutes, 11.3% 45 to 60 minutes, 12.5% 60 minutes or more (2000)

SURFSIDE (town). Covers a land area of 0.505 square miles and a water area of 0.460 square miles. Located at 25.87° N. Lat.; 80.12° W. Long. Elevation is 10 feet.

Population: 4,108 (1990); 4,909 (2000); 4,955 (2007); 4,940 (2012 projected); Race: 93.8% White, 1.1% Black, 1.2% Asian, 50.8% Hispanic of any race (2007); Density: 9,812.9 persons per square mile (2007); Average household size: 2.25 (2007); Median age: 47.3 (2007); Males per 100 females: 88.5 (2007); Marriage status: 22.5% never married, 55.9% now married, 8.1% widowed, 13.5% divorced (2000); Foreign born: 50.7% (2000); Ancestry (includes multiple ancestries): 46.4% Other groups, 8.2% German, 6.8% Italian, 6.7% Polish, 6.7% Russian (2000).
Economy: Single-family building permits issued: 0 (2006); Multi-family building permits issued: 0 (2006); Employment by occupation: 23.2% management, 29.1% professional, 9.9% services, 28.4% sales, 0.0% farming, 5.8% construction, 3.6% production (2000).
Income: Per capita income: $43,754 (2007); Median household income: $62,288 (2007); Average household income: $97,922 (2007); Percent of households with income of $100,000 or more: 31.1% (2007); Poverty rate: 11.5% (2000).
Education: Percent of population age 25 and over with: High school diploma (including GED) or higher: 86.8% (2007); Bachelor's degree or higher: 40.8% (2007); Master's degree or higher: 19.7% (2007).
Housing: Homeownership rate: 70.1% (2007); Median home value: $428,485 (2007); Median rent: $613 per month (2000); Median age of housing: 38 years (2000).
Safety: Violent crime rate: 83.5 per 10,000 population; Property crime rate: 258.9 per 10,000 population (2006).
Newspapers: The Tropical Tribune (General - Circulation 30,000)
Transportation: Commute to work: 88.7% car, 2.1% public transportation, 2.5% walk, 5.4% work from home (2000); Travel time to work: 16.3% less than 15 minutes, 32.4% 15 to 30 minutes, 30.1% 30 to 45 minutes, 12.7% 45 to 60 minutes, 8.4% 60 minutes or more (2000)

SWEETWATER (city). Covers a land area of 0.816 square miles and a water area of 0 square miles. Located at 25.76° N. Lat.; 80.37° W. Long. Elevation is 8 feet.

Population: 13,909 (1990); 14,226 (2000); 13,839 (2007); 13,926 (2012 projected); Race: 90.4% White, 0.8% Black, 0.2% Asian, 93.2% Hispanic of any race (2007); Density: 16,965.3 persons per square mile (2007); Average household size: 3.32 (2007); Median age: 38.9 (2007); Males per 100 females: 93.1 (2007); Marriage status: 24.2% never married, 59.6% now married, 6.5% widowed, 9.6% divorced (2000); Foreign born: 74.7% (2000); Ancestry (includes multiple ancestries): 85.0% Other groups, 2.3% United States or American, 0.5% Italian, 0.4% Irish, 0.4% Nigerian (2000).
Economy: Single-family building permits issued: 4 (2006); Multi-family building permits issued: 0 (2006); Employment by occupation: 6.5% management, 10.2% professional, 18.3% services, 36.9% sales, 0.1% farming, 12.5% construction, 15.4% production (2000).
Income: Per capita income: $12,676 (2007); Median household income: $32,284 (2007); Average household income: $42,087 (2007); Percent of households with income of $100,000 or more: 6.9% (2007); Poverty rate: 18.1% (2000).
Education: Percent of population age 25 and over with: High school diploma (including GED) or higher: 52.7% (2007); Bachelor's degree or higher: 12.8% (2007); Master's degree or higher: 6.0% (2007).
Vocational/Technical School(s)
Universal Massage and Beauty Institute (Private, For-profit)
  Fall 2006 Enrollment: 101 . . . . (305) 485-7700
  2006-07 Tuition: $10,600

Housing: Homeownership rate: 49.9% (2007); Median home value: $209,369 (2007); Median rent: $581 per month (2000); Median age of housing: 24 years (2000).
Safety: Violent crime rate: 19.3 per 10,000 population; Property crime rate: 165.3 per 10,000 population (2006).
Transportation: Commute to work: 91.1% car, 5.2% public transportation, 3.0% walk, 0.5% work from home (2000); Travel time to work: 13.0% less than 15 minutes, 39.9% 15 to 30 minutes, 30.3% 30 to 45 minutes, 10.0% 45 to 60 minutes, 6.8% 60 minutes or more (2000)
Additional Information Contacts
City of Sweetwater. . . . . (305) 485-4528
  http://www.cityofsweetwater.fl.gov

TAMIAMI (CDP). Covers a land area of 7.343 square miles and a water area of 0.230 square miles. Located at 25.75° N. Lat.; 80.40° W. Long. Elevation is 3 feet.
Population: 39,068 (1990); 54,788 (2000); 59,567 (2007); 63,487 (2012 projected); Race: 90.4% White, 1.0% Black, 0.6% Asian, 87.9% Hispanic of any race (2007); Density: 8,112.2 persons per square mile (2007); Average household size: 3.38 (2007); Median age: 39.2 (2007); Males per 100 females: 90.9 (2007); Marriage status: 23.3% never married, 60.2% now married, 6.2% widowed, 10.2% divorced (2000); Foreign born: 65.5% (2000); Ancestry (includes multiple ancestries): 88.0% Other groups, 1.9% United States or American, 1.3% Italian, 0.9% Irish, 0.9% German (2000).
Economy: Employment by occupation: 15.7% management, 16.0% professional, 13.2% services, 35.8% sales, 0.2% farming, 8.4% construction, 10.7% production (2000).
Income: Per capita income: $20,111 (2007); Median household income: $54,451 (2007); Average household income: $67,147 (2007); Percent of households with income of $100,000 or more: 18.2% (2007); Poverty rate: 9.4% (2000).
Education: Percent of population age 25 and over with: High school diploma (including GED) or higher: 71.1% (2007); Bachelor's degree or higher: 21.5% (2007); Master's degree or higher: 9.1% (2007).
Housing: Homeownership rate: 84.6% (2007); Median home value: $282,054 (2007); Median rent: $743 per month (2000); Median age of housing: 16 years (2000).
Transportation: Commute to work: 95.9% car, 0.7% public transportation, 0.6% walk, 2.2% work from home (2000); Travel time to work: 10.7% less than 15 minutes, 31.2% 15 to 30 minutes, 32.1% 30 to 45 minutes, 15.3% 45 to 60 minutes, 10.6% 60 minutes or more (2000)

THE CROSSINGS (CDP). Covers a land area of 3.736 square miles and a water area of 0.035 square miles. Located at 25.66° N. Lat.; 80.40° W. Long. Elevation is 7 feet.
Population: 22,290 (1990); 23,557 (2000); 26,784 (2007); 29,193 (2012 projected); Race: 85.6% White, 4.2% Black, 3.0% Asian, 64.7% Hispanic of any race (2007); Density: 7,168.6 persons per square mile (2007); Average household size: 2.90 (2007); Median age: 38.0 (2007); Males per 100 females: 88.4 (2007); Marriage status: 25.7% never married, 56.2% now married, 4.5% widowed, 13.5% divorced (2000); Foreign born: 46.5% (2000); Ancestry (includes multiple ancestries): 67.1% Other groups, 4.8% German, 4.6% Irish, 4.6% Italian, 3.5% United States or American (2000).
Economy: Employment by occupation: 19.8% management, 23.0% professional, 11.4% services, 35.7% sales, 0.2% farming, 5.5% construction, 4.5% production (2000).
Income: Per capita income: $26,441 (2007); Median household income: $60,302 (2007); Average household income: $76,411 (2007); Percent of households with income of $100,000 or more: 24.3% (2007); Poverty rate: 6.5% (2000).
Education: Percent of population age 25 and over with: High school diploma (including GED) or higher: 90.0% (2007); Bachelor's degree or higher: 35.7% (2007); Master's degree or higher: 13.5% (2007).
Housing: Homeownership rate: 80.8% (2007); Median home value: $266,474 (2007); Median rent: $869 per month (2000); Median age of housing: 19 years (2000).
Transportation: Commute to work: 92.8% car, 2.0% public transportation, 0.4% walk, 3.8% work from home (2000); Travel time to work: 14.6% less than 15 minutes, 27.9% 15 to 30 minutes, 24.2% 30 to 45 minutes, 17.5% 45 to 60 minutes, 15.8% 60 minutes or more (2000)

THE HAMMOCKS (CDP). Covers a land area of 7.861 square miles and a water area of 0.172 square miles. Located at 25.67° N. Lat.; 80.43° W. Long. Elevation is 3 feet.

Population: 26,829 (1990); 47,379 (2000); 54,648 (2007); 60,063 (2012 projected); Race: 79.4% White, 5.7% Black, 2.9% Asian, 72.3% Hispanic of any race (2007); Density: 6,952.0 persons per square mile (2007); Average household size: 3.19 (2007); Median age: 33.8 (2007); Males per 100 females: 90.6 (2007); Marriage status: 26.6% never married, 58.4% now married, 4.4% widowed, 10.6% divorced (2000); Foreign born: 52.4% (2000); Ancestry (includes multiple ancestries): 75.5% Other groups, 4.0% Italian, 3.1% United States or American, 3.0% German, 3.0% Jamaican (2000).
Economy: Employment by occupation: 17.6% management, 19.6% professional, 12.4% services, 36.2% sales, 0.0% farming, 6.3% construction, 8.0% production (2000).
Income: Per capita income: $21,784 (2007); Median household income: $58,115 (2007); Average household income: $69,012 (2007); Percent of households with income of $100,000 or more: 18.3% (2007); Poverty rate: 8.6% (2000).
Education: Percent of population age 25 and over with: High school diploma (including GED) or higher: 87.2% (2007); Bachelor's degree or higher: 31.2% (2007); Master's degree or higher: 10.8% (2007).
Housing: Homeownership rate: 63.7% (2007); Median home value: $285,305 (2007); Median rent: $758 per month (2000); Median age of housing: 12 years (2000).
Transportation: Commute to work: 93.4% car, 2.2% public transportation, 0.6% walk, 2.9% work from home (2000); Travel time to work: 12.8% less than 15 minutes, 23.7% 15 to 30 minutes, 27.6% 30 to 45 minutes, 17.5% 45 to 60 minutes, 18.3% 60 minutes or more (2000)

THREE LAKES (CDP). Covers a land area of 3.263 square miles and a water area of 0.543 square miles. Located at 25.63° N. Lat.; 80.39° W. Long. Elevation is 7 feet.
Population: 2,336 (1990); 6,955 (2000); 10,516 (2007); 12,895 (2012 projected); Race: 74.0% White, 13.8% Black, 3.5% Asian, 58.4% Hispanic of any race (2007); Density: 3,222.7 persons per square mile (2007); Average household size: 2.91 (2007); Median age: 33.0 (2007); Males per 100 females: 91.4 (2007); Marriage status: 26.2% never married, 61.1% now married, 3.0% widowed, 9.6% divorced (2000); Foreign born: 37.5% (2000); Ancestry (includes multiple ancestries): 60.0% Other groups, 7.6% German, 7.2% Jamaican, 6.7% Irish, 4.8% Italian (2000).
Economy: Employment by occupation: 17.6% management, 23.9% professional, 12.8% services, 33.6% sales, 0.4% farming, 4.9% construction, 6.7% production (2000).
Income: Per capita income: $26,430 (2007); Median household income: $63,325 (2007); Average household income: $76,953 (2007); Percent of households with income of $100,000 or more: 23.6% (2007); Poverty rate: 8.0% (2000).
Education: Percent of population age 25 and over with: High school diploma (including GED) or higher: 90.6% (2007); Bachelor's degree or higher: 32.2% (2007); Master's degree or higher: 13.6% (2007).
Housing: Homeownership rate: 70.4% (2007); Median home value: $265,030 (2007); Median rent: $863 per month (2000); Median age of housing: 7 years (2000).
Transportation: Commute to work: 92.6% car, 3.3% public transportation, 0.4% walk, 2.9% work from home (2000); Travel time to work: 15.1% less than 15 minutes, 25.2% 15 to 30 minutes, 23.5% 30 to 45 minutes, 19.2% 45 to 60 minutes, 16.9% 60 minutes or more (2000)

UNIVERSITY PARK (CDP). Covers a land area of 4.061 square miles and a water area of 0.039 square miles. Located at 25.74° N. Lat.; 80.36° W. Long. Elevation is 3 feet.
Population: 24,524 (1990); 26,538 (2000); 26,222 (2007); 26,365 (2012 projected); Race: 88.2% White, 4.6% Black, 1.4% Asian, 82.2% Hispanic of any race (2007); Density: 6,457.3 persons per square mile (2007); Average household size: 3.03 (2007); Median age: 40.7 (2007); Males per 100 females: 84.4 (2007); Marriage status: 27.3% never married, 53.5% now married, 8.3% widowed, 10.9% divorced (2000); Foreign born: 66.6% (2000); Ancestry (includes multiple ancestries): 82.8% Other groups, 2.3% Italian, 1.4% United States or American, 1.0% German, 0.9% English (2000).
Economy: Employment by occupation: 14.0% management, 16.9% professional, 15.4% services, 33.7% sales, 0.1% farming, 10.2% construction, 9.6% production (2000).
Income: Per capita income: $20,012 (2007); Median household income: $45,608 (2007); Average household income: $59,891 (2007); Percent of households with income of $100,000 or more: 16.6% (2007); Poverty rate: 14.4% (2000).

diploma (including GED) or higher: 69.5% (2007); Bachelor's degree or higher: 22.8% (2007); Master's degree or higher: 8.6% (2007).
Housing: Homeownership rate: 62.3% (2007); Median home value: $324,010 (2007); Median rent: $600 per month (2000); Median age of housing: 23 years (2000).
Transportation: Commute to work: 91.8% car, 1.8% public transportation, 2.5% walk, 2.4% work from home (2000); Travel time to work: 13.5% less than 15 minutes, 32.1% 15 to 30 minutes, 32.8% 30 to 45 minutes, 14.2% 45 to 60 minutes, 7.4% 60 minutes or more (2000)

VIRGINIA GARDENS (village).
Covers a land area of 0.300 square miles and a water area of 0 square miles. Located at 25.80° N. Lat.; 80.29° W. Long. Elevation is 3 feet.
Population: 2,212 (1990); 2,348 (2000); 2,398 (2007); 2,379 (2012 projected); Race: 84.2% White, 2.4% Black, 1.2% Asian, 75.2% Hispanic of any race (2007); Density: 7,987.1 persons per square mile (2007); Average household size: 2.72 (2007); Median age: 40.0 (2007); Males per 100 females: 97.4 (2007); Marriage status: 20.2% never married, 57.4% now married, 6.9% widowed, 15.5% divorced (2000); Foreign born: 50.3% (2000); Ancestry (includes multiple ancestries): 69.6% Other groups, 6.1% English, 5.9% Italian, 5.6% Irish, 5.6% United States or American (2000).
Economy: Single-family building permits issued: 0 (2006); Multi-family building permits issued: 0 (2006); Employment by occupation: 11.9% management, 14.3% professional, 14.1% services, 35.6% sales, 0.0% farming, 10.8% construction, 13.3% production (2000).
Income: Per capita income: $21,932 (2007); Median household income: $47,579 (2007); Average household income: $58,992 (2007); Percent of households with income of $100,000 or more: 12.9% (2007); Poverty rate: 11.3% (2000).
Education: Percent of population age 25 and over with: High school diploma (including GED) or higher: 77.0% (2007); Bachelor's degree or higher: 22.5% (2007); Master's degree or higher: 7.8% (2007).
Housing: Homeownership rate: 50.5% (2007); Median home value: $286,916 (2007); Median rent: $579 per month (2000); Median age of housing: 41 years (2000).
Safety: Violent crime rate: 13.1 per 10,000 population; Property crime rate: 130.5 per 10,000 population (2006).
Transportation: Commute to work: 90.1% car, 4.9% public transportation, 1.9% walk, 2.3% work from home (2000); Travel time to work: 24.8% less than 15 minutes, 45.0% 15 to 30 minutes, 18.7% 30 to 45 minutes, 4.1% 45 to 60 minutes, 7.4% 60 minutes or more (2000)

WEST LITTLE RIVER (CDP).
Covers a land area of 4.582 square miles and a water area of 0.047 square miles. Located at 25.85° N. Lat.; 80.23° W. Long. Elevation is 7 feet.
Population: 33,575 (1990); 32,498 (2000); 31,580 (2007); 31,473 (2012 projected); Race: 38.0% White, 49.4% Black, 0.2% Asian, 47.9% Hispanic of any race (2007); Density: 6,892.9 persons per square mile (2007); Average household size: 3.43 (2007); Median age: 34.7 (2007); Males per 100 females: 95.2 (2007); Marriage status: 34.2% never married, 47.5% now married, 6.9% widowed, 11.4% divorced (2000); Foreign born: 35.0% (2000); Ancestry (includes multiple ancestries): 71.5% Other groups, 5.2% Haitian, 4.7% United States or American, 1.7% Jamaican, 1.7% African (2000).
Economy: Employment by occupation: 4.4% management, 9.0% professional, 23.7% services, 27.2% sales, 0.5% farming, 13.2% construction, 22.0% production (2000).
Income: Per capita income: $11,957 (2007); Median household income: $29,381 (2007); Average household income: $40,531 (2007); Percent of households with income of $100,000 or more: 6.2% (2007); Poverty rate: 29.0% (2000).
Education: Percent of population age 25 and over with: High school diploma (including GED) or higher: 50.9% (2007); Bachelor's degree or higher: 5.6% (2007); Master's degree or higher: 2.2% (2007).
Housing: Homeownership rate: 63.7% (2007); Median home value: $171,516 (2007); Median rent: $468 per month (2000); Median age of housing: 41 years (2000).
Transportation: Commute to work: 88.1% car, 8.0% public transportation, 1.3% walk, 0.4% work from home (2000); Travel time to work: 11.4% less than 15 minutes, 39.0% 15 to 30 minutes, 32.2% 30 to 45 minutes, 7.1% 45 to 60 minutes, 10.4% 60 minutes or more (2000)

WEST MIAMI (city).
Covers a land area of 0.711 square miles and a water area of 0 square miles. Located at 25.75° N. Lat.; 80.29° W. Long. Elevation is 10 feet.
Population: 5,727 (1990); 5,863 (2000); 5,758 (2007); 5,848 (2012 projected); Race: 92.7% White, 0.8% Black, 0.5% Asian, 86.2% Hispanic of any race (2007); Density: 8,093.9 persons per square mile (2007); Average household size: 2.88 (2007); Median age: 45.4 (2007); Males per 100 females: 84.4 (2007); Marriage status: 20.4% never married, 56.7% now married, 10.1% widowed, 12.8% divorced (2000); Foreign born: 68.5% (2000); Ancestry (includes multiple ancestries): 83.6% Other groups, 2.7% United States or American, 2.4% Italian, 2.0% German, 1.5% English (2000).
Economy: Single-family building permits issued: 0 (2006); Multi-family building permits issued: 0 (2006); Employment by occupation: 11.7% management, 14.6% professional, 12.8% services, 37.0% sales, 0.4% farming, 11.5% construction, 12.0% production (2000).
Income: Per capita income: $19,554 (2007); Median household income: $40,988 (2007); Average household income: $55,305 (2007); Percent of households with income of $100,000 or more: 13.2% (2007); Poverty rate: 9.5% (2000).
Education: Percent of population age 25 and over with: High school diploma (including GED) or higher: 63.5% (2007); Bachelor's degree or higher: 18.0% (2007); Master's degree or higher: 7.2% (2007).
Housing: Homeownership rate: 68.1% (2007); Median home value: $317,990 (2007); Median rent: $570 per month (2000); Median age of housing: 47 years (2000).
Safety: Violent crime rate: 28.7 per 10,000 population; Property crime rate: 261.5 per 10,000 population (2006).
Transportation: Commute to work: 94.1% car, 2.5% public transportation, 0.9% walk, 2.0% work from home (2000); Travel time to work: 13.1% less than 15 minutes, 44.9% 15 to 30 minutes, 30.8% 30 to 45 minutes, 6.8% 45 to 60 minutes, 4.3% 60 minutes or more (2000)
Additional Information Contacts
City of West Miami . . . . (305) 266-1122

WEST PERRINE (CDP).
Covers a land area of 1.731 square miles and a water area of 0 square miles. Located at 25.60° N. Lat.; 80.36° W. Long. Elevation is 10 feet.
Population: 8,798 (1990); 8,600 (2000); 8,947 (2007); 9,317 (2012 projected); Race: 20.8% White, 69.3% Black, 1.1% Asian, 21.9% Hispanic of any race (2007); Density: 5,167.3 persons per square mile (2007); Average household size: 3.35 (2007); Median age: 30.0 (2007); Males per 100 females: 89.3 (2007); Marriage status: 41.4% never married, 39.5% now married, 8.1% widowed, 11.0% divorced (2000); Foreign born: 20.2% (2000); Ancestry (includes multiple ancestries): 68.1% Other groups, 4.8% Jamaican, 3.2% Haitian, 2.4% Trinidadian and Tobagonian, 2.4% English (2000).
Economy: Employment by occupation: 7.8% management, 16.4% professional, 26.0% services, 28.8% sales, 0.0% farming, 7.7% construction, 13.2% production (2000).
Income: Per capita income: $13,362 (2007); Median household income: $31,912 (2007); Average household income: $44,272 (2007); Percent of households with income of $100,000 or more: 10.7% (2007); Poverty rate: 34.4% (2000).
Education: Percent of population age 25 and over with: High school diploma (including GED) or higher: 68.0% (2007); Bachelor's degree or higher: 12.3% (2007); Master's degree or higher: 4.9% (2007).
Housing: Homeownership rate: 64.3% (2007); Median home value: $194,444 (2007); Median rent: $388 per month (2000); Median age of housing: 31 years (2000).
Transportation: Commute to work: 87.4% car, 6.1% public transportation, 2.0% walk, 1.4% work from home (2000); Travel time to work: 19.5% less than 15 minutes, 39.8% 15 to 30 minutes, 16.9% 30 to 45 minutes, 13.9% 45 to 60 minutes, 9.8% 60 minutes or more (2000)

WESTCHESTER (CDP).
Covers a land area of 4.015 square miles and a water area of 0 square miles. Located at 25.74° N. Lat.; 80.33° W. Long. Elevation is 3 feet.
Population: 29,883 (1990); 30,271 (2000); 29,390 (2007); 29,191 (2012 projected); Race: 94.5% White, 0.7% Black, 0.5% Asian, 86.9% Hispanic of any race (2007); Density: 7,320.5 persons per square mile (2007); Average household size: 3.09 (2007); Median age: 45.2 (2007); Males per 100 females: 88.0 (2007); Marriage status: 21.2% never married, 57.0% now married, 9.9% widowed, 11.9% divorced (2000); Foreign born: 69.0%

(2000); Ancestry (includes multiple ancestries): 85.8% Other groups, 2.4% United States or American, 1.6% Italian, 1.1% English, 1.0% German (2000).

Economy: Employment by occupation: 13.5% management, 14.6% professional, 15.5% services, 34.7% sales, 0.6% farming, 10.1% construction, 10.9% production (2000).

Income: Per capita income: $19,816 (2007); Median household income: $46,125 (2007); Average household income: $60,196 (2007); Percent of households with income of $100,000 or more: 15.0% (2007); Poverty rate: 11.8% (2000).

Education: Percent of population age 25 and over with: High school diploma (including GED) or higher: 63.8% (2007); Bachelor's degree or higher: 21.5% (2007); Master's degree or higher: 9.3% (2007).

Housing: Homeownership rate: 69.0% (2007); Median home value: $325,738 (2007); Median rent: $629 per month (2000); Median age of housing: 37 years (2000).

Transportation: Commute to work: 93.7% car, 2.1% public transportation, 0.6% walk, 2.6% work from home (2000); Travel time to work: 13.7% less than 15 minutes, 40.0% 15 to 30 minutes, 28.1% 30 to 45 minutes, 10.8% 45 to 60 minutes, 7.4% 60 minutes or more (2000)

WESTVIEW (CDP). Covers a land area of 3.117 square miles and a water area of 0.110 square miles. Located at 25.88° N. Lat.; 80.23° W. Long. Elevation is 3 feet.

Population: 9,668 (1990); 9,692 (2000); 9,720 (2007); 9,871 (2012 projected); Race: 18.5% White, 72.8% Black, 0.4% Asian, 22.6% Hispanic of any race (2007); Density: 3,118.2 persons per square mile (2007); Average household size: 3.35 (2007); Median age: 31.6 (2007); Males per 100 females: 89.1 (2007); Marriage status: 39.1% never married, 40.2% now married, 7.0% widowed, 13.7% divorced (2000); Foreign born: 30.3% (2000); Ancestry (includes multiple ancestries): 58.9% Other groups, 10.0% Haitian, 7.2% United States or American, 6.9% Jamaican, 1.7% African (2000).

Economy: Employment by occupation: 6.2% management, 13.8% professional, 26.7% services, 27.0% sales, 0.0% farming, 9.8% construction, 16.4% production (2000).

Income: Per capita income: $11,805 (2007); Median household income: $30,737 (2007); Average household income: $39,064 (2007); Percent of households with income of $100,000 or more: 4.2% (2007); Poverty rate: 26.0% (2000).

Education: Percent of population age 25 and over with: High school diploma (including GED) or higher: 60.9% (2007); Bachelor's degree or higher: 9.1% (2007); Master's degree or higher: 3.5% (2007).

Housing: Homeownership rate: 63.2% (2007); Median home value: $173,254 (2007); Median rent: $478 per month (2000); Median age of housing: 37 years (2000).

Transportation: Commute to work: 86.5% car, 11.2% public transportation, 1.0% walk, 0.8% work from home (2000); Travel time to work: 11.3% less than 15 minutes, 34.6% 15 to 30 minutes, 34.6% 30 to 45 minutes, 9.3% 45 to 60 minutes, 10.2% 60 minutes or more (2000)

WESTWOOD LAKES (CDP). Covers a land area of 1.723 square miles and a water area of 0.091 square miles. Located at 25.72° N. Lat.; 80.36° W. Long. Elevation is 3 feet.

Population: 11,522 (1990); 12,005 (2000); 11,750 (2007); 11,748 (2012 projected); Race: 93.6% White, 0.7% Black, 0.9% Asian, 81.1% Hispanic of any race (2007); Density: 6,819.5 persons per square mile (2007); Average household size: 3.48 (2007); Median age: 41.9 (2007); Males per 100 females: 92.4 (2007); Marriage status: 20.8% never married, 60.6% now married, 7.5% widowed, 11.1% divorced (2000); Foreign born: 58.1% (2000); Ancestry (includes multiple ancestries): 74.3% Other groups, 4.3% United States or American, 3.7% Irish, 3.5% German, 2.6% English (2000).

Economy: Employment by occupation: 11.1% management, 12.2% professional, 17.6% services, 35.0% sales, 0.6% farming, 12.9% construction, 10.4% production (2000).

Income: Per capita income: $18,515 (2007); Median household income: $51,570 (2007); Average household income: $62,347 (2007); Percent of households with income of $100,000 or more: 15.8% (2007); Poverty rate: 9.6% (2000).

Education: Percent of population age 25 and over with: High school diploma (including GED) or higher: 66.2% (2007); Bachelor's degree or higher: 14.2% (2007); Master's degree or higher: 7.2% (2007).

Housing: Homeownership rate: 86.6% (2007); Median home value: $303,524 (2007); Median rent: $854 per month (2000); Median age of housing: 43 years (2000).

Transportation: Commute to work: 94.7% car, 1.6% public transportation, 0.8% walk, 2.6% work from home (2000); Travel time to work: 17.0% less than 15 minutes, 36.4% 15 to 30 minutes, 26.7% 30 to 45 minutes, 11.3% 45 to 60 minutes, 8.6% 60 minutes or more (2000)

Monroe County

Located in southern Florida, at the tip of a peninsula; Everglades area, with Cape Sable and Whitewater Bay; includes most of the Florida Keys, enclosing Florida Bay. Covers a land area of 996.91 square miles, a water area of 2,740.24 square miles, and is located in the Eastern Time Zone. The county was founded in 1823. County seat is Key West.

Monroe County is part of the Key West, FL Micropolitan Statistical Area. The entire metro area includes: Monroe County, FL

Weather Station: Flamingo Ranger Station   Elevation: 0 feet

	Jan	Feb	Mar	Apr	May	Jun	Jul	Aug	Sep	Oct	Nov	Dec
High	77	77	79	83	86	88	89	90	89	86	82	78
Low	56	57	60	64	69	73	74	74	73	69	64	59
Precip	2.0	1.6	1.9	2.1	5.0	7.3	4.9	7.5	7.3	4.3	2.5	1.5
Snow	0.0	0.0	0.0	0.0	0.0	0.0	0.0	0.0	0.0	0.0	0.0	0.0

High and Low temperatures in degrees Fahrenheit; Precipitation and Snow in inches

Weather Station: Key West Int'l Airport   Elevation: 3 feet

	Jan	Feb	Mar	Apr	May	Jun	Jul	Aug	Sep	Oct	Nov	Dec
High	75	76	79	82	85	88	89	89	88	85	80	77
Low	65	66	69	72	76	79	80	79	78	76	72	67
Precip	2.5	1.6	1.9	2.0	3.5	4.5	3.5	5.2	5.5	4.4	2.6	2.1
Snow	0.0	0.0	0.0	0.0	0.0	0.0	0.0	0.0	0.0	0.0	0.0	0.0

High and Low temperatures in degrees Fahrenheit; Precipitation and Snow in inches

Weather Station: Tavernier   Elevation: 6 feet

	Jan	Feb	Mar	Apr	May	Jun	Jul	Aug	Sep	Oct	Nov	Dec
High	77	78	80	84	87	89	91	90	89	86	82	78
Low	63	64	67	70	74	77	78	78	77	74	70	66
Precip	2.5	2.0	2.3	1.9	3.9	6.8	3.3	5.1	6.7	5.4	3.0	2.0
Snow	0.0	0.0	0.0	0.0	0.0	0.0	0.0	0.0	0.0	0.0	0.0	0.0

High and Low temperatures in degrees Fahrenheit; Precipitation and Snow in inches

Population: 78,024 (1990); 79,589 (2000); 78,715 (2007); 80,490 (2012 projected); Race: 89.7% White, 5.2% Black, 1.1% Asian, 18.2% Hispanic of any race (2007); Density: 79.0 persons per square mile (2007); Average household size: 2.26 (2007); Median age: 46.9 (2007); Males per 100 females: 113.3 (2007).

Religion: Five largest groups: 16.4% Catholic Church, 4.0% Southern Baptist Convention, 2.1% The United Methodist Church, 1.3% Episcopal Church, 1.2% Seventh-day Adventist Church (2000).

Economy: Unemployment rate: 3.0% (11/2007); Total civilian labor force: 43,394 (11/2007); Leading industries: 35.4% accommodation & food services; 21.0% retail trade; 14.7% hotels (exc casino hotels) & motels (2005); Farms: 18 totaling 102 acres (2002); Companies that employ 500 or more persons: 1 (2005); Companies that employ 100 to 499 persons: 30 (2005); Companies that employ less than 100 persons: 3,715 (2005); Black-owned businesses: 347 (2002); Hispanic-owned businesses: 1,286 (2002); Asian-owned businesses: 130 (2002); Women-owned businesses: 2,681 (2002); Retail sales per capita: $23,323 (2007). Single-family building permits issued: 430 (2006); Multi-family building permits issued: 27 (2006).

Income: Per capita income: $31,292 (2007); Median household income: $50,715 (2007); Average household income: $70,158 (2007); Percent of households with income of $100,000 or more: 18.6% (2007); Poverty rate: 10.6% (2005); Bankruptcy rate: 0.67% (2006).

Education: Percent of population age 25 and over with: High school diploma (including GED) or higher: 84.8% (2007); Bachelor's degree or higher: 25.5% (2007); Master's degree or higher: 8.7% (2007).

Housing: Homeownership rate: 62.9% (2007); Median home value: $652,739 (2007); Median rent: $735 per month (2000); Median age of housing: 23 years (2000).

Health: Birth rate: 102.0 per 10,000 population (2006); Death rate: 97.3 per 10,000 population (2006); Age-adjusted cancer mortality rate: 193.6 deaths per 100,000 population (2004); Number of physicians: 25.7 per 10,000 population (2004); Hospital beds: 27.6 per 10,000 population (2004); Hospital admissions: 960.8 per 10,000 population (2004).

Elections: 2004 Presidential election results: 49.2% Bush, 49.7% Kerry, 0.7% Nader, 0.2% Badnarik

National and State Parks: Bahia Honda State Park; Crocodile Lake National Wildlife Refuge; Curry Hammock State Park; Dry Tortugas National Park; Everglades National Park; Fort Zachary Taylor Historic State Park; Great White Heron National Wildlife Refuge; Indian Key Historic State Park; John Pennekamp Coral Reef State Park; Key Largo Hammocks Botanical State Park; Key Largo National Marine Sanctuary; Key West National Wildlife Refuge; Lignumvitae Key Botanical State Park; Long Key State Park; Looe Key National Marine Sanctuary; National Key Deer Refuge; Windley Key Fossil Reef Geological State Park

Additional Information Contacts

Monroe County Government . . . . (305) 294-4641
   http://monroecofl.virtualtownhall.net
Big Pine Key Chamber of Commerce . . . . (305) 872-2411
   http://www.lowerkeyschamber.com
Greater Marathon Chamber of Commerce . . . . (305) 743-5417
   http://www.floridakeysmarathon.com
Islamorada Chamber of Commerce. . . . . (305) 664-4503
   http://www.islamoradachamber.com
Key Largo Chamber of Commerce . . . . (305) 451-4747
   http://www.keylargo.org
Key West Chamber of Commerce . . . . (305) 294-2587
   http://www.keywestchamber.org
Ocean Reef Business Council . . . . (305) 367-3646
Village of Islamorada . . . . (305) 664-6400
   http://www.islamorada.fl.us

Monroe County Communities

BIG COPPITT KEY (CDP). Covers a land area of 1.377 square miles and a water area of 0.096 square miles. Located at 24.59° N. Lat.; 81.65° W. Long. Elevation is 3 feet.
Population: 2,388 (1990); 2,595 (2000); 2,581 (2007); 2,658 (2012 projected); Race: 92.6% White, 1.0% Black, 1.8% Asian, 18.9% Hispanic of any race (2007); Density: 1,875.0 persons per square mile (2007); Average household size: 2.37 (2007); Median age: 45.4 (2007); Males per 100 females: 116.5 (2007); Marriage status: 19.9% never married, 53.4% now married, 6.7% widowed, 20.0% divorced (2000); Foreign born: 13.5% (2000); Ancestry (includes multiple ancestries): 28.4% Other groups, 11.8% German, 11.0% English, 10.7% Irish, 8.1% United States or American (2000).
Economy: Employment by occupation: 10.6% management, 15.6% professional, 20.2% services, 25.1% sales, 5.1% farming, 13.4% construction, 9.8% production (2000).
Income: Per capita income: $28,755 (2007); Median household income: $55,969 (2007); Average household income: $68,277 (2007); Percent of households with income of $100,000 or more: 19.6% (2007); Poverty rate: 8.6% (2000).
Education: Percent of population age 25 and over with: High school diploma (including GED) or higher: 81.8% (2007); Bachelor's degree or higher: 19.3% (2007); Master's degree or higher: 8.1% (2007).
Housing: Homeownership rate: 67.2% (2007); Median home value: $633,249 (2007); Median rent: $746 per month (2000); Median age of housing: 18 years (2000).
Transportation: Commute to work: 93.1% car, 0.0% public transportation, 0.5% walk, 2.1% work from home (2000); Travel time to work: 33.3% less than 15 minutes, 49.7% 15 to 30 minutes, 13.5% 30 to 45 minutes, 1.0% 45 to 60 minutes, 2.5% 60 minutes or more (2000)

BIG PINE KEY (CDP). Covers a land area of 9.765 square miles and a water area of 0.183 square miles. Located at 24.68° N. Lat.; 81.36° W. Long. Elevation is 3 feet.
Population: 4,206 (1990); 5,032 (2000); 5,037 (2007); 5,191 (2012 projected); Race: 93.8% White, 1.4% Black, 0.8% Asian, 8.3% Hispanic of any race (2007); Density: 515.8 persons per square mile (2007); Average household size: 2.21 (2007); Median age: 48.5 (2007); Males per 100 females: 109.1 (2007); Marriage status: 19.1% never married, 64.3% now married, 4.5% widowed, 12.1% divorced (2000); Foreign born: 9.5% (2000); Ancestry (includes multiple ancestries): 21.8% German, 17.0% English, 15.1% Other groups, 13.8% Irish, 8.8% Italian (2000).
Economy: Employment by occupation: 10.2% management, 13.1% professional, 22.0% services, 27.2% sales, 3.1% farming, 15.1% construction, 9.2% production (2000).
Income: Per capita income: $28,043 (2007); Median household income: $51,481 (2007); Average household income: $61,456 (2007); Percent of

households with income of $100,000 or more: 14.1% (2007); Poverty rate: 9.5% (2000).
Education: Percent of population age 25 and over with: High school diploma (including GED) or higher: 86.8% (2007); Bachelor's degree or higher: 24.9% (2007); Master's degree or higher: 5.8% (2007).
School District(s)
Monroe County School District (PK-12)
   2005-06 Enrollment: 8,677 . . . . (305) 293-1400
Housing: Homeownership rate: 76.8% (2007); Median home value: $544,975 (2007); Median rent: $836 per month (2000); Median age of housing: 19 years (2000).
Transportation: Commute to work: 85.9% car, 0.7% public transportation, 1.0% walk, 5.5% work from home (2000); Travel time to work: 30.7% less than 15 minutes, 14.1% 15 to 30 minutes, 27.9% 30 to 45 minutes, 20.9% 45 to 60 minutes, 6.4% 60 minutes or more (2000)
Additional Information Contacts
Big Pine Key Chamber of Commerce . . . . (305) 872-2411
   http://www.lowerkeyschamber.com

CUDJOE KEY (CDP). Covers a land area of 5.238 square miles and a water area of 0.393 square miles. Located at 24.66° N. Lat.; 81.48° W. Long.
Population: 1,714 (1990); 1,695 (2000); 1,726 (2007); 1,786 (2012 projected); Race: 94.8% White, 1.5% Black, 1.7% Asian, 7.0% Hispanic of any race (2007); Density: 329.5 persons per square mile (2007); Average household size: 2.10 (2007); Median age: 52.1 (2007); Males per 100 females: 106.5 (2007); Marriage status: 20.2% never married, 62.5% now married, 3.3% widowed, 14.1% divorced (2000); Foreign born: 6.0% (2000); Ancestry (includes multiple ancestries): 23.9% Irish, 21.3% German, 16.0% English, 14.5% Other groups, 8.1% United States or American (2000).
Economy: Employment by occupation: 13.2% management, 13.6% professional, 13.9% services, 29.7% sales, 2.8% farming, 18.3% construction, 8.5% production (2000).
Income: Per capita income: $38,776 (2007); Median household income: $68,617 (2007); Average household income: $81,420 (2007); Percent of households with income of $100,000 or more: 27.4% (2007); Poverty rate: 5.8% (2000).
Education: Percent of population age 25 and over with: High school diploma (including GED) or higher: 92.6% (2007); Bachelor's degree or higher: 21.5% (2007); Master's degree or higher: 9.3% (2007).
Housing: Homeownership rate: 82.6% (2007); Median home value: $754,496 (2007); Median rent: $935 per month (2000); Median age of housing: 15 years (2000).
Transportation: Commute to work: 89.4% car, 0.0% public transportation, 0.0% walk, 5.0% work from home (2000); Travel time to work: 29.1% less than 15 minutes, 19.0% 15 to 30 minutes, 38.9% 30 to 45 minutes, 9.8% 45 to 60 minutes, 3.2% 60 minutes or more (2000)

DUCK KEY (CDP). Covers a land area of 0.862 square miles and a water area of 0.045 square miles. Located at 24.77° N. Lat.; 80.91° W. Long. Elevation is 3 feet.
Population: 529 (1990); 443 (2000); 492 (2007); 533 (2012 projected); Race: 98.8% White, 0.2% Black, 0.4% Asian, 2.2% Hispanic of any race (2007); Density: 571.1 persons per square mile (2007); Average household size: 1.88 (2007); Median age: 57.0 (2007); Males per 100 females: 101.6 (2007); Marriage status: 10.4% never married, 79.3% now married, 7.5% widowed, 2.9% divorced (2000); Foreign born: 2.0% (2000); Ancestry (includes multiple ancestries): 26.4% Irish, 23.5% English, 17.7% German, 17.4% Russian, 9.2% Italian (2000).
Economy: Employment by occupation: 23.7% management, 22.5% professional, 11.9% services, 14.6% sales, 13.0% farming, 5.5% construction, 8.7% production (2000).
Income: Per capita income: $47,475 (2007); Median household income: $44,545 (2007); Average household income: $89,151 (2007); Percent of households with income of $100,000 or more: 26.0% (2007); Poverty rate: 16.6% (2000).
Education: Percent of population age 25 and over with: High school diploma (including GED) or higher: 98.4% (2007); Bachelor's degree or higher: 49.9% (2007); Master's degree or higher: 30.7% (2007).
Housing: Homeownership rate: 78.2% (2007); Median home value: $1 million+ (2007); Median rent: $779 per month (2000); Median age of housing: 12 years (2000).
Transportation: Commute to work: 70.9% car, 0.0% public transportation, 3.3% walk, 15.2% work from home (2000); Travel time to work: 43.0% less

than 15 minutes, 36.2% 15 to 30 minutes, 9.2% 30 to 45 minutes, 0.0% 45 to 60 minutes, 11.6% 60 minutes or more (2000)

ISLAMORADA (village). Covers a land area of 7.113 square miles and a water area of 0.141 square miles. Located at 24.93° N. Lat.; 80.61° W. Long. Elevation is 5 feet.

History: Islamorada, on the Upper Matecumbe Key, was the location of a camp of veterans working on the Overseas Highway when the devastating hurricane struck in 1935. The Hurricane Memorial was erected here in memory of the men who lost their lives in that storm.

Population: 6,720 (1990); 6,846 (2000); 6,815 (2007); 7,004 (2012 projected); Race: 96.3% White, 0.5% Black, 0.9% Asian, 7.4% Hispanic of any race (2007); Density: 958.1 persons per square mile (2007); Average household size: 2.13 (2007); Median age: 50.2 (2007); Males per 100 females: 112.2 (2007); Marriage status: 23.1% never married, 57.6% now married, 5.7% widowed, 13.6% divorced (2000); Foreign born: 6.7% (2000); Ancestry (includes multiple ancestries): 21.1% Irish, 19.3% German, 18.5% English, 9.8% Other groups, 8.0% United States or American (2000).

Economy: Single-family building permits issued: 99 (2006); Multi-family building permits issued: 0 (2006); Employment by occupation: 11.6% management, 16.4% professional, 20.1% services, 30.0% sales, 3.9% farming, 7.0% construction, 10.9% production (2000).

Income: Per capita income: $35,435 (2007); Median household income: $46,276 (2007); Average household income: $75,262 (2007); Percent of households with income of $100,000 or more: 20.3% (2007); Poverty rate: 6.9% (2000).

Education: Percent of population age 25 and over with: High school diploma (including GED) or higher: 91.9% (2007); Bachelor's degree or higher: 28.8% (2007); Master's degree or higher: 9.7% (2007).

Housing: Homeownership rate: 71.8% (2007); Median home value: $735,595 (2007); Median rent: $709 per month (2000); Median age of housing: 20 years (2000).

Transportation: Commute to work: 82.7% car, 0.1% public transportation, 7.8% walk, 7.3% work from home (2000); Travel time to work: 52.1% less than 15 minutes, 25.1% 15 to 30 minutes, 6.9% 30 to 45 minutes, 3.6% 45 to 60 minutes, 12.3% 60 minutes or more (2000)

Additional Information Contacts
Islamorada Chamber of Commerce . . . . (305) 664-4503
    http://www.islamoradachamber.com
Village of Islamorada . . . . (305) 664-6400
    http://www.islamorada.fl.us

KEY COLONY BEACH (city). Covers a land area of 0.508 square miles and a water area of 0.162 square miles. Located at 24.72° N. Lat.; 81.01° W. Long. Elevation is 3 feet.

Population: 993 (1990); 788 (2000); 779 (2007); 790 (2012 projected); Race: 98.8% White, 0.6% Black, 0.0% Asian, 6.4% Hispanic of any race (2007); Density: 1,532.1 persons per square mile (2007); Average household size: 1.85 (2007); Median age: 60.9 (2007); Males per 100 females: 102.3 (2007); Marriage status: 7.2% never married, 63.6% now married, 13.5% widowed, 15.8% divorced (2000); Foreign born: 11.8% (2000); Ancestry (includes multiple ancestries): 25.3% German, 22.0% English, 17.2% Irish, 14.2% Other groups, 7.3% French (except Basque) (2000).

Economy: Single-family building permits issued: 8 (2006); Multi-family building permits issued: 5 (2006); Employment by occupation: 14.4% management, 18.7% professional, 21.0% services, 32.7% sales, 2.3% farming, 6.2% construction, 4.7% production (2000).

Income: Per capita income: $41,672 (2007); Median household income: $49,444 (2007); Average household income: $77,292 (2007); Percent of households with income of $100,000 or more: 19.3% (2007); Poverty rate: 7.4% (2000).

Education: Percent of population age 25 and over with: High school diploma (including GED) or higher: 92.7% (2007); Bachelor's degree or higher: 35.4% (2007); Master's degree or higher: 8.9% (2007).

Housing: Homeownership rate: 73.1% (2007); Median home value: $889,583 (2007); Median rent: $831 per month (2000); Median age of housing: 25 years (2000).

Safety: Violent crime rate: 12.4 per 10,000 population; Property crime rate: 197.8 per 10,000 population (2006).

Transportation: Commute to work: 82.0% car, 0.0% public transportation, 4.7% walk, 6.7% work from home (2000); Travel time to work: 74.8% less than 15 minutes, 13.9% 15 to 30 minutes, 6.7% 30 to 45 minutes, 2.1% 45 to 60 minutes, 2.5% 60 minutes or more (2000)

KEY LARGO (CDP). Covers a land area of 12.152 square miles and a water area of 3.136 square miles. Located at 25.10° N. Lat.; 80.43° W. Long. Elevation is 7 feet.

Population: 11,302 (1990); 11,886 (2000); 11,646 (2007); 11,791 (2012 projected); Race: 93.4% White, 2.3% Black, 0.7% Asian, 20.9% Hispanic of any race (2007); Density: 958.4 persons per square mile (2007); Average household size: 2.29 (2007); Median age: 47.0 (2007); Males per 100 females: 107.2 (2007); Marriage status: 20.0% never married, 59.1% now married, 6.2% widowed, 14.7% divorced (2000); Foreign born: 15.9% (2000); Ancestry (includes multiple ancestries): 25.5% Other groups, 19.0% German, 14.4% English, 13.3% Irish, 8.5% Italian (2000).

Economy: Employment by occupation: 12.7% management, 14.5% professional, 20.6% services, 25.3% sales, 2.1% farming, 15.0% construction, 9.7% production (2000).

Income: Per capita income: $30,476 (2007); Median household income: $50,943 (2007); Average household income: $69,513 (2007); Percent of households with income of $100,000 or more: 18.5% (2007); Poverty rate: 8.3% (2000).

Education: Percent of population age 25 and over with: High school diploma (including GED) or higher: 84.2% (2007); Bachelor's degree or higher: 24.4% (2007); Master's degree or higher: 8.3% (2007).

School District(s)
Monroe County School District (PK-12)
    2005-06 Enrollment: 8,677 . . . . (305) 293-1400

Housing: Homeownership rate: 70.6% (2007); Median home value: $477,303 (2007); Median rent: $668 per month (2000); Median age of housing: 20 years (2000).

Transportation: Commute to work: 88.9% car, 1.1% public transportation, 2.3% walk, 3.9% work from home (2000); Travel time to work: 43.0% less than 15 minutes, 26.8% 15 to 30 minutes, 11.7% 30 to 45 minutes, 5.8% 45 to 60 minutes, 12.7% 60 minutes or more (2000)

Airports: Ocean Reef Club

Additional Information Contacts
Key Largo Chamber of Commerce . . . . (305) 451-4747
    http://www.keylargo.org
Ocean Reef Business Council . . . . (305) 367-3646

KEY WEST (city). County seat. Covers a land area of 5.946 square miles and a water area of 1.459 square miles. Located at 24.55° N. Lat.; 81.78° W. Long. Elevation is 3 feet.

History: Key West, at the tip of the string of coral islands off the southern coast of Florida, was visited by explorers and adventurers for several centuries before a permanent settlement was established after 1823. Families from New England, Virginia, and South Carolina came, and many turned to salvaging cargoes from vessels wrecked on the reefs. Fort Taylor was built here during the Mexican War of 1846-1848, and strengthened at the beginning of the Civil War. Though Key West citizens were Confederate sympathizers, the city was held by Federal forces throughout the war. For a time, Key West was the world's largest cigar manufacturer. The Overseas Extension of the Florida East Coast Railway was completed in 1912 to link Key West over the other keys with the mainland, but a 1935 hurricane destroyed it. In 1938 the Overseas Highway was built along the same route.

Population: 24,842 (1990); 25,478 (2000); 24,472 (2007); 24,552 (2012 projected); Race: 83.9% White, 10.0% Black, 1.5% Asian, 16.6% Hispanic of any race (2007); Density: 4,115.8 persons per square mile (2007); Average household size: 2.28 (2007); Median age: 43.4 (2007); Males per 100 females: 122.1 (2007); Marriage status: 33.8% never married, 45.5% now married, 5.4% widowed, 15.2% divorced (2000); Foreign born: 15.8% (2000); Ancestry (includes multiple ancestries): 27.4% Other groups, 12.4% English, 12.2% German, 11.3% Irish, 6.8% Italian (2000).

Economy: Unemployment rate: 2.7% (11/2007); Total civilian labor force: 14,176 (11/2007); Single-family building permits issued: 30 (2006); Multi-family building permits issued: 0 (2006); Employment by occupation: 14.7% management, 15.1% professional, 26.7% services, 26.2% sales, 2.2% farming, 9.1% construction, 6.0% production (2000).

Income: Per capita income: $31,889 (2007); Median household income: $52,547 (2007); Average household income: $71,690 (2007); Percent of households with income of $100,000 or more: 19.2% (2007); Poverty rate: 10.2% (2000).

Taxes: Total city taxes per capita: $936 (2005); City property taxes per capita: $492 (2005).

Education: Percent of population age 25 and over with: High school diploma (including GED) or higher: 84.7% (2007); Bachelor's degree or higher: 27.4% (2007); Master's degree or higher: 10.0% (2007).

School District(s)

Monroe County School District (PK-12)

    2005-06 Enrollment: 8,677 . . . . (305) 293-1400

Two-year College(s)

Florida Keys Community College (Public)

    Fall 2006 Enrollment: 965 . . . . (305) 296-9081

    2006-07 Tuition: In-state $2,250; Out-of-state $6,991

Housing: Homeownership rate: 46.8% (2007); Median home value: $846,215 (2007); Median rent: $822 per month (2000); Median age of housing: 39 years (2000).

Hospitals: Lower Keys Medical Center (169 beds)

Safety: Violent crime rate: 85.0 per 10,000 population; Property crime rate: 668.5 per 10,000 population (2006).

Newspapers: Key West Citizen (Circulation 9,265)

Transportation: Commute to work: 66.7% car, 1.2% public transportation, 8.0% walk, 5.7% work from home (2000); Travel time to work: 64.7% less than 15 minutes, 29.3% 15 to 30 minutes, 3.8% 30 to 45 minutes, 0.8% 45 to 60 minutes, 1.4% 60 minutes or more (2000)

Airports: Key West International (primary service)

Additional Information Contacts

Key West Chamber of Commerce . . . . (305) 294-2587

    http://www.keywestchamber.org

LAYTON (city).
Aka Long Key. Covers a land area of 0.216 square miles and a water area of 0.028 square miles. Located at 24.82° N. Lat.; 80.81° W. Long. Elevation is 3 feet.

Population: 183 (1990); 186 (2000); 166 (2007); 174 (2012 projected); Race: 99.4% White, 0.0% Black, 0.6% Asian, 1.8% Hispanic of any race (2007); Density: 767.6 persons per square mile (2007); Average household size: 2.21 (2007); Median age: 54.7 (2007); Males per 100 females: 90.8 (2007); Marriage status: 28.9% never married, 55.0% now married, 7.3% widowed, 8.7% divorced (2000); Foreign born: 19.6% (2000); Ancestry (includes multiple ancestries): 34.6% English, 24.6% German, 17.1% French (except Basque), 17.1% Irish, 12.5% Other groups (2000).

Economy: Single-family building permits issued: 1 (2006); Multi-family building permits issued: 0 (2006); Employment by occupation: 23.1% management, 14.5% professional, 26.5% services, 26.5% sales, 0.0% farming, 7.7% construction, 1.7% production (2000).

Income: Per capita income: $32,771 (2007); Median household income: $57,000 (2007); Average household income: $72,533 (2007); Percent of households with income of $100,000 or more: 24.0% (2007); Poverty rate: 15.4% (2000).

Education: Percent of population age 25 and over with: High school diploma (including GED) or higher: 88.1% (2007); Bachelor's degree or higher: 21.0% (2007); Master's degree or higher: 4.9% (2007).

Housing: Homeownership rate: 66.7% (2007); Median home value: $779,412 (2007); Median rent: $600 per month (2000); Median age of housing: 25 years (2000).

Transportation: Commute to work: 76.9% car, 0.0% public transportation, 8.5% walk, 0.0% work from home (2000); Travel time to work: 45.3% less than 15 minutes, 28.2% 15 to 30 minutes, 8.5% 30 to 45 minutes, 8.5% 45 to 60 minutes, 9.4% 60 minutes or more (2000)

MARATHON (city).
Covers a land area of 8.646 square miles and a water area of 0.997 square miles. Located at 24.72° N. Lat.; 81.04° W. Long. Elevation is 3 feet.

History: Marathon became the trading center of Key Vaca, chosen by settlers for its fertile land and fresh-water wells.

Population: 10,728 (1990); 10,255 (2000); 10,191 (2007); 10,418 (2012 projected); Race: 90.2% White, 5.0% Black, 0.6% Asian, 26.6% Hispanic of any race (2007); Density: 1,178.7 persons per square mile (2007); Average household size: 2.21 (2007); Median age: 48.1 (2007); Males per 100 females: 110.6 (2007); Marriage status: 20.7% never married, 57.6% now married, 6.1% widowed, 15.6% divorced (2000); Foreign born: 19.8% (2000); Ancestry (includes multiple ancestries): 28.8% Other groups, 17.2% German, 15.7% Irish, 12.7% English, 5.8% United States or American (2000).

Economy: Single-family building permits issued: 96 (2006); Multi-family building permits issued: 8 (2006); Employment by occupation: 10.0% management, 12.5% professional, 25.3% services, 22.1% sales, 4.1% farming, 15.0% construction, 11.1% production (2000).

Income: Per capita income: $27,577 (2007); Median household income: $41,713 (2007); Average household income: $60,563 (2007); Percent of households with income of $100,000 or more: 14.0% (2007); Poverty rate: 14.2% (2000).

Education: Percent of population age 25 and over with: High school diploma (including GED) or higher: 80.4% (2007); Bachelor's degree or higher: 20.7% (2007); Master's degree or higher: 5.6% (2007).

School District(s)

Monroe County School District (PK-12)

    2005-06 Enrollment: 8,677 . . . . (305) 293-1400

Housing: Homeownership rate: 63.2% (2007); Median home value: $481,538 (2007); Median rent: $628 per month (2000); Median age of housing: 24 years (2000).

Hospitals: Fishermen's Hospital (58 beds)

Newspapers: Florida Keys Keynoter (General - Circulation 11,000)

Transportation: Commute to work: 78.6% car, 2.2% public transportation, 8.0% walk, 3.6% work from home (2000); Travel time to work: 69.0% less than 15 minutes, 18.1% 15 to 30 minutes, 4.3% 30 to 45 minutes, 3.9% 45 to 60 minutes, 4.7% 60 minutes or more (2000)

Airports: The Florida Keys Marathon

Additional Information Contacts

Greater Marathon Chamber of Commerce . . . . (305) 743-5417

    http://www.floridakeysmarathon.com

NORTH KEY LARGO (CDP).
Covers a land area of 18.774 square miles and a water area of 0.889 square miles. Located at 25.29° N. Lat.; 80.30° W. Long.

Population: 1,490 (1990); 1,049 (2000); 802 (2007); 690 (2012 projected); Race: 98.3% White, 0.7% Black, 0.5% Asian, 2.2% Hispanic of any race (2007); Density: 42.7 persons per square mile (2007); Average household size: 1.83 (2007); Median age: 64.3 (2007); Males per 100 females: 93.3 (2007); Marriage status: 7.2% never married, 72.2% now married, 9.5% widowed, 11.2% divorced (2000); Foreign born: 4.3% (2000); Ancestry (includes multiple ancestries): 31.4% English, 20.9% German, 13.5% Irish, 7.1% Italian, 5.4% French (except Basque) (2000).

Economy: Employment by occupation: 40.2% management, 16.8% professional, 11.5% services, 17.1% sales, 2.4% farming, 11.9% construction, 0.0% production (2000).

Income: Per capita income: $74,458 (2007); Median household income: $95,991 (2007); Average household income: $136,025 (2007); Percent of households with income of $100,000 or more: 48.1% (2007); Poverty rate: 0.5% (2000).

Education: Percent of population age 25 and over with: High school diploma (including GED) or higher: 97.7% (2007); Bachelor's degree or higher: 57.7% (2007); Master's degree or higher: 20.4% (2007).

Housing: Homeownership rate: 85.2% (2007); Median home value: $1 million+ (2007); Median rent: $390 per month (2000); Median age of housing: 22 years (2000).

Transportation: Commute to work: 44.3% car, 0.0% public transportation, 13.3% walk, 32.2% work from home (2000); Travel time to work: 68.2% less than 15 minutes, 22.5% 15 to 30 minutes, 5.2% 30 to 45 minutes, 0.0% 45 to 60 minutes, 4.0% 60 minutes or more (2000)

STOCK ISLAND (CDP).
Covers a land area of 0.896 square miles and a water area of 0.014 square miles. Located at 24.57° N. Lat.; 81.73° W. Long. Elevation is 3 feet.

Population: 3,613 (1990); 4,410 (2000); 4,970 (2007); 5,471 (2012 projected); Race: 78.9% White, 12.2% Black, 1.4% Asian, 48.9% Hispanic of any race (2007); Density: 5,543.8 persons per square mile (2007); Average household size: 2.60 (2007); Median age: 40.4 (2007); Males per 100 females: 116.4 (2007); Marriage status: 30.5% never married, 47.0% now married, 4.6% widowed, 17.9% divorced (2000); Foreign born: 28.1% (2000); Ancestry (includes multiple ancestries): 52.2% Other groups, 8.7% United States or American, 7.5% English, 6.6% German, 5.8% Irish (2000).

Economy: Employment by occupation: 5.7% management, 9.7% professional, 29.1% services, 19.2% sales, 7.5% farming, 16.9% construction, 11.8% production (2000).

Income: Per capita income: $17,332 (2007); Median household income: $37,807 (2007); Average household income: $44,216 (2007); Percent of households with income of $100,000 or more: 7.5% (2007); Poverty rate: 20.5% (2000).

Education: Percent of population age 25 and over with: High school diploma (including GED) or higher: 66.8% (2007); Bachelor's degree or higher: 9.7% (2007); Master's degree or higher: 3.1% (2007).

Housing: Homeownership rate: 49.3% (2007); Median home value: $244,792 (2007); Median rent: $617 per month (2000); Median age of housing: 25 years (2000).
Transportation: Commute to work: 76.1% car, 2.3% public transportation, 4.7% walk, 1.2% work from home (2000); Travel time to work: 56.3% less than 15 minutes, 38.6% 15 to 30 minutes, 4.8% 30 to 45 minutes, 0.0% 45 to 60 minutes, 0.4% 60 minutes or more (2000)

SUMMERLAND KEY (unincorporated postal area, zip code 33042). Covers a land area of 27.945 square miles and a water area of 9.627 square miles. Located at 24.66° N. Lat.; 81.48° W. Long. Elevation is 10 feet.
Population: 6,097 (2000); Race: 97.0% White, 0.8% Black, 0.2% Asian, 6.3% Hispanic of any race (2000); Density: 218.2 persons per square mile (2000); Age: 15.7% under 18, 14.3% over 64 (2000); Marriage status: 17.0% never married, 65.4% now married, 2.6% widowed, 15.1% divorced (2000); Foreign born: 7.1% (2000); Ancestry (includes multiple ancestries): 20.9% Irish, 20.0% German, 17.4% English, 15.8% Other groups, 8.6% Italian (2000).
Economy: Employment by occupation: 12.2% management, 16.5% professional, 16.1% services, 29.2% sales, 3.0% farming, 14.9% construction, 8.0% production (2000).
Income: Per capita income: $28,353 (2000); Median household income: $53,409 (2000); Poverty rate: 6.6% (2000).
Education: Percent of population age 25 and over with: High school diploma (including GED) or higher: 89.6% (2000); Bachelor's degree or higher: 26.8% (2000).

School District(s)
Monroe County School District (PK-12)
    2005-06 Enrollment: 8,677 . . . . (305) 293-1400
Housing: Homeownership rate: 80.1% (2000); Median home value: $270,600 (2000); Median rent: $834 per month (2000); Median age of housing: 16 years (2000).
Transportation: Commute to work: 90.5% car, 0.5% public transportation, 0.0% walk, 5.1% work from home (2000); Travel time to work: 26.7% less than 15 minutes, 23.5% 15 to 30 minutes, 36.2% 30 to 45 minutes, 9.8% 45 to 60 minutes, 3.9% 60 minutes or more (2000)

TAVERNIER (CDP). Covers a land area of 2.611 square miles and a water area of 0.094 square miles. Located at 25.01° N. Lat.; 80.51° W. Long. Elevation is 7 feet.
History: Tavernier, on the southern end of Key Largo, was named for a pirate friend of Jean La Fitte, who was said to have used this area as a hiding place. The land boom of the 1920's brought growth to Tavernier.
Population: 2,433 (1990); 2,173 (2000); 1,800 (2007); 1,620 (2012 projected); Race: 96.8% White, 0.9% Black, 0.6% Asian, 22.7% Hispanic of any race (2007); Density: 689.3 persons per square mile (2007); Average household size: 2.36 (2007); Median age: 47.2 (2007); Males per 100 females: 102.5 (2007); Marriage status: 16.4% never married, 62.4% now married, 5.4% widowed, 15.7% divorced (2000); Foreign born: 14.9% (2000); Ancestry (includes multiple ancestries): 29.2% Other groups, 20.5% Irish, 18.3% English, 17.3% German, 8.8% United States or American (2000).
Economy: Employment by occupation: 7.7% management, 12.5% professional, 21.1% services, 23.4% sales, 5.3% farming, 17.9% construction, 12.1% production (2000).
Income: Per capita income: $26,907 (2007); Median household income: $49,709 (2007); Average household income: $63,060 (2007); Percent of households with income of $100,000 or more: 13.9% (2007); Poverty rate: 9.9% (2000).
Education: Percent of population age 25 and over with: High school diploma (including GED) or higher: 87.7% (2007); Bachelor's degree or higher: 19.9% (2007); Master's degree or higher: 4.2% (2007).

School District(s)
Monroe County School District (PK-12)
    2005-06 Enrollment: 8,677 . . . . (305) 293-1400
Housing: Homeownership rate: 65.5% (2007); Median home value: $570,866 (2007); Median rent: $638 per month (2000); Median age of housing: 19 years (2000).
Hospitals: Mariners Hospital (42 beds)
Newspapers: CBA: The Reporter (General - Circulation 8,000)
Transportation: Commute to work: 89.8% car, 0.0% public transportation, 1.8% walk, 4.4% work from home (2000); Travel time to work: 38.8% less than 15 minutes, 36.0% 15 to 30 minutes, 9.8% 30 to 45 minutes, 2.5% 45 to 60 minutes, 12.9% 60 minutes or more (2000)

Nassau County

Located in northeastern Florida; bounded on the east by the Atlantic Ocean, and on the north by the St. Marys River and the Georgia border; includes Amelia Barrier Island. Covers a land area of 651.55 square miles, a water area of 74.30 square miles, and is located in the Eastern Time Zone. The county was founded in 1824. County seat is Fernandina Beach.

Nassau County is part of the Jacksonville, FL Metropolitan Statistical Area. The entire metro area includes: Baker County, FL; Clay County, FL; Duval County, FL; Nassau County, FL; St. Johns County, FL

Weather Station: Fernandina Beach   Elevation: 13 feet

	Jan	Feb	Mar	Apr	May	Jun	Jul	Aug	Sep	Oct	Nov	Dec
High	62	65	71	77	82	87	90	88	85	78	71	65
Low	43	46	51	58	65	71	74	74	72	64	54	47
Precip	3.9	3.3	4.2	2.8	3.0	5.3	5.9	5.5	7.4	4.5	2.5	2.7
Snow	tr	tr	tr	0.0	0.0	0.0	0.0	0.0	0.0	0.0	0.0	0.0

High and Low temperatures in degrees Fahrenheit; Precipitation and Snow in inches

Population: 43,941 (1990); 57,663 (2000); 67,326 (2007); 74,594 (2012 projected); Race: 89.7% White, 7.4% Black, 0.8% Asian, 2.1% Hispanic of any race (2007); Density: 103.3 persons per square mile (2007); Average household size: 2.58 (2007); Median age: 40.8 (2007); Males per 100 females: 97.6 (2007).
Religion: Five largest groups: 29.2% Southern Baptist Convention, 5.2% Catholic Church, 3.7% The United Methodist Church, 2.1% Church of God (Cleveland, Tennessee), 1.7% Presbyterian Church (U.S.A.) (2000).
Economy: Unemployment rate: 3.6% (11/2007); Total civilian labor force: 34,567 (11/2007); Leading industries: 24.3% accommodation & food services; 19.2% retail trade; 11.9% hotels (exc casino hotels) & motels (2005); Farms: 315 totaling n/a acres (2002); Companies that employ 500 or more persons: 3 (2005); Companies that employ 100 to 499 persons: 17 (2005); Companies that employ less than 100 persons: 1,587 (2005); Black-owned businesses: n/a (2002); Hispanic-owned businesses: 104 (2002); Asian-owned businesses: n/a (2002); Women-owned businesses: 1,431 (2002); Retail sales per capita: $10,623 (2007). Single-family building permits issued: 986 (2006); Multi-family building permits issued: 250 (2006).
Income: Per capita income: $28,020 (2007); Median household income: $55,705 (2007); Average household income: $71,764 (2007); Percent of households with income of $100,000 or more: 19.1% (2007); Poverty rate: 9.2% (2005); Bankruptcy rate: 2.13% (2006).
Education: Percent of population age 25 and over with: High school diploma (including GED) or higher: 81.9% (2007); Bachelor's degree or higher: 20.5% (2007); Master's degree or higher: 7.1% (2007).
Housing: Homeownership rate: 81.2% (2007); Median home value: $199,753 (2007); Median rent: $450 per month (2000); Median age of housing: 16 years (2000).
Health: Birth rate: 104.8 per 10,000 population (2006); Death rate: 89.9 per 10,000 population (2006); Age-adjusted cancer mortality rate: 245.4 deaths per 100,000 population (2004); Air Quality Index: 99.1% good, 0.9% moderate, 0.0% unhealthy for sensitive individuals, 0.0% unhealthy (percent of days in 2006); Number of physicians: 11.9 per 10,000 population (2005); Hospital beds: 5.1 per 10,000 population (2004); Hospital admissions: 402.5 per 10,000 population (2004).
Elections: 2004 Presidential election results: 72.6% Bush, 26.2% Kerry, 0.6% Nader, 0.2% Badnarik
National and State Parks: Amelia Island State Park; Cary State Forest; Fernandina Plaza Historic State Park; Fort Clinch State Park; Nassau Sound Fishing Pier State Park
Additional Information Contacts
Nassau County Government . . . . (904) 548-4600
    http://www.nassauclerk.org
City of Fernandina Beach . . . . (904) 277-7305
    http://www.fbfl.us
Fernandina Beach Chamber of Commerce . . . . (904) 261-3248
    http://islandchamber.com

Nassau County Communities

BRYCEVILLE (unincorporated postal area, zip code 32009). Covers a land area of 91.626 square miles and a water area of 0.023 square miles. Located at 30.42° N. Lat.; 81.95° W. Long. Elevation is 70 feet.

History: Bryceville developed as a livestock and dairying center. Razorback hogs, allowed to roam the woods, were rounded up like cattle here.
Population: 2,730 (2000); Race: 97.8% White, 1.1% Black, 0.0% Asian, 0.5% Hispanic of any race (2000); Density: 29.8 persons per square mile (2000); Age: 30.1% under 18, 5.5% over 64 (2000); Marriage status: 18.2% never married, 69.6% now married, 3.1% widowed, 9.2% divorced (2000); Foreign born: 0.8% (2000); Ancestry (includes multiple ancestries): 25.4% United States or American, 7.3% English, 6.3% Irish, 6.0% Other groups, 5.4% German (2000).
Economy: Employment by occupation: 10.2% management, 13.6% professional, 11.9% services, 31.0% sales, 0.8% farming, 20.0% construction, 12.6% production (2000).
Income: Per capita income: $19,213 (2000); Median household income: $45,359 (2000); Poverty rate: 7.3% (2000).
Education: Percent of population age 25 and over with: High school diploma (including GED) or higher: 78.6% (2000); Bachelor's degree or higher: 8.7% (2000).

School District(s)
Nassau County School District (PK-12)
2005-06 Enrollment: 10,748 . . . . (904) 491-9901
Housing: Homeownership rate: 88.9% (2000); Median home value: $115,400 (2000); Median rent: $450 per month (2000); Median age of housing: 11 years (2000).
Transportation: Commute to work: 97.1% car, 0.0% public transportation, 0.0% walk, 2.1% work from home (2000); Travel time to work: 7.0% less than 15 minutes, 17.5% 15 to 30 minutes, 39.0% 30 to 45 minutes, 18.7% 45 to 60 minutes, 17.7% 60 minutes or more (2000)

CALLAHAN (town).
Covers a land area of 1.327 square miles and a water area of 0 square miles. Located at 30.56° N. Lat.; 81.83° W. Long. Elevation is 20 feet.
History: Callahan was the site in 1778 of an attack by 300 American cavalry under Colonel Elijah Clarke on a larger group of British troops, in which the Americans lost 13 men and were forced to withdraw.
Population: 946 (1990); 962 (2000); 994 (2007); 1,022 (2012 projected); Race: 83.0% White, 13.4% Black, 0.5% Asian, 2.3% Hispanic of any race (2007); Density: 749.0 persons per square mile (2007); Average household size: 2.33 (2007); Median age: 32.3 (2007); Males per 100 females: 84.1 (2007); Marriage status: 25.6% never married, 47.4% now married, 14.6% widowed, 12.4% divorced (2000); Foreign born: 0.6% (2000); Ancestry (includes multiple ancestries): 24.8% United States or American, 15.9% Other groups, 12.1% Irish, 8.6% English, 6.2% German (2000).
Economy: Single-family building permits issued: 21 (2006); Multi-family building permits issued: 0 (2006); Employment by occupation: 8.0% management, 16.3% professional, 19.0% services, 28.1% sales, 0.0% farming, 10.7% construction, 17.9% production (2000).
Income: Per capita income: $19,615 (2007); Median household income: $32,167 (2007); Average household income: $45,446 (2007); Percent of households with income of $100,000 or more: 11.0% (2007); Poverty rate: 21.9% (2000).
Education: Percent of population age 25 and over with: High school diploma (including GED) or higher: 69.8% (2007); Bachelor's degree or higher: 12.5% (2007); Master's degree or higher: 3.8% (2007).

School District(s)
Nassau County School District (PK-12)
2005-06 Enrollment: 10,748 . . . . (904) 491-9901
Housing: Homeownership rate: 47.9% (2007); Median home value: $143,919 (2007); Median rent: $327 per month (2000); Median age of housing: 19 years (2000).
Newspapers: Nassau County Record (General - Circulation 5,000)
Transportation: Commute to work: 88.2% car, 0.0% public transportation, 7.8% walk, 2.4% work from home (2000); Travel time to work: 23.7% less than 15 minutes, 33.6% 15 to 30 minutes, 26.7% 30 to 45 minutes, 12.9% 45 to 60 minutes, 3.0% 60 minutes or more (2000)

FERNANDINA BEACH (city).
County seat. Covers a land area of 10.716 square miles and a water area of 0.003 square miles. Located at 30.66° N. Lat.; 81.45° W. Long. Elevation is 10 feet.
History: Named for Don Domingo Fernandez, who obtained a land grant in 1785. A Spanish post stood on the site of Fernandina Beach in the 1680s, when the island was called Santa Maria. It was renamed Amelia Island in 1735 by General James Oglethorpe of Georgia, when he established a fort here. When Florida was returned to Spain, a land grant given to Fernandez included the village of Fernandina. An important port in the 1800s,

Fernandina Beach became an industrial city with shrimp and menhaden fisheries and pulp mills.
Population: 8,887 (1990); 10,549 (2000); 11,501 (2007); 12,358 (2012 projected); Race: 82.5% White, 14.5% Black, 0.9% Asian, 3.3% Hispanic of any race (2007); Density: 1,073.3 persons per square mile (2007); Average household size: 2.28 (2007); Median age: 45.1 (2007); Males per 100 females: 92.7 (2007); Marriage status: 22.1% never married, 58.0% now married, 9.0% widowed, 10.9% divorced (2000); Foreign born: 5.4% (2000); Ancestry (includes multiple ancestries): 19.1% Other groups, 16.4% English, 13.4% United States or American, 12.4% Irish, 11.4% German (2000).
Economy: Single-family building permits issued: 158 (2006); Multi-family building permits issued: 0 (2006); Employment by occupation: 15.3% management, 23.0% professional, 16.3% services, 23.6% sales, 0.3% farming, 10.5% construction, 11.2% production (2000).
Income: Per capita income: $28,718 (2007); Median household income: $47,463 (2007); Average household income: $64,226 (2007); Percent of households with income of $100,000 or more: 15.1% (2007); Poverty rate: 10.2% (2000).
Education: Percent of population age 25 and over with: High school diploma (including GED) or higher: 87.9% (2007); Bachelor's degree or higher: 33.4% (2007); Master's degree or higher: 12.5% (2007).

School District(s)
Nassau County School District (PK-12)
2005-06 Enrollment: 10,748 . . . . (904) 491-9901
Housing: Homeownership rate: 68.8% (2007); Median home value: $269,407 (2007); Median rent: $556 per month (2000); Median age of housing: 21 years (2000).
Hospitals: Baptist Medical Center Nassau (54 beds)
Safety: Violent crime rate: 42.8 per 10,000 population; Property crime rate: 445.3 per 10,000 population (2006).
Newspapers: News-Leader (General - Circulation 10,500)
Transportation: Commute to work: 91.0% car, 0.9% public transportation, 2.1% walk, 2.9% work from home (2000); Travel time to work: 50.3% less than 15 minutes, 20.3% 15 to 30 minutes, 12.3% 30 to 45 minutes, 10.6% 45 to 60 minutes, 6.5% 60 minutes or more (2000)
Airports: Fernandina Beach Municipal
Additional Information Contacts
City of Fernandina Beach . . . . (904) 277-7305
http://www.fbfl.us
Fernandina Beach Chamber of Commerce . . . . (904) 261-3248
http://islandchamber.com

HILLIARD (town).
Covers a land area of 5.495 square miles and a water area of 0 square miles. Located at 30.68° N. Lat.; 81.92° W. Long. Elevation is 59 feet.
History: Hilliard began as a trading post in the early 1800's, when cotton and tobacco were the leading crops.
Population: 2,486 (1990); 2,702 (2000); 2,716 (2007); 2,833 (2012 projected); Race: 82.0% White, 14.2% Black, 0.9% Asian, 1.1% Hispanic of any race (2007); Density: 494.3 persons per square mile (2007); Average household size: 2.81 (2007); Median age: 34.1 (2007); Males per 100 females: 88.0 (2007); Marriage status: 18.2% never married, 63.0% now married, 7.9% widowed, 10.9% divorced (2000); Foreign born: 1.0% (2000); Ancestry (includes multiple ancestries): 19.6% United States or American, 13.7% Irish, 12.7% Other groups, 11.0% English, 6.7% German (2000).
Economy: Single-family building permits issued: 6 (2006); Multi-family building permits issued: 0 (2006); Employment by occupation: 4.5% management, 8.0% professional, 17.4% services, 29.6% sales, 1.9% farming, 14.7% construction, 23.8% production (2000).
Income: Per capita income: $18,546 (2007); Median household income: $43,870 (2007); Average household income: $51,414 (2007); Percent of households with income of $100,000 or more: 10.3% (2007); Poverty rate: 11.7% (2000).
Taxes: Total city taxes per capita: $266 (2005); City property taxes per capita: $11 (2005).
Education: Percent of population age 25 and over with: High school diploma (including GED) or higher: 67.9% (2007); Bachelor's degree or higher: 5.5% (2007); Master's degree or higher: 1.9% (2007).

School District(s)
Nassau County School District (PK-12)
2005-06 Enrollment: 10,748 . . . . (904) 491-9901

$120,109 (2007); Median rent: $396 per month (2000); Median age of housing: 23 years (2000).
Transportation: Commute to work: 92.3% car, 0.0% public transportation, 2.2% walk, 2.5% work from home (2000); Travel time to work: 25.7% less than 15 minutes, 8.2% 15 to 30 minutes, 26.6% 30 to 45 minutes, 19.3% 45 to 60 minutes, 20.2% 60 minutes or more (2000)

NASSAU VILLAGE-RATLIFF (CDP). Covers a land area of 14.812 square miles and a water area of 0 square miles. Located at 30.51° N. Lat.; 81.79° W. Long.
Population: 4,047 (1990); 4,667 (2000); 4,471 (2007); 4,485 (2012 projected); Race: 96.9% White, 0.4% Black, 0.5% Asian, 1.2% Hispanic of any race (2007); Density: 301.8 persons per square mile (2007); Average household size: 2.81 (2007); Median age: 38.5 (2007); Males per 100 females: 101.0 (2007); Marriage status: 18.5% never married, 66.8% now married, 5.8% widowed, 8.9% divorced (2000); Foreign born: 0.4% (2000); Ancestry (includes multiple ancestries): 35.7% United States or American, 8.8% English, 7.1% Other groups, 6.8% German, 6.5% Irish (2000).
Economy: Employment by occupation: 7.0% management, 9.5% professional, 14.1% services, 32.1% sales, 0.0% farming, 18.8% construction, 18.4% production (2000).
Income: Per capita income: $18,546 (2007); Median household income: $47,276 (2007); Average household income: $52,085 (2007); Percent of households with income of $100,000 or more: 6.2% (2007); Poverty rate: 6.8% (2000).
Education: Percent of population age 25 and over with: High school diploma (including GED) or higher: 72.6% (2007); Bachelor's degree or higher: 6.3% (2007); Master's degree or higher: 0.9% (2007).
Housing: Homeownership rate: 90.6% (2007); Median home value: $144,473 (2007); Median rent: $460 per month (2000); Median age of housing: 17 years (2000).
Transportation: Commute to work: 96.9% car, 0.0% public transportation, 1.5% walk, 1.6% work from home (2000); Travel time to work: 16.6% less than 15 minutes, 32.0% 15 to 30 minutes, 33.7% 30 to 45 minutes, 11.1% 45 to 60 minutes, 6.5% 60 minutes or more (2000)

YULEE (CDP). Covers a land area of 22.982 square miles and a water area of 0.020 square miles. Located at 30.63° N. Lat.; 81.57° W. Long. Elevation is 36 feet.
History: Yulee was named for David L. Yulee, U.S. Senator from Florida (1845-1851 and 1855-1861), whose name before his election was David Levy. After the Civil War, Yulee was arrested for aiding in the escape of Jefferson Davis, and was imprisoned briefly at Fort Pulaski, Georgia.
Population: 6,751 (1990); 8,392 (2000); 8,729 (2007); 9,197 (2012 projected); Race: 88.5% White, 7.8% Black, 0.8% Asian, 2.0% Hispanic of any race (2007); Density: 379.8 persons per square mile (2007); Average household size: 2.67 (2007); Median age: 37.3 (2007); Males per 100 females: 100.8 (2007); Marriage status: 18.5% never married, 63.9% now married, 5.2% widowed, 12.4% divorced (2000); Foreign born: 1.7% (2000); Ancestry (includes multiple ancestries): 18.5% Other groups, 17.8% United States or American, 10.1% Irish, 8.0% German, 6.8% English (2000).
Economy: Employment by occupation: 9.6% management, 11.8% professional, 15.5% services, 25.6% sales, 0.5% farming, 15.7% construction, 21.3% production (2000).
Income: Per capita income: $21,449 (2007); Median household income: $47,532 (2007); Average household income: $57,274 (2007); Percent of households with income of $100,000 or more: 11.1% (2007); Poverty rate: 10.6% (2000).
Education: Percent of population age 25 and over with: High school diploma (including GED) or higher: 78.7% (2007); Bachelor's degree or higher: 7.4% (2007); Master's degree or higher: 2.4% (2007).

School District(s)
Nassau County School District (PK-12)
    2005-06 Enrollment: 10,748 . . . . (904) 491-9901
Housing: Homeownership rate: 82.2% (2007); Median home value: $165,033 (2007); Median rent: $398 per month (2000); Median age of housing: 15 years (2000).
Transportation: Commute to work: 94.3% car, 0.0% public transportation, 0.3% walk, 3.6% work from home (2000); Travel time to work: 14.1% less than 15 minutes, 45.7% 15 to 30 minutes, 23.2% 30 to 45 minutes, 12.9% 45 to 60 minutes, 4.2% 60 minutes or more (2000)

Located in northwestern Florida; bounded on the north by Alabama, and on the south by the Gulf of Mexico; drained by the Blackwater, Yellow, and Shoal Rivers; includes part of Choctawhatchee National Forest. Covers a land area of 935.63 square miles, a water area of 146.37 square miles, and is located in the Central Time Zone. The county was founded in 1915. County seat is Crestview.

Okaloosa County is part of the Fort Walton Beach-Crestview-Destin, FL Metropolitan Statistical Area. The entire metro area includes: Okaloosa County, FL

Population: 143,776 (1990); 170,498 (2000); 190,265 (2007); 205,569 (2012 projected); Race: 82.1% White, 9.5% Black, 2.7% Asian, 5.5% Hispanic of any race (2007); Density: 203.4 persons per square mile (2007); Average household size: 2.50 (2007); Median age: 38.3 (2007); Males per 100 females: 101.5 (2007).
Religion: Five largest groups: 20.2% Southern Baptist Convention, 6.7% The United Methodist Church, 6.7% Catholic Church, 2.2% Assemblies of God, 1.3% Episcopal Church (2000).
Economy: Unemployment rate: 3.2% (11/2007); Total civilian labor force: 100,049 (11/2007); Leading industries: 21.1% retail trade; 16.6% accommodation & food services; 12.6% health care and social assistance (2005); Farms: 465 totaling 55,119 acres (2002); Companies that employ 500 or more persons: 10 (2005); Companies that employ 100 to 499 persons: 75 (2005); Companies that employ less than 100 persons: 5,567 (2005); Black-owned businesses: 399 (2002); Hispanic-owned businesses: 633 (2002); Asian-owned businesses: 461 (2002); Women-owned businesses: 4,207 (2002); Retail sales per capita: $20,034 (2007). Single-family building permits issued: 1,699 (2006); Multi-family building permits issued: 91 (2006).
Income: Per capita income: $26,486 (2007); Median household income: $51,459 (2007); Average household income: $65,309 (2007); Percent of households with income of $100,000 or more: 16.5% (2007); Poverty rate: 9.8% (2005); Bankruptcy rate: 1.11% (2006).
Taxes: Total county taxes per capita: $307 (2005); County property taxes per capita: $224 (2005).
Education: Percent of population age 25 and over with: High school diploma (including GED) or higher: 87.9% (2007); Bachelor's degree or higher: 24.2% (2007); Master's degree or higher: 9.2% (2007).
Housing: Homeownership rate: 67.2% (2007); Median home value: $196,783 (2007); Median rent: $502 per month (2000); Median age of housing: 18 years (2000).
Health: Birth rate: 164.3 per 10,000 population (2006); Death rate: 80.9 per 10,000 population (2006); Age-adjusted cancer mortality rate: 187.2 deaths per 100,000 population (2004); Number of physicians: 24.9 per 10,000 population (2005); Hospital beds: 26.2 per 10,000 population (2004); Hospital admissions: 1,366.4 per 10,000 population (2004).
Elections: 2004 Presidential election results: 77.6% Bush, 21.6% Kerry, 0.4% Nader, 0.2% Badnarik
National and State Parks: Fred Gannon Rocky Bayou State Park; Henderson Beach State Park; Rocky Bayou State Park Aquatic Preserve
Additional Information Contacts
Okaloosa County Government. . . . . (850) 689-5030
    http://www.co.okaloosa.fl.us
City of Niceville . . . . (850) 729-4008
    http://cityofniceville.org
City of Valparaiso. . . . . (850) 729-5402
    http://www.valp.org
Crestview Chamber of Commerce. . . . . (850) 682-3212
    http://www.crestviewchamber.com
Destin Chamber of Commerce . . . . (850) 837-6241
    http://www.destinchamber.com
Greater Fort Walton Bch Chamber . . . . (850) 244-8191
    http://www.fwbchamber.org
Valparaiso Chamber of Commerce . . . . (850) 678-2323
    http://www.nicevillechamber.org

Okaloosa County Communities

BAKER (unincorporated postal area, zip code 32531). Covers a land area of 229.191 square miles and a water area of 1.242 square miles. Located at 30.87° N. Lat.; 86.68° W. Long. Elevation is 249 feet.
Population: 4,278 (2000); Race: 95.4% White, 1.9% Black, 0.3% Asian, 0.4% Hispanic of any race (2000); Density: 18.7 persons per square mile

(2000); Age: 26.7% under 18, 12.3% over 64 (2000); Marriage status: 16.1% never married, 73.1% now married, 3.9% widowed, 6.9% divorced (2000); Foreign born: 0.8% (2000); Ancestry (includes multiple ancestries): 17.0% United States or American, 14.4% Other groups, 13.0% Irish, 9.3% English, 7.6% German (2000).

Economy: Employment by occupation: 9.3% management, 17.9% professional, 14.0% services, 20.9% sales, 1.4% farming, 21.9% construction, 14.7% production (2000).

Income: Per capita income: $16,276 (2000); Median household income: $36,019 (2000); Poverty rate: 8.1% (2000).

Education: Percent of population age 25 and over with: High school diploma (including GED) or higher: 80.7% (2000); Bachelor's degree or higher: 12.4% (2000).

School District(s)
Okaloosa County School District (PK-12)
   2005-06 Enrollment: 31,756 . . . . (850) 833-3109

Housing: Homeownership rate: 83.0% (2000); Median home value: $79,400 (2000); Median rent: $401 per month (2000); Median age of housing: 21 years (2000).

Transportation: Commute to work: 97.2% car, 0.0% public transportation, 1.3% walk, 1.5% work from home (2000); Travel time to work: 12.9% less than 15 minutes, 36.8% 15 to 30 minutes, 19.7% 30 to 45 minutes, 18.3% 45 to 60 minutes, 12.2% 60 minutes or more (2000)

CINCO BAYOU (town). Covers a land area of 0.178 square miles and a water area of 0 square miles. Located at 30.42° N. Lat.; 86.60° W. Long. Elevation is 13 feet.

Population: 322 (1990); 377 (2000); 403 (2007); 428 (2012 projected); Race: 76.4% White, 16.1% Black, 4.7% Asian, 4.7% Hispanic of any race (2007); Density: 2,261.9 persons per square mile (2007); Average household size: 1.74 (2007); Median age: 44.5 (2007); Males per 100 females: 98.5 (2007); Marriage status: 28.2% never married, 43.3% now married, 3.3% widowed, 25.2% divorced (2000); Foreign born: 7.2% (2000); Ancestry (includes multiple ancestries): 35.6% Other groups, 12.2% German, 11.9% United States or American, 10.2% English, 9.9% Irish (2000).

Economy: Employment by occupation: 11.7% management, 12.2% professional, 25.0% services, 31.7% sales, 0.0% farming, 16.7% construction, 2.8% production (2000).

Income: Per capita income: $32,144 (2007); Median household income: $35,435 (2007); Average household income: $55,216 (2007); Percent of households with income of $100,000 or more: 8.6% (2007); Poverty rate: 15.5% (2000).

Education: Percent of population age 25 and over with: High school diploma (including GED) or higher: 90.8% (2007); Bachelor's degree or higher: 18.1% (2007); Master's degree or higher: 6.2% (2007).

Housing: Homeownership rate: 48.7% (2007); Median home value: $185,156 (2007); Median rent: $432 per month (2000); Median age of housing: 18 years (2000).

Transportation: Commute to work: 90.3% car, 1.0% public transportation, 1.0% walk, 6.6% work from home (2000); Travel time to work: 33.3% less than 15 minutes, 42.6% 15 to 30 minutes, 15.3% 30 to 45 minutes, 0.0% 45 to 60 minutes, 8.7% 60 minutes or more (2000)

CRESTVIEW (city). County seat. Covers a land area of 12.799 square miles and a water area of 0.029 square miles. Located at 30.75° N. Lat.; 86.57° W. Long. Elevation is 236 feet.

History: '

Population: 10,471 (1990); 14,766 (2000); 18,675 (2007); 21,312 (2012 projected); Race: 73.4% White, 18.0% Black, 3.1% Asian, 4.9% Hispanic of any race (2007); Density: 1,459.1 persons per square mile (2007); Average household size: 2.74 (2007); Median age: 34.0 (2007); Males per 100 females: 94.4 (2007); Marriage status: 23.7% never married, 58.3% now married, 6.9% widowed, 11.1% divorced (2000); Foreign born: 5.1% (2000); Ancestry (includes multiple ancestries): 25.7% Other groups, 14.3% United States or American, 11.1% German, 8.8% Irish, 8.6% English (2000).

Economy: Single-family building permits issued: 692 (2006); Multi-family building permits issued: 0 (2006); Employment by occupation: 8.5% management, 17.5% professional, 23.2% services, 27.7% sales, 0.1% farming, 13.2% construction, 9.8% production (2000).

Income: Per capita income: $19,763 (2007); Median household income: $43,474 (2007); Average household income: $53,228 (2007); Percent of households with income of $100,000 or more: 10.4% (2007); Poverty rate: 16.7% (2000).

Education: Percent of population age 25 and over with: High school diploma (including GED) or higher: 79.8% (2007); Bachelor's degree or higher: 14.1% (2007); Master's degree or higher: 4.8% (2007).

School District(s)
Okaloosa County School District (PK-12)
   2005-06 Enrollment: 31,756 . . . . (850) 833-3109

Housing: Homeownership rate: 67.3% (2007); Median home value: $167,752 (2007); Median rent: $367 per month (2000); Median age of housing: 15 years (2000).

Hospitals: North Okaloosa Medical Center (110 beds)

Safety: Violent crime rate: 54.4 per 10,000 population; Property crime rate: 396.5 per 10,000 population (2006).

Newspapers: Crestview News Bulletin (General - Circulation 2,500); News Extra (General - Circulation 12,361)

Transportation: Commute to work: 96.9% car, 0.2% public transportation, 0.7% walk, 1.0% work from home (2000); Travel time to work: 30.1% less than 15 minutes, 24.0% 15 to 30 minutes, 26.1% 30 to 45 minutes, 13.8% 45 to 60 minutes, 6.1% 60 minutes or more (2000); Amtrak: Service available.

Airports: Bob Sikes

Additional Information Contacts
Crestview Chamber of Commerce. (850) 682-3212
   http://www.crestviewchamber.com

DESTIN (city). Covers a land area of 7.528 square miles and a water area of 0.650 square miles. Located at 30.39° N. Lat.; 86.47° W. Long. Elevation is 26 feet.

Population: 7,689 (1990); 11,119 (2000); 13,165 (2007); 14,647 (2012 projected); Race: 95.7% White, 0.3% Black, 1.2% Asian, 3.9% Hispanic of any race (2007); Density: 1,748.9 persons per square mile (2007); Average household size: 2.21 (2007); Median age: 46.2 (2007); Males per 100 females: 102.2 (2007); Marriage status: 19.1% never married, 60.1% now married, 6.6% widowed, 14.2% divorced (2000); Foreign born: 5.1% (2000); Ancestry (includes multiple ancestries): 16.6% German, 14.8% English, 12.5% Irish, 11.1% United States or American, 10.9% Other groups (2000).

Economy: Single-family building permits issued: 166 (2006); Multi-family building permits issued: 3 (2006); Employment by occupation: 19.2% management, 17.1% professional, 14.6% services, 28.4% sales, 2.0% farming, 10.7% construction, 8.1% production (2000).

Income: Per capita income: $39,598 (2007); Median household income: $65,101 (2007); Average household income: $87,216 (2007); Percent of households with income of $100,000 or more: 25.1% (2007); Poverty rate: 5.5% (2000).

Education: Percent of population age 25 and over with: High school diploma (including GED) or higher: 91.9% (2007); Bachelor's degree or higher: 31.7% (2007); Master's degree or higher: 9.8% (2007).

School District(s)
Okaloosa County School District (PK-12)
   2005-06 Enrollment: 31,756 . . . . (850) 833-3109

Housing: Homeownership rate: 75.3% (2007); Median home value: $329,444 (2007); Median rent: $678 per month (2000); Median age of housing: 14 years (2000).

Hospitals: Sacred Heart Hospital on the Emerald Coast

Newspapers: Destin Log (General - Circulation 8,000)

Transportation: Commute to work: 92.9% car, 0.3% public transportation, 1.8% walk, 3.0% work from home (2000); Travel time to work: 41.5% less than 15 minutes, 33.3% 15 to 30 minutes, 17.1% 30 to 45 minutes, 3.5% 45 to 60 minutes, 4.5% 60 minutes or more (2000)

Airports: Destin-Fort Walton Beach

Additional Information Contacts
Destin Chamber of Commerce . . . . (850) 837-6241
   http://www.destinchamber.com

EGLIN AFB (CDP). Covers a land area of 3.061 square miles and a water area of 0.138 square miles. Located at 30.45° N. Lat.; 86.55° W. Long.

Population: 8,347 (1990); 8,082 (2000); 8,248 (2007); 8,499 (2012 projected); Race: 72.5% White, 12.7% Black, 2.5% Asian, 15.2% Hispanic of any race (2007); Density: 2,694.3 persons per square mile (2007); Average household size: 3.44 (2007); Median age: 21.1 (2007); Males per 100 females: 100.8 (2007); Marriage status: 7.6% never married, 89.2% now married, 0.4% widowed, 2.7% divorced (2000); Foreign born: 4.7% (2000); Ancestry (includes multiple ancestries): 36.1% Other groups,

English (2000).

Economy: Employment by occupation: 8.4% management, 18.8% professional, 25.6% services, 30.8% sales, 0.0% farming, 9.1% construction, 7.3% production (2000).

Income: Per capita income: $13,072 (2007); Median household income: $38,076 (2007); Average household income: $44,331 (2007); Percent of households with income of $100,000 or more: 3.8% (2007); Poverty rate: 4.5% (2000).

Education: Percent of population age 25 and over with: High school diploma (including GED) or higher: 96.1% (2007); Bachelor's degree or higher: 19.4% (2007); Master's degree or higher: 6.0% (2007).

School District(s)
Okaloosa County School District (PK-12)

    2005-06 Enrollment: 31,756 . . . . (850) 833-3109

Housing: Homeownership rate: 1.1% (2007); Median home value: $190,972 (2007); Median rent: $543 per month (2000); Median age of housing: 40 years (2000).

Transportation: Commute to work: 93.5% car, 0.5% public transportation, 0.9% walk, 2.6% work from home (2000); Travel time to work: 48.2% less than 15 minutes, 35.1% 15 to 30 minutes, 14.1% 30 to 45 minutes, 1.8% 45 to 60 minutes, 0.8% 60 minutes or more (2000)

FORT WALTON BEACH (city).
Covers a land area of 7.444 square miles and a water area of 0.761 square miles. Located at 30.42° N. Lat.; 86.61° W. Long. Elevation is 7 feet.

History: The city grew around a fort constructed during the Seminole War (1835—1842). Its main growth came after 1941, when it developed as a resort center and the air force base was expanded. A national historic landmark here includes a Museum of Native American culture. Incorporated 1941.

Population: 21,548 (1990); 19,973 (2000); 20,186 (2007); 20,621 (2012 projected); Race: 77.9% White, 13.4% Black, 2.8% Asian, 5.1% Hispanic of any race (2007); Density: 2,711.7 persons per square mile (2007); Average household size: 2.29 (2007); Median age: 41.3 (2007); Males per 100 females: 96.7 (2007); Marriage status: 23.2% never married, 55.0% now married, 7.5% widowed, 14.3% divorced (2000); Foreign born: 5.7% (2000); Ancestry (includes multiple ancestries): 24.7% Other groups, 13.9% German, 12.3% English, 9.7% Irish, 9.3% United States or American (2000).

Economy: Single-family building permits issued: 34 (2006); Multi-family building permits issued: 17 (2006); Employment by occupation: 12.1% management, 18.2% professional, 21.6% services, 27.0% sales, 0.1% farming, 10.9% construction, 10.1% production (2000).

Income: Per capita income: $25,817 (2007); Median household income: $47,552 (2007); Average household income: $58,856 (2007); Percent of households with income of $100,000 or more: 14.1% (2007); Poverty rate: 9.9% (2000).

Education: Percent of population age 25 and over with: High school diploma (including GED) or higher: 89.1% (2007); Bachelor's degree or higher: 21.4% (2007); Master's degree or higher: 7.4% (2007).

School District(s)
Okaloosa County School District (PK-12)

    2005-06 Enrollment: 31,756 . . . . (850) 833-3109

Two-year College(s)
Okaloosa Applied Technology Center (Public)

    Fall 2006 Enrollment: 293 . . . . (850) 833-3500

Housing: Homeownership rate: 63.6% (2007); Median home value: $178,542 (2007); Median rent: $482 per month (2000); Median age of housing: 31 years (2000).

Hospitals: Fort Walton Beach Medical Center (247 beds); Gulf Coast Treatment Center (24 beds)

Safety: Violent crime rate: 68.5 per 10,000 population; Property crime rate: 418.8 per 10,000 population (2006).

Newspapers: Northwest Florida Daily News (Circulation 40,562)

Transportation: Commute to work: 94.1% car, 0.2% public transportation, 2.3% walk, 1.8% work from home (2000); Travel time to work: 43.2% less than 15 minutes, 36.9% 15 to 30 minutes, 12.3% 30 to 45 minutes, 3.1% 45 to 60 minutes, 4.5% 60 minutes or more (2000)

Additional Information Contacts

Greater Fort Walton Bch Chamber . . . . (850) 244-8191
    http://www.fwbchamber.org

HOLT (unincorporated postal area, zip code 32564).
Aka Holts. Covers a land area of 72.217 square miles and a water area of 0.083 square miles. Located at 30.71° N. Lat.; 86.77° W. Long. Elevation is 200 feet.

Population: 2,331 (2000); Race: 93.7% White, 0.3% Black, 1.0% Asian, 2.7% Hispanic of any race (2000); Density: 32.3 persons per square mile (2000); Age: 24.7% under 18, 12.7% over 64 (2000); Marriage status: 24.0% never married, 55.5% now married, 7.3% widowed, 13.3% divorced (2000); Foreign born: 1.7% (2000); Ancestry (includes multiple ancestries): 23.2% Other groups, 22.3% United States or American, 12.5% Irish, 10.0% English, 6.7% German (2000).

Economy: Employment by occupation: 7.2% management, 4.9% professional, 26.5% services, 23.3% sales, 0.7% farming, 23.1% construction, 14.2% production (2000).

Income: Per capita income: $13,694 (2000); Median household income: $35,385 (2000); Poverty rate: 16.2% (2000).

Education: Percent of population age 25 and over with: High school diploma (including GED) or higher: 68.6% (2000); Bachelor's degree or higher: 7.5% (2000).

School District(s)
Santa Rosa County School District (PK-12)

    2005-06 Enrollment: 25,038 . . . . (850) 983-5010

Housing: Homeownership rate: 93.8% (2000); Median home value: $56,800 (2000); Median rent: $129 per month (2000); Median age of housing: 16 years (2000).

Transportation: Commute to work: 96.0% car, 1.1% public transportation, 0.0% walk, 0.0% work from home (2000); Travel time to work: 10.4% less than 15 minutes, 42.5% 15 to 30 minutes, 15.8% 30 to 45 minutes, 21.2% 45 to 60 minutes, 10.1% 60 minutes or more (2000)

HURLBURT FIELD (unincorporated postal area, zip code 32544).
Aka Eglin Auxiliary Field No. 9. Covers a land area of 252.353 square miles and a water area of 0.154 square miles. Located at 30.42° N. Lat.; 86.69° W. Long.

Population: 3,093 (2000); Race: 66.8% White, 18.4% Black, 2.7% Asian, 8.8% Hispanic of any race (2000); Density: 12.3 persons per square mile (2000); Age: 31.3% under 18, 0.3% over 64 (2000); Marriage status: 33.6% never married, 62.4% now married, 0.0% widowed, 4.0% divorced (2000); Foreign born: 4.5% (2000); Ancestry (includes multiple ancestries): 38.4% Other groups, 12.8% Irish, 12.7% German, 8.8% English, 7.8% United States or American (2000).

Economy: Employment by occupation: 8.5% management, 9.6% professional, 28.2% services, 36.8% sales, 0.0% farming, 12.7% construction, 4.2% production (2000).

Income: Per capita income: $11,879 (2000); Median household income: $32,163 (2000); Poverty rate: 5.6% (2000).

Education: Percent of population age 25 and over with: High school diploma (including GED) or higher: 97.6% (2000); Bachelor's degree or higher: 14.4% (2000).

Housing: Homeownership rate: 2.0% (2000); Median home value: $n/a (2000); Median rent: $581 per month (2000); Median age of housing: 14 years (2000).

Transportation: Commute to work: 81.5% car, 0.5% public transportation, 11.9% walk, 2.1% work from home (2000); Travel time to work: 71.6% less than 15 minutes, 21.4% 15 to 30 minutes, 4.7% 30 to 45 minutes, 1.3% 45 to 60 minutes, 1.0% 60 minutes or more (2000)

LAKE LORRAINE (CDP).
Covers a land area of 2.040 square miles and a water area of 0.317 square miles. Located at 30.44° N. Lat.; 86.57° W. Long. Elevation is 26 feet.

Population: 6,779 (1990); 7,106 (2000); 7,172 (2007); 7,337 (2012 projected); Race: 81.9% White, 8.9% Black, 3.1% Asian, 7.2% Hispanic of any race (2007); Density: 3,515.5 persons per square mile (2007); Average household size: 2.35 (2007); Median age: 41.5 (2007); Males per 100 females: 96.7 (2007); Marriage status: 22.4% never married, 59.5% now married, 5.2% widowed, 12.8% divorced (2000); Foreign born: 6.1% (2000); Ancestry (includes multiple ancestries): 21.6% Other groups, 13.5% German, 13.3% United States or American, 10.9% English, 9.0% Irish (2000).

Economy: Employment by occupation: 10.6% management, 20.3% professional, 23.6% services, 30.1% sales, 0.5% farming, 8.8% construction, 6.1% production (2000).

Income: Per capita income: $29,593 (2007); Median household income: $58,576 (2007); Average household income: $69,541 (2007); Percent of

diploma (including GED) or higher: 91.8% (2007); Bachelor's degree or higher: 30.0% (2007); Master's degree or higher: 14.1% (2007).

Housing: Homeownership rate: 65.1% (2007); Median home value: $250,116 (2007); Median rent: $575 per month (2000); Median age of housing: 21 years (2000).

Transportation: Commute to work: 94.5% car, 0.7% public transportation, 0.6% walk, 2.1% work from home (2000); Travel time to work: 30.2% less than 15 minutes, 53.3% 15 to 30 minutes, 9.7% 30 to 45 minutes, 3.7% 45 to 60 minutes, 3.1% 60 minutes or more (2000)

LAUREL HILL (city).
Covers a land area of 3.139 square miles and a water area of 0 square miles. Located at 30.96° N. Lat.; 86.45° W. Long. Elevation is 282 feet.

Population: 556 (1990); 549 (2000); 629 (2007); 687 (2012 projected); Race: 81.7% White, 16.7% Black, 0.0% Asian, 1.7% Hispanic of any race (2007); Density: 200.4 persons per square mile (2007); Average household size: 2.40 (2007); Median age: 41.3 (2007); Males per 100 females: 91.8 (2007); Marriage status: 17.2% never married, 64.4% now married, 8.5% widowed, 9.8% divorced (2000); Foreign born: 2.0% (2000); Ancestry (includes multiple ancestries): 29.7% United States or American, 26.4% Other groups, 7.3% Irish, 6.0% German, 4.0% Scottish (2000).

Economy: Employment by occupation: 11.9% management, 9.1% professional, 14.2% services, 26.0% sales, 1.8% farming, 22.8% construction, 14.2% production (2000).

Income: Per capita income: $16,753 (2007); Median household income: $33,000 (2007); Average household income: $40,219 (2007); Percent of households with income of $100,000 or more: 5.0% (2007); Poverty rate: 21.6% (2000).

Education: Percent of population age 25 and over with: High school diploma (including GED) or higher: 62.2% (2007); Bachelor's degree or higher: 4.8% (2007); Master's degree or higher: 1.2% (2007).

School District(s)
Okaloosa County School District (PK-12)
    2005-06 Enrollment: 31,756 . . . . (850) 833-3109

Housing: Homeownership rate: 80.5% (2007); Median home value: $91,923 (2007); Median rent: $263 per month (2000); Median age of housing: 24 years (2000).

Transportation: Commute to work: 85.1% car, 0.0% public transportation, 7.0% walk, 1.9% work from home (2000); Travel time to work: 13.7% less than 15 minutes, 18.0% 15 to 30 minutes, 24.6% 30 to 45 minutes, 11.4% 45 to 60 minutes, 32.2% 60 minutes or more (2000)

MARY ESTHER (city).
Covers a land area of 1.539 square miles and a water area of 0 square miles. Located at 30.41° N. Lat.; 86.65° W. Long. Elevation is 23 feet.

Population: 4,139 (1990); 4,055 (2000); 4,215 (2007); 4,386 (2012 projected); Race: 82.8% White, 6.4% Black, 4.1% Asian, 5.1% Hispanic of any race (2007); Density: 2,738.9 persons per square mile (2007); Average household size: 2.43 (2007); Median age: 41.6 (2007); Males per 100 females: 102.2 (2007); Marriage status: 17.6% never married, 66.7% now married, 4.0% widowed, 11.8% divorced (2000); Foreign born: 6.7% (2000); Ancestry (includes multiple ancestries): 19.8% Other groups, 13.7% Irish, 13.3% German, 12.6% English, 11.8% United States or American (2000).

Economy: Employment by occupation: 11.4% management, 18.1% professional, 19.4% services, 32.7% sales, 0.0% farming, 9.4% construction, 9.0% production (2000).

Income: Per capita income: $26,845 (2007); Median household income: $52,175 (2007); Average household income: $65,142 (2007); Percent of households with income of $100,000 or more: 17.1% (2007); Poverty rate: 5.7% (2000).

Education: Percent of population age 25 and over with: High school diploma (including GED) or higher: 92.0% (2007); Bachelor's degree or higher: 22.5% (2007); Master's degree or higher: 8.1% (2007).

School District(s)
Okaloosa County School District (PK-12)
    2005-06 Enrollment: 31,756 . . . . (850) 833-3109

Housing: Homeownership rate: 74.6% (2007); Median home value: $182,292 (2007); Median rent: $521 per month (2000); Median age of housing: 27 years (2000).

Transportation: Commute to work: 94.8% car, 0.4% public transportation, 0.7% walk, 1.8% work from home (2000); Travel time to work: 48.4% less

NICEVILLE (city).
Covers a land area of 10.922 square miles and a water area of 0.407 square miles. Located at 30.51° N. Lat.; 86.47° W. Long. Elevation is 36 feet.

Population: 10,878 (1990); 11,684 (2000); 12,788 (2007); 13,667 (2012 projected); Race: 86.2% White, 4.6% Black, 3.5% Asian, 4.4% Hispanic of any race (2007); Density: 1,170.9 persons per square mile (2007); Average household size: 2.46 (2007); Median age: 42.2 (2007); Males per 100 females: 97.6 (2007); Marriage status: 21.4% never married, 63.4% now married, 5.2% widowed, 10.1% divorced (2000); Foreign born: 6.3% (2000); Ancestry (includes multiple ancestries): 21.6% Other groups, 14.4% German, 12.9% Irish, 12.9% United States or American, 11.4% English (2000).

Economy: Single-family building permits issued: 83 (2006); Multi-family building permits issued: 26 (2006); Employment by occupation: 12.6% management, 19.9% professional, 22.2% services, 27.0% sales, 0.1% farming, 10.4% construction, 7.8% production (2000).

Income: Per capita income: $27,122 (2007); Median household income: $56,624 (2007); Average household income: $66,412 (2007); Percent of households with income of $100,000 or more: 19.3% (2007); Poverty rate: 9.6% (2000).

Education: Percent of population age 25 and over with: High school diploma (including GED) or higher: 88.9% (2007); Bachelor's degree or higher: 26.3% (2007); Master's degree or higher: 11.3% (2007).

School District(s)
Okaloosa County School District (PK-12)
    2005-06 Enrollment: 31,756 . . . . (850) 833-3109

Four-year College(s)
Okaloosa-Walton College (Public)
    Fall 2006 Enrollment: 6,742 . . . . (850) 678-5111
    2006-07 Tuition: In-state $1,763; Out-of-state $6,730

Housing: Homeownership rate: 71.9% (2007); Median home value: $211,181 (2007); Median rent: $460 per month (2000); Median age of housing: 20 years (2000).

Hospitals: Twin Cities Hospital (65 beds)

Safety: Violent crime rate: 15.6 per 10,000 population; Property crime rate: 135.2 per 10,000 population (2006).

Newspapers: Bay Beacon (General - Circulation 2,000); Beacon Express (General - Circulation 13,250)

Transportation: Commute to work: 95.9% car, 0.3% public transportation, 0.7% walk, 1.3% work from home (2000); Travel time to work: 28.9% less than 15 minutes, 46.0% 15 to 30 minutes, 19.2% 30 to 45 minutes, 3.1% 45 to 60 minutes, 2.8% 60 minutes or more (2000)

Additional Information Contacts
City of Niceville . . . . (850) 729-4008
    http://cityofniceville.org

OCEAN CITY (CDP).
Covers a land area of 1.601 square miles and a water area of 0.308 square miles. Located at 30.44° N. Lat.; 86.60° W. Long. Elevation is 10 feet.

Population: 5,431 (1990); 5,594 (2000); 5,541 (2007); 5,630 (2012 projected); Race: 81.7% White, 7.8% Black, 3.6% Asian, 5.7% Hispanic of any race (2007); Density: 3,460.4 persons per square mile (2007); Average household size: 2.21 (2007); Median age: 40.7 (2007); Males per 100 females: 97.8 (2007); Marriage status: 23.5% never married, 54.6% now married, 7.2% widowed, 14.6% divorced (2000); Foreign born: 5.2% (2000); Ancestry (includes multiple ancestries): 18.5% Other groups, 13.8% United States or American, 11.7% German, 11.3% English, 10.3% Irish (2000).

Economy: Employment by occupation: 8.9% management, 20.3% professional, 19.4% services, 27.4% sales, 1.0% farming, 11.2% construction, 11.7% production (2000).

Income: Per capita income: $26,522 (2007); Median household income: $42,775 (2007); Average household income: $58,543 (2007); Percent of households with income of $100,000 or more: 10.6% (2007); Poverty rate: 8.6% (2000).

Education: Percent of population age 25 and over with: High school diploma (including GED) or higher: 90.4% (2007); Bachelor's degree or higher: 21.0% (2007); Master's degree or higher: 5.5% (2007).

Housing: Homeownership rate: 60.3% (2007); Median home value: $169,121 (2007); Median rent: $501 per month (2000); Median age of housing: 32 years (2000).

SHALIMAR (town). Covers a land area of 0.294 square miles and a water area of 0 square miles. Located at 30.44° N. Lat.; 86.58° W. Long. Elevation is 13 feet.

Population: 345 (1990); 718 (2000); 708 (2007); 713 (2012 projected); Race: 86.3% White, 8.2% Black, 2.8% Asian, 2.3% Hispanic of any race (2007); Density: 2,407.6 persons per square mile (2007); Average household size: 2.42 (2007); Median age: 44.1 (2007); Males per 100 females: 94.0 (2007); Marriage status: 18.1% never married, 60.7% now married, 6.9% widowed, 14.3% divorced (2000); Foreign born: 4.8% (2000); Ancestry (includes multiple ancestries): 17.7% Other groups, 16.0% United States or American, 12.3% German, 10.9% Irish, 10.5% English (2000).

Economy: Employment by occupation: 27.6% management, 25.8% professional, 12.4% services, 24.2% sales, 0.0% farming, 3.9% construction, 6.1% production (2000).

Income: Per capita income: $39,057 (2007); Median household income: $75,490 (2007); Average household income: $94,700 (2007); Percent of households with income of $100,000 or more: 32.9% (2007); Poverty rate: 3.1% (2000).

Education: Percent of population age 25 and over with: High school diploma (including GED) or higher: 95.5% (2007); Bachelor's degree or higher: 47.7% (2007); Master's degree or higher: 20.9% (2007).

School District(s)

Okaloosa County School District (PK-12)

    2005-06 Enrollment: 31,756 . . . . (850) 833-3109

Housing: Homeownership rate: 81.8% (2007); Median home value: $338,690 (2007); Median rent: $769 per month (2000); Median age of housing: 10 years (2000).

Transportation: Commute to work: 95.0% car, 0.3% public transportation, 2.5% walk, 2.2% work from home (2000); Travel time to work: 44.8% less than 15 minutes, 42.8% 15 to 30 minutes, 7.1% 30 to 45 minutes, 3.4% 45 to 60 minutes, 2.0% 60 minutes or more (2000)

VALPARAISO (city). Covers a land area of 11.937 square miles and a water area of 0.811 square miles. Located at 30.50° N. Lat.; 86.49° W. Long. Elevation is 46 feet.

Population: 4,654 (1990); 6,408 (2000); 6,401 (2007); 6,527 (2012 projected); Race: 76.2% White, 12.7% Black, 2.5% Asian, 13.7% Hispanic of any race (2007); Density: 536.2 persons per square mile (2007); Average household size: 3.09 (2007); Median age: 35.1 (2007); Males per 100 females: 154.6 (2007); Marriage status: 34.6% never married, 47.8% now married, 4.6% widowed, 13.0% divorced (2000); Foreign born: 6.7% (2000); Ancestry (includes multiple ancestries): 25.9% Other groups, 12.7% German, 12.5% Irish, 11.3% English, 8.6% United States or American (2000).

Economy: Single-family building permits issued: 11 (2006); Multi-family building permits issued: 0 (2006); Employment by occupation: 11.4% management, 22.9% professional, 19.3% services, 26.0% sales, 0.3% farming, 11.8% construction, 8.4% production (2000).

Income: Per capita income: $21,967 (2007); Median household income: $46,335 (2007); Average household income: $55,242 (2007); Percent of households with income of $100,000 or more: 10.9% (2007); Poverty rate: 6.7% (2000).

Education: Percent of population age 25 and over with: High school diploma (including GED) or higher: 90.4% (2007); Bachelor's degree or higher: 20.5% (2007); Master's degree or higher: 9.8% (2007).

School District(s)

Okaloosa County School District (PK-12)

    2005-06 Enrollment: 31,756 . . . . (850) 833-3109

Housing: Homeownership rate: 69.5% (2007); Median home value: $166,763 (2007); Median rent: $379 per month (2000); Median age of housing: 28 years (2000).

Safety: Violent crime rate: 17.0 per 10,000 population; Property crime rate: 139.1 per 10,000 population (2006).

Transportation: Commute to work: 91.4% car, 0.8% public transportation, 4.3% walk, 1.4% work from home (2000); Travel time to work: 53.5% less than 15 minutes, 26.1% 15 to 30 minutes, 14.7% 30 to 45 minutes, 4.3% 45 to 60 minutes, 1.4% 60 minutes or more (2000)

Airports: Eglin AFB (primary service/small hub)

Additional Information Contacts

WRIGHT (CDP). Covers a land area of 5.469 square miles and a water area of 0.069 square miles. Located at 30.44° N. Lat.; 86.63° W. Long. Elevation is 43 feet.

Population: 18,927 (1990); 21,697 (2000); 23,784 (2007); 25,443 (2012 projected); Race: 72.9% White, 15.6% Black, 3.8% Asian, 6.8% Hispanic of any race (2007); Density: 4,348.6 persons per square mile (2007); Average household size: 2.30 (2007); Median age: 36.0 (2007); Males per 100 females: 101.2 (2007); Marriage status: 27.2% never married, 52.2% now married, 5.8% widowed, 14.8% divorced (2000); Foreign born: 7.2% (2000); Ancestry (includes multiple ancestries): 28.5% Other groups, 13.0% German, 12.3% Irish, 9.4% United States or American, 9.4% English (2000).

Economy: Employment by occupation: 10.8% management, 17.7% professional, 18.8% services, 26.9% sales, 0.4% farming, 14.2% construction, 11.2% production (2000).

Income: Per capita income: $23,893 (2007); Median household income: $45,500 (2007); Average household income: $54,267 (2007); Percent of households with income of $100,000 or more: 10.2% (2007); Poverty rate: 10.9% (2000).

Education: Percent of population age 25 and over with: High school diploma (including GED) or higher: 87.6% (2007); Bachelor's degree or higher: 21.0% (2007); Master's degree or higher: 7.2% (2007).

Housing: Homeownership rate: 55.1% (2007); Median home value: $168,002 (2007); Median rent: $496 per month (2000); Median age of housing: 16 years (2000).

Transportation: Commute to work: 95.1% car, 0.7% public transportation, 1.6% walk, 1.2% work from home (2000); Travel time to work: 44.4% less than 15 minutes, 39.3% 15 to 30 minutes, 9.5% 30 to 45 minutes, 3.1% 45 to 60 minutes, 3.7% 60 minutes or more (2000)

Okeechobee County

Located in central Florida; bounded on the west by the Kissimmee River, and on the south by Lake Okeechobee; contains many small lakes and swamps. Covers a land area of 773.94 square miles, a water area of 117.63 square miles, and is located in the Eastern Time Zone. The county was founded in 1917. County seat is Okeechobee.

Okeechobee County is part of the Okeechobee, FL Micropolitan Statistical Area. The entire metro area includes: Okeechobee County, FL

Weather Station: Fort Drum 5 NW   Elevation: 68 feet

	Jan	Feb	Mar	Apr	May	Jun	Jul	Aug	Sep	Oct	Nov	Dec
High	75	76	80	84	88	90	91	91	90	86	80	76
Low	50	51	55	58	63	69	71	72	70	65	58	52
Precip	2.4	2.5	3.9	2.4	4.5	8.1	7.8	7.2	6.7	3.7	2.3	1.9
Snow	tr	0.0	0.0	0.0	0.0	0.0	0.0	0.0	0.0	0.0	0.0	0.0

High and Low temperatures in degrees Fahrenheit; Precipitation and Snow in inches

Population: 29,601 (1990); 35,910 (2000); 39,562 (2007); 41,396 (2012 projected); Race: 76.7% White, 7.8% Black, 1.0% Asian, 22.3% Hispanic of any race (2007); Density: 51.1 persons per square mile (2007); Average household size: 2.83 (2007); Median age: 36.2 (2007); Males per 100 females: 116.5 (2007).

Religion: Five largest groups: 15.9% Southern Baptist Convention, 7.7% Catholic Church, 1.9% The United Methodist Church, 1.7% Church of God (Cleveland, Tennessee), 1.3% Lutheran Church—Missouri Synod (2000).

Economy: Unemployment rate: 5.5% (11/2007); Total civilian labor force: 18,338 (11/2007); Leading industries: 23.8% retail trade; 22.3% health care and social assistance; 13.3% accommodation & food services (2005); Farms: 638 totaling 392,495 acres (2002); Companies that employ 500 or more persons: 0 (2005); Companies that employ 100 to 499 persons: 9 (2005); Companies that employ less than 100 persons: 778 (2005); Black-owned businesses: n/a (2002); Hispanic-owned businesses: n/a (2002); Asian-owned businesses: n/a (2002); Women-owned businesses: 508 (2002); Retail sales per capita: $11,705 (2007). Single-family building permits issued: 202 (2006); Multi-family building permits issued: 0 (2006).

Income: Per capita income: $16,955 (2007); Median household income: $35,266 (2007); Average household income: $47,133 (2007); Percent of households with income of $100,000 or more: 8.0% (2007); Poverty rate: 18.1% (2005); Bankruptcy rate: 1.24% (2006).

Health: Birth rate: 154.4 per 10,000 population (2006); Death rate: 118.3 per 10,000 population (2006); Age-adjusted cancer mortality rate: 207.9 deaths per 100,000 population (2004); Number of physicians: 12.1 per 10,000 population (2005); Hospital beds: 25.9 per 10,000 population (2004); Hospital admissions: 1,303.0 per 10,000 population (2004).

Elections: 2004 Presidential election results: 57.2% Bush, 42.3% Kerry, 0.3% Nader, 0.1% Badnarik

National and State Parks: Kissimmee Prairie Preserve State Park

Additional Information Contacts

Okeechobee County Government . . . . (863) 763-6441
    http://www.co.okeechobee.fl.us
City of Okeechobee . . . . (863) 763-3372
    http://www.cityofokeechobee.com
Okeechobee Chamber of Commerce . . . . (863) 763-6464
    http://www.okeechobeechamberofcommerce.com

Okeechobee County Communities

CYPRESS QUARTERS (CDP). Covers a land area of 2.706 square miles and a water area of 0 square miles. Located at 27.24° N. Lat.; 80.81° W. Long. Elevation is 26 feet.

Population: 1,343 (1990); 1,150 (2000); 1,102 (2007); 1,066 (2012 projected); Race: 38.7% White, 51.6% Black, 0.5% Asian, 10.3% Hispanic of any race (2007); Density: 407.3 persons per square mile (2007); Average household size: 2.68 (2007); Median age: 31.0 (2007); Males per 100 females: 95.0 (2007); Marriage status: 36.3% never married, 46.0% now married, 8.5% widowed, 9.2% divorced (2000); Foreign born: 2.3% (2000); Ancestry (includes multiple ancestries): 47.0% Other groups, 11.2% Irish, 6.5% English, 3.9% German, 3.0% United States or American (2000).

Economy: Employment by occupation: 7.1% management, 14.7% professional, 18.4% services, 25.3% sales, 7.1% farming, 12.4% construction, 14.9% production (2000).

Income: Per capita income: $18,411 (2007); Median household income: $36,500 (2007); Average household income: $49,136 (2007); Percent of households with income of $100,000 or more: 5.1% (2007); Poverty rate: 30.5% (2000).

Education: Percent of population age 25 and over with: High school diploma (including GED) or higher: 58.4% (2007); Bachelor's degree or higher: 7.8% (2007); Master's degree or higher: 2.9% (2007).

Housing: Homeownership rate: 70.3% (2007); Median home value: $119,423 (2007); Median rent: $242 per month (2000); Median age of housing: 29 years (2000).

Transportation: Commute to work: 92.0% car, 1.3% public transportation, 2.2% walk, 0.0% work from home (2000); Travel time to work: 47.1% less than 15 minutes, 24.2% 15 to 30 minutes, 4.9% 30 to 45 minutes, 6.0% 45 to 60 minutes, 17.8% 60 minutes or more (2000)

OKEECHOBEE (city). County seat. Covers a land area of 4.126 square miles and a water area of 0.037 square miles. Located at 27.24° N. Lat.; 80.83° W. Long. Elevation is 26 feet.

History: Okeechobee developed as a commercial center for the surrounding area of poultry and frog farms, and as the seat of Okeechobee County. The breeding of bullfrogs for the frog-leg market was a major early industry.

Population: 4,945 (1990); 5,376 (2000); 5,596 (2007); 5,766 (2012 projected); Race: 78.4% White, 8.2% Black, 1.4% Asian, 19.1% Hispanic of any race (2007); Density: 1,356.2 persons per square mile (2007); Average household size: 2.92 (2007); Median age: 35.7 (2007); Males per 100 females: 102.2 (2007); Marriage status: 21.4% never married, 53.8% now married, 10.2% widowed, 14.7% divorced (2000); Foreign born: 7.4% (2000); Ancestry (includes multiple ancestries): 25.2% Other groups, 11.8% Irish, 11.2% United States or American, 10.7% German, 10.3% English (2000).

Economy: Single-family building permits issued: 33 (2006); Multi-family building permits issued: 0 (2006); Employment by occupation: 7.7% management, 14.6% professional, 23.9% services, 24.3% sales, 6.3% farming, 10.6% construction, 12.6% production (2000).

---

diploma (including GED) or higher: 60.2% (2007); Bachelor's degree or higher: 10.3% (2007); Master's degree or higher: 4.8% (2007).

School District(s)

Dozier/Okeechobee (PK-12)
    2005-06 Enrollment: 420 . . . . (850) 638-6222
Okeechobee County School District (PK-12)
    2005-06 Enrollment: 7,348 . . . . (863) 462-5000

Housing: Homeownership rate: 71.4% (2007); Median home value: $153,490 (2007); Median rent: $416 per month (2000); Median age of housing: 23 years (2000).

Hospitals: Raulerson Hospital (101 beds)

Safety: Violent crime rate: 71.7 per 10,000 population; Property crime rate: 520.0 per 10,000 population (2006).

Newspapers: Indiantown News (General - Circulation 10,000); Okeechobee News (Circulation 4,000)

Transportation: Commute to work: 92.3% car, 1.2% public transportation, 1.7% walk, 2.6% work from home (2000); Travel time to work: 55.6% less than 15 minutes, 20.4% 15 to 30 minutes, 11.9% 30 to 45 minutes, 3.5% 45 to 60 minutes, 8.5% 60 minutes or more (2000); Amtrak: Service available.

Additional Information Contacts

City of Okeechobee . . . . (863) 763-3372
    http://www.cityofokeechobee.com
Okeechobee Chamber of Commerce . . . . (863) 763-6464
    http://www.okeechobeechamberofcommerce.com

TAYLOR CREEK (CDP). Covers a land area of 3.996 square miles and a water area of 0.150 square miles. Located at 27.21° N. Lat.; 80.79° W. Long. Elevation is 16 feet.

Population: 4,081 (1990); 4,289 (2000); 4,548 (2007); 4,630 (2012 projected); Race: 92.4% White, 0.3% Black, 0.9% Asian, 6.9% Hispanic of any race (2007); Density: 1,138.1 persons per square mile (2007); Average household size: 2.13 (2007); Median age: 52.8 (2007); Males per 100 females: 104.3 (2007); Marriage status: 12.6% never married, 58.4% now married, 13.5% widowed, 15.4% divorced (2000); Foreign born: 6.6% (2000); Ancestry (includes multiple ancestries): 18.7% Other groups, 16.2% German, 13.7% English, 12.2% United States or American, 11.6% Irish (2000).

Economy: Employment by occupation: 7.6% management, 11.7% professional, 15.2% services, 28.9% sales, 4.6% farming, 21.0% construction, 11.1% production (2000).

Income: Per capita income: $19,305 (2007); Median household income: $28,587 (2007); Average household income: $40,677 (2007); Percent of households with income of $100,000 or more: 7.2% (2007); Poverty rate: 15.2% (2000).

Education: Percent of population age 25 and over with: High school diploma (including GED) or higher: 67.0% (2007); Bachelor's degree or higher: 6.1% (2007); Master's degree or higher: 1.3% (2007).

Housing: Homeownership rate: 81.0% (2007); Median home value: $118,568 (2007); Median rent: $445 per month (2000); Median age of housing: 20 years (2000).

Transportation: Commute to work: 95.2% car, 0.0% public transportation, 0.0% walk, 1.5% work from home (2000); Travel time to work: 42.9% less than 15 minutes, 24.4% 15 to 30 minutes, 12.9% 30 to 45 minutes, 4.7% 45 to 60 minutes, 15.1% 60 minutes or more (2000)

Orange County

Located in central Florida; bounded on the east by the St. Johns River; includes part of Lake Apopka. Covers a land area of 907.45 square miles, a water area of 96.74 square miles, and is located in the Eastern Time Zone. The county was founded in 1824. County seat is Orlando.

Orange County is part of the Orlando-Kissimmee, FL Metropolitan Statistical Area. The entire metro area includes: Lake County, FL; Orange County, FL; Osceola County, FL; Seminole County, FL

Population: 677,491 (1990); 896,344 (2000); 1,072,519 (2007); 1,204,568 (2012 projected); Race: 63.4% White, 19.8% Black, 4.2% Asian, 24.1% Hispanic of any race (2007); Density: 1,181.9 persons per square mile (2007); Average household size: 2.64 (2007); Median age: 34.7 (2007); Males per 100 females: 98.7 (2007).

Religion: Five largest groups: 13.2% Catholic Church, 8.2% Southern Baptist Convention, 3.3% The United Methodist Church, 2.5% Assemblies of God, 1.6% Presbyterian Church (U.S.A.) (2000).

Economy: Unemployment rate: 4.0% (11/2007); Total civilian labor force: 601,374 (11/2007); Leading industries: 14.9% accommodation & food services; 11.2% retail trade; 9.1% administration, support, waste management, remediation services (2005); Farms: 901 totaling 146,637 acres (2002); Companies that employ 500 or more persons: 139 (2005); Companies that employ 100 to 499 persons: 851 (2005); Companies that employ less than 100 persons: 30,943 (2005); Black-owned businesses: 7,835 (2002); Hispanic-owned businesses: 12,738 (2002); Asian-owned businesses: 4,220 (2002); Women-owned businesses: 22,286 (2002); Retail sales per capita: $18,980 (2007). Single-family building permits issued: 9,527 (2006); Multi-family building permits issued: 4,619 (2006).

Income: Per capita income: $24,376 (2007); Median household income: $47,426 (2007); Average household income: $63,754 (2007); Percent of households with income of $100,000 or more: 15.5% (2007); Poverty rate: 12.7% (2005); Bankruptcy rate: 1.14% (2006).

Taxes: Total county taxes per capita: $794 (2005); County property taxes per capita: $477 (2005).

Education: Percent of population age 25 and over with: High school diploma (including GED) or higher: 82.2% (2007); Bachelor's degree or higher: 26.5% (2007); Master's degree or higher: 7.9% (2007).

Housing: Homeownership rate: 61.5% (2007); Median home value: $206,102 (2007); Median rent: $605 per month (2000); Median age of housing: 18 years (2000).

Health: Birth rate: 157.6 per 10,000 population (2006); Death rate: 64.8 per 10,000 population (2006); Age-adjusted cancer mortality rate: 186.2 deaths per 100,000 population (2004); Air Quality Index: 82.5% good, 17.3% moderate, 0.3% unhealthy for sensitive individuals, 0.0% unhealthy (percent of days in 2006); Number of physicians: 26.4 per 10,000 population (2005); Hospital beds: 35.5 per 10,000 population (2004); Hospital admissions: 1,930.7 per 10,000 population (2004).

Elections: 2004 Presidential election results: 49.6% Bush, 49.8% Kerry, 0.3% Nader, 0.2% Badnarik

National and State Parks: Rock Springs Run State Reserve; Wekiwa Springs State Park; William Beardall Tosohatchee State Preserve

Additional Information Contacts

Orange County Government	(407) 836-7350
http://www.orangecountyfl.net	
African American Chamber of Commerce	(407) 420-4870
http://www.blackcommerce.org	
Apopka Chamber of Commerce	(407) 886-1441
http://www.apopkachamber.org	
Brazilian-American Chamber of Commerce	(407) 363-0906
http://www.cfbacc.com	
City of Apopka	(407) 703-1700
http://www.apopka.net	
City of Belle Isle	(407) 851-7730
http://www.cityofbelleislefl.org	
City of Maitland	(407) 539-6200
http://www.ci.maitland.fl.us	
City of Ocoee	(407) 905-3100
http://www.ci.ocoee.fl.us	
City of Winter Garden	(407) 656-4111
http://www.cwgdn.com	
City of Winter Park	(407) 599-3399
http://www.ci.winter-park.fl.us	
Downtown Orlando Partnership	(407) 228-3891
http://www.downtownorlandopartnership.com	
East Orange Chamber of Commerce	(407) 277-5951
Maitland Chamber of Commerce	(407) 644-0741
http://www.maitlandchamber.com	

Orange County Communities

APOPKA (city). Covers a land area of 24.042 square miles and a water area of 0.891 square miles. Located at 28.67° N. Lat.; 81.51° W. Long. Elevation is 131 feet.

History: Named for the Greek translations of "potato" and "eating place". Apopka was settled in 1856 when it was called The Lodge, for a Masonic lodge building erected here. Apopka became a trading and shipping center for fern growers.

Population: 17,031 (1990); 26,642 (2000); 35,213 (2007); 41,281 (2012 projected); Race: 67.3% White, 19.5% Black, 2.3% Asian, 24.0% Hispanic of any race (2007); Density: 1,464.6 persons per square mile (2007); Average household size: 2.76 (2007); Median age: 34.6 (2007); Males per 100 females: 94.8 (2007); Marriage status: 22.1% never married, 59.6% now married, 5.1% widowed, 13.2% divorced (2000); Foreign born: 11.8% (2000); Ancestry (includes multiple ancestries): 30.1% Other groups, 12.6% German, 10.9% Irish, 8.9% United States or American, 7.9% English (2000).

Economy: Unemployment rate: 3.8% (11/2007); Total civilian labor force: 20,172 (11/2007); Single-family building permits issued: 754 (2006); Multi-family building permits issued: 130 (2006); Employment by occupation: 15.0% management, 18.8% professional, 12.8% services, 31.6% sales, 1.8% farming, 8.8% construction, 11.3% production (2000).

Income: Per capita income: $22,570 (2007); Median household income: $49,601 (2007); Average household income: $61,933 (2007); Percent of households with income of $100,000 or more: 14.4% (2007); Poverty rate: 9.5% (2000).

Taxes: Total city taxes per capita: $428 (2005); City property taxes per capita: $146 (2005).

Education: Percent of population age 25 and over with: High school diploma (including GED) or higher: 82.0% (2007); Bachelor's degree or higher: 22.6% (2007); Master's degree or higher: 7.5% (2007).

School District(s)

Orange County School District (PK-12)	
2005-06 Enrollment: 173,331	(407) 317-3202
Seminole County School District (PK-12)	
2005-06 Enrollment: 66,692	(407) 320-0006

Housing: Homeownership rate: 77.2% (2007); Median home value: $193,358 (2007); Median rent: $577 per month (2000); Median age of housing: 11 years (2000).

Hospitals: Florida Hospital Apopka (50 beds)

Safety: Violent crime rate: 111.3 per 10,000 population; Property crime rate: 499.0 per 10,000 population (2006).

Newspapers: Apopka Chief (General - Circulation 3,800); The Planter (General - Circulation 10,000)

Transportation: Commute to work: 94.6% car, 1.3% public transportation, 0.6% walk, 2.6% work from home (2000); Travel time to work: 18.6% less than 15 minutes, 30.4% 15 to 30 minutes, 30.5% 30 to 45 minutes, 12.4% 45 to 60 minutes, 8.2% 60 minutes or more (2000)

Additional Information Contacts

Apopka Chamber of Commerce	(407) 886-1441
http://www.apopkachamber.org	
City of Apopka	(407) 703-1700
http://www.apopka.net	

AZALEA PARK (CDP). Covers a land area of 3.210 square miles and a water area of 0.031 square miles. Located at 28.54° N. Lat.; 81.29° W. Long. Elevation is 95 feet.

Population: 8,924 (1990); 11,073 (2000); 11,538 (2007); 12,065 (2012 projected); Race: 61.4% White, 9.7% Black, 4.3% Asian, 50.5% Hispanic of any race (2007); Density: 3,594.9 persons per square mile (2007); Average household size: 2.77 (2007); Median age: 32.8 (2007); Males per 100 females: 98.4 (2007); Marriage status: 33.0% never married, 50.9% now married, 6.6% widowed, 9.4% divorced (2000); Foreign born: 15.2% (2000); Ancestry (includes multiple ancestries): 43.8% Other groups, 9.9% United States or American, 7.9% German, 7.2% English, 6.9% Irish (2000).

Income: Per capita income: $14,294 (2007); Median household income: $33,249 (2007); Average household income: $38,810 (2007); Percent of households with income of $100,000 or more: 1.8% (2007); Poverty rate: 11.5% (2000).

Education: Percent of population age 25 and over with: High school diploma (including GED) or higher: 75.2% (2007); Bachelor's degree or higher: 13.3% (2007); Master's degree or higher: 3.3% (2007).

Housing: Homeownership rate: 55.5% (2007); Median home value: $156,096 (2007); Median rent: $611 per month (2000); Median age of housing: 26 years (2000).

Transportation: Commute to work: 92.9% car, 1.8% public transportation, 2.1% walk, 1.9% work from home (2000); Travel time to work: 16.2% less than 15 minutes, 41.8% 15 to 30 minutes, 26.7% 30 to 45 minutes, 9.9% 45 to 60 minutes, 5.3% 60 minutes or more (2000)

BAY HILL (CDP). Covers a land area of 2.540 square miles and a water area of 0.059 square miles. Located at 28.45° N. Lat.; 81.50° W. Long. Elevation is 98 feet.

Population: 4,262 (1990); 5,177 (2000); 6,549 (2007); 7,540 (2012 projected); Race: 83.4% White, 2.7% Black, 10.0% Asian, 6.2% Hispanic of any race (2007); Density: 2,578.2 persons per square mile (2007); Average household size: 2.84 (2007); Median age: 44.0 (2007); Males per 100 females: 96.9 (2007); Marriage status: 21.0% never married, 71.0% now married, 2.4% widowed, 5.6% divorced (2000); Foreign born: 15.3% (2000); Ancestry (includes multiple ancestries): 21.2% Other groups, 13.4% German, 12.8% English, 11.8% Irish, 11.0% Italian (2000).

Economy: Employment by occupation: 34.5% management, 20.3% professional, 9.6% services, 30.4% sales, 0.3% farming, 1.3% construction, 3.6% production (2000).

Income: Per capita income: $53,774 (2007); Median household income: $110,304 (2007); Average household income: $152,586 (2007); Percent of households with income of $100,000 or more: 55.3% (2007); Poverty rate: 4.3% (2000).

Education: Percent of population age 25 and over with: High school diploma (including GED) or higher: 92.6% (2007); Bachelor's degree or higher: 50.9% (2007); Master's degree or higher: 14.9% (2007).

Housing: Homeownership rate: 92.7% (2007); Median home value: $524,439 (2007); Median rent: $1,500 per month (2000); Median age of housing: 15 years (2000).

Transportation: Commute to work: 92.4% car, 0.3% public transportation, 0.0% walk, 4.6% work from home (2000); Travel time to work: 23.8% less than 15 minutes, 45.6% 15 to 30 minutes, 18.4% 30 to 45 minutes, 5.5% 45 to 60 minutes, 6.7% 60 minutes or more (2000)

BAY LAKE (city). Covers a land area of 19.927 square miles and a water area of 1.193 square miles. Located at 28.39° N. Lat.; 81.56° W. Long. Elevation is 92 feet.

Population: 0 (1990); 23 (2000); 51 (2007); 69 (2012 projected); Race: 94.1% White, 5.9% Black, 0.0% Asian, 0.0% Hispanic of any race (2007); Density: 2.6 persons per square mile (2007); Average household size: 2.43 (2007); Median age: 43.5 (2007); Males per 100 females: 155.0 (2007); Marriage status: 33.3% never married, 59.3% now married, 0.0% widowed, 7.4% divorced (2000); Foreign born: 0.0% (2000); Ancestry (includes multiple ancestries): 59.0% Irish, 35.9% French (except Basque), 20.5% English, 20.5% German, 10.3% Other groups (2000).

Economy: Single-family building permits issued: 0 (2006); Multi-family building permits issued: 0 (2006); Employment by occupation: 0.0% management, 8.7% professional, 21.7% services, 43.5% sales, 0.0% farming, 13.0% construction, 13.0% production (2000).

Income: Per capita income: $52,451 (2007); Median household income: $94,643 (2007); Average household income: $127,381 (2007); Percent of households with income of $100,000 or more: 42.9% (2007); Poverty rate: 0.0% (2000).

Education: Percent of population age 25 and over with: High school diploma (including GED) or higher: 92.1% (2007); Bachelor's degree or higher: 10.5% (2007); Master's degree or higher: 2.6% (2007).

Housing: Homeownership rate: 85.7% (2007); Median home value: $76,250 (2007); Median rent: $n/a per month (2000); Median age of housing: 16 years (2000).

Transportation: Commute to work: 100.0% car, 0.0% public transportation, 0.0% walk, 0.0% work from home (2000); Travel time to

---

BELLE ISLE (city). Covers a land area of 1.925 square miles and a water area of 2.706 square miles. Located at 28.46° N. Lat.; 81.35° W. Long. Elevation is 95 feet.

Population: 5,243 (1990); 5,531 (2000); 5,754 (2007); 6,045 (2012 projected); Race: 93.3% White, 2.0% Black, 1.2% Asian, 8.1% Hispanic of any race (2007); Density: 2,989.1 persons per square mile (2007); Average household size: 2.44 (2007); Median age: 43.5 (2007); Males per 100 females: 100.6 (2007); Marriage status: 18.0% never married, 65.7% now married, 6.1% widowed, 10.2% divorced (2000); Foreign born: 6.3% (2000); Ancestry (includes multiple ancestries): 18.1% German, 15.6% English, 14.1% Irish, 12.2% Other groups, 8.5% United States or American (2000).

Economy: Employment by occupation: 18.4% management, 21.9% professional, 16.7% services, 26.0% sales, 0.0% farming, 7.4% construction, 9.6% production (2000).

Income: Per capita income: $35,776 (2007); Median household income: $74,804 (2007); Average household income: $87,116 (2007); Percent of households with income of $100,000 or more: 31.1% (2007); Poverty rate: 2.9% (2000).

Education: Percent of population age 25 and over with: High school diploma (including GED) or higher: 92.3% (2007); Bachelor's degree or higher: 36.7% (2007); Master's degree or higher: 15.2% (2007).

Housing: Homeownership rate: 88.7% (2007); Median home value: $291,829 (2007); Median rent: $475 per month (2000); Median age of housing: 29 years (2000).

Transportation: Commute to work: 91.7% car, 2.4% public transportation, 1.0% walk, 3.5% work from home (2000); Travel time to work: 16.8% less than 15 minutes, 53.6% 15 to 30 minutes, 18.3% 30 to 45 minutes, 8.0% 45 to 60 minutes, 3.3% 60 minutes or more (2000)

Additional Information Contacts

City of Belle Isle . . . . (407) 851-7730
   http://www.cityofbelleislefl.org

BITHLO (CDP). Covers a land area of 10.672 square miles and a water area of 0.203 square miles. Located at 28.55° N. Lat.; 81.10° W. Long. Elevation is 62 feet.

History: Derived from Native American word for "canoe."

Population: 4,834 (1990); 4,626 (2000); 6,495 (2007); 7,784 (2012 projected); Race: 91.6% White, 1.4% Black, 0.4% Asian, 11.5% Hispanic of any race (2007); Density: 608.6 persons per square mile (2007); Average household size: 2.76 (2007); Median age: 35.1 (2007); Males per 100 females: 106.1 (2007); Marriage status: 30.0% never married, 48.6% now married, 3.5% widowed, 17.9% divorced (2000); Foreign born: 1.5% (2000); Ancestry (includes multiple ancestries): 28.2% United States or American, 11.8% German, 11.8% Other groups, 8.5% Irish, 7.3% English (2000).

Economy: Employment by occupation: 6.6% management, 3.2% professional, 19.2% services, 27.3% sales, 0.4% farming, 27.1% construction, 16.0% production (2000).

Income: Per capita income: $18,199 (2007); Median household income: $42,511 (2007); Average household income: $50,276 (2007); Percent of households with income of $100,000 or more: 8.2% (2007); Poverty rate: 21.5% (2000).

Education: Percent of population age 25 and over with: High school diploma (including GED) or higher: 60.9% (2007); Bachelor's degree or higher: 2.2% (2007); Master's degree or higher: 0.0% (2007).

Housing: Homeownership rate: 73.0% (2007); Median home value: $116,667 (2007); Median rent: $427 per month (2000); Median age of housing: 20 years (2000).

Transportation: Commute to work: 95.3% car, 1.2% public transportation, 0.0% walk, 2.4% work from home (2000); Travel time to work: 15.0% less than 15 minutes, 22.3% 15 to 30 minutes, 26.4% 30 to 45 minutes, 20.4% 45 to 60 minutes, 15.8% 60 minutes or more (2000)

CHRISTMAS (CDP). Covers a land area of 3.572 square miles and a water area of 0 square miles. Located at 28.53° N. Lat.; 80.99° W. Long. Elevation is 43 feet.

Population: 1,121 (1990); 1,162 (2000); 1,627 (2007); 1,943 (2012 projected); Race: 94.3% White, 0.6% Black, 1.0% Asian, 2.1% Hispanic of any race (2007); Density: 455.5 persons per square mile (2007); Average household size: 2.69 (2007); Median age: 39.7 (2007); Males per 100 females: 104.9 (2007); Marriage status: 24.6% never married, 48.8% now

professional, 26.3% services, 25.7% sales, 0.0% farming, 25.3% construction, 10.4% production (2000).

Income: Per capita income: $16,919 (2007); Median household income: $37,753 (2007); Average household income: $45,575 (2007); Percent of households with income of $100,000 or more: 6.8% (2007); Poverty rate: 12.3% (2000).

Education: Percent of population age 25 and over with: High school diploma (including GED) or higher: 67.4% (2007); Bachelor's degree or higher: 4.7% (2007); Master's degree or higher: 1.6% (2007).

Housing: Homeownership rate: 80.8% (2007); Median home value: $109,810 (2007); Median rent: $460 per month (2000); Median age of housing: 16 years (2000).

Transportation: Commute to work: 90.1% car, 1.5% public transportation, 0.0% walk, 8.4% work from home (2000); Travel time to work: 4.3% less than 15 minutes, 33.6% 15 to 30 minutes, 30.0% 30 to 45 minutes, 18.7% 45 to 60 minutes, 13.4% 60 minutes or more (2000)

CONWAY (CDP). Covers a land area of 3.450 square miles and a water area of 0.172 square miles. Located at 28.49° N. Lat.; 81.33° W. Long. Elevation is 108 feet.

Population: 13,101 (1990); 14,394 (2000); 14,634 (2007); 15,065 (2012 projected); Race: 87.3% White, 3.5% Black, 2.3% Asian, 14.3% Hispanic of any race (2007); Density: 4,241.2 persons per square mile (2007); Average household size: 2.68 (2007); Median age: 40.1 (2007); Males per 100 females: 97.1 (2007); Marriage status: 22.7% never married, 62.9% now married, 5.1% widowed, 9.3% divorced (2000); Foreign born: 6.7% (2000); Ancestry (includes multiple ancestries): 23.3% Other groups, 16.6% English, 15.3% German, 12.8% Irish, 8.9% United States or American (2000).

Economy: Employment by occupation: 17.1% management, 23.3% professional, 11.3% services, 30.0% sales, 0.3% farming, 8.8% construction, 9.3% production (2000).

Income: Per capita income: $28,856 (2007); Median household income: $61,692 (2007); Average household income: $77,241 (2007); Percent of households with income of $100,000 or more: 23.3% (2007); Poverty rate: 5.0% (2000).

Education: Percent of population age 25 and over with: High school diploma (including GED) or higher: 89.2% (2007); Bachelor's degree or higher: 31.7% (2007); Master's degree or higher: 9.2% (2007).

Housing: Homeownership rate: 81.6% (2007); Median home value: $230,094 (2007); Median rent: $668 per month (2000); Median age of housing: 28 years (2000).

Transportation: Commute to work: 92.8% car, 1.3% public transportation, 2.0% walk, 3.2% work from home (2000); Travel time to work: 18.3% less than 15 minutes, 45.1% 15 to 30 minutes, 29.0% 30 to 45 minutes, 4.6% 45 to 60 minutes, 3.0% 60 minutes or more (2000)

DOCTOR PHILLIPS (CDP). Covers a land area of 3.400 square miles and a water area of 1.455 square miles. Located at 28.45° N. Lat.; 81.49° W. Long. Elevation is 121 feet.

Population: 7,594 (1990); 9,548 (2000); 11,400 (2007); 12,793 (2012 projected); Race: 80.4% White, 3.4% Black, 10.7% Asian, 9.7% Hispanic of any race (2007); Density: 3,353.1 persons per square mile (2007); Average household size: 2.73 (2007); Median age: 41.2 (2007); Males per 100 females: 95.1 (2007); Marriage status: 23.9% never married, 64.9% now married, 3.0% widowed, 8.2% divorced (2000); Foreign born: 19.3% (2000); Ancestry (includes multiple ancestries): 20.8% Other groups, 15.6% German, 13.4% Irish, 12.1% English, 12.1% Italian (2000).

Economy: Employment by occupation: 23.7% management, 21.8% professional, 14.2% services, 33.5% sales, 0.0% farming, 1.8% construction, 5.0% production (2000).

Income: Per capita income: $38,513 (2007); Median household income: $81,732 (2007); Average household income: $105,287 (2007); Percent of households with income of $100,000 or more: 38.4% (2007); Poverty rate: 4.4% (2000).

Education: Percent of population age 25 and over with: High school diploma (including GED) or higher: 93.8% (2007); Bachelor's degree or higher: 50.4% (2007); Master's degree or higher: 17.4% (2007).

Transportation: ... than 15 minutes, 49.3% 15 to 30 minutes, 16.8% 30 to 45 minutes, 5.5% 45 to 60 minutes, 4.0% 60 minutes or more (2000)

EATONVILLE (town). Covers a land area of 0.985 square miles and a water area of 0.101 square miles. Located at 28.61° N. Lat.; 81.38° W. Long. Elevation is 95 feet.

History: Eatonville was founded in 1886 and named for Captain Josiah Eaton of nearby Maitland. This was the home of novelist Zora Neale Hurston, author of "Their Eyes Were Watching God" (1937).

Population: 2,256 (1990); 2,432 (2000); 2,401 (2007); 2,413 (2012 projected); Race: 7.2% White, 88.7% Black, 0.4% Asian, 4.0% Hispanic of any race (2007); Density: 2,438.1 persons per square mile (2007); Average household size: 3.11 (2007); Median age: 31.1 (2007); Males per 100 females: 90.7 (2007); Marriage status: 43.0% never married, 39.7% now married, 5.9% widowed, 11.4% divorced (2000); Foreign born: 4.2% (2000); Ancestry (includes multiple ancestries): 78.6% Other groups, 3.9% United States or American, 2.6% African, 1.6% Dutch, 1.1% French (except Basque) (2000).

Economy: Single-family building permits issued: 8 (2006); Multi-family building permits issued: 0 (2006); Employment by occupation: 4.0% management, 14.9% professional, 24.4% services, 26.9% sales, 0.0% farming, 11.0% construction, 18.8% production (2000).

Income: Per capita income: $13,724 (2007); Median household income: $33,611 (2007); Average household income: $41,680 (2007); Percent of households with income of $100,000 or more: 6.5% (2007); Poverty rate: 25.0% (2000).

Education: Percent of population age 25 and over with: High school diploma (including GED) or higher: 67.2% (2007); Bachelor's degree or higher: 11.9% (2007); Master's degree or higher: 1.6% (2007).

School District(s)

Orange County School District (PK-12)

2005-06 Enrollment: 173,331 . . . . (407) 317-3202

Housing: Homeownership rate: 49.7% (2007); Median home value: $129,790 (2007); Median rent: $459 per month (2000); Median age of housing: 30 years (2000).

Safety: Violent crime rate: 234.6 per 10,000 population; Property crime rate: 358.0 per 10,000 population (2006).

Transportation: Commute to work: 86.7% car, 7.1% public transportation, 2.5% walk, 2.5% work from home (2000); Travel time to work: 36.3% less than 15 minutes, 35.6% 15 to 30 minutes, 17.3% 30 to 45 minutes, 1.2% 45 to 60 minutes, 9.6% 60 minutes or more (2000)

EDGEWOOD (city). Covers a land area of 1.214 square miles and a water area of 0.265 square miles. Located at 28.48° N. Lat.; 81.37° W. Long. Elevation is 95 feet.

Population: 1,738 (1990); 1,901 (2000); 1,983 (2007); 2,065 (2012 projected); Race: 83.5% White, 8.4% Black, 2.8% Asian, 10.3% Hispanic of any race (2007); Density: 1,633.7 persons per square mile (2007); Average household size: 2.34 (2007); Median age: 45.0 (2007); Males per 100 females: 97.3 (2007); Marriage status: 13.7% never married, 67.7% now married, 6.1% widowed, 12.5% divorced (2000); Foreign born: 7.3% (2000); Ancestry (includes multiple ancestries): 20.5% Other groups, 17.9% English, 12.9% Irish, 12.4% German, 5.8% United States or American (2000).

Economy: Single-family building permits issued: 0 (2006); Multi-family building permits issued: 0 (2006); Employment by occupation: 17.5% management, 28.1% professional, 9.6% services, 36.1% sales, 0.0% farming, 1.3% construction, 7.4% production (2000).

Income: Per capita income: $42,566 (2007); Median household income: $63,088 (2007); Average household income: $99,287 (2007); Percent of households with income of $100,000 or more: 29.1% (2007); Poverty rate: 6.2% (2000).

Education: Percent of population age 25 and over with: High school diploma (including GED) or higher: 93.4% (2007); Bachelor's degree or higher: 39.8% (2007); Master's degree or higher: 14.1% (2007).

Housing: Homeownership rate: 80.3% (2007); Median home value: $279,386 (2007); Median rent: $559 per month (2000); Median age of housing: 26 years (2000).

Safety: Violent crime rate: 46.9 per 10,000 population; Property crime rate: 595.4 per 10,000 population (2006).

FAIRVIEW SHORES (CDP). Covers a land area of 3.914 square miles and a water area of 0.548 square miles. Located at 28.59° N. Lat.; 81.39° W. Long. Elevation is 89 feet.

Population: 13,330 (1990); 13,898 (2000); 13,183 (2007); 12,939 (2012 projected); Race: 70.9% White, 17.6% Black, 3.5% Asian, 12.2% Hispanic of any race (2007); Density: 3,368.2 persons per square mile (2007); Average household size: 2.32 (2007); Median age: 37.6 (2007); Males per 100 females: 99.2 (2007); Marriage status: 29.4% never married, 44.8% now married, 8.5% widowed, 17.3% divorced (2000); Foreign born: 7.6% (2000); Ancestry (includes multiple ancestries): 27.0% Other groups, 15.0% German, 11.7% English, 11.3% Irish, 7.7% United States or American (2000).

Economy: Employment by occupation: 15.5% management, 15.9% professional, 15.4% services, 31.4% sales, 0.0% farming, 9.9% construction, 12.0% production (2000).

Income: Per capita income: $22,683 (2007); Median household income: $39,915 (2007); Average household income: $51,975 (2007); Percent of households with income of $100,000 or more: 10.5% (2007); Poverty rate: 13.6% (2000).

Education: Percent of population age 25 and over with: High school diploma (including GED) or higher: 82.7% (2007); Bachelor's degree or higher: 20.4% (2007); Master's degree or higher: 5.0% (2007).

Housing: Homeownership rate: 56.4% (2007); Median home value: $180,649 (2007); Median rent: $531 per month (2000); Median age of housing: 38 years (2000).

Transportation: Commute to work: 90.5% car, 3.1% public transportation, 1.3% walk, 3.1% work from home (2000); Travel time to work: 28.3% less than 15 minutes, 43.6% 15 to 30 minutes, 18.6% 30 to 45 minutes, 4.4% 45 to 60 minutes, 5.1% 60 minutes or more (2000)

GOLDENROD (CDP). Aka Golden Rod. Covers a land area of 2.593 square miles and a water area of 0.131 square miles. Located at 28.61° N. Lat.; 81.29° W. Long. Elevation is 85 feet.

Population: 12,380 (1990); 12,871 (2000); 12,336 (2007); 12,256 (2012 projected); Race: 75.8% White, 7.7% Black, 3.5% Asian, 24.9% Hispanic of any race (2007); Density: 4,756.9 persons per square mile (2007); Average household size: 2.31 (2007); Median age: 35.3 (2007); Males per 100 females: 103.4 (2007); Marriage status: 35.2% never married, 47.7% now married, 5.0% widowed, 12.1% divorced (2000); Foreign born: 9.8% (2000); Ancestry (includes multiple ancestries): 28.8% Other groups, 13.6% German, 13.3% Irish, 11.9% English, 6.8% Italian (2000).

Economy: Employment by occupation: 10.4% management, 20.8% professional, 15.4% services, 32.2% sales, 0.4% farming, 10.9% construction, 9.9% production (2000).

Income: Per capita income: $23,165 (2007); Median household income: $45,416 (2007); Average household income: $53,142 (2007); Percent of households with income of $100,000 or more: 9.9% (2007); Poverty rate: 10.9% (2000).

Education: Percent of population age 25 and over with: High school diploma (including GED) or higher: 89.5% (2007); Bachelor's degree or higher: 27.8% (2007); Master's degree or higher: 7.7% (2007).

Housing: Homeownership rate: 48.5% (2007); Median home value: $189,606 (2007); Median rent: $627 per month (2000); Median age of housing: 24 years (2000).

Transportation: Commute to work: 92.5% car, 1.8% public transportation, 1.4% walk, 3.1% work from home (2000); Travel time to work: 22.7% less than 15 minutes, 37.6% 15 to 30 minutes, 26.2% 30 to 45 minutes, 7.5% 45 to 60 minutes, 5.9% 60 minutes or more (2000)

Additional Information Contacts

Goldenrod Chamber of Commerce . . . . (407) 677-5980
http://www.goldenrodchamber.com

GOTHA (CDP). Covers a land area of 1.760 square miles and a water area of 0.200 square miles. Located at 28.53° N. Lat.; 81.52° W. Long. Elevation is 121 feet.

Population: 265 (1990); 731 (2000); 1,104 (2007); 1,356 (2012 projected); Race: 84.3% White, 6.1% Black, 4.8% Asian, 9.7% Hispanic of any race (2007); Density: 627.4 persons per square mile (2007); Average household size: 2.89 (2007); Median age: 37.8 (2007); Males per 100 females: 97.5 (2007); Marriage status: 25.8% never married, 60.8% now married, 3.0%

construction, 5.8% production (2000).

Income: Per capita income: $36,156 (2007); Median household income: $65,488 (2007); Average household income: $104,116 (2007); Percent of households with income of $100,000 or more: 32.5% (2007); Poverty rate: 20.0% (2000).

Education: Percent of population age 25 and over with: High school diploma (including GED) or higher: 100.0% (2007); Bachelor's degree or higher: 32.3% (2007); Master's degree or higher: 11.3% (2007).

Housing: Homeownership rate: 85.9% (2007); Median home value: $453,922 (2007); Median rent: $521 per month (2000); Median age of housing: 14 years (2000).

Transportation: Commute to work: 94.1% car, 0.0% public transportation, 0.0% walk, 5.9% work from home (2000); Travel time to work: 11.5% less than 15 minutes, 41.9% 15 to 30 minutes, 16.7% 30 to 45 minutes, 7.9% 45 to 60 minutes, 21.9% 60 minutes or more (2000)

HOLDEN HEIGHTS (CDP). Covers a land area of 1.273 square miles and a water area of 0.395 square miles. Located at 28.50° N. Lat.; 81.38° W. Long. Elevation is 95 feet.

Population: 3,916 (1990); 3,856 (2000); 3,790 (2007); 3,818 (2012 projected); Race: 65.3% White, 22.3% Black, 3.4% Asian, 18.6% Hispanic of any race (2007); Density: 2,978.1 persons per square mile (2007); Average household size: 2.71 (2007); Median age: 42.5 (2007); Males per 100 females: 103.0 (2007); Marriage status: 23.1% never married, 58.4% now married, 5.9% widowed, 12.7% divorced (2000); Foreign born: 13.3% (2000); Ancestry (includes multiple ancestries): 26.1% Other groups, 11.6% German, 11.5% United States or American, 9.1% English, 8.3% Irish (2000).

Economy: Employment by occupation: 14.6% management, 19.8% professional, 14.6% services, 27.8% sales, 0.0% farming, 11.7% construction, 11.5% production (2000).

Income: Per capita income: $23,107 (2007); Median household income: $52,793 (2007); Average household income: $59,492 (2007); Percent of households with income of $100,000 or more: 11.6% (2007); Poverty rate: 16.6% (2000).

Education: Percent of population age 25 and over with: High school diploma (including GED) or higher: 81.0% (2007); Bachelor's degree or higher: 23.5% (2007); Master's degree or higher: 3.8% (2007).

Housing: Homeownership rate: 69.9% (2007); Median home value: $197,656 (2007); Median rent: $511 per month (2000); Median age of housing: 30 years (2000).

Transportation: Commute to work: 90.8% car, 3.8% public transportation, 0.9% walk, 2.8% work from home (2000); Travel time to work: 29.4% less than 15 minutes, 40.4% 15 to 30 minutes, 18.1% 30 to 45 minutes, 3.3% 45 to 60 minutes, 8.8% 60 minutes or more (2000)

HUNTERS CREEK (CDP). Covers a land area of 4.305 square miles and a water area of 0.003 square miles. Located at 28.35° N. Lat.; 81.42° W. Long. Elevation is 89 feet.

Population: 1,241 (1990); 9,369 (2000); 12,503 (2007); 14,713 (2012 projected); Race: 78.2% White, 5.8% Black, 9.3% Asian, 14.4% Hispanic of any race (2007); Density: 2,904.5 persons per square mile (2007); Average household size: 2.71 (2007); Median age: 37.0 (2007); Males per 100 females: 97.4 (2007); Marriage status: 23.0% never married, 65.7% now married, 3.3% widowed, 8.0% divorced (2000); Foreign born: 19.9% (2000); Ancestry (includes multiple ancestries): 28.3% Other groups, 16.4% Irish, 15.6% German, 11.1% Italian, 10.8% English (2000).

Economy: Employment by occupation: 30.8% management, 21.0% professional, 13.9% services, 26.9% sales, 0.0% farming, 2.8% construction, 4.6% production (2000).

Income: Per capita income: $36,275 (2007); Median household income: $80,208 (2007); Average household income: $98,178 (2007); Percent of households with income of $100,000 or more: 36.4% (2007); Poverty rate: 4.2% (2000).

Education: Percent of population age 25 and over with: High school diploma (including GED) or higher: 93.3% (2007); Bachelor's degree or higher: 45.0% (2007); Master's degree or higher: 14.1% (2007).

Housing: Homeownership rate: 55.8% (2007); Median home value: $345,332 (2007); Median rent: $869 per month (2000); Median age of housing: 5 years (2000).

LAKE BUENA VISTA (city). Covers a land area of 4.808 square miles and a water area of 0.088 square miles. Located at 28.37° N. Lat.; 81.52° W. Long. Elevation is 95 feet.

Population: 6 (1990); 16 (2000); 36 (2007); 51 (2012 projected); Race: 100.0% White, 0.0% Black, 0.0% Asian, 0.0% Hispanic of any race (2007); Density: 7.5 persons per square mile (2007); Average household size: 1.71 (2007); Median age: 54.3 (2007); Males per 100 females: 111.8 (2007); Marriage status: 0.0% never married, 68.8% now married, 18.8% widowed, 12.5% divorced (2000); Foreign born: 0.0% (2000); Ancestry (includes multiple ancestries): 37.5% German, 18.8% Irish, 18.8% United States or American, 12.5% French (except Basque) (2000).

Economy: Single-family building permits issued: 0 (2006); Multi-family building permits issued: 0 (2006); Employment by occupation: 0.0% management, 40.0% professional, 40.0% services, 20.0% sales, 0.0% farming, 0.0% construction, 0.0% production (2000).

Income: Per capita income: $26,528 (2007); Median household income: $42,500 (2007); Average household income: $45,476 (2007); Percent of households with income of $100,000 or more: 0.0% (2007); Poverty rate: 0.0% (2000).

Education: Percent of population age 25 and over with: High school diploma (including GED) or higher: 100.0% (2007); Bachelor's degree or higher: 26.7% (2007); Master's degree or higher: 13.3% (2007).

Housing: Homeownership rate: 90.5% (2007); Median home value: $156,250 (2007); Median rent: $475 per month (2000); Median age of housing: 14 years (2000).

Transportation: Commute to work: 100.0% car, 0.0% public transportation, 0.0% walk, 0.0% work from home (2000); Travel time to work: 40.0% less than 15 minutes, 0.0% 15 to 30 minutes, 60.0% 30 to 45 minutes, 0.0% 45 to 60 minutes, 0.0% 60 minutes or more (2000)

LAKE BUTLER (CDP). Covers a land area of 12.949 square miles and a water area of 7.545 square miles. Located at 28.49° N. Lat.; 81.53° W. Long. Elevation is 98 feet.

Population: 4,050 (1990); 7,062 (2000); 11,799 (2007); 14,954 (2012 projected); Race: 88.9% White, 3.2% Black, 4.7% Asian, 5.2% Hispanic of any race (2007); Density: 911.2 persons per square mile (2007); Average household size: 3.11 (2007); Median age: 37.5 (2007); Males per 100 females: 99.0 (2007); Marriage status: 14.7% never married, 77.7% now married, 3.2% widowed, 4.5% divorced (2000); Foreign born: 8.1% (2000); Ancestry (includes multiple ancestries): 19.2% German, 16.9% English, 15.1% Irish, 11.7% Other groups, 7.6% United States or American (2000).

Economy: Employment by occupation: 34.8% management, 25.1% professional, 8.1% services, 27.8% sales, 0.0% farming, 1.4% construction, 2.8% production (2000).

Income: Per capita income: $58,843 (2007); Median household income: $137,114 (2007); Average household income: $182,804 (2007); Percent of households with income of $100,000 or more: 65.1% (2007); Poverty rate: 1.8% (2000).

Education: Percent of population age 25 and over with: High school diploma (including GED) or higher: 96.1% (2007); Bachelor's degree or higher: 56.3% (2007); Master's degree or higher: 20.2% (2007).

Housing: Homeownership rate: 96.1% (2007); Median home value: $654,313 (2007); Median rent: $629 per month (2000); Median age of housing: 10 years (2000).

Transportation: Commute to work: 91.2% car, 0.0% public transportation, 0.3% walk, 7.6% work from home (2000); Travel time to work: 17.7% less than 15 minutes, 42.6% 15 to 30 minutes, 30.1% 30 to 45 minutes, 4.9% 45 to 60 minutes, 4.8% 60 minutes or more (2000)

LAKE HART (CDP). Covers a land area of 1.368 square miles and a water area of 0.484 square miles. Located at 28.38° N. Lat.; 81.22° W. Long. Elevation is 69 feet.

Population: 559 (1990); 557 (2000); 1,220 (2007); 1,656 (2012 projected); Race: 92.5% White, 0.4% Black, 2.2% Asian, 5.6% Hispanic of any race (2007); Density: 891.5 persons per square mile (2007); Average household size: 2.39 (2007); Median age: 44.9 (2007); Males per 100 females: 108.9 (2007); Marriage status: 28.9% never married, 58.0% now married, 0.0% widowed, 13.0% divorced (2000); Foreign born: 3.9% (2000); Ancestry (includes multiple ancestries): 17.1% English, 17.1% United States or American, 16.2% German, 15.6% Irish, 15.4% Other groups (2000).

households with income of $100,000 or more: 24.5% (2007); Poverty rate: 6.9% (2000).

Education: Percent of population age 25 and over with: High school diploma (including GED) or higher: 87.7% (2007); Bachelor's degree or higher: 29.8% (2007); Master's degree or higher: 8.9% (2007).

Housing: Homeownership rate: 72.2% (2007); Median home value: $388,889 (2007); Median rent: $438 per month (2000); Median age of housing: 19 years (2000).

Transportation: Commute to work: 87.5% car, 0.0% public transportation, 3.4% walk, 9.2% work from home (2000); Travel time to work: 12.7% less than 15 minutes, 35.4% 15 to 30 minutes, 34.7% 30 to 45 minutes, 7.1% 45 to 60 minutes, 10.1% 60 minutes or more (2000)

LOCKHART (CDP). Covers a land area of 4.368 square miles and a water area of 0.195 square miles. Located at 28.62° N. Lat.; 81.43° W. Long. Elevation is 85 feet.

Population: 11,636 (1990); 12,944 (2000); 14,395 (2007); 15,630 (2012 projected); Race: 65.8% White, 21.2% Black, 2.9% Asian, 21.1% Hispanic of any race (2007); Density: 3,295.8 persons per square mile (2007); Average household size: 2.75 (2007); Median age: 33.9 (2007); Males per 100 females: 98.9 (2007); Marriage status: 25.4% never married, 55.9% now married, 4.6% widowed, 14.1% divorced (2000); Foreign born: 9.7% (2000); Ancestry (includes multiple ancestries): 30.8% Other groups, 12.8% German, 10.5% Irish, 10.5% United States or American, 7.4% English (2000).

Economy: Employment by occupation: 11.2% management, 14.9% professional, 15.1% services, 29.7% sales, 0.1% farming, 14.6% construction, 14.4% production (2000).

Income: Per capita income: $18,833 (2007); Median household income: $43,439 (2007); Average household income: $51,512 (2007); Percent of households with income of $100,000 or more: 8.2% (2007); Poverty rate: 11.3% (2000).

Education: Percent of population age 25 and over with: High school diploma (including GED) or higher: 78.8% (2007); Bachelor's degree or higher: 15.5% (2007); Master's degree or higher: 4.1% (2007).

Housing: Homeownership rate: 69.2% (2007); Median home value: $161,391 (2007); Median rent: $557 per month (2000); Median age of housing: 21 years (2000).

Transportation: Commute to work: 95.9% car, 1.0% public transportation, 0.8% walk, 1.3% work from home (2000); Travel time to work: 20.5% less than 15 minutes, 37.7% 15 to 30 minutes, 25.8% 30 to 45 minutes, 10.4% 45 to 60 minutes, 5.6% 60 minutes or more (2000)

MAITLAND (city). Aka Lake Maitland. Covers a land area of 4.642 square miles and a water area of 1.033 square miles. Located at 28.62° N. Lat.; 81.36° W. Long. Elevation is 89 feet.

History: Maitland was established on the site of Fort Maitland, built in 1838 and named for Captain William S. Maitland of the U.S. Army. The town was incorporated in 1884.

Population: 10,220 (1990); 12,019 (2000); 13,168 (2007); 14,188 (2012 projected); Race: 81.7% White, 11.0% Black, 3.3% Asian, 8.5% Hispanic of any race (2007); Density: 2,836.6 persons per square mile (2007); Average household size: 2.45 (2007); Median age: 40.8 (2007); Males per 100 females: 91.0 (2007); Marriage status: 23.1% never married, 57.2% now married, 7.4% widowed, 12.3% divorced (2000); Foreign born: 7.4% (2000); Ancestry (includes multiple ancestries): 20.2% Other groups, 16.7% English, 14.2% German, 11.0% Irish, 7.5% United States or American (2000).

Economy: Single-family building permits issued: 48 (2006); Multi-family building permits issued: 219 (2006); Employment by occupation: 22.9% management, 28.1% professional, 10.0% services, 28.1% sales, 0.0% farming, 3.3% construction, 7.6% production (2000).

Income: Per capita income: $39,781 (2007); Median household income: $61,665 (2007); Average household income: $96,640 (2007); Percent of households with income of $100,000 or more: 29.5% (2007); Poverty rate: 6.4% (2000).

Education: Percent of population age 25 and over with: High school diploma (including GED) or higher: 93.1% (2007); Bachelor's degree or higher: 50.7% (2007); Master's degree or higher: 19.1% (2007).

School District(s)
Orange County School District (PK-12)
2005-06 Enrollment: 173,331 . . . . (407) 317-3202
Four-year College(s)
Florida College of Natural Health (Private, For-profit)
Fall 2006 Enrollment: 366 . . . . (407) 261-0319
University of Phoenix-Central Florida Campus (Private, For-profit)
Fall 2006 Enrollment: 2,068. (407) 667-0555
2006-07 Tuition: In-state $10,808; Out-of-state $10,808
Housing: Homeownership rate: 70.3% (2007); Median home value: $345,887 (2007); Median rent: $612 per month (2000); Median age of housing: 27 years (2000).
Safety: Violent crime rate: 28.5 per 10,000 population; Property crime rate: 270.8 per 10,000 population (2006).
Transportation: Commute to work: 89.9% car, 1.6% public transportation, 1.3% walk, 5.7% work from home (2000); Travel time to work: 23.9% less than 15 minutes, 47.7% 15 to 30 minutes, 17.3% 30 to 45 minutes, 4.9% 45 to 60 minutes, 6.1% 60 minutes or more (2000)
Additional Information Contacts
City of Maitland . . . . (407) 539-6200
http://www.ci.maitland.fl.us
Maitland Chamber of Commerce. . . . . (407) 644-0741
http://www.maitlandchamber.com

MEADOW WOODS (CDP). Covers a land area of 11.373 square miles and a water area of 0.036 square miles. Located at 28.37° N. Lat.; 81.36° W. Long. Elevation is 75 feet.
Population: 5,514 (1990); 11,286 (2000); 18,017 (2007); 22,560 (2012 projected); Race: 65.6% White, 13.4% Black, 2.6% Asian, 61.5% Hispanic of any race (2007); Density: 1,584.2 persons per square mile (2007); Average household size: 3.27 (2007); Median age: 34.4 (2007); Males per 100 females: 94.6 (2007); Marriage status: 26.6% never married, 60.4% now married, 3.5% widowed, 9.5% divorced (2000); Foreign born: 20.5% (2000); Ancestry (includes multiple ancestries): 61.5% Other groups, 6.9% German, 6.5% Irish, 5.4% Italian, 4.3% English (2000).
Economy: Employment by occupation: 9.4% management, 13.7% professional, 21.9% services, 36.3% sales, 0.0% farming, 7.5% construction, 11.2% production (2000).
Income: Per capita income: $17,104 (2007); Median household income: $49,251 (2007); Average household income: $56,008 (2007); Percent of households with income of $100,000 or more: 8.7% (2007); Poverty rate: 7.5% (2000).
Education: Percent of population age 25 and over with: High school diploma (including GED) or higher: 81.1% (2007); Bachelor's degree or higher: 16.5% (2007); Master's degree or higher: 4.3% (2007).
Housing: Homeownership rate: 78.8% (2007); Median home value: $198,860 (2007); Median rent: $761 per month (2000); Median age of housing: 8 years (2000).
Transportation: Commute to work: 95.9% car, 1.2% public transportation, 0.2% walk, 2.2% work from home (2000); Travel time to work: 11.4% less than 15 minutes, 49.1% 15 to 30 minutes, 28.0% 30 to 45 minutes, 7.3% 45 to 60 minutes, 4.2% 60 minutes or more (2000)

OAK RIDGE (CDP). Covers a land area of 4.161 square miles and a water area of 0.153 square miles. Located at 28.47° N. Lat.; 81.42° W. Long. Elevation is 89 feet.
Population: 15,388 (1990); 22,349 (2000); 25,063 (2007); 27,304 (2012 projected); Race: 37.1% White, 31.1% Black, 5.8% Asian, 45.6% Hispanic of any race (2007); Density: 6,023.1 persons per square mile (2007); Average household size: 3.05 (2007); Median age: 30.7 (2007); Males per 100 females: 101.2 (2007); Marriage status: 33.0% never married, 52.8% now married, 3.4% widowed, 10.8% divorced (2000); Foreign born: 35.5% (2000); Ancestry (includes multiple ancestries): 58.3% Other groups, 10.0% Haitian, 4.4% United States or American, 3.9% German, 3.5% Irish (2000).
Economy: Employment by occupation: 5.9% management, 8.9% professional, 30.8% services, 28.2% sales, 0.2% farming, 10.9% construction, 15.2% production (2000).
Income: Per capita income: $12,109 (2007); Median household income: $30,582 (2007); Average household income: $36,778 (2007); Percent of households with income of $100,000 or more: 2.9% (2007); Poverty rate: 19.6% (2000).
Education: Percent of population age 25 and over with: High school diploma (including GED) or higher: 66.9% (2007); Bachelor's degree or higher: 10.4% (2007); Master's degree or higher: 3.5% (2007).

Housing: Homeownership rate: 38.1% (2007); Median home value: $153,699 (2007); Median rent: $588 per month (2000); Median age of housing: 19 years (2000).
Transportation: Commute to work: 87.7% car, 7.4% public transportation, 1.6% walk, 1.4% work from home (2000); Travel time to work: 21.7% less than 15 minutes, 44.4% 15 to 30 minutes, 25.0% 30 to 45 minutes, 4.9% 45 to 60 minutes, 4.0% 60 minutes or more (2000)

OAKLAND (city). Covers a land area of 1.630 square miles and a water area of 0.002 square miles. Located at 28.55° N. Lat.; 81.63° W. Long. Elevation is 121 feet.
History: Oakland was founded in 1854 by settlers from South Carolina, and became an early industrial center with sawmills, sugar mills, and cotton gins. It was named for the large oak trees on the site.
Population: 783 (1990); 936 (2000); 1,151 (2007); 1,303 (2012 projected); Race: 71.2% White, 24.0% Black, 1.7% Asian, 3.6% Hispanic of any race (2007); Density: 706.0 persons per square mile (2007); Average household size: 2.70 (2007); Median age: 40.2 (2007); Males per 100 females: 92.8 (2007); Marriage status: 20.5% never married, 62.8% now married, 8.1% widowed, 8.5% divorced (2000); Foreign born: 1.6% (2000); Ancestry (includes multiple ancestries): 31.5% Other groups, 13.6% United States or American, 13.3% English, 9.8% German, 9.3% Irish (2000).
Economy: Employment by occupation: 17.2% management, 22.2% professional, 16.6% services, 26.3% sales, 1.6% farming, 8.6% construction, 7.5% production (2000).
Income: Per capita income: $28,905 (2007); Median household income: $66,447 (2007); Average household income: $77,916 (2007); Percent of households with income of $100,000 or more: 23.9% (2007); Poverty rate: 5.9% (2000).
Education: Percent of population age 25 and over with: High school diploma (including GED) or higher: 81.1% (2007); Bachelor's degree or higher: 26.1% (2007); Master's degree or higher: 4.9% (2007).
School District(s)
Orange County School District (PK-12)
2005-06 Enrollment: 173,331 . . . . (407) 317-3202
Housing: Homeownership rate: 81.5% (2007); Median home value: $270,588 (2007); Median rent: $363 per month (2000); Median age of housing: 21 years (2000).
Safety: Violent crime rate: 27.0 per 10,000 population; Property crime rate: 351.0 per 10,000 population (2006).
Transportation: Commute to work: 94.6% car, 2.8% public transportation, 1.2% walk, 1.4% work from home (2000); Travel time to work: 20.8% less than 15 minutes, 28.1% 15 to 30 minutes, 37.6% 30 to 45 minutes, 8.3% 45 to 60 minutes, 5.2% 60 minutes or more (2000)

OCOEE (city). Covers a land area of 13.234 square miles and a water area of 0.819 square miles. Located at 28.57° N. Lat.; 81.53° W. Long. Elevation is 121 feet.
History: Named for the Cherokee translation of "apricot-vine place." Ocoee grew up around a camp established by Dr. J.S. Starke on the shore of Lake Starke. The settlement was called Starke until a town was platted in 1886.
Population: 14,479 (1990); 24,391 (2000); 30,821 (2007); 35,430 (2012 projected); Race: 74.8% White, 9.6% Black, 4.5% Asian, 17.9% Hispanic of any race (2007); Density: 2,329.0 persons per square mile (2007); Average household size: 2.95 (2007); Median age: 34.6 (2007); Males per 100 females: 98.0 (2007); Marriage status: 22.5% never married, 65.4% now married, 3.4% widowed, 8.8% divorced (2000); Foreign born: 12.4% (2000); Ancestry (includes multiple ancestries): 26.2% Other groups, 14.1% German, 11.3% Irish, 10.0% English, 9.9% United States or American (2000).
Economy: Unemployment rate: 3.2% (11/2007); Total civilian labor force: 18,422 (11/2007); Single-family building permits issued: 556 (2006); Multi-family building permits issued: 0 (2006); Employment by occupation: 15.5% management, 16.3% professional, 15.5% services, 29.7% sales, 0.7% farming, 12.0% construction, 10.1% production (2000).
Income: Per capita income: $26,534 (2007); Median household income: $66,959 (2007); Average household income: $77,954 (2007); Percent of households with income of $100,000 or more: 23.3% (2007); Poverty rate: 5.6% (2000).
Education: Percent of population age 25 and over with: High school diploma (including GED) or higher: 82.7% (2007); Bachelor's degree or higher: 25.2% (2007); Master's degree or higher: 6.0% (2007).
School District(s)
Orange County School District (PK-12)
2005-06 Enrollment: 173,331 . . . . (407) 317-3202

Housing: Homeownership rate: 85.2% (2007); Median home value: $243,473 (2007); Median rent: $633 per month (2000); Median age of housing: 10 years (2000).
Hospitals: Health Central (171 beds)
Safety: Violent crime rate: 50.7 per 10,000 population; Property crime rate: 496.5 per 10,000 population (2006).
Transportation: Commute to work: 95.1% car, 0.6% public transportation, 0.6% walk, 3.0% work from home (2000); Travel time to work: 16.8% less than 15 minutes, 33.9% 15 to 30 minutes, 34.5% 30 to 45 minutes, 8.4% 45 to 60 minutes, 6.5% 60 minutes or more (2000)
Additional Information Contacts
City of Ocoee . . . . (407) 905-3100
   http://www.ci.ocoee.fl.us

ORLANDO (city). County seat. Covers a land area of 93.495 square miles and a water area of 7.459 square miles. Located at 28.53° N. Lat.; 81.37° W. Long. Elevation is 98 feet.

History: Orlando began in 1850 as Jernigan, an outgrowth of Fort Gatlin which had been abandoned by the army in 1848. The first residents were cattlemen who had been occupying the area for some years. Jernigan became the seat of Orange County in 1856, and was incorporated in 1875. The town's name was later changed to Orlando, perhaps for Shakespeare's hero in "As You Like It." The first commercial citrus grove near Orlando was planted by W.H. Holden in 1865, and citrus orchards soon replaced cattle lands.
Population: 161,172 (1990); 185,951 (2000); 212,477 (2007); 233,698 (2012 projected); Race: 56.2% White, 28.0% Black, 3.4% Asian, 22.9% Hispanic of any race (2007); Density: 2,272.6 persons per square mile (2007); Average household size: 2.24 (2007); Median age: 34.7 (2007); Males per 100 females: 95.7 (2007); Marriage status: 35.8% never married, 44.2% now married, 6.1% widowed, 13.8% divorced (2000); Foreign born: 14.4% (2000); Ancestry (includes multiple ancestries): 39.5% Other groups, 9.8% German, 8.7% Irish, 7.9% English, 6.7% United States or American (2000).
Economy: Unemployment rate: 3.9% (11/2007); Total civilian labor force: 130,517 (11/2007); Single-family building permits issued: 1,563 (2006); Multi-family building permits issued: 2,790 (2006); Employment by occupation: 14.4% management, 18.9% professional, 19.2% services, 30.0% sales, 0.2% farming, 7.5% construction, 9.8% production (2000).
Income: Per capita income: $24,412 (2007); Median household income: $40,086 (2007); Average household income: $54,151 (2007); Percent of households with income of $100,000 or more: 10.6% (2007); Poverty rate: 15.9% (2000).
Taxes: Total city taxes per capita: $715 (2005); City property taxes per capita: $367 (2005).
Education: Percent of population age 25 and over with: High school diploma (including GED) or higher: 82.6% (2007); Bachelor's degree or higher: 28.5% (2007); Master's degree or higher: 8.3% (2007).

School District(s)
Florida Virtual School (PK-12)
   2005-06 Enrollment: 3,904 . . . . (407) 317-3326
Orange County School District (PK-12)
   2005-06 Enrollment: 173,331 . . . . (407) 317-3202

Four-year College(s)
DeVry University-Florida (Private, For-profit)
   Fall 2006 Enrollment: 2,940 . . . . (407) 345-2800
   2006-07 Tuition: In-state $13,370; Out-of-state $13,370
Florida College of Integrative Medicine (Private, For-profit)
   Fall 2006 Enrollment: 128 . . . . (407) 888-8689
Florida Hospital College of Health Sciences (Private, Not-for-profit, Seventh Day Adventists)
   Fall 2006 Enrollment: 2,086 . . . . (407) 303-7742
   2006-07 Tuition: In-state $7,720; Out-of-state $7,720
Florida Metropolitan University-North Orlando (Private, For-profit)
   Fall 2006 Enrollment: 1,088 . . . . (407) 628-5870
   2006-07 Tuition: In-state $10,440; Out-of-state $10,440
Florida Metropolitan University-South Orlando (Private, For-profit)
   Fall 2006 Enrollment: 3,772 . . . . (407) 851-2525
   2006-07 Tuition: In-state $10,440; Out-of-state $10,440
International Academy of Design and Technology (Private, For-profit)
   Fall 2006 Enrollment: 1,158 . . . . (407) 857-2300
   2006-07 Tuition: In-state $15,672; Out-of-state $15,672
University of Central Florida (Public)
   Fall 2006 Enrollment: 46,646 . . . . (407) 823-2000
   2006-07 Tuition: In-state $3,492; Out-of-state $17,017

Two-year College(s)
Florida Technical College (Private, For-profit)
   Fall 2006 Enrollment: 831 . . . . (407) 447-7300
High-Tech Institute-Orlando (Private, For-profit)
   Fall 2006 Enrollment: 1,084 . . . . (407) 893-7400
Mid Florida Tech (Public)
   Fall 2006 Enrollment: 2,042 . . . . (407) 855-5880
Orlando Culinary Academy (Private, For-profit)
   Fall 2006 Enrollment: 810 . . . . (407) 888-4000
Polytechnic Institute of America (Private, For-profit)
   Fall 2006 Enrollment: 68 . . . . (407) 275-9696
Stenotype Institute of Jacksonville Inc (Private, For-profit)
   Fall 2006 Enrollment: 200 . . . . (407) 816-5573
Universal Technical Institute-Automotive Motorcycle & Marine Mechanics (Private, For-profit)
   Fall 2006 Enrollment: 3,744 . . . . (407) 240-2422
Valencia Community College (Public)
   Fall 2006 Enrollment: 30,245 . . . . (407) 299-2187
   2006-07 Tuition: In-state $2,100; Out-of-state $7,858

Vocational/Technical School(s)
Audio Recording Technology Institute (Private, For-profit)
   Fall 2006 Enrollment: 65 . . . . (402) 423-2784
   2006-07 Tuition: $18,300
Career Training Institute (Private, For-profit)
   Fall 2006 Enrollment: 301 . . . . (407) 884-1816
   2006-07 Tuition: $12,000
Orlando Tech (Public)
   Fall 2006 Enrollment: 709 . . . . (407) 317-3431
   2006-07 Tuition: $1,193
Housing: Homeownership rate: 39.6% (2007); Median home value: $195,344 (2007); Median rent: $606 per month (2000); Median age of housing: 22 years (2000).
Hospitals: Arnold Palmer Hospital for Children & Women (301 beds); Florida Hospital E Orlando (123 beds); Florida Hospital Orlando (1783 beds); Orlando Regional Healthcare (1572 beds); Orlando Regional Medical Center (267 beds); Sand Lake Hospital (153 beds)
Safety: Violent crime rate: 198.3 per 10,000 population; Property crime rate: 844.9 per 10,000 population (2006).
Newspapers: Central Florida Advocate (Black - Circulation 15,000); Latino International - Orlando Edition (Hispanic - Circulation 45,000); Orlando Times (Black - Circulation 10,000); Orlando Weekly (Alternative, General - Circulation 50,000); The Orlando Sentinel (Circulation 269,269)
Transportation: Commute to work: 90.1% car, 4.1% public transportation, 1.9% walk, 2.2% work from home (2000); Travel time to work: 21.7% less than 15 minutes, 43.7% 15 to 30 minutes, 23.6% 30 to 45 minutes, 5.9% 45 to 60 minutes, 5.1% 60 minutes or more (2000); Amtrak: Service available.
Airports: Executive; Kissimmee Municipal; Orlando International (primary service/large hub); Orlando Sanford (primary service/small hub)
Additional Information Contacts
African American Chamber of Commerce . . . . (407) 420-4870
   http://www.blackcommerce.org
Brazilian-American Chamber of Commerce . . . . (407) 363-0906
   http://www.cfbacc.com
Downtown Orlando Partnership . . . . (407) 228-3891
   http://www.downtownorlandopartnership.com
East Orange Chamber of Commerce . . . . (407) 277-5951
Orlando Chamber of Commerce . . . . (407) 425-1234
   http://www.orlando.org
South Orange Chamber of Commerce . . . . (407) 854-4246

ORLOVISTA (CDP). Covers a land area of 1.930 square miles and a water area of 0.033 square miles. Located at 28.54° N. Lat.; 81.46° W. Long. Elevation is 112 feet.

History: Orlovista came into existence during the real estate boom of the 1920's. Near Orlovista was Deer Island Pit, constructed as a center for cock fighting.
Population: 5,438 (1990); 6,047 (2000); 5,958 (2007); 6,004 (2012 projected); Race: 46.4% White, 34.3% Black, 4.5% Asian, 19.0% Hispanic of any race (2007); Density: 3,087.0 persons per square mile (2007); Average household size: 2.86 (2007); Median age: 34.1 (2007); Males per 100 females: 99.0 (2007); Marriage status: 36.1% never married, 43.1% now married, 6.9% widowed, 13.8% divorced (2000); Foreign born: 14.3% (2000); Ancestry (includes multiple ancestries): 43.9% Other groups, 14.9% United States or American, 7.2% German, 6.3% Irish, 4.3% Italian (2000).

Income: Per capita income: $16,053 (2007); Median household income: $38,588 (2007); Average household income: $42,186 (2007); Percent of households with income of $100,000 or more: 4.6% (2007); Poverty rate: 16.8% (2000).

Education: Percent of population age 25 and over with: High school diploma (including GED) or higher: 62.9% (2007); Bachelor's degree or higher: 5.9% (2007); Master's degree or higher: 1.9% (2007).

Housing: Homeownership rate: 60.8% (2007); Median home value: $131,813 (2007); Median rent: $553 per month (2000); Median age of housing: 28 years (2000).

Transportation: Commute to work: 93.2% car, 2.4% public transportation, 0.8% walk, 1.5% work from home (2000); Travel time to work: 21.9% less than 15 minutes, 34.3% 15 to 30 minutes, 27.3% 30 to 45 minutes, 9.5% 45 to 60 minutes, 7.0% 60 minutes or more (2000)

PARADISE HEIGHTS (CDP).

Covers a land area of 0.472 square miles and a water area of 0 square miles. Located at 28.62° N. Lat.; 81.54° W. Long. Elevation is 98 feet.

Population: 1,677 (1990); 1,310 (2000); 1,708 (2007); 2,015 (2012 projected); Race: 71.5% White, 5.9% Black, 0.6% Asian, 33.6% Hispanic of any race (2007); Density: 3,622.3 persons per square mile (2007); Average household size: 2.77 (2007); Median age: 31.3 (2007); Males per 100 females: 109.8 (2007); Marriage status: 29.3% never married, 52.7% now married, 9.2% widowed, 8.7% divorced (2000); Foreign born: 15.1% (2000); Ancestry (includes multiple ancestries): 31.1% Other groups, 30.6% United States or American, 11.6% Irish, 9.3% English, 8.6% German (2000).

Economy: Employment by occupation: 4.0% management, 5.3% professional, 18.8% services, 21.1% sales, 6.2% farming, 29.0% construction, 15.7% production (2000).

Income: Per capita income: $16,583 (2007); Median household income: $40,482 (2007); Average household income: $45,535 (2007); Percent of households with income of $100,000 or more: 4.5% (2007); Poverty rate: 14.9% (2000).

Education: Percent of population age 25 and over with: High school diploma (including GED) or higher: 61.3% (2007); Bachelor's degree or higher: 0.8% (2007); Master's degree or higher: 0.8% (2007).

Housing: Homeownership rate: 56.6% (2007); Median home value: $140,278 (2007); Median rent: $505 per month (2000); Median age of housing: 33 years (2000).

Transportation: Commute to work: 92.6% car, 0.0% public transportation, 1.9% walk, 1.0% work from home (2000); Travel time to work: 19.3% less than 15 minutes, 44.1% 15 to 30 minutes, 21.0% 30 to 45 minutes, 12.3% 45 to 60 minutes, 3.3% 60 minutes or more (2000)

PINE CASTLE (CDP).

Covers a land area of 2.616 square miles and a water area of 0.213 square miles. Located at 28.46° N. Lat.; 81.37° W. Long. Elevation is 98 feet.

Population: 8,188 (1990); 8,803 (2000); 9,545 (2007); 10,251 (2012 projected); Race: 63.1% White, 15.3% Black, 2.8% Asian, 43.1% Hispanic of any race (2007); Density: 3,648.1 persons per square mile (2007); Average household size: 2.83 (2007); Median age: 34.3 (2007); Males per 100 females: 103.5 (2007); Marriage status: 27.2% never married, 56.6% now married, 4.2% widowed, 12.0% divorced (2000); Foreign born: 29.6% (2000); Ancestry (includes multiple ancestries): 38.7% Other groups, 8.1% German, 7.8% Irish, 7.2% English, 6.3% United States or American (2000).

Economy: Employment by occupation: 7.2% management, 9.9% professional, 21.9% services, 24.6% sales, 0.0% farming, 15.6% construction, 20.9% production (2000).

Income: Per capita income: $16,876 (2007); Median household income: $38,686 (2007); Average household income: $47,767 (2007); Percent of households with income of $100,000 or more: 6.6% (2007); Poverty rate: 15.0% (2000).

Education: Percent of population age 25 and over with: High school diploma (including GED) or higher: 72.2% (2007); Bachelor's degree or higher: 12.0% (2007); Master's degree or higher: 3.2% (2007).

Housing: Homeownership rate: 52.4% (2007); Median home value: $159,172 (2007); Median rent: $519 per month (2000); Median age of housing: 29 years (2000).

Transportation: Commute to work: 89.2% car, 4.5% public transportation, 2.0% walk, 2.4% work from home (2000); Travel time to work: 27.6% less

PINE HILLS (CDP).

Covers a land area of 7.682 square miles and a water area of 0.241 square miles. Located at 28.57° N. Lat.; 81.45° W. Long. Elevation is 115 feet.

Population: 34,712 (1990); 41,764 (2000); 42,104 (2007); 43,135 (2012 projected); Race: 24.0% White, 58.9% Black, 3.1% Asian, 15.6% Hispanic of any race (2007); Density: 5,481.0 persons per square mile (2007); Average household size: 3.14 (2007); Median age: 30.6 (2007); Males per 100 females: 93.7 (2007); Marriage status: 32.1% never married, 51.3% now married, 5.3% widowed, 11.2% divorced (2000); Foreign born: 22.4% (2000); Ancestry (includes multiple ancestries): 45.9% Other groups, 11.5% Haitian, 6.6% United States or American, 4.8% German, 4.2% Irish (2000).

Economy: Employment by occupation: 6.8% management, 11.4% professional, 23.7% services, 28.3% sales, 0.5% farming, 13.6% construction, 15.6% production (2000).

Income: Per capita income: $13,401 (2007); Median household income: $34,560 (2007); Average household income: $41,426 (2007); Percent of households with income of $100,000 or more: 4.2% (2007); Poverty rate: 18.5% (2000).

Education: Percent of population age 25 and over with: High school diploma (including GED) or higher: 71.3% (2007); Bachelor's degree or higher: 10.5% (2007); Master's degree or higher: 3.1% (2007).

Housing: Homeownership rate: 64.9% (2007); Median home value: $151,395 (2007); Median rent: $551 per month (2000); Median age of housing: 27 years (2000).

Transportation: Commute to work: 91.8% car, 4.6% public transportation, 0.8% walk, 1.2% work from home (2000); Travel time to work: 13.8% less than 15 minutes, 37.7% 15 to 30 minutes, 30.9% 30 to 45 minutes, 10.6% 45 to 60 minutes, 7.0% 60 minutes or more (2000)

SKY LAKE (CDP).

Covers a land area of 1.260 square miles and a water area of 0.009 square miles. Located at 28.46° N. Lat.; 81.39° W. Long. Elevation is 98 feet.

Population: 6,202 (1990); 5,651 (2000); 6,651 (2007); 7,373 (2012 projected); Race: 62.8% White, 14.4% Black, 2.8% Asian, 44.7% Hispanic of any race (2007); Density: 5,277.3 persons per square mile (2007); Average household size: 2.92 (2007); Median age: 37.9 (2007); Males per 100 females: 95.4 (2007); Marriage status: 28.5% never married, 51.5% now married, 7.8% widowed, 12.2% divorced (2000); Foreign born: 21.3% (2000); Ancestry (includes multiple ancestries): 40.6% Other groups, 11.7% German, 11.4% Irish, 7.9% English, 4.4% United States or American (2000).

Economy: Employment by occupation: 5.6% management, 11.1% professional, 26.9% services, 34.6% sales, 0.4% farming, 8.8% construction, 12.7% production (2000).

Income: Per capita income: $16,868 (2007); Median household income: $39,057 (2007); Average household income: $47,779 (2007); Percent of households with income of $100,000 or more: 7.1% (2007); Poverty rate: 12.9% (2000).

Education: Percent of population age 25 and over with: High school diploma (including GED) or higher: 72.8% (2007); Bachelor's degree or higher: 12.3% (2007); Master's degree or higher: 3.6% (2007).

Housing: Homeownership rate: 71.8% (2007); Median home value: $161,014 (2007); Median rent: $549 per month (2000); Median age of housing: 33 years (2000).

Transportation: Commute to work: 90.9% car, 4.5% public transportation, 2.7% walk, 1.1% work from home (2000); Travel time to work: 25.8% less than 15 minutes, 40.9% 15 to 30 minutes, 22.0% 30 to 45 minutes, 4.5% 45 to 60 minutes, 6.8% 60 minutes or more (2000)

SOUTH APOPKA (CDP).

Covers a land area of 2.747 square miles and a water area of 0.071 square miles. Located at 28.65° N. Lat.; 81.50° W. Long. Elevation is 125 feet.

Population: 5,584 (1990); 5,800 (2000); 5,942 (2007); 6,093 (2012 projected); Race: 26.1% White, 64.9% Black, 0.1% Asian, 14.8% Hispanic of any race (2007); Density: 2,162.9 persons per square mile (2007); Average household size: 3.22 (2007); Median age: 28.8 (2007); Males per 100 females: 94.8 (2007); Marriage status: 39.4% never married, 43.6% now married, 6.8% widowed, 10.2% divorced (2000); Foreign born: 6.8% (2000); Ancestry (includes multiple ancestries): 61.5% Other groups, 4.3% African, 4.2% United States or American, 3.5% English, 3.1% Irish (2000).

households with income of $100,000 or more: 5.0% (2007); Poverty rate: 34.9% (2000).
Education: Percent of population age 25 and over with: High school diploma (including GED) or higher: 49.3% (2007); Bachelor's degree or higher: 5.8% (2007); Master's degree or higher: 1.2% (2007).
Housing: Homeownership rate: 65.6% (2007); Median home value: $134,235 (2007); Median rent: $343 per month (2000); Median age of housing: 29 years (2000).
Transportation: Commute to work: 88.7% car, 5.8% public transportation, 2.5% walk, 0.4% work from home (2000); Travel time to work: 21.0% less than 15 minutes, 31.8% 15 to 30 minutes, 27.2% 30 to 45 minutes, 7.0% 45 to 60 minutes, 13.0% 60 minutes or more (2000)

SOUTHCHASE (CDP). Covers a land area of 2.171 square miles and a water area of 0 square miles. Located at 28.39° N. Lat.; 81.38° W. Long. Elevation is 89 feet.
Population: 441 (1990); 4,633 (2000); 6,130 (2007); 7,189 (2012 projected); Race: 49.8% White, 17.5% Black, 12.3% Asian, 42.5% Hispanic of any race (2007); Density: 2,823.4 persons per square mile (2007); Average household size: 3.42 (2007); Median age: 33.2 (2007); Males per 100 females: 95.5 (2007); Marriage status: 24.5% never married, 67.3% now married, 2.5% widowed, 5.7% divorced (2000); Foreign born: 14.6% (2000); Ancestry (includes multiple ancestries): 53.3% Other groups, 10.7% German, 8.5% Irish, 5.2% Italian, 5.0% English (2000).
Economy: Employment by occupation: 13.4% management, 18.3% professional, 12.4% services, 38.9% sales, 0.0% farming, 9.1% construction, 7.9% production (2000).
Income: Per capita income: $22,274 (2007); Median household income: $71,177 (2007); Average household income: $76,281 (2007); Percent of households with income of $100,000 or more: 20.1% (2007); Poverty rate: 3.0% (2000).
Education: Percent of population age 25 and over with: High school diploma (including GED) or higher: 90.1% (2007); Bachelor's degree or higher: 26.2% (2007); Master's degree or higher: 4.9% (2007).
Housing: Homeownership rate: 93.4% (2007); Median home value: $283,505 (2007); Median rent: $988 per month (2000); Median age of housing: 5 years (2000).
Transportation: Commute to work: 97.3% car, 0.0% public transportation, 1.2% walk, 1.5% work from home (2000); Travel time to work: 13.8% less than 15 minutes, 48.4% 15 to 30 minutes, 31.3% 30 to 45 minutes, 4.0% 45 to 60 minutes, 2.4% 60 minutes or more (2000)

TAFT (CDP). Covers a land area of 1.016 square miles and a water area of 0.027 square miles. Located at 28.42° N. Lat.; 81.36° W. Long. Elevation is 95 feet.
Population: 1,781 (1990); 1,938 (2000); 2,206 (2007); 2,409 (2012 projected); Race: 81.1% White, 4.7% Black, 2.9% Asian, 28.6% Hispanic of any race (2007); Density: 2,171.1 persons per square mile (2007); Average household size: 2.84 (2007); Median age: 36.3 (2007); Males per 100 females: 110.9 (2007); Marriage status: 25.4% never married, 51.8% now married, 7.3% widowed, 15.5% divorced (2000); Foreign born: 10.5% (2000); Ancestry (includes multiple ancestries): 23.8% Other groups, 18.7% United States or American, 10.2% German, 7.4% Irish, 5.3% Polish (2000).
Economy: Employment by occupation: 8.5% management, 8.1% professional, 14.1% services, 29.8% sales, 0.0% farming, 22.1% construction, 17.4% production (2000).
Income: Per capita income: $17,120 (2007); Median household income: $37,377 (2007); Average household income: $48,607 (2007); Percent of households with income of $100,000 or more: 7.5% (2007); Poverty rate: 14.3% (2000).
Education: Percent of population age 25 and over with: High school diploma (including GED) or higher: 59.4% (2007); Bachelor's degree or higher: 7.4% (2007); Master's degree or higher: 2.4% (2007).
School District(s)
Orange County School District (PK-12)
  2005-06 Enrollment: 173,331 . . . . (407) 317-3202
Housing: Homeownership rate: 68.6% (2007); Median home value: $136,353 (2007); Median rent: $433 per month (2000); Median age of housing: 22 years (2000).

TANGELO PARK (CDP). Covers a land area of 0.342 square miles and a water area of 0 square miles. Located at 28.45° N. Lat.; 81.44° W. Long. Elevation is 95 feet.
Population: 2,663 (1990); 2,430 (2000); 2,220 (2007); 2,118 (2012 projected); Race: 5.8% White, 89.9% Black, 0.3% Asian, 2.4% Hispanic of any race (2007); Density: 6,500.1 persons per square mile (2007); Average household size: 3.14 (2007); Median age: 30.2 (2007); Males per 100 females: 94.7 (2007); Marriage status: 39.4% never married, 42.0% now married, 7.0% widowed, 11.6% divorced (2000); Foreign born: 12.3% (2000); Ancestry (includes multiple ancestries): 73.3% Other groups, 6.2% Jamaican, 3.3% Haitian, 2.0% Ethiopian, 2.0% United States or American (2000).
Economy: Employment by occupation: 2.9% management, 4.9% professional, 25.5% services, 32.2% sales, 0.0% farming, 16.0% construction, 18.5% production (2000).
Income: Per capita income: $11,669 (2007); Median household income: $33,065 (2007); Average household income: $36,693 (2007); Percent of households with income of $100,000 or more: 1.0% (2007); Poverty rate: 13.9% (2000).
Education: Percent of population age 25 and over with: High school diploma (including GED) or higher: 70.7% (2007); Bachelor's degree or higher: 8.3% (2007); Master's degree or higher: 2.6% (2007).
Housing: Homeownership rate: 77.1% (2007); Median home value: $131,944 (2007); Median rent: $552 per month (2000); Median age of housing: 36 years (2000).
Transportation: Commute to work: 92.2% car, 4.5% public transportation, 0.8% walk, 1.6% work from home (2000); Travel time to work: 25.5% less than 15 minutes, 37.7% 15 to 30 minutes, 26.9% 30 to 45 minutes, 2.1% 45 to 60 minutes, 7.8% 60 minutes or more (2000)

TANGERINE (CDP). Covers a land area of 1.154 square miles and a water area of 0.649 square miles. Located at 28.75° N. Lat.; 81.63° W. Long. Elevation is 151 feet.
Population: 830 (1990); 826 (2000); 942 (2007); 1,029 (2012 projected); Race: 91.1% White, 2.8% Black, 1.9% Asian, 10.4% Hispanic of any race (2007); Density: 816.4 persons per square mile (2007); Average household size: 2.49 (2007); Median age: 42.4 (2007); Males per 100 females: 96.7 (2007); Marriage status: 8.9% never married, 80.2% now married, 2.6% widowed, 8.3% divorced (2000); Foreign born: 3.5% (2000); Ancestry (includes multiple ancestries): 20.7% English, 20.0% Other groups, 20.0% Irish, 8.7% German, 7.9% French (except Basque) (2000).
Economy: Employment by occupation: 18.4% management, 24.0% professional, 16.1% services, 22.9% sales, 2.1% farming, 14.1% construction, 2.4% production (2000).
Income: Per capita income: $26,338 (2007); Median household income: $54,259 (2007); Average household income: $65,635 (2007); Percent of households with income of $100,000 or more: 14.6% (2007); Poverty rate: 2.7% (2000).
Education: Percent of population age 25 and over with: High school diploma (including GED) or higher: 89.5% (2007); Bachelor's degree or higher: 30.7% (2007); Master's degree or higher: 7.5% (2007).
Housing: Homeownership rate: 91.3% (2007); Median home value: $237,687 (2007); Median rent: $n/a per month (2000); Median age of housing: 42 years (2000).
Transportation: Commute to work: 98.0% car, 0.0% public transportation, 0.0% walk, 2.0% work from home (2000); Travel time to work: 12.5% less than 15 minutes, 29.7% 15 to 30 minutes, 30.8% 30 to 45 minutes, 18.5% 45 to 60 minutes, 8.5% 60 minutes or more (2000)

TILDENVILLE (CDP). Covers a land area of 0.350 square miles and a water area of 0.058 square miles. Located at 28.53° N. Lat.; 81.60° W. Long. Elevation is 102 feet.
Population: 534 (1990); 513 (2000); 2,213 (2007); 3,328 (2012 projected); Race: 31.8% White, 57.0% Black, 0.0% Asian, 23.5% Hispanic of any race (2007); Density: 6,323.0 persons per square mile (2007); Average household size: 2.96 (2007); Median age: 33.7 (2007); Males per 100 females: 94.8 (2007); Marriage status: 34.3% never married, 52.8% now married, 0.0% widowed, 12.9% divorced (2000); Foreign born: 1.8% (2000); Ancestry (includes multiple ancestries): 86.1% Other groups, 6.9% African, 4.0% United States or American, 1.8% Jamaican (2000).

Income: Per capita income: $16,622 (2007); Median household income: $47,440 (2007); Average household income: $49,244 (2007); Percent of households with income of $100,000 or more: 4.8% (2007); Poverty rate: 11.7% (2000).
Education: Percent of population age 25 and over with: High school diploma (including GED) or higher: 61.4% (2007); Bachelor's degree or higher: 7.7% (2007); Master's degree or higher: 0.0% (2007).
Housing: Homeownership rate: 79.9% (2007); Median home value: $141,764 (2007); Median rent: $382 per month (2000); Median age of housing: 12 years (2000).
Transportation: Commute to work: 85.9% car, 9.8% public transportation, 0.0% walk, 4.3% work from home (2000); Travel time to work: 20.8% less than 15 minutes, 21.2% 15 to 30 minutes, 46.9% 30 to 45 minutes, 11.0% 45 to 60 minutes, 0.0% 60 minutes or more (2000)

UNION PARK (CDP). Covers a land area of 2.987 square miles and a water area of 0.034 square miles. Located at 28.56° N. Lat.; 81.23° W. Long. Elevation is 82 feet.
Population: 6,861 (1990); 10,191 (2000); 11,756 (2007); 12,987 (2012 projected); Race: 68.9% White, 7.9% Black, 4.2% Asian, 36.2% Hispanic of any race (2007); Density: 3,935.4 persons per square mile (2007); Average household size: 2.71 (2007); Median age: 33.2 (2007); Males per 100 females: 100.6 (2007); Marriage status: 32.2% never married, 52.4% now married, 3.6% widowed, 11.8% divorced (2000); Foreign born: 10.2% (2000); Ancestry (includes multiple ancestries): 38.7% Other groups, 12.3% German, 10.5% Irish, 8.1% English, 6.8% United States or American (2000).
Economy: Employment by occupation: 10.2% management, 20.3% professional, 15.3% services, 30.7% sales, 0.3% farming, 11.8% construction, 11.4% production (2000).
Income: Per capita income: $21,094 (2007); Median household income: $49,309 (2007); Average household income: $57,028 (2007); Percent of households with income of $100,000 or more: 11.2% (2007); Poverty rate: 11.3% (2000).
Education: Percent of population age 25 and over with: High school diploma (including GED) or higher: 84.1% (2007); Bachelor's degree or higher: 21.1% (2007); Master's degree or higher: 4.9% (2007).
Housing: Homeownership rate: 65.8% (2007); Median home value: $180,695 (2007); Median rent: $675 per month (2000); Median age of housing: 17 years (2000).
Transportation: Commute to work: 96.8% car, 0.4% public transportation, 0.1% walk, 1.4% work from home (2000); Travel time to work: 16.2% less than 15 minutes, 34.7% 15 to 30 minutes, 32.9% 30 to 45 minutes, 11.3% 45 to 60 minutes, 4.9% 60 minutes or more (2000)

WEDGEFIELD (CDP). Covers a land area of 23.421 square miles and a water area of 0.079 square miles. Located at 28.48° N. Lat.; 81.08° W. Long. Elevation is 69 feet.
Population: 1,091 (1990); 2,700 (2000); 4,101 (2007); 5,081 (2012 projected); Race: 74.0% White, 10.2% Black, 10.4% Asian, 12.1% Hispanic of any race (2007); Density: 175.1 persons per square mile (2007); Average household size: 2.83 (2007); Median age: 40.1 (2007); Males per 100 females: 103.9 (2007); Marriage status: 18.7% never married, 67.5% now married, 4.3% widowed, 9.6% divorced (2000); Foreign born: 15.2% (2000); Ancestry (includes multiple ancestries): 25.6% Other groups, 17.7% Irish, 13.9% German, 10.1% English, 10.1% United States or American (2000).
Economy: Employment by occupation: 21.2% management, 17.6% professional, 15.6% services, 30.6% sales, 0.0% farming, 7.7% construction, 7.2% production (2000).
Income: Per capita income: $27,421 (2007); Median household income: $69,303 (2007); Average household income: $77,500 (2007); Percent of households with income of $100,000 or more: 24.6% (2007); Poverty rate: 5.8% (2000).
Education: Percent of population age 25 and over with: High school diploma (including GED) or higher: 86.3% (2007); Bachelor's degree or higher: 24.4% (2007); Master's degree or higher: 9.3% (2007).
Housing: Homeownership rate: 83.1% (2007); Median home value: $261,949 (2007); Median rent: $888 per month (2000); Median age of housing: 10 years (2000).
Transportation: Commute to work: 94.8% car, 1.1% public transportation, 0.5% walk, 3.6% work from home (2000); Travel time to work: 3.0% less

WILLIAMSBURG (CDP). Covers a land area of 3.680 square miles and a water area of 0.066 square miles. Located at 28.41° N. Lat.; 81.44° W. Long. Elevation is 89 feet.
Population: 5,160 (1990); 6,736 (2000); 7,623 (2007); 8,364 (2012 projected); Race: 86.1% White, 2.4% Black, 5.5% Asian, 12.3% Hispanic of any race (2007); Density: 2,071.5 persons per square mile (2007); Average household size: 2.02 (2007); Median age: 50.0 (2007); Males per 100 females: 90.1 (2007); Marriage status: 21.0% never married, 57.2% now married, 10.4% widowed, 11.4% divorced (2000); Foreign born: 15.7% (2000); Ancestry (includes multiple ancestries): 21.6% Other groups, 14.8% German, 13.1% Italian, 12.5% Irish, 9.7% English (2000).
Economy: Employment by occupation: 16.6% management, 17.8% professional, 23.8% services, 32.4% sales, 0.6% farming, 3.7% construction, 5.1% production (2000).
Income: Per capita income: $30,260 (2007); Median household income: $52,430 (2007); Average household income: $61,235 (2007); Percent of households with income of $100,000 or more: 12.8% (2007); Poverty rate: 4.0% (2000).
Education: Percent of population age 25 and over with: High school diploma (including GED) or higher: 87.4% (2007); Bachelor's degree or higher: 29.7% (2007); Master's degree or higher: 9.0% (2007).
Housing: Homeownership rate: 86.5% (2007); Median home value: $231,034 (2007); Median rent: $797 per month (2000); Median age of housing: 14 years (2000).
Transportation: Commute to work: 97.0% car, 0.8% public transportation, 0.2% walk, 1.5% work from home (2000); Travel time to work: 24.6% less than 15 minutes, 56.4% 15 to 30 minutes, 13.4% 30 to 45 minutes, 3.7% 45 to 60 minutes, 2.0% 60 minutes or more (2000)

WINDERMERE (town). Covers a land area of 1.124 square miles and a water area of 0.002 square miles. Located at 28.49° N. Lat.; 81.53° W. Long. Elevation is 121 feet.
Population: 1,643 (1990); 1,897 (2000); 2,127 (2007); 2,327 (2012 projected); Race: 93.8% White, 2.2% Black, 2.6% Asian, 4.7% Hispanic of any race (2007); Density: 1,892.9 persons per square mile (2007); Average household size: 2.67 (2007); Median age: 41.8 (2007); Males per 100 females: 104.3 (2007); Marriage status: 18.9% never married, 67.9% now married, 5.5% widowed, 7.7% divorced (2000); Foreign born: 7.0% (2000); Ancestry (includes multiple ancestries): 21.8% German, 18.6% English, 14.4% Irish, 11.7% Other groups, 8.2% United States or American (2000).
Economy: Employment by occupation: 31.5% management, 26.2% professional, 8.9% services, 25.6% sales, 0.0% farming, 3.9% construction, 3.9% production (2000).
Income: Per capita income: $53,212 (2007); Median household income: $94,355 (2007); Average household income: $142,189 (2007); Percent of households with income of $100,000 or more: 47.4% (2007); Poverty rate: 3.1% (2000).
Taxes: Total city taxes per capita: $865 (2005); City property taxes per capita: $472 (2005).
Education: Percent of population age 25 and over with: High school diploma (including GED) or higher: 97.2% (2007); Bachelor's degree or higher: 54.7% (2007); Master's degree or higher: 17.5% (2007).

School District(s)
Orange County School District (PK-12)
  2005-06 Enrollment: 173,331 . . . . (407) 317-3202
Housing: Homeownership rate: 89.1% (2007); Median home value: $726,955 (2007); Median rent: $817 per month (2000); Median age of housing: 27 years (2000).
Safety: Violent crime rate: 4.9 per 10,000 population; Property crime rate: 127.6 per 10,000 population (2006).
Transportation: Commute to work: 91.2% car, 0.6% public transportation, 1.2% walk, 6.2% work from home (2000); Travel time to work: 17.6% less than 15 minutes, 50.2% 15 to 30 minutes, 24.8% 30 to 45 minutes, 3.9% 45 to 60 minutes, 3.5% 60 minutes or more (2000)

WINTER GARDEN (city). Covers a land area of 12.057 square miles and a water area of 0.024 square miles. Located at 28.56° N. Lat.; 81.58° W. Long. Elevation is 125 feet.
History: Named for being a place to escape from cold winters. Winter Garden developed around citrus fruit packing plants.
Population: 11,437 (1990); 14,351 (2000); 25,470 (2007); 32,804 (2012 projected); Race: 73.1% White, 13.3% Black, 1.4% Asian, 23.2% Hispanic

11.6% English, 11.4% German, 11.0% United States or American, 10.0% Irish (2000).

Economy: Single-family building permits issued: 865 (2006); Multi-family building permits issued: 0 (2006); Employment by occupation: 10.9% management, 16.4% professional, 19.5% services, 27.1% sales, 0.7% farming, 13.3% construction, 12.2% production (2000).

Income: Per capita income: $23,129 (2007); Median household income: $47,399 (2007); Average household income: $59,673 (2007); Percent of households with income of $100,000 or more: 15.0% (2007); Poverty rate: 12.0% (2000).

Education: Percent of population age 25 and over with: High school diploma (including GED) or higher: 78.5% (2007); Bachelor's degree or higher: 19.8% (2007); Master's degree or higher: 5.3% (2007).

School District(s)

Orange County School District (PK-12)

2005-06 Enrollment: 173,331 . . . . (407) 317-3202

Two-year College(s)

Westside Tech (Public)

Fall 2006 Enrollment: 618 . . . . (407) 905-2018

Housing: Homeownership rate: 65.4% (2007); Median home value: $185,699 (2007); Median rent: $523 per month (2000); Median age of housing: 16 years (2000).

Safety: Violent crime rate: 107.2 per 10,000 population; Property crime rate: 432.3 per 10,000 population (2006).

Newspapers: The West Orange Times (General - Circulation 9,000)

Transportation: Commute to work: 94.9% car, 1.1% public transportation, 1.6% walk, 0.8% work from home (2000); Travel time to work: 22.5% less than 15 minutes, 37.8% 15 to 30 minutes, 29.3% 30 to 45 minutes, 6.1% 45 to 60 minutes, 4.3% 60 minutes or more (2000)

Additional Information Contacts

City of Winter Garden . . . . (407) 656-4111
http://www.cwgdn.com
Winter Garden Chamber of Commerce . . . . (407) 656-1304
http://www.wochamber.com

WINTER PARK (city). Covers a land area of 7.341 square miles and a water area of 1.313 square miles. Located at 28.59° N. Lat.; 81.34° W. Long. Elevation is 92 feet.

History: Named for being a place to escape from cold winters. Winter Park began as Lakeview, founded in 1858. The name was changed to Osceola in 1870, and to Winter Park in 1881 when a new townsite was laid out by a group of New Englanders. The town developed around Rollins College, founded in 1885 by the General Congregational Association.

Population: 24,339 (1990); 24,090 (2000); 24,809 (2007); 25,729 (2012 projected); Race: 84.2% White, 11.1% Black, 1.6% Asian, 5.6% Hispanic of any race (2007); Density: 3,379.5 persons per square mile (2007); Average household size: 2.21 (2007); Median age: 43.8 (2007); Males per 100 females: 85.8 (2007); Marriage status: 25.9% never married, 52.6% now married, 10.1% widowed, 11.4% divorced (2000); Foreign born: 6.6% (2000); Ancestry (includes multiple ancestries): 17.9% English, 17.3% Other groups, 15.3% German, 12.1% Irish, 6.1% United States or American (2000).

Economy: Unemployment rate: 3.1% (11/2007); Total civilian labor force: 14,970 (11/2007); Single-family building permits issued: 112 (2006); Multi-family building permits issued: 6 (2006); Employment by occupation: 22.0% management, 31.4% professional, 9.6% services, 27.3% sales, 0.0% farming, 4.2% construction, 5.5% production (2000).

Income: Per capita income: $44,353 (2007); Median household income: $56,046 (2007); Average household income: $97,150 (2007); Percent of households with income of $100,000 or more: 28.3% (2007); Poverty rate: 7.8% (2000).

Taxes: Total city taxes per capita: $811 (2005); City property taxes per capita: $427 (2005).

Education: Percent of population age 25 and over with: High school diploma (including GED) or higher: 92.0% (2007); Bachelor's degree or higher: 49.0% (2007); Master's degree or higher: 19.2% (2007).

School District(s)

Orange County School District (PK-12)

2005-06 Enrollment: 173,331 . . . . (407) 317-3202

2006-07 Tuition: In-state $43,995; Out-of-state $43,995
Herzing College (Private, For-profit)

Fall 2006 Enrollment: 182 . . . . (407) 478-0500

2006-07 Tuition: In-state $12,240; Out-of-state $12,240
Rollins College (Private, Not-for-profit)

Fall 2006 Enrollment: 3,478 . . . . (407) 646-2000

2006-07 Tuition: In-state $30,860; Out-of-state $30,860

Two-year College(s)

Central Florida College (Private, For-profit)

Fall 2006 Enrollment: 333 . . . . (407) 843-3984
Winter Park Tech (Public)

Fall 2006 Enrollment: 574 . . . . (407) 622-2900

Vocational/Technical School(s)

Florida Institute of Animal Arts (Private, For-profit)

Fall 2006 Enrollment: 201 . . . . (407) 657-5033

2006-07 Tuition: $9,300
Southern Technical Institute (Private, For-profit)

Fall 2006 Enrollment: 8 . . . . (407) 478-5300

2006-07 Tuition: $7,520

Housing: Homeownership rate: 64.6% (2007); Median home value: $381,255 (2007); Median rent: $584 per month (2000); Median age of housing: 36 years (2000).

Hospitals: Winter Park Memorial Hospital (334 beds)

Safety: Violent crime rate: 31.4 per 10,000 population; Property crime rate: 340.6 per 10,000 population (2006).

Transportation: Commute to work: 87.6% car, 1.6% public transportation, 4.0% walk, 5.5% work from home (2000); Travel time to work: 30.7% less than 15 minutes, 42.3% 15 to 30 minutes, 19.7% 30 to 45 minutes, 4.1% 45 to 60 minutes, 3.1% 60 minutes or more (2000); Amtrak: Service available.

Additional Information Contacts

City of Winter Park . . . . (407) 599-3399
http://www.ci.winter-park.fl.us
Winter Park Chamber of Commerce . . . . (407) 644-8281
http://www.winterpark.org

ZELLWOOD (CDP). Covers a land area of 3.888 square miles and a water area of 0.184 square miles. Located at 28.72° N. Lat.; 81.59° W. Long. Elevation is 98 feet.

History: Zellwood was settled and named by Elwood Zell, a Philadelphia publisher, and became a winter destination for northern visitors.

Population: 2,813 (1990); 2,540 (2000); 2,780 (2007); 3,003 (2012 projected); Race: 93.2% White, 2.6% Black, 0.0% Asian, 12.6% Hispanic of any race (2007); Density: 715.0 persons per square mile (2007); Average household size: 1.96 (2007); Median age: 64.0 (2007); Males per 100 females: 88.0 (2007); Marriage status: 11.3% never married, 68.5% now married, 14.6% widowed, 5.6% divorced (2000); Foreign born: 9.1% (2000); Ancestry (includes multiple ancestries): 18.0% German, 15.4% Other groups, 14.6% English, 14.6% Irish, 8.8% United States or American (2000).

Economy: Employment by occupation: 12.8% management, 8.7% professional, 17.5% services, 33.7% sales, 1.2% farming, 11.6% construction, 14.4% production (2000).

Income: Per capita income: $23,213 (2007); Median household income: $32,438 (2007); Average household income: $44,239 (2007); Percent of households with income of $100,000 or more: 7.7% (2007); Poverty rate: 11.9% (2000).

Education: Percent of population age 25 and over with: High school diploma (including GED) or higher: 71.2% (2007); Bachelor's degree or higher: 11.9% (2007); Master's degree or higher: 1.3% (2007).

School District(s)

Orange County School District (PK-12)

2005-06 Enrollment: 173,331 . . . . (407) 317-3202

Housing: Homeownership rate: 89.8% (2007); Median home value: $129,020 (2007); Median rent: $443 per month (2000); Median age of housing: 17 years (2000).

Transportation: Commute to work: 87.3% car, 2.3% public transportation, 7.9% walk, 1.4% work from home (2000); Travel time to work: 20.7% less than 15 minutes, 20.3% 15 to 30 minutes, 41.9% 30 to 45 minutes, 3.0% 45 to 60 minutes, 14.1% 60 minutes or more (2000)

Located in central Florida; lowland area, includes Lakes Kissimmee, Tohopekaliga, East Tohopekaliga, and other lakes. Covers a land area of 1,321.90 square miles, a water area of 184.45 square miles, and is located in the Eastern Time Zone. The county was founded in 1887. County seat is Kissimmee.

Osceola County is part of the Orlando-Kissimmee, FL Metropolitan Statistical Area. The entire metro area includes: Lake County, FL; Orange County, FL; Osceola County, FL; Seminole County, FL

Weather Station: Kissimmee 2   Elevation: 59 feet

	Jan	Feb	Mar	Apr	May	Jun	Jul	Aug	Sep	Oct	Nov	Dec
High	73	75	79	83	88	91	92	92	90	85	80	75
Low	50	51	56	59	65	71	72	73	72	65	58	52
Precip	2.4	2.8	3.6	2.0	3.9	6.0	6.6	7.2	5.9	3.2	2.4	2.2
Snow	0.0	0.0	0.0	0.0	0.0	0.0	0.0	0.0	0.0	0.0	0.0	0.0

High and Low temperatures in degrees Fahrenheit; Precipitation and Snow in inches

Population: 107,728 (1990); 172,493 (2000); 251,103 (2007); 308,498 (2012 projected); Race: 70.6% White, 9.4% Black, 2.6% Asian, 39.6% Hispanic of any race (2007); Density: 190.0 persons per square mile (2007); Average household size: 2.81 (2007); Median age: 34.8 (2007); Males per 100 females: 98.7 (2007).
Religion: Five largest groups: 11.0% Catholic Church, 5.3% Southern Baptist Convention, 2.1% The United Methodist Church, 1.5% Christian Churches and Churches of Christ, 1.2% Assemblies of God (2000).
Economy: Unemployment rate: 4.6% (11/2007); Total civilian labor force: 127,043 (11/2007); Leading industries: 20.0% accommodation & food services; 18.8% retail trade; 11.3% health care and social assistance (2005); Farms: 519 totaling 652,673 acres (2002); Companies that employ 500 or more persons: 9 (2005); Companies that employ 100 to 499 persons: 83 (2005); Companies that employ less than 100 persons: 4,801 (2005); Black-owned businesses: 1,082 (2002); Hispanic-owned businesses: 3,339 (2002); Asian-owned businesses: n/a (2002); Women-owned businesses: 3,974 (2002); Retail sales per capita: $12,984 (2007). Single-family building permits issued: 5,772 (2006); Multi-family building permits issued: 2,234 (2006).
Income: Per capita income: $19,424 (2007); Median household income: $43,500 (2007); Average household income: $54,097 (2007); Percent of households with income of $100,000 or more: 9.9% (2007); Poverty rate: 13.9% (2005); Bankruptcy rate: 1.22% (2006).
Taxes: Total county taxes per capita: $764 (2005); County property taxes per capita: $356 (2005).
Education: Percent of population age 25 and over with: High school diploma (including GED) or higher: 79.6% (2007); Bachelor's degree or higher: 16.3% (2007); Master's degree or higher: 5.0% (2007).
Housing: Homeownership rate: 68.1% (2007); Median home value: $188,530 (2007); Median rent: $610 per month (2000); Median age of housing: 13 years (2000).
Health: Birth rate: 144.4 per 10,000 population (2006); Death rate: 62.0 per 10,000 population (2006); Age-adjusted cancer mortality rate: 181.6 deaths per 100,000 population (2004); Air Quality Index: 96.4% good, 3.6% moderate, 0.0% unhealthy for sensitive individuals, 0.0% unhealthy (percent of days in 2006); Number of physicians: 10.6 per 10,000 population (2005); Hospital beds: 13.6 per 10,000 population (2004); Hospital admissions: 673.5 per 10,000 population (2004).
Elections: 2004 Presidential election results: 52.5% Bush, 47.0% Kerry, 0.3% Nader, 0.1% Badnarik
Additional Information Contacts
Osceola County Government . . . . (407) 847-1200
   http://www.osceola.org
City of Kissimmee . . . . (407) 847-2821
   http://www.kissimmee.org
City of Saint Cloud . . . . (407) 957-7300
   http://www.stcloud.org
Kissimmee Osceola Chamber of Commerce . . . . (407) 847-3174
   http://www.kissimmeechamber.com
St. Cloud/Greater Osceola Co. Chamber . . . . (407) 892-3671
   http://stcloudflchamber.com

Osceola County Communities

CAMPBELL (CDP). Covers a land area of 1.873 square miles and a water area of 0.027 square miles. Located at 28.26° N. Lat.; 81.45° W. Long. Elevation is 75 feet.
Population: 3,353 (1990); 2,677 (2000); 3,415 (2007); 3,962 (2012 projected); Race: 90.9% White, 1.6% Black, 1.4% Asian, 7.0% Hispanic of any race (2007); Density: 1,822.9 persons per square mile (2007); Average household size: 1.96 (2007); Median age: 65.4 (2007); Males per 100 females: 75.9 (2007); Marriage status: 16.1% never married, 49.4% now married, 24.7% widowed, 9.9% divorced (2000); Foreign born: 5.4% (2000); Ancestry (includes multiple ancestries): 20.0% English, 13.9% German, 10.4% United States or American, 10.1% Other groups, 7.4% Irish (2000).
Economy: Employment by occupation: 5.4% management, 6.7% professional, 25.9% services, 34.0% sales, 1.0% farming, 15.1% construction, 11.8% production (2000).
Income: Per capita income: $19,980 (2007); Median household income: $33,351 (2007); Average household income: $38,369 (2007); Percent of households with income of $100,000 or more: 5.2% (2007); Poverty rate: 13.5% (2000).
Education: Percent of population age 25 and over with: High school diploma (including GED) or higher: 76.4% (2007); Bachelor's degree or higher: 13.3% (2007); Master's degree or higher: 5.6% (2007).
Housing: Homeownership rate: 55.1% (2007); Median home value: $84,643 (2007); Median rent: $702 per month (2000); Median age of housing: 24 years (2000).
Transportation: Commute to work: 88.3% car, 0.0% public transportation, 0.0% walk, 4.4% work from home (2000); Travel time to work: 21.2% less than 15 minutes, 39.4% 15 to 30 minutes, 21.2% 30 to 45 minutes, 7.7% 45 to 60 minutes, 10.6% 60 minutes or more (2000)

CELEBRATION (CDP). Covers a land area of 10.669 square miles and a water area of 0.028 square miles. Located at 28.32° N. Lat.; 81.54° W. Long. Elevation is 82 feet.
Population: 1,245 (1990); 2,736 (2000); 4,521 (2007); 5,737 (2012 projected); Race: 91.4% White, 2.7% Black, 3.2% Asian, 10.5% Hispanic of any race (2007); Density: 423.7 persons per square mile (2007); Average household size: 2.79 (2007); Median age: 36.7 (2007); Males per 100 females: 95.6 (2007); Marriage status: 22.2% never married, 67.6% now married, 5.8% widowed, 4.4% divorced (2000); Foreign born: 7.8% (2000); Ancestry (includes multiple ancestries): 16.9% Irish, 14.7% German, 14.5% Other groups, 11.6% Italian, 11.3% English (2000).
Economy: Employment by occupation: 33.5% management, 23.1% professional, 15.0% services, 18.2% sales, 0.0% farming, 4.7% construction, 5.5% production (2000).
Income: Per capita income: $52,321 (2007); Median household income: $95,155 (2007); Average household income: $145,217 (2007); Percent of households with income of $100,000 or more: 46.3% (2007); Poverty rate: 6.2% (2000).
Education: Percent of population age 25 and over with: High school diploma (including GED) or higher: 93.8% (2007); Bachelor's degree or higher: 57.5% (2007); Master's degree or higher: 21.7% (2007).
School District(s)
Osceola County School District (PK-12)
   2005-06 Enrollment: 47,446 . . . . (407) 870-4008
Housing: Homeownership rate: 62.7% (2007); Median home value: $857,681 (2007); Median rent: $873 per month (2000); Median age of housing: 3 years (2000).
Transportation: Commute to work: 76.6% car, 0.0% public transportation, 5.6% walk, 15.9% work from home (2000); Travel time to work: 45.2% less than 15 minutes, 30.7% 15 to 30 minutes, 18.2% 30 to 45 minutes, 2.0% 45 to 60 minutes, 4.0% 60 minutes or more (2000)

KENANSVILLE (unincorporated postal area, zip code 34739). Covers a land area of 353.332 square miles and a water area of 12.101 square miles. Located at 27.93° N. Lat.; 81.09° W. Long. Elevation is 74 feet.
Population: 828 (2000); Race: 97.5% White, 0.0% Black, 0.0% Asian, 9.4% Hispanic of any race (2000); Density: 2.3 persons per square mile (2000); Age: 20.5% under 18, 22.5% over 64 (2000); Marriage status: 17.7% never married, 64.8% now married, 8.4% widowed, 9.2% divorced (2000); Foreign born: 8.2% (2000); Ancestry (includes multiple ancestries): 19.2% Other groups, 15.3% Irish, 14.3% United States or American, 13.5% English, 10.5% German (2000).

Income: Per capita income: $19,293 (2000); Median household income: $36,645 (2000); Poverty rate: 13.4% (2000).

Education: Percent of population age 25 and over with: High school diploma (including GED) or higher: 73.5% (2000); Bachelor's degree or higher: 9.2% (2000).

Housing: Homeownership rate: 75.2% (2000); Median home value: $133,300 (2000); Median rent: $310 per month (2000); Median age of housing: 17 years (2000).

Transportation: Commute to work: 82.3% car, 0.0% public transportation, 9.9% walk, 4.1% work from home (2000); Travel time to work: 29.5% less than 15 minutes, 23.8% 15 to 30 minutes, 15.7% 30 to 45 minutes, 10.7% 45 to 60 minutes, 20.3% 60 minutes or more (2000)

KISSIMMEE (city). County seat. Covers a land area of 16.680 square miles and a water area of 0.636 square miles. Located at 28.30° N. Lat.; 81.41° W. Long. Elevation is 66 feet.

History: Named for the Seminole-Creek translation of "mulberry". The area around Kissimmee was settled by cattle ranchers who acquired Spanish land grants in the early 1800s. There was a trading post here in 1881, when the railroad was built from Orlando. Soon sugarcane plantations and sugar mills were established, and the settlement flourished.

Population: 32,042 (1990); 47,814 (2000); 62,875 (2007); 74,419 (2012 projected); Race: 59.1% White, 11.3% Black, 3.7% Asian, 56.5% Hispanic of any race (2007); Density: 3,769.6 persons per square mile (2007); Average household size: 2.77 (2007); Median age: 31.7 (2007); Males per 100 females: 100.4 (2007); Marriage status: 30.4% never married, 52.6% now married, 4.6% widowed, 12.4% divorced (2000); Foreign born: 19.5% (2000); Ancestry (includes multiple ancestries): 49.4% Other groups, 8.8% German, 7.1% Irish, 6.3% United States or American, 6.3% English (2000).

Economy: Unemployment rate: 3.9% (11/2007); Total civilian labor force: 34,260 (11/2007); Single-family building permits issued: 397 (2006); Multi-family building permits issued: 2 (2006); Employment by occupation: 8.9% management, 11.8% professional, 27.9% services, 29.7% sales, 0.2% farming, 11.2% construction, 10.3% production (2000).

Income: Per capita income: $15,804 (2007); Median household income: $35,796 (2007); Average household income: $43,483 (2007); Percent of households with income of $100,000 or more: 4.8% (2007); Poverty rate: 15.4% (2000).

Taxes: Total city taxes per capita: $322 (2005); City property taxes per capita: $142 (2005).

Education: Percent of population age 25 and over with: High school diploma (including GED) or higher: 78.8% (2007); Bachelor's degree or higher: 17.0% (2007); Master's degree or higher: 4.7% (2007).

School District(s)
Osceola County School District (PK-12)
    2005-06 Enrollment: 47,446 . . . . (407) 870-4008

Four-year College(s)
Florida Christian College Inc (Private, Not-for-profit, Christian Churches and Churches of Christ)
    Fall 2006 Enrollment: 255 . . . . (407) 847-8966
    2006-07 Tuition: In-state $10,812; Out-of-state $10,812

Vocational/Technical School(s)
Technical Education Center-Osceola (Public)
    Fall 2006 Enrollment: 268 . . . . (407) 344-5080
    2006-07 Tuition: $3,857

Housing: Homeownership rate: 42.8% (2007); Median home value: $180,034 (2007); Median rent: $619 per month (2000); Median age of housing: 14 years (2000).

Hospitals: Florida Hospital Kissimmee (50 beds); Osceola Regional Medical Center (231 beds)

Safety: Violent crime rate: 78.9 per 10,000 population; Property crime rate: 389.1 per 10,000 population (2006).

Newspapers: Osceola News-Gazette (General - Circulation 29,000); South Orange News (General - Circulation 21,000)

Transportation: Commute to work: 93.3% car, 2.0% public transportation, 1.9% walk, 1.2% work from home (2000); Travel time to work: 21.8% less than 15 minutes, 41.2% 15 to 30 minutes, 25.2% 30 to 45 minutes, 6.6% 45 to 60 minutes, 5.2% 60 minutes or more (2000); Amtrak: Service available.

Additional Information Contacts
City of Kissimmee . . . . (407) 847-2821
    http://www.kissimmee.org

POINCIANA (CDP). Covers a land area of 35.106 square miles and a water area of 0.238 square miles. Located at 28.15° N. Lat.; 81.47° W. Long. Elevation is 66 feet.

Population: 4,687 (1990); 13,647 (2000); 28,499 (2007); 38,705 (2012 projected); Race: 57.6% White, 21.9% Black, 0.9% Asian, 50.1% Hispanic of any race (2007); Density: 811.8 persons per square mile (2007); Average household size: 3.29 (2007); Median age: 30.7 (2007); Males per 100 females: 96.8 (2007); Marriage status: 25.1% never married, 62.3% now married, 3.9% widowed, 8.7% divorced (2000); Foreign born: 15.2% (2000); Ancestry (includes multiple ancestries): 49.1% Other groups, 9.8% German, 8.6% Irish, 7.2% Italian, 4.4% English (2000).

Economy: Employment by occupation: 9.3% management, 10.3% professional, 28.2% services, 29.3% sales, 0.0% farming, 11.4% construction, 11.6% production (2000).

Income: Per capita income: $13,110 (2007); Median household income: $39,166 (2007); Average household income: $43,164 (2007); Percent of households with income of $100,000 or more: 2.7% (2007); Poverty rate: 12.8% (2000).

Education: Percent of population age 25 and over with: High school diploma (including GED) or higher: 77.7% (2007); Bachelor's degree or higher: 9.8% (2007); Master's degree or higher: 3.4% (2007).

Housing: Homeownership rate: 79.2% (2007); Median home value: $179,640 (2007); Median rent: $618 per month (2000); Median age of housing: 8 years (2000).

Transportation: Commute to work: 97.4% car, 0.7% public transportation, 0.4% walk, 0.3% work from home (2000); Travel time to work: 7.8% less than 15 minutes, 19.9% 15 to 30 minutes, 40.0% 30 to 45 minutes, 22.1% 45 to 60 minutes, 10.0% 60 minutes or more (2000)

SAINT CLOUD (city). Covers a land area of 9.163 square miles and a water area of 0.009 square miles. Located at 28.24° N. Lat.; 81.28° W. Long. Elevation is 75 feet.

History: Named for Saint Cloud, 524-560, grandson of King Clovis I of France. St. Cloud was founded in the early 1880s as a cattle shipping center. In 1909 many veterans of the Grand Army of the Republic settled here, bringing the nickname of the G.A.R. Town to St. Cloud. The town was the center of a reclamation project that drained swamps to form pasture and crop lands.

Population: 13,703 (1990); 20,074 (2000); 24,946 (2007); 28,825 (2012 projected); Race: 84.8% White, 3.1% Black, 1.2% Asian, 23.2% Hispanic of any race (2007); Density: 2,722.5 persons per square mile (2007); Average household size: 2.61 (2007); Median age: 36.3 (2007); Males per 100 females: 93.5 (2007); Marriage status: 17.5% never married, 60.6% now married, 8.7% widowed, 13.2% divorced (2000); Foreign born: 6.2% (2000); Ancestry (includes multiple ancestries): 20.9% Other groups, 17.2% German, 16.4% Irish, 10.6% English, 8.8% United States or American (2000).

Economy: Single-family building permits issued: 1,310 (2006); Multi-family building permits issued: 0 (2006); Employment by occupation: 9.4% management, 13.9% professional, 21.2% services, 29.6% sales, 0.3% farming, 12.9% construction, 12.7% production (2000).

Income: Per capita income: $20,318 (2007); Median household income: $44,368 (2007); Average household income: $52,592 (2007); Percent of households with income of $100,000 or more: 8.8% (2007); Poverty rate: 8.1% (2000).

Education: Percent of population age 25 and over with: High school diploma (including GED) or higher: 79.4% (2007); Bachelor's degree or higher: 14.0% (2007); Master's degree or higher: 3.7% (2007).

School District(s)
Osceola County School District (PK-12)
    2005-06 Enrollment: 47,446 . . . . (407) 870-4008

Housing: Homeownership rate: 71.0% (2007); Median home value: $179,897 (2007); Median rent: $516 per month (2000); Median age of housing: 19 years (2000).

Hospitals: Orlando Regional St. Cloud Hospital (84 beds)

Safety: Violent crime rate: 74.3 per 10,000 population; Property crime rate: 502.4 per 10,000 population (2006).

Transportation: Commute to work: 94.3% car, 0.7% public transportation, 1.3% walk, 1.6% work from home (2000); Travel time to work: 24.1% less than 15 minutes, 26.1% 15 to 30 minutes, 31.5% 30 to 45 minutes, 11.0% 45 to 60 minutes, 7.3% 60 minutes or more (2000)

Additional Information Contacts

YEEHAW JUNCTION (CDP). Covers a land area of 5.596 square miles and a water area of 0.023 square miles. Located at 28.33° N. Lat.; 81.35° W. Long. Elevation is 62 feet.

Population: 14,383 (1990); 21,778 (2000); 28,809 (2007); 34,173 (2012 projected); Race: 55.2% White, 14.4% Black, 2.7% Asian, 64.4% Hispanic of any race (2007); Density: 5,148.5 persons per square mile (2007); Average household size: 3.14 (2007); Median age: 33.7 (2007); Males per 100 females: 95.1 (2007); Marriage status: 25.3% never married, 59.4% now married, 5.6% widowed, 9.7% divorced (2000); Foreign born: 19.8% (2000); Ancestry (includes multiple ancestries): 59.0% Other groups, 5.6% Irish, 5.1% German, 4.8% United States or American, 4.3% Italian (2000).

Economy: Employment by occupation: 8.9% management, 10.5% professional, 23.5% services, 31.7% sales, 0.2% farming, 11.5% construction, 13.8% production (2000).

Income: Per capita income: $16,472 (2007); Median household income: $42,530 (2007); Average household income: $51,284 (2007); Percent of households with income of $100,000 or more: 8.1% (2007); Poverty rate: 10.2% (2000).

Education: Percent of population age 25 and over with: High school diploma (including GED) or higher: 74.8% (2007); Bachelor's degree or higher: 13.2% (2007); Master's degree or higher: 3.5% (2007).

Housing: Homeownership rate: 73.7% (2007); Median home value: $178,467 (2007); Median rent: $653 per month (2000); Median age of housing: 13 years (2000).

Transportation: Commute to work: 96.2% car, 0.7% public transportation, 0.7% walk, 1.0% work from home (2000); Travel time to work: 12.4% less than 15 minutes, 45.7% 15 to 30 minutes, 30.6% 30 to 45 minutes, 5.1% 45 to 60 minutes, 6.2% 60 minutes or more (2000)

Palm Beach County

Located in southeastern Florida; bounded on the east by the Atlantic Ocean; includes Lake Okeechobee. Covers a land area of 1,974.11 square miles, a water area of 412.22 square miles, and is located in the Eastern Time Zone. The county was founded in 1909. County seat is West Palm Beach.

Palm Beach County is part of the Miami-Fort Lauderdale-Pompano Beach, FL Metropolitan Statistical Area. The entire metro area includes: Fort Lauderdale-Pompano Beach-Deerfield Beach, FL Metropolitan Division (Broward County, FL); Miami-Miami Beach-Kendall, FL Metropolitan Division (Miami-Dade County, FL); West Palm Beach-Boca Raton-Boynton Beach, FL Metropolitan Division (Palm Beach County, FL)

Weather Station: Belle Glade Exp. Station   Elevation: 13 feet

	Jan	Feb	Mar	Apr	May	Jun	Jul	Aug	Sep	Oct	Nov	Dec
High	75	76	80	84	87	90	91	91	90	86	81	76
Low	52	52	57	59	65	70	71	71	70	66	60	54
Precip	2.6	1.9	3.1	2.2	5.2	7.4	7.4	7.4	7.1	3.5	2.8	1.8
Snow	tr	0.0	0.0	0.0	0.0	0.0	0.0	0.0	0.0	0.0	0.0	0.0

High and Low temperatures in degrees Fahrenheit; Precipitation and Snow in inches

Weather Station: Canal Point USDA   Elevation: 29 feet

	Jan	Feb	Mar	Apr	May	Jun	Jul	Aug	Sep	Oct	Nov	Dec
High	74	76	80	84	88	90	92	92	90	86	81	76
Low	53	54	58	61	66	70	71	71	71	67	61	56
Precip	2.7	2.3	3.8	2.2	4.8	7.5	6.3	7.0	7.0	3.9	2.9	2.1
Snow	0.0	0.0	0.0	0.0	0.0	0.0	0.0	0.0	0.0	0.0	0.0	0.0

High and Low temperatures in degrees Fahrenheit; Precipitation and Snow in inches

Weather Station: West Palm Beach Int'l Airport   Elevation: 16 feet

	Jan	Feb	Mar	Apr	May	Jun	Jul	Aug	Sep	Oct	Nov	Dec
High	75	76	79	82	86	89	90	90	89	85	80	77
Low	57	58	62	65	70	74	75	75	75	71	66	60
Precip	3.9	2.6	4.0	3.5	5.6	7.8	5.9	6.7	8.1	5.4	5.4	3.1
Snow	tr	0.0	tr	0.0	0.0	0.0	0.0	tr	0.0	0.0	0.0	0.0

High and Low temperatures in degrees Fahrenheit; Precipitation and Snow in inches

Population: 863,518 (1990); 1,131,184 (2000); 1,302,553 (2007); 1,424,456 (2012 projected); Race: 75.6% White, 15.3% Black, 2.0% Asian, 16.9% Hispanic of any race (2007); Density: 659.8 persons per square mile

Economy: Unemployment rate: 4.5% (11/2007); Total civilian labor force: 648,759 (11/2007); Leading industries: 15.2% retail trade; 13.6% health care and social assistance; 11.3% accommodation & food services (2005); Farms: 1,110 totaling 535,965 acres (2002); Companies that employ 500 or more persons: 68 (2005); Companies that employ 100 to 499 persons: 696 (2005); Companies that employ less than 100 persons: 41,884 (2005); Black-owned businesses: 8,169 (2002); Hispanic-owned businesses: 13,267 (2002); Asian-owned businesses: 3,010 (2002); Women-owned businesses: 37,808 (2002); Retail sales per capita: $17,228 (2007). Single-family building permits issued: 4,652 (2006); Multi-family building permits issued: 3,725 (2006).

Income: Per capita income: $32,256 (2007); Median household income: $51,457 (2007); Average household income: $76,672 (2007); Percent of households with income of $100,000 or more: 21.1% (2007); Poverty rate: 11.0% (2005); Bankruptcy rate: 0.80% (2006).

Taxes: Total county taxes per capita: $682 (2005); County property taxes per capita: $478 (2005).

Education: Percent of population age 25 and over with: High school diploma (including GED) or higher: 83.9% (2007); Bachelor's degree or higher: 28.1% (2007); Master's degree or higher: 10.3% (2007).

Housing: Homeownership rate: 75.3% (2007); Median home value: $264,178 (2007); Median rent: $648 per month (2000); Median age of housing: 19 years (2000).

Health: Birth rate: 126.4 per 10,000 population (2006); Death rate: 110.3 per 10,000 population (2006); Age-adjusted cancer mortality rate: 169.2 deaths per 100,000 population (2004); Air Quality Index: 89.9% good, 10.1% moderate, 0.0% unhealthy for sensitive individuals, 0.0% unhealthy (percent of days in 2006); Number of physicians: 28.8 per 10,000 population (2005); Hospital beds: 28.4 per 10,000 population (2004); Hospital admissions: 1,379.1 per 10,000 population (2004).

Elections: 2004 Presidential election results: 39.1% Bush, 60.4% Kerry, 0.3% Nader, 0.1% Badnarik.

National and State Parks: John D MacArthur Beach State Park; Loxahatchee National Wildlife Refuge; Mar-A-Lago National Historical Site; Pahokee State Park; Palm Beach Pines State Recreation Area

Additional Information Contacts

Palm Beach County Government . . . . (561) 355-2001
   http://www.co.palm-beach.fl.us
Belle Glade Chamber of Commerce . . . . (561) 996-2745
   http://www.belleglladechamber.com
Boca Raton Chamber of Commerce . . . . (561) 395-4433
   http://www.bocaratonchamber.com
Boynton Beach Chamber of Commerce . . . . (561) 732-9501
   http://www.boyntonbeach.org
City of Belle Glade . . . . (561) 996-0100
   http://belleglade-fl.com
City of Boca Raton . . . . (561) 393-7700
   http://www.ci.boca-raton.fl.us
City of Boynton Beach . . . . (561) 742-6000
   http://www.boynton-beach.org
City of Delray Beach . . . . (561) 243-7000
   http://mydelraybeach.com
City of Greenacres . . . . (561) 642-2000
   http://www.ci.greenacres.fl.us
City of Lake Worth . . . . (561) 586-1662
   http://www.lakeworth.org
City of Pahokee . . . . (561) 924-5534
   http://www.pahokeeflorida.com
City of Palm Beach Gardens . . . . (561) 799-4100
   http://www.pbgfl.com
City of Riviera Beach . . . . (561) 845-4000
   http://www.rivierabch.com
City of West Palm Beach . . . . (561) 822-1210
   http://www.cityofwpb.com
Delray Beach Chamber of Commerce . . . . (561) 278-0424
   http://www.delraybeach.com
Hispanic Chamber of Commerce . . . . (561) 832-1986
   http://www.palmbeachhispanicchamber.com
Jupiter Chamber of Commerce . . . . (561) 746-7111
   http://www.jupiterfl.org

http://www.palmbeaches.org

Palm Beach Gardens Chamber of Commerce . . . . (561) 694-2300
http://www.npbchamber.com
Town of Jupiter . . . . (561) 746-5134
http://www.jupiter.fl.us
Town of Lake Park . . . . (561) 881-3300
http://www.lakeparkflorida.net
Town of Lantana . . . . (561) 540-5000
http://www.lantana.org
Town of Palm Beach . . . . (561) 838-5400
http://palmbeach.govoffice.com
Village of North Palm Beach . . . . (561) 841-3380
http://www.village-npb.org
Village of Royal Palm Beach . . . . (561) 790-5100
http://royalpalmbeach.com
Village of Wellington . . . . (561) 791-4000
http://www.wellvillage.com
West Palm Beach Chamber of Commerce . . . . (561) 833-3711
http://www.palmbeaches.org

Palm Beach County Communities

ATLANTIS (city). Covers a land area of 1.371 square miles and a water area of 0.041 square miles. Located at 26.59° N. Lat.; 80.10° W. Long. Elevation is 13 feet.

Population: 1,658 (1990); 2,005 (2000); 2,147 (2007); 2,266 (2012 projected); Race: 96.4% White, 0.8% Black, 2.3% Asian, 3.1% Hispanic of any race (2007); Density: 1,566.5 persons per square mile (2007); Average household size: 1.92 (2007); Median age: 65.3 (2007); Males per 100 females: 87.3 (2007); Marriage status: 10.7% never married, 71.7% now married, 13.8% widowed, 3.8% divorced (2000); Foreign born: 12.6% (2000); Ancestry (includes multiple ancestries): 21.7% German, 18.1% English, 13.5% Irish, 10.0% Italian, 6.9% Other groups (2000).

Economy: Single-family building permits issued: 2 (2006); Multi-family building permits issued: 0 (2006); Employment by occupation: 21.6% management, 23.7% professional, 16.7% services, 29.9% sales, 0.8% farming, 4.3% construction, 2.9% production (2000).

Income: Per capita income: $56,294 (2007); Median household income: $77,105 (2007); Average household income: $107,817 (2007); Percent of households with income of $100,000 or more: 34.0% (2007); Poverty rate: 4.0% (2000).

Taxes: Total city taxes per capita: $1,328 (2005); City property taxes per capita: $1,011 (2005).

Education: Percent of population age 25 and over with: High school diploma (including GED) or higher: 93.7% (2007); Bachelor's degree or higher: 40.2% (2007); Master's degree or higher: 18.5% (2007).

Housing: Homeownership rate: 95.4% (2007); Median home value: $479,319 (2007); Median rent: $675 per month (2000); Median age of housing: 24 years (2000).

Hospitals: JFK Medical Center (424 beds)

Safety: Violent crime rate: 45.9 per 10,000 population; Property crime rate: 188.2 per 10,000 population (2006).

Transportation: Commute to work: 94.0% car, 0.0% public transportation, 0.0% walk, 6.0% work from home (2000); Travel time to work: 41.9% less than 15 minutes, 36.8% 15 to 30 minutes, 13.7% 30 to 45 minutes, 5.1% 45 to 60 minutes, 2.5% 60 minutes or more (2000)

BELLE GLADE (city). Covers a land area of 4.649 square miles and a water area of 0.009 square miles. Located at 26.68° N. Lat.; 80.67° W. Long. Elevation is 16 feet.

History: Named for a tourist's comment in 1921 — "belle of the Glades" referring to the Everglade section of the state. Belle Glade sprang into existence in 1925 and was destroyed just as quickly in 1928 by a hurricane. The town was rebuilt and grew as a trading center for a truck-farming area.

Population: 16,429 (1990); 14,906 (2000); 14,915 (2007); 15,021 (2012 projected); Race: 31.2% White, 49.4% Black, 0.2% Asian, 32.5% Hispanic of any race (2007); Density: 3,208.1 persons per square mile (2007);

building permits issued: 2 (2006); Employment by occupation: 6.0% management, 16.1% professional, 15.3% services, 19.6% sales, 15.1% farming, 11.5% construction, 16.2% production (2000).

Income: Per capita income: $12,352 (2007); Median household income: $25,645 (2007); Average household income: $37,299 (2007); Percent of households with income of $100,000 or more: 5.6% (2007); Poverty rate: 32.9% (2000).

Education: Percent of population age 25 and over with: High school diploma (including GED) or higher: 47.3% (2007); Bachelor's degree or higher: 10.2% (2007); Master's degree or higher: 3.8% (2007).

School District(s)

Palm Beach County School District (PK-12)
    2005-06 Enrollment: 175,076 . . . . (561) 434-8200

Housing: Homeownership rate: 42.6% (2007); Median home value: $145,906 (2007); Median rent: $319 per month (2000); Median age of housing: 31 years (2000).

Hospitals: Glades General Hospital (73 beds)

Safety: Violent crime rate: 130.1 per 10,000 population; Property crime rate: 506.3 per 10,000 population (2006).

Transportation: Commute to work: 79.7% car, 14.3% public transportation, 3.0% walk, 0.9% work from home (2000); Travel time to work: 43.0% less than 15 minutes, 21.8% 15 to 30 minutes, 16.0% 30 to 45 minutes, 5.8% 45 to 60 minutes, 13.4% 60 minutes or more (2000)

Additional Information Contacts

Belle Glade Chamber of Commerce . . . . (561) 996-2745
http://www.belleglade chamber.com
City of Belle Glade . . . . (561) 996-0100
http://belleglade-fl.com

BELLE GLADE CAMP (CDP). Covers a land area of 0.479 square miles and a water area of 0 square miles. Located at 26.66° N. Lat.; 80.68° W. Long. Elevation is 10 feet.

Population: 1,616 (1990); 1,141 (2000); 937 (2007); 822 (2012 projected); Race: 24.5% White, 50.2% Black, 0.0% Asian, 41.5% Hispanic of any race (2007); Density: 1,954.7 persons per square mile (2007); Average household size: 3.94 (2007); Median age: 21.0 (2007); Males per 100 females: 90.8 (2007); Marriage status: 52.6% never married, 30.1% now married, 6.7% widowed, 10.6% divorced (2000); Foreign born: 21.9% (2000); Ancestry (includes multiple ancestries): 48.3% Other groups, 22.5% Haitian, 5.0% Jamaican, 2.1% United States or American, 1.6% African (2000).

Economy: Employment by occupation: 0.0% management, 9.3% professional, 17.6% services, 9.3% sales, 39.3% farming, 0.0% construction, 24.5% production (2000).

Income: Per capita income: $5,704 (2007); Median household income: $20,217 (2007); Average household income: $22,458 (2007); Percent of households with income of $100,000 or more: 0.0% (2007); Poverty rate: 62.1% (2000).

Education: Percent of population age 25 and over with: High school diploma (including GED) or higher: 25.2% (2007); Bachelor's degree or higher: 5.0% (2007); Master's degree or higher: 0.0% (2007).

Housing: Homeownership rate: 0.0% (2007); Median home value: $n/a (2007); Median rent: $308 per month (2000); Median age of housing: 28 years (2000).

Transportation: Commute to work: 75.5% car, 22.9% public transportation, 0.0% walk, 0.0% work from home (2000); Travel time to work: 21.7% less than 15 minutes, 18.0% 15 to 30 minutes, 22.3% 30 to 45 minutes, 12.7% 45 to 60 minutes, 25.4% 60 minutes or more (2000)

BOCA DEL MAR (CDP). Covers a land area of 4.021 square miles and a water area of 0 square miles. Located at 26.34° N. Lat.; 80.14° W. Long. Elevation is 13 feet.

Population: 17,754 (1990); 21,832 (2000); 22,152 (2007); 22,678 (2012 projected); Race: 93.2% White, 1.6% Black, 2.1% Asian, 11.8% Hispanic of any race (2007); Density: 5,509.7 persons per square mile (2007); Average household size: 1.97 (2007); Median age: 47.2 (2007); Males per 100 females: 84.8 (2007); Marriage status: 20.6% never married, 53.4% now married, 12.7% widowed, 13.3% divorced (2000); Foreign born: 16.4%

(2000); Ancestry (includes multiple ancestries): 18.2% Other groups, 14.0% Italian, 12.7% German, 9.6% Irish, 9.5% Russian (2000).
Economy: Employment by occupation: 20.5% management, 24.0% professional, 13.0% services, 34.9% sales, 0.0% farming, 3.3% construction, 4.3% production (2000).
Income: Per capita income: $39,366 (2007); Median household income: $56,713 (2007); Average household income: $75,475 (2007); Percent of households with income of $100,000 or more: 23.0% (2007); Poverty rate: 4.3% (2000).
Education: Percent of population age 25 and over with: High school diploma (including GED) or higher: 94.9% (2007); Bachelor's degree or higher: 41.8% (2007); Master's degree or higher: 16.2% (2007).
Housing: Homeownership rate: 62.1% (2007); Median home value: $321,531 (2007); Median rent: $926 per month (2000); Median age of housing: 15 years (2000).
Transportation: Commute to work: 92.3% car, 0.3% public transportation, 0.3% walk, 5.9% work from home (2000); Travel time to work: 27.3% less than 15 minutes, 46.6% 15 to 30 minutes, 16.0% 30 to 45 minutes, 5.7% 45 to 60 minutes, 4.4% 60 minutes or more (2000)

BOCA POINTE (CDP). Covers a land area of 1.151 square miles and a water area of 0 square miles. Located at 26.33° N. Lat.; 80.16° W. Long. Elevation is 13 feet.
Population: 2,147 (1990); 3,302 (2000); 3,703 (2007); 3,859 (2012 projected); Race: 98.1% White, 0.5% Black, 0.9% Asian, 5.2% Hispanic of any race (2007); Density: 3,216.0 persons per square mile (2007); Average household size: 1.81 (2007); Median age: 64.2 (2007); Males per 100 females: 79.6 (2007); Marriage status: 7.3% never married, 70.3% now married, 14.3% widowed, 8.1% divorced (2000); Foreign born: 11.5% (2000); Ancestry (includes multiple ancestries): 17.7% Russian, 16.6% Other groups, 12.1% United States or American, 10.9% Polish, 6.7% German (2000).
Economy: Employment by occupation: 25.4% management, 22.2% professional, 7.8% services, 44.0% sales, 0.0% farming, 0.6% construction, 0.0% production (2000).
Income: Per capita income: $78,850 (2007); Median household income: $103,722 (2007); Average household income: $142,360 (2007); Percent of households with income of $100,000 or more: 51.6% (2007); Poverty rate: 2.0% (2000).
Education: Percent of population age 25 and over with: High school diploma (including GED) or higher: 96.7% (2007); Bachelor's degree or higher: 39.5% (2007); Master's degree or higher: 15.2% (2007).
Housing: Homeownership rate: 94.4% (2007); Median home value: $484,865 (2007); Median rent: $1,511 per month (2000); Median age of housing: 14 years (2000).
Transportation: Commute to work: 83.7% car, 0.7% public transportation, 0.8% walk, 14.8% work from home (2000); Travel time to work: 38.1% less than 15 minutes, 34.5% 15 to 30 minutes, 14.9% 30 to 45 minutes, 5.5% 45 to 60 minutes, 7.1% 60 minutes or more (2000)

BOCA RATON (city). Covers a land area of 27.189 square miles and a water area of 1.931 square miles. Located at 26.36° N. Lat.; 80.10° W. Long. Elevation is 13 feet.
History: The Mediterranean architecture of Boca Raton was planned by architect Addison Mizner as his dream city during the 1920's land boom. The city's name comes from the Spanish for "mouth of rats," referring to the sharp rocks guarding the anchorage.
Population: 61,401 (1990); 74,764 (2000); 78,047 (2007); 81,130 (2012 projected); Race: 88.8% White, 4.5% Black, 2.2% Asian, 12.1% Hispanic of any race (2007); Density: 2,870.5 persons per square mile (2007); Average household size: 2.33 (2007); Median age: 44.3 (2007); Males per 100 females: 95.8 (2007); Marriage status: 22.1% never married, 60.6% now married, 7.4% widowed, 10.0% divorced (2000); Foreign born: 18.0% (2000); Ancestry (includes multiple ancestries): 15.5% Other groups, 14.4% German, 12.4% Italian, 12.0% Irish, 9.4% English (2000).
Economy: Unemployment rate: 3.4% (11/2007); Total civilian labor force: 47,690 (11/2007); Single-family building permits issued: 55 (2006); Multi-family building permits issued: 247 (2006); Employment by occupation: 23.3% management, 22.3% professional, 13.4% services, 30.9% sales, 0.1% farming, 5.2% construction, 4.8% production (2000).
Income: Per capita income: $51,713 (2007); Median household income: $68,764 (2007); Average household income: $118,706 (2007); Percent of households with income of $100,000 or more: 35.6% (2007); Poverty rate: 6.7% (2000).

Taxes: Total city taxes per capita: $998 (2005); City property taxes per capita: $543 (2005).
Education: Percent of population age 25 and over with: High school diploma (including GED) or higher: 91.8% (2007); Bachelor's degree or higher: 43.9% (2007); Master's degree or higher: 16.9% (2007).
School District(s)
Florida Atlantic University Laboratory School (PK-12)
    2005-06 Enrollment: 639 . . . . (561) 367-3970
Palm Beach County School District (PK-12)
    2005-06 Enrollment: 175,076 . . . . (561) 434-8200
Four-year College(s)
Everglades University (Private, Not-for-profit)
    Fall 2006 Enrollment: 644 . . . . (561) 912-1211
    2006-07 Tuition: In-state $11,920; Out-of-state $11,920
Florida Atlantic University (Public)
    Fall 2006 Enrollment: 25,325. (561) 297-3000
    2006-07 Tuition: In-state $2,662; Out-of-state $13,113
Lynn University (Private, Not-for-profit)
    Fall 2006 Enrollment: 2,715. . . . . (561) 237-7000
    2006-07 Tuition: In-state $26,200; Out-of-state $26,200
Housing: Homeownership rate: 75.2% (2007); Median home value: $459,017 (2007); Median rent: $770 per month (2000); Median age of housing: 23 years (2000).
Hospitals: West Boca Medical Center (185 beds)
Safety: Violent crime rate: 27.0 per 10,000 population; Property crime rate: 335.0 per 10,000 population (2006).
Newspapers: Boca Raton News (Circulation 23,105); Globe (General - Circulation 1,516,823); National Enquirer (General - Circulation 2,076,032); National Examiner (General - Circulation 600,000); Weekly World News (General - Circulation 380,000)
Transportation: Commute to work: 89.2% car, 0.9% public transportation, 2.0% walk, 6.1% work from home (2000); Travel time to work: 40.7% less than 15 minutes, 36.4% 15 to 30 minutes, 14.0% 30 to 45 minutes, 4.4% 45 to 60 minutes, 4.4% 60 minutes or more (2000)
Airports: Boca Raton
Additional Information Contacts
Boca Raton Chamber of Commerce . . . . (561) 395-4433
    http://www.bocaratonchamber.com
City of Boca Raton . . . . (561) 393-7700
    http://www.ci.boca-raton.fl.us

BOYNTON BEACH (city). Covers a land area of 15.877 square miles and a water area of 0.373 square miles. Located at 26.52° N. Lat.; 80.07° W. Long. Elevation is 20 feet.
History: Named for Major N.S. Boynton, who built a hotel on a local beach. Incorporated 1920 as Boynton.
Population: 48,285 (1990); 60,389 (2000); 67,948 (2007); 73,600 (2012 projected); Race: 65.3% White, 25.7% Black, 2.1% Asian, 13.0% Hispanic of any race (2007); Density: 4,279.6 persons per square mile (2007); Average household size: 2.29 (2007); Median age: 42.5 (2007); Males per 100 females: 89.3 (2007); Marriage status: 21.5% never married, 55.6% now married, 11.1% widowed, 11.8% divorced (2000); Foreign born: 17.4% (2000); Ancestry (includes multiple ancestries): 22.8% Other groups, 11.8% German, 11.6% Irish, 9.7% Italian, 9.0% English (2000).
Economy: Unemployment rate: 4.2% (11/2007); Total civilian labor force: 34,953 (11/2007); Single-family building permits issued: 453 (2006); Multi-family building permits issued: 7 (2006); Employment by occupation: 12.4% management, 17.2% professional, 21.1% services, 29.7% sales, 0.6% farming, 10.6% construction, 8.3% production (2000).
Income: Per capita income: $25,625 (2007); Median household income: $44,299 (2007); Average household income: $57,995 (2007); Percent of households with income of $100,000 or more: 11.9% (2007); Poverty rate: 10.2% (2000).
Taxes: Total city taxes per capita: $639 (2005); City property taxes per capita: $381 (2005).
Education: Percent of population age 25 and over with: High school diploma (including GED) or higher: 80.9% (2007); Bachelor's degree or higher: 21.2% (2007); Master's degree or higher: 6.7% (2007).
School District(s)
Palm Beach County School District (PK-12)
    2005-06 Enrollment: 175,076 . . . . (561) 434-8200
Four-year College(s)
Saint Vincent de Paul Regional Seminary (Private, Not-for-profit, Roman Catholic)
    Fall 2006 Enrollment: 89 . . . . (561) 732-4424

Housing: Homeownership rate: 73.0% (2007); Median home value: $192,607 (2007); Median rent: $707 per month (2000); Median age of housing: 21 years (2000).
Hospitals: Bethesda Memorial Hospital (362 beds)
Safety: Violent crime rate: 97.0 per 10,000 population; Property crime rate: 501.7 per 10,000 population (2006).
Transportation: Commute to work: 93.7% car, 1.5% public transportation, 1.1% walk, 2.6% work from home (2000); Travel time to work: 23.8% less than 15 minutes, 41.1% 15 to 30 minutes, 23.4% 30 to 45 minutes, 7.1% 45 to 60 minutes, 4.7% 60 minutes or more (2000)
Additional Information Contacts
Boynton Beach Chamber of Commerce . . . . (561) 732-9501
    http://www.boyntonbeach.org
City of Boynton Beach . . . . (561) 742-6000
    http://www.boynton-beach.org

BRINY BREEZES (town). Covers a land area of 0.070 square miles and a water area of 0.024 square miles. Located at 26.50° N. Lat.; 80.05° W. Long. Elevation is 13 feet.
Population: 390 (1990); 411 (2000); 420 (2007); 432 (2012 projected); Race: 99.0% White, 0.0% Black, 0.7% Asian, 0.7% Hispanic of any race (2007); Density: 6,042.0 persons per square mile (2007); Average household size: 1.52 (2007); Median age: 71.1 (2007); Males per 100 females: 80.3 (2007); Marriage status: 8.3% never married, 57.3% now married, 23.2% widowed, 11.2% divorced (2000); Foreign born: 3.6% (2000); Ancestry (includes multiple ancestries): 22.3% English, 20.3% Irish, 18.2% German, 6.5% French (except Basque), 5.3% Other groups (2000).
Economy: Single-family building permits issued: 0 (2006); Multi-family building permits issued: 0 (2006); Employment by occupation: 11.2% management, 29.2% professional, 20.2% services, 25.8% sales, 0.0% farming, 4.5% construction, 9.0% production (2000).
Income: Per capita income: $35,851 (2007); Median household income: $38,684 (2007); Average household income: $54,556 (2007); Percent of households with income of $100,000 or more: 12.3% (2007); Poverty rate: 6.6% (2000).
Education: Percent of population age 25 and over with: High school diploma (including GED) or higher: 87.7% (2007); Bachelor's degree or higher: 30.1% (2007); Master's degree or higher: 15.7% (2007).
Housing: Homeownership rate: 91.7% (2007); Median home value: $148,750 (2007); Median rent: $495 per month (2000); Median age of housing: 27 years (2000).
Transportation: Commute to work: 84.5% car, 0.0% public transportation, 2.4% walk, 0.0% work from home (2000); Travel time to work: 27.4% less than 15 minutes, 38.1% 15 to 30 minutes, 20.2% 30 to 45 minutes, 3.6% 45 to 60 minutes, 10.7% 60 minutes or more (2000)

CANAL POINT (CDP). Covers a land area of 1.547 square miles and a water area of 0 square miles. Located at 26.86° N. Lat.; 80.63° W. Long. Elevation is 13 feet.
History: Canal Point was built below the dike and along both banks of the West Palm Beach Canal. A sugar mill was the early industry here.
Population: 472 (1990); 525 (2000); 595 (2007); 646 (2012 projected); Race: 52.3% White, 10.4% Black, 0.5% Asian, 51.6% Hispanic of any race (2007); Density: 384.6 persons per square mile (2007); Average household size: 2.67 (2007); Median age: 34.0 (2007); Males per 100 females: 96.4 (2007); Marriage status: 19.9% never married, 57.0% now married, 11.9% widowed, 11.2% divorced (2000); Foreign born: 28.0% (2000); Ancestry (includes multiple ancestries): 58.7% Other groups, 15.6% United States or American, 7.3% English, 5.1% Jamaican, 4.2% Irish (2000).
Economy: Employment by occupation: 11.8% management, 16.3% professional, 11.8% services, 14.4% sales, 0.0% farming, 15.7% construction, 30.1% production (2000).
Income: Per capita income: $21,693 (2007); Median household income: $39,583 (2007); Average household income: $57,881 (2007); Percent of households with income of $100,000 or more: 11.2% (2007); Poverty rate: 14.4% (2000).
Education: Percent of population age 25 and over with: High school diploma (including GED) or higher: 54.4% (2007); Bachelor's degree or higher: 6.4% (2007); Master's degree or higher: 1.7% (2007).
School District(s)
Palm Beach County School District (PK-12)
    2005-06 Enrollment: 175,076 . . . . (561) 434-8200
Housing: Homeownership rate: 48.0% (2007); Median home value: $139,375 (2007); Median rent: $349 per month (2000); Median age of housing: 41 years (2000).

Transportation: Commute to work: 100.0% car, 0.0% public transportation, 0.0% walk, 0.0% work from home (2000); Travel time to work: 40.5% less than 15 minutes, 39.9% 15 to 30 minutes, 3.9% 30 to 45 minutes, 15.7% 45 to 60 minutes, 0.0% 60 minutes or more (2000)

CENTURY VILLAGE (CDP). Covers a land area of 1.004 square miles and a water area of 0.073 square miles. Located at 26.71° N. Lat.; 80.12° W. Long. Elevation is 16 feet.
Population: 8,528 (1990); 7,616 (2000); 6,642 (2007); 6,105 (2012 projected); Race: 97.6% White, 0.6% Black, 0.7% Asian, 5.2% Hispanic of any race (2007); Density: 6,617.6 persons per square mile (2007); Average household size: 1.34 (2007); Median age: 79.5 (2007); Males per 100 females: 60.5 (2007); Marriage status: 5.8% never married, 45.8% now married, 36.7% widowed, 11.7% divorced (2000); Foreign born: 16.3% (2000); Ancestry (includes multiple ancestries): 22.0% Other groups, 14.9% Russian, 9.3% Polish, 9.2% Italian, 5.7% United States or American (2000).
Economy: Employment by occupation: 5.2% management, 11.4% professional, 27.7% services, 42.1% sales, 0.0% farming, 5.6% construction, 8.0% production (2000).
Income: Per capita income: $20,949 (2007); Median household income: $20,401 (2007); Average household income: $28,103 (2007); Percent of households with income of $100,000 or more: 2.8% (2007); Poverty rate: 12.3% (2000).
Education: Percent of population age 25 and over with: High school diploma (including GED) or higher: 78.6% (2007); Bachelor's degree or higher: 13.7% (2007); Master's degree or higher: 5.0% (2007).
Housing: Homeownership rate: 91.4% (2007); Median home value: $49,628 (2007); Median rent: $420 per month (2000); Median age of housing: 26 years (2000).
Transportation: Commute to work: 87.0% car, 5.4% public transportation, 1.0% walk, 3.9% work from home (2000); Travel time to work: 27.3% less than 15 minutes, 43.9% 15 to 30 minutes, 14.4% 30 to 45 minutes, 9.8% 45 to 60 minutes, 4.5% 60 minutes or more (2000)

CLOUD LAKE (town). Covers a land area of 0.063 square miles and a water area of 0 square miles. Located at 26.67° N. Lat.; 80.07° W. Long. Elevation is 10 feet.
Population: 121 (1990); 167 (2000); 139 (2007); 142 (2012 projected); Race: 78.4% White, 5.8% Black, 13.7% Asian, 46.0% Hispanic of any race (2007); Density: 2,207.2 persons per square mile (2007); Average household size: 2.73 (2007); Median age: 37.5 (2007); Males per 100 females: 85.3 (2007); Marriage status: 18.0% never married, 63.1% now married, 6.3% widowed, 12.6% divorced (2000); Foreign born: 13.0% (2000); Ancestry (includes multiple ancestries): 24.4% Irish, 17.1% Other groups, 11.4% English, 10.6% United States or American, 10.6% German (2000).
Economy: Single-family building permits issued: 0 (2006); Multi-family building permits issued: 0 (2006); Employment by occupation: 2.2% management, 15.2% professional, 22.8% services, 28.3% sales, 0.0% farming, 28.3% construction, 3.3% production (2000).
Income: Per capita income: $24,442 (2007); Median household income: $63,214 (2007); Average household income: $66,618 (2007); Percent of households with income of $100,000 or more: 19.6% (2007); Poverty rate: 0.0% (2000).
Education: Percent of population age 25 and over with: High school diploma (including GED) or higher: 86.8% (2007); Bachelor's degree or higher: 14.3% (2007); Master's degree or higher: 8.8% (2007).
Housing: Homeownership rate: 58.8% (2007); Median home value: $196,875 (2007); Median rent: $450 per month (2000); Median age of housing: 47 years (2000).
Transportation: Commute to work: 94.6% car, 5.4% public transportation, 0.0% walk, 0.0% work from home (2000); Travel time to work: 26.1% less than 15 minutes, 48.9% 15 to 30 minutes, 25.0% 30 to 45 minutes, 0.0% 45 to 60 minutes, 0.0% 60 minutes or more (2000)

CYPRESS LAKES (CDP). Covers a land area of 0.427 square miles and a water area of 0.026 square miles. Located at 26.72° N. Lat.; 80.12° W. Long. Elevation is 16 feet.
Population: 1,177 (1990); 1,468 (2000); 1,721 (2007); 1,905 (2012 projected); Race: 96.2% White, 2.7% Black, 0.9% Asian, 3.3% Hispanic of any race (2007); Density: 4,031.6 persons per square mile (2007); Average household size: 1.69 (2007); Median age: 74.2 (2007); Males per 100 females: 78.9 (2007); Marriage status: 4.5% never married, 73.4% now married, 18.8% widowed, 3.3% divorced (2000); Foreign born: 5.4%

(2000); Ancestry (includes multiple ancestries): 21.5% Italian, 17.2% Other groups, 11.3% United States or American, 9.3% Irish, 9.1% Russian (2000).
Economy: Employment by occupation: 34.5% management, 0.0% professional, 15.9% services, 33.6% sales, 0.0% farming, 0.0% construction, 15.9% production (2000).
Income: Per capita income: $29,425 (2007); Median household income: $31,238 (2007); Average household income: $49,696 (2007); Percent of households with income of $100,000 or more: 6.8% (2007); Poverty rate: 4.3% (2000).
Education: Percent of population age 25 and over with: High school diploma (including GED) or higher: 80.6% (2007); Bachelor's degree or higher: 11.5% (2007); Master's degree or higher: 3.0% (2007).
Housing: Homeownership rate: 97.3% (2007); Median home value: $202,500 (2007); Median rent: $n/a per month (2000); Median age of housing: 13 years (2000).
Transportation: Commute to work: 90.5% car, 0.0% public transportation, 0.0% walk, 9.5% work from home (2000); Travel time to work: 48.8% less than 15 minutes, 26.7% 15 to 30 minutes, 15.1% 30 to 45 minutes, 9.3% 45 to 60 minutes, 0.0% 60 minutes or more (2000)

DELRAY BEACH (city). Covers a land area of 15.368 square miles and a water area of 0.525 square miles. Located at 26.45° N. Lat.; 80.08° W. Long. Elevation is 16 feet.
History: Named, perhaps, for the Spanish translation of "of the king". Delray Beach was settled in 1895, and grew as a tourist resort area and the center of an agricultural area producing beans, peppers, tomatoes, sugar cane, and citrus fruit.
Population: 47,833 (1990); 60,020 (2000); 65,731 (2007); 70,195 (2012 projected); Race: 62.8% White, 28.4% Black, 1.5% Asian, 9.5% Hispanic of any race (2007); Density: 4,277.2 persons per square mile (2007); Average household size: 2.24 (2007); Median age: 44.7 (2007); Males per 100 females: 93.1 (2007); Marriage status: 24.6% never married, 51.6% now married, 11.5% widowed, 12.3% divorced (2000); Foreign born: 21.5% (2000); Ancestry (includes multiple ancestries): 21.5% Other groups, 10.6% Haitian, 10.5% German, 10.3% Irish, 8.1% English (2000).
Economy: Unemployment rate: 4.2% (11/2007); Total civilian labor force: 32,759 (11/2007); Single-family building permits issued: 116 (2006); Multi-family building permits issued: 264 (2006); Employment by occupation: 14.8% management, 18.8% professional, 22.1% services, 26.9% sales, 0.5% farming, 7.9% construction, 9.0% production (2000).
Income: Per capita income: $32,412 (2007); Median household income: $49,226 (2007); Average household income: $72,174 (2007); Percent of households with income of $100,000 or more: 19.7% (2007); Poverty rate: 11.8% (2000).
Education: Percent of population age 25 and over with: High school diploma (including GED) or higher: 80.8% (2007); Bachelor's degree or higher: 29.3% (2007); Master's degree or higher: 10.1% (2007).

School District(s)
Palm Beach County School District (PK-12)
    2005-06 Enrollment: 175,076 . . . . (561) 434-8200

Vocational/Technical School(s)
Levin School of Health Care (Private, For-profit)
    Fall 2006 Enrollment: n/a . . . . (561) 274-9663
Housing: Homeownership rate: 69.4% (2007); Median home value: $234,116 (2007); Median rent: $704 per month (2000); Median age of housing: 22 years (2000).
Hospitals: Delray Medical Center (343 beds); Delray Medical Center (343 beds); Pinecrest Rehabilitation Hospital (90 beds)
Safety: Violent crime rate: 103.0 per 10,000 population; Property crime rate: 506.0 per 10,000 population (2006).
Transportation: Commute to work: 90.5% car, 1.7% public transportation, 1.8% walk, 4.3% work from home (2000); Travel time to work: 32.9% less than 15 minutes, 41.5% 15 to 30 minutes, 15.4% 30 to 45 minutes, 5.2% 45 to 60 minutes, 5.0% 60 minutes or more (2000); Amtrak: Service available.
Additional Information Contacts
City of Delray Beach . . . . (561) 243-7000
    http://mydelraybeach.com
Delray Beach Chamber of Commerce . . . . (561) 278-0424
    http://www.delraybeach.com

DUNES ROAD (CDP). Covers a land area of 0.517 square miles and a water area of 0 square miles. Located at 26.48° N. Lat.; 80.11° W. Long. Elevation is 16 feet.

Population: 391 (1990); 391 (2000); 469 (2007); 523 (2012 projected); Race: 84.6% White, 12.6% Black, 1.1% Asian, 5.3% Hispanic of any race (2007); Density: 906.8 persons per square mile (2007); Average household size: 2.88 (2007); Median age: 38.1 (2007); Males per 100 females: 102.2 (2007); Marriage status: 10.1% never married, 55.9% now married, 11.4% widowed, 22.5% divorced (2000); Foreign born: 4.2% (2000); Ancestry (includes multiple ancestries): 48.2% German, 22.0% Palestinian, 19.7% Italian, 13.1% Czechoslovakian, 10.6% English (2000).
Economy: Employment by occupation: 44.9% management, 14.1% professional, 3.0% services, 27.8% sales, 0.0% farming, 5.1% construction, 5.1% production (2000).
Income: Per capita income: $43,657 (2007); Median household income: $104,375 (2007); Average household income: $125,613 (2007); Percent of households with income of $100,000 or more: 52.1% (2007); Poverty rate: 3.4% (2000).
Education: Percent of population age 25 and over with: High school diploma (including GED) or higher: 98.9% (2007); Bachelor's degree or higher: 27.3% (2007); Master's degree or higher: 6.4% (2007).
Housing: Homeownership rate: 96.9% (2007); Median home value: $585,106 (2007); Median rent: $n/a per month (2000); Median age of housing: 14 years (2000).
Transportation: Commute to work: 97.0% car, 0.0% public transportation, 0.0% walk, 3.0% work from home (2000); Travel time to work: 37.5% less than 15 minutes, 40.1% 15 to 30 minutes, 12.0% 30 to 45 minutes, 2.6% 45 to 60 minutes, 7.8% 60 minutes or more (2000)

FREMD VILLAGE-PADGETT ISLAND (CDP). Covers a land area of 1.182 square miles and a water area of 0 square miles. Located at 26.80° N. Lat.; 80.65° W. Long.
Population: 2,181 (1990); 2,264 (2000); 2,516 (2007); 2,708 (2012 projected); Race: 3.0% White, 91.4% Black, 0.1% Asian, 8.0% Hispanic of any race (2007); Density: 2,128.3 persons per square mile (2007); Average household size: 3.31 (2007); Median age: 20.9 (2007); Males per 100 females: 76.9 (2007); Marriage status: 57.5% never married, 30.3% now married, 5.9% widowed, 6.3% divorced (2000); Foreign born: 7.3% (2000); Ancestry (includes multiple ancestries): 75.2% Other groups, 1.8% United States or American, 1.6% Jamaican, 0.4% West Indian, 0.4% African (2000).
Economy: Employment by occupation: 2.9% management, 12.4% professional, 29.5% services, 24.1% sales, 7.2% farming, 3.1% construction, 20.8% production (2000).
Income: Per capita income: $7,888 (2007); Median household income: $16,609 (2007); Average household income: $26,078 (2007); Percent of households with income of $100,000 or more: 3.8% (2007); Poverty rate: 55.7% (2000).
Education: Percent of population age 25 and over with: High school diploma (including GED) or higher: 50.5% (2007); Bachelor's degree or higher: 6.1% (2007); Master's degree or higher: 0.0% (2007).
Housing: Homeownership rate: 8.9% (2007); Median home value: $132,353 (2007); Median rent: $269 per month (2000); Median age of housing: 27 years (2000).
Transportation: Commute to work: 81.0% car, 7.9% public transportation, 3.9% walk, 0.0% work from home (2000); Travel time to work: 39.0% less than 15 minutes, 27.5% 15 to 30 minutes, 9.2% 30 to 45 minutes, 14.9% 45 to 60 minutes, 9.5% 60 minutes or more (2000)

GLEN RIDGE (town). Covers a land area of 0.226 square miles and a water area of 0 square miles. Located at 26.67° N. Lat.; 80.07° W. Long. Elevation is 10 feet.
Population: 207 (1990); 276 (2000); 228 (2007); 231 (2012 projected); Race: 72.8% White, 14.5% Black, 0.0% Asian, 19.3% Hispanic of any race (2007); Density: 1,010.2 persons per square mile (2007); Average household size: 2.96 (2007); Median age: 35.0 (2007); Males per 100 females: 103.6 (2007); Marriage status: 21.3% never married, 42.6% now married, 11.1% widowed, 25.0% divorced (2000); Foreign born: 7.4% (2000); Ancestry (includes multiple ancestries): 19.9% Irish, 17.7% English, 17.3% French (except Basque), 13.3% German, 8.5% Other groups (2000).
Economy: Single-family building permits issued: 0 (2006); Multi-family building permits issued: 0 (2006); Employment by occupation: 14.0% management, 15.7% professional, 14.9% services, 32.2% sales, 0.0% farming, 11.6% construction, 11.6% production (2000).
Income: Per capita income: $19,441 (2007); Median household income: $44,583 (2007); Average household income: $57,565 (2007); Percent of

households with income of $100,000 or more: 13.0% (2007); Poverty rate: 4.8% (2000).
Education: Percent of population age 25 and over with: High school diploma (including GED) or higher: 83.2% (2007); Bachelor's degree or higher: 13.1% (2007); Master's degree or higher: 2.2% (2007).
Housing: Homeownership rate: 87.0% (2007); Median home value: $334,000 (2007); Median rent: $436 per month (2000); Median age of housing: 42 years (2000).
Transportation: Commute to work: 93.2% car, 0.0% public transportation, 0.0% walk, 4.2% work from home (2000); Travel time to work: 38.9% less than 15 minutes, 34.5% 15 to 30 minutes, 23.0% 30 to 45 minutes, 0.0% 45 to 60 minutes, 3.5% 60 minutes or more (2000)

GOLDEN LAKES (CDP). Covers a land area of 2.365 square miles and a water area of 0 square miles. Located at 26.70° N. Lat.; 80.16° W. Long. Elevation is 16 feet.
Population: 3,867 (1990); 6,694 (2000); 7,314 (2007); 7,805 (2012 projected); Race: 56.9% White, 31.3% Black, 1.6% Asian, 26.4% Hispanic of any race (2007); Density: 3,093.2 persons per square mile (2007); Average household size: 2.18 (2007); Median age: 35.7 (2007); Males per 100 females: 87.8 (2007); Marriage status: 21.2% never married, 52.3% now married, 16.0% widowed, 10.5% divorced (2000); Foreign born: 21.0% (2000); Ancestry (includes multiple ancestries): 38.5% Other groups, 9.5% German, 6.2% Russian, 5.9% Irish, 5.5% Italian (2000).
Economy: Employment by occupation: 8.5% management, 17.9% professional, 26.2% services, 28.7% sales, 1.1% farming, 10.0% construction, 7.6% production (2000).
Income: Per capita income: $19,289 (2007); Median household income: $29,759 (2007); Average household income: $42,051 (2007); Percent of households with income of $100,000 or more: 6.7% (2007); Poverty rate: 13.0% (2000).
Education: Percent of population age 25 and over with: High school diploma (including GED) or higher: 75.1% (2007); Bachelor's degree or higher: 16.6% (2007); Master's degree or higher: 6.8% (2007).
Housing: Homeownership rate: 54.9% (2007); Median home value: $91,364 (2007); Median rent: $636 per month (2000); Median age of housing: 16 years (2000).
Transportation: Commute to work: 93.6% car, 2.9% public transportation, 0.0% walk, 2.1% work from home (2000); Travel time to work: 18.8% less than 15 minutes, 42.6% 15 to 30 minutes, 24.3% 30 to 45 minutes, 5.2% 45 to 60 minutes, 9.1% 60 minutes or more (2000)

GOLF (village). Covers a land area of 0.830 square miles and a water area of 0.014 square miles. Located at 26.50° N. Lat.; 80.10° W. Long. Elevation is 13 feet.
Population: 234 (1990); 230 (2000); 249 (2007); 263 (2012 projected); Race: 95.2% White, 1.6% Black, 0.0% Asian, 3.2% Hispanic of any race (2007); Density: 300.1 persons per square mile (2007); Average household size: 1.92 (2007); Median age: 66.0 (2007); Males per 100 females: 96.1 (2007); Marriage status: 7.0% never married, 80.4% now married, 10.3% widowed, 2.3% divorced (2000); Foreign born: 5.0% (2000); Ancestry (includes multiple ancestries): 38.1% English, 23.8% Irish, 15.9% German, 10.5% Scottish, 6.7% Italian (2000).
Economy: Single-family building permits issued: 30 (2006); Multi-family building permits issued: 0 (2006); Employment by occupation: 28.6% management, 31.4% professional, 8.6% services, 31.4% sales, 0.0% farming, 0.0% construction, 0.0% production (2000).
Income: Per capita income: $153,554 (2007); Median household income: $242,857 (2007); Average household income: $294,115 (2007); Percent of households with income of $100,000 or more: 76.9% (2007); Poverty rate: 1.7% (2000).
Education: Percent of population age 25 and over with: High school diploma (including GED) or higher: 99.0% (2007); Bachelor's degree or higher: 76.7% (2007); Master's degree or higher: 27.2% (2007).
Housing: Homeownership rate: 94.6% (2007); Median home value: $1 million+ (2007); Median rent: $n/a per month (2000); Median age of housing: 25 years (2000).
Transportation: Commute to work: 84.3% car, 0.0% public transportation, 0.0% walk, 15.7% work from home (2000); Travel time to work: 30.5% less than 15 minutes, 50.8% 15 to 30 minutes, 11.9% 30 to 45 minutes, 0.0% 45 to 60 minutes, 6.8% 60 minutes or more (2000)

GREENACRES (city). Aka Greenacres City. Covers a land area of 4.659 square miles and a water area of 0.011 square miles. Located at 26.62° N. Lat.; 80.13° W. Long. Elevation is 23 feet.

Population: 20,225 (1990); 27,569 (2000); 32,159 (2007); 35,423 (2012 projected); Race: 76.3% White, 9.1% Black, 2.6% Asian, 32.1% Hispanic of any race (2007); Density: 6,902.8 persons per square mile (2007); Average household size: 2.28 (2007); Median age: 39.5 (2007); Males per 100 females: 90.1 (2007); Marriage status: 19.8% never married, 55.6% now married, 10.6% widowed, 14.1% divorced (2000); Foreign born: 19.3% (2000); Ancestry (includes multiple ancestries): 30.9% Other groups, 13.1% Italian, 12.0% German, 10.9% Irish, 7.4% English (2000).
Economy: Unemployment rate: 4.2% (11/2007); Total civilian labor force: 16,435 (11/2007); Single-family building permits issued: 276 (2006); Multi-family building permits issued: 0 (2006); Employment by occupation: 10.4% management, 14.4% professional, 21.4% services, 28.4% sales, 0.3% farming, 13.7% construction, 11.2% production (2000).
Income: Per capita income: $20,708 (2007); Median household income: $38,687 (2007); Average household income: $47,118 (2007); Percent of households with income of $100,000 or more: 6.5% (2007); Poverty rate: 7.2% (2000).
Education: Percent of population age 25 and over with: High school diploma (including GED) or higher: 80.3% (2007); Bachelor's degree or higher: 18.2% (2007); Master's degree or higher: 7.5% (2007).
School District(s)
Palm Beach County School District (PK-12)
    2005-06 Enrollment: 175,076 . . . . (561) 434-8200
Two-year College(s)
Keiser Career College-Greenacres (Private, For-profit)
    Fall 2006 Enrollment: 716 . . . . (561) 433-2330
    2006-07 Tuition: In-state $12,440; Out-of-state $12,440
Housing: Homeownership rate: 70.5% (2007); Median home value: $158,659 (2007); Median rent: $660 per month (2000); Median age of housing: 15 years (2000).
Safety: Violent crime rate: 100.4 per 10,000 population; Property crime rate: 372.5 per 10,000 population (2006).
Transportation: Commute to work: 95.0% car, 0.5% public transportation, 0.3% walk, 1.9% work from home (2000); Travel time to work: 17.3% less than 15 minutes, 40.4% 15 to 30 minutes, 28.5% 30 to 45 minutes, 7.9% 45 to 60 minutes, 5.9% 60 minutes or more (2000)
Additional Information Contacts
City of Greenacres . . . . (561) 642-2000
    http://www.ci.greenacres.fl.us

GULF STREAM (town). Covers a land area of 0.751 square miles and a water area of 0.080 square miles. Located at 26.49° N. Lat.; 80.06° W. Long. Elevation is 7 feet.
Population: 653 (1990); 716 (2000); 777 (2007); 812 (2012 projected); Race: 94.2% White, 1.4% Black, 1.9% Asian, 4.5% Hispanic of any race (2007); Density: 1,035.0 persons per square mile (2007); Average household size: 2.06 (2007); Median age: 56.5 (2007); Males per 100 females: 93.3 (2007); Marriage status: 14.6% never married, 64.8% now married, 10.1% widowed, 10.4% divorced (2000); Foreign born: 9.6% (2000); Ancestry (includes multiple ancestries): 22.6% English, 17.8% Irish, 16.8% German, 8.4% United States or American, 7.5% Italian (2000).
Economy: Employment by occupation: 34.4% management, 19.2% professional, 8.3% services, 27.5% sales, 1.4% farming, 7.6% construction, 1.4% production (2000).
Income: Per capita income: $108,642 (2007); Median household income: $160,484 (2007); Average household income: $223,912 (2007); Percent of households with income of $100,000 or more: 62.9% (2007); Poverty rate: 2.5% (2000).
Education: Percent of population age 25 and over with: High school diploma (including GED) or higher: 95.6% (2007); Bachelor's degree or higher: 58.2% (2007); Master's degree or higher: 23.8% (2007).
Housing: Homeownership rate: 91.2% (2007); Median home value: $1 million+ (2007); Median rent: $963 per month (2000); Median age of housing: 28 years (2000).
Safety: Violent crime rate: 13.1 per 10,000 population; Property crime rate: 104.7 per 10,000 population (2006).
Transportation: Commute to work: 69.3% car, 1.1% public transportation, 4.0% walk, 23.4% work from home (2000); Travel time to work: 36.2% less than 15 minutes, 33.8% 15 to 30 minutes, 18.1% 30 to 45 minutes, 5.7% 45 to 60 minutes, 6.2% 60 minutes or more (2000)

GUN CLUB ESTATES (CDP). Covers a land area of 0.118 square miles and a water area of 0 square miles. Located at 26.67° N. Lat.; 80.10° W. Long. Elevation is 13 feet.

Population: 593 (1990); 711 (2000); 748 (2007); 747 (2012 projected); Race: 85.4% White, 1.3% Black, 0.1% Asian, 59.8% Hispanic of any race (2007); Density: 6,323.5 persons per square mile (2007); Average household size: 2.92 (2007); Median age: 35.7 (2007); Males per 100 females: 109.5 (2007); Marriage status: 38.1% never married, 37.9% now married, 1.6% widowed, 22.4% divorced (2000); Foreign born: 32.2% (2000); Ancestry (includes multiple ancestries): 46.8% Other groups, 10.9% West Indian, 8.4% Italian, 7.6% German, 6.6% Irish (2000).

Economy: Employment by occupation: 9.1% management, 5.5% professional, 20.8% services, 35.2% sales, 0.0% farming, 20.3% construction, 9.1% production (2000).

Income: Per capita income: $14,629 (2007); Median household income: $34,211 (2007); Average household income: $42,744 (2007); Percent of households with income of $100,000 or more: 4.3% (2007); Poverty rate: 3.7% (2000).

Education: Percent of population age 25 and over with: High school diploma (including GED) or higher: 53.5% (2007); Bachelor's degree or higher: 0.0% (2007); Master's degree or higher: 0.0% (2007).

Housing: Homeownership rate: 87.1% (2007); Median home value: $157,955 (2007); Median rent: $570 per month (2000); Median age of housing: 45 years (2000).

Transportation: Commute to work: 97.4% car, 0.0% public transportation, 0.0% walk, 2.6% work from home (2000); Travel time to work: 14.6% less than 15 minutes, 69.4% 15 to 30 minutes, 7.7% 30 to 45 minutes, 8.2% 45 to 60 minutes, 0.0% 60 minutes or more (2000)

HAMPTONS AT BOCA RATON (CDP).

Covers a land area of 2.486 square miles and a water area of 0.182 square miles. Located at 26.38° N. Lat.; 80.18° W. Long. Elevation is 16 feet.

Population: 11,686 (1990); 11,306 (2000); 10,653 (2007); 10,351 (2012 projected); Race: 93.2% White, 2.4% Black, 1.4% Asian, 7.1% Hispanic of any race (2007); Density: 4,284.5 persons per square mile (2007); Average household size: 1.76 (2007); Median age: 73.6 (2007); Males per 100 females: 71.6 (2007); Marriage status: 9.4% never married, 56.6% now married, 27.9% widowed, 6.1% divorced (2000); Foreign born: 16.9% (2000); Ancestry (includes multiple ancestries): 24.2% Other groups, 10.0% Polish, 9.1% Russian, 8.3% United States or American, 7.6% Italian (2000).

Economy: Employment by occupation: 15.3% management, 19.1% professional, 15.5% services, 34.7% sales, 0.0% farming, 6.9% construction, 8.6% production (2000).

Income: Per capita income: $28,375 (2007); Median household income: $34,583 (2007); Average household income: $49,964 (2007); Percent of households with income of $100,000 or more: 11.3% (2007); Poverty rate: 7.3% (2000).

Education: Percent of population age 25 and over with: High school diploma (including GED) or higher: 82.1% (2007); Bachelor's degree or higher: 19.1% (2007); Master's degree or higher: 7.6% (2007).

Housing: Homeownership rate: 87.4% (2007); Median home value: $134,271 (2007); Median rent: $622 per month (2000); Median age of housing: 17 years (2000).

Transportation: Commute to work: 93.4% car, 1.4% public transportation, 0.0% walk, 3.7% work from home (2000); Travel time to work: 16.7% less than 15 minutes, 43.9% 15 to 30 minutes, 23.4% 30 to 45 minutes, 5.7% 45 to 60 minutes, 10.4% 60 minutes or more (2000)

HAVERHILL (town).

Covers a land area of 0.574 square miles and a water area of 0 square miles. Located at 26.69° N. Lat.; 80.12° W. Long. Elevation is 16 feet.

Population: 1,127 (1990); 1,454 (2000); 1,426 (2007); 1,412 (2012 projected); Race: 67.7% White, 19.0% Black, 1.8% Asian, 33.0% Hispanic of any race (2007); Density: 2,485.9 persons per square mile (2007); Average household size: 2.77 (2007); Median age: 36.8 (2007); Males per 100 females: 101.7 (2007); Marriage status: 25.7% never married, 57.1% now married, 6.3% widowed, 10.9% divorced (2000); Foreign born: 19.3% (2000); Ancestry (includes multiple ancestries): 30.2% Other groups, 12.7% Irish, 12.3% German, 10.7% English, 7.6% United States or American (2000).

Economy: Single-family building permits issued: 1 (2006); Multi-family building permits issued: 0 (2006); Employment by occupation: 15.2% management, 17.6% professional, 18.0% services, 25.0% sales, 0.0% farming, 16.7% construction, 7.6% production (2000).

Income: Per capita income: $26,096 (2007); Median household income: $52,647 (2007); Average household income: $72,257 (2007); Percent of

households with income of $100,000 or more: 16.1% (2007); Poverty rate: 8.3% (2000).

Education: Percent of population age 25 and over with: High school diploma (including GED) or higher: 83.7% (2007); Bachelor's degree or higher: 23.2% (2007); Master's degree or higher: 8.0% (2007).

Housing: Homeownership rate: 81.4% (2007); Median home value: $257,552 (2007); Median rent: $588 per month (2000); Median age of housing: 27 years (2000).

Transportation: Commute to work: 93.0% car, 0.8% public transportation, 0.7% walk, 5.6% work from home (2000); Travel time to work: 24.1% less than 15 minutes, 41.7% 15 to 30 minutes, 21.9% 30 to 45 minutes, 7.2% 45 to 60 minutes, 5.1% 60 minutes or more (2000)

HIGH POINT (CDP).

Covers a land area of 0.593 square miles and a water area of 0 square miles. Located at 26.46° N. Lat.; 80.12° W. Long. Elevation is 20 feet.

Population: 2,003 (1990); 2,191 (2000); 2,148 (2007); 2,168 (2012 projected); Race: 87.2% White, 11.0% Black, 0.4% Asian, 3.6% Hispanic of any race (2007); Density: 3,621.4 persons per square mile (2007); Average household size: 1.67 (2007); Median age: 74.5 (2007); Males per 100 females: 79.3 (2007); Marriage status: 7.4% never married, 61.4% now married, 24.8% widowed, 6.4% divorced (2000); Foreign born: 9.6% (2000); Ancestry (includes multiple ancestries): 23.0% Other groups, 15.0% Russian, 9.5% Italian, 7.9% United States or American, 6.9% Polish (2000).

Economy: Employment by occupation: 11.6% management, 15.4% professional, 21.9% services, 49.2% sales, 0.0% farming, 0.0% construction, 1.9% production (2000).

Income: Per capita income: $23,933 (2007); Median household income: $34,427 (2007); Average household income: $39,882 (2007); Percent of households with income of $100,000 or more: 5.8% (2007); Poverty rate: 6.6% (2000).

Education: Percent of population age 25 and over with: High school diploma (including GED) or higher: 88.4% (2007); Bachelor's degree or higher: 18.2% (2007); Master's degree or higher: 6.5% (2007).

Housing: Homeownership rate: 89.4% (2007); Median home value: $115,587 (2007); Median rent: $707 per month (2000); Median age of housing: 16 years (2000).

Transportation: Commute to work: 96.1% car, 0.0% public transportation, 0.0% walk, 3.9% work from home (2000); Travel time to work: 19.1% less than 15 minutes, 58.9% 15 to 30 minutes, 16.1% 30 to 45 minutes, 2.7% 45 to 60 minutes, 3.3% 60 minutes or more (2000)

HIGHLAND BEACH (town).

Covers a land area of 0.490 square miles and a water area of 0.641 square miles. Located at 26.40° N. Lat.; 80.06° W. Long. Elevation is 13 feet.

Population: 3,209 (1990); 3,775 (2000); 4,194 (2007); 4,516 (2012 projected); Race: 97.8% White, 0.5% Black, 0.5% Asian, 4.7% Hispanic of any race (2007); Density: 8,560.9 persons per square mile (2007); Average household size: 1.68 (2007); Median age: 66.7 (2007); Males per 100 females: 88.4 (2007); Marriage status: 8.7% never married, 68.0% now married, 15.8% widowed, 7.5% divorced (2000); Foreign born: 13.1% (2000); Ancestry (includes multiple ancestries): 12.0% German, 11.5% Russian, 11.0% Italian, 10.0% Other groups, 10.0% United States or American (2000).

Economy: Single-family building permits issued: 1 (2006); Multi-family building permits issued: 0 (2006); Employment by occupation: 33.7% management, 29.7% professional, 5.4% services, 24.4% sales, 0.0% farming, 3.0% construction, 3.8% production (2000).

Income: Per capita income: $68,932 (2007); Median household income: $79,480 (2007); Average household income: $114,925 (2007); Percent of households with income of $100,000 or more: 39.1% (2007); Poverty rate: 2.1% (2000).

Education: Percent of population age 25 and over with: High school diploma (including GED) or higher: 94.5% (2007); Bachelor's degree or higher: 48.0% (2007); Master's degree or higher: 21.9% (2007).

Housing: Homeownership rate: 83.1% (2007); Median home value: $505,411 (2007); Median rent: $1,539 per month (2000); Median age of housing: 21 years (2000).

Safety: Violent crime rate: 11.9 per 10,000 population; Property crime rate: 93.0 per 10,000 population (2006).

Transportation: Commute to work: 84.4% car, 0.0% public transportation, 0.9% walk, 12.6% work from home (2000); Travel time to work: 34.8% less than 15 minutes, 45.7% 15 to 30 minutes, 13.2% 30 to 45 minutes, 1.1% 45 to 60 minutes, 5.3% 60 minutes or more (2000)

HYPOLUXO (town).
Covers a land area of 0.595 square miles and a water area of 0.229 square miles. Located at 26.56° N. Lat.; 80.05° W. Long. Elevation is 7 feet.

History: Hypoluxo was settled in 1873 on Lake Worth. The name is of Indian origin meaning "round mound."

Population: 791 (1990); 2,015 (2000); 2,579 (2007); 2,977 (2012 projected); Race: 87.1% White, 4.8% Black, 2.6% Asian, 8.3% Hispanic of any race (2007); Density: 4,337.9 persons per square mile (2007); Average household size: 1.83 (2007); Median age: 48.5 (2007); Males per 100 females: 97.9 (2007); Marriage status: 19.8% never married, 54.9% now married, 9.6% widowed, 15.7% divorced (2000); Foreign born: 18.3% (2000); Ancestry (includes multiple ancestries): 19.8% German, 17.0% Irish, 13.8% English, 11.1% Italian, 10.9% Other groups (2000).

Economy: Single-family building permits issued: 0 (2006); Multi-family building permits issued: 0 (2006); Employment by occupation: 21.9% management, 24.3% professional, 12.7% services, 31.9% sales, 0.0% farming, 3.0% construction, 6.2% production (2000).

Income: Per capita income: $44,082 (2007); Median household income: $61,113 (2007); Average household income: $80,687 (2007); Percent of households with income of $100,000 or more: 25.8% (2007); Poverty rate: 7.1% (2000).

Education: Percent of population age 25 and over with: High school diploma (including GED) or higher: 91.8% (2007); Bachelor's degree or higher: 38.4% (2007); Master's degree or higher: 13.6% (2007).

School District(s)
Palm Beach County School District (PK-12)
   2005-06 Enrollment: 175,076 . . . . (561) 434-8200

Housing: Homeownership rate: 61.0% (2007); Median home value: $266,972 (2007); Median rent: $926 per month (2000); Median age of housing: 8 years (2000).

Safety: Violent crime rate: 18.8 per 10,000 population; Property crime rate: 128.0 per 10,000 population (2006).

Transportation: Commute to work: 94.0% car, 0.9% public transportation, 0.5% walk, 4.3% work from home (2000); Travel time to work: 18.1% less than 15 minutes, 43.8% 15 to 30 minutes, 23.4% 30 to 45 minutes, 6.7% 45 to 60 minutes, 8.0% 60 minutes or more (2000)

JUNO BEACH (town).
Covers a land area of 1.395 square miles and a water area of 0.474 square miles. Located at 26.87° N. Lat.; 80.05° W. Long. Elevation is 23 feet.

Population: 2,340 (1990); 3,262 (2000); 3,536 (2007); 3,768 (2012 projected); Race: 97.2% White, 0.7% Black, 0.6% Asian, 5.4% Hispanic of any race (2007); Density: 2,535.6 persons per square mile (2007); Average household size: 1.81 (2007); Median age: 60.0 (2007); Males per 100 females: 86.6 (2007); Marriage status: 12.8% never married, 60.7% now married, 14.7% widowed, 11.8% divorced (2000); Foreign born: 7.3% (2000); Ancestry (includes multiple ancestries): 19.3% Irish, 18.2% German, 15.9% Italian, 13.4% English, 6.3% French (except Basque) (2000).

Economy: Single-family building permits issued: 0 (2006); Multi-family building permits issued: 0 (2006); Employment by occupation: 27.3% management, 19.0% professional, 13.5% services, 28.3% sales, 0.0% farming, 1.7% construction, 10.1% production (2000).

Income: Per capita income: $52,653 (2007); Median household income: $60,690 (2007); Average household income: $95,146 (2007); Percent of households with income of $100,000 or more: 26.3% (2007); Poverty rate: 4.5% (2000).

Education: Percent of population age 25 and over with: High school diploma (including GED) or higher: 94.6% (2007); Bachelor's degree or higher: 40.9% (2007); Master's degree or higher: 14.5% (2007).

School District(s)
Palm Beach County School District (PK-12)
   2005-06 Enrollment: 175,076 . . . . (561) 434-8200

Housing: Homeownership rate: 74.7% (2007); Median home value: $385,650 (2007); Median rent: $1,174 per month (2000); Median age of housing: 17 years (2000).

Safety: Violent crime rate: 11.6 per 10,000 population; Property crime rate: 298.4 per 10,000 population (2006).

Transportation: Commute to work: 84.5% car, 0.6% public transportation, 1.8% walk, 10.7% work from home (2000); Travel time to work: 31.4% less than 15 minutes, 44.2% 15 to 30 minutes, 10.4% 30 to 45 minutes, 11.1% 45 to 60 minutes, 2.9% 60 minutes or more (2000)

JUNO RIDGE (CDP).
Covers a land area of 0.145 square miles and a water area of 0 square miles. Located at 26.84° N. Lat.; 80.06° W. Long. Elevation is 13 feet.

Population: 802 (1990); 742 (2000); 693 (2007); 673 (2012 projected); Race: 91.8% White, 2.6% Black, 0.7% Asian, 7.8% Hispanic of any race (2007); Density: 4,763.9 persons per square mile (2007); Average household size: 1.83 (2007); Median age: 37.5 (2007); Males per 100 females: 118.6 (2007); Marriage status: 29.2% never married, 40.3% now married, 8.0% widowed, 22.6% divorced (2000); Foreign born: 10.8% (2000); Ancestry (includes multiple ancestries): 19.7% Irish, 18.7% Other groups, 13.7% English, 10.1% German, 7.2% Italian (2000).

Economy: Employment by occupation: 11.6% management, 14.0% professional, 20.9% services, 26.4% sales, 0.0% farming, 16.5% construction, 10.6% production (2000).

Income: Per capita income: $26,699 (2007); Median household income: $45,435 (2007); Average household income: $48,948 (2007); Percent of households with income of $100,000 or more: 5.6% (2007); Poverty rate: 9.4% (2000).

Education: Percent of population age 25 and over with: High school diploma (including GED) or higher: 91.9% (2007); Bachelor's degree or higher: 12.5% (2007); Master's degree or higher: 2.3% (2007).

Housing: Homeownership rate: 33.6% (2007); Median home value: $213,281 (2007); Median rent: $647 per month (2000); Median age of housing: 30 years (2000).

Transportation: Commute to work: 91.7% car, 0.0% public transportation, 5.8% walk, 1.6% work from home (2000); Travel time to work: 40.1% less than 15 minutes, 31.3% 15 to 30 minutes, 23.8% 30 to 45 minutes, 1.1% 45 to 60 minutes, 3.6% 60 minutes or more (2000)

JUPITER (town).
Covers a land area of 19.999 square miles and a water area of 1.125 square miles. Located at 26.92° N. Lat.; 80.10° W. Long. Elevation is 3 feet.

Population: 30,117 (1990); 39,328 (2000); 49,232 (2007); 55,968 (2012 projected); Race: 92.9% White, 1.4% Black, 1.6% Asian, 11.7% Hispanic of any race (2007); Density: 2,461.8 persons per square mile (2007); Average household size: 2.34 (2007); Median age: 42.9 (2007); Males per 100 females: 98.4 (2007); Marriage status: 18.9% never married, 62.3% now married, 6.5% widowed, 12.3% divorced (2000); Foreign born: 10.5% (2000); Ancestry (includes multiple ancestries): 18.6% Irish, 17.9% German, 16.8% Italian, 13.6% English, 12.2% Other groups (2000).

Economy: Unemployment rate: 3.3% (11/2007); Total civilian labor force: 27,350 (11/2007); Single-family building permits issued: 313 (2006); Multi-family building permits issued: 159 (2006); Employment by occupation: 18.5% management, 21.9% professional, 16.0% services, 28.8% sales, 0.3% farming, 7.8% construction, 6.7% production (2000).

Income: Per capita income: $39,718 (2007); Median household income: $64,028 (2007); Average household income: $93,011 (2007); Percent of households with income of $100,000 or more: 28.8% (2007); Poverty rate: 4.8% (2000).

Education: Percent of population age 25 and over with: High school diploma (including GED) or higher: 91.9% (2007); Bachelor's degree or higher: 36.3% (2007); Master's degree or higher: 13.0% (2007).

School District(s)
Palm Beach County School District (PK-12)
   2005-06 Enrollment: 175,076 . . . . (561) 434-8200

Housing: Homeownership rate: 81.6% (2007); Median home value: $329,737 (2007); Median rent: $779 per month (2000); Median age of housing: 15 years (2000).

Hospitals: Jupiter Medical Center (156 beds)

Safety: Violent crime rate: 33.5 per 10,000 population; Property crime rate: 277.7 per 10,000 population (2006).

Newspapers: The Jupiter Courier (General - Circulation 8,000)

Transportation: Commute to work: 92.0% car, 0.4% public transportation, 0.8% walk, 4.9% work from home (2000); Travel time to work: 30.9% less than 15 minutes, 38.8% 15 to 30 minutes, 20.4% 30 to 45 minutes, 5.0% 45 to 60 minutes, 4.9% 60 minutes or more (2000)

Additional Information Contacts
Jupiter Chamber of Commerce . . . . (561) 746-7111
   http://www.jupiterfl.org
Town of Jupiter . . . . (561) 746-5134
   http://www.jupiter.fl.us

JUPITER INLET COLONY (town).
Covers a land area of 0.176 square miles and a water area of 0.052 square miles. Located at 26.94° N. Lat.; 80.07° W. Long. Elevation is 7 feet.

Population: 434 (1990); 368 (2000); 415 (2007); 450 (2012 projected); Race: 99.8% White, 0.0% Black, 0.0% Asian, 0.0% Hispanic of any race (2007); Density: 2,357.1 persons per square mile (2007); Average household size: 2.01 (2007); Median age: 60.2 (2007); Males per 100 females: 99.5 (2007); Marriage status: 6.7% never married, 74.2% now married, 9.7% widowed, 9.4% divorced (2000); Foreign born: 6.2% (2000); Ancestry (includes multiple ancestries): 29.8% English, 20.2% Irish, 18.4% German, 12.2% Italian, 10.6% United States or American (2000).

Economy: Single-family building permits issued: 3 (2006); Multi-family building permits issued: 0 (2006); Employment by occupation: 29.1% management, 40.7% professional, 7.0% services, 17.4% sales, 0.0% farming, 0.0% construction, 5.8% production (2000).

Income: Per capita income: $62,373 (2007); Median household income: $67,000 (2007); Average household income: $125,655 (2007); Percent of households with income of $100,000 or more: 41.7% (2007); Poverty rate: 3.9% (2000).

Education: Percent of population age 25 and over with: High school diploma (including GED) or higher: 97.7% (2007); Bachelor's degree or higher: 56.3% (2007); Master's degree or higher: 21.6% (2007).

Housing: Homeownership rate: 94.7% (2007); Median home value: $997,222 (2007); Median rent: $2,000+ per month (2000); Median age of housing: 34 years (2000).

Safety: Violent crime rate: 0.0 per 10,000 population; Property crime rate: 251.9 per 10,000 population (2006).

Transportation: Commute to work: 91.4% car, 0.0% public transportation, 0.0% walk, 8.6% work from home (2000); Travel time to work: 23.0% less than 15 minutes, 44.6% 15 to 30 minutes, 21.6% 30 to 45 minutes, 5.4% 45 to 60 minutes, 5.4% 60 minutes or more (2000)

KINGS POINT (CDP).
Covers a land area of 1.822 square miles and a water area of 0 square miles. Located at 26.44° N. Lat.; 80.14° W. Long. Elevation is 16 feet.

Population: 12,428 (1990); 12,207 (2000); 12,212 (2007); 12,470 (2012 projected); Race: 98.8% White, 0.4% Black, 0.3% Asian, 1.8% Hispanic of any race (2007); Density: 6,701.3 persons per square mile (2007); Average household size: 1.49 (2007); Median age: 78.5 (2007); Males per 100 females: 66.5 (2007); Marriage status: 4.5% never married, 57.6% now married, 32.0% widowed, 5.9% divorced (2000); Foreign born: 10.8% (2000); Ancestry (includes multiple ancestries): 21.9% Other groups, 16.2% Russian, 10.9% Polish, 9.8% United States or American, 7.2% Italian (2000).

Economy: Employment by occupation: 9.5% management, 14.9% professional, 17.2% services, 43.6% sales, 0.6% farming, 2.0% construction, 12.2% production (2000).

Income: Per capita income: $24,866 (2007); Median household income: $28,567 (2007); Average household income: $36,961 (2007); Percent of households with income of $100,000 or more: 4.4% (2007); Poverty rate: 7.4% (2000).

Education: Percent of population age 25 and over with: High school diploma (including GED) or higher: 82.6% (2007); Bachelor's degree or higher: 13.0% (2007); Master's degree or higher: 5.1% (2007).

Housing: Homeownership rate: 91.2% (2007); Median home value: $90,474 (2007); Median rent: $523 per month (2000); Median age of housing: 22 years (2000).

Transportation: Commute to work: 94.2% car, 1.0% public transportation, 0.0% walk, 4.8% work from home (2000); Travel time to work: 37.0% less than 15 minutes, 41.5% 15 to 30 minutes, 16.4% 30 to 45 minutes, 2.3% 45 to 60 minutes, 2.7% 60 minutes or more (2000)

LAKE BELVEDERE ESTATES (CDP).
Covers a land area of 0.579 square miles and a water area of 0.001 square miles. Located at 26.68° N. Lat.; 80.13° W. Long. Elevation is 16 feet.

Population: 1,445 (1990); 1,525 (2000); 1,570 (2007); 1,525 (2012 projected); Race: 48.3% White, 41.7% Black, 1.6% Asian, 18.4% Hispanic of any race (2007); Density: 2,712.7 persons per square mile (2007); Average household size: 3.27 (2007); Median age: 33.9 (2007); Males per 100 females: 102.3 (2007); Marriage status: 31.9% never married, 49.3% now married, 4.5% widowed, 14.4% divorced (2000); Foreign born: 17.1% (2000); Ancestry (includes multiple ancestries): 32.4% Other groups, 11.7% German, 8.8% English, 8.2% Italian, 6.2% United States or American (2000).

professional, 17.4% services, 38.7% sales, 2.3% farming, 9.4% construction, 11.2% production (2000).

Income: Per capita income: $17,498 (2007); Median household income: $49,103 (2007); Average household income: $57,234 (2007); Percent of households with income of $100,000 or more: 8.1% (2007); Poverty rate: 17.9% (2000).

Education: Percent of population age 25 and over with: High school diploma (including GED) or higher: 76.6% (2007); Bachelor's degree or higher: 16.0% (2007); Master's degree or higher: 4.5% (2007).

Housing: Homeownership rate: 91.0% (2007); Median home value: $194,402 (2007); Median rent: $725 per month (2000); Median age of housing: 33 years (2000).

Transportation: Commute to work: 95.1% car, 1.1% public transportation, 0.7% walk, 3.1% work from home (2000); Travel time to work: 8.3% less than 15 minutes, 57.1% 15 to 30 minutes, 23.1% 30 to 45 minutes, 3.3% 45 to 60 minutes, 8.2% 60 minutes or more (2000)

LAKE CLARKE SHORES (town).
Covers a land area of 0.975 square miles and a water area of 0.077 square miles. Located at 26.64° N. Lat.; 80.07° W. Long. Elevation is 13 feet.

Population: 3,364 (1990); 3,451 (2000); 3,452 (2007); 3,481 (2012 projected); Race: 90.2% White, 1.4% Black, 2.4% Asian, 26.6% Hispanic of any race (2007); Density: 3,539.9 persons per square mile (2007); Average household size: 2.41 (2007); Median age: 45.3 (2007); Males per 100 females: 100.0 (2007); Marriage status: 18.5% never married, 65.0% now married, 6.0% widowed, 10.5% divorced (2000); Foreign born: 19.5% (2000); Ancestry (includes multiple ancestries): 21.0% Other groups, 16.6% English, 15.1% German, 13.1% Irish, 8.8% Italian (2000).

Economy: Single-family building permits issued: 3 (2006); Multi-family building permits issued: 0 (2006); Employment by occupation: 21.5% management, 25.3% professional, 13.0% services, 25.1% sales, 0.0% farming, 7.7% construction, 7.4% production (2000).

Income: Per capita income: $34,014 (2007); Median household income: $67,415 (2007); Average household income: $82,051 (2007); Percent of households with income of $100,000 or more: 25.6% (2007); Poverty rate: 4.0% (2000).

Education: Percent of population age 25 and over with: High school diploma (including GED) or higher: 89.8% (2007); Bachelor's degree or higher: 44.6% (2007); Master's degree or higher: 12.1% (2007).

Housing: Homeownership rate: 90.0% (2007); Median home value: $318,427 (2007); Median rent: $585 per month (2000); Median age of housing: 28 years (2000).

Safety: Violent crime rate: 2.8 per 10,000 population; Property crime rate: 136.4 per 10,000 population (2006).

Transportation: Commute to work: 91.8% car, 1.6% public transportation, 0.0% walk, 4.8% work from home (2000); Travel time to work: 28.3% less than 15 minutes, 48.6% 15 to 30 minutes, 17.3% 30 to 45 minutes, 4.5% 45 to 60 minutes, 1.3% 60 minutes or more (2000)

LAKE HARBOR (CDP).
Covers a land area of 1.312 square miles and a water area of 0 square miles. Located at 26.68° N. Lat.; 80.80° W. Long. Elevation is 13 feet.

Population: 178 (1990); 195 (2000); 160 (2007); 141 (2012 projected); Race: 49.4% White, 33.8% Black, 3.8% Asian, 7.5% Hispanic of any race (2007); Density: 122.0 persons per square mile (2007); Average household size: 2.96 (2007); Median age: 39.0 (2007); Males per 100 females: 105.1 (2007); Marriage status: 24.7% never married, 59.7% now married, 0.0% widowed, 15.6% divorced (2000); Foreign born: 30.1% (2000); Ancestry (includes multiple ancestries): 33.3% Other groups, 31.2% African, 8.6% Scottish, 8.6% English, 3.2% Jamaican (2000).

Economy: Employment by occupation: 0.0% management, 0.0% professional, 16.7% services, 0.0% sales, 55.6% farming, 0.0% construction, 27.8% production (2000).

Income: Per capita income: $12,844 (2007); Median household income: $38,750 (2007); Average household income: $38,056 (2007); Percent of households with income of $100,000 or more: 0.0% (2007); Poverty rate: 9.7% (2000).

Education: Percent of population age 25 and over with: High school diploma (including GED) or higher: 51.0% (2007); Bachelor's degree or higher: 0.0% (2007); Master's degree or higher: 0.0% (2007).

Housing: Homeownership rate: 35.2% (2007); Median home value: $73,214 (2007); Median rent: $325 per month (2000); Median age of housing: 37 years (2000).

minutes, 0.0% 45 to 60 minutes, 16.7% 60 minutes or more (2000)

LAKE PARK (town). Covers a land area of 2.170 square miles and a water area of 0.176 square miles. Located at 26.80° N. Lat.; 80.06° W. Long. Elevation is 13 feet.

Population: 7,362 (1990); 8,721 (2000); 9,082 (2007); 9,435 (2012 projected); Race: 34.0% White, 54.8% Black, 3.1% Asian, 7.6% Hispanic of any race (2007); Density: 4,185.1 persons per square mile (2007); Average household size: 2.62 (2007); Median age: 35.1 (2007); Males per 100 females: 97.6 (2007); Marriage status: 31.9% never married, 49.2% now married, 7.2% widowed, 11.6% divorced (2000); Foreign born: 24.8% (2000); Ancestry (includes multiple ancestries): 26.8% Other groups, 14.4% Haitian, 8.9% United States or American, 8.3% German, 7.4% Irish (2000).

Economy: Single-family building permits issued: 0 (2006); Multi-family building permits issued: 0 (2006); Employment by occupation: 10.8% management, 13.5% professional, 29.1% services, 24.5% sales, 0.6% farming, 10.5% construction, 11.0% production (2000).

Income: Per capita income: $18,728 (2007); Median household income: $36,422 (2007); Average household income: $48,105 (2007); Percent of households with income of $100,000 or more: 7.1% (2007); Poverty rate: 16.8% (2000).

Education: Percent of population age 25 and over with: High school diploma (including GED) or higher: 74.2% (2007); Bachelor's degree or higher: 15.8% (2007); Master's degree or higher: 6.2% (2007).

School District(s)

Palm Beach County School District (PK-12)
    2005-06 Enrollment: 175,076 . . . . (561) 434-8200

Housing: Homeownership rate: 46.0% (2007); Median home value: $207,613 (2007); Median rent: $596 per month (2000); Median age of housing: 31 years (2000).

Safety: Violent crime rate: 88.1 per 10,000 population; Property crime rate: 713.7 per 10,000 population (2006).

Newspapers: WeekDay (General - Circulation 11,500)

Transportation: Commute to work: 93.8% car, 1.9% public transportation, 1.1% walk, 1.4% work from home (2000); Travel time to work: 28.6% less than 15 minutes, 45.1% 15 to 30 minutes, 16.3% 30 to 45 minutes, 4.4% 45 to 60 minutes, 5.6% 60 minutes or more (2000)

Additional Information Contacts

Town of Lake Park. . . . . (561) 881-3300
    http://www.lakeparkflorida.net

LAKE WORTH (city). Covers a land area of 5.643 square miles and a water area of 0.820 square miles. Located at 26.62° N. Lat.; 80.05° W. Long. Elevation is 16 feet.

History: Named for General William Jenkins Worth, who saw service in the Seminole and Mexican Wars. The town of Lake Worth developed as a tourist town along both shores of the lake. The lake, too, was named for General Worth.

Population: 29,083 (1990); 35,133 (2000); 36,163 (2007); 37,299 (2012 projected); Race: 59.9% White, 19.5% Black, 0.8% Asian, 39.8% Hispanic of any race (2007); Density: 6,408.0 persons per square mile (2007); Average household size: 2.56 (2007); Median age: 36.1 (2007); Males per 100 females: 109.3 (2007); Marriage status: 31.9% never married, 47.4% now married, 7.3% widowed, 13.4% divorced (2000); Foreign born: 35.6% (2000); Ancestry (includes multiple ancestries): 34.6% Other groups, 8.7% German, 8.5% Irish, 7.8% Haitian, 6.1% English (2000).

Economy: Unemployment rate: 4.0% (11/2007); Total civilian labor force: 19,891 (11/2007); Single-family building permits issued: 40 (2006); Multi-family building permits issued: 94 (2006); Employment by occupation: 7.5% management, 14.4% professional, 25.3% services, 22.8% sales, 2.4% farming, 17.3% construction, 10.4% production (2000).

Income: Per capita income: $17,743 (2007); Median household income: $33,875 (2007); Average household income: $44,357 (2007); Percent of households with income of $100,000 or more: 6.8% (2007); Poverty rate: 20.0% (2000).

Education: Percent of population age 25 and over with: High school diploma (including GED) or higher: 66.1% (2007); Bachelor's degree or higher: 16.3% (2007); Master's degree or higher: 5.4% (2007).

School District(s)

Palm Beach County School District (PK-12)
    2005-06 Enrollment: 175,076 . . . . (561) 434-8200

2006-07 Tuition: In-state $2,300; Out-of-state $8,500

Vocational/Technical School(s)

Academy of Healing Arts Massage & Facial Skin Care (Private, For-profit)
    Fall 2006 Enrollment: 21 . . . . (561) 965-5550
    2006-07 Tuition: $8,950

Housing: Homeownership rate: 52.9% (2007); Median home value: $172,407 (2007); Median rent: $484 per month (2000); Median age of housing: 38 years (2000).

Safety: Violent crime rate: 179.7 per 10,000 population; Property crime rate: 772.8 per 10,000 population (2006).

Newspapers: Beachcomber (General - Circulation 3,500); Coastal Observer (General - Circulation 38,000); Lake Worth Herald Press (General - Circulation 38,000)

Transportation: Commute to work: 90.7% car, 2.4% public transportation, 1.7% walk, 2.6% work from home (2000); Travel time to work: 19.4% less than 15 minutes, 43.9% 15 to 30 minutes, 23.4% 30 to 45 minutes, 6.5% 45 to 60 minutes, 6.8% 60 minutes or more (2000)

Additional Information Contacts

City of Lake Worth . . . . (561) 586-1662
    http://www.lakeworth.org
Lake Worth Chamber of Commerce . . . . (561) 582-4401
    http://www.lwchamber.com

LAKE WORTH CORRIDOR (CDP). Covers a land area of 3.423 square miles and a water area of 0 square miles. Located at 26.62° N. Lat.; 80.10° W. Long. Elevation is 13 feet.

Population: 14,533 (1990); 18,663 (2000); 19,774 (2007); 20,749 (2012 projected); Race: 52.0% White, 17.3% Black, 1.3% Asian, 54.5% Hispanic of any race (2007); Density: 5,777.3 persons per square mile (2007); Average household size: 3.20 (2007); Median age: 28.7 (2007); Males per 100 females: 115.1 (2007); Marriage status: 35.0% never married, 46.1% now married, 3.9% widowed, 15.0% divorced (2000); Foreign born: 29.9% (2000); Ancestry (includes multiple ancestries): 46.5% Other groups, 9.4% Irish, 8.1% German, 5.3% Italian, 5.0% United States or American (2000).

Economy: Employment by occupation: 5.6% management, 7.9% professional, 24.7% services, 23.2% sales, 2.7% farming, 23.2% construction, 12.6% production (2000).

Income: Per capita income: $13,271 (2007); Median household income: $34,644 (2007); Average household income: $41,630 (2007); Percent of households with income of $100,000 or more: 4.2% (2007); Poverty rate: 20.0% (2000).

Education: Percent of population age 25 and over with: High school diploma (including GED) or higher: 60.2% (2007); Bachelor's degree or higher: 6.4% (2007); Master's degree or higher: 2.2% (2007).

Housing: Homeownership rate: 40.8% (2007); Median home value: $171,158 (2007); Median rent: $564 per month (2000); Median age of housing: 27 years (2000).

Transportation: Commute to work: 92.3% car, 2.7% public transportation, 1.4% walk, 1.0% work from home (2000); Travel time to work: 17.1% less than 15 minutes, 39.5% 15 to 30 minutes, 30.9% 30 to 45 minutes, 6.2% 45 to 60 minutes, 6.3% 60 minutes or more (2000)

LAKESIDE GREEN (CDP). Covers a land area of 0.545 square miles and a water area of 0 square miles. Located at 26.73° N. Lat.; 80.11° W. Long. Elevation is 13 feet.

Population: 2,994 (1990); 3,311 (2000); 3,615 (2007); 3,863 (2012 projected); Race: 66.4% White, 21.5% Black, 3.8% Asian, 13.7% Hispanic of any race (2007); Density: 6,635.6 persons per square mile (2007); Average household size: 2.34 (2007); Median age: 40.8 (2007); Males per 100 females: 85.9 (2007); Marriage status: 25.8% never married, 48.5% now married, 10.2% widowed, 15.5% divorced (2000); Foreign born: 12.5% (2000); Ancestry (includes multiple ancestries): 40.2% Other groups, 12.1% Irish, 11.4% Italian, 10.1% German, 6.3% English (2000).

Economy: Employment by occupation: 13.7% management, 30.9% professional, 18.2% services, 26.4% sales, 0.0% farming, 5.9% construction, 4.9% production (2000).

Income: Per capita income: $24,638 (2007); Median household income: $46,837 (2007); Average household income: $53,519 (2007); Percent of households with income of $100,000 or more: 10.2% (2007); Poverty rate: 6.7% (2000).

Education: Percent of population age 25 and over with: High school diploma (including GED) or higher: 89.7% (2007); Bachelor's degree or higher: 31.4% (2007); Master's degree or higher: 10.1% (2007).

Housing: Homeownership rate: 69.3% (2007); Median home value: $201,802 (2007); Median rent: $791 per month (2000); Median age of housing: 15 years (2000).

Transportation: Commute to work: 94.4% car, 0.3% public transportation, 1.3% walk, 3.6% work from home (2000); Travel time to work: 23.3% less than 15 minutes, 48.2% 15 to 30 minutes, 19.0% 30 to 45 minutes, 4.3% 45 to 60 minutes, 5.2% 60 minutes or more (2000)

LANTANA (town).
Covers a land area of 2.282 square miles and a water area of 0.624 square miles. Located at 26.58° N. Lat.; 80.05° W. Long. Elevation is 10 feet.

History: Lantana, a tourist community on Lake Worth, was named for a flowering shrub, common throughout Florida, called lantana.

Population: 8,392 (1990); 9,437 (2000); 10,819 (2007); 11,807 (2012 projected); Race: 72.3% White, 14.6% Black, 1.1% Asian, 25.4% Hispanic of any race (2007); Density: 4,740.4 persons per square mile (2007); Average household size: 2.49 (2007); Median age: 38.0 (2007); Males per 100 females: 105.8 (2007); Marriage status: 28.1% never married, 52.5% now married, 6.4% widowed, 13.1% divorced (2000); Foreign born: 21.5% (2000); Ancestry (includes multiple ancestries): 19.8% Other groups, 13.7% German, 13.7% Irish, 9.5% English, 6.5% Italian (2000).

Economy: Single-family building permits issued: 2 (2006); Multi-family building permits issued: 0 (2006); Employment by occupation: 7.9% management, 16.4% professional, 23.0% services, 26.8% sales, 1.2% farming, 15.2% construction, 9.5% production (2000).

Income: Per capita income: $23,650 (2007); Median household income: $40,198 (2007); Average household income: $58,372 (2007); Percent of households with income of $100,000 or more: 10.8% (2007); Poverty rate: 8.3% (2000).

Education: Percent of population age 25 and over with: High school diploma (including GED) or higher: 75.5% (2007); Bachelor's degree or higher: 16.2% (2007); Master's degree or higher: 6.6% (2007).

School District(s)
Palm Beach County School District (PK-12)
　　2005-06 Enrollment: 175,076 . . . . (561) 434-8200

Housing: Homeownership rate: 67.9% (2007); Median home value: $188,688 (2007); Median rent: $530 per month (2000); Median age of housing: 31 years (2000).

Hospitals: A.G. Holley State Hospital (100 beds)

Safety: Violent crime rate: 75.9 per 10,000 population; Property crime rate: 510.5 per 10,000 population (2006).

Transportation: Commute to work: 93.0% car, 2.4% public transportation, 0.6% walk, 2.1% work from home (2000); Travel time to work: 24.8% less than 15 minutes, 40.4% 15 to 30 minutes, 25.4% 30 to 45 minutes, 4.3% 45 to 60 minutes, 5.1% 60 minutes or more (2000)

Additional Information Contacts
Town of Lantana . . . . (561) 540-5000
　　http://www.lantana.org

LIMESTONE CREEK (CDP).
Covers a land area of 0.453 square miles and a water area of 0 square miles. Located at 26.94° N. Lat.; 80.14° W. Long. Elevation is 10 feet.

Population: 424 (1990); 569 (2000); 651 (2007); 707 (2012 projected); Race: 9.4% White, 86.5% Black, 0.8% Asian, 8.8% Hispanic of any race (2007); Density: 1,437.8 persons per square mile (2007); Average household size: 3.56 (2007); Median age: 25.7 (2007); Males per 100 females: 100.3 (2007); Marriage status: 27.7% never married, 49.0% now married, 13.7% widowed, 9.6% divorced (2000); Foreign born: 0.0% (2000); Ancestry (includes multiple ancestries): 72.4% Other groups, 14.5% Irish, 11.5% English, 6.0% United States or American (2000).

Economy: Employment by occupation: 22.8% management, 0.0% professional, 29.7% services, 19.0% sales, 0.0% farming, 16.5% construction, 12.0% production (2000).

Income: Per capita income: $12,012 (2007); Median household income: $33,952 (2007); Average household income: $42,732 (2007); Percent of households with income of $100,000 or more: 5.5% (2007); Poverty rate: 8.5% (2000).

Education: Percent of population age 25 and over with: High school diploma (including GED) or higher: 71.0% (2007); Bachelor's degree or higher: 0.0% (2007); Master's degree or higher: 0.0% (2007).

Housing: Homeownership rate: 84.7% (2007); Median home value: $184,722 (2007); Median rent: $n/a per month (2000); Median age of housing: 4 years (2000).

Transportation: Commute to work: 100.0% car, 0.0% public transportation, 0.0% walk, 0.0% work from home (2000); Travel time to work: 32.9% less than 15 minutes, 58.2% 15 to 30 minutes, 0.0% 30 to 45 minutes, 8.9% 45 to 60 minutes, 0.0% 60 minutes or more (2000)

LOXAHATCHEE (unincorporated postal area, zip code 33470).
Covers a land area of 422.292 square miles and a water area of 0.300 square miles. Located at 26.75° N. Lat.; 80.30° W. Long. Elevation is 22 feet.

Population: 19,103 (2000); Race: 87.8% White, 5.6% Black, 1.2% Asian, 10.9% Hispanic of any race (2000); Density: 45.2 persons per square mile (2000); Age: 31.6% under 18, 4.6% over 64 (2000); Marriage status: 20.9% never married, 66.8% now married, 3.4% widowed, 8.8% divorced (2000); Foreign born: 10.0% (2000); Ancestry (includes multiple ancestries): 19.6% Other groups, 15.8% Irish, 15.4% German, 12.0% Italian, 8.2% English (2000).

Economy: Employment by occupation: 13.5% management, 16.0% professional, 14.9% services, 25.8% sales, 1.3% farming, 19.2% construction, 9.3% production (2000).

Income: Per capita income: $22,526 (2000); Median household income: $61,644 (2000); Poverty rate: 4.5% (2000).

Education: Percent of population age 25 and over with: High school diploma (including GED) or higher: 85.3% (2000); Bachelor's degree or higher: 15.7% (2000).

School District(s)
Palm Beach County School District (PK-12)
　　2005-06 Enrollment: 175,076 . . . . (561) 434-8200

Housing: Homeownership rate: 94.6% (2000); Median home value: $140,300 (2000); Median rent: $1,052 per month (2000); Median age of housing: 6 years (2000).

Hospitals: Palms West Hospital (175 beds)

Transportation: Commute to work: 94.3% car, 0.2% public transportation, 1.0% walk, 3.8% work from home (2000); Travel time to work: 9.4% less than 15 minutes, 20.2% 15 to 30 minutes, 29.4% 30 to 45 minutes, 18.0% 45 to 60 minutes, 23.0% 60 minutes or more (2000)

Additional Information Contacts
Loxahatchee Chamber of Commerce . . . . (561) 790-6200
　　http://www.palmswest.com

MANALAPAN (town).
Covers a land area of 0.450 square miles and a water area of 1.983 square miles. Located at 26.56° N. Lat.; 80.04° W. Long. Elevation is 3 feet.

Population: 312 (1990); 321 (2000); 356 (2007); 382 (2012 projected); Race: 96.6% White, 0.0% Black, 2.8% Asian, 4.2% Hispanic of any race (2007); Density: 790.4 persons per square mile (2007); Average household size: 1.90 (2007); Median age: 61.4 (2007); Males per 100 females: 96.7 (2007); Marriage status: 6.9% never married, 69.3% now married, 18.5% widowed, 5.3% divorced (2000); Foreign born: 15.5% (2000); Ancestry (includes multiple ancestries): 20.7% German, 18.0% Irish, 13.3% English, 7.1% Other groups, 5.3% Scottish (2000).

Economy: Single-family building permits issued: 4 (2006); Multi-family building permits issued: 0 (2006); Employment by occupation: 46.8% management, 24.7% professional, 7.8% services, 14.3% sales, 0.0% farming, 6.5% construction, 0.0% production (2000).

Income: Per capita income: $122,746 (2007); Median household income: $157,500 (2007); Average household income: $233,676 (2007); Percent of households with income of $100,000 or more: 61.0% (2007); Poverty rate: 5.9% (2000).

Education: Percent of population age 25 and over with: High school diploma (including GED) or higher: 97.5% (2007); Bachelor's degree or higher: 43.7% (2007); Master's degree or higher: 17.0% (2007).

Housing: Homeownership rate: 95.7% (2007); Median home value: $1 million+ (2007); Median rent: $2,000+ per month (2000); Median age of housing: 26 years (2000).

Safety: Violent crime rate: 144.1 per 10,000 population; Property crime rate: 288.2 per 10,000 population (2006).

Transportation: Commute to work: 79.2% car, 0.0% public transportation, 3.9% walk, 16.9% work from home (2000); Travel time to work: 15.6% less than 15 minutes, 48.4% 15 to 30 minutes, 23.4% 30 to 45 minutes, 9.4% 45 to 60 minutes, 3.1% 60 minutes or more (2000)

MANGONIA PARK (town).
Covers a land area of 0.709 square miles and a water area of 0 square miles. Located at 26.75° N. Lat.; 80.07° W. Long. Elevation is 16 feet.

Population: 1,453 (1990); 1,283 (2000); 1,622 (2007); 1,851 (2012 projected); Race: 10.6% White, 78.7% Black, 0.4% Asian, 11.3% Hispanic of any race (2007); Density: 2,287.9 persons per square mile (2007); Average household size: 2.95 (2007); Median age: 31.9 (2007); Males per 100 females: 89.7 (2007); Marriage status: 42.2% never married, 41.0% now married, 4.8% widowed, 12.0% divorced (2000); Foreign born: 24.7% (2000); Ancestry (includes multiple ancestries): 62.9% Other groups, 9.0% Haitian, 4.4% Irish, 3.9% Jamaican, 3.6% United States or American (2000).

Economy: Single-family building permits issued: 0 (2006); Multi-family building permits issued: 0 (2006); Employment by occupation: 4.2% management, 13.2% professional, 24.0% services, 29.3% sales, 1.7% farming, 12.5% construction, 15.1% production (2000).

Income: Per capita income: $19,254 (2007); Median household income: $45,488 (2007); Average household income: $56,782 (2007); Percent of households with income of $100,000 or more: 11.6% (2007); Poverty rate: 19.2% (2000).

Education: Percent of population age 25 and over with: High school diploma (including GED) or higher: 71.5% (2007); Bachelor's degree or higher: 8.5% (2007); Master's degree or higher: 0.9% (2007).

Housing: Homeownership rate: 50.9% (2007); Median home value: $150,000 (2007); Median rent: $554 per month (2000); Median age of housing: 28 years (2000).

Safety: Violent crime rate: 743.3 per 10,000 population; Property crime rate: 2,812.3 per 10,000 population (2006).

Transportation: Commute to work: 86.8% car, 8.6% public transportation, 3.5% walk, 0.5% work from home (2000); Travel time to work: 37.8% less than 15 minutes, 36.3% 15 to 30 minutes, 16.0% 30 to 45 minutes, 5.5% 45 to 60 minutes, 4.4% 60 minutes or more (2000)

MISSION BAY (CDP).
Covers a land area of 0.773 square miles and a water area of 0 square miles. Located at 26.36° N. Lat.; 80.21° W. Long. Elevation is 13 feet.

Population: 1,227 (1990); 2,926 (2000); 3,868 (2007); 4,498 (2012 projected); Race: 89.9% White, 1.8% Black, 3.7% Asian, 13.7% Hispanic of any race (2007); Density: 5,004.1 persons per square mile (2007); Average household size: 2.93 (2007); Median age: 37.9 (2007); Males per 100 females: 93.9 (2007); Marriage status: 16.8% never married, 73.3% now married, 3.6% widowed, 6.3% divorced (2000); Foreign born: 19.4% (2000); Ancestry (includes multiple ancestries): 26.7% Other groups, 15.7% Italian, 8.2% United States or American, 8.0% Irish, 7.5% Polish (2000).

Economy: Employment by occupation: 25.4% management, 31.8% professional, 8.2% services, 25.5% sales, 0.0% farming, 4.8% construction, 4.2% production (2000).

Income: Per capita income: $45,147 (2007); Median household income: $104,812 (2007); Average household income: $132,496 (2007); Percent of households with income of $100,000 or more: 53.5% (2007); Poverty rate: 2.3% (2000).

Education: Percent of population age 25 and over with: High school diploma (including GED) or higher: 97.7% (2007); Bachelor's degree or higher: 50.5% (2007); Master's degree or higher: 20.9% (2007).

Housing: Homeownership rate: 90.6% (2007); Median home value: $422,646 (2007); Median rent: $1,688 per month (2000); Median age of housing: 9 years (2000).

Transportation: Commute to work: 91.1% car, 1.7% public transportation, 0.0% walk, 5.1% work from home (2000); Travel time to work: 13.8% less than 15 minutes, 44.1% 15 to 30 minutes, 28.0% 30 to 45 minutes, 7.2% 45 to 60 minutes, 6.9% 60 minutes or more (2000)

NORTH PALM BEACH (village).
Covers a land area of 3.561 square miles and a water area of 2.243 square miles. Located at 26.81° N. Lat.; 80.06° W. Long. Elevation is 10 feet.

Population: 12,009 (1990); 12,064 (2000); 12,764 (2007); 13,395 (2012 projected); Race: 94.6% White, 1.5% Black, 1.8% Asian, 5.2% Hispanic of any race (2007); Density: 3,584.6 persons per square mile (2007); Average household size: 1.91 (2007); Median age: 51.6 (2007); Males per 100 females: 95.4 (2007); Marriage status: 18.2% never married, 58.3% now married, 10.9% widowed, 12.6% divorced (2000); Foreign born: 8.7% (2000); Ancestry (includes multiple ancestries): 22.1% Irish, 20.4% German, 15.1% English, 11.5% Italian, 7.3% Other groups (2000).

building permits issued: 0 (2006); Employment by occupation: 18.2% management, 23.8% professional, 13.8% services, 30.1% sales, 0.2% farming, 8.6% construction, 5.4% production (2000).

Income: Per capita income: $46,224 (2007); Median household income: $61,357 (2007); Average household income: $88,375 (2007); Percent of households with income of $100,000 or more: 27.1% (2007); Poverty rate: 3.9% (2000).

Education: Percent of population age 25 and over with: High school diploma (including GED) or higher: 92.6% (2007); Bachelor's degree or higher: 35.8% (2007); Master's degree or higher: 12.2% (2007).

School District(s)
Palm Beach County School District (PK-12)

   2005-06 Enrollment: 175,076 . . . . (561) 434-8200

Housing: Homeownership rate: 77.0% (2007); Median home value: $292,822 (2007); Median rent: $723 per month (2000); Median age of housing: 28 years (2000).

Safety: Violent crime rate: 39.7 per 10,000 population; Property crime rate: 269.3 per 10,000 population (2006).

Transportation: Commute to work: 91.7% car, 0.4% public transportation, 1.3% walk, 5.4% work from home (2000); Travel time to work: 37.1% less than 15 minutes, 41.3% 15 to 30 minutes, 13.3% 30 to 45 minutes, 3.5% 45 to 60 minutes, 4.8% 60 minutes or more (2000)

Additional Information Contacts

Village of North Palm Beach . . . . (561) 841-3380
   http://www.village-npb.org

OCEAN RIDGE (town).
Covers a land area of 0.857 square miles and a water area of 1.141 square miles. Located at 26.52° N. Lat.; 80.05° W. Long. Elevation is 7 feet.

Population: 1,570 (1990); 1,636 (2000); 1,616 (2007); 1,647 (2012 projected); Race: 97.7% White, 0.2% Black, 0.5% Asian, 3.7% Hispanic of any race (2007); Density: 1,886.3 persons per square mile (2007); Average household size: 1.82 (2007); Median age: 57.5 (2007); Males per 100 females: 95.4 (2007); Marriage status: 11.9% never married, 63.3% now married, 13.1% widowed, 11.7% divorced (2000); Foreign born: 15.1% (2000); Ancestry (includes multiple ancestries): 19.7% Irish, 18.6% German, 14.2% English, 10.1% Italian, 8.5% Other groups (2000).

Economy: Single-family building permits issued: 4 (2006); Multi-family building permits issued: 0 (2006); Employment by occupation: 32.7% management, 18.6% professional, 10.2% services, 32.9% sales, 0.0% farming, 2.8% construction, 2.9% production (2000).

Income: Per capita income: $78,951 (2007); Median household income: $73,333 (2007); Average household income: $143,354 (2007); Percent of households with income of $100,000 or more: 41.9% (2007); Poverty rate: 4.7% (2000).

Education: Percent of population age 25 and over with: High school diploma (including GED) or higher: 94.4% (2007); Bachelor's degree or higher: 42.4% (2007); Master's degree or higher: 19.1% (2007).

Housing: Homeownership rate: 84.4% (2007); Median home value: $790,509 (2007); Median rent: $746 per month (2000); Median age of housing: 30 years (2000).

Safety: Violent crime rate: 5.8 per 10,000 population; Property crime rate: 306.7 per 10,000 population (2006).

Transportation: Commute to work: 78.8% car, 0.0% public transportation, 0.0% walk, 20.4% work from home (2000); Travel time to work: 26.9% less than 15 minutes, 39.9% 15 to 30 minutes, 21.6% 30 to 45 minutes, 4.6% 45 to 60 minutes, 7.0% 60 minutes or more (2000)

PAHOKEE (city).
Covers a land area of 5.395 square miles and a water area of 0 square miles. Located at 26.82° N. Lat.; 80.66° W. Long. Elevation is 13 feet.

History: Pahokee developed on Lake Okeechobee as a shipping point for winter vegetables.

Population: 6,898 (1990); 5,985 (2000); 6,333 (2007); 6,625 (2012 projected); Race: 22.7% White, 52.7% Black, 0.6% Asian, 38.0% Hispanic of any race (2007); Density: 1,173.9 persons per square mile (2007); Average household size: 3.58 (2007); Median age: 25.7 (2007); Males per 100 females: 105.3 (2007); Marriage status: 33.1% never married, 49.3% now married, 9.5% widowed, 8.1% divorced (2000); Foreign born: 19.5% (2000); Ancestry (includes multiple ancestries): 67.8% Other groups, 5.6% United States or American, 2.4% Jamaican, 2.0% English, 1.5% Irish (2000).

Economy: Single-family building permits issued: 36 (2006); Multi-family building permits issued: 0 (2006); Employment by occupation: 7.1%

management, 10.2% professional, 21.8% services, 19.0% sales, 12.8% farming, 9.3% construction, 19.8% production (2000).
Income: Per capita income: $11,639 (2007); Median household income: $29,577 (2007); Average household income: $40,994 (2007); Percent of households with income of $100,000 or more: 6.8% (2007); Poverty rate: 32.0% (2000).
Education: Percent of population age 25 and over with: High school diploma (including GED) or higher: 46.3% (2007); Bachelor's degree or higher: 6.4% (2007); Master's degree or higher: 1.6% (2007).
School District(s)
Palm Beach County School District (PK-12)
    2005-06 Enrollment: 175,076 . . . . (561) 434-8200
Housing: Homeownership rate: 57.8% (2007); Median home value: $114,161 (2007); Median rent: $249 per month (2000); Median age of housing: 30 years (2000).
Safety: Violent crime rate: 211.6 per 10,000 population; Property crime rate: 520.6 per 10,000 population (2006).
Transportation: Commute to work: 83.2% car, 8.6% public transportation, 4.4% walk, 0.6% work from home (2000); Travel time to work: 33.7% less than 15 minutes, 30.8% 15 to 30 minutes, 10.6% 30 to 45 minutes, 11.2% 45 to 60 minutes, 13.6% 60 minutes or more (2000)
Additional Information Contacts
City of Pahokee . . . . (561) 924-5534
    http://www.pahokeeflorida.com
Pahokee Chamber of Commerce . . . . (561) 924-5579
    http://www.pahokee.com

PALM BEACH (town). Covers a land area of 3.922 square miles and a water area of 6.518 square miles. Located at 26.71° N. Lat.; 80.03° W. Long. Elevation is 7 feet.
History: The first families to settle in what is now Palm Beach came in 1873 to the island formed by Lake Worth on the west and the Atlantic Ocean on the east. Captain Elisha Newton Dimick, who built a house on the island in 1876, is credited with being the founder of the town. In 1880 the Palm City post office was established, and soon the name was changed to Palm Beach. Luxurious hotels and lavish private residences made Palm Beach into an exclusive resort town.
Population: 9,814 (1990); 10,468 (2000); 10,613 (2007); 10,871 (2012 projected); Race: 94.3% White, 3.9% Black, 0.7% Asian, 3.1% Hispanic of any race (2007); Density: 2,706.2 persons per square mile (2007); Average household size: 1.79 (2007); Median age: 67.2 (2007); Males per 100 females: 79.9 (2007); Marriage status: 10.3% never married, 61.1% now married, 18.3% widowed, 10.4% divorced (2000); Foreign born: 15.4% (2000); Ancestry (includes multiple ancestries): 12.9% Other groups, 12.8% English, 11.5% German, 10.5% Russian, 8.7% Irish (2000).
Economy: Single-family building permits issued: 26 (2006); Multi-family building permits issued: 7 (2006); Employment by occupation: 32.0% management, 24.8% professional, 10.6% services, 30.7% sales, 0.0% farming, 1.2% construction, 0.7% production (2000).
Income: Per capita income: $103,845 (2007); Median household income: $110,941 (2007); Average household income: $185,835 (2007); Percent of households with income of $100,000 or more: 53.4% (2007); Poverty rate: 5.3% (2000).
Education: Percent of population age 25 and over with: High school diploma (including GED) or higher: 95.7% (2007); Bachelor's degree or higher: 53.4% (2007); Master's degree or higher: 22.2% (2007).
Housing: Homeownership rate: 83.8% (2007); Median home value: $1 million+ (2007); Median rent: $844 per month (2000); Median age of housing: 29 years (2000).
Safety: Violent crime rate: 6.0 per 10,000 population; Property crime rate: 211.6 per 10,000 population (2006).
Newspapers: Palm Beach Daily News (Circulation 7,500)
Transportation: Commute to work: 67.4% car, 0.4% public transportation, 9.5% walk, 20.3% work from home (2000); Travel time to work: 51.4% less than 15 minutes, 30.2% 15 to 30 minutes, 10.3% 30 to 45 minutes, 4.8% 45 to 60 minutes, 3.3% 60 minutes or more (2000)
Additional Information Contacts
Palm Beach Chamber of Commerce . . . . (561) 833-3711
    http://www.palmbeaches.org
Town of Palm Beach . . . . (561) 838-5400
    http://palmbeach.govoffice.com

PALM BEACH GARDENS (city). Covers a land area of 55.683 square miles and a water area of 0.251 square miles. Located at 26.82° N. Lat.; 80.11° W. Long. Elevation is 16 feet.

Population: 24,518 (1990); 35,058 (2000); 49,851 (2007); 59,560 (2012 projected); Race: 92.2% White, 3.1% Black, 2.6% Asian, 8.1% Hispanic of any race (2007); Density: 895.3 persons per square mile (2007); Average household size: 2.22 (2007); Median age: 46.1 (2007); Males per 100 females: 91.1 (2007); Marriage status: 18.4% never married, 60.2% now married, 8.1% widowed, 13.4% divorced (2000); Foreign born: 10.8% (2000); Ancestry (includes multiple ancestries): 17.2% German, 15.2% Irish, 13.7% Other groups, 13.3% English, 12.9% Italian (2000).
Economy: Unemployment rate: 3.0% (11/2007); Total civilian labor force: 27,561 (11/2007); Single-family building permits issued: 224 (2006); Multi-family building permits issued: 274 (2006); Employment by occupation: 21.4% management, 25.5% professional, 12.3% services, 30.3% sales, 0.2% farming, 4.6% construction, 5.7% production (2000).
Income: Per capita income: $48,198 (2007); Median household income: $68,646 (2007); Average household income: $106,463 (2007); Percent of households with income of $100,000 or more: 31.5% (2007); Poverty rate: 5.6% (2000).
Education: Percent of population age 25 and over with: High school diploma (including GED) or higher: 94.2% (2007); Bachelor's degree or higher: 44.2% (2007); Master's degree or higher: 17.7% (2007).
School District(s)
Palm Beach County School District (PK-12)
    2005-06 Enrollment: 175,076 . . . . (561) 434-8200
Housing: Homeownership rate: 80.6% (2007); Median home value: $326,212 (2007); Median rent: $846 per month (2000); Median age of housing: 14 years (2000).
Hospitals: Palm Beach Gardens Medical Center (204 beds)
Safety: Violent crime rate: 28.5 per 10,000 population; Property crime rate: 364.1 per 10,000 population (2006).
Transportation: Commute to work: 92.3% car, 0.3% public transportation, 1.1% walk, 5.4% work from home (2000); Travel time to work: 29.5% less than 15 minutes, 47.3% 15 to 30 minutes, 15.3% 30 to 45 minutes, 3.7% 45 to 60 minutes, 4.2% 60 minutes or more (2000)
Additional Information Contacts
City of Palm Beach Gardens . . . . (561) 799-4100
    http://www.pbgfl.com
Palm Beach Gardens Chamber of Commerce . . . . (561) 694-2300
    http://www.npbchamber.com

PALM BEACH SHORES (town). Covers a land area of 0.253 square miles and a water area of 0.126 square miles. Located at 26.77° N. Lat.; 80.03° W. Long. Elevation is 10 feet.
Population: 1,040 (1990); 1,269 (2000); 1,544 (2007); 1,738 (2012 projected); Race: 82.6% White, 14.7% Black, 0.7% Asian, 3.6% Hispanic of any race (2007); Density: 6,096.3 persons per square mile (2007); Average household size: 1.79 (2007); Median age: 54.2 (2007); Males per 100 females: 101.6 (2007); Marriage status: 21.2% never married, 49.5% now married, 13.2% widowed, 16.1% divorced (2000); Foreign born: 12.8% (2000); Ancestry (includes multiple ancestries): 18.9% German, 16.5% Irish, 16.0% English, 7.3% Other groups, 7.2% Italian (2000).
Economy: Single-family building permits issued: 0 (2006); Multi-family building permits issued: 77 (2006); Employment by occupation: 18.5% management, 19.3% professional, 12.9% services, 32.6% sales, 0.0% farming, 10.6% construction, 6.2% production (2000).
Income: Per capita income: $42,647 (2007); Median household income: $51,429 (2007); Average household income: $76,389 (2007); Percent of households with income of $100,000 or more: 19.1% (2007); Poverty rate: 5.7% (2000).
Education: Percent of population age 25 and over with: High school diploma (including GED) or higher: 91.8% (2007); Bachelor's degree or higher: 34.8% (2007); Master's degree or higher: 14.3% (2007).
Housing: Homeownership rate: 69.3% (2007); Median home value: $387,908 (2007); Median rent: $608 per month (2000); Median age of housing: 38 years (2000).
Safety: Violent crime rate: 19.5 per 10,000 population; Property crime rate: 545.1 per 10,000 population (2006).
Transportation: Commute to work: 76.9% car, 1.7% public transportation, 7.4% walk, 11.0% work from home (2000); Travel time to work: 29.4% less than 15 minutes, 38.6% 15 to 30 minutes, 19.4% 30 to 45 minutes, 5.0% 45 to 60 minutes, 7.6% 60 minutes or more (2000)

PALM SPRINGS (village). Covers a land area of 1.611 square miles and a water area of 0.047 square miles. Located at 26.64° N. Lat.; 80.09° W. Long. Elevation is 13 feet.

Population: 10,799 (1990); 11,699 (2000); 12,303 (2007); 12,823 (2012 projected); Race: 78.6% White, 9.1% Black, 1.4% Asian, 37.7% Hispanic of any race (2007); Density: 7,636.0 persons per square mile (2007); Average household size: 2.30 (2007); Median age: 37.7 (2007); Males per 100 females: 92.1 (2007); Marriage status: 25.3% never married, 50.3% now married, 8.7% widowed, 15.7% divorced (2000); Foreign born: 26.2% (2000); Ancestry (includes multiple ancestries): 30.7% Other groups, 11.6% Irish, 11.2% German, 9.4% English, 8.6% Italian (2000).
Economy: Single-family building permits issued: 69 (2006); Multi-family building permits issued: 2 (2006); Employment by occupation: 10.6% management, 14.8% professional, 17.0% services, 30.7% sales, 0.0% farming, 12.8% construction, 14.1% production (2000).
Income: Per capita income: $20,265 (2007); Median household income: $38,175 (2007); Average household income: $46,662 (2007); Percent of households with income of $100,000 or more: 7.4% (2007); Poverty rate: 7.9% (2000).
Education: Percent of population age 25 and over with: High school diploma (including GED) or higher: 82.2% (2007); Bachelor's degree or higher: 16.5% (2007); Master's degree or higher: 6.3% (2007).

School District(s)
Palm Beach County School District (PK-12)
 2005-06 Enrollment: 175,076 . . . . (561) 434-8200
Two-year College(s)
Medvance Institute-West Palm (Private, For-profit)
 Fall 2006 Enrollment: 363 . . . . (561) 304-3466
Housing: Homeownership rate: 64.5% (2007); Median home value: $142,860 (2007); Median rent: $610 per month (2000); Median age of housing: 24 years (2000).
Safety: Violent crime rate: 61.8 per 10,000 population; Property crime rate: 625.5 per 10,000 population (2006).
Transportation: Commute to work: 94.6% car, 0.6% public transportation, 1.3% walk, 1.9% work from home (2000); Travel time to work: 21.6% less than 15 minutes, 44.1% 15 to 30 minutes, 22.4% 30 to 45 minutes, 6.9% 45 to 60 minutes, 5.1% 60 minutes or more (2000)

PLANTATION MOBILE HOME PARK (CDP). Covers a land area of 0.257 square miles and a water area of 0.006 square miles. Located at 26.70° N. Lat.; 80.13° W. Long. Elevation is 16 feet.
Population: 1,114 (1990); 1,218 (2000); 1,241 (2007); 1,222 (2012 projected); Race: 62.0% White, 18.7% Black, 0.5% Asian, 27.5% Hispanic of any race (2007); Density: 4,823.9 persons per square mile (2007); Average household size: 2.45 (2007); Median age: 34.3 (2007); Males per 100 females: 102.1 (2007); Marriage status: 34.0% never married, 47.9% now married, 7.4% widowed, 10.7% divorced (2000); Foreign born: 13.8% (2000); Ancestry (includes multiple ancestries): 21.7% Other groups, 15.5% German, 13.5% Irish, 12.4% United States or American, 9.2% English (2000).
Economy: Employment by occupation: 8.1% management, 9.1% professional, 27.5% services, 18.6% sales, 0.0% farming, 20.6% construction, 16.1% production (2000).
Income: Per capita income: $16,666 (2007); Median household income: $34,342 (2007); Average household income: $40,794 (2007); Percent of households with income of $100,000 or more: 3.9% (2007); Poverty rate: 20.8% (2000).
Education: Percent of population age 25 and over with: High school diploma (including GED) or higher: 68.8% (2007); Bachelor's degree or higher: 4.9% (2007); Master's degree or higher: 1.9% (2007).
Housing: Homeownership rate: 52.5% (2007); Median home value: $84,167 (2007); Median rent: $557 per month (2000); Median age of housing: 24 years (2000).
Transportation: Commute to work: 97.0% car, 0.8% public transportation, 2.2% walk, 0.0% work from home (2000); Travel time to work: 30.7% less than 15 minutes, 48.5% 15 to 30 minutes, 16.4% 30 to 45 minutes, 1.0% 45 to 60 minutes, 3.4% 60 minutes or more (2000)

RIVIERA BEACH (city). Covers a land area of 8.335 square miles and a water area of 1.515 square miles. Located at 26.78° N. Lat.; 80.06° W. Long. Elevation is 13 feet.
History: Named for the French coastal district. Incorporated 1922.
Population: 27,791 (1990); 29,884 (2000); 35,017 (2007); 38,624 (2012 projected); Race: 26.7% White, 67.8% Black, 1.4% Asian, 6.5% Hispanic of any race (2007); Density: 4,201.1 persons per square mile (2007); Average household size: 2.60 (2007); Median age: 35.6 (2007); Males per 100 females: 92.8 (2007); Marriage status: 32.3% never married, 46.4% now married, 8.5% widowed, 12.8% divorced (2000); Foreign born: 10.1%

(2000); Ancestry (includes multiple ancestries): 57.1% Other groups, 4.4% German, 4.1% English, 3.8% Irish, 3.4% United States or American (2000).
Economy: Unemployment rate: 5.5% (11/2007); Total civilian labor force: 15,804 (11/2007); Single-family building permits issued: 275 (2006); Multi-family building permits issued: 432 (2006); Employment by occupation: 8.8% management, 15.7% professional, 25.1% services, 26.1% sales, 0.2% farming, 9.3% construction, 14.7% production (2000).
Income: Per capita income: $22,067 (2007); Median household income: $37,717 (2007); Average household income: $56,840 (2007); Percent of households with income of $100,000 or more: 13.2% (2007); Poverty rate: 23.0% (2000).
Education: Percent of population age 25 and over with: High school diploma (including GED) or higher: 73.6% (2007); Bachelor's degree or higher: 18.6% (2007); Master's degree or higher: 6.3% (2007).
School District(s)
Palm Beach County School District (PK-12)
 2005-06 Enrollment: 175,076 . . . . (561) 434-8200
Housing: Homeownership rate: 61.1% (2007); Median home value: $198,736 (2007); Median rent: $503 per month (2000); Median age of housing: 27 years (2000).
Safety: Violent crime rate: 262.9 per 10,000 population; Property crime rate: 917.0 per 10,000 population (2006).
Transportation: Commute to work: 88.8% car, 4.3% public transportation, 2.2% walk, 2.3% work from home (2000); Travel time to work: 27.8% less than 15 minutes, 41.1% 15 to 30 minutes, 21.3% 30 to 45 minutes, 3.6% 45 to 60 minutes, 6.2% 60 minutes or more (2000)
Additional Information Contacts
City of Riviera Beach . . . . (561) 845-4000
 http://www.rivierabch.com

ROYAL PALM BEACH (village). Covers a land area of 9.891 square miles and a water area of 0.179 square miles. Located at 26.70° N. Lat.; 80.22° W. Long. Elevation is 16 feet.
Population: 15,662 (1990); 21,523 (2000); 32,529 (2007); 39,697 (2012 projected); Race: 71.7% White, 18.4% Black, 3.5% Asian, 16.6% Hispanic of any race (2007); Density: 3,288.7 persons per square mile (2007); Average household size: 2.83 (2007); Median age: 37.3 (2007); Males per 100 females: 93.1 (2007); Marriage status: 19.4% never married, 65.3% now married, 7.6% widowed, 7.7% divorced (2000); Foreign born: 14.7% (2000); Ancestry (includes multiple ancestries): 24.4% Other groups, 14.0% German, 13.3% Italian, 11.8% Irish, 8.5% United States or American (2000).
Economy: Unemployment rate: 3.4% (11/2007); Total civilian labor force: 18,555 (11/2007); Single-family building permits issued: 51 (2006); Multi-family building permits issued: 0 (2006); Employment by occupation: 14.0% management, 20.4% professional, 13.5% services, 30.5% sales, 0.4% farming, 11.4% construction, 9.8% production (2000).
Income: Per capita income: $25,186 (2007); Median household income: $63,357 (2007); Average household income: $71,260 (2007); Percent of households with income of $100,000 or more: 20.2% (2007); Poverty rate: 4.3% (2000).
Education: Percent of population age 25 and over with: High school diploma (including GED) or higher: 87.5% (2007); Bachelor's degree or higher: 24.3% (2007); Master's degree or higher: 7.8% (2007).
School District(s)
Palm Beach County School District (PK-12)
 2005-06 Enrollment: 175,076 . . . . (561) 434-8200
Housing: Homeownership rate: 89.7% (2007); Median home value: $244,280 (2007); Median rent: $778 per month (2000); Median age of housing: 15 years (2000).
Safety: Violent crime rate: 27.7 per 10,000 population; Property crime rate: 270.0 per 10,000 population (2006).
Newspapers: The Observer (General - Circulation 21,000)
Transportation: Commute to work: 95.6% car, 0.1% public transportation, 0.8% walk, 2.4% work from home (2000); Travel time to work: 12.9% less than 15 minutes, 28.0% 15 to 30 minutes, 36.2% 30 to 45 minutes, 13.4% 45 to 60 minutes, 9.5% 60 minutes or more (2000)
Additional Information Contacts
Village of Royal Palm Beach . . . . (561) 790-5100
 http://royalpalmbeach.com

ROYAL PALM ESTATES (CDP). Covers a land area of 0.805 square miles and a water area of 0 square miles. Located at 26.68° N. Lat.; 80.12° W. Long. Elevation is 16 feet.

Average household size: 3.26 (2007); Median age: 31.7 (2007); Males per 100 females: 107.0 (2007); Marriage status: 40.5% never married, 40.7% now married, 2.6% widowed, 16.2% divorced (2000); Foreign born: 23.6% (2000); Ancestry (includes multiple ancestries): 45.2% Other groups, 8.1% United States or American, 7.6% Irish, 6.7% Italian, 4.6% German (2000).
Economy: Employment by occupation: 5.3% management, 12.9% professional, 21.1% services, 26.8% sales, 0.0% farming, 21.1% construction, 12.8% production (2000).
Income: Per capita income: $16,744 (2007); Median household income: $32,332 (2007); Average household income: $53,874 (2007); Percent of households with income of $100,000 or more: 7.5% (2007); Poverty rate: 22.2% (2000).
Education: Percent of population age 25 and over with: High school diploma (including GED) or higher: 66.5% (2007); Bachelor's degree or higher: 10.1% (2007); Master's degree or higher: 4.4% (2007).
Housing: Homeownership rate: 49.8% (2007); Median home value: $169,977 (2007); Median rent: $526 per month (2000); Median age of housing: 23 years (2000).
Transportation: Commute to work: 92.1% car, 1.7% public transportation, 0.8% walk, 1.5% work from home (2000); Travel time to work: 16.5% less than 15 minutes, 47.2% 15 to 30 minutes, 25.1% 30 to 45 minutes, 6.4% 45 to 60 minutes, 4.9% 60 minutes or more (2000)

SANDALFOOT COVE (CDP).
Covers a land area of 2.968 square miles and a water area of 0 square miles. Located at 26.33° N. Lat.; 80.18° W. Long. Elevation is 13 feet.
Population: 14,221 (1990); 16,582 (2000); 15,671 (2007); 15,207 (2012 projected); Race: 82.2% White, 5.6% Black, 3.8% Asian, 22.6% Hispanic of any race (2007); Density: 5,280.0 persons per square mile (2007); Average household size: 2.38 (2007); Median age: 40.5 (2007); Males per 100 females: 92.4 (2007); Marriage status: 20.7% never married, 58.7% now married, 7.0% widowed, 13.6% divorced (2000); Foreign born: 22.4% (2000); Ancestry (includes multiple ancestries): 22.7% Other groups, 15.0% Italian, 10.7% Irish, 10.7% German, 6.9% United States or American (2000).
Economy: Employment by occupation: 14.4% management, 19.4% professional, 15.1% services, 34.6% sales, 0.1% farming, 8.6% construction, 7.8% production (2000).
Income: Per capita income: $25,792 (2007); Median household income: $48,661 (2007); Average household income: $61,345 (2007); Percent of households with income of $100,000 or more: 13.9% (2007); Poverty rate: 5.0% (2000).
Education: Percent of population age 25 and over with: High school diploma (including GED) or higher: 84.3% (2007); Bachelor's degree or higher: 19.9% (2007); Master's degree or higher: 6.8% (2007).
Housing: Homeownership rate: 79.4% (2007); Median home value: $210,344 (2007); Median rent: $922 per month (2000); Median age of housing: 18 years (2000).
Transportation: Commute to work: 94.8% car, 0.6% public transportation, 0.3% walk, 3.3% work from home (2000); Travel time to work: 21.1% less than 15 minutes, 44.5% 15 to 30 minutes, 22.3% 30 to 45 minutes, 5.6% 45 to 60 minutes, 6.6% 60 minutes or more (2000)

SCHALL CIRCLE (CDP).
Covers a land area of 0.318 square miles and a water area of 0 square miles. Located at 26.71° N. Lat.; 80.11° W. Long. Elevation is 13 feet.
Population: 733 (1990); 965 (2000); 951 (2007); 952 (2012 projected); Race: 52.7% White, 36.8% Black, 0.7% Asian, 20.7% Hispanic of any race (2007); Density: 2,991.6 persons per square mile (2007); Average household size: 2.43 (2007); Median age: 30.0 (2007); Males per 100 females: 91.7 (2007); Marriage status: 44.1% never married, 41.2% now married, 3.5% widowed, 11.2% divorced (2000); Foreign born: 12.9% (2000); Ancestry (includes multiple ancestries): 47.6% Other groups, 10.4% Irish, 10.1% German, 9.0% United States or American, 4.1% English (2000).
Economy: Employment by occupation: 5.4% management, 8.6% professional, 51.7% services, 11.4% sales, 4.5% farming, 15.3% construction, 3.0% production (2000).
Income: Per capita income: $10,899 (2007); Median household income: $20,431 (2007); Average household income: $26,509 (2007); Percent of households with income of $100,000 or more: 0.0% (2007); Poverty rate: 33.0% (2000).

Housing: Homeownership rate: 44.5% (2007); Median home value: $135,938 (2007); Median rent: $387 per month (2000); Median age of housing: 28 years (2000).
Transportation: Commute to work: 76.5% car, 13.6% public transportation, 4.5% walk, 5.4% work from home (2000); Travel time to work: 25.3% less than 15 minutes, 63.3% 15 to 30 minutes, 6.4% 30 to 45 minutes, 1.4% 45 to 60 minutes, 3.6% 60 minutes or more (2000)

SEMINOLE MANOR (CDP).
Covers a land area of 0.407 square miles and a water area of 0 square miles. Located at 26.58° N. Lat.; 80.10° W. Long. Elevation is 13 feet.
Population: 1,972 (1990); 2,546 (2000); 2,561 (2007); 2,598 (2012 projected); Race: 59.0% White, 22.6% Black, 1.1% Asian, 40.3% Hispanic of any race (2007); Density: 6,299.3 persons per square mile (2007); Average household size: 2.98 (2007); Median age: 32.8 (2007); Males per 100 females: 94.8 (2007); Marriage status: 27.2% never married, 53.3% now married, 3.7% widowed, 15.9% divorced (2000); Foreign born: 15.1% (2000); Ancestry (includes multiple ancestries): 29.0% Other groups, 10.5% Irish, 9.0% German, 8.9% Italian, 8.4% Haitian (2000).
Economy: Employment by occupation: 6.5% management, 10.5% professional, 22.2% services, 27.1% sales, 0.3% farming, 21.5% construction, 11.8% production (2000).
Income: Per capita income: $17,135 (2007); Median household income: $39,860 (2007); Average household income: $51,145 (2007); Percent of households with income of $100,000 or more: 7.0% (2007); Poverty rate: 12.3% (2000).
Education: Percent of population age 25 and over with: High school diploma (including GED) or higher: 70.2% (2007); Bachelor's degree or higher: 8.9% (2007); Master's degree or higher: 3.1% (2007).
Housing: Homeownership rate: 77.6% (2007); Median home value: $155,616 (2007); Median rent: $622 per month (2000); Median age of housing: 31 years (2000).
Transportation: Commute to work: 96.3% car, 2.3% public transportation, 0.7% walk, 0.6% work from home (2000); Travel time to work: 25.0% less than 15 minutes, 33.4% 15 to 30 minutes, 23.6% 30 to 45 minutes, 9.6% 45 to 60 minutes, 8.4% 60 minutes or more (2000)

SOUTH BAY (city).
Covers a land area of 2.707 square miles and a water area of 1.004 square miles. Located at 26.66° N. Lat.; 80.71° W. Long. Elevation is 20 feet.
History: South Bay was established on the shores of Lake Okeechobee, and developed as the terminus of the Atlantic Coast Line and Florida East Coast Railway lines. Much of the town was destroyed in 1938 by a hurricane which blew waters inland from the lake.
Population: 3,614 (1990); 3,859 (2000); 4,120 (2007); 4,320 (2012 projected); Race: 26.2% White, 66.3% Black, 0.2% Asian, 18.6% Hispanic of any race (2007); Density: 1,521.8 persons per square mile (2007); Average household size: 4.81 (2007); Median age: 32.2 (2007); Males per 100 females: 178.2 (2007); Marriage status: 45.1% never married, 44.0% now married, 5.6% widowed, 5.4% divorced (2000); Foreign born: 11.5% (2000); Ancestry (includes multiple ancestries): 48.3% Other groups, 3.3% United States or American, 2.4% Jamaican, 0.5% African, 0.4% Bahamian (2000).
Economy: Single-family building permits issued: 0 (2006); Multi-family building permits issued: 0 (2006); Employment by occupation: 5.0% management, 16.2% professional, 18.2% services, 20.3% sales, 7.3% farming, 10.3% construction, 22.6% production (2000).
Income: Per capita income: $11,041 (2007); Median household income: $28,380 (2007); Average household income: $41,673 (2007); Percent of households with income of $100,000 or more: 7.7% (2007); Poverty rate: 36.7% (2000).
Education: Percent of population age 25 and over with: High school diploma (including GED) or higher: 55.3% (2007); Bachelor's degree or higher: 7.3% (2007); Master's degree or higher: 2.0% (2007).
School District(s)
Palm Beach County School District (PK-12)
    2005-06 Enrollment: 175,076 . . . . (561) 434-8200
Housing: Homeownership rate: 58.4% (2007); Median home value: $144,118 (2007); Median rent: $300 per month (2000); Median age of housing: 25 years (2000).
Safety: Violent crime rate: 162.3 per 10,000 population; Property crime rate: 351.3 per 10,000 population (2006).

SOUTH PALM BEACH (town).
Covers a land area of 0.134 square miles and a water area of 0.199 square miles. Located at 26.59° N. Lat.; 80.03° W. Long. Elevation is 3 feet.
Population: 1,480 (1990); 699 (2000); 721 (2007); 748 (2012 projected); Race: 98.9% White, 0.0% Black, 0.8% Asian, 4.0% Hispanic of any race (2007); Density: 5,368.1 persons per square mile (2007); Average household size: 1.51 (2007); Median age: 67.4 (2007); Males per 100 females: 76.3 (2007); Marriage status: 13.4% never married, 50.0% now married, 12.4% widowed, 24.2% divorced (2000); Foreign born: 20.9% (2000); Ancestry (includes multiple ancestries): 14.9% German, 14.6% Irish, 10.4% Other groups, 9.4% Russian, 8.0% Italian (2000).
Economy: Single-family building permits issued: 0 (2006); Multi-family building permits issued: 0 (2006); Employment by occupation: 19.8% management, 9.7% professional, 22.8% services, 40.9% sales, 0.0% farming, 4.2% construction, 2.5% production (2000).
Income: Per capita income: $39,494 (2007); Median household income: $41,293 (2007); Average household income: $59,447 (2007); Percent of households with income of $100,000 or more: 12.5% (2007); Poverty rate: 15.7% (2000).
Education: Percent of population age 25 and over with: High school diploma (including GED) or higher: 91.0% (2007); Bachelor's degree or higher: 40.2% (2007); Master's degree or higher: 18.2% (2007).
Housing: Homeownership rate: 85.2% (2007); Median home value: $208,772 (2007); Median rent: $760 per month (2000); Median age of housing: 25 years (2000).
Safety: Violent crime rate: 0.0 per 10,000 population; Property crime rate: 83.5 per 10,000 population (2006).
Transportation: Commute to work: 94.8% car, 0.0% public transportation, 5.2% walk, 0.0% work from home (2000); Travel time to work: 21.3% less than 15 minutes, 59.6% 15 to 30 minutes, 11.7% 30 to 45 minutes, 5.2% 45 to 60 minutes, 2.2% 60 minutes or more (2000)

STACEY STREET (CDP).
Covers a land area of 0.115 square miles and a water area of 0 square miles. Located at 26.69° N. Lat.; 80.12° W. Long. Elevation is 16 feet.
Population: 759 (1990); 958 (2000); 998 (2007); 1,003 (2012 projected); Race: 44.2% White, 50.8% Black, 0.4% Asian, 42.9% Hispanic of any race (2007); Density: 8,703.5 persons per square mile (2007); Average household size: 3.79 (2007); Median age: 26.3 (2007); Males per 100 females: 110.5 (2007); Marriage status: 49.3% never married, 37.0% now married, 2.1% widowed, 11.5% divorced (2000); Foreign born: 41.4% (2000); Ancestry (includes multiple ancestries): 58.6% Other groups, 13.4% Irish, 7.1% Jamaican, 6.0% Bahamian, 4.2% German (2000).
Economy: Employment by occupation: 3.1% management, 13.2% professional, 36.7% services, 21.0% sales, 0.0% farming, 17.6% construction, 8.4% production (2000).
Income: Per capita income: $9,311 (2007); Median household income: $27,197 (2007); Average household income: $34,458 (2007); Percent of households with income of $100,000 or more: 4.6% (2007); Poverty rate: 35.1% (2000).
Education: Percent of population age 25 and over with: High school diploma (including GED) or higher: 60.2% (2007); Bachelor's degree or higher: 6.6% (2007); Master's degree or higher: 4.4% (2007).
Housing: Homeownership rate: 8.0% (2007); Median home value: $123,214 (2007); Median rent: $603 per month (2000); Median age of housing: 21 years (2000).
Transportation: Commute to work: 81.1% car, 8.0% public transportation, 2.6% walk, 6.0% work from home (2000); Travel time to work: 17.0% less than 15 minutes, 46.8% 15 to 30 minutes, 18.2% 30 to 45 minutes, 4.9% 45 to 60 minutes, 13.1% 60 minutes or more (2000)

TEQUESTA (village).
Covers a land area of 1.750 square miles and a water area of 0.458 square miles. Located at 26.96° N. Lat.; 80.09° W. Long. Elevation is 10 feet.
Population: 4,996 (1990); 5,273 (2000); 5,562 (2007); 5,815 (2012 projected); Race: 97.5% White, 0.6% Black, 1.0% Asian, 3.2% Hispanic of any race (2007); Density: 3,179.1 persons per square mile (2007); Average household size: 2.23 (2007); Median age: 48.8 (2007); Males per 100 females: 90.5 (2007); Marriage status: 15.6% never married, 63.5% now married, 11.4% widowed, 9.6% divorced (2000); Foreign born: 7.5%

management, 25.3% professional, 14.0% services, 34.7% sales, 0.2% farming, 6.0% construction, 4.6% production (2000).
Income: Per capita income: $42,325 (2007); Median household income: $66,731 (2007); Average household income: $93,947 (2007); Percent of households with income of $100,000 or more: 29.5% (2007); Poverty rate: 3.2% (2000).
Education: Percent of population age 25 and over with: High school diploma (including GED) or higher: 95.4% (2007); Bachelor's degree or higher: 36.7% (2007); Master's degree or higher: 11.9% (2007).
Housing: Homeownership rate: 83.5% (2007); Median home value: $345,045 (2007); Median rent: $867 per month (2000); Median age of housing: 24 years (2000).
Safety: Violent crime rate: 24.6 per 10,000 population; Property crime rate: 172.4 per 10,000 population (2006).
Transportation: Commute to work: 91.2% car, 0.5% public transportation, 1.6% walk, 4.9% work from home (2000); Travel time to work: 36.9% less than 15 minutes, 28.7% 15 to 30 minutes, 20.2% 30 to 45 minutes, 7.3% 45 to 60 minutes, 6.9% 60 minutes or more (2000)

VILLAGES OF ORIOLE (CDP).
Covers a land area of 1.026 square miles and a water area of 0 square miles. Located at 26.45° N. Lat.; 80.15° W. Long. Elevation is 20 feet.
Population: 5,698 (1990); 4,758 (2000); 4,216 (2007); 4,066 (2012 projected); Race: 98.9% White, 0.5% Black, 0.0% Asian, 0.7% Hispanic of any race (2007); Density: 4,109.2 persons per square mile (2007); Average household size: 1.50 (2007); Median age: 78.7 (2007); Males per 100 females: 67.6 (2007); Marriage status: 2.8% never married, 63.2% now married, 29.4% widowed, 4.6% divorced (2000); Foreign born: 9.8% (2000); Ancestry (includes multiple ancestries): 25.0% Other groups, 17.5% Russian, 12.1% United States or American, 11.7% Polish, 4.3% Italian (2000).
Economy: Employment by occupation: 15.9% management, 3.5% professional, 21.5% services, 46.7% sales, 0.0% farming, 9.1% construction, 3.3% production (2000).
Income: Per capita income: $28,035 (2007); Median household income: $33,392 (2007); Average household income: $41,988 (2007); Percent of households with income of $100,000 or more: 4.7% (2007); Poverty rate: 7.0% (2000).
Education: Percent of population age 25 and over with: High school diploma (including GED) or higher: 87.7% (2007); Bachelor's degree or higher: 16.4% (2007); Master's degree or higher: 7.4% (2007).
Housing: Homeownership rate: 95.2% (2007); Median home value: $160,316 (2007); Median rent: $554 per month (2000); Median age of housing: 17 years (2000).
Transportation: Commute to work: 92.0% car, 0.0% public transportation, 2.2% walk, 5.8% work from home (2000); Travel time to work: 33.7% less than 15 minutes, 48.1% 15 to 30 minutes, 8.2% 30 to 45 minutes, 7.7% 45 to 60 minutes, 2.3% 60 minutes or more (2000)

WELLINGTON (village).
Covers a land area of 31.053 square miles and a water area of 0.313 square miles. Located at 26.65° N. Lat.; 80.25° W. Long. Elevation is 16 feet.
Population: 22,555 (1990); 38,216 (2000); 56,529 (2007); 68,431 (2012 projected); Race: 84.6% White, 7.5% Black, 2.4% Asian, 16.8% Hispanic of any race (2007); Density: 1,820.4 persons per square mile (2007); Average household size: 2.93 (2007); Median age: 36.6 (2007); Males per 100 females: 95.7 (2007); Marriage status: 20.3% never married, 67.6% now married, 3.8% widowed, 8.3% divorced (2000); Foreign born: 13.4% (2000); Ancestry (includes multiple ancestries): 19.0% Other groups, 15.1% Irish, 14.6% Italian, 13.6% German, 11.2% English (2000).
Economy: Unemployment rate: 3.3% (11/2007); Total civilian labor force: 30,568 (11/2007); Single-family building permits issued: 224 (2006); Multi-family building permits issued: 0 (2006); Employment by occupation: 19.4% management, 24.9% professional, 13.5% services, 30.7% sales, 0.6% farming, 5.0% construction, 5.8% production (2000).
Income: Per capita income: $34,004 (2007); Median household income: $76,632 (2007); Average household income: $99,534 (2007); Percent of households with income of $100,000 or more: 34.5% (2007); Poverty rate: 4.3% (2000).

Education: Percent of population age 25 and over with: High school diploma (including GED) or higher: 92.3% (2007); Bachelor's degree or higher: 37.7% (2007); Master's degree or higher: 13.5% (2007).

School District(s)

Palm Beach County School District (PK-12)
  2005-06 Enrollment: 175,076 . . . . (561) 434-8200
Housing: Homeownership rate: 82.8% (2007); Median home value: $360,414 (2007); Median rent: $867 per month (2000); Median age of housing: 11 years (2000).
Hospitals: Wellington Regional Medical Center (143 beds)
Safety: Violent crime rate: 29.9 per 10,000 population; Property crime rate: 315.5 per 10,000 population (2006).
Newspapers: Greenacres/Lake Worth/Lantana Forum (General - Circulation 27,000); Town Crier (General - Circulation 20,500)
Transportation: Commute to work: 90.9% car, 0.6% public transportation, 0.6% walk, 6.6% work from home (2000); Travel time to work: 23.2% less than 15 minutes, 22.5% 15 to 30 minutes, 29.1% 30 to 45 minutes, 15.8% 45 to 60 minutes, 9.4% 60 minutes or more (2000)

Additional Information Contacts

Village of Wellington . . . . (561) 791-4000
  http://www.wellvillage.com

WEST PALM BEACH (city). County seat. Covers a land area of 55.142 square miles and a water area of 3.059 square miles. Located at 26.71° N. Lat.; 80.06° W. Long. Elevation is 13 feet.

History: West Palm Beach was established on the western shore of Lake Worth, and grew as the business and railroad center for Palm Beach on the opposite shore. Later, West Palm Beach became a winter resort as well. West Palm Beach was developed by Henry Flagler, pioneer railroad builder, in the 1890's. When Palm Beach County was carved out of Dade County, West Palm Beach was chosen as the county seat.
Population: 68,172 (1990); 82,103 (2000); 100,705 (2007); 113,381 (2012 projected); Race: 53.4% White, 34.6% Black, 2.0% Asian, 21.8% Hispanic of any race (2007); Density: 1,826.3 persons per square mile (2007); Average household size: 2.34 (2007); Median age: 37.4 (2007); Males per 100 females: 98.5 (2007); Marriage status: 33.2% never married, 45.3% now married, 8.5% widowed, 13.0% divorced (2000); Foreign born: 24.7% (2000); Ancestry (includes multiple ancestries): 40.1% Other groups, 7.5% German, 7.0% Irish, 6.2% English, 5.2% United States or American (2000).
Economy: Unemployment rate: 4.5% (11/2007); Total civilian labor force: 53,275 (11/2007); Single-family building permits issued: 131 (2006); Multi-family building permits issued: 1,177 (2006); Employment by occupation: 12.4% management, 19.8% professional, 22.4% services, 25.7% sales, 0.8% farming, 9.0% construction, 10.0% production (2000).
Income: Per capita income: $26,760 (2007); Median household income: $41,163 (2007); Average household income: $61,181 (2007); Percent of households with income of $100,000 or more: 14.8% (2007); Poverty rate: 18.9% (2000).
Taxes: Total city taxes per capita: $969 (2005); City property taxes per capita: $559 (2005).
Education: Percent of population age 25 and over with: High school diploma (including GED) or higher: 75.9% (2007); Bachelor's degree or higher: 27.2% (2007); Master's degree or higher: 10.4% (2007).

School District(s)

Palm Beach County School District (PK-12)
  2005-06 Enrollment: 175,076 . . . . (561) 434-8200

Four-year College(s)

Lincoln College of Technology (Private, For-profit)
  Fall 2006 Enrollment: 1,137. (561) 842-8324
  2006-07 Tuition: In-state $11,177; Out-of-state $11,177
Northwood University-Florida Education Center (Private, Not-for-profit)
  Fall 2006 Enrollment: 911 . . . . (561) 478-5500
  2006-07 Tuition: In-state $15,801; Out-of-state $15,801
Palm Beach Atlantic University-West Palm Beach (Private, Not-for-profit, Interdenominational)
  Fall 2006 Enrollment: 3,264. . . . . (561) 803-2000
  2006-07 Tuition: In-state $18,740; Out-of-state $18,740
South University-West Palm Beach (Private, For-profit)
  Fall 2006 Enrollment: 593 . . . . (561) 697-9200
  2006-07 Tuition: In-state $11,850; Out-of-state $11,850

Vocational/Technical School(s)

Academy for Practical Nursing & Health Occupations (Private, Not-for-profit)
  Fall 2006 Enrollment: 378 . . . . (561) 683-1400
  2006-07 Tuition: $15,053

Medical Career Institute of South Florida (Private, For-profit)
  Fall 2006 Enrollment: 412 . . . . (561) 296-0824
  2006-07 Tuition: $11,500
Ross Medical Education Center (Private, For-profit)
  Fall 2006 Enrollment: 48 . . . . (561) 433-1288
  2006-07 Tuition: $9,430
The Beauty Institute (Private, For-profit)
  Fall 2006 Enrollment: 126 . . . . (561) 688-0225
  2006-07 Tuition: $7,621
Housing: Homeownership rate: 51.8% (2007); Median home value: $220,599 (2007); Median rent: $582 per month (2000); Median age of housing: 26 years (2000).
Hospitals: Columbia Hospital (250 beds); Good Samaritan Medical Center (341 beds); St. Mary's Medical Center (460 beds); West Palm Beach Veterans Affairs Medical Center (270 beds)
Safety: Violent crime rate: 118.4 per 10,000 population; Property crime rate: 739.5 per 10,000 population (2006).
Newspapers: El Latino Semanal (Hispanic - Circulation 36,000); Palm Beach Daily Business Review (Circulation 9,072); Palm Beach Gazette (Black - Circulation 3,000); Palm Beach Jewish News (Jewish - Circulation 23,000); Semanario Accion (Hispanic - Circulation 25,000); The Palm Beach Post (Circulation 181,312)
Transportation: Commute to work: 89.8% car, 2.8% public transportation, 2.8% walk, 2.3% work from home (2000); Travel time to work: 29.6% less than 15 minutes, 44.1% 15 to 30 minutes, 17.3% 30 to 45 minutes, 4.1% 45 to 60 minutes, 4.9% 60 minutes or more (2000); Amtrak: Service available.
Airports: North Palm Beach County General Aviation; Palm Beach County Park; Palm Beach International (primary service/medium hub)

Additional Information Contacts

City of West Palm Beach . . . . (561) 822-1210
  http://www.cityofwpb.com
Hispanic Chamber of Commerce . . . . (561) 832-1986
  http://www.palmbeachhispanicchamber.com
West Palm Beach Chamber of Commerce . . . . (561) 833-3711
  http://www.palmbeaches.org

WESTGATE-BELVEDERE HOMES (CDP). Covers a land area of 2.062 square miles and a water area of 0 square miles. Located at 26.69° N. Lat.; 80.09° W. Long.

Population: 6,880 (1990); 8,134 (2000); 7,740 (2007); 7,569 (2012 projected); Race: 53.1% White, 29.8% Black, 0.8% Asian, 43.5% Hispanic of any race (2007); Density: 3,753.7 persons per square mile (2007); Average household size: 2.97 (2007); Median age: 30.7 (2007); Males per 100 females: 102.6 (2007); Marriage status: 31.6% never married, 49.6% now married, 4.4% widowed, 14.3% divorced (2000); Foreign born: 26.5% (2000); Ancestry (includes multiple ancestries): 45.4% Other groups, 9.5% United States or American, 7.1% Haitian, 7.0% Irish, 6.2% English (2000).
Economy: Employment by occupation: 5.7% management, 9.1% professional, 26.0% services, 23.8% sales, 3.1% farming, 18.9% construction, 13.3% production (2000).
Income: Per capita income: $13,091 (2007); Median household income: $30,898 (2007); Average household income: $38,899 (2007); Percent of households with income of $100,000 or more: 3.8% (2007); Poverty rate: 20.8% (2000).
Education: Percent of population age 25 and over with: High school diploma (including GED) or higher: 57.2% (2007); Bachelor's degree or higher: 7.0% (2007); Master's degree or higher: 2.3% (2007).
Housing: Homeownership rate: 56.3% (2007); Median home value: $138,778 (2007); Median rent: $534 per month (2000); Median age of housing: 31 years (2000).
Transportation: Commute to work: 93.0% car, 1.4% public transportation, 2.0% walk, 1.4% work from home (2000); Travel time to work: 22.7% less than 15 minutes, 43.8% 15 to 30 minutes, 20.0% 30 to 45 minutes, 5.6% 45 to 60 minutes, 8.0% 60 minutes or more (2000)

WHISPER WALK (CDP). Covers a land area of 1.002 square miles and a water area of 0 square miles. Located at 26.39° N. Lat.; 80.18° W. Long. Elevation is 16 feet.

Population: 3,037 (1990); 5,135 (2000); 5,543 (2007); 5,870 (2012 projected); Race: 92.0% White, 2.8% Black, 3.3% Asian, 7.7% Hispanic of any race (2007); Density: 5,530.9 persons per square mile (2007); Average household size: 2.13 (2007); Median age: 60.7 (2007); Males per 100 females: 85.7 (2007); Marriage status: 8.1% never married, 74.8% now married, 11.8% widowed, 5.3% divorced (2000); Foreign born: 12.0%

(2000); Ancestry (includes multiple ancestries): 21.3% Other groups, 12.6% Russian, 11.4% Italian, 11.2% Polish, 8.0% United States or American (2000).
Economy: Employment by occupation: 21.1% management, 19.9% professional, 13.0% services, 38.9% sales, 0.0% farming, 2.8% construction, 4.3% production (2000).
Income: Per capita income: $31,900 (2007); Median household income: $50,706 (2007); Average household income: $67,826 (2007); Percent of households with income of $100,000 or more: 19.8% (2007); Poverty rate: 4.7% (2000).
Education: Percent of population age 25 and over with: High school diploma (including GED) or higher: 87.0% (2007); Bachelor's degree or higher: 24.9% (2007); Master's degree or higher: 8.0% (2007).
Housing: Homeownership rate: 95.2% (2007); Median home value: $219,712 (2007); Median rent: $1,130 per month (2000); Median age of housing: 12 years (2000).
Transportation: Commute to work: 90.7% car, 0.0% public transportation, 0.0% walk, 9.3% work from home (2000); Travel time to work: 27.8% less than 15 minutes, 37.9% 15 to 30 minutes, 23.8% 30 to 45 minutes, 6.9% 45 to 60 minutes, 3.6% 60 minutes or more (2000)

Pasco County

Located in west central Florida; bounded on the west by the Gulf of Mexico; includes many small lakes. Covers a land area of 744.85 square miles, a water area of 123.10 square miles, and is located in the Eastern Time Zone. The county was founded in 1887. County seat is Dade City.

Pasco County is part of the Tampa-St. Petersburg-Clearwater, FL Metropolitan Statistical Area. The entire metro area includes: Hernando County, FL; Hillsborough County, FL; Pasco County, FL; Pinellas County, FL

Weather Station: Saint Leo   Elevation: 187 feet

	Jan	Feb	Mar	Apr	May	Jun	Jul	Aug	Sep	Oct	Nov	Dec
High	72	74	79	84	89	91	92	92	91	85	79	74
Low	49	51	55	59	65	70	72	72	71	64	57	51
Precip	3.5	3.6	4.3	2.4	4.1	6.9	7.7	7.4	6.5	2.9	2.5	2.7
Snow	tr	0.0	0.0	0.0	0.0	0.0	0.0	0.0	0.0	0.0	0.0	0.0

High and Low temperatures in degrees Fahrenheit; Precipitation and Snow in inches

Population: 281,131 (1990); 344,765 (2000); 439,510 (2007); 498,583 (2012 projected); Race: 90.3% White, 3.4% Black, 1.6% Asian, 9.0% Hispanic of any race (2007); Density: 590.1 persons per square mile (2007); Average household size: 2.35 (2007); Median age: 42.6 (2007); Males per 100 females: 93.8 (2007).
Religion: Five largest groups: 16.1% Catholic Church, 4.4% Southern Baptist Convention, 2.2% The United Methodist Church, 1.3% Assemblies of God, 0.9% Church of God (Cleveland, Tennessee) (2000).
Economy: Unemployment rate: 5.2% (11/2007); Total civilian labor force: 192,848 (11/2007); Leading industries: 23.2% retail trade; 19.3% health care and social assistance; 12.6% accommodation & food services (2005); Farms: 1,222 totaling 168,716 acres (2002); Companies that employ 500 or more persons: 11 (2005); Companies that employ 100 to 499 persons: 93 (2005); Companies that employ less than 100 persons: 7,829 (2005); Black-owned businesses: n/a (2002); Hispanic-owned businesses: n/a (2002); Asian-owned businesses: 539 (2002); Women-owned businesses: 6,626 (2002); Retail sales per capita: $11,024 (2007). Single-family building permits issued: 5,007 (2006); Multi-family building permits issued: 862 (2006).
Income: Per capita income: $22,685 (2007); Median household income: $41,050 (2007); Average household income: $52,900 (2007); Percent of households with income of $100,000 or more: 10.3% (2007); Poverty rate: 11.3% (2005); Bankruptcy rate: 2.00% (2006).
Taxes: Total county taxes per capita: $467 (2005); County property taxes per capita: $308 (2005).
Education: Percent of population age 25 and over with: High school diploma (including GED) or higher: 78.6% (2007); Bachelor's degree or higher: 14.4% (2007); Master's degree or higher: 4.7% (2007).
Housing: Homeownership rate: 83.4% (2007); Median home value: $141,505 (2007); Median rent: $432 per month (2000); Median age of housing: 19 years (2000).
Health: Birth rate: 108.9 per 10,000 population (2006); Death rate: 121.0 per 10,000 population (2006); Age-adjusted cancer mortality rate: 201.7 deaths per 100,000 population (2004); Air Quality Index: 91.8% good, 7.9% moderate, 0.3% unhealthy for sensitive individuals, 0.0% unhealthy

(percent of days in 2006); Number of physicians: 14.1 per 10,000 population (2005); Hospital beds: 25.8 per 10,000 population (2004); Hospital admissions: 1,252.8 per 10,000 population (2004).
Elections: 2004 Presidential election results: 54.1% Bush, 44.4% Kerry, 0.8% Nader, 0.3% Badnarik
National and State Parks: Anclote Key Preserve State Park; Anclote National Wildlife Refuge; Werner-Boyce Salt Springs State Park; Withlacoochee State Forest
Additional Information Contacts

Pasco County Government . . . . (727) 847-8100
    http://www.pascocountyfl.net
City of Dade City . . . . (352) 523-5050
    http://www.dadecityfl.com
City of New Port Richey. . . . . (727) 853-1016
    http://www.cityofnewportrichey.org
City of Zephyrhills . . . . (813) 780-0000
    http://www.ci.zephyrhills.fl.us
Dade City Chamber of Commerce. . . . . (352) 567-3769
    http://www.dadecitychamber.org
Land O' Lakes Chamber of Commerce . . . . (813) 909-2722
    http://www.centralpascochamber.com
New Port Richey Chamber of Commerce . . . . (727) 842-7651
    http://www.westpasco.com

Pasco County Communities

BAYONET POINT (CDP). Covers a land area of 5.604 square miles and a water area of 0.076 square miles. Located at 28.32° N. Lat.; 82.68° W. Long. Elevation is 30 feet.
Population: 21,860 (1990); 23,577 (2000); 24,576 (2007); 25,322 (2012 projected); Race: 94.8% White, 1.4% Black, 0.9% Asian, 5.9% Hispanic of any race (2007); Density: 4,385.5 persons per square mile (2007); Average household size: 2.08 (2007); Median age: 52.7 (2007); Males per 100 females: 85.1 (2007); Marriage status: 12.9% never married, 59.6% now married, 18.9% widowed, 8.7% divorced (2000); Foreign born: 6.3% (2000); Ancestry (includes multiple ancestries): 21.5% German, 17.3% Irish, 16.2% Italian, 12.9% English, 7.6% Other groups (2000).
Economy: Employment by occupation: 8.9% management, 15.2% professional, 21.5% services, 30.8% sales, 0.2% farming, 13.1% construction, 10.4% production (2000).
Income: Per capita income: $19,322 (2007); Median household income: $32,844 (2007); Average household income: $39,597 (2007); Percent of households with income of $100,000 or more: 3.5% (2007); Poverty rate: 11.6% (2000).
Education: Percent of population age 25 and over with: High school diploma (including GED) or higher: 75.7% (2007); Bachelor's degree or higher: 10.2% (2007); Master's degree or higher: 3.8% (2007).
Housing: Homeownership rate: 84.7% (2007); Median home value: $119,021 (2007); Median rent: $468 per month (2000); Median age of housing: 22 years (2000).
Transportation: Commute to work: 95.7% car, 0.4% public transportation, 1.3% walk, 1.8% work from home (2000); Travel time to work: 36.6% less than 15 minutes, 32.5% 15 to 30 minutes, 13.2% 30 to 45 minutes, 6.2% 45 to 60 minutes, 11.5% 60 minutes or more (2000)

BEACON SQUARE (CDP). Aka Beacon Squier. Covers a land area of 1.999 square miles and a water area of 0.037 square miles. Located at 28.21° N. Lat.; 82.74° W. Long. Elevation is 7 feet.
Population: 6,265 (1990); 7,263 (2000); 7,653 (2007); 7,933 (2012 projected); Race: 92.0% White, 2.2% Black, 1.2% Asian, 6.8% Hispanic of any race (2007); Density: 3,828.5 persons per square mile (2007); Average household size: 2.09 (2007); Median age: 46.0 (2007); Males per 100 females: 86.3 (2007); Marriage status: 16.8% never married, 57.3% now married, 13.6% widowed, 12.2% divorced (2000); Foreign born: 8.1% (2000); Ancestry (includes multiple ancestries): 19.1% German, 16.6% Irish, 15.2% Italian, 10.6% English, 10.0% Other groups (2000).
Economy: Employment by occupation: 10.4% management, 16.1% professional, 18.4% services, 32.3% sales, 0.0% farming, 11.5% construction, 11.3% production (2000).
Income: Per capita income: $19,320 (2007); Median household income: $32,245 (2007); Average household income: $40,321 (2007); Percent of households with income of $100,000 or more: 4.4% (2007); Poverty rate: 9.5% (2000).

Education: Percent of population age 25 and over with: High school diploma (including GED) or higher: 77.4% (2007); Bachelor's degree or higher: 11.6% (2007); Master's degree or higher: 3.4% (2007).
Housing: Homeownership rate: 86.2% (2007); Median home value: $106,070 (2007); Median rent: $499 per month (2000); Median age of housing: 27 years (2000).
Transportation: Commute to work: 94.4% car, 0.3% public transportation, 0.5% walk, 2.9% work from home (2000); Travel time to work: 25.8% less than 15 minutes, 32.5% 15 to 30 minutes, 17.7% 30 to 45 minutes, 14.3% 45 to 60 minutes, 9.8% 60 minutes or more (2000)

CRYSTAL SPRINGS (CDP).

Covers a land area of 5.553 square miles and a water area of 0 square miles. Located at 28.18° N. Lat.; 82.16° W. Long. Elevation is 75 feet.
Population: 1,028 (1990); 1,175 (2000); 1,301 (2007); 1,383 (2012 projected); Race: 88.3% White, 1.3% Black, 0.0% Asian, 9.7% Hispanic of any race (2007); Density: 234.3 persons per square mile (2007); Average household size: 2.72 (2007); Median age: 34.4 (2007); Males per 100 females: 103.0 (2007); Marriage status: 17.6% never married, 65.7% now married, 2.3% widowed, 14.4% divorced (2000); Foreign born: 0.5% (2000); Ancestry (includes multiple ancestries): 20.6% Irish, 18.3% United States or American, 15.9% Other groups, 15.8% English, 13.1% German (2000).
Economy: Employment by occupation: 3.0% management, 6.5% professional, 17.4% services, 33.2% sales, 1.8% farming, 16.5% construction, 21.6% production (2000).
Income: Per capita income: $21,214 (2007); Median household income: $47,614 (2007); Average household income: $57,620 (2007); Percent of households with income of $100,000 or more: 10.6% (2007); Poverty rate: 9.8% (2000).
Education: Percent of population age 25 and over with: High school diploma (including GED) or higher: 65.8% (2007); Bachelor's degree or higher: 3.6% (2007); Master's degree or higher: 1.1% (2007).
Housing: Homeownership rate: 82.5% (2007); Median home value: $114,965 (2007); Median rent: $439 per month (2000); Median age of housing: 16 years (2000).
Transportation: Commute to work: 86.1% car, 1.1% public transportation, 6.5% walk, 3.4% work from home (2000); Travel time to work: 20.8% less than 15 minutes, 35.4% 15 to 30 minutes, 19.9% 30 to 45 minutes, 7.3% 45 to 60 minutes, 16.7% 60 minutes or more (2000)

DADE CITY (city).

County seat. Covers a land area of 3.282 square miles and a water area of 0.096 square miles. Located at 28.36° N. Lat.; 82.19° W. Long. Elevation is 118 feet.
History: Dade City began as a trading post and became the commercial center of a truck-farming and citrus-fruit district.
Population: 5,702 (1990); 6,188 (2000); 6,655 (2007); 6,980 (2012 projected); Race: 53.1% White, 28.9% Black, 0.8% Asian, 25.2% Hispanic of any race (2007); Density: 2,027.6 persons per square mile (2007); Average household size: 2.51 (2007); Median age: 33.5 (2007); Males per 100 females: 92.4 (2007); Marriage status: 25.6% never married, 48.9% now married, 12.3% widowed, 13.3% divorced (2000); Foreign born: 6.2% (2000); Ancestry (includes multiple ancestries): 45.4% Other groups, 11.0% German, 10.0% Irish, 9.2% English, 6.0% United States or American (2000).
Economy: Single-family building permits issued: 37 (2006); Multi-family building permits issued: 6 (2006); Employment by occupation: 7.9% management, 17.3% professional, 19.5% services, 22.6% sales, 5.0% farming, 12.2% construction, 15.5% production (2000).
Income: Per capita income: $18,506 (2007); Median household income: $33,704 (2007); Average household income: $45,026 (2007); Percent of households with income of $100,000 or more: 6.8% (2007); Poverty rate: 15.8% (2000).
Education: Percent of population age 25 and over with: High school diploma (including GED) or higher: 72.7% (2007); Bachelor's degree or higher: 17.3% (2007); Master's degree or higher: 6.8% (2007).
School District(s)
Pasco County School District (PK-12)
    2005-06 Enrollment: 60,846 . . . . (813) 794-2651
Housing: Homeownership rate: 57.6% (2007); Median home value: $117,974 (2007); Median rent: $416 per month (2000); Median age of housing: 26 years (2000).
Hospitals: Pasco Community Hospital (120 beds)
Safety: Violent crime rate: 129.7 per 10,000 population; Property crime rate: 510.2 per 10,000 population (2006).

Newspapers: Pasco News (General - Circulation 5,500); Wesley Chapel Connection (General - Circulation 36,000); Zephyr Hills Sun (General - Circulation 36,000)
Transportation: Commute to work: 91.7% car, 0.6% public transportation, 3.5% walk, 3.2% work from home (2000); Travel time to work: 43.3% less than 15 minutes, 24.6% 15 to 30 minutes, 14.0% 30 to 45 minutes, 8.4% 45 to 60 minutes, 9.8% 60 minutes or more (2000); Amtrak: Service available.
Additional Information Contacts
City of Dade City . . . . (352) 523-5050
    http://www.dadecityfl.com
Dade City Chamber of Commerce . . . . (352) 567-3769
    http://www.dadecitychamber.org

DADE CITY NORTH (CDP).

Covers a land area of 1.819 square miles and a water area of 0.018 square miles. Located at 28.37° N. Lat.; 82.19° W. Long. Elevation is 92 feet.
Population: 3,052 (1990); 3,319 (2000); 3,523 (2007); 3,634 (2012 projected); Race: 45.4% White, 12.9% Black, 0.1% Asian, 71.7% Hispanic of any race (2007); Density: 1,936.4 persons per square mile (2007); Average household size: 3.65 (2007); Median age: 27.3 (2007); Males per 100 females: 123.1 (2007); Marriage status: 34.1% never married, 53.9% now married, 4.8% widowed, 7.2% divorced (2000); Foreign born: 33.5% (2000); Ancestry (includes multiple ancestries): 60.6% Other groups, 10.8% United States or American, 5.0% Irish, 3.0% English, 2.3% Dutch (2000).
Economy: Employment by occupation: 1.3% management, 3.4% professional, 14.3% services, 11.1% sales, 25.7% farming, 27.3% construction, 16.8% production (2000).
Income: Per capita income: $12,296 (2007); Median household income: $31,067 (2007); Average household income: $42,962 (2007); Percent of households with income of $100,000 or more: 5.0% (2007); Poverty rate: 29.1% (2000).
Education: Percent of population age 25 and over with: High school diploma (including GED) or higher: 30.5% (2007); Bachelor's degree or higher: 0.8% (2007); Master's degree or higher: 0.1% (2007).
Housing: Homeownership rate: 52.6% (2007); Median home value: $76,250 (2007); Median rent: $299 per month (2000); Median age of housing: 32 years (2000).
Transportation: Commute to work: 98.0% car, 0.0% public transportation, 1.5% walk, 0.0% work from home (2000); Travel time to work: 24.4% less than 15 minutes, 28.6% 15 to 30 minutes, 19.3% 30 to 45 minutes, 4.5% 45 to 60 minutes, 23.2% 60 minutes or more (2000)

ELFERS (CDP).

Covers a land area of 3.510 square miles and a water area of 0.024 square miles. Located at 28.21° N. Lat.; 82.72° W. Long. Elevation is 39 feet.
Population: 12,153 (1990); 13,161 (2000); 14,237 (2007); 14,962 (2012 projected); Race: 92.0% White, 1.9% Black, 1.4% Asian, 7.9% Hispanic of any race (2007); Density: 4,055.7 persons per square mile (2007); Average household size: 2.33 (2007); Median age: 42.5 (2007); Males per 100 females: 85.2 (2007); Marriage status: 16.5% never married, 56.1% now married, 15.8% widowed, 11.6% divorced (2000); Foreign born: 6.0% (2000); Ancestry (includes multiple ancestries): 17.6% German, 16.4% Irish, 13.4% Italian, 13.1% English, 12.7% Other groups (2000).
Economy: Employment by occupation: 8.8% management, 11.1% professional, 20.3% services, 33.0% sales, 0.2% farming, 12.8% construction, 13.8% production (2000).
Income: Per capita income: $17,256 (2007); Median household income: $33,034 (2007); Average household income: $39,669 (2007); Percent of households with income of $100,000 or more: 3.4% (2007); Poverty rate: 12.9% (2000).
Education: Percent of population age 25 and over with: High school diploma (including GED) or higher: 72.7% (2007); Bachelor's degree or higher: 6.9% (2007); Master's degree or higher: 2.0% (2007).
School District(s)
Pasco County School District (PK-12)
    2005-06 Enrollment: 60,846 . . . . (813) 794-2651
Housing: Homeownership rate: 85.4% (2007); Median home value: $104,610 (2007); Median rent: $460 per month (2000); Median age of housing: 26 years (2000).
Transportation: Commute to work: 93.1% car, 0.5% public transportation, 1.6% walk, 2.3% work from home (2000); Travel time to work: 29.2% less than 15 minutes, 29.2% 15 to 30 minutes, 18.5% 30 to 45 minutes, 12.1% 45 to 60 minutes, 11.0% 60 minutes or more (2000)

HOLIDAY

HOLIDAY (CDP). Covers a land area of 5.382 square miles and a water area of 0.345 square miles. Located at 28.18° N. Lat.; 82.74° W. Long. Elevation is 16 feet.

Population: 20,286 (1990); 21,904 (2000); 24,352 (2007); 25,946 (2012 projected); Race: 91.4% White, 3.1% Black, 1.5% Asian, 6.7% Hispanic of any race (2007); Density: 4,525.0 persons per square mile (2007); Average household size: 2.12 (2007); Median age: 44.8 (2007); Males per 100 females: 91.0 (2007); Marriage status: 16.9% never married, 57.9% now married, 13.5% widowed, 11.7% divorced (2000); Foreign born: 10.2% (2000); Ancestry (includes multiple ancestries): 18.6% German, 16.9% Irish, 11.5% Italian, 11.0% English, 9.2% Other groups (2000).

Economy: Employment by occupation: 6.5% management, 14.3% professional, 19.3% services, 31.5% sales, 0.2% farming, 14.7% construction, 13.5% production (2000).

Income: Per capita income: $19,235 (2007); Median household income: $32,692 (2007); Average household income: $40,713 (2007); Percent of households with income of $100,000 or more: 3.5% (2007); Poverty rate: 11.4% (2000).

Education: Percent of population age 25 and over with: High school diploma (including GED) or higher: 74.4% (2007); Bachelor's degree or higher: 7.3% (2007); Master's degree or higher: 2.0% (2007).

School District(s)
Pasco County School District (PK-12)
   2005-06 Enrollment: 60,846 . . . . (813) 794-2651

Four-year College(s)
Webster College (Private, For-profit)
   Fall 2006 Enrollment: 346 . . . . (727) 942-0069
   2006-07 Tuition: In-state $10,205; Out-of-state $10,205

Housing: Homeownership rate: 82.7% (2007); Median home value: $106,162 (2007); Median rent: $464 per month (2000); Median age of housing: 27 years (2000).

Transportation: Commute to work: 94.5% car, 0.0% public transportation, 0.3% walk, 3.3% work from home (2000); Travel time to work: 24.7% less than 15 minutes, 31.3% 15 to 30 minutes, 21.0% 30 to 45 minutes, 13.4% 45 to 60 minutes, 9.5% 60 minutes or more (2000)

HUDSON

HUDSON (CDP). Covers a land area of 6.365 square miles and a water area of 0.018 square miles. Located at 28.36° N. Lat.; 82.68° W. Long. Elevation is 10 feet.

Population: 10,731 (1990); 12,765 (2000); 14,529 (2007); 15,659 (2012 projected); Race: 95.3% White, 0.7% Black, 1.3% Asian, 4.1% Hispanic of any race (2007); Density: 2,282.5 persons per square mile (2007); Average household size: 2.04 (2007); Median age: 56.0 (2007); Males per 100 females: 93.2 (2007); Marriage status: 13.4% never married, 62.0% now married, 13.8% widowed, 10.8% divorced (2000); Foreign born: 7.9% (2000); Ancestry (includes multiple ancestries): 19.9% German, 17.8% Irish, 13.3% English, 12.0% Italian, 7.8% Other groups (2000).

Economy: Employment by occupation: 10.5% management, 17.7% professional, 22.2% services, 25.4% sales, 0.5% farming, 14.6% construction, 9.1% production (2000).

Income: Per capita income: $24,150 (2007); Median household income: $39,535 (2007); Average household income: $48,965 (2007); Percent of households with income of $100,000 or more: 7.0% (2007); Poverty rate: 9.9% (2000).

Education: Percent of population age 25 and over with: High school diploma (including GED) or higher: 76.0% (2007); Bachelor's degree or higher: 13.1% (2007); Master's degree or higher: 4.4% (2007).

School District(s)
Pasco County School District (PK-12)
   2005-06 Enrollment: 60,846 . . . . (813) 794-2651

Housing: Homeownership rate: 80.9% (2007); Median home value: $162,142 (2007); Median rent: $449 per month (2000); Median age of housing: 18 years (2000).

Hospitals: Regional Medical Center Bayonet Point (290 beds)

Transportation: Commute to work: 90.4% car, 0.8% public transportation, 1.4% walk, 3.9% work from home (2000); Travel time to work: 39.3% less than 15 minutes, 27.6% 15 to 30 minutes, 10.7% 30 to 45 minutes, 8.6% 45 to 60 minutes, 13.9% 60 minutes or more (2000)

JASMINE ESTATES

JASMINE ESTATES (CDP). Covers a land area of 3.574 square miles and a water area of 0.064 square miles. Located at 28.29° N. Lat.; 82.69° W. Long. Elevation is 3 feet.

Population: 17,133 (1990); 18,213 (2000); 19,258 (2007); 19,986 (2012 projected); Race: 91.0% White, 2.9% Black, 1.3% Asian, 9.8% Hispanic of household size: 2.17 (2007); Median age: 42.4 (2007); Males per 100 females: 88.4 (2007); Marriage status: 19.1% never married, 55.2% now married, 13.8% widowed, 11.9% divorced (2000); Foreign born: 8.5% (2000); Ancestry (includes multiple ancestries): 19.0% Italian, 16.4% German, 15.8% Irish, 11.3% Other groups, 8.2% United States or American (2000).

Economy: Employment by occupation: 8.2% management, 14.3% professional, 20.4% services, 35.6% sales, 0.0% farming, 10.0% construction, 11.5% production (2000).

Income: Per capita income: $16,346 (2007); Median household income: $29,722 (2007); Average household income: $35,469 (2007); Percent of households with income of $100,000 or more: 2.5% (2007); Poverty rate: 14.3% (2000).

Education: Percent of population age 25 and over with: High school diploma (including GED) or higher: 72.7% (2007); Bachelor's degree or higher: 8.3% (2007); Master's degree or higher: 2.6% (2007).

Housing: Homeownership rate: 77.0% (2007); Median home value: $118,092 (2007); Median rent: $473 per month (2000); Median age of housing: 22 years (2000).

Transportation: Commute to work: 96.0% car, 0.8% public transportation, 0.5% walk, 1.1% work from home (2000); Travel time to work: 35.1% less than 15 minutes, 31.4% 15 to 30 minutes, 12.7% 30 to 45 minutes, 8.8% 45 to 60 minutes, 12.1% 60 minutes or more (2000)

LACOOCHEE

LACOOCHEE (CDP). Covers a land area of 2.852 square miles and a water area of 0 square miles. Located at 28.46° N. Lat.; 82.17° W. Long. Elevation is 72 feet.

Population: 2,072 (1990); 1,345 (2000); 1,205 (2007); 1,211 (2012 projected); Race: 63.0% White, 24.6% Black, 0.1% Asian, 48.0% Hispanic of any race (2007); Density: 422.5 persons per square mile (2007); Average household size: 3.17 (2007); Median age: 25.6 (2007); Males per 100 females: 101.8 (2007); Marriage status: 14.9% never married, 62.8% now married, 11.8% widowed, 10.5% divorced (2000); Foreign born: 16.5% (2000); Ancestry (includes multiple ancestries): 52.2% Other groups, 12.7% United States or American, 9.4% English, 7.4% Irish, 2.7% Scottish (2000).

Economy: Employment by occupation: 8.9% management, 10.5% professional, 22.0% services, 6.4% sales, 14.3% farming, 16.2% construction, 21.7% production (2000).

Income: Per capita income: $7,633 (2007); Median household income: $18,621 (2007); Average household income: $24,204 (2007); Percent of households with income of $100,000 or more: 2.4% (2007); Poverty rate: 51.2% (2000).

Education: Percent of population age 25 and over with: High school diploma (including GED) or higher: 40.5% (2007); Bachelor's degree or higher: 4.4% (2007); Master's degree or higher: 2.4% (2007).

School District(s)
Hernando County School District (PK-12)
   2005-06 Enrollment: 20,666 . . . . (352) 797-7001

Housing: Homeownership rate: 46.6% (2007); Median home value: $66,176 (2007); Median rent: $230 per month (2000); Median age of housing: 26 years (2000).

Transportation: Commute to work: 98.6% car, 0.0% public transportation, 1.4% walk, 0.0% work from home (2000); Travel time to work: 12.5% less than 15 minutes, 40.6% 15 to 30 minutes, 24.0% 30 to 45 minutes, 5.9% 45 to 60 minutes, 17.0% 60 minutes or more (2000)

LAND O' LAKES

LAND O' LAKES (CDP). Covers a land area of 18.616 square miles and a water area of 2.497 square miles. Located at 28.20° N. Lat.; 82.44° W. Long. Elevation is 75 feet.

Population: 13,062 (1990); 20,971 (2000); 32,805 (2007); 40,014 (2012 projected); Race: 90.5% White, 3.8% Black, 1.9% Asian, 12.5% Hispanic of any race (2007); Density: 1,762.2 persons per square mile (2007); Average household size: 2.71 (2007); Median age: 37.6 (2007); Males per 100 females: 97.5 (2007); Marriage status: 17.5% never married, 67.4% now married, 4.9% widowed, 10.2% divorced (2000); Foreign born: 4.2% (2000); Ancestry (includes multiple ancestries): 20.3% German, 18.9% Other groups, 14.7% Irish, 13.8% English, 8.7% United States or American (2000).

Economy: Employment by occupation: 14.7% management, 23.8% professional, 10.5% services, 31.7% sales, 0.1% farming, 11.0% construction, 8.2% production (2000).

Income: Per capita income: $29,005 (2007); Median household income: $68,665 (2007); Average household income: $78,484 (2007); Percent of

diploma (including GED) or higher: 89.7% (2007); Bachelor's degree or higher: 27.8% (2007); Master's degree or higher: 9.2% (2007).

School District(s)
Pasco County School District (PK-12)
  2005-06 Enrollment: 60,846 .... (813) 794-2651
Housing: Homeownership rate: 86.0% (2007); Median home value: $230,036 (2007); Median rent: $527 per month (2000); Median age of housing: 13 years (2000).
Transportation: Commute to work: 93.6% car, 0.4% public transportation, 0.8% walk, 4.1% work from home (2000); Travel time to work: 15.9% less than 15 minutes, 22.0% 15 to 30 minutes, 34.2% 30 to 45 minutes, 17.9% 45 to 60 minutes, 9.9% 60 minutes or more (2000)
Additional Information Contacts
Land O' Lakes Chamber of Commerce .... (813) 909-2722
  http://www.centralpascochamber.com

NEW PORT RICHEY (city). Covers a land area of 4.510 square miles and a water area of 0.069 square miles. Located at 28.24° N. Lat.; 82.71° W. Long. Elevation is 16 feet.
History: Named for Old Port Richey, which was named for A.M. Richey, first settler and postmaster. New Port Richey developed as a resort town, about a mile from the Old Port Richey, which in the 1880s was a port of call for schooners between Cedar Keys and Key West.
Population: 14,615 (1990); 16,117 (2000); 17,309 (2007); 18,057 (2012 projected); Race: 90.6% White, 1.9% Black, 1.4% Asian, 9.0% Hispanic of any race (2007); Density: 3,837.6 persons per square mile (2007); Average household size: 2.21 (2007); Median age: 42.8 (2007); Males per 100 females: 90.4 (2007); Marriage status: 20.7% never married, 49.5% now married, 14.5% widowed, 15.3% divorced (2000); Foreign born: 9.3% (2000); Ancestry (includes multiple ancestries): 18.0% German, 16.8% Irish, 13.3% English, 11.8% Other groups, 11.2% Italian (2000).
Economy: Single-family building permits issued: 47 (2006); Multi-family building permits issued: 0 (2006); Employment by occupation: 7.0% management, 14.0% professional, 25.4% services, 26.1% sales, 0.3% farming, 13.6% construction, 13.6% production (2000).
Income: Per capita income: $18,612 (2007); Median household income: $29,996 (2007); Average household income: $39,638 (2007); Percent of households with income of $100,000 or more: 4.5% (2007); Poverty rate: 16.6% (2000).
Taxes: Total city taxes per capita: $554 (2005); City property taxes per capita: $257 (2005).
Education: Percent of population age 25 and over with: High school diploma (including GED) or higher: 73.6% (2007); Bachelor's degree or higher: 7.7% (2007); Master's degree or higher: 2.7% (2007).

School District(s)
Pasco County School District (PK-12)
  2005-06 Enrollment: 60,846 .... (813) 794-2651
Two-year College(s)
Pasco-Hernando Community College (Public)
  Fall 2006 Enrollment: 7,547 .... (727) 847-2727
  2006-07 Tuition: In-state $1,967; Out-of-state $7,368
Vocational/Technical School(s)
Benes International School of Beauty (Private, For-profit)
  Fall 2006 Enrollment: 144 .... (727) 848-8415
  2006-07 Tuition: $12,200
Housing: Homeownership rate: 65.4% (2007); Median home value: $106,286 (2007); Median rent: $390 per month (2000); Median age of housing: 25 years (2000).
Hospitals: Community Hospital (414 beds); North Bay Medical Center (122 beds)
Safety: Violent crime rate: 126.6 per 10,000 population; Property crime rate: 581.0 per 10,000 population (2006).
Newspapers: The Suncoast News (General - Circulation 182,200); West Pasco Press (General - Circulation 1,500)
Transportation: Commute to work: 91.8% car, 0.2% public transportation, 4.7% walk, 1.0% work from home (2000); Travel time to work: 38.1% less than 15 minutes, 26.4% 15 to 30 minutes, 14.4% 30 to 45 minutes, 10.2% 45 to 60 minutes, 10.9% 60 minutes or more (2000)
Airports: Tampa Bay Executive
Additional Information Contacts
City of New Port Richey .... (727) 853-1016
  http://www.cityofnewportrichey.org

NEW PORT RICHEY EAST (CDP). Covers a land area of 3.608 square miles and a water area of 0.056 square miles. Located at 28.26° N. Lat.; 82.69° W. Long.
Population: 9,300 (1990); 9,916 (2000); 10,116 (2007); 10,311 (2012 projected); Race: 92.9% White, 1.9% Black, 1.8% Asian, 7.5% Hispanic of any race (2007); Density: 2,803.4 persons per square mile (2007); Average household size: 2.19 (2007); Median age: 41.2 (2007); Males per 100 females: 91.4 (2007); Marriage status: 20.2% never married, 54.4% now married, 13.2% widowed, 12.2% divorced (2000); Foreign born: 6.2% (2000); Ancestry (includes multiple ancestries): 21.0% German, 16.8% Irish, 12.8% Italian, 10.9% Other groups, 10.1% English (2000).
Economy: Employment by occupation: 10.7% management, 15.6% professional, 16.1% services, 36.7% sales, 0.4% farming, 9.0% construction, 11.6% production (2000).
Income: Per capita income: $19,879 (2007); Median household income: $33,868 (2007); Average household income: $43,225 (2007); Percent of households with income of $100,000 or more: 5.2% (2007); Poverty rate: 10.8% (2000).
Education: Percent of population age 25 and over with: High school diploma (including GED) or higher: 81.9% (2007); Bachelor's degree or higher: 13.0% (2007); Master's degree or higher: 3.8% (2007).
Housing: Homeownership rate: 66.5% (2007); Median home value: $137,197 (2007); Median rent: $487 per month (2000); Median age of housing: 18 years (2000).
Transportation: Commute to work: 95.0% car, 0.0% public transportation, 1.0% walk, 2.5% work from home (2000); Travel time to work: 38.4% less than 15 minutes, 29.0% 15 to 30 minutes, 15.5% 30 to 45 minutes, 7.7% 45 to 60 minutes, 9.5% 60 minutes or more (2000)

ODESSA (CDP). Covers a land area of 5.298 square miles and a water area of 0.335 square miles. Located at 28.18° N. Lat.; 82.56° W. Long. Elevation is 56 feet.
Population: 2,900 (1990); 3,173 (2000); 7,993 (2007); 10,940 (2012 projected); Race: 94.8% White, 1.0% Black, 1.1% Asian, 9.5% Hispanic of any race (2007); Density: 1,508.7 persons per square mile (2007); Average household size: 2.56 (2007); Median age: 41.0 (2007); Males per 100 females: 109.8 (2007); Marriage status: 19.1% never married, 63.9% now married, 6.8% widowed, 10.3% divorced (2000); Foreign born: 3.3% (2000); Ancestry (includes multiple ancestries): 16.0% Other groups, 11.3% United States or American, 10.5% German, 10.2% English, 9.7% Irish (2000).
Economy: Employment by occupation: 16.0% management, 13.8% professional, 13.6% services, 28.0% sales, 0.0% farming, 17.6% construction, 11.0% production (2000).
Income: Per capita income: $28,842 (2007); Median household income: $57,023 (2007); Average household income: $73,843 (2007); Percent of households with income of $100,000 or more: 22.8% (2007); Poverty rate: 6.7% (2000).
Education: Percent of population age 25 and over with: High school diploma (including GED) or higher: 80.8% (2007); Bachelor's degree or higher: 18.3% (2007); Master's degree or higher: 5.1% (2007).
School District(s)
Hillsborough County School District (PK-12)
  2005-06 Enrollment: 189,469 .... (813) 272-4050
Housing: Homeownership rate: 88.2% (2007); Median home value: $195,042 (2007); Median rent: $434 per month (2000); Median age of housing: 17 years (2000).
Transportation: Commute to work: 91.8% car, 1.9% public transportation, 0.0% walk, 5.5% work from home (2000); Travel time to work: 10.3% less than 15 minutes, 33.0% 15 to 30 minutes, 33.1% 30 to 45 minutes, 16.8% 45 to 60 minutes, 6.8% 60 minutes or more (2000)

PORT RICHEY (city). Covers a land area of 2.107 square miles and a water area of 0.630 square miles. Located at 28.27° N. Lat.; 82.72° W. Long. Elevation is 10 feet.
Population: 2,608 (1990); 3,021 (2000); 3,248 (2007); 3,364 (2012 projected); Race: 93.9% White, 1.2% Black, 1.8% Asian, 3.8% Hispanic of any race (2007); Density: 1,541.6 persons per square mile (2007); Average household size: 2.06 (2007); Median age: 48.0 (2007); Males per 100 females: 100.1 (2007); Marriage status: 17.1% never married, 52.2% now married, 14.8% widowed, 15.9% divorced (2000); Foreign born: 3.7%

farming, 16.1% construction, 8.7% production (2000).

Income: Per capita income: $21,984 (2007); Median household income: $31,331 (2007); Average household income: $43,842 (2007); Percent of households with income of $100,000 or more: 7.7% (2007); Poverty rate: 16.1% (2000).

Education: Percent of population age 25 and over with: High school diploma (including GED) or higher: 78.2% (2007); Bachelor's degree or higher: 13.4% (2007); Master's degree or higher: 5.8% (2007).

School District(s)

Pasco County School District (PK-12)

   2005-06 Enrollment: 60,846 . . . . (813) 794-2651

Housing: Homeownership rate: 68.1% (2007); Median home value: $168,527 (2007); Median rent: $395 per month (2000); Median age of housing: 23 years (2000).

Safety: Violent crime rate: 100.3 per 10,000 population; Property crime rate: 929.5 per 10,000 population (2006).

Transportation: Commute to work: 91.7% car, 0.0% public transportation, 1.7% walk, 4.6% work from home (2000); Travel time to work: 34.0% less than 15 minutes, 29.1% 15 to 30 minutes, 17.9% 30 to 45 minutes, 9.8% 45 to 60 minutes, 9.2% 60 minutes or more (2000)

SAINT LEO (town). Covers a land area of 1.609 square miles and a water area of 0.264 square miles. Located at 28.33° N. Lat.; 82.25° W. Long. Elevation is 187 feet.

History: St. Leo grew around an abbey established in 1889 by Benedictine monks and named for Pope Leo I.

Population: 1,241 (1990); 595 (2000); 719 (2007); 757 (2012 projected); Race: 80.3% White, 11.8% Black, 2.8% Asian, 14.5% Hispanic of any race (2007); Density: 446.9 persons per square mile (2007); Average household size: 11.79 (2007); Median age: 20.6 (2007); Males per 100 females: 94.3 (2007); Marriage status: 83.9% never married, 15.4% now married, 0.0% widowed, 0.7% divorced (2000); Foreign born: 6.4% (2000); Ancestry (includes multiple ancestries): 19.2% German, 17.6% United States or American, 15.3% Other groups, 14.3% Irish, 13.0% English (2000).

Economy: Single-family building permits issued: 12 (2006); Multi-family building permits issued: 0 (2006); Employment by occupation: 2.8% management, 27.1% professional, 19.4% services, 45.5% sales, 0.7% farming, 0.0% construction, 4.5% production (2000).

Income: Per capita income: $10,767 (2007); Median household income: $44,167 (2007); Average household income: $75,533 (2007); Percent of households with income of $100,000 or more: 26.2% (2007); Poverty rate: 19.9% (2000).

Education: Percent of population age 25 and over with: High school diploma (including GED) or higher: 86.3% (2007); Bachelor's degree or higher: 41.1% (2007); Master's degree or higher: 9.5% (2007).

Four-year College(s)

Saint Leo University (Private, Not-for-profit, Roman Catholic)

   Fall 2006 Enrollment: 14,179. (352) 588-8200

   2006-07 Tuition: In-state $14,996; Out-of-state $14,996

Housing: Homeownership rate: 73.8% (2007); Median home value: $446,429 (2007); Median rent: $267 per month (2000); Median age of housing: 17 years (2000).

Transportation: Commute to work: 35.3% car, 0.7% public transportation, 45.3% walk, 14.7% work from home (2000); Travel time to work: 74.7% less than 15 minutes, 13.9% 15 to 30 minutes, 7.6% 30 to 45 minutes, 1.3% 45 to 60 minutes, 2.5% 60 minutes or more (2000)

SAN ANTONIO (city). Covers a land area of 1.231 square miles and a water area of 0 square miles. Located at 28.33° N. Lat.; 82.27° W. Long. Elevation is 167 feet.

History: San Antonio was founded in the 1880's by Judge Edmund F. Dunne, former Chief Justice of Arizona, who named the town for the saint to whom he prayed when he was lost in the Arizona desert while prospecting for silver.

Population: 788 (1990); 655 (2000); 834 (2007); 942 (2012 projected); Race: 95.9% White, 0.0% Black, 1.9% Asian, 10.9% Hispanic of any race (2007); Density: 677.7 persons per square mile (2007); Average household size: 2.41 (2007); Median age: 35.6 (2007); Males per 100 females: 94.9 (2007); Marriage status: 21.2% never married, 65.4% now married, 3.9% widowed, 9.5% divorced (2000); Foreign born: 2.4% (2000); Ancestry

farming, 12.5% construction, 7.1% production (2000).

Income: Per capita income: $25,902 (2007); Median household income: $48,621 (2007); Average household income: $62,435 (2007); Percent of households with income of $100,000 or more: 18.2% (2007); Poverty rate: 10.1% (2000).

Education: Percent of population age 25 and over with: High school diploma (including GED) or higher: 92.2% (2007); Bachelor's degree or higher: 28.3% (2007); Master's degree or higher: 8.4% (2007).

School District(s)

Pasco County School District (PK-12)

   2005-06 Enrollment: 60,846 . . . . (813) 794-2651

Housing: Homeownership rate: 73.4% (2007); Median home value: $172,619 (2007); Median rent: $384 per month (2000); Median age of housing: 18 years (2000).

Transportation: Commute to work: 93.6% car, 0.0% public transportation, 3.5% walk, 2.9% work from home (2000); Travel time to work: 36.8% less than 15 minutes, 26.2% 15 to 30 minutes, 19.5% 30 to 45 minutes, 13.2% 45 to 60 minutes, 4.3% 60 minutes or more (2000)

SHADY HILLS (CDP). Covers a land area of 26.170 square miles and a water area of 1.225 square miles. Located at 28.40° N. Lat.; 82.54° W. Long. Elevation is 52 feet.

Population: 7,197 (1990); 7,798 (2000); 9,042 (2007); 9,828 (2012 projected); Race: 95.3% White, 1.2% Black, 0.2% Asian, 5.7% Hispanic of any race (2007); Density: 345.5 persons per square mile (2007); Average household size: 2.72 (2007); Median age: 37.1 (2007); Males per 100 females: 97.5 (2007); Marriage status: 20.4% never married, 62.5% now married, 6.9% widowed, 10.1% divorced (2000); Foreign born: 4.6% (2000); Ancestry (includes multiple ancestries): 17.7% German, 16.2% Irish, 15.5% United States or American, 11.1% Other groups, 9.8% English (2000).

Economy: Employment by occupation: 9.8% management, 12.6% professional, 22.4% services, 24.2% sales, 0.2% farming, 16.9% construction, 13.9% production (2000).

Income: Per capita income: $18,538 (2007); Median household income: $42,170 (2007); Average household income: $50,336 (2007); Percent of households with income of $100,000 or more: 8.3% (2007); Poverty rate: 13.6% (2000).

Education: Percent of population age 25 and over with: High school diploma (including GED) or higher: 76.1% (2007); Bachelor's degree or higher: 7.7% (2007); Master's degree or higher: 2.4% (2007).

Housing: Homeownership rate: 86.9% (2007); Median home value: $145,304 (2007); Median rent: $404 per month (2000); Median age of housing: 16 years (2000).

Transportation: Commute to work: 93.1% car, 0.4% public transportation, 1.2% walk, 2.5% work from home (2000); Travel time to work: 10.5% less than 15 minutes, 28.5% 15 to 30 minutes, 28.5% 30 to 45 minutes, 12.2% 45 to 60 minutes, 20.3% 60 minutes or more (2000)

TRINITY (CDP). Covers a land area of 4.721 square miles and a water area of 0 square miles. Located at 28.17° N. Lat.; 82.67° W. Long. Elevation is 20 feet.

Population: 1,141 (1990); 4,279 (2000); 6,581 (2007); 7,991 (2012 projected); Race: 93.8% White, 2.2% Black, 2.4% Asian, 3.8% Hispanic of any race (2007); Density: 1,393.9 persons per square mile (2007); Average household size: 2.49 (2007); Median age: 46.0 (2007); Males per 100 females: 92.3 (2007); Marriage status: 11.8% never married, 76.9% now married, 6.9% widowed, 4.3% divorced (2000); Foreign born: 9.4% (2000); Ancestry (includes multiple ancestries): 20.1% Italian, 17.6% Irish, 15.8% German, 14.7% English, 9.2% Other groups (2000).

Economy: Employment by occupation: 20.2% management, 25.4% professional, 8.9% services, 35.6% sales, 0.5% farming, 3.2% construction, 6.2% production (2000).

Income: Per capita income: $39,364 (2007); Median household income: $76,424 (2007); Average household income: $97,868 (2007); Percent of households with income of $100,000 or more: 34.7% (2007); Poverty rate: 2.1% (2000).

Education: Percent of population age 25 and over with: High school diploma (including GED) or higher: 92.4% (2007); Bachelor's degree or higher: 34.2% (2007); Master's degree or higher: 12.3% (2007).

Trinity College of Florida (Private, Not-for-profit, Interdenominational)
    Fall 2006 Enrollment: 182 . . . . (727) 376-6911
    2006-07 Tuition: In-state $9,120; Out-of-state $9,120
Housing: Homeownership rate: 98.0% (2007); Median home value: $373,923 (2007); Median rent: $1,110 per month (2000); Median age of housing: 3 years (2000).
Transportation: Commute to work: 93.8% car, 0.0% public transportation, 0.0% walk, 4.2% work from home (2000); Travel time to work: 11.5% less than 15 minutes, 29.1% 15 to 30 minutes, 26.7% 30 to 45 minutes, 23.2% 45 to 60 minutes, 9.5% 60 minutes or more (2000)

WESLEY CHAPEL (CDP).
Covers a land area of 6.057 square miles and a water area of 0.027 square miles. Located at 28.17° N. Lat.; 82.35° W. Long. Elevation is 108 feet.
Population: 1,928 (1990); 5,691 (2000); 12,775 (2007); 17,121 (2012 projected); Race: 68.1% White, 14.8% Black, 8.4% Asian, 19.2% Hispanic of any race (2007); Density: 2,109.0 persons per square mile (2007); Average household size: 2.84 (2007); Median age: 34.4 (2007); Males per 100 females: 95.8 (2007); Marriage status: 16.1% never married, 73.0% now married, 3.8% widowed, 7.0% divorced (2000); Foreign born: 11.5% (2000); Ancestry (includes multiple ancestries): 26.3% Other groups, 15.5% German, 14.4% Irish, 10.1% Italian, 9.1% English (2000).
Economy: Employment by occupation: 22.3% management, 30.2% professional, 8.5% services, 31.3% sales, 0.6% farming, 3.1% construction, 4.0% production (2000).
Income: Per capita income: $33,608 (2007); Median household income: $84,344 (2007); Average household income: $95,580 (2007); Percent of households with income of $100,000 or more: 34.5% (2007); Poverty rate: 1.9% (2000).
Education: Percent of population age 25 and over with: High school diploma (including GED) or higher: 95.4% (2007); Bachelor's degree or higher: 42.5% (2007); Master's degree or higher: 14.8% (2007).
School District(s)
Pasco County School District (PK-12)
    2005-06 Enrollment: 60,846 . . . . (813) 794-2651
Housing: Homeownership rate: 97.4% (2007); Median home value: $266,234 (2007); Median rent: $1,069 per month (2000); Median age of housing: 4 years (2000).
Transportation: Commute to work: 96.8% car, 0.0% public transportation, 0.3% walk, 2.1% work from home (2000); Travel time to work: 10.6% less than 15 minutes, 31.2% 15 to 30 minutes, 31.4% 30 to 45 minutes, 13.2% 45 to 60 minutes, 13.6% 60 minutes or more (2000)

WESLEY CHAPEL SOUTH (CDP).
Covers a land area of 11.131 square miles and a water area of 0.032 square miles. Located at 28.24° N. Lat.; 82.32° W. Long.
Population: 1,656 (1990); 3,245 (2000); 8,399 (2007); 11,564 (2012 projected); Race: 90.0% White, 2.4% Black, 2.7% Asian, 8.9% Hispanic of any race (2007); Density: 754.6 persons per square mile (2007); Average household size: 2.55 (2007); Median age: 40.1 (2007); Males per 100 females: 98.7 (2007); Marriage status: 18.5% never married, 66.0% now married, 4.1% widowed, 11.5% divorced (2000); Foreign born: 7.3% (2000); Ancestry (includes multiple ancestries): 20.4% Other groups, 19.0% German, 16.3% English, 14.5% United States or American, 13.4% Irish (2000).
Economy: Employment by occupation: 15.0% management, 21.9% professional, 15.3% services, 25.2% sales, 0.4% farming, 11.9% construction, 10.4% production (2000).
Income: Per capita income: $32,290 (2007); Median household income: $65,243 (2007); Average household income: $82,358 (2007); Percent of households with income of $100,000 or more: 23.7% (2007); Poverty rate: 6.6% (2000).
Education: Percent of population age 25 and over with: High school diploma (including GED) or higher: 86.8% (2007); Bachelor's degree or higher: 24.9% (2007); Master's degree or higher: 9.6% (2007).
Housing: Homeownership rate: 92.0% (2007); Median home value: $214,991 (2007); Median rent: $506 per month (2000); Median age of housing: 11 years (2000).
Transportation: Commute to work: 91.4% car, 0.0% public transportation, 0.0% walk, 4.9% work from home (2000); Travel time to work: 16.1% less than 15 minutes, 33.0% 15 to 30 minutes, 29.7% 30 to 45 minutes, 12.2% 45 to 60 minutes, 9.0% 60 minutes or more (2000)

ZEPHYRHILLS (city).
Covers a land area of 6.268 square miles and a water area of 0.074 square miles. Located at 28.23° N. Lat.; 82.18° W. Long. Elevation is 95 feet.
History: The site of Zephyrhills was chosen by Captain H.B. Jefferies, a Union army officer, as a home for veterans. The town was known as Abbott's Station until 1915.
Population: 8,770 (1990); 10,833 (2000); 11,931 (2007); 12,614 (2012 projected); Race: 87.8% White, 5.0% Black, 1.8% Asian, 8.6% Hispanic of any race (2007); Density: 1,903.4 persons per square mile (2007); Average household size: 2.17 (2007); Median age: 43.7 (2007); Males per 100 females: 85.5 (2007); Marriage status: 12.6% never married, 59.2% now married, 14.7% widowed, 13.5% divorced (2000); Foreign born: 6.2% (2000); Ancestry (includes multiple ancestries): 19.2% German, 16.6% English, 13.0% United States or American, 12.6% Irish, 12.3% Other groups (2000).
Economy: Single-family building permits issued: 107 (2006); Multi-family building permits issued: 4 (2006); Employment by occupation: 9.8% management, 13.0% professional, 20.1% services, 34.0% sales, 0.9% farming, 10.6% construction, 11.6% production (2000).
Income: Per capita income: $20,026 (2007); Median household income: $31,673 (2007); Average household income: $42,234 (2007); Percent of households with income of $100,000 or more: 5.1% (2007); Poverty rate: 12.1% (2000).
Taxes: Total city taxes per capita: $503 (2005); City property taxes per capita: $239 (2005).
Education: Percent of population age 25 and over with: High school diploma (including GED) or higher: 74.5% (2007); Bachelor's degree or higher: 9.8% (2007); Master's degree or higher: 3.6% (2007).
School District(s)
Pasco County School District (PK-12)
    2005-06 Enrollment: 60,846 . . . . (813) 794-2651
Housing: Homeownership rate: 69.9% (2007); Median home value: $119,911 (2007); Median rent: $376 per month (2000); Median age of housing: 21 years (2000).
Hospitals: East Pasco Medical Center (154 beds)
Safety: Violent crime rate: 51.3 per 10,000 population; Property crime rate: 654.6 per 10,000 population (2006).
Newspapers: Zephyrhills News (General - Circulation 5,000)
Transportation: Commute to work: 94.0% car, 0.1% public transportation, 2.7% walk, 2.5% work from home (2000); Travel time to work: 35.9% less than 15 minutes, 23.8% 15 to 30 minutes, 20.6% 30 to 45 minutes, 10.1% 45 to 60 minutes, 9.5% 60 minutes or more (2000)
Additional Information Contacts
City of Zephyrhills . . . . (813) 780-0000
    http://www.ci.zephyrhills.fl.us

ZEPHYRHILLS NORTH (CDP).
Covers a land area of 1.078 square miles and a water area of 0 square miles. Located at 28.25° N. Lat.; 82.16° W. Long.
Population: 2,272 (1990); 2,544 (2000); 2,754 (2007); 2,883 (2012 projected); Race: 91.0% White, 1.6% Black, 2.1% Asian, 6.1% Hispanic of any race (2007); Density: 2,554.8 persons per square mile (2007); Average household size: 1.93 (2007); Median age: 62.0 (2007); Males per 100 females: 81.7 (2007); Marriage status: 12.6% never married, 66.9% now married, 13.3% widowed, 7.2% divorced (2000); Foreign born: 5.1% (2000); Ancestry (includes multiple ancestries): 20.5% German, 15.9% English, 13.4% United States or American, 9.7% Irish, 8.4% French (except Basque) (2000).
Economy: Employment by occupation: 6.0% management, 13.9% professional, 17.2% services, 34.2% sales, 0.0% farming, 7.5% construction, 21.2% production (2000).
Income: Per capita income: $20,682 (2007); Median household income: $35,909 (2007); Average household income: $39,998 (2007); Percent of households with income of $100,000 or more: 4.6% (2007); Poverty rate: 10.7% (2000).
Education: Percent of population age 25 and over with: High school diploma (including GED) or higher: 75.4% (2007); Bachelor's degree or higher: 7.8% (2007); Master's degree or higher: 2.9% (2007).
Housing: Homeownership rate: 84.7% (2007); Median home value: $83,776 (2007); Median rent: $356 per month (2000); Median age of housing: 18 years (2000).
Transportation: Commute to work: 93.3% car, 0.0% public transportation, 3.5% walk, 0.0% work from home (2000); Travel time to work: 45.2% less

ZEPHYRHILLS SOUTH (CDP).

Covers a land area of 1.918 square miles and a water area of 0 square miles. Located at 28.21° N. Lat.; 82.18° W. Long.

Population: 3,461 (1990); 4,435 (2000); 5,486 (2007); 6,169 (2012 projected); Race: 93.9% White, 1.6% Black, 0.4% Asian, 4.6% Hispanic of any race (2007); Density: 2,859.7 persons per square mile (2007); Average household size: 1.98 (2007); Median age: 58.9 (2007); Males per 100 females: 93.0 (2007); Marriage status: 8.0% never married, 67.2% now married, 13.4% widowed, 11.4% divorced (2000); Foreign born: 6.9% (2000); Ancestry (includes multiple ancestries): 15.7% German, 13.8% English, 12.5% Irish, 9.7% Other groups, 8.9% United States or American (2000).

Economy: Employment by occupation: 7.2% management, 10.7% professional, 19.7% services, 31.4% sales, 1.8% farming, 10.7% construction, 18.4% production (2000).

Income: Per capita income: $16,886 (2007); Median household income: $26,479 (2007); Average household income: $33,459 (2007); Percent of households with income of $100,000 or more: 2.2% (2007); Poverty rate: 12.5% (2000).

Education: Percent of population age 25 and over with: High school diploma (including GED) or higher: 70.1% (2007); Bachelor's degree or higher: 6.3% (2007); Master's degree or higher: 1.7% (2007).

Housing: Homeownership rate: 88.4% (2007); Median home value: $68,043 (2007); Median rent: $356 per month (2000); Median age of housing: 17 years (2000).

Transportation: Commute to work: 93.5% car, 0.5% public transportation, 2.9% walk, 1.8% work from home (2000); Travel time to work: 33.2% less than 15 minutes, 28.9% 15 to 30 minutes, 20.1% 30 to 45 minutes, 11.9% 45 to 60 minutes, 5.8% 60 minutes or more (2000)

ZEPHYRHILLS WEST (CDP).

Covers a land area of 2.656 square miles and a water area of 0 square miles. Located at 28.23° N. Lat.; 82.20° W. Long.

Population: 4,746 (1990); 5,242 (2000); 5,855 (2007); 6,259 (2012 projected); Race: 96.2% White, 0.5% Black, 0.9% Asian, 3.9% Hispanic of any race (2007); Density: 2,204.2 persons per square mile (2007); Average household size: 1.87 (2007); Median age: 66.1 (2007); Males per 100 females: 86.6 (2007); Marriage status: 6.6% never married, 67.9% now married, 16.8% widowed, 8.7% divorced (2000); Foreign born: 6.8% (2000); Ancestry (includes multiple ancestries): 20.4% English, 18.0% German, 14.7% United States or American, 9.6% Irish, 5.7% French (except Basque) (2000).

Economy: Employment by occupation: 10.0% management, 10.3% professional, 20.8% services, 30.4% sales, 0.8% farming, 17.3% construction, 10.4% production (2000).

Income: Per capita income: $20,671 (2007); Median household income: $30,293 (2007); Average household income: $38,716 (2007); Percent of households with income of $100,000 or more: 3.6% (2007); Poverty rate: 10.7% (2000).

Education: Percent of population age 25 and over with: High school diploma (including GED) or higher: 74.7% (2007); Bachelor's degree or higher: 12.0% (2007); Master's degree or higher: 2.6% (2007).

Housing: Homeownership rate: 89.9% (2007); Median home value: $96,812 (2007); Median rent: $407 per month (2000); Median age of housing: 21 years (2000).

Transportation: Commute to work: 90.0% car, 0.0% public transportation, 2.1% walk, 4.9% work from home (2000); Travel time to work: 49.2% less than 15 minutes, 17.6% 15 to 30 minutes, 14.6% 30 to 45 minutes, 7.9% 45 to 60 minutes, 10.7% 60 minutes or more (2000)

Pinellas County

Located in western Florida; on the Pinellas Peninsula, bounded on the west by the Gulf of Mexico, and on the east by Tampa Bay; includes Long Key and a chain of barrier islands, and Butler Lake. Covers a land area of 279.92 square miles, a water area of 327.75 square miles, and is located in the Eastern Time Zone. The county was founded in 1911. County seat is Clearwater.

Pinellas County is part of the Tampa-St. Petersburg-Clearwater, FL Metropolitan Statistical Area. The entire metro area includes: Hernando

Weather Station: Saint Petersburg — Elevation: 6 feet

	Jan	Feb	Mar	Apr	May	Jun	Jul	Aug	Sep	Oct	Nov	Dec
High	70	72	76	81	86	89	91	90	89	84	77	72
Low	54	56	60	65	71	75	77	77	76	70	63	57
Precip	2.8	3.0	3.5	1.9	2.9	6.0	6.3	8.1	7.5	2.7	2.0	2.6
Snow	tr	0.0	0.0	0.0	0.0	0.0	0.0	0.0	0.0	0.0	0.0	0.0

High and Low temperatures in degrees Fahrenheit; Precipitation and Snow in inches

Weather Station: Tarpon Springs Sewage Plant — Elevation: 6 feet

	Jan	Feb	Mar	Apr	May	Jun	Jul	Aug	Sep	Oct	Nov	Dec
High	71	73	77	82	87	90	91	91	90	85	79	74
Low	50	52	56	61	67	72	73	73	72	65	58	52
Precip	3.3	3.3	4.1	2.0	3.2	5.7	6.7	8.3	7.0	3.4	2.4	3.0
Snow	0.0	0.0	0.0	0.0	0.0	0.0	0.0	0.0	0.0	0.0	0.0	0.0

High and Low temperatures in degrees Fahrenheit; Precipitation and Snow in inches

Population: 851,659 (1990); 921,482 (2000); 938,397 (2007); 958,280 (2012 projected); Race: 83.0% White, 10.1% Black, 2.7% Asian, 6.6% Hispanic of any race (2007); Density: 3,352.4 persons per square mile (2007); Average household size: 2.22 (2007); Median age: 44.9 (2007); Males per 100 females: 92.2 (2007).

Religion: Five largest groups: 12.2% Catholic Church, 4.4% The United Methodist Church, 3.9% Southern Baptist Convention, 2.6% Jewish Estimate, 1.3% Presbyterian Church (U.S.A.) (2000).

Economy: Unemployment rate: 4.2% (11/2007); Total civilian labor force: 489,207 (11/2007); Leading industries: 16.8% health care and social assistance; 14.2% retail trade; 10.2% accommodation & food services (2005); Farms: 111 totaling 1,589 acres (2002); Companies that employ 500 or more persons: 74 (2005); Companies that employ 100 to 499 persons: 574 (2005); Companies that employ less than 100 persons: 27,634 (2005); Black-owned businesses: 3,085 (2002); Hispanic-owned businesses: 2,884 (2002); Asian-owned businesses: 2,224 (2002); Women-owned businesses: 23,631 (2002); Retail sales per capita: $17,700 (2007). Single-family building permits issued: 1,786 (2006); Multi-family building permits issued: 394 (2006).

Income: Per capita income: $27,789 (2007); Median household income: $43,584 (2007); Average household income: $60,763 (2007); Percent of households with income of $100,000 or more: 14.3% (2007); Poverty rate: 11.2% (2005); Bankruptcy rate: 1.87% (2006).

Taxes: Total county taxes per capita: $545 (2005); County property taxes per capita: $410 (2005).

Education: Percent of population age 25 and over with: High school diploma (including GED) or higher: 84.2% (2007); Bachelor's degree or higher: 23.2% (2007); Master's degree or higher: 8.0% (2007).

Housing: Homeownership rate: 70.8% (2007); Median home value: $171,177 (2007); Median rent: $524 per month (2000); Median age of housing: 27 years (2000).

Health: Birth rate: 104.4 per 10,000 population (2006); Death rate: 132.2 per 10,000 population (2006); Age-adjusted cancer mortality rate: 192.5 deaths per 100,000 population (2004); Air Quality Index: 87.1% good, 12.1% moderate, 0.8% unhealthy for sensitive individuals, 0.0% unhealthy (percent of days in 2006); Number of physicians: 30.1 per 10,000 population (2005); Hospital beds: 45.1 per 10,000 population (2004); Hospital admissions: 1,736.5 per 10,000 population (2004).

Elections: 2004 Presidential election results: 49.6% Bush, 49.5% Kerry, 0.5% Nader, 0.2% Badnarik

National and State Parks: Caladesi Island State Park; Honeymoon Island State Park; Pinellas County State Aquatic Preserve; Pinellas National Wildlife Refuge; Weedon Island State Preserve

Additional Information Contacts

Pinellas County Government . . . . (727) 464-3377
   http://www.pinellascounty.org
City of Dunedin . . . . (727) 298-3034
   http://www.dunedingov.com
City of Gulfport . . . . (727) 893-1000
   http://www.ci.gulfport.fl.us
City of Indian Rocks Beach . . . . (727) 595-2517
   http://www.indian-rocks-beach.com
City of Largo . . . . (727) 587-6700
   http://www.largo.com
City of Oldsmar . . . . (813) 749-1115
   http://ci.oldsmar.fl.us
City of Pinellas Park . . . . (727) 541-0700
   http://www.pinellas-park.com

City of Safety Harbor . . . . (727) 724-1555
   http://www.cityofsafetyharbor.com
City of Saint Pete Beach . . . . (727) 367-2735
   http://www.stpetebeach.org
City of Seminole . . . . (727) 391-0204
   http://www.city-seminole.org
City of South Pasadena . . . . (727) 347-4171
   http://ci.south-pasadena.fl.us
City of Tarpon Springs . . . . (727) 938-3711
   http://www.tarponsprings.com
City of Treasure Island . . . . (727) 547-4575
   http://www.ci.treasure-island.fl.us
Clearwater Beach Chamber . . . . (727) 447-7600
   http://www.beachchamber.com
Clearwater Chamber of Commerce . . . . (727) 461-0011
   http://www.clearwaterflorida.org
Dunedin Chamber of Commerce . . . . (727) 733-3197
   http://www.dunedin-fl.com
Gulf Beaches Chamber of Commerce . . . . (727) 595-4575
Gulf Beaches-Tampa Bay Chamber . . . . (727) 360-6957
   http://www.tampabaybeaches.com
Largo Chamber of Commerce . . . . (727) 584-2321
   http://www.largochamber.com
Oldsmar Chamber of Commerce . . . . (813) 855-4233
   http://www.oldsmarchamber.org
Palm Harbor Area Chamber of Commerce . . . . (727) 784-4287
   http://www.palmharborcc.org
Pinellas Park Chamber of Commerce . . . . (727) 544-4777
   http://www.pinellasparkchamber.com
Safety Harbor Chamber of Commerce . . . . (727) 726-2890
   http://www.safetyharborchamber.com
Seminole Chamber of Commerce . . . . (727) 392-3245
   http://seminolechamber.net
St. Petersburg Chamber of Commerce . . . . (727) 821-4069
   http://www.stpete.com
Suncoast Welcome Center . . . . (727) 726-1547
   http://www.visitclearwaterflorida.com/visitor_center.php
Tarpon Springs Chamber of Commerce . . . . (727) 937-6109
   http://www.tarponspringschamber.org

Pinellas County Communities

BAY PINES (CDP). Covers a land area of 1.394 square miles and a water area of 0.856 square miles. Located at 27.81° N. Lat.; 82.77° W. Long. Elevation is 10 feet.
Population: 3,698 (1990); 3,065 (2000); 2,811 (2007); 2,686 (2012 projected); Race: 97.4% White, 0.2% Black, 0.5% Asian, 3.2% Hispanic of any race (2007); Density: 2,016.7 persons per square mile (2007); Average household size: 2.07 (2007); Median age: 51.6 (2007); Males per 100 females: 92.1 (2007); Marriage status: 15.9% never married, 59.0% now married, 10.8% widowed, 14.3% divorced (2000); Foreign born: 5.9% (2000); Ancestry (includes multiple ancestries): 19.7% German, 16.0% Irish, 13.0% English, 11.6% Italian, 8.3% Other groups (2000).
Economy: Employment by occupation: 14.1% management, 20.3% professional, 14.7% services, 29.1% sales, 0.0% farming, 11.7% construction, 10.2% production (2000).
Income: Per capita income: $26,103 (2007); Median household income: $40,571 (2007); Average household income: $54,111 (2007); Percent of households with income of $100,000 or more: 10.5% (2007); Poverty rate: 3.5% (2000).
Education: Percent of population age 25 and over with: High school diploma (including GED) or higher: 87.1% (2007); Bachelor's degree or higher: 21.5% (2007); Master's degree or higher: 6.2% (2007).
Housing: Homeownership rate: 91.8% (2007); Median home value: $169,252 (2007); Median rent: $479 per month (2000); Median age of housing: 32 years (2000).
Hospitals: Bay Pines VA Healthcare System (469 beds)
Transportation: Commute to work: 93.8% car, 1.1% public transportation, 0.9% walk, 1.2% work from home (2000); Travel time to work: 30.6% less than 15 minutes, 45.4% 15 to 30 minutes, 18.4% 30 to 45 minutes, 3.8% 45 to 60 minutes, 1.8% 60 minutes or more (2000)

BELLEAIR (town). Covers a land area of 1.795 square miles and a water area of 1.019 square miles. Located at 27.93° N. Lat.; 82.81° W. Long. Elevation is 46 feet.

History: Belleair was incorporated in 1925, but the Belleview Hotel was built here in 1896 by Henry Plant with a spur of the Atlantic Coast Line Railroad running to the hotel entrance.
Population: 3,951 (1990); 4,067 (2000); 4,273 (2007); 4,454 (2012 projected); Race: 97.8% White, 0.2% Black, 0.5% Asian, 3.5% Hispanic of any race (2007); Density: 2,380.6 persons per square mile (2007); Average household size: 2.08 (2007); Median age: 53.5 (2007); Males per 100 females: 86.5 (2007); Marriage status: 13.2% never married, 65.4% now married, 13.7% widowed, 7.6% divorced (2000); Foreign born: 8.6% (2000); Ancestry (includes multiple ancestries): 21.9% English, 20.0% German, 15.9% Irish, 9.4% Other groups, 7.8% United States or American (2000).
Economy: Single-family building permits issued: 6 (2006); Multi-family building permits issued: 0 (2006); Employment by occupation: 24.4% management, 27.5% professional, 7.5% services, 32.4% sales, 0.0% farming, 3.4% construction, 4.8% production (2000).
Income: Per capita income: $60,375 (2007); Median household income: $79,861 (2007); Average household income: $122,515 (2007); Percent of households with income of $100,000 or more: 40.8% (2007); Poverty rate: 4.0% (2000).
Taxes: Total city taxes per capita: $994 (2005); City property taxes per capita: $654 (2005).
Education: Percent of population age 25 and over with: High school diploma (including GED) or higher: 95.8% (2007); Bachelor's degree or higher: 48.6% (2007); Master's degree or higher: 18.9% (2007).
Housing: Homeownership rate: 88.7% (2007); Median home value: $372,085 (2007); Median rent: $723 per month (2000); Median age of housing: 32 years (2000).
Safety: Violent crime rate: 2.4 per 10,000 population; Property crime rate: 132.1 per 10,000 population (2006).
Transportation: Commute to work: 87.7% car, 1.0% public transportation, 0.0% walk, 10.7% work from home (2000); Travel time to work: 41.7% less than 15 minutes, 31.4% 15 to 30 minutes, 11.9% 30 to 45 minutes, 8.2% 45 to 60 minutes, 6.8% 60 minutes or more (2000)

BELLEAIR BEACH (city). Covers a land area of 0.577 square miles and a water area of 1.152 square miles. Located at 27.92° N. Lat.; 82.83° W. Long. Elevation is 3 feet.
Population: 2,070 (1990); 1,751 (2000); 1,801 (2007); 1,853 (2012 projected); Race: 95.6% White, 0.3% Black, 2.1% Asian, 3.6% Hispanic of any race (2007); Density: 3,123.9 persons per square mile (2007); Average household size: 2.08 (2007); Median age: 53.8 (2007); Males per 100 females: 101.5 (2007); Marriage status: 12.6% never married, 68.7% now married, 6.6% widowed, 12.2% divorced (2000); Foreign born: 16.5% (2000); Ancestry (includes multiple ancestries): 23.8% German, 18.3% Irish, 15.2% English, 10.6% United States or American, 7.9% Other groups (2000).
Economy: Employment by occupation: 31.3% management, 20.6% professional, 13.1% services, 29.7% sales, 0.0% farming, 1.0% construction, 4.3% production (2000).
Income: Per capita income: $58,194 (2007); Median household income: $77,902 (2007); Average household income: $121,305 (2007); Percent of households with income of $100,000 or more: 38.5% (2007); Poverty rate: 7.8% (2000).
Education: Percent of population age 25 and over with: High school diploma (including GED) or higher: 95.3% (2007); Bachelor's degree or higher: 52.4% (2007); Master's degree or higher: 17.6% (2007).
Housing: Homeownership rate: 87.6% (2007); Median home value: $468,667 (2007); Median rent: $981 per month (2000); Median age of housing: 27 years (2000).
Safety: Violent crime rate: 6.0 per 10,000 population; Property crime rate: 96.7 per 10,000 population (2006).
Transportation: Commute to work: 96.0% car, 0.0% public transportation, 0.0% walk, 1.4% work from home (2000); Travel time to work: 24.8% less than 15 minutes, 44.8% 15 to 30 minutes, 17.4% 30 to 45 minutes, 10.3% 45 to 60 minutes, 2.8% 60 minutes or more (2000)

BELLEAIR BLUFFS (city). Covers a land area of 0.462 square miles and a water area of 0.164 square miles. Located at 27.92° N. Lat.; 82.81° W. Long. Elevation is 46 feet.
Population: 2,128 (1990); 2,243 (2000); 2,172 (2007); 2,125 (2012 projected); Race: 97.1% White, 0.2% Black, 1.5% Asian, 1.7% Hispanic of any race (2007); Density: 4,703.9 persons per square mile (2007); Average household size: 1.67 (2007); Median age: 59.7 (2007); Males per 100 females: 78.9 (2007); Marriage status: 15.5% never married, 50.9% now

married, 17.3% widowed, 16.3% divorced (2000); Foreign born: 6.7% (2000); Ancestry (includes multiple ancestries): 18.9% English, 16.9% Irish, 16.9% German, 5.8% Italian, 5.5% United States or American (2000).
Economy: Employment by occupation: 19.2% management, 21.9% professional, 17.3% services, 26.8% sales, 0.0% farming, 6.8% construction, 8.1% production (2000).
Income: Per capita income: $35,173 (2007); Median household income: $37,013 (2007); Average household income: $58,615 (2007); Percent of households with income of $100,000 or more: 11.6% (2007); Poverty rate: 6.1% (2000).
Education: Percent of population age 25 and over with: High school diploma (including GED) or higher: 90.1% (2007); Bachelor's degree or higher: 28.0% (2007); Master's degree or higher: 9.1% (2007).
Housing: Homeownership rate: 68.3% (2007); Median home value: $203,299 (2007); Median rent: $475 per month (2000); Median age of housing: 30 years (2000).
Safety: Violent crime rate: 53.1 per 10,000 population; Property crime rate: 234.3 per 10,000 population (2006).
Transportation: Commute to work: 89.0% car, 0.5% public transportation, 3.3% walk, 5.6% work from home (2000); Travel time to work: 35.2% less than 15 minutes, 38.9% 15 to 30 minutes, 12.4% 30 to 45 minutes, 9.1% 45 to 60 minutes, 4.4% 60 minutes or more (2000)

CLEARWATER (city). County seat. Covers a land area of 25.287 square miles and a water area of 12.437 square miles. Located at 27.97° N. Lat.; 82.76° W. Long. Elevation is 30 feet.
History: Named for the local waters of the Gulf of Mexico. Clearwater had its beginning in Fort Harrison, established here in 1841. The town was incorporated as Clearwater in 1891, and grew as a center for fruit and fruit juice canning. When Pinellas County was separated out from Hillsborough County in 1912, Clearwater acted faster than St. Petersburg in providing a courthouse, and became the county seat.
Population: 100,872 (1990); 108,787 (2000); 108,660 (2007); 109,635 (2012 projected); Race: 81.0% White, 10.6% Black, 2.0% Asian, 13.5% Hispanic of any race (2007); Density: 4,297.0 persons per square mile (2007); Average household size: 2.25 (2007); Median age: 43.5 (2007); Males per 100 females: 93.2 (2007); Marriage status: 24.4% never married, 50.9% now married, 9.9% widowed, 14.8% divorced (2000); Foreign born: 13.2% (2000); Ancestry (includes multiple ancestries): 21.5% Other groups, 16.9% German, 13.8% Irish, 11.9% English, 8.0% Italian (2000).
Economy: Unemployment rate: 3.8% (11/2007); Total civilian labor force: 58,760 (11/2007); Single-family building permits issued: 108 (2006); Multi-family building permits issued: 2 (2006); Employment by occupation: 14.5% management, 19.6% professional, 16.3% services, 31.0% sales, 0.3% farming, 7.8% construction, 10.5% production (2000).
Income: Per capita income: $26,570 (2007); Median household income: $42,974 (2007); Average household income: $58,296 (2007); Percent of households with income of $100,000 or more: 13.5% (2007); Poverty rate: 12.3% (2000).
Taxes: Total city taxes per capita: $552 (2005); City property taxes per capita: $342 (2005).
Education: Percent of population age 25 and over with: High school diploma (including GED) or higher: 84.6% (2007); Bachelor's degree or higher: 24.1% (2007); Master's degree or higher: 8.5% (2007).

School District(s)
Pinellas County School District (PK-12)
    2005-06 Enrollment: 113,651 . . . . (727) 588-6011
Four-year College(s)
Clearwater Christian College (Private, Not-for-profit, Undenominational)
    Fall 2006 Enrollment: 586 . . . . (727) 726-1153
    2006-07 Tuition: In-state $11,860; Out-of-state $11,860
Florida Metropolitan University-Pinellas (Private, For-profit)
    Fall 2006 Enrollment: 838 . . . . (727) 725-2688
    2006-07 Tuition: In-state $10,440; Out-of-state $10,440
St Petersburg College (Public)
    Fall 2006 Enrollment: 24,558. . . . . (727) 341-4772
    2006-07 Tuition: In-state $2,091; Out-of-state $7,559
Two-year College(s)
Edutech Centers (Private, For-profit)
    Fall 2006 Enrollment: 532 . . . . (727) 724-1037
    2006-07 Tuition: In-state $8,460; Out-of-state $8,460
National Aviation Academy A & P School (Private, For-profit)
    Fall 2006 Enrollment: 233 . . . . (727) 531-2080
Pinellas Technical Education Center-Clearwater (Public)
    Fall 2006 Enrollment: 969 . . . . (727) 538-7167

Vocational/Technical School(s)
Sunstate Academy (Private, For-profit)
    Fall 2006 Enrollment: 113 . . . . (727) 538-3827
    2006-07 Tuition: $13,975
Ultimate Medical Academy (Private, For-profit)
    Fall 2006 Enrollment: 210 . . . . (727) 298-8685
    2006-07 Tuition: $8,488
Housing: Homeownership rate: 62.2% (2007); Median home value: $181,218 (2007); Median rent: $538 per month (2000); Median age of housing: 27 years (2000).
Hospitals: Morton Plant Health System Rehabilitation Center (120 beds); Morton Plant Hospital (687 beds); Windmoor Healthcare of Clearwater (163 beds)
Safety: Violent crime rate: 78.0 per 10,000 population; Property crime rate: 437.7 per 10,000 population (2006).
Newspapers: Clearwater Gazette and Beach Views (General - Circulation 17,000)
Transportation: Commute to work: 86.7% car, 3.9% public transportation, 3.0% walk, 4.1% work from home (2000); Travel time to work: 31.1% less than 15 minutes, 39.6% 15 to 30 minutes, 18.8% 30 to 45 minutes, 6.0% 45 to 60 minutes, 4.5% 60 minutes or more (2000)
Additional Information Contacts
Clearwater Beach Chamber. . . . . (727) 447-7600
    http://www.beachchamber.com
Clearwater Chamber of Commerce . . . . (727) 461-0011
    http://www.clearwaterflorida.org
Suncoast Welcome Center . . . . (727) 726-1547
    http://www.visitclearwaterflorida.com/visitor_center.php

CLEARWATER BEACH (unincorporated postal area, zip code 33767). Covers a land area of 3.084 square miles and a water area of 0 square miles. Located at 27.96° N. Lat.; 82.82° W. Long. Elevation is 5 feet.
Population: 9,765 (2000); Race: 98.7% White, 0.0% Black, 0.3% Asian, 2.1% Hispanic of any race (2000); Density: 3,166.3 persons per square mile (2000); Age: 6.6% under 18, 36.9% over 64 (2000); Marriage status: 12.5% never married, 62.5% now married, 9.4% widowed, 15.6% divorced (2000); Foreign born: 14.2% (2000); Ancestry (includes multiple ancestries): 19.8% German, 16.6% Irish, 15.1% English, 8.8% Italian, 5.4% Other groups (2000).
Economy: Employment by occupation: 30.0% management, 20.5% professional, 9.6% services, 31.7% sales, 0.0% farming, 3.4% construction, 4.8% production (2000).
Income: Per capita income: $45,617 (2000); Median household income: $51,069 (2000); Poverty rate: 6.6% (2000).
Education: Percent of population age 25 and over with: High school diploma (including GED) or higher: 90.8% (2000); Bachelor's degree or higher: 37.6% (2000).
Housing: Homeownership rate: 72.1% (2000); Median home value: $331,200 (2000); Median rent: $765 per month (2000); Median age of housing: 24 years (2000).
Transportation: Commute to work: 75.8% car, 0.9% public transportation, 4.7% walk, 13.7% work from home (2000); Travel time to work: 25.2% less than 15 minutes, 33.4% 15 to 30 minutes, 20.6% 30 to 45 minutes, 13.0% 45 to 60 minutes, 7.8% 60 minutes or more (2000)

DUNEDIN (city). Covers a land area of 10.381 square miles and a water area of 17.825 square miles. Located at 28.02° N. Lat.; 82.77° W. Long. Elevation is 30 feet.
History: Dunedin was settled in the late 1850s and was called Jonesboro until the post office was established in 1878. The name of Dunedin was chosen by J.L. Douglas and James Somerville who had come from Dunedin, Scotland. Dunedin was an early Gulf port where fruits and vegetables were shipped by schooner.
Population: 34,496 (1990); 35,691 (2000); 36,654 (2007); 37,551 (2012 projected); Race: 93.0% White, 2.7% Black, 1.6% Asian, 4.8% Hispanic of any race (2007); Density: 3,530.9 persons per square mile (2007); Average household size: 2.04 (2007); Median age: 49.8 (2007); Males per 100 females: 85.9 (2007); Marriage status: 18.6% never married, 53.6% now married, 12.8% widowed, 15.0% divorced (2000); Foreign born: 9.7% (2000); Ancestry (includes multiple ancestries): 21.3% German, 17.2% Irish, 14.6% English, 10.9% Other groups, 10.2% Italian (2000).
Economy: Unemployment rate: 3.8% (11/2007); Total civilian labor force: 18,729 (11/2007); Single-family building permits issued: 36 (2006); Multi-family building permits issued: 6 (2006); Employment by occupation:

households with income of $100,000 or more: 12.8% (2007); Poverty rate: 8.2% (2000).

Education: Percent of population age 25 and over with: High school diploma (including GED) or higher: 86.6% (2007); Bachelor's degree or higher: 22.3% (2007); Master's degree or higher: 7.1% (2007).

School District(s)

Pinellas County School District (PK-12)
2005-06 Enrollment: 113,651 . . . . (727) 588-6011

Housing: Homeownership rate: 71.5% (2007); Median home value: $169,752 (2007); Median rent: $501 per month (2000); Median age of housing: 26 years (2000).

Safety: Violent crime rate: 35.1 per 10,000 population; Property crime rate: 243.1 per 10,000 population (2006).

Transportation: Commute to work: 91.3% car, 1.1% public transportation, 2.1% walk, 3.8% work from home (2000); Travel time to work: 31.4% less than 15 minutes, 35.9% 15 to 30 minutes, 20.3% 30 to 45 minutes, 6.8% 45 to 60 minutes, 5.5% 60 minutes or more (2000)

Additional Information Contacts

City of Dunedin . . . . (727) 298-3034
http://www.dunedingov.com
Dunedin Chamber of Commerce . . . . (727) 733-3197
http://www.dunedin-fl.com

EAST LAKE (CDP). Covers a land area of 29.782 square miles and a water area of 1.983 square miles. Located at 28.10° N. Lat.; 82.69° W. Long. Elevation is 13 feet.

Population: 12,669 (1990); 29,394 (2000); 34,890 (2007); 38,722 (2012 projected); Race: 92.9% White, 1.6% Black, 3.3% Asian, 5.6% Hispanic of any race (2007); Density: 1,171.5 persons per square mile (2007); Average household size: 2.52 (2007); Median age: 44.5 (2007); Males per 100 females: 94.7 (2007); Marriage status: 16.6% never married, 69.4% now married, 6.2% widowed, 7.8% divorced (2000); Foreign born: 9.6% (2000); Ancestry (includes multiple ancestries): 21.2% German, 16.7% Irish, 14.1% English, 13.9% Italian, 10.9% Other groups (2000).

Economy: Employment by occupation: 24.9% management, 24.2% professional, 11.5% services, 32.7% sales, 0.0% farming, 2.0% construction, 4.7% production (2000).

Income: Per capita income: $43,961 (2007); Median household income: $83,492 (2007); Average household income: $110,453 (2007); Percent of households with income of $100,000 or more: 40.4% (2007); Poverty rate: 3.9% (2000).

Education: Percent of population age 25 and over with: High school diploma (including GED) or higher: 94.0% (2007); Bachelor's degree or higher: 42.3% (2007); Master's degree or higher: 14.4% (2007).

Housing: Homeownership rate: 84.4% (2007); Median home value: $347,801 (2007); Median rent: $703 per month (2000); Median age of housing: 10 years (2000).

Transportation: Commute to work: 91.6% car, 0.4% public transportation, 0.6% walk, 5.8% work from home (2000); Travel time to work: 16.1% less than 15 minutes, 38.8% 15 to 30 minutes, 25.9% 30 to 45 minutes, 13.6% 45 to 60 minutes, 5.6% 60 minutes or more (2000)

FEATHER SOUND (CDP). Covers a land area of 4.211 square miles and a water area of 9.877 square miles. Located at 27.90° N. Lat.; 82.67° W. Long.

Population: 2,690 (1990); 3,597 (2000); 4,537 (2007); 5,164 (2012 projected); Race: 91.9% White, 3.1% Black, 3.2% Asian, 4.9% Hispanic of any race (2007); Density: 1,077.3 persons per square mile (2007); Average household size: 1.85 (2007); Median age: 41.9 (2007); Males per 100 females: 97.4 (2007); Marriage status: 28.9% never married, 52.5% now married, 3.1% widowed, 15.5% divorced (2000); Foreign born: 10.6% (2000); Ancestry (includes multiple ancestries): 17.7% German, 17.0% Irish, 14.9% Other groups, 12.2% Italian, 11.3% English (2000).

Economy: Employment by occupation: 28.3% management, 27.7% professional, 6.2% services, 32.9% sales, 0.0% farming, 1.9% construction, 3.2% production (2000).

Income: Per capita income: $64,616 (2007); Median household income: $82,251 (2007); Average household income: $119,513 (2007); Percent of households with income of $100,000 or more: 39.0% (2007); Poverty rate: 2.2% (2000).

$325,740 (2007); Median rent: $788 per month (2000); Median age of housing: 14 years (2000).

Transportation: Commute to work: 92.7% car, 0.5% public transportation, 1.6% walk, 3.8% work from home (2000); Travel time to work: 27.8% less than 15 minutes, 44.7% 15 to 30 minutes, 16.0% 30 to 45 minutes, 6.1% 45 to 60 minutes, 5.2% 60 minutes or more (2000)

GANDY (CDP). Covers a land area of 2.548 square miles and a water area of 14.006 square miles. Located at 27.86° N. Lat.; 82.62° W. Long.

Population: 3,016 (1990); 2,031 (2000); 2,282 (2007); 2,521 (2012 projected); Race: 87.8% White, 4.3% Black, 3.2% Asian, 5.9% Hispanic of any race (2007); Density: 895.6 persons per square mile (2007); Average household size: 1.59 (2007); Median age: 49.6 (2007); Males per 100 females: 115.1 (2007); Marriage status: 19.1% never married, 41.4% now married, 13.6% widowed, 25.9% divorced (2000); Foreign born: 7.4% (2000); Ancestry (includes multiple ancestries): 16.9% German, 14.9% Irish, 12.7% United States or American, 11.8% Other groups, 10.6% English (2000).

Economy: Employment by occupation: 12.9% management, 24.0% professional, 15.5% services, 25.7% sales, 0.0% farming, 10.4% construction, 11.5% production (2000).

Income: Per capita income: $28,842 (2007); Median household income: $35,844 (2007); Average household income: $45,962 (2007); Percent of households with income of $100,000 or more: 7.3% (2007); Poverty rate: 5.2% (2000).

Education: Percent of population age 25 and over with: High school diploma (including GED) or higher: 79.3% (2007); Bachelor's degree or higher: 21.3% (2007); Master's degree or higher: 5.5% (2007).

Housing: Homeownership rate: 57.9% (2007); Median home value: $17,523 (2007); Median rent: $675 per month (2000); Median age of housing: 24 years (2000).

Transportation: Commute to work: 95.0% car, 3.0% public transportation, 0.0% walk, 2.0% work from home (2000); Travel time to work: 21.4% less than 15 minutes, 51.9% 15 to 30 minutes, 22.3% 30 to 45 minutes, 3.8% 45 to 60 minutes, 0.6% 60 minutes or more (2000)

GULFPORT (city). Aka Gulf Port. Covers a land area of 2.833 square miles and a water area of 1.009 square miles. Located at 27.75° N. Lat.; 82.70° W. Long. Elevation is 16 feet.

History: Named for its location on the Gulf of Mexico. Settled 1843. Incorporated 1913.

Population: 11,857 (1990); 12,527 (2000); 12,544 (2007); 12,679 (2012 projected); Race: 85.8% White, 9.8% Black, 0.6% Asian, 4.8% Hispanic of any race (2007); Density: 4,428.3 persons per square mile (2007); Average household size: 2.01 (2007); Median age: 49.6 (2007); Males per 100 females: 89.4 (2007); Marriage status: 23.0% never married, 50.5% now married, 11.8% widowed, 14.8% divorced (2000); Foreign born: 9.2% (2000); Ancestry (includes multiple ancestries): 17.3% German, 14.0% Other groups, 13.3% Irish, 12.8% English, 8.3% Italian (2000).

Economy: Single-family building permits issued: 30 (2006); Multi-family building permits issued: 0 (2006); Employment by occupation: 12.4% management, 16.6% professional, 17.8% services, 31.5% sales, 0.3% farming, 9.8% construction, 11.6% production (2000).

Income: Per capita income: $27,216 (2007); Median household income: $34,920 (2007); Average household income: $54,381 (2007); Percent of households with income of $100,000 or more: 11.3% (2007); Poverty rate: 13.3% (2000).

Education: Percent of population age 25 and over with: High school diploma (including GED) or higher: 81.4% (2007); Bachelor's degree or higher: 19.7% (2007); Master's degree or higher: 8.3% (2007).

School District(s)

Pinellas County School District (PK-12)
2005-06 Enrollment: 113,651 . . . . (727) 588-6011

Housing: Homeownership rate: 71.8% (2007); Median home value: $138,993 (2007); Median rent: $456 per month (2000); Median age of housing: 38 years (2000).

Safety: Violent crime rate: 44.3 per 10,000 population; Property crime rate: 486.2 per 10,000 population (2006).

Transportation: Commute to work: 89.9% car, 2.3% public transportation, 2.3% walk, 2.4% work from home (2000); Travel time to work: 32.2% less

HARBOR BLUFFS (CDP). Covers a land area of 0.696 square miles and a water area of 0.258 square miles. Located at 27.90° N. Lat.; 82.82° W. Long. Elevation is 10 feet.

Population: 2,614 (1990); 2,807 (2000); 2,861 (2007); 2,926 (2012 projected); Race: 95.8% White, 0.1% Black, 2.5% Asian, 2.3% Hispanic of any race (2007); Density: 4,107.9 persons per square mile (2007); Average household size: 2.41 (2007); Median age: 48.9 (2007); Males per 100 females: 94.8 (2007); Marriage status: 17.6% never married, 68.2% now married, 8.9% widowed, 5.3% divorced (2000); Foreign born: 7.0% (2000); Ancestry (includes multiple ancestries): 21.3% English, 20.9% Irish, 19.6% German, 9.7% United States or American, 6.5% Italian (2000).

Economy: Employment by occupation: 18.7% management, 27.2% professional, 10.2% services, 35.1% sales, 0.0% farming, 3.6% construction, 5.2% production (2000).

Income: Per capita income: $46,830 (2007); Median household income: $69,444 (2007); Average household income: $112,858 (2007); Percent of households with income of $100,000 or more: 31.3% (2007); Poverty rate: 5.7% (2000).

Education: Percent of population age 25 and over with: High school diploma (including GED) or higher: 93.3% (2007); Bachelor's degree or higher: 44.8% (2007); Master's degree or higher: 18.3% (2007).

Housing: Homeownership rate: 94.4% (2007); Median home value: $311,981 (2007); Median rent: $858 per month (2000); Median age of housing: 35 years (2000).

Transportation: Commute to work: 90.7% car, 0.0% public transportation, 0.9% walk, 7.0% work from home (2000); Travel time to work: 35.3% less than 15 minutes, 35.0% 15 to 30 minutes, 18.9% 30 to 45 minutes, 8.7% 45 to 60 minutes, 2.0% 60 minutes or more (2000)

INDIAN ROCKS BEACH (city). Covers a land area of 0.930 square miles and a water area of 0.465 square miles. Located at 27.89° N. Lat.; 82.84° W. Long. Elevation is 10 feet.

Population: 3,963 (1990); 5,072 (2000); 5,295 (2007); 5,504 (2012 projected); Race: 96.3% White, 0.4% Black, 0.8% Asian, 4.1% Hispanic of any race (2007); Density: 5,694.4 persons per square mile (2007); Average household size: 1.85 (2007); Median age: 50.9 (2007); Males per 100 females: 102.4 (2007); Marriage status: 16.9% never married, 56.3% now married, 6.9% widowed, 19.9% divorced (2000); Foreign born: 10.8% (2000); Ancestry (includes multiple ancestries): 26.3% German, 18.5% Irish, 17.5% English, 10.4% Italian, 9.2% Other groups (2000).

Economy: Single-family building permits issued: 0 (2006); Multi-family building permits issued: 0 (2006); Employment by occupation: 20.8% management, 22.5% professional, 13.8% services, 33.3% sales, 0.0% farming, 4.6% construction, 5.0% production (2000).

Income: Per capita income: $49,180 (2007); Median household income: $66,313 (2007); Average household income: $90,861 (2007); Percent of households with income of $100,000 or more: 28.7% (2007); Poverty rate: 4.7% (2000).

Education: Percent of population age 25 and over with: High school diploma (including GED) or higher: 94.5% (2007); Bachelor's degree or higher: 39.0% (2007); Master's degree or higher: 13.0% (2007).

Housing: Homeownership rate: 66.6% (2007); Median home value: $376,782 (2007); Median rent: $713 per month (2000); Median age of housing: 19 years (2000).

Safety: Violent crime rate: 31.8 per 10,000 population; Property crime rate: 257.8 per 10,000 population (2006).

Transportation: Commute to work: 87.4% car, 0.6% public transportation, 0.6% walk, 10.8% work from home (2000); Travel time to work: 25.0% less than 15 minutes, 37.4% 15 to 30 minutes, 19.4% 30 to 45 minutes, 7.8% 45 to 60 minutes, 10.3% 60 minutes or more (2000)

Additional Information Contacts

City of Indian Rocks Beach . . . . (727) 595-2517
    http://www.indian-rocks-beach.com
Gulf Beaches Chamber of Commerce . . . . (727) 595-4575

INDIAN SHORES (town). Aka Indian Rocks Beach South Shore. Covers a land area of 0.334 square miles and a water area of 0.611 square miles. Located at 27.85° N. Lat.; 82.84° W. Long. Elevation is 3 feet.

(2000); Ancestry (includes multiple ancestries): 22.6% German, 19.1% English, 17.9% Irish, 8.4% United States or American, 8.2% Italian (2000).

Economy: Single-family building permits issued: 1 (2006); Multi-family building permits issued: 27 (2006); Employment by occupation: 23.7% management, 23.5% professional, 13.8% services, 26.8% sales, 0.0% farming, 6.2% construction, 6.1% production (2000).

Income: Per capita income: $45,071 (2007); Median household income: $52,846 (2007); Average household income: $76,628 (2007); Percent of households with income of $100,000 or more: 23.2% (2007); Poverty rate: 6.9% (2000).

Education: Percent of population age 25 and over with: High school diploma (including GED) or higher: 89.6% (2007); Bachelor's degree or higher: 33.8% (2007); Master's degree or higher: 14.0% (2007).

Housing: Homeownership rate: 60.8% (2007); Median home value: $330,690 (2007); Median rent: $648 per month (2000); Median age of housing: 22 years (2000).

Safety: Violent crime rate: 17.9 per 10,000 population; Property crime rate: 188.9 per 10,000 population (2006).

Transportation: Commute to work: 87.6% car, 1.2% public transportation, 1.4% walk, 6.8% work from home (2000); Travel time to work: 23.8% less than 15 minutes, 29.9% 15 to 30 minutes, 28.7% 30 to 45 minutes, 10.5% 45 to 60 minutes, 7.1% 60 minutes or more (2000)

KENNETH CITY (town). Covers a land area of 0.715 square miles and a water area of 0.004 square miles. Located at 27.81° N. Lat.; 82.71° W. Long. Elevation is 20 feet.

Population: 4,549 (1990); 4,400 (2000); 4,233 (2007); 4,149 (2012 projected); Race: 82.2% White, 5.3% Black, 7.1% Asian, 8.3% Hispanic of any race (2007); Density: 5,921.6 persons per square mile (2007); Average household size: 2.31 (2007); Median age: 46.2 (2007); Males per 100 females: 81.6 (2007); Marriage status: 19.0% never married, 53.5% now married, 15.8% widowed, 11.7% divorced (2000); Foreign born: 9.2% (2000); Ancestry (includes multiple ancestries): 17.5% Other groups, 17.2% Irish, 17.0% German, 12.1% English, 9.7% Italian (2000).

Economy: Single-family building permits issued: 12 (2006); Multi-family building permits issued: 0 (2006); Employment by occupation: 8.7% management, 15.0% professional, 11.8% services, 31.1% sales, 1.6% farming, 14.8% construction, 17.0% production (2000).

Income: Per capita income: $22,415 (2007); Median household income: $39,405 (2007); Average household income: $49,685 (2007); Percent of households with income of $100,000 or more: 8.9% (2007); Poverty rate: 9.4% (2000).

Education: Percent of population age 25 and over with: High school diploma (including GED) or higher: 81.4% (2007); Bachelor's degree or higher: 13.2% (2007); Master's degree or higher: 4.1% (2007).

Housing: Homeownership rate: 78.0% (2007); Median home value: $137,313 (2007); Median rent: $477 per month (2000); Median age of housing: 37 years (2000).

Safety: Violent crime rate: 69.0 per 10,000 population; Property crime rate: 413.9 per 10,000 population (2006).

Transportation: Commute to work: 95.6% car, 0.4% public transportation, 1.3% walk, 2.1% work from home (2000); Travel time to work: 29.8% less than 15 minutes, 49.1% 15 to 30 minutes, 13.6% 30 to 45 minutes, 4.6% 45 to 60 minutes, 2.9% 60 minutes or more (2000)

LARGO (city). Covers a land area of 15.663 square miles and a water area of 0.463 square miles. Located at 27.90° N. Lat.; 82.77° W. Long. Elevation is 33 feet.

History: Named for the Spanish translation of "long." Largo developed as a shipping center for citrus and truck gardeners, with citrus packing plants and fruit juice canneries.

Population: 70,008 (1990); 69,371 (2000); 70,489 (2007); 71,951 (2012 projected); Race: 90.0% White, 3.9% Black, 2.2% Asian, 6.1% Hispanic of any race (2007); Density: 4,500.5 persons per square mile (2007); Average household size: 2.04 (2007); Median age: 48.1 (2007); Males per 100 females: 88.6 (2007); Marriage status: 19.5% never married, 52.3% now married, 13.6% widowed, 14.7% divorced (2000); Foreign born: 9.4% (2000); Ancestry (includes multiple ancestries): 18.3% German, 15.4% Irish, 13.9% English, 11.2% Other groups, 9.6% Italian (2000).

37,411 (11/2007); Single-family building permits issued: 36 (2006); Multi-family building permits issued: 134 (2006); Employment by occupation: 10.7% management, 18.5% professional, 16.6% services, 32.7% sales, 0.1% farming, 9.0% construction, 12.4% production (2000).
Income: Per capita income: $23,831 (2007); Median household income: $36,781 (2007); Average household income: $47,514 (2007); Percent of households with income of $100,000 or more: 7.3% (2007); Poverty rate: 9.1% (2000).
Education: Percent of population age 25 and over with: High school diploma (including GED) or higher: 83.4% (2007); Bachelor's degree or higher: 16.3% (2007); Master's degree or higher: 5.7% (2007).

School District(s)
Pinellas County School District (PK-12)
   2005-06 Enrollment: 113,651 . . . . (727) 588-6011
Four-year College(s)
Remington College-Largo Campus (Private, For-profit)
   Fall 2006 Enrollment: 325 . . . . (727) 532-1999
Schiller International University (Private, For-profit)
   Fall 2006 Enrollment: 192 . . . . (727) 736-5082
   2006-07 Tuition: In-state $16,880; Out-of-state $16,880
Two-year College(s)
Central Florida College (Private, For-profit)
   Fall 2006 Enrollment: 202 . . . . (727) 531-5900
Vocational/Technical School(s)
American Institute of Beauty (Private, For-profit)
   Fall 2006 Enrollment: 76 . . . . (727) 532-2125
   2006-07 Tuition: $9,850

Housing: Homeownership rate: 67.5% (2007); Median home value: $124,267 (2007); Median rent: $539 per month (2000); Median age of housing: 25 years (2000).
Hospitals: Largo Medical Center (256 beds); Sun Coast Hospital (300 beds)
Safety: Violent crime rate: 58.0 per 10,000 population; Property crime rate: 360.9 per 10,000 population (2006).
Newspapers: Bellair Bee (General - Circulation 8,300); Clearwater Leader (General - Circulation 12,988); Largo Leader (General - Circulation 20,500); Seminole Beacon (General - Circulation 35,000)
Transportation: Commute to work: 92.7% car, 1.3% public transportation, 2.0% walk, 2.2% work from home (2000); Travel time to work: 30.1% less than 15 minutes, 40.7% 15 to 30 minutes, 18.6% 30 to 45 minutes, 5.0% 45 to 60 minutes, 5.6% 60 minutes or more (2000)
Additional Information Contacts
City of Largo. . . . . (727) 587-6700
   http://www.largo.com
Largo Chamber of Commerce . . . . (727) 584-2321
   http://www.largochamber.com

MADEIRA BEACH (city).
Covers a land area of 1.027 square miles and a water area of 2.244 square miles. Located at 27.79° N. Lat.; 82.79° W. Long. Elevation is 3 feet.
Population: 4,229 (1990); 4,511 (2000); 4,484 (2007); 4,522 (2012 projected); Race: 96.4% White, 0.3% Black, 0.5% Asian, 2.6% Hispanic of any race (2007); Density: 4,365.7 persons per square mile (2007); Average household size: 1.75 (2007); Median age: 51.2 (2007); Males per 100 females: 112.0 (2007); Marriage status: 23.7% never married, 47.9% now married, 7.5% widowed, 20.9% divorced (2000); Foreign born: 6.4% (2000); Ancestry (includes multiple ancestries): 19.7% German, 16.2% Irish, 13.5% English, 10.2% Italian, 7.4% Other groups (2000).
Economy: Employment by occupation: 18.2% management, 12.2% professional, 22.1% services, 28.9% sales, 0.7% farming, 10.6% construction, 7.2% production (2000).
Income: Per capita income: $38,598 (2007); Median household income: $45,345 (2007); Average household income: $67,712 (2007); Percent of households with income of $100,000 or more: 17.8% (2007); Poverty rate: 9.8% (2000).
Education: Percent of population age 25 and over with: High school diploma (including GED) or higher: 87.3% (2007); Bachelor's degree or higher: 22.2% (2007); Master's degree or higher: 6.1% (2007).

School District(s)
Pinellas County School District (PK-12)
   2005-06 Enrollment: 113,651 . . . . (727) 588-6011
Housing: Homeownership rate: 57.5% (2007); Median home value: $339,359 (2007); Median rent: $486 per month (2000); Median age of housing: 35 years (2000).

rate: 700.6 per 10,000 population (2006).
Transportation: Commute to work: 84.2% car, 1.6% public transportation, 3.8% walk, 7.4% work from home (2000); Travel time to work: 29.6% less than 15 minutes, 34.1% 15 to 30 minutes, 26.6% 30 to 45 minutes, 6.2% 45 to 60 minutes, 3.5% 60 minutes or more (2000)

NORTH REDINGTON BEACH (town).
Covers a land area of 0.303 square miles and a water area of 0.717 square miles. Located at 27.82° N. Lat.; 82.82° W. Long. Elevation is 3 feet.
Population: 1,135 (1990); 1,474 (2000); 1,476 (2007); 1,497 (2012 projected); Race: 95.3% White, 0.3% Black, 1.5% Asian, 4.4% Hispanic of any race (2007); Density: 4,873.2 persons per square mile (2007); Average household size: 1.84 (2007); Median age: 58.9 (2007); Males per 100 females: 86.8 (2007); Marriage status: 10.7% never married, 63.1% now married, 12.4% widowed, 13.8% divorced (2000); Foreign born: 8.9% (2000); Ancestry (includes multiple ancestries): 23.4% German, 16.1% English, 15.1% Italian, 13.5% Irish, 12.0% Other groups (2000).
Economy: Employment by occupation: 20.1% management, 23.5% professional, 14.7% services, 28.5% sales, 0.0% farming, 5.7% construction, 7.4% production (2000).
Income: Per capita income: $43,985 (2007); Median household income: $55,347 (2007); Average household income: $80,850 (2007); Percent of households with income of $100,000 or more: 25.9% (2007); Poverty rate: 4.2% (2000).
Education: Percent of population age 25 and over with: High school diploma (including GED) or higher: 92.2% (2007); Bachelor's degree or higher: 33.7% (2007); Master's degree or higher: 14.3% (2007).
Housing: Homeownership rate: 55.7% (2007); Median home value: $487,500 (2007); Median rent: $732 per month (2000); Median age of housing: 26 years (2000).
Safety: Violent crime rate: 0.0 per 10,000 population; Property crime rate: 194.4 per 10,000 population (2006).
Transportation: Commute to work: 77.8% car, 1.2% public transportation, 6.4% walk, 8.3% work from home (2000); Travel time to work: 19.8% less than 15 minutes, 33.1% 15 to 30 minutes, 28.5% 30 to 45 minutes, 14.1% 45 to 60 minutes, 4.5% 60 minutes or more (2000)

OLDSMAR (city).
Covers a land area of 8.916 square miles and a water area of 0.751 square miles. Located at 28.04° N. Lat.; 82.67° W. Long. Elevation is 7 feet.
Population: 8,104 (1990); 11,910 (2000); 13,592 (2007); 14,794 (2012 projected); Race: 87.0% White, 3.8% Black, 4.0% Asian, 9.2% Hispanic of any race (2007); Density: 1,524.5 persons per square mile (2007); Average household size: 2.60 (2007); Median age: 37.4 (2007); Males per 100 females: 94.0 (2007); Marriage status: 21.0% never married, 60.1% now married, 6.3% widowed, 12.6% divorced (2000); Foreign born: 11.6% (2000); Ancestry (includes multiple ancestries): 22.5% German, 18.9% Irish, 14.4% Other groups, 13.2% Italian, 12.1% English (2000).
Economy: Single-family building permits issued: 25 (2006); Multi-family building permits issued: 0 (2006); Employment by occupation: 19.1% management, 17.3% professional, 10.8% services, 33.9% sales, 0.0% farming, 7.0% construction, 11.9% production (2000).
Income: Per capita income: $25,647 (2007); Median household income: $58,959 (2007); Average household income: $66,387 (2007); Percent of households with income of $100,000 or more: 15.7% (2007); Poverty rate: 4.8% (2000).
Education: Percent of population age 25 and over with: High school diploma (including GED) or higher: 86.6% (2007); Bachelor's degree or higher: 23.7% (2007); Master's degree or higher: 5.4% (2007).

School District(s)
Pinellas County School District (PK-12)
   2005-06 Enrollment: 113,651 . . . . (727) 588-6011
Housing: Homeownership rate: 76.7% (2007); Median home value: $182,540 (2007); Median rent: $652 per month (2000); Median age of housing: 13 years (2000).
Safety: Violent crime rate: 40.6 per 10,000 population; Property crime rate: 383.1 per 10,000 population (2006).
Transportation: Commute to work: 93.3% car, 0.3% public transportation, 2.2% walk, 3.0% work from home (2000); Travel time to work: 26.2% less than 15 minutes, 34.4% 15 to 30 minutes, 25.9% 30 to 45 minutes, 9.0% 45 to 60 minutes, 4.5% 60 minutes or more (2000)
Additional Information Contacts
City of Oldsmar . . . . (813) 749-1115
   http://ci.oldsmar.fl.us

PALM HARBOR (CDP).

Covers a land area of 17.917 square miles and a water area of 8.669 square miles. Located at 28.08° N. Lat.; 82.75° W. Long. Elevation is 49 feet.

History: Named for its abundance of palm trees. Palm Harbor was founded by real estate promoters in the 1880s, and was first called Sutherland, in the unfulfilled hope that the Duke of Sutherland, who lived in nearby Tarpon Springs, would lend financial support.

Population: 50,255 (1990); 59,248 (2000); 60,162 (2007); 61,329 (2012 projected); Race: 94.3% White, 1.4% Black, 1.8% Asian, 4.8% Hispanic of any race (2007); Density: 3,357.8 persons per square mile (2007); Average household size: 2.29 (2007); Median age: 45.3 (2007); Males per 100 females: 89.4 (2007); Marriage status: 18.2% never married, 61.6% now married, 10.3% widowed, 9.8% divorced (2000); Foreign born: 8.4% (2000); Ancestry (includes multiple ancestries): 19.5% German, 16.5% Irish, 13.9% English, 12.8% Italian, 8.9% Other groups (2000).

Economy: Employment by occupation: 17.7% management, 22.7% professional, 12.8% services, 32.7% sales, 0.1% farming, 7.0% construction, 7.0% production (2000).

Income: Per capita income: $31,225 (2007); Median household income: $51,691 (2007); Average household income: $70,400 (2007); Percent of households with income of $100,000 or more: 18.7% (2007); Poverty rate: 5.5% (2000).

Education: Percent of population age 25 and over with: High school diploma (including GED) or higher: 90.3% (2007); Bachelor's degree or higher: 28.3% (2007); Master's degree or higher: 9.5% (2007).

School District(s)
Pinellas County School District (PK-12)
    2005-06 Enrollment: 113,651 . . . . (727) 588-6011

Vocational/Technical School(s)
Central Florida Institute Inc (Private, For-profit)
    Fall 2006 Enrollment: 439 . . . . (727) 786-4707
    2006-07 Tuition: $9,979

Housing: Homeownership rate: 77.9% (2007); Median home value: $217,793 (2007); Median rent: $697 per month (2000); Median age of housing: 16 years (2000).

Transportation: Commute to work: 92.3% car, 0.8% public transportation, 0.9% walk, 4.9% work from home (2000); Travel time to work: 24.5% less than 15 minutes, 32.7% 15 to 30 minutes, 26.5% 30 to 45 minutes, 10.3% 45 to 60 minutes, 6.0% 60 minutes or more (2000)

Additional Information Contacts
Palm Harbor Area Chamber of Commerce . . . . (727) 784-4287
    http://www.palmharborcc.org

PINELLAS PARK (city).

Covers a land area of 14.748 square miles and a water area of 0.190 square miles. Located at 27.85° N. Lat.; 82.70° W. Long. Elevation is 13 feet.

History: Named for the Spanish translation of "point of pines". Incorporated 1915.

Population: 45,348 (1990); 45,658 (2000); 46,613 (2007); 47,697 (2012 projected); Race: 85.1% White, 2.9% Black, 5.8% Asian, 8.8% Hispanic of any race (2007); Density: 3,160.6 persons per square mile (2007); Average household size: 2.34 (2007); Median age: 42.3 (2007); Males per 100 females: 92.3 (2007); Marriage status: 20.6% never married, 54.5% now married, 10.8% widowed, 14.1% divorced (2000); Foreign born: 9.5% (2000); Ancestry (includes multiple ancestries): 18.5% German, 17.8% Other groups, 15.8% Irish, 11.6% English, 8.4% Italian (2000).

Economy: Unemployment rate: 4.3% (11/2007); Total civilian labor force: 25,228 (11/2007); Single-family building permits issued: 213 (2006); Multi-family building permits issued: 5 (2006); Employment by occupation: 9.9% management, 13.3% professional, 15.1% services, 32.5% sales, 0.3% farming, 10.8% construction, 18.1% production (2000).

Income: Per capita income: $20,915 (2007); Median household income: $39,881 (2007); Average household income: $47,973 (2007); Percent of households with income of $100,000 or more: 6.7% (2007); Poverty rate: 9.3% (2000).

Education: Percent of population age 25 and over with: High school diploma (including GED) or higher: 80.2% (2007); Bachelor's degree or higher: 11.9% (2007); Master's degree or higher: 3.5% (2007).

School District(s)
Pinellas County School District (PK-12)
    2005-06 Enrollment: 113,651 . . . . (727) 588-6011

2006-07 Tuition: $10,245

Housing: Homeownership rate: 74.9% (2007); Median home value: $134,528 (2007); Median rent: $508 per month (2000); Median age of housing: 25 years (2000).

Safety: Violent crime rate: 52.8 per 10,000 population; Property crime rate: 553.3 per 10,000 population (2006).

Transportation: Commute to work: 92.7% car, 1.1% public transportation, 1.7% walk, 2.2% work from home (2000); Travel time to work: 31.5% less than 15 minutes, 47.3% 15 to 30 minutes, 13.5% 30 to 45 minutes, 3.9% 45 to 60 minutes, 3.7% 60 minutes or more (2000)

Additional Information Contacts
City of Pinellas Park . . . . (727) 541-0700
    http://www.pinellas-park.com
Pinellas Park Chamber of Commerce . . . . (727) 544-4777
    http://www.pinellasparkchamber.com

REDINGTON BEACH (town).

Covers a land area of 0.364 square miles and a water area of 0.934 square miles. Located at 27.81° N. Lat.; 82.81° W. Long. Elevation is 3 feet.

Population: 1,626 (1990); 1,539 (2000); 1,586 (2007); 1,636 (2012 projected); Race: 96.0% White, 0.8% Black, 1.9% Asian, 4.2% Hispanic of any race (2007); Density: 4,357.6 persons per square mile (2007); Average household size: 2.14 (2007); Median age: 52.2 (2007); Males per 100 females: 86.2 (2007); Marriage status: 21.1% never married, 56.3% now married, 8.6% widowed, 14.0% divorced (2000); Foreign born: 12.5% (2000); Ancestry (includes multiple ancestries): 18.4% English, 18.3% German, 13.3% Irish, 8.0% Italian, 7.4% French (except Basque) (2000).

Economy: Employment by occupation: 23.1% management, 23.7% professional, 12.7% services, 25.1% sales, 0.0% farming, 6.4% construction, 8.9% production (2000).

Income: Per capita income: $45,449 (2007); Median household income: $66,279 (2007); Average household income: $97,146 (2007); Percent of households with income of $100,000 or more: 32.7% (2007); Poverty rate: 5.7% (2000).

Education: Percent of population age 25 and over with: High school diploma (including GED) or higher: 88.3% (2007); Bachelor's degree or higher: 40.3% (2007); Master's degree or higher: 18.2% (2007).

Housing: Homeownership rate: 88.8% (2007); Median home value: $354,508 (2007); Median rent: $832 per month (2000); Median age of housing: 41 years (2000).

Safety: Violent crime rate: 19.3 per 10,000 population; Property crime rate: 174.1 per 10,000 population (2006).

Transportation: Commute to work: 91.0% car, 0.6% public transportation, 0.9% walk, 3.1% work from home (2000); Travel time to work: 20.2% less than 15 minutes, 35.7% 15 to 30 minutes, 25.1% 30 to 45 minutes, 12.5% 45 to 60 minutes, 6.5% 60 minutes or more (2000)

REDINGTON SHORES (town).

Covers a land area of 0.393 square miles and a water area of 0.807 square miles. Located at 27.82° N. Lat.; 82.83° W. Long. Elevation is 3 feet.

Population: 2,366 (1990); 2,338 (2000); 2,359 (2007); 2,414 (2012 projected); Race: 96.8% White, 0.4% Black, 0.6% Asian, 4.0% Hispanic of any race (2007); Density: 6,008.9 persons per square mile (2007); Average household size: 1.78 (2007); Median age: 56.9 (2007); Males per 100 females: 96.4 (2007); Marriage status: 18.1% never married, 54.0% now married, 11.9% widowed, 16.0% divorced (2000); Foreign born: 6.8% (2000); Ancestry (includes multiple ancestries): 20.9% German, 18.6% English, 16.1% Irish, 8.2% Italian, 6.0% Polish (2000).

Economy: Single-family building permits issued: 21 (2006); Multi-family building permits issued: 0 (2006); Employment by occupation: 15.7% management, 20.5% professional, 16.7% services, 32.0% sales, 0.3% farming, 8.3% construction, 6.6% production (2000).

Income: Per capita income: $38,194 (2007); Median household income: $48,063 (2007); Average household income: $68,154 (2007); Percent of households with income of $100,000 or more: 17.1% (2007); Poverty rate: 8.2% (2000).

Education: Percent of population age 25 and over with: High school diploma (including GED) or higher: 93.0% (2007); Bachelor's degree or higher: 27.2% (2007); Master's degree or higher: 6.4% (2007).

Housing: Homeownership rate: 75.2% (2007); Median home value: $312,602 (2007); Median rent: $704 per month (2000); Median age of housing: 26 years (2000).

RIDGECREST (CDP). Covers a land area of 0.563 square miles and a water area of 0.007 square miles. Located at 27.89° N. Lat.; 82.80° W. Long. Elevation is 56 feet.
Population: 2,932 (1990); 2,453 (2000); 2,408 (2007); 2,423 (2012 projected); Race: 13.0% White, 83.8% Black, 0.1% Asian, 4.3% Hispanic of any race (2007); Density: 4,274.7 persons per square mile (2007); Average household size: 3.11 (2007); Median age: 27.5 (2007); Males per 100 females: 83.4 (2007); Marriage status: 39.4% never married, 46.1% now married, 9.6% widowed, 5.0% divorced (2000); Foreign born: 1.1% (2000); Ancestry (includes multiple ancestries): 71.9% Other groups, 3.2% German, 2.0% Irish, 1.3% English, 0.8% African (2000).
Economy: Employment by occupation: 2.3% management, 14.2% professional, 27.5% services, 33.9% sales, 0.0% farming, 10.9% construction, 11.2% production (2000).
Income: Per capita income: $16,297 (2007); Median household income: $37,269 (2007); Average household income: $44,339 (2007); Percent of households with income of $100,000 or more: 7.5% (2007); Poverty rate: 22.7% (2000).
Education: Percent of population age 25 and over with: High school diploma (including GED) or higher: 68.5% (2007); Bachelor's degree or higher: 12.1% (2007); Master's degree or higher: 9.1% (2007).
Housing: Homeownership rate: 63.5% (2007); Median home value: $124,474 (2007); Median rent: $427 per month (2000); Median age of housing: 27 years (2000).
Transportation: Commute to work: 91.6% car, 3.6% public transportation, 1.1% walk, 0.7% work from home (2000); Travel time to work: 29.5% less than 15 minutes, 33.9% 15 to 30 minutes, 31.2% 30 to 45 minutes, 2.1% 45 to 60 minutes, 3.4% 60 minutes or more (2000)

SAFETY HARBOR (city). Covers a land area of 4.917 square miles and a water area of 0.132 square miles. Located at 28.00° N. Lat.; 82.69° W. Long. Elevation is 20 feet.
History: Named for its location as a sheltered harbor for seamen and ships. Safety Harbor, at the head of Old Tampa Bay, grew up around the mineral springs. Odet Philippe, a surgeon in Napoleon's navy, settled here in 1823. He planted citrus groves, grew tobacco, and made cigars.
Population: 16,155 (1990); 17,203 (2000); 17,544 (2007); 17,959 (2012 projected); Race: 91.2% White, 4.2% Black, 2.3% Asian, 4.6% Hispanic of any race (2007); Density: 3,567.7 persons per square mile (2007); Average household size: 2.40 (2007); Median age: 44.6 (2007); Males per 100 females: 91.6 (2007); Marriage status: 18.8% never married, 61.4% now married, 8.2% widowed, 11.6% divorced (2000); Foreign born: 7.3% (2000); Ancestry (includes multiple ancestries): 19.3% German, 16.2% Irish, 12.8% Other groups, 12.4% English, 9.7% Italian (2000).
Economy: Single-family building permits issued: 22 (2006); Multi-family building permits issued: 0 (2006); Employment by occupation: 16.8% management, 27.7% professional, 11.2% services, 31.9% sales, 0.1% farming, 5.3% construction, 7.1% production (2000).
Income: Per capita income: $33,474 (2007); Median household income: $59,916 (2007); Average household income: $78,688 (2007); Percent of households with income of $100,000 or more: 24.9% (2007); Poverty rate: 5.6% (2000).
Education: Percent of population age 25 and over with: High school diploma (including GED) or higher: 89.6% (2007); Bachelor's degree or higher: 34.4% (2007); Master's degree or higher: 11.9% (2007).

School District(s)
Pinellas County School District (PK-12)
  2005-06 Enrollment: 113,651 . . . . (727) 588-6011
Housing: Homeownership rate: 84.6% (2007); Median home value: $233,017 (2007); Median rent: $613 per month (2000); Median age of housing: 18 years (2000).
Hospitals: Mease Countryside Hospital (205 beds)
Safety: Violent crime rate: 22.5 per 10,000 population; Property crime rate: 160.0 per 10,000 population (2006).
Transportation: Commute to work: 92.5% car, 0.5% public transportation, 1.7% walk, 3.4% work from home (2000); Travel time to work: 23.5% less than 15 minutes, 37.8% 15 to 30 minutes, 28.0% 30 to 45 minutes, 7.3% 45 to 60 minutes, 3.4% 60 minutes or more (2000)
Additional Information Contacts

SAINT PETE BEACH (city). Aka Saint Petersburg Beach. Covers a land area of 2.247 square miles and a water area of 17.632 square miles. Located at 27.72° N. Lat.; 82.74° W. Long. Elevation is 3 feet.
Population: 9,200 (1990); 9,929 (2000); 10,377 (2007); 10,767 (2012 projected); Race: 96.7% White, 1.1% Black, 0.7% Asian, 3.4% Hispanic of any race (2007); Density: 4,617.1 persons per square mile (2007); Average household size: 1.87 (2007); Median age: 55.6 (2007); Males per 100 females: 100.4 (2007); Marriage status: 16.3% never married, 56.5% now married, 12.8% widowed, 14.4% divorced (2000); Foreign born: 13.0% (2000); Ancestry (includes multiple ancestries): 18.5% German, 18.0% English, 17.9% Irish, 9.7% Italian, 7.0% Other groups (2000).
Economy: Single-family building permits issued: 15 (2006); Multi-family building permits issued: 0 (2006); Employment by occupation: 20.4% management, 22.8% professional, 15.2% services, 28.3% sales, 0.5% farming, 5.8% construction, 7.0% production (2000).
Income: Per capita income: $46,482 (2007); Median household income: $60,534 (2007); Average household income: $86,054 (2007); Percent of households with income of $100,000 or more: 23.3% (2007); Poverty rate: 7.4% (2000).
Education: Percent of population age 25 and over with: High school diploma (including GED) or higher: 87.3% (2007); Bachelor's degree or higher: 34.4% (2007); Master's degree or higher: 11.6% (2007).
Housing: Homeownership rate: 69.9% (2007); Median home value: $361,233 (2007); Median rent: $566 per month (2000); Median age of housing: 32 years (2000).
Safety: Violent crime rate: 50.3 per 10,000 population; Property crime rate: 532.6 per 10,000 population (2006).
Transportation: Commute to work: 84.4% car, 1.7% public transportation, 5.5% walk, 5.6% work from home (2000); Travel time to work: 34.3% less than 15 minutes, 32.9% 15 to 30 minutes, 16.7% 30 to 45 minutes, 9.1% 45 to 60 minutes, 6.9% 60 minutes or more (2000)
Additional Information Contacts
City of Saint Pete Beach . . . . (727) 367-2735
  http://www.stpetebeach.org

SAINT PETERSBURG (city). Covers a land area of 59.627 square miles and a water area of 73.451 square miles. Located at 27.78° N. Lat.; 82.66° W. Long. Elevation is 43 feet.
History: St. Petersburg was founded by John C. Williams of Detroit, who bought land here in 1876. In 1888 he convinced Peter Demens to build a railroad, called the Orange Belt Line, to the community, which was named by Demens for the city in his native Russia. St. Petersburg, incorporated in 1892, was designed and promoted as a winter resort, capitalizing on its many days of sunshine each year.
Population: 238,846 (1990); 248,232 (2000); 250,583 (2007); 254,508 (2012 projected); Race: 67.1% White, 24.9% Black, 3.4% Asian, 5.7% Hispanic of any race (2007); Density: 4,202.5 persons per square mile (2007); Average household size: 2.27 (2007); Median age: 40.9 (2007); Males per 100 females: 92.6 (2007); Marriage status: 27.8% never married, 48.3% now married, 9.0% widowed, 14.9% divorced (2000); Foreign born: 9.1% (2000); Ancestry (includes multiple ancestries): 27.8% Other groups, 14.7% German, 12.4% Irish, 11.1% English, 6.8% Italian (2000).
Economy: Unemployment rate: 4.2% (11/2007); Total civilian labor force: 135,159 (11/2007); Single-family building permits issued: 496 (2006); Multi-family building permits issued: 164 (2006); Employment by occupation: 13.2% management, 20.8% professional, 16.7% services, 28.3% sales, 0.1% farming, 8.2% construction, 12.7% production (2000).
Income: Per capita income: $24,742 (2007); Median household income: $40,466 (2007); Average household income: $55,310 (2007); Percent of households with income of $100,000 or more: 11.9% (2007); Poverty rate: 13.3% (2000).
Taxes: Total city taxes per capita: $491 (2005); City property taxes per capita: $298 (2005).
Education: Percent of population age 25 and over with: High school diploma (including GED) or higher: 82.1% (2007); Bachelor's degree or higher: 23.1% (2007); Master's degree or higher: 8.1% (2007).
School District(s)
Pinellas County School District (PK-12)
  2005-06 Enrollment: 113,651 . . . . (727) 588-6011

Two-year College(s)

Galen Health Institute-Tampa Bay (Private, For-profit)
Fall 2006 Enrollment: 74 . . . . (727) 577-1497
Pinellas Technical Education Center (Public)
Fall 2006 Enrollment: 2,614 . . . . (727) 893-2500

Vocational/Technical School(s)

Career Institute of Florida (Private, For-profit)
Fall 2006 Enrollment: 121 . . . . (727) 576-9597
2006-07 Tuition: $7,500
Loraines Academy Inc (Private, For-profit)
Fall 2006 Enrollment: 253 . . . . (727) 347-4247
2006-07 Tuition: $13,615

Housing: Homeownership rate: 63.0% (2007); Median home value: $158,831 (2007); Median rent: $478 per month (2000); Median age of housing: 37 years (2000).

Hospitals: All Children's Hospital (216 beds); Bayfront Medical Center (502 beds); Edward White Hospital (167 beds); Kindred Hospital-St. Petersburg (82 beds); Northside Hospital (288 beds); Palms of Pasadena Hospital (307 beds); Saint Petersburg General Hospital (219 beds); St. Anthony's Hospital (405 beds)

Safety: Violent crime rate: 148.2 per 10,000 population; Property crime rate: 647.9 per 10,000 population (2006).

Newspapers: Pinellas News (General - Circulation 2,800); St. Petersburg Times (Circulation 311,680); Weekly Challenger (Black - Circulation 35,500)

Transportation: Commute to work: 90.0% car, 2.9% public transportation, 2.2% walk, 3.1% work from home (2000); Travel time to work: 30.8% less than 15 minutes, 41.1% 15 to 30 minutes, 17.9% 30 to 45 minutes, 5.7% 45 to 60 minutes, 4.5% 60 minutes or more (2000); Amtrak: Service available.

Airports: St Petersburg-Clearwater International (primary service)

Additional Information Contacts

Gulf Beaches-Tampa Bay Chamber . . . . (727) 360-6957
http://www.tampabaybeaches.com
St. Petersburg Chamber of Commerce . . . . (727) 821-4069
http://www.stpete.com

SEMINOLE (city).

Covers a land area of 2.474 square miles and a water area of 0.243 square miles. Located at 27.83° N. Lat.; 82.78° W. Long. Elevation is 36 feet.

Population: 10,345 (1990); 10,890 (2000); 10,695 (2007); 10,750 (2012 projected); Race: 95.3% White, 0.7% Black, 1.2% Asian, 3.2% Hispanic of any race (2007); Density: 4,323.3 persons per square mile (2007); Average household size: 1.80 (2007); Median age: 59.2 (2007); Males per 100 females: 77.8 (2007); Marriage status: 15.9% never married, 48.7% now married, 22.1% widowed, 13.3% divorced (2000); Foreign born: 7.3% (2000); Ancestry (includes multiple ancestries): 22.2% German, 15.9% Irish, 14.6% English, 9.6% Italian, 7.4% United States or American (2000).

Economy: Single-family building permits issued: 49 (2006); Multi-family building permits issued: 0 (2006); Employment by occupation: 12.6% management, 14.4% professional, 17.6% services, 33.2% sales, 0.4% farming, 10.5% construction, 11.3% production (2000).

Income: Per capita income: $25,172 (2007); Median household income: $34,958 (2007); Average household income: $44,887 (2007); Percent of households with income of $100,000 or more: 7.1% (2007); Poverty rate: 9.0% (2000).

Education: Percent of population age 25 and over with: High school diploma (including GED) or higher: 80.9% (2007); Bachelor's degree or higher: 16.0% (2007); Master's degree or higher: 5.8% (2007).

School District(s)

Pinellas County School District (PK-12)
2005-06 Enrollment: 113,651 . . . . (727) 588-6011

Housing: Homeownership rate: 77.4% (2007); Median home value: $131,310 (2007); Median rent: $577 per month (2000); Median age of housing: 28 years (2000).

Safety: Violent crime rate: 37.2 per 10,000 population; Property crime rate: 360.8 per 10,000 population (2006).

Seminole Chamber of Commerce . . . . (727) 392-3245
http://seminolechamber.net

SOUTH HIGHPOINT (CDP).

Covers a land area of 2.176 square miles and a water area of 0 square miles. Located at 27.90° N. Lat.; 82.71° W. Long. Elevation is 13 feet.

Population: 7,103 (1990); 8,839 (2000); 8,485 (2007); 8,364 (2012 projected); Race: 60.2% White, 28.7% Black, 4.5% Asian, 14.0% Hispanic of any race (2007); Density: 3,900.2 persons per square mile (2007); Average household size: 4.15 (2007); Median age: 32.7 (2007); Males per 100 females: 166.6 (2007); Marriage status: 31.1% never married, 47.3% now married, 4.3% widowed, 17.3% divorced (2000); Foreign born: 9.6% (2000); Ancestry (includes multiple ancestries): 24.6% Other groups, 8.6% German, 8.0% English, 6.6% Irish, 5.6% United States or American (2000).

Economy: Employment by occupation: 6.5% management, 12.6% professional, 19.6% services, 34.1% sales, 0.9% farming, 8.7% construction, 17.6% production (2000).

Income: Per capita income: $10,960 (2007); Median household income: $32,763 (2007); Average household income: $42,898 (2007); Percent of households with income of $100,000 or more: 6.6% (2007); Poverty rate: 22.2% (2000).

Education: Percent of population age 25 and over with: High school diploma (including GED) or higher: 70.2% (2007); Bachelor's degree or higher: 4.9% (2007); Master's degree or higher: 1.6% (2007).

Housing: Homeownership rate: 47.6% (2007); Median home value: $113,151 (2007); Median rent: $465 per month (2000); Median age of housing: 23 years (2000).

Transportation: Commute to work: 88.2% car, 3.2% public transportation, 2.0% walk, 2.7% work from home (2000); Travel time to work: 29.4% less than 15 minutes, 41.5% 15 to 30 minutes, 19.1% 30 to 45 minutes, 3.9% 45 to 60 minutes, 6.1% 60 minutes or more (2000)

SOUTH PASADENA (city).

Aka Coreytown. Covers a land area of 0.677 square miles and a water area of 0.470 square miles. Located at 27.75° N. Lat.; 82.74° W. Long. Elevation is 3 feet.

Population: 5,644 (1990); 5,778 (2000); 5,739 (2007); 5,778 (2012 projected); Race: 97.8% White, 0.2% Black, 1.0% Asian, 2.3% Hispanic of any race (2007); Density: 8,473.0 persons per square mile (2007); Average household size: 1.57 (2007); Median age: 70.3 (2007); Males per 100 females: 66.0 (2007); Marriage status: 9.7% never married, 52.0% now married, 24.2% widowed, 14.1% divorced (2000); Foreign born: 13.0% (2000); Ancestry (includes multiple ancestries): 19.2% German, 16.8% Irish, 14.7% English, 8.2% Italian, 4.9% Other groups (2000).

Economy: Single-family building permits issued: 3 (2006); Multi-family building permits issued: 3 (2006); Employment by occupation: 16.4% management, 17.8% professional, 15.2% services, 39.8% sales, 0.0% farming, 4.5% construction, 6.3% production (2000).

Income: Per capita income: $30,743 (2007); Median household income: $31,255 (2007); Average household income: $47,136 (2007); Percent of households with income of $100,000 or more: 7.5% (2007); Poverty rate: 8.6% (2000).

Education: Percent of population age 25 and over with: High school diploma (including GED) or higher: 85.8% (2007); Bachelor's degree or higher: 21.3% (2007); Master's degree or higher: 6.0% (2007).

Housing: Homeownership rate: 62.3% (2007); Median home value: $174,186 (2007); Median rent: $545 per month (2000); Median age of housing: 25 years (2000).

Safety: Violent crime rate: 18.9 per 10,000 population; Property crime rate: 454.3 per 10,000 population (2006).

Transportation: Commute to work: 86.5% car, 0.0% public transportation, 9.0% walk, 3.2% work from home (2000); Travel time to work: 29.6% less than 15 minutes, 40.4% 15 to 30 minutes, 16.9% 30 to 45 minutes, 8.4% 45 to 60 minutes, 4.6% 60 minutes or more (2000)

Additional Information Contacts

City of South Pasadena . . . . (727) 347-4171
http://ci.south-pasadena.fl.us

TARPON SPRINGS (city). Covers a land area of 9.143 square miles and a water area of 7.743 square miles. Located at 28.14° N. Lat.; 82.75° W. Long. Elevation is 23 feet.

History: Tarpon Springs was founded in 1876 and named for the mistaken belief that the fish that spawned in Spring Bayou were tarpon. A resort hotel was built here in the 1880s by Hamilton Disston, a manufacturer from Philadelphia. For several years, the Duke of Sutherland, cousin to Queen Victoria, was a neighbor.

Population: 18,361 (1990); 21,003 (2000); 22,982 (2007); 24,496 (2012 projected); Race: 89.0% White, 6.0% Black, 1.4% Asian, 6.6% Hispanic of any race (2007); Density: 2,513.5 persons per square mile (2007); Average household size: 2.28 (2007); Median age: 46.3 (2007); Males per 100 females: 93.1 (2007); Marriage status: 17.6% never married, 60.7% now married, 10.6% widowed, 11.0% divorced (2000); Foreign born: 10.1% (2000); Ancestry (includes multiple ancestries): 17.7% German, 14.9% Irish, 12.6% Other groups, 12.3% English, 11.8% Greek (2000).

Economy: Single-family building permits issued: 337 (2006); Multi-family building permits issued: 0 (2006); Employment by occupation: 14.2% management, 17.5% professional, 17.2% services, 30.8% sales, 0.2% farming, 10.1% construction, 9.9% production (2000).

Income: Per capita income: $27,774 (2007); Median household income: $46,553 (2007); Average household income: $62,943 (2007); Percent of households with income of $100,000 or more: 13.5% (2007); Poverty rate: 9.8% (2000).

Education: Percent of population age 25 and over with: High school diploma (including GED) or higher: 81.8% (2007); Bachelor's degree or higher: 20.4% (2007); Master's degree or higher: 7.2% (2007).

School District(s)

Pinellas County School District (PK-12)

    2005-06 Enrollment: 113,651 . . . . (727) 588-6011

Housing: Homeownership rate: 78.3% (2007); Median home value: $185,947 (2007); Median rent: $447 per month (2000); Median age of housing: 22 years (2000).

Hospitals: Helen Ellis Memorial Hospital (168 beds)

Safety: Violent crime rate: 92.5 per 10,000 population; Property crime rate: 338.6 per 10,000 population (2006).

Transportation: Commute to work: 91.2% car, 1.6% public transportation, 2.5% walk, 2.9% work from home (2000); Travel time to work: 27.0% less than 15 minutes, 29.2% 15 to 30 minutes, 22.0% 30 to 45 minutes, 12.4% 45 to 60 minutes, 9.3% 60 minutes or more (2000)

Additional Information Contacts

City of Tarpon Springs . . . . (727) 938-3711
    http://www.tarponsprings.com

Tarpon Springs Chamber of Commerce . . . . (727) 937-6109
    http://www.tarponspringschamber.org

TIERRA VERDE (CDP). Covers a land area of 1.471 square miles and a water area of 3.076 square miles. Located at 27.68° N. Lat.; 82.72° W. Long. Elevation is 3 feet.

Population: 2,186 (1990); 3,574 (2000); 4,718 (2007); 5,481 (2012 projected); Race: 94.5% White, 2.5% Black, 1.2% Asian, 4.6% Hispanic of any race (2007); Density: 3,208.0 persons per square mile (2007); Average household size: 2.10 (2007); Median age: 51.2 (2007); Males per 100 females: 101.0 (2007); Marriage status: 15.7% never married, 67.5% now married, 3.1% widowed, 13.7% divorced (2000); Foreign born: 7.8% (2000); Ancestry (includes multiple ancestries): 23.2% German, 18.4% Irish, 13.1% English, 12.9% Italian, 10.7% Other groups (2000).

Economy: Employment by occupation: 30.0% management, 26.9% professional, 8.1% services, 30.5% sales, 0.0% farming, 2.1% construction, 2.5% production (2000).

Income: Per capita income: $62,421 (2007); Median household income: $98,690 (2007); Average household income: $131,065 (2007); Percent of households with income of $100,000 or more: 49.2% (2007); Poverty rate: 3.9% (2000).

Education: Percent of population age 25 and over with: High school diploma (including GED) or higher: 93.9% (2007); Bachelor's degree or higher: 47.8% (2007); Master's degree or higher: 14.3% (2007).

Housing: Homeownership rate: 86.8% (2007); Median home value: $435,758 (2007); Median rent: $996 per month (2000); Median age of housing: 13 years (2000).

Transportation: Commute to work: 90.9% car, 0.4% public transportation, 0.8% walk, 6.0% work from home (2000); Travel time to work: 14.1% less than 15 minutes, 46.4% 15 to 30 minutes, 25.2% 30 to 45 minutes, 7.1% 45 to 60 minutes, 7.2% 60 minutes or more (2000)

TREASURE ISLAND (city). Covers a land area of 1.592 square miles and a water area of 3.730 square miles. Located at 27.76° N. Lat.; 82.76° W. Long. Elevation is 3 feet.

Population: 7,266 (1990); 7,450 (2000); 7,634 (2007); 7,852 (2012 projected); Race: 97.0% White, 0.4% Black, 0.8% Asian, 3.0% Hispanic of any race (2007); Density: 4,794.6 persons per square mile (2007); Average household size: 1.77 (2007); Median age: 54.3 (2007); Males per 100 females: 96.6 (2007); Marriage status: 15.1% never married, 57.5% now married, 8.8% widowed, 18.6% divorced (2000); Foreign born: 7.8% (2000); Ancestry (includes multiple ancestries): 23.2% German, 19.5% Irish, 15.8% English, 9.6% Italian, 7.2% Other groups (2000).

Economy: Single-family building permits issued: 5 (2006); Multi-family building permits issued: 16 (2006); Employment by occupation: 19.5% management, 23.7% professional, 13.2% services, 32.0% sales, 0.5% farming, 6.4% construction, 4.8% production (2000).

Income: Per capita income: $41,661 (2007); Median household income: $48,591 (2007); Average household income: $73,825 (2007); Percent of households with income of $100,000 or more: 21.3% (2007); Poverty rate: 5.6% (2000).

Education: Percent of population age 25 and over with: High school diploma (including GED) or higher: 89.5% (2007); Bachelor's degree or higher: 30.7% (2007); Master's degree or higher: 11.1% (2007).

Housing: Homeownership rate: 64.6% (2007); Median home value: $378,618 (2007); Median rent: $586 per month (2000); Median age of housing: 29 years (2000).

Safety: Violent crime rate: 19.6 per 10,000 population; Property crime rate: 367.7 per 10,000 population (2006).

Transportation: Commute to work: 87.5% car, 0.0% public transportation, 2.2% walk, 9.1% work from home (2000); Travel time to work: 26.7% less than 15 minutes, 42.1% 15 to 30 minutes, 15.4% 30 to 45 minutes, 7.8% 45 to 60 minutes, 8.0% 60 minutes or more (2000)

Additional Information Contacts

City of Treasure Island . . . . (727) 547-4575
    http://www.ci.treasure-island.fl.us

WEST AND EAST LEALMAN (CDP). Covers a land area of 4.729 square miles and a water area of 0.030 square miles. Located at 27.82° N. Lat.; 82.68° W. Long. Elevation is 49 feet.

Population: 21,350 (1990); 21,753 (2000); 21,043 (2007); 20,772 (2012 projected); Race: 83.7% White, 4.7% Black, 5.7% Asian, 6.9% Hispanic of any race (2007); Density: 4,449.3 persons per square mile (2007); Average household size: 2.22 (2007); Median age: 42.3 (2007); Males per 100 females: 99.9 (2007); Marriage status: 21.0% never married, 48.6% now married, 11.7% widowed, 18.8% divorced (2000); Foreign born: 7.9% (2000); Ancestry (includes multiple ancestries): 17.8% Other groups, 17.0% German, 15.2% Irish, 12.5% English, 9.3% United States or American (2000).

Economy: Employment by occupation: 9.1% management, 10.1% professional, 17.4% services, 30.5% sales, 0.3% farming, 12.6% construction, 20.0% production (2000).

Income: Per capita income: $17,613 (2007); Median household income: $30,409 (2007); Average household income: $38,692 (2007); Percent of households with income of $100,000 or more: 4.4% (2007); Poverty rate: 17.4% (2000).

Education: Percent of population age 25 and over with: High school diploma (including GED) or higher: 67.6% (2007); Bachelor's degree or higher: 8.5% (2007); Master's degree or higher: 3.0% (2007).

Housing: Homeownership rate: 66.6% (2007); Median home value: $107,047 (2007); Median rent: $427 per month (2000); Median age of housing: 35 years (2000).

Transportation: Commute to work: 90.3% car, 2.4% public transportation, 2.3% walk, 2.3% work from home (2000); Travel time to work: 30.6% less than 15 minutes, 43.9% 15 to 30 minutes, 15.8% 30 to 45 minutes, 3.8% 45 to 60 minutes, 5.9% 60 minutes or more (2000)

Polk County

Located in central Florida; bounded on the east by the Kissimmee River, and on the north by the Withlacoochee River; drained by the Peace River. Covers a land area of 1,874.38 square miles, a water area of 135.60 square miles, and is located in the Eastern Time Zone. The county was founded in 1861. County seat is Bartow.

Weather Station: Bartow — Elevation: 124 feet

	Jan	Feb	Mar	Apr	May	Jun	Jul	Aug	Sep	Oct	Nov	Dec
High	73	75	80	84	89	91	92	92	90	85	80	75
Low	50	52	56	60	66	71	72	73	72	65	59	52
Precip	2.6	2.9	3.3	2.5	4.0	6.8	8.4	6.6	6.6	2.7	2.2	2.4
Snow	0.0	0.0	0.0	0.0	0.0	0.0	0.0	0.0	0.0	0.0	0.0	0.0

High and Low temperatures in degrees Fahrenheit; Precipitation and Snow in inches

Weather Station: Lake Alfred Exp. Station — Elevation: 137 feet

	Jan	Feb	Mar	Apr	May	Jun	Jul	Aug	Sep	Oct	Nov	Dec
High	72	74	79	84	89	91	93	93	91	86	80	74
Low	47	49	54	58	64	70	72	72	70	63	56	50
Precip	2.6	2.8	3.7	2.0	4.2	6.9	7.2	7.3	6.5	3.0	2.3	2.2
Snow	tr	0.0	0.0	0.0	0.0	0.0	0.0	0.0	0.0	0.0	0.0	0.0

High and Low temperatures in degrees Fahrenheit; Precipitation and Snow in inches

Weather Station: Lakeland Linder Airport — Elevation: 209 feet

	Jan	Feb	Mar	Apr	May	Jun	Jul	Aug	Sep	Oct	Nov	Dec
High	72	74	80	84	89	92	93	92	91	85	79	74
Low	50	52	57	61	66	71	73	73	72	65	59	53
Precip	2.5	2.8	3.6	2.0	4.2	7.1	7.8	7.4	6.1	2.3	2.3	2.1
Snow	tr	0.0	0.0	0.0	0.0	0.0	0.0	0.0	0.0	0.0	0.0	0.0

High and Low temperatures in degrees Fahrenheit; Precipitation and Snow in inches

Weather Station: Mountain Lake — Elevation: 124 feet

	Jan	Feb	Mar	Apr	May	Jun	Jul	Aug	Sep	Oct	Nov	Dec
High	74	76	81	85	90	92	93	92	90	86	80	75
Low	49	50	55	59	64	70	71	71	70	64	57	51
Precip	2.4	2.5	3.3	2.0	4.0	7.5	7.5	6.6	5.8	2.5	2.2	2.1
Snow	tr	0.0	0.0	0.0	0.0	0.0	0.0	0.0	0.0	0.0	0.0	0.0

High and Low temperatures in degrees Fahrenheit; Precipitation and Snow in inches

Population: 405,382 (1990); 483,924 (2000); 559,664 (2007); 612,505 (2012 projected); Race: 76.5% White, 13.9% Black, 1.3% Asian, 14.2% Hispanic of any race (2007); Density: 298.6 persons per square mile (2007); Average household size: 2.57 (2007); Median age: 38.5 (2007); Males per 100 females: 96.9 (2007).

Religion: Five largest groups: 14.0% Southern Baptist Convention, 7.8% Catholic Church, 3.9% The United Methodist Church, 2.8% Assemblies of God, 1.6% Church of God (Cleveland, Tennessee) (2000).

Economy: Unemployment rate: 4.6% (11/2007); Total civilian labor force: 276,851 (11/2007); Leading industries: 14.4% retail trade; 12.9% health care and social assistance; 10.1% transportation & warehousing (2005); Farms: 3,114 totaling 626,634 acres (2002); Companies that employ 500 or more persons: 29 (2005); Companies that employ 100 to 499 persons: 262 (2005); Companies that employ less than 100 persons: 10,987 (2005); Black-owned businesses: 1,609 (2002); Hispanic-owned businesses: 1,425 (2002); Asian-owned businesses: 886 (2002); Women-owned businesses: 7,874 (2002); Retail sales per capita: $10,501 (2007); Single-family building permits issued: 7,609 (2006); Multi-family building permits issued: 1,714 (2006).

Income: Per capita income: $21,517 (2007); Median household income: $41,821 (2007); Average household income: $54,625 (2007); Percent of households with income of $100,000 or more: 10.9% (2007); Poverty rate: 13.9% (2005); Bankruptcy rate: 1.91% (2006).

Taxes: Total county taxes per capita: $421 (2005); County property taxes per capita: $264 (2005).

Education: Percent of population age 25 and over with: High school diploma (including GED) or higher: 75.1% (2007); Bachelor's degree or higher: 15.1% (2007); Master's degree or higher: 4.9% (2007).

Housing: Homeownership rate: 74.6% (2007); Median home value: $113,583 (2007); Median rent: $400 per month (2000); Median age of housing: 20 years (2000).

Health: Birth rate: 137.0 per 10,000 population (2006); Death rate: 102.2 per 10,000 population (2006); Age-adjusted cancer mortality rate: 191.2 deaths per 100,000 population (2004); Air Quality Index: 89.3% good, 10.4% moderate, 0.3% unhealthy for sensitive individuals, 0.0% unhealthy (percent of days in 2006); Number of physicians: 15.4 per 10,000 population (2005); Hospital beds: 27.7 per 10,000 population (2004); Hospital admissions: 1,338.3 per 10,000 population (2004).

Elections: 2004 Presidential election results: 58.6% Bush, 40.8% Kerry, 0.4% Nader, 0.1% Badnarik

National and State Parks: Lake Kissimmee State Park

Additional Information Contacts

http://auburndalefl.com
Bartow Chamber of Commerce . . . . (863) 533-7125
   http://www.bartowchamber.com
City of Fort Meade . . . . (863) 285-1100
Davenport Chamber of Commerce . . . . (863) 422-3975
   http://polk-county.com
Dundee Area Chamber of Commerce . . . . (863) 439-3261
   http://www.dundeechamber.com
Eagle Lake Chamber of Commerce. . . . . (941) 299-3164
   http://www.eaglelake-fla.com
Fort Meade Chamber of Commerce . . . . (941) 285-8253
   http://www.eog.state.fl.us/ftmeade
Frostproof Chamber of Commerce . . . . (863) 635-9112
   http://www.frostproofchamber.com
Greater Mulberry Chamber of Commerce . . . . (863) 425-4414
   http://www.mulberrychamber.org
Haines City Chamber of Commerce . . . . (941) 422-3751
   http://www.hainescity.com
Lake Wales Chamber of Commerce . . . . (863) 676-3445
   http://www.lakewaleschamber.com
Lakeland Chamber of Commerce . . . . (863) 688-8551
   http://www.lakelandchamber.com
Lakeland Economic Development Council . . . . (863) 687-3788
   http://www.lakelandedc.com
Winter Haven Chamber of Commerce. . . . . (863) 293-2138
   http://winterhavenfl.com

Polk County Communities

AUBURNDALE (city). Covers a land area of 5.220 square miles and a water area of 4.078 square miles. Located at 28.06° N. Lat.; 81.79° W. Long. Elevation is 164 feet.

History: Auburndale was founded by a group seeking a healthful climate, who named the community Sanitaria. Later residents from Auburndale, Massachusetts, renamed the town.

Population: 9,597 (1990); 11,032 (2000); 12,301 (2007); 12,976 (2012 projected); Race: 76.7% White, 14.1% Black, 1.1% Asian, 11.9% Hispanic of any race (2007); Density: 2,356.6 persons per square mile (2007); Average household size: 2.66 (2007); Median age: 35.2 (2007); Males per 100 females: 93.7 (2007); Marriage status: 22.7% never married, 56.2% now married, 8.7% widowed, 12.4% divorced (2000); Foreign born: 5.8% (2000); Ancestry (includes multiple ancestries): 19.5% Other groups, 17.7% United States or American, 10.2% English, 9.6% German, 8.0% Irish (2000).

Economy: Single-family building permits issued: 292 (2006); Multi-family building permits issued: 40 (2006); Employment by occupation: 10.8% management, 13.4% professional, 18.3% services, 26.4% sales, 2.9% farming, 10.3% construction, 17.9% production (2000).

Income: Per capita income: $18,581 (2007); Median household income: $39,373 (2007); Average household income: $48,903 (2007); Percent of households with income of $100,000 or more: 9.2% (2007); Poverty rate: 17.3% (2000).

Education: Percent of population age 25 and over with: High school diploma (including GED) or higher: 70.1% (2007); Bachelor's degree or higher: 11.7% (2007); Master's degree or higher: 3.5% (2007).

School District(s)

Polk County School District (PK-12)
   2005-06 Enrollment: 86,292 . . . . (863) 534-0521

Housing: Homeownership rate: 68.1% (2007); Median home value: $112,529 (2007); Median rent: $372 per month (2000); Median age of housing: 25 years (2000).

Safety: Violent crime rate: 69.1 per 10,000 population; Property crime rate: 607.6 per 10,000 population (2006).

Transportation: Commute to work: 95.3% car, 1.3% public transportation, 0.7% walk, 1.0% work from home (2000); Travel time to work: 28.4% less than 15 minutes, 39.8% 15 to 30 minutes, 21.1% 30 to 45 minutes, 6.5% 45 to 60 minutes, 4.2% 60 minutes or more (2000)

Additional Information Contacts

Auburndale Chamber of Commerce . . . . (863) 967-3400
   http://auburndalefl.com

BABSON PARK (CDP). Covers a land area of 1.494 square miles and a water area of 0 square miles. Located at 27.83° N. Lat.; 81.52° W. Long. Elevation is 144 feet.

History: Babson Park was first called Crooked Lake for the nearby lake, but was renamed by Roger Babson who purchased the land in 1923.

Population: 1,125 (1990); 1,182 (2000); 1,309 (2007); 1,394 (2012 projected); Race: 79.4% White, 13.6% Black, 2.2% Asian, 9.5% Hispanic of any race (2007); Density: 876.5 persons per square mile (2007); Average household size: 3.17 (2007); Median age: 27.7 (2007); Males per 100 females: 103.9 (2007); Marriage status: 19.2% never married, 63.5% now married, 5.3% widowed, 12.0% divorced (2000); Foreign born: 1.3% (2000); Ancestry (includes multiple ancestries): 24.6% Other groups, 15.2% Irish, 13.9% English, 6.9% German, 5.2% Scottish (2000).

Economy: Employment by occupation: 5.9% management, 10.0% professional, 23.3% services, 27.9% sales, 10.2% farming, 13.6% construction, 9.2% production (2000).

Income: Per capita income: $13,560 (2007); Median household income: $34,363 (2007); Average household income: $40,914 (2007); Percent of households with income of $100,000 or more: 5.6% (2007); Poverty rate: 10.3% (2000).

Education: Percent of population age 25 and over with: High school diploma (including GED) or higher: 75.9% (2007); Bachelor's degree or higher: 16.2% (2007); Master's degree or higher: 8.5% (2007).

School District(s)
Polk County School District (PK-12)
   2005-06 Enrollment: 86,292 . . . . (863) 534-0521

Four-year College(s)
Webber International University (Private, Not-for-profit)
   Fall 2006 Enrollment: 617 . . . . (863) 638-1431
   2006-07 Tuition: In-state $15,900; Out-of-state $15,900

Housing: Homeownership rate: 78.9% (2007); Median home value: $109,459 (2007); Median rent: $310 per month (2000); Median age of housing: 23 years (2000).

Transportation: Commute to work: 95.2% car, 0.0% public transportation, 0.0% walk, 4.8% work from home (2000); Travel time to work: 23.1% less than 15 minutes, 56.1% 15 to 30 minutes, 13.0% 30 to 45 minutes, 7.9% 45 to 60 minutes, 0.0% 60 minutes or more (2000)

BARTOW (city). County seat. Covers a land area of 11.226 square miles and a water area of 0.141 square miles. Located at 27.89° N. Lat.; 81.84° W. Long. Elevation is 121 feet.

History: The area around Bartow was settled in 1851 by planters on the site of Fort Blount, built during the Seminole Wars. The town was named in 1867 for Confederate General Francis Bartow.

Population: 14,829 (1990); 15,340 (2000); 16,270 (2007); 16,977 (2012 projected); Race: 65.9% White, 26.2% Black, 1.3% Asian, 12.3% Hispanic of any race (2007); Density: 1,449.4 persons per square mile (2007); Average household size: 2.73 (2007); Median age: 36.0 (2007); Males per 100 females: 100.7 (2007); Marriage status: 24.3% never married, 53.1% now married, 10.2% widowed, 12.4% divorced (2000); Foreign born: 5.4% (2000); Ancestry (includes multiple ancestries): 33.4% Other groups, 11.2% United States or American, 9.1% English, 7.7% Irish, 7.3% German (2000).

Economy: Single-family building permits issued: 173 (2006); Multi-family building permits issued: 0 (2006); Employment by occupation: 10.6% management, 19.1% professional, 15.1% services, 26.4% sales, 0.7% farming, 8.9% construction, 19.1% production (2000).

Income: Per capita income: $22,856 (2007); Median household income: $45,273 (2007); Average household income: $59,169 (2007); Percent of households with income of $100,000 or more: 12.3% (2007); Poverty rate: 13.1% (2000).

Taxes: Total city taxes per capita: $446 (2005); City property taxes per capita: $120 (2005).

Education: Percent of population age 25 and over with: High school diploma (including GED) or higher: 78.4% (2007); Bachelor's degree or higher: 16.9% (2007); Master's degree or higher: 5.4% (2007).

School District(s)
Polk County School District (PK-12)
   2005-06 Enrollment: 86,292 . . . . (863) 534-0521

Housing: Homeownership rate: 70.7% (2007); Median home value: $109,493 (2007); Median rent: $386 per month (2000); Median age of housing: 33 years (2000).

Hospitals: Bartow Regioanl Medical Center (56 beds)

rate: 641.0 per 10,000 population (2006).

Newspapers: The Polk County Democrat (General - Circulation 4,405)

Transportation: Commute to work: 94.1% car, 0.3% public transportation, 3.3% walk, 1.0% work from home (2000); Travel time to work: 44.7% less than 15 minutes, 30.3% 15 to 30 minutes, 17.1% 30 to 45 minutes, 3.8% 45 to 60 minutes, 4.0% 60 minutes or more (2000)

Airports: Bartow Municipal

Additional Information Contacts
Bartow Chamber of Commerce . . . . (863) 533-7125
   http://www.bartowchamber.com

COMBEE SETTLEMENT (CDP). Covers a land area of 2.121 square miles and a water area of 0 square miles. Located at 28.05° N. Lat.; 81.90° W. Long. Elevation is 131 feet.

Population: 5,477 (1990); 5,436 (2000); 5,243 (2007); 5,178 (2012 projected); Race: 82.9% White, 7.9% Black, 0.7% Asian, 10.7% Hispanic of any race (2007); Density: 2,472.3 persons per square mile (2007); Average household size: 2.43 (2007); Median age: 35.4 (2007); Males per 100 females: 102.4 (2007); Marriage status: 22.1% never married, 52.8% now married, 9.2% widowed, 15.9% divorced (2000); Foreign born: 4.0% (2000); Ancestry (includes multiple ancestries): 20.2% United States or American, 18.7% Other groups, 12.0% Irish, 11.2% German, 10.8% English (2000).

Economy: Employment by occupation: 5.7% management, 13.3% professional, 17.0% services, 28.5% sales, 1.1% farming, 15.7% construction, 18.7% production (2000).

Income: Per capita income: $17,036 (2007); Median household income: $35,000 (2007); Average household income: $41,351 (2007); Percent of households with income of $100,000 or more: 4.9% (2007); Poverty rate: 19.5% (2000).

Education: Percent of population age 25 and over with: High school diploma (including GED) or higher: 75.4% (2007); Bachelor's degree or higher: 5.8% (2007); Master's degree or higher: 2.3% (2007).

Housing: Homeownership rate: 62.6% (2007); Median home value: $91,000 (2007); Median rent: $398 per month (2000); Median age of housing: 33 years (2000).

Transportation: Commute to work: 91.8% car, 0.9% public transportation, 3.0% walk, 0.8% work from home (2000); Travel time to work: 21.5% less than 15 minutes, 42.0% 15 to 30 minutes, 23.2% 30 to 45 minutes, 5.9% 45 to 60 minutes, 7.3% 60 minutes or more (2000)

CROOKED LAKE PARK (CDP). Covers a land area of 0.562 square miles and a water area of 0 square miles. Located at 27.83° N. Lat.; 81.59° W. Long. Elevation is 125 feet.

Population: 1,427 (1990); 1,682 (2000); 2,283 (2007); 2,674 (2012 projected); Race: 87.8% White, 5.6% Black, 0.3% Asian, 9.7% Hispanic of any race (2007); Density: 4,058.9 persons per square mile (2007); Average household size: 2.57 (2007); Median age: 37.8 (2007); Males per 100 females: 85.9 (2007); Marriage status: 21.3% never married, 59.3% now married, 11.1% widowed, 8.3% divorced (2000); Foreign born: 3.3% (2000); Ancestry (includes multiple ancestries): 24.8% United States or American, 12.3% English, 12.3% German, 11.7% Other groups, 10.4% Irish (2000).

Economy: Employment by occupation: 5.8% management, 21.5% professional, 12.3% services, 32.2% sales, 2.5% farming, 10.7% construction, 15.1% production (2000).

Income: Per capita income: $23,862 (2007); Median household income: $45,699 (2007); Average household income: $60,936 (2007); Percent of households with income of $100,000 or more: 10.8% (2007); Poverty rate: 5.3% (2000).

Education: Percent of population age 25 and over with: High school diploma (including GED) or higher: 79.0% (2007); Bachelor's degree or higher: 16.2% (2007); Master's degree or higher: 1.5% (2007).

Housing: Homeownership rate: 85.7% (2007); Median home value: $92,581 (2007); Median rent: $419 per month (2000); Median age of housing: 26 years (2000).

Transportation: Commute to work: 95.5% car, 0.0% public transportation, 4.0% walk, 0.5% work from home (2000); Travel time to work: 44.1% less than 15 minutes, 36.2% 15 to 30 minutes, 10.9% 30 to 45 minutes, 7.3% 45 to 60 minutes, 1.5% 60 minutes or more (2000)

CRYSTAL LAKE (CDP). Aka Lake Holloway. Covers a land area of 2.692 square miles and a water area of 0.118 square miles. Located at 28.03° N. Lat.; 81.91° W. Long. Elevation is 151 feet.

Average household size: 2.48 (2007); Median age: 34.1 (2007); Males per 100 females: 97.6 (2007); Marriage status: 27.3% never married, 52.9% now married, 8.2% widowed, 11.6% divorced (2000); Foreign born: 6.9% (2000); Ancestry (includes multiple ancestries): 27.3% Other groups, 17.7% United States or American, 11.1% German, 9.8% English, 6.6% Irish (2000).

Economy: Employment by occupation: 5.3% management, 14.5% professional, 18.7% services, 30.0% sales, 0.0% farming, 14.0% construction, 17.5% production (2000).

Income: Per capita income: $17,624 (2007); Median household income: $34,886 (2007); Average household income: $43,669 (2007); Percent of households with income of $100,000 or more: 6.0% (2007); Poverty rate: 16.4% (2000).

Education: Percent of population age 25 and over with: High school diploma (including GED) or higher: 72.3% (2007); Bachelor's degree or higher: 9.4% (2007); Master's degree or higher: 2.7% (2007).

Housing: Homeownership rate: 56.6% (2007); Median home value: $85,349 (2007); Median rent: $418 per month (2000); Median age of housing: 28 years (2000).

Transportation: Commute to work: 94.3% car, 0.3% public transportation, 1.6% walk, 0.9% work from home (2000); Travel time to work: 29.9% less than 15 minutes, 42.7% 15 to 30 minutes, 17.9% 30 to 45 minutes, 2.3% 45 to 60 minutes, 7.2% 60 minutes or more (2000)

CYPRESS GARDENS (CDP).
Covers a land area of 3.798 square miles and a water area of 0.491 square miles. Located at 28.00° N. Lat.; 81.69° W. Long. Elevation is 167 feet.

Population: 7,822 (1990); 8,844 (2000); 9,666 (2007); 10,286 (2012 projected); Race: 92.1% White, 2.8% Black, 1.9% Asian, 4.0% Hispanic of any race (2007); Density: 2,545.0 persons per square mile (2007); Average household size: 2.49 (2007); Median age: 45.2 (2007); Males per 100 females: 88.5 (2007); Marriage status: 14.3% never married, 65.2% now married, 9.9% widowed, 10.6% divorced (2000); Foreign born: 4.3% (2000); Ancestry (includes multiple ancestries): 19.5% German, 15.5% English, 13.7% Irish, 12.7% United States or American, 11.0% Other groups (2000).

Economy: Employment by occupation: 13.7% management, 27.2% professional, 12.7% services, 29.4% sales, 0.0% farming, 7.9% construction, 9.0% production (2000).

Income: Per capita income: $27,478 (2007); Median household income: $54,465 (2007); Average household income: $67,649 (2007); Percent of households with income of $100,000 or more: 16.5% (2007); Poverty rate: 3.2% (2000).

Education: Percent of population age 25 and over with: High school diploma (including GED) or higher: 87.2% (2007); Bachelor's degree or higher: 28.5% (2007); Master's degree or higher: 9.7% (2007).

Housing: Homeownership rate: 88.3% (2007); Median home value: $146,019 (2007); Median rent: $547 per month (2000); Median age of housing: 26 years (2000).

Transportation: Commute to work: 96.0% car, 0.0% public transportation, 1.0% walk, 2.3% work from home (2000); Travel time to work: 36.6% less than 15 minutes, 39.0% 15 to 30 minutes, 11.9% 30 to 45 minutes, 5.6% 45 to 60 minutes, 6.8% 60 minutes or more (2000)

DAVENPORT (city).
Covers a land area of 1.564 square miles and a water area of 0.062 square miles. Located at 28.16° N. Lat.; 81.60° W. Long. Elevation is 138 feet.

History: Davenport developed as the center of a citrus region, with fruit-packing and canning plants. A citrus candy factory here made crystallized fruit peel.

Population: 1,625 (1990); 1,924 (2000); 2,127 (2007); 2,366 (2012 projected); Race: 88.2% White, 3.6% Black, 0.6% Asian, 14.3% Hispanic of any race (2007); Density: 1,360.4 persons per square mile (2007); Average household size: 2.56 (2007); Median age: 50.6 (2007); Males per 100 females: 90.3 (2007); Marriage status: 15.9% never married, 62.5% now married, 14.3% widowed, 7.3% divorced (2000); Foreign born: 5.9% (2000); Ancestry (includes multiple ancestries): 19.5% Other groups, 15.1% United States or American, 13.6% English, 12.8% German, 6.1% Irish (2000).

Economy: Single-family building permits issued: 86 (2006); Multi-family building permits issued: 0 (2006); Employment by occupation: 12.9%

$34,671 (2007); Average household income: $43,843 (2007); Percent of households with income of $100,000 or more: 5.8% (2007); Poverty rate: 10.8% (2000).

Education: Percent of population age 25 and over with: High school diploma (including GED) or higher: 71.0% (2007); Bachelor's degree or higher: 10.2% (2007); Master's degree or higher: 2.1% (2007).

School District(s)
Osceola County School District (PK-12)
   2005-06 Enrollment: 47,446 . . . . (407) 870-4008
Polk County School District (PK-12)
   2005-06 Enrollment: 86,292 . . . . (863) 534-0521

Housing: Homeownership rate: 89.5% (2007); Median home value: $96,500 (2007); Median rent: $565 per month (2000); Median age of housing: 14 years (2000).

Hospitals: Heart of Florida Regional Medical Center (142 beds)

Safety: Violent crime rate: 34.1 per 10,000 population; Property crime rate: 351.0 per 10,000 population (2006).

Transportation: Commute to work: 96.3% car, 1.3% public transportation, 0.0% walk, 1.1% work from home (2000); Travel time to work: 16.7% less than 15 minutes, 36.5% 15 to 30 minutes, 27.6% 30 to 45 minutes, 10.9% 45 to 60 minutes, 8.2% 60 minutes or more (2000)

Additional Information Contacts
Davenport Chamber of Commerce . . . . (863) 422-3975
  http://polk-county.com

DUNDEE (town).
Covers a land area of 3.931 square miles and a water area of 0.380 square miles. Located at 28.02° N. Lat.; 81.62° W. Long. Elevation is 161 feet.

History: Dundee grew as a community of citrus growers, whose groves are in the surrounding area.

Population: 2,342 (1990); 2,912 (2000); 3,364 (2007); 3,694 (2012 projected); Race: 63.9% White, 24.0% Black, 1.5% Asian, 17.4% Hispanic of any race (2007); Density: 855.7 persons per square mile (2007); Average household size: 2.58 (2007); Median age: 38.9 (2007); Males per 100 females: 93.3 (2007); Marriage status: 18.8% never married, 61.2% now married, 8.7% widowed, 11.3% divorced (2000); Foreign born: 7.2% (2000); Ancestry (includes multiple ancestries): 23.0% Other groups, 11.9% English, 11.4% United States or American, 10.3% Irish, 9.4% German (2000).

Economy: Single-family building permits issued: 44 (2006); Multi-family building permits issued: 0 (2006); Employment by occupation: 5.2% management, 10.1% professional, 20.0% services, 29.1% sales, 4.0% farming, 15.5% construction, 16.1% production (2000).

Income: Per capita income: $16,893 (2007); Median household income: $33,768 (2007); Average household income: $42,690 (2007); Percent of households with income of $100,000 or more: 5.2% (2007); Poverty rate: 12.8% (2000).

Education: Percent of population age 25 and over with: High school diploma (including GED) or higher: 66.6% (2007); Bachelor's degree or higher: 5.2% (2007); Master's degree or higher: 1.1% (2007).

School District(s)
Polk County School District (PK-12)
   2005-06 Enrollment: 86,292 . . . . (863) 534-0521

Housing: Homeownership rate: 79.6% (2007); Median home value: $97,541 (2007); Median rent: $343 per month (2000); Median age of housing: 21 years (2000).

Safety: Violent crime rate: 112.3 per 10,000 population; Property crime rate: 638.6 per 10,000 population (2006).

Transportation: Commute to work: 96.2% car, 0.0% public transportation, 0.3% walk, 1.2% work from home (2000); Travel time to work: 27.2% less than 15 minutes, 48.8% 15 to 30 minutes, 10.6% 30 to 45 minutes, 6.6% 45 to 60 minutes, 6.8% 60 minutes or more (2000)

EAGLE LAKE (city).
Covers a land area of 1.386 square miles and a water area of 0.046 square miles. Located at 27.98° N. Lat.; 81.75° W. Long. Elevation is 167 feet.

Population: 2,025 (1990); 2,496 (2000); 2,653 (2007); 2,777 (2012 projected); Race: 75.3% White, 6.5% Black, 0.3% Asian, 31.1% Hispanic of any race (2007); Density: 1,913.8 persons per square mile (2007); Average household size: 2.86 (2007); Median age: 32.9 (2007); Males per 100 females: 97.4 (2007); Marriage status: 23.0% never married, 58.1% now married, 8.1% widowed, 10.9% divorced (2000); Foreign born: 15.9%

16.4% United States or American, 8.7% German, 7.5% English, 6.9% Irish (2000).

Economy: Single-family building permits issued: 26 (2006); Multi-family building permits issued: 0 (2006); Employment by occupation: 6.4% management, 12.1% professional, 14.5% services, 20.2% sales, 8.2% farming, 17.1% construction, 21.5% production (2000).

Income: Per capita income: $15,781 (2007); Median household income: $35,648 (2007); Average household income: $44,828 (2007); Percent of households with income of $100,000 or more: 7.0% (2007); Poverty rate: 17.9% (2000).

Education: Percent of population age 25 and over with: High school diploma (including GED) or higher: 61.1% (2007); Bachelor's degree or higher: 9.1% (2007); Master's degree or higher: 3.4% (2007).

School District(s)
Polk County School District (PK-12)

  2005-06 Enrollment: 86,292 . . . . (863) 534-0521

Housing: Homeownership rate: 67.9% (2007); Median home value: $91,029 (2007); Median rent: $353 per month (2000); Median age of housing: 28 years (2000).

Transportation: Commute to work: 91.8% car, 0.7% public transportation, 5.1% walk, 1.5% work from home (2000); Travel time to work: 34.7% less than 15 minutes, 33.1% 15 to 30 minutes, 23.4% 30 to 45 minutes, 4.1% 45 to 60 minutes, 4.7% 60 minutes or more (2000)

Additional Information Contacts

Eagle Lake Chamber of Commerce . . . . (941) 299-3164
  http://www.eaglelake-fla.com

FORT MEADE (city).
Covers a land area of 4.975 square miles and a water area of 0.047 square miles. Located at 27.75° N. Lat.; 81.79° W. Long. Elevation is 138 feet.

History: The original Fort Meade was a military post built on the banks of the Peace River during the Seminole War, and named for Lieutenant George Gordon Meade, later acclaimed in the battle of Gettysburg. Stonewall Jackson was stationed at Fort Meade in 1851. The settlement here became a trading post with a traffic in alligator hides, with an order in 1881 for 5,000 hides from a Paris leather firm.

Population: 5,323 (1990); 5,691 (2000); 5,801 (2007); 5,927 (2012 projected); Race: 65.6% White, 21.1% Black, 0.2% Asian, 22.7% Hispanic of any race (2007); Density: 1,165.9 persons per square mile (2007); Average household size: 2.72 (2007); Median age: 34.4 (2007); Males per 100 females: 96.0 (2007); Marriage status: 23.6% never married, 54.7% now married, 10.4% widowed, 11.3% divorced (2000); Foreign born: 10.5% (2000); Ancestry (includes multiple ancestries): 35.0% Other groups, 15.6% United States or American, 6.6% Irish, 5.6% English, 4.9% German (2000).

Economy: Single-family building permits issued: 22 (2006); Multi-family building permits issued: 0 (2006); Employment by occupation: 9.0% management, 10.0% professional, 13.7% services, 25.0% sales, 3.4% farming, 16.5% construction, 22.4% production (2000).

Income: Per capita income: $18,038 (2007); Median household income: $38,641 (2007); Average household income: $48,874 (2007); Percent of households with income of $100,000 or more: 8.3% (2007); Poverty rate: 18.3% (2000).

Education: Percent of population age 25 and over with: High school diploma (including GED) or higher: 67.8% (2007); Bachelor's degree or higher: 6.0% (2007); Master's degree or higher: 2.3% (2007).

School District(s)
Polk County School District (PK-12)

  2005-06 Enrollment: 86,292 . . . . (863) 534-0521

Housing: Homeownership rate: 74.2% (2007); Median home value: $83,455 (2007); Median rent: $303 per month (2000); Median age of housing: 31 years (2000).

Safety: Violent crime rate: 53.1 per 10,000 population; Property crime rate: 376.8 per 10,000 population (2006).

Newspapers: The Fort Meade Leader (General - Circulation 1,394)

Transportation: Commute to work: 95.3% car, 0.4% public transportation, 0.4% walk, 0.0% work from home (2000); Travel time to work: 29.8% less than 15 minutes, 28.4% 15 to 30 minutes, 21.1% 30 to 45 minutes, 10.8% 45 to 60 minutes, 9.9% 60 minutes or more (2000)

Additional Information Contacts

City of Fort Meade . . . . (863) 285-1100
Fort Meade Chamber of Commerce . . . . (941) 285-8253
  http://www.eog.state.fl.us/ftmeade

FROSTPROOF (city).
Covers a land area of 2.486 square miles and a water area of 0.004 square miles. Located at 27.74° N. Lat.; 81.53° W. Long. Elevation is 112 feet.

History: Frostproof was named by early settlers who hoped that frost would never damage their citrus crops. Such was not the case, but the town grew around citrus packing and canning plants.

Population: 2,825 (1990); 2,975 (2000); 3,069 (2007); 3,214 (2012 projected); Race: 69.9% White, 4.6% Black, 0.1% Asian, 31.4% Hispanic of any race (2007); Density: 1,234.6 persons per square mile (2007); Average household size: 2.69 (2007); Median age: 32.2 (2007); Males per 100 females: 103.0 (2007); Marriage status: 22.8% never married, 60.0% now married, 7.4% widowed, 9.8% divorced (2000); Foreign born: 13.2% (2000); Ancestry (includes multiple ancestries): 30.6% Other groups, 17.6% United States or American, 8.0% English, 7.9% German, 6.7% Irish (2000).

Economy: Single-family building permits issued: 2 (2006); Multi-family building permits issued: 0 (2006); Employment by occupation: 7.9% management, 10.2% professional, 14.4% services, 30.1% sales, 7.1% farming, 11.1% construction, 19.2% production (2000).

Income: Per capita income: $18,143 (2007); Median household income: $36,395 (2007); Average household income: $48,757 (2007); Percent of households with income of $100,000 or more: 7.9% (2007); Poverty rate: 16.8% (2000).

Education: Percent of population age 25 and over with: High school diploma (including GED) or higher: 63.2% (2007); Bachelor's degree or higher: 10.6% (2007); Master's degree or higher: 4.4% (2007).

School District(s)
Polk County School District (PK-12)

  2005-06 Enrollment: 86,292 . . . . (863) 534-0521

Housing: Homeownership rate: 68.4% (2007); Median home value: $80,357 (2007); Median rent: $334 per month (2000); Median age of housing: 27 years (2000).

Safety: Violent crime rate: 16.7 per 10,000 population; Property crime rate: 340.0 per 10,000 population (2006).

Transportation: Commute to work: 92.1% car, 0.6% public transportation, 3.6% walk, 3.3% work from home (2000); Travel time to work: 45.0% less than 15 minutes, 15.1% 15 to 30 minutes, 23.0% 30 to 45 minutes, 7.7% 45 to 60 minutes, 9.2% 60 minutes or more (2000)

Additional Information Contacts

Frostproof Chamber of Commerce . . . . (863) 635-9112
  http://www.frostproofchamber.com

FUSSELS CORNER (CDP).
Covers a land area of 7.058 square miles and a water area of 0 square miles. Located at 28.06° N. Lat.; 81.85° W. Long. Elevation is 112 feet.

Population: 4,329 (1990); 5,313 (2000); 6,312 (2007); 7,007 (2012 projected); Race: 87.5% White, 4.3% Black, 0.2% Asian, 8.4% Hispanic of any race (2007); Density: 894.3 persons per square mile (2007); Average household size: 2.33 (2007); Median age: 44.8 (2007); Males per 100 females: 100.1 (2007); Marriage status: 15.6% never married, 65.7% now married, 8.6% widowed, 10.0% divorced (2000); Foreign born: 6.5% (2000); Ancestry (includes multiple ancestries): 16.2% Other groups, 14.9% English, 13.4% German, 11.9% Irish, 9.6% United States or American (2000).

Economy: Employment by occupation: 5.6% management, 10.5% professional, 17.4% services, 30.9% sales, 0.8% farming, 12.0% construction, 22.8% production (2000).

Income: Per capita income: $23,256 (2007); Median household income: $42,416 (2007); Average household income: $54,167 (2007); Percent of households with income of $100,000 or more: 9.8% (2007); Poverty rate: 13.7% (2000).

Education: Percent of population age 25 and over with: High school diploma (including GED) or higher: 69.3% (2007); Bachelor's degree or higher: 11.3% (2007); Master's degree or higher: 3.9% (2007).

Housing: Homeownership rate: 82.9% (2007); Median home value: $80,391 (2007); Median rent: $325 per month (2000); Median age of housing: 10 years (2000).

Transportation: Commute to work: 95.5% car, 0.5% public transportation, 1.9% walk, 1.3% work from home (2000); Travel time to work: 26.0% less than 15 minutes, 45.5% 15 to 30 minutes, 17.5% 30 to 45 minutes, 5.1% 45 to 60 minutes, 5.8% 60 minutes or more (2000)

GIBSONIA (CDP).

Covers a land area of 2.578 square miles and a water area of 0.648 square miles. Located at 28.11° N. Lat.; 81.97° W. Long. Elevation is 171 feet.

Population: 4,542 (1990); 4,507 (2000); 5,278 (2007); 5,825 (2012 projected); Race: 90.9% White, 3.7% Black, 0.9% Asian, 10.2% Hispanic of any race (2007); Density: 2,047.0 persons per square mile (2007); Average household size: 2.52 (2007); Median age: 38.7 (2007); Males per 100 females: 96.9 (2007); Marriage status: 18.8% never married, 63.0% now married, 6.6% widowed, 11.6% divorced (2000); Foreign born: 5.1% (2000); Ancestry (includes multiple ancestries): 21.0% Other groups, 14.8% German, 14.2% United States or American, 13.2% Irish, 8.2% English (2000).

Economy: Employment by occupation: 11.3% management, 13.2% professional, 17.3% services, 31.8% sales, 0.3% farming, 13.6% construction, 12.5% production (2000).

Income: Per capita income: $20,831 (2007); Median household income: $43,168 (2007); Average household income: $51,858 (2007); Percent of households with income of $100,000 or more: 8.7% (2007); Poverty rate: 10.6% (2000).

Education: Percent of population age 25 and over with: High school diploma (including GED) or higher: 83.7% (2007); Bachelor's degree or higher: 15.3% (2007); Master's degree or higher: 4.6% (2007).

Housing: Homeownership rate: 76.0% (2007); Median home value: $127,961 (2007); Median rent: $457 per month (2000); Median age of housing: 23 years (2000).

Transportation: Commute to work: 89.6% car, 0.5% public transportation, 2.1% walk, 5.3% work from home (2000); Travel time to work: 31.6% less than 15 minutes, 38.4% 15 to 30 minutes, 15.8% 30 to 45 minutes, 6.4% 45 to 60 minutes, 7.8% 60 minutes or more (2000)

HAINES CITY (city).

Covers a land area of 8.292 square miles and a water area of 0.646 square miles. Located at 28.11° N. Lat.; 81.62° W. Long. Elevation is 167 feet.

History: First called Clay Cut, the community adopted the name of Haines City in 1887, in honor of Henry Haines. After this honor, Haines, a South Florida Railroad official, arranged for the railroad to erect a station here.

Population: 11,063 (1990); 13,174 (2000); 16,434 (2007); 18,631 (2012 projected); Race: 51.2% White, 30.6% Black, 0.5% Asian, 32.4% Hispanic of any race (2007); Density: 1,981.9 persons per square mile (2007); Average household size: 2.79 (2007); Median age: 34.1 (2007); Males per 100 females: 97.1 (2007); Marriage status: 22.8% never married, 57.3% now married, 9.1% widowed, 10.7% divorced (2000); Foreign born: 18.1% (2000); Ancestry (includes multiple ancestries): 47.6% Other groups, 8.8% German, 8.7% United States or American, 5.7% English, 4.9% Irish (2000).

Economy: Single-family building permits issued: 441 (2006); Multi-family building permits issued: 0 (2006); Employment by occupation: 5.4% management, 10.2% professional, 31.0% services, 21.9% sales, 5.1% farming, 12.2% construction, 14.1% production (2000).

Income: Per capita income: $15,094 (2007); Median household income: $30,776 (2007); Average household income: $41,750 (2007); Percent of households with income of $100,000 or more: 5.4% (2007); Poverty rate: 18.6% (2000).

Education: Percent of population age 25 and over with: High school diploma (including GED) or higher: 58.9% (2007); Bachelor's degree or higher: 8.8% (2007); Master's degree or higher: 2.9% (2007).

School District(s)

Polk County School District (PK-12)
    2005-06 Enrollment: 86,292 . . . . (863) 534-0521

Housing: Homeownership rate: 64.8% (2007); Median home value: $84,326 (2007); Median rent: $361 per month (2000); Median age of housing: 22 years (2000).

Safety: Violent crime rate: 59.5 per 10,000 population; Property crime rate: 559.9 per 10,000 population (2006).

Transportation: Commute to work: 91.6% car, 1.5% public transportation, 2.8% walk, 1.9% work from home (2000); Travel time to work: 28.3% less than 15 minutes, 26.1% 15 to 30 minutes, 32.1% 30 to 45 minutes, 6.8% 45 to 60 minutes, 6.6% 60 minutes or more (2000)

Additional Information Contacts

Dundee Area Chamber of Commerce . . . . (863) 439-3261
    http://www.dundeechamber.com
Haines City Chamber of Commerce . . . . (941) 422-3751
    http://www.hainescity.com

HIGHLAND CITY (CDP).

Aka Highlands City. Covers a land area of 0.829 square miles and a water area of 0 square miles. Located at 27.96° N. Lat.; 81.87° W. Long. Elevation is 118 feet.

Population: 1,919 (1990); 2,051 (2000); 2,117 (2007); 2,185 (2012 projected); Race: 77.9% White, 13.9% Black, 0.9% Asian, 20.5% Hispanic of any race (2007); Density: 2,554.3 persons per square mile (2007); Average household size: 2.68 (2007); Median age: 31.0 (2007); Males per 100 females: 93.2 (2007); Marriage status: 23.6% never married, 57.1% now married, 4.7% widowed, 14.6% divorced (2000); Foreign born: 1.8% (2000); Ancestry (includes multiple ancestries): 26.1% Other groups, 11.2% United States or American, 11.1% German, 10.6% Irish, 9.1% English (2000).

Economy: Employment by occupation: 5.3% management, 15.4% professional, 16.5% services, 39.6% sales, 0.0% farming, 9.3% construction, 14.0% production (2000).

Income: Per capita income: $14,689 (2007); Median household income: $35,399 (2007); Average household income: $39,314 (2007); Percent of households with income of $100,000 or more: 3.7% (2007); Poverty rate: 13.5% (2000).

Education: Percent of population age 25 and over with: High school diploma (including GED) or higher: 78.8% (2007); Bachelor's degree or higher: 5.2% (2007); Master's degree or higher: 2.3% (2007).

Housing: Homeownership rate: 64.2% (2007); Median home value: $96,118 (2007); Median rent: $358 per month (2000); Median age of housing: 19 years (2000).

Transportation: Commute to work: 93.8% car, 0.0% public transportation, 0.8% walk, 4.2% work from home (2000); Travel time to work: 33.0% less than 15 minutes, 41.5% 15 to 30 minutes, 18.6% 30 to 45 minutes, 0.9% 45 to 60 minutes, 6.0% 60 minutes or more (2000)

HIGHLAND PARK (village).

Covers a land area of 0.448 square miles and a water area of 0.271 square miles. Located at 27.86° N. Lat.; 81.56° W. Long. Elevation is 131 feet.

Population: 155 (1990); 244 (2000); 259 (2007); 273 (2012 projected); Race: 91.9% White, 0.8% Black, 5.8% Asian, 1.5% Hispanic of any race (2007); Density: 577.6 persons per square mile (2007); Average household size: 2.14 (2007); Median age: 50.4 (2007); Males per 100 females: 94.7 (2007); Marriage status: 9.7% never married, 71.9% now married, 7.6% widowed, 10.8% divorced (2000); Foreign born: 3.8% (2000); Ancestry (includes multiple ancestries): 25.4% German, 19.9% English, 13.6% Scottish, 13.1% Irish, 9.3% Other groups (2000).

Economy: Employment by occupation: 17.3% management, 30.9% professional, 11.1% services, 23.5% sales, 0.0% farming, 3.7% construction, 13.6% production (2000).

Income: Per capita income: $34,730 (2007); Median household income: $44,167 (2007); Average household income: $74,339 (2007); Percent of households with income of $100,000 or more: 19.8% (2007); Poverty rate: 3.9% (2000).

Education: Percent of population age 25 and over with: High school diploma (including GED) or higher: 92.3% (2007); Bachelor's degree or higher: 41.3% (2007); Master's degree or higher: 18.4% (2007).

Housing: Homeownership rate: 85.1% (2007); Median home value: $126,786 (2007); Median rent: $567 per month (2000); Median age of housing: 29 years (2000).

Transportation: Commute to work: 87.7% car, 0.0% public transportation, 0.0% walk, 9.9% work from home (2000); Travel time to work: 45.2% less than 15 minutes, 32.9% 15 to 30 minutes, 6.8% 30 to 45 minutes, 2.7% 45 to 60 minutes, 12.3% 60 minutes or more (2000)

HILLCREST HEIGHTS (town).

Covers a land area of 0.162 square miles and a water area of 0 square miles. Located at 27.82° N. Lat.; 81.53° W. Long. Elevation is 236 feet.

Population: 221 (1990); 266 (2000); 305 (2007); 334 (2012 projected); Race: 95.1% White, 2.3% Black, 1.3% Asian, 3.6% Hispanic of any race (2007); Density: 1,880.7 persons per square mile (2007); Average household size: 2.70 (2007); Median age: 40.3 (2007); Males per 100 females: 93.0 (2007); Marriage status: 15.1% never married, 70.7% now married, 5.9% widowed, 8.3% divorced (2000); Foreign born: 3.3% (2000); Ancestry (includes multiple ancestries): 26.2% English, 24.4% German, 10.7% Irish, 9.2% United States or American, 7.0% French (except Basque) (2000).

Economy: Employment by occupation: 23.0% management, 23.8% professional, 12.7% services, 24.6% sales, 0.8% farming, 10.3% construction, 4.8% production (2000).

Income: Per capita income: $30,107 (2007); Median household income: $72,717 (2007); Average household income: $81,261 (2007); Percent of households with income of $100,000 or more: 15.9% (2007); Poverty rate: 1.5% (2000).
Education: Percent of population age 25 and over with: High school diploma (including GED) or higher: 87.3% (2007); Bachelor's degree or higher: 26.0% (2007); Master's degree or higher: 10.3% (2007).
Housing: Homeownership rate: 87.6% (2007); Median home value: $167,083 (2007); Median rent: $420 per month (2000); Median age of housing: 40 years (2000).
Transportation: Commute to work: 99.2% car, 0.0% public transportation, 0.0% walk, 0.0% work from home (2000); Travel time to work: 30.6% less than 15 minutes, 52.4% 15 to 30 minutes, 7.3% 30 to 45 minutes, 6.5% 45 to 60 minutes, 3.2% 60 minutes or more (2000)

INWOOD (CDP). Aka West Winter Haven. Covers a land area of 1.917 square miles and a water area of 0.088 square miles. Located at 28.03° N. Lat.; 81.76° W. Long. Elevation is 144 feet.
Population: 6,764 (1990); 6,925 (2000); 6,792 (2007); 6,798 (2012 projected); Race: 59.1% White, 29.7% Black, 1.2% Asian, 11.8% Hispanic of any race (2007); Density: 3,542.7 persons per square mile (2007); Average household size: 2.45 (2007); Median age: 34.1 (2007); Males per 100 females: 98.1 (2007); Marriage status: 27.0% never married, 49.3% now married, 9.9% widowed, 13.8% divorced (2000); Foreign born: 9.9% (2000); Ancestry (includes multiple ancestries): 26.1% Other groups, 15.1% United States or American, 10.6% Irish, 7.7% German, 6.5% Haitian (2000).
Economy: Employment by occupation: 5.3% management, 12.0% professional, 24.0% services, 19.9% sales, 1.4% farming, 17.5% construction, 19.8% production (2000).
Income: Per capita income: $14,616 (2007); Median household income: $28,860 (2007); Average household income: $35,826 (2007); Percent of households with income of $100,000 or more: 3.2% (2007); Poverty rate: 19.1% (2000).
Education: Percent of population age 25 and over with: High school diploma (including GED) or higher: 66.2% (2007); Bachelor's degree or higher: 5.9% (2007); Master's degree or higher: 2.4% (2007).
Housing: Homeownership rate: 57.7% (2007); Median home value: $78,963 (2007); Median rent: $398 per month (2000); Median age of housing: 34 years (2000).
Transportation: Commute to work: 94.7% car, 0.3% public transportation, 1.0% walk, 1.6% work from home (2000); Travel time to work: 35.5% less than 15 minutes, 33.1% 15 to 30 minutes, 17.5% 30 to 45 minutes, 10.1% 45 to 60 minutes, 3.8% 60 minutes or more (2000)

JAN PHYL VILLAGE (CDP). Covers a land area of 4.716 square miles and a water area of 0.113 square miles. Located at 28.01° N. Lat.; 81.77° W. Long. Elevation is 154 feet.
Population: 5,308 (1990); 5,633 (2000); 6,146 (2007); 6,541 (2012 projected); Race: 66.0% White, 24.2% Black, 2.2% Asian, 10.6% Hispanic of any race (2007); Density: 1,303.3 persons per square mile (2007); Average household size: 2.92 (2007); Median age: 32.4 (2007); Males per 100 females: 91.6 (2007); Marriage status: 22.9% never married, 61.5% now married, 6.6% widowed, 9.1% divorced (2000); Foreign born: 6.4% (2000); Ancestry (includes multiple ancestries): 29.4% Other groups, 21.6% United States or American, 10.6% English, 9.4% German, 8.5% Irish (2000).
Economy: Employment by occupation: 9.6% management, 14.4% professional, 13.3% services, 29.9% sales, 0.6% farming, 12.8% construction, 19.4% production (2000).
Income: Per capita income: $19,318 (2007); Median household income: $47,843 (2007); Average household income: $56,431 (2007); Percent of households with income of $100,000 or more: 11.1% (2007); Poverty rate: 8.5% (2000).
Education: Percent of population age 25 and over with: High school diploma (including GED) or higher: 77.2% (2007); Bachelor's degree or higher: 11.4% (2007); Master's degree or higher: 2.9% (2007).
Housing: Homeownership rate: 78.5% (2007); Median home value: $108,309 (2007); Median rent: $411 per month (2000); Median age of housing: 23 years (2000).
Transportation: Commute to work: 95.7% car, 0.0% public transportation, 0.0% walk, 3.5% work from home (2000); Travel time to work: 27.7% less than 15 minutes, 40.5% 15 to 30 minutes, 25.4% 30 to 45 minutes, 3.3% 45 to 60 minutes, 3.0% 60 minutes or more (2000)

KATHLEEN (CDP). Covers a land area of 3.325 square miles and a water area of 0 square miles. Located at 28.12° N. Lat.; 82.02° W. Long. Elevation is 144 feet.
Population: 2,743 (1990); 3,280 (2000); 4,025 (2007); 4,525 (2012 projected); Race: 90.2% White, 2.7% Black, 0.3% Asian, 12.4% Hispanic of any race (2007); Density: 1,210.4 persons per square mile (2007); Average household size: 2.81 (2007); Median age: 35.2 (2007); Males per 100 females: 99.2 (2007); Marriage status: 20.7% never married, 58.9% now married, 7.2% widowed, 13.2% divorced (2000); Foreign born: 4.9% (2000); Ancestry (includes multiple ancestries): 31.4% United States or American, 14.4% Other groups, 12.2% Irish, 9.7% English, 8.5% German (2000).
Economy: Employment by occupation: 12.9% management, 12.0% professional, 13.1% services, 26.1% sales, 0.5% farming, 16.2% construction, 19.3% production (2000).
Income: Per capita income: $19,229 (2007); Median household income: $45,934 (2007); Average household income: $54,049 (2007); Percent of households with income of $100,000 or more: 11.7% (2007); Poverty rate: 10.1% (2000).
Education: Percent of population age 25 and over with: High school diploma (including GED) or higher: 67.8% (2007); Bachelor's degree or higher: 7.6% (2007); Master's degree or higher: 3.8% (2007).
Housing: Homeownership rate: 83.0% (2007); Median home value: $106,512 (2007); Median rent: $376 per month (2000); Median age of housing: 18 years (2000).
Transportation: Commute to work: 95.7% car, 0.0% public transportation, 0.0% walk, 2.5% work from home (2000); Travel time to work: 14.3% less than 15 minutes, 52.4% 15 to 30 minutes, 15.4% 30 to 45 minutes, 8.0% 45 to 60 minutes, 9.9% 60 minutes or more (2000)

LAKE ALFRED (city). Covers a land area of 4.902 square miles and a water area of 3.684 square miles. Located at 28.09° N. Lat.; 81.72° W. Long. Elevation is 174 feet.
History: Lake Alfred was named for Alfred Parslow, an early landowner and franchiser for a local railroad. The town grew in an area of citrus groves, and was earlier known as Barton Junction, Chubb, and Fargo.
Population: 3,747 (1990); 3,890 (2000); 3,911 (2007); 3,955 (2012 projected); Race: 76.7% White, 17.4% Black, 0.9% Asian, 9.1% Hispanic of any race (2007); Density: 797.9 persons per square mile (2007); Average household size: 2.56 (2007); Median age: 37.5 (2007); Males per 100 females: 89.3 (2007); Marriage status: 19.2% never married, 62.4% now married, 7.2% widowed, 11.1% divorced (2000); Foreign born: 5.9% (2000); Ancestry (includes multiple ancestries): 25.7% Other groups, 13.7% German, 12.1% English, 12.0% United States or American, 11.7% Irish (2000).
Economy: Single-family building permits issued: 64 (2006); Multi-family building permits issued: 0 (2006); Employment by occupation: 13.6% management, 18.2% professional, 16.3% services, 24.7% sales, 1.7% farming, 11.8% construction, 13.8% production (2000).
Income: Per capita income: $21,065 (2007); Median household income: $42,969 (2007); Average household income: $53,171 (2007); Percent of households with income of $100,000 or more: 9.4% (2007); Poverty rate: 14.0% (2000).
Education: Percent of population age 25 and over with: High school diploma (including GED) or higher: 74.6% (2007); Bachelor's degree or higher: 15.7% (2007); Master's degree or higher: 5.4% (2007).
School District(s)
Polk County School District (PK-12)
    2005-06 Enrollment: 86,292 . . . . (863) 534-0521
Housing: Homeownership rate: 72.2% (2007); Median home value: $118,784 (2007); Median rent: $397 per month (2000); Median age of housing: 28 years (2000).
Safety: Violent crime rate: 30.0 per 10,000 population; Property crime rate: 325.3 per 10,000 population (2006).
Transportation: Commute to work: 94.2% car, 0.3% public transportation, 2.3% walk, 1.4% work from home (2000); Travel time to work: 31.1% less than 15 minutes, 32.3% 15 to 30 minutes, 18.3% 30 to 45 minutes, 8.0% 45 to 60 minutes, 10.3% 60 minutes or more (2000)

LAKE HAMILTON (town). Covers a land area of 3.032 square miles and a water area of 0.881 square miles. Located at 28.04° N. Lat.; 81.62° W. Long. Elevation is 148 feet.
History: Lake Hamilton, on the shores of the lake for which it was named, grew around a citrus packing plant.

Population: 1,128 (1990); 1,304 (2000); 1,398 (2007); 1,469 (2012 projected); Race: 67.6% White, 26.3% Black, 0.6% Asian, 7.7% Hispanic of any race (2007); Density: 461.0 persons per square mile (2007); Average household size: 2.71 (2007); Median age: 37.0 (2007); Males per 100 females: 91.8 (2007); Marriage status: 23.9% never married, 63.2% now married, 6.5% widowed, 6.5% divorced (2000); Foreign born: 3.1% (2000); Ancestry (includes multiple ancestries): 36.1% Other groups, 10.2% English, 10.0% United States or American, 9.0% Irish, 8.4% German (2000).
Economy: Single-family building permits issued: 3 (2006); Multi-family building permits issued: 0 (2006); Employment by occupation: 9.9% management, 12.8% professional, 19.5% services, 18.3% sales, 4.1% farming, 16.6% construction, 18.9% production (2000).
Income: Per capita income: $19,068 (2007); Median household income: $37,870 (2007); Average household income: $48,573 (2007); Percent of households with income of $100,000 or more: 8.2% (2007); Poverty rate: 21.5% (2000).
Education: Percent of population age 25 and over with: High school diploma (including GED) or higher: 65.6% (2007); Bachelor's degree or higher: 12.0% (2007); Master's degree or higher: 3.9% (2007).
Housing: Homeownership rate: 75.0% (2007); Median home value: $119,811 (2007); Median rent: $355 per month (2000); Median age of housing: 33 years (2000).
Safety: Violent crime rate: 41.7 per 10,000 population; Property crime rate: 632.8 per 10,000 population (2006).
Transportation: Commute to work: 96.5% car, 1.4% public transportation, 0.6% walk, 0.6% work from home (2000); Travel time to work: 22.9% less than 15 minutes, 38.0% 15 to 30 minutes, 25.8% 30 to 45 minutes, 7.1% 45 to 60 minutes, 6.2% 60 minutes or more (2000)

LAKE WALES (city).
Covers a land area of 13.345 square miles and a water area of 0.665 square miles. Located at 27.90° N. Lat.; 81.58° W. Long. Elevation is 148 feet.
History: Lake Wales grew as a resort town on the lake of the same name. The name was originally Waels, for the Waels family who settled here in the early 1900's. The spelling was changed when the town was platted in 1911.
Population: 10,130 (1990); 10,194 (2000); 13,294 (2007); 15,311 (2012 projected); Race: 56.4% White, 35.5% Black, 0.7% Asian, 15.0% Hispanic of any race (2007); Density: 996.2 persons per square mile (2007); Average household size: 2.52 (2007); Median age: 34.9 (2007); Males per 100 females: 90.2 (2007); Marriage status: 24.7% never married, 49.7% now married, 13.2% widowed, 12.4% divorced (2000); Foreign born: 7.9% (2000); Ancestry (includes multiple ancestries): 38.2% Other groups, 11.2% United States or American, 8.6% English, 7.8% German, 7.7% Irish (2000).
Economy: Single-family building permits issued: 103 (2006); Multi-family building permits issued: 0 (2006); Employment by occupation: 6.6% management, 18.3% professional, 17.8% services, 23.7% sales, 8.3% farming, 9.0% construction, 16.3% production (2000).
Income: Per capita income: $18,659 (2007); Median household income: $30,658 (2007); Average household income: $45,818 (2007); Percent of households with income of $100,000 or more: 8.4% (2007); Poverty rate: 21.4% (2000).
Education: Percent of population age 25 and over with: High school diploma (including GED) or higher: 73.4% (2007); Bachelor's degree or higher: 18.3% (2007); Master's degree or higher: 6.3% (2007).
School District(s)
Polk County School District (PK-12)
    2005-06 Enrollment: 86,292 . . . . (863) 534-0521
Four-year College(s)
Warner Southern College (Private, Not-for-profit, Church of God)
    Fall 2006 Enrollment: 1,043. . . . . (863) 638-1426
    2006-07 Tuition: In-state $13,210; Out-of-state $13,210
Housing: Homeownership rate: 54.1% (2007); Median home value: $107,596 (2007); Median rent: $325 per month (2000); Median age of housing: 28 years (2000).
Hospitals: Lake Wales Medical Center (154 beds)
Safety: Violent crime rate: 41.0 per 10,000 population; Property crime rate: 535.5 per 10,000 population (2006).
Newspapers: The Lake Wales News (General - Circulation 3,200)
Transportation: Commute to work: 90.7% car, 1.5% public transportation, 3.1% walk, 3.4% work from home (2000); Travel time to work: 44.8% less than 15 minutes, 23.6% 15 to 30 minutes, 15.5% 30 to 45 minutes, 8.0% 45 to 60 minutes, 7.9% 60 minutes or more (2000)

Additional Information Contacts
Lake Wales Chamber of Commerce . . . . (863) 676-3445
    http://www.lakewaleschamber.com

LAKELAND (city).
Covers a land area of 45.842 square miles and a water area of 5.610 square miles. Located at 28.04° N. Lat.; 81.95° W. Long. Elevation is 197 feet.
History: Lakeland began when the South Florida Railroad was built here in 1884, and the town was incorporated in 1885. In 1894 Lakeland absorbed the town of Acton, established nearby by a group of Englishmen and named for British historian Lord Acton. Lakeland grew as the headquarters of the Florida Citrus Commission, and the location of many citrus producing and shipping companies.
Population: 73,375 (1990); 78,452 (2000); 82,493 (2007); 85,983 (2012 projected); Race: 70.9% White, 22.0% Black, 1.8% Asian, 9.4% Hispanic of any race (2007); Density: 1,799.5 persons per square mile (2007); Average household size: 2.32 (2007); Median age: 39.4 (2007); Males per 100 females: 88.5 (2007); Marriage status: 24.0% never married, 52.9% now married, 10.6% widowed, 12.5% divorced (2000); Foreign born: 5.7% (2000); Ancestry (includes multiple ancestries): 29.4% Other groups, 12.5% German, 11.1% English, 10.3% Irish, 9.9% United States or American (2000).
Economy: Unemployment rate: 3.9% (11/2007); Total civilian labor force: 44,293 (11/2007); Single-family building permits issued: 844 (2006); Multi-family building permits issued: 851 (2006); Employment by occupation: 11.3% management, 19.5% professional, 16.9% services, 28.6% sales, 0.4% farming, 7.6% construction, 15.7% production (2000).
Income: Per capita income: $22,301 (2007); Median household income: $37,586 (2007); Average household income: $50,797 (2007); Percent of households with income of $100,000 or more: 9.5% (2007); Poverty rate: 15.0% (2000).
Taxes: Total city taxes per capita: $471 (2005); City property taxes per capita: $161 (2005).
Education: Percent of population age 25 and over with: High school diploma (including GED) or higher: 79.7% (2007); Bachelor's degree or higher: 21.3% (2007); Master's degree or higher: 7.7% (2007).
School District(s)
Polk County School District (PK-12)
    2005-06 Enrollment: 86,292 . . . . (863) 534-0521
Four-year College(s)
Florida Metropolitan University-Lakeland (Private, For-profit)
    Fall 2006 Enrollment: 687 . . . . (863) 686-1444
    2006-07 Tuition: In-state $10,440; Out-of-state $10,440
Florida Southern College (Private, Not-for-profit, United Methodist)
    Fall 2006 Enrollment: 2,441. . . . . (863) 680-4111
    2006-07 Tuition: In-state $20,175; Out-of-state $20,175
Southeastern University (Private, Not-for-profit, Assemblies of God Church)
    Fall 2006 Enrollment: 2,901. . . . . (863) 667-5000
    2006-07 Tuition: In-state $12,280; Out-of-state $12,280
Two-year College(s)
Traviss Career Center (Public)
    Fall 2006 Enrollment: 780 . . . . (863) 499-2700
    2006-07 Tuition: In-state $2,000; Out-of-state $8,600
Housing: Homeownership rate: 61.0% (2007); Median home value: $114,810 (2007); Median rent: $423 per month (2000); Median age of housing: 25 years (2000).
Hospitals: Lakeland Regional Medical Center (851 beds)
Safety: Violent crime rate: 65.7 per 10,000 population; Property crime rate: 571.8 per 10,000 population (2006).
Newspapers: The Ledger (Circulation 75,140)
Transportation: Commute to work: 91.9% car, 1.8% public transportation, 2.7% walk, 2.2% work from home (2000); Travel time to work: 37.1% less than 15 minutes, 39.4% 15 to 30 minutes, 13.0% 30 to 45 minutes, 5.3% 45 to 60 minutes, 5.2% 60 minutes or more (2000); Amtrak: Service available.
Airports: Lakeland Linder Regional
Additional Information Contacts
Lakeland Chamber of Commerce . . . . (863) 688-8551
    http://www.lakelandchamber.com
Lakeland Economic Development Council . . . . (863) 687-3788
    http://www.lakelandedc.com

LAKELAND HIGHLANDS (CDP).
Covers a land area of 5.584 square miles and a water area of 0.574 square miles. Located at 27.96° N. Lat.; 81.94° W. Long. Elevation is 223 feet.

Population: 9,972 (1990); 12,557 (2000); 14,468 (2007); 15,813 (2012 projected); Race: 92.5% White, 3.3% Black, 2.1% Asian, 4.7% Hispanic of any race (2007); Density: 2,591.0 persons per square mile (2007); Average household size: 2.78 (2007); Median age: 41.8 (2007); Males per 100 females: 94.7 (2007); Marriage status: 17.3% never married, 70.9% now married, 5.8% widowed, 6.1% divorced (2000); Foreign born: 6.2% (2000); Ancestry (includes multiple ancestries): 17.3% German, 15.2% United States or American, 13.3% Irish, 13.3% English, 12.5% Other groups (2000).
Economy: Employment by occupation: 19.2% management, 30.4% professional, 10.1% services, 25.3% sales, 0.0% farming, 7.6% construction, 7.5% production (2000).
Income: Per capita income: $36,426 (2007); Median household income: $73,655 (2007); Average household income: $101,197 (2007); Percent of households with income of $100,000 or more: 31.5% (2007); Poverty rate: 3.3% (2000).
Education: Percent of population age 25 and over with: High school diploma (including GED) or higher: 92.9% (2007); Bachelor's degree or higher: 40.0% (2007); Master's degree or higher: 15.7% (2007).
Housing: Homeownership rate: 92.3% (2007); Median home value: $197,033 (2007); Median rent: $582 per month (2000); Median age of housing: 18 years (2000).
Transportation: Commute to work: 96.9% car, 0.0% public transportation, 0.1% walk, 2.3% work from home (2000); Travel time to work: 22.7% less than 15 minutes, 54.3% 15 to 30 minutes, 13.0% 30 to 45 minutes, 4.9% 45 to 60 minutes, 5.1% 60 minutes or more (2000)

LOUGHMAN (CDP).

Covers a land area of 3.723 square miles and a water area of 0.046 square miles. Located at 28.24° N. Lat.; 81.56° W. Long. Elevation is 102 feet.
Population: 1,239 (1990); 1,385 (2000); 2,077 (2007); 2,518 (2012 projected); Race: 82.8% White, 8.6% Black, 0.7% Asian, 16.9% Hispanic of any race (2007); Density: 557.9 persons per square mile (2007); Average household size: 2.49 (2007); Median age: 37.6 (2007); Males per 100 females: 93.6 (2007); Marriage status: 26.4% never married, 56.8% now married, 7.3% widowed, 9.5% divorced (2000); Foreign born: 8.5% (2000); Ancestry (includes multiple ancestries): 28.3% Other groups, 17.3% German, 15.7% United States or American, 13.3% Irish, 8.4% English (2000).
Economy: Employment by occupation: 10.0% management, 12.1% professional, 25.4% services, 17.3% sales, 0.0% farming, 21.7% construction, 13.5% production (2000).
Income: Per capita income: $16,793 (2007); Median household income: $38,500 (2007); Average household income: $41,823 (2007); Percent of households with income of $100,000 or more: 6.1% (2007); Poverty rate: 18.0% (2000).
Education: Percent of population age 25 and over with: High school diploma (including GED) or higher: 67.3% (2007); Bachelor's degree or higher: 16.0% (2007); Master's degree or higher: 3.4% (2007).
Housing: Homeownership rate: 79.3% (2007); Median home value: $58,026 (2007); Median rent: $244 per month (2000); Median age of housing: 9 years (2000).
Transportation: Commute to work: 91.7% car, 0.0% public transportation, 1.6% walk, 4.0% work from home (2000); Travel time to work: 14.2% less than 15 minutes, 60.1% 15 to 30 minutes, 12.5% 30 to 45 minutes, 9.6% 45 to 60 minutes, 3.6% 60 minutes or more (2000)

MEDULLA (CDP).

Covers a land area of 5.676 square miles and a water area of 0.018 square miles. Located at 27.96° N. Lat.; 81.98° W. Long. Elevation is 161 feet.
Population: 3,977 (1990); 6,637 (2000); 8,108 (2007); 9,109 (2012 projected); Race: 82.1% White, 12.3% Black, 0.9% Asian, 8.3% Hispanic of any race (2007); Density: 1,428.5 persons per square mile (2007); Average household size: 2.59 (2007); Median age: 34.6 (2007); Males per 100 females: 99.8 (2007); Marriage status: 25.1% never married, 61.6% now married, 4.0% widowed, 9.2% divorced (2000); Foreign born: 3.3% (2000); Ancestry (includes multiple ancestries): 17.8% United States or American, 17.2% Other groups, 12.7% German, 12.2% Irish, 8.7% English (2000).
Economy: Employment by occupation: 16.6% management, 20.7% professional, 14.6% services, 25.0% sales, 0.2% farming, 10.0% construction, 12.9% production (2000).
Income: Per capita income: $25,255 (2007); Median household income: $52,414 (2007); Average household income: $65,189 (2007); Percent of households with income of $100,000 or more: 17.3% (2007); Poverty rate: 6.0% (2000).

Education: Percent of population age 25 and over with: High school diploma (including GED) or higher: 87.6% (2007); Bachelor's degree or higher: 20.7% (2007); Master's degree or higher: 6.5% (2007).
Housing: Homeownership rate: 63.9% (2007); Median home value: $166,007 (2007); Median rent: $493 per month (2000); Median age of housing: 14 years (2000).
Transportation: Commute to work: 92.7% car, 0.7% public transportation, 0.8% walk, 4.1% work from home (2000); Travel time to work: 27.9% less than 15 minutes, 42.8% 15 to 30 minutes, 18.6% 30 to 45 minutes, 6.6% 45 to 60 minutes, 4.2% 60 minutes or more (2000)

MULBERRY (city).

Covers a land area of 3.067 square miles and a water area of 0.141 square miles. Located at 27.89° N. Lat.; 81.97° W. Long. Elevation is 112 feet.
History: Mulberry grew up around a railroad loading station noted for a large mulberry tree growing beside the tracks where freight was unloaded. Pebble phosphate was mined here, and for several decades in the late 1800's and early 1900's Mulberry resembled a gold-mining town of the west.
Population: 3,084 (1990); 3,230 (2000); 3,719 (2007); 4,030 (2012 projected); Race: 78.2% White, 17.0% Black, 0.4% Asian, 6.7% Hispanic of any race (2007); Density: 1,212.7 persons per square mile (2007); Average household size: 2.39 (2007); Median age: 40.5 (2007); Males per 100 females: 93.7 (2007); Marriage status: 16.7% never married, 58.6% now married, 12.9% widowed, 11.8% divorced (2000); Foreign born: 3.6% (2000); Ancestry (includes multiple ancestries): 28.0% Other groups, 16.3% United States or American, 11.6% German, 10.2% English, 9.6% Irish (2000).
Economy: Single-family building permits issued: 3 (2006); Multi-family building permits issued: 0 (2006); Employment by occupation: 6.5% management, 14.4% professional, 15.7% services, 23.0% sales, 7.9% farming, 14.4% construction, 18.0% production (2000).
Income: Per capita income: $17,802 (2007); Median household income: $32,900 (2007); Average household income: $42,494 (2007); Percent of households with income of $100,000 or more: 5.1% (2007); Poverty rate: 16.6% (2000).
Education: Percent of population age 25 and over with: High school diploma (including GED) or higher: 72.5% (2007); Bachelor's degree or higher: 7.3% (2007); Master's degree or higher: 2.0% (2007).

School District(s)
Polk County School District (PK-12)
    2005-06 Enrollment: 86,292 . . . . (863) 534-0521

Vocational/Technical School(s)
Florida Career Institute Inc (Private, For-profit)
    Fall 2006 Enrollment: 100 . . . . (863) 646-1400
    2006-07 Tuition: In-state $11,211; Out-of-state $11,211
Housing: Homeownership rate: 75.9% (2007); Median home value: $74,651 (2007); Median rent: $340 per month (2000); Median age of housing: 20 years (2000).
Safety: Violent crime rate: 76.0 per 10,000 population; Property crime rate: 806.0 per 10,000 population (2006).
Newspapers: Polk County Press-Mulberry Edition (General - Circulation 3,000)
Transportation: Commute to work: 96.1% car, 0.0% public transportation, 0.6% walk, 1.8% work from home (2000); Travel time to work: 25.5% less than 15 minutes, 32.9% 15 to 30 minutes, 22.8% 30 to 45 minutes, 7.6% 45 to 60 minutes, 11.1% 60 minutes or more (2000)
Additional Information Contacts
Greater Mulberry Chamber of Commerce . . . . (863) 425-4414
    http://www.mulberrychamber.org

POLK CITY (town).

Covers a land area of 0.771 square miles and a water area of 0 square miles. Located at 28.18° N. Lat.; 81.82° W. Long. Elevation is 171 feet.
History: Polk City was founded in 1922 by Isasac Van Horn on the northern shore of Lake Agnes, one of many small lakes in the area.
Population: 1,493 (1990); 1,516 (2000); 1,711 (2007); 1,842 (2012 projected); Race: 92.0% White, 2.2% Black, 0.6% Asian, 13.6% Hispanic of any race (2007); Density: 2,219.1 persons per square mile (2007); Average household size: 2.78 (2007); Median age: 34.0 (2007); Males per 100 females: 98.3 (2007); Marriage status: 16.2% never married, 59.9% now married, 7.1% widowed, 16.8% divorced (2000); Foreign born: 2.1% (2000); Ancestry (includes multiple ancestries): 15.2% Other groups, 13.5% Irish, 12.6% English, 8.8% United States or American, 7.2% German (2000).

Economy: Single-family building permits issued: 10 (2006); Multi-family building permits issued: 6 (2006); Employment by occupation: 4.9% management, 8.9% professional, 17.4% services, 25.4% sales, 0.6% farming, 18.6% construction, 24.2% production (2000).
Income: Per capita income: $17,653 (2007); Median household income: $41,641 (2007); Average household income: $49,114 (2007); Percent of households with income of $100,000 or more: 5.0% (2007); Poverty rate: 13.4% (2000).
Education: Percent of population age 25 and over with: High school diploma (including GED) or higher: 69.7% (2007); Bachelor's degree or higher: 6.1% (2007); Master's degree or higher: 1.0% (2007).

School District(s)
Polk County School District (PK-12)
   2005-06 Enrollment: 86,292 . . . . (863) 534-0521
Housing: Homeownership rate: 77.1% (2007); Median home value: $91,500 (2007); Median rent: $325 per month (2000); Median age of housing: 16 years (2000).
Transportation: Commute to work: 94.9% car, 0.0% public transportation, 0.4% walk, 4.6% work from home (2000); Travel time to work: 14.4% less than 15 minutes, 32.6% 15 to 30 minutes, 37.3% 30 to 45 minutes, 8.3% 45 to 60 minutes, 7.4% 60 minutes or more (2000)

WAHNETA (CDP). Covers a land area of 2.421 square miles and a water area of 0 square miles. Located at 27.95° N. Lat.; 81.72° W. Long. Elevation is 131 feet.
Population: 4,050 (1990); 4,731 (2000); 4,957 (2007); 5,156 (2012 projected); Race: 58.2% White, 1.4% Black, 0.0% Asian, 63.5% Hispanic of any race (2007); Density: 2,047.6 persons per square mile (2007); Average household size: 3.61 (2007); Median age: 27.8 (2007); Males per 100 females: 119.9 (2007); Marriage status: 26.8% never married, 58.1% now married, 4.7% widowed, 10.3% divorced (2000); Foreign born: 24.0% (2000); Ancestry (includes multiple ancestries): 49.5% Other groups, 12.6% United States or American, 7.7% Irish, 4.7% English, 3.5% German (2000).
Economy: Employment by occupation: 7.9% management, 3.6% professional, 10.6% services, 13.3% sales, 14.9% farming, 24.1% construction, 25.7% production (2000).
Income: Per capita income: $9,055 (2007); Median household income: $24,580 (2007); Average household income: $32,715 (2007); Percent of households with income of $100,000 or more: 3.1% (2007); Poverty rate: 29.1% (2000).
Education: Percent of population age 25 and over with: High school diploma (including GED) or higher: 33.1% (2007); Bachelor's degree or higher: 1.0% (2007); Master's degree or higher: 0.7% (2007).
Housing: Homeownership rate: 62.1% (2007); Median home value: $60,978 (2007); Median rent: $376 per month (2000); Median age of housing: 27 years (2000).
Transportation: Commute to work: 93.0% car, 1.8% public transportation, 1.3% walk, 0.5% work from home (2000); Travel time to work: 30.4% less than 15 minutes, 31.0% 15 to 30 minutes, 16.6% 30 to 45 minutes, 3.7% 45 to 60 minutes, 18.3% 60 minutes or more (2000)

WAVERLY (CDP). Covers a land area of 3.544 square miles and a water area of 0.038 square miles. Located at 27.96° N. Lat.; 81.62° W. Long. Elevation is 128 feet.
Population: 1,994 (1990); 1,927 (2000); 2,250 (2007); 2,488 (2012 projected); Race: 68.3% White, 24.4% Black, 0.2% Asian, 6.8% Hispanic of any race (2007); Density: 635.0 persons per square mile (2007); Average household size: 2.19 (2007); Median age: 57.1 (2007); Males per 100 females: 92.5 (2007); Marriage status: 9.2% never married, 69.8% now married, 10.4% widowed, 10.7% divorced (2000); Foreign born: 2.3% (2000); Ancestry (includes multiple ancestries): 24.2% Other groups, 15.1% United States or American, 12.5% German, 10.0% Irish, 7.8% English (2000).
Economy: Employment by occupation: 1.5% management, 8.5% professional, 17.2% services, 38.6% sales, 1.4% farming, 11.9% construction, 20.8% production (2000).
Income: Per capita income: $17,888 (2007); Median household income: $24,344 (2007); Average household income: $39,228 (2007); Percent of households with income of $100,000 or more: 7.4% (2007); Poverty rate: 15.2% (2000).
Education: Percent of population age 25 and over with: High school diploma (including GED) or higher: 64.6% (2007); Bachelor's degree or higher: 7.3% (2007); Master's degree or higher: 1.5% (2007).

Housing: Homeownership rate: 88.8% (2007); Median home value: $68,237 (2007); Median rent: $236 per month (2000); Median age of housing: 10 years (2000).
Transportation: Commute to work: 95.2% car, 0.0% public transportation, 1.6% walk, 1.6% work from home (2000); Travel time to work: 30.6% less than 15 minutes, 37.2% 15 to 30 minutes, 13.6% 30 to 45 minutes, 11.4% 45 to 60 minutes, 7.2% 60 minutes or more (2000)

WILLOW OAK (CDP). Covers a land area of 3.216 square miles and a water area of 0 square miles. Located at 27.92° N. Lat.; 82.02° W. Long. Elevation is 112 feet.
Population: 2,607 (1990); 4,917 (2000); 5,655 (2007); 6,194 (2012 projected); Race: 77.3% White, 8.2% Black, 0.9% Asian, 32.5% Hispanic of any race (2007); Density: 1,758.7 persons per square mile (2007); Average household size: 2.78 (2007); Median age: 31.6 (2007); Males per 100 females: 105.9 (2007); Marriage status: 22.9% never married, 61.5% now married, 3.9% widowed, 11.8% divorced (2000); Foreign born: 10.7% (2000); Ancestry (includes multiple ancestries): 32.4% Other groups, 20.7% United States or American, 11.4% German, 10.0% Irish, 5.5% English (2000).
Economy: Employment by occupation: 8.5% management, 11.9% professional, 15.0% services, 24.7% sales, 2.4% farming, 13.4% construction, 24.0% production (2000).
Income: Per capita income: $19,704 (2007); Median household income: $45,031 (2007); Average household income: $54,727 (2007); Percent of households with income of $100,000 or more: 9.3% (2007); Poverty rate: 13.4% (2000).
Education: Percent of population age 25 and over with: High school diploma (including GED) or higher: 73.5% (2007); Bachelor's degree or higher: 10.8% (2007); Master's degree or higher: 4.3% (2007).
Housing: Homeownership rate: 54.8% (2007); Median home value: $99,640 (2007); Median rent: $443 per month (2000); Median age of housing: 13 years (2000).
Transportation: Commute to work: 95.8% car, 0.0% public transportation, 0.0% walk, 3.2% work from home (2000); Travel time to work: 16.3% less than 15 minutes, 48.4% 15 to 30 minutes, 18.0% 30 to 45 minutes, 6.7% 45 to 60 minutes, 10.6% 60 minutes or more (2000)

WINSTON (CDP). Covers a land area of 5.449 square miles and a water area of 0.001 square miles. Located at 28.03° N. Lat.; 82.00° W. Long. Elevation is 138 feet.
Population: 9,033 (1990); 9,024 (2000); 9,137 (2007); 9,286 (2012 projected); Race: 54.1% White, 29.8% Black, 0.3% Asian, 23.5% Hispanic of any race (2007); Density: 1,677.0 persons per square mile (2007); Average household size: 2.76 (2007); Median age: 30.8 (2007); Males per 100 females: 98.9 (2007); Marriage status: 27.0% never married, 49.0% now married, 6.7% widowed, 17.3% divorced (2000); Foreign born: 9.0% (2000); Ancestry (includes multiple ancestries): 42.1% Other groups, 12.2% United States or American, 8.0% Irish, 6.8% German, 5.4% English (2000).
Economy: Employment by occupation: 5.1% management, 7.3% professional, 17.6% services, 24.6% sales, 0.9% farming, 16.4% construction, 28.1% production (2000).
Income: Per capita income: $13,613 (2007); Median household income: $29,394 (2007); Average household income: $37,126 (2007); Percent of households with income of $100,000 or more: 4.4% (2007); Poverty rate: 26.0% (2000).
Education: Percent of population age 25 and over with: High school diploma (including GED) or higher: 58.9% (2007); Bachelor's degree or higher: 4.8% (2007); Master's degree or higher: 1.9% (2007).
Housing: Homeownership rate: 60.6% (2007); Median home value: $67,527 (2007); Median rent: $370 per month (2000); Median age of housing: 27 years (2000).
Transportation: Commute to work: 92.7% car, 1.2% public transportation, 2.4% walk, 1.4% work from home (2000); Travel time to work: 31.0% less than 15 minutes, 42.1% 15 to 30 minutes, 15.0% 30 to 45 minutes, 6.9% 45 to 60 minutes, 5.0% 60 minutes or more (2000)

WINTER HAVEN (city). Covers a land area of 17.678 square miles and a water area of 7.738 square miles. Located at 28.03° N. Lat.; 81.72° W. Long. Elevation is 167 feet.
History: Winter Haven grew in the middle of citrus groves and a cluster of 97 lakes within a five-mile radius. The town developed around citrus packing houses and canneries.

Population: 26,334 (1990); 26,487 (2000); 28,765 (2007); 30,564 (2012 projected); Race: 67.9% White, 24.6% Black, 1.4% Asian, 7.3% Hispanic of any race (2007); Density: 1,627.2 persons per square mile (2007); Average household size: 2.23 (2007); Median age: 44.0 (2007); Males per 100 females: 87.2 (2007); Marriage status: 20.0% never married, 52.3% now married, 15.3% widowed, 12.5% divorced (2000); Foreign born: 5.9% (2000); Ancestry (includes multiple ancestries): 23.1% Other groups, 14.6% United States or American, 11.5% German, 10.6% English, 9.5% Irish (2000).

Economy: Unemployment rate: 4.8% (11/2007); Total civilian labor force: 13,384 (11/2007); Single-family building permits issued: 684 (2006); Multi-family building permits issued: 350 (2006); Employment by occupation: 10.9% management, 15.4% professional, 19.1% services, 29.2% sales, 1.2% farming, 10.2% construction, 14.1% production (2000).

Income: Per capita income: $22,140 (2007); Median household income: $36,098 (2007); Average household income: $48,431 (2007); Percent of households with income of $100,000 or more: 8.4% (2007); Poverty rate: 15.0% (2000).

Taxes: Total city taxes per capita: $579 (2005); City property taxes per capita: $269 (2005).

Education: Percent of population age 25 and over with: High school diploma (including GED) or higher: 75.9% (2007); Bachelor's degree or higher: 16.8% (2007); Master's degree or higher: 5.7% (2007).

School District(s)
Polk County School District (PK-12)
    2005-06 Enrollment: 86,292 . . . . (863) 534-0521
Two-year College(s)
Polk Community College (Public)
    Fall 2006 Enrollment: 6,872. . . . . (863) 297-1000
    2006-07 Tuition: In-state $1,890; Out-of-state $7,050
Ridge Career Center (Public)
    Fall 2006 Enrollment: 714 . . . . (863) 419-3060
    2006-07 Tuition: In-state $1,850; Out-of-state $7,300

Housing: Homeownership rate: 59.6% (2007); Median home value: $98,617 (2007); Median rent: $387 per month (2000); Median age of housing: 27 years (2000).

Hospitals: Winter Haven Hospital (579 beds)

Safety: Violent crime rate: 75.3 per 10,000 population; Property crime rate: 680.0 per 10,000 population (2006).

Newspapers: Homefinder (General - Circulation 14,500); Senior Lifestyles (General, Senior Citizen - Circulation 14,500); The News Chief (Circulation 11,226)

Transportation: Commute to work: 95.6% car, 0.8% public transportation, 1.0% walk, 1.1% work from home (2000); Travel time to work: 37.5% less than 15 minutes, 34.7% 15 to 30 minutes, 17.4% 30 to 45 minutes, 5.1% 45 to 60 minutes, 5.2% 60 minutes or more (2000); Amtrak: Service available.

Additional Information Contacts
Winter Haven Chamber of Commerce. . . . . (863) 293-2138
    http://winterhavenfl.com

Putnam County

Located in northern Florida; swampy area, drained by the St. Johns River; includes Lake George and Crescent Lake. Covers a land area of 721.89 square miles, a water area of 105.27 square miles, and is located in the Eastern Time Zone. The county was founded in 1849. County seat is Palatka.

Putnam County is part of the Palatka, FL Micropolitan Statistical Area. The entire metro area includes: Putnam County, FL

Population: 65,070 (1990); 70,423 (2000); 74,438 (2007); 77,346 (2012 projected); Race: 76.6% White, 17.3% Black, 0.6% Asian, 7.8% Hispanic of any race (2007); Density: 103.1 persons per square mile (2007); Average household size: 2.50 (2007); Median age: 40.8 (2007); Males per 100 females: 97.6 (2007).

Religion: Five largest groups: 21.9% Southern Baptist Convention, 3.5% The United Methodist Church, 3.2% Catholic Church, 1.8% International Pentecostal Holiness Church, 1.5% The Church of Jesus Christ of Latter-day Saints (2000).

Economy: Unemployment rate: 4.9% (11/2007); Total civilian labor force: 32,083 (11/2007); Leading industries: 20.5% retail trade; 18.8% manufacturing; 15.6% health care and social assistance (2005); Farms: 466 totaling 92,619 acres (2002); Companies that employ 500 or more

persons: 3 (2005); Companies that employ 100 to 499 persons: 13 (2005); Companies that employ less than 100 persons: 1,417 (2005); Black-owned businesses: 439 (2002); Hispanic-owned businesses: n/a (2002); Asian-owned businesses: n/a (2002); Women-owned businesses: 1,077 (2002); Retail sales per capita: $8,965 (2007). Single-family building permits issued: 282 (2006); Multi-family building permits issued: 57 (2006).

Income: Per capita income: $18,408 (2007); Median household income: $32,966 (2007); Average household income: $45,459 (2007); Percent of households with income of $100,000 or more: 7.8% (2007); Poverty rate: 20.9% (2005); Bankruptcy rate: 1.59% (2006).

Taxes: Total county taxes per capita: $545 (2005); County property taxes per capita: $366 (2005).

Education: Percent of population age 25 and over with: High school diploma (including GED) or higher: 70.4% (2007); Bachelor's degree or higher: 9.5% (2007); Master's degree or higher: 3.7% (2007).

Housing: Homeownership rate: 79.9% (2007); Median home value: $89,082 (2007); Median rent: $300 per month (2000); Median age of housing: 21 years (2000).

Health: Birth rate: 134.2 per 10,000 population (2006); Death rate: 127.0 per 10,000 population (2006); Age-adjusted cancer mortality rate: 253.7 deaths per 100,000 population (2004); Air Quality Index: 97.3% good, 2.7% moderate, 0.0% unhealthy for sensitive individuals, 0.0% unhealthy (percent of days in 2006); Number of physicians: 10.6 per 10,000 population (2005); Hospital beds: 19.5 per 10,000 population (2004); Hospital admissions: 956.0 per 10,000 population (2004).

Elections: 2004 Presidential election results: 59.1% Bush, 40.1% Kerry, 0.4% Nader, 0.2% Badnarik

National and State Parks: Ocala National Recreation Trail; Ravine Gardens State Park

Additional Information Contacts
Putnam County Government . . . . (386) 329-0200
    http://www.putnam-fl.com/
Palatka Chamber of Commerce. (386) 328-1503
    http://www.putnamcountychamber.org
Putnam County Chamber of Commerce . . . . (386) 698-1657
    http://www.putnamcountychamber.org

Putnam County Communities

CRESCENT CITY (city). Covers a land area of 1.834 square miles and a water area of 0.303 square miles. Located at 29.43° N. Lat.; 81.51° W. Long. Elevation is 52 feet.

Population: 1,869 (1990); 1,776 (2000); 1,840 (2007); 1,875 (2012 projected); Race: 56.2% White, 33.5% Black, 1.1% Asian, 20.7% Hispanic of any race (2007); Density: 1,003.5 persons per square mile (2007); Average household size: 2.67 (2007); Median age: 37.4 (2007); Males per 100 females: 88.5 (2007); Marriage status: 27.4% never married, 47.5% now married, 13.6% widowed, 11.5% divorced (2000); Foreign born: 11.0% (2000); Ancestry (includes multiple ancestries): 46.9% Other groups, 12.7% English, 7.8% German, 5.9% United States or American, 5.5% Irish (2000).

Economy: Employment by occupation: 6.4% management, 13.0% professional, 18.9% services, 30.0% sales, 10.3% farming, 6.2% construction, 15.2% production (2000).

Income: Per capita income: $14,100 (2007); Median household income: $24,444 (2007); Average household income: $36,522 (2007); Percent of households with income of $100,000 or more: 7.1% (2007); Poverty rate: 27.9% (2000).

Education: Percent of population age 25 and over with: High school diploma (including GED) or higher: 62.7% (2007); Bachelor's degree or higher: 13.8% (2007); Master's degree or higher: 4.4% (2007).

School District(s)
Putnam County School District (PK-12)
    2005-06 Enrollment: 12,456 . . . . (386) 329-0510

Housing: Homeownership rate: 60.9% (2007); Median home value: $110,317 (2007); Median rent: $220 per month (2000); Median age of housing: 34 years (2000).

Safety: Violent crime rate: 194.8 per 10,000 population; Property crime rate: 595.2 per 10,000 population (2006).

Newspapers: Courier-Journal (General - Circulation 3,000)

Transportation: Commute to work: 91.4% car, 0.5% public transportation, 2.9% walk, 3.1% work from home (2000); Travel time to work: 43.5% less than 15 minutes, 15.9% 15 to 30 minutes, 21.5% 30 to 45 minutes, 6.5% 45 to 60 minutes, 12.6% 60 minutes or more (2000)

Additional Information Contacts

EAST PALATKA

EAST PALATKA (CDP). Covers a land area of 3.207 square miles and a water area of 1.297 square miles. Located at 29.65° N. Lat.; 81.59° W. Long. Elevation is 16 feet.

History: East Palatka, established on the east bank of the St. Johns River, was the northern terminal of the St. Johns & Halifax Railway in 1886. When Henry Flagler purchased the railway in 1889, he extended the line to Ormond and Daytona, and began passenger service.

Population: 1,989 (1990); 1,707 (2000); 1,648 (2007); 1,699 (2012 projected); Race: 57.5% White, 38.8% Black, 1.8% Asian, 2.1% Hispanic of any race (2007); Density: 513.9 persons per square mile (2007); Average household size: 3.19 (2007); Median age: 36.9 (2007); Males per 100 females: 159.1 (2007); Marriage status: 37.8% never married, 46.4% now married, 5.1% widowed, 10.8% divorced (2000); Foreign born: 2.1% (2000); Ancestry (includes multiple ancestries): 24.6% Other groups, 12.4% United States or American, 8.2% English, 7.7% Irish, 5.9% German (2000).

Economy: Employment by occupation: 9.7% management, 14.9% professional, 16.5% services, 32.7% sales, 2.1% farming, 10.1% construction, 14.0% production (2000).

Income: Per capita income: $21,345 (2007); Median household income: $44,875 (2007); Average household income: $64,449 (2007); Percent of households with income of $100,000 or more: 19.3% (2007); Poverty rate: 17.4% (2000).

Education: Percent of population age 25 and over with: High school diploma (including GED) or higher: 64.4% (2007); Bachelor's degree or higher: 8.2% (2007); Master's degree or higher: 2.5% (2007).

School District(s)
Putnam County School District (PK-12)

    2005-06 Enrollment: 12,456 . . . . (386) 329-0510

Housing: Homeownership rate: 78.3% (2007); Median home value: $97,051 (2007); Median rent: $349 per month (2000); Median age of housing: 32 years (2000).

Transportation: Commute to work: 96.1% car, 0.0% public transportation, 1.8% walk, 0.0% work from home (2000); Travel time to work: 57.5% less than 15 minutes, 22.9% 15 to 30 minutes, 9.9% 30 to 45 minutes, 3.6% 45 to 60 minutes, 6.1% 60 minutes or more (2000)

FLORAHOME

FLORAHOME (unincorporated postal area, zip code 32140). Covers a land area of 43.241 square miles and a water area of 1.336 square miles. Located at 29.76° N. Lat.; 81.85° W. Long. Elevation is 125 feet.

Population: 1,589 (2000); Race: 93.9% White, 1.6% Black, 0.0% Asian, 1.6% Hispanic of any race (2000); Density: 36.7 persons per square mile (2000); Age: 22.1% under 18, 10.1% over 64 (2000); Marriage status: 13.0% never married, 69.2% now married, 5.4% widowed, 12.4% divorced (2000); Foreign born: 0.7% (2000); Ancestry (includes multiple ancestries): 20.1% United States or American, 19.9% German, 12.9% Irish, 9.9% English, 8.0% Other groups (2000).

Economy: Employment by occupation: 16.7% management, 4.9% professional, 6.1% services, 24.3% sales, 2.8% farming, 25.6% construction, 19.6% production (2000).

Income: Per capita income: $16,733 (2000); Median household income: $32,955 (2000); Poverty rate: 9.7% (2000).

Education: Percent of population age 25 and over with: High school diploma (including GED) or higher: 64.2% (2000); Bachelor's degree or higher: 5.7% (2000).

School District(s)
Putnam County School District (PK-12)

    2005-06 Enrollment: 12,456 . . . . (386) 329-0510

Housing: Homeownership rate: 93.6% (2000); Median home value: $59,900 (2000); Median rent: $467 per month (2000); Median age of housing: 17 years (2000).

Transportation: Commute to work: 97.8% car, 0.0% public transportation, 0.0% walk, 2.2% work from home (2000); Travel time to work: 8.8% less than 15 minutes, 30.8% 15 to 30 minutes, 29.2% 30 to 45 minutes, 11.4% 45 to 60 minutes, 19.8% 60 minutes or more (2000)

GEORGETOWN

GEORGETOWN (unincorporated postal area, zip code 32139). Covers a land area of 7.787 square miles and a water area of 0.329 square miles. Located at 29.38° N. Lat.; 81.61° W. Long. Elevation is 24 feet.

Population: 607 (2000); Race: 77.8% White, 8.4% Black, 0.0% Asian, 13.8% Hispanic of any race (2000); Density: 78.0 persons per square mile (2000); Age: 11.9% under 18, 31.0% over 64 (2000); Marriage status:

English, 2.7% Welsh (2000).

Economy: Employment by occupation: 0.0% management, 4.5% professional, 9.6% services, 24.9% sales, 22.0% farming, 18.1% construction, 20.9% production (2000).

Income: Per capita income: $39,665 (2000); Median household income: $25,508 (2000); Poverty rate: 15.2% (2000).

Education: Percent of population age 25 and over with: High school diploma (including GED) or higher: 61.9% (2000); Bachelor's degree or higher: 4.2% (2000).

Housing: Homeownership rate: 96.6% (2000); Median home value: $84,000 (2000); Median rent: $275 per month (2000); Median age of housing: 15 years (2000).

Transportation: Commute to work: 96.4% car, 0.0% public transportation, 0.0% walk, 3.6% work from home (2000); Travel time to work: 11.3% less than 15 minutes, 43.1% 15 to 30 minutes, 19.4% 30 to 45 minutes, 11.9% 45 to 60 minutes, 14.4% 60 minutes or more (2000)

INTERLACHEN

INTERLACHEN (town). Covers a land area of 5.805 square miles and a water area of 0.646 square miles. Located at 29.62° N. Lat.; 81.89° W. Long. Elevation is 105 feet.

Population: 1,160 (1990); 1,475 (2000); 1,588 (2007); 1,646 (2012 projected); Race: 74.4% White, 5.5% Black, 0.4% Asian, 28.0% Hispanic of any race (2007); Density: 273.5 persons per square mile (2007); Average household size: 2.72 (2007); Median age: 35.5 (2007); Males per 100 females: 93.2 (2007); Marriage status: 24.3% never married, 57.4% now married, 7.8% widowed, 10.4% divorced (2000); Foreign born: 2.1% (2000); Ancestry (includes multiple ancestries): 35.5% Other groups, 12.6% United States or American, 7.1% English, 6.0% German, 5.4% Irish (2000).

Economy: Employment by occupation: 6.0% management, 16.1% professional, 14.6% services, 25.9% sales, 2.8% farming, 19.1% construction, 15.6% production (2000).

Income: Per capita income: $15,982 (2007); Median household income: $31,406 (2007); Average household income: $43,459 (2007); Percent of households with income of $100,000 or more: 6.7% (2007); Poverty rate: 27.5% (2000).

Education: Percent of population age 25 and over with: High school diploma (including GED) or higher: 62.8% (2007); Bachelor's degree or higher: 7.1% (2007); Master's degree or higher: 2.5% (2007).

School District(s)
Putnam County School District (PK-12)

    2005-06 Enrollment: 12,456 . . . . (386) 329-0510

Housing: Homeownership rate: 82.7% (2007); Median home value: $69,559 (2007); Median rent: $286 per month (2000); Median age of housing: 22 years (2000).

Transportation: Commute to work: 92.0% car, 0.0% public transportation, 2.4% walk, 4.3% work from home (2000); Travel time to work: 20.4% less than 15 minutes, 22.2% 15 to 30 minutes, 24.0% 30 to 45 minutes, 9.7% 45 to 60 minutes, 23.8% 60 minutes or more (2000)

MELROSE

MELROSE (unincorporated postal area, zip code 32666). Covers a land area of 25.258 square miles and a water area of 3.534 square miles. Located at 29.73° N. Lat.; 82.01° W. Long. Elevation is 161 feet.

History: Melrose was settled in 1879 by Scottish pioneers who planted citrus groves on the shores of Santa Fe Lake. The town was named for Melrose, Scotland.

Population: 4,669 (2000); Race: 89.4% White, 6.5% Black, 1.2% Asian, 1.3% Hispanic of any race (2000); Density: 184.9 persons per square mile (2000); Age: 16.1% under 18, 22.9% over 64 (2000); Marriage status: 19.8% never married, 53.6% now married, 9.8% widowed, 16.8% divorced (2000); Foreign born: 2.7% (2000); Ancestry (includes multiple ancestries): 16.3% English, 16.0% United States or American, 12.4% Irish, 11.5% German, 10.3% Other groups (2000).

Economy: Employment by occupation: 13.9% management, 20.4% professional, 17.8% services, 22.2% sales, 0.7% farming, 12.8% construction, 12.1% production (2000).

Income: Per capita income: $22,637 (2000); Median household income: $36,903 (2000); Poverty rate: 8.0% (2000).

Education: Percent of population age 25 and over with: High school diploma (including GED) or higher: 85.6% (2000); Bachelor's degree or higher: 18.2% (2000).

School District(s)

Putnam County School District (PK-12)

    2005-06 Enrollment: 12,456 . . . . (386) 329-0510

Housing: Homeownership rate: 87.7% (2000); Median home value: $98,200 (2000); Median rent: $426 per month (2000); Median age of housing: 22 years (2000).

Transportation: Commute to work: 92.7% car, 0.3% public transportation, 1.0% walk, 3.8% work from home (2000); Travel time to work: 13.7% less than 15 minutes, 19.0% 15 to 30 minutes, 32.9% 30 to 45 minutes, 17.4% 45 to 60 minutes, 17.0% 60 minutes or more (2000)

PALATKA (city). County seat. Covers a land area of 6.957 square miles and a water area of 0.577 square miles. Located at 29.64° N. Lat.; 81.65° W. Long. Elevation is 20 feet.

History: Palatka began as a trading post established in 1821 on the St. Johns River. The name is of Indian origin meaning "crossing over." Palatka became an important port in the 1870's, shipping citrus fruit and lumber from its cypress mill, as well as being a resort called on by passenger steamers from as far as the Mississippi River.

Population: 10,826 (1990); 10,033 (2000); 10,354 (2007); 10,517 (2012 projected); Race: 44.3% White, 52.5% Black, 0.7% Asian, 3.5% Hispanic of any race (2007); Density: 1,488.3 persons per square mile (2007); Average household size: 2.53 (2007); Median age: 33.5 (2007); Males per 100 females: 84.6 (2007); Marriage status: 31.1% never married, 44.5% now married, 11.9% widowed, 12.5% divorced (2000); Foreign born: 2.0% (2000); Ancestry (includes multiple ancestries): 40.2% Other groups, 10.2% United States or American, 5.5% English, 5.4% Irish, 4.4% German (2000).

Economy: Single-family building permits issued: 16 (2006); Multi-family building permits issued: 0 (2006); Employment by occupation: 6.6% management, 16.8% professional, 19.1% services, 26.1% sales, 2.4% farming, 10.5% construction, 18.4% production (2000).

Income: Per capita income: $12,923 (2007); Median household income: $20,178 (2007); Average household income: $30,896 (2007); Percent of households with income of $100,000 or more: 3.7% (2007); Poverty rate: 33.1% (2000).

Education: Percent of population age 25 and over with: High school diploma (including GED) or higher: 66.8% (2007); Bachelor's degree or higher: 10.5% (2007); Master's degree or higher: 4.5% (2007).

School District(s)

Putnam County School District (PK-12)

    2005-06 Enrollment: 12,456 . . . . (386) 329-0510

Two-year College(s)

Saint Johns River Community College (Public)

    Fall 2006 Enrollment: 5,096. (386) 312-4200

    2006-07 Tuition: In-state $1,974; Out-of-state $6,954

Housing: Homeownership rate: 51.0% (2007); Median home value: $86,028 (2007); Median rent: $273 per month (2000); Median age of housing: 30 years (2000).

Hospitals: Putnam Community Medical Center (141 beds)

Safety: Violent crime rate: 172.6 per 10,000 population; Property crime rate: 820.5 per 10,000 population (2006).

Newspapers: Daily News (Circulation 11,372)

Transportation: Commute to work: 90.9% car, 3.1% public transportation, 2.7% walk, 2.2% work from home (2000); Travel time to work: 51.6% less than 15 minutes, 28.3% 15 to 30 minutes, 9.6% 30 to 45 minutes, 4.4% 45 to 60 minutes, 6.2% 60 minutes or more (2000); Amtrak: Service available.

Additional Information Contacts

Palatka Chamber of Commerce. . . . . (386) 328-1503

    http://www.putnamcountychamber.org

POMONA PARK (town). Covers a land area of 2.930 square miles and a water area of 0.403 square miles. Located at 29.49° N. Lat.; 81.60° W. Long. Elevation is 43 feet.

Population: 663 (1990); 789 (2000); 755 (2007); 767 (2012 projected); Race: 85.2% White, 11.0% Black, 0.0% Asian, 6.4% Hispanic of any race (2007); Density: 257.7 persons per square mile (2007); Average household size: 2.26 (2007); Median age: 45.2 (2007); Males per 100 females: 97.1 (2007); Marriage status: 16.9% never married, 54.2% now married, 12.5% widowed, 16.3% divorced (2000); Foreign born: 5.8% (2000); Ancestry (includes multiple ancestries): 22.1% Other groups, 14.9% Irish, 13.9% German, 11.7% United States or American, 9.4% English (2000).

Economy: Employment by occupation: 9.6% management, 14.9% professional, 14.2% services, 31.0% sales, 4.6% farming, 7.7% construction, 18.0% production (2000).

Income: Per capita income: $19,583 (2007); Median household income: $30,690 (2007); Average household income: $41,796 (2007); Percent of households with income of $100,000 or more: 6.3% (2007); Poverty rate: 25.5% (2000).

Taxes: Total city taxes per capita: $358 (2005); City property taxes per capita: $171 (2005).

Education: Percent of population age 25 and over with: High school diploma (including GED) or higher: 67.7% (2007); Bachelor's degree or higher: 9.8% (2007); Master's degree or higher: 4.5% (2007).

Housing: Homeownership rate: 82.6% (2007); Median home value: $67,600 (2007); Median rent: $291 per month (2000); Median age of housing: 25 years (2000).

Transportation: Commute to work: 94.4% car, 0.0% public transportation, 2.4% walk, 0.8% work from home (2000); Travel time to work: 17.0% less than 15 minutes, 17.4% 15 to 30 minutes, 25.9% 30 to 45 minutes, 11.3% 45 to 60 minutes, 28.3% 60 minutes or more (2000)

SAN MATEO (unincorporated postal area, zip code 32187). Covers a land area of 24.116 square miles and a water area of 0.168 square miles. Located at 29.59° N. Lat.; 81.57° W. Long. Elevation is 85 feet.

History: San Mateo was established in a region of orange groves, where the land had been cultivated for more than a century. Between 1765 and 1783, a town called Rollestown, or Charlotia, existed near the site of San Mateo. Rolleston was founded by Denys Rolle, a member of the British parliament, who brought a group of people from the London slums, planning to rehabilitate them in the Utopia he created. In 1783 Rolles moved to the Bahamas.

Population: 2,037 (2000); Race: 77.9% White, 22.1% Black, 0.0% Asian, 1.2% Hispanic of any race (2000); Density: 84.5 persons per square mile (2000); Age: 26.4% under 18, 15.4% over 64 (2000); Marriage status: 19.9% never married, 62.3% now married, 7.1% widowed, 10.6% divorced (2000); Foreign born: 1.0% (2000); Ancestry (includes multiple ancestries): 27.0% Other groups, 15.6% United States or American, 13.8% English, 11.2% Irish, 7.3% German (2000).

Economy: Employment by occupation: 5.3% management, 19.8% professional, 18.5% services, 21.8% sales, 5.7% farming, 13.4% construction, 15.6% production (2000).

Income: Per capita income: $14,920 (2000); Median household income: $30,273 (2000); Poverty rate: 22.5% (2000).

Education: Percent of population age 25 and over with: High school diploma (including GED) or higher: 75.1% (2000); Bachelor's degree or higher: 10.6% (2000).

School District(s)

Putnam County School District (PK-12)

    2005-06 Enrollment: 12,456 . . . . (386) 329-0510

Housing: Homeownership rate: 87.3% (2000); Median home value: $78,000 (2000); Median rent: $330 per month (2000); Median age of housing: 20 years (2000).

Transportation: Commute to work: 95.4% car, 2.2% public transportation, 1.0% walk, 1.4% work from home (2000); Travel time to work: 15.2% less than 15 minutes, 50.7% 15 to 30 minutes, 20.8% 30 to 45 minutes, 5.7% 45 to 60 minutes, 7.5% 60 minutes or more (2000)

SATSUMA (unincorporated postal area, zip code 32189). Covers a land area of 34.070 square miles and a water area of 0.267 square miles. Located at 29.55° N. Lat.; 81.64° W. Long. Elevation is 74 feet.

History: Satsuma developed as a trading center in a citrus and truck-farm area. The town was named for the Satsuma orange, a variety that withstands low temperatures.

Population: 5,866 (2000); Race: 92.7% White, 4.6% Black, 0.2% Asian, 2.2% Hispanic of any race (2000); Density: 172.2 persons per square mile (2000); Age: 17.8% under 18, 25.8% over 64 (2000); Marriage status: 11.3% never married, 63.7% now married, 9.5% widowed, 15.5% divorced (2000); Foreign born: 1.8% (2000); Ancestry (includes multiple ancestries): 17.0% United States or American, 13.4% Other groups, 12.1% Irish, 10.8% English, 9.6% German (2000).

Economy: Employment by occupation: 8.3% management, 10.9% professional, 17.8% services, 27.3% sales, 1.4% farming, 16.4% construction, 17.9% production (2000).

Income: Per capita income: $16,481 (2000); Median household income: $26,670 (2000); Poverty rate: 16.6% (2000).

Education: Percent of population age 25 and over with: High school diploma (including GED) or higher: 69.6% (2000); Bachelor's degree or higher: 7.1% (2000).

WELAKA (town). Covers a land area of 1.358 square miles and a water area of 0.043 square miles. Located at 29.48° N. Lat.; 81.67° W. Long. Elevation is 26 feet.

Population: 534 (1990); 586 (2000); 610 (2007); 630 (2012 projected); Race: 73.8% White, 21.5% Black, 0.0% Asian, 5.4% Hispanic of any race (2007); Density: 449.0 persons per square mile (2007); Average household size: 2.09 (2007); Median age: 52.2 (2007); Males per 100 females: 87.1 (2007); Marriage status: 15.2% never married, 58.8% now married, 12.1% widowed, 14.0% divorced (2000); Foreign born: 2.0% (2000); Ancestry (includes multiple ancestries): 22.3% Other groups, 14.2% United States or American, 7.7% English, 7.3% German, 7.0% Irish (2000).

Economy: Single-family building permits issued: 16 (2006); Multi-family building permits issued: 57 (2006); Employment by occupation: 8.7% management, 6.6% professional, 28.4% services, 29.0% sales, 3.8% farming, 12.0% construction, 11.5% production (2000).

Income: Per capita income: $19,348 (2007); Median household income: $32,174 (2007); Average household income: $39,872 (2007); Percent of households with income of $100,000 or more: 3.4% (2007); Poverty rate: 25.0% (2000).

Education: Percent of population age 25 and over with: High school diploma (including GED) or higher: 70.8% (2007); Bachelor's degree or higher: 10.5% (2007); Master's degree or higher: 1.3% (2007).

Housing: Homeownership rate: 73.6% (2007); Median home value: $72,955 (2007); Median rent: $250 per month (2000); Median age of housing: 19 years (2000).

Safety: Violent crime rate: 16.0 per 10,000 population; Property crime rate: 160.0 per 10,000 population (2006).

Transportation: Commute to work: 93.6% car, 0.0% public transportation, 3.5% walk, 1.7% work from home (2000); Travel time to work: 18.3% less than 15 minutes, 33.7% 15 to 30 minutes, 21.9% 30 to 45 minutes, 7.1% 45 to 60 minutes, 18.9% 60 minutes or more (2000)

Santa Rosa County

Located in northwestern Florida; bounded on the north by Georgia, on the south by the Gulf of Mexico, and on the west by the Escambia River; includes part of Pensacola Bay and Santa Rosa Sound; drained by the Blackwater and Yellow Rivers. Covers a land area of 1,016.93 square miles, a water area of 156.65 square miles, and is located in the Central Time Zone. The county was founded in 1842. County seat is Milton.

Santa Rosa County is part of the Pensacola-Ferry Pass-Brent, FL Metropolitan Statistical Area. The entire metro area includes: Escambia County, FL; Santa Rosa County, FL

Weather Station: Milton Experiment Station   Elevation: 216 feet

	Jan	Feb	Mar	Apr	May	Jun	Jul	Aug	Sep	Oct	Nov	Dec
High	61	65	72	78	85	90	92	91	88	80	71	64
Low	39	42	49	54	62	69	71	71	67	55	47	42
Precip	6.4	5.1	7.4	4.3	5.1	7.4	8.1	6.7	6.1	4.0	5.2	4.4
Snow	0.1	0.1	tr	0.0	0.0	0.0	0.0	0.0	0.0	0.0	0.0	0.0

High and Low temperatures in degrees Fahrenheit; Precipitation and Snow in inches

Population: 81,965 (1990); 117,743 (2000); 146,426 (2007); 163,756 (2012 projected); Race: 89.7% White, 4.9% Black, 1.5% Asian, 3.3% Hispanic of any race (2007); Density: 144.0 persons per square mile (2007); Average household size: 2.65 (2007); Median age: 38.9 (2007); Males per 100 females: 99.7 (2007).

Religion: Five largest groups: 16.7% Southern Baptist Convention, 7.9% The United Methodist Church, 5.7% Assemblies of God, 5.3% Catholic Church, 0.9% The Church of Jesus Christ of Latter-day Saints (2000).

Economy: Unemployment rate: 3.8% (11/2007); Total civilian labor force: 68,680 (11/2007); Leading industries: 19.8% retail trade; 14.3% construction; 13.9% health care and social assistance (2005); Farms: 505 totaling 83,790 acres (2002); Companies that employ 500 or more persons: 1 (2005); Companies that employ 100 to 499 persons: 25 (2005); Companies that employ less than 100 persons: 2,557 (2005); Black-owned businesses: 208 (2002); Hispanic-owned businesses: 319 (2002);

per capita: $259 (2005).

Education: Percent of population age 25 and over with: High school diploma (including GED) or higher: 85.9% (2007); Bachelor's degree or higher: 23.1% (2007); Master's degree or higher: 8.0% (2007).

Housing: Homeownership rate: 80.7% (2007); Median home value: $178,643 (2007); Median rent: $441 per month (2000); Median age of housing: 15 years (2000).

Health: Birth rate: 122.4 per 10,000 population (2006); Death rate: 77.2 per 10,000 population (2006); Age-adjusted cancer mortality rate: 208.9 deaths per 100,000 population (2004); Air Quality Index: 87.3% good, 12.4% moderate, 0.3% unhealthy for sensitive individuals, 0.0% unhealthy (percent of days in 2006); Number of physicians: 18.7 per 10,000 population (2005); Hospital beds: 16.1 per 10,000 population (2004); Hospital admissions: 653.8 per 10,000 population (2004).

Elections: 2004 Presidential election results: 77.3% Bush, 21.8% Kerry, 0.4% Nader, 0.1% Badnarik

National and State Parks: Blackwater Heritage Trail State Park; Blackwater River State Forest; Blackwater River State Park; Navarre Beach State Park

Additional Information Contacts

Santa Rosa County Government	(850) 623-0135
http://www.co.santa-rosa.fl.us	
City of Gulf Breeze	(850) 934-5100
http://www.cityofgulfbreeze.com	
City of Milton	(850) 983-5400
http://www.ci.milton.fl.us	
Gulf Breeze Area Chamber of Commerce	(850) 932-7888
http://www.gulfbreezechamber.com	
Gulf Breeze Chamber of Commerce	(850) 932-1500
http://www.gulfbreezechamber.com	
Milton Chamber of Commerce	(850) 623-2339
http://www.srcchamber.com	
Pace Area Chamber of Commerce	(850) 994-9633
http://www.pacechamber.com	

Santa Rosa County Communities

BAGDAD (CDP). Covers a land area of 3.520 square miles and a water area of 0.718 square miles. Located at 30.59° N. Lat.; 87.03° W. Long. Elevation is 13 feet.

History: Bagdad grew around the Bagdad Lumber Company, where pine and cypress were cut and shipped to New Orleans in the early 1850's.

Population: 1,457 (1990); 1,490 (2000); 1,916 (2007); 2,166 (2012 projected); Race: 82.2% White, 10.4% Black, 0.7% Asian, 1.9% Hispanic of any race (2007); Density: 544.4 persons per square mile (2007); Average household size: 2.47 (2007); Median age: 41.1 (2007); Males per 100 females: 95.1 (2007); Marriage status: 22.0% never married, 49.2% now married, 13.3% widowed, 15.5% divorced (2000); Foreign born: 1.0% (2000); Ancestry (includes multiple ancestries): 34.7% Other groups, 11.8% United States or American, 9.2% English, 7.6% Irish, 7.3% German (2000).

Economy: Employment by occupation: 5.4% management, 15.8% professional, 19.4% services, 24.3% sales, 0.0% farming, 18.9% construction, 16.2% production (2000).

Income: Per capita income: $19,669 (2007); Median household income: $39,417 (2007); Average household income: $47,603 (2007); Percent of households with income of $100,000 or more: 9.2% (2007); Poverty rate: 22.5% (2000).

Education: Percent of population age 25 and over with: High school diploma (including GED) or higher: 68.5% (2007); Bachelor's degree or higher: 12.4% (2007); Master's degree or higher: 2.2% (2007).

School District(s)

Santa Rosa County School District (PK-12)

  2005-06 Enrollment: 25,038 . . . . (850) 983-5010

Housing: Homeownership rate: 78.7% (2007); Median home value: $128,125 (2007); Median rent: $408 per month (2000); Median age of housing: 31 years (2000).

Transportation: Commute to work: 96.9% car, 0.0% public transportation, 0.0% walk, 1.7% work from home (2000); Travel time to work: 31.7% less than 15 minutes, 48.6% 15 to 30 minutes, 12.8% 30 to 45 minutes, 3.8% 45 to 60 minutes, 3.2% 60 minutes or more (2000)

GULF BREEZE (city). Covers a land area of 4.752 square miles and a water area of 18.795 square miles. Located at 30.36° N. Lat.; 87.17° W. Long. Elevation is 16 feet.
Population: 5,530 (1990); 5,665 (2000); 6,497 (2007); 6,999 (2012 projected); Race: 97.1% White, 0.4% Black, 0.7% Asian, 1.6% Hispanic of any race (2007); Density: 1,367.1 persons per square mile (2007); Average household size: 2.33 (2007); Median age: 48.7 (2007); Males per 100 females: 90.2 (2007); Marriage status: 17.6% never married, 65.7% now married, 7.9% widowed, 8.8% divorced (2000); Foreign born: 3.0% (2000); Ancestry (includes multiple ancestries): 19.5% German, 16.7% English, 12.9% Irish, 10.6% Other groups, 9.7% United States or American (2000).
Economy: Employment by occupation: 20.9% management, 32.4% professional, 9.5% services, 26.3% sales, 0.0% farming, 6.1% construction, 4.9% production (2000).
Income: Per capita income: $40,353 (2007); Median household income: $56,372 (2007); Average household income: $92,262 (2007); Percent of households with income of $100,000 or more: 24.0% (2007); Poverty rate: 4.2% (2000).
Taxes: Total city taxes per capita: $631 (2005); City property taxes per capita: $184 (2005).
Education: Percent of population age 25 and over with: High school diploma (including GED) or higher: 95.8% (2007); Bachelor's degree or higher: 48.7% (2007); Master's degree or higher: 20.3% (2007).

School District(s)
Santa Rosa County School District (PK-12)
    2005-06 Enrollment: 25,038 . . . . (850) 983-5010
Housing: Homeownership rate: 82.1% (2007); Median home value: $285,015 (2007); Median rent: $582 per month (2000); Median age of housing: 28 years (2000).
Hospitals: Friary (30 beds); Gulf Breeze Hospital (60 beds); Twelve Oaks Alcohol & Drug Recovery Center (58 beds)
Safety: Violent crime rate: 7.6 per 10,000 population; Property crime rate: 272.7 per 10,000 population (2006).
Transportation: Commute to work: 91.7% car, 0.0% public transportation, 0.3% walk, 6.2% work from home (2000); Travel time to work: 23.4% less than 15 minutes, 52.3% 15 to 30 minutes, 16.7% 30 to 45 minutes, 2.1% 45 to 60 minutes, 5.5% 60 minutes or more (2000)
Additional Information Contacts
City of Gulf Breeze . . . . (850) 934-5100
    http://www.cityofgulfbreeze.com
Gulf Breeze Area Chamber of Commerce . . . . (850) 932-7888
    http://www.gulfbreezechamber.com
Gulf Breeze Chamber of Commerce . . . . (850) 932-1500
    http://www.gulfbreezechamber.com

JAY (town). Covers a land area of 1.583 square miles and a water area of 0 square miles. Located at 30.95° N. Lat.; 87.15° W. Long. Elevation is 256 feet.
Population: 666 (1990); 579 (2000); 551 (2007); 547 (2012 projected); Race: 96.9% White, 0.7% Black, 0.4% Asian, 3.4% Hispanic of any race (2007); Density: 348.1 persons per square mile (2007); Average household size: 2.47 (2007); Median age: 42.6 (2007); Males per 100 females: 90.0 (2007); Marriage status: 18.4% never married, 54.0% now married, 12.5% widowed, 15.1% divorced (2000); Foreign born: 1.7% (2000); Ancestry (includes multiple ancestries): 40.1% United States or American, 10.5% Other groups, 8.8% English, 5.9% German, 4.4% Irish (2000).
Economy: Employment by occupation: 8.5% management, 21.8% professional, 19.7% services, 12.2% sales, 1.1% farming, 12.2% construction, 24.5% production (2000).
Income: Per capita income: $15,616 (2007); Median household income: $28,472 (2007); Average household income: $38,330 (2007); Percent of households with income of $100,000 or more: 5.8% (2007); Poverty rate: 16.5% (2000).
Education: Percent of population age 25 and over with: High school diploma (including GED) or higher: 63.6% (2007); Bachelor's degree or higher: 13.9% (2007); Master's degree or higher: 6.5% (2007).

School District(s)
Santa Rosa County School District (PK-12)
    2005-06 Enrollment: 25,038 . . . . (850) 983-5010

Housing: Homeownership rate: 62.3% (2007); Median home value: $90,714 (2007); Median rent: $281 per month (2000); Median age of housing: 35 years (2000).
Hospitals: Jay Hospital (55 beds)
Transportation: Commute to work: 86.2% car, 0.0% public transportation, 4.3% walk, 5.9% work from home (2000); Travel time to work: 55.9% less than 15 minutes, 13.6% 15 to 30 minutes, 10.7% 30 to 45 minutes, 14.7% 45 to 60 minutes, 5.1% 60 minutes or more (2000)

MILTON (city). County seat. Covers a land area of 4.373 square miles and a water area of 0.210 square miles. Located at 30.63° N. Lat.; 87.04° W. Long. Elevation is 33 feet.
History: Milton began in 1825 as a trading post on the Blackwater River. A community grew up around several sawmills, and became a cotton shipping port during the Civil War.
Population: 7,537 (1990); 7,045 (2000); 7,455 (2007); 7,704 (2012 projected); Race: 76.0% White, 17.2% Black, 2.0% Asian, 4.9% Hispanic of any race (2007); Density: 1,704.9 persons per square mile (2007); Average household size: 2.59 (2007); Median age: 34.6 (2007); Males per 100 females: 88.1 (2007); Marriage status: 21.7% never married, 54.7% now married, 10.0% widowed, 13.5% divorced (2000); Foreign born: 3.1% (2000); Ancestry (includes multiple ancestries): 28.8% Other groups, 14.0% Irish, 12.4% German, 10.9% United States or American, 9.6% English (2000).
Economy: Employment by occupation: 7.1% management, 15.2% professional, 18.9% services, 28.0% sales, 0.0% farming, 13.4% construction, 17.4% production (2000).
Income: Per capita income: $17,486 (2007); Median household income: $34,883 (2007); Average household income: $43,557 (2007); Percent of households with income of $100,000 or more: 5.4% (2007); Poverty rate: 16.6% (2000).
Education: Percent of population age 25 and over with: High school diploma (including GED) or higher: 79.8% (2007); Bachelor's degree or higher: 15.9% (2007); Master's degree or higher: 4.2% (2007).

School District(s)
Okaloosa County School District (PK-12)
    2005-06 Enrollment: 31,756 . . . . (850) 833-3109
Santa Rosa County School District (PK-12)
    2005-06 Enrollment: 25,038 . . . . (850) 983-5010
Two-year College(s)
Radford M Locklin Technical Center (Public)
    Fall 2006 Enrollment: 368 . . . . (850) 983-5700
    2006-07 Tuition: In-state $1,446; Out-of-state $5,886
Housing: Homeownership rate: 56.9% (2007); Median home value: $122,150 (2007); Median rent: $364 per month (2000); Median age of housing: 33 years (2000).
Hospitals: Santa Rosa Medical Center (129 beds); West Florida Community Care Center (100 beds)
Safety: Violent crime rate: 65.3 per 10,000 population; Property crime rate: 541.8 per 10,000 population (2006).
Newspapers: Press Gazette (General - Circulation 7,000); Santa Rosa Free Press (General - Circulation 7,000)
Transportation: Commute to work: 94.3% car, 0.3% public transportation, 1.9% walk, 1.3% work from home (2000); Travel time to work: 36.7% less than 15 minutes, 27.9% 15 to 30 minutes, 22.5% 30 to 45 minutes, 7.4% 45 to 60 minutes, 5.5% 60 minutes or more (2000)
Additional Information Contacts
City of Milton . . . . (850) 983-5400
    http://www.ci.milton.fl.us
Milton Chamber of Commerce . . . . (850) 623-2339
    http://www.srcchamber.com

PACE (CDP). Covers a land area of 9.382 square miles and a water area of 0 square miles. Located at 30.59° N. Lat.; 87.15° W. Long. Elevation is 66 feet.
Population: 6,277 (1990); 7,393 (2000); 8,558 (2007); 9,259 (2012 projected); Race: 92.7% White, 2.0% Black, 1.3% Asian, 2.5% Hispanic of any race (2007); Density: 912.2 persons per square mile (2007); Average household size: 2.62 (2007); Median age: 36.9 (2007); Males per 100 females: 95.3 (2007); Marriage status: 19.7% never married, 62.9% now married, 4.7% widowed, 12.7% divorced (2000); Foreign born: 2.8% (2000); Ancestry (includes multiple ancestries): 19.6% United States or American, 17.5% Other groups, 14.2% Irish, 10.2% German, 8.2% English (2000).

Economy: Employment by occupation: 10.2% management, 18.0% professional, 15.6% services, 26.3% sales, 0.5% farming, 17.1% construction, 12.3% production (2000).

Income: Per capita income: $19,058 (2007); Median household income: $41,093 (2007); Average household income: $49,877 (2007); Percent of households with income of $100,000 or more: 9.2% (2007); Poverty rate: 12.3% (2000).

Education: Percent of population age 25 and over with: High school diploma (including GED) or higher: 85.5% (2007); Bachelor's degree or higher: 13.6% (2007); Master's degree or higher: 4.4% (2007).

School District(s)

Santa Rosa County School District (PK-12)

2005-06 Enrollment: 25,038 . . . . (850) 983-5010

Housing: Homeownership rate: 76.7% (2007); Median home value: $146,521 (2007); Median rent: $377 per month (2000); Median age of housing: 19 years (2000).

Transportation: Commute to work: 94.6% car, 0.2% public transportation, 0.5% walk, 2.8% work from home (2000); Travel time to work: 22.4% less than 15 minutes, 43.8% 15 to 30 minutes, 21.9% 30 to 45 minutes, 7.0% 45 to 60 minutes, 4.9% 60 minutes or more (2000)

Additional Information Contacts

Pace Area Chamber of Commerce . . . . (850) 994-9633
http://www.pacechamber.com

Sarasota County

Located in southwestern Florida; bounded on the west by the Gulf of Mexico, with barrier beaches and Sarasota Bay; lowland area, drained by the Myakka River. Covers a land area of 571.55 square miles, a water area of 153.63 square miles, and is located in the Eastern Time Zone. The county was founded in 1921. County seat is Sarasota.

Sarasota County is part of the Sarasota-Bradenton-Venice, FL Metropolitan Statistical Area. The entire metro area includes: Manatee County, FL; Sarasota County, FL

Weather Station: Myakka River State Park   Elevation: 19 feet

	Jan	Feb	Mar	Apr	May	Jun	Jul	Aug	Sep	Oct	Nov	Dec
High	75	77	81	86	91	92	93	93	91	87	81	76
Low	49	51	55	58	63	69	71	72	71	65	58	52
Precip	3.2	2.9	3.6	2.1	3.4	8.9	9.6	9.6	8.1	3.2	2.2	2.3
Snow	0.0	0.0	0.0	0.0	0.0	0.0	0.0	0.0	0.0	0.0	0.0	tr

High and Low temperatures in degrees Fahrenheit; Precipitation and Snow in inches

Weather Station: Venice   Elevation: 6 feet

	Jan	Feb	Mar	Apr	May	Jun	Jul	Aug	Sep	Oct	Nov	Dec
High	72	74	77	82	86	90	91	91	90	86	80	74
Low	51	52	57	61	67	72	73	74	73	66	59	54
Precip	2.7	2.2	3.6	1.9	2.3	6.7	6.6	8.3	7.4	3.1	2.1	2.3
Snow	tr	0.0	0.0	0.0	0.0	0.0	0.0	0.0	0.0	0.0	0.0	0.0

High and Low temperatures in degrees Fahrenheit; Precipitation and Snow in inches

Population: 277,776 (1990); 325,957 (2000); 378,581 (2007); 416,537 (2012 projected); Race: 91.3% White, 4.4% Black, 1.1% Asian, 6.7% Hispanic of any race (2007); Density: 662.4 persons per square mile (2007); Average household size: 2.17 (2007); Median age: 49.9 (2007); Males per 100 females: 91.7 (2007).

Religion: Five largest groups: 19.9% Catholic Church, 4.9% Southern Baptist Convention, 4.1% Jewish Estimate, 3.4% The United Methodist Church, 3.0% Presbyterian Church (U.S.A.) (2000).

Economy: Unemployment rate: 4.8% (11/2007); Total civilian labor force: 184,858 (11/2007); Leading industries: 17.0% retail trade; 16.4% health care and social assistance; 11.3% accommodation & food services (2005); Farms: 371 totaling 121,310 acres (2002); Companies that employ 500 or more persons: 9 (2005); Companies that employ 100 to 499 persons: 207 (2005); Companies that employ less than 100 persons: 13,247 (2005); Black-owned businesses: n/a (2002); Hispanic-owned businesses: 1,301 (2002); Asian-owned businesses: 745 (2002); Women-owned businesses: 9,948 (2002); Retail sales per capita: $18,357 (2007). Single-family building permits issued: 3,418 (2006); Multi-family building permits issued: 687 (2006).

Income: Per capita income: $32,670 (2007); Median household income: $48,649 (2007); Average household income: $70,126 (2007); Percent of households with income of $100,000 or more: 17.3% (2007); Poverty rate: 9.1% (2005); Bankruptcy rate: 1.20% (2006).

Taxes: Total county taxes per capita: $749 (2005); County property taxes per capita: $463 (2005).

Education: Percent of population age 25 and over with: High school diploma (including GED) or higher: 87.1% (2007); Bachelor's degree or higher: 26.8% (2007); Master's degree or higher: 10.1% (2007).

Housing: Homeownership rate: 80.1% (2007); Median home value: $244,877 (2007); Median rent: $626 per month (2000); Median age of housing: 21 years (2000).

Health: Birth rate: 82.6 per 10,000 population (2006); Death rate: 133.7 per 10,000 population (2006); Age-adjusted cancer mortality rate: 164.0 deaths per 100,000 population (2004); Air Quality Index: 88.5% good, 11.2% moderate, 0.3% unhealthy for sensitive individuals, 0.0% unhealthy (percent of days in 2006); Number of physicians: 30.5 per 10,000 population (2005); Hospital beds: 30.2 per 10,000 population (2004); Hospital admissions: 1,423.4 per 10,000 population (2004).

Elections: 2004 Presidential election results: 53.5% Bush, 45.2% Kerry, 0.6% Nader, 0.3% Badnarik

National and State Parks: Myakka River State Park; Oscar Scherer State Park

Additional Information Contacts

Sarasota County Government . . . . (941) 951-5344
http://www.co.sarasota.fl.us
Committee for Economic Development . . . . (941) 309-1200
http://www.edcsarasotacounty.com
Englewood Area Chamber of Commerce . . . . (941) 474-5511
http://www.englewoodchamber.com
Longboat Key Chamber of Commerce . . . . (941) 383-2466
http://www.longboatkeychamber.com
North Port Chamber of Commerce . . . . (941) 426-8744
http://www.northportareachamber.com
Sarasota Chamber of Commerce . . . . (941) 955-8187
http://www.sarasotachamber.org
Siesta Key Chamber of Commerce . . . . (941) 349-3800
http://www.siestakeychamber.com
Town of Longboat Key . . . . (941) 316-1999
http://www.longboatkey.org
Venice Chamber of Commerce . . . . (941) 488-2236
http://www.venicechamber.com

Sarasota County Communities

BEE RIDGE (CDP). Covers a land area of 3.907 square miles and a water area of 0 square miles. Located at 27.28° N. Lat.; 82.47° W. Long. Elevation is 33 feet.

Population: 6,406 (1990); 8,744 (2000); 10,043 (2007); 10,978 (2012 projected); Race: 96.3% White, 1.1% Black, 1.0% Asian, 4.8% Hispanic of any race (2007); Density: 2,570.5 persons per square mile (2007); Average household size: 2.24 (2007); Median age: 51.9 (2007); Males per 100 females: 82.2 (2007); Marriage status: 15.5% never married, 59.9% now married, 15.1% widowed, 9.5% divorced (2000); Foreign born: 8.0% (2000); Ancestry (includes multiple ancestries): 24.6% German, 14.4% English, 13.6% Irish, 9.4% Other groups, 8.6% Italian (2000).

Economy: Employment by occupation: 13.3% management, 23.0% professional, 19.3% services, 28.3% sales, 1.1% farming, 8.2% construction, 6.8% production (2000).

Income: Per capita income: $32,930 (2007); Median household income: $56,405 (2007); Average household income: $72,818 (2007); Percent of households with income of $100,000 or more: 22.0% (2007); Poverty rate: 5.5% (2000).

Education: Percent of population age 25 and over with: High school diploma (including GED) or higher: 89.0% (2007); Bachelor's degree or higher: 29.8% (2007); Master's degree or higher: 11.2% (2007).

Housing: Homeownership rate: 85.0% (2007); Median home value: $294,864 (2007); Median rent: $865 per month (2000); Median age of housing: 15 years (2000).

Transportation: Commute to work: 90.7% car, 1.2% public transportation, 2.0% walk, 4.9% work from home (2000); Travel time to work: 34.5% less than 15 minutes, 48.1% 15 to 30 minutes, 12.9% 30 to 45 minutes, 1.5% 45 to 60 minutes, 3.0% 60 minutes or more (2000)

DESOTO LAKES (CDP). Covers a land area of 1.261 square miles and a water area of 0 square miles. Located at 27.37° N. Lat.; 82.49° W. Long. Elevation is 30 feet.

Population: 2,533 (1990); 3,198 (2000); 3,510 (2007); 3,726 (2012 projected); Race: 91.6% White, 4.4% Black, 1.4% Asian, 6.1% Hispanic of

any race (2007); Density: 2,784.5 persons per square mile (2007); Average household size: 2.44 (2007); Median age: 42.6 (2007); Males per 100 females: 93.9 (2007); Marriage status: 17.8% never married, 63.4% now married, 5.2% widowed, 13.6% divorced (2000); Foreign born: 8.3% (2000); Ancestry (includes multiple ancestries): 18.3% German, 14.7% Other groups, 14.4% Irish, 12.8% English, 6.3% French (except Basque) (2000).

Economy: Employment by occupation: 15.3% management, 26.7% professional, 16.6% services, 25.8% sales, 0.0% farming, 7.6% construction, 8.0% production (2000).

Income: Per capita income: $31,684 (2007); Median household income: $61,067 (2007); Average household income: $77,285 (2007); Percent of households with income of $100,000 or more: 21.5% (2007); Poverty rate: 3.8% (2000).

Education: Percent of population age 25 and over with: High school diploma (including GED) or higher: 90.7% (2007); Bachelor's degree or higher: 29.0% (2007); Master's degree or higher: 9.5% (2007).

Housing: Homeownership rate: 89.1% (2007); Median home value: $242,687 (2007); Median rent: $751 per month (2000); Median age of housing: 19 years (2000).

Transportation: Commute to work: 95.3% car, 0.6% public transportation, 0.0% walk, 3.6% work from home (2000); Travel time to work: 31.8% less than 15 minutes, 48.3% 15 to 30 minutes, 14.6% 30 to 45 minutes, 1.8% 45 to 60 minutes, 3.6% 60 minutes or more (2000)

ENGLEWOOD (CDP).
Covers a land area of 9.830 square miles and a water area of 3.001 square miles. Located at 26.96° N. Lat.; 82.35° W. Long. Elevation is 10 feet.

Population: 15,032 (1990); 16,196 (2000); 16,666 (2007); 17,180 (2012 projected); Race: 97.7% White, 0.2% Black, 0.5% Asian, 2.5% Hispanic of any race (2007); Density: 1,695.4 persons per square mile (2007); Average household size: 1.93 (2007); Median age: 63.0 (2007); Males per 100 females: 89.7 (2007); Marriage status: 9.5% never married, 65.8% now married, 14.8% widowed, 10.0% divorced (2000); Foreign born: 5.9% (2000); Ancestry (includes multiple ancestries): 24.3% German, 19.3% English, 14.5% Irish, 6.5% United States or American, 6.3% Italian (2000).

Economy: Employment by occupation: 11.1% management, 15.6% professional, 21.4% services, 27.6% sales, 0.6% farming, 13.9% construction, 9.8% production (2000).

Income: Per capita income: $26,019 (2007); Median household income: $35,775 (2007); Average household income: $49,861 (2007); Percent of households with income of $100,000 or more: 8.4% (2007); Poverty rate: 8.7% (2000).

Education: Percent of population age 25 and over with: High school diploma (including GED) or higher: 85.2% (2007); Bachelor's degree or higher: 16.0% (2007); Master's degree or higher: 6.2% (2007).

School District(s)
Charlotte County School District (PK-12)
    2005-06 Enrollment: 17,507 . . . . (941) 255-0808
Sarasota County School District (PK-12)
    2005-06 Enrollment: 41,405 . . . . (941) 927-9000

Housing: Homeownership rate: 85.4% (2007); Median home value: $172,897 (2007); Median rent: $488 per month (2000); Median age of housing: 21 years (2000).

Hospitals: Englewood Community Hospital (100 beds)

Newspapers: Englewood Review (General - Circulation 6,000); Englewood Sun (Circulation 31,000)

Transportation: Commute to work: 94.2% car, 0.7% public transportation, 1.3% walk, 0.8% work from home (2000); Travel time to work: 41.4% less than 15 minutes, 28.2% 15 to 30 minutes, 18.8% 30 to 45 minutes, 5.0% 45 to 60 minutes, 6.6% 60 minutes or more (2000)

Additional Information Contacts
Englewood Area Chamber of Commerce . . . . (941) 474-5511
    http://www.englewoodchamber.com

FRUITVILLE (CDP).
Covers a land area of 7.039 square miles and a water area of 0 square miles. Located at 27.33° N. Lat.; 82.46° W. Long. Elevation is 30 feet.

Population: 9,570 (1990); 12,741 (2000); 14,860 (2007); 16,392 (2012 projected); Race: 93.8% White, 1.6% Black, 1.9% Asian, 6.2% Hispanic of any race (2007); Density: 2,110.9 persons per square mile (2007); Average household size: 2.40 (2007); Median age: 39.1 (2007); Males per 100 females: 96.6 (2007); Marriage status: 21.2% never married, 61.6% now married, 7.6% widowed, 9.6% divorced (2000); Foreign born: 7.3% (2000);

Ancestry (includes multiple ancestries): 23.3% German, 15.0% Irish, 13.3% English, 10.1% Other groups, 9.6% Italian (2000).

Economy: Employment by occupation: 14.0% management, 21.7% professional, 14.7% services, 29.5% sales, 0.3% farming, 11.4% construction, 8.5% production (2000).

Income: Per capita income: $29,200 (2007); Median household income: $56,085 (2007); Average household income: $69,560 (2007); Percent of households with income of $100,000 or more: 16.7% (2007); Poverty rate: 4.7% (2000).

Education: Percent of population age 25 and over with: High school diploma (including GED) or higher: 89.3% (2007); Bachelor's degree or higher: 29.2% (2007); Master's degree or higher: 8.8% (2007).

Housing: Homeownership rate: 73.4% (2007); Median home value: $264,805 (2007); Median rent: $715 per month (2000); Median age of housing: 13 years (2000).

Transportation: Commute to work: 95.0% car, 0.2% public transportation, 0.7% walk, 3.1% work from home (2000); Travel time to work: 32.1% less than 15 minutes, 48.4% 15 to 30 minutes, 12.4% 30 to 45 minutes, 2.2% 45 to 60 minutes, 4.8% 60 minutes or more (2000)

GULF GATE ESTATES (CDP).
Covers a land area of 2.811 square miles and a water area of 0 square miles. Located at 27.25° N. Lat.; 82.50° W. Long. Elevation is 13 feet.

Population: 11,622 (1990); 11,647 (2000); 11,706 (2007); 11,959 (2012 projected); Race: 95.2% White, 1.2% Black, 1.1% Asian, 5.2% Hispanic of any race (2007); Density: 4,163.7 persons per square mile (2007); Average household size: 1.91 (2007); Median age: 51.0 (2007); Males per 100 females: 84.1 (2007); Marriage status: 18.9% never married, 52.2% now married, 14.4% widowed, 14.5% divorced (2000); Foreign born: 11.0% (2000); Ancestry (includes multiple ancestries): 19.4% German, 15.0% English, 13.9% Irish, 9.4% Italian, 8.4% Other groups (2000).

Economy: Employment by occupation: 11.5% management, 16.6% professional, 18.0% services, 34.9% sales, 0.0% farming, 9.7% construction, 9.2% production (2000).

Income: Per capita income: $28,098 (2007); Median household income: $38,899 (2007); Average household income: $53,468 (2007); Percent of households with income of $100,000 or more: 9.7% (2007); Poverty rate: 5.9% (2000).

Education: Percent of population age 25 and over with: High school diploma (including GED) or higher: 87.9% (2007); Bachelor's degree or higher: 25.1% (2007); Master's degree or higher: 10.3% (2007).

Housing: Homeownership rate: 65.2% (2007); Median home value: $214,297 (2007); Median rent: $672 per month (2000); Median age of housing: 25 years (2000).

Transportation: Commute to work: 92.4% car, 0.6% public transportation, 1.7% walk, 3.9% work from home (2000); Travel time to work: 39.1% less than 15 minutes, 41.9% 15 to 30 minutes, 14.6% 30 to 45 minutes, 1.2% 45 to 60 minutes, 3.2% 60 minutes or more (2000)

KENSINGTON PARK (CDP).
Covers a land area of 1.345 square miles and a water area of 0 square miles. Located at 27.35° N. Lat.; 82.49° W. Long. Elevation is 20 feet.

Population: 3,165 (1990); 3,720 (2000); 4,023 (2007); 4,275 (2012 projected); Race: 79.0% White, 10.1% Black, 2.1% Asian, 18.4% Hispanic of any race (2007); Density: 2,990.5 persons per square mile (2007); Average household size: 2.41 (2007); Median age: 41.8 (2007); Males per 100 females: 92.8 (2007); Marriage status: 19.9% never married, 55.2% now married, 9.5% widowed, 15.4% divorced (2000); Foreign born: 16.8% (2000); Ancestry (includes multiple ancestries): 24.1% Other groups, 17.0% German, 12.6% Irish, 10.9% English, 9.3% United States or American (2000).

Economy: Employment by occupation: 12.7% management, 13.3% professional, 19.8% services, 30.9% sales, 0.6% farming, 11.5% construction, 11.3% production (2000).

Income: Per capita income: $23,279 (2007); Median household income: $45,906 (2007); Average household income: $56,145 (2007); Percent of households with income of $100,000 or more: 11.7% (2007); Poverty rate: 10.0% (2000).

Education: Percent of population age 25 and over with: High school diploma (including GED) or higher: 84.2% (2007); Bachelor's degree or higher: 20.1% (2007); Master's degree or higher: 7.3% (2007).

Housing: Homeownership rate: 88.1% (2007); Median home value: $182,832 (2007); Median rent: $740 per month (2000); Median age of housing: 34 years (2000).

LAKE SARASOTA (CDP). Covers a land area of 1.368 square miles and a water area of 0 square miles. Located at 27.29° N. Lat.; 82.43° W. Long. Elevation is 30 feet.

Population: 3,898 (1990); 4,458 (2000); 4,777 (2007); 5,044 (2012 projected); Race: 94.9% White, 1.1% Black, 0.3% Asian, 6.2% Hispanic of any race (2007); Density: 3,491.4 persons per square mile (2007); Average household size: 2.86 (2007); Median age: 36.0 (2007); Males per 100 females: 100.4 (2007); Marriage status: 21.3% never married, 60.3% now married, 3.4% widowed, 15.0% divorced (2000); Foreign born: 5.2% (2000); Ancestry (includes multiple ancestries): 23.1% German, 16.2% Irish, 13.3% Other groups, 10.8% English, 7.6% Italian (2000).

Economy: Employment by occupation: 10.1% management, 19.2% professional, 23.2% services, 27.1% sales, 0.0% farming, 12.7% construction, 7.6% production (2000).

Income: Per capita income: $22,056 (2007); Median household income: $54,049 (2007); Average household income: $63,052 (2007); Percent of households with income of $100,000 or more: 12.9% (2007); Poverty rate: 3.0% (2000).

Education: Percent of population age 25 and over with: High school diploma (including GED) or higher: 90.6% (2007); Bachelor's degree or higher: 21.6% (2007); Master's degree or higher: 5.8% (2007).

Housing: Homeownership rate: 80.0% (2007); Median home value: $238,775 (2007); Median rent: $909 per month (2000); Median age of housing: 16 years (2000).

Transportation: Commute to work: 94.6% car, 0.8% public transportation, 0.4% walk, 2.9% work from home (2000); Travel time to work: 26.9% less than 15 minutes, 46.7% 15 to 30 minutes, 14.5% 30 to 45 minutes, 6.7% 45 to 60 minutes, 5.1% 60 minutes or more (2000)

LAUREL (CDP). Covers a land area of 5.215 square miles and a water area of 0.864 square miles. Located at 27.14° N. Lat.; 82.46° W. Long. Elevation is 10 feet.

Population: 8,245 (1990); 8,393 (2000); 8,506 (2007); 8,728 (2012 projected); Race: 95.4% White, 1.6% Black, 1.1% Asian, 2.1% Hispanic of any race (2007); Density: 1,631.2 persons per square mile (2007); Average household size: 1.96 (2007); Median age: 58.3 (2007); Males per 100 females: 92.0 (2007); Marriage status: 10.6% never married, 63.7% now married, 13.9% widowed, 11.8% divorced (2000); Foreign born: 6.2% (2000); Ancestry (includes multiple ancestries): 23.0% German, 18.5% English, 12.9% Irish, 8.5% Other groups, 8.4% United States or American (2000).

Economy: Employment by occupation: 11.9% management, 20.4% professional, 15.5% services, 32.4% sales, 0.9% farming, 9.3% construction, 9.6% production (2000).

Income: Per capita income: $38,285 (2007); Median household income: $51,057 (2007); Average household income: $75,174 (2007); Percent of households with income of $100,000 or more: 17.7% (2007); Poverty rate: 8.4% (2000).

Education: Percent of population age 25 and over with: High school diploma (including GED) or higher: 87.8% (2007); Bachelor's degree or higher: 25.2% (2007); Master's degree or higher: 9.5% (2007).

Housing: Homeownership rate: 85.5% (2007); Median home value: $272,590 (2007); Median rent: $556 per month (2000); Median age of housing: 24 years (2000).

Transportation: Commute to work: 91.5% car, 0.7% public transportation, 1.0% walk, 5.9% work from home (2000); Travel time to work: 41.4% less than 15 minutes, 35.1% 15 to 30 minutes, 16.6% 30 to 45 minutes, 2.9% 45 to 60 minutes, 3.9% 60 minutes or more (2000)

LONGBOAT KEY (town). Covers a land area of 4.916 square miles and a water area of 12.150 square miles. Located at 27.39° N. Lat.; 82.64° W. Long.

Population: 5,937 (1990); 7,603 (2000); 7,529 (2007); 7,576 (2012 projected); Race: 99.0% White, 0.1% Black, 0.6% Asian, 0.8% Hispanic of any race (2007); Density: 1,531.4 persons per square mile (2007); Average household size: 1.75 (2007); Median age: 68.6 (2007); Males per 100 females: 86.9 (2007); Marriage status: 4.4% never married, 77.7% now married, 13.1% widowed, 4.8% divorced (2000); Foreign born: 11.2% (2000); Ancestry (includes multiple ancestries): 17.1% German, 14.8% English, 13.0% Irish, 10.3% Russian, 6.5% Other groups (2000).

$103,241 (2007); Average household income: $160,769 (2007); Percent of households with income of $100,000 or more: 51.3% (2007); Poverty rate: 2.9% (2000).

Education: Percent of population age 25 and over with: High school diploma (including GED) or higher: 94.4% (2007); Bachelor's degree or higher: 52.8% (2007); Master's degree or higher: 24.6% (2007).

Housing: Homeownership rate: 91.7% (2007); Median home value: $809,575 (2007); Median rent: $875 per month (2000); Median age of housing: 22 years (2000).

Safety: Violent crime rate: 1.3 per 10,000 population; Property crime rate: 123.2 per 10,000 population (2006).

Newspapers: The Longboat Observer (General - Circulation 20,000)

Transportation: Commute to work: 66.4% car, 1.5% public transportation, 4.6% walk, 20.1% work from home (2000); Travel time to work: 40.2% less than 15 minutes, 27.1% 15 to 30 minutes, 19.2% 30 to 45 minutes, 4.8% 45 to 60 minutes, 8.8% 60 minutes or more (2000)

Additional Information Contacts

Longboat Key Chamber of Commerce . . . . (941) 383-2466
   http://www.longboatkeychamber.com
Town of Longboat Key . . . . (941) 316-1999
   http://www.longboatkey.org

NOKOMIS (CDP). Covers a land area of 1.668 square miles and a water area of 0.315 square miles. Located at 27.12° N. Lat.; 82.43° W. Long. Elevation is 10 feet.

History: The name of Nokomis is of Indian origin meaning "my grandmother."

Population: 3,301 (1990); 3,334 (2000); 3,460 (2007); 3,554 (2012 projected); Race: 96.8% White, 0.9% Black, 0.4% Asian, 3.4% Hispanic of any race (2007); Density: 2,074.1 persons per square mile (2007); Average household size: 2.11 (2007); Median age: 47.3 (2007); Males per 100 females: 100.8 (2007); Marriage status: 17.8% never married, 55.8% now married, 10.6% widowed, 15.7% divorced (2000); Foreign born: 2.7% (2000); Ancestry (includes multiple ancestries): 24.8% German, 15.0% English, 14.9% Irish, 9.2% United States or American, 8.5% Other groups (2000).

Economy: Employment by occupation: 8.4% management, 17.9% professional, 18.5% services, 30.3% sales, 1.2% farming, 16.3% construction, 7.3% production (2000).

Income: Per capita income: $27,835 (2007); Median household income: $40,050 (2007); Average household income: $58,510 (2007); Percent of households with income of $100,000 or more: 13.2% (2007); Poverty rate: 12.9% (2000).

Education: Percent of population age 25 and over with: High school diploma (including GED) or higher: 80.6% (2007); Bachelor's degree or higher: 13.1% (2007); Master's degree or higher: 6.1% (2007).

School District(s)

Sarasota County School District (PK-12)
   2005-06 Enrollment: 41,405 . . . . (941) 927-9000

Housing: Homeownership rate: 79.1% (2007); Median home value: $159,559 (2007); Median rent: $452 per month (2000); Median age of housing: 26 years (2000).

Transportation: Commute to work: 93.6% car, 0.0% public transportation, 1.6% walk, 3.4% work from home (2000); Travel time to work: 37.8% less than 15 minutes, 35.8% 15 to 30 minutes, 16.0% 30 to 45 minutes, 4.1% 45 to 60 minutes, 6.2% 60 minutes or more (2000)

NORTH PORT (city). Aka North Port Charlotte. Covers a land area of 74.772 square miles and a water area of 0.766 square miles. Located at 27.06° N. Lat.; 82.17° W. Long. Elevation is 10 feet.

Population: 11,987 (1990); 22,797 (2000); 48,730 (2007); 65,229 (2012 projected); Race: 90.7% White, 5.2% Black, 0.7% Asian, 5.0% Hispanic of any race (2007); Density: 651.7 persons per square mile (2007); Average household size: 2.62 (2007); Median age: 38.2 (2007); Males per 100 females: 95.3 (2007); Marriage status: 15.6% never married, 63.8% now married, 9.5% widowed, 11.0% divorced (2000); Foreign born: 12.1% (2000); Ancestry (includes multiple ancestries): 21.8% German, 15.8% Irish, 11.9% English, 10.4% Other groups, 8.5% Italian (2000).

Economy: Unemployment rate: 6.1% (11/2007); Total civilian labor force: 22,087 (11/2007); Single-family building permits issued: 2,094 (2006);

Multi-family building permits issued: 122 (2006); Employment by occupation: 8.4% management, 14.4% professional, 21.5% services, 29.8% sales, 0.1% farming, 14.8% construction, 11.0% production (2000).
Income: Per capita income: $20,469 (2007); Median household income: $46,733 (2007); Average household income: $53,295 (2007); Percent of households with income of $100,000 or more: 8.4% (2007); Poverty rate: 8.3% (2000).
Education: Percent of population age 25 and over with: High school diploma (including GED) or higher: 82.4% (2007); Bachelor's degree or higher: 11.4% (2007); Master's degree or higher: 3.7% (2007).

School District(s)

Sarasota County School District (PK-12)

   2005-06 Enrollment: 41,405 . . . . (941) 927-9000
Housing: Homeownership rate: 89.6% (2007); Median home value: $199,793 (2007); Median rent: $540 per month (2000); Median age of housing: 14 years (2000).
Safety: Violent crime rate: 34.9 per 10,000 population; Property crime rate: 277.7 per 10,000 population (2006).
Newspapers: North Port Sun (Circulation 5,500)
Transportation: Commute to work: 95.0% car, 0.4% public transportation, 0.4% walk, 2.5% work from home (2000); Travel time to work: 17.8% less than 15 minutes, 35.6% 15 to 30 minutes, 28.5% 30 to 45 minutes, 11.0% 45 to 60 minutes, 7.1% 60 minutes or more (2000)
Additional Information Contacts
North Port Chamber of Commerce . . . . (941) 426-8744
   http://www.northportareachamber.com

NORTH SARASOTA (CDP).
Covers a land area of 3.783 square miles and a water area of 0 square miles. Located at 27.36° N. Lat.; 82.51° W. Long. Elevation is 36 feet.
Population: 6,702 (1990); 6,738 (2000); 6,694 (2007); 6,821 (2012 projected); Race: 59.9% White, 32.7% Black, 0.5% Asian, 14.6% Hispanic of any race (2007); Density: 1,769.6 persons per square mile (2007); Average household size: 2.40 (2007); Median age: 41.1 (2007); Males per 100 females: 94.0 (2007); Marriage status: 22.2% never married, 54.5% now married, 8.1% widowed, 15.2% divorced (2000); Foreign born: 8.9% (2000); Ancestry (includes multiple ancestries): 33.0% Other groups, 14.1% German, 10.2% United States or American, 8.8% Irish, 8.3% English (2000).
Economy: Employment by occupation: 8.2% management, 13.1% professional, 23.2% services, 26.0% sales, 1.0% farming, 11.3% construction, 17.1% production (2000).
Income: Per capita income: $20,079 (2007); Median household income: $37,589 (2007); Average household income: $48,106 (2007); Percent of households with income of $100,000 or more: 9.3% (2007); Poverty rate: 17.2% (2000).
Education: Percent of population age 25 and over with: High school diploma (including GED) or higher: 73.7% (2007); Bachelor's degree or higher: 12.7% (2007); Master's degree or higher: 4.3% (2007).
Housing: Homeownership rate: 80.0% (2007); Median home value: $141,330 (2007); Median rent: $480 per month (2000); Median age of housing: 23 years (2000).
Transportation: Commute to work: 91.8% car, 0.9% public transportation, 0.4% walk, 2.6% work from home (2000); Travel time to work: 35.6% less than 15 minutes, 42.1% 15 to 30 minutes, 16.9% 30 to 45 minutes, 2.3% 45 to 60 minutes, 3.0% 60 minutes or more (2000)

OSPREY (CDP).
Covers a land area of 5.455 square miles and a water area of 0.611 square miles. Located at 27.19° N. Lat.; 82.48° W. Long. Elevation is 10 feet.
History: Osprey developed as a fishing settlement. The town was named for the osprey, or fish hawk.
Population: 2,886 (1990); 4,143 (2000); 4,941 (2007); 5,508 (2012 projected); Race: 96.7% White, 0.3% Black, 1.4% Asian, 2.3% Hispanic of any race (2007); Density: 905.7 persons per square mile (2007); Average household size: 2.09 (2007); Median age: 54.8 (2007); Males per 100 females: 95.1 (2007); Marriage status: 11.1% never married, 71.5% now married, 7.3% widowed, 10.1% divorced (2000); Foreign born: 10.3% (2000); Ancestry (includes multiple ancestries): 24.2% German, 18.3% English, 14.5% Irish, 8.5% Italian, 7.2% United States or American (2000).
Economy: Employment by occupation: 14.8% management, 14.7% professional, 22.3% services, 33.6% sales, 0.0% farming, 9.6% construction, 5.1% production (2000).
Income: Per capita income: $56,902 (2007); Median household income: $71,992 (2007); Average household income: $118,680 (2007); Percent of

households with income of $100,000 or more: 35.2% (2007); Poverty rate: 6.5% (2000).
Education: Percent of population age 25 and over with: High school diploma (including GED) or higher: 88.5% (2007); Bachelor's degree or higher: 35.5% (2007); Master's degree or higher: 13.0% (2007).

School District(s)

Sarasota County School District (PK-12)

   2005-06 Enrollment: 41,405 . . . . (941) 927-9000
Housing: Homeownership rate: 88.8% (2007); Median home value: $476,439 (2007); Median rent: $525 per month (2000); Median age of housing: 15 years (2000).
Transportation: Commute to work: 83.8% car, 0.6% public transportation, 0.0% walk, 12.6% work from home (2000); Travel time to work: 24.7% less than 15 minutes, 50.0% 15 to 30 minutes, 18.4% 30 to 45 minutes, 2.2% 45 to 60 minutes, 4.7% 60 minutes or more (2000)

PLANTATION (CDP).
Covers a land area of 2.448 square miles and a water area of 0.004 square miles. Located at 27.06° N. Lat.; 82.37° W. Long. Elevation is 10 feet.
Population: 1,885 (1990); 4,168 (2000); 5,632 (2007); 6,611 (2012 projected); Race: 98.3% White, 0.2% Black, 0.4% Asian, 1.3% Hispanic of any race (2007); Density: 2,300.8 persons per square mile (2007); Average household size: 1.93 (2007); Median age: 67.9 (2007); Males per 100 females: 88.0 (2007); Marriage status: 5.7% never married, 82.3% now married, 7.8% widowed, 4.2% divorced (2000); Foreign born: 10.4% (2000); Ancestry (includes multiple ancestries): 24.8% German, 19.8% English, 19.7% Irish, 8.4% Italian, 6.5% Polish (2000).
Economy: Employment by occupation: 19.7% management, 22.1% professional, 12.7% services, 30.6% sales, 0.0% farming, 3.7% construction, 11.2% production (2000).
Income: Per capita income: $38,408 (2007); Median household income: $59,145 (2007); Average household income: $74,004 (2007); Percent of households with income of $100,000 or more: 17.7% (2007); Poverty rate: 0.9% (2000).
Education: Percent of population age 25 and over with: High school diploma (including GED) or higher: 94.4% (2007); Bachelor's degree or higher: 30.9% (2007); Master's degree or higher: 11.8% (2007).
Housing: Homeownership rate: 96.5% (2007); Median home value: $355,302 (2007); Median rent: $744 per month (2000); Median age of housing: 10 years (2000).
Transportation: Commute to work: 94.6% car, 0.0% public transportation, 0.9% walk, 4.5% work from home (2000); Travel time to work: 33.3% less than 15 minutes, 42.0% 15 to 30 minutes, 16.8% 30 to 45 minutes, 5.2% 45 to 60 minutes, 2.7% 60 minutes or more (2000)

RIDGE WOOD HEIGHTS (CDP).
Covers a land area of 1.429 square miles and a water area of 0.026 square miles. Located at 27.29° N. Lat.; 82.51° W. Long. Elevation is 23 feet.
Population: 4,851 (1990); 5,028 (2000); 5,110 (2007); 5,246 (2012 projected); Race: 94.1% White, 1.3% Black, 1.2% Asian, 7.3% Hispanic of any race (2007); Density: 3,575.3 persons per square mile (2007); Average household size: 2.20 (2007); Median age: 40.8 (2007); Males per 100 females: 102.0 (2007); Marriage status: 23.0% never married, 54.8% now married, 4.8% widowed, 17.3% divorced (2000); Foreign born: 6.2% (2000); Ancestry (includes multiple ancestries): 27.7% German, 18.5% Irish, 15.2% English, 10.1% Other groups, 8.2% Italian (2000).
Economy: Employment by occupation: 12.6% management, 17.1% professional, 18.2% services, 28.8% sales, 0.0% farming, 14.0% construction, 9.4% production (2000).
Income: Per capita income: $26,253 (2007); Median household income: $49,156 (2007); Average household income: $57,874 (2007); Percent of households with income of $100,000 or more: 13.8% (2007); Poverty rate: 6.0% (2000).
Education: Percent of population age 25 and over with: High school diploma (including GED) or higher: 86.1% (2007); Bachelor's degree or higher: 21.2% (2007); Master's degree or higher: 5.8% (2007).
Housing: Homeownership rate: 71.5% (2007); Median home value: $204,483 (2007); Median rent: $621 per month (2000); Median age of housing: 25 years (2000).
Transportation: Commute to work: 94.4% car, 0.9% public transportation, 1.1% walk, 1.1% work from home (2000); Travel time to work: 38.3% less than 15 minutes, 46.1% 15 to 30 minutes, 8.6% 30 to 45 minutes, 3.1% 45 to 60 minutes, 3.9% 60 minutes or more (2000)

SARASOTA (city). County seat. Covers a land area of 14.892 square miles and a water area of 11.037 square miles. Located at 27.33° N. Lat.; 82.53° W. Long. Elevation is 23 feet.

History: Sarasota was settled in 1884 by sixty Scottish families, who kept the name of Sarasota by which the area had previously been known. A golf course was built in 1886, and with golf and fishing, Sarasota became popular as a winter resort. When Sarasota County was carved out of Manatee County by the legislature in 1921, Sarasota was named the county seat. John Ringling selected Sarasota as winter quarters for his circus in 1929 and made his home here.

Population: 51,400 (1990); 52,715 (2000); 53,931 (2007); 55,633 (2012 projected); Race: 73.6% White, 16.2% Black, 1.4% Asian, 19.2% Hispanic of any race (2007); Density: 3,621.5 persons per square mile (2007); Average household size: 2.21 (2007); Median age: 41.3 (2007); Males per 100 females: 96.6 (2007); Marriage status: 27.2% never married, 46.2% now married, 11.3% widowed, 15.4% divorced (2000); Foreign born: 13.9% (2000); Ancestry (includes multiple ancestries): 27.0% Other groups, 14.0% German, 10.5% English, 10.5% Irish, 6.2% United States or American (2000).

Economy: Unemployment rate: 4.5% (11/2007); Total civilian labor force: 28,739 (11/2007); Single-family building permits issued: 111 (2006); Multi-family building permits issued: 14 (2006); Employment by occupation: 11.2% management, 17.8% professional, 23.1% services, 26.6% sales, 0.4% farming, 11.1% construction, 9.8% production (2000).

Income: Per capita income: $26,319 (2007); Median household income: $38,211 (2007); Average household income: $56,569 (2007); Percent of households with income of $100,000 or more: 11.6% (2007); Poverty rate: 16.7% (2000).

Taxes: Total city taxes per capita: $835 (2005); City property taxes per capita: $320 (2005).

Education: Percent of population age 25 and over with: High school diploma (including GED) or higher: 80.1% (2007); Bachelor's degree or higher: 25.4% (2007); Master's degree or higher: 9.1% (2007).

School District(s)
Manatee County School District (PK-12)
    2005-06 Enrollment: 41,351 . . . . (941) 708-8770
Sarasota County School District (PK-12)
    2005-06 Enrollment: 41,405 . . . . (941) 927-9000

Four-year College(s)
Argosy University-Sarasota Campus (Private, For-profit)
    Fall 2006 Enrollment: 1,801. . . . . (941) 379-0404
East West College of Natural Medicine (Private, For-profit)
    Fall 2006 Enrollment: 121 . . . . (941) 355-9080
New College of Florida (Public)
    Fall 2006 Enrollment: 746 . . . . (941) 487-5000
    2006-07 Tuition: In-state $3,800; Out-of-state $20,500
Ringling School of Art and Design (Private, Not-for-profit)
    Fall 2006 Enrollment: 1,090. . . . . (800) 255-7695
    2006-07 Tuition: In-state $24,710; Out-of-state $24,710

Two-year College(s)
Sarasota County Technical Institute (Public)
    Fall 2006 Enrollment: 688 . . . . (941) 924-1365

Vocational/Technical School(s)
Fashion Focus Hair Academy (Private, For-profit)
    Fall 2006 Enrollment: 73 . . . . (941) 921-4877
    2006-07 Tuition: $8,650
Sarasota School of Massage Therapy (Private, For-profit)
    Fall 2006 Enrollment: 123 . . . . (941) 957-0577
    2006-07 Tuition: $8,325
Sunstate Academy (Private, For-profit)
    Fall 2006 Enrollment: 93 . . . . (941) 377-4880
    2006-07 Tuition: $11,550

Housing: Homeownership rate: 58.2% (2007); Median home value: $212,641 (2007); Median rent: $566 per month (2000); Median age of housing: 30 years (2000).

Hospitals: Bayside Center for Behavioral Health at Sarasota Memorial (82 beds); Doctors Hospital of Sarasota (168 beds); HealthSouth Rehabilitation Hospital of Sarasota (75 beds); Sarasota Memorial Health Care Systems (845 beds)

Safety: Violent crime rate: 103.4 per 10,000 population; Property crime rate: 656.0 per 10,000 population (2006).

Newspapers: Herald Tribune (General - Circulation 15,000); New York Staats Zeitung (Ethnic - Circulation 20,000); Pelican Press (General - Circulation 24,000); Sarasota Herald-Tribune (Circulation 116,044); Tempo 50,000)

Transportation: Commute to work: 88.2% car, 2.5% public transportation, 2.7% walk, 3.5% work from home (2000); Travel time to work: 39.0% less than 15 minutes, 40.2% 15 to 30 minutes, 14.0% 30 to 45 minutes, 3.2% 45 to 60 minutes, 3.6% 60 minutes or more (2000); Amtrak: Service available.

Airports: Sarasota/Bradenton International (primary service/small hub)

Additional Information Contacts
Committee for Economic Development . . . . (941) 309-1200
    http://www.edcsarasotacounty.com
Sarasota Chamber of Commerce . . . . (941) 955-8187
    http://www.sarasotachamber.org
Siesta Key Chamber of Commerce . . . . (941) 349-3800
    http://www.siestakeychamber.com

SARASOTA SPRINGS (CDP). Covers a land area of 3.617 square miles and a water area of 0 square miles. Located at 27.31° N. Lat.; 82.47° W. Long. Elevation is 23 feet.

Population: 16,088 (1990); 15,875 (2000); 15,676 (2007); 15,814 (2012 projected); Race: 93.8% White, 1.0% Black, 1.1% Asian, 7.9% Hispanic of any race (2007); Density: 4,334.5 persons per square mile (2007); Average household size: 2.36 (2007); Median age: 42.1 (2007); Males per 100 females: 93.5 (2007); Marriage status: 19.8% never married, 58.1% now married, 9.3% widowed, 12.8% divorced (2000); Foreign born: 5.9% (2000); Ancestry (includes multiple ancestries): 22.2% German, 14.1% Irish, 13.0% English, 11.0% Other groups, 9.3% United States or American (2000).

Economy: Employment by occupation: 10.8% management, 17.6% professional, 19.4% services, 30.6% sales, 0.3% farming, 12.7% construction, 8.7% production (2000).

Income: Per capita income: $24,473 (2007); Median household income: $45,609 (2007); Average household income: $57,655 (2007); Percent of households with income of $100,000 or more: 10.8% (2007); Poverty rate: 6.9% (2000).

Education: Percent of population age 25 and over with: High school diploma (including GED) or higher: 89.0% (2007); Bachelor's degree or higher: 20.1% (2007); Master's degree or higher: 6.4% (2007).

Housing: Homeownership rate: 83.0% (2007); Median home value: $201,897 (2007); Median rent: $675 per month (2000); Median age of housing: 25 years (2000).

Transportation: Commute to work: 95.5% car, 0.3% public transportation, 0.8% walk, 2.3% work from home (2000); Travel time to work: 30.2% less than 15 minutes, 50.7% 15 to 30 minutes, 12.5% 30 to 45 minutes, 2.1% 45 to 60 minutes, 4.4% 60 minutes or more (2000)

SIESTA KEY (CDP). Covers a land area of 2.292 square miles and a water area of 1.163 square miles. Located at 27.27° N. Lat.; 82.55° W. Long. Elevation is 3 feet.

Population: 7,772 (1990); 7,150 (2000); 6,738 (2007); 6,497 (2012 projected); Race: 98.0% White, 0.1% Black, 0.8% Asian, 2.5% Hispanic of any race (2007); Density: 2,940.3 persons per square mile (2007); Average household size: 1.86 (2007); Median age: 60.2 (2007); Males per 100 females: 91.8 (2007); Marriage status: 11.1% never married, 66.4% now married, 11.7% widowed, 10.9% divorced (2000); Foreign born: 10.5% (2000); Ancestry (includes multiple ancestries): 21.4% German, 18.6% English, 15.1% Irish, 6.4% Other groups, 5.5% United States or American (2000).

Economy: Employment by occupation: 26.2% management, 28.7% professional, 10.7% services, 28.5% sales, 0.3% farming, 2.4% construction, 3.2% production (2000).

Income: Per capita income: $67,462 (2007); Median household income: $83,669 (2007); Average household income: $125,568 (2007); Percent of households with income of $100,000 or more: 40.6% (2007); Poverty rate: 4.4% (2000).

Education: Percent of population age 25 and over with: High school diploma (including GED) or higher: 95.7% (2007); Bachelor's degree or higher: 51.7% (2007); Master's degree or higher: 22.0% (2007).

Housing: Homeownership rate: 82.5% (2007); Median home value: $767,695 (2007); Median rent: $942 per month (2000); Median age of housing: 26 years (2000).

Transportation: Commute to work: 80.6% car, 0.3% public transportation, 3.6% walk, 12.2% work from home (2000); Travel time to work: 31.9% less than 15 minutes, 46.2% 15 to 30 minutes, 14.0% 30 to 45 minutes, 1.4% 45 to 60 minutes, 6.5% 60 minutes or more (2000)

SOUTH GATE RIDGE (CDP).
Covers a land area of 1.811 square miles and a water area of 0 square miles. Located at 27.28° N. Lat.; 82.49° W. Long. Elevation is 30 feet.

Population: 5,924 (1990); 5,655 (2000); 5,636 (2007); 5,719 (2012 projected); Race: 91.7% White, 0.8% Black, 2.8% Asian, 9.2% Hispanic of any race (2007); Density: 3,112.0 persons per square mile (2007); Average household size: 2.23 (2007); Median age: 43.5 (2007); Males per 100 females: 93.5 (2007); Marriage status: 19.4% never married, 56.7% now married, 9.3% widowed, 14.7% divorced (2000); Foreign born: 8.4% (2000); Ancestry (includes multiple ancestries): 17.9% German, 14.7% Irish, 14.3% English, 13.4% Italian, 11.2% Other groups (2000).

Economy: Employment by occupation: 14.6% management, 20.9% professional, 20.9% services, 22.9% sales, 0.0% farming, 12.9% construction, 7.9% production (2000).

Income: Per capita income: $30,675 (2007); Median household income: $53,206 (2007); Average household income: $68,018 (2007); Percent of households with income of $100,000 or more: 18.6% (2007); Poverty rate: 4.5% (2000).

Education: Percent of population age 25 and over with: High school diploma (including GED) or higher: 90.7% (2007); Bachelor's degree or higher: 28.6% (2007); Master's degree or higher: 10.1% (2007).

Housing: Homeownership rate: 75.2% (2007); Median home value: $221,622 (2007); Median rent: $670 per month (2000); Median age of housing: 24 years (2000).

Transportation: Commute to work: 93.8% car, 0.5% public transportation, 0.0% walk, 4.6% work from home (2000); Travel time to work: 36.3% less than 15 minutes, 44.3% 15 to 30 minutes, 11.8% 30 to 45 minutes, 2.3% 45 to 60 minutes, 5.3% 60 minutes or more (2000)

SOUTH SARASOTA (CDP).
Covers a land area of 1.951 square miles and a water area of 0.372 square miles. Located at 27.28° N. Lat.; 82.53° W. Long. Elevation is 13 feet.

Population: 5,174 (1990); 5,314 (2000); 5,313 (2007); 5,382 (2012 projected); Race: 94.0% White, 0.4% Black, 1.7% Asian, 6.3% Hispanic of any race (2007); Density: 2,723.7 persons per square mile (2007); Average household size: 2.06 (2007); Median age: 49.1 (2007); Males per 100 females: 96.4 (2007); Marriage status: 19.8% never married, 57.0% now married, 8.1% widowed, 15.1% divorced (2000); Foreign born: 8.5% (2000); Ancestry (includes multiple ancestries): 22.4% German, 18.2% English, 15.2% Irish, 9.5% Other groups, 8.1% Italian (2000).

Economy: Employment by occupation: 15.2% management, 24.2% professional, 14.6% services, 31.0% sales, 0.0% farming, 8.4% construction, 6.6% production (2000).

Income: Per capita income: $51,789 (2007); Median household income: $62,662 (2007); Average household income: $106,731 (2007); Percent of households with income of $100,000 or more: 32.5% (2007); Poverty rate: 6.6% (2000).

Education: Percent of population age 25 and over with: High school diploma (including GED) or higher: 90.4% (2007); Bachelor's degree or higher: 42.7% (2007); Master's degree or higher: 17.0% (2007).

Housing: Homeownership rate: 80.1% (2007); Median home value: $374,611 (2007); Median rent: $598 per month (2000); Median age of housing: 26 years (2000).

Transportation: Commute to work: 85.5% car, 0.9% public transportation, 5.2% walk, 6.3% work from home (2000); Travel time to work: 42.9% less than 15 minutes, 37.1% 15 to 30 minutes, 13.0% 30 to 45 minutes, 1.8% 45 to 60 minutes, 5.1% 60 minutes or more (2000)

SOUTH VENICE (CDP).
Covers a land area of 6.213 square miles and a water area of 0.371 square miles. Located at 27.04° N. Lat.; 82.41° W. Long. Elevation is 13 feet.

Population: 11,999 (1990); 13,539 (2000); 14,461 (2007); 15,260 (2012 projected); Race: 96.9% White, 0.7% Black, 0.6% Asian, 2.9% Hispanic of any race (2007); Density: 2,327.6 persons per square mile (2007); Average household size: 2.28 (2007); Median age: 45.5 (2007); Males per 100 females: 95.4 (2007); Marriage status: 15.6% never married, 63.3% now married, 7.9% widowed, 13.2% divorced (2000); Foreign born: 5.2% (2000); Ancestry (includes multiple ancestries): 20.8% German, 17.6% Irish, 17.4% English, 9.6% Italian, 8.5% Other groups (2000).

Economy: Employment by occupation: 8.6% management, 15.2% professional, 22.1% services, 28.7% sales, 0.0% farming, 12.5% construction, 12.9% production (2000).

Income: Per capita income: $22,756 (2007); Median household income: $41,366 (2007); Average household income: $51,888 (2007); Percent of

---

5.7% (2000).

Education: Percent of population age 25 and over with: High school diploma (including GED) or higher: 82.7% (2007); Bachelor's degree or higher: 14.5% (2007); Master's degree or higher: 4.5% (2007).

Housing: Homeownership rate: 88.8% (2007); Median home value: $181,537 (2007); Median rent: $561 per month (2000); Median age of housing: 22 years (2000).

Transportation: Commute to work: 95.8% car, 0.3% public transportation, 0.8% walk, 2.2% work from home (2000); Travel time to work: 36.0% less than 15 minutes, 33.8% 15 to 30 minutes, 19.5% 30 to 45 minutes, 5.3% 45 to 60 minutes, 5.3% 60 minutes or more (2000)

SOUTHGATE (CDP).
Aka Sarasota Southeast. Covers a land area of 2.044 square miles and a water area of 0.036 square miles. Located at 27.30° N. Lat.; 82.51° W. Long.

Population: 7,267 (1990); 7,455 (2000); 7,562 (2007); 7,697 (2012 projected); Race: 94.5% White, 1.3% Black, 1.3% Asian, 10.2% Hispanic of any race (2007); Density: 3,700.2 persons per square mile (2007); Average household size: 2.03 (2007); Median age: 48.2 (2007); Males per 100 females: 91.3 (2007); Marriage status: 15.0% never married, 59.6% now married, 9.0% widowed, 16.4% divorced (2000); Foreign born: 9.8% (2000); Ancestry (includes multiple ancestries): 24.0% German, 16.3% English, 13.3% Irish, 11.9% Other groups, 8.1% Italian (2000).

Economy: Employment by occupation: 12.4% management, 17.4% professional, 21.3% services, 31.3% sales, 0.5% farming, 9.6% construction, 7.5% production (2000).

Income: Per capita income: $28,211 (2007); Median household income: $44,880 (2007); Average household income: $56,885 (2007); Percent of households with income of $100,000 or more: 13.0% (2007); Poverty rate: 6.8% (2000).

Education: Percent of population age 25 and over with: High school diploma (including GED) or higher: 87.4% (2007); Bachelor's degree or higher: 24.7% (2007); Master's degree or higher: 9.6% (2007).

Housing: Homeownership rate: 79.1% (2007); Median home value: $241,024 (2007); Median rent: $605 per month (2000); Median age of housing: 33 years (2000).

Transportation: Commute to work: 91.0% car, 0.7% public transportation, 2.0% walk, 4.3% work from home (2000); Travel time to work: 43.7% less than 15 minutes, 38.9% 15 to 30 minutes, 12.0% 30 to 45 minutes, 2.0% 45 to 60 minutes, 3.4% 60 minutes or more (2000)

THE MEADOWS (CDP).
Covers a land area of 2.316 square miles and a water area of 0 square miles. Located at 27.36° N. Lat.; 82.47° W. Long. Elevation is 26 feet.

Population: 3,665 (1990); 4,423 (2000); 4,936 (2007); 5,336 (2012 projected); Race: 95.1% White, 2.3% Black, 1.1% Asian, 2.0% Hispanic of any race (2007); Density: 2,131.2 persons per square mile (2007); Average household size: 1.79 (2007); Median age: 69.5 (2007); Males per 100 females: 80.6 (2007); Marriage status: 8.4% never married, 68.0% now married, 15.7% widowed, 7.9% divorced (2000); Foreign born: 12.8% (2000); Ancestry (includes multiple ancestries): 15.2% German, 15.0% English, 14.7% Irish, 8.5% Other groups, 8.5% Italian (2000).

Economy: Employment by occupation: 26.2% management, 21.0% professional, 14.8% services, 34.4% sales, 0.0% farming, 0.0% construction, 3.5% production (2000).

Income: Per capita income: $45,608 (2007); Median household income: $61,108 (2007); Average household income: $80,309 (2007); Percent of households with income of $100,000 or more: 24.1% (2007); Poverty rate: 3.4% (2000).

Education: Percent of population age 25 and over with: High school diploma (including GED) or higher: 96.5% (2007); Bachelor's degree or higher: 46.2% (2007); Master's degree or higher: 17.6% (2007).

Housing: Homeownership rate: 81.3% (2007); Median home value: $278,103 (2007); Median rent: $938 per month (2000); Median age of housing: 16 years (2000).

Transportation: Commute to work: 88.8% car, 0.0% public transportation, 0.7% walk, 9.9% work from home (2000); Travel time to work: 31.4% less than 15 minutes, 52.2% 15 to 30 minutes, 12.9% 30 to 45 minutes, 0.0% 45 to 60 minutes, 3.5% 60 minutes or more (2000)

VAMO (CDP).
Covers a land area of 1.773 square miles and a water area of 0.316 square miles. Located at 27.22° N. Lat.; 82.49° W. Long. Elevation is 13 feet.

Population: 3,325 (1990); 5,285 (2000); 5,729 (2007); 6,058 (2012 projected); Race: 95.5% White, 1.2% Black, 1.7% Asian, 6.1% Hispanic of any race (2007); Density: 3,231.8 persons per square mile (2007); Average household size: 1.99 (2007); Median age: 49.7 (2007); Males per 100 females: 84.7 (2007); Marriage status: 19.9% never married, 50.4% now married, 15.3% widowed, 14.4% divorced (2000); Foreign born: 8.7% (2000); Ancestry (includes multiple ancestries): 17.0% German, 16.6% English, 13.9% Irish, 9.1% United States or American, 7.0% Other groups (2000).
Economy: Employment by occupation: 15.3% management, 17.8% professional, 23.4% services, 28.0% sales, 0.0% farming, 4.6% construction, 10.8% production (2000).
Income: Per capita income: $41,936 (2007); Median household income: $53,230 (2007); Average household income: $76,654 (2007); Percent of households with income of $100,000 or more: 21.0% (2007); Poverty rate: 5.6% (2000).
Education: Percent of population age 25 and over with: High school diploma (including GED) or higher: 92.5% (2007); Bachelor's degree or higher: 42.4% (2007); Master's degree or higher: 17.7% (2007).
Housing: Homeownership rate: 53.9% (2007); Median home value: $279,020 (2007); Median rent: $825 per month (2000); Median age of housing: 18 years (2000).
Transportation: Commute to work: 90.9% car, 0.3% public transportation, 2.8% walk, 2.5% work from home (2000); Travel time to work: 27.3% less than 15 minutes, 44.4% 15 to 30 minutes, 20.1% 30 to 45 minutes, 5.0% 45 to 60 minutes, 3.1% 60 minutes or more (2000)

VENICE (city).
Covers a land area of 9.115 square miles and a water area of 0.548 square miles. Located at 27.09° N. Lat.; 82.43° W. Long. Elevation is 10 feet.
History: Venice came into existence during the Florida land boom of the 1920's. It was built by the Brotherhood of Locomotive Engineers, who laid out a city that had few residents until the mid-1930's.
Population: 18,380 (1990); 17,764 (2000); 20,900 (2007); 23,108 (2012 projected); Race: 97.6% White, 0.6% Black, 0.6% Asian, 1.7% Hispanic of any race (2007); Density: 2,292.9 persons per square mile (2007); Average household size: 1.79 (2007); Median age: 69.1 (2007); Males per 100 females: 77.4 (2007); Marriage status: 8.7% never married, 62.5% now married, 19.3% widowed, 9.5% divorced (2000); Foreign born: 6.8% (2000); Ancestry (includes multiple ancestries): 20.8% German, 19.1% English, 17.4% Irish, 7.9% Italian, 6.6% United States or American (2000).
Economy: Single-family building permits issued: 140 (2006); Multi-family building permits issued: 142 (2006); Employment by occupation: 14.0% management, 21.3% professional, 22.3% services, 29.1% sales, 0.1% farming, 6.5% construction, 6.6% production (2000).
Income: Per capita income: $33,276 (2007); Median household income: $41,991 (2007); Average household income: $57,874 (2007); Percent of households with income of $100,000 or more: 13.0% (2007); Poverty rate: 5.7% (2000).
Education: Percent of population age 25 and over with: High school diploma (including GED) or higher: 89.9% (2007); Bachelor's degree or higher: 28.1% (2007); Master's degree or higher: 10.3% (2007).

School District(s)
Sarasota County School District (PK-12)
    2005-06 Enrollment: 41,405 . . . . (941) 927-9000
Housing: Homeownership rate: 77.9% (2007); Median home value: $233,963 (2007); Median rent: $640 per month (2000); Median age of housing: 24 years (2000).
Hospitals: Bon Secours Venice Hospital (312 beds)
Safety: Violent crime rate: 24.8 per 10,000 population; Property crime rate: 280.9 per 10,000 population (2006).
Newspapers: The Venice Gondolier (General - Circulation 12,000)
Transportation: Commute to work: 87.6% car, 0.2% public transportation, 3.4% walk, 6.2% work from home (2000); Travel time to work: 46.2% less than 15 minutes, 27.1% 15 to 30 minutes, 17.3% 30 to 45 minutes, 4.6% 45 to 60 minutes, 4.7% 60 minutes or more (2000)
Additional Information Contacts
Venice Chamber of Commerce . . . . (941) 488-2236
    http://www.venicechamber.com

VENICE GARDENS (CDP).
Covers a land area of 2.499 square miles and a water area of 0.188 square miles. Located at 27.07° N. Lat.; 82.40° W. Long. Elevation is 13 feet.
Population: 7,795 (1990); 7,466 (2000); 7,535 (2007); 7,689 (2012 projected); Race: 96.4% White, 0.6% Black, 1.9% Asian, 2.3% Hispanic of

any race (2007); Density: 3,015.5 persons per square mile (2007); Average household size: 2.11 (2007); Median age: 55.4 (2007); Males per 100 females: 88.0 (2007); Marriage status: 12.1% never married, 64.0% now married, 12.6% widowed, 11.3% divorced (2000); Foreign born: 6.4% (2000); Ancestry (includes multiple ancestries): 21.0% German, 18.9% Irish, 17.9% English, 7.8% Other groups, 7.7% Italian (2000).
Economy: Employment by occupation: 8.7% management, 13.6% professional, 22.1% services, 33.2% sales, 0.0% farming, 13.6% construction, 8.7% production (2000).
Income: Per capita income: $25,552 (2007); Median household income: $44,405 (2007); Average household income: $53,872 (2007); Percent of households with income of $100,000 or more: 9.7% (2007); Poverty rate: 5.8% (2000).
Education: Percent of population age 25 and over with: High school diploma (including GED) or higher: 86.7% (2007); Bachelor's degree or higher: 19.2% (2007); Master's degree or higher: 7.0% (2007).
Housing: Homeownership rate: 87.1% (2007); Median home value: $209,945 (2007); Median rent: $577 per month (2000); Median age of housing: 26 years (2000).
Transportation: Commute to work: 92.9% car, 0.2% public transportation, 1.6% walk, 3.9% work from home (2000); Travel time to work: 38.6% less than 15 minutes, 36.3% 15 to 30 minutes, 14.7% 30 to 45 minutes, 7.3% 45 to 60 minutes, 3.0% 60 minutes or more (2000)

WARM MINERAL SPRINGS (CDP).
Covers a land area of 2.623 square miles and a water area of 0.283 square miles. Located at 27.04° N. Lat.; 82.26° W. Long. Elevation is 3 feet.
Population: 4,027 (1990); 4,811 (2000); 5,756 (2007); 6,441 (2012 projected); Race: 98.1% White, 0.7% Black, 0.4% Asian, 1.4% Hispanic of any race (2007); Density: 2,194.4 persons per square mile (2007); Average household size: 1.75 (2007); Median age: 71.8 (2007); Males per 100 females: 83.8 (2007); Marriage status: 4.3% never married, 73.7% now married, 16.3% widowed, 5.7% divorced (2000); Foreign born: 13.6% (2000); Ancestry (includes multiple ancestries): 18.9% German, 15.7% English, 14.8% Irish, 7.3% Polish, 7.1% Italian (2000).
Economy: Employment by occupation: 6.4% management, 3.8% professional, 18.4% services, 46.4% sales, 0.0% farming, 11.4% construction, 13.6% production (2000).
Income: Per capita income: $27,241 (2007); Median household income: $35,597 (2007); Average household income: $47,804 (2007); Percent of households with income of $100,000 or more: 7.4% (2007); Poverty rate: 7.6% (2000).
Education: Percent of population age 25 and over with: High school diploma (including GED) or higher: 83.8% (2007); Bachelor's degree or higher: 19.1% (2007); Master's degree or higher: 6.9% (2007).
Housing: Homeownership rate: 93.0% (2007); Median home value: $146,276 (2007); Median rent: $477 per month (2000); Median age of housing: 17 years (2000).
Transportation: Commute to work: 92.3% car, 1.2% public transportation, 1.3% walk, 2.5% work from home (2000); Travel time to work: 22.6% less than 15 minutes, 45.0% 15 to 30 minutes, 22.7% 30 to 45 minutes, 3.0% 45 to 60 minutes, 6.7% 60 minutes or more (2000)

Seminole County

Located in east central Florida; bounded on the north and east by the St. Johns River; includes many lakes. Covers a land area of 308.20 square miles, a water area of 36.67 square miles, and is located in the Eastern Time Zone. The county was founded in 1913. County seat is Sanford.

Seminole County is part of the Orlando-Kissimmee, FL Metropolitan Statistical Area. The entire metro area includes: Lake County, FL; Orange County, FL; Osceola County, FL; Seminole County, FL

Weather Station: Sanford Experiment Station										Elevation: 13 feet	
	Jan	Feb	Mar	Apr	May	Jun	Jul	Aug	Sep	Oct	Nov	Dec
High	70	72	77	82	87	90	92	92	89	84	78	72
Low	48	49	54	58	64	70	72	72	71	64	57	51
Precip	3.0	3.1	3.9	2.6	3.6	6.5	6.8	7.4	5.7	3.7	3.0	2.6
Snow	0.0	0.0	0.0	0.0	0.0	0.0	0.0	0.0	0.0	0.0	0.0	0.0

High and Low temperatures in degrees Fahrenheit; Precipitation and Snow in inches

Population: 287,529 (1990); 365,196 (2000); 417,992 (2007); 459,295 (2012 projected); Race: 79.0% White, 10.6% Black, 3.3% Asian, 14.4% Hispanic of any race (2007); Density: 1,356.2 persons per square mile

(2007); Average household size: 2.59 (2007); Median age: 38.5 (2007); Males per 100 females: 96.8 (2007).

Religion: Five largest groups: 16.5% Catholic Church, 5.3% Southern Baptist Convention, 2.6% The United Methodist Church, 2.6% Independent, Non-Charismatic Churches, 1.3% Lutheran Church—Missouri Synod (2000).

Economy: Unemployment rate: 3.8% (11/2007); Total civilian labor force: 246,642 (11/2007); Leading industries: 17.4% retail trade; 12.6% construction; 9.3% accommodation & food services (2005); Farms: 376 totaling 27,987 acres (2002); Companies that employ 500 or more persons: 17 (2005); Companies that employ 100 to 499 persons: 245 (2005); Companies that employ less than 100 persons: 12,692 (2005); Black-owned businesses: 1,340 (2002); Hispanic-owned businesses: 2,898 (2002); Asian-owned businesses: 1,498 (2002); Women-owned businesses: 8,803 (2002); Retail sales per capita: $19,172 (2007). Single-family building permits issued: 2,710 (2006); Multi-family building permits issued: 13 (2006).

Income: Per capita income: $29,536 (2007); Median household income: $57,362 (2007); Average household income: $76,088 (2007); Percent of households with income of $100,000 or more: 22.5% (2007); Poverty rate: 8.2% (2005); Bankruptcy rate: 1.14% (2006).

Taxes: Total county taxes per capita: $472 (2005); County property taxes per capita: $326 (2005).

Education: Percent of population age 25 and over with: High school diploma (including GED) or higher: 88.8% (2007); Bachelor's degree or higher: 31.2% (2007); Master's degree or higher: 10.0% (2007).

Housing: Homeownership rate: 70.3% (2007); Median home value: $223,317 (2007); Median rent: $633 per month (2000); Median age of housing: 17 years (2000).

Health: Birth rate: 125.2 per 10,000 population (2006); Death rate: 69.7 per 10,000 population (2006); Age-adjusted cancer mortality rate: 183.1 deaths per 100,000 population (2004); Air Quality Index: 87.7% good, 12.1% moderate, 0.3% unhealthy for sensitive individuals, 0.0% unhealthy (percent of days in 2006); Number of physicians: 19.0 per 10,000 population (2005); Hospital beds: 11.1 per 10,000 population (2004); Hospital admissions: 450.4 per 10,000 population (2004).

Elections: 2004 Presidential election results: 58.1% Bush, 41.3% Kerry, 0.3% Nader, 0.2% Badnarik.

National and State Parks: Lower Wekiva River Preserve State Park

Additional Information Contacts

Seminole County Government . . . . (407) 665-7219
 http://www.seminolecountyfl.gov
City of Altamonte Springs . . . . (407) 585-1423
 http://www.altamonte.org
City of Casselberry. . . . . (407) 262-7700
 http://www.casselberry.org
City of Lake Mary. . . . . (407) 585-1400
 http://www.lakemaryfl.com
City of Longwood . . . . (407) 260-3440
 http://www.ci.longwood.fl.us
City of Oviedo . . . . (407) 971-5555
 http://www.ci.oviedo.fl.us
City of Sanford . . . . (407) 330-5600
 http://www.ci.sanford.fl.us
City of Winter Springs . . . . (407) 327-1800
 http://www.winterspringsfl.org
Goldenrod Chamber of Commerce . . . . (407) 677-5980
 http://www.goldenrodchamber.com
Lake Mary-Heathrow Chamber of Commerce . . . . (407) 333-4748
 http://www.seminolebusiness.org
Longwood Chamber of Commerce . . . . (407) 333-4748
Sanford Chamber of Commerce . . . . (407) 322-2212
 http://www.sanfordchamber.com
Seminole County Regional Chamber of Commerce . . . . . (407) 333-4748
 http://www.seminolebusiness.org

Seminole County Communities

ALTAMONTE SPRINGS (city). Covers a land area of 8.896 square miles and a water area of 0.557 square miles. Located at 28.66° N. Lat.; 81.39° W. Long. Elevation is 85 feet.

Population: 36,355 (1990); 41,200 (2000); 41,840 (2007); 43,089 (2012 projected); Race: 73.8% White, 11.7% Black, 3.9% Asian, 21.2% Hispanic of any race (2007); Density: 4,703.0 persons per square mile (2007); Average household size: 2.15 (2007); Median age: 37.0 (2007); Males per

100 females: 94.1 (2007); Marriage status: 31.1% never married, 47.0% now married, 6.1% widowed, 15.8% divorced (2000); Foreign born: 12.7% (2000); Ancestry (includes multiple ancestries): 30.7% Other groups, 14.4% German, 12.5% Irish, 9.8% English, 8.3% Italian (2000).

Economy: Unemployment rate: 3.5% (11/2007); Total civilian labor force: 28,447 (11/2007); Single-family building permits issued: 9 (2006); Multi-family building permits issued: 7 (2006); Employment by occupation: 13.7% management, 25.3% professional, 13.4% services, 32.5% sales, 0.0% farming, 7.6% construction, 7.6% production (2000).

Income: Per capita income: $26,856 (2007); Median household income: $46,716 (2007); Average household income: $57,391 (2007); Percent of households with income of $100,000 or more: 12.4% (2007); Poverty rate: 7.4% (2000).

Education: Percent of population age 25 and over with: High school diploma (including GED) or higher: 89.9% (2007); Bachelor's degree or higher: 31.4% (2007); Master's degree or higher: 9.1% (2007).

School District(s)
Seminole County School District (PK-12)
 2005-06 Enrollment: 66,692 . . . . (407) 320-0006

Two-year College(s)
Golf Academy of the South (Private, For-profit)
 Fall 2006 Enrollment: 220 . . . . (800) 342-7342
 2006-07 Tuition: In-state $9,813; Out-of-state $9,813

Vocational/Technical School(s)
Galiano Career Academy (Private, For-profit)
 Fall 2006 Enrollment: 279 . . . . (407) 331-3900
 2006-07 Tuition: $8,050

Housing: Homeownership rate: 41.0% (2007); Median home value: $194,716 (2007); Median rent: $646 per month (2000); Median age of housing: 18 years (2000).

Hospitals: Florida Hospital Altamonte (258 beds)

Safety: Violent crime rate: 50.8 per 10,000 population; Property crime rate: 401.9 per 10,000 population (2006).

Transportation: Commute to work: 93.5% car, 1.2% public transportation, 1.7% walk, 2.7% work from home (2000); Travel time to work: 25.5% less than 15 minutes, 39.6% 15 to 30 minutes, 22.5% 30 to 45 minutes, 7.8% 45 to 60 minutes, 4.6% 60 minutes or more (2000)

Additional Information Contacts

City of Altamonte Springs . . . . (407) 585-1423
 http://www.altamonte.org
Seminole County Regional Chamber of Commerce . . . . . (407) 333-4748
 http://www.seminolebusiness.org

CASSELBERRY (city). Covers a land area of 6.662 square miles and a water area of 0.431 square miles. Located at 28.66° N. Lat.; 81.32° W. Long. Elevation is 56 feet.

Population: 21,488 (1990); 22,629 (2000); 23,788 (2007); 24,931 (2012 projected); Race: 81.5% White, 6.8% Black, 2.4% Asian, 20.2% Hispanic of any race (2007); Density: 3,570.5 persons per square mile (2007); Average household size: 2.27 (2007); Median age: 39.6 (2007); Males per 100 females: 94.8 (2007); Marriage status: 26.4% never married, 50.7% now married, 7.4% widowed, 15.5% divorced (2000); Foreign born: 10.0% (2000); Ancestry (includes multiple ancestries): 25.0% Other groups, 15.9% German, 14.4% Irish, 12.3% English, 8.5% Italian (2000).

Economy: Unemployment rate: 3.7% (11/2007); Total civilian labor force: 15,221 (11/2007); Single-family building permits issued: 183 (2006); Multi-family building permits issued: 0 (2006); Employment by occupation: 12.7% management, 15.6% professional, 15.9% services, 35.4% sales, 0.2% farming, 11.1% construction, 9.1% production (2000).

Income: Per capita income: $22,652 (2007); Median household income: $43,166 (2007); Average household income: $51,066 (2007); Percent of households with income of $100,000 or more: 9.1% (2007); Poverty rate: 8.8% (2000).

Education: Percent of population age 25 and over with: High school diploma (including GED) or higher: 84.7% (2007); Bachelor's degree or higher: 19.1% (2007); Master's degree or higher: 6.1% (2007).

School District(s)
Seminole County School District (PK-12)
 2005-06 Enrollment: 66,692 . . . . (407) 320-0006

Two-year College(s)
City College (Private, Not-for-profit)
 Fall 2006 Enrollment: 99 . . . . (407) 831-9816
 2006-07 Tuition: In-state $9,840; Out-of-state $9,840

Vocational/Technical School(s)

Paul Mitchell the School (Private, For-profit)
   Fall 2006 Enrollment: 239 . . . . (801) 302-8801
   2006-07 Tuition: $13,425

Housing: Homeownership rate: 61.0% (2007); Median home value: $158,100 (2007); Median rent: $625 per month (2000); Median age of housing: 22 years (2000).

Safety: Violent crime rate: 52.2 per 10,000 population; Property crime rate: 390.6 per 10,000 population (2006).

Transportation: Commute to work: 94.1% car, 1.1% public transportation, 1.9% walk, 1.9% work from home (2000); Travel time to work: 23.4% less than 15 minutes, 35.3% 15 to 30 minutes, 25.8% 30 to 45 minutes, 8.3% 45 to 60 minutes, 7.1% 60 minutes or more (2000)

Additional Information Contacts

City of Casselberry. . . . . (407) 262-7700
   http://www.casselberry.org

CHULUOTA (CDP). Covers a land area of 1.804 square miles and a water area of 0.392 square miles. Located at 28.64° N. Lat.; 81.12° W. Long. Elevation is 59 feet.

Population: 1,398 (1990); 1,921 (2000); 3,262 (2007); 4,148 (2012 projected); Race: 93.9% White, 0.4% Black, 0.7% Asian, 5.7% Hispanic of any race (2007); Density: 1,807.8 persons per square mile (2007); Average household size: 2.76 (2007); Median age: 37.4 (2007); Males per 100 females: 94.2 (2007); Marriage status: 22.5% never married, 55.8% now married, 4.9% widowed, 16.8% divorced (2000); Foreign born: 2.8% (2000); Ancestry (includes multiple ancestries): 22.5% Other groups, 20.8% German, 14.7% Irish, 11.0% English, 9.9% United States or American (2000).

Economy: Employment by occupation: 10.1% management, 18.9% professional, 18.3% services, 21.8% sales, 0.0% farming, 20.3% construction, 10.6% production (2000).

Income: Per capita income: $19,913 (2007); Median household income: $51,272 (2007); Average household income: $54,863 (2007); Percent of households with income of $100,000 or more: 7.7% (2007); Poverty rate: 5.1% (2000).

Education: Percent of population age 25 and over with: High school diploma (including GED) or higher: 88.3% (2007); Bachelor's degree or higher: 12.9% (2007); Master's degree or higher: 1.5% (2007).

School District(s)

Seminole County School District (PK-12)
   2005-06 Enrollment: 66,692 . . . . (407) 320-0006

Housing: Homeownership rate: 84.7% (2007); Median home value: $183,684 (2007); Median rent: $511 per month (2000); Median age of housing: 20 years (2000).

Transportation: Commute to work: 96.9% car, 0.0% public transportation, 0.0% walk, 2.0% work from home (2000); Travel time to work: 4.4% less than 15 minutes, 33.5% 15 to 30 minutes, 22.0% 30 to 45 minutes, 24.9% 45 to 60 minutes, 15.2% 60 minutes or more (2000)

FERN PARK (CDP). Covers a land area of 2.051 square miles and a water area of 0.290 square miles. Located at 28.64° N. Lat.; 81.34° W. Long. Elevation is 95 feet.

Population: 8,080 (1990); 8,318 (2000); 8,173 (2007); 8,222 (2012 projected); Race: 80.9% White, 9.6% Black, 2.0% Asian, 16.2% Hispanic of any race (2007); Density: 3,984.6 persons per square mile (2007); Average household size: 2.27 (2007); Median age: 41.9 (2007); Males per 100 females: 93.4 (2007); Marriage status: 24.8% never married, 53.7% now married, 8.5% widowed, 13.0% divorced (2000); Foreign born: 10.1% (2000); Ancestry (includes multiple ancestries): 21.4% Other groups, 14.5% German, 14.1% Irish, 11.0% English, 8.6% United States or American (2000).

Economy: Employment by occupation: 11.2% management, 22.6% professional, 11.5% services, 39.0% sales, 0.1% farming, 8.1% construction, 7.5% production (2000).

Income: Per capita income: $28,326 (2007); Median household income: $50,330 (2007); Average household income: $64,159 (2007); Percent of households with income of $100,000 or more: 16.8% (2007); Poverty rate: 7.8% (2000).

Education: Percent of population age 25 and over with: High school diploma (including GED) or higher: 85.1% (2007); Bachelor's degree or higher: 30.1% (2007); Master's degree or higher: 9.1% (2007).

School District(s)

Seminole County School District (PK-12)
   2005-06 Enrollment: 66,692 . . . . (407) 320-0006

Two-year College(s)

Americare School of Nursing (Private, For-profit)
   Fall 2006 Enrollment: 319 . . . . (407) 673-7406

Housing: Homeownership rate: 65.2% (2007); Median home value: $209,775 (2007); Median rent: $485 per month (2000); Median age of housing: 27 years (2000).

Transportation: Commute to work: 88.8% car, 3.3% public transportation, 1.2% walk, 3.7% work from home (2000); Travel time to work: 19.9% less than 15 minutes, 44.0% 15 to 30 minutes, 21.1% 30 to 45 minutes, 8.9% 45 to 60 minutes, 6.0% 60 minutes or more (2000)

FOREST CITY (CDP). Covers a land area of 4.271 square miles and a water area of 0.647 square miles. Located at 28.66° N. Lat.; 81.44° W. Long. Elevation is 95 feet.

Population: 10,471 (1990); 12,612 (2000); 14,051 (2007); 15,249 (2012 projected); Race: 81.3% White, 6.1% Black, 4.6% Asian, 19.5% Hispanic of any race (2007); Density: 3,290.2 persons per square mile (2007); Average household size: 2.62 (2007); Median age: 38.5 (2007); Males per 100 females: 97.6 (2007); Marriage status: 23.1% never married, 61.0% now married, 5.4% widowed, 10.5% divorced (2000); Foreign born: 14.1% (2000); Ancestry (includes multiple ancestries): 23.2% Other groups, 15.2% German, 13.9% Irish, 11.5% English, 7.3% Italian (2000).

Economy: Employment by occupation: 16.9% management, 22.1% professional, 12.6% services, 30.9% sales, 0.6% farming, 9.1% construction, 7.6% production (2000).

Income: Per capita income: $29,572 (2007); Median household income: $57,639 (2007); Average household income: $76,587 (2007); Percent of households with income of $100,000 or more: 22.3% (2007); Poverty rate: 6.0% (2000).

Education: Percent of population age 25 and over with: High school diploma (including GED) or higher: 87.2% (2007); Bachelor's degree or higher: 26.4% (2007); Master's degree or higher: 8.8% (2007).

Housing: Homeownership rate: 69.0% (2007); Median home value: $204,326 (2007); Median rent: $662 per month (2000); Median age of housing: 18 years (2000).

Transportation: Commute to work: 92.7% car, 0.7% public transportation, 1.5% walk, 3.4% work from home (2000); Travel time to work: 20.1% less than 15 minutes, 37.4% 15 to 30 minutes, 26.7% 30 to 45 minutes, 8.5% 45 to 60 minutes, 7.3% 60 minutes or more (2000)

GENEVA (CDP). Covers a land area of 11.390 square miles and a water area of 1.036 square miles. Located at 28.73° N. Lat.; 81.11° W. Long. Elevation is 62 feet.

Population: 2,097 (1990); 2,601 (2000); 2,815 (2007); 3,006 (2012 projected); Race: 94.5% White, 2.2% Black, 1.4% Asian, 2.1% Hispanic of any race (2007); Density: 247.1 persons per square mile (2007); Average household size: 2.78 (2007); Median age: 42.1 (2007); Males per 100 females: 103.0 (2007); Marriage status: 21.0% never married, 66.2% now married, 4.2% widowed, 8.7% divorced (2000); Foreign born: 3.1% (2000); Ancestry (includes multiple ancestries): 22.0% German, 15.9% English, 13.4% Other groups, 12.5% Irish, 8.4% United States or American (2000).

Economy: Employment by occupation: 14.6% management, 20.0% professional, 13.1% services, 23.3% sales, 1.1% farming, 18.5% construction, 9.4% production (2000).

Income: Per capita income: $27,786 (2007); Median household income: $57,162 (2007); Average household income: $77,214 (2007); Percent of households with income of $100,000 or more: 27.1% (2007); Poverty rate: 4.8% (2000).

Education: Percent of population age 25 and over with: High school diploma (including GED) or higher: 87.3% (2007); Bachelor's degree or higher: 21.0% (2007); Master's degree or higher: 8.7% (2007).

School District(s)

Seminole County School District (PK-12)
   2005-06 Enrollment: 66,692 . . . . (407) 320-0006

Housing: Homeownership rate: 89.9% (2007); Median home value: $253,058 (2007); Median rent: $471 per month (2000); Median age of housing: 17 years (2000).

Transportation: Commute to work: 86.7% car, 1.6% public transportation, 2.2% walk, 6.4% work from home (2000); Travel time to work: 8.8% less than 15 minutes, 29.3% 15 to 30 minutes, 29.0% 30 to 45 minutes, 14.4% 45 to 60 minutes, 18.6% 60 minutes or more (2000)

HEATHROW (CDP). Covers a land area of 2.774 square miles and a water area of 0.531 square miles. Located at 28.77° N. Lat.; 81.37° W. Long. Elevation is 49 feet.

Population: 1,013 (1990); 4,068 (2000); 5,486 (2007); 6,482 (2012 projected); Race: 85.8% White, 4.5% Black, 6.4% Asian, 8.7% Hispanic of any race (2007); Density: 1,977.8 persons per square mile (2007); Average household size: 2.24 (2007); Median age: 44.4 (2007); Males per 100 females: 94.8 (2007); Marriage status: 17.4% never married, 68.6% now married, 4.7% widowed, 9.3% divorced (2000); Foreign born: 14.6% (2000); Ancestry (includes multiple ancestries): 19.2% Irish, 16.1% English, 14.0% German, 13.4% Other groups, 9.9% Italian (2000).
Economy: Employment by occupation: 37.2% management, 24.9% professional, 4.8% services, 29.3% sales, 0.0% farming, 1.4% construction, 2.4% production (2000).
Income: Per capita income: $67,361 (2007); Median household income: $104,745 (2007); Average household income: $150,650 (2007); Percent of households with income of $100,000 or more: 51.9% (2007); Poverty rate: 2.1% (2000).
Education: Percent of population age 25 and over with: High school diploma (including GED) or higher: 95.3% (2007); Bachelor's degree or higher: 52.5% (2007); Master's degree or higher: 20.1% (2007).
Housing: Homeownership rate: 73.3% (2007); Median home value: $423,594 (2007); Median rent: $966 per month (2000); Median age of housing: 5 years (2000).
Transportation: Commute to work: 94.2% car, 0.6% public transportation, 0.5% walk, 3.8% work from home (2000); Travel time to work: 28.1% less than 15 minutes, 39.5% 15 to 30 minutes, 21.1% 30 to 45 minutes, 4.4% 45 to 60 minutes, 6.9% 60 minutes or more (2000)

LAKE MARY (city). Covers a land area of 8.610 square miles and a water area of 1.063 square miles. Located at 28.75° N. Lat.; 81.32° W. Long. Elevation is 62 feet.
Population: 6,203 (1990); 11,458 (2000); 15,567 (2007); 18,451 (2012 projected); Race: 85.5% White, 4.8% Black, 5.4% Asian, 8.6% Hispanic of any race (2007); Density: 1,808.1 persons per square mile (2007); Average household size: 2.69 (2007); Median age: 41.0 (2007); Males per 100 females: 97.5 (2007); Marriage status: 17.8% never married, 68.6% now married, 5.3% widowed, 8.2% divorced (2000); Foreign born: 8.3% (2000); Ancestry (includes multiple ancestries): 22.4% German, 15.9% Other groups, 14.4% English, 14.0% Irish, 10.1% Italian (2000).
Economy: Single-family building permits issued: 214 (2006); Multi-family building permits issued: 0 (2006); Employment by occupation: 21.0% management, 23.1% professional, 9.9% services, 33.0% sales, 0.1% farming, 7.5% construction, 5.3% production (2000).
Income: Per capita income: $38,383 (2007); Median household income: $86,269 (2007); Average household income: $102,633 (2007); Percent of households with income of $100,000 or more: 40.5% (2007); Poverty rate: 2.9% (2000).
Education: Percent of population age 25 and over with: High school diploma (including GED) or higher: 92.3% (2007); Bachelor's degree or higher: 38.6% (2007); Master's degree or higher: 13.3% (2007).
School District(s)
Seminole County School District (PK-12)
    2005-06 Enrollment: 66,692 . . . . (407) 320-0006
Four-year College(s)
ITT Technical Institute-Lake Mary (Private, For-profit)
    Fall 2006 Enrollment: 510 . . . . (407) 660-2900
    2006-07 Tuition: In-state $14,880; Out-of-state $14,880
Housing: Homeownership rate: 83.6% (2007); Median home value: $331,006 (2007); Median rent: $683 per month (2000); Median age of housing: 10 years (2000).
Safety: Violent crime rate: 20.8 per 10,000 population; Property crime rate: 199.5 per 10,000 population (2006).
Transportation: Commute to work: 93.0% car, 0.1% public transportation, 1.2% walk, 3.8% work from home (2000); Travel time to work: 30.8% less than 15 minutes, 30.8% 15 to 30 minutes, 20.8% 30 to 45 minutes, 10.7% 45 to 60 minutes, 6.9% 60 minutes or more (2000)
Additional Information Contacts
City of Lake Mary. . . . . (407) 585-1400
    http://www.lakemaryfl.com
Lake Mary-Heathrow Chamber of Commerce . . . . (407) 333-4748
    http://www.seminolebusiness.org

LONGWOOD (city). Covers a land area of 5.320 square miles and a water area of 0.291 square miles. Located at 28.70° N. Lat.; 81.34° W. Long. Elevation is 72 feet.
History: Named for a district in Boston, home to E.W. Henck. Has experienced major growth since 1975.

Population: 13,724 (1990); 13,745 (2000); 13,914 (2007); 14,229 (2012 projected); Race: 83.2% White, 4.4% Black, 3.2% Asian, 14.8% Hispanic of any race (2007); Density: 2,615.5 persons per square mile (2007); Average household size: 2.67 (2007); Median age: 40.3 (2007); Males per 100 females: 94.5 (2007); Marriage status: 24.3% never married, 55.7% now married, 7.2% widowed, 12.7% divorced (2000); Foreign born: 10.5% (2000); Ancestry (includes multiple ancestries): 20.6% Other groups, 18.0% German, 16.0% Irish, 13.2% English, 9.2% Italian (2000).
Economy: Single-family building permits issued: 69 (2006); Multi-family building permits issued: 0 (2006); Employment by occupation: 14.7% management, 19.3% professional, 12.9% services, 30.4% sales, 0.0% farming, 11.4% construction, 11.3% production (2000).
Income: Per capita income: $25,998 (2007); Median household income: $59,271 (2007); Average household income: $68,723 (2007); Percent of households with income of $100,000 or more: 18.4% (2007); Poverty rate: 6.6% (2000).
Education: Percent of population age 25 and over with: High school diploma (including GED) or higher: 86.0% (2007); Bachelor's degree or higher: 21.5% (2007); Master's degree or higher: 6.1% (2007).
School District(s)
Seminole County School District (PK-12)
    2005-06 Enrollment: 66,692 . . . . (407) 320-0006
Vocational/Technical School(s)
Cambridge Institute of Allied Health (Private, For-profit)
    Fall 2006 Enrollment: 120 . . . . (407) 265-8383
    2006-07 Tuition: $599
Housing: Homeownership rate: 74.6% (2007); Median home value: $189,616 (2007); Median rent: $629 per month (2000); Median age of housing: 22 years (2000).
Hospitals: Orlando Regional - South Seminole Hospital (206 beds)
Safety: Violent crime rate: 68.8 per 10,000 population; Property crime rate: 490.3 per 10,000 population (2006).
Newspapers: La Prensa (Hispanic - Circulation 30,000)
Transportation: Commute to work: 93.6% car, 0.2% public transportation, 0.3% walk, 3.6% work from home (2000); Travel time to work: 27.2% less than 15 minutes, 38.3% 15 to 30 minutes, 21.6% 30 to 45 minutes, 7.6% 45 to 60 minutes, 5.3% 60 minutes or more (2000)
Additional Information Contacts
City of Longwood . . . . (407) 260-3440
    http://www.ci.longwood.fl.us
Longwood Chamber of Commerce . . . . (407) 333-4748

MIDWAY (CDP). Covers a land area of 1.391 square miles and a water area of 0 square miles. Located at 28.79° N. Lat.; 81.22° W. Long. Elevation is 23 feet.
Population: 2,024 (1990); 1,714 (2000); 1,604 (2007); 1,563 (2012 projected); Race: 6.5% White, 89.8% Black, 1.1% Asian, 1.6% Hispanic of any race (2007); Density: 1,153.0 persons per square mile (2007); Average household size: 2.86 (2007); Median age: 34.0 (2007); Males per 100 females: 86.3 (2007); Marriage status: 37.8% never married, 32.6% now married, 12.9% widowed, 16.7% divorced (2000); Foreign born: 0.0% (2000); Ancestry (includes multiple ancestries): 75.3% Other groups, 2.5% African, 2.2% United States or American (2000).
Economy: Employment by occupation: 1.7% management, 4.8% professional, 25.3% services, 19.2% sales, 0.0% farming, 13.8% construction, 35.2% production (2000).
Income: Per capita income: $14,928 (2007); Median household income: $35,608 (2007); Average household income: $42,683 (2007); Percent of households with income of $100,000 or more: 3.4% (2007); Poverty rate: 26.0% (2000).
Education: Percent of population age 25 and over with: High school diploma (including GED) or higher: 51.7% (2007); Bachelor's degree or higher: 4.8% (2007); Master's degree or higher: 1.7% (2007).
Housing: Homeownership rate: 70.4% (2007); Median home value: $98,226 (2007); Median rent: $423 per month (2000); Median age of housing: 31 years (2000).
Transportation: Commute to work: 91.6% car, 6.8% public transportation, 0.0% walk, 0.3% work from home (2000); Travel time to work: 16.3% less than 15 minutes, 47.7% 15 to 30 minutes, 21.8% 30 to 45 minutes, 5.8% 45 to 60 minutes, 8.4% 60 minutes or more (2000)

OVIEDO (city). Covers a land area of 15.134 square miles and a water area of 0.320 square miles. Located at 28.66° N. Lat.; 81.19° W. Long. Elevation is 49 feet.

History: Named for the capital city of the Spanish province of Asturias. Incorporated 1925.
Population: 11,588 (1990); 26,316 (2000); 32,172 (2007); 36,509 (2012 projected); Race: 81.9% White, 8.3% Black, 3.2% Asian, 16.5% Hispanic of any race (2007); Density: 2,125.8 persons per square mile (2007); Average household size: 3.11 (2007); Median age: 34.5 (2007); Males per 100 females: 98.5 (2007); Marriage status: 22.9% never married, 67.1% now married, 3.1% widowed, 6.9% divorced (2000); Foreign born: 9.2% (2000); Ancestry (includes multiple ancestries): 24.0% Other groups, 18.1% German, 13.4% Irish, 11.7% English, 11.6% Italian (2000).
Economy: Unemployment rate: 2.8% (11/2007); Total civilian labor force: 18,615 (11/2007); Single-family building permits issued: 169 (2006); Multi-family building permits issued: 0 (2006); Employment by occupation: 17.9% management, 25.9% professional, 12.7% services, 30.1% sales, 0.1% farming, 6.7% construction, 6.5% production (2000).
Income: Per capita income: $29,399 (2007); Median household income: $77,575 (2007); Average household income: $91,356 (2007); Percent of households with income of $100,000 or more: 32.6% (2007); Poverty rate: 4.6% (2000).
Education: Percent of population age 25 and over with: High school diploma (including GED) or higher: 93.4% (2007); Bachelor's degree or higher: 40.8% (2007); Master's degree or higher: 13.2% (2007).

School District(s)
Seminole County School District (PK-12)
    2005-06 Enrollment: 66,692 . . . . (407) 320-0006
Housing: Homeownership rate: 86.5% (2007); Median home value: $254,608 (2007); Median rent: $776 per month (2000); Median age of housing: 8 years (2000).
Safety: Violent crime rate: 23.1 per 10,000 population; Property crime rate: 150.6 per 10,000 population (2006).
Newspapers: The Oviedo Voice (General - Circulation 4,500)
Transportation: Commute to work: 93.4% car, 0.1% public transportation, 0.4% walk, 4.1% work from home (2000); Travel time to work: 18.3% less than 15 minutes, 30.8% 15 to 30 minutes, 29.1% 30 to 45 minutes, 15.1% 45 to 60 minutes, 6.7% 60 minutes or more (2000)
Additional Information Contacts
City of Oviedo . . . . (407) 971-5555
    http://www.ci.oviedo.fl.us

SANFORD (city). County seat. Covers a land area of 19.107 square miles and a water area of 3.494 square miles. Located at 28.79° N. Lat.; 81.27° W. Long. Elevation is 30 feet.
History: Named for General Henry Shelton Sanford, President Lincoln's minister to Belgium. Sanford had its beginning as Mellonville, a trading post established in 1837 near Fort Mellon. The land on which the town was founded was purchased in 1871 by General Sanford, who planted citrus groves.
Population: 33,887 (1990); 38,291 (2000); 48,913 (2007); 56,391 (2012 projected); Race: 54.8% White, 34.2% Black, 1.4% Asian, 14.2% Hispanic of any race (2007); Density: 2,560.0 persons per square mile (2007); Average household size: 2.62 (2007); Median age: 34.3 (2007); Males per 100 females: 100.1 (2007); Marriage status: 30.6% never married, 47.6% now married, 6.5% widowed, 15.3% divorced (2000); Foreign born: 5.9% (2000); Ancestry (includes multiple ancestries): 38.8% Other groups, 10.7% German, 9.2% Irish, 9.1% English, 6.2% United States or American (2000).
Economy: Unemployment rate: 4.7% (11/2007); Total civilian labor force: 24,855 (11/2007); Single-family building permits issued: 825 (2006); Multi-family building permits issued: 6 (2006); Employment by occupation: 9.3% management, 15.8% professional, 18.3% services, 29.3% sales, 0.3% farming, 12.1% construction, 15.0% production (2000).
Income: Per capita income: $18,482 (2007); Median household income: $37,666 (2007); Average household income: $47,228 (2007); Percent of households with income of $100,000 or more: 7.9% (2007); Poverty rate: 17.8% (2000).
Taxes: Total city taxes per capita: $590 (2005); City property taxes per capita: $215 (2005).
Education: Percent of population age 25 and over with: High school diploma (including GED) or higher: 77.6% (2007); Bachelor's degree or higher: 14.6% (2007); Master's degree or higher: 4.2% (2007).

School District(s)
Seminole County School District (PK-12)
    2005-06 Enrollment: 66,692 . . . . (407) 320-0006

Two-year College(s)
Seminole Community College (Public)
    Fall 2006 Enrollment: 11,655. . . . . (407) 708-4722
    2006-07 Tuition: In-state $2,180; Out-of-state $7,668
Vocational/Technical School(s)
Delta Connection Academy (Private, For-profit)
    Fall 2006 Enrollment: n/a. . . . . (407) 330-7020
Housing: Homeownership rate: 55.1% (2007); Median home value: $142,785 (2007); Median rent: $508 per month (2000); Median age of housing: 23 years (2000).
Hospitals: Central Florida Regional Hospital (226 beds)
Safety: Violent crime rate: 48.7 per 10,000 population; Property crime rate: 722.9 per 10,000 population (2006).
Newspapers: The Seminole Herald (General - Circulation 4,500)
Transportation: Commute to work: 93.2% car, 1.2% public transportation, 1.6% walk, 2.2% work from home (2000); Travel time to work: 28.7% less than 15 minutes, 35.1% 15 to 30 minutes, 19.8% 30 to 45 minutes, 8.4% 45 to 60 minutes, 8.0% 60 minutes or more (2000); Amtrak: Service available.
Additional Information Contacts
City of Sanford . . . . (407) 330-5600
    http://www.ci.sanford.fl.us
Sanford Chamber of Commerce . . . . (407) 322-2212
    http://www.sanfordchamber.com

WEKIWA SPRINGS (CDP). Aka Wekiva Springs. Covers a land area of 8.641 square miles and a water area of 0.520 square miles. Located at 28.69° N. Lat.; 81.42° W. Long. Elevation is 52 feet.
Population: 23,024 (1990); 23,169 (2000); 23,894 (2007); 24,821 (2012 projected); Race: 93.2% White, 1.7% Black, 2.8% Asian, 6.3% Hispanic of any race (2007); Density: 2,765.1 persons per square mile (2007); Average household size: 2.58 (2007); Median age: 44.8 (2007); Males per 100 females: 95.0 (2007); Marriage status: 20.6% never married, 66.8% now married, 4.7% widowed, 8.0% divorced (2000); Foreign born: 7.8% (2000); Ancestry (includes multiple ancestries): 19.4% German, 15.7% English, 14.9% Irish, 12.9% Other groups, 8.9% Italian (2000).
Economy: Employment by occupation: 24.3% management, 26.3% professional, 7.9% services, 33.1% sales, 0.0% farming, 4.3% construction, 4.1% production (2000).
Income: Per capita income: $40,904 (2007); Median household income: $77,146 (2007); Average household income: $105,218 (2007); Percent of households with income of $100,000 or more: 36.0% (2007); Poverty rate: 2.6% (2000).
Education: Percent of population age 25 and over with: High school diploma (including GED) or higher: 96.0% (2007); Bachelor's degree or higher: 49.3% (2007); Master's degree or higher: 17.3% (2007).
Housing: Homeownership rate: 79.8% (2007); Median home value: $294,407 (2007); Median rent: $908 per month (2000); Median age of housing: 18 years (2000).
Transportation: Commute to work: 91.2% car, 0.1% public transportation, 0.2% walk, 8.0% work from home (2000); Travel time to work: 18.3% less than 15 minutes, 37.5% 15 to 30 minutes, 28.4% 30 to 45 minutes, 10.1% 45 to 60 minutes, 5.6% 60 minutes or more (2000)

WINTER SPRINGS (city). Aka North Orlando. Covers a land area of 14.346 square miles and a water area of 0.138 square miles. Located at 28.69° N. Lat.; 81.27° W. Long. Elevation is 52 feet.
Population: 22,280 (1990); 31,666 (2000); 34,337 (2007); 36,791 (2012 projected); Race: 86.1% White, 5.5% Black, 2.4% Asian, 13.8% Hispanic of any race (2007); Density: 2,393.5 persons per square mile (2007); Average household size: 2.66 (2007); Median age: 39.9 (2007); Males per 100 females: 94.9 (2007); Marriage status: 20.9% never married, 64.1% now married, 5.2% widowed, 9.8% divorced (2000); Foreign born: 8.1% (2000); Ancestry (includes multiple ancestries): 19.0% Other groups, 18.2% German, 15.6% Irish, 12.8% English, 10.8% Italian (2000).
Economy: Unemployment rate: 3.6% (11/2007); Total civilian labor force: 19,591 (11/2007); Single-family building permits issued: 274 (2006); Multi-family building permits issued: 0 (2006); Employment by occupation: 18.8% management, 24.5% professional, 11.7% services, 30.4% sales, 0.1% farming, 7.6% construction, 6.9% production (2000).
Income: Per capita income: $31,763 (2007); Median household income: $63,675 (2007); Average household income: $84,502 (2007); Percent of households with income of $100,000 or more: 29.2% (2007); Poverty rate: 4.2% (2000).

Education: Percent of population age 25 and over with: High school diploma (including GED) or higher: 92.4% (2007); Bachelor's degree or higher: 37.1% (2007); Master's degree or higher: 13.1% (2007).

School District(s)

Seminole County School District (PK-12)

    2005-06 Enrollment: 66,692 . . . . (407) 320-0006

Housing: Homeownership rate: 81.2% (2007); Median home value: $238,234 (2007); Median rent: $631 per month (2000); Median age of housing: 15 years (2000).

Safety: Violent crime rate: 29.0 per 10,000 population; Property crime rate: 190.7 per 10,000 population (2006).

Transportation: Commute to work: 93.8% car, 0.3% public transportation, 0.3% walk, 4.5% work from home (2000); Travel time to work: 17.1% less than 15 minutes, 37.8% 15 to 30 minutes, 28.2% 30 to 45 minutes, 10.5% 45 to 60 minutes, 6.4% 60 minutes or more (2000)

Additional Information Contacts

City of Winter Springs . . . . (407) 327-1800
    http://www.winterspringsfl.org

Saint Johns County

Located in northeastern Florida; bounded on the west by the St. Johns River, and on the east by the Atlantic Ocean; lowland area, includes Anastasia Island and the Matanzas River. Covers a land area of 609.01 square miles, a water area of 212.42 square miles, and is located in the Eastern Time Zone. The county was founded in 1822. County seat is Saint Augustine.

Saint Johns County is part of the Jacksonville, FL Metropolitan Statistical Area. The entire metro area includes: Baker County, FL; Clay County, FL; Duval County, FL; Nassau County, FL; St. Johns County, FL

Weather Station: Saint Augustine   Elevation: 6 feet

	Jan	Feb	Mar	Apr	May	Jun	Jul	Aug	Sep	Oct	Nov	Dec
High	67	69	74	79	84	88	91	89	86	81	75	68
Low	46	48	53	58	65	71	72	72	71	64	56	49
Precip	3.2	3.0	3.7	2.7	3.2	5.2	4.6	5.9	6.6	4.6	2.3	2.9
Snow	tr	0.0	tr	0.0	0.0	0.0	0.0	0.0	0.0	0.0	0.0	0.0

High and Low temperatures in degrees Fahrenheit; Precipitation and Snow in inches

Population: 83,829 (1990); 123,135 (2000); 170,190 (2007); 202,038 (2012 projected); Race: 90.3% White, 5.8% Black, 1.6% Asian, 3.9% Hispanic of any race (2007); Density: 279.5 persons per square mile (2007); Average household size: 2.47 (2007); Median age: 41.4 (2007); Males per 100 females: 96.3 (2007).

Religion: Five largest groups: 16.3% Catholic Church, 8.7% Southern Baptist Convention, 4.5% Episcopal Church, 1.8% The United Methodist Church, 1.3% Presbyterian Church in America (2000).

Economy: Unemployment rate: 3.6% (11/2007); Total civilian labor force: 88,434 (11/2007); Leading industries: 19.0% retail trade; 18.6% accommodation & food services; 12.8% health care and social assistance (2005); Farms: 204 totaling 37,653 acres (2002); Companies that employ 500 or more persons: 8 (2005); Companies that employ 100 to 499 persons: 55 (2005); Companies that employ less than 100 persons: 4,544 (2005); Black-owned businesses: n/a (2002); Hispanic-owned businesses: n/a (2002); Asian-owned businesses: 286 (2002); Women-owned businesses: 3,628 (2002); Retail sales per capita: $13,155 (2007). Single-family building permits issued: 2,502 (2006); Multi-family building permits issued: 508 (2006).

Income: Per capita income: $34,054 (2007); Median household income: $58,986 (2007); Average household income: $83,605 (2007); Percent of households with income of $100,000 or more: 25.3% (2007); Poverty rate: 7.5% (2005); Bankruptcy rate: 1.03% (2006).

Taxes: Total county taxes per capita: $708 (2005); County property taxes per capita: $528 (2005).

Education: Percent of population age 25 and over with: High school diploma (including GED) or higher: 87.1% (2007); Bachelor's degree or higher: 32.2% (2007); Master's degree or higher: 10.8% (2007).

Housing: Homeownership rate: 78.0% (2007); Median home value: $283,339 (2007); Median rent: $632 per month (2000); Median age of housing: 15 years (2000).

Health: Birth rate: 95.6 per 10,000 population (2006); Death rate: 75.7 per 10,000 population (2006); Age-adjusted cancer mortality rate: 204.5 deaths per 100,000 population (2004); Number of physicians: 30.1 per 10,000 population (2005); Hospital beds: 19.7 per 10,000 population (2004); Hospital admissions: 960.1 per 10,000 population (2004).

Elections: 2004 Presidential election results: 68.6% Bush, 30.6% Kerry, 0.5% Nader, 0.3% Badnarik

National and State Parks: Anastasia State Park; Butler Beach State Park; Castillo de San Marcos National Monument; Faver-Dykes State Park; Fort Matanzas National Monument; Guana River State Park

Additional Information Contacts

Saint Johns County Government . . . . (904) 209-0300
    http://www.sjcfl.us
St. Augustine Chamber of Commerce . . . . (904) 829-5681
    http://www.staugustinechamber.com

Saint Johns County Communities

BUTLER BEACH (CDP). Covers a land area of 2.488 square miles and a water area of 0 square miles. Located at 29.80° N. Lat.; 81.26° W. Long. Elevation is 3 feet.

Population: 3,349 (1990); 4,436 (2000); 5,626 (2007); 6,463 (2012 projected); Race: 97.1% White, 0.3% Black, 1.2% Asian, 1.8% Hispanic of any race (2007); Density: 2,261.3 persons per square mile (2007); Average household size: 2.00 (2007); Median age: 55.9 (2007); Males per 100 females: 95.9 (2007); Marriage status: 12.2% never married, 69.0% now married, 9.5% widowed, 9.3% divorced (2000); Foreign born: 6.6% (2000); Ancestry (includes multiple ancestries): 19.5% German, 17.9% Irish, 16.8% English, 10.4% Italian, 8.9% United States or American (2000).

Economy: Employment by occupation: 16.1% management, 26.2% professional, 14.7% services, 27.9% sales, 0.0% farming, 9.5% construction, 5.6% production (2000).

Income: Per capita income: $38,582 (2007); Median household income: $52,745 (2007); Average household income: $77,000 (2007); Percent of households with income of $100,000 or more: 18.1% (2007); Poverty rate: 6.3% (2000).

Education: Percent of population age 25 and over with: High school diploma (including GED) or higher: 95.0% (2007); Bachelor's degree or higher: 38.6% (2007); Master's degree or higher: 13.4% (2007).

Housing: Homeownership rate: 82.3% (2007); Median home value: $337,446 (2007); Median rent: $720 per month (2000); Median age of housing: 14 years (2000).

Transportation: Commute to work: 91.4% car, 0.5% public transportation, 2.3% walk, 5.4% work from home (2000); Travel time to work: 20.1% less than 15 minutes, 40.8% 15 to 30 minutes, 14.6% 30 to 45 minutes, 13.0% 45 to 60 minutes, 11.5% 60 minutes or more (2000)

CRESCENT BEACH (CDP). Covers a land area of 1.524 square miles and a water area of 0 square miles. Located at 29.76° N. Lat.; 81.25° W. Long. Elevation is 7 feet.

Population: 1,081 (1990); 985 (2000); 1,232 (2007); 1,410 (2012 projected); Race: 96.8% White, 0.1% Black, 0.6% Asian, 0.8% Hispanic of any race (2007); Density: 808.3 persons per square mile (2007); Average household size: 1.80 (2007); Median age: 58.9 (2007); Males per 100 females: 106.7 (2007); Marriage status: 20.2% never married, 47.9% now married, 6.8% widowed, 25.2% divorced (2000); Foreign born: 1.4% (2000); Ancestry (includes multiple ancestries): 19.4% German, 19.3% English, 17.0% Irish, 9.8% United States or American, 7.7% Scottish (2000).

Economy: Employment by occupation: 27.1% management, 15.1% professional, 5.5% services, 24.9% sales, 3.4% farming, 15.8% construction, 8.2% production (2000).

Income: Per capita income: $41,607 (2007); Median household income: $52,013 (2007); Average household income: $100,000 or more: 8.2% (2007); Poverty rate: 8.9% (2000).

Education: Percent of population age 25 and over with: High school diploma (including GED) or higher: 83.0% (2007); Bachelor's degree or higher: 29.8% (2007); Master's degree or higher: 11.2% (2007).

Housing: Homeownership rate: 74.8% (2007); Median home value: $240,079 (2007); Median rent: $669 per month (2000); Median age of housing: 19 years (2000).

Transportation: Commute to work: 81.1% car, 0.0% public transportation, 7.9% walk, 7.7% work from home (2000); Travel time to work: 27.4% less than 15 minutes, 40.3% 15 to 30 minutes, 22.8% 30 to 45 minutes, 0.0% 45 to 60 minutes, 9.4% 60 minutes or more (2000)

ELKTON (unincorporated postal area, zip code 32033). Covers a land area of 78.595 square miles and a water area of 0.091 square miles. Located at 29.78° N. Lat.; 81.44° W. Long. Elevation is 36 feet.

Population: 2,171 (2000); Race: 87.0% White, 10.2% Black, 1.3% Asian, 3.6% Hispanic of any race (2000); Density: 27.6 persons per square mile (2000); Age: 20.7% under 18, 19.7% over 64 (2000); Marriage status: 15.0% never married, 67.1% now married, 10.7% widowed, 7.2% divorced (2000); Foreign born: 2.8% (2000); Ancestry (includes multiple ancestries): 21.3% Other groups, 18.0% Irish, 16.3% German, 11.6% English, 7.6% Italian (2000).
Economy: Employment by occupation: 13.2% management, 16.9% professional, 17.4% services, 31.3% sales, 0.6% farming, 13.3% construction, 7.4% production (2000).
Income: Per capita income: $20,047 (2000); Median household income: $40,156 (2000); Poverty rate: 12.2% (2000).
Education: Percent of population age 25 and over with: High school diploma (including GED) or higher: 80.4% (2000); Bachelor's degree or higher: 20.8% (2000).
Housing: Homeownership rate: 91.6% (2000); Median home value: $104,800 (2000); Median rent: $552 per month (2000); Median age of housing: 8 years (2000).
Transportation: Commute to work: 99.2% car, 0.0% public transportation, 0.8% walk, 0.0% work from home (2000); Travel time to work: 16.0% less than 15 minutes, 51.7% 15 to 30 minutes, 18.2% 30 to 45 minutes, 8.4% 45 to 60 minutes, 5.8% 60 minutes or more (2000)

FRUIT COVE (CDP).
Covers a land area of 17.860 square miles and a water area of 0.005 square miles. Located at 30.10° N. Lat.; 81.61° W. Long. Elevation is 10 feet.
Population: 5,904 (1990); 16,077 (2000); 27,773 (2007); 35,371 (2012 projected); Race: 92.3% White, 3.0% Black, 2.7% Asian, 3.9% Hispanic of any race (2007); Density: 1,555.0 persons per square mile (2007); Average household size: 3.08 (2007); Median age: 37.5 (2007); Males per 100 females: 101.5 (2007); Marriage status: 16.7% never married, 73.3% now married, 3.9% widowed, 6.1% divorced (2000); Foreign born: 4.0% (2000); Ancestry (includes multiple ancestries): 18.9% German, 16.6% Irish, 14.7% English, 10.9% Other groups, 10.4% United States or American (2000).
Economy: Employment by occupation: 25.5% management, 23.8% professional, 9.6% services, 30.7% sales, 0.2% farming, 4.7% construction, 5.4% production (2000).
Income: Per capita income: $37,635 (2007); Median household income: $100,479 (2007); Average household income: $115,679 (2007); Percent of households with income of $100,000 or more: 50.4% (2007); Poverty rate: 1.9% (2000).
Education: Percent of population age 25 and over with: High school diploma (including GED) or higher: 96.0% (2007); Bachelor's degree or higher: 42.6% (2007); Master's degree or higher: 11.9% (2007).
School District(s)
St. Johns County School District (PK-12)
    2005-06 Enrollment: 24,403 . . . . (904) 819-7502
Housing: Homeownership rate: 93.3% (2007); Median home value: $353,274 (2007); Median rent: $990 per month (2000); Median age of housing: 5 years (2000).
Transportation: Commute to work: 96.6% car, 0.3% public transportation, 0.0% walk, 2.5% work from home (2000); Travel time to work: 9.7% less than 15 minutes, 28.3% 15 to 30 minutes, 43.5% 30 to 45 minutes, 14.0% 45 to 60 minutes, 4.6% 60 minutes or more (2000)

HASTINGS (town).
Covers a land area of 0.659 square miles and a water area of 0 square miles. Located at 29.71° N. Lat.; 81.50° W. Long. Elevation is 7 feet.
History: Hastings developed as a potato market town. In 1918 Hastings harvested a particularly large potato crop while the rest of the country had small crops, and the town was crowded with buyers paying cash for the potatoes. The town officials had to call out the Home Guards to protect the bank building because of the unusually large number of deposits.
Population: 595 (1990); 521 (2000); 577 (2007); 610 (2012 projected); Race: 51.3% White, 40.4% Black, 0.0% Asian, 10.4% Hispanic of any race (2007); Density: 875.5 persons per square mile (2007); Average household size: 2.38 (2007); Median age: 37.5 (2007); Males per 100 females: 87.3 (2007); Marriage status: 24.5% never married, 51.2% now married, 10.0% widowed, 14.3% divorced (2000); Foreign born: 4.7% (2000); Ancestry (includes multiple ancestries): 46.6% Other groups, 11.4% English, 7.5% United States or American, 7.5% German, 5.6% Irish (2000).
Economy: Employment by occupation: 7.3% management, 13.6% professional, 32.0% services, 22.3% sales, 5.3% farming, 12.1% construction, 7.3% production (2000).

Income: Per capita income: $17,153 (2007); Median household income: $31,500 (2007); Average household income: $40,806 (2007); Percent of households with income of $100,000 or more: 8.3% (2007); Poverty rate: 21.0% (2000).
Education: Percent of population age 25 and over with: High school diploma (including GED) or higher: 75.5% (2007); Bachelor's degree or higher: 13.8% (2007); Master's degree or higher: 4.7% (2007).
School District(s)
St. Johns County School District (PK-12)
    2005-06 Enrollment: 24,403 . . . . (904) 819-7502
Housing: Homeownership rate: 76.0% (2007); Median home value: $106,429 (2007); Median rent: $379 per month (2000); Median age of housing: 33 years (2000).
Transportation: Commute to work: 92.1% car, 0.0% public transportation, 5.0% walk, 3.0% work from home (2000); Travel time to work: 18.4% less than 15 minutes, 30.1% 15 to 30 minutes, 35.2% 30 to 45 minutes, 6.1% 45 to 60 minutes, 10.2% 60 minutes or more (2000)

PALM VALLEY (CDP).
Covers a land area of 13.412 square miles and a water area of 0.586 square miles. Located at 30.20° N. Lat.; 81.38° W. Long. Elevation is 7 feet.
Population: 9,960 (1990); 19,860 (2000); 23,249 (2007); 25,753 (2012 projected); Race: 94.5% White, 1.5% Black, 2.1% Asian, 4.2% Hispanic of any race (2007); Density: 1,733.5 persons per square mile (2007); Average household size: 2.44 (2007); Median age: 41.1 (2007); Males per 100 females: 95.2 (2007); Marriage status: 19.5% never married, 64.7% now married, 4.2% widowed, 11.5% divorced (2000); Foreign born: 6.8% (2000); Ancestry (includes multiple ancestries): 18.1% English, 17.9% German, 17.0% Irish, 11.5% Other groups, 8.7% Italian (2000).
Economy: Employment by occupation: 26.7% management, 21.8% professional, 13.6% services, 28.8% sales, 0.0% farming, 4.8% construction, 4.3% production (2000).
Income: Per capita income: $50,744 (2007); Median household income: $82,388 (2007); Average household income: $123,001 (2007); Percent of households with income of $100,000 or more: 40.3% (2007); Poverty rate: 3.5% (2000).
Education: Percent of population age 25 and over with: High school diploma (including GED) or higher: 96.2% (2007); Bachelor's degree or higher: 53.6% (2007); Master's degree or higher: 17.7% (2007).
Housing: Homeownership rate: 68.6% (2007); Median home value: $516,721 (2007); Median rent: $784 per month (2000); Median age of housing: 10 years (2000).
Transportation: Commute to work: 92.1% car, 0.3% public transportation, 0.9% walk, 5.0% work from home (2000); Travel time to work: 30.5% less than 15 minutes, 27.8% 15 to 30 minutes, 28.8% 30 to 45 minutes, 8.7% 45 to 60 minutes, 4.2% 60 minutes or more (2000)

SAINT AUGUSTINE (city).
County seat. Covers a land area of 8.372 square miles and a water area of 2.356 square miles. Located at 29.89° N. Lat.; 81.31° W. Long. Elevation is 5 feet.
History: Named for the saint's day, August 28, 1565, when land was first sighted by the Spaniards. St. Augustine is recognized as the oldest permanent European settlement in the United States. The site was chosen by the Spanish in 1565 because it could be easily defended, and the Spanish flavor has influenced successive groups of non-Spanish settlers. Don Pedro Menendez de Aviles, Spanish admiral, is credited with founding and naming St. Augustine. The town sustained a series of attacks by the British until 1763, when the Spanish fled and Florida came under British rule. During the Revolution, the city was a center of British operations against the southern colonies. After another period of Spanish rule, St. Augustine became an American town with the transfer of Florida to the United States.
Population: 11,874 (1990); 11,592 (2000); 12,198 (2007); 12,818 (2012 projected); Race: 81.5% White, 13.7% Black, 1.0% Asian, 4.2% Hispanic of any race (2007); Density: 1,457.0 persons per square mile (2007); Average household size: 2.25 (2007); Median age: 41.2 (2007); Males per 100 females: 85.0 (2007); Marriage status: 32.0% never married, 42.3% now married, 11.5% widowed, 14.2% divorced (2000); Foreign born: 5.8% (2000); Ancestry (includes multiple ancestries): 20.6% Other groups, 14.6% German, 13.8% Irish, 13.6% English, 6.6% United States or American (2000).
Economy: Single-family building permits issued: 34 (2006); Multi-family building permits issued: 44 (2006); Employment by occupation: 13.7% management, 18.3% professional, 21.0% services, 28.7% sales, 0.7% farming, 7.7% construction, 9.9% production (2000).

Income: Per capita income: $25,869 (2007); Median household income: $36,827 (2007); Average household income: $56,690 (2007); Percent of households with income of $100,000 or more: 13.9% (2007); Poverty rate: 15.8% (2000).
Education: Percent of population age 25 and over with: High school diploma (including GED) or higher: 82.0% (2007); Bachelor's degree or higher: 28.5% (2007); Master's degree or higher: 10.9% (2007).

School District(s)
Florida School for the Deaf and the Blind (PK-12)
    2005-06 Enrollment: 745 . . . . (904) 827-2210
St. Johns County School District (PK-12)
    2005-06 Enrollment: 24,403 . . . . (904) 819-7502

Four-year College(s)
Flagler College (Private, Not-for-profit)
    Fall 2006 Enrollment: 2,246 . . . . (904) 829-6481
    2006-07 Tuition: In-state $9,450; Out-of-state $9,450

Two-year College(s)
First Coast Technical Institute (Public)
    Fall 2006 Enrollment: 763 . . . . (904) 824-4401
Housing: Homeownership rate: 60.6% (2007); Median home value: $235,109 (2007); Median rent: $545 per month (2000); Median age of housing: 48 years (2000).
Hospitals: Flagler Hospital (321 beds)
Safety: Violent crime rate: 96.2 per 10,000 population; Property crime rate: 661.6 per 10,000 population (2006).
Newspapers: St. Augustine Record (Circulation 15,804)
Transportation: Commute to work: 78.2% car, 1.3% public transportation, 12.0% walk, 4.0% work from home (2000); Travel time to work: 57.7% less than 15 minutes, 22.8% 15 to 30 minutes, 8.6% 30 to 45 minutes, 6.1% 45 to 60 minutes, 4.8% 60 minutes or more (2000)
Airports: St Augustine
Additional Information Contacts
St. Augustine Chamber of Commerce . . . . (904) 829-5681
    http://www.staugustinechamber.com

SAINT AUGUSTINE BEACH (city).
Covers a land area of 1.941 square miles and a water area of 0 square miles. Located at 29.84° N. Lat.; 81.27° W. Long. Elevation is 7 feet.
History: There has been a lighthouse at St. Augustine Beach since the 1500's. In 1586 Sir Francis Drake sighted the Spanish signal-tower at this spot.
Population: 3,696 (1990); 4,683 (2000); 5,593 (2007); 6,230 (2012 projected); Race: 95.7% White, 0.3% Black, 1.9% Asian, 3.4% Hispanic of any race (2007); Density: 2,882.0 persons per square mile (2007); Average household size: 2.04 (2007); Median age: 43.6 (2007); Males per 100 females: 96.2 (2007); Marriage status: 25.9% never married, 53.1% now married, 5.1% widowed, 15.9% divorced (2000); Foreign born: 7.7% (2000); Ancestry (includes multiple ancestries): 19.7% German, 17.6% Irish, 17.1% English, 10.3% Other groups, 7.7% Italian (2000).
Economy: Single-family building permits issued: 76 (2006); Multi-family building permits issued: 0 (2006); Employment by occupation: 14.5% management, 21.5% professional, 18.4% services, 31.1% sales, 0.0% farming, 7.8% construction, 6.6% production (2000).
Income: Per capita income: $34,889 (2007); Median household income: $48,750 (2007); Average household income: $71,061 (2007); Percent of households with income of $100,000 or more: 16.2% (2007); Poverty rate: 8.7% (2000).
Education: Percent of population age 25 and over with: High school diploma (including GED) or higher: 94.7% (2007); Bachelor's degree or higher: 42.9% (2007); Master's degree or higher: 18.4% (2007).
Housing: Homeownership rate: 61.2% (2007); Median home value: $300,309 (2007); Median rent: $647 per month (2000); Median age of housing: 16 years (2000).
Safety: Violent crime rate: 34.2 per 10,000 population; Property crime rate: 271.8 per 10,000 population (2006).
Transportation: Commute to work: 89.5% car, 0.2% public transportation, 2.1% walk, 4.4% work from home (2000); Travel time to work: 35.4% less than 15 minutes, 36.9% 15 to 30 minutes, 11.5% 30 to 45 minutes, 7.4% 45 to 60 minutes, 8.9% 60 minutes or more (2000)

SAINT AUGUSTINE SHORES (CDP).
Covers a land area of 3.438 square miles and a water area of 0.030 square miles. Located at 29.81° N. Lat.; 81.31° W. Long. Elevation is 26 feet.
Population: 4,411 (1990); 4,922 (2000); 6,071 (2007); 6,880 (2012 projected); Race: 94.4% White, 2.1% Black, 1.6% Asian, 4.5% Hispanic of

any race (2007); Density: 1,765.8 persons per square mile (2007); Average household size: 2.10 (2007); Median age: 51.2 (2007); Males per 100 females: 85.6 (2007); Marriage status: 12.6% never married, 66.3% now married, 11.7% widowed, 9.4% divorced (2000); Foreign born: 7.6% (2000); Ancestry (includes multiple ancestries): 18.3% Irish, 16.1% German, 14.2% English, 9.9% United States or American, 9.1% Other groups (2000).
Economy: Employment by occupation: 13.1% management, 19.1% professional, 20.5% services, 32.7% sales, 0.0% farming, 7.5% construction, 7.0% production (2000).
Income: Per capita income: $25,401 (2007); Median household income: $46,081 (2007); Average household income: $53,235 (2007); Percent of households with income of $100,000 or more: 8.6% (2007); Poverty rate: 6.9% (2000).
Education: Percent of population age 25 and over with: High school diploma (including GED) or higher: 89.1% (2007); Bachelor's degree or higher: 23.2% (2007); Master's degree or higher: 9.8% (2007).
Housing: Homeownership rate: 82.9% (2007); Median home value: $193,107 (2007); Median rent: $712 per month (2000); Median age of housing: 19 years (2000).
Transportation: Commute to work: 93.6% car, 0.6% public transportation, 2.4% walk, 2.8% work from home (2000); Travel time to work: 33.0% less than 15 minutes, 47.5% 15 to 30 minutes, 9.6% 30 to 45 minutes, 7.8% 45 to 60 minutes, 2.1% 60 minutes or more (2000)

SAINT AUGUSTINE SOUTH (CDP).
Covers a land area of 1.720 square miles and a water area of 0 square miles. Located at 29.84° N. Lat.; 81.31° W. Long.
Population: 4,218 (1990); 5,035 (2000); 5,624 (2007); 6,086 (2012 projected); Race: 96.0% White, 1.2% Black, 1.4% Asian, 4.1% Hispanic of any race (2007); Density: 3,269.7 persons per square mile (2007); Average household size: 2.54 (2007); Median age: 42.1 (2007); Males per 100 females: 92.6 (2007); Marriage status: 20.4% never married, 66.9% now married, 5.4% widowed, 7.2% divorced (2000); Foreign born: 6.0% (2000); Ancestry (includes multiple ancestries): 21.5% English, 16.1% Irish, 14.7% United States or American, 12.7% German, 11.4% Other groups (2000).
Economy: Employment by occupation: 12.6% management, 21.6% professional, 17.2% services, 29.1% sales, 0.5% farming, 8.4% construction, 10.6% production (2000).
Income: Per capita income: $26,184 (2007); Median household income: $56,645 (2007); Average household income: $65,542 (2007); Percent of households with income of $100,000 or more: 13.7% (2007); Poverty rate: 4.1% (2000).
Education: Percent of population age 25 and over with: High school diploma (including GED) or higher: 89.3% (2007); Bachelor's degree or higher: 21.9% (2007); Master's degree or higher: 6.1% (2007).
Housing: Homeownership rate: 89.7% (2007); Median home value: $216,536 (2007); Median rent: $832 per month (2000); Median age of housing: 17 years (2000).
Transportation: Commute to work: 96.9% car, 0.0% public transportation, 0.0% walk, 2.2% work from home (2000); Travel time to work: 35.6% less than 15 minutes, 33.8% 15 to 30 minutes, 7.6% 30 to 45 minutes, 9.8% 45 to 60 minutes, 13.2% 60 minutes or more (2000)

SAWGRASS (CDP).
Covers a land area of 3.088 square miles and a water area of 0.143 square miles. Located at 30.19° N. Lat.; 81.37° W. Long. Elevation is 3 feet.
Population: 2,999 (1990); 4,942 (2000); 5,410 (2007); 5,812 (2012 projected); Race: 96.2% White, 0.7% Black, 1.6% Asian, 2.7% Hispanic of any race (2007); Density: 1,751.9 persons per square mile (2007); Average household size: 1.99 (2007); Median age: 54.2 (2007); Males per 100 females: 87.4 (2007); Marriage status: 12.8% never married, 66.7% now married, 7.2% widowed, 13.4% divorced (2000); Foreign born: 5.2% (2000); Ancestry (includes multiple ancestries): 19.4% English, 16.4% German, 14.8% Irish, 7.8% Other groups, 7.0% United States or American (2000).
Economy: Employment by occupation: 35.9% management, 22.4% professional, 5.9% services, 30.3% sales, 0.0% farming, 1.9% construction, 3.7% production (2000).
Income: Per capita income: $69,492 (2007); Median household income: $95,278 (2007); Average household income: $138,014 (2007); Percent of households with income of $100,000 or more: 47.1% (2007); Poverty rate: 2.5% (2000).

Education: Percent of population age 25 and over with: High school diploma (including GED) or higher: 97.8% (2007); Bachelor's degree or higher: 61.2% (2007); Master's degree or higher: 19.7% (2007).

Housing: Homeownership rate: 80.2% (2007); Median home value: $589,709 (2007); Median rent: $965 per month (2000); Median age of housing: 13 years (2000).

Transportation: Commute to work: 93.8% car, 0.0% public transportation, 1.2% walk, 3.8% work from home (2000); Travel time to work: 25.8% less than 15 minutes, 23.8% 15 to 30 minutes, 39.2% 30 to 45 minutes, 9.4% 45 to 60 minutes, 1.8% 60 minutes or more (2000)

VILLANO BEACH (CDP).

Covers a land area of 1.794 square miles and a water area of 0 square miles. Located at 29.93° N. Lat.; 81.30° W. Long. Elevation is 10 feet.

Population: 1,867 (1990); 2,533 (2000); 3,393 (2007); 3,949 (2012 projected); Race: 96.4% White, 0.6% Black, 1.4% Asian, 1.3% Hispanic of any race (2007); Density: 1,891.1 persons per square mile (2007); Average household size: 2.08 (2007); Median age: 48.2 (2007); Males per 100 females: 92.3 (2007); Marriage status: 19.7% never married, 62.2% now married, 6.1% widowed, 11.9% divorced (2000); Foreign born: 4.4% (2000); Ancestry (includes multiple ancestries): 19.9% German, 15.7% English, 12.8% Irish, 11.7% Italian, 10.4% Other groups (2000).

Economy: Employment by occupation: 16.5% management, 24.3% professional, 18.5% services, 26.9% sales, 0.0% farming, 10.0% construction, 3.9% production (2000).

Income: Per capita income: $47,187 (2007); Median household income: $67,453 (2007); Average household income: $97,361 (2007); Percent of households with income of $100,000 or more: 34.8% (2007); Poverty rate: 4.9% (2000).

Education: Percent of population age 25 and over with: High school diploma (including GED) or higher: 92.0% (2007); Bachelor's degree or higher: 41.6% (2007); Master's degree or higher: 11.9% (2007).

Housing: Homeownership rate: 77.3% (2007); Median home value: $367,961 (2007); Median rent: $539 per month (2000); Median age of housing: 16 years (2000).

Transportation: Commute to work: 93.3% car, 0.0% public transportation, 1.1% walk, 2.8% work from home (2000); Travel time to work: 31.0% less than 15 minutes, 33.9% 15 to 30 minutes, 17.9% 30 to 45 minutes, 9.5% 45 to 60 minutes, 7.7% 60 minutes or more (2000)

Saint Lucie County

Located in southeastern Florida; swampy, lowland area bounded on the east by the Atlantic Ocean, with a barrier beach enclosing Indian River lagoon. Covers a land area of 572.45 square miles, a water area of 115.63 square miles, and is located in the Eastern Time Zone. The county was founded in 1844. County seat is Fort Pierce.

Saint Lucie County is part of the Port St. Lucie, FL Metropolitan Statistical Area. The entire metro area includes: Martin County, FL; St. Lucie County, FL

Weather Station: Fort Pierce   Elevation: 22 feet

	Jan	Feb	Mar	Apr	May	Jun	Jul	Aug	Sep	Oct	Nov	Dec
High	74	75	79	82	86	89	91	91	89	85	80	76
Low	52	53	57	61	67	71	72	72	72	67	61	54
Precip	2.8	3.0	3.4	2.7	4.6	5.8	5.7	6.4	8.1	5.9	3.5	2.3
Snow	tr	0.0	0.0	0.0	0.0	0.0	0.0	0.0	0.0	0.0	0.0	0.0

High and Low temperatures in degrees Fahrenheit; Precipitation and Snow in inches

Population: 150,171 (1990); 192,695 (2000); 255,824 (2007); 299,621 (2012 projected); Race: 76.1% White, 16.0% Black, 1.3% Asian, 13.3% Hispanic of any race (2007); Density: 446.9 persons per square mile (2007); Average household size: 2.48 (2007); Median age: 41.3 (2007); Males per 100 females: 96.3 (2007).

Religion: Five largest groups: 23.4% Catholic Church, 4.3% Southern Baptist Convention, 2.0% The United Methodist Church, 1.6% Jewish Estimate, 0.7% Presbyterian Church (U.S.A.) (2000).

Economy: Unemployment rate: 6.3% (11/2007); Total civilian labor force: 120,205 (11/2007); Leading industries: 19.8% retail trade; 15.2% health care and social assistance; 10.5% accommodation & food services (2005); Farms: 477 totaling 221,537 acres (2002); Companies that employ 500 or more persons: 7 (2005); Companies that employ 100 to 499 persons: 80 (2005); Companies that employ less than 100 persons: 4,884 (2005); Black-owned businesses: 856 (2002); Hispanic-owned businesses: 827 (2002); Asian-owned businesses: 549 (2002); Women-owned businesses:

4,475 (2002); Retail sales per capita: $12,394 (2007). Single-family building permits issued: 4,636 (2006); Multi-family building permits issued: 728 (2006).

Income: Per capita income: $22,857 (2007); Median household income: $43,471 (2007); Average household income: $56,371 (2007); Percent of households with income of $100,000 or more: 11.4% (2007); Poverty rate: 12.3% (2005); Bankruptcy rate: 0.99% (2006).

Taxes: Total county taxes per capita: $479 (2005); County property taxes per capita: $393 (2005).

Education: Percent of population age 25 and over with: High school diploma (including GED) or higher: 79.3% (2007); Bachelor's degree or higher: 15.5% (2007); Master's degree or higher: 5.4% (2007).

Housing: Homeownership rate: 80.1% (2007); Median home value: $186,482 (2007); Median rent: $518 per month (2000); Median age of housing: 16 years (2000).

Health: Birth rate: 124.4 per 10,000 population (2006); Death rate: 101.0 per 10,000 population (2006); Age-adjusted cancer mortality rate: 185.1 deaths per 100,000 population (2004); Air Quality Index: 93.6% good, 6.4% moderate, 0.0% unhealthy for sensitive individuals, 0.0% unhealthy (percent of days in 2006); Number of physicians: 13.5 per 10,000 population (2005); Hospital beds: 33.7 per 10,000 population (2004); Hospital admissions: 1,371.3 per 10,000 population (2004).

Elections: 2004 Presidential election results: 47.6% Bush, 51.8% Kerry, 0.4% Nader, 0.1% Badnarik

National and State Parks: Avalon State Park; Fort Pierce Inlet State Park; Pepper Beach State Recreation Area; Savannas Preserve State Park

Additional Information Contacts

Saint Lucie County Government . . . . (772) 462-1400
   http://www.stlucieco.gov

St. Lucie County Chamber of Commerce . . . . (772) 340-1333
   http://www.stluciechamber.org

Saint Lucie County Communities

FORT PIERCE (city).

County seat. Covers a land area of 14.742 square miles and a water area of 6.021 square miles. Located at 27.43° N. Lat.; 80.33° W. Long. Elevation is 16 feet.

History: The original Fort Pierce was built in 1838 as a link in a chain of east coast defenses. The town of Fort Pierce developed as a citrus and vegetable shipping center.

Population: 38,676 (1990); 37,516 (2000); 37,993 (2007); 39,007 (2012 projected); Race: 43.6% White, 42.9% Black, 1.0% Asian, 23.7% Hispanic of any race (2007); Density: 2,577.2 persons per square mile (2007); Average household size: 2.59 (2007); Median age: 33.8 (2007); Males per 100 females: 98.9 (2007); Marriage status: 29.7% never married, 48.0% now married, 10.0% widowed, 12.3% divorced (2000); Foreign born: 18.4% (2000); Ancestry (includes multiple ancestries): 42.8% Other groups, 8.2% Irish, 7.9% German, 6.9% English, 6.6% United States or American (2000).

Economy: Unemployment rate: 7.8% (11/2007); Total civilian labor force: 18,127 (11/2007); Single-family building permits issued: 216 (2006); Multi-family building permits issued: 325 (2006); Employment by occupation: 6.7% management, 13.2% professional, 19.3% services, 20.5% sales, 9.0% farming, 15.8% construction, 15.5% production (2000).

Income: Per capita income: $16,693 (2007); Median household income: $28,864 (2007); Average household income: $42,581 (2007); Percent of households with income of $100,000 or more: 7.1% (2007); Poverty rate: 30.9% (2000).

Taxes: Total city taxes per capita: $465 (2005); City property taxes per capita: $247 (2005).

Education: Percent of population age 25 and over with: High school diploma (including GED) or higher: 60.6% (2007); Bachelor's degree or higher: 12.9% (2007); Master's degree or higher: 4.7% (2007).

School District(s)

Palm Beach County School District (PK-12)
   2005-06 Enrollment: 175,076 . . . . (561) 434-8200
St. Lucie County School District (PK-12)
   2005-06 Enrollment: 34,912 . . . . (772) 429-3925

Two-year College(s)

Indian River Community College (Public)
   Fall 2006 Enrollment: 13,270 . . . . (772) 462-4722
   2006-07 Tuition: In-state $1,756; Out-of-state $6,410

Vocational/Technical School(s)

Ari Ben Aviator (Private, For-profit)
   Fall 2006 Enrollment: 66 . . . . (772) 466-4822
   2006-07 Tuition: $35,995

housing: 27 years (2000).
Hospitals: Lawnwood Pavilion (36 beds); New Horizons of the Treasure Coast (30 beds)
Safety: Violent crime rate: 204.1 per 10,000 population; Property crime rate: 746.4 per 10,000 population (2006).
Newspapers: Tribune (Circulation 29,280)
Transportation: Commute to work: 89.9% car, 4.0% public transportation, 1.9% walk, 2.0% work from home (2000); Travel time to work: 30.9% less than 15 minutes, 31.9% 15 to 30 minutes, 25.2% 30 to 45 minutes, 4.1% 45 to 60 minutes, 7.8% 60 minutes or more (2000)
Airports: St Lucie County International
Additional Information Contacts
St. Lucie County Chamber of Commerce . . . . (772) 340-1333
   http://www.stluciechamber.org

FORT PIERCE NORTH (CDP).
Covers a land area of 4.470 square miles and a water area of 0.095 square miles. Located at 27.46° N. Lat.; 80.35° W. Long.
Population: 8,065 (1990); 7,386 (2000); 6,865 (2007); 6,666 (2012 projected); Race: 15.9% White, 78.1% Black, 0.0% Asian, 8.7% Hispanic of any race (2007); Density: 1,535.8 persons per square mile (2007); Average household size: 2.84 (2007); Median age: 33.0 (2007); Males per 100 females: 93.3 (2007); Marriage status: 32.7% never married, 47.8% now married, 7.9% widowed, 11.6% divorced (2000); Foreign born: 6.9% (2000); Ancestry (includes multiple ancestries): 52.3% Other groups, 9.2% African, 5.9% United States or American, 3.0% Irish, 2.8% German (2000).
Economy: Employment by occupation: 5.4% management, 15.2% professional, 25.8% services, 21.0% sales, 5.5% farming, 10.4% construction, 16.6% production (2000).
Income: Per capita income: $13,443 (2007); Median household income: $29,212 (2007); Average household income: $37,979 (2007); Percent of households with income of $100,000 or more: 4.4% (2007); Poverty rate: 22.1% (2000).
Education: Percent of population age 25 and over with: High school diploma (including GED) or higher: 59.1% (2007); Bachelor's degree or higher: 10.3% (2007); Master's degree or higher: 4.2% (2007).
Housing: Homeownership rate: 74.7% (2007); Median home value: $104,280 (2007); Median rent: $475 per month (2000); Median age of housing: 26 years (2000).
Transportation: Commute to work: 95.8% car, 2.3% public transportation, 1.2% walk, 0.0% work from home (2000); Travel time to work: 34.1% less than 15 minutes, 34.5% 15 to 30 minutes, 17.7% 30 to 45 minutes, 7.2% 45 to 60 minutes, 6.5% 60 minutes or more (2000)

FORT PIERCE SOUTH (CDP).
Covers a land area of 4.503 square miles and a water area of 0 square miles. Located at 27.41° N. Lat.; 80.35° W. Long. Elevation is 13 feet.
Population: 4,899 (1990); 5,672 (2000); 5,853 (2007); 6,123 (2012 projected); Race: 65.4% White, 18.7% Black, 1.7% Asian, 31.4% Hispanic of any race (2007); Density: 1,299.7 persons per square mile (2007); Average household size: 2.81 (2007); Median age: 32.5 (2007); Males per 100 females: 97.9 (2007); Marriage status: 25.9% never married, 54.7% now married, 6.7% widowed, 12.8% divorced (2000); Foreign born: 14.1% (2000); Ancestry (includes multiple ancestries): 27.6% Other groups, 12.0% United States or American, 11.9% English, 10.3% Irish, 9.4% German (2000).
Economy: Employment by occupation: 8.3% management, 15.2% professional, 18.0% services, 22.8% sales, 3.3% farming, 17.4% construction, 15.0% production (2000).
Income: Per capita income: $18,782 (2007); Median household income: $34,234 (2007); Average household income: $52,638 (2007); Percent of households with income of $100,000 or more: 10.7% (2007); Poverty rate: 17.6% (2000).
Education: Percent of population age 25 and over with: High school diploma (including GED) or higher: 68.3% (2007); Bachelor's degree or higher: 12.3% (2007); Master's degree or higher: 4.9% (2007).
Housing: Homeownership rate: 64.1% (2007); Median home value: $134,696 (2007); Median rent: $470 per month (2000); Median age of housing: 27 years (2000).

HUTCHINSON ISLAND SOUTH (CDP).
Covers a land area of 4.512 square miles and a water area of 43.560 square miles. Located at 27.28° N. Lat.; 80.22° W. Long.
Population: 3,893 (1990); 4,846 (2000); 5,186 (2007); 5,514 (2012 projected); Race: 98.7% White, 0.1% Black, 0.2% Asian, 1.4% Hispanic of any race (2007); Density: 1,149.4 persons per square mile (2007); Average household size: 1.67 (2007); Median age: 70.0 (2007); Males per 100 females: 88.0 (2007); Marriage status: 4.9% never married, 72.4% now married, 15.6% widowed, 7.0% divorced (2000); Foreign born: 9.0% (2000); Ancestry (includes multiple ancestries): 20.2% German, 19.8% English, 15.5% Irish, 11.4% Italian, 5.8% United States or American (2000).
Economy: Employment by occupation: 10.9% management, 23.9% professional, 15.7% services, 34.3% sales, 0.0% farming, 8.4% construction, 6.8% production (2000).
Income: Per capita income: $47,225 (2007); Median household income: $50,649 (2007); Average household income: $78,977 (2007); Percent of households with income of $100,000 or more: 20.2% (2007); Poverty rate: 4.5% (2000).
Education: Percent of population age 25 and over with: High school diploma (including GED) or higher: 87.7% (2007); Bachelor's degree or higher: 24.6% (2007); Master's degree or higher: 10.6% (2007).
Housing: Homeownership rate: 90.6% (2007); Median home value: $263,259 (2007); Median rent: $843 per month (2000); Median age of housing: 15 years (2000).
Transportation: Commute to work: 76.6% car, 0.0% public transportation, 9.3% walk, 11.0% work from home (2000); Travel time to work: 28.6% less than 15 minutes, 37.4% 15 to 30 minutes, 20.6% 30 to 45 minutes, 6.1% 45 to 60 minutes, 7.3% 60 minutes or more (2000)

INDIAN RIVER ESTATES (CDP).
Covers a land area of 5.537 square miles and a water area of 0.208 square miles. Located at 27.36° N. Lat.; 80.30° W. Long. Elevation is 13 feet.
Population: 4,872 (1990); 5,793 (2000); 5,971 (2007); 6,202 (2012 projected); Race: 92.7% White, 3.7% Black, 0.5% Asian, 6.5% Hispanic of any race (2007); Density: 1,078.3 persons per square mile (2007); Average household size: 2.42 (2007); Median age: 43.6 (2007); Males per 100 females: 96.9 (2007); Marriage status: 13.8% never married, 66.8% now married, 8.5% widowed, 10.9% divorced (2000); Foreign born: 6.1% (2000); Ancestry (includes multiple ancestries): 17.7% German, 16.0% Irish, 11.6% English, 10.9% Italian, 10.9% United States or American (2000).
Economy: Employment by occupation: 13.1% management, 14.7% professional, 13.8% services, 33.2% sales, 0.6% farming, 15.9% construction, 8.7% production (2000).
Income: Per capita income: $20,234 (2007); Median household income: $42,832 (2007); Average household income: $48,609 (2007); Percent of households with income of $100,000 or more: 6.8% (2007); Poverty rate: 7.7% (2000).
Education: Percent of population age 25 and over with: High school diploma (including GED) or higher: 75.7% (2007); Bachelor's degree or higher: 8.9% (2007); Master's degree or higher: 2.9% (2007).
Housing: Homeownership rate: 91.9% (2007); Median home value: $168,506 (2007); Median rent: $558 per month (2000); Median age of housing: 15 years (2000).
Transportation: Commute to work: 93.8% car, 0.3% public transportation, 0.6% walk, 4.4% work from home (2000); Travel time to work: 21.3% less than 15 minutes, 50.1% 15 to 30 minutes, 18.5% 30 to 45 minutes, 4.6% 45 to 60 minutes, 5.5% 60 minutes or more (2000)

LAKEWOOD PARK (CDP).
Covers a land area of 6.697 square miles and a water area of 0.224 square miles. Located at 27.54° N. Lat.; 80.39° W. Long. Elevation is 20 feet.
Population: 9,240 (1990); 10,458 (2000); 11,069 (2007); 11,666 (2012 projected); Race: 88.1% White, 7.5% Black, 0.8% Asian, 4.6% Hispanic of any race (2007); Density: 1,652.8 persons per square mile (2007); Average household size: 2.27 (2007); Median age: 45.0 (2007); Males per 100 females: 95.4 (2007); Marriage status: 15.6% never married, 64.1% now married, 9.7% widowed, 10.5% divorced (2000); Foreign born: 5.2% (2000); Ancestry (includes multiple ancestries): 16.9% Irish, 16.4%

German, 13.2% English, 12.9% Other groups, 10.9% United States or American (2000).
Economy: Employment by occupation: 11.9% management, 12.4% professional, 16.1% services, 30.4% sales, 1.3% farming, 16.0% construction, 11.9% production (2000).
Income: Per capita income: $22,002 (2007); Median household income: $41,010 (2007); Average household income: $49,721 (2007); Percent of households with income of $100,000 or more: 8.0% (2007); Poverty rate: 9.5% (2000).
Education: Percent of population age 25 and over with: High school diploma (including GED) or higher: 81.0% (2007); Bachelor's degree or higher: 11.6% (2007); Master's degree or higher: 3.1% (2007).
Housing: Homeownership rate: 84.4% (2007); Median home value: $141,494 (2007); Median rent: $505 per month (2000); Median age of housing: 16 years (2000).
Transportation: Commute to work: 96.1% car, 0.0% public transportation, 0.7% walk, 1.5% work from home (2000); Travel time to work: 16.5% less than 15 minutes, 55.0% 15 to 30 minutes, 20.9% 30 to 45 minutes, 2.2% 45 to 60 minutes, 5.5% 60 minutes or more (2000)

PORT SAINT LUCIE (city). Covers a land area of 75.541 square miles and a water area of 1.149 square miles. Located at 27.27° N. Lat.; 80.35° W. Long. Elevation is 16 feet.
Population: 55,843 (1990); 88,769 (2000); 142,771 (2007); 178,736 (2012 projected); Race: 81.8% White, 10.6% Black, 1.7% Asian, 12.8% Hispanic of any race (2007); Density: 1,890.0 persons per square mile (2007); Average household size: 2.58 (2007); Median age: 39.5 (2007); Males per 100 females: 95.7 (2007); Marriage status: 18.4% never married, 64.3% now married, 6.9% widowed, 10.5% divorced (2000); Foreign born: 9.6% (2000); Ancestry (includes multiple ancestries): 17.4% Irish, 16.9% German, 15.7% Italian, 15.4% Other groups, 11.5% English (2000).
Economy: Unemployment rate: 5.6% (11/2007); Total civilian labor force: 70,615 (11/2007); Single-family building permits issued: 4,067 (2006); Multi-family building permits issued: 116 (2006); Employment by occupation: 10.6% management, 16.0% professional, 17.6% services, 32.0% sales, 0.5% farming, 12.5% construction, 10.7% production (2000).
Income: Per capita income: $21,642 (2007); Median household income: $46,921 (2007); Average household income: $55,580 (2007); Percent of households with income of $100,000 or more: 10.5% (2007); Poverty rate: 7.9% (2000).
Taxes: Total city taxes per capita: $365 (2005); City property taxes per capita: $152 (2005).
Education: Percent of population age 25 and over with: High school diploma (including GED) or higher: 83.9% (2007); Bachelor's degree or higher: 15.0% (2007); Master's degree or higher: 4.9% (2007).
School District(s)
St. Lucie County School District (PK-12)
    2005-06 Enrollment: 34,912 . . . . (772) 429-3925
Housing: Homeownership rate: 84.2% (2007); Median home value: $200,684 (2007); Median rent: $627 per month (2000); Median age of housing: 12 years (2000).
Hospitals: Savannas Hospital (75 beds); St. Lucie Medical Center (194 beds)
Safety: Violent crime rate: 25.4 per 10,000 population; Property crime rate: 266.1 per 10,000 population (2006).
Transportation: Commute to work: 95.8% car, 0.3% public transportation, 0.5% walk, 2.2% work from home (2000); Travel time to work: 18.2% less than 15 minutes, 41.9% 15 to 30 minutes, 23.8% 30 to 45 minutes, 8.8% 45 to 60 minutes, 7.3% 60 minutes or more (2000)

PORT SAINT LUCIE-RIVER PARK (CDP). Covers a land area of 2.336 square miles and a water area of 0.176 square miles. Located at 27.32° N. Lat.; 80.33° W. Long.
Population: 4,954 (1990); 5,175 (2000); 6,814 (2007); 7,980 (2012 projected); Race: 86.1% White, 7.3% Black, 1.2% Asian, 12.9% Hispanic of any race (2007); Density: 2,917.2 persons per square mile (2007); Average household size: 2.13 (2007); Median age: 48.7 (2007); Males per 100 females: 94.1 (2007); Marriage status: 14.8% never married, 54.9% now married, 17.7% widowed, 12.5% divorced (2000); Foreign born: 7.2% (2000); Ancestry (includes multiple ancestries): 16.1% Italian, 15.6% German, 15.2% English, 14.2% Irish, 11.4% Other groups (2000).
Economy: Employment by occupation: 5.8% management, 13.3% professional, 19.5% services, 35.2% sales, 1.1% farming, 14.4% construction, 10.6% production (2000).

Income: Per capita income: $22,449 (2007); Median household income: $33,675 (2007); Average household income: $47,690 (2007); Percent of households with income of $100,000 or more: 8.3% (2007); Poverty rate: 9.2% (2000).
Education: Percent of population age 25 and over with: High school diploma (including GED) or higher: 78.0% (2007); Bachelor's degree or higher: 13.2% (2007); Master's degree or higher: 4.3% (2007).
Housing: Homeownership rate: 82.1% (2007); Median home value: $125,269 (2007); Median rent: $532 per month (2000); Median age of housing: 26 years (2000).
Transportation: Commute to work: 96.0% car, 0.0% public transportation, 0.1% walk, 3.2% work from home (2000); Travel time to work: 19.7% less than 15 minutes, 45.1% 15 to 30 minutes, 21.6% 30 to 45 minutes, 6.4% 45 to 60 minutes, 7.2% 60 minutes or more (2000)

SAINT LUCIE (village). Covers a land area of 0.810 square miles and a water area of 0 square miles. Located at 27.49° N. Lat.; 80.34° W. Long. Elevation is 7 feet.
Population: 634 (1990); 604 (2000); 603 (2007); 546 (2012 projected); Race: 95.5% White, 1.5% Black, 0.0% Asian, 5.0% Hispanic of any race (2007); Density: 744.9 persons per square mile (2007); Average household size: 2.15 (2007); Median age: 45.0 (2007); Males per 100 females: 103.7 (2007); Marriage status: 24.8% never married, 52.0% now married, 8.2% widowed, 15.1% divorced (2000); Foreign born: 1.9% (2000); Ancestry (includes multiple ancestries): 22.8% German, 17.7% Irish, 16.7% English, 9.1% Italian, 7.8% United States or American (2000).
Economy: Single-family building permits issued: 0 (2006); Multi-family building permits issued: 0 (2006); Employment by occupation: 15.9% management, 17.6% professional, 16.7% services, 25.6% sales, 0.6% farming, 17.0% construction, 6.6% production (2000).
Income: Per capita income: $34,221 (2007); Median household income: $48,889 (2007); Average household income: $73,696 (2007); Percent of households with income of $100,000 or more: 20.7% (2007); Poverty rate: 4.0% (2000).
Education: Percent of population age 25 and over with: High school diploma (including GED) or higher: 81.9% (2007); Bachelor's degree or higher: 24.4% (2007); Master's degree or higher: 7.7% (2007).
Housing: Homeownership rate: 75.4% (2007); Median home value: $252,273 (2007); Median rent: $504 per month (2000); Median age of housing: 33 years (2000).
Transportation: Commute to work: 93.8% car, 0.0% public transportation, 0.6% walk, 2.6% work from home (2000); Travel time to work: 33.8% less than 15 minutes, 40.2% 15 to 30 minutes, 15.7% 30 to 45 minutes, 3.0% 45 to 60 minutes, 7.3% 60 minutes or more (2000)

WHITE CITY (CDP). Covers a land area of 7.062 square miles and a water area of 0 square miles. Located at 27.38° N. Lat.; 80.33° W. Long. Elevation is 13 feet.
History: White City was settled in the 1890's by Danish immigrants from Chicago, interested in the citrus orchards.
Population: 3,792 (1990); 4,221 (2000); 5,531 (2007); 6,455 (2012 projected); Race: 90.0% White, 3.7% Black, 1.4% Asian, 8.7% Hispanic of any race (2007); Density: 783.2 persons per square mile (2007); Average household size: 2.68 (2007); Median age: 37.8 (2007); Males per 100 females: 99.7 (2007); Marriage status: 20.8% never married, 61.5% now married, 6.3% widowed, 11.4% divorced (2000); Foreign born: 4.4% (2000); Ancestry (includes multiple ancestries): 22.3% Irish, 17.5% English, 15.2% United States or American, 13.2% German, 11.6% Other groups (2000).
Economy: Employment by occupation: 10.1% management, 21.1% professional, 14.4% services, 23.9% sales, 1.4% farming, 17.1% construction, 11.9% production (2000).
Income: Per capita income: $26,463 (2007); Median household income: $50,625 (2007); Average household income: $70,378 (2007); Percent of households with income of $100,000 or more: 20.7% (2007); Poverty rate: 11.1% (2000).
Education: Percent of population age 25 and over with: High school diploma (including GED) or higher: 80.4% (2007); Bachelor's degree or higher: 17.8% (2007); Master's degree or higher: 6.5% (2007).
Housing: Homeownership rate: 84.2% (2007); Median home value: $204,468 (2007); Median rent: $514 per month (2000); Median age of housing: 25 years (2000).
Transportation: Commute to work: 95.9% car, 0.0% public transportation, 0.2% walk, 2.3% work from home (2000); Travel time to work: 35.8% less

Located in central Florida; bounded partly on the west and south by the Withlacoochee River; includes Lake Panasoffkee and many other lakes. Covers a land area of 545.73 square miles, a water area of 34.58 square miles, and is located in the Eastern Time Zone. The county was founded in 1853. County seat is Bushnell.

Sumter County is part of the The Villages, FL Micropolitan Statistical Area. The entire metro area includes: Sumter County, FL

Population: 31,577 (1990); 53,345 (2000); 73,997 (2007); 92,171 (2012 projected); Race: 83.2% White, 12.6% Black, 0.6% Asian, 8.0% Hispanic of any race (2007); Density: 135.6 persons per square mile (2007); Average household size: 2.50 (2007); Median age: 43.8 (2007); Males per 100 females: 115.8 (2007).
Religion: Five largest groups: 14.9% Southern Baptist Convention, 3.0% Church of God (Cleveland, Tennessee), 2.8% The United Methodist Church, 2.1% Assemblies of God, 2.1% Catholic Church (2000).
Economy: Unemployment rate: 3.2% (11/2007); Total civilian labor force: 34,898 (11/2007); Leading industries: 29.8% construction; 15.5% retail trade; 10.9% accommodation & food services (2005); Farms: 902 totaling 187,373 acres (2002); Companies that employ 500 or more persons: 2 (2005); Companies that employ 100 to 499 persons: 17 (2005); Companies that employ less than 100 persons: 805 (2005); Black-owned businesses: n/a (2002); Hispanic-owned businesses: n/a (2002); Asian-owned businesses: n/a (2002); Women-owned businesses: 932 (2002); Retail sales per capita: $6,903 (2007). Single-family building permits issued: 3,558 (2006); Multi-family building permits issued: 18 (2006).
Income: Per capita income: $20,403 (2007); Median household income: $38,622 (2007); Average household income: $48,888 (2007); Percent of households with income of $100,000 or more: 8.6% (2007); Poverty rate: 14.4% (2005); Bankruptcy rate: 0.81% (2006).
Education: Percent of population age 25 and over with: High school diploma (including GED) or higher: 79.3% (2007); Bachelor's degree or higher: 13.8% (2007); Master's degree or higher: 5.3% (2007).
Housing: Homeownership rate: 88.4% (2007); Median home value: $177,722 (2007); Median rent: $321 per month (2000); Median age of housing: 13 years (2000).
Health: Birth rate: 79.1 per 10,000 population (2006); Death rate: 119.1 per 10,000 population (2006); Age-adjusted cancer mortality rate: 197.3 deaths per 100,000 population (2004); Number of physicians: 3.4 per 10,000 population (2005); Hospital beds: 9.9 per 10,000 population (2004); Hospital admissions: 951.0 per 10,000 population (2004).
Elections: 2004 Presidential election results: 62.2% Bush, 36.4% Kerry, 0.8% Nader, 0.1% Badnarik
National and State Parks: Dade Battlefield Historic State Park
Additional Information Contacts
Sumter County Government . . . . (352) 793-0200
   http://www.sumtercountyfl.gov
Sumter County Chamber of Commerce. . . . . (352) 793-3099
   http://www.sumterchamber.org

Sumter County Communities

BUSHNELL (city). County seat. Covers a land area of 2.352 square miles and a water area of <.001 square miles. Located at 28.66° N. Lat.; 82.11° W. Long. Elevation is 79 feet.
History: Bushnell was named for the engineer who surveyed the railroad right-of-way through the area. The town developed as a shipping center for the surrounding citrus and agricultural area, and as the seat of Sumter County.
Population: 2,036 (1990); 2,050 (2000); 2,516 (2007); 2,997 (2012 projected); Race: 82.6% White, 12.7% Black, 1.1% Asian, 5.1% Hispanic of any race (2007); Density: 1,069.8 persons per square mile (2007); Average household size: 2.50 (2007); Median age: 34.0 (2007); Males per 100 females: 107.6 (2007); Marriage status: 13.2% never married, 64.1% now married, 12.4% widowed, 10.3% divorced (2000); Foreign born: 2.5% (2000); Ancestry (includes multiple ancestries): 18.1% Other groups, 13.4% United States or American, 11.2% German, 10.0% English, 8.8% Irish (2000).

households with income of $100,000 or more: 3.4% (2007); Poverty rate: 14.7% (2000).
Education: Percent of population age 25 and over with: High school diploma (including GED) or higher: 72.1% (2007); Bachelor's degree or higher: 10.0% (2007); Master's degree or higher: 2.4% (2007).
School District(s)
Sumter County School District (PK-12)
   2005-06 Enrollment: 7,157 . . . . (352) 793-2315
Housing: Homeownership rate: 67.0% (2007); Median home value: $109,046 (2007); Median rent: $313 per month (2000); Median age of housing: 17 years (2000).
Safety: Violent crime rate: 88.2 per 10,000 population; Property crime rate: 556.8 per 10,000 population (2006).
Newspapers: Sumter County Times (General - Circulation 5,000)
Transportation: Commute to work: 92.5% car, 0.0% public transportation, 2.5% walk, 1.9% work from home (2000); Travel time to work: 40.1% less than 15 minutes, 21.4% 15 to 30 minutes, 13.9% 30 to 45 minutes, 8.0% 45 to 60 minutes, 16.6% 60 minutes or more (2000)
Additional Information Contacts
Sumter County Chamber of Commerce. . . . . (352) 793-3099
   http://www.sumterchamber.org

CENTER HILL (city). Covers a land area of 1.711 square miles and a water area of 0.057 square miles. Located at 28.64° N. Lat.; 81.99° W. Long. Elevation is 98 feet.
History: Center Hill was settled in 1883 and became a shipping center for strawberries, watermelons, and green beans.
Population: 735 (1990); 910 (2000); 958 (2007); 1,054 (2012 projected); Race: 77.8% White, 3.8% Black, 0.9% Asian, 39.6% Hispanic of any race (2007); Density: 559.8 persons per square mile (2007); Average household size: 3.23 (2007); Median age: 26.7 (2007); Males per 100 females: 118.2 (2007); Marriage status: 24.2% never married, 59.4% now married, 7.0% widowed, 9.4% divorced (2000); Foreign born: 18.0% (2000); Ancestry (includes multiple ancestries): 40.0% Other groups, 9.5% Irish, 6.8% German, 6.0% English, 4.8% United States or American (2000).
Economy: Employment by occupation: 8.1% management, 11.8% professional, 18.0% services, 18.5% sales, 9.8% farming, 14.3% construction, 19.4% production (2000).
Income: Per capita income: $16,469 (2007); Median household income: $35,214 (2007); Average household income: $52,896 (2007); Percent of households with income of $100,000 or more: 10.4% (2007); Poverty rate: 26.2% (2000).
Education: Percent of population age 25 and over with: High school diploma (including GED) or higher: 58.6% (2007); Bachelor's degree or higher: 5.5% (2007); Master's degree or higher: 1.2% (2007).
Housing: Homeownership rate: 75.8% (2007); Median home value: $86,304 (2007); Median rent: $303 per month (2000); Median age of housing: 28 years (2000).
Safety: Violent crime rate: 154.0 per 10,000 population; Property crime rate: 71.9 per 10,000 population (2006).
Transportation: Commute to work: 92.3% car, 0.0% public transportation, 4.5% walk, 2.6% work from home (2000); Travel time to work: 27.4% less than 15 minutes, 25.9% 15 to 30 minutes, 21.0% 30 to 45 minutes, 6.7% 45 to 60 minutes, 19.0% 60 minutes or more (2000)

COLEMAN (city). Covers a land area of 1.454 square miles and a water area of 0 square miles. Located at 28.80° N. Lat.; 82.06° W. Long. Elevation is 66 feet.
Population: 880 (1990); 647 (2000); 602 (2007); 594 (2012 projected); Race: 62.0% White, 32.6% Black, 0.2% Asian, 5.0% Hispanic of any race (2007); Density: 414.0 persons per square mile (2007); Average household size: 2.47 (2007); Median age: 26.9 (2007); Males per 100 females: 96.1 (2007); Marriage status: 23.3% never married, 44.9% now married, 13.0% widowed, 18.7% divorced (2000); Foreign born: 1.0% (2000); Ancestry (includes multiple ancestries): 40.6% Other groups, 15.5% United States or American, 9.5% English, 9.3% Irish, 5.0% German (2000).
Economy: Employment by occupation: 8.8% management, 10.3% professional, 28.6% services, 23.1% sales, 1.1% farming, 9.9% construction, 18.3% production (2000).

Income: Per capita income: $15,590 (2007); Median household income: $27,857 (2007); Average household income: $38,463 (2007); Percent of households with income of $100,000 or more: 7.4% (2007); Poverty rate: 22.7% (2000).

Education: Percent of population age 25 and over with: High school diploma (including GED) or higher: 64.4% (2007); Bachelor's degree or higher: 7.3% (2007); Master's degree or higher: 2.5% (2007).

Housing: Homeownership rate: 76.6% (2007); Median home value: $98,929 (2007); Median rent: $297 per month (2000); Median age of housing: 29 years (2000).

Safety: Violent crime rate: 0.0 per 10,000 population; Property crime rate: 87.0 per 10,000 population (2006).

Transportation: Commute to work: 93.6% car, 0.7% public transportation, 1.5% walk, 4.1% work from home (2000); Travel time to work: 29.7% less than 15 minutes, 39.8% 15 to 30 minutes, 14.8% 30 to 45 minutes, 9.0% 45 to 60 minutes, 6.6% 60 minutes or more (2000)

LAKE PANASOFFKEE (CDP). Aka Panasoffkee. Covers a land area of 4.031 square miles and a water area of 0.014 square miles. Located at 28.79° N. Lat.; 82.13° W. Long. Elevation is 59 feet.

Population: 2,705 (1990); 3,413 (2000); 4,149 (2007); 4,865 (2012 projected); Race: 96.3% White, 1.0% Black, 0.8% Asian, 1.0% Hispanic of any race (2007); Density: 1,029.2 persons per square mile (2007); Average household size: 2.07 (2007); Median age: 40.9 (2007); Males per 100 females: 96.3 (2007); Marriage status: 11.3% never married, 63.0% now married, 10.6% widowed, 15.1% divorced (2000); Foreign born: 1.7% (2000); Ancestry (includes multiple ancestries): 21.5% United States or American, 17.1% Irish, 17.0% English, 16.1% German, 9.6% Other groups (2000).

Economy: Employment by occupation: 4.4% management, 9.6% professional, 26.0% services, 22.7% sales, 0.0% farming, 17.5% construction, 19.8% production (2000).

Income: Per capita income: $20,512 (2007); Median household income: $32,107 (2007); Average household income: $42,509 (2007); Percent of households with income of $100,000 or more: 6.5% (2007); Poverty rate: 12.0% (2000).

Education: Percent of population age 25 and over with: High school diploma (including GED) or higher: 68.5% (2007); Bachelor's degree or higher: 4.2% (2007); Master's degree or higher: 1.4% (2007).

School District(s)
Sumter County School District (PK-12)
   2005-06 Enrollment: 7,157 . . . . (352) 793-2315

Housing: Homeownership rate: 84.4% (2007); Median home value: $95,826 (2007); Median rent: $302 per month (2000); Median age of housing: 22 years (2000).

Transportation: Commute to work: 93.6% car, 0.0% public transportation, 1.7% walk, 3.7% work from home (2000); Travel time to work: 20.8% less than 15 minutes, 31.3% 15 to 30 minutes, 20.1% 30 to 45 minutes, 9.1% 45 to 60 minutes, 18.8% 60 minutes or more (2000)

OXFORD (unincorporated postal area, zip code 34484). Covers a land area of 42.698 square miles and a water area of 0.237 square miles. Located at 28.90° N. Lat.; 82.06° W. Long. Elevation is 114 feet.

Population: 2,282 (2000); Race: 91.9% White, 6.3% Black, 0.0% Asian, 0.9% Hispanic of any race (2000); Density: 53.4 persons per square mile (2000); Age: 26.9% under 18, 13.2% over 64 (2000); Marriage status: 22.2% never married, 63.5% now married, 5.7% widowed, 8.7% divorced (2000); Foreign born: 0.3% (2000); Ancestry (includes multiple ancestries): 19.3% Other groups, 18.8% Irish, 15.4% United States or American, 11.1% English, 10.4% German (2000).

Economy: Employment by occupation: 10.8% management, 14.4% professional, 18.0% services, 24.7% sales, 1.6% farming, 17.3% construction, 13.2% production (2000).

Income: Per capita income: $18,201 (2000); Median household income: $37,741 (2000); Poverty rate: 11.5% (2000).

Education: Percent of population age 25 and over with: High school diploma (including GED) or higher: 82.6% (2000); Bachelor's degree or higher: 9.0% (2000).

Housing: Homeownership rate: 86.4% (2000); Median home value: $92,500 (2000); Median rent: $358 per month (2000); Median age of housing: 18 years (2000).

Transportation: Commute to work: 94.1% car, 0.0% public transportation, 0.8% walk, 4.0% work from home (2000); Travel time to work: 26.7% less than 15 minutes, 28.5% 15 to 30 minutes, 29.6% 30 to 45 minutes, 7.3% 45 to 60 minutes, 7.8% 60 minutes or more (2000)

SUMTERVILLE (unincorporated postal area, zip code 33585). Covers a land area of 17.122 square miles and a water area of 0.104 square miles. Located at 28.73° N. Lat.; 82.06° W. Long. Elevation is 75 feet.

Population: 777 (2000); Race: 83.5% White, 9.4% Black, 2.2% Asian, 6.8% Hispanic of any race (2000); Density: 45.4 persons per square mile (2000); Age: 22.2% under 18, 14.8% over 64 (2000); Marriage status: 16.7% never married, 62.7% now married, 9.9% widowed, 10.7% divorced (2000); Foreign born: 3.0% (2000); Ancestry (includes multiple ancestries): 25.5% United States or American, 24.1% Other groups, 11.6% Irish, 9.8% English, 9.5% German (2000).

Economy: Employment by occupation: 5.2% management, 9.6% professional, 13.0% services, 36.4% sales, 0.0% farming, 20.7% construction, 15.1% production (2000).

Income: Per capita income: $13,088 (2000); Median household income: $25,388 (2000); Poverty rate: 16.4% (2000).

Education: Percent of population age 25 and over with: High school diploma (including GED) or higher: 72.7% (2000); Bachelor's degree or higher: 10.2% (2000).

Housing: Homeownership rate: 78.9% (2000); Median home value: $51,400 (2000); Median rent: $302 per month (2000); Median age of housing: 20 years (2000).

Transportation: Commute to work: 93.8% car, 0.0% public transportation, 2.6% walk, 0.0% work from home (2000); Travel time to work: 33.2% less than 15 minutes, 33.6% 15 to 30 minutes, 13.7% 30 to 45 minutes, 6.2% 45 to 60 minutes, 13.4% 60 minutes or more (2000)

THE VILLAGES (CDP). Covers a land area of 5.190 square miles and a water area of 0.388 square miles. Located at 28.93° N. Lat.; 81.97° W. Long. Elevation is 66 feet.

Population: 627 (1990); 8,333 (2000); 18,145 (2007); 25,876 (2012 projected); Race: 97.7% White, 0.8% Black, 0.8% Asian, 1.6% Hispanic of any race (2007); Density: 3,496.0 persons per square mile (2007); Average household size: 1.88 (2007); Median age: 67.0 (2007); Males per 100 females: 87.2 (2007); Marriage status: 2.3% never married, 85.2% now married, 9.0% widowed, 3.6% divorced (2000); Foreign born: 5.8% (2000); Ancestry (includes multiple ancestries): 25.6% German, 20.0% English, 18.7% Irish, 10.6% Italian, 4.6% French (except Basque) (2000).

Economy: Employment by occupation: 9.8% management, 20.2% professional, 27.0% services, 34.1% sales, 0.0% farming, 4.7% construction, 4.3% production (2000).

Income: Per capita income: $32,828 (2007); Median household income: $48,559 (2007); Average household income: $61,483 (2007); Percent of households with income of $100,000 or more: 13.3% (2007); Poverty rate: 3.7% (2000).

Education: Percent of population age 25 and over with: High school diploma (including GED) or higher: 89.7% (2007); Bachelor's degree or higher: 23.6% (2007); Master's degree or higher: 10.0% (2007).

School District(s)
Sumter County School District (PK-12)
   2005-06 Enrollment: 7,157 . . . . (352) 793-2315

Housing: Homeownership rate: 98.3% (2007); Median home value: $305,820 (2007); Median rent: $1,013 per month (2000); Median age of housing: 3 years (2000).

Hospitals: Villages Regional Hospital (60 beds)

Transportation: Commute to work: 87.8% car, 0.0% public transportation, 0.0% walk, 5.6% work from home (2000); Travel time to work: 52.0% less than 15 minutes, 23.0% 15 to 30 minutes, 14.2% 30 to 45 minutes, 3.0% 45 to 60 minutes, 7.8% 60 minutes or more (2000)

WEBSTER (city). Covers a land area of 1.324 square miles and a water area of 0 square miles. Located at 28.61° N. Lat.; 82.05° W. Long. Elevation is 89 feet.

Population: 773 (1990); 805 (2000); 907 (2007); 1,037 (2012 projected); Race: 54.4% White, 33.4% Black, 0.4% Asian, 19.6% Hispanic of any race (2007); Density: 685.3 persons per square mile (2007); Average household size: 2.77 (2007); Median age: 29.5 (2007); Males per 100 females: 90.5 (2007); Marriage status: 28.0% never married, 45.6% now married, 11.7% widowed, 14.7% divorced (2000); Foreign born: 5.3% (2000); Ancestry (includes multiple ancestries): 46.9% Other groups, 12.9% United States or American, 7.8% German, 3.7% English, 3.1% Irish (2000).

Economy: Employment by occupation: 5.9% management, 8.9% professional, 27.4% services, 19.3% sales, 4.1% farming, 6.7% construction, 27.8% production (2000).

Income: Per capita income: $10,584 (2007); Median household income: $20,400 (2007); Average household income: $29,146 (2007); Percent of households with income of $100,000 or more: 2.1% (2007); Poverty rate: 30.6% (2000).

Education: Percent of population age 25 and over with: High school diploma (including GED) or higher: 51.6% (2007); Bachelor's degree or higher: 5.4% (2007); Master's degree or higher: 1.5% (2007).

School District(s)

Sumter County School District (PK-12)

  2005-06 Enrollment: 7,157 . . . . (352) 793-2315

Housing: Homeownership rate: 68.0% (2007); Median home value: $89,375 (2007); Median rent: $246 per month (2000); Median age of housing: 20 years (2000).

Safety: Violent crime rate: 164.3 per 10,000 population; Property crime rate: 328.6 per 10,000 population (2006).

Transportation: Commute to work: 96.3% car, 0.0% public transportation, 0.0% walk, 2.6% work from home (2000); Travel time to work: 38.5% less than 15 minutes, 20.2% 15 to 30 minutes, 16.4% 30 to 45 minutes, 10.3% 45 to 60 minutes, 14.5% 60 minutes or more (2000)

WILDWOOD (city). Covers a land area of 5.165 square miles and a water area of 0.003 square miles. Located at 28.85° N. Lat.; 82.03° W. Long. Elevation is 66 feet.

History: Wildwood was named in 1878 by the telegraph operator at a station in the forest who headed his dispatches "Wildwood." The community developed around the Seaboard Air Line railroad yards.

Population: 3,622 (1990); 3,924 (2000); 3,713 (2007); 3,777 (2012 projected); Race: 64.8% White, 32.2% Black, 0.2% Asian, 3.4% Hispanic of any race (2007); Density: 718.8 persons per square mile (2007); Average household size: 2.38 (2007); Median age: 36.6 (2007); Males per 100 females: 83.5 (2007); Marriage status: 15.6% never married, 61.2% now married, 8.7% widowed, 14.6% divorced (2000); Foreign born: 1.9% (2000); Ancestry (includes multiple ancestries): 33.5% Other groups, 12.9% United States or American, 12.7% German, 11.1% English, 7.3% Irish (2000).

Economy: Single-family building permits issued: 60 (2006); Multi-family building permits issued: 18 (2006); Employment by occupation: 6.3% management, 11.3% professional, 20.6% services, 32.6% sales, 1.1% farming, 13.0% construction, 15.1% production (2000).

Income: Per capita income: $13,455 (2007); Median household income: $25,288 (2007); Average household income: $31,632 (2007); Percent of households with income of $100,000 or more: 1.5% (2007); Poverty rate: 21.7% (2000).

Education: Percent of population age 25 and over with: High school diploma (including GED) or higher: 68.1% (2007); Bachelor's degree or higher: 9.0% (2007); Master's degree or higher: 2.6% (2007).

School District(s)

Sumter County School District (PK-12)

  2005-06 Enrollment: 7,157 . . . . (352) 793-2315

Housing: Homeownership rate: 77.7% (2007); Median home value: $61,042 (2007); Median rent: $331 per month (2000); Median age of housing: 16 years (2000).

Safety: Violent crime rate: 203.7 per 10,000 population; Property crime rate: 570.9 per 10,000 population (2006).

Transportation: Commute to work: 95.3% car, 0.5% public transportation, 2.5% walk, 0.9% work from home (2000); Travel time to work: 31.9% less than 15 minutes, 37.5% 15 to 30 minutes, 14.1% 30 to 45 minutes, 11.3% 45 to 60 minutes, 5.2% 60 minutes or more (2000); Amtrak: Service available.

Suwannee County

Located in northern Florida; bounded on the west and south by the Suwannee River and on the south by the Santa Fe River; includes several lakes. Covers a land area of 687.64 square miles, a water area of 4.26 square miles, and is located in the Eastern Time Zone. The county was founded in 1858. County seat is Live Oak.

Weather Station: Live Oak — Elevation: 118 feet

	Jan	Feb	Mar	Apr	May	Jun	Jul	Aug	Sep	Oct	Nov	Dec
High	67	71	77	82	88	92	93	92	90	83	76	69
Low	42	44	50	55	62	69	71	71	68	58	51	44
Precip	5.0	4.0	5.4	3.5	3.3	6.1	6.5	6.6	4.3	3.3	2.4	3.1
Snow	tr	tr	tr	0.0	0.0	0.0	0.0	0.0	0.0	0.0	0.0	0.1

High and Low temperatures in degrees Fahrenheit; Precipitation and Snow in inches

Population: 26,780 (1990); 34,844 (2000); 39,363 (2007); 42,411 (2012 projected); Race: 84.7% White, 11.4% Black, 0.7% Asian, 7.5% Hispanic of any race (2007); Density: 57.2 persons per square mile (2007); Average household size: 2.55 (2007); Median age: 39.9 (2007); Males per 100 females: 96.6 (2007).

Religion: Five largest groups: 34.3% Southern Baptist Convention, 3.1% Catholic Church, 3.0% The United Methodist Church, 2.6% Church of God (Cleveland, Tennessee), 1.5% The Church of Jesus Christ of Latter-day Saints (2000).

Economy: Unemployment rate: 3.9% (11/2007); Total civilian labor force: 17,669 (11/2007); Leading industries: 22.8% manufacturing; 20.3% retail trade; 15.5% health care and social assistance (2005); Farms: 1,054 totaling 170,149 acres (2002); Companies that employ 500 or more persons: 1 (2005); Companies that employ 100 to 499 persons: 6 (2005); Companies that employ less than 100 persons: 687 (2005); Black-owned businesses: n/a (2002); Hispanic-owned businesses: n/a (2002); Asian-owned businesses: n/a (2002); Women-owned businesses: 468 (2002); Retail sales per capita: $8,741 (2007). Single-family building permits issued: 172 (2006); Multi-family building permits issued: 102 (2006).

Income: Per capita income: $17,439 (2007); Median household income: $34,444 (2007); Average household income: $44,098 (2007); Percent of households with income of $100,000 or more: 6.7% (2007); Poverty rate: 17.5% (2005); Bankruptcy rate: 0.78% (2006).

Education: Percent of population age 25 and over with: High school diploma (including GED) or higher: 73.3% (2007); Bachelor's degree or higher: 10.4% (2007); Master's degree or higher: 3.3% (2007).

Housing: Homeownership rate: 81.4% (2007); Median home value: $125,089 (2007); Median rent: $280 per month (2000); Median age of housing: 17 years (2000).

Health: Birth rate: 144.1 per 10,000 population (2006); Death rate: 133.4 per 10,000 population (2006); Age-adjusted cancer mortality rate: 259.1 deaths per 100,000 population (2004); Number of physicians: 2.9 per 10,000 population (2005); Hospital beds: 4.0 per 10,000 population (2004); Hospital admissions: 147.2 per 10,000 population (2004).

Elections: 2004 Presidential election results: 70.6% Bush, 28.6% Kerry, 0.5% Nader, 0.2% Badnarik

National and State Parks: Ichetucknee Springs State Park; Peacock Springs State Park

Additional Information Contacts

Suwannee County Government. (386) 364-3450

City of Live Oak . . . . (386) 362-2276
  http://www.cityofliveoak.org
Live Oak Chamber of Commerce . . . . (386) 362-3071
  http://www.suwanneechamber.com

Suwannee County Communities

BRANFORD (town). Covers a land area of 0.829 square miles and a water area of 0 square miles. Located at 29.96° N. Lat.; 82.92° W. Long. Elevation is 43 feet.

Population: 670 (1990); 695 (2000); 779 (2007); 834 (2012 projected); Race: 86.9% White, 5.4% Black, 0.4% Asian, 16.4% Hispanic of any race (2007); Density: 939.9 persons per square mile (2007); Average household size: 2.55 (2007); Median age: 32.8 (2007); Males per 100 females: 94.3 (2007); Marriage status: 25.8% never married, 43.7% now married, 16.7% widowed, 13.8% divorced (2000); Foreign born: 7.5% (2000); Ancestry (includes multiple ancestries): 21.9% United States or American, 15.9% Other groups, 9.6% Irish, 8.0% German, 5.1% English (2000).

Economy: Employment by occupation: 7.1% management, 13.4% professional, 21.2% services, 19.7% sales, 13.8% farming, 8.6% construction, 16.4% production (2000).

Income: Per capita income: $15,181 (2007); Median household income: $28,804 (2007); Average household income: $38,402 (2007); Percent of households with income of $100,000 or more: 5.2% (2007); Poverty rate: 21.0% (2000).

Education: Percent of population age 25 and over with: High school diploma (including GED) or higher: 63.8% (2007); Bachelor's degree or higher: 10.8% (2007); Master's degree or higher: 3.7% (2007).

School District(s)

Suwannee County School District (PK-12)

  2005-06 Enrollment: 5,834 . . . . (386) 364-2604

Housing: Homeownership rate: 54.4% (2007); Median home value: $112,162 (2007); Median rent: $214 per month (2000); Median age of housing: 29 years (2000).
Newspapers: Branford News (General - Circulation 2,000)
Transportation: Commute to work: 87.9% car, 0.0% public transportation, 10.2% walk, 0.0% work from home (2000); Travel time to work: 40.9% less than 15 minutes, 7.6% 15 to 30 minutes, 31.8% 30 to 45 minutes, 11.4% 45 to 60 minutes, 8.3% 60 minutes or more (2000)

LIVE OAK (city). County seat. Covers a land area of 6.955 square miles and a water area of 0.002 square miles. Located at 30.29° N. Lat.; 82.98° W. Long. Elevation is 105 feet.
History: Live Oak was the location of a large bright-leaf tobacco market, with auction warehouses. The town's name referred to a large live oak tree near the place where the railroad station was later built. Live-oak timber was shipped from here in the 1830's.
Population: 6,346 (1990); 6,480 (2000); 6,906 (2007); 7,205 (2012 projected); Race: 58.4% White, 36.5% Black, 0.9% Asian, 14.2% Hispanic of any race (2007); Density: 992.9 persons per square mile (2007); Average household size: 2.70 (2007); Median age: 34.9 (2007); Males per 100 females: 96.5 (2007); Marriage status: 23.7% never married, 54.0% now married, 9.6% widowed, 12.7% divorced (2000); Foreign born: 6.9% (2000); Ancestry (includes multiple ancestries): 38.6% Other groups, 14.0% United States or American, 5.4% Irish, 5.1% English, 3.3% German (2000).
Economy: Single-family building permits issued: 7 (2006); Multi-family building permits issued: 102 (2006); Employment by occupation: 6.3% management, 15.1% professional, 20.8% services, 22.8% sales, 4.7% farming, 10.4% construction, 19.8% production (2000).
Income: Per capita income: $14,115 (2007); Median household income: $27,813 (2007); Average household income: $37,009 (2007); Percent of households with income of $100,000 or more: 4.9% (2007); Poverty rate: 23.9% (2000).
Education: Percent of population age 25 and over with: High school diploma (including GED) or higher: 68.7% (2007); Bachelor's degree or higher: 12.0% (2007); Master's degree or higher: 3.3% (2007).

School District(s)
Suwannee County School District (PK-12)
    2005-06 Enrollment: 5,834 . . . . (386) 364-2604
Vocational/Technical School(s)
Suwannee-Hamilton Technical Center (Public)
    Fall 2006 Enrollment: 120 . . . . (386) 364-2750
    2006-07 Tuition: $2,593
Housing: Homeownership rate: 65.8% (2007); Median home value: $110,650 (2007); Median rent: $250 per month (2000); Median age of housing: 31 years (2000).
Hospitals: Shands Live Oak (30 beds)
Safety: Violent crime rate: 79.6 per 10,000 population; Property crime rate: 444.7 per 10,000 population (2006).
Newspapers: Suwannee Democrat (General - Circulation 5,400)
Transportation: Commute to work: 95.2% car, 0.0% public transportation, 2.6% walk, 1.5% work from home (2000); Travel time to work: 45.4% less than 15 minutes, 28.2% 15 to 30 minutes, 19.4% 30 to 45 minutes, 2.3% 45 to 60 minutes, 4.8% 60 minutes or more (2000)
Additional Information Contacts
City of Live Oak . . . . (386) 362-2276
    http://www.cityofliveoak.org
Live Oak Chamber of Commerce . . . . (386) 362-3071
    http://www.suwanneechamber.com

MCALPIN (unincorporated postal area, zip code 32062). Covers a land area of 60.398 square miles and a water area of 0.008 square miles. Located at 30.13° N. Lat.; 82.98° W. Long. Elevation is 101 feet.
Population: 1,994 (2000); Race: 92.1% White, 3.7% Black, 0.0% Asian, 5.4% Hispanic of any race (2000); Density: 33.0 persons per square mile (2000); Age: 29.8% under 18, 16.4% over 64 (2000); Marriage status: 21.0% never married, 64.6% now married, 6.8% widowed, 7.6% divorced (2000); Foreign born: 6.3% (2000); Ancestry (includes multiple ancestries): 22.3% United States or American, 13.8% Irish, 11.9% Other groups, 11.5% German, 11.3% English (2000).
Economy: Employment by occupation: 13.5% management, 25.6% professional, 12.9% services, 15.7% sales, 7.1% farming, 13.8% construction, 11.3% production (2000).
Income: Per capita income: $14,305 (2000); Median household income: $32,604 (2000); Poverty rate: 19.2% (2000).

Education: Percent of population age 25 and over with: High school diploma (including GED) or higher: 77.9% (2000); Bachelor's degree or higher: 11.0% (2000).
Housing: Homeownership rate: 89.5% (2000); Median home value: $70,900 (2000); Median rent: $303 per month (2000); Median age of housing: 16 years (2000).
Transportation: Commute to work: 87.2% car, 0.0% public transportation, 6.6% walk, 4.8% work from home (2000); Travel time to work: 18.6% less than 15 minutes, 29.5% 15 to 30 minutes, 28.9% 30 to 45 minutes, 10.2% 45 to 60 minutes, 12.8% 60 minutes or more (2000)

O'BRIEN (unincorporated postal area, zip code 32071). Covers a land area of 108.768 square miles and a water area of 0.007 square miles. Located at 30.03° N. Lat.; 82.94° W. Long. Elevation is 62 feet.
Population: 3,111 (2000); Race: 95.1% White, 3.5% Black, 0.5% Asian, 3.2% Hispanic of any race (2000); Density: 28.6 persons per square mile (2000); Age: 21.5% under 18, 14.0% over 64 (2000); Marriage status: 15.3% never married, 63.5% now married, 5.8% widowed, 15.4% divorced (2000); Foreign born: 3.1% (2000); Ancestry (includes multiple ancestries): 18.7% United States or American, 12.0% Irish, 11.7% Other groups, 11.6% German, 8.5% English (2000).
Economy: Employment by occupation: 9.2% management, 20.8% professional, 14.3% services, 21.2% sales, 4.3% farming, 16.6% construction, 13.6% production (2000).
Income: Per capita income: $16,202 (2000); Median household income: $32,237 (2000); Poverty rate: 11.4% (2000).
Education: Percent of population age 25 and over with: High school diploma (including GED) or higher: 75.2% (2000); Bachelor's degree or higher: 10.1% (2000).
Housing: Homeownership rate: 86.6% (2000); Median home value: $62,900 (2000); Median rent: $340 per month (2000); Median age of housing: 15 years (2000).
Transportation: Commute to work: 92.3% car, 0.0% public transportation, 0.0% walk, 6.4% work from home (2000); Travel time to work: 16.7% less than 15 minutes, 25.9% 15 to 30 minutes, 29.3% 30 to 45 minutes, 12.6% 45 to 60 minutes, 15.4% 60 minutes or more (2000)

WELLBORN (unincorporated postal area, zip code 32094). Covers a land area of 56.035 square miles and a water area of 0.469 square miles. Located at 30.20° N. Lat.; 82.81° W. Long. Elevation is 195 feet.
Population: 2,597 (2000); Race: 89.7% White, 5.1% Black, 0.0% Asian, 2.3% Hispanic of any race (2000); Density: 46.3 persons per square mile (2000); Age: 20.6% under 18, 16.1% over 64 (2000); Marriage status: 15.2% never married, 66.4% now married, 10.8% widowed, 7.6% divorced (2000); Foreign born: 1.8% (2000); Ancestry (includes multiple ancestries): 22.7% United States or American, 19.9% Other groups, 11.8% English, 9.3% German, 6.1% Irish (2000).
Economy: Employment by occupation: 7.2% management, 17.4% professional, 15.1% services, 22.3% sales, 4.0% farming, 20.9% construction, 13.1% production (2000).
Income: Per capita income: $16,257 (2000); Median household income: $31,745 (2000); Poverty rate: 16.7% (2000).
Education: Percent of population age 25 and over with: High school diploma (including GED) or higher: 75.2% (2000); Bachelor's degree or higher: 6.9% (2000).
Housing: Homeownership rate: 89.7% (2000); Median home value: $84,700 (2000); Median rent: $138 per month (2000); Median age of housing: 17 years (2000).
Transportation: Commute to work: 94.2% car, 0.0% public transportation, 1.1% walk, 3.1% work from home (2000); Travel time to work: 16.3% less than 15 minutes, 36.7% 15 to 30 minutes, 27.9% 30 to 45 minutes, 10.0% 45 to 60 minutes, 9.0% 60 minutes or more (2000)

Taylor County

Located in northern Florida; bounded on the south by the Gulf of Mexico, and on the west by the Aucilla River; includes many small lakes. Covers a land area of 1,041.91 square miles, a water area of 190.10 square miles, and is located in the Eastern Time Zone. The county was founded in 1856. County seat is Perry.

Weather Station: Perry   Elevation: 42 feet

	Jan	Feb	Mar	Apr	May	Jun	Jul	Aug	Sep	Oct	Nov	Dec
High	67	70	76	82	88	91	93	92	90	84	76	70
Low	41	43	49	54	62	68	71	70	67	57	49	43
Precip	4.9	4.0	5.6	3.4	3.5	6.0	8.5	8.9	5.0	3.2	2.7	3.4
Snow	tr	0.0	0.0	0.0	0.0	0.0	0.0	0.0	0.0	0.0	0.0	0.0

High and Low temperatures in degrees Fahrenheit; Precipitation and Snow in inches

Population: 17,117 (1990); 19,256 (2000); 20,808 (2007); 22,507 (2012 projected); Race: 78.0% White, 19.0% Black, 0.5% Asian, 2.0% Hispanic of any race (2007); Density: 20.0 persons per square mile (2007); Average household size: 2.64 (2007); Median age: 38.8 (2007); Males per 100 females: 109.6 (2007).

Religion: Five largest groups: 34.0% Southern Baptist Convention, 3.3% The United Methodist Church, 1.9% Catholic Church, 1.8% Churches of Christ, 1.6% Church of God (Cleveland, Tennessee) (2000).

Economy: Unemployment rate: 4.5% (11/2007); Total civilian labor force: 9,068 (11/2007); Leading industries: 32.0% manufacturing; 19.4% retail trade; 14.1% health care and social assistance (2005); Farms: 101 totaling 53,720 acres (2002); Companies that employ 500 or more persons: 1 (2005); Companies that employ 100 to 499 persons: 8 (2005); Companies that employ less than 100 persons: 417 (2005); Black-owned businesses: n/a (2002); Hispanic-owned businesses: n/a (2002); Asian-owned businesses: n/a (2002); Women-owned businesses: n/a (2002); Retail sales per capita: $13,877 (2007). Single-family building permits issued: 75 (2006); Multi-family building permits issued: 0 (2006).

Income: Per capita income: $18,210 (2007); Median household income: $34,808 (2007); Average household income: $44,726 (2007); Percent of households with income of $100,000 or more: 8.3% (2007); Poverty rate: 18.4% (2005); Bankruptcy rate: 1.11% (2006).

Education: Percent of population age 25 and over with: High school diploma (including GED) or higher: 69.9% (2007); Bachelor's degree or higher: 8.8% (2007); Master's degree or higher: 3.6% (2007).

Housing: Homeownership rate: 80.2% (2007); Median home value: $116,429 (2007); Median rent: $263 per month (2000); Median age of housing: 21 years (2000).

Health: Birth rate: 124.0 per 10,000 population (2006); Death rate: 113.4 per 10,000 population (2006); Age-adjusted cancer mortality rate: 239.5 deaths per 100,000 population (2004); Number of physicians: 9.2 per 10,000 population (2005); Hospital beds: 24.9 per 10,000 population (2004); Hospital admissions: 1,156.8 per 10,000 population (2004).

Elections: 2004 Presidential election results: 63.7% Bush, 35.5% Kerry, 0.5% Nader, 0.1% Badnarik

National and State Parks: Econfina River State Park; Forest Capital Museum State Park

Additional Information Contacts
Taylor County Government . . . . (850) 838-3500

City of Perry . . . . (850) 584-7940
Perry Chamber of Commerce . . . . (850) 584-5366
    http://www.taylorcountychamber.com

Taylor County Communities

PERRY (city). County seat. Covers a land area of 9.287 square miles and a water area of 0 square miles. Located at 30.11° N. Lat.; 83.58° W. Long. Elevation is 46 feet.

History: Perry developed as a lumber town with sawmills along the railroad sidings. The post office was established in 1869. Prior to that the community was called Rosehead.

Population: 7,151 (1990); 6,847 (2000); 7,076 (2007); 7,346 (2012 projected); Race: 60.0% White, 37.0% Black, 0.6% Asian, 2.2% Hispanic of any race (2007); Density: 761.9 persons per square mile (2007); Average household size: 2.53 (2007); Median age: 35.4 (2007); Males per 100 females: 93.0 (2007); Marriage status: 28.1% never married, 49.1% now married, 9.2% widowed, 13.7% divorced (2000); Foreign born: 1.3% (2000); Ancestry (includes multiple ancestries): 40.2% Other groups, 10.3% United States or American, 7.3% Irish, 5.6% German, 5.4% English (2000).

Economy: Single-family building permits issued: 17 (2006); Multi-family building permits issued: 0 (2006); Employment by occupation: 9.1% management, 10.2% professional, 19.7% services, 22.1% sales, 4.0% farming, 10.1% construction, 24.8% production (2000).

Income: Per capita income: $15,650 (2007); Median household income: $30,407 (2007); Average household income: $39,281 (2007); Percent of

households with income of $100,000 or more: 7.5% (2007); Poverty rate: 28.0% (2000).

Education: Percent of population age 25 and over with: High school diploma (including GED) or higher: 67.4% (2007); Bachelor's degree or higher: 9.7% (2007); Master's degree or higher: 4.2% (2007).

School District(s)
Taylor County School District (PK-12)
    2005-06 Enrollment: 3,501 . . . . (850) 838-2500
Two-year College(s)
Taylor Technical Institute (Public)
    Fall 2006 Enrollment: 326 . . . . (850) 838-2545
    2006-07 Tuition: In-state $1,624; Out-of-state $6,439

Housing: Homeownership rate: 67.5% (2007); Median home value: $119,485 (2007); Median rent: $233 per month (2000); Median age of housing: 32 years (2000).

Hospitals: Doctors Memorial Hospital (48 beds)

Safety: Violent crime rate: 179.6 per 10,000 population; Property crime rate: 242.4 per 10,000 population (2006).

Newspapers: Perry News-Herald (General - Circulation 5,200); Taco Times (General - Circulation 5,200)

Transportation: Commute to work: 92.1% car, 0.0% public transportation, 3.0% walk, 1.3% work from home (2000); Travel time to work: 63.8% less than 15 minutes, 22.2% 15 to 30 minutes, 6.8% 30 to 45 minutes, 1.3% 45 to 60 minutes, 5.8% 60 minutes or more (2000)

Airports: Perry-Foley

Additional Information Contacts
City of Perry . . . . (850) 584-7940
Perry Chamber of Commerce . . . . (850) 584-5366
    http://www.taylorcountychamber.com

SALEM (unincorporated postal area, zip code 32356). Covers a land area of 7.431 square miles and a water area of 0 square miles. Located at 29.90° N. Lat.; 83.42° W. Long. Elevation is 41 feet.

Population: 95 (2000); Race: 100.0% White, 0.0% Black, 0.0% Asian, 0.0% Hispanic of any race (2000); Density: 12.8 persons per square mile (2000); Age: 9.3% under 18, 14.7% over 64 (2000); Marriage status: 28.0% never married, 65.3% now married, 6.7% widowed, 0.0% divorced (2000); Foreign born: 0.0% (2000); Ancestry (includes multiple ancestries): 16.0% United States or American, 8.0% Scottish, 6.7% Other groups (2000).

Economy: Employment by occupation: 13.3% management, 0.0% professional, 31.1% services, 11.1% sales, 0.0% farming, 13.3% construction, 31.1% production (2000).

Income: Per capita income: $20,405 (2000); Median household income: $66,406 (2000); Poverty rate: 6.7% (2000).

Education: Percent of population age 25 and over with: High school diploma (including GED) or higher: 88.9% (2000); Bachelor's degree or higher: 11.1% (2000).

Housing: Homeownership rate: 100.0% (2000); Median home value: $n/a (2000); Median rent: $n/a per month (2000); Median age of housing: 29 years (2000).

Transportation: Commute to work: 86.7% car, 0.0% public transportation, 0.0% walk, 13.3% work from home (2000); Travel time to work: 0.0% less than 15 minutes, 35.9% 15 to 30 minutes, 48.7% 30 to 45 minutes, 0.0% 45 to 60 minutes, 15.4% 60 minutes or more (2000)

STEINHATCHEE (unincorporated postal area, zip code 32359). Aka Stephensville. Covers a land area of 88.776 square miles and a water area of 0.179 square miles. Located at 29.67° N. Lat.; 83.38° W. Long. Elevation is 15 feet.

Population: 1,453 (2000); Race: 98.7% White, 1.3% Black, 0.0% Asian, 0.4% Hispanic of any race (2000); Density: 16.4 persons per square mile (2000); Age: 15.3% under 18, 26.3% over 64 (2000); Marriage status: 11.5% never married, 63.4% now married, 12.1% widowed, 13.1% divorced (2000); Foreign born: 3.3% (2000); Ancestry (includes multiple ancestries): 19.9% United States or American, 13.5% Irish, 12.9% English, 10.4% German, 6.5% Other groups (2000).

Economy: Employment by occupation: 6.1% management, 15.9% professional, 28.3% services, 13.3% sales, 10.4% farming, 13.3% construction, 12.7% production (2000).

Income: Per capita income: $18,536 (2000); Median household income: $26,188 (2000); Poverty rate: 12.0% (2000).

Education: Percent of population age 25 and over with: High school diploma (including GED) or higher: 72.4% (2000); Bachelor's degree or higher: 12.1% (2000).

Taylor County School District (PK-12)

2005-06 Enrollment: 3,501 . . . . (850) 838-2500

Housing: Homeownership rate: 93.3% (2000); Median home value: $80,000 (2000); Median rent: $244 per month (2000); Median age of housing: 18 years (2000).

Transportation: Commute to work: 80.8% car, 2.7% public transportation, 7.2% walk, 4.4% work from home (2000); Travel time to work: 44.2% less than 15 minutes, 17.7% 15 to 30 minutes, 12.8% 30 to 45 minutes, 12.2% 45 to 60 minutes, 13.1% 60 minutes or more (2000)

Union County

Located in northern Florida; includes several lakes. Covers a land area of 240.29 square miles, a water area of 9.42 square miles, and is located in the Eastern Time Zone. The county was founded in 1921. County seat is Lake Butler.

Population: 10,252 (1990); 13,442 (2000); 15,402 (2007); 16,845 (2012 projected); Race: 73.1% White, 23.3% Black, 0.4% Asian, 4.1% Hispanic of any race (2007); Density: 64.1 persons per square mile (2007); Average household size: 4.15 (2007); Median age: 36.4 (2007); Males per 100 females: 203.0 (2007).

Religion: Five largest groups: 19.5% Southern Baptist Convention, 2.8% The Church of Jesus Christ of Latter-day Saints, 2.2% Independent, Non-Charismatic Churches, 1.6% Christian Churches and Churches of Christ, 1.5% National Association of Free Wi

Economy: Unemployment rate: 3.3% (11/2007); Total civilian labor force: 5,274 (11/2007); Leading industries: 25.5% health care and social assistance; 9.7% retail trade; 7.8% accommodation & food services (2005); Farms: 275 totaling 59,635 acres (2002); Companies that employ 500 or more persons: 0 (2005); Companies that employ 100 to 499 persons: 3 (2005); Companies that employ less than 100 persons: 135 (2005); Black-owned businesses: n/a (2002); Hispanic-owned businesses: n/a (2002); Asian-owned businesses: n/a (2002); Women-owned businesses: n/a (2002); Retail sales per capita: $5,242 (2007). Single-family building permits issued: 71 (2006); Multi-family building permits issued: 0 (2006).

Income: Per capita income: $14,019 (2007); Median household income: $39,811 (2007); Average household income: $48,398 (2007); Percent of households with income of $100,000 or more: 7.3% (2007); Poverty rate: 20.3% (2005); Bankruptcy rate: 1.28% (2006).

Education: Percent of population age 25 and over with: High school diploma (including GED) or higher: 72.5% (2007); Bachelor's degree or higher: 7.5% (2007); Master's degree or higher: 2.7% (2007).

Housing: Homeownership rate: 75.1% (2007); Median home value: $124,550 (2007); Median rent: $278 per month (2000); Median age of housing: 18 years (2000).

Health: Birth rate: 107.1 per 10,000 population (2006); Death rate: 86.9 per 10,000 population (2006); Age-adjusted cancer mortality rate: 450.1 deaths per 100,000 population (2004); Number of physicians: 10.1 per 10,000 population (2005); Hospital beds: 140.3 per 10,000 population (2004); Hospital admissions: 3,834.1 per 10,000 population (2004).

Elections: 2004 Presidential election results: 72.6% Bush, 26.8% Kerry, 0.3% Nader, 0.0% Badnarik

National and State Parks: Olustee Battlefield Historic State Park

Additional Information Contacts

Union County Government . . . . (386) 496-4241

Union County Communities

LAKE BUTLER (city). County seat. Covers a land area of 1.719 square miles and a water area of 0.109 square miles. Located at 30.02° N. Lat.; 82.34° W. Long. Elevation is 141 feet.

History: The town of Lake Butler was named for Colonel Robert Butler who accepted East Florida from Spain in 1821. The principal early industry was the production of naval stores (rosin and turpentine originally used for calking ships).

Population: 2,116 (1990); 1,927 (2000); 2,007 (2007); 2,010 (2012 projected); Race: 63.0% White, 32.4% Black, 1.8% Asian, 4.3% Hispanic of any race (2007); Density: 1,167.8 persons per square mile (2007); Average household size: 2.62 (2007); Median age: 27.2 (2007); Males per 100 females: 85.3 (2007); Marriage status: 26.4% never married, 50.3% now married, 8.7% widowed, 14.6% divorced (2000); Foreign born: 3.1% (2000); Ancestry (includes multiple ancestries): 30.0% Other groups,

29.5% United States or American, 5.4% German, 5.0% Irish, 5.0% English (2000).

Economy: Employment by occupation: 9.5% management, 13.4% professional, 30.5% services, 23.1% sales, 2.8% farming, 6.1% construction, 14.5% production (2000).

Income: Per capita income: $18,431 (2007); Median household income: $32,254 (2007); Average household income: $47,718 (2007); Percent of households with income of $100,000 or more: 9.1% (2007); Poverty rate: 25.6% (2000).

Education: Percent of population age 25 and over with: High school diploma (including GED) or higher: 71.8% (2007); Bachelor's degree or higher: 9.3% (2007); Master's degree or higher: 4.8% (2007).

Union County School District (PK-12)

2005-06 Enrollment: 2,204 . . . . (386) 496-2045

Housing: Homeownership rate: 51.8% (2007); Median home value: $126,786 (2007); Median rent: $266 per month (2000); Median age of housing: 25 years (2000).

Hospitals: Lake Butler Hospital (27 beds); North Florida Reception Center Hospital (153 beds)

Newspapers: Union County Times (General - Circulation 2,500)

Transportation: Commute to work: 93.2% car, 0.0% public transportation, 2.5% walk, 3.2% work from home (2000); Travel time to work: 46.4% less than 15 minutes, 15.7% 15 to 30 minutes, 19.6% 30 to 45 minutes, 9.3% 45 to 60 minutes, 9.0% 60 minutes or more (2000)

RAIFORD (town). Covers a land area of 0.524 square miles and a water area of 0 square miles. Located at 30.06° N. Lat.; 82.23° W. Long. Elevation is 131 feet.

Population: 198 (1990); 187 (2000); 198 (2007); 197 (2012 projected); Race: 80.8% White, 17.7% Black, 0.0% Asian, 0.0% Hispanic of any race (2007); Density: 377.6 persons per square mile (2007); Average household size: 2.71 (2007); Median age: 30.4 (2007); Males per 100 females: 83.3 (2007); Marriage status: 23.1% never married, 62.7% now married, 6.7% widowed, 7.5% divorced (2000); Foreign born: 1.0% (2000); Ancestry (includes multiple ancestries): 31.3% United States or American, 16.2% Other groups, 12.1% German, 8.1% Irish, 6.6% English (2000).

Economy: Employment by occupation: 15.3% management, 18.6% professional, 30.5% services, 11.9% sales, 0.0% farming, 10.2% construction, 13.6% production (2000).

Income: Per capita income: $19,634 (2007); Median household income: $34,643 (2007); Average household income: $53,253 (2007); Percent of households with income of $100,000 or more: 6.8% (2007); Poverty rate: 36.4% (2000).

Education: Percent of population age 25 and over with: High school diploma (including GED) or higher: 58.6% (2007); Bachelor's degree or higher: 8.1% (2007); Master's degree or higher: 0.0% (2007).

Bradford County School District (PK-12)

2005-06 Enrollment: 3,831 . . . . (904) 966-6018

Union County School District (PK-12)

2005-06 Enrollment: 2,204 . . . . (386) 496-2045

Housing: Homeownership rate: 78.1% (2007); Median home value: $108,594 (2007); Median rent: $240 per month (2000); Median age of housing: 34 years (2000).

Transportation: Commute to work: 93.4% car, 0.0% public transportation, 3.3% walk, 0.0% work from home (2000); Travel time to work: 29.5% less than 15 minutes, 42.6% 15 to 30 minutes, 14.8% 30 to 45 minutes, 6.6% 45 to 60 minutes, 6.6% 60 minutes or more (2000)

WORTHINGTON SPRINGS (town). Aka Worthington. Covers a land area of 0.360 square miles and a water area of 0 square miles. Located at 29.93° N. Lat.; 82.42° W. Long. Elevation is 118 feet.

Population: 178 (1990); 193 (2000); 232 (2007); 258 (2012 projected); Race: 85.8% White, 8.6% Black, 0.0% Asian, 3.0% Hispanic of any race (2007); Density: 645.1 persons per square mile (2007); Average household size: 2.67 (2007); Median age: 32.1 (2007); Males per 100 females: 95.0 (2007); Marriage status: 16.9% never married, 61.3% now married, 7.3% widowed, 14.5% divorced (2000); Foreign born: 0.0% (2000); Ancestry (includes multiple ancestries): 28.3% United States or American, 13.9% Other groups, 11.4% Irish, 11.4% English, 4.2% European (2000).

Economy: Employment by occupation: 9.4% management, 14.1% professional, 23.4% services, 23.4% sales, 0.0% farming, 20.3% construction, 9.4% production (2000).

Income: Per capita income: $14,806 (2007); Median household income: $26,944 (2007); Average household income: $39,483 (2007); Percent of households with income of $100,000 or more: 11.5% (2007); Poverty rate: 22.3% (2000).

Education: Percent of population age 25 and over with: High school diploma (including GED) or higher: 65.5% (2007); Bachelor's degree or higher: 16.5% (2007); Master's degree or higher: 8.6% (2007).

Housing: Homeownership rate: 69.0% (2007); Median home value: $96,000 (2007); Median rent: $317 per month (2000); Median age of housing: 23 years (2000).

Transportation: Commute to work: 85.9% car, 0.0% public transportation, 6.3% walk, 0.0% work from home (2000); Travel time to work: 39.1% less than 15 minutes, 39.1% 15 to 30 minutes, 15.6% 30 to 45 minutes, 0.0% 45 to 60 minutes, 6.3% 60 minutes or more (2000)

Volusia County

Located in northeastern Florida; bounded on the west by the St. Johns River, and on the east by the Atlantic Ocean; lowland area, with many lakes and lagoons, including Mosquito Lagoon. Covers a land area of 1,103.25 square miles, a water area of 329.19 square miles, and is located in the Eastern Time Zone. The county was founded in 1854. County seat is De Land.

Volusia County is part of the Deltona-Daytona Beach-Ormond Beach, FL Metropolitan Statistical Area. The entire metro area includes: Volusia County, FL

Weather Station: Daytona Beach Regional Airport   Elevation: 26 feet

	Jan	Feb	Mar	Apr	May	Jun	Jul	Aug	Sep	Oct	Nov	Dec
High	69	70	75	80	85	88	90	90	87	82	76	71
Low	48	49	54	59	65	71	73	73	72	66	57	51
Precip	3.2	2.8	3.7	2.6	3.2	5.7	5.1	6.1	6.3	4.6	3.0	2.7
Snow	tr	0.0	tr	0.0	0.0	tr	0.0	tr	0.0	0.0	0.0	tr

High and Low temperatures in degrees Fahrenheit; Precipitation and Snow in inches

Population: 370,712 (1990); 443,343 (2000); 505,685 (2007); 551,752 (2012 projected); Race: 84.1% White, 9.8% Black, 1.3% Asian, 9.6% Hispanic of any race (2007); Density: 458.4 persons per square mile (2007); Average household size: 2.39 (2007); Median age: 43.0 (2007); Males per 100 females: 95.4 (2007).

Religion: Five largest groups: 15.2% Catholic Church, 6.8% Southern Baptist Convention, 3.1% The United Methodist Church, 1.7% Jewish Estimate, 1.3% Presbyterian Church (U.S.A.) (2000).

Economy: Unemployment rate: 4.4% (11/2007); Total civilian labor force: 254,388 (11/2007); Leading industries: 18.8% retail trade; 15.9% health care and social assistance; 13.7% accommodation & food services (2005); Farms: 1,114 totaling 93,842 acres (2002); Companies that employ 500 or more persons: 18 (2005); Companies that employ 100 to 499 persons: 193 (2005); Companies that employ less than 100 persons: 12,764 (2005); Black-owned businesses: 868 (2002); Hispanic-owned businesses: 1,513 (2002); Asian-owned businesses: 598 (2002); Women-owned businesses: 10,202 (2002); Retail sales per capita: $13,796 (2007). Single-family building permits issued: 2,906 (2006); Multi-family building permits issued: 909 (2006).

Income: Per capita income: $23,375 (2007); Median household income: $41,584 (2007); Average household income: $55,137 (2007); Percent of households with income of $100,000 or more: 11.4% (2007); Poverty rate: 11.6% (2005); Bankruptcy rate: 1.68% (2006).

Taxes: Total county taxes per capita: $423 (2005); County property taxes per capita: $352 (2005).

Education: Percent of population age 25 and over with: High school diploma (including GED) or higher: 82.4% (2007); Bachelor's degree or higher: 17.9% (2007); Master's degree or higher: 6.1% (2007).

Housing: Homeownership rate: 76.5% (2007); Median home value: $165,442 (2007); Median rent: $498 per month (2000); Median age of housing: 21 years (2000).

Health: Birth rate: 100.3 per 10,000 population (2006); Death rate: 129.7 per 10,000 population (2006); Age-adjusted cancer mortality rate: 213.5 deaths per 100,000 population (2004); Air Quality Index: 91.8% good, 8.2% moderate, 0.0% unhealthy for sensitive individuals, 0.0% unhealthy (percent of days in 2006); Number of physicians: 18.8 per 10,000 population (2005); Hospital beds: 29.4 per 10,000 population (2004); Hospital admissions: 1,367.3 per 10,000 population (2004).

Elections: 2004 Presidential election results: 48.9% Bush, 50.5% Kerry, 0.4% Nader, 0.1% Badnarik

National and State Parks: Addison Blockhouse Historic State Park; Blue Spring State Park; Bulow Creek State Park; De Leon Springs State Park; Haw Creek Preserve State Park; Lake Woodruff National Wildlife Refuge; New Smyrna Sugar Mill Ruins State Historic Site; North Peninsula State Park; Ormond Tomb State Park; Tomoka State Park

Additional Information Contacts

Volusia County Government . . . . (386) 736-5920
  http://www.volusia.org
City of De Bary. . . . . (386) 668-2040
  http://debary.org
City of Edgewater. . . . . (386) 424-2400
  http://www.cityofedgewater.org
City of Orange City. . . . . (386) 775-5400
  http://www.ci.orange-city.fl.us
City of Port Orange . . . . (386) 506-5500
  http://www.port-orange.org
City of South Daytona . . . . (386) 322-3000
  http://www.southdaytona.org
Daytona Beach Chamber of Commerce . . . . (904) 255-0981
  http://www.daytonachamber.com
Daytona Beach Shores Chamber . . . . (904) 761-7163
  http://www.pschamber.com
De Land Chamber of Commerce . . . . (904) 734-4331
  http://www.delandchamber.org
Deltona Chamber of Commerce . . . . (386) 775-2793
  http://www.chamberofcommerceofwestvolusia.com
New Smyrna Beach Chamber of Commerce. . . . . (904) 428-2449
  http://www.sevchamber.com
Orange City Chamber of Commerce . . . . (386) 775-2793
  http://www.chamberofcommerceofwestvolusia.com
Ormond Beach Chamber of Commerce . . . . (386) 677-3454
  http://www.ormondchamber.com

Volusia County Communities

DAYTONA BEACH (city). Covers a land area of 58.677 square miles and a water area of 6.254 square miles. Located at 29.20° N. Lat.; 81.03° W. Long. Elevation is 13 feet.

History: The town of Daytona Beach was laid out about 1870 in an area along the Halifax River (a tidewater lagoon on the Atlantic Ocean) where American colonists from Georgia had established plantations. The town was platted by Mathias Day, who named it Daytona. Transportation was a problem until 1887 when a bridge across the Halifax River made access to the ocean peninsula easier, and a bridge over the Tomoka River allowed the railroad to enter Daytona. Daytona developed as a resort, with some citrus industry. In 1926 the communities of Seabreeze and Daytona Beach, on the east shore of the peninsula, united with Daytona under the name of Daytona Beach. By this time, the Beach had become a motor speedway, with the cream of world racers breaking speed records here.

Population: 62,186 (1990); 64,112 (2000); 64,929 (2007); 66,404 (2012 projected); Race: 59.2% White, 34.4% Black, 2.4% Asian, 4.7% Hispanic of any race (2007); Density: 1,106.6 persons per square mile (2007); Average household size: 2.22 (2007); Median age: 37.5 (2007); Males per 100 females: 101.8 (2007); Marriage status: 34.7% never married, 41.9% now married, 9.6% widowed, 13.8% divorced (2000); Foreign born: 7.7% (2000); Ancestry (includes multiple ancestries): 33.1% Other groups, 11.0% German, 10.4% Irish, 8.3% English, 5.9% Italian (2000).

Economy: Unemployment rate: 4.5% (11/2007); Total civilian labor force: 33,649 (11/2007); Single-family building permits issued: 363 (2006); Multi-family building permits issued: 10 (2006); Employment by occupation: 8.9% management, 17.2% professional, 23.3% services, 29.4% sales, 0.2% farming, 8.4% construction, 12.6% production (2000).

Income: Per capita income: $19,666 (2007); Median household income: $29,044 (2007); Average household income: $42,353 (2007); Percent of households with income of $100,000 or more: 7.6% (2007); Poverty rate: 23.6% (2000).

Taxes: Total city taxes per capita: $621 (2005); City property taxes per capita: $325 (2005).

Education: Percent of population age 25 and over with: High school diploma (including GED) or higher: 80.6% (2007); Bachelor's degree or higher: 19.5% (2007); Master's degree or higher: 6.4% (2007).

School District(s)
Flagler County School District (PK-12)
  2005-06 Enrollment: 9,698 . . . . (386) 437-7526

Volusia County School District (PK-12)
   2005-06 Enrollment: 65,281 . . . . (386) 734-7190
Four-year College(s)
Bethune Cookman College (Private, Not-for-profit, Historically black, United Methodist)
   Fall 2006 Enrollment: 3,111. . . . . (386) 481-2000
   2006-07 Tuition: In-state $11,792; Out-of-state $11,792
Daytona Beach Community College (Public)
   Fall 2006 Enrollment: 12,064. (386) 506-3000
   2006-07 Tuition: In-state $2,103; Out-of-state $7,954
Embry Riddle Aeronautical University-Daytona Beach (Private, Not-for-profit)
   Fall 2006 Enrollment: 4,863. . . . . (800) 222-3728
   2006-07 Tuition: In-state $25,490; Out-of-state $25,490
Embry Riddle Aeronautical University-Worldwide (Private, Not-for-profit)
   Fall 2006 Enrollment: 15,570. (800) 522-6787
   2006-07 Tuition: In-state $4,674; Out-of-state $4,674
Housing: Homeownership rate: 48.2% (2007); Median home value: $149,445 (2007); Median rent: $460 per month (2000); Median age of housing: 30 years (2000).
Hospitals: Halifax Medical Center (764 beds)
Safety: Violent crime rate: 136.8 per 10,000 population; Property crime rate: 783.4 per 10,000 population (2006).
Newspapers: Daytona Times (Black - Circulation 15,000); The Daytona Beach News-Journal (Circulation 107,251)
Transportation: Commute to work: 85.2% car, 3.8% public transportation, 5.7% walk, 2.1% work from home (2000); Travel time to work: 42.4% less than 15 minutes, 40.0% 15 to 30 minutes, 9.7% 30 to 45 minutes, 2.4% 45 to 60 minutes, 5.5% 60 minutes or more (2000); Amtrak: Service available.
Airports: Daytona Beach International (primary service)
Additional Information Contacts
Daytona Beach Chamber of Commerce . . . . (904) 255-0981
   http://www.daytonachamber.com
Daytona Beach Shores Chamber . . . . (904) 761-7163
   http://www.pschamber.com

DAYTONA BEACH SHORES (city). Aka Cottage Colony. Covers a land area of 0.910 square miles and a water area of 0.027 square miles. Located at 29.17° N. Lat.; 80.98° W. Long. Elevation is 16 feet.
Population: 2,813 (1990); 4,299 (2000); 5,243 (2007); 5,892 (2012 projected); Race: 95.6% White, 1.0% Black, 2.0% Asian, 1.3% Hispanic of any race (2007); Density: 5,759.1 persons per square mile (2007); Average household size: 1.74 (2007); Median age: 65.1 (2007); Males per 100 females: 90.2 (2007); Marriage status: 11.4% never married, 64.9% now married, 11.3% widowed, 12.5% divorced (2000); Foreign born: 13.6% (2000); Ancestry (includes multiple ancestries): 19.9% German, 17.8% English, 13.6% Irish, 8.9% Italian, 7.2% United States or American (2000).
Economy: Single-family building permits issued: 1 (2006); Multi-family building permits issued: 161 (2006); Employment by occupation: 20.8% management, 12.8% professional, 17.4% services, 35.9% sales, 0.8% farming, 6.2% construction, 6.1% production (2000).
Income: Per capita income: $41,360 (2007); Median household income: $50,018 (2007); Average household income: $72,164 (2007); Percent of households with income of $100,000 or more: 20.7% (2007); Poverty rate: 6.8% (2000).
Education: Percent of population age 25 and over with: High school diploma (including GED) or higher: 89.5% (2007); Bachelor's degree or higher: 24.9% (2007); Master's degree or higher: 9.0% (2007).
Housing: Homeownership rate: 80.3% (2007); Median home value: $269,782 (2007); Median rent: $731 per month (2000); Median age of housing: 15 years (2000).
Safety: Violent crime rate: 59.2 per 10,000 population; Property crime rate: 577.8 per 10,000 population (2006).
Transportation: Commute to work: 73.0% car, 0.7% public transportation, 10.9% walk, 13.9% work from home (2000); Travel time to work: 33.6% less than 15 minutes, 44.1% 15 to 30 minutes, 14.6% 30 to 45 minutes, 2.3% 45 to 60 minutes, 5.4% 60 minutes or more (2000)

DE BARY (city). Covers a land area of 18.223 square miles and a water area of 3.217 square miles. Located at 28.88° N. Lat.; 81.31° W. Long. Elevation is 72 feet.
Population: 9,671 (1990); 15,559 (2000); 18,906 (2007); 21,263 (2012 projected); Race: 93.1% White, 2.7% Black, 1.6% Asian, 5.9% Hispanic of any race (2007); Density: 1,037.5 persons per square mile (2007); Average household size: 2.42 (2007); Median age: 46.1 (2007); Males per 100

females: 93.4 (2007); Marriage status: 15.8% never married, 65.3% now married, 9.5% widowed, 9.5% divorced (2000); Foreign born: 5.0% (2000); Ancestry (includes multiple ancestries): 19.0% German, 15.3% English, 15.2% Irish, 10.5% Other groups, 10.4% United States or American (2000).
Economy: Employment by occupation: 15.6% management, 16.7% professional, 14.5% services, 29.8% sales, 0.0% farming, 13.1% construction, 10.4% production (2000).
Income: Per capita income: $27,726 (2007); Median household income: $52,968 (2007); Average household income: $67,005 (2007); Percent of households with income of $100,000 or more: 17.4% (2007); Poverty rate: 6.9% (2000).
Education: Percent of population age 25 and over with: High school diploma (including GED) or higher: 82.8% (2007); Bachelor's degree or higher: 17.8% (2007); Master's degree or higher: 5.6% (2007).
Housing: Homeownership rate: 88.1% (2007); Median home value: $172,183 (2007); Median rent: $524 per month (2000); Median age of housing: 16 years (2000).
Transportation: Commute to work: 94.1% car, 0.5% public transportation, 0.3% walk, 3.8% work from home (2000); Travel time to work: 17.7% less than 15 minutes, 31.5% 15 to 30 minutes, 27.0% 30 to 45 minutes, 12.1% 45 to 60 minutes, 11.7% 60 minutes or more (2000)
Additional Information Contacts
City of De Bary . . . . (386) 668-2040
   http://debary.org

DE LAND (city). County seat. Covers a land area of 15.871 square miles and a water area of 0.186 square miles. Located at 29.02° N. Lat.; 81.30° W. Long. Elevation is 39 feet.
History: De Land was founded in 1876 by Henry A. DeLand, a baking powder manufacturer, who planted trees along all the proposed streets. DeLand also founded Stetson University (first called DeLand University) in 1886, with the financial backing of John B. Stetson, the hat manufacturer. Lue Gim Gong, known as the Luther Burbank of Florida, settled here in 1886 and gained recognition as a citrus culturist.
Population: 17,979 (1990); 20,904 (2000); 24,637 (2007); 27,183 (2012 projected); Race: 72.0% White, 19.8% Black, 1.1% Asian, 13.4% Hispanic of any race (2007); Density: 1,552.3 persons per square mile (2007); Average household size: 2.50 (2007); Median age: 35.9 (2007); Males per 100 females: 86.0 (2007); Marriage status: 23.2% never married, 51.7% now married, 13.0% widowed, 12.0% divorced (2000); Foreign born: 7.3% (2000); Ancestry (includes multiple ancestries): 27.7% Other groups, 12.1% German, 10.4% Irish, 10.2% English, 7.0% United States or American (2000).
Economy: Single-family building permits issued: 458 (2006); Multi-family building permits issued: 32 (2006); Employment by occupation: 10.5% management, 17.6% professional, 18.9% services, 24.6% sales, 2.0% farming, 10.8% construction, 15.6% production (2000).
Income: Per capita income: $19,102 (2007); Median household income: $34,097 (2007); Average household income: $44,938 (2007); Percent of households with income of $100,000 or more: 7.2% (2007); Poverty rate: 19.0% (2000).
Education: Percent of population age 25 and over with: High school diploma (including GED) or higher: 78.1% (2007); Bachelor's degree or higher: 18.5% (2007); Master's degree or higher: 8.0% (2007).
School District(s)
Volusia County School District (PK-12)
   2005-06 Enrollment: 65,281 . . . . (386) 734-7190
Four-year College(s)
Stetson University (Private, Not-for-profit)
   Fall 2006 Enrollment: 3,762. . . . . (386) 822-7000
   2006-07 Tuition: In-state $27,010; Out-of-state $27,010
Two-year College(s)
Angley College (Private, For-profit)
   Fall 2006 Enrollment: 101 . . . . (386) 740-1215
Housing: Homeownership rate: 53.9% (2007); Median home value: $133,855 (2007); Median rent: $458 per month (2000); Median age of housing: 27 years (2000).
Hospitals: Florida Hospital DeLand (156 beds)
Safety: Violent crime rate: 83.1 per 10,000 population; Property crime rate: 845.6 per 10,000 population (2006).
Newspapers: The DeLand Beacon (General - Circulation 8,000); The Deltona Beacon (General - Circulation 8,000)
Transportation: Commute to work: 90.1% car, 1.0% public transportation, 4.4% walk, 3.0% work from home (2000); Travel time to work: 43.1% less than 15 minutes, 26.4% 15 to 30 minutes, 16.1% 30 to 45 minutes, 7.1%

DE LAND SOUTHWEST (CDP).

Covers a land area of 0.628 square miles and a water area of 0 square miles. Located at 29.00° N. Lat.; 81.31° W. Long.

Population: 1,166 (1990); 1,169 (2000); 1,197 (2007); 1,235 (2012 projected); Race: 28.0% White, 65.5% Black, 0.5% Asian, 11.8% Hispanic of any race (2007); Density: 1,907.5 persons per square mile (2007); Average household size: 2.98 (2007); Median age: 37.2 (2007); Males per 100 females: 80.3 (2007); Marriage status: 32.5% never married, 33.6% now married, 19.8% widowed, 14.2% divorced (2000); Foreign born: 5.8% (2000); Ancestry (includes multiple ancestries): 47.3% Other groups, 3.9% African, 3.0% Jamaican, 0.9% West Indian, 0.6% Swedish (2000).

Economy: Employment by occupation: 2.3% management, 13.9% professional, 36.1% services, 20.0% sales, 1.9% farming, 12.9% construction, 12.9% production (2000).

Income: Per capita income: $10,038 (2007); Median household income: $17,075 (2007); Average household income: $24,981 (2007); Percent of households with income of $100,000 or more: 1.2% (2007); Poverty rate: 45.7% (2000).

Education: Percent of population age 25 and over with: High school diploma (including GED) or higher: 55.4% (2007); Bachelor's degree or higher: 8.1% (2007); Master's degree or higher: 4.5% (2007).

Housing: Homeownership rate: 61.9% (2007); Median home value: $105,250 (2007); Median rent: $340 per month (2000); Median age of housing: 33 years (2000).

Transportation: Commute to work: 89.0% car, 0.0% public transportation, 3.5% walk, 7.4% work from home (2000); Travel time to work: 31.0% less than 15 minutes, 48.8% 15 to 30 minutes, 17.8% 30 to 45 minutes, 0.0% 45 to 60 minutes, 2.4% 60 minutes or more (2000)

DE LEON SPRINGS (CDP).

Covers a land area of 2.631 square miles and a water area of 0 square miles. Located at 29.12° N. Lat.; 81.35° W. Long. Elevation is 49 feet.

History: The village of De Leon Springs was established near the Ponce de Leon Springs, where the Spanish had erected a sugar mill previous to 1763. The site of the village was plantation land planted in corn, sugar cane, and indigo when Florida became a Territory in 1819.

Population: 1,467 (1990); 2,358 (2000); 2,361 (2007); 2,396 (2012 projected); Race: 48.8% White, 4.6% Black, 0.3% Asian, 64.4% Hispanic of any race (2007); Density: 897.4 persons per square mile (2007); Average household size: 3.24 (2007); Median age: 29.2 (2007); Males per 100 females: 102.0 (2007); Marriage status: 22.6% never married, 62.9% now married, 5.6% widowed, 8.8% divorced (2000); Foreign born: 24.0% (2000); Ancestry (includes multiple ancestries): 44.9% Other groups, 9.5% United States or American, 8.4% Irish, 5.5% English, 5.2% German (2000).

Economy: Employment by occupation: 6.4% management, 6.8% professional, 19.9% services, 18.4% sales, 13.5% farming, 15.5% construction, 19.5% production (2000).

Income: Per capita income: $14,175 (2007); Median household income: $33,587 (2007); Average household income: $45,972 (2007); Percent of households with income of $100,000 or more: 7.8% (2007); Poverty rate: 17.2% (2000).

Education: Percent of population age 25 and over with: High school diploma (including GED) or higher: 59.6% (2007); Bachelor's degree or higher: 7.3% (2007); Master's degree or higher: 2.6% (2007).

School District(s)

Volusia County School District (PK-12)

    2005-06 Enrollment: 65,281 . . . . (386) 734-7190

Housing: Homeownership rate: 79.9% (2007); Median home value: $132,692 (2007); Median rent: $315 per month (2000); Median age of housing: 19 years (2000).

Transportation: Commute to work: 99.6% car, 0.0% public transportation, 0.0% walk, 0.0% work from home (2000); Travel time to work: 12.4% less than 15 minutes, 51.3% 15 to 30 minutes, 26.2% 30 to 45 minutes, 2.1% 45 to 60 minutes, 7.9% 60 minutes or more (2000)

DELTONA (city).

Covers a land area of 35.778 square miles and a water area of 2.543 square miles. Located at 28.90° N. Lat.; 81.21° W. Long. Elevation is 30 feet.

(2000); Ancestry (includes multiple ancestries): 27.1% Other groups, 15.8% German, 14.5% Irish, 9.8% Italian, 9.7% English (2000).

Economy: Unemployment rate: 4.8% (11/2007); Total civilian labor force: 45,636 (11/2007); Single-family building permits issued: 512 (2006); Multi-family building permits issued: 0 (2006); Employment by occupation: 10.6% management, 16.0% professional, 16.0% services, 31.1% sales, 0.1% farming, 13.8% construction, 12.4% production (2000).

Income: Per capita income: $19,065 (2007); Median household income: $45,403 (2007); Average household income: $53,720 (2007); Percent of households with income of $100,000 or more: 8.7% (2007); Poverty rate: 8.1% (2000).

Education: Percent of population age 25 and over with: High school diploma (including GED) or higher: 82.6% (2007); Bachelor's degree or higher: 13.4% (2007); Master's degree or higher: 3.8% (2007).

School District(s)

Volusia County School District (PK-12)

    2005-06 Enrollment: 65,281 . . . . (386) 734-7190

Housing: Homeownership rate: 87.3% (2007); Median home value: $161,458 (2007); Median rent: $580 per month (2000); Median age of housing: 15 years (2000).

Transportation: Commute to work: 95.6% car, 0.5% public transportation, 0.3% walk, 2.5% work from home (2000); Travel time to work: 14.8% less than 15 minutes, 28.5% 15 to 30 minutes, 27.6% 30 to 45 minutes, 14.7% 45 to 60 minutes, 14.5% 60 minutes or more (2000)

Additional Information Contacts

Deltona Chamber of Commerce . . . . (386) 775-2793

    http://www.chamberofcommerceofwestvolusia.com

EDGEWATER (city).

Covers a land area of 9.969 square miles and a water area of 0.374 square miles. Located at 28.96° N. Lat.; 80.90° W. Long. Elevation is 3 feet.

Population: 15,689 (1990); 18,668 (2000); 21,674 (2007); 23,882 (2012 projected); Race: 95.1% White, 2.0% Black, 0.7% Asian, 3.0% Hispanic of any race (2007); Density: 2,174.1 persons per square mile (2007); Average household size: 2.43 (2007); Median age: 42.8 (2007); Males per 100 females: 93.2 (2007); Marriage status: 17.2% never married, 61.9% now married, 8.8% widowed, 12.2% divorced (2000); Foreign born: 3.4% (2000); Ancestry (includes multiple ancestries): 16.9% German, 16.5% Irish, 14.1% English, 10.1% Other groups, 9.9% Italian (2000).

Economy: Single-family building permits issued: 103 (2006); Multi-family building permits issued: 0 (2006); Employment by occupation: 9.5% management, 15.9% professional, 20.2% services, 27.9% sales, 0.3% farming, 13.9% construction, 12.2% production (2000).

Income: Per capita income: $20,842 (2007); Median household income: $42,183 (2007); Average household income: $50,396 (2007); Percent of households with income of $100,000 or more: 7.2% (2007); Poverty rate: 9.2% (2000).

Education: Percent of population age 25 and over with: High school diploma (including GED) or higher: 82.0% (2007); Bachelor's degree or higher: 10.6% (2007); Master's degree or higher: 3.9% (2007).

Housing: Homeownership rate: 83.7% (2007); Median home value: $154,347 (2007); Median rent: $494 per month (2000); Median age of housing: 17 years (2000).

Safety: Violent crime rate: 34.0 per 10,000 population; Property crime rate: 293.7 per 10,000 population (2006).

Transportation: Commute to work: 94.8% car, 0.7% public transportation, 0.4% walk, 1.6% work from home (2000); Travel time to work: 31.8% less than 15 minutes, 31.1% 15 to 30 minutes, 22.6% 30 to 45 minutes, 7.5% 45 to 60 minutes, 6.9% 60 minutes or more (2000)

Additional Information Contacts

City of Edgewater. . . . . (386) 424-2400

    http://www.cityofedgewater.org

GLENCOE (CDP).

Covers a land area of 7.646 square miles and a water area of 0.048 square miles. Located at 29.01° N. Lat.; 80.96° W. Long. Elevation is 20 feet.

Population: 1,908 (1990); 2,485 (2000); 3,178 (2007); 3,650 (2012 projected); Race: 97.3% White, 1.4% Black, 0.1% Asian, 1.0% Hispanic of any race (2007); Density: 415.6 persons per square mile (2007); Average

household size: 2.50 (2007); Median age: 43.4 (2007); Males per 100 females: 99.4 (2007); Marriage status: 18.3% never married, 64.1% now married, 6.1% widowed, 11.5% divorced (2000); Foreign born: 2.5% (2000); Ancestry (includes multiple ancestries): 21.1% German, 18.8% English, 16.3% Irish, 11.7% United States or American, 7.5% Other groups (2000).
Economy: Employment by occupation: 12.4% management, 18.5% professional, 20.0% services, 24.0% sales, 0.5% farming, 14.8% construction, 9.9% production (2000).
Income: Per capita income: $24,985 (2007); Median household income: $45,556 (2007); Average household income: $62,469 (2007); Percent of households with income of $100,000 or more: 15.7% (2007); Poverty rate: 5.6% (2000).
Education: Percent of population age 25 and over with: High school diploma (including GED) or higher: 83.8% (2007); Bachelor's degree or higher: 19.1% (2007); Master's degree or higher: 6.8% (2007).
Housing: Homeownership rate: 92.9% (2007); Median home value: $186,523 (2007); Median rent: $585 per month (2000); Median age of housing: 18 years (2000).
Transportation: Commute to work: 91.4% car, 0.7% public transportation, 0.5% walk, 3.7% work from home (2000); Travel time to work: 39.1% less than 15 minutes, 30.8% 15 to 30 minutes, 21.6% 30 to 45 minutes, 2.1% 45 to 60 minutes, 6.3% 60 minutes or more (2000)

HOLLY HILL (city). Covers a land area of 3.892 square miles and a water area of 0.631 square miles. Located at 29.24° N. Lat.; 81.04° W. Long. Elevation is 13 feet.
History: Holly Hill was settled on the Turnbull land grant, and was named for the holly trees that once grew here. The town developed as a suburb of Daytona Beach.
Population: 11,401 (1990); 12,119 (2000); 12,606 (2007); 13,152 (2012 projected); Race: 82.9% White, 12.0% Black, 1.2% Asian, 5.7% Hispanic of any race (2007); Density: 3,238.6 persons per square mile (2007); Average household size: 2.14 (2007); Median age: 42.1 (2007); Males per 100 females: 93.1 (2007); Marriage status: 21.6% never married, 48.7% now married, 12.4% widowed, 17.2% divorced (2000); Foreign born: 4.9% (2000); Ancestry (includes multiple ancestries): 17.1% Other groups, 13.7% German, 12.1% Irish, 11.7% English, 11.3% United States or American (2000).
Economy: Single-family building permits issued: 20 (2006); Multi-family building permits issued: 6 (2006); Employment by occupation: 6.0% management, 13.7% professional, 23.6% services, 24.9% sales, 0.2% farming, 16.2% construction, 15.5% production (2000).
Income: Per capita income: $18,371 (2007); Median household income: $30,153 (2007); Average household income: $38,198 (2007); Percent of households with income of $100,000 or more: 4.0% (2007); Poverty rate: 16.5% (2000).
Education: Percent of population age 25 and over with: High school diploma (including GED) or higher: 75.6% (2007); Bachelor's degree or higher: 9.6% (2007); Master's degree or higher: 2.9% (2007).
School District(s)
Volusia County School District (PK-12)
    2005-06 Enrollment: 65,281 . . . . (386) 734-7190
Housing: Homeownership rate: 60.0% (2007); Median home value: $116,506 (2007); Median rent: $482 per month (2000); Median age of housing: 32 years (2000).
Safety: Violent crime rate: 91.9 per 10,000 population; Property crime rate: 674.3 per 10,000 population (2006).
Transportation: Commute to work: 90.6% car, 1.6% public transportation, 1.4% walk, 2.2% work from home (2000); Travel time to work: 41.1% less than 15 minutes, 36.0% 15 to 30 minutes, 14.6% 30 to 45 minutes, 3.0% 45 to 60 minutes, 5.4% 60 minutes or more (2000)

LAKE HELEN (city). Covers a land area of 4.219 square miles and a water area of 0.103 square miles. Located at 28.98° N. Lat.; 81.23° W. Long. Elevation is 66 feet.
Population: 2,415 (1990); 2,743 (2000); 2,776 (2007); 2,862 (2012 projected); Race: 84.1% White, 12.5% Black, 0.3% Asian, 4.7% Hispanic of any race (2007); Density: 657.9 persons per square mile (2007); Average household size: 2.46 (2007); Median age: 43.2 (2007); Males per 100 females: 90.3 (2007); Marriage status: 18.9% never married, 59.9% now married, 8.4% widowed, 12.9% divorced (2000); Foreign born: 0.5% (2000); Ancestry (includes multiple ancestries): 19.9% English, 18.9% German, 14.4% Other groups, 13.0% Irish, 8.2% United States or American (2000).

Economy: Single-family building permits issued: 15 (2006); Multi-family building permits issued: 0 (2006); Employment by occupation: 11.6% management, 20.9% professional, 14.9% services, 20.2% sales, 1.1% farming, 13.4% construction, 17.8% production (2000).
Income: Per capita income: $19,201 (2007); Median household income: $41,618 (2007); Average household income: $47,170 (2007); Percent of households with income of $100,000 or more: 5.5% (2007); Poverty rate: 9.7% (2000).
Education: Percent of population age 25 and over with: High school diploma (including GED) or higher: 79.3% (2007); Bachelor's degree or higher: 13.4% (2007); Master's degree or higher: 2.1% (2007).
School District(s)
Volusia County School District (PK-12)
    2005-06 Enrollment: 65,281 . . . . (386) 734-7190
Housing: Homeownership rate: 86.0% (2007); Median home value: $132,118 (2007); Median rent: $471 per month (2000); Median age of housing: 24 years (2000).
Safety: Violent crime rate: 14.0 per 10,000 population; Property crime rate: 241.0 per 10,000 population (2006).
Transportation: Commute to work: 90.2% car, 1.7% public transportation, 2.5% walk, 4.1% work from home (2000); Travel time to work: 18.6% less than 15 minutes, 50.6% 15 to 30 minutes, 17.6% 30 to 45 minutes, 9.5% 45 to 60 minutes, 3.6% 60 minutes or more (2000)

NEW SMYRNA BEACH (city). Covers a land area of 27.686 square miles and a water area of 3.090 square miles. Located at 29.03° N. Lat.; 80.92° W. Long. Elevation is 7 feet.
History: Incorporated 1903.
Population: 18,261 (1990); 20,048 (2000); 22,180 (2007); 23,854 (2012 projected); Race: 91.4% White, 5.9% Black, 0.7% Asian, 2.1% Hispanic of any race (2007); Density: 801.1 persons per square mile (2007); Average household size: 2.01 (2007); Median age: 54.6 (2007); Males per 100 females: 90.4 (2007); Marriage status: 17.5% never married, 57.6% now married, 11.6% widowed, 13.3% divorced (2000); Foreign born: 5.5% (2000); Ancestry (includes multiple ancestries): 18.4% German, 16.9% English, 16.3% Irish, 11.5% Other groups, 8.8% Italian (2000).
Economy: Single-family building permits issued: 118 (2006); Multi-family building permits issued: 283 (2006); Employment by occupation: 14.1% management, 17.1% professional, 20.2% services, 26.4% sales, 0.3% farming, 11.0% construction, 10.9% production (2000).
Income: Per capita income: $29,045 (2007); Median household income: $42,774 (2007); Average household income: $58,005 (2007); Percent of households with income of $100,000 or more: 12.7% (2007); Poverty rate: 10.8% (2000).
Education: Percent of population age 25 and over with: High school diploma (including GED) or higher: 85.3% (2007); Bachelor's degree or higher: 23.2% (2007); Master's degree or higher: 8.8% (2007).
School District(s)
Volusia County School District (PK-12)
    2005-06 Enrollment: 65,281 . . . . (386) 734-7190
Housing: Homeownership rate: 74.9% (2007); Median home value: $201,758 (2007); Median rent: $497 per month (2000); Median age of housing: 24 years (2000).
Hospitals: Bert Fish Medical Center (116 beds)
Safety: Violent crime rate: 55.9 per 10,000 population; Property crime rate: 354.1 per 10,000 population (2006).
Newspapers: The Observer (Circulation 5,000)
Transportation: Commute to work: 89.6% car, 0.1% public transportation, 1.7% walk, 4.7% work from home (2000); Travel time to work: 40.1% less than 15 minutes, 26.8% 15 to 30 minutes, 18.8% 30 to 45 minutes, 5.6% 45 to 60 minutes, 8.6% 60 minutes or more (2000)
Airports: New Smyrna Beach Municipal
Additional Information Contacts
New Smyrna Beach Chamber of Commerce . . . . (904) 428-2449
    http://www.sevchamber.com

NORTH DE LAND (CDP). Covers a land area of 0.589 square miles and a water area of 0 square miles. Located at 29.04° N. Lat.; 81.29° W. Long. Elevation is 79 feet.
Population: 1,379 (1990); 1,327 (2000); 1,532 (2007); 1,687 (2012 projected); Race: 88.4% White, 3.7% Black, 2.0% Asian, 11.2% Hispanic of any race (2007); Density: 2,601.8 persons per square mile (2007); Average household size: 2.52 (2007); Median age: 37.6 (2007); Males per 100 females: 96.2 (2007); Marriage status: 17.5% never married, 52.8% now married, 8.8% widowed, 20.9% divorced (2000); Foreign born: 9.0%

(2000); Ancestry (includes multiple ancestries): 14.1% Other groups, 12.2% Irish, 11.0% German, 11.0% United States or American, 10.5% English (2000).
Economy: Employment by occupation: 12.6% management, 17.1% professional, 8.2% services, 28.1% sales, 2.1% farming, 11.2% construction, 20.7% production (2000).
Income: Per capita income: $20,103 (2007); Median household income: $35,403 (2007); Average household income: $50,571 (2007); Percent of households with income of $100,000 or more: 10.8% (2007); Poverty rate: 11.8% (2000).
Education: Percent of population age 25 and over with: High school diploma (including GED) or higher: 75.1% (2007); Bachelor's degree or higher: 15.8% (2007); Master's degree or higher: 6.2% (2007).
Housing: Homeownership rate: 78.0% (2007); Median home value: $130,845 (2007); Median rent: $483 per month (2000); Median age of housing: 39 years (2000).
Transportation: Commute to work: 92.9% car, 0.0% public transportation, 1.7% walk, 3.4% work from home (2000); Travel time to work: 51.5% less than 15 minutes, 20.0% 15 to 30 minutes, 10.5% 30 to 45 minutes, 3.9% 45 to 60 minutes, 14.2% 60 minutes or more (2000)

OAK HILL (city). Covers a land area of 6.377 square miles and a water area of 4.876 square miles. Located at 28.88° N. Lat.; 80.84° W. Long. Elevation is 13 feet.
History: Oak Hill developed as a shipping center for citrus fruit grown in the area, and for orange and palmetto honey from local apiaries.
Population: 1,164 (1990); 1,378 (2000); 1,453 (2007); 1,521 (2012 projected); Race: 84.4% White, 12.9% Black, 0.3% Asian, 1.1% Hispanic of any race (2007); Density: 227.8 persons per square mile (2007); Average household size: 2.47 (2007); Median age: 41.8 (2007); Males per 100 females: 107.0 (2007); Marriage status: 19.4% never married, 62.1% now married, 6.8% widowed, 11.7% divorced (2000); Foreign born: 5.0% (2000); Ancestry (includes multiple ancestries): 30.8% Other groups, 12.0% English, 9.7% German, 8.7% Irish, 8.3% United States or American (2000).
Economy: Single-family building permits issued: 10 (2006); Multi-family building permits issued: 0 (2006); Employment by occupation: 7.7% management, 12.5% professional, 21.5% services, 18.4% sales, 3.6% farming, 19.7% construction, 16.7% production (2000).
Income: Per capita income: $21,783 (2007); Median household income: $38,906 (2007); Average household income: $53,735 (2007); Percent of households with income of $100,000 or more: 9.0% (2007); Poverty rate: 14.4% (2000).
Taxes: Total city taxes per capita: $328 (2005); City property taxes per capita: $183 (2005).
Education: Percent of population age 25 and over with: High school diploma (including GED) or higher: 71.4% (2007); Bachelor's degree or higher: 8.3% (2007); Master's degree or higher: 1.7% (2007).
School District(s)
Volusia County School District (PK-12)
    2005-06 Enrollment: 65,281 . . . . (386) 734-7190
Housing: Homeownership rate: 80.1% (2007); Median home value: $138,929 (2007); Median rent: $369 per month (2000); Median age of housing: 23 years (2000).
Safety: Violent crime rate: 92.8 per 10,000 population; Property crime rate: 371.1 per 10,000 population (2006).
Transportation: Commute to work: 91.2% car, 0.0% public transportation, 3.7% walk, 3.5% work from home (2000); Travel time to work: 22.2% less than 15 minutes, 33.9% 15 to 30 minutes, 23.6% 30 to 45 minutes, 14.1% 45 to 60 minutes, 6.3% 60 minutes or more (2000)

ORANGE CITY (city). Covers a land area of 6.051 square miles and a water area of 0.065 square miles. Located at 28.94° N. Lat.; 81.29° W. Long. Elevation is 33 feet.
History: Orange City was founded in the 1870's by three families from Eau Claire, Wisconsin, who wanted to raise citrus crops. The settlement was first known as Wisconsin Settlement.
Population: 5,621 (1990); 6,604 (2000); 7,488 (2007); 8,145 (2012 projected); Race: 90.8% White, 4.5% Black, 0.7% Asian, 8.0% Hispanic of any race (2007); Density: 1,237.5 persons per square mile (2007); Average household size: 2.11 (2007); Median age: 49.0 (2007); Males per 100 females: 87.7 (2007); Marriage status: 13.7% never married, 61.1% now married, 12.1% widowed, 13.0% divorced (2000); Foreign born: 4.2% (2000); Ancestry (includes multiple ancestries): 17.8% German, 15.6%

Irish, 15.1% English, 11.7% United States or American, 11.4% Other groups (2000).
Economy: Single-family building permits issued: 60 (2006); Multi-family building permits issued: 96 (2006); Employment by occupation: 10.5% management, 13.3% professional, 17.9% services, 31.9% sales, 0.0% farming, 11.2% construction, 15.2% production (2000).
Income: Per capita income: $18,687 (2007); Median household income: $30,894 (2007); Average household income: $38,806 (2007); Percent of households with income of $100,000 or more: 4.7% (2007); Poverty rate: 9.9% (2000).
Education: Percent of population age 25 and over with: High school diploma (including GED) or higher: 80.2% (2007); Bachelor's degree or higher: 12.7% (2007); Master's degree or higher: 3.6% (2007).
School District(s)
Volusia County School District (PK-12)
    2005-06 Enrollment: 65,281 . . . . (386) 734-7190
Housing: Homeownership rate: 75.0% (2007); Median home value: $111,898 (2007); Median rent: $417 per month (2000); Median age of housing: 20 years (2000).
Hospitals: Florida Hospital Fish Memorial (139 beds)
Safety: Violent crime rate: 117.6 per 10,000 population; Property crime rate: 1,096.9 per 10,000 population (2006).
Transportation: Commute to work: 92.8% car, 0.4% public transportation, 1.3% walk, 2.8% work from home (2000); Travel time to work: 28.9% less than 15 minutes, 32.3% 15 to 30 minutes, 19.9% 30 to 45 minutes, 12.3% 45 to 60 minutes, 6.6% 60 minutes or more (2000)
Additional Information Contacts
City of Orange City. . . . . (386) 775-5400
    http://www.ci.orange-city.fl.us
Orange City Chamber of Commerce . . . . (386) 775-2793
    http://www.chamberofcommerceofwestvolusia.com

ORMOND BEACH (city). Aka Ormond. Covers a land area of 25.750 square miles and a water area of 3.320 square miles. Located at 29.28° N. Lat.; 81.07° W. Long. Elevation is 7 feet.
History: Development began at Ormond Beach in 1875 when John Anderson built a home here which was later purchased by Henry M. Flagler, pioneer railroad and resort promoter. John D. Rockefeller (1839-1937) had a winter home in Ormond Beach, and spent much time here in his later years.
Population: 32,157 (1990); 36,301 (2000); 38,780 (2007); 40,683 (2012 projected); Race: 93.4% White, 2.8% Black, 1.9% Asian, 3.0% Hispanic of any race (2007); Density: 1,506.0 persons per square mile (2007); Average household size: 2.29 (2007); Median age: 48.6 (2007); Males per 100 females: 89.3 (2007); Marriage status: 17.4% never married, 61.0% now married, 10.1% widowed, 11.4% divorced (2000); Foreign born: 7.0% (2000); Ancestry (includes multiple ancestries): 17.6% German, 16.9% English, 14.8% Irish, 10.1% Other groups, 9.7% United States or American (2000).
Economy: Unemployment rate: 3.6% (11/2007); Total civilian labor force: 20,087 (11/2007); Single-family building permits issued: 115 (2006); Multi-family building permits issued: 0 (2006); Employment by occupation: 16.1% management, 24.3% professional, 14.9% services, 30.2% sales, 0.1% farming, 7.7% construction, 6.8% production (2000).
Income: Per capita income: $30,887 (2007); Median household income: $50,017 (2007); Average household income: $70,064 (2007); Percent of households with income of $100,000 or more: 18.4% (2007); Poverty rate: 6.1% (2000).
Education: Percent of population age 25 and over with: High school diploma (including GED) or higher: 88.1% (2007); Bachelor's degree or higher: 29.0% (2007); Master's degree or higher: 10.7% (2007).
School District(s)
Volusia County School District (PK-12)
    2005-06 Enrollment: 65,281 . . . . (386) 734-7190
Two-year College(s)
Daytona College (Private, For-profit)
    Fall 2006 Enrollment: 58 . . . . (386) 267-0565
Vocational/Technical School(s)
Wyotech (Private, For-profit)
    Fall 2006 Enrollment: 285 . . . . (386) 255-0295
    2006-07 Tuition: $11,990
Housing: Homeownership rate: 81.8% (2007); Median home value: $197,955 (2007); Median rent: $621 per month (2000); Median age of housing: 21 years (2000).

Hospitals: Florida Hospital - Ormond Memorial (205 beds); Memorial Hospital - Oceanside (119 beds)
Safety: Violent crime rate: 31.3 per 10,000 population; Property crime rate: 295.4 per 10,000 population (2006).
Transportation: Commute to work: 92.8% car, 0.9% public transportation, 1.1% walk, 3.4% work from home (2000); Travel time to work: 35.5% less than 15 minutes, 45.0% 15 to 30 minutes, 11.7% 30 to 45 minutes, 3.1% 45 to 60 minutes, 4.7% 60 minutes or more (2000)
Airports: Ormond Beach Municipal
Additional Information Contacts
Ormond Beach Chamber of Commerce . . . . (386) 677-3454
   http://www.ormondchamber.com

ORMOND-BY-THE-SEA (CDP).
Covers a land area of 1.986 square miles and a water area of 0.005 square miles. Located at 29.33° N. Lat.; 81.06° W. Long. Elevation is 13 feet.
Population: 8,141 (1990); 8,430 (2000); 7,863 (2007); 7,630 (2012 projected); Race: 96.7% White, 0.5% Black, 0.7% Asian, 3.2% Hispanic of any race (2007); Density: 3,959.9 persons per square mile (2007); Average household size: 1.93 (2007); Median age: 55.6 (2007); Males per 100 females: 88.7 (2007); Marriage status: 14.2% never married, 56.8% now married, 16.0% widowed, 13.0% divorced (2000); Foreign born: 7.1% (2000); Ancestry (includes multiple ancestries): 19.2% Irish, 19.0% German, 14.8% English, 12.6% Italian, 8.3% Other groups (2000).
Economy: Employment by occupation: 10.6% management, 21.8% professional, 18.1% services, 25.1% sales, 0.6% farming, 12.7% construction, 11.0% production (2000).
Income: Per capita income: $27,566 (2007); Median household income: $40,661 (2007); Average household income: $52,873 (2007); Percent of households with income of $100,000 or more: 9.8% (2007); Poverty rate: 9.8% (2000).
Education: Percent of population age 25 and over with: High school diploma (including GED) or higher: 85.7% (2007); Bachelor's degree or higher: 21.5% (2007); Master's degree or higher: 7.0% (2007).
Housing: Homeownership rate: 81.9% (2007); Median home value: $181,433 (2007); Median rent: $601 per month (2000); Median age of housing: 30 years (2000).
Transportation: Commute to work: 93.2% car, 0.4% public transportation, 1.3% walk, 2.7% work from home (2000); Travel time to work: 21.9% less than 15 minutes, 41.4% 15 to 30 minutes, 25.7% 30 to 45 minutes, 4.7% 45 to 60 minutes, 6.2% 60 minutes or more (2000)

OSTEEN (unincorporated postal area, zip code 32764).
Covers a land area of 65.127 square miles and a water area of 0.929 square miles. Located at 28.83° N. Lat.; 81.09° W. Long. Elevation is 50 feet.
Population: 2,441 (2000); Race: 94.0% White, 4.4% Black, 0.0% Asian, 2.7% Hispanic of any race (2000); Density: 37.5 persons per square mile (2000); Age: 20.1% under 18, 26.2% over 64 (2000); Marriage status: 11.2% never married, 66.7% now married, 10.5% widowed, 11.6% divorced (2000); Foreign born: 3.7% (2000); Ancestry (includes multiple ancestries): 17.4% United States or American, 13.9% Irish, 13.5% English, 13.2% Other groups, 10.5% German (2000).
Economy: Employment by occupation: 14.9% management, 9.7% professional, 19.1% services, 23.9% sales, 0.8% farming, 17.4% construction, 14.2% production (2000).
Income: Per capita income: $23,566 (2000); Median household income: $36,830 (2000); Poverty rate: 10.4% (2000).
Education: Percent of population age 25 and over with: High school diploma (including GED) or higher: 82.8% (2000); Bachelor's degree or higher: 15.4% (2000).

School District(s)
Volusia County School District (PK-12)
   2005-06 Enrollment: 65,281 . . . . (386) 734-7190
Housing: Homeownership rate: 92.5% (2000); Median home value: $102,700 (2000); Median rent: $347 per month (2000); Median age of housing: 18 years (2000).
Transportation: Commute to work: 94.9% car, 0.0% public transportation, 2.3% walk, 1.3% work from home (2000); Travel time to work: 4.2% less than 15 minutes, 29.5% 15 to 30 minutes, 37.9% 30 to 45 minutes, 12.6% 45 to 60 minutes, 15.8% 60 minutes or more (2000)

PIERSON (town).
Covers a land area of 8.136 square miles and a water area of 0.604 square miles. Located at 29.24° N. Lat.; 81.45° W. Long. Elevation is 75 feet.
Population: 3,407 (1990); 2,596 (2000); 2,655 (2007); 2,723 (2012 projected); Race: 88.5% White, 3.4% Black, 0.0% Asian, 75.9% Hispanic of any race (2007); Density: 326.3 persons per square mile (2007); Average household size: 5.10 (2007); Median age: 28.8 (2007); Males per 100 females: 140.3 (2007); Marriage status: 15.6% never married, 73.8% now married, 5.6% widowed, 5.1% divorced (2000); Foreign born: 22.5% (2000); Ancestry (includes multiple ancestries): 33.0% Other groups, 4.5% English, 3.6% German, 3.6% United States or American, 2.7% Irish (2000).
Economy: Single-family building permits issued: 2 (2006); Multi-family building permits issued: 0 (2006); Employment by occupation: 6.2% management, 7.3% professional, 13.9% services, 14.1% sales, 36.9% farming, 10.6% construction, 11.0% production (2000).
Income: Per capita income: $13,927 (2007); Median household income: $31,071 (2007); Average household income: $41,272 (2007); Percent of households with income of $100,000 or more: 5.2% (2007); Poverty rate: 33.6% (2000).
Education: Percent of population age 25 and over with: High school diploma (including GED) or higher: 33.9% (2007); Bachelor's degree or higher: 4.4% (2007); Master's degree or higher: 1.5% (2007).

School District(s)
Volusia County School District (PK-12)
   2005-06 Enrollment: 65,281 . . . . (386) 734-7190
Housing: Homeownership rate: 70.2% (2007); Median home value: $135,000 (2007); Median rent: $319 per month (2000); Median age of housing: 31 years (2000).
Transportation: Commute to work: 95.7% car, 0.0% public transportation, 0.9% walk, 2.7% work from home (2000); Travel time to work: 32.8% less than 15 minutes, 33.9% 15 to 30 minutes, 19.8% 30 to 45 minutes, 6.5% 45 to 60 minutes, 7.0% 60 minutes or more (2000)

PONCE INLET (town).
Aka Ponce Park. Covers a land area of 4.332 square miles and a water area of 10.341 square miles. Located at 29.09° N. Lat.; 80.94° W. Long. Elevation is 13 feet.
Population: 1,704 (1990); 2,513 (2000); 3,441 (2007); 4,081 (2012 projected); Race: 97.5% White, 0.9% Black, 0.6% Asian, 2.0% Hispanic of any race (2007); Density: 794.4 persons per square mile (2007); Average household size: 2.04 (2007); Median age: 58.2 (2007); Males per 100 females: 95.2 (2007); Marriage status: 13.1% never married, 70.6% now married, 6.6% widowed, 9.7% divorced (2000); Foreign born: 7.0% (2000); Ancestry (includes multiple ancestries): 20.3% German, 15.1% Irish, 13.8% Italian, 13.4% English, 11.1% United States or American (2000).
Economy: Single-family building permits issued: 24 (2006); Multi-family building permits issued: 0 (2006); Employment by occupation: 24.6% management, 23.6% professional, 12.5% services, 28.5% sales, 0.2% farming, 4.9% construction, 5.8% production (2000).
Income: Per capita income: $43,040 (2007); Median household income: $60,796 (2007); Average household income: $87,893 (2007); Percent of households with income of $100,000 or more: 26.8% (2007); Poverty rate: 5.1% (2000).
Education: Percent of population age 25 and over with: High school diploma (including GED) or higher: 92.2% (2007); Bachelor's degree or higher: 32.0% (2007); Master's degree or higher: 12.9% (2007).
Housing: Homeownership rate: 90.8% (2007); Median home value: $328,070 (2007); Median rent: $1,000 per month (2000); Median age of housing: 14 years (2000).
Safety: Violent crime rate: 15.4 per 10,000 population; Property crime rate: 135.1 per 10,000 population (2006).
Transportation: Commute to work: 86.3% car, 1.2% public transportation, 1.6% walk, 8.2% work from home (2000); Travel time to work: 14.9% less than 15 minutes, 48.6% 15 to 30 minutes, 18.9% 30 to 45 minutes, 9.4% 45 to 60 minutes, 8.3% 60 minutes or more (2000)

PORT ORANGE (city).
Covers a land area of 24.706 square miles and a water area of 1.969 square miles. Located at 29.11° N. Lat.; 81.00° W. Long. Elevation is 7 feet.
History: Port Orange was established in 1861 and developed as a shrimp and oyster center on the west bank of the Halifax River. The Dunlawton Sugar Mill was built here in the 1700's and was still used as late as 1880.
Population: 37,779 (1990); 45,823 (2000); 55,451 (2007); 62,447 (2012 projected); Race: 94.1% White, 2.2% Black, 1.6% Asian, 3.4% Hispanic of any race (2007); Density: 2,244.4 persons per square mile (2007); Average household size: 2.31 (2007); Median age: 45.4 (2007); Males per 100 females: 92.1 (2007); Marriage status: 18.1% never married, 60.1% now married, 9.7% widowed, 12.1% divorced (2000); Foreign born: 5.7%

(2000); Ancestry (includes multiple ancestries): 18.2% German, 15.7% Irish, 14.0% English, 11.1% Italian, 8.3% Other groups (2000).
Economy: Unemployment rate: 3.5% (11/2007); Total civilian labor force: 29,405 (11/2007); Single-family building permits issued: 246 (2006); Multi-family building permits issued: 8 (2006); Employment by occupation: 12.5% management, 17.6% professional, 17.6% services, 31.4% sales, 0.3% farming, 11.1% construction, 9.5% production (2000).
Income: Per capita income: $24,939 (2007); Median household income: $46,159 (2007); Average household income: $56,954 (2007); Percent of households with income of $100,000 or more: 11.8% (2007); Poverty rate: 7.6% (2000).
Education: Percent of population age 25 and over with: High school diploma (including GED) or higher: 84.9% (2007); Bachelor's degree or higher: 17.6% (2007); Master's degree or higher: 5.8% (2007).

School District(s)
Volusia County School District (PK-12)
    2005-06 Enrollment: 65,281 . . . . (386) 734-7190
Housing: Homeownership rate: 82.6% (2007); Median home value: $173,744 (2007); Median rent: $580 per month (2000); Median age of housing: 17 years (2000).
Safety: Violent crime rate: 13.0 per 10,000 population; Property crime rate: 227.3 per 10,000 population (2006).
Transportation: Commute to work: 95.0% car, 0.5% public transportation, 0.8% walk, 2.2% work from home (2000); Travel time to work: 28.0% less than 15 minutes, 48.4% 15 to 30 minutes, 13.8% 30 to 45 minutes, 3.0% 45 to 60 minutes, 6.7% 60 minutes or more (2000)
Additional Information Contacts
City of Port Orange . . . . (386) 506-5500
    http://www.port-orange.org

SAMSULA-SPRUCE CREEK (CDP). Covers a land area of 19.918 square miles and a water area of 0.012 square miles. Located at 29.06° N. Lat.; 81.05° W. Long.
Population: 2,929 (1990); 4,877 (2000); 7,299 (2007); 9,001 (2012 projected); Race: 96.3% White, 0.6% Black, 1.0% Asian, 2.1% Hispanic of any race (2007); Density: 366.4 persons per square mile (2007); Average household size: 2.45 (2007); Median age: 49.1 (2007); Males per 100 females: 97.6 (2007); Marriage status: 15.8% never married, 68.2% now married, 5.8% widowed, 10.2% divorced (2000); Foreign born: 5.0% (2000); Ancestry (includes multiple ancestries): 24.4% German, 19.9% English, 13.0% Irish, 7.4% Other groups, 6.8% Italian (2000).
Economy: Employment by occupation: 16.3% management, 18.1% professional, 12.1% services, 26.1% sales, 2.2% farming, 14.2% construction, 11.0% production (2000).
Income: Per capita income: $46,772 (2007); Median household income: $83,093 (2007); Average household income: $114,598 (2007); Percent of households with income of $100,000 or more: 40.1% (2007); Poverty rate: 5.4% (2000).
Education: Percent of population age 25 and over with: High school diploma (including GED) or higher: 90.4% (2007); Bachelor's degree or higher: 31.4% (2007); Master's degree or higher: 10.7% (2007).
Housing: Homeownership rate: 91.7% (2007); Median home value: $366,100 (2007); Median rent: $535 per month (2000); Median age of housing: 13 years (2000).
Transportation: Commute to work: 89.0% car, 0.0% public transportation, 0.4% walk, 8.2% work from home (2000); Travel time to work: 16.9% less than 15 minutes, 53.1% 15 to 30 minutes, 20.7% 30 to 45 minutes, 2.1% 45 to 60 minutes, 7.2% 60 minutes or more (2000)

SEVILLE (unincorporated postal area, zip code 32190). Covers a land area of 28.726 square miles and a water area of 3.739 square miles. Located at 29.33° N. Lat.; 81.50° W. Long. Elevation is 55 feet.
History: Seville was named for the small Seville orange which grew wild here. The trees, not native to the area, were reportedly planted by the Spaniards.
Population: 1,090 (2000); Race: 66.1% White, 19.5% Black, 0.0% Asian, 19.7% Hispanic of any race (2000); Density: 37.9 persons per square mile (2000); Age: 23.1% under 18, 19.6% over 64 (2000); Marriage status: 11.8% never married, 71.4% now married, 8.6% widowed, 8.2% divorced (2000); Foreign born: 8.1% (2000); Ancestry (includes multiple ancestries): 31.3% Other groups, 18.1% English, 13.6% Irish, 10.8% United States or American, 8.1% German (2000).
Economy: Employment by occupation: 9.8% management, 6.6% professional, 13.7% services, 24.9% sales, 15.1% farming, 5.9% construction, 23.8% production (2000).

Income: Per capita income: $14,029 (2000); Median household income: $29,821 (2000); Poverty rate: 10.1% (2000).
Education: Percent of population age 25 and over with: High school diploma (including GED) or higher: 75.1% (2000); Bachelor's degree or higher: 2.8% (2000).

School District(s)
Volusia County School District (PK-12)
    2005-06 Enrollment: 65,281 . . . . (386) 734-7190
Housing: Homeownership rate: 84.3% (2000); Median home value: $70,600 (2000); Median rent: $200 per month (2000); Median age of housing: 28 years (2000).
Transportation: Commute to work: 92.6% car, 0.0% public transportation, 4.6% walk, 2.8% work from home (2000); Travel time to work: 41.1% less than 15 minutes, 36.1% 15 to 30 minutes, 10.7% 30 to 45 minutes, 5.5% 45 to 60 minutes, 6.7% 60 minutes or more (2000)

SOUTH DAYTONA (city). Aka Blake. Covers a land area of 3.563 square miles and a water area of 1.277 square miles. Located at 29.16° N. Lat.; 81.00° W. Long. Elevation is 10 feet.
Population: 12,549 (1990); 13,177 (2000); 13,379 (2007); 13,668 (2012 projected); Race: 85.5% White, 10.4% Black, 1.5% Asian, 3.8% Hispanic of any race (2007); Density: 3,754.8 persons per square mile (2007); Average household size: 2.24 (2007); Median age: 40.4 (2007); Males per 100 females: 93.8 (2007); Marriage status: 24.4% never married, 51.2% now married, 8.6% widowed, 15.9% divorced (2000); Foreign born: 6.3% (2000); Ancestry (includes multiple ancestries): 16.5% Irish, 14.7% English, 14.5% German, 14.0% Other groups, 10.8% United States or American (2000).
Economy: Single-family building permits issued: 4 (2006); Multi-family building permits issued: 186 (2006); Employment by occupation: 11.4% management, 15.9% professional, 20.4% services, 31.2% sales, 0.4% farming, 9.9% construction, 10.8% production (2000).
Income: Per capita income: $20,344 (2007); Median household income: $35,670 (2007); Average household income: $45,387 (2007); Percent of households with income of $100,000 or more: 5.4% (2007); Poverty rate: 10.7% (2000).
Education: Percent of population age 25 and over with: High school diploma (including GED) or higher: 83.4% (2007); Bachelor's degree or higher: 14.2% (2007); Master's degree or higher: 4.0% (2007).

School District(s)
Volusia County School District (PK-12)
    2005-06 Enrollment: 65,281 . . . . (386) 734-7190
Vocational/Technical School(s)
International Academy (Private, For-profit)
    Fall 2006 Enrollment: 239 . . . . (386) 767-4600
    2006-07 Tuition: $14,400
Housing: Homeownership rate: 68.4% (2007); Median home value: $151,903 (2007); Median rent: $498 per month (2000); Median age of housing: 26 years (2000).
Safety: Violent crime rate: 43.0 per 10,000 population; Property crime rate: 392.4 per 10,000 population (2006).
Transportation: Commute to work: 93.8% car, 0.8% public transportation, 1.7% walk, 2.2% work from home (2000); Travel time to work: 34.3% less than 15 minutes, 48.7% 15 to 30 minutes, 10.3% 30 to 45 minutes, 2.1% 45 to 60 minutes, 4.6% 60 minutes or more (2000)
Additional Information Contacts
City of South Daytona . . . . (386) 322-3000
    http://www.southdaytona.org

WEST DE LAND (CDP). Covers a land area of 2.337 square miles and a water area of 0 square miles. Located at 29.01° N. Lat.; 81.32° W. Long. Elevation is 49 feet.
Population: 3,302 (1990); 3,424 (2000); 3,245 (2007); 3,180 (2012 projected); Race: 84.1% White, 9.5% Black, 0.5% Asian, 10.1% Hispanic of any race (2007); Density: 1,388.4 persons per square mile (2007); Average household size: 2.63 (2007); Median age: 37.5 (2007); Males per 100 females: 100.1 (2007); Marriage status: 23.1% never married, 57.0% now married, 9.6% widowed, 10.3% divorced (2000); Foreign born: 7.2% (2000); Ancestry (includes multiple ancestries): 19.5% German, 18.5% Irish, 15.3% Other groups, 14.0% English, 10.4% United States or American (2000).
Economy: Employment by occupation: 9.7% management, 15.1% professional, 13.6% services, 31.6% sales, 0.8% farming, 15.4% construction, 13.7% production (2000).

Income: Per capita income: $20,899 (2007); Median household income: $41,437 (2007); Average household income: $54,019 (2007); Percent of households with income of $100,000 or more: 10.4% (2007); Poverty rate: 9.4% (2000).
Education: Percent of population age 25 and over with: High school diploma (including GED) or higher: 81.7% (2007); Bachelor's degree or higher: 17.0% (2007); Master's degree or higher: 7.9% (2007).
Housing: Homeownership rate: 83.6% (2007); Median home value: $136,292 (2007); Median rent: $440 per month (2000); Median age of housing: 32 years (2000).
Transportation: Commute to work: 94.5% car, 0.7% public transportation, 0.9% walk, 3.4% work from home (2000); Travel time to work: 41.2% less than 15 minutes, 28.2% 15 to 30 minutes, 12.3% 30 to 45 minutes, 7.6% 45 to 60 minutes, 10.7% 60 minutes or more (2000)

Wakulla County

Located in northwestern Florida; bounded on the south by Apalachee Bay of the Gulf of Mexico; drained by the St. Marks and Wakulla Rivers; includes part of Apalachicola National Forest. Covers a land area of 606.66 square miles, a water area of 129.08 square miles, and is located in the Eastern Time Zone. The county was founded in 1843. County seat is Crawfordville.

Wakulla County is part of the Tallahassee, FL Metropolitan Statistical Area. The entire metro area includes: Gadsden County, FL; Jefferson County, FL; Leon County, FL; Wakulla County, FL

Population: 14,202 (1990); 22,863 (2000); 28,812 (2007); 32,594 (2012 projected); Race: 85.7% White, 11.7% Black, 0.5% Asian, 2.8% Hispanic of any race (2007); Density: 47.5 persons per square mile (2007); Average household size: 2.69 (2007); Median age: 38.7 (2007); Males per 100 females: 112.1 (2007).
Religion: Five largest groups: 12.1% Southern Baptist Convention, 3.8% The United Methodist Church, 2.4% National Primitive Baptist Convention, USA, 1.5% The Church of Jesus Christ of Latter-day Saints, 1.2% Assemblies of God (2000).
Economy: Unemployment rate: 3.1% (11/2007); Total civilian labor force: 15,160 (11/2007); Leading industries: 17.5% retail trade; 13.0% accommodation & food services; 11.9% construction (2005); Farms: 126 totaling 10,900 acres (2002); Companies that employ 500 or more persons: 0 (2005); Companies that employ 100 to 499 persons: 3 (2005); Companies that employ less than 100 persons: 425 (2005); Black-owned businesses: n/a (2002); Hispanic-owned businesses: n/a (2002); Asian-owned businesses: n/a (2002); Women-owned businesses: 633 (2002); Retail sales per capita: $4,121 (2007). Single-family building permits issued: 571 (2006); Multi-family building permits issued: 0 (2006).
Income: Per capita income: $20,828 (2007); Median household income: $42,929 (2007); Average household income: $53,336 (2007); Percent of households with income of $100,000 or more: 10.7% (2007); Poverty rate: 11.8% (2005); Bankruptcy rate: 1.86% (2006).
Education: Percent of population age 25 and over with: High school diploma (including GED) or higher: 78.1% (2007); Bachelor's degree or higher: 15.8% (2007); Master's degree or higher: 5.7% (2007).
Housing: Homeownership rate: 84.2% (2007); Median home value: $145,467 (2007); Median rent: $383 per month (2000); Median age of housing: 15 years (2000).
Health: Birth rate: 114.8 per 10,000 population (2006); Death rate: 64.3 per 10,000 population (2006); Age-adjusted cancer mortality rate: 145.8 deaths per 100,000 population (2004); Air Quality Index: 95.6% good, 4.4% moderate, 0.0% unhealthy for sensitive individuals, 0.0% unhealthy (percent of days in 2006); Number of physicians: 4.3 per 10,000 population (2005); Hospital beds: 0.0 per 10,000 population (2004); Hospital admissions: 0.0 per 10,000 population (2004).
Elections: 2004 Presidential election results: 57.6% Bush, 41.6% Kerry, 0.4% Nader, 0.2% Badnarik
National and State Parks: Apalachicola National Forest; Edward Ball Wakulla Springs State Park; Ochlockonee River State Park; Saint Marks National Wildlife Refuge; San Marcos De Apalache Historic State Park
Additional Information Contacts
Wakulla County Government . . . . (850) 926-0919
  http://www.wakullacounty.org
Crawfordville Chamber of Commerce . . . . (850) 926-1848
  http://www.wakullacounty.org

Wakulla County Communities

PANACEA (unincorporated postal area, zip code 32346). Covers a land area of 39.879 square miles and a water area of 1.821 square miles. Located at 29.98° N. Lat.; 84.38° W. Long. Elevation is 5 feet.
History: Panacea was known as Smith Springs until 1893, when the land around the five springs was purchased by settlers from Boston and renamed for the curative properties of the spring waters. A salt plant was operated here during the Civil War.
Population: 2,165 (2000); Race: 92.5% White, 6.4% Black, 0.6% Asian, 0.3% Hispanic of any race (2000); Density: 54.3 persons per square mile (2000); Age: 20.5% under 18, 16.2% over 64 (2000); Marriage status: 16.9% never married, 53.4% now married, 9.3% widowed, 20.5% divorced (2000); Foreign born: 1.7% (2000); Ancestry (includes multiple ancestries): 19.9% United States or American, 19.6% Other groups, 12.5% English, 8.5% German, 6.2% Irish (2000).
Economy: Employment by occupation: 16.8% management, 10.2% professional, 16.2% services, 25.5% sales, 3.7% farming, 14.3% construction, 13.2% production (2000).
Income: Per capita income: $17,336 (2000); Median household income: $28,875 (2000); Poverty rate: 16.2% (2000).
Education: Percent of population age 25 and over with: High school diploma (including GED) or higher: 76.8% (2000); Bachelor's degree or higher: 20.0% (2000).
Housing: Homeownership rate: 79.6% (2000); Median home value: $119,900 (2000); Median rent: $354 per month (2000); Median age of housing: 22 years (2000).
Transportation: Commute to work: 89.6% car, 0.6% public transportation, 1.7% walk, 8.1% work from home (2000); Travel time to work: 34.3% less than 15 minutes, 21.2% 15 to 30 minutes, 7.7% 30 to 45 minutes, 11.3% 45 to 60 minutes, 25.5% 60 minutes or more (2000)

SAINT MARKS (city). Covers a land area of 1.929 square miles and a water area of 0.013 square miles. Located at 30.15° N. Lat.; 84.20° W. Long. Elevation is 10 feet.
History: St. Marks grew as a fishing village on an inlet of Apalachee Bay. Nearby was St. Marks Fort, built in 1739 by the Spanish and later used by the English.
Population: 307 (1990); 272 (2000); 322 (2007); 347 (2012 projected); Race: 93.8% White, 2.2% Black, 0.6% Asian, 0.6% Hispanic of any race (2007); Density: 166.9 persons per square mile (2007); Average household size: 1.96 (2007); Median age: 48.1 (2007); Males per 100 females: 107.7 (2007); Marriage status: 14.3% never married, 56.7% now married, 13.8% widowed, 15.2% divorced (2000); Foreign born: 2.5% (2000); Ancestry (includes multiple ancestries): 19.1% English, 13.0% German, 13.0% Irish, 10.5% Other groups, 7.9% United States or American (2000).
Economy: Employment by occupation: 17.9% management, 22.8% professional, 17.9% services, 10.6% sales, 1.6% farming, 17.9% construction, 11.4% production (2000).
Income: Per capita income: $18,230 (2007); Median household income: $28,000 (2007); Average household income: $35,793 (2007); Percent of households with income of $100,000 or more: 3.7% (2007); Poverty rate: 19.5% (2000).
Education: Percent of population age 25 and over with: High school diploma (including GED) or higher: 74.9% (2007); Bachelor's degree or higher: 10.6% (2007); Master's degree or higher: 4.3% (2007).
School District(s)
Wakulla County School District (PK-12)
  2005-06 Enrollment: 4,884 . . . . (850) 926-0065
Housing: Homeownership rate: 72.0% (2007); Median home value: $122,222 (2007); Median rent: $298 per month (2000); Median age of housing: 30 years (2000).
Transportation: Commute to work: 86.2% car, 0.0% public transportation, 8.1% walk, 4.1% work from home (2000); Travel time to work: 22.9% less than 15 minutes, 10.2% 15 to 30 minutes, 29.7% 30 to 45 minutes, 19.5% 45 to 60 minutes, 17.8% 60 minutes or more (2000)

SOPCHOPPY (city). Covers a land area of 1.519 square miles and a water area of 0 square miles. Located at 30.06° N. Lat.; 84.49° W. Long. Elevation is 30 feet.
History: Sopchoppy developed around a lumber mill on the Sopchoppy River.
Population: 427 (1990); 426 (2000); 502 (2007); 548 (2012 projected); Race: 77.1% White, 17.7% Black, 1.6% Asian, 5.6% Hispanic of any race (2007); Density: 330.4 persons per square mile (2007); Average household

size: 2.35 (2007); Median age: 39.6 (2007); Males per 100 females: 88.7 (2007); Marriage status: 23.7% never married, 59.9% now married, 10.9% widowed, 5.4% divorced (2000); Foreign born: 0.0% (2000); Ancestry (includes multiple ancestries): 25.9% Other groups, 14.6% United States or American, 12.4% English, 6.1% German, 5.4% Irish (2000).

Economy: Employment by occupation: 6.8% management, 19.3% professional, 20.5% services, 24.2% sales, 1.9% farming, 15.5% construction, 11.8% production (2000).

Income: Per capita income: $21,579 (2007); Median household income: $34,091 (2007); Average household income: $50,619 (2007); Percent of households with income of $100,000 or more: 7.9% (2007); Poverty rate: 17.1% (2000).

Education: Percent of population age 25 and over with: High school diploma (including GED) or higher: 69.9% (2007); Bachelor's degree or higher: 9.9% (2007); Master's degree or higher: 4.2% (2007).

School District(s)

Wakulla County School District (PK-12)

   2005-06 Enrollment: 4,884 . . . . (850) 926-0065

Housing: Homeownership rate: 74.8% (2007); Median home value: $100,000 (2007); Median rent: $373 per month (2000); Median age of housing: 30 years (2000).

Transportation: Commute to work: 94.3% car, 0.0% public transportation, 3.8% walk, 1.9% work from home (2000); Travel time to work: 23.7% less than 15 minutes, 37.2% 15 to 30 minutes, 14.1% 30 to 45 minutes, 13.5% 45 to 60 minutes, 11.5% 60 minutes or more (2000).

Walton County

Located in northwestern Florida; bounded on the east by the Choctawhatchee River, on the north by Alabama, and on the south by Choctawhatchee Bay on the Gulf of Mexico; includes the highest point in the state (345 ft), and part of Choctawhatchee Nati onal Forest. Covers a land area of 1,057.56 square miles, a water area of 180.47 square miles, and is located in the Central Time Zone. The county was founded in 1824. County seat is De Funiak Springs.

Weather Station: De Funiak Springs   Elevation: 229 feet

	Jan	Feb	Mar	Apr	May	Jun	Jul	Aug	Sep	Oct	Nov	Dec
High	62	66	73	79	86	90	92	91	88	80	71	65
Low	38	41	47	52	60	67	70	70	65	54	45	41
Precip	5.4	5.8	6.4	4.0	5.0	6.9	8.0	7.0	5.9	3.6	4.7	4.4
Snow	tr	tr	tr	0.0	0.0	0.0	0.0	0.0	0.0	0.0	0.0	0.0

High and Low temperatures in degrees Fahrenheit; Precipitation and Snow in inches

Population: 27,760 (1990); 40,601 (2000); 55,706 (2007); 66,949 (2012 projected); Race: 88.2% White, 6.8% Black, 0.7% Asian, 3.0% Hispanic of any race (2007); Density: 52.7 persons per square mile (2007); Average household size: 2.39 (2007); Median age: 40.8 (2007); Males per 100 females: 103.2 (2007).

Religion: Five largest groups: 20.2% Southern Baptist Convention, 4.7% The United Methodist Church, 2.5% Catholic Church, 1.5% Assemblies of God, 1.2% Presbyterian Church (U.S.A.) (2000).

Economy: Unemployment rate: 2.6% (11/2007); Total civilian labor force: 35,076 (11/2007); Leading industries: 22.2% accommodation & food services; 18.9% retail trade; 12.6% construction (2005); Farms: 540 totaling 79,910 acres (2002); Companies that employ 500 or more persons: 2 (2005); Companies that employ 100 to 499 persons: 15 (2005); Companies that employ less than 100 persons: 1,462 (2005); Black-owned businesses: n/a (2002); Hispanic-owned businesses: n/a (2002); Asian-owned businesses: n/a (2002); Women-owned businesses: 1,371 (2002); Retail sales per capita: $16,505 (2007). Single-family building permits issued: 1,032 (2006); Multi-family building permits issued: 245 (2006).

Income: Per capita income: $23,539 (2007); Median household income: $41,185 (2007); Average household income: $55,904 (2007); Percent of households with income of $100,000 or more: 11.2% (2007); Poverty rate: 13.0% (2005); Bankruptcy rate: 0.90% (2006).

Taxes: Total county taxes per capita: $1,097 (2005); County property taxes per capita: $647 (2005).

Education: Percent of population age 25 and over with: High school diploma (including GED) or higher: 77.9% (2007); Bachelor's degree or higher: 18.2% (2007); Master's degree or higher: 6.8% (2007).

Housing: Homeownership rate: 79.0% (2007); Median home value: $182,915 (2007); Median rent: $383 per month (2000); Median age of housing: 14 years (2000).

Health: Birth rate: 115.4 per 10,000 population (2006); Death rate: 103.9 per 10,000 population (2006); Age-adjusted cancer mortality rate: 226.3 deaths per 100,000 population (2004); Number of physicians: 8.3 per 10,000 population (2005); Hospital beds: 20.7 per 10,000 population (2004); Hospital admissions: 867.0 per 10,000 population (2004).

Elections: 2004 Presidential election results: 73.2% Bush, 25.9% Kerry, 0.5% Nader, 0.1% Badnarik

National and State Parks: Basin Bayou State Recreation Area; Deer Lake State Park; Eden Gardens State Park; Grayton Beach State Park; Topsail Hill Preserve State Park

Additional Information Contacts

Walton County Government. . . . . (850) 892-8115
   http://www.co.walton.fl.us
City of De Funiak Springs . . . . (850) 892-8500
   http://www.defuniaksprings.net
Walton County Chamber of Commerce. . . . . (850) 267-0683
   http://www.waltoncountychamber.com

Walton County Communities

DE FUNIAK SPRINGS (city). County seat. Covers a land area of 10.967 square miles and a water area of 0.276 square miles. Located at 30.72° N. Lat.; 86.11° W. Long. Elevation is 259 feet.

History: De Funiak Springs was named for Colonel Fred DeFuniak, an official of the Louisville & Nashville Railroad. A Confederate monument was erected in 1871 in De Funiak Springs.

Population: 5,173 (1990); 5,089 (2000); 5,618 (2007); 6,080 (2012 projected); Race: 70.4% White, 23.1% Black, 0.8% Asian, 5.1% Hispanic of any race (2007); Density: 512.2 persons per square mile (2007); Average household size: 2.41 (2007); Median age: 36.7 (2007); Males per 100 females: 88.2 (2007); Marriage status: 23.7% never married, 49.1% now married, 12.6% widowed, 14.6% divorced (2000); Foreign born: 4.0% (2000); Ancestry (includes multiple ancestries): 34.1% Other groups, 13.8% United States or American, 9.9% Irish, 7.6% German, 6.6% English (2000).

Economy: Single-family building permits issued: 15 (2006); Multi-family building permits issued: 0 (2006); Employment by occupation: 6.0% management, 14.7% professional, 22.0% services, 30.2% sales, 0.6% farming, 11.9% construction, 14.5% production (2000).

Income: Per capita income: $17,503 (2007); Median household income: $30,245 (2007); Average household income: $41,129 (2007); Percent of households with income of $100,000 or more: 6.8% (2007); Poverty rate: 18.4% (2000).

Education: Percent of population age 25 and over with: High school diploma (including GED) or higher: 71.6% (2007); Bachelor's degree or higher: 12.7% (2007); Master's degree or higher: 4.5% (2007).

School District(s)

Walton County School District (PK-12)

   2005-06 Enrollment: 6,557 . . . . (850) 892-1100

Housing: Homeownership rate: 63.4% (2007); Median home value: $139,946 (2007); Median rent: $277 per month (2000); Median age of housing: 36 years (2000).

Newspapers: Beach Breeze (General - Circulation 6,000); De Funiak Springs Herald-Breeze (General - Circulation 6,300)

Transportation: Commute to work: 90.2% car, 1.0% public transportation, 5.3% walk, 1.6% work from home (2000); Travel time to work: 43.6% less than 15 minutes, 12.6% 15 to 30 minutes, 9.9% 30 to 45 minutes, 21.5% 45 to 60 minutes, 12.5% 60 minutes or more (2000)

Airports: Defuniak Springs

Additional Information Contacts

City of De Funiak Springs . . . . (850) 892-8500
   http://www.defuniaksprings.net
Walton County Chamber of Commerce. . . . . (850) 267-0683
   http://www.waltoncountychamber.com

FREEPORT (city). Covers a land area of 10.782 square miles and a water area of 0.027 square miles. Located at 30.50° N. Lat.; 86.13° W. Long. Elevation is 33 feet.

Population: 917 (1990); 1,190 (2000); 1,571 (2007); 1,867 (2012 projected); Race: 93.3% White, 2.4% Black, 0.2% Asian, 1.7% Hispanic of any race (2007); Density: 145.7 persons per square mile (2007); Average household size: 2.37 (2007); Median age: 35.4 (2007); Males per 100 females: 100.9 (2007); Marriage status: 18.5% never married, 59.6% now married, 11.1% widowed, 10.8% divorced (2000); Foreign born: 1.1% (2000); Ancestry (includes multiple ancestries): 22.2% United States or

American, 18.0% Other groups, 13.4% Irish, 9.3% English, 5.8% German (2000).
Economy: Employment by occupation: 6.4% management, 10.0% professional, 22.3% services, 28.9% sales, 0.4% farming, 18.6% construction, 13.3% production (2000).
Income: Per capita income: $16,848 (2007); Median household income: $30,270 (2007); Average household income: $39,861 (2007); Percent of households with income of $100,000 or more: 6.5% (2007); Poverty rate: 21.4% (2000).
Education: Percent of population age 25 and over with: High school diploma (including GED) or higher: 63.8% (2007); Bachelor's degree or higher: 8.1% (2007); Master's degree or higher: 3.0% (2007).

School District(s)
Walton County School District (PK-12)
    2005-06 Enrollment: 6,557 . . . . (850) 892-1100
Housing: Homeownership rate: 67.6% (2007); Median home value: $124,128 (2007); Median rent: $282 per month (2000); Median age of housing: 18 years (2000).
Transportation: Commute to work: 91.9% car, 0.0% public transportation, 1.0% walk, 4.6% work from home (2000); Travel time to work: 28.3% less than 15 minutes, 18.7% 15 to 30 minutes, 35.0% 30 to 45 minutes, 10.4% 45 to 60 minutes, 7.6% 60 minutes or more (2000)

MIRAMAR BEACH (CDP). Covers a land area of 4.598 square miles and a water area of 0.120 square miles. Located at 30.38° N. Lat.; 86.35° W. Long. Elevation is 20 feet.
Population: 1,644 (1990); 2,435 (2000); 3,777 (2007); 4,691 (2012 projected); Race: 95.4% White, 0.9% Black, 1.8% Asian, 1.8% Hispanic of any race (2007); Density: 821.4 persons per square mile (2007); Average household size: 1.95 (2007); Median age: 52.9 (2007); Males per 100 females: 99.0 (2007); Marriage status: 11.6% never married, 72.0% now married, 5.9% widowed, 10.6% divorced (2000); Foreign born: 4.7% (2000); Ancestry (includes multiple ancestries): 21.0% German, 15.4% Irish, 14.5% English, 14.0% United States or American, 8.1% Other groups (2000).
Economy: Employment by occupation: 23.8% management, 16.9% professional, 17.9% services, 33.6% sales, 0.0% farming, 3.8% construction, 3.9% production (2000).
Income: Per capita income: $35,342 (2007); Median household income: $54,502 (2007); Average household income: $68,267 (2007); Percent of households with income of $100,000 or more: 18.3% (2007); Poverty rate: 6.9% (2000).
Education: Percent of population age 25 and over with: High school diploma (including GED) or higher: 92.3% (2007); Bachelor's degree or higher: 40.5% (2007); Master's degree or higher: 13.7% (2007).
Housing: Homeownership rate: 80.3% (2007); Median home value: $391,076 (2007); Median rent: $775 per month (2000); Median age of housing: 10 years (2000).
Transportation: Commute to work: 89.0% car, 0.0% public transportation, 1.9% walk, 6.3% work from home (2000); Travel time to work: 45.5% less than 15 minutes, 37.7% 15 to 30 minutes, 10.3% 30 to 45 minutes, 3.8% 45 to 60 minutes, 2.7% 60 minutes or more (2000)

PAXTON (town). Covers a land area of 3.907 square miles and a water area of 0.066 square miles. Located at 30.97° N. Lat.; 86.31° W. Long. Elevation is 318 feet.
Population: 600 (1990); 656 (2000); 651 (2007); 658 (2012 projected); Race: 91.7% White, 2.8% Black, 0.0% Asian, 2.6% Hispanic of any race (2007); Density: 166.6 persons per square mile (2007); Average household size: 2.45 (2007); Median age: 38.3 (2007); Males per 100 females: 89.2 (2007); Marriage status: 17.1% never married, 57.8% now married, 9.6% widowed, 15.6% divorced (2000); Foreign born: 0.9% (2000); Ancestry (includes multiple ancestries): 30.0% United States or American, 14.8% Other groups, 13.6% Irish, 10.0% English, 2.3% Scotch-Irish (2000).
Economy: Employment by occupation: 5.5% management, 18.8% professional, 20.7% services, 19.6% sales, 3.0% farming, 17.3% construction, 15.1% production (2000).
Income: Per capita income: $16,863 (2007); Median household income: $30,714 (2007); Average household income: $41,269 (2007); Percent of households with income of $100,000 or more: 4.1% (2007); Poverty rate: 12.3% (2000).
Education: Percent of population age 25 and over with: High school diploma (including GED) or higher: 55.9% (2007); Bachelor's degree or higher: 6.4% (2007); Master's degree or higher: 0.9% (2007).

School District(s)
Walton County School District (PK-12)
    2005-06 Enrollment: 6,557 . . . . (850) 892-1100
Housing: Homeownership rate: 86.8% (2007); Median home value: $90,385 (2007); Median rent: $314 per month (2000); Median age of housing: 29 years (2000).
Transportation: Commute to work: 94.3% car, 0.0% public transportation, 3.4% walk, 1.1% work from home (2000); Travel time to work: 37.6% less than 15 minutes, 10.5% 15 to 30 minutes, 24.0% 30 to 45 minutes, 15.9% 45 to 60 minutes, 12.0% 60 minutes or more (2000)

SANTA ROSA BEACH (unincorporated postal area, zip code 32459). Aka Santa Rosa. Covers a land area of 64.998 square miles and a water area of 0.823 square miles. Located at 30.36° N. Lat.; 86.18° W. Long. Elevation is 4 feet.
Population: 6,210 (2000); Race: 93.3% White, 0.0% Black, 0.8% Asian, 2.1% Hispanic of any race (2000); Density: 95.5 persons per square mile (2000); Age: 19.5% under 18, 14.4% over 64 (2000); Marriage status: 20.9% never married, 58.1% now married, 6.0% widowed, 15.0% divorced (2000); Foreign born: 4.3% (2000); Ancestry (includes multiple ancestries): 25.1% English, 18.0% German, 16.4% Irish, 13.3% Other groups, 10.9% United States or American (2000).
Economy: Employment by occupation: 16.2% management, 13.8% professional, 24.6% services, 25.6% sales, 2.0% farming, 12.2% construction, 5.6% production (2000).
Income: Per capita income: $28,132 (2000); Median household income: $42,359 (2000); Poverty rate: 6.8% (2000).
Education: Percent of population age 25 and over with: High school diploma (including GED) or higher: 90.0% (2000); Bachelor's degree or higher: 31.5% (2000).

School District(s)
Walton County School District (PK-12)
    2005-06 Enrollment: 6,557 . . . . (850) 892-1100
Housing: Homeownership rate: 76.0% (2000); Median home value: $161,500 (2000); Median rent: $637 per month (2000); Median age of housing: 10 years (2000).
Newspapers: The Walton Sun (General - Circulation 14,000)
Transportation: Commute to work: 91.3% car, 0.4% public transportation, 1.5% walk, 4.4% work from home (2000); Travel time to work: 40.4% less than 15 minutes, 34.1% 15 to 30 minutes, 12.5% 30 to 45 minutes, 9.5% 45 to 60 minutes, 3.4% 60 minutes or more (2000)

Washington County

Located in northwestern Florida; bounded on the west by the Choctawhatchee River; includes many small lakes. Covers a land area of 579.93 square miles, a water area of 35.86 square miles, and is located in the Central Time Zone. The county was founded in 1825. County seat is Chipley.

Weather Station: Chipley 3 E   Elevation: 127 feet

	Jan	Feb	Mar	Apr	May	Jun	Jul	Aug	Sep	Oct	Nov	Dec
High	60	65	72	78	85	90	91	91	88	80	71	63
Low	38	40	47	53	61	68	71	70	66	54	45	40
Precip	6.1	5.0	6.2	3.8	4.3	5.3	6.9	5.5	4.6	3.1	3.9	3.8
Snow	tr	0.0	0.0	0.0	0.0	0.0	0.0	0.0	0.0	0.0	0.0	0.0

High and Low temperatures in degrees Fahrenheit; Precipitation and Snow in inches

Population: 16,919 (1990); 20,973 (2000); 23,141 (2007); 24,981 (2012 projected); Race: 81.6% White, 13.8% Black, 0.6% Asian, 2.4% Hispanic of any race (2007); Density: 39.9 persons per square mile (2007); Average household size: 2.62 (2007); Median age: 39.5 (2007); Males per 100 females: 110.3 (2007).
Religion: Five largest groups: 24.8% Southern Baptist Convention, 4.2% Assemblies of God, 3.5% The United Methodist Church, 3.2% Catholic Church, 1.4% National Association of Free Will Baptists (2000).
Economy: Unemployment rate: 3.9% (11/2007); Total civilian labor force: 9,985 (11/2007); Leading industries: 21.3% health care and social assistance; 18.5% retail trade; 8.7% accommodation & food services (2005); Farms: 391 totaling 53,251 acres (2002); Companies that employ 500 or more persons: 1 (2005); Companies that employ 100 to 499 persons: 5 (2005); Companies that employ less than 100 persons: 379 (2005); Black-owned businesses: n/a (2002); Hispanic-owned businesses: n/a (2002); Asian-owned businesses: n/a (2002); Women-owned businesses: 424 (2002); Retail sales per capita: $8,149 (2007).

Single-family building permits issued: 125 (2006); Multi-family building permits issued: 0 (2006).
Income: Per capita income: $17,369 (2007); Median household income: $32,618 (2007); Average household income: $44,696 (2007); Percent of households with income of $100,000 or more: 7.5% (2007); Poverty rate: 18.8% (2005); Bankruptcy rate: 0.75% (2006).
Education: Percent of population age 25 and over with: High school diploma (including GED) or higher: 71.1% (2007); Bachelor's degree or higher: 9.1% (2007); Master's degree or higher: 3.4% (2007).
Housing: Homeownership rate: 82.5% (2007); Median home value: $146,191 (2007); Median rent: $278 per month (2000); Median age of housing: 20 years (2000).
Health: Birth rate: 109.2 per 10,000 population (2006); Death rate: 109.6 per 10,000 population (2006); Age-adjusted cancer mortality rate: 238.6 deaths per 100,000 population (2004); Number of physicians: 6.3 per 10,000 population (2005); Hospital beds: 26.9 per 10,000 population (2004); Hospital admissions: 168.2 per 10,000 population (2004).
Elections: 2004 Presidential election results: 71.1% Bush, 28.1% Kerry, 0.5% Nader, 0.1% Badnarik
National and State Parks: Falling Waters State Park
Additional Information Contacts
Washington County Government . . . . (850) 638-6200
  http://www.washingtonfl.com
Chipley Chamber of Commerce . . . . (850) 638-4157
  http://www.washcomall.com
Washington County Chamber of Commerce . . . . (850) 638-4157
  http://www.washcomall.com

Washington County Communities

CARYVILLE (town). Covers a land area of 3.023 square miles and a water area of 0.128 square miles. Located at 30.77° N. Lat.; 85.81° W. Long. Elevation is 52 feet.
Population: 660 (1990); 218 (2000); 170 (2007); 180 (2012 projected); Race: 70.6% White, 20.6% Black, 0.0% Asian, 8.8% Hispanic of any race (2007); Density: 56.2 persons per square mile (2007); Average household size: 2.50 (2007); Median age: 33.9 (2007); Males per 100 females: 123.7 (2007); Marriage status: 22.4% never married, 48.3% now married, 16.7% widowed, 12.6% divorced (2000); Foreign born: 1.9% (2000); Ancestry (includes multiple ancestries): 28.5% United States or American, 17.8% Other groups, 9.8% German, 9.3% Irish, 4.7% Dutch (2000).
Economy: Employment by occupation: 0.0% management, 5.2% professional, 23.4% services, 23.4% sales, 0.0% farming, 28.6% construction, 19.5% production (2000).
Income: Per capita income: $12,015 (2007); Median household income: $25,000 (2007); Average household income: $30,037 (2007); Percent of households with income of $100,000 or more: 2.9% (2007); Poverty rate: 37.3% (2000).
Education: Percent of population age 25 and over with: High school diploma (including GED) or higher: 53.3% (2007); Bachelor's degree or higher: 2.8% (2007); Master's degree or higher: 0.0% (2007).
Housing: Homeownership rate: 79.4% (2007); Median home value: $90,000 (2007); Median rent: $275 per month (2000); Median age of housing: 18 years (2000).
Transportation: Commute to work: 93.5% car, 0.0% public transportation, 0.0% walk, 2.6% work from home (2000); Travel time to work: 26.7% less than 15 minutes, 25.3% 15 to 30 minutes, 26.7% 30 to 45 minutes, 2.7% 45 to 60 minutes, 18.7% 60 minutes or more (2000)

CHIPLEY (city). County seat. Covers a land area of 4.117 square miles and a water area of 0 square miles. Located at 30.77° N. Lat.; 85.53° W. Long. Elevation is 105 feet.
History: Chipley was founded in 1882 when the Pensacola & Atlantic Railroad arrived in the area. First called Orange, the town was later named for railroad official Colonel William D. Chipley.
Population: 3,894 (1990); 3,592 (2000); 3,600 (2007); 3,722 (2012 projected); Race: 65.8% White, 30.1% Black, 1.1% Asian, 1.4% Hispanic of any race (2007); Density: 874.4 persons per square mile (2007); Average household size: 2.49 (2007); Median age: 39.6 (2007); Males per 100 females: 89.0 (2007); Marriage status: 24.6% never married, 54.1% now married, 13.7% widowed, 7.6% divorced (2000); Foreign born: 1.0% (2000); Ancestry (includes multiple ancestries): 27.7% Other groups, 16.4% United States or American, 9.6% Irish, 7.7% English, 5.0% German (2000).

Economy: Employment by occupation: 6.9% management, 20.8% professional, 21.7% services, 19.6% sales, 2.9% farming, 14.9% construction, 13.1% production (2000).
Income: Per capita income: $14,814 (2007); Median household income: $25,019 (2007); Average household income: $36,852 (2007); Percent of households with income of $100,000 or more: 6.3% (2007); Poverty rate: 27.7% (2000).
Education: Percent of population age 25 and over with: High school diploma (including GED) or higher: 65.7% (2007); Bachelor's degree or higher: 12.3% (2007); Master's degree or higher: 5.6% (2007).
School District(s)
Washington County School District (PK-12)
  2005-06 Enrollment: 3,490 . . . . (850) 638-6222
Two-year College(s)
Washington-Holmes Technical Center (Public)
  Fall 2006 Enrollment: 494 . . . . (850) 638-1180
Housing: Homeownership rate: 63.5% (2007); Median home value: $124,213 (2007); Median rent: $273 per month (2000); Median age of housing: 36 years (2000).
Hospitals: Northwest Florida Community Hospital (59 beds)
Safety: Violent crime rate: 64.1 per 10,000 population; Property crime rate: 339.2 per 10,000 population (2006).
Newspapers: Washington County News (General - Circulation 4,200)
Transportation: Commute to work: 93.7% car, 0.0% public transportation, 0.9% walk, 3.3% work from home (2000); Travel time to work: 54.2% less than 15 minutes, 17.7% 15 to 30 minutes, 7.5% 30 to 45 minutes, 9.7% 45 to 60 minutes, 10.9% 60 minutes or more (2000); Amtrak: Service available.
Additional Information Contacts
Chipley Chamber of Commerce . . . . (850) 638-4157
  http://www.washcomall.com

EBRO (town). Covers a land area of 3.150 square miles and a water area of 0.050 square miles. Located at 30.44° N. Lat.; 85.88° W. Long. Elevation is 75 feet.
Population: 257 (1990); 250 (2000); 241 (2007); 244 (2012 projected); Race: 76.8% White, 2.9% Black, 0.0% Asian, 4.6% Hispanic of any race (2007); Density: 76.5 persons per square mile (2007); Average household size: 2.41 (2007); Median age: 38.8 (2007); Males per 100 females: 95.9 (2007); Marriage status: 26.2% never married, 48.9% now married, 6.2% widowed, 18.7% divorced (2000); Foreign born: 1.5% (2000); Ancestry (includes multiple ancestries): 26.2% United States or American, 18.1% English, 17.7% Other groups, 16.2% Irish, 2.6% French (except Basque) (2000).
Economy: Employment by occupation: 15.3% management, 6.6% professional, 16.1% services, 25.5% sales, 2.2% farming, 13.9% construction, 20.4% production (2000).
Income: Per capita income: $17,541 (2007); Median household income: $32,500 (2007); Average household income: $42,275 (2007); Percent of households with income of $100,000 or more: 7.0% (2007); Poverty rate: 21.0% (2000).
Education: Percent of population age 25 and over with: High school diploma (including GED) or higher: 69.8% (2007); Bachelor's degree or higher: 2.4% (2007); Master's degree or higher: 2.4% (2007).
Housing: Homeownership rate: 73.0% (2007); Median home value: $109,821 (2007); Median rent: $266 per month (2000); Median age of housing: 17 years (2000).
Transportation: Commute to work: 88.9% car, 1.5% public transportation, 4.4% walk, 3.7% work from home (2000); Travel time to work: 40.0% less than 15 minutes, 8.5% 15 to 30 minutes, 21.5% 30 to 45 minutes, 17.7% 45 to 60 minutes, 12.3% 60 minutes or more (2000)

VERNON (city). Covers a land area of 4.723 square miles and a water area of 0.003 square miles. Located at 30.62° N. Lat.; 85.71° W. Long. Elevation is 43 feet.
Population: 778 (1990); 743 (2000); 779 (2007); 805 (2012 projected); Race: 77.9% White, 15.0% Black, 0.8% Asian, 1.9% Hispanic of any race (2007); Density: 164.9 persons per square mile (2007); Average household size: 2.49 (2007); Median age: 36.8 (2007); Males per 100 females: 87.3 (2007); Marriage status: 19.3% never married, 59.6% now married, 10.7% widowed, 10.4% divorced (2000); Foreign born: 0.7% (2000); Ancestry (includes multiple ancestries): 27.1% Other groups, 18.3% United States or American, 13.3% Irish, 10.3% German, 9.0% English (2000).

Economy: Employment by occupation: 8.3% management, 19.8% professional, 21.7% services, 18.2% sales, 3.6% farming, 13.8% construction, 14.6% production (2000).

Income: Per capita income: $15,546 (2007); Median household income: $24,015 (2007); Average household income: $36,925 (2007); Percent of households with income of $100,000 or more: 8.0% (2007); Poverty rate: 28.5% (2000).

Education: Percent of population age 25 and over with: High school diploma (including GED) or higher: 60.0% (2007); Bachelor's degree or higher: 10.8% (2007); Master's degree or higher: 4.3% (2007).

School District(s)

Washington County School District (PK-12)

   2005-06 Enrollment: 3,490 . . . . (850) 638-6222

Housing: Homeownership rate: 73.8% (2007); Median home value: $102,841 (2007); Median rent: $289 per month (2000); Median age of housing: 30 years (2000).

Transportation: Commute to work: 97.2% car, 0.0% public transportation, 0.8% walk, 0.8% work from home (2000); Travel time to work: 28.0% less than 15 minutes, 31.3% 15 to 30 minutes, 15.4% 30 to 45 minutes, 8.5% 45 to 60 minutes, 16.7% 60 minutes or more (2000)

Additional Information Contacts

Washington County Chamber of Commerce . . . . (850) 638-4157
   http://www.washcomall.com

WAUSAU (town). Covers a land area of 1.131 square miles and a water area of 0 square miles. Located at 30.63° N. Lat.; 85.58° W. Long. Elevation is 95 feet.

Population: 332 (1990); 398 (2000); 418 (2007); 433 (2012 projected); Race: 95.0% White, 0.2% Black, 0.2% Asian, 2.6% Hispanic of any race (2007); Density: 369.4 persons per square mile (2007); Average household size: 2.39 (2007); Median age: 36.5 (2007); Males per 100 females: 100.0 (2007); Marriage status: 17.1% never married, 57.3% now married, 9.2% widowed, 16.4% divorced (2000); Foreign born: 1.0% (2000); Ancestry (includes multiple ancestries): 24.9% United States or American, 11.6% Other groups, 11.1% Irish, 8.1% German, 7.1% French (except Basque) (2000).

Economy: Employment by occupation: 7.0% management, 17.5% professional, 17.5% services, 13.2% sales, 2.6% farming, 31.6% construction, 10.5% production (2000).

Income: Per capita income: $11,980 (2007); Median household income: $23,700 (2007); Average household income: $28,614 (2007); Percent of households with income of $100,000 or more: 2.3% (2007); Poverty rate: 29.2% (2000).

Education: Percent of population age 25 and over with: High school diploma (including GED) or higher: 59.7% (2007); Bachelor's degree or higher: 4.9% (2007); Master's degree or higher: 1.5% (2007).

Housing: Homeownership rate: 75.4% (2007); Median home value: $100,000 (2007); Median rent: $288 per month (2000); Median age of housing: 21 years (2000).

Transportation: Commute to work: 83.3% car, 0.0% public transportation, 11.1% walk, 0.0% work from home (2000); Travel time to work: 22.2% less than 15 minutes, 47.2% 15 to 30 minutes, 7.4% 30 to 45 minutes, 7.4% 45 to 60 minutes, 15.7% 60 minutes or more (2000);

CDP = Census Designated Place

CDP = Census Designated Place

CDP = Census Designated Place

CDP = Census Designated Place

Spring Hill CDP *Hernando County*, 77
Spring Lake CDP *Hernando County*, 77
Springfield city *Bay County*, 8
Stacey Street CDP *Palm Beach County*, 194
Starke city *Bradford County*, 10
Steinhatchee postal area *Taylor County*, 247
Stock Island CDP *Monroe County*, 157
Stuart city *Martin County*, 132
Sugarmill Woods CDP *Citrus County*, 45
Summerland Key postal area *Monroe County*, 158
Sumter County, 243 - 244
Sumterville postal area *Sumter County*, 244
Suncoast Estates CDP *Lee County*, 115
Sunny Isles Beach city *Miami-Dade County*, 151
Sunrise city *Broward County*, 34
Sunset CDP *Miami-Dade County*, 151
Sunshine Acres CDP *Broward County*, 34
Sunshine Ranches CDP *Broward County*, 34
Surfside town *Miami-Dade County*, 151
Suwannee County, 245
Sweetwater city *Miami-Dade County*, 151
Sylvan Shores CDP *Highlands County*, 80

T

Taft CDP *Orange County*, 174
Tallahassee city *Leon County*, 116
Tamarac city *Broward County*, 34
Tamiami CDP *Miami-Dade County*, 152
Tampa city *Hillsborough County*, 86
Tangelo Park CDP *Orange County*, 174
Tangerine CDP *Orange County*, 174
Tarpon Springs city *Pinellas County*, 211
Tavares city *Lake County*, 106
Tavernier CDP *Monroe County*, 158
Taylor County, 246 - 247
Taylor Creek CDP *Okeechobee County*, 165
Tedder CDP *Broward County*, 35
Temple Terrace city *Hillsborough County*, 87
Tequesta village *Palm Beach County*, 194
Terra Mar CDP *Broward County*, 35
The Crossings CDP *Miami-Dade County*, 152
The Hammocks CDP *Miami-Dade County*, 152
The Meadows CDP *Sarasota County*, 231
The Villages CDP *Sumter County*, 244
Thonotosassa CDP *Hillsborough County*, 88
Three Lakes CDP *Miami-Dade County*, 152
Three Oaks CDP *Lee County*, 115
Tice CDP *Lee County*, 115
Tierra Verde CDP *Pinellas County*, 211
Tildenville CDP *Orange County*, 174
Timber Pines CDP *Hernando County*, 77
Titusville city *Brevard County*, 16
Town 'n' Country CDP *Hillsborough County*, 88
Treasure Island city *Pinellas County*, 211
Trenton city *Gilchrist County*, 67
Trinity CDP *Pasco County*, 200
Twin Lakes CDP *Broward County*, 35
Tyndall AFB CDP *Bay County*, 8

U

Umatilla city *Lake County*, 106
Union County, 248
Union Park CDP *Orange County*, 175
University Park CDP *Miami-Dade County*, 152
University CDP *Hillsborough County*, 88
Upper Grand Lagoon CDP *Bay County*, 8
Utopia CDP *Broward County*, 35

V

Valparaiso city *Okaloosa County*, 164
Valrico CDP *Hillsborough County*, 88
Vamo CDP *Sarasota County*, 231
Venice Gardens CDP *Sarasota County*, 232
Venice city *Sarasota County*, 232
Venus postal area *Highlands County*, 80
Vernon city *Washington County*, 259
Vero Beach South CDP *Indian River County*, 93
Vero Beach city *Indian River County*, 93
Village Park CDP *Broward County*, 35
Villages of Oriole CDP *Palm Beach County*, 194
Villano Beach CDP *Saint Johns County*, 240
Villas CDP *Lee County*, 115
Vineyards CDP *Collier County*, 51
Virginia Gardens village *Miami-Dade County*, 153
Volusia County, 249 - 255

W

Wabasso Beach CDP *Indian River County*, 93
Wabasso CDP *Indian River County*, 93
Wahneta CDP *Polk County*, 220
Wakulla County, 256
Waldo city *Alachua County*, 3
Walton County, 257
Warm Mineral Springs CDP *Sarasota County*, 232
Warrington CDP *Escambia County*, 61
Washington County, 258 - 260
Washington Park CDP *Broward County*, 36
Watertown CDP *Columbia County*, 53
Wauchula city *Hardee County*, 71
Wausau town *Washington County*, 260
Waverly CDP *Polk County*, 220
Webster city *Sumter County*, 244
Wedgefield CDP *Orange County*, 175
Weeki Wachee Gardens CDP *Hernando County*, 77
Weeki Wachee city *Hernando County*, 77
Weirsdale postal area *Marion County*, 130
Wekiwa Springs CDP *Seminole County*, 236
Welaka town *Putnam County*, 224
Wellborn postal area *Suwannee County*, 246
Wellington village *Palm Beach County*, 194
Wesley Chapel South CDP *Pasco County*, 201
Wesley Chapel CDP *Pasco County*, 201
West and East Lealman CDP *Pinellas County*, 211
West Bradenton CDP *Manatee County*, 126

West De Land CDP *Volusia County*, 255
West Ken-Lark CDP *Broward County*, 36
West Little River CDP *Miami-Dade County*, 153
West Melbourne city *Brevard County*, 17
West Miami city *Miami-Dade County*, 153
West Palm Beach city *Palm Beach County*, 195
West Pensacola CDP *Escambia County*, 61
West Perrine CDP *Miami-Dade County*, 153
West Samoset CDP *Manatee County*, 126
West Vero Corridor CDP *Indian River County*, 94
Westchase CDP *Hillsborough County*, 88
Westchester CDP *Miami-Dade County*, 153
Westgate-Belvedere Homes CDP *Palm Beach County*, 195
Weston city *Broward County*, 36
Westview CDP *Miami-Dade County*, 154
Westville town *Holmes County*, 90
Westwood Lakes CDP *Miami-Dade County*, 154
Wewahitchka city *Gulf County*, 69
Whiskey Creek CDP *Lee County*, 115
Whisper Walk CDP *Palm Beach County*, 195
White City CDP *Saint Lucie County*, 242
White Springs town *Hamilton County*, 70
Whitfield CDP *Manatee County*, 127
Wildwood city *Sumter County*, 245
Williamsburg CDP *Orange County*, 175
Williston Highlands CDP *Levy County*, 120
Williston city *Levy County*, 120
Willow Oak CDP *Polk County*, 220
Wilton Manors city *Broward County*, 36
Wimauma CDP *Hillsborough County*, 89
Windermere town *Orange County*, 175
Winston CDP *Polk County*, 220
Winter Beach CDP *Indian River County*, 94
Winter Garden city *Orange County*, 175
Winter Haven city *Polk County*, 220
Winter Park city *Orange County*, 176
Winter Springs city *Seminole County*, 236
Woodville CDP *Leon County*, 117
Worthington Springs town *Union County*, 248
Wright CDP *Okaloosa County*, 164

Y

Yalaha CDP *Lake County*, 106
Yankeetown town *Levy County*, 120
Yeehaw Junction CDP *Osceola County*, 179
Youngstown postal area *Bay County*, 9
Yulee CDP *Nassau County*, 160

Z

Zellwood CDP *Orange County*, 176
Zephyrhills North CDP *Pasco County*, 201
Zephyrhills South CDP *Pasco County*, 202
Zephyrhills West CDP *Pasco County*, 202
Zephyrhills city *Pasco County*, 201
Zolfo Springs town *Hardee County*, 71

CDP = Census Designated Place

Comparative Statistics

Place	1990	2000	2007 Estimate	2012 Projection
Altamonte Springs city *Seminole Co.*	36,355	41,200	41,840	43,089
Apopka city *Orange Co.*	17,031	26,642	35,213	41,281
Boca Raton city *Palm Beach Co.*	61,401	74,764	78,047	81,130
Bonita Springs city *Lee Co.*	17,511	32,797	40,311	45,953
Boynton Beach city *Palm Beach Co.*	48,285	60,389	67,948	73,600
Bradenton city *Manatee Co.*	43,699	49,504	54,934	59,082
Brandon CDP *Hillsborough Co.*	57,304	77,895	95,468	107,570
Cape Coral city *Lee Co.*	75,507	102,286	153,992	189,594
Carol City CDP *Miami-Dade Co.*	53,331	59,443	62,519	65,440
Clearwater city *Pinellas Co.*	100,872	108,787	108,660	109,635
Coconut Creek city *Broward Co.*	27,509	43,566	49,339	52,965
Coral Gables city *Miami-Dade Co.*	41,660	42,249	43,172	44,433
Coral Springs city *Broward Co.*	78,602	117,549	129,132	136,677
Country Club CDP *Miami-Dade Co.*	23,164	36,310	41,861	46,032
Davie town *Broward Co.*	54,493	75,720	85,081	91,137
Daytona Beach city *Volusia Co.*	62,186	64,112	64,929	66,404
Deerfield Beach city *Broward Co.*	55,289	64,583	65,940	67,072
Delray Beach city *Palm Beach Co.*	47,833	60,020	65,731	70,195
Deltona city *Volusia Co.*	49,242	69,543	86,568	98,387
Dunedin city *Pinellas Co.*	34,496	35,691	36,654	37,551
East Lake CDP *Pinellas Co.*	12,669	29,394	34,890	38,722
Egypt Lake-Leto CDP *Hillsborough Co.*	28,830	32,782	35,830	38,183
Fort Lauderdale city *Broward Co.*	149,908	152,397	166,763	176,239
Fort Myers city *Lee Co.*	45,222	48,208	55,227	60,968
Fort Pierce city *Saint Lucie Co.*	38,676	37,516	37,993	39,007
Fountainbleau CDP *Miami-Dade Co.*	46,661	59,549	64,389	68,359
Gainesville city *Alachua Co.*	90,519	95,447	97,244	101,406
Golden Glades CDP *Miami-Dade Co.*	25,312	32,623	33,426	34,349
Greater Carrollwood CDP *Hillsborough Co.*	29,062	33,519	35,861	37,812
Greenacres city *Palm Beach Co.*	20,225	27,569	32,159	35,423
Hallandale city *Broward Co.*	30,997	34,282	35,594	36,590
Hialeah city *Miami-Dade Co.*	188,005	226,419	219,483	217,593
Hollywood city *Broward Co.*	121,944	139,357	144,774	148,736
Homestead city *Miami-Dade Co.*	28,451	31,909	46,428	56,016
Jacksonville special city *Duval Co.*	635,221	735,617	814,629	882,596
Jupiter town *Palm Beach Co.*	30,117	39,328	49,232	55,968
Kendale Lakes CDP *Miami-Dade Co.*	48,524	56,901	57,577	58,813
Kendall CDP *Miami-Dade Co.*	69,644	75,226	74,666	75,254
Kendall West CDP *Miami-Dade Co.*	16,857	38,034	47,803	54,570
Kissimmee city *Osceola Co.*	32,042	47,814	62,875	74,419
Lake Worth city *Palm Beach Co.*	29,083	35,133	36,163	37,299
Lakeland city *Polk Co.*	73,375	78,452	82,493	85,983
Lakeside CDP *Clay Co.*	29,137	30,927	33,811	36,215
Land O' Lakes CDP *Pasco Co.*	13,062	20,971	32,805	40,014
Largo city *Pinellas Co.*	70,008	69,371	70,489	71,951
Lauderdale Lakes city *Broward Co.*	27,341	31,705	32,461	32,914
Lauderhill city *Broward Co.*	49,135	57,585	59,078	60,156
Lehigh Acres CDP *Lee Co.*	22,352	33,430	47,986	58,233
Margate city *Broward Co.*	42,985	53,909	55,768	57,095
Melbourne city *Brevard Co.*	61,834	71,382	77,266	81,907

Place	1990	2000	2007 Estimate	2012 Projection
Merritt Island CDP *Brevard Co.*	32,886	36,090	37,565	38,955
Miami city *Miami-Dade Co.*	358,843	362,470	398,228	426,446
Miami Beach city *Miami-Dade Co.*	92,639	87,933	88,233	89,932
Miramar city *Broward Co.*	40,663	72,739	114,073	139,680
North Fort Myers CDP *Lee Co.*	34,213	40,214	46,669	51,779
North Lauderdale city *Broward Co.*	26,844	32,264	36,089	38,584
North Miami city *Miami-Dade Co.*	50,721	59,880	57,614	56,907
North Miami Beach city *Miami-Dade Co.*	34,812	40,786	39,548	39,235
North Port city *Sarasota Co.*	11,987	22,797	48,730	65,229
Oakland Park city *Broward Co.*	26,326	30,966	31,834	32,427
Ocala city *Marion Co.*	42,851	45,943	50,721	54,553
Orlando city *Orange Co.*	161,172	185,951	212,477	233,698
Ormond Beach city *Volusia Co.*	32,157	36,301	38,780	40,683
Oviedo city *Seminole Co.*	11,588	26,316	32,172	36,509
Palm Bay city *Brevard Co.*	62,587	79,413	97,251	109,542
Palm Beach Gardens city *Palm Beach Co.*	24,518	35,058	49,851	59,560
Palm Coast city *Flagler Co.*	16,998	32,732	58,540	77,162
Palm Harbor CDP *Pinellas Co.*	50,255	59,248	60,162	61,329
Panama City city *Bay Co.*	36,193	36,417	36,923	37,375
Pembroke Pines city *Broward Co.*	66,095	137,427	149,322	157,001
Pensacola city *Escambia Co.*	58,906	56,255	53,700	52,303
Pine Hills CDP *Orange Co.*	34,712	41,764	42,104	43,135
Pinellas Park city *Pinellas Co.*	45,348	45,658	46,613	47,697
Plant City city *Hillsborough Co.*	23,296	29,915	31,872	33,456
Plantation city *Broward Co.*	66,997	82,934	85,549	87,416
Pompano Beach city *Broward Co.*	72,400	78,191	81,277	83,506
Port Charlotte CDP *Charlotte Co.*	41,534	46,451	47,745	48,841
Port Orange city *Volusia Co.*	37,779	45,823	55,451	62,447
Port Saint Lucie city *Saint Lucie Co.*	55,843	88,769	142,771	178,736
Richmond West CDP *Miami-Dade Co.*	6,224	28,082	36,786	42,751
Riviera Beach city *Palm Beach Co.*	27,791	29,884	35,017	38,624
Royal Palm Beach village *Palm Beach Co.*	15,662	21,523	32,529	39,697
Saint Petersburg city *Pinellas Co.*	238,846	248,232	250,583	254,508
Sanford city *Seminole Co.*	33,887	38,291	48,913	56,391
Sarasota city *Sarasota Co.*	51,400	52,715	53,931	55,633
South Miami Heights CDP *Miami-Dade Co.*	30,030	33,522	35,794	37,792
Spring Hill CDP *Hernando Co.*	50,663	69,078	90,586	103,687
Sunrise city *Broward Co.*	64,675	85,779	90,378	93,484
Tallahassee city *Leon Co.*	128,014	150,624	166,141	182,811
Tamarac city *Broward Co.*	45,366	55,588	60,269	63,445
Tamiami CDP *Miami-Dade Co.*	39,068	54,788	59,567	63,487
Tampa city *Hillsborough Co.*	279,960	303,447	332,025	354,374
The Hammocks CDP *Miami-Dade Co.*	26,829	47,379	54,648	60,063
Titusville city *Brevard Co.*	39,970	40,670	44,760	47,890
Town 'n' Country CDP *Hillsborough Co.*	60,978	72,523	78,961	84,039
University CDP *Hillsborough Co.*	23,760	30,736	32,339	33,800
Wellington village *Palm Beach Co.*	22,555	38,216	56,529	68,431
West Palm Beach city *Palm Beach Co.*	68,172	82,103	100,705	113,381
Weston city *Broward Co.*	10,099	49,286	67,538	78,734
Winter Springs city *Seminole Co.*	22,280	31,666	34,337	36,791

Physical Characteristics

Place	Density (persons per square mile)	Land Area (square miles)	Water Area (square miles)	Elevation (feet)
Altamonte Springs city *Seminole Co.*	4,703.0	8.90	0.56	85
Apopka city *Orange Co.*	1,464.6	24.04	0.89	131
Boca Raton city *Palm Beach Co.*	2,870.5	27.19	1.93	13
Bonita Springs city *Lee Co.*	1,142.3	35.29	5.72	10
Boynton Beach city *Palm Beach Co.*	4,279.6	15.88	0.37	20
Bradenton city *Manatee Co.*	4,537.0	12.11	2.33	3
Brandon CDP *Hillsborough Co.*	3,324.2	28.72	0.57	46
Cape Coral city *Lee Co.*	1,464.0	105.19	9.91	3
Carol City CDP *Miami-Dade Co.*	8,199.4	7.62	0.11	7
Clearwater city *Pinellas Co.*	4,297.0	25.29	12.44	30
Coconut Creek city *Broward Co.*	4,273.2	11.55	0.24	7
Coral Gables city *Miami-Dade Co.*	3,287.2	13.13	24.02	10
Coral Springs city *Broward Co.*	5,401.0	23.91	0.24	10
Country Club CDP *Miami-Dade Co.*	9,707.8	4.31	0.20	3
Davie town *Broward Co.*	2,545.2	33.43	0.74	3
Daytona Beach city *Volusia Co.*	1,106.6	58.68	6.25	13
Deerfield Beach city *Broward Co.*	4,911.7	13.43	1.50	13
Delray Beach city *Palm Beach Co.*	4,277.2	15.37	0.53	16
Deltona city *Volusia Co.*	2,419.6	35.78	2.54	30
Dunedin city *Pinellas Co.*	3,530.9	10.38	17.83	30
East Lake CDP *Pinellas Co.*	1,171.5	29.78	1.98	13
Egypt Lake-Leto CDP *Hillsborough Co.*	6,002.3	5.97	0.22	43
Fort Lauderdale city *Broward Co.*	5,255.9	31.73	4.29	3
Fort Myers city *Lee Co.*	1,735.1	31.83	8.59	10
Fort Pierce city *Saint Lucie Co.*	2,577.2	14.74	6.02	16
Fountainbleau CDP *Miami-Dade Co.*	14,623.9	4.40	0.11	3
Gainesville city *Alachua Co.*	2,018.2	48.18	0.92	177
Golden Glades CDP *Miami-Dade Co.*	6,798.3	4.92	0.06	3
Greater Carrollwood CDP *Hillsborough Co.*	3,747.5	9.57	0.71	n/a
Greenacres city *Palm Beach Co.*	6,902.8	4.66	0.01	23
Hallandale city *Broward Co.*	8,454.7	4.21	0.34	10
Hialeah city *Miami-Dade Co.*	11,406.8	19.24	0.50	7
Hollywood city *Broward Co.*	5,295.3	27.34	3.46	10
Homestead city *Miami-Dade Co.*	3,250.4	14.28	0.09	3
Jacksonville special city *Duval Co.*	1,075.2	757.68	116.65	16
Jupiter town *Palm Beach Co.*	2,461.8	20.00	1.13	3
Kendale Lakes CDP *Miami-Dade Co.*	7,045.1	8.17	0.43	3
Kendall CDP *Miami-Dade Co.*	4,630.1	16.13	0.22	13
Kendall West CDP *Miami-Dade Co.*	14,100.1	3.39	0.26	n/a
Kissimmee city *Osceola Co.*	3,769.6	16.68	0.64	66
Lake Worth city *Palm Beach Co.*	6,408.0	5.64	0.82	16
Lakeland city *Polk Co.*	1,799.5	45.84	5.61	197
Lakeside CDP *Clay Co.*	2,231.1	15.15	2.26	66
Land O' Lakes CDP *Pasco Co.*	1,762.2	18.62	2.50	75
Largo city *Pinellas Co.*	4,500.5	15.66	0.46	33
Lauderdale Lakes city *Broward Co.*	9,042.7	3.59	0.05	7
Lauderhill city *Broward Co.*	8,097.5	7.30	0.04	3
Lehigh Acres CDP *Lee Co.*	505.7	94.89	1.09	20
Margate city *Broward Co.*	6,331.6	8.81	0.17	10
Melbourne city *Brevard Co.*	2,558.7	30.20	5.29	20

Place	Density (persons per square mile)	Land Area (square miles)	Water Area (square miles)	Elevation (feet)
Merritt Island CDP *Brevard Co.*	2,128.2	17.65	29.40	3
Miami city *Miami-Dade Co.*	11,163.3	35.67	19.59	7
Miami Beach city *Miami-Dade Co.*	12,544.7	7.03	11.67	3
Miramar city *Broward Co.*	3,867.0	29.50	1.50	7
North Fort Myers CDP *Lee Co.*	886.9	52.62	1.97	3
North Lauderdale city *Broward Co.*	9,305.4	3.88	0.03	10
North Miami city *Miami-Dade Co.*	6,812.0	8.46	1.53	7
North Miami Beach city *Miami-Dade Co.*	7,980.8	4.96	0.34	10
North Port city *Sarasota Co.*	651.7	74.77	0.77	10
Oakland Park city *Broward Co.*	5,052.4	6.30	0.60	3
Ocala city *Marion Co.*	1,312.9	38.63	0.00	69
Orlando city *Orange Co.*	2,272.6	93.50	7.46	98
Ormond Beach city *Volusia Co.*	1,506.0	25.75	3.32	7
Oviedo city *Seminole Co.*	2,125.8	15.13	0.32	49
Palm Bay city *Brevard Co.*	1,528.0	63.65	3.10	16
Palm Beach Gardens city *Palm Beach Co.*	895.3	55.68	0.25	16
Palm Coast city *Flagler Co.*	1,154.3	50.72	0.98	3
Palm Harbor CDP *Pinellas Co.*	3,357.8	17.92	8.67	49
Panama City city *Bay Co.*	1,799.5	20.52	6.17	26
Pembroke Pines city *Broward Co.*	4,517.5	33.05	1.38	7
Pensacola city *Escambia Co.*	2,366.1	22.70	16.96	102
Pine Hills CDP *Orange Co.*	5,481.0	7.68	0.24	115
Pinellas Park city *Pinellas Co.*	3,160.6	14.75	0.19	13
Plant City city *Hillsborough Co.*	1,408.4	22.63	0.12	128
Plantation city *Broward Co.*	3,935.5	21.74	0.19	3
Pompano Beach city *Broward Co.*	3,954.6	20.55	1.60	13
Port Charlotte CDP *Charlotte Co.*	2,144.0	22.27	1.59	3
Port Orange city *Volusia Co.*	2,244.4	24.71	1.97	7
Port Saint Lucie city *Saint Lucie Co.*	1,890.0	75.54	1.15	16
Richmond West CDP *Miami-Dade Co.*	8,803.5	4.18	0.09	7
Riviera Beach city *Palm Beach Co.*	4,201.1	8.34	1.51	13
Royal Palm Beach village *Palm Beach Co.*	3,288.7	9.89	0.18	16
Saint Petersburg city *Pinellas Co.*	4,202.5	59.63	73.45	43
Sanford city *Seminole Co.*	2,560.0	19.11	3.49	30
Sarasota city *Sarasota Co.*	3,621.5	14.89	11.04	23
South Miami Heights CDP *Miami-Dade Co.*	7,261.3	4.93	0.00	10
Spring Hill CDP *Hernando Co.*	1,704.9	53.13	1.71	213
Sunrise city *Broward Co.*	4,965.2	18.20	0.23	5
Tallahassee city *Leon Co.*	1,735.9	95.71	2.54	203
Tamarac city *Broward Co.*	5,290.7	11.39	0.50	10
Tamiami CDP *Miami-Dade Co.*	8,112.2	7.34	0.23	3
Tampa city *Hillsborough Co.*	2,962.8	112.07	58.53	3
The Hammocks CDP *Miami-Dade Co.*	6,952.0	7.86	0.17	3
Titusville city *Brevard Co.*	2,105.8	21.26	4.65	10
Town 'n' Country CDP *Hillsborough Co.*	3,335.4	23.67	0.74	3
University CDP *Hillsborough Co.*	8,355.5	3.87	0.01	n/a
Wellington village *Palm Beach Co.*	1,820.4	31.05	0.31	16
West Palm Beach city *Palm Beach Co.*	1,826.3	55.14	3.06	13
Weston city *Broward Co.*	2,842.3	23.76	2.52	3
Winter Springs city *Seminole Co.*	2,393.5	14.35	0.14	52

NOTE: Population Density figures as of 2007; Land Area and Water Area figures as of 2000.

Population by Race/Hispanic Origin

Place	White Alone (%)	Black Alone (%)	Asian Alone (%)	Hispanic (%)
Altamonte Springs city *Seminole Co.*	73.8	11.7	3.9	21.2
Apopka city *Orange Co.*	67.3	19.5	2.3	24.0
Boca Raton city *Palm Beach Co.*	88.8	4.5	2.2	12.1
Bonita Springs city *Lee Co.*	83.4	0.6	0.5	28.3
Boynton Beach city *Palm Beach Co.*	65.3	25.7	2.1	13.0
Bradenton city *Manatee Co.*	75.6	15.5	1.1	15.2
Brandon CDP *Hillsborough Co.*	75.2	13.3	3.0	17.6
Cape Coral city *Lee Co.*	88.7	3.3	1.2	15.0
Carol City CDP *Miami-Dade Co.*	40.1	49.5	0.5	45.9
Clearwater city *Pinellas Co.*	81.0	10.6	2.0	13.5
Coconut Creek city *Broward Co.*	78.3	10.3	3.6	18.2
Coral Gables city *Miami-Dade Co.*	91.7	3.3	1.7	48.6
Coral Springs city *Broward Co.*	74.1	13.5	4.5	22.1
Country Club CDP *Miami-Dade Co.*	62.7	21.3	2.0	65.6
Davie town *Broward Co.*	82.4	6.2	3.6	26.9
Daytona Beach city *Volusia Co.*	59.2	34.4	2.4	4.7
Deerfield Beach city *Broward Co.*	75.1	15.9	1.8	12.5
Delray Beach city *Palm Beach Co.*	62.8	28.4	1.5	9.5
Deltona city *Volusia Co.*	78.4	9.6	1.2	26.1
Dunedin city *Pinellas Co.*	93.0	2.7	1.6	4.8
East Lake CDP *Pinellas Co.*	92.9	1.6	3.3	5.6
Egypt Lake-Leto CDP *Hillsborough Co.*	71.1	9.8	4.4	54.6
Fort Lauderdale city *Broward Co.*	61.0	30.4	1.2	11.6
Fort Myers city *Lee Co.*	50.6	35.7	1.3	20.8
Fort Pierce city *Saint Lucie Co.*	43.6	42.9	1.0	23.7
Fountainbleau CDP *Miami-Dade Co.*	87.3	2.0	1.8	87.6
Gainesville city *Alachua Co.*	65.1	25.0	5.3	7.3
Golden Glades CDP *Miami-Dade Co.*	20.0	68.1	1.3	16.9
Greater Carrollwood CDP *Hillsborough Co.*	80.9	7.1	4.2	24.5
Greenacres city *Palm Beach Co.*	76.3	9.1	2.6	32.1
Hallandale city *Broward Co.*	72.8	18.1	1.3	26.3
Hialeah city *Miami-Dade Co.*	88.1	2.6	0.4	91.5
Hollywood city *Broward Co.*	71.9	15.3	2.5	31.3
Homestead city *Miami-Dade Co.*	63.2	20.1	0.9	57.0
Jacksonville special city *Duval Co.*	60.4	31.4	3.4	5.7
Jupiter town *Palm Beach Co.*	92.9	1.4	1.6	11.7
Kendale Lakes CDP *Miami-Dade Co.*	87.6	1.9	1.6	82.0
Kendall CDP *Miami-Dade Co.*	87.0	3.6	2.8	58.1
Kendall West CDP *Miami-Dade Co.*	84.6	3.1	1.1	84.4
Kissimmee city *Osceola Co.*	59.1	11.3	3.7	56.5
Lake Worth city *Palm Beach Co.*	59.9	19.5	0.8	39.8
Lakeland city *Polk Co.*	70.9	22.0	1.8	9.4
Lakeside CDP *Clay Co.*	81.9	9.7	2.9	7.1
Land O' Lakes CDP *Pasco Co.*	90.5	3.8	1.9	12.5
Largo city *Pinellas Co.*	90.0	3.9	2.2	6.1
Lauderdale Lakes city *Broward Co.*	16.3	74.1	1.0	6.0
Lauderhill city *Broward Co.*	26.6	64.6	1.7	8.3
Lehigh Acres CDP *Lee Co.*	76.5	12.6	1.1	23.2
Margate city *Broward Co.*	69.1	17.9	3.7	21.7
Melbourne city *Brevard Co.*	81.8	10.6	2.8	7.6

Place	White Alone (%)	Black Alone (%)	Asian Alone (%)	Hispanic (%)
Merritt Island CDP *Brevard Co.*	89.4	5.2	2.0	5.1
Miami city *Miami-Dade Co.*	68.7	19.7	0.7	67.8
Miami Beach city *Miami-Dade Co.*	87.6	3.3	1.4	56.7
Miramar city *Broward Co.*	41.4	43.6	3.6	37.5
North Fort Myers CDP *Lee Co.*	94.0	1.8	0.7	5.4
North Lauderdale city *Broward Co.*	37.9	44.9	3.0	25.1
North Miami city *Miami-Dade Co.*	31.1	57.9	1.7	23.6
North Miami Beach city *Miami-Dade Co.*	43.7	40.9	3.9	33.8
North Port city *Sarasota Co.*	90.7	5.2	0.7	5.0
Oakland Park city *Broward Co.*	55.2	30.5	2.2	22.2
Ocala city *Marion Co.*	71.2	21.9	1.9	8.4
Orlando city *Orange Co.*	56.2	28.0	3.4	22.9
Ormond Beach city *Volusia Co.*	93.4	2.8	1.9	3.0
Oviedo city *Seminole Co.*	81.9	8.3	3.2	16.5
Palm Bay city *Brevard Co.*	77.1	14.1	1.9	11.9
Palm Beach Gardens city *Palm Beach Co.*	92.2	3.1	2.6	8.1
Palm Coast city *Flagler Co.*	83.2	11.2	2.1	8.6
Palm Harbor CDP *Pinellas Co.*	94.3	1.4	1.8	4.8
Panama City city *Bay Co.*	71.7	22.8	1.6	4.4
Pembroke Pines city *Broward Co.*	68.0	17.9	4.6	38.3
Pensacola city *Escambia Co.*	64.1	30.9	1.9	2.2
Pine Hills CDP *Orange Co.*	24.0	58.9	3.1	15.6
Pinellas Park city *Pinellas Co.*	85.1	2.9	5.8	8.8
Plant City city *Hillsborough Co.*	67.9	15.1	1.1	23.7
Plantation city *Broward Co.*	71.0	18.7	3.7	17.4
Pompano Beach city *Broward Co.*	65.8	25.1	1.0	14.2
Port Charlotte CDP *Charlotte Co.*	86.4	8.5	1.4	7.3
Port Orange city *Volusia Co.*	94.1	2.2	1.6	3.4
Port Saint Lucie city *Saint Lucie Co.*	81.8	10.6	1.7	12.8
Richmond West CDP *Miami-Dade Co.*	77.4	7.7	1.9	77.2
Riviera Beach city *Palm Beach Co.*	26.7	67.8	1.4	6.5
Royal Palm Beach village *Palm Beach Co.*	71.7	18.4	3.5	16.6
Saint Petersburg city *Pinellas Co.*	67.1	24.9	3.4	5.7
Sanford city *Seminole Co.*	54.8	34.2	1.4	14.2
Sarasota city *Sarasota Co.*	73.6	16.2	1.4	19.2
South Miami Heights CDP *Miami-Dade Co.*	57.1	27.7	1.7	61.4
Spring Hill CDP *Hernando Co.*	91.4	4.0	1.1	10.3
Sunrise city *Broward Co.*	61.4	25.5	3.8	23.3
Tallahassee city *Leon Co.*	57.8	35.6	3.2	4.9
Tamarac city *Broward Co.*	73.4	16.2	1.9	21.6
Tamiami CDP *Miami-Dade Co.*	90.4	1.0	0.6	87.9
Tampa city *Hillsborough Co.*	60.8	27.3	2.9	22.6
The Hammocks CDP *Miami-Dade Co.*	79.4	5.7	2.9	72.3
Titusville city *Brevard Co.*	81.5	14.3	1.1	4.6
Town 'n' Country CDP *Hillsborough Co.*	73.4	9.8	4.0	37.1
University CDP *Hillsborough Co.*	45.0	37.5	4.4	23.6
Wellington village *Palm Beach Co.*	84.6	7.5	2.4	16.8
West Palm Beach city *Palm Beach Co.*	53.4	34.6	2.0	21.8
Weston city *Broward Co.*	83.9	5.2	4.1	38.4
Winter Springs city *Seminole Co.*	86.1	5.5	2.4	13.8

NOTE: Data as of 2007; (1) Figures are not in combination with any other race; (2) Persons of Hispanic Origin may be of any race

Avg. Household Size, Median Age, Male/Female Ratio & Foreign Born

Place	Average Household Size (persons)	Median Age (years)	Male/Female Ratio (males per 100 females)	Foreign Born (%)
Altamonte Springs city *Seminole Co.*	2.15	37.0	94.1	12.7
Apopka city *Orange Co.*	2.76	34.6	94.8	11.8
Boca Raton city *Palm Beach Co.*	2.33	44.3	95.8	18.0
Bonita Springs city *Lee Co.*	2.19	53.1	105.2	16.0
Boynton Beach city *Palm Beach Co.*	2.29	42.5	89.3	17.4
Bradenton city *Manatee Co.*	2.31	40.5	92.4	8.5
Brandon CDP *Hillsborough Co.*	2.64	35.4	95.2	7.6
Cape Coral city *Lee Co.*	2.51	39.8	96.1	8.7
Carol City CDP *Miami-Dade Co.*	3.64	33.2	92.6	37.2
Clearwater city *Pinellas Co.*	2.25	43.5	93.2	13.2
Coconut Creek city *Broward Co.*	2.24	41.6	88.5	18.3
Coral Gables city *Miami-Dade Co.*	2.51	40.5	88.0	37.9
Coral Springs city *Broward Co.*	2.99	34.5	95.6	21.3
Country Club CDP *Miami-Dade Co.*	2.85	32.3	90.7	47.0
Davie town *Broward Co.*	2.70	36.2	96.0	17.5
Daytona Beach city *Volusia Co.*	2.22	37.5	101.8	7.7
Deerfield Beach city *Broward Co.*	2.07	45.4	88.5	22.7
Delray Beach city *Palm Beach Co.*	2.24	44.7	93.1	21.5
Deltona city *Volusia Co.*	2.83	37.0	95.0	7.1
Dunedin city *Pinellas Co.*	2.04	49.8	85.9	9.7
East Lake CDP *Pinellas Co.*	2.52	44.5	94.7	9.6
Egypt Lake-Leto CDP *Hillsborough Co.*	2.39	34.0	96.6	27.3
Fort Lauderdale city *Broward Co.*	2.21	41.4	110.8	21.7
Fort Myers city *Lee Co.*	2.49	31.7	100.6	13.4
Fort Pierce city *Saint Lucie Co.*	2.59	33.8	98.9	18.4
Fountainbleau CDP *Miami-Dade Co.*	2.87	37.6	87.6	73.1
Gainesville city *Alachua Co.*	2.49	27.6	95.8	8.7
Golden Glades CDP *Miami-Dade Co.*	3.39	32.6	89.6	45.3
Greater Carrollwood CDP *Hillsborough Co.*	2.35	38.8	92.7	13.5
Greenacres city *Palm Beach Co.*	2.28	39.5	90.1	19.3
Hallandale city *Broward Co.*	1.94	52.0	87.1	36.1
Hialeah city *Miami-Dade Co.*	3.24	40.0	93.0	72.1
Hollywood city *Broward Co.*	2.39	40.3	95.6	26.3
Homestead city *Miami-Dade Co.*	3.12	29.4	103.2	36.0
Jacksonville special city *Duval Co.*	2.54	35.4	94.5	5.9
Jupiter town *Palm Beach Co.*	2.34	42.9	98.4	10.5
Kendale Lakes CDP *Miami-Dade Co.*	3.19	37.7	90.2	58.8
Kendall CDP *Miami-Dade Co.*	2.67	39.7	89.0	42.6
Kendall West CDP *Miami-Dade Co.*	3.35	33.5	90.4	59.4
Kissimmee city *Osceola Co.*	2.77	31.7	100.4	19.5
Lake Worth city *Palm Beach Co.*	2.56	36.1	109.3	35.6
Lakeland city *Polk Co.*	2.32	39.4	88.5	5.7
Lakeside CDP *Clay Co.*	2.77	36.8	96.2	5.7
Land O' Lakes CDP *Pasco Co.*	2.71	37.6	97.5	4.2
Largo city *Pinellas Co.*	2.04	48.1	88.6	9.4
Lauderdale Lakes city *Broward Co.*	2.67	34.6	83.9	40.5
Lauderhill city *Broward Co.*	2.53	36.0	86.3	33.8
Lehigh Acres CDP *Lee Co.*	2.68	35.3	97.0	9.3
Margate city *Broward Co.*	2.41	41.1	91.5	22.0
Melbourne city *Brevard Co.*	2.28	41.1	95.3	7.8

Place	Average Household Size (persons)	Median Age (years)	Male/Female Ratio (males per 100 females)	Foreign Born (%)
Merritt Island CDP *Brevard Co.*	2.38	44.8	96.2	6.4
Miami city *Miami-Dade Co.*	2.69	40.0	99.2	59.5
Miami Beach city *Miami-Dade Co.*	1.93	42.6	105.1	55.5
Miramar city *Broward Co.*	3.23	32.1	92.6	40.7
North Fort Myers CDP *Lee Co.*	2.00	59.1	92.3	4.2
North Lauderdale city *Broward Co.*	3.04	31.3	95.0	34.9
North Miami city *Miami-Dade Co.*	3.01	33.5	92.8	48.5
North Miami Beach city *Miami-Dade Co.*	2.99	36.2	92.2	49.7
North Port city *Sarasota Co.*	2.62	38.2	95.3	12.1
Oakland Park city *Broward Co.*	2.32	37.5	108.9	29.6
Ocala city *Marion Co.*	2.48	37.5	92.6	4.6
Orlando city *Orange Co.*	2.24	34.7	95.7	14.4
Ormond Beach city *Volusia Co.*	2.29	48.6	89.3	7.0
Oviedo city *Seminole Co.*	3.11	34.5	98.5	9.2
Palm Bay city *Brevard Co.*	2.58	38.0	95.7	9.5
Palm Beach Gardens city *Palm Beach Co.*	2.22	46.1	91.1	10.8
Palm Coast city *Flagler Co.*	2.39	44.8	93.2	12.5
Palm Harbor CDP *Pinellas Co.*	2.29	45.3	89.4	8.4
Panama City city *Bay Co.*	2.43	37.8	95.7	3.2
Pembroke Pines city *Broward Co.*	2.67	38.1	88.0	29.0
Pensacola city *Escambia Co.*	2.24	42.1	88.9	3.6
Pine Hills CDP *Orange Co.*	3.14	30.6	93.7	22.4
Pinellas Park city *Pinellas Co.*	2.34	42.3	92.3	9.5
Plant City city *Hillsborough Co.*	2.73	33.3	94.9	9.8
Plantation city *Broward Co.*	2.50	39.3	91.5	22.4
Pompano Beach city *Broward Co.*	2.21	43.7	98.4	20.3
Port Charlotte CDP *Charlotte Co.*	2.29	47.5	88.9	9.6
Port Orange city *Volusia Co.*	2.31	45.4	92.1	5.7
Port Saint Lucie city *Saint Lucie Co.*	2.58	39.5	95.7	9.6
Richmond West CDP *Miami-Dade Co.*	3.69	31.8	95.6	45.6
Riviera Beach city *Palm Beach Co.*	2.60	35.6	92.8	10.1
Royal Palm Beach village *Palm Beach Co.*	2.83	37.3	93.1	14.7
Saint Petersburg city *Pinellas Co.*	2.27	40.9	92.6	9.1
Sanford city *Seminole Co.*	2.62	34.3	100.1	5.9
Sarasota city *Sarasota Co.*	2.21	41.3	96.6	13.9
South Miami Heights CDP *Miami-Dade Co.*	3.44	32.8	93.4	44.1
Spring Hill CDP *Hernando Co.*	2.42	44.6	91.2	6.7
Sunrise city *Broward Co.*	2.58	37.7	89.7	28.1
Tallahassee city *Leon Co.*	2.30	29.2	90.8	5.5
Tamarac city *Broward Co.*	2.05	49.8	83.0	21.3
Tamiami CDP *Miami-Dade Co.*	3.38	39.2	90.9	65.5
Tampa city *Hillsborough Co.*	2.41	35.6	97.3	12.2
The Hammocks CDP *Miami-Dade Co.*	3.19	33.8	90.6	52.4
Titusville city *Brevard Co.*	2.32	42.2	91.7	4.8
Town 'n' Country CDP *Hillsborough Co.*	2.46	36.9	96.1	17.6
University CDP *Hillsborough Co.*	2.23	28.8	99.6	15.0
Wellington village *Palm Beach Co.*	2.93	36.6	95.7	13.4
West Palm Beach city *Palm Beach Co.*	2.34	37.4	98.5	24.7
Weston city *Broward Co.*	3.07	34.7	94.4	28.0
Winter Springs city *Seminole Co.*	2.66	39.9	94.9	8.1

NOTE: Average Household Size, Median Age, and Male/Female Ratio figures as of 2007. Foreign Born figures as of 2000.

Five Largest Ancestry Groups

Place	Group 1	Group 2	Group 3	Group 4	Group 5
Altamonte Springs city *Seminole Co.*	Other (30.7%)	German (14.4%)	Irish (12.5%)	English (9.8%)	Italian (8.3%)
Apopka city *Orange Co.*	Other (30.1%)	German (12.6%)	Irish (10.9%)	American (8.9%)	English (7.9%)
Boca Raton city *Palm Beach Co.*	Other (15.5%)	German (14.4%)	Italian (12.4%)	Irish (12.0%)	English (9.4%)
Bonita Springs city *Lee Co.*	German (20.5%)	Other (19.4%)	English (14.8%)	Irish (13.6%)	American (6.2%)
Boynton Beach city *Palm Beach Co.*	Other (22.8%)	German (11.8%)	Irish (11.6%)	Italian (9.7%)	English (9.0%)
Bradenton city *Manatee Co.*	Other (24.8%)	German (14.9%)	English (12.0%)	Irish (10.9%)	American (6.7%)
Brandon CDP *Hillsborough Co.*	Other (27.1%)	German (14.4%)	Irish (12.5%)	English (11.4%)	American (8.5%)
Cape Coral city *Lee Co.*	German (20.9%)	Irish (15.9%)	Other (13.5%)	Italian (13.1%)	English (11.9%)
Carol City CDP *Miami-Dade Co.*	Other (70.8%)	Jamaican (5.2%)	American (4.8%)	Haitian (2.3%)	African (0.8%)
Clearwater city *Pinellas Co.*	Other (21.5%)	German (16.9%)	Irish (13.8%)	English (11.9%)	Italian (8.0%)
Coconut Creek city *Broward Co.*	Other (24.4%)	Italian (13.5%)	German (10.7%)	Irish (10.2%)	Polish (6.8%)
Coral Gables city *Miami-Dade Co.*	Other (54.0%)	English (7.4%)	German (7.0%)	Irish (5.7%)	Italian (5.3%)
Coral Springs city *Broward Co.*	Other (26.8%)	Italian (14.2%)	German (11.9%)	Irish (11.3%)	American (6.5%)
Country Club CDP *Miami-Dade Co.*	Other (72.7%)	American (3.8%)	Haitian (3.1%)	Irish (2.1%)	Italian (2.1%)
Davie town *Broward Co.*	Other (28.2%)	Irish (14.0%)	German (13.7%)	Italian (12.5%)	English (7.5%)
Daytona Beach city *Volusia Co.*	Other (33.1%)	German (11.0%)	Irish (10.4%)	English (8.3%)	Italian (5.9%)
Deerfield Beach city *Broward Co.*	Other (23.2%)	Irish (10.8%)	Italian (10.6%)	German (9.6%)	English (7.2%)
Delray Beach city *Palm Beach Co.*	Other (21.5%)	Haitian (10.6%)	German (10.5%)	Irish (10.3%)	English (8.1%)
Deltona city *Volusia Co.*	Other (27.1%)	German (15.8%)	Irish (14.5%)	Italian (9.8%)	English (9.7%)
Dunedin city *Pinellas Co.*	German (21.3%)	Irish (17.2%)	English (14.6%)	Other (10.9%)	Italian (10.2%)
East Lake CDP *Pinellas Co.*	German (21.2%)	Irish (16.7%)	English (14.1%)	Italian (13.9%)	Other (10.9%)
Egypt Lake-Leto CDP *Hillsborough Co.*	Other (54.6%)	German (7.6%)	Irish (6.8%)	Italian (6.3%)	American (5.5%)
Fort Lauderdale city *Broward Co.*	Other (27.5%)	German (10.4%)	Irish (10.3%)	English (8.2%)	Italian (7.6%)
Fort Myers city *Lee Co.*	Other (38.5%)	German (10.7%)	English (8.0%)	Irish (7.7%)	American (6.4%)
Fort Pierce city *Saint Lucie Co.*	Other (42.8%)	Irish (8.2%)	German (7.9%)	English (6.9%)	American (6.6%)
Fountainbleau CDP *Miami-Dade Co.*	Other (86.2%)	American (2.5%)	Italian (1.7%)	German (0.8%)	Irish (0.5%)
Gainesville city *Alachua Co.*	Other (31.1%)	German (12.6%)	Irish (10.7%)	English (9.9%)	American (5.6%)
Golden Glades CDP *Miami-Dade Co.*	Other (36.4%)	Haitian (32.0%)	Jamaican (5.4%)	American (5.2%)	German (1.9%)
Greater Carrollwood CDP *Hillsborough Co.*	Other (31.0%)	German (13.9%)	Irish (12.7%)	English (10.2%)	Italian (8.9%)
Greenacres city *Palm Beach Co.*	Other (30.9%)	Italian (13.1%)	German (12.0%)	Irish (10.9%)	English (7.4%)
Hallandale city *Broward Co.*	Other (33.9%)	Italian (9.2%)	German (5.9%)	American (5.4%)	Russian (5.1%)
Hialeah city *Miami-Dade Co.*	Other (85.0%)	American (2.6%)	Italian (0.7%)	German (0.6%)	Irish (0.5%)
Hollywood city *Broward Co.*	Other (33.5%)	Italian (9.5%)	Irish (9.1%)	German (8.6%)	American (7.0%)
Homestead city *Miami-Dade Co.*	Other (62.2%)	American (5.2%)	Haitian (4.8%)	Irish (4.2%)	German (4.0%)
Jacksonville special city *Duval Co.*	Other (35.5%)	German (9.6%)	American (9.3%)	Irish (9.0%)	English (8.5%)
Jupiter town *Palm Beach Co.*	Irish (18.6%)	German (17.9%)	Italian (16.8%)	English (13.6%)	Other (12.2%)
Kendale Lakes CDP *Miami-Dade Co.*	Other (79.4%)	American (2.8%)	Italian (2.3%)	German (1.8%)	English (1.7%)
Kendall CDP *Miami-Dade Co.*	Other (59.3%)	German (5.7%)	American (5.4%)	Italian (5.1%)	Irish (5.0%)
Kendall West CDP *Miami-Dade Co.*	Other (82.8%)	American (2.5%)	Italian (2.1%)	German (1.6%)	English (1.2%)
Kissimmee city *Osceola Co.*	Other (49.4%)	German (8.8%)	Irish (7.1%)	American (6.3%)	English (6.3%)
Lake Worth city *Palm Beach Co.*	Other (34.6%)	German (8.7%)	Irish (8.5%)	Haitian (7.8%)	English (6.1%)
Lakeland city *Polk Co.*	Other (29.4%)	German (12.5%)	English (11.1%)	Irish (10.3%)	American (9.9%)
Lakeside CDP *Clay Co.*	Other (20.8%)	German (14.7%)	Irish (12.4%)	American (11.9%)	English (10.9%)
Land O' Lakes CDP *Pasco Co.*	German (20.3%)	Other (18.9%)	Irish (14.7%)	English (13.8%)	American (8.7%)
Largo city *Pinellas Co.*	German (18.3%)	Irish (15.4%)	English (13.9%)	Other (11.2%)	Italian (9.6%)
Lauderdale Lakes city *Broward Co.*	Other (35.3%)	Jamaican (17.9%)	Haitian (15.0%)	American (5.7%)	Italian (2.5%)
Lauderhill city *Broward Co.*	Other (33.8%)	Jamaican (17.0%)	Haitian (8.8%)	American (7.5%)	Italian (3.8%)
Lehigh Acres CDP *Lee Co.*	Other (22.4%)	German (15.1%)	Irish (12.4%)	American (11.9%)	English (10.6%)
Margate city *Broward Co.*	Other (27.6%)	Italian (12.8%)	German (11.2%)	Irish (11.2%)	English (6.5%)
Melbourne city *Brevard Co.*	Other (20.2%)	German (16.7%)	Irish (14.7%)	English (12.8%)	Italian (8.2%)

Place	Group 1	Group 2	Group 3	Group 4	Group 5
Merritt Island CDP *Brevard Co.*	German (19.6%)	English (16.0%)	Irish (15.5%)	Other (14.4%)	Italian (8.7%)
Miami city *Miami-Dade Co.*	Other (71.3%)	Haitian (5.0%)	American (3.1%)	Italian (1.4%)	German (1.2%)
Miami Beach city *Miami-Dade Co.*	Other (54.1%)	Italian (5.0%)	American (5.0%)	German (4.3%)	Russian (3.7%)
Miramar city *Broward Co.*	Other (47.8%)	Jamaican (15.5%)	Haitian (6.0%)	American (4.9%)	German (3.9%)
North Fort Myers CDP *Lee Co.*	German (20.0%)	English (15.7%)	Irish (14.0%)	American (10.0%)	Other (8.1%)
North Lauderdale city *Broward Co.*	Other (36.9%)	Jamaican (11.4%)	American (8.0%)	Italian (6.9%)	Haitian (6.9%)
North Miami city *Miami-Dade Co.*	Other (34.2%)	Haitian (31.1%)	American (5.5%)	Jamaican (3.1%)	German (2.4%)
North Miami Beach city *Miami-Dade Co.*	Other (43.2%)	Haitian (19.3%)	American (6.0%)	Jamaican (5.4%)	Italian (3.0%)
North Port city *Sarasota Co.*	German (21.8%)	Irish (15.8%)	English (11.9%)	Other (10.4%)	Italian (8.5%)
Oakland Park city *Broward Co.*	Other (32.4%)	German (10.3%)	Irish (9.6%)	Italian (8.0%)	Haitian (7.4%)
Ocala city *Marion Co.*	Other (26.9%)	German (13.2%)	Irish (11.8%)	English (11.1%)	American (6.8%)
Orlando city *Orange Co.*	Other (39.5%)	German (9.8%)	Irish (8.7%)	English (7.9%)	American (6.7%)
Ormond Beach city *Volusia Co.*	German (17.6%)	English (16.9%)	Irish (14.8%)	Other (10.1%)	American (9.7%)
Oviedo city *Seminole Co.*	Other (24.0%)	German (18.1%)	Irish (13.4%)	English (11.7%)	Italian (11.6%)
Palm Bay city *Brevard Co.*	Other (21.9%)	German (17.9%)	Irish (14.6%)	English (10.1%)	Italian (9.2%)
Palm Beach Gardens city *Palm Beach Co.*	German (17.2%)	Irish (15.2%)	Other (13.7%)	English (13.3%)	Italian (12.9%)
Palm Coast city *Flagler Co.*	Other (17.5%)	Irish (16.9%)	German (15.9%)	Italian (15.3%)	English (11.9%)
Palm Harbor CDP *Pinellas Co.*	German (19.5%)	Irish (16.5%)	English (13.9%)	Italian (12.8%)	Other (8.9%)
Panama City city *Bay Co.*	Other (25.9%)	American (12.9%)	Irish (10.3%)	German (9.8%)	English (9.1%)
Pembroke Pines city *Broward Co.*	Other (42.2%)	Italian (9.4%)	Irish (8.2%)	German (8.1%)	American (6.1%)
Pensacola city *Escambia Co.*	Other (33.4%)	English (11.0%)	German (10.5%)	Irish (10.0%)	American (7.7%)
Pine Hills CDP *Orange Co.*	Other (45.9%)	Haitian (11.5%)	American (6.6%)	German (4.8%)	Irish (4.2%)
Pinellas Park city *Pinellas Co.*	German (18.5%)	Other (17.8%)	Irish (15.8%)	English (11.6%)	Italian (8.4%)
Plant City city *Hillsborough Co.*	Other (37.4%)	Irish (11.3%)	German (11.0%)	English (10.7%)	American (9.2%)
Plantation city *Broward Co.*	Other (26.8%)	German (10.8%)	Irish (10.2%)	Italian (8.9%)	American (8.0%)
Pompano Beach city *Broward Co.*	Other (29.3%)	German (9.7%)	Irish (9.7%)	Italian (8.9%)	English (6.5%)
Port Charlotte CDP *Charlotte Co.*	German (19.3%)	Irish (15.9%)	English (12.6%)	Other (12.4%)	Italian (10.4%)
Port Orange city *Volusia Co.*	German (18.2%)	Irish (15.7%)	English (14.0%)	Italian (11.1%)	Other (8.3%)
Port Saint Lucie city *Saint Lucie Co.*	Irish (17.4%)	German (16.9%)	Italian (15.7%)	Other (15.4%)	English (11.5%)
Richmond West CDP *Miami-Dade Co.*	Other (79.4%)	American (5.4%)	Jamaican (3.4%)	Italian (2.7%)	Irish (2.2%)
Riviera Beach city *Palm Beach Co.*	Other (57.1%)	German (4.4%)	English (4.1%)	Irish (3.8%)	American (3.4%)
Royal Palm Beach village *Palm Beach Co.*	Other (24.4%)	German (14.0%)	Italian (13.3%)	Irish (11.8%)	American (8.5%)
Saint Petersburg city *Pinellas Co.*	Other (27.8%)	German (14.7%)	Irish (12.4%)	English (11.1%)	Italian (6.8%)
Sanford city *Seminole Co.*	Other (38.8%)	German (10.7%)	Irish (9.2%)	English (9.1%)	American (6.2%)
Sarasota city *Sarasota Co.*	Other (27.0%)	German (14.0%)	English (10.5%)	Irish (10.5%)	American (6.2%)
South Miami Heights CDP *Miami-Dade Co.*	Other (71.3%)	Jamaican (5.7%)	American (4.4%)	English (1.7%)	German (1.6%)
Spring Hill CDP *Hernando Co.*	German (19.7%)	Italian (18.0%)	Irish (17.0%)	Other (12.8%)	English (11.0%)
Sunrise city *Broward Co.*	Other (33.8%)	Italian (10.3%)	Jamaican (8.0%)	Irish (7.4%)	German (7.4%)
Tallahassee city *Leon Co.*	Other (34.1%)	German (9.4%)	English (9.2%)	Irish (8.8%)	American (5.3%)
Tamarac city *Broward Co.*	Other (29.8%)	Italian (10.9%)	American (9.1%)	Irish (7.9%)	German (7.7%)
Tamiami CDP *Miami-Dade Co.*	Other (88.0%)	American (1.9%)	Italian (1.3%)	Irish (0.9%)	German (0.9%)
Tampa city *Hillsborough Co.*	Other (42.3%)	German (9.2%)	Irish (8.4%)	English (7.7%)	American (6.2%)
The Hammocks CDP *Miami-Dade Co.*	Other (75.5%)	Italian (4.0%)	American (3.1%)	German (3.0%)	Jamaican (3.0%)
Titusville city *Brevard Co.*	Other (19.4%)	German (16.7%)	Irish (13.4%)	English (12.4%)	American (8.9%)
Town 'n' Country CDP *Hillsborough Co.*	Other (39.9%)	German (13.2%)	Irish (10.3%)	English (8.2%)	Italian (7.3%)
University CDP *Hillsborough Co.*	Other (46.8%)	German (6.7%)	Irish (6.1%)	American (4.5%)	English (4.1%)
Wellington village *Palm Beach Co.*	Other (19.0%)	Irish (15.1%)	Italian (14.6%)	German (13.6%)	English (11.2%)
West Palm Beach city *Palm Beach Co.*	Other (40.1%)	German (7.5%)	Irish (7.0%)	English (6.2%)	American (5.2%)
Weston city *Broward Co.*	Other (40.7%)	Italian (9.8%)	German (9.2%)	Irish (7.9%)	American (6.8%)
Winter Springs city *Seminole Co.*	Other (19.0%)	German (18.2%)	Irish (15.6%)	English (12.8%)	Italian (10.8%)

NOTE: Data as of 2000; "Other" includes Hispanic and race groups; "French" excludes Basque; Please refer to the Explanation of Data for more information.

Marriage Status

Place	Never Married (%)	Now Married (%)	Widowed (%)	Divorced (%)
Altamonte Springs city *Seminole Co.*	31.1	47.0	6.1	15.8
Apopka city *Orange Co.*	22.1	59.6	5.1	13.2
Boca Raton city *Palm Beach Co.*	22.1	60.6	7.4	10.0
Bonita Springs city *Lee Co.*	14.0	68.8	8.1	9.1
Boynton Beach city *Palm Beach Co.*	21.5	55.6	11.1	11.8
Bradenton city *Manatee Co.*	22.4	52.7	12.3	12.6
Brandon CDP *Hillsborough Co.*	22.9	62.3	4.4	10.4
Cape Coral city *Lee Co.*	17.0	64.6	7.1	11.3
Carol City CDP *Miami-Dade Co.*	33.2	50.9	4.9	10.9
Clearwater city *Pinellas Co.*	24.4	50.9	9.9	14.8
Coconut Creek city *Broward Co.*	17.6	60.3	11.4	10.7
Coral Gables city *Miami-Dade Co.*	32.0	51.4	6.0	10.6
Coral Springs city *Broward Co.*	25.5	60.2	4.1	10.3
Country Club CDP *Miami-Dade Co.*	29.3	55.3	4.0	11.5
Davie town *Broward Co.*	25.5	55.1	5.7	13.6
Daytona Beach city *Volusia Co.*	34.7	41.9	9.6	13.8
Deerfield Beach city *Broward Co.*	23.5	50.8	13.5	12.3
Delray Beach city *Palm Beach Co.*	24.6	51.6	11.5	12.3
Deltona city *Volusia Co.*	21.1	61.6	6.5	10.8
Dunedin city *Pinellas Co.*	18.6	53.6	12.8	15.0
East Lake CDP *Pinellas Co.*	16.6	69.4	6.2	7.8
Egypt Lake-Leto CDP *Hillsborough Co.*	29.9	50.1	5.2	14.8
Fort Lauderdale city *Broward Co.*	35.3	43.3	7.3	14.0
Fort Myers city *Lee Co.*	33.6	43.2	8.8	14.5
Fort Pierce city *Saint Lucie Co.*	29.7	48.0	10.0	12.3
Fountainbleau CDP *Miami-Dade Co.*	26.3	55.3	6.0	12.3
Gainesville city *Alachua Co.*	49.1	37.1	4.7	9.1
Golden Glades CDP *Miami-Dade Co.*	35.6	46.7	6.9	10.9
Greater Carrollwood CDP *Hillsborough Co.*	23.9	58.5	4.4	13.2
Greenacres city *Palm Beach Co.*	19.8	55.6	10.6	14.1
Hallandale city *Broward Co.*	20.4	50.3	16.4	12.9
Hialeah city *Miami-Dade Co.*	22.3	58.5	7.3	11.8
Hollywood city *Broward Co.*	25.5	50.7	9.5	14.4
Homestead city *Miami-Dade Co.*	36.7	48.5	4.8	10.0
Jacksonville special city *Duval Co.*	26.5	53.9	6.3	13.3
Jupiter town *Palm Beach Co.*	18.9	62.3	6.5	12.3
Kendale Lakes CDP *Miami-Dade Co.*	23.9	58.4	6.4	11.4
Kendall CDP *Miami-Dade Co.*	25.8	55.7	6.1	12.4
Kendall West CDP *Miami-Dade Co.*	25.1	59.6	4.0	11.4
Kissimmee city *Osceola Co.*	30.4	52.6	4.6	12.4
Lake Worth city *Palm Beach Co.*	31.9	47.4	7.3	13.4
Lakeland city *Polk Co.*	24.0	52.9	10.6	12.5
Lakeside CDP *Clay Co.*	20.7	64.4	4.4	10.6
Land O' Lakes CDP *Pasco Co.*	17.5	67.4	4.9	10.2
Largo city *Pinellas Co.*	19.5	52.3	13.6	14.7
Lauderdale Lakes city *Broward Co.*	32.2	45.9	11.0	10.9
Lauderhill city *Broward Co.*	30.3	48.5	9.7	11.5
Lehigh Acres CDP *Lee Co.*	17.3	63.2	9.2	10.3
Margate city *Broward Co.*	21.7	56.4	11.3	10.6
Melbourne city *Brevard Co.*	24.3	53.3	9.0	13.5

Place	Never Married (%)	Now Married (%)	Widowed (%)	Divorced (%)
Merritt Island CDP *Brevard Co.*	19.6	58.3	9.0	13.1
Miami city *Miami-Dade Co.*	32.2	46.7	8.3	12.8
Miami Beach city *Miami-Dade Co.*	35.4	41.8	8.8	14.0
Miramar city *Broward Co.*	27.6	58.1	4.2	10.1
North Fort Myers CDP *Lee Co.*	11.6	64.4	13.2	10.8
North Lauderdale city *Broward Co.*	32.9	51.6	4.7	10.8
North Miami city *Miami-Dade Co.*	37.2	47.1	6.3	9.4
North Miami Beach city *Miami-Dade Co.*	31.6	49.9	7.2	11.3
North Port city *Sarasota Co.*	15.6	63.8	9.5	11.0
Oakland Park city *Broward Co.*	35.6	43.9	5.2	15.2
Ocala city *Marion Co.*	23.7	51.5	10.1	14.6
Orlando city *Orange Co.*	35.8	44.2	6.1	13.8
Ormond Beach city *Volusia Co.*	17.4	61.0	10.1	11.4
Oviedo city *Seminole Co.*	22.9	67.1	3.1	6.9
Palm Bay city *Brevard Co.*	21.5	59.9	6.5	12.0
Palm Beach Gardens city *Palm Beach Co.*	18.4	60.2	8.1	13.4
Palm Coast city *Flagler Co.*	12.9	70.8	9.2	7.2
Palm Harbor CDP *Pinellas Co.*	18.2	61.6	10.3	9.8
Panama City city *Bay Co.*	23.5	53.8	8.2	14.5
Pembroke Pines city *Broward Co.*	20.9	60.7	7.8	10.6
Pensacola city *Escambia Co.*	29.6	48.0	8.7	13.6
Pine Hills CDP *Orange Co.*	32.1	51.3	5.3	11.2
Pinellas Park city *Pinellas Co.*	20.6	54.5	10.8	14.1
Plant City city *Hillsborough Co.*	22.5	58.0	7.4	12.1
Plantation city *Broward Co.*	25.2	57.7	6.5	10.7
Pompano Beach city *Broward Co.*	27.0	49.8	10.5	12.7
Port Charlotte CDP *Charlotte Co.*	15.8	61.8	11.8	10.5
Port Orange city *Volusia Co.*	18.1	60.1	9.7	12.1
Port Saint Lucie city *Saint Lucie Co.*	18.4	64.3	6.9	10.5
Richmond West CDP *Miami-Dade Co.*	20.5	68.0	3.0	8.4
Riviera Beach city *Palm Beach Co.*	32.3	46.4	8.5	12.8
Royal Palm Beach village *Palm Beach Co.*	19.4	65.3	7.6	7.7
Saint Petersburg city *Pinellas Co.*	27.8	48.3	9.0	14.9
Sanford city *Seminole Co.*	30.6	47.6	6.5	15.3
Sarasota city *Sarasota Co.*	27.2	46.2	11.3	15.4
South Miami Heights CDP *Miami-Dade Co.*	30.8	51.2	6.2	11.8
Spring Hill CDP *Hernando Co.*	16.0	64.7	10.1	9.2
Sunrise city *Broward Co.*	24.1	55.2	10.0	10.7
Tallahassee city *Leon Co.*	49.2	37.2	4.3	9.3
Tamarac city *Broward Co.*	17.3	55.7	16.0	11.0
Tamiami CDP *Miami-Dade Co.*	23.3	60.2	6.2	10.2
Tampa city *Hillsborough Co.*	31.0	47.4	7.6	14.0
The Hammocks CDP *Miami-Dade Co.*	26.6	58.4	4.4	10.6
Titusville city *Brevard Co.*	20.0	56.7	10.0	13.3
Town 'n' Country CDP *Hillsborough Co.*	27.2	54.2	5.3	13.3
University CDP *Hillsborough Co.*	49.1	31.7	6.4	12.8
Wellington village *Palm Beach Co.*	20.3	67.6	3.8	8.3
West Palm Beach city *Palm Beach Co.*	33.2	45.3	8.5	13.0
Weston city *Broward Co.*	19.2	70.6	3.3	6.9
Winter Springs city *Seminole Co.*	20.9	64.1	5.2	9.8

NOTE: Data as of 2000

Employment and Building Permits Issued

Place	Unemployment Rate (%)	Total Civilian Labor Force	Single-Family Building Permits	Multi-Family Building Permits
Altamonte Springs city *Seminole Co.*	3.5	28,447	9	7
Apopka city *Orange Co.*	3.8	20,172	754	130
Boca Raton city *Palm Beach Co.*	3.4	47,690	55	247
Bonita Springs city *Lee Co.*	4.2	19,892	747	329
Boynton Beach city *Palm Beach Co.*	4.2	34,953	453	7
Bradenton city *Manatee Co.*	4.0	27,446	221	38
Brandon CDP *Hillsborough Co.*	n/a	n/a	n/a	n/a
Cape Coral city *Lee Co.*	5.4	83,691	3,727	770
Carol City CDP *Miami-Dade Co.*	n/a	n/a	n/a	n/a
Clearwater city *Pinellas Co.*	3.8	58,760	108	2
Coconut Creek city *Broward Co.*	3.5	27,203	132	0
Coral Gables city *Miami-Dade Co.*	2.2	25,857	63	153
Coral Springs city *Broward Co.*	3.4	77,595	76	22
Country Club CDP *Miami-Dade Co.*	n/a	n/a	n/a	n/a
Davie town *Broward Co.*	3.3	50,735	510	71
Daytona Beach city *Volusia Co.*	4.5	33,649	363	10
Deerfield Beach city *Broward Co.*	3.6	39,762	138	0
Delray Beach city *Palm Beach Co.*	4.2	32,759	116	264
Deltona city *Volusia Co.*	4.8	45,636	512	0
Dunedin city *Pinellas Co.*	3.8	18,729	36	6
East Lake CDP *Pinellas Co.*	n/a	n/a	n/a	n/a
Egypt Lake-Leto CDP *Hillsborough Co.*	n/a	n/a	n/a	n/a
Fort Lauderdale city *Broward Co.*	3.8	95,186	289	1,021
Fort Myers city *Lee Co.*	4.6	31,580	1,435	1,188
Fort Pierce city *Saint Lucie Co.*	7.8	18,127	216	325
Fountainbleau CDP *Miami-Dade Co.*	n/a	n/a	n/a	n/a
Gainesville city *Alachua Co.*	3.0	59,483	147	576
Golden Glades CDP *Miami-Dade Co.*	n/a	n/a	n/a	n/a
Greater Carrollwood CDP *Hillsborough Co.*	n/a	n/a	n/a	n/a
Greenacres city *Palm Beach Co.*	4.2	16,435	276	0
Hallandale city *Broward Co.*	4.5	17,372	12	181
Hialeah city *Miami-Dade Co.*	4.8	101,015	12	231
Hollywood city *Broward Co.*	4.0	81,830	69	106
Homestead city *Miami-Dade Co.*	3.2	21,675	991	662
Jacksonville special city *Duval Co.*	4.1	417,148	6,291	3,521
Jupiter town *Palm Beach Co.*	3.3	27,350	313	159
Kendale Lakes CDP *Miami-Dade Co.*	n/a	n/a	n/a	n/a
Kendall CDP *Miami-Dade Co.*	n/a	n/a	n/a	n/a
Kendall West CDP *Miami-Dade Co.*	n/a	n/a	n/a	n/a
Kissimmee city *Osceola Co.*	3.9	34,260	397	2
Lake Worth city *Palm Beach Co.*	4.0	19,891	40	94
Lakeland city *Polk Co.*	3.9	44,293	844	851
Lakeside CDP *Clay Co.*	n/a	n/a	n/a	n/a
Land O' Lakes CDP *Pasco Co.*	n/a	n/a	n/a	n/a
Largo city *Pinellas Co.*	4.0	37,411	36	134
Lauderdale Lakes city *Broward Co.*	4.7	14,809	0	0
Lauderhill city *Broward Co.*	4.4	31,002	163	0
Lehigh Acres CDP *Lee Co.*	n/a	n/a	n/a	n/a
Margate city *Broward Co.*	4.0	30,721	10	0
Melbourne city *Brevard Co.*	4.5	39,818	315	197

Place	Unemployment Rate (%)	Total Civilian Labor Force	Single-Family Building Permits	Multi-Family Building Permits
Merritt Island CDP *Brevard Co.*	n/a	n/a	n/a	n/a
Miami city *Miami-Dade Co.*	4.0	173,413	133	7,348
Miami Beach city *Miami-Dade Co.*	2.8	50,354	23	285
Miramar city *Broward Co.*	4.0	59,278	397	566
North Fort Myers CDP *Lee Co.*	n/a	n/a	n/a	n/a
North Lauderdale city *Broward Co.*	3.5	24,214	243	0
North Miami city *Miami-Dade Co.*	4.0	28,363	3	3
North Miami Beach city *Miami-Dade Co.*	4.2	19,456	84	0
North Port city *Sarasota Co.*	6.1	22,087	2,094	122
Oakland Park city *Broward Co.*	3.6	20,573	166	0
Ocala city *Marion Co.*	4.1	24,043	612	192
Orlando city *Orange Co.*	3.9	130,517	1,563	2,790
Ormond Beach city *Volusia Co.*	3.6	20,087	115	0
Oviedo city *Seminole Co.*	2.8	18,615	169	0
Palm Bay city *Brevard Co.*	5.3	48,306	1,764	7
Palm Beach Gardens city *Palm Beach Co.*	3.0	27,561	224	274
Palm Coast city *Flagler Co.*	5.8	27,812	1,283	298
Palm Harbor CDP *Pinellas Co.*	n/a	n/a	n/a	n/a
Panama City city *Bay Co.*	4.0	18,560	n/a	n/a
Pembroke Pines city *Broward Co.*	3.5	85,079	5	103
Pensacola city *Escambia Co.*	3.7	26,648	104	0
Pine Hills CDP *Orange Co.*	n/a	n/a	n/a	n/a
Pinellas Park city *Pinellas Co.*	4.3	25,228	213	5
Plant City city *Hillsborough Co.*	4.3	15,403	328	15
Plantation city *Broward Co.*	3.2	53,917	38	201
Pompano Beach city *Broward Co.*	3.8	52,733	334	178
Port Charlotte CDP *Charlotte Co.*	n/a	n/a	n/a	n/a
Port Orange city *Volusia Co.*	3.5	29,405	246	8
Port Saint Lucie city *Saint Lucie Co.*	5.6	70,615	4,067	116
Richmond West CDP *Miami-Dade Co.*	n/a	n/a	n/a	n/a
Riviera Beach city *Palm Beach Co.*	5.5	15,804	275	432
Royal Palm Beach village *Palm Beach Co.*	3.4	18,555	51	0
Saint Petersburg city *Pinellas Co.*	4.2	135,159	496	164
Sanford city *Seminole Co.*	4.7	24,855	825	6
Sarasota city *Sarasota Co.*	4.5	28,739	111	14
South Miami Heights CDP *Miami-Dade Co.*	n/a	n/a	n/a	n/a
Spring Hill CDP *Hernando Co.*	n/a	n/a	n/a	n/a
Sunrise city *Broward Co.*	3.8	50,620	18	500
Tallahassee city *Leon Co.*	3.3	91,396	804	588
Tamarac city *Broward Co.*	4.5	29,382	254	26
Tamiami CDP *Miami-Dade Co.*	n/a	n/a	n/a	n/a
Tampa city *Hillsborough Co.*	4.4	167,604	1,940	985
The Hammocks CDP *Miami-Dade Co.*	n/a	n/a	n/a	n/a
Titusville city *Brevard Co.*	4.3	20,914	288	72
Town 'n' Country CDP *Hillsborough Co.*	n/a	n/a	n/a	n/a
University CDP *Hillsborough Co.*	n/a	n/a	n/a	n/a
Wellington village *Palm Beach Co.*	3.3	30,568	224	0
West Palm Beach city *Palm Beach Co.*	4.5	53,275	131	1,177
Weston city *Broward Co.*	2.9	35,828	11	0
Winter Springs city *Seminole Co.*	3.6	19,591	274	0

NOTE: Unemployment Rate and Civilian Labor Force as of November 2007; Building permit data covers 2006; n/a not available.

Place	Sales	Prof.	Mgmt	Services	Production	Constr.
Altamonte Springs city *Seminole Co.*	32.5	25.3	13.7	13.4	7.6	7.6
Apopka city *Orange Co.*	31.6	18.8	15.0	12.8	11.3	8.8
Boca Raton city *Palm Beach Co.*	30.9	22.3	23.3	13.4	4.8	5.2
Bonita Springs city *Lee Co.*	27.2	11.4	13.2	21.7	6.8	18.0
Boynton Beach city *Palm Beach Co.*	29.7	17.2	12.4	21.1	8.3	10.6
Bradenton city *Manatee Co.*	26.3	18.0	10.0	19.5	13.7	10.6
Brandon CDP *Hillsborough Co.*	34.9	21.5	15.3	12.1	8.7	7.2
Cape Coral city *Lee Co.*	32.3	16.3	12.2	16.5	9.5	12.8
Carol City CDP *Miami-Dade Co.*	29.9	13.2	6.6	19.6	18.9	11.6
Clearwater city *Pinellas Co.*	31.0	19.6	14.5	16.3	10.5	7.8
Coconut Creek city *Broward Co.*	33.8	19.7	17.9	12.9	6.7	8.7
Coral Gables city *Miami-Dade Co.*	25.3	34.8	25.1	9.4	2.9	2.5
Coral Springs city *Broward Co.*	32.9	20.8	18.7	12.8	7.0	7.6
Country Club CDP *Miami-Dade Co.*	35.4	17.3	14.2	13.9	11.5	7.6
Davie town *Broward Co.*	30.0	19.3	14.8	15.3	8.8	11.6
Daytona Beach city *Volusia Co.*	29.4	17.2	8.9	23.3	12.6	8.4
Deerfield Beach city *Broward Co.*	30.3	15.4	15.3	18.8	9.4	10.3
Delray Beach city *Palm Beach Co.*	26.9	18.8	14.8	22.1	9.0	7.9
Deltona city *Volusia Co.*	31.1	16.0	10.6	16.0	12.4	13.8
Dunedin city *Pinellas Co.*	33.0	20.1	15.1	16.5	7.3	7.8
East Lake CDP *Pinellas Co.*	32.7	24.2	24.9	11.5	4.7	2.0
Egypt Lake-Leto CDP *Hillsborough Co.*	35.4	14.8	11.2	15.5	13.7	9.1
Fort Lauderdale city *Broward Co.*	27.4	17.9	15.5	20.1	9.8	9.1
Fort Myers city *Lee Co.*	27.5	17.5	8.1	23.4	9.8	12.7
Fort Pierce city *Saint Lucie Co.*	20.5	13.2	6.7	19.3	15.5	15.8
Fountainbleau CDP *Miami-Dade Co.*	37.6	14.4	13.0	15.7	12.4	6.7
Gainesville city *Alachua Co.*	26.3	35.2	10.7	17.6	5.5	4.4
Golden Glades CDP *Miami-Dade Co.*	29.0	14.9	7.0	25.7	12.6	10.6
Greater Carrollwood CDP *Hillsborough Co.*	33.8	25.4	18.8	10.5	6.7	4.6
Greenacres city *Palm Beach Co.*	28.4	14.4	10.4	21.4	11.2	13.7
Hallandale city *Broward Co.*	32.4	15.3	12.4	20.5	11.0	8.3
Hialeah city *Miami-Dade Co.*	30.7	9.0	7.5	14.2	24.0	14.3
Hollywood city *Broward Co.*	29.7	18.4	13.0	16.9	10.0	11.6
Homestead city *Miami-Dade Co.*	21.4	10.3	7.0	19.7	9.8	17.5
Jacksonville special city *Duval Co.*	32.6	17.6	13.6	14.0	12.4	9.5
Jupiter town *Palm Beach Co.*	28.8	21.9	18.5	16.0	6.7	7.8
Kendale Lakes CDP *Miami-Dade Co.*	37.9	16.8	14.6	13.1	9.5	7.9
Kendall CDP *Miami-Dade Co.*	32.8	26.2	18.7	11.8	5.3	5.2
Kendall West CDP *Miami-Dade Co.*	37.6	15.0	12.5	15.7	9.4	9.7
Kissimmee city *Osceola Co.*	29.7	11.8	8.9	27.9	10.3	11.2
Lake Worth city *Palm Beach Co.*	22.8	14.4	7.5	25.3	10.4	17.3
Lakeland city *Polk Co.*	28.6	19.5	11.3	16.9	15.7	7.6
Lakeside CDP *Clay Co.*	32.8	19.3	15.1	12.2	9.2	11.4
Land O' Lakes CDP *Pasco Co.*	31.7	23.8	14.7	10.5	8.2	11.0
Largo city *Pinellas Co.*	32.7	18.5	10.7	16.6	12.4	9.0
Lauderdale Lakes city *Broward Co.*	27.3	14.8	5.3	26.8	13.8	11.7
Lauderhill city *Broward Co.*	32.3	16.1	10.1	20.0	10.8	10.4
Lehigh Acres CDP *Lee Co.*	30.5	12.9	9.0	19.0	12.1	16.3
Margate city *Broward Co.*	34.5	15.4	12.1	15.4	9.9	12.5
Melbourne city *Brevard Co.*	28.9	20.5	10.9	18.2	11.0	10.2

Place	Sales	Prof.	Mgmt	Services	Production	Constr.
Merritt Island CDP *Brevard Co.*	25.9	25.6	13.9	15.6	9.5	9.1
Miami city *Miami-Dade Co.*	26.2	13.4	10.4	22.1	13.8	13.6
Miami Beach city *Miami-Dade Co.*	26.9	22.5	17.7	21.1	6.8	4.8
Miramar city *Broward Co.*	33.1	18.4	12.9	16.3	9.9	9.2
North Fort Myers CDP *Lee Co.*	30.6	14.0	9.4	17.2	11.7	16.7
North Lauderdale city *Broward Co.*	31.7	13.4	10.2	19.1	11.7	13.8
North Miami city *Miami-Dade Co.*	28.5	15.0	9.2	25.0	13.8	8.4
North Miami Beach city *Miami-Dade Co.*	32.1	13.0	9.0	22.6	13.0	10.2
North Port city *Sarasota Co.*	29.8	14.4	8.4	21.5	11.0	14.8
Oakland Park city *Broward Co.*	27.0	16.2	10.3	21.3	13.2	11.8
Ocala city *Marion Co.*	27.1	20.1	11.7	18.9	12.0	9.4
Orlando city *Orange Co.*	30.0	18.9	14.4	19.2	9.8	7.5
Ormond Beach city *Volusia Co.*	30.2	24.3	16.1	14.9	6.8	7.7
Oviedo city *Seminole Co.*	30.1	25.9	17.9	12.7	6.5	6.7
Palm Bay city *Brevard Co.*	27.5	19.8	9.6	18.8	12.1	12.1
Palm Beach Gardens city *Palm Beach Co.*	30.3	25.5	21.4	12.3	5.7	4.6
Palm Coast city *Flagler Co.*	29.9	15.6	12.5	20.6	10.8	10.6
Palm Harbor CDP *Pinellas Co.*	32.7	22.7	17.7	12.8	7.0	7.0
Panama City city *Bay Co.*	27.7	21.2	10.9	20.8	10.4	8.6
Pembroke Pines city *Broward Co.*	32.2	22.3	18.4	12.5	7.2	7.3
Pensacola city *Escambia Co.*	26.8	25.0	13.3	17.9	8.7	7.7
Pine Hills CDP *Orange Co.*	28.3	11.4	6.8	23.7	15.6	13.6
Pinellas Park city *Pinellas Co.*	32.5	13.3	9.9	15.1	18.1	10.8
Plant City city *Hillsborough Co.*	28.1	14.6	10.9	15.3	18.5	10.1
Plantation city *Broward Co.*	32.2	24.2	18.7	12.0	6.2	6.5
Pompano Beach city *Broward Co.*	30.0	15.1	13.5	18.5	11.0	11.4
Port Charlotte CDP *Charlotte Co.*	29.5	17.1	8.0	22.4	9.8	13.1
Port Orange city *Volusia Co.*	31.4	17.6	12.5	17.6	9.5	11.1
Port Saint Lucie city *Saint Lucie Co.*	32.0	16.0	10.6	17.6	10.7	12.5
Richmond West CDP *Miami-Dade Co.*	36.7	16.7	15.1	14.5	7.9	8.7
Riviera Beach city *Palm Beach Co.*	26.1	15.7	8.8	25.1	14.7	9.3
Royal Palm Beach village *Palm Beach Co.*	30.5	20.4	14.0	13.5	9.8	11.4
Saint Petersburg city *Pinellas Co.*	28.3	20.8	13.2	16.7	12.7	8.2
Sanford city *Seminole Co.*	29.3	15.8	9.3	18.3	15.0	12.1
Sarasota city *Sarasota Co.*	26.6	17.8	11.2	23.1	9.8	11.1
South Miami Heights CDP *Miami-Dade Co.*	30.8	9.8	8.5	22.6	13.5	14.2
Spring Hill CDP *Hernando Co.*	30.7	17.5	8.2	19.3	11.3	12.5
Sunrise city *Broward Co.*	34.1	18.6	13.1	15.7	9.5	8.9
Tallahassee city *Leon Co.*	28.7	30.7	15.3	15.4	5.2	4.6
Tamarac city *Broward Co.*	36.0	15.2	13.2	15.7	9.0	10.6
Tamiami CDP *Miami-Dade Co.*	35.8	16.0	15.7	13.2	10.7	8.4
Tampa city *Hillsborough Co.*	30.1	20.2	13.8	16.3	10.9	8.6
The Hammocks CDP *Miami-Dade Co.*	36.2	19.6	17.6	12.4	8.0	6.3
Titusville city *Brevard Co.*	25.9	23.5	10.1	16.7	13.0	10.8
Town 'n' Country CDP *Hillsborough Co.*	34.5	17.1	14.2	14.4	11.9	7.8
University CDP *Hillsborough Co.*	32.5	19.5	7.5	20.9	9.5	9.7
Wellington village *Palm Beach Co.*	30.7	24.9	19.4	13.5	5.8	5.0
West Palm Beach city *Palm Beach Co.*	25.7	19.8	12.4	22.4	10.0	9.0
Weston city *Broward Co.*	30.5	23.6	28.1	10.1	4.6	3.2
Winter Springs city *Seminole Co.*	30.4	24.5	18.8	11.7	6.9	7.6

NOTE: Data as of 2000

Educational Attainment

Place	Percent of Population 25 Years and Over with:		
	High School Diploma including Equivalency	Bachelor's Degree or Higher	Masters's Degree or Higher
Altamonte Springs city *Seminole Co.*	89.9	31.4	9.1
Apopka city *Orange Co.*	82.0	22.6	7.5
Boca Raton city *Palm Beach Co.*	91.8	43.9	16.9
Bonita Springs city *Lee Co.*	84.6	27.5	10.1
Boynton Beach city *Palm Beach Co.*	80.9	21.2	6.7
Bradenton city *Manatee Co.*	80.4	20.8	7.4
Brandon CDP *Hillsborough Co.*	89.2	26.0	7.5
Cape Coral city *Lee Co.*	85.5	17.3	5.6
Carol City CDP *Miami-Dade Co.*	61.1	9.7	3.7
Clearwater city *Pinellas Co.*	84.6	24.1	8.5
Coconut Creek city *Broward Co.*	87.8	27.9	9.2
Coral Gables city *Miami-Dade Co.*	91.6	58.2	30.8
Coral Springs city *Broward Co.*	89.8	34.5	11.9
Country Club CDP *Miami-Dade Co.*	80.2	23.2	7.4
Davie town *Broward Co.*	84.5	26.2	9.8
Daytona Beach city *Volusia Co.*	80.6	19.5	6.4
Deerfield Beach city *Broward Co.*	79.5	21.2	6.6
Delray Beach city *Palm Beach Co.*	80.8	29.3	10.1
Deltona city *Volusia Co.*	82.6	13.4	3.8
Dunedin city *Pinellas Co.*	86.6	22.3	7.1
East Lake CDP *Pinellas Co.*	94.0	42.3	14.4
Egypt Lake-Leto CDP *Hillsborough Co.*	76.6	19.0	6.7
Fort Lauderdale city *Broward Co.*	78.8	27.8	10.4
Fort Myers city *Lee Co.*	70.9	18.0	6.4
Fort Pierce city *Saint Lucie Co.*	60.6	12.9	4.7
Fountainbleau CDP *Miami-Dade Co.*	70.0	22.2	10.4
Gainesville city *Alachua Co.*	87.9	43.2	22.2
Golden Glades CDP *Miami-Dade Co.*	63.4	12.4	4.8
Greater Carrollwood CDP *Hillsborough Co.*	91.8	42.3	14.7
Greenacres city *Palm Beach Co.*	80.3	18.2	7.5
Hallandale city *Broward Co.*	73.2	19.8	8.1
Hialeah city *Miami-Dade Co.*	50.0	10.4	4.4
Hollywood city *Broward Co.*	79.5	21.8	8.4
Homestead city *Miami-Dade Co.*	53.8	11.1	3.5
Jacksonville special city *Duval Co.*	82.7	21.5	6.6
Jupiter town *Palm Beach Co.*	91.9	36.3	13.0
Kendale Lakes CDP *Miami-Dade Co.*	78.6	22.9	9.9
Kendall CDP *Miami-Dade Co.*	88.2	40.4	17.4
Kendall West CDP *Miami-Dade Co.*	76.9	21.8	8.7
Kissimmee city *Osceola Co.*	78.8	17.0	4.7
Lake Worth city *Palm Beach Co.*	66.1	16.3	5.4
Lakeland city *Polk Co.*	79.7	21.3	7.7
Lakeside CDP *Clay Co.*	90.0	21.8	7.0
Land O' Lakes CDP *Pasco Co.*	89.7	27.8	9.2
Largo city *Pinellas Co.*	83.4	16.3	5.7
Lauderdale Lakes city *Broward Co.*	67.9	12.7	4.4
Lauderhill city *Broward Co.*	76.2	16.4	5.4
Lehigh Acres CDP *Lee Co.*	77.1	11.2	4.3
Margate city *Broward Co.*	80.2	17.1	5.7
Melbourne city *Brevard Co.*	85.6	21.9	7.6

Place	Percent of Population 25 Years and Over with:		
	High School Diploma including Equivalency	Bachelor's Degree or Higher	Masters's Degree or Higher
Merritt Island CDP *Brevard Co.*	88.6	28.8	10.4
Miami city *Miami-Dade Co.*	53.3	16.7	8.0
Miami Beach city *Miami-Dade Co.*	78.8	33.5	15.8
Miramar city *Broward Co.*	83.3	22.8	7.1
North Fort Myers CDP *Lee Co.*	80.2	14.3	5.9
North Lauderdale city *Broward Co.*	77.7	13.6	3.1
North Miami city *Miami-Dade Co.*	66.9	15.8	6.8
North Miami Beach city *Miami-Dade Co.*	68.6	14.3	5.9
North Port city *Sarasota Co.*	82.4	11.4	3.7
Oakland Park city *Broward Co.*	78.2	21.4	6.6
Ocala city *Marion Co.*	79.6	19.6	7.6
Orlando city *Orange Co.*	82.6	28.5	8.3
Ormond Beach city *Volusia Co.*	88.1	29.0	10.7
Oviedo city *Seminole Co.*	93.4	40.8	13.2
Palm Bay city *Brevard Co.*	83.8	16.6	4.8
Palm Beach Gardens city *Palm Beach Co.*	94.2	44.2	17.7
Palm Coast city *Flagler Co.*	85.6	19.3	7.0
Palm Harbor CDP *Pinellas Co.*	90.3	28.3	9.5
Panama City city *Bay Co.*	79.6	19.2	7.5
Pembroke Pines city *Broward Co.*	87.8	28.6	10.1
Pensacola city *Escambia Co.*	85.0	32.9	12.0
Pine Hills CDP *Orange Co.*	71.3	10.5	3.1
Pinellas Park city *Pinellas Co.*	80.2	11.9	3.5
Plant City city *Hillsborough Co.*	71.4	16.8	5.5
Plantation city *Broward Co.*	91.0	36.6	13.5
Pompano Beach city *Broward Co.*	77.6	22.0	7.2
Port Charlotte CDP *Charlotte Co.*	79.2	14.8	6.0
Port Orange city *Volusia Co.*	84.9	17.6	5.8
Port Saint Lucie city *Saint Lucie Co.*	83.9	15.0	4.9
Richmond West CDP *Miami-Dade Co.*	83.0	22.5	7.7
Riviera Beach city *Palm Beach Co.*	73.6	18.6	6.3
Royal Palm Beach village *Palm Beach Co.*	87.5	24.3	7.8
Saint Petersburg city *Pinellas Co.*	82.1	23.1	8.1
Sanford city *Seminole Co.*	77.6	14.6	4.2
Sarasota city *Sarasota Co.*	80.1	25.4	9.1
South Miami Heights CDP *Miami-Dade Co.*	61.3	9.1	3.4
Spring Hill CDP *Hernando Co.*	79.2	11.9	4.1
Sunrise city *Broward Co.*	84.0	20.3	6.6
Tallahassee city *Leon Co.*	89.9	45.1	19.7
Tamarac city *Broward Co.*	83.8	17.0	5.8
Tamiami CDP *Miami-Dade Co.*	71.1	21.5	9.1
Tampa city *Hillsborough Co.*	77.7	26.5	9.5
The Hammocks CDP *Miami-Dade Co.*	87.2	31.2	10.8
Titusville city *Brevard Co.*	84.6	19.5	6.0
Town 'n' Country CDP *Hillsborough Co.*	83.0	24.1	6.9
University CDP *Hillsborough Co.*	75.0	22.2	7.3
Wellington village *Palm Beach Co.*	92.3	37.7	13.5
West Palm Beach city *Palm Beach Co.*	75.9	27.2	10.4
Weston city *Broward Co.*	95.7	52.7	22.0
Winter Springs city *Seminole Co.*	92.4	37.1	13.1

NOTE: Data as of 2007

Income and Poverty

Place	Average Household Income ($)	Median Household Income ($)	Per Capita Income ($)	Households w/$100,000+ Income (%)	Poverty Rate (%)
Altamonte Springs city *Seminole Co.*	57,391	46,716	26,856	12.4	7.4
Apopka city *Orange Co.*	61,933	49,601	22,570	14.4	9.5
Boca Raton city *Palm Beach Co.*	118,706	68,764	51,713	35.6	6.7
Bonita Springs city *Lee Co.*	93,212	58,633	42,609	25.2	6.7
Boynton Beach city *Palm Beach Co.*	57,995	44,299	25,625	11.9	10.2
Bradenton city *Manatee Co.*	50,683	39,876	22,790	8.7	13.6
Brandon CDP *Hillsborough Co.*	68,852	58,602	26,296	17.6	5.4
Cape Coral city *Lee Co.*	64,047	52,607	25,641	14.0	7.0
Carol City CDP *Miami-Dade Co.*	50,921	42,896	14,237	8.1	16.5
Clearwater city *Pinellas Co.*	58,296	42,974	26,570	13.5	12.3
Coconut Creek city *Broward Co.*	65,896	52,395	29,515	17.9	7.1
Coral Gables city *Miami-Dade Co.*	130,013	78,045	52,464	40.4	6.9
Coral Springs city *Broward Co.*	85,989	66,396	28,946	28.4	8.0
Country Club CDP *Miami-Dade Co.*	52,778	41,844	18,595	8.9	13.1
Davie town *Broward Co.*	73,743	55,254	27,403	23.1	9.8
Daytona Beach city *Volusia Co.*	42,353	29,044	19,666	7.6	23.6
Deerfield Beach city *Broward Co.*	54,540	39,456	26,746	12.4	12.5
Delray Beach city *Palm Beach Co.*	72,174	49,226	32,412	19.7	11.8
Deltona city *Volusia Co.*	53,720	45,403	19,065	8.7	8.1
Dunedin city *Pinellas Co.*	56,150	40,859	28,127	12.8	8.2
East Lake CDP *Pinellas Co.*	110,453	83,492	43,961	40.4	3.9
Egypt Lake-Leto CDP *Hillsborough Co.*	48,211	38,969	20,175	7.7	14.4
Fort Lauderdale city *Broward Co.*	70,455	45,479	32,371	18.4	17.7
Fort Myers city *Lee Co.*	47,395	32,425	19,605	9.1	21.8
Fort Pierce city *Saint Lucie Co.*	42,581	28,864	16,693	7.1	30.9
Fountainbleau CDP *Miami-Dade Co.*	48,487	40,212	16,899	7.8	14.2
Gainesville city *Alachua Co.*	48,650	32,466	20,195	10.9	26.7
Golden Glades CDP *Miami-Dade Co.*	40,617	30,995	12,251	5.6	20.9
Greater Carrollwood CDP *Hillsborough Co.*	74,332	55,613	31,685	21.1	5.0
Greenacres city *Palm Beach Co.*	47,118	38,687	20,708	6.5	7.2
Hallandale city *Broward Co.*	47,637	33,331	24,938	9.4	16.8
Hialeah city *Miami-Dade Co.*	41,988	32,595	13,295	6.1	18.6
Hollywood city *Broward Co.*	60,137	43,310	25,377	14.3	13.2
Homestead city *Miami-Dade Co.*	40,914	30,916	13,409	6.2	31.8
Jacksonville special city *Duval Co.*	61,475	47,137	24,492	14.5	12.2
Jupiter town *Palm Beach Co.*	93,011	64,028	39,718	28.8	4.8
Kendale Lakes CDP *Miami-Dade Co.*	62,295	49,363	19,697	14.6	10.3
Kendall CDP *Miami-Dade Co.*	82,127	57,060	31,133	24.9	8.6
Kendall West CDP *Miami-Dade Co.*	57,018	44,008	17,115	12.9	15.4
Kissimmee city *Osceola Co.*	43,483	35,796	15,804	4.8	15.4
Lake Worth city *Palm Beach Co.*	44,357	33,875	17,743	6.8	20.0
Lakeland city *Polk Co.*	50,797	37,586	22,301	9.5	15.0
Lakeside CDP *Clay Co.*	66,128	56,496	23,944	17.1	4.5
Land O' Lakes CDP *Pasco Co.*	78,484	68,665	29,005	25.4	4.9
Largo city *Pinellas Co.*	47,514	36,781	23,831	7.3	9.1
Lauderdale Lakes city *Broward Co.*	38,725	30,181	14,738	4.5	22.5
Lauderhill city *Broward Co.*	46,679	35,593	18,722	7.9	17.8
Lehigh Acres CDP *Lee Co.*	54,282	46,708	20,386	8.6	7.7
Margate city *Broward Co.*	54,716	44,496	22,772	11.8	8.4
Melbourne city *Brevard Co.*	51,320	39,542	22,888	10.1	11.5

Place	Average Household Income ($)	Median Household Income ($)	Per Capita Income ($)	Households w/$100,000+ Income (%)	Poverty Rate (%)
Merritt Island CDP *Brevard Co.*	67,942	50,654	28,838	19.9	9.4
Miami city *Miami-Dade Co.*	46,332	27,277	17,720	9.6	28.5
Miami Beach city *Miami-Dade Co.*	64,446	35,994	33,734	16.1	21.8
Miramar city *Broward Co.*	72,174	61,503	22,422	21.4	8.2
North Fort Myers CDP *Lee Co.*	49,071	39,150	24,672	8.4	9.9
North Lauderdale city *Broward Co.*	50,384	43,376	16,555	7.3	13.7
North Miami city *Miami-Dade Co.*	45,494	31,860	15,361	7.8	23.9
North Miami Beach city *Miami-Dade Co.*	46,489	34,619	15,677	7.3	20.5
North Port city *Sarasota Co.*	53,295	46,733	20,469	8.4	8.3
Oakland Park city *Broward Co.*	50,550	41,028	22,071	9.2	16.5
Ocala city *Marion Co.*	49,684	35,601	20,735	9.7	18.1
Orlando city *Orange Co.*	54,151	40,086	24,412	10.6	15.9
Ormond Beach city *Volusia Co.*	70,064	50,017	30,887	18.4	6.1
Oviedo city *Seminole Co.*	91,356	77,575	29,399	32.6	4.6
Palm Bay city *Brevard Co.*	50,922	42,480	19,843	8.1	9.5
Palm Beach Gardens city *Palm Beach Co.*	106,463	68,646	48,198	31.5	5.6
Palm Coast city *Flagler Co.*	61,893	49,371	26,030	13.5	7.5
Palm Harbor CDP *Pinellas Co.*	70,400	51,691	31,225	18.7	5.5
Panama City city *Bay Co.*	51,039	37,292	21,357	10.3	17.2
Pembroke Pines city *Broward Co.*	75,031	61,542	28,210	24.7	5.4
Pensacola city *Escambia Co.*	57,173	40,622	25,627	12.6	16.1
Pine Hills CDP *Orange Co.*	41,426	34,560	13,401	4.2	18.5
Pinellas Park city *Pinellas Co.*	47,973	39,881	20,915	6.7	9.3
Plant City city *Hillsborough Co.*	60,592	46,389	22,301	13.2	14.7
Plantation city *Broward Co.*	82,200	62,619	33,025	27.2	6.4
Pompano Beach city *Broward Co.*	59,059	41,622	27,475	14.0	17.0
Port Charlotte CDP *Charlotte Co.*	47,503	37,346	20,850	8.1	10.1
Port Orange city *Volusia Co.*	56,954	46,159	24,939	11.8	7.6
Port Saint Lucie city *Saint Lucie Co.*	55,580	46,921	21,642	10.5	7.9
Richmond West CDP *Miami-Dade Co.*	77,904	67,679	21,097	22.0	5.6
Riviera Beach city *Palm Beach Co.*	56,840	37,717	22,067	13.2	23.0
Royal Palm Beach village *Palm Beach Co.*	71,260	63,357	25,186	20.2	4.3
Saint Petersburg city *Pinellas Co.*	55,310	40,466	24,742	11.9	13.3
Sanford city *Seminole Co.*	47,228	37,666	18,482	7.9	17.8
Sarasota city *Sarasota Co.*	56,569	38,211	26,319	11.6	16.7
South Miami Heights CDP *Miami-Dade Co.*	47,781	39,642	13,962	8.7	17.2
Spring Hill CDP *Hernando Co.*	49,925	39,792	20,769	7.5	9.5
Sunrise city *Broward Co.*	54,525	46,371	21,214	11.4	9.7
Tallahassee city *Leon Co.*	51,781	35,236	22,960	12.1	24.7
Tamarac city *Broward Co.*	49,558	38,780	24,337	9.1	8.9
Tamiami CDP *Miami-Dade Co.*	67,147	54,451	20,111	18.2	9.4
Tampa city *Hillsborough Co.*	60,794	40,377	25,634	14.3	18.1
The Hammocks CDP *Miami-Dade Co.*	69,012	58,115	21,784	18.3	8.6
Titusville city *Brevard Co.*	52,105	40,852	22,712	11.4	12.4
Town 'n' Country CDP *Hillsborough Co.*	59,393	46,901	24,196	12.8	8.6
University CDP *Hillsborough Co.*	30,195	23,986	14,621	2.5	31.3
Wellington village *Palm Beach Co.*	99,534	76,632	34,004	34.5	4.3
West Palm Beach city *Palm Beach Co.*	61,181	41,163	26,760	14.8	18.9
Weston city *Broward Co.*	134,580	98,168	43,902	49.0	5.0
Winter Springs city *Seminole Co.*	84,502	63,675	31,763	29.2	4.2

NOTE: Data as of 2007 except for Poverty Rate which is from 2000; (1) Percentage of population with income below the poverty level

Taxes

Place	Total City Taxes Per Capita ($)	City Property Taxes Per Capita ($)
Altamonte Springs city *Seminole Co.*	n/a	n/a
Apopka city *Orange Co.*	428	146
Boca Raton city *Palm Beach Co.*	998	543
Bonita Springs city *Lee Co.*	n/a	n/a
Boynton Beach city *Palm Beach Co.*	639	381
Bradenton city *Manatee Co.*	n/a	n/a
Brandon CDP *Hillsborough Co.*	n/a	n/a
Cape Coral city *Lee Co.*	589	314
Carol City CDP *Miami-Dade Co.*	n/a	n/a
Clearwater city *Pinellas Co.*	552	342
Coconut Creek city *Broward Co.*	n/a	n/a
Coral Gables city *Miami-Dade Co.*	1,694	1,119
Coral Springs city *Broward Co.*	357	212
Country Club CDP *Miami-Dade Co.*	n/a	n/a
Davie town *Broward Co.*	552	317
Daytona Beach city *Volusia Co.*	621	325
Deerfield Beach city *Broward Co.*	n/a	n/a
Delray Beach city *Palm Beach Co.*	n/a	n/a
Deltona city *Volusia Co.*	n/a	n/a
Dunedin city *Pinellas Co.*	n/a	n/a
East Lake CDP *Pinellas Co.*	n/a	n/a
Egypt Lake-Leto CDP *Hillsborough Co.*	n/a	n/a
Fort Lauderdale city *Broward Co.*	880	535
Fort Myers city *Lee Co.*	775	411
Fort Pierce city *Saint Lucie Co.*	465	247
Fountainbleau CDP *Miami-Dade Co.*	n/a	n/a
Gainesville city *Alachua Co.*	337	166
Golden Glades CDP *Miami-Dade Co.*	n/a	n/a
Greater Carrollwood CDP *Hillsborough Co.*	n/a	n/a
Greenacres city *Palm Beach Co.*	n/a	n/a
Hallandale city *Broward Co.*	n/a	n/a
Hialeah city *Miami-Dade Co.*	485	210
Hollywood city *Broward Co.*	590	365
Homestead city *Miami-Dade Co.*	421	150
Jacksonville special city *Duval Co.*	829	416
Jupiter town *Palm Beach Co.*	n/a	n/a
Kendale Lakes CDP *Miami-Dade Co.*	n/a	n/a
Kendall CDP *Miami-Dade Co.*	n/a	n/a
Kendall West CDP *Miami-Dade Co.*	n/a	n/a
Kissimmee city *Osceola Co.*	322	142
Lake Worth city *Palm Beach Co.*	n/a	n/a
Lakeland city *Polk Co.*	471	161
Lakeside CDP *Clay Co.*	n/a	n/a
Land O' Lakes CDP *Pasco Co.*	n/a	n/a
Largo city *Pinellas Co.*	n/a	n/a
Lauderdale Lakes city *Broward Co.*	n/a	n/a
Lauderhill city *Broward Co.*	n/a	n/a
Lehigh Acres CDP *Lee Co.*	n/a	n/a
Margate city *Broward Co.*	n/a	n/a
Melbourne city *Brevard Co.*	469	180

Place	Total City Taxes Per Capita ($)	City Property Taxes Per Capita ($)
Merritt Island CDP *Brevard Co.*	n/a	n/a
Miami city *Miami-Dade Co.*	841	489
Miami Beach city *Miami-Dade Co.*	1,911	1,078
Miramar city *Broward Co.*	n/a	n/a
North Fort Myers CDP *Lee Co.*	n/a	n/a
North Lauderdale city *Broward Co.*	n/a	n/a
North Miami city *Miami-Dade Co.*	405	244
North Miami Beach city *Miami-Dade Co.*	n/a	n/a
North Port city *Sarasota Co.*	n/a	n/a
Oakland Park city *Broward Co.*	n/a	n/a
Ocala city *Marion Co.*	513	282
Orlando city *Orange Co.*	715	367
Ormond Beach city *Volusia Co.*	n/a	n/a
Oviedo city *Seminole Co.*	n/a	n/a
Palm Bay city *Brevard Co.*	433	188
Palm Beach Gardens city *Palm Beach Co.*	n/a	n/a
Palm Coast city *Flagler Co.*	n/a	n/a
Palm Harbor CDP *Pinellas Co.*	n/a	n/a
Panama City city *Bay Co.*	645	210
Pembroke Pines city *Broward Co.*	465	215
Pensacola city *Escambia Co.*	614	251
Pine Hills CDP *Orange Co.*	n/a	n/a
Pinellas Park city *Pinellas Co.*	n/a	n/a
Plant City city *Hillsborough Co.*	396	211
Plantation city *Broward Co.*	461	276
Pompano Beach city *Broward Co.*	615	342
Port Charlotte CDP *Charlotte Co.*	n/a	n/a
Port Orange city *Volusia Co.*	n/a	n/a
Port Saint Lucie city *Saint Lucie Co.*	365	152
Richmond West CDP *Miami-Dade Co.*	n/a	n/a
Riviera Beach city *Palm Beach Co.*	n/a	n/a
Royal Palm Beach village *Palm Beach Co.*	n/a	n/a
Saint Petersburg city *Pinellas Co.*	491	298
Sanford city *Seminole Co.*	590	215
Sarasota city *Sarasota Co.*	835	320
South Miami Heights CDP *Miami-Dade Co.*	n/a	n/a
Spring Hill CDP *Hernando Co.*	n/a	n/a
Sunrise city *Broward Co.*	579	309
Tallahassee city *Leon Co.*	425	134
Tamarac city *Broward Co.*	n/a	n/a
Tamiami CDP *Miami-Dade Co.*	n/a	n/a
Tampa city *Hillsborough Co.*	748	348
The Hammocks CDP *Miami-Dade Co.*	n/a	n/a
Titusville city *Brevard Co.*	352	183
Town 'n' Country CDP *Hillsborough Co.*	n/a	n/a
University CDP *Hillsborough Co.*	n/a	n/a
Wellington village *Palm Beach Co.*	n/a	n/a
West Palm Beach city *Palm Beach Co.*	969	559
Weston city *Broward Co.*	383	119
Winter Springs city *Seminole Co.*	n/a	n/a

NOTE: Data as of 2005.

Housing

Place	Homeownership Rate (%)	Median Home Value ($)	Median Age of Housing (years)	Median Rent ($/month)
Altamonte Springs city *Seminole Co.*	41.0	194,716	18	646
Apopka city *Orange Co.*	77.2	193,358	11	577
Boca Raton city *Palm Beach Co.*	75.2	459,017	23	770
Bonita Springs city *Lee Co.*	83.6	315,941	11	631
Boynton Beach city *Palm Beach Co.*	73.0	192,607	21	707
Bradenton city *Manatee Co.*	61.3	189,179	23	562
Brandon CDP *Hillsborough Co.*	70.4	189,666	16	630
Cape Coral city *Lee Co.*	80.4	248,494	15	588
Carol City CDP *Miami-Dade Co.*	82.4	191,317	27	620
Clearwater city *Pinellas Co.*	62.2	181,218	27	538
Coconut Creek city *Broward Co.*	74.5	210,716	13	824
Coral Gables city *Miami-Dade Co.*	65.2	732,933	42	694
Coral Springs city *Broward Co.*	65.6	365,318	14	806
Country Club CDP *Miami-Dade Co.*	44.9	217,470	14	726
Davie town *Broward Co.*	76.5	255,629	17	711
Daytona Beach city *Volusia Co.*	48.2	149,445	30	460
Deerfield Beach city *Broward Co.*	70.8	172,610	23	718
Delray Beach city *Palm Beach Co.*	69.4	234,116	22	704
Deltona city *Volusia Co.*	87.3	161,458	15	580
Dunedin city *Pinellas Co.*	71.5	169,752	26	501
East Lake CDP *Pinellas Co.*	84.4	347,801	10	703
Egypt Lake-Leto CDP *Hillsborough Co.*	44.3	157,142	22	559
Fort Lauderdale city *Broward Co.*	54.9	317,292	35	577
Fort Myers city *Lee Co.*	37.8	167,703	26	508
Fort Pierce city *Saint Lucie Co.*	53.9	118,997	27	413
Fountainbleau CDP *Miami-Dade Co.*	51.3	184,245	18	705
Gainesville city *Alachua Co.*	48.5	145,197	26	457
Golden Glades CDP *Miami-Dade Co.*	53.2	203,602	35	549
Greater Carrollwood CDP *Hillsborough Co.*	70.3	209,161	17	646
Greenacres city *Palm Beach Co.*	70.5	158,659	15	660
Hallandale city *Broward Co.*	66.5	176,781	28	578
Hialeah city *Miami-Dade Co.*	50.8	226,794	27	537
Hollywood city *Broward Co.*	62.5	233,506	32	619
Homestead city *Miami-Dade Co.*	40.8	179,059	19	444
Jacksonville special city *Duval Co.*	64.2	153,560	25	501
Jupiter town *Palm Beach Co.*	81.6	329,737	15	779
Kendale Lakes CDP *Miami-Dade Co.*	79.2	233,658	21	755
Kendall CDP *Miami-Dade Co.*	66.1	325,039	24	712
Kendall West CDP *Miami-Dade Co.*	64.3	249,464	13	691
Kissimmee city *Osceola Co.*	42.8	180,034	14	619
Lake Worth city *Palm Beach Co.*	52.9	172,407	38	484
Lakeland city *Polk Co.*	61.0	114,810	25	423
Lakeside CDP *Clay Co.*	77.3	155,393	18	609
Land O' Lakes CDP *Pasco Co.*	86.0	230,036	13	527
Largo city *Pinellas Co.*	67.5	124,267	25	539
Lauderdale Lakes city *Broward Co.*	62.4	124,097	25	596
Lauderhill city *Broward Co.*	60.8	154,539	23	614
Lehigh Acres CDP *Lee Co.*	84.0	184,616	17	513
Margate city *Broward Co.*	79.9	188,109	22	720
Melbourne city *Brevard Co.*	62.0	175,175	21	510

Place	Homeownership Rate (%)	Median Home Value ($)	Median Age of Housing (years)	Median Rent ($/month)
Merritt Island CDP *Brevard Co.*	75.4	258,938	30	503
Miami city *Miami-Dade Co.*	35.0	267,085	37	473
Miami Beach city *Miami-Dade Co.*	36.7	324,455	37	581
Miramar city *Broward Co.*	81.6	283,994	16	694
North Fort Myers CDP *Lee Co.*	86.9	124,823	18	480
North Lauderdale city *Broward Co.*	63.9	198,033	21	696
North Miami city *Miami-Dade Co.*	50.5	186,207	35	547
North Miami Beach city *Miami-Dade Co.*	61.7	193,064	36	573
North Port city *Sarasota Co.*	89.6	199,793	14	540
Oakland Park city *Broward Co.*	51.3	217,900	29	606
Ocala city *Marion Co.*	56.3	127,923	24	430
Orlando city *Orange Co.*	39.6	195,344	22	606
Ormond Beach city *Volusia Co.*	81.8	197,955	21	621
Oviedo city *Seminole Co.*	86.5	254,608	8	776
Palm Bay city *Brevard Co.*	75.8	168,061	15	536
Palm Beach Gardens city *Palm Beach Co.*	80.6	326,212	14	846
Palm Coast city *Flagler Co.*	85.9	220,115	10	659
Palm Harbor CDP *Pinellas Co.*	77.9	217,793	16	697
Panama City city *Bay Co.*	57.6	145,210	31	435
Pembroke Pines city *Broward Co.*	80.7	272,847	10	856
Pensacola city *Escambia Co.*	63.9	148,639	33	455
Pine Hills CDP *Orange Co.*	64.9	151,395	27	551
Pinellas Park city *Pinellas Co.*	74.9	134,528	25	508
Plant City city *Hillsborough Co.*	65.9	161,412	20	445
Plantation city *Broward Co.*	71.7	307,854	19	851
Pompano Beach city *Broward Co.*	63.1	215,872	27	630
Port Charlotte CDP *Charlotte Co.*	80.5	165,862	21	535
Port Orange city *Volusia Co.*	82.6	173,744	17	580
Port Saint Lucie city *Saint Lucie Co.*	84.2	200,684	12	627
Richmond West CDP *Miami-Dade Co.*	93.8	270,039	4	929
Riviera Beach city *Palm Beach Co.*	61.1	198,736	27	503
Royal Palm Beach village *Palm Beach Co.*	89.7	244,280	15	778
Saint Petersburg city *Pinellas Co.*	63.0	158,831	37	478
Sanford city *Seminole Co.*	55.1	142,785	23	508
Sarasota city *Sarasota Co.*	58.2	212,641	30	566
South Miami Heights CDP *Miami-Dade Co.*	62.5	197,553	25	518
Spring Hill CDP *Hernando Co.*	86.6	158,712	14	510
Sunrise city *Broward Co.*	73.6	212,751	19	759
Tallahassee city *Leon Co.*	44.2	167,326	21	490
Tamarac city *Broward Co.*	80.5	198,011	21	720
Tamiami CDP *Miami-Dade Co.*	84.6	282,054	16	743
Tampa city *Hillsborough Co.*	54.8	163,856	34	486
The Hammocks CDP *Miami-Dade Co.*	63.7	285,305	12	758
Titusville city *Brevard Co.*	68.5	155,173	27	445
Town 'n' Country CDP *Hillsborough Co.*	64.2	164,997	19	626
University CDP *Hillsborough Co.*	11.9	100,820	20	481
Wellington village *Palm Beach Co.*	82.8	360,414	11	867
West Palm Beach city *Palm Beach Co.*	51.8	220,599	26	582
Weston city *Broward Co.*	83.6	454,205	5	969
Winter Springs city *Seminole Co.*	81.2	238,234	15	631

NOTE: Homeownership Rate and Median Home Value as of 2007; Median Rent and Median Age of Housing as of 2000.

Commute to Work

Place	Automobile (%)	Public Transportation (%)	Walk (%)	Work from Home (%)
Altamonte Springs city *Seminole Co.*	93.5	1.2	1.7	2.7
Apopka city *Orange Co.*	94.6	1.3	0.6	2.6
Boca Raton city *Palm Beach Co.*	89.2	0.9	2.0	6.1
Bonita Springs city *Lee Co.*	89.6	0.5	1.6	5.8
Boynton Beach city *Palm Beach Co.*	93.7	1.5	1.1	2.6
Bradenton city *Manatee Co.*	93.1	1.0	1.4	2.3
Brandon CDP *Hillsborough Co.*	94.8	0.5	1.0	3.1
Cape Coral city *Lee Co.*	94.7	0.5	0.7	2.8
Carol City CDP *Miami-Dade Co.*	94.1	3.2	0.4	0.9
Clearwater city *Pinellas Co.*	86.7	3.9	3.0	4.1
Coconut Creek city *Broward Co.*	95.1	0.7	0.5	2.8
Coral Gables city *Miami-Dade Co.*	83.7	2.9	6.7	5.5
Coral Springs city *Broward Co.*	92.7	1.0	1.2	3.9
Country Club CDP *Miami-Dade Co.*	94.8	1.7	0.7	1.9
Davie town *Broward Co.*	93.7	0.9	1.2	2.6
Daytona Beach city *Volusia Co.*	85.2	3.8	5.7	2.1
Deerfield Beach city *Broward Co.*	93.4	1.2	1.4	2.4
Delray Beach city *Palm Beach Co.*	90.5	1.7	1.8	4.3
Deltona city *Volusia Co.*	95.6	0.5	0.3	2.5
Dunedin city *Pinellas Co.*	91.3	1.1	2.1	3.8
East Lake CDP *Pinellas Co.*	91.6	0.4	0.6	5.8
Egypt Lake-Leto CDP *Hillsborough Co.*	94.6	0.9	1.6	1.9
Fort Lauderdale city *Broward Co.*	86.5	4.9	2.4	3.8
Fort Myers city *Lee Co.*	90.0	2.3	3.4	1.8
Fort Pierce city *Saint Lucie Co.*	89.9	4.0	1.9	2.0
Fountainbleau CDP *Miami-Dade Co.*	92.0	3.0	1.2	2.1
Gainesville city *Alachua Co.*	82.0	3.2	5.6	3.1
Golden Glades CDP *Miami-Dade Co.*	88.0	8.7	0.7	1.4
Greater Carrollwood CDP *Hillsborough Co.*	94.3	0.6	1.0	3.0
Greenacres city *Palm Beach Co.*	95.0	0.5	0.3	1.9
Hallandale city *Broward Co.*	88.2	4.3	2.8	3.2
Hialeah city *Miami-Dade Co.*	93.1	2.9	1.6	1.1
Hollywood city *Broward Co.*	90.8	3.1	1.8	2.8
Homestead city *Miami-Dade Co.*	90.2	2.9	1.6	1.0
Jacksonville special city *Duval Co.*	92.6	2.1	1.8	1.9
Jupiter town *Palm Beach Co.*	92.0	0.4	0.8	4.9
Kendale Lakes CDP *Miami-Dade Co.*	93.1	2.1	1.1	3.3
Kendall CDP *Miami-Dade Co.*	89.5	4.5	1.0	4.2
Kendall West CDP *Miami-Dade Co.*	92.3	3.1	0.6	2.1
Kissimmee city *Osceola Co.*	93.3	2.0	1.9	1.2
Lake Worth city *Palm Beach Co.*	90.7	2.4	1.7	2.6
Lakeland city *Polk Co.*	91.9	1.8	2.7	2.2
Lakeside CDP *Clay Co.*	94.3	0.2	0.8	2.9
Land O' Lakes CDP *Pasco Co.*	93.6	0.4	0.8	4.1
Largo city *Pinellas Co.*	92.7	1.3	2.0	2.2
Lauderdale Lakes city *Broward Co.*	90.2	7.1	1.2	0.8
Lauderhill city *Broward Co.*	90.9	5.3	1.0	1.5
Lehigh Acres CDP *Lee Co.*	95.2	0.4	0.7	2.5
Margate city *Broward Co.*	94.4	1.3	0.9	1.8
Melbourne city *Brevard Co.*	94.3	0.3	1.9	1.9

Place	Automobile (%)	Public Transportation (%)	Walk (%)	Work from Home (%)
Merritt Island CDP *Brevard Co.*	94.2	0.3	1.2	2.8
Miami city *Miami-Dade Co.*	80.8	11.4	3.7	2.1
Miami Beach city *Miami-Dade Co.*	67.7	11.4	10.3	5.4
Miramar city *Broward Co.*	94.7	1.5	0.9	1.9
North Fort Myers CDP *Lee Co.*	92.2	0.9	1.2	3.5
North Lauderdale city *Broward Co.*	94.1	2.6	0.6	1.9
North Miami city *Miami-Dade Co.*	83.2	10.6	2.7	2.0
North Miami Beach city *Miami-Dade Co.*	86.6	9.5	1.3	1.6
North Port city *Sarasota Co.*	95.0	0.4	0.4	2.5
Oakland Park city *Broward Co.*	89.9	4.4	2.3	2.0
Ocala city *Marion Co.*	93.1	0.4	2.1	2.6
Orlando city *Orange Co.*	90.1	4.1	1.9	2.2
Ormond Beach city *Volusia Co.*	92.8	0.9	1.1	3.4
Oviedo city *Seminole Co.*	93.4	0.1	0.4	4.1
Palm Bay city *Brevard Co.*	95.6	0.4	0.4	2.1
Palm Beach Gardens city *Palm Beach Co.*	92.3	0.3	1.1	5.4
Palm Coast city *Flagler Co.*	94.2	0.7	0.7	2.9
Palm Harbor CDP *Pinellas Co.*	92.3	0.8	0.9	4.9
Panama City city *Bay Co.*	93.9	0.7	1.6	2.2
Pembroke Pines city *Broward Co.*	94.6	0.9	0.6	3.0
Pensacola city *Escambia Co.*	91.6	2.1	1.7	3.0
Pine Hills CDP *Orange Co.*	91.8	4.6	0.8	1.2
Pinellas Park city *Pinellas Co.*	92.7	1.1	1.7	2.2
Plant City city *Hillsborough Co.*	94.7	0.4	1.2	2.0
Plantation city *Broward Co.*	93.9	1.2	0.6	3.4
Pompano Beach city *Broward Co.*	89.7	2.7	2.2	2.6
Port Charlotte CDP *Charlotte Co.*	95.0	0.3	0.6	2.4
Port Orange city *Volusia Co.*	95.0	0.5	0.8	2.2
Port Saint Lucie city *Saint Lucie Co.*	95.8	0.3	0.5	2.2
Richmond West CDP *Miami-Dade Co.*	95.8	1.1	0.2	2.3
Riviera Beach city *Palm Beach Co.*	88.8	4.3	2.2	2.3
Royal Palm Beach village *Palm Beach Co.*	95.6	0.1	0.8	2.4
Saint Petersburg city *Pinellas Co.*	90.0	2.9	2.2	3.1
Sanford city *Seminole Co.*	93.2	1.2	1.6	2.2
Sarasota city *Sarasota Co.*	88.2	2.5	2.7	3.5
South Miami Heights CDP *Miami-Dade Co.*	91.0	3.9	1.8	1.7
Spring Hill CDP *Hernando Co.*	96.3	0.1	0.5	2.2
Sunrise city *Broward Co.*	94.8	1.7	1.1	1.8
Tallahassee city *Leon Co.*	91.3	2.4	2.6	2.4
Tamarac city *Broward Co.*	94.2	1.7	1.0	1.9
Tamiami CDP *Miami-Dade Co.*	95.9	0.7	0.6	2.2
Tampa city *Hillsborough Co.*	90.3	2.7	2.3	2.6
The Hammocks CDP *Miami-Dade Co.*	93.4	2.2	0.6	2.9
Titusville city *Brevard Co.*	94.6	0.3	1.8	2.0
Town 'n' Country CDP *Hillsborough Co.*	93.7	1.3	1.1	2.3
University CDP *Hillsborough Co.*	87.0	3.3	5.6	0.8
Wellington village *Palm Beach Co.*	90.9	0.6	0.6	6.6
West Palm Beach city *Palm Beach Co.*	89.8	2.8	2.8	2.3
Weston city *Broward Co.*	91.9	0.6	0.8	5.7
Winter Springs city *Seminole Co.*	93.8	0.3	0.3	4.5

NOTE: Data as of 2000

Travel Time to Work

Place	Less than 15 Minutes (%)	15 to 30 Minutes (%)	30 to 45 Minutes (%)	45 to 60 Minutes (%)	60 Minutes or More (%)
Altamonte Springs city *Seminole Co.*	25.5	39.6	22.5	7.8	4.6
Apopka city *Orange Co.*	18.6	30.4	30.5	12.4	8.2
Boca Raton city *Palm Beach Co.*	40.7	36.4	14.0	4.4	4.4
Bonita Springs city *Lee Co.*	30.9	35.2	23.4	6.1	4.5
Boynton Beach city *Palm Beach Co.*	23.8	41.1	23.4	7.1	4.7
Bradenton city *Manatee Co.*	30.5	41.7	17.3	5.4	5.0
Brandon CDP *Hillsborough Co.*	22.9	34.5	25.8	10.8	6.0
Cape Coral city *Lee Co.*	25.5	41.4	21.1	5.8	6.2
Carol City CDP *Miami-Dade Co.*	11.7	33.5	33.8	11.5	9.4
Clearwater city *Pinellas Co.*	31.1	39.6	18.8	6.0	4.5
Coconut Creek city *Broward Co.*	17.3	43.2	27.4	7.4	4.7
Coral Gables city *Miami-Dade Co.*	29.1	40.2	21.1	5.9	3.7
Coral Springs city *Broward Co.*	23.5	30.0	28.0	11.1	7.4
Country Club CDP *Miami-Dade Co.*	12.4	31.3	32.4	14.7	9.2
Davie town *Broward Co.*	19.1	36.4	26.6	9.9	8.0
Daytona Beach city *Volusia Co.*	42.4	40.0	9.7	2.4	5.5
Deerfield Beach city *Broward Co.*	24.3	45.0	20.9	5.4	4.4
Delray Beach city *Palm Beach Co.*	32.9	41.5	15.4	5.2	5.0
Deltona city *Volusia Co.*	14.8	28.5	27.6	14.7	14.5
Dunedin city *Pinellas Co.*	31.4	35.9	20.3	6.8	5.5
East Lake CDP *Pinellas Co.*	16.1	38.8	25.9	13.6	5.6
Egypt Lake-Leto CDP *Hillsborough Co.*	27.5	42.0	21.5	5.3	3.7
Fort Lauderdale city *Broward Co.*	29.7	38.5	19.7	5.8	6.4
Fort Myers city *Lee Co.*	33.5	38.9	15.6	5.8	6.1
Fort Pierce city *Saint Lucie Co.*	30.9	31.9	25.2	4.1	7.8
Fountainbleau CDP *Miami-Dade Co.*	15.9	41.5	27.0	9.6	6.0
Gainesville city *Alachua Co.*	43.2	43.2	7.7	2.6	3.3
Golden Glades CDP *Miami-Dade Co.*	14.5	35.0	31.1	9.9	9.5
Greater Carrollwood CDP *Hillsborough Co.*	19.1	41.1	27.5	8.2	4.1
Greenacres city *Palm Beach Co.*	17.3	40.4	28.5	7.9	5.9
Hallandale city *Broward Co.*	24.2	34.7	23.7	8.8	8.7
Hialeah city *Miami-Dade Co.*	18.4	38.4	27.8	8.4	6.9
Hollywood city *Broward Co.*	22.5	37.4	24.5	9.1	6.5
Homestead city *Miami-Dade Co.*	23.8	27.7	22.9	10.0	15.5
Jacksonville special city *Duval Co.*	21.2	43.7	24.1	6.4	4.6
Jupiter town *Palm Beach Co.*	30.9	38.8	20.4	5.0	4.9
Kendale Lakes CDP *Miami-Dade Co.*	11.2	26.4	28.7	17.3	16.5
Kendall CDP *Miami-Dade Co.*	17.4	29.7	25.3	14.8	12.8
Kendall West CDP *Miami-Dade Co.*	8.5	20.8	30.4	19.5	20.7
Kissimmee city *Osceola Co.*	21.8	41.2	25.2	6.6	5.2
Lake Worth city *Palm Beach Co.*	19.4	43.9	23.4	6.5	6.8
Lakeland city *Polk Co.*	37.1	39.4	13.0	5.3	5.2
Lakeside CDP *Clay Co.*	17.9	26.8	28.9	18.1	8.3
Land O' Lakes CDP *Pasco Co.*	15.9	22.0	34.2	17.9	9.9
Largo city *Pinellas Co.*	30.1	40.7	18.6	5.0	5.6
Lauderdale Lakes city *Broward Co.*	11.5	42.5	29.5	8.3	8.2
Lauderhill city *Broward Co.*	14.2	40.2	28.9	9.5	7.1
Lehigh Acres CDP *Lee Co.*	18.9	30.7	32.3	11.1	7.0
Margate city *Broward Co.*	18.6	36.4	30.2	9.0	5.8
Melbourne city *Brevard Co.*	36.2	43.3	11.5	4.0	5.0

Place	Less than 15 Minutes (%)	15 to 30 Minutes (%)	30 to 45 Minutes (%)	45 to 60 Minutes (%)	60 Minutes or More (%)
Merritt Island CDP *Brevard Co.*	33.0	38.4	16.7	5.8	6.2
Miami city *Miami-Dade Co.*	20.0	38.9	24.8	6.6	9.6
Miami Beach city *Miami-Dade Co.*	27.5	37.3	22.5	6.0	6.8
Miramar city *Broward Co.*	12.1	32.0	31.9	14.3	9.6
North Fort Myers CDP *Lee Co.*	23.0	43.4	19.7	7.2	6.7
North Lauderdale city *Broward Co.*	13.9	40.1	31.3	7.5	7.3
North Miami city *Miami-Dade Co.*	15.6	32.9	32.0	10.3	9.1
North Miami Beach city *Miami-Dade Co.*	18.3	32.1	28.5	11.1	10.0
North Port city *Sarasota Co.*	17.8	35.6	28.5	11.0	7.1
Oakland Park city *Broward Co.*	26.1	42.7	19.2	6.3	5.7
Ocala city *Marion Co.*	45.0	38.8	8.4	3.1	4.7
Orlando city *Orange Co.*	21.7	43.7	23.6	5.9	5.1
Ormond Beach city *Volusia Co.*	35.5	45.0	11.7	3.1	4.7
Oviedo city *Seminole Co.*	18.3	30.8	29.1	15.1	6.7
Palm Bay city *Brevard Co.*	19.4	47.1	21.0	6.7	5.8
Palm Beach Gardens city *Palm Beach Co.*	29.5	47.3	15.3	3.7	4.2
Palm Coast city *Flagler Co.*	36.6	29.1	20.0	6.7	7.6
Palm Harbor CDP *Pinellas Co.*	24.5	32.7	26.5	10.3	6.0
Panama City city *Bay Co.*	44.1	40.2	10.3	2.6	2.8
Pembroke Pines city *Broward Co.*	13.4	29.5	31.2	16.7	9.1
Pensacola city *Escambia Co.*	39.4	41.8	11.6	2.7	4.5
Pine Hills CDP *Orange Co.*	13.8	37.7	30.9	10.6	7.0
Pinellas Park city *Pinellas Co.*	31.5	47.3	13.5	3.9	3.7
Plant City city *Hillsborough Co.*	34.6	30.6	21.8	7.5	5.5
Plantation city *Broward Co.*	22.1	37.0	25.9	9.2	5.8
Pompano Beach city *Broward Co.*	25.9	41.5	21.5	5.4	5.7
Port Charlotte CDP *Charlotte Co.*	42.6	35.0	10.1	6.7	5.6
Port Orange city *Volusia Co.*	28.0	48.4	13.8	3.0	6.7
Port Saint Lucie city *Saint Lucie Co.*	18.2	41.9	23.8	8.8	7.3
Richmond West CDP *Miami-Dade Co.*	8.5	22.8	27.6	17.4	23.7
Riviera Beach city *Palm Beach Co.*	27.8	41.1	21.3	3.6	6.2
Royal Palm Beach village *Palm Beach Co.*	12.9	28.0	36.2	13.4	9.5
Saint Petersburg city *Pinellas Co.*	30.8	41.1	17.9	5.7	4.5
Sanford city *Seminole Co.*	28.7	35.1	19.8	8.4	8.0
Sarasota city *Sarasota Co.*	39.0	40.2	14.0	3.2	3.6
South Miami Heights CDP *Miami-Dade Co.*	17.3	31.4	23.5	12.8	14.9
Spring Hill CDP *Hernando Co.*	27.6	36.6	16.0	7.1	12.8
Sunrise city *Broward Co.*	20.3	33.2	28.2	10.9	7.3
Tallahassee city *Leon Co.*	37.6	45.4	12.3	2.0	2.7
Tamarac city *Broward Co.*	19.9	36.2	29.2	8.3	6.4
Tamiami CDP *Miami-Dade Co.*	10.7	31.2	32.1	15.3	10.6
Tampa city *Hillsborough Co.*	30.1	41.6	18.5	4.9	4.9
The Hammocks CDP *Miami-Dade Co.*	12.8	23.7	27.6	17.5	18.3
Titusville city *Brevard Co.*	35.4	30.1	19.2	8.8	6.6
Town 'n' Country CDP *Hillsborough Co.*	21.1	39.8	24.8	8.1	6.2
University CDP *Hillsborough Co.*	26.4	33.7	23.8	9.2	6.9
Wellington village *Palm Beach Co.*	23.2	22.5	29.1	15.8	9.4
West Palm Beach city *Palm Beach Co.*	29.6	44.1	17.3	4.1	4.9
Weston city *Broward Co.*	17.3	25.9	29.6	16.9	10.4
Winter Springs city *Seminole Co.*	17.1	37.8	28.2	10.5	6.4

NOTE: Data as of 2000

Crime

Place	Violent Crime Rate (crimes per 10,000 population)	Property Crime Rate (crimes per 10,000 population)
Altamonte Springs city *Seminole Co.*	50.8	401.9
Apopka city *Orange Co.*	111.3	499.0
Boca Raton city *Palm Beach Co.*	27.0	335.0
Bonita Springs city *Lee Co.*	n/a	n/a
Boynton Beach city *Palm Beach Co.*	97.0	501.7
Bradenton city *Manatee Co.*	74.8	481.5
Brandon CDP *Hillsborough Co.*	n/a	n/a
Cape Coral city *Lee Co.*	28.5	344.7
Carol City CDP *Miami-Dade Co.*	n/a	n/a
Clearwater city *Pinellas Co.*	78.0	437.7
Coconut Creek city *Broward Co.*	20.7	219.9
Coral Gables city *Miami-Dade Co.*	27.1	489.3
Coral Springs city *Broward Co.*	22.3	225.2
Country Club CDP *Miami-Dade Co.*	n/a	n/a
Davie town *Broward Co.*	34.5	334.6
Daytona Beach city *Volusia Co.*	136.8	783.4
Deerfield Beach city *Broward Co.*	72.3	333.7
Delray Beach city *Palm Beach Co.*	103.0	506.0
Deltona city *Volusia Co.*	n/a	n/a
Dunedin city *Pinellas Co.*	35.1	243.1
East Lake CDP *Pinellas Co.*	n/a	n/a
Egypt Lake-Leto CDP *Hillsborough Co.*	n/a	n/a
Fort Lauderdale city *Broward Co.*	98.9	583.8
Fort Myers city *Lee Co.*	157.7	489.8
Fort Pierce city *Saint Lucie Co.*	204.1	746.4
Fountainbleau CDP *Miami-Dade Co.*	n/a	n/a
Gainesville city *Alachua Co.*	99.1	523.9
Golden Glades CDP *Miami-Dade Co.*	n/a	n/a
Greater Carrollwood CDP *Hillsborough Co.*	n/a	n/a
Greenacres city *Palm Beach Co.*	100.4	372.5
Hallandale city *Broward Co.*	104.0	418.7
Hialeah city *Miami-Dade Co.*	56.3	386.9
Hollywood city *Broward Co.*	49.8	422.3
Homestead city *Miami-Dade Co.*	229.6	688.5
Jacksonville special city *Duval Co.*	83.7	541.6
Jupiter town *Palm Beach Co.*	33.5	277.7
Kendale Lakes CDP *Miami-Dade Co.*	n/a	n/a
Kendall CDP *Miami-Dade Co.*	n/a	n/a
Kendall West CDP *Miami-Dade Co.*	n/a	n/a
Kissimmee city *Osceola Co.*	78.9	389.1
Lake Worth city *Palm Beach Co.*	179.7	772.8
Lakeland city *Polk Co.*	65.7	571.8
Lakeside CDP *Clay Co.*	n/a	n/a
Land O' Lakes CDP *Pasco Co.*	n/a	n/a
Largo city *Pinellas Co.*	58.0	360.9
Lauderdale Lakes city *Broward Co.*	125.5	439.7
Lauderhill city *Broward Co.*	104.1	387.0
Lehigh Acres CDP *Lee Co.*	n/a	n/a
Margate city *Broward Co.*	34.4	169.6
Melbourne city *Brevard Co.*	113.4	514.5

Place	Violent Crime Rate (crimes per 10,000 population)	Property Crime Rate (crimes per 10,000 population)
Merritt Island CDP *Brevard Co.*	n/a	n/a
Miami city *Miami-Dade Co.*	150.9	516.3
Miami Beach city *Miami-Dade Co.*	124.7	848.0
Miramar city *Broward Co.*	51.2	296.9
North Fort Myers CDP *Lee Co.*	n/a	n/a
North Lauderdale city *Broward Co.*	74.5	218.3
North Miami city *Miami-Dade Co.*	111.2	623.1
North Miami Beach city *Miami-Dade Co.*	104.5	552.5
North Port city *Sarasota Co.*	34.9	277.7
Oakland Park city *Broward Co.*	156.3	760.0
Ocala city *Marion Co.*	141.9	649.0
Orlando city *Orange Co.*	198.3	844.9
Ormond Beach city *Volusia Co.*	31.3	295.4
Oviedo city *Seminole Co.*	23.1	150.6
Palm Bay city *Brevard Co.*	63.7	332.7
Palm Beach Gardens city *Palm Beach Co.*	28.5	364.1
Palm Coast city *Flagler Co.*	n/a	n/a
Palm Harbor CDP *Pinellas Co.*	n/a	n/a
Panama City city *Bay Co.*	106.0	563.3
Pembroke Pines city *Broward Co.*	23.7	319.5
Pensacola city *Escambia Co.*	92.1	530.0
Pine Hills CDP *Orange Co.*	n/a	n/a
Pinellas Park city *Pinellas Co.*	52.8	553.3
Plant City city *Hillsborough Co.*	98.8	568.8
Plantation city *Broward Co.*	30.0	420.3
Pompano Beach city *Broward Co.*	129.0	470.6
Port Charlotte CDP *Charlotte Co.*	n/a	n/a
Port Orange city *Volusia Co.*	13.0	227.3
Port Saint Lucie city *Saint Lucie Co.*	25.4	266.1
Richmond West CDP *Miami-Dade Co.*	n/a	n/a
Riviera Beach city *Palm Beach Co.*	262.9	917.0
Royal Palm Beach village *Palm Beach Co.*	27.7	270.0
Saint Petersburg city *Pinellas Co.*	148.2	647.9
Sanford city *Seminole Co.*	48.7	722.9
Sarasota city *Sarasota Co.*	103.4	656.0
South Miami Heights CDP *Miami-Dade Co.*	n/a	n/a
Spring Hill CDP *Hernando Co.*	n/a	n/a
Sunrise city *Broward Co.*	46.2	362.9
Tallahassee city *Leon Co.*	100.2	478.3
Tamarac city *Broward Co.*	27.4	200.4
Tamiami CDP *Miami-Dade Co.*	n/a	n/a
Tampa city *Hillsborough Co.*	115.8	566.8
The Hammocks CDP *Miami-Dade Co.*	n/a	n/a
Titusville city *Brevard Co.*	80.0	364.5
Town 'n' Country CDP *Hillsborough Co.*	n/a	n/a
University CDP *Hillsborough Co.*	n/a	n/a
Wellington village *Palm Beach Co.*	29.9	315.5
West Palm Beach city *Palm Beach Co.*	118.4	739.5
Weston city *Broward Co.*	14.4	144.8
Winter Springs city *Seminole Co.*	29.0	190.7

NOTE: Data as of 2006.

Education

Florida Public School Educational Profile

Category	Value	Category	Value
Schools (2005-2006)	3,766	**Diploma Recipients** (2004-2005)	133,318
Instructional Level		White, Non-Hispanic	77,144
Primary	1,925	Black, Non-Hispanic	26,569
Middle	558	Asian/Pacific Islander	3,724
High	584	American Indian/Alaskan Native	551
Other Level	571	Hispanic	25,330
Curriculum		**High School Drop-out Rate** (%) (2001-2002)	3.7
Regular	2,977	White, Non-Hispanic	3.0
Special Education	128	Black, Non-Hispanic	4.9
Vocational	34	Asian/Pacific Islander	1.9
Alternative	499	American Indian/Alaskan Native	3.5
Type		Hispanic	4.5
Magnet	266	**Staff** (2005-2006)	
Charter	298	Teachers	158,962.0
Title I Eligible	1,389	Average Salary[1] ($)	43,095
School-wide Title I	1,346	Librarians/Media Specialists	2,783.0
Students (2005-2006)	2,675,024	Guidance Counselors	5,584.0
Gender (%)		**Ratios** (2005-2006)	
Male	51.4	Student/Teacher Ratio	16.8 to 1
Female	48.6	Student/Librarian Ratio	961.2 to 1
Race/Ethnicity (%)		Student/Counselor Ratio	479.1 to 1
White, Non-Hispanic	49.6	**College Entrance Exam Scores** (2006)	
Black, Non-Hispanic	23.9	SAT Reasoning Test™	
Asian/Pacific Islander	2.2	Participation Rate (%)	65
American Indian/Alaskan Native	0.3	Mean SAT Critical Reading Score	496
Hispanic	23.9	Mean SAT Writing Score	480
Classification (%)		Mean SAT Math Score	497
Individual Education Program (IEP)	14.9	American College Testing Program (ACT)	
Migrant (2004-2005)	1.0	Participation Rate (%)	45
English Language Learner (ELL)	8.3	Average Composite Score	20.3
Eligible for Free Lunch Program	37.1	Average English Score	19.6
Eligible for Reduced-Price Lunch Program	8.7	Average Math Score	20.3
Current Spending ($ per student in FY 2005)	7,207	Average Reading Score	20.9
Instruction	4,261	Average Science Score	19.9
Support Services	2,600		

Note: For an explanation of data, please refer to the User's Guide in the front of the book; (1) Includes extra-duty pay

Number of Schools

Rank	Number	District Name	City
1	394	Dade County SD	Miami
2	285	Broward County SD	Fort Lauderdale
3	261	Hillsborough County SD	Tampa
4	236	Palm Beach County SD	West Palm Beach
5	211	Orange County SD	Orlando
6	182	Duval County SD	Jacksonville
7	173	Pinellas County SD	Largo
8	153	Polk County SD	Bartow
9	117	Brevard County SD	Viera
10	101	Lee County SD	Fort Myers
11	94	Volusia County SD	Deland
12	79	Escambia County SD	Pensacola
13	77	Seminole County SD	Sanford
14	76	Manatee County SD	Bradenton
14	76	Pasco County SD	Land O' Lakes
16	72	Alachua County SD	Gainesville
17	63	Osceola County SD	Kissimmee
18	62	Collier County SD	Naples
18	62	Marion County SD	Ocala
20	59	Sarasota County SD	Sarasota
21	58	Okaloosa County SD	Ft Walton Bch
22	57	Lake County SD	Tavares
22	57	Leon County SD	Tallahassee
24	48	Bay County SD	Panama City
25	46	Saint Lucie County SD	Fort Pierce
26	37	Saint Johns County SD	Saint Augustine
26	37	Santa Rosa County SD	Milton
28	36	Clay County SD	Green Cove Spgs
29	34	Martin County SD	Stuart
30	28	Indian River County SD	Vero Beach
31	25	Citrus County SD	Inverness
32	24	Charlotte County SD	Port Charlotte
32	24	Hernando County SD	Brooksville
34	23	Putnam County SD	Palatka
35	22	Gadsden County SD	Quincy
36	20	Jackson County SD	Marianna
36	20	Monroe County SD	Key West
36	20	Okeechobee County SD	Okeechobee
39	19	Highlands County SD	Sebring
39	19	Nassau County SD	Fernandina Bch
41	18	Walton County SD	Defuniak Spgs
42	16	Levy County SD	Bronson
43	15	Columbia County SD	Lake City
43	15	Sumter County SD	Bushnell
45	14	Hendry County SD	La Belle
46	13	Desoto County SD	Arcadia
46	13	Flagler County SD	Bunnell
48	11	Bradford County SD	Starke
48	11	Suwannee County SD	Live Oak
48	11	Wakulla County SD	Crawfordville
51	10	Madison County SD	Madison
52	9	Hardee County SD	Wauchula
52	9	Holmes County SD	Bonifay
52	9	Taylor County SD	Perry
55	8	Baker County SD	Macclenny
55	8	Gulf County SD	Port Saint Joe
55	8	Washington County SD	Chipley
58	7	Calhoun County SD	Blountstown
58	7	Hamilton County SD	Jasper
60	6	Union County SD	Lake Butler
61	5	Dixie County SD	Cross City
61	5	Gilchrist County SD	Trenton
63	2	Florida State Univ Lab School	Tallahassee
63	2	Florida Virtual School	Orlando

Number of Teachers

Rank	Number	District Name	City
1	20,606	Dade County SD	Miami
2	15,717	Broward County SD	Fort Lauderdale
3	10,924	Hillsborough County SD	Tampa
4	10,737	Orange County SD	Orlando
5	10,084	Palm Beach County SD	West Palm Beach
6	7,526	Duval County SD	Jacksonville
7	6,799	Pinellas County SD	Largo
8	6,046	Polk County SD	Bartow
9	4,489	Brevard County SD	Viera
10	4,322	Lee County SD	Fort Myers
11	4,202	Volusia County SD	Deland
12	4,039	Seminole County SD	Sanford
13	3,956	Pasco County SD	Land O' Lakes
14	2,833	Sarasota County SD	Sarasota
15	2,761	Escambia County SD	Pensacola
16	2,671	Osceola County SD	Kissimmee
17	2,547	Collier County SD	Naples

Rank	Number	District Name	City
18	2,544	Manatee County SD	Bradenton
19	2,439	Marion County SD	Ocala
20	2,270	Lake County SD	Tavares
21	2,174	Clay County SD	Green Cove Spgs
22	1,951	Leon County SD	Tallahassee
23	1,878	Saint Lucie County SD	Fort Pierce
24	1,844	Okaloosa County SD	Ft Walton Bch
25	1,714	Bay County SD	Panama City
26	1,683	Alachua County SD	Gainesville
27	1,499	Santa Rosa County SD	Milton
28	1,436	Hernando County SD	Brooksville
29	1,423	Saint Johns County SD	Saint Augustine
30	1,057	Martin County SD	Stuart
31	1,028	Indian River County SD	Vero Beach
32	999	Citrus County SD	Inverness
33	991	Charlotte County SD	Port Charlotte
34	802	Highlands County SD	Sebring
35	761	Flagler County SD	Bunnell
36	700	Putnam County SD	Palatka
37	642	Columbia County SD	Lake City
38	632	Nassau County SD	Fernandina Bch
39	596	Monroe County SD	Key West
40	444	Jackson County SD	Marianna
41	439	Walton County SD	Defuniak Spgs
42	434	Sumter County SD	Bushnell
43	425	Gadsden County SD	Quincy
44	420	Okeechobee County SD	Okeechobee
45	417	Hendry County SD	La Belle
46	386	Levy County SD	Bronson
47	355	Suwannee County SD	Live Oak
48	329	Hardee County SD	Wauchula
49	296	Desoto County SD	Arcadia
50	289	Wakulla County SD	Crawfordville
51	280	Baker County SD	Macclenny
52	252	Bradford County SD	Starke
53	249	Washington County SD	Chipley
54	216	Holmes County SD	Bonifay
55	212	Taylor County SD	Perry
56	191	Union County SD	Lake Butler
57	183	Florida Virtual School	Orlando
58	177	Gilchrist County SD	Trenton
59	170	Madison County SD	Madison
60	164	Calhoun County SD	Blountstown
61	149	Florida State Univ Lab School	Tallahassee
62	136	Gulf County SD	Port Saint Joe
63	127	Dixie County SD	Cross City
64	121	Hamilton County SD	Jasper

Number of Students

Rank	Number	District Name	City
1	362,070	Dade County SD	Miami
2	271,630	Broward County SD	Fort Lauderdale
3	193,757	Hillsborough County SD	Tampa
4	175,609	Orange County SD	Orlando
5	174,935	Palm Beach County SD	West Palm Beach
6	126,662	Duval County SD	Jacksonville
7	112,174	Pinellas County SD	Largo
8	89,443	Polk County SD	Bartow
9	75,634	Lee County SD	Fort Myers
10	75,233	Brevard County SD	Viera
11	67,530	Seminole County SD	Sanford
12	65,627	Volusia County SD	Deland
13	62,768	Pasco County SD	Land O' Lakes
14	49,798	Osceola County SD	Kissimmee
15	43,460	Escambia County SD	Pensacola
16	43,292	Collier County SD	Naples
17	42,370	Manatee County SD	Bradenton
18	42,035	Marion County SD	Ocala
19	41,890	Sarasota County SD	Sarasota
20	38,060	Lake County SD	Tavares
21	36,201	Saint Lucie County SD	Fort Pierce
22	34,169	Clay County SD	Green Cove Spgs
23	32,327	Leon County SD	Tallahassee
24	31,011	Okaloosa County SD	Ft Walton Bch
25	29,109	Alachua County SD	Gainesville
26	27,618	Bay County SD	Panama City
27	25,757	Saint Johns County SD	Saint Augustine
28	25,188	Santa Rosa County SD	Milton
29	21,707	Hernando County SD	Brooksville
30	18,156	Martin County SD	Stuart
31	17,907	Charlotte County SD	Port Charlotte
32	17,239	Indian River County SD	Vero Beach
33	15,812	Citrus County SD	Inverness
34	12,274	Putnam County SD	Palatka
35	12,136	Highlands County SD	Sebring
36	11,053	Flagler County SD	Bunnell
37	10,866	Nassau County SD	Fernandina Bch

Rank	Number	District Name	City
38	10,188	Columbia County SD	Lake City
39	8,594	Monroe County SD	Key West
40	7,578	Hendry County SD	La Belle
41	7,457	Jackson County SD	Marianna
42	7,416	Sumter County SD	Bushnell
43	7,329	Okeechobee County SD	Okeechobee
44	6,896	Walton County SD	Defuniak Spgs
45	6,515	Gadsden County SD	Quincy
46	6,256	Levy County SD	Bronson
47	5,954	Suwannee County SD	Live Oak
48	5,373	Florida Virtual School	Orlando
49	5,019	Desoto County SD	Arcadia
50	4,967	Hardee County SD	Wauchula
51	4,914	Wakulla County SD	Crawfordville
52	4,903	Baker County SD	Macclenny
53	3,779	Bradford County SD	Starke
54	3,560	Washington County SD	Chipley
55	3,439	Holmes County SD	Bonifay
56	3,378	Taylor County SD	Perry
57	3,032	Madison County SD	Madison
58	2,892	Gilchrist County SD	Trenton
59	2,290	Union County SD	Lake Butler
60	2,274	Calhoun County SD	Blountstown
61	2,238	Dixie County SD	Cross City
62	2,206	Florida State Univ Lab School	Tallahassee
63	2,179	Gulf County SD	Port Saint Joe
64	2,010	Hamilton County SD	Jasper

Male Students

Rank	Percent	District Name	City
1	53.9	Madison County SD	Madison
2	53.8	Desoto County SD	Arcadia
3	53.0	Putnam County SD	Palatka
4	52.8	Gulf County SD	Port Saint Joe
5	52.6	Holmes County SD	Bonifay
6	52.3	Baker County SD	Macclenny
7	52.2	Wakulla County SD	Crawfordville
8	52.2	Hardee County SD	Wauchula
9	52.1	Okaloosa County SD	Ft Walton Bch
10	52.0	Walton County SD	Defuniak Spgs
11	52.0	Monroe County SD	Key West
12	52.0	Flagler County SD	Bunnell
13	51.9	Sumter County SD	Bushnell
14	51.8	Okeechobee County SD	Okeechobee
15	51.8	Santa Rosa County SD	Milton
16	51.8	Saint Johns County SD	Saint Augustine
17	51.8	Hamilton County SD	Jasper
18	51.7	Suwannee County SD	Live Oak
19	51.7	Union County SD	Lake Butler
20	51.7	Levy County SD	Bronson
21	51.7	Highlands County SD	Sebring
22	51.7	Polk County SD	Bartow
23	51.7	Martin County SD	Stuart
24	51.7	Nassau County SD	Fernandina Bch
25	51.6	Indian River County SD	Vero Beach
26	51.6	Jackson County SD	Marianna
27	51.6	Citrus County SD	Inverness
28	51.5	Broward County SD	Fort Lauderdale
29	51.5	Marion County SD	Ocala
30	51.5	Columbia County SD	Lake City
31	51.4	Pasco County SD	Land O' Lakes
32	51.4	Brevard County SD	Viera
33	51.4	Washington County SD	Chipley
34	51.4	Palm Beach County SD	West Palm Beach
35	51.4	Collier County SD	Naples
36	51.4	Volusia County SD	Deland
37	51.4	Orange County SD	Orlando
38	51.4	Clay County SD	Green Cove Spgs
39	51.4	Bradford County SD	Starke
40	51.4	Lee County SD	Fort Myers
40	51.4	Pinellas County SD	Largo
42	51.4	Osceola County SD	Kissimmee
43	51.3	Sarasota County SD	Sarasota
44	51.3	Bay County SD	Panama City
45	51.3	Hernando County SD	Brooksville
46	51.3	Manatee County SD	Bradenton
47	51.2	Alachua County SD	Gainesville
48	51.2	Hendry County SD	La Belle
49	51.2	Seminole County SD	Sanford
50	51.2	Hillsborough County SD	Tampa
51	51.1	Escambia County SD	Pensacola
52	51.1	Lake County SD	Tavares
53	51.1	Dade County SD	Miami
54	50.9	Saint Lucie County SD	Fort Pierce
55	50.9	Charlotte County SD	Port Charlotte
56	50.9	Dixie County SD	Cross City
57	50.8	Leon County SD	Tallahassee

Rank	Percent	District Name	City
58	50.7	Calhoun County SD	Blountstown
59	50.6	Gadsden County SD	Quincy
60	50.6	Duval County SD	Jacksonville
61	50.5	Gilchrist County SD	Trenton
62	50.4	Taylor County SD	Perry
63	49.3	Florida State Univ Lab School	Tallahassee
64	42.4	Florida Virtual School	Orlando

Female Students

Rank	Percent	District Name	City
1	57.5	Florida Virtual School	Orlando
2	50.6	Florida State Univ Lab School	Tallahassee
3	49.5	Taylor County SD	Perry
4	49.4	Gilchrist County SD	Trenton
5	49.3	Duval County SD	Jacksonville
6	49.3	Gadsden County SD	Quincy
7	49.2	Calhoun County SD	Blountstown
8	49.1	Leon County SD	Tallahassee
9	49.0	Dixie County SD	Cross City
10	49.0	Charlotte County SD	Port Charlotte
11	49.0	Saint Lucie County SD	Fort Pierce
12	48.8	Dade County SD	Miami
13	48.8	Lake County SD	Tavares
14	48.8	Escambia County SD	Pensacola
15	48.7	Hillsborough County SD	Tampa
16	48.7	Seminole County SD	Sanford
17	48.7	Hendry County SD	La Belle
18	48.7	Alachua County SD	Gainesville
19	48.6	Manatee County SD	Bradenton
20	48.6	Hernando County SD	Brooksville
21	48.6	Bay County SD	Panama City
22	48.6	Sarasota County SD	Sarasota
23	48.5	Osceola County SD	Kissimmee
24	48.5	Lee County SD	Fort Myers
24	48.5	Pinellas County SD	Largo
26	48.5	Bradford County SD	Starke
27	48.5	Clay County SD	Green Cove Spgs
28	48.5	Orange County SD	Orlando
29	48.5	Volusia County SD	Deland
30	48.5	Collier County SD	Naples
31	48.5	Palm Beach County SD	West Palm Beach
32	48.5	Washington County SD	Chipley
33	48.5	Brevard County SD	Viera
34	48.5	Pasco County SD	Land O' Lakes
35	48.4	Columbia County SD	Lake City
36	48.4	Marion County SD	Ocala
37	48.4	Broward County SD	Fort Lauderdale
38	48.3	Citrus County SD	Inverness
39	48.3	Jackson County SD	Marianna
40	48.3	Indian River County SD	Vero Beach
41	48.2	Nassau County SD	Fernandina Bch
42	48.2	Martin County SD	Stuart
43	48.2	Polk County SD	Bartow
44	48.2	Highlands County SD	Sebring
45	48.2	Levy County SD	Bronson
46	48.2	Union County SD	Lake Butler
47	48.2	Suwannee County SD	Live Oak
48	48.1	Hamilton County SD	Jasper
49	48.1	Saint Johns County SD	Saint Augustine
50	48.1	Santa Rosa County SD	Milton
51	48.1	Okeechobee County SD	Okeechobee
52	48.0	Sumter County SD	Bushnell
53	47.9	Flagler County SD	Bunnell
54	47.9	Monroe County SD	Key West
55	47.9	Walton County SD	Defuniak Spgs
56	47.8	Okaloosa County SD	Ft Walton Bch
57	47.7	Hardee County SD	Wauchula
58	47.7	Wakulla County SD	Crawfordville
59	47.6	Baker County SD	Macclenny
60	47.3	Holmes County SD	Bonifay
61	47.1	Gulf County SD	Port Saint Joe
62	46.9	Putnam County SD	Palatka
63	46.1	Desoto County SD	Arcadia
64	46.0	Madison County SD	Madison

Individual Education Program Students

Rank	Percent	District Name	City
1	27.0	Gilchrist County SD	Trenton
2	24.3	Madison County SD	Madison
3	23.8	Bradford County SD	Starke
4	23.3	Levy County SD	Bronson
5	22.4	Calhoun County SD	Blountstown
6	21.5	Okeechobee County SD	Okeechobee
7	21.3	Dixie County SD	Cross City
8	20.0	Wakulla County SD	Crawfordville
9	19.8	Alachua County SD	Gainesville
10	19.6	Gulf County SD	Port Saint Joe
11	19.1	Charlotte County SD	Port Charlotte
12	18.9	Hardee County SD	Wauchula
13	18.8	Jackson County SD	Marianna
14	18.7	Columbia County SD	Lake City
14	18.7	Taylor County SD	Perry
16	18.4	Pasco County SD	Land O' Lakes
17	18.2	Bay County SD	Panama City
17	18.2	Desoto County SD	Arcadia
19	18.1	Clay County SD	Green Cove Spgs
19	18.1	Monroe County SD	Key West
19	18.1	Putnam County SD	Palatka
19	18.1	Volusia County SD	Deland
23	17.9	Manatee County SD	Bradenton
24	17.7	Leon County SD	Tallahassee
25	17.6	Union County SD	Lake Butler
26	17.2	Brevard County SD	Viera
26	17.2	Citrus County SD	Inverness
28	17.1	Escambia County SD	Pensacola
28	17.1	Marion County SD	Ocala
30	16.5	Hendry County SD	La Belle
30	16.5	Pinellas County SD	Largo
32	16.4	Highlands County SD	Sebring
32	16.4	Martin County SD	Stuart
32	16.4	Sarasota County SD	Sarasota
35	16.3	Hamilton County SD	Jasper
36	16.1	Hernando County SD	Brooksville
37	16.0	Gadsden County SD	Quincy
38	15.9	Okaloosa County SD	Ft Walton Bch
39	15.6	Santa Rosa County SD	Milton
40	15.4	Holmes County SD	Bonifay
40	15.4	Lake County SD	Tavares
42	15.3	Duval County SD	Jacksonville
42	15.3	Sumter County SD	Bushnell
44	15.2	Hillsborough County SD	Tampa
45	15.1	Washington County SD	Chipley
46	14.8	Orange County SD	Orlando
47	14.7	Nassau County SD	Fernandina Bch
47	14.7	Osceola County SD	Kissimmee
49	14.6	Flagler County SD	Bunnell
49	14.6	Palm Beach County SD	West Palm Beach
51	14.5	Saint Johns County SD	Saint Augustine
52	14.4	Lee County SD	Fort Myers
53	14.2	Collier County SD	Naples
54	14.1	Polk County SD	Bartow
55	13.7	Indian River County SD	Vero Beach
56	13.4	Walton County SD	Defuniak Spgs
57	13.3	Saint Lucie County SD	Fort Pierce
58	12.9	Seminole County SD	Sanford
59	12.7	Suwannee County SD	Live Oak
60	11.8	Dade County SD	Miami
61	11.7	Broward County SD	Fort Lauderdale
62	10.8	Baker County SD	Macclenny
63	9.1	Florida State Univ Lab School	Tallahassee
64	0.0	Florida Virtual School	Orlando

English Language Learner Students

Rank	Percent	District Name	City
1	17.8	Orange County SD	Orlando
2	16.8	Osceola County SD	Kissimmee
3	16.0	Dade County SD	Miami
4	15.5	Collier County SD	Naples
5	11.3	Palm Beach County SD	West Palm Beach
6	10.6	Hillsborough County SD	Tampa
7	10.2	Lee County SD	Fort Myers
7	10.2	Martin County SD	Stuart
9	9.8	Broward County SD	Fort Lauderdale
10	8.5	Desoto County SD	Arcadia
11	8.0	Manatee County SD	Bradenton
12	7.3	Hendry County SD	La Belle
13	6.9	Gadsden County SD	Quincy
14	6.5	Polk County SD	Bartow
15	6.2	Hardee County SD	Wauchula
16	5.9	Lake County SD	Tavares
17	5.7	Okeechobee County SD	Okeechobee
17	5.7	Saint Lucie County SD	Fort Pierce
19	5.6	Monroe County SD	Key West
20	4.7	Highlands County SD	Sebring
21	4.5	Sarasota County SD	Sarasota
22	4.4	Indian River County SD	Vero Beach
22	4.4	Sumter County SD	Bushnell
24	4.1	Hamilton County SD	Jasper
24	4.1	Putnam County SD	Palatka
26	3.9	Marion County SD	Ocala
27	3.8	Volusia County SD	Deland
28	3.6	Seminole County SD	Sanford
29	3.1	Flagler County SD	Bunnell
30	3.0	Pasco County SD	Land O' Lakes
30	3.0	Pinellas County SD	Largo
32	2.8	Duval County SD	Jacksonville
33	2.3	Suwannee County SD	Live Oak
34	1.8	Brevard County SD	Viera
35	1.7	Florida State Univ Lab School	Tallahassee
36	1.6	Hernando County SD	Brooksville
36	1.6	Levy County SD	Bronson
38	1.5	Alachua County SD	Gainesville
38	1.5	Walton County SD	Defuniak Spgs
40	1.4	Okaloosa County SD	Ft Walton Bch
41	1.1	Bay County SD	Panama City
42	1.0	Charlotte County SD	Port Charlotte
42	1.0	Leon County SD	Tallahassee
44	0.9	Gilchrist County SD	Trenton
45	0.8	Clay County SD	Green Cove Spgs
45	0.8	Escambia County SD	Pensacola
47	0.7	Columbia County SD	Lake City
47	0.7	Jackson County SD	Marianna
49	0.6	Citrus County SD	Inverness
49	0.6	Nassau County SD	Fernandina Bch
51	0.5	Madison County SD	Madison
51	0.5	Santa Rosa County SD	Milton
53	0.4	Calhoun County SD	Blountstown
53	0.4	Saint Johns County SD	Saint Augustine
55	0.2	Baker County SD	Macclenny
55	0.2	Bradford County SD	Starke
55	0.2	Holmes County SD	Bonifay
55	0.2	Taylor County SD	Perry
59	0.1	Union County SD	Lake Butler
60	0.0	Gulf County SD	Port Saint Joe
60	0.0	Wakulla County SD	Crawfordville
62	0.0	Dixie County SD	Cross City
62	0.0	Florida Virtual School	Orlando
62	0.0	Washington County SD	Chipley

Migrant Students

Rank	Percent	District Name	City
1	26.2	Hendry County SD	La Belle
2	14.0	Hardee County SD	Wauchula
3	10.1	Collier County SD	Naples
4	10.0	Highlands County SD	Sebring
5	9.4	Gadsden County SD	Quincy
6	7.8	Desoto County SD	Arcadia
7	7.5	Okeechobee County SD	Okeechobee
8	5.9	Sumter County SD	Bushnell
9	4.5	Putnam County SD	Palatka
10	4.2	Suwannee County SD	Live Oak
11	3.9	Hamilton County SD	Jasper
12	3.8	Manatee County SD	Bradenton
13	3.4	Indian River County SD	Vero Beach
14	2.5	Lee County SD	Fort Myers
15	2.4	Alachua County SD	Gainesville
16	2.0	Levy County SD	Bronson
17	1.9	Gilchrist County SD	Trenton
18	1.8	Polk County SD	Bartow
19	1.6	Madison County SD	Madison
19	1.6	Saint Lucie County SD	Fort Pierce
21	1.1	Calhoun County SD	Blountstown
21	1.1	Union County SD	Lake Butler
23	1.0	Volusia County SD	Deland
24	0.9	Hillsborough County SD	Tampa
24	0.9	Palm Beach County SD	West Palm Beach
24	0.9	Walton County SD	Defuniak Spgs
27	0.8	Dixie County SD	Cross City
27	0.8	Escambia County SD	Pensacola
29	0.6	Dade County SD	Miami
29	0.6	Jackson County SD	Marianna
29	0.6	Pasco County SD	Land O' Lakes
32	0.5	Bay County SD	Panama City
32	0.5	Holmes County SD	Bonifay
34	0.4	Florida State Univ Lab School	Tallahassee
34	0.4	Monroe County SD	Key West
36	0.3	Broward County SD	Fort Lauderdale
36	0.3	Citrus County SD	Inverness
36	0.3	Orange County SD	Orlando
36	0.3	Washington County SD	Chipley
40	0.2	Baker County SD	Macclenny
40	0.2	Bradford County SD	Starke
40	0.2	Clay County SD	Green Cove Spgs
40	0.2	Flagler County SD	Bunnell
40	0.2	Lake County SD	Tavares
40	0.2	Martin County SD	Stuart
40	0.2	Osceola County SD	Kissimmee
40	0.2	Sarasota County SD	Sarasota
48	0.1	Marion County SD	Ocala
48	0.1	Nassau County SD	Fernandina Bch

48	0.1	Okaloosa County SD	Ft Walton Bch
48	0.1	Saint Johns County SD	Saint Augustine
52	0.0	Brevard County SD	Viera
52	0.0	Columbia County SD	Lake City
52	0.0	Duval County SD	Jacksonville
52	0.0	Leon County SD	Tallahassee
52	0.0	Santa Rosa County SD	Milton
57	0.0	Charlotte County SD	Port Charlotte
57	0.0	Florida Virtual School	Orlando
57	0.0	Gulf County SD	Port Saint Joe
57	0.0	Hernando County SD	Brooksville
57	0.0	Pinellas County SD	Largo
57	0.0	Seminole County SD	Sanford
57	0.0	Taylor County SD	Perry
57	0.0	Wakulla County SD	Crawfordville

Students Eligible for Free Lunch

Rank	Percent	District Name	City
1	69.0	Gadsden County SD	Quincy
2	62.5	Madison County SD	Madison
3	61.2	Hendry County SD	La Belle
4	57.4	Putnam County SD	Palatka
5	55.6	Dixie County SD	Cross City
5	55.6	Hardee County SD	Wauchula
7	51.6	Dade County SD	Miami
8	50.2	Desoto County SD	Arcadia
9	49.4	Escambia County SD	Pensacola
10	49.0	Taylor County SD	Perry
11	47.9	Highlands County SD	Sebring
12	47.6	Polk County SD	Bartow
13	44.6	Hamilton County SD	Jasper
14	44.4	Levy County SD	Bronson
15	43.9	Holmes County SD	Bonifay
15	43.9	Suwannee County SD	Live Oak
17	43.2	Columbia County SD	Lake City
17	43.2	Jackson County SD	Marianna
19	43.1	Osceola County SD	Kissimmee
20	42.1	Marion County SD	Ocala
21	41.8	Bradford County SD	Starke
22	41.6	Washington County SD	Chipley
23	41.5	Saint Lucie County SD	Fort Pierce
24	41.4	Sumter County SD	Bushnell
25	40.9	Okeechobee County SD	Okeechobee
26	40.3	Hillsborough County SD	Tampa
27	40.0	Alachua County SD	Gainesville
28	39.1	Calhoun County SD	Blountstown
29	37.8	Orange County SD	Orlando
30	37.7	Gilchrist County SD	Trenton
31	36.7	Manatee County SD	Bradenton
32	36.5	Walton County SD	Defuniak Spgs
33	35.3	Palm Beach County SD	West Palm Beach
34	35.2	Bay County SD	Panama City
35	35.0	Lee County SD	Fort Myers
36	34.8	Baker County SD	Macclenny
36	34.8	Union County SD	Lake Butler
38	34.5	Collier County SD	Naples
39	34.1	Gulf County SD	Port Saint Joe
39	34.1	Pasco County SD	Land O' Lakes
41	33.9	Hernando County SD	Brooksville
42	33.6	Duval County SD	Jacksonville
43	33.0	Citrus County SD	Inverness
44	32.8	Broward County SD	Fort Lauderdale
45	32.6	Lake County SD	Tavares
46	32.2	Volusia County SD	Deland
47	32.1	Indian River County SD	Vero Beach
48	31.7	Pinellas County SD	Largo
49	31.5	Monroe County SD	Key West
50	30.9	Leon County SD	Tallahassee
51	28.1	Charlotte County SD	Port Charlotte
52	27.3	Flagler County SD	Bunnell
53	27.2	Wakulla County SD	Crawfordville
54	25.0	Nassau County SD	Fernandina Bch
55	24.3	Santa Rosa County SD	Milton
56	24.0	Brevard County SD	Viera
57	22.9	Seminole County SD	Sanford
58	22.4	Sarasota County SD	Sarasota
59	21.6	Martin County SD	Stuart
60	20.8	Okaloosa County SD	Ft Walton Bch
61	17.6	Clay County SD	Green Cove Spgs
62	13.7	Saint Johns County SD	Saint Augustine
63	12.7	Florida State Univ Lab School	Tallahassee
64	0.0	Florida Virtual School	Orlando

Students Eligible for Reduced-Price Lunch

Rank	Percent	District Name	City

1	13.0	Dixie County SD	Cross City
1	13.0	Holmes County SD	Bonifay
3	12.8	Calhoun County SD	Blountstown
3	12.8	Washington County SD	Chipley
5	12.4	Escambia County SD	Pensacola
6	12.3	Osceola County SD	Kissimmee
7	12.2	Gilchrist County SD	Trenton
8	11.5	Sumter County SD	Bushnell
9	11.4	Charlotte County SD	Port Charlotte
9	11.4	Levy County SD	Bronson
11	11.3	Hamilton County SD	Jasper
11	11.3	Okeechobee County SD	Okeechobee
13	11.2	Gadsden County SD	Quincy
14	11.0	Bradford County SD	Starke
14	11.0	Saint Lucie County SD	Fort Pierce
14	11.0	Walton County SD	Defuniak Spgs
17	10.9	Madison County SD	Madison
18	10.8	Gulf County SD	Port Saint Joe
19	10.6	Columbia County SD	Lake City
20	10.5	Bay County SD	Panama City
21	10.4	Marion County SD	Ocala
22	10.0	Polk County SD	Bartow
23	9.8	Hernando County SD	Brooksville
24	9.7	Volusia County SD	Deland
25	9.6	Citrus County SD	Inverness
26	9.5	Dade County SD	Miami
26	9.5	Jackson County SD	Marianna
26	9.5	Union County SD	Lake Butler
29	9.4	Highlands County SD	Sebring
29	9.4	Pasco County SD	Land O' Lakes
31	9.3	Lee County SD	Fort Myers
32	9.2	Lake County SD	Tavares
33	9.1	Desoto County SD	Arcadia
33	9.1	Hillsborough County SD	Tampa
35	9.0	Suwannee County SD	Live Oak
36	8.7	Broward County SD	Fort Lauderdale
37	8.6	Orange County SD	Orlando
37	8.6	Pinellas County SD	Largo
39	8.5	Nassau County SD	Fernandina Bch
39	8.5	Putnam County SD	Palatka
41	8.4	Hardee County SD	Wauchula
41	8.4	Hendry County SD	La Belle
43	8.2	Wakulla County SD	Crawfordville
44	8.1	Duval County SD	Jacksonville
44	8.1	Taylor County SD	Perry
46	8.0	Baker County SD	Macclenny
46	8.0	Santa Rosa County SD	Milton
48	7.9	Monroe County SD	Key West
49	7.7	Flagler County SD	Bunnell
50	7.5	Florida State Univ Lab School	Tallahassee
50	7.5	Seminole County SD	Sanford
52	7.4	Okaloosa County SD	Ft Walton Bch
53	7.3	Indian River County SD	Vero Beach
54	7.1	Clay County SD	Green Cove Spgs
55	6.8	Collier County SD	Naples
55	6.8	Manatee County SD	Bradenton
57	6.5	Alachua County SD	Gainesville
57	6.5	Sarasota County SD	Sarasota
59	6.4	Palm Beach County SD	West Palm Beach
60	6.0	Brevard County SD	Viera
61	5.7	Leon County SD	Tallahassee
62	5.0	Martin County SD	Stuart
63	4.1	Saint Johns County SD	Saint Augustine
64	0.0	Florida Virtual School	Orlando

Student/Teacher Ratio

Rank	Ratio	District Name	City
1	29.4	Florida Virtual School	Orlando
2	19.3	Saint Lucie County SD	Fort Pierce
3	18.6	Osceola County SD	Kissimmee
4	18.2	Hendry County SD	La Belle
5	18.1	Charlotte County SD	Port Charlotte
5	18.1	Saint Johns County SD	Saint Augustine
7	17.8	Madison County SD	Madison
8	17.7	Hillsborough County SD	Tampa
9	17.6	Dade County SD	Miami
9	17.6	Dixie County SD	Cross City
11	17.5	Baker County SD	Macclenny
11	17.5	Lee County SD	Fort Myers
11	17.5	Okeechobee County SD	Okeechobee
11	17.5	Putnam County SD	Palatka
15	17.3	Alachua County SD	Gainesville
15	17.3	Broward County SD	Fort Lauderdale
15	17.3	Palm Beach County SD	West Palm Beach
18	17.2	Marion County SD	Ocala
18	17.2	Martin County SD	Stuart
18	17.2	Nassau County SD	Fernandina Bch

21	17.1	Sumter County SD	Bushnell
22	17.0	Collier County SD	Naples
22	17.0	Desoto County SD	Arcadia
22	17.0	Wakulla County SD	Crawfordville
25	16.8	Brevard County SD	Viera
25	16.8	Duval County SD	Jacksonville
25	16.8	Indian River County SD	Vero Beach
25	16.8	Jackson County SD	Marianna
25	16.8	Lake County SD	Tavares
25	16.8	Okaloosa County SD	Ft Walton Bch
25	16.8	Santa Rosa County SD	Milton
25	16.8	Suwannee County SD	Live Oak
33	16.7	Manatee County SD	Bradenton
33	16.7	Seminole County SD	Sanford
35	16.6	Hamilton County SD	Jasper
35	16.6	Leon County SD	Tallahassee
37	16.5	Pinellas County SD	Largo
38	16.4	Orange County SD	Orlando
39	16.3	Gilchrist County SD	Trenton
40	16.2	Levy County SD	Bronson
41	16.1	Bay County SD	Panama City
42	16.0	Gulf County SD	Port Saint Joe
43	15.9	Columbia County SD	Lake City
43	15.9	Holmes County SD	Bonifay
43	15.9	Pasco County SD	Land O' Lakes
43	15.9	Taylor County SD	Perry
47	15.8	Citrus County SD	Inverness
48	15.7	Clay County SD	Green Cove Spgs
48	15.7	Escambia County SD	Pensacola
48	15.7	Walton County SD	Defuniak Spgs
51	15.6	Volusia County SD	Deland
52	15.3	Gadsden County SD	Quincy
53	15.1	Hardee County SD	Wauchula
53	15.1	Hernando County SD	Brooksville
53	15.1	Highlands County SD	Sebring
56	15.0	Bradford County SD	Starke
57	14.8	Florida State Univ Lab School	Tallahassee
57	14.8	Polk County SD	Bartow
57	14.8	Sarasota County SD	Sarasota
60	14.5	Flagler County SD	Bunnell
61	14.4	Monroe County SD	Key West
62	14.3	Washington County SD	Chipley
63	13.9	Calhoun County SD	Blountstown
64	12.0	Union County SD	Lake Butler

Student/Librarian Ratio

Rank	Ratio	District Name	City
1	2,238.0	Dixie County SD	Cross City
2	2,204.7	Sarasota County SD	Sarasota
3	2,148.5	Monroe County SD	Key West
4	1,579.0	Flagler County SD	Bunnell
5	1,570.5	Seminole County SD	Sanford
6	1,350.6	Lee County SD	Fort Myers
7	1,276.9	Osceola County SD	Kissimmee
8	1,190.0	Palm Beach County SD	West Palm Beach
9	1,153.3	Hillsborough County SD	Tampa
10	1,141.3	Broward County SD	Fort Lauderdale
11	1,126.0	Taylor County SD	Perry
12	1,103.0	Florida State Univ Lab School	Tallahassee
13	1,064.3	Orange County SD	Orlando
14	1,010.7	Madison County SD	Madison
15	1,005.0	Hamilton County SD	Jasper
16	1,000.4	Okaloosa County SD	Ft Walton Bch
17	986.7	Hernando County SD	Brooksville
18	986.6	Dade County SD	Miami
19	952.7	Saint Lucie County SD	Fort Pierce
20	937.5	Volusia County SD	Deland
21	899.6	Santa Rosa County SD	Milton
22	895.4	Charlotte County SD	Port Charlotte
23	894.4	Marion County SD	Ocala
24	888.2	Saint Johns County SD	Saint Augustine
25	885.7	Duval County SD	Jacksonville
26	882.7	Manatee County SD	Bradenton
27	865.8	Collier County SD	Naples
28	854.2	Clay County SD	Green Cove Spgs
29	850.6	Suwannee County SD	Live Oak
30	845.8	Lake County SD	Tavares
31	843.4	Pinellas County SD	Largo
32	836.5	Desoto County SD	Arcadia
33	820.9	Indian River County SD	Vero Beach
34	819.0	Wakulla County SD	Crawfordville
35	818.3	Putnam County SD	Palatka
36	817.8	Brevard County SD	Viera
37	817.2	Baker County SD	Macclenny
38	814.3	Okeechobee County SD	Okeechobee
39	809.1	Highlands County SD	Sebring
40	804.7	Pasco County SD	Land O' Lakes

41	783.7	Columbia County SD	Lake City
42	767.2	Bay County SD	Panama City
43	763.3	Union County SD	Lake Butler
44	757.8	Hendry County SD	La Belle
45	756.5	Martin County SD	Stuart
46	753.0	Citrus County SD	Inverness
47	751.8	Leon County SD	Tallahassee
48	739.2	Polk County SD	Bartow
49	724.3	Escambia County SD	Pensacola
50	723.0	Gilchrist County SD	Trenton
51	674.2	Sumter County SD	Bushnell
52	639.2	Nassau County SD	Fernandina Bch
53	629.8	Bradford County SD	Starke
54	621.4	Jackson County SD	Marianna
55	620.9	Hardee County SD	Wauchula
56	593.3	Washington County SD	Chipley
57	574.7	Walton County SD	Defuniak Spgs
58	568.7	Levy County SD	Bronson
59	559.8	Alachua County SD	Gainesville
60	544.8	Gulf County SD	Port Saint Joe
61	491.3	Holmes County SD	Bonifay
62	465.4	Gadsden County SD	Quincy
63	324.9	Calhoun County SD	Blountstown
64	n/a	Florida Virtual School	Orlando

Student/Counselor Ratio

Rank	Ratio	District Name	City
1	6,458.6	Hillsborough County SD	Tampa
2	767.6	Florida Virtual School	Orlando
3	663.0	Indian River County SD	Vero Beach
4	627.4	Desoto County SD	Arcadia
5	606.4	Madison County SD	Madison
6	577.2	Seminole County SD	Sanford
7	563.0	Taylor County SD	Perry
8	552.1	Lee County SD	Fort Myers
9	551.5	Florida State Univ Lab School	Tallahassee
10	548.8	Orange County SD	Orlando
11	546.0	Wakulla County SD	Crawfordville
12	543.6	Duval County SD	Jacksonville
13	529.7	Sumter County SD	Bushnell
14	525.6	Okaloosa County SD	Ft Walton Bch
15	518.7	Osceola County SD	Kissimmee
16	503.8	Santa Rosa County SD	Milton
17	502.4	Flagler County SD	Bunnell
18	492.6	Walton County SD	Defuniak Spgs
19	490.3	Baker County SD	Macclenny
20	488.6	Okeechobee County SD	Okeechobee
21	485.4	Highlands County SD	Sebring
22	478.0	Palm Beach County SD	West Palm Beach
23	477.8	Martin County SD	Stuart
24	473.6	Hendry County SD	La Belle
25	465.1	Broward County SD	Fort Lauderdale
26	463.5	Pinellas County SD	Largo
27	458.7	Brevard County SD	Viera
28	458.0	Union County SD	Lake Butler
29	454.6	Putnam County SD	Palatka
30	451.5	Hardee County SD	Wauchula
31	447.7	Charlotte County SD	Port Charlotte
32	447.6	Dixie County SD	Cross City
33	447.2	Marion County SD	Ocala
34	442.8	Polk County SD	Bartow
35	436.6	Saint Johns County SD	Saint Augustine
36	436.4	Sarasota County SD	Sarasota
37	435.8	Gulf County SD	Port Saint Joe
38	432.9	Collier County SD	Naples
39	431.0	Leon County SD	Tallahassee
40	430.3	Escambia County SD	Pensacola
41	429.7	Monroe County SD	Key West
42	428.1	Alachua County SD	Gainesville
43	425.3	Suwannee County SD	Live Oak
44	423.7	Manatee County SD	Bradenton
45	406.8	Saint Lucie County SD	Fort Pierce
46	405.4	Citrus County SD	Inverness
47	402.4	Nassau County SD	Fernandina Bch
48	402.0	Hamilton County SD	Jasper
49	395.6	Washington County SD	Chipley
50	392.3	Pasco County SD	Land O' Lakes
51	391.0	Levy County SD	Bronson
52	388.4	Lake County SD	Tavares
53	388.3	Clay County SD	Green Cove Spgs
54	383.8	Volusia County SD	Deland
55	382.1	Holmes County SD	Bonifay
56	379.0	Calhoun County SD	Blountstown
57	377.9	Bradford County SD	Starke
58	377.3	Columbia County SD	Lake City
59	371.4	Dade County SD	Miami
60	361.5	Gilchrist County SD	Trenton
61	355.9	Hernando County SD	Brooksville
62	349.6	Bay County SD	Panama City
63	342.9	Gadsden County SD	Quincy
64	324.2	Jackson County SD	Marianna

Current Spending per Student in FY2003

Rank	Dollars	District Name	City
1	9,548	Monroe County SD	Key West
2	9,219	Washington County SD	Chipley
3	9,205	Desoto County SD	Arcadia
4	8,513	Sarasota County SD	Sarasota
5	8,425	Collier County SD	Naples
6	8,118	Taylor County SD	Perry
7	8,038	Hamilton County SD	Jasper
8	7,900	Dixie County SD	Cross City
9	7,869	Dade County SD	Miami
10	7,824	Gulf County SD	Port Saint Joe
11	7,747	Gadsden County SD	Quincy
12	7,708	Palm Beach County SD	West Palm Beach
13	7,674	Gilchrist County SD	Trenton
14	7,659	Holmes County SD	Bonifay
15	7,577	Walton County SD	Defuniak Spgs
16	7,537	Highlands County SD	Sebring
17	7,494	Martin County SD	Stuart
18	7,457	Hendry County SD	La Belle
19	7,408	Bradford County SD	Starke
19	7,408	Hardee County SD	Wauchula
21	7,356	Charlotte County SD	Port Charlotte
22	7,330	Union County SD	Lake Butler
23	7,321	Escambia County SD	Pensacola
24	7,309	Broward County SD	Fort Lauderdale
25	7,304	Alachua County SD	Gainesville
26	7,299	Polk County SD	Bartow
27	7,291	Lee County SD	Fort Myers
28	7,287	Suwannee County SD	Live Oak
29	7,242	Levy County SD	Bronson
30	7,200	Manatee County SD	Bradenton
31	7,198	Citrus County SD	Inverness
32	7,185	Jackson County SD	Marianna
33	7,126	Okeechobee County SD	Okeechobee
34	7,121	Pinellas County SD	Largo
35	7,102	Madison County SD	Madison
36	7,085	Leon County SD	Tallahassee
37	7,028	Indian River County SD	Vero Beach
38	7,007	Volusia County SD	Deland
39	6,978	Flagler County SD	Bunnell
40	6,958	Bay County SD	Panama City
40	6,958	Marion County SD	Ocala
42	6,948	Lake County SD	Tavares
43	6,932	Columbia County SD	Lake City
44	6,882	Duval County SD	Jacksonville
45	6,868	Saint Johns County SD	Saint Augustine
46	6,821	Sumter County SD	Bushnell
47	6,797	Brevard County SD	Viera
48	6,793	Calhoun County SD	Blountstown
49	6,785	Putnam County SD	Palatka
50	6,755	Okaloosa County SD	Ft Walton Bch
51	6,717	Osceola County SD	Kissimmee
52	6,712	Orange County SD	Orlando
53	6,704	Saint Lucie County SD	Fort Pierce
54	6,693	Wakulla County SD	Crawfordville
55	6,677	Hillsborough County SD	Tampa
56	6,635	Pasco County SD	Land O' Lakes
57	6,596	Baker County SD	Macclenny
58	6,491	Hernando County SD	Brooksville
59	6,454	Santa Rosa County SD	Milton
60	6,377	Seminole County SD	Sanford
61	6,242	Clay County SD	Green Cove Spgs
62	6,235	Nassau County SD	Fernandina Bch
63	n/a	Florida State Univ Lab School	Tallahassee
63	n/a	Florida Virtual School	Orlando

Number of Diploma Recipients

Rank	Number	District Name	City
1	16,638	Dade County SD	Miami
2	11,654	Broward County SD	Fort Lauderdale
3	7,968	Hillsborough County SD	Tampa
4	7,687	Palm Beach County SD	West Palm Beach
5	7,361	Orange County SD	Orlando
6	5,413	Pinellas County SD	Largo
7	5,260	Duval County SD	Jacksonville
8	3,815	Polk County SD	Bartow
9	3,578	Brevard County SD	Viera
10	3,420	Seminole County SD	Sanford
11	3,386	Volusia County SD	Deland
12	2,846	Lee County SD	Fort Myers
13	2,453	Pasco County SD	Land O' Lakes
14	2,320	Escambia County SD	Pensacola
15	1,978	Okaloosa County SD	Ft Walton Bch
16	1,960	Marion County SD	Ocala
17	1,895	Sarasota County SD	Sarasota
18	1,853	Osceola County SD	Kissimmee
19	1,788	Leon County SD	Tallahassee
20	1,711	Collier County SD	Naples
21	1,709	Manatee County SD	Bradenton
22	1,651	Alachua County SD	Gainesville
23	1,627	Clay County SD	Green Cove Spgs
24	1,531	Lake County SD	Tavares
25	1,333	Santa Rosa County SD	Milton
26	1,258	Saint Lucie County SD	Fort Pierce
27	1,230	Bay County SD	Panama City
28	1,097	Saint Johns County SD	Saint Augustine
29	1,076	Charlotte County SD	Port Charlotte
30	923	Hernando County SD	Brooksville
31	842	Martin County SD	Stuart
32	830	Citrus County SD	Inverness
33	821	Indian River County SD	Vero Beach
34	577	Nassau County SD	Fernandina Bch
35	561	Highlands County SD	Sebring
36	486	Monroe County SD	Key West
37	447	Putnam County SD	Palatka
38	441	Columbia County SD	Lake City
39	409	Jackson County SD	Marianna
40	385	Flagler County SD	Bunnell
41	346	Gadsden County SD	Quincy
42	339	Okeechobee County SD	Okeechobee
43	301	Levy County SD	Bronson
44	290	Hendry County SD	La Belle
45	284	Suwannee County SD	Live Oak
46	261	Sumter County SD	Bushnell
47	246	Walton County SD	Defuniak Spgs
48	233	Wakulla County SD	Crawfordville
49	223	Baker County SD	Macclenny
50	214	Bradford County SD	Starke
51	213	Hardee County SD	Wauchula
52	204	Desoto County SD	Arcadia
53	203	Holmes County SD	Bonifay
53	203	Taylor County SD	Perry
55	191	Washington County SD	Chipley
56	180	Madison County SD	Madison
57	150	Dixie County SD	Cross City
58	141	Gilchrist County SD	Trenton
59	129	Union County SD	Lake Butler
60	119	Hamilton County SD	Jasper
61	117	Gulf County SD	Port Saint Joe
62	106	Calhoun County SD	Blountstown
63	93	Florida State Univ Lab School	Tallahassee
64	n/a	Florida Virtual School	Orlando

High School Drop-out Rate

Rank	Percent	District Name	City
1	9.0	Lee County SD	Fort Myers
2	7.5	Hardee County SD	Wauchula
3	6.8	Madison County SD	Madison
4	6.7	Duval County SD	Jacksonville
5	6.3	Pinellas County SD	Largo
6	6.1	Alachua County SD	Gainesville
6	6.1	Hendry County SD	La Belle
6	6.1	Walton County SD	Defuniak Spgs
9	5.7	Wakulla County SD	Crawfordville
10	5.6	Okeechobee County SD	Okeechobee
10	5.6	Osceola County SD	Kissimmee
12	5.5	Lake County SD	Tavares
13	5.4	Gadsden County SD	Quincy
14	5.3	Highlands County SD	Sebring
15	4.8	Citrus County SD	Inverness
15	4.8	Dade County SD	Miami
17	4.7	Baker County SD	Macclenny
18	4.4	Collier County SD	Naples
19	4.3	Bradford County SD	Starke
20	4.2	Charlotte County SD	Port Charlotte
20	4.2	Monroe County SD	Key West
20	4.2	Pasco County SD	Land O' Lakes
23	4.0	Nassau County SD	Fernandina Bch
24	3.7	Desoto County SD	Arcadia
24	3.7	Leon County SD	Tallahassee
24	3.7	Manatee County SD	Bradenton
27	3.6	Dixie County SD	Cross City
27	3.6	Levy County SD	Bronson
27	3.6	Okaloosa County SD	Ft Walton Bch
27	3.6	Polk County SD	Bartow
27	3.6	Sarasota County SD	Sarasota
32	3.5	Marion County SD	Ocala

32	3.5	Suwannee County SD	Live Oak
34	3.4	Orange County SD	Orlando
35	3.2	Calhoun County SD	Blountstown
35	3.2	Washington County SD	Chipley
37	3.1	Holmes County SD	Bonifay
37	3.1	Palm Beach County SD	West Palm Beach
39	3.0	Taylor County SD	Perry
40	2.9	Gilchrist County SD	Trenton
41	2.8	Clay County SD	Green Cove Spgs
41	2.8	Escambia County SD	Pensacola
41	2.8	Hamilton County SD	Jasper
41	2.8	Hillsborough County SD	Tampa
41	2.8	Sumter County SD	Bushnell
46	2.7	Jackson County SD	Marianna
47	2.5	Putnam County SD	Palatka
47	2.5	Saint Johns County SD	Saint Augustine
49	2.3	Flagler County SD	Bunnell
49	2.3	Hernando County SD	Brooksville
51	2.1	Santa Rosa County SD	Milton
52	1.9	Florida State Univ Lab School	Tallahassee
52	1.9	Union County SD	Lake Butler
52	1.9	Volusia County SD	Deland
55	1.8	Bay County SD	Panama City
55	1.8	Indian River County SD	Vero Beach
57	1.7	Columbia County SD	Lake City
58	1.6	Broward County SD	Fort Lauderdale
58	1.6	Saint Lucie County SD	Fort Pierce
60	1.5	Seminole County SD	Sanford
61	0.9	Brevard County SD	Viera
62	0.6	Martin County SD	Stuart
63	0.5	Gulf County SD	Port Saint Joe
64	n/a	Florida Virtual School	Orlando

:ies NATIONAL CENTER FOR EDUCATION STATISTICS
Institute of Education Sciences
NCES 2007-495FL4

The Nation's Report Card

Mathematics 2007
State Snapshot Report

Florida
Grade 4
Public Schools

The National Assessment of Educational Progress (NAEP) assesses mathematics in five content areas: number properties and operations; measurement; geometry; data analysis and probability; and algebra. The NAEP mathematics scale ranges from 0 to 500.

Overall Mathematics Results for Florida

- In 2007, the average scale score for fourth-grade students in Florida was 242. This was higher than their average score in 2005 (239) and was higher than their average score in 1992 (214).[1]
- Florida's average score (242) in 2007 was higher than that of the nation's public schools (239).
- Of the 52 states and other jurisdictions that participated in the 2007 fourth-grade assessment, students' average scale score in Florida was higher than those in 25 jurisdictions, not significantly different from those in 18 jurisdictions, and lower than those in 8 jurisdictions.[2]
- The percentage of students in Florida who performed at or above the NAEP *Proficient* level was 40 percent in 2007. This percentage was greater than that in 2005 (37 percent) and was greater than that in 1992 (13 percent).
- The percentage of students in Florida who performed at or above the NAEP *Basic* level was 86 percent in 2007. This percentage was greater than that in 2005 (82 percent) and was greater than that in 1992 (52 percent).

Percentages at NAEP Achievement Levels and Average Score

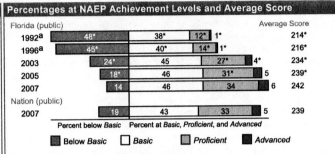

	Average Score
Florida (public)	
1992[a] 48* 38* 12* 1*	214*
1996[a] 45* 40* 14* 1*	216*
2003 24* 45 27* 4*	234*
2005 18* 46 31* 5	239*
2007 14 46 34 6	242
Nation (public)	
2007 19 43 33 5	239

Percent below *Basic*   Percent at *Basic, Proficient,* and *Advanced*

■ Below *Basic*   □ *Basic*   ▨ *Proficient*   ■ *Advanced*

[a] Accommodations were not permitted for this assessment.

NOTE: The NAEP grade 4 mathematics achievement levels correspond to the following scale points: Below *Basic*, 213 or lower; *Basic*, 214–248; *Proficient*, 249–281; *Advanced*, 282 or above.

Performance of NAEP Reporting Groups in Florida: 2007

Reporting groups	Percent of students	Average score	Percent below *Basic*	Percent of students at or above *Basic*	Percent of students at or above *Proficient*	Percent *Advanced*
Male	51	243 ↑	13 ↓	87 ↑	43 ↑	7
Female	49	241 ↑	14 ↓	86 ↑	38	5
White	48	250	6 ↓	94 ↑	54	8
Black	21	225	29	71	15	1
Hispanic	25	238 ↑	17 ↓	83 ↑	33	3
Asian/Pacific Islander	2	255	7	93	59	17
American Indian/Alaska Native	#	‡	‡	‡	‡	‡
Eligible for National School Lunch Program	48	233 ↑	21 ↓	79 ↑	25	2
Not eligible for National School Lunch Program	51	251	7	93	55	9

Average Score Gaps Between Selected Groups

- In 2007, male students in Florida had an average score that was higher than that of female students by 3 points. In 1992, there was no significant difference between the average score of male and female students.
- In 2007, Black students had an average score that was lower than that of White students by 25 points. This performance gap was narrower than that of 1992 (34 points).
- In 2007, Hispanic students had an average score that was lower than that of White students by 13 points. In 1992, the average score for Hispanic students was lower than that of White students by 16 points.
- In 2007, students who were eligible for free/reduced-price school lunch, a proxy for poverty, had an average score that was lower than that of students who were not eligible for free/reduced-price school lunch by 18 points. This performance gap was narrower than that of 1996 (24 points).
- In 2007, the score gap between students at the 75th percentile and students at the 25th percentile was 35 points. This performance gap was narrower than that of 1992 (42 points).

Mathematics Scores at Selected Percentiles

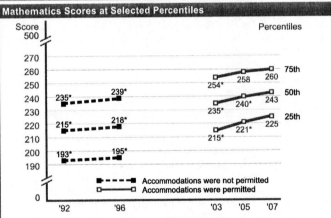

Score	Percentiles
75th	254* 258 260
50th	235* 239* 235* 240* 243
25th	215* 218* 215* 221* 225
	193* 195*

■---■ Accommodations were not permitted
□---□ Accommodations were permitted

'92 '96 '03 '05 '07

NOTE: Scores at selected percentiles on the NAEP mathematics scale indicate how well students at lower, middle, and higher levels performed.

\# Rounds to zero.

‡ Reporting standards not met.

* Significantly different from 2007.

↑ Significantly higher than 2005. ↓ Significantly lower than 2005.

[1] Comparisons (higher/lower/narrower/wider/not different) are based on statistical tests. The .05 level was used for testing statistical significance. Statistical comparisons are calculated on the basis of unrounded scale scores or percentages. Comparisons across jurisdictions and comparisons with the nation or within a jurisdiction across years may be affected by differences in exclusion rates for students with disabilities (SD) and English language learners (ELL). The exclusion rates for SD and ELL in Florida were 2 percent and 2 percent in 2007, respectively.For more information on NAEP significance testing see http://nces.ed.gov/nationsreportcard/mathematics/interpret-results.asp#statistical.

[2] "Jurisdictions" refers to states and the District of Columbia and the Department of Defense Education Activity schools.

NOTE: Detail may not sum to totals because of rounding and because the "Information not available" category for the National School Lunch Program, which provides free and reduced-price lunches, and the "Unclassified" category for race/ethnicity are not displayed. Visit http://nces.ed.gov/nationsreportcard/states/ for additional results and detailed information.

SOURCE: U.S. Department of Education, Institute of Education Sciences, National Center for Education Statistics, National Assessment of Educational Progress (NAEP), various years, 1992–2007 Mathematics Assessments.

NCES 2007-497FL4

The Nation's Report Card

Reading 2007
State Snapshot Report

Florida
Grade 4
Public Schools

The National Assessment of Educational Progress (NAEP) assesses reading in two content areas in grade 4: reading for literary experience and to gain information. The NAEP reading scale ranges from 0 to 500.

Overall Reading Results for Florida

- In 2007, the average scale score for fourth-grade students in Florida was 224. This was higher than their average score in 2005 (219) and was higher than their average score in 1992 (208).[1]
- Florida's average score (224) in 2007 was higher than that of the nation's public schools (220).
- Of the 52 states and other jurisdictions that participated in the 2007 fourth-grade assessment, students' average scale score in Florida was higher than those in 22 jurisdictions, not significantly different from those in 19 jurisdictions, and lower than those in 10 jurisdictions.[2]
- The percentage of students in Florida who performed at or above the NAEP *Proficient* level was 34 percent in 2007. This percentage was greater than that in 2005 (30 percent) and was greater than that in 1992 (21 percent).
- The percentage of students in Florida who performed at or above the NAEP *Basic* level was 70 percent in 2007. This percentage was greater than that in 2005 (65 percent) and was greater than that in 1992 (53 percent).

Percentages at NAEP Achievement Levels and Average Score

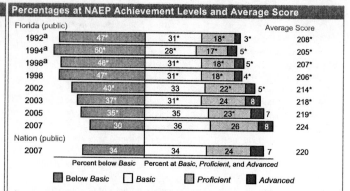

Florida (public)

Year				Average Score
1992ᵃ	47*	31*	18* 3*	208*
1994ᵃ	50*	28*	17* 5*	205*
1998ᵃ	46*	31*	18* 5*	207*
1998	47*	31*	18* 4*	206*
2002	40*	33	22* 5*	214*
2003	37*	31*	24 8	218*
2005	35*	35	23* 7	219*
2007	30	36	26 8	224

Nation (public)

Year				
2007	34	34	24 7	220

Percent below *Basic*   Percent at *Basic, Proficient,* and *Advanced*

■ Below *Basic*   □ *Basic*   ▨ *Proficient*   ■ *Advanced*

ᵃ Accommodations were not permitted for this assessment.

NOTE: The NAEP grade 4 reading achievement levels correspond to the following scale points: Below *Basic*, 207 or lower; *Basic*, 208–237; *Proficient*, 238–267; *Advanced*, 268 or above.

Performance of NAEP Reporting Groups in Florida: 2007

Reporting groups	Percent of students	Average score	Percent below *Basic*	Percent of students at or above *Basic*	Percent of students at or above *Proficient*	Percent *Advanced*
Male	51	220	34 ↓	66	30	6
Female	49	227 ↑	25 ↓	75	38 ↑	10
White	47	232	19 ↓	81	44	11
Black	21	208	48	52	16	2
Hispanic	25	218	36	64	28	6
Asian/Pacific Islander	2	241	14	86	57	18
American Indian/Alaska Native	#	‡	‡	‡	‡	‡
Eligible for National School Lunch Program	49	213 ↑	41 ↓	59	22	3
Not eligible for National School Lunch Program	50	234 ↑	18 ↓	82	46	12

Average Score Gaps Between Selected Groups

- In 2007, male students in Florida had an average score that was lower than that of female students by 8 points. In 1992, the average score for male students was lower than that of female students by 6 points.
- In 2007, Black students had an average score that was lower than that of White students by 24 points. This performance gap was narrower than that of 1992 (33 points).
- In 2007, Hispanic students had an average score that was lower than that of White students by 14 points. In 1992, the average score for Hispanic students was lower than that of White students by 15 points.
- In 2007, students who were eligible for free/reduced-price school lunch, a proxy for poverty, had an average score that was lower than that of students who were not eligible for free/reduced-price school lunch by 21 points. This performance gap was narrower than that of 1998 (29 points).
- In 2007, the score gap between students at the 75th percentile and students at the 25th percentile was 43 points. This performance gap was narrower than that of 1992 (49 points).

Reading Scores at Selected Percentiles

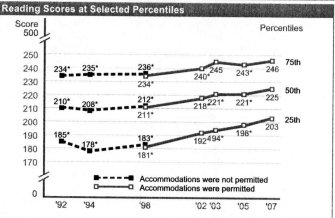

NOTE: Scores at selected percentiles on the NAEP reading scale indicate how well students at lower, middle, and higher levels performed.

\# Rounds to zero.
* Significantly different from 2007.
‡ Reporting standards not met.
↑ Significantly higher than 2005. ↓ Significantly lower than 2005.

[1] Comparisons (higher/lower/narrower/wider/not different) are based on statistical tests. The .05 level was used for testing statistical significance. Statistical comparisons are calculated on the basis of unrounded scale scores or percentages. Comparisons across jurisdictions and comparisons with the nation or within a jurisdiction across years may be affected by differences in exclusion rates for students with disabilities (SD) and English language learners (ELL). The exclusion rates for SD and ELL in Florida were 4 percent and 4 percent in 2007, respectively. For more information on NAEP significance testing see http://nces.ed.gov/nationsreportcard/reading/interpret-results.asp#statistical.

[2] "Jurisdictions" refers to states and the District of Columbia and the Department of Defense Education Activity schools.

NOTE: Detail may not sum to totals because of rounding and because the "Information not available" category for the National School Lunch Program, which provides free and reduced-price lunches, and the "Unclassified" category for race/ethnicity are not displayed. Visit http://nces.ed.gov/nationsreportcard/states/ for additional results and detailed information.

SOURCE: U.S. Department of Education, Institute of Education Sciences, National Center for Education Statistics, National Assessment of Educational Progress (NAEP), various years, 1992–2007 Reading Assessments.

Writing 2002

The writing assessment of the National Assessment of Educational Progress (NAEP) measures narrative, informative, and persuasive writing–three purposes identified in the NAEP framework. The NAEP writing scale ranges from 0 to 300.

Overall Writing Results for Florida

- The average scale score for fourth-grade students in Florida was 158.

- Florida's average score (158) was higher[1] than that of the nation's public schools (153).

- Students' average scale scores in Florida were higher than those in 26 jurisdictions[2], not significantly different from those in 17 jurisdictions, and lower than those in 4 jurisdictions.

- The percentage of students who performed at or above the NAEP *Proficient* level was 33 percent. The percentage of students who performed at or above the *Basic* level was 86 percent.

Student Percentage at Each Achievement Level

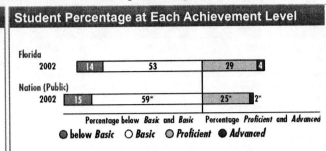

Florida
2002 | 14 | 53 | 29 | 4

Nation (Public)
2002 | 15 | 59* | 25* | 2*

Percentage below *Basic* and *Basic*   Percentage *Proficient* and *Advanced*
● below *Basic*   ○ *Basic*   ◑ *Proficient*   ● *Advanced*

Performance of NAEP Reporting Groups in Florida

Reporting groups	Percentage of students	Average Score	Percentage of students at			
			Below *Basic*	*Basic*	*Proficient*	*Advanced*
Male	51	149 ↑	18	59	21 ↑	2
Female	49	168 ↑	9	48 ↓	37 ↑	6 ↑
White	51	165 ↑	9	52 ↓	34 ↑	5 ↑
Black	24	144 ↑	21	58	18 ↑	2
Hispanic	22	154 ↑	17 ↓	54	27 ↑	3 ↑
Asian/Pacific Islander	2	---	---	---	---	---
American Indian/Alaska Native	#	---	---	---	---	---
Free/reduced-priced school lunch						
Eligible	55	149 ↑	19 ↓	57 ↓	22 ↑	2 ↑
Not eligible	43	169 ↑	7	49 ↓	38 ↑	6 ↑
Information not available	2	---	---	---	---	---

Average Score Gaps Between Selected Groups

- Female students in Florida had an average score that was higher than that of male students (19 points). This performance gap was not significantly different from that of the Nation (18 points).

- White students had an average score that was higher than that of Black students (20 points). This performance gap was not significantly different from that of the Nation (20 points).

- White students had an average score that was higher than that of Hispanic students (11 points). This performance gap was narrower than that of the Nation (19 points).

- Students who were not eligible for free/reduced-price school lunch had an average score that was higher than that of students who were eligible (21 points). This performance gap was not significantly different from that of the Nation (22 points).

Writing Scale Scores at Selected Percentiles

Scale Score Distribution

	25th Percentile	50th Percentile	75th Percentile
Florida	131	159 ↑	185 ↑
Nation (Public)	128	153	178

An examination of scores at different percentiles on the 0-300 NAEP writing scale at each grade indicates how well students at lower, middle, and higher levels of the distribution performed. For example, the data above shows that 75 percent of students in public schools nationally scored below *178*, while 75 percent of students in Florida scored below *185*.

Percentage rounds to zero.   --- Reporting standards not met; sample size insufficient to permit a reliable estimate.
* Significantly different from Florida.   ↑ Significantly higher than, ↓ lower than appropriate subgroup in the nation (public).
[1] Comparisons (higher/lower/not different) are based on statistical tests. The .05 level was used for testing statistical significance.
[2] "Jurisdictions" includes participating states and other jurisdictions (such as Guam or the District of Columbia).
NOTE: Detail may not sum to totals because of rounding. Score gaps are calculated based on differences between unrounded average scale scores.
Visit http://nces.ed.gov/nationsreportcard/states/ for additional results and detailed information.
SOURCE: U.S. Department of Education, Institute of Education Sciences, National Center for Education Statistics, National Assessment of Educational Progress (NAEP), 2002 Writing Assessment.

The Nation's Report Card
State **Science** 2005
Snapshot Report

Florida
Grade 4
Public Schools
NCES 2006-467FL4

The National Assessment of Educational Progress (NAEP) assesses science in two major dimensions: Fields of Science (Earth, Physical, and Life) and Knowing and Doing Science (Conceptual Understanding, Scientific Investigation, and Practical Reasoning). The NAEP science scale ranges from 0 to 300. Scales are created separately for each grade.

Overall Science Results for Florida

- Florida's average score (150) in 2005 was not significantly different from that of the nation's public schools (149).[1]
- Of the 44 states and one jurisdiction that participated in the 2005 fourth-grade assessment, students' average scale score in Florida was higher than those in 10 jurisdictions, not significantly different from those in 12 jurisdictions, and lower than those in 22 jurisdictions.[2]
- The percentage of students in Florida who performed at or above the NAEP *Proficient* level was 26 percent in 2005. This percentage was not significantly different from that in the nation (27 percent).
- The percentage of students in Florida who performed at or above the NAEP *Basic* level was 68 percent in 2005. This percentage was greater than that in the nation (66 percent).

Student Percentages at NAEP Achievement Levels

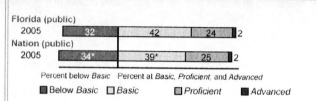

Percent below *Basic*   Percent at *Basic*, *Proficient*, and *Advanced*

■ Below *Basic*   □ *Basic*   ▨ *Proficient*   ■ *Advanced*

NOTE: The NAEP grade 4 science achievement levels correspond to the following scale points: Below *Basic*, 137 or lower; *Basic*, 138–169; *Proficient*, 170–204; *Advanced*, 205 or above.

Performance of NAEP Reporting Groups in Florida: 2005

Reporting groups	Percent of students	Average score	Percent below *Basic*	Percent of students at or above *Basic*	Percent of students at or above *Proficient*	Percent *Advanced*
Male	51	151	31	69	28	2
Female	49	149	33↓	67↑	23	1
White	49↓	161	17	83	38	3
Black	22↑	130	61	39	7	#
Hispanic	24↑	144↑	38↓	62↑	17↑	1
Asian/Pacific Islander	2↓	162	15↓	85↑	35	5
American Indian/Alaska Native	#↓	‡	‡	‡	‡	‡
Eligible for free/reduced-price school lunch	51↑	139↑	46↓	54↑	13	1
Not eligible for free/reduced-price school lunch	48↓	162	17	83	39	3

Average Score Gaps Between Selected Groups

- In 2005, male students in Florida had an average score that was higher than that of female students by 2 points. In the nation, the average score for male students was higher than that of female students by 4 points.
- In 2005, Black students had an average score that was lower than that of White students by 31 points. In the nation, the average score for Black students was lower than that of White students by 33 points.
- In 2005, Hispanic students had an average score that was lower than that of White students by 17 points. This performance gap was narrower than that of the nation (29 points).
- In 2005, students who were eligible for free/reduced-price school lunch, an indicator of poverty, had an average score that was lower than that of students who were not eligible for free/reduced-price school lunch by 22 points. This performance gap was narrower than that of the nation (27 points).
- In 2005, the score gap between students at the 75th percentile and students at the 25th percentile was 39 points. This performance gap was narrower than that of the nation (43 points).

Science Scale Scores at Selected Percentiles

	Scale Score Distribution		
	25th Percentile	50th Percentile	75th Percentile
Florida	131	152	170
Nation (public)	129 *	152	172

Scores at selected percentiles on the NAEP science scale indicate how well students at lower, middle, and higher levels performed. For example, the data above shows that 75 percent of students in public schools nationally scored below 172, while 75 percent of students in Florida scored below 170.

The estimate rounds to zero.   ‡ Reporting standards not met.

* Significantly different from Florida.   ↑ Significantly higher than nation (public).   ↓ Significantly lower than nation (public).

[1] Comparisons (higher/lower/not different) are based on statistical tests. The .05 level was used for testing statistical significance. Comparisons across jurisdictions and comparisons with the nation or within a jurisdiction across years may be affected by differences in exclusion rates for students with disabilities (SD) and English language learners (ELL). The exclusion rates for SD and ELL in Florida were 2 percent and 1 percent in 2005, respectively. Statistical comparisons are calculated on the basis of unrounded scale scores or percentages.
[2] "Jurisdiction" refers to states and the Department of Defense Education Activity schools.
NOTE: Detail may not sum to totals because of rounding and because the "Information not available" category for free/reduced-price school lunch and the "Unclassifed" category for race/ethnicity are not displayed. Visit http://nces.ed.gov/nationsreportcard/states/ for additional results and detailed information.
SOURCE: U.S. Department of Education, Institute of Education Sciences, National Center for Education Statistics, National Assessment of Educational Progress (NAEP), 2005 Science Assessment.

<ies NATIONAL CENTER FOR EDUCATION STATISTICS
Institute of Education Sciences

NCES 2007-495FL8

The Nation's Report Card

Mathematics 2007
State Snapshot Report

Florida
Grade 8
Public Schools

The National Assessment of Educational Progress (NAEP) assesses mathematics in five content areas: number properties and operations; measurement; geometry; data analysis and probability; and algebra. The NAEP mathematics scale ranges from 0 to 500.

Overall Mathematics Results for Florida

- In 2007, the average scale score for eighth-grade students in Florida was 277. This was not significantly different from their average score in 2005 (274) and was higher than their average score in 1990 (255).[1]
- Florida's average score (277) in 2007 was lower than that of the nation's public schools (280).
- Of the 52 states and other jurisdictions that participated in the 2007 eighth-grade assessment, students' average scale score in Florida was higher than those in 9 jurisdictions, not significantly different from those in 11 jurisdictions, and lower than those in 31 jurisdictions.[2]
- The percentage of students in Florida who performed at or above the NAEP *Proficient* level was 27 percent in 2007. This percentage was not significantly different from that in 2005 (26 percent) and was greater than that in 1990 (12 percent).
- The percentage of students in Florida who performed at or above the NAEP *Basic* level was 68 percent in 2007. This percentage was not significantly different from that in 2005 (65 percent) and was greater than that in 1990 (43 percent).

Percentages at NAEP Achievement Levels and Average Score

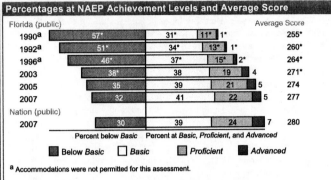

a Accommodations were not permitted for this assessment.

NOTE: The NAEP grade 8 mathematics achievement levels correspond to the following scale points: Below *Basic*, 261 or lower; *Basic*, 262–298; *Proficient*, 299–332; *Advanced*, 333 or above.

Performance of NAEP Reporting Groups in Florida: 2007

Reporting groups	Percent of students	Average score	Percent below *Basic*	Percent of students at or above *Basic*	*Proficient*	Percent *Advanced*
Male	49 ↓	278	32	68	29	6
Female	51 ↑	277 ↑	32	68	26	5
White	48	289	20	80	37	8
Black	23	259 ↑	52 ↓	48 ↑	11	1
Hispanic	24	270	39	61	21	3
Asian/Pacific Islander	2	293	20	80	48	14
American Indian/Alaska Native	#	‡	‡	‡	‡	‡
Eligible for National School Lunch Program	44	265 ↑	45	55	16	1
Not eligible for National School Lunch Program	56	287	22	78	37	9

Average Score Gaps Between Selected Groups

- In 2007, male students in Florida had an average score that was not significantly different from that of female students. In 1990, there was no significant difference between the average score of male and female students.
- In 2007, Black students had an average score that was lower than that of White students by 29 points. In 1990, the average score for Black students was lower than that of White students by 34 points.
- In 2007, Hispanic students had an average score that was lower than that of White students by 18 points. In 1990, the average score for Hispanic students was lower than that of White students by 19 points.
- In 2007, students who were eligible for free/reduced-price school lunch, a proxy for poverty, had an average score that was lower than that of students who were not eligible for free/reduced-price school lunch by 23 points. In 1996, the average score for students who were eligible for free/reduced-price school lunch was lower than the score of those not eligible by 27 points.
- In 2007, the score gap between students at the 75th percentile and students at the 25th percentile was 47 points. In 1990, the score gap between students at the 75th percentile and students at the 25th percentile was 49 points.

Mathematics Scores at Selected Percentiles

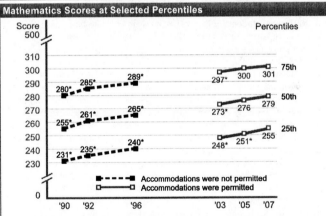

NOTE: Scores at selected percentiles on the NAEP mathematics scale indicate how well students at lower, middle, and higher levels performed.

Rounds to zero.   ‡ Reporting standards not met.
* Significantly different from 2007.   ↑ Significantly higher than 2005. ↓ Significantly lower than 2005.
[1] Comparisons (higher/lower/narrower/wider/not different) are based on statistical tests. The .05 level was used for testing statistical significance. Statistical comparisons are calculated on the basis of unrounded scale scores or percentages. Comparisons across jurisdictions and comparisons with the nation or within a jurisdiction across years may be affected by differences in exclusion rates for students with disabilities (SD) and English language learners (ELL). The exclusion rates for SD and ELL in Florida were 2 percent and 1 percent in 2007, respectively. For more information on NAEP significance testing see http://nces.ed.gov/nationsreportcard/mathematics/interpret-results.asp#statistical.
[2] "Jurisdictions" refers to states and the District of Columbia and the Department of Defense Education Activity schools.
NOTE: Detail may not sum to totals because of rounding and because the "Information not available" category for the National School Lunch Program, which provides free and reduced-price lunches, and the "Unclassified" category for race/ethnicity are not displayed. Visit http://nces.ed.gov/nationsreportcard/states/ for additional results and detailed information.
SOURCE: U.S. Department of Education, Institute of Education Sciences, National Center for Education Statistics, National Assessment of Educational Progress (NAEP), various years, 1990–2007 Mathematics Assessments.

The National Assessment of Educational Progress (NAEP) assesses reading in three content areas in grade 8: reading for literary experience, to gain information, and to perform a task. The NAEP reading scale ranges from 0 to 500.

Overall Reading Results for Florida

- In 2007, the average scale score for eighth-grade students in Florida was 260. This was higher than their average score in 2005 (256) and was higher than their average score in 1998 (255).[1]
- Florida's average score (260) in 2007 was not significantly different from that of the nation's public schools (261).
- Of the 52 states and other jurisdictions that participated in the 2007 eighth-grade assessment, students' average scale score in Florida was higher than those in 10 jurisdictions, not significantly different from those in 13 jurisdictions, and lower than those in 28 jurisdictions.[2]
- The percentage of students in Florida who performed at or above the NAEP *Proficient* level was 28 percent in 2007. This percentage was not significantly different from that in 2005 (25 percent) and was greater than that in 1998 (23 percent).
- The percentage of students in Florida who performed at or above the NAEP *Basic* level was 71 percent in 2007. This percentage was greater than that in 2005 (66 percent) and was greater than that in 1998 (67 percent).

Percentages at NAEP Achievement Levels and Average Score

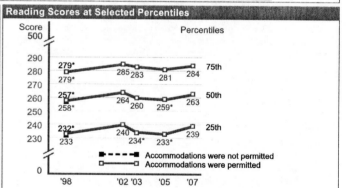

Florida (public)					Average Score
1998[a]	35*	43	22*	1*	253*
1998	33*	44	21*	1*	255*
2002	28	43	27	2	261
2003	32*	41	24	2	257
2005	34*	41	23	2	256*
2007	29	43	26	2	260
Nation (public)					
2007	27	43	27	2	261

Percent below *Basic*   Percent at *Basic*, *Proficient*, and *Advanced*

■ Below *Basic*   □ *Basic*   ▨ *Proficient*   ■ *Advanced*

[a] Accommodations were not permitted for this assessment.

NOTE: The NAEP grade 8 reading achievement levels correspond to the following scale points: Below *Basic*, 242 or lower; *Basic*, 243–280; *Proficient*, 281–322; *Advanced*, 323 or above.

Performance of NAEP Reporting Groups in Florida: 2007

Reporting groups	Percent of students	Average score	Percent below *Basic*	Percent of students at or above *Basic*	*Proficient*	Percent *Advanced*
Male	52 ↑	254 ↑	34 ↓	66 ↑	22	1
Female	48 ↓	266 ↑	22 ↓	78 ↑	34	3
White	49	268	20	80	36	3
Black	23	244	45	55	13	#
Hispanic	23	256	33	67	23	1
Asian/Pacific Islander	3	278	9	91	46	5
American Indian/Alaska Native	#	‡	‡	‡	‡	‡
Eligible for National School Lunch Program	42	249	39 ↓	61 ↑	17	1
Not eligible for National School Lunch Program	57	268	21 ↓	79	36	3

Average Score Gaps Between Selected Groups

- In 2007, male students in Florida had an average score that was lower than that of female students by 12 points. In 1998, the average score for male students was lower than that of female students by 13 points.
- In 2007, Black students had an average score that was lower than that of White students by 24 points. In 1998, the average score for Black students was lower than that of White students by 28 points.
- In 2007, Hispanic students had an average score that was lower than that of White students by 12 points. In 1998, the average score for Hispanic students was lower than that of White students by 17 points.
- In 2007, students who were eligible for free/reduced-price school lunch, a proxy for poverty, had an average score that was lower than that of students who were not eligible for free/reduced-price school lunch by 18 points. In 1998, the average score for students who were eligible for free/reduced-price school lunch was lower than the score of those not eligible by 24 points.
- In 2007, the score gap between students at the 75th percentile and students at the 25th percentile was 45 points. In 1998, the score gap between students at the 75th percentile and students at the 25th percentile was 46 points.

Reading Scores at Selected Percentiles

Score

Percentiles

75th: 279* 279* 285 283 281 284
50th: 257* 258* 264 260 259* 263
25th: 232* 233 240 234* 233* 239

■--- Accommodations were not permitted
□— Accommodations were permitted

'98   '02 '03   '05   '07

NOTE: Scores at selected percentiles on the NAEP reading scale indicate how well students at lower, middle, and higher levels performed.

Rounds to zero.   ‡ Reporting standards not met.

* Significantly different from 2007.   ↑ Significantly higher than 2005. ↓ Significantly lower than 2005.

[1] Comparisons (higher/lower/narrower/wider/not different) are based on statistical tests. The .05 level was used for testing statistical significance. Statistical comparisons are calculated on the basis of unrounded scale scores or percentages. Comparisons across jurisdictions and comparisons with the nation or within a jurisdiction across years may be affected by differences in exclusion rates for students with disabilities (SD) and English language learners (ELL). The exclusion rates for SD and ELL in Florida were 3 percent and 3 percent in 2007, respectively. For more information on NAEP significance testing see http://nces.ed.gov/nationsreportcard/reading/interpret-results.asp#statistical.

[2] "Jurisdictions" refers to states and the District of Columbia and the Department of Defense Education Activity schools.

NOTE: Detail may not sum to totals because of rounding and because the "Information not available" category for the National School Lunch Program, which provides free and reduced-price lunches, and the "Unclassified" category for race/ethnicity are not displayed. Visit http://nces.ed.gov/nationsreportcard/states/ for additional results and detailed information.

SOURCE: U.S. Department of Education, Institute of Education Sciences, National Center for Education Statistics, National Assessment of Educational Progress (NAEP), various years, 1998–2007 Reading Assessments.

Writing 2002

Public School

Snapshot Report

NCES 2003-532FL6

The writing assessment of the National Assessment of Educational Progress (NAEP) measures narrative, informative, and persuasive writing–three purposes identified in the NAEP framework. The NAEP writing scale ranges from 0 to 300.

Overall Writing Results for Florida

- The average scale score for eighth-grade students in Florida was 154. This was higher[1] than the average score (142) in 1998.

- Florida's average score (154) was not found to be significantly different from that of the nation's public schools (152).

- Students' average scale scores in Florida were higher than those in 20 jurisdictions[2], not significantly different from those in 19 jurisdictions, and lower than those in 7 jurisdictions.

- The percentage of students who performed at or above the NAEP *Proficient* level was 32 percent. This percentage was greater than 1998 (19).

Student Percentage at Each Achievement Level

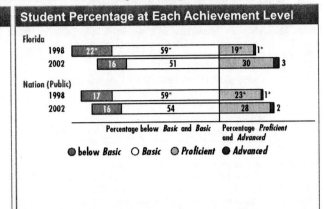

Performance of NAEP Reporting Groups in Florida

Reporting groups	Percentage of students	Average Score	Percentage of students at			
			Below *Basic*	*Basic*	*Proficient*	*Advanced*
Male	50	141 ↑	24 ↓	56	19 ↑	1
Female	50	166 ↑	8 ↓	47 ↓	40 ↑	5 ↑
White	55	163 ↑	10 ↓	50 ↓	36 ↑	4 ↑
Black	23	137 ↑	26 ↓	58	16 ↑	1
Hispanic	18	144 ↑	24	50	25 ↑	1
Asian/Pacific Islander	2	167	9	44	42	5
American Indian/Alaska Native	#	---	---	---	---	---
Free/reduced-priced school lunch						
Eligible	43	141 ↑	24 ↓	56	19 ↑	1
Not eligible	52	163 ↑	10	48 ↓	38 ↑	4 ↑
Information not available	5	162	11	50	34	5

Average Score Gaps Between Selected Groups

- Female students in Florida had an average score that was higher than that of male students (25 points). This performance gap was not significantly different from that of 1998 (22 points).

- White students had an average score that was higher than that of Black students (26 points). This performance gap was not significantly different from that of 1998 (24 points).

- White students had an average score that was higher than that of Hispanic students (19 points). This performance gap was not significantly different from that of 1998 (14 points).

- Students who were not eligible for free/reduced-price school lunch had an average score that was higher than that of students who were eligible (22 points). This performance gap was not significantly different from that of 1998 (23 points).

Writing Scale Scores at Selected Percentiles

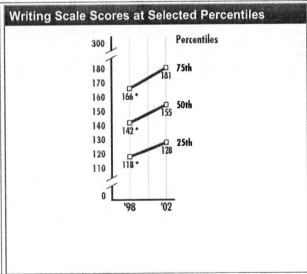

Percentage rounds to zero.   --- Reporting standards not met; sample size insufficient to permit a reliable estimate.

* Significantly different from 2002.   ↑ Statistically significantly higher than 1998.   ↓ Statistically significantly lower than 1998.

[1] Comparisons (higher/lower/not different) are based on statistical tests. The .05 level was used for testing statistical significance.

[2] "Jurisdictions" includes participating states and other jurisdictions (such as Guam or the District of Columbia).

NOTE: Detail may not sum to totals because of rounding. Score gaps are calculated based on differences between unrounded average scale scores. Performance changes across years should be interpreted in the context of changes in rates of exclusion of special-needs students, which occurred in some states. See *The Nation's Report Card: Writing 2002* for additional information.

Visit http://nces.ed.gov/nationsreportcard/states/ for additional results and detailed information.

SOURCE: U.S. Department of Education, Institute of Education Sciences, National Center for Education Statistics, National Assessment of Educational Progress (NAEP), 1998 and 2002 Writing Assessments.

The National Assessment of Educational Progress (NAEP) assesses science in two major dimensions: Fields of Science (Earth, Physical, and Life) and Knowing and Doing Science (Conceptual Understanding, Scientific Investigation, and Practical Reasoning). The NAEP science scale ranges from 0 to 300. Scales are created separately for each grade.

Overall Science Results for Florida

- In 2005, the average scale score for eighth-grade students in Florida was 141. This was not significantly different from their average score in 1996 (142).[1]
- Florida's average score (141) in 2005 was lower than that of the nation's public schools (147).
- Of the 44 states and one jurisdiction that participated in the 2005 eighth-grade assessment, students' average scale score in Florida was higher than those in 3 jurisdictions, not significantly different from those in 8 jurisdictions, and lower than those in 33 jurisdictions.[2]
- The percentage of students in Florida who performed at or above the NAEP *Proficient* level was 21 percent in 2005. This percentage was not significantly different from that in 1996 (21 percent).
- The percentage of students in Florida who performed at or above the NAEP *Basic* level was 51 percent in 2005. This percentage was not significantly different from that in 1996 (51 percent).

Student Percentages at NAEP Achievement Levels

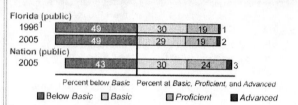

Percent below *Basic*   Percent at *Basic*, *Proficient*, and *Advanced*

■ Below *Basic*   □ *Basic*   ▨ *Proficient*   ■ *Advanced*

[1] Accommodations were not permitted for this assessment.

NOTE: The NAEP grade 8 science achievement levels correspond to the following scale points: Below *Basic*, 142 or lower; *Basic*, 143–169; *Proficient*, 170–207; *Advanced*, 208 or above.

Performance of NAEP Reporting Groups in Florida: 2005

Reporting groups	Percent of students	Average score	Percent below *Basic*	Percent of students at or above		Percent *Advanced*
				Basic	*Proficient*	
Male	49↓	142	48	52	24	3
Female	51↑	140	51	49	19	1
White	50↓	155	32	68	32	3
Black	24	118	76	24	6	#
Hispanic	22	131	62	38	14	1
Asian/Pacific Islander	2	149	43	57	29	2
American Indian/Alaska Native	#	‡	‡	‡	‡	‡
Eligible for free/reduced-price school lunch	46↑	128	64	36	12	1
Not eligible for free/reduced-price school lunch	53	152	36	64	30	3

Average Score Gaps Between Selected Groups

- In 2005, male students in Florida had an average score that was not significantly different from that of female students. In 1996, there was no significant difference between the average score of male and female students.
- In 2005, Black students had an average score that was lower than that of White students by 37 points. In 1996, the average score for Black students was lower than that of White students by 37 points.
- In 2005, Hispanic students had an average score that was lower than that of White students by 24 points. In 1996, the average score for Hispanic students was lower than that of White students by 23 points.
- In 2005, students who were eligible for free/reduced-price school lunch, an indicator of poverty, had an average score that was lower than that of students who were not eligible for free/reduced-price school lunch by 24 points. In 1996, the average score for students who were eligible for free/reduced-price school lunch was lower than the score of those not eligible by 27 points.
- In 2005, the score gap between students at the 75th percentile and students at the 25th percentile was 49 points. In 1996, the score gap between students at the 75th percentile and students at the 25th percentile was 46 points.

Science Scale Scores at Selected Percentiles

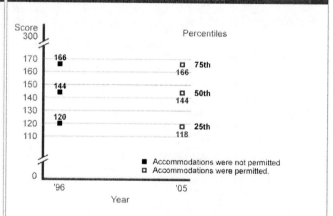

Scores at selected percentiles on the NAEP science scale indicate how well students at lower, middle, and higher levels performed.

The estimate rounds to zero.   ‡ Reporting standards not met.

* Significantly different from 2005.   ↑ Significantly higher than 1996. ↓ Significantly lower than 1996.

[1] Comparisons (higher/lower/not different) are based on statistical tests. The .05 level was used for testing statistical significance. Comparisons across jurisdictions and comparisons with the nation or within a jurisdiction across years may be affected by differences in exclusion rates for students with disabilities (SD) and English language learners (ELL). The exclusion rates for SD and ELL in Florida were 2 percent and 1 percent in 2005, respectively. Statistical comparisons are calculated on the basis of unrounded scale scores or percentages.

[2] "Jurisdiction" refers to states and the Department of Defense Education Activity schools.

NOTE: Detail may not sum to totals because of rounding and because the "Information not available" category for free/reduced-price school lunch and the "Unclassifed" category for race/ethnicity are not displayed. Visit http://nces.ed.gov/nationsreportcard/states/ for additional results and detailed information.

SOURCE: U.S. Department of Education, Institute of Education Sciences, National Center for Education Statistics, National Assessment of Educational Progress (NAEP), 1996 and 2005 Science Assessments.

Mathematics Scores
Statewide Comparison for 2001 to 2007
FCAT Mathematics – Sunshine State Standards Test[1]

Grade	Year	Number of Students	Developmental Scale Score	Mean Scale Score	1	2	3	4	5	Achievement Level 3 & Above
3	2001	186,336	1258	291	24	24	33	16	3	52
	2002	188,606	1309	302	21	20	34	20	5	59
	2003	188,487	1335	308	19	19	34	22	7	63
	2004	206,534	1346	310	17	19	34	23	7	64
	2005	203,037	1380	317	15	17	34	25	9	68
	2006	204,402	1409	324	12	16	34	27	10	72
	2007	201,862	1428	328	12	14	33	28	13	74
4	2001	188,633	1394	286	31	24	29	13	3	45
	2002	192,366	1428	294	26	24	32	15	4	51
	2003	193,503	1446	298	22	23	34	16	4	54
	2004	176,316	1508	312	15	21	37	20	6	64
	2005	195,866	1509	312	15	21	38	21	6	64
	2006	192,610	1534	318	14	19	36	23	8	67
	2007	196,632	1540	319	13	18	37	23	8	69
5	2001	187,623	1579	314	27	25	22	20	6	48
	2002	192,472	1598	318	25	27	23	19	6	48
	2003	192,692	1607	320	23	26	24	21	7	52
	2004	196,233	1616	322	21	27	24	21	7	52
	2005	181,434	1648	329	16	27	27	24	6	57
	2006	197,076	1649	329	17	27	26	24	7	57
	2007	192,369	1662	332	15	26	26	25	8	59
6	2001	187,054	1592	291	39	21	24	12	4	40
	2002	193,948	1622	298	35	22	25	13	5	43
	2003	196,134	1642	302	31	22	27	14	6	47
	2004	198,905	1637	301	33	22	26	14	5	46
	2005	201,550	1653	305	31	22	26	15	6	47
	2006	186,792	1681	312	26	21	28	17	8	53
	2007	198,195	1663	307	28	22	28	16	7	50
7	2001	183,131	1724	290	35	20	24	15	6	45
	2002	191,786	1734	292	33	21	26	14	7	47
	2003	197,161	1747	296	31	21	26	15	6	47
	2004	201,188	1760	299	30	21	27	16	7	50
	2005	202,361	1778	303	26	22	28	17	8	53
	2006	202,303	1791	307	23	22	30	18	7	55
	2007	188,619	1811	312	20	21	32	19	8	59
8	2001	174,067	1847	308	24	21	31	14	10	55
	2002	184,379	1837	305	25	22	31	14	8	53
	2003	191,656	1856	310	22	22	32	14	10	56
	2004	197,646	1858	311	23	21	31	15	11	56
	2005	201,488	1866	313	21	20	32	15	11	59
	2006	200,431	1872	314	20	20	33	16	11	60
	2007	199,297	1885	318	18	19	34	17	12	63
9	2001	191,094	1863	284	30	24	24	15	7	46
	2002	203,911	1871	286	28	24	26	15	6	47
	2003	205,079	1892	293	23	25	28	17	6	51
	2004	214,168	1903	296	22	23	28	19	8	55
	2005	214,360	1918	300	20	21	30	20	9	59
	2006	212,359	1924	302	18	23	30	20	9	59
	2007	207,364	1925	302	17	22	31	21	8	60
10	2001	144,236	1975	321	20	21	24	25	10	59
	2002	149,782	1967	319	19	21	25	27	8	60
	2003	165,624	1970	320	19	20	24	27	9	60
	2004	166,227	1982	323	16	21	26	29	9	63
	2005	178,530	1979	322	15	22	27	28	8	63
	2006	184,635	1987	324	15	19	26	31	8	65
	2007	185,346	1983	323	14	20	28	30	7	65

Percent of Students by Achievement Level

NOTE: Achievement Level information was not reported in May 2001 for grades 3, 4, 6, 7, and 9. The data shown here reflect retroactive application of the Achievement Level criteria.

[1] Data are for all students tested in all curriculum groups.

Source: Florida Department of Education, May 2007

Grades 3-10

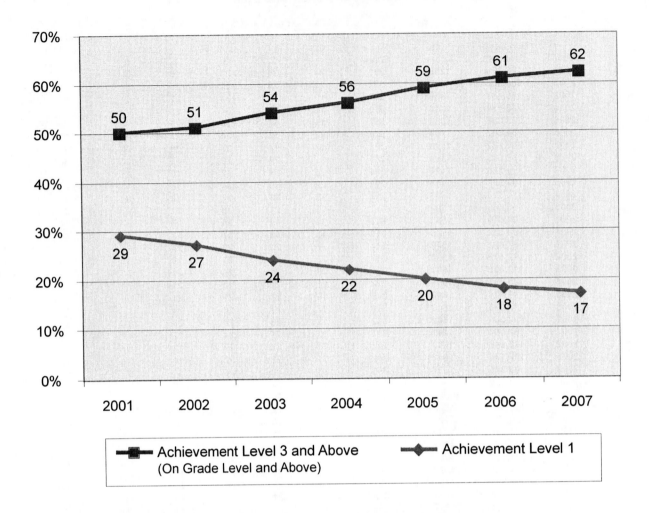

In 2007, 62 percent of all students in Grades 3-10 were performing at or above Achievement Level 3 (on grade level and above) on FCAT Mathematics. This is an increase from 50 percent in 2001, 51 percent in 2002, 54 percent in 2003, 56 percent in 2004, 59 percent in 2005, and 61 percent in 2006. In 2007, 17 percent of all students in Grades 3-10 were performing at Achievement Level 1 on FCAT Mathematics. This is a decrease from 29 percent in 2001, 27 percent in 2002, 24 percent in 2003, 22 percent in 2004, 20 percent in 2005, and 18 percent in 2006.

Source: Florida Department of Education, May 2007

FCAT Mathematics Achievement Level 3 and Above
(On Grade Level and Above)
Grades 3-10

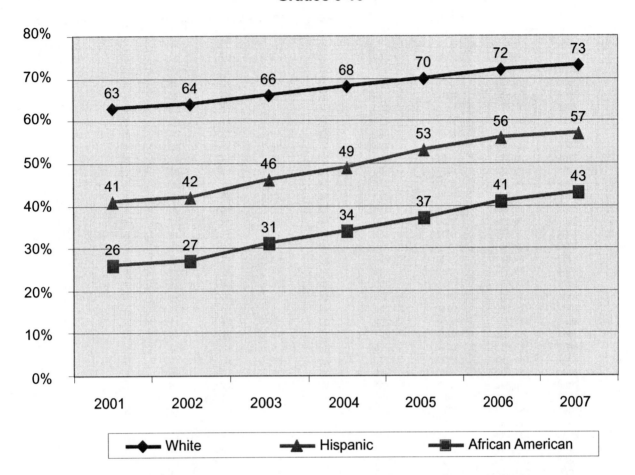

In 2007, 73 percent of White students in Grades 3-10 were performing at or above Achievement Level 3 (on grade level and above) on FCAT Mathematics. This is an increase from 63 percent in 2001, 64 percent in 2002, 66 percent in 2003, 68 percent in 2004, 70 percent in 2005, and 72 percent in 2006. In 2007, 57 percent of Hispanic students in Grades 3-10 were performing at or above Achievement Level 3 (on grade level and above) on FCAT Mathematics. This is an increase from 41 percent in 2001, 42 percent in 2002, 46 percent in 2003, 49 percent in 2004, 53 percent in 2005, and 56 percent in 2006. In 2007, 43 percent of African American students in Grades 3-10 were performing at or above Achievement Level 3 (on grade level and above) on FCAT Mathematics. This is an increase from 26 percent in 2001, 27 percent in 2002, 31 percent in 2003, 34 percent in 2004, 37 percent in 2005, and 41 percent in 2006.

Source: Florida Department of Education, May 2007

Reading Scores
Statewide Comparison for 2001 to 2007
FCAT Reading – Sunshine State Standards Test[1]

Grade	Year	Number of Students	Develop-mental Scale Score	Mean Scale Score	Percent of Students by Achievement Level 1	2	3	4	5	Achievement Level 3 & Above
3	2001	186,139	1233	289	29	14	32	21	4	57
	2002	188,387	1257	293	27	14	32	23	5	60
	2003	188,107	1290	298	23	15	33	25	5	63
	2004	206,435	1315	303	22	13	33	26	6	66
	2005	202,975	1333	305	20	13	33	28	6	67
	2006	204,238	1382	313	14	11	37	33	5	75
	2007	201,894	1356	309	19	13	33	28	8	69
4	2001	188,696	1455	298	31	16	28	18	7	53
	2002	191,866	1463	299	30	15	28	21	6	55
	2003	193,391	1497	305	25	15	31	23	6	60
	2004	176,148	1571	318	16	14	35	27	7	70
	2005	195,678	1575	319	15	13	35	29	8	71
	2006	192,480	1547	314	19	16	34	26	7	66
	2007	196,512	1558	316	18	14	33	27	8	68
5	2001	187,570	1493	282	31	17	29	18	5	52
	2002	192,604	1507	285	28	18	30	19	4	53
	2003	192,881	1540	290	25	18	33	21	4	58
	2004	196,343	1562	294	24	17	31	22	6	59
	2005	181,651	1611	303	18	16	34	25	7	66
	2006	197,054	1619	304	17	16	35	26	7	67
	2007	192,289	1647	310	14	15	36	29	6	72
6	2001	187,234	1604	292	30	18	29	18	5	52
	2002	194,125	1601	291	30	18	28	18	5	51
	2003	196,333	1619	295	28	18	30	18	5	53
	2004	199,083	1634	297	26	20	31	18	6	54
	2005	201,609	1644	299	25	20	31	19	5	56
	2006	186,948	1709	311	18	17	33	25	6	64
	2007	198,295	1683	306	19	19	35	21	6	62
7	2001	183,272	1677	292	32	21	28	14	5	47
	2002	191,991	1690	294	29	21	29	16	5	50
	2003	197,417	1704	297	28	21	29	17	6	52
	2004	201,346	1710	298	27	20	30	17	6	53
	2005	202,520	1712	299	27	21	30	17	5	53
	2006	202,438	1773	310	19	21	34	21	6	61
	2007	188,700	1786	313	17	20	35	20	7	63
8	2001	174,016	1814	295	30	27	26	13	4	43
	2002	184,483	1813	295	29	26	28	14	3	45
	2003	192,116	1842	301	26	26	30	16	3	49
	2004	197,778	1815	295	30	26	26	14	4	45
	2005	201,758	1824	297	27	30	30	12	2	44
	2006	200,421	1834	299	24	30	32	13	2	46
	2007	199,456	1850	303	22	29	33	14	2	49
9	2001	191,518	1781	286	46	26	16	7	5	28
	2002	204,728	1789	287	44	27	17	8	4	29
	2003	205,965	1807	291	43	27	18	8	5	31
	2004	214,994	1830	295	39	29	19	8	5	32
	2005	214,984	1860	301	35	28	21	10	6	36
	2006	212,904	1890	306	30	30	24	11	5	40
	2007	207,794	1900	308	28	31	25	11	5	41
10	2001	144,471	1964	307	31	31	20	8	9	37
	2002	150,131	1942	303	32	33	21	8	7	36
	2003	167,396	1939	302	33	32	20	8	8	36
	2004	166,955	1927	300	37	29	17	7	10	34
	2005	179,354	1906	296	39	29	17	7	8	32
	2006	185,568	1918	298	38	29	17	7	9	32
	2007	186,048	1927	300	39	28	16	7	11	34

NOTE: Achievement Level information was not reported in May 2001 for grades 3, 4, 6, 7, and 9. The data shown here reflect retroactive application of the Achievement Level criteria.

[1]Data are for all students tested in all curriculum groups.

Source: Florida Department of Education, May 2007

FCAT Reading by Achievement Level
Grades 3-10

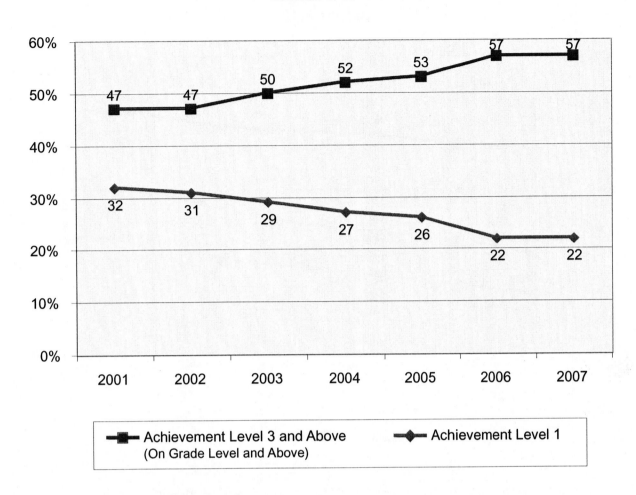

In 2007, 57 percent of all students in Grades 3-10 were performing at or above Achievement Level 3 (on grade level and above) on FCAT Reading. This is an increase from 47 percent in 2001, 47 percent in 2002, 50 percent in 2003, 52 percent in 2004, 53 percent in 2005, and is equal to 57 percent in 2006. In 2007, 22 percent of all students in Grades 3-10 were performing at Achievement Level 1 on FCAT Reading. This is a decrease from 32 percent in 2001, 31 percent in 2002, 29 percent in 2003, 27 percent in 2004, 26 percent in 2005, and is equal to 22 percent in 2006.

Source: Florida Department of Education, May 2007

FCAT Reading Achievement Level 3 and Above
(On Grade Level and Above)
Grades 3-10

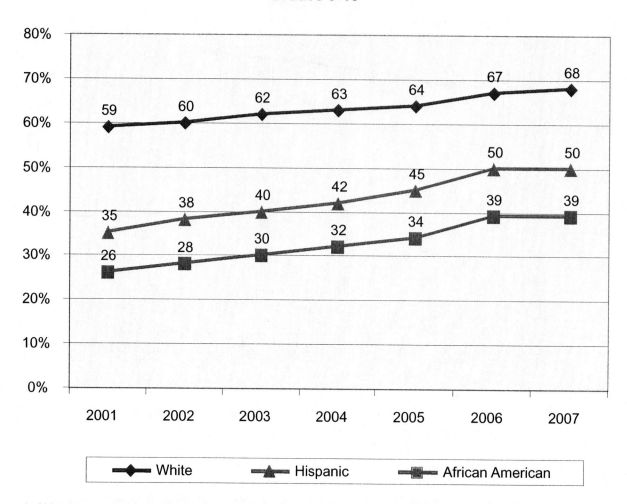

In 2007, 68 percent of White students in Grades 3-10 were performing at or above Achievement Level 3 (on grade level and above) on FCAT Reading. This is an increase from 59 percent in 2001, 60 percent in 2002, 62 percent in 2003, 63 percent in 2004, 64 percent in 2005, and 67 percent in 2006. In 2007, 50 percent of Hispanic students in Grades 3-10 were performing at or above Achievement Level 3 (on grade level and above) on FCAT Reading. This is an increase from 35 percent in 2001, 38 percent in 2002, 40 percent in 2003, 42 percent in 2004, 45 percent in 2005, and is equal to 50 percent in 2006. In 2007, 39 percent of African American students in Grades 3-10 were performing at or above Achievement Level 3 (on grade level and above) on FCAT Reading. This is an increase from 26 percent in 2001, 28 percent in 2002, 30 percent in 2003, 32 percent in 2004, 34 percent in 2005, and is equal to 39 percent in 2006.

Source: Florida Department of Education, May 2007

Science Scores - Grades 5, 8, and 11*
Statewide Results for 2003 to 2007

FCAT Science – Sunshine State Standards Test[1]

				Percent of Students by Achievement Level[2]						Mean Points Earned by Content Area			
Grade	Year	Number of Students	Average Mean Scale Score	1	2	3	4	5	Achievement Level 3 and Above[2]	Physical and Chemical	Earth and Space	Life and Environmental	Scientific Thinking
5	2003	191,470	285	38	34	22	4	1	28	7/12	6/12	8/13	7/12
5	2004	195,700	286	37	34	24	4	1	29	8/13	5/11	8/13	6/12
5	2005	180,453	296	29	38	27	5	1	33	8/13	7/13	8/13	7/12
5	2006	195,877	299	29	36	27	6	2	35	7/12	7/14	7/13	7/12
5	2007	191,789	306	25	33	31	8	2	42	7/12	8/15	7/12	6/12
8	2003	189,425	287	36	37	24	3	0	28	5/12	8/13	6/13	7/13
8	2004	195,351	286	36	36	25	3	0	28	8/14	6/11	8/14	5/12
8	2005	198,670	291	36	32	26	5	1	33	7/13	6/12	7/13	6/13
8	2006	198,142	289	35	33	26	5	1	32	5/11	7/13	8/13	6/14
8	2007	197,536	298	31	31	30	7	1	38	6/14	7/12	7/13	7/12
10	2003	154,263	290	42	29	23	5	1	29	5/12	6/13	8/13	6/13
10	2004	163,546	287	40	30	24	5	1	30	6/14	6/11	7/15	7/11
11	2005	142,353	293	36	31	27	5	1	33	6/14	6/11	6/14	7/12
11	2006	149,848	298	32	33	30	4	0	35	6/13	6/11	8/15	7/12
11	2007	164,580	302	30	33	31	5	1	37	5/13	7/12	6/12	7/14

* The high school Science assessment was moved from grade 10 to grade 11 in 2005.
[1]Data are for all students tested in all curriculum groups.

[2] Percentages may not add to 100 due to rounding.

Source: Florida Department of Education, May 2007

Statewide Comparison of FCAT Writing Average Scores[1]
Grades 4, 8, and 10
1993-2007*

Grade 4

Category/Year	1993	1994	1995	1996	1997	1998	1999	2000	2001	2002	2003	2004	2005	2006	2007
Writing to Explain	1.7	2.1	2.1	2.2	2.5	3.0	2.9	3.2	3.5	3.3	3.5	3.6	3.7	4.0	3.8
Writing to Tell a Story	2.3	2.3	2.7	2.8	2.8	3.1	3.2	3.2	3.4	3.5	3.8	3.7	3.7	3.7	3.8
Grade 4 Combined	2.0	2.2	2.4	2.5	2.6	3.0	3.1	3.2	3.4	3.4	3.6	3.7	3.7	3.9	3.9[2]

Grade 8

Category/Year	1993	1994	1995	1996	1997	1998	1999	2000	2001	2002	2003	2004	2005	2006	2007
Writing to Explain	3.2	2.7	3.1	3.7	3.4	3.4	3.5	3.8	3.8	3.8	3.9	3.9	3.9	4.0	4.1
Writing to Convince	2.8	2.8	3.0	3.3	3.3	3.2	3.4	3.5	3.5	3.8	3.8	3.7	3.7	3.9	4.1
Grade 8 Combined	3.0	2.7	3.1	3.5	3.4	3.3	3.4	3.7	3.7	3.8	3.9	3.8	3.8	4.0	4.1[2]

Grade 10

Category/Year	1993	1994	1995	1996	1997	1998	1999	2000	2001	2002	2003	2004	2005	2006	2007
Writing to Explain	NA	2.9	3.3	3.2	3.7	3.6	3.6	3.9	4.0	4.0	3.8	3.8	3.7	3.9	3.8
Writing to Convince	NA	2.9	3.2	3.4	3.5	3.5	3.5	3.8	3.7	3.7	3.7	3.9	4.0	3.8	4.0
Grade 10 Combined	NA	2.9	3.3	3.3	3.6	3.6	3.6	3.9	3.8	3.8	3.8	3.8	3.8	3.9	3.9[2]

- Beginning in 2000, averages are for all curriculum groups combined. Previous averages are for standard curriculum students only.

[1] FCAT Writing+, formerly FCAT Writing, is also known as the Florida Writing Assessment Program and Florida Writes!

[2] Combined essay averages include students with overall scores only. Individual essay averages include all students who completed the essay.

FCAT Writing+ Average Essay Scores 1993-2007

Grade-level scores have become similar over time.

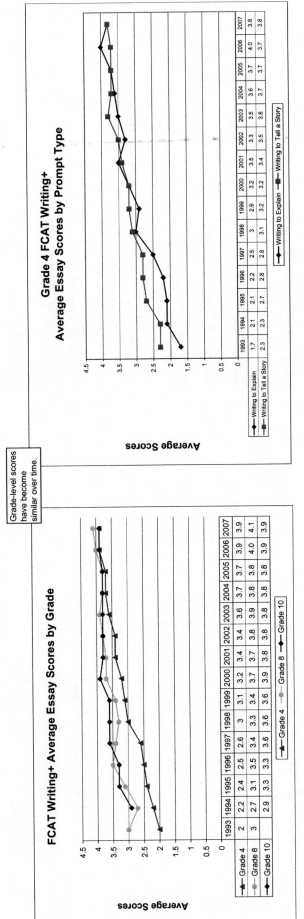

FCAT Writing+ Average Essay Scores by Grade

	1993	1994	1995	1996	1997	1998	1999	2000	2001	2002	2003	2004	2005	2006	2007
Grade 4	2	2.2	2.4	2.5	2.6	3	3.1	3.2	3.4	3.4	3.6	3.7	3.7	3.9	3.9
Grade 8	3	2.7	3.1	3.5	3.4	3.3	3.4	3.7	3.7	3.8	3.9	3.8	3.8	4.0	4.1
Grade 10		2.9	3.3	3.3	3.6	3.6	3.6	3.8	3.8	3.8	3.8	3.8	3.8	3.9	3.9

Grade 4 FCAT Writing+ Average Essay Scores by Prompt Type

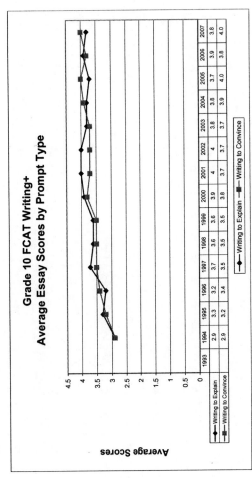

	1993	1994	1995	1996	1997	1998	1999	2000	2001	2002	2003	2004	2005	2006	2007
Writing to Explain	1.7	2.1	2.1	2.2	2.5	3	2.9	3.2	3.4	3.3	3.5	3.6	3.7	4.0	3.8
Writing to Tell a Story	2.3	2.3	2.7	2.8	2.8	3.1	3.2	3.2	3.4	3.5	3.8	3.7	3.7	3.7	3.8

Grade 8 FCAT Writing+ Average Essay Scores by Prompt Type

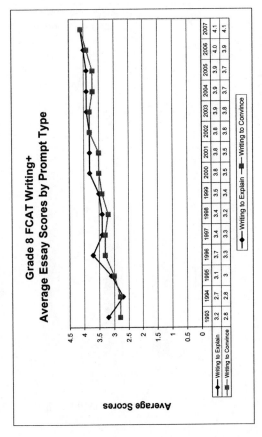

	1993	1994	1995	1996	1997	1998	1999	2000	2001	2002	2003	2004	2005	2006	2007
Writing to Explain	3.2	2.7	3.1	3.3	3.4	3.4	3.5	3.5	3.8	3.8	3.8	3.9	3.9	4.0	4.1
Writing to Convince	2.8	2.8	3	3.3	3.3	3.2	3.4	3.4	3.5	3.8	3.8	3.7	3.7	3.9	4.1

Grade 10 FCAT Writing+ Average Essay Scores by Prompt Type

	1993	1994	1995	1996	1997	1998	1999	2000	2001	2002	2003	2004	2005	2006	2007
Writing to Explain		2.9	3.3	3.2	3.7	3.6	3.6	3.9	4	4	3.8	3.8	3.7	3.9	3.8
Writing to Convince		2.9	3.2	3.4	3.5	3.5	3.5	3.8	3.7	3.7	3.7	3.9	4.0	3.8	4.0

FCAT Writing+ 1999-2007 Percent Scoring at and Above 3.5 and 4

In 2007, the percent of students scoring 3.5 and above increased in Grades 4, 8, and 10.

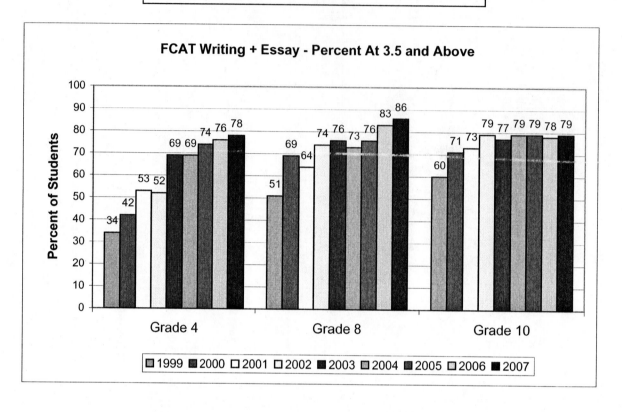

In 2007, the percent of students scoring 4 and above increased in Grades 4, 8, and 10.

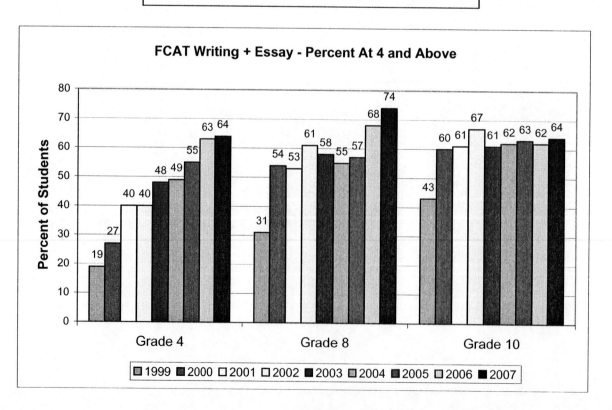

FCAT Writing+ 1999-2007 Percent Scoring At and Above 3.5 and 4

In 2007, the percent of students scoring 3.5 and above increased in Grades 4 8, and 10.

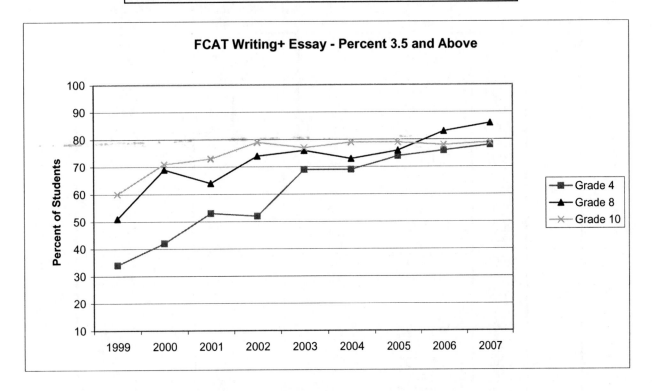

In 2007, the percent of students scoring 4 and above increased in Grades 4, 8, and 10.

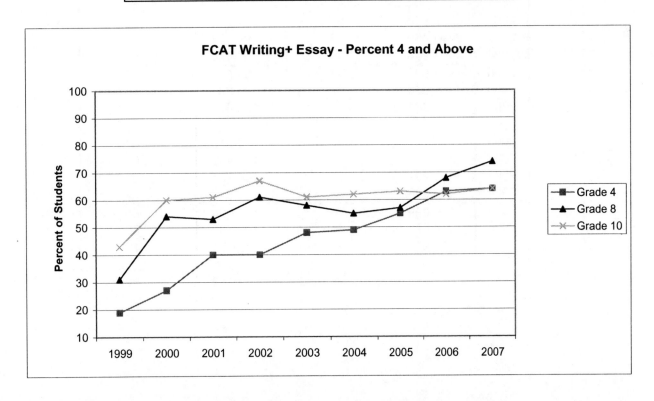

| Grade | Year | READING | | MATHEMATICS | |
		Number of Students	Median NPR	Number of Students	Median NPR
3	2001	185,991	56	186,080	59
	2002	187,965	57	188,192	62
	2003	187,526	61	187,665	66
	2004	205,797	62	205,804	68
	2005	201,925	50	201,794	62
	2006	203,784	61	203,436	67
	2007	201,432	62	200,939	69
4	2001	188,270	56	188,260	59
	2002	191,874	57	191,906	62
	2003	192,378	58	192,485	64
	2004	175,579	63	175,629	69
	2005	194,474	55	194,444	63
	2006	191,431	70	191,214	71
	2007	195,735	63	195,380	77
5	2001	187,249	51	187,290	59
	2002	192,300	52	192,256	61
	2003	191,775	55	191,867	63
	2004	195,541	56	195,535	63
	2005	180,422	61	180,332	64
	2006	196,076	69	195,845	71
	2007	191,585	74	191,156	75
6	2001	186,894	49	186,800	61
	2002	193,916	52	193,776	63
	2003	194,460	53	194,324	64
	2004	197,279	54	197,130	66
	2005	198,657	54	198,535	61
	2006	185,390	67	185,234	67
	2007	196,601	66	196,479	66
7	2001	182,777	54	182,613	61
	2002	191,668	56	191,442	65
	2003	194,997	57	194,795	66
	2004	199,038	57	198,949	67
	2005	199,099	56	198,994	65
	2006	199,870	65	199,730	69
	2007	186,548	66	186,371	73

Grade	Year	READING		ATHEMATICS	
		Number of Students	Median NPR	Number of Students	Median NPR
8	2001	173,687	59	173,432	62
	2002	184,347	60	184,185	64
	2003	190,020	58	189,913	65
	2004	195,605	60	195,564	66
	2005	198,138	67	198,064	67
	2006	198,152	65	198,010	73
	2007	197,104	67	197,007	74
9	2001	189,333	44	188,997	63
	2002	200,173	44	199,749	65
	2003	195,145	44	194,843	66
	2004	204,032	44	203,775	69
	2005	204,543	63	204,314	71
	2006	202,847	65	202,656	74
	2007	198,078	71	197,848	74
10	2001	142,538	49	142,311	64
	2002	144,781	50	144,596	67
	2003	153,503	46	153,363	66
	2004	160,636	45	160,458	66
	2005	172,934	61	172,738	58
	2006	178,378	67	178,160	70
	2007	178,598	60	178,349	67

NOTE: The 2005, 2006, and 2007 FCAT Norm-Referenced Tests are custom forms of the Stanford 10®. Prior to that, the Stanford 9® was used.
May 2007 Florida Department of Education, Assessment and School Performance

Ancestry

Top 10 Places Sorted by Number
Based on all places, regardless of population

Place (place type) County	Number	%
Jacksonville (special city) Duval	179	0.02
Tallahassee (city) Leon	70	0.05
Pensacola (city) Escambia	59	0.10
Palm Harbor (cdp) Pinellas	53	0.09
Weston (city) Broward	49	0.10
Rockledge (city) Brevard	47	0.23
Tampa (city) Hillsborough	47	0.02
Bellview (cdp) Escambia	42	0.20
Palm Valley (cdp) St. Johns	39	0.20
Gainesville (city) Alachua	37	0.04

Top 10 Places Sorted by Percent
Based on all places, regardless of population

Place (place type) County	Number	%
Southchase (cdp) Orange	33	0.73
Freeport (city) Walton	8	0.65
Sharpes (cdp) Brevard	20	0.57
Belleair Beach (city) Pinellas	9	0.54
Inglis (town) Levy	6	0.40
Southgate (cdp) Sarasota	29	0.39
Cedar Key (city) Levy	3	0.39
Harbor Bluffs (cdp) Pinellas	11	0.38
Zellwood (cdp) Orange	9	0.37
Plantation Mobile Home Park (cdp) Palm Beach	5	0.37

Top 10 Places Sorted by Percent
Based on places with populations of 10,000 or more

Place (place type) County	Number	%
Gonzalez (cdp) Escambia	30	0.26
Rockledge (city) Brevard	47	0.23
Bellview (cdp) Escambia	42	0.20
Palm Valley (cdp) St. Johns	39	0.20
Niceville (city) Okaloosa	21	0.18
Wilton Manors (city) Broward	20	0.16
Callaway (city) Bay	21	0.15
Destin (city) Okaloosa	16	0.14
South Miami (city) Miami-Dade	14	0.13
Casselberry (city) Seminole	27	0.12

Afghan

Top 10 Places Sorted by Number
Based on all places, regardless of population

Place (place type) County	Number	%
Jacksonville (special city) Duval	205	0.03
Dunedin (city) Pinellas	31	0.09
Bellair-Meadowbrook Terrace (cdp) Clay	14	0.08
Palm Beach Gardens (city) Palm Beach	14	0.04
Davie (town) Broward	13	0.02
Weston (city) Broward	11	0.02
Bonita Springs (city) Lee	10	0.03
Lake Mary (city) Seminole	8	0.07
Titusville (city) Brevard	8	0.02
Fort Lauderdale (city) Broward	7	0.00

Top 10 Places Sorted by Percent
Based on all places, regardless of population

Place (place type) County	Number	%
Royal Palm Estates (cdp) Palm Beach	6	0.17
Dunedin (city) Pinellas	31	0.09
Bellair-Meadowbrook Terrace (cdp) Clay	14	0.08
Lake Mary (city) Seminole	8	0.07
Villas (cdp) Lee	6	0.05
Doctor Phillips (cdp) Orange	5	0.05
Palm Beach Gardens (city) Palm Beach	14	0.04
Jacksonville (special city) Duval	205	0.03
Bonita Springs (city) Lee	10	0.03
Davie (town) Broward	13	0.02

Based on places with populations of 10,000 or more

Place (place type) County	Number	%
Dunedin (city) Pinellas	31	0.09
Bellair-Meadowbrook Terrace (cdp) Clay	14	0.08
Lake Mary (city) Seminole	8	0.07
Villas (cdp) Lee	6	0.05
Palm Beach Gardens (city) Palm Beach	14	0.04
Jacksonville (special city) Duval	205	0.03
Bonita Springs (city) Lee	10	0.03
Davie (town) Broward	13	0.02
Weston (city) Broward	11	0.02
Titusville (city) Brevard	8	0.02

African American/Black

Top 10 Places Sorted by Number
Based on all places, regardless of population

Place (place type) County	Number	%
Jacksonville (special city) Duval	218,451	29.70
Miami (city) Miami-Dade	87,857	24.24
Tampa (city) Hillsborough	82,470	27.18
St. Petersburg (city) Pinellas	57,483	23.16
Orlando (city) Orange	52,652	28.31
Tallahassee (city) Leon	52,611	34.93
Fort Lauderdale (city) Broward	48,033	31.52
Lauderhill (city) Broward	35,657	61.92
North Miami (city) Miami-Dade	34,778	58.08
Miramar (city) Broward	33,627	46.23

Top 10 Places Sorted by Percent
Based on all places, regardless of population

Place (place type) County	Number	%
Washington Park (cdp) Broward	1,250	99.44
Franklin Park (cdp) Broward	933	98.94
Roosevelt Gardens (cdp) Broward	1,894	98.49
West Ken-Lark (cdp) Broward	3,358	98.42
Broward Estates (cdp) Broward	3,360	98.36
St. George (cdp) Broward	2,405	98.16
Rock Island (cdp) Broward	3,000	97.53
Bunche Park (cdp) Miami-Dade	3,865	97.28
Carver Ranches (cdp) Broward	4,165	96.88
Golden Heights (cdp) Broward	485	96.81

Top 10 Places Sorted by Percent
Based on places with populations of 10,000 or more

Place (place type) County	Number	%
Scott Lake (cdp) Miami-Dade	13,445	93.36
Brownsville (cdp) Miami-Dade	13,249	92.05
Norland (cdp) Miami-Dade	18,992	82.59
Gladeview (cdp) Miami-Dade	11,323	78.26
Pinewood (cdp) Miami-Dade	12,422	75.18
Lauderdale Lakes (city) Broward	22,834	72.02
Opa-locka (city) Miami-Dade	10,705	71.60
Golden Glades (cdp) Miami-Dade	22,922	70.26
Riviera Beach (city) Palm Beach	20,735	69.38
Lauderhill (city) Broward	35,657	61.92

African American/Black: Not Hispanic

Top 10 Places Sorted by Number
Based on all places, regardless of population

Place (place type) County	Number	%
Jacksonville (special city) Duval	215,484	29.29
Tampa (city) Hillsborough	79,161	26.09
Miami (city) Miami-Dade	77,247	21.31
St. Petersburg (city) Pinellas	56,642	22.82
Tallahassee (city) Leon	51,926	34.47
Orlando (city) Orange	50,745	27.29
Fort Lauderdale (city) Broward	47,272	31.02
Lauderhill (city) Broward	35,041	60.85
North Miami (city) Miami-Dade	33,411	55.80

Top 10 Places Sorted by Percent
Based on all places, regardless of population

Place (place type) County	Number	%
Washington Park (cdp) Broward	1,243	98.89
Roosevelt Gardens (cdp) Broward	1,891	98.34
Franklin Park (cdp) Broward	924	97.99
St. George (cdp) Broward	2,394	97.71
Broward Estates (cdp) Broward	3,335	97.63
West Ken-Lark (cdp) Broward	3,329	97.57
Rock Island (cdp) Broward	2,990	97.20
Carver Ranches (cdp) Broward	4,146	96.44
Golden Heights (cdp) Broward	483	96.41
Bunche Park (cdp) Miami-Dade	3,820	96.17

Top 10 Places Sorted by Percent
Based on places with populations of 10,000 or more

Place (place type) County	Number	%
Scott Lake (cdp) Miami-Dade	13,177	91.50
Brownsville (cdp) Miami-Dade	13,069	90.80
Norland (cdp) Miami-Dade	18,523	80.55
Gladeview (cdp) Miami-Dade	11,085	76.62
Pinewood (cdp) Miami-Dade	12,043	72.89
Lauderdale Lakes (city) Broward	22,531	71.06
Riviera Beach (city) Palm Beach	20,476	68.52
Opa-locka (city) Miami-Dade	10,127	67.73
Golden Glades (cdp) Miami-Dade	22,079	67.68
Lauderhill (city) Broward	35,041	60.85

African American/Black: Hispanic

Top 10 Places Sorted by Number
Based on all places, regardless of population

Place (place type) County	Number	%
Miami (city) Miami-Dade	10,610	2.93
Hialeah (city) Miami-Dade	4,321	1.91
Tampa (city) Hillsborough	3,309	1.09
Jacksonville (special city) Duval	2,967	0.40
Orlando (city) Orange	1,907	1.03
Carol City (cdp) Miami-Dade	1,882	3.17
Miami Beach (city) Miami-Dade	1,456	1.66
North Miami (city) Miami-Dade	1,367	2.28
Miramar (city) Broward	1,310	1.80
Hollywood (city) Broward	1,235	0.89

Top 10 Places Sorted by Percent
Based on all places, regardless of population

Place (place type) County	Number	%
Opa-locka (city) Miami-Dade	578	3.87
Carol City (cdp) Miami-Dade	1,882	3.17
Homestead Base (cdp) Miami-Dade	14	3.14
Cloud Lake (town) Palm Beach	5	2.99
Miami (city) Miami-Dade	10,610	2.93
Miami Gardens (cdp) Broward	79	2.92
Stacey Street (cdp) Palm Beach	28	2.92
West Little River (cdp) Miami-Dade	923	2.84
El Portal (village) Miami-Dade	70	2.79
Oak Ridge (cdp) Orange	606	2.71

Top 10 Places Sorted by Percent
Based on places with populations of 10,000 or more

Place (place type) County	Number	%
Opa-locka (city) Miami-Dade	578	3.87
Carol City (cdp) Miami-Dade	1,882	3.17
Miami (city) Miami-Dade	10,610	2.93
West Little River (cdp) Miami-Dade	923	2.84
Oak Ridge (cdp) Orange	606	2.71
South Miami Heights (cdp) Miami-Dade	876	2.61
Poinciana (cdp) Osceola	354	2.59
Golden Glades (cdp) Miami-Dade	843	2.58
Yeehaw Junction (cdp) Osceola	550	2.53

Notes: (cdp) census designated place; Refer to the User's Guide in the front of the book for more detailed information.

Palmetto Estates (cdp) Miami-Dade	340	2.49

African, sub-Saharan

Top 10 Places Sorted by Number
Based on all places, regardless of population

Place (place type) County	Number	%
Jacksonville (special city) Duval	8,010	1.09
Miami (city) Miami-Dade	2,816	0.78
Tampa (city) Hillsborough	2,718	0.90
St. Petersburg (city) Pinellas	2,394	0.97
Tallahassee (city) Leon	2,240	1.49
Fort Lauderdale (city) Broward	1,802	1.18
Orlando (city) Orange	1,786	0.96
Gainesville (city) Alachua	1,630	1.70
Pine Hills (cdp) Orange	964	2.30
Hollywood (city) Broward	961	0.69

Top 10 Places Sorted by Percent
Based on all places, regardless of population

Place (place type) County	Number	%
Lake Harbor (cdp) Palm Beach	29	31.18
Century (town) Escambia	162	9.41
Fort Pierce North (cdp) St. Lucie	673	9.17
Tildenville (cdp) Orange	34	6.85
South Brooksville (cdp) Hernando	85	6.35
Franklin Park (cdp) Broward	56	5.10
Coleman (city) Sumter	32	4.59
Penney Farms (town) Clay	23	4.28
South Apopka (cdp) Orange	259	4.26
Graceville (city) Jackson	103	4.24

Top 10 Places Sorted by Percent
Based on places with populations of 10,000 or more

Place (place type) County	Number	%
Leesburg (city) Lake	417	2.63
Norland (cdp) Miami-Dade	531	2.31
Pine Hills (cdp) Orange	964	2.30
Brownsville (cdp) Miami-Dade	307	2.12
Princeton (cdp) Miami-Dade	194	1.91
University (cdp) Hillsborough	574	1.87
Gainesville (city) Alachua	1,630	1.70
West Little River (cdp) Miami-Dade	539	1.67
Crestview (city) Okaloosa	247	1.67
Sanford (city) Seminole	607	1.61

African, Subsaharan: African

Top 10 Places Sorted by Number
Based on all places, regardless of population

Place (place type) County	Number	%
Jacksonville (special city) Duval	6,995	0.95
Miami (city) Miami-Dade	2,661	0.73
Tampa (city) Hillsborough	2,282	0.75
St. Petersburg (city) Pinellas	2,107	0.85
Tallahassee (city) Leon	1,726	1.15
Orlando (city) Orange	1,598	0.86
Fort Lauderdale (city) Broward	1,594	1.05
Gainesville (city) Alachua	1,249	1.31
Pine Hills (cdp) Orange	903	2.15
West Palm Beach (city) Palm Beach	705	0.86

Top 10 Places Sorted by Percent
Based on all places, regardless of population

Place (place type) County	Number	%
Lake Harbor (cdp) Palm Beach	29	31.18
Century (town) Escambia	162	9.41
Fort Pierce North (cdp) St. Lucie	673	9.17
Tildenville (cdp) Orange	34	6.85
Franklin Park (cdp) Broward	56	5.10
Coleman (city) Sumter	32	4.59
Penney Farms (town) Clay	23	4.28

South Apopka (cdp) Orange	259	4.26
Graceville (city) Jackson	103	4.24
Goulding (cdp) Escambia	176	3.94

Top 10 Places Sorted by Percent
Based on places with populations of 10,000 or more

Place (place type) County	Number	%
Leesburg (city) Lake	417	2.63
Pine Hills (cdp) Orange	903	2.15
Norland (cdp) Miami-Dade	487	2.12
Brownsville (cdp) Miami-Dade	307	2.12
Princeton (cdp) Miami-Dade	194	1.91
West Little River (cdp) Miami-Dade	539	1.67
Crestview (city) Okaloosa	247	1.67
Sanford (city) Seminole	607	1.61
Fort Pierce (city) St. Lucie	542	1.45
University (cdp) Hillsborough	439	1.43

African, Subsaharan: Cape Verdean

Top 10 Places Sorted by Number
Based on all places, regardless of population

Place (place type) County	Number	%
Poinciana (cdp) Osceola	90	0.66
Orlando (city) Orange	84	0.05
Jacksonville (special city) Duval	72	0.01
Coral Springs (city) Broward	66	0.06
Kissimmee (city) Osceola	56	0.12
Bloomingdale (cdp) Hillsborough	53	0.27
Coconut Creek (city) Broward	52	0.12
Largo (city) Pinellas	41	0.06
Palm Bay (city) Brevard	39	0.05
Citrus Park (cdp) Hillsborough	35	0.17

Top 10 Places Sorted by Percent
Based on all places, regardless of population

Place (place type) County	Number	%
Poinciana (cdp) Osceola	90	0.66
Kendall Green (cdp) Broward	9	0.29
Chambers Estates (cdp) Broward	10	0.28
Bloomingdale (cdp) Hillsborough	53	0.27
Charlotte Park (cdp) Charlotte	6	0.26
Upper Grand Lagoon (cdp) Bay	28	0.25
Micco (cdp) Brevard	22	0.23
Richmond Heights (cdp) Miami-Dade	15	0.18
Citrus Park (cdp) Hillsborough	35	0.17
West Pensacola (cdp) Escambia	32	0.15

Top 10 Places Sorted by Percent
Based on places with populations of 10,000 or more

Place (place type) County	Number	%
Poinciana (cdp) Osceola	90	0.66
Bloomingdale (cdp) Hillsborough	53	0.27
Upper Grand Lagoon (cdp) Bay	28	0.25
Citrus Park (cdp) Hillsborough	35	0.17
West Pensacola (cdp) Escambia	32	0.15
Meadow Woods (cdp) Orange	16	0.14
Kissimmee (city) Osceola	56	0.12
Coconut Creek (city) Broward	52	0.12
Royal Palm Beach (village) Palm Beach	18	0.08
Lake Wales (city) Polk	8	0.08

African, Subsaharan: Ethiopian

Top 10 Places Sorted by Number
Based on all places, regardless of population

Place (place type) County	Number	%
Gainesville (city) Alachua	135	0.14
Tampa (city) Hillsborough	106	0.03
Jacksonville (special city) Duval	99	0.01
Boca Raton (city) Palm Beach	55	0.07
Fairview Shores (cdp) Orange	50	0.37

Tangelo Park (cdp) Orange	46	1.99
Margate (city) Broward	36	0.07
North Miami (city) Miami-Dade	36	0.06
Sarasota (city) Sarasota	28	0.05
Town 'n' Country (cdp) Hillsborough	28	0.04

Top 10 Places Sorted by Percent
Based on all places, regardless of population

Place (place type) County	Number	%
Tangelo Park (cdp) Orange	46	1.99
Esto (town) Holmes	3	0.86
Fairview Shores (cdp) Orange	50	0.37
Sunny Isles Beach (city) Miami-Dade	24	0.16
Gainesville (city) Alachua	135	0.14
Pine Castle (cdp) Orange	9	0.11
Thonotosassa (cdp) Hillsborough	6	0.10
Egypt Lake-Leto (cdp) Hillsborough	26	0.08
Greater Northdale (cdp) Hillsborough	16	0.08
Boca Raton (city) Palm Beach	55	0.07

Top 10 Places Sorted by Percent
Based on places with populations of 10,000 or more

Place (place type) County	Number	%
Fairview Shores (cdp) Orange	50	0.37
Sunny Isles Beach (city) Miami-Dade	24	0.16
Gainesville (city) Alachua	135	0.14
Egypt Lake-Leto (cdp) Hillsborough	26	0.08
Greater Northdale (cdp) Hillsborough	16	0.08
Boca Raton (city) Palm Beach	55	0.07
Margate (city) Broward	36	0.07
Pinewood (cdp) Miami-Dade	11	0.07
Palmetto (city) Manatee	9	0.07
North Miami (city) Miami-Dade	36	0.06

African, Subsaharan: Ghanian

Top 10 Places Sorted by Number
Based on all places, regardless of population

Place (place type) County	Number	%
Tampa (city) Hillsborough	126	0.04
Jacksonville (special city) Duval	112	0.02
Deerfield Beach (city) Broward	105	0.16
Tallahassee (city) Leon	82	0.05
Pembroke Pines (city) Broward	69	0.05
Lakeside (cdp) Clay	28	0.09
Wellington (village) Palm Beach	28	0.07
North Miami Beach (city) Miami-Dade	26	0.06
St. Augustine (city) St. Johns	23	0.20
St. Petersburg (city) Pinellas	22	0.01

Top 10 Places Sorted by Percent
Based on all places, regardless of population

Place (place type) County	Number	%
Mangonia Park (town) Palm Beach	8	0.62
Tedder (cdp) Broward	7	0.35
Pebble Creek (cdp) Hillsborough	10	0.21
St. Augustine (city) St. Johns	23	0.20
Deerfield Beach (city) Broward	105	0.16
Doctor Phillips (cdp) Orange	11	0.11
Niceville (city) Okaloosa	12	0.10
Lakeside (cdp) Clay	28	0.09
Lakeland Highlands (cdp) Polk	12	0.09
Wellington (village) Palm Beach	28	0.07

Top 10 Places Sorted by Percent
Based on places with populations of 10,000 or more

Place (place type) County	Number	%
St. Augustine (city) St. Johns	23	0.20
Deerfield Beach (city) Broward	105	0.16
Niceville (city) Okaloosa	12	0.10
Lakeside (cdp) Clay	28	0.09
Lakeland Highlands (cdp) Polk	12	0.09

Notes: (cdp) census designated place; Refer to the User's Guide in the front of the book for more detailed information.

Place (place type) County	Number	%
Wellington (village) Palm Beach	28	0.07
North Miami Beach (city) Miami-Dade	26	0.06
Tallahassee (city) Leon	82	0.05
Pembroke Pines (city) Broward	69	0.05
Tampa (city) Hillsborough	126	0.04

African, Subsaharan: Kenyan

Top 10 Places Sorted by Number
Based on all places, regardless of population

Place (place type) County	Number	%
Ocala (city) Marion	53	0.12
Gainesville (city) Alachua	30	0.03
Pompano Beach (city) Broward	29	0.04
Plantation (city) Broward	28	0.03
Ives Estates (cdp) Miami-Dade	26	0.15
Forest City (cdp) Seminole	23	0.18
Miami Shores (village) Miami-Dade	22	0.21
Heathrow (cdp) Seminole	15	0.38
Daytona Beach (city) Volusia	10	0.02
Clearwater (city) Pinellas	10	0.01

Top 10 Places Sorted by Percent
Based on all places, regardless of population

Place (place type) County	Number	%
Heathrow (cdp) Seminole	15	0.38
Stacey Street (cdp) Palm Beach	2	0.24
Miami Shores (village) Miami-Dade	22	0.21
Forest City (cdp) Seminole	23	0.18
Ives Estates (cdp) Miami-Dade	26	0.15
Ocala (city) Marion	53	0.12
Lantana (town) Palm Beach	7	0.07
Pompano Beach (city) Broward	29	0.04
Gainesville (city) Alachua	30	0.03
Plantation (city) Broward	28	0.03

Top 10 Places Sorted by Percent
Based on places with populations of 10,000 or more

Place (place type) County	Number	%
Miami Shores (village) Miami-Dade	22	0.21
Forest City (cdp) Seminole	23	0.18
Ives Estates (cdp) Miami-Dade	26	0.15
Ocala (city) Marion	53	0.12
Pompano Beach (city) Broward	29	0.04
Gainesville (city) Alachua	30	0.03
Plantation (city) Broward	28	0.03
Vero Beach South (cdp) Indian River	7	0.03
Daytona Beach (city) Volusia	10	0.02
Fort Myers (city) Lee	8	0.02

African, Subsaharan: Liberian

Top 10 Places Sorted by Number
Based on all places, regardless of population

Place (place type) County	Number	%
Boynton Beach (city) Palm Beach	85	0.14
Royal Palm Beach (village) Palm Beach	61	0.28
Daytona Beach (city) Volusia	41	0.06
Delray Beach (city) Palm Beach	37	0.06
Hollywood (city) Broward	37	0.03
Parkland (city) Broward	24	0.17
Cape Coral (city) Lee	22	0.02
Greater Carrollwood (cdp) Hillsborough	12	0.04
Jacksonville (special city) Duval	10	0.00
Punta Gorda (city) Charlotte	9	0.06

Top 10 Places Sorted by Percent
Based on all places, regardless of population

Place (place type) County	Number	%
Royal Palm Beach (village) Palm Beach	61	0.28
Parkland (city) Broward	24	0.17
Boynton Beach (city) Palm Beach	85	0.14

Place (place type) County	Number	%
Daytona Beach (city) Volusia	41	0.06
Delray Beach (city) Palm Beach	37	0.06
Punta Gorda (city) Charlotte	9	0.06
Greater Carrollwood (cdp) Hillsborough	12	0.04
Hollywood (city) Broward	37	0.03
Cape Coral (city) Lee	22	0.02
North Lauderdale (city) Broward	8	0.02

Top 10 Places Sorted by Percent
Based on places with populations of 10,000 or more

Place (place type) County	Number	%
Royal Palm Beach (village) Palm Beach	61	0.28
Parkland (city) Broward	24	0.17
Boynton Beach (city) Palm Beach	85	0.14
Daytona Beach (city) Volusia	41	0.06
Delray Beach (city) Palm Beach	37	0.06
Punta Gorda (city) Charlotte	9	0.06
Greater Carrollwood (cdp) Hillsborough	12	0.04
Hollywood (city) Broward	37	0.03
Cape Coral (city) Lee	22	0.02
North Lauderdale (city) Broward	8	0.02

African, Subsaharan: Nigerian

Top 10 Places Sorted by Number
Based on all places, regardless of population

Place (place type) County	Number	%
Hollywood (city) Broward	285	0.20
Jacksonville (special city) Duval	281	0.04
Miramar (city) Broward	267	0.37
Tallahassee (city) Leon	250	0.17
Pembroke Pines (city) Broward	188	0.14
St. Petersburg (city) Pinellas	136	0.05
Melbourne (city) Brevard	124	0.17
Golden Glades (cdp) Miami-Dade	118	0.37
Rockledge (city) Brevard	115	0.57
University (cdp) Hillsborough	108	0.35

Top 10 Places Sorted by Percent
Based on all places, regardless of population

Place (place type) County	Number	%
South Brooksville (cdp) Hernando	77	5.75
Homestead Base (cdp) Miami-Dade	12	2.96
Tangelo Park (cdp) Orange	33	1.42
Wesley Chapel (cdp) Pasco	65	1.10
Heathrow (cdp) Seminole	39	1.00
Country Walk (cdp) Miami-Dade	81	0.76
Andover (cdp) Miami-Dade	62	0.72
Rockledge (city) Brevard	115	0.57
Eatonville (town) Orange	12	0.50
Wimauma (cdp) Hillsborough	19	0.45

Top 10 Places Sorted by Percent
Based on places with populations of 10,000 or more

Place (place type) County	Number	%
Country Walk (cdp) Miami-Dade	81	0.76
Rockledge (city) Brevard	115	0.57
Cooper City (city) Broward	107	0.39
Miramar (city) Broward	267	0.37
Golden Glades (cdp) Miami-Dade	118	0.37
Sweetwater (city) Miami-Dade	52	0.36
University (cdp) Hillsborough	108	0.35
Richmond West (cdp) Miami-Dade	91	0.32
Scott Lake (cdp) Miami-Dade	31	0.22
Gladeview (cdp) Miami-Dade	30	0.21

African, Subsaharan: Senegalese

Top 10 Places Sorted by Number
Based on all places, regardless of population

Place (place type) County	Number	%
Coconut Creek (city) Broward	32	0.07

Place (place type) County	Number	%
Pompano Beach (city) Broward	24	0.03
North Miami Beach (city) Miami-Dade	6	0.01

Top 10 Places Sorted by Percent
Based on all places, regardless of population

Place (place type) County	Number	%
Coconut Creek (city) Broward	32	0.07
Pompano Beach (city) Broward	24	0.03
North Miami Beach (city) Miami-Dade	6	0.01

Top 10 Places Sorted by Percent
Based on places with populations of 10,000 or more

Place (place type) County	Number	%
Coconut Creek (city) Broward	32	0.07
Pompano Beach (city) Broward	24	0.03
North Miami Beach (city) Miami-Dade	6	0.01

African, Subsaharan: Sierra Leonean

Top 10 Places Sorted by Number
Based on all places, regardless of population

Place (place type) County	Number	%
Jacksonville (special city) Duval	49	0.01
Kendale Lakes (cdp) Miami-Dade	29	0.05
Riverview (cdp) Hillsborough	15	0.12
Orlando (city) Orange	12	0.01
Egypt Lake-Leto (cdp) Hillsborough	10	0.03
Wedgefield (cdp) Orange	8	0.28
Golden Gate (cdp) Collier	8	0.04
Lake Magdalene (cdp) Hillsborough	8	0.03
Golden Glades (cdp) Miami-Dade	8	0.02
St. Petersburg (city) Pinellas	7	0.00

Top 10 Places Sorted by Percent
Based on all places, regardless of population

Place (place type) County	Number	%
Wedgefield (cdp) Orange	8	0.28
Riverview (cdp) Hillsborough	15	0.12
Kendale Lakes (cdp) Miami-Dade	29	0.05
Golden Gate (cdp) Collier	8	0.04
Egypt Lake-Leto (cdp) Hillsborough	10	0.03
Lake Magdalene (cdp) Hillsborough	8	0.03
Country Walk (cdp) Miami-Dade	3	0.03
Golden Glades (cdp) Miami-Dade	8	0.02
Greenacres (city) Palm Beach	5	0.02
Jacksonville (special city) Duval	49	0.01

Top 10 Places Sorted by Percent
Based on places with populations of 10,000 or more

Place (place type) County	Number	%
Riverview (cdp) Hillsborough	15	0.12
Kendale Lakes (cdp) Miami-Dade	29	0.05
Golden Gate (cdp) Collier	8	0.04
Egypt Lake-Leto (cdp) Hillsborough	10	0.03
Lake Magdalene (cdp) Hillsborough	8	0.03
Country Walk (cdp) Miami-Dade	3	0.03
Golden Glades (cdp) Miami-Dade	8	0.02
Greenacres (city) Palm Beach	5	0.02
Jacksonville (special city) Duval	49	0.01
Orlando (city) Orange	12	0.01

African, Subsaharan: Somalian

Top 10 Places Sorted by Number
Based on all places, regardless of population

Place (place type) County	Number	%
Pembroke Pines (city) Broward	22	0.02
Deerfield Beach (city) Broward	18	0.03
Tampa (city) Hillsborough	11	0.00
Miami Beach (city) Miami-Dade	9	0.01

Notes: (cdp) census designated place; Refer to the User's Guide in the front of the book for more detailed information.

Top 10 Places Sorted by Percent
Based on all places, regardless of population

Place (place type) County	Number	%
Deerfield Beach (city) Broward	18	0.03
Pembroke Pines (city) Broward	22	0.02
Miami Beach (city) Miami-Dade	9	0.01
Tampa (city) Hillsborough	11	0.00

Top 10 Places Sorted by Percent
Based on places with populations of 10,000 or more

Place (place type) County	Number	%
Deerfield Beach (city) Broward	18	0.03
Pembroke Pines (city) Broward	22	0.02
Miami Beach (city) Miami-Dade	9	0.01
Tampa (city) Hillsborough	11	0.00

African, Subsaharan: South African

Top 10 Places Sorted by Number
Based on all places, regardless of population

Place (place type) County	Number	%
Weston (city) Broward	210	0.43
Boca Raton (city) Palm Beach	163	0.22
Jacksonville (special city) Duval	154	0.02
Tampa (city) Hillsborough	139	0.05
Fort Lauderdale (city) Broward	120	0.08
Plantation (city) Broward	119	0.14
Coral Springs (city) Broward	114	0.10
Deerfield Beach (city) Broward	104	0.16
Boca Del Mar (cdp) Palm Beach	89	0.42
Aventura (city) Miami-Dade	88	0.35

Top 10 Places Sorted by Percent
Based on all places, regardless of population

Place (place type) County	Number	%
Gotha (cdp) Orange	31	4.14
Melbourne Beach (town) Brevard	41	1.24
Harbor Bluffs (cdp) Pinellas	21	0.73
Wesley Chapel South (cdp) Pasco	18	0.55
Three Oaks (cdp) Lee	12	0.53
Sandalfoot Cove (cdp) Palm Beach	85	0.51
Big Coppitt Key (cdp) Monroe	13	0.50
Chuluota (cdp) Seminole	9	0.45
North Andrews Gardens (cdp) Broward	42	0.44
Weston (city) Broward	210	0.43

Top 10 Places Sorted by Percent
Based on places with populations of 10,000 or more

Place (place type) County	Number	%
Sandalfoot Cove (cdp) Palm Beach	85	0.51
Weston (city) Broward	210	0.43
Boca Del Mar (cdp) Palm Beach	89	0.42
Aventura (city) Miami-Dade	88	0.35
Lakeland Highlands (cdp) Polk	44	0.35
Sunny Isles Beach (city) Miami-Dade	38	0.25
Boca Raton (city) Palm Beach	163	0.22
Ojus (cdp) Miami-Dade	36	0.22
Parkland (city) Broward	31	0.22
Winter Springs (city) Seminole	66	0.21

African, Subsaharan: Sudanese

Top 10 Places Sorted by Number
Based on all places, regardless of population

Place (place type) County	Number	%
Jacksonville (special city) Duval	64	0.01
Pembroke Pines (city) Broward	44	0.03
Clearwater (city) Pinellas	19	0.02
Jasmine Estates (cdp) Pasco	16	0.09
Miramar (city) Broward	16	0.02
Plant City (city) Hillsborough	10	0.03

Place (place type) County	Number	%
North Miami (city) Miami-Dade	10	0.02
Plantation (city) Broward	10	0.01
Fort Lauderdale (city) Broward	8	0.01
Tampa (city) Hillsborough	7	0.00

Top 10 Places Sorted by Percent
Based on all places, regardless of population

Place (place type) County	Number	%
Jasmine Estates (cdp) Pasco	16	0.09
Pembroke Pines (city) Broward	44	0.03
Plant City (city) Hillsborough	10	0.03
Clearwater (city) Pinellas	19	0.02
Miramar (city) Broward	16	0.02
North Miami (city) Miami-Dade	10	0.02
Jacksonville (special city) Duval	64	0.01
Plantation (city) Broward	10	0.01
Fort Lauderdale (city) Broward	8	0.01
Tampa (city) Hillsborough	7	0.00

Top 10 Places Sorted by Percent
Based on places with populations of 10,000 or more

Place (place type) County	Number	%
Jasmine Estates (cdp) Pasco	16	0.09
Pembroke Pines (city) Broward	44	0.03
Plant City (city) Hillsborough	10	0.03
Clearwater (city) Pinellas	19	0.02
Miramar (city) Broward	16	0.02
North Miami (city) Miami-Dade	10	0.02
Jacksonville (special city) Duval	64	0.01
Plantation (city) Broward	10	0.01
Fort Lauderdale (city) Broward	8	0.01
Tampa (city) Hillsborough	7	0.00

African, Subsaharan: Ugandan

Top 10 Places Sorted by Number
Based on all places, regardless of population

Place (place type) County	Number	%
Tampa (city) Hillsborough	22	0.01
North Miami Beach (city) Miami-Dade	20	0.05
Fort Lauderdale (city) Broward	13	0.01
Hallandale (city) Broward	7	0.02

Top 10 Places Sorted by Percent
Based on all places, regardless of population

Place (place type) County	Number	%
North Miami Beach (city) Miami-Dade	20	0.05
Hallandale (city) Broward	7	0.02
Tampa (city) Hillsborough	22	0.01
Fort Lauderdale (city) Broward	13	0.01

Top 10 Places Sorted by Percent
Based on places with populations of 10,000 or more

Place (place type) County	Number	%
North Miami Beach (city) Miami-Dade	20	0.05
Hallandale (city) Broward	7	0.02
Tampa (city) Hillsborough	22	0.01
Fort Lauderdale (city) Broward	13	0.01

African, Subsaharan: Zairian

Top 10 Places Sorted by Number
Based on all places, regardless of population

Place (place type) County	Number	%
Miami Beach (city) Miami-Dade	12	0.01
Orlando (city) Orange	10	0.01
Miami (city) Miami-Dade	7	0.00

Top 10 Places Sorted by Percent
Based on all places, regardless of population

Place (place type) County	Number	%
Miami Beach (city) Miami-Dade	12	0.01
Orlando (city) Orange	10	0.01
Miami (city) Miami-Dade	7	0.00

Top 10 Places Sorted by Percent
Based on places with populations of 10,000 or more

Place (place type) County	Number	%
Miami Beach (city) Miami-Dade	12	0.01
Orlando (city) Orange	10	0.01
Miami (city) Miami-Dade	7	0.00

African, Subsaharan: Zimbabwean

Top 10 Places Sorted by Number
Based on all places, regardless of population

Place (place type) County	Number	%
Fort Lauderdale (city) Broward	36	0.02
Gainesville (city) Alachua	33	0.03
St. Petersburg (city) Pinellas	19	0.01
Bradenton (city) Manatee	14	0.03
Miami (city) Miami-Dade	12	0.00
Hunters Creek (cdp) Orange	10	0.11
Bloomingdale (cdp) Hillsborough	10	0.05
Orlando (city) Orange	10	0.01
Port St. Lucie (city) St. Lucie	8	0.01
West Palm Beach (city) Palm Beach	7	0.01

Top 10 Places Sorted by Percent
Based on all places, regardless of population

Place (place type) County	Number	%
Layton (city) Monroe	4	1.67
Hunters Creek (cdp) Orange	10	0.11
Bloomingdale (cdp) Hillsborough	10	0.05
Gainesville (city) Alachua	33	0.03
Bradenton (city) Manatee	14	0.03
Fort Lauderdale (city) Broward	36	0.02
St. Petersburg (city) Pinellas	19	0.01
Orlando (city) Orange	10	0.01
Port St. Lucie (city) St. Lucie	8	0.01
West Palm Beach (city) Palm Beach	7	0.01

Top 10 Places Sorted by Percent
Based on places with populations of 10,000 or more

Place (place type) County	Number	%
Bloomingdale (cdp) Hillsborough	10	0.05
Gainesville (city) Alachua	33	0.03
Bradenton (city) Manatee	14	0.03
Fort Lauderdale (city) Broward	36	0.02
St. Petersburg (city) Pinellas	19	0.01
Orlando (city) Orange	10	0.01
Port St. Lucie (city) St. Lucie	8	0.01
West Palm Beach (city) Palm Beach	7	0.01
Miami (city) Miami-Dade	12	0.00

African, Subsaharan: Other

Top 10 Places Sorted by Number
Based on all places, regardless of population

Place (place type) County	Number	%
Jacksonville (special city) Duval	167	0.02
Tallahassee (city) Leon	120	0.08
The Hammocks (cdp) Miami-Dade	57	0.12
Kissimmee (city) Osceola	46	0.10
Daytona Beach (city) Volusia	36	0.06
Clearwater (city) Pinellas	34	0.03
Westchase (cdp) Hillsborough	32	0.29
Orlando (city) Orange	31	0.02
Lockhart (cdp) Orange	30	0.24

Notes: (cdp) census designated place; Refer to the User's Guide in the front of the book for more detailed information.

Place (place type) County	Number	%
Tedder (cdp) Broward	14	0.70
Westchase (cdp) Hillsborough	32	0.29
Plantation Mobile Home Park (cdp) Palm Beach	4	0.29
Pebble Creek (cdp) Hillsborough	13	0.27
Broward Estates (cdp) Broward	9	0.26
Lockhart (cdp) Orange	30	0.24
South Patrick Shores (cdp) Brevard	17	0.18
The Hammocks (cdp) Miami-Dade	57	0.12
Lake Mary (city) Seminole	12	0.11
Kissimmee (city) Osceola	46	0.10

Top 10 Places Sorted by Percent
Based on places with populations of 10,000 or more

Place (place type) County	Number	%
Westchase (cdp) Hillsborough	32	0.29
Lockhart (cdp) Orange	30	0.24
The Hammocks (cdp) Miami-Dade	57	0.12
Lake Mary (city) Seminole	12	0.11
Kissimmee (city) Osceola	46	0.10
Tallahassee (city) Leon	120	0.08
Doral (cdp) Miami-Dade	14	0.07
Ojus (cdp) Miami-Dade	12	0.07
North Palm Beach (village) Palm Beach	8	0.07
Daytona Beach (city) Volusia	36	0.06

Alaska Native tribes, specified

Top 10 Places Sorted by Number
Based on all places, regardless of population

Place (place type) County	Number	%
Jacksonville (special city) Duval	46	0.01
Fort Lauderdale (city) Broward	25	0.02
Tampa (city) Hillsborough	22	0.01
Tallahassee (city) Leon	14	0.01
North Miami (city) Miami-Dade	13	0.02
Largo (city) Pinellas	11	0.01
Miami (city) Miami-Dade	11	0.00
Palm Bay (city) Brevard	9	0.01
Port St. Lucie (city) St. Lucie	8	0.01
Orlando (city) Orange	8	0.00

Top 10 Places Sorted by Percent
Based on all places, regardless of population

Place (place type) County	Number	%
Three Oaks (cdp) Lee	3	0.13
Grand Ridge (town) Jackson	1	0.13
Palm Shores (town) Brevard	1	0.13
El Portal (village) Miami-Dade	3	0.12
Watertown (cdp) Columbia	3	0.11
North River Shores (cdp) Martin	3	0.10
Feather Sound (cdp) Pinellas	3	0.08
Crystal Lake (cdp) Polk	4	0.07
Palm Springs North (cdp) Miami-Dade	4	0.07
Mary Esther (city) Okaloosa	3	0.07

Top 10 Places Sorted by Percent
Based on places with populations of 10,000 or more

Place (place type) County	Number	%
Villas (cdp) Lee	6	0.05
Fernandina Beach (city) Nassau	5	0.05
Bartow (city) Polk	6	0.04
Poinciana (cdp) Osceola	6	0.04
Niceville (city) Okaloosa	5	0.04
Lakewood Park (cdp) St. Lucie	3	0.03
Fort Lauderdale (city) Broward	25	0.02
North Miami (city) Miami-Dade	13	0.02
Largo (city) Pinellas	11	0.02

Top 10 Places Sorted by Number
Based on all places, regardless of population

Place (place type) County	Number	%
Tampa (city) Hillsborough	7	0.00
Panama City (city) Bay	6	0.02
Jacksonville (special city) Duval	5	0.00
Spring Hill (cdp) Hernando	4	0.01
Orlando (city) Orange	4	0.00
Watertown (cdp) Columbia	3	0.11
Lauderdale Lakes (city) Broward	3	0.01
Miami Beach (city) Miami-Dade	3	0.00
Bay Pines (cdp) Pinellas	2	0.07
Pretty Bayou (cdp) Bay	2	0.06

Top 10 Places Sorted by Percent
Based on all places, regardless of population

Place (place type) County	Number	%
Watertown (cdp) Columbia	3	0.11
Bay Pines (cdp) Pinellas	2	0.07
North Brooksville (cdp) Hernando	1	0.07
South Brooksville (cdp) Hernando	1	0.07
Pretty Bayou (cdp) Bay	2	0.06
Eastpoint (cdp) Franklin	1	0.05
Gibsonia (cdp) Polk	2	0.04
Ocean City (cdp) Okaloosa	2	0.04
Apollo Beach (cdp) Hillsborough	2	0.03
Panama City (city) Bay	6	0.02

Top 10 Places Sorted by Percent
Based on places with populations of 10,000 or more

Place (place type) County	Number	%
Panama City (city) Bay	6	0.02
Spring Hill (cdp) Hernando	4	0.01
Lauderdale Lakes (city) Broward	3	0.01
Myrtle Grove (cdp) Escambia	2	0.01
Callaway (city) Bay	1	0.01
Gulfport (city) Pinellas	1	0.01
Holly Hill (city) Volusia	1	0.01
Immokalee (cdp) Collier	1	0.01
Lutz (cdp) Hillsborough	1	0.01
Lynn Haven (city) Bay	1	0.01

Alaska Native: Aleut

Top 10 Places Sorted by Number
Based on all places, regardless of population

Place (place type) County	Number	%
Jacksonville (special city) Duval	11	0.00
Tallahassee (city) Leon	4	0.00
Three Oaks (cdp) Lee	3	0.13
North River Shores (cdp) Martin	3	0.10
Feather Sound (cdp) Pinellas	3	0.08
Rotonda (cdp) Charlotte	3	0.05
Collier Manor-Cresthaven (cdp) Broward	3	0.04
Titusville (city) Brevard	3	0.01
Fort Lauderdale (city) Broward	3	0.00
Pompano Beach (city) Broward	3	0.00

Top 10 Places Sorted by Percent
Based on all places, regardless of population

Place (place type) County	Number	%
Three Oaks (cdp) Lee	3	0.13
North River Shores (cdp) Martin	3	0.10
Feather Sound (cdp) Pinellas	3	0.08
Rotonda (cdp) Charlotte	3	0.05
Collier Manor-Cresthaven (cdp) Broward	3	0.04
Graceville (city) Jackson	1	0.04
Villas (cdp) Lee	2	0.02

Top 10 Places Sorted by Percent
Based on places with populations of 10,000 or more

Place (place type) County	Number	%
Villas (cdp) Lee	2	0.02
Titusville (city) Brevard	3	0.01
West Pensacola (cdp) Escambia	2	0.01
Bartow (city) Polk	1	0.01
Belle Glade (city) Palm Beach	1	0.01
Conway (cdp) Orange	1	0.01
Edgewater (city) Volusia	1	0.01
Ives Estates (cdp) Miami-Dade	1	0.01
Lady Lake (town) Lake	1	0.01
Lakewood Park (cdp) St. Lucie	1	0.01

Alaska Native: Eskimo

Top 10 Places Sorted by Number
Based on all places, regardless of population

Place (place type) County	Number	%
Jacksonville (special city) Duval	12	0.00
Tampa (city) Hillsborough	12	0.00
Tallahassee (city) Leon	9	0.01
Poinciana (cdp) Osceola	6	0.04
Largo (city) Pinellas	6	0.01
Palm Bay (city) Brevard	6	0.01
Bartow (city) Polk	5	0.03
Davie (town) Broward	5	0.01
Fort Lauderdale (city) Broward	5	0.00
Miami (city) Miami-Dade	5	0.00

Top 10 Places Sorted by Percent
Based on all places, regardless of population

Place (place type) County	Number	%
Laguna Beach (cdp) Bay	2	0.07
Five Points (cdp) Columbia	1	0.07
Anna Maria (city) Manatee	1	0.06
Gandy (cdp) Pinellas	1	0.05
Poinciana (cdp) Osceola	6	0.04
Fernandina Beach (city) Nassau	4	0.04
Villas (cdp) Lee	4	0.04
Combee Settlement (cdp) Polk	2	0.04
Bartow (city) Polk	5	0.03
High Springs (city) Alachua	1	0.03

Top 10 Places Sorted by Percent
Based on places with populations of 10,000 or more

Place (place type) County	Number	%
Poinciana (cdp) Osceola	6	0.04
Fernandina Beach (city) Nassau	4	0.04
Villas (cdp) Lee	4	0.04
Bartow (city) Polk	5	0.03
Fort Walton Beach (city) Okaloosa	3	0.02
Jasmine Estates (cdp) Pasco	3	0.02
Iona (cdp) Lee	2	0.02
Tallahassee (city) Leon	9	0.01
Largo (city) Pinellas	6	0.01
Palm Bay (city) Brevard	6	0.01

Alaska Native: Tlingit-Haida

Top 10 Places Sorted by Number
Based on all places, regardless of population

Place (place type) County	Number	%
Jacksonville (special city) Duval	17	0.00
Fort Lauderdale (city) Broward	16	0.01
North Miami (city) Miami-Dade	13	0.02
Port St. Lucie (city) St. Lucie	7	0.01
Lauderhill (city) Broward	6	0.01

Notes: (cdp) census designated place; Refer to the User's Guide in the front of the book for more detailed information.

Place (place type) County	Number	%
Miami (city) Miami-Dade	6	0.00
Niceville (city) Okaloosa	5	0.04
Golden Glades (cdp) Miami-Dade	5	0.02
Bradenton (city) Manatee	4	0.01
El Portal (village) Miami-Dade	3	0.12

Top 10 Places Sorted by Percent
Based on all places, regardless of population

Place (place type) County	Number	%
Grand Ridge (town) Jackson	1	0.13
El Portal (village) Miami-Dade	3	0.12
Mary Esther (city) Okaloosa	3	0.07
Palm Springs North (cdp) Miami-Dade	3	0.05
Niceville (city) Okaloosa	5	0.04
Boyette (cdp) Hillsborough	2	0.03
Lake Lorraine (cdp) Okaloosa	2	0.03
Sharpes (cdp) Brevard	1	0.03
West Ken-Lark (cdp) Broward	1	0.03
North Miami (city) Miami-Dade	13	0.02

Top 10 Places Sorted by Percent
Based on places with populations of 10,000 or more

Place (place type) County	Number	%
Niceville (city) Okaloosa	5	0.04
North Miami (city) Miami-Dade	13	0.02
Golden Glades (cdp) Miami-Dade	5	0.02
Cypress Lake (cdp) Lee	2	0.02
Fort Lauderdale (city) Broward	16	0.01
Port St. Lucie (city) St. Lucie	7	0.01
Lauderhill (city) Broward	6	0.01
Bradenton (city) Manatee	4	0.01
Lauderdale Lakes (city) Broward	3	0.01
Merritt Island (cdp) Brevard	3	0.01

Alaska Native: All other tribes

Top 10 Places Sorted by Number
Based on all places, regardless of population

Place (place type) County	Number	%
Crystal Lake (cdp) Polk	3	0.06
Azalea Park (cdp) Orange	2	0.02
Lakewood Park (cdp) St. Lucie	2	0.02
Orlando (city) Orange	2	0.00
Palm Shores (town) Brevard	1	0.13
Wedgefield (cdp) Orange	1	0.04
Vero Beach (city) Indian River	1	0.01
Brent (cdp) Escambia	1	0.00
Jacksonville (special city) Duval	1	0.00
Largo (city) Pinellas	1	0.00

Top 10 Places Sorted by Percent
Based on all places, regardless of population

Place (place type) County	Number	%
Palm Shores (town) Brevard	1	0.13
Crystal Lake (cdp) Polk	3	0.06
Wedgefield (cdp) Orange	1	0.04
Azalea Park (cdp) Orange	2	0.02
Lakewood Park (cdp) St. Lucie	2	0.02
Vero Beach (city) Indian River	1	0.01
Orlando (city) Orange	2	0.00
Brent (cdp) Escambia	1	0.00
Jacksonville (special city) Duval	1	0.00
Largo (city) Pinellas	1	0.00

Top 10 Places Sorted by Percent
Based on places with populations of 10,000 or more

Place (place type) County	Number	%
Azalea Park (cdp) Orange	2	0.02
Lakewood Park (cdp) St. Lucie	2	0.02
Vero Beach (city) Indian River	1	0.01
Orlando (city) Orange	2	0.00
Brent (cdp) Escambia	1	0.00

Place (place type) County	Number	%
Jacksonville (special city) Duval	1	0.00
Largo (city) Pinellas	1	0.00
Naples (city) Collier	1	0.00
Palm Bay (city) Brevard	1	0.00
South Miami Heights (cdp) Miami-Dade	1	0.00

Alaska Native tribes, not specified

Top 10 Places Sorted by Number
Based on all places, regardless of population

Place (place type) County	Number	%
Jacksonville (special city) Duval	9	0.00
Tampa (city) Hillsborough	8	0.00
St. Petersburg (city) Pinellas	6	0.00
Orange Park (town) Clay	4	0.04
Daytona Beach (city) Volusia	4	0.01
Melbourne (city) Brevard	4	0.01
Combee Settlement (cdp) Polk	2	0.04
Williamsburg (cdp) Orange	2	0.03
Hollywood (city) Broward	2	0.00
Largo (city) Pinellas	2	0.00

Top 10 Places Sorted by Percent
Based on all places, regardless of population

Place (place type) County	Number	%
Grand Ridge (town) Jackson	1	0.13
North Brooksville (cdp) Hernando	1	0.07
South Brooksville (cdp) Hernando	1	0.07
Chuluota (cdp) Seminole	1	0.05
Orange Park (town) Clay	4	0.04
Combee Settlement (cdp) Polk	2	0.04
Tyndall AFB (cdp) Bay	1	0.04
Williamsburg (cdp) Orange	2	0.03
Pretty Bayou (cdp) Bay	1	0.03
Dade City (city) Pasco	1	0.02

Top 10 Places Sorted by Percent
Based on places with populations of 10,000 or more

Place (place type) County	Number	%
Daytona Beach (city) Volusia	4	0.01
Melbourne (city) Brevard	4	0.01
De Bary (city) Volusia	1	0.01
Gulfport (city) Pinellas	1	0.01
Lakeland Highlands (cdp) Polk	1	0.01
St. Augustine (city) St. Johns	1	0.01
Upper Grand Lagoon (cdp) Bay	1	0.01
Villas (cdp) Lee	1	0.01
Zephyrhills (city) Pasco	1	0.01
Jacksonville (special city) Duval	9	0.00

American Indian or Alaska Native, not specified

Top 10 Places Sorted by Number
Based on all places, regardless of population

Place (place type) County	Number	%
Jacksonville (special city) Duval	1,954	0.27
Tampa (city) Hillsborough	1,030	0.34
Miami (city) Miami-Dade	897	0.25
St. Petersburg (city) Pinellas	709	0.29
Orlando (city) Orange	499	0.27
Tallahassee (city) Leon	333	0.22
Hialeah (city) Miami-Dade	327	0.14
Fort Lauderdale (city) Broward	325	0.21
Hollywood (city) Broward	314	0.23
Clearwater (city) Pinellas	260	0.24

Top 10 Places Sorted by Percent
Based on all places, regardless of population

Place (place type) County	Number	%
Hillsboro Ranches (cdp) Broward	1	2.13
Istachatta (cdp) Hernando	1	1.54

Place (place type) County	Number	%
Caryville (town) Washington	3	1.38
Waldo (city) Alachua	11	1.34
Center Hill (city) Sumter	11	1.21
Vernon (city) Washington	9	1.21
Ebro (town) Washington	3	1.20
Esto (town) Holmes	4	1.12
St. Marks (city) Wakulla	3	1.10
Gotha (cdp) Orange	8	1.09

Top 10 Places Sorted by Percent
Based on places with populations of 10,000 or more

Place (place type) County	Number	%
West Pensacola (cdp) Escambia	130	0.59
Oak Ridge (cdp) Orange	117	0.52
Ensley (cdp) Escambia	97	0.52
Myrtle Grove (cdp) Escambia	90	0.52
Wright (cdp) Okaloosa	110	0.51
Bellview (cdp) Escambia	109	0.51
Meadow Woods (cdp) Orange	57	0.51
Niceville (city) Okaloosa	58	0.50
Cocoa (city) Brevard	79	0.48
Kissimmee (city) Osceola	227	0.47

Albanian

Top 10 Places Sorted by Number
Based on all places, regardless of population

Place (place type) County	Number	%
Jacksonville (special city) Duval	855	0.12
Largo (city) Pinellas	312	0.45
St. Petersburg (city) Pinellas	311	0.13
Clearwater (city) Pinellas	211	0.20
Dunedin (city) Pinellas	199	0.55
Fort Lauderdale (city) Broward	158	0.10
Orlando (city) Orange	114	0.06
Palm Harbor (cdp) Pinellas	105	0.18
Oldsmar (city) Pinellas	75	0.64
Tampa (city) Hillsborough	65	0.02

Top 10 Places Sorted by Percent
Based on all places, regardless of population

Place (place type) County	Number	%
Green Meadow (cdp) Broward	14	0.76
Cudjoe Key (cdp) Monroe	13	0.75
Oldsmar (city) Pinellas	75	0.64
Dunedin (city) Pinellas	199	0.55
Buckingham (cdp) Lee	20	0.51
Briny Breezes (town) Palm Beach	2	0.48
Largo (city) Pinellas	312	0.45
Islamorada (village) Monroe	29	0.42
South Pasadena (city) Pinellas	24	0.41
Atlantis (city) Palm Beach	8	0.38

Top 10 Places Sorted by Percent
Based on places with populations of 10,000 or more

Place (place type) County	Number	%
Oldsmar (city) Pinellas	75	0.64
Dunedin (city) Pinellas	199	0.55
Largo (city) Pinellas	312	0.45
Fruitville (cdp) Sarasota	40	0.31
Lake Worth Corridor (cdp) Palm Beach	49	0.27
Clearwater (city) Pinellas	211	0.20
Holiday (cdp) Pasco	41	0.19
Palm Harbor (cdp) Pinellas	105	0.18
Kings Point (cdp) Palm Beach	22	0.18
Seminole (city) Pinellas	19	0.18

Notes: (cdp) census designated place; Refer to the User's Guide in the front of the book for more detailed information.

Alsatian

Top 10 Places Sorted by Number
Based on all places, regardless of population

Place (place type) County	Number	%
Jacksonville (special city) Duval	43	0.01
Gainesville (city) Alachua	38	0.04
Greenacres (city) Palm Beach	30	0.11
Altamonte Springs (city) Seminole	23	0.06
Boynton Beach (city) Palm Beach	21	0.04
Boca Raton (city) Palm Beach	19	0.03
Coral Springs (city) Broward	17	0.01
Cape Coral (city) Lee	16	0.02
Lakeland (city) Polk	15	0.02
Naples (city) Collier	14	0.07

Top 10 Places Sorted by Percent
Based on all places, regardless of population

Place (place type) County	Number	%
Placid Lakes (cdp) Highlands	11	0.36
North Redington Beach (town) Pinellas	4	0.29
Sharpes (cdp) Brevard	9	0.25
Howey-in-the-Hills (town) Lake	2	0.20
Holmes Beach (city) Manatee	9	0.18
West Bradenton (cdp) Manatee	7	0.16
North Sarasota (cdp) Sarasota	10	0.14
Pelican Bay (cdp) Collier	8	0.14
Fort Myers Beach (town) Lee	8	0.12
Greenacres (city) Palm Beach	30	0.11

Top 10 Places Sorted by Percent
Based on places with populations of 10,000 or more

Place (place type) County	Number	%
Greenacres (city) Palm Beach	30	0.11
Gulf Gate Estates (cdp) Sarasota	11	0.10
Jensen Beach (cdp) Martin	9	0.08
Lighthouse Point (city) Broward	9	0.08
Naples (city) Collier	14	0.07
Atlantic Beach (city) Duval	9	0.07
Hudson (cdp) Pasco	9	0.07
Altamonte Springs (city) Seminole	23	0.06
Englewood (cdp) Sarasota	9	0.06
North Palm Beach (village) Palm Beach	7	0.06

American Indian tribes, specified

Top 10 Places Sorted by Number
Based on all places, regardless of population

Place (place type) County	Number	%
Jacksonville (special city) Duval	3,545	0.48
Tampa (city) Hillsborough	1,559	0.51
St. Petersburg (city) Pinellas	1,364	0.55
Miami (city) Miami-Dade	825	0.23
Orlando (city) Orange	807	0.43
Tallahassee (city) Leon	595	0.40
Clearwater (city) Pinellas	494	0.45
Hollywood (city) Broward	483	0.35
Brandon (cdp) Hillsborough	471	0.60
Pensacola (city) Escambia	454	0.81

Top 10 Places Sorted by Percent
Based on all places, regardless of population

Place (place type) County	Number	%
Ebro (town) Washington	48	19.20
Esto (town) Holmes	16	4.49
Waldo (city) Alachua	36	4.38
Vernon (city) Washington	28	3.77
Freeport (city) Walton	40	3.36
Ponce de Leon (town) Holmes	14	3.06
Lacoochee (cdp) Pasco	41	3.05
Bagdad (cdp) Santa Rosa	45	3.02
Paxton (town) Walton	19	2.90
Indiantown (cdp) Martin	160	2.86

Top 10 Places Sorted by Percent
Based on places with populations of 10,000 or more

Place (place type) County	Number	%
Warrington (cdp) Escambia	293	1.93
West Pensacola (cdp) Escambia	370	1.69
Bellview (cdp) Escambia	327	1.54
Myrtle Grove (cdp) Escambia	245	1.42
Middleburg (cdp) Clay	145	1.40
Ensley (cdp) Escambia	248	1.32
Gonzalez (cdp) Escambia	148	1.30
Lake Worth (city) Palm Beach	412	1.17
Upper Grand Lagoon (cdp) Bay	124	1.14
Brent (cdp) Escambia	246	1.11

American Indian: Apache

Top 10 Places Sorted by Number
Based on all places, regardless of population

Place (place type) County	Number	%
Jacksonville (special city) Duval	97	0.01
Tampa (city) Hillsborough	66	0.02
St. Petersburg (city) Pinellas	28	0.01
Orlando (city) Orange	24	0.01
Tallahassee (city) Leon	23	0.02
Clearwater (city) Pinellas	20	0.02
Warrington (cdp) Escambia	12	0.08
Palm Bay (city) Brevard	12	0.02
Cape Coral (city) Lee	12	0.01
Port St. Lucie (city) St. Lucie	12	0.01

Top 10 Places Sorted by Percent
Based on all places, regardless of population

Place (place type) County	Number	%
Esto (town) Holmes	4	1.12
Cottondale (town) Jackson	5	0.58
North Redington Beach (town) Pinellas	6	0.41
St. Marks (city) Wakulla	1	0.37
Lee (town) Madison	1	0.28
Cinco Bayou (town) Okaloosa	1	0.27
Jennings (town) Hamilton	2	0.24
Molino (cdp) Escambia	3	0.23
Rolling Oaks (cdp) Broward	3	0.23
East Bronson (cdp) Levy	2	0.19

Top 10 Places Sorted by Percent
Based on places with populations of 10,000 or more

Place (place type) County	Number	%
Middleburg (cdp) Clay	10	0.10
Warrington (cdp) Escambia	12	0.08
St. Augustine (city) St. Johns	9	0.08
Destin (city) Okaloosa	7	0.06
Union Park (cdp) Orange	6	0.06
Bayonet Point (cdp) Pasco	11	0.05
Elfers (cdp) Pasco	7	0.05
Upper Grand Lagoon (cdp) Bay	5	0.05
Zephyrhills (city) Pasco	5	0.05
Land O' Lakes (cdp) Pasco	9	0.04

American Indian: Blackfeet

Top 10 Places Sorted by Number
Based on all places, regardless of population

Place (place type) County	Number	%
Jacksonville (special city) Duval	186	0.03
Tampa (city) Hillsborough	86	0.03
St. Petersburg (city) Pinellas	76	0.03
Orlando (city) Orange	41	0.02
Palm Bay (city) Brevard	35	0.04
Port St. Lucie (city) St. Lucie	32	0.04
Davie (town) Broward	31	0.04
Deltona (city) Volusia	31	0.04
Clearwater (city) Pinellas	28	0.03

| Brandon (cdp) Hillsborough | 26 | 0.03 |

Top 10 Places Sorted by Percent
Based on all places, regardless of population

Place (place type) County	Number	%
Branford (town) Suwannee	6	0.86
Otter Creek (town) Levy	1	0.83
Edgewater (cdp) Broward	4	0.50
North Beach (cdp) Indian River	1	0.41
Lake Mack-Forest Hills (cdp) Lake	4	0.40
Ebro (town) Washington	1	0.40
South Brooksville (cdp) Hernando	5	0.36
Zephyrhills South (cdp) Pasco	13	0.29
Lee (town) Madison	1	0.28
Suncoast Estates (cdp) Lee	11	0.23

Top 10 Places Sorted by Percent
Based on places with populations of 10,000 or more

Place (place type) County	Number	%
Princeton (cdp) Miami-Dade	13	0.13
Gulfport (city) Pinellas	15	0.12
Callaway (city) Bay	14	0.10
Wright (cdp) Okaloosa	19	0.09
New Port Richey (city) Pasco	15	0.09
Zephyrhills (city) Pasco	9	0.08
West and East Lealman (cdp) Pinellas	16	0.07
Temple Terrace (city) Hillsborough	14	0.07
Fort Walton Beach (city) Okaloosa	13	0.07
Palmetto (city) Manatee	9	0.07

American Indian: Cherokee

Top 10 Places Sorted by Number
Based on all places, regardless of population

Place (place type) County	Number	%
Jacksonville (special city) Duval	1,717	0.23
Tampa (city) Hillsborough	651	0.21
St. Petersburg (city) Pinellas	619	0.25
Orlando (city) Orange	349	0.19
Melbourne (city) Brevard	243	0.34
Tallahassee (city) Leon	237	0.16
Brandon (cdp) Hillsborough	219	0.28
Deltona (city) Volusia	188	0.27
Pensacola (city) Escambia	184	0.33
Gainesville (city) Alachua	184	0.19

Top 10 Places Sorted by Percent
Based on all places, regardless of population

Place (place type) County	Number	%
Waldo (city) Alachua	33	4.02
Ebro (town) Washington	7	2.80
Golden Heights (cdp) Broward	10	2.00
Bagdad (cdp) Santa Rosa	23	1.54
Greenwood (town) Jackson	10	1.36
Callahan (town) Nassau	12	1.25
Vernon (city) Washington	9	1.21
Cottondale (town) Jackson	10	1.15
Esto (town) Holmes	4	1.12
Lake Mack-Forest Hills (cdp) Lake	11	1.11

Top 10 Places Sorted by Percent
Based on places with populations of 10,000 or more

Place (place type) County	Number	%
Warrington (cdp) Escambia	116	0.76
Middleburg (cdp) Clay	77	0.74
West Pensacola (cdp) Escambia	112	0.51
Wright (cdp) Okaloosa	111	0.51
Port St. John (cdp) Brevard	61	0.50
St. Augustine (city) St. Johns	57	0.49
Bellair-Meadowbrook Terrace (cdp) Clay	80	0.48
West and East Lealman (cdp) Pinellas	103	0.47
Upper Grand Lagoon (cdp) Bay	51	0.47

Notes: (cdp) census designated place; Refer to the User's Guide in the front of the book for more detailed information.

Place (place type) County	Number	%
Niceville (city) Okaloosa	52	0.45

American Indian: Cheyenne

Top 10 Places Sorted by Number
Based on all places, regardless of population

Place (place type) County	Number	%
Jacksonville (special city) Duval	15	0.00
Melbourne (city) Brevard	7	0.01
Desoto Lakes (cdp) Sarasota	4	0.13
Gonzalez (cdp) Escambia	4	0.04
Wright (cdp) Okaloosa	4	0.02
Daytona Beach (city) Volusia	4	0.01
Greenacres (city) Palm Beach	4	0.01
Pinellas Park (city) Pinellas	4	0.01
Port St. Lucie (city) St. Lucie	4	0.00
St. Petersburg (city) Pinellas	4	0.00

Top 10 Places Sorted by Percent
Based on all places, regardless of population

Place (place type) County	Number	%
McIntosh (town) Marion	1	0.22
Desoto Lakes (cdp) Sarasota	4	0.13
Waldo (city) Alachua	1	0.12
Estates of Fort Lauderdale (cdp) Broward	2	0.11
Boulevard Gardens (cdp) Broward	1	0.07
Gonzalez (cdp) Escambia	4	0.04
Ocean City (cdp) Okaloosa	2	0.04
Big Coppitt Key (cdp) Monroe	1	0.04
Placid Lakes (cdp) Highlands	1	0.03
Wright (cdp) Okaloosa	4	0.02

Top 10 Places Sorted by Percent
Based on places with populations of 10,000 or more

Place (place type) County	Number	%
Gonzalez (cdp) Escambia	4	0.04
Wright (cdp) Okaloosa	4	0.02
Oldsmar (city) Pinellas	2	0.02
Melbourne (city) Brevard	7	0.01
Daytona Beach (city) Volusia	4	0.01
Greenacres (city) Palm Beach	4	0.01
Pinellas Park (city) Pinellas	4	0.01
Dunedin (city) Pinellas	3	0.01
Bayshore Gardens (cdp) Manatee	2	0.01
Callaway (city) Bay	2	0.01

American Indian: Chickasaw

Top 10 Places Sorted by Number
Based on all places, regardless of population

Place (place type) County	Number	%
Jacksonville (special city) Duval	23	0.00
Port St. Lucie (city) St. Lucie	12	0.01
Tampa (city) Hillsborough	9	0.00
Titusville (city) Brevard	7	0.02
Palm Bay (city) Brevard	7	0.01
Clearwater (city) Pinellas	6	0.01
St. Petersburg (city) Pinellas	6	0.00
Cypress Quarters (cdp) Okeechobee	5	0.43
Bellair-Meadowbrook Terrace (cdp) Clay	5	0.03
Altamonte Springs (city) Seminole	5	0.01

Top 10 Places Sorted by Percent
Based on all places, regardless of population

Place (place type) County	Number	%
Lazy Lake (village) Broward	1	2.63
Cypress Quarters (cdp) Okeechobee	5	0.43
Lely Resort (cdp) Collier	4	0.28
Sneads (town) Jackson	3	0.16
Bagdad (cdp) Santa Rosa	2	0.13
Chipley (city) Washington	3	0.08
Taft (cdp) Orange	1	0.05

Place (place type) County	Number	%
Panama City Beach (city) Bay	3	0.04
Asbury Lake (cdp) Clay	1	0.04
Groveland (city) Lake	1	0.04

Top 10 Places Sorted by Percent
Based on places with populations of 10,000 or more

Place (place type) County	Number	%
Bellair-Meadowbrook Terrace (cdp) Clay	5	0.03
Titusville (city) Brevard	7	0.02
San Carlos Park (cdp) Lee	4	0.02
Wekiwa Springs (cdp) Seminole	4	0.02
Wright (cdp) Okaloosa	4	0.02
Gulfport (city) Pinellas	3	0.02
Keystone (cdp) Hillsborough	3	0.02
South Daytona (city) Volusia	3	0.02
Destin (city) Okaloosa	2	0.02
Lady Lake (town) Lake	2	0.02

American Indian: Chippewa

Top 10 Places Sorted by Number
Based on all places, regardless of population

Place (place type) County	Number	%
Jacksonville (special city) Duval	97	0.01
St. Petersburg (city) Pinellas	52	0.02
Tampa (city) Hillsborough	36	0.01
Orlando (city) Orange	27	0.01
Port Charlotte (cdp) Charlotte	26	0.06
Cape Coral (city) Lee	26	0.03
Largo (city) Pinellas	24	0.03
Port St. Lucie (city) St. Lucie	22	0.02
Palm Bay (city) Brevard	18	0.02
Sarasota (city) Sarasota	17	0.03

Top 10 Places Sorted by Percent
Based on all places, regardless of population

Place (place type) County	Number	%
Pine Island Center (cdp) Lee	6	0.35
Crooked Lake Park (cdp) Polk	4	0.24
Lochmoor Waterway Estates (cdp) Lee	8	0.21
Weeki Wachee Gardens (cdp) Hernando	2	0.18
Samsula-Spruce Creek (cdp) Volusia	8	0.16
Yankeetown (town) Levy	1	0.16
Micanopy (town) Alachua	1	0.15
Inverness Highlands North (cdp) Citrus	2	0.14
Loughman (cdp) Polk	2	0.14
Branford (town) Suwannee	1	0.14

Top 10 Places Sorted by Percent
Based on places with populations of 10,000 or more

Place (place type) County	Number	%
Upper Grand Lagoon (cdp) Bay	14	0.13
Homosassa Springs (cdp) Citrus	9	0.07
Holly Hill (city) Volusia	8	0.07
Port Charlotte (cdp) Charlotte	26	0.06
Holiday (cdp) Pasco	14	0.06
Conway (cdp) Orange	8	0.06
Punta Gorda (city) Charlotte	8	0.06
Port St. John (cdp) Brevard	6	0.05
Zephyrhills (city) Pasco	5	0.05
North Fort Myers (cdp) Lee	16	0.04

American Indian: Choctaw

Top 10 Places Sorted by Number
Based on all places, regardless of population

Place (place type) County	Number	%
Jacksonville (special city) Duval	131	0.02
St. Petersburg (city) Pinellas	52	0.02
Tampa (city) Hillsborough	34	0.01
Orlando (city) Orange	32	0.02
Clearwater (city) Pinellas	23	0.02

Place (place type) County	Number	%
Gainesville (city) Alachua	23	0.02
Brandon (cdp) Hillsborough	22	0.03
Cape Coral (city) Lee	22	0.02
Fort Lauderdale (city) Broward	22	0.01
Hollywood (city) Broward	21	0.02

Top 10 Places Sorted by Percent
Based on all places, regardless of population

Place (place type) County	Number	%
Cypress Quarters (cdp) Okeechobee	5	0.43
Lacoochee (cdp) Pasco	5	0.37
Micanopy (town) Alachua	2	0.31
Woodville (cdp) Leon	7	0.23
Tavernier (cdp) Monroe	5	0.23
Cottondale (town) Jackson	2	0.23
Sopchoppy (city) Wakulla	1	0.23
North Redington Beach (town) Pinellas	3	0.20
Hernando Beach (cdp) Hernando	4	0.18
Laurel Hill (city) Okaloosa	1	0.18

Top 10 Places Sorted by Percent
Based on places with populations of 10,000 or more

Place (place type) County	Number	%
Bellview (cdp) Escambia	20	0.09
Warrington (cdp) Escambia	14	0.09
Destin (city) Okaloosa	10	0.09
Niceville (city) Okaloosa	10	0.09
Brent (cdp) Escambia	16	0.07
Edgewater (city) Volusia	13	0.07
Ferry Pass (cdp) Escambia	15	0.06
Eustis (city) Lake	9	0.06
Winter Garden (city) Orange	8	0.06
Lakeland Highlands (cdp) Polk	7	0.06

American Indian: Colville

Top 10 Places Sorted by Number
Based on all places, regardless of population

Place (place type) County	Number	%
Jacksonville (special city) Duval	3	0.00
Orlando (city) Orange	2	0.00
North Sarasota (cdp) Sarasota	1	0.01
Warrington (cdp) Escambia	1	0.01
Bellview (cdp) Escambia	1	0.00
St. Petersburg (city) Pinellas	1	0.00
Tampa (city) Hillsborough	1	0.00

Top 10 Places Sorted by Percent
Based on all places, regardless of population

Place (place type) County	Number	%
North Sarasota (cdp) Sarasota	1	0.01
Warrington (cdp) Escambia	1	0.01
Jacksonville (special city) Duval	3	0.00
Orlando (city) Orange	2	0.00
Bellview (cdp) Escambia	1	0.00
St. Petersburg (city) Pinellas	1	0.00
Tampa (city) Hillsborough	1	0.00

Top 10 Places Sorted by Percent
Based on places with populations of 10,000 or more

Place (place type) County	Number	%
Warrington (cdp) Escambia	1	0.01
Jacksonville (special city) Duval	3	0.00
Orlando (city) Orange	2	0.00
Bellview (cdp) Escambia	1	0.00
St. Petersburg (city) Pinellas	1	0.00
Tampa (city) Hillsborough	1	0.00

Notes: (cdp) census designated place; Refer to the User's Guide in the front of the book for more detailed information.

American Indian: Comanche

Top 10 Places Sorted by Number
Based on all places, regardless of population

Place (place type) County	Number	%
Jacksonville (special city) Duval	12	0.00
St. Petersburg (city) Pinellas	12	0.00
Tallahassee (city) Leon	5	0.00
Tampa (city) Hillsborough	5	0.00
Mango (cdp) Hillsborough	4	0.05
Atlantic Beach (city) Duval	4	0.03
Dania Beach (city) Broward	4	0.02
New Smyrna Beach (city) Volusia	4	0.02
Palm River-Clair Mel (cdp) Hillsborough	4	0.02
West and East Lealman (cdp) Pinellas	4	0.02

Top 10 Places Sorted by Percent
Based on all places, regardless of population

Place (place type) County	Number	%
Masaryktown (cdp) Hernando	1	0.11
Geneva (cdp) Seminole	2	0.08
Rolling Oaks (cdp) Broward	1	0.08
St. Augustine Beach (city) St. Johns	3	0.06
Baldwin (town) Duval	1	0.06
Mango (cdp) Hillsborough	4	0.05
Dunnellon (city) Marion	1	0.05
Bithlo (cdp) Orange	2	0.04
Parker (city) Bay	2	0.04
Mount Plymouth (cdp) Lake	1	0.04

Top 10 Places Sorted by Percent
Based on places with populations of 10,000 or more

Place (place type) County	Number	%
Atlantic Beach (city) Duval	4	0.03
Dania Beach (city) Broward	4	0.02
New Smyrna Beach (city) Volusia	4	0.02
Palm River-Clair Mel (cdp) Hillsborough	4	0.02
West and East Lealman (cdp) Pinellas	4	0.02
Conway (cdp) Orange	3	0.02
Gulfport (city) Pinellas	3	0.02
Myrtle Grove (cdp) Escambia	3	0.02
Riverview (cdp) Hillsborough	3	0.02
Zephyrhills (city) Pasco	2	0.02

American Indian: Cree

Top 10 Places Sorted by Number
Based on all places, regardless of population

Place (place type) County	Number	%
Jacksonville (special city) Duval	10	0.00
St. Petersburg (city) Pinellas	10	0.00
Tampa (city) Hillsborough	9	0.00
Egypt Lake-Leto (cdp) Hillsborough	8	0.02
Pinellas Park (city) Pinellas	7	0.02
Lake Lorraine (cdp) Okaloosa	6	0.08
Cape Coral (city) Lee	6	0.01
Melbourne (city) Brevard	5	0.01
Pace (cdp) Santa Rosa	4	0.05
Daytona Beach (city) Volusia	4	0.01

Top 10 Places Sorted by Percent
Based on all places, regardless of population

Place (place type) County	Number	%
Micanopy (town) Alachua	2	0.31
Juno Ridge (cdp) Palm Beach	1	0.13
Blountstown (city) Calhoun	3	0.12
Dover (cdp) Hillsborough	3	0.11
Mexico Beach (city) Bay	1	0.10
Weeki Wachee Gardens (cdp) Hernando	1	0.09
Lake Lorraine (cdp) Okaloosa	6	0.08
Lower Grand Lagoon (cdp) Bay	3	0.07
Pace (cdp) Santa Rosa	4	0.05
Belle Isle (city) Orange	2	0.04

Top 10 Places Sorted by Percent
Based on places with populations of 10,000 or more

Place (place type) County	Number	%
Destin (city) Okaloosa	3	0.03
Egypt Lake-Leto (cdp) Hillsborough	8	0.02
Pinellas Park (city) Pinellas	7	0.02
Marathon (city) Monroe	2	0.02
St. Augustine (city) St. Johns	2	0.02
Cape Coral (city) Lee	6	0.01
Melbourne (city) Brevard	5	0.01
Daytona Beach (city) Volusia	4	0.01
Ferry Pass (cdp) Escambia	4	0.01
Panama City (city) Bay	4	0.01

American Indian: Creek

Top 10 Places Sorted by Number
Based on all places, regardless of population

Place (place type) County	Number	%
Jacksonville (special city) Duval	188	0.03
Pensacola (city) Escambia	160	0.28
West Pensacola (cdp) Escambia	150	0.68
Bellview (cdp) Escambia	135	0.64
Ensley (cdp) Escambia	125	0.67
Ferry Pass (cdp) Escambia	108	0.40
Tallahassee (city) Leon	107	0.07
Brent (cdp) Escambia	98	0.44
Warrington (cdp) Escambia	89	0.59
Pace (cdp) Santa Rosa	88	1.19

Top 10 Places Sorted by Percent
Based on all places, regardless of population

Place (place type) County	Number	%
Ebro (town) Washington	37	14.80
Freeport (city) Walton	34	2.86
Ponce de Leon (town) Holmes	9	1.97
Esto (town) Holmes	7	1.97
Vernon (city) Washington	14	1.88
Paxton (town) Walton	12	1.83
Pittman (cdp) Lake	3	1.56
Grand Ridge (town) Jackson	12	1.52
Wausau (town) Washington	5	1.26
Pace (cdp) Santa Rosa	88	1.19

Top 10 Places Sorted by Percent
Based on places with populations of 10,000 or more

Place (place type) County	Number	%
West Pensacola (cdp) Escambia	150	0.68
Ensley (cdp) Escambia	125	0.67
Bellview (cdp) Escambia	135	0.64
Gonzalez (cdp) Escambia	71	0.62
Warrington (cdp) Escambia	89	0.59
Brent (cdp) Escambia	98	0.44
Myrtle Grove (cdp) Escambia	76	0.44
Ferry Pass (cdp) Escambia	108	0.40
Lynn Haven (city) Bay	44	0.35
Pensacola (city) Escambia	160	0.28

American Indian: Crow

Top 10 Places Sorted by Number
Based on all places, regardless of population

Place (place type) County	Number	%
Jacksonville (special city) Duval	7	0.00
Lake City (city) Columbia	5	0.05
Fort Pierce (city) St. Lucie	5	0.01
Hollywood (city) Broward	5	0.00
St. Petersburg (city) Pinellas	5	0.00
Lake Worth Corridor (cdp) Palm Beach	4	0.02
Lake Worth (city) Palm Beach	3	0.01
Sanford (city) Seminole	3	0.01
The Crossings (cdp) Miami-Dade	3	0.01

(Vero Beach / Delaware column)

Place (place type) County	Number	%
Vero Beach South (cdp) Indian River	3	0.01

Top 10 Places Sorted by Percent
Based on all places, regardless of population

Place (place type) County	Number	%
Oak Hill (city) Volusia	1	0.07
Lake City (city) Columbia	5	0.05
Pine Manor (cdp) Lee	2	0.05
Fish Hawk (cdp) Hillsborough	1	0.05
Tedder (cdp) Broward	1	0.05
Fort Pierce South (cdp) St. Lucie	2	0.04
Harlem (cdp) Hendry	1	0.04
Lake Worth Corridor (cdp) Palm Beach	4	0.02
Hernando (cdp) Citrus	2	0.02
Middleburg (cdp) Clay	2	0.02

Top 10 Places Sorted by Percent
Based on places with populations of 10,000 or more

Place (place type) County	Number	%
Lake Worth Corridor (cdp) Palm Beach	4	0.02
Middleburg (cdp) Clay	2	0.02
Riverview (cdp) Hillsborough	2	0.02
Fort Pierce (city) St. Lucie	5	0.01
Lake Worth (city) Palm Beach	3	0.01
Sanford (city) Seminole	3	0.01
The Crossings (cdp) Miami-Dade	3	0.01
Vero Beach South (cdp) Indian River	3	0.01
Bellair-Meadowbrook Terrace (cdp) Clay	2	0.01
Fruit Cove (cdp) St. Johns	2	0.01

American Indian: Delaware

Top 10 Places Sorted by Number
Based on all places, regardless of population

Place (place type) County	Number	%
St. Petersburg (city) Pinellas	12	0.00
Jacksonville (special city) Duval	10	0.00
Tallahassee (city) Leon	9	0.01
Port Orange (city) Volusia	7	0.02
Deltona (city) Volusia	7	0.01
Union Park (cdp) Orange	5	0.05
Elfers (cdp) Pasco	5	0.04
Cape Coral (city) Lee	5	0.01
Tyndall AFB (cdp) Bay	4	0.15
Cape Canaveral (city) Brevard	4	0.05

Top 10 Places Sorted by Percent
Based on all places, regardless of population

Place (place type) County	Number	%
Tyndall AFB (cdp) Bay	4	0.15
Hilliard (town) Nassau	3	0.11
Gandy (cdp) Pinellas	2	0.10
Big Coppitt Key (cdp) Monroe	2	0.08
Astatula (town) Lake	1	0.08
Inverness Highlands North (cdp) Citrus	1	0.07
Pompano Estates (cdp) Broward	2	0.06
Sharpes (cdp) Brevard	2	0.06
Union Park (cdp) Orange	5	0.05
Cape Canaveral (city) Brevard	4	0.05

Top 10 Places Sorted by Percent
Based on places with populations of 10,000 or more

Place (place type) County	Number	%
Union Park (cdp) Orange	5	0.05
Elfers (cdp) Pasco	5	0.04
Port Orange (city) Volusia	7	0.02
New Port Richey (city) Pasco	3	0.02
Palm Valley (cdp) St. Johns	3	0.02
Sebastian (city) Indian River	3	0.02
Fruitville (cdp) Sarasota	2	0.02
Gulfport (city) Pinellas	2	0.02
Oldsmar (city) Pinellas	2	0.02

Notes: (cdp) census designated place; Refer to the User's Guide in the front of the book for more detailed information.

American Indian: Houma

Top 10 Places Sorted by Number
Based on all places, regardless of population

Place (place type) County	Number	%
Jacksonville (special city) Duval	14	0.00
Bellview (cdp) Escambia	11	0.05
Warrington (cdp) Escambia	5	0.03
Gainesville (city) Alachua	5	0.01
Tampa (city) Hillsborough	5	0.00
Auburndale (city) Polk	4	0.04
Brent (cdp) Escambia	4	0.02
West Pensacola (cdp) Escambia	4	0.02
Riverland Village (cdp) Broward	3	0.14
Panama City Beach (city) Bay	3	0.04

Top 10 Places Sorted by Percent
Based on all places, regardless of population

Place (place type) County	Number	%
Riverland Village (cdp) Broward	3	0.14
North De Land (cdp) Volusia	1	0.08
Bellview (cdp) Escambia	11	0.05
Auburndale (city) Polk	4	0.04
Panama City Beach (city) Bay	3	0.04
Villano Beach (cdp) St. Johns	1	0.04
Warrington (cdp) Escambia	5	0.03
High Point (cdp) Hernando	1	0.03
Wesley Chapel South (cdp) Pasco	1	0.03
Brent (cdp) Escambia	4	0.02

Top 10 Places Sorted by Percent
Based on places with populations of 10,000 or more

Place (place type) County	Number	%
Bellview (cdp) Escambia	11	0.05
Auburndale (city) Polk	4	0.04
Warrington (cdp) Escambia	5	0.03
Brent (cdp) Escambia	4	0.02
West Pensacola (cdp) Escambia	4	0.02
Myrtle Grove (cdp) Escambia	3	0.02
Lynn Haven (city) Bay	2	0.02
Gainesville (city) Alachua	5	0.01
Wellington (village) Palm Beach	3	0.01
Bayonet Point (cdp) Pasco	2	0.01

American Indian: Iroquois

Top 10 Places Sorted by Number
Based on all places, regardless of population

Place (place type) County	Number	%
Jacksonville (special city) Duval	131	0.02
Tampa (city) Hillsborough	77	0.03
St. Petersburg (city) Pinellas	67	0.03
Orlando (city) Orange	41	0.02
Cape Coral (city) Lee	38	0.04
West and East Lealman (cdp) Pinellas	37	0.17
Clearwater (city) Pinellas	36	0.03
Palm Bay (city) Brevard	32	0.04
Pinellas Park (city) Pinellas	31	0.07
Largo (city) Pinellas	31	0.04

Top 10 Places Sorted by Percent
Based on all places, regardless of population

Place (place type) County	Number	%
East Williston (cdp) Levy	10	1.04
Ebro (town) Washington	1	0.40
Big Coppitt Key (cdp) Monroe	9	0.35
Mexico Beach (city) Bay	3	0.29
Webster (city) Sumter	2	0.25
Lake Panasoffkee (cdp) Sumter	8	0.23
Fruitland Park (city) Lake	7	0.22

Top 10 Places Sorted by Percent
Based on places with populations of 10,000 or more

Place (place type) County	Number	%
West and East Lealman (cdp) Pinellas	37	0.17
New Smyrna Beach (city) Volusia	16	0.08
Myrtle Grove (cdp) Escambia	13	0.08
Middleburg (cdp) Clay	8	0.08
Pinellas Park (city) Pinellas	31	0.07
Wright (cdp) Okaloosa	15	0.07
Lockhart (cdp) Orange	9	0.07
Port Orange (city) Volusia	29	0.06
Titusville (city) Brevard	24	0.06
Lehigh Acres (cdp) Lee	20	0.06

American Indian: Kiowa

Top 10 Places Sorted by Number
Based on all places, regardless of population

Place (place type) County	Number	%
Destin (city) Okaloosa	8	0.07
Jacksonville (special city) Duval	6	0.00
Orlovista (cdp) Orange	3	0.05
Palm Bay (city) Brevard	3	0.00
St. Petersburg (city) Pinellas	3	0.00
Citrus Park (cdp) Hillsborough	2	0.01
Fruit Cove (cdp) St. Johns	2	0.01
Lakeside (cdp) Clay	2	0.01
Merritt Island (cdp) Brevard	2	0.01
New Smyrna Beach (city) Volusia	2	0.01

Top 10 Places Sorted by Percent
Based on all places, regardless of population

Place (place type) County	Number	%
Destin (city) Okaloosa	8	0.07
Orlovista (cdp) Orange	3	0.05
Charlotte Harbor (cdp) Charlotte	1	0.03
Woodville (cdp) Leon	1	0.03
Live Oak (city) Suwannee	1	0.02
Citrus Park (cdp) Hillsborough	2	0.01
Fruit Cove (cdp) St. Johns	2	0.01
Lakeside (cdp) Clay	2	0.01
Merritt Island (cdp) Brevard	2	0.01
New Smyrna Beach (city) Volusia	2	0.01

Top 10 Places Sorted by Percent
Based on places with populations of 10,000 or more

Place (place type) County	Number	%
Destin (city) Okaloosa	8	0.07
Citrus Park (cdp) Hillsborough	2	0.01
Fruit Cove (cdp) St. Johns	2	0.01
Lakeside (cdp) Clay	2	0.01
Merritt Island (cdp) Brevard	2	0.01
New Smyrna Beach (city) Volusia	2	0.01
Sebastian (city) Indian River	2	0.01
Holly Hill (city) Volusia	1	0.01
Hudson (cdp) Pasco	1	0.01
Miami Shores (village) Miami-Dade	1	0.01

American Indian: Latin American Indians

Top 10 Places Sorted by Number
Based on all places, regardless of population

Place (place type) County	Number	%
Miami (city) Miami-Dade	535	0.15
Lake Worth (city) Palm Beach	318	0.91
West Palm Beach (city) Palm Beach	265	0.32
Tampa (city) Hillsborough	226	0.07
Hialeah (city) Miami-Dade	178	0.08

(continued)

	Number	%
Southeast Arcadia (cdp) De Soto	118	1.95
Homestead (city) Miami-Dade	104	0.33

Top 10 Places Sorted by Percent
Based on all places, regardless of population

Place (place type) County	Number	%
Indiantown (cdp) Martin	156	2.79
Southeast Arcadia (cdp) De Soto	118	1.95
Lake Worth (city) Palm Beach	318	0.91
Eagle Lake (city) Polk	22	0.88
Wimauma (cdp) Hillsborough	31	0.73
Tice (cdp) Lee	30	0.66
Wabasso (cdp) Indian River	6	0.65
Dover (cdp) Hillsborough	18	0.64
North De Land (cdp) Volusia	7	0.53
Lacoochee (cdp) Pasco	7	0.52

Top 10 Places Sorted by Percent
Based on places with populations of 10,000 or more

Place (place type) County	Number	%
Lake Worth (city) Palm Beach	318	0.91
Lake Worth Corridor (cdp) Palm Beach	64	0.34
Homestead (city) Miami-Dade	104	0.33
West Palm Beach (city) Palm Beach	265	0.32
Princeton (cdp) Miami-Dade	24	0.24
Yeehaw Junction (cdp) Osceola	50	0.23
Golden Gate (cdp) Collier	44	0.21
Meadow Woods (cdp) Orange	22	0.19
Goldenrod (cdp) Seminole	23	0.18
Stuart (city) Martin	25	0.17

American Indian: Lumbee

Top 10 Places Sorted by Number
Based on all places, regardless of population

Place (place type) County	Number	%
Jacksonville (special city) Duval	108	0.01
St. Petersburg (city) Pinellas	22	0.01
Tampa (city) Hillsborough	18	0.01
Lakeside (cdp) Clay	10	0.03
Ocala (city) Marion	10	0.02
Merritt Island (cdp) Brevard	9	0.02
Port Orange (city) Volusia	9	0.02
Cocoa (city) Brevard	8	0.05
Ensley (cdp) Escambia	8	0.04
Clearwater (city) Pinellas	8	0.01

Top 10 Places Sorted by Percent
Based on all places, regardless of population

Place (place type) County	Number	%
Winter Beach (cdp) Indian River	4	0.41
Lake Placid (town) Highlands	6	0.36
Davenport (city) Polk	6	0.31
Branford (town) Suwannee	2	0.29
Webster (city) Sumter	2	0.25
Placid Lakes (cdp) Highlands	5	0.16
Pine Lakes (cdp) Lake	1	0.13
Woodville (cdp) Leon	3	0.10
East Lake-Orient Park (cdp) Hillsborough	5	0.09
Newberry (city) Alachua	3	0.09

Top 10 Places Sorted by Percent
Based on places with populations of 10,000 or more

Place (place type) County	Number	%
Cocoa (city) Brevard	8	0.05
Warrington (cdp) Escambia	7	0.05
Gonzalez (cdp) Escambia	6	0.05
Ensley (cdp) Escambia	8	0.04
Lynn Haven (city) Bay	5	0.04

Notes: (cdp) census designated place; Refer to the User's Guide in the front of the book for more detailed information.

Place (place type) County	Number	%
Lakeside (cdp) Clay	10	0.03
North Port (city) Sarasota	7	0.03
St. Cloud (city) Osceola	6	0.03
Fort Walton Beach (city) Okaloosa	5	0.03
Palmetto (city) Manatee	4	0.03

American Indian: Menominee

Top 10 Places Sorted by Number
Based on all places, regardless of population

Place (place type) County	Number	%
Gibsonton (cdp) Hillsborough	5	0.06
Middleburg (cdp) Clay	4	0.04
New Port Richey (city) Pasco	3	0.02
Kissimmee (city) Osceola	3	0.01
North Miami (city) Miami-Dade	3	0.01
Tallahassee (city) Leon	3	0.00
Land O' Lakes (cdp) Pasco	2	0.01
Rockledge (city) Brevard	2	0.01
Sanford (city) Seminole	2	0.01
Wellington (village) Palm Beach	2	0.01

Top 10 Places Sorted by Percent
Based on all places, regardless of population

Place (place type) County	Number	%
Gibsonton (cdp) Hillsborough	5	0.06
Anna Maria (city) Manatee	1	0.06
Middleburg (cdp) Clay	4	0.04
High Springs (city) Alachua	1	0.03
New Port Richey (city) Pasco	3	0.02
Butler Beach (cdp) St. Johns	1	0.02
Floral City (cdp) Citrus	1	0.02
June Park (cdp) Brevard	1	0.02
Zephyrhills West (cdp) Pasco	1	0.02
Kissimmee (city) Osceola	3	0.01

Top 10 Places Sorted by Percent
Based on places with populations of 10,000 or more

Place (place type) County	Number	%
Middleburg (cdp) Clay	4	0.04
New Port Richey (city) Pasco	3	0.02
Kissimmee (city) Osceola	3	0.01
North Miami (city) Miami-Dade	3	0.01
Land O' Lakes (cdp) Pasco	2	0.01
Rockledge (city) Brevard	2	0.01
Sanford (city) Seminole	2	0.01
Wellington (village) Palm Beach	2	0.01
Azalea Park (cdp) Orange	1	0.01
Forest City (cdp) Seminole	1	0.01

American Indian: Navajo

Top 10 Places Sorted by Number
Based on all places, regardless of population

Place (place type) County	Number	%
Jacksonville (special city) Duval	64	0.01
Tampa (city) Hillsborough	18	0.01
Bellair-Meadowbrook Terrace (cdp) Clay	12	0.07
Palm Bay (city) Brevard	12	0.00
Myrtle Grove (cdp) Escambia	10	0.06
Gainesville (city) Alachua	10	0.01
Sarasota (city) Sarasota	9	0.02
West Palm Beach (city) Palm Beach	9	0.01
St. Petersburg (city) Pinellas	9	0.00
Bellview (cdp) Escambia	8	0.04

Top 10 Places Sorted by Percent
Based on all places, regardless of population

Place (place type) County	Number	%
Pine Manor (cdp) Lee	4	0.11
Bronson (town) Levy	1	0.10
Schall Circle (cdp) Palm Beach	1	0.10

Place (place type) County	Number	%
Eglin AFB (cdp) Okaloosa	7	0.09
Leisureville (cdp) Broward	1	0.09
Chipley (city) Washington	3	0.08
Lauderdale-by-the-Sea (town) Broward	2	0.08
Molino (cdp) Escambia	1	0.08
Bellair-Meadowbrook Terrace (cdp) Clay	12	0.07
Lakewood Park (cdp) St. Lucie	7	0.07

Top 10 Places Sorted by Percent
Based on places with populations of 10,000 or more

Place (place type) County	Number	%
Bellair-Meadowbrook Terrace (cdp) Clay	12	0.07
Lakewood Park (cdp) St. Lucie	7	0.07
Myrtle Grove (cdp) Escambia	10	0.06
Lockhart (cdp) Orange	6	0.05
Bellview (cdp) Escambia	8	0.04
Callaway (city) Bay	5	0.04
Lakeside (cdp) Clay	8	0.03
Brent (cdp) Escambia	6	0.03
Bartow (city) Polk	5	0.03
Palm Bay (city) Brevard	12	0.02

American Indian: Osage

Top 10 Places Sorted by Number
Based on all places, regardless of population

Place (place type) County	Number	%
Jacksonville (special city) Duval	14	0.00
Tampa (city) Hillsborough	14	0.00
St. Petersburg (city) Pinellas	11	0.00
Deltona (city) Volusia	5	0.01
Zephyrhills (city) Pasco	4	0.04
Wright (cdp) Okaloosa	4	0.02
Lauderdale Lakes (city) Broward	4	0.01
Pinellas Park (city) Pinellas	4	0.01
Port St. Lucie (city) St. Lucie	4	0.00
Nassau Village-Ratliff (cdp) Nassau	3	0.06

Top 10 Places Sorted by Percent
Based on all places, regardless of population

Place (place type) County	Number	%
Captiva (cdp) Lee	1	0.26
Greenwood (town) Jackson	1	0.14
Gun Club Estates (cdp) Palm Beach	1	0.14
Nassau Village-Ratliff (cdp) Nassau	3	0.06
Riverland Village (cdp) Broward	1	0.05
Zephyrhills (city) Pasco	4	0.04
South Patrick Shores (cdp) Brevard	3	0.03
Longboat Key (town) Sarasota	2	0.03
Milton (city) Santa Rosa	2	0.03
Indian River Shores (town) Indian River	1	0.03

Top 10 Places Sorted by Percent
Based on places with populations of 10,000 or more

Place (place type) County	Number	%
Zephyrhills (city) Pasco	4	0.04
Wright (cdp) Okaloosa	4	0.02
Florida Ridge (cdp) Indian River	3	0.02
Cocoa Beach (city) Brevard	2	0.02
Deltona (city) Volusia	5	0.01
Lauderdale Lakes (city) Broward	4	0.01
Pinellas Park (city) Pinellas	4	0.01
De Land (city) Volusia	3	0.01
Fort Myers (city) Lee	3	0.01
Kissimmee (city) Osceola	3	0.01

American Indian: Ottawa

Top 10 Places Sorted by Number
Based on all places, regardless of population

Place (place type) County	Number	%
Jacksonville (special city) Duval	12	0.00

Place (place type) County	Number	%
Clearwater (city) Pinellas	8	0.01
Frostproof (city) Polk	5	0.17
Punta Gorda (city) Charlotte	5	0.03
Tyndall AFB (cdp) Bay	4	0.15
Inverness Highlands South (cdp) Citrus	4	0.07
Hudson (cdp) Pasco	4	0.03
Valparaiso (city) Okaloosa	3	0.05
Jasmine Estates (cdp) Pasco	3	0.02
Apopka (city) Orange	3	0.01

Top 10 Places Sorted by Percent
Based on all places, regardless of population

Place (place type) County	Number	%
Matlacha Isles-Matlacha Shores (cdp) Lee	1	0.33
Frostproof (city) Polk	5	0.17
Tyndall AFB (cdp) Bay	4	0.15
Gotha (cdp) Orange	1	0.14
Lake Kathryn (cdp) Lake	1	0.12
Eagle Lake (city) Polk	2	0.08
Seminole Manor (cdp) Palm Beach	2	0.08
Inverness Highlands South (cdp) Citrus	4	0.07
Belleair Beach (city) Pinellas	1	0.06
Valparaiso (city) Okaloosa	3	0.05

Top 10 Places Sorted by Percent
Based on places with populations of 10,000 or more

Place (place type) County	Number	%
Punta Gorda (city) Charlotte	5	0.03
Hudson (cdp) Pasco	4	0.03
Jasmine Estates (cdp) Pasco	3	0.02
Iona (cdp) Lee	2	0.02
Westchase (cdp) Hillsborough	2	0.02
Wilton Manors (city) Broward	2	0.02
Clearwater (city) Pinellas	8	0.01
Apopka (city) Orange	3	0.01
North Fort Myers (cdp) Lee	3	0.01
Tamarac (city) Broward	3	0.01

American Indian: Paiute

Top 10 Places Sorted by Number
Based on all places, regardless of population

Place (place type) County	Number	%
Jacksonville (special city) Duval	6	0.00
Bellview (cdp) Escambia	4	0.02
Warrington (cdp) Escambia	3	0.02
West Pensacola (cdp) Escambia	3	0.01
Hollywood (city) Broward	3	0.00
Orlando (city) Orange	3	0.00
Davie (town) Broward	2	0.00
Pinellas Park (city) Pinellas	2	0.00
St. Petersburg (city) Pinellas	2	0.00
Sarasota (city) Sarasota	2	0.00

Top 10 Places Sorted by Percent
Based on all places, regardless of population

Place (place type) County	Number	%
Malone (town) Jackson	1	0.05
Bellview (cdp) Escambia	4	0.02
Warrington (cdp) Escambia	3	0.02
Sky Lake (cdp) Orange	1	0.02
Vamo (cdp) Sarasota	1	0.02
West Pensacola (cdp) Escambia	3	0.01
Callaway (city) Bay	1	0.01
Cutler (cdp) Miami-Dade	1	0.01
Homosassa Springs (cdp) Citrus	1	0.01
Hudson (cdp) Pasco	1	0.01

Top 10 Places Sorted by Percent
Based on places with populations of 10,000 or more

Place (place type) County	Number	%
Bellview (cdp) Escambia	4	0.02

Notes: (cdp) census designated place; Refer to the User's Guide in the front of the book for more detailed information.

Place (place type) County	Number	%
Warrington (cdp) Escambia	3	0.02
West Pensacola (cdp) Escambia	3	0.01
Callaway (city) Bay	1	0.01
Cutler (cdp) Miami-Dade	1	0.01
Homosassa Springs (cdp) Citrus	1	0.01
Hudson (cdp) Pasco	1	0.01
Pinecrest (village) Miami-Dade	1	0.01
Winter Garden (city) Orange	1	0.01
Jacksonville (special city) Duval	6	0.00

American Indian: Pima

Top 10 Places Sorted by Number
Based on all places, regardless of population

Place (place type) County	Number	%
Goulding (cdp) Escambia	3	0.07
Auburndale (city) Polk	3	0.03
Big Coppitt Key (cdp) Monroe	2	0.08
Ormond Beach (city) Volusia	2	0.01
Riviera Beach (city) Palm Beach	2	0.01
Jacksonville (special city) Duval	2	0.00
Indian River Estates (cdp) St. Lucie	1	0.02
Lake Worth Corridor (cdp) Palm Beach	1	0.01
Miami (city) Miami-Dade	1	0.00
North Miami (city) Miami-Dade	1	0.00

Top 10 Places Sorted by Percent
Based on all places, regardless of population

Place (place type) County	Number	%
Big Coppitt Key (cdp) Monroe	2	0.08
Goulding (cdp) Escambia	3	0.07
Auburndale (city) Polk	3	0.03
Indian River Estates (cdp) St. Lucie	1	0.02
Ormond Beach (city) Volusia	2	0.01
Riviera Beach (city) Palm Beach	2	0.01
Lake Worth Corridor (cdp) Palm Beach	1	0.01
Jacksonville (special city) Duval	2	0.00
Miami (city) Miami-Dade	1	0.00
North Miami (city) Miami-Dade	1	0.00

Top 10 Places Sorted by Percent
Based on places with populations of 10,000 or more

Place (place type) County	Number	%
Auburndale (city) Polk	3	0.03
Ormond Beach (city) Volusia	2	0.01
Riviera Beach (city) Palm Beach	2	0.01
Lake Worth Corridor (cdp) Palm Beach	1	0.01
Jacksonville (special city) Duval	2	0.00
Miami (city) Miami-Dade	1	0.00
North Miami (city) Miami-Dade	1	0.00
Tampa (city) Hillsborough	1	0.00

American Indian: Potawatomi

Top 10 Places Sorted by Number
Based on all places, regardless of population

Place (place type) County	Number	%
Cape Coral (city) Lee	13	0.01
Jacksonville (special city) Duval	11	0.00
St. Petersburg (city) Pinellas	8	0.00
Town 'n' Country (cdp) Hillsborough	6	0.01
Goldenrod (cdp) Seminole	5	0.04
Wekiwa Springs (cdp) Seminole	5	0.02
Palm Bay (city) Brevard	5	0.01
Sorrento (cdp) Lake	4	0.52
Beacon Square (cdp) Pasco	4	0.06
Southgate (cdp) Sarasota	4	0.05

Top 10 Places Sorted by Percent
Based on all places, regardless of population

Place (place type) County	Number	%
Sorrento (cdp) Lake	4	0.52

Place (place type) County	Number	%
Three Oaks (cdp) Lee	3	0.13
Palm Shores (town) Brevard	1	0.13
Chuluota (cdp) Seminole	2	0.10
De Land Southwest (cdp) Volusia	1	0.09
Freeport (city) Walton	1	0.08
Zephyrhills South (cdp) Pasco	3	0.07
Frostproof (city) Polk	2	0.07
Beacon Square (cdp) Pasco	4	0.06
Odessa (cdp) Hillsborough	2	0.06

Top 10 Places Sorted by Percent
Based on places with populations of 10,000 or more

Place (place type) County	Number	%
Goldenrod (cdp) Seminole	5	0.04
Niceville (city) Okaloosa	3	0.03
Wekiwa Springs (cdp) Seminole	5	0.02
Bellair-Meadowbrook Terrace (cdp) Clay	4	0.02
Myrtle Grove (cdp) Escambia	4	0.02
New Smyrna Beach (city) Volusia	4	0.02
Fruitville (cdp) Sarasota	2	0.02
Cape Coral (city) Lee	13	0.01
Town 'n' Country (cdp) Hillsborough	6	0.01
Palm Bay (city) Brevard	5	0.01

American Indian: Pueblo

Top 10 Places Sorted by Number
Based on all places, regardless of population

Place (place type) County	Number	%
Miami (city) Miami-Dade	42	0.01
Pinewood (cdp) Miami-Dade	12	0.07
Tampa (city) Hillsborough	11	0.00
Merritt Island (cdp) Brevard	10	0.03
Hialeah (city) Miami-Dade	10	0.00
Gainesville (city) Alachua	9	0.01
Jacksonville (special city) Duval	9	0.00
Titusville (city) Brevard	8	0.02
Orlando (city) Orange	8	0.00
St. Petersburg (city) Pinellas	8	0.00

Top 10 Places Sorted by Percent
Based on all places, regardless of population

Place (place type) County	Number	%
Homestead Base (cdp) Miami-Dade	1	0.22
Lacoochee (cdp) Pasco	2	0.15
Bithlo (cdp) Orange	5	0.11
Sharpes (cdp) Brevard	3	0.09
St. Augustine South (cdp) St. Johns	4	0.08
Pinewood (cdp) Miami-Dade	12	0.07
Westgate-Belvedere Homes (cdp) Palm Beach	5	0.06
Century (town) Escambia	1	0.06
Roseland (cdp) Indian River	1	0.06
West Samoset (cdp) Manatee	3	0.05

Top 10 Places Sorted by Percent
Based on places with populations of 10,000 or more

Place (place type) County	Number	%
Pinewood (cdp) Miami-Dade	12	0.07
Palmetto (city) Manatee	5	0.04
Jensen Beach (cdp) Martin	4	0.04
Merritt Island (cdp) Brevard	10	0.03
Holiday (cdp) Pasco	6	0.03
Parkland (city) Broward	4	0.03
Titusville (city) Brevard	8	0.02
Lake Worth (city) Palm Beach	7	0.02
Golden Glades (cdp) Miami-Dade	6	0.02
Royal Palm Beach (village) Palm Beach	5	0.02

American Indian: Puget Sound Salish

Top 10 Places Sorted by Number
Based on all places, regardless of population

Place (place type) County	Number	%
Bellview (cdp) Escambia	6	0.03
Bloomingdale (cdp) Hillsborough	6	0.03
Tampa (city) Hillsborough	6	0.00
Panama City (city) Bay	3	0.01
Odessa (cdp) Hillsborough	2	0.06
Eglin AFB (cdp) Okaloosa	2	0.02
Brent (cdp) Escambia	2	0.01
Altamonte Springs (city) Seminole	2	0.00
Cape Coral (city) Lee	2	0.00
Daytona Beach (city) Volusia	2	0.00

Top 10 Places Sorted by Percent
Based on all places, regardless of population

Place (place type) County	Number	%
Odessa (cdp) Hillsborough	2	0.06
Lake Helen (city) Volusia	1	0.04
Bellview (cdp) Escambia	6	0.03
Bloomingdale (cdp) Hillsborough	6	0.03
Eglin AFB (cdp) Okaloosa	2	0.02
Starke (city) Bradford	1	0.02
Panama City (city) Bay	3	0.01
Brent (cdp) Escambia	2	0.01
Port St. John (cdp) Brevard	1	0.01
Princeton (cdp) Miami-Dade	1	0.01

Top 10 Places Sorted by Percent
Based on places with populations of 10,000 or more

Place (place type) County	Number	%
Bellview (cdp) Escambia	6	0.03
Bloomingdale (cdp) Hillsborough	6	0.03
Panama City (city) Bay	3	0.01
Brent (cdp) Escambia	2	0.01
Port St. John (cdp) Brevard	1	0.01
Princeton (cdp) Miami-Dade	1	0.01
South Venice (cdp) Sarasota	1	0.01
Warrington (cdp) Escambia	1	0.01
Tampa (city) Hillsborough	6	0.00
Altamonte Springs (city) Seminole	2	0.00

American Indian: Seminole

Top 10 Places Sorted by Number
Based on all places, regardless of population

Place (place type) County	Number	%
Jacksonville (special city) Duval	124	0.02
Immokalee (cdp) Collier	123	0.62
Tampa (city) Hillsborough	74	0.02
St. Petersburg (city) Pinellas	41	0.02
Hollywood (city) Broward	38	0.03
Orlando (city) Orange	36	0.02
East Lake-Orient Park (cdp) Hillsborough	35	0.61
Davie (town) Broward	27	0.04
Brandon (cdp) Hillsborough	26	0.03
Okeechobee (city) Okeechobee	22	0.41

Top 10 Places Sorted by Percent
Based on all places, regardless of population

Place (place type) County	Number	%
La Crosse (town) Alachua	1	0.70
Immokalee (cdp) Collier	123	0.62
East Lake-Orient Park (cdp) Hillsborough	35	0.61
Reddick (town) Marion	3	0.53
Okeechobee (city) Okeechobee	22	0.41
Paisley (cdp) Lake	3	0.41
St. Lucie (village) St. Lucie	2	0.33
Bell (town) Gilchrist	1	0.29
East Bronson (cdp) Levy	3	0.28
Vernon (city) Washington	2	0.27

Notes: (cdp) census designated place; Refer to the User's Guide in the front of the book for more detailed information.

Top 10 Places Sorted by Percent
Based on places with populations of 10,000 or more

Place (place type) County	Number	%
Immokalee (cdp) Collier	123	0.62
Holly Hill (city) Volusia	8	0.07
Ocoee (city) Orange	14	0.06
Riverview (cdp) Hillsborough	7	0.06
Lake Wales (city) Polk	6	0.06
Middleburg (cdp) Clay	6	0.06
Cocoa Beach (city) Brevard	6	0.05
Upper Grand Lagoon (cdp) Bay	5	0.05
Davie (town) Broward	27	0.04
Sanford (city) Seminole	15	0.04

American Indian: Shoshone

Top 10 Places Sorted by Number
Based on all places, regardless of population

Place (place type) County	Number	%
Jacksonville (special city) Duval	7	0.00
Tampa (city) Hillsborough	7	0.00
Miami (city) Miami-Dade	6	0.00
Longwood (city) Seminole	5	0.04
Pinellas Park (city) Pinellas	5	0.01
Mount Plymouth (cdp) Lake	4	0.14
New Smyrna Beach (city) Volusia	4	0.02
Iona (cdp) Lee	3	0.03
Oldsmar (city) Pinellas	3	0.03
Jupiter (town) Palm Beach	3	0.01

Top 10 Places Sorted by Percent
Based on all places, regardless of population

Place (place type) County	Number	%
Webster (city) Sumter	2	0.25
Page Park (cdp) Lee	1	0.19
Mount Plymouth (cdp) Lake	4	0.14
Hawthorne (city) Alachua	2	0.14
Andrews (cdp) Levy	1	0.14
Christmas (cdp) Orange	1	0.09
Dunnellon (city) Marion	1	0.05
Taft (cdp) Orange	1	0.05
Longwood (city) Seminole	5	0.04
Iona (cdp) Lee	3	0.03

Top 10 Places Sorted by Percent
Based on places with populations of 10,000 or more

Place (place type) County	Number	%
Longwood (city) Seminole	5	0.04
Iona (cdp) Lee	3	0.03
Oldsmar (city) Pinellas	3	0.03
New Smyrna Beach (city) Volusia	4	0.02
Cypress Lake (cdp) Lee	2	0.02
Fernandina Beach (city) Nassau	2	0.02
Pinellas Park (city) Pinellas	5	0.01
Jupiter (town) Palm Beach	3	0.01
Citrus Ridge (cdp) Lake	1	0.01
Conway (cdp) Orange	1	0.01

American Indian: Sioux

Top 10 Places Sorted by Number
Based on all places, regardless of population

Place (place type) County	Number	%
Jacksonville (special city) Duval	108	0.01
St. Petersburg (city) Pinellas	53	0.02
Tampa (city) Hillsborough	44	0.01
Cape Coral (city) Lee	32	0.03
Brandon (cdp) Hillsborough	28	0.04
Melbourne (city) Brevard	25	0.04
Orlando (city) Orange	23	0.01
Tallahassee (city) Leon	21	0.01
Hollywood (city) Broward	18	0.01

| **Sarasota** (city) Sarasota | 17 | 0.03 |

Top 10 Places Sorted by Percent
Based on all places, regardless of population

Place (place type) County	Number	%
Caryville (town) Washington	2	0.92
Christmas (cdp) Orange	4	0.34
Dunes Road (cdp) Palm Beach	1	0.26
Ponce de Leon (town) Holmes	1	0.22
Paxton (town) Walton	1	0.15
Pretty Bayou (cdp) Bay	5	0.14
Greenwood (town) Jackson	1	0.14
Matlacha (cdp) Lee	1	0.14
Apalachicola (city) Franklin	3	0.13
Pine Lakes (cdp) Lake	1	0.13

Top 10 Places Sorted by Percent
Based on places with populations of 10,000 or more

Place (place type) County	Number	%
Gonzalez (cdp) Escambia	10	0.09
Safety Harbor (city) Pinellas	12	0.07
Warrington (cdp) Escambia	11	0.07
South Daytona (city) Volusia	9	0.07
West Pensacola (cdp) Escambia	14	0.06
Lynn Haven (city) Bay	8	0.06
Lakeland Highlands (cdp) Polk	7	0.06
Port St. John (cdp) Brevard	7	0.06
Riverview (cdp) Hillsborough	7	0.06
Bellview (cdp) Escambia	10	0.05

American Indian: Tohono O'Odham

Top 10 Places Sorted by Number
Based on all places, regardless of population

Place (place type) County	Number	%
Big Coppitt Key (cdp) Monroe	7	0.27
Merritt Island (cdp) Brevard	4	0.01
Poinciana (cdp) Osceola	3	0.02
Margate (city) Broward	3	0.01
Deltona (city) Volusia	3	0.00
Fort Pierce (city) St. Lucie	2	0.01
Plantation Mobile Home Park (cdp) Palm Beach	1	0.08
Lakeside Green (cdp) Palm Beach	1	0.03
Fort Walton Beach (city) Okaloosa	1	0.01
Lake Park (town) Palm Beach	1	0.01

Top 10 Places Sorted by Percent
Based on all places, regardless of population

Place (place type) County	Number	%
Big Coppitt Key (cdp) Monroe	7	0.27
Plantation Mobile Home Park (cdp) Palm Beach	1	0.08
Lakeside Green (cdp) Palm Beach	1	0.03
Poinciana (cdp) Osceola	3	0.02
Merritt Island (cdp) Brevard	4	0.01
Margate (city) Broward	3	0.01
Fort Pierce (city) St. Lucie	2	0.01
Fort Walton Beach (city) Okaloosa	1	0.01
Lake Park (town) Palm Beach	1	0.01
Myrtle Grove (cdp) Escambia	1	0.01

Top 10 Places Sorted by Percent
Based on places with populations of 10,000 or more

Place (place type) County	Number	%
Poinciana (cdp) Osceola	3	0.02
Merritt Island (cdp) Brevard	4	0.01
Margate (city) Broward	3	0.01
Fort Pierce (city) St. Lucie	2	0.01
Fort Walton Beach (city) Okaloosa	1	0.01
Myrtle Grove (cdp) Escambia	1	0.01
Deltona (city) Volusia	3	0.00
Bonita Springs (city) Lee	1	0.00
Brandon (cdp) Hillsborough	1	0.00

| **Fort Myers** (city) Lee | 1 | 0.00 |

American Indian: Ute

Top 10 Places Sorted by Number
Based on all places, regardless of population

Place (place type) County	Number	%
Sunrise (city) Broward	4	0.00
Upper Grand Lagoon (cdp) Bay	3	0.03
Poinciana (cdp) Osceola	3	0.02
New Smyrna Beach (city) Volusia	3	0.01
Jacksonville (special city) Duval	3	0.00
Lakeland (city) Polk	3	0.00
Cutler Ridge (cdp) Miami-Dade	2	0.01
Daytona Beach (city) Volusia	2	0.00
Bushnell (city) Sumter	1	0.05
Asbury Lake (cdp) Clay	1	0.04

Top 10 Places Sorted by Percent
Based on all places, regardless of population

Place (place type) County	Number	%
Bushnell (city) Sumter	1	0.05
Asbury Lake (cdp) Clay	1	0.04
Blountstown (city) Calhoun	1	0.04
Upper Grand Lagoon (cdp) Bay	3	0.03
Poinciana (cdp) Osceola	3	0.02
New Smyrna Beach (city) Volusia	3	0.01
Cutler Ridge (cdp) Miami-Dade	2	0.01
Crestview (city) Okaloosa	1	0.01
Gulf Gate Estates (cdp) Sarasota	1	0.01
Lighthouse Point (city) Broward	1	0.01

Top 10 Places Sorted by Percent
Based on places with populations of 10,000 or more

Place (place type) County	Number	%
Upper Grand Lagoon (cdp) Bay	3	0.03
Poinciana (cdp) Osceola	3	0.02
New Smyrna Beach (city) Volusia	3	0.01
Cutler Ridge (cdp) Miami-Dade	2	0.01
Crestview (city) Okaloosa	1	0.01
Gulf Gate Estates (cdp) Sarasota	1	0.01
Lighthouse Point (city) Broward	1	0.01
Niceville (city) Okaloosa	1	0.01
Sunrise (city) Broward	4	0.00
Jacksonville (special city) Duval	3	0.00

American Indian: Yakama

Top 10 Places Sorted by Number
Based on all places, regardless of population

Place (place type) County	Number	%
Fort Myers (city) Lee	6	0.01
Lauderdale Lakes (city) Broward	4	0.01
Sanford (city) Seminole	3	0.01
Palm River-Clair Mel (cdp) Hillsborough	2	0.01
Masarytown (cdp) Hernando	1	0.11
Hilliard (town) Nassau	1	0.04
Eustis (city) Lake	1	0.01
Riverview (cdp) Hillsborough	1	0.01
Sebastian (city) Indian River	1	0.01
Springfield (city) Bay	1	0.01

Top 10 Places Sorted by Percent
Based on all places, regardless of population

Place (place type) County	Number	%
Masarytown (cdp) Hernando	1	0.11
Hilliard (town) Nassau	1	0.04
Fort Myers (city) Lee	6	0.01
Lauderdale Lakes (city) Broward	4	0.01
Sanford (city) Seminole	3	0.01
Palm River-Clair Mel (cdp) Hillsborough	2	0.01
Eustis (city) Lake	1	0.01

Notes: (cdp) census designated place; Refer to the User's Guide in the front of the book for more detailed information.

Place (place type) County	Number	%
Riverview (cdp) Hillsborough	1	0.01
Sebastian (city) Indian River	1	0.01
Springfield (city) Bay	1	0.01

Top 10 Places Sorted by Percent
Based on places with populations of 10,000 or more

Place (place type) County	Number	%
Fort Myers (city) Lee	6	0.01
Lauderdale Lakes (city) Broward	4	0.01
Sanford (city) Seminole	3	0.01
Palm River-Clair Mel (cdp) Hillsborough	2	0.01
Eustis (city) Lake	1	0.01
Riverview (cdp) Hillsborough	1	0.01
Sebastian (city) Indian River	1	0.01
Winter Garden (city) Orange	1	0.01
Daytona Beach (city) Volusia	1	0.00
Deerfield Beach (city) Broward	1	0.00

American Indian: Yaqui

Top 10 Places Sorted by Number
Based on all places, regardless of population

Place (place type) County	Number	%
Jacksonville (special city) Duval	12	0.00
Casselberry (city) Seminole	11	0.05
West Vero Corridor (cdp) Indian River	6	0.08
Orlando (city) Orange	6	0.00
Hudson (cdp) Pasco	4	0.03
Daytona Beach (city) Volusia	4	0.01
Melbourne (city) Brevard	4	0.01
St. Augustine Shores (cdp) St. Johns	3	0.06
Eglin AFB (cdp) Okaloosa	3	0.04
Hallandale (city) Broward	3	0.01

Top 10 Places Sorted by Percent
Based on all places, regardless of population

Place (place type) County	Number	%
West Vero Corridor (cdp) Indian River	6	0.08
Laguna Beach (cdp) Bay	2	0.07
St. Augustine Shores (cdp) St. Johns	3	0.06
Casselberry (city) Seminole	11	0.05
Eglin AFB (cdp) Okaloosa	3	0.04
Hudson (cdp) Pasco	4	0.03
Medulla (cdp) Polk	2	0.03
Bay Hill (cdp) Orange	1	0.02
Labelle (city) Hendry	1	0.02
North Weeki Wachee (cdp) Hernando	1	0.02

Top 10 Places Sorted by Percent
Based on places with populations of 10,000 or more

Place (place type) County	Number	%
Casselberry (city) Seminole	11	0.05
Hudson (cdp) Pasco	4	0.03
Daytona Beach (city) Volusia	4	0.01
Melbourne (city) Brevard	4	0.01
Hallandale (city) Broward	3	0.01
Palm Harbor (cdp) Pinellas	3	0.01
Greenacres (city) Palm Beach	2	0.01
Naples (city) Collier	2	0.01
Sanford (city) Seminole	2	0.01
Azalea Park (cdp) Orange	1	0.01

American Indian: Yuman

Top 10 Places Sorted by Number
Based on all places, regardless of population

Place (place type) County	Number	%
Tampa (city) Hillsborough	3	0.00
Ebro (town) Washington	2	0.80
North Fort Myers (cdp) Lee	2	0.00
West Palm Beach (city) Palm Beach	2	0.00
St. Augustine South (cdp) St. Johns	1	0.02

Place (place type) County	Number	%
Cape Canaveral (city) Brevard	1	0.01
Fern Park (cdp) Seminole	1	0.01
Indian Harbour Beach (city) Brevard	1	0.01
Lockhart (cdp) Orange	1	0.01
Palm Springs (village) Palm Beach	1	0.01

Top 10 Places Sorted by Percent
Based on all places, regardless of population

Place (place type) County	Number	%
Ebro (town) Washington	2	0.80
St. Augustine South (cdp) St. Johns	1	0.02
Cape Canaveral (city) Brevard	1	0.01
Fern Park (cdp) Seminole	1	0.01
Indian Harbour Beach (city) Brevard	1	0.01
Lockhart (cdp) Orange	1	0.01
Palm Springs (village) Palm Beach	1	0.01
Tampa (city) Hillsborough	3	0.00
North Fort Myers (cdp) Lee	2	0.00
West Palm Beach (city) Palm Beach	2	0.00

Top 10 Places Sorted by Percent
Based on places with populations of 10,000 or more

Place (place type) County	Number	%
Lockhart (cdp) Orange	1	0.01
Palm Springs (village) Palm Beach	1	0.01
Tampa (city) Hillsborough	3	0.00
North Fort Myers (cdp) Lee	2	0.00
West Palm Beach (city) Palm Beach	2	0.00
Clearwater (city) Pinellas	1	0.00
Coconut Creek (city) Broward	1	0.00
Deltona (city) Volusia	1	0.00
Fort Lauderdale (city) Broward	1	0.00
Jacksonville (special city) Duval	1	0.00

American Indian: All other tribes

Top 10 Places Sorted by Number
Based on all places, regardless of population

Place (place type) County	Number	%
Jacksonville (special city) Duval	275	0.04
St. Petersburg (city) Pinellas	141	0.06
Tampa (city) Hillsborough	87	0.03
Miami (city) Miami-Dade	70	0.02
Orlando (city) Orange	67	0.04
Brandon (cdp) Hillsborough	42	0.05
Port St. Lucie (city) St. Lucie	40	0.05
Fort Lauderdale (city) Broward	40	0.03
Palm Bay (city) Brevard	37	0.05
Clearwater (city) Pinellas	36	0.03

Top 10 Places Sorted by Percent
Based on all places, regardless of population

Place (place type) County	Number	%
Beverly Beach (town) Flagler	3	0.55
Wausau (town) Washington	2	0.50
Williston (city) Levy	10	0.44
Ponce de Leon (town) Holmes	2	0.44
Crescent Beach (cdp) St. Johns	4	0.41
South Brooksville (cdp) Hernando	5	0.36
Mary Esther (city) Okaloosa	14	0.35
Chula Vista (cdp) Broward	2	0.35
Interlachen (town) Putnam	5	0.34
Crooked Lake Park (cdp) Polk	5	0.30

Top 10 Places Sorted by Percent
Based on places with populations of 10,000 or more

Place (place type) County	Number	%
Middleburg (cdp) Clay	16	0.15
Homosassa Springs (cdp) Citrus	18	0.14
Bloomingdale (cdp) Hillsborough	25	0.13
West Pensacola (cdp) Escambia	24	0.11
South Bradenton (cdp) Manatee	23	0.11

Place (place type) County	Number	%
Callaway (city) Bay	15	0.11
San Carlos Park (cdp) Lee	17	0.10
Elfers (cdp) Pasco	13	0.10
Gulfport (city) Pinellas	12	0.10
Riverview (cdp) Hillsborough	12	0.10

American Indian tribes, not specified

Top 10 Places Sorted by Number
Based on all places, regardless of population

Place (place type) County	Number	%
Jacksonville (special city) Duval	288	0.04
Tampa (city) Hillsborough	172	0.06
Miami (city) Miami-Dade	157	0.04
St. Petersburg (city) Pinellas	103	0.04
Orlando (city) Orange	102	0.05
Gainesville (city) Alachua	65	0.07
Hialeah (city) Miami-Dade	59	0.03
Tallahassee (city) Leon	58	0.04
Lakeland (city) Polk	56	0.07
Fort Lauderdale (city) Broward	54	0.04

Top 10 Places Sorted by Percent
Based on all places, regardless of population

Place (place type) County	Number	%
Noma (town) Holmes	3	1.41
Glen Ridge (town) Palm Beach	3	1.09
Lawtey (city) Bradford	7	1.07
Chokoloskee (cdp) Collier	4	0.99
Beverly Beach (town) Flagler	4	0.73
Fort White (town) Columbia	3	0.73
Bristol (city) Liberty	6	0.71
Lake Kathryn (cdp) Lake	4	0.47
Alva (cdp) Lee	10	0.46
Glen St. Mary (town) Baker	2	0.42

Top 10 Places Sorted by Percent
Based on places with populations of 10,000 or more

Place (place type) County	Number	%
Brent (cdp) Escambia	43	0.19
Fort Walton Beach (city) Okaloosa	30	0.15
Callaway (city) Bay	18	0.13
Poinciana (cdp) Osceola	17	0.12
Lockhart (cdp) Orange	16	0.12
South Miami Heights (cdp) Miami-Dade	32	0.10
West and East Lealman (cdp) Pinellas	21	0.10
Lake Worth Corridor (cdp) Palm Beach	18	0.10
Seminole (city) Pinellas	11	0.10
Golden Gate (cdp) Collier	19	0.09

Arab

Top 10 Places Sorted by Number
Based on all places, regardless of population

Place (place type) County	Number	%
Jacksonville (special city) Duval	5,861	0.80
Miami (city) Miami-Dade	1,864	0.51
Orlando (city) Orange	1,693	0.91
Kendall (cdp) Miami-Dade	1,315	1.75
Coral Springs (city) Broward	1,247	1.06
Pembroke Pines (city) Broward	1,230	0.90
St. Petersburg (city) Pinellas	1,229	0.50
Hollywood (city) Broward	1,183	0.85
Tampa (city) Hillsborough	1,118	0.37
Miami Beach (city) Miami-Dade	934	1.06

Top 10 Places Sorted by Percent
Based on all places, regardless of population

Place (place type) County	Number	%
Dunes Road (cdp) Palm Beach	104	21.99
Cloud Lake (town) Palm Beach	5	4.07
Belleair Beach (city) Pinellas	65	3.88

Notes: (cdp) census designated place; Refer to the User's Guide in the front of the book for more detailed information.

Place (place type) County	Number	%
Lake Belvedere Estates (cdp) Palm Beach	49	3.28
Tierra Verde (cdp) Pinellas	116	3.27
Gulf Stream (town) Palm Beach	22	3.18
Wesley Chapel (cdp) Pasco	186	3.16
Doctor Phillips (cdp) Orange	302	3.13
Gateway (cdp) Lee	82	2.70
Surfside (town) Miami-Dade	128	2.50

Top 10 Places Sorted by Percent
Based on places with populations of 10,000 or more

Place (place type) County	Number	%
Pinecrest (village) Miami-Dade	477	2.49
Sunny Isles Beach (city) Miami-Dade	380	2.49
Ojus (cdp) Miami-Dade	365	2.19
Temple Terrace (city) Hillsborough	428	2.05
Aventura (city) Miami-Dade	505	2.00
Kendall (cdp) Miami-Dade	1,315	1.75
Miami Lakes (cdp) Miami-Dade	396	1.74
Ives Estates (cdp) Miami-Dade	297	1.71
Azalea Park (cdp) Orange	189	1.70
Lake Magdalene (cdp) Hillsborough	436	1.51

Arab: Arab/Arabic

Top 10 Places Sorted by Number
Based on all places, regardless of population

Place (place type) County	Number	%
Jacksonville (special city) Duval	1,602	0.22
Tampa (city) Hillsborough	333	0.11
Miami (city) Miami-Dade	333	0.09
Miami Lakes (cdp) Miami-Dade	261	1.15
Orlando (city) Orange	254	0.14
Temple Terrace (city) Hillsborough	231	1.11
Palm Bay (city) Brevard	226	0.28
Pembroke Pines (city) Broward	220	0.16
Kissimmee (city) Osceola	201	0.42
The Hammocks (cdp) Miami-Dade	199	0.42

Top 10 Places Sorted by Percent
Based on all places, regardless of population

Place (place type) County	Number	%
Port La Belle (cdp) Hendry	58	1.79
Wesley Chapel (cdp) Pasco	86	1.46
Palm Shores (town) Brevard	11	1.39
Placid Lakes (cdp) Highlands	35	1.16
Gulf Stream (town) Palm Beach	8	1.16
Miami Lakes (cdp) Miami-Dade	261	1.15
Gateway (cdp) Lee	35	1.15
Shady Hills (cdp) Pasco	87	1.12
Temple Terrace (city) Hillsborough	231	1.11
Haverhill (town) Palm Beach	15	0.98

Top 10 Places Sorted by Percent
Based on places with populations of 10,000 or more

Place (place type) County	Number	%
Miami Lakes (cdp) Miami-Dade	261	1.15
Temple Terrace (city) Hillsborough	231	1.11
Belle Glade (city) Palm Beach	115	0.77
Ives Estates (cdp) Miami-Dade	127	0.73
Sunny Isles Beach (city) Miami-Dade	88	0.58
Sunset (cdp) Miami-Dade	92	0.54
Conway (cdp) Orange	70	0.49
Cooper City (city) Broward	127	0.46
Kissimmee (city) Osceola	201	0.42
The Hammocks (cdp) Miami-Dade	199	0.42

Arab: Egyptian

Top 10 Places Sorted by Number
Based on all places, regardless of population

Place (place type) County	Number	%
Altamonte Springs (city) Seminole	204	0.49

Place (place type) County	Number	%
Coral Springs (city) Broward	189	0.16
Jacksonville (special city) Duval	167	0.02
Ojus (cdp) Miami-Dade	164	0.98
Palm Harbor (cdp) Pinellas	129	0.22
Ormond Beach (city) Volusia	119	0.33
Clearwater (city) Pinellas	119	0.11
Cocoa Beach (city) Brevard	103	0.83
Miami Beach (city) Miami-Dade	100	0.11
Fort Lauderdale (city) Broward	97	0.06

Top 10 Places Sorted by Percent
Based on all places, regardless of population

Place (place type) County	Number	%
Belleair Beach (city) Pinellas	46	2.75
Rolling Oaks (cdp) Broward	23	1.62
Manalapan (town) Palm Beach	5	1.55
Butler Beach (cdp) St. Johns	63	1.39
Ojus (cdp) Miami-Dade	164	0.98
Tierra Verde (cdp) Pinellas	34	0.96
Fern Park (cdp) Seminole	79	0.95
Redington Beach (town) Pinellas	15	0.91
Kendall Green (cdp) Broward	27	0.86
Cocoa Beach (city) Brevard	103	0.83

Top 10 Places Sorted by Percent
Based on places with populations of 10,000 or more

Place (place type) County	Number	%
Ojus (cdp) Miami-Dade	164	0.98
Cocoa Beach (city) Brevard	103	0.83
Sunny Isles Beach (city) Miami-Dade	87	0.57
Altamonte Springs (city) Seminole	204	0.49
Eustis (city) Lake	62	0.40
Pinecrest (village) Miami-Dade	74	0.39
Lake Wales (city) Polk	38	0.37
Cypress Lake (cdp) Lee	44	0.36
Ormond Beach (city) Volusia	119	0.33
Atlantic Beach (city) Duval	44	0.33

Arab: Iraqi

Top 10 Places Sorted by Number
Based on all places, regardless of population

Place (place type) County	Number	%
Jacksonville (special city) Duval	169	0.02
Miami (city) Miami-Dade	89	0.02
Cocoa Beach (city) Brevard	41	0.33
Miami Beach (city) Miami-Dade	41	0.05
West Palm Beach (city) Palm Beach	41	0.05
Clearwater (city) Pinellas	36	0.03
St. Petersburg (city) Pinellas	34	0.01
Cooper City (city) Broward	32	0.12
Meadow Woods (cdp) Orange	30	0.26
Miami Springs (city) Miami-Dade	29	0.21

Top 10 Places Sorted by Percent
Based on all places, regardless of population

Place (place type) County	Number	%
Sea Ranch Lakes (village) Broward	5	0.36
Cocoa Beach (city) Brevard	41	0.33
Meadow Woods (cdp) Orange	30	0.26
Miami Springs (city) Miami-Dade	29	0.21
Palm Beach (town) Palm Beach	21	0.20
Golden Beach (town) Miami-Dade	2	0.19
Cooper City (city) Broward	32	0.12
Fort Myers Beach (town) Lee	8	0.12
Aventura (city) Miami-Dade	27	0.11
Dania Beach (city) Broward	22	0.11

Top 10 Places Sorted by Percent
Based on places with populations of 10,000 or more

Place (place type) County	Number	%
Cocoa Beach (city) Brevard	41	0.33

Place (place type) County	Number	%
Meadow Woods (cdp) Orange	30	0.26
Miami Springs (city) Miami-Dade	29	0.21
Palm Beach (town) Palm Beach	21	0.20
Cooper City (city) Broward	32	0.12
Aventura (city) Miami-Dade	27	0.11
Dania Beach (city) Broward	22	0.11
Cocoa (city) Brevard	16	0.10
Lighthouse Point (city) Broward	9	0.08
Maitland (city) Orange	9	0.08

Arab: Jordanian

Top 10 Places Sorted by Number
Based on all places, regardless of population

Place (place type) County	Number	%
Hollywood (city) Broward	100	0.07
Ojus (cdp) Miami-Dade	91	0.55
Jacksonville (special city) Duval	81	0.01
Lakes by the Bay (cdp) Miami-Dade	64	0.71
Ferry Pass (cdp) Escambia	55	0.20
Oviedo (city) Seminole	55	0.20
Miami (city) Miami-Dade	55	0.02
Coral Springs (city) Broward	53	0.05
University (cdp) Hillsborough	44	0.14
Fort Lauderdale (city) Broward	44	0.03

Top 10 Places Sorted by Percent
Based on all places, regardless of population

Place (place type) County	Number	%
Lake Belvedere Estates (cdp) Palm Beach	35	2.34
Lakes by the Bay (cdp) Miami-Dade	64	0.71
Gulf Stream (town) Palm Beach	4	0.58
Ojus (cdp) Miami-Dade	91	0.55
Golden Lakes (cdp) Palm Beach	22	0.33
Wahneta (cdp) Polk	13	0.27
Ferry Pass (cdp) Escambia	55	0.20
Oviedo (city) Seminole	55	0.20
Sweetwater (city) Miami-Dade	24	0.17
Bay Hill (cdp) Orange	8	0.15

Top 10 Places Sorted by Percent
Based on places with populations of 10,000 or more

Place (place type) County	Number	%
Ojus (cdp) Miami-Dade	91	0.55
Ferry Pass (cdp) Escambia	55	0.20
Oviedo (city) Seminole	55	0.20
Sweetwater (city) Miami-Dade	24	0.17
University (cdp) Hillsborough	44	0.14
Ocoee (city) Orange	32	0.14
Winter Springs (city) Seminole	42	0.13
New Port Richey East (cdp) Pasco	12	0.12
Lake Magdalene (cdp) Hillsborough	29	0.10
North Port (city) Sarasota	23	0.10

Arab: Lebanese

Top 10 Places Sorted by Number
Based on all places, regardless of population

Place (place type) County	Number	%
Jacksonville (special city) Duval	1,623	0.22
Miami (city) Miami-Dade	855	0.24
Kendall (cdp) Miami-Dade	755	1.00
Orlando (city) Orange	587	0.32
St. Petersburg (city) Pinellas	565	0.23
Coral Springs (city) Broward	511	0.43
Hialeah (city) Miami-Dade	429	0.19
Pembroke Pines (city) Broward	421	0.31
Coral Gables (city) Miami-Dade	402	0.95
Hollywood (city) Broward	394	0.28

Notes: (cdp) census designated place; Refer to the User's Guide in the front of the book for more detailed information.

Top 10 Places Sorted by Percent
Based on all places, regardless of population

Place (place type) County	Number	%
Cloud Lake (town) Palm Beach	5	4.07
Leisureville (cdp) Broward	25	2.31
Tierra Verde (cdp) Pinellas	74	2.09
Biscayne Park (village) Miami-Dade	62	1.87
Chula Vista (cdp) Broward	9	1.54
Ocean Ridge (town) Palm Beach	24	1.47
Gulf Stream (town) Palm Beach	10	1.45
Vineyards (cdp) Collier	32	1.41
Wabasso Beach (cdp) Indian River	15	1.34
Shalimar (town) Okaloosa	8	1.13

Top 10 Places Sorted by Percent
Based on places with populations of 10,000 or more

Place (place type) County	Number	%
Doral (cdp) Miami-Dade	225	1.10
Pinecrest (village) Miami-Dade	209	1.09
Kendall (cdp) Miami-Dade	755	1.00
Coral Gables (city) Miami-Dade	402	0.95
Lake Magdalene (cdp) Hillsborough	235	0.82
Sunset (cdp) Miami-Dade	128	0.75
Azalea Park (cdp) Orange	79	0.71
Lake Mary (city) Seminole	76	0.67
The Crossings (cdp) Miami-Dade	155	0.66
Greater Northdale (cdp) Hillsborough	132	0.65

Arab: Moroccan

Top 10 Places Sorted by Number
Based on all places, regardless of population

Place (place type) County	Number	%
Orlando (city) Orange	272	0.15
Kissimmee (city) Osceola	249	0.52
Sarasota (city) Sarasota	128	0.24
Miami Beach (city) Miami-Dade	120	0.14
Sunny Isles Beach (city) Miami-Dade	108	0.71
Hollywood (city) Broward	107	0.08
Pembroke Pines (city) Broward	99	0.07
Clearwater (city) Pinellas	96	0.09
Jacksonville (special city) Duval	94	0.01
St. Petersburg (city) Pinellas	87	0.04

Top 10 Places Sorted by Percent
Based on all places, regardless of population

Place (place type) County	Number	%
Williamsburg (cdp) Orange	76	1.10
Bay Harbor Islands (town) Miami-Dade	41	0.80
Sunny Isles Beach (city) Miami-Dade	108	0.71
Hastings (town) St. Johns	3	0.64
Indian Harbour Beach (city) Brevard	49	0.60
Kissimmee (city) Osceola	249	0.52
Bal Harbour (village) Miami-Dade	17	0.51
St. Leo (town) Pasco	3	0.49
Three Lakes (cdp) Miami-Dade	27	0.39
Hobe Sound (cdp) Martin	42	0.38

Top 10 Places Sorted by Percent
Based on places with populations of 10,000 or more

Place (place type) County	Number	%
Sunny Isles Beach (city) Miami-Dade	108	0.71
Kissimmee (city) Osceola	249	0.52
Hobe Sound (cdp) Martin	42	0.38
Country Walk (cdp) Miami-Dade	41	0.38
Aventura (city) Miami-Dade	76	0.30
Poinciana (cdp) Osceola	39	0.29
Sarasota (city) Sarasota	128	0.24
Land O' Lakes (cdp) Pasco	49	0.24
Citrus Ridge (cdp) Lake	27	0.24
South Miami (city) Miami-Dade	24	0.22

Arab: Palestinian

Top 10 Places Sorted by Number
Based on all places, regardless of population

Place (place type) County	Number	%
Jacksonville (special city) Duval	789	0.11
Orlando (city) Orange	169	0.09
Plantation (city) Broward	156	0.19
Brandon (cdp) Hillsborough	149	0.19
West Palm Beach (city) Palm Beach	149	0.18
St. Petersburg (city) Pinellas	127	0.05
Miami (city) Miami-Dade	119	0.03
The Hammocks (cdp) Miami-Dade	112	0.24
Palm Harbor (cdp) Pinellas	105	0.18
Dunes Road (cdp) Palm Beach	104	21.99

Top 10 Places Sorted by Percent
Based on all places, regardless of population

Place (place type) County	Number	%
Dunes Road (cdp) Palm Beach	104	21.99
Molino (cdp) Escambia	18	1.27
Doctor Phillips (cdp) Orange	80	0.83
Wesley Chapel (cdp) Pasco	48	0.82
Bay Hill (cdp) Orange	38	0.71
Bay Pines (cdp) Pinellas	21	0.63
Surfside (town) Miami-Dade	27	0.53
Holden Heights (cdp) Orange	17	0.44
South Daytona (city) Volusia	53	0.40
Fruitville (cdp) Sarasota	52	0.40

Top 10 Places Sorted by Percent
Based on places with populations of 10,000 or more

Place (place type) County	Number	%
South Daytona (city) Volusia	53	0.40
Fruitville (cdp) Sarasota	52	0.40
Meadow Woods (cdp) Orange	44	0.38
Marco Island (city) Collier	49	0.33
Coral Terrace (cdp) Miami-Dade	69	0.28
Greater Northdale (cdp) Hillsborough	55	0.27
Punta Gorda (city) Charlotte	39	0.27
Parkland (city) Broward	37	0.26
The Hammocks (cdp) Miami-Dade	112	0.24
Egypt Lake-Leto (cdp) Hillsborough	75	0.23

Arab: Syrian

Top 10 Places Sorted by Number
Based on all places, regardless of population

Place (place type) County	Number	%
Jacksonville (special city) Duval	1,182	0.16
Kendall (cdp) Miami-Dade	335	0.45
Spring Hill (cdp) Hernando	239	0.35
Miami (city) Miami-Dade	236	0.07
Orlando (city) Orange	204	0.11
Hollywood (city) Broward	186	0.13
Aventura (city) Miami-Dade	182	0.72
Pembroke Pines (city) Broward	155	0.11
St. Petersburg (city) Pinellas	153	0.06
Sunrise (city) Broward	123	0.14

Top 10 Places Sorted by Percent
Based on all places, regardless of population

Place (place type) County	Number	%
Atlantis (city) Palm Beach	28	1.32
Surfside (town) Miami-Dade	50	0.98
Manalapan (town) Palm Beach	3	0.93
Polk City (town) Polk	13	0.87
Gateway (cdp) Lee	25	0.82
Briny Breezes (town) Palm Beach	3	0.73
Aventura (city) Miami-Dade	182	0.72
Bonnie Lock-Woodsetter North (cdp) Broward	28	0.65
Belleair Beach (city) Pinellas	10	0.60
East Palatka (cdp) Putnam	10	0.58

Top 10 Places Sorted by Percent
Based on places with populations of 10,000 or more

Place (place type) County	Number	%
Aventura (city) Miami-Dade	182	0.72
Oldsmar (city) Pinellas	65	0.55
Holiday (cdp) Pasco	117	0.53
Kendall (cdp) Miami-Dade	335	0.45
Lynn Haven (city) Bay	55	0.45
Ives Estates (cdp) Miami-Dade	74	0.42
East Lake (cdp) Pinellas	117	0.40
Wekiwa Springs (cdp) Seminole	93	0.40
Sunny Isles Beach (city) Miami-Dade	57	0.37
Spring Hill (cdp) Hernando	239	0.35

Arab: Other

Top 10 Places Sorted by Number
Based on all places, regardless of population

Place (place type) County	Number	%
Jacksonville (special city) Duval	154	0.02
Pembroke Pines (city) Broward	142	0.10
Miami Beach (city) Miami-Dade	138	0.16
Tampa (city) Hillsborough	131	0.04
Coral Springs (city) Broward	111	0.09
Temple Terrace (city) Hillsborough	98	0.47
Orlando (city) Orange	97	0.05
Melbourne (city) Brevard	94	0.13
The Hammocks (cdp) Miami-Dade	91	0.19
Hallandale (city) Broward	89	0.26

Top 10 Places Sorted by Percent
Based on all places, regardless of population

Place (place type) County	Number	%
Golden Beach (town) Miami-Dade	12	1.14
Yankeetown (town) Levy	4	0.62
Cypress Lakes (cdp) Palm Beach	7	0.51
Temple Terrace (city) Hillsborough	98	0.47
Azalea Park (cdp) Orange	46	0.41
Glenvar Heights (cdp) Miami-Dade	51	0.32
South Beach (cdp) Indian River	11	0.32
Live Oak (city) Suwannee	19	0.29
Feather Sound (cdp) Pinellas	11	0.27
Hallandale (city) Broward	89	0.26

Top 10 Places Sorted by Percent
Based on places with populations of 10,000 or more

Place (place type) County	Number	%
Temple Terrace (city) Hillsborough	98	0.47
Azalea Park (cdp) Orange	46	0.41
Glenvar Heights (cdp) Miami-Dade	51	0.32
Hallandale (city) Broward	89	0.26
Upper Grand Lagoon (cdp) Bay	26	0.24
Boca Del Mar (cdp) Palm Beach	49	0.23
Myrtle Grove (cdp) Escambia	40	0.23
Pinecrest (village) Miami-Dade	43	0.22
The Hammocks (cdp) Miami-Dade	91	0.19
Belle Glade (city) Palm Beach	26	0.17

Armenian

Top 10 Places Sorted by Number
Based on all places, regardless of population

Place (place type) County	Number	%
Jacksonville (special city) Duval	397	0.05
Tampa (city) Hillsborough	222	0.07
Coral Springs (city) Broward	191	0.16
Fort Lauderdale (city) Broward	171	0.11
Clearwater (city) Pinellas	152	0.14
St. Petersburg (city) Pinellas	146	0.06
Miami (city) Miami-Dade	138	0.04
Lake Mary (city) Seminole	132	1.17
Boca Raton (city) Palm Beach	132	0.17

Notes: (cdp) census designated place; Refer to the User's Guide in the front of the book for more detailed information.

Place (place type) County	Number	%
Orlando (city) Orange	126	0.07

Top 10 Places Sorted by Percent
Based on all places, regardless of population

Place (place type) County	Number	%
Lake Mary (city) Seminole	132	1.17
Punta Rassa (cdp) Lee	19	1.13
Hillcrest Heights (town) Polk	3	1.11
Terra Mar (cdp) Broward	29	1.08
Yankeetown (town) Levy	6	0.93
Pine Ridge (cdp) Collier	15	0.81
Parkland (city) Broward	105	0.75
Pine Island Ridge (cdp) Broward	39	0.73
West Bradenton (cdp) Manatee	32	0.71
Bay Harbor Islands (town) Miami-Dade	36	0.70

Top 10 Places Sorted by Percent
Based on places with populations of 10,000 or more

Place (place type) County	Number	%
Lake Mary (city) Seminole	132	1.17
Parkland (city) Broward	105	0.75
Key West (city) Monroe	93	0.36
Marco Island (city) Collier	51	0.34
Key Largo (cdp) Monroe	39	0.33
Miami Shores (village) Miami-Dade	32	0.31
East Lake (cdp) Pinellas	89	0.30
Sarasota Springs (cdp) Sarasota	44	0.28
Palm Beach Gardens (city) Palm Beach	92	0.27
Kings Point (cdp) Palm Beach	32	0.26

Asian

Top 10 Places Sorted by Number
Based on all places, regardless of population

Place (place type) County	Number	%
Jacksonville (special city) Duval	25,465	3.46
Tampa (city) Hillsborough	8,363	2.76
St. Petersburg (city) Pinellas	8,101	3.26
Pembroke Pines (city) Broward	6,553	4.77
Orlando (city) Orange	6,259	3.37
Gainesville (city) Alachua	4,976	5.21
Coral Springs (city) Broward	4,925	4.19
Tallahassee (city) Leon	4,417	2.93
Hollywood (city) Broward	3,469	2.49
Sunrise (city) Broward	3,294	3.84

Top 10 Places Sorted by Percent
Based on all places, regardless of population

Place (place type) County	Number	%
Bay Hill (cdp) Orange	560	10.82
Southchase (cdp) Orange	493	10.64
Doctor Phillips (cdp) Orange	909	9.52
Ivanhoe Estates (cdp) Broward	26	9.32
Wedgefield (cdp) Orange	236	8.74
Hunters Creek (cdp) Orange	771	8.23
Cloud Lake (town) Palm Beach	13	7.78
Pebble Creek (cdp) Hillsborough	344	7.13
Oak Ridge (cdp) Orange	1,525	6.82
Myrtle Grove (cdp) Escambia	1,107	6.43

Top 10 Places Sorted by Percent
Based on places with populations of 10,000 or more

Place (place type) County	Number	%
Oak Ridge (cdp) Orange	1,525	6.82
Myrtle Grove (cdp) Escambia	1,107	6.43
Ives Estates (cdp) Miami-Dade	1,024	5.82
Doral (cdp) Miami-Dade	1,168	5.71
Wright (cdp) Okaloosa	1,162	5.36
Pinecrest (village) Miami-Dade	1,019	5.35
Gainesville (city) Alachua	4,976	5.21
North Miami Beach (city) Miami-Dade	2,031	4.98
Niceville (city) Okaloosa	579	4.96

Place (place type) County	Number	%
Callaway (city) Bay	701	4.93

Asian: Bangladeshi

Top 10 Places Sorted by Number
Based on all places, regardless of population

Place (place type) County	Number	%
Boynton Beach (city) Palm Beach	50	0.08
Delray Beach (city) Palm Beach	49	0.08
Miami Beach (city) Miami-Dade	49	0.06
Lake Worth Corridor (cdp) Palm Beach	44	0.24
Kissimmee (city) Osceola	44	0.09
North Miami Beach (city) Miami-Dade	36	0.09
Deerfield Beach (city) Broward	34	0.05
Fort Lauderdale (city) Broward	34	0.02
Pompano Beach (city) Broward	32	0.04
Plantation (city) Broward	30	0.04

Top 10 Places Sorted by Percent
Based on all places, regardless of population

Place (place type) County	Number	%
North Brooksville (cdp) Hernando	5	0.34
Pompano Beach Highlands (cdp) Broward	19	0.29
Loch Lomond (cdp) Broward	10	0.28
Twin Lakes (cdp) Broward	5	0.27
Lake Worth Corridor (cdp) Palm Beach	44	0.24
Chambers Estates (cdp) Broward	8	0.22
Broadview-Pompano Park (cdp) Broward	11	0.21
Edgewood (city) Orange	4	0.21
Hypoluxo (town) Palm Beach	4	0.20
Dover (cdp) Hillsborough	5	0.18

Top 10 Places Sorted by Percent
Based on places with populations of 10,000 or more

Place (place type) County	Number	%
Lake Worth Corridor (cdp) Palm Beach	44	0.24
Sandalfoot Cove (cdp) Palm Beach	22	0.13
Oak Ridge (cdp) Orange	25	0.11
Kissimmee (city) Osceola	44	0.09
North Miami Beach (city) Miami-Dade	36	0.09
Longwood (city) Seminole	13	0.09
Country Walk (cdp) Miami-Dade	10	0.09
Boynton Beach (city) Palm Beach	50	0.08
Delray Beach (city) Palm Beach	49	0.08
Oakland Park (city) Broward	26	0.08

Asian: Cambodian

Top 10 Places Sorted by Number
Based on all places, regardless of population

Place (place type) County	Number	%
Jacksonville (special city) Duval	1,064	0.14
St. Petersburg (city) Pinellas	538	0.22
West and East Lealman (cdp) Pinellas	65	0.30
Pinellas Park (city) Pinellas	58	0.13
Oak Ridge (cdp) Orange	50	0.22
Port St. Lucie (city) St. Lucie	44	0.05
Brent (cdp) Escambia	41	0.18
Gainesville (city) Alachua	32	0.03
South Bradenton (cdp) Manatee	30	0.14
Orlando (city) Orange	29	0.02

Top 10 Places Sorted by Percent
Based on all places, regardless of population

Place (place type) County	Number	%
Kenneth City (town) Pinellas	26	0.59
West and East Lealman (cdp) Pinellas	65	0.30
Southchase (cdp) Orange	12	0.26
Williamsburg (cdp) Orange	17	0.25
St. Petersburg (city) Pinellas	538	0.22
Oak Ridge (cdp) Orange	50	0.22
Brent (cdp) Escambia	41	0.18

Place (place type) County	Number	%
Goulding (cdp) Escambia	7	0.16
Jacksonville (special city) Duval	1,064	0.14
South Bradenton (cdp) Manatee	30	0.14

Top 10 Places Sorted by Percent
Based on places with populations of 10,000 or more

Place (place type) County	Number	%
West and East Lealman (cdp) Pinellas	65	0.30
St. Petersburg (city) Pinellas	538	0.22
Oak Ridge (cdp) Orange	50	0.22
Brent (cdp) Escambia	41	0.18
Jacksonville (special city) Duval	1,064	0.14
South Bradenton (cdp) Manatee	30	0.14
Pinellas Park (city) Pinellas	58	0.13
Bayshore Gardens (cdp) Manatee	21	0.12
Lake Mary (city) Seminole	10	0.09
Meadow Woods (cdp) Orange	10	0.09

Asian: Chinese, except Taiwanese

Top 10 Places Sorted by Number
Based on all places, regardless of population

Place (place type) County	Number	%
Jacksonville (special city) Duval	1,879	0.26
Pembroke Pines (city) Broward	1,622	1.18
Gainesville (city) Alachua	1,411	1.48
Tallahassee (city) Leon	1,118	0.74
Coral Springs (city) Broward	1,092	0.93
Miami (city) Miami-Dade	1,021	0.28
Kendall (cdp) Miami-Dade	990	1.32
Tampa (city) Hillsborough	895	0.29
Orlando (city) Orange	873	0.47
Sunrise (city) Broward	832	0.97

Top 10 Places Sorted by Percent
Based on all places, regardless of population

Place (place type) County	Number	%
Godfrey Road (cdp) Broward	5	2.91
Ivanhoe Estates (cdp) Broward	8	2.87
Pinecrest (village) Miami-Dade	405	2.13
Doral (cdp) Miami-Dade	398	1.95
Country Walk (cdp) Miami-Dade	198	1.86
Pebble Creek (cdp) Hillsborough	83	1.72
Three Lakes (cdp) Miami-Dade	119	1.71
Doctor Phillips (cdp) Orange	162	1.70
North Miami Beach (city) Miami-Dade	677	1.66
The Crossings (cdp) Miami-Dade	382	1.62

Top 10 Places Sorted by Percent
Based on places with populations of 10,000 or more

Place (place type) County	Number	%
Pinecrest (village) Miami-Dade	405	2.13
Doral (cdp) Miami-Dade	398	1.95
Country Walk (cdp) Miami-Dade	198	1.86
North Miami Beach (city) Miami-Dade	677	1.66
The Crossings (cdp) Miami-Dade	382	1.62
The Hammocks (cdp) Miami-Dade	764	1.61
Cutler (cdp) Miami-Dade	271	1.56
Ives Estates (cdp) Miami-Dade	273	1.55
Gainesville (city) Alachua	1,411	1.48
Parkland (city) Broward	189	1.37

Asian: Filipino

Top 10 Places Sorted by Number
Based on all places, regardless of population

Place (place type) County	Number	%
Jacksonville (special city) Duval	12,295	1.67
Tampa (city) Hillsborough	1,450	0.48
Orlando (city) Orange	1,138	0.61
Pembroke Pines (city) Broward	1,062	0.77
St. Petersburg (city) Pinellas	1,030	0.41

Notes: (cdp) census designated place; Refer to the User's Guide in the front of the book for more detailed information.

Place (place type) County	Number	%
Wedgefield (cdp) Orange	165	6.11
Myrtle Grove (cdp) Escambia	683	3.97
Highland Park (village) Polk	8	3.28
Southchase (cdp) Orange	146	3.15
Eglin AFB (cdp) Okaloosa	242	2.99
Bellview (cdp) Escambia	585	2.76
Tyndall AFB (cdp) Bay	75	2.72
Bellair-Meadowbrook Terrace (cdp) Clay	436	2.64
Lakeside (cdp) Clay	659	2.13
Mary Esther (city) Okaloosa	86	2.12

Top 10 Places Sorted by Percent
Based on places with populations of 10,000 or more

Place (place type) County	Number	%
Myrtle Grove (cdp) Escambia	683	3.97
Bellview (cdp) Escambia	585	2.76
Bellair-Meadowbrook Terrace (cdp) Clay	436	2.64
Lakeside (cdp) Clay	659	2.13
Wright (cdp) Okaloosa	418	1.93
Niceville (city) Okaloosa	224	1.92
Callaway (city) Bay	257	1.81
Crestview (city) Okaloosa	249	1.69
Jacksonville (special city) Duval	12,295	1.67
Atlantic Beach (city) Duval	221	1.65

Asian: Hmong

Top 10 Places Sorted by Number
Based on all places, regardless of population

Place (place type) County	Number	%
Clearwater (city) Pinellas	27	0.02
South Highpoint (cdp) Pinellas	14	0.16
Fort Myers Beach (town) Lee	10	0.15
Jacksonville (special city) Duval	10	0.00
Safety Harbor (city) Pinellas	8	0.05
Riverview (cdp) Hillsborough	6	0.05
Longwood (city) Seminole	6	0.04
Bloomingdale (cdp) Hillsborough	6	0.03
Orlando (city) Orange	5	0.00
Westchase (cdp) Hillsborough	4	0.04

Top 10 Places Sorted by Percent
Based on all places, regardless of population

Place (place type) County	Number	%
South Highpoint (cdp) Pinellas	14	0.16
Fort Myers Beach (town) Lee	10	0.15
Safety Harbor (city) Pinellas	8	0.05
Riverview (cdp) Hillsborough	6	0.05
Longwood (city) Seminole	6	0.04
Westchase (cdp) Hillsborough	4	0.04
Bloomingdale (cdp) Hillsborough	6	0.03
Dade City North (cdp) Pasco	1	0.03
Clearwater (city) Pinellas	27	0.02
Jan Phyl Village (cdp) Polk	1	0.02

Top 10 Places Sorted by Percent
Based on places with populations of 10,000 or more

Place (place type) County	Number	%
Safety Harbor (city) Pinellas	8	0.05
Riverview (cdp) Hillsborough	6	0.05
Longwood (city) Seminole	6	0.04
Westchase (cdp) Hillsborough	4	0.04
Bloomingdale (cdp) Hillsborough	6	0.03

Top 10 Places Sorted by Number
Based on all places, regardless of population

Place (place type) County	Number	%
Jacksonville (special city) Duval	3,163	0.43
Pembroke Pines (city) Broward	2,237	1.63
Coral Springs (city) Broward	2,149	1.83
Tampa (city) Hillsborough	1,955	0.64
Orlando (city) Orange	1,464	0.79
Hollywood (city) Broward	1,410	1.01
Plantation (city) Broward	1,230	1.48
Sunrise (city) Broward	1,217	1.42
Gainesville (city) Alachua	1,185	1.24
Tallahassee (city) Leon	1,098	0.73

Top 10 Places Sorted by Percent
Based on all places, regardless of population

Place (place type) County	Number	%
Cloud Lake (town) Palm Beach	12	7.19
Bay Hill (cdp) Orange	303	5.85
Ivanhoe Estates (cdp) Broward	14	5.02
Golden Heights (cdp) Broward	20	3.99
Doctor Phillips (cdp) Orange	375	3.93
Black Diamond (cdp) Citrus	25	3.60
Gotha (cdp) Orange	23	3.15
Lake Harbor (cdp) Palm Beach	6	3.08
Hunters Creek (cdp) Orange	244	2.60
Southchase (cdp) Orange	107	2.31

Top 10 Places Sorted by Percent
Based on places with populations of 10,000 or more

Place (place type) County	Number	%
Palmetto Estates (cdp) Miami-Dade	301	2.20
Cooper City (city) Broward	545	1.95
Ives Estates (cdp) Miami-Dade	337	1.92
Coral Springs (city) Broward	2,149	1.83
Pembroke Pines (city) Broward	2,237	1.63
University (cdp) Hillsborough	470	1.53
South Miami Heights (cdp) Miami-Dade	511	1.52
Ocoee (city) Orange	368	1.51
Plantation (city) Broward	1,230	1.48
North Lauderdale (city) Broward	472	1.46

Asian: Indonesian

Top 10 Places Sorted by Number
Based on all places, regardless of population

Place (place type) County	Number	%
Jacksonville (special city) Duval	44	0.01
Tampa (city) Hillsborough	41	0.01
St. Petersburg (city) Pinellas	40	0.02
Miami (city) Miami-Dade	39	0.01
Miami Beach (city) Miami-Dade	28	0.03
Gainesville (city) Alachua	24	0.03
Coral Springs (city) Broward	24	0.02
Brandon (cdp) Hillsborough	19	0.02
Palm Bay (city) Brevard	19	0.02
Sunrise (city) Broward	19	0.02

Top 10 Places Sorted by Percent
Based on all places, regardless of population

Place (place type) County	Number	%
Leisureville (cdp) Broward	3	0.26
Ravenswood Estates (cdp) Broward	2	0.21
Green Meadow (cdp) Broward	3	0.16

Top 10 Places Sorted by Percent
Based on places with populations of 10,000 or more

Place (place type) County	Number	%
Lake Mary (city) Seminole	10	0.09
Brent (cdp) Escambia	16	0.07
Temple Terrace (city) Hillsborough	14	0.07
Ives Estates (cdp) Miami-Dade	13	0.07
Sunny Isles Beach (city) Miami-Dade	9	0.06
Union Park (cdp) Orange	6	0.06
Hallandale (city) Broward	16	0.05
Lutz (cdp) Hillsborough	9	0.05
Lockhart (cdp) Orange	6	0.05
University (cdp) Hillsborough	11	0.04

Asian: Japanese

Top 10 Places Sorted by Number
Based on all places, regardless of population

Place (place type) County	Number	%
Jacksonville (special city) Duval	930	0.13
Orlando (city) Orange	447	0.24
Tampa (city) Hillsborough	410	0.14
Tallahassee (city) Leon	306	0.20
St. Petersburg (city) Pinellas	296	0.12
Gainesville (city) Alachua	293	0.31
Kendall (cdp) Miami-Dade	196	0.26
Doral (cdp) Miami-Dade	193	0.94
Pembroke Pines (city) Broward	188	0.14
Melbourne (city) Brevard	177	0.25

Top 10 Places Sorted by Percent
Based on all places, regardless of population

Place (place type) County	Number	%
Fisher Island (cdp) Miami-Dade	6	1.28
Tyndall AFB (cdp) Bay	28	1.02
Doral (cdp) Miami-Dade	193	0.94
Westville (town) Holmes	2	0.90
Highland Park (village) Polk	2	0.82
North Beach (cdp) Indian River	2	0.82
Mary Esther (city) Okaloosa	32	0.79
Williamsburg (cdp) Orange	49	0.73
Eglin AFB (cdp) Okaloosa	53	0.66
Mission Bay (cdp) Palm Beach	19	0.65

Top 10 Places Sorted by Percent
Based on places with populations of 10,000 or more

Place (place type) County	Number	%
Doral (cdp) Miami-Dade	193	0.94
Niceville (city) Okaloosa	69	0.59
Wright (cdp) Okaloosa	118	0.54
Fort Walton Beach (city) Okaloosa	92	0.46
Callaway (city) Bay	58	0.41
Myrtle Grove (cdp) Escambia	68	0.40
The Crossings (cdp) Miami-Dade	91	0.39
Bellair-Meadowbrook Terrace (cdp) Clay	61	0.37
Union Park (cdp) Orange	36	0.35
Bellview (cdp) Escambia	73	0.34

Asian: Korean

Top 10 Places Sorted by Number
Based on all places, regardless of population

Place (place type) County	Number	%
Jacksonville (special city) Duval	1,366	0.19

Notes: (cdp) census designated place; Refer to the User's Guide in the front of the book for more detailed information.

Tampa (city) Hillsborough		772	0.25
Gainesville (city) Alachua		564	0.59
Orlando (city) Orange		524	0.28
Tallahassee (city) Leon		508	0.34
Town 'n' Country (cdp) Hillsborough		444	0.61
Pembroke Pines (city) Broward		428	0.31
St. Petersburg (city) Pinellas		393	0.16
Coral Springs (city) Broward		357	0.30
Brandon (cdp) Hillsborough		313	0.40

Top 10 Places Sorted by Percent
Based on all places, regardless of population

Place (place type) County	Number	%
Royal Palm Ranches (cdp) Broward	4	1.36
Forest City (cdp) Seminole	163	1.29
Tyndall AFB (cdp) Bay	33	1.20
Lake Lorraine (cdp) Okaloosa	75	1.06
Heathrow (cdp) Seminole	41	1.01
Bay Hill (cdp) Orange	48	0.93
Callaway (city) Bay	125	0.88
Niceville (city) Okaloosa	101	0.86
Black Diamond (cdp) Citrus	6	0.86
Wright (cdp) Okaloosa	182	0.84

Top 10 Places Sorted by Percent
Based on places with populations of 10,000 or more

Place (place type) County	Number	%
Forest City (cdp) Seminole	163	1.29
Callaway (city) Bay	125	0.88
Niceville (city) Okaloosa	101	0.86
Wright (cdp) Okaloosa	182	0.84
Citrus Park (cdp) Hillsborough	142	0.70
Greater Northdale (cdp) Hillsborough	139	0.68
Westchase (cdp) Hillsborough	69	0.62
Town 'n' Country (cdp) Hillsborough	444	0.61
Gainesville (city) Alachua	564	0.59
Crestview (city) Okaloosa	87	0.59

Asian: Laotian

Top 10 Places Sorted by Number
Based on all places, regardless of population

Place (place type) County	Number	%
St. Petersburg (city) Pinellas	1,178	0.47
Pinellas Park (city) Pinellas	296	0.65
Jacksonville (special city) Duval	273	0.04
West and East Lealman (cdp) Pinellas	120	0.55
Deltona (city) Volusia	73	0.10
Lake Park (town) Palm Beach	55	0.63
Oak Ridge (cdp) Orange	52	0.23
Clearwater (city) Pinellas	52	0.05
Bartow (city) Polk	42	0.27
North Fort Myers (cdp) Lee	42	0.10

Top 10 Places Sorted by Percent
Based on all places, regardless of population

Place (place type) County	Number	%
Pinellas Park (city) Pinellas	296	0.65
Lake Park (town) Palm Beach	55	0.63
West and East Lealman (cdp) Pinellas	120	0.55
St. Petersburg (city) Pinellas	1,178	0.47
South Highpoint (cdp) Pinellas	40	0.45
Fort Myers Shores (cdp) Lee	21	0.36
Olga (cdp) Lee	5	0.36
De Leon Springs (cdp) Volusia	8	0.34
Three Oaks (cdp) Lee	7	0.31
Crescent City (city) Putnam	5	0.28

Top 10 Places Sorted by Percent
Based on places with populations of 10,000 or more

Place (place type) County	Number	%
Pinellas Park (city) Pinellas	296	0.65

West and East Lealman (cdp) Pinellas		120	0.55
St. Petersburg (city) Pinellas		1,178	0.47
Bartow (city) Polk		42	0.27
Oak Ridge (cdp) Orange		52	0.23
Longwood (city) Seminole		28	0.20
Princeton (cdp) Miami-Dade		14	0.14
Leisure City (cdp) Miami-Dade		25	0.11
Oldsmar (city) Pinellas		13	0.11
Deltona (city) Volusia		73	0.10

Asian: Malaysian

Top 10 Places Sorted by Number
Based on all places, regardless of population

Place (place type) County	Number	%
Jacksonville (special city) Duval	56	0.01
Gainesville (city) Alachua	21	0.02
St. Petersburg (city) Pinellas	12	0.00
Pinellas Park (city) Pinellas	11	0.02
Deltona (city) Volusia	10	0.01
Bellview (cdp) Escambia	9	0.04
Atlantic Beach (city) Duval	8	0.06
Tallahassee (city) Leon	8	0.01
Deerfield Beach (city) Broward	7	0.01
Hollywood (city) Broward	7	0.01

Top 10 Places Sorted by Percent
Based on all places, regardless of population

Place (place type) County	Number	%
Page Park (cdp) Lee	1	0.19
Wedgefield (cdp) Orange	4	0.15
Broadview Park (cdp) Broward	6	0.09
Bay Hill (cdp) Orange	4	0.08
Atlantic Beach (city) Duval	8	0.06
Gibsonton (cdp) Hillsborough	5	0.06
Arcadia (city) De Soto	4	0.06
Biscayne Park (village) Miami-Dade	2	0.06
Pompano Estates (cdp) Broward	2	0.06
South Miami (city) Miami-Dade	5	0.05

Top 10 Places Sorted by Percent
Based on places with populations of 10,000 or more

Place (place type) County	Number	%
Atlantic Beach (city) Duval	8	0.06
South Miami (city) Miami-Dade	5	0.05
Bellview (cdp) Escambia	9	0.04
Longwood (city) Seminole	5	0.04
Gainesville (city) Alachua	21	0.02
Pinellas Park (city) Pinellas	11	0.02
Key West (city) Monroe	5	0.02
Oak Ridge (cdp) Orange	4	0.02
Goldenrod (cdp) Seminole	3	0.02
Cocoa Beach (city) Brevard	2	0.02

Asian: Pakistani

Top 10 Places Sorted by Number
Based on all places, regardless of population

Place (place type) County	Number	%
Pembroke Pines (city) Broward	307	0.22
Coral Springs (city) Broward	239	0.20
Orlando (city) Orange	190	0.10
Sunrise (city) Broward	187	0.22
Kissimmee (city) Osceola	178	0.37
Hollywood (city) Broward	166	0.12
Kendale Lakes (cdp) Miami-Dade	158	0.28
Davie (town) Broward	155	0.20
Kendall (cdp) Miami-Dade	153	0.20
Tampa (city) Hillsborough	150	0.05

Top 10 Places Sorted by Percent
Based on all places, regardless of population

Place (place type) County	Number	%
Jupiter Island (town) Martin	8	1.29
Bay Hill (cdp) Orange	62	1.20
Roseland (cdp) Indian River	16	0.90
Doctor Phillips (cdp) Orange	53	0.56
Ives Estates (cdp) Miami-Dade	93	0.53
Green Meadow (cdp) Broward	10	0.53
Hunters Creek (cdp) Orange	48	0.51
Southchase (cdp) Orange	20	0.43
Ravenswood Estates (cdp) Broward	4	0.42
Kissimmee (city) Osceola	178	0.37

Top 10 Places Sorted by Percent
Based on places with populations of 10,000 or more

Place (place type) County	Number	%
Ives Estates (cdp) Miami-Dade	93	0.53
Kissimmee (city) Osceola	178	0.37
Kendale Lakes (cdp) Miami-Dade	158	0.28
The Crossings (cdp) Miami-Dade	64	0.27
Westwood Lakes (cdp) Miami-Dade	32	0.27
Miami Lakes (cdp) Miami-Dade	60	0.26
The Hammocks (cdp) Miami-Dade	120	0.25
Country Club (cdp) Miami-Dade	89	0.25
Glenvar Heights (cdp) Miami-Dade	37	0.23
Pembroke Pines (city) Broward	307	0.22

Asian: Sri Lankan

Top 10 Places Sorted by Number
Based on all places, regardless of population

Place (place type) County	Number	%
Jacksonville (special city) Duval	27	0.00
Orlando (city) Orange	21	0.01
University (cdp) Hillsborough	19	0.06
Daytona Beach (city) Volusia	19	0.03
Coral Springs (city) Broward	18	0.02
Boca Raton (city) Palm Beach	17	0.02
Gainesville (city) Alachua	16	0.02
Lakeland (city) Polk	16	0.02
Kissimmee (city) Osceola	13	0.03
Tampa (city) Hillsborough	13	0.00

Top 10 Places Sorted by Percent
Based on all places, regardless of population

Place (place type) County	Number	%
Hillsboro Pines (cdp) Broward	1	0.25
Pebble Creek (cdp) Hillsborough	8	0.17
Bonnie Lock-Woodsetter North (cdp) Broward	7	0.16
Tedder (cdp) Broward	3	0.14
Juno Ridge (cdp) Palm Beach	1	0.13
Babson Park (cdp) Polk	1	0.08
Osprey (cdp) Sarasota	3	0.07
Ramblewood East (cdp) Broward	1	0.07
University (cdp) Hillsborough	19	0.06
South Beach (cdp) Indian River	2	0.06

Top 10 Places Sorted by Percent
Based on places with populations of 10,000 or more

Place (place type) County	Number	%
University (cdp) Hillsborough	19	0.06
Port Salerno (cdp) Martin	5	0.05
Bellair-Meadowbrook Terrace (cdp) Clay	7	0.04
Glenvar Heights (cdp) Miami-Dade	7	0.04
Sandalfoot Cove (cdp) Palm Beach	6	0.04
Atlantic Beach (city) Duval	5	0.04
Daytona Beach (city) Volusia	19	0.03
Kissimmee (city) Osceola	13	0.03
Wellington (village) Palm Beach	10	0.03
Greater Carrollwood (cdp) Hillsborough	9	0.03

Notes: (cdp) census designated place; Refer to the User's Guide in the front of the book for more detailed information.

Asian: Taiwanese

Top 10 Places Sorted by Number
Based on all places, regardless of population

Place (place type) County	Number	%
Tallahassee (city) Leon	106	0.07
Jacksonville (special city) Duval	96	0.01
Gainesville (city) Alachua	87	0.09
Tampa (city) Hillsborough	66	0.02
Coral Springs (city) Broward	47	0.04
Davie (town) Broward	45	0.06
Pembroke Pines (city) Broward	45	0.03
Miami (city) Miami-Dade	33	0.01
Temple Terrace (city) Hillsborough	32	0.15
Plantation (city) Broward	30	0.04

Top 10 Places Sorted by Percent
Based on all places, regardless of population

Place (place type) County	Number	%
Godfrey Road (cdp) Broward	2	1.16
Cinco Bayou (town) Okaloosa	2	0.53
Hunters Creek (cdp) Orange	23	0.25
Carrabelle (city) Franklin	3	0.23
Mission Bay (cdp) Palm Beach	6	0.21
Bagdad (cdp) Santa Rosa	3	0.20
Wesley Chapel (cdp) Pasco	11	0.19
Big Coppitt Key (cdp) Monroe	5	0.19
Pebble Creek (cdp) Hillsborough	8	0.17
Green Meadow (cdp) Broward	3	0.16

Top 10 Places Sorted by Percent
Based on places with populations of 10,000 or more

Place (place type) County	Number	%
Temple Terrace (city) Hillsborough	32	0.15
Pinecrest (village) Miami-Dade	24	0.13
Conway (cdp) Orange	19	0.13
Meadow Woods (cdp) Orange	13	0.12
Gainesville (city) Alachua	87	0.09
Doral (cdp) Miami-Dade	19	0.09
Miami Shores (village) Miami-Dade	9	0.09
Keystone (cdp) Hillsborough	12	0.08
Citrus Ridge (cdp) Lake	10	0.08
Tallahassee (city) Leon	106	0.07

Asian: Thai

Top 10 Places Sorted by Number
Based on all places, regardless of population

Place (place type) County	Number	%
Tampa (city) Hillsborough	376	0.12
Jacksonville (special city) Duval	271	0.04
Wright (cdp) Okaloosa	193	0.89
St. Petersburg (city) Pinellas	191	0.08
Melbourne (city) Brevard	158	0.22
Brandon (cdp) Hillsborough	140	0.18
Fort Walton Beach (city) Okaloosa	133	0.67
Gainesville (city) Alachua	121	0.13
Orlando (city) Orange	112	0.06
Fort Lauderdale (city) Broward	104	0.07

Top 10 Places Sorted by Percent
Based on all places, regardless of population

Place (place type) County	Number	%
Ocean City (cdp) Okaloosa	64	1.14
Wright (cdp) Okaloosa	193	0.89
Mary Esther (city) Okaloosa	31	0.76
Fort Walton Beach (city) Okaloosa	133	0.67
Palm Shores (town) Brevard	5	0.63
Springfield (city) Bay	48	0.54
Callaway (city) Bay	76	0.53
Lake Lorraine (cdp) Okaloosa	38	0.53
Cinco Bayou (town) Okaloosa	2	0.53
Niceville (city) Okaloosa	60	0.51

Top 10 Places Sorted by Percent
Based on places with populations of 10,000 or more

Place (place type) County	Number	%
Wright (cdp) Okaloosa	193	0.89
Fort Walton Beach (city) Okaloosa	133	0.67
Callaway (city) Bay	76	0.53
Niceville (city) Okaloosa	60	0.51
Crestview (city) Okaloosa	36	0.24
Destin (city) Okaloosa	27	0.24
Wilton Manors (city) Broward	29	0.23
Palm Springs (village) Palm Beach	27	0.23
Melbourne (city) Brevard	158	0.22
Pinecrest (village) Miami-Dade	42	0.22

Asian: Vietnamese

Top 10 Places Sorted by Number
Based on all places, regardless of population

Place (place type) County	Number	%
Jacksonville (special city) Duval	2,566	0.35
St. Petersburg (city) Pinellas	2,108	0.85
Tampa (city) Hillsborough	1,677	0.55
Orlando (city) Orange	939	0.50
Pinellas Park (city) Pinellas	839	1.84
Town 'n' Country (cdp) Hillsborough	807	1.11
Oak Ridge (cdp) Orange	706	3.16
Pine Hills (cdp) Orange	646	1.55
West and East Lealman (cdp) Pinellas	584	2.68
Egypt Lake-Leto (cdp) Hillsborough	458	1.40

Top 10 Places Sorted by Percent
Based on all places, regardless of population

Place (place type) County	Number	%
Oak Ridge (cdp) Orange	706	3.16
Springfield (city) Bay	254	2.88
Kenneth City (town) Pinellas	124	2.82
West and East Lealman (cdp) Pinellas	584	2.68
Village Park (cdp) Broward	22	2.46
Southchase (cdp) Orange	97	2.09
West Pensacola (cdp) Escambia	412	1.88
South Highpoint (cdp) Pinellas	164	1.86
Pinellas Park (city) Pinellas	839	1.84
Orlovista (cdp) Orange	97	1.60

Top 10 Places Sorted by Percent
Based on places with populations of 10,000 or more

Place (place type) County	Number	%
Oak Ridge (cdp) Orange	706	3.16
West and East Lealman (cdp) Pinellas	584	2.68
West Pensacola (cdp) Escambia	412	1.88
Pinellas Park (city) Pinellas	839	1.84
Azalea Park (cdp) Orange	174	1.57
Pine Hills (cdp) Orange	646	1.55
Fairview Shores (cdp) Orange	213	1.53
Egypt Lake-Leto (cdp) Hillsborough	458	1.40
North Lauderdale (city) Broward	360	1.12
Town 'n' Country (cdp) Hillsborough	807	1.11

Asian: Other Asian, specified

Top 10 Places Sorted by Number
Based on all places, regardless of population

Place (place type) County	Number	%
Jacksonville (special city) Duval	152	0.02
Tampa (city) Hillsborough	45	0.01
Tallahassee (city) Leon	38	0.03
Orlando (city) Orange	34	0.02
St. Petersburg (city) Pinellas	34	0.01
Miami (city) Miami-Dade	26	0.01
Gainesville (city) Alachua	23	0.02
Coral Springs (city) Broward	19	0.02
Deerfield Beach (city) Broward	17	0.03

(Asian: Other Asian, specified — continued)

Place (place type) County	Number	%
Plantation (city) Broward	16	0.02

Top 10 Places Sorted by Percent
Based on all places, regardless of population

Place (place type) County	Number	%
De Leon Springs (cdp) Volusia	6	0.25
Willow Oak (cdp) Polk	10	0.20
West De Land (cdp) Volusia	7	0.20
Manattee Road (cdp) Levy	3	0.15
North Brooksville (cdp) Hernando	2	0.14
Lake Clarke Shores (town) Palm Beach	4	0.12
El Portal (village) Miami-Dade	3	0.12
Malabar (town) Brevard	3	0.11
Wabasso (cdp) Indian River	1	0.11
Southeast Arcadia (cdp) De Soto	6	0.10

Top 10 Places Sorted by Percent
Based on places with populations of 10,000 or more

Place (place type) County	Number	%
Iona (cdp) Lee	9	0.08
Palm Springs (village) Palm Beach	9	0.08
Westchase (cdp) Hillsborough	9	0.08
Key Largo (cdp) Monroe	8	0.07
Wilton Manors (city) Broward	7	0.06
Key West (city) Monroe	14	0.05
Palm Valley (cdp) St. Johns	10	0.05
Fort Walton Beach (city) Okaloosa	9	0.05
Jensen Beach (cdp) Martin	5	0.05
Cocoa (city) Brevard	7	0.04

Asian: Other Asian, not specified

Top 10 Places Sorted by Number
Based on all places, regardless of population

Place (place type) County	Number	%
Jacksonville (special city) Duval	1,110	0.15
Tampa (city) Hillsborough	441	0.15
St. Petersburg (city) Pinellas	407	0.16
Orlando (city) Orange	368	0.20
Miami (city) Miami-Dade	298	0.08
Pembroke Pines (city) Broward	268	0.20
Tallahassee (city) Leon	237	0.16
Fort Lauderdale (city) Broward	176	0.12
Coral Springs (city) Broward	175	0.15
Gainesville (city) Alachua	167	0.17

Top 10 Places Sorted by Percent
Based on all places, regardless of population

Place (place type) County	Number	%
Lake Harbor (cdp) Palm Beach	2	1.03
Hillcrest Heights (town) Polk	2	0.75
Glen Ridge (town) Palm Beach	2	0.72
Doctor Phillips (cdp) Orange	65	0.68
Homestead Base (cdp) Miami-Dade	3	0.67
Fisher Island (cdp) Miami-Dade	3	0.64
Windermere (town) Orange	11	0.58
Midway (cdp) Seminole	10	0.58
Christmas (cdp) Orange	6	0.52
Leisureville (cdp) Broward	6	0.52

Top 10 Places Sorted by Percent
Based on places with populations of 10,000 or more

Place (place type) County	Number	%
Ives Estates (cdp) Miami-Dade	69	0.39
North Miami Beach (city) Miami-Dade	128	0.31
Oak Ridge (cdp) Orange	68	0.30
Bellair-Meadowbrook Terrace (cdp) Clay	49	0.30
Wright (cdp) Okaloosa	61	0.28
The Crossings (cdp) Miami-Dade	62	0.26
Greater Northdale (cdp) Hillsborough	52	0.25
Kissimmee (city) Osceola	116	0.24
Pine Hills (cdp) Orange	100	0.24

Notes: (cdp) census designated place; Refer to the User's Guide in the front of the book for more detailed information.

Altamonte Springs (city) Seminole ... 99 ... 0.24

Assyrian/Chaldean/Syriac

Top 10 Places Sorted by Number
Based on all places, regardless of population

Place (place type) County	Number	%
North Miami Beach (city) Miami-Dade	75	0.18
Big Pine Key (cdp) Monroe	38	0.75
Jacksonville (special city) Duval	29	0.00
St. Augustine Shores (cdp) St. Johns	18	0.35
Jupiter (town) Palm Beach	16	0.04
Ferry Pass (cdp) Escambia	14	0.05
Pompano Beach (city) Broward	12	0.02
Hialeah (city) Miami-Dade	10	0.00
Englewood (cdp) Sarasota	9	0.06
Titusville (city) Brevard	9	0.02

Top 10 Places Sorted by Percent
Based on all places, regardless of population

Place (place type) County	Number	%
Big Pine Key (cdp) Monroe	38	0.75
St. Augustine Shores (cdp) St. Johns	18	0.35
North Miami Beach (city) Miami-Dade	75	0.18
Juno Beach (town) Palm Beach	5	0.16
Ponce Inlet (town) Volusia	4	0.16
Perry (city) Taylor	7	0.10
Gifford (cdp) Indian River	7	0.09
Englewood (cdp) Sarasota	9	0.06
Lakewood Park (cdp) St. Lucie	6	0.06
Ferry Pass (cdp) Escambia	14	0.05

Top 10 Places Sorted by Percent
Based on places with populations of 10,000 or more

Place (place type) County	Number	%
North Miami Beach (city) Miami-Dade	75	0.18
Englewood (cdp) Sarasota	9	0.06
Lakewood Park (cdp) St. Lucie	6	0.06
Ferry Pass (cdp) Escambia	14	0.05
Greater Sun Center (cdp) Hillsborough	8	0.05
Marco Island (city) Collier	8	0.05
Jupiter (town) Palm Beach	16	0.04
Rockledge (city) Brevard	8	0.04
Pompano Beach (city) Broward	12	0.02
Titusville (city) Brevard	9	0.02

Australian

Top 10 Places Sorted by Number
Based on all places, regardless of population

Place (place type) County	Number	%
Jacksonville (special city) Duval	137	0.02
Fort Lauderdale (city) Broward	94	0.06
Miami (city) Miami-Dade	94	0.03
Tallahassee (city) Leon	86	0.06
St. Petersburg (city) Pinellas	84	0.03
Clearwater (city) Pinellas	70	0.06
West Palm Beach (city) Palm Beach	64	0.08
Tampa (city) Hillsborough	64	0.02
Orlando (city) Orange	63	0.03
Hollywood (city) Broward	61	0.04

Top 10 Places Sorted by Percent
Based on all places, regardless of population

Place (place type) County	Number	%
Molino (cdp) Escambia	23	1.62
Atlantis (city) Palm Beach	26	1.22
Cudjoe Key (cdp) Monroe	21	1.21
Tyndall AFB (cdp) Bay	23	0.83
Sunshine Acres (cdp) Broward	8	0.76
Tierra Verde (cdp) Pinellas	22	0.62
North Key Largo (cdp) Monroe	6	0.59

Fort Myers Shores (cdp) Lee	33	0.57
Apollo Beach (cdp) Hillsborough	41	0.55
Samsula-Spruce Creek (cdp) Volusia	23	0.47

Top 10 Places Sorted by Percent
Based on places with populations of 10,000 or more

Place (place type) County	Number	%
Lake Mary (city) Seminole	38	0.34
Key Biscayne (village) Miami-Dade	35	0.33
Wright (cdp) Okaloosa	59	0.27
Fairview Shores (cdp) Orange	30	0.22
Palm Valley (cdp) St. Johns	41	0.21
Destin (city) Okaloosa	21	0.19
Ferry Pass (cdp) Escambia	47	0.17
Poinciana (cdp) Osceola	22	0.16
St. Augustine (city) St. Johns	17	0.15
East Lake (cdp) Pinellas	37	0.13

Austrian

Top 10 Places Sorted by Number
Based on all places, regardless of population

Place (place type) County	Number	%
Jacksonville (special city) Duval	1,086	0.15
St. Petersburg (city) Pinellas	931	0.38
Tamarac (city) Broward	862	1.54
Pembroke Pines (city) Broward	837	0.61
Coral Springs (city) Broward	821	0.70
Miami Beach (city) Miami-Dade	816	0.93
Fort Lauderdale (city) Broward	816	0.54
Hollywood (city) Broward	790	0.57
Boca Raton (city) Palm Beach	786	1.04
Plantation (city) Broward	735	0.88

Top 10 Places Sorted by Percent
Based on all places, regardless of population

Place (place type) County	Number	%
Indian Creek (village) Miami-Dade	2	5.88
Oak Point (cdp) Broward	9	5.70
Highland Beach (town) Palm Beach	152	4.21
Golf (village) Palm Beach	10	4.18
High Point (cdp) Palm Beach	83	3.76
Villages of Oriole (cdp) Palm Beach	174	3.67
Hamptons at Boca Raton (cdp) Palm Beach	391	3.42
Kings Point (cdp) Palm Beach	420	3.39
Boca Pointe (cdp) Palm Beach	106	3.21
Burnt Store Marina (cdp) Lee	34	2.81

Top 10 Places Sorted by Percent
Based on places with populations of 10,000 or more

Place (place type) County	Number	%
Hamptons at Boca Raton (cdp) Palm Beach	391	3.42
Kings Point (cdp) Palm Beach	420	3.39
Palm Beach (town) Palm Beach	224	2.16
Pinecrest (village) Miami-Dade	351	1.83
Aventura (city) Miami-Dade	422	1.67
Tamarac (city) Broward	862	1.54
Hallandale (city) Broward	490	1.42
Boca Del Mar (cdp) Palm Beach	281	1.31
Sandalfoot Cove (cdp) Palm Beach	210	1.27
Coconut Creek (city) Broward	491	1.13

Basque

Top 10 Places Sorted by Number
Based on all places, regardless of population

Place (place type) County	Number	%
Miami (city) Miami-Dade	118	0.03
Cutler (cdp) Miami-Dade	96	0.54
Coral Gables (city) Miami-Dade	82	0.19
Miami Beach (city) Miami-Dade	77	0.09
Tampa (city) Hillsborough	76	0.03

Doral (cdp) Miami-Dade	69	0.34
Kendall (cdp) Miami-Dade	69	0.09
Fort Lauderdale (city) Broward	59	0.04
Jacksonville (special city) Duval	49	0.01
Port St. Lucie (city) St. Lucie	45	0.05

Top 10 Places Sorted by Percent
Based on all places, regardless of population

Place (place type) County	Number	%
Fisher Island (cdp) Miami-Dade	6	1.77
Madison (city) Madison	20	0.61
Cutler (cdp) Miami-Dade	96	0.54
Ocean Ridge (town) Palm Beach	6	0.37
Doral (cdp) Miami-Dade	69	0.34
Key Biscayne (village) Miami-Dade	35	0.33
Lake Clarke Shores (town) Palm Beach	11	0.31
Three Lakes (cdp) Miami-Dade	16	0.23
Belleview (city) Marion	8	0.23
Harbour Heights (cdp) Charlotte	7	0.23

Top 10 Places Sorted by Percent
Based on places with populations of 10,000 or more

Place (place type) County	Number	%
Cutler (cdp) Miami-Dade	96	0.54
Doral (cdp) Miami-Dade	69	0.34
Key Biscayne (village) Miami-Dade	35	0.33
Coral Gables (city) Miami-Dade	82	0.19
Glenvar Heights (cdp) Miami-Dade	31	0.19
Fernandina Beach (city) Nassau	14	0.14
Winter Park (city) Orange	31	0.13
Marco Island (city) Collier	19	0.13
Westchester (cdp) Miami-Dade	32	0.11
Wilton Manors (city) Broward	14	0.11

Belgian

Top 10 Places Sorted by Number
Based on all places, regardless of population

Place (place type) County	Number	%
Jacksonville (special city) Duval	645	0.09
St. Petersburg (city) Pinellas	269	0.11
Miami Beach (city) Miami-Dade	201	0.23
Cape Coral (city) Lee	160	0.16
Fort Lauderdale (city) Broward	153	0.10
Fort Pierce (city) St. Lucie	146	0.39
Orlando (city) Orange	144	0.08
Tallahassee (city) Leon	134	0.09
Brandon (cdp) Hillsborough	132	0.17
Spring Hill (cdp) Hernando	128	0.18

Top 10 Places Sorted by Percent
Based on all places, regardless of population

Place (place type) County	Number	%
Sunshine Acres (cdp) Broward	25	2.38
Riverland Village (cdp) Broward	30	1.46
Lochmoor Waterway Estates (cdp) Lee	49	1.27
Weeki Wachee Gardens (cdp) Hernando	13	1.12
Celebration (cdp) Osceola	27	0.98
Estates of Fort Lauderdale (cdp) Broward	18	0.98
Ocean Breeze Park (town) Martin	4	0.89
Cudjoe Key (cdp) Monroe	15	0.86
Palmona Park (cdp) Lee	10	0.78
Osprey (cdp) Sarasota	31	0.75

Top 10 Places Sorted by Percent
Based on places with populations of 10,000 or more

Place (place type) County	Number	%
South Venice (cdp) Sarasota	89	0.66
South Miami (city) Miami-Dade	67	0.61
Cypress Lake (cdp) Lee	73	0.60
Atlantic Beach (city) Duval	77	0.57
Port St. John (cdp) Brevard	62	0.52

Notes: (cdp) census designated place; Refer to the User's Guide in the front of the book for more detailed information.

Place (place type) County	Number	%
Zephyrhills (city) Pasco	55	0.51
Jensen Beach (cdp) Martin	56	0.50
Lake Mary (city) Seminole	54	0.48
Englewood (cdp) Sarasota	76	0.47
Land O' Lakes (cdp) Pasco	93	0.45

Brazilian

Top 10 Places Sorted by Number
Based on all places, regardless of population

Place (place type) County	Number	%
Deerfield Beach (city) Broward	2,307	3.56
Miami Beach (city) Miami-Dade	1,949	2.21
Orlando (city) Orange	1,355	0.73
Pompano Beach (city) Broward	919	1.17
Fort Lauderdale (city) Broward	917	0.60
Coral Springs (city) Broward	901	0.77
Miami (city) Miami-Dade	802	0.22
Boca Raton (city) Palm Beach	788	1.04
Pembroke Pines (city) Broward	751	0.55
Hollywood (city) Broward	731	0.52

Top 10 Places Sorted by Percent
Based on all places, regardless of population

Place (place type) County	Number	%
Loch Lomond (cdp) Broward	469	14.12
Indian Creek (village) Miami-Dade	4	11.76
North Bay Village (city) Miami-Dade	419	6.22
Bonnie Lock-Woodsetter North (cdp) Broward	238	5.52
Deerfield Beach (city) Broward	2,307	3.56
Pompano Beach Highlands (cdp) Broward	178	2.74
Doral (cdp) Miami-Dade	535	2.61
Palm Aire (cdp) Broward	34	2.60
Country Estates (cdp) Broward	48	2.58
Kendall Green (cdp) Broward	73	2.32

Top 10 Places Sorted by Percent
Based on places with populations of 10,000 or more

Place (place type) County	Number	%
Deerfield Beach (city) Broward	2,307	3.56
Doral (cdp) Miami-Dade	535	2.61
Oakland Park (city) Broward	704	2.26
Miami Beach (city) Miami-Dade	1,949	2.21
Sandalfoot Cove (cdp) Palm Beach	340	2.05
Aventura (city) Miami-Dade	463	1.83
Key Biscayne (village) Miami-Dade	180	1.72
Ojus (cdp) Miami-Dade	268	1.61
The Crossings (cdp) Miami-Dade	362	1.54
Sunny Isles Beach (city) Miami-Dade	222	1.45

British

Top 10 Places Sorted by Number
Based on all places, regardless of population

Place (place type) County	Number	%
Jacksonville (special city) Duval	3,160	0.43
St. Petersburg (city) Pinellas	1,607	0.65
Tampa (city) Hillsborough	1,535	0.51
Tallahassee (city) Leon	1,136	0.75
Orlando (city) Orange	1,080	0.58
Fort Lauderdale (city) Broward	882	0.58
Clearwater (city) Pinellas	877	0.81
Gainesville (city) Alachua	759	0.79
Melbourne (city) Brevard	656	0.92
Coral Springs (city) Broward	653	0.56

Top 10 Places Sorted by Percent
Based on all places, regardless of population

Place (place type) County	Number	%
Pineland (cdp) Lee	26	5.49
Jupiter Island (town) Martin	26	4.19
Indian River Shores (town) Indian River	133	4.04
Golf (village) Palm Beach	9	3.77
Taft (cdp) Orange	64	3.34
Homosassa (cdp) Citrus	75	3.31
Wabasso Beach (cdp) Indian River	35	3.13
La Crosse (town) Alachua	4	3.08
Cedar Key (city) Levy	23	2.97
Belleair (town) Pinellas	114	2.80

Top 10 Places Sorted by Percent
Based on places with populations of 10,000 or more

Place (place type) County	Number	%
Lighthouse Point (city) Broward	173	1.62
Citrus Ridge (cdp) Lake	175	1.53
Winter Park (city) Orange	348	1.44
Vero Beach (city) Indian River	239	1.34
Pinecrest (village) Miami-Dade	249	1.30
Sunny Isles Beach (city) Miami-Dade	189	1.24
Punta Gorda (city) Charlotte	176	1.22
Wekiwa Springs (cdp) Seminole	275	1.18
Oviedo (city) Seminole	307	1.14
Naples (city) Collier	238	1.13

Bulgarian

Top 10 Places Sorted by Number
Based on all places, regardless of population

Place (place type) County	Number	%
St. Petersburg (city) Pinellas	268	0.11
Greater Carrollwood (cdp) Hillsborough	129	0.38
Miami Beach (city) Miami-Dade	91	0.10
Fort Lauderdale (city) Broward	85	0.06
Gainesville (city) Alachua	80	0.08
Boca Raton (city) Palm Beach	75	0.10
Miami (city) Miami-Dade	74	0.02
Tampa (city) Hillsborough	61	0.02
Clearwater (city) Pinellas	58	0.05
Hollywood (city) Broward	58	0.04

Top 10 Places Sorted by Percent
Based on all places, regardless of population

Place (place type) County	Number	%
Chambers Estates (cdp) Broward	42	1.18
Burnt Store Marina (cdp) Lee	11	0.91
Solana (cdp) Charlotte	6	0.61
Manattee Road (cdp) Levy	10	0.47
Country Estates (cdp) Broward	8	0.43
Trinity (cdp) Pasco	19	0.42
Greater Carrollwood (cdp) Hillsborough	129	0.38
Marathon (city) Monroe	37	0.36
Bal Harbour (village) Miami-Dade	12	0.36
North Redington Beach (town) Pinellas	5	0.36

Top 10 Places Sorted by Percent
Based on places with populations of 10,000 or more

Place (place type) County	Number	%
Greater Carrollwood (cdp) Hillsborough	129	0.38
Marathon (city) Monroe	37	0.36
Palm Springs (village) Palm Beach	35	0.30
Maitland (city) Orange	30	0.25
Winter Garden (city) Orange	33	0.24
Sunny Isles Beach (city) Miami-Dade	34	0.22
Apopka (city) Orange	55	0.21
New Port Richey (city) Pasco	29	0.18
Gulf Gate Estates (cdp) Sarasota	21	0.18
Meadow Woods (cdp) Orange	20	0.17

Canadian

Top 10 Places Sorted by Number
Based on all places, regardless of population

Place (place type) County	Number	%
Jacksonville (special city) Duval	1,400	0.19

Place (place type) County	Number	%
Hollywood (city) Broward	1,156	0.83
St. Petersburg (city) Pinellas	963	0.39
Deerfield Beach (city) Broward	708	1.09
Largo (city) Pinellas	699	1.01
Fort Lauderdale (city) Broward	655	0.43
Coral Springs (city) Broward	599	0.51
Boca Raton (city) Palm Beach	582	0.77
Clearwater (city) Pinellas	570	0.53
Pembroke Pines (city) Broward	544	0.40

Top 10 Places Sorted by Percent
Based on all places, regardless of population

Place (place type) County	Number	%
Ravenswood Estates (cdp) Broward	100	10.72
Village Park (cdp) Broward	82	7.56
North Beach (cdp) Indian River	12	5.43
Dunes Road (cdp) Palm Beach	20	4.23
Estates of Fort Lauderdale (cdp) Broward	66	3.58
Andrews (cdp) Levy	23	3.05
Pembroke Park (town) Broward	191	3.01
Hypoluxo (town) Palm Beach	58	2.87
Orangetree (cdp) Collier	27	2.62
Layton (city) Monroe	6	2.50

Top 10 Places Sorted by Percent
Based on places with populations of 10,000 or more

Place (place type) County	Number	%
Englewood (cdp) Sarasota	244	1.50
Hallandale (city) Broward	475	1.37
North Palm Beach (village) Palm Beach	153	1.26
East Lake (cdp) Pinellas	369	1.25
Hudson (cdp) Pasco	149	1.17
Deerfield Beach (city) Broward	708	1.09
Dunedin (city) Pinellas	374	1.04
Holiday (cdp) Pasco	227	1.04
Largo (city) Pinellas	699	1.01
Venice (city) Sarasota	179	1.00

Carpatho Rusyn

Top 10 Places Sorted by Number
Based on all places, regardless of population

Place (place type) County	Number	%
Orlando (city) Orange	17	0.01
Port St. Lucie (city) St. Lucie	16	0.02
Hobe Sound (cdp) Martin	15	0.13
Roseland (cdp) Indian River	11	0.61
Coral Springs (city) Broward	11	0.01
Fort Lauderdale (city) Broward	10	0.01
Country Club (cdp) Miami-Dade	9	0.02
Gifford (cdp) Indian River	8	0.11
Tallahassee (city) Leon	8	0.01
Jacksonville (special city) Duval	8	0.00

Top 10 Places Sorted by Percent
Based on all places, regardless of population

Place (place type) County	Number	%
Roseland (cdp) Indian River	11	0.61
Briny Breezes (town) Palm Beach	2	0.48
Hobe Sound (cdp) Martin	15	0.13
Gifford (cdp) Indian River	8	0.11
Winter Garden (city) Orange	7	0.05
Doral (cdp) Miami-Dade	7	0.03
Port St. Lucie (city) St. Lucie	16	0.02
Country Club (cdp) Miami-Dade	9	0.02
Orlando (city) Orange	17	0.01
Coral Springs (city) Broward	11	0.01

Top 10 Places Sorted by Percent
Based on places with populations of 10,000 or more

Place (place type) County	Number	%
Hobe Sound (cdp) Martin	15	0.13

Place (place type) County	Number	%
Winter Garden (city) Orange	7	0.05
Doral (cdp) Miami-Dade	7	0.03
Port St. Lucie (city) St. Lucie	16	0.02
Country Club (cdp) Miami-Dade	9	0.02
Orlando (city) Orange	17	0.01
Coral Springs (city) Broward	11	0.01
Fort Lauderdale (city) Broward	10	0.01
Tallahassee (city) Leon	8	0.01
Spring Hill (cdp) Hernando	7	0.01

Celtic

Top 10 Places Sorted by Number
Based on all places, regardless of population

Place (place type) County	Number	%
Jacksonville (special city) Duval	195	0.03
Tallahassee (city) Leon	125	0.08
Tampa (city) Hillsborough	111	0.04
Gainesville (city) Alachua	86	0.09
Callaway (city) Bay	64	0.45
Chuluota (cdp) Seminole	58	2.92
Melbourne (city) Brevard	44	0.06
West Bradenton (cdp) Manatee	41	0.91
St. Petersburg (city) Pinellas	41	0.02
Clearwater (city) Pinellas	39	0.04

Top 10 Places Sorted by Percent
Based on all places, regardless of population

Place (place type) County	Number	%
Chuluota (cdp) Seminole	58	2.92
St. Leo (town) Pasco	12	1.97
Jay (town) Santa Rosa	6	1.10
South Beach (cdp) Indian River	32	0.94
West Bradenton (cdp) Manatee	41	0.91
Melbourne Village (town) Brevard	6	0.89
St. George (cdp) Broward	19	0.79
Bradenton Beach (city) Manatee	9	0.61
Manasota Key (cdp) Charlotte	8	0.61
North Key Largo (cdp) Monroe	5	0.49

Top 10 Places Sorted by Percent
Based on places with populations of 10,000 or more

Place (place type) County	Number	%
Callaway (city) Bay	64	0.45
St. Augustine (city) St. Johns	31	0.27
Lakeland Highlands (cdp) Polk	32	0.25
Leesburg (city) Lake	31	0.20
Lockhart (cdp) Orange	21	0.17
Holly Hill (city) Volusia	18	0.15
Fruit Cove (cdp) St. Johns	16	0.10
Palmetto (city) Manatee	12	0.10
Lake Wales (city) Polk	10	0.10
Gainesville (city) Alachua	86	0.09

Croatian

Top 10 Places Sorted by Number
Based on all places, regardless of population

Place (place type) County	Number	%
Jacksonville (special city) Duval	659	0.09
Cape Coral (city) Lee	298	0.29
St. Petersburg (city) Pinellas	284	0.11
Tampa (city) Hillsborough	247	0.08
Palm Harbor (cdp) Pinellas	216	0.37
Largo (city) Pinellas	178	0.26
Orlando (city) Orange	145	0.08
Pinellas Park (city) Pinellas	138	0.30
Port Orange (city) Volusia	131	0.29
Hollywood (city) Broward	121	0.09

Top 10 Places Sorted by Percent
Based on all places, regardless of population

Place (place type) County	Number	%
North Redington Beach (town) Pinellas	24	1.75
Feather Sound (cdp) Pinellas	51	1.24
Harbour Heights (cdp) Charlotte	31	1.04
Pine Castle (cdp) Orange	77	0.94
Terra Mar (cdp) Broward	23	0.86
Holmes Beach (city) Manatee	42	0.85
Rio (cdp) Martin	9	0.85
Bay Hill (cdp) Orange	41	0.76
Lecanto (cdp) Citrus	33	0.70
Palmona Park (cdp) Lee	9	0.70

Top 10 Places Sorted by Percent
Based on places with populations of 10,000 or more

Place (place type) County	Number	%
Oldsmar (city) Pinellas	65	0.55
Niceville (city) Okaloosa	61	0.52
Marco Island (city) Collier	67	0.45
New Port Richey (city) Pasco	68	0.43
Seminole (city) Pinellas	42	0.39
Iona (cdp) Lee	45	0.38
Palm Harbor (cdp) Pinellas	216	0.37
Cypress Lake (cdp) Lee	44	0.36
Oakland Park (city) Broward	105	0.34
Bloomingdale (cdp) Hillsborough	68	0.34

Cypriot

Top 10 Places Sorted by Number
Based on all places, regardless of population

Place (place type) County	Number	%
Boca Raton (city) Palm Beach	52	0.07
Jacksonville (special city) Duval	35	0.00
Palm Harbor (cdp) Pinellas	30	0.05
Oldsmar (city) Pinellas	25	0.21
Wellington (village) Palm Beach	20	0.05
Brandon (cdp) Hillsborough	17	0.02
Palm Bay (city) Brevard	16	0.02
Fort Lauderdale (city) Broward	14	0.01
Boca Del Mar (cdp) Palm Beach	12	0.06
Bonita Springs (city) Lee	12	0.04

Top 10 Places Sorted by Percent
Based on all places, regardless of population

Place (place type) County	Number	%
Osprey (cdp) Sarasota	11	0.27
Oldsmar (city) Pinellas	25	0.21
Boca Raton (city) Palm Beach	52	0.07
Port St. John (cdp) Brevard	8	0.07
Miami Shores (village) Miami-Dade	7	0.07
Boca Del Mar (cdp) Palm Beach	12	0.06
Palm Harbor (cdp) Pinellas	30	0.05
Wellington (village) Palm Beach	20	0.05
Bonita Springs (city) Lee	12	0.04
Hallandale (city) Broward	11	0.03

Top 10 Places Sorted by Percent
Based on places with populations of 10,000 or more

Place (place type) County	Number	%
Oldsmar (city) Pinellas	25	0.21
Boca Raton (city) Palm Beach	52	0.07
Port St. John (cdp) Brevard	8	0.07
Miami Shores (village) Miami-Dade	7	0.07
Boca Del Mar (cdp) Palm Beach	12	0.06
Palm Harbor (cdp) Pinellas	30	0.05
Wellington (village) Palm Beach	20	0.05
Bonita Springs (city) Lee	12	0.04
Hallandale (city) Broward	11	0.03
Oakland Park (city) Broward	9	0.03

Czech

Top 10 Places Sorted by Number
Based on all places, regardless of population

Place (place type) County	Number	%
Jacksonville (special city) Duval	1,244	0.17
St. Petersburg (city) Pinellas	990	0.40
Tampa (city) Hillsborough	592	0.20
Cape Coral (city) Lee	509	0.50
Fort Lauderdale (city) Broward	508	0.33
Clearwater (city) Pinellas	489	0.45
Coral Springs (city) Broward	441	0.38
Boca Raton (city) Palm Beach	396	0.52
Daytona Beach (city) Volusia	393	0.61
Palm Harbor (cdp) Pinellas	366	0.62

Top 10 Places Sorted by Percent
Based on all places, regardless of population

Place (place type) County	Number	%
Goodland (cdp) Collier	25	11.31
Pine Island (cdp) Hernando	5	9.09
Anna Maria (city) Manatee	83	4.55
Solana (cdp) Charlotte	26	2.63
Cloud Lake (town) Palm Beach	3	2.44
Juno Ridge (cdp) Palm Beach	14	1.86
Wabasso Beach (cdp) Indian River	20	1.79
Jupiter Island (town) Martin	11	1.77
Duck Key (cdp) Monroe	9	1.66
High Point (cdp) Hernando	50	1.65

Top 10 Places Sorted by Percent
Based on places with populations of 10,000 or more

Place (place type) County	Number	%
Hudson (cdp) Pasco	191	1.50
Wilton Manors (city) Broward	109	0.86
Bonita Springs (city) Lee	276	0.84
Jasmine Estates (cdp) Pasco	143	0.79
Venice (city) Sarasota	138	0.77
Tarpon Springs (city) Pinellas	160	0.76
Merritt Island (cdp) Brevard	266	0.74
Oldsmar (city) Pinellas	85	0.72
Westchase (cdp) Hillsborough	78	0.70
Lake Magdalene (cdp) Hillsborough	199	0.69

Czechoslovakian

Top 10 Places Sorted by Number
Based on all places, regardless of population

Place (place type) County	Number	%
Jacksonville (special city) Duval	741	0.10
St. Petersburg (city) Pinellas	493	0.20
Hollywood (city) Broward	330	0.24
Spring Hill (cdp) Hernando	327	0.47
Tampa (city) Hillsborough	308	0.10
Clearwater (city) Pinellas	289	0.27
Cape Coral (city) Lee	239	0.23
Palm Harbor (cdp) Pinellas	222	0.38
Plantation (city) Broward	216	0.26
Melbourne (city) Brevard	199	0.28

Top 10 Places Sorted by Percent
Based on all places, regardless of population

Place (place type) County	Number	%
Dunes Road (cdp) Palm Beach	62	13.11
Lazy Lake (village) Broward	2	5.13
Goodland (cdp) Collier	11	4.98
Black Diamond (cdp) Citrus	30	4.60
Okahumpka (cdp) Lake	9	4.41
Ferndale (cdp) Lake	12	4.17
Cloud Lake (town) Palm Beach	5	4.07
Juno Ridge (cdp) Palm Beach	14	1.86
Lely Resort (cdp) Collier	24	1.68
Matlacha (cdp) Lee	13	1.64

Notes: (cdp) census designated place; Refer to the User's Guide in the front of the book for more detailed information.

Top 10 Places Sorted by Percent
Based on places with populations of 10,000 or more

Place (place type) County	Number	%
Seminole (city) Pinellas	100	0.93
Lighthouse Point (city) Broward	71	0.67
Fruit Cove (cdp) St. Johns	96	0.60
Greater Northdale (cdp) Hillsborough	107	0.53
Boca Del Mar (cdp) Palm Beach	112	0.52
Greater Sun Center (cdp) Hillsborough	84	0.52
Hudson (cdp) Pasco	66	0.52
De Bary (city) Volusia	77	0.49
Englewood (cdp) Sarasota	78	0.48
Cocoa Beach (city) Brevard	59	0.48

Danish

Top 10 Places Sorted by Number
Based on all places, regardless of population

Place (place type) County	Number	%
Jacksonville (special city) Duval	1,337	0.18
St. Petersburg (city) Pinellas	906	0.37
Tampa (city) Hillsborough	591	0.19
Fort Lauderdale (city) Broward	570	0.37
Palm Harbor (cdp) Pinellas	531	0.90
Orlando (city) Orange	514	0.28
Cape Coral (city) Lee	473	0.46
Tallahassee (city) Leon	421	0.28
Clearwater (city) Pinellas	405	0.38
Largo (city) Pinellas	379	0.55

Top 10 Places Sorted by Percent
Based on all places, regardless of population

Place (place type) County	Number	%
North Beach (cdp) Indian River	6	2.71
Burnt Store Marina (cdp) Lee	26	2.15
Loughman (cdp) Polk	27	2.11
Melbourne Village (town) Brevard	14	2.08
June Park (cdp) Brevard	97	2.07
Matlacha (cdp) Lee	16	2.02
Laguna Beach (cdp) Bay	56	1.90
Butler Beach (cdp) St. Johns	85	1.88
Matlacha Isles-Matlacha Shores (cdp) Lee	5	1.85
Worthington Springs (town) Union	3	1.81

Top 10 Places Sorted by Percent
Based on places with populations of 10,000 or more

Place (place type) County	Number	%
Punta Gorda (city) Charlotte	150	1.04
Palm City (cdp) Martin	183	0.91
Marco Island (city) Collier	137	0.91
Palm Harbor (cdp) Pinellas	531	0.90
Wekiwa Springs (cdp) Seminole	208	0.89
Gonzalez (cdp) Escambia	95	0.81
Naples (city) Collier	168	0.80
Seminole (city) Pinellas	85	0.79
Pinecrest (village) Miami-Dade	150	0.78
New Smyrna Beach (city) Volusia	156	0.77

Dutch

Top 10 Places Sorted by Number
Based on all places, regardless of population

Place (place type) County	Number	%
Jacksonville (special city) Duval	7,635	1.04
St. Petersburg (city) Pinellas	4,000	1.61
Tampa (city) Hillsborough	3,035	1.00
Orlando (city) Orange	2,223	1.20
Cape Coral (city) Lee	1,991	1.95
Clearwater (city) Pinellas	1,684	1.56
Palm Bay (city) Brevard	1,671	2.10
Melbourne (city) Brevard	1,624	2.28
Port St. Lucie (city) St. Lucie	1,624	1.83

| Tallahassee (city) Leon | 1,586 | 1.05 |

Top 10 Places Sorted by Percent
Based on all places, regardless of population

Place (place type) County	Number	%
Islandia (city) Miami-Dade	3	50.00
Indian Creek (village) Miami-Dade	7	20.59
Pine Island (cdp) Hernando	11	20.00
Lazy Lake (village) Broward	6	15.38
Solana (cdp) Charlotte	84	8.50
North De Land (cdp) Volusia	106	7.79
Matlacha Isles-Matlacha Shores (cdp) Lee	21	7.75
Hillsboro Pines (cdp) Broward	32	6.60
Duck Key (cdp) Monroe	35	6.47
Gotha (cdp) Orange	45	6.01

Top 10 Places Sorted by Percent
Based on places with populations of 10,000 or more

Place (place type) County	Number	%
Englewood (cdp) Sarasota	564	3.47
Homosassa Springs (cdp) Citrus	413	3.24
Zephyrhills (city) Pasco	330	3.09
Seminole (city) Pinellas	331	3.07
Elfers (cdp) Pasco	401	3.04
North Palm Beach (village) Palm Beach	363	2.99
South Bradenton (cdp) Manatee	591	2.76
North Fort Myers (cdp) Lee	1,098	2.72
Port Salerno (cdp) Martin	274	2.71
Lutz (cdp) Hillsborough	456	2.67

Eastern European

Top 10 Places Sorted by Number
Based on all places, regardless of population

Place (place type) County	Number	%
Plantation (city) Broward	525	0.63
Boca Raton (city) Palm Beach	518	0.69
Coral Springs (city) Broward	508	0.43
Hollywood (city) Broward	494	0.35
Miami Beach (city) Miami-Dade	414	0.47
Weston (city) Broward	328	0.67
Jacksonville (special city) Duval	323	0.04
Kendall (cdp) Miami-Dade	316	0.42
Aventura (city) Miami-Dade	297	1.18
Boca Del Mar (cdp) Palm Beach	250	1.17

Top 10 Places Sorted by Percent
Based on all places, regardless of population

Place (place type) County	Number	%
Mission Bay (cdp) Palm Beach	70	2.28
Celebration (cdp) Osceola	48	1.75
Boca Pointe (cdp) Palm Beach	55	1.67
Odessa (cdp) Hillsborough	46	1.38
Bay Harbor Islands (town) Miami-Dade	65	1.26
Whisper Walk (cdp) Palm Beach	62	1.21
Chambers Estates (cdp) Broward	43	1.21
Aventura (city) Miami-Dade	297	1.18
Boca Del Mar (cdp) Palm Beach	250	1.17
Ojus (cdp) Miami-Dade	157	0.94

Top 10 Places Sorted by Percent
Based on places with populations of 10,000 or more

Place (place type) County	Number	%
Aventura (city) Miami-Dade	297	1.18
Boca Del Mar (cdp) Palm Beach	250	1.17
Ojus (cdp) Miami-Dade	157	0.94
Sandalfoot Cove (cdp) Palm Beach	129	0.78
Cutler (cdp) Miami-Dade	132	0.75
Maitland (city) Orange	88	0.74
Cooper City (city) Broward	202	0.73
Parkland (city) Broward	100	0.71
Boca Raton (city) Palm Beach	518	0.69

| Wekiwa Springs (cdp) Seminole | 158 | 0.68 |

English

Top 10 Places Sorted by Number
Based on all places, regardless of population

Place (place type) County	Number	%
Jacksonville (special city) Duval	62,798	8.54
St. Petersburg (city) Pinellas	27,556	11.12
Tampa (city) Hillsborough	23,319	7.68
Orlando (city) Orange	14,663	7.88
Tallahassee (city) Leon	13,888	9.22
Clearwater (city) Pinellas	12,820	11.88
Fort Lauderdale (city) Broward	12,456	8.19
Cape Coral (city) Lee	12,127	11.87
Port St. Lucie (city) St. Lucie	10,173	11.46
Largo (city) Pinellas	9,669	13.92

Top 10 Places Sorted by Percent
Based on all places, regardless of population

Place (place type) County	Number	%
Bayport (cdp) Hernando	16	66.67
Golf (village) Palm Beach	91	38.08
Captiva (cdp) Lee	140	35.71
Layton (city) Monroe	83	34.58
North Key Largo (cdp) Monroe	317	31.36
Orchid (town) Indian River	42	30.43
Punta Rassa (cdp) Lee	502	29.97
Jupiter Inlet Colony (town) Palm Beach	115	29.79
Penney Farms (town) Clay	155	28.86
Jupiter Island (town) Martin	177	28.50

Top 10 Places Sorted by Percent
Based on places with populations of 10,000 or more

Place (place type) County	Number	%
Greater Sun Center (cdp) Hillsborough	3,336	20.48
Englewood (cdp) Sarasota	3,140	19.32
Venice (city) Sarasota	3,402	19.06
Naples (city) Collier	3,920	18.68
Lady Lake (town) Lake	2,130	18.24
Palm Valley (cdp) St. Johns	3,584	18.05
Winter Park (city) Orange	4,347	17.94
Punta Gorda (city) Charlotte	2,556	17.71
Cypress Lake (cdp) Lee	2,121	17.53
South Venice (cdp) Sarasota	2,345	17.36

Estonian

Top 10 Places Sorted by Number
Based on all places, regardless of population

Place (place type) County	Number	%
Wellington (village) Palm Beach	49	0.13
Dania Beach (city) Broward	43	0.21
Orlando (city) Orange	38	0.02
Jacksonville (special city) Duval	28	0.00
North Miami Beach (city) Miami-Dade	26	0.06
Sunny Isles Beach (city) Miami-Dade	25	0.16
Ormond Beach (city) Volusia	25	0.07
Greenacres (city) Palm Beach	22	0.08
Merritt Island (cdp) Brevard	22	0.06
Boca Raton (city) Palm Beach	21	0.03

Top 10 Places Sorted by Percent
Based on all places, regardless of population

Place (place type) County	Number	%
East Palatka (cdp) Putnam	6	0.35
Lower Grand Lagoon (cdp) Bay	13	0.32
Carrabelle (city) Franklin	4	0.31
Orlovista (cdp) Orange	16	0.26
St. James City (cdp) Lee	9	0.22
Dania Beach (city) Broward	43	0.21
Baldwin (town) Duval	3	0.18

Notes: (cdp) census designated place; Refer to the User's Guide in the front of the book for more detailed information.

Place (place type) County	Number	%
Osprey (cdp) Sarasota	7	0.17
Sunny Isles Beach (city) Miami-Dade	25	0.16
Cypress Lake (cdp) Lee	18	0.15

Top 10 Places Sorted by Percent
Based on places with populations of 10,000 or more

Place (place type) County	Number	%
Dania Beach (city) Broward	43	0.21
Sunny Isles Beach (city) Miami-Dade	25	0.16
Cypress Lake (cdp) Lee	18	0.15
Wellington (village) Palm Beach	49	0.13
Kings Point (cdp) Palm Beach	16	0.13
Venice (city) Sarasota	16	0.09
Riverview (cdp) Hillsborough	11	0.09
Palm Beach (town) Palm Beach	9	0.09
Greenacres (city) Palm Beach	22	0.08
Ormond Beach (city) Volusia	25	0.07

European

Top 10 Places Sorted by Number
Based on all places, regardless of population

Place (place type) County	Number	%
Jacksonville (special city) Duval	5,173	0.70
Tampa (city) Hillsborough	1,958	0.65
Tallahassee (city) Leon	1,416	0.94
St. Petersburg (city) Pinellas	1,372	0.55
Orlando (city) Orange	1,110	0.60
Gainesville (city) Alachua	1,024	1.07
Miami Beach (city) Miami-Dade	988	1.12
Coral Springs (city) Broward	944	0.80
Hollywood (city) Broward	872	0.63
Brandon (cdp) Hillsborough	856	1.10

Top 10 Places Sorted by Percent
Based on all places, regardless of population

Place (place type) County	Number	%
Edgewater (cdp) Broward	78	11.00
Ivanhoe Estates (cdp) Broward	19	7.51
San Antonio (city) Pasco	39	6.34
Fisher Island (cdp) Miami-Dade	20	5.90
Wewahitchka (city) Gulf	102	5.86
Worthington Springs (town) Union	7	4.22
Indialantic (town) Brevard	107	3.64
North Brooksville (cdp) Hernando	52	3.52
Geneva (cdp) Seminole	98	3.49
Lake Lorraine (cdp) Okaloosa	230	3.24

Top 10 Places Sorted by Percent
Based on places with populations of 10,000 or more

Place (place type) County	Number	%
Niceville (city) Okaloosa	251	2.13
Maitland (city) Orange	247	2.07
Ojus (cdp) Miami-Dade	320	1.92
Cutler (cdp) Miami-Dade	319	1.81
Pinecrest (village) Miami-Dade	315	1.64
Wekiwa Springs (cdp) Seminole	378	1.62
Palm Beach Gardens (city) Palm Beach	458	1.33
Fruit Cove (cdp) St. Johns	202	1.26
Goldenrod (cdp) Seminole	165	1.26
Jacksonville Beach (city) Duval	260	1.24

Finnish

Top 10 Places Sorted by Number
Based on all places, regardless of population

Place (place type) County	Number	%
Lake Worth (city) Palm Beach	1,026	2.91
Jacksonville (special city) Duval	665	0.09
Lantana (town) Palm Beach	570	5.97
St. Petersburg (city) Pinellas	407	0.16
Orlando (city) Orange	330	0.18

Place (place type) County	Number	%
Clearwater (city) Pinellas	317	0.29
Cape Coral (city) Lee	315	0.31
Greenacres (city) Palm Beach	232	0.85
Port Charlotte (cdp) Charlotte	227	0.49
Tampa (city) Hillsborough	227	0.07

Top 10 Places Sorted by Percent
Based on all places, regardless of population

Place (place type) County	Number	%
Lantana (town) Palm Beach	570	5.97
South Palm Beach (town) Palm Beach	30	4.14
Hypoluxo (town) Palm Beach	77	3.81
Lake Worth (city) Palm Beach	1,026	2.91
Manalapan (town) Palm Beach	9	2.79
Riverland Village (cdp) Broward	32	1.55
Wabasso (cdp) Indian River	12	1.44
Bokeelia (cdp) Lee	24	1.24
Melbourne Village (town) Brevard	8	1.19
Hutchinson Island South (cdp) St. Lucie	56	1.18

Top 10 Places Sorted by Percent
Based on places with populations of 10,000 or more

Place (place type) County	Number	%
Lake Worth (city) Palm Beach	1,026	2.91
Sebastian (city) Indian River	156	0.95
Greenacres (city) Palm Beach	232	0.85
Marco Island (city) Collier	127	0.85
North Palm Beach (village) Palm Beach	84	0.69
Lake Worth Corridor (cdp) Palm Beach	109	0.59
Hobe Sound (cdp) Martin	64	0.57
Lighthouse Point (city) Broward	61	0.57
Zephyrhills (city) Pasco	61	0.57
Port Charlotte (cdp) Charlotte	227	0.49

French, except Basque

Top 10 Places Sorted by Number
Based on all places, regardless of population

Place (place type) County	Number	%
Jacksonville (special city) Duval	16,196	2.20
St. Petersburg (city) Pinellas	9,438	3.81
Tampa (city) Hillsborough	7,198	2.37
Orlando (city) Orange	4,327	2.33
Cape Coral (city) Lee	4,300	4.21
Fort Lauderdale (city) Broward	4,153	2.73
Clearwater (city) Pinellas	3,814	3.53
Hollywood (city) Broward	3,601	2.59
Port St. Lucie (city) St. Lucie	3,402	3.83
Tallahassee (city) Leon	3,382	2.25

Top 10 Places Sorted by Percent
Based on all places, regardless of population

Place (place type) County	Number	%
Bay Lake (city) Orange	14	35.90
Glen Ridge (town) Palm Beach	47	17.34
Layton (city) Monroe	41	17.08
Lake Buena Vista (city) Orange	2	12.50
Hampton (city) Bradford	57	11.59
Weeki Wachee (city) Hernando	1	11.11
Page Park (cdp) Lee	60	10.70
Matlacha Isles-Matlacha Shores (cdp) Lee	29	10.70
Ravenswood Estates (cdp) Broward	98	10.50
Belleview (city) Marion	358	10.07

Top 10 Places Sorted by Percent
Based on places with populations of 10,000 or more

Place (place type) County	Number	%
South Venice (cdp) Sarasota	838	6.20
Middleburg (cdp) Clay	610	5.86
Lady Lake (town) Lake	640	5.48
Lakewood Park (cdp) St. Lucie	562	5.40
Cocoa Beach (city) Brevard	648	5.22

Place (place type) County	Number	%
Elfers (cdp) Pasco	686	5.20
Port Charlotte (cdp) Charlotte	2,390	5.14
Villas (cdp) Lee	571	5.11
Edgewater (city) Volusia	960	5.09
Key Largo (cdp) Monroe	606	5.06

French Canadian

Top 10 Places Sorted by Number
Based on all places, regardless of population

Place (place type) County	Number	%
Jacksonville (special city) Duval	4,238	0.58
St. Petersburg (city) Pinellas	2,528	1.02
Tampa (city) Hillsborough	1,892	0.62
Hollywood (city) Broward	1,696	1.22
Port St. Lucie (city) St. Lucie	1,357	1.53
Clearwater (city) Pinellas	1,290	1.20
Palm Bay (city) Brevard	1,257	1.58
Orlando (city) Orange	1,240	0.67
Fort Lauderdale (city) Broward	1,163	0.76
Largo (city) Pinellas	1,079	1.55

Top 10 Places Sorted by Percent
Based on all places, regardless of population

Place (place type) County	Number	%
Godfrey Road (cdp) Broward	18	8.45
Matlacha Isles-Matlacha Shores (cdp) Lee	15	5.54
Hypoluxo (town) Palm Beach	101	4.99
Crescent Beach (cdp) St. Johns	39	4.91
Pembroke Park (town) Broward	296	4.67
Rio (cdp) Martin	49	4.60
Ridge Manor (cdp) Hernando	176	4.27
Ravenswood Estates (cdp) Broward	38	4.07
Highland Park (village) Polk	9	3.81
East Bronson (cdp) Levy	38	3.57

Top 10 Places Sorted by Percent
Based on places with populations of 10,000 or more

Place (place type) County	Number	%
Hallandale (city) Broward	934	2.70
De Bary (city) Volusia	400	2.54
Dania Beach (city) Broward	491	2.44
Hobe Sound (cdp) Martin	256	2.29
Iona (cdp) Lee	251	2.12
Greater Sun Center (cdp) Hillsborough	332	2.04
Stuart (city) Martin	297	2.02
Edgewater (city) Volusia	363	1.92
Palm City (cdp) Martin	382	1.90
Upper Grand Lagoon (cdp) Bay	208	1.89

German

Top 10 Places Sorted by Number
Based on all places, regardless of population

Place (place type) County	Number	%
Jacksonville (special city) Duval	70,440	9.58
St. Petersburg (city) Pinellas	36,327	14.66
Tampa (city) Hillsborough	27,990	9.22
Cape Coral (city) Lee	21,385	20.92
Orlando (city) Orange	18,259	9.82
Clearwater (city) Pinellas	18,191	16.86
Fort Lauderdale (city) Broward	15,857	10.42
Port St. Lucie (city) St. Lucie	14,983	16.87
Palm Bay (city) Brevard	14,240	17.92
Tallahassee (city) Leon	14,091	9.36

Top 10 Places Sorted by Percent
Based on all places, regardless of population

Place (place type) County	Number	%
Pine Island (cdp) Hernando	28	50.91
Islandia (city) Miami-Dade	3	50.00
Dunes Road (cdp) Palm Beach	228	48.20

Place	Number	%
Bayport (cdp) Hernando	10	41.67
Lake Buena Vista (city) Orange	6	37.50
Istachatta (cdp) Hernando	22	36.07
Matlacha Isles-Matlacha Shores (cdp) Lee	94	34.69
Royal Palm Ranches (cdp) Broward	97	32.23
Captiva (cdp) Lee	118	30.10
Matlacha (cdp) Lee	234	29.55

Top 10 Places Sorted by Percent
Based on places with populations of 10,000 or more

Place (place type) County	Number	%
San Carlos Park (cdp) Lee	4,108	25.48
Iona (cdp) Lee	2,970	25.06
Englewood (cdp) Sarasota	3,952	24.32
Punta Gorda (city) Charlotte	3,419	23.69
Marco Island (city) Collier	3,498	23.35
Fruitville (cdp) Sarasota	3,000	23.27
Cypress Lake (cdp) Lee	2,793	23.08
Greater Sun Center (cdp) Hillsborough	3,737	22.95
Oldsmar (city) Pinellas	2,641	22.50
Lake Mary (city) Seminole	2,528	22.39

German Russian

Top 10 Places Sorted by Number
Based on all places, regardless of population

Place (place type) County	Number	%
Melrose Park (cdp) Broward	29	0.41
Hollywood (city) Broward	20	0.01
Hallandale (city) Broward	17	0.05
Plantation (city) Broward	14	0.02
Palm Bay (city) Brevard	11	0.01
Port St. Lucie (city) St. Lucie	11	0.01
Leesburg (city) Lake	9	0.06
Orlando (city) Orange	9	0.00
Kendall West (cdp) Miami-Dade	8	0.02
Titusville (city) Brevard	8	0.02

Top 10 Places Sorted by Percent
Based on all places, regardless of population

Place (place type) County	Number	%
Melrose Park (cdp) Broward	29	0.41
Leesburg (city) Lake	9	0.06
Hallandale (city) Broward	17	0.05
Gulfport (city) Pinellas	5	0.04
Bayshore Gardens (cdp) Manatee	6	0.03
West Pensacola (cdp) Escambia	6	0.03
Plantation (city) Broward	14	0.02
Kendall West (cdp) Miami-Dade	8	0.02
Titusville (city) Brevard	8	0.02
Panama City (city) Bay	7	0.02

Top 10 Places Sorted by Percent
Based on places with populations of 10,000 or more

Place (place type) County	Number	%
Leesburg (city) Lake	9	0.06
Hallandale (city) Broward	17	0.05
Gulfport (city) Pinellas	5	0.04
Bayshore Gardens (cdp) Manatee	6	0.03
West Pensacola (cdp) Escambia	6	0.03
Plantation (city) Broward	14	0.02
Kendall West (cdp) Miami-Dade	8	0.02
Titusville (city) Brevard	8	0.02
Panama City (city) Bay	7	0.02
Hollywood (city) Broward	20	0.01

Greek

Top 10 Places Sorted by Number
Based on all places, regardless of population

Place (place type) County	Number	%
Tarpon Springs (city) Pinellas	2,479	11.77
Jacksonville (special city) Duval	2,314	0.31
Clearwater (city) Pinellas	1,934	1.79
Palm Harbor (cdp) Pinellas	1,707	2.89
St. Petersburg (city) Pinellas	1,436	0.58
Holiday (cdp) Pasco	1,247	5.69
Hollywood (city) Broward	1,097	0.79
Boca Raton (city) Palm Beach	1,065	1.41
Fort Lauderdale (city) Broward	1,038	0.68
Tampa (city) Hillsborough	1,022	0.34

Top 10 Places Sorted by Percent
Based on all places, regardless of population

Place (place type) County	Number	%
Tarpon Springs (city) Pinellas	2,479	11.77
Holiday (cdp) Pasco	1,247	5.69
Fisher Island (cdp) Miami-Dade	18	5.31
East Lake (cdp) Pinellas	868	2.95
Beacon Square (cdp) Pasco	212	2.92
Palm Harbor (cdp) Pinellas	1,707	2.89
Twin Lakes (cdp) Broward	47	2.75
Miramar Beach (cdp) Walton	56	2.30
Indian Rocks Beach (city) Pinellas	109	2.15
Sea Ranch Lakes (village) Broward	28	2.03

Top 10 Places Sorted by Percent
Based on places with populations of 10,000 or more

Place (place type) County	Number	%
Tarpon Springs (city) Pinellas	2,479	11.77
Holiday (cdp) Pasco	1,247	5.69
East Lake (cdp) Pinellas	868	2.95
Palm Harbor (cdp) Pinellas	1,707	2.89
Lakewood Park (cdp) St. Lucie	204	1.96
New Port Richey East (cdp) Pasco	188	1.86
Clearwater (city) Pinellas	1,934	1.79
Dunedin (city) Pinellas	591	1.65
North Palm Beach (village) Palm Beach	183	1.51
Elfers (cdp) Pasco	196	1.48

Guyanese

Top 10 Places Sorted by Number
Based on all places, regardless of population

Place (place type) County	Number	%
Pembroke Pines (city) Broward	508	0.37
Miramar (city) Broward	469	0.65
Pine Hills (cdp) Orange	385	0.92
Jacksonville (special city) Duval	358	0.05
Town 'n' Country (cdp) Hillsborough	354	0.49
South Miami Heights (cdp) Miami-Dade	337	1.00
Hollywood (city) Broward	281	0.20
Tampa (city) Hillsborough	220	0.07
Sunrise (city) Broward	218	0.25
Lauderhill (city) Broward	217	0.38

Top 10 Places Sorted by Percent
Based on all places, regardless of population

Place (place type) County	Number	%
Wedgefield (cdp) Orange	91	3.23
Broadview-Pompano Park (cdp) Broward	72	1.40
Pine Castle (cdp) Orange	100	1.22
Southchase (cdp) Orange	54	1.19
South Miami Heights (cdp) Miami-Dade	337	1.00
Riverland Village (cdp) Broward	20	0.97
Pine Hills (cdp) Orange	385	0.92
Melrose Park (cdp) Broward	65	0.92
Silver Springs Shores (cdp) Marion	60	0.92
Palmetto Estates (cdp) Miami-Dade	113	0.83

Top 10 Places Sorted by Percent
Based on places with populations of 10,000 or more

Place (place type) County	Number	%
South Miami Heights (cdp) Miami-Dade	337	1.00

Place	Number	%
Pine Hills (cdp) Orange	385	0.92
Palmetto Estates (cdp) Miami-Dade	113	0.83
Miramar (city) Broward	469	0.65
Lauderdale Lakes (city) Broward	163	0.52
Citrus Park (cdp) Hillsborough	105	0.52
Poinciana (cdp) Osceola	70	0.52
Richmond West (cdp) Miami-Dade	139	0.50
Town 'n' Country (cdp) Hillsborough	354	0.49
Temple Terrace (city) Hillsborough	102	0.49

Hawaii Native/Pacific Islander

Top 10 Places Sorted by Number
Based on all places, regardless of population

Place (place type) County	Number	%
Jacksonville (special city) Duval	1,290	0.18
Miami (city) Miami-Dade	681	0.19
Tampa (city) Hillsborough	643	0.21
Orlando (city) Orange	487	0.26
St. Petersburg (city) Pinellas	369	0.15
Fort Lauderdale (city) Broward	274	0.18
West Palm Beach (city) Palm Beach	262	0.32
Hollywood (city) Broward	260	0.19
Delray Beach (city) Palm Beach	255	0.42
Miramar (city) Broward	251	0.35

Top 10 Places Sorted by Percent
Based on all places, regardless of population

Place (place type) County	Number	%
Ebro (town) Washington	5	2.00
Pine Island (cdp) Hernando	1	1.56
Center Hill (city) Sumter	12	1.32
Sky Lake (cdp) Orange	64	1.13
Webster (city) Sumter	9	1.12
Indiantown (cdp) Martin	62	1.11
Lake Harbor (cdp) Palm Beach	2	1.03
Hillsboro Pines (cdp) Broward	4	0.99
Gun Club Estates (cdp) Palm Beach	7	0.98
Belle Glade (city) Palm Beach	145	0.97

Top 10 Places Sorted by Percent
Based on places with populations of 10,000 or more

Place (place type) County	Number	%
Belle Glade (city) Palm Beach	145	0.97
Oak Ridge (cdp) Orange	141	0.63
Myrtle Grove (cdp) Escambia	102	0.59
Wright (cdp) Okaloosa	102	0.47
Brent (cdp) Escambia	103	0.46
Delray Beach (city) Palm Beach	255	0.42
North Miami (city) Miami-Dade	247	0.41
Pine Hills (cdp) Orange	165	0.40
West Pensacola (cdp) Escambia	88	0.40
Poinciana (cdp) Osceola	55	0.40

Hawaii Native/Pacific Islander: Melanesian

Top 10 Places Sorted by Number
Based on all places, regardless of population

Place (place type) County	Number	%
St. Petersburg (city) Pinellas	10	0.00
Hobe Sound (cdp) Martin	6	0.05
Deltona (city) Volusia	4	0.01
Kissimmee (city) Osceola	4	0.01
Melbourne (city) Brevard	4	0.01
Sky Lake (cdp) Orange	3	0.05
Port Salerno (cdp) Martin	3	0.03
Fairview Shores (cdp) Orange	3	0.02
Boca Del Mar (cdp) Palm Beach	3	0.01
Brent (cdp) Escambia	3	0.01

Notes: (cdp) census designated place; Refer to the User's Guide in the front of the book for more detailed information.

Place (place type) County	Number	%
Hobe Sound (cdp) Martin	6	0.05
Sky Lake (cdp) Orange	3	0.05
Port Salerno (cdp) Martin	3	0.03
Charlotte Harbor (cdp) Charlotte	1	0.03
Fairview Shores (cdp) Orange	3	0.02
Eglin AFB (cdp) Okaloosa	2	0.02
Mount Dora (city) Lake	2	0.02
Bay Hill (cdp) Orange	1	0.02
Deltona (city) Volusia	4	0.01
Kissimmee (city) Osceola	4	0.01

Top 10 Places Sorted by Percent

Based on places with populations of 10,000 or more

Place (place type) County	Number	%
Hobe Sound (cdp) Martin	6	0.05
Port Salerno (cdp) Martin	3	0.03
Fairview Shores (cdp) Orange	3	0.02
Deltona (city) Volusia	4	0.01
Kissimmee (city) Osceola	4	0.01
Melbourne (city) Brevard	4	0.01
Boca Del Mar (cdp) Palm Beach	3	0.01
Brent (cdp) Escambia	3	0.01
Oak Ridge (cdp) Orange	3	0.01
Palm Coast (city) Flagler	2	0.01

Hawaii Native/Pacific Islander: Fijian

Top 10 Places Sorted by Number

Based on all places, regardless of population

Place (place type) County	Number	%
St. Petersburg (city) Pinellas	10	0.00
Deltona (city) Volusia	4	0.01
Kissimmee (city) Osceola	4	0.01
Melbourne (city) Brevard	4	0.01
Sky Lake (cdp) Orange	3	0.05
Port Salerno (cdp) Martin	3	0.03
Boca Del Mar (cdp) Palm Beach	3	0.01
Oak Ridge (cdp) Orange	3	0.01
Kendall (cdp) Miami-Dade	3	0.00
Orlando (city) Orange	3	0.00

Top 10 Places Sorted by Percent

Based on all places, regardless of population

Place (place type) County	Number	%
Sky Lake (cdp) Orange	3	0.05
Port Salerno (cdp) Martin	3	0.03
Charlotte Harbor (cdp) Charlotte	1	0.03
Eglin AFB (cdp) Okaloosa	2	0.02
Deltona (city) Volusia	4	0.01
Kissimmee (city) Osceola	4	0.01
Melbourne (city) Brevard	4	0.01
Boca Del Mar (cdp) Palm Beach	3	0.01
Oak Ridge (cdp) Orange	3	0.01
Wellington (village) Palm Beach	2	0.01

Top 10 Places Sorted by Percent

Based on places with populations of 10,000 or more

Place (place type) County	Number	%
Port Salerno (cdp) Martin	3	0.03
Deltona (city) Volusia	4	0.01
Kissimmee (city) Osceola	4	0.01
Melbourne (city) Brevard	4	0.01
Boca Del Mar (cdp) Palm Beach	3	0.01
Oak Ridge (cdp) Orange	3	0.01
Wellington (village) Palm Beach	2	0.01
Forest City (cdp) Seminole	1	0.01
Glenvar Heights (cdp) Miami-Dade	1	0.01
Sandalfoot Cove (cdp) Palm Beach	1	0.01

Hawaii Native/Pacific Islander: Other Melanesian

Top 10 Places Sorted by Number

Based on all places, regardless of population

Place (place type) County	Number	%
Hobe Sound (cdp) Martin	6	0.05
Fairview Shores (cdp) Orange	3	0.02
Brent (cdp) Escambia	3	0.01
West Palm Beach (city) Palm Beach	3	0.00
Mount Dora (city) Lake	2	0.02
Palm Coast (city) Flagler	2	0.01
Bay Hill (cdp) Orange	1	0.02
Sebring (city) Highlands	1	0.01
South Daytona (city) Volusia	1	0.01
Ferry Pass (cdp) Escambia	1	0.00

Top 10 Places Sorted by Percent

Based on all places, regardless of population

Place (place type) County	Number	%
Hobe Sound (cdp) Martin	6	0.05
Fairview Shores (cdp) Orange	3	0.02
Mount Dora (city) Lake	2	0.02
Bay Hill (cdp) Orange	1	0.02
Brent (cdp) Escambia	3	0.01
Palm Coast (city) Flagler	2	0.01
Sebring (city) Highlands	1	0.01
South Daytona (city) Volusia	1	0.01
West Palm Beach (city) Palm Beach	3	0.00
Ferry Pass (cdp) Escambia	1	0.00

Top 10 Places Sorted by Percent

Based on places with populations of 10,000 or more

Place (place type) County	Number	%
Hobe Sound (cdp) Martin	6	0.05
Fairview Shores (cdp) Orange	3	0.02
Brent (cdp) Escambia	3	0.01
Palm Coast (city) Flagler	2	0.01
South Daytona (city) Volusia	1	0.01
West Palm Beach (city) Palm Beach	3	0.00
Ferry Pass (cdp) Escambia	1	0.00
Fountainbleau (cdp) Miami-Dade	1	0.00
Jacksonville (special city) Duval	1	0.00
Lake Magdalene (cdp) Hillsborough	1	0.00

Hawaii Native/Pacific Islander: Micronesian

Top 10 Places Sorted by Number

Based on all places, regardless of population

Place (place type) County	Number	%
Jacksonville (special city) Duval	300	0.04
Tampa (city) Hillsborough	168	0.06
West Palm Beach (city) Palm Beach	98	0.12
Orlando (city) Orange	71	0.04
Brent (cdp) Escambia	64	0.29
Indiantown (cdp) Martin	55	0.98
Miami (city) Miami-Dade	48	0.01
Fort Myers (city) Lee	47	0.10
Immokalee (cdp) Collier	41	0.21
Cocoa (city) Brevard	38	0.23

Top 10 Places Sorted by Percent

Based on all places, regardless of population

Place (place type) County	Number	%
Pine Island (cdp) Hernando	1	1.56
Ebro (town) Washington	3	1.20
Indiantown (cdp) Martin	55	0.98
Noma (town) Holmes	2	0.94
Palm Shores (town) Brevard	6	0.76
Paradise Heights (cdp) Orange	9	0.69
Juno Ridge (cdp) Palm Beach	4	0.54
Chula Vista (cdp) Broward	3	0.52

| Broadview Park (cdp) Broward | 34 | 0.50 |
| Center Hill (city) Sumter | 4 | 0.44 |

Top 10 Places Sorted by Percent

Based on places with populations of 10,000 or more

Place (place type) County	Number	%
Brent (cdp) Escambia	64	0.29
Cocoa (city) Brevard	38	0.23
Immokalee (cdp) Collier	41	0.21
Myrtle Grove (cdp) Escambia	31	0.18
Port St. John (cdp) Brevard	21	0.17
Wright (cdp) Okaloosa	33	0.15
Golden Gate (cdp) Collier	31	0.15
Upper Grand Lagoon (cdp) Bay	14	0.13
West Palm Beach (city) Palm Beach	98	0.12
Lake Worth Corridor (cdp) Palm Beach	22	0.12

Hawaii Native/Pacific Islander: Guamanian or Chamorro

Top 10 Places Sorted by Number

Based on all places, regardless of population

Place (place type) County	Number	%
Jacksonville (special city) Duval	263	0.04
West Palm Beach (city) Palm Beach	98	0.12
Tampa (city) Hillsborough	72	0.02
Indiantown (cdp) Martin	55	0.98
Miami (city) Miami-Dade	45	0.01
Brent (cdp) Escambia	44	0.20
Fort Myers (city) Lee	43	0.09
Immokalee (cdp) Collier	41	0.21
Cocoa (city) Brevard	38	0.23
Broadview Park (cdp) Broward	34	0.50

Top 10 Places Sorted by Percent

Based on all places, regardless of population

Place (place type) County	Number	%
Pine Island (cdp) Hernando	1	1.56
Ebro (town) Washington	3	1.20
Indiantown (cdp) Martin	55	0.98
Noma (town) Holmes	2	0.94
Palm Shores (town) Brevard	6	0.76
Paradise Heights (cdp) Orange	9	0.69
Juno Ridge (cdp) Palm Beach	4	0.54
Chula Vista (cdp) Broward	3	0.52
Broadview Park (cdp) Broward	34	0.50
Center Hill (city) Sumter	4	0.44

Top 10 Places Sorted by Percent

Based on places with populations of 10,000 or more

Place (place type) County	Number	%
Cocoa (city) Brevard	38	0.23
Immokalee (cdp) Collier	41	0.21
Brent (cdp) Escambia	44	0.20
Myrtle Grove (cdp) Escambia	27	0.16
Golden Gate (cdp) Collier	31	0.15
Port St. John (cdp) Brevard	18	0.15
Wright (cdp) Okaloosa	30	0.14
Upper Grand Lagoon (cdp) Bay	14	0.13
West Palm Beach (city) Palm Beach	98	0.12
Bellview (cdp) Escambia	24	0.11

Hawaii Native/Pacific Islander: Other Micronesian

Top 10 Places Sorted by Number

Based on all places, regardless of population

Place (place type) County	Number	%
Tampa (city) Hillsborough	96	0.03
Orlando (city) Orange	38	0.02
Jacksonville (special city) Duval	37	0.01
Brent (cdp) Escambia	20	0.09

Notes: (cdp) census designated place; Refer to the User's Guide in the front of the book for more detailed information.

Place (place type) County	Number	%
Largo (city) Pinellas	18	0.03
North Fort Myers (cdp) Lee	12	0.03
Oak Ridge (cdp) Orange	11	0.05
Holiday (cdp) Pasco	8	0.04
Hollywood (city) Broward	8	0.01
Osprey (cdp) Sarasota	5	0.12

Top 10 Places Sorted by Percent
Based on all places, regardless of population

Place (place type) County	Number	%
Edgewater (cdp) Broward	2	0.25
Reddick (town) Marion	1	0.18
Osprey (cdp) Sarasota	5	0.12
Brent (cdp) Escambia	20	0.09
Minneola (city) Lake	5	0.09
Freeport (city) Walton	1	0.08
Southchase (cdp) Orange	3	0.06
Oak Ridge (cdp) Orange	11	0.05
Kensington Park (cdp) Sarasota	2	0.05
Holiday (cdp) Pasco	8	0.04

Top 10 Places Sorted by Percent
Based on places with populations of 10,000 or more

Place (place type) County	Number	%
Brent (cdp) Escambia	20	0.09
Oak Ridge (cdp) Orange	11	0.05
Holiday (cdp) Pasco	8	0.04
Tampa (city) Hillsborough	96	0.03
Largo (city) Pinellas	18	0.03
North Fort Myers (cdp) Lee	12	0.03
Warrington (cdp) Escambia	5	0.03
Orlando (city) Orange	38	0.02
Dania Beach (city) Broward	4	0.02
Key West (city) Monroe	4	0.02

Hawaii Native/Pacific Islander: Polynesian

Top 10 Places Sorted by Number
Based on all places, regardless of population

Place (place type) County	Number	%
Jacksonville (special city) Duval	493	0.07
Tampa (city) Hillsborough	189	0.06
St. Petersburg (city) Pinellas	155	0.06
Orlando (city) Orange	149	0.08
Miami (city) Miami-Dade	103	0.03
Tallahassee (city) Leon	91	0.06
Hollywood (city) Broward	87	0.06
Fort Lauderdale (city) Broward	81	0.05
Cape Coral (city) Lee	69	0.07
Brandon (cdp) Hillsborough	66	0.08

Top 10 Places Sorted by Percent
Based on all places, regardless of population

Place (place type) County	Number	%
Webster (city) Sumter	8	0.99
Pine Lakes (cdp) Lake	7	0.93
Charleston Park (cdp) Lee	3	0.73
Sky Lake (cdp) Orange	40	0.71
Hastings (town) St. Johns	3	0.58
Mexico Beach (city) Bay	5	0.49
Eglin AFB (cdp) Okaloosa	39	0.48
Taft (cdp) Orange	7	0.36
Plantation Mobile Home Park (cdp) Palm Beach	4	0.33
Matlacha Isles-Matlacha Shores (cdp) Lee	1	0.33

Top 10 Places Sorted by Percent
Based on places with populations of 10,000 or more

Place (place type) County	Number	%
Oak Ridge (cdp) Orange	65	0.29
Myrtle Grove (cdp) Escambia	48	0.28
Meadow Woods (cdp) Orange	29	0.26
West Pensacola (cdp) Escambia	50	0.23

Place (place type) County	Number	%
Lynn Haven (city) Bay	26	0.21
Wright (cdp) Okaloosa	42	0.19
Crestview (city) Okaloosa	25	0.17
Poinciana (cdp) Osceola	23	0.17
Callaway (city) Bay	23	0.16
Niceville (city) Okaloosa	18	0.15

Hawaii Native/Pacific Islander: Native Hawaiian

Top 10 Places Sorted by Number
Based on all places, regardless of population

Place (place type) County	Number	%
Jacksonville (special city) Duval	369	0.05
Tampa (city) Hillsborough	117	0.04
Orlando (city) Orange	103	0.06
St. Petersburg (city) Pinellas	71	0.03
Miami (city) Miami-Dade	71	0.02
Cape Coral (city) Lee	62	0.06
Tallahassee (city) Leon	52	0.03
Hollywood (city) Broward	51	0.04
Fort Lauderdale (city) Broward	50	0.03
Clearwater (city) Pinellas	41	0.04

Top 10 Places Sorted by Percent
Based on all places, regardless of population

Place (place type) County	Number	%
Webster (city) Sumter	8	0.99
Pine Lakes (cdp) Lake	6	0.79
Mexico Beach (city) Bay	5	0.49
Eglin AFB (cdp) Okaloosa	32	0.40
Sky Lake (cdp) Orange	22	0.39
Plantation Mobile Home Park (cdp) Palm Beach	4	0.33
Howey-in-the-Hills (town) Lake	3	0.31
Manalapan (town) Palm Beach	1	0.31
Keystone Heights (city) Clay	4	0.30
Bowling Green (city) Hardee	8	0.28

Top 10 Places Sorted by Percent
Based on places with populations of 10,000 or more

Place (place type) County	Number	%
Wright (cdp) Okaloosa	39	0.18
Lynn Haven (city) Bay	23	0.18
Crestview (city) Okaloosa	25	0.17
Meadow Woods (cdp) Orange	19	0.17
West Pensacola (cdp) Escambia	33	0.15
Callaway (city) Bay	21	0.15
Niceville (city) Okaloosa	17	0.15
Myrtle Grove (cdp) Escambia	23	0.13
Bellair-Meadowbrook Terrace (cdp) Clay	21	0.13
Bellview (cdp) Escambia	23	0.11

Hawaii Native/Pacific Islander: Samoan

Top 10 Places Sorted by Number
Based on all places, regardless of population

Place (place type) County	Number	%
Jacksonville (special city) Duval	105	0.01
Tampa (city) Hillsborough	64	0.02
Tallahassee (city) Leon	32	0.02
Gainesville (city) Alachua	28	0.03
Orlando (city) Orange	28	0.02
St. Petersburg (city) Pinellas	28	0.01
Delray Beach (city) Palm Beach	27	0.04
West Palm Beach (city) Palm Beach	25	0.03
Miami (city) Miami-Dade	25	0.01
Myrtle Grove (cdp) Escambia	23	0.13

Top 10 Places Sorted by Percent
Based on all places, regardless of population

Place (place type) County	Number	%
Hastings (town) St. Johns	3	0.58

Place (place type) County	Number	%
Matlacha Isles-Matlacha Shores (cdp) Lee	1	0.33
St. Leo (town) Pasco	1	0.17
Myrtle Grove (cdp) Escambia	23	0.13
Pine Lakes (cdp) Lake	1	0.13
Lake Forest (cdp) Broward	6	0.12
Zolfo Springs (town) Hardee	2	0.12
Sky Lake (cdp) Orange	6	0.11
South Highpoint (cdp) Pinellas	9	0.10
Pine Ridge (cdp) Collier	2	0.10

Top 10 Places Sorted by Percent
Based on places with populations of 10,000 or more

Place (place type) County	Number	%
Myrtle Grove (cdp) Escambia	23	0.13
West Pensacola (cdp) Escambia	17	0.08
Brent (cdp) Escambia	16	0.07
New Port Richey (city) Pasco	11	0.07
Poinciana (cdp) Osceola	9	0.07
Bartow (city) Polk	9	0.06
Yeehaw Junction (cdp) Osceola	10	0.05
Ives Estates (cdp) Miami-Dade	8	0.05
Winter Garden (city) Orange	7	0.05
Delray Beach (city) Palm Beach	27	0.04

Hawaii Native/Pacific Islander: Tongan

Top 10 Places Sorted by Number
Based on all places, regardless of population

Place (place type) County	Number	%
St. Petersburg (city) Pinellas	33	0.01
Oak Ridge (cdp) Orange	31	0.14
Largo (city) Pinellas	24	0.03
Hollywood (city) Broward	18	0.01
Pine Castle (cdp) Orange	9	0.10
Deltona (city) Volusia	6	0.01
Palm Bay (city) Brevard	6	0.01
Orlando (city) Orange	6	0.00
Poinciana (cdp) Osceola	5	0.04
Bradenton (city) Manatee	5	0.01

Top 10 Places Sorted by Percent
Based on all places, regardless of population

Place (place type) County	Number	%
Page Park (cdp) Lee	1	0.19
Oak Ridge (cdp) Orange	31	0.14
Pine Castle (cdp) Orange	9	0.10
Lochmoor Waterway Estates (cdp) Lee	4	0.10
Gandy (cdp) Pinellas	2	0.10
Holden Heights (cdp) Orange	3	0.08
Carrabelle (city) Franklin	1	0.08
Citrus Springs (cdp) Citrus	3	0.07
Port Richey (city) Pasco	2	0.07
North Redington Beach (town) Pinellas	1	0.07

Top 10 Places Sorted by Percent
Based on places with populations of 10,000 or more

Place (place type) County	Number	%
Oak Ridge (cdp) Orange	31	0.14
Poinciana (cdp) Osceola	5	0.04
Largo (city) Pinellas	24	0.03
Hudson (cdp) Pasco	2	0.02
St. Petersburg (city) Pinellas	33	0.01
Hollywood (city) Broward	18	0.01
Deltona (city) Volusia	6	0.01
Palm Bay (city) Brevard	6	0.01
Bradenton (city) Manatee	5	0.01
Dunedin (city) Pinellas	5	0.01

Notes: (cdp) census designated place; Refer to the User's Guide in the front of the book for more detailed information.

Hawaii Native/Pacific Islander: Other Polynesian

Top 10 Places Sorted by Number
Based on all places, regardless of population

Place (place type) County	Number	%
St. Petersburg (city) Pinellas	23	0.01
Jacksonville (special city) Duval	17	0.00
Largo (city) Pinellas	12	0.02
Orlando (city) Orange	12	0.01
Sky Lake (cdp) Orange	11	0.19
Fort Lauderdale (city) Broward	11	0.01
Brandon (cdp) Hillsborough	10	0.01
Coral Springs (city) Broward	9	0.01
Plantation (city) Broward	8	0.01
Tampa (city) Hillsborough	7	0.00

Top 10 Places Sorted by Percent
Based on all places, regardless of population

Place (place type) County	Number	%
Charleston Park (cdp) Lee	3	0.73
Sky Lake (cdp) Orange	11	0.19
Pine Castle (cdp) Orange	4	0.05
Doctor Phillips (cdp) Orange	4	0.04
Meadow Woods (cdp) Orange	4	0.04
Tavares (city) Lake	4	0.04
Golden Lakes (cdp) Palm Beach	3	0.04
Malabar (town) Brevard	1	0.04
Oak Ridge (cdp) Orange	6	0.03
Winter Garden (city) Orange	4	0.03

Top 10 Places Sorted by Percent
Based on places with populations of 10,000 or more

Place (place type) County	Number	%
Meadow Woods (cdp) Orange	4	0.04
Oak Ridge (cdp) Orange	6	0.03
Winter Garden (city) Orange	4	0.03
Azalea Park (cdp) Orange	3	0.03
Largo (city) Pinellas	12	0.02
Ocoee (city) Orange	5	0.02
Bayshore Gardens (cdp) Manatee	4	0.02
Cutler Ridge (cdp) Miami-Dade	4	0.02
Lynn Haven (city) Bay	2	0.02
Miami Shores (village) Miami-Dade	2	0.02

Hawaii Native/Pacific Islander: Other Pacific Islander, specified

Top 10 Places Sorted by Number
Based on all places, regardless of population

Place (place type) County	Number	%
Jacksonville (special city) Duval	59	0.01
St. Petersburg (city) Pinellas	26	0.01
Tampa (city) Hillsborough	25	0.01
Miami (city) Miami-Dade	21	0.01
Tallahassee (city) Leon	21	0.01
Gainesville (city) Alachua	16	0.02
Delray Beach (city) Palm Beach	14	0.02
Lauderhill (city) Broward	14	0.02
Orlando (city) Orange	13	0.01
Willow Oak (cdp) Polk	10	0.20

Top 10 Places Sorted by Percent
Based on all places, regardless of population

Place (place type) County	Number	%
De Leon Springs (cdp) Volusia	6	0.25
Willow Oak (cdp) Polk	10	0.20
Manattee Road (cdp) Levy	3	0.15
North Brooksville (cdp) Hernando	2	0.14
Southeast Arcadia (cdp) De Soto	6	0.10
Perry (city) Taylor	6	0.09
Goulding (cdp) Escambia	4	0.09
Williston (city) Levy	2	0.09

Place (place type) County	Number	%
Graceville (city) Jackson	2	0.08
Ridgecrest (cdp) Pinellas	2	0.08

Top 10 Places Sorted by Percent
Based on places with populations of 10,000 or more

Place (place type) County	Number	%
Kings Point (cdp) Palm Beach	5	0.04
Wilton Manors (city) Broward	5	0.04
Middleburg (cdp) Clay	4	0.04
Riviera Beach (city) Palm Beach	8	0.03
Fort Walton Beach (city) Okaloosa	6	0.03
Hamptons at Boca Raton (cdp) Palm Beach	3	0.03
Gainesville (city) Alachua	16	0.02
Delray Beach (city) Palm Beach	14	0.02
Lauderhill (city) Broward	14	0.02
Daytona Beach (city) Volusia	10	0.02

Hawaii Native/Pacific Islander: Other Pacific Islander, not specified

Top 10 Places Sorted by Number
Based on all places, regardless of population

Place (place type) County	Number	%
Miami (city) Miami-Dade	509	0.14
Jacksonville (special city) Duval	437	0.06
Tampa (city) Hillsborough	260	0.09
Orlando (city) Orange	251	0.13
North Miami (city) Miami-Dade	209	0.35
Miramar (city) Broward	209	0.29
Delray Beach (city) Palm Beach	183	0.30
Sunrise (city) Broward	174	0.20
Lauderhill (city) Broward	152	0.26
Fort Lauderdale (city) Broward	149	0.10

Top 10 Places Sorted by Percent
Based on all places, regardless of population

Place (place type) County	Number	%
Lake Harbor (cdp) Palm Beach	2	1.03
Hillsboro Pines (cdp) Broward	4	0.99
Gun Club Estates (cdp) Palm Beach	7	0.98
Belle Glade (city) Palm Beach	138	0.93
Center Hill (city) Sumter	8	0.88
Ebro (town) Washington	2	0.80
Sunshine Acres (cdp) Broward	6	0.73
St. Leo (town) Pasco	3	0.50
Watertown (cdp) Columbia	14	0.49
Tangerine (cdp) Orange	4	0.48

Top 10 Places Sorted by Percent
Based on places with populations of 10,000 or more

Place (place type) County	Number	%
Belle Glade (city) Palm Beach	138	0.93
North Miami (city) Miami-Dade	209	0.35
Pine Hills (cdp) Orange	138	0.33
Palmetto Estates (cdp) Miami-Dade	45	0.33
Delray Beach (city) Palm Beach	183	0.30
Norland (cdp) Miami-Dade	70	0.30
Miramar (city) Broward	209	0.29
Golden Glades (cdp) Miami-Dade	93	0.29
Pinewood (cdp) Miami-Dade	46	0.28
North Miami Beach (city) Miami-Dade	110	0.27

Hispanic or Latino

Top 10 Places Sorted by Number
Based on all places, regardless of population

Place (place type) County	Number	%
Miami (city) Miami-Dade	238,351	65.76
Hialeah (city) Miami-Dade	204,543	90.34
Tampa (city) Hillsborough	58,522	19.29
Fountainbleau (cdp) Miami-Dade	51,948	87.24
Tamiami (cdp) Miami-Dade	47,654	86.98

Place (place type) County	Number	%
Miami Beach (city) Miami-Dade	47,000	53.45
Kendale Lakes (cdp) Miami-Dade	43,574	76.58
Pembroke Pines (city) Broward	38,700	28.16
Kendall (cdp) Miami-Dade	37,549	49.91
Orlando (city) Orange	32,510	17.48

Top 10 Places Sorted by Percent
Based on all places, regardless of population

Place (place type) County	Number	%
Sweetwater (city) Miami-Dade	13,253	93.16
Hialeah (city) Miami-Dade	204,543	90.34
Hialeah Gardens (city) Miami-Dade	17,324	89.78
Fountainbleau (cdp) Miami-Dade	51,948	87.24
Tamiami (cdp) Miami-Dade	47,654	86.98
Westchester (cdp) Miami-Dade	25,824	85.31
West Miami (city) Miami-Dade	4,927	84.04
University Park (cdp) Miami-Dade	21,945	82.69
Coral Terrace (cdp) Miami-Dade	20,015	82.10
Kendall West (cdp) Miami-Dade	30,060	79.03

Top 10 Places Sorted by Percent
Based on places with populations of 10,000 or more

Place (place type) County	Number	%
Sweetwater (city) Miami-Dade	13,253	93.16
Hialeah (city) Miami-Dade	204,543	90.34
Hialeah Gardens (city) Miami-Dade	17,324	89.78
Fountainbleau (cdp) Miami-Dade	51,948	87.24
Tamiami (cdp) Miami-Dade	47,654	86.98
Westchester (cdp) Miami-Dade	25,824	85.31
University Park (cdp) Miami-Dade	21,945	82.69
Coral Terrace (cdp) Miami-Dade	20,015	82.10
Kendall West (cdp) Miami-Dade	30,060	79.03
Kendale Lakes (cdp) Miami-Dade	43,574	76.58

Hispanic: Central American

Top 10 Places Sorted by Number
Based on all places, regardless of population

Place (place type) County	Number	%
Miami (city) Miami-Dade	40,158	11.08
Hialeah (city) Miami-Dade	14,668	6.48
Fountainbleau (cdp) Miami-Dade	7,342	12.33
Kendale Lakes (cdp) Miami-Dade	3,640	6.40
Tamiami (cdp) Miami-Dade	3,451	6.30
Kendall (cdp) Miami-Dade	3,310	4.40
Miami Beach (city) Miami-Dade	3,096	3.52
Lake Worth (city) Palm Beach	2,965	8.44
Sweetwater (city) Miami-Dade	2,818	19.81
West Palm Beach (city) Palm Beach	2,745	3.34

Top 10 Places Sorted by Percent
Based on all places, regardless of population

Place (place type) County	Number	%
Sweetwater (city) Miami-Dade	2,818	19.81
Indiantown (cdp) Martin	985	17.63
Fountainbleau (cdp) Miami-Dade	7,342	12.33
Miami (city) Miami-Dade	40,158	11.08
Canal Point (cdp) Palm Beach	50	9.52
Lake Worth (city) Palm Beach	2,965	8.44
Homestead (city) Miami-Dade	2,595	8.13
West Little River (cdp) Miami-Dade	2,528	7.78
Hialeah Gardens (city) Miami-Dade	1,472	7.63
Broadview Park (cdp) Broward	481	7.08

Top 10 Places Sorted by Percent
Based on places with populations of 10,000 or more

Place (place type) County	Number	%
Sweetwater (city) Miami-Dade	2,818	19.81
Fountainbleau (cdp) Miami-Dade	7,342	12.33
Miami (city) Miami-Dade	40,158	11.08
Lake Worth (city) Palm Beach	2,965	8.44
Homestead (city) Miami-Dade	2,595	8.13

Notes: (cdp) census designated place; Refer to the User's Guide in the front of the book for more detailed information.

Place (place type) County	Number	%
West Little River (cdp) Miami-Dade	2,528	7.78
Hialeah Gardens (city) Miami-Dade	1,472	7.63
Richmond West (cdp) Miami-Dade	1,963	6.99
Kendall West (cdp) Miami-Dade	2,511	6.60
Hialeah (city) Miami-Dade	14,668	6.48

Hispanic: Costa Rican

Top 10 Places Sorted by Number
Based on all places, regardless of population

Place (place type) County	Number	%
Miami (city) Miami-Dade	775	0.21
Hialeah (city) Miami-Dade	473	0.21
Miami Beach (city) Miami-Dade	293	0.33
Jacksonville (special city) Duval	259	0.04
Hollywood (city) Broward	256	0.18
Tampa (city) Hillsborough	233	0.08
Pembroke Pines (city) Broward	227	0.17
Kendall (cdp) Miami-Dade	171	0.23
Fountainbleau (cdp) Miami-Dade	153	0.26
Carol City (cdp) Miami-Dade	128	0.22

Top 10 Places Sorted by Percent
Based on all places, regardless of population

Place (place type) County	Number	%
Medley (town) Miami-Dade	10	0.91
Miami Springs (city) Miami-Dade	109	0.79
Virginia Gardens (village) Miami-Dade	18	0.77
Golden Beach (town) Miami-Dade	7	0.76
Hillcrest Heights (town) Polk	2	0.75
Callahan (town) Nassau	7	0.73
Naples Park (cdp) Collier	33	0.49
Utopia (cdp) Broward	3	0.42
North Beach (cdp) Indian River	1	0.41
El Portal (village) Miami-Dade	10	0.40

Top 10 Places Sorted by Percent
Based on places with populations of 10,000 or more

Place (place type) County	Number	%
Miami Springs (city) Miami-Dade	109	0.79
Miami Beach (city) Miami-Dade	293	0.33
Doral (cdp) Miami-Dade	66	0.32
Glenvar Heights (cdp) Miami-Dade	52	0.32
Westwood Lakes (cdp) Miami-Dade	37	0.31
Princeton (cdp) Miami-Dade	30	0.30
Richmond West (cdp) Miami-Dade	82	0.29
Key Biscayne (village) Miami-Dade	30	0.29
Kendall West (cdp) Miami-Dade	105	0.28
The Hammocks (cdp) Miami-Dade	126	0.27

Hispanic: Guatemalan

Top 10 Places Sorted by Number
Based on all places, regardless of population

Place (place type) County	Number	%
Miami (city) Miami-Dade	2,475	0.68
West Palm Beach (city) Palm Beach	1,841	2.24
Lake Worth (city) Palm Beach	1,711	4.87
Homestead (city) Miami-Dade	1,059	3.32
Indiantown (cdp) Martin	923	16.52
Immokalee (cdp) Collier	861	4.36
Hialeah (city) Miami-Dade	823	0.36
Fort Lauderdale (city) Broward	477	0.31
Fort Myers (city) Lee	475	0.99
Lake Worth Corridor (cdp) Palm Beach	459	2.46

Top 10 Places Sorted by Percent
Based on all places, regardless of population

Place (place type) County	Number	%
Indiantown (cdp) Martin	923	16.52
Lake Worth (city) Palm Beach	1,711	4.87
Immokalee (cdp) Collier	861	4.36

Place (place type) County	Number	%
Tice (cdp) Lee	191	4.21
Mangonia Park (town) Palm Beach	49	3.82
Homestead (city) Miami-Dade	1,059	3.32
Westgate-Belvedere Homes (cdp) Palm Beach	265	3.26
Jennings (town) Hamilton	25	3.00
Lake Worth Corridor (cdp) Palm Beach	459	2.46
Fanning Springs (city) Levy	17	2.31

Top 10 Places Sorted by Percent
Based on places with populations of 10,000 or more

Place (place type) County	Number	%
Lake Worth (city) Palm Beach	1,711	4.87
Immokalee (cdp) Collier	861	4.36
Homestead (city) Miami-Dade	1,059	3.32
Lake Worth Corridor (cdp) Palm Beach	459	2.46
West Palm Beach (city) Palm Beach	1,841	2.24
Stuart (city) Martin	186	1.27
Bonita Springs (city) Lee	393	1.20
West Little River (cdp) Miami-Dade	391	1.20
Marathon (city) Monroe	120	1.17
Jupiter (town) Palm Beach	427	1.09

Hispanic: Honduran

Top 10 Places Sorted by Number
Based on all places, regardless of population

Place (place type) County	Number	%
Miami (city) Miami-Dade	12,118	3.34
Hialeah (city) Miami-Dade	2,593	1.15
Miami Beach (city) Miami-Dade	1,062	1.21
Tampa (city) Hillsborough	778	0.26
West Little River (cdp) Miami-Dade	709	2.18
Fountainbleau (cdp) Miami-Dade	650	1.09
North Miami (city) Miami-Dade	565	0.94
Lake Worth (city) Palm Beach	559	1.59
Carol City (cdp) Miami-Dade	428	0.72
Hollywood (city) Broward	418	0.30

Top 10 Places Sorted by Percent
Based on all places, regardless of population

Place (place type) County	Number	%
Loch Lomond (cdp) Broward	128	3.62
Miami (city) Miami-Dade	12,118	3.34
Broadview Park (cdp) Broward	182	2.68
Canal Point (cdp) Palm Beach	13	2.48
West Little River (cdp) Miami-Dade	709	2.18
Bonnie Lock-Woodsetter North (cdp) Broward	73	1.71
Pinewood (cdp) Miami-Dade	276	1.67
Lake Worth (city) Palm Beach	559	1.59
Medley (town) Miami-Dade	17	1.55
Gladeview (cdp) Miami-Dade	223	1.54

Top 10 Places Sorted by Percent
Based on places with populations of 10,000 or more

Place (place type) County	Number	%
Miami (city) Miami-Dade	12,118	3.34
West Little River (cdp) Miami-Dade	709	2.18
Pinewood (cdp) Miami-Dade	276	1.67
Lake Worth (city) Palm Beach	559	1.59
Gladeview (cdp) Miami-Dade	223	1.54
Sweetwater (city) Miami-Dade	187	1.31
Miami Beach (city) Miami-Dade	1,062	1.21
Hialeah Gardens (city) Miami-Dade	223	1.16
Lake Worth Corridor (cdp) Palm Beach	216	1.16
Hialeah (city) Miami-Dade	2,593	1.15

Hispanic: Nicaraguan

Top 10 Places Sorted by Number
Based on all places, regardless of population

Place (place type) County	Number	%
Miami (city) Miami-Dade	20,543	5.67

Place (place type) County	Number	%
Hialeah (city) Miami-Dade	9,211	4.07
Fountainbleau (cdp) Miami-Dade	5,624	9.44
Kendale Lakes (cdp) Miami-Dade	2,612	4.59
Tamiami (cdp) Miami-Dade	2,551	4.66
Sweetwater (city) Miami-Dade	2,366	16.63
Kendall (cdp) Miami-Dade	1,869	2.48
Kendall West (cdp) Miami-Dade	1,670	4.39
The Hammocks (cdp) Miami-Dade	1,364	2.88
Carol City (cdp) Miami-Dade	1,305	2.20

Top 10 Places Sorted by Percent
Based on all places, regardless of population

Place (place type) County	Number	%
Sweetwater (city) Miami-Dade	2,366	16.63
Fountainbleau (cdp) Miami-Dade	5,624	9.44
Canal Point (cdp) Palm Beach	32	6.10
Miami (city) Miami-Dade	20,543	5.67
Hialeah Gardens (city) Miami-Dade	939	4.87
Tamiami (cdp) Miami-Dade	2,551	4.66
Kendale Lakes (cdp) Miami-Dade	2,612	4.59
Kendall West (cdp) Miami-Dade	1,670	4.39
Richmond West (cdp) Miami-Dade	1,178	4.19
Hialeah (city) Miami-Dade	9,211	4.07

Top 10 Places Sorted by Percent
Based on places with populations of 10,000 or more

Place (place type) County	Number	%
Sweetwater (city) Miami-Dade	2,366	16.63
Fountainbleau (cdp) Miami-Dade	5,624	9.44
Miami (city) Miami-Dade	20,543	5.67
Hialeah Gardens (city) Miami-Dade	939	4.87
Tamiami (cdp) Miami-Dade	2,551	4.66
Kendale Lakes (cdp) Miami-Dade	2,612	4.59
Kendall West (cdp) Miami-Dade	1,670	4.39
Richmond West (cdp) Miami-Dade	1,178	4.19
Hialeah (city) Miami-Dade	9,211	4.07
Gladeview (cdp) Miami-Dade	536	3.70

Hispanic: Panamanian

Top 10 Places Sorted by Number
Based on all places, regardless of population

Place (place type) County	Number	%
Miami (city) Miami-Dade	657	0.18
Jacksonville (special city) Duval	461	0.06
Tampa (city) Hillsborough	407	0.13
Hialeah (city) Miami-Dade	379	0.17
Pembroke Pines (city) Broward	367	0.27
Miramar (city) Broward	336	0.46
Fountainbleau (cdp) Miami-Dade	293	0.49
Kendall (cdp) Miami-Dade	268	0.36
Hollywood (city) Broward	241	0.17
Country Club (cdp) Miami-Dade	240	0.66

Top 10 Places Sorted by Percent
Based on all places, regardless of population

Place (place type) County	Number	%
Indian Creek (village) Miami-Dade	1	3.03
Lisbon (cdp) Lake	5	1.83
Miami Gardens (cdp) Broward	29	1.07
Doral (cdp) Miami-Dade	192	0.94
Richmond West (cdp) Miami-Dade	210	0.75
Lakes by the Bay (cdp) Miami-Dade	65	0.72
Tyndall AFB (cdp) Bay	19	0.69
Country Club (cdp) Miami-Dade	240	0.66
Palmetto Estates (cdp) Miami-Dade	80	0.59
Eglin AFB (cdp) Okaloosa	41	0.51

Top 10 Places Sorted by Percent
Based on places with populations of 10,000 or more

Place (place type) County	Number	%
Doral (cdp) Miami-Dade	192	0.94

Notes: (cdp) census designated place; Refer to the User's Guide in the front of the book for more detailed information.

Place (place type) County	Number	%
Richmond West (cdp) Miami-Dade	210	0.75
Country Club (cdp) Miami-Dade	240	0.66
Palmetto Estates (cdp) Miami-Dade	80	0.59
Fountainbleau (cdp) Miami-Dade	293	0.49
The Hammocks (cdp) Miami-Dade	226	0.48
Miramar (city) Broward	336	0.46
Poinciana (cdp) Osceola	58	0.43
Ives Estates (cdp) Miami-Dade	70	0.40
Country Walk (cdp) Miami-Dade	43	0.40

Hispanic: Salvadoran

Top 10 Places Sorted by Number
Based on all places, regardless of population

Place (place type) County	Number	%
Miami (city) Miami-Dade	2,482	0.68
Homestead (city) Miami-Dade	859	2.69
Hialeah (city) Miami-Dade	763	0.34
Fort Lauderdale (city) Broward	674	0.44
Lake Worth (city) Palm Beach	433	1.23
Oakland Park (city) Broward	425	1.37
Tampa (city) Hillsborough	362	0.12
Kendall (cdp) Miami-Dade	337	0.45
North Lauderdale (city) Broward	336	1.04
Leisure City (cdp) Miami-Dade	286	1.29

Top 10 Places Sorted by Percent
Based on all places, regardless of population

Place (place type) County	Number	%
Clewiston (city) Hendry	200	3.10
Homestead (city) Miami-Dade	859	2.69
Belle Glade Camp (cdp) Palm Beach	20	1.75
Florida City (city) Miami-Dade	129	1.64
North Andrews Gardens (cdp) Broward	157	1.63
Greensboro (town) Gadsden	10	1.62
Quincy (city) Gadsden	110	1.58
Caryville (town) Washington	3	1.38
Oakland Park (city) Broward	425	1.37
Leisure City (cdp) Miami-Dade	286	1.29

Top 10 Places Sorted by Percent
Based on places with populations of 10,000 or more

Place (place type) County	Number	%
Homestead (city) Miami-Dade	859	2.69
Oakland Park (city) Broward	425	1.37
Leisure City (cdp) Miami-Dade	286	1.29
Lake Worth Corridor (cdp) Palm Beach	235	1.26
Lake Worth (city) Palm Beach	433	1.23
North Lauderdale (city) Broward	336	1.04
Miami (city) Miami-Dade	2,482	0.68
South Miami Heights (cdp) Miami-Dade	218	0.65
Key Biscayne (village) Miami-Dade	67	0.64
Kissimmee (city) Osceola	276	0.58

Hispanic: Other Central American

Top 10 Places Sorted by Number
Based on all places, regardless of population

Place (place type) County	Number	%
Miami (city) Miami-Dade	1,108	0.31
Hialeah (city) Miami-Dade	426	0.19
Fountainbleau (cdp) Miami-Dade	143	0.24
Tamiami (cdp) Miami-Dade	95	0.17
West Little River (cdp) Miami-Dade	90	0.28
Kendale Lakes (cdp) Miami-Dade	90	0.16
Tampa (city) Hillsborough	90	0.03
Miami Beach (city) Miami-Dade	83	0.09
Kendall (cdp) Miami-Dade	79	0.11
Lake Worth (city) Palm Beach	75	0.21

Top 10 Places Sorted by Percent
Based on all places, regardless of population

Place (place type) County	Number	%
Godfrey Road (cdp) Broward	1	0.58
Village Park (cdp) Broward	5	0.56
Broadview Park (cdp) Broward	36	0.53
Sweetwater (city) Miami-Dade	68	0.48
Homestead Base (cdp) Miami-Dade	2	0.45
Miami Gardens (cdp) Broward	12	0.44
Belle Glade Camp (cdp) Palm Beach	5	0.44
Indiantown (cdp) Martin	23	0.41
Mangonia Park (town) Palm Beach	5	0.39
Loch Lomond (cdp) Broward	13	0.37

Top 10 Places Sorted by Percent
Based on places with populations of 10,000 or more

Place (place type) County	Number	%
Sweetwater (city) Miami-Dade	68	0.48
Gladeview (cdp) Miami-Dade	47	0.32
Miami (city) Miami-Dade	1,108	0.31
West Little River (cdp) Miami-Dade	90	0.28
Hialeah Gardens (city) Miami-Dade	48	0.25
Fountainbleau (cdp) Miami-Dade	143	0.24
Richmond West (cdp) Miami-Dade	63	0.22
Doral (cdp) Miami-Dade	44	0.22
Westwood Lakes (cdp) Miami-Dade	26	0.22
Princeton (cdp) Miami-Dade	22	0.22

Hispanic: Cuban

Top 10 Places Sorted by Number
Based on all places, regardless of population

Place (place type) County	Number	%
Hialeah (city) Miami-Dade	140,651	62.12
Miami (city) Miami-Dade	123,763	34.14
Tamiami (cdp) Miami-Dade	31,029	56.63
Fountainbleau (cdp) Miami-Dade	22,206	37.29
Kendale Lakes (cdp) Miami-Dade	21,953	38.58
Westchester (cdp) Miami-Dade	19,886	65.69
Miami Beach (city) Miami-Dade	18,038	20.51
Kendall (cdp) Miami-Dade	16,029	21.31
University Park (cdp) Miami-Dade	15,871	59.80
Coral Terrace (cdp) Miami-Dade	15,084	61.87

Top 10 Places Sorted by Percent
Based on all places, regardless of population

Place (place type) County	Number	%
Westchester (cdp) Miami-Dade	19,886	65.69
Hialeah (city) Miami-Dade	140,651	62.12
Coral Terrace (cdp) Miami-Dade	15,084	61.87
West Miami (city) Miami-Dade	3,612	61.61
University Park (cdp) Miami-Dade	15,871	59.80
Olympia Heights (cdp) Miami-Dade	7,755	57.65
Tamiami (cdp) Miami-Dade	31,029	56.63
Westwood Lakes (cdp) Miami-Dade	6,730	56.06
Hialeah Gardens (city) Miami-Dade	10,480	54.31
Medley (town) Miami-Dade	570	51.91

Top 10 Places Sorted by Percent
Based on places with populations of 10,000 or more

Place (place type) County	Number	%
Westchester (cdp) Miami-Dade	19,886	65.69
Hialeah (city) Miami-Dade	140,651	62.12
Coral Terrace (cdp) Miami-Dade	15,084	61.87
University Park (cdp) Miami-Dade	15,871	59.80
Olympia Heights (cdp) Miami-Dade	7,755	57.65
Tamiami (cdp) Miami-Dade	31,029	56.63
Westwood Lakes (cdp) Miami-Dade	6,730	56.06
Hialeah Gardens (city) Miami-Dade	10,480	54.31
Sweetwater (city) Miami-Dade	7,101	49.92
Sunset (cdp) Miami-Dade	7,989	46.58

Hispanic: Dominican Republic

Top 10 Places Sorted by Number
Based on all places, regardless of population

Place (place type) County	Number	%
Miami (city) Miami-Dade	6,370	1.76
Hialeah (city) Miami-Dade	4,106	1.81
Carol City (cdp) Miami-Dade	1,785	3.00
Fountainbleau (cdp) Miami-Dade	1,779	2.99
Hollywood (city) Broward	1,681	1.21
Pembroke Pines (city) Broward	1,637	1.19
Miramar (city) Broward	1,439	1.98
Tampa (city) Hillsborough	1,397	0.46
Country Club (cdp) Miami-Dade	1,309	3.61
Orlando (city) Orange	1,191	0.64

Top 10 Places Sorted by Percent
Based on all places, regardless of population

Place (place type) County	Number	%
Miami Gardens (cdp) Broward	125	4.62
Lake Forest (cdp) Broward	198	3.96
Country Club (cdp) Miami-Dade	1,309	3.61
Oak Ridge (cdp) Orange	677	3.03
Carol City (cdp) Miami-Dade	1,785	3.00
Fountainbleau (cdp) Miami-Dade	1,779	2.99
Hialeah Gardens (city) Miami-Dade	551	2.86
Yeehaw Junction (cdp) Osceola	609	2.80
Doral (cdp) Miami-Dade	540	2.64
Opa-locka (city) Miami-Dade	387	2.59

Top 10 Places Sorted by Percent
Based on places with populations of 10,000 or more

Place (place type) County	Number	%
Country Club (cdp) Miami-Dade	1,309	3.61
Oak Ridge (cdp) Orange	677	3.03
Carol City (cdp) Miami-Dade	1,785	3.00
Fountainbleau (cdp) Miami-Dade	1,779	2.99
Hialeah Gardens (city) Miami-Dade	551	2.86
Yeehaw Junction (cdp) Osceola	609	2.80
Doral (cdp) Miami-Dade	540	2.64
Opa-locka (city) Miami-Dade	387	2.59
Kendall West (cdp) Miami-Dade	982	2.58
South Miami Heights (cdp) Miami-Dade	851	2.54

Hispanic: Mexican

Top 10 Places Sorted by Number
Based on all places, regardless of population

Place (place type) County	Number	%
Immokalee (cdp) Collier	11,354	57.45
Homestead (city) Miami-Dade	7,279	22.81
Tampa (city) Hillsborough	6,272	2.07
Jacksonville (special city) Duval	6,076	0.83
Leisure City (cdp) Miami-Dade	5,259	23.74
Clearwater (city) Pinellas	4,771	4.39
Fort Pierce (city) St. Lucie	4,311	11.49
Bonita Springs (city) Lee	3,955	12.06
Plant City (city) Hillsborough	3,681	12.30
Miami (city) Miami-Dade	3,669	1.01

Top 10 Places Sorted by Percent
Based on all places, regardless of population

Place (place type) County	Number	%
Fellsmere (city) Indian River	2,585	67.79
Wimauma (cdp) Hillsborough	2,816	66.32
Pierson (town) Volusia	1,593	61.36
Immokalee (cdp) Collier	11,354	57.45
Naples Manor (cdp) Collier	2,601	50.15
Dade City North (cdp) Pasco	1,616	48.69
Wahneta (cdp) Polk	2,028	42.87
Zolfo Springs (town) Hardee	702	42.78
Southeast Arcadia (cdp) De Soto	2,542	41.92
Dover (cdp) Hillsborough	1,162	41.53

Notes: (cdp) census designated place; Refer to the User's Guide in the front of the book for more detailed information.

Place (place type) County	Number	%
Leisure City (cdp) Miami-Dade	5,259	23.74
Homestead (city) Miami-Dade	7,279	22.81
Palmetto (city) Manatee	2,821	22.44
Haines City (city) Polk	2,309	17.53
Golden Gate (cdp) Collier	3,529	16.84
Lake Worth Corridor (cdp) Palm Beach	3,032	16.25
Belle Glade (city) Palm Beach	2,302	15.44
Plant City (city) Hillsborough	3,681	12.30
Bonita Springs (city) Lee	3,955	12.06

Hispanic: Puerto Rican

Top 10 Places Sorted by Number
Based on all places, regardless of population

Place (place type) County	Number	%
Tampa (city) Hillsborough	17,527	5.78
Orlando (city) Orange	17,029	9.16
Kissimmee (city) Osceola	11,312	23.66
Jacksonville (special city) Duval	11,066	1.50
Miami (city) Miami-Dade	10,257	2.83
Deltona (city) Volusia	9,136	13.14
Yeehaw Junction (cdp) Osceola	7,980	36.64
Town 'n' Country (cdp) Hillsborough	7,505	10.35
Hollywood (city) Broward	7,463	5.36
Pembroke Pines (city) Broward	6,887	5.01

Top 10 Places Sorted by Percent
Based on all places, regardless of population

Place (place type) County	Number	%
Harlem Heights (cdp) Lee	396	37.18
Yeehaw Junction (cdp) Osceola	7,980	36.64
Meadow Woods (cdp) Orange	3,772	33.42
Poinciana (cdp) Osceola	3,789	27.76
Azalea Park (cdp) Orange	2,745	24.79
Kissimmee (city) Osceola	11,312	23.66
Oak Ridge (cdp) Orange	4,249	19.01
Southchase (cdp) Orange	880	18.99
Interlachen (town) Putnam	252	17.08
Union Park (cdp) Orange	1,730	16.98

Top 10 Places Sorted by Percent
Based on places with populations of 10,000 or more

Place (place type) County	Number	%
Yeehaw Junction (cdp) Osceola	7,980	36.64
Meadow Woods (cdp) Orange	3,772	33.42
Poinciana (cdp) Osceola	3,789	27.76
Azalea Park (cdp) Orange	2,745	24.79
Kissimmee (city) Osceola	11,312	23.66
Oak Ridge (cdp) Orange	4,249	19.01
Union Park (cdp) Orange	1,730	16.98
Deltona (city) Volusia	9,136	13.14
Egypt Lake-Leto (cdp) Hillsborough	3,559	10.86
Town 'n' Country (cdp) Hillsborough	7,505	10.35

Hispanic: South American

Top 10 Places Sorted by Number
Based on all places, regardless of population

Place (place type) County	Number	%
Miami (city) Miami-Dade	15,076	4.16
Hialeah (city) Miami-Dade	12,510	5.53
Miami Beach (city) Miami-Dade	11,589	13.18
The Hammocks (cdp) Miami-Dade	9,494	20.04
Pembroke Pines (city) Broward	8,292	6.03
Fountainbleau (cdp) Miami-Dade	8,100	13.60
Kendall (cdp) Miami-Dade	7,961	10.58
Kendale Lakes (cdp) Miami-Dade	7,076	12.44
Kendall West (cdp) Miami-Dade	7,073	18.60

Place (place type) County	Number	%
Doral (cdp) Miami-Dade	4,989	24.41
The Hammocks (cdp) Miami-Dade	9,494	20.04
Kendall West (cdp) Miami-Dade	7,073	18.60
Key Biscayne (village) Miami-Dade	1,793	17.06
North Bay Village (city) Miami-Dade	1,087	16.14
Virginia Gardens (village) Miami-Dade	345	14.69
The Crossings (cdp) Miami-Dade	3,326	14.12
Sunny Isles Beach (city) Miami-Dade	2,150	14.04
Fountainbleau (cdp) Miami-Dade	8,100	13.60
Bay Harbor Islands (town) Miami-Dade	699	13.58

Top 10 Places Sorted by Percent
Based on places with populations of 10,000 or more

Place (place type) County	Number	%
Doral (cdp) Miami-Dade	4,989	24.41
The Hammocks (cdp) Miami-Dade	9,494	20.04
Kendall West (cdp) Miami-Dade	7,073	18.60
Key Biscayne (village) Miami-Dade	1,793	17.06
The Crossings (cdp) Miami-Dade	3,326	14.12
Sunny Isles Beach (city) Miami-Dade	2,150	14.04
Fountainbleau (cdp) Miami-Dade	8,100	13.60
Weston (city) Broward	6,620	13.43
Country Club (cdp) Miami-Dade	4,843	13.34
Miami Beach (city) Miami-Dade	11,589	13.18

Hispanic: Argentinean

Top 10 Places Sorted by Number
Based on all places, regardless of population

Place (place type) County	Number	%
Miami Beach (city) Miami-Dade	2,680	3.05
Miami (city) Miami-Dade	1,669	0.46
Hialeah (city) Miami-Dade	632	0.28
Kendall (cdp) Miami-Dade	605	0.80
Fountainbleau (cdp) Miami-Dade	518	0.87
Coral Springs (city) Broward	498	0.42
Pembroke Pines (city) Broward	463	0.34
Hollywood (city) Broward	456	0.33
Aventura (city) Miami-Dade	424	1.68
The Hammocks (cdp) Miami-Dade	401	0.85

Top 10 Places Sorted by Percent
Based on all places, regardless of population

Place (place type) County	Number	%
North Bay Village (city) Miami-Dade	252	3.74
Miami Beach (city) Miami-Dade	2,680	3.05
Bay Harbor Islands (town) Miami-Dade	157	3.05
Key Biscayne (village) Miami-Dade	282	2.68
Sunny Isles Beach (city) Miami-Dade	371	2.42
Surfside (town) Miami-Dade	117	2.38
Bal Harbour (village) Miami-Dade	74	2.24
Fisher Island (cdp) Miami-Dade	8	1.71
Aventura (city) Miami-Dade	424	1.68
Biscayne Park (village) Miami-Dade	52	1.59

Top 10 Places Sorted by Percent
Based on places with populations of 10,000 or more

Place (place type) County	Number	%
Miami Beach (city) Miami-Dade	2,680	3.05
Key Biscayne (village) Miami-Dade	282	2.68
Sunny Isles Beach (city) Miami-Dade	371	2.42
Aventura (city) Miami-Dade	424	1.68
Ojus (cdp) Miami-Dade	249	1.50
Doral (cdp) Miami-Dade	262	1.28
Ives Estates (cdp) Miami-Dade	183	1.04
The Crossings (cdp) Miami-Dade	233	0.99
Fountainbleau (cdp) Miami-Dade	518	0.87

Top 10 Places Sorted by Number
Based on all places, regardless of population

Place (place type) County	Number	%
Miami (city) Miami-Dade	355	0.10
Miami Beach (city) Miami-Dade	176	0.20
Kendall (cdp) Miami-Dade	170	0.23
Fountainbleau (cdp) Miami-Dade	153	0.26
Hialeah (city) Miami-Dade	113	0.05
Hollywood (city) Broward	100	0.07
Kendale Lakes (cdp) Miami-Dade	96	0.17
The Hammocks (cdp) Miami-Dade	93	0.20
Tamiami (cdp) Miami-Dade	82	0.15
Kendall West (cdp) Miami-Dade	79	0.21

Top 10 Places Sorted by Percent
Based on all places, regardless of population

Place (place type) County	Number	%
North Bay Village (city) Miami-Dade	31	0.46
Medley (town) Miami-Dade	5	0.46
Lely Resort (cdp) Collier	5	0.35
Golden Beach (town) Miami-Dade	3	0.33
Naples Park (cdp) Collier	21	0.31
The Crossings (cdp) Miami-Dade	69	0.29
Fountainbleau (cdp) Miami-Dade	153	0.26
Key Biscayne (village) Miami-Dade	27	0.26
Bay Harbor Islands (town) Miami-Dade	13	0.25
Kendall (cdp) Miami-Dade	170	0.23

Top 10 Places Sorted by Percent
Based on places with populations of 10,000 or more

Place (place type) County	Number	%
The Crossings (cdp) Miami-Dade	69	0.29
Fountainbleau (cdp) Miami-Dade	153	0.26
Key Biscayne (village) Miami-Dade	27	0.26
Kendall (cdp) Miami-Dade	170	0.23
Miami Springs (city) Miami-Dade	31	0.23
Doral (cdp) Miami-Dade	45	0.22
Sunset (cdp) Miami-Dade	37	0.22
Kendall West (cdp) Miami-Dade	79	0.21
Miami Beach (city) Miami-Dade	176	0.20
The Hammocks (cdp) Miami-Dade	93	0.20

Hispanic: Chilean

Top 10 Places Sorted by Number
Based on all places, regardless of population

Place (place type) County	Number	%
Miami (city) Miami-Dade	939	0.26
Miami Beach (city) Miami-Dade	623	0.71
Hialeah (city) Miami-Dade	611	0.27
Fountainbleau (cdp) Miami-Dade	550	0.92
Kendall (cdp) Miami-Dade	479	0.64
The Hammocks (cdp) Miami-Dade	409	0.86
Kendale Lakes (cdp) Miami-Dade	381	0.67
Hollywood (city) Broward	302	0.22
Pembroke Pines (city) Broward	298	0.22
Tamiami (cdp) Miami-Dade	262	0.48

Top 10 Places Sorted by Percent
Based on all places, regardless of population

Place (place type) County	Number	%
Doral (cdp) Miami-Dade	224	1.10
North Bay Village (city) Miami-Dade	68	1.01
Fountainbleau (cdp) Miami-Dade	550	0.92
The Crossings (cdp) Miami-Dade	212	0.90
Chula Vista (cdp) Broward	5	0.87
The Hammocks (cdp) Miami-Dade	409	0.86
Country Walk (cdp) Miami-Dade	83	0.78

Notes: (cdp) census designated place; Refer to the User's Guide in the front of the book for more detailed information.

Cutler (cdp) Miami-Dade		129	0.74
Key Biscayne (village) Miami-Dade		76	0.72
Miami Beach (city) Miami-Dade		623	0.71

Top 10 Places Sorted by Percent
Based on places with populations of 10,000 or more

Place (place type) County	Number	%
Doral (cdp) Miami-Dade	224	1.10
Fountainbleau (cdp) Miami-Dade	550	0.92
The Crossings (cdp) Miami-Dade	212	0.90
The Hammocks (cdp) Miami-Dade	409	0.86
Country Walk (cdp) Miami-Dade	83	0.78
Cutler (cdp) Miami-Dade	129	0.74
Key Biscayne (village) Miami-Dade	76	0.72
Miami Beach (city) Miami-Dade	623	0.71
Glenvar Heights (cdp) Miami-Dade	116	0.71
Kendale Lakes (cdp) Miami-Dade	381	0.67

Hispanic: Colombian

Top 10 Places Sorted by Number
Based on all places, regardless of population

Place (place type) County	Number	%
Hialeah (city) Miami-Dade	7,152	3.16
Miami (city) Miami-Dade	5,784	1.60
The Hammocks (cdp) Miami-Dade	4,749	10.02
Pembroke Pines (city) Broward	4,124	3.00
Miami Beach (city) Miami-Dade	3,872	4.40
Kendall West (cdp) Miami-Dade	3,778	9.93
Kendale Lakes (cdp) Miami-Dade	3,619	6.36
Kendall (cdp) Miami-Dade	3,429	4.56
Fountainbleau (cdp) Miami-Dade	3,153	5.29
Hollywood (city) Broward	3,152	2.26

Top 10 Places Sorted by Percent
Based on all places, regardless of population

Place (place type) County	Number	%
The Hammocks (cdp) Miami-Dade	4,749	10.02
Kendall West (cdp) Miami-Dade	3,778	9.93
Doral (cdp) Miami-Dade	1,780	8.71
Country Club (cdp) Miami-Dade	3,134	8.63
Virginia Gardens (village) Miami-Dade	168	7.16
Key Biscayne (village) Miami-Dade	743	7.07
Kendale Lakes (cdp) Miami-Dade	3,619	6.36
Weston (city) Broward	3,052	6.19
The Crossings (cdp) Miami-Dade	1,454	6.17
Sunny Isles Beach (city) Miami-Dade	930	6.07

Top 10 Places Sorted by Percent
Based on places with populations of 10,000 or more

Place (place type) County	Number	%
The Hammocks (cdp) Miami-Dade	4,749	10.02
Kendall West (cdp) Miami-Dade	3,778	9.93
Doral (cdp) Miami-Dade	1,780	8.71
Country Club (cdp) Miami-Dade	3,134	8.63
Key Biscayne (village) Miami-Dade	743	7.07
Kendale Lakes (cdp) Miami-Dade	3,619	6.36
Weston (city) Broward	3,052	6.19
The Crossings (cdp) Miami-Dade	1,454	6.17
Sunny Isles Beach (city) Miami-Dade	930	6.07
Country Walk (cdp) Miami-Dade	594	5.58

Hispanic: Ecuadorian

Top 10 Places Sorted by Number
Based on all places, regardless of population

Place (place type) County	Number	%
Miami (city) Miami-Dade	1,408	0.39
Hialeah (city) Miami-Dade	1,159	0.51
Pembroke Pines (city) Broward	734	0.53
Hollywood (city) Broward	592	0.42
Fountainbleau (cdp) Miami-Dade	564	0.95

The Hammocks (cdp) Miami-Dade		522	1.10
Miami Beach (city) Miami-Dade		493	0.56
Coral Springs (city) Broward		441	0.38
Kendall West (cdp) Miami-Dade		417	1.10
Kendall (cdp) Miami-Dade		415	0.55

Top 10 Places Sorted by Percent
Based on all places, regardless of population

Place (place type) County	Number	%
Virginia Gardens (village) Miami-Dade	31	1.32
Doral (cdp) Miami-Dade	241	1.18
The Hammocks (cdp) Miami-Dade	522	1.10
Kendall West (cdp) Miami-Dade	417	1.10
Key Biscayne (village) Miami-Dade	102	0.97
Fountainbleau (cdp) Miami-Dade	564	0.95
Country Club (cdp) Miami-Dade	326	0.90
Country Walk (cdp) Miami-Dade	93	0.87
Sunshine Acres (cdp) Broward	7	0.85
Meadow Woods (cdp) Orange	95	0.84

Top 10 Places Sorted by Percent
Based on places with populations of 10,000 or more

Place (place type) County	Number	%
Doral (cdp) Miami-Dade	241	1.18
The Hammocks (cdp) Miami-Dade	522	1.10
Kendall West (cdp) Miami-Dade	417	1.10
Key Biscayne (village) Miami-Dade	102	0.97
Fountainbleau (cdp) Miami-Dade	564	0.95
Country Club (cdp) Miami-Dade	326	0.90
Country Walk (cdp) Miami-Dade	93	0.87
Meadow Woods (cdp) Orange	95	0.84
Hialeah Gardens (city) Miami-Dade	161	0.83
Miami Lakes (cdp) Miami-Dade	170	0.75

Hispanic: Paraguayan

Top 10 Places Sorted by Number
Based on all places, regardless of population

Place (place type) County	Number	%
Miami Beach (city) Miami-Dade	64	0.07
Miami (city) Miami-Dade	45	0.01
Kendall (cdp) Miami-Dade	31	0.04
Coral Gables (city) Miami-Dade	26	0.06
Fountainbleau (cdp) Miami-Dade	23	0.04
Doral (cdp) Miami-Dade	21	0.10
Pembroke Pines (city) Broward	20	0.01
The Crossings (cdp) Miami-Dade	18	0.08
Hialeah (city) Miami-Dade	16	0.01
Hollywood (city) Broward	15	0.01

Top 10 Places Sorted by Percent
Based on all places, regardless of population

Place (place type) County	Number	%
Fisher Island (cdp) Miami-Dade	3	0.64
Golden Beach (town) Miami-Dade	5	0.54
Ramblewood East (cdp) Broward	7	0.50
Hypoluxo (town) Palm Beach	3	0.15
North Bay Village (city) Miami-Dade	9	0.13
Key Biscayne (village) Miami-Dade	13	0.12
Village Park (cdp) Broward	1	0.11
Doral (cdp) Miami-Dade	21	0.10
Harbour Heights (cdp) Charlotte	3	0.10
Bal Harbour (village) Miami-Dade	3	0.09

Top 10 Places Sorted by Percent
Based on places with populations of 10,000 or more

Place (place type) County	Number	%
Key Biscayne (village) Miami-Dade	13	0.12
Doral (cdp) Miami-Dade	21	0.10
The Crossings (cdp) Miami-Dade	18	0.08
Sunny Isles Beach (city) Miami-Dade	12	0.08
Miami Beach (city) Miami-Dade	64	0.07

Coral Gables (city) Miami-Dade		26	0.06
Cutler Ridge (cdp) Miami-Dade		12	0.05
Sandalfoot Cove (cdp) Palm Beach		9	0.05
Miami Springs (city) Miami-Dade		7	0.05
South Miami (city) Miami-Dade		5	0.05

Hispanic: Peruvian

Top 10 Places Sorted by Number
Based on all places, regardless of population

Place (place type) County	Number	%
Miami (city) Miami-Dade	2,447	0.68
Miami Beach (city) Miami-Dade	1,630	1.85
The Hammocks (cdp) Miami-Dade	1,591	3.36
Kendall (cdp) Miami-Dade	1,512	2.01
Hollywood (city) Broward	1,466	1.05
Hialeah (city) Miami-Dade	1,418	0.63
Kendale Lakes (cdp) Miami-Dade	1,157	2.03
Kendall West (cdp) Miami-Dade	1,084	2.85
Pembroke Pines (city) Broward	1,082	0.79
Fountainbleau (cdp) Miami-Dade	1,044	1.75

Top 10 Places Sorted by Percent
Based on all places, regardless of population

Place (place type) County	Number	%
The Hammocks (cdp) Miami-Dade	1,591	3.36
Virginia Gardens (village) Miami-Dade	76	3.24
Bay Harbor Islands (town) Miami-Dade	160	3.11
Doral (cdp) Miami-Dade	602	2.95
Kendall West (cdp) Miami-Dade	1,084	2.85
The Crossings (cdp) Miami-Dade	634	2.69
Key Biscayne (village) Miami-Dade	261	2.48
Ojus (cdp) Miami-Dade	381	2.29
North Bay Village (city) Miami-Dade	146	2.17
Kendale Lakes (cdp) Miami-Dade	1,157	2.03

Top 10 Places Sorted by Percent
Based on places with populations of 10,000 or more

Place (place type) County	Number	%
The Hammocks (cdp) Miami-Dade	1,591	3.36
Doral (cdp) Miami-Dade	602	2.95
Kendall West (cdp) Miami-Dade	1,084	2.85
The Crossings (cdp) Miami-Dade	634	2.69
Key Biscayne (village) Miami-Dade	261	2.48
Ojus (cdp) Miami-Dade	381	2.29
Kendale Lakes (cdp) Miami-Dade	1,157	2.03
Kendall (cdp) Miami-Dade	1,512	2.01
Miami Springs (city) Miami-Dade	260	1.90
Miami Beach (city) Miami-Dade	1,630	1.85

Hispanic: Uruguayan

Top 10 Places Sorted by Number
Based on all places, regardless of population

Place (place type) County	Number	%
Miami Beach (city) Miami-Dade	222	0.25
Miami (city) Miami-Dade	221	0.06
Hialeah (city) Miami-Dade	118	0.05
Hollywood (city) Broward	113	0.08
Kendale Lakes (cdp) Miami-Dade	100	0.18
Coral Springs (city) Broward	99	0.08
North Andrews Gardens (cdp) Broward	93	0.96
Sunrise (city) Broward	92	0.11
The Hammocks (cdp) Miami-Dade	79	0.17
Pembroke Pines (city) Broward	78	0.06

Top 10 Places Sorted by Percent
Based on all places, regardless of population

Place (place type) County	Number	%
Cloud Lake (town) Palm Beach	2	1.20
North Andrews Gardens (cdp) Broward	93	0.96
Twin Lakes (cdp) Broward	10	0.53

Notes: (cdp) census designated place; Refer to the User's Guide in the front of the book for more detailed information.

Golden Beach (town) Miami-Dade	4	0.44
Sunshine Acres (cdp) Broward	3	0.36
Glen Ridge (town) Palm Beach	1	0.36
North Bay Village (city) Miami-Dade	22	0.33
Bay Harbor Islands (town) Miami-Dade	17	0.33
Palm Aire (cdp) Broward	4	0.26
Miami Beach (city) Miami-Dade	222	0.25

Top 10 Places Sorted by Percent
Based on places with populations of 10,000 or more

Place (place type) County	Number	%
Miami Beach (city) Miami-Dade	222	0.25
The Crossings (cdp) Miami-Dade	48	0.20
Ojus (cdp) Miami-Dade	31	0.19
Sunny Isles Beach (city) Miami-Dade	29	0.19
Kendale Lakes (cdp) Miami-Dade	100	0.18
The Hammocks (cdp) Miami-Dade	79	0.17
Greenacres (city) Palm Beach	48	0.17
Doral (cdp) Miami-Dade	35	0.17
Country Club (cdp) Miami-Dade	56	0.15
Glenvar Heights (cdp) Miami-Dade	24	0.15

Hispanic: Venezuelan

Top 10 Places Sorted by Number
Based on all places, regardless of population

Place (place type) County	Number	%
Weston (city) Broward	2,020	4.10
Miami (city) Miami-Dade	1,959	0.54
Fountainbleau (cdp) Miami-Dade	1,868	3.14
Doral (cdp) Miami-Dade	1,680	8.22
Miami Beach (city) Miami-Dade	1,572	1.79
The Hammocks (cdp) Miami-Dade	1,488	3.14
Pembroke Pines (city) Broward	1,242	0.90
Hialeah (city) Miami-Dade	1,117	0.49
Kendall (cdp) Miami-Dade	1,108	1.47
Kendall West (cdp) Miami-Dade	1,015	2.67

Top 10 Places Sorted by Percent
Based on all places, regardless of population

Place (place type) County	Number	%
Doral (cdp) Miami-Dade	1,680	8.22
Weston (city) Broward	2,020	4.10
Fisher Island (cdp) Miami-Dade	19	4.07
Fountainbleau (cdp) Miami-Dade	1,868	3.14
The Hammocks (cdp) Miami-Dade	1,488	3.14
Kendall West (cdp) Miami-Dade	1,015	2.67
Lazy Lake (village) Broward	1	2.63
Key Biscayne (village) Miami-Dade	248	2.36
North Bay Village (city) Miami-Dade	145	2.15
Glenvar Heights (cdp) Miami-Dade	332	2.04

Top 10 Places Sorted by Percent
Based on places with populations of 10,000 or more

Place (place type) County	Number	%
Doral (cdp) Miami-Dade	1,680	8.22
Weston (city) Broward	2,020	4.10
Fountainbleau (cdp) Miami-Dade	1,868	3.14
The Hammocks (cdp) Miami-Dade	1,488	3.14
Kendall West (cdp) Miami-Dade	1,015	2.67
Key Biscayne (village) Miami-Dade	248	2.36
Glenvar Heights (cdp) Miami-Dade	332	2.04
Sunny Isles Beach (city) Miami-Dade	300	1.96
The Crossings (cdp) Miami-Dade	453	1.92
Miami Beach (city) Miami-Dade	1,572	1.79

Hispanic: Other South American

Top 10 Places Sorted by Number
Based on all places, regardless of population

Place (place type) County	Number	%
Miami Beach (city) Miami-Dade	257	0.29

Miami (city) Miami-Dade	249	0.07
Hollywood (city) Broward	188	0.13
Pembroke Pines (city) Broward	185	0.13
Hialeah (city) Miami-Dade	174	0.08
The Hammocks (cdp) Miami-Dade	157	0.33
Fountainbleau (cdp) Miami-Dade	156	0.26
Coral Springs (city) Broward	156	0.13
Kendall (cdp) Miami-Dade	147	0.20
Weston (city) Broward	130	0.26

Top 10 Places Sorted by Percent
Based on all places, regardless of population

Place (place type) County	Number	%
Surfside (town) Miami-Dade	30	0.61
Village Park (cdp) Broward	5	0.56
Doral (cdp) Miami-Dade	99	0.48
Biscayne Park (village) Miami-Dade	14	0.43
The Crossings (cdp) Miami-Dade	83	0.35
The Hammocks (cdp) Miami-Dade	157	0.33
Key Biscayne (village) Miami-Dade	35	0.33
Bay Harbor Islands (town) Miami-Dade	17	0.33
Bronson (town) Levy	3	0.31
Richmond West (cdp) Miami-Dade	84	0.30

Top 10 Places Sorted by Percent
Based on places with populations of 10,000 or more

Place (place type) County	Number	%
Doral (cdp) Miami-Dade	99	0.48
The Crossings (cdp) Miami-Dade	83	0.35
The Hammocks (cdp) Miami-Dade	157	0.33
Key Biscayne (village) Miami-Dade	35	0.33
Richmond West (cdp) Miami-Dade	84	0.30
Miami Beach (city) Miami-Dade	257	0.29
Kendall West (cdp) Miami-Dade	103	0.27
Fountainbleau (cdp) Miami-Dade	156	0.26
Weston (city) Broward	130	0.26
Ojus (cdp) Miami-Dade	43	0.26

Hispanic: Other

Top 10 Places Sorted by Number
Based on all places, regardless of population

Place (place type) County	Number	%
Miami (city) Miami-Dade	39,058	10.78
Hialeah (city) Miami-Dade	24,305	10.73
Tampa (city) Hillsborough	13,499	4.45
Fountainbleau (cdp) Miami-Dade	9,962	16.73
Miami Beach (city) Miami-Dade	8,414	9.57
Kendale Lakes (cdp) Miami-Dade	7,479	13.14
Pembroke Pines (city) Broward	7,127	5.19
Kendall (cdp) Miami-Dade	6,548	8.70
The Hammocks (cdp) Miami-Dade	6,367	13.44
Tamiami (cdp) Miami-Dade	6,257	11.42

Top 10 Places Sorted by Percent
Based on all places, regardless of population

Place (place type) County	Number	%
Fountainbleau (cdp) Miami-Dade	9,962	16.73
Sweetwater (city) Miami-Dade	2,264	15.91
Kendall West (cdp) Miami-Dade	5,815	15.29
The Hammocks (cdp) Miami-Dade	6,367	13.44
Doral (cdp) Miami-Dade	2,727	13.34
Hialeah Gardens (city) Miami-Dade	2,571	13.32
Kendale Lakes (cdp) Miami-Dade	7,479	13.14
Richmond West (cdp) Miami-Dade	3,557	12.67
Virginia Gardens (village) Miami-Dade	297	12.65
Country Club (cdp) Miami-Dade	4,563	12.57

Top 10 Places Sorted by Percent
Based on places with populations of 10,000 or more

Place (place type) County	Number	%
Fountainbleau (cdp) Miami-Dade	9,962	16.73

Sweetwater (city) Miami-Dade	2,264	15.91
Kendall West (cdp) Miami-Dade	5,815	15.29
The Hammocks (cdp) Miami-Dade	6,367	13.44
Doral (cdp) Miami-Dade	2,727	13.34
Hialeah Gardens (city) Miami-Dade	2,571	13.32
Kendale Lakes (cdp) Miami-Dade	7,479	13.14
Richmond West (cdp) Miami-Dade	3,557	12.67
Country Club (cdp) Miami-Dade	4,563	12.57
Tamiami (cdp) Miami-Dade	6,257	11.42

Hungarian

Top 10 Places Sorted by Number
Based on all places, regardless of population

Place (place type) County	Number	%
Jacksonville (special city) Duval	2,485	0.34
Hollywood (city) Broward	1,703	1.22
St. Petersburg (city) Pinellas	1,673	0.68
Tampa (city) Hillsborough	1,218	0.40
Fort Lauderdale (city) Broward	1,161	0.76
Coral Springs (city) Broward	1,134	0.97
Plantation (city) Broward	1,070	1.28
Boca Raton (city) Palm Beach	1,054	1.39
Pembroke Pines (city) Broward	1,052	0.77
Port St. Lucie (city) St. Lucie	973	1.10

Top 10 Places Sorted by Percent
Based on all places, regardless of population

Place (place type) County	Number	%
Godfrey Road (cdp) Broward	38	17.84
Layton (city) Monroe	24	10.00
Indian Creek (village) Miami-Dade	2	5.88
Boca Pointe (cdp) Palm Beach	149	4.52
Yalaha (cdp) Lake	46	4.14
Chokoloskee (cdp) Collier	18	3.50
Cypress Lakes (cdp) Palm Beach	48	3.48
South Palm Beach (town) Palm Beach	24	3.31
Century Village (cdp) Palm Beach	246	3.24
Lakeside Green (cdp) Palm Beach	113	3.19

Top 10 Places Sorted by Percent
Based on places with populations of 10,000 or more

Place (place type) County	Number	%
Kings Point (cdp) Palm Beach	341	2.75
Gulf Gate Estates (cdp) Sarasota	222	1.92
Palm Beach Gardens (city) Palm Beach	643	1.87
Hallandale (city) Broward	644	1.86
Boca Del Mar (cdp) Palm Beach	382	1.78
Hamptons at Boca Raton (cdp) Palm Beach	187	1.64
Gulfport (city) Pinellas	194	1.54
Seminole (city) Pinellas	166	1.54
Aventura (city) Miami-Dade	378	1.50
Cooper City (city) Broward	411	1.48

Icelander

Top 10 Places Sorted by Number
Based on all places, regardless of population

Place (place type) County	Number	%
Orlando (city) Orange	91	0.05
Tallahassee (city) Leon	90	0.06
Jacksonville (special city) Duval	64	0.01
Miami (city) Miami-Dade	36	0.01
Longwood (city) Seminole	35	0.26
Placid Lakes (cdp) Highlands	34	1.13
St. Petersburg (city) Pinellas	29	0.01
Palm Harbor (cdp) Pinellas	26	0.04
Miami Springs (city) Miami-Dade	24	0.18
Palm Coast (city) Flagler	24	0.07

Notes: (cdp) census designated place; Refer to the User's Guide in the front of the book for more detailed information.

Place (place type) County	Number	%
Placid Lakes (cdp) Highlands	34	1.13
Southchase (cdp) Orange	22	0.48
Callahan (town) Nassau	3	0.32
Zephyrhills South (cdp) Pasco	14	0.30
Longwood (city) Seminole	35	0.26
Cape Canaveral (city) Brevard	23	0.26
West De Land (cdp) Volusia	8	0.23
Lake Butler (cdp) Orange	15	0.21
Miami Springs (city) Miami-Dade	24	0.18
Warm Mineral Springs (cdp) Sarasota	9	0.18

Top 10 Places Sorted by Percent
Based on places with populations of 10,000 or more

Place (place type) County	Number	%
Longwood (city) Seminole	35	0.26
Miami Springs (city) Miami-Dade	24	0.18
Lynn Haven (city) Bay	15	0.12
Lakewood Park (cdp) St. Lucie	13	0.12
Lighthouse Point (city) Broward	13	0.12
Gulf Gate Estates (cdp) Sarasota	12	0.10
Opa-locka (city) Miami-Dade	13	0.09
Gonzalez (cdp) Escambia	11	0.09
Key Biscayne (village) Miami-Dade	9	0.09
Palm Valley (cdp) St. Johns	16	0.08

Iranian

Top 10 Places Sorted by Number
Based on all places, regardless of population

Place (place type) County	Number	%
Jacksonville (special city) Duval	407	0.06
Sunrise (city) Broward	252	0.29
Coral Springs (city) Broward	247	0.21
Gainesville (city) Alachua	216	0.23
The Crossings (cdp) Miami-Dade	202	0.86
Boca Raton (city) Palm Beach	202	0.27
Parkland (city) Broward	167	1.19
Kendall (cdp) Miami-Dade	167	0.22
Weston (city) Broward	157	0.32
Plantation (city) Broward	149	0.18

Top 10 Places Sorted by Percent
Based on all places, regardless of population

Place (place type) County	Number	%
Fisher Island (cdp) Miami-Dade	30	8.85
Naranja (cdp) Miami-Dade	63	1.50
Pebble Creek (cdp) Hillsborough	61	1.26
Parkland (city) Broward	167	1.19
Malabar (town) Brevard	31	1.10
Hillsboro Beach (town) Broward	20	0.92
Hunters Creek (cdp) Orange	81	0.91
The Crossings (cdp) Miami-Dade	202	0.86
Cutler (cdp) Miami-Dade	132	0.75
Heathrow (cdp) Seminole	25	0.64

Top 10 Places Sorted by Percent
Based on places with populations of 10,000 or more

Place (place type) County	Number	%
Parkland (city) Broward	167	1.19
The Crossings (cdp) Miami-Dade	202	0.86
Cutler (cdp) Miami-Dade	132	0.75
Gonzalez (cdp) Escambia	63	0.54
Greater Northdale (cdp) Hillsborough	105	0.52
Keystone (cdp) Hillsborough	73	0.50
Doral (cdp) Miami-Dade	91	0.44
Ormond Beach (city) Volusia	137	0.38
Greater Carrollwood (cdp) Hillsborough	119	0.35
Lakeland Highlands (cdp) Polk	44	0.35

Top 10 Places Sorted by Number
Based on all places, regardless of population

Place (place type) County	Number	%
Jacksonville (special city) Duval	66,148	8.99
St. Petersburg (city) Pinellas	30,759	12.41
Tampa (city) Hillsborough	25,499	8.40
Cape Coral (city) Lee	16,271	15.92
Orlando (city) Orange	16,241	8.73
Fort Lauderdale (city) Broward	15,639	10.28
Port St. Lucie (city) St. Lucie	15,466	17.42
Clearwater (city) Pinellas	14,935	13.84
Tallahassee (city) Leon	13,276	8.82
Coral Springs (city) Broward	13,257	11.28

Top 10 Places Sorted by Percent
Based on all places, regardless of population

Place (place type) County	Number	%
Bay Lake (city) Orange	23	58.97
Godfrey Road (cdp) Broward	70	32.86
Lake Kathryn (cdp) Lake	215	30.63
Istachatta (cdp) Hernando	18	29.51
Lazy Lake (village) Broward	11	28.21
Three Oaks (cdp) Lee	607	26.93
Duck Key (cdp) Monroe	143	26.43
Cloud Lake (town) Palm Beach	30	24.39
Cudjoe Key (cdp) Monroe	415	23.89
Golf (village) Palm Beach	57	23.85

Top 10 Places Sorted by Percent
Based on places with populations of 10,000 or more

Place (place type) County	Number	%
North Palm Beach (village) Palm Beach	2,686	22.15
Jensen Beach (cdp) Martin	2,214	19.94
Vero Beach South (cdp) Indian River	3,954	19.41
Marco Island (city) Collier	2,892	19.31
Lighthouse Point (city) Broward	2,023	18.96
Oldsmar (city) Pinellas	2,223	18.94
Jupiter (town) Palm Beach	7,303	18.58
Cocoa Beach (city) Brevard	2,300	18.53
Vero Beach (city) Indian River	3,191	17.88
Hudson (cdp) Pasco	2,259	17.75

Israeli

Top 10 Places Sorted by Number
Based on all places, regardless of population

Place (place type) County	Number	%
Hollywood (city) Broward	742	0.53
Aventura (city) Miami-Dade	580	2.30
Plantation (city) Broward	439	0.53
Sunrise (city) Broward	434	0.51
Coral Springs (city) Broward	320	0.27
Ojus (cdp) Miami-Dade	295	1.77
Sunny Isles Beach (city) Miami-Dade	260	1.70
Boca Raton (city) Palm Beach	237	0.31
Miami Beach (city) Miami-Dade	237	0.27
Cooper City (city) Broward	233	0.84

Top 10 Places Sorted by Percent
Based on all places, regardless of population

Place (place type) County	Number	%
Golden Beach (town) Miami-Dade	46	4.39
Estates of Fort Lauderdale (cdp) Broward	61	3.31
Aventura (city) Miami-Dade	580	2.30
Ojus (cdp) Miami-Dade	295	1.77
Sunny Isles Beach (city) Miami-Dade	260	1.70
Mission Bay (cdp) Palm Beach	50	1.63
Cooper City (city) Broward	233	0.84
Hamptons at Boca Raton (cdp) Palm Beach	96	0.84
Ramblewood East (cdp) Broward	9	0.71
Ives Estates (cdp) Miami-Dade	116	0.67

Place (place type) County	Number	%
Aventura (city) Miami-Dade	580	2.30
Ojus (cdp) Miami-Dade	295	1.77
Sunny Isles Beach (city) Miami-Dade	260	1.70
Cooper City (city) Broward	233	0.84
Hamptons at Boca Raton (cdp) Palm Beach	96	0.84
Ives Estates (cdp) Miami-Dade	116	0.67
Hollywood (city) Broward	742	0.53
Plantation (city) Broward	439	0.53
Sunrise (city) Broward	434	0.51
Lakewood Park (cdp) St. Lucie	52	0.50

Italian

Top 10 Places Sorted by Number
Based on all places, regardless of population

Place (place type) County	Number	%
Jacksonville (special city) Duval	25,385	3.45
Tampa (city) Hillsborough	17,096	5.63
St. Petersburg (city) Pinellas	16,736	6.75
Coral Springs (city) Broward	16,709	14.22
Port St. Lucie (city) St. Lucie	13,966	15.73
Cape Coral (city) Lee	13,437	13.15
Hollywood (city) Broward	13,206	9.48
Pembroke Pines (city) Broward	12,850	9.37
Spring Hill (cdp) Hernando	12,431	17.96
Fort Lauderdale (city) Broward	11,512	7.57

Top 10 Places Sorted by Percent
Based on all places, regardless of population

Place (place type) County	Number	%
Hillsboro Pines (cdp) Broward	149	30.72
Godfrey Road (cdp) Broward	56	26.29
Estates of Fort Lauderdale (cdp) Broward	398	21.57
Cypress Lakes (cdp) Palm Beach	296	21.48
Trinity (cdp) Pasco	902	20.12
Dunes Road (cdp) Palm Beach	93	19.66
Jasmine Estates (cdp) Pasco	3,432	19.01
Ferndale (cdp) Lake	53	18.40
Inverness Highlands South (cdp) Citrus	1,057	18.29
Ivanhoe Estates (cdp) Broward	46	18.18

Top 10 Places Sorted by Percent
Based on places with populations of 10,000 or more

Place (place type) County	Number	%
Jasmine Estates (cdp) Pasco	3,432	19.01
Spring Hill (cdp) Hernando	12,431	17.96
Lighthouse Point (city) Broward	1,891	17.73
Jupiter (town) Palm Beach	6,586	16.75
Parkland (city) Broward	2,293	16.39
Bayonet Point (cdp) Pasco	3,823	16.15
Port St. Lucie (city) St. Lucie	13,966	15.73
Palm Coast (city) Flagler	5,128	15.31
Sandalfoot Cove (cdp) Palm Beach	2,489	15.00
Palm City (cdp) Martin	2,992	14.88

Latvian

Top 10 Places Sorted by Number
Based on all places, regardless of population

Place (place type) County	Number	%
St. Petersburg (city) Pinellas	350	0.14
Jacksonville (special city) Duval	103	0.01
Coral Springs (city) Broward	99	0.08
St. Pete Beach (city) Pinellas	97	0.98
Miami Beach (city) Miami-Dade	96	0.11
North Miami (city) Miami-Dade	89	0.15
Hollywood (city) Broward	89	0.06
Miami (city) Miami-Dade	81	0.02
Davie (town) Broward	79	0.10

Notes: (cdp) census designated place; Refer to the User's Guide in the front of the book for more detailed information.

Place (place type) County	Number	%
Orchid (town) Indian River	3	2.17
Palm Beach Shores (town) Palm Beach	13	1.07
St. Pete Beach (city) Pinellas	97	0.98
Longboat Key (town) Sarasota	49	0.65
Cypress Lakes (cdp) Palm Beach	9	0.65
Pine Island Ridge (cdp) Broward	32	0.60
Surfside (town) Miami-Dade	25	0.49
Villages of Oriole (cdp) Palm Beach	23	0.49
South Pasadena (city) Pinellas	27	0.46
St. Augustine South (cdp) St. Johns	22	0.44

Top 10 Places Sorted by Percent
Based on places with populations of 10,000 or more

Place (place type) County	Number	%
Hamptons at Boca Raton (cdp) Palm Beach	46	0.40
Oldsmar (city) Pinellas	41	0.35
Sunny Isles Beach (city) Miami-Dade	39	0.26
Palm Beach (town) Palm Beach	19	0.18
Jupiter (town) Palm Beach	65	0.17
Punta Gorda (city) Charlotte	23	0.16
Villas (cdp) Lee	18	0.16
North Miami (city) Miami-Dade	89	0.15
Wellington (village) Palm Beach	56	0.15
St. Petersburg (city) Pinellas	350	0.14

Lithuanian

Top 10 Places Sorted by Number
Based on all places, regardless of population

Place (place type) County	Number	%
Jacksonville (special city) Duval	1,014	0.14
St. Petersburg (city) Pinellas	873	0.35
Hollywood (city) Broward	490	0.35
Coral Springs (city) Broward	450	0.38
Clearwater (city) Pinellas	446	0.41
Cape Coral (city) Lee	398	0.39
Pembroke Pines (city) Broward	390	0.28
Spring Hill (cdp) Hernando	388	0.56
Fort Lauderdale (city) Broward	386	0.25
St. Pete Beach (city) Pinellas	375	3.78

Top 10 Places Sorted by Percent
Based on all places, regardless of population

Place (place type) County	Number	%
Juno Ridge (cdp) Palm Beach	41	5.44
Pine Lakes (cdp) Lake	23	3.85
St. Pete Beach (city) Pinellas	375	3.78
Paisley (cdp) Lake	22	3.26
Pineland (cdp) Lee	14	2.95
Royal Palm Ranches (cdp) Broward	8	2.66
Belleview (city) Marion	75	2.11
Sea Ranch Lakes (village) Broward	28	2.03
Juno Beach (town) Palm Beach	59	1.89
North Key Largo (cdp) Monroe	19	1.88

Top 10 Places Sorted by Percent
Based on places with populations of 10,000 or more

Place (place type) County	Number	%
Palm Beach (town) Palm Beach	155	1.49
Hudson (cdp) Pasco	137	1.08
Gulfport (city) Pinellas	115	0.91
Jupiter (town) Palm Beach	310	0.79
Edgewater (city) Volusia	147	0.78
Parkland (city) Broward	109	0.78
Lutz (cdp) Hillsborough	131	0.77
Union Park (cdp) Orange	78	0.76
Kings Point (cdp) Palm Beach	93	0.75

Top 10 Places Sorted by Number
Based on all places, regardless of population

Place (place type) County	Number	%
Clearwater (city) Pinellas	122	0.11
Bee Ridge (cdp) Sarasota	47	0.53
Coral Gables (city) Miami-Dade	47	0.11
Jacksonville (special city) Duval	42	0.01
Sunrise (city) Broward	37	0.04
Dunedin (city) Pinellas	26	0.07
Fort Lauderdale (city) Broward	26	0.02
Keystone (cdp) Hillsborough	22	0.15
Venice (city) Sarasota	19	0.11
Melbourne (city) Brevard	19	0.03

Top 10 Places Sorted by Percent
Based on places with populations of 10,000 or more

Place (place type) County	Number	%
Howey-in-the-Hills (town) Lake	7	0.70
Bee Ridge (cdp) Sarasota	47	0.53
Charlotte Park (cdp) Charlotte	7	0.31
Kensington Park (cdp) Sarasota	11	0.30
Brookridge (cdp) Hernando	9	0.29
Lake Lorraine (cdp) Okaloosa	16	0.23
Heathrow (cdp) Seminole	9	0.23
Indian Shores (town) Pinellas	4	0.23
St. Augustine Beach (city) St. Johns	8	0.17
Warm Mineral Springs (cdp) Sarasota	8	0.16

Macedonian

Top 10 Places Sorted by Number
Based on all places, regardless of population

Place (place type) County	Number	%
Hollywood (city) Broward	73	0.05
Boca Raton (city) Palm Beach	70	0.09
Fort Lauderdale (city) Broward	66	0.04
Plantation (city) Broward	45	0.05
Clearwater (city) Pinellas	37	0.03
Boynton Beach (city) Palm Beach	34	0.06
Cooper City (city) Broward	30	0.11
Greater Sun Center (cdp) Hillsborough	29	0.18
East Lake (cdp) Pinellas	27	0.09
Spring Hill (cdp) Hernando	25	0.04

Top 10 Places Sorted by Percent
Based on all places, regardless of population

Place (place type) County	Number	%
Pine Ridge (cdp) Collier	14	0.75
Belleair Bluffs (city) Pinellas	8	0.36
Redington Beach (town) Pinellas	4	0.24
Greater Sun Center (cdp) Hillsborough	29	0.18
Pelican Bay (cdp) Collier	10	0.18
West Melbourne (city) Brevard	15	0.15
Indian River Estates (cdp) St. Lucie	8	0.14

Top 10 Places Sorted by Percent
Based on places with populations of 10,000 or more

Place (place type) County	Number	%
Greater Sun Center (cdp) Hillsborough	29	0.18
Cooper City (city) Broward	30	0.11
Boca Raton (city) Palm Beach	70	0.09
East Lake (cdp) Pinellas	27	0.09
Dania Beach (city) Broward	18	0.09
Lighthouse Point (city) Broward	9	0.08
Boca Del Mar (cdp) Palm Beach	15	0.07
Elfers (cdp) Pasco	9	0.07
Boynton Beach (city) Palm Beach	34	0.06
Winter Springs (city) Seminole	20	0.06

Maltese

Top 10 Places Sorted by Number
Based on all places, regardless of population

Place (place type) County	Number	%
Cape Coral (city) Lee	141	0.14
Ormond Beach (city) Volusia	87	0.24
Shady Hills (cdp) Pasco	57	0.73
Clearwater (city) Pinellas	53	0.05
Coconut Creek (city) Broward	49	0.11
Boca Raton (city) Palm Beach	45	0.06
Palm Harbor (cdp) Pinellas	44	0.07
Coral Springs (city) Broward	37	0.03
Melbourne (city) Brevard	36	0.05
Bayonet Point (cdp) Pasco	34	0.14

Top 10 Places Sorted by Percent
Based on all places, regardless of population

Place (place type) County	Number	%
Shady Hills (cdp) Pasco	57	0.73
Sawgrass (cdp) St. Johns	28	0.57
Pebble Creek (cdp) Hillsborough	25	0.52
North De Land (cdp) Volusia	6	0.44
Country Estates (cdp) Broward	8	0.43
North Weeki Wachee (cdp) Hernando	12	0.29
Lochmoor Waterway Estates (cdp) Lee	11	0.29
Nokomis (cdp) Sarasota	9	0.27
Naples Park (cdp) Collier	18	0.26
Holden Heights (cdp) Orange	10	0.26

Top 10 Places Sorted by Percent
Based on places with populations of 10,000 or more

Place (place type) County	Number	%
Ormond Beach (city) Volusia	87	0.24
Cutler (cdp) Miami-Dade	31	0.18
Jensen Beach (cdp) Martin	18	0.16
Lighthouse Point (city) Broward	17	0.16
Cape Coral (city) Lee	141	0.14
Bayonet Point (cdp) Pasco	34	0.14
Palm Beach (town) Palm Beach	12	0.12
Coconut Creek (city) Broward	49	0.11
Jasmine Estates (cdp) Pasco	19	0.11
Dania Beach (city) Broward	21	0.10

New Zealander

Top 10 Places Sorted by Number
Based on all places, regardless of population

Place (place type) County	Number	%
Fort Lauderdale (city) Broward	59	0.04
Palm Coast (city) Flagler	48	0.14
St. Petersburg (city) Pinellas	43	0.02
Jacksonville (special city) Duval	31	0.00
Cape Coral (city) Lee	23	0.02

Notes: (cdp) census designated place; Refer to the User's Guide in the front of the book for more detailed information.

Place (place type) County	Number	%
Pompano Beach (city) Broward	22	0.03
Coral Springs (city) Broward	19	0.02
Treasure Island (city) Pinellas	18	0.24
Surfside (town) Miami-Dade	17	0.33
St. Pete Beach (city) Pinellas	17	0.17

Top 10 Places Sorted by Percent
Based on all places, regardless of population

Place (place type) County	Number	%
Chokoloskee (cdp) Collier	8	1.55
Surfside (town) Miami-Dade	17	0.33
Nokomis (cdp) Sarasota	10	0.30
Biscayne Park (village) Miami-Dade	9	0.27
Treasure Island (city) Pinellas	18	0.24
Thonotosassa (cdp) Hillsborough	12	0.20
St. Pete Beach (city) Pinellas	17	0.17
Bay Harbor Islands (town) Miami-Dade	9	0.17
Palm Coast (city) Flagler	48	0.14
Inverness (city) Citrus	7	0.10

Top 10 Places Sorted by Percent
Based on places with populations of 10,000 or more

Place (place type) County	Number	%
Palm Coast (city) Flagler	48	0.14
Riverview (cdp) Hillsborough	10	0.08
St. Augustine (city) St. Johns	7	0.06
Key West (city) Monroe	12	0.05
Tarpon Springs (city) Pinellas	11	0.05
Pinecrest (village) Miami-Dade	9	0.05
Fort Lauderdale (city) Broward	59	0.04
Jupiter (town) Palm Beach	15	0.04
Wekiwa Springs (cdp) Seminole	10	0.04
Vero Beach South (cdp) Indian River	8	0.04

Northern European

Top 10 Places Sorted by Number
Based on all places, regardless of population

Place (place type) County	Number	%
Jacksonville (special city) Duval	188	0.03
Gainesville (city) Alachua	137	0.14
East Lake (cdp) Pinellas	124	0.42
St. Petersburg (city) Pinellas	111	0.04
Lakeland (city) Polk	92	0.12
Orlando (city) Orange	89	0.05
Tallahassee (city) Leon	84	0.06
Winter Park (city) Orange	82	0.34
Fort Lauderdale (city) Broward	81	0.05
Tampa (city) Hillsborough	81	0.03

Top 10 Places Sorted by Percent
Based on all places, regardless of population

Place (place type) County	Number	%
McIntosh (town) Marion	8	1.86
Trinity (cdp) Pasco	47	1.05
Tedder (cdp) Broward	18	0.91
Edgewood (city) Orange	13	0.71
Pine Ridge (cdp) Collier	13	0.70
Orange Park (town) Clay	62	0.69
Ridge Wood Heights (cdp) Sarasota	33	0.64
South Pasadena (city) Pinellas	30	0.51
Boyette (cdp) Hillsborough	29	0.47
East Lake (cdp) Pinellas	124	0.42

Top 10 Places Sorted by Percent
Based on places with populations of 10,000 or more

Place (place type) County	Number	%
East Lake (cdp) Pinellas	124	0.42
Winter Park (city) Orange	82	0.34
Oviedo (city) Seminole	77	0.28
Crestview (city) Okaloosa	42	0.28
Wekiwa Springs (cdp) Seminole	55	0.24

Place (place type) County	Number	%
Homosassa Springs (cdp) Citrus	28	0.22
Niceville (city) Okaloosa	26	0.22
Fernandina Beach (city) Nassau	23	0.22
Port Salerno (cdp) Martin	20	0.20
Titusville (city) Brevard	77	0.19

Norwegian

Top 10 Places Sorted by Number
Based on all places, regardless of population

Place (place type) County	Number	%
Jacksonville (special city) Duval	4,816	0.65
St. Petersburg (city) Pinellas	2,489	1.00
Tampa (city) Hillsborough	1,786	0.59
Cape Coral (city) Lee	1,299	1.27
Clearwater (city) Pinellas	1,234	1.14
Orlando (city) Orange	1,225	0.66
Fort Lauderdale (city) Broward	1,204	0.79
Largo (city) Pinellas	1,128	1.62
Port St. Lucie (city) St. Lucie	977	1.10
Tallahassee (city) Leon	961	0.64

Top 10 Places Sorted by Percent
Based on all places, regardless of population

Place (place type) County	Number	%
Islandia (city) Miami-Dade	1	16.67
Lake Lindsey (cdp) Hernando	7	15.91
North Beach (cdp) Indian River	24	10.86
Nobleton (cdp) Hernando	9	6.82
Orchid (town) Indian River	9	6.52
Otter Creek (town) Levy	6	5.50
Beverly Beach (town) Flagler	27	5.49
Plantation Island (cdp) Collier	9	4.23
Duck Key (cdp) Monroe	22	4.07
Goodland (cdp) Collier	9	4.07

Top 10 Places Sorted by Percent
Based on places with populations of 10,000 or more

Place (place type) County	Number	%
Niceville (city) Okaloosa	275	2.33
Punta Gorda (city) Charlotte	316	2.19
Naples (city) Collier	428	2.04
Marco Island (city) Collier	294	1.96
Azalea Park (cdp) Orange	204	1.83
Keystone (cdp) Hillsborough	259	1.76
Lake Mary (city) Seminole	184	1.63
Largo (city) Pinellas	1,128	1.62
Cocoa Beach (city) Brevard	198	1.60
Villas (cdp) Lee	174	1.56

Pennsylvania German

Top 10 Places Sorted by Number
Based on all places, regardless of population

Place (place type) County	Number	%
Jacksonville (special city) Duval	217	0.03
Clearwater (city) Pinellas	134	0.12
Spring Hill (cdp) Hernando	132	0.19
Cape Coral (city) Lee	110	0.11
Bradenton (city) Manatee	109	0.22
Fort Lauderdale (city) Broward	93	0.06
Tampa (city) Hillsborough	92	0.03
Melbourne (city) Brevard	78	0.11
Sarasota (city) Sarasota	72	0.14
Deltona (city) Volusia	70	0.10

Top 10 Places Sorted by Percent
Based on all places, regardless of population

Place (place type) County	Number	%
Nobleton (cdp) Hernando	7	5.30
Matlacha Isles-Matlacha Shores (cdp) Lee	6	2.21
Sorrento (cdp) Lake	15	2.02

Place (place type) County	Number	%
Ellenton (cdp) Manatee	61	1.98
Matlacha (cdp) Lee	15	1.89
Plantation Mobile Home Park (cdp) Palm Beach	25	1.84
Beverly Beach (town) Flagler	9	1.83
Dunnellon (city) Marion	23	1.20
Orangetree (cdp) Collier	12	1.16
Odessa (cdp) Hillsborough	27	0.81

Top 10 Places Sorted by Percent
Based on places with populations of 10,000 or more

Place (place type) County	Number	%
Hobe Sound (cdp) Martin	32	0.29
St. Cloud (city) Osceola	53	0.26
Citrus Ridge (cdp) Lake	29	0.25
De Bary (city) Volusia	38	0.24
San Carlos Park (cdp) Lee	38	0.24
South Daytona (city) Volusia	32	0.24
Gulfport (city) Pinellas	29	0.23
Villas (cdp) Lee	26	0.23
Westchase (cdp) Hillsborough	26	0.23
Bradenton (city) Manatee	109	0.22

Polish

Top 10 Places Sorted by Number
Based on all places, regardless of population

Place (place type) County	Number	%
Jacksonville (special city) Duval	10,500	1.43
St. Petersburg (city) Pinellas	7,542	3.04
Coral Springs (city) Broward	6,741	5.74
Tampa (city) Hillsborough	5,130	1.69
Cape Coral (city) Lee	5,055	4.95
Hollywood (city) Broward	5,026	3.61
Pembroke Pines (city) Broward	4,881	3.56
Boca Raton (city) Palm Beach	4,521	5.98
Port St. Lucie (city) St. Lucie	4,487	5.05
Fort Lauderdale (city) Broward	4,344	2.86

Top 10 Places Sorted by Percent
Based on all places, regardless of population

Place (place type) County	Number	%
Hillsboro Pines (cdp) Broward	57	11.75
Villages of Oriole (cdp) Palm Beach	553	11.68
Whisper Walk (cdp) Palm Beach	573	11.16
Boca Pointe (cdp) Palm Beach	359	10.88
Kings Point (cdp) Palm Beach	1,345	10.86
Spring Lake (cdp) Hernando	29	10.82
Hernando Beach (cdp) Hernando	231	10.74
Oak Point (cdp) Broward	16	10.13
Hamptons at Boca Raton (cdp) Palm Beach	1,143	10.01
Century Village (cdp) Palm Beach	705	9.29

Top 10 Places Sorted by Percent
Based on places with populations of 10,000 or more

Place (place type) County	Number	%
Kings Point (cdp) Palm Beach	1,345	10.86
Hamptons at Boca Raton (cdp) Palm Beach	1,143	10.01
Aventura (city) Miami-Dade	1,893	7.49
Boca Del Mar (cdp) Palm Beach	1,604	7.49
Jasmine Estates (cdp) Pasco	1,287	7.13
Coconut Creek (city) Broward	2,954	6.82
Bayonet Point (cdp) Pasco	1,492	6.30
Parkland (city) Broward	877	6.27
Boca Raton (city) Palm Beach	4,521	5.98
Spring Hill (cdp) Hernando	4,108	5.94

Portuguese

Top 10 Places Sorted by Number
Based on all places, regardless of population

Place (place type) County	Number	%
Jacksonville (special city) Duval	1,184	0.16

Notes: (cdp) census designated place; Refer to the User's Guide in the front of the book for more detailed information.

Place (place type) County	Number	%
St. Petersburg (city) Pinellas	882	0.36
Coral Springs (city) Broward	848	0.72
Deerfield Beach (city) Broward	655	1.01
Miami Beach (city) Miami-Dade	655	0.74
Tampa (city) Hillsborough	618	0.20
Pembroke Pines (city) Broward	592	0.43
Hollywood (city) Broward	588	0.42
Port St. Lucie (city) St. Lucie	537	0.60
Cape Coral (city) Lee	536	0.52

Top 10 Places Sorted by Percent
Based on all places, regardless of population

Place (place type) County	Number	%
Pine Lakes (cdp) Lake	44	7.36
Jupiter Island (town) Martin	35	5.64
Sunshine Ranches (cdp) Broward	77	4.24
Bokeelia (cdp) Lee	52	2.69
Citrus Hills (cdp) Citrus	99	2.45
Ivanhoe Estates (cdp) Broward	6	2.37
Chambers Estates (cdp) Broward	82	2.30
Ravenswood Estates (cdp) Broward	21	2.25
High Point (cdp) Hernando	53	1.75
Chula Vista (cdp) Broward	10	1.71

Top 10 Places Sorted by Percent
Based on places with populations of 10,000 or more

Place (place type) County	Number	%
Palm Coast (city) Flagler	486	1.45
Sebastian (city) Indian River	210	1.28
Doral (cdp) Miami-Dade	259	1.26
Oldsmar (city) Pinellas	131	1.12
Lakewood Park (cdp) St. Lucie	106	1.02
Deerfield Beach (city) Broward	655	1.01
Ocoee (city) Orange	232	0.98
North Port (city) Sarasota	207	0.91
Citrus Ridge (cdp) Lake	102	0.89
San Carlos Park (cdp) Lee	134	0.83

Romanian

Top 10 Places Sorted by Number
Based on all places, regardless of population

Place (place type) County	Number	%
Hollywood (city) Broward	1,613	1.16
Hallandale (city) Broward	1,056	3.06
Jacksonville (special city) Duval	707	0.10
Pembroke Pines (city) Broward	684	0.50
Coral Springs (city) Broward	611	0.52
Sunrise (city) Broward	559	0.65
Plantation (city) Broward	469	0.56
Tamarac (city) Broward	452	0.81
Aventura (city) Miami-Dade	446	1.77
Davie (town) Broward	407	0.54

Top 10 Places Sorted by Percent
Based on all places, regardless of population

Place (place type) County	Number	%
Hallandale (city) Broward	1,056	3.06
Fisher Island (cdp) Miami-Dade	8	2.36
Villages of Oriole (cdp) Palm Beach	107	2.26
Century Village (cdp) Palm Beach	159	2.10
Kings Point (cdp) Palm Beach	239	1.93
Whisper Walk (cdp) Palm Beach	99	1.93
Aventura (city) Miami-Dade	446	1.77
Boca Pointe (cdp) Palm Beach	57	1.73
Hamptons at Boca Raton (cdp) Palm Beach	183	1.60
Sunny Isles Beach (city) Miami-Dade	219	1.43

Top 10 Places Sorted by Percent
Based on places with populations of 10,000 or more

Place (place type) County	Number	%
Hallandale (city) Broward	1,056	3.06

Place (place type) County	Number	%
Kings Point (cdp) Palm Beach	239	1.93
Aventura (city) Miami-Dade	446	1.77
Hamptons at Boca Raton (cdp) Palm Beach	183	1.60
Sunny Isles Beach (city) Miami-Dade	219	1.43
Hollywood (city) Broward	1,613	1.16
Cutler (cdp) Miami-Dade	201	1.14
Ojus (cdp) Miami-Dade	177	1.06
Palm Beach (town) Palm Beach	102	0.98
Boca Del Mar (cdp) Palm Beach	208	0.97

Russian

Top 10 Places Sorted by Number
Based on all places, regardless of population

Place (place type) County	Number	%
Coral Springs (city) Broward	5,710	4.86
Hollywood (city) Broward	4,464	3.21
Pembroke Pines (city) Broward	4,179	3.05
Boca Raton (city) Palm Beach	4,066	5.38
Jacksonville (special city) Duval	3,705	0.50
Sunrise (city) Broward	3,533	4.13
Tamarac (city) Broward	3,431	6.12
Plantation (city) Broward	3,428	4.12
Miami Beach (city) Miami-Dade	3,286	3.73
Aventura (city) Miami-Dade	2,998	11.87

Top 10 Places Sorted by Percent
Based on all places, regardless of population

Place (place type) County	Number	%
Marineland (town) Flagler	5	71.43
Boca Pointe (cdp) Palm Beach	584	17.70
Villages of Oriole (cdp) Palm Beach	829	17.50
Duck Key (cdp) Monroe	94	17.38
Kings Point (cdp) Palm Beach	2,005	16.19
Fisher Island (cdp) Miami-Dade	54	15.93
High Point (cdp) Palm Beach	330	14.97
Century Village (cdp) Palm Beach	1,129	14.88
Oak Point (cdp) Broward	22	13.92
Ramblewood East (cdp) Broward	165	13.01

Top 10 Places Sorted by Percent
Based on places with populations of 10,000 or more

Place (place type) County	Number	%
Kings Point (cdp) Palm Beach	2,005	16.19
Aventura (city) Miami-Dade	2,998	11.87
Palm Beach (town) Palm Beach	1,089	10.50
Sunny Isles Beach (city) Miami-Dade	1,447	9.47
Boca Del Mar (cdp) Palm Beach	2,027	9.46
Hamptons at Boca Raton (cdp) Palm Beach	1,035	9.06
Ojus (cdp) Miami-Dade	1,256	7.53
Parkland (city) Broward	976	6.98
Pinecrest (village) Miami-Dade	1,331	6.94
Coconut Creek (city) Broward	2,804	6.47

Scandinavian

Top 10 Places Sorted by Number
Based on all places, regardless of population

Place (place type) County	Number	%
Jacksonville (special city) Duval	560	0.08
Tampa (city) Hillsborough	294	0.10
Clearwater (city) Pinellas	226	0.21
St. Petersburg (city) Pinellas	210	0.08
Orlando (city) Orange	192	0.10
Tallahassee (city) Leon	189	0.13
Port St. Lucie (city) St. Lucie	168	0.19
Coral Springs (city) Broward	152	0.13
Cape Coral (city) Lee	144	0.14
Pembroke Pines (city) Broward	139	0.10

Top 10 Places Sorted by Percent
Based on all places, regardless of population

Place (place type) County	Number	%
Cloud Lake (town) Palm Beach	3	2.44
Masaryktown (cdp) Hernando	15	1.70
Pine Island Ridge (cdp) Broward	86	1.61
Crescent Beach (cdp) St. Johns	11	1.39
Lochmoor Waterway Estates (cdp) Lee	46	1.19
Indian River Shores (town) Indian River	37	1.12
Inwood (cdp) Polk	75	1.11
Geneva (cdp) Seminole	29	1.03
Gibsonia (cdp) Polk	48	0.99
Ellenton (cdp) Manatee	28	0.91

Top 10 Places Sorted by Percent
Based on places with populations of 10,000 or more

Place (place type) County	Number	%
Wilton Manors (city) Broward	67	0.53
Stuart (city) Martin	77	0.52
Riverview (cdp) Hillsborough	51	0.42
Union Park (cdp) Orange	43	0.42
St. Augustine (city) St. Johns	47	0.41
Vero Beach South (cdp) Indian River	78	0.38
Homosassa Springs (cdp) Citrus	47	0.37
East Lake (cdp) Pinellas	106	0.36
Safety Harbor (city) Pinellas	62	0.36
Lynn Haven (city) Bay	44	0.36

Scotch-Irish

Top 10 Places Sorted by Number
Based on all places, regardless of population

Place (place type) County	Number	%
Jacksonville (special city) Duval	13,064	1.78
St. Petersburg (city) Pinellas	4,625	1.87
Tampa (city) Hillsborough	4,497	1.48
Tallahassee (city) Leon	3,309	2.20
Orlando (city) Orange	2,634	1.42
Gainesville (city) Alachua	2,223	2.33
Clearwater (city) Pinellas	2,091	1.94
Cape Coral (city) Lee	1,735	1.70
Lakeland (city) Polk	1,645	2.10
Largo (city) Pinellas	1,632	2.35

Top 10 Places Sorted by Percent
Based on all places, regardless of population

Place (place type) County	Number	%
Bayport (cdp) Hernando	6	25.00
Lee (town) Madison	31	8.86
Matlacha Isles-Matlacha Shores (cdp) Lee	18	6.64
Highland Park (village) Polk	15	6.36
Pineland (cdp) Lee	30	6.33
Country Estates (cdp) Broward	116	6.24
Silver Lake (cdp) Lake	116	6.21
Penney Farms (town) Clay	33	6.15
Chuluota (cdp) Seminole	120	6.05
Yankeetown (town) Levy	39	6.03

Top 10 Places Sorted by Percent
Based on places with populations of 10,000 or more

Place (place type) County	Number	%
Cocoa Beach (city) Brevard	471	3.79
St. Augustine (city) St. Johns	407	3.54
Ferry Pass (cdp) Escambia	951	3.50
Greater Sun Center (cdp) Hillsborough	557	3.42
Upper Grand Lagoon (cdp) Bay	373	3.40
Warrington (cdp) Escambia	511	3.37
Merritt Island (cdp) Brevard	1,199	3.32
Naples (city) Collier	670	3.19
Maitland (city) Orange	377	3.16
Niceville (city) Okaloosa	371	3.15

Notes: (cdp) census designated place; Refer to the User's Guide in the front of the book for more detailed information.

Top 10 Places Sorted by Number
Based on all places, regardless of population

Place (place type) County	Number	%
Jacksonville (special city) Duval	13,558	1.84
St. Petersburg (city) Pinellas	6,317	2.55
Tampa (city) Hillsborough	5,312	1.75
Tallahassee (city) Leon	3,513	2.33
Orlando (city) Orange	3,164	1.70
Fort Lauderdale (city) Broward	2,689	1.77
Clearwater (city) Pinellas	2,555	2.37
Gainesville (city) Alachua	2,298	2.40
Largo (city) Pinellas	2,040	2.94
Cape Coral (city) Lee	2,012	1.97

Top 10 Places Sorted by Percent
Based on all places, regardless of population

Place (place type) County	Number	%
Highland Park (village) Polk	32	13.56
Golf (village) Palm Beach	25	10.46
Lazy Lake (village) Broward	4	10.26
Manasota Key (cdp) Charlotte	134	10.24
Captiva (cdp) Lee	38	9.69
Pine Island (cdp) Hernando	5	9.09
Punta Rassa (cdp) Lee	149	8.90
Lake Harbor (cdp) Palm Beach	8	8.60
Crescent Beach (cdp) St. Johns	61	7.68
Goodland (cdp) Collier	16	7.24

Top 10 Places Sorted by Percent
Based on places with populations of 10,000 or more

Place (place type) County	Number	%
Winter Park (city) Orange	1,229	5.07
Atlantic Beach (city) Duval	613	4.55
Naples (city) Collier	921	4.39
Palm Valley (cdp) St. Johns	858	4.32
Destin (city) Okaloosa	477	4.24
Venice (city) Sarasota	744	4.17
Greater Sun Center (cdp) Hillsborough	672	4.13
Dunedin (city) Pinellas	1,413	3.93
Keystone (cdp) Hillsborough	571	3.88
Jacksonville Beach (city) Duval	783	3.73

Serbian

Top 10 Places Sorted by Number
Based on all places, regardless of population

Place (place type) County	Number	%
St. Petersburg (city) Pinellas	206	0.08
Jacksonville (special city) Duval	155	0.02
Hollywood (city) Broward	117	0.08
Orlando (city) Orange	105	0.06
Cape Coral (city) Lee	101	0.10
Pinellas Park (city) Pinellas	94	0.21
Warm Mineral Springs (cdp) Sarasota	90	1.83
Tampa (city) Hillsborough	85	0.03
Palm Coast (city) Flagler	83	0.25
Coral Springs (city) Broward	78	0.07

Top 10 Places Sorted by Percent
Based on all places, regardless of population

Place (place type) County	Number	%
Warm Mineral Springs (cdp) Sarasota	90	1.83
Edgewater (cdp) Broward	6	0.85
Ramblewood East (cdp) Broward	10	0.79
Macclenny (city) Baker	33	0.75
Howey-in-the-Hills (town) Lake	7	0.70
Doctor Phillips (cdp) Orange	66	0.68
Alva (cdp) Lee	13	0.64
Belleair Beach (city) Pinellas	10	0.60
Brooker (town) Bradford	2	0.58
Tequesta (village) Palm Beach	28	0.54

Based on places with populations of 10,000 or more

Place (place type) County	Number	%
Palm Beach (town) Palm Beach	36	0.35
Palm Coast (city) Flagler	83	0.25
Elfers (cdp) Pasco	33	0.25
Casselberry (city) Seminole	49	0.22
Palm Valley (cdp) St. Johns	43	0.22
New Port Richey (city) Pasco	35	0.22
Pinellas Park (city) Pinellas	94	0.21
North Port (city) Sarasota	47	0.21
Westchase (cdp) Hillsborough	23	0.21
Haines City (city) Polk	26	0.20

Slavic

Top 10 Places Sorted by Number
Based on all places, regardless of population

Place (place type) County	Number	%
Jacksonville (special city) Duval	227	0.03
St. Petersburg (city) Pinellas	116	0.05
Tampa (city) Hillsborough	114	0.04
Hudson (cdp) Pasco	109	0.86
Neptune Beach (city) Duval	90	1.24
Kendall (cdp) Miami-Dade	65	0.09
Coral Springs (city) Broward	65	0.06
Pembroke Pines (city) Broward	63	0.05
Palm City (cdp) Martin	60	0.30
Gainesville (city) Alachua	59	0.06

Top 10 Places Sorted by Percent
Based on all places, regardless of population

Place (place type) County	Number	%
Fisher Island (cdp) Miami-Dade	11	3.24
Matlacha Isles-Matlacha Shores (cdp) Lee	6	2.21
Wedgefield (cdp) Orange	48	1.71
Neptune Beach (city) Duval	90	1.24
Hudson (cdp) Pasco	109	0.86
South Palm Beach (town) Palm Beach	6	0.83
Glencoe (cdp) Volusia	18	0.71
Naples Park (cdp) Collier	44	0.65
Indian River Estates (cdp) St. Lucie	35	0.60
Tierra Verde (cdp) Pinellas	20	0.56

Top 10 Places Sorted by Percent
Based on places with populations of 10,000 or more

Place (place type) County	Number	%
Hudson (cdp) Pasco	109	0.86
North Palm Beach (village) Palm Beach	37	0.31
Palm City (cdp) Martin	60	0.30
St. Augustine (city) St. Johns	35	0.30
Lakeland Highlands (cdp) Polk	36	0.28
Fruit Cove (cdp) St. Johns	38	0.24
Boca Del Mar (cdp) Palm Beach	40	0.19
Lynn Haven (city) Bay	23	0.19
Vero Beach South (cdp) Indian River	36	0.18
South Venice (cdp) Sarasota	24	0.18

Slovak

Top 10 Places Sorted by Number
Based on all places, regardless of population

Place (place type) County	Number	%
Jacksonville (special city) Duval	564	0.08
St. Petersburg (city) Pinellas	530	0.21
Cape Coral (city) Lee	529	0.52
Port St. Lucie (city) St. Lucie	429	0.48
Spring Hill (cdp) Hernando	320	0.46
Clearwater (city) Pinellas	280	0.26
Fort Lauderdale (city) Broward	265	0.17
Margate (city) Broward	252	0.47
Orlando (city) Orange	246	0.13

Top 10 Places Sorted by Percent
Based on all places, regardless of population

Place (place type) County	Number	%
Winter Beach (cdp) Indian River	59	5.26
Matlacha (cdp) Lee	33	4.17
Masaryktown (cdp) Hernando	35	3.97
Layton (city) Monroe	5	2.08
Ponce Inlet (town) Volusia	49	1.95
Jupiter Island (town) Martin	12	1.93
Edgewood (city) Orange	33	1.80
Crescent Beach (cdp) St. Johns	13	1.64
Desoto Lakes (cdp) Sarasota	51	1.57
Olga (cdp) Lee	23	1.56

Top 10 Places Sorted by Percent
Based on places with populations of 10,000 or more

Place (place type) County	Number	%
Seminole (city) Pinellas	83	0.77
Lake Mary (city) Seminole	85	0.75
Longwood (city) Seminole	101	0.74
Iona (cdp) Lee	76	0.64
Goldenrod (cdp) Seminole	82	0.63
Forest City (cdp) Seminole	80	0.63
Hobe Sound (cdp) Martin	69	0.62
East Lake (cdp) Pinellas	181	0.61
Sarasota Springs (cdp) Sarasota	97	0.61
Gulf Gate Estates (cdp) Sarasota	70	0.61

Slovene

Top 10 Places Sorted by Number
Based on all places, regardless of population

Place (place type) County	Number	%
Jacksonville (special city) Duval	163	0.02
Cape Coral (city) Lee	138	0.14
Fort Lauderdale (city) Broward	113	0.07
St. Petersburg (city) Pinellas	92	0.04
Dunedin (city) Pinellas	89	0.25
Melbourne (city) Brevard	74	0.10
Spring Hill (cdp) Hernando	72	0.10
Samsula-Spruce Creek (cdp) Volusia	67	1.35
Port St. Lucie (city) St. Lucie	63	0.07
Ormond Beach (city) Volusia	55	0.15

Top 10 Places Sorted by Percent
Based on all places, regardless of population

Place (place type) County	Number	%
Samsula-Spruce Creek (cdp) Volusia	67	1.35
Lely (cdp) Collier	34	0.89
Palm Beach Shores (town) Palm Beach	9	0.74
Crooked Lake Park (cdp) Polk	12	0.65
Hernando (cdp) Citrus	49	0.58
Charlotte Park (cdp) Charlotte	13	0.57
Umatilla (city) Lake	12	0.55
Country Estates (cdp) Broward	10	0.54
Hernando Beach (cdp) Hernando	11	0.51
North Redington Beach (town) Pinellas	7	0.51

Top 10 Places Sorted by Percent
Based on places with populations of 10,000 or more

Place (place type) County	Number	%
Jensen Beach (cdp) Martin	37	0.33
Dunedin (city) Pinellas	89	0.25
Maitland (city) Orange	29	0.24
Lighthouse Point (city) Broward	23	0.22
Villas (cdp) Lee	23	0.21
New Smyrna Beach (city) Volusia	39	0.19
Marathon (city) Monroe	19	0.19
Stuart (city) Martin	25	0.17
Bellair-Meadowbrook Terrace (cdp) Clay	26	0.16

Notes: (cdp) census designated place; Refer to the User's Guide in the front of the book for more detailed information.

Top 10 Places Sorted by Number
Based on all places, regardless of population

Place (place type) County	Number	%
Boca Del Mar (cdp) Palm Beach	15	0.07
Cocoa Beach (city) Brevard	10	0.08
Aventura (city) Miami-Dade	7	0.03
Lake Magdalene (cdp) Hillsborough	7	0.02
St. Pete Beach (city) Pinellas	5	0.05
Myrtle Grove (cdp) Escambia	5	0.03

Top 10 Places Sorted by Percent
Based on all places, regardless of population

Place (place type) County	Number	%
Cocoa Beach (city) Brevard	10	0.08
Boca Del Mar (cdp) Palm Beach	15	0.07
St. Pete Beach (city) Pinellas	5	0.05
Aventura (city) Miami-Dade	7	0.03
Myrtle Grove (cdp) Escambia	5	0.03
Lake Magdalene (cdp) Hillsborough	7	0.02

Top 10 Places Sorted by Percent
Based on places with populations of 10,000 or more

Place (place type) County	Number	%
Cocoa Beach (city) Brevard	10	0.08
Boca Del Mar (cdp) Palm Beach	15	0.07
Aventura (city) Miami-Dade	7	0.03
Myrtle Grove (cdp) Escambia	5	0.03
Lake Magdalene (cdp) Hillsborough	7	0.02

Swedish

Top 10 Places Sorted by Number
Based on all places, regardless of population

Place (place type) County	Number	%
Jacksonville (special city) Duval	4,774	0.65
St. Petersburg (city) Pinellas	3,150	1.27
Tampa (city) Hillsborough	2,521	0.83
Clearwater (city) Pinellas	1,863	1.73
Cape Coral (city) Lee	1,598	1.56
Orlando (city) Orange	1,552	0.83
Fort Lauderdale (city) Broward	1,518	1.00
Coral Springs (city) Broward	1,324	1.13
Palm Harbor (cdp) Pinellas	1,264	2.14
Gainesville (city) Alachua	1,241	1.30

Top 10 Places Sorted by Percent
Based on all places, regardless of population

Place (place type) County	Number	%
Pine Island (cdp) Hernando	12	21.82
Plantation Island (cdp) Collier	15	7.04
Reddick (town) Marion	36	6.35
Pineland (cdp) Lee	28	5.91
Lake Kathryn (cdp) Lake	40	5.70
Royal Palm Ranches (cdp) Broward	16	5.32
Briny Breezes (town) Palm Beach	21	5.08
Homosassa (cdp) Citrus	109	4.82
Hillsboro Pines (cdp) Broward	23	4.74
Celebration (cdp) Osceola	120	4.37

Top 10 Places Sorted by Percent
Based on places with populations of 10,000 or more

Place (place type) County	Number	%
Naples (city) Collier	654	3.12
Sarasota Springs (cdp) Sarasota	469	2.96
Marco Island (city) Collier	437	2.92
Englewood (cdp) Sarasota	462	2.84
Palm City (cdp) Martin	542	2.70

Vero Beach South (cdp) Indian River	466	2.29

Swiss

Top 10 Places Sorted by Number
Based on all places, regardless of population

Place (place type) County	Number	%
Jacksonville (special city) Duval	1,064	0.14
St. Petersburg (city) Pinellas	615	0.25
Tampa (city) Hillsborough	549	0.18
Hollywood (city) Broward	421	0.30
Clearwater (city) Pinellas	414	0.38
Orlando (city) Orange	377	0.20
Tallahassee (city) Leon	339	0.23
Fort Lauderdale (city) Broward	339	0.22
Cape Coral (city) Lee	336	0.33
Sarasota (city) Sarasota	280	0.53

Top 10 Places Sorted by Percent
Based on all places, regardless of population

Place (place type) County	Number	%
Pittman (cdp) Lake	11	14.10
Lazy Lake (village) Broward	4	10.26
Crescent Beach (cdp) St. Johns	27	3.40
Highland Park (village) Polk	7	2.97
Orangetree (cdp) Collier	29	2.81
Punta Rassa (cdp) Lee	41	2.45
Vineyards (cdp) Collier	55	2.42
Williston Highlands (cdp) Levy	31	2.33
Samsula-Spruce Creek (cdp) Volusia	106	2.14
Wausau (town) Washington	8	2.02

Top 10 Places Sorted by Percent
Based on places with populations of 10,000 or more

Place (place type) County	Number	%
Punta Gorda (city) Charlotte	164	1.14
Naples (city) Collier	213	1.01
Cypress Lake (cdp) Lee	122	1.01
Gulf Gate Estates (cdp) Sarasota	114	0.99
Key Biscayne (village) Miami-Dade	104	0.99
Greater Sun Center (cdp) Hillsborough	142	0.87
Fruitville (cdp) Sarasota	108	0.84
South Venice (cdp) Sarasota	100	0.74
Marco Island (city) Collier	109	0.73
Palm City (cdp) Martin	131	0.65

Turkish

Top 10 Places Sorted by Number
Based on all places, regardless of population

Place (place type) County	Number	%
Miami Beach (city) Miami-Dade	342	0.39
Jacksonville (special city) Duval	324	0.04
Hollywood (city) Broward	218	0.16
Tampa (city) Hillsborough	208	0.07
Coral Springs (city) Broward	192	0.16
Coconut Creek (city) Broward	186	0.43
Weston (city) Broward	183	0.37
Pompano Beach (city) Broward	165	0.21
Gainesville (city) Alachua	163	0.17
Miami (city) Miami-Dade	160	0.04

Top 10 Places Sorted by Percent
Based on all places, regardless of population

Place (place type) County	Number	%
Royal Palm Ranches (cdp) Broward	14	4.65
Palm Shores (town) Brevard	15	1.90
Bay Harbor Islands (town) Miami-Dade	70	1.36

Cudjoe Key (cdp) Monroe	10	0.58
Madeira Beach (city) Pinellas	25	0.56
Aventura (city) Miami-Dade	140	0.55

Top 10 Places Sorted by Percent
Based on places with populations of 10,000 or more

Place (place type) County	Number	%
Ojus (cdp) Miami-Dade	132	0.79
Kings Point (cdp) Palm Beach	85	0.69
Aventura (city) Miami-Dade	140	0.55
Coconut Creek (city) Broward	186	0.43
Oakland Park (city) Broward	131	0.42
Miami Beach (city) Miami-Dade	342	0.39
Sunny Isles Beach (city) Miami-Dade	59	0.39
North Palm Beach (village) Palm Beach	46	0.38
Weston (city) Broward	183	0.37
Cutler (cdp) Miami-Dade	65	0.37

Ukrainian

Top 10 Places Sorted by Number
Based on all places, regardless of population

Place (place type) County	Number	%
Jacksonville (special city) Duval	1,294	0.18
St. Petersburg (city) Pinellas	943	0.38
Hollywood (city) Broward	753	0.54
North Port (city) Sarasota	612	2.69
Tampa (city) Hillsborough	551	0.18
Clearwater (city) Pinellas	507	0.47
Fort Lauderdale (city) Broward	467	0.31
Miami Beach (city) Miami-Dade	460	0.52
Spring Hill (cdp) Hernando	444	0.64
Coral Springs (city) Broward	428	0.36

Top 10 Places Sorted by Percent
Based on all places, regardless of population

Place (place type) County	Number	%
Oak Point (cdp) Broward	40	25.32
North Beach (cdp) Indian River	17	7.69
Paisley (cdp) Lake	23	3.41
Warm Mineral Springs (cdp) Sarasota	139	2.83
North Port (city) Sarasota	612	2.69
Ferndale (cdp) Lake	7	2.43
Pine Ridge (cdp) Collier	45	2.42
Ponce Inlet (town) Volusia	55	2.19
St. Leo (town) Pasco	12	1.97
Plantation (cdp) Sarasota	77	1.94

Top 10 Places Sorted by Percent
Based on places with populations of 10,000 or more

Place (place type) County	Number	%
North Port (city) Sarasota	612	2.69
Gulfport (city) Pinellas	216	1.71
Sunny Isles Beach (city) Miami-Dade	203	1.33
Ojus (cdp) Miami-Dade	206	1.23
Boca Del Mar (cdp) Palm Beach	244	1.14
Kings Point (cdp) Palm Beach	138	1.11
Goldenrod (cdp) Seminole	127	0.97
Palm Coast (city) Flagler	307	0.92
Hudson (cdp) Pasco	106	0.83
Hamptons at Boca Raton (cdp) Palm Beach	93	0.81

United States or American

Top 10 Places Sorted by Number
Based on all places, regardless of population

Place (place type) County	Number	%
Jacksonville (special city) Duval	68,488	9.31

Notes: (cdp) census designated place; Refer to the User's Guide in the front of the book for more detailed information.

Place	Number	
Tampa (city) Hillsborough	18,834	6.21
St. Petersburg (city) Pinellas	14,062	5.67
Orlando (city) Orange	12,426	6.68
Miami (city) Miami-Dade	11,317	3.12
Hollywood (city) Broward	9,762	7.01
Fort Lauderdale (city) Broward	8,904	5.85
Pembroke Pines (city) Broward	8,380	6.11
Tallahassee (city) Leon	7,976	5.30
Cape Coral (city) Lee	7,841	7.67

Top 10 Places Sorted by Percent
Based on all places, regardless of population

Place (place type) County	Number	%
Chokoloskee (cdp) Collier	259	50.29
Westville (town) Holmes	95	41.13
Jay (town) Santa Rosa	218	40.07
Bristol (city) Liberty	319	39.73
Altha (town) Calhoun	212	39.70
Nassau Village-Ratliff (cdp) Nassau	1,631	35.74
Glen St. Mary (town) Baker	155	34.44
Islandia (city) Miami-Dade	2	33.33
Sneads (town) Jackson	613	31.65
Kathleen (cdp) Polk	1,061	31.44

Top 10 Places Sorted by Percent
Based on places with populations of 10,000 or more

Place (place type) County	Number	%
Auburndale (city) Polk	1,984	17.69
Upper Grand Lagoon (cdp) Bay	1,822	16.59
Lakeland Highlands (cdp) Polk	1,943	15.24
Lynn Haven (city) Bay	1,838	14.88
Winter Haven (city) Polk	3,798	14.64
Warrington (cdp) Escambia	2,204	14.51
Middleburg (cdp) Clay	1,502	14.43
Crestview (city) Okaloosa	2,121	14.31
Callaway (city) Bay	1,977	13.87
Bellview (cdp) Escambia	2,863	13.59

Welsh

Top 10 Places Sorted by Number
Based on all places, regardless of population

Place (place type) County	Number	%
Jacksonville (special city) Duval	3,699	0.50
St. Petersburg (city) Pinellas	1,985	0.80
Tampa (city) Hillsborough	1,346	0.44
Tallahassee (city) Leon	1,061	0.70
Fort Lauderdale (city) Broward	1,050	0.69
Orlando (city) Orange	1,046	0.56
Cape Coral (city) Lee	773	0.76
Palm Bay (city) Brevard	719	0.90
Gainesville (city) Alachua	636	0.67
Clearwater (city) Pinellas	616	0.57

Top 10 Places Sorted by Percent
Based on all places, regardless of population

Place (place type) County	Number	%
Marineland (town) Flagler	2	28.57
Matlacha (cdp) Lee	45	5.68
Penney Farms (town) Clay	25	4.66
Pine Lakes (cdp) Lake	26	4.35
Indialantic (town) Brevard	108	3.67
Sorrento (cdp) Lake	27	3.64
Goodland (cdp) Collier	8	3.62
Chokoloskee (cdp) Collier	16	3.11
Hillcrest Heights (town) Polk	8	2.95
North Key Largo (cdp) Monroe	29	2.87

Top 10 Places Sorted by Percent
Based on places with populations of 10,000 or more

Place (place type) County	Number	%
Lady Lake (town) Lake	187	1.60

Place	Number	
Greater Sun Center (cdp) Hillsborough	253	1.55
Stuart (city) Martin	218	1.48
Bellair-Meadowbrook Terrace (cdp) Clay	241	1.45
Naples (city) Collier	303	1.44
Zephyrhills (city) Pasco	148	1.38
New Smyrna Beach (city) Volusia	279	1.37
Land O' Lakes (cdp) Pasco	281	1.35
Gulf Gate Estates (cdp) Sarasota	151	1.31
Winter Park (city) Orange	309	1.28

West Indian, excluding Hispanic

Top 10 Places Sorted by Number
Based on all places, regardless of population

Place (place type) County	Number	%
Miami (city) Miami-Dade	22,904	6.32
North Miami (city) Miami-Dade	22,034	36.70
Miramar (city) Broward	18,445	25.38
Lauderhill (city) Broward	16,626	29.04
Fort Lauderdale (city) Broward	14,964	9.84
Golden Glades (cdp) Miami-Dade	13,197	41.01
Pembroke Pines (city) Broward	12,327	8.99
Lauderdale Lakes (city) Broward	11,455	36.35
North Miami Beach (city) Miami-Dade	11,041	27.15
Sunrise (city) Broward	11,027	12.88

Top 10 Places Sorted by Percent
Based on all places, regardless of population

Place (place type) County	Number	%
Melrose Park (cdp) Broward	2,918	41.17
Golden Glades (cdp) Miami-Dade	13,197	41.01
Norland (cdp) Miami-Dade	8,976	38.98
North Miami (city) Miami-Dade	22,034	36.70
Lauderdale Lakes (city) Broward	11,455	36.35
Pompano Estates (cdp) Broward	1,172	33.82
El Portal (village) Miami-Dade	813	32.30
Pinewood (cdp) Miami-Dade	5,402	32.12
Lauderhill (city) Broward	16,626	29.04
Belle Glade Camp (cdp) Palm Beach	355	28.09

Top 10 Places Sorted by Percent
Based on places with populations of 10,000 or more

Place (place type) County	Number	%
Golden Glades (cdp) Miami-Dade	13,197	41.01
Norland (cdp) Miami-Dade	8,976	38.98
North Miami (city) Miami-Dade	22,034	36.70
Lauderdale Lakes (city) Broward	11,455	36.35
Pinewood (cdp) Miami-Dade	5,402	32.12
Lauderhill (city) Broward	16,626	29.04
North Miami Beach (city) Miami-Dade	11,041	27.15
Palmetto Estates (cdp) Miami-Dade	3,497	25.57
Miramar (city) Broward	18,445	25.38
Scott Lake (cdp) Miami-Dade	3,269	22.72

West Indian: Bahamian, excluding Hispanic

Top 10 Places Sorted by Number
Based on all places, regardless of population

Place (place type) County	Number	%
Miami (city) Miami-Dade	1,470	0.41
North Miami (city) Miami-Dade	675	1.12
Fort Lauderdale (city) Broward	607	0.40
Miramar (city) Broward	578	0.80
Golden Glades (cdp) Miami-Dade	541	1.68
Pembroke Pines (city) Broward	518	0.38
Norland (cdp) Miami-Dade	513	2.23
Lauderhill (city) Broward	473	0.83
North Miami Beach (city) Miami-Dade	441	1.08
Carol City (cdp) Miami-Dade	437	0.74

Top 10 Places Sorted by Percent
Based on all places, regardless of population

Place (place type) County	Number	%
Stacey Street (cdp) Palm Beach	50	6.02
Andover (cdp) Miami-Dade	295	3.41
Bunche Park (cdp) Miami-Dade	131	3.29
Lake Lucerne (cdp) Miami-Dade	237	2.59
Carver Ranches (cdp) Broward	109	2.54
Norland (cdp) Miami-Dade	513	2.23
El Portal (village) Miami-Dade	53	2.11
Brownsville (cdp) Miami-Dade	279	1.93
Lake Forest (cdp) Broward	92	1.85
Goulds (cdp) Miami-Dade	140	1.84

Top 10 Places Sorted by Percent
Based on places with populations of 10,000 or more

Place (place type) County	Number	%
Norland (cdp) Miami-Dade	513	2.23
Brownsville (cdp) Miami-Dade	279	1.93
Pinewood (cdp) Miami-Dade	304	1.81
Golden Glades (cdp) Miami-Dade	541	1.68
Scott Lake (cdp) Miami-Dade	223	1.55
North Miami (city) Miami-Dade	675	1.12
North Miami Beach (city) Miami-Dade	441	1.08
Key West (city) Monroe	269	1.06
West Little River (cdp) Miami-Dade	339	1.05
Gladeview (cdp) Miami-Dade	138	0.95

West Indian: Barbadian, excluding Hispanic

Top 10 Places Sorted by Number
Based on all places, regardless of population

Place (place type) County	Number	%
St. Petersburg (city) Pinellas	240	0.10
Lauderhill (city) Broward	168	0.29
Orlando (city) Orange	156	0.08
North Miami (city) Miami-Dade	149	0.25
Miramar (city) Broward	139	0.19
Pine Hills (cdp) Orange	112	0.27
Tampa (city) Hillsborough	99	0.03
Palm Bay (city) Brevard	92	0.12
Hollywood (city) Broward	86	0.06
Fort Lauderdale (city) Broward	84	0.06

Top 10 Places Sorted by Percent
Based on all places, regardless of population

Place (place type) County	Number	%
Harlem (cdp) Hendry	34	1.20
St. George (cdp) Broward	24	1.00
Mangonia Park (town) Palm Beach	11	0.85
Melrose Park (cdp) Broward	54	0.76
Belle Glade Camp (cdp) Palm Beach	8	0.63
Samsula-Spruce Creek (cdp) Volusia	30	0.61
De Land Southwest (cdp) Volusia	6	0.53
Three Lakes (cdp) Miami-Dade	31	0.44
Waverly (cdp) Polk	8	0.43
Indiantown (cdp) Martin	22	0.41

Top 10 Places Sorted by Percent
Based on places with populations of 10,000 or more

Place (place type) County	Number	%
Azalea Park (cdp) Orange	45	0.40
Palmetto Estates (cdp) Miami-Dade	50	0.37
Meadow Woods (cdp) Orange	41	0.36
Poinciana (cdp) Osceola	44	0.32
Lauderhill (city) Broward	168	0.29
Pine Hills (cdp) Orange	112	0.27
North Miami (city) Miami-Dade	149	0.25
Norland (cdp) Miami-Dade	57	0.25
Golden Glades (cdp) Miami-Dade	67	0.21
Fairview Shores (cdp) Orange	27	0.20

Notes: (cdp) census designated place; Refer to the User's Guide in the front of the book for more detailed information.

West Indian: Belizean, excluding Hispanic

Top 10 Places Sorted by Number
Based on all places, regardless of population

Place (place type) County	Number	%
Jacksonville (special city) Duval	122	0.02
Pine Manor (cdp) Lee	119	3.06
Miami (city) Miami-Dade	105	0.03
Plantation (city) Broward	91	0.11
North Miami Beach (city) Miami-Dade	85	0.21
Carol City (cdp) Miami-Dade	85	0.14
Tamarac (city) Broward	59	0.11
North Miami (city) Miami-Dade	56	0.09
Collier Manor-Cresthaven (cdp) Broward	55	0.69
Pembroke Pines (city) Broward	54	0.04

Top 10 Places Sorted by Percent
Based on all places, regardless of population

Place (place type) County	Number	%
Pine Manor (cdp) Lee	119	3.06
Royal Palm Estates (cdp) Palm Beach	45	1.30
Collier Manor-Cresthaven (cdp) Broward	55	0.69
Rock Island (cdp) Broward	17	0.54
Roosevelt Gardens (cdp) Broward	10	0.54
Bithlo (cdp) Orange	20	0.45
Golden Lakes (cdp) Palm Beach	28	0.42
Washington Park (cdp) Broward	5	0.40
Meadow Woods (cdp) Orange	45	0.39
Tangelo Park (cdp) Orange	7	0.30

Top 10 Places Sorted by Percent
Based on places with populations of 10,000 or more

Place (place type) County	Number	%
Meadow Woods (cdp) Orange	45	0.39
Palmetto Estates (cdp) Miami-Dade	40	0.29
Upper Grand Lagoon (cdp) Bay	28	0.25
Brownsville (cdp) Miami-Dade	33	0.23
North Miami Beach (city) Miami-Dade	85	0.21
Casselberry (city) Seminole	39	0.18
Miami Springs (city) Miami-Dade	25	0.18
Oakland Park (city) Broward	46	0.15
Longwood (city) Seminole	20	0.15
Carol City (cdp) Miami-Dade	85	0.14

West Indian: Bermudan, excluding Hispanic

Top 10 Places Sorted by Number
Based on all places, regardless of population

Place (place type) County	Number	%
Jacksonville (special city) Duval	90	0.01
Lake Mary (city) Seminole	46	0.41
Fern Park (cdp) Seminole	38	0.46
Sunrise (city) Broward	30	0.04
Celebration (cdp) Osceola	24	0.87
Punta Gorda (city) Charlotte	24	0.17
Springfield (city) Bay	20	0.22
Gainesville (city) Alachua	19	0.02
Cape Coral (city) Lee	17	0.02
Casselberry (city) Seminole	16	0.07

Top 10 Places Sorted by Percent
Based on all places, regardless of population

Place (place type) County	Number	%
Celebration (cdp) Osceola	24	0.87
Lawtey (city) Bradford	3	0.53
Fern Park (cdp) Seminole	38	0.46
Lake Mary (city) Seminole	46	0.41
Springfield (city) Bay	20	0.22
Pompano Estates (cdp) Broward	7	0.20
Port La Belle (cdp) Hendry	6	0.19
Punta Gorda (city) Charlotte	24	0.17
South Bay (city) Palm Beach	5	0.13

Live Oak (city) Suwannee	7	0.11

Top 10 Places Sorted by Percent
Based on places with populations of 10,000 or more

Place (place type) County	Number	%
Lake Mary (city) Seminole	46	0.41
Punta Gorda (city) Charlotte	24	0.17
Casselberry (city) Seminole	16	0.07
Sebastian (city) Indian River	12	0.07
Hobe Sound (cdp) Martin	8	0.07
Riverview (cdp) Hillsborough	8	0.07
Sunrise (city) Broward	30	0.04
Palm Beach Gardens (city) Palm Beach	15	0.04
Pinellas Park (city) Pinellas	13	0.03
North Fort Myers (cdp) Lee	12	0.03

West Indian: British West Indian, excluding Hispanic

Top 10 Places Sorted by Number
Based on all places, regardless of population

Place (place type) County	Number	%
Miramar (city) Broward	428	0.59
Carol City (cdp) Miami-Dade	327	0.55
Norland (cdp) Miami-Dade	305	1.32
Orlando (city) Orange	279	0.15
Pembroke Pines (city) Broward	270	0.20
Lauderhill (city) Broward	254	0.44
North Miami (city) Miami-Dade	246	0.41
Lauderdale Lakes (city) Broward	238	0.76
Hollywood (city) Broward	224	0.16
Fort Lauderdale (city) Broward	209	0.14

Top 10 Places Sorted by Percent
Based on all places, regardless of population

Place (place type) County	Number	%
Utopia (cdp) Broward	29	4.00
Bunche Park (cdp) Miami-Dade	63	1.58
Royal Palm Estates (cdp) Palm Beach	46	1.33
Norland (cdp) Miami-Dade	305	1.32
Pembroke Park (town) Broward	66	1.04
Scott Lake (cdp) Miami-Dade	134	0.93
Golden Lakes (cdp) Palm Beach	56	0.84
Loch Lomond (cdp) Broward	26	0.78
Lake Lucerne (cdp) Miami-Dade	70	0.77
Lauderdale Lakes (city) Broward	238	0.76

Top 10 Places Sorted by Percent
Based on places with populations of 10,000 or more

Place (place type) County	Number	%
Norland (cdp) Miami-Dade	305	1.32
Scott Lake (cdp) Miami-Dade	134	0.93
Lauderdale Lakes (city) Broward	238	0.76
Golden Glades (cdp) Miami-Dade	197	0.61
Miramar (city) Broward	428	0.59
Sandalfoot Cove (cdp) Palm Beach	93	0.56
Carol City (cdp) Miami-Dade	327	0.55
Lauderhill (city) Broward	254	0.44
Pine Hills (cdp) Orange	176	0.42
North Miami (city) Miami-Dade	246	0.41

West Indian: Dutch West Indian, excluding Hispanic

Top 10 Places Sorted by Number
Based on all places, regardless of population

Place (place type) County	Number	%
Palm Bay (city) Brevard	59	0.07
Plantation (city) Broward	50	0.06
Royal Palm Beach (village) Palm Beach	42	0.19
Kendale Lakes (cdp) Miami-Dade	40	0.07
Forest City (cdp) Seminole	37	0.29

Jacksonville (special city) Duval	37	0.01
Tampa (city) Hillsborough	34	0.01
Brandon (cdp) Hillsborough	32	0.04
Opa-locka (city) Miami-Dade	28	0.18
Miami (city) Miami-Dade	27	0.01

Top 10 Places Sorted by Percent
Based on all places, regardless of population

Place (place type) County	Number	%
Edgewood (city) Orange	6	0.33
Forest City (cdp) Seminole	37	0.29
Samoset (cdp) Manatee	8	0.24
Chambers Estates (cdp) Broward	8	0.22
Westchase (cdp) Hillsborough	23	0.21
Daytona Beach Shores (city) Volusia	9	0.21
Princeton (cdp) Miami-Dade	20	0.20
Royal Palm Beach (village) Palm Beach	42	0.19
Opa-locka (city) Miami-Dade	28	0.18
Boyette (cdp) Hillsborough	10	0.16

Top 10 Places Sorted by Percent
Based on places with populations of 10,000 or more

Place (place type) County	Number	%
Forest City (cdp) Seminole	37	0.29
Westchase (cdp) Hillsborough	23	0.21
Princeton (cdp) Miami-Dade	20	0.20
Royal Palm Beach (village) Palm Beach	42	0.19
Opa-locka (city) Miami-Dade	28	0.18
Miami Shores (village) Miami-Dade	14	0.13
Elfers (cdp) Pasco	14	0.11
Villas (cdp) Lee	12	0.11
Norland (cdp) Miami-Dade	19	0.08
Palm Bay (city) Brevard	59	0.07

West Indian: Haitian, excluding Hispanic

Top 10 Places Sorted by Number
Based on all places, regardless of population

Place (place type) County	Number	%
North Miami (city) Miami-Dade	18,656	31.07
Miami (city) Miami-Dade	18,309	5.05
Fort Lauderdale (city) Broward	10,869	7.14
Golden Glades (cdp) Miami-Dade	10,284	31.95
North Miami Beach (city) Miami-Dade	7,864	19.33
Delray Beach (city) Palm Beach	6,351	10.60
Lauderhill (city) Broward	5,034	8.79
Pine Hills (cdp) Orange	4,817	11.47
Lauderdale Lakes (city) Broward	4,732	15.01
Pompano Beach (city) Broward	4,718	6.03

Top 10 Places Sorted by Percent
Based on all places, regardless of population

Place (place type) County	Number	%
Golden Glades (cdp) Miami-Dade	10,284	31.95
Pompano Estates (cdp) Broward	1,083	31.26
North Miami (city) Miami-Dade	18,656	31.07
Pinewood (cdp) Miami-Dade	4,315	25.66
Tedder (cdp) Broward	499	25.11
Kendall Green (cdp) Broward	724	23.04
Belle Glade Camp (cdp) Palm Beach	284	22.47
El Portal (village) Miami-Dade	556	22.09
Bonnie Lock-Woodsetter North (cdp) Broward	872	20.24
North Miami Beach (city) Miami-Dade	7,864	19.33

Top 10 Places Sorted by Percent
Based on places with populations of 10,000 or more

Place (place type) County	Number	%
Golden Glades (cdp) Miami-Dade	10,284	31.95
North Miami (city) Miami-Dade	18,656	31.07
Pinewood (cdp) Miami-Dade	4,315	25.66
North Miami Beach (city) Miami-Dade	7,864	19.33
Lauderdale Lakes (city) Broward	4,732	15.01

Notes: (cdp) census designated place; Refer to the User's Guide in the front of the book for more detailed information.

Place (place type) County	Number	%
Pine Hills (cdp) Orange	4,617	11.47
Immokalee (cdp) Collier	2,095	10.79
Delray Beach (city) Palm Beach	6,351	10.60

West Indian: Jamaican, excluding Hispanic

Top 10 Places Sorted by Number
Based on all places, regardless of population

Place (place type) County	Number	%
Miramar (city) Broward	11,263	15.50
Lauderhill (city) Broward	9,723	16.98
Pembroke Pines (city) Broward	7,648	5.58
Sunrise (city) Broward	6,888	8.04
Lauderdale Lakes (city) Broward	5,646	17.91
Norland (cdp) Miami-Dade	4,849	21.06
North Lauderdale (city) Broward	3,688	11.41
Plantation (city) Broward	3,657	4.39
Carol City (cdp) Miami-Dade	3,111	5.23
Hollywood (city) Broward	3,105	2.23

Top 10 Places Sorted by Percent
Based on all places, regardless of population

Place (place type) County	Number	%
Melrose Park (cdp) Broward	1,596	22.52
Norland (cdp) Miami-Dade	4,849	21.06
Lauderdale Lakes (city) Broward	5,646	17.91
Palmetto Estates (cdp) Miami-Dade	2,359	17.25
Lauderhill (city) Broward	9,723	16.98
Andover (cdp) Miami-Dade	1,433	16.55
Miramar (city) Broward	11,263	15.50
Scott Lake (cdp) Miami-Dade	1,870	13.00
Utopia (cdp) Broward	91	12.55
North Lauderdale (city) Broward	3,688	11.41

Top 10 Places Sorted by Percent
Based on places with populations of 10,000 or more

Place (place type) County	Number	%
Norland (cdp) Miami-Dade	4,849	21.06
Lauderdale Lakes (city) Broward	5,646	17.91
Palmetto Estates (cdp) Miami-Dade	2,359	17.25
Lauderhill (city) Broward	9,723	16.98
Miramar (city) Broward	11,263	15.50
Scott Lake (cdp) Miami-Dade	1,870	13.00
North Lauderdale (city) Broward	3,688	11.41
Sunrise (city) Broward	6,888	8.04
Ives Estates (cdp) Miami-Dade	1,000	5.74
South Miami Heights (cdp) Miami-Dade	1,909	5.69

West Indian: Trinidadian and Tobagonian, excluding Hispanic

Top 10 Places Sorted by Number
Based on all places, regardless of population

Place (place type) County	Number	%
Miramar (city) Broward	897	1.23
Hollywood (city) Broward	727	0.52
Sunrise (city) Broward	694	0.81
Pembroke Pines (city) Broward	592	0.43
Lauderhill (city) Broward	480	0.84
Plantation (city) Broward	461	0.55
Coral Springs (city) Broward	433	0.37
Palmetto Estates (cdp) Miami-Dade	413	3.02
Tampa (city) Hillsborough	359	0.12
North Lauderdale (city) Broward	357	1.10

Top 10 Places Sorted by Percent
Based on all places, regardless of population

Place (place type) County	Number	%
Palmetto Estates (cdp) Miami-Dade	413	3.02

Place (place type) County	Number	%
Loch Lomond (cdp) Broward	63	1.90
Country Walk (cdp) Miami-Dade	190	1.78
East Perrine (cdp) Miami-Dade	121	1.77
Ramblewood East (cdp) Broward	21	1.66
Bonnie Lock-Woodsetter North (cdp) Broward	65	1.51
Norland (cdp) Miami-Dade	328	1.42
Surfside (town) Miami-Dade	73	1.42

Top 10 Places Sorted by Percent
Based on places with populations of 10,000 or more

Place (place type) County	Number	%
Palmetto Estates (cdp) Miami-Dade	413	3.02
Country Walk (cdp) Miami-Dade	190	1.78
Norland (cdp) Miami-Dade	328	1.42
Miramar (city) Broward	897	1.23
North Lauderdale (city) Broward	357	1.10
Lauderhill (city) Broward	480	0.84
Sunrise (city) Broward	694	0.81
Princeton (cdp) Miami-Dade	80	0.79
Poinciana (cdp) Osceola	102	0.75
Scott Lake (cdp) Miami-Dade	104	0.72

West Indian: U.S. Virgin Islander, excluding Hispanic

Top 10 Places Sorted by Number
Based on all places, regardless of population

Place (place type) County	Number	%
Miramar (city) Broward	207	0.28
St. Petersburg (city) Pinellas	197	0.08
Orlando (city) Orange	166	0.09
Lauderdale Lakes (city) Broward	159	0.50
Tallahassee (city) Leon	153	0.10
Deltona (city) Volusia	123	0.18
Tampa (city) Hillsborough	108	0.04
Miami (city) Miami-Dade	107	0.03
Jacksonville (special city) Duval	107	0.01
Pine Hills (cdp) Orange	100	0.24

Top 10 Places Sorted by Percent
Based on all places, regardless of population

Place (place type) County	Number	%
Utopia (cdp) Broward	15	2.07
Opa-locka North (cdp) Miami-Dade	94	1.51
Silver Springs Shores (cdp) Marion	40	0.61
Scott Lake (cdp) Miami-Dade	85	0.59
Pembroke Park (town) Broward	36	0.57
Golden Lakes (cdp) Palm Beach	34	0.51
Lauderdale Lakes (city) Broward	159	0.50
Naples Manor (cdp) Collier	22	0.43
Westview (cdp) Miami-Dade	39	0.41
Lake Lucerne (cdp) Miami-Dade	36	0.39

Top 10 Places Sorted by Percent
Based on places with populations of 10,000 or more

Place (place type) County	Number	%
Scott Lake (cdp) Miami-Dade	85	0.59
Lauderdale Lakes (city) Broward	159	0.50
Miramar (city) Broward	207	0.28
Pine Hills (cdp) Orange	100	0.24
Yeehaw Junction (cdp) Osceola	50	0.23
North Lauderdale (city) Broward	65	0.20
Deltona (city) Volusia	123	0.18
Ives Estates (cdp) Miami-Dade	32	0.18
Lauderhill (city) Broward	82	0.14
Country Club (cdp) Miami-Dade	52	0.14

Top 10 Places Sorted by Number
Based on all places, regardless of population

Place (place type) County	Number	%
Jacksonville (special city) Duval	750	0.10
Pembroke Pines (city) Broward	522	0.38
Miramar (city) Broward	493	0.68
Tampa (city) Hillsborough	415	0.14
Orlando (city) Orange	369	0.20
Lauderhill (city) Broward	365	0.64
Miami (city) Miami-Dade	350	0.10
Sunrise (city) Broward	337	0.39
Hollywood (city) Broward	324	0.23
North Lauderdale (city) Broward	307	0.95

Top 10 Places Sorted by Percent
Based on all places, regardless of population

Place (place type) County	Number	%
Gun Club Estates (cdp) Palm Beach	92	10.86
Chula Vista (cdp) Broward	20	3.42
Lake Belvedere Estates (cdp) Palm Beach	27	1.81
St. Leo (town) Pasco	10	1.64
Orlovista (cdp) Orange	95	1.56
East Perrine (cdp) Miami-Dade	102	1.49
Roosevelt Gardens (cdp) Broward	26	1.39
Sky Lake (cdp) Orange	81	1.37
Loch Lomond (cdp) Broward	41	1.23
Poinciana (cdp) Osceola	162	1.19

Top 10 Places Sorted by Percent
Based on places with populations of 10,000 or more

Place (place type) County	Number	%
Poinciana (cdp) Osceola	162	1.19
North Lauderdale (city) Broward	307	0.95
Meadow Woods (cdp) Orange	93	0.81
Yeehaw Junction (cdp) Osceola	156	0.70
Opa-locka (city) Miami-Dade	105	0.69
Miramar (city) Broward	493	0.68
Pine Hills (cdp) Orange	275	0.65
Lauderhill (city) Broward	365	0.64
Apopka (city) Orange	165	0.63
Ives Estates (cdp) Miami-Dade	101	0.58

West Indian: Other, excluding Hispanic

Top 10 Places Sorted by Number
Based on all places, regardless of population

Place (place type) County	Number	%
St. Petersburg (city) Pinellas	74	0.03
Greater Northdale (cdp) Hillsborough	59	0.29
Davie (town) Broward	42	0.06
Jacksonville (special city) Duval	42	0.01
Tampa (city) Hillsborough	38	0.01
Fort Lauderdale (city) Broward	37	0.02
Orlando (city) Orange	37	0.02
Carol City (cdp) Miami-Dade	34	0.06
University (cdp) Hillsborough	32	0.10
Miami Beach (city) Miami-Dade	29	0.03

Top 10 Places Sorted by Percent
Based on all places, regardless of population

Place (place type) County	Number	%
Seffner (cdp) Hillsborough	28	0.50
Fussels Corner (cdp) Polk	16	0.31
Greater Northdale (cdp) Hillsborough	59	0.29
Madeira Beach (city) Pinellas	10	0.22
East Perrine (cdp) Miami-Dade	12	0.18
Flagler Beach (city) Flagler	9	0.18
Pinewood (cdp) Miami-Dade	19	0.11
De Bary (city) Volusia	18	0.11
University (cdp) Hillsborough	32	0.10

Notes: (cdp) census designated place; Refer to the User's Guide in the front of the book for more detailed information.

Place (place type) County	Number	%
Greater Northdale (cdp) Hillsborough	59	0.29
Pinewood (cdp) Miami-Dade	19	0.11
De Bary (city) Volusia	18	0.11
University (cdp) Hillsborough	32	0.10
Atlantic Beach (city) Duval	13	0.10
Poinciana (cdp) Osceola	12	0.09
De Land (city) Volusia	16	0.08
Upper Grand Lagoon (cdp) Bay	9	0.08
South Miami Heights (cdp) Miami-Dade	24	0.07
Citrus Park (cdp) Hillsborough	15	0.07

White

Top 10 Places Sorted by Number
Based on all places, regardless of population

Place (place type) County	Number	%
Jacksonville (special city) Duval	485,785	66.04
Miami (city) Miami-Dade	251,993	69.52
Hialeah (city) Miami-Dade	206,539	91.22
Tampa (city) Hillsborough	201,268	66.33
St. Petersburg (city) Pinellas	181,278	73.03
Orlando (city) Orange	117,957	63.43
Hollywood (city) Broward	112,460	80.70
Pembroke Pines (city) Broward	107,142	77.96
Fort Lauderdale (city) Broward	99,898	65.55
Coral Springs (city) Broward	97,897	83.28

Top 10 Places Sorted by Percent
Based on all places, regardless of population

Place (place type) County	Number	%
Plantation Island (cdp) Collier	202	100.00
Nobleton (cdp) Hernando	160	100.00
Orchid (town) Indian River	140	100.00
Bascom (town) Jackson	106	100.00
Lake Lindsey (cdp) Hernando	49	100.00
Indian Creek (village) Miami-Dade	33	100.00
Lake Buena Vista (city) Orange	16	100.00
Weeki Wachee (city) Hernando	12	100.00
Islandia (city) Miami-Dade	6	100.00
Marineland (town) Flagler	6	100.00

Top 10 Places Sorted by Percent
Based on places with populations of 10,000 or more

Place (place type) County	Number	%
Kings Point (cdp) Palm Beach	12,134	99.40
Greater Sun Center (cdp) Hillsborough	16,181	99.14
Englewood (cdp) Sarasota	15,995	98.76
Venice (city) Sarasota	17,519	98.62
Marco Island (city) Collier	14,650	98.46
South Venice (cdp) Sarasota	13,319	98.38
Lighthouse Point (city) Broward	10,562	98.10
Iona (cdp) Lee	11,524	98.03
Hudson (cdp) Pasco	12,512	98.02
Seminole (city) Pinellas	10,652	97.81

White: Not Hispanic

Top 10 Places Sorted by Number
Based on all places, regardless of population

Place (place type) County	Number	%
Jacksonville (special city) Duval	467,111	63.50
St. Petersburg (city) Pinellas	173,878	70.05
Tampa (city) Hillsborough	158,426	52.21
Orlando (city) Orange	96,921	52.12
Cape Coral (city) Lee	90,436	88.41
Fort Lauderdale (city) Broward	88,757	58.24
Tallahassee (city) Leon	88,527	58.77

Based on all places, regardless of population

Place (place type) County	Number	%
Bascom (town) Jackson	106	100.00
Lake Lindsey (cdp) Hernando	49	100.00
Lake Buena Vista (city) Orange	16	100.00
Weeki Wachee (city) Hernando	12	100.00
Islandia (city) Miami-Dade	6	100.00
Marineland (town) Flagler	6	100.00
Jupiter Inlet Colony (town) Palm Beach	367	99.73
Orchid (town) Indian River	139	99.29
Punta Rassa (cdp) Lee	1,715	99.08
Briny Breezes (town) Palm Beach	407	99.03

Top 10 Places Sorted by Percent
Based on places with populations of 10,000 or more

Place (place type) County	Number	%
Kings Point (cdp) Palm Beach	12,007	98.36
Greater Sun Center (cdp) Hillsborough	16,012	98.11
Venice (city) Sarasota	17,360	97.73
Englewood (cdp) Sarasota	15,819	97.67
South Venice (cdp) Sarasota	13,140	97.05
Seminole (city) Pinellas	10,458	96.03
Homosassa Springs (cdp) Citrus	11,942	95.86
Hudson (cdp) Pasco	12,232	95.82
Edgewater (city) Volusia	17,874	95.75
Cocoa Beach (city) Brevard	11,911	95.43

White: Hispanic

Top 10 Places Sorted by Number
Based on all places, regardless of population

Place (place type) County	Number	%
Miami (city) Miami-Dade	207,888	57.35
Hialeah (city) Miami-Dade	187,865	82.97
Fountainbleau (cdp) Miami-Dade	47,111	79.11
Tamiami (cdp) Miami-Dade	44,572	81.35
Tampa (city) Hillsborough	42,842	14.12
Miami Beach (city) Miami-Dade	42,181	47.97
Kendale Lakes (cdp) Miami-Dade	40,249	70.74
Kendall (cdp) Miami-Dade	35,083	46.64
Pembroke Pines (city) Broward	33,066	24.06
The Hammocks (cdp) Miami-Dade	27,479	58.00

Top 10 Places Sorted by Percent
Based on all places, regardless of population

Place (place type) County	Number	%
Sweetwater (city) Miami-Dade	12,056	84.75
Hialeah (city) Miami-Dade	187,865	82.97
Hialeah Gardens (city) Miami-Dade	15,954	82.68
Westchester (cdp) Miami-Dade	24,773	81.84
Tamiami (cdp) Miami-Dade	44,572	81.35
West Miami (city) Miami-Dade	4,660	79.48
Fountainbleau (cdp) Miami-Dade	47,111	79.11
University Park (cdp) Miami-Dade	20,825	78.47
Coral Terrace (cdp) Miami-Dade	19,121	78.43
Olympia Heights (cdp) Miami-Dade	9,836	73.12

Top 10 Places Sorted by Percent
Based on places with populations of 10,000 or more

Place (place type) County	Number	%
Sweetwater (city) Miami-Dade	12,056	84.75
Hialeah (city) Miami-Dade	187,865	82.97
Hialeah Gardens (city) Miami-Dade	15,954	82.68
Westchester (cdp) Miami-Dade	24,773	81.84
Tamiami (cdp) Miami-Dade	44,572	81.35
Fountainbleau (cdp) Miami-Dade	47,111	79.11
University Park (cdp) Miami-Dade	20,825	78.47

Top 10 Places Sorted by Number
Based on all places, regardless of population

Place (place type) County	Number	%
Jacksonville (special city) Duval	2,655	0.36
St. Petersburg (city) Pinellas	1,459	0.59
Clearwater (city) Pinellas	585	0.54
Tampa (city) Hillsborough	345	0.11
Pinellas Park (city) Pinellas	338	0.74
Hollywood (city) Broward	245	0.18
Coral Springs (city) Broward	183	0.16
New Port Richey (city) Pasco	164	1.05
Jupiter (town) Palm Beach	141	0.36
Miami Beach (city) Miami-Dade	135	0.15

Top 10 Places Sorted by Percent
Based on all places, regardless of population

Place (place type) County	Number	%
Goodland (cdp) Collier	11	4.98
Plantation Island (cdp) Collier	8	3.76
Cudjoe Key (cdp) Monroe	27	1.55
New Port Richey (city) Pasco	164	1.05
Gulf Gate Estates (cdp) Sarasota	121	1.05
Pine Castle (cdp) Orange	78	0.95
Wewahitchka (city) Gulf	14	0.80
Pinellas Park (city) Pinellas	338	0.74
Desoto Lakes (cdp) Sarasota	24	0.74
South Sarasota (cdp) Sarasota	35	0.68

Top 10 Places Sorted by Percent
Based on places with populations of 10,000 or more

Place (place type) County	Number	%
New Port Richey (city) Pasco	164	1.05
Gulf Gate Estates (cdp) Sarasota	121	1.05
Pinellas Park (city) Pinellas	338	0.74
St. Petersburg (city) Pinellas	1,459	0.59
Clearwater (city) Pinellas	585	0.54
Casselberry (city) Seminole	110	0.50
West and East Lealman (cdp) Pinellas	94	0.43
Lockhart (cdp) Orange	50	0.40
Lakewood Park (cdp) St. Lucie	39	0.37
Jacksonville (special city) Duval	2,655	0.36

Notes: (cdp) census designated place; Refer to the User's Guide in the front of the book for more detailed information.

Hispanic Population

Total Population
Top 10 Places Sorted by Number

Place (place type) County	Number
Jacksonville (city) Duval	735,503
Miami (city) Miami-Dade	362,563
Tampa (city) Hillsborough	303,512
St. Petersburg (city) Pinellas	247,793
Hialeah (city) Miami-Dade	226,411
Orlando (city) Orange	185,984
Fort Lauderdale (city) Broward	152,125
Tallahassee (city) Leon	150,581
Hollywood (city) Broward	139,261
Pembroke Pines (city) Broward	137,112

Hispanic
Top 10 Places Sorted by Number

Place (place type) County	Number
Miami (city) Miami-Dade	238,461
Hialeah (city) Miami-Dade	204,808
Tampa (city) Hillsborough	58,571
Fountainbleau (cdp) Miami-Dade	51,833
Tamiami (cdp) Miami-Dade	47,691
Miami Beach (city) Miami-Dade	46,980
Kendale Lakes (cdp) Miami-Dade	43,588
Pembroke Pines (city) Broward	38,348
Kendall (cdp) Miami-Dade	37,640
Orlando (city) Orange	32,897

Hispanic
Top 10 Places Sorted by Percent of Total Population

Place (place type) County	Percent
Sweetwater (city) Miami-Dade	93.61
Hialeah (city) Miami-Dade	90.46
Hialeah Gardens (city) Miami-Dade	90.13
Tamiami (cdp) Miami-Dade	87.11
Fountainbleau (cdp) Miami-Dade	87.09
Westchester (cdp) Miami-Dade	85.43
University Park (cdp) Miami-Dade	82.77
Coral Terrace (cdp) Miami-Dade	81.92
Kendall West (cdp) Miami-Dade	79.15
Kendale Lakes (cdp) Miami-Dade	76.62

Argentinian
Top 10 Places Sorted by Number

Place (place type) County	Number
Miami Beach (city) Miami-Dade	3,031
Miami (city) Miami-Dade	2,029
Kendall (cdp) Miami-Dade	655
Sunny Isles Beach (city) Miami-Dade	571
Hollywood (city) Broward	559
Fountainbleau (cdp) Miami-Dade	440
Hialeah (city) Miami-Dade	429

Argentinian
Top 10 Places Sorted by Percent of Hispanic Population

Place (place type) County	Percent
Sunny Isles Beach (city) Miami-Dade	10.19
Miami Beach (city) Miami-Dade	6.45
Hollywood (city) Broward	1.78
Kendall (cdp) Miami-Dade	1.74
Fountainbleau (cdp) Miami-Dade	0.85
Miami (city) Miami-Dade	0.85
Hialeah (city) Miami-Dade	0.21

Argentinian
Top 10 Places Sorted by Percent of Total Population

Place (place type) County	Percent
Sunny Isles Beach (city) Miami-Dade	3.74
Miami Beach (city) Miami-Dade	3.44
Kendall (cdp) Miami-Dade	0.87

Miami (city) Miami-Dade	
Hollywood (city) Broward	0.40
Hialeah (city) Miami-Dade	0.19

Bolivian
Top 10 Places Sorted by Number

Place (place type) County	Number
No places met population threshold.	

Bolivian
Top 10 Places Sorted by Percent of Hispanic Population

Place (place type) County	Percent
No places met population threshold.	

Bolivian
Top 10 Places Sorted by Percent of Total Population

Place (place type) County	Percent
No places met population threshold.	

Central American
Top 10 Places Sorted by Number

Place (place type) County	Number
Miami (city) Miami-Dade	43,925
Hialeah (city) Miami-Dade	15,904
Fountainbleau (cdp) Miami-Dade	8,161
Kendale Lakes (cdp) Miami-Dade	4,079
Tamiami (cdp) Miami-Dade	3,850
Kendall (cdp) Miami-Dade	3,845
Homestead (city) Miami-Dade	3,418
Tampa (city) Hillsborough	3,229
Lake Worth (city) Palm Beach	3,204
Miami Beach (city) Miami-Dade	2,823

Central American
Top 10 Places Sorted by Percent of Hispanic Population

Place (place type) County	Percent
Gladeview (cdp) Miami-Dade	33.13
Lake Worth (city) Palm Beach	30.78
Brownsville (cdp) Miami-Dade	29.13
Palmetto Estates (cdp) Miami-Dade	23.77
Oakland Park (city) Broward	21.52
Homestead (city) Miami-Dade	19.95
Pinewood (cdp) Miami-Dade	19.77
West Little River (cdp) Miami-Dade	19.30
Sweetwater (city) Miami-Dade	19.19
West Palm Beach (city) Palm Beach	18.66

Central American
Top 10 Places Sorted by Percent of Total Population

Place (place type) County	Percent
Sweetwater (city) Miami-Dade	17.97
Fountainbleau (cdp) Miami-Dade	13.71
Miami (city) Miami-Dade	12.12
Homestead (city) Miami-Dade	10.67
Lake Worth (city) Palm Beach	9.09
West Little River (cdp) Miami-Dade	7.74
Kendale Lakes (cdp) Miami-Dade	7.17
Gladeview (cdp) Miami-Dade	7.03
Tamiami (cdp) Miami-Dade	7.03
Hialeah (city) Miami-Dade	7.02

Chilean
Top 10 Places Sorted by Number

Place (place type) County	Number
Miami (city) Miami-Dade	897
Hialeah (city) Miami-Dade	750
Miami Beach (city) Miami-Dade	739
Fountainbleau (cdp) Miami-Dade	703
Kendall (cdp) Miami-Dade	480
Hollywood (city) Broward	377

Place (place type) County	Percent
Miami Beach (city) Miami-Dade	1.57
Fountainbleau (cdp) Miami-Dade	1.36
Kendall (cdp) Miami-Dade	1.28
Hollywood (city) Broward	1.20
Miami (city) Miami-Dade	0.38
Hialeah (city) Miami-Dade	0.37

Chilean
Top 10 Places Sorted by Percent of Total Population

Place (place type) County	Percent
Fountainbleau (cdp) Miami-Dade	1.18
Miami Beach (city) Miami-Dade	0.84
Kendall (cdp) Miami-Dade	0.64
Hialeah (city) Miami-Dade	0.33
Hollywood (city) Broward	0.27
Miami (city) Miami-Dade	0.25

Colombian
Top 10 Places Sorted by Number

Place (place type) County	Number
Hialeah (city) Miami-Dade	7,715
Miami (city) Miami-Dade	6,006
The Hammocks (cdp) Miami-Dade	4,988
Miami Beach (city) Miami-Dade	4,493
Kendall West (cdp) Miami-Dade	4,368
Kendall (cdp) Miami-Dade	4,130
Kendale Lakes (cdp) Miami-Dade	4,003
Country Club (cdp) Miami-Dade	3,669
Pembroke Pines (city) Broward	3,463
Hollywood (city) Broward	3,312

Colombian
Top 10 Places Sorted by Percent of Hispanic Population

Place (place type) County	Percent
Weston (city) Broward	19.92
Aventura (city) Miami-Dade	19.46
Plantation (city) Broward	19.44
Sandalfoot Cove (cdp) Palm Beach	17.24
Sunrise (city) Broward	16.92
Country Club (cdp) Miami-Dade	16.61
The Hammocks (cdp) Miami-Dade	16.07
Tamarac (city) Broward	15.75
Key Biscayne (village) Miami-Dade	15.34
Sunny Isles Beach (city) Miami-Dade	15.02

Colombian
Top 10 Places Sorted by Percent of Total Population

Place (place type) County	Percent
Kendall West (cdp) Miami-Dade	11.51
The Hammocks (cdp) Miami-Dade	10.52
Country Club (cdp) Miami-Dade	10.08
Doral (cdp) Miami-Dade	7.74
The Crossings (cdp) Miami-Dade	7.72
Key Biscayne (village) Miami-Dade	7.64
Kendale Lakes (cdp) Miami-Dade	7.04
Weston (city) Broward	6.11
Sunny Isles Beach (city) Miami-Dade	5.51
Kendall (cdp) Miami-Dade	5.49

Costa Rican
Top 10 Places Sorted by Number

Place (place type) County	Number
Miami (city) Miami-Dade	816
Hialeah (city) Miami-Dade	523

Costa Rican
Top 10 Places Sorted by Percent of Hispanic Population

Place (place type) County	Percent
Miami (city) Miami-Dade	0.34

Notes: Please refer to the User's Guide for an explanation of data; tables include places with populations > 9,999 and reflect only those areas that meet Summary File 4 population thresholds, therefore there may be less than 10 places listed

Hialeah (city) Miami-Dade ... 0.26

Costa Rican
Top 10 Places Sorted by Percent of Total Population

Place (place type) County	Percent
Hialeah (city) Miami-Dade	0.23
Miami (city) Miami-Dade	0.23

Cuban
Top 10 Places Sorted by Number

Place (place type) County	Number
Hialeah (city) Miami-Dade	141,302
Miami (city) Miami-Dade	124,734
Tamiami (cdp) Miami-Dade	32,381
Fountainbleau (cdp) Miami-Dade	22,301
Kendale Lakes (cdp) Miami-Dade	22,057
Westchester (cdp) Miami-Dade	20,420
Miami Beach (city) Miami-Dade	18,241
Kendall (cdp) Miami-Dade	15,868
University Park (cdp) Miami-Dade	15,699
Coral Terrace (cdp) Miami-Dade	15,063

Cuban
Top 10 Places Sorted by Percent of Hispanic Population

Place (place type) County	Percent
Westchester (cdp) Miami-Dade	78.98
Coral Terrace (cdp) Miami-Dade	75.48
Olympia Heights (cdp) Miami-Dade	75.21
Westwood Lakes (cdp) Miami-Dade	74.82
University Park (cdp) Miami-Dade	71.64
Sunset (cdp) Miami-Dade	69.36
Hialeah (city) Miami-Dade	68.99
Tamiami (cdp) Miami-Dade	67.90
Miami Lakes (cdp) Miami-Dade	63.74
Key Largo (cdp) Monroe	63.33

Cuban
Top 10 Places Sorted by Percent of Total Population

Place (place type) County	Percent
Westchester (cdp) Miami-Dade	67.48
Hialeah (city) Miami-Dade	62.41
Coral Terrace (cdp) Miami-Dade	61.84
University Park (cdp) Miami-Dade	59.30
Tamiami (cdp) Miami-Dade	59.15
Olympia Heights (cdp) Miami-Dade	57.28
Westwood Lakes (cdp) Miami-Dade	57.26
Hialeah Gardens (city) Miami-Dade	57.02
Sweetwater (city) Miami-Dade	53.92
Sunset (cdp) Miami-Dade	48.24

Dominican
Top 10 Places Sorted by Number

Place (place type) County	Number
Miami (city) Miami-Dade	7,270
Hialeah (city) Miami-Dade	4,886
Fountainbleau (cdp) Miami-Dade	1,928
Carol City (cdp) Miami-Dade	1,883
Pembroke Pines (city) Broward	1,809
Hollywood (city) Broward	1,688
The Hammocks (cdp) Miami-Dade	1,519
Tampa (city) Hillsborough	1,426
Miramar (city) Broward	1,412
Miami Beach (city) Miami-Dade	1,396

Dominican
Top 10 Places Sorted by Percent of Hispanic Population

Place (place type) County	Percent
Golden Glades (cdp) Miami-Dade	10.41
West Little River (cdp) Miami-Dade	7.74
North Miami (city) Miami-Dade	7.67
North Miami Beach (city) Miami-Dade	7.59
Carol City (cdp) Miami-Dade	7.54

Place (place type) County	Percent
Cape Coral (city) Lee	6.97
Oak Ridge (cdp) Orange	6.85
Miramar (city) Broward	6.56
Country Club (cdp) Miami-Dade	6.20
Kissimmee (city) Osceola	5.88

Dominican
Top 10 Places Sorted by Percent of Total Population

Place (place type) County	Percent
Country Club (cdp) Miami-Dade	3.76
Hialeah Gardens (city) Miami-Dade	3.45
Fountainbleau (cdp) Miami-Dade	3.24
The Hammocks (cdp) Miami-Dade	3.20
Carol City (cdp) Miami-Dade	3.17
Richmond West (cdp) Miami-Dade	3.14
West Little River (cdp) Miami-Dade	3.10
South Miami Heights (cdp) Miami-Dade	2.91
Oak Ridge (cdp) Orange	2.87
Yeehaw Junction (cdp) Osceola	2.64

Ecuadorian
Top 10 Places Sorted by Number

Place (place type) County	Number
Miami (city) Miami-Dade	1,755
Hialeah (city) Miami-Dade	1,233
Coral Springs (city) Broward	942
Fountainbleau (cdp) Miami-Dade	799
Miami Beach (city) Miami-Dade	662
Hollywood (city) Broward	628
Sunrise (city) Broward	529
Pembroke Pines (city) Broward	486
Tampa (city) Hillsborough	418

Ecuadorian
Top 10 Places Sorted by Percent of Hispanic Population

Place (place type) County	Percent
Coral Springs (city) Broward	5.15
Sunrise (city) Broward	3.64
Hollywood (city) Broward	2.00
Fountainbleau (cdp) Miami-Dade	1.54
Miami Beach (city) Miami-Dade	1.41
Pembroke Pines (city) Broward	1.27
Miami (city) Miami-Dade	0.74
Tampa (city) Hillsborough	0.71
Hialeah (city) Miami-Dade	0.60

Ecuadorian
Top 10 Places Sorted by Percent of Total Population

Place (place type) County	Percent
Fountainbleau (cdp) Miami-Dade	1.34
Coral Springs (city) Broward	0.80
Miami Beach (city) Miami-Dade	0.75
Sunrise (city) Broward	0.62
Hialeah (city) Miami-Dade	0.54
Miami (city) Miami-Dade	0.48
Hollywood (city) Broward	0.45
Pembroke Pines (city) Broward	0.35
Tampa (city) Hillsborough	0.14

Guatelmalan
Top 10 Places Sorted by Number

Place (place type) County	Number
Miami (city) Miami-Dade	2,851
West Palm Beach (city) Palm Beach	2,060
Lake Worth (city) Palm Beach	1,966
Homestead (city) Miami-Dade	1,435
Immokalee (cdp) Collier	1,154
Hialeah (city) Miami-Dade	842
Fort Myers (city) Lee	393
Fort Lauderdale (city) Broward	371
Bonita Springs (city) Lee	369

Guatelmalan
Top 10 Places Sorted by Percent of Hispanic Population

Place (place type) County	Percent
Lake Worth (city) Palm Beach	18.89
West Palm Beach (city) Palm Beach	13.73
Immokalee (cdp) Collier	8.44
Homestead (city) Miami-Dade	8.37
Bonita Springs (city) Lee	6.53
Fort Myers (city) Lee	5.75
Fort Lauderdale (city) Broward	2.67
Miami (city) Miami-Dade	1.20
Hialeah (city) Miami-Dade	0.41

Guatelmalan
Top 10 Places Sorted by Percent of Total Population

Place (place type) County	Percent
Immokalee (cdp) Collier	5.95
Lake Worth (city) Palm Beach	5.58
Homestead (city) Miami-Dade	4.48
West Palm Beach (city) Palm Beach	2.53
Bonita Springs (city) Lee	1.12
Fort Myers (city) Lee	0.82
Miami (city) Miami-Dade	0.79
Hialeah (city) Miami-Dade	0.37
Fort Lauderdale (city) Broward	0.24

Honduran
Top 10 Places Sorted by Number

Place (place type) County	Number
Miami (city) Miami-Dade	13,660
Hialeah (city) Miami-Dade	2,651
West Little River (cdp) Miami-Dade	975
Tampa (city) Hillsborough	894
Miami Beach (city) Miami-Dade	810
Fountainbleau (cdp) Miami-Dade	642
North Miami (city) Miami-Dade	590
Kendale Lakes (cdp) Miami-Dade	557
Carol City (cdp) Miami-Dade	518
North Miami Beach (city) Miami-Dade	509

Honduran
Top 10 Places Sorted by Percent of Hispanic Population

Place (place type) County	Percent
West Little River (cdp) Miami-Dade	7.53
Miami (city) Miami-Dade	5.73
Lake Worth (city) Palm Beach	4.65
North Miami Beach (city) Miami-Dade	4.13
North Miami (city) Miami-Dade	4.12
Carol City (cdp) Miami-Dade	2.07
Miami Beach (city) Miami-Dade	1.72
Tampa (city) Hillsborough	1.53
Hollywood (city) Broward	1.41
Hialeah (city) Miami-Dade	1.29

Honduran
Top 10 Places Sorted by Percent of Total Population

Place (place type) County	Percent
Miami (city) Miami-Dade	3.77
West Little River (cdp) Miami-Dade	3.02
Lake Worth (city) Palm Beach	1.37
North Miami Beach (city) Miami-Dade	1.25
Hialeah (city) Miami-Dade	1.17
Fountainbleau (cdp) Miami-Dade	1.08
Kendale Lakes (cdp) Miami-Dade	0.98
North Miami (city) Miami-Dade	0.98
Miami Beach (city) Miami-Dade	0.92
Carol City (cdp) Miami-Dade	0.87

Mexican
Top 10 Places Sorted by Number

Place (place type) County	Number
Immokalee (cdp) Collier	10,817
Tampa (city) Hillsborough	7,216

Notes: Please refer to the User's Guide for an explanation of data; tables include places with populations > 9,999 and reflect only those areas that meet Summary File 4 population thresholds, therefore there may be less than 10 places listed

Place (place type) County	Number
Homestead (city) Miami-Dade	7,106
Jacksonville (city) Duval	5,521
Leisure City (cdp) Miami-Dade	5,441
Clearwater (city) Pinellas	4,211
Fort Pierce (city) Saint Lucie	4,177
Golden Gate (cdp) Collier	3,689
Bradenton (city) Manatee	3,625
Sarasota (city) Sarasota	3,545

Mexican
Top 10 Places Sorted by Percent of Hispanic Population

Place (place type) County	Percent
Palmetto (city) Manatee	80.37
Immokalee (cdp) Collier	79.13
Haines City (city) Polk	75.16
Auburndale (city) Polk	74.73
Fort Pierce (city) Saint Lucie	71.81
Plant City (city) Hillsborough	67.40
Bradenton (city) Manatee	64.52
Lake Wales (city) Polk	64.31
Bonita Springs (city) Lee	59.18
De Land (city) Volusia	58.30

Mexican
Top 10 Places Sorted by Percent of Total Population

Place (place type) County	Percent
Immokalee (cdp) Collier	55.73
Leisure City (cdp) Miami-Dade	24.99
Homestead (city) Miami-Dade	22.17
Palmetto (city) Manatee	20.97
Lake Worth Corridor (cdp) Palm Beach	17.58
Golden Gate (cdp) Collier	17.56
Haines City (city) Polk	17.49
Belle Glade (city) Palm Beach	15.47
Plant City (city) Hillsborough	11.61
Fort Pierce (city) Saint Lucie	11.14

Nicaraguan
Top 10 Places Sorted by Number

Place (place type) County	Number
Miami (city) Miami-Dade	22,571
Hialeah (city) Miami-Dade	10,161
Fountainbleau (cdp) Miami-Dade	6,120
Kendale Lakes (cdp) Miami-Dade	2,847
Tamiami (cdp) Miami-Dade	2,757
Sweetwater (city) Miami-Dade	2,404
Kendall (cdp) Miami-Dade	2,232
Kendall West (cdp) Miami-Dade	1,598
The Hammocks (cdp) Miami-Dade	1,526
Carol City (cdp) Miami-Dade	1,448

Nicaraguan
Top 10 Places Sorted by Percent of Hispanic Population

Place (place type) County	Percent
Gladeview (cdp) Miami-Dade	26.78
Sweetwater (city) Miami-Dade	18.00
Pinewood (cdp) Miami-Dade	15.00
Fountainbleau (cdp) Miami-Dade	11.81
Palmetto Estates (cdp) Miami-Dade	11.63
Miami (city) Miami-Dade	9.47
West Little River (cdp) Miami-Dade	8.75
Kendale Lakes (cdp) Miami-Dade	6.53
Richmond West (cdp) Miami-Dade	6.17
Kendall (cdp) Miami-Dade	5.93

Nicaraguan
Top 10 Places Sorted by Percent of Total Population

Place (place type) County	Percent
Sweetwater (city) Miami-Dade	16.85
Fountainbleau (cdp) Miami-Dade	10.28
Miami (city) Miami-Dade	6.23
Gladeview (cdp) Miami-Dade	5.69
Tamiami (cdp) Miami-Dade	5.04

Place (place type) County	Percent
Kendale Lakes (cdp) Miami-Dade	5.00
Hialeah (city) Miami-Dade	4.49
Hialeah Gardens (city) Miami-Dade	4.38
Richmond West (cdp) Miami-Dade	4.32
Kendall West (cdp) Miami-Dade	4.21

Panamanian
Top 10 Places Sorted by Number

Place (place type) County	Number
Miami (city) Miami-Dade	883
Tampa (city) Hillsborough	632
Jacksonville (city) Duval	581
Fountainbleau (cdp) Miami-Dade	522
Miramar (city) Broward	367

Panamanian
Top 10 Places Sorted by Percent of Hispanic Population

Place (place type) County	Percent
Jacksonville (city) Duval	1.91
Miramar (city) Broward	1.70
Tampa (city) Hillsborough	1.08
Fountainbleau (cdp) Miami-Dade	1.01
Miami (city) Miami-Dade	0.37

Panamanian
Top 10 Places Sorted by Percent of Total Population

Place (place type) County	Percent
Fountainbleau (cdp) Miami-Dade	0.88
Miramar (city) Broward	0.50
Miami (city) Miami-Dade	0.24
Tampa (city) Hillsborough	0.21
Jacksonville (city) Duval	0.08

Paraguayan
Top 10 Places Sorted by Number

Place (place type) County	Number
No places met population threshold.	

Paraguayan
Top 10 Places Sorted by Percent of Hispanic Population

Place (place type) County	Percent
No places met population threshold.	

Paraguayan
Top 10 Places Sorted by Percent of Total Population

Place (place type) County	Percent
No places met population threshold.	

Peruvian
Top 10 Places Sorted by Number

Place (place type) County	Number
Miami (city) Miami-Dade	2,767
Miami Beach (city) Miami-Dade	1,898
The Hammocks (cdp) Miami-Dade	1,821
Pembroke Pines (city) Broward	1,505
Hialeah (city) Miami-Dade	1,459
Kendall (cdp) Miami-Dade	1,370
Hollywood (city) Broward	1,337
Fountainbleau (cdp) Miami-Dade	1,181
Kendall West (cdp) Miami-Dade	1,147
Kendale Lakes (cdp) Miami-Dade	967

Peruvian
Top 10 Places Sorted by Percent of Hispanic Population

Place (place type) County	Percent
North Lauderdale (city) Broward	7.92
North Miami Beach (city) Miami-Dade	6.36
The Hammocks (cdp) Miami-Dade	5.87
Coral Springs (city) Broward	5.21
Weston (city) Broward	4.79

Place (place type) County	Percent
Plantation (city) Broward	4.59
Davie (town) Broward	4.49
The Crossings (cdp) Miami-Dade	4.48
Hollywood (city) Broward	4.26
Sunrise (city) Broward	4.08

Peruvian
Top 10 Places Sorted by Percent of Total Population

Place (place type) County	Percent
The Hammocks (cdp) Miami-Dade	3.84
Kendall West (cdp) Miami-Dade	3.02
Doral (cdp) Miami-Dade	2.66
The Crossings (cdp) Miami-Dade	2.55
Miami Beach (city) Miami-Dade	2.16
Fountainbleau (cdp) Miami-Dade	1.98
North Miami Beach (city) Miami-Dade	1.93
Richmond West (cdp) Miami-Dade	1.86
Kendall (cdp) Miami-Dade	1.82
North Lauderdale (city) Broward	1.72

Puerto Rican
Top 10 Places Sorted by Number

Place (place type) County	Number
Orlando (city) Orange	16,701
Tampa (city) Hillsborough	15,837
Kissimmee (city) Osceola	12,079
Jacksonville (city) Duval	10,924
Miami (city) Miami-Dade	10,138
Deltona (city) Volusia	9,488
Yeehaw Junction (cdp) Osceola	8,357
Town 'n' Country (cdp) Hillsborough	7,453
Pembroke Pines (city) Broward	7,370
Hialeah (city) Miami-Dade	6,971

Puerto Rican
Top 10 Places Sorted by Percent of Hispanic Population

Place (place type) County	Percent
Poinciana (cdp) Osceola	78.45
Deltona (city) Volusia	73.81
Zephyrhills (city) Pasco	72.73
Yeehaw Junction (cdp) Osceola	68.99
St. Cloud (city) Osceola	66.40
Lockhart (cdp) Orange	65.55
Spring Hill (cdp) Hernando	62.80
Meadow Woods (cdp) Orange	62.60
Azalea Park (cdp) Orange	61.54
Kissimmee (city) Osceola	61.46

Puerto Rican
Top 10 Places Sorted by Percent of Total Population

Place (place type) County	Percent
Yeehaw Junction (cdp) Osceola	37.71
Meadow Woods (cdp) Orange	33.14
Poinciana (cdp) Osceola	31.19
Kissimmee (city) Osceola	25.40
Azalea Park (cdp) Orange	23.90
Oak Ridge (cdp) Orange	17.35
Union Park (cdp) Orange	16.24
Deltona (city) Volusia	13.59
Egypt Lake-Leto (cdp) Hillsborough	10.35
Town 'n' Country (cdp) Hillsborough	10.29

Salvadoran
Top 10 Places Sorted by Number

Place (place type) County	Number
Miami (city) Miami-Dade	2,394
Homestead (city) Miami-Dade	1,120
Hialeah (city) Miami-Dade	950
Oakland Park (city) Broward	775
Fort Lauderdale (city) Broward	664
Lake Worth (city) Palm Beach	527

Notes: Please refer to the User's Guide for an explanation of data; tables include places with populations > 9,999 and reflect only those areas that meet Summary File 4 population thresholds, therefore there may be less than 10 places listed

Salvadoran
Top 10 Places Sorted by Percent of Hispanic Population

Place (place type) County	Percent
Oakland Park (city) Broward	13.79
Homestead (city) Miami-Dade	6.54
Lake Worth (city) Palm Beach	5.06
Fort Lauderdale (city) Broward	4.78
Miami (city) Miami-Dade	1.00
Hialeah (city) Miami-Dade	0.46

Salvadoran
Top 10 Places Sorted by Percent of Total Population

Place (place type) County	Percent
Homestead (city) Miami-Dade	3.49
Oakland Park (city) Broward	2.48
Lake Worth (city) Palm Beach	1.50
Miami (city) Miami-Dade	0.66
Fort Lauderdale (city) Broward	0.44
Hialeah (city) Miami-Dade	0.42

South American
Top 10 Places Sorted by Number

Place (place type) County	Number
Miami (city) Miami-Dade	15,956
Miami Beach (city) Miami-Dade	12,984
Hialeah (city) Miami-Dade	12,903
The Hammocks (cdp) Miami-Dade	9,791
Kendall (cdp) Miami-Dade	8,700
Fountainbleau (cdp) Miami-Dade	8,376
Pembroke Pines (city) Broward	7,815
Kendall West (cdp) Miami-Dade	7,733
Hollywood (city) Broward	7,347
Kendale Lakes (cdp) Miami-Dade	7,318

South American
Top 10 Places Sorted by Percent of Hispanic Population

Place (place type) County	Percent
Aventura (city) Miami-Dade	45.30
Weston (city) Broward	43.67
Sunny Isles Beach (city) Miami-Dade	40.74
Doral (cdp) Miami-Dade	37.28
Sandalfoot Cove (cdp) Palm Beach	35.73
Plantation (city) Broward	35.29
Ojus (cdp) Miami-Dade	34.77
Key Biscayne (village) Miami-Dade	34.75
Boca Raton (city) Palm Beach	32.74
The Hammocks (cdp) Miami-Dade	31.54

South American
Top 10 Places Sorted by Percent of Total Population

Place (place type) County	Percent
Doral (cdp) Miami-Dade	24.76
The Hammocks (cdp) Miami-Dade	20.64
Kendall West (cdp) Miami-Dade	20.37
Key Biscayne (village) Miami-Dade	17.30
The Crossings (cdp) Miami-Dade	16.83
Sunny Isles Beach (city) Miami-Dade	14.95
Country Club (cdp) Miami-Dade	14.78
Miami Beach (city) Miami-Dade	14.74
Fountainbleau (cdp) Miami-Dade	14.07
Weston (city) Broward	13.39

Spaniard
Top 10 Places Sorted by Number

Place (place type) County	Number
Miami (city) Miami-Dade	951
Tampa (city) Hillsborough	733
Miami Beach (city) Miami-Dade	573
Hialeah (city) Miami-Dade	509

Spaniard
Top 10 Places Sorted by Percent of Hispanic Population

Place (place type) County	Percent
Tampa (city) Hillsborough	1.25
Miami Beach (city) Miami-Dade	1.22
Miami (city) Miami-Dade	0.40
Hialeah (city) Miami-Dade	0.25

Spaniard
Top 10 Places Sorted by Percent of Total Population

Place (place type) County	Percent
Miami Beach (city) Miami-Dade	0.65
Miami (city) Miami-Dade	0.26
Tampa (city) Hillsborough	0.24
Hialeah (city) Miami-Dade	0.22

Uruguayan
Top 10 Places Sorted by Number

Place (place type) County	Number
No places met population threshold.	

Uruguayan
Top 10 Places Sorted by Percent of Hispanic Population

Place (place type) County	Percent
No places met population threshold.	

Uruguayan
Top 10 Places Sorted by Percent of Total Population

Place (place type) County	Percent
No places met population threshold.	

Venezuelan
Top 10 Places Sorted by Number

Place (place type) County	Number
Fountainbleau (cdp) Miami-Dade	2,084
Weston (city) Broward	1,969
Doral (cdp) Miami-Dade	1,841
Miami (city) Miami-Dade	1,760
The Hammocks (cdp) Miami-Dade	1,668
Pembroke Pines (city) Broward	1,480
Miami Beach (city) Miami-Dade	1,456
Kendall (cdp) Miami-Dade	1,453
Kendall West (cdp) Miami-Dade	1,160
Hialeah (city) Miami-Dade	955

Venezuelan
Top 10 Places Sorted by Percent of Hispanic Population

Place (place type) County	Percent
Doral (cdp) Miami-Dade	13.51
Weston (city) Broward	13.07
The Hammocks (cdp) Miami-Dade	5.37
Plantation (city) Broward	4.89
The Crossings (cdp) Miami-Dade	4.64
Fountainbleau (cdp) Miami-Dade	4.02
Kendall (cdp) Miami-Dade	3.86
Kendall West (cdp) Miami-Dade	3.86
Pembroke Pines (city) Broward	3.86
Richmond West (cdp) Miami-Dade	3.12

Venezuelan
Top 10 Places Sorted by Percent of Total Population

Place (place type) County	Percent
Doral (cdp) Miami-Dade	8.97
Weston (city) Broward	4.01
The Hammocks (cdp) Miami-Dade	3.52
Fountainbleau (cdp) Miami-Dade	3.50
Kendall West (cdp) Miami-Dade	3.06
The Crossings (cdp) Miami-Dade	2.64
Richmond West (cdp) Miami-Dade	2.18
Kendall (cdp) Miami-Dade	1.93
Miami Beach (city) Miami-Dade	1.65

Kendale Lakes (cdp) Miami-Dade	1.53

Other Hispanic
Top 10 Places Sorted by Number

Place (place type) County	Number
Miami (city) Miami-Dade	32,320
Hialeah (city) Miami-Dade	20,725
Tampa (city) Hillsborough	12,266
Fountainbleau (cdp) Miami-Dade	8,566
Kendale Lakes (cdp) Miami-Dade	6,905
Miami Beach (city) Miami-Dade	6,425
Pembroke Pines (city) Broward	5,783
The Hammocks (cdp) Miami-Dade	5,769
Hollywood (city) Broward	5,716
Jacksonville (city) Duval	5,400

Other Hispanic
Top 10 Places Sorted by Percent of Hispanic Population

Place (place type) County	Percent
Lake Magdalene (cdp) Hillsborough	24.72
Lakeside (cdp) Clay	24.42
Sandalfoot Cove (cdp) Palm Beach	24.04
Tamarac (city) Broward	23.72
Greater Northdale (cdp) Hillsborough	23.07
North Miami (city) Miami-Dade	22.86
Greater Carrollwood (cdp) Hillsborough	22.34
North Miami Beach (city) Miami-Dade	21.59
Country Walk (cdp) Miami-Dade	21.57
Norland (cdp) Miami-Dade	21.46

Other Hispanic
Top 10 Places Sorted by Percent of Total Population

Place (place type) County	Percent
Fountainbleau (cdp) Miami-Dade	14.39
Sweetwater (city) Miami-Dade	12.97
Kendall West (cdp) Miami-Dade	12.57
Richmond West (cdp) Miami-Dade	12.25
Country Walk (cdp) Miami-Dade	12.17
The Hammocks (cdp) Miami-Dade	12.16
Kendale Lakes (cdp) Miami-Dade	12.14
Doral (cdp) Miami-Dade	11.84
Hialeah Gardens (city) Miami-Dade	11.17
Country Club (cdp) Miami-Dade	10.98

Median Age

Total Population
Top 10 Places Sorted by Number

Place (place type) County	Years
Hamptons at Boca Raton (cdp) Palm Beach	73.0
Naples (city) Collier	60.6
North Fort Myers (cdp) Lee	60.3
Marco Island (city) Collier	59.5
Bayonet Point (cdp) Pasco	57.9
Cypress Lake (cdp) Lee	56.5
Bonita Springs (city) Lee	53.8
Aventura (city) Miami-Dade	52.8
Hallandale (city) Broward	52.8
Tamarac (city) Broward	51.9

Hispanic
Top 10 Places Sorted by Number

Place (place type) County	Years
Palm Coast (city) Flagler	45.4
Westchester (cdp) Miami-Dade	44.4
University Park (cdp) Miami-Dade	43.2
Coral Terrace (cdp) Miami-Dade	42.6
Naples (city) Collier	42.1
Lakeland Highlands (cdp) Polk	41.3
Olympia Heights (cdp) Miami-Dade	41.3
Sunny Isles Beach (city) Miami-Dade	40.2
Miami (city) Miami-Dade	40.0
Coral Gables (city) Miami-Dade	39.7

Notes: Please refer to the User's Guide for an explanation of data; tables include places with populations > 9,999 and reflect only those areas that meet Summary File 4 population thresholds, therefore there may be less than 10 places listed

Argentinian
Top 10 Places Sorted by Number

Place (place type) County	Years
Sunny Isles Beach (city) Miami-Dade	43.3
Hollywood (city) Broward	35.9
Hialeah (city) Miami-Dade	35.0
Kendall (cdp) Miami-Dade	34.8
Fountainbleau (cdp) Miami-Dade	33.6
Miami (city) Miami-Dade	33.6
Miami Beach (city) Miami-Dade	29.4

Bolivian
Top 10 Places Sorted by Number

Place (place type) County	Years
No places met population threshold.	

Central American
Top 10 Places Sorted by Number

Place (place type) County	Years
The Crossings (cdp) Miami-Dade	37.2
Pinecrest (village) Miami-Dade	37.1
Doral (cdp) Miami-Dade	35.7
Deerfield Beach (city) Broward	35.3
Cutler Ridge (cdp) Miami-Dade	34.7
Glenvar Heights (cdp) Miami-Dade	34.6
Sunset (cdp) Miami-Dade	34.6
University Park (cdp) Miami-Dade	34.5
Coral Gables (city) Miami-Dade	34.2
Carol City (cdp) Miami-Dade	33.6

Chilean
Top 10 Places Sorted by Number

Place (place type) County	Years
Hollywood (city) Broward	42.1
Miami (city) Miami-Dade	40.8
Hialeah (city) Miami-Dade	36.4
Miami Beach (city) Miami-Dade	36.0
Kendall (cdp) Miami-Dade	35.5
Fountainbleau (cdp) Miami-Dade	33.7

Colombian
Top 10 Places Sorted by Number

Place (place type) County	Years
Cutler Ridge (cdp) Miami-Dade	40.8
Westchester (cdp) Miami-Dade	40.2
University Park (cdp) Miami-Dade	38.5
Davie (town) Broward	38.1
Miami Springs (city) Miami-Dade	38.1
Margate (city) Broward	37.4
Hialeah (city) Miami-Dade	37.2
Plantation (city) Broward	37.0
Cooper City (city) Broward	36.9
Greater Carrollwood (cdp) Hillsborough	36.8

Costa Rican
Top 10 Places Sorted by Number

Place (place type) County	Years
Miami (city) Miami-Dade	31.3
Hialeah (city) Miami-Dade	30.6

Cuban
Top 10 Places Sorted by Number

Place (place type) County	Years
Sunny Isles Beach (city) Miami-Dade	59.2
Miami Beach (city) Miami-Dade	54.6
Miami (city) Miami-Dade	52.8
Clearwater (city) Pinellas	52.6
Aventura (city) Miami-Dade	50.7
Hallandale (city) Broward	49.8
Key Biscayne (village) Miami-Dade	49.8
Opa-locka (city) Miami-Dade	49.4
University Park (cdp) Miami-Dade	48.6

Brownsville (cdp) Miami-Dade	48.3

Dominican
Top 10 Places Sorted by Number

Place (place type) County	Years
South Miami Heights (cdp) Miami-Dade	38.1
Cape Coral (city) Lee	37.4
Coral Springs (city) Broward	37.1
Tamiami (cdp) Miami-Dade	36.9
Miami Beach (city) Miami-Dade	36.4
Golden Glades (cdp) Miami-Dade	35.1
Hialeah Gardens (city) Miami-Dade	35.0
Miramar (city) Broward	35.0
Miami (city) Miami-Dade	34.8
West Palm Beach (city) Palm Beach	34.8

Ecuadorian
Top 10 Places Sorted by Number

Place (place type) County	Years
Hialeah (city) Miami-Dade	40.7
Tampa (city) Hillsborough	38.5
Miami (city) Miami-Dade	37.4
Pembroke Pines (city) Broward	36.1
Miami Beach (city) Miami-Dade	34.4
Hollywood (city) Broward	33.1
Coral Springs (city) Broward	32.4
Sunrise (city) Broward	30.5
Fountainbleau (cdp) Miami-Dade	28.5

Guatelmalan
Top 10 Places Sorted by Number

Place (place type) County	Years
Miami (city) Miami-Dade	32.6
Hialeah (city) Miami-Dade	30.4
Fort Lauderdale (city) Broward	30.0
Immokalee (cdp) Collier	26.0
Homestead (city) Miami-Dade	24.5
Bonita Springs (city) Lee	24.3
West Palm Beach (city) Palm Beach	24.3
Fort Myers (city) Lee	22.9
Lake Worth (city) Palm Beach	22.3

Honduran
Top 10 Places Sorted by Number

Place (place type) County	Years
Hollywood (city) Broward	35.8
Carol City (cdp) Miami-Dade	34.1
Miami Beach (city) Miami-Dade	32.4
North Miami (city) Miami-Dade	32.4
Tamiami (cdp) Miami-Dade	31.8
Miami (city) Miami-Dade	31.7
Fountainbleau (cdp) Miami-Dade	30.0
North Miami Beach (city) Miami-Dade	29.8
Kendale Lakes (cdp) Miami-Dade	29.7
Hialeah (city) Miami-Dade	29.2

Mexican
Top 10 Places Sorted by Number

Place (place type) County	Years
Doral (cdp) Miami-Dade	33.1
Largo (city) Pinellas	33.1
Pembroke Pines (city) Broward	33.1
Miami Beach (city) Miami-Dade	32.9
Tamiami (cdp) Miami-Dade	32.3
The Hammocks (cdp) Miami-Dade	31.4
Hollywood (city) Broward	30.9
Fountainbleau (cdp) Miami-Dade	30.6
Deerfield Beach (city) Broward	30.5
Hialeah (city) Miami-Dade	29.1

Nicaraguan
Top 10 Places Sorted by Number

Place (place type) County	Years
The Crossings (cdp) Miami-Dade	37.3
Coral Gables (city) Miami-Dade	35.8
Miami Springs (city) Miami-Dade	34.9
University Park (cdp) Miami-Dade	34.8
Miami Beach (city) Miami-Dade	34.3
Pinewood (cdp) Miami-Dade	34.2
North Miami (city) Miami-Dade	33.7
Carol City (cdp) Miami-Dade	33.2
Kendale Lakes (cdp) Miami-Dade	32.9
Coral Terrace (cdp) Miami-Dade	32.5

Panamanian
Top 10 Places Sorted by Number

Place (place type) County	Years
Miami (city) Miami-Dade	36.3
Fountainbleau (cdp) Miami-Dade	33.0
Miramar (city) Broward	32.1
Tampa (city) Hillsborough	31.5
Jacksonville (city) Duval	28.4

Paraguayan
Top 10 Places Sorted by Number

Place (place type) County	Years
No places met population threshold.	

Peruvian
Top 10 Places Sorted by Number

Place (place type) County	Years
Fort Lauderdale (city) Broward	37.1
Miami Beach (city) Miami-Dade	37.0
Miami (city) Miami-Dade	36.8
Davie (town) Broward	36.5
Sunrise (city) Broward	36.4
The Crossings (cdp) Miami-Dade	36.3
Fountainbleau (cdp) Miami-Dade	36.0
Kendale Lakes (cdp) Miami-Dade	35.2
Richmond West (cdp) Miami-Dade	35.2
Hialeah (city) Miami-Dade	34.9

Puerto Rican
Top 10 Places Sorted by Number

Place (place type) County	Years
Ojus (cdp) Miami-Dade	40.4
Westchester (cdp) Miami-Dade	39.6
Coral Terrace (cdp) Miami-Dade	39.5
Land O' Lakes (cdp) Pasco	39.2
Spring Hill (cdp) Hernando	39.0
Palm Coast (city) Flagler	38.5
Forest City (cdp) Seminole	38.1
Miami Lakes (cdp) Miami-Dade	37.8
Jupiter (town) Palm Beach	37.7
Sarasota (city) Sarasota	37.5

Salvadoran
Top 10 Places Sorted by Number

Place (place type) County	Years
Miami (city) Miami-Dade	31.3
Hialeah (city) Miami-Dade	29.5
Oakland Park (city) Broward	26.5
Fort Lauderdale (city) Broward	26.2
Homestead (city) Miami-Dade	24.7
Lake Worth (city) Palm Beach	24.0

South American
Top 10 Places Sorted by Number

Place (place type) County	Years
Westwood Lakes (cdp) Miami-Dade	40.6
Olympia Heights (cdp) Miami-Dade	40.3
West Little River (cdp) Miami-Dade	40.0

Notes: Please refer to the User's Guide for an explanation of data; tables include places with populations > 9,999 and reflect only those areas that meet Summary File 4 population thresholds, therefore there may be less than 10 places listed

Place	Value
Sweetwater (city) Miami-Dade	39.6
Parkland (city) Broward	39.4
Coral Terrace (cdp) Miami-Dade	39.3
Sarasota (city) Sarasota	39.0
Palm Bay (city) Brevard	38.2
Cutler Ridge (cdp) Miami-Dade	37.6
Delray Beach (city) Palm Beach	37.6

Spaniard
Top 10 Places Sorted by Number

Place (place type) County	Years
Hialeah (city) Miami-Dade	55.3
Tampa (city) Hillsborough	54.5
Miami (city) Miami-Dade	54.0
Miami Beach (city) Miami-Dade	40.5

Uruguayan
Top 10 Places Sorted by Number

Place (place type) County	Years
No places met population threshold.	

Venezuelan
Top 10 Places Sorted by Number

Place (place type) County	Years
Miami (city) Miami-Dade	35.1
Kendale Lakes (cdp) Miami-Dade	32.7
Coral Springs (city) Broward	32.4
Kendall West (cdp) Miami-Dade	32.4
Weston (city) Broward	32.4
Pembroke Pines (city) Broward	31.3
Miami Beach (city) Miami-Dade	31.1
Tamiami (cdp) Miami-Dade	31.1
Coral Gables (city) Miami-Dade	30.5
Doral (cdp) Miami-Dade	30.5

Other Hispanic
Top 10 Places Sorted by Number

Place (place type) County	Years
Key West (city) Monroe	40.3
Aventura (city) Miami-Dade	39.3
Spring Hill (cdp) Hernando	38.7
Hallandale (city) Broward	36.8
Boca Raton (city) Palm Beach	36.7
Pompano Beach (city) Broward	36.4
Ojus (cdp) Miami-Dade	35.8
Tampa (city) Hillsborough	35.5
Miami Beach (city) Miami-Dade	35.4
Sunny Isles Beach (city) Miami-Dade	35.0

Average Household Size

Total Population
Top 10 Places Sorted by Number

Place (place type) County	Number
Immokalee (cdp) Collier	3.90
Leisure City (cdp) Miami-Dade	3.65
Princeton (cdp) Miami-Dade	3.60
Scott Lake (cdp) Miami-Dade	3.58
Carol City (cdp) Miami-Dade	3.57
Richmond West (cdp) Miami-Dade	3.57
Westwood Lakes (cdp) Miami-Dade	3.42
Hialeah Gardens (city) Miami-Dade	3.38
West Little River (cdp) Miami-Dade	3.38
Palmetto Estates (cdp) Miami-Dade	3.35

Hispanic
Top 10 Places Sorted by Number

Place (place type) County	Number
Scott Lake (cdp) Miami-Dade	4.60
Fort Pierce (city) Saint Lucie	4.37
Immokalee (cdp) Collier	4.36
Palmetto (city) Manatee	4.34

Place	Value
De Land (city) Volusia	4.33
Zephyrhills (city) Pasco	4.11
Bonita Springs (city) Lee	4.07
Golden Gate (cdp) Collier	4.06
Lake Worth Corridor (cdp) Palm Beach	4.05
Eustis (city) Lake	4.02

Argentinian
Top 10 Places Sorted by Number

Place (place type) County	Number
Hialeah (city) Miami-Dade	3.71
Hollywood (city) Broward	3.31
Kendall (cdp) Miami-Dade	2.82
Fountainbleau (cdp) Miami-Dade	2.67
Miami (city) Miami-Dade	2.57
Miami Beach (city) Miami-Dade	2.34
Sunny Isles Beach (city) Miami-Dade	2.24

Bolivian
Top 10 Places Sorted by Number

Place (place type) County	Number
No places met population threshold.	

Central American
Top 10 Places Sorted by Number

Place (place type) County	Number
Immokalee (cdp) Collier	6.66
Palmetto Estates (cdp) Miami-Dade	4.94
Coral Terrace (cdp) Miami-Dade	4.81
West Palm Beach (city) Palm Beach	4.64
Lake Worth Corridor (cdp) Palm Beach	4.52
South Miami Heights (cdp) Miami-Dade	4.42
West Little River (cdp) Miami-Dade	4.39
Fort Myers (city) Lee	4.35
Pinewood (cdp) Miami-Dade	4.34
Princeton (cdp) Miami-Dade	4.33

Chilean
Top 10 Places Sorted by Number

Place (place type) County	Number
Fountainbleau (cdp) Miami-Dade	3.71
Hollywood (city) Broward	3.31
Miami (city) Miami-Dade	3.30
Hialeah (city) Miami-Dade	3.10
Kendall (cdp) Miami-Dade	3.05
Miami Beach (city) Miami-Dade	1.87

Colombian
Top 10 Places Sorted by Number

Place (place type) County	Number
Meadow Woods (cdp) Orange	4.69
South Miami Heights (cdp) Miami-Dade	4.61
Yeehaw Junction (cdp) Osceola	4.53
Richmond West (cdp) Miami-Dade	4.42
Carol City (cdp) Miami-Dade	4.20
Sandalfoot Cove (cdp) Palm Beach	4.12
Kendale Lakes (cdp) Miami-Dade	4.03
Cutler Ridge (cdp) Miami-Dade	3.99
Cape Coral (city) Lee	3.83
Hialeah Gardens (city) Miami-Dade	3.81

Costa Rican
Top 10 Places Sorted by Number

Place (place type) County	Number
Hialeah (city) Miami-Dade	3.98
Miami (city) Miami-Dade	2.46

Cuban
Top 10 Places Sorted by Number

Place (place type) County	Number
Westwood Lakes (cdp) Miami-Dade	3.68

Place	Value
Pinecrest (village) Miami-Dade	3.56
Cooper City (city) Broward	3.55
Princeton (cdp) Miami-Dade	3.53
Carol City (cdp) Miami-Dade	3.48
Citrus Park (cdp) Hillsborough	3.48
West Little River (cdp) Miami-Dade	3.48
Golden Gate (cdp) Collier	3.47
Cutler (cdp) Miami-Dade	3.44
Greater Northdale (cdp) Hillsborough	3.43

Dominican
Top 10 Places Sorted by Number

Place (place type) County	Number
Weston (city) Broward	4.27
Carol City (cdp) Miami-Dade	4.13
Hialeah Gardens (city) Miami-Dade	4.13
Miramar (city) Broward	4.12
South Miami Heights (cdp) Miami-Dade	4.01
Kendall West (cdp) Miami-Dade	3.98
The Hammocks (cdp) Miami-Dade	3.97
West Little River (cdp) Miami-Dade	3.93
North Miami Beach (city) Miami-Dade	3.85
Richmond West (cdp) Miami-Dade	3.84

Ecuadorian
Top 10 Places Sorted by Number

Place (place type) County	Number
Fountainbleau (cdp) Miami-Dade	4.32
Coral Springs (city) Broward	4.05
Hialeah (city) Miami-Dade	3.64
Sunrise (city) Broward	3.39
Pembroke Pines (city) Broward	3.38
Hollywood (city) Broward	3.26
Miami (city) Miami-Dade	2.88
Tampa (city) Hillsborough	2.72
Miami Beach (city) Miami-Dade	2.15

Guatelmalan
Top 10 Places Sorted by Number

Place (place type) County	Number
Immokalee (cdp) Collier	7.17
West Palm Beach (city) Palm Beach	5.27
Fort Myers (city) Lee	4.96
Lake Worth (city) Palm Beach	4.41
Homestead (city) Miami-Dade	4.17
Bonita Springs (city) Lee	4.02
Fort Lauderdale (city) Broward	3.61
Hialeah (city) Miami-Dade	3.59
Miami (city) Miami-Dade	3.37

Honduran
Top 10 Places Sorted by Number

Place (place type) County	Number
Fountainbleau (cdp) Miami-Dade	4.40
West Little River (cdp) Miami-Dade	4.24
North Miami Beach (city) Miami-Dade	4.17
Kendale Lakes (cdp) Miami-Dade	4.09
Lake Worth (city) Palm Beach	3.93
Hialeah (city) Miami-Dade	3.72
Carol City (cdp) Miami-Dade	3.71
Miami (city) Miami-Dade	3.50
Tamiami (cdp) Miami-Dade	3.49
North Miami (city) Miami-Dade	3.41

Mexican
Top 10 Places Sorted by Number

Place (place type) County	Number
De Land (city) Volusia	5.23
Golden Gate (cdp) Collier	5.18
Lake Worth Corridor (cdp) Palm Beach	5.00
South Miami Heights (cdp) Miami-Dade	4.97
North Lauderdale (city) Broward	4.86
Fort Pierce (city) Saint Lucie	4.84

Notes: Please refer to the User's Guide for an explanation of data; tables include places with populations > 9,999 and reflect only those areas that meet Summary File 4 population thresholds, therefore there may be less than 10 places listed

Place (place type) County	Number
Palmetto (city) Manatee	4.76
Leisure City (cdp) Miami-Dade	4.75
Apopka (city) Orange	4.65
Coconut Creek (city) Broward	4.59

Nicaraguan
Top 10 Places Sorted by Number

Place (place type) County	Number
Palmetto Estates (cdp) Miami-Dade	5.38
Coral Terrace (cdp) Miami-Dade	5.10
South Miami Heights (cdp) Miami-Dade	4.67
West Little River (cdp) Miami-Dade	4.57
Pinewood (cdp) Miami-Dade	4.53
Carol City (cdp) Miami-Dade	4.48
Sweetwater (city) Miami-Dade	4.46
Richmond West (cdp) Miami-Dade	4.29
Miramar (city) Broward	4.28
Tamiami (cdp) Miami-Dade	4.19

Panamanian
Top 10 Places Sorted by Number

Place (place type) County	Number
Miramar (city) Broward	3.15
Fountainbleau (cdp) Miami-Dade	2.83
Jacksonville (city) Duval	2.72
Miami (city) Miami-Dade	2.61
Tampa (city) Hillsborough	2.57

Paraguayan
Top 10 Places Sorted by Number

Place (place type) County	Number
No places met population threshold.	

Peruvian
Top 10 Places Sorted by Number

Place (place type) County	Number
Miramar (city) Broward	4.36
Richmond West (cdp) Miami-Dade	4.10
Hialeah (city) Miami-Dade	4.01
The Hammocks (cdp) Miami-Dade	3.97
Kendall West (cdp) Miami-Dade	3.95
North Lauderdale (city) Broward	3.95
Coral Springs (city) Broward	3.72
Kendall (cdp) Miami-Dade	3.68
Pembroke Pines (city) Broward	3.48
Sunrise (city) Broward	3.47

Puerto Rican
Top 10 Places Sorted by Number

Place (place type) County	Number
Forest City (cdp) Seminole	4.27
West Little River (cdp) Miami-Dade	4.25
Zephyrhills (city) Pasco	4.20
Pinewood (cdp) Miami-Dade	4.08
University Park (cdp) Miami-Dade	4.05
Poinciana (cdp) Osceola	3.93
Palmetto Estates (cdp) Miami-Dade	3.87
Oviedo (city) Seminole	3.79
Longwood (city) Seminole	3.73
Carol City (cdp) Miami-Dade	3.72

Salvadoran
Top 10 Places Sorted by Number

Place (place type) County	Number
Homestead (city) Miami-Dade	4.13
Fort Lauderdale (city) Broward	3.79
Oakland Park (city) Broward	3.52
Lake Worth (city) Palm Beach	3.38
Hialeah (city) Miami-Dade	3.20
Miami (city) Miami-Dade	2.96

South American
Top 10 Places Sorted by Number

Place (place type) County	Number
Meadow Woods (cdp) Orange	4.79
Leisure City (cdp) Miami-Dade	4.60
West Little River (cdp) Miami-Dade	4.43
Carol City (cdp) Miami-Dade	4.30
Yeehaw Junction (cdp) Osceola	4.20
Richmond West (cdp) Miami-Dade	4.18
Pinecrest (village) Miami-Dade	4.17
Westwood Lakes (cdp) Miami-Dade	4.14
Sweetwater (city) Miami-Dade	4.10
Sandalfoot Cove (cdp) Palm Beach	3.95

Spaniard
Top 10 Places Sorted by Number

Place (place type) County	Number
Hialeah (city) Miami-Dade	3.36
Miami Beach (city) Miami-Dade	2.35
Miami (city) Miami-Dade	2.22
Tampa (city) Hillsborough	1.69

Uruguayan
Top 10 Places Sorted by Number

Place (place type) County	Number
No places met population threshold.	

Venezuelan
Top 10 Places Sorted by Number

Place (place type) County	Number
Tamiami (cdp) Miami-Dade	4.17
Richmond West (cdp) Miami-Dade	3.93
Coral Springs (city) Broward	3.68
Plantation (city) Broward	3.48
The Crossings (cdp) Miami-Dade	3.45
Kendall West (cdp) Miami-Dade	3.37
Weston (city) Broward	3.28
Tampa (city) Hillsborough	3.19
Doral (cdp) Miami-Dade	3.18
Pembroke Pines (city) Broward	3.16

Other Hispanic
Top 10 Places Sorted by Number

Place (place type) County	Number
Leisure City (cdp) Miami-Dade	5.58
Immokalee (cdp) Collier	4.61
Opa-locka (city) Miami-Dade	4.46
West Little River (cdp) Miami-Dade	4.32
Olympia Heights (cdp) Miami-Dade	4.30
Bonita Springs (city) Lee	4.17
Richmond West (cdp) Miami-Dade	4.08
Gladeview (cdp) Miami-Dade	3.88
Plant City (city) Hillsborough	3.84
Hialeah Gardens (city) Miami-Dade	3.82

Language Spoken at Home: English Only

Total Population 5 Years and Over Who Speak English-Only at Home
Top 10 Places Sorted by Number

Place (place type) County	Number
Jacksonville (city) Duval	616,988
Tampa (city) Hillsborough	218,362
St. Petersburg (city) Pinellas	206,489
Tallahassee (city) Leon	130,526
Orlando (city) Orange	130,439
Fort Lauderdale (city) Broward	108,442
Hollywood (city) Broward	87,182
Miami (city) Miami-Dade	86,669
Clearwater (city) Pinellas	85,394
Cape Coral (city) Lee	83,549

Total Population 5 Years and Over Who Speak English-Only at Home
Top 10 Places Sorted by Percent

Place (place type) County	Percent
Port St. John (cdp) Brevard	95.01
North Fort Myers (cdp) Lee	94.07
Pensacola (city) Escambia	93.77
Bellview (cdp) Escambia	93.50
Jensen Beach (cdp) Martin	93.45
Titusville (city) Brevard	93.44
Leesburg (city) Lake	93.42
Jacksonville Beach (city) Duval	93.08
Rockledge (city) Brevard	92.94
Ferry Pass (cdp) Escambia	92.93

Hispanics 5 Years and Over Who Speak English-Only at Home
Top 10 Places Sorted by Number

Place (place type) County	Number
Miami (city) Miami-Dade	12,945
Tampa (city) Hillsborough	10,107
Hialeah (city) Miami-Dade	8,606
Jacksonville (city) Duval	8,444
Pembroke Pines (city) Broward	4,010
Orlando (city) Orange	4,005
Hollywood (city) Broward	3,667
Miami Beach (city) Miami-Dade	3,150
St. Petersburg (city) Pinellas	2,724
Kendall (cdp) Miami-Dade	2,704

Hispanics 5 Years and Over Who Speak English-Only at Home
Top 10 Places Sorted by Percent

Place (place type) County	Percent
Callaway (city) Bay	61.01
Port St. John (cdp) Brevard	59.24
Wright (cdp) Okaloosa	56.56
Warrington (cdp) Escambia	53.30
Bayonet Point (cdp) Pasco	50.77
Myrtle Grove (cdp) Escambia	49.57
Titusville (city) Brevard	47.39
Ferry Pass (cdp) Escambia	46.36
West Pensacola (cdp) Escambia	42.83
Pensacola (city) Escambia	41.97

Argentinians 5 Years and Over Who Speak English-Only at Home
Top 10 Places Sorted by Number

Place (place type) County	Number
Miami Beach (city) Miami-Dade	84
Miami (city) Miami-Dade	75
Sunny Isles Beach (city) Miami-Dade	51
Hollywood (city) Broward	36
Kendall (cdp) Miami-Dade	35
Fountainbleau (cdp) Miami-Dade	6
Hialeah (city) Miami-Dade	0

Argentinians 5 Years and Over Who Speak English-Only at Home
Top 10 Places Sorted by Percent

Place (place type) County	Percent
Sunny Isles Beach (city) Miami-Dade	9.17
Hollywood (city) Broward	6.56
Kendall (cdp) Miami-Dade	5.55
Miami (city) Miami-Dade	3.93
Miami Beach (city) Miami-Dade	2.87
Fountainbleau (cdp) Miami-Dade	1.39
Hialeah (city) Miami-Dade	0.00

Notes: Please refer to the User's Guide for an explanation of data; tables include places with populations > 9,999 and reflect only those areas that meet Summary File 4 population thresholds, therefore there may be less than 10 places listed

Bolivians 5 Years and Over Who Speak English-Only at Home
Top 10 Places Sorted by Number

Place (place type) County	Number
No places met population threshold.	

Bolivians 5 Years and Over Who Speak English-Only at Home
Top 10 Places Sorted by Percent

Place (place type) County	Percent
No places met population threshold.	

Central Americans 5 Years and Over Who Speak English-Only at Home
Top 10 Places Sorted by Number

Place (place type) County	Number
Miami (city) Miami-Dade	1,726
Tampa (city) Hillsborough	638
Hialeah (city) Miami-Dade	460
Fountainbleau (cdp) Miami-Dade	378
Jacksonville (city) Duval	348
Kendall (cdp) Miami-Dade	252
Homestead (city) Miami-Dade	204
Miami Beach (city) Miami-Dade	176
Pembroke Pines (city) Broward	156
Hollywood (city) Broward	150

Central Americans 5 Years and Over Who Speak English-Only at Home
Top 10 Places Sorted by Percent

Place (place type) County	Percent
Brandon (cdp) Hillsborough	25.41
Plantation (city) Broward	23.06
Tampa (city) Hillsborough	21.03
Jacksonville (city) Duval	20.64
Yeehaw Junction (cdp) Osceola	14.32
Coral Springs (city) Broward	13.36
Margate (city) Broward	13.35
Boynton Beach (city) Palm Beach	12.67
Opa-locka (city) Miami-Dade	12.58
Bonita Springs (city) Lee	11.42

Chileans 5 Years and Over Who Speak English-Only at Home
Top 10 Places Sorted by Number

Place (place type) County	Number
Miami Beach (city) Miami-Dade	104
Hialeah (city) Miami-Dade	67
Kendall (cdp) Miami-Dade	38
Miami (city) Miami-Dade	26
Hollywood (city) Broward	7
Fountainbleau (cdp) Miami-Dade	0

Chileans 5 Years and Over Who Speak English-Only at Home
Top 10 Places Sorted by Percent

Place (place type) County	Percent
Miami Beach (city) Miami-Dade	14.40
Hialeah (city) Miami-Dade	8.93
Kendall (cdp) Miami-Dade	8.12
Miami (city) Miami-Dade	2.96
Hollywood (city) Broward	1.99
Fountainbleau (cdp) Miami-Dade	0.00

Colombians 5 Years and Over Who Speak English-Only at Home
Top 10 Places Sorted by Number

Place (place type) County	Number
Miami (city) Miami-Dade	255
Miami Beach (city) Miami-Dade	236
Hialeah (city) Miami-Dade	212
Hollywood (city) Broward	205
Pembroke Pines (city) Broward	179
Plantation (city) Broward	175
Jacksonville (city) Duval	167
Tampa (city) Hillsborough	126
Kendall (cdp) Miami-Dade	124
Fountainbleau (cdp) Miami-Dade	117

Colombians 5 Years and Over Who Speak English-Only at Home
Top 10 Places Sorted by Percent

Place (place type) County	Percent
Cooper City (city) Broward	20.70
Jacksonville (city) Duval	13.15
Pompano Beach (city) Broward	12.34
Cape Coral (city) Lee	11.11
Sandalfoot Cove (cdp) Palm Beach	10.38
University Park (cdp) Miami-Dade	8.96
Fort Lauderdale (city) Broward	8.85
Plantation (city) Broward	8.50
Coconut Creek (city) Broward	8.26
Cutler Ridge (cdp) Miami-Dade	8.21

Costa Ricans 5 Years and Over Who Speak English-Only at Home
Top 10 Places Sorted by Number

Place (place type) County	Number
Miami (city) Miami-Dade	57
Hialeah (city) Miami-Dade	0

Costa Ricans 5 Years and Over Who Speak English-Only at Home
Top 10 Places Sorted by Percent

Place (place type) County	Percent
Miami (city) Miami-Dade	7.17
Hialeah (city) Miami-Dade	0.00

Cubans 5 Years and Over Who Speak English-Only at Home
Top 10 Places Sorted by Number

Place (place type) County	Number
Miami (city) Miami-Dade	6,769
Hialeah (city) Miami-Dade	6,190
Tampa (city) Hillsborough	1,971
Miami Beach (city) Miami-Dade	1,325
Kendall (cdp) Miami-Dade	1,179
Pembroke Pines (city) Broward	1,143
Tamiami (cdp) Miami-Dade	1,136
Westchester (cdp) Miami-Dade	912
Kendale Lakes (cdp) Miami-Dade	868
Hollywood (city) Broward	815

Cubans 5 Years and Over Who Speak English-Only at Home
Top 10 Places Sorted by Percent

Place (place type) County	Percent
Gainesville (city) Alachua	36.31
Brandon (cdp) Hillsborough	32.71
Lake Magdalene (cdp) Hillsborough	31.81
Pompano Beach (city) Broward	28.81
Spring Hill (cdp) Hernando	26.09
Tallahassee (city) Leon	25.60
Greater Northdale (cdp) Hillsborough	25.24
Royal Palm Beach (village) Palm Beach	24.89
Weston (city) Broward	24.77
Key West (city) Monroe	23.54

Dominicans 5 Years and Over Who Speak English-Only at Home
Top 10 Places Sorted by Number

Place (place type) County	Number
Miami (city) Miami-Dade	482
Hollywood (city) Broward	118
Hialeah (city) Miami-Dade	109
Orlando (city) Orange	106
Carol City (cdp) Miami-Dade	79
Kissimmee (city) Osceola	63
The Hammocks (cdp) Miami-Dade	60
Coral Springs (city) Broward	57
Weston (city) Broward	54
Pembroke Pines (city) Broward	52

Dominicans 5 Years and Over Who Speak English-Only at Home
Top 10 Places Sorted by Percent

Place (place type) County	Percent
Weston (city) Broward	14.10
Coral Springs (city) Broward	10.78
Orlando (city) Orange	9.15
Egypt Lake-Leto (cdp) Hillsborough	8.92
West Palm Beach (city) Palm Beach	8.56
Jacksonville (city) Duval	8.24
Hollywood (city) Broward	7.41
Miami (city) Miami-Dade	7.01
Sunrise (city) Broward	6.09
Kissimmee (city) Osceola	5.83

Ecuadorians 5 Years and Over Who Speak English-Only at Home
Top 10 Places Sorted by Number

Place (place type) County	Number
Miami (city) Miami-Dade	134
Coral Springs (city) Broward	67
Hollywood (city) Broward	54
Miami Beach (city) Miami-Dade	46
Tampa (city) Hillsborough	34
Hialeah (city) Miami-Dade	33
Sunrise (city) Broward	29
Fountainbleau (cdp) Miami-Dade	24
Pembroke Pines (city) Broward	23

Ecuadorians 5 Years and Over Who Speak English-Only at Home
Top 10 Places Sorted by Percent

Place (place type) County	Percent
Hollywood (city) Broward	8.87
Tampa (city) Hillsborough	8.85
Miami (city) Miami-Dade	7.92
Coral Springs (city) Broward	7.49
Miami Beach (city) Miami-Dade	7.13
Sunrise (city) Broward	5.75
Pembroke Pines (city) Broward	4.79
Fountainbleau (cdp) Miami-Dade	3.12
Hialeah (city) Miami-Dade	2.75

Guatelmalans 5 Years and Over Who Speak English-Only at Home
Top 10 Places Sorted by Number

Place (place type) County	Number
Miami (city) Miami-Dade	140
West Palm Beach (city) Palm Beach	134
Immokalee (cdp) Collier	99
Homestead (city) Miami-Dade	77
Lake Worth (city) Palm Beach	35
Fort Myers (city) Lee	21
Fort Lauderdale (city) Broward	8
Bonita Springs (city) Lee	0
Hialeah (city) Miami-Dade	0

Guatelmalans 5 Years and Over Who Speak English-Only at Home
Top 10 Places Sorted by Percent

Place (place type) County	Percent
Immokalee (cdp) Collier	9.45
West Palm Beach (city) Palm Beach	6.99

Place (place type) County	
Fort Myers (city) Lee	6.02
Homestead (city) Miami-Dade	5.77
Miami (city) Miami-Dade	5.24
Fort Lauderdale (city) Broward	2.22
Lake Worth (city) Palm Beach	2.05
Bonita Springs (city) Lee	0.00
Hialeah (city) Miami-Dade	0.00

Hondurans 5 Years and Over Who Speak English-Only at Home
Top 10 Places Sorted by Number

Place (place type) County	Number
Miami (city) Miami-Dade	581
Tampa (city) Hillsborough	168
Hialeah (city) Miami-Dade	67
North Miami Beach (city) Miami-Dade	49
North Miami (city) Miami-Dade	34
Carol City (cdp) Miami-Dade	33
Miami Beach (city) Miami-Dade	33
Fountainbleau (cdp) Miami-Dade	15
Hollywood (city) Broward	14
West Little River (cdp) Miami-Dade	14

Hondurans 5 Years and Over Who Speak English-Only at Home
Top 10 Places Sorted by Percent

Place (place type) County	Percent
Tampa (city) Hillsborough	20.82
North Miami Beach (city) Miami-Dade	9.90
Carol City (cdp) Miami-Dade	6.55
North Miami (city) Miami-Dade	5.92
Miami (city) Miami-Dade	4.49
Miami Beach (city) Miami-Dade	4.27
Hollywood (city) Broward	3.48
Hialeah (city) Miami-Dade	2.64
Fountainbleau (cdp) Miami-Dade	2.40
Kendale Lakes (cdp) Miami-Dade	1.58

Mexicans 5 Years and Over Who Speak English-Only at Home
Top 10 Places Sorted by Number

Place (place type) County	Number
Jacksonville (city) Duval	2,601
Tampa (city) Hillsborough	1,251
Immokalee (cdp) Collier	803
St. Petersburg (city) Pinellas	740
Golden Gate (cdp) Collier	559
Clearwater (city) Pinellas	555
Orlando (city) Orange	531
Bradenton (city) Manatee	495
Palmetto (city) Manatee	466
Port St. Lucie (city) Saint Lucie	402

Mexicans 5 Years and Over Who Speak English-Only at Home
Top 10 Places Sorted by Percent

Place (place type) County	Percent
Wright (cdp) Okaloosa	62.57
Panama City (city) Bay	56.02
Jacksonville (city) Duval	53.17
Largo (city) Pinellas	52.27
Palm Bay (city) Brevard	51.29
Gainesville (city) Alachua	47.29
St. Petersburg (city) Pinellas	47.04
Tallahassee (city) Leon	44.74
Plantation (city) Broward	42.88
Port St. Lucie (city) Saint Lucie	40.85

Nicaraguans 5 Years and Over Who Speak English-Only at Home
Top 10 Places Sorted by Number

Place (place type) County	Number
Miami (city) Miami-Dade	758
Hialeah (city) Miami-Dade	316
Fountainbleau (cdp) Miami-Dade	310
Tampa (city) Hillsborough	119
Miami Beach (city) Miami-Dade	110
Kendall (cdp) Miami-Dade	102
Kendale Lakes (cdp) Miami-Dade	95
Sweetwater (city) Miami-Dade	81
Carol City (cdp) Miami-Dade	77
Kendall West (cdp) Miami-Dade	76

Nicaraguans 5 Years and Over Who Speak English-Only at Home
Top 10 Places Sorted by Percent

Place (place type) County	Percent
Tampa (city) Hillsborough	26.21
Miami Beach (city) Miami-Dade	11.17
North Miami (city) Miami-Dade	7.81
Miramar (city) Broward	6.57
Carol City (cdp) Miami-Dade	5.61
Coral Terrace (cdp) Miami-Dade	5.53
Pinewood (cdp) Miami-Dade	5.36
Hollywood (city) Broward	5.34
Fountainbleau (cdp) Miami-Dade	5.26
South Miami Heights (cdp) Miami-Dade	5.04

Panamanians 5 Years and Over Who Speak English-Only at Home
Top 10 Places Sorted by Number

Place (place type) County	Number
Tampa (city) Hillsborough	170
Jacksonville (city) Duval	149
Miramar (city) Broward	81
Fountainbleau (cdp) Miami-Dade	36
Miami (city) Miami-Dade	10

Panamanians 5 Years and Over Who Speak English-Only at Home
Top 10 Places Sorted by Percent

Place (place type) County	Percent
Tampa (city) Hillsborough	27.91
Jacksonville (city) Duval	26.05
Miramar (city) Broward	23.48
Fountainbleau (cdp) Miami-Dade	7.05
Miami (city) Miami-Dade	1.17

Paraguayans 5 Years and Over Who Speak English-Only at Home
Top 10 Places Sorted by Number

Place (place type) County	Number
No places met population threshold.	

Paraguayans 5 Years and Over Who Speak English-Only at Home
Top 10 Places Sorted by Percent

Place (place type) County	Percent
No places met population threshold.	

Peruvians 5 Years and Over Who Speak English-Only at Home
Top 10 Places Sorted by Number

Place (place type) County	Number
Miami (city) Miami-Dade	104
Pembroke Pines (city) Broward	98
Hollywood (city) Broward	96
Kendall (cdp) Miami-Dade	72
Kendale Lakes (cdp) Miami-Dade	70
Kendall West (cdp) Miami-Dade	59
Miami Beach (city) Miami-Dade	46
North Lauderdale (city) Broward	44
Weston (city) Broward	44
Davie (town) Broward	43

Peruvians 5 Years and Over Who Speak English-Only at Home
Top 10 Places Sorted by Percent

Place (place type) County	Percent
Orlando (city) Orange	9.07
Fort Lauderdale (city) Broward	8.97
North Lauderdale (city) Broward	8.09
Hollywood (city) Broward	7.74
Richmond West (cdp) Miami-Dade	7.61
Kendale Lakes (cdp) Miami-Dade	7.51
Pembroke Pines (city) Broward	7.19
Davie (town) Broward	7.18
Sunrise (city) Broward	6.38
Weston (city) Broward	6.25

Puerto Ricans 5 Years and Over Who Speak English-Only at Home
Top 10 Places Sorted by Number

Place (place type) County	Number
Jacksonville (city) Duval	2,459
Tampa (city) Hillsborough	2,273
Orlando (city) Orange	1,824
Deltona (city) Volusia	1,502
Pembroke Pines (city) Broward	1,302
Kissimmee (city) Osceola	1,293
Hollywood (city) Broward	1,198
Town 'n' Country (cdp) Hillsborough	1,008
Coral Springs (city) Broward	982
Brandon (cdp) Hillsborough	893

Puerto Ricans 5 Years and Over Who Speak English-Only at Home
Top 10 Places Sorted by Percent

Place (place type) County	Percent
Dunedin (city) Pinellas	46.39
Titusville (city) Brevard	42.76
Tallahassee (city) Leon	42.41
Lakeside (cdp) Clay	42.01
Jasmine Estates (cdp) Pasco	41.72
Port Orange (city) Volusia	39.79
Merritt Island (cdp) Brevard	39.51
Boca Raton (city) Palm Beach	39.43
North Fort Myers (cdp) Lee	36.53
Pompano Beach (city) Broward	34.84

Salvadorans 5 Years and Over Who Speak English-Only at Home
Top 10 Places Sorted by Number

Place (place type) County	Number
Miami (city) Miami-Dade	123
Homestead (city) Miami-Dade	42
Fort Lauderdale (city) Broward	23
Hialeah (city) Miami-Dade	9
Lake Worth (city) Palm Beach	0
Oakland Park (city) Broward	0

Salvadorans 5 Years and Over Who Speak English-Only at Home
Top 10 Places Sorted by Percent

Place (place type) County	Percent
Miami (city) Miami-Dade	5.40
Homestead (city) Miami-Dade	4.45
Fort Lauderdale (city) Broward	3.57
Hialeah (city) Miami-Dade	1.01
Lake Worth (city) Palm Beach	0.00
Oakland Park (city) Broward	0.00

South Americans 5 Years and Over Who Speak English-Only at Home
Top 10 Places Sorted by Number

Place (place type) County	Number
Miami (city) Miami-Dade	713

Notes: Please refer to the User's Guide for an explanation of data; tables include places with populations > 9,999 and reflect only those areas that meet Summary File 4 population thresholds, therefore there may be less than 10 places listed

Place (place type) County	Number
Miami Beach (city) Miami-Dade	608
Hollywood (city) Broward	443
Pembroke Pines (city) Broward	439
Kendall (cdp) Miami-Dade	384
Hialeah (city) Miami-Dade	334
Tallahassee (city) Leon	324
Jacksonville (city) Duval	310
Fort Lauderdale (city) Broward	309
Plantation (city) Broward	294

South Americans 5 Years and Over Who Speak English-Only at Home
Top 10 Places Sorted by Percent

Place (place type) County	Percent
Tallahassee (city) Leon	42.13
Palm Bay (city) Brevard	25.40
Deltona (city) Volusia	21.92
Cooper City (city) Broward	19.14
Gainesville (city) Alachua	15.14
Jacksonville (city) Duval	12.80
Delray Beach (city) Palm Beach	12.56
St. Petersburg (city) Pinellas	11.82
Brandon (cdp) Hillsborough	11.11
Coconut Creek (city) Broward	10.95

Spaniards 5 Years and Over Who Speak English-Only at Home
Top 10 Places Sorted by Number

Place (place type) County	Number
Tampa (city) Hillsborough	185
Miami (city) Miami-Dade	37
Miami Beach (city) Miami-Dade	36
Hialeah (city) Miami-Dade	25

Spaniards 5 Years and Over Who Speak English-Only at Home
Top 10 Places Sorted by Percent

Place (place type) County	Percent
Tampa (city) Hillsborough	26.43
Miami Beach (city) Miami-Dade	6.41
Hialeah (city) Miami-Dade	5.10
Miami (city) Miami-Dade	3.98

Uruguayans 5 Years and Over Who Speak English-Only at Home
Top 10 Places Sorted by Number

Place (place type) County	Number
No places met population threshold.

Uruguayans 5 Years and Over Who Speak English-Only at Home
Top 10 Places Sorted by Percent

Place (place type) County	Percent
No places met population threshold.

Venezuelans 5 Years and Over Who Speak English-Only at Home
Top 10 Places Sorted by Number

Place (place type) County	Number
Tampa (city) Hillsborough	87
Miami (city) Miami-Dade	81
Kendall (cdp) Miami-Dade	77
Coral Springs (city) Broward	62
The Hammocks (cdp) Miami-Dade	61
Hollywood (city) Broward	41
Miami Beach (city) Miami-Dade	40
Orlando (city) Orange	38
Plantation (city) Broward	37
Pembroke Pines (city) Broward	35

Venezuelans 5 Years and Over Who Speak English-Only at Home
Top 10 Places Sorted by Percent

Place (place type) County	Percent
Tampa (city) Hillsborough	15.59
Coral Springs (city) Broward	12.89
Plantation (city) Broward	7.58
Hollywood (city) Broward	7.00
Kendall (cdp) Miami-Dade	5.60
Orlando (city) Orange	5.19
Miami (city) Miami-Dade	4.80
The Hammocks (cdp) Miami-Dade	3.90
Kendale Lakes (cdp) Miami-Dade	3.38
Miami Beach (city) Miami-Dade	2.84

Other Hispanics 5 Years and Over Who Speak English-Only at Home
Top 10 Places Sorted by Number

Place (place type) County	Number
Tampa (city) Hillsborough	3,466
Miami (city) Miami-Dade	2,036
Jacksonville (city) Duval	1,868
Hialeah (city) Miami-Dade	1,023
Town 'n' Country (cdp) Hillsborough	766
Orlando (city) Orange	655
Hollywood (city) Broward	631
Pembroke Pines (city) Broward	619
Egypt Lake-Leto (cdp) Hillsborough	609
St. Petersburg (city) Pinellas	581

Other Hispanics 5 Years and Over Who Speak English-Only at Home
Top 10 Places Sorted by Percent

Place (place type) County	Percent
Tallahassee (city) Leon	50.76
Greater Northdale (cdp) Hillsborough	48.37
St. Petersburg (city) Pinellas	44.18
Greater Carrollwood (cdp) Hillsborough	42.83
Apopka (city) Orange	40.29
Brandon (cdp) Hillsborough	40.21
Jacksonville (city) Duval	39.99
Spring Hill (cdp) Hernando	39.76
University (cdp) Hillsborough	39.05
Key West (city) Monroe	38.60

Language Spoken at Home: Spanish

Total Population 5 Years and Over Who Speak Spanish at Home
Top 10 Places Sorted by Number

Place (place type) County	Number
Miami (city) Miami-Dade	227,293
Hialeah (city) Miami-Dade	195,884
Fountainbleau (cdp) Miami-Dade	50,247
Tampa (city) Hillsborough	50,106
Tamiami (cdp) Miami-Dade	47,435
Miami Beach (city) Miami-Dade	46,174
Kendale Lakes (cdp) Miami-Dade	43,425
Kendall (cdp) Miami-Dade	36,760
Pembroke Pines (city) Broward	35,320
The Hammocks (cdp) Miami-Dade	30,890

Total Population 5 Years and Over Who Speak Spanish at Home
Top 10 Places Sorted by Percent

Place (place type) County	Percent
Hialeah Gardens (city) Miami-Dade	95.13
Sweetwater (city) Miami-Dade	92.39
Tamiami (cdp) Miami-Dade	91.91
Hialeah (city) Miami-Dade	91.88
Fountainbleau (cdp) Miami-Dade	90.14
Westchester (cdp) Miami-Dade	87.99
University Park (cdp) Miami-Dade	85.61

Coral Terrace (cdp) Miami-Dade	84.04
Kendall West (cdp) Miami-Dade	83.05
Kendale Lakes (cdp) Miami-Dade	81.46

Hispanics 5 Years and Over Who Speak Spanish at Home
Top 10 Places Sorted by Number

Place (place type) County	Number
Miami (city) Miami-Dade	213,295
Hialeah (city) Miami-Dade	185,933
Fountainbleau (cdp) Miami-Dade	47,278
Tamiami (cdp) Miami-Dade	43,701
Tampa (city) Hillsborough	43,611
Miami Beach (city) Miami-Dade	41,617
Kendale Lakes (cdp) Miami-Dade	39,673
Kendall (cdp) Miami-Dade	32,456
Pembroke Pines (city) Broward	31,076
The Hammocks (cdp) Miami-Dade	27,580

Hispanics 5 Years and Over Who Speak Spanish at Home
Top 10 Places Sorted by Percent

Place (place type) County	Percent
Hialeah Gardens (city) Miami-Dade	97.34
Kendale Lakes (cdp) Miami-Dade	96.11
Tamiami (cdp) Miami-Dade	96.09
Fountainbleau (cdp) Miami-Dade	96.01
Olympia Heights (cdp) Miami-Dade	95.49
Hialeah (city) Miami-Dade	95.46
Westchester (cdp) Miami-Dade	95.22
University Park (cdp) Miami-Dade	95.20
Country Club (cdp) Miami-Dade	94.95
Doral (cdp) Miami-Dade	94.91

Argentinians 5 Years and Over Who Speak Spanish at Home
Top 10 Places Sorted by Number

Place (place type) County	Number
Miami Beach (city) Miami-Dade	2,783
Miami (city) Miami-Dade	1,810
Kendall (cdp) Miami-Dade	587
Sunny Isles Beach (city) Miami-Dade	505
Hollywood (city) Broward	496
Fountainbleau (cdp) Miami-Dade	402
Hialeah (city) Miami-Dade	389

Argentinians 5 Years and Over Who Speak Spanish at Home
Top 10 Places Sorted by Percent

Place (place type) County	Percent
Hialeah (city) Miami-Dade	100.00
Miami Beach (city) Miami-Dade	95.15
Miami (city) Miami-Dade	94.96
Fountainbleau (cdp) Miami-Dade	93.27
Kendall (cdp) Miami-Dade	93.03
Sunny Isles Beach (city) Miami-Dade	90.83
Hollywood (city) Broward	90.35

Bolivians 5 Years and Over Who Speak Spanish at Home
Top 10 Places Sorted by Number

Place (place type) County	Number
No places met population threshold.

Bolivians 5 Years and Over Who Speak Spanish at Home
Top 10 Places Sorted by Percent

Place (place type) County	Percent
No places met population threshold.

Notes: Please refer to the User's Guide for an explanation of data; tables include places with populations > 9,999 and reflect only those areas that meet Summary File 4 population thresholds, therefore there may be less than 10 places listed

Central Americans 5 Years and Over Who Speak Spanish at Home
Top 10 Places Sorted by Number

Place (place type) County	Number
Miami (city) Miami-Dade	39,899
Hialeah (city) Miami-Dade	14,810
Fountainbleau (cdp) Miami-Dade	7,389
Kendale Lakes (cdp) Miami-Dade	3,776
Tamiami (cdp) Miami-Dade	3,520
Kendall (cdp) Miami-Dade	3,425
Homestead (city) Miami-Dade	2,908
Miami Beach (city) Miami-Dade	2,546
Lake Worth (city) Palm Beach	2,428
Kendall West (cdp) Miami-Dade	2,403

Central Americans 5 Years and Over Who Speak Spanish at Home
Top 10 Places Sorted by Percent

Place (place type) County	Percent
Hialeah Gardens (city) Miami-Dade	98.75
Country Walk (cdp) Miami-Dade	98.21
University Park (cdp) Miami-Dade	98.09
The Hammocks (cdp) Miami-Dade	98.03
Bradenton (city) Manatee	97.97
Country Club (cdp) Miami-Dade	97.57
West Little River (cdp) Miami-Dade	97.46
Kendale Lakes (cdp) Miami-Dade	97.34
Gladeview (cdp) Miami-Dade	97.24
Lake Worth Corridor (cdp) Palm Beach	97.08

Chileans 5 Years and Over Who Speak Spanish at Home
Top 10 Places Sorted by Number

Place (place type) County	Number
Miami (city) Miami-Dade	843
Hialeah (city) Miami-Dade	683
Fountainbleau (cdp) Miami-Dade	626
Miami Beach (city) Miami-Dade	618
Kendall (cdp) Miami-Dade	424
Hollywood (city) Broward	345

Chileans 5 Years and Over Who Speak Spanish at Home
Top 10 Places Sorted by Percent

Place (place type) County	Percent
Fountainbleau (cdp) Miami-Dade	98.12
Hollywood (city) Broward	98.01
Miami (city) Miami-Dade	95.90
Hialeah (city) Miami-Dade	91.07
Kendall (cdp) Miami-Dade	90.60
Miami Beach (city) Miami-Dade	85.60

Colombians 5 Years and Over Who Speak Spanish at Home
Top 10 Places Sorted by Number

Place (place type) County	Number
Hialeah (city) Miami-Dade	7,273
Miami (city) Miami-Dade	5,496
The Hammocks (cdp) Miami-Dade	4,684
Miami Beach (city) Miami-Dade	4,050
Kendall West (cdp) Miami-Dade	3,963
Kendall (cdp) Miami-Dade	3,795
Kendale Lakes (cdp) Miami-Dade	3,743
Country Club (cdp) Miami-Dade	3,401
Pembroke Pines (city) Broward	3,083
Hollywood (city) Broward	2,960

Colombians 5 Years and Over Who Speak Spanish at Home
Top 10 Places Sorted by Percent

Place (place type) County	Percent
Deerfield Beach (city) Broward	100.00

Place (place type) County	
Oak Ridge (cdp) Orange	100.00
Doral (cdp) Miami-Dade	98.50
Kendale Lakes (cdp) Miami-Dade	98.34
Tamiami (cdp) Miami-Dade	98.28
Sunset (cdp) Miami-Dade	98.27
The Hammocks (cdp) Miami-Dade	97.77
Aventura (city) Miami-Dade	97.71
Country Club (cdp) Miami-Dade	97.48
Tamarac (city) Broward	97.46

Costa Ricans 5 Years and Over Who Speak Spanish at Home
Top 10 Places Sorted by Number

Place (place type) County	Number
Miami (city) Miami-Dade	728
Hialeah (city) Miami-Dade	515

Costa Ricans 5 Years and Over Who Speak Spanish at Home
Top 10 Places Sorted by Percent

Place (place type) County	Percent
Hialeah (city) Miami-Dade	100.00
Miami (city) Miami-Dade	91.57

Cubans 5 Years and Over Who Speak Spanish at Home
Top 10 Places Sorted by Number

Place (place type) County	Number
Hialeah (city) Miami-Dade	129,600
Miami (city) Miami-Dade	114,426
Tamiami (cdp) Miami-Dade	30,022
Fountainbleau (cdp) Miami-Dade	20,915
Kendale Lakes (cdp) Miami-Dade	20,107
Westchester (cdp) Miami-Dade	18,859
Miami Beach (city) Miami-Dade	16,439
University Park (cdp) Miami-Dade	14,574
Kendall (cdp) Miami-Dade	13,857
Coral Terrace (cdp) Miami-Dade	13,775

Cubans 5 Years and Over Who Speak Spanish at Home
Top 10 Places Sorted by Percent

Place (place type) County	Percent
Hialeah Gardens (city) Miami-Dade	97.83
Fountainbleau (cdp) Miami-Dade	96.26
Tamiami (cdp) Miami-Dade	96.26
Glenvar Heights (cdp) Miami-Dade	96.20
South Miami Heights (cdp) Miami-Dade	96.02
Kendale Lakes (cdp) Miami-Dade	95.78
Olympia Heights (cdp) Miami-Dade	95.60
University Park (cdp) Miami-Dade	95.40
West Little River (cdp) Miami-Dade	95.38
Hialeah (city) Miami-Dade	95.37

Dominicans 5 Years and Over Who Speak Spanish at Home
Top 10 Places Sorted by Number

Place (place type) County	Number
Miami (city) Miami-Dade	6,386
Hialeah (city) Miami-Dade	4,582
Fountainbleau (cdp) Miami-Dade	1,821
Carol City (cdp) Miami-Dade	1,677
Pembroke Pines (city) Broward	1,608
Hollywood (city) Broward	1,475
The Hammocks (cdp) Miami-Dade	1,343
Miami Beach (city) Miami-Dade	1,317
Miramar (city) Broward	1,276
Country Club (cdp) Miami-Dade	1,255

Dominicans 5 Years and Over Who Speak Spanish at Home
Top 10 Places Sorted by Percent

Place (place type) County	Percent
Country Club (cdp) Miami-Dade	100.00
Fountainbleau (cdp) Miami-Dade	99.24
Hialeah Gardens (city) Miami-Dade	99.08
Kendale Lakes (cdp) Miami-Dade	98.58
Kendall West (cdp) Miami-Dade	98.15
North Miami Beach (city) Miami-Dade	97.94
Hialeah (city) Miami-Dade	97.68
Yeehaw Junction (cdp) Osceola	97.66
Miramar (city) Broward	97.03
Oak Ridge (cdp) Orange	96.93

Ecuadorians 5 Years and Over Who Speak Spanish at Home
Top 10 Places Sorted by Number

Place (place type) County	Number
Miami (city) Miami-Dade	1,558
Hialeah (city) Miami-Dade	1,167
Coral Springs (city) Broward	827
Fountainbleau (cdp) Miami-Dade	746
Miami Beach (city) Miami-Dade	599
Hollywood (city) Broward	555
Sunrise (city) Broward	475
Pembroke Pines (city) Broward	457
Tampa (city) Hillsborough	337

Ecuadorians 5 Years and Over Who Speak Spanish at Home
Top 10 Places Sorted by Percent

Place (place type) County	Percent
Hialeah (city) Miami-Dade	97.25
Fountainbleau (cdp) Miami-Dade	96.88
Pembroke Pines (city) Broward	95.21
Sunrise (city) Broward	94.25
Miami Beach (city) Miami-Dade	92.87
Coral Springs (city) Broward	92.51
Miami (city) Miami-Dade	92.08
Hollywood (city) Broward	91.13
Tampa (city) Hillsborough	87.76

Guatelmalans 5 Years and Over Who Speak Spanish at Home
Top 10 Places Sorted by Number

Place (place type) County	Number
Miami (city) Miami-Dade	2,534
West Palm Beach (city) Palm Beach	1,548
Lake Worth (city) Palm Beach	1,367
Homestead (city) Miami-Dade	1,244
Immokalee (cdp) Collier	902
Hialeah (city) Miami-Dade	819
Fort Lauderdale (city) Broward	353
Fort Myers (city) Lee	292
Bonita Springs (city) Lee	233

Guatelmalans 5 Years and Over Who Speak Spanish at Home
Top 10 Places Sorted by Percent

Place (place type) County	Percent
Hialeah (city) Miami-Dade	100.00
Fort Lauderdale (city) Broward	97.78
Miami (city) Miami-Dade	94.76
Homestead (city) Miami-Dade	93.18
Immokalee (cdp) Collier	86.07
Fort Myers (city) Lee	83.67
West Palm Beach (city) Palm Beach	80.71
Lake Worth (city) Palm Beach	80.13
Bonita Springs (city) Lee	79.79

Notes: Please refer to the User's Guide for an explanation of data; tables include places with populations > 9,999 and reflect only those areas that meet Summary File 4 population thresholds, therefore there may be less than 10 places listed

Hondurans 5 Years and Over Who Speak Spanish at Home
Top 10 Places Sorted by Number

Place (place type) County	Number
Miami (city) Miami-Dade	12,285
Hialeah (city) Miami-Dade	2,474
West Little River (cdp) Miami-Dade	872
Miami Beach (city) Miami-Dade	740
Tampa (city) Hillsborough	639
Fountainbleau (cdp) Miami-Dade	610
North Miami (city) Miami-Dade	513
Kendale Lakes (cdp) Miami-Dade	498
Carol City (cdp) Miami-Dade	462
North Miami Beach (city) Miami-Dade	446

Hondurans 5 Years and Over Who Speak Spanish at Home
Top 10 Places Sorted by Percent

Place (place type) County	Percent
Lake Worth (city) Palm Beach	100.00
Tamiami (cdp) Miami-Dade	100.00
Kendale Lakes (cdp) Miami-Dade	98.42
West Little River (cdp) Miami-Dade	98.42
Fountainbleau (cdp) Miami-Dade	97.60
Hialeah (city) Miami-Dade	97.36
Miami Beach (city) Miami-Dade	95.73
Miami (city) Miami-Dade	95.03
Hollywood (city) Broward	93.28
Carol City (cdp) Miami-Dade	91.67

Mexicans 5 Years and Over Who Speak Spanish at Home
Top 10 Places Sorted by Number

Place (place type) County	Number
Immokalee (cdp) Collier	8,739
Homestead (city) Miami-Dade	5,717
Tampa (city) Hillsborough	5,120
Leisure City (cdp) Miami-Dade	4,443
Fort Pierce (city) Saint Lucie	3,484
Clearwater (city) Pinellas	3,117
Sarasota (city) Sarasota	3,005
Golden Gate (cdp) Collier	2,788
Bonita Springs (city) Lee	2,742
Plant City (city) Hillsborough	2,718

Mexicans 5 Years and Over Who Speak Spanish at Home
Top 10 Places Sorted by Percent

Place (place type) County	Percent
Fountainbleau (cdp) Miami-Dade	96.41
Doral (cdp) Miami-Dade	96.33
Sarasota (city) Sarasota	95.46
De Land (city) Volusia	94.90
Bonita Springs (city) Lee	94.72
The Hammocks (cdp) Miami-Dade	94.48
Fort Pierce (city) Saint Lucie	94.39
Hialeah (city) Miami-Dade	94.39
Homestead (city) Miami-Dade	94.05
Auburndale (city) Polk	93.90

Nicaraguans 5 Years and Over Who Speak Spanish at Home
Top 10 Places Sorted by Number

Place (place type) County	Number
Miami (city) Miami-Dade	20,705
Hialeah (city) Miami-Dade	9,424
Fountainbleau (cdp) Miami-Dade	5,503
Kendale Lakes (cdp) Miami-Dade	2,619
Tamiami (cdp) Miami-Dade	2,514
Sweetwater (city) Miami-Dade	2,196
Kendall (cdp) Miami-Dade	2,020
Kendall West (cdp) Miami-Dade	1,486
The Hammocks (cdp) Miami-Dade	1,444
Carol City (cdp) Miami-Dade	1,285

Nicaraguans 5 Years and Over Who Speak Spanish at Home
Top 10 Places Sorted by Percent

Place (place type) County	Percent
The Crossings (cdp) Miami-Dade	100.00
Hialeah Gardens (city) Miami-Dade	99.25
The Hammocks (cdp) Miami-Dade	98.37
West Little River (cdp) Miami-Dade	98.36
Country Club (cdp) Miami-Dade	97.92
Tamiami (cdp) Miami-Dade	97.40
Palmetto Estates (cdp) Miami-Dade	97.16
University Park (cdp) Miami-Dade	97.12
Coral Gables (city) Miami-Dade	96.81
Hialeah (city) Miami-Dade	96.76

Panamanians 5 Years and Over Who Speak Spanish at Home
Top 10 Places Sorted by Number

Place (place type) County	Number
Miami (city) Miami-Dade	848
Fountainbleau (cdp) Miami-Dade	475
Tampa (city) Hillsborough	439
Jacksonville (city) Duval	423
Miramar (city) Broward	264

Panamanians 5 Years and Over Who Speak Spanish at Home
Top 10 Places Sorted by Percent

Place (place type) County	Percent
Miami (city) Miami-Dade	98.83
Fountainbleau (cdp) Miami-Dade	92.95
Miramar (city) Broward	76.52
Jacksonville (city) Duval	73.95
Tampa (city) Hillsborough	72.09

Paraguayans 5 Years and Over Who Speak Spanish at Home
Top 10 Places Sorted by Number

Place (place type) County	Number
No places met population threshold.	

Paraguayans 5 Years and Over Who Speak Spanish at Home
Top 10 Places Sorted by Percent

Place (place type) County	Percent
No places met population threshold.	

Peruvians 5 Years and Over Who Speak Spanish at Home
Top 10 Places Sorted by Number

Place (place type) County	Number
Miami (city) Miami-Dade	2,506
Miami Beach (city) Miami-Dade	1,754
The Hammocks (cdp) Miami-Dade	1,712
Hialeah (city) Miami-Dade	1,386
Pembroke Pines (city) Broward	1,265
Kendall (cdp) Miami-Dade	1,180
Hollywood (city) Broward	1,145
Fountainbleau (cdp) Miami-Dade	1,109
Kendall West (cdp) Miami-Dade	1,049
Kendale Lakes (cdp) Miami-Dade	862

Peruvians 5 Years and Over Who Speak Spanish at Home
Top 10 Places Sorted by Percent

Place (place type) County	Percent
Hialeah (city) Miami-Dade	100.00
North Miami Beach (city) Miami-Dade	100.00
Plantation (city) Broward	98.23

Place (place type) County	
Fountainbleau (cdp) Miami-Dade	98.05
The Hammocks (cdp) Miami-Dade	98.05
Doral (cdp) Miami-Dade	96.99
Miami Beach (city) Miami-Dade	96.32
Miramar (city) Broward	95.02
The Crossings (cdp) Miami-Dade	94.97
Miami (city) Miami-Dade	94.78

Puerto Ricans 5 Years and Over Who Speak Spanish at Home
Top 10 Places Sorted by Number

Place (place type) County	Number
Orlando (city) Orange	13,487
Tampa (city) Hillsborough	12,075
Kissimmee (city) Osceola	9,753
Miami (city) Miami-Dade	8,662
Jacksonville (city) Duval	7,382
Deltona (city) Volusia	7,308
Yeehaw Junction (cdp) Osceola	6,972
Hialeah (city) Miami-Dade	6,105
Town 'n' Country (cdp) Hillsborough	5,835
Pembroke Pines (city) Broward	5,539

Puerto Ricans 5 Years and Over Who Speak Spanish at Home
Top 10 Places Sorted by Percent

Place (place type) County	Percent
Opa-locka (city) Miami-Dade	98.68
Tamiami (cdp) Miami-Dade	98.39
Doral (cdp) Miami-Dade	97.61
The Crossings (cdp) Miami-Dade	96.99
West Little River (cdp) Miami-Dade	96.46
Fountainbleau (cdp) Miami-Dade	95.59
Kendale Lakes (cdp) Miami-Dade	95.49
University Park (cdp) Miami-Dade	95.43
Hialeah Gardens (city) Miami-Dade	94.68
Meadow Woods (cdp) Orange	93.98

Salvadorans 5 Years and Over Who Speak Spanish at Home
Top 10 Places Sorted by Number

Place (place type) County	Number
Miami (city) Miami-Dade	2,155
Homestead (city) Miami-Dade	902
Hialeah (city) Miami-Dade	881
Oakland Park (city) Broward	739
Fort Lauderdale (city) Broward	622
Lake Worth (city) Palm Beach	493

Salvadorans 5 Years and Over Who Speak Spanish at Home
Top 10 Places Sorted by Percent

Place (place type) County	Percent
Lake Worth (city) Palm Beach	100.00
Oakland Park (city) Broward	100.00
Hialeah (city) Miami-Dade	98.99
Fort Lauderdale (city) Broward	96.43
Homestead (city) Miami-Dade	95.55
Miami (city) Miami-Dade	94.60

South Americans 5 Years and Over Who Speak Spanish at Home
Top 10 Places Sorted by Number

Place (place type) County	Number
Miami (city) Miami-Dade	14,456
Hialeah (city) Miami-Dade	12,158
Miami Beach (city) Miami-Dade	11,781
The Hammocks (cdp) Miami-Dade	9,112
Kendall (cdp) Miami-Dade	7,847
Fountainbleau (cdp) Miami-Dade	7,745
Kendall West (cdp) Miami-Dade	7,122
Kendale Lakes (cdp) Miami-Dade	6,876
Pembroke Pines (city) Broward	6,811

Notes: Please refer to the User's Guide for an explanation of data; tables include places with populations > 9,999 and reflect only those areas that meet Summary File 4 population thresholds, therefore there may be less than 10 places listed

Hollywood (city) Broward   6,494

South Americans 5 Years and Over Who Speak Spanish at Home
Top 10 Places Sorted by Percent

Place (place type) County	Percent
Olympia Heights (cdp) Miami-Dade	100.00
Palm Beach Gardens (city) Palm Beach	100.00
Altamonte Springs (city) Seminole	99.12
West Little River (cdp) Miami-Dade	98.77
Sarasota (city) Sarasota	98.42
Westchester (cdp) Miami-Dade	98.07
Doral (cdp) Miami-Dade	97.97
Golden Glades (cdp) Miami-Dade	97.72
Hialeah Gardens (city) Miami-Dade	97.70
Greater Carrollwood (cdp) Hillsborough	97.66

Spaniards 5 Years and Over Who Speak Spanish at Home
Top 10 Places Sorted by Number

Place (place type) County	Number
Miami (city) Miami-Dade	888
Miami Beach (city) Miami-Dade	526
Tampa (city) Hillsborough	506
Hialeah (city) Miami-Dade	465

Spaniards 5 Years and Over Who Speak Spanish at Home
Top 10 Places Sorted by Percent

Place (place type) County	Percent
Miami (city) Miami-Dade	95.48
Hialeah (city) Miami-Dade	94.90
Miami Beach (city) Miami-Dade	93.59
Tampa (city) Hillsborough	72.29

Uruguayans 5 Years and Over Who Speak Spanish at Home
Top 10 Places Sorted by Number

Place (place type) County	Number

No places met population threshold.

Uruguayans 5 Years and Over Who Speak Spanish at Home
Top 10 Places Sorted by Percent

Place (place type) County	Percent

No places met population threshold.

Venezuelans 5 Years and Over Who Speak Spanish at Home
Top 10 Places Sorted by Number

Place (place type) County	Number
Fountainbleau (cdp) Miami-Dade	1,970
Weston (city) Broward	1,860
Doral (cdp) Miami-Dade	1,649
Miami (city) Miami-Dade	1,549
The Hammocks (cdp) Miami-Dade	1,471
Miami Beach (city) Miami-Dade	1,344
Kendall (cdp) Miami-Dade	1,287
Pembroke Pines (city) Broward	1,283
Kendall West (cdp) Miami-Dade	1,114
Hialeah (city) Miami-Dade	908

Venezuelans 5 Years and Over Who Speak Spanish at Home
Top 10 Places Sorted by Percent

Place (place type) County	Percent
Tamiami (cdp) Miami-Dade	100.00
The Crossings (cdp) Miami-Dade	100.00
Weston (city) Broward	99.04
Fountainbleau (cdp) Miami-Dade	98.85
Kendall West (cdp) Miami-Dade	97.72

Place (place type) County	Percent
Hialeah (city) Miami-Dade	97.63
Richmond West (cdp) Miami-Dade	97.36
Doral (cdp) Miami-Dade	97.23
Kendale Lakes (cdp) Miami-Dade	96.62
Miami Beach (city) Miami-Dade	95.39

Other Hispanics 5 Years and Over Who Speak Spanish at Home
Top 10 Places Sorted by Number

Place (place type) County	Number
Miami (city) Miami-Dade	25,944
Hialeah (city) Miami-Dade	16,817
Tampa (city) Hillsborough	7,687
Fountainbleau (cdp) Miami-Dade	7,249
Kendale Lakes (cdp) Miami-Dade	5,941
Miami Beach (city) Miami-Dade	5,184
The Hammocks (cdp) Miami-Dade	4,598
Hollywood (city) Broward	4,426
Pembroke Pines (city) Broward	4,220
Tamiami (cdp) Miami-Dade	4,196

Other Hispanics 5 Years and Over Who Speak Spanish at Home
Top 10 Places Sorted by Percent

Place (place type) County	Percent
Sunny Isles Beach (city) Miami-Dade	99.16
Olympia Heights (cdp) Miami-Dade	97.04
Kendale Lakes (cdp) Miami-Dade	95.81
Fountainbleau (cdp) Miami-Dade	95.53
Poinciana (cdp) Osceola	95.44
Gladeview (cdp) Miami-Dade	94.76
Ives Estates (cdp) Miami-Dade	94.67
Sweetwater (city) Miami-Dade	94.52
Tamiami (cdp) Miami-Dade	94.44
Palmetto Estates (cdp) Miami-Dade	94.11

Foreign Born

Total Population
Top 10 Places Sorted by Number

Place (place type) County	Number
Miami (city) Miami-Dade	215,739
Hialeah (city) Miami-Dade	163,256
Miami Beach (city) Miami-Dade	48,852
Jacksonville (city) Duval	43,661
Fountainbleau (cdp) Miami-Dade	43,496
Pembroke Pines (city) Broward	39,727
Tampa (city) Hillsborough	37,027
Hollywood (city) Broward	36,562
Tamiami (cdp) Miami-Dade	35,850
Kendale Lakes (cdp) Miami-Dade	33,460

Total Population
Top 10 Places Sorted by Percent

Place (place type) County	Percent
Sweetwater (city) Miami-Dade	74.68
Fountainbleau (cdp) Miami-Dade	73.08
Hialeah (city) Miami-Dade	72.11
Hialeah Gardens (city) Miami-Dade	70.11
Westchester (cdp) Miami-Dade	69.00
University Park (cdp) Miami-Dade	66.62
Coral Terrace (cdp) Miami-Dade	66.12
Tamiami (cdp) Miami-Dade	65.49
Doral (cdp) Miami-Dade	62.55
Miami (city) Miami-Dade	59.50

Hispanic
Top 10 Places Sorted by Number

Place (place type) County	Number
Miami (city) Miami-Dade	188,008
Hialeah (city) Miami-Dade	160,779
Fountainbleau (cdp) Miami-Dade	41,125
Miami Beach (city) Miami-Dade	36,211

Place (place type) County	Number
Tamiami (cdp) Miami-Dade	34,857
Kendale Lakes (cdp) Miami-Dade	30,802
Kendall (cdp) Miami-Dade	24,625
Tampa (city) Hillsborough	21,240
Kendall West (cdp) Miami-Dade	20,522
Westchester (cdp) Miami-Dade	20,394

Hispanic
Top 10 Places Sorted by Percent

Place (place type) County	Percent
Marco Island (city) Collier	82.30
Aventura (city) Miami-Dade	81.08
Sunny Isles Beach (city) Miami-Dade	80.73
Fountainbleau (cdp) Miami-Dade	79.34
Westchester (cdp) Miami-Dade	78.88
Miami (city) Miami-Dade	78.84
Sweetwater (city) Miami-Dade	78.51
Hialeah (city) Miami-Dade	78.50
Coral Terrace (cdp) Miami-Dade	77.22
Miami Beach (city) Miami-Dade	77.08

Argentinian
Top 10 Places Sorted by Number

Place (place type) County	Number
Miami Beach (city) Miami-Dade	2,809
Miami (city) Miami-Dade	1,801
Kendall (cdp) Miami-Dade	547
Sunny Isles Beach (city) Miami-Dade	543
Hollywood (city) Broward	491
Hialeah (city) Miami-Dade	395
Fountainbleau (cdp) Miami-Dade	360

Argentinian
Top 10 Places Sorted by Percent

Place (place type) County	Percent
Sunny Isles Beach (city) Miami-Dade	95.10
Miami Beach (city) Miami-Dade	92.68
Hialeah (city) Miami-Dade	92.07
Miami (city) Miami-Dade	88.76
Hollywood (city) Broward	87.84
Kendall (cdp) Miami-Dade	83.51
Fountainbleau (cdp) Miami-Dade	81.82

Bolivian
Top 10 Places Sorted by Number

Place (place type) County	Number

No places met population threshold.

Bolivian
Top 10 Places Sorted by Percent

Place (place type) County	Percent

No places met population threshold.

Central American
Top 10 Places Sorted by Number

Place (place type) County	Number
Miami (city) Miami-Dade	38,302
Hialeah (city) Miami-Dade	13,832
Fountainbleau (cdp) Miami-Dade	6,984
Kendale Lakes (cdp) Miami-Dade	3,409
Tamiami (cdp) Miami-Dade	3,130
Kendall (cdp) Miami-Dade	3,037
Homestead (city) Miami-Dade	2,836
Miami Beach (city) Miami-Dade	2,478
Lake Worth (city) Palm Beach	2,403
West Palm Beach (city) Palm Beach	2,397

Central American
Top 10 Places Sorted by Percent

Place (place type) County	Percent
Deerfield Beach (city) Broward	89.88

Notes: Please refer to the User's Guide for an explanation of data; tables include places with populations > 9,999 and reflect only those areas that meet Summary File 4 population thresholds, therefore there may be less than 10 places listed

Place (place type) County	
Gladeview (cdp) Miami-Dade	89.88
Golden Gate (cdp) Collier	89.07
North Miami (city) Miami-Dade	88.69
Opa-locka (city) Miami-Dade	88.46
Jupiter (town) Palm Beach	88.00
Miami Beach (city) Miami-Dade	87.78
Pinewood (cdp) Miami-Dade	87.67
Margate (city) Broward	87.61
Coral Gables (city) Miami-Dade	87.57

Chilean
Top 10 Places Sorted by Number

Place (place type) County	Number
Miami (city) Miami-Dade	811
Hialeah (city) Miami-Dade	722
Fountainbleau (cdp) Miami-Dade	638
Miami Beach (city) Miami-Dade	612
Kendall (cdp) Miami-Dade	435
Hollywood (city) Broward	320

Chilean
Top 10 Places Sorted by Percent

Place (place type) County	Percent
Hialeah (city) Miami-Dade	96.27
Fountainbleau (cdp) Miami-Dade	90.75
Kendall (cdp) Miami-Dade	90.63
Miami (city) Miami-Dade	90.41
Hollywood (city) Broward	84.88
Miami Beach (city) Miami-Dade	82.81

Colombian
Top 10 Places Sorted by Number

Place (place type) County	Number
Hialeah (city) Miami-Dade	6,687
Miami (city) Miami-Dade	5,243
The Hammocks (cdp) Miami-Dade	4,210
Miami Beach (city) Miami-Dade	3,937
Kendall West (cdp) Miami-Dade	3,541
Kendall (cdp) Miami-Dade	3,491
Kendale Lakes (cdp) Miami-Dade	3,204
Country Club (cdp) Miami-Dade	2,962
Pembroke Pines (city) Broward	2,699
Hollywood (city) Broward	2,681

Colombian
Top 10 Places Sorted by Percent

Place (place type) County	Percent
Deerfield Beach (city) Broward	92.06
Sunny Isles Beach (city) Miami-Dade	90.50
University Park (cdp) Miami-Dade	90.50
Tamarac (city) Broward	90.44
Glenvar Heights (cdp) Miami-Dade	89.04
Fountainbleau (cdp) Miami-Dade	88.39
Kissimmee (city) Osceola	88.03
Doral (cdp) Miami-Dade	87.78
Miami Beach (city) Miami-Dade	87.63
Miami (city) Miami-Dade	87.30

Costa Rican
Top 10 Places Sorted by Number

Place (place type) County	Number
Miami (city) Miami-Dade	667
Hialeah (city) Miami-Dade	451

Costa Rican
Top 10 Places Sorted by Percent

Place (place type) County	Percent
Hialeah (city) Miami-Dade	86.23
Miami (city) Miami-Dade	81.74

Cuban
Top 10 Places Sorted by Number

Place (place type) County	Number
Hialeah (city) Miami-Dade	119,595
Miami (city) Miami-Dade	108,492
Tamiami (cdp) Miami-Dade	24,750
Fountainbleau (cdp) Miami-Dade	19,287
Westchester (cdp) Miami-Dade	16,690
Kendale Lakes (cdp) Miami-Dade	16,265
Miami Beach (city) Miami-Dade	15,214
University Park (cdp) Miami-Dade	12,655
Coral Terrace (cdp) Miami-Dade	12,393
Kendall (cdp) Miami-Dade	10,264

Cuban
Top 10 Places Sorted by Percent

Place (place type) County	Percent
Sunny Isles Beach (city) Miami-Dade	89.81
Brownsville (cdp) Miami-Dade	88.68
Miami (city) Miami-Dade	86.98
Fountainbleau (cdp) Miami-Dade	86.48
Hialeah (city) Miami-Dade	84.64
Golden Gate (cdp) Collier	84.34
Pinewood (cdp) Miami-Dade	83.89
Miami Beach (city) Miami-Dade	83.41
Belle Glade (city) Palm Beach	83.13
Hialeah Gardens (city) Miami-Dade	82.92

Dominican
Top 10 Places Sorted by Number

Place (place type) County	Number
Miami (city) Miami-Dade	5,723
Hialeah (city) Miami-Dade	3,813
Fountainbleau (cdp) Miami-Dade	1,568
Carol City (cdp) Miami-Dade	1,274
Miami Beach (city) Miami-Dade	1,212
The Hammocks (cdp) Miami-Dade	1,130
Pembroke Pines (city) Broward	1,072
Hollywood (city) Broward	998
Miramar (city) Broward	997
Country Club (cdp) Miami-Dade	951

Dominican
Top 10 Places Sorted by Percent

Place (place type) County	Percent
Hialeah Gardens (city) Miami-Dade	92.01
Miami Beach (city) Miami-Dade	86.82
Doral (cdp) Miami-Dade	83.02
Fountainbleau (cdp) Miami-Dade	81.33
Miami (city) Miami-Dade	78.72
Hialeah (city) Miami-Dade	78.04
West Little River (cdp) Miami-Dade	75.85
The Hammocks (cdp) Miami-Dade	74.39
North Miami Beach (city) Miami-Dade	72.91
Golden Glades (cdp) Miami-Dade	72.83

Ecuadorian
Top 10 Places Sorted by Number

Place (place type) County	Number
Miami (city) Miami-Dade	1,459
Hialeah (city) Miami-Dade	1,076
Coral Springs (city) Broward	673
Fountainbleau (cdp) Miami-Dade	635
Miami Beach (city) Miami-Dade	514
Hollywood (city) Broward	443
Pembroke Pines (city) Broward	396
Sunrise (city) Broward	386
Tampa (city) Hillsborough	338

Ecuadorian
Top 10 Places Sorted by Percent

Place (place type) County	Percent
Hialeah (city) Miami-Dade	87.27
Miami (city) Miami-Dade	83.13
Pembroke Pines (city) Broward	81.48
Tampa (city) Hillsborough	80.86
Fountainbleau (cdp) Miami-Dade	79.47
Miami Beach (city) Miami-Dade	77.64
Sunrise (city) Broward	72.97
Coral Springs (city) Broward	71.44
Hollywood (city) Broward	70.54

Guatelmalan
Top 10 Places Sorted by Number

Place (place type) County	Number
Miami (city) Miami-Dade	2,400
West Palm Beach (city) Palm Beach	1,781
Lake Worth (city) Palm Beach	1,382
Homestead (city) Miami-Dade	1,224
Immokalee (cdp) Collier	833
Hialeah (city) Miami-Dade	682
Fort Lauderdale (city) Broward	331
Fort Myers (city) Lee	309
Bonita Springs (city) Lee	281

Guatelmalan
Top 10 Places Sorted by Percent

Place (place type) County	Percent
Fort Lauderdale (city) Broward	89.22
West Palm Beach (city) Palm Beach	86.46
Homestead (city) Miami-Dade	85.30
Miami (city) Miami-Dade	84.18
Hialeah (city) Miami-Dade	81.00
Fort Myers (city) Lee	78.63
Bonita Springs (city) Lee	76.15
Immokalee (cdp) Collier	72.18
Lake Worth (city) Palm Beach	70.30

Honduran
Top 10 Places Sorted by Number

Place (place type) County	Number
Miami (city) Miami-Dade	12,099
Hialeah (city) Miami-Dade	2,290
West Little River (cdp) Miami-Dade	797
Miami Beach (city) Miami-Dade	739
Tampa (city) Hillsborough	639
Fountainbleau (cdp) Miami-Dade	585
North Miami (city) Miami-Dade	532
Kendale Lakes (cdp) Miami-Dade	444
North Miami Beach (city) Miami-Dade	415
Lake Worth (city) Palm Beach	404

Honduran
Top 10 Places Sorted by Percent

Place (place type) County	Percent
Miami Beach (city) Miami-Dade	91.23
Fountainbleau (cdp) Miami-Dade	91.12
North Miami (city) Miami-Dade	90.17
Miami (city) Miami-Dade	88.57
Hialeah (city) Miami-Dade	86.38
Tamiami (cdp) Miami-Dade	86.31
Lake Worth (city) Palm Beach	83.47
West Little River (cdp) Miami-Dade	81.74
North Miami Beach (city) Miami-Dade	81.53
Kendale Lakes (cdp) Miami-Dade	79.71

Mexican
Top 10 Places Sorted by Number

Place (place type) County	Number
Immokalee (cdp) Collier	5,667
Tampa (city) Hillsborough	3,769
Homestead (city) Miami-Dade	3,731

Notes: Please refer to the User's Guide for an explanation of data; tables include places with populations > 9,999 and reflect only those areas that meet Summary File 4 population thresholds, therefore there may be less than 10 places listed

Place (place type) County	
Clearwater (city) Pinellas	2,953
Fort Pierce (city) Saint Lucie	2,925
Sarasota (city) Sarasota	2,776
Golden Gate (cdp) Collier	2,760
Leisure City (cdp) Miami-Dade	2,572
Bonita Springs (city) Lee	2,191
Lake Worth Corridor (cdp) Palm Beach	2,128

Mexican
Top 10 Places Sorted by Percent

Place (place type) County	Percent
Oak Ridge (cdp) Orange	79.70
Kendall West (cdp) Miami-Dade	78.41
Sarasota (city) Sarasota	78.31
Doral (cdp) Miami-Dade	76.29
Golden Gate (cdp) Collier	74.82
Fountainbleau (cdp) Miami-Dade	73.86
Oakland Park (city) Broward	72.87
Clearwater (city) Pinellas	70.13
Fort Pierce (city) Saint Lucie	70.03
Boca Raton (city) Palm Beach	69.51

Nicaraguan
Top 10 Places Sorted by Number

Place (place type) County	Number
Miami (city) Miami-Dade	19,647
Hialeah (city) Miami-Dade	8,960
Fountainbleau (cdp) Miami-Dade	5,271
Kendale Lakes (cdp) Miami-Dade	2,384
Tamiami (cdp) Miami-Dade	2,184
Sweetwater (city) Miami-Dade	2,071
Kendall (cdp) Miami-Dade	1,752
Kendall West (cdp) Miami-Dade	1,426
The Hammocks (cdp) Miami-Dade	1,322
Carol City (cdp) Miami-Dade	1,193

Nicaraguan
Top 10 Places Sorted by Percent

Place (place type) County	Percent
Palmetto Estates (cdp) Miami-Dade	92.78
Miramar (city) Broward	91.47
Miami Beach (city) Miami-Dade	90.52
Pinewood (cdp) Miami-Dade	90.36
West Little River (cdp) Miami-Dade	90.29
Gladeview (cdp) Miami-Dade	90.16
Kendall West (cdp) Miami-Dade	89.24
Coral Terrace (cdp) Miami-Dade	89.11
The Crossings (cdp) Miami-Dade	88.49
Hialeah (city) Miami-Dade	88.18

Panamanian
Top 10 Places Sorted by Number

Place (place type) County	Number
Miami (city) Miami-Dade	759
Fountainbleau (cdp) Miami-Dade	396
Tampa (city) Hillsborough	344
Jacksonville (city) Duval	290
Miramar (city) Broward	288

Panamanian
Top 10 Places Sorted by Percent

Place (place type) County	Percent
Miami (city) Miami-Dade	85.96
Miramar (city) Broward	78.47
Fountainbleau (cdp) Miami-Dade	75.86
Tampa (city) Hillsborough	54.43
Jacksonville (city) Duval	49.91

Paraguayan
Top 10 Places Sorted by Number

Place (place type) County	Number
No places met population threshold.	

Paraguayan
Top 10 Places Sorted by Percent

Place (place type) County	Percent
No places met population threshold.	

Peruvian
Top 10 Places Sorted by Number

Place (place type) County	Number
Miami (city) Miami-Dade	2,373
Miami Beach (city) Miami-Dade	1,704
The Hammocks (cdp) Miami-Dade	1,423
Hialeah (city) Miami-Dade	1,280
Kendall (cdp) Miami-Dade	1,105
Pembroke Pines (city) Broward	1,060
Hollywood (city) Broward	1,052
Kendall West (cdp) Miami-Dade	1,049
Fountainbleau (cdp) Miami-Dade	1,036
Coral Springs (city) Broward	870

Peruvian
Top 10 Places Sorted by Percent

Place (place type) County	Percent
Doral (cdp) Miami-Dade	91.74
Kendall West (cdp) Miami-Dade	91.46
Coral Springs (city) Broward	91.29
Miami Beach (city) Miami-Dade	89.78
The Crossings (cdp) Miami-Dade	89.68
North Miami Beach (city) Miami-Dade	89.66
Hialeah (city) Miami-Dade	87.73
Fountainbleau (cdp) Miami-Dade	87.72
Weston (city) Broward	87.66
Richmond West (cdp) Miami-Dade	86.18

Puerto Rican
Top 10 Places Sorted by Number

Place (place type) County	Number
Miami (city) Miami-Dade	335
Town 'n' Country (cdp) Hillsborough	232
Orlando (city) Orange	219
Hialeah (city) Miami-Dade	197
Tampa (city) Hillsborough	192
Kissimmee (city) Osceola	175
Jacksonville (city) Duval	167
Carol City (cdp) Miami-Dade	140
Fort Lauderdale (city) Broward	112
Cutler Ridge (cdp) Miami-Dade	101

Puerto Rican
Top 10 Places Sorted by Percent

Place (place type) County	Percent
Miami Springs (city) Miami-Dade	12.41
Westchester (cdp) Miami-Dade	12.00
Glenvar Heights (cdp) Miami-Dade	10.66
Wekiwa Springs (cdp) Seminole	7.46
Delray Beach (city) Palm Beach	6.55
Lake Worth Corridor (cdp) Palm Beach	6.28
Cutler Ridge (cdp) Miami-Dade	6.25
Lauderhill (city) Broward	5.93
Hallandale (city) Broward	5.90
Hialeah Gardens (city) Miami-Dade	5.19

Salvadoran
Top 10 Places Sorted by Number

Place (place type) County	Number
Miami (city) Miami-Dade	2,130
Homestead (city) Miami-Dade	908
Hialeah (city) Miami-Dade	765
Oakland Park (city) Broward	626
Fort Lauderdale (city) Broward	529
Lake Worth (city) Palm Beach	444

Salvadoran
Top 10 Places Sorted by Percent

Place (place type) County	Percent
Miami (city) Miami-Dade	88.97
Lake Worth (city) Palm Beach	84.25
Homestead (city) Miami-Dade	81.07
Oakland Park (city) Broward	80.77
Hialeah (city) Miami-Dade	80.53
Fort Lauderdale (city) Broward	79.67

South American
Top 10 Places Sorted by Number

Place (place type) County	Number
Miami (city) Miami-Dade	13,962
Miami Beach (city) Miami-Dade	11,585
Hialeah (city) Miami-Dade	11,377
The Hammocks (cdp) Miami-Dade	8,110
Fountainbleau (cdp) Miami-Dade	7,308
Kendall (cdp) Miami-Dade	7,294
Kendall West (cdp) Miami-Dade	6,484
Kendale Lakes (cdp) Miami-Dade	6,097
Pembroke Pines (city) Broward	6,074
Hollywood (city) Broward	5,885

South American
Top 10 Places Sorted by Percent

Place (place type) County	Percent
Oakland Park (city) Broward	93.30
Sunny Isles Beach (city) Miami-Dade	93.12
Oak Ridge (cdp) Orange	92.67
Deerfield Beach (city) Broward	91.34
Doral (cdp) Miami-Dade	89.88
Miami Beach (city) Miami-Dade	89.23
Pinecrest (village) Miami-Dade	88.84
Hialeah (city) Miami-Dade	88.17
Sunset (cdp) Miami-Dade	88.15
Aventura (city) Miami-Dade	87.89

Spaniard
Top 10 Places Sorted by Number

Place (place type) County	Number
Miami (city) Miami-Dade	819
Miami Beach (city) Miami-Dade	498
Hialeah (city) Miami-Dade	410
Tampa (city) Hillsborough	191

Spaniard
Top 10 Places Sorted by Percent

Place (place type) County	Percent
Miami Beach (city) Miami-Dade	86.91
Miami (city) Miami-Dade	86.12
Hialeah (city) Miami-Dade	80.55
Tampa (city) Hillsborough	26.06

Uruguayan
Top 10 Places Sorted by Number

Place (place type) County	Number
No places met population threshold.	

Uruguayan
Top 10 Places Sorted by Percent

Place (place type) County	Percent
No places met population threshold.	

Venezuelan
Top 10 Places Sorted by Number

Place (place type) County	Number
Fountainbleau (cdp) Miami-Dade	1,876
Weston (city) Broward	1,779
Doral (cdp) Miami-Dade	1,685
Miami (city) Miami-Dade	1,619

Notes: Please refer to the User's Guide for an explanation of data; tables include places with populations > 9,999 and reflect only those areas that meet Summary File 4 population thresholds, therefore there may be less than 10 places listed

Place (place type) County	Number
The Hammocks (cdp) Miami-Dade	1,413
Miami Beach (city) Miami-Dade	1,331
Pembroke Pines (city) Broward	1,292
Kendall (cdp) Miami-Dade	1,212
Kendall West (cdp) Miami-Dade	982
Hialeah (city) Miami-Dade	876

Venezuelan
Top 10 Places Sorted by Percent

Place (place type) County	Percent
Tamiami (cdp) Miami-Dade	93.94
Miami (city) Miami-Dade	91.99
Hialeah (city) Miami-Dade	91.73
Doral (cdp) Miami-Dade	91.53
Miami Beach (city) Miami-Dade	91.41
Orlando (city) Orange	90.65
Weston (city) Broward	90.35
Fountainbleau (cdp) Miami-Dade	90.02
Kendale Lakes (cdp) Miami-Dade	89.78
Tampa (city) Hillsborough	87.66

Other Hispanic
Top 10 Places Sorted by Number

Place (place type) County	Number
Miami (city) Miami-Dade	18,266
Hialeah (city) Miami-Dade	10,487
Fountainbleau (cdp) Miami-Dade	5,455
Miami Beach (city) Miami-Dade	4,494
Kendale Lakes (cdp) Miami-Dade	3,847
Hollywood (city) Broward	3,150
The Hammocks (cdp) Miami-Dade	2,910
Kendall (cdp) Miami-Dade	2,833
Pembroke Pines (city) Broward	2,763
Kendall West (cdp) Miami-Dade	2,708

Other Hispanic
Top 10 Places Sorted by Percent

Place (place type) County	Percent
Aventura (city) Miami-Dade	83.65
Gladeview (cdp) Miami-Dade	73.99
Key Biscayne (village) Miami-Dade	71.48
Miami Beach (city) Miami-Dade	69.95
Doral (cdp) Miami-Dade	68.95
Delray Beach (city) Palm Beach	68.87
Ojus (cdp) Miami-Dade	68.08
Golden Gate (cdp) Collier	66.18
Jupiter (town) Palm Beach	64.27
Fountainbleau (cdp) Miami-Dade	63.68

Foreign-Born Naturalized Citizens

Total Population
Top 10 Places Sorted by Number

Place (place type) County	Number
Miami (city) Miami-Dade	89,727
Hialeah (city) Miami-Dade	70,331
Pembroke Pines (city) Broward	22,597
Miami Beach (city) Miami-Dade	21,744
Jacksonville (city) Duval	20,786
Tamiami (cdp) Miami-Dade	20,633
Fountainbleau (cdp) Miami-Dade	18,348
Kendale Lakes (cdp) Miami-Dade	17,856
Kendall (cdp) Miami-Dade	16,474
Hollywood (city) Broward	16,136

Total Population
Top 10 Places Sorted by Percent

Place (place type) County	Percent
Westchester (cdp) Miami-Dade	41.34
University Park (cdp) Miami-Dade	40.38
Tamiami (cdp) Miami-Dade	37.69
Coral Terrace (cdp) Miami-Dade	36.41
Olympia Heights (cdp) Miami-Dade	36.14

Place (place type) County	Percent
Westwood Lakes (cdp) Miami-Dade	33.37
Sunset (cdp) Miami-Dade	32.98
Miami Lakes (cdp) Miami-Dade	32.32
Kendale Lakes (cdp) Miami-Dade	31.39
Hialeah (city) Miami-Dade	31.06

Hispanic
Top 10 Places Sorted by Number

Place (place type) County	Number
Miami (city) Miami-Dade	79,264
Hialeah (city) Miami-Dade	69,014
Tamiami (cdp) Miami-Dade	20,107
Fountainbleau (cdp) Miami-Dade	17,610
Miami Beach (city) Miami-Dade	16,432
Kendale Lakes (cdp) Miami-Dade	16,336
Kendall (cdp) Miami-Dade	13,071
Westchester (cdp) Miami-Dade	12,212
Pembroke Pines (city) Broward	10,874
University Park (cdp) Miami-Dade	10,263

Hispanic
Top 10 Places Sorted by Percent

Place (place type) County	Percent
Westchester (cdp) Miami-Dade	47.23
University Park (cdp) Miami-Dade	46.83
Coral Gables (city) Miami-Dade	45.23
Olympia Heights (cdp) Miami-Dade	45.19
Miami Lakes (cdp) Miami-Dade	44.06
Sunset (cdp) Miami-Dade	43.93
Coral Terrace (cdp) Miami-Dade	42.28
Westwood Lakes (cdp) Miami-Dade	42.22
Tamiami (cdp) Miami-Dade	42.16
South Miami (city) Miami-Dade	38.70

Argentinian
Top 10 Places Sorted by Number

Place (place type) County	Number
Miami Beach (city) Miami-Dade	548
Miami (city) Miami-Dade	473
Kendall (cdp) Miami-Dade	211
Sunny Isles Beach (city) Miami-Dade	166
Fountainbleau (cdp) Miami-Dade	136
Hollywood (city) Broward	120
Hialeah (city) Miami-Dade	84

Argentinian
Top 10 Places Sorted by Percent

Place (place type) County	Percent
Kendall (cdp) Miami-Dade	32.21
Fountainbleau (cdp) Miami-Dade	30.91
Sunny Isles Beach (city) Miami-Dade	29.07
Miami (city) Miami-Dade	23.31
Hollywood (city) Broward	21.47
Hialeah (city) Miami-Dade	19.58
Miami Beach (city) Miami-Dade	18.08

Bolivian
Top 10 Places Sorted by Number

Place (place type) County	Number
No places met population threshold.	

Bolivian
Top 10 Places Sorted by Percent

Place (place type) County	Percent
No places met population threshold.	

Central American
Top 10 Places Sorted by Number

Place (place type) County	Number
Miami (city) Miami-Dade	5,529
Hialeah (city) Miami-Dade	2,654

Place (place type) County	Number
Fountainbleau (cdp) Miami-Dade	1,921
Kendall (cdp) Miami-Dade	1,231
Tamiami (cdp) Miami-Dade	1,215
Kendale Lakes (cdp) Miami-Dade	1,132
The Hammocks (cdp) Miami-Dade	823
Miami Beach (city) Miami-Dade	756
Tampa (city) Hillsborough	715
Pembroke Pines (city) Broward	702

Central American
Top 10 Places Sorted by Percent

Place (place type) County	Percent
Gladeview (cdp) Miami-Dade	42.73
The Crossings (cdp) Miami-Dade	41.07
Sunset (cdp) Miami-Dade	39.92
Pembroke Pines (city) Broward	36.41
Richmond West (cdp) Miami-Dade	34.85
Egypt Lake-Leto (cdp) Hillsborough	34.31
Miramar (city) Broward	33.77
The Hammocks (cdp) Miami-Dade	33.35
North Miami Beach (city) Miami-Dade	33.21
Doral (cdp) Miami-Dade	33.06

Chilean
Top 10 Places Sorted by Number

Place (place type) County	Number
Kendall (cdp) Miami-Dade	216
Hialeah (city) Miami-Dade	213
Miami Beach (city) Miami-Dade	206
Miami (city) Miami-Dade	202
Fountainbleau (cdp) Miami-Dade	159
Hollywood (city) Broward	91

Chilean
Top 10 Places Sorted by Percent

Place (place type) County	Percent
Kendall (cdp) Miami-Dade	45.00
Hialeah (city) Miami-Dade	28.40
Miami Beach (city) Miami-Dade	27.88
Hollywood (city) Broward	24.14
Fountainbleau (cdp) Miami-Dade	22.62
Miami (city) Miami-Dade	22.52

Colombian
Top 10 Places Sorted by Number

Place (place type) County	Number
Hialeah (city) Miami-Dade	2,567
Miami (city) Miami-Dade	1,681
The Hammocks (cdp) Miami-Dade	1,537
Kendall West (cdp) Miami-Dade	1,237
Kendale Lakes (cdp) Miami-Dade	1,233
Kendall (cdp) Miami-Dade	1,173
Miami Beach (city) Miami-Dade	1,151
Pembroke Pines (city) Broward	1,114
Country Club (cdp) Miami-Dade	994
Hollywood (city) Broward	917

Colombian
Top 10 Places Sorted by Percent

Place (place type) County	Percent
Carol City (cdp) Miami-Dade	43.11
Miami Springs (city) Miami-Dade	42.57
Greater Carrollwood (cdp) Hillsborough	39.23
Coral Gables (city) Miami-Dade	38.52
Westchester (cdp) Miami-Dade	38.43
University Park (cdp) Miami-Dade	37.63
Tamiami (cdp) Miami-Dade	37.32
Hallandale (city) Broward	37.06
Country Walk (cdp) Miami-Dade	36.03
The Crossings (cdp) Miami-Dade	34.12

Notes: Please refer to the User's Guide for an explanation of data; tables include places with populations > 9,999 and reflect only those areas that meet Summary File 4 population thresholds, therefore there may be less than 10 places listed

Costa Rican
Top 10 Places Sorted by Number

Place (place type) County	Number
Miami (city) Miami-Dade	193
Hialeah (city) Miami-Dade	179

Costa Rican
Top 10 Places Sorted by Percent

Place (place type) County	Percent
Hialeah (city) Miami-Dade	34.23
Miami (city) Miami-Dade	23.65

Cuban
Top 10 Places Sorted by Number

Place (place type) County	Number
Miami (city) Miami-Dade	61,227
Hialeah (city) Miami-Dade	56,623
Tamiami (cdp) Miami-Dade	15,736
Fountainbleau (cdp) Miami-Dade	11,226
Westchester (cdp) Miami-Dade	10,668
Kendale Lakes (cdp) Miami-Dade	10,627
Miami Beach (city) Miami-Dade	10,266
University Park (cdp) Miami-Dade	8,683
Kendall (cdp) Miami-Dade	7,647
Coral Terrace (cdp) Miami-Dade	7,193

Cuban
Top 10 Places Sorted by Percent

Place (place type) County	Percent
Sunny Isles Beach (city) Miami-Dade	67.92
Key Biscayne (village) Miami-Dade	60.99
Hallandale (city) Broward	58.80
Coral Gables (city) Miami-Dade	58.04
Miami Lakes (cdp) Miami-Dade	57.06
Aventura (city) Miami-Dade	56.98
Miami Beach (city) Miami-Dade	56.28
Tamarac (city) Broward	55.80
University Park (cdp) Miami-Dade	55.31
Port St. Lucie (city) Saint Lucie	53.26

Dominican
Top 10 Places Sorted by Number

Place (place type) County	Number
Miami (city) Miami-Dade	2,182
Hialeah (city) Miami-Dade	1,718
Fountainbleau (cdp) Miami-Dade	717
Pembroke Pines (city) Broward	638
Carol City (cdp) Miami-Dade	617
The Hammocks (cdp) Miami-Dade	584
Hollywood (city) Broward	513
Miramar (city) Broward	498
Miami Beach (city) Miami-Dade	490
Country Club (cdp) Miami-Dade	401

Dominican
Top 10 Places Sorted by Percent

Place (place type) County	Percent
Tamiami (cdp) Miami-Dade	59.97
Town 'n' Country (cdp) Hillsborough	46.13
Jacksonville (city) Duval	42.69
Kendale Lakes (cdp) Miami-Dade	42.59
Hialeah Gardens (city) Miami-Dade	39.82
West Palm Beach (city) Palm Beach	38.97
The Hammocks (cdp) Miami-Dade	38.45
Fountainbleau (cdp) Miami-Dade	37.19
Cape Coral (city) Lee	37.11
Weston (city) Broward	36.61

Ecuadorian
Top 10 Places Sorted by Number

Place (place type) County	Number
Miami (city) Miami-Dade	559
Hialeah (city) Miami-Dade	465
Pembroke Pines (city) Broward	302
Coral Springs (city) Broward	278
Tampa (city) Hillsborough	213
Miami Beach (city) Miami-Dade	197
Sunrise (city) Broward	191
Hollywood (city) Broward	189
Fountainbleau (cdp) Miami-Dade	166

Ecuadorian
Top 10 Places Sorted by Percent

Place (place type) County	Percent
Pembroke Pines (city) Broward	62.14
Tampa (city) Hillsborough	50.96
Hialeah (city) Miami-Dade	37.71
Sunrise (city) Broward	36.11
Miami (city) Miami-Dade	31.85
Hollywood (city) Broward	30.10
Miami Beach (city) Miami-Dade	29.76
Coral Springs (city) Broward	29.51
Fountainbleau (cdp) Miami-Dade	20.78

Guatelmalan
Top 10 Places Sorted by Number

Place (place type) County	Number
Miami (city) Miami-Dade	533
Hialeah (city) Miami-Dade	160
Lake Worth (city) Palm Beach	90
Fort Lauderdale (city) Broward	86
West Palm Beach (city) Palm Beach	46
Homestead (city) Miami-Dade	38
Immokalee (cdp) Collier	33
Bonita Springs (city) Lee	11
Fort Myers (city) Lee	6

Guatelmalan
Top 10 Places Sorted by Percent

Place (place type) County	Percent
Fort Lauderdale (city) Broward	23.18
Hialeah (city) Miami-Dade	19.00
Miami (city) Miami-Dade	18.70
Lake Worth (city) Palm Beach	4.58
Bonita Springs (city) Lee	2.98
Immokalee (cdp) Collier	2.86
Homestead (city) Miami-Dade	2.65
West Palm Beach (city) Palm Beach	2.23
Fort Myers (city) Lee	1.53

Honduran
Top 10 Places Sorted by Number

Place (place type) County	Number
Miami (city) Miami-Dade	1,767
Hialeah (city) Miami-Dade	465
North Miami (city) Miami-Dade	208
Tampa (city) Hillsborough	206
West Little River (cdp) Miami-Dade	191
Miami Beach (city) Miami-Dade	177
Tamiami (cdp) Miami-Dade	165
Carol City (cdp) Miami-Dade	163
Kendale Lakes (cdp) Miami-Dade	137
Fountainbleau (cdp) Miami-Dade	123

Honduran
Top 10 Places Sorted by Percent

Place (place type) County	Percent
Tamiami (cdp) Miami-Dade	36.42
North Miami (city) Miami-Dade	35.25
Carol City (cdp) Miami-Dade	31.47
Kendale Lakes (cdp) Miami-Dade	24.60
Hollywood (city) Broward	24.55
Tampa (city) Hillsborough	23.04
Miami Beach (city) Miami-Dade	21.85
North Miami Beach (city) Miami-Dade	20.04

| West Little River (cdp) Miami-Dade | 19.59 |
| Fountainbleau (cdp) Miami-Dade | 19.16 |

Mexican
Top 10 Places Sorted by Number

Place (place type) County	Number
Immokalee (cdp) Collier	1,030
Tampa (city) Hillsborough	637
Bradenton (city) Manatee	478
Leisure City (cdp) Miami-Dade	427
Homestead (city) Miami-Dade	359
Plant City (city) Hillsborough	358
Jacksonville (city) Duval	355
Fort Pierce (city) Saint Lucie	345
Haines City (city) Polk	340
Clearwater (city) Pinellas	292

Mexican
Top 10 Places Sorted by Percent

Place (place type) County	Percent
Kendale Lakes (cdp) Miami-Dade	22.81
San Carlos Park (cdp) Lee	22.41
Plantation (city) Broward	20.86
Miami Beach (city) Miami-Dade	19.57
Tamiami (cdp) Miami-Dade	19.22
Margate (city) Broward	17.34
Ocoee (city) Orange	17.09
Davie (town) Broward	16.71
Fountainbleau (cdp) Miami-Dade	16.18
Hialeah (city) Miami-Dade	15.42

Nicaraguan
Top 10 Places Sorted by Number

Place (place type) County	Number
Miami (city) Miami-Dade	2,209
Hialeah (city) Miami-Dade	1,484
Fountainbleau (cdp) Miami-Dade	1,414
Kendale Lakes (cdp) Miami-Dade	780
Kendall (cdp) Miami-Dade	769
Tamiami (cdp) Miami-Dade	728
The Hammocks (cdp) Miami-Dade	459
Sweetwater (city) Miami-Dade	409
Kendall West (cdp) Miami-Dade	363
Gladeview (cdp) Miami-Dade	355

Nicaraguan
Top 10 Places Sorted by Percent

Place (place type) County	Percent
The Crossings (cdp) Miami-Dade	48.11
Gladeview (cdp) Miami-Dade	43.13
Miami Beach (city) Miami-Dade	35.38
Kendall (cdp) Miami-Dade	34.45
Miramar (city) Broward	33.49
The Hammocks (cdp) Miami-Dade	30.08
Palmetto Estates (cdp) Miami-Dade	28.88
Richmond West (cdp) Miami-Dade	27.87
Kendale Lakes (cdp) Miami-Dade	27.40
Tamiami (cdp) Miami-Dade	26.41

Panamanian
Top 10 Places Sorted by Number

Place (place type) County	Number
Miami (city) Miami-Dade	255
Tampa (city) Hillsborough	149
Jacksonville (city) Duval	144
Fountainbleau (cdp) Miami-Dade	99
Miramar (city) Broward	94

Panamanian
Top 10 Places Sorted by Percent

Place (place type) County	Percent
Miami (city) Miami-Dade	28.88

Notes: Please refer to the User's Guide for an explanation of data; tables include places with populations > 9,999 and reflect only those areas that meet Summary File 4 population thresholds, therefore there may be less than 10 places listed

Place (place type) County	Number
Miramar (city) Broward	25.61
Jacksonville (city) Duval	24.78
Tampa (city) Hillsborough	23.58
Fountainbleau (cdp) Miami-Dade	18.97

Paraguayan
Top 10 Places Sorted by Number

Place (place type) County	Number
No places met population threshold.	

Paraguayan
Top 10 Places Sorted by Percent

Place (place type) County	Percent
No places met population threshold.	

Peruvian
Top 10 Places Sorted by Number

Place (place type) County	Number
Miami (city) Miami-Dade	756
The Hammocks (cdp) Miami-Dade	448
Miami Beach (city) Miami-Dade	434
Pembroke Pines (city) Broward	425
Hialeah (city) Miami-Dade	393
Kendale Lakes (cdp) Miami-Dade	351
Fountainbleau (cdp) Miami-Dade	329
Hollywood (city) Broward	288
Sunrise (city) Broward	265
Miramar (city) Broward	248

Peruvian
Top 10 Places Sorted by Percent

Place (place type) County	Percent
Sunrise (city) Broward	44.61
Miramar (city) Broward	37.46
Kendale Lakes (cdp) Miami-Dade	36.30
The Crossings (cdp) Miami-Dade	35.44
Weston (city) Broward	32.18
Richmond West (cdp) Miami-Dade	31.09
Plantation (city) Broward	30.50
North Lauderdale (city) Broward	29.50
Pembroke Pines (city) Broward	28.24
Fountainbleau (cdp) Miami-Dade	27.86

Puerto Rican
Top 10 Places Sorted by Number

Place (place type) County	Number
Miami (city) Miami-Dade	228
Carol City (cdp) Miami-Dade	105
Town 'n' Country (cdp) Hillsborough	105
Pembroke Pines (city) Broward	75
Hialeah (city) Miami-Dade	73
Tampa (city) Hillsborough	71
Deltona (city) Volusia	69
Egypt Lake-Leto (cdp) Hillsborough	64
Jacksonville (city) Duval	62
Kendale Lakes (cdp) Miami-Dade	45

Puerto Rican
Top 10 Places Sorted by Percent

Place (place type) County	Percent
Westchester (cdp) Miami-Dade	8.47
Glenvar Heights (cdp) Miami-Dade	8.45
Delray Beach (city) Palm Beach	6.00
The Crossings (cdp) Miami-Dade	4.45
Lauderhill (city) Broward	4.40
Carol City (cdp) Miami-Dade	3.76
Hialeah Gardens (city) Miami-Dade	3.76
Miami Springs (city) Miami-Dade	3.42
Tamiami (cdp) Miami-Dade	3.42
Hallandale (city) Broward	3.34

Salvadoran
Top 10 Places Sorted by Number

Place (place type) County	Number
Miami (city) Miami-Dade	407
Hialeah (city) Miami-Dade	208
Fort Lauderdale (city) Broward	120
Oakland Park (city) Broward	62
Lake Worth (city) Palm Beach	52
Homestead (city) Miami-Dade	38

Salvadoran
Top 10 Places Sorted by Percent

Place (place type) County	Percent
Hialeah (city) Miami-Dade	21.89
Fort Lauderdale (city) Broward	18.07
Miami (city) Miami-Dade	17.00
Lake Worth (city) Palm Beach	9.87
Oakland Park (city) Broward	8.00
Homestead (city) Miami-Dade	3.39

South American
Top 10 Places Sorted by Number

Place (place type) County	Number
Miami (city) Miami-Dade	4,188
Hialeah (city) Miami-Dade	4,027
Miami Beach (city) Miami-Dade	3,005
The Hammocks (cdp) Miami-Dade	2,614
Kendale Lakes (cdp) Miami-Dade	2,444
Pembroke Pines (city) Broward	2,334
Kendall (cdp) Miami-Dade	2,258
Kendall West (cdp) Miami-Dade	1,910
Fountainbleau (cdp) Miami-Dade	1,906
Hollywood (city) Broward	1,814

South American
Top 10 Places Sorted by Percent

Place (place type) County	Percent
Citrus Park (cdp) Hillsborough	47.65
Golden Glades (cdp) Miami-Dade	46.42
Palm Beach Gardens (city) Palm Beach	43.15
Parkland (city) Broward	39.89
Sweetwater (city) Miami-Dade	39.77
Cutler (cdp) Miami-Dade	39.75
Port St. Lucie (city) Saint Lucie	39.60
Olympia Heights (cdp) Miami-Dade	39.30
South Miami (city) Miami-Dade	39.05
Delray Beach (city) Palm Beach	38.23

Spaniard
Top 10 Places Sorted by Number

Place (place type) County	Number
Miami (city) Miami-Dade	450
Hialeah (city) Miami-Dade	220
Miami Beach (city) Miami-Dade	137
Tampa (city) Hillsborough	78

Spaniard
Top 10 Places Sorted by Percent

Place (place type) County	Percent
Miami (city) Miami-Dade	47.32
Hialeah (city) Miami-Dade	43.22
Miami Beach (city) Miami-Dade	23.91
Tampa (city) Hillsborough	10.64

Uruguayan
Top 10 Places Sorted by Number

Place (place type) County	Number
No places met population threshold.	

Uruguayan
Top 10 Places Sorted by Percent

Place (place type) County	Percent
No places met population threshold.	

Venezuelan
Top 10 Places Sorted by Number

Place (place type) County	Number
Fountainbleau (cdp) Miami-Dade	258
Miami (city) Miami-Dade	243
The Hammocks (cdp) Miami-Dade	241
Kendall (cdp) Miami-Dade	217
Miami Beach (city) Miami-Dade	202
Tampa (city) Hillsborough	199
Pembroke Pines (city) Broward	186
Hialeah (city) Miami-Dade	181
Kendall West (cdp) Miami-Dade	180
Kendale Lakes (cdp) Miami-Dade	165

Venezuelan
Top 10 Places Sorted by Percent

Place (place type) County	Percent
Tampa (city) Hillsborough	31.89
Richmond West (cdp) Miami-Dade	24.02
Hialeah (city) Miami-Dade	18.95
Kendale Lakes (cdp) Miami-Dade	18.94
Coral Springs (city) Broward	17.94
The Crossings (cdp) Miami-Dade	17.52
Coral Gables (city) Miami-Dade	17.30
Hollywood (city) Broward	16.06
Kendall West (cdp) Miami-Dade	15.52
Kendall (cdp) Miami-Dade	14.93

Other Hispanic
Top 10 Places Sorted by Number

Place (place type) County	Number
Miami (city) Miami-Dade	5,188
Hialeah (city) Miami-Dade	3,451
Fountainbleau (cdp) Miami-Dade	1,673
Miami Beach (city) Miami-Dade	1,553
Kendale Lakes (cdp) Miami-Dade	1,523
Kendall (cdp) Miami-Dade	1,420
Tamiami (cdp) Miami-Dade	1,246
Hollywood (city) Broward	1,132
Pembroke Pines (city) Broward	1,079
The Hammocks (cdp) Miami-Dade	1,051

Other Hispanic
Top 10 Places Sorted by Percent

Place (place type) County	Percent
Norland (cdp) Miami-Dade	40.51
Ojus (cdp) Miami-Dade	34.31
Hallandale (city) Broward	30.16
Lauderhill (city) Broward	28.78
Palm Bay (city) Brevard	28.12
Margate (city) Broward	27.92
Coral Terrace (cdp) Miami-Dade	27.19
Kendall (cdp) Miami-Dade	26.36
Palm Springs (village) Palm Beach	26.21
Coral Gables (city) Miami-Dade	26.12

Educational Attainment: High School Graduates

Total Population 25 Years and Over Who are High School Graduates
Top 10 Places Sorted by Number

Place (place type) County	Number
Jacksonville (city) Duval	385,300
Tampa (city) Hillsborough	153,114
St. Petersburg (city) Pinellas	143,458
Miami (city) Miami-Dade	133,069

Notes: Please refer to the User's Guide for an explanation of data; tables include places with populations > 9,999 and reflect only those areas that meet Summary File 4 population thresholds, therefore there may be less than 10 places listed

Place (place type) County	
Orlando (city) Orange	103,129
Fort Lauderdale (city) Broward	87,921
Pembroke Pines (city) Broward	82,419
Hollywood (city) Broward	79,650
Hialeah (city) Miami-Dade	77,548
Tallahassee (city) Leon	71,754

Total Population 25 Years and Over Who are High School Graduates
Top 10 Places Sorted by Percent

Place (place type) County	Percent
Westchase (cdp) Hillsborough	96.62
Wekiwa Springs (cdp) Seminole	96.03
Weston (city) Broward	95.47
Key Biscayne (village) Miami-Dade	94.99
Boca Del Mar (cdp) Palm Beach	94.88
Keystone (cdp) Hillsborough	94.87
Bloomingdale (cdp) Hillsborough	94.79
Pinecrest (village) Miami-Dade	94.24
Parkland (city) Broward	94.07
Palm Beach Gardens (city) Palm Beach	94.03

Hispanics 25 Years and Over Who are High School Graduates
Top 10 Places Sorted by Number

Place (place type) County	Number
Miami (city) Miami-Dade	83,405
Hialeah (city) Miami-Dade	70,397
Miami Beach (city) Miami-Dade	25,722
Fountainbleau (cdp) Miami-Dade	24,867
Tamiami (cdp) Miami-Dade	23,414
Kendale Lakes (cdp) Miami-Dade	22,385
Tampa (city) Hillsborough	22,246
Kendall (cdp) Miami-Dade	21,481
Pembroke Pines (city) Broward	21,009
The Hammocks (cdp) Miami-Dade	16,989

Hispanics 25 Years and Over Who are High School Graduates
Top 10 Places Sorted by Percent

Place (place type) County	Percent
East Lake (cdp) Pinellas	97.21
Westchase (cdp) Hillsborough	96.16
Weston (city) Broward	92.90
Boca Del Mar (cdp) Palm Beach	92.71
Key Biscayne (village) Miami-Dade	92.16
Keystone (cdp) Hillsborough	91.80
Land O' Lakes (cdp) Pasco	91.23
Parkland (city) Broward	90.60
Gainesville (city) Alachua	90.24
Callaway (city) Bay	90.11

Argentinians 25 Years and Over Who are High School Graduates
Top 10 Places Sorted by Number

Place (place type) County	Number
Miami Beach (city) Miami-Dade	1,670
Miami (city) Miami-Dade	1,063
Kendall (cdp) Miami-Dade	461
Sunny Isles Beach (city) Miami-Dade	375
Hollywood (city) Broward	298
Fountainbleau (cdp) Miami-Dade	278
Hialeah (city) Miami-Dade	180

Argentinians 25 Years and Over Who are High School Graduates
Top 10 Places Sorted by Percent

Place (place type) County	Percent
Kendall (cdp) Miami-Dade	93.70
Miami Beach (city) Miami-Dade	80.02
Sunny Isles Beach (city) Miami-Dade	77.96
Hollywood (city) Broward	77.40
Fountainbleau (cdp) Miami-Dade	76.16

Place (place type) County	
Miami (city) Miami-Dade	73.41
Hialeah (city) Miami-Dade	61.64

Bolivians 25 Years and Over Who are High School Graduates
Top 10 Places Sorted by Number

Place (place type) County	Number
No places met population threshold.	

Bolivians 25 Years and Over Who are High School Graduates
Top 10 Places Sorted by Percent

Place (place type) County	Percent
No places met population threshold.	

Central Americans 25 Years and Over Who are High School Graduates
Top 10 Places Sorted by Number

Place (place type) County	Number
Miami (city) Miami-Dade	11,896
Hialeah (city) Miami-Dade	4,920
Fountainbleau (cdp) Miami-Dade	3,896
Kendale Lakes (cdp) Miami-Dade	2,117
Kendall (cdp) Miami-Dade	2,098
Tamiami (cdp) Miami-Dade	1,846
The Hammocks (cdp) Miami-Dade	1,589
Miami Beach (city) Miami-Dade	1,542
Kendall West (cdp) Miami-Dade	1,268
Tampa (city) Hillsborough	1,258

Central Americans 25 Years and Over Who are High School Graduates
Top 10 Places Sorted by Percent

Place (place type) County	Percent
Doral (cdp) Miami-Dade	94.66
Brandon (cdp) Hillsborough	90.45
The Hammocks (cdp) Miami-Dade	90.34
The Crossings (cdp) Miami-Dade	90.15
Country Walk (cdp) Miami-Dade	88.81
Plantation (city) Broward	88.74
Kendall (cdp) Miami-Dade	81.60
Pembroke Pines (city) Broward	79.81
Coral Gables (city) Miami-Dade	79.50
Kendale Lakes (cdp) Miami-Dade	79.44

Chileans 25 Years and Over Who are High School Graduates
Top 10 Places Sorted by Number

Place (place type) County	Number
Miami (city) Miami-Dade	521
Miami Beach (city) Miami-Dade	488
Hialeah (city) Miami-Dade	358
Fountainbleau (cdp) Miami-Dade	346
Kendall (cdp) Miami-Dade	301
Hollywood (city) Broward	191

Chileans 25 Years and Over Who are High School Graduates
Top 10 Places Sorted by Percent

Place (place type) County	Percent
Kendall (cdp) Miami-Dade	100.00
Miami Beach (city) Miami-Dade	85.76
Fountainbleau (cdp) Miami-Dade	73.31
Miami (city) Miami-Dade	72.26
Hollywood (city) Broward	67.25
Hialeah (city) Miami-Dade	66.92

Colombians 25 Years and Over Who are High School Graduates
Top 10 Places Sorted by Number

Place (place type) County	Number
Hialeah (city) Miami-Dade	3,604
Miami (city) Miami-Dade	3,124
The Hammocks (cdp) Miami-Dade	2,697
Miami Beach (city) Miami-Dade	2,614
Kendall (cdp) Miami-Dade	2,372
Kendale Lakes (cdp) Miami-Dade	2,110
Pembroke Pines (city) Broward	2,040
Kendall West (cdp) Miami-Dade	2,013
Country Club (cdp) Miami-Dade	1,947
Hollywood (city) Broward	1,752

Colombians 25 Years and Over Who are High School Graduates
Top 10 Places Sorted by Percent

Place (place type) County	Percent
Clearwater (city) Pinellas	95.97
The Crossings (cdp) Miami-Dade	94.83
Weston (city) Broward	93.55
Key Biscayne (village) Miami-Dade	91.18
Sandalfoot Cove (cdp) Palm Beach	91.04
Country Walk (cdp) Miami-Dade	90.91
Doral (cdp) Miami-Dade	90.17
Aventura (city) Miami-Dade	89.68
Pembroke Pines (city) Broward	89.32
Coral Springs (city) Broward	88.97

Costa Ricans 25 Years and Over Who are High School Graduates
Top 10 Places Sorted by Number

Place (place type) County	Number
Miami (city) Miami-Dade	380
Hialeah (city) Miami-Dade	167

Costa Ricans 25 Years and Over Who are High School Graduates
Top 10 Places Sorted by Percent

Place (place type) County	Percent
Miami (city) Miami-Dade	64.08
Hialeah (city) Miami-Dade	54.93

Cubans 25 Years and Over Who are High School Graduates
Top 10 Places Sorted by Number

Place (place type) County	Number
Hialeah (city) Miami-Dade	49,639
Miami (city) Miami-Dade	48,348
Tamiami (cdp) Miami-Dade	16,494
Kendale Lakes (cdp) Miami-Dade	11,881
Fountainbleau (cdp) Miami-Dade	11,258
Westchester (cdp) Miami-Dade	10,120
Miami Beach (city) Miami-Dade	9,885
Kendall (cdp) Miami-Dade	9,687
Coral Gables (city) Miami-Dade	8,336
University Park (cdp) Miami-Dade	8,150

Cubans 25 Years and Over Who are High School Graduates
Top 10 Places Sorted by Percent

Place (place type) County	Percent
Weston (city) Broward	92.88
Key Biscayne (village) Miami-Dade	92.49
Gainesville (city) Alachua	92.10
Pinecrest (village) Miami-Dade	91.83
Cutler (cdp) Miami-Dade	91.77
Brandon (cdp) Hillsborough	91.31
Miami Shores (village) Miami-Dade	89.97
Coral Springs (city) Broward	89.43
Doral (cdp) Miami-Dade	87.30

Notes: Please refer to the User's Guide for an explanation of data; tables include places with populations > 9,999 and reflect only those areas that meet Summary File 4 population thresholds, therefore there may be less than 10 places listed

Place (place type) County	
Coral Gables (city) Miami-Dade	87.28

Dominicans 25 Years and Over Who are High School Graduates
Top 10 Places Sorted by Number

Place (place type) County	Number
Miami (city) Miami-Dade	2,196
Hialeah (city) Miami-Dade	1,952
Pembroke Pines (city) Broward	916
Fountainbleau (cdp) Miami-Dade	914
The Hammocks (cdp) Miami-Dade	862
Miami Beach (city) Miami-Dade	770
Hollywood (city) Broward	726
Miramar (city) Broward	642
Country Club (cdp) Miami-Dade	616
Orlando (city) Orange	537

Dominicans 25 Years and Over Who are High School Graduates
Top 10 Places Sorted by Percent

Place (place type) County	Percent
Weston (city) Broward	87.90
The Hammocks (cdp) Miami-Dade	86.81
Doral (cdp) Miami-Dade	85.15
Coral Springs (city) Broward	83.68
Pembroke Pines (city) Broward	82.97
Kendall West (cdp) Miami-Dade	80.19
Jacksonville (city) Duval	78.24
Tamiami (cdp) Miami-Dade	78.21
Richmond West (cdp) Miami-Dade	76.28
Town 'n' Country (cdp) Hillsborough	76.17

Ecuadorians 25 Years and Over Who are High School Graduates
Top 10 Places Sorted by Number

Place (place type) County	Number
Miami (city) Miami-Dade	719
Hialeah (city) Miami-Dade	525
Coral Springs (city) Broward	511
Fountainbleau (cdp) Miami-Dade	423
Miami Beach (city) Miami-Dade	422
Pembroke Pines (city) Broward	365
Sunrise (city) Broward	346
Hollywood (city) Broward	325
Tampa (city) Hillsborough	268

Ecuadorians 25 Years and Over Who are High School Graduates
Top 10 Places Sorted by Percent

Place (place type) County	Percent
Pembroke Pines (city) Broward	97.33
Sunrise (city) Broward	89.41
Hollywood (city) Broward	87.84
Fountainbleau (cdp) Miami-Dade	87.58
Coral Springs (city) Broward	83.50
Miami Beach (city) Miami-Dade	80.38
Tampa (city) Hillsborough	80.00
Hialeah (city) Miami-Dade	61.40
Miami (city) Miami-Dade	57.94

Guatelmalans 25 Years and Over Who are High School Graduates
Top 10 Places Sorted by Number

Place (place type) County	Number
Miami (city) Miami-Dade	677
Hialeah (city) Miami-Dade	245
West Palm Beach (city) Palm Beach	141
Lake Worth (city) Palm Beach	113
Immokalee (cdp) Collier	68
Fort Lauderdale (city) Broward	63
Homestead (city) Miami-Dade	40
Bonita Springs (city) Lee	32
Fort Myers (city) Lee	0

Guatelmalans 25 Years and Over Who are High School Graduates
Top 10 Places Sorted by Percent

Place (place type) County	Percent
Hialeah (city) Miami-Dade	49.70
Miami (city) Miami-Dade	34.49
Fort Lauderdale (city) Broward	30.29
Bonita Springs (city) Lee	21.19
West Palm Beach (city) Palm Beach	14.49
Lake Worth (city) Palm Beach	13.12
Immokalee (cdp) Collier	11.35
Homestead (city) Miami-Dade	5.86
Fort Myers (city) Lee	0.00

Hondurans 25 Years and Over Who are High School Graduates
Top 10 Places Sorted by Number

Place (place type) County	Number
Miami (city) Miami-Dade	3,353
Hialeah (city) Miami-Dade	783
Miami Beach (city) Miami-Dade	373
Fountainbleau (cdp) Miami-Dade	278
West Little River (cdp) Miami-Dade	239
Tampa (city) Hillsborough	235
Hollywood (city) Broward	233
Kendale Lakes (cdp) Miami-Dade	226
Tamiami (cdp) Miami-Dade	224
North Miami (city) Miami-Dade	207

Hondurans 25 Years and Over Who are High School Graduates
Top 10 Places Sorted by Percent

Place (place type) County	Percent
Tamiami (cdp) Miami-Dade	72.03
Fountainbleau (cdp) Miami-Dade	70.74
Kendale Lakes (cdp) Miami-Dade	69.54
North Miami Beach (city) Miami-Dade	67.60
Hollywood (city) Broward	67.34
Miami Beach (city) Miami-Dade	63.76
North Miami (city) Miami-Dade	54.91
Hialeah (city) Miami-Dade	48.85
West Little River (cdp) Miami-Dade	46.50
Tampa (city) Hillsborough	40.94

Mexicans 25 Years and Over Who are High School Graduates
Top 10 Places Sorted by Number

Place (place type) County	Number
Jacksonville (city) Duval	2,066
Tampa (city) Hillsborough	1,801
Miami (city) Miami-Dade	1,007
Clearwater (city) Pinellas	955
Immokalee (cdp) Collier	867
Orlando (city) Orange	796
Sarasota (city) Sarasota	618
St. Petersburg (city) Pinellas	601
Miami Beach (city) Miami-Dade	576
Homestead (city) Miami-Dade	573

Mexicans 25 Years and Over Who are High School Graduates
Top 10 Places Sorted by Percent

Place (place type) County	Percent
The Hammocks (cdp) Miami-Dade	94.70
Doral (cdp) Miami-Dade	94.31
Gainesville (city) Alachua	86.31
Pembroke Pines (city) Broward	84.18
Panama City (city) Bay	84.03
Largo (city) Pinellas	82.70
Weston (city) Broward	82.13
Wright (cdp) Okaloosa	81.50
Palm Bay (city) Brevard	79.95
Fountainbleau (cdp) Miami-Dade	75.51

Nicaraguans 25 Years and Over Who are High School Graduates
Top 10 Places Sorted by Number

Place (place type) County	Number
Miami (city) Miami-Dade	6,285
Hialeah (city) Miami-Dade	3,100
Fountainbleau (cdp) Miami-Dade	2,750
Kendale Lakes (cdp) Miami-Dade	1,493
Tamiami (cdp) Miami-Dade	1,221
Kendall (cdp) Miami-Dade	1,150
The Hammocks (cdp) Miami-Dade	1,039
Sweetwater (city) Miami-Dade	906
Kendall West (cdp) Miami-Dade	759
Richmond West (cdp) Miami-Dade	607

Nicaraguans 25 Years and Over Who are High School Graduates
Top 10 Places Sorted by Percent

Place (place type) County	Percent
The Hammocks (cdp) Miami-Dade	91.06
The Crossings (cdp) Miami-Dade	89.42
Miami Beach (city) Miami-Dade	85.78
Coral Gables (city) Miami-Dade	84.59
Kendale Lakes (cdp) Miami-Dade	80.75
Kendall (cdp) Miami-Dade	80.48
Hollywood (city) Broward	79.89
University Park (cdp) Miami-Dade	79.16
Tamiami (cdp) Miami-Dade	73.87
Kendall West (cdp) Miami-Dade	73.83

Panamanians 25 Years and Over Who are High School Graduates
Top 10 Places Sorted by Number

Place (place type) County	Number
Miami (city) Miami-Dade	449
Fountainbleau (cdp) Miami-Dade	369
Tampa (city) Hillsborough	367
Jacksonville (city) Duval	323
Miramar (city) Broward	171

Panamanians 25 Years and Over Who are High School Graduates
Top 10 Places Sorted by Percent

Place (place type) County	Percent
Jacksonville (city) Duval	96.71
Fountainbleau (cdp) Miami-Dade	92.95
Tampa (city) Hillsborough	84.17
Miami (city) Miami-Dade	73.73
Miramar (city) Broward	72.77

Paraguayans 25 Years and Over Who are High School Graduates
Top 10 Places Sorted by Number

Place (place type) County	Number
No places met population threshold.	

Paraguayans 25 Years and Over Who are High School Graduates
Top 10 Places Sorted by Percent

Place (place type) County	Percent
No places met population threshold.	

Peruvians 25 Years and Over Who are High School Graduates
Top 10 Places Sorted by Number

Place (place type) County	Number
Miami (city) Miami-Dade	1,471
The Hammocks (cdp) Miami-Dade	1,201
Miami Beach (city) Miami-Dade	1,159
Pembroke Pines (city) Broward	890
Kendall (cdp) Miami-Dade	849

Notes: Please refer to the User's Guide for an explanation of data; tables include places with populations > 9,999 and reflect only those areas that meet Summary File 4 population thresholds, therefore there may be less than 10 places listed

Place (place type) County	Number
Fountainbleau (cdp) Miami-Dade	796
Hollywood (city) Broward	784
Hialeah (city) Miami-Dade	754
Kendall West (cdp) Miami-Dade	714
Kendale Lakes (cdp) Miami-Dade	578

Peruvians 25 Years and Over Who are High School Graduates
Top 10 Places Sorted by Percent

Place (place type) County	Percent
Plantation (city) Broward	96.60
Weston (city) Broward	95.95
Kendale Lakes (cdp) Miami-Dade	95.22
Kendall (cdp) Miami-Dade	95.18
Richmond West (cdp) Miami-Dade	94.82
The Hammocks (cdp) Miami-Dade	94.34
Coral Springs (city) Broward	94.01
Pembroke Pines (city) Broward	93.88
Sunrise (city) Broward	93.84
North Lauderdale (city) Broward	92.47

Puerto Ricans 25 Years and Over Who are High School Graduates
Top 10 Places Sorted by Number

Place (place type) County	Number
Orlando (city) Orange	7,158
Tampa (city) Hillsborough	5,350
Kissimmee (city) Osceola	4,774
Jacksonville (city) Duval	4,413
Deltona (city) Volusia	4,070
Pembroke Pines (city) Broward	3,956
Yeehaw Junction (cdp) Osceola	3,409
Miami (city) Miami-Dade	3,366
Town 'n' Country (cdp) Hillsborough	3,089
Hollywood (city) Broward	2,749

Puerto Ricans 25 Years and Over Who are High School Graduates
Top 10 Places Sorted by Percent

Place (place type) County	Percent
Coral Gables (city) Miami-Dade	96.22
Weston (city) Broward	95.68
Wekiwa Springs (cdp) Seminole	94.09
Cooper City (city) Broward	93.17
Tallahassee (city) Leon	92.59
Longwood (city) Seminole	91.34
Oviedo (city) Seminole	91.23
Doral (cdp) Miami-Dade	90.94
The Hammocks (cdp) Miami-Dade	90.78
Port Orange (city) Volusia	89.93

Salvadorans 25 Years and Over Who are High School Graduates
Top 10 Places Sorted by Number

Place (place type) County	Number
Miami (city) Miami-Dade	528
Hialeah (city) Miami-Dade	317
Fort Lauderdale (city) Broward	102
Oakland Park (city) Broward	84
Lake Worth (city) Palm Beach	83
Homestead (city) Miami-Dade	31

Salvadorans 25 Years and Over Who are High School Graduates
Top 10 Places Sorted by Percent

Place (place type) County	Percent
Hialeah (city) Miami-Dade	53.55
Lake Worth (city) Palm Beach	34.73
Miami (city) Miami-Dade	31.41
Fort Lauderdale (city) Broward	29.91
Oakland Park (city) Broward	19.91
Homestead (city) Miami-Dade	5.66

South Americans 25 Years and Over Who are High School Graduates
Top 10 Places Sorted by Number

Place (place type) County	Number
Miami (city) Miami-Dade	8,224
Miami Beach (city) Miami-Dade	7,679
Hialeah (city) Miami-Dade	5,994
The Hammocks (cdp) Miami-Dade	5,653
Kendall (cdp) Miami-Dade	5,284
Pembroke Pines (city) Broward	4,740
Fountainbleau (cdp) Miami-Dade	4,585
Kendale Lakes (cdp) Miami-Dade	4,052
Hollywood (city) Broward	3,982
Weston (city) Broward	3,957

South Americans 25 Years and Over Who are High School Graduates
Top 10 Places Sorted by Percent

Place (place type) County	Percent
Tallahassee (city) Leon	98.79
Clearwater (city) Pinellas	96.96
Weston (city) Broward	95.17
Gainesville (city) Alachua	94.47
Key Biscayne (village) Miami-Dade	93.79
South Miami (city) Miami-Dade	93.03
Aventura (city) Miami-Dade	92.40
Sandalfoot Cove (cdp) Palm Beach	92.34
Pembroke Pines (city) Broward	91.49
Coconut Creek (city) Broward	91.20

Spaniards 25 Years and Over Who are High School Graduates
Top 10 Places Sorted by Number

Place (place type) County	Number
Tampa (city) Hillsborough	518
Miami Beach (city) Miami-Dade	414
Miami (city) Miami-Dade	408
Hialeah (city) Miami-Dade	144

Spaniards 25 Years and Over Who are High School Graduates
Top 10 Places Sorted by Percent

Place (place type) County	Percent
Miami Beach (city) Miami-Dade	86.97
Tampa (city) Hillsborough	81.57
Miami (city) Miami-Dade	49.94
Hialeah (city) Miami-Dade	36.09

Uruguayans 25 Years and Over Who are High School Graduates
Top 10 Places Sorted by Number

Place (place type) County	Number
No places met population threshold.	

Uruguayans 25 Years and Over Who are High School Graduates
Top 10 Places Sorted by Percent

Place (place type) County	Percent
No places met population threshold.	

Venezuelans 25 Years and Over Who are High School Graduates
Top 10 Places Sorted by Number

Place (place type) County	Number
Weston (city) Broward	1,221
Fountainbleau (cdp) Miami-Dade	1,117
Doral (cdp) Miami-Dade	1,115
Miami (city) Miami-Dade	912
Miami Beach (city) Miami-Dade	907
Kendall (cdp) Miami-Dade	906
The Hammocks (cdp) Miami-Dade	906
Pembroke Pines (city) Broward	893
Kendall West (cdp) Miami-Dade	580
Kendale Lakes (cdp) Miami-Dade	464

Venezuelans 25 Years and Over Who are High School Graduates
Top 10 Places Sorted by Percent

Place (place type) County	Percent
The Crossings (cdp) Miami-Dade	98.03
Weston (city) Broward	96.45
Coral Gables (city) Miami-Dade	95.27
Pembroke Pines (city) Broward	94.30
Kendall (cdp) Miami-Dade	93.79
Doral (cdp) Miami-Dade	93.70
Plantation (city) Broward	92.09
Richmond West (cdp) Miami-Dade	91.67
Miami Beach (city) Miami-Dade	90.43
Tamiami (cdp) Miami-Dade	90.03

Other Hispanics 25 Years and Over Who are High School Graduates
Top 10 Places Sorted by Number

Place (place type) County	Number
Miami (city) Miami-Dade	7,960
Tampa (city) Hillsborough	5,240
Hialeah (city) Miami-Dade	4,769
Fountainbleau (cdp) Miami-Dade	2,973
Miami Beach (city) Miami-Dade	2,950
Kendale Lakes (cdp) Miami-Dade	2,699
Pembroke Pines (city) Broward	2,383
Kendall (cdp) Miami-Dade	2,220
Jacksonville (city) Duval	2,151
Hollywood (city) Broward	2,096

Other Hispanics 25 Years and Over Who are High School Graduates
Top 10 Places Sorted by Percent

Place (place type) County	Percent
Key Biscayne (village) Miami-Dade	94.55
Greater Northdale (cdp) Hillsborough	93.00
Lake Magdalene (cdp) Hillsborough	92.20
Lakeside (cdp) Clay	91.83
Glenvar Heights (cdp) Miami-Dade	89.80
Daytona Beach (city) Volusia	89.52
Weston (city) Broward	88.83
Country Walk (cdp) Miami-Dade	88.64
St. Petersburg (city) Pinellas	88.46
Gainesville (city) Alachua	87.82

Educational Attainment: Four-Year College Graduates

Total Population 25 Years and Over Who are Four-Year College Graduates
Top 10 Places Sorted by Number

Place (place type) County	Number
Jacksonville (city) Duval	98,991
Tampa (city) Hillsborough	50,471
Miami (city) Miami-Dade	41,004
St. Petersburg (city) Pinellas	39,987
Tallahassee (city) Leon	35,901
Orlando (city) Orange	35,396
Fort Lauderdale (city) Broward	31,059
Pembroke Pines (city) Broward	26,847
Coral Springs (city) Broward	24,489
Boca Raton (city) Palm Beach	24,362

Total Population 25 Years and Over Who are Four-Year College Graduates
Top 10 Places Sorted by Percent

Place (place type) County	Percent
Key Biscayne (village) Miami-Dade	64.95
Pinecrest (village) Miami-Dade	61.56

Notes: Please refer to the User's Guide for an explanation of data; tables include places with populations > 9,999 and reflect only those areas that meet Summary File 4 population thresholds, therefore there may be less than 10 places listed

Place (place type) County	
Coral Gables (city) Miami-Dade	58.28
Cutler (cdp) Miami-Dade	55.75
Parkland (city) Broward	52.79
Maitland (city) Orange	51.78
Weston (city) Broward	50.87
Winter Park (city) Orange	50.14
Wekiwa Springs (cdp) Seminole	49.62
Westchase (cdp) Hillsborough	49.04

Hispanics 25 Years and Over Who are Four-Year College Graduates
Top 10 Places Sorted by Number

Place (place type) County	Number
Miami (city) Miami-Dade	23,714
Hialeah (city) Miami-Dade	14,660
Miami Beach (city) Miami-Dade	9,176
Kendall (cdp) Miami-Dade	8,729
Coral Gables (city) Miami-Dade	7,706
Fountainbleau (cdp) Miami-Dade	7,698
Pembroke Pines (city) Broward	7,101
Tamiami (cdp) Miami-Dade	7,028
Kendale Lakes (cdp) Miami-Dade	6,174
The Hammocks (cdp) Miami-Dade	5,424

Hispanics 25 Years and Over Who are Four-Year College Graduates
Top 10 Places Sorted by Percent

Place (place type) County	Percent
Key Biscayne (village) Miami-Dade	60.96
Parkland (city) Broward	56.93
Coral Gables (city) Miami-Dade	52.09
Pinecrest (village) Miami-Dade	50.38
Gainesville (city) Alachua	46.92
Weston (city) Broward	46.16
Cutler (cdp) Miami-Dade	44.95
Wekiwa Springs (cdp) Seminole	44.31
Aventura (city) Miami-Dade	44.24
Doral (cdp) Miami-Dade	44.17

Argentinians 25 Years and Over Who are Four-Year College Graduates
Top 10 Places Sorted by Number

Place (place type) County	Number
Miami Beach (city) Miami-Dade	604
Miami (city) Miami-Dade	433
Kendall (cdp) Miami-Dade	205
Sunny Isles Beach (city) Miami-Dade	73
Hollywood (city) Broward	67
Hialeah (city) Miami-Dade	57
Fountainbleau (cdp) Miami-Dade	54

Argentinians 25 Years and Over Who are Four-Year College Graduates
Top 10 Places Sorted by Percent

Place (place type) County	Percent
Kendall (cdp) Miami-Dade	41.67
Miami (city) Miami-Dade	29.90
Miami Beach (city) Miami-Dade	28.94
Hialeah (city) Miami-Dade	19.52
Hollywood (city) Broward	17.40
Sunny Isles Beach (city) Miami-Dade	15.18
Fountainbleau (cdp) Miami-Dade	14.79

Bolivians 25 Years and Over Who are Four-Year College Graduates
Top 10 Places Sorted by Number

Place (place type) County	Number
No places met population threshold.	

Bolivians 25 Years and Over Who are Four-Year College Graduates
Top 10 Places Sorted by Percent

Place (place type) County	Percent
No places met population threshold.	

Central Americans 25 Years and Over Who are Four-Year College Graduates
Top 10 Places Sorted by Number

Place (place type) County	Number
Miami (city) Miami-Dade	2,228
Fountainbleau (cdp) Miami-Dade	966
Hialeah (city) Miami-Dade	875
Kendall (cdp) Miami-Dade	687
Kendale Lakes (cdp) Miami-Dade	537
Tamiami (cdp) Miami-Dade	491
The Hammocks (cdp) Miami-Dade	483
Miami Beach (city) Miami-Dade	417
Pembroke Pines (city) Broward	355
Kendall West (cdp) Miami-Dade	343

Central Americans 25 Years and Over Who are Four-Year College Graduates
Top 10 Places Sorted by Percent

Place (place type) County	Percent
Doral (cdp) Miami-Dade	51.55
Coral Gables (city) Miami-Dade	40.72
Pinecrest (village) Miami-Dade	37.85
The Crossings (cdp) Miami-Dade	32.88
Plantation (city) Broward	30.80
The Hammocks (cdp) Miami-Dade	27.46
Glenvar Heights (cdp) Miami-Dade	27.00
Kendall (cdp) Miami-Dade	26.72
Coral Springs (city) Broward	26.34
Pembroke Pines (city) Broward	25.97

Chileans 25 Years and Over Who are Four-Year College Graduates
Top 10 Places Sorted by Number

Place (place type) County	Number
Miami (city) Miami-Dade	147
Miami Beach (city) Miami-Dade	117
Fountainbleau (cdp) Miami-Dade	107
Kendall (cdp) Miami-Dade	74
Hialeah (city) Miami-Dade	45
Hollywood (city) Broward	42

Chileans 25 Years and Over Who are Four-Year College Graduates
Top 10 Places Sorted by Percent

Place (place type) County	Percent
Kendall (cdp) Miami-Dade	24.58
Fountainbleau (cdp) Miami-Dade	22.67
Miami Beach (city) Miami-Dade	20.56
Miami (city) Miami-Dade	20.39
Hollywood (city) Broward	14.79
Hialeah (city) Miami-Dade	8.41

Colombians 25 Years and Over Who are Four-Year College Graduates
Top 10 Places Sorted by Number

Place (place type) County	Number
Miami (city) Miami-Dade	1,060
Weston (city) Broward	1,058
Miami Beach (city) Miami-Dade	1,027
Kendall (cdp) Miami-Dade	991
The Hammocks (cdp) Miami-Dade	886
Pembroke Pines (city) Broward	762
Doral (cdp) Miami-Dade	623
Hialeah (city) Miami-Dade	611
Kendale Lakes (cdp) Miami-Dade	533
Plantation (city) Broward	531

Colombians 25 Years and Over Who are Four-Year College Graduates
Top 10 Places Sorted by Percent

Place (place type) County	Percent
Key Biscayne (village) Miami-Dade	63.04
Weston (city) Broward	57.85
Doral (cdp) Miami-Dade	56.18
Aventura (city) Miami-Dade	53.00
Coral Gables (city) Miami-Dade	47.35
Glenvar Heights (cdp) Miami-Dade	34.94
Kendall (cdp) Miami-Dade	34.94
Cooper City (city) Broward	33.97
Clearwater (city) Pinellas	33.70
Pembroke Pines (city) Broward	33.36

Costa Ricans 25 Years and Over Who are Four-Year College Graduates
Top 10 Places Sorted by Number

Place (place type) County	Number
Miami (city) Miami-Dade	77
Hialeah (city) Miami-Dade	21

Costa Ricans 25 Years and Over Who are Four-Year College Graduates
Top 10 Places Sorted by Percent

Place (place type) County	Percent
Miami (city) Miami-Dade	12.98
Hialeah (city) Miami-Dade	6.91

Cubans 25 Years and Over Who are Four-Year College Graduates
Top 10 Places Sorted by Number

Place (place type) County	Number
Miami (city) Miami-Dade	14,926
Hialeah (city) Miami-Dade	10,997
Tamiami (cdp) Miami-Dade	5,056
Coral Gables (city) Miami-Dade	5,031
Kendall (cdp) Miami-Dade	4,215
Miami Beach (city) Miami-Dade	3,847
Fountainbleau (cdp) Miami-Dade	3,668
Westchester (cdp) Miami-Dade	3,462
Kendale Lakes (cdp) Miami-Dade	3,310
University Park (cdp) Miami-Dade	2,916

Cubans 25 Years and Over Who are Four-Year College Graduates
Top 10 Places Sorted by Percent

Place (place type) County	Percent
Key Biscayne (village) Miami-Dade	58.47
Pinecrest (village) Miami-Dade	57.56
Coral Gables (city) Miami-Dade	52.68
Gainesville (city) Alachua	49.86
Miami Shores (village) Miami-Dade	47.04
Tallahassee (city) Leon	44.91
Cutler (cdp) Miami-Dade	44.58
Boynton Beach (city) Palm Beach	43.50
Weston (city) Broward	42.81
Boca Raton (city) Palm Beach	38.47

Dominicans 25 Years and Over Who are Four-Year College Graduates
Top 10 Places Sorted by Number

Place (place type) County	Number
Miami (city) Miami-Dade	428
Hialeah (city) Miami-Dade	402
Pembroke Pines (city) Broward	353
Fountainbleau (cdp) Miami-Dade	341
The Hammocks (cdp) Miami-Dade	308
Miami Beach (city) Miami-Dade	241
Doral (cdp) Miami-Dade	186
Hollywood (city) Broward	156
Country Club (cdp) Miami-Dade	127

Notes: Please refer to the User's Guide for an explanation of data; tables include places with populations > 9,999 and reflect only those areas that meet Summary File 4 population thresholds, therefore there may be less than 10 places listed

Miramar (city) Broward	123

Dominicans 25 Years and Over Who are Four-Year College Graduates
Top 10 Places Sorted by Percent

Place (place type) County	Percent
Doral (cdp) Miami-Dade	52.10
Weston (city) Broward	37.50
Pembroke Pines (city) Broward	31.97
The Hammocks (cdp) Miami-Dade	31.02
Fountainbleau (cdp) Miami-Dade	28.35
Richmond West (cdp) Miami-Dade	23.72
Miami Beach (city) Miami-Dade	22.50
Kendall (cdp) Miami-Dade	21.65
Tamiami (cdp) Miami-Dade	19.83
Kendale Lakes (cdp) Miami-Dade	19.43

Ecuadorians 25 Years and Over Who are Four-Year College Graduates
Top 10 Places Sorted by Number

Place (place type) County	Number
Miami (city) Miami-Dade	213
Coral Springs (city) Broward	176
Miami Beach (city) Miami-Dade	165
Hialeah (city) Miami-Dade	118
Pembroke Pines (city) Broward	107
Fountainbleau (cdp) Miami-Dade	97
Tampa (city) Hillsborough	83
Hollywood (city) Broward	56
Sunrise (city) Broward	42

Ecuadorians 25 Years and Over Who are Four-Year College Graduates
Top 10 Places Sorted by Percent

Place (place type) County	Percent
Miami Beach (city) Miami-Dade	31.43
Coral Springs (city) Broward	28.76
Pembroke Pines (city) Broward	28.53
Tampa (city) Hillsborough	24.78
Fountainbleau (cdp) Miami-Dade	20.08
Miami (city) Miami-Dade	17.16
Hollywood (city) Broward	15.14
Hialeah (city) Miami-Dade	13.80
Sunrise (city) Broward	10.85

Guatelmalans 25 Years and Over Who are Four-Year College Graduates
Top 10 Places Sorted by Number

Place (place type) County	Number
Miami (city) Miami-Dade	140
Lake Worth (city) Palm Beach	42
Hialeah (city) Miami-Dade	17
West Palm Beach (city) Palm Beach	15
Bonita Springs (city) Lee	5
Fort Lauderdale (city) Broward	0
Fort Myers (city) Lee	0
Homestead (city) Miami-Dade	0
Immokalee (cdp) Collier	0

Guatelmalans 25 Years and Over Who are Four-Year College Graduates
Top 10 Places Sorted by Percent

Place (place type) County	Percent
Miami (city) Miami-Dade	7.13
Lake Worth (city) Palm Beach	4.88
Hialeah (city) Miami-Dade	3.45
Bonita Springs (city) Lee	3.31
West Palm Beach (city) Palm Beach	1.54
Fort Lauderdale (city) Broward	0.00
Fort Myers (city) Lee	0.00
Homestead (city) Miami-Dade	0.00
Immokalee (cdp) Collier	0.00

Hondurans 25 Years and Over Who are Four-Year College Graduates
Top 10 Places Sorted by Number

Place (place type) County	Number
Miami (city) Miami-Dade	468
Hialeah (city) Miami-Dade	92
Miami Beach (city) Miami-Dade	82
Tamiami (cdp) Miami-Dade	50
Fountainbleau (cdp) Miami-Dade	46
Hollywood (city) Broward	40
Kendale Lakes (cdp) Miami-Dade	36
Tampa (city) Hillsborough	26
Carol City (cdp) Miami-Dade	22
Lake Worth (city) Palm Beach	22

Hondurans 25 Years and Over Who are Four-Year College Graduates
Top 10 Places Sorted by Percent

Place (place type) County	Percent
Tamiami (cdp) Miami-Dade	16.08
Miami Beach (city) Miami-Dade	14.02
Fountainbleau (cdp) Miami-Dade	11.70
Hollywood (city) Broward	11.56
Kendale Lakes (cdp) Miami-Dade	11.08
Lake Worth (city) Palm Beach	8.59
Carol City (cdp) Miami-Dade	6.96
Hialeah (city) Miami-Dade	5.74
Miami (city) Miami-Dade	5.00
Tampa (city) Hillsborough	4.53

Mexicans 25 Years and Over Who are Four-Year College Graduates
Top 10 Places Sorted by Number

Place (place type) County	Number
Jacksonville (city) Duval	436
Miami (city) Miami-Dade	401
Tampa (city) Hillsborough	393
Doral (cdp) Miami-Dade	287
Orlando (city) Orange	271
Miami Beach (city) Miami-Dade	211
Clearwater (city) Pinellas	183
Pembroke Pines (city) Broward	156
The Hammocks (cdp) Miami-Dade	153
Fort Lauderdale (city) Broward	152

Mexicans 25 Years and Over Who are Four-Year College Graduates
Top 10 Places Sorted by Percent

Place (place type) County	Percent
Doral (cdp) Miami-Dade	65.38
Gainesville (city) Alachua	52.98
The Hammocks (cdp) Miami-Dade	47.66
Weston (city) Broward	45.36
Melbourne (city) Brevard	30.77
Tallahassee (city) Leon	25.93
Pembroke Pines (city) Broward	25.70
Miami Beach (city) Miami-Dade	25.27
Plantation (city) Broward	24.59
Miramar (city) Broward	23.96

Nicaraguans 25 Years and Over Who are Four-Year College Graduates
Top 10 Places Sorted by Number

Place (place type) County	Number
Miami (city) Miami-Dade	1,247
Fountainbleau (cdp) Miami-Dade	697
Hialeah (city) Miami-Dade	661
Kendale Lakes (cdp) Miami-Dade	379
Kendall (cdp) Miami-Dade	342
Tamiami (cdp) Miami-Dade	316
The Hammocks (cdp) Miami-Dade	272
Sweetwater (city) Miami-Dade	228
Kendall West (cdp) Miami-Dade	193

Richmond West (cdp) Miami-Dade	160

Nicaraguans 25 Years and Over Who are Four-Year College Graduates
Top 10 Places Sorted by Percent

Place (place type) County	Percent
Coral Gables (city) Miami-Dade	34.05
The Crossings (cdp) Miami-Dade	30.48
Kendall (cdp) Miami-Dade	23.93
The Hammocks (cdp) Miami-Dade	23.84
Miami Beach (city) Miami-Dade	22.64
Kendale Lakes (cdp) Miami-Dade	20.50
Hialeah Gardens (city) Miami-Dade	20.36
North Miami (city) Miami-Dade	19.60
Tamiami (cdp) Miami-Dade	19.12
Richmond West (cdp) Miami-Dade	19.09

Panamanians 25 Years and Over Who are Four-Year College Graduates
Top 10 Places Sorted by Number

Place (place type) County	Number
Miami (city) Miami-Dade	121
Fountainbleau (cdp) Miami-Dade	103
Tampa (city) Hillsborough	52
Jacksonville (city) Duval	44
Miramar (city) Broward	27

Panamanians 25 Years and Over Who are Four-Year College Graduates
Top 10 Places Sorted by Percent

Place (place type) County	Percent
Fountainbleau (cdp) Miami-Dade	25.94
Miami (city) Miami-Dade	19.87
Jacksonville (city) Duval	13.17
Tampa (city) Hillsborough	11.93
Miramar (city) Broward	11.49

Paraguayans 25 Years and Over Who are Four-Year College Graduates
Top 10 Places Sorted by Number

Place (place type) County	Number
No places met population threshold.	

Paraguayans 25 Years and Over Who are Four-Year College Graduates
Top 10 Places Sorted by Percent

Place (place type) County	Percent
No places met population threshold.	

Peruvians 25 Years and Over Who are Four-Year College Graduates
Top 10 Places Sorted by Number

Place (place type) County	Number
Miami (city) Miami-Dade	464
Pembroke Pines (city) Broward	403
Kendall (cdp) Miami-Dade	383
The Hammocks (cdp) Miami-Dade	330
Fountainbleau (cdp) Miami-Dade	280
Miami Beach (city) Miami-Dade	277
Weston (city) Broward	201
Kendall West (cdp) Miami-Dade	191
Kendale Lakes (cdp) Miami-Dade	177
Hollywood (city) Broward	176

Peruvians 25 Years and Over Who are Four-Year College Graduates
Top 10 Places Sorted by Percent

Place (place type) County	Percent
Plantation (city) Broward	44.48
Kendall (cdp) Miami-Dade	42.94
Pembroke Pines (city) Broward	42.51

Notes: Please refer to the User's Guide for an explanation of data; tables include places with populations > 9,999 and reflect only those areas that meet Summary File 4 population thresholds, therefore there may be less than 10 places listed

Place (place type) County	
Weston (city) Broward	38.73
Doral (cdp) Miami-Dade	34.48
Fountainbleau (cdp) Miami-Dade	31.32
Fort Lauderdale (city) Broward	29.43
Kendale Lakes (cdp) Miami-Dade	29.16
Sunrise (city) Broward	28.67
Coral Springs (city) Broward	28.13

Puerto Ricans 25 Years and Over Who are Four-Year College Graduates
Top 10 Places Sorted by Number

Place (place type) County	Number
Orlando (city) Orange	1,395
Pembroke Pines (city) Broward	1,165
Jacksonville (city) Duval	978
Miami (city) Miami-Dade	964
Tampa (city) Hillsborough	902
Kissimmee (city) Osceola	744
Coral Springs (city) Broward	742
Yeehaw Junction (cdp) Osceola	647
Weston (city) Broward	616
Miami Beach (city) Miami-Dade	604

Puerto Ricans 25 Years and Over Who are Four-Year College Graduates
Top 10 Places Sorted by Percent

Place (place type) County	Percent
Coral Gables (city) Miami-Dade	63.52
Glenvar Heights (cdp) Miami-Dade	57.33
Weston (city) Broward	53.20
Doral (cdp) Miami-Dade	45.31
Tallahassee (city) Leon	43.21
Wekiwa Springs (cdp) Seminole	42.73
Gainesville (city) Alachua	38.56
Miami Lakes (cdp) Miami-Dade	37.18
Cooper City (city) Broward	36.12
Plantation (city) Broward	35.98

Salvadorans 25 Years and Over Who are Four-Year College Graduates
Top 10 Places Sorted by Number

Place (place type) County	Number
Miami (city) Miami-Dade	128
Fort Lauderdale (city) Broward	14
Oakland Park (city) Broward	14
Lake Worth (city) Palm Beach	13
Homestead (city) Miami-Dade	12
Hialeah (city) Miami-Dade	9

Salvadorans 25 Years and Over Who are Four-Year College Graduates
Top 10 Places Sorted by Percent

Place (place type) County	Percent
Miami (city) Miami-Dade	7.61
Lake Worth (city) Palm Beach	5.44
Fort Lauderdale (city) Broward	4.11
Oakland Park (city) Broward	3.32
Homestead (city) Miami-Dade	2.19
Hialeah (city) Miami-Dade	1.52

South Americans 25 Years and Over Who are Four-Year College Graduates
Top 10 Places Sorted by Number

Place (place type) County	Number
Miami (city) Miami-Dade	2,864
Miami Beach (city) Miami-Dade	2,651
Kendall (cdp) Miami-Dade	2,238
Weston (city) Broward	2,127
Pembroke Pines (city) Broward	1,921
The Hammocks (cdp) Miami-Dade	1,729
Doral (cdp) Miami-Dade	1,497
Fountainbleau (cdp) Miami-Dade	1,478
Hialeah (city) Miami-Dade	1,106
Hollywood (city) Broward	1,076

South Americans 25 Years and Over Who are Four-Year College Graduates
Top 10 Places Sorted by Percent

Place (place type) County	Percent
Key Biscayne (village) Miami-Dade	59.61
Parkland (city) Broward	54.84
Gainesville (city) Alachua	54.38
Coral Gables (city) Miami-Dade	53.13
Aventura (city) Miami-Dade	52.13
Weston (city) Broward	51.15
Pinecrest (village) Miami-Dade	48.18
South Miami (city) Miami-Dade	45.30
Doral (cdp) Miami-Dade	43.98
Tallahassee (city) Leon	41.40

Spaniards 25 Years and Over Who are Four-Year College Graduates
Top 10 Places Sorted by Number

Place (place type) County	Number
Tampa (city) Hillsborough	244
Miami Beach (city) Miami-Dade	228
Miami (city) Miami-Dade	164
Hialeah (city) Miami-Dade	8

Spaniards 25 Years and Over Who are Four-Year College Graduates
Top 10 Places Sorted by Percent

Place (place type) County	Percent
Miami Beach (city) Miami-Dade	47.90
Tampa (city) Hillsborough	38.43
Miami (city) Miami-Dade	20.07
Hialeah (city) Miami-Dade	2.01

Uruguayans 25 Years and Over Who are Four-Year College Graduates
Top 10 Places Sorted by Number

Place (place type) County	Number
No places met population threshold.	

Uruguayans 25 Years and Over Who are Four-Year College Graduates
Top 10 Places Sorted by Percent

Place (place type) County	Percent
No places met population threshold.	

Venezuelans 25 Years and Over Who are Four-Year College Graduates
Top 10 Places Sorted by Number

Place (place type) County	Number
Weston (city) Broward	656
Doral (cdp) Miami-Dade	582
Kendall (cdp) Miami-Dade	484
Pembroke Pines (city) Broward	468
Fountainbleau (cdp) Miami-Dade	408
Miami (city) Miami-Dade	378
The Hammocks (cdp) Miami-Dade	348
Miami Beach (city) Miami-Dade	338
Coral Gables (city) Miami-Dade	214
Orlando (city) Orange	192

Venezuelans 25 Years and Over Who are Four-Year College Graduates
Top 10 Places Sorted by Percent

Place (place type) County	Percent
Coral Gables (city) Miami-Dade	63.31
Weston (city) Broward	51.82
Coral Springs (city) Broward	50.18
Kendall (cdp) Miami-Dade	50.10
Pembroke Pines (city) Broward	49.42

Place (place type) County	
Doral (cdp) Miami-Dade	48.91
Tampa (city) Hillsborough	45.65
Tamiami (cdp) Miami-Dade	45.62
Richmond West (cdp) Miami-Dade	43.01
Orlando (city) Orange	41.74

Other Hispanics 25 Years and Over Who are Four-Year College Graduates
Top 10 Places Sorted by Number

Place (place type) County	Number
Miami (city) Miami-Dade	1,739
Tampa (city) Hillsborough	1,360
Miami Beach (city) Miami-Dade	977
Hialeah (city) Miami-Dade	850
Fountainbleau (cdp) Miami-Dade	827
Pembroke Pines (city) Broward	761
Kendale Lakes (cdp) Miami-Dade	758
Kendall (cdp) Miami-Dade	750
Doral (cdp) Miami-Dade	637
Jacksonville (city) Duval	595

Other Hispanics 25 Years and Over Who are Four-Year College Graduates
Top 10 Places Sorted by Percent

Place (place type) County	Percent
Key Biscayne (village) Miami-Dade	66.46
Cutler (cdp) Miami-Dade	54.55
Doral (cdp) Miami-Dade	45.37
Gainesville (city) Alachua	45.33
Coral Gables (city) Miami-Dade	43.41
Temple Terrace (city) Hillsborough	42.65
Aventura (city) Miami-Dade	38.61
Greater Carrollwood (cdp) Hillsborough	36.53
Sandalfoot Cove (cdp) Palm Beach	35.51
Cooper City (city) Broward	35.02

Median Household Income

Total Population
Top 10 Places Sorted by Number

Place (place type) County	Dollars
Pinecrest (village) Miami-Dade	107,507
Cutler (cdp) Miami-Dade	106,432
Parkland (city) Broward	102,624
Key Biscayne (village) Miami-Dade	86,599
Weston (city) Broward	80,920
Keystone (cdp) Hillsborough	80,677
Westchase (cdp) Hillsborough	79,561
Cooper City (city) Broward	75,166
Wekiwa Springs (cdp) Seminole	71,839
Wellington (village) Palm Beach	70,271

Hispanic
Top 10 Places Sorted by Number

Place (place type) County	Dollars
Cutler (cdp) Miami-Dade	109,352
Pinecrest (village) Miami-Dade	97,084
Lake Mary (city) Seminole	91,247
Wekiwa Springs (cdp) Seminole	90,000
Parkland (city) Broward	89,876
Key Biscayne (village) Miami-Dade	83,752
Westchase (cdp) Hillsborough	76,380
Cooper City (city) Broward	74,952
Keystone (cdp) Hillsborough	72,083
Bloomingdale (cdp) Hillsborough	66,500

Argentinian
Top 10 Places Sorted by Number

Place (place type) County	Dollars
Kendall (cdp) Miami-Dade	40,938
Hialeah (city) Miami-Dade	39,688
Miami (city) Miami-Dade	36,289
Fountainbleau (cdp) Miami-Dade	31,944

Notes: Please refer to the User's Guide for an explanation of data; tables include places with populations > 9,999 and reflect only those areas that meet Summary File 4 population thresholds, therefore there may be less than 10 places listed

Place (place type) County	Dollars
Hollywood (city) Broward	27,857
Sunny Isles Beach (city) Miami-Dade	23,750
Miami Beach (city) Miami-Dade	22,154

Bolivian
Top 10 Places Sorted by Number

Place (place type) County	Dollars

No places met population threshold.

Central American
Top 10 Places Sorted by Number

Place (place type) County	Dollars
Country Walk (cdp) Miami-Dade	72,396
Sunset (cdp) Miami-Dade	64,821
Pembroke Pines (city) Broward	60,969
Plantation (city) Broward	60,139
The Crossings (cdp) Miami-Dade	60,114
Jupiter (town) Palm Beach	57,500
Richmond West (cdp) Miami-Dade	57,250
The Hammocks (cdp) Miami-Dade	55,882
Doral (cdp) Miami-Dade	55,000
Miramar (city) Broward	54,671

Chilean
Top 10 Places Sorted by Number

Place (place type) County	Dollars
Fountainbleau (cdp) Miami-Dade	40,395
Kendall (cdp) Miami-Dade	36,719
Hollywood (city) Broward	36,667
Miami (city) Miami-Dade	28,667
Hialeah (city) Miami-Dade	25,195
Miami Beach (city) Miami-Dade	21,875

Colombian
Top 10 Places Sorted by Number

Place (place type) County	Dollars
Meadow Woods (cdp) Orange	60,880
Cooper City (city) Broward	60,476
Miami Lakes (cdp) Miami-Dade	57,422
Key Biscayne (village) Miami-Dade	55,469
Wellington (village) Palm Beach	55,441
Richmond West (cdp) Miami-Dade	54,286
South Miami Heights (cdp) Miami-Dade	53,092
Sunset (cdp) Miami-Dade	52,115
Coral Gables (city) Miami-Dade	51,118
Plantation (city) Broward	50,263

Costa Rican
Top 10 Places Sorted by Number

Place (place type) County	Dollars
Miami (city) Miami-Dade	28,405
Hialeah (city) Miami-Dade	25,769

Cuban
Top 10 Places Sorted by Number

Place (place type) County	Dollars
Pinecrest (village) Miami-Dade	136,566
Cutler (cdp) Miami-Dade	125,198
Key Biscayne (village) Miami-Dade	97,344
Weston (city) Broward	94,463
Cooper City (city) Broward	88,617
Coral Gables (city) Miami-Dade	73,830
Wellington (village) Palm Beach	68,438
Plantation (city) Broward	68,167
Miami Lakes (cdp) Miami-Dade	67,143
Miami Shores (village) Miami-Dade	64,750

Dominican
Top 10 Places Sorted by Number

Place (place type) County	Dollars
The Hammocks (cdp) Miami-Dade	57,228

Place (place type) County	Dollars
Weston (city) Broward	57,014
Pembroke Pines (city) Broward	52,050
Sunrise (city) Broward	50,375
Kendale Lakes (cdp) Miami-Dade	43,259
Miramar (city) Broward	43,000
Richmond West (cdp) Miami-Dade	42,414
Tamiami (cdp) Miami-Dade	41,429
Town 'n' Country (cdp) Hillsborough	40,536
Hialeah Gardens (city) Miami-Dade	40,313

Ecuadorian
Top 10 Places Sorted by Number

Place (place type) County	Dollars
Coral Springs (city) Broward	69,444
Pembroke Pines (city) Broward	58,333
Hollywood (city) Broward	37,578
Sunrise (city) Broward	37,250
Hialeah (city) Miami-Dade	35,169
Fountainbleau (cdp) Miami-Dade	32,426
Miami (city) Miami-Dade	25,664
Miami Beach (city) Miami-Dade	24,375
Tampa (city) Hillsborough	20,294

Guatelmalan
Top 10 Places Sorted by Number

Place (place type) County	Dollars
Immokalee (cdp) Collier	47,679
Fort Myers (city) Lee	45,625
West Palm Beach (city) Palm Beach	37,313
Lake Worth (city) Palm Beach	32,292
Bonita Springs (city) Lee	32,222
Fort Lauderdale (city) Broward	31,250
Miami (city) Miami-Dade	28,583
Homestead (city) Miami-Dade	25,657
Hialeah (city) Miami-Dade	24,189

Honduran
Top 10 Places Sorted by Number

Place (place type) County	Dollars
Fountainbleau (cdp) Miami-Dade	45,500
Lake Worth (city) Palm Beach	40,750
North Miami (city) Miami-Dade	35,699
Carol City (cdp) Miami-Dade	35,063
Hollywood (city) Broward	33,929
Hialeah (city) Miami-Dade	30,958
Tamiami (cdp) Miami-Dade	26,667
West Little River (cdp) Miami-Dade	26,667
Tampa (city) Hillsborough	26,324
Miami (city) Miami-Dade	23,233

Mexican
Top 10 Places Sorted by Number

Place (place type) County	Dollars
Doral (cdp) Miami-Dade	76,197
Pembroke Pines (city) Broward	73,047
Weston (city) Broward	71,538
Key West (city) Monroe	58,333
Miramar (city) Broward	56,339
Sunrise (city) Broward	52,308
The Hammocks (cdp) Miami-Dade	51,250
Davie (town) Broward	50,662
South Miami Heights (cdp) Miami-Dade	46,000
Brandon (cdp) Hillsborough	45,500

Nicaraguan
Top 10 Places Sorted by Number

Place (place type) County	Dollars
The Crossings (cdp) Miami-Dade	59,821
Miramar (city) Broward	58,935
The Hammocks (cdp) Miami-Dade	58,347
Richmond West (cdp) Miami-Dade	57,344
Coral Gables (city) Miami-Dade	53,917
Tamiami (cdp) Miami-Dade	52,188

Place (place type) County	Dollars
Kendall (cdp) Miami-Dade	49,375
Palmetto Estates (cdp) Miami-Dade	46,250
South Miami Heights (cdp) Miami-Dade	44,318
Kendale Lakes (cdp) Miami-Dade	44,047

Panamanian
Top 10 Places Sorted by Number

Place (place type) County	Dollars
Fountainbleau (cdp) Miami-Dade	55,231
Jacksonville (city) Duval	47,969
Miramar (city) Broward	35,855
Miami (city) Miami-Dade	32,054
Tampa (city) Hillsborough	24,671

Paraguayan
Top 10 Places Sorted by Number

Place (place type) County	Dollars

No places met population threshold.

Peruvian
Top 10 Places Sorted by Number

Place (place type) County	Dollars
The Crossings (cdp) Miami-Dade	64,000
Weston (city) Broward	58,750
Doral (cdp) Miami-Dade	58,077
Pembroke Pines (city) Broward	56,808
Miramar (city) Broward	56,591
The Hammocks (cdp) Miami-Dade	55,917
Richmond West (cdp) Miami-Dade	53,000
Sunrise (city) Broward	44,821
Kendall West (cdp) Miami-Dade	41,932
Fort Lauderdale (city) Broward	40,882

Puerto Rican
Top 10 Places Sorted by Number

Place (place type) County	Dollars
Wekiwa Springs (cdp) Seminole	86,365
Weston (city) Broward	70,703
Richmond West (cdp) Miami-Dade	67,279
Coral Gables (city) Miami-Dade	65,720
Cooper City (city) Broward	64,259
Coconut Creek (city) Broward	61,250
Royal Palm Beach (village) Palm Beach	60,417
Palmetto Estates (cdp) Miami-Dade	59,716
The Crossings (cdp) Miami-Dade	58,750
Miami Lakes (cdp) Miami-Dade	58,438

Salvadoran
Top 10 Places Sorted by Number

Place (place type) County	Dollars
Homestead (city) Miami-Dade	32,639
Fort Lauderdale (city) Broward	29,792
Oakland Park (city) Broward	25,542
Lake Worth (city) Palm Beach	24,615
Miami (city) Miami-Dade	21,797
Hialeah (city) Miami-Dade	21,500

South American
Top 10 Places Sorted by Number

Place (place type) County	Dollars
Cutler (cdp) Miami-Dade	85,412
Parkland (city) Broward	65,417
Cooper City (city) Broward	61,190
Meadow Woods (cdp) Orange	60,909
Key Biscayne (village) Miami-Dade	60,000
Weston (city) Broward	55,945
Wellington (village) Palm Beach	55,737
Miami Lakes (cdp) Miami-Dade	55,481
Richmond West (cdp) Miami-Dade	54,663
Coral Terrace (cdp) Miami-Dade	52,946

Notes: Please refer to the User's Guide for an explanation of data; tables include places with populations > 9,999 and reflect only those areas that meet Summary File 4 population thresholds, therefore there may be less than 10 places listed

Spaniard
Top 10 Places Sorted by Number

Place (place type) County	Dollars
Miami Beach (city) Miami-Dade	43,906
Hialeah (city) Miami-Dade	38,359
Tampa (city) Hillsborough	31,625
Miami (city) Miami-Dade	25,134

Uruguayan
Top 10 Places Sorted by Number

Place (place type) County	Dollars
No places met population threshold.	

Venezuelan
Top 10 Places Sorted by Number

Place (place type) County	Dollars
Richmond West (cdp) Miami-Dade	60,658
Coral Gables (city) Miami-Dade	56,875
Weston (city) Broward	55,513
Plantation (city) Broward	55,227
Kendall (cdp) Miami-Dade	47,216
Coral Springs (city) Broward	46,719
Tamiami (cdp) Miami-Dade	43,864
Pembroke Pines (city) Broward	42,386
Doral (cdp) Miami-Dade	41,333
The Hammocks (cdp) Miami-Dade	41,094

Other Hispanic
Top 10 Places Sorted by Number

Place (place type) County	Dollars
Cooper City (city) Broward	77,028
Greater Northdale (cdp) Hillsborough	59,583
Temple Terrace (city) Hillsborough	59,286
Miami Lakes (cdp) Miami-Dade	57,083
Richmond West (cdp) Miami-Dade	56,767
Key Biscayne (village) Miami-Dade	56,071
Miami Shores (village) Miami-Dade	55,972
Coral Terrace (cdp) Miami-Dade	55,694
Country Walk (cdp) Miami-Dade	54,948
Miramar (city) Broward	54,330

Per Capita Income

Total Population
Top 10 Places Sorted by Number

Place (place type) County	Dollars
Naples (city) Collier	61,141
Key Biscayne (village) Miami-Dade	54,213
Pinecrest (village) Miami-Dade	51,181
Coral Gables (city) Miami-Dade	46,163
Boca Raton (city) Palm Beach	45,628
Cutler (cdp) Miami-Dade	42,986
Palm Beach Gardens (city) Palm Beach	42,975
Marco Island (city) Collier	42,875
Parkland (city) Broward	41,896
Aventura (city) Miami-Dade	41,092

Hispanic
Top 10 Places Sorted by Number

Place (place type) County	Dollars
Key Biscayne (village) Miami-Dade	46,682
Coral Gables (city) Miami-Dade	41,997
Westchase (cdp) Hillsborough	41,823
Pinecrest (village) Miami-Dade	40,784
Cutler (cdp) Miami-Dade	36,802
Parkland (city) Broward	36,728
Lake Mary (city) Seminole	32,302
Aventura (city) Miami-Dade	31,980
Maitland (city) Orange	27,579
Miami Lakes (cdp) Miami-Dade	27,543

Argentinian
Top 10 Places Sorted by Number

Place (place type) County	Dollars
Kendall (cdp) Miami-Dade	21,551
Miami (city) Miami-Dade	20,737
Miami Beach (city) Miami-Dade	17,211
Sunny Isles Beach (city) Miami-Dade	16,962
Fountainbleau (cdp) Miami-Dade	15,238
Hialeah (city) Miami-Dade	14,892
Hollywood (city) Broward	14,713

Bolivian
Top 10 Places Sorted by Number

Place (place type) County	Dollars
No places met population threshold.	

Central American
Top 10 Places Sorted by Number

Place (place type) County	Dollars
Pinecrest (village) Miami-Dade	32,446
Kissimmee (city) Osceola	30,814
Coral Gables (city) Miami-Dade	27,046
Doral (cdp) Miami-Dade	26,410
Plantation (city) Broward	24,614
The Crossings (cdp) Miami-Dade	22,224
Pembroke Pines (city) Broward	20,872
Richmond West (cdp) Miami-Dade	19,882
The Hammocks (cdp) Miami-Dade	18,882
Coral Springs (city) Broward	18,668

Chilean
Top 10 Places Sorted by Number

Place (place type) County	Dollars
Hollywood (city) Broward	41,421
Kendall (cdp) Miami-Dade	18,805
Miami (city) Miami-Dade	16,787
Miami Beach (city) Miami-Dade	16,063
Fountainbleau (cdp) Miami-Dade	11,869
Hialeah (city) Miami-Dade	11,676

Colombian
Top 10 Places Sorted by Number

Place (place type) County	Dollars
Greater Carrollwood (cdp) Hillsborough	39,919
Key Biscayne (village) Miami-Dade	39,675
Miami Lakes (cdp) Miami-Dade	34,692
Deerfield Beach (city) Broward	32,633
Coral Gables (city) Miami-Dade	31,909
Doral (cdp) Miami-Dade	30,236
Aventura (city) Miami-Dade	26,011
Jacksonville (city) Duval	25,440
Ojus (cdp) Miami-Dade	24,060
Weston (city) Broward	21,914

Costa Rican
Top 10 Places Sorted by Number

Place (place type) County	Dollars
Miami (city) Miami-Dade	11,901
Hialeah (city) Miami-Dade	10,481

Cuban
Top 10 Places Sorted by Number

Place (place type) County	Dollars
Key Biscayne (village) Miami-Dade	65,854
Pinecrest (village) Miami-Dade	53,282
Coral Gables (city) Miami-Dade	48,094
Cutler (cdp) Miami-Dade	47,146
Boca Raton (city) Palm Beach	42,127
Weston (city) Broward	37,503
Lake Magdalene (cdp) Hillsborough	37,023
Glenvar Heights (cdp) Miami-Dade	36,948
Altamonte Springs (city) Seminole	33,321

Doral (cdp) Miami-Dade	32,899

Dominican
Top 10 Places Sorted by Number

Place (place type) County	Dollars
The Hammocks (cdp) Miami-Dade	19,896
Weston (city) Broward	19,856
Coral Springs (city) Broward	19,051
Tamiami (cdp) Miami-Dade	18,429
Doral (cdp) Miami-Dade	17,829
Pembroke Pines (city) Broward	16,807
Tampa (city) Hillsborough	15,739
Richmond West (cdp) Miami-Dade	14,875
Town 'n' Country (cdp) Hillsborough	14,740
Hialeah Gardens (city) Miami-Dade	14,546

Ecuadorian
Top 10 Places Sorted by Number

Place (place type) County	Dollars
Pembroke Pines (city) Broward	25,478
Coral Springs (city) Broward	19,023
Miami Beach (city) Miami-Dade	17,788
Sunrise (city) Broward	16,225
Miami (city) Miami-Dade	14,825
Hialeah (city) Miami-Dade	13,189
Hollywood (city) Broward	12,036
Tampa (city) Hillsborough	10,737
Fountainbleau (cdp) Miami-Dade	10,453

Guatelmalan
Top 10 Places Sorted by Number

Place (place type) County	Dollars
Fort Lauderdale (city) Broward	11,372
Miami (city) Miami-Dade	10,887
Immokalee (cdp) Collier	10,409
West Palm Beach (city) Palm Beach	9,018
Bonita Springs (city) Lee	8,989
Fort Myers (city) Lee	8,650
Hialeah (city) Miami-Dade	7,641
Homestead (city) Miami-Dade	7,234
Lake Worth (city) Palm Beach	7,210

Honduran
Top 10 Places Sorted by Number

Place (place type) County	Dollars
Hollywood (city) Broward	15,868
Carol City (cdp) Miami-Dade	14,697
Miami Beach (city) Miami-Dade	12,407
Tamiami (cdp) Miami-Dade	11,964
Tampa (city) Hillsborough	11,016
Fountainbleau (cdp) Miami-Dade	10,874
Hialeah (city) Miami-Dade	10,504
North Miami Beach (city) Miami-Dade	9,819
Lake Worth (city) Palm Beach	9,633
Miami (city) Miami-Dade	9,228

Mexican
Top 10 Places Sorted by Number

Place (place type) County	Dollars
Doral (cdp) Miami-Dade	27,236
Pembroke Pines (city) Broward	24,223
Plantation (city) Broward	21,763
Weston (city) Broward	20,312
Orlando (city) Orange	20,044
Miami Beach (city) Miami-Dade	19,765
Melbourne (city) Brevard	19,303
The Hammocks (cdp) Miami-Dade	18,123
Sunrise (city) Broward	17,747
Miramar (city) Broward	17,715

Notes: Please refer to the User's Guide for an explanation of data; tables include places with populations > 9,999 and reflect only those areas that meet Summary File 4 population thresholds, therefore there may be less than 10 places listed

Nicaraguan
Top 10 Places Sorted by Number

Place (place type) County	Dollars
The Crossings (cdp) Miami-Dade	23,575
Coral Gables (city) Miami-Dade	21,491
The Hammocks (cdp) Miami-Dade	20,046
Miramar (city) Broward	19,507
Tampa (city) Hillsborough	17,344
Richmond West (cdp) Miami-Dade	17,110
Kendale Lakes (cdp) Miami-Dade	16,729
Kendall (cdp) Miami-Dade	16,571
Hollywood (city) Broward	16,534
Miami Beach (city) Miami-Dade	14,632

Panamanian
Top 10 Places Sorted by Number

Place (place type) County	Dollars
Miami (city) Miami-Dade	23,014
Fountainbleau (cdp) Miami-Dade	17,102
Jacksonville (city) Duval	15,532
Tampa (city) Hillsborough	11,665
Miramar (city) Broward	11,234

Paraguayan
Top 10 Places Sorted by Number

Place (place type) County	Dollars
No places met population threshold.	

Peruvian
Top 10 Places Sorted by Number

Place (place type) County	Dollars
Weston (city) Broward	24,906
Kendale Lakes (cdp) Miami-Dade	22,421
Orlando (city) Orange	22,045
Plantation (city) Broward	20,234
The Hammocks (cdp) Miami-Dade	20,131
The Crossings (cdp) Miami-Dade	20,023
Miami (city) Miami-Dade	19,081
Doral (cdp) Miami-Dade	17,508
Hialeah (city) Miami-Dade	16,658
Fountainbleau (cdp) Miami-Dade	16,513

Puerto Rican
Top 10 Places Sorted by Number

Place (place type) County	Dollars
Coral Gables (city) Miami-Dade	42,008
Weston (city) Broward	29,363
Deerfield Beach (city) Broward	29,214
Miami Lakes (cdp) Miami-Dade	27,535
Wekiwa Springs (cdp) Seminole	27,388
Lake Magdalene (cdp) Hillsborough	26,128
The Crossings (cdp) Miami-Dade	26,066
Glenvar Heights (cdp) Miami-Dade	25,124
Doral (cdp) Miami-Dade	23,838
Coconut Creek (city) Broward	23,518

Salvadoran
Top 10 Places Sorted by Number

Place (place type) County	Dollars
Fort Lauderdale (city) Broward	10,466
Miami (city) Miami-Dade	10,207
Oakland Park (city) Broward	10,067
Homestead (city) Miami-Dade	9,794
Lake Worth (city) Palm Beach	9,326
Hialeah (city) Miami-Dade	9,042

South American
Top 10 Places Sorted by Number

Place (place type) County	Dollars
Cutler (cdp) Miami-Dade	37,651
Key Biscayne (village) Miami-Dade	36,450
Coral Gables (city) Miami-Dade	32,634

Place (place type) County	Dollars
Aventura (city) Miami-Dade	29,891
Delray Beach (city) Palm Beach	28,413
Miami Lakes (cdp) Miami-Dade	28,403
Greater Carrollwood (cdp) Hillsborough	27,633
Boca Raton (city) Palm Beach	26,302
Deerfield Beach (city) Broward	24,204
Doral (cdp) Miami-Dade	23,359

Spaniard
Top 10 Places Sorted by Number

Place (place type) County	Dollars
Tampa (city) Hillsborough	26,392
Miami Beach (city) Miami-Dade	25,841
Miami (city) Miami-Dade	17,083
Hialeah (city) Miami-Dade	13,312

Uruguayan
Top 10 Places Sorted by Number

Place (place type) County	Dollars
No places met population threshold.	

Venezuelan
Top 10 Places Sorted by Number

Place (place type) County	Dollars
Coral Gables (city) Miami-Dade	36,827
Weston (city) Broward	24,539
Miami Beach (city) Miami-Dade	24,212
The Crossings (cdp) Miami-Dade	21,774
Pembroke Pines (city) Broward	20,022
Doral (cdp) Miami-Dade	19,591
Miami (city) Miami-Dade	19,488
Coral Springs (city) Broward	18,516
Kendall (cdp) Miami-Dade	16,144
Richmond West (cdp) Miami-Dade	15,721

Other Hispanic
Top 10 Places Sorted by Number

Place (place type) County	Dollars
Golden Gate (cdp) Collier	30,936
Key Biscayne (village) Miami-Dade	30,118
Aventura (city) Miami-Dade	29,609
Greater Carrollwood (cdp) Hillsborough	29,288
Boca Raton (city) Palm Beach	28,953
Temple Terrace (city) Hillsborough	28,529
Coral Gables (city) Miami-Dade	27,641
Pinecrest (village) Miami-Dade	23,213
Greater Northdale (cdp) Hillsborough	20,999
Key West (city) Monroe	19,820

Poverty Status

Total Population with Income Below Poverty Level
Top 10 Places Sorted by Number

Place (place type) County	Number
Miami (city) Miami-Dade	100,405
Jacksonville (city) Duval	87,691
Tampa (city) Hillsborough	53,425
Hialeah (city) Miami-Dade	41,537
Tallahassee (city) Leon	33,978
St. Petersburg (city) Pinellas	32,127
Orlando (city) Orange	29,029
Fort Lauderdale (city) Broward	26,158
Gainesville (city) Alachua	22,559
Miami Beach (city) Miami-Dade	19,003

Total Population with Income Below Poverty Level
Top 10 Places Sorted by Percent

Place (place type) County	Percent
Gladeview (cdp) Miami-Dade	52.77
Brownsville (cdp) Miami-Dade	42.71
Immokalee (cdp) Collier	39.84
Opa-locka (city) Miami-Dade	35.20

Place (place type) County	
Pinewood (cdp) Miami-Dade	33.46
Belle Glade (city) Palm Beach	32.87
Homestead (city) Miami-Dade	31.77
University (cdp) Hillsborough	31.34
Fort Pierce (city) Saint Lucie	30.91
West Little River (cdp) Miami-Dade	29.04

Hispanics with Income Below Poverty Level
Top 10 Places Sorted by Number

Place (place type) County	Number
Miami (city) Miami-Dade	62,475
Hialeah (city) Miami-Dade	38,013
Tampa (city) Hillsborough	13,275
Miami Beach (city) Miami-Dade	12,069
Fountainbleau (cdp) Miami-Dade	7,568
Orlando (city) Orange	6,545
Homestead (city) Miami-Dade	5,795
Kendall West (cdp) Miami-Dade	5,128
Immokalee (cdp) Collier	5,062
Hollywood (city) Broward	4,910

Hispanics with Income Below Poverty Level
Top 10 Places Sorted by Percent

Place (place type) County	Percent
Gladeview (cdp) Miami-Dade	60.15
West Pensacola (cdp) Escambia	44.07
Auburndale (city) Polk	41.95
Brownsville (cdp) Miami-Dade	40.05
University (cdp) Hillsborough	39.56
De Land (city) Volusia	39.05
Fort Pierce (city) Saint Lucie	38.51
Immokalee (cdp) Collier	38.08
Gainesville (city) Alachua	38.04
Brent (cdp) Escambia	36.47

Argentinians with Income Below Poverty Level
Top 10 Places Sorted by Number

Place (place type) County	Number
Miami Beach (city) Miami-Dade	1,029
Miami (city) Miami-Dade	672
Hollywood (city) Broward	207
Sunny Isles Beach (city) Miami-Dade	121
Fountainbleau (cdp) Miami-Dade	106
Kendall (cdp) Miami-Dade	106
Hialeah (city) Miami-Dade	70

Argentinians with Income Below Poverty Level
Top 10 Places Sorted by Percent

Place (place type) County	Percent
Hollywood (city) Broward	37.03
Miami Beach (city) Miami-Dade	33.95
Miami (city) Miami-Dade	33.37
Fountainbleau (cdp) Miami-Dade	24.09
Sunny Isles Beach (city) Miami-Dade	21.19
Hialeah (city) Miami-Dade	16.75
Kendall (cdp) Miami-Dade	16.72

Bolivians with Income Below Poverty Level
Top 10 Places Sorted by Number

Place (place type) County	Number
No places met population threshold.	

Bolivians with Income Below Poverty Level
Top 10 Places Sorted by Percent

Place (place type) County	Percent
No places met population threshold.	

Central Americans with Income Below Poverty Level
Top 10 Places Sorted by Number

Place (place type) County	Number
Miami (city) Miami-Dade	12,437

Notes: Please refer to the User's Guide for an explanation of data; tables include places with populations > 9,999 and reflect only those areas that meet Summary File 4 population thresholds, therefore there may be less than 10 places listed

Place (place type) County	Number
Hialeah (city) Miami-Dade	2,956
West Palm Beach (city) Palm Beach	1,013
Lake Worth (city) Palm Beach	1,002
Homestead (city) Miami-Dade	922
Fountainbleau (cdp) Miami-Dade	794
West Little River (cdp) Miami-Dade	789
Miami Beach (city) Miami-Dade	691
Tampa (city) Hillsborough	684
Kendall West (cdp) Miami-Dade	655

Central Americans with Income Below Poverty Level
Top 10 Places Sorted by Percent

Place (place type) County	Percent
Gladeview (cdp) Miami-Dade	57.17
Immokalee (cdp) Collier	54.24
Leisure City (cdp) Miami-Dade	36.48
West Palm Beach (city) Palm Beach	36.41
Oakland Park (city) Broward	35.60
Pinewood (cdp) Miami-Dade	34.82
Brownsville (cdp) Miami-Dade	32.83
Lake Worth (city) Palm Beach	32.09
Bonita Springs (city) Lee	32.07
West Little River (cdp) Miami-Dade	31.85

Chileans with Income Below Poverty Level
Top 10 Places Sorted by Number

Place (place type) County	Number
Miami Beach (city) Miami-Dade	226
Miami (city) Miami-Dade	220
Fountainbleau (cdp) Miami-Dade	147
Hialeah (city) Miami-Dade	112
Kendall (cdp) Miami-Dade	64
Hollywood (city) Broward	41

Chileans with Income Below Poverty Level
Top 10 Places Sorted by Percent

Place (place type) County	Percent
Miami Beach (city) Miami-Dade	30.58
Miami (city) Miami-Dade	24.53
Fountainbleau (cdp) Miami-Dade	20.91
Hialeah (city) Miami-Dade	15.20
Kendall (cdp) Miami-Dade	13.33
Hollywood (city) Broward	10.88

Colombians with Income Below Poverty Level
Top 10 Places Sorted by Number

Place (place type) County	Number
Miami (city) Miami-Dade	1,751
Hialeah (city) Miami-Dade	1,489
Miami Beach (city) Miami-Dade	1,471
Kendall West (cdp) Miami-Dade	1,291
The Hammocks (cdp) Miami-Dade	983
Kendall (cdp) Miami-Dade	913
Kendale Lakes (cdp) Miami-Dade	781
Hollywood (city) Broward	746
Country Club (cdp) Miami-Dade	694
Fountainbleau (cdp) Miami-Dade	629

Colombians with Income Below Poverty Level
Top 10 Places Sorted by Percent

Place (place type) County	Percent
Oak Ridge (cdp) Orange	43.90
Egypt Lake-Leto (cdp) Hillsborough	38.10
Clearwater (city) Pinellas	35.42
Sunny Isles Beach (city) Miami-Dade	33.37
Miami Beach (city) Miami-Dade	32.89
West Palm Beach (city) Palm Beach	31.02
Kendall West (cdp) Miami-Dade	29.77
Miami (city) Miami-Dade	29.56
Kissimmee (city) Osceola	27.93
Davie (town) Broward	27.76

Costa Ricans with Income Below Poverty Level
Top 10 Places Sorted by Number

Place (place type) County	Number
Miami (city) Miami-Dade	263
Hialeah (city) Miami-Dade	83

Costa Ricans with Income Below Poverty Level
Top 10 Places Sorted by Percent

Place (place type) County	Percent
Miami (city) Miami-Dade	32.23
Hialeah (city) Miami-Dade	15.87

Cubans with Income Below Poverty Level
Top 10 Places Sorted by Number

Place (place type) County	Number
Miami (city) Miami-Dade	30,214
Hialeah (city) Miami-Dade	25,322
Miami Beach (city) Miami-Dade	4,465
Fountainbleau (cdp) Miami-Dade	3,214
Tamiami (cdp) Miami-Dade	2,923
Tampa (city) Hillsborough	2,906
Westchester (cdp) Miami-Dade	2,326
Kendale Lakes (cdp) Miami-Dade	1,965
Carol City (cdp) Miami-Dade	1,892
University Park (cdp) Miami-Dade	1,836

Cubans with Income Below Poverty Level
Top 10 Places Sorted by Percent

Place (place type) County	Percent
Gladeview (cdp) Miami-Dade	65.72
Gainesville (city) Alachua	44.03
Brownsville (cdp) Miami-Dade	43.22
Tallahassee (city) Leon	38.10
Homestead (city) Miami-Dade	32.94
Pinewood (cdp) Miami-Dade	31.90
Opa-locka (city) Miami-Dade	31.06
Boynton Beach (city) Palm Beach	26.49
West Little River (cdp) Miami-Dade	26.33
Miami Beach (city) Miami-Dade	24.85

Dominicans with Income Below Poverty Level
Top 10 Places Sorted by Number

Place (place type) County	Number
Miami (city) Miami-Dade	1,959
Hialeah (city) Miami-Dade	991
West Little River (cdp) Miami-Dade	377
Orlando (city) Orange	339
Miami Beach (city) Miami-Dade	314
Hollywood (city) Broward	311
Tampa (city) Hillsborough	277
Carol City (cdp) Miami-Dade	262
South Miami Heights (cdp) Miami-Dade	250
Fountainbleau (cdp) Miami-Dade	241

Dominicans with Income Below Poverty Level
Top 10 Places Sorted by Percent

Place (place type) County	Percent
West Little River (cdp) Miami-Dade	37.97
Oak Ridge (cdp) Orange	30.32
Egypt Lake-Leto (cdp) Hillsborough	28.26
Town 'n' Country (cdp) Hillsborough	27.87
Orlando (city) Orange	27.43
Miami (city) Miami-Dade	27.21
Hialeah Gardens (city) Miami-Dade	26.95
Golden Glades (cdp) Miami-Dade	26.06
South Miami Heights (cdp) Miami-Dade	25.83
Miami Beach (city) Miami-Dade	22.59

Ecuadorians with Income Below Poverty Level
Top 10 Places Sorted by Number

Place (place type) County	Number
Miami (city) Miami-Dade	441
Hialeah (city) Miami-Dade	147
Fountainbleau (cdp) Miami-Dade	102
Miami Beach (city) Miami-Dade	102
Tampa (city) Hillsborough	78
Hollywood (city) Broward	44
Sunrise (city) Broward	29
Coral Springs (city) Broward	19
Pembroke Pines (city) Broward	18

Ecuadorians with Income Below Poverty Level
Top 10 Places Sorted by Percent

Place (place type) County	Percent
Miami (city) Miami-Dade	25.23
Tampa (city) Hillsborough	18.66
Miami Beach (city) Miami-Dade	15.41
Fountainbleau (cdp) Miami-Dade	12.77
Hialeah (city) Miami-Dade	11.92
Hollywood (city) Broward	7.01
Sunrise (city) Broward	5.48
Pembroke Pines (city) Broward	3.70
Coral Springs (city) Broward	2.02

Guatelmalans with Income Below Poverty Level
Top 10 Places Sorted by Number

Place (place type) County	Number
West Palm Beach (city) Palm Beach	831
Lake Worth (city) Palm Beach	779
Miami (city) Miami-Dade	686
Immokalee (cdp) Collier	592
Homestead (city) Miami-Dade	433
Hialeah (city) Miami-Dade	204
Bonita Springs (city) Lee	188
Fort Lauderdale (city) Broward	124
Fort Myers (city) Lee	68

Guatelmalans with Income Below Poverty Level
Top 10 Places Sorted by Percent

Place (place type) County	Percent
Immokalee (cdp) Collier	53.87
Bonita Springs (city) Lee	50.95
Lake Worth (city) Palm Beach	40.96
West Palm Beach (city) Palm Beach	40.56
Fort Lauderdale (city) Broward	33.42
Homestead (city) Miami-Dade	30.17
Hialeah (city) Miami-Dade	24.58
Miami (city) Miami-Dade	24.15
Fort Myers (city) Lee	17.85

Hondurans with Income Below Poverty Level
Top 10 Places Sorted by Number

Place (place type) County	Number
Miami (city) Miami-Dade	4,077
Hialeah (city) Miami-Dade	438
Tampa (city) Hillsborough	352
West Little River (cdp) Miami-Dade	287
Miami Beach (city) Miami-Dade	199
Fountainbleau (cdp) Miami-Dade	129
Lake Worth (city) Palm Beach	78
Tamiami (cdp) Miami-Dade	74
North Miami Beach (city) Miami-Dade	70
North Miami (city) Miami-Dade	63

Hondurans with Income Below Poverty Level
Top 10 Places Sorted by Percent

Place (place type) County	Percent
Tampa (city) Hillsborough	39.37
Miami (city) Miami-Dade	30.03
West Little River (cdp) Miami-Dade	29.71
Miami Beach (city) Miami-Dade	24.84
Fountainbleau (cdp) Miami-Dade	20.35
Hialeah (city) Miami-Dade	16.84
Lake Worth (city) Palm Beach	16.74
Tamiami (cdp) Miami-Dade	16.70

Notes: Please refer to the User's Guide for an explanation of data; tables include places with populations > 9,999 and reflect only those areas that meet Summary File 4 population thresholds, therefore there may be less than 10 places listed

North Miami Beach (city) Miami-Dade	13.86
North Miami (city) Miami-Dade	11.31

Mexicans with Income Below Poverty Level
Top 10 Places Sorted by Number

Place (place type) County	Number
Immokalee (cdp) Collier	3,982
Homestead (city) Miami-Dade	2,590
Tampa (city) Hillsborough	1,925
Fort Pierce (city) Saint Lucie	1,451
Leisure City (cdp) Miami-Dade	1,429
Bradenton (city) Manatee	1,127
Sarasota (city) Sarasota	1,005
Lake Worth (city) Palm Beach	912
Pompano Beach (city) Broward	891
Clearwater (city) Pinellas	824

Mexicans with Income Below Poverty Level
Top 10 Places Sorted by Percent

Place (place type) County	Percent
Gainesville (city) Alachua	49.73
University (cdp) Hillsborough	45.87
De Land (city) Volusia	44.01
Ocala (city) Marion	42.48
Auburndale (city) Polk	41.71
Kendall West (cdp) Miami-Dade	41.33
Immokalee (cdp) Collier	37.94
Homestead (city) Miami-Dade	36.55
Fort Pierce (city) Saint Lucie	35.63
Pompano Beach (city) Broward	35.22

Nicaraguans with Income Below Poverty Level
Top 10 Places Sorted by Number

Place (place type) County	Number
Miami (city) Miami-Dade	6,476
Hialeah (city) Miami-Dade	1,803
Gladeview (cdp) Miami-Dade	476
Fountainbleau (cdp) Miami-Dade	401
Sweetwater (city) Miami-Dade	399
West Little River (cdp) Miami-Dade	347
Kendall West (cdp) Miami-Dade	344
Pinewood (cdp) Miami-Dade	220
Carol City (cdp) Miami-Dade	209
Miami Beach (city) Miami-Dade	207

Nicaraguans with Income Below Poverty Level
Top 10 Places Sorted by Percent

Place (place type) County	Percent
Gladeview (cdp) Miami-Dade	57.84
Pinewood (cdp) Miami-Dade	39.29
West Little River (cdp) Miami-Dade	30.98
Miami (city) Miami-Dade	28.94
Kendall West (cdp) Miami-Dade	21.53
Miami Beach (city) Miami-Dade	20.87
North Miami (city) Miami-Dade	19.34
Hialeah (city) Miami-Dade	17.83
Westchester (cdp) Miami-Dade	16.73
Sweetwater (city) Miami-Dade	16.60

Panamanians with Income Below Poverty Level
Top 10 Places Sorted by Number

Place (place type) County	Number
Miami (city) Miami-Dade	199
Tampa (city) Hillsborough	93
Jacksonville (city) Duval	81
Fountainbleau (cdp) Miami-Dade	68
Miramar (city) Broward	46

Panamanians with Income Below Poverty Level
Top 10 Places Sorted by Percent

Place (place type) County	Percent
Miami (city) Miami-Dade	22.74

Tampa (city) Hillsborough	14.72
Jacksonville (city) Duval	14.34
Fountainbleau (cdp) Miami-Dade	13.03
Miramar (city) Broward	12.53

Paraguayans with Income Below Poverty Level
Top 10 Places Sorted by Number

Place (place type) County	Number
No places met population threshold.	

Paraguayans with Income Below Poverty Level
Top 10 Places Sorted by Percent

Place (place type) County	Percent
No places met population threshold.	

Peruvians with Income Below Poverty Level
Top 10 Places Sorted by Number

Place (place type) County	Number
Miami (city) Miami-Dade	650
Miami Beach (city) Miami-Dade	617
Hollywood (city) Broward	281
North Lauderdale (city) Broward	266
Hialeah (city) Miami-Dade	246
Kendall West (cdp) Miami-Dade	192
Coral Springs (city) Broward	166
Fountainbleau (cdp) Miami-Dade	158
The Hammocks (cdp) Miami-Dade	133
North Miami Beach (city) Miami-Dade	128

Peruvians with Income Below Poverty Level
Top 10 Places Sorted by Percent

Place (place type) County	Percent
North Lauderdale (city) Broward	47.84
Miami Beach (city) Miami-Dade	32.58
Miami (city) Miami-Dade	23.75
Hollywood (city) Broward	21.02
Coral Springs (city) Broward	17.42
Fort Lauderdale (city) Broward	17.09
Hialeah (city) Miami-Dade	16.97
Kendall West (cdp) Miami-Dade	16.74
Orlando (city) Orange	16.70
North Miami Beach (city) Miami-Dade	16.35

Puerto Ricans with Income Below Poverty Level
Top 10 Places Sorted by Number

Place (place type) County	Number
Tampa (city) Hillsborough	4,353
Miami (city) Miami-Dade	3,783
Orlando (city) Orange	3,339
Kissimmee (city) Osceola	2,507
Jacksonville (city) Duval	1,766
Hialeah (city) Miami-Dade	1,337
University (cdp) Hillsborough	1,302
Hollywood (city) Broward	1,206
Deltona (city) Volusia	1,010
Yeehaw Junction (cdp) Osceola	983

Puerto Ricans with Income Below Poverty Level
Top 10 Places Sorted by Percent

Place (place type) County	Percent
Fort Pierce (city) Saint Lucie	59.47
University (cdp) Hillsborough	46.63
Winter Haven (city) Polk	39.14
Miami (city) Miami-Dade	38.57
Gainesville (city) Alachua	38.09
West Little River (cdp) Miami-Dade	37.38
Homestead (city) Miami-Dade	37.29
Lake Worth Corridor (cdp) Palm Beach	36.87
Lake Worth (city) Palm Beach	36.04
West and East Lealman (cdp) Pinellas	35.01

Salvadorans with Income Below Poverty Level
Top 10 Places Sorted by Number

Place (place type) County	Number
Miami (city) Miami-Dade	484
Homestead (city) Miami-Dade	323
Hialeah (city) Miami-Dade	247
Oakland Park (city) Broward	233
Lake Worth (city) Palm Beach	145
Fort Lauderdale (city) Broward	127

Salvadorans with Income Below Poverty Level
Top 10 Places Sorted by Percent

Place (place type) County	Percent
Oakland Park (city) Broward	30.06
Homestead (city) Miami-Dade	29.07
Lake Worth (city) Palm Beach	27.51
Hialeah (city) Miami-Dade	26.00
Miami (city) Miami-Dade	20.62
Fort Lauderdale (city) Broward	19.54

South Americans with Income Below Poverty Level
Top 10 Places Sorted by Number

Place (place type) County	Number
Miami (city) Miami-Dade	4,425
Miami Beach (city) Miami-Dade	3,940
Hialeah (city) Miami-Dade	2,347
Kendall West (cdp) Miami-Dade	1,816
The Hammocks (cdp) Miami-Dade	1,557
Hollywood (city) Broward	1,545
Fountainbleau (cdp) Miami-Dade	1,521
Kendall (cdp) Miami-Dade	1,488
Kendale Lakes (cdp) Miami-Dade	1,124
Doral (cdp) Miami-Dade	1,098

South Americans with Income Below Poverty Level
Top 10 Places Sorted by Percent

Place (place type) County	Percent
Tallahassee (city) Leon	36.90
Homestead (city) Miami-Dade	35.75
Egypt Lake-Leto (cdp) Hillsborough	35.36
Gainesville (city) Alachua	33.23
Oak Ridge (cdp) Orange	32.79
Altamonte Springs (city) Seminole	30.81
Miami Beach (city) Miami-Dade	30.40
Dania Beach (city) Broward	29.04
Miami (city) Miami-Dade	28.01
Tampa (city) Hillsborough	26.47

Spaniards with Income Below Poverty Level
Top 10 Places Sorted by Number

Place (place type) County	Number
Miami (city) Miami-Dade	175
Miami Beach (city) Miami-Dade	88
Tampa (city) Hillsborough	87
Hialeah (city) Miami-Dade	78

Spaniards with Income Below Poverty Level
Top 10 Places Sorted by Percent

Place (place type) County	Percent
Miami (city) Miami-Dade	18.98
Hialeah (city) Miami-Dade	15.60
Miami Beach (city) Miami-Dade	15.36
Tampa (city) Hillsborough	11.87

Uruguayans with Income Below Poverty Level
Top 10 Places Sorted by Number

Place (place type) County	Number
No places met population threshold.	

Notes: Please refer to the User's Guide for an explanation of data; tables include places with populations > 9,999 and reflect only those areas that meet Summary File 4 population thresholds, therefore there may be less than 10 places listed

Uruguayans with Income Below Poverty Level
Top 10 Places Sorted by Percent

Place (place type) County	Percent
No places met population threshold.	

Venezuelans with Income Below Poverty Level
Top 10 Places Sorted by Number

Place (place type) County	Number
Miami (city) Miami-Dade	496
Doral (cdp) Miami-Dade	401
Miami Beach (city) Miami-Dade	370
The Hammocks (cdp) Miami-Dade	347
Tampa (city) Hillsborough	346
Fountainbleau (cdp) Miami-Dade	342
Weston (city) Broward	263
Hialeah (city) Miami-Dade	257
Orlando (city) Orange	239
Kendall (cdp) Miami-Dade	207

Venezuelans with Income Below Poverty Level
Top 10 Places Sorted by Percent

Place (place type) County	Percent
Tampa (city) Hillsborough	55.45
Orlando (city) Orange	31.08
Miami (city) Miami-Dade	28.59
Hialeah (city) Miami-Dade	26.91
Miami Beach (city) Miami-Dade	25.41
Hollywood (city) Broward	23.39
Doral (cdp) Miami-Dade	21.78
Plantation (city) Broward	21.75
The Hammocks (cdp) Miami-Dade	20.93
Tamiami (cdp) Miami-Dade	19.27

Other Hispanics with Income Below Poverty Level
Top 10 Places Sorted by Number

Place (place type) County	Number
Miami (city) Miami-Dade	8,670
Hialeah (city) Miami-Dade	4,588
Tampa (city) Hillsborough	2,095
Miami Beach (city) Miami-Dade	1,663
Fountainbleau (cdp) Miami-Dade	1,300
Orlando (city) Orange	1,030
Kendale Lakes (cdp) Miami-Dade	816
Hollywood (city) Broward	799
Jacksonville (city) Duval	743
Country Club (cdp) Miami-Dade	660

Other Hispanics with Income Below Poverty Level
Top 10 Places Sorted by Percent

Place (place type) County	Percent
Gladeview (cdp) Miami-Dade	48.75
Plant City (city) Hillsborough	42.02
Pine Hills (cdp) Orange	39.53
Sarasota (city) Sarasota	38.20
Daytona Beach (city) Volusia	35.92
Tallahassee (city) Leon	35.08
Homestead (city) Miami-Dade	34.34
Lake Worth Corridor (cdp) Palm Beach	32.90
Immokalee (cdp) Collier	30.31
Lake Worth (city) Palm Beach	29.98

Homeownership

Total Population Who Own Their Own Homes
Top 10 Places Sorted by Number

Place (place type) County	Number
Jacksonville (city) Duval	179,782
St. Petersburg (city) Pinellas	69,697
Tampa (city) Hillsborough	68,753
Miami (city) Miami-Dade	46,847
Pembroke Pines (city) Broward	41,636
Fort Lauderdale (city) Broward	37,927
Hollywood (city) Broward	37,102
Hialeah (city) Miami-Dade	35,963
Orlando (city) Orange	33,052
Cape Coral (city) Lee	32,663

Total Population Who Own Their Own Homes
Top 10 Places Sorted by Percent

Place (place type) County	Percent
Keystone (cdp) Hillsborough	94.74
Richmond West (cdp) Miami-Dade	93.84
Lakeland Highlands (cdp) Polk	92.63
Cooper City (city) Broward	92.24
Country Walk (cdp) Miami-Dade	92.05
Cutler (cdp) Miami-Dade	88.65
Miami Shores (village) Miami-Dade	88.63
De Bary (city) Volusia	88.33
Royal Palm Beach (village) Palm Beach	88.31
Westchase (cdp) Hillsborough	88.29

Hispanics Who Own Their Own Homes
Top 10 Places Sorted by Number

Place (place type) County	Number
Hialeah (city) Miami-Dade	33,368
Miami (city) Miami-Dade	29,933
Tamiami (cdp) Miami-Dade	12,432
Kendale Lakes (cdp) Miami-Dade	10,917
Tampa (city) Hillsborough	10,742
Fountainbleau (cdp) Miami-Dade	9,941
Pembroke Pines (city) Broward	9,565
Kendall (cdp) Miami-Dade	8,115
Miami Beach (city) Miami-Dade	7,288
The Hammocks (cdp) Miami-Dade	6,353

Hispanics Who Own Their Own Homes
Top 10 Places Sorted by Percent

Place (place type) County	Percent
Lakeland Highlands (cdp) Polk	100.00
Keystone (cdp) Hillsborough	97.59
Hamptons at Boca Raton (cdp) Palm Beach	96.07
Land O' Lakes (cdp) Pasco	95.35
Richmond West (cdp) Miami-Dade	94.10
Country Walk (cdp) Miami-Dade	93.37
Palm Coast (cdp) Flagler	89.94
Cooper City (city) Broward	89.41
Royal Palm Beach (village) Palm Beach	88.18
Bloomingdale (cdp) Hillsborough	87.31

Argentinians Who Own Their Own Homes
Top 10 Places Sorted by Number

Place (place type) County	Number
Miami Beach (city) Miami-Dade	405
Miami (city) Miami-Dade	306
Kendall (cdp) Miami-Dade	191
Sunny Isles Beach (city) Miami-Dade	110
Hialeah (city) Miami-Dade	108
Hollywood (city) Broward	83
Fountainbleau (cdp) Miami-Dade	52

Argentinians Who Own Their Own Homes
Top 10 Places Sorted by Percent

Place (place type) County	Percent
Hialeah (city) Miami-Dade	70.59
Kendall (cdp) Miami-Dade	57.01
Sunny Isles Beach (city) Miami-Dade	49.33
Hollywood (city) Broward	47.43
Miami (city) Miami-Dade	39.08
Miami Beach (city) Miami-Dade	28.76
Fountainbleau (cdp) Miami-Dade	27.08

Bolivians Who Own Their Own Homes
Top 10 Places Sorted by Number

Place (place type) County	Number
No places met population threshold.	

Bolivians Who Own Their Own Homes
Top 10 Places Sorted by Percent

Place (place type) County	Percent
No places met population threshold.	

Central Americans Who Own Their Own Homes
Top 10 Places Sorted by Number

Place (place type) County	Number
Miami (city) Miami-Dade	1,802
Hialeah (city) Miami-Dade	1,226
Fountainbleau (cdp) Miami-Dade	1,092
Kendale Lakes (cdp) Miami-Dade	780
Tamiami (cdp) Miami-Dade	666
Richmond West (cdp) Miami-Dade	581
Carol City (cdp) Miami-Dade	566
Kendall (cdp) Miami-Dade	559
Tampa (city) Hillsborough	442
Kendall West (cdp) Miami-Dade	413

Central Americans Who Own Their Own Homes
Top 10 Places Sorted by Percent

Place (place type) County	Percent
Richmond West (cdp) Miami-Dade	97.32
Country Walk (cdp) Miami-Dade	94.59
Palmetto Estates (cdp) Miami-Dade	86.21
Carol City (cdp) Miami-Dade	85.89
Miramar (city) Broward	78.00
South Miami Heights (cdp) Miami-Dade	77.80
The Crossings (cdp) Miami-Dade	73.56
Tamiami (cdp) Miami-Dade	71.92
Pembroke Pines (city) Broward	70.69
Princeton (cdp) Miami-Dade	70.64

Chileans Who Own Their Own Homes
Top 10 Places Sorted by Number

Place (place type) County	Number
Hialeah (city) Miami-Dade	143
Miami (city) Miami-Dade	132
Miami Beach (city) Miami-Dade	119
Hollywood (city) Broward	89
Kendall (cdp) Miami-Dade	89
Fountainbleau (cdp) Miami-Dade	67

Chileans Who Own Their Own Homes
Top 10 Places Sorted by Percent

Place (place type) County	Percent
Hollywood (city) Broward	60.54
Kendall (cdp) Miami-Dade	58.55
Hialeah (city) Miami-Dade	45.83
Miami Beach (city) Miami-Dade	32.16
Miami (city) Miami-Dade	31.28
Fountainbleau (cdp) Miami-Dade	28.39

Colombians Who Own Their Own Homes
Top 10 Places Sorted by Number

Place (place type) County	Number
Hialeah (city) Miami-Dade	1,082
The Hammocks (cdp) Miami-Dade	856
Pembroke Pines (city) Broward	758
Kendale Lakes (cdp) Miami-Dade	714
Miami (city) Miami-Dade	670
Kendall West (cdp) Miami-Dade	613
Kendall (cdp) Miami-Dade	582
Country Club (cdp) Miami-Dade	574
Hollywood (city) Broward	568
Miami Beach (city) Miami-Dade	548

Notes: Please refer to the User's Guide for an explanation of data; tables include places with populations > 9,999 and reflect only those areas that meet Summary File 4 population thresholds, therefore there may be less than 10 places listed

Colombians Who Own Their Own Homes
Top 10 Places Sorted by Percent

Place (place type) County	Percent
Country Walk (cdp) Miami-Dade	93.42
Richmond West (cdp) Miami-Dade	91.40
Carol City (cdp) Miami-Dade	83.06
Tamiami (cdp) Miami-Dade	82.01
Miramar (city) Broward	76.62
South Miami Heights (cdp) Miami-Dade	76.56
Margate (city) Broward	75.51
Lauderhill (city) Broward	74.52
Cooper City (city) Broward	73.33
University Park (cdp) Miami-Dade	72.53

Costa Ricans Who Own Their Own Homes
Top 10 Places Sorted by Number

Place (place type) County	Number
Hialeah (city) Miami-Dade	69
Miami (city) Miami-Dade	59

Costa Ricans Who Own Their Own Homes
Top 10 Places Sorted by Percent

Place (place type) County	Percent
Hialeah (city) Miami-Dade	52.67
Miami (city) Miami-Dade	22.52

Cubans Who Own Their Own Homes
Top 10 Places Sorted by Number

Place (place type) County	Number
Hialeah (city) Miami-Dade	26,589
Miami (city) Miami-Dade	22,008
Tamiami (cdp) Miami-Dade	9,444
Kendale Lakes (cdp) Miami-Dade	6,799
Fountainbleau (cdp) Miami-Dade	6,416
Westchester (cdp) Miami-Dade	4,956
Kendall (cdp) Miami-Dade	4,472
Miami Beach (city) Miami-Dade	4,204
Pembroke Pines (city) Broward	4,094
University Park (cdp) Miami-Dade	4,012

Cubans Who Own Their Own Homes
Top 10 Places Sorted by Percent

Place (place type) County	Percent
Royal Palm Beach (village) Palm Beach	100.00
Country Walk (cdp) Miami-Dade	94.23
Cooper City (city) Broward	93.32
Richmond West (cdp) Miami-Dade	93.31
Miramar (city) Broward	91.46
Palm River-Clair Mel (cdp) Hillsborough	90.79
Cutler (cdp) Miami-Dade	90.00
Pinecrest (village) Miami-Dade	89.30
The Crossings (cdp) Miami-Dade	88.58
Weston (city) Broward	88.55

Dominicans Who Own Their Own Homes
Top 10 Places Sorted by Number

Place (place type) County	Number
Miami (city) Miami-Dade	658
Hialeah (city) Miami-Dade	628
Carol City (cdp) Miami-Dade	387
Pembroke Pines (city) Broward	381
Miramar (city) Broward	339
Hollywood (city) Broward	337
The Hammocks (cdp) Miami-Dade	335
Fountainbleau (cdp) Miami-Dade	284
South Miami Heights (cdp) Miami-Dade	245
Richmond West (cdp) Miami-Dade	222

Dominicans Who Own Their Own Homes
Top 10 Places Sorted by Percent

Place (place type) County	Percent
Weston (city) Broward	91.96

Richmond West (cdp) Miami-Dade	88.45
Yeehaw Junction (cdp) Osceola	82.63
Miramar (city) Broward	80.71
Carol City (cdp) Miami-Dade	77.71
Tamiami (cdp) Miami-Dade	77.43
Pembroke Pines (city) Broward	75.90
The Hammocks (cdp) Miami-Dade	72.20
South Miami Heights (cdp) Miami-Dade	71.22
Kendall West (cdp) Miami-Dade	67.96

Ecuadorians Who Own Their Own Homes
Top 10 Places Sorted by Number

Place (place type) County	Number
Hialeah (city) Miami-Dade	212
Miami (city) Miami-Dade	202
Pembroke Pines (city) Broward	171
Coral Springs (city) Broward	129
Hollywood (city) Broward	101
Sunrise (city) Broward	100
Fountainbleau (cdp) Miami-Dade	96
Tampa (city) Hillsborough	84
Miami Beach (city) Miami-Dade	64

Ecuadorians Who Own Their Own Homes
Top 10 Places Sorted by Percent

Place (place type) County	Percent
Pembroke Pines (city) Broward	73.39
Hollywood (city) Broward	61.59
Sunrise (city) Broward	60.98
Coral Springs (city) Broward	56.83
Tampa (city) Hillsborough	50.91
Hialeah (city) Miami-Dade	49.07
Fountainbleau (cdp) Miami-Dade	48.00
Miami (city) Miami-Dade	31.08
Miami Beach (city) Miami-Dade	19.16

Guatelmalans Who Own Their Own Homes
Top 10 Places Sorted by Number

Place (place type) County	Number
Miami (city) Miami-Dade	136
Hialeah (city) Miami-Dade	100
Fort Lauderdale (city) Broward	37
Lake Worth (city) Palm Beach	36
West Palm Beach (city) Palm Beach	32
Homestead (city) Miami-Dade	31
Immokalee (cdp) Collier	18
Bonita Springs (city) Lee	11
Fort Myers (city) Lee	5

Guatelmalans Who Own Their Own Homes
Top 10 Places Sorted by Percent

Place (place type) County	Percent
Hialeah (city) Miami-Dade	40.00
Fort Lauderdale (city) Broward	25.00
Miami (city) Miami-Dade	14.20
Bonita Springs (city) Lee	12.09
Immokalee (cdp) Collier	11.76
Lake Worth (city) Palm Beach	8.98
Homestead (city) Miami-Dade	8.59
West Palm Beach (city) Palm Beach	6.91
Fort Myers (city) Lee	5.56

Hondurans Who Own Their Own Homes
Top 10 Places Sorted by Number

Place (place type) County	Number
Miami (city) Miami-Dade	498
Hialeah (city) Miami-Dade	185
Carol City (cdp) Miami-Dade	126
West Little River (cdp) Miami-Dade	112
Tampa (city) Hillsborough	110
North Miami Beach (city) Miami-Dade	84
Kendale Lakes (cdp) Miami-Dade	79
North Miami (city) Miami-Dade	57

Tamiami (cdp) Miami-Dade	53
Fountainbleau (cdp) Miami-Dade	52

Hondurans Who Own Their Own Homes
Top 10 Places Sorted by Percent

Place (place type) County	Percent
Carol City (cdp) Miami-Dade	84.56
Kendale Lakes (cdp) Miami-Dade	78.22
North Miami Beach (city) Miami-Dade	55.63
Tamiami (cdp) Miami-Dade	55.21
West Little River (cdp) Miami-Dade	46.09
Fountainbleau (cdp) Miami-Dade	44.83
Tampa (city) Hillsborough	38.87
North Miami (city) Miami-Dade	33.53
Hollywood (city) Broward	32.65
Hialeah (city) Miami-Dade	25.55

Mexicans Who Own Their Own Homes
Top 10 Places Sorted by Number

Place (place type) County	Number
Immokalee (cdp) Collier	939
Tampa (city) Hillsborough	719
Jacksonville (city) Duval	705
Leisure City (cdp) Miami-Dade	503
Fort Pierce (city) Saint Lucie	392
Bonita Springs (city) Lee	336
Plant City (city) Hillsborough	280
Haines City (city) Polk	267
Ocoee (city) Orange	248
Belle Glade (city) Palm Beach	247

Mexicans Who Own Their Own Homes
Top 10 Places Sorted by Percent

Place (place type) County	Percent
Weston (city) Broward	93.53
Lehigh Acres (cdp) Lee	83.26
Kendale Lakes (cdp) Miami-Dade	79.20
Deltona (city) Volusia	72.06
Davie (town) Broward	71.18
Ocoee (city) Orange	69.66
Pembroke Pines (city) Broward	66.27
Miramar (city) Broward	65.34
Coconut Creek (city) Broward	63.58
Apopka (city) Orange	60.81

Nicaraguans Who Own Their Own Homes
Top 10 Places Sorted by Number

Place (place type) County	Number
Fountainbleau (cdp) Miami-Dade	809
Miami (city) Miami-Dade	802
Hialeah (city) Miami-Dade	727
Kendale Lakes (cdp) Miami-Dade	543
Tamiami (cdp) Miami-Dade	453
Kendall (cdp) Miami-Dade	320
Richmond West (cdp) Miami-Dade	308
Carol City (cdp) Miami-Dade	300
Kendall West (cdp) Miami-Dade	299
The Hammocks (cdp) Miami-Dade	291

Nicaraguans Who Own Their Own Homes
Top 10 Places Sorted by Percent

Place (place type) County	Percent
Richmond West (cdp) Miami-Dade	97.16
Miramar (city) Broward	88.15
Carol City (cdp) Miami-Dade	87.21
South Miami Heights (cdp) Miami-Dade	79.51
The Crossings (cdp) Miami-Dade	78.57
Palmetto Estates (cdp) Miami-Dade	73.08
Tamiami (cdp) Miami-Dade	72.36
Kendale Lakes (cdp) Miami-Dade	69.44
North Miami (city) Miami-Dade	65.10
Hialeah Gardens (city) Miami-Dade	62.65

Notes: Please refer to the User's Guide for an explanation of data; tables include places with populations > 9,999 and reflect only those areas that meet Summary File 4 population thresholds, therefore there may be less than 10 places listed

Place (place type) County	Number
Fountainbleau (cdp) Miami-Dade	103
Miami (city) Miami-Dade	89
Jacksonville (city) Duval	88
Tampa (city) Hillsborough	87
Miramar (city) Broward	68

Panamanians Who Own Their Own Homes
Top 10 Places Sorted by Percent

Place (place type) County	Percent
Miramar (city) Broward	52.31
Fountainbleau (cdp) Miami-Dade	49.05
Jacksonville (city) Duval	47.57
Tampa (city) Hillsborough	46.28
Miami (city) Miami-Dade	24.45

Paraguayans Who Own Their Own Homes
Top 10 Places Sorted by Number

Place (place type) County	Number

No places met population threshold.

Paraguayans Who Own Their Own Homes
Top 10 Places Sorted by Percent

Place (place type) County	Percent

No places met population threshold.

Peruvians Who Own Their Own Homes
Top 10 Places Sorted by Number

Place (place type) County	Number
The Hammocks (cdp) Miami-Dade	357
Pembroke Pines (city) Broward	321
Hialeah (city) Miami-Dade	241
Kendale Lakes (cdp) Miami-Dade	214
Miami (city) Miami-Dade	210
Kendall (cdp) Miami-Dade	209
Fountainbleau (cdp) Miami-Dade	180
Miami Beach (city) Miami-Dade	158
North Miami Beach (city) Miami-Dade	157
Kendall West (cdp) Miami-Dade	155

Peruvians Who Own Their Own Homes
Top 10 Places Sorted by Percent

Place (place type) County	Percent
Miramar (city) Broward	89.15
Pembroke Pines (city) Broward	86.52
Richmond West (cdp) Miami-Dade	84.21
The Crossings (cdp) Miami-Dade	73.62
Weston (city) Broward	69.10
The Hammocks (cdp) Miami-Dade	66.85
Sunrise (city) Broward	66.84
Doral (cdp) Miami-Dade	61.19
Kendall (cdp) Miami-Dade	57.42
Kendale Lakes (cdp) Miami-Dade	57.37

Puerto Ricans Who Own Their Own Homes
Top 10 Places Sorted by Number

Place (place type) County	Number
Deltona (city) Volusia	2,523
Tampa (city) Hillsborough	2,288
Pembroke Pines (city) Broward	1,783
Yeehaw Junction (cdp) Osceola	1,737
Orlando (city) Orange	1,718
Jacksonville (city) Duval	1,677
Kissimmee (city) Osceola	1,465
Town 'n' Country (cdp) Hillsborough	1,370
Hollywood (city) Broward	1,214
Miami (city) Miami-Dade	1,168

Place (place type) County	Percent
Richmond West (cdp) Miami-Dade	100.00
Land O' Lakes (cdp) Pasco	96.88
Country Walk (cdp) Miami-Dade	94.12
Oviedo (city) Seminole	94.10
Wekiwa Springs (cdp) Seminole	90.91
Palm Coast (city) Flagler	89.84
Longwood (city) Seminole	89.41
Cooper City (city) Broward	86.92
Deltona (city) Volusia	85.73
Meadow Woods (cdp) Orange	85.46

Salvadorans Who Own Their Own Homes
Top 10 Places Sorted by Number

Place (place type) County	Number
Miami (city) Miami-Dade	177
Homestead (city) Miami-Dade	58
Hialeah (city) Miami-Dade	57
Oakland Park (city) Broward	57
Lake Worth (city) Palm Beach	38
Fort Lauderdale (city) Broward	35

Salvadorans Who Own Their Own Homes
Top 10 Places Sorted by Percent

Place (place type) County	Percent
Oakland Park (city) Broward	28.08
Lake Worth (city) Palm Beach	23.90
Hialeah (city) Miami-Dade	23.55
Fort Lauderdale (city) Broward	22.29
Miami (city) Miami-Dade	22.26
Homestead (city) Miami-Dade	18.83

South Americans Who Own Their Own Homes
Top 10 Places Sorted by Number

Place (place type) County	Number
Hialeah (city) Miami-Dade	1,943
Pembroke Pines (city) Broward	1,850
Miami (city) Miami-Dade	1,824
The Hammocks (cdp) Miami-Dade	1,720
Miami Beach (city) Miami-Dade	1,503
Kendale Lakes (cdp) Miami-Dade	1,498
Kendall (cdp) Miami-Dade	1,447
Weston (city) Broward	1,300
Hollywood (city) Broward	1,195
Kendall West (cdp) Miami-Dade	1,148

South Americans Who Own Their Own Homes
Top 10 Places Sorted by Percent

Place (place type) County	Percent
Citrus Park (cdp) Hillsborough	91.45
Richmond West (cdp) Miami-Dade	91.27
Country Walk (cdp) Miami-Dade	91.25
Olympia Heights (cdp) Miami-Dade	83.81
Carol City (cdp) Miami-Dade	83.79
West Little River (cdp) Miami-Dade	82.48
Parkland (city) Broward	81.13
Tamiami (cdp) Miami-Dade	80.95
Cooper City (city) Broward	80.20
Miramar (city) Broward	79.35

Spaniards Who Own Their Own Homes
Top 10 Places Sorted by Number

Place (place type) County	Number
Tampa (city) Hillsborough	295
Miami (city) Miami-Dade	251
Miami Beach (city) Miami-Dade	150
Hialeah (city) Miami-Dade	114

Place (place type) County	Percent
Hialeah (city) Miami-Dade	84.44
Tampa (city) Hillsborough	74.68
Miami (city) Miami-Dade	54.09
Miami Beach (city) Miami-Dade	47.02

Uruguayans Who Own Their Own Homes
Top 10 Places Sorted by Number

Place (place type) County	Number

No places met population threshold.

Uruguayans Who Own Their Own Homes
Top 10 Places Sorted by Percent

Place (place type) County	Percent

No places met population threshold.

Venezuelans Who Own Their Own Homes
Top 10 Places Sorted by Number

Place (place type) County	Number
Weston (city) Broward	487
Doral (cdp) Miami-Dade	361
Pembroke Pines (city) Broward	328
Kendall (cdp) Miami-Dade	282
Miami (city) Miami-Dade	222
The Hammocks (cdp) Miami-Dade	215
Miami Beach (city) Miami-Dade	168
Kendall West (cdp) Miami-Dade	166
The Crossings (cdp) Miami-Dade	154
Kendale Lakes (cdp) Miami-Dade	135

Venezuelans Who Own Their Own Homes
Top 10 Places Sorted by Percent

Place (place type) County	Percent
Richmond West (cdp) Miami-Dade	92.25
Tamiami (cdp) Miami-Dade	85.52
Weston (city) Broward	71.20
Pembroke Pines (city) Broward	69.49
The Crossings (cdp) Miami-Dade	63.11
Kendale Lakes (cdp) Miami-Dade	61.64
Kendall (cdp) Miami-Dade	58.51
Doral (cdp) Miami-Dade	56.94
Kendall West (cdp) Miami-Dade	47.16
Coral Springs (city) Broward	47.06

Other Hispanics Who Own Their Own Homes
Top 10 Places Sorted by Number

Place (place type) County	Number
Tampa (city) Hillsborough	3,019
Miami (city) Miami-Dade	1,997
Hialeah (city) Miami-Dade	1,687
Kendale Lakes (cdp) Miami-Dade	1,058
Pembroke Pines (city) Broward	868
Fountainbleau (cdp) Miami-Dade	867
Kendall (cdp) Miami-Dade	796
The Hammocks (cdp) Miami-Dade	770
Hollywood (city) Broward	767
Jacksonville (city) Duval	758

Other Hispanics Who Own Their Own Homes
Top 10 Places Sorted by Percent

Place (place type) County	Percent
Miami Shores (village) Miami-Dade	100.00
Spring Hill (cdp) Hernando	96.43
Richmond West (cdp) Miami-Dade	93.71
Country Walk (cdp) Miami-Dade	93.48
Palmetto Estates (cdp) Miami-Dade	92.23
Carol City (cdp) Miami-Dade	89.70
Cooper City (city) Broward	88.33
Ojus (cdp) Miami-Dade	85.86
Citrus Park (cdp) Hillsborough	84.88

Notes: Please refer to the User's Guide for an explanation of data; tables include places with populations > 9,999 and reflect only those areas that meet Summary File 4 population thresholds, therefore there may be less than 10 places listed

Poinciana (cdp) Osceola — 84.62

Median Gross Rent

All Specified Renter-Occupied Housing Units
Top 10 Places Sorted by Number

Place (place type) County	Dollars/Month
Key Biscayne (village) Miami-Dade	1,674
Aventura (city) Miami-Dade	1,256
Parkland (city) Broward	1,128
Richmond West (cdp) Miami-Dade	1,084
Weston (city) Broward	1,084
Country Walk (cdp) Miami-Dade	1,017
Wekiwa Springs (cdp) Seminole	1,014
Boca Del Mar (cdp) Palm Beach	1,010
Sandalfoot Cove (cdp) Palm Beach	996
Wellington (village) Palm Beach	989

Specified Housing Units Rented by Hispanics
Top 10 Places Sorted by Number

Place (place type) County	Dollars/Month
Key Biscayne (village) Miami-Dade	1,822
Aventura (city) Miami-Dade	1,261
Land O' Lakes (cdp) Pasco	1,250
Parkland (city) Broward	1,169
Richmond West (cdp) Miami-Dade	1,056
Weston (city) Broward	1,028
Wekiwa Springs (cdp) Seminole	990
Pembroke Pines (city) Broward	969
Wellington (village) Palm Beach	965
Westwood Lakes (cdp) Miami-Dade	959

Specified Housing Units Rented by Argentinians
Top 10 Places Sorted by Number

Place (place type) County	Dollars/Month
Sunny Isles Beach (city) Miami-Dade	870
Hialeah (city) Miami-Dade	819
Kendall (cdp) Miami-Dade	807
Fountainbleau (cdp) Miami-Dade	800
Miami (city) Miami-Dade	769
Hollywood (city) Broward	741
Miami Beach (city) Miami-Dade	632

Specified Housing Units Rented by Bolivians
Top 10 Places Sorted by Number

Place (place type) County	Dollars/Month

No places met population threshold.

Specified Housing Units Rented by Central Americans
Top 10 Places Sorted by Number

Place (place type) County	Dollars/Month
Richmond West (cdp) Miami-Dade	1,278
Doral (cdp) Miami-Dade	1,071
Country Walk (cdp) Miami-Dade	950
The Crossings (cdp) Miami-Dade	922
Pembroke Pines (city) Broward	903
The Hammocks (cdp) Miami-Dade	895
Coral Terrace (cdp) Miami-Dade	868
Princeton (cdp) Miami-Dade	850
Kendale Lakes (cdp) Miami-Dade	841
Carol City (cdp) Miami-Dade	835

Specified Housing Units Rented by Chileans
Top 10 Places Sorted by Number

Place (place type) County	Dollars/Month
Kendall (cdp) Miami-Dade	843
Fountainbleau (cdp) Miami-Dade	831
Hollywood (city) Broward	715
Miami (city) Miami-Dade	693
Miami Beach (city) Miami-Dade	676
Hialeah (city) Miami-Dade	647

Specified Housing Units Rented by Colombians
Top 10 Places Sorted by Number

Place (place type) County	Dollars/Month
Key Biscayne (village) Miami-Dade	2,001
Aventura (city) Miami-Dade	1,190
Meadow Woods (cdp) Orange	1,139
Cooper City (city) Broward	1,100
Weston (city) Broward	1,068
Wellington (village) Palm Beach	1,048
Carol City (cdp) Miami-Dade	1,015
Sandalfoot Cove (cdp) Palm Beach	989
Pembroke Pines (city) Broward	981
Plantation (city) Broward	970

Specified Housing Units Rented by Costa Ricans
Top 10 Places Sorted by Number

Place (place type) County	Dollars/Month
Hialeah (city) Miami-Dade	713
Miami (city) Miami-Dade	666

Specified Housing Units Rented by Cubans
Top 10 Places Sorted by Number

Place (place type) County	Dollars/Month
Key Biscayne (village) Miami-Dade	1,736
Aventura (city) Miami-Dade	1,236
Country Walk (cdp) Miami-Dade	1,167
Weston (city) Broward	1,114
Richmond West (cdp) Miami-Dade	1,085
Westwood Lakes (cdp) Miami-Dade	1,002
Sunrise (city) Broward	969
The Crossings (cdp) Miami-Dade	969
Wellington (village) Palm Beach	964
Pembroke Pines (city) Broward	955

Specified Housing Units Rented by Dominicans
Top 10 Places Sorted by Number

Place (place type) County	Dollars/Month
Doral (cdp) Miami-Dade	1,174
Tamiami (cdp) Miami-Dade	1,065
Richmond West (cdp) Miami-Dade	1,059
Pembroke Pines (city) Broward	962
Weston (city) Broward	850
Sunrise (city) Broward	849
The Hammocks (cdp) Miami-Dade	830
Fountainbleau (cdp) Miami-Dade	813
Country Club (cdp) Miami-Dade	804
Kendale Lakes (cdp) Miami-Dade	791

Specified Housing Units Rented by Ecuadorians
Top 10 Places Sorted by Number

Place (place type) County	Dollars/Month
Pembroke Pines (city) Broward	1,053
Coral Springs (city) Broward	953
Sunrise (city) Broward	853
Fountainbleau (cdp) Miami-Dade	833
Hialeah (city) Miami-Dade	711
Hollywood (city) Broward	698
Miami (city) Miami-Dade	581
Miami Beach (city) Miami-Dade	558
Tampa (city) Hillsborough	439

Specified Housing Units Rented by Guatemalans
Top 10 Places Sorted by Number

Place (place type) County	Dollars/Month
Bonita Springs (city) Lee	690
West Palm Beach (city) Palm Beach	639
Hialeah (city) Miami-Dade	638
Fort Lauderdale (city) Broward	630
Lake Worth (city) Palm Beach	615
Homestead (city) Miami-Dade	605
Immokalee (cdp) Collier	580
Fort Myers (city) Lee	556
Miami (city) Miami-Dade	530

Specified Housing Units Rented by Hondurans
Top 10 Places Sorted by Number

Place (place type) County	Dollars/Month
Kendale Lakes (cdp) Miami-Dade	1,125
Fountainbleau (cdp) Miami-Dade	855
Carol City (cdp) Miami-Dade	823
Tamiami (cdp) Miami-Dade	749
Hialeah (city) Miami-Dade	698
North Miami Beach (city) Miami-Dade	667
Hollywood (city) Broward	664
North Miami (city) Miami-Dade	658
Lake Worth (city) Palm Beach	609
Miami Beach (city) Miami-Dade	589

Specified Housing Units Rented by Mexicans
Top 10 Places Sorted by Number

Place (place type) County	Dollars/Month
Doral (cdp) Miami-Dade	1,155
Pembroke Pines (city) Broward	1,149
Plantation (city) Broward	1,023
Weston (city) Broward	950
Key West (city) Monroe	933
Sunrise (city) Broward	904
Tamiami (cdp) Miami-Dade	878
Coral Springs (city) Broward	847
Coconut Creek (city) Broward	822
Kendale Lakes (cdp) Miami-Dade	813

Specified Housing Units Rented by Nicaraguans
Top 10 Places Sorted by Number

Place (place type) County	Dollars/Month
Richmond West (cdp) Miami-Dade	1,375
South Miami Heights (cdp) Miami-Dade	929
The Crossings (cdp) Miami-Dade	922
The Hammocks (cdp) Miami-Dade	900
Miramar (city) Broward	894
Carol City (cdp) Miami-Dade	888
Coral Terrace (cdp) Miami-Dade	877
Kendale Lakes (cdp) Miami-Dade	845
Fountainbleau (cdp) Miami-Dade	806
Kendall West (cdp) Miami-Dade	805

Specified Housing Units Rented by Panamanians
Top 10 Places Sorted by Number

Place (place type) County	Dollars/Month
Miramar (city) Broward	829
Fountainbleau (cdp) Miami-Dade	775
Jacksonville (city) Duval	732
Tampa (city) Hillsborough	568
Miami (city) Miami-Dade	545

Specified Housing Units Rented by Paraguayans
Top 10 Places Sorted by Number

Place (place type) County	Dollars/Month

No places met population threshold.

Specified Housing Units Rented by Peruvians
Top 10 Places Sorted by Number

Place (place type) County	Dollars/Month
Miramar (city) Broward	1,219
Weston (city) Broward	1,146
Richmond West (cdp) Miami-Dade	1,125
Pembroke Pines (city) Broward	1,000
Plantation (city) Broward	995
Doral (cdp) Miami-Dade	959
The Hammocks (cdp) Miami-Dade	952
Coral Springs (city) Broward	907
North Lauderdale (city) Broward	890
Kendale Lakes (cdp) Miami-Dade	854

Notes: Please refer to the User's Guide for an explanation of data; tables include places with populations > 9,999 and reflect only those areas that meet Summary File 4 population thresholds, therefore there may be less than 10 places listed

Specified Housing Units Rented by Puerto Ricans
Top 10 Places Sorted by Number

Place (place type) County	Dollars/Month
Wellington (village) Palm Beach	1,054
Pembroke Pines (city) Broward	965
Wekiwa Springs (cdp) Seminole	950
Tamiami (cdp) Miami-Dade	948
The Crossings (cdp) Miami-Dade	947
Miami Lakes (cdp) Miami-Dade	938
Plantation (city) Broward	929
Weston (city) Broward	897
Coconut Creek (city) Broward	886
Doral (cdp) Miami-Dade	878

Specified Housing Units Rented by Salvadorans
Top 10 Places Sorted by Number

Place (place type) County	Dollars/Month
Oakland Park (city) Broward	670
Hialeah (city) Miami-Dade	623
Fort Lauderdale (city) Broward	576
Lake Worth (city) Palm Beach	547
Homestead (city) Miami-Dade	542
Miami (city) Miami-Dade	534

Specified Housing Units Rented by South Americans
Top 10 Places Sorted by Number

Place (place type) County	Dollars/Month
Key Biscayne (village) Miami-Dade	1,736
Aventura (city) Miami-Dade	1,316
Parkland (city) Broward	1,179
Meadow Woods (cdp) Orange	1,135
Cooper City (city) Broward	1,100
Richmond West (cdp) Miami-Dade	1,063
Weston (city) Broward	1,047
Sandalfoot Cove (cdp) Palm Beach	1,030
Wellington (village) Palm Beach	1,030
Pembroke Pines (city) Broward	988

Specified Housing Units Rented by Spaniards
Top 10 Places Sorted by Number

Place (place type) County	Dollars/Month
Miami Beach (city) Miami-Dade	703
Hialeah (city) Miami-Dade	671
Tampa (city) Hillsborough	573
Miami (city) Miami-Dade	509

Specified Housing Units Rented by Uruguayans
Top 10 Places Sorted by Number

Place (place type) County	Dollars/Month
No places met population threshold.	

Specified Housing Units Rented by Venezuelans
Top 10 Places Sorted by Number

Place (place type) County	Dollars/Month
Richmond West (cdp) Miami-Dade	1,375
Coral Springs (city) Broward	1,058
Tamiami (cdp) Miami-Dade	1,031
Weston (city) Broward	1,017
Pembroke Pines (city) Broward	996
The Crossings (cdp) Miami-Dade	979
Plantation (city) Broward	970
Doral (cdp) Miami-Dade	937
The Hammocks (cdp) Miami-Dade	846
Fountainbleau (cdp) Miami-Dade	820

Specified Housing Units Rented by Other Hispanics
Top 10 Places Sorted by Number

Place (place type) County	Dollars/Month
Cooper City (city) Broward	2,001
Key Biscayne (village) Miami-Dade	2,001
Aventura (city) Miami-Dade	1,267
Palmetto Estates (cdp) Miami-Dade	1,125
Plantation (city) Broward	1,028
Doral (cdp) Miami-Dade	988
The Crossings (cdp) Miami-Dade	988
Pembroke Pines (city) Broward	984
Weston (city) Broward	958
Wellington (village) Palm Beach	956

Median Home Value

All Specified Owner-Occupied Housing Units
Top 10 Places Sorted by Number

Place (place type) County	Dollars
Key Biscayne (village) Miami-Dade	615,500
Naples (city) Collier	416,000
Pinecrest (village) Miami-Dade	393,900
Coral Gables (city) Miami-Dade	336,800
Miami Beach (city) Miami-Dade	334,400
Parkland (city) Broward	309,700
Sunny Isles Beach (city) Miami-Dade	298,400
Marco Island (city) Collier	291,100
Cutler (cdp) Miami-Dade	266,800
Key West (city) Monroe	265,800

Specified Housing Units Owned and Occupied by Hispanics
Top 10 Places Sorted by Number

Place (place type) County	Dollars
Key Biscayne (village) Miami-Dade	612,400
Sunny Isles Beach (city) Miami-Dade	426,900
Pinecrest (village) Miami-Dade	418,100
Coral Gables (city) Miami-Dade	319,100
Cutler (cdp) Miami-Dade	283,800
Key West (city) Monroe	255,100
Miami Beach (city) Miami-Dade	246,600
Parkland (city) Broward	239,400
Glenvar Heights (cdp) Miami-Dade	238,600
East Lake (cdp) Pinellas	215,200

Specified Housing Units Owned and Occupied by Argentinians
Top 10 Places Sorted by Number

Place (place type) County	Dollars
Miami Beach (city) Miami-Dade	384,400
Sunny Isles Beach (city) Miami-Dade	272,700
Kendall (cdp) Miami-Dade	150,600
Miami (city) Miami-Dade	145,800
Fountainbleau (cdp) Miami-Dade	100,000
Hialeah (city) Miami-Dade	88,400
Hollywood (city) Broward	85,400

Specified Housing Units Owned and Occupied by Bolivians
Top 10 Places Sorted by Number

Place (place type) County	Dollars
No places met population threshold.	

Specified Housing Units Owned and Occupied by Central Americans
Top 10 Places Sorted by Number

Place (place type) County	Dollars
Miami Beach (city) Miami-Dade	445,200
Key West (city) Monroe	337,500
Coral Gables (city) Miami-Dade	325,000
Pinecrest (village) Miami-Dade	297,200
Glenvar Heights (cdp) Miami-Dade	180,900
Westchester (cdp) Miami-Dade	164,400
Plantation (city) Broward	159,600
Coral Springs (city) Broward	158,400
Doral (cdp) Miami-Dade	155,700
Sunset (cdp) Miami-Dade	153,100

Specified Housing Units Owned and Occupied by Chileans
Top 10 Places Sorted by Number

Place (place type) County	Dollars
Miami Beach (city) Miami-Dade	531,300
Kendall (cdp) Miami-Dade	165,300
Miami (city) Miami-Dade	149,200
Fountainbleau (cdp) Miami-Dade	122,900
Hialeah (city) Miami-Dade	99,300
Hollywood (city) Broward	92,000

Specified Housing Units Owned and Occupied by Colombians
Top 10 Places Sorted by Number

Place (place type) County	Dollars
Key Biscayne (village) Miami-Dade	875,000
Miami Beach (city) Miami-Dade	403,800
Aventura (city) Miami-Dade	350,000
Coral Gables (city) Miami-Dade	319,700
Ojus (cdp) Miami-Dade	240,600
Doral (cdp) Miami-Dade	171,900
Weston (city) Broward	171,300
Miami Springs (city) Miami-Dade	168,800
Coral Springs (city) Broward	167,600
Miami Lakes (cdp) Miami-Dade	167,200

Specified Housing Units Owned and Occupied by Costa Ricans
Top 10 Places Sorted by Number

Place (place type) County	Dollars
Miami (city) Miami-Dade	136,700
Hialeah (city) Miami-Dade	111,900

Specified Housing Units Owned and Occupied by Cubans
Top 10 Places Sorted by Number

Place (place type) County	Dollars
Key Biscayne (village) Miami-Dade	601,400
Sunny Isles Beach (city) Miami-Dade	517,900
Pinecrest (village) Miami-Dade	412,000
Coral Gables (city) Miami-Dade	316,300
Cutler (cdp) Miami-Dade	271,900
Key West (city) Monroe	268,000
Glenvar Heights (cdp) Miami-Dade	263,700
Miami Beach (city) Miami-Dade	231,300
Miami Shores (village) Miami-Dade	216,700
Weston (city) Broward	207,400

Specified Housing Units Owned and Occupied by Dominicans
Top 10 Places Sorted by Number

Place (place type) County	Dollars
Miami Beach (city) Miami-Dade	371,400
Weston (city) Broward	169,800
Doral (cdp) Miami-Dade	141,800
Tamiami (cdp) Miami-Dade	138,700
Pembroke Pines (city) Broward	138,000
The Hammocks (cdp) Miami-Dade	128,700
Coral Springs (city) Broward	127,700
Richmond West (cdp) Miami-Dade	125,300
Kendall (cdp) Miami-Dade	118,500
Miami (city) Miami-Dade	117,100

Specified Housing Units Owned and Occupied by Ecuadorians
Top 10 Places Sorted by Number

Place (place type) County	Dollars
Miami Beach (city) Miami-Dade	450,000
Miami (city) Miami-Dade	154,700
Coral Springs (city) Broward	148,500
Pembroke Pines (city) Broward	136,700
Hialeah (city) Miami-Dade	111,800

Notes: Please refer to the User's Guide for an explanation of data; tables include places with populations > 9,999 and reflect only those areas that meet Summary File 4 population thresholds, therefore there may be less than 10 places listed

Sunrise (city) Broward	105,600
Hollywood (city) Broward	92,500
Fountainbleau (cdp) Miami-Dade	89,100
Tampa (city) Hillsborough	70,000

Specified Housing Units Owned and Occupied by Guatelmalans
Top 10 Places Sorted by Number

Place (place type) County	Dollars
Miami (city) Miami-Dade	116,000
Bonita Springs (city) Lee	112,500
Hialeah (city) Miami-Dade	96,400
Fort Lauderdale (city) Broward	85,000
Homestead (city) Miami-Dade	78,100
West Palm Beach (city) Palm Beach	69,400
Fort Myers (city) Lee	65,000
Immokalee (cdp) Collier	65,000
Lake Worth (city) Palm Beach	54,100

Specified Housing Units Owned and Occupied by Hondurans
Top 10 Places Sorted by Number

Place (place type) County	Dollars
Miami Beach (city) Miami-Dade	450,000
Kendale Lakes (cdp) Miami-Dade	135,200
Miami (city) Miami-Dade	100,000
Fountainbleau (cdp) Miami-Dade	99,500
North Miami Beach (city) Miami-Dade	98,900
Tamiami (cdp) Miami-Dade	92,900
Hialeah (city) Miami-Dade	87,800
North Miami (city) Miami-Dade	87,400
Carol City (cdp) Miami-Dade	87,300
Hollywood (city) Broward	78,600

Specified Housing Units Owned and Occupied by Mexicans
Top 10 Places Sorted by Number

Place (place type) County	Dollars
Weston (city) Broward	192,100
Boca Raton (city) Palm Beach	181,700
Doral (cdp) Miami-Dade	172,800
Coral Springs (city) Broward	159,300
Plantation (city) Broward	152,500
Pembroke Pines (city) Broward	144,100
Coconut Creek (city) Broward	139,500
Auburndale (city) Polk	137,500
The Hammocks (cdp) Miami-Dade	135,600
Miami (city) Miami-Dade	134,600

Specified Housing Units Owned and Occupied by Nicaraguans
Top 10 Places Sorted by Number

Place (place type) County	Dollars
Coral Gables (city) Miami-Dade	234,500
Westchester (cdp) Miami-Dade	185,700
Miami Springs (city) Miami-Dade	154,700
Kendall (cdp) Miami-Dade	138,900
Miramar (city) Miami-Dade	133,400
The Hammocks (cdp) Miami-Dade	132,600
Tamiami (cdp) Miami-Dade	129,300
Coral Terrace (cdp) Miami-Dade	128,900
Kendall West (cdp) Miami-Dade	127,300
The Crossings (cdp) Miami-Dade	126,400

Specified Housing Units Owned and Occupied by Panamanians
Top 10 Places Sorted by Number

Place (place type) County	Dollars
Miramar (city) Broward	137,500
Miami (city) Miami-Dade	126,300
Fountainbleau (cdp) Miami-Dade	94,300
Jacksonville (city) Duval	80,000
Tampa (city) Hillsborough	67,900

Specified Housing Units Owned and Occupied by Paraguayans
Top 10 Places Sorted by Number

Place (place type) County	Dollars
No places met population threshold.	

Specified Housing Units Owned and Occupied by Peruvians
Top 10 Places Sorted by Number

Place (place type) County	Dollars
Weston (city) Broward	220,000
Doral (cdp) Miami-Dade	190,900
Miami Beach (city) Miami-Dade	175,000
Miramar (city) Broward	158,600
Kendall (cdp) Miami-Dade	147,700
Miami (city) Miami-Dade	143,300
Richmond West (cdp) Miami-Dade	139,400
The Hammocks (cdp) Miami-Dade	137,300
Pembroke Pines (city) Broward	137,100
Coral Springs (city) Broward	134,100

Specified Housing Units Owned and Occupied by Puerto Ricans
Top 10 Places Sorted by Number

Place (place type) County	Dollars
Coral Gables (city) Miami-Dade	313,300
Doral (cdp) Miami-Dade	186,900
Boca Raton (city) Palm Beach	177,500
Weston (city) Broward	177,000
Miami Lakes (cdp) Miami-Dade	169,600
Miami Beach (city) Miami-Dade	161,800
Coral Springs (city) Broward	158,500
Kendall (cdp) Miami-Dade	158,300
Wellington (village) Palm Beach	150,800
Coconut Creek (city) Broward	147,300

Specified Housing Units Owned and Occupied by Salvadorans
Top 10 Places Sorted by Number

Place (place type) County	Dollars
Miami (city) Miami-Dade	122,800
Oakland Park (city) Broward	112,500
Hialeah (city) Miami-Dade	87,700
Lake Worth (city) Palm Beach	74,400
Fort Lauderdale (city) Broward	66,300
Homestead (city) Miami-Dade	66,100

Specified Housing Units Owned and Occupied by South Americans
Top 10 Places Sorted by Number

Place (place type) County	Dollars
Key Biscayne (village) Miami-Dade	564,300
Pinecrest (village) Miami-Dade	541,700
Miami Beach (city) Miami-Dade	376,400
Coral Gables (city) Miami-Dade	329,200
Cutler (cdp) Miami-Dade	301,300
Sunny Isles Beach (city) Miami-Dade	295,500
Parkland (city) Broward	260,000
Boca Raton (city) Palm Beach	233,800
Ojus (cdp) Miami-Dade	209,400
Aventura (city) Miami-Dade	188,900

Specified Housing Units Owned and Occupied by Spaniards
Top 10 Places Sorted by Number

Place (place type) County	Dollars
Miami Beach (city) Miami-Dade	190,600
Miami (city) Miami-Dade	119,100
Hialeah (city) Miami-Dade	109,500
Tampa (city) Hillsborough	83,300

Specified Housing Units Owned and Occupied by Uruguayans
Top 10 Places Sorted by Number

Place (place type) County	Dollars
No places met population threshold.	

Specified Housing Units Owned and Occupied by Venezuelans
Top 10 Places Sorted by Number

Place (place type) County	Dollars
Coral Gables (city) Miami-Dade	420,000
Miami Beach (city) Miami-Dade	365,400
Coral Springs (city) Broward	189,600
Miami (city) Miami-Dade	182,500
Weston (city) Broward	174,500
Doral (cdp) Miami-Dade	170,800
Hollywood (city) Broward	162,200
Pembroke Pines (city) Broward	152,800
The Hammocks (cdp) Miami-Dade	146,200
The Crossings (cdp) Miami-Dade	144,600

Specified Housing Units Owned and Occupied by Other Hispanics
Top 10 Places Sorted by Number

Place (place type) County	Dollars
Key Biscayne (village) Miami-Dade	666,700
Pinecrest (village) Miami-Dade	386,400
Coral Gables (city) Miami-Dade	298,900
Cutler (cdp) Miami-Dade	271,700
Key West (city) Monroe	210,500
Miami Beach (city) Miami-Dade	210,000
Glenvar Heights (cdp) Miami-Dade	201,400
Miami Lakes (cdp) Miami-Dade	194,000
Weston (city) Broward	175,900
Aventura (city) Miami-Dade	172,900

Notes: Please refer to the User's Guide for an explanation of data; tables include places with populations > 9,999 and reflect only those areas that meet Summary File 4 population thresholds, therefore there may be less than 10 places listed

Asian Population

Population

Total Population
Top 10 Places Sorted by Number

Place (place type) County	Number
Jacksonville (city) Duval	735,503
Miami (city) Miami-Dade	362,563
Tampa (city) Hillsborough	303,512
St. Petersburg (city) Pinellas	247,793
Hialeah (city) Miami-Dade	226,411
Orlando (city) Orange	185,984
Fort Lauderdale (city) Broward	152,125
Tallahassee (city) Leon	150,581
Hollywood (city) Broward	139,261
Pembroke Pines (city) Broward	137,112

Asian
Top 10 Places Sorted by Number

Place (place type) County	Number
Jacksonville (city) Duval	19,838
St. Petersburg (city) Pinellas	6,729
Tampa (city) Hillsborough	6,415
Pembroke Pines (city) Broward	5,004
Orlando (city) Orange	4,823
Gainesville (city) Alachua	4,399
Coral Springs (city) Broward	3,985
Tallahassee (city) Leon	3,466
Hollywood (city) Broward	2,940
Sunrise (city) Broward	2,915

Asian
Top 10 Places Sorted by Percent of Total Population

Place (place type) County	Percent
Hunters Creek (cdp) Orange	8.61
Doctor Phillips (cdp) Orange	7.99
Oak Ridge (cdp) Orange	5.83
Springfield (city) Bay	5.81
Doral (cdp) Miami-Dade	5.78
Ives Estates (cdp) Miami-Dade	4.77
Myrtle Grove (cdp) Escambia	4.69
Pinecrest (village) Miami-Dade	4.61
Gainesville (city) Alachua	4.60
Westchase (cdp) Hillsborough	4.57

Native Hawaiian and Other Pacific Islander
Top 10 Places Sorted by Number

Place (place type) County	Number
Jacksonville (city) Duval	497

Native Hawaiian and Other Pacific Islander
Top 10 Places Sorted by Percent of Asian Population

Place (place type) County	Percent
Jacksonville (city) Duval	100.00

Native Hawaiian and Other Pacific Islander
Top 10 Places Sorted by Percent of Total Population

Place (place type) County	Percent
Jacksonville (city) Duval	0.07

Asian Indian
Top 10 Places Sorted by Number

Place (place type) County	Number
Jacksonville (city) Duval	2,730
Coral Springs (city) Broward	1,855
Pembroke Pines (city) Broward	1,752
Orlando (city) Orange	1,460
Tampa (city) Hillsborough	1,408
Hollywood (city) Broward	1,269
Tallahassee (city) Leon	1,109
Plantation (city) Broward	1,105
Gainesville (city) Alachua	1,056
Sunrise (city) Broward	990

Asian Indian
Top 10 Places Sorted by Percent of Asian Population

Place (place type) County	Percent
East Lake (cdp) Pinellas	66.57
Plantation (city) Broward	49.86
West Palm Beach (city) Palm Beach	48.62
Cooper City (city) Broward	47.78
Coral Springs (city) Broward	46.55
Altamonte Springs (city) Seminole	46.35
Doctor Phillips (cdp) Orange	45.01
Hollywood (city) Broward	43.16
Lakeland (city) Polk	42.42
Miami (city) Miami-Dade	39.79

Asian Indian
Top 10 Places Sorted by Percent of Total Population

Place (place type) County	Percent
Doctor Phillips (cdp) Orange	3.60
Cooper City (city) Broward	2.14
East Lake (cdp) Pinellas	1.60
Coral Springs (city) Broward	1.58
Altamonte Springs (city) Seminole	1.38
Plantation (city) Broward	1.33
Pembroke Pines (city) Broward	1.28
Sunrise (city) Broward	1.16
Weston (city) Broward	1.13
Gainesville (city) Alachua	1.10

Bangladeshi
Top 10 Places Sorted by Number

Place (place type) County	Number
No places met population threshold.	

Bangladeshi
Top 10 Places Sorted by Percent of Asian Population

Place (place type) County	Percent
No places met population threshold.	

Bangladeshi
Top 10 Places Sorted by Percent of Total Population

Place (place type) County	Percent
No places met population threshold.	

Cambodian
Top 10 Places Sorted by Number

Place (place type) County	Number
Jacksonville (city) Duval	1,001
St. Petersburg (city) Pinellas	516

Cambodian
Top 10 Places Sorted by Percent of Asian Population

Place (place type) County	Percent
St. Petersburg (city) Pinellas	7.67
Jacksonville (city) Duval	5.05

Cambodian
Top 10 Places Sorted by Percent of Total Population

Place (place type) County	Percent
St. Petersburg (city) Pinellas	0.21
Jacksonville (city) Duval	0.14

Chinese (except Taiwanese)
Top 10 Places Sorted by Number

Place (place type) County	Number
Jacksonville (city) Duval	1,629
Gainesville (city) Alachua	1,456
Pembroke Pines (city) Broward	1,153
Sunrise (city) Broward	903
Coral Springs (city) Broward	893
Tallahassee (city) Leon	753
North Miami Beach (city) Miami-Dade	741
St. Petersburg (city) Pinellas	731
Tampa (city) Hillsborough	672
Hollywood (city) Broward	649

Chinese (except Taiwanese)
Top 10 Places Sorted by Percent of Asian Population

Place (place type) County	Percent
North Miami Beach (city) Miami-Dade	43.43
Gainesville (city) Alachua	33.10
Margate (city) Broward	32.13
Sunrise (city) Broward	30.98
Davie (town) Broward	30.37
The Hammocks (cdp) Miami-Dade	28.62
Kendall (cdp) Miami-Dade	26.75
Miramar (city) Broward	24.14
Pembroke Pines (city) Broward	23.04
Miami (city) Miami-Dade	22.74

Chinese (except Taiwanese)
Top 10 Places Sorted by Percent of Total Population

Place (place type) County	Percent
North Miami Beach (city) Miami-Dade	1.82
Gainesville (city) Alachua	1.52
Sunrise (city) Broward	1.05
Margate (city) Broward	1.01
The Hammocks (cdp) Miami-Dade	0.89
Pembroke Pines (city) Broward	0.84
Davie (town) Broward	0.83
Kendall (cdp) Miami-Dade	0.83
Coral Springs (city) Broward	0.76
Miramar (city) Broward	0.70

Fijian
Top 10 Places Sorted by Number

Place (place type) County	Number
No places met population threshold.	

Fijian
Top 10 Places Sorted by Percent of Asian Population

Place (place type) County	Percent
No places met population threshold.	

Fijian
Top 10 Places Sorted by Percent of Total Population

Place (place type) County	Percent
No places met population threshold.	

Filipino
Top 10 Places Sorted by Number

Place (place type) County	Number
Jacksonville (city) Duval	9,783
Tampa (city) Hillsborough	970
Pembroke Pines (city) Broward	927
St. Petersburg (city) Pinellas	870
Orlando (city) Orange	724
Cape Coral (city) Lee	683
Lakeside (cdp) Clay	571
Miramar (city) Broward	476
Myrtle Grove (cdp) Escambia	471
Clearwater (city) Pinellas	451

Filipino
Top 10 Places Sorted by Percent of Asian Population

Place (place type) County	Percent
Lakeside (cdp) Clay	73.39
Cape Coral (city) Lee	59.70
Yeehaw Junction (cdp) Osceola	59.10
Myrtle Grove (cdp) Escambia	58.00
Bellview (cdp) Escambia	52.35
Jacksonville (city) Duval	49.31
Clearwater (city) Pinellas	28.47
Miramar (city) Broward	22.53

Notes: Please refer to the User's Guide for an explanation of data; tables reflect only those areas that meet Summary File 4 population thresholds, therefore there may be less than 10 places listed

Pembroke Pines (city) Broward — 18.53
Tampa (city) Hillsborough — 15.12

Filipino
Top 10 Places Sorted by Percent of Total Population

Place (place type) County	Percent
Myrtle Grove (cdp) Escambia	2.72
Bellview (cdp) Escambia	1.96
Lakeside (cdp) Clay	1.85
Yeehaw Junction (cdp) Osceola	1.54
Jacksonville (city) Duval	1.33
Pembroke Pines (city) Broward	0.68
Cape Coral (city) Lee	0.67
Miramar (city) Broward	0.65
Clearwater (city) Pinellas	0.42
Orlando (city) Orange	0.39

Guamanian or Chamorro
Top 10 Places Sorted by Number

Place (place type) County	Number
No places met population threshold.	

Guamanian or Chamorro
Top 10 Places Sorted by Percent of Asian Population

Place (place type) County	Percent
No places met population threshold.	

Guamanian or Chamorro
Top 10 Places Sorted by Percent of Total Population

Place (place type) County	Percent
No places met population threshold.	

Hawaiian, Native
Top 10 Places Sorted by Number

Place (place type) County	Number
No places met population threshold.	

Hawaiian, Native
Top 10 Places Sorted by Percent of Asian Population

Place (place type) County	Percent
No places met population threshold.	

Hawaiian, Native
Top 10 Places Sorted by Percent of Total Population

Place (place type) County	Percent
No places met population threshold.	

Hmong
Top 10 Places Sorted by Number

Place (place type) County	Number
No places met population threshold.	

Hmong
Top 10 Places Sorted by Percent of Asian Population

Place (place type) County	Percent
No places met population threshold.	

Hmong
Top 10 Places Sorted by Percent of Total Population

Place (place type) County	Percent
No places met population threshold.	

Indonesian
Top 10 Places Sorted by Number

Place (place type) County	Number
No places met population threshold.	

Indonesian
Top 10 Places Sorted by Percent of Asian Population

Place (place type) County	Percent
No places met population threshold.	

Indonesian
Top 10 Places Sorted by Percent of Total Population

Place (place type) County	Percent
No places met population threshold.	

Japanese
Top 10 Places Sorted by Number

Place (place type) County	Number
Jacksonville (city) Duval	531

Japanese
Top 10 Places Sorted by Percent of Asian Population

Place (place type) County	Percent
Jacksonville (city) Duval	2.68

Japanese
Top 10 Places Sorted by Percent of Total Population

Place (place type) County	Percent
Jacksonville (city) Duval	0.07

Korean
Top 10 Places Sorted by Number

Place (place type) County	Number
Tampa (city) Hillsborough	963
Jacksonville (city) Duval	940
Orlando (city) Orange	550
Gainesville (city) Alachua	501

Korean
Top 10 Places Sorted by Percent of Asian Population

Place (place type) County	Percent
Tampa (city) Hillsborough	15.01
Orlando (city) Orange	11.40
Gainesville (city) Alachua	11.39
Jacksonville (city) Duval	4.74

Korean
Top 10 Places Sorted by Percent of Total Population

Place (place type) County	Percent
Gainesville (city) Alachua	0.52
Tampa (city) Hillsborough	0.32
Orlando (city) Orange	0.30
Jacksonville (city) Duval	0.13

Laotian
Top 10 Places Sorted by Number

Place (place type) County	Number
St. Petersburg (city) Pinellas	1,133

Laotian
Top 10 Places Sorted by Percent of Asian Population

Place (place type) County	Percent
St. Petersburg (city) Pinellas	16.84

Laotian
Top 10 Places Sorted by Percent of Total Population

Place (place type) County	Percent
St. Petersburg (city) Pinellas	0.46

Malaysian
Top 10 Places Sorted by Number

Place (place type) County	Number
No places met population threshold.	

Malaysian
Top 10 Places Sorted by Percent of Asian Population

Place (place type) County	Percent
No places met population threshold.	

Malaysian
Top 10 Places Sorted by Percent of Total Population

Place (place type) County	Percent
No places met population threshold.	

Pakistani
Top 10 Places Sorted by Number

Place (place type) County	Number
No places met population threshold.	

Pakistani
Top 10 Places Sorted by Percent of Asian Population

Place (place type) County	Percent
No places met population threshold.	

Pakistani
Top 10 Places Sorted by Percent of Total Population

Place (place type) County	Percent
No places met population threshold.	

Samoan
Top 10 Places Sorted by Number

Place (place type) County	Number
No places met population threshold.	

Samoan
Top 10 Places Sorted by Percent of Asian Population

Place (place type) County	Percent
No places met population threshold.	

Samoan
Top 10 Places Sorted by Percent of Total Population

Place (place type) County	Percent
No places met population threshold.	

Sri Lankan
Top 10 Places Sorted by Number

Place (place type) County	Number
No places met population threshold.	

Sri Lankan
Top 10 Places Sorted by Percent of Asian Population

Place (place type) County	Percent
No places met population threshold.	

Sri Lankan
Top 10 Places Sorted by Percent of Total Population

Place (place type) County	Percent
No places met population threshold.	

Taiwanese
Top 10 Places Sorted by Number

Place (place type) County	Number
No places met population threshold.	

Taiwanese
Top 10 Places Sorted by Percent of Asian Population

Place (place type) County	Percent
No places met population threshold.	

Notes: Please refer to the User's Guide for an explanation of data; tables reflect only those areas that meet Summary File 4 population thresholds, therefore there may be less than 10 places listed

Taiwanese
Top 10 Places Sorted by Percent of Total Population

Place (place type) County	Percent
No places met population threshold.	

Thai
Top 10 Places Sorted by Number

Place (place type) County	Number
No places met population threshold.	

Thai
Top 10 Places Sorted by Percent of Asian Population

Place (place type) County	Percent
No places met population threshold.	

Thai
Top 10 Places Sorted by Percent of Total Population

Place (place type) County	Percent
No places met population threshold.	

Tongan
Top 10 Places Sorted by Number

Place (place type) County	Number
No places met population threshold.	

Tongan
Top 10 Places Sorted by Percent of Asian Population

Place (place type) County	Percent
No places met population threshold.	

Tongan
Top 10 Places Sorted by Percent of Total Population

Place (place type) County	Percent
No places met population threshold.	

Vietnamese
Top 10 Places Sorted by Number

Place (place type) County	Number
Jacksonville (city) Duval	2,051
St. Petersburg (city) Pinellas	1,610
Tampa (city) Hillsborough	1,379
Orlando (city) Orange	694
Town 'n' Country (cdp) Hillsborough	686
Pine Hills (cdp) Orange	641
Oak Ridge (cdp) Orange	527
Pinellas Park (city) Pinellas	526
West and East Lealman (cdp) Pinellas	457

Vietnamese
Top 10 Places Sorted by Percent of Asian Population

Place (place type) County	Percent
West and East Lealman (cdp) Pinellas	58.59
Pine Hills (cdp) Orange	54.79
Oak Ridge (cdp) Orange	40.35
Town 'n' Country (cdp) Hillsborough	30.10
Pinellas Park (city) Pinellas	29.04
St. Petersburg (city) Pinellas	23.93
Tampa (city) Hillsborough	21.50
Orlando (city) Orange	14.39
Jacksonville (city) Duval	10.34

Vietnamese
Top 10 Places Sorted by Percent of Total Population

Place (place type) County	Percent
Oak Ridge (cdp) Orange	2.35
West and East Lealman (cdp) Pinellas	2.09
Pine Hills (cdp) Orange	1.53
Pinellas Park (city) Pinellas	1.16
Town 'n' Country (cdp) Hillsborough	0.95
St. Petersburg (city) Pinellas	0.65

Tampa (city) Hillsborough	0.45
Orlando (city) Orange	0.37
Jacksonville (city) Duval	0.28

Median Age

Total Population
Top 10 Places Sorted by Number

Place (place type) County	Years
Tamarac (city) Broward	51.9
Palm Coast (city) Flagler	50.7
Ormond Beach (city) Volusia	47.6
Largo (city) Pinellas	47.5
Spring Hill (cdp) Hernando	47.5
Palm Beach Gardens (city) Palm Beach	44.7
Deerfield Beach (city) Broward	44.2
Delray Beach (city) Palm Beach	44.0
Palm Harbor (cdp) Pinellas	43.3
Merritt Island (cdp) Brevard	42.9

Asian
Top 10 Places Sorted by Number

Place (place type) County	Years
Hialeah (city) Miami-Dade	45.3
Kendale Lakes (cdp) Miami-Dade	42.9
Lakeside (cdp) Clay	42.6
Fort Walton Beach (city) Okaloosa	42.4
Niceville (city) Okaloosa	41.8
Wright (cdp) Okaloosa	40.9
Golden Glades (cdp) Miami-Dade	40.3
Bellair-Meadowbrook Terrace (cdp) Clay	39.5
Titusville (city) Brevard	39.5
Cape Coral (city) Lee	39.4

Native Hawaiian and Other Pacific Islander
Top 10 Places Sorted by Number

Place (place type) County	Years
Jacksonville (city) Duval	25.7

Asian Indian
Top 10 Places Sorted by Number

Place (place type) County	Years
Doctor Phillips (cdp) Orange	39.6
Cooper City (city) Broward	38.5
Lakeland (city) Polk	38.1
Sunrise (city) Broward	37.6
Davie (town) Broward	35.6
The Hammocks (cdp) Miami-Dade	35.5
Coral Springs (city) Broward	35.4
Hollywood (city) Broward	35.4
Boca Raton (city) Palm Beach	34.5
Miramar (city) Broward	34.3

Bangladeshi
Top 10 Places Sorted by Number

Place (place type) County	Years
No places met population threshold.	

Cambodian
Top 10 Places Sorted by Number

Place (place type) County	Years
Jacksonville (city) Duval	28.9
St. Petersburg (city) Pinellas	21.4

Chinese (except Taiwanese)
Top 10 Places Sorted by Number

Place (place type) County	Years
Miami (city) Miami-Dade	52.2
North Miami Beach (city) Miami-Dade	41.0
Coral Springs (city) Broward	39.8
The Hammocks (cdp) Miami-Dade	39.7
Pembroke Pines (city) Broward	37.7

Sunrise (city) Broward	37.7
Orlando (city) Orange	37.6
Davie (town) Broward	37.0
Hollywood (city) Broward	37.0
Kendall (cdp) Miami-Dade	36.8

Fijian
Top 10 Places Sorted by Number

Place (place type) County	Years
No places met population threshold.	

Filipino
Top 10 Places Sorted by Number

Place (place type) County	Years
Lakeside (cdp) Clay	43.5
Bellview (cdp) Escambia	41.6
Cape Coral (city) Lee	40.3
Pembroke Pines (city) Broward	39.9
Yeehaw Junction (cdp) Osceola	38.4
Myrtle Grove (cdp) Escambia	36.9
Miramar (city) Broward	36.0
St. Petersburg (city) Pinellas	35.5
Jacksonville (city) Duval	35.2
Tampa (city) Hillsborough	35.1

Guamanian or Chamorro
Top 10 Places Sorted by Number

Place (place type) County	Years
No places met population threshold.	

Hawaiian, Native
Top 10 Places Sorted by Number

Place (place type) County	Years
No places met population threshold.	

Hmong
Top 10 Places Sorted by Number

Place (place type) County	Years
No places met population threshold.	

Indonesian
Top 10 Places Sorted by Number

Place (place type) County	Years
No places met population threshold.	

Japanese
Top 10 Places Sorted by Number

Place (place type) County	Years
Jacksonville (city) Duval	36.5

Korean
Top 10 Places Sorted by Number

Place (place type) County	Years
Jacksonville (city) Duval	37.1
Tampa (city) Hillsborough	37.0
Orlando (city) Orange	33.4
Gainesville (city) Alachua	28.8

Laotian
Top 10 Places Sorted by Number

Place (place type) County	Years
St. Petersburg (city) Pinellas	30.3

Malaysian
Top 10 Places Sorted by Number

Place (place type) County	Years
No places met population threshold.	

Notes: Please refer to the User's Guide for an explanation of data; tables reflect only those areas that meet Summary File 4 population thresholds, therefore there may be less than 10 places listed

Pakistani
Top 10 Places Sorted by Number

Place (place type) County	Years
No places met population threshold.	

Samoan
Top 10 Places Sorted by Number

Place (place type) County	Years
No places met population threshold.	

Sri Lankan
Top 10 Places Sorted by Number

Place (place type) County	Years
No places met population threshold.	

Taiwanese
Top 10 Places Sorted by Number

Place (place type) County	Years
No places met population threshold.	

Thai
Top 10 Places Sorted by Number

Place (place type) County	Years
No places met population threshold.	

Tongan
Top 10 Places Sorted by Number

Place (place type) County	Years
No places met population threshold.	

Vietnamese
Top 10 Places Sorted by Number

Place (place type) County	Years
Orlando (city) Orange	35.4
Town 'n' Country (cdp) Hillsborough	34.6
St. Petersburg (city) Pinellas	33.3
Oak Ridge (cdp) Orange	31.2
Pinellas Park (city) Pinellas	30.8
West and East Lealman (cdp) Pinellas	30.5
Pine Hills (cdp) Orange	29.9
Jacksonville (city) Duval	29.5
Tampa (city) Hillsborough	29.5

Average Household Size

Total Population
Top 10 Places Sorted by Number

Place (place type) County	Number
Richmond West (cdp) Miami-Dade	3.57
South Miami Heights (cdp) Miami-Dade	3.34
Golden Glades (cdp) Miami-Dade	3.23
Kendall West (cdp) Miami-Dade	3.22
Yeehaw Junction (cdp) Osceola	3.17
Miramar (city) Broward	3.16
Hialeah (city) Miami-Dade	3.15
Kendale Lakes (cdp) Miami-Dade	3.14
Oviedo (city) Seminole	3.11
Pine Hills (cdp) Orange	3.10

Asian
Top 10 Places Sorted by Number

Place (place type) County	Number
Sunset (cdp) Miami-Dade	3.98
East Lake (cdp) Pinellas	3.93
Springfield (city) Bay	3.79
Weston (city) Broward	3.79
Greater Northdale (cdp) Hillsborough	3.72
Doctor Phillips (cdp) Orange	3.62
West and East Lealman (cdp) Pinellas	3.61
Cooper City (city) Broward	3.58

Pensacola (city) Escambia	3.52
Brandon (cdp) Hillsborough	3.51

Native Hawaiian and Other Pacific Islander
Top 10 Places Sorted by Number

Place (place type) County	Number
Jacksonville (city) Duval	3.24

Asian Indian
Top 10 Places Sorted by Number

Place (place type) County	Number
East Lake (cdp) Pinellas	4.18
Weston (city) Broward	4.16
The Hammocks (cdp) Miami-Dade	3.89
Cooper City (city) Broward	3.41
Sunrise (city) Broward	3.29
Coral Springs (city) Broward	3.25
Doctor Phillips (cdp) Orange	3.22
Miramar (city) Broward	3.19
West Palm Beach (city) Palm Beach	3.17
Hollywood (city) Broward	3.14

Bangladeshi
Top 10 Places Sorted by Number

Place (place type) County	Number
No places met population threshold.	

Cambodian
Top 10 Places Sorted by Number

Place (place type) County	Number
Jacksonville (city) Duval	4.11
St. Petersburg (city) Pinellas	3.95

Chinese (except Taiwanese)
Top 10 Places Sorted by Number

Place (place type) County	Number
Sunrise (city) Broward	3.64
Margate (city) Broward	3.37
North Miami Beach (city) Miami-Dade	3.29
Davie (town) Broward	3.26
Miramar (city) Broward	3.22
Pembroke Pines (city) Broward	2.89
Jacksonville (city) Duval	2.68
St. Petersburg (city) Pinellas	2.64
Coral Springs (city) Broward	2.51
Hollywood (city) Broward	2.50

Fijian
Top 10 Places Sorted by Number

Place (place type) County	Number
No places met population threshold.	

Filipino
Top 10 Places Sorted by Number

Place (place type) County	Number
Miramar (city) Broward	4.04
Yeehaw Junction (cdp) Osceola	3.71
Cape Coral (city) Lee	3.23
Lakeside (cdp) Clay	3.23
Jacksonville (city) Duval	3.20
Pembroke Pines (city) Broward	3.17
Bellview (cdp) Escambia	3.13
Clearwater (city) Pinellas	2.83
Orlando (city) Orange	2.65
St. Petersburg (city) Pinellas	2.65

Guamanian or Chamorro
Top 10 Places Sorted by Number

Place (place type) County	Number
No places met population threshold.	

Hawaiian, Native
Top 10 Places Sorted by Number

Place (place type) County	Number
No places met population threshold.	

Hmong
Top 10 Places Sorted by Number

Place (place type) County	Number
No places met population threshold.	

Indonesian
Top 10 Places Sorted by Number

Place (place type) County	Number
No places met population threshold.	

Japanese
Top 10 Places Sorted by Number

Place (place type) County	Number
Jacksonville (city) Duval	1.96

Korean
Top 10 Places Sorted by Number

Place (place type) County	Number
Tampa (city) Hillsborough	2.82
Jacksonville (city) Duval	2.74
Orlando (city) Orange	2.54
Gainesville (city) Alachua	2.15

Laotian
Top 10 Places Sorted by Number

Place (place type) County	Number
St. Petersburg (city) Pinellas	4.23

Malaysian
Top 10 Places Sorted by Number

Place (place type) County	Number
No places met population threshold.	

Pakistani
Top 10 Places Sorted by Number

Place (place type) County	Number
No places met population threshold.	

Samoan
Top 10 Places Sorted by Number

Place (place type) County	Number
No places met population threshold.	

Sri Lankan
Top 10 Places Sorted by Number

Place (place type) County	Number
No places met population threshold.	

Taiwanese
Top 10 Places Sorted by Number

Place (place type) County	Number
No places met population threshold.	

Thai
Top 10 Places Sorted by Number

Place (place type) County	Number
No places met population threshold.	

Tongan
Top 10 Places Sorted by Number

Place (place type) County	Number
No places met population threshold.	

Notes: Please refer to the User's Guide for an explanation of data; tables reflect only those areas that meet Summary File 4 population thresholds, therefore there may be less than 10 places listed

Vietnamese
Top 10 Places Sorted by Number

Place (place type) County	Number
Town 'n' Country (cdp) Hillsborough	5.26
Oak Ridge (cdp) Orange	3.65
West and East Lealman (cdp) Pinellas	3.58
St. Petersburg (city) Pinellas	3.48
Tampa (city) Hillsborough	3.26
Jacksonville (city) Duval	3.24
Pinellas Park (city) Pinellas	3.23
Pine Hills (cdp) Orange	3.18
Orlando (city) Orange	2.97

Language Spoken at Home: English Only

Total Population 5 Years and Over Who Speak English-Only at Home
Top 10 Places Sorted by Number

Place (place type) County	Number
Jacksonville (city) Duval	616,988
Tampa (city) Hillsborough	218,362
St. Petersburg (city) Pinellas	206,489
Tallahassee (city) Leon	130,526
Orlando (city) Orange	130,439
Fort Lauderdale (city) Broward	108,442
Hollywood (city) Broward	87,182
Miami (city) Miami-Dade	86,669
Clearwater (city) Pinellas	85,394
Cape Coral (city) Lee	83,549

Total Population 5 Years and Over Who Speak English-Only at Home
Top 10 Places Sorted by Percent

Place (place type) County	Percent
Ensley (cdp) Escambia	95.13
Pensacola (city) Escambia	93.77
Bellview (cdp) Escambia	93.50
Titusville (city) Brevard	93.44
Jacksonville Beach (city) Duval	93.08
Ferry Pass (cdp) Escambia	92.93
Panama City (city) Bay	92.78
West Pensacola (cdp) Escambia	92.54
Callaway (city) Bay	92.05
Merritt Island (cdp) Brevard	91.84

Asians 5 Years and Over Who Speak English-Only at Home
Top 10 Places Sorted by Number

Place (place type) County	Number
Jacksonville (city) Duval	4,610
Pembroke Pines (city) Broward	1,377
Tampa (city) Hillsborough	1,286
Coral Springs (city) Broward	1,223
Hollywood (city) Broward	1,205
Orlando (city) Orange	1,157
St. Petersburg (city) Pinellas	1,025
Tallahassee (city) Leon	889
Gainesville (city) Alachua	854
Plantation (city) Broward	833

Asians 5 Years and Over Who Speak English-Only at Home
Top 10 Places Sorted by Percent

Place (place type) County	Percent
South Miami Heights (cdp) Miami-Dade	95.38
Richmond West (cdp) Miami-Dade	49.51
Jacksonville Beach (city) Duval	45.86
Lake Magdalene (cdp) Hillsborough	44.72
Hollywood (city) Broward	44.58
Sanford (city) Seminole	42.70
Tamarac (city) Broward	42.69
Deltona (city) Volusia	42.37
Coconut Creek (city) Broward	41.32

Place	
Pompano Beach (city) Broward	41.09

Native Hawaiian and Other Pacific Islanders 5 Years and Over Who Speak English-Only at Home
Top 10 Places Sorted by Number

Place (place type) County	Number
Jacksonville (city) Duval	250

Native Hawaiian and Other Pacific Islanders 5 Years and Over Who Speak English-Only at Home
Top 10 Places Sorted by Percent

Place (place type) County	Percent
Jacksonville (city) Duval	59.95

Asian Indians 5 Years and Over Who Speak English-Only at Home
Top 10 Places Sorted by Number

Place (place type) County	Number
Hollywood (city) Broward	765
Coral Springs (city) Broward	750
Pembroke Pines (city) Broward	665
Plantation (city) Broward	583
Sunrise (city) Broward	481
Jacksonville (city) Duval	436
Tallahassee (city) Leon	420
Miramar (city) Broward	332
Miami (city) Miami-Dade	311
Tampa (city) Hillsborough	307

Asian Indians 5 Years and Over Who Speak English-Only at Home
Top 10 Places Sorted by Percent

Place (place type) County	Percent
Hollywood (city) Broward	67.94
Miramar (city) Broward	60.04
Plantation (city) Broward	55.47
Sunrise (city) Broward	51.50
Kendall (cdp) Miami-Dade	45.13
North Miami Beach (city) Miami-Dade	44.29
The Hammocks (cdp) Miami-Dade	43.91
Coral Springs (city) Broward	43.71
Fort Lauderdale (city) Broward	42.86
Pembroke Pines (city) Broward	42.63

Bangladeshis 5 Years and Over Who Speak English-Only at Home
Top 10 Places Sorted by Number

Place (place type) County	Number
No places met population threshold.	

Bangladeshis 5 Years and Over Who Speak English-Only at Home
Top 10 Places Sorted by Percent

Place (place type) County	Percent
No places met population threshold.	

Cambodians 5 Years and Over Who Speak English-Only at Home
Top 10 Places Sorted by Number

Place (place type) County	Number
Jacksonville (city) Duval	106
St. Petersburg (city) Pinellas	41

Cambodians 5 Years and Over Who Speak English-Only at Home
Top 10 Places Sorted by Percent

Place (place type) County	Percent
Jacksonville (city) Duval	11.22
St. Petersburg (city) Pinellas	8.22

Chinese (except Taiwanese) 5 Years and Over Who Speak English-Only at Home
Top 10 Places Sorted by Number

Place (place type) County	Number
Kendall (cdp) Miami-Dade	299
Pembroke Pines (city) Broward	288
Miramar (city) Broward	211
Jacksonville (city) Duval	210
Coral Springs (city) Broward	177
Hollywood (city) Broward	153
Sunrise (city) Broward	143
Tampa (city) Hillsborough	134
Gainesville (city) Alachua	110
Orlando (city) Orange	95

Chinese (except Taiwanese) 5 Years and Over Who Speak English-Only at Home
Top 10 Places Sorted by Percent

Place (place type) County	Percent
Kendall (cdp) Miami-Dade	48.54
Miramar (city) Broward	45.38
Pembroke Pines (city) Broward	27.88
Hollywood (city) Broward	24.52
Coral Springs (city) Broward	20.97
Tampa (city) Hillsborough	20.71
The Hammocks (cdp) Miami-Dade	20.10
Orlando (city) Orange	19.59
Margate (city) Broward	18.75
Sunrise (city) Broward	17.25

Fijians 5 Years and Over Who Speak English-Only at Home
Top 10 Places Sorted by Number

Place (place type) County	Number
No places met population threshold.	

Fijians 5 Years and Over Who Speak English-Only at Home
Top 10 Places Sorted by Percent

Place (place type) County	Percent
No places met population threshold.	

Filipinos 5 Years and Over Who Speak English-Only at Home
Top 10 Places Sorted by Number

Place (place type) County	Number
Jacksonville (city) Duval	3,124
Tampa (city) Hillsborough	285
Orlando (city) Orange	274
Pembroke Pines (city) Broward	216
St. Petersburg (city) Pinellas	183
Myrtle Grove (cdp) Escambia	175
Cape Coral (city) Lee	169
Bellview (cdp) Escambia	155
Lakeside (cdp) Clay	155
Clearwater (city) Pinellas	142

Filipinos 5 Years and Over Who Speak English-Only at Home
Top 10 Places Sorted by Percent

Place (place type) County	Percent
Bellview (cdp) Escambia	38.37
Orlando (city) Orange	38.06
Myrtle Grove (cdp) Escambia	37.88
Jacksonville (city) Duval	33.40
Clearwater (city) Pinellas	33.02
Miramar (city) Broward	30.92
Tampa (city) Hillsborough	30.06
Yeehaw Junction (cdp) Osceola	28.88
Lakeside (cdp) Clay	27.43
Cape Coral (city) Lee	26.16

Notes: Please refer to the User's Guide for an explanation of data; tables reflect only those areas that meet Summary File 4 population thresholds, therefore there may be less than 10 places listed

Guamanians or Chamorros 5 Years and Over Who Speak English-Only at Home
Top 10 Places Sorted by Number

Place (place type) County	Number
No places met population threshold.	

Guamanians or Chamorros 5 Years and Over Who Speak English-Only at Home
Top 10 Places Sorted by Percent

Place (place type) County	Percent
No places met population threshold.	

Hawaiian Natives 5 Years and Over Who Speak English-Only at Home
Top 10 Places Sorted by Number

Place (place type) County	Number
No places met population threshold.	

Hawaiian Natives 5 Years and Over Who Speak English-Only at Home
Top 10 Places Sorted by Percent

Place (place type) County	Percent
No places met population threshold.	

Hmongs 5 Years and Over Who Speak English-Only at Home
Top 10 Places Sorted by Number

Place (place type) County	Number
No places met population threshold.	

Hmongs 5 Years and Over Who Speak English-Only at Home
Top 10 Places Sorted by Percent

Place (place type) County	Percent
No places met population threshold.	

Indonesians 5 Years and Over Who Speak English-Only at Home
Top 10 Places Sorted by Number

Place (place type) County	Number
No places met population threshold.	

Indonesians 5 Years and Over Who Speak English-Only at Home
Top 10 Places Sorted by Percent

Place (place type) County	Percent
No places met population threshold.	

Japanese 5 Years and Over Who Speak English-Only at Home
Top 10 Places Sorted by Number

Place (place type) County	Number
Jacksonville (city) Duval	224

Japanese 5 Years and Over Who Speak English-Only at Home
Top 10 Places Sorted by Percent

Place (place type) County	Percent
Jacksonville (city) Duval	43.33

Koreans 5 Years and Over Who Speak English-Only at Home
Top 10 Places Sorted by Number

Place (place type) County	Number
Jacksonville (city) Duval	147
Tampa (city) Hillsborough	144
Orlando (city) Orange	122
Gainesville (city) Alachua	48

Koreans 5 Years and Over Who Speak English-Only at Home
Top 10 Places Sorted by Percent

Place (place type) County	Percent
Orlando (city) Orange	24.02
Jacksonville (city) Duval	16.42
Tampa (city) Hillsborough	15.43
Gainesville (city) Alachua	10.55

Laotians 5 Years and Over Who Speak English-Only at Home
Top 10 Places Sorted by Number

Place (place type) County	Number
St. Petersburg (city) Pinellas	36

Laotians 5 Years and Over Who Speak English-Only at Home
Top 10 Places Sorted by Percent

Place (place type) County	Percent
St. Petersburg (city) Pinellas	3.34

Malaysians 5 Years and Over Who Speak English-Only at Home
Top 10 Places Sorted by Number

Place (place type) County	Number
No places met population threshold.	

Malaysians 5 Years and Over Who Speak English-Only at Home
Top 10 Places Sorted by Percent

Place (place type) County	Percent
No places met population threshold.	

Pakistanis 5 Years and Over Who Speak English-Only at Home
Top 10 Places Sorted by Number

Place (place type) County	Number
No places met population threshold.	

Pakistanis 5 Years and Over Who Speak English-Only at Home
Top 10 Places Sorted by Percent

Place (place type) County	Percent
No places met population threshold.	

Samoans 5 Years and Over Who Speak English-Only at Home
Top 10 Places Sorted by Number

Place (place type) County	Number
No places met population threshold.	

Samoans 5 Years and Over Who Speak English-Only at Home
Top 10 Places Sorted by Percent

Place (place type) County	Percent
No places met population threshold.	

Sri Lankans 5 Years and Over Who Speak English-Only at Home
Top 10 Places Sorted by Number

Place (place type) County	Number
No places met population threshold.	

Sri Lankans 5 Years and Over Who Speak English-Only at Home
Top 10 Places Sorted by Percent

Place (place type) County	Percent
No places met population threshold.	

Taiwanese 5 Years and Over Who Speak English-Only at Home
Top 10 Places Sorted by Number

Place (place type) County	Number
No places met population threshold.	

Taiwanese 5 Years and Over Who Speak English-Only at Home
Top 10 Places Sorted by Percent

Place (place type) County	Percent
No places met population threshold.	

Thais 5 Years and Over Who Speak English-Only at Home
Top 10 Places Sorted by Number

Place (place type) County	Number
No places met population threshold.	

Thais 5 Years and Over Who Speak English-Only at Home
Top 10 Places Sorted by Percent

Place (place type) County	Percent
No places met population threshold.	

Tongans 5 Years and Over Who Speak English-Only at Home
Top 10 Places Sorted by Number

Place (place type) County	Number
No places met population threshold.	

Tongans 5 Years and Over Who Speak English-Only at Home
Top 10 Places Sorted by Percent

Place (place type) County	Percent
No places met population threshold.	

Vietnamese 5 Years and Over Who Speak English-Only at Home
Top 10 Places Sorted by Number

Place (place type) County	Number
Jacksonville (city) Duval	123
Orlando (city) Orange	85
Tampa (city) Hillsborough	83
St. Petersburg (city) Pinellas	76
West and East Lealman (cdp) Pinellas	63
Town 'n' Country (cdp) Hillsborough	55
Pine Hills (cdp) Orange	51
Pinellas Park (city) Pinellas	26
Oak Ridge (cdp) Orange	7

Vietnamese 5 Years and Over Who Speak English-Only at Home
Top 10 Places Sorted by Percent

Place (place type) County	Percent
West and East Lealman (cdp) Pinellas	14.52
Orlando (city) Orange	12.96
Pine Hills (cdp) Orange	8.59
Town 'n' Country (cdp) Hillsborough	8.12
Jacksonville (city) Duval	6.57
Tampa (city) Hillsborough	6.39
Pinellas Park (city) Pinellas	5.32
St. Petersburg (city) Pinellas	4.96
Oak Ridge (cdp) Orange	1.51

Foreign Born

Total Population
Top 10 Places Sorted by Number

Place (place type) County	Number
Miami (city) Miami-Dade	215,739

Notes: Please refer to the User's Guide for an explanation of data; tables reflect only those areas that meet Summary File 4 population thresholds, therefore there may be less than 10 places listed

Hialeah (city) Miami-Dade	163,256
Miami Beach (city) Miami-Dade	48,852
Jacksonville (city) Duval	43,661
Fountainbleau (cdp) Miami-Dade	43,496
Pembroke Pines (city) Broward	39,727
Tampa (city) Hillsborough	37,027
Hollywood (city) Broward	36,562
Kendale Lakes (cdp) Miami-Dade	33,460
Fort Lauderdale (city) Broward	32,938

Total Population
Top 10 Places Sorted by Percent

Place (place type) County	Percent
Fountainbleau (cdp) Miami-Dade	73.08
Hialeah (city) Miami-Dade	72.11
Doral (cdp) Miami-Dade	62.55
Miami (city) Miami-Dade	59.50
Kendall West (cdp) Miami-Dade	59.41
Kendale Lakes (cdp) Miami-Dade	58.82
Miami Beach (city) Miami-Dade	55.48
The Hammocks (cdp) Miami-Dade	52.44
Sunset (cdp) Miami-Dade	50.66
North Miami Beach (city) Miami-Dade	49.67

Asian
Top 10 Places Sorted by Number

Place (place type) County	Number
Jacksonville (city) Duval	13,857
St. Petersburg (city) Pinellas	5,185
Tampa (city) Hillsborough	5,046
Pembroke Pines (city) Broward	3,758
Orlando (city) Orange	3,740
Gainesville (city) Alachua	3,191
Coral Springs (city) Broward	3,064
Tallahassee (city) Leon	2,632
Sunrise (city) Broward	2,268
Hollywood (city) Broward	2,218

Asian
Top 10 Places Sorted by Percent

Place (place type) County	Percent
Pine Hills (cdp) Orange	88.55
Sunset (cdp) Miami-Dade	86.31
Doral (cdp) Miami-Dade	85.16
Boca Raton (city) Palm Beach	84.33
Fountainbleau (cdp) Miami-Dade	84.22
Palm Bay (city) Brevard	83.20
Deerfield Beach (city) Broward	83.07
Bellair-Meadowbrook Terrace (cdp) Clay	82.83
Kendall (cdp) Miami-Dade	82.35
University (cdp) Hillsborough	82.24

Native Hawaiian and Other Pacific Islander
Top 10 Places Sorted by Number

Place (place type) County	Number
Jacksonville (city) Duval	36

Native Hawaiian and Other Pacific Islander
Top 10 Places Sorted by Percent

Place (place type) County	Percent
Jacksonville (city) Duval	7.24

Asian Indian
Top 10 Places Sorted by Number

Place (place type) County	Number
Jacksonville (city) Duval	2,055
Coral Springs (city) Broward	1,422
Pembroke Pines (city) Broward	1,346
Orlando (city) Orange	1,198
Tampa (city) Hillsborough	1,039
Hollywood (city) Broward	1,003
Plantation (city) Broward	853
Tallahassee (city) Leon	852

Sunrise (city) Broward	815
St. Petersburg (city) Pinellas	723

Asian Indian
Top 10 Places Sorted by Percent

Place (place type) County	Percent
Boca Raton (city) Palm Beach	94.23
Lakeland (city) Polk	87.86
Melbourne (city) Brevard	86.78
Fort Lauderdale (city) Broward	82.77
Kendall (cdp) Miami-Dade	82.76
Sunrise (city) Broward	82.32
Orlando (city) Orange	82.05
Cooper City (city) Broward	81.11
St. Petersburg (city) Pinellas	80.60
West Palm Beach (city) Palm Beach	79.38

Bangladeshi
Top 10 Places Sorted by Number

Place (place type) County	Number
No places met population threshold.	

Bangladeshi
Top 10 Places Sorted by Percent

Place (place type) County	Percent
No places met population threshold.	

Cambodian
Top 10 Places Sorted by Number

Place (place type) County	Number
Jacksonville (city) Duval	725
St. Petersburg (city) Pinellas	369

Cambodian
Top 10 Places Sorted by Percent

Place (place type) County	Percent
Jacksonville (city) Duval	72.43
St. Petersburg (city) Pinellas	71.51

Chinese (except Taiwanese)
Top 10 Places Sorted by Number

Place (place type) County	Number
Gainesville (city) Alachua	1,193
Jacksonville (city) Duval	1,091
Pembroke Pines (city) Broward	847
Coral Springs (city) Broward	695
Sunrise (city) Broward	655
St. Petersburg (city) Pinellas	608
Tallahassee (city) Leon	602
North Miami Beach (city) Miami-Dade	591
Kendall (cdp) Miami-Dade	538
Tampa (city) Hillsborough	496

Chinese (except Taiwanese)
Top 10 Places Sorted by Percent

Place (place type) County	Percent
Kendall (cdp) Miami-Dade	85.94
Orlando (city) Orange	85.57
St. Petersburg (city) Pinellas	83.17
Gainesville (city) Alachua	81.94
Tallahassee (city) Leon	79.95
North Miami Beach (city) Miami-Dade	79.76
Coral Springs (city) Broward	77.83
Miami (city) Miami-Dade	77.19
Miramar (city) Broward	77.06
Davie (town) Broward	76.36

Fijian
Top 10 Places Sorted by Number

Place (place type) County	Number
No places met population threshold.	

Fijian
Top 10 Places Sorted by Percent

Place (place type) County	Percent
No places met population threshold.	

Filipino
Top 10 Places Sorted by Number

Place (place type) County	Number
Jacksonville (city) Duval	6,587
Tampa (city) Hillsborough	783
Pembroke Pines (city) Broward	754
St. Petersburg (city) Pinellas	647
Cape Coral (city) Lee	490
Orlando (city) Orange	471
Lakeside (cdp) Clay	463
Clearwater (city) Pinellas	317
Myrtle Grove (cdp) Escambia	317
Miramar (city) Broward	311

Filipino
Top 10 Places Sorted by Percent

Place (place type) County	Percent
Pembroke Pines (city) Broward	81.34
Lakeside (cdp) Clay	81.09
Tampa (city) Hillsborough	80.72
St. Petersburg (city) Pinellas	74.37
Yeehaw Junction (cdp) Osceola	72.43
Cape Coral (city) Lee	71.74
Clearwater (city) Pinellas	70.29
Jacksonville (city) Duval	67.33
Myrtle Grove (cdp) Escambia	67.30
Miramar (city) Broward	65.34

Guamanian or Chamorro
Top 10 Places Sorted by Number

Place (place type) County	Number
No places met population threshold.	

Guamanian or Chamorro
Top 10 Places Sorted by Percent

Place (place type) County	Percent
No places met population threshold.	

Hawaiian, Native
Top 10 Places Sorted by Number

Place (place type) County	Number
No places met population threshold.	

Hawaiian, Native
Top 10 Places Sorted by Percent

Place (place type) County	Percent
No places met population threshold.	

Hmong
Top 10 Places Sorted by Number

Place (place type) County	Number
No places met population threshold.	

Hmong
Top 10 Places Sorted by Percent

Place (place type) County	Percent
No places met population threshold.	

Indonesian
Top 10 Places Sorted by Number

Place (place type) County	Number
No places met population threshold.	

Notes: Please refer to the User's Guide for an explanation of data; tables reflect only those areas that meet Summary File 4 population thresholds, therefore there may be less than 10 places listed

Indonesian
Top 10 Places Sorted by Percent

Place (place type) County	Percent
No places met population threshold.	

Japanese
Top 10 Places Sorted by Number

Place (place type) County	Number
Jacksonville (city) Duval	343

Japanese
Top 10 Places Sorted by Percent

Place (place type) County	Percent
Jacksonville (city) Duval	64.60

Korean
Top 10 Places Sorted by Number

Place (place type) County	Number
Jacksonville (city) Duval	771
Tampa (city) Hillsborough	737
Orlando (city) Orange	416
Gainesville (city) Alachua	388

Korean
Top 10 Places Sorted by Percent

Place (place type) County	Percent
Jacksonville (city) Duval	82.02
Gainesville (city) Alachua	77.45
Tampa (city) Hillsborough	76.53
Orlando (city) Orange	75.64

Laotian
Top 10 Places Sorted by Number

Place (place type) County	Number
St. Petersburg (city) Pinellas	898

Laotian
Top 10 Places Sorted by Percent

Place (place type) County	Percent
St. Petersburg (city) Pinellas	79.26

Malaysian
Top 10 Places Sorted by Number

Place (place type) County	Number
No places met population threshold.	

Malaysian
Top 10 Places Sorted by Percent

Place (place type) County	Percent
No places met population threshold.	

Pakistani
Top 10 Places Sorted by Number

Place (place type) County	Number
No places met population threshold.	

Pakistani
Top 10 Places Sorted by Percent

Place (place type) County	Percent
No places met population threshold.	

Samoan
Top 10 Places Sorted by Number

Place (place type) County	Number
No places met population threshold.	

Samoan
Top 10 Places Sorted by Percent

Place (place type) County	Percent
No places met population threshold.	

Sri Lankan
Top 10 Places Sorted by Number

Place (place type) County	Number
No places met population threshold.	

Sri Lankan
Top 10 Places Sorted by Percent

Place (place type) County	Percent
No places met population threshold.	

Taiwanese
Top 10 Places Sorted by Number

Place (place type) County	Number
No places met population threshold.	

Taiwanese
Top 10 Places Sorted by Percent

Place (place type) County	Percent
No places met population threshold.	

Thai
Top 10 Places Sorted by Number

Place (place type) County	Number
No places met population threshold.	

Thai
Top 10 Places Sorted by Percent

Place (place type) County	Percent
No places met population threshold.	

Tongan
Top 10 Places Sorted by Number

Place (place type) County	Number
No places met population threshold.	

Tongan
Top 10 Places Sorted by Percent

Place (place type) County	Percent
No places met population threshold.	

Vietnamese
Top 10 Places Sorted by Number

Place (place type) County	Number
Jacksonville (city) Duval	1,535
St. Petersburg (city) Pinellas	1,248
Tampa (city) Hillsborough	1,244
Town 'n' Country (cdp) Hillsborough	595
Pine Hills (cdp) Orange	569
Orlando (city) Orange	568
Oak Ridge (cdp) Orange	450
Pinellas Park (city) Pinellas	391
West and East Lealman (cdp) Pinellas	365

Vietnamese
Top 10 Places Sorted by Percent

Place (place type) County	Percent
Tampa (city) Hillsborough	90.21
Pine Hills (cdp) Orange	88.77
Town 'n' Country (cdp) Hillsborough	86.73
Oak Ridge (cdp) Orange	85.39
Orlando (city) Orange	81.84
West and East Lealman (cdp) Pinellas	79.87
St. Petersburg (city) Pinellas	77.52
Jacksonville (city) Duval	74.84
Pinellas Park (city) Pinellas	74.33

Foreign-Born Naturalized Citizens

Total Population
Top 10 Places Sorted by Number

Place (place type) County	Number
Miami (city) Miami-Dade	89,727
Hialeah (city) Miami-Dade	70,331
Pembroke Pines (city) Broward	22,597
Miami Beach (city) Miami-Dade	21,744
Jacksonville (city) Duval	20,786
Fountainbleau (cdp) Miami-Dade	18,348
Kendale Lakes (cdp) Miami-Dade	17,856
Kendall (cdp) Miami-Dade	16,474
Hollywood (city) Broward	16,136
Tampa (city) Hillsborough	14,683

Total Population
Top 10 Places Sorted by Percent

Place (place type) County	Percent
Sunset (cdp) Miami-Dade	32.98
Miami Lakes (cdp) Miami-Dade	32.32
Kendale Lakes (cdp) Miami-Dade	31.39
Hialeah (city) Miami-Dade	31.06
Fountainbleau (cdp) Miami-Dade	30.83
Miami (city) Miami-Dade	24.75
Miami Beach (city) Miami-Dade	24.69
Kendall West (cdp) Miami-Dade	24.63
Coral Gables (city) Miami-Dade	24.38
The Hammocks (cdp) Miami-Dade	24.16

Asian
Top 10 Places Sorted by Number

Place (place type) County	Number
Jacksonville (city) Duval	7,673
St. Petersburg (city) Pinellas	2,206
Tampa (city) Hillsborough	2,080
Pembroke Pines (city) Broward	2,069
Orlando (city) Orange	1,750
Coral Springs (city) Broward	1,392
Sunrise (city) Broward	1,184
Hollywood (city) Broward	1,034
Tallahassee (city) Leon	977
Gainesville (city) Alachua	897

Asian
Top 10 Places Sorted by Percent

Place (place type) County	Percent
Kendale Lakes (cdp) Miami-Dade	54.45
Ferry Pass (cdp) Escambia	54.19
Yeehaw Junction (cdp) Osceola	49.74
North Lauderdale (city) Broward	49.70
South Miami Heights (cdp) Miami-Dade	49.42
Royal Palm Beach (village) Palm Beach	49.24
Lakeside (cdp) Clay	49.10
Niceville (city) Okaloosa	48.78
Doctor Phillips (cdp) Orange	48.77
Fort Walton Beach (city) Okaloosa	48.72

Native Hawaiian and Other Pacific Islander
Top 10 Places Sorted by Number

Place (place type) County	Number
Jacksonville (city) Duval	15

Native Hawaiian and Other Pacific Islander
Top 10 Places Sorted by Percent

Place (place type) County	Percent
Jacksonville (city) Duval	3.02

Notes: Please refer to the User's Guide for an explanation of data; tables reflect only those areas that meet Summary File 4 population thresholds, therefore there may be less than 10 places listed

Asian Indian
Top 10 Places Sorted by Number

Place (place type) County	Number
Pembroke Pines (city) Broward	683
Jacksonville (city) Duval	660
Orlando (city) Orange	593
Coral Springs (city) Broward	549
Sunrise (city) Broward	357
Hollywood (city) Broward	346
Plantation (city) Broward	331
Tallahassee (city) Leon	318
Tampa (city) Hillsborough	313
Kendall (cdp) Miami-Dade	308

Asian Indian
Top 10 Places Sorted by Percent

Place (place type) County	Percent
Cooper City (city) Broward	51.10
Davie (town) Broward	46.78
Altamonte Springs (city) Seminole	46.76
Doctor Phillips (cdp) Orange	43.23
Melbourne (city) Brevard	42.22
Kendall (cdp) Miami-Dade	42.13
Orlando (city) Orange	40.62
Fort Lauderdale (city) Broward	40.07
Pembroke Pines (city) Broward	38.98
East Lake (cdp) Pinellas	36.17

Bangladeshi
Top 10 Places Sorted by Number

Place (place type) County	Number
No places met population threshold.	

Bangladeshi
Top 10 Places Sorted by Percent

Place (place type) County	Percent
No places met population threshold.	

Cambodian
Top 10 Places Sorted by Number

Place (place type) County	Number
Jacksonville (city) Duval	349
St. Petersburg (city) Pinellas	136

Cambodian
Top 10 Places Sorted by Percent

Place (place type) County	Percent
Jacksonville (city) Duval	34.87
St. Petersburg (city) Pinellas	26.36

Chinese (except Taiwanese)
Top 10 Places Sorted by Number

Place (place type) County	Number
Jacksonville (city) Duval	639
Pembroke Pines (city) Broward	497
Sunrise (city) Broward	427
Coral Springs (city) Broward	376
North Miami Beach (city) Miami-Dade	360
Kendall (cdp) Miami-Dade	306
Hollywood (city) Broward	296
Miami (city) Miami-Dade	272
Margate (city) Broward	263
Tampa (city) Hillsborough	237

Chinese (except Taiwanese)
Top 10 Places Sorted by Percent

Place (place type) County	Percent
Miami (city) Miami-Dade	55.40
Kendall (cdp) Miami-Dade	48.88
North Miami Beach (city) Miami-Dade	48.58
Margate (city) Broward	48.43
Sunrise (city) Broward	47.29

Miramar (city) Broward	45.88
Hollywood (city) Broward	45.61
Pembroke Pines (city) Broward	43.10
Coral Springs (city) Broward	42.11
Orlando (city) Orange	40.68

Fijian
Top 10 Places Sorted by Number

Place (place type) County	Number
No places met population threshold.	

Fijian
Top 10 Places Sorted by Percent

Place (place type) County	Percent
No places met population threshold.	

Filipino
Top 10 Places Sorted by Number

Place (place type) County	Number
Jacksonville (city) Duval	4,406
Pembroke Pines (city) Broward	460
Tampa (city) Hillsborough	365
St. Petersburg (city) Pinellas	363
Lakeside (cdp) Clay	318
Orlando (city) Orange	265
Cape Coral (city) Lee	261
Myrtle Grove (cdp) Escambia	239
Bellview (cdp) Escambia	205
Miramar (city) Broward	203

Filipino
Top 10 Places Sorted by Percent

Place (place type) County	Percent
Lakeside (cdp) Clay	55.69
Myrtle Grove (cdp) Escambia	50.74
Bellview (cdp) Escambia	49.76
Pembroke Pines (city) Broward	49.62
Yeehaw Junction (cdp) Osceola	48.97
Jacksonville (city) Duval	45.04
Miramar (city) Broward	42.65
St. Petersburg (city) Pinellas	41.72
Cape Coral (city) Lee	38.21
Tampa (city) Hillsborough	37.63

Guamanian or Chamorro
Top 10 Places Sorted by Number

Place (place type) County	Number
No places met population threshold.	

Guamanian or Chamorro
Top 10 Places Sorted by Percent

Place (place type) County	Percent
No places met population threshold.	

Hawaiian, Native
Top 10 Places Sorted by Number

Place (place type) County	Number
No places met population threshold.	

Hawaiian, Native
Top 10 Places Sorted by Percent

Place (place type) County	Percent
No places met population threshold.	

Hmong
Top 10 Places Sorted by Number

Place (place type) County	Number
No places met population threshold.	

Hmong
Top 10 Places Sorted by Percent

Place (place type) County	Percent
No places met population threshold.	

Indonesian
Top 10 Places Sorted by Number

Place (place type) County	Number
No places met population threshold.	

Indonesian
Top 10 Places Sorted by Percent

Place (place type) County	Percent
No places met population threshold.	

Japanese
Top 10 Places Sorted by Number

Place (place type) County	Number
Jacksonville (city) Duval	154

Japanese
Top 10 Places Sorted by Percent

Place (place type) County	Percent
Jacksonville (city) Duval	29.00

Korean
Top 10 Places Sorted by Number

Place (place type) County	Number
Jacksonville (city) Duval	416
Tampa (city) Hillsborough	252
Orlando (city) Orange	126
Gainesville (city) Alachua	53

Korean
Top 10 Places Sorted by Percent

Place (place type) County	Percent
Jacksonville (city) Duval	44.26
Tampa (city) Hillsborough	26.17
Orlando (city) Orange	22.91
Gainesville (city) Alachua	10.58

Laotian
Top 10 Places Sorted by Number

Place (place type) County	Number
St. Petersburg (city) Pinellas	377

Laotian
Top 10 Places Sorted by Percent

Place (place type) County	Percent
St. Petersburg (city) Pinellas	33.27

Malaysian
Top 10 Places Sorted by Number

Place (place type) County	Number
No places met population threshold.	

Malaysian
Top 10 Places Sorted by Percent

Place (place type) County	Percent
No places met population threshold.	

Pakistani
Top 10 Places Sorted by Number

Place (place type) County	Number
No places met population threshold.	

Notes: Please refer to the User's Guide for an explanation of data; tables reflect only those areas that meet Summary File 4 population thresholds, therefore there may be less than 10 places listed

Pakistani
Top 10 Places Sorted by Percent

Place (place type) County	Percent
No places met population threshold.	

Samoan
Top 10 Places Sorted by Number

Place (place type) County	Number
No places met population threshold.	

Samoan
Top 10 Places Sorted by Percent

Place (place type) County	Percent
No places met population threshold.	

Sri Lankan
Top 10 Places Sorted by Number

Place (place type) County	Number
No places met population threshold.	

Sri Lankan
Top 10 Places Sorted by Percent

Place (place type) County	Percent
No places met population threshold.	

Taiwanese
Top 10 Places Sorted by Number

Place (place type) County	Number
No places met population threshold.	

Taiwanese
Top 10 Places Sorted by Percent

Place (place type) County	Percent
No places met population threshold.	

Thai
Top 10 Places Sorted by Number

Place (place type) County	Number
No places met population threshold.	

Thai
Top 10 Places Sorted by Percent

Place (place type) County	Percent
No places met population threshold.	

Tongan
Top 10 Places Sorted by Number

Place (place type) County	Number
No places met population threshold.	

Tongan
Top 10 Places Sorted by Percent

Place (place type) County	Percent
No places met population threshold.	

Vietnamese
Top 10 Places Sorted by Number

Place (place type) County	Number
Jacksonville (city) Duval	714
Tampa (city) Hillsborough	521
St. Petersburg (city) Pinellas	500
Town 'n' Country (cdp) Hillsborough	296
Orlando (city) Orange	295
Oak Ridge (cdp) Orange	226
Pinellas Park (city) Pinellas	159
Pine Hills (cdp) Orange	142
West and East Lealman (cdp) Pinellas	108

Vietnamese
Top 10 Places Sorted by Percent

Place (place type) County	Percent
Town 'n' Country (cdp) Hillsborough	43.15
Oak Ridge (cdp) Orange	42.88
Orlando (city) Orange	42.51
Tampa (city) Hillsborough	37.78
Jacksonville (city) Duval	34.81
St. Petersburg (city) Pinellas	31.06
Pinellas Park (city) Pinellas	30.23
West and East Lealman (cdp) Pinellas	23.63
Pine Hills (cdp) Orange	22.15

Educational Attainment: High School Graduates

Total Populations 25 Years and Over Who are High School Graduates
Top 10 Places Sorted by Number

Place (place type) County	Number
Jacksonville (city) Duval	385,300
Tampa (city) Hillsborough	153,114
St. Petersburg (city) Pinellas	143,458
Miami (city) Miami-Dade	133,069
Orlando (city) Orange	103,129
Fort Lauderdale (city) Broward	87,921
Pembroke Pines (city) Broward	82,419
Hollywood (city) Broward	79,650
Hialeah (city) Miami-Dade	77,548
Tallahassee (city) Leon	71,754

Total Populations 25 Years and Over Who are High School Graduates
Top 10 Places Sorted by Percent

Place (place type) County	Percent
Westchase (cdp) Hillsborough	96.62
Wekiwa Springs (cdp) Seminole	96.03
Weston (city) Broward	95.47
Pinecrest (village) Miami-Dade	94.24
Palm Beach Gardens (city) Palm Beach	94.03
East Lake (cdp) Pinellas	93.96
Doctor Phillips (cdp) Orange	93.86
Oviedo (city) Seminole	93.33
Hunters Creek (cdp) Orange	93.32
Wellington (village) Palm Beach	92.16

Asians 25 Years and Over Who are High School Graduates
Top 10 Places Sorted by Number

Place (place type) County	Number
Jacksonville (city) Duval	10,604
Tampa (city) Hillsborough	3,596
Orlando (city) Orange	3,005
Pembroke Pines (city) Broward	2,957
St. Petersburg (city) Pinellas	2,903
Gainesville (city) Alachua	2,232
Coral Springs (city) Broward	2,215
Tallahassee (city) Leon	2,108
Hollywood (city) Broward	1,496
Sunrise (city) Broward	1,373

Asians 25 Years and Over Who are High School Graduates
Top 10 Places Sorted by Percent

Place (place type) County	Percent
Oviedo (city) Seminole	97.65
Gainesville (city) Alachua	95.79
Temple Terrace (city) Hillsborough	93.75
University (cdp) Hillsborough	93.57
Palm Harbor (cdp) Pinellas	92.42
Tamarac (city) Broward	92.10
Citrus Park (cdp) Hillsborough	92.05
Royal Palm Beach (village) Palm Beach	91.93
Tallahassee (city) Leon	91.61
Weston (city) Broward	91.14

Native Hawaiian and Other Pacific Islanders 25 Years and Over Who are High School Graduates
Top 10 Places Sorted by Number

Place (place type) County	Number
Jacksonville (city) Duval	210

Native Hawaiian and Other Pacific Islanders 25 Years and Over Who are High School Graduates
Top 10 Places Sorted by Percent

Place (place type) County	Percent
Jacksonville (city) Duval	76.09

Asian Indians 25 Years and Over Who are High School Graduates
Top 10 Places Sorted by Number

Place (place type) County	Number
Jacksonville (city) Duval	1,661
Pembroke Pines (city) Broward	1,059
Coral Springs (city) Broward	1,018
Orlando (city) Orange	951
Tampa (city) Hillsborough	747
Tallahassee (city) Leon	664
Hollywood (city) Broward	575
St. Petersburg (city) Pinellas	572
Plantation (city) Broward	541
Miami (city) Miami-Dade	526

Asian Indians 25 Years and Over Who are High School Graduates
Top 10 Places Sorted by Percent

Place (place type) County	Percent
Gainesville (city) Alachua	96.90
Lakeland (city) Polk	96.10
Davie (town) Broward	96.08
Tallahassee (city) Leon	95.68
Kendall (cdp) Miami-Dade	93.57
Orlando (city) Orange	92.51
St. Petersburg (city) Pinellas	92.26
Jacksonville (city) Duval	91.97
Pembroke Pines (city) Broward	91.85
Weston (city) Broward	91.40

Bangladeshis 25 Years and Over Who are High School Graduates
Top 10 Places Sorted by Number

Place (place type) County	Number
No places met population threshold.	

Bangladeshis 25 Years and Over Who are High School Graduates
Top 10 Places Sorted by Percent

Place (place type) County	Percent
No places met population threshold.	

Cambodians 25 Years and Over Who are High School Graduates
Top 10 Places Sorted by Number

Place (place type) County	Number
Jacksonville (city) Duval	249
St. Petersburg (city) Pinellas	103

Cambodians 25 Years and Over Who are High School Graduates
Top 10 Places Sorted by Percent

Place (place type) County	Percent
Jacksonville (city) Duval	46.89
St. Petersburg (city) Pinellas	42.39

Notes: Please refer to the User's Guide for an explanation of data; tables reflect only those areas that meet Summary File 4 population thresholds, therefore there may be less than 10 places listed

Chinese (except Taiwanese) 25 Years and Over Who are High School Graduates
Top 10 Places Sorted by Number

Place (place type) County	Number
Gainesville (city) Alachua	874
Jacksonville (city) Duval	870
Tallahassee (city) Leon	551
Pembroke Pines (city) Broward	532
Coral Springs (city) Broward	516
Tampa (city) Hillsborough	427
Kendall (cdp) Miami-Dade	400
St. Petersburg (city) Pinellas	396
Orlando (city) Orange	342
Sunrise (city) Broward	334

Chinese (except Taiwanese) 25 Years and Over Who are High School Graduates
Top 10 Places Sorted by Percent

Place (place type) County	Percent
Gainesville (city) Alachua	98.09
Tallahassee (city) Leon	97.35
Miramar (city) Broward	92.07
Tampa (city) Hillsborough	85.06
Jacksonville (city) Duval	83.41
Orlando (city) Orange	82.21
Kendall (cdp) Miami-Dade	82.14
Davie (town) Broward	77.92
Margate (city) Broward	77.78
Coral Springs (city) Broward	77.01

Fijians 25 Years and Over Who are High School Graduates
Top 10 Places Sorted by Number

Place (place type) County	Number
No places met population threshold.	

Fijians 25 Years and Over Who are High School Graduates
Top 10 Places Sorted by Percent

Place (place type) County	Percent
No places met population threshold.	

Filipinos 25 Years and Over Who are High School Graduates
Top 10 Places Sorted by Number

Place (place type) County	Number
Jacksonville (city) Duval	5,771
Pembroke Pines (city) Broward	655
Tampa (city) Hillsborough	583
St. Petersburg (city) Pinellas	542
Orlando (city) Orange	464
Cape Coral (city) Lee	420
Lakeside (cdp) Clay	394
Myrtle Grove (cdp) Escambia	275
Miramar (city) Broward	272
Clearwater (city) Pinellas	267

Filipinos 25 Years and Over Who are High School Graduates
Top 10 Places Sorted by Percent

Place (place type) County	Percent
Orlando (city) Orange	95.47
Yeehaw Junction (cdp) Osceola	94.20
Pembroke Pines (city) Broward	93.57
Tampa (city) Hillsborough	89.55
Miramar (city) Broward	88.60
Clearwater (city) Pinellas	88.41
Jacksonville (city) Duval	88.11
Lakeside (cdp) Clay	86.40
Cape Coral (city) Lee	84.34
St. Petersburg (city) Pinellas	84.03

Guamanians or Chamorros 25 Years and Over Who are High School Graduates
Top 10 Places Sorted by Number

Place (place type) County	Number
No places met population threshold.	

Guamanians or Chamorros 25 Years and Over Who are High School Graduates
Top 10 Places Sorted by Percent

Place (place type) County	Percent
No places met population threshold.	

Hawaiian Natives 25 Years and Over Who are High School Graduates
Top 10 Places Sorted by Number

Place (place type) County	Number
No places met population threshold.	

Hawaiian Natives 25 Years and Over Who are High School Graduates
Top 10 Places Sorted by Percent

Place (place type) County	Percent
No places met population threshold.	

Hmongs 25 Years and Over Who are High School Graduates
Top 10 Places Sorted by Number

Place (place type) County	Number
No places met population threshold.	

Hmongs 25 Years and Over Who are High School Graduates
Top 10 Places Sorted by Percent

Place (place type) County	Percent
No places met population threshold.	

Indonesians 25 Years and Over Who are High School Graduates
Top 10 Places Sorted by Number

Place (place type) County	Number
No places met population threshold.	

Indonesians 25 Years and Over Who are High School Graduates
Top 10 Places Sorted by Percent

Place (place type) County	Percent
No places met population threshold.	

Japanese 25 Years and Over Who are High School Graduates
Top 10 Places Sorted by Number

Place (place type) County	Number
Jacksonville (city) Duval	371

Japanese 25 Years and Over Who are High School Graduates
Top 10 Places Sorted by Percent

Place (place type) County	Percent
Jacksonville (city) Duval	84.32

Koreans 25 Years and Over Who are High School Graduates
Top 10 Places Sorted by Number

Place (place type) County	Number
Tampa (city) Hillsborough	539
Jacksonville (city) Duval	497
Orlando (city) Orange	341
Gainesville (city) Alachua	270

Koreans 25 Years and Over Who are High School Graduates
Top 10 Places Sorted by Percent

Place (place type) County	Percent
Gainesville (city) Alachua	96.43
Orlando (city) Orange	86.33
Tampa (city) Hillsborough	82.67
Jacksonville (city) Duval	75.76

Laotians 25 Years and Over Who are High School Graduates
Top 10 Places Sorted by Number

Place (place type) County	Number
St. Petersburg (city) Pinellas	343

Laotians 25 Years and Over Who are High School Graduates
Top 10 Places Sorted by Percent

Place (place type) County	Percent
St. Petersburg (city) Pinellas	51.89

Malaysians 25 Years and Over Who are High School Graduates
Top 10 Places Sorted by Number

Place (place type) County	Number
No places met population threshold.	

Malaysians 25 Years and Over Who are High School Graduates
Top 10 Places Sorted by Percent

Place (place type) County	Percent
No places met population threshold.	

Pakistanis 25 Years and Over Who are High School Graduates
Top 10 Places Sorted by Number

Place (place type) County	Number
No places met population threshold.	

Pakistanis 25 Years and Over Who are High School Graduates
Top 10 Places Sorted by Percent

Place (place type) County	Percent
No places met population threshold.	

Samoans 25 Years and Over Who are High School Graduates
Top 10 Places Sorted by Number

Place (place type) County	Number
No places met population threshold.	

Samoans 25 Years and Over Who are High School Graduates
Top 10 Places Sorted by Percent

Place (place type) County	Percent
No places met population threshold.	

Sri Lankans 25 Years and Over Who are High School Graduates
Top 10 Places Sorted by Number

Place (place type) County	Number
No places met population threshold.	

Sri Lankans 25 Years and Over Who are High School Graduates
Top 10 Places Sorted by Percent

Place (place type) County	Percent
No places met population threshold.	

Notes: Please refer to the User's Guide for an explanation of data; tables reflect only those areas that meet Summary File 4 population thresholds, therefore there may be less than 10 places listed

Place (place type) County	Number
No places met population threshold.

Taiwanese 25 Years and Over Who are High School Graduates
Top 10 Places Sorted by Percent

Place (place type) County	Percent
No places met population threshold.

Thais 25 Years and Over Who are High School Graduates
Top 10 Places Sorted by Number

Place (place type) County	Number
No places met population threshold.

Thais 25 Years and Over Who are High School Graduates
Top 10 Places Sorted by Percent

Place (place type) County	Percent
No places met population threshold.

Tongans 25 Years and Over Who are High School Graduates
Top 10 Places Sorted by Number

Place (place type) County	Number
No places met population threshold.

Tongans 25 Years and Over Who are High School Graduates
Top 10 Places Sorted by Percent

Place (place type) County	Percent
No places met population threshold.

Vietnamese 25 Years and Over Who are High School Graduates
Top 10 Places Sorted by Number

Place (place type) County	Number
Tampa (city) Hillsborough	677
Jacksonville (city) Duval	608
St. Petersburg (city) Pinellas	505
Orlando (city) Orange	329
Town 'n' Country (cdp) Hillsborough	327
Pinellas Park (city) Pinellas	278
Pine Hills (cdp) Orange	242
Oak Ridge (cdp) Orange	154
West and East Lealman (cdp) Pinellas	86

Vietnamese 25 Years and Over Who are High School Graduates
Top 10 Places Sorted by Percent

Place (place type) County	Percent
Pinellas Park (city) Pinellas	75.75
Tampa (city) Hillsborough	70.08
Town 'n' Country (cdp) Hillsborough	68.55
Orlando (city) Orange	66.87
Pine Hills (cdp) Orange	58.03
St. Petersburg (city) Pinellas	50.45
Jacksonville (city) Duval	48.76
Oak Ridge (cdp) Orange	38.21
West and East Lealman (cdp) Pinellas	29.86

Total Populations 25 Years and Over Who are Four-Year College Graduates
Top 10 Places Sorted by Number

Place (place type) County	Number
Jacksonville (city) Duval	98,991
Tampa (city) Hillsborough	50,471
Miami (city) Miami-Dade	41,004
St. Petersburg (city) Pinellas	39,987
Tallahassee (city) Leon	35,901
Orlando (city) Orange	35,396
Fort Lauderdale (city) Broward	31,059
Pembroke Pines (city) Broward	26,847
Coral Springs (city) Broward	24,489
Boca Raton (city) Palm Beach	24,362

Total Populations 25 Years and Over Who are Four-Year College Graduates
Top 10 Places Sorted by Percent

Place (place type) County	Percent
Pinecrest (village) Miami-Dade	61.56
Coral Gables (city) Miami-Dade	58.28
Weston (city) Broward	50.87
Wekiwa Springs (cdp) Seminole	49.62
Doctor Phillips (cdp) Orange	49.54
Westchase (cdp) Hillsborough	49.04
Doral (cdp) Miami-Dade	47.61
Hunters Creek (cdp) Orange	44.99
Tallahassee (city) Leon	44.96
Boca Raton (city) Palm Beach	44.18

Asians 25 Years and Over Who are Four-Year College Graduates
Top 10 Places Sorted by Number

Place (place type) County	Number
Jacksonville (city) Duval	4,517
Gainesville (city) Alachua	1,874
Pembroke Pines (city) Broward	1,762
Tampa (city) Hillsborough	1,756
Tallahassee (city) Leon	1,540
Orlando (city) Orange	1,465
St. Petersburg (city) Pinellas	1,069
Coral Springs (city) Broward	1,026
Kendall (cdp) Miami-Dade	856
Miami (city) Miami-Dade	721

Asians 25 Years and Over Who are Four-Year College Graduates
Top 10 Places Sorted by Percent

Place (place type) County	Percent
Gainesville (city) Alachua	80.43
University (cdp) Hillsborough	75.64
Tallahassee (city) Leon	66.93
Temple Terrace (city) Hillsborough	65.28
Weston (city) Broward	61.48
Glenvar Heights (cdp) Miami-Dade	61.32
Country Club (cdp) Miami-Dade	60.78
Fountainbleau (cdp) Miami-Dade	59.71
Coral Gables (city) Miami-Dade	59.63
Palm Harbor (cdp) Pinellas	59.57

Native Hawaiian and Other Pacific Islanders 25 Years and Over Who are Four-Year College Graduates
Top 10 Places Sorted by Number

Place (place type) County	Number
Jacksonville (city) Duval	42

Place (place type) County	Percent
Jacksonville (city) Duval	15.22

Asian Indians 25 Years and Over Who are Four-Year College Graduates
Top 10 Places Sorted by Number

Place (place type) County	Number
Jacksonville (city) Duval	1,245
Pembroke Pines (city) Broward	653
Tallahassee (city) Leon	552
Orlando (city) Orange	543
Tampa (city) Hillsborough	491
Coral Springs (city) Broward	471
Gainesville (city) Alachua	361
St. Petersburg (city) Pinellas	341
Plantation (city) Broward	331
Miami (city) Miami-Dade	305

Asian Indians 25 Years and Over Who are Four-Year College Graduates
Top 10 Places Sorted by Percent

Place (place type) County	Percent
Gainesville (city) Alachua	85.95
Tallahassee (city) Leon	79.54
Lakeland (city) Polk	69.16
Jacksonville (city) Duval	68.94
Town 'n' Country (cdp) Hillsborough	67.35
Altamonte Springs (city) Seminole	64.96
Kendall (cdp) Miami-Dade	64.30
Davie (town) Broward	60.84
Cooper City (city) Broward	58.17
Melbourne (city) Brevard	56.75

Bangladeshis 25 Years and Over Who are Four-Year College Graduates
Top 10 Places Sorted by Number

Place (place type) County	Number
No places met population threshold.

Bangladeshis 25 Years and Over Who are Four-Year College Graduates
Top 10 Places Sorted by Percent

Place (place type) County	Percent
No places met population threshold.

Cambodians 25 Years and Over Who are Four-Year College Graduates
Top 10 Places Sorted by Number

Place (place type) County	Number
Jacksonville (city) Duval	32
St. Petersburg (city) Pinellas	6

Cambodians 25 Years and Over Who are Four-Year College Graduates
Top 10 Places Sorted by Percent

Place (place type) County	Percent
Jacksonville (city) Duval	6.03
St. Petersburg (city) Pinellas	2.47

Chinese (except Taiwanese) 25 Years and Over Who are Four-Year College Graduates
Top 10 Places Sorted by Number

Place (place type) County	Number
Gainesville (city) Alachua	825
Jacksonville (city) Duval	458
Tallahassee (city) Leon	448
Pembroke Pines (city) Broward	262
Coral Springs (city) Broward	253

Notes: Please refer to the User's Guide for an explanation of data; tables reflect only those areas that meet Summary File 4 population thresholds, therefore there may be less than 10 places listed

Place (place type) County	
Tampa (city) Hillsborough	248
Kendall (cdp) Miami-Dade	242
Orlando (city) Orange	218
St. Petersburg (city) Pinellas	173
Davie (town) Broward	165

Chinese (except Taiwanese) 25 Years and Over Who are Four-Year College Graduates
Top 10 Places Sorted by Percent

Place (place type) County	Percent
Gainesville (city) Alachua	92.59
Tallahassee (city) Leon	79.15
The Hammocks (cdp) Miami-Dade	54.76
Orlando (city) Orange	52.40
Kendall (cdp) Miami-Dade	49.69
Tampa (city) Hillsborough	49.40
Jacksonville (city) Duval	43.91
Davie (town) Broward	42.86
Coral Springs (city) Broward	37.76
Pembroke Pines (city) Broward	33.98

Fijians 25 Years and Over Who are Four-Year College Graduates
Top 10 Places Sorted by Number

Place (place type) County	Number
No places met population threshold.	

Fijians 25 Years and Over Who are Four-Year College Graduates
Top 10 Places Sorted by Percent

Place (place type) County	Percent
No places met population threshold.	

Filipinos 25 Years and Over Who are Four-Year College Graduates
Top 10 Places Sorted by Number

Place (place type) County	Number
Jacksonville (city) Duval	2,111
Pembroke Pines (city) Broward	411
Tampa (city) Hillsborough	305
St. Petersburg (city) Pinellas	263
Cape Coral (city) Lee	229
Orlando (city) Orange	202
Lakeside (cdp) Clay	152
Miramar (city) Broward	141
Yeehaw Junction (cdp) Osceola	128
Clearwater (city) Pinellas	127

Filipinos 25 Years and Over Who are Four-Year College Graduates
Top 10 Places Sorted by Percent

Place (place type) County	Percent
Yeehaw Junction (cdp) Osceola	61.84
Pembroke Pines (city) Broward	58.71
Tampa (city) Hillsborough	46.85
Cape Coral (city) Lee	45.98
Miramar (city) Broward	45.93
Clearwater (city) Pinellas	42.05
Orlando (city) Orange	41.56
St. Petersburg (city) Pinellas	40.78
Lakeside (cdp) Clay	33.33
Jacksonville (city) Duval	32.23

Guamanians or Chamorros 25 Years and Over Who are Four-Year College Graduates
Top 10 Places Sorted by Number

Place (place type) County	Number
No places met population threshold.	

Guamanians or Chamorros 25 Years and Over Who are Four-Year College Graduates
Top 10 Places Sorted by Percent

Place (place type) County	Percent
No places met population threshold.	

Hawaiian Natives 25 Years and Over Who are Four-Year College Graduates
Top 10 Places Sorted by Number

Place (place type) County	Number
No places met population threshold.	

Hawaiian Natives 25 Years and Over Who are Four-Year College Graduates
Top 10 Places Sorted by Percent

Place (place type) County	Percent
No places met population threshold.	

Hmongs 25 Years and Over Who are Four-Year College Graduates
Top 10 Places Sorted by Number

Place (place type) County	Number
No places met population threshold.	

Hmongs 25 Years and Over Who are Four-Year College Graduates
Top 10 Places Sorted by Percent

Place (place type) County	Percent
No places met population threshold.	

Indonesians 25 Years and Over Who are Four-Year College Graduates
Top 10 Places Sorted by Number

Place (place type) County	Number
No places met population threshold.	

Indonesians 25 Years and Over Who are Four-Year College Graduates
Top 10 Places Sorted by Percent

Place (place type) County	Percent
No places met population threshold.	

Japanese 25 Years and Over Who are Four-Year College Graduates
Top 10 Places Sorted by Number

Place (place type) County	Number
Jacksonville (city) Duval	47

Japanese 25 Years and Over Who are Four-Year College Graduates
Top 10 Places Sorted by Percent

Place (place type) County	Percent
Jacksonville (city) Duval	10.68

Koreans 25 Years and Over Who are Four-Year College Graduates
Top 10 Places Sorted by Number

Place (place type) County	Number
Tampa (city) Hillsborough	319
Gainesville (city) Alachua	215
Orlando (city) Orange	133
Jacksonville (city) Duval	107

Koreans 25 Years and Over Who are Four-Year College Graduates
Top 10 Places Sorted by Percent

Place (place type) County	Percent
Gainesville (city) Alachua	76.79

Place (place type) County	
Tampa (city) Hillsborough	48.93
Orlando (city) Orange	33.67
Jacksonville (city) Duval	16.31

Laotians 25 Years and Over Who are Four-Year College Graduates
Top 10 Places Sorted by Number

Place (place type) County	Number
St. Petersburg (city) Pinellas	26

Laotians 25 Years and Over Who are Four-Year College Graduates
Top 10 Places Sorted by Percent

Place (place type) County	Percent
St. Petersburg (city) Pinellas	3.93

Malaysians 25 Years and Over Who are Four-Year College Graduates
Top 10 Places Sorted by Number

Place (place type) County	Number
No places met population threshold.	

Malaysians 25 Years and Over Who are Four-Year College Graduates
Top 10 Places Sorted by Percent

Place (place type) County	Percent
No places met population threshold.	

Pakistanis 25 Years and Over Who are Four-Year College Graduates
Top 10 Places Sorted by Number

Place (place type) County	Number
No places met population threshold.	

Pakistanis 25 Years and Over Who are Four-Year College Graduates
Top 10 Places Sorted by Percent

Place (place type) County	Percent
No places met population threshold.	

Samoans 25 Years and Over Who are Four-Year College Graduates
Top 10 Places Sorted by Number

Place (place type) County	Number
No places met population threshold.	

Samoans 25 Years and Over Who are Four-Year College Graduates
Top 10 Places Sorted by Percent

Place (place type) County	Percent
No places met population threshold.	

Sri Lankans 25 Years and Over Who are Four-Year College Graduates
Top 10 Places Sorted by Number

Place (place type) County	Number
No places met population threshold.	

Sri Lankans 25 Years and Over Who are Four-Year College Graduates
Top 10 Places Sorted by Percent

Place (place type) County	Percent
No places met population threshold.	

Notes: Please refer to the User's Guide for an explanation of data; tables reflect only those areas that meet Summary File 4 population thresholds, therefore there may be less than 10 places listed

Taiwanese 25 Years and Over Who are Four-Year College Graduates
Top 10 Places Sorted by Number

Place (place type) County	Number
No places met population threshold.	

Taiwanese 25 Years and Over Who are Four-Year College Graduates
Top 10 Places Sorted by Percent

Place (place type) County	Percent
No places met population threshold.	

Thais 25 Years and Over Who are Four-Year College Graduates
Top 10 Places Sorted by Number

Place (place type) County	Number
No places met population threshold.	

Thais 25 Years and Over Who are Four-Year College Graduates
Top 10 Places Sorted by Percent

Place (place type) County	Percent
No places met population threshold.	

Tongans 25 Years and Over Who are Four-Year College Graduates
Top 10 Places Sorted by Number

Place (place type) County	Number
No places met population threshold.	

Tongans 25 Years and Over Who are Four-Year College Graduates
Top 10 Places Sorted by Percent

Place (place type) County	Percent
No places met population threshold.	

Vietnamese 25 Years and Over Who are Four-Year College Graduates
Top 10 Places Sorted by Number

Place (place type) County	Number
Jacksonville (city) Duval	215
Tampa (city) Hillsborough	163
Orlando (city) Orange	137
St. Petersburg (city) Pinellas	50
West and East Lealman (cdp) Pinellas	44
Town 'n' Country (cdp) Hillsborough	42
Pine Hills (cdp) Orange	41
Pinellas Park (city) Pinellas	29
Oak Ridge (cdp) Orange	9

Vietnamese 25 Years and Over Who are Four-Year College Graduates
Top 10 Places Sorted by Percent

Place (place type) County	Percent
Orlando (city) Orange	27.85
Jacksonville (city) Duval	17.24
Tampa (city) Hillsborough	16.87
West and East Lealman (cdp) Pinellas	15.28
Pine Hills (cdp) Orange	9.83
Town 'n' Country (cdp) Hillsborough	8.81
Pinellas Park (city) Pinellas	7.90
St. Petersburg (city) Pinellas	5.00
Oak Ridge (cdp) Orange	2.23

Median Household Income

Total Population
Top 10 Places Sorted by Number

Place (place type) County	Dollars
Pinecrest (village) Miami-Dade	107,507

Weston (city) Broward	80,920
Westchase (cdp) Hillsborough	79,561
Cooper City (city) Broward	75,166
Wekiwa Springs (cdp) Seminole	71,839
Doctor Phillips (cdp) Orange	70,754
Wellington (village) Palm Beach	70,271
Hunters Creek (cdp) Orange	67,775
East Lake (cdp) Pinellas	67,546
Coral Gables (city) Miami-Dade	66,839

Asian
Top 10 Places Sorted by Number

Place (place type) County	Dollars
East Lake (cdp) Pinellas	91,877
Hunters Creek (cdp) Orange	83,827
Weston (city) Broward	82,682
Ocoee (city) Orange	80,085
Ormond Beach (city) Volusia	76,832
Wellington (village) Palm Beach	76,445
Wekiwa Springs (cdp) Seminole	75,783
Oviedo (city) Seminole	75,244
Richmond West (cdp) Miami-Dade	75,190
Citrus Park (cdp) Hillsborough	72,022

Native Hawaiian and Other Pacific Islander
Top 10 Places Sorted by Number

Place (place type) County	Dollars
Jacksonville (city) Duval	38,750

Asian Indian
Top 10 Places Sorted by Number

Place (place type) County	Dollars
East Lake (cdp) Pinellas	100,000
Davie (town) Broward	69,083
Doctor Phillips (cdp) Orange	68,571
Altamonte Springs (city) Seminole	62,143
Weston (city) Broward	61,042
Pembroke Pines (city) Broward	60,294
Sunrise (city) Broward	60,144
Jacksonville (city) Duval	58,835
Lakeland (city) Polk	58,750
The Hammocks (cdp) Miami-Dade	58,214

Bangladeshi
Top 10 Places Sorted by Number

Place (place type) County	Dollars
No places met population threshold.	

Cambodian
Top 10 Places Sorted by Number

Place (place type) County	Dollars
Jacksonville (city) Duval	42,292
St. Petersburg (city) Pinellas	34,261

Chinese (except Taiwanese)
Top 10 Places Sorted by Number

Place (place type) County	Dollars
Kendall (cdp) Miami-Dade	53,750
Pembroke Pines (city) Broward	50,469
Jacksonville (city) Duval	49,306
Miramar (city) Broward	46,111
St. Petersburg (city) Pinellas	45,199
Davie (town) Broward	42,045
Coral Springs (city) Broward	40,417
Hollywood (city) Broward	38,125
Sunrise (city) Broward	36,434
Orlando (city) Orange	35,347

Fijian
Top 10 Places Sorted by Number

Place (place type) County	Dollars
No places met population threshold.	

Filipino
Top 10 Places Sorted by Number

Place (place type) County	Dollars
Miramar (city) Broward	88,334
Pembroke Pines (city) Broward	68,906
Yeehaw Junction (cdp) Osceola	68,882
Lakeside (cdp) Clay	63,365
Jacksonville (city) Duval	54,035
Bellview (cdp) Escambia	47,083
Orlando (city) Orange	46,607
Cape Coral (city) Lee	45,417
Tampa (city) Hillsborough	40,662
St. Petersburg (city) Pinellas	36,667

Guamanian or Chamorro
Top 10 Places Sorted by Number

Place (place type) County	Dollars
No places met population threshold.	

Hawaiian, Native
Top 10 Places Sorted by Number

Place (place type) County	Dollars
No places met population threshold.	

Hmong
Top 10 Places Sorted by Number

Place (place type) County	Dollars
No places met population threshold.	

Indonesian
Top 10 Places Sorted by Number

Place (place type) County	Dollars
No places met population threshold.	

Japanese
Top 10 Places Sorted by Number

Place (place type) County	Dollars
Jacksonville (city) Duval	35,375

Korean
Top 10 Places Sorted by Number

Place (place type) County	Dollars
Jacksonville (city) Duval	39,688
Tampa (city) Hillsborough	31,500
Orlando (city) Orange	20,833
Gainesville (city) Alachua	11,506

Laotian
Top 10 Places Sorted by Number

Place (place type) County	Dollars
St. Petersburg (city) Pinellas	48,092

Malaysian
Top 10 Places Sorted by Number

Place (place type) County	Dollars
No places met population threshold.	

Pakistani
Top 10 Places Sorted by Number

Place (place type) County	Dollars
No places met population threshold.	

Samoan
Top 10 Places Sorted by Number

Place (place type) County	Dollars
No places met population threshold.	

Notes: Please refer to the User's Guide for an explanation of data; tables reflect only those areas that meet Summary File 4 population thresholds, therefore there may be less than 10 places listed

Sri Lankan
Top 10 Places Sorted by Number

Place (place type) County	Dollars
No places met population threshold.	

Taiwanese
Top 10 Places Sorted by Number

Place (place type) County	Dollars
No places met population threshold.	

Thai
Top 10 Places Sorted by Number

Place (place type) County	Dollars
No places met population threshold.	

Tongan
Top 10 Places Sorted by Number

Place (place type) County	Dollars
No places met population threshold.	

Vietnamese
Top 10 Places Sorted by Number

Place (place type) County	Dollars
Town 'n' Country (cdp) Hillsborough	56,250
St. Petersburg (city) Pinellas	41,154
Orlando (city) Orange	40,278
Oak Ridge (cdp) Orange	39,293
West and East Lealman (cdp) Pinellas	38,281
Pinellas Park (city) Pinellas	34,196
Jacksonville (city) Duval	31,842
Pine Hills (cdp) Orange	26,853
Tampa (city) Hillsborough	25,789

Per Capita Income

Total Population
Top 10 Places Sorted by Number

Place (place type) County	Dollars
Pinecrest (village) Miami-Dade	51,181
Coral Gables (city) Miami-Dade	46,163
Boca Raton (city) Palm Beach	45,628
Palm Beach Gardens (city) Palm Beach	42,975
Westchase (cdp) Hillsborough	37,630
East Lake (cdp) Pinellas	36,206
Wekiwa Springs (cdp) Seminole	36,196
Weston (city) Broward	35,490
Jupiter (town) Palm Beach	35,088
Doctor Phillips (cdp) Orange	31,197

Asian
Top 10 Places Sorted by Number

Place (place type) County	Dollars
Pinecrest (village) Miami-Dade	58,647
Ormond Beach (city) Volusia	46,372
Wellington (village) Palm Beach	37,821
Wekiwa Springs (cdp) Seminole	36,200
East Lake (cdp) Pinellas	34,938
Greater Carrollwood (cdp) Hillsborough	34,513
Palm Beach Gardens (city) Palm Beach	34,389
Palm Harbor (cdp) Pinellas	30,541
Jupiter (town) Palm Beach	29,586
Coral Gables (city) Miami-Dade	29,400

Native Hawaiian and Other Pacific Islander
Top 10 Places Sorted by Number

Place (place type) County	Dollars
Jacksonville (city) Duval	14,953

Asian Indian
Top 10 Places Sorted by Number

Place (place type) County	Dollars
Doctor Phillips (cdp) Orange	39,901
East Lake (cdp) Pinellas	35,452
Tallahassee (city) Leon	31,654
Town 'n' Country (cdp) Hillsborough	30,345
Jacksonville (city) Duval	29,608
Kendall (cdp) Miami-Dade	27,955
St. Petersburg (city) Pinellas	27,702
Tampa (city) Hillsborough	26,153
Davie (town) Broward	25,698
West Palm Beach (city) Palm Beach	23,139

Bangladeshi
Top 10 Places Sorted by Number

Place (place type) County	Dollars
No places met population threshold.	

Cambodian
Top 10 Places Sorted by Number

Place (place type) County	Dollars
Jacksonville (city) Duval	11,706
St. Petersburg (city) Pinellas	9,283

Chinese (except Taiwanese)
Top 10 Places Sorted by Number

Place (place type) County	Dollars
Hollywood (city) Broward	39,812
Coral Springs (city) Broward	29,188
Orlando (city) Orange	27,271
Kendall (cdp) Miami-Dade	26,510
Tampa (city) Hillsborough	23,278
Jacksonville (city) Duval	22,836
St. Petersburg (city) Pinellas	22,766
The Hammocks (cdp) Miami-Dade	21,633
Davie (town) Broward	20,205
Tallahassee (city) Leon	19,956

Fijian
Top 10 Places Sorted by Number

Place (place type) County	Dollars
No places met population threshold.	

Filipino
Top 10 Places Sorted by Number

Place (place type) County	Dollars
Pembroke Pines (city) Broward	25,764
St. Petersburg (city) Pinellas	24,537
Miramar (city) Broward	22,974
Yeehaw Junction (cdp) Osceola	21,033
Jacksonville (city) Duval	19,773
Tampa (city) Hillsborough	18,175
Orlando (city) Orange	18,137
Lakeside (cdp) Clay	17,771
Clearwater (city) Pinellas	16,165
Bellview (cdp) Escambia	15,612

Guamanian or Chamorro
Top 10 Places Sorted by Number

Place (place type) County	Dollars
No places met population threshold.	

Hawaiian, Native
Top 10 Places Sorted by Number

Place (place type) County	Dollars
No places met population threshold.	

Hmong
Top 10 Places Sorted by Number

Place (place type) County	Dollars
No places met population threshold.	

Indonesian
Top 10 Places Sorted by Number

Place (place type) County	Dollars
No places met population threshold.	

Japanese
Top 10 Places Sorted by Number

Place (place type) County	Dollars
Jacksonville (city) Duval	14,228

Korean
Top 10 Places Sorted by Number

Place (place type) County	Dollars
Tampa (city) Hillsborough	15,615
Jacksonville (city) Duval	15,344
Orlando (city) Orange	13,416
Gainesville (city) Alachua	7,384

Laotian
Top 10 Places Sorted by Number

Place (place type) County	Dollars
St. Petersburg (city) Pinellas	12,356

Malaysian
Top 10 Places Sorted by Number

Place (place type) County	Dollars
No places met population threshold.	

Pakistani
Top 10 Places Sorted by Number

Place (place type) County	Dollars
No places met population threshold.	

Samoan
Top 10 Places Sorted by Number

Place (place type) County	Dollars
No places met population threshold.	

Sri Lankan
Top 10 Places Sorted by Number

Place (place type) County	Dollars
No places met population threshold.	

Taiwanese
Top 10 Places Sorted by Number

Place (place type) County	Dollars
No places met population threshold.	

Thai
Top 10 Places Sorted by Number

Place (place type) County	Dollars
No places met population threshold.	

Tongan
Top 10 Places Sorted by Number

Place (place type) County	Dollars
No places met population threshold.	

Vietnamese
Top 10 Places Sorted by Number

Place (place type) County	Dollars
Orlando (city) Orange	20,441

Notes: Please refer to the User's Guide for an explanation of data; tables reflect only those areas that meet Summary File 4 population thresholds, therefore there may be less than 10 places listed

Place (place type) County	
Pinellas Park (city) Pinellas	15,915
Jacksonville (city) Duval	13,762
St. Petersburg (city) Pinellas	13,092
Town 'n' Country (cdp) Hillsborough	12,451
Tampa (city) Hillsborough	12,346
Oak Ridge (cdp) Orange	11,864
West and East Lealman (cdp) Pinellas	10,405
Pine Hills (cdp) Orange	9,166

Poverty Status

Total Populations with Income Below Poverty Level
Top 10 Places Sorted by Number

Place (place type) County	Number
Miami (city) Miami-Dade	100,405
Jacksonville (city) Duval	87,691
Tampa (city) Hillsborough	53,425
Hialeah (city) Miami-Dade	41,537
Tallahassee (city) Leon	33,978
St. Petersburg (city) Pinellas	32,127
Orlando (city) Orange	29,029
Fort Lauderdale (city) Broward	26,158
Gainesville (city) Alachua	22,559
Miami Beach (city) Miami-Dade	19,003

Total Populations with Income Below Poverty Level
Top 10 Places Sorted by Percent

Place (place type) County	Percent
University (cdp) Hillsborough	31.34
Miami (city) Miami-Dade	28.45
Gainesville (city) Alachua	26.69
West Pensacola (cdp) Escambia	25.33
Tallahassee (city) Leon	24.70
North Miami (city) Miami-Dade	23.92
Daytona Beach (city) Volusia	23.61
Miami Beach (city) Miami-Dade	21.84
Fort Myers (city) Lee	21.77
Springfield (city) Bay	21.49

Asians with Income Below Poverty Level
Top 10 Places Sorted by Number

Place (place type) County	Number
Jacksonville (city) Duval	1,585
Gainesville (city) Alachua	1,476
Tampa (city) Hillsborough	1,145
Tallahassee (city) Leon	629
Orlando (city) Orange	582
North Miami Beach (city) Miami-Dade	537
Miami (city) Miami-Dade	525
Coral Springs (city) Broward	512
St. Petersburg (city) Pinellas	500
Hollywood (city) Broward	356

Asians with Income Below Poverty Level
Top 10 Places Sorted by Percent

Place (place type) County	Percent
Ocala (city) Marion	37.93
Gainesville (city) Alachua	37.84
South Miami Heights (cdp) Miami-Dade	34.62
University (cdp) Hillsborough	32.59
North Miami Beach (city) Miami-Dade	31.95
Daytona Beach (city) Volusia	28.77
Oakland Park (city) Broward	28.10
Miami Beach (city) Miami-Dade	26.58
Ensley (cdp) Escambia	24.69
Miami (city) Miami-Dade	24.43

Native Hawaiian and Other Pacific Islanders with Income Below Poverty Level
Top 10 Places Sorted by Number

Place (place type) County	Number
Jacksonville (city) Duval	47

Native Hawaiian and Other Pacific Islanders with Income Below Poverty Level
Top 10 Places Sorted by Percent

Place (place type) County	Percent
Jacksonville (city) Duval	9.98

Asian Indians with Income Below Poverty Level
Top 10 Places Sorted by Number

Place (place type) County	Number
Gainesville (city) Alachua	362
Jacksonville (city) Duval	220
Miami (city) Miami-Dade	209
North Miami Beach (city) Miami-Dade	175
Tampa (city) Hillsborough	169
Coral Springs (city) Broward	162
Hollywood (city) Broward	156
East Lake (cdp) Pinellas	153
Fort Lauderdale (city) Broward	143
Plantation (city) Broward	131

Asian Indians with Income Below Poverty Level
Top 10 Places Sorted by Percent

Place (place type) County	Percent
North Miami Beach (city) Miami-Dade	44.19
Gainesville (city) Alachua	41.51
East Lake (cdp) Pinellas	32.55
Fort Lauderdale (city) Broward	26.78
Miami (city) Miami-Dade	24.33
Boca Raton (city) Palm Beach	23.18
West Palm Beach (city) Palm Beach	16.56
Kendall (cdp) Miami-Dade	15.87
Miramar (city) Broward	15.45
Melbourne (city) Brevard	13.55

Bangladeshis with Income Below Poverty Level
Top 10 Places Sorted by Number

Place (place type) County	Number
No places met population threshold.	

Bangladeshis with Income Below Poverty Level
Top 10 Places Sorted by Percent

Place (place type) County	Percent
No places met population threshold.	

Cambodians with Income Below Poverty Level
Top 10 Places Sorted by Number

Place (place type) County	Number
St. Petersburg (city) Pinellas	81
Jacksonville (city) Duval	69

Cambodians with Income Below Poverty Level
Top 10 Places Sorted by Percent

Place (place type) County	Percent
St. Petersburg (city) Pinellas	16.53
Jacksonville (city) Duval	6.93

Chinese (except Taiwanese) with Income Below Poverty Level
Top 10 Places Sorted by Number

Place (place type) County	Number
Gainesville (city) Alachua	462
Sunrise (city) Broward	205
Jacksonville (city) Duval	191
Coral Springs (city) Broward	188
North Miami Beach (city) Miami-Dade	160
Miami (city) Miami-Dade	157
Pembroke Pines (city) Broward	132
Hollywood (city) Broward	130
Tampa (city) Hillsborough	123
The Hammocks (cdp) Miami-Dade	86

Chinese (except Taiwanese) with Income Below Poverty Level
Top 10 Places Sorted by Percent

Place (place type) County	Percent
Gainesville (city) Alachua	34.71
Miami (city) Miami-Dade	31.98
Sunrise (city) Broward	22.70
North Miami Beach (city) Miami-Dade	21.80
Coral Springs (city) Broward	21.05
The Hammocks (cdp) Miami-Dade	20.67
Hollywood (city) Broward	20.03
Tampa (city) Hillsborough	18.30
Margate (city) Broward	15.65
Jacksonville (city) Duval	11.85

Fijians with Income Below Poverty Level
Top 10 Places Sorted by Number

Place (place type) County	Number
No places met population threshold.	

Fijians with Income Below Poverty Level
Top 10 Places Sorted by Percent

Place (place type) County	Percent
No places met population threshold.	

Filipinos with Income Below Poverty Level
Top 10 Places Sorted by Number

Place (place type) County	Number
Jacksonville (city) Duval	543
Tampa (city) Hillsborough	86
Cape Coral (city) Lee	81
Orlando (city) Orange	78
Pembroke Pines (city) Broward	71
St. Petersburg (city) Pinellas	71
Clearwater (city) Pinellas	38
Bellview (cdp) Escambia	24
Yeehaw Junction (cdp) Osceola	7
Myrtle Grove (cdp) Escambia	6

Filipinos with Income Below Poverty Level
Top 10 Places Sorted by Percent

Place (place type) County	Percent
Cape Coral (city) Lee	11.86
Orlando (city) Orange	11.13
Tampa (city) Hillsborough	9.18
Clearwater (city) Pinellas	8.43
St. Petersburg (city) Pinellas	8.16
Pembroke Pines (city) Broward	7.66
Bellview (cdp) Escambia	5.83
Jacksonville (city) Duval	5.65
Yeehaw Junction (cdp) Osceola	2.05
Myrtle Grove (cdp) Escambia	1.38

Guamanians or Chamorros with Income Below Poverty Level
Top 10 Places Sorted by Number

Place (place type) County	Number
No places met population threshold.	

Guamanians or Chamorros with Income Below Poverty Level
Top 10 Places Sorted by Percent

Place (place type) County	Percent
No places met population threshold.	

Hawaiian Natives with Income Below Poverty Level
Top 10 Places Sorted by Number

Place (place type) County	Number
No places met population threshold.	

Notes: Please refer to the User's Guide for an explanation of data; tables reflect only those areas that meet Summary File 4 population thresholds, therefore there may be less than 10 places listed

Hawaiian Natives with Income Below Poverty Level
Top 10 Places Sorted by Percent

Place (place type) County	Percent
No places met population threshold.	

Hmongs with Income Below Poverty Level
Top 10 Places Sorted by Number

Place (place type) County	Number
No places met population threshold.	

Hmongs with Income Below Poverty Level
Top 10 Places Sorted by Percent

Place (place type) County	Percent
No places met population threshold.	

Indonesians with Income Below Poverty Level
Top 10 Places Sorted by Number

Place (place type) County	Number
No places met population threshold.	

Indonesians with Income Below Poverty Level
Top 10 Places Sorted by Percent

Place (place type) County	Percent
No places met population threshold.	

Japanese with Income Below Poverty Level
Top 10 Places Sorted by Number

Place (place type) County	Number
Jacksonville (city) Duval	72

Japanese with Income Below Poverty Level
Top 10 Places Sorted by Percent

Place (place type) County	Percent
Jacksonville (city) Duval	13.85

Koreans with Income Below Poverty Level
Top 10 Places Sorted by Number

Place (place type) County	Number
Tampa (city) Hillsborough	291
Gainesville (city) Alachua	243
Orlando (city) Orange	107
Jacksonville (city) Duval	102

Koreans with Income Below Poverty Level
Top 10 Places Sorted by Percent

Place (place type) County	Percent
Gainesville (city) Alachua	51.59
Tampa (city) Hillsborough	30.22
Orlando (city) Orange	19.45
Jacksonville (city) Duval	11.22

Laotians with Income Below Poverty Level
Top 10 Places Sorted by Number

Place (place type) County	Number
St. Petersburg (city) Pinellas	49

Laotians with Income Below Poverty Level
Top 10 Places Sorted by Percent

Place (place type) County	Percent
St. Petersburg (city) Pinellas	4.32

Malaysians with Income Below Poverty Level
Top 10 Places Sorted by Number

Place (place type) County	Number
No places met population threshold.	

Malaysians with Income Below Poverty Level
Top 10 Places Sorted by Percent

Place (place type) County	Percent
No places met population threshold.	

Pakistanis with Income Below Poverty Level
Top 10 Places Sorted by Number

Place (place type) County	Number
No places met population threshold.	

Pakistanis with Income Below Poverty Level
Top 10 Places Sorted by Percent

Place (place type) County	Percent
No places met population threshold.	

Samoans with Income Below Poverty Level
Top 10 Places Sorted by Number

Place (place type) County	Number
No places met population threshold.	

Samoans with Income Below Poverty Level
Top 10 Places Sorted by Percent

Place (place type) County	Percent
No places met population threshold.	

Sri Lankans with Income Below Poverty Level
Top 10 Places Sorted by Number

Place (place type) County	Number
No places met population threshold.	

Sri Lankans with Income Below Poverty Level
Top 10 Places Sorted by Percent

Place (place type) County	Percent
No places met population threshold.	

Taiwanese with Income Below Poverty Level
Top 10 Places Sorted by Number

Place (place type) County	Number
No places met population threshold.	

Taiwanese with Income Below Poverty Level
Top 10 Places Sorted by Percent

Place (place type) County	Percent
No places met population threshold.	

Thais with Income Below Poverty Level
Top 10 Places Sorted by Number

Place (place type) County	Number
No places met population threshold.	

Thais with Income Below Poverty Level
Top 10 Places Sorted by Percent

Place (place type) County	Percent
No places met population threshold.	

Tongans with Income Below Poverty Level
Top 10 Places Sorted by Number

Place (place type) County	Number
No places met population threshold.	

Tongans with Income Below Poverty Level
Top 10 Places Sorted by Percent

Place (place type) County	Percent
No places met population threshold.	

Vietnamese with Income Below Poverty Level
Top 10 Places Sorted by Number

Place (place type) County	Number
Jacksonville (city) Duval	347
Tampa (city) Hillsborough	322
St. Petersburg (city) Pinellas	110
Pinellas Park (city) Pinellas	84
West and East Lealman (cdp) Pinellas	70
Pine Hills (cdp) Orange	65
Orlando (city) Orange	59
Oak Ridge (cdp) Orange	41
Town 'n' Country (cdp) Hillsborough	14

Vietnamese with Income Below Poverty Level
Top 10 Places Sorted by Percent

Place (place type) County	Percent
Tampa (city) Hillsborough	23.35
Jacksonville (city) Duval	17.10
Pinellas Park (city) Pinellas	15.97
West and East Lealman (cdp) Pinellas	15.35
Pine Hills (cdp) Orange	10.14
Orlando (city) Orange	8.50
Oak Ridge (cdp) Orange	7.78
St. Petersburg (city) Pinellas	6.90
Town 'n' Country (cdp) Hillsborough	2.04

Homeownership

Total Populations Who Own Their Own Homes
Top 10 Places Sorted by Number

Place (place type) County	Number
Jacksonville (city) Duval	179,782
St. Petersburg (city) Pinellas	69,697
Tampa (city) Hillsborough	68,753
Miami (city) Miami-Dade	46,847
Pembroke Pines (city) Broward	41,636
Fort Lauderdale (city) Broward	37,927
Hollywood (city) Broward	37,102
Hialeah (city) Miami-Dade	35,963
Orlando (city) Orange	33,052
Cape Coral (city) Lee	32,663

Total Populations Who Own Their Own Homes
Top 10 Places Sorted by Percent

Place (place type) County	Percent
Richmond West (cdp) Miami-Dade	93.84
Cooper City (city) Broward	92.24
Royal Palm Beach (village) Palm Beach	88.31
Westchase (cdp) Hillsborough	88.29
Deltona (city) Volusia	87.19
Palm Coast (city) Flagler	86.37
Spring Hill (cdp) Hernando	86.24
Oviedo (city) Seminole	85.75
Ocoee (city) Orange	84.30
East Lake (cdp) Pinellas	83.68

Asians Who Own Their Own Homes
Top 10 Places Sorted by Number

Place (place type) County	Number
Jacksonville (city) Duval	3,753
St. Petersburg (city) Pinellas	1,299
Pembroke Pines (city) Broward	1,099
Tampa (city) Hillsborough	864
Coral Springs (city) Broward	813
Orlando (city) Orange	654
Sunrise (city) Broward	609
Hollywood (city) Broward	568
Kendall (cdp) Miami-Dade	516
Miramar (city) Broward	493

Asians Who Own Their Own Homes
Top 10 Places Sorted by Percent

Place (place type) County	Percent
Ocoee (city) Orange	93.26
Deltona (city) Volusia	93.15
Richmond West (cdp) Miami-Dade	92.27
Royal Palm Beach (village) Palm Beach	89.68
Cooper City (city) Broward	89.32
Westchase (cdp) Hillsborough	87.84
Oviedo (city) Seminole	86.67
Merritt Island (cdp) Brevard	86.16
Miramar (city) Broward	85.00
Palm Coast (city) Flagler	84.11

Native Hawaiian and Other Pacific Islanders Who Own Their Own Homes
Top 10 Places Sorted by Number

Place (place type) County	Number
Jacksonville (city) Duval	63

Native Hawaiian and Other Pacific Islanders Who Own Their Own Homes
Top 10 Places Sorted by Percent

Place (place type) County	Percent
Jacksonville (city) Duval	42.28

Asian Indians Who Own Their Own Homes
Top 10 Places Sorted by Number

Place (place type) County	Number
Coral Springs (city) Broward	400
Jacksonville (city) Duval	397
Pembroke Pines (city) Broward	345
Sunrise (city) Broward	251
Orlando (city) Orange	216
Hollywood (city) Broward	212
Kendall (cdp) Miami-Dade	201
Tallahassee (city) Leon	192
Plantation (city) Broward	179
Miramar (city) Broward	162

Asian Indians Who Own Their Own Homes
Top 10 Places Sorted by Percent

Place (place type) County	Percent
Miramar (city) Broward	86.63
Davie (town) Broward	83.15
Weston (city) Broward	83.15
Cooper City (city) Broward	78.95
Sunrise (city) Broward	78.68
Coral Springs (city) Broward	77.37
Doctor Phillips (cdp) Orange	75.45
Pembroke Pines (city) Broward	65.84
Kendall (cdp) Miami-Dade	63.61
The Hammocks (cdp) Miami-Dade	63.48

Bangladeshis Who Own Their Own Homes
Top 10 Places Sorted by Number

Place (place type) County	Number
No places met population threshold.	

Bangladeshis Who Own Their Own Homes
Top 10 Places Sorted by Percent

Place (place type) County	Percent
No places met population threshold.	

Cambodians Who Own Their Own Homes
Top 10 Places Sorted by Number

Place (place type) County	Number
Jacksonville (city) Duval	172
St. Petersburg (city) Pinellas	118

Cambodians Who Own Their Own Homes
Top 10 Places Sorted by Percent

Place (place type) County	Percent
St. Petersburg (city) Pinellas	82.52
Jacksonville (city) Duval	74.14

Chinese (except Taiwanese) Who Own Their Own Homes
Top 10 Places Sorted by Number

Place (place type) County	Number
Jacksonville (city) Duval	307
Pembroke Pines (city) Broward	286
Coral Springs (city) Broward	249
Sunrise (city) Broward	212
Kendall (cdp) Miami-Dade	182
St. Petersburg (city) Pinellas	182
Hollywood (city) Broward	179
North Miami Beach (city) Miami-Dade	175
Margate (city) Broward	151
Tampa (city) Hillsborough	133

Chinese (except Taiwanese) Who Own Their Own Homes
Top 10 Places Sorted by Percent

Place (place type) County	Percent
Miramar (city) Broward	91.61
Sunrise (city) Broward	89.83
Margate (city) Broward	87.79
Coral Springs (city) Broward	80.32
North Miami Beach (city) Miami-Dade	79.55
Pembroke Pines (city) Broward	78.36
Davie (town) Broward	75.64
Hollywood (city) Broward	73.97
Kendall (cdp) Miami-Dade	67.66
The Hammocks (cdp) Miami-Dade	65.92

Fijians Who Own Their Own Homes
Top 10 Places Sorted by Number

Place (place type) County	Number
No places met population threshold.	

Fijians Who Own Their Own Homes
Top 10 Places Sorted by Percent

Place (place type) County	Percent
No places met population threshold.	

Filipinos Who Own Their Own Homes
Top 10 Places Sorted by Number

Place (place type) County	Number
Jacksonville (city) Duval	2,124
Pembroke Pines (city) Broward	244
St. Petersburg (city) Pinellas	203
Tampa (city) Hillsborough	128
Cape Coral (city) Lee	108
Myrtle Grove (cdp) Escambia	101
Lakeside (cdp) Clay	95
Miramar (city) Broward	95
Bellview (cdp) Escambia	88
Orlando (city) Orange	80

Filipinos Who Own Their Own Homes
Top 10 Places Sorted by Percent

Place (place type) County	Percent
Miramar (city) Broward	95.00
Pembroke Pines (city) Broward	85.92
Yeehaw Junction (cdp) Osceola	85.11
Jacksonville (city) Duval	77.83
Cape Coral (city) Lee	76.06
Lakeside (cdp) Clay	76.00
Bellview (cdp) Escambia	73.95
St. Petersburg (city) Pinellas	61.89
Myrtle Grove (cdp) Escambia	58.72

Tampa (city) Hillsborough   46.21

Guamanians or Chamorros Who Own Their Own Homes
Top 10 Places Sorted by Number

Place (place type) County	Number
No places met population threshold.	

Guamanians or Chamorros Who Own Their Own Homes
Top 10 Places Sorted by Percent

Place (place type) County	Percent
No places met population threshold.	

Hawaiian Natives Who Own Their Own Homes
Top 10 Places Sorted by Number

Place (place type) County	Number
No places met population threshold.	

Hawaiian Natives Who Own Their Own Homes
Top 10 Places Sorted by Percent

Place (place type) County	Percent
No places met population threshold.	

Hmongs Who Own Their Own Homes
Top 10 Places Sorted by Number

Place (place type) County	Number
No places met population threshold.	

Hmongs Who Own Their Own Homes
Top 10 Places Sorted by Percent

Place (place type) County	Percent
No places met population threshold.	

Indonesians Who Own Their Own Homes
Top 10 Places Sorted by Number

Place (place type) County	Number
No places met population threshold.	

Indonesians Who Own Their Own Homes
Top 10 Places Sorted by Percent

Place (place type) County	Percent
No places met population threshold.	

Japanese Who Own Their Own Homes
Top 10 Places Sorted by Number

Place (place type) County	Number
Jacksonville (city) Duval	102

Japanese Who Own Their Own Homes
Top 10 Places Sorted by Percent

Place (place type) County	Percent
Jacksonville (city) Duval	62.20

Koreans Who Own Their Own Homes
Top 10 Places Sorted by Number

Place (place type) County	Number
Jacksonville (city) Duval	144
Tampa (city) Hillsborough	129
Orlando (city) Orange	60
Gainesville (city) Alachua	31

Koreans Who Own Their Own Homes
Top 10 Places Sorted by Percent

Place (place type) County	Percent
Jacksonville (city) Duval	55.17
Tampa (city) Hillsborough	44.95
Orlando (city) Orange	27.27

Notes: Please refer to the User's Guide for an explanation of data; tables reflect only those areas that meet Summary File 4 population thresholds, therefore there may be less than 10 places listed

Gainesville (city) Alachua 14.90

Laotians Who Own Their Own Homes
Top 10 Places Sorted by Number

Place (place type) County	Number
St. Petersburg (city) Pinellas	219

Laotians Who Own Their Own Homes
Top 10 Places Sorted by Percent

Place (place type) County	Percent
St. Petersburg (city) Pinellas	79.64

Malaysians Who Own Their Own Homes
Top 10 Places Sorted by Number

Place (place type) County	Number
No places met population threshold.	

Malaysians Who Own Their Own Homes
Top 10 Places Sorted by Percent

Place (place type) County	Percent
No places met population threshold.	

Pakistanis Who Own Their Own Homes
Top 10 Places Sorted by Number

Place (place type) County	Number
No places met population threshold.	

Pakistanis Who Own Their Own Homes
Top 10 Places Sorted by Percent

Place (place type) County	Percent
No places met population threshold.	

Samoans Who Own Their Own Homes
Top 10 Places Sorted by Number

Place (place type) County	Number
No places met population threshold.	

Samoans Who Own Their Own Homes
Top 10 Places Sorted by Percent

Place (place type) County	Percent
No places met population threshold.	

Sri Lankans Who Own Their Own Homes
Top 10 Places Sorted by Number

Place (place type) County	Number
No places met population threshold.	

Sri Lankans Who Own Their Own Homes
Top 10 Places Sorted by Percent

Place (place type) County	Percent
No places met population threshold.	

Taiwanese Who Own Their Own Homes
Top 10 Places Sorted by Number

Place (place type) County	Number
No places met population threshold.	

Taiwanese Who Own Their Own Homes
Top 10 Places Sorted by Percent

Place (place type) County	Percent
No places met population threshold.	

Thais Who Own Their Own Homes
Top 10 Places Sorted by Number

Place (place type) County	Number
No places met population threshold.	

Thais Who Own Their Own Homes
Top 10 Places Sorted by Percent

Place (place type) County	Percent
No places met population threshold.	

Tongans Who Own Their Own Homes
Top 10 Places Sorted by Number

Place (place type) County	Number
No places met population threshold.	

Tongans Who Own Their Own Homes
Top 10 Places Sorted by Percent

Place (place type) County	Percent
No places met population threshold.	

Vietnamese Who Own Their Own Homes
Top 10 Places Sorted by Number

Place (place type) County	Number
Jacksonville (city) Duval	274
St. Petersburg (city) Pinellas	273
Pinellas Park (city) Pinellas	158
Tampa (city) Hillsborough	143
Town 'n' Country (cdp) Hillsborough	137
Oak Ridge (cdp) Orange	129
Orlando (city) Orange	112
Pine Hills (cdp) Orange	100
West and East Lealman (cdp) Pinellas	82

Vietnamese Who Own Their Own Homes
Top 10 Places Sorted by Percent

Place (place type) County	Percent
Town 'n' Country (cdp) Hillsborough	89.54
Oak Ridge (cdp) Orange	88.97
Pinellas Park (city) Pinellas	80.61
West and East Lealman (cdp) Pinellas	67.77
St. Petersburg (city) Pinellas	63.05
Pine Hills (cdp) Orange	60.61
Jacksonville (city) Duval	48.32
Orlando (city) Orange	41.79
Tampa (city) Hillsborough	38.75

Median Gross Rent

All Specified Renter-Occupied Housing Units
Top 10 Places Sorted by Number

Place (place type) County	Dollars/Month
Doctor Phillips (cdp) Orange	1,150
Richmond West (cdp) Miami-Dade	1,084
Weston (city) Broward	1,084
Wekiwa Springs (cdp) Seminole	1,014
Wellington (village) Palm Beach	989
Cooper City (city) Broward	988
Hunters Creek (cdp) Orange	972
Doral (cdp) Miami-Dade	968
Pembroke Pines (city) Broward	945
Palm Beach Gardens (city) Palm Beach	939

Specified Housing Units Rented by Asians
Top 10 Places Sorted by Number

Place (place type) County	Dollars/Month
Hunters Creek (cdp) Orange	1,139
Kendale Lakes (cdp) Miami-Dade	1,139
Doctor Phillips (cdp) Orange	1,060
Jupiter (town) Palm Beach	1,031
Palm Coast (city) Flagler	1,014
Richmond West (cdp) Miami-Dade	1,014
Wellington (village) Palm Beach	989
Westchase (cdp) Hillsborough	982
Weston (city) Broward	969
Royal Palm Beach (village) Palm Beach	950

Specified Housing Units Rented by Native Hawaiian and Other Pacific Islanders
Top 10 Places Sorted by Number

Place (place type) County	Dollars/Month
Jacksonville (city) Duval	575

Specified Housing Units Rented by Asian Indians
Top 10 Places Sorted by Number

Place (place type) County	Dollars/Month
Doctor Phillips (cdp) Orange	1,125
Pembroke Pines (city) Broward	922
Plantation (city) Broward	921
Coral Springs (city) Broward	919
Weston (city) Broward	841
North Miami Beach (city) Miami-Dade	830
Boca Raton (city) Palm Beach	815
West Palm Beach (city) Palm Beach	793
Orlando (city) Orange	772
Miramar (city) Broward	767

Specified Housing Units Rented by Bangladeshis
Top 10 Places Sorted by Number

Place (place type) County	Dollars/Month
No places met population threshold.	

Specified Housing Units Rented by Cambodians
Top 10 Places Sorted by Number

Place (place type) County	Dollars/Month
St. Petersburg (city) Pinellas	467
Jacksonville (city) Duval	384

Specified Housing Units Rented by Chinese (except Taiwanese)
Top 10 Places Sorted by Number

Place (place type) County	Dollars/Month
Pembroke Pines (city) Broward	945
Coral Springs (city) Broward	910
The Hammocks (cdp) Miami-Dade	873
Miramar (city) Broward	850
Hollywood (city) Broward	819
Davie (town) Broward	808
Orlando (city) Orange	769
Margate (city) Broward	740
Kendall (cdp) Miami-Dade	701
Sunrise (city) Broward	680

Specified Housing Units Rented by Fijians
Top 10 Places Sorted by Number

Place (place type) County	Dollars/Month
No places met population threshold.	

Specified Housing Units Rented by Filipinos
Top 10 Places Sorted by Number

Place (place type) County	Dollars/Month
Miramar (city) Broward	1,375
Pembroke Pines (city) Broward	859
Yeehaw Junction (cdp) Osceola	750
Orlando (city) Orange	697
Cape Coral (city) Lee	694
Bellview (cdp) Escambia	665
Jacksonville (city) Duval	642
St. Petersburg (city) Pinellas	586
Tampa (city) Hillsborough	585
Clearwater (city) Pinellas	565

Specified Housing Units Rented by Guamanians or Chamorros
Top 10 Places Sorted by Number

Place (place type) County	Dollars/Month
No places met population threshold.	

Notes: Please refer to the User's Guide for an explanation of data; tables reflect only those areas that meet Summary File 4 population thresholds, therefore there may be less than 10 places listed

Specified Housing Units Rented by Hawaiian Natives
Top 10 Places Sorted by Number

Place (place type) County	Dollars/Month
No places met population threshold.	

Specified Housing Units Rented by Hmongs
Top 10 Places Sorted by Number

Place (place type) County	Dollars/Month
No places met population threshold.	

Specified Housing Units Rented by Indonesians
Top 10 Places Sorted by Number

Place (place type) County	Dollars/Month
No places met population threshold.	

Specified Housing Units Rented by Japanese
Top 10 Places Sorted by Number

Place (place type) County	Dollars/Month
Jacksonville (city) Duval	464

Specified Housing Units Rented by Koreans
Top 10 Places Sorted by Number

Place (place type) County	Dollars/Month
Orlando (city) Orange	811
Jacksonville (city) Duval	631
Tampa (city) Hillsborough	489
Gainesville (city) Alachua	488

Specified Housing Units Rented by Laotians
Top 10 Places Sorted by Number

Place (place type) County	Dollars/Month
St. Petersburg (city) Pinellas	708

Specified Housing Units Rented by Malaysians
Top 10 Places Sorted by Number

Place (place type) County	Dollars/Month
No places met population threshold.	

Specified Housing Units Rented by Pakistanis
Top 10 Places Sorted by Number

Place (place type) County	Dollars/Month
No places met population threshold.	

Specified Housing Units Rented by Samoans
Top 10 Places Sorted by Number

Place (place type) County	Dollars/Month
No places met population threshold.	

Specified Housing Units Rented by Sri Lankans
Top 10 Places Sorted by Number

Place (place type) County	Dollars/Month
No places met population threshold.	

Specified Housing Units Rented by Taiwanese
Top 10 Places Sorted by Number

Place (place type) County	Dollars/Month
No places met population threshold.	

Specified Housing Units Rented by Thais
Top 10 Places Sorted by Number

Place (place type) County	Dollars/Month
No places met population threshold.	

Specified Housing Units Rented by Tongans
Top 10 Places Sorted by Number

Place (place type) County	Dollars/Month
No places met population threshold.	

Specified Housing Units Rented by Vietnamese
Top 10 Places Sorted by Number

Place (place type) County	Dollars/Month
Orlando (city) Orange	630
Pinellas Park (city) Pinellas	603
Oak Ridge (cdp) Orange	600
Town 'n' Country (cdp) Hillsborough	536
Tampa (city) Hillsborough	517
Jacksonville (city) Duval	495
Pine Hills (cdp) Orange	489
West and East Lealman (cdp) Pinellas	473
St. Petersburg (city) Pinellas	407

Median Home Value

All Specified Owner-Occupied Housing Units
Top 10 Places Sorted by Number

Place (place type) County	Dollars
Pinecrest (village) Miami-Dade	393,900
Coral Gables (city) Miami-Dade	336,800
Miami Beach (city) Miami-Dade	334,400
Boca Raton (city) Palm Beach	230,200
Glenvar Heights (cdp) Miami-Dade	215,000
Weston (city) Broward	202,000
East Lake (cdp) Pinellas	197,700
Doral (cdp) Miami-Dade	178,500
Kendall (cdp) Miami-Dade	175,700
Coral Springs (city) Broward	175,500

Specified Housing Units Owned and Occupied by Asians
Top 10 Places Sorted by Number

Place (place type) County	Dollars
Miami Beach (city) Miami-Dade	440,000
East Lake (cdp) Pinellas	254,800
Westchase (cdp) Hillsborough	223,100
Weston (city) Broward	215,600
Pinecrest (village) Miami-Dade	202,800
Coral Gables (city) Miami-Dade	200,000
Ormond Beach (city) Volusia	200,000
Hunters Creek (cdp) Orange	186,700
Doctor Phillips (cdp) Orange	186,400
Wekiwa Springs (cdp) Seminole	186,100

Specified Housing Units Owned and Occupied by Native Hawaiian and Other Pacific Islanders
Top 10 Places Sorted by Number

Place (place type) County	Dollars
Jacksonville (city) Duval	68,300

Specified Housing Units Owned and Occupied by Asian Indians
Top 10 Places Sorted by Number

Place (place type) County	Dollars
East Lake (cdp) Pinellas	288,600
Davie (town) Broward	229,300
Weston (city) Broward	221,900
Kendall (cdp) Miami-Dade	214,000
Orlando (city) Orange	191,100
Doctor Phillips (cdp) Orange	184,600
Plantation (city) Broward	179,800
Miami (city) Miami-Dade	169,100
Tampa (city) Hillsborough	163,800
Jacksonville (city) Duval	162,000

Specified Housing Units Owned and Occupied by Bangladeshis
Top 10 Places Sorted by Number

Place (place type) County	Dollars
No places met population threshold.	

Specified Housing Units Owned and Occupied by Cambodians
Top 10 Places Sorted by Number

Place (place type) County	Dollars
Jacksonville (city) Duval	83,900
St. Petersburg (city) Pinellas	72,700

Specified Housing Units Owned and Occupied by Chinese (except Taiwanese)
Top 10 Places Sorted by Number

Place (place type) County	Dollars
Miami (city) Miami-Dade	225,000
Pembroke Pines (city) Broward	159,000
Tallahassee (city) Leon	158,300
Davie (town) Broward	157,600
Coral Springs (city) Broward	141,000
Orlando (city) Orange	136,700
Jacksonville (city) Duval	135,900
Gainesville (city) Alachua	134,700
Miramar (city) Broward	130,800
The Hammocks (cdp) Miami-Dade	128,800

Specified Housing Units Owned and Occupied by Fijians
Top 10 Places Sorted by Number

Place (place type) County	Dollars
No places met population threshold.	

Specified Housing Units Owned and Occupied by Filipinos
Top 10 Places Sorted by Number

Place (place type) County	Dollars
Pembroke Pines (city) Broward	167,400
Miramar (city) Broward	143,800
Yeehaw Junction (cdp) Osceola	133,200
Clearwater (city) Pinellas	130,000
Orlando (city) Orange	125,000
Cape Coral (city) Lee	113,700
Jacksonville (city) Duval	100,900
Tampa (city) Hillsborough	89,300
Bellview (cdp) Escambia	87,800
Myrtle Grove (cdp) Escambia	80,900

Specified Housing Units Owned and Occupied by Guamanians or Chamorros
Top 10 Places Sorted by Number

Place (place type) County	Dollars
No places met population threshold.	

Specified Housing Units Owned and Occupied by Hawaiian Natives
Top 10 Places Sorted by Number

Place (place type) County	Dollars
No places met population threshold.	

Specified Housing Units Owned and Occupied by Hmongs
Top 10 Places Sorted by Number

Place (place type) County	Dollars
No places met population threshold.	

Specified Housing Units Owned and Occupied by Indonesians
Top 10 Places Sorted by Number

Place (place type) County	Dollars
No places met population threshold.	

Notes: Please refer to the User's Guide for an explanation of data; tables reflect only those areas that meet Summary File 4 population thresholds, therefore there may be less than 10 places listed

Specified Housing Units Owned and Occupied by Japanese
Top 10 Places Sorted by Number

Place (place type) County	Dollars
Jacksonville (city) Duval	85,000

Specified Housing Units Owned and Occupied by Koreans
Top 10 Places Sorted by Number

Place (place type) County	Dollars
Orlando (city) Orange	173,500
Tampa (city) Hillsborough	154,200
Gainesville (city) Alachua	137,500
Jacksonville (city) Duval	125,300

Specified Housing Units Owned and Occupied by Laotians
Top 10 Places Sorted by Number

Place (place type) County	Dollars
St. Petersburg (city) Pinellas	68,400

Specified Housing Units Owned and Occupied by Malaysians
Top 10 Places Sorted by Number

Place (place type) County	Dollars
No places met population threshold.	

Specified Housing Units Owned and Occupied by Pakistanis
Top 10 Places Sorted by Number

Place (place type) County	Dollars
No places met population threshold.	

Specified Housing Units Owned and Occupied by Samoans
Top 10 Places Sorted by Number

Place (place type) County	Dollars
No places met population threshold.	

Specified Housing Units Owned and Occupied by Sri Lankans
Top 10 Places Sorted by Number

Place (place type) County	Dollars
No places met population threshold.	

Specified Housing Units Owned and Occupied by Taiwanese
Top 10 Places Sorted by Number

Place (place type) County	Dollars
No places met population threshold.	

Specified Housing Units Owned and Occupied by Thais
Top 10 Places Sorted by Number

Place (place type) County	Dollars
No places met population threshold.	

Specified Housing Units Owned and Occupied by Tongans
Top 10 Places Sorted by Number

Place (place type) County	Dollars
No places met population threshold.	

Specified Housing Units Owned and Occupied by Vietnamese
Top 10 Places Sorted by Number

Place (place type) County	Dollars
Orlando (city) Orange	93,300
Oak Ridge (cdp) Orange	85,900
Pine Hills (cdp) Orange	84,100
Town 'n' Country (cdp) Hillsborough	81,600
Pinellas Park (city) Pinellas	80,300
West and East Lealman (cdp) Pinellas	75,000
Jacksonville (city) Duval	72,900
Tampa (city) Hillsborough	68,200
St. Petersburg (city) Pinellas	64,500

Notes: Please refer to the User's Guide for an explanation of data; tables reflect only those areas that meet Summary File 4 population thresholds, therefore there may be less than 10 places listed

Climate

PHYSICAL FEATURES. Florida, situated between latitudes 24° 30' and 31° N., and longitudes 80° and 87° 30' W., is largely a lowland peninsula comprising about 54,100 square miles of land area and is surrounded on three sides by the waters of the Atlantic Ocean and the Gulf of Mexico. Countless shallow lakes, which exist particularly on the peninsula and range in size from small cypress ponds to that of Lake Okeechobee, account for approximately 4,400 square miles of additional water area.

No point in the State is more than 70 miles from salt water, and the highest natural land in the Northwest Division is only 345 feet above sea level. Coastal areas are low and flat and are indented by many small bays or inlets. Many small islands dot the shorelines. The elevation of most of the interior ranges from 50 to 100 feet above sea level, though gentle hills in the interior of the peninsula and across the northern and western portions of the State rise above 200 feet.

A large portion of the southern one-third of the peninsula is the swampland known as the Everglades. An ill-defined divide of low, rolling hills, extending north-to-south near the middle of the peninsula and terminating north of Lake Okeechobee, gives rise to most peninsula streams, chains of lakes, and many springs. Stream gradients are slight and often insufficient to handle the runoff following heavy rainfall. Consequently, there are sizable areas of swamp and marshland near these streams.

GENERAL CLIMATE. Climate is probably Florida's greatest natural resource. General climatic conditions range from a zone of transition between temperate and subtropical conditions in the extreme northern interior portion of the State to the tropical conditions found on the Florida Keys. The chief factors of climatic control are: latitude, proximity to the Atlantic Ocean and Gulf of Mexico, and numerous inland lakes.

Summers throughout the State are long, warm, and relatively humid; winters, although punctuated with periodic invasions of cool to occasionally cold air from the north, are mild because of the southern latitude and relatively warm adjacent ocean waters. The Gulf Stream, which flows around the western tip of Cuba, through the Straits of Florida, and northward along the lower east coast, exerts a warming influence to the southern east coast largely because the predominate wind direction is from the east. Coastal weather stations throughout the State average slightly warmer in winter and cooler in summer than do inland weather stations at the same latitude.

Florida enjoys abundant rainfall. Except for the northwestern portion of the State, the average year can be divided into two seasons—the so-called "rainy season" and the long, relatively dry season. On the peninsula, generally more than one-half of the precipitation for an average year can be expected to fall during the four-month period, June through September. In northwest Florida, there is a secondary rainfall maximum in late winter and in early spring.

The summer heat is tempered by sea breezes along the coast and by frequent afternoon or early evening thunderstorms in all areas. During the warm season, sea breezes are felt almost daily within several miles of the coast and occasionally 20 to 30 miles inland. Thundershowers, which on the average occur about one-half of the days in summer, frequently are accompanied by as much as a rapid 10 to 20°F. drop in temperature, resulting in comfortable weather for the remainder of the day. Gentle breezes occur almost daily in all areas and serve to mitigate further the oppressiveness that otherwise would accompany the prevailing summer temperature and humidity conditions. Because most of the large-scale wind patterns affecting Florida have passed over water surfaces, hot drying winds seldom occur.

Most of the summer rainfall is derived from "local" showers or thundershowers. Many weather stations average more than 80 thundershowers per year, and some average more than 100. Showers are often heavy, usually lasting only one or two hours, and generally occur near the hottest part of the day. The more severe thundershowers are occasionally attended by hail or locally strong winds which may inflict serious local damage to crops and property. Day-long summer rains are usually associated with tropical disturbances and are infrequent. Even in the wet season, the rainfall duration is generally less than 10 percent of the time.

DROUGHTS. Florida is not immune from drought, even though annual rainfall amounts are relatively large. Prolonged periods of deficient rainfall are occasionally experienced even during the time of the expected rainy season. Several such dry periods, in the course of one or two years, can lead to significantly lowered water tables and lake levels which, in turn, may cause serious water shortages for those communities that depend upon lakes and shallow wells for their water supply. Statewide droughts during summer are rare, but it is not unusual during a drought in one portion of the State for other portions to receive generous rainfall. In a few instances, individual weather stations have experienced periods of a month or more without rainfall.

SNOW. Snowfall in Florida is unusual, although measurable amounts have fallen in the northern portions at irregular intervals, and a trace of snow has been recorded as far south as Fort Myers.

WIND. Prevailing winds over the southern peninsula are southeast and east. Over the remainder of the State, wind directions are influenced locally by convectional forces inland and by the land-and-sea-breeze-effect near the coast. Consequently, prevailing directions are somewhat erratic, but, in general, follow a pattern from the north in winter and from the south in summer. The windiest months are March and April. High local winds of short duration occur occasionally in connection with thunderstorms in summer and with cold fronts moving across the State in other seasons. Tornadoes, funnel clouds, and waterspouts also occur, averaging 10 to 15 in a year. Tornadoes have occurred in all seasons, but are most frequent in spring; they also occur in connection with tropical storms. Generally, tornado paths in Florida are short. Occasionally, waterspouts come inland, but they usually dissipate soon after reaching land and affect only very small areas.

TROPICAL STORMS. Storms that produce high winds and are often destructive are usually tropical in origin. Florida, jutting out into the ocean between the subtropical Atlantic and the Gulf of Mexico, is the most exposed of all States to these storms. In particular, hurricanes can approach from the Atlantic Ocean to the east, from the Caribbean Sea to the south, and from the Gulf of Mexico to the west.

The vulnerability of the State to tropical storms varies with the progress of the hurricane season. In August and early September, tropical storms normally approach the State from the east or southeast, but as the season progresses into late September and October, the region of maximum hurricane activity (insofar as Florida is concerned) shifts to the western Caribbean. Most of those storms that move into Florida approach the State from the south or southwest, entering the Keys, the Miami area, or along the west coast. Some of the world's heaviest rainfalls have occurred within tropical cyclones. Rainfall over 20 inches in 24 hours is not uncommon. The intensity of the rainfall, however, does not seem to bear any relation to the intensity of the wind circulation.

OTHER CLIMATIC ELEMENTS. The climate of Florida is humid. Inland areas with greater temperature extremes enjoy slightly lower relative humidity, especially during times of hot weather. On the average, variations in relative humidity from one place to another are small; humidities range from about 50 to 65 percent during the afternoon hours to about 85 to 95 percent during the night and early morning hours.

Heavy fogs are usually confined to the night and early morning hours in the late fall, winter, and early spring months. On the average, they occur about 35 to 40 days in a year over the extreme northern portion; about 25 to 30 days in a year over the central portion; and less than 10 days in a year over the extreme southern portion of the State. These fogs usually dissipate or thin soon after sunrise; heavy daytime fog is seldom observed in Florida.

Florida has been nicknamed the Sunshine State. Sunshine measurements made at widely separated stations in the State indicate the sun shines about two-thirds of the possible sunlight hours during the year, ranging from slightly more than 60 percent of possible in December and January to more than 70 percent of possible in April and May. In general, southern Florida enjoys a higher percentage of possible sunshine hours than does northern Florida. The length of day operates to Florida's advantage. In winter, when sunshine is highly valued, the sun can shine longer in Florida than in the more northern latitudes. In summer, the situation reverses itself with longer days returning to the north.

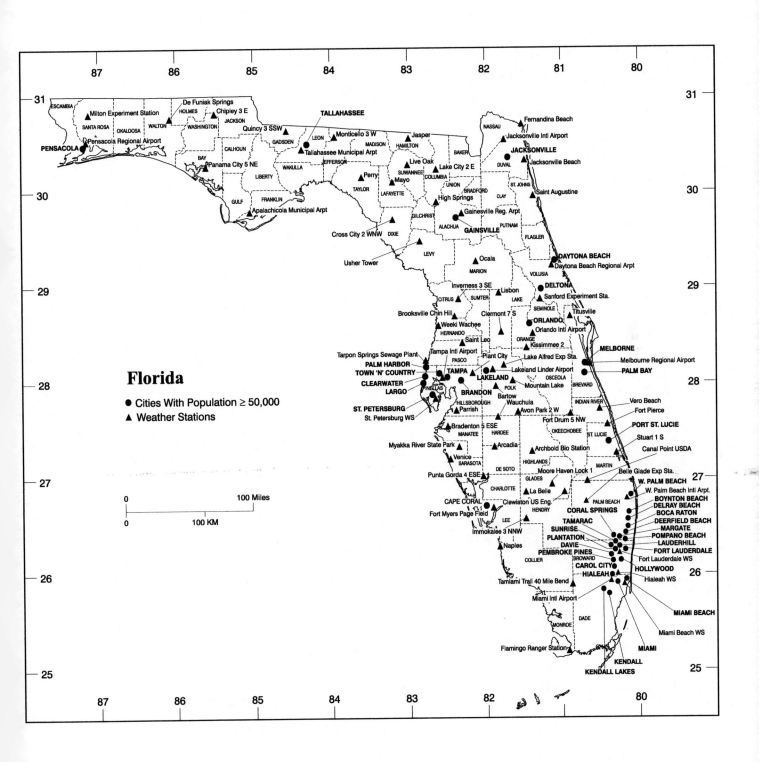

Florida

● Cities With Population ≥ 50,000
▲ Weather Stations

Florida Weather Stations by County

County	Station Name
Alachua	Gainesville Regional Airport
	High Springs
Bay	Panama City 5 NE
Brevard	Melbourne Regional Airport
	Titusville
Broward	Fort Lauderdale
Charlotte	Punta Gorda 4 ESE
Citrus	Inverness 3 SE
Collier	Immokalee 3 NNW
	Naples
Columbia	Lake City 2 E
Dade	Hialeah
	Miami Beach
	Miami Int'l Airport
	Tamiami Trail 40 Mile Bend
Desoto	Arcadia
Dixie	Cross City 2 WNW
Duval	Jacksonville Beach
	Jacksonville Int'l Airport
Escambia	Pensacola Regional Airport
Franklin	Apalachicola Municipal Airport
Gadsden	Quincy 3 SSW
Glades	Moore Haven Lock 1
Hamilton	Jasper
Hardee	Wauchula
Hendry	Clewiston U.S. Engineers
	La Belle
Hernando	Brooksville Chin Hill
	Weeki Wachee
Highlands	Archbold Bio Station
	Avon Park 2 W
Hillsborough	Plant City
	Tampa Int'l Airport
Indian River	Vero Beach
Jefferson	Monticello 3 W
Lafayette	Mayo
Lake	Clermont 7 S
	Lisbon

County	Station Name
Lee	Fort Myers Page Field
Leon	Tallahassee Municipal Airport
Levy	Usher Tower
Manatee	Bradenton 5 ESE
	Parrish
Marion	Ocala
Martin	Stuart 1 S
Monroe	Flamingo Ranger Station
	Key West Int'l Airport
	Tavernier
Nassau	Fernandina Beach
Okeechobee	Fort Drum 5 NW
Orange	Orlando Int'l Airport
Osceola	Kissimmee 2
Palm Beach	Belle Glade Exp. Station
	Canal Point USDA
	West Palm Beach Int'l Airport
Pasco	Saint Leo
Pinellas	Saint Petersburg
	Tarpon Springs Sewage Plant
Polk	Bartow
	Lake Alfred Exp. Station
	Lakeland Linder Airport
	Mountain Lake
Santa Rosa	Milton Experiment Station
Sarasota	Myakka River State Park
	Venice
Seminole	Sanford Experiment Station
St. Johns	Saint Augustine
St. Lucie	Fort Pierce
Suwannee	Live Oak
Taylor	Perry
Volusia	Daytona Beach Regional Airport
Walton	De Funiak Springs
Washington	Chipley 3 E

Florida Weather Stations by City

City	Station Name	Miles
Boca Raton	Fort Lauderdale	19
Boynton Beach	West Palm Beach Int'l Airport	11
Brandon	Plant City	11
	Tampa Int'l Airport	15
Cape Coral	Fort Myers Page Field	6
Carol City	Fort Lauderdale	12
	Hialeah	8
	Miami Beach	14
	Miami Int'l Airport	9
Clearwater	Saint Petersburg	17
	Tampa Int'l Airport	14
	Tarpon Springs Sewage Plant	12
Coral Springs	Fort Lauderdale	12
Davie	Fort Lauderdale	5
	Hialeah	17
	Miami Int'l Airport	18
Daytona Beach	Daytona Beach Reg Airport	2
Deerfield Beach	Fort Lauderdale	15
Delray Beach	West Palm Beach Int'l Airport	16
Deltona	Sanford Experiment Station	7
Fort Lauderdale	Fort Lauderdale	5
Gainesville	High Springs	19
	Gainesville Regional Airport	4
Hialeah	Fort Lauderdale	18
	Hialeah	2
	Miami Beach	12
	Miami Int'l Airport	3
Hollywood	Fort Lauderdale	6
	Hialeah	14
	Miami Beach	17
	Miami Int'l Airport	16
Jacksonville	Jacksonville Int'l Airport	14
	Jacksonville Beach	15
Kendale Lakes	Hialeah	12
	Miami Beach	18
	Miami Int'l Airport	10
Kendall	Hialeah	12
	Miami Beach	15
	Miami Int'l Airport	10
Lakeland	Bartow	11
	Lake Alfred Exp. Station	15
	Lakeland Linder Airport	0
	Plant City	11
Largo	Saint Petersburg	13

City	Station Name	Miles
Largo (cont.)	Tampa Int'l Airport	16
	Tarpon Springs Sewage Plant	17
Lauderhill	Fort Lauderdale	5
Margate	Fort Lauderdale	10
Melbourne	Melbourne Regional Airport	1
Miami	Hialeah	5
	Miami Beach	6
	Miami Int'l Airport	5
Miami Beach	Hialeah	9
	Miami Beach	2
	Miami Int'l Airport	10
Orlando	Kissimmee 2	18
	Orlando Int'l Airport	7
Palm Bay	Melbourne Regional Airport	7
Palm Harbor	Tampa Int'l Airport	15
	Tarpon Springs Sewage Plant	5
Pembroke Pines	Fort Lauderdale	8
	Hialeah	12
	Miami Beach	18
	Miami Int'l Airport	14
Pensacola	Pensacola Regional Airport	2
Plantation	Fort Lauderdale	4
Pompano Beach	Fort Lauderdale	10
Port St. Lucie	Fort Pierce	13
	Stuart 1 S	10
St. Petersburg	Saint Petersburg	2
	Tampa Int'l Airport	15
Sunrise	Fort Lauderdale	6
Tallahassee	Quincy 3 SSW	19
	Tallahassee Municipal Airport	6
Tamarac	Fort Lauderdale	8
Tampa	Saint Petersburg	17
	Tampa Int'l Airport	4
Town 'n' Country	Saint Petersburg	17
	Tampa Int'l Airport	4
	Tarpon Springs Sewage Plant	14
West Palm Beach	West Palm Beach Int'l Airport	3

Note: Miles is the distance between the geographic center of the city and the weather station.

Florida Weather Stations by Elevation

Feet	Station Name
242	Quincy 3 SSW
239	Brooksville Chin Hill
229	De Funiak Springs
216	Milton Experiment Station
209	Lakeland Linder Airport
193	Lake City 2 E
187	Saint Leo
150	Avon Park 2 W
144	Jasper
144	Monticello 3 W
137	Archbold Bio Station
137	Lake Alfred Exp. Station
131	Gainesville Regional Airport
127	Chipley 3 E
124	Bartow
124	Mountain Lake
118	Live Oak
118	Plant City
111	Pensacola Regional Airport
108	Clermont 7 S
95	Orlando Int'l Airport
72	Ocala
68	Fort Drum 5 NW
65	Lisbon
62	Arcadia
62	High Springs
62	Mayo
59	Kissimmee 2
59	Parrish
59	Wauchula
52	Tallahassee Municipal Airport
42	Perry
39	Cross City 2 WNW
39	Inverness 3 SE
32	Immokalee 3 NNW
32	Melbourne Regional Airport
32	Miami Int'l Airport
32	Moore Haven Lock 1
32	Usher Tower
29	Canal Point USDA
29	Panama City 5 NE
29	Titusville
26	Daytona Beach Regional Airport
22	Fort Pierce
22	Jacksonville Int'l Airport
19	Apalachicola Municipal Airport
19	Bradenton 5 ESE
19	Clewiston U.S. Engineers
19	Myakka River State Park
19	Punta Gorda 4 ESE
19	Vero Beach
19	Weeki Wachee
16	Tampa Int'l Airport
16	West Palm Beach Int'l Airport
13	Belle Glade Exp. Station

Feet	Station Name
13	Fernandina Beach
13	Fort Lauderdale
13	Fort Myers Page Field
13	La Belle
13	Sanford Experiment Station
13	Tamiami Trail 40 Mile Bend
9	Hialeah
9	Jacksonville Beach
9	Stuart 1 S
6	Saint Augustine
6	Saint Petersburg
6	Tarpon Springs Sewage Plant
6	Tavernier
6	Venice
3	Key West Int'l Airport
3	Miami Beach
3	Naples
0	Flamingo Ranger Station

Apalachicola Municipal Airport

Apalachicola is located in a coastal area that is low and flat and bordered by the Gulf of Mexico from the east-northeast through the south to the west-southwest. There are many rivers, creeks, lakes, and bays to the north. Apalachicola is situated at the mouth of the Apalachicola River and on the Apalachicola Bay. Several islands to the east and south offer very good protection from the occasionally rough seas of the Gulf. The land area is generally sandy, and is heavily covered with pine and cypress forests and scattered palmetto palms.

The climate of this locality is typical of that experienced on the northern Gulf of Mexico. Because of the moderating effect of the surrounding Gulf, temperatures are usually mild and subtropical in nature, but are subject to occasional wide winter variations.

Average annual rainfall is about 57 inches, but actual monthly and yearly totals vary widely. Sandy soil and generally adequate drainage allow rapid absorption and runoff during occasional tropical downpours. Thunderstorms occur in all months. About three-fourths of the average annual number occur during the summer months. Very few tropical storms affect Apalachicola.

Hail has fallen on occasions, but averages less than one occurrence a year. There is no record of sleet or glaze. Snow has fallen on rare occasions, but generally melted as it fell. A measurable amount of snow is rare.

Apalachicola Municipal Airport *Franklin Co.*   Elevation: 19 ft.   Latitude: 29° 44' N   Longitude: 85° 02' W

	JAN	FEB	MAR	APR	MAY	JUN	JUL	AUG	SEP	OCT	NOV	DEC	YEAR
Mean Maximum Temp. (°F)	62.1	64.6	69.9	76.1	83.1	88.2	89.7	89.3	86.9	79.9	71.9	65.1	77.2
Mean Temp. (°F)	53.1	55.6	61.1	67.1	74.3	80.1	81.9	81.8	79.2	70.6	62.4	55.9	68.6
Mean Minimum Temp. (°F)	44.1	46.6	52.4	58.0	65.5	71.9	74.2	74.1	71.3	61.3	52.8	46.6	59.9
Extreme Maximum Temp. (°F)	80	80	85	90	98	100	101	103	97	92	85	83	103
Extreme Minimum Temp. (°F)	9	19	22	36	47	48	63	62	52	33	27	14	9
Days Maximum Temp. ≥ 90°F	0	0	0	0	2	10	16	14	7	1	0	0	50
Days Maximum Temp. ≤ 32°F	0	0	0	0	0	0	0	0	0	0	0	0	0
Days Minimum Temp. ≤ 32°F	5	2	0	0	0	0	0	0	0	0	0	3	10
Days Minimum Temp. ≤ 0°F	0	0	0	0	0	0	0	0	0	0	0	0	0
Heating Degree Days (base 65°F)	368	268	151	40	1	0	0	0	0	20	135	294	1,277
Cooling Degree Days (base 65°F)	6	11	39	105	300	462	542	534	427	208	67	20	2,721
Mean Precipitation (in.)	4.92	3.82	5.00	3.05	2.86	4.26	7.10	7.89	6.59	4.39	3.45	3.58	56.91
Maximum Precipitation (in.)	20.8	8.9	13.5	12.1	12.1	18.3	18.1	21.1	18.3	11.2	6.7	9.7	88.2
Minimum Precipitation (in.)	0.8	0.5	0.7	0.1	0.3	0.3	0.8	2.3	0.6	0.1	0.5	0.9	38.1
Maximum 24-hr. Precipitation (in.)	4.0	4.4	8.2	6.2	6.8	4.2	6.3	5.4	7.7	6.2	4.2	3.6	8.2
Days With ≥ 0.1" Precipitation	7	5	6	4	3	6	9	9	8	4	5	6	72
Days With ≥ 1.0" Precipitation	2	1	2	1	1	1	2	2	2	1	1	1	17
Mean Snowfall (in.)	trace	trace	trace	0.0	0.0	0.0	0.0	0.0	0.0	0.0	0.0	trace	trace
Maximum Snowfall (in.)	trace	trace	trace	0	0	0	0	0	0	0	0	trace	trace
Maximum 24-hr. Snowfall (in.)	trace	trace	trace	0	0	0	0	0	0	0	0	trace	trace
Days With ≥ 1.0" Snow Depth	0	0	0	0	0	0	0	0	0	0	0	0	0
Thunderstorm Days	2	3	4	3	5	11	17	17	10	2	2	2	78
Foggy Days	17	15	17	14	12	8	7	8	9	11	13	16	147
Predominant Sky Cover	OVR	OVR	OVR	CLR	SCT	SCT	SCT	SCT	SCT	CLR	CLR	OVR	OVR
Mean Relative Humidity 7am (%)	83	86	88	87	87	87	89	91	89	86	86	85	87
Mean Relative Humidity 4pm (%)	62	64	66	62	65	67	70	69	67	60	64	65	65
Mean Dewpoint (°F)	42	47	53	58	66	71	74	74	70	60	54	47	60
Prevailing Wind Direction	N	SE	SE	SE	S	SW	SW	SE	NE	NE	NE	N	SE
Prevailing Wind Speed (mph)	10	9	10	10	8	8	7	9	8	8	8	10	9
Maximum Wind Gust (mph)	41	49	41	43	61	38	41	68	68	44	85	47	85

Daytona Beach Regional Airport

Daytona Beach is located on the Atlantic Ocean. The Halifax River, part of the Florida Inland Waterway, runs through the city. The terrain in the area is flat and the soil is mostly sandy. Elevations in the area range from three to 15 feet above mean sea level near the ocean to about 31 feet at the airport and on a ridge running along the western city limits.

Nearness to the ocean results in a climate tempered by the effect of land and sea breezes. In the summer, while maximum temperatures reach 90 degrees or above during the late morning or early afternoon, the number of hours of 90 degrees or above is relatively small due to the beginning of the sea breeze near midday and the occurrence of local afternoon convective thunderstorms which lower the temperature to the comfortable 80s. Winters, although subject to invasions of cold air, are relatively mild due to the nearness of the ocean and latitudinal location.

The rainy season from June through mid-October produces 60 percent of the annual rainfall. The major portion of the summer rainfall occurs in the form of local convective thunderstorms which are occasionally heavy and produce as much as two or three inches of rain. The more severe thunderstorms may be attended by strong gusty winds. Almost all rainfall during the winter months is associated with frontal passages.

Long periods of cloudiness and rain are infrequent, usually not lasting over two or three days. These periods are usually associated with a stationary front, a so-called northeaster, or a tropical disturbance.

Tropical disturbances or hurricanes are not considered a great threat to this area of the state. Generally hurricanes in this latitude tend to pass well offshore or lose much of their intensity while crossing the state before reaching this area. Only in gusts have hurricane-force winds been recorded at this station.

Heavy fog occurs mostly during the winter and early spring. These fogs usually form by radiational cooling at night and dissipate soon after sunrise. On rare occasions sea fog moves in from the ocean and persists for two or three days. There is no significant source in the area for air pollution.

Daytona Beach Regional Airport *Volusia Co.*   Elevation: 26 ft.   Latitude: 29° 11' N   Longitude: 81° 04' W

	JAN	FEB	MAR	APR	MAY	JUN	JUL	AUG	SEP	OCT	NOV	DEC	YEAR
Mean Maximum Temp. (°F)	68.7	70.4	75.2	79.7	84.7	88.5	90.5	89.6	87.3	82.0	76.0	70.9	80.3
Mean Temp. (°F)	58.2	59.9	64.6	69.2	74.9	79.8	81.6	81.3	79.7	73.9	66.6	60.8	70.9
Mean Minimum Temp. (°F)	47.5	49.2	54.1	58.7	65.0	71.0	72.7	73.0	72.0	65.7	57.2	50.6	61.4
Extreme Maximum Temp. (°F)	87	89	92	94	97	101	102	100	96	93	88	88	102
Extreme Minimum Temp. (°F)	15	26	26	36	44	52	60	65	53	41	30	19	15
Days Maximum Temp. ≥ 90°F	0	0	0	2	5	11	19	15	7	1	0	0	60
Days Maximum Temp. ≤ 32°F	0	0	0	0	0	0	0	0	0	0	0	0	0
Days Minimum Temp. ≤ 32°F	2	1	0	0	0	0	0	0	0	0	0	1	4
Days Minimum Temp. ≤ 0°F	0	0	0	0	0	0	0	0	0	0	0	0	0
Heating Degree Days (base 65°F)	242	181	95	26	1	0	0	0	0	6	67	179	797
Cooling Degree Days (base 65°F)	31	45	83	149	308	450	525	517	439	288	127	53	3,015
Mean Precipitation (in.)	3.20	2.84	3.68	2.57	3.18	5.67	5.12	6.10	6.28	4.58	3.00	2.70	48.92
Maximum Precipitation (in.)	7.2	9.1	8.1	7.1	12.3	15.2	14.4	19.9	15.2	13.0	12.9	12.0	79.3
Minimum Precipitation (in.)	0.1	0.6	0.3	trace	0.1	1.0	0.2	2.0	0.4	0.2	trace	0.1	31.4
Maximum 24-hr. Precipitation (in.)	5.7	3.6	5.0	4.0	4.0	6.1	3.3	4.4	6.2	9.1	9.0	3.6	9.1
Days With ≥ 0.1" Precipitation	5	5	5	3	5	8	8	10	8	6	4	5	72
Days With ≥ 1.0" Precipitation	1	1	1	1	1	2	1	2	2	1	1	1	15
Mean Snowfall (in.)	trace	0.0	trace	0.0	0.0	trace	0.0	trace	0.0	0.0	0.0	trace	trace
Maximum Snowfall (in.)	trace	trace	0	0	0	0	0	0	0	0	0	trace	trace
Maximum 24-hr. Snowfall (in.)	trace	trace	0	0	0	0	0	0	0	0	0	trace	trace
Days With ≥ 1.0" Snow Depth	0	0	0	0	0	0	0	0	0	0	0	0	0
Thunderstorm Days	1	2	3	4	8	14	17	15	9	3	1	1	78
Foggy Days	15	12	12	10	10	10	8	9	8	9	12	14	129
Predominant Sky Cover	OVR	OVR	CLR	CLR	SCT	SCT	SCT	SCT	SCT	SCT	CLR	OVR	SCT
Mean Relative Humidity 7am (%)	87	86	86	85	85	87	89	91	90	87	87	87	87
Mean Relative Humidity 4pm (%)	61	59	57	56	61	68	69	71	71	66	64	63	64
Mean Dewpoint (°F)	49	50	54	58	65	70	72	73	71	65	57	52	61
Prevailing Wind Direction	NW	N	WSW	ESE	ESE	E	SW	E	ENE	ENE	NW	NW	E
Prevailing Wind Speed (mph)	9	12	12	12	12	10	7	10	12	12	8	8	10
Maximum Wind Gust (mph)	62	58	77	58	69	74	67	68	55	56	55	60	77

Fort Myers Page Field

Located on the south bank of the Caloosahatchee River, about 15 miles from the Gulf of Mexico, Fort Myers has a climate characterized as subtropical, with temperature extremes of both summer and winter tempered by the marine influence of the Gulf.

Temperatures generally range from the low 60s in winter to the low 80s in summer. Winters are mild, with many bright, warm days and moderately cool nights. Occasional cold snaps bring temperatures in the 30s, but only rarely do temperatures drop into the 20s. Frost occurs in the farming areas on only a few occasions each year, and usually is light and scattered. In the summer, temperatures have reached 100 degrees, but these occurrences are very rare.

About two-thirds of annual precipitation occurs during June through September. There are frequent long periods during the winter when only very light, or no rain falls. Most rain during the summer occurs as late afternoon or early evening thunderstorms, which bring welcome cooling on hot summer days. These showers seldom last long, even though they yield large amounts of rain. Exceptions are during the late summer or fall when tropical storms or hurricanes may pass near the Fort Myers area. These may result in heavy downpours that may reach torrential proportions. 24 hour amounts of from six to over 10 inches may occur.

The prevailing wind direction is east and, except during the passage of tropical storms, high velocities are not experienced. During winter and spring there are usually a few days with 20 to 30 mph winds and thunderstorms are sometimes accompanied by strong gusts for brief periods. Winds approximating 100 mph have been experienced with the passage of hurricanes during the fall months.

Thunderstorms have occurred during every month, but are infrequent from November to April. From June through September they occur on 2 out of every 3 days on an average, and as a general rule, in the late afternoons or early evenings. Heavy fog is rather infrequent, occurring mostly in winter during the early mornings. There is seldom a day without sunshine at some time.

Relative humidity is high during the night, dropping off in the middle of the day.

Fort Myers Page Field *Lee County*   Elevation: 13 ft.   Latitude: 26° 35' N   Longitude: 81° 52' W

	JAN	FEB	MAR	APR	MAY	JUN	JUL	AUG	SEP	OCT	NOV	DEC	YEAR
Mean Maximum Temp. (°F)	74.8	76.1	80.2	84.6	88.8	91.1	91.7	91.7	90.3	86.4	81.4	76.7	84.5
Mean Temp. (°F)	64.5	65.5	69.5	73.6	78.5	82.1	83.1	83.3	82.2	77.6	71.8	66.4	74.9
Mean Minimum Temp. (°F)	54.1	54.9	58.9	62.7	68.0	73.2	74.5	74.8	74.2	68.8	62.2	56.2	65.2
Extreme Maximum Temp. (°F)	88	91	93	96	99	103	98	98	96	95	95	90	103
Extreme Minimum Temp. (°F)	28	32	33	42	52	60	67	69	64	48	34	27	27
Days Maximum Temp. ≥ 90°F	0	0	1	4	14	21	25	25	20	7	1	0	118
Days Maximum Temp. ≤ 32°F	0	0	0	0	0	0	0	0	0	0	0	0	0
Days Minimum Temp. ≤ 32°F	0	0	0	0	0	0	0	0	0	0	0	0	0
Days Minimum Temp. ≤ 0°F	0	0	0	0	0	0	0	0	0	0	0	0	0
Heating Degree Days (base 65°F)	107	76	26	3	0	0	0	0	0	1	17	73	303
Cooling Degree Days (base 65°F)	93	112	176	275	434	539	578	582	532	410	239	128	4,098
Mean Precipitation (in.)	2.36	2.12	3.27	1.62	3.56	9.68	9.00	9.58	7.80	2.49	1.79	1.59	54.86
Maximum Precipitation (in.)	7.9	10.8	18.6	5.7	10.3	20.1	16.7	16.7	16.6	11.9	8.1	5.2	74.8
Minimum Precipitation (in.)	0	0.1	trace	trace	0.3	2.0	2.3	4.0	1.9	0	trace	trace	32.8
Maximum 24-hr. Precipitation (in.)	2.6	2.6	5.6	3.8	7.8	5.7	7.3	5.1	5.5	6.2	3.6	3.0	7.8
Days With ≥ 0.1" Precipitation	3	3	4	3	5	11	13	13	11	4	3	3	76
Days With ≥ 1.0" Precipitation	1	1	1	0	1	3	3	3	2	1	0	0	16
Mean Snowfall (in.)	0.0	0.0	0.0	0.0	0.0	0.0	0.0	0.0	0.0	0.0	0.0	0.0	0.0
Maximum Snowfall (in.)	0	0	0	0	0	0	0	0	0	0	0	0	0
Maximum 24-hr. Snowfall (in.)	0	0	0	0	0	0	0	0	0	0	0	0	0
Days With ≥ 1.0" Snow Depth	0	0	0	0	0	0	0	0	0	0	0	0	0
Thunderstorm Days	1	1	2	3	6	16	22	21	14	4	1	1	92
Foggy Days	15	12	13	10	9	6	3	3	4	8	11	13	107
Predominant Sky Cover	CLR	CLR	CLR	CLR	SCT	SCT	BRK	BRK	SCT	SCT	SCT	CLR	SCT
Mean Relative Humidity 7am (%)	90	89	89	88	87	89	90	91	92	90	90	90	90
Mean Relative Humidity 4pm (%)	56	54	52	50	53	64	68	67	66	59	58	57	59
Mean Dewpoint (°F)	55	55	58	61	66	72	73	74	73	67	61	57	64
Prevailing Wind Direction	NE	NE	ENE	E	E	E	E	E	ENE	NE	NE	NE	ENE
Prevailing Wind Speed (mph)	8	9	9	9	8	7	7	7	7	9	8	8	8
Maximum Wind Gust (mph)	45	46	39	38	45	71	45	48	41	40	37	47	71

Gainesville Regional Airport

Gainsville lies in the north central part of the Florida peninsula, almost midway between the coasts of the Atlantic Ocean and the Gulf of Mexico. The terrain is fairly level with several nearby lakes to the east and south. Due to its centralized location, maritime influences are somewhat less than they would be along coastlines at the same latitude.

Maximum temperatures in summer average slightly more than 90 degrees. From June to September, the number of days when temperatures exceed 89 degrees is 84 on average. Record high temperatures are in excess of 100 degrees. Minimum temperatures in winter average a little more than 44 degrees. The average number of days per year when temperatures are freezing or below is 18. Record lows occur in the teens. Low temperatures are a consequence of cold winds from the north or nighttime radiational cooling of the ground in contact with rather calm air.

Rainfall is appreciable in every month but is most abundant from showers and thunderstorms in summer. The average number of thunderstorm hours yearly is approximately 160. In winter, large-scale cyclone and frontal activity is responsible for some of the precipitation. Monthly average values range from about two inches in November to about eight inches in August. Snowfall is practically unknown.

Because of its inland location, Gainesville does not have serious problems with hurricanes. An occasional hurricane will cross the Gulf or Atlantic coast and head toward Gainesville, but before it arrives it is weakened by surface friction and a depletion of water vapor.

Gainesville Regional Airport *Alachua Co.*   Elevation: 131 ft.   Latitude: 29° 42' N   Longitude: 82° 17' W

	JAN	FEB	MAR	APR	MAY	JUN	JUL	AUG	SEP	OCT	NOV	DEC	YEAR
Mean Maximum Temp. (°F)	na	na	na	na	na	na	na	na	na	na	na	na	na
Mean Temp. (°F)	na	na	na	na	na	na	na	na	na	na	na	na	na
Mean Minimum Temp. (°F)	na	na	na	na	na	na	na	na	na	na	na	na	na
Extreme Maximum Temp. (°F)	na	na	na	na	na	na	na	na	na	na	na	na	na
Extreme Minimum Temp. (°F)	na	na	na	na	na	na	na	na	na	na	na	na	na
Days Maximum Temp. ≥ 90°F	na	na	na	na	na	na	na	na	na	na	na	na	na
Days Maximum Temp. ≤ 32°F	na	na	na	na	na	na	na	na	na	na	na	na	na
Days Minimum Temp. ≤ 32°F	na	na	na	na	na	na	na	na	na	na	na	na	na
Days Minimum Temp. ≤ 0°F	na	na	na	na	na	na	na	na	na	na	na	na	na
Heating Degree Days (base 65°F)	na	na	na	na	na	na	na	na	na	na	na	na	na
Cooling Degree Days (base 65°F)	*17*	*29*	*63*	*130*	*312*	*443*	*511*	*497*	*405*	*214*	*83*	*25*	*2,729*
Mean Precipitation (in.)	na	na	na	na	na	na	na	na	na	na	na	na	na
Maximum Precipitation (in.)	9.0	6.9	9.8	6.0	7.2	14.8	12.2	15.8	12.0	8.0	4.5	6.4	70.8
Minimum Precipitation (in.)	0.5	0.3	0.7	0.4	0.2	2.2	1.5	2.5	1.9	trace	0.3	0.2	40.5
Maximum 24-hr. Precipitation (in.)	2.2	2.6	3.3	2.8	3.5	4.3	3.2	3.8	6.2	5.1	2.0	2.3	6.2
Days With ≥ 0.1" Precipitation	na	na	na	na	na	na	na	na	na	na	na	na	na
Days With ≥ 1.0" Precipitation	na	na	na	na	na	na	na	na	na	na	na	na	na
Mean Snowfall (in.)	na	na	na	na	na	na	na	na	na	na	na	na	na
Maximum Snowfall (in.)	0	trace	0	0	0	0	0	0	0	0	0	trace	trace
Maximum 24-hr. Snowfall (in.)	0	trace	0	0	0	0	0	0	0	0	0	trace	trace
Days With ≥ 1.0" Snow Depth	na	na	na	na	na	na	na	na	na	na	na	na	na
Thunderstorm Days	1	2	3	3	6	13	20	17	8	3	1	1	78
Foggy Days	19	17	20	21	22	23	21	24	23	21	21	19	251
Predominant Sky Cover	OVR	OVR	CLR	CLR	SCT	BRK	SCT	BRK	SCT	CLR	CLR	OVR	SCT
Mean Relative Humidity 7am (%)	90	90	92	92	91	93	94	96	96	94	94	92	93
Mean Relative Humidity 4pm (%)	60	55	52	50	51	61	67	67	67	63	63	61	60
Mean Dewpoint (°F)	47	49	53	56	63	70	73	73	70	63	57	49	60
Prevailing Wind Direction	WNW	W	W	W	ESE	WSW	WSW	E	E	NE	NE	NW	E
Prevailing Wind Speed (mph)	9	10	10	9	9	9	9	7	8	9	9	8	9
Maximum Wind Gust (mph)	na	na	na	na	na	na	na	na	na	na	na	na	na

Jacksonville Int'l Airport

Jacksonville, a very large metropolitan area covering 840 square miles, extends from the Atlantic Ocean to about 40 miles inland. Downtown Jacksonville is located some 16 miles inland on the St. Johns River. The surrounding terrain is level. Easterly winds blowing about 40 percent of the time produce a maritime influence that modifies to some extent the heat of summer and the cold of winter. Summers are long, warm and relatively humid. Winters, although punctuated with periodic invasions of cool to occasionally cold air from the north, are mild because of the southern latitude and the proximity to the warm Atlantic Ocean waters. Because of the nearness to the ocean, climatic features across the city vary. For example, during the summer months temperatures at Jacksonville International Airport, located 17 miles inland, usually reach into the low and mid-90s before being tempered by sea breezes. Temperatures along the beaches rarely exceed 90 degrees. Summer thunderstorms usually occur before the noon hour along the beaches, while afternoon thunderstorms are the rule inland.

The annual temperature for Jacksonville is between 68 and 69 degrees. June, July, and August are the hottest months, with temperatures averaging near 80 degrees. December, January, and February are the coolest months, with temperatures near the middle 50s. Temperatures exceed 95 degrees only about ten times a year. Night temperatures in summer are usually comfortable, rarely failing to drop below 80 degrees.

The greatest rainfall, mostly in the form of local thundershowers, occurs during the summer months when a measurable amount can be expected one day in two. Rainfall of one inch or more in 24 hours normally occurs about fourteen times a year, and very infrequently heavy rains, associated with tropical storms, reach amounts of several inches with durations of more than 24 hours.

The atmosphere is moist, with an average relative humidity of about 75 percent, ranging from about 90 percent in early morning hours to about 55 percent during the afternoon.

Prevailing winds are northeasterly in the fall and winter months, and southwesterly in spring and summer. Wind movement, which averages slightly less than nine mph, is two to three mph higher in the early afternoon than the early morning hours, and slightly higher in spring than in other seasons of the year. Although this area is in the Hurricane Belt, this section of the coast has been very fortunate in escaping hurricane-force winds. Most hurricanes reaching this latitude have tended to move parallel to the coastline, keeping well out to sea.

Jacksonville Int'l Airport *Duval County*   Elevation: 22 ft.   Latitude: 30° 30' N   Longitude: 81° 42' W

	JAN	FEB	MAR	APR	MAY	JUN	JUL	AUG	SEP	OCT	NOV	DEC	YEAR
Mean Maximum Temp. (°F)	64.6	67.7	73.9	79.5	85.1	89.7	92.1	90.6	87.4	80.2	73.4	66.9	79.3
Mean Temp. (°F)	53.2	56.0	61.9	67.2	73.8	79.6	82.3	81.5	78.5	70.1	62.1	55.7	68.5
Mean Minimum Temp. (°F)	41.8	44.3	49.9	55.0	62.5	69.4	72.5	72.3	69.4	59.9	50.8	44.4	57.7
Extreme Maximum Temp. (°F)	84	86	91	94	98	103	103	102	98	94	88	84	103
Extreme Minimum Temp. (°F)	7	19	23	34	45	47	61	63	48	36	21	11	7
Days Maximum Temp. ≥ 90°F	0	0	0	1	6	16	24	20	10	1	0	0	78
Days Maximum Temp. ≤ 32°F	0	0	0	0	0	0	0	0	0	0	0	0	0
Days Minimum Temp. ≤ 32°F	7	4	1	0	0	0	0	0	0	0	1	5	18
Days Minimum Temp. ≤ 0°F	0	0	0	0	0	0	0	0	0	0	0	0	0
Heating Degree Days (base 65°F)	373	269	150	51	4	0	0	0	0	27	146	305	1,325
Cooling Degree Days (base 65°F)	12	25	60	125	289	459	557	528	405	198	70	22	2,750
Mean Precipitation (in.)	3.73	3.40	4.21	3.11	3.51	5.37	6.04	6.99	7.62	3.98	2.28	2.64	52.88
Maximum Precipitation (in.)	10.2	8.8	10.2	11.6	10.4	14.0	16.2	16.2	19.4	13.4	5.0	7.1	79.6
Minimum Precipitation (in.)	0.1	0.5	0.7	0.1	0.2	1.6	2.0	2.2	1.0	0.3	trace	trace	31.2
Maximum 24-hr. Precipitation (in.)	2.9	4.9	7.1	7.3	5.4	5.9	7.3	7.8	10.+	7.8	2.8	2.9	10.+
Days With ≥ 0.1" Precipitation	6	5	6	4	5	9	10	10	9	5	4	5	78
Days With ≥ 1.0" Precipitation	1	1	1	1	1	1	2	2	2	1	1	1	15
Mean Snowfall (in.)	trace	trace	trace	trace	0.0	trace	trace	0.0	0.0	0.0	0.0	trace	trace
Maximum Snowfall (in.)	trace	2	1	0	0	0	0	0	0	0	0	1	2
Maximum 24-hr. Snowfall (in.)	trace	2	1	0	0	0	0	0	0	0	0	1	2
Days With ≥ 1.0" Snow Depth	0	0	0	0	0	0	0	0	0	0	0	0	0
Thunderstorm Days	1	2	3	4	6	11	16	13	7	2	1	1	67
Foggy Days	18	14	15	13	14	13	11	15	16	17	16	17	179
Predominant Sky Cover	OVR	OVR	OVR	CLR	SCT	BRK	BRK	SCT	SCT	CLR	CLR	OVR	OVR
Mean Relative Humidity 7am (%)	87	86	87	87	87	88	89	92	92	91	90	88	89
Mean Relative Humidity 4pm (%)	57	53	50	49	54	61	64	66	67	62	59	59	58
Mean Dewpoint (°F)	44	46	50	56	63	70	72	73	70	62	53	47	59
Prevailing Wind Direction	NW	NW	WSW	SE	SE	SW	SW	SW	NE	NE	NW	NW	SW
Prevailing Wind Speed (mph)	9	10	10	10	10	8	7	7	10	12	8	9	9
Maximum Wind Gust (mph)	64	62	66	67	71	67	69	66	59	43	49	61	71

Key West Int'l Airport

Key West is located at the end of the Overseas Highway and near the western end of the Florida Keys, which are a chain of islands swinging in a southwesterly arc from the southeast coast of the Florida peninsula. The nearest point of the mainland is about 60 statute miles to the northeast, while Cuba at its closest point is 98 miles south. The city occupies the island of the same name which is three and a half miles long and one mile wide. Its mean elevation is around eight feet. The maximum elevation of 18 feet covers only about one acre in the western portion. Soil is a thin layer of sand, or marlfill, overlying a stratum of Oolitic limestone. Vegetation on the eastern end of the island is scanty, chiefly of low growth. The western end, where settlement and landscaping are older, has a little heavier growth. The airport and Weather Service Office are located on the southeast shore on partially filled mangrove swamp.

The waters surrounding the key are quite shallow up to the mainland on the northeast and for six miles to the reef on the south. There is little wave action because the reef disrupts any established wave pattern.

Because of the nearness of the Gulf Stream in the Straits of Florida, about 12 miles south and southeast, and the tempering effects of the Gulf of Mexico to the west and north, Key West has a notably mild, tropical-maritime climate in which the average temperatures during the winter are about 14 degrees lower than in summer. Cold fronts are strongly modified by the warm water as they move in from northerly quadrants in winter. There is no known record of frost, ice, sleet, or snow in Key West. Prevailing easterly tradewinds and sea breezes suppress the usual summertime heating. Diurnal variations throughout the year average only about 10 degrees.

Precipitation is characterized by dry and wet seasons. The period of December through April receives abundant sunshine and slightly less than 25 percent of the annual rainfall. This rainfall usually occurs in advance of cold fronts in a few heavy showers, or occasionally five to eight light showers per month. June through October is normally the wet season, receiving approximately 53 percent of the yearly total in numerous showers and thunderstorms. Early morning is the favored time for diurnal showers. Easterly waves during this season occasionally bring excessive rainfall, while infrequent hurricanes may be accompanied by unusually heavy amounts. Humidity remains relatively high during the entire year.

Key West Int'l Airport *Monroe County*   Elevation: 3 ft.   Latitude: 24° 33' N   Longitude: 81° 45' W

	JAN	FEB	MAR	APR	MAY	JUN	JUL	AUG	SEP	OCT	NOV	DEC	YEAR
Mean Maximum Temp. (°F)	75.2	75.8	78.7	81.9	85.3	88.0	89.3	89.4	88.1	84.7	80.5	76.8	82.8
Mean Temp. (°F)	70.2	70.7	73.7	77.1	80.6	83.4	84.5	84.3	83.3	80.3	76.2	72.1	78.0
Mean Minimum Temp. (°F)	65.1	65.6	68.8	72.3	75.9	78.7	79.6	79.2	78.4	75.7	71.9	67.3	73.2
Extreme Maximum Temp. (°F)	86	85	88	90	91	93	94	98	93	91	89	86	98
Extreme Minimum Temp. (°F)	41	45	47	48	64	70	71	71	69	65	50	44	41
Days Maximum Temp. ≥ 90°F	0	0	0	0	1	7	15	16	7	0	0	0	46
Days Maximum Temp. ≤ 32°F	0	0	0	0	0	0	0	0	0	0	0	0	0
Days Minimum Temp. ≤ 32°F	0	0	0	0	0	0	0	0	0	0	0	0	0
Days Minimum Temp. ≤ 0°F	0	0	0	0	0	0	0	0	0	0	0	0	0
Heating Degree Days (base 65°F)	25	17	6	0	0	0	0	0	0	0	0	13	61
Cooling Degree Days (base 65°F)	186	199	272	363	491	566	616	612	557	482	348	234	4,926
Mean Precipitation (in.)	2.47	1.56	1.88	1.99	3.52	4.52	3.53	5.24	5.50	4.40	2.63	2.08	39.32
Maximum Precipitation (in.)	17.6	4.5	9.7	10.6	12.9	14.4	11.7	10.4	18.4	21.6	27.7	11.2	62.9
Minimum Precipitation (in.)	trace	trace	trace	0	0.3	0.3	0.4	2.2	1.7	0.7	trace	0.1	20.0
Maximum 24-hr. Precipitation (in.)	6.4	2.5	5.3	6.2	7.2	5.1	3.0	3.3	6.1	6.5	23.+	6.7	23.+
Days With ≥ 0.1" Precipitation	4	3	3	3	4	7	7	9	10	6	3	3	62
Days With ≥ 1.0" Precipitation	1	0	0	1	1	1	1	2	1	1	1	1	11
Mean Snowfall (in.)	0.0	0.0	0.0	0.0	0.0	0.0	0.0	0.0	0.0	0.0	0.0	0.0	0.0
Maximum Snowfall (in.)	0	0	0	0	0	0	0	0	0	0	0	0	0
Maximum 24-hr. Snowfall (in.)	0	0	0	0	0	0	0	0	0	0	0	0	0
Days With ≥ 1.0" Snow Depth	0	0	0	0	0	0	0	0	0	0	0	0	0
Thunderstorm Days	1	1	2	2	4	10	13	15	12	4	1	1	66
Foggy Days	3	1	1	< 1	< 1	< 1	< 1	< 1	< 1	< 1	1	1	7
Predominant Sky Cover	SCT	SCT	SCT	SCT	SCT	SCT	SCT	SCT	SCT	SCT	SCT	SCT	SCT
Mean Relative Humidity 7am (%)	82	81	79	76	76	78	76	78	81	82	83	82	79
Mean Relative Humidity 4pm (%)	69	67	66	63	65	68	66	67	69	69	70	70	68
Mean Dewpoint (°F)	62	62	64	66	70	74	74	74	74	71	67	63	69
Prevailing Wind Direction	NE	NE	SE	ESE	ESE	SE	ESE	ESE	ESE	ENE	NE	NE	ESE
Prevailing Wind Speed (mph)	12	12	13	14	13	10	12	12	12	13	13	12	12
Maximum Wind Gust (mph)	58	55	75	78	53	70	67	56	87	90	69	54	90

Miami Int'l Airport

Miami is located on the lower east coast of Florida. To the east of the city lies Biscayne Bay, an arm of the ocean, about 15 miles long and three miles wide. East of the bay is the island of Miami Beach, a mile or less wide and about 10 miles long, and beyond Miami Beach is the Atlantic Ocean. The surrounding countryside is level and sparsely wooded.

The climate of Miami is essentially subtropical marine, featured by a long and warm summer, with abundant rainfall, followed by a mild, dry winter. The marine influence is evidenced by the low daily range of temperature and the rapid warming of cold air masses which pass to the east of the state. The Miami area is subject to winds from the east or southeast about half the time, and in several specific respects has a climate whose features differ from those farther inland.

One of these features is the annual precipitation for the area. During the early morning hours more rainfall occurs at Miami Beach than at the airport, while during the afternoon the reverse is true. The airport office is about nine miles inland.

An even more striking difference appears in the annual number of days with temperatures reaching 90 degrees or higher, with inland stations having about four times more than the beach. Minimum temperature contrasts also are particularly marked under proper conditions, with the difference between inland locations and the Miami Beach station frequently reaching to 15 degrees or more, especially in winter.

Freezing temperatures occur occasionally in the suburbs and farming districts southwest, west, and northwest of the city, but rarely near the ocean.

Hurricanes occasionally affect the area. The months of greatest frequency are September and October. Destructive tornadoes are very rare. Funnel clouds are occasionally sighted and a few touch the ground briefly but significant damage is seldom reported. Waterspouts are often visible from the beaches during the summer months, however, significant damage is seldom reported. June, July, and August have the highest frequency of dangerous lightning events.

Miami Int'l Airport *Miami-Dade County*   Elevation: 32 ft.   Latitude: 25° 49' N   Longitude: 80° 18' W

	JAN	FEB	MAR	APR	MAY	JUN	JUL	AUG	SEP	OCT	NOV	DEC	YEAR
Mean Maximum Temp. (°F)	75.9	76.8	79.6	82.8	86.0	88.4	89.7	89.7	88.3	85.1	80.9	77.4	83.4
Mean Temp. (°F)	68.0	69.0	72.1	75.6	79.3	82.0	83.3	83.4	82.3	79.0	74.4	70.1	76.6
Mean Minimum Temp. (°F)	60.1	61.1	64.7	68.4	72.5	75.6	76.9	77.0	76.2	72.8	67.9	62.8	69.7
Extreme Maximum Temp. (°F)	88	89	92	96	96	98	98	98	97	95	89	87	98
Extreme Minimum Temp. (°F)	30	37	32	46	56	60	69	69	68	53	40	30	30
Days Maximum Temp. ≥ 90°F	0	0	0	2	5	11	17	17	11	3	0	0	66
Days Maximum Temp. ≤ 32°F	0	0	0	0	0	0	0	0	0	0	0	0	0
Days Minimum Temp. ≤ 32°F	0	0	0	0	0	0	0	0	0	0	0	0	0
Days Minimum Temp. ≤ 0°F	0	0	0	0	0	0	0	0	0	0	0	0	0
Heating Degree Days (base 65°F)	58	37	14	1	0	0	0	0	0	0	5	36	151
Cooling Degree Days (base 65°F)	157	170	237	321	454	530	590	589	533	455	306	201	4,543
Mean Precipitation (in.)	1.95	2.09	2.64	3.28	5.82	8.55	5.77	8.51	8.32	5.67	3.42	1.98	58.00
Maximum Precipitation (in.)	6.7	8.1	10.6	10.2	18.5	22.4	11.2	16.6	24.4	21.6	13.8	6.4	89.3
Minimum Precipitation (in.)	trace	0.1	trace	0	0.4	2.0	1.8	1.6	2.6	1.3	0.1	0.1	37.0
Maximum 24-hr. Precipitation (in.)	2.4	4.5	7.1	7.3	12.+	6.6	4.5	6.6	6.1	9.9	7.6	4.4	12.+
Days With ≥ 0.1" Precipitation	4	4	4	4	8	11	11	12	12	8	5	3	86
Days With ≥ 1.0" Precipitation	0	0	1	1	2	3	2	2	3	2	1	0	17
Mean Snowfall (in.)	0.0	0.0	0.0	0.0	trace	0.0	0.0	0.0	0.0	0.0	0.0	0.0	trace
Maximum Snowfall (in.)	0	0	0	0	0	0	0	0	0	0	0	0	0
Maximum 24-hr. Snowfall (in.)	0	0	0	0	0	0	0	0	0	0	0	0	0
Days With ≥ 1.0" Snow Depth	0	0	0	0	0	0	0	0	0	0	0	0	0
Thunderstorm Days	1	1	2	3	6	12	15	16	12	5	1	1	75
Foggy Days	7	5	4	3	3	1	1	1	1	3	5	6	40
Predominant Sky Cover	SCT	SCT	SCT	SCT	SCT	SCT	SCT	SCT	SCT	SCT	SCT	SCT	SCT
Mean Relative Humidity 7am (%)	85	84	82	80	81	84	84	86	88	87	85	84	84
Mean Relative Humidity 4pm (%)	60	58	57	57	61	68	66	67	69	65	63	60	63
Mean Dewpoint (°F)	58	58	60	63	68	72	73	74	73	69	64	59	66
Prevailing Wind Direction	NNW	ESE	SE	ESE	ESE	ESE	ESE	ESE	E	ENE	ENE	NNW	ESE
Prevailing Wind Speed (mph)	9	12	12	12	10	10	9	9	9	12	13	9	10
Maximum Wind Gust (mph)	58	61	60	78	62	68	56	115	94	125	53	46	125

Orlando Int'l Airport

Orlando is located in the central section of the Florida peninsula, surrounded by many lakes. Relative humidities remain high the year-round, with values near 90 percent at night and 40 to 50 percent in the afternoon. On some winter days, the humidity may drop to 20 percent.

The rainy season extends from June through September, sometimes through October when tropical storms are near. During this period, scattered afternoon thunderstorms are an almost daily occurrence, and these bring a drop in temperature to make the climate bearable. Summer temperatures above 95 degrees are rather rare. There is usually a breeze which contributes to the general comfort.

During the winter months rainfall is light. While temperatures, on infrequent occasion, may drop at night to near freezing, they rise rapidly during the day and, in brilliant sunshine, afternoons are pleasant.

Frozen precipitation in the form of snowflakes, snow pellets, or sleet is rare. However, hail is occasionally reported during thunderstorms.

Hurricanes are usually not considered a great threat to Orlando, since, to reach this area, they must pass over a substantial stretch of land and, in so doing, lose much of their punch. Sustained hurricane winds of 75 mph or higher rarely occur. Orlando, being inland, is relatively safe from high water, although heavy rains sometimes briefly flood sections of the city.

Orlando Int'l Airport *Orange County*   Elevation: 95 ft.   Latitude: 28° 26' N   Longitude: 81° 20' W

	JAN	FEB	MAR	APR	MAY	JUN	JUL	AUG	SEP	OCT	NOV	DEC	YEAR
Mean Maximum Temp. (°F)	70.9	73.8	78.3	82.8	87.9	90.8	91.9	91.6	89.8	84.5	78.6	72.9	82.8
Mean Temp. (°F)	59.9	62.6	67.0	71.4	77.1	81.3	82.6	82.7	81.2	75.2	68.7	62.5	72.7
Mean Minimum Temp. (°F)	48.9	51.3	55.7	59.9	66.2	71.8	73.3	73.8	72.5	65.8	58.6	52.2	62.5
Extreme Maximum Temp. (°F)	87	89	92	95	97	100	101	100	98	95	89	90	101
Extreme Minimum Temp. (°F)	19	26	25	38	48	53	64	65	57	44	35	20	19
Days Maximum Temp. ≥ 90°F	0	0	0	3	12	20	25	25	19	4	0	0	108
Days Maximum Temp. ≤ 32°F	0	0	0	0	0	0	0	0	0	0	0	0	0
Days Minimum Temp. ≤ 32°F	2	1	0	0	0	0	0	0	0	0	0	1	4
Days Minimum Temp. ≤ 0°F	0	0	0	0	0	0	0	0	0	0	0	0	0
Heating Degree Days (base 65°F)	197	126	59	9	1	0	0	0	0	3	42	141	578
Cooling Degree Days (base 65°F)	50	67	124	203	382	498	559	562	491	336	160	75	3,507
Mean Precipitation (in.)	2.51	2.43	3.70	2.51	3.85	7.42	7.36	6.38	5.89	2.87	2.44	2.34	49.70
Maximum Precipitation (in.)	7.2	8.3	11.4	9.1	10.4	15.3	13.3	11.6	10.3	5.6	10.3	5.3	67.8
Minimum Precipitation (in.)	0.2	0.1	1.1	0.1	0.5	3.5	2.6	2.9	2.5	0.4	0.2	0.2	31.7
Maximum 24-hr. Precipitation (in.)	4.2	2.4	4.1	5.1	3.1	4.4	4.1	3.0	3.6	2.4	3.8	2.8	5.1
Days With ≥ 0.1" Precipitation	4	4	5	3	6	10	11	11	9	5	4	4	76
Days With ≥ 1.0" Precipitation	1	1	1	1	1	2	2	2	2	1	1	1	16
Mean Snowfall (in.)	trace	0.0	trace	trace	trace	0.0	trace	trace	0.0	0.0	0.0	0.0	trace
Maximum Snowfall (in.)	trace	0	0	0	0	0	0	0	0	0	0	0	trace
Maximum 24-hr. Snowfall (in.)	trace	0	0	0	0	0	0	0	0	0	0	0	trace
Days With ≥ 1.0" Snow Depth	0	0	0	0	0	0	0	0	0	0	0	0	0
Thunderstorm Days	1	2	3	3	8	16	19	19	11	3	1	1	87
Foggy Days	16	14	15	13	13	12	10	9	11	14	16	17	160
Predominant Sky Cover	OVR	OVR	OVR	CLR	SCT	BRK	BRK	BRK	BRK	SCT	OVR	OVR	BRK
Mean Relative Humidity 7am (%)	88	89	90	88	89	91	91	93	93	91	91	90	90
Mean Relative Humidity 4pm (%)	54	50	48	47	51	61	64	66	65	59	58	58	57
Mean Dewpoint (°F)	50	51	55	58	65	71	72	73	72	65	59	53	62
Prevailing Wind Direction	N	N	S	E	E	S	S	E	NE	N	N	N	N
Prevailing Wind Speed (mph)	9	9	10	9	9	8	8	8	8	8	9	9	9
Maximum Wind Gust (mph)	48	51	62	56	68	62	74	62	56	40	49	44	74

Pensacola Regional Airport

Pensacola is situated on a somewhat hilly, sandy slope which borders Pensacola Bay, an expanse of deep water several miles in width. The bay is separated from the Gulf of Mexico by a long, narrow island that forms a natural breakwater for the harbor. Elevations in the city range from a few feet above sea level to more than 100 feet in portions of the residential sections, and most of the city is well above storm tides.

The Gulf of Mexico, about six miles distant, moderates the climate of Pensacola by tempering the cold Northers of winter and causing cool and refreshing sea breezes during the daytime in summer.

The average temperature for the summer months is around 80 degrees with an average daily range of 12.5 degrees. Temperatures of 90 degrees or higher occur on the average of 39 times yearly. A temperature of 100 degrees or higher occurs occasionally. The average winter temperature is in the low to mid 50s with an average daily range of 15.7 degrees. On the average, the temperature falls to freezing or below on only nine days of the year. The average occurrence of the last temperature as low as 32 degrees in spring is mid-February, and the average earliest occurrence in autumn is early December, making the average growing season 292 days. Severe cold waves are rather infrequent.

Rainfall is usually well distributed through the year with the greatest frequency normally being in July and August. The greatest monthly rainfall occurs, on average, in July and least in October. Much of the rainfall in summer occurs during the daylight hours and comes in the form of thunderstorms, often producing excessive amounts. Winter rains are frequently lighter, but extend over longer periods. Snow has occurred in about 30 percent of the winters but measurable amounts are less frequent.

A moderate sea breeze usually blows off the Gulf of Mexico during most of the day in summer. Seriously destructive hurricanes are occasionally experienced in this vicinity but loss of life is rare. Hurricanes have occurred from early July to mid-October.

Pensacola Regional Airport *Escambia Co.*   Elevation: 111 ft.   Latitude: 30° 29' N   Longitude: 87° 11' W

	JAN	FEB	MAR	APR	MAY	JUN	JUL	AUG	SEP	OCT	NOV	DEC	YEAR
Mean Maximum Temp. (°F)	60.8	64.1	70.0	76.3	83.4	89.0	90.5	90.0	87.1	79.3	70.3	63.6	77.0
Mean Temp. (°F)	51.7	54.6	60.9	67.1	74.6	80.6	82.5	82.1	78.9	69.6	60.7	54.3	68.1
Mean Minimum Temp. (°F)	42.6	45.1	51.7	57.9	65.8	72.1	74.5	74.2	70.6	59.8	51.0	45.0	59.2
Extreme Maximum Temp. (°F)	80	82	86	96	98	101	106	104	98	92	85	81	106
Extreme Minimum Temp. (°F)	5	15	22	33	48	56	66	62	49	32	25	11	5
Days Maximum Temp. ≥ 90°F	0	0	0	0	3	13	19	18	10	0	0	0	63
Days Maximum Temp. ≤ 32°F	0	0	0	0	0	0	0	0	0	0	0	0	0
Days Minimum Temp. ≤ 32°F	6	3	1	0	0	0	0	0	0	0	1	4	15
Days Minimum Temp. ≤ 0°F	0	0	0	0	0	0	0	0	0	0	0	0	0
Heating Degree Days (base 65°F)	415	297	166	44	1	0	0	0	1	32	172	344	1,472
Cooling Degree Days (base 65°F)	6	11	41	106	302	473	552	541	413	179	48	18	2,690
Mean Precipitation (in.)	5.44	4.90	6.53	3.90	4.65	6.59	8.03	7.01	5.57	4.35	4.23	3.98	65.18
Maximum Precipitation (in.)	18.8	11.7	13.0	15.5	10.3	21.1	20.4	14.1	15.7	14.8	12.0	15.3	92.7
Minimum Precipitation (in.)	0.6	0.5	0.8	0.4	0.1	0.3	1.7	0.9	0.4	0	0.3	0.6	28.5
Maximum 24-hr. Precipitation (in.)	5.4	4.7	11.+	5.9	4.9	6.4	5.1	6.3	9.3	5.0	3.3	3.5	11.+
Days With ≥ 0.1" Precipitation	7	6	7	5	5	7	10	9	6	4	5	6	77
Days With ≥ 1.0" Precipitation	2	1	2	1	2	2	2	2	2	1	1	1	19
Mean Snowfall (in.)	trace	trace	trace	0.0	0.0	0.0	trace	0.0	0.0	0.0	0.0	trace	trace
Maximum Snowfall (in.)	3	2	2	0	0	0	0	0	0	0	0	trace	3
Maximum 24-hr. Snowfall (in.)	2	2	2	0	0	0	0	0	0	0	0	trace	2
Days With ≥ 1.0" Snow Depth	0	0	0	0	0	0	0	0	0	0	0	0	0
Thunderstorm Days	2	3	4	4	5	10	15	14	7	2	2	1	69
Foggy Days	18	15	18	16	15	13	12	15	14	14	14	17	181
Predominant Sky Cover	OVR	OVR	OVR	CLR	SCT	SCT	SCT	SCT	SCT	CLR	CLR	OVR	SCT
Mean Relative Humidity 7am (%)	84	84	82	80	78	79	81	83	83	81	83	85	82
Mean Relative Humidity 4pm (%)	64	62	60	59	61	63	67	67	64	59	63	67	63
Mean Dewpoint (°F)	44	47	50	56	65	71	73	73	68	59	51	46	58
Prevailing Wind Direction	NNW	N	NNW	SE	SSE	SSW	SW	NE	N	N	NNW	N	N
Prevailing Wind Speed (mph)	10	10	12	12	10	9	8	7	8	8	10	9	9
Maximum Wind Gust (mph)	na	na	na	na	na	na	na	na	na	na	na	na	na

Tallahassee Municipal Airport

Located about 20 miles from the Gulf of Mexico, Tallahassee has a mild, moist climate of the Gulf States. In contrast to the southern part of the Florida Peninsula, there is a definite march of the four seasons with considerable winter rainfall and quite a bit less winter sunshine. The annual average temperature is about 68 degrees.

During the winter, topographic effects and cold air drainage into lower elevations produce a wide variation of low temperatures on cold, clear and calm nights. Freezing temperatures at the airport and surrounding suburban areas average about thirty-six occurrences each winter, but freezing temperatures in the city are about half that number. Temperatures of 25 degrees or lower in the suburban areas average about twelve times per winter, with temperatures dropping into the teens on occasions. Below zero temperatures are rarely recorded. Snow in Tallahassee is infrequent. The date for the last occurrence of 32 degrees is February 28, but has been as late as April 8. The date of the first occurrence of 32 degrees in the fall is November 25, but has been as early as October 18. This gives an average growing season of some 270 days.

Summer is the least pleasant time of the year. Thunderstorms occur every other day. Rather high temperatures and very high humidities cause considerable discomfort. Occurrences of temperatures of 90 degrees or higher average about 90 days per year, but only about 22 of these days have readings as high as 95 degrees. Temperatures reach 100 degrees once or twice in less than half the years. In general, summertime cloudiness holds the high temperatures about 90 degrees.

July is the wettest month followed by August, September, and June. The driest months are October, November, and April.

Extended droughts are infrequent, shorter droughts are rather common, but both are significant. Droughts, or rainfall deficiencies, when extended over months or years, cause the disappearance of large lakes and cypress ponds. Droughts of shorter duration create fire danger in the nearby forests.

High winds are infrequent and of short duration, usually associated with strong cold fronts in the late winter and early spring months. The likelihood of a hurricane occurrence in our coastal area is about once every 17 years with fringe effects felt about once every five years.

Tallahassee Municipal Airport *Leon County*   Elevation: 52 ft.   Latitude: 30° 24' N   Longitude: 84° 21' W

	JAN	FEB	MAR	APR	MAY	JUN	JUL	AUG	SEP	OCT	NOV	DEC	YEAR
Mean Maximum Temp. (°F)	63.5	67.2	73.8	80.1	86.3	90.8	91.8	91.3	88.7	81.2	72.9	66.1	79.5
Mean Temp. (°F)	51.3	54.2	60.5	66.0	73.6	79.6	81.6	81.4	78.4	68.7	60.0	53.6	67.4
Mean Minimum Temp. (°F)	39.1	41.1	47.1	51.8	60.9	68.4	71.3	71.4	68.1	56.3	47.0	41.2	55.3
Extreme Maximum Temp. (°F)	82	85	89	95	99	103	103	103	99	94	87	84	103
Extreme Minimum Temp. (°F)	6	14	20	29	34	46	59	57	45	30	13	13	6
Days Maximum Temp. ≥ 90°F	0	0	0	1	8	19	24	23	16	2	0	0	93
Days Maximum Temp. ≤ 32°F	0	0	0	0	0	0	0	0	0	0	0	0	0
Days Minimum Temp. ≤ 32°F	11	7	3	0	0	0	0	0	0	0	4	9	34
Days Minimum Temp. ≤ 0°F	0	0	0	0	0	0	0	0	0	0	0	0	0
Heating Degree Days (base 65°F)	427	312	180	67	5	0	0	0	1	45	193	362	1,592
Cooling Degree Days (base 65°F)	6	15	46	101	288	457	533	526	406	181	53	15	2,627
Mean Precipitation (in.)	5.49	4.74	6.74	3.67	5.09	6.99	8.41	7.06	4.78	3.38	3.84	4.12	64.31
Maximum Precipitation (in.)	18.9	11.5	16.5	13.1	11.7	17.4	20.1	15.7	20.3	12.3	10.4	12.6	104.
Minimum Precipitation (in.)	0.2	0.8	1.0	0.3	trace	2.1	2.3	2.4	0.1	trace	0.4	0.9	31.0
Maximum 24-hr. Precipitation (in.)	4.9	5.6	7.1	4.9	5.1	6.7	8.2	7.1	8.9	6.6	4.9	5.0	8.9
Days With ≥ 0.1" Precipitation	7	6	6	4	6	9	11	10	7	4	4	6	80
Days With ≥ 1.0" Precipitation	2	2	2	1	2	2	2	2	1	1	1	1	19
Mean Snowfall (in.)	trace	trace	trace	0.0	*0.0*	trace	trace	0.0	trace	0.0	0.0	trace	*trace*
Maximum Snowfall (in.)	trace	3	trace	0	0	0	0	0	0	0	0	1	3
Maximum 24-hr. Snowfall (in.)	trace	2	trace	0	0	0	0	0	0	0	0	1	2
Days With ≥ 1.0" Snow Depth	0	0	0	0	0	0	0	0	0	0	0	0	0
Thunderstorm Days	2	2	4	4	8	14	19	16	8	2	2	2	83
Foggy Days	17	16	18	17	19	18	17	19	18	16	16	17	208
Predominant Sky Cover	OVR	OVR	OVR	CLR	SCT	SCT	BRK	SCT	SCT	CLR	CLR	OVR	OVR
Mean Relative Humidity 7am (%)	87	87	88	89	89	91	93	94	92	90	89	87	90
Mean Relative Humidity 4pm (%)	54	51	49	46	50	58	66	64	60	51	52	55	55
Mean Dewpoint (°F)	42	44	49	55	62	69	72	72	69	58	49	44	57
Prevailing Wind Direction	N	N	S	S	S	S	S	E	ENE	N	N	N	N
Prevailing Wind Speed (mph)	8	9	10	10	9	8	7	6	8	7	8	8	8
Maximum Wind Gust (mph)	53	51	53	54	81	76	67	64	83	58	68	43	83

Tampa Int'l Airport

Tampa is on west central coast of the Florida Peninsula. Very near the Gulf of Mexico at the upper end of Tampa Bay, land and sea breezes modify the subtropical climate. Major rivers flowing into the area are the Hillsborough, the Alafia, and the Little Manatee.

Winters are mild. Summers are long, rather warm, and humid. Low temperatures are about 50 degrees in the winter and 70 degrees during the summer. Afternoon highs range from the low 70s in the winter to around 90 degrees from June through September. Invasions of cold northern air produce an occasional cool winter morning. Freezing temperatures occur on one or two mornings per year during December, January, and February. In some years no freezing temperatures occur. Temperatures rarely fail to recover to the 60s on the cooler winter days. Temperatures above the low 90s are uncommon because of the afternoon sea breezes and thunderstorms. An outstanding feature of the Tampa climate is the summer thunderstorm season. Most of the thunderstorms occur in the late afternoon hours from June through September. The resulting sudden drop in temperature from about 90 degrees to around 70 degrees makes for a pleasant change. Between a dry spring and a dry fall, some 30 inches of rain, about 60 percent of the annual total, falls during the summer months. Snowfall is very rare.

A large part of the generally flat sandy land near the coast has an elevation of under 15 feet above sea level. This does make the area vulnerable to tidal surges. Tropical storms threaten the area on a few occasions most years. The greatest risk of hurricanes has been during the months of June and October. Many hurricanes, by replenishing the soil moisture and raising the water table, do far more good than harm. The heaviest rains in a 24-hour period, around 12 inches, have been associated with hurricanes.

Fittingly named the Suncoast, the sun shines more than 65 percent of the possible, with the sunniest months being April and May. Afternoon humidities are usually 60 percent or higher in the summer months, but range from 50 to 60 percent the remainder of the year.

Night ground fogs occur frequently during the cooler winter months. Prevailing winds are easterly, but westerly afternoon and early evening sea breezes occur most months of the year. Winds in excess of 25 mph are not common and usually occur only with thunderstorms or tropical disturbances.

Based on the 1951-1980 period, the average first occurrence of 32 degrees Fahrenheit in the fall is December 26 and the average last occurrence in the spring is February 3.

Tampa Int'l Airport *Hillsborough County*   Elevation: 16 ft.   Latitude: 27° 58' N   Longitude: 82° 32' W

	JAN	FEB	MAR	APR	MAY	JUN	JUL	AUG	SEP	OCT	NOV	DEC	YEAR
Mean Maximum Temp. (°F)	70.5	72.2	76.9	81.5	87.2	89.9	90.7	90.6	89.3	84.4	78.2	72.6	82.0
Mean Temp. (°F)	60.6	62.2	67.0	71.5	77.6	81.7	82.8	82.8	81.3	75.4	68.5	62.8	72.8
Mean Minimum Temp. (°F)	50.6	52.1	56.9	61.4	68.0	73.5	74.8	74.8	73.3	66.3	58.8	53.0	63.6
Extreme Maximum Temp. (°F)	86	88	89	93	98	99	97	98	96	94	90	86	99
Extreme Minimum Temp. (°F)	21	25	29	40	49	53	63	67	57	44	23	19	19
Days Maximum Temp. ≥ 90°F	0	0	0	1	8	17	22	22	17	3	0	0	90
Days Maximum Temp. ≤ 32°F	0	0	0	0	0	0	0	0	0	0	0	0	0
Days Minimum Temp. ≤ 32°F	1	1	0	0	0	0	0	0	0	0	0	1	3
Days Minimum Temp. ≤ 0°F	0	0	0	0	0	0	0	0	0	0	0	0	0
Heating Degree Days (base 65°F)	187	134	61	11	0	0	0	0	0	3	47	139	582
Cooling Degree Days (base 65°F)	54	70	124	209	405	513	561	562	494	337	166	80	3,575
Mean Precipitation (in.)	2.31	2.80	3.03	1.81	2.99	5.42	6.31	7.70	6.50	2.32	1.59	2.29	45.07
Maximum Precipitation (in.)	8.0	7.9	12.6	6.6	17.6	13.8	20.6	18.6	14.0	7.4	6.7	6.7	76.6
Minimum Precipitation (in.)	trace	0.2	0.1	trace	0.1	1.9	1.6	2.3	1.3	0.1	trace	0.1	28.9
Maximum 24-hr. Precipitation (in.)	3.3	3.1	4.3	3.3	11.+	5.5	9.1	4.9	4.4	2.7	3.8	2.7	11.+
Days With ≥ 0.1" Precipitation	4	4	4	3	4	8	10	11	8	4	3	4	67
Days With ≥ 1.0" Precipitation	1	1	1	0	1	2	2	3	2	1	0	1	15
Mean Snowfall (in.)	trace	0.0	trace	trace	0.0	0.0	trace	0.0	0.0	0.0	0.0	trace	trace
Maximum Snowfall (in.)	trace	trace	trace	0	0	0	0	0	0	0	0	trace	trace
Maximum 24-hr. Snowfall (in.)	trace	trace	trace	0	0	0	0	0	0	0	0	trace	trace
Days With ≥ 1.0" Snow Depth	0	0	0	0	0	0	0	0	0	0	0	0	0
Thunderstorm Days	1	2	3	3	5	14	21	20	12	3	1	1	86
Foggy Days	15	13	13	10	10	8	6	8	9	9	12	14	127
Predominant Sky Cover	OVR	OVR	SCT	CLR	SCT	SCT	BRK	BRK	SCT	SCT	CLR	CLR	SCT
Mean Relative Humidity 7am (%)	87	87	87	86	85	86	88	90	91	89	88	87	88
Mean Relative Humidity 4pm (%)	57	55	54	51	52	60	65	66	64	57	56	58	58
Mean Dewpoint (°F)	51	52	56	60	65	71	73	73	72	65	58	53	62
Prevailing Wind Direction	NE	E	E	E	E	W	E	E	ENE	NE	NE	NE	ENE
Prevailing Wind Speed (mph)	8	8	8	9	9	10	7	7	8	9	8	8	8
Maximum Wind Gust (mph)	55	73	58	56	99	78	67	59	75	53	54	60	99

Vero Beach

Vero Beach is located on the southeast coast of Florida, separated from the Atlantic Ocean by the Inland Waterway and a narrow island offshore. Its climate is strongly influenced by this maritime location. Temperatures in summer rarely reach 100 degrees. The average maximum temperature in July and August is about 90 degrees. In winter the average minimum temperature is slightly above 50 degrees with record lows near 20 degrees. On average, only one day a year experiences freezing temperatures, usually in January.

Rainfall occurs in all seasons but most abundantly in summer when showers are common. Thunderstorms are present approximately 70 to 80 days a year. Monthly precipitation amounts in winter are about half those in summer, and are due in part to cold frontal systems traversing the region. Throughout the year, relative humidity at 7 A.M. tends to range from 80 to 90 percent. The 1 P.M. humidity ranges from 60 to 70 percent with lower values occurring in midafternoon when temperatures are the highest.

Vero Beach lies at the northern boundary of a tropical rainy region. Within that region during summer and fall there may be hurricane activity. Of those hurricanes that pass close to Vero Beach, many move northward offshore, some cross the peninsula of Florida moving generally eastward but being weakened by their passage over land, and some enter the coastal area from the Atlantic Ocean. The frequency of the latter group has been small, about five in 114 years.

Vero Beach *Indian River County*   Elevation: 19 ft.   Latitude: 27° 38' N   Longitude: 80° 27' W

	JAN	FEB	MAR	APR	MAY	JUN	JUL	AUG	SEP	OCT	NOV	DEC	YEAR
Mean Maximum Temp. (°F)	73.1	74.1	77.9	81.5	85.6	88.6	90.4	90.3	88.6	84.5	79.5	74.8	82.4
Mean Temp. (°F)	61.9	63.0	67.1	70.8	75.6	79.5	81.1	81.2	80.1	75.5	69.7	64.1	72.5
Mean Minimum Temp. (°F)	50.6	51.8	56.2	60.1	65.5	70.4	71.7	72.1	71.5	66.5	59.9	53.5	62.5
Extreme Maximum Temp. (°F)	86	89	92	95	97	98	99	97	96	93	90	87	99
Extreme Minimum Temp. (°F)	23	29	26	37	46	56	62	63	63	44	31	24	23
Days Maximum Temp. ≥ 90°F	0	0	0	2	5	13	21	21	13	2	0	0	77
Days Maximum Temp. ≤ 32°F	0	0	0	0	0	0	0	0	0	0	0	0	0
Days Minimum Temp. ≤ 32°F	1	1	0	0	0	0	0	0	0	0	0	0	2
Days Minimum Temp. ≤ 0°F	0	0	0	0	0	0	0	0	0	0	0	0	0
Heating Degree Days (base 65°F)	152	117	55	13	1	0	0	0	0	2	32	107	479
Cooling Degree Days (base 65°F)	61	73	123	188	334	448	515	516	459	342	185	89	3,333
Mean Precipitation (in.)	2.79	2.98	3.96	2.49	4.46	6.94	6.18	6.95	7.24	5.61	3.83	2.28	55.71
Maximum Precipitation (in.)	8.9	6.8	12.8	8.8	5.8	10.8	11.1	11.7	15.4	12.4	11.8	5.9	66.7
Minimum Precipitation (in.)	0.3	0.3	0.2	trace	0.3	1.5	2.9	2.0	1.7	0.8	0.3	0.2	35.2
Maximum 24-hr. Precipitation (in.)	2.8	2.5	6.8	4.1	2.7	2.6	3.4	6.4	7.2	4.5	4.8	2.6	7.2
Days With ≥ 0.1" Precipitation	5	5	5	5	7	9	10	10	11	8	5	4	84
Days With ≥ 1.0" Precipitation	1	1	1	1	1	2	2	2	2	1	1	0	15
Mean Snowfall (in.)	trace	0.0	0.0	0.0	0.0	0.0	0.0	0.0	0.0	0.0	0.0	0.0	trace
Maximum Snowfall (in.)	0	0	0	0	0	0	0	0	0	0	0	0	0
Maximum 24-hr. Snowfall (in.)	0	0	0	0	0	0	0	0	0	0	0	0	0
Days With ≥ 1.0" Snow Depth	0	0	0	0	0	0	0	0	0	0	0	0	0
Thunderstorm Days	1	1	3	4	6	12	16	15	10	4	1	< 1	73
Foggy Days	12	12	12	10	10	8	7	9	7	9	11	12	119
Predominant Sky Cover	SCT	SCT	SCT	SCT	SCT	SCT	SCT	SCT	SCT	SCT	SCT	SCT	SCT
Mean Relative Humidity 7am (%)	89	88	86	84	83	86	88	90	90	87	87	88	87
Mean Relative Humidity 4pm (%)	63	60	59	58	62	69	69	70	70	68	66	64	65
Mean Dewpoint (°F)	56	56	58	61	67	72	73	74	73	68	62	56	65
Prevailing Wind Direction	NW	ESE	SE	ESE	ESE	ESE	ESE	ESE	ENE	NE	NW	NW	ESE
Prevailing Wind Speed (mph)	10	12	14	12	12	12	10	10	10	12	9	9	12
Maximum Wind Gust (mph)	na	na	na	na	na	na	na	na	na	na	na	na	na

West Palm Beach Int'l Airport

West Palm Beach and Palm Beach, both located on the coastal sand ridge of southeastern Florida, are separated by Lake Worth, a portion of the Inland Waterway. The entire coastal ridge is only about five miles wide and in early times the Everglades reached to its western edge. Now most of the swampland has been drained and is devoted to agriculture, the peat-like muck soil being very fertile when fortified with certain lacking minerals. The Atlantic Ocean forms the eastern edge of Palm Beach, and the Gulf Stream flows northward about two miles offshore, its nearest approach to the Florida coast.

Because of its southerly location and marine influences, the Palm Beach area has a notably equable climate. Cold continental air must either travel over water or flow down the Florida Peninsula to reach the area, and in either case its cold is appreciably modified. Actually, the coldest weather, with infrequent frosts, is experienced the second or third night after the arrival of the cold air, due to the loss of heat through radiation cooling. The frequency of temperatures as low as the freezing mark is about one per three years at the National Weather Service Office, but in the farmlands farther from the coast the frequency of light freezes is much higher.

Summer temperatures are tempered by the ocean breeze, and by the frequent formation of cumulus clouds, which shade the land somewhat without completely obscuring the sun. Temperatures of 89 degrees or higher have occurred in all months of the year, but the 100 degree mark has rarely occurred. August is the warmest month and has an average maximum temperature of about 90 degrees. The occurrence of 90 degree temperatures in August is so common that such can be expected on more than two-thirds of the days. However, temperatures as high as 100 degrees rarely occur.

The moist, unstable air in this area results in frequent showers, usually of short duration. Thunderstorms are frequent during the summer, occurring every other day. Rainfall is heaviest during the summer and fall, the fall rainfall occurring from occasional heavy rains accompanying tropical disturbances. High winds, associated with hurricanes, have been estimated at about 140 mph in the city.

Flying weather is usually very good in this area, with instrument weather occurring only rarely. Heavy fog occurs on an average of only one morning a month in the winter and spring, and almost never in the summer and fall.

W. Palm Beach Int'l Airport *Palm Beach Co.*   Elevation: 16 ft.   Latitude: 26° 41' N   Longitude: 80° 06' W

	JAN	FEB	MAR	APR	MAY	JUN	JUL	AUG	SEP	OCT	NOV	DEC	YEAR
Mean Maximum Temp. (°F)	75.0	76.1	79.0	82.2	85.8	88.6	90.1	90.1	88.6	85.1	80.4	76.6	83.1
Mean Temp. (°F)	66.1	67.1	70.4	73.8	78.2	81.1	82.6	82.8	81.6	78.2	73.0	68.3	75.3
Mean Minimum Temp. (°F)	57.1	58.0	61.8	65.5	70.5	73.7	75.0	75.4	74.7	71.3	65.6	60.0	67.4
Extreme Maximum Temp. (°F)	87	89	94	99	96	98	99	97	95	95	91	88	99
Extreme Minimum Temp. (°F)	27	32	30	43	51	61	68	69	67	48	37	28	27
Days Maximum Temp. ≥ 90°F	0	0	0	2	4	11	19	20	11	2	0	0	69
Days Maximum Temp. ≤ 32°F	0	0	0	0	0	0	0	0	0	0	0	0	0
Days Minimum Temp. ≤ 32°F	0	0	0	0	0	0	0	0	0	0	0	0	0
Days Minimum Temp. ≤ 0°F	0	0	0	0	0	0	0	0	0	0	0	0	0
Heating Degree Days (base 65°F)	84	59	26	3	0	0	0	0	0	0	11	55	238
Cooling Degree Days (base 65°F)	122	137	196	274	416	501	561	564	512	426	266	164	4,139
Mean Precipitation (in.)	3.86	2.63	4.01	3.47	5.57	7.75	5.86	6.73	8.12	5.37	5.38	3.06	61.81
Maximum Precipitation (in.)	11.0	8.7	16.8	12.6	15.2	17.9	13.3	20.1	24.9	18.7	14.6	11.7	85.9
Minimum Precipitation (in.)	0.2	0.3	0.3	trace	0.4	1.1	1.2	1.7	1.8	1.2	0.2	0.1	37.3
Maximum 24-hr. Precipitation (in.)	6.8	2.9	5.6	6.5	7.0	4.9	5.3	8.0	5.7	7.1	7.4	6.4	8.0
Days With ≥ 0.1" Precipitation	5	5	5	4	7	11	10	11	12	8	6	5	89
Days With ≥ 1.0" Precipitation	1	1	1	1	2	3	1	2	3	1	2	1	19
Mean Snowfall (in.)	trace	0.0	trace	0.0	0.0	0.0	0.0	trace	0.0	0.0	0.0	0.0	trace
Maximum Snowfall (in.)	trace	0	0	0	0	0	0	0	0	0	0	0	trace
Maximum 24-hr. Snowfall (in.)	trace	0	0	0	0	0	0	0	0	0	0	0	trace
Days With ≥ 1.0" Snow Depth	0	0	0	0	0	0	0	0	0	0	0	0	0
Thunderstorm Days	1	1	3	4	7	13	16	16	11	4	2	1	79
Foggy Days	7	6	6	4	3	3	2	2	2	4	5	6	50
Predominant Sky Cover	SCT	SCT	SCT	SCT	SCT	SCT	SCT	SCT	SCT	SCT	SCT	SCT	SCT
Mean Relative Humidity 7am (%)	84	84	83	79	80	84	85	86	87	85	84	84	84
Mean Relative Humidity 4pm (%)	61	59	58	58	63	69	68	68	70	66	64	62	64
Mean Dewpoint (°F)	56	57	59	62	67	72	73	73	73	68	63	58	65
Prevailing Wind Direction	NW	NW	SE	SE	ESE	ESE	ESE	ESE	E	ENE	E	NW	E
Prevailing Wind Speed (mph)	10	10	13	13	12	10	10	10	12	14	14	10	12
Maximum Wind Gust (mph)	62	52	74	63	74	92	59	66	75	49	47	53	92

Arcadia *Desoto County*   Elevation: 62 ft.   Latitude: 27° 14' N   Longitude: 81° 51' W

	JAN	FEB	MAR	APR	MAY	JUN	JUL	AUG	SEP	OCT	NOV	DEC	YEAR
Mean Maximum Temp. (°F)	73.8	75.4	80.1	84.3	89.2	91.1	91.8	91.5	89.8	85.5	79.8	75.1	83.9
Mean Temp. (°F)	61.4	62.6	67.2	70.9	76.4	79.9	81.3	81.3	80.0	74.9	68.5	63.4	72.3
Mean Minimum Temp. (°F)	49.0	49.6	54.2	57.4	63.3	68.7	70.7	71.1	70.2	64.4	57.0	51.7	60.6
Extreme Maximum Temp. (°F)	88	92	94	98	100	104	100	98	97	98	92	89	104
Extreme Minimum Temp. (°F)	18	24	26	32	43	52	61	62	56	41	23	22	18
Days Maximum Temp. ≥ 90°F	0	0	1	5	16	22	26	26	19	5	0	0	120
Days Maximum Temp. ≤ 32°F	0	0	0	0	0	0	0	0	0	0	0	0	0
Days Minimum Temp. ≤ 32°F	3	2	0	0	0	0	0	0	0	0	0	2	7
Days Minimum Temp. ≤ 0°F	0	0	0	0	0	0	0	0	0	0	0	0	0
Heating Degree Days (base 65°F)	164	124	56	14	0	0	0	0	0	3	40	122	523
Cooling Degree Days (base 65°F)	51	64	121	189	364	460	519	515	457	326	154	79	3,299
Mean Precipitation (in.)	2.20	2.55	3.28	1.74	4.15	8.04	7.39	6.96	6.75	2.85	2.11	1.80	49.82
Days With ≥ 0.1" Precipitation	3	3	4	3	5	9	10	10	9	4	3	3	66
Days With ≥ 1.0" Precipitation	1	1	1	1	1	3	2	2	2	1	1	1	17
Mean Snowfall (in.)	0.0	0.0	0.0	0.0	0.0	0.0	0.0	0.0	0.0	0.0	0.0	0.0	0.0
Days With ≥ 1.0" Snow Depth	0	0	0	0	0	0	0	0	0	0	0	0	0

Archbold Bio Station *Highlands County*   Elevation: 137 ft.   Latitude: 27° 11' N   Longitude: 81° 21' W

	JAN	FEB	MAR	APR	MAY	JUN	JUL	AUG	SEP	OCT	NOV	DEC	YEAR
Mean Maximum Temp. (°F)	74.3	76.3	80.8	85.3	89.8	91.9	93.0	92.8	91.0	86.6	81.0	75.8	84.9
Mean Temp. (°F)	61.0	62.3	66.8	70.5	75.7	79.6	80.7	81.1	79.9	74.8	68.9	63.2	72.0
Mean Minimum Temp. (°F)	47.6	48.3	52.7	55.6	61.6	67.2	68.4	69.2	68.7	63.0	56.8	50.5	59.1
Extreme Maximum Temp. (°F)	87	91	94	98	100	102	103	99	98	96	96	90	103
Extreme Minimum Temp. (°F)	13	21	24	27	36	50	58	60	56	38	28	18	13
Days Maximum Temp. ≥ 90°F	0	0	2	7	17	23	28	28	23	8	1	0	137
Days Maximum Temp. ≤ 32°F	0	0	0	0	0	0	0	0	0	0	0	0	0
Days Minimum Temp. ≤ 32°F	4	3	1	0	0	0	0	0	0	0	0	2	10
Days Minimum Temp. ≤ 0°F	0	0	0	0	0	0	0	0	0	0	0	0	0
Heating Degree Days (base 65°F)	177	136	67	23	1	0	0	0	0	4	40	129	577
Cooling Degree Days (base 65°F)	58	72	125	189	337	451	501	511	451	319	163	79	3,256
Mean Precipitation (in.)	2.44	2.48	3.48	2.28	4.11	7.90	7.79	7.50	6.40	3.06	2.06	1.94	51.44
Days With ≥ 0.1" Precipitation	4	4	4	4	6	11	11	11	10	5	3	3	76
Days With ≥ 1.0" Precipitation	1	1	1	1	2	3	3	2	2	1	1	1	19
Mean Snowfall (in.)	trace	0.0	0.0	0.0	0.0	0.0	0.0	0.0	0.0	0.0	0.0	0.0	trace
Days With ≥ 1.0" Snow Depth	0	0	0	0	0	0	0	0	0	0	0	0	0

Avon Park 2 W *Highlands County*   Elevation: 150 ft.   Latitude: 27° 36' N   Longitude: 81° 32' W

	JAN	FEB	MAR	APR	MAY	JUN	JUL	AUG	SEP	OCT	NOV	DEC	YEAR
Mean Maximum Temp. (°F)	72.3	75.1	79.2	83.8	88.5	90.8	91.8	91.6	89.9	85.2	79.4	74.5	83.5
Mean Temp. (°F)	60.0	62.7	67.0	71.5	76.7	80.4	81.7	81.7	80.3	74.9	68.3	62.9	72.3
Mean Minimum Temp. (°F)	47.7	50.3	54.7	59.1	64.9	70.0	71.5	71.8	70.7	64.5	57.3	51.3	61.1
Extreme Maximum Temp. (°F)	88	92	93	95	98	101	100	99	99	96	92	88	101
Extreme Minimum Temp. (°F)	18	26	23	34	44	50	62	59	58	43	29	23	18
Days Maximum Temp. ≥ 90°F	0	0	0	4	13	21	26	25	19	5	0	0	113
Days Maximum Temp. ≤ 32°F	0	0	0	0	0	0	0	0	0	0	0	0	0
Days Minimum Temp. ≤ 32°F	3	1	0	0	0	0	0	0	0	0	0	1	5
Days Minimum Temp. ≤ 0°F	0	0	0	0	0	0	0	0	0	0	0	0	0
Heating Degree Days (base 65°F)	201	126	62	14	1	0	0	0	0	4	45	137	590
Cooling Degree Days (base 65°F)	49	74	122	203	366	470	526	526	462	319	149	75	3,341
Mean Precipitation (in.)	2.57	2.47	3.16	2.16	3.75	8.23	7.10	7.21	5.99	3.10	2.28	1.84	49.86
Days With ≥ 0.1" Precipitation	4	4	4	3	6	10	11	11	9	5	3	3	73
Days With ≥ 1.0" Precipitation	1	1	1	1	1	3	2	2	2	1	1	1	17
Mean Snowfall (in.)	trace	0.0	0.0	0.0	0.0	0.0	0.0	0.0	0.0	0.0	0.0	0.0	trace
Days With ≥ 1.0" Snow Depth	0	0	0	0	0	0	0	0	0	0	0	0	0

Bartow *Polk County*   Elevation: 124 ft.   Latitude: 27° 54' N   Longitude: 81° 51' W

	JAN	FEB	MAR	APR	MAY	JUN	JUL	AUG	SEP	OCT	NOV	DEC	YEAR
Mean Maximum Temp. (°F)	73.4	75.2	80.0	84.3	88.9	91.4	92.3	92.3	90.4	85.4	79.7	74.7	84.0
Mean Temp. (°F)	61.8	63.4	67.9	72.2	77.5	81.3	82.4	82.5	81.0	75.2	69.2	63.5	73.2
Mean Minimum Temp. (°F)	50.1	51.6	55.8	60.1	66.0	71.2	72.4	72.7	71.5	64.9	58.6	52.2	62.3
Extreme Maximum Temp. (°F)	86	89	93	96	98	103	101	99	96	94	93	90	103
Extreme Minimum Temp. (°F)	20	23	23	39	49	59	63	63	56	42	32	22	20
Days Maximum Temp. ≥ 90°F	0	0	1	4	14	23	27	27	21	4	0	0	121
Days Maximum Temp. ≤ 32°F	0	0	0	0	0	0	0	0	0	0	0	0	0
Days Minimum Temp. ≤ 32°F	2	1	0	0	0	0	0	0	0	0	0	1	4
Days Minimum Temp. ≤ 0°F	0	0	0	0	0	0	0	0	0	0	0	0	0
Heating Degree Days (base 65°F)	158	112	47	7	0	0	0	0	0	2	36	121	483
Cooling Degree Days (base 65°F)	62	85	143	232	402	510	563	568	496	339	176	83	3,659
Mean Precipitation (in.)	2.58	2.89	3.31	2.54	3.95	6.76	8.44	6.56	6.62	2.74	2.17	2.38	50.94
Days With ≥ 0.1" Precipitation	4	4	5	4	5	9	12	11	9	5	4	4	76
Days With ≥ 1.0" Precipitation	1	1	1	1	1	2	3	2	2	1	1	1	17
Mean Snowfall (in.)	0.0	0.0	0.0	0.0	0.0	0.0	0.0	0.0	0.0	0.0	0.0	0.0	0.0
Days With ≥ 1.0" Snow Depth	0	0	0	0	0	0	0	0	0	0	0	0	0

Belle Glade Exp. Station *Palm Beach County*   Elevation: 13 ft.   Latitude: 26° 39' N   Longitude: 80° 38' W

	JAN	FEB	MAR	APR	MAY	JUN	JUL	AUG	SEP	OCT	NOV	DEC	YEAR
Mean Maximum Temp. (°F)	75.0	76.4	79.9	83.6	87.3	89.8	91.2	91.2	89.7	85.9	80.9	76.5	84.0
Mean Temp. (°F)	63.5	64.5	68.2	71.5	76.1	79.9	81.2	81.3	80.1	75.8	70.4	65.5	73.2
Mean Minimum Temp. (°F)	51.9	52.5	56.6	59.4	64.9	70.0	71.1	71.3	70.5	65.6	60.0	54.4	62.3
Extreme Maximum Temp. (°F)	88	90	92	95	97	98	97	98	97	96	91	89	98
Extreme Minimum Temp. (°F)	21	29	29	34	45	55	64	65	60	39	36	24	21
Days Maximum Temp. ≥ 90°F	0	0	1	3	8	17	24	25	18	5	0	0	101
Days Maximum Temp. ≤ 32°F	0	0	0	0	0	0	0	0	0	0	0	0	0
Days Minimum Temp. ≤ 32°F	1	0	0	0	0	0	0	0	0	0	0	1	2
Days Minimum Temp. ≤ 0°F	0	0	0	0	0	0	0	0	0	0	0	0	0
Heating Degree Days (base 65°F)	124	93	41	11	0	0	0	0	0	2	22	87	380
Cooling Degree Days (base 65°F)	80	93	144	210	350	464	516	519	460	351	196	107	3,490
Mean Precipitation (in.)	2.58	1.93	3.07	2.17	5.16	7.40	7.44	7.44	7.13	3.50	2.78	1.81	52.41
Days With ≥ 0.1" Precipitation	4	4	4	4	7	10	11	11	11	6	4	3	79
Days With ≥ 1.0" Precipitation	1	0	1	1	2	2	2	2	2	1	1	0	15
Mean Snowfall (in.)	trace	0.0	0.0	0.0	0.0	0.0	0.0	0.0	0.0	0.0	0.0	0.0	trace
Days With ≥ 1.0" Snow Depth	0	0	0	0	0	0	0	0	0	0	0	0	0

Bradenton 5 ESE *Manatee County*   Elevation: 19 ft.   Latitude: 27° 27' N   Longitude: 82° 28' W

	JAN	FEB	MAR	APR	MAY	JUN	JUL	AUG	SEP	OCT	NOV	DEC	YEAR
Mean Maximum Temp. (°F)	72.5	74.0	78.1	82.3	87.4	90.3	91.5	91.5	90.0	85.3	79.5	74.3	83.1
Mean Temp. (°F)	61.3	62.8	67.0	70.9	76.3	80.5	82.0	82.2	80.9	75.2	68.9	63.3	72.6
Mean Minimum Temp. (°F)	50.0	51.5	55.9	59.4	65.1	70.6	72.3	72.9	71.8	65.1	58.2	52.3	62.1
Extreme Maximum Temp. (°F)	89	88	90	94	95	100	100	99	97	95	90	89	100
Extreme Minimum Temp. (°F)	23	24	30	38	46	52	62	60	59	44	29	20	20
Days Maximum Temp. ≥ 90°F	0	0	0	1	10	20	25	25	19	5	0	0	105
Days Maximum Temp. ≤ 32°F	0	0	0	0	0	0	0	0	0	0	0	0	0
Days Minimum Temp. ≤ 32°F	1	1	0	0	0	0	0	0	0	0	0	1	3
Days Minimum Temp. ≤ 0°F	0	0	0	0	0	0	0	0	0	0	0	0	0
Heating Degree Days (base 65°F)	173	125	59	14	0	0	0	0	0	3	42	128	544
Cooling Degree Days (base 65°F)	62	78	129	202	368	486	548	554	489	341	175	86	3,518
Mean Precipitation (in.)	2.99	2.72	3.52	1.79	2.96	7.42	8.50	9.43	7.17	2.99	2.34	2.44	54.27
Days With ≥ 0.1" Precipitation	4	4	4	3	4	9	12	13	10	4	3	4	74
Days With ≥ 1.0" Precipitation	1	1	1	0	1	3	3	3	2	1	1	1	18
Mean Snowfall (in.)	0.0	0.0	0.0	0.0	0.0	0.0	0.0	0.0	0.0	0.0	0.0	0.0	0.0
Days With ≥ 1.0" Snow Depth	0	0	0	0	0	0	0	0	0	0	0	0	0

Brooksville Chin Hill *Hernando County*   Elevation: 239 ft.   Latitude: 28° 37' N   Longitude: 82° 22' W

	JAN	FEB	MAR	APR	MAY	JUN	JUL	AUG	SEP	OCT	NOV	DEC	YEAR
Mean Maximum Temp. (°F)	70.8	72.7	78.2	82.3	**87.6**	89.9	90.7	90.2	89.1	83.9	77.9	72.5	**82.1**
Mean Temp. (°F)	59.7	61.2	66.5	70.7	**76.3**	80.0	81.2	81.1	79.8	73.9	67.1	61.7	**71.6**
Mean Minimum Temp. (°F)	48.5	49.6	54.8	59.2	**64.8**	70.1	71.7	71.8	70.4	63.9	56.3	50.8	**61.0**
Extreme Maximum Temp. (°F)	89	89	90	96	100	104	100	99	96	94	89	86	104
Extreme Minimum Temp. (°F)	13	21	20	36	48	55	61	62	55	40	22	15	13
Days Maximum Temp. ≥ 90°F	0	0	0	2	9	**17**	21	21	15	2	0	0	**87**
Days Maximum Temp. ≤ 32°F	0	0	0	0	0	0	0	0	0	0	0	0	0
Days Minimum Temp. ≤ 32°F	2	1	0	0	0	0	0	0	0	0	0	1	4
Days Minimum Temp. ≤ 0°F	0	0	0	0	0	0	0	0	0	0	0	0	0
Heating Degree Days (base 65°F)	209	150	62	15	**1**	0	0	0	0	4	57	157	**655**
Cooling Degree Days (base 65°F)	45	53	109	187	**361**	458	513	**511**	449	290	131	60	**3,167**
Mean Precipitation (in.)	3.36	3.36	4.36	2.65	3.44	7.04	6.86	8.47	6.13	2.44	2.36	2.47	52.94
Days With ≥ 0.1" Precipitation	5	4	5	3	5	9	10	11	8	4	3	4	71
Days With ≥ 1.0" Precipitation	1	1	1	1	1	2	2	3	2	1	1	1	17
Mean Snowfall (in.)	0.0	0.0	0.0	0.0	0.0	0.0	0.0	0.0	0.0	0.0	0.0	0.0	0.0
Days With ≥ 1.0" Snow Depth	0	0	0	0	0	0	0	0	0	0	0	0	0

Canal Point USDA *Palm Beach County*   Elevation: 29 ft.   Latitude: 26° 52' N   Longitude: 80° 37' W

	JAN	FEB	MAR	APR	MAY	JUN	JUL	AUG	SEP	OCT	NOV	DEC	YEAR
Mean Maximum Temp. (°F)	74.4	75.7	79.8	84.1	87.9	90.3	91.8	91.6	90.3	86.4	81.0	76.1	84.1
Mean Temp. (°F)	63.7	64.9	68.8	72.5	76.8	80.3	81.4	81.5	80.6	76.9	71.3	65.9	73.7
Mean Minimum Temp. (°F)	52.9	54.1	57.8	60.9	65.6	70.2	71.0	71.4	70.8	67.2	61.4	55.8	63.3
Extreme Maximum Temp. (°F)	89	90	92	95	97	98	100	98	98	96	91	89	100
Extreme Minimum Temp. (°F)	25	29	31	41	48	54	62	61	60	42	39	25	25
Days Maximum Temp. ≥ 90°F	0	0	1	3	11	20	26	26	21	7	0	0	115
Days Maximum Temp. ≤ 32°F	0	0	0	0	0	0	0	0	0	0	0	0	0
Days Minimum Temp. ≤ 32°F	0	0	0	0	0	0	0	0	0	0	0	0	0
Days Minimum Temp. ≤ 0°F	0	0	0	0	0	0	0	0	0	0	0	0	0
Heating Degree Days (base 65°F)	108	79	30	4	0	0	0	0	0	1	14	72	308
Cooling Degree Days (base 65°F)	73	96	158	238	376	473	524	527	478	385	218	111	3,657
Mean Precipitation (in.)	2.68	2.34	3.83	2.18	4.80	7.46	6.27	7.00	7.04	3.94	2.94	2.05	52.53
Days With ≥ 0.1" Precipitation	4	4	5	3	6	10	10	11	10	6	4	4	77
Days With ≥ 1.0" Precipitation	1	1	1	1	2	2	2	2	2	1	1	1	17
Mean Snowfall (in.)	0.0	0.0	0.0	0.0	0.0	0.0	0.0	0.0	0.0	0.0	0.0	0.0	0.0
Days With ≥ 1.0" Snow Depth	0	0	0	0	0	0	0	0	0	0	0	0	0

Chipley 3 E *Washington County*   Elevation: 127 ft.   Latitude: 30° 47' N   Longitude: 85° 29' W

	JAN	FEB	MAR	APR	MAY	JUN	JUL	AUG	SEP	OCT	NOV	DEC	YEAR
Mean Maximum Temp. (°F)	60.2	64.5	71.7	78.4	85.1	89.7	91.4	90.8	87.6	79.7	70.7	63.5	77.8
Mean Temp. (°F)	48.9	52.5	59.4	65.6	72.9	78.7	81.1	80.5	76.7	66.8	58.1	51.7	66.1
Mean Minimum Temp. (°F)	37.6	40.4	47.0	52.7	60.6	67.8	70.7	70.1	65.8	53.9	45.5	39.9	54.3
Extreme Maximum Temp. (°F)	81	83	88	94	100	104	104	102	98	94	88	85	104
Extreme Minimum Temp. (°F)	2	13	20	31	39	47	61	55	43	29	17	10	2
Days Maximum Temp. ≥ 90°F	0	0	0	1	6	16	22	21	13	1	0	0	80
Days Maximum Temp. ≤ 32°F	0	0	0	0	0	0	0	0	0	0	0	0	0
Days Minimum Temp. ≤ 32°F	11	7	2	0	0	0	0	0	0	0	3	10	33
Days Minimum Temp. ≤ 0°F	0	0	0	0	0	0	0	0	0	0	0	0	0
Heating Degree Days (base 65°F)	499	358	206	75	6	0	0	0	2	66	234	421	1,867
Cooling Degree Days (base 65°F)	5	12	35	92	260	421	509	488	344	133	33	13	2,345
Mean Precipitation (in.)	6.11	5.04	6.18	3.80	4.31	5.32	6.88	5.47	4.62	3.11	3.93	3.84	58.61
Days With ≥ 0.1" Precipitation	8	6	7	5	6	8	10	8	6	4	5	6	79
Days With ≥ 1.0" Precipitation	2	2	2	1	1	2	2	2	1	1	1	1	18
Mean Snowfall (in.)	trace	0.0	0.0	0.0	0.0	0.0	0.0	0.0	0.0	0.0	0.0	0.0	trace
Days With ≥ 1.0" Snow Depth	0	0	0	0	0	0	0	0	0	0	0	0	0

Clermont 7 S *Lake County*   Elevation: 108 ft.   Latitude: 28° 27' N   Longitude: 81° 45' W

	JAN	FEB	MAR	APR	MAY	JUN	JUL	AUG	SEP	OCT	NOV	DEC	YEAR
Mean Maximum Temp. (°F)	70.3	72.9	78.2	83.0	87.6	90.1	91.6	91.0	88.9	83.3	77.1	71.8	82.2
Mean Temp. (°F)	59.9	61.8	66.8	71.1	76.3	80.3	81.8	81.8	80.2	74.3	67.5	61.8	71.9
Mean Minimum Temp. (°F)	49.3	50.6	55.4	59.1	65.0	70.4	71.9	72.5	71.4	65.2	57.8	51.7	61.7
Extreme Maximum Temp. (°F)	86	89	91	94	99	101	101	98	96	94	88	87	101
Extreme Minimum Temp. (°F)	18	27	25	39	49	51	62	64	55	41	28	19	18
Days Maximum Temp. ≥ 90°F	0	0	0	3	10	17	24	21	15	2	0	0	92
Days Maximum Temp. ≤ 32°F	0	0	0	0	0	0	0	0	0	0	0	0	0
Days Minimum Temp. ≤ 32°F	2	1	0	0	0	0	0	0	0	0	0	1	4
Days Minimum Temp. ≤ 0°F	0	0	0	0	0	0	0	0	0	0	0	0	0
Heating Degree Days (base 65°F)	199	139	61	13	0	0	0	0	0	4	51	150	617
Cooling Degree Days (base 65°F)	43	60	115	189	351	463	531	528	453	301	139	59	3,232
Mean Precipitation (in.)	3.15	2.73	3.96	2.17	3.76	7.91	6.76	6.85	5.75	2.48	2.37	2.43	50.32
Days With ≥ 0.1" Precipitation	5	5	5	3	5	10	11	11	8	4	3	4	74
Days With ≥ 1.0" Precipitation	1	1	1	1	1	2	2	2	1	1	1	1	15
Mean Snowfall (in.)	trace	trace	0.0	0.0	0.0	0.0	0.0	0.0	0.0	0.0	0.0	0.0	trace
Days With ≥ 1.0" Snow Depth	0	0	0	0	0	0	0	0	0	0	0	0	0

Clewiston U.S. Engineers *Hendry County*   Elevation: 19 ft.   Latitude: 26° 45' N   Longitude: 80° 55' W

	JAN	FEB	MAR	APR	MAY	JUN	JUL	AUG	SEP	OCT	NOV	DEC	YEAR
Mean Maximum Temp. (°F)	73.4	75.3	79.8	83.7	87.6	90.1	91.8	91.3	89.8	85.2	80.0	74.9	83.6
Mean Temp. (°F)	63.8	65.4	69.6	73.3	77.7	81.0	82.2	82.3	81.5	77.3	71.9	66.1	74.3
Mean Minimum Temp. (°F)	54.2	55.6	59.2	62.9	67.8	71.9	72.5	73.1	73.1	69.4	63.7	57.4	65.1
Extreme Maximum Temp. (°F)	90	92	95	98	98	101	101	101	98	97	93	90	101
Extreme Minimum Temp. (°F)	26	32	29	40	51	62	66	67	65	49	35	26	26
Days Maximum Temp. ≥ 90°F	0	0	2	4	9	17	24	23	17	4	1	0	101
Days Maximum Temp. ≤ 32°F	0	0	0	0	0	0	0	0	0	0	0	0	0
Days Minimum Temp. ≤ 32°F	1	0	0	0	0	0	0	0	0	0	0	0	1
Days Minimum Temp. ≤ 0°F	0	0	0	0	0	0	0	0	0	0	0	0	0
Heating Degree Days (base 65°F)	120	81	31	6	0	0	0	0	0	1	17	79	335
Cooling Degree Days (base 65°F)	84	114	176	260	410	500	548	551	501	397	245	119	3,905
Mean Precipitation (in.)	2.18	2.07	3.02	2.13	4.65	7.19	6.53	6.36	4.93	2.97	2.25	1.51	45.79
Days With ≥ 0.1" Precipitation	4	4	4	3	5	9	9	10	8	4	3	3	66
Days With ≥ 1.0" Precipitation	1	1	1	1	1	2	2	2	1	1	1	0	14
Mean Snowfall (in.)	0.0	0.0	0.0	0.0	0.0	0.0	0.0	0.0	0.0	0.0	0.0	0.0	0.0
Days With ≥ 1.0" Snow Depth	0	0	0	0	0	0	0	0	0	0	0	0	0

Cross City 2 WNW *Dixie County*   Elevation: 39 ft.   Latitude: 29° 39' N   Longitude: 83° 10' W

	JAN	FEB	MAR	APR	MAY	JUN	JUL	AUG	SEP	OCT	NOV	DEC	YEAR
Mean Maximum Temp. (°F)	65.1	67.9	73.9	79.2	85.5	89.5	90.4	90.1	88.0	81.8	74.3	67.7	79.4
Mean Temp. (°F)	52.6	55.4	61.3	66.3	73.0	78.5	80.4	80.2	77.8	69.8	62.0	55.3	67.7
Mean Minimum Temp. (°F)	39.8	42.9	48.7	53.4	60.5	67.4	70.3	70.4	67.7	57.4	49.2	42.4	55.8
Extreme Maximum Temp. (°F)	84	84	90	92	100	100	101	100	96	96	89	85	101
Extreme Minimum Temp. (°F)	10	16	20	31	38	50	57	55	49	31	15	13	10
Days Maximum Temp. ≥ 90°F	0	0	0	0	5	16	20	19	13	2	0	0	75
Days Maximum Temp. ≤ 32°F	0	0	0	0	0	0	0	0	0	0	0	0	0
Days Minimum Temp. ≤ 32°F	9	5	1	0	0	0	0	0	0	0	2	7	24
Days Minimum Temp. ≤ 0°F	0	0	0	0	0	0	0	0	0	0	0	0	0
Heating Degree Days (base 65°F)	389	278	158	59	5	0	0	0	0	33	150	319	1,391
Cooling Degree Days (base 65°F)	9	18	49	96	264	416	486	487	385	198	70	21	2,499
Mean Precipitation (in.)	4.49	3.59	4.70	3.51	3.20	6.27	8.91	9.79	5.78	3.02	2.40	3.37	59.03
Days With ≥ 0.1" Precipitation	7	5	5	4	5	8	11	12	8	4	4	5	78
Days With ≥ 1.0" Precipitation	1	1	2	1	1	2	3	3	2	1	1	1	19
Mean Snowfall (in.)	0.0	0.0	0.0	0.0	0.0	0.0	0.0	0.0	0.0	0.0	0.0	0.0	0.0
Days With ≥ 1.0" Snow Depth	0	0	0	0	0	0	0	0	0	0	0	0	0

De Funiak Springs *Walton County*   Elevation: 229 ft.   Latitude: 30° 44' N   Longitude: 86° 04' W

	JAN	FEB	MAR	APR	MAY	JUN	JUL	AUG	SEP	OCT	NOV	DEC	YEAR
Mean Maximum Temp. (°F)	62.5	66.0	72.7	79.2	85.6	90.4	91.8	91.2	88.1	80.5	71.3	64.5	78.6
Mean Temp. (°F)	50.4	53.5	59.9	65.7	73.0	78.7	81.0	80.4	76.8	67.2	58.2	52.6	66.4
Mean Minimum Temp. (°F)	38.2	40.9	47.1	52.2	60.3	67.0	70.1	69.5	65.4	53.9	45.1	40.6	54.2
Extreme Maximum Temp. (°F)	81	82	90	95	99	104	105	101	99	93	88	83	105
Extreme Minimum Temp. (°F)	3	12	19	28	35	44	55	58	40	28	16	7	3
Days Maximum Temp. ≥ 90°F	0	0	0	1	6	17	23	22	14	1	0	0	84
Days Maximum Temp. ≤ 32°F	0	0	0	0	0	0	0	0	0	0	0	0	0
Days Minimum Temp. ≤ 32°F	12	7	3	0	0	0	0	0	0	0	4	9	35
Days Minimum Temp. ≤ 0°F	0	0	0	0	0	0	0	0	0	0	0	0	0
Heating Degree Days (base 65°F)	455	330	191	69	5	0	0	0	2	55	228	395	1,730
Cooling Degree Days (base 65°F)	4	12	36	90	262	425	510	490	353	139	29	15	2,365
Mean Precipitation (in.)	5.39	5.75	6.40	3.96	5.03	6.93	7.95	7.04	5.91	3.60	4.68	4.42	67.06
Days With ≥ 0.1" Precipitation	7	7	7	5	6	10	12	10	7	3	5	6	85
Days With ≥ 1.0" Precipitation	2	2	3	1	1	2	2	2	2	1	2	1	21
Mean Snowfall (in.)	trace	trace	trace	0.0	0.0	0.0	0.0	0.0	0.0	0.0	0.0	0.0	trace
Days With ≥ 1.0" Snow Depth	0	0	0	0	0	0	0	0	0	0	0	0	0

Fernandina Beach *Nassau County*   Elevation: 13 ft.   Latitude: 30° 40' N   Longitude: 81° 28' W

	JAN	FEB	MAR	APR	MAY	JUN	JUL	AUG	SEP	OCT	NOV	DEC	YEAR
Mean Maximum Temp. (°F)	62.2	65.1	70.9	76.6	82.5	87.4	89.9	88.5	85.5	78.5	71.4	65.1	77.0
Mean Temp. (°F)	52.7	55.5	61.2	67.1	73.7	79.3	81.9	81.1	78.6	71.1	62.9	56.1	68.4
Mean Minimum Temp. (°F)	43.2	45.9	51.4	57.6	65.0	71.2	73.7	73.7	71.6	63.7	54.4	47.1	59.9
Extreme Maximum Temp. (°F)	88	85	88	94	96	102	102	101	99	94	87	85	102
Extreme Minimum Temp. (°F)	4	20	22	37	40	51	63	61	52	41	24	12	4
Days Maximum Temp. ≥ 90°F	0	0	0	1	3	10	16	11	4	1	0	0	46
Days Maximum Temp. ≤ 32°F	0	0	0	0	0	0	0	0	0	0	0	0	0
Days Minimum Temp. ≤ 32°F	4	2	0	0	0	0	0	0	0	0	0	2	8
Days Minimum Temp. ≤ 0°F	0	0	0	0	0	0	0	0	0	0	0	0	0
Heating Degree Days (base 65°F)	383	276	156	49	3	0	0	0	0	17	125	288	1,297
Cooling Degree Days (base 65°F)	8	16	43	111	282	445	539	515	411	217	71	19	2,677
Mean Precipitation (in.)	3.85	3.32	4.17	2.78	2.98	5.31	5.92	5.46	7.37	4.45	2.52	2.74	50.87
Days With ≥ 0.1" Precipitation	7	6	6	4	5	8	9	8	9	5	4	5	76
Days With ≥ 1.0" Precipitation	1	1	1	1	1	1	2	2	2	1	1	1	15
Mean Snowfall (in.)	trace	trace	trace	0.0	0.0	0.0	0.0	0.0	0.0	0.0	0.0	0.0	trace
Days With ≥ 1.0" Snow Depth	0	0	0	0	0	0	0	0	0	0	0	0	0

Flamingo Ranger Station *Monroe County*   Elevation: 0 ft.   Latitude: 25° 09' N   Longitude: 80° 55' W

	JAN	FEB	MAR	APR	MAY	JUN	JUL	AUG	SEP	OCT	NOV	DEC	YEAR
Mean Maximum Temp. (°F)	76.6	77.2	79.5	82.9	86.0	88.2	89.3	89.8	88.9	86.1	82.3	78.4	83.8
Mean Temp. (°F)	66.3	67.1	69.9	73.5	77.3	80.8	81.7	81.9	81.1	77.6	73.2	68.5	74.9
Mean Minimum Temp. (°F)	56.0	56.9	60.2	64.1	68.7	73.3	74.1	74.0	73.3	69.1	63.9	58.5	66.0
Extreme Maximum Temp. (°F)	88	92	88	94	96	104	100	97	101	99	91	89	104
Extreme Minimum Temp. (°F)	27	24	33	44	48	58	62	28	60	41	36	25	24
Days Maximum Temp. ≥ 90°F	0	0	0	0	3	9	16	19	13	2	0	0	62
Days Maximum Temp. ≤ 32°F	0	0	0	0	0	0	0	0	0	0	0	0	0
Days Minimum Temp. ≤ 32°F	0	0	0	0	0	0	0	0	0	0	0	0	0
Days Minimum Temp. ≤ 0°F	0	0	0	0	0	0	0	0	0	0	0	0	0
Heating Degree Days (base 65°F)	71	53	21	2	0	0	0	0	0	0	6	38	191
Cooling Degree Days (base 65°F)	117	132	180	268	396	489	535	535	490	410	265	160	3,977
Mean Precipitation (in.)	2.02	1.61	1.87	2.06	5.01	7.29	4.93	7.53	7.25	4.27	2.46	1.51	47.81
Days With ≥ 0.1" Precipitation	4	3	3	3	6	9	9	10	11	6	4	3	71
Days With ≥ 1.0" Precipitation	0	0	0	0	2	2	1	2	2	1	1	0	11
Mean Snowfall (in.)	0.0	0.0	0.0	0.0	0.0	0.0	0.0	0.0	0.0	0.0	0.0	0.0	0.0
Days With ≥ 1.0" Snow Depth	0	0	0	0	0	0	0	0	0	0	0	0	0

Fort Drum 5 NW *Okeechobee County*   Elevation: 68 ft.   Latitude: 27° 35' N   Longitude: 80° 50' W

	JAN	FEB	MAR	APR	MAY	JUN	JUL	AUG	SEP	OCT	NOV	DEC	YEAR
Mean Maximum Temp. (°F)	74.7	75.9	79.7	83.7	87.8	90.4	91.5	91.5	89.8	85.5	80.4	75.6	83.9
Mean Temp. (°F)	62.4	63.4	67.2	70.9	75.7	79.9	81.1	81.5	80.1	75.4	69.4	64.0	72.6
Mean Minimum Temp. (°F)	50.1	51.0	54.7	58.0	63.5	69.3	70.8	71.5	70.4	65.2	58.5	52.3	61.3
Extreme Maximum Temp. (°F)	89	88	92	97	98	102	101	99	97	98	93	87	102
Extreme Minimum Temp. (°F)	17	20	27	32	42	55	60	62	60	41	24	22	17
Days Maximum Temp. ≥ 90°F	0	0	0	3	9	17	22	23	18	4	0	0	96
Days Maximum Temp. ≤ 32°F	0	0	0	0	0	0	0	0	0	0	0	0	0
Days Minimum Temp. ≤ 32°F	2	1	0	0	0	0	0	0	0	0	0	1	4
Days Minimum Temp. ≤ 0°F	0	0	0	0	0	0	0	0	0	0	0	0	0
Heating Degree Days (base 65°F)	139	108	48	10	0	0	0	0	0	2	30	109	446
Cooling Degree Days (base 65°F)	67	78	123	194	341	464	522	530	463	345	181	82	3,390
Mean Precipitation (in.)	2.35	2.51	3.89	2.38	4.53	8.06	7.78	7.16	6.71	3.65	2.31	1.89	53.22
Days With ≥ 0.1" Precipitation	2	4	3	3	5	9	8	8	8	4	3	3	60
Days With ≥ 1.0" Precipitation	0	1	1	1	1	3	3	2	2	1	1	0	16
Mean Snowfall (in.)	trace	0.0	0.0	0.0	0.0	0.0	0.0	0.0	0.0	0.0	0.0	0.0	trace
Days With ≥ 1.0" Snow Depth	0	0	0	0	0	0	0	0	0	0	0	0	0

Fort Lauderdale *Broward County*   Elevation: 13 ft.   Latitude: 26° 06' N   Longitude: 80° 12' W

	JAN	FEB	MAR	APR	MAY	JUN	JUL	AUG	SEP	OCT	NOV	DEC	YEAR
Mean Maximum Temp. (°F)	76.2	76.8	79.4	82.5	85.6	88.3	89.5	89.8	88.6	85.5	81.1	77.6	83.4
Mean Temp. (°F)	67.4	67.9	71.1	74.4	78.2	81.2	82.4	82.8	81.7	78.5	73.8	69.4	75.7
Mean Minimum Temp. (°F)	58.6	59.0	62.7	66.3	70.7	74.1	75.3	75.6	74.8	71.6	66.4	61.3	68.0
Extreme Maximum Temp. (°F)	88	89	92	94	97	97	99	97	98	95	89	88	99
Extreme Minimum Temp. (°F)	28	34	32	42	54	63	64	66	65	47	36	30	28
Days Maximum Temp. ≥ 90°F	0	0	0	1	4	10	15	18	9	2	0	0	59
Days Maximum Temp. ≤ 32°F	0	0	0	0	0	0	0	0	0	0	0	0	0
Days Minimum Temp. ≤ 32°F	0	0	0	0	0	0	0	0	0	0	0	0	0
Days Minimum Temp. ≤ 0°F	0	0	0	0	0	0	0	0	0	0	0	0	0
Heating Degree Days (base 65°F)	62	45	17	2	0	0	0	0	0	0	7	39	172
Cooling Degree Days (base 65°F)	149	154	213	295	423	500	557	567	514	442	291	190	4,295
Mean Precipitation (in.)	3.03	2.79	3.02	3.77	6.43	9.92	6.59	6.95	8.34	6.21	4.55	2.53	64.13
Days With ≥ 0.1" Precipitation	5	4	4	4	8	11	10	11	12	9	6	4	88
Days With ≥ 1.0" Precipitation	1	1	1	1	2	3	2	2	2	2	1	1	19
Mean Snowfall (in.)	0.0	0.0	0.0	0.0	0.0	0.0	0.0	0.0	0.0	0.0	0.0	0.0	0.0
Days With ≥ 1.0" Snow Depth	0	0	0	0	0	0	0	0	0	0	0	0	0

Fort Pierce *St. Lucie County*   Elevation: 22 ft.   Latitude: 27° 28' N   Longitude: 80° 21' W

	JAN	FEB	MAR	APR	MAY	JUN	JUL	AUG	SEP	OCT	NOV	DEC	YEAR
Mean Maximum Temp. (°F)	74.3	75.3	78.9	82.3	86.3	89.4	91.2	90.9	89.4	85.4	80.4	76.0	83.3
Mean Temp. (°F)	63.0	64.1	68.0	71.8	76.7	80.3	81.7	81.7	80.6	76.5	70.5	65.2	73.3
Mean Minimum Temp. (°F)	51.7	52.8	57.2	61.4	67.0	71.0	72.2	72.4	71.8	67.5	60.7	54.4	63.3
Extreme Maximum Temp. (°F)	89	89	92	97	98	100	101	98	99	96	92	88	101
Extreme Minimum Temp. (°F)	19	25	26	33	45	56	64	61	63	42	31	19	19
Days Maximum Temp. ≥ 90°F	0	0	1	2	6	14	24	24	16	4	0	0	91
Days Maximum Temp. ≤ 32°F	0	0	0	0	0	0	0	0	0	0	0	0	0
Days Minimum Temp. ≤ 32°F	1	0	0	0	0	0	0	0	0	0	0	1	2
Days Minimum Temp. ≤ 0°F	0	0	0	0	0	0	0	0	0	0	0	0	0
Heating Degree Days (base 65°F)	134	101	48	9	0	0	0	0	0	2	25	95	414
Cooling Degree Days (base 65°F)	73	87	140	213	371	471	533	528	474	365	199	105	3,559
Mean Precipitation (in.)	2.75	3.03	3.43	2.66	4.62	5.75	5.65	6.38	8.07	5.92	3.53	2.29	54.08
Days With ≥ 0.1" Precipitation	5	5	5	4	7	9	8	10	11	8	5	4	81
Days With ≥ 1.0" Precipitation	1	1	1	1	1	2	2	2	2	2	1	0	16
Mean Snowfall (in.)	trace	0.0	0.0	0.0	0.0	0.0	0.0	0.0	0.0	0.0	0.0	0.0	trace
Days With ≥ 1.0" Snow Depth	0	0	0	0	0	0	0	0	0	0	0	0	0

Hialeah *Dade County*   Elevation: 9 ft.   Latitude: 25° 50' N   Longitude: 80° 17' W

	JAN	FEB	MAR	APR	MAY	JUN	JUL	AUG	SEP	OCT	NOV	DEC	YEAR
Mean Maximum Temp. (°F)	77.2	77.5	80.5	83.3	86.8	89.1	90.8	90.8	89.5	86.2	82.0	78.3	84.3
Mean Temp. (°F)	68.1	68.5	72.4	75.1	79.1	81.8	83.4	83.5	82.4	78.8	74.3	69.8	76.4
Mean Minimum Temp. (°F)	58.5	59.5	63.9	66.9	71.3	74.5	75.9	76.0	75.2	71.3	66.6	61.2	68.4
Extreme Maximum Temp. (°F)	89	90	92	95	97	99	100	99	97	95	91	90	100
Extreme Minimum Temp. (°F)	28	36	32	40	55	60	62	60	62	51	38	30	28
Days Maximum Temp. ≥ 90°F	0	0	0	2	7	14	22	23	16	5	0	0	89
Days Maximum Temp. ≤ 32°F	0	0	0	0	0	0	0	0	0	0	0	0	0
Days Minimum Temp. ≤ 32°F	0	0	0	0	0	0	0	0	0	0	0	0	0
Days Minimum Temp. ≤ 0°F	0	0	0	0	0	0	0	0	0	0	0	0	0
Heating Degree Days (base 65°F)	55	42	14	2	0	0	0	0	0	0	6	36	155
Cooling Degree Days (base 65°F)	166	169	255	320	458	527	595	597	539	448	307	205	4,586
Mean Precipitation (in.)	2.47	2.25	3.20	3.82	6.32	10.37	6.95	9.00	8.89	6.43	3.81	2.41	65.92
Days With ≥ 0.1" Precipitation	5	4	4	4	8	12	11	12	13	9	6	4	92
Days With ≥ 1.0" Precipitation	1	1	1	1	2	3	2	3	3	2	1	1	21
Mean Snowfall (in.)	0.0	0.0	0.0	0.0	0.0	0.0	0.0	0.0	0.0	0.0	0.0	0.0	0.0
Days With ≥ 1.0" Snow Depth	0	0	0	0	0	0	0	0	0	0	0	0	0

High Springs *Alachua County*   Elevation: 62 ft.   Latitude: 29° 50' N   Longitude: 82° 36' W

	JAN	FEB	MAR	APR	MAY	JUN	JUL	AUG	SEP	OCT	NOV	DEC	YEAR
Mean Maximum Temp. (°F)	68.0	71.9	77.9	83.3	88.6	91.6	92.5	92.0	89.8	83.4	76.8	70.5	82.2
Mean Temp. (°F)	54.1	57.6	63.5	68.4	75.1	80.1	81.5	81.3	78.7	70.5	63.2	56.9	69.2
Mean Minimum Temp. (°F)	40.2	43.1	48.9	53.4	61.6	68.5	70.6	70.6	67.6	57.8	49.4	43.2	56.2
Extreme Maximum Temp. (°F)	87	88	92	96	101	104	107	104	99	99	90	89	107
Extreme Minimum Temp. (°F)	9	17	20	30	*41*	45	55	59	49	29	26	8	*8*
Days Maximum Temp. ≥ 90°F	0	0	0	4	*15*	*22*	25	24	18	3	0	0	*111*
Days Maximum Temp. ≤ 32°F	0	0	0	0	0	0	0	0	0	0	0	0	0
Days Minimum Temp. ≤ 32°F	9	5	1	0	0	0	0	0	0	0	2	6	23
Days Minimum Temp. ≤ 0°F	0	0	0	0	0	0	0	0	0	0	0	0	0
Heating Degree Days (base 65°F)	*344*	225	114	38	*1*	0	0	0	0	23	125	269	*1,139*
Cooling Degree Days (base 65°F)	13	27	68	135	327	461	528	523	413	203	79	24	2,801
Mean Precipitation (in.)	4.42	3.80	4.52	3.36	3.81	6.81	7.34	8.19	4.37	3.05	2.19	2.72	54.58
Days With ≥ 0.1" Precipitation	6	5	6	4	6	9	11	11	7	4	4	4	77
Days With ≥ 1.0" Precipitation	2	1	2	1	1	2	2	3	1	1	1	1	18
Mean Snowfall (in.)	trace	0.0	0.0	0.0	0.0	0.0	0.0	0.0	0.0	0.0	0.0	0.0	trace
Days With ≥ 1.0" Snow Depth	0	0	0	0	0	0	0	0	0	0	0	0	0

Immokalee 3 NNW *Collier County* Elevation: 32 ft. Latitude: 26° 28' N Longitude: 81° 26' W

	JAN	FEB	MAR	APR	MAY	JUN	JUL	AUG	SEP	OCT	NOV	DEC	YEAR
Mean Maximum Temp. (°F)	76.5	78.0	81.6	84.9	89.0	90.8	91.6	91.4	89.9	86.4	81.5	77.6	84.9
Mean Temp. (°F)	64.3	65.3	69.0	72.0	76.9	80.4	81.7	82.0	80.9	76.4	70.8	66.0	73.8
Mean Minimum Temp. (°F)	52.0	52.6	56.4	59.1	64.7	69.9	71.7	72.5	71.8	66.3	60.1	54.3	62.6
Extreme Maximum Temp. (°F)	88	90	99	96	99	101	98	100	96	94	91	89	101
Extreme Minimum Temp. (°F)	20	25	30	38	49	54	63	64	64	45	27	24	20
Days Maximum Temp. ≥ 90°F	0	0	1	5	14	20	26	25	19	6	0	0	116
Days Maximum Temp. ≤ 32°F	0	0	0	0	0	0	0	0	0	0	0	0	0
Days Minimum Temp. ≤ 32°F	1	1	0	0	0	0	0	0	0	0	0	1	3
Days Minimum Temp. ≤ 0°F	0	0	0	0	0	0	0	0	0	0	0	0	0
Heating Degree Days (base 65°F)	106	81	32	7	0	0	0	0	0	1	21	75	323
Cooling Degree Days (base 65°F)	86	104	162	226	374	479	529	539	483	366	210	113	3,671
Mean Precipitation (in.)	2.34	2.30	2.98	2.42	4.23	7.92	7.04	7.53	6.43	2.82	2.31	1.76	50.08
Days With ≥ 0.1" Precipitation	4	4	4	3	6	10	12	13	10	5	3	3	77
Days With ≥ 1.0" Precipitation	1	1	1	1	1	3	2	2	2	1	1	1	17
Mean Snowfall (in.)	0.0	0.0	0.0	0.0	0.0	0.0	0.0	0.0	0.0	0.0	0.0	0.0	0.0
Days With ≥ 1.0" Snow Depth	0	0	0	0	0	0	0	0	0	0	0	0	0

Inverness 3 SE *Citrus County* Elevation: 39 ft. Latitude: 28° 48' N Longitude: 82° 19' W

	JAN	FEB	MAR	APR	MAY	JUN	JUL	AUG	SEP	OCT	NOV	DEC	YEAR
Mean Maximum Temp. (°F)	69.6	71.7	77.2	82.1	87.6	90.5	91.7	91.1	89.6	83.7	77.3	72.1	82.0
Mean Temp. (°F)	56.9	58.7	64.2	69.2	75.4	80.2	81.6	81.4	79.6	72.7	65.2	59.4	70.4
Mean Minimum Temp. (°F)	44.1	45.6	51.2	56.3	63.1	69.7	71.4	71.6	69.6	61.6	53.1	46.6	58.7
Extreme Maximum Temp. (°F)	85	89	92	94	100	101	100	99	101	94	92	89	101
Extreme Minimum Temp. (°F)	15	21	24	32	42	52	61	61	51	33	24	15	15
Days Maximum Temp. ≥ 90°F	0	0	0	3	10	19	24	23	18	4	0	0	101
Days Maximum Temp. ≤ 32°F	0	0	0	0	0	0	0	0	0	0	0	0	0
Days Minimum Temp. ≤ 32°F	5	4	1	0	0	0	0	0	0	0	1	3	14
Days Minimum Temp. ≤ 0°F	0	0	0	0	0	0	0	0	0	0	0	0	0
Heating Degree Days (base 65°F)	277	207	106	29	1	0	0	0	0	11	89	209	929
Cooling Degree Days (base 65°F)	24	36	76	145	320	456	514	513	431	258	104	39	2,916
Mean Precipitation (in.)	3.61	3.08	4.26	2.41	3.48	7.30	6.90	7.76	5.89	2.73	2.26	2.56	52.24
Days With ≥ 0.1" Precipitation	5	4	5	3	5	9	11	12	9	4	4	4	75
Days With ≥ 1.0" Precipitation	1	1	1	1	1	2	2	2	2	1	1	1	16
Mean Snowfall (in.)	0.0	0.0	0.0	0.0	0.0	0.0	0.0	0.0	0.0	0.0	0.0	0.0	0.0
Days With ≥ 1.0" Snow Depth	0	0	0	0	0	0	0	0	0	0	0	0	0

Jacksonville Beach *Duval County* Elevation: 9 ft. Latitude: 30° 17' N Longitude: 81° 24' W

	JAN	FEB	MAR	APR	MAY	JUN	JUL	AUG	SEP	OCT	NOV	DEC	YEAR
Mean Maximum Temp. (°F)	63.8	65.9	71.4	76.9	82.7	87.1	89.8	88.5	86.0	79.8	72.3	66.5	77.6
Mean Temp. (°F)	54.9	57.0	62.5	68.1	74.5	79.5	81.7	81.3	79.4	72.7	64.1	58.1	69.5
Mean Minimum Temp. (°F)	46.0	48.0	53.6	59.3	66.2	71.7	73.7	74.1	72.9	65.5	55.8	49.6	61.4
Extreme Maximum Temp. (°F)	85	85	89	94	97	99	103	102	98	93	88	85	103
Extreme Minimum Temp. (°F)	14	21	24	37	50	55	63	64	53	40	25	15	14
Days Maximum Temp. ≥ 90°F	0	0	0	1	2	8	14	9	3	1	0	0	38
Days Maximum Temp. ≤ 32°F	0	0	0	0	0	0	0	0	0	0	0	0	0
Days Minimum Temp. ≤ 32°F	3	2	0	0	0	0	0	0	0	0	0	1	6
Days Minimum Temp. ≤ 0°F	0	0	0	0	0	0	0	0	0	0	0	0	0
Heating Degree Days (base 65°F)	320	238	123	31	1	0	0	0	0	9	102	235	1,059
Cooling Degree Days (base 65°F)	9	18	50	128	305	445	533	522	437	259	76	28	2,810
Mean Precipitation (in.)	3.66	3.04	4.11	2.84	3.09	5.69	5.18	6.10	7.06	5.17	2.30	2.77	51.01
Days With ≥ 0.1" Precipitation	6	5	6	4	5	8	8	8	9	6	4	5	74
Days With ≥ 1.0" Precipitation	1	1	1	1	1	2	2	2	2	1	1	1	16
Mean Snowfall (in.)	trace	trace	0.0	0.0	0.0	0.0	0.0	0.0	0.0	0.0	0.0	trace	trace
Days With ≥ 1.0" Snow Depth	0	0	0	0	0	0	0	0	0	0	0	0	0

Jasper *Hamilton County* Elevation: 144 ft. Latitude: 30° 31' N Longitude: 82° 57' W

	JAN	FEB	MAR	APR	MAY	JUN	JUL	AUG	SEP	OCT	NOV	DEC	YEAR
Mean Maximum Temp. (°F)	64.0	66.9	73.8	79.4	85.5	90.0	91.6	91.2	88.8	81.2	73.7	66.3	79.4
Mean Temp. (°F)	51.2	54.0	60.6	66.1	72.9	78.6	80.9	80.4	77.4	68.3	60.4	53.5	67.0
Mean Minimum Temp. (°F)	38.4	41.3	47.4	52.7	60.2	67.2	70.1	69.6	66.0	55.3	47.1	40.5	54.6
Extreme Maximum Temp. (°F)	83	84	90	93	97	103	102	103	102	94	89	86	103
Extreme Minimum Temp. (°F)	4	14	19	33	39	47	59	59	45	31	15	12	4
Days Maximum Temp. ≥ 90°F	0	0	0	1	6	18	24	22	15	2	0	0	88
Days Maximum Temp. ≤ 32°F	0	0	0	0	0	0	0	0	0	0	0	0	0
Days Minimum Temp. ≤ 32°F	11	6	2	0	0	0	0	0	0	0	3	9	31
Days Minimum Temp. ≤ 0°F	0	0	0	0	0	0	0	0	0	0	0	0	0
Heating Degree Days (base 65°F)	432	316	175	66	6	0	0	0	0	47	182	367	1,591
Cooling Degree Days (base 65°F)	6	14	45	101	260	421	506	489	368	160	54	16	2,440
Mean Precipitation (in.)	4.96	4.14	5.28	3.46	3.42	5.99	5.74	6.47	3.88	2.92	2.78	3.45	52.49
Days With ≥ 0.1" Precipitation	7	6	6	4	5	9	10	10	6	3	4	5	75
Days With ≥ 1.0" Precipitation	2	1	2	1	1	2	2	2	1	1	1	1	17
Mean Snowfall (in.)	trace	trace	trace	0.0	0.0	0.0	0.0	0.0	0.0	0.0	0.0	trace	trace
Days With ≥ 1.0" Snow Depth	0	0	0	0	0	0	0	0	0	0	0	0	0

Kissimmee 2 *Osceola County*   Elevation: 59 ft.   Latitude: 28° 17' N   Longitude: 81° 25' W

	JAN	FEB	MAR	APR	MAY	JUN	JUL	AUG	SEP	OCT	NOV	DEC	YEAR
Mean Maximum Temp. (°F)	73.4	75.2	79.3	83.2	87.5	90.7	91.8	91.6	89.8	85.0	79.8	74.7	83.5
Mean Temp. (°F)	61.6	63.1	67.5	71.3	76.3	80.7	82.1	82.2	80.7	75.2	68.9	63.2	72.8
Mean Minimum Temp. (°F)	49.8	51.0	55.6	59.3	65.1	70.8	72.4	72.8	71.6	65.3	58.0	51.7	62.0
Extreme Maximum Temp. (°F)	85	89	91	98	97	101	101	100	97	95	89	88	101
Extreme Minimum Temp. (°F)	19	27	25	38	46	53	63	65	56	42	29	20	19
Days Maximum Temp. ≥ 90°F	0	0	0	2	9	20	26	25	18	4	0	0	104
Days Maximum Temp. ≤ 32°F	0	0	0	0	0	0	0	0	0	0	0	0	0
Days Minimum Temp. ≤ 32°F	2	1	0	0	0	0	0	0	0	0	0	1	4
Days Minimum Temp. ≤ 0°F	0	0	0	0	0	0	0	0	0	0	0	0	0
Heating Degree Days (base 65°F)	159	113	52	10	0	0	0	0	0	3	37	123	497
Cooling Degree Days (base 65°F)	57	72	130	201	360	484	550	551	478	335	168	77	3,463
Mean Precipitation (in.)	2.42	2.80	3.58	2.04	3.91	6.03	6.59	7.23	5.91	3.20	2.41	2.22	48.34
Days With ≥ 0.1" Precipitation	4	4	5	3	6	9	11	11	9	5	3	4	74
Days With ≥ 1.0" Precipitation	1	1	1	0	1	2	2	2	2	1	1	1	15
Mean Snowfall (in.)	0.0	0.0	0.0	0.0	0.0	0.0	0.0	0.0	0.0	0.0	0.0	0.0	0.0
Days With ≥ 1.0" Snow Depth	0	0	0	0	0	0	0	0	0	0	0	0	0

La Belle *Hendry County*   Elevation: 13 ft.   Latitude: 26° 45' N   Longitude: 81° 26' W

	JAN	FEB	MAR	APR	MAY	JUN	JUL	AUG	SEP	OCT	NOV	DEC	YEAR
Mean Maximum Temp. (°F)	na	77.9	*81.8*	85.9	na	92.0	na	na	na	*87.0*	na	na	na
Mean Temp. (°F)	na	64.9	*68.5*	72.2	na	80.6	na	na	na	*76.1*	na	na	na
Mean Minimum Temp. (°F)	na	51.8	*55.0*	58.6	63.8	69.1	na	na	na	65.2	na	na	na
Extreme Maximum Temp. (°F)	90	92	95	98	104	102	101	*99*	97	96	94	90	*104*
Extreme Minimum Temp. (°F)	19	24	28	37	47	55	61	*62*	60	42	27	*24*	*19*
Days Maximum Temp. ≥ 90°F	0	1	3	7	14	22	23	*24*	19	8	1	0	*122*
Days Maximum Temp. ≤ 32°F	0	0	0	0	0	0	0	0	0	0	0	0	0
Days Minimum Temp. ≤ 32°F	1	1	0	0	0	0	0	0	0	0	0	1	3
Days Minimum Temp. ≤ 0°F	0	0	0	0	0	0	0	0	0	0	0	0	0
Heating Degree Days (base 65°F)	na	91	*45*	9	na	0	na	na	na	1	na	na	na
Cooling Degree Days (base 65°F)	na	103	na	229	na	485	na	na	*488*	357	na	na	na
Mean Precipitation (in.)	2.44	2.23	3.30	2.27	4.10	8.86	7.73	7.79	6.26	3.36	2.30	1.68	52.32
Days With ≥ 0.1" Precipitation	3	3	4	3	5	9	10	9	8	4	2	2	62
Days With ≥ 1.0" Precipitation	1	1	1	1	1	2	2	2	2	1	1	0	15
Mean Snowfall (in.)	trace	0.0	0.0	0.0	0.0	0.0	0.0	0.0	0.0	0.0	0.0	0.0	trace
Days With ≥ 1.0" Snow Depth	0	0	0	0	0	0	0	0	0	0	0	0	0

Lake Alfred Exp. Station *Polk County*   Elevation: 137 ft.   Latitude: 28° 06' N   Longitude: 81° 43' W

	JAN	FEB	MAR	APR	MAY	JUN	JUL	AUG	SEP	OCT	NOV	DEC	YEAR
Mean Maximum Temp. (°F)	72.1	74.2	78.7	83.5	88.6	91.4	92.8	92.8	90.8	85.8	79.8	74.0	83.7
Mean Temp. (°F)	59.6	61.6	66.5	70.9	76.4	80.8	82.3	82.3	80.4	74.5	68.1	62.0	72.1
Mean Minimum Temp. (°F)	47.1	49.0	54.1	58.2	64.3	70.1	71.8	71.7	70.0	63.2	56.5	50.0	60.5
Extreme Maximum Temp. (°F)	88	89	93	96	99	104	103	101	98	95	90	88	104
Extreme Minimum Temp. (°F)	19	25	24	35	45	50	61	60	54	38	26	19	19
Days Maximum Temp. ≥ 90°F	0	0	1	4	14	22	27	27	21	6	0	0	122
Days Maximum Temp. ≤ 32°F	0	0	0	0	0	0	0	0	0	0	0	0	0
Days Minimum Temp. ≤ 32°F	3	1	0	0	0	0	0	0	0	0	0	2	6
Days Minimum Temp. ≤ 0°F	0	0	0	0	0	0	0	0	0	0	0	0	0
Heating Degree Days (base 65°F)	211	150	72	18	0	0	0	0	0	5	51	155	662
Cooling Degree Days (base 65°F)	46	66	119	196	366	484	551	548	466	317	157	72	3,388
Mean Precipitation (in.)	2.57	2.81	3.66	1.99	4.20	6.89	7.23	7.27	6.47	2.99	2.28	2.24	50.60
Days With ≥ 0.1" Precipitation	4	5	5	3	6	9	11	11	9	4	3	3	73
Days With ≥ 1.0" Precipitation	1	1	1	1	1	2	2	2	2	1	1	1	16
Mean Snowfall (in.)	trace	0.0	0.0	0.0	0.0	0.0	0.0	0.0	0.0	0.0	0.0	0.0	trace
Days With ≥ 1.0" Snow Depth	0	0	0	0	0	0	0	0	0	0	0	0	0

Lake City 2 E *Columbia County*   Elevation: 193 ft.   Latitude: 30° 11' N   Longitude: 82° 36' W

	JAN	FEB	MAR	APR	MAY	JUN	JUL	AUG	SEP	OCT	NOV	DEC	YEAR
Mean Maximum Temp. (°F)	64.4	67.7	74.1	79.6	85.8	89.8	91.4	90.7	87.9	80.8	73.6	67.0	79.4
Mean Temp. (°F)	53.1	56.0	62.0	67.1	73.8	79.2	81.2	80.7	77.9	69.8	62.3	55.8	68.2
Mean Minimum Temp. (°F)	41.8	44.3	49.8	54.8	61.8	68.5	71.0	70.7	68.0	58.7	50.9	44.5	57.1
Extreme Maximum Temp. (°F)	84	88	89	96	96	104	102	104	97	93	87	91	104
Extreme Minimum Temp. (°F)	7	16	19	34	41	49	57	62	47	34	18	9	7
Days Maximum Temp. ≥ 90°F	0	0	0	1	7	17	23	22	13	1	0	0	84
Days Maximum Temp. ≤ 32°F	0	0	0	0	0	0	0	0	0	0	0	0	0
Days Minimum Temp. ≤ 32°F	8	4	1	0	0	0	0	0	0	0	2	5	20
Days Minimum Temp. ≤ 0°F	0	0	0	0	0	0	0	0	0	0	0	0	0
Heating Degree Days (base 65°F)	377	269	150	53	4	0	0	0	0	30	146	304	1,333
Cooling Degree Days (base 65°F)	13	23	62	125	295	448	522	507	390	190	76	26	2,677
Mean Precipitation (in.)	4.53	3.79	5.06	3.25	3.84	6.76	6.70	7.36	4.59	2.88	2.39	3.00	54.15
Days With ≥ 0.1" Precipitation	7	5	6	4	6	9	10	11	7	4	3	5	77
Days With ≥ 1.0" Precipitation	2	1	2	1	1	2	2	2	1	1	1	1	17
Mean Snowfall (in.)	trace	0.0	0.0	0.0	0.0	0.0	0.0	0.0	0.0	0.0	0.0	0.0	trace
Days With ≥ 1.0" Snow Depth	0	0	0	0	0	0	0	0	0	0	0	0	0

Lakeland Linder Airport *Polk County*   Elevation: 209 ft.   Latitude: 28° 02' N   Longitude: 81° 57' W

	JAN	FEB	MAR	APR	MAY	JUN	JUL	AUG	SEP	OCT	NOV	DEC	YEAR
Mean Maximum Temp. (°F)	72.0	74.5	79.7	84.0	88.9	91.7	92.9	92.5	90.8	85.2	78.9	73.7	83.7
Mean Temp. (°F)	61.3	63.2	68.2	72.3	77.7	81.5	82.7	82.8	81.3	75.4	68.9	63.2	73.2
Mean Minimum Temp. (°F)	50.4	51.9	56.7	60.6	66.4	71.4	72.6	73.0	71.8	65.5	58.8	52.7	62.6
Extreme Maximum Temp. (°F)	87	90	92	95	103	105	100	100	98	96	93	87	105
Extreme Minimum Temp. (°F)	20	27	25	35	47	52	64	66	57	42	28	21	20
Days Maximum Temp. ≥ 90°F	0	0	1	4	14	22	26	26	20	5	0	0	118
Days Maximum Temp. ≤ 32°F	0	0	0	0	0	0	0	0	0	0	0	0	0
Days Minimum Temp. ≤ 32°F	1	1	0	0	0	0	0	0	0	0	0	1	3
Days Minimum Temp. ≤ 0°F	0	0	0	0	0	0	0	0	0	0	0	0	0
Heating Degree Days (base 65°F)	173	117	44	7	0	0	0	0	0	2	44	127	514
Cooling Degree Days (base 65°F)	62	86	154	237	419	523	578	579	508	351	184	81	3,762
Mean Precipitation (in.)	2.54	2.77	3.59	1.95	4.24	7.08	7.80	7.41	6.10	2.26	2.25	2.12	50.11
Days With ≥ 0.1" Precipitation	4	4	5	4	5	10	12	11	9	3	3	4	74
Days With ≥ 1.0" Precipitation	1	1	1	1	1	2	3	2	2	1	1	0	16
Mean Snowfall (in.)	trace	0.0	0.0	0.0	0.0	0.0	0.0	0.0	0.0	0.0	0.0	0.0	trace
Days With ≥ 1.0" Snow Depth	0	0	0	0	0	0	0	0	0	0	0	0	0

Lisbon *Lake County*   Elevation: 65 ft.   Latitude: 28° 52' N   Longitude: 81° 47' W

	JAN	FEB	MAR	APR	MAY	JUN	JUL	AUG	SEP	OCT	NOV	DEC	YEAR
Mean Maximum Temp. (°F)	68.7	71.2	76.6	81.3	86.5	89.8	91.3	91.1	89.0	83.0	76.2	70.2	81.3
Mean Temp. (°F)	57.7	60.0	65.1	69.7	75.7	80.2	81.9	81.7	79.9	73.2	65.6	59.6	70.9
Mean Minimum Temp. (°F)	46.7	48.6	53.5	58.3	64.9	70.5	72.3	72.3	70.7	63.4	55.0	49.0	60.4
Extreme Maximum Temp. (°F)	86	89	91	95	98	100	100	101	100	97	89	86	101
Extreme Minimum Temp. (°F)	16	24	25	39	46	53	62	61	52	39	24	18	16
Days Maximum Temp. ≥ 90°F	0	0	0	1	8	17	23	23	15	2	0	0	89
Days Maximum Temp. ≤ 32°F	0	0	0	0	0	0	0	0	0	0	0	0	0
Days Minimum Temp. ≤ 32°F	3	2	0	0	0	0	0	0	0	0	0	2	7
Days Minimum Temp. ≤ 0°F	0	0	0	0	0	0	0	0	0	0	0	0	0
Heating Degree Days (base 65°F)	254	175	89	22	1	0	0	0	0	8	79	202	830
Cooling Degree Days (base 65°F)	26	41	84	159	336	468	539	536	446	265	100	36	3,036
Mean Precipitation (in.)	3.41	3.03	4.16	2.83	4.18	6.12	5.51	6.25	5.61	2.63	2.51	2.64	48.88
Days With ≥ 0.1" Precipitation	5	4	5	4	6	9	10	11	8	5	4	5	76
Days With ≥ 1.0" Precipitation	1	1	2	1	1	2	1	2	2	1	1	1	16
Mean Snowfall (in.)	trace	trace	0.0	0.0	0.0	0.0	0.0	0.0	0.0	0.0	0.0	0.0	trace
Days With ≥ 1.0" Snow Depth	0	0	0	0	0	0	0	0	0	0	0	0	0

Live Oak *Suwannee County*   Elevation: 118 ft.   Latitude: 30° 14' N   Longitude: 82° 58' W

	JAN	FEB	MAR	APR	MAY	JUN	JUL	AUG	SEP	OCT	NOV	DEC	YEAR
Mean Maximum Temp. (°F)	67.1	70.5	76.7	82.2	88.3	91.9	93.1	92.4	89.9	83.1	75.8	69.0	81.7
Mean Temp. (°F)	54.7	57.4	63.2	68.5	75.2	80.2	82.2	81.7	79.0	70.8	63.2	56.6	69.4
Mean Minimum Temp. (°F)	42.1	44.1	49.7	54.7	62.0	68.5	71.1	70.9	68.0	58.5	50.5	44.2	57.0
Extreme Maximum Temp. (°F)	86	88	91	96	100	106	104	103	99	95	88	86	106
Extreme Minimum Temp. (°F)	6	16	19	31	40	47	60	60	46	29	15	13	6
Days Maximum Temp. ≥ 90°F	0	0	0	2	12	22	27	26	19	4	0	0	112
Days Maximum Temp. ≤ 32°F	0	0	0	0	0	0	0	0	0	0	0	0	0
Days Minimum Temp. ≤ 32°F	8	5	2	0	0	0	0	0	0	0	2	6	23
Days Minimum Temp. ≤ 0°F	0	0	0	0	0	0	0	0	0	0	0	0	0
Heating Degree Days (base 65°F)	335	237	123	39	2	0	0	0	0	25	131	281	1,173
Cooling Degree Days (base 65°F)	16	32	74	151	333	473	550	533	420	220	87	30	2,919
Mean Precipitation (in.)	5.00	3.98	5.42	3.47	3.33	6.08	6.54	6.63	4.33	3.32	2.43	3.09	53.62
Days With ≥ 0.1" Precipitation	7	5	6	4	5	9	9	9	6	3	4	5	72
Days With ≥ 1.0" Precipitation	2	1	2	1	1	2	2	2	1	1	1	1	17
Mean Snowfall (in.)	trace	trace	trace	0.0	0.0	0.0	0.0	0.0	0.0	0.0	0.0	0.1	0.1
Days With ≥ 1.0" Snow Depth	0	0	0	0	0	0	0	0	0	0	0	0	0

Mayo *Lafayette County*   Elevation: 62 ft.   Latitude: 30° 03' N   Longitude: 83° 10' W

	JAN	FEB	MAR	APR	MAY	JUN	JUL	AUG	SEP	OCT	NOV	DEC	YEAR
Mean Maximum Temp. (°F)	65.1	68.6	75.2	80.8	87.0	90.8	92.2	91.7	89.3	82.3	74.7	67.4	80.4
Mean Temp. (°F)	52.7	55.7	62.2	67.4	74.4	79.7	81.8	81.3	78.5	69.5	61.9	54.9	68.3
Mean Minimum Temp. (°F)	40.2	42.7	49.1	54.0	61.7	68.6	71.3	70.8	67.6	56.7	49.2	42.4	56.2
Extreme Maximum Temp. (°F)	86	86	91	96	98	104	103	103	99	96	90	86	104
Extreme Minimum Temp. (°F)	7	12	19	32	41	47	60	60	46	32	25	12	7
Days Maximum Temp. ≥ 90°F	0	0	0	2	10	20	25	24	18	3	0	0	102
Days Maximum Temp. ≤ 32°F	0	0	0	0	0	0	0	0	0	0	0	0	0
Days Minimum Temp. ≤ 32°F	9	6	1	0	0	0	0	0	0	0	2	7	25
Days Minimum Temp. ≤ 0°F	0	0	0	0	0	0	0	0	0	0	0	0	0
Heating Degree Days (base 65°F)	390	277	148	52	4	0	0	0	0	38	156	329	1,394
Cooling Degree Days (base 65°F)	12	23	63	128	307	456	535	520	405	195	74	26	2,744
Mean Precipitation (in.)	5.01	3.74	5.14	3.16	3.23	5.86	7.67	8.12	4.73	3.05	2.57	3.31	55.59
Days With ≥ 0.1" Precipitation	6	6	6	4	5	9	11	11	7	3	4	5	77
Days With ≥ 1.0" Precipitation	2	1	2	1	1	2	3	2	1	1	1	1	18
Mean Snowfall (in.)	trace	0.0	0.0	0.0	0.0	0.0	0.0	0.0	0.0	0.0	0.0	0.0	trace
Days With ≥ 1.0" Snow Depth	0	0	0	0	0	0	0	0	0	0	0	0	0

Melbourne Regional Airport *Brevard County*   Elevation: 32 ft.   Latitude: 28° 07' N   Longitude: 80° 39' W

	JAN	FEB	MAR	APR	MAY	JUN	JUL	AUG	SEP	OCT	NOV	DEC	YEAR
Mean Maximum Temp. (°F)	71.7	72.9	77.2	80.6	85.1	88.7	90.5	89.9	88.1	83.3	78.1	73.4	81.6
Mean Temp. (°F)	61.5	62.5	66.8	70.8	76.0	80.0	81.4	81.4	80.1	75.5	69.4	63.6	72.4
Mean Minimum Temp. (°F)	51.2	52.0	56.5	60.9	66.8	71.2	72.3	72.9	72.2	67.6	60.5	53.7	63.2
Extreme Maximum Temp. (°F)	88	88	93	97	97	101	102	101	98	93	91	89	102
Extreme Minimum Temp. (°F)	17	28	25	25	47	55	60	60	58	41	31	21	17
Days Maximum Temp. ≥ 90°F	0	0	1	2	5	12	19	17	9	2	0	0	67
Days Maximum Temp. ≤ 32°F	0	0	0	0	0	0	0	0	0	0	0	0	0
Days Minimum Temp. ≤ 32°F	1	1	0	0	0	0	0	0	0	0	0	1	3
Days Minimum Temp. ≤ 0°F	0	0	0	0	0	0	0	0	0	0	0	0	0
Heating Degree Days (base 65°F)	164	127	61	16	0	0	0	0	0	3	36	122	529
Cooling Degree Days (base 65°F)	56	70	115	187	346	464	521	520	461	347	178	83	3,348
Mean Precipitation (in.)	2.54	2.52	3.01	2.05	4.05	5.67	5.35	5.70	7.15	4.72	3.11	2.29	48.16
Days With ≥ 0.1" Precipitation	4	5	4	3	6	9	8	9	9	7	4	4	72
Days With ≥ 1.0" Precipitation	1	1	1	0	1	2	2	2	2	1	1	1	15
Mean Snowfall (in.)	0.0	0.0	0.0	0.0	0.0	0.0	0.0	0.0	0.0	0.0	0.0	0.0	0.0
Days With ≥ 1.0" Snow Depth	0	0	0	0	0	0	0	0	0	0	0	0	0

Miami Beach *Dade County*   Elevation: 3 ft.   Latitude: 25° 47' N   Longitude: 80° 08' W

	JAN	FEB	MAR	APR	MAY	JUN	JUL	AUG	SEP	OCT	NOV	DEC	YEAR
Mean Maximum Temp. (°F)	74.2	74.8	76.7	79.4	82.7	85.8	87.4	87.6	86.3	83.2	79.1	75.7	81.1
Mean Temp. (°F)	68.6	69.2	71.8	74.9	78.4	81.3	82.9	83.1	82.0	79.0	74.8	70.7	76.4
Mean Minimum Temp. (°F)	63.0	63.5	66.8	70.2	74.0	76.7	78.4	78.5	77.7	74.8	70.5	65.6	71.6
Extreme Maximum Temp. (°F)	84	88	92	94	95	97	98	98	96	95	89	85	98
Extreme Minimum Temp. (°F)	32	37	32	46	58	66	66	67	67	54	39	32	32
Days Maximum Temp. ≥ 90°F	0	0	0	0	1	3	5	5	2	1	0	0	17
Days Maximum Temp. ≤ 32°F	0	0	0	0	0	0	0	0	0	0	0	0	0
Days Minimum Temp. ≤ 32°F	0	0	0	0	0	0	0	0	0	0	0	0	0
Days Minimum Temp. ≤ 0°F	0	0	0	0	0	0	0	0	0	0	0	0	0
Heating Degree Days (base 65°F)	48	32	14	2	0	0	0	0	0	0	4	30	130
Cooling Degree Days (base 65°F)	169	173	226	303	425	503	574	579	524	452	316	218	4,462
Mean Precipitation (in.)	2.49	2.18	2.20	2.66	5.04	6.91	3.31	5.24	6.85	4.57	3.35	1.95	46.75
Days With ≥ 0.1" Precipitation	4	4	4	4	6	9	7	9	9	7	5	3	71
Days With ≥ 1.0" Precipitation	1	1	1	1	2	2	1	1	2	1	1	1	15
Mean Snowfall (in.)	0.0	0.0	0.0	0.0	0.0	0.0	0.0	0.0	0.0	0.0	0.0	0.0	0.0
Days With ≥ 1.0" Snow Depth	0	0	0	0	0	0	0	0	0	0	0	0	0

Milton Experiment Stn. *Santa Rosa County*   Elevation: 216 ft.   Latitude: 30° 47' N   Longitude: 87° 08' W

	JAN	FEB	MAR	APR	MAY	JUN	JUL	AUG	SEP	OCT	NOV	DEC	YEAR
Mean Maximum Temp. (°F)	61.0	64.9	71.6	78.2	85.0	90.1	91.5	91.4	88.3	80.4	71.1	63.9	78.1
Mean Temp. (°F)	50.1	53.3	60.1	66.1	73.5	79.4	81.4	81.0	77.4	67.8	59.2	52.8	66.8
Mean Minimum Temp. (°F)	39.1	41.6	48.6	54.0	61.9	68.7	71.2	70.6	66.5	55.1	47.2	41.7	55.5
Extreme Maximum Temp. (°F)	79	83	88	94	99	102	103	101	102	93	88	82	103
Extreme Minimum Temp. (°F)	3	12	20	30	39	50	61	57	45	31	19	8	3
Days Maximum Temp. ≥ 90°F	0	0	0	0	6	18	22	23	15	2	0	0	86
Days Maximum Temp. ≤ 32°F	0	0	0	0	0	0	0	0	0	0	0	0	0
Days Minimum Temp. ≤ 32°F	10	6	2	0	0	0	0	0	0	0	3	8	29
Days Minimum Temp. ≤ 0°F	0	0	0	0	0	0	0	0	0	0	0	0	0
Heating Degree Days (base 65°F)	465	335	186	65	4	0	0	0	2	56	208	389	1,710
Cooling Degree Days (base 65°F)	5	12	38	98	274	441	519	510	374	149	40	15	2,475
Mean Precipitation (in.)	6.40	5.14	7.37	4.31	5.08	7.39	8.12	6.70	6.08	4.02	5.22	4.37	70.20
Days With ≥ 0.1" Precipitation	8	6	7	5	6	8	11	10	7	4	6	6	84
Days With ≥ 1.0" Precipitation	2	2	2	1	1	2	2	2	2	1	2	1	20
Mean Snowfall (in.)	0.1	0.1	trace	0.0	0.0	0.0	0.0	0.0	0.0	0.0	0.0	0.0	0.2
Days With ≥ 1.0" Snow Depth	0	0	0	0	0	0	0	0	0	0	0	0	0

Monticello 3 W *Jefferson County*   Elevation: 144 ft.   Latitude: 30° 32' N   Longitude: 83° 55' W

	JAN	FEB	MAR	APR	MAY	JUN	JUL	AUG	SEP	OCT	NOV	DEC	YEAR
Mean Maximum Temp. (°F)	61.7	65.9	72.3	78.2	84.5	89.3	90.6	89.9	87.2	79.7	71.8	64.8	78.0
Mean Temp. (°F)	49.8	53.2	59.9	65.3	72.3	78.2	80.2	79.7	76.4	66.8	59.0	52.4	66.1
Mean Minimum Temp. (°F)	37.8	40.5	47.4	52.4	60.1	67.1	69.9	69.4	65.6	53.9	46.1	39.9	54.2
Extreme Maximum Temp. (°F)	83	85	90	93	96	103	102	100	97	93	87	84	103
Extreme Minimum Temp. (°F)	4	14	18	31	38	44	58	58	43	31	13	11	4
Days Maximum Temp. ≥ 90°F	0	0	0	0	4	15	20	18	10	1	0	0	68
Days Maximum Temp. ≤ 32°F	0	0	0	0	0	0	0	0	0	0	0	0	0
Days Minimum Temp. ≤ 32°F	12	7	2	0	0	0	0	0	0	0	4	10	35
Days Minimum Temp. ≤ 0°F	0	0	0	0	0	0	0	0	0	0	0	0	0
Heating Degree Days (base 65°F)	471	338	193	77	8	0	0	0	2	64	216	398	1,767
Cooling Degree Days (base 65°F)	4	13	39	90	249	414	492	472	344	137	46	14	2,314
Mean Precipitation (in.)	5.63	4.62	6.02	3.63	4.06	5.71	6.65	6.75	4.47	3.41	3.57	3.89	58.41
Days With ≥ 0.1" Precipitation	7	5	6	4	6	8	10	10	6	4	4	5	75
Days With ≥ 1.0" Precipitation	2	1	2	1	1	2	2	2	1	1	1	1	17
Mean Snowfall (in.)	trace	trace	trace	0.0	0.0	0.0	0.0	0.0	0.0	0.0	0.0	trace	trace
Days With ≥ 1.0" Snow Depth	0	0	0	0	0	0	0	0	0	0	0	0	0

Moore Haven Lock 1 *Glades County*　Elevation: 32 ft.　　Latitude: 26° 50' N　　Longitude: 81° 05' W

	JAN	FEB	MAR	APR	MAY	JUN	JUL	AUG	SEP	OCT	NOV	DEC	YEAR
Mean Maximum Temp. (°F)	74.0	75.6	79.5	83.4	87.7	90.4	91.7	91.3	89.5	85.2	79.9	75.4	83.6
Mean Temp. (°F)	62.8	63.9	68.1	72.0	76.8	80.6	81.9	82.0	80.9	76.2	70.2	64.8	73.4
Mean Minimum Temp. (°F)	51.6	52.3	56.5	60.6	65.8	70.7	72.1	72.6	72.3	67.2	60.5	54.2	63.0
Extreme Maximum Temp. (°F)	88	90	93	97	98	101	100	98	99	95	91	89	101
Extreme Minimum Temp. (°F)	23	29	26	39	44	57	62	63	62	45	32	23	23
Days Maximum Temp. ≥ 90°F	0	0	1	4	11	18	25	24	17	5	0	0	105
Days Maximum Temp. ≤ 32°F	0	0	0	0	0	0	0	0	0	0	0	0	0
Days Minimum Temp. ≤ 32°F	1	0	0	0	0	0	0	0	0	0	0	1	2
Days Minimum Temp. ≤ 0°F	0	0	0	0	0	0	0	0	0	0	0	0	0
Heating Degree Days (base 65°F)	138	104	46	9	0	0	0	0	0	1	27	99	424
Cooling Degree Days (base 65°F)	76	90	149	223	378	483	540	544	487	364	194	101	3,629
Mean Precipitation (in.)	2.13	2.12	3.29	2.21	3.78	7.15	6.71	6.94	6.13	3.06	1.90	1.63	47.05
Days With ≥ 0.1" Precipitation	4	3	4	4	6	11	10	11	8	5	3	3	72
Days With ≥ 1.0" Precipitation	1	1	1	1	1	2	2	2	2	1	0	0	14
Mean Snowfall (in.)	0.0	0.0	0.0	0.0	0.0	0.0	0.0	0.0	0.0	0.0	0.0	0.0	0.0
Days With ≥ 1.0" Snow Depth	0	0	0	0	0	0	0	0	0	0	0	0	0

Mountain Lake *Polk County*　Elevation: 124 ft.　　Latitude: 27° 56' N　　Longitude: 81° 36' W

	JAN	FEB	MAR	APR	MAY	JUN	JUL	AUG	SEP	OCT	NOV	DEC	YEAR
Mean Maximum Temp. (°F)	73.8	76.0	80.6	84.9	89.5	92.0	92.8	92.5	90.5	85.7	79.7	75.1	84.4
Mean Temp. (°F)	61.4	63.1	67.7	71.8	76.9	80.8	81.8	82.0	80.5	74.8	68.3	63.1	72.7
Mean Minimum Temp. (°F)	49.0	50.1	54.7	58.6	64.2	69.6	70.8	71.5	70.4	63.9	56.9	51.2	60.9
Extreme Maximum Temp. (°F)	89	91	95	96	99	101	105	100	98	96	91	89	105
Extreme Minimum Temp. (°F)	16	24	25	34	44	50	53	62	57	40	24	19	16
Days Maximum Temp. ≥ 90°F	0	0	3	7	16	22	27	27	20	6	0	0	128
Days Maximum Temp. ≤ 32°F	0	0	0	0	0	0	0	0	0	0	0	0	0
Days Minimum Temp. ≤ 32°F	3	1	0	0	0	0	0	0	0	0	0	2	6
Days Minimum Temp. ≤ 0°F	0	0	0	0	0	0	0	0	0	0	0	0	0
Heating Degree Days (base 65°F)	169	120	53	10	0	0	0	0	0	3	44	127	526
Cooling Degree Days (base 65°F)	57	74	128	212	371	481	526	535	464	314	149	71	3,382
Mean Precipitation (in.)	2.44	2.49	3.27	2.02	4.02	7.47	7.52	6.61	5.81	2.51	2.22	2.14	48.52
Days With ≥ 0.1" Precipitation	4	4	5	3	6	10	12	10	8	5	4	4	75
Days With ≥ 1.0" Precipitation	1	1	1	1	1	2	2	2	2	1	1	1	16
Mean Snowfall (in.)	trace	0.0	0.0	0.0	0.0	0.0	0.0	0.0	0.0	0.0	0.0	0.0	trace
Days With ≥ 1.0" Snow Depth	0	0	0	0	0	0	0	0	0	0	0	0	0

Myakka River State Park *Sarasota County*　Elevation: 19 ft.　　Latitude: 27° 14' N　　Longitude: 82° 19' W

	JAN	FEB	MAR	APR	MAY	JUN	JUL	AUG	SEP	OCT	NOV	DEC	YEAR
Mean Maximum Temp. (°F)	74.7	76.8	81.4	85.7	90.9	92.4	93.0	92.9	91.4	87.1	81.3	76.3	85.3
Mean Temp. (°F)	62.1	63.7	68.2	71.9	77.1	80.8	82.0	82.6	81.4	76.0	69.5	64.2	73.3
Mean Minimum Temp. (°F)	49.4	50.6	54.9	58.0	63.2	69.1	71.0	72.2	71.3	64.8	57.6	52.0	61.2
Extreme Maximum Temp. (°F)	89	91	93	98	104	105	101	104	103	97	95	90	105
Extreme Minimum Temp. (°F)	18	22	28	34	43	50	63	63	58	42	24	22	18
Days Maximum Temp. ≥ 90°F	0	0	2	8	21	25	28	28	23	11	1	0	147
Days Maximum Temp. ≤ 32°F	0	0	0	0	0	0	0	0	0	0	0	0	0
Days Minimum Temp. ≤ 32°F	2	1	0	0	0	0	0	0	0	0	0	1	4
Days Minimum Temp. ≤ 0°F	0	0	0	0	0	0	0	0	0	0	0	0	0
Heating Degree Days (base 65°F)	148	107	43	9	0	0	0	0	0	2	33	108	450
Cooling Degree Days (base 65°F)	66	90	148	223	388	493	542	562	501	360	183	96	3,652
Mean Precipitation (in.)	3.16	2.91	3.61	2.11	3.37	8.92	9.63	9.61	8.05	3.21	2.23	2.30	59.11
Days With ≥ 0.1" Precipitation	4	4	4	3	5	10	13	13	10	5	4	3	78
Days With ≥ 1.0" Precipitation	1	1	1	1	1	3	3	3	3	1	1	1	20
Mean Snowfall (in.)	0.0	0.0	0.0	0.0	0.0	0.0	0.0	0.0	0.0	0.0	0.0	trace	trace
Days With ≥ 1.0" Snow Depth	0	0	0	0	0	0	0	0	0	0	0	0	0

Naples *Collier County*　Elevation: 3 ft.　　Latitude: 26° 10' N　　Longitude: 81° 47' W

	JAN	FEB	MAR	APR	MAY	JUN	JUL	AUG	SEP	OCT	NOV	DEC	YEAR
Mean Maximum Temp. (°F)	76.6	77.6	80.9	84.4	88.0	90.4	91.7	91.9	90.9	87.6	82.9	78.3	85.1
Mean Temp. (°F)	65.3	66.2	69.7	73.2	77.5	81.1	82.1	82.5	81.8	77.9	72.4	67.3	74.8
Mean Minimum Temp. (°F)	54.0	54.7	58.4	62.0	67.0	71.7	72.5	73.1	72.7	68.0	61.8	56.2	64.4
Extreme Maximum Temp. (°F)	88	89	91	93	95	98	98	97	99	95	91	89	99
Extreme Minimum Temp. (°F)	26	28	33	39	52	59	62	63	59	48	31	27	26
Days Maximum Temp. ≥ 90°F	0	0	0	2	9	20	27	28	24	9	1	0	120
Days Maximum Temp. ≤ 32°F	0	0	0	0	0	0	0	0	0	0	0	0	0
Days Minimum Temp. ≤ 32°F	1	0	0	0	0	0	0	0	0	0	0	0	1
Days Minimum Temp. ≤ 0°F	0	0	0	0	0	0	0	0	0	0	0	0	0
Heating Degree Days (base 65°F)	88	64	24	4	0	0	0	0	0	0	11	58	249
Cooling Degree Days (base 65°F)	100	114	175	257	399	497	546	557	512	416	243	137	3,953
Mean Precipitation (in.)	2.06	2.21	2.49	1.95	4.33	8.20	7.98	7.68	8.22	3.69	2.00	1.52	52.33
Days With ≥ 0.1" Precipitation	3	4	3	3	5	10	12	12	11	5	3	3	74
Days With ≥ 1.0" Precipitation	1	1	1	0	2	3	3	2	2	1	1	0	17
Mean Snowfall (in.)	0.0	0.0	0.0	0.0	0.0	0.0	0.0	0.0	0.0	0.0	0.0	0.0	0.0
Days With ≥ 1.0" Snow Depth	0	0	0	0	0	0	0	0	0	0	0	0	0

Ocala *Marion County* Elevation: 72 ft. Latitude: 29° 12' N Longitude: 82° 05' W

	JAN	FEB	MAR	APR	MAY	JUN	JUL	AUG	SEP	OCT	NOV	DEC	YEAR
Mean Maximum Temp. (°F)	70.3	72.8	78.3	83.0	88.3	91.1	92.3	91.7	89.9	84.2	77.5	72.0	82.6
Mean Temp. (°F)	57.9	59.9	65.3	69.6	75.7	80.2	81.7	81.3	79.4	72.8	65.7	59.7	70.8
Mean Minimum Temp. (°F)	45.6	46.9	52.3	56.2	63.0	69.2	71.1	70.8	68.7	61.3	53.6	47.4	58.8
Extreme Maximum Temp. (°F)	86	89	91	97	101	105	100	100	97	95	89	88	105
Extreme Minimum Temp. (°F)	11	20	23	33	45	48	58	60	45	32	23	15	11
Days Maximum Temp. ≥ 90°F	0	0	0	3	12	21	26	24	19	4	0	0	109
Days Maximum Temp. ≤ 32°F	0	0	0	0	0	0	0	0	0	0	0	0	0
Days Minimum Temp. ≤ 32°F	5	3	1	0	0	0	0	0	0	0	1	3	13
Days Minimum Temp. ≤ 0°F	0	0	0	0	0	0	0	0	0	0	0	0	0
Heating Degree Days (base 65°F)	250	181	90	25	1	0	0	0	0	11	81	202	841
Cooling Degree Days (base 65°F)	32	47	98	168	339	465	531	518	430	258	111	44	3,041
Mean Precipitation (in.)	3.64	3.28	4.18	2.87	3.81	7.11	6.39	6.05	5.46	2.77	2.43	2.69	50.68
Days With ≥ 0.1" Precipitation	6	5	6	4	5	9	11	12	8	4	4	4	78
Days With ≥ 1.0" Precipitation	1	1	1	1	1	2	2	1	2	1	1	1	15
Mean Snowfall (in.)	trace	trace	0.0	0.0	0.0	0.0	0.0	0.0	0.0	0.0	0.0	0.0	trace
Days With ≥ 1.0" Snow Depth	0	0	0	0	0	0	0	0	0	0	0	0	0

Panama City 5 NE *Bay County* Elevation: 29 ft. Latitude: 30° 13' N Longitude: 85° 36' W

	JAN	FEB	MAR	APR	MAY	JUN	JUL	AUG	SEP	OCT	NOV	DEC	YEAR
Mean Maximum Temp. (°F)	62.7	65.4	71.1	77.2	83.6	88.5	89.9	90.0	87.8	80.4	72.5	64.9	77.8
Mean Temp. (°F)	51.2	53.7	59.8	65.5	72.7	78.7	80.9	80.7	77.8	68.3	60.5	53.2	66.9
Mean Minimum Temp. (°F)	39.7	42.1	48.3	53.9	61.7	68.9	71.8	71.4	67.8	56.3	48.4	41.4	56.0
Extreme Maximum Temp. (°F)	80	82	87	93	100	100	101	100	98	93	91	82	101
Extreme Minimum Temp. (°F)	6	15	23	34	40	46	60	59	45	33	26	11	6
Days Maximum Temp. ≥ 90°F	0	0	0	0	3	13	18	19	12	1	0	0	66
Days Maximum Temp. ≤ 32°F	0	0	0	0	0	0	0	0	0	0	0	0	0
Days Minimum Temp. ≤ 32°F	10	6	2	0	0	0	0	0	0	0	2	8	28
Days Minimum Temp. ≤ 0°F	0	0	0	0	0	0	0	0	0	0	0	0	0
Heating Degree Days (base 65°F)	428	322	190	65	5	0	0	0	1	43	179	375	1,608
Cooling Degree Days (base 65°F)	5	12	32	82	249	416	498	497	384	162	47	15	2,399
Mean Precipitation (in.)	5.95	4.90	6.23	3.93	4.03	6.12	8.86	7.52	6.19	3.67	4.57	4.10	66.07
Days With ≥ 0.1" Precipitation	7	6	7	4	5	8	11	11	7	4	5	6	81
Days With ≥ 1.0" Precipitation	2	2	2	1	1	2	3	2	2	1	1	1	20
Mean Snowfall (in.)	trace	trace	0.0	0.0	0.0	0.0	0.0	0.0	0.0	0.0	0.0	0.0	trace
Days With ≥ 1.0" Snow Depth	0	0	0	0	0	0	0	0	0	0	0	0	0

Parrish *Manatee County* Elevation: 59 ft. Latitude: 27° 37' N Longitude: 82° 21' W

	JAN	FEB	MAR	APR	MAY	JUN	JUL	AUG	SEP	OCT	NOV	DEC	YEAR
Mean Maximum Temp. (°F)	72.9	74.4	78.4	82.7	87.6	90.2	91.2	91.1	89.9	85.4	79.6	74.5	83.2
Mean Temp. (°F)	61.5	62.6	66.8	70.7	75.9	80.2	81.6	81.8	80.6	75.1	68.8	63.3	72.4
Mean Minimum Temp. (°F)	50.0	50.8	55.1	58.7	64.2	70.2	72.0	72.4	71.3	64.8	57.9	52.0	61.6
Extreme Maximum Temp. (°F)	86	88	91	93	97	101	98	101	99	93	91	87	101
Extreme Minimum Temp. (°F)	18	24	29	36	41	51	62	64	57	44	25	23	18
Days Maximum Temp. ≥ 90°F	0	0	0	1	9	20	25	24	20	5	0	0	104
Days Maximum Temp. ≤ 32°F	0	0	0	0	0	0	0	0	0	0	0	0	0
Days Minimum Temp. ≤ 32°F	2	1	0	0	0	0	0	0	0	0	0	1	4
Days Minimum Temp. ≤ 0°F	0	0	0	0	0	0	0	0	0	0	0	0	0
Heating Degree Days (base 65°F)	167	125	61	16	1	0	0	0	0	4	40	129	543
Cooling Degree Days (base 65°F)	55	67	111	182	336	466	522	526	470	326	158	79	3,298
Mean Precipitation (in.)	2.85	3.19	3.23	2.03	3.18	7.15	7.45	8.68	7.39	2.86	2.31	2.26	52.58
Days With ≥ 0.1" Precipitation	4	4	4	3	4	9	11	12	9	4	3	3	70
Days With ≥ 1.0" Precipitation	1	1	1	1	1	3	2	3	2	1	1	1	18
Mean Snowfall (in.)	trace	0.0	0.0	0.0	0.0	0.0	0.0	0.0	0.0	0.0	0.0	0.0	trace
Days With ≥ 1.0" Snow Depth	0	0	0	0	0	0	0	0	0	0	0	0	0

Perry *Taylor County* Elevation: 42 ft. Latitude: 30° 06' N Longitude: 83° 34' W

	JAN	FEB	MAR	APR	MAY	JUN	JUL	AUG	SEP	OCT	NOV	DEC	YEAR
Mean Maximum Temp. (°F)	67.0	70.3	76.2	81.8	87.8	91.4	92.7	92.2	90.3	83.6	76.4	69.7	81.6
Mean Temp. (°F)	54.2	56.9	62.5	67.7	74.7	79.7	81.7	81.4	78.9	70.5	62.8	56.5	69.0
Mean Minimum Temp. (°F)	41.4	43.4	48.8	53.6	61.5	67.9	70.7	70.4	67.5	57.2	49.1	43.2	56.2
Extreme Maximum Temp. (°F)	85	87	90	94	99	103	104	102	99	94	90	86	104
Extreme Minimum Temp. (°F)	7	14	19	29	40	46	59	59	45	28	14	12	7
Days Maximum Temp. ≥ 90°F	0	0	0	2	11	22	26	25	20	4	0	0	110
Days Maximum Temp. ≤ 32°F	0	0	0	0	0	0	0	0	0	0	0	0	0
Days Minimum Temp. ≤ 32°F	8	5	2	0	0	0	0	0	0	0	3	7	25
Days Minimum Temp. ≤ 0°F	0	0	0	0	0	0	0	0	0	0	0	0	0
Heating Degree Days (base 65°F)	343	244	132	45	2	0	0	0	0	26	136	282	1,210
Cooling Degree Days (base 65°F)	12	25	60	126	309	446	526	518	414	208	80	27	2,751
Mean Precipitation (in.)	4.91	4.00	5.59	3.35	3.52	6.02	8.48	8.86	5.01	3.15	2.70	3.38	58.97
Days With ≥ 0.1" Precipitation	7	6	6	4	6	8	12	11	7	4	4	6	81
Days With ≥ 1.0" Precipitation	2	1	2	1	1	2	2	3	2	1	1	1	19
Mean Snowfall (in.)	trace	0.0	0.0	0.0	0.0	0.0	0.0	0.0	0.0	0.0	0.0	0.0	trace
Days With ≥ 1.0" Snow Depth	0	0	0	0	0	0	0	0	0	0	0	0	0

Plant City *Hillsborough County*   Elevation: 118 ft.   Latitude: 28° 01' N   Longitude: 82° 08' W

	JAN	FEB	MAR	APR	MAY	JUN	JUL	AUG	SEP	OCT	NOV	DEC	YEAR
Mean Maximum Temp. (°F)	73.0	74.7	79.4	83.6	88.5	90.8	91.8	91.4	90.2	85.5	79.5	74.6	83.6
Mean Temp. (°F)	61.2	62.6	67.2	71.2	76.6	80.6	81.8	81.9	80.5	75.0	68.3	63.0	72.5
Mean Minimum Temp. (°F)	49.3	50.5	54.9	58.9	64.6	70.4	71.8	72.2	70.8	64.6	57.1	51.3	61.4
Extreme Maximum Temp. (°F)	87	89	91	96	99	102	102	99	98	94	92	89	102
Extreme Minimum Temp. (°F)	17	25	24	35	43	49	62	63	55	39	21	20	17
Days Maximum Temp. ≥ 90°F	0	0	1	3	12	21	26	25	20	5	0	0	113
Days Maximum Temp. ≤ 32°F	0	0	0	0	0	0	0	0	0	0	0	0	0
Days Minimum Temp. ≤ 32°F	2	1	0	0	0	0	0	0	0	0	0	1	4
Days Minimum Temp. ≤ 0°F	0	0	0	0	0	0	0	0	0	0	0	0	0
Heating Degree Days (base 65°F)	176	127	60	15	0	0	0	0	0	4	47	133	562
Cooling Degree Days (base 65°F)	56	76	126	203	370	483	535	536	468	321	155	75	3,404
Mean Precipitation (in.)	2.74	3.17	3.56	2.13	3.81	7.01	7.35	7.83	6.56	2.41	2.11	2.55	51.23
Days With ≥ 0.1" Precipitation	4	4	5	4	5	9	11	12	9	4	3	4	74
Days With ≥ 1.0" Precipitation	1	1	1	1	1	2	2	2	2	1	1	1	16
Mean Snowfall (in.)	0.0	0.0	0.0	0.0	0.0	0.0	0.0	0.0	0.0	0.0	0.0	0.0	0.0
Days With ≥ 1.0" Snow Depth	0	0	0	0	0	0	0	0	0	0	0	0	0

Punta Gorda 4 ESE *Charlotte County*   Elevation: 19 ft.   Latitude: 26° 55' N   Longitude: 82° 00' W

	JAN	FEB	MAR	APR	MAY	JUN	JUL	AUG	SEP	OCT	NOV	DEC	YEAR
Mean Maximum Temp. (°F)	74.3	75.9	80.2	84.4	89.1	91.5	92.2	92.2	90.7	86.3	80.8	76.2	84.5
Mean Temp. (°F)	63.0	64.4	68.6	72.4	77.5	81.4	82.6	82.8	81.6	76.4	70.2	65.1	73.8
Mean Minimum Temp. (°F)	51.7	52.9	56.9	60.4	65.9	71.2	72.9	73.3	72.4	66.4	59.5	54.0	63.1
Extreme Maximum Temp. (°F)	89	92	91	94	98	101	99	97	95	94	93	89	101
Extreme Minimum Temp. (°F)	23	27	29	38	49	57	63	65	61	46	28	25	23
Days Maximum Temp. ≥ 90°F	0	0	1	3	14	23	27	27	22	6	0	0	123
Days Maximum Temp. ≤ 32°F	0	0	0	0	0	0	0	0	0	0	0	0	0
Days Minimum Temp. ≤ 32°F	1	0	0	0	0	0	0	0	0	0	0	1	2
Days Minimum Temp. ≤ 0°F	0	0	0	0	0	0	0	0	0	0	0	0	0
Heating Degree Days (base 65°F)	130	91	35	4	0	0	0	0	0	1	25	88	374
Cooling Degree Days (base 65°F)	79	94	154	241	401	512	566	571	510	375	197	105	3,805
Mean Precipitation (in.)	2.33	2.35	3.01	1.69	3.35	8.46	7.72	7.76	6.58	3.12	1.86	1.78	50.01
Days With ≥ 0.1" Precipitation	4	4	4	3	5	10	13	11	10	5	3	3	75
Days With ≥ 1.0" Precipitation	1	1	1	0	1	3	2	2	2	1	0	1	15
Mean Snowfall (in.)	0.0	0.0	0.0	0.0	0.0	0.0	0.0	0.0	0.0	0.0	0.0	0.0	0.0
Days With ≥ 1.0" Snow Depth	0	0	0	0	0	0	0	0	0	0	0	0	0

Quincy 3 SSW *Gadsden County*   Elevation: 242 ft.   Latitude: 30° 36' N   Longitude: 84° 33' W

	JAN	FEB	MAR	APR	MAY	JUN	JUL	AUG	SEP	OCT	NOV	DEC	YEAR
Mean Maximum Temp. (°F)	61.7	65.7	72.1	78.4	84.9	89.4	90.7	90.0	87.4	79.8	71.7	65.0	78.1
Mean Temp. (°F)	50.8	53.9	60.3	66.1	73.3	79.1	80.8	80.4	77.3	68.3	60.3	53.9	67.0
Mean Minimum Temp. (°F)	39.8	42.0	48.6	53.7	61.6	68.5	70.9	70.7	67.1	56.7	48.8	42.7	55.9
Extreme Maximum Temp. (°F)	83	85	90	92	99	102	102	101	98	93	86	84	102
Extreme Minimum Temp. (°F)	4	0	19	33	36	49	62	59	48	33	20	12	0
Days Maximum Temp. ≥ 90°F	0	0	0	0	5	15	21	18	11	1	0	0	71
Days Maximum Temp. ≤ 32°F	0	0	0	0	0	0	0	0	0	0	0	0	0
Days Minimum Temp. ≤ 32°F	9	6	1	0	0	0	0	0	0	0	2	6	24
Days Minimum Temp. ≤ 0°F	0	0	0	0	0	0	0	0	0	0	0	0	0
Heating Degree Days (base 65°F)	442	320	183	67	6	0	0	0	1	44	183	356	1,602
Cooling Degree Days (base 65°F)	6	14	41	101	272	440	510	496	370	159	49	16	2,474
Mean Precipitation (in.)	5.68	4.49	6.21	3.64	4.81	5.59	6.85	5.64	3.74	3.43	3.53	3.59	57.20
Days With ≥ 0.1" Precipitation	7	6	7	4	6	8	10	9	6	4	4	6	77
Days With ≥ 1.0" Precipitation	2	1	2	1	2	2	2	1	1	1	1	1	17
Mean Snowfall (in.)	trace	trace	trace	0.0	0.0	0.0	0.0	0.0	0.0	0.0	0.0	0.0	trace
Days With ≥ 1.0" Snow Depth	0	0	0	0	0	0	0	0	0	0	0	0	0

Saint Augustine *St. Johns County*   Elevation: 6 ft.   Latitude: 29° 54' N   Longitude: 81° 19' W

	JAN	FEB	MAR	APR	MAY	JUN	JUL	AUG	SEP	OCT	NOV	DEC	YEAR
Mean Maximum Temp. (°F)	66.8	69.2	73.6	78.7	83.9	88.1	90.6	89.2	86.5	80.7	74.6	68.3	79.2
Mean Temp. (°F)	56.4	58.5	63.3	68.4	74.4	79.4	81.5	80.8	78.9	72.4	65.4	58.6	69.8
Mean Minimum Temp. (°F)	46.0	47.8	52.9	58.0	64.9	70.5	72.4	72.4	71.2	64.0	56.1	48.8	60.4
Extreme Maximum Temp. (°F)	86	87	93	95	97	101	103	101	98	94	88	86	103
Extreme Minimum Temp. (°F)	10	21	23	34	45	52	59	61	51	36	31	16	10
Days Maximum Temp. ≥ 90°F	0	0	0	1	4	11	18	13	6	1	0	0	54
Days Maximum Temp. ≤ 32°F	0	0	0	0	0	0	0	0	0	0	0	0	0
Days Minimum Temp. ≤ 32°F	3	2	0	0	0	0	0	0	0	0	0	2	7
Days Minimum Temp. ≤ 0°F	0	0	0	0	0	0	0	0	0	0	0	0	0
Heating Degree Days (base 65°F)	278	202	109	29	1	0	0	0	0	9	81	224	933
Cooling Degree Days (base 65°F)	16	25	55	134	296	439	521	501	413	251	98	32	2,781
Mean Precipitation (in.)	3.21	2.96	3.73	2.69	3.17	5.24	4.57	5.92	6.57	4.58	2.27	2.90	47.81
Days With ≥ 0.1" Precipitation	5	5	5	4	5	8	7	9	9	6	4	5	72
Days With ≥ 1.0" Precipitation	1	1	1	1	1	1	1	2	2	1	0	1	13
Mean Snowfall (in.)	trace	0.0	trace	0.0	0.0	0.0	0.0	0.0	0.0	0.0	0.0	0.0	trace
Days With ≥ 1.0" Snow Depth	0	0	0	0	0	0	0	0	0	0	0	0	0

Saint Leo *Pasco County* Elevation: 187 ft.   Latitude: 28° 20' N   Longitude: 82° 16' W

	JAN	FEB	MAR	APR	MAY	JUN	JUL	AUG	SEP	OCT	NOV	DEC	YEAR
Mean Maximum Temp. (°F)	71.7	74.3	79.2	83.8	89.1	91.5	92.4	92.1	90.7	85.4	79.2	74.0	83.6
Mean Temp. (°F)	60.2	62.5	67.2	71.6	77.1	81.0	82.2	82.1	80.6	74.7	68.1	62.7	72.5
Mean Minimum Temp. (°F)	48.7	50.6	55.2	59.4	65.1	70.5	71.9	72.0	70.5	63.9	57.1	51.4	61.4
Extreme Maximum Temp. (°F)	87	90	92	95	99	103	100	99	98	96	92	88	103
Extreme Minimum Temp. (°F)	18	22	24	38	46	54	64	63	53	39	27	20	18
Days Maximum Temp. ≥ 90°F	0	0	1	4	16	22	27	26	21	6	0	0	123
Days Maximum Temp. ≤ 32°F	0	0	0	0	0	0	0	0	0	0	0	0	0
Days Minimum Temp. ≤ 32°F	2	1	0	0	0	0	0	0	0	0	0	1	4
Days Minimum Temp. ≤ 0°F	0	0	0	0	0	0	0	0	0	0	0	0	0
Heating Degree Days (base 65°F)	193	130	58	10	0	0	0	0	0	3	48	138	580
Cooling Degree Days (base 65°F)	53	75	130	215	395	497	551	547	476	316	157	75	3,487
Mean Precipitation (in.)	3.48	3.55	4.25	2.37	4.10	6.94	7.66	7.40	6.52	2.86	2.49	2.67	54.29
Days With ≥ 0.1" Precipitation	5	5	5	3	5	9	12	12	9	4	4	4	77
Days With ≥ 1.0" Precipitation	1	1	2	1	1	2	3	2	2	1	1	1	18
Mean Snowfall (in.)	trace	0.0	0.0	0.0	0.0	0.0	0.0	0.0	0.0	0.0	0.0	0.0	trace
Days With ≥ 1.0" Snow Depth	0	0	0	0	0	0	0	0	0	0	0	0	0

Saint Petersburg *Pinellas County* Elevation: 6 ft.   Latitude: 27° 46' N   Longitude: 82° 38' W

	JAN	FEB	MAR	APR	MAY	JUN	JUL	AUG	SEP	OCT	NOV	DEC	YEAR
Mean Maximum Temp. (°F)	70.0	71.6	76.0	80.8	86.2	89.5	90.6	90.2	88.7	83.7	77.3	72.0	81.4
Mean Temp. (°F)	62.2	63.6	68.2	73.0	78.6	82.4	83.7	83.4	82.1	76.9	70.1	64.4	74.1
Mean Minimum Temp. (°F)	54.3	55.6	60.3	65.2	71.0	75.4	76.7	76.6	75.6	70.1	62.9	56.8	66.7
Extreme Maximum Temp. (°F)	88	90	88	93	96	99	100	99	97	92	89	88	100
Extreme Minimum Temp. (°F)	27	28	34	46	55	61	69	67	61	51	35	24	24
Days Maximum Temp. ≥ 90°F	0	0	0	0	5	16	22	21	13	2	0	0	79
Days Maximum Temp. ≤ 32°F	0	0	0	0	0	0	0	0	0	0	0	0	0
Days Minimum Temp. ≤ 32°F	0	0	0	0	0	0	0	0	0	0	0	0	0
Days Minimum Temp. ≤ 0°F	0	0	0	0	0	0	0	0	0	0	0	0	0
Heating Degree Days (base 65°F)	140	97	38	4	0	0	0	0	0	1	26	97	403
Cooling Degree Days (base 65°F)	50	68	133	237	428	529	586	582	515	375	184	83	3,770
Mean Precipitation (in.)	2.78	2.99	3.52	1.92	2.90	5.99	6.25	8.09	7.51	2.69	2.03	2.62	49.29
Days With ≥ 0.1" Precipitation	5	4	5	3	4	7	10	11	9	4	3	4	69
Days With ≥ 1.0" Precipitation	1	1	1	0	1	2	2	3	2	1	1	1	16
Mean Snowfall (in.)	trace	0.0	0.0	0.0	0.0	0.0	0.0	0.0	0.0	0.0	0.0	0.0	trace
Days With ≥ 1.0" Snow Depth	0	0	0	0	0	0	0	0	0	0	0	0	0

Sanford Experiment Station *Seminole County* Elevation: 13 ft.   Latitude: 28° 48' N   Longitude: 81° 14' W

	JAN	FEB	MAR	APR	MAY	JUN	JUL	AUG	SEP	OCT	NOV	DEC	YEAR
Mean Maximum Temp. (°F)	70.4	72.2	77.1	81.6	87.0	90.5	92.0	91.6	89.2	83.6	77.6	72.0	82.1
Mean Temp. (°F)	59.1	60.7	65.6	69.7	75.3	80.1	81.8	81.8	80.0	74.0	67.4	61.5	71.4
Mean Minimum Temp. (°F)	47.7	49.1	54.0	57.8	63.6	69.6	71.6	72.0	70.7	64.3	57.2	50.8	60.7
Extreme Maximum Temp. (°F)	89	89	92	96	100	102	103	100	98	95	92	87	103
Extreme Minimum Temp. (°F)	19	26	27	36	45	52	60	65	52	39	30	19	19
Days Maximum Temp. ≥ 90°F	0	0	0	2	10	18	25	24	16	3	0	0	98
Days Maximum Temp. ≤ 32°F	0	0	0	0	0	0	0	0	0	0	0	0	0
Days Minimum Temp. ≤ 32°F	2	1	0	0	0	0	0	0	0	0	0	1	4
Days Minimum Temp. ≤ 0°F	0	0	0	0	0	0	0	0	0	0	0	0	0
Heating Degree Days (base 65°F)	220	161	79	22	1	0	0	0	0	5	54	162	704
Cooling Degree Days (base 65°F)	36	48	97	164	327	461	536	533	450	296	139	58	3,145
Mean Precipitation (in.)	3.01	3.07	3.92	2.57	3.64	6.46	6.80	7.35	5.72	3.65	2.96	2.58	51.73
Days With ≥ 0.1" Precipitation	4	4	5	3	5	9	9	10	7	6	3	4	69
Days With ≥ 1.0" Precipitation	1	1	1	1	1	2	2	2	2	1	1	1	16
Mean Snowfall (in.)	0.0	0.0	0.0	0.0	0.0	0.0	0.0	0.0	0.0	0.0	0.0	0.0	0.0
Days With ≥ 1.0" Snow Depth	0	0	0	0	0	0	0	0	0	0	0	0	0

Stuart 1 S *Martin County* Elevation: 9 ft.   Latitude: 27° 10' N   Longitude: 80° 14' W

	JAN	FEB	MAR	APR	MAY	JUN	JUL	AUG	SEP	OCT	NOV	DEC	YEAR
Mean Maximum Temp. (°F)	75.3	76.2	79.0	82.2	85.5	88.6	90.0	90.1	89.0	85.5	80.5	76.8	83.2
Mean Temp. (°F)	65.2	65.8	69.5	73.0	77.1	80.6	82.0	82.3	81.5	77.5	72.0	67.5	74.5
Mean Minimum Temp. (°F)	55.1	55.5	59.8	63.7	68.7	72.7	73.9	74.4	73.9	69.5	63.5	58.2	65.7
Extreme Maximum Temp. (°F)	89	89	93	95	96	98	101	99	97	96	89	89	101
Extreme Minimum Temp. (°F)	23	28	26	37	45	55	63	61	65	44	33	27	23
Days Maximum Temp. ≥ 90°F	0	0	0	2	5	11	17	18	13	3	0	0	69
Days Maximum Temp. ≤ 32°F	0	0	0	0	0	0	0	0	0	0	0	0	0
Days Minimum Temp. ≤ 32°F	1	0	0	0	0	0	0	0	0	0	0	0	1
Days Minimum Temp. ≤ 0°F	0	0	0	0	0	0	0	0	0	0	0	0	0
Heating Degree Days (base 65°F)	87	67	28	5	0	0	0	0	0	1	12	55	255
Cooling Degree Days (base 65°F)	105	109	170	252	395	489	550	558	511	411	246	148	3,944
Mean Precipitation (in.)	3.12	3.35	4.57	2.78	5.43	6.93	6.25	6.43	8.16	6.42	4.18	2.72	60.34
Days With ≥ 0.1" Precipitation	5	5	6	6	8	11	11	11	11	9	6	5	94
Days With ≥ 1.0" Precipitation	1	1	1	1	2	2	2	2	2	1	1	1	18
Mean Snowfall (in.)	0.0	0.0	0.0	0.0	0.0	0.0	0.0	0.0	0.0	0.0	0.0	0.0	0.0
Days With ≥ 1.0" Snow Depth	0	0	0	0	0	0	0	0	0	0	0	0	0

Tamiami Trail 40 Mile Bend *Dade County*   Elevation: 13 ft.   Latitude: 25° 46' N   Longitude: 80° 49' W

	JAN	FEB	MAR	APR	MAY	JUN	JUL	AUG	SEP	OCT	NOV	DEC	YEAR
Mean Maximum Temp. (°F)	77.6	78.7	82.0	85.6	89.1	91.0	92.2	92.4	90.9	87.1	82.6	78.7	85.7
Mean Temp. (°F)	67.4	68.0	70.9	74.2	78.2	81.5	83.2	83.7	82.8	79.1	74.1	69.1	76.0
Mean Minimum Temp. (°F)	57.0	57.3	59.8	62.7	67.2	71.9	74.2	75.0	74.6	71.1	65.5	59.4	66.3
Extreme Maximum Temp. (°F)	89	90	92	98	98	102	99	101	97	97	93	95	102
Extreme Minimum Temp. (°F)	28	33	34	42	45	59	63	64	65	52	36	28	28
Days Maximum Temp. ≥ 90°F	0	0	1	6	14	22	27	27	22	9	0	0	129
Days Maximum Temp. ≤ 32°F	0	0	0	0	0	0	0	0	0	0	0	0	0
Days Minimum Temp. ≤ 32°F	0	0	0	0	0	0	0	0	0	0	0	0	0
Days Minimum Temp. ≤ 0°F	0	0	0	0	0	0	0	0	0	0	0	0	0
Heating Degree Days (base 65°F)	61	43	16	3	0	0	0	0	0	0	6	39	168
Cooling Degree Days (base 65°F)	140	153	216	298	427	513	588	603	545	457	295	177	4,412
Mean Precipitation (in.)	1.90	2.00	2.30	2.38	4.96	8.54	7.60	6.91	6.56	4.46	2.28	1.63	51.52
Days With ≥ 0.1" Precipitation	3	3	3	4	7	11	11	11	10	6	3	3	75
Days With ≥ 1.0" Precipitation	0	0	0	1	1	3	2	2	2	1	1	0	13
Mean Snowfall (in.)	0.0	0.0	0.0	0.0	0.0	0.0	0.0	0.0	0.0	0.0	0.0	0.0	0.0
Days With ≥ 1.0" Snow Depth	0	0	0	0	0	0	0	0	0	0	0	0	0

Tarpon Springs Sewage Plant *Pinellas County*   Elevation: 6 ft.   Latitude: 28° 09' N   Longitude: 82° 45' W

	JAN	FEB	MAR	APR	MAY	JUN	JUL	AUG	SEP	OCT	NOV	DEC	YEAR
Mean Maximum Temp. (°F)	71.1	72.8	77.4	81.6	86.9	90.0	91.4	91.5	90.2	85.2	79.0	73.5	82.5
Mean Temp. (°F)	60.6	62.2	66.9	71.2	76.8	81.0	82.5	82.5	81.0	75.2	68.6	62.8	72.6
Mean Minimum Temp. (°F)	50.1	51.6	56.3	60.8	66.6	71.9	73.5	73.5	71.9	65.1	58.2	52.1	62.6
Extreme Maximum Temp. (°F)	87	88	89	92	97	100	102	99	97	93	90	87	102
Extreme Minimum Temp. (°F)	19	23	31	37	45	51	64	64	55	42	28	21	19
Days Maximum Temp. ≥ 90°F	0	0	0	1	8	18	24	24	19	5	0	0	99
Days Maximum Temp. ≤ 32°F	0	0	0	0	0	0	0	0	0	0	0	0	0
Days Minimum Temp. ≤ 32°F	2	1	0	0	0	0	0	0	0	0	0	1	4
Days Minimum Temp. ≤ 0°F	0	0	0	0	0	0	0	0	0	0	0	0	0
Heating Degree Days (base 65°F)	183	132	58	10	0	0	0	0	0	3	43	137	566
Cooling Degree Days (base 65°F)	56	69	123	208	388	501	562	566	497	338	173	82	3,563
Mean Precipitation (in.)	3.26	3.31	4.05	1.95	3.15	5.67	6.72	8.31	7.04	3.41	2.36	3.01	52.24
Days With ≥ 0.1" Precipitation	5	4	5	3	4	8	10	11	9	5	4	4	72
Days With ≥ 1.0" Precipitation	1	1	2	1	1	2	2	3	2	1	1	1	18
Mean Snowfall (in.)	0.0	0.0	0.0	0.0	0.0	0.0	0.0	0.0	0.0	0.0	0.0	0.0	0.0
Days With ≥ 1.0" Snow Depth	0	0	0	0	0	0	0	0	0	0	0	0	0

Tavernier *Monroe County*   Elevation: 6 ft.   Latitude: 25° 00' N   Longitude: 80° 31' W

	JAN	FEB	MAR	APR	MAY	JUN	JUL	AUG	SEP	OCT	NOV	DEC	YEAR
Mean Maximum Temp. (°F)	76.6	77.5	80.5	83.6	86.7	88.8	90.9	90.4	89.0	85.7	81.5	77.9	84.1
Mean Temp. (°F)	70.0	70.7	73.8	77.0	80.3	82.8	84.6	84.2	83.0	79.9	75.9	71.8	77.8
Mean Minimum Temp. (°F)	63.3	63.8	67.0	70.3	73.9	76.7	78.2	77.9	77.0	74.1	70.2	65.7	71.5
Extreme Maximum Temp. (°F)	86	87	90	94	93	96	97	97	95	94	90	89	97
Extreme Minimum Temp. (°F)	35	39	40	51	62	68	69	69	66	57	42	35	35
Days Maximum Temp. ≥ 90°F	0	0	0	1	4	12	20	20	13	3	0	0	73
Days Maximum Temp. ≤ 32°F	0	0	0	0	0	0	0	0	0	0	0	0	0
Days Minimum Temp. ≤ 32°F	0	0	0	0	0	0	0	0	0	0	0	0	0
Days Minimum Temp. ≤ 0°F	0	0	0	0	0	0	0	0	0	0	0	0	0
Heating Degree Days (base 65°F)	33	19	7	0	0	0	0	0	0	0	2	20	81
Cooling Degree Days (base 65°F)	191	201	276	362	487	552	622	606	551	473	341	237	4,899
Mean Precipitation (in.)	2.50	1.97	2.26	1.94	3.91	6.80	3.25	5.11	6.74	5.36	2.99	1.99	44.82
Days With ≥ 0.1" Precipitation	3	3	3	3	5	8	5	8	9	7	4	3	61
Days With ≥ 1.0" Precipitation	1	1	1	1	1	2	1	1	2	1	1	1	14
Mean Snowfall (in.)	0.0	0.0	0.0	0.0	0.0	0.0	0.0	0.0	0.0	0.0	0.0	0.0	0.0
Days With ≥ 1.0" Snow Depth	0	0	0	0	0	0	0	0	0	0	0	0	0

Titusville *Brevard County*   Elevation: 29 ft.   Latitude: 28° 37' N   Longitude: 80° 50' W

	JAN	FEB	MAR	APR	MAY	JUN	JUL	AUG	SEP	OCT	NOV	DEC	YEAR
Mean Maximum Temp. (°F)	70.4	72.3	77.3	81.2	86.3	89.6	91.5	91.1	88.7	83.4	77.5	72.5	81.8
Mean Temp. (°F)	59.4	61.1	66.3	70.2	75.8	79.9	81.7	81.5	79.9	74.3	67.7	62.0	71.6
Mean Minimum Temp. (°F)	48.3	49.8	55.1	59.1	65.2	70.2	71.7	71.9	71.0	65.2	57.8	51.4	61.4
Extreme Maximum Temp. (°F)	88	88	92	96	101	103	101	100	98	98	93	88	103
Extreme Minimum Temp. (°F)	19	23	26	35	45	56	62	62	57	40	30	19	19
Days Maximum Temp. ≥ 90°F	0	0	1	2	8	16	23	22	13	3	0	0	88
Days Maximum Temp. ≤ 32°F	0	0	0	0	0	0	0	0	0	0	0	0	0
Days Minimum Temp. ≤ 32°F	2	1	0	0	0	0	0	0	0	0	0	1	4
Days Minimum Temp. ≤ 0°F	0	0	0	0	0	0	0	0	0	0	0	0	0
Heating Degree Days (base 65°F)	212	153	71	18	0	0	0	0	0	4	52	153	663
Cooling Degree Days (base 65°F)	34	50	111	171	339	456	531	521	446	303	143	65	3,170
Mean Precipitation (in.)	2.54	2.81	3.80	2.81	3.66	6.17	7.27	7.52	6.80	4.40	3.47	2.54	53.79
Days With ≥ 0.1" Precipitation	4	5	5	4	6	10	10	11	10	7	5	5	82
Days With ≥ 1.0" Precipitation	1	1	1	1	1	2	3	2	2	1	1	1	17
Mean Snowfall (in.)	trace	0.0	0.0	0.0	0.0	0.0	0.0	0.0	0.0	0.0	0.0	0.0	trace
Days With ≥ 1.0" Snow Depth	0	0	0	0	0	0	0	0	0	0	0	0	0

£sher Tower *Levy County*   Elevation: 32 ft.   Latitude: 29° 25' N   Longitude: 82° 49' W

	JAN	FEB	MAR	APR	MAY	JUN	JUL	AUG	SEP	OCT	NOV	DEC	YEAR
Mean Maximum Temp. (°F)	68.2	71.0	77.0	82.3	87.8	91.0	91.9	91.3	89.7	83.8	76.2	70.2	81.7
Mean Temp. (°F)	55.8	58.3	63.8	68.7	74.7	79.5	81.1	81.1	79.1	71.5	63.6	57.7	69.6
Mean Minimum Temp. (°F)	43.4	45.6	50.6	55.1	61.5	67.9	70.2	70.8	68.5	59.3	51.1	45.2	57.4
Extreme Maximum Temp. (°F)	87	86	92	96	102	105	102	100	99	96	92	86	105
Extreme Minimum Temp. (°F)	9	17	22	32	42	44	59	61	48	32	17	12	9
Days Maximum Temp. ≥ 90°F	0	0	0	2	11	21	25	23	18	3	0	0	103
Days Maximum Temp. ≤ 32°F	0	0	0	0	0	0	0	0	0	0	0	0	0
Days Minimum Temp. ≤ 32°F	6	4	1	0	0	0	0	0	0	0	1	5	17
Days Minimum Temp. ≤ 0°F	0	0	0	0	0	0	0	0	0	0	0	0	0
Heating Degree Days (base 65°F)	299	210	107	29	1	0	0	0	0	16	118	249	1,029
Cooling Degree Days (base 65°F)	17	30	75	149	313	445	515	511	424	233	90	32	2,834
Mean Precipitation (in.)	4.57	3.52	4.81	3.66	3.09	6.72	8.49	10.22	6.38	2.99	2.54	3.32	60.31
Days With ≥ 0.1" Precipitation	7	5	6	4	5	9	12	14	9	4	4	5	84
Days With ≥ 1.0" Precipitation	2	1	2	1	1	2	2	3	2	1	1	1	19
Mean Snowfall (in.)	0.0	trace	0.0	0.0	0.0	0.0	0.0	0.0	0.0	0.0	0.0	0.0	trace
Days With ≥ 1.0" Snow Depth	0	0	0	0	0	0	0	0	0	0	0	0	0

Venice *Sarasota County*   Elevation: 6 ft.   Latitude: 27° 06' N   Longitude: 82° 26' W

	JAN	FEB	MAR	APR	MAY	JUN	JUL	AUG	SEP	OCT	NOV	DEC	YEAR
Mean Maximum Temp. (°F)	71.8	73.6	77.4	81.5	86.4	89.5	91.0	91.2	90.0	85.6	79.8	74.4	82.7
Mean Temp. (°F)	61.4	63.0	67.3	71.4	76.7	80.9	82.2	82.5	81.4	75.9	69.5	64.4	73.1
Mean Minimum Temp. (°F)	51.0	52.3	57.2	61.1	66.9	72.2	73.4	73.8	72.8	66.3	59.1	54.1	63.4
Extreme Maximum Temp. (°F)	89	89	90	95	98	100	99	99	99	95	91	89	100
Extreme Minimum Temp. (°F)	23	26	33	41	51	56	62	65	61	45	29	24	23
Days Maximum Temp. ≥ 90°F	0	0	0	1	7	14	22	23	18	4	0	0	89
Days Maximum Temp. ≤ 32°F	0	0	0	0	0	0	0	0	0	0	0	0	0
Days Minimum Temp. ≤ 32°F	1	0	0	0	0	0	0	0	0	0	0	1	2
Days Minimum Temp. ≤ 0°F	0	0	0	0	0	0	0	0	0	0	0	0	0
Heating Degree Days (base 65°F)	166	117	50	9	0	0	0	0	0	2	31	115	490
Cooling Degree Days (base 65°F)	59	79	133	205	374	498	559	568	513	364	176	109	3,637
Mean Precipitation (in.)	2.73	2.15	3.60	1.85	2.28	6.74	6.64	8.30	7.39	3.12	2.09	2.34	49.23
Days With ≥ 0.1" Precipitation	4	4	4	3	4	8	10	12	10	4	3	3	69
Days With ≥ 1.0" Precipitation	1	1	1	1	1	2	2	2	2	1	1	1	16
Mean Snowfall (in.)	trace	0.0	0.0	0.0	0.0	0.0	0.0	0.0	0.0	0.0	0.0	0.0	trace
Days With ≥ 1.0" Snow Depth	0	0	0	0	0	0	0	0	0	0	0	0	0

Wauchula *Hardee County*   Elevation: 59 ft.   Latitude: 27° 33' N   Longitude: 81° 48' W

	JAN	FEB	MAR	APR	MAY	JUN	JUL	AUG	SEP	OCT	NOV	DEC	YEAR
Mean Maximum Temp. (°F)	74.1	75.9	80.3	84.4	89.1	91.3	92.4	92.3	90.7	85.9	80.2	75.4	84.3
Mean Temp. (°F)	61.9	63.3	67.4	71.2	76.6	80.6	81.9	82.2	80.8	75.3	68.8	63.6	72.8
Mean Minimum Temp. (°F)	49.7	50.6	54.5	57.9	64.1	69.8	71.4	72.0	70.7	64.5	57.3	51.7	61.2
Extreme Maximum Temp. (°F)	87	90	94	96	99	102	100	98	96	95	90	92	102
Extreme Minimum Temp. (°F)	20	25	23	35	44	51	62	64	58	39	26	22	20
Days Maximum Temp. ≥ 90°F	0	0	1	5	15	22	27	27	22	6	0	0	125
Days Maximum Temp. ≤ 32°F	0	0	0	0	0	0	0	0	0	0	0	0	0
Days Minimum Temp. ≤ 32°F	2	1	0	0	0	0	0	0	0	0	0	1	4
Days Minimum Temp. ≤ 0°F	0	0	0	0	0	0	0	0	0	0	0	0	0
Heating Degree Days (base 65°F)	157	117	55	12	0	0	0	0	0	3	40	121	505
Cooling Degree Days (base 65°F)	63	81	127	196	364	479	538	545	477	331	161	80	3,442
Mean Precipitation (in.)	2.41	2.71	3.47	2.33	4.00	8.01	8.07	7.32	6.03	2.73	2.08	1.98	51.14
Days With ≥ 0.1" Precipitation	4	4	5	3	5	10	11	12	9	4	3	3	73
Days With ≥ 1.0" Precipitation	1	1	1	1	1	2	3	2	2	1	0	1	16
Mean Snowfall (in.)	trace	0.0	0.0	0.0	0.0	0.0	0.0	0.0	0.0	0.0	0.0	0.0	trace
Days With ≥ 1.0" Snow Depth	0	0	0	0	0	0	0	0	0	0	0	0	0

Weeki Wachee *Hernando County*   Elevation: 19 ft.   Latitude: 28° 31' N   Longitude: 82° 35' W

	JAN	FEB	MAR	APR	MAY	JUN	JUL	AUG	SEP	OCT	NOV	DEC	YEAR
Mean Maximum Temp. (°F)	70.3	72.2	77.2	82.2	87.1	90.2	91.6	91.5	90.3	85.0	78.7	72.8	82.4
Mean Temp. (°F)	57.4	59.2	64.3	69.1	74.8	79.8	81.2	81.1	79.6	73.1	66.1	59.6	70.4
Mean Minimum Temp. (°F)	44.5	46.1	51.4	55.9	62.4	69.2	70.8	70.7	68.8	61.0	53.3	46.4	58.4
Extreme Maximum Temp. (°F)	88	91	92	96	100	100	100	98	98	97	91	90	100
Extreme Minimum Temp. (°F)	13	22	21	34	44	47	60	63	48	36	23	19	13
Days Maximum Temp. ≥ 90°F	0	0	0	2	9	19	25	25	19	5	0	0	104
Days Maximum Temp. ≤ 32°F	0	0	0	0	0	0	0	0	0	0	0	0	0
Days Minimum Temp. ≤ 32°F	5	3	1	0	0	0	0	0	0	0	0	3	12
Days Minimum Temp. ≤ 0°F	0	0	0	0	0	0	0	0	0	0	0	0	0
Heating Degree Days (base 65°F)	264	197	106	30	1	0	0	0	0	9	76	208	891
Cooling Degree Days (base 65°F)	34	45	89	161	321	464	525	519	444	276	127	52	3,057
Mean Precipitation (in.)	3.84	3.20	4.24	2.51	2.95	5.92	8.31	7.60	6.46	2.29	2.12	2.50	51.94
Days With ≥ 0.1" Precipitation	5	4	4	3	4	7	11	10	7	3	3	4	65
Days With ≥ 1.0" Precipitation	1	1	1	1	1	2	3	2	2	1	1	1	17
Mean Snowfall (in.)	0.0	0.0	0.0	0.0	0.0	0.0	0.0	0.0	0.0	0.0	0.0	0.0	0.0
Days With ≥ 1.0" Snow Depth	0	0	0	0	0	0	0	0	0	0	0	0	0

Note: See Appendix D for explanation of data.

Annual Extreme Maximum Temperature

	Highest			Lowest	
Rank	Station Name	°F	Rank	Station Name	°F
1	High Springs	107	1	Tavernier	**97**
2	Live Oak	106	2	Belle Glade Exp. Station	98
2	Pensacola Regional Airport	106	2	Key West Int'l Airport	98
4	De Funiak Springs	**105**	2	Miami Beach	98
4	Lakeland Linder Airport	**105**	2	Miami Int'l Airport	98
4	Mountain Lake	105	6	Fort Lauderdale	99
4	Myakka River State Park	105	6	Naples	99
4	Ocala	105	6	Tampa Int'l Airport	99
4	Usher Tower	105	6	Vero Beach	99
10	Arcadia	104	6	West Palm Beach Int'l Airport	99
10	Brooksville Chin Hill	104	11	Bradenton 5 ESE	100
10	Chipley 3 E	104	11	Canal Point USDA	100
10	Flamingo Ranger Station	104	11	Hialeah	100
10	La Belle	**104**	11	Saint Petersburg	100
10	Lake Alfred Exp. Station	104	11	Venice	**100**
10	Lake City 2 E	104	11	Weeki Wachee	100
10	Mayo	104	17	Avon Park 2 W	101
10	Perry	104	17	Clermont 7 S	101
19	Apalachicola Municipal Airport	103	17	Clewiston U.S. Engineers	101
19	Archbold Bio Station	103	17	Cross City 2 WNW	101
19	Bartow	103	17	Fort Pierce	101
19	Fort Myers Page Field	**103**	17	Immokalee 3 NNW	101
19	Jacksonville Beach	103	17	Inverness 3 SE	101
19	Jacksonville Int'l Airport	103	17	Kissimmee 2	101
19	Jasper	103	17	Lisbon	101

Annual Mean Maximum Temperature

	Highest			Lowest	
Rank	Station Name	°F	Rank	Station Name	°F
1	Tamiami Trail 40 Mile Bend	**85.7**	1	Fernandina Beach	77.0
2	Myakka River State Park	85.3	1	Pensacola Regional Airport	77.0
3	Naples	85.1	3	Apalachicola Municipal Airport	77.2
4	Archbold Bio Station	84.9	4	Jacksonville Beach	**77.6**
4	Immokalee 3 NNW	84.9	5	Chipley 3 E	77.8
6	Fort Myers Page Field	84.5	5	Panama City 5 NE	77.8
6	Punta Gorda 4 ESE	84.5	7	Monticello 3 W	78.0
8	Mountain Lake	84.4	8	Milton Experiment Station	78.1
9	Hialeah	84.3	8	Quincy 3 SSW	78.1
9	Wauchula	84.3	10	De Funiak Springs	78.6
11	Canal Point USDA	84.1	11	Saint Augustine	**79.2**
11	Tavernier	**84.1**	12	Jacksonville Int'l Airport	79.3
13	Bartow	84.0	13	Cross City 2 WNW	**79.4**
13	Belle Glade Exp. Station	84.0	13	Jasper	79.4
15	Arcadia	83.9	13	Lake City 2 E	79.4
15	Fort Drum 5 NW	**83.9**	16	Tallahassee Municipal Airport	79.5
17	Flamingo Ranger Station	83.8	17	Daytona Beach Regional Airport	80.3
18	Lake Alfred Exp. Station	83.7	18	Mayo	80.4
18	Lakeland Linder Airport	**83.7**	19	Miami Beach	81.1
20	Clewiston U.S. Engineers	**83.6**	20	Lisbon	81.3
20	Moore Haven Lock 1	83.6	21	Saint Petersburg	81.4
20	Plant City	83.6	22	Melbourne Regional Airport	81.6
20	Saint Leo	83.6	22	Perry	81.6
24	Avon Park 2 W	83.5	24	Live Oak	81.7
24	Kissimmee 2	83.5	24	Usher Tower	81.7

Annual Mean Temperature

	Highest			Lowest	
Rank	Station Name	°F	Rank	Station Name	°F
1	Key West Int'l Airport	78.0	1	Chipley 3 E	66.1
2	Tavernier	*77.8*	1	Monticello 3 W	66.1
3	Miami Int'l Airport	76.6	3	De Funiak Springs	66.4
4	Hialeah	76.4	4	Milton Experiment Station	66.8
4	Miami Beach	76.4	5	Panama City 5 NE	66.9
6	Tamiami Trail 40 Mile Bend	*76.0*	6	Jasper	67.0
7	Fort Lauderdale	75.7	6	Quincy 3 SSW	67.0
8	West Palm Beach Int'l Airport	75.3	8	Tallahassee Municipal Airport	67.4
9	Flamingo Ranger Station	74.9	9	Cross City 2 WNW	*67.7*
9	Fort Myers Page Field	74.9	10	Pensacola Regional Airport	68.1
11	Naples	74.8	11	Lake City 2 E	68.2
12	Stuart 1 S	74.5	12	Mayo	68.3
13	Clewiston U.S. Engineers	*74.3*	13	Fernandina Beach	68.4
14	Saint Petersburg	74.1	14	Jacksonville Int'l Airport	68.5
15	Immokalee 3 NNW	73.8	15	Apalachicola Municipal Airport	68.6
15	Punta Gorda 4 ESE	73.8	16	Perry	69.0
17	Canal Point USDA	73.7	17	High Springs	69.2
18	Moore Haven Lock 1	73.4	18	Live Oak	69.4
19	Fort Pierce	73.3	19	Jacksonville Beach	*69.5*
19	Myakka River State Park	73.3	20	Usher Tower	69.6
21	Bartow	73.2	21	Saint Augustine	*69.8*
21	Belle Glade Exp. Station	73.2	22	Inverness 3 SE	70.4
21	Lakeland Linder Airport	*73.2*	22	Weeki Wachee	70.4
24	Venice	*73.1*	24	Ocala	70.8
25	Kissimmee 2	72.8	25	Daytona Beach Regional Airport	70.9

Annual Mean Minimum Temperature

	Highest			Lowest	
Rank	Station Name	°F	Rank	Station Name	°F
1	Key West Int'l Airport	73.2	1	De Funiak Springs	54.2
2	Miami Beach	71.6	1	Monticello 3 W	54.2
3	Tavernier	*71.5*	3	Chipley 3 E	54.3
4	Miami Int'l Airport	69.7	4	Jasper	54.6
5	Hialeah	68.4	5	Tallahassee Municipal Airport	55.3
6	Fort Lauderdale	68.0	6	Milton Experiment Station	55.5
7	West Palm Beach Int'l Airport	67.4	7	Cross City 2 WNW	*55.8*
8	Saint Petersburg	66.7	8	Quincy 3 SSW	55.9
9	Tamiami Trail 40 Mile Bend	*66.3*	9	Panama City 5 NE	56.0
10	Flamingo Ranger Station	66.0	10	High Springs	56.2
11	Stuart 1 S	65.7	10	Mayo	56.2
12	Fort Myers Page Field	65.2	10	Perry	56.2
13	Clewiston U.S. Engineers	*65.1*	13	Live Oak	57.0
14	Naples	64.4	14	Lake City 2 E	57.1
15	Tampa Int'l Airport	63.6	15	Usher Tower	57.4
16	Venice	*63.4*	16	Jacksonville Int'l Airport	57.7
17	Canal Point USDA	63.3	17	Weeki Wachee	58.4
17	Fort Pierce	63.3	18	Inverness 3 SE	58.7
19	Melbourne Regional Airport	63.2	19	Ocala	58.8
20	Punta Gorda 4 ESE	63.1	20	Archbold Bio Station	59.1
21	Moore Haven Lock 1	63.0	21	Pensacola Regional Airport	59.2
22	Immokalee 3 NNW	62.6	22	Apalachicola Municipal Airport	59.9
22	Lakeland Linder Airport	*62.6*	22	Fernandina Beach	59.9
22	Tarpon Springs Sewage Plant	62.6	24	Lisbon	60.4
25	Orlando Int'l Airport	*62.5*	24	Saint Augustine	*60.4*

Annual Extreme Minimum Temperature

	Highest				Lowest	
Rank	Station Name	°F		Rank	Station Name	°F
1	Key West Int'l Airport	41		1	Quincy 3 SSW	0
2	Tavernier	*35*		2	Chipley 3 E	2
3	Miami Beach	32		3	De Funiak Springs	*3*
4	Miami Int'l Airport	30		3	Milton Experiment Station	3
5	Fort Lauderdale	28		5	Fernandina Beach	4
5	Hialeah	28		5	Jasper	4
5	Tamiami Trail 40 Mile Bend	28		5	Monticello 3 W	4
8	Fort Myers Page Field	*27*		8	Pensacola Regional Airport	5
8	West Palm Beach Int'l Airport	27		9	Live Oak	6
10	Clewiston U.S. Engineers	26		9	Panama City 5 NE	6
10	Naples	26		9	Tallahassee Municipal Airport	6
12	Canal Point USDA	25		12	Jacksonville Int'l Airport	7
13	Flamingo Ranger Station	24		12	Lake City 2 E	7
13	Saint Petersburg	24		12	Mayo	7
15	Moore Haven Lock 1	23		12	Perry	7
15	Punta Gorda 4 ESE	23		16	High Springs	*8*
15	Stuart 1 S	23		17	Apalachicola Municipal Airport	9
15	Venice	*23*		17	Usher Tower	9
15	Vero Beach	23		19	Cross City 2 WNW	10
20	Belle Glade Exp. Station	21		19	Saint Augustine	*10*
21	Bartow	20		21	Ocala	11
21	Bradenton 5 ESE	20		22	Archbold Bio Station	13
21	Immokalee 3 NNW	20		22	Brooksville Chin Hill	13
21	Lakeland Linder Airport	*20*		22	Weeki Wachee	13
21	Wauchula	20		25	Jacksonville Beach	14

July Mean Maximum Temperature

	Highest				Lowest	
Rank	Station Name	°F		Rank	Station Name	°F
1	Live Oak	93.1		1	Miami Beach	87.4
2	Archbold Bio Station	93.0		2	Flamingo Ranger Station	89.3
2	Myakka River State Park	93.0		2	Key West Int'l Airport	89.3
4	Lakeland Linder Airport	92.9		4	Fort Lauderdale	89.5
5	Lake Alfred Exp. Station	92.8		5	Apalachicola Municipal Airport	89.7
5	Mountain Lake	92.8		5	Miami Int'l Airport	89.7
7	Perry	92.7		7	Jacksonville Beach	89.8
8	High Springs	92.5		8	Fernandina Beach	89.9
9	Saint Leo	92.4		8	Panama City 5 NE	89.9
9	Wauchula	92.4		10	Stuart 1 S	90.0
11	Bartow	92.3		11	West Palm Beach Int'l Airport	90.1
11	Ocala	92.3		12	Cross City 2 WNW	*90.4*
13	Mayo	92.2		12	Vero Beach	90.4
13	Punta Gorda 4 ESE	92.2		14	Daytona Beach Regional Airport	90.5
13	Tamiami Trail 40 Mile Bend	92.2		14	Melbourne Regional Airport	90.5
16	Jacksonville Int'l Airport	92.1		14	Pensacola Regional Airport	90.5
17	Sanford Experiment Station	92.0		17	Monticello 3 W	90.6
18	Orlando Int'l Airport	91.9		17	Saint Augustine	90.6
18	Usher Tower	91.9		17	Saint Petersburg	90.6
20	Arcadia	91.8		20	Brooksville Chin Hill	90.7
20	Avon Park 2 W	91.8		20	Quincy 3 SSW	90.7
20	Canal Point USDA	91.8		20	Tampa Int'l Airport	90.7
20	Clewiston U.S. Engineers	91.8		23	Hialeah	90.8
20	De Funiak Springs	91.8		24	Tavernier	*90.9*
20	Kissimmee 2	91.8		25	Venice	*91.0*

January Mean Minimum Temperature

	Highest			Lowest	
Rank	**Station Name**	**°F**	**Rank**	**Station Name**	**°F**
1	Key West Int'l Airport	65.1	1	Chipley 3 E	37.6
2	Tavernier	63.3	2	Monticello 3 W	37.8
3	Miami Beach	63.0	3	De Funiak Springs	38.2
4	Miami Int'l Airport	60.1	4	Jasper	38.4
5	Fort Lauderdale	58.6	5	Milton Experiment Station	39.1
6	Hialeah	58.5	5	Tallahassee Municipal Airport	39.1
7	West Palm Beach Int'l Airport	57.1	7	Panama City 5 NE	39.7
8	Tamiami Trail 40 Mile Bend	57.0	8	Cross City 2 WNW	39.8
9	Flamingo Ranger Station	56.0	8	Quincy 3 SSW	39.8
10	Stuart 1 S	55.1	10	High Springs	40.2
11	Saint Petersburg	54.3	10	Mayo	40.2
12	Clewiston U.S. Engineers	54.2	12	Perry	41.4
13	Fort Myers Page Field	54.1	13	Jacksonville Int'l Airport	41.8
14	Naples	54.0	13	Lake City 2 E	41.8
15	Canal Point USDA	52.9	15	Live Oak	42.1
16	Immokalee 3 NNW	52.0	16	Pensacola Regional Airport	42.6
17	Belle Glade Exp. Station	51.9	17	Fernandina Beach	43.2
18	Fort Pierce	51.7	18	Usher Tower	43.4
18	Punta Gorda 4 ESE	51.7	19	Apalachicola Municipal Airport	44.1
20	Moore Haven Lock 1	51.6	19	Inverness 3 SE	44.1
21	Melbourne Regional Airport	51.2	21	Weeki Wachee	44.5
22	Venice	51.0	22	Ocala	45.6
23	Tampa Int'l Airport	50.6	23	Jacksonville Beach	46.0
23	Vero Beach	50.6	23	Saint Augustine	*46.0*
25	Lakeland Linder Airport	50.4	25	Lisbon	46.7

Number of Annual Heating Degree Days

	Highest			Lowest	
Rank	**Station Name**	**Num.**	**Rank**	**Station Name**	**Num.**
1	Chipley 3 E	1,867	1	Key West Int'l Airport	61
2	Monticello 3 W	1,767	2	Tavernier	*81*
3	De Funiak Springs	1,730	3	Miami Beach	130
4	Milton Experiment Station	1,710	4	Miami Int'l Airport	151
5	Panama City 5 NE	1,608	5	Hialeah	155
6	Quincy 3 SSW	1,602	6	Tamiami Trail 40 Mile Bend	*168*
7	Tallahassee Municipal Airport	1,592	7	Fort Lauderdale	172
8	Jasper	1,591	8	Flamingo Ranger Station	191
9	Pensacola Regional Airport	1,472	9	West Palm Beach Int'l Airport	238
10	Mayo	1,394	10	Naples	249
11	Cross City 2 WNW	*1,391*	11	Stuart 1 S	255
12	Lake City 2 E	1,333	12	Fort Myers Page Field	303
13	Jacksonville Int'l Airport	1,325	13	Canal Point USDA	308
14	Fernandina Beach	1,297	14	Immokalee 3 NNW	323
15	Apalachicola Municipal Airport	1,277	15	Clewiston U.S. Engineers	*335*
16	Perry	1,210	16	Punta Gorda 4 ESE	374
17	Live Oak	1,173	17	Belle Glade Exp. Station	380
18	High Springs	*1,139*	18	Saint Petersburg	403
19	Jacksonville Beach	*1,059*	19	Fort Pierce	414
20	Usher Tower	1,029	20	Moore Haven Lock 1	424
21	Saint Augustine	*933*	21	Fort Drum 5 NW	*446*
22	Inverness 3 SE	929	22	Myakka River State Park	450
23	Weeki Wachee	891	23	Vero Beach	479
24	Ocala	841	24	Bartow	483
25	Lisbon	830	25	Venice	*490*

Number of Annual Cooling Degree Days

	Highest			Lowest	
Rank	Station Name	Num.	Rank	Station Name	Num.
1	Key West Int'l Airport	4,926	1	Monticello 3 W	2,314
2	Tavernier	4,899	2	Chipley 3 E	2,345
3	Hialeah	4,586	3	De Funiak Springs	2,365
4	Miami Int'l Airport	4,543	4	Panama City 5 NE	2,399
5	Miami Beach	4,462	5	Jasper	2,440
6	Tamiami Trail 40 Mile Bend	4,412	6	Quincy 3 SSW	2,474
7	Fort Lauderdale	4,295	7	Milton Experiment Station	2,475
8	West Palm Beach Int'l Airport	4,139	8	Cross City 2 WNW	2,499
9	Fort Myers Page Field	4,098	9	Tallahassee Municipal Airport	2,627
10	Flamingo Ranger Station	3,977	10	Fernandina Beach	2,677
11	Naples	3,953	10	Lake City 2 E	2,677
12	Stuart 1 S	3,944	12	Pensacola Regional Airport	2,690
13	Clewiston U.S. Engineers	3,905	13	Apalachicola Municipal Airport	2,721
14	Punta Gorda 4 ESE	3,805	14	Gainesville Regional Airport	2,729
15	Saint Petersburg	3,770	15	Mayo	2,744
16	Lakeland Linder Airport	3,762	16	Jacksonville Int'l Airport	2,750
17	Immokalee 3 NNW	3,671	17	Perry	2,751
18	Bartow	3,659	18	Saint Augustine	2,781
19	Canal Point USDA	3,657	19	High Springs	2,801
20	Myakka River State Park	3,652	20	Jacksonville Beach	2,810
21	Venice	3,637	21	Usher Tower	2,834
22	Moore Haven Lock 1	3,629	22	Inverness 3 SE	2,916
23	Tampa Int'l Airport	3,575	23	Live Oak	2,919
24	Tarpon Springs Sewage Plant	3,563	24	Daytona Beach Regional Airport	3,015
25	Fort Pierce	3,559	25	Lisbon	3,036

Annual Precipitation

	Highest			Lowest	
Rank	Station Name	Inches	Rank	Station Name	Inches
1	Milton Experiment Station	70.20	1	Key West Int'l Airport	39.32
2	De Funiak Springs	67.06	2	Tavernier	44.82
3	Panama City 5 NE	66.07	3	Tampa Int'l Airport	45.07
4	Hialeah	65.92	4	Clewiston U.S. Engineers	45.79
5	Pensacola Regional Airport	65.18	5	Miami Beach	46.75
6	Tallahassee Municipal Airport	64.31	6	Moore Haven Lock 1	47.05
7	Fort Lauderdale	64.13	7	Flamingo Ranger Station	47.81
8	West Palm Beach Int'l Airport	61.81	7	Saint Augustine	47.81
9	Stuart 1 S	60.34	9	Melbourne Regional Airport	48.16
10	Usher Tower	60.31	10	Kissimmee 2	48.34
11	Myakka River State Park	59.11	11	Mountain Lake	48.52
12	Cross City 2 WNW	59.03	12	Lisbon	48.88
13	Perry	58.97	13	Daytona Beach Regional Airport	48.92
14	Chipley 3 E	58.61	14	Venice	49.23
15	Monticello 3 W	58.41	15	Saint Petersburg	49.29
16	Miami Int'l Airport	58.00	16	Orlando Int'l Airport	49.70
17	Quincy 3 SSW	57.20	17	Arcadia	49.82
18	Apalachicola Municipal Airport	56.91	18	Avon Park 2 W	49.86
19	Vero Beach	55.71	19	Punta Gorda 4 ESE	50.01
20	Mayo	55.59	20	Immokalee 3 NNW	50.08
21	Fort Myers Page Field	54.86	21	Lakeland Linder Airport	50.11
22	High Springs	54.58	22	Clermont 7 S	50.32
23	Saint Leo	54.29	23	Lake Alfred Exp. Station	50.60
24	Bradenton 5 ESE	54.27	24	Ocala	50.68
25	Lake City 2 E	54.15	25	Fernandina Beach	50.87

Number of Days Annually With ≥ 0.1″ Precipitation

	Highest			Lowest	
Rank	**Station Name**	**Days**	**Rank**	**Station Name**	**Days**
1	Stuart 1 S	94	1	Fort Drum 5 NW	60
2	Hialeah	92	2	Tavernier	61
3	West Palm Beach Int'l Airport	89	3	Key West Int'l Airport	62
4	Fort Lauderdale	88	3	La Belle	62
5	Miami Int'l Airport	86	5	Weeki Wachee	65
6	De Funiak Springs	85	6	Arcadia	66
7	Milton Experiment Station	84	6	Clewiston U.S. Engineers	66
7	Usher Tower	84	8	Tampa Int'l Airport	67
7	Vero Beach	84	9	Saint Petersburg	69
10	Titusville	82	9	Sanford Experiment Station	69
11	Fort Pierce	81	9	Venice	69
11	Panama City 5 NE	81	12	Parrish	70
11	Perry	81	13	Brooksville Chin Hill	71
14	Tallahassee Municipal Airport	80	13	Flamingo Ranger Station	71
15	Belle Glade Exp. Station	79	13	Miami Beach	71
15	Chipley 3 E	79	16	Apalachicola Municipal Airport	72
17	Cross City 2 WNW	78	16	Daytona Beach Regional Airport	72
17	Jacksonville Int'l Airport	78	16	Live Oak	72
17	Myakka River State Park	78	16	Melbourne Regional Airport	72
17	Ocala	78	16	Moore Haven Lock 1	72
21	Canal Point USDA	77	16	Saint Augustine	72
21	High Springs	77	16	Tarpon Springs Sewage Plant	72
21	Immokalee 3 NNW	77	23	Avon Park 2 W	73
21	Lake City 2 E	77	23	Lake Alfred Exp. Station	73
21	Mayo	77	23	Wauchula	73

Number of Days Annually With ≥ 0.1″ Precipitation

	Highest			Lowest	
Rank	**Station Name**	**Days**	**Rank**	**Station Name**	**Days**
1	De Funiak Springs	21	1	Flamingo Ranger Station	11
1	Hialeah	21	1	Key West Int'l Airport	11
3	Milton Experiment Station	20	3	Saint Augustine	13
3	Myakka River State Park	20	3	Tamiami Trail 40 Mile Bend	13
3	Panama City 5 NE	20	5	Clewiston U.S. Engineers	14
6	Archbold Bio Station	19	5	Moore Haven Lock 1	14
6	Cross City 2 WNW	19	5	Tavernier	14
6	Fort Lauderdale	19	8	Belle Glade Exp. Station	15
6	Pensacola Regional Airport	19	8	Clermont 7 S	15
6	Perry	19	8	Daytona Beach Regional Airport	15
6	Tallahassee Municipal Airport	19	8	Fernandina Beach	15
6	Usher Tower	19	8	Jacksonville Int'l Airport	15
6	West Palm Beach Int'l Airport	19	8	Kissimmee 2	15
14	Bradenton 5 ESE	18	8	La Belle	15
14	Chipley 3 E	18	8	Melbourne Regional Airport	15
14	High Springs	18	8	Miami Beach	15
14	Mayo	18	8	Ocala	15
14	Parrish	18	8	Punta Gorda 4 ESE	15
14	Saint Leo	18	8	Tampa Int'l Airport	15
14	Stuart 1 S	18	8	Vero Beach	15
14	Tarpon Springs Sewage Plant	18	21	Fort Drum 5 NW	16
22	Apalachicola Municipal Airport	17	21	Fort Myers Page Field	16
22	Arcadia	17	21	Fort Pierce	16
22	Avon Park 2 W	17	21	Inverness 3 SE	16
22	Bartow	17	21	Jacksonville Beach	16

Annual Snowfall

Highest			Lowest		
Rank	Station Name	Inches	Rank	Station Name	Inches
1	Milton Experiment Station	0.2	1	Arcadia	0.0
2	Live Oak	0.1	1	Bartow	0.0
3	Apalachicola Municipal Airport	Trace	1	Bradenton 5 ESE	0.0
3	Archbold Bio Station	Trace	1	Brooksville Chin Hill	0.0
3	Avon Park 2 W	Trace	1	Canal Point USDA	0.0
3	Belle Glade Exp. Station	Trace	1	Clewiston U.S. Engineers	0.0
3	Chipley 3 E	Trace	1	Cross City 2 WNW	0.0
3	Clermont 7 S	Trace	1	Flamingo Ranger Station	0.0
3	Daytona Beach Regional Airport	Trace	1	Fort Lauderdale	0.0
3	De Funiak Springs	Trace	1	Fort Myers Page Field	*0.0*
3	Fernandina Beach	Trace	1	Hialeah	0.0
3	Fort Drum 5 NW	Trace	1	Immokalee 3 NNW	0.0
3	Fort Pierce	Trace	1	Inverness 3 SE	0.0
3	High Springs	Trace	1	Key West Int'l Airport	0.0
3	Jacksonville Beach	Trace	1	Kissimmee 2	0.0
3	Jacksonville Int'l Airport	Trace	1	Melbourne Regional Airport	0.0
3	Jasper	Trace	1	Miami Beach	0.0
3	La Belle	Trace	1	Moore Haven Lock 1	0.0
3	Lake Alfred Exp. Station	Trace	1	Naples	0.0
3	Lake City 2 E	Trace	1	Plant City	0.0
3	Lakeland Linder Airport	*Trace*	1	Punta Gorda 4 ESE	0.0
3	Lisbon	Trace	1	Sanford Experiment Station	0.0
3	Mayo	Trace	1	Stuart 1 S	0.0
3	Miami Int'l Airport	Trace	1	Tamiami Trail 40 Mile Bend	0.0
3	Monticello 3 W	Trace	1	Tarpon Springs Sewage Plant	0.0

Note: See User's Guide for explanation of data.

Deadliest Storm Events in Florida: Septmeber 1982 - August 2007

Rank	Location or County	Date	Storm Event	Fatalities	Injuries	Property Damage ($mil.)	Crop Damage ($mil.)
1	Northwest Florida	3/12/1993	Tornadoes, Tstm Wind, Hail ("Storm of the Century")	25	0	1,600.0	2.5
2	Intercession City	2/23/1998	Tornado (F3)	25	145	50.0	0.0
3	Turpentine	2/2/2007	Tornado (F3)	13	9	46.0	0.0
4	Longwood	2/23/1998	Tornado (F3)	12	36	30.0	0.0
5	Coastal Areas	3/13/1993	Storm Surge	10	0	50.0	0.0
6	South, East-Central, and Northeast Florida	11/13/1994	Tropical Storm Gordon	8	43	0.5	0.5
7	Lady Lake	2/2/2007	Tornado (F3)	8	10	52.0	0.0
8	Charlotte, De Soto, Lee, Manatee, and Sarasota Counties	8/13/2004	Hurricane Charley	7	780	5,400.0	285.0
9	Escambia, Okaloosa, and Santa Rosa Counties	9/13/2004	Hurricane Ivan	7	0	4,000.0	25.0
10	Inlet Beach	6/8/2003	Rip Current	6	0	0.0	0.0
11	Bay, Calhoun, Dixie, Franklin, Gadsden, Gulf, Holmes, Jackson, Jefferson, Lafayette, Leon, Liberty, Madison, Taylor, Wakulla, Walton, and Washington Counties	9/15/2004	Hurricane Ivan	6	16	90.4	0.0
12	Palm Beach, Broward, and Miami-Dade Counties	8/25/2005	Hurricane Katrina	6	0	100.0	423.0
13	Broward, Collier, Miami-Dade, and Palm Beach Counties	10/24/2005	Hurricane Wilma	5	0	10,000.0	0.0
14	Madison County	4/19/1988	Tornado (F3)	4	18	25.0	0.0
15	Orange, Osceola, Seminole Counties	8/13/2004	High Wind (91 kts.)	4	0	1,300.0	0.0
16	Alachua, Baker, Bradford, Clay, Columbia, Duval, Flagler, Gilchrist, Hamilton, Marion, Nassau, Putnam, St. Johns, Suwannee, and Union Counties	9/4/2004	Tropical Storm Frances	4	0	0.0	0.0
17	Blountstown	9/15/2004	Tornado (F2)	4	5	2.5	0.0
18	Citrus County	4/9/1983	Tornado (F3)	3	2	2.5	0.0
19	Franklin County	6/8/1989	Tornado (F2)	3	4	2.5	0.0
20	Pinellas County	10/3/1992	Tornado (F3)	3	75	25.0	0.0
21	Chiefland	3/12/1993	Tornado (F2)	3	10	50.0	0.0
22	Brevard, Osceola, Orange, and Indian River Counties	8/2/1995	Hurricane Erin	3	0	0.0	130.0
23	Winter Garden	2/22/1998	Tornado (F3)	3	70	15.0	0.0
24	Coastal Broward and Coastal Palm Beach Counties	11/11/2003	Heavy Surf/High Surf	3	0	0.0	0.0

Source: National Climatic Data Center, Storm Events Database

Most Destructive Storm Events in Florida: Septmeber 1982 - August 2007

Rank	Location or County	Date	Storm Event	Fatalities	Injuries	Property Damage ($mil.)	Crop Damage ($mil.)
1	Broward, Collier, Miami-Dade, and Palm Beach Counties	10/24/2005	Hurricane Wilma	5	0	10,000.0	0.0
2	Charlotte, De Soto, Lee, Manatee, and Sarasota Counties	8/13/2004	Hurricane Charley	7	780	5,400.0	285.0
3	Brevard, Indian River, Martin, St. Lucie, and Volusia Counties	9/4/2004	Hurricane Frances	0	0	4,800.0	93.2
4	Escambia, Okaloosa, and Santa Rosa Counties	9/13/2004	Hurricane Ivan	7	0	4,000.0	25.0
5	Northwest Florida	10/3/1995	Hurricane Opal	1	0	2,100.0	5.0
6	Northwest Florida	3/12/1993	Tornadoes, Tstm Wind, Hail ("Storm of the Century")	25	0	1,600.0	2.5
7	Escambia, Okaloosa, and Santa Rosa Counties	7/9/2005	Hurricane Dennis	0	0	1,500.0	0.3
8	Orange, Osceola, and Seminole Counties	8/13/2004	High Wind (91 kts.)	4	0	1,300.0	0.0
9	Northwest Florida	10/4/1995	Hurricane Opal	0	0	1,000.0	0.0
10	Hardee, Highlands, and Polk Counties	8/13/2004	High Wind (94kts.)	1	12	929.0	175.0
11	Highlands and Polk Counties	9/25/2004	High Wind (61kts.)	0	0	702.0	0.0
12	Broward, Collier, Glades, Hendry, Miami-Dade, and Palm Beach Counties	9/4/2004	Hurricane Frances	0	0	621.0	90.0
13	Southeast Broward and Miami-Dade Counties	10/3/2000	Flood	0	0	450.0	500.0
14	Brevard, Indian River, Martin, St. Lucie, Volusia	9/25/2004	Hurricane Jeanne	0	0	379.9	8.7
15	Calhoun, Franklin, Gadsden, Gulf, Holmes, Jackson, Walton, and Jackson Counties	3/10/1998	Flood	0	0	367.0	0.0
16	Broward, Glades, Hendry, Miami-Dade, and Palm Beach Counties	9/25/2004	Hurricane Jeanne	0	0	323.0	30.0
17	Palm Beach, Broward, and Miami-Dade Counties	10/14/1999	Hurricane Irene	0	4	262.0	338.0
18	Miami-Dade and Monroe Counties	9/25/1998	Hurricane Georges	0	0	255.0	15.0
19	Northwest Florida	8/3/1995	Hurricane Erin	0	0	230.0	5.0
20	Brevard County	7/1/1998	Wild/Forest Fire	0	52	200.0	0.0

Source: National Climatic Data Center, Storm Events Database

Demographic and Reference Maps

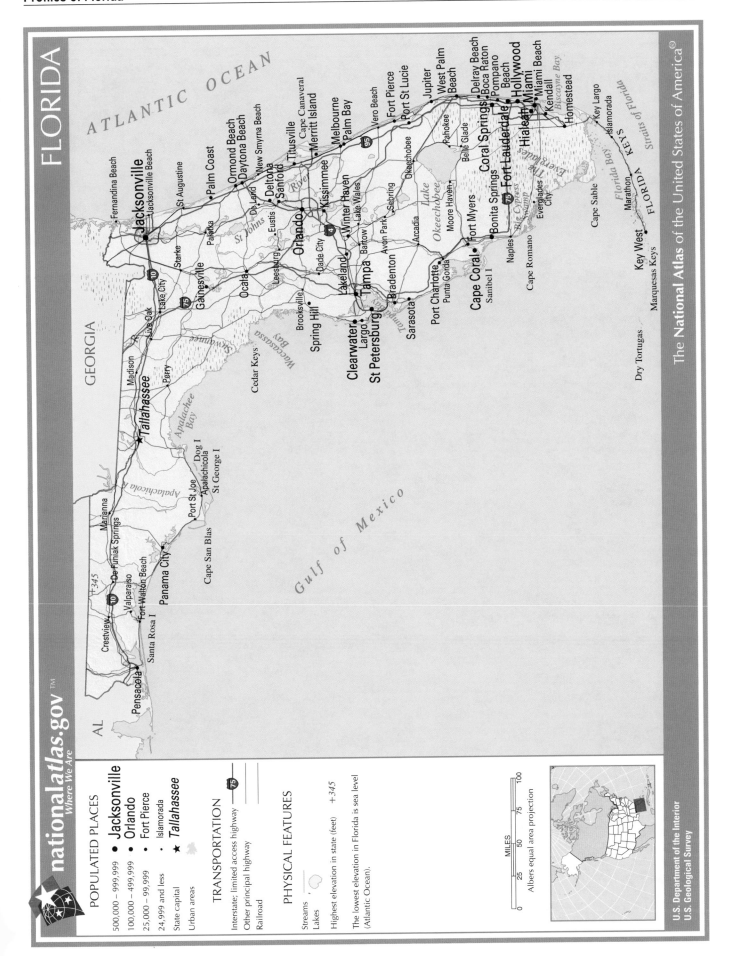

FLORIDA - Core Based Statistical Areas and Counties

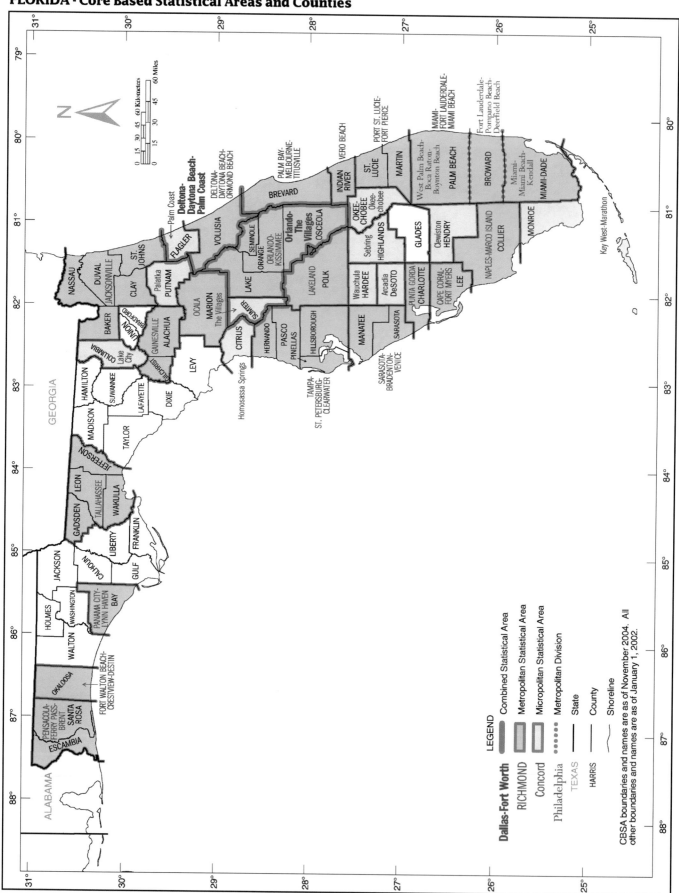

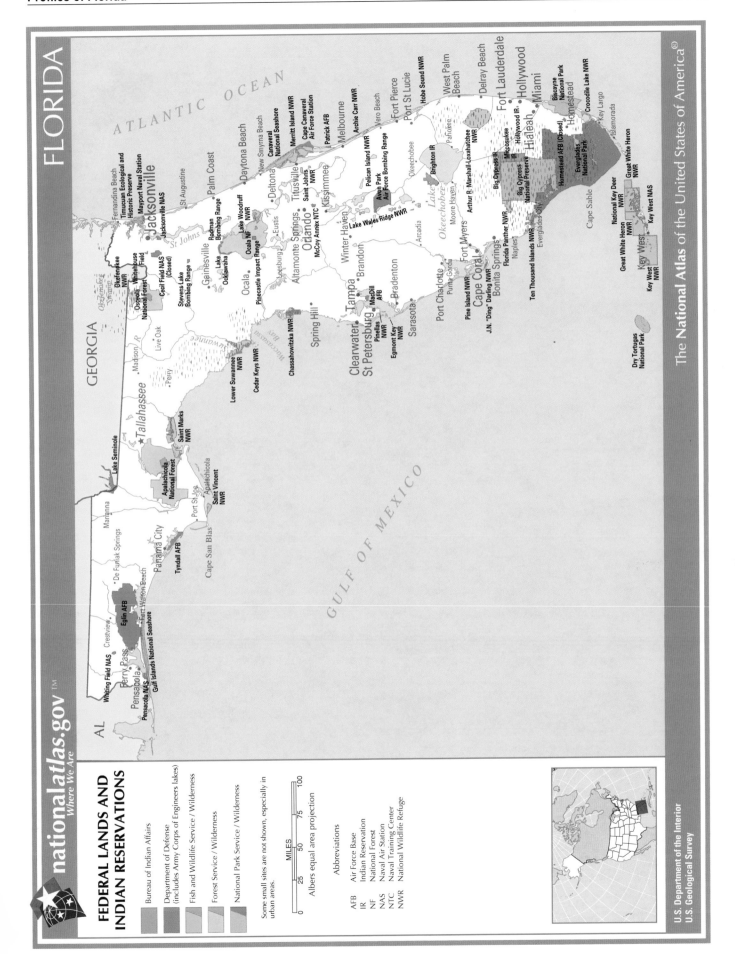

FLORIDA

nationalatlas.gov ™
Where We Are

FEDERAL LANDS AND INDIAN RESERVATIONS

Bureau of Indian Affairs

Department of Defense
(includes Army Corps of Engineers lakes)

Fish and Wildlife Service / Wilderness

Forest Service / Wilderness

National Park Service / Wilderness

Some small sites are not shown, especially in urban areas.

MILES
0   25   50   75   100

Albers equal area projection

Abbreviations

AFB   Air Force Base
IR   Indian Reservation
NF   National Forest
NAS   Naval Air Station
NTC   Naval Training Center
NWR   National Wildlife Refuge

The **National Atlas** of the United States of America®

U.S. Department of the Interior
U.S. Geological Survey

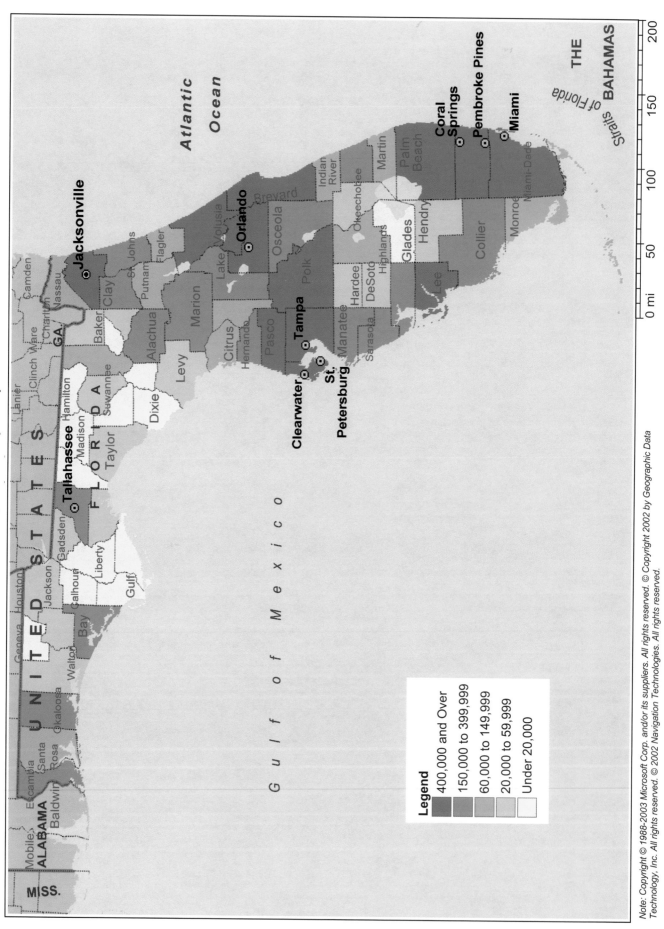

Population (2007)

Legend
- 400,000 and Over
- 150,000 to 399,999
- 60,000 to 149,999
- 20,000 to 59,999
- Under 20,000

Percent White (2007)

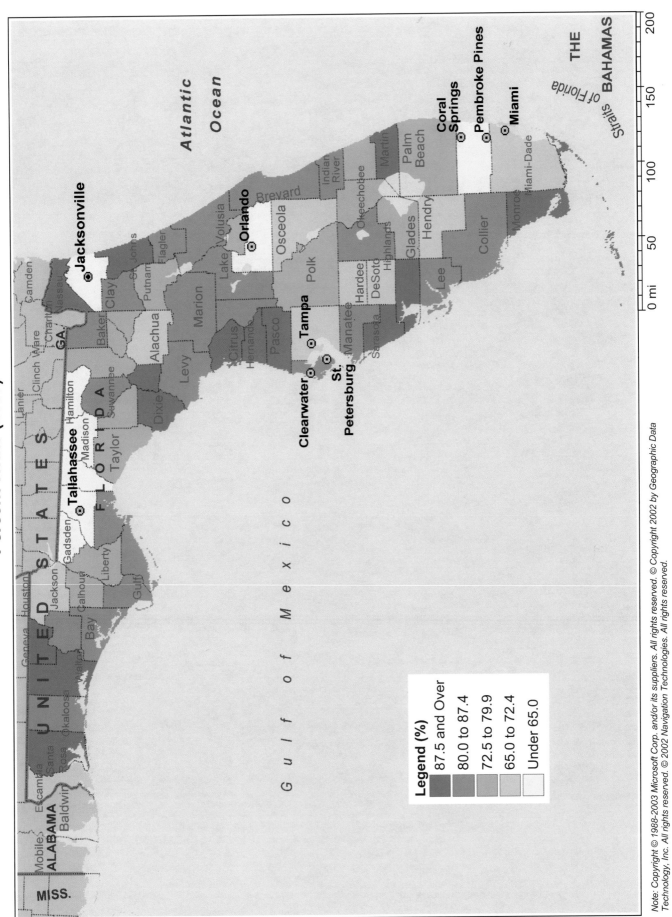

Legend (%)

- 87.5 and Over
- 80.0 to 87.4
- 72.5 to 79.9
- 65.0 to 72.4
- Under 65.0

Percent Black (2007)

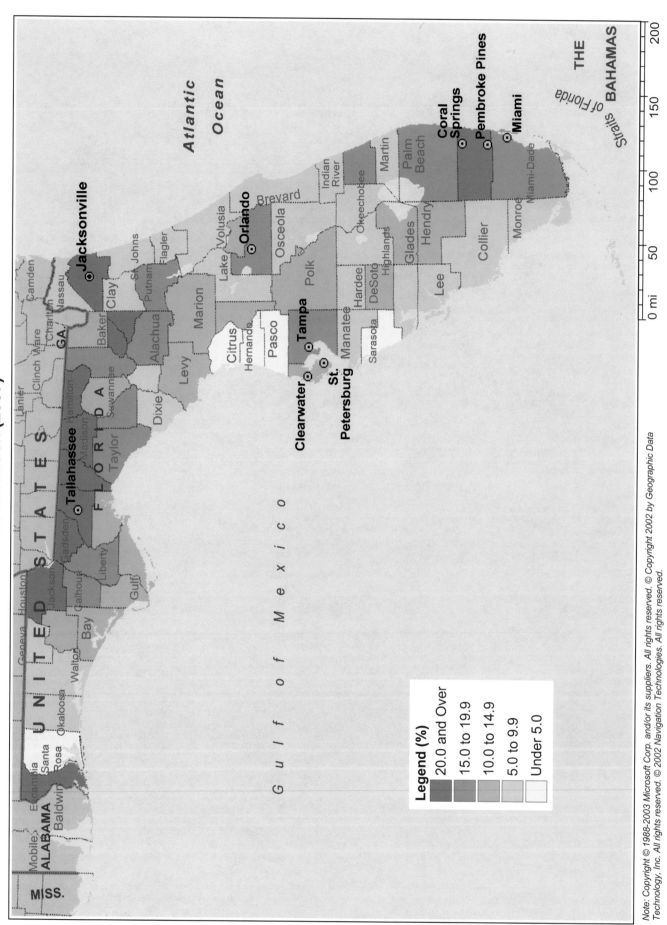

Legend (%)

- 20.0 and Over
- 15.0 to 19.9
- 10.0 to 14.9
- 5.0 to 9.9
- Under 5.0

Percent Asian (2007)

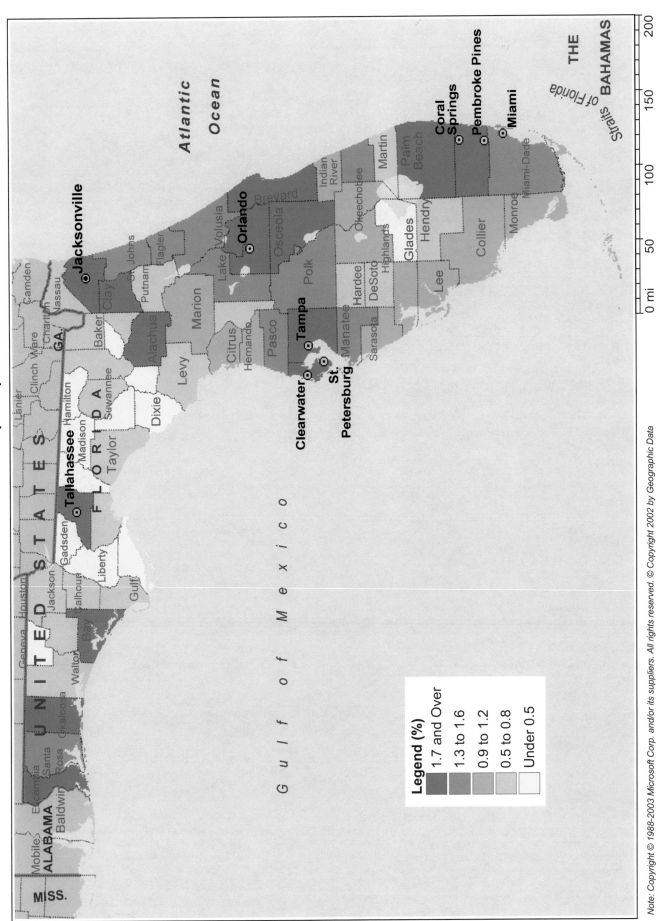

Legend (%)

- 1.7 and Over
- 1.3 to 1.6
- 0.9 to 1.2
- 0.5 to 0.8
- Under 0.5

Percent Hispanic (2007)

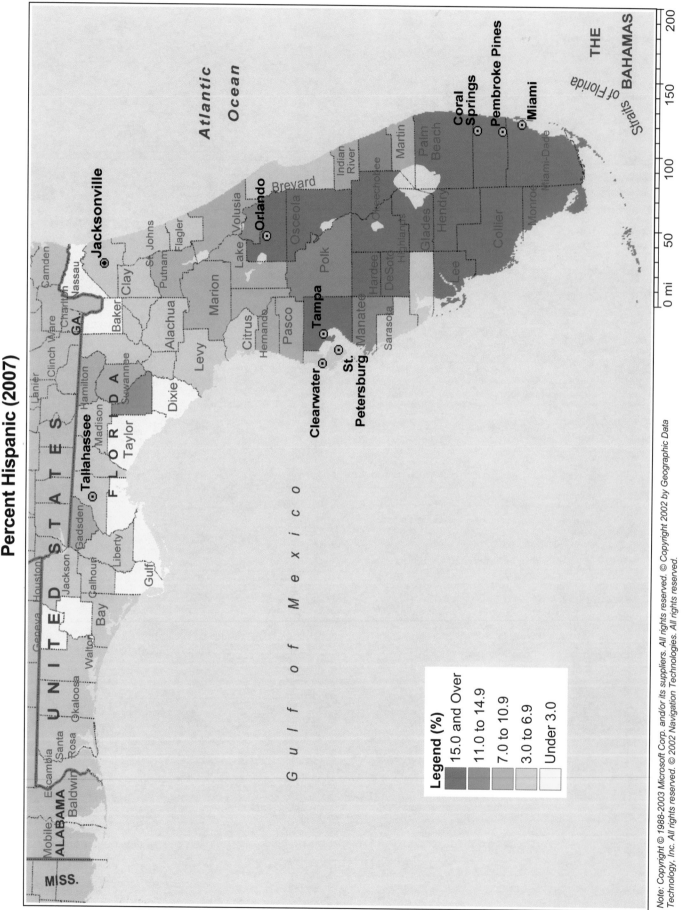

Legend (%)
- 15.0 and Over
- 11.0 to 14.9
- 7.0 to 10.9
- 3.0 to 6.9
- Under 3.0

Median Age (2007)

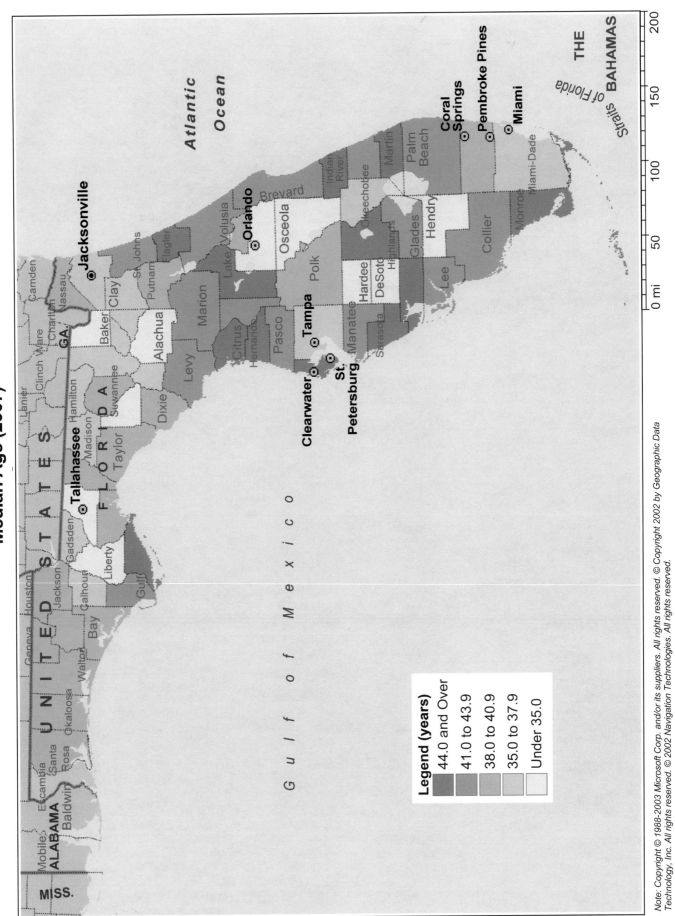

Legend (years)
- 44.0 and Over
- 41.0 to 43.9
- 38.0 to 40.9
- 35.0 to 37.9
- Under 35.0

Median Household Income (2007)

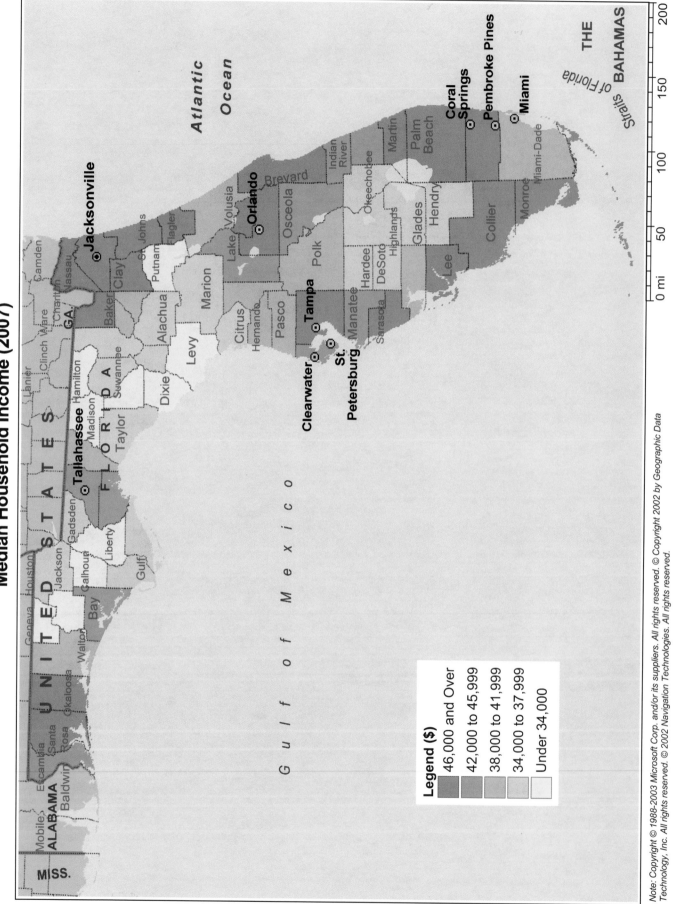

Legend ($)

- 46,000 and Over
- 42,000 to 45,999
- 38,000 to 41,999
- 34,000 to 37,999
- Under 34,000

Percent of Population Living Below Poverty Level (2005)

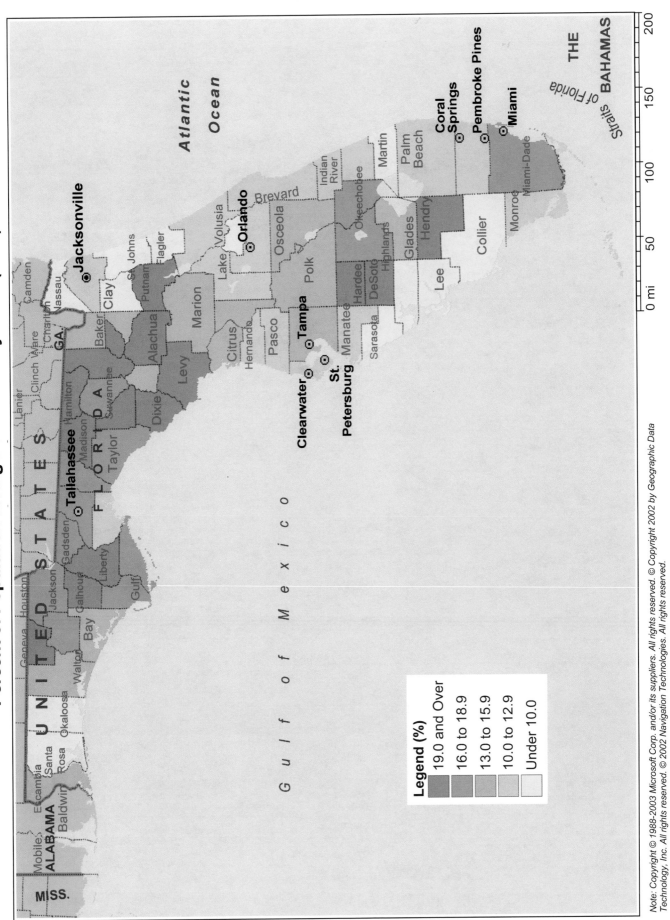

Legend (%)
- 19.0 and Over
- 16.0 to 18.9
- 13.0 to 15.9
- 10.0 to 12.9
- Under 10.0

Median Home Value (2007)

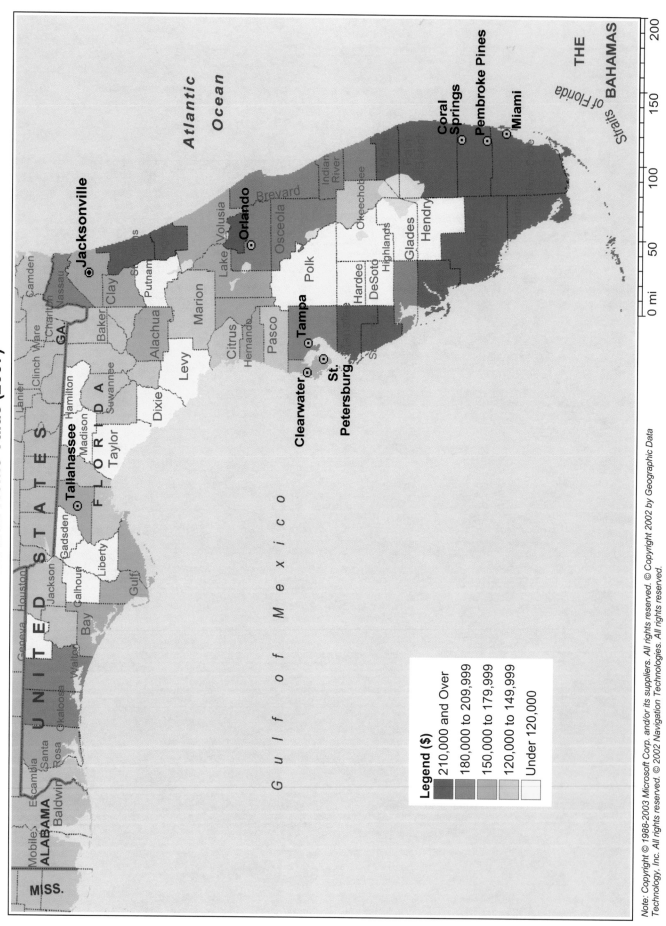

Legend ($)

- 210,000 and Over
- 180,000 to 209,999
- 150,000 to 179,999
- 120,000 to 149,999
- Under 120,000

Percent of Population Who are Homeowners (2007)

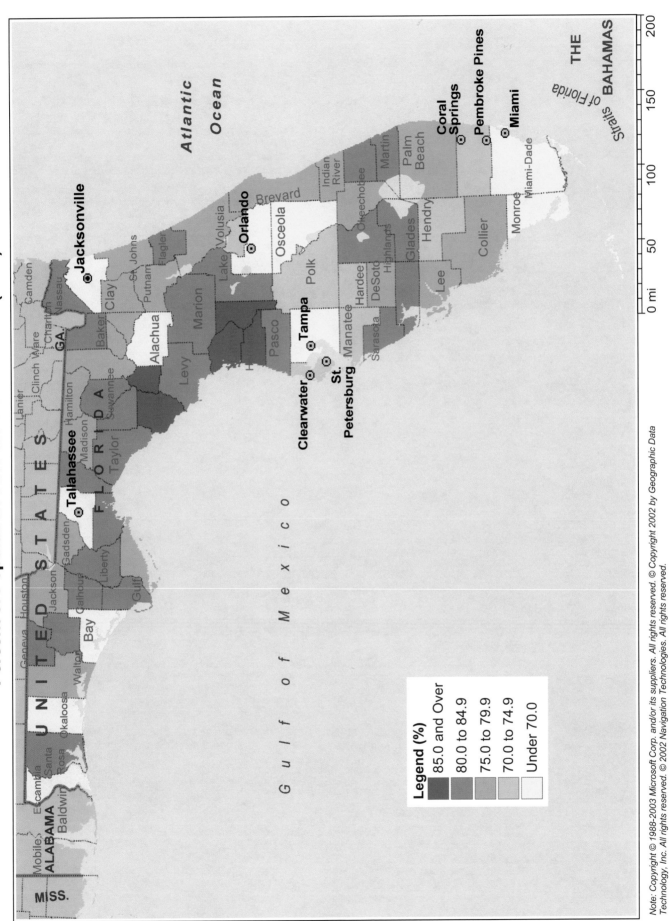

Legend (%)

- 85.0 and Over
- 80.0 to 84.9
- 75.0 to 79.9
- 70.0 to 74.9
- Under 70.0

High School Graduates* (2007)

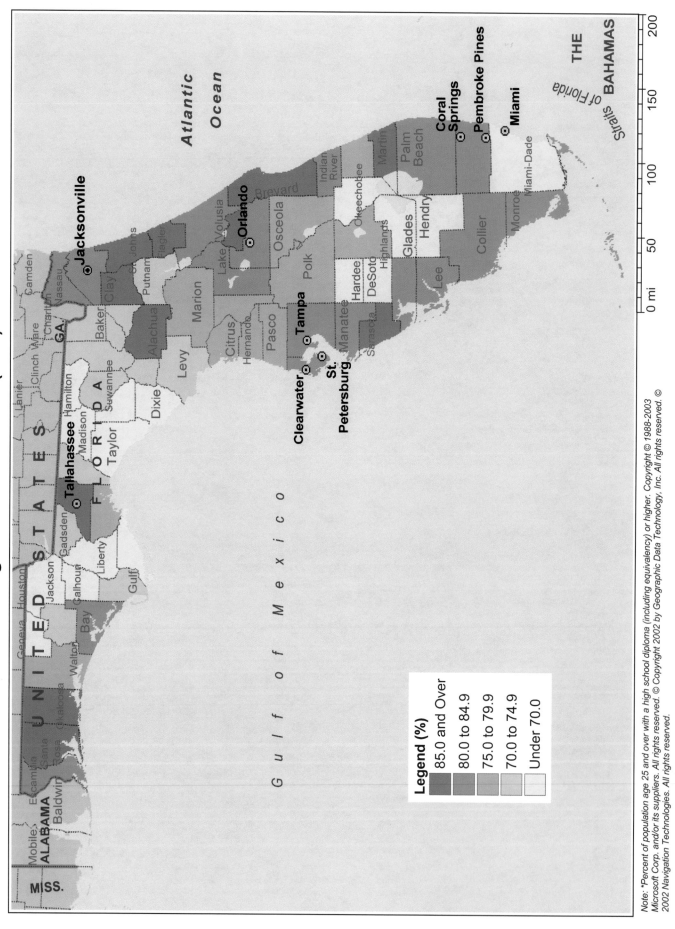

Legend (%)

- 85.0 and Over
- 80.0 to 84.9
- 75.0 to 79.9
- 70.0 to 74.9
- Under 70.0

Note: *Percent of population age 25 and over with a high school diploma (including equivalency) or higher. Copyright © 1988-2003 Microsoft Corp. and/or its suppliers. All rights reserved. © Copyright 2002 by Geographic Data Technology, Inc. All rights reserved. © 2002 Navigation Technologies. All rights reserved.

College Graduates* (2007)

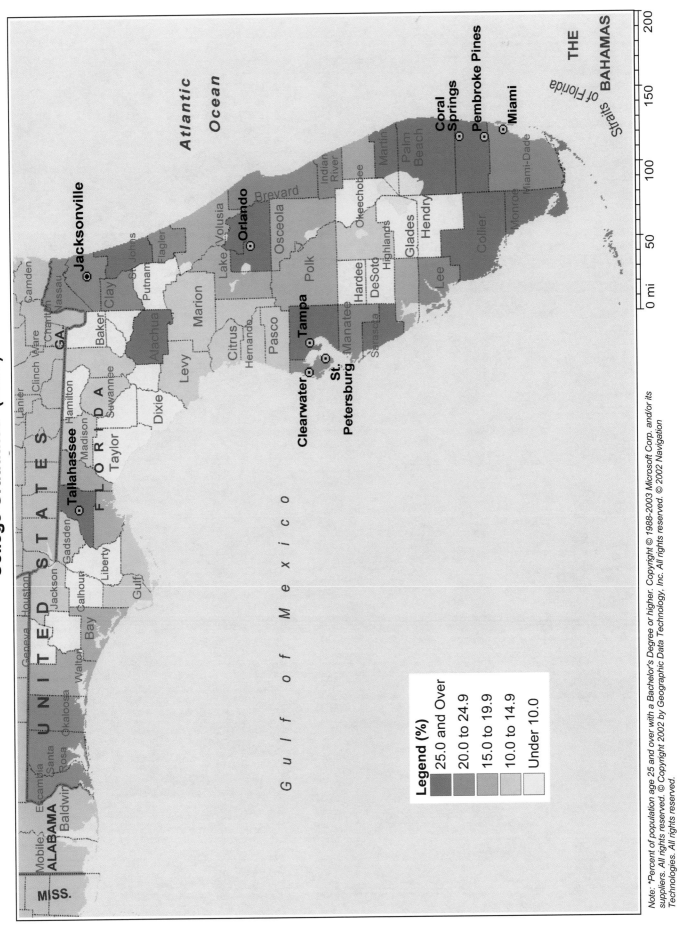

Legend (%)

- 25.0 and Over
- 20.0 to 24.9
- 15.0 to 19.9
- 10.0 to 14.9
- Under 10.0

Percent of Population Who Voted for George Bush in 2004

Legend (%)
- 60.0 and Over
- 55.0 to 59.9
- 50.0 to 54.9
- 45.0 to 49.9
- 40.0 to 44.9
- Under 40.0

Business Information ◆ Ratings Guides ◆ General Reference ◆ Education ◆
Statistics ◆ Demographics ◆ Health Information ◆ Canadian Information

Grey House
Publishing

The Directory of Business Information Resources, 2008

With 100% verification, over 1,000 new listings and more than 12,000 updates, *The Directory of Business Information Resources* is the most up-to-date source for contacts in over 98 business areas – from advertising and agriculture to utilities and wholesalers. This carefully researched volume details: the Associations representing each industry; the Newsletters that keep members current; the Magazines and Journals - with their "Special Issues" - that are important to the trade, the Conventions that are "must attends," Databases, Directories and Industry Web Sites that provide access to must-have marketing resources. Includes contact names, phone & fax numbers, web sites and e-mail addresses. This one-volume resource is a gold mine of information and would be a welcome addition to any reference collection.

"This is a most useful and easy-to-use addition to any researcher's library." –The Information Professionals Institute

Softcover ISBN 978-1-59237-193-8, 2,500 pages, $195.00 | Online Database $495.00

Nations of the World, 2007/08 A Political, Economic and Business Handbook

This completely revised edition covers all the nations of the world in an easy-to-use, single volume. Each nation is profiled in a single chapter that includes Key Facts, Political & Economic Issues, a Country Profile and Business Information. In this fast-changing world, it is extremely important to make sure that the most up-to-date information is included in your reference collection. This edition is just the answer. Each of the 200+ country chapters have been carefully reviewed by a political expert to make sure that the text reflects the most current information on Politics, Travel Advisories, Economics and more. You'll find such vital information as a Country Map, Population Characteristics, Inflation, Agricultural Production, Foreign Debt, Political History, Foreign Policy, Regional Insecurity, Economics, Trade & Tourism, Historical Profile, Political Systems, Ethnicity, Languages, Media, Climate, Hotels, Chambers of Commerce, Banking, Travel Information and more. Five Regional Chapters follow the main text and include a Regional Map, an Introductory Article, Key Indicators and Currencies for the Region. As an added bonus, an all-inclusive CD-ROM is available as a companion to the printed text. Noted for its sophisticated, up-to-date and reliable compilation of political, economic and business information, this brand new edition will be an important acquisition to any public, academic or special library reference collection.

"A useful addition to both general reference collections and business collections." –RUSQ

Softcover ISBN 978-1-59237-177-8, 1,700 pages, $155.00

The Directory of Venture Capital & Private Equity Firms, 2008

This edition has been extensively updated and broadly expanded to offer direct access to over 2,800 Domestic and International Venture Capital Firms, including address, phone & fax numbers, e-mail addresses and web sites for both primary and branch locations. Entries include details on the firm's Mission Statement, Industry Group Preferences, Geographic Preferences, Average and Minimum Investments and Investment Criteria. You'll also find details that are available nowhere else, including the Firm's Portfolio Companies and extensive information on each of the firm's Managing Partners, such as Education, Professional Background and Directorships held, along with the Partner's E-mail Address. *The Directory of Venture Capital & Private Equity Firms* offers five important indexes: Geographic Index, Executive Name Index, Portfolio Company Index, Industry Preference Index and College & University Index. With its comprehensive coverage and detailed, extensive information on each company, The Directory of Venture Capital & Private Equity Firms is an important addition to any finance collection.

"The sheer number of listings, the descriptive information and the outstanding indexing make this directory a better value than ...Pratt's Guide to Venture Capital Sources. Recommended for business collections in large public, academic and business libraries." –Choice

Softcover ISBN 978-1-59237-272-0, 1,300 pages, $565/$450 Library | Online Database $889.00

The Directory of Mail Order Catalogs, 2008

Published since 1981, *The Directory of Mail Order Catalogs* is the premier source of information on the mail order catalog industry. It is the source that business professionals and librarians have come to rely on for the thousands of catalog companies in the US. Since the 2007 edition, *The Directory of Mail Order Catalogs* has been combined with its companion volume, *The Directory of Business to Business Catalogs*, to offer all 13,000 catalog companies in one easy-to-use volume. Section I: Consumer Catalogs, covers over 9,000 consumer catalog companies in 44 different product chapters from Animals to Toys & Games. Section II: Business to Business Catalogs, details 5,000 business catalogs, everything from computers to laboratory supplies, building construction and much more. Listings contain detailed contact information including mailing address, phone & fax numbers, web sites, e-mail addresses and key contacts along with important business details such as product descriptions, employee size, years in business, sales volume, catalog size, number of catalogs mailed and more. Three indexes are included for easy access to information: Catalog & Company Name Index, Geographic Index and Product Index. *The Directory of Mail Order Catalogs*, now with its expanded business to business catalogs, is the largest and most comprehensive resource covering this billion-dollar industry. It is the standard in its field. This important resource is a useful tool for entrepreneurs searching for catalogs to pick up their product, vendors looking to expand their customer base in the catalog industry, market researchers, small businesses investigating new supply vendors, along with the library patron who is exploring the available catalogs in their areas of interest.

"This is a godsend for those looking for information." –Reference Book Review

Softcover ISBN 978-1-59237-202-7, 1,700 pages, $350/$250 Library | Online Database $495.00

Business Information ♦ Ratings Guides ♦ General Reference ♦ Education ♦
Statistics ♦ Demographics ♦ Health Information ♦ Canadian Information

The Encyclopedia of Emerging Industries

*Published under an exclusive license from the Gale Group, Inc.

The fifth edition of the *Encyclopedia of Emerging Industries* details the inception, emergence, and current status of nearly 120 flourishing U.S. industries and industry segments. These focused essays unearth for users a wealth of relevant, current, factual data previously accessible only through a diverse variety of sources. This volume provides broad-based, highly-readable, industry information under such headings as Industry Snapshot, Organization & Structure, Background & Development, Industry Leaders, Current Conditions, America and the World, Pioneers, and Research & Technology. Essays in this new edition, arranged alphabetically for easy use, have been completely revised, with updated statistics and the most current information on industry trends and developments. In addition, there are new essays on some of the most interesting and influential new business fields, including Application Service Providers, Concierge Services, Entrepreneurial Training, Fuel Cells, Logistics Outsourcing Services, Pharmacogenomics, and Tissue Engineering. Two indexes, General and Industry, provide immediate access to this wealth of information. Plus, two conversion tables for SIC and NAICS codes, along with Suggested Further Readings, are provided to aid the user. *The Encyclopedia of Emerging Industries* pinpoints emerging industries while they are still in the spotlight. This important resource will be an important acquisition to any business reference collection.

> *"This well-designed source...should become another standard business source, nicely complementing Standard & Poor's Industry Surveys. It contains more information on each industry than Hoover's Handbook of Emerging Companies, is broader in scope than The Almanac of American Employers 1998-1999, but is less expansive than the Encyclopedia of Careers & Vocational Guidance. Highly recommended for all academic libraries and specialized business collections." –Library Journal*

Hardcover ISBN 978-1-59237-242-3, 1,400 pages, $325.00

Encyclopedia of American Industries

*Published under an exclusive license from the Gale Group, Inc.

The Encyclopedia of American Industries is a major business reference tool that provides detailed, comprehensive information on a wide range of industries in every realm of American business. A two volume set, Volume I provides separate coverage of nearly 500 manufacturing industries, while Volume II presents nearly 600 essays covering the vast array of services and other non-manufacturing industries in the United States. Combined, these two volumes provide individual essays on every industry recognized by the U.S. Standard Industrial Classification (SIC) system. Both volumes are arranged numerically by SIC code, for easy use. Additionally, each entry includes the corresponding NAICS code(s). The *Encyclopedia's* business coverage includes information on historical events of consequence, as well as current trends and statistics. Essays include an Industry Snapshot, Organization & Structure, Background & Development, Current Conditions, Industry Leaders, Workforce, America and the World, Research & Technology along with Suggested Further Readings. Both SIC and NAICS code conversion tables and an all-encompassing Subject Index, with cross-references, complete the text. With its detailed, comprehensive information on a wide range of industries, this resource will be an important tool for both the industry newcomer and the seasoned professional.

> *"Encyclopedia of American Industries contains detailed, signed essays on virtually every industry in contemporary society. ... Highly recommended for all but the smallest libraries." -American Reference Books Annual*

Two Volumes, Hardcover ISBN 978-1-59237-244-7, 3,000 pages, $650.00

Encyclopedia of Global Industries

*Published under an exclusive license from the Gale Group, Inc.

This fourth edition of the acclaimed *Encyclopedia of Global Industries* presents a thoroughly revised and expanded look at more than 125 business sectors of global significance. Detailed, insightful articles discuss the origins, development, trends, key statistics and current international character of the world's most lucrative, dynamic and widely researched industries – including hundreds of profiles of leading international corporations. Beginning researchers will gain from this book a solid understanding of how each industry operates and which countries and companies are significant participants, while experienced researchers will glean current and historical figures for comparison and analysis. The industries profiled in previous editions have been updated, and in some cases, expanded to reflect recent industry trends. Additionally, this edition provides both SIC and NAICS codes for all industries profiled. As in the original volumes, *The Encyclopedia of Global Industries* offers thorough studies of some of the biggest and most frequently researched industry sectors, including Aircraft, Biotechnology, Computers, Internet Services, Motor Vehicles, Pharmaceuticals, Semiconductors, Software and Telecommunications. An SIC and NAICS conversion table and an all-encompassing Subject Index, with cross-references, are provided to ensure easy access to this wealth of information. These and many others make the *Encyclopedia of Global Industries* the authoritative reference for studies of international industries.

> *"Provides detailed coverage of the history, development, and current status of 115 of "the world's most lucrative and high-profile industries." It far surpasses the Department of Commerce's U.S. Global Trade Outlook 1995-2000 (GPO, 1995) in scope and coverage. Recommended for comprehensive public and academic library business collections." -Booklist*

Hardcover ISBN 978-1-59237-243-0, 1,400 pages, $495.00

Business Information ◆ Ratings Guides ◆ General Reference ◆ Education ◆
Statistics ◆ Demographics ◆ Health Information ◆ Canadian Information

Grey House Publishing

Sports Market Place Directory, 2008

For over 20 years, this comprehensive, up-to-date directory has offered direct access to the Who, What, When & Where of the Sports Industry. With over 20,000 updates and enhancements, the *Sports Market Place Directory* is the most detailed, comprehensive and current sports business reference source available. In 1,800 information-packed pages, *Sports Market Place Directory* profiles contact information and key executives for: Single Sport Organizations, Professional Leagues, Multi-Sport Organizations, Disabled Sports, High School & Youth Sports, Military Sports, Olympic Organizations, Media, Sponsors, Sponsorship & Marketing Event Agencies, Event & Meeting Calendars, Professional Services, College Sports, Manufacturers & Retailers, Facilities and much more. The Sports Market Place Directory provides organization's contact information with detailed descriptions including: Key Contacts, physical, mailing, email and web addresses plus phone and fax numbers. *Sports Market Place Directory* provides a one-stop resources for this billion-dollar industry. This will be an important resource for large public libraries, university libraries, university athletic programs, career services or job placement organizations, and is a must for anyone doing research on or marketing to the US and Canadian sports industry.

"Grey House is the new publisher and has produced an excellent edition...highly recommended for public libraries and academic libraries with sports management programs or strong interest in athletics." -Booklist

Softcover ISBN 978-1-59237-348-2, 1,800 pages, $225.00 | Online Database $479.00

Food and Beverage Market Place, 2008

Food and Beverage Market Place is bigger and better than ever with thousands of new companies, thousands of updates to existing companies and two revised and enhanced product category indexes. This comprehensive directory profiles over 18,000 Food & Beverage Manufacturers, 12,000 Equipment & Supply Companies, 2,200 Transportation & Warehouse Companies, 2,000 Brokers & Wholesalers, 8,000 Importers & Exporters, 900 Industry Resources and hundreds of Mail Order Catalogs. Listings include detailed Contact Information, Sales Volumes, Key Contacts, Brand & Product Information, Packaging Details and much more. *Food and Beverage Market Place* is available as a three-volume printed set, a subscription-based Online Database via the Internet, on CD-ROM, as well as mailing lists and a licensable database.

"An essential purchase for those in the food industry but will also be useful in public libraries where needed. Much of the information will be difficult and time consuming to locate without this handy three-volume ready-reference source." –ARBA

3 Vol Set, Softcover ISBN 978-1-59237-198-3, 8,500 pages, $595 | Online Database $795 | Online Database & 3 Vol Set Combo, $995

The Grey House Performing Arts Directory, 2007

The Grey House Performing Arts Directory is the most comprehensive resource covering the Performing Arts. This important directory provides current information on over 8,500 Dance Companies, Instrumental Music Programs, Opera Companies, Choral Groups, Theater Companies, Performing Arts Series and Performing Arts Facilities. Plus, this edition now contains a brand new section on Artist Management Groups. In addition to mailing address, phone & fax numbers, e-mail addresses and web sites, dozens of other fields of available information include mission statement, key contacts, facilities, seating capacity, season, attendance and more. This directory also provides an important Information Resources section that covers hundreds of Performing Arts Associations, Magazines, Newsletters, Trade Shows, Directories, Databases and Industry Web Sites. Five indexes provide immediate access to this wealth of information: Entry Name, Executive Name, Performance Facilities, Geographic and Information Resources. *The Grey House Performing Arts Directory* pulls together thousands of Performing Arts Organizations, Facilities and Information Resources into an easy-to-use source – this kind of comprehensiveness and extensive detail is not available in any resource on the market place today.

"Immensely useful and user-friendly … recommended for public, academic and certain special library reference collections." –Booklist

Softcover ISBN 978-1-59237-138-9, 1,500 pages, $185.00 | Online Database $335.00

New York State Directory, 2007/08

The New York State Directory, published annually since 1983, is a comprehensive and easy-to-use guide to accessing public officials and private sector organizations and individuals who influence public policy in the state of New York. *The New York State Directory* includes important information on all New York state legislators and congressional representatives, including biographies and key committee assignments. It also includes staff rosters for all branches of New York state government and for federal agencies and departments that impact the state policy process. Following the state government section are 25 chapters covering policy areas from agriculture through veterans' affairs. Each chapter identifies the state, local and federal agencies and officials that formulate or implement policy. In addition, each chapter contains a roster of private sector experts and advocates who influence the policy process. The directory also offers appendices that include statewide party officials; chambers of commerce; lobbying organizations; public and private universities and colleges; television, radio and print media; and local government agencies and officials.

"This comprehensive directory covers not only New York State government offices and key personnel but pertinent U.S. government agencies and non-governmental entities. This directory is all encompassing... recommended." -Choice

New York State Directory - Softcover ISBN 978-1-59237-190-7, 800 pages, $145.00
New York State Directory with *Profiles of New York* – 2 Volumes, Softcover ISBN 978-1-59237-191-4, 1,600 pages, $225.00

Business Information ◆ Ratings Guides ◆ General Reference ◆ Education ◆
Statistics ◆ Demographics ◆ Health Information ◆ Canadian Information

The Grey House Homeland Security Directory, 2008

This updated edition features the latest contact information for government and private organizations involved with Homeland Security along with the latest product information and provides detailed profiles of nearly 1,000 Federal & State Organizations & Agencies and over 3,000 Officials and Key Executives involved with Homeland Security. These listings are incredibly detailed and include Mailing Address, Phone & Fax Numbers, Email Addresses & Web Sites, a complete Description of the Agency and a complete list of the Officials and Key Executives associated with the Agency. Next, *The Grey House Homeland Security Directory* provides the go-to source for Homeland Security Products & Services. This section features over 2,000 Companies that provide Consulting, Products or Services. With this Buyer's Guide at their fingertips, users can locate suppliers of everything from Training Materials to Access Controls, from Perimeter Security to BioTerrorism Countermeasures and everything in between – complete with contact information and product descriptions. A handy Product Locator Index is provided to quickly and easily locate suppliers of a particular product. This comprehensive, information-packed resource will be a welcome tool for any company or agency that is in need of Homeland Security information and will be a necessary acquisition for the reference collection of all public libraries and large school districts.

"Compiles this information in one place and is discerning in content. A useful purchase for public and academic libraries." –Booklist

Softcover ISBN 978-1-59237-196-6, 800 pages, $195.00 | Online Database $385.00

The Grey House Safety & Security Directory, 2008

The Grey House Safety & Security Directory is the most comprehensive reference tool and buyer's guide for the safety and security industry. Arranged by safety topic, each chapter begins with OSHA regulations for the topic, followed by Training Articles written by top professionals in the field and Self-Inspection Checklists. Next, each topic contains Buyer's Guide sections that feature related products and services. Topics include Administration, Insurance, Loss Control & Consulting, Protective Equipment & Apparel, Noise & Vibration, Facilities Monitoring & Maintenance, Employee Health Maintenance & Ergonomics, Retail Food Services, Machine Guards, Process Guidelines & Tool Handling, Ordinary Materials Handling, Hazardous Materials Handling, Workplace Preparation & Maintenance, Electrical Lighting & Safety, Fire & Rescue and Security. Six important indexes make finding information and product manufacturers quick and easy: Geographical Index of Manufacturers and Distributors, Company Profile Index, Brand Name Index, Product Index, Index of Web Sites and Index of Advertisers. This comprehensive, up-to-date reference will provide every tool necessary to make sure a business is in compliance with OSHA regulations and locate the products and services needed to meet those regulations.

"Presents industrial safety information for engineers, plant managers, risk managers, and construction site supervisors..." –Choice

Softcover ISBN 978-1-59237-205-8, 1,500 pages, $165.00

The Grey House Transportation Security Directory & Handbook

This is the only reference of its kind that brings together current data on Transportation Security. With information on everything from Regulatory Authorities to Security Equipment, this top-flight database brings together the relevant information necessary for creating and maintaining a security plan for a wide range of transportation facilities. With this current, comprehensive directory at the ready you'll have immediate access to: Regulatory Authorities & Legislation; Information Resources; Sample Security Plans & Checklists; Contact Data for Major Airports, Seaports, Railroads, Trucking Companies and Oil Pipelines; Security Service Providers; Recommended Equipment & Product Information and more. Using the *Grey House Transportation Security Directory & Handbook*, managers will be able to quickly and easily assess their current security plans; develop contacts to create and maintain new security procedures; and source the products and services necessary to adequately maintain a secure environment. This valuable resource is a must for all Security Managers at Airports, Seaports, Railroads, Trucking Companies and Oil Pipelines.

"Highly recommended. Library collections that support all levels of readers, including professionals/practitioners; and schools/organizations offering education and training in transportation security." -Choice

Softcover ISBN 978-1-59237-075-7, 800 pages, $195.00

The Grey House Biometric Information Directory

This edition offers a complete, current overview of biometric companies and products – one of the fastest growing industries in today's economy. Detailed profiles of manufacturers of the latest biometric technology, including Finger, Voice, Face, Hand, Signature, Iris, Vein and Palm Identification systems. Data on the companies include key executives, company size and a detailed, indexed description of their product line. Information in the directory includes: Editorial on Advancements in Biometrics; Profiles of 700+ companies listed with contact information; Organizations, Trade & Educational Associations, Publications, Conferences, Trade Shows and Expositions Worldwide; Web Site Index; Biometric & Vendors Services Index by Types of Biometrics; and a Glossary of Biometric Terms. This resource will be an important source for anyone who is considering the use of a biometric product, investing in the development of biometric technology, support existing marketing and sales efforts and will be an important acquisition for the business reference collection for large public and business libraries.

"This book should prove useful to agencies or businesses seeking companies that deal with biometric technology. Summing Up: Recommended. Specialized collections serving researchers/faculty and professionals/practitioners." -Choice

Softcover ISBN 978-1-59237-121-1, 800 pages, $225.00

Business Information ◆ **Ratings Guides** ◆ **General Reference** ◆ **Education** ◆
Statistics ◆ **Demographics** ◆ **Health Information** ◆ **Canadian Information**

The Environmental Resource Handbook, 2007/08

The Environmental Resource Handbook is the most up-to-date and comprehensive source for Environmental Resources and Statistics. Section I: Resources provides detailed contact information for thousands of information sources, including Associations & Organizations, Awards & Honors, Conferences, Foundations & Grants, Environmental Health, Government Agencies, National Parks & Wildlife Refuges, Publications, Research Centers, Educational Programs, Green Product Catalogs, Consultants and much more. Section II: Statistics, provides statistics and rankings on hundreds of important topics, including Children's Environmental Index, Municipal Finances, Toxic Chemicals, Recycling, Climate, Air & Water Quality and more. This kind of up-to-date environmental data, all in one place, is not available anywhere else on the market place today. This vast compilation of resources and statistics is a must-have for all public and academic libraries as well as any organization with a primary focus on the environment.

"...the intrinsic value of the information make it worth consideration by libraries with environmental collections and environmentally concerned users." –Booklist

Softcover ISBN 978-1-59237-195-2, 1,000 pages, $155.00 | Online Database $300.00

The Rauch Guide to the US Adhesives & Sealants, Cosmetics & Toiletries, Ink, Paint, Plastics, Pulp & Paper and Rubber Industries

The Rauch Guides save time and money by organizing widely scattered information and providing estimates for important business decisions, some of which are available nowhere else. Within each Guide, after a brief introduction, the ECONOMICS section provides data on industry shipments; long-term growth and forecasts; prices; company performance; employment, expenditures, and productivity; transportation and geographical patterns; packaging; foreign trade; and government regulations. Next, TECHNOLOGY & RAW MATERIALS provide market, technical, and raw material information for chemicals, equipment and related materials, including market size and leading suppliers, prices, end uses, and trends. PRODUCTS & MARKETS provide information for each major industry product, including market size and historical trends, leading suppliers, five-year forecasts, industry structure, and major end uses. Next, the COMPANY DIRECTORY profiles major industry companies, both public and private. Information includes complete contact information, web address, estimated total and domestic sales, product description, and recent mergers and acquisitions. *The Rauch Guides* will prove to be an invaluable source of market information, company data, trends and forecasts that anyone in these fast-paced industries.

"An invaluable and affordable publication. The comprehensive nature of the data and text offers considerable insights into the industry, market sizes, company activities, and applications of the products of the industry. The additions that have been made have certainly enhanced the value of the Guide." –Adhesives & Sealants Newsletter of the Rauch Guide to the US Adhesives & Sealants Industry

Paint Industry: Softcover ISBN 978-1-59237-127-3 $595 | Plastics Industry: Softcover ISBN 978-1-59237-128-0 $595 | Adhesives and Sealants Industry: Softcover ISBN 978-1-59237-129-7 $595 | Ink Industry: Softcover ISBN 978-1-59237-126-6 $595 | Rubber Industry: Softcover ISBN 978-1-59237-130-3 $595 | Pulp and Paper Industry: Softcover ISBN 978-1-59237-131-0 $595 | Cosmetic & Toiletries Industry: Softcover ISBN 978-1-59237-132-7 $895

Research Services Directory: Commercial & Corporate Research Centers

This ninth edition provides access to well over 8,000 independent Commercial Research Firms, Corporate Research Centers and Laboratories offering contract services for hands-on, basic or applied research. Research Services Directory covers the thousands of types of research companies, including Biotechnology & Pharmaceutical Developers, Consumer Product Research, Defense Contractors, Electronics & Software Engineers, Think Tanks, Forensic Investigators, Independent Commercial Laboratories, Information Brokers, Market & Survey Research Companies, Medical Diagnostic Facilities, Product Research & Development Firms and more. Each entry provides the company's name, mailing address, phone & fax numbers, key contacts, web site, e-mail address, as well as a company description and research and technical fields served. Four indexes provide immediate access to this wealth of information: Research Firms Index, Geographic Index, Personnel Name Index and Subject Index.

"An important source for organizations in need of information about laboratories, individuals and other facilities." –ARBA

Softcover ISBN 978-1-59237-003-0, 1,400 pages, $465.00

International Business and Trade Directories

Completely updated, the Third Edition of *International Business and Trade Directories* now contains more than 10,000 entries, over 2,000 more than the last edition, making this directory the most comprehensive resource of the worlds business and trade directories. Entries include content descriptions, price, publisher's name and address, web site and e-mail addresses, phone and fax numbers and editorial staff. Organized by industry group, and then by region, this resource puts over 10,000 industry-specific business and trade directories at the reader's fingertips. Three indexes are included for quick access to information: Geographic Index, Publisher Index and Title Index. Public, college and corporate libraries, as well as individuals and corporations seeking critical market information will want to add this directory to their marketing collection.

"Reasonably priced for a work of this type, this directory should appeal to larger academic, public and corporate libraries with an international focus." –Library Journal

Softcover ISBN 978-1-930956-63-6, 1,800 pages, $225.00

Business Information ♦ **Ratings Guides** ♦ General Reference ♦ Education ♦
Statistics ♦ Demographics ♦ Health Information ♦ Canadian Information

Grey House Publishing

TheStreet.com Ratings Guide to Health Insurers

TheStreet.com Ratings Guide to Health Insurers is the first and only source to cover the financial stability of the nation's health care system, rating the financial safety of more than 6,000 health insurance providers, health maintenance organizations (HMOs) and all of the Blue Cross Blue Shield plans – updated quarterly to ensure the most accurate information. The Guide also provides a complete listing of all the major health insurers, including all Long-Term Care and Medigap insurers. Our *Guide to Health Insurers* includes comprehensive, timely coverage on the financial stability of HMOs and health insurers; the most accurate insurance company ratings available–the same quality ratings heralded by the U.S. General Accounting Office; separate listings for those companies offering Medigap and long-term care policies; the number of serious consumer complaints filed against most HMOs so you can see who is actually providing the best (or worst) service and more. The easy-to-use layout gives you a one-line summary analysis for each company that we track, followed by an in-depth, detailed analysis of all HMOs and the largest health insurers. The guide also includes a list of TheStreet.com Ratings Recommended Companies with information on how to contact them, and the reasoning behind any rating upgrades or downgrades.

> *"With 20 years behind its insurance-advocacy research [the rating guide] continues to offer a wealth of information that helps consumers weigh their healthcare options now and in the future." -Today's Librarian*

Issues published quarterly, Softcover, 550 pages, $499.00 for four quarterly issues, $249.00 for a single issue

TheStreet.com Ratings Guide to Life & Annuity Insurers

TheStreet.com Safety Ratings are the most reliable source for evaluating an insurer's financial solvency risk. Consequently, policy-holders have come to rely on TheStreet.com's flagship publication, *TheStreet.com Ratings Guide to Life & Annuity Insurers*, to help them identify the safest companies to do business with. Each easy-to-use edition delivers TheStreet.com's independent ratings and analyses on more than 1,100 insurers, updated every quarter. Plus, your patrons will find a complete list of TheStreet.com Recommended Companies, including contact information, and the reasoning behind any rating upgrades or downgrades. This guide is perfect for those who are considering the purchase of a life insurance policy, placing money in an annuity, or advising clients about insurance and annuities. A life or health insurance policy or annuity is only as secure as the insurance company issuing it. Therefore, make sure your patrons have what they need to periodically monitor the financial condition of the companies with whom they have an investment. The TheStreet.com Ratings product line is designed to help them in their evaluations.

> *"Weiss has an excellent reputation and this title is held by hundreds of libraries. This guide is recommended for public and academic libraries " -ARBA*

Issues published quarterly, Softcover, 360 pages, $499.00 for four quarterly issues, $249.00 for a single issue

TheStreet.com Ratings Guide to Property & Casualty Insurers

TheStreet.com Ratings Guide to Property and Casualty Insurers provides the most extensive coverage of insurers writing policies, helping consumers and businesses avoid financial headaches. Updated quarterly, this easy-to-use publication delivers the independent, unbiased TheStreet.com Safety Ratings and supporting analyses on more than 2,800 U.S. insurance companies, offering auto & homeowners insurance, business insurance, worker's compensation insurance, product liability insurance, medical malpractice and other professional liability insurance. Each edition includes a list of TheStreet.com Recommended Companies by type of insurance, including a contact number, plus helpful information about the coverage provided by the State Guarantee Associations.

> *"In contrast to the other major insurance rating agencies...Weiss does not have a financial relationship worth the companies it rates. A GAO study found that Weiss identified financial vulnerability earlier than the other rating agencies." -ARBA*

Issues published quarterly, Softcover, 455 pages, $499.00 for four quarterly issues, $249.00 for a single issue

TheStreet.com Ratings Consumer Box Set

Deliver the critical information your patrons need to safeguard their personal finances with *TheStreet.com Ratings' Consumer Guide Box Set*. Each of the eight guides is packed with accurate, unbiased information and recommendations to help your patrons make sound financial decisions. TheStreet.com Ratings Consumer Guide Box Set provides your patrons with easy to understand guidance on important personal finance topics, including: *Consumer Guide to Variable Annuities, Consumer Guide to Medicare Supplement Insurance, Consumer Guide to Elder Care Choices, Consumer Guide to Automobile Insurance, Consumer Guide to Long-Term Care Insurance, Consumer Guide to Homeowners Insurance, Consumer Guide to Term Life Insurance, and Consumer Guide to Medicare Prescription Drug Coverage*. Each guide provides an easy-to-read overview of the topic, what to look out for when selecting a company or insurance plan to do business with, who are the recommended companies to work with and how to navigate through these often-times difficult decisions. Custom worksheets and step-by-step directions make these resources accessible to all types of users. Packaged in a handy custom display box, these helpful guides will prove to be a much-used addition to any reference collection.

Issues published twice per year, Softcover, 600 pages, $499.00 for two biennial issues

Business Information ◆ **Ratings Guides** ◆ General Reference ◆ Education ◆
Statistics ◆ Demographics ◆ Health Information ◆ Canadian Information

TheStreet.com Ratings Guide to Stock Mutual Funds

TheStreet.com Ratings Guide to Stock Mutual Funds offers ratings and analyses on more than 8,800 equity mutual funds – more than any other publication. The exclusive TheStreet.com Investment Ratings combine an objective evaluation of each fund's performance and risk to provide a single, user-friendly, composite rating, giving your patrons a better handle on a mutual fund's risk-adjusted performance. Each edition identifies the top-performing mutual funds based on risk category, type of fund, and overall risk-adjusted performance. TheStreet.com's unique investment rating system makes it easy to see exactly which stocks are on the rise and which ones should be avoided. For those investors looking to tailor their mutual fund selections based on age, income, and tolerance for risk, we've also assigned two component ratings to each fund: a performance rating and a risk rating. With these, you can identify those funds that are best suited to meet your - or your client's – individual needs and goals. Plus, we include a handy Risk Profile Quiz to help you assess your personal tolerance for risk. So whether you're an investing novice or professional, the *Guide to Stock Mutual Funds* gives you everything you need to find a mutual fund that is right for you.

"There is tremendous need for information such as that provided by this Weiss publication. This reasonably priced guide is recommended for public and academic libraries serving investors." -ARBA

Issues published quarterly, Softcover, 655 pages, $499 for four quarterly issues, $249 for a single issue

TheStreet.com Ratings Guide to Exchange-Traded Funds

TheStreet.com Ratings editors analyze hundreds of mutual funds each quarter, condensing all of the available data into a single composite opinion of each fund's risk-adjusted performance. The intuitive, consumer-friendly ratings allow investors to instantly identify those funds that have historically done well and those that have under-performed the market. Each quarterly edition identifies the top-performing exchange-traded funds based on risk category, type of fund, and overall risk-adjusted performance. The rating scale, A through F, gives you a better handle on an exchange-traded fund's risk-adjusted performance. Other features include Top & Bottom 200 Exchange-Traded Funds; Performance and Risk: 100 Best and Worst Exchange- Traded Funds; Investor Profile Quiz; Performance Benchmarks and Fund Type Descriptions. With the growing popularity of mutual fund investing, consumers need a reliable source to help them track and evaluate the performance of their mutual fund holdings. Plus, they need a way of identifying and monitoring other funds as potential new investments. Unfortunately, the hundreds of performance and risk measures available, multiplied by the vast number of mutual fund investments on the market today, can make this a daunting task for even the most sophisticated investor. This Guide will serve as a useful tool for both the first-time and seasoned investor.

Editions published quarterly, Softcover, 440 pages, $499.00 for four quarterly issues, $249.00 for a single issue

TheStreet.com Ratings Guide to Bond & Money Market Mutual Funds

TheStreet.com Ratings Guide to Bond & Money Market Mutual Funds has everything your patrons need to easily identify the top-performing fixed income funds on the market today. Each quarterly edition contains TheStreet.com's independent ratings and analyses on more than 4,600 fixed income funds – more than any other publication, including corporate bond funds, high-yield bond funds, municipal bond funds, mortgage security funds, money market funds, global bond funds and government bond funds. In addition, the fund's risk rating is combined with its three-year performance rating to get an overall picture of the fund's risk-adjusted performance. The resulting TheStreet.com Investment Rating gives a single, user-friendly, objective evaluation that makes it easy to compare one fund to another and select the right fund based on the level of risk tolerance. Most investors think of fixed income mutual funds as "safe" investments. That's not always the case, however, depending on the credit risk, interest rate risk, and prepayment risk of the securities owned by the fund. TheStreet.com Ratings assesses each of these risks and assigns each fund a risk rating to help investors quickly evaluate the fund's risk component. Plus, we include a handy Risk Profile Quiz to help you assess your personal tolerance for risk. So whether you're an investing novice or professional, the *Guide to Bond and Money Market Mutual Funds* gives you everything you need to find a mutual fund that is right for you.

"Comprehensive... It is easy to use and consumer-oriented, and can be recommended for larger public and academic libraries." -ARBA

Issues published quarterly, Softcover, 470 pages, $499.00 for four quarterly issues, $249.00 for a single issue

TheStreet.com Ratings Guide to Banks & Thrifts

Updated quarterly, for the most up-to-date information, *TheStreet.com Ratings Guide to Banks and Thrifts* offers accurate, intuitive safety ratings your patrons can trust; supporting ratios and analyses that show an institution's strong & weak points; identification of the TheStreet.com Recommended Companies with branches in your area; a complete list of institutions receiving upgrades/downgrades; and comprehensive coverage of every bank and thrift in the nation – more than 9,000. TheStreet.com Safety Ratings are then based on the analysts' review of publicly available information collected by the federal banking regulators. The easy-to-use layout gives you: the institution's TheStreet.com Safety Rating for the last 3 years; the five key indexes used to evaluate each institution; along with the primary ratios and statistics used in determining the company's rating. *TheStreet.com Ratings Guide to Banks & Thrifts* will be a must for individuals who are concerned about the safety of their CD or savings account; need to be sure that an existing line of credit will be there when they need it; or simply want to avoid the hassles of dealing with a failing or troubled institution.

"Large public and academic libraries most definitely need to acquire the work. Likewise, special libraries in large corporations will find this title indispensable." -ARBA

Issues published quarterly, Softcover, 370 pages, $499.00 for four quarterly issues, $249.00 for a single issue

Business Information ◆ <u>Ratings Guides</u> ◆ General Reference ◆ Education ◆ Statistics ◆ Demographics ◆ Health Information ◆ Canadian Information

TheStreet.com Ratings Guide to Common Stocks

TheStreet.com Ratings Guide to Common Stocks gives your patrons reliable insight into the risk-adjusted performance of common stocks listed on the NYSE, AMEX, and Nasdaq – over 5,800 stocks in all – more than any other publication. TheStreet.com's unique investment rating system makes it easy to see exactly which stocks are on the rise and which ones should be avoided. In addition, your patrons also get supporting analysis showing growth trends, profitability, debt levels, valuation levels, the top-rated stocks within each industry, and more. Plus, each stock is ranked with the easy-to-use buy-hold-sell equivalents commonly used by Wall Street. Whether they're selecting their own investments or checking up on a broker's recommendation, TheStreet.com Ratings can help them in their evaluations.

"Users... will find the information succinct and the explanations readable, easy to understand, and helpful to a novice." -Library Journal

Issues published quarterly, Softcover, 440 pages, $499.00 for four quarterly issues, $249.00 for a single issue

TheStreet.com Ratings Ultimate Guided Tour of Stock Investing

This important reference guide from TheStreet.com Ratings is just what librarians around the country have asked for: a step-by-step introduction to stock investing for the beginning to intermediate investor. This easy-to-navigate guide explores the basics of stock investing and includes the intuitive TheStreet.com Investment Rating on more than 5,800 stocks, complete with real-world investing information that can be put to use immediately with stocks that fit the concepts discussed in the guide; informative charts, graphs and worksheets; easy-to-understand explanations on topics like P/E, compound interest, marked indices, diversifications, brokers, and much more; along with financial safety ratings for every stock on the NYSE, American Stock Exchange and the Nasdaq. This consumer-friendly guide offers complete how-to information on stock investing that can be put to use right away; a friendly format complete with our "Wise Guide" who leads the reader on a safari to learn about the investing jungle; helpful charts, graphs and simple worksheets; the intuitive TheStreet.com Investment rating on over 6,000 stocks — every stock found on the NYSE, American Stock Exchange and the NASDAQ; and much more.

"Provides investors with an alternative to stock broker recommendations, which recently have been tarnished by conflicts of interest. In summary, the guide serves as a welcome addition for all public library collections." -ARBA

Issues published quarterly, Softcover, 370 pages, $499.00 for four quarterly issues, $249.00 for a single issue

TheStreet.com Ratings' Reports & Services

- Ratings Online — An on-line summary covering an individual company's TheStreet.com Financial Strength Rating or an investment's unique TheStreet.com Investment Rating with the factors contributing to that rating; available 24 hours a day by visiting www.thestreet.com/tscratings or calling (800) 289-9222.
- Unlimited Ratings Research — The ultimate research tool providing fast, easy online access to the very latest TheStreet.com Financial Strength Ratings and Investment Ratings. Price: $559 per industry.

Contact TheStreet.com for more information about Reports & Services at www.thestreet.com/tscratings or call (800) 289-9222

TheStreet.com Ratings' Custom Reports

TheStreet.com Ratings is pleased to offer two customized options for receiving ratings data. Each taps into TheStreet.com's vast data repositories and is designed to provide exactly the data you need. Choose from a variety of industries, companies, data variables, and delivery formats including print, Excel, SQL, Text or Access.

- Customized Reports - get right to the heart of your company's research and data needs with a report customized to your specifications.
- Complete Database Download – TheStreet.com will design and deliver the database; from there you can sort it, recalculate it, and format your results to suit your specific needs.

Contact TheStreet.com for more information about Custom Reports at www.thestreet.com/tscratings or call (800) 289-9222

Business Information ◆ Ratings Guides ◆ <u>General Reference</u> ◆ Education ◆
Statistics ◆ Demographics ◆ Health Information ◆ Canadian Information

The Value of a Dollar 1600-1859, The Colonial Era to The Civil War

Following the format of the widely acclaimed, *The Value of a Dollar, 1860-2004, The Value of a Dollar 1600-1859, The Colonial Era to The Civil War* records the actual prices of thousands of items that consumers purchased from the Colonial Era to the Civil War. Our editorial department had been flooded with requests from users of our *Value of a Dollar* for the same type of information, just from an earlier time period. This new volume is just the answer – with pricing data from 1600 to 1859. Arranged into five-year chapters, each 5-year chapter includes a Historical Snapshot, Consumer Expenditures, Investments, Selected Income, Income/Standard Jobs, Food Basket, Standard Prices and Miscellany. There is also a section on Trends. This informative section charts the change in price over time and provides added detail on the reasons prices changed within the time period, including industry developments, changes in consumer attitudes and important historical facts. This fascinating survey will serve a wide range of research needs and will be useful in all high school, public and academic library reference collections.

"The Value of a Dollar: Colonial Era to the Civil War, 1600-1865 will find a happy audience among students, researchers, and general browsers. It offers a fascinating and detailed look at early American history from the viewpoint of everyday people trying to make ends meet. This title and the earlier publication, The Value of a Dollar, 1860-2004, complement each other very well, and readers will appreciate finding them side-by-side on the shelf." -Booklist

Hardcover ISBN 978-1-59237-094-8, 600 pages, $145.00 | Ebook ISBN 978-1-59237-169-3 www.gale.com/gvrl/partners/grey.htm

The Value of a Dollar 1860-2004, Third Edition

A guide to practical economy, *The Value of a Dollar* records the actual prices of thousands of items that consumers purchased from the Civil War to the present, along with facts about investment options and income opportunities. This brand new Third Edition boasts a brand new addition to each five-year chapter, a section on Trends. This informative section charts the change in price over time and provides added detail on the reasons prices changed within the time period, including industry developments, changes in consumer attitudes and important historical facts. Plus, a brand new chapter for 2000-2004 has been added. Each 5-year chapter includes a Historical Snapshot, Consumer Expenditures, Investments, Selected Income, Income/Standard Jobs, Food Basket, Standard Prices and Miscellany. This interesting and useful publication will be widely used in any reference collection.

"Business historians, reporters, writers and students will find this source... very helpful for historical research. Libraries will want to purchase it." –ARBA

Hardcover ISBN 978-1-59237-074-0, 600 pages, $145.00 | Ebook ISBN 978-1-59237-173-0 www.gale.com/gvrl/partners/grey.htm

Working Americans 1880-1999
Volume I: The Working Class, Volume II: The Middle Class, Volume III: The Upper Class

Each of the volumes in the *Working Americans* series focuses on a particular class of Americans, The Working Class, The Middle Class and The Upper Class over the last 120 years. Chapters in each volume focus on one decade and profile three to five families. Family Profiles include real data on Income & Job Descriptions, Selected Prices of the Times, Annual Income, Annual Budgets, Family Finances, Life at Work, Life at Home, Life in the Community, Working Conditions, Cost of Living, Amusements and much more. Each chapter also contains an Economic Profile with Average Wages of other Professions, a selection of Typical Pricing, Key Events & Inventions, News Profiles, Articles from Local Media and Illustrations. The *Working Americans* series captures the lifestyles of each of the classes from the last twelve decades, covers a vast array of occupations and ethnic backgrounds and travels the entire nation. These interesting and useful compilations of portraits of the American Working, Middle and Upper Classes during the last 120 years will be an important addition to any high school, public or academic library reference collection.

"These interesting, unique compilations of economic and social facts, figures and graphs will support multiple research needs. They will engage and enlighten patrons in high school, public and academic library collections." –Booklist

Volume I: The Working Class Hardcover ISBN 978-1-891482-81-6, 558 pages, $145.00 | Volume II: The Middle Class Hardcover ISBN 978-1-891482-72-4, 591 pages, $145.00 | Volume III: The Upper Class Hardcover ISBN 978-1-930956-38-4, 567 pages, $145.00 | Ebooks www.gale.com/gvrl/partners/grey.htm

Working Americans 1880-1999 Volume IV: Their Children

This Fourth Volume in the highly successful *Working Americans* series focuses on American children, decade by decade from 1880 to 1999. This interesting and useful volume introduces the reader to three children in each decade, one from each of the Working, Middle and Upper classes. Like the first three volumes in the series, the individual profiles are created from interviews, diaries, statistical studies, biographies and news reports. Profiles cover a broad range of ethnic backgrounds, geographic area and lifestyles – everything from an orphan in Memphis in 1882, following the Yellow Fever epidemic of 1878 to an eleven-year-old nephew of a beer baron and owner of the New York Yankees in New York City in 1921. Chapters also contain important supplementary materials including News Features as well as information on everything from Schools to Parks, Infectious Diseases to Childhood Fears along with Entertainment, Family Life and much more to provide an informative overview of the lifestyles of children from each decade. This interesting account of what life was like for Children in the Working, Middle and Upper Classes will be a welcome addition to the reference collection of any high school, public or academic library.

Hardcover ISBN 978-1-930956-35-3, 600 pages, $145.00 | Ebook ISBN 978-1-59237-166-2 www.gale.com/gvrl/partners/grey.htm

Business Information ♦ Ratings Guides ♦ **General Reference** ♦ Education ♦
Statistics ♦ Demographics ♦ Health Information ♦ Canadian Information

Working Americans 1880-2003 Volume V: Americans At War

Working Americans 1880-2003 Volume V: Americans At War is divided into 11 chapters, each covering a decade from 1880-2003 and examines the lives of Americans during the time of war, including declared conflicts, one-time military actions, protests, and preparations for war. Each decade includes several personal profiles, whether on the battlefield or on the homefront, that tell the stories of civilians, soldiers, and officers during the decade. The profiles examine: Life at Home; Life at Work; and Life in the Community. Each decade also includes an Economic Profile with statistical comparisons, a Historical Snapshot, News Profiles, local News Articles, and Illustrations that provide a solid historical background to the decade being examined. Profiles range widely not only geographically, but also emotionally, from that of a girl whose leg was torn off in a blast during WWI, to the boredom of being stationed in the Dakotas as the Indian Wars were drawing to a close. As in previous volumes of the *Working Americans* series, information is presented in narrative form, but hard facts and real-life situations back up each story. The basis of the profiles come from diaries, private print books, personal interviews, family histories, estate documents and magazine articles. For easy reference, *Working Americans 1880-2003 Volume V: Americans At War* includes an in-depth Subject Index. The Working Americans series has become an important reference for public libraries, academic libraries and high school libraries. This fifth volume will be a welcome addition to all of these types of reference collections.

Hardcover ISBN 978-1-59237-024-5, 600 pages, $145.00 | Ebook ISBN 978-1-59237-167-9 www.gale.com/gvrl/partners/grey.htm

Working Americans 1880-2005 Volume VI: Women at Work

Unlike any other volume in the *Working Americans* series, this Sixth Volume, is the first to focus on a particular gender of Americans. *Volume VI: Women at Work*, traces what life was like for working women from the 1860's to the present time. Beginning with the life of a maid in 1890 and a store clerk in 1900 and ending with the life and times of the modern working women, this text captures the struggle, strengths and changing perception of the American woman at work. Each chapter focuses on one decade and profiles three to five women with real data on Income & Job Descriptions, Selected Prices of the Times, Annual Income, Annual Budgets, Family Finances, Life at Work, Life at Home, Life in the Community, Working Conditions, Cost of Living, Amusements and much more. For even broader access to the events, economics and attitude towards women throughout the past 130 years, each chapter is supplemented with News Profiles, Articles from Local Media, Illustrations, Economic Profiles, Typical Pricing, Key Events, Inventions and more. This important volume illustrates what life was like for working women over time and allows the reader to develop an understanding of the changing role of women at work. These interesting and useful compilations of portraits of women at work will be an important addition to any high school, public or academic library reference collection.

Hardcover ISBN 978-1-59237-063-4, 600 pages, $145.00 | Ebook ISBN 978-1-59237-168-6 www.gale.com/gvrl/partners/grey.htm

Working Americans 1880-2005 Volume VII: Social Movements

Working Americans series, Volume VII: Social Movements explores how Americans sought and fought for change from the 1880s to the present time. Following the format of previous volumes in the Working Americans series, the text examines the lives of 34 individuals who have worked -- often behind the scenes --- to bring about change. Issues include topics as diverse as the Anti-smoking movement of 1901 to efforts by Native Americans to reassert their long lost rights. Along the way, the book will profile individuals brave enough to demand suffrage for Kansas women in 1912 or demand an end to lynching during a March on Washington in 1923. Each profile is enriched with real data on Income & Job Descriptions, Selected Prices of the Times, Annual Incomes & Budgets, Life at Work, Life at Home, Life in the Community, along with News Features, Key Events, and Illustrations. The depth of information contained in each profile allow the user to explore the private, financial and public lives of these subjects, deepening our understanding of how calls for change took place in our society. A must-purchase for the reference collections of high school libraries, public libraries and academic libraries.

Hardcover ISBN 978-1-59237-101-3, 600 pages, $145.00 | Ebook ISBN 978-1-59237-174-7 www.gale.com/gvrl/partners/grey.htm

Working Americans 1880-2005 Volume VIII: Immigrants

Working Americans 1880-2007 Volume VIII: Immigrants illustrates what life was like for families leaving their homeland and creating a new life in the United States. Each chapter covers one decade and introduces the reader to three immigrant families. Family profiles cover what life was like in their homeland, in their community in the United States, their home life, working conditions and so much more. As the reader moves through these pages, the families and individuals come to life, painting a picture of why they left their homeland, their experiences in setting roots in a new country, their struggles and triumphs, stretching from the 1800s to the present time. Profiles include a seven-year-old Swedish girl who meets her father for the first time at Ellis Island; a Chinese photographer's assistant; an Armenian who flees the genocide of his country to build Ford automobiles in Detroit; a 38-year-old German bachelor cigar maker who settles in Newark NJ, but contemplates tobacco farming in Virginia; a 19-year-old Irish domestic servant who is amazed at the easy life of American dogs; a 19-year-old Filipino who came to Hawaii against his parent's wishes to farm sugar cane; a French-Canadian who finds success as a boxer in Maine and many more. As in previous volumes, information is presented in narrative form, but hard facts and real-life situations back up each story. With the topic of immigration being so hotly debated in this country, this timely resource will prove to be a useful source for students, researchers, historians and library patrons to discover the issues facing immigrants in the United States. This title will be a useful addition to reference collections of public libraries, university libraries and high schools.

Hardcover ISBN 978-1-59237-197-6, 600 pages, $145.00 | Ebook ISBN 978-1-59237-232-4 www.gale.com/gvrl/partners/grey.htm

The Encyclopedia of Warrior Peoples & Fighting Groups

Many military groups throughout the world have excelled in their craft either by fortuitous circumstances, outstanding leadership, or intense training. This new second edition of *The Encyclopedia of Warrior Peoples and Fighting Groups* explores the origins and leadership of these outstanding combat forces, chronicles their conquests and accomplishments, examines the circumstances surrounding their decline or disbanding, and assesses their influence on the groups and methods of warfare that followed. Readers will encounter ferocious tribes, charismatic leaders, and daring militias, from ancient times to the present, including Amazons, Buffalo Soldiers, Green Berets, Iron Brigade, Kamikazes, Peoples of the Sea, Polish Winged Hussars, Teutonic Knights, and Texas Rangers. With over 100 alphabetical entries, numerous cross-references and illustrations, a comprehensive bibliography, and index, the *Encyclopedia of Warrior Peoples and Fighting Groups* is a valuable resource for readers seeking insight into the bold history of distinguished fighting forces.

"Especially useful for high school students, undergraduates, and general readers with an interest in military history." –Library Journal

Hardcover ISBN 978-1-59237-116-7, 660 pages, $135.00 | Ebook ISBN 978-1-59237-172-3 www.gale.com/gvrl/partners/grey.htm

The Encyclopedia of Invasions & Conquests, From the Ancient Times to the Present

This second edition of the popular *Encyclopedia of Invasions & Conquests*, a comprehensive guide to over 150 invasions, conquests, battles and occupations from ancient times to the present, takes readers on a journey that includes the Roman conquest of Britain, the Portuguese colonization of Brazil, and the Iraqi invasion of Kuwait, to name a few. New articles will explore the late 20th and 21st centuries, with a specific focus on recent conflicts in Afghanistan, Kuwait, Iraq, Yugoslavia, Grenada and Chechnya. In addition to covering the military aspects of invasions and conquests, entries cover some of the political, economic, and cultural aspects, for example, the effects of a conquest on the invade country's political and monetary system and in its language and religion. The entries on leaders – among them Sargon, Alexander the Great, William the Conqueror, and Adolf Hitler – deal with the people who sought to gain control, expand power, or exert religious or political influence over others through military means. Revised and updated for this second edition, entries are arranged alphabetically within historical periods. Each chapter provides a map to help readers locate key areas and geographical features, and bibliographical references appear at the end of each entry. Other useful features include cross-references, a cumulative bibliography and a comprehensive subject index. This authoritative, well-organized, lucidly written volume will prove invaluable for a variety of readers, including high school students, military historians, members of the armed forces, history buffs and hobbyists.

"Engaging writing, sensible organization, nice illustrations, interesting and obscure facts, and useful maps make this book a pleasure to read." –ARBA

Hardcover ISBN 978-1-59237-114-3, 598 pages, $135.00 | Ebook ISBN 978-1-59237-171-6 www.gale.com/gvrl/partners/grey.htm

Encyclopedia of Prisoners of War & Internment

This authoritative second edition provides a valuable overview of the history of prisoners of war and interned civilians, from earliest times to the present. Written by an international team of experts in the field of POW studies, this fascinating and thought-provoking volume includes entries on a wide range of subjects including the Crusades, Plains Indian Warfare, concentration camps, the two world wars, and famous POWs throughout history, as well as atrocities, escapes, and much more. Written in a clear and easily understandable style, this informative reference details over 350 entries, 30% larger than the first edition, that survey the history of prisoners of war and interned civilians from the earliest times to the present, with emphasis on the 19th and 20th centuries. Medical conditions, international law, exchanges of prisoners, organizations working on behalf of POWs, and trials associated with the treatment of captives are just some of the themes explored. Entries are arranged alphabetically, plus illustrations and maps are provided for easy reference. The text also includes an introduction, bibliography, appendix of selected documents, and end-of-entry reading suggestions. This one-of-a-kind reference will be a helpful addition to the reference collections of all public libraries, high schools, and university libraries and will prove invaluable to historians and military enthusiasts.

"Thorough and detailed yet accessible to the lay reader.
Of special interest to subject specialists and historians; recommended for public and academic libraries." - Library Journal

Hardcover ISBN 978-1-59237-120-4, 676 pages, $135.00 | Ebook ISBN 978-1-59237-170-9 www.gale.com/gvrl/partners/grey.htm

The Encyclopedia of Rural America: the Land & People

History, sociology, anthropology, and public policy are combined to deliver the encyclopedia destined to become the standard reference work in American rural studies. From irrigation and marriage to games and mental health, this encyclopedia is the first to explore the contemporary landscape of rural America, placed in historical perspective. With over 300 articles prepared by leading experts from across the nation, this timely encyclopedia documents and explains the major themes, concepts, industries, concerns, and everyday life of the people and land who make up rural America. Entries range from the industrial sector and government policy to arts and humanities and social and family concerns. Articles explore every aspect of life in rural America. *Encyclopedia of Rural America*, with its broad range of coverage, will appeal to high school and college students as well as graduate students, faculty, scholars, and people whose work pertains to rural areas.

"This exemplary encyclopedia is guaranteed to educate our highly urban society about the uniqueness of rural America. Recommended for public and academic libraries." -Library Journal

Two Volumes, Hardcover, ISBN 978-1-59237-115-0, 800 pages, $195.00

To preview any of our Directories Risk-Free for 30 days, call (800) 562-2139 or fax (518) 789-0556
www.greyhouse.com books@greyhouse.com

Business Information ♦ Ratings Guides ♦ <u>General Reference</u> ♦ Education ♦
Statistics ♦ Demographics ♦ Health Information ♦ Canadian Information

The Religious Right, A Reference Handbook

Timely and unbiased, this third edition updates and expands its examination of the religious right and its influence on our government, citizens, society, and politics. From the fight to outlaw the teaching of Darwin's theory of evolution to the struggle to outlaw abortion, the religious right is continually exerting an influence on public policy. This text explores the influence of religion on legislation and society, while examining the alignment of the religious right with the political right. A historical survey of the movement highlights the shift to "hands-on" approach to politics and the struggle to present a unified front. The coverage offers a critical historical survey of the religious right movement, focusing on its increased involvement in the political arena, attempts to forge coalitions, and notable successes and failures. The text offers complete coverage of biographies of the men and women who have advanced the cause and an up to date chronology illuminate the movement's goals, including their accomplishments and failures. This edition offers an extensive update to all sections along with several brand new entries. Two new sections complement this third edition, a chapter on legal issues and court decisions and a chapter on demographic statistics and electoral patterns. To aid in further research, *The Religious Right*, offers an entire section of annotated listings of print and non-print resources, as well as of organizations affiliated with the religious right, and those opposing it. Comprehensive in its scope, this work offers easy-to-read, pertinent information for those seeking to understand the religious right and its evolving role in American society. A must for libraries of all sizes, university religion departments, activists, high schools and for those interested in the evolving role of the religious right.

" Recommended for all public and academic libraries." - Library Journal

Hardcover ISBN 978-1-59237-113-6, 600 pages, $135.00 | Ebook ISBN 978-1-59237-226-3 www.gale.com/gvrl/partners/grey.htm

From Suffrage to the Senate, America's Political Women

From Suffrage to the Senate is a comprehensive and valuable compendium of biographies of leading women in U.S. politics, past and present, and an examination of the wide range of women's movements. Up to date through 2006, this dynamically illustrated reference work explores American women's path to political power and social equality from the struggle for the right to vote and the abolition of slavery to the first African American woman in the U.S. Senate and beyond. This new edition includes over 150 new entries and a brand new section on trends and demographics of women in politics. The in-depth coverage also traces the political heritage of the abolition, labor, suffrage, temperance, and reproductive rights movements. The alphabetically arranged entries include biographies of every woman from across the political spectrum who has served in the U.S. House and Senate, along with women in the Judiciary and the U.S. Cabinet and, new to this edition, biographies of activists and political consultants. Bibliographical references follow each entry. For easy reference, a handy chronology is provided detailing 150 years of women's history. This up-to-date reference will be a must-purchase for women's studies departments, high schools and public libraries and will be a handy resource for those researching the key players in women's politics, past and present.

"An engaging tool that would be useful in high school, public, and academic libraries looking for an overview of the political history of women in the US." –Booklist

Two Volumes, Hardcover ISBN 978-1-59237-117-4, 1,160 pages, $195.00 | Ebook ISBN 978-1-59237-227-0
www.gale.com/gvrl/partners/grey.htm

An African Biographical Dictionary

This landmark second edition is the only biographical dictionary to bring together, in one volume, cultural, social and political leaders – both historical and contemporary – of the sub-Saharan region. Over 800 biographical sketches of prominent Africans, as well as foreigners who have affected the continent's history, are featured, 150 more than the previous edition. The wide spectrum of leaders includes religious figures, writers, politicians, scientists, entertainers, sports personalities and more. Access to these fascinating individuals is provided in a user-friendly format. The biographies are arranged alphabetically, cross-referenced and indexed. Entries include the country or countries in which the person was significant and the commonly accepted dates of birth and death. Each biographical sketch is chronologically written; entries for cultural personalities add an evaluation of their work. This information is followed by a selection of references often found in university and public libraries, including autobiographies and principal biographical works. Appendixes list each individual by country and by field of accomplishment – rulers, musicians, explorers, missionaries, businessmen, physicists – nearly thirty categories in all. Another convenient appendix lists heads of state since independence by country. Up-to-date and representative of African societies as a whole, An African Biographical Dictionary provides a wealth of vital information for students of African culture and is an indispensable reference guide for anyone interested in African affairs.

"An unquestionable convenience to have these concise, informative biographies gathered into one source, indexed, and analyzed by appendixes listing entrants by nation and occupational field." –Wilson Library Bulletin

Hardcover ISBN 978-1-59237-112-9, 667 pages, $135.00 | Ebook ISBN 978-1-59237-229-4 www.gale.com/gvrl/partners/grey.htm

Business Information ✦ Ratings Guides ✦ <u>General Reference</u> ✦ Education ✦
Statistics ✦ Demographics ✦ Health Information ✦ Canadian Information

Grey House Publishing

American Environmental Leaders, From Colonial Times to the Present

A comprehensive and diverse award winning collection of biographies of the most important figures in American environmentalism. Few subjects arouse the passions the way the environment does. How will we feed an ever-increasing population and how can that food be made safe for consumption? Who decides how land is developed? How can environmental policies be made fair for everyone, including multiethnic groups, women, children, and the poor? *American Environmental Leaders* presents more than 350 biographies of men and women who have devoted their lives to studying, debating, and organizing these and other controversial issues over the last 200 years. In addition to the scientists who have analyzed how human actions affect nature, we are introduced to poets, landscape architects, presidents, painters, activists, even sanitation engineers, and others who have forever altered how we think about the environment. The easy to use A–Z format provides instant access to these fascinating individuals, and frequent cross references indicate others with whom individuals worked (and sometimes clashed). End of entry references provide users with a starting point for further research.

"Highly recommended for high school, academic, and public libraries needing environmental biographical information." –Library Journal/Starred Review

Two Volumes, Hardcover ISBN 978-1-59237-119-8, 900 pages $195.00 | Ebook ISBN 978-1-59237-230-0
www.gale.com/gvrl/partners/grey.htm

World Cultural Leaders of the Twentieth & Twenty-First Centuries

World Cultural Leaders of the Twentieth & Twenty-First Centuries is a window into the arts, performances, movements, and music that shaped the world's cultural development since 1900. A remarkable around-the-world look at one-hundred-plus years of cultural development through the eyes of those that set the stage and stayed to play. This second edition offers over 120 new biographies along with a complete update of existing biographies. To further aid the reader, a handy fold-out timeline traces important events in all six cultural categories from 1900 through the present time. Plus, a new section of detailed material and resources for 100 selected individuals is also new to this edition, with further data on museums, homesteads, websites, artwork and more. This remarkable compilation will answer a wide range of questions. Who was the originator of the term "documentary"? Which poet married the daughter of the famed novelist Thomas Mann in order to help her escape Nazi Germany? Which British writer served as an agent in Russia against the Bolsheviks before the 1917 revolution? A handy two-volume set that makes it easy to look up 450 worldwide cultural icons: novelists, poets, playwrights, painters, sculptors, architects, dancers, choreographers, actors, directors, filmmakers, singers, composers, and musicians. *World Cultural Leaders of the Twentieth & Twenty-First Centuries* provides entries (many of them illustrated) covering the person's works, achievements, and professional career in a thorough essay and offers interesting facts and statistics. Entries are fully cross-referenced so that readers can learn how various individuals influenced others. An index of leaders by occupation, a useful glossary and a thorough general index complete the coverage. This remarkable resource will be an important acquisition for the reference collections of public libraries, university libraries and high schools.

"Fills a need for handy, concise information on a wide array of international cultural figures."-ARBA

Two Volumes, Hardcover ISBN 978-1-59237-118-1, 900 pages, $195.00 | Ebook ISBN 978-1-59237-231-7
www.gale.com/gvrl/partners/grey.htm

Political Corruption in America: An Encyclopedia of Scandals, Power, and Greed

The complete scandal-filled history of American political corruption, focusing on the infamous people and cases, as well as society's electoral and judicial reactions. Since colonial times, there has been no shortage of politicians willing to take a bribe, skirt campaign finance laws, or act in their own interests. Corruption like the Whiskey Ring, Watergate, and Whitewater cases dominate American life, making political scandal a leading U.S. industry. From judges to senators, presidents to mayors, *Political Corruption in America* discusses the infamous people throughout history who have been accused of and implicated in crooked behavior. In this new second edition, more than 250 A–Z entries explore the people, crimes, investigations, and court cases behind 200 years of American political scandals. This unbiased volume also delves into the issues surrounding Koreagate, the Chinese campaign scandal, and other ethical lapses. Relevant statutes and terms, including the Independent Counsel Statute and impeachment as a tool of political punishment, are examined as well. Students, scholars, and other readers interested in American history, political science, and ethics will appreciate this survey of a wide range of corrupting influences. This title focuses on how politicians from all parties have fallen because of their greed and hubris, and how society has used electoral and judicial means against those who tested the accepted standards of political conduct. A full range of illustrations including political cartoons, photos of key figures such as Abe Fortas and Archibald Cox, graphs of presidential pardons, and tables showing the number of expulsions and censures in both the House and Senate round out the text. In addition, a comprehensive chronology of major political scandals in U.S. history from colonial times until the present. For further reading, an extensive bibliography lists sources including archival letters, newspapers, and private manuscript collections from the United States and Great Britain. With its comprehensive coverage of this interesting topic, *Political Corruption in America: An Encyclopedia of Scandals, Power, and Greed* will prove to be a useful addition to the reference collections of all public libraries, university libraries, history collections, political science collections and high schools.

"...this encyclopedia is a useful contribution to the field. Highly recommended." - CHOICE
"Political Corruption should be useful in most academic, high school, and public libraries." Booklist

Hardcover ISBN 978-1-59237-297-3, 500 pages, $135.00

To preview any of our Directories Risk-Free for 30 days, call (800) 562-2139 or fax (518) 789-0556
www.greyhouse.com books@greyhouse.com

Religion and Law: A Dictionary

This informative, easy-to-use reference work covers a wide range of legal issues that affect the roles of religion and law in American society. Extensive A–Z entries provide coverage of key court decisions, case studies, concepts, individuals, religious groups, organizations, and agencies shaping religion and law in today's society. This *Dictionary* focuses on topics involved with the constitutional theory and interpretation of religion and the law; terms providing a historical explanation of the ways in which America's ever increasing ethnic and religious diversity contributed to our current understanding of the mandates of the First and Fourteenth Amendments; terms and concepts describing the development of religion clause jurisprudence; an analytical examination of the distinct vocabulary used in this area of the law; the means by which American courts have attempted to balance religious liberty against other important individual and social interests in a wide variety of physical and regulatory environments, including the classroom, the workplace, the courtroom, religious group organization and structure, taxation, the clash of "secular" and "religious" values, and the relationship of the generalized idea of individual autonomy of the specific concept of religious liberty. Important legislation and legal cases affecting religion and society are thoroughly covered in this timely volume, including a detailed Table of Cases and Table of Statutes for more detailed research. A guide to further reading and an index are also included. This useful resource will be an important acquisition for the reference collections of all public libraries, university libraries, religion reference collections and high schools.

Hardcover ISBN 978-1-59237-298-0, 500 pages, $135.00

Human Rights in the United States: A Dictionary and Documents

This two volume set offers easy to grasp explanations of the basic concepts, laws, and case law in the field, with emphasis on human rights in the historical, political, and legal experience of the United States. Human rights is a term not fully understood by many Americans. Addressing this gap, the new second edition of *Human Rights in the United States: A Dictionary and Documents* offers a comprehensive introduction that places the history of human rights in the United States in an international context. It surveys the legal protection of human dignity in the United States, examines the sources of human rights norms, cites key legal cases, explains the role of international governmental and non-governmental organizations, and charts global, regional, and U.N. human rights measures. Over 240 dictionary entries of human rights terms are detailed—ranging from asylum and cultural relativism to hate crimes and torture. Each entry discusses the significance of the term, gives examples, and cites appropriate documents and court decisions. In addition, a Documents section is provided that contains 59 conventions, treaties, and protocols related to the most up to date international action on ethnic cleansing; freedom of expression and religion; violence against women; and much more. A bibliography, extensive glossary, and comprehensive index round out this indispensable volume. This comprehensive, timely volume is a must for large public libraries, university libraries and social science departments, along with high school libraries.

> "...invaluable for anyone interested in human rights issues ... highly recommended for all reference collections."
> - American Reference Books Annual

Two Volumes, Hardcover ISBN 978-1-59237-290-4, 750 pages, $225.00

Business Information ✦ Ratings Guides ✦ General Reference ✦ **Education** ✦
Statistics ✦ Demographics ✦ Health Information ✦ Canadian Information

Grey House
Publishing

The Comparative Guide to American Elementary & Secondary Schools, 2008

The only guide of its kind, this award winning compilation offers a snapshot profile of every public school district in the United States serving 1,500 or more students – more than 5,900 districts are covered. Organized alphabetically by district within state, each chapter begins with a Statistical Overview of the state. Each district listing includes contact information (name, address, phone number and web site) plus Grades Served, the Numbers of Students and Teachers and the Number of Regular, Special Education, Alternative and Vocational Schools in the district along with statistics on Student/Classroom Teacher Ratios, Drop Out Rates, Ethnicity, the Numbers of Librarians and Guidance Counselors and District Expenditures per student. As an added bonus, *The Comparative Guide to American Elementary and Secondary Schools* provides important ranking tables, both by state and nationally, for each data element. For easy navigation through this wealth of information, this handbook contains a useful City Index that lists all districts that operate schools within a city. These important comparative statistics are necessary for anyone considering relocation or doing comparative research on their own district and would be a perfect acquisition for any public library or school district library.

"This straightforward guide is an easy way to find general information. Valuable for academic and large public library collections." –ARBA

Softcover ISBN 978-1-59237-223-2, 2,400 pages, $125.00 | Ebook ISBN 978-1-59237-238-6 www.gale.com/gvrl/partners/grey.htm

The Complete Learning Disabilities Directory, 2008

The Complete Learning Disabilities Directory is the most comprehensive database of Programs, Services, Curriculum Materials, Professional Meetings & Resources, Camps, Newsletters and Support Groups for teachers, students and families concerned with learning disabilities. This information-packed directory includes information about Associations & Organizations, Schools, Colleges & Testing Materials, Government Agencies, Legal Resources and much more. For quick, easy access to information, this directory contains four indexes: Entry Name Index, Subject Index and Geographic Index. With every passing year, the field of learning disabilities attracts more attention and the network of caring, committed and knowledgeable professionals grows every day. This directory is an invaluable research tool for these parents, students and professionals.

"Due to its wealth and depth of coverage, parents, teachers and others… should find this an invaluable resource." -Booklist

Softcover ISBN 978-1-59237-207-2, 900 pages, $145.00 | Online Database $195.00 | Online Database & Directory Combo $280.00

Educators Resource Directory, 2007/08

Educators Resource Directory is a comprehensive resource that provides the educational professional with thousands of resources and statistical data for professional development. This directory saves hours of research time by providing immediate access to Associations & Organizations, Conferences & Trade Shows, Educational Research Centers, Employment Opportunities & Teaching Abroad, School Library Services, Scholarships, Financial Resources, Professional Consultants, Computer Software & Testing Resources and much more. Plus, this comprehensive directory also includes a section on Statistics and Rankings with over 100 tables, including statistics on Average Teacher Salaries, SAT/ACT scores, Revenues & Expenditures and more. These important statistics will allow the user to see how their school rates among others, make relocation decisions and so much more. For quick access to information, this directory contains four indexes: Entry & Publisher Index, Geographic Index, a Subject & Grade Index and Web Sites Index. *Educators Resource Directory* will be a well-used addition to the reference collection of any school district, education department or public library.

"Recommended for all collections that serve elementary and secondary school professionals." –Choice

Softcover ISBN 978-1-59237-179-2, 800 pages, $145.00 | Online Database $195.00 | Online Database & Directory Combo $280.00

Profiles of New York | Profiles of Florida | Profiles of Texas | Profiles of Illinois | Profiles of Michigan | Profiles of Ohio | Profiles of New Jersey | Profiles of Massachusetts | Profiles of Pennsylvania | Profiles of Wisconsin | Profiles of Connecticut & Rhode Island | Profiles of Indiana | Profiles of North Carolina & South Carolina | Profiles of Virginia | Profiles of California

The careful layout gives the user an easy-to-read snapshot of every single place and county in the state, from the biggest metropolis to the smallest unincorporated hamlet. The richness of each place or county profile is astounding in its depth, from history to weather, all packed in an easy-to-navigate, compact format. Each profile contains data on History, Geography, Climate, Population, Vital Statistics, Economy, Income, Taxes, Education, Housing, Health & Environment, Public Safety, Newspapers, Transportation, Presidential Election Results, Information Contacts and Chambers of Commerce. As an added bonus, there is a section on Selected Statistics, where data from the 100 largest towns and cities is arranged into easy-to-use charts. Each of 22 different data points has its own two-page spread with the cities listed in alpha order so researchers can easily compare and rank cities. A remarkable compilation that offers overviews and insights into each corner of the state, each volume goes beyond Census statistics, beyond metro area coverage, beyond the 100 best places to live. Drawn from official census information, other government statistics and original research, you will have at your fingertips data that's available nowhere else in one single source.

"The publisher claims that this is the 'most comprehensive portrait of the state of Florida ever published,' and this reviewer is inclined to believe it...Recommended. All levels." –Choice on Profiles of Florida

Each Profiles of... title ranges from 400-800 pages, priced at $149.00 each

America's Top-Rated Cities, 2008

America's Top-Rated Cities provides current, comprehensive statistical information and other essential data in one easy-to-use source on the 100 "top" cities that have been cited as the best for business and living in the U.S. This handbook allows readers to see, at a glance, a concise social, business, economic, demographic and environmental profile of each city, including brief evaluative comments. In addition to detailed data on Cost of Living, Finances, Real Estate, Education, Major Employers, Media, Crime and Climate, city reports now include Housing Vacancies, Tax Audits, Bankruptcy, Presidential Election Results and more. This outstanding source of information will be widely used in any reference collection.

"The only source of its kind that brings together all of this information into one easy-to-use source. It will be beneficial to many business and public libraries." –ARBA

Four Volumes, Softcover ISBN 978-1-59237-349-9, 2,500 pages, $195.00 | Ebook ISBN 978-1-59237-233-1
www.gale.com/gvrl/partners/grey.htm

America's Top-Rated Smaller Cities, 2008/09

A perfect companion to *America's Top-Rated Cities, America's Top-Rated Smaller Cities* provides current, comprehensive business and living profiles of smaller cities (population 25,000-99,999) that have been cited as the best for business and living in the United States. Sixty cities make up this 2004 edition of America's Top-Rated Smaller Cities, all are top-ranked by Population Growth, Median Income, Unemployment Rate and Crime Rate. City reports reflect the most current data available on a wide-range of statistics, including Employment & Earnings, Household Income, Unemployment Rate, Population Characteristics, Taxes, Cost of Living, Education, Health Care, Public Safety, Recreation, Media, Air & Water Quality and much more. Plus, each city report contains a Background of the City, and an Overview of the State Finances. *America's Top-Rated Smaller Cities* offers a reliable, one-stop source for statistical data that, before now, could only be found scattered in hundreds of sources. This volume is designed for a wide range of readers: individuals considering relocating a residence or business; professionals considering expanding their business or changing careers; general and market researchers; real estate consultants; human resource personnel; urban planners and investors.

"Provides current, comprehensive statistical information in one easy-to-use source... Recommended for public and academic libraries and specialized collections." –Library Journal

Two Volumes, Softcover ISBN 978-1-59237-284-3, 1,100 pages, $195.00 | Ebook ISBN 978-1-59237-234-8
www.gale.com/gvrl/partners/grey.htm

Profiles of America: Facts, Figures & Statistics for Every Populated Place in the United States

Profiles of America is the only source that pulls together, in one place, statistical, historical and descriptive information about every place in the United States in an easy-to-use format. This award winning reference set, now in its second edition, compiles statistics and data from over 20 different sources – the latest census information has been included along with more than nine brand new statistical topics. This Four-Volume Set details over 40,000 places, from the biggest metropolis to the smallest unincorporated hamlet, and provides statistical details and information on over 50 different topics including Geography, Climate, Population, Vital Statistics, Economy, Income, Taxes, Education, Housing, Health & Environment, Public Safety, Newspapers, Transportation, Presidential Election Results and Information Contacts or Chambers of Commerce. Profiles are arranged, for ease-of-use, by state and then by county. Each county begins with a County-Wide Overview and is followed by information for each Community in that particular county. The Community Profiles within the county are arranged alphabetically. *Profiles of America* is a virtual snapshot of America at your fingertips and a unique compilation of information that will be widely used in any reference collection.

A Library Journal Best Reference Book "An outstanding compilation." –Library Journal

Four Volumes, Softcover ISBN 978-1-891482-80-9, 10,000 pages, $595.00

To preview any of our Directories Risk-Free for 30 days, call (800) 562-2139 or fax (518) 789-0556
www.greyhouse.com books@greyhouse.com

Business Information ✦ Ratings Guides ✦ General Reference ✦ Education ✦
Statistics ✦ **Demographics** ✦ Health Information ✦ Canadian Information

The Comparative Guide to American Suburbs, 2007/08

The Comparative Guide to American Suburbs is a one-stop source for Statistics on the 2,000+ suburban communities surrounding the 50 largest metropolitan areas – their population characteristics, income levels, economy, school system and important data on how they compare to one another. Organized into 50 Metropolitan Area chapters, each chapter contains an overview of the Metropolitan Area, a detailed Map followed by a comprehensive Statistical Profile of each Suburban Community, including Contact Information, Physical Characteristics, Population Characteristics, Income, Economy, Unemployment Rate, Cost of Living, Education, Chambers of Commerce and more. Next, statistical data is sorted into Ranking Tables that rank the suburbs by twenty different criteria, including Population, Per Capita Income, Unemployment Rate, Crime Rate, Cost of Living and more. *The Comparative Guide to American Suburbs* is the best source for locating data on suburbs. Those looking to relocate, as well as those doing preliminary market research, will find this an invaluable timesaving resource.

> *"Public and academic libraries will find this compilation useful…The work draws together figures from many sources and will be especially helpful for job relocation decisions." – Booklist*

Softcover ISBN 978-1-59237-180-8, 1,700 pages, $130.00 | Ebook ISBN 978-1-59237-235-5 www.gale.com/gvrl/partners/grey.htm

The American Tally: Statistics & Comparative Rankings for U.S. Cities with Populations over 10,000

This important statistical handbook compiles, all in one place, comparative statistics on all U.S. cities and towns with a 10,000+ population. *The American Tally* provides statistical details on over 4,000 cities and towns and profiles how they compare with one another in Population Characteristics, Education, Language & Immigration, Income & Employment and Housing. Each section begins with an alphabetical listing of cities by state, allowing for quick access to both the statistics and relative rankings of any city. Next, the highest and lowest cities are listed in each statistic. These important, informative lists provide quick reference to which cities are at both extremes of the spectrum for each statistic. Unlike any other reference, *The American Tally* provides quick, easy access to comparative statistics – a must-have for any reference collection.

> *"A solid library reference." -Bookwatch*

Softcover ISBN 978-1-930956-29-2, 500 pages, $125.00 | Ebook ISBN 978-1-59237-241-6 www.gale.com/gvrl/partners/grey.htm

The Asian Databook: Statistics for all US Counties & Cities with Over 10,000 Population

This is the first-ever resource that compiles statistics and rankings on the US Asian population. *The Asian Databook* presents over 20 statistical data points for each city and county, arranged alphabetically by state, then alphabetically by place name. Data reported for each place includes Population, Languages Spoken at Home, Foreign-Born, Educational Attainment, Income Figures, Poverty Status, Homeownership, Home Values & Rent, and more. Next, in the Rankings Section, the top 75 places are listed for each data element. These easy-to-access ranking tables allow the user to quickly determine trends and population characteristics. This kind of comparative data can not be found elsewhere, in print or on the web, in a format that's as easy-to-use or more concise. A useful resource for those searching for demographics data, career search and relocation information and also for market research. With data ranging from Ancestry to Education, *The Asian Databook* presents a useful compilation of information that will be a much-needed resource in the reference collection of any public or academic library along with the marketing collection of any company whose primary focus in on the Asian population.

> *"This useful resource will help those searching for demographics data, and market research or relocation information… Accurate and clearly laid out, the publication is recommended for large public library and research collections." -Booklist*

Softcover ISBN 978-1-59237-044-3, 1,000 pages, $150.00

The Hispanic Databook: Statistics for all US Counties & Cities with Over 10,000 Population

Previously published by Toucan Valley Publications, this second edition has been completely updated with figures from the latest census and has been broadly expanded to include dozens of new data elements and a brand new Rankings section. The Hispanic population in the United States has increased over 42% in the last 10 years and accounts for 12.5% of the total US population. For ease-of-use, *The Hispanic Databook* presents over 20 statistical data points for each city and county, arranged alphabetically by state, then alphabetically by place name. Data reported for each place includes Population, Languages Spoken at Home, Foreign-Born, Educational Attainment, Income Figures, Poverty Status, Homeownership, Home Values & Rent, and more. Next, in the Rankings Section, the top 75 places are listed for each data element. These easy-to-access ranking tables allow the user to quickly determine trends and population characteristics. This kind of comparative data can not be found elsewhere, in print or on the web, in a format that's as easy-to-use or more concise. A useful resource for those searching for demographics data, career search and relocation information and also for market research. With data ranging from Ancestry to Education, *The Hispanic Databook* presents a useful compilation of information that will be a much-needed resource in the reference collection of any public or academic library along with the marketing collection of any company whose primary focus in on the Hispanic population.

> *"This accurate, clearly presented volume of selected Hispanic demographics is recommended for large public libraries and research collections."-Library Journal*

Softcover ISBN 978-1-59237-008-5, 1,000 pages, $150.00

Business Information ◆ Ratings Guides ◆ General Reference ◆ Education ◆
Statistics ◆ Demographics ◆ Health Information ◆ Canadian Information

Grey House
Publishing

Ancestry in America: A Comparative Guide to Over 200 Ethnic Backgrounds

This brand new reference work pulls together thousands of comparative statistics on the Ethnic Backgrounds of all populated places in the United States with populations over 10,000. Never before has this kind of information been reported in a single volume. Section One, Statistics by Place, is made up of a list of over 200 ancestry and race categories arranged alphabetically by each of the 5,000 different places with populations over 10,000. The population number of the ancestry group in that city or town is provided along with the percent that group represents of the total population. This informative city-by-city section allows the user to quickly and easily explore the ethnic makeup of all major population bases in the United States. Section Two, Comparative Rankings, contains three tables for each ethnicity and race. In the first table, the top 150 populated places are ranked by population number for that particular ancestry group, regardless of population. In the second table, the top 150 populated places are ranked by the percent of the total population for that ancestry group. In the third table, those top 150 populated places with 10,000 population are ranked by population number for each ancestry group. These easy-to-navigate tables allow users to see ancestry population patterns and make city-by-city comparisons as well. This brand new, information-packed resource will serve a wide-range or research requests for demographics, population characteristics, relocation information and much more. *Ancestry in America: A Comparative Guide to Over 200 Ethnic Backgrounds* will be an important acquisition to all reference collections.

"This compilation will serve a wide range of research requests for population characteristics … it offers much more detail than other sources." –Booklist

Softcover ISBN 978-1-59237-029-0, 1,500 pages, $225.00

Weather America, A Thirty-Year Summary of Statistical Weather Data and Rankings

This valuable resource provides extensive climatological data for over 4,000 National and Cooperative Weather Stations throughout the United States. Weather America begins with a new Major Storms section that details major storm events of the nation and a National Rankings section that details rankings for several data elements, such as Maximum Temperature and Precipitation. The main body of Weather America is organized into 50 state sections. Each section provides a Data Table on each Weather Station, organized alphabetically, that provides statistics on Maximum and Minimum Temperatures, Precipitation, Snowfall, Extreme Temperatures, Foggy Days, Humidity and more. State sections contain two brand new features in this edition – a City Index and a narrative Description of the climatic conditions of the state. Each section also includes a revised Map of the State that includes not only weather stations, but cities and towns.

"Best Reference Book of the Year." –Library Journal

Softcover ISBN 978-1-891482-29-8, 2,013 pages, $175.00 | Ebook ISBN 978-1-59237-237-9 www.gale.com/gvrl/partners/grey.htm

Crime in America's Top-Rated Cities

This volume includes over 20 years of crime statistics in all major crime categories: violent crimes, property crimes and total crime. *Crime in America's Top-Rated Cities* is conveniently arranged by city and covers 76 top-rated cities. Crime in America's Top-Rated Cities offers details that compare the number of crimes and crime rates for the city, suburbs and metro area along with national crime trends for violent, property and total crimes. Also, this handbook contains important information and statistics on Anti-Crime Programs, Crime Risk, Hate Crimes, Illegal Drugs, Law Enforcement, Correctional Facilities, Death Penalty Laws and much more. A much-needed resource for people who are relocating, business professionals, general researchers, the press, law enforcement officials and students of criminal justice.

"Data is easy to access and will save hours of searching." –Global Enforcement Review

Softcover ISBN 978-1-891482-84-7, 832 pages, $155.00

Business Information ◆ Ratings Guides ◆ General Reference ◆ Education ◆
Statistics ◆ Demographics ◆ Health Information ◆ Canadian Information

The Complete Directory for People with Disabilities, 2008

A wealth of information, now in one comprehensive sourcebook. Completely updated, this edition contains more information than ever before, including thousands of new entries and enhancements to existing entries and thousands of additional web sites and e-mail addresses. This up-to-date directory is the most comprehensive resource available for people with disabilities, detailing Independent Living Centers, Rehabilitation Facilities, State & Federal Agencies, Associations, Support Groups, Periodicals & Books, Assistive Devices, Employment & Education Programs, Camps and Travel Groups. Each year, more libraries, schools, colleges, hospitals, rehabilitation centers and individuals add *The Complete Directory for People with Disabilities* to their collections, making sure that this information is readily available to the families, individuals and professionals who can benefit most from the amazing wealth of resources cataloged here.

"No other reference tool exists to meet the special needs of the disabled in one convenient resource for information." –Library Journal

Softcover ISBN 978-1-59237-194-5, 1,200 pages, $165.00 | Online Database $215.00 | Online Database & Directory Combo $300.00

The Complete Learning Disabilities Directory, 2008

The Complete Learning Disabilities Directory is the most comprehensive database of Programs, Services, Curriculum Materials, Professional Meetings & Resources, Camps, Newsletters and Support Groups for teachers, students and families concerned with learning disabilities. This information-packed directory includes information about Associations & Organizations, Schools, Colleges & Testing Materials, Government Agencies, Legal Resources and much more. For quick, easy access to information, this directory contains four indexes: Entry Name Index, Subject Index and Geographic Index. With every passing year, the field of learning disabilities attracts more attention and the network of caring, committed and knowledgeable professionals grows every day. This directory is an invaluable research tool for these parents, students and professionals.

"Due to its wealth and depth of coverage, parents, teachers and others… should find this an invaluable resource." -Booklist

Softcover ISBN 978-1-59237-207-2, 900 pages, $145.00 | Online Database $195.00 | Online Database & Directory Combo $280.00

The Complete Directory for People with Chronic Illness, 2007/08

Thousands of hours of research have gone into this completely updated edition – several new chapters have been added along with thousands of new entries and enhancements to existing entries. Plus, each chronic illness chapter has been reviewed by a medical expert in the field. This widely-hailed directory is structured around the 90 most prevalent chronic illnesses – from Asthma to Cancer to Wilson's Disease – and provides a comprehensive overview of the support services and information resources available for people diagnosed with a chronic illness. Each chronic illness has its own chapter and contains a brief description in layman's language, followed by important resources for National & Local Organizations, State Agencies, Newsletters, Books & Periodicals, Libraries & Research Centers, Support Groups & Hotlines, Web Sites and much more. This directory is an important resource for health care professionals, the collections of hospital and health care libraries, as well as an invaluable tool for people with a chronic illness and their support network.

"A must purchase for all hospital and health care libraries and is strongly recommended for all public library reference departments." –ARBA

Softcover ISBN 978-1-59237-183-9, 1,200 pages, $165.00 | Online Database $215.00 | Online Database & Directory Combo $300.00

The Complete Mental Health Directory, 2008/09

This is the most comprehensive resource covering the field of behavioral health, with critical information for both the layman and the mental health professional. For the layman, this directory offers understandable descriptions of 25 Mental Health Disorders as well as detailed information on Associations, Media, Support Groups and Mental Health Facilities. For the professional, The Complete Mental Health Directory offers critical and comprehensive information on Managed Care Organizations, Information Systems, Government Agencies and Provider Organizations. This comprehensive volume of needed information will be widely used in any reference collection.

"… the strength of this directory is that it consolidates widely dispersed information into a single volume." –Booklist

Softcover ISBN 978-1-59237-285-0, 800 pages, $165.00 | Online Database $215.00 | Online & Directory Combo $300.00

Business Information ◆ Ratings Guides ◆ General Reference ◆ Education ◆ Statistics ◆ Demographics ◆ Health Information ◆ Canadian Information

Grey House Publishing

The Comparative Guide to American Hospitals, Second Edition

This new second edition compares all of the nation's hospitals by 24 measures of quality in the treatment of heart attack, heart failure, pneumonia, and, new to this edition, surgical procedures and pregnancy care. Plus, this second edition is now available in regional volumes, to make locating information about hospitals in your area quicker and easier than ever before. The Comparative Guide to American Hospitals provides a snapshot profile of each of the nations 4,200+ hospitals. These informative profiles illustrate how the hospital rates when providing 24 different treatments within four broad categories: Heart Attack Care, Heart Failure Care, Surgical Infection Prevention (NEW), and Pregnancy Care measures (NEW). Each profile includes the raw percentage for that hospital, the state average, the US average and data on the top hospital. For easy access to contact information, each profile includes the hospital's address, phone and fax numbers, email and web addresses, type and accreditation along with 5 top key administrations. These profiles will allow the user to quickly identify the quality of the hospital and have the necessary information at their fingertips to make contact with that hospital. Most importantly, *The Comparative Guide to American Hospitals* provides easy-to-use Regional State by State Statistical Summary Tables for each of the data elements to allow the user to quickly locate hospitals with the best level of service. Plus, a new 30-Day Mortality Chart, Glossary of Terms and Regional Hospital Profile Index make this a must-have source. This new, expanded edition will be a must for the reference collection at all public, medical and academic libraries.

> *"These data will help those with heart conditions and pneumonia make informed decisions about their healthcare and encourage hospitals to improve the quality of care they provide. Large medical, hospital, and public libraries are most likely to benefit from this weighty resource."*-Library Journal

Four Volumes Softcover ISBN 978-1-59237-182-2, 3,500 pages, $325.00 | Regional Volumes $135.00 | Ebook ISBN 978-1-59237-239-3 www.gale.com/gvrl/partners/grey.htm

Older Americans Information Directory, 2007

Completely updated for 2007, this sixth edition has been completely revised and now contains 1,000 new listings, over 8,000 updates to existing listings and over 3,000 brand new e-mail addresses and web sites. You'll find important resources for Older Americans including National, Regional, State & Local Organizations, Government Agencies, Research Centers, Libraries & Information Centers, Legal Resources, Discount Travel Information, Continuing Education Programs, Disability Aids & Assistive Devices, Health, Print Media and Electronic Media. Three indexes: Entry Index, Subject Index and Geographic Index make it easy to find just the right source of information. This comprehensive guide to resources for Older Americans will be a welcome addition to any reference collection.

> *"Highly recommended for academic, public, health science and consumer libraries…"* –Choice

1,200 pages; Softcover ISBN 978-1-59237-136-5, $165.00 | Online Database $215.00 | Online Database & Directory Combo $300.00

The Complete Directory for Pediatric Disorders, 2008

This important directory provides parents and caregivers with information about Pediatric Conditions, Disorders, Diseases and Disabilities, including Blood Disorders, Bone & Spinal Disorders, Brain Defects & Abnormalities, Chromosomal Disorders, Congenital Heart Defects, Movement Disorders, Neuromuscular Disorders and Pediatric Tumors & Cancers. This carefully written directory offers: understandable Descriptions of 15 major bodily systems; Descriptions of more than 200 Disorders and a Resources Section, detailing National Agencies & Associations, State Associations, Online Services, Libraries & Resource Centers, Research Centers, Support Groups & Hotlines, Camps, Books and Periodicals. This resource will provide immediate access to information crucial to families and caregivers when coping with children's illnesses.

> *"Recommended for public and consumer health libraries."* –Library Journal

Softcover ISBN 978-1-59237-150-1, 1,200 pages, $165.00 | Online Database $215.00 | Online Database & Directory Combo $300.00

The Directory of Drug & Alcohol Residential Rehabilitation Facilities

This brand new directory is the first-ever resource to bring together, all in one place, data on the thousands of drug and alcohol residential rehabilitation facilities in the United States. The Directory of Drug & Alcohol Residential Rehabilitation Facilities covers over 1,000 facilities, with detailed contact information for each one, including mailing address, phone and fax numbers, email addresses and web sites, mission statement, type of treatment programs, cost, average length of stay, numbers of residents and counselors, accreditation, insurance plans accepted, type of environment, religious affiliation, education components and much more. It also contains a helpful chapter on General Resources that provides contact information for Associations, Print & Electronic Media, Support Groups and Conferences. Multiple indexes allow the user to pinpoint the facilities that meet very specific criteria. This time-saving tool is what so many counselors, parents and medical professionals have been asking for. The Directory of Drug & Alcohol Residential Rehabilitation Facilities will be a helpful tool in locating the right source for treatment for a wide range of individuals. This comprehensive directory will be an important acquisition for all reference collections: public and academic libraries, case managers, social workers, state agencies and many more.

> *"This is an excellent, much needed directory that fills an important gap…"* –Booklist

Softcover ISBN 978-1-59237-031-3, 300 pages, $135.00

Business Information ◆ Ratings Guides ◆ General Reference ◆ Education ◆
Statistics ◆ Demographics ◆ <u>Health Information</u> ◆ Canadian Information

The Directory of Hospital Personnel, 2008

The Directory of Hospital Personnel is the best resource you can have at your fingertips when researching or marketing a product or service to the hospital market. A "Who's Who" of the hospital universe, this directory puts you in touch with over 150,000 key decision-makers. With 100% verification of data you can rest assured that you will reach the right person with just one call. Every hospital in the U.S. is profiled, listed alphabetically by city within state. Plus, three easy-to-use, cross-referenced indexes put the facts at your fingertips faster and more easily than any other directory: Hospital Name Index, Bed Size Index and Personnel Index. *The Directory of Hospital Personnel* is the only complete source for key hospital decision-makers by name. Whether you want to define or restructure sales territories... locate hospitals with the purchasing power to accept your proposals... keep track of important contacts or colleagues... or find information on which insurance plans are accepted, *The Directory of Hospital Personnel* gives you the information you need – easily, efficiently, effectively and accurately.

"Recommended for college, university and medical libraries." -ARBA

Softcover ISBN 978-1-59237-286-7, 2,500 pages, $325.00 | Online Database $545.00 | Online Database & Directory Combo, $650.00

The Directory of Health Care Group Purchasing Organizations, 2008

This comprehensive directory provides the important data you need to get in touch with over 800 Group Purchasing Organizations. By providing in-depth information on this growing market and its members, *The Directory of Health Care Group Purchasing Organizations* fills a major need for the most accurate and comprehensive information on over 800 GPOs – Mailing Address, Phone & Fax Numbers, E-mail Addresses, Key Contacts, Purchasing Agents, Group Descriptions, Membership Categorization, Standard Vendor Proposal Requirements, Membership Fees & Terms, Expanded Services, Total Member Beds & Outpatient Visits represented and more. Five Indexes provide a number of ways to locate the right GPO: Alphabetical Index, Expanded Services Index, Organization Type Index, Geographic Index and Member Institution Index. With its comprehensive and detailed information on each purchasing organization, *The Directory of Health Care Group Purchasing Organizations* is the go-to source for anyone looking to target this market.

"The information is clearly arranged and easy to access...recommended for those needing this very specialized information." –ARBA

1,000 pages; Softcover ISBN 978-1-59237-287-4, $325.00 | Online Database, $650.00 | Online Database & Directory Combo, $750.00

The HMO/PPO Directory, 2008

The HMO/PPO Directory is a comprehensive source that provides detailed information about Health Maintenance Organizations and Preferred Provider Organizations nationwide. This comprehensive directory details more information about more managed health care organizations than ever before. Over 1,100 HMOs, PPOs, Medicare Advantage Plans and affiliated companies are listed, arranged alphabetically by state. Detailed listings include Key Contact Information, Prescription Drug Benefits, Enrollment, Geographical Areas served, Affiliated Physicians & Hospitals, Federal Qualifications, Status, Year Founded, Managed Care Partners, Employer References, Fees & Payment Information and more. Plus, five years of historical information is included related to Revenues, Net Income, Medical Loss Ratios, Membership Enrollment and Number of Patient Complaints. Five easy-to-use, cross-referenced indexes will put this vast array of information at your fingertips immediately: HMO Index, PPO Index, Other Providers Index, Personnel Index and Enrollment Index. *The HMO/PPO Directory* provides the most comprehensive data on the most companies available on the market place today.

"Helpful to individuals requesting certain HMO/PPO issues such as co-payment costs, subscription costs and patient complaints. Individuals concerned (or those with questions) about their insurance may find this text to be of use to them." -ARBA

Softcover ISBN 978-1-59237-204-1, 600 pages, $325.00 | Online Database, $495.00 | Online Database & Directory Combo, $600.00

Medical Device Register, 2008

The only one-stop resource of every medical supplier licensed to sell products in the US. This award-winning directory offers immediate access to over 13,000 companies - and more than 65,000 products – in two information-packed volumes. This comprehensive resource saves hours of time and trouble when searching for medical equipment and supplies and the manufacturers who provide them. Volume I: The Product Directory, provides essential information for purchasing or specifying medical supplies for every medical device, supply, and diagnostic available in the US. Listings provide FDA codes & Federal Procurement Eligibility, Contact information for every manufacturer of the product along with Prices and Product Specifications. Volume 2 - Supplier Profiles, offers the most complete and important data about Suppliers, Manufacturers and Distributors. Company Profiles detail the number of employees, ownership, method of distribution, sales volume, net income, key executives detailed contact information medical products the company supplies, plus the medical specialties they cover. Four indexes provide immediate access to this wealth of information: Keyword Index, Trade Name Index, Supplier Geographical Index and OEM (Original Equipment Manufacturer) Index. *Medical Device Register* is the only one-stop source for locating suppliers and products; looking for new manufacturers or hard-to-find medical devices; comparing products and companies; know who's selling what and who to buy from cost effectively. This directory has become the standard in its field and will be a welcome addition to the reference collection of any medical library, large public library, university library along with the collections that serve the medical community.

"A wealth of information on medical devices, medical device companies... and key personnel in the industry is provide in this comprehensive reference work... A valuable reference work, one of the best hardcopy compilations available." -Doody Publishing

Two Volumes, Hardcover ISBN 978-1-59237-206-5, 3,000 pages, $325.00

Business Information ◆ Ratings Guides ◆ General Reference ◆ Education ◆
Statistics ◆ Demographics ◆ Health Information ◆ Canadian Information

Grey House
Publishing

Canadian Almanac & Directory, 2008

The Canadian Almanac & Directory contains sixteen directories in one – giving you all the facts and figures you will ever need about Canada. No other single source provides users with the quality and depth of up-to-date information for all types of research. This national directory and guide gives you access to statistics, images and over 100,000 names and addresses for everything from Airlines to Zoos - updated every year. It's Ten Directories in One! Each section is a directory in itself, providing robust information on business and finance, communications, government, associations, arts and culture (museums, zoos, libraries, etc.), health, transportation, law, education, and more. Government information includes federal, provincial and territorial - and includes an easy-to-use quick index to find key information. A separate municipal government section includes every municipality in Canada, with full profiles of Canada's largest urban centers. A complete legal directory lists judges and judicial officials, court locations and law firms across the country. A wealth of general information, the *Canadian Almanac & Directory* also includes national statistics on population, employment, imports and exports, and more. National awards and honors are presented, along with forms of address, Commonwealth information and full color photos of Canadian symbols. Postal information, weights, measures, distances and other useful charts are also incorporated. Complete almanac information includes perpetual calendars, five-year holiday planners and astronomical information. Published continuously for 160 years, *The Canadian Almanac & Directory* is the best single reference source for business executives, managers and assistants; government and public affairs executives; lawyers; marketing, sales and advertising executives; researchers, editors and journalists.

Hardcover ISBN 978-1-59237-220-1, 1,600 pages, $315.00

Associations Canada, 2008

The Most Powerful Fact-Finder to Business, Trade, Professional and Consumer Organizations
Associations Canada covers Canadian organizations and international groups including industry, commercial and professional associations, registered charities, special interest and common interest organizations. This annually revised compendium provides detailed listings and abstracts for nearly 20,000 regional, national and international organizations. This popular volume provides the most comprehensive picture of Canada's non-profit sector. Detailed listings enable users to identify an organization's budget, founding date, scope of activity, licensing body, sources of funding, executive information, full address and complete contact information, just to name a few. Powerful indexes help researchers find information quickly and easily. The following indexes are included: subject, acronym, geographic, budget, executive name, conferences & conventions, mailing list, defunct and unreachable associations and registered charitable organizations. In addition to annual spending of over $1 billion on transportation and conventions alone, Canadian associations account for many millions more in pursuit of membership interests. *Associations Canada* provides complete access to this highly lucrative market. *Associations Canada* is a strong source of prospects for sales and marketing executives, tourism and convention officials, researchers, government officials - anyone who wants to locate non-profit interest groups and trade associations.

Hardcover ISBN 978-1-59237-277-5, 1,600 pages, $315.00

Financial Services Canada, 2008/09

Financial Services Canada is the only master file of current contacts and information that serves the needs of the entire financial services industry in Canada. With over 18,000 organizations and hard-to-find business information, Financial Services Canada is the most up-to-date source for names and contact numbers of industry professionals, senior executives, portfolio managers, financial advisors, agency bureaucrats and elected representatives. Financial Services Canada incorporates the latest changes in the industry to provide you with the most current details on each company, including: name, title, organization, telephone and fax numbers, e-mail and web addresses. *Financial Services Canada* also includes private company listings never before compiled, government agencies, association and consultant services - to ensure that you'll never miss a client or a contact. Current listings include: banks and branches, non-depository institutions, stock exchanges and brokers, investment management firms, insurance companies, major accounting and law firms, government agencies and financial associations. Powerful indexes assist researchers with locating the vital financial information they need. The following indexes are included: alphabetic, geographic, executive name, corporate web site/e-mail, government quick reference and subject. *Financial Services Canada* is a valuable resource for financial executives, bankers, financial planners, sales and marketing professionals, lawyers and chartered accountants, government officials, investment dealers, journalists, librarians and reference specialists.

Hardcover ISBN 978-1-59237-278-2, 900 pages, $315.00

Directory of Libraries in Canada, 2008/09

The Directory of Libraries in Canada brings together almost 7,000 listings including libraries and their branches, information resource centers, archives and library associations and learning centers. The directory offers complete and comprehensive information on Canadian libraries, resource centers, business information centers, professional associations, regional library systems, archives, library schools and library technical programs. *The Directory of Libraries in Canada* includes important features of each library and service, including library information; personnel details, including contact names and e-mail addresses; collection information; services available to users; acquisitions budgets; and computers and automated systems. Useful information on each library's electronic access is also included, such as Internet browser, connectivity and public Internet/CD-ROM/subscription database access. The directory also provides powerful indexes for subject, location, personal name and Web site/e-mail to assist researchers with locating the crucial information they need. *The Directory of Libraries in Canada* is a vital reference tool for publishers, advocacy groups, students, research institutions, computer hardware suppliers, and other diverse groups that provide products and services to this unique market.

Hardcover ISBN 978-1-59237-279-9, 850 pages, $315.00

Canadian Environmental Directory, 2008 /09

The Canadian Environmental Directory is Canada's most complete and only national listing of environmental associations and organizations, government regulators and purchasing groups, product and service companies, special libraries, and more! The extensive Products and Services section provides detailed listings enabling users to identify the company name, address, phone, fax, e-mail, Web address, firm type, contact names (and titles), product and service information, affiliations, trade information, branch and affiliate data. The Government section gives you all the contact information you need at every government level – federal, provincial and municipal. We also include descriptions of current environmental initiatives, programs and agreements, names of environment-related acts administered by each ministry or department PLUS information and tips on who to contact and how to sell to governments in Canada. The Associations section provides complete contact information and a brief description of activities. Included are Canadian environmental organizations and international groups including industry, commercial and professional associations, registered charities, special interest and common interest organizations. All the Information you need about the Canadian environmental industry: directory of products and services, special libraries and resource, conferences, seminars and tradeshows, chronology of environmental events, law firms and major Canadian companies, *The Canadian Environmental Directory* is ideal for business, government, engineers and anyone conducting research on the environment.

Softcover ISBN 978-1-59237-224-9, 900 pages, $315.00

Canadian Parliamentary Guide, 2008

An indispensable guide to government in Canada, the annual *Canadian Parliamentary Guide* provides information on both federal and provincial governments, courts, and their elected and appointed members. The Guide is completely bilingual, with each record appearing both in English and then in French. The Guide contains biographical sketches of members of the Governor General's Household, the Privy Council, members of Canadian legislatures (federal, including both the House of Commons and the Senate, provincial and territorial), members of the federal superior courts (Supreme, Federal, Federal Appeal, Court Martial Appeal and Tax Courts) and the senior staff for these institutions. Biographies cover personal data, political career, private career and contact information. In addition, the Guide provides descriptions of each of the institutions, including brief historical information in text and chart format and significant facts (i.e. number of members and their salaries). The Guide covers the results of all federal general elections and by-elections from Confederations to the present and the results of the most recent provincial elections. A complete name index rounds out the text, making information easy to find. No other resources presents a more up-to-date, more complete picture of Canadian government and her political leaders.   A must-have resource for all Canadian reference collections.

Hardcover ISBN 978-1-59237-310-9, 800 pages, $184.00